**ISBN 0-918417-78-3**



The data in this book have been prepared using generally accepted statistical techniques. CACI Marketing Systems cannot and does not warrant that the data collected in this book are completely error free.

# TABLE OF CONTENTS

# Introduction

CACI is an international information systems and high-technology services corporation. With sales in excess of $442 million, CACI employs more than 4,300 people in 90 offices throughout North America and Western Europe.

The scope of CACI Marketing Systems includes demographics, consumer classification, market research, site evaluation, sales forecasting, direct mail profiling, custom demographic and economic research, and other areas.

CACI Marketing Systems offers custom application services in retail planning, site modeling, and customer profiling. Our consultants, professional analysts, demographers, and programmers help clients define and target their markets. CACI can assist clients to evaluate new sites, investigate market potential for new products, and determine customer profiles using comprehensive forecasts.

CACI Marketing Systems maintains an extensive data library that includes census data, forecasts, and consumer surveys, with information on population, age, sex, Hispanic origin, race, income, housing, and consumer expenditures. Data are available in census, postal, media, and customized geographies.

CACI Marketing Systems also offers:

**Reports**: Demographics (Current-Year Updates, Five-Year Projections, and 1990 Census), sales potential, purchase potential, ACORN lifestyles, business data, crime, traffic volumes, drivetimes and shopping center data.

**Sourcebooks**: Demographics for ZIP Codes and counties. More than 150 characteristics such as age, race, income, and households. Also available on CD-ROM.

**Maps**: Customized maps portray multiple demographic or business characteristics for a wide selection of geographies such as DMAs, counties, census tracts, and ZIP Codes. Available in sizes ranging from 8 ½" x 11" and 34" x 44".

**Diskettes**: Thousands of demographic variables are arranged into population and housing files. Age, sex, income, race, housing units, households, and more. In Excel, dBASE, and other formats.

**CD-ROM**: Demographic characteristics for various geographies on CD-ROM. Includes menu-driven software that allows text retrieval, simple searches, querying, sorting, and data exporting.

**Software Solutions**: CACI's software packages are cost-effective solutions that meet a variety of market research and site selection needs. Easy-to-use mapping and reporting functions are available so you can instantly see the areas you're researching and get the data you need, all on your desktop in minutes.

For more information visit the following websites:

**www.demographics.caci.com** - For a complete list of CACI's products and services.

**www.infods.com** - For accurate demographic site reports, instantly, On-the-Web.

Or you can reach us at:

East Coast:
1100 N.Glebe Road
Arlington, VA 22201
(800) 292-2224
Fax: (703) 243-6272

West Coast:
3252 Holiday Court
LaJolla, CA 92037
(800) 394-3690
Fax: (858) 677-5420

# Site Reporter™

## The Low Cost PC-Based Solution to Your Business and Marketing Needs

- Generate reports automatically
- Simple to learn and use (No training necessary)
- Entire U.S. on one CD-ROM
- Point and click to browse data
- Display and demographic information on a map
- Full custom mapping capabilities for the entire U.S.
- Save reports as spreadsheets
- Effortless import/export of data
- Features the "Industry Standard" CACI Demographic and Income Forecast
- Creates reports directly from any address or street intersection
- Block group level data retrieval for circles and polygons
- Up to ten trade areas per site
- Aggregate any standard geographic unit
- Self-guided site analysis report and maps
- TIGER '95 Streets/Highways
- Also includes Places, Shopping Centers (w/750,000 GLA), Airports and Interstate Highways
- "Go-To" function allows instant location of cities, ZIP Codes, lat/longs, etc.
- 3-digit ZIP Code boundaries
- Map templates with inserts

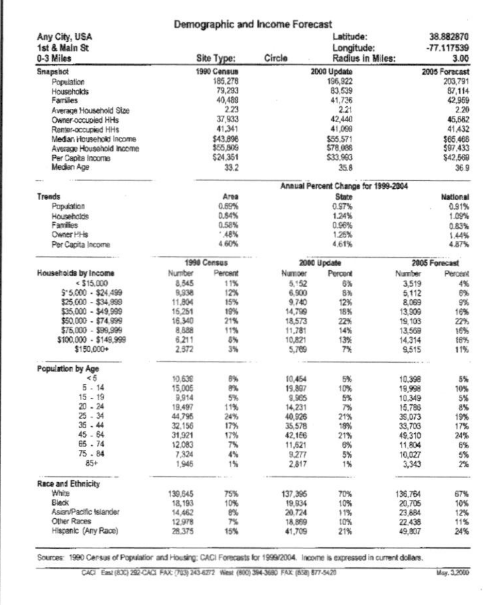

**Demographic and Income Forecast**

| Any City, USA | | | Latitude: | 38.882870 |
|---|---|---|---|---|
| 1st & Main St | | | Longitude: | -77.117539 |
| 0-3 Miles | Site Type: | Circle | Radius in Miles: | 3.00 |

| Snapshot | 1990 Census | 2000 Update | 2005 Forecast |
|---|---|---|---|
| Population | 185,278 | 196,922 | 203,791 |
| Households | 79,293 | 83,539 | 87,114 |
| Families | 40,489 | 41,736 | 42,959 |
| Average Household Size | 2.23 | 2.21 | 2.20 |
| Owner-occupied HHs | 37,933 | 42,440 | 45,682 |
| Renter-occupied HHs | 41,341 | 41,099 | 41,432 |
| Median Household Income | $43,898 | $55,571 | $65,468 |
| Average Household Income | $55,809 | $78,088 | $97,433 |
| Per Capita Income | $24,351 | $33,993 | $42,569 |
| Median Age | 33.2 | 35.8 | 36.9 |

| | Annual Percent Change for 1999-2004 | | |
|---|---|---|---|
| Trends | Area | State | National |
| Population | 0.69% | 0.97% | 0.91% |
| Households | 0.84% | 1.24% | 1.09% |
| Families | 0.58% | 0.96% | 0.83% |
| Owner HHs | '.48% | 1.26% | 1.44% |
| Per Capita Income | 4.60% | 4.61% | 4.87% |

| | 1990 Census | | 2000 Update | | 2005 Forecast | |
|---|---|---|---|---|---|---|
| Households by Income | Number | Percent | Number | Percent | Number | Percent |
| < $15,000 | 8,645 | 11% | 5,152 | 6% | 3,519 | 4% |
| $15,000 - $24,499 | 9,938 | 12% | 6,900 | 8% | 5,112 | 6% |
| $25,000 - $34,999 | 11,804 | 15% | 9,740 | 12% | 8,069 | 9% |
| $35,000 - $49,999 | 15,251 | 19% | 14,799 | 18% | 13,909 | 16% |
| $50,000 - $74,999 | 16,340 | 21% | 18,573 | 22% | 19,103 | 22% |
| $75,000 - $99,999 | 8,888 | 11% | 11,781 | 14% | 13,569 | 16% |
| $100,000 - $149,999 | 6,211 | 8% | 10,821 | 13% | 14,314 | 16% |
| $150,000+ | 2,572 | 3% | 5,769 | 7% | 9,515 | 11% |
| **Population by Age** | | | | | | |
| < 5 | 10,638 | 6% | 10,454 | 5% | 10,398 | 5% |
| 5 - 14 | 15,005 | 8% | 19,897 | 10% | 19,998 | 10% |
| 15 - 19 | 9,914 | 5% | 9,965 | 5% | 10,349 | 5% |
| 20 - 24 | 19,497 | 11% | 14,231 | 7% | 15,786 | 8% |
| 25 - 34 | 44,795 | 24% | 40,926 | 21% | 39,073 | 19% |
| 35 - 44 | 32,156 | 17% | 35,578 | 18% | 33,703 | 17% |
| 45 - 64 | 31,921 | 17% | 42,156 | 21% | 49,310 | 24% |
| 65 - 74 | 12,083 | 7% | 11,621 | 6% | 11,804 | 6% |
| 75 - 84 | 7,324 | 4% | 9,277 | 5% | 10,027 | 5% |
| 85+ | 1,946 | 1% | 2,817 | 1% | 3,343 | 2% |
| **Race and Ethnicity** | | | | | | |
| White | 139,645 | 75% | 137,395 | 70% | 136,764 | 67% |
| Black | 18,193 | 10% | 19,934 | 10% | 20,705 | 10% |
| Asian/Pacific Islander | 14,462 | 8% | 20,724 | 11% | 23,884 | 12% |
| Other Races | 12,978 | 7% | 18,869 | 10% | 22,438 | 11% |
| Hispanic (Any Race) | 28,375 | 15% | 41,709 | 21% | 49,807 | 24% |

Sources: 1990 Census of Population and Housing; CACI Forecasts for 1999/2004. Income is expressed in current dollars.

CACI East (800) 292-CACI FAX: (703) 243-6272 West (800) 394-3690 FAX: (858) 877-5420 May. 3,2000

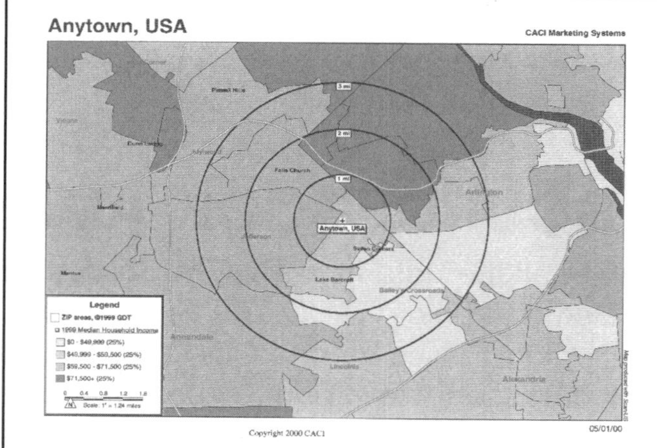


Standard and add-on databases include:

- ACORN®
- Businesses
- Crime Data
- Demographics
- Drive Time Module
- Retail Spending
- Senior Living
- Traffic Volumes

## CACI Coder/Plus™

You can instantly geocode an unlimited number of addresses anywhere in the U.S. by assigning lat/long coordinates and geographic IDs, all in a single pass.

System requirement: Windows 95 or higher, 8MB RAM, 30 MB hard disk space, Microsoft Excel, Microsoft Word, CD-ROM player, printer accessible from Windows.

For more information call (800) 292-2224/East Coast or (800) 394-3690/West Coast or visit us on the web at www.demographics.caci.com

# Site Reports

**With CACI instant demographics, data in hard-copy report format is just a phone call away! CACI data include:**

**Demographic Reports, Updates and Forecasts** - See where your market is headed and plan how to achieve success.

**Expenditure Reports** - Combine the power of the Consumer Expenditure Survey and the Simmons Market Research Bureau data to reveal the amount spent for a product or service relative to the national average.

**Business Reports** - CACI's Business Reports incorporate InfoUSA business data on nearly ten million businesses to help you make informed and sound business decisions.

**Shopping Center Reports** - Learn as much as the owner or developer and add to your knowledge base with these three annually updated reports. The National Research Bureau (NRB) provides data on over 35,000 shopping centers for these powerful reports, covering nearly everyone in the shopping center industry.

Crime Watch

| | Any City, USA 1st & Main St 0-1 Mile | Any City, USA 1st & Main St 0-3 Miles | Any City, USA 1st & Main St 0-5 Miles |
|---|---|---|---|
| **Demographics** | | | |
| 1990 Population | 24,635 | 194,134 | 492,938 |
| 2000 Population | 25,807 | 205,021 | 499,067 |
| 2005 Population | 26,566 | 211,748 | 508,560 |
| 2000 - 2005 Annual Change | 0.6% | 0.6% | 0.4% |
| 1990 Median HH Income | $43,357 | $43,232 | $42,972 |
| 2000 Median HH Income | $56,562 | $54,902 | $54,544 |
| 2005 Median HH Income | $67,543 | $64,741 | $63,440 |
| 2000 - 2005 Annual Change | 3.6% | 3.4% | 3.1% |
| | | **1990 Crime Indexes** | |
| Overall CAP Index | 122 | 90 | 84 |
| Crimes Against Persons | 95 | 72 | 69 |
| Homicide | 91 | 75 | 79 |
| Rape | 71 | 76 | 78 |
| Robbery | 160 | 132 | 134 |
| Aggravated Assault | 65 | 41 | 35 |
| Crimes Against Property | 126 | 92 | 86 |
| Burglary | 123 | 93 | 82 |
| Larceny | 133 | 95 | 90 |
| Auto Theft | 91 | 77 | 67 |
| | | **2000 Crime Indexes** | |
| Overall CAP Index | 117 | 89 | 76 |
| Crimes Against Persons | 92 | 72 | 61 |
| Homicide | 93 | 74 | 68 |
| Rape | 74 | 76 | 65 |
| Robbery | 156 | 132 | 118 |
| Aggravated Assault | 60 | 40 | 32 |
| Crimes Against Property | 121 | 91 | 78 |
| Burglary | 119 | 92 | 73 |
| Larceny | 129 | 94 | 83 |
| Auto Theft | 83 | 75 | 64 |
| | | **2005 Crime Indexes** | |
| Overall CAP Index | 113 | 88 | 73 |
| Crimes Against Persons | 88 | 71 | 58 |
| Homicide | 87 | 69 | 62 |
| Rape | 70 | 73 | 59 |
| Robbery | 149 | 130 | 111 |
| Aggravated Assault | 58 | 40 | 31 |
| Crimes Against Property | 117 | 90 | 75 |
| Burglary | 111 | 88 | 66 |
| Larceny | 126 | 93 | 80 |
| Auto Theft | 82 | 76 | 64 |

CAPCrime scores indicate the risk of crime for each site compared to a national average of 100. Data are not reported by CAP Index, Inc. for tracts with fewer than 20 people.
CAPCrime is a product of CAP Index, Inc., King of Prussia, PA. Copyright 1999 CAP Index, Inc. All rights reserved.

Demographic Data Sources: U.S. Bureau of the Census, 1990 census data. CACI 1999/2004 forecasts.
Copyright 2000 CACI East (800) 292-CACI FAX: (703) 243-8272 West (800) 394-3690 FAX: (858) 677-5420

ACORN Area Update

Any City, USA
1st & Main St
0-3 Miles
Site Type: Circle
Latitude: 38.882870
Longitude: -77.117539
Radius in Miles: 3.00

| ACORN Type | ACORN Description | Population 2000 Number | Population 2000 Percent | Base Percent | Area Index |
|---|---|---|---|---|---|
| 1A | Top One Percent | 9,199 | 4.7% | 1.1% | 407 |
| 1B | Wealthy Seaboard Suburbs | 40,905 | 20.8% | 2.5% | 830 |
| 1C | Upper Income Empty Nesters | 551 | 0.3% | 2.0% | 14 |
| 1D | Successful Suburbanites | 0 | 0.0% | 2.5% | - |
| 1E | Prosperous Baby Boomers | 0 | 0.0% | 4.3% | - |
| 1F | Semirural Lifestyle | 0 | 0.0% | 5.2% | - |
| 2A | Urban Professional Couples | 14,713 | 7.5% | 3.7% | 199 |
| 2B | Baby Boomers with Children | 0 | 0.0% | 4.5% | - |
| 2C | Thriving Immigrants | 7,260 | 3.7% | 1.9% | 192 |
| 2D | Pacific Heights | 10 | 0.0% | 0.8% | 1 |
| 2E | Older, Settled Married Couples | 0 | 0.0% | 4.4% | - |
| 3A | High Rise Renters | 65,392 | 33.2% | 1.5% | 2149 |
| 3B | Enterprising Young Singles | 4,808 | 2.4% | 3.0% | 81 |
| 4A | Retirement Communities | 3,419 | 1.7% | 1.1% | 161 |
| 4B | Active Senior Singles | 1,941 | 1.0% | 2.4% | 41 |
| 4C | Prosperous Older Couples | 0 | 0.0% | 3.0% | - |
| 4D | Wealthiest Seniors | 0 | 0.0% | 0.8% | - |
| 4E | Rural Resort Dwellers | 0 | 0.0% | 1.0% | - |
| 4F | Senior Sun Seekers | 2 | 0.0% | 1.6% | |
| 5A | Twentysomethings | 303 | 0.2% | 1.5% | 10 |
| 5B | College Campuses | 3,757 | 1.9% | 1.3% | 148 |
| 5C | Military Proximity | 4,643 | 2.4% | 2.4% | 99 |
| 6A | East Coast Immigrants | 31,800 | 16.1% | 1.9% | 859 |
| 6B | Working Class Families | 2,964 | 1.5% | 1.1% | 140 |
| 6C | Newly Formed Households | 0 | 0.0% | 4.8% | - |
| 6D | Southwestern Families | 0 | 0.0% | 3.1% | - |
| 6E | West Coast Immigrants | 0 | 0.0% | 1.7% | - |
| 6F | Low Income: Young and Old | 0 | 0.0% | 2.3% | - |
| 7A | Middle America | 0 | 0.0% | 8.1% | - |
| 7B | Young, Frequent Movers | 0 | 0.0% | 3.2% | - |
| 7C | Rural Industrial Workers | 0 | 0.0% | 5.4% | - |
| 7D | Prairie Farmers | 0 | 0.0% | 0.9% | - |
| 7E | Small Town Working Families | 0 | 0.0% | 1.7% | - |
| 7F | Rustbelt Neighborhoods | 0 | 0.0% | 3.1% | - |
| 7G | Heartland Communities | 0 | 0.0% | 3.3% | - |
| 8A | Young Immigrant Families | 4,240 | 2.2% | 1.3% | 166 |
| 8B | Social Security Dependents | 1,032 | 0.5% | 0.7% | 72 |
| 8C | Distressed Neighborhoods | 3 | 0.0% | 1.2% | |
| 8D | Hardtimes | 0 | 0.0% | 1.5% | - |
| 8E | Urban Working Families | 0 | 0.0% | 1.8% | - |
| 9A | Business Districts | 0 | 0.0% | 0.0% | - |
| 9B | Institutional Populations | 0 | 0.0% | 0.1% | - |
| | Total | 196,942 | 100% | 100% | |

Base: U.S.

**Note:** ACORN type 9C, "Unpopulated Areas", is not shown.

Copyright 2000 CACI East (800) 292-CACI FAX: (703) 243-6272 West (800) 394-3690 FAX: (858) 677-5420 May.8,2000

Businesses by Employee Size
Sorted by SIC Code

Any City, USA
1st & Main St
0-3 Miles
Site Type: Circle
Latitude: 38.882870
Longitude: -77.115754
Radius in miles: 3.00

Total Businesses: 6,424
Total Daytime Business Population: 82,167
Total Sales ($000): $8,428,967
Residential Population: 196,247
Daytime Business/Residential Ratio: 0.42 : 1

| SIC Code | Description | Businesses Number | Businesses Percent | Employees Number | Employees Percent | Sales ($000) Amount | Sales ($000) Percent | 1-4 | 5-9 | 10-49 | 50-100 | 100+ |
|---|---|---|---|---|---|---|---|---|---|---|---|---|
| 07 | Agricultural Services | 36 | 0.6% | 181 | 0.2% | $8,148 | 0.1% | 23 | 7 | 6 | 0 | 0 |
| 13 | Oil and Gas Extraction | 1 | 0.0% | 1 | 0.0% | $75 | 0.0% | 1 | 0 | 0 | 0 | 0 |
| 14 | Mining and Quarrying of Nonmetallic Minerals, Except Fuels | 1 | 0.0% | 1 | 0.0% | $75 | 0.0% | 1 | 0 | 0 | 0 | 0 |
| 15 | Building Cnstrctn - General Contractors & Operative Builders | 104 | 1.6% | 568 | 0.7% | $99,992 | 1.2% | 77 | 12 | 14 | 0 | 1 |
| 16 | Heavy Cnstrctn, Except Building Construction - Contractors | 13 | 0.2% | 39 | 0.0% | $6,588 | 0.1% | 9 | 4 | 0 | 0 | 0 |
| 17 | Construction - Special Trade Contractors | 142 | 2.2% | 1,234 | 1.5% | $167,157 | 1.3% | 94 | 12 | 30 | 4 | 2 |
| 20 | Food and Kindred Products | 1 | 0.0% | 31 | 0.0% | $3,813 | 0.0% | 0 | 0 | 1 | 0 | 0 |
| 21 | Tobacco Products | 1 | 0.0% | 2 | 0.0% | $1,060 | 0.0% | 1 | 0 | 0 | 0 | 0 |
| 22 | Textile Mill Products | 2 | 0.0% | 16 | 0.0% | $1,880 | 0.0% | 1 | 0 | 1 | 0 | 0 |
| 23 | Apparel, Finished Prdcts from Fabrics & Similar Materials | 2 | 0.0% | 17 | 0.0% | $1,126 | 0.0% | 1 | 0 | 1 | 0 | 0 |
| 26 | Paper and Allied Products | 1 | 0.0% | 13 | 0.0% | $191,000 | 2.3% | 0 | 0 | 1 | 0 | 0 |
| 27 | Printing, Publishing and Allied Industries | 132 | 2.1% | 2,394 | 2.9% | $188,414 | 2.2% | 84 | 17 | 26 | 2 | 3 |
| 28 | Chemicals and Allied Products | 2 | 0.0% | 3 | 0.0% | $1,001 | 0.0% | 2 | 0 | 0 | 0 | 0 |
| 32 | Stone, Clay, Glass, and Concrete Products | 1 | 0.0% | 10 | 0.0% | $870 | 0.0% | 0 | 0 | 1 | 0 | 0 |
| 34 | Fabricated Metal Prdcts, Except Machinery & Transport Eqpmnt | 6 | 0.1% | 16 | 0.0% | $3,064 | 0.0% | 5 | 1 | 0 | 0 | 0 |
| 35 | Industrial and Commercial Machinery and Computer Equipment | 11 | 0.2% | 45 | 0.1% | $9,712 | 0.1% | 7 | 3 | 1 | 0 | 0 |

Source: Business data provided by InfoUSA, Omaha NE Copyright 1998, all rights reserved. CACI 1999/2004 forecasts.

Copyright 2000 CACI East (800) 292-CACI FAX: (703) 243-6272 West (800) 394-3690 FAX: (858) 677-5420 May. 8,2000

For more information call (800) 292-2224/East Coast or (800) 394-3690/West Coast or visit us on the web at www.demographics.caci.com

# Site Reports

Choose from 70 different reports for any study area of any size or shape - anywhere in the U.S.

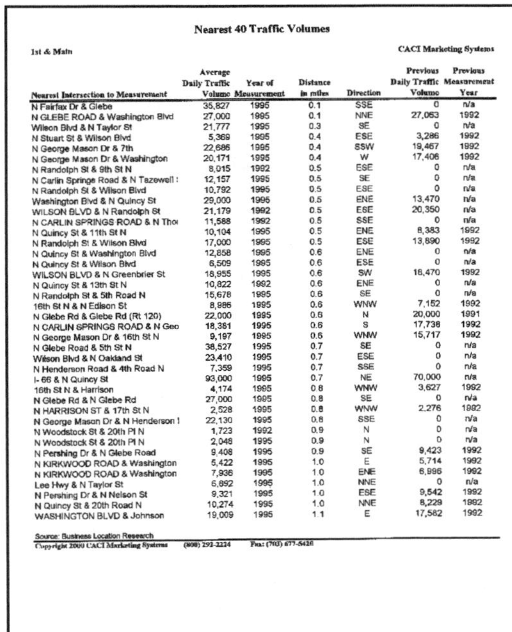

**Nearest 40 Traffic Volumes**

1st & Main — CACI Marketing Systems

| Nearest Intersection to Measurement | Average Daily Traffic Volume | Year of Measurement | Distance in miles | Direction | Previous Daily Traffic Volume | Previous Measurement Year |
|---|---|---|---|---|---|---|
| N Fairfax Dr & Glebe | 35,827 | 1995 | 0.1 | SSE | 0 | n/a |
| N GLEBE ROAD & Washington Blvd | 27,000 | 1995 | 0.1 | NNE | 27,063 | 1992 |
| Wilson Blvd & N Taylor St | 21,777 | 1995 | 0.3 | SE | 0 | n/a |
| N Stuart St & Wilson Blvd | 5,369 | 1995 | 0.4 | ESE | 3,286 | 1992 |
| N George Mason Dr & 7th | 22,686 | 1995 | 0.4 | SSW | 19,467 | 1992 |
| N George Mason Dr & Washington | 20,171 | 1995 | 0.4 | W | 17,406 | 1992 |
| N Randolph St & 9th St N | 8,015 | 1992 | 0.5 | ESE | 0 | n/a |
| N Carlin Springs Road & N Tazewell : | 12,157 | 1995 | 0.5 | SE | 0 | n/a |
| N Randolph St & Wilson Blvd | 10,792 | 1995 | 0.5 | ESE | 0 | n/a |
| Washington Blvd & N Quincy St | 29,000 | 1995 | 0.5 | ENE | 13,470 | n/a |
| WILSON BLVD & N Randolph St | 21,179 | 1992 | 0.5 | ESE | 20,350 | n/a |
| N CARLIN SPRINGS ROAD & N Tho | 11,588 | 1992 | 0.5 | SSE | 0 | n/a |
| N Quincy St & 11th St N | 10,104 | 1995 | 0.5 | ENE | 8,383 | 1992 |
| N Randolph St & Wilson Blvd | 17,000 | 1995 | 0.5 | ESE | 13,890 | 1992 |
| N Quincy St & Washington Blvd | 12,858 | 1995 | 0.6 | ENE | 0 | n/a |
| N Quincy St & Wilson Blvd | 6,509 | 1995 | 0.6 | ESE | 0 | n/a |
| WILSON BLVD & N Greenbrier St | 18,955 | 1995 | 0.6 | SW | 18,470 | 1992 |
| N Quincy St & 13th St N | 10,822 | 1992 | 0.6 | ENE | 0 | n/a |
| N Randolph St & 5th Road N | 15,678 | 1995 | 0.6 | SE | 0 | n/a |
| 16th St N & N Edison St | 8,986 | 1995 | 0.6 | WNW | 7,152 | 1992 |
| N Glebe Rd & Glebe Rd (Rt 120) | 22,000 | 1995 | 0.6 | N | 20,000 | 1991 |
| N CARLIN SPRINGS ROAD & N Geo | 18,361 | 1995 | 0.6 | S | 17,736 | 1992 |
| N George Mason Dr & 16th St N | 9,197 | 1995 | 0.6 | WNW | 15,717 | 1992 |
| N Glebe Road & 5th St N | 38,527 | 1995 | 0.7 | SE | 0 | n/a |
| Wilson Blvd & N Oakland St | 23,410 | 1995 | 0.7 | ESE | 0 | n/a |
| N Henderson Road & 4th Road N | 7,359 | 1995 | 0.7 | SSE | 0 | n/a |
| I-66 & N Quincy St | 93,000 | 1995 | 0.7 | NE | 70,000 | n/a |
| 16th St N & Harrison | 4,174 | 1995 | 0.8 | WNW | 3,627 | 1992 |
| N Glebe Rd & N Glebe Rd | 27,000 | 1995 | 0.8 | SE | 0 | n/a |
| N HARRISON ST & 17th St N | 2,528 | 1995 | 0.8 | WNW | 2,276 | 1992 |
| N George Mason Dr & N Henderson I | 22,130 | 1995 | 0.8 | SSE | 0 | n/a |
| N Woodstock St & 20th Pl N | 1,723 | 1992 | 0.9 | N | 0 | n/a |
| N Woodstock St & 20th Pl N | 2,048 | 1995 | 0.9 | N | 0 | n/a |
| N Pershing Dr & N Glebe Road | 9,408 | 1995 | 0.9 | SE | 9,423 | 1992 |
| N KIRKWOOD ROAD & Washington | 5,422 | 1995 | 1.0 | E | 5,714 | 1992 |
| N KIRKWOOD ROAD & Washington | 7,936 | 1995 | 1.0 | ENE | 6,986 | 1992 |
| Lee Hwy & N Taylor St | 6,892 | 1995 | 1.0 | NNE | 0 | n/a |
| N Pershing Dr & N Nelson St | 9,321 | 1995 | 1.0 | ESE | 9,542 | 1992 |
| N Quincy St & 20th Road N | 10,274 | 1995 | 1.0 | NNE | 8,229 | 1992 |
| WASHINGTON BLVD & Johnson | 19,009 | 1995 | 1.1 | E | 17,582 | 1992 |

Source: Business Location Research



**Marketing Tools** - CACI offers creative tools to solve your business problems, including:

- Information on the growth potential for a specific market area
- ZIP Codes surrounding any specific areas
- Details on a county or a metropolitan area
- Top 50 of anything
- And more!

**Consumer Profiling/Geocoding** - Consumer profiling is geocoding, enhancing and analyzing your customer file to help you better understand your business. To profile your customers, CACI offers reports that can tell you who your customers are and what their product preferences are.

For more information on these reports, visit our web site at **www.demographics.caci.com** to view samples of these reports and order our products and services online.

**Demographic and Income Forecast**

Any City, USA
1st & Main St
0-3 Miles

Site Type: Circle — Latitude: 38.882870 — Longitude: -77.117539 — Radius in Miles: 3.00

| Snapshot | 1990 Census | 2000 Update | 2005 Forecast |
|---|---|---|---|
| Population | 185,278 | 196,922 | 203,791 |
| Households | 79,293 | 83,539 | 87,114 |
| Families | 40,489 | 41,736 | 42,959 |
| Average Household Size | 2.23 | 2.21 | 2.20 |
| Owner-occupied HHs | 37,933 | 42,440 | 45,682 |
| Renter-occupied HHs | 41,341 | 41,099 | 41,432 |
| Median Household Income | $43,898 | $55,571 | $65,466 |
| Average Household Income | $55,809 | $78,088 | $97,433 |
| Per Capita Income | $24,351 | $33,993 | $42,569 |
| Median Age | 33.2 | 35.8 | 36.9 |

Annual Percent Change for 1999-2004

| Trends | Area | State | National |
|---|---|---|---|
| Population | 0.69% | 0.97% | 0.91% |
| Households | 0.84% | 1.24% | 1.09% |
| Families | 0.58% | 0.96% | 0.83% |
| Owner HHs | 1.48% | 1.25% | 1.44% |
| Per Capita Income | 4.60% | 4.61% | 4.87% |

| | 1990 Census | | 2000 Update | | 2005 Forecast | |
|---|---|---|---|---|---|---|
| Households by Income | Number | Percent | Number | Percent | Number | Percent |
| < $15,000 | 8,545 | 11% | 5,152 | 6% | 3,519 | 4% |
| $15,000 - $24,499 | 9,938 | 12% | 6,900 | 8% | 5,112 | 6% |
| $25,000 - $34,999 | 11,804 | 15% | 9,740 | 12% | 8,069 | 9% |
| $35,000 - $49,999 | 15,251 | 19% | 14,799 | 18% | 13,909 | 16% |
| $50,000 - $74,999 | 16,340 | 21% | 18,573 | 22% | 19,103 | 22% |
| $75,000 - $99,999 | 8,888 | 11% | 11,781 | 14% | 13,569 | 16% |
| $100,000 - $149,999 | 6,211 | 8% | 10,821 | 13% | 14,314 | 16% |
| $150,000+ | 2,672 | 3% | 5,769 | 7% | 9,515 | 11% |
| **Population by Age** | | | | | | |
| < 5 | 10,639 | 6% | 10,454 | 5% | 10,398 | 5% |
| 5 - 14 | 15,005 | 8% | 19,897 | 10% | 19,998 | 10% |
| 15 - 19 | 9,914 | 5% | 9,965 | 5% | 10,349 | 5% |
| 20 - 24 | 19,497 | 11% | 14,231 | 7% | 15,786 | 8% |
| 25 - 34 | 44,795 | 24% | 40,926 | 21% | 39,073 | 19% |
| 35 - 44 | 32,156 | 17% | 35,578 | 18% | 33,703 | 17% |
| 45 - 64 | 31,921 | 17% | 42,156 | 21% | 49,310 | 24% |
| 65 - 74 | 12,083 | 7% | 11,621 | 6% | 11,804 | 6% |
| 75 - 84 | 7,324 | 4% | 9,277 | 5% | 10,027 | 5% |
| 85+ | 1,946 | 1% | 2,817 | 1% | 3,343 | 2% |
| **Race and Ethnicity** | | | | | | |
| White | 139,645 | 75% | 137,395 | 70% | 136,764 | 67% |
| Black | 18,193 | 10% | 19,934 | 10% | 20,705 | 10% |
| Asian/Pacific Islander | 14,462 | 8% | 20,724 | 11% | 23,884 | 12% |
| Other Races | 12,978 | 7% | 18,869 | 10% | 22,438 | 11% |
| Hispanic (Any Race) | 28,375 | 15% | 41,709 | 21% | 49,807 | 24% |

Sources: 1990 Census of Population and Housing; CACI Forecasts for 1999/2004. Income is expressed in current dollars.

 May. 8,2000

**Disposable Income and Net Worth Forecast**

Any City, USA
1st & Main St
0-3 Miles

Site Type: Circle — Latitude: 38.882870 — Longitude: -77.117539 — Radius in Miles: 3.00

| | 1990 Census | 2000 | 2005 | 2000-2005 Change | Annual Change |
|---|---|---|---|---|---|
| Population | 185,278 | 196,922 | 203,791 | 6,869 | 0.7% |
| Median Age | 33.2 | 35.8 | 36.9 | 1.1 | 0.6% |
| Households | 79,293 | 83,539 | 87,114 | 3,575 | 0.8% |
| Average Household Size | 2.23 | 2.21 | 2.20 | -0.01 | -0.1% |
| Median Household Income | $43,898 | $55,571 | $65,466 | $9,895 | 3.3% |

**2000 Households by Disposable Income**

| | Number | Percent |
|---|---|---|
| Total | 83,535 | 100% |
| < $15,000 | 7,252 | 8.7% |
| $15,000 - $24,999 | 11,272 | 13.5% |
| $25,000 - $34,999 | 13,946 | 16.7% |
| $35,000 - $49,999 | 17,373 | 20.8% |
| $50,000 - $74,999 | 20,557 | 24.6% |
| $75,000 - $99,999 | 7,475 | 8.9% |
| $100,000 - $149,999 | 3,439 | 4.1% |
| $150,000+ | 2,221 | 2.7% |
| Median Disposable Income | $41,584 | |
| Average Disposable Income | $52,416 | |

**2000 Disposable Income by Age of Householder**

Number of Households

| | < 35 | 35-44 | 45-54 | 55-64 | 65-74 | 75+ |
|---|---|---|---|---|---|---|
| Total | 24,158 | 21,557 | 16,509 | 7,458 | 7,239 | 6,613 |
| < $15,000 | 2,379 | 1,265 | 846 | 496 | 891 | 1,373 |
| $15,000 - $24,999 | 4,056 | 2,553 | 1,311 | 888 | 1,338 | 1,126 |
| $25,000 - $34,999 | 5,321 | 3,533 | 1,957 | 902 | 1,132 | 1,101 |
| $35,000 - $49,999 | 5,359 | 4,583 | 3,207 | 1,543 | 1,370 | 1,310 |
| $50,000 - $74,999 | 5,281 | 6,160 | 4,792 | 1,692 | 1,587 | 1,044 |
| $75,000 - $99,999 | 1,246 | 1,890 | 2,271 | 1,188 | 513 | 366 |
| $100,000+ | 517 | 1,573 | 2,124 | 746 | 408 | 292 |
| Median Disposable Income | $35,588 | $45,066 | $53,033 | $48,617 | $37,039 | $31,656 |
| Average Disposable Income | $41,154 | $52,758 | $62,718 | $58,181 | $46,359 | $40,941 |

* **Disposable Income** is after-tax household income. Disposable income forecasts are based on the Current Population Survey, U.S. Bureau of the Census.

 May. 8,2000

For more information call (800) 292-2224/East Coast or (800) 394-3690/West Coast or visit us on the web at www.demographics.caci.com

# Your One-Stop Internet Connection for Demographics

If you prefer to browse at your leisure, visit our comprehensive and integrated web site at www.demographics.caci.com to see our products and services.

**CACI's Web Site Offers...**

- An extensive list and samples of our products and services
- Samples of our reports and maps
- Download demos of Site Reporter, Sourcebook America, ACORN User's Guide, and ZIP Tracts
- Daily Fun Facts - interesting demographics facts about the U.S. population that change each time you log on to our site
- Free ZIP Code Data - 15 facts about any U.S. ZIP Code
- Order products and services online
- Forum for industry-related questions
- Free electronic newsletter

Visit www.demographics.caci.com for all of your business and marketing needs. If you'd like to speak to one of our account representatives, please call 800-292-2224/East or 800-394-3690/West.

# Preface
# Thirteenth Edition

In 1986, CACI created the *Sourcebook of County Demographics*, a desktop resource guide of county data, for marketing professionals, advertising agencies, libraries and researchers. The Sourcebook was instantly acclaimed as the premier guide for county demographics and marketing information.

CACI has produced the 13th edition of the Sourcebook to coincide with its release of 2000/2005 projections of key population and income characteristics to provide you with the most accurate demographic information. The Sourcebook contains updated data for population, households, families, income, race, age and spending potential for various products. Some of the features of the new edition include:

**Every U.S. County** - each county is profiled with over 70 demographic variables. MSA and DMA codes for each county are listed.

**Five Profile Sections** - the variables are arranged by page into Population Change, Population Composition, Households, Income and Spending Potential Profiles. The updated demographics include: Population, Age, Race, Hispanic Origin, Household Type, Household Income, and Disposable Income.

**Business Data** - information about each county's predominant industry provides total business and total employment data.

**Summaries** - state and national summaries provide quick comparison of a county to state and national information.

**Demographic Update Methodology** - the new methodology statement explains how population and income data are forecast from the 1990 Census base.

**Explanation of Variables** - the variables and key terms used in the Sourcebook are defined to help you understand and explain your findings.

CACI Marketing Systems continues its commitment to accuracy and quality. Every methodology is reviewed and tested to assure the highest data integrity.

If you would like more information about our products and services, please call:

East Coast:
1100 N. Glebe Rd.
Arlington, VA 22201
(800) 292-2224
Fax: (703) 243-6272

West Coast:
3252 Holiday Ct.
LaJolla, CA 92037
(800) 394-3690
Fax: (858) 677-5420

# CACI MARKETING SYSTEMS UPDATE METHODOLOGY: 2000-2005

The U.S. population continues to grow by about one percent annually to over 275 million in 2000. Moderate national growth is a composite that incorporates slow change in the Northeast and Midwest and high growth in the West and South, a decline in the number of young adults aged 20 to 34 years old and a surge in the middle (40-54 years) and oldest (85+ years) ages, low fertility and high rates of immigration. National averages disguise the variation in population change evident regionally and locally.

The fastest growing states are in the West: Nevada leads with an average annual rate of 4.6 percent from 1990 through 2000, followed by Arizona with 2.9 percent, and Idaho, Utah and Colorado at 2.3 percent. The traditionally slower pace of change in the Northeast continues, with population growth less than one percent for most states and a slight decline in population for Rhode Island.

According to the U.S. Bureau of the Census Press Briefing on September 30, 1999, households in the United States experienced an annual increase in their income for the fourth straight year. Nationally, household income is forecast to increase from a median of $30,056 in 1990 to $49,127 in 2005.

CACI Marketing Systems presents 2000/2005 forecasts of population and income that include age by sex, race by Hispanic origin, households and families, housing by occupancy and tenure and home value, income, including household and family income distributions, household income by age of householder, and per capita income. Updates of household income are also extended to provide after-tax (disposable) income and a measure of household wealth, net worth.[1]

CACI's forecasts are revised annually to incorporate the latest trends and their impact on local populations. Changes in the forecasts are a result of annual fluctuations in trends and improvements in the techniques for measuring those trends. Time series' analysis is an integral part of forecasting; however, changes in the historic databases and improvements in modeling preclude comparison to updates from previous years.

For example, 2000 population updates reflect not only population change through 1999, but also revisions in the time series of county population estimates, 1991-98.[2] CACI also refined its forecast methodology in 2000 to track changes at the block group level. The combined impact of revised data sources and improved techniques distinguishes the 2000/2005 forecasts from previous years.

Forecasts are developed from the 1990 census base. Changes in the population since 1990 are captured from a variety of data sources and applied to provide the most accurate update for the current year, 2000. This change is then extrapolated five years, to 2005. The 2000 update represents current events; the 2005 forecast illustrates the effects of current events if continued for the next five years. Following is a description of CACI's forecast methodology.

## DEMOGRAPHIC UPDATE METHODOLOGY

Forecasts are prepared initially for counties and block groups (BGs). From the county database, forecasts are aggregated to metropolitan areas, Nielsen's Designated Market Areas (DMAs), states or higher levels. From the block group database, forecasts can be retrieved for census tracts, places, ZIP Codes, or any user-defined site, circle, or polygon.

### *Total Population: Counties*

The change in total population is a function of the changes in household population and the population in group quarters, which are subject to different trends. The addition of a prison, for example, produces a sudden increase in the group quarters population that is unlikely to yield an attendant change in the household population—or the projected population growth of a county. A military base closing effects an immediate decrease in the household population with the reduction not only of military personnel, but also their families and civilian personnel; however, this drop is also unlikely to continue.

The disparity of trends in household versus group quarters population is accommodated by separate projections. The group quarters population is estimated for the current year, 2000, from combined sources. Beginning with the Census Bureau's estimates of group quarters at the county level, CACI also adds local data sources to uncover more recent changes in group quarters.

Forecasting change in the size and distribution of the household population begins at the county level with the latest estimates, 1991-1999, and extensive analysis. Testing after the 1990 census covered the rules of thumb on projection accuracy such as the effects of population size, rate of change, and length of projection interval.[3] County testing also featured another rule of thumb—the unlikely continuation of extreme rates of change—and emphasized the importance of assumptions regarding the likely course of future change. One way or another, the population at a future date, including July 1, 2000, must be extrapolated from the past. The future may

1 All forecasts are mid-year, for July 1 of the forecast year.

2 Annual estimate series for states and counties are produced by the Census Bureau and States through the Federal-State Cooperative Program for Population Estimates. County estimates for 1999 were released March, 2000.

3 A copy of CACI's test results of 1990 forecasts against the 1990 Census, *Evaluating Population Projections*, is available upon request.

be projected simply as an illustration of a past trend, or base line such as population change from 1980 to 1990. Or, the most likely course of change may be plotted from a review of the past.

Selection of an appropriate trend line for a county depends upon population size, past change, and the projection date, one, five or ten years in the future. For example, projections for smaller counties (less than 5,000) or counties that are experiencing a loss of population, benefit from a longer trend line, characteristic of several years of change rather than one or two years. More recent data provide more accurate forecasts for areas that are growing rapidly, at least in the short run.[4]

Choice of the best projection technique is also guided by testing. Past studies have not shown more complex methods to be more accurate; however, the measure of population change, whether total or by component, can make a difference in projection accuracy. As noted earlier, rapid rates of change, positive or negative, do not continue indefinitely. In fact, small areas like counties can experience sharp annual fluctuations in rates of change. More conservative measures, such as a linear "model", tend to be more accurate for the extremes than techniques that can exaggerate the amount of change, like exponential extrapolation.

To calculate 2000 and 2005 county forecasts, CACI applies test results to the data from the Bureau of the Census' county population estimates, 1991-1999.[4] State population totals are not derived independently. County populations are summed to represent state forecasts. Controlling county projections to state totals was a common practice, derived from the belief that projection accuracy for smaller areas could be improved by controlling the totals to independently calculated totals for parent areas. Recent testing disproved the accuracy of this assumption for counties and states. CACI's 1999 updates differed from the Census Bureau's 1999 estimates by less than one percent at the county level and 0.1 percent at the state level.

### *Total Population: Block Groups*

Forecasts of subcounty population trends are built primarily from an analysis of recent (1990-99) change and at the block group level. Current trends are measured from local estimates and time series analysis of the changes in residential delivery statistics from the U.S. Postal Service.

To capture recent (1990-1999) trends, CACI has incorporated a variety of data sources: special censuses, subcounty estimates of change from the Census Bureau's latest (1998) estimates for places and MCDs, local sources of information about change, where applicable, and surveys of residential address changes through 1999. The U.S. Postal Service publishes and sells counts of residential deliveries for every postal carrier route. Post office delivery counts are not the same as housing units in a carrier route, especially in rural areas. Sparsely populated areas tend to have post office box ZIPs because there are few rural addressing systems and little comparability to urban, street delivery. However, a time series analysis of postal carrier routes and the corresponding delivery statistics provides a useful estimate of local change—from the development of a new housing subdivision to the demolition of an old housing complex.

The first step in calculating local demographic change is the derivation of correspondence files. The correspondence between 1990 census statistical areas and postal carrier routes is developed using databases from Geographic Data Technology and R. L. Polk—updated annually. The correspondence between block groups and places is developed from the 1990 census data at the block level. Demographic analysis of population and housing among small areas complements the geographic data. The combined geodemographic database treats the distribution of the population as continuous, not discrete or unique to a statistical area. This combination also clarifies the relationship between 1980 and 1990 geography and provides a consistent 1980 database in 1990 geography.

The comprehensive analysis of 1980-1990 change also addressed the best techniques for capturing demographic trends for small areas. Analysis was conducted in both 1980 and 1990 geography to study not only current population change, but also its antecedents. Reaching back to the 1970s, the study revealed a pattern of change in subcounty areas that was remarkably similar to counties and larger areas.

The rules of thumb on projection accuracy apply to block groups, too. Population size and rate of change show similar effects. The probability of extremes in population change, loss or growth, is also unlikely to continue among block groups. From the 1970s to the 1980s, for example, rapid change was likely to shift to a more moderate pace in three out of four tracts/CSDs. By extension, more recent data also improve forecast accuracy at the BG level—especially among growing areas.

Testing also identifies the best techniques for extrapolating population change for small areas. Like counties, forecasts for block groups improve when conservative measures of extreme trends are used instead of techniques that can exaggerate the amount of change, like exponential extrapolation. Specific to the block groups, however, is the stabilizing influence of controlling projections to independent totals for larger areas. Projection accuracy improves with use of a technique that relates local change to county change.

4 Lynn Wombold, 1992, *The Long and Short of Population Forecasting: A Test of County Populations against the 1990 Census*, paper presented at the 1992 Annual Meeting of the Population Association of America.

5 Annual, postcensal estimate series for states and counties are produced jointly by the Census Bureau and States through the Federal State Cooperative Program for Population Estimates.

The best techniques are also derived from a combination of models. An average of local data is used for most block groups to estimate current population change. Averages reduce overall error, bias, and the occurrence of outliers, extremely high or very low projections. Discrepant trends are checked against local sources. The group quarters population is tracked independently from the 1990 census to 2000 by locating the sites of new institutions or group quarters by block groups. Finally, totals for block groups are controlled to the county projections.

***Population Characteristics***

The population by age and sex is projected via a cohort survival model that calculates the components of population change separately, by age and sex. Applying survival rates specific to the population characteristics of the block groups carries the 1990 population for each block group forward. Changes in the population by age/sex diverge at the BG level. For example, an area that is losing population can age more rapidly with the loss of population in prime migrant ages, 20-35 years—unless there is a college nearby. An influx of college students can offset the loss of youthful outmigrants. To capture these variations, CACI's model is keyed to the size and characteristics of the population. This stratification identifies several different patterns of change by age and sex that are applied in the cohort survival model. Births are projected from area-specific, child-woman ratios. Migration is computed as a residual, the difference between the survived population and independent projections of total BG populations.

Forecasts of the population by age-sex at the block group level are controlled to independent forecasts by county and state.

Adjustments for age misreporting in the 1990 census are incorporated primarily through census survival rates in place of life table survival rates. Census survival rates measure mortality and the differences between the 1980 and 1990 censuses in coverage and in reporting errors. Usually, these rates are not computed for the population born during the decade. Birth cohorts were adjusted for age misreporting separately, using data from the 1990 Census Block Group file, STP171.

Forecasts by race and Hispanic origin are combined in the 2000/2005 updates. Using 1998 estimates produced by the Census Bureau, CACI estimates race by Hispanic origin at the county level first.[6] Local trends in the distribution of the population by race and Hispanic origin are incorporated in the model. The Census Bureau's 1990-98 estimates reveal recent change, although some adjustment is necessary to adapt the Census Bureau's estimates, which are consistent with the classification of race by the Office of Management and Budget, to four of the summary races reported in the 1990 census data. County-level analysis is then merged with estimates from the Census Bureau's March 1999 Current Population Survey (CPS). Forecasts by BG combine local changes in the distributions by race and projected change for counties. Block group distributions are controlled finally to county projections. Data are reported by Hispanic origin for five race groups that are consistent with 1990 census tabulations.

***Households***

Analysis of the composition of households is predicated upon local patterns of change, which are controlled to the more constant trends for states and counties. Nationally, household change has stabilized in the 1990s. The dramatic shifts in size and distribution in the 1970s and 1980s were created by the Baby Boom as they entered their twenties and formed households. Fertility rates declined with fewer births and delayed childbearing. Divorce rates increased. Single-person and single-parent households expanded. Average household size dropped. As a result, households increased more rapidly than the population, and families, especially the traditional married-couple family, decreased proportionately. But the pace has slackened as the Baby Boom, and the rest of the population, age. State changes in household characteristics estimated by the Census Bureau, combined with regional changes in households and families from the March 1999 CPS, show that the long-term decline in average household size continues, but at a much slower pace. The household formation stage of the Baby Boom is over: Few states show any growth in households among 15 to 34 year olds. [7]

Local change, however, is affected more by the singular composition of the population, and trends often vary from the national norm. Few block groups represent a cross-section of U.S. households. In areas that gained population from immigration in the 1980s, the trend in average household size actually reversed and increased. To distinguish local variation, CACI's model is keyed to the characteristics of households at the block group level. This stratification identifies several different patterns of change by household type that are applied to forecast trends in the characteristics of households—both family composition and tenure. Local change is emphasized in the 2000/2005 forecasts of households, families, and tenure for counties and block groups. National trends are monitored and applied as controls.

***Housing***

CACI housing updates include housing units, tenure and home value. Housing units are updated from the 1990 census base by recorded changes in the housing inventory, building permits and residential demolitions. Estimates of housing change for permit-issuing places are extended to block groups from the time series of USPS residential counts. Vacant units

[6] U.S. Bureau of the Census, Estimates of the Population of Counties by Race/Hispanic Origin: 1990-1998, released September, 1999.

[7] U.S. Bureau of the Census, Estimates of Housing Units, Households, Households by Age of Householder, and Persons Per Household of States: Annual Time Series July 1, 1991 to July 1, 1998, revised December 8, 1999.

**Table 1.**
**Sources of Differences between Bureau of Economic Analysis and Census Bureau Income Estimates**

| | **BEA** | **Census Bureau** |
|---|---|---|
| 1. Income definition | Personal income | Money income |
| 2. Collection method | Administrative records | Survey of households |
| 3. Place of tabulation | Business/ tax address with a residence adjustment | Residential address |

are calculated as a residual, the difference between total housing units and households (occupied housing units).

Tenure, owner versus renter occupancy, is modeled from analysis of local occupancy rates, housing development and state changes in tenure from the March 1999 CPS. Again, CACI's model is keyed to the characteristics of households at the block group level and then controlled to independent forecasts of change in tenure for states. Owner occupancy increased in the U.S. from 64 percent in 1990 to 67.5 percent in 2000. Locally, the rates vary more, from 91 percent in affluent neighborhoods to 21 percent in economically distressed areas. The changes in owner versus renter occupancy are projected independently and then controlled to the total number of occupied units forecast for the block groups. Finally, tenure by block group is controlled to independent state estimates of change in tenure.

Home value is updated for *specified* owner-occupied housing units: single-family homes excluding mobile homes, houses on ten acres or more and houses with a business or medical office. Data collected in the 1990 Census of Population and Housing represent the homeowner's estimate of current value. Without another census of homeowners, an alternative estimate of market value must be used. CACI employs the median price of recently sold homes to represent the change in home value since 1990. The National Association of Realtors compiles data from sales of single-family homes.

Change in median home value among block groups is derived from the trends assessed for larger markets. The distribution of home value is then modeled to reflect current change in median existing home sales price. From 1990 to 2000, home value increased by over 2.5 percent annually—slightly less than the rate of inflation—and down from the growth of 5.3 percent annually in the 1980s. The most rapid increase in home value was evident in Western states with rapid population growth, like Utah, Colorado, Oregon and Idaho and Midwestern states with below average home values in 1990, like Minnesota, Wisconsin and Iowa. Home value declined slightly in states with some of the highest home values in 1990, like Hawaii and Connecticut. Five-year forecasts reflect the assumption that trends from 1990 through 2000 will continue.

## INCOME UPDATE METHODOLOGY

### *Data Sources*

To estimate household income, CACI uses several governmental and independent sources, including: (i) the Bureau of Economic Analysis (BEA), U.S. Department of Commerce; (ii) the National Planning Association Data Service (NPA Data Service), Washington D.C.; (iii) the U.S. Bureau of the Census' Current Population Survey (CPS) and State and County Income Estimates; and (iv) the 1980 and 1990 Censuses of Population and Housing.

Every year, BEA releases new personal income data for every county in the U.S. These data are the best source of intercensal income estimates. NPA Data Service updates BEA's data to the current year and forecasts income for counties with an econometric model. The model incorporates conditions in local labor markets, including employment by type and by industry, earnings by industry, and the components of personal income.

CACI's projection base is the income reported in the 1990 Census. Technically, 1990 income data represent income in 1989 because the Census Bureau tabulates income received in the "last year" before the census. The income that is reported in the 1990 census is expressed in 1989 dollars. Similarly, CACI's 2000 income updates represent income received in 1999, expressed in 1999 dollars. Projections for 2005 are also in current (2004) dollars, assuming an annual three-percent rate of inflation.

Income forecasts are not comparable to previous years. First, the forecasts are made at the block group level. Second, the distribution of income is expanded to display all of the income intervals that were originally reported in 1990 Census tabulations and extended to estimate households earning up to $500,000 and over.

[8] Lois Fonseca and Jeff Tayman, 1989, *Postcensal Estimates of Household Income Distributions*, Demography 26:149-159.
[9] U.S. Bureau of the Census, 1989, 1993, 1995, 1996 State and County Income estimates, released February, 2000. Bureau of Economic Analysis, 1994 to Q3 1999 State Personal Income estimates, released January 26, 2000.

### *Income Methods*

CACI first estimates county income distributions and then the distributions for block groups. The 2000 county income forecasts are the result of a three-step process. The first step applies the lognormal probability distribution to represent the distribution of income within each county. This technique is a modification of the method presented by Fonseca and Tayman.[8] The model is calibrated against the 1990 census income distribution.

The second step calculates rates of change in per capita personal income and in median household income. Using NPA Data Service's forecasts of personal income, CACI derives a rate of change for every county in the U.S. These rates are adjusted by the historical relationship between change in per capita personal income and change in median household income and then applied to generate a preliminary distribution of income.

The third and final step combines results to derive the predicted distributions. Results are compared to the income reported from the March 1999 Current Population Survey and recently released estimates of median household income by state and county.[9] The Census Bureau's data are used to check and adjust the income estimates, producing the income distributions for every county. CPS income data ensure the inclusion of current trends in labor markets, industry, and the economy.

To estimate the income distributions for block groups, CACI employs the rates-of-change approach, as for the counties. The lognormal probability model is not used for BGs since this method is more appropriate for geographic areas with more households or families. The resulting BG estimates are adjusted via iterative proportional fitting to match the county income distributions. The Pareto function is employed to extend the upper interval of the income distribution from $150,000 to $500,000.

### *Differences from Other Sources of Income Data*

CACI uses income data from the Bureau of Economic Analysis and the Census Bureau. There are, however, substantial differences between BEA and Census Bureau estimates of income. Care should be taken when comparing CACI estimates with other data sources, since many income estimates are based solely on BEA data. Table 1 summarizes the differences:

Different definitions and methods of data collection generate different counts and measures of income. BEA calculates **personal income** as part of its mission to produce national income accounting estimates such as the gross national product (GNP). The Census Bureau collects **money income** statistics to satisfy its objective to enumerate and describe the population of the United States.

**Personal income** includes wages and salaries, proprietors' income, dividends, interest, rent, and transfer payments. Personal income excludes personal contributions to social insurance, and includes a "residence adjustment" to adjust income that is not earned in the county of residence.

**Money income** includes the incomes covered by BEA's personal income, but contributions to social insurance are not subtracted, and no residence adjustment is needed since the data are collected from the household directly. To learn more about the techniques employed by each data source, consult the Census Bureau's glossary and BEA's publication, *Local Area Personal Income*. CACI uses the Census Bureau's definition of household income, which enables direct comparison of income updates and decennial census data. The methods employed by CACI are designed to adjust the BEA data to match, as closely as possible, the Census Bureau's estimates of income.

### *Disposable Income*

Disposable income represents an estimate of a household's purchasing power or, simply, after-tax income. The proportion of household income left after taxes is estimated from special studies conducted by the Census Bureau to simulate household taxes.[10] Four types of taxes are deducted: Federal individual income taxes, State individual income taxes, FICA (Social Security) and Federal retirement payroll taxes, and property taxes for owner-occupied housing. Capital gains/losses are excluded from CACI's estimates.

Using the Current Population Survey with a sample size of about 65,000 households, CACI applies the proportions of after-tax income to income intervals that are cross-tabulated by age of householder for each state. State-specific proportions account for the variation in taxes by state. The proportions, or multipliers, are then applied to CACI's age by income forecasts for block groups and counties to calculate disposable income.

### *Net Worth*

Net worth represents total household wealth less any debts (unsecured or secured by assets). Assets include real estate (own home or rental property), own business, IRAs and Keogh accounts, stocks, mutual funds, and motor vehicles. Examples of secured debt include home mortgages and vehicle loans, unsecured debt, credit card and other bills or certain bank loans. Not included in net worth are equity in pension plans and the value of home furnishings. Data on household wealth are collected from the Census Bureau's Survey of Income and Program Participation (SIPP) from a sample of about 21,000 households.[11] CACI first obtains the relationship of net worth to household income by age and race of householder. Estimates are differentiated by tenure since home ownership is a major factor in household net worth.

10 For a more complete discussion of the Census Bureau's estimates of household taxes, please see Current Population Reports, Series P-60, Number 182RD, *Measuring the Effect of Benefits and Taxes on Income and Poverty: 1979-1991*, U.S. Government Printing Office, Washington, DC, 1992.

11 A discussion of household wealth is available from the Census Bureau, Current Population Reports, Series P-60, Number 179, *Income, Poverty, and Wealth in the United States: A Chartbook*, U.S. Government Printing Office, 1992.

The 1990 income distribution has been extended to estimate net worth. The Pareto function is employed to extend the upper interval of the income distribution from $150,000 to $500,000. This estimate enables the calculation of net worth for wealthy households.

***Use of Projections***

Projections are necessarily based upon past events. The past and the present are known; the future must be extrapolated from this knowledge base. While projections represent the unknown, they are not uninformed. Guidelines to the development of projections also inform the use of those projections:

1. The recent past provides a reasonable clue to the course of future events, especially if that information is tempered with a historical perspective.

2. A stable rate of growth is easier to anticipate than rapid growth or decline.

3. The risk inherent in projections is inversely related to the size of an area: the smaller the area, the greater the risk.

4. The risk increases with the length of the projection interval. Any deviation of the projected trends from actual events is amplified over time.

5. Due to a maturing population and economy, growth is slowing in the United States. Rates of growth for 1990–2000 are likely to be smaller than 1980–1990 rates.

CACI revises its projections annually to draw upon the most recent estimates and projections of local trends. However, this data can be complemented with personal knowledge of an area to provide the qualitative, anecdotal detail that is not captured in a national database. It is incumbent upon the data user, also the producers, to incorporate as much information as possible when assessing local trends, especially areas that are subject to "boom-bust" cycles.

# SPENDING POTENTIAL INDEXES METHODOLOGY

*Spending potential data measure the likely expenditure for a product or service in a county, ZIP Code, or other trade area. CACI's database includes average expenditure per consumer household, total expenditure and a Spending Potential Index (SPI) for about 400 goods and services. The Sourcebook shows the SPIs for twenty key products/services. The SPI compares the average expenditure per consumer household for a specific product/service in the trade area with the average expenditure for that product/service nationally. The index is tabulated to represent a value of 100 as the average spending, a value of more than 100 as high spending, and a value of less than 100 as low spending, relative to the U.S. For example, an index of 120 estimates that spending in the trade area is likely to be 20 percent higher than the U.S. average; an index of 85, 15 percent lower.*

## Methodology

Data for CACI's consumer spending reports are calculated from the Bureau of Labor Statistics' Consumer Expenditure Surveys (CEX). CACI extracted demographic and economic data for households from the CEX Interview Surveys, 1993 and 1994, to construct a conditional probability model. The model links the spending of consumer units or households surveyed in the CEX to all households with similar socioeconomic characteristics. Spending patterns are further differentiated by geography—region of the U.S., urban v. rural, and metropolitan v. nonmetropolitan—and updated to current prices using the annual Consumer Price Index. Expenditures represent annual averages or total expenditures.

## Computation of a Spending Potential Index

For any trade area, the expenditure per consumer household for a particular product or service can be computed by linking the expenditure data to the demographic characteristics of the population. The SPI is defined as the ratio of the local average to the U.S. average expenditure. The following equation shows how the index is derived:

$$\text{SPI} = \frac{\text{Local Average Expenditure}}{\text{U.S. Average Expenditure}} \times 100$$

## How High is High?

The SPI exhibits different ranges of values for different products/services. In general, products pertaining to specific lifestyles or income levels will show a wider range of SPI values than products or services which are purchased by everybody.

The SPI has an average value of 100, but the distribution of SPIs among counties varies by product. Below is a table showing the upper range of values for select SPIs by county. This is a rough guide for determining "how high is high":

**Medians and Percentiles of Spending Potential Indexes: All U.S. Counties**

| | | Somewhat High | Very High | Extremely High |
|---|---|---|---|---|
| | | ***Percentiles*** | | |
| | ***Median*** | ***75th*** | ***90th*** | ***95th*** |
| **Financial Services:** | | | | |
| Auto Loan | 97 | 99 | 100 | 102 |
| Home Loan | 76 | 87 | 98 | 105 |
| Investments | 82 | 91 | 98 | 103 |
| Retirement Plans | 83 | 89 | 97 | 103 |
| **The Home:** | | | | |
| ***Home Improvements*** | | | | |
| Home Repair | 94 | 98 | 101 | 102 |
| Lawn & Garden | 92 | 95 | 100 | 103 |
| Remodeling | 109 | 112 | 114 | 115 |
| ***Furnishings*** | | | | |
| Appliances | 96 | 98 | 100 | 102 |
| Electronics | 93 | 95 | 99 | 103 |
| Furniture | 83 | 91 | 99 | 105 |
| **Entertainment:** | | | | |
| Restaurants | 85 | 92 | 101 | 107 |
| Sporting Goods | 95 | 97 | 100 | 102 |
| Theater & Concerts | 86 | 92 | 98 | 102 |
| Toys & Hobbies | 96 | 99 | 101 | 103 |
| Travel | 78 | 85 | 92 | 97 |
| Video Rental | 98 | 100 | 101 | 102 |
| **Personal:** | | | | |
| Apparel | 85 | 91 | 99 | 105 |
| Auto Aftermarket | 91 | 94 | 100 | 104 |
| Health Insurance | 101 | 103 | 105 | 106 |
| Pets & Supplies | 97 | 100 | 102 | 103 |

## Variable Definitions

**Following are the definitions of the 2000 Sourcebook Spending Potential Indexes:**

### *Financial Services*

**Auto Loan**
Lease payments, finance charges, and principal paid for cars, trucks and vans (new and used).

**Home Loan**
Interest on mortgage and home equity loans, principal reduction of mortgage and home equity loans, and special or lump-sum mortgage and home equity payments.

**Investments**
Purchase price of stocks, bonds, or mutual funds (including broker fees).

**Retirement Plans**
Deductions for government retirement, railroad retirement, private pensions, and self-employment retirement plan.

### *The Home*

*Home Improvements*

**Home Repair**
Contractor labor and material costs associated with painting or papering, plumbing or water heating installation or repair, heating, air conditioning or electrical work, roofing and gutters, and other repair and maintenance work, materials and supplies for repairing outdoor patios, walks, fences, driveways or permanent swimming pools, plastering or paneling, roofing and gutters, siding and installation, repair or replacement of window panes, screens, storm doors, awnings, etc., replacement or repair of appliances, repair or replacement of hard-surfaced flooring, replacement of installed wall-to-wall carpeting, materials and equipment for painting and wallpapering, and materials and supplies for plumbing, water heating installation and repairs, electrical work, heating and air conditioning jobs, hard-surfaced flooring.

**Lawn & Garden**
Gardening and lawn care services, lawn mowing equipment and other yard machinery, power and non-power tools, rental and repair of lawn equipment and tools, fresh flowers, potted plants, and other landscaping supplies.

**Remodeling**
Improvement-type upkeep and other managerial services, contractors, labor and material costs, cost of supplies rented for additions, maintenance and repairs, new construction, appliances provided by contractor for additions, alterations and new constructions, materials and supplies purchased for insulation, dwellings under construction, additions, finishing, remodeling, landscaping, building outdoor patios, walks, fences or other enclosures, driveways, or permanent swimming pools, capital improvements, and installed or noninstalled wall-to-wall carpeting.

*Furnishings*

**Appliances**
Purchase and installation of refrigerators, home freezers, clothes washers and dryers, stoves and ovens, microwave ovens, portable dishwashers, and other small electrical kitchen appliances.

**Electronics**
Radios, phonographs, tape recorders and players, sound components and component systems, accessories and other sound equipment. Records, tapes, CDs (including those purchased from club), and needles. Televisions (including black and white, color, and large screen color TV projection equipment), VCRs, video disc players and video cameras, video cassettes, tapes, discs, and video game hardware and software. Computers, computer hardware, software and accessories for non-business use.

**Furniture**
Mattresses and springs, other bedroom furniture, sofas, living room chairs and tables, kitchen and dining room furniture, modular wall units, shelves, cabinets, other living/family room furniture, and office furniture for home use.

### *Entertainment*

**Restaurants**
Dining out at restaurants (including alcoholic beverages).

**Sporting Goods**
Ping-pong, pool tables, other similar items, general sports equipment, health and exercise equipment, bicycles, camping equipment, hunting and fishing equipment, winter sports equipment, water sports and other miscellaneous equipment.

**Theater/Concerts**
Entertainment admission fees including movies, theater, concert, opera, other musical series, and season tickets.

**Toys & Hobbies**
Toys, games, hobbies, tricycles, and battery powered riders.

**Travel**
Airline fares, lodging away from home, and auto and truck rental (out-of-town trips).

**Video Rental**
Rental of video cassettes, tapes, and discs.

## *Personal*

**Apparel**
Men's suits, sport coats, coats and jackets, underwear, socks, nightwear, sweaters and vests, activewear, shirts, pants, shorts, and accessories. Women's coats and jackets, dresses, sport coats and tailored jackets, sweaters and vests, shirts and blouses, skirts and culottes, pants, shorts, activewear, nightwear, undergarments, hosiery, suits, and accessories. Boys' and girls' coats and jackets, sweaters, shirts, underwear, nightwear, socks and hosiery, suits, dresses and skirts, shirts and blouses, sport coats, vests, pants, shorts and short sets, activewear, uniforms, and accessories. Infants' coats, rompers, dresses, sweaters, underwear (including diapers), sleepwear, and accessories. Men's, women's, boy's and girl's footwear. Watches and jewelry.

**Auto Aftermarket**
Motor oil, motor tune-up, lubrication and oil changes, tires (new, used, or recapped), shock absorber replacement, clutch and transmission repair, motor repair and replacement, and brake work (including brake adjustment).

**Health Insurance**
Commercial health insurance, Blue Cross or Blue Shield, health maintenance plans, Medicare payments, commercial Medicare supplements, dental insurance, and other health insurance.

**Pets & Supplies**
Pets, pet supplies, and medicine for pets.

# BUSINESS DATA NOTE

CACI's business data are extracted from a comprehensive list of businesses licensed from *Info*USA. The *Info*USA business list contains data on about ten million U.S. businesses including name and location, franchise code, Standard Industrial Classification (SIC) code, number of employees and sales volume.

**Data Sources**

*Info*USA collects and maintains its business database by referencing several sources, including directory listings (yellow pages and business white pages), annual reports, 10K's and SEC information, federal, state, and municipal government data, business magazines, newsletters and newspapers, and U.S. Postal Service information. *Info*USA conducts telephone verification with each business annually to ensure accurate and complete information.

CACI provides reports and file extracts from *Info*-USA database that include the number of businesses by SIC code and employment size or sales volume, total employment, and total sales, where available. Industry classifications include the standard two- and four-digit SIC codes, *Info*USA proprietary six-digit industry codes plus a special industry code for select SICs that provides more detailed information, such as the number of rooms in hotels/motels or the number of beds in hospitals and nursing homes. Sales data are reported for business locations.

The Business Data Section shows the total number of companies and employees by county for all industries. Also shown is the top industry, determined by total employment for each county. Industries are represented by two-digit SIC codes. A complete list of the two-digit codes for the Standard Industrial Classification (SIC) system is included in Appendix VI.

**Business Locations**

*Info*USA compiles an address list of businesses from its sources and telephone verification. The addresses are then geocoded to assign a latitude/longitude coordinate to the business site and to append a census geographic code. Most businesses are coded at the address level and assigned to a census block group. Of course, the quality of the local address system varies: address matching is more likely in an urban area with street-level address systems than in rural areas. Overall, 82 percent of the businesses are coded at the address level; 84 percent are assigned to a census block group. If a business cannot be assigned to a block group, it is assigned to a census tract or county.

# EXPLANATION OF VARIABLES*

## Age
Age is reported for five-year age groups and select summary groups such as 18 years/over. CACI projections for 2000.

### *Median Age*
Median age is calculated from the distribution of age by five-year groups. 1990 census and CACI projections for 2000. (See also Median)

## Average Disposable Income
See Disposable Income.

## Average Household Size
See Household.

## County
Counties are the primary political and administrative subdivisions of a state and are identified by a two-digit state FIPS code and a three-digit county FIPS code. (See also FIPS Code)

## DMA
A Designated Market Area is a television market defined by Nielsen Media Research. DMAs are revised annually. Current definitions are 1999-2000 series.

## Disposable Income
Disposable income represents an estimate of a household's purchasing power or, simply, after-tax income. The proportion of household income left after taxes is estimated from special studies conducted by the Census Bureau to simulate household taxes. Four types of taxes are deducted: Federal individual income taxes, State individual income taxes, FICA (Social Security) and Federal retirement payroll taxes, and property taxes for owner-occupied housing. Capital gains/losses are excluded from CACI's estimates. CACI projections for 2000. (See also Income)

### *Average Disposable Income*
Average disposable income is calculated from the distribution of disposable income.

## Family
A household in which the householder and one or more persons in the household are related by birth, marriage, or adoption. The census tabulates only one family per household. 1990 census and CACI projections for 2000.

## FIPS Code
Federal Information Processing Standards for numeric codes used to identify states and counties.

## Hispanic Origin
Defined by self-identification, Hispanic origin refers to ethnicity, not race. Persons of Hispanic origin may be of any race. 1990 census and CACI projections for 2000.

## Household
A household is an occupied housing unit. Household type is identified by the presence of relatives and the number of persons: family households (with or without children) include married couples and other families—a male or female householder with no spouse present. Nonfamily households may be a group (2 to 9) of unrelated persons or a single person living along. (A unit with 10+ unrelated persons is classified as group quarters.) 1990 census and CACI projections for 2000 and 2005.

### *Average Household Size*
Average size is calculated by dividing the number of persons in households by the number of households.

## Householder
One person in each household is designated as the householder. In most cases, this is the person, or one of the persons, in whose name the home is owned, being bought, or rented. If no such person in the household exists, any adult household member 15 years old and over is designated as the householder.

## Household Income
See Income.

## Income
Income in 2000 and 2005 is a forecast based upon 1990 census income tabulations. Income amounts are expressed in current dollars, including an adjustment for inflation or cost-of-living increases. For a discussion of income projections, see Update Methodology. CACI projections for 2000 and 2005.

### *Household Income Base*
The sum of the household income distribution.

### *Median Household Income*
The value that divides the distribution of household income into two equal parts. Pareto interpolation is used if the median falls in any income intervals with a width of $5,000 or more, except for the lowest income interval. For income intervals with a width of $2,500 and the lowest interval, <$5,000, linear interpolation is used. If the median falls in the upper income interval, $500,000+, it is represented by the value $500,001.

### *Per Capita Income*
The average income for all persons, calculated from the aggregate income of persons 15 years and older.

### *Rank*
Counties are ranked on 2000 median household income within each state and nationally.

## Male/Female Ratio
The number of males divided by the number of females, multiplied by 100. CACI projections for 2000.

* Note: For further information about 1990 Census data, please see 1990 Census of Population and Housing, Summary Tape Files 1 and 3 Technical Documentation prepared by the Bureau of the Census.

## Median
A value that divides a distribution into two equal parts. A median is a positional measure that is unaffected by extremely high or low values in a distribution that can affect an average.

## MSA
The Metropolitan Statistical Areas in this edition represent June 30, 1999 metropolitan areas defined by the Office of Management and Budget. MSAs are represented by counties that meet specific criteria regarding population size, density and commuting sites. Generally, MSAs include a central city or urbanized area of 50,000 with a total area population of 100,000. MSAs are identified by four-digit FIPS codes that are independent of state/county codes since many MSAs cross state lines.

The Metropolitan Areas presented here include MSAs, PMSAs or Primary Metropolitan Statistical Areas, and NECMAs or New England County Metropolitan Areas. When a Metropolitan Area has a million or more residents, PMSAs may be delineated. NECMAs are the county equivalents of Metropolitan Areas in New England, which are actually defined by cities and towns.

## Per Capita Income
See Income.

## Population
The total number of residents of an area. Residence refers to the "usual place" where a person lives, which is not necessarily the legal residence. For example, college students are counted where they attend school. 1980 census (revised), 1990 census and CACI projections for 2000 and 2005.

## Race
Defined by self-identification, race detail from the 1990 Census includes 25 groups with the addition of ten more Asian or Pacific Islander groups in 1990. The race categories presented here are White, Black, and Asian or Pacific Islander. CACI forecasts race for White, Black, American Indian or Alaska Native, Asian or Pacific Islander and Other Races populations that are consistent with 1990 Census tabulations. 1990 Census and CACI projections for 2000.

## Rate, Annual Percent
Calculated as an average annual compound rate of change from 1990 to 2000 for population, households, and families. For example:

$$\text{Rate} = 100 \times [(P_{00} / P_{90})^{1/10.25} - 1]$$

Counties are ranked on the rate of population change, 1990-2000, within each state.

## Spending Potential Index
See Spending Potential Indexes Methodology.

## State
States are identified by a two-digit FIPS code. The District of Columbia is included as a state-equivalent area in CACI's database. (See also FIPS Code)

# SUMMARY MAPS

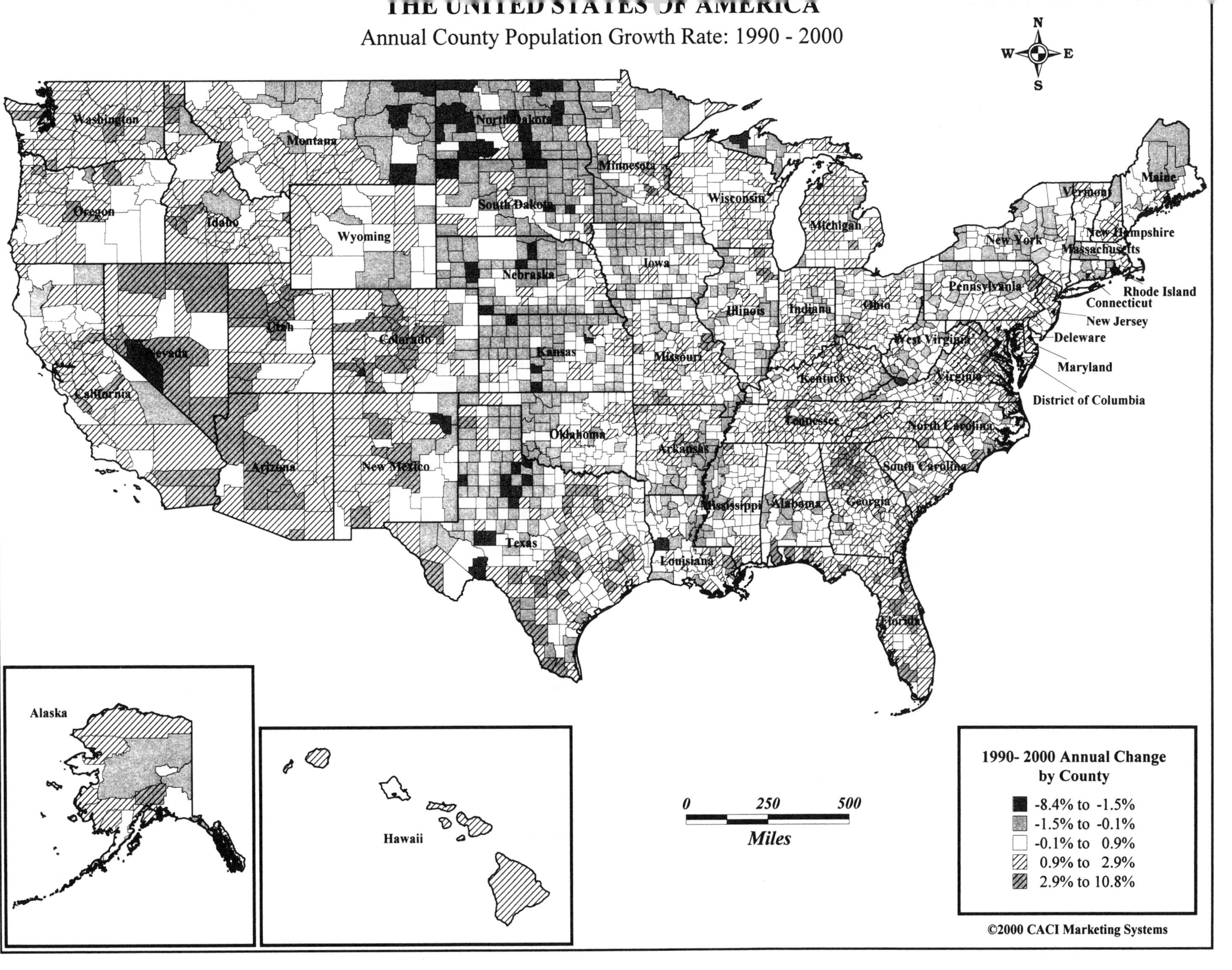
THE UNITED STATES OF AMERICA
Annual County Population Growth Rate: 1990 - 2000
N
W
E
S
Washington
Oregon
California
Idaho
Nevada
Montana
Wyoming
Utah
Arizona
Colorado
New Mexico
North Dakota
South Dakota
Nebraska
Kansas
Oklahoma
Texas
Minnesota
Iowa
Missouri
Arkansas
Louisiana
Wisconsin
Illinois
Michigan
Indiana
Ohio
Kentucky
Tennessee
Mississippi
Alabama
Georgia
Florida
South Carolina
North Carolina
Virginia
West Virginia
Pennsylvania
New York
Vermont
Maine
New Hampshire
Massachusetts
Rhode Island
Connecticut
New Jersey
Deleware
Maryland
District of Columbia
Alaska
Hawaii
0
250
500
Miles
1990- 2000 Annual Change by County
-8.4% to -1.5%
-1.5% to -0.1%
-0.1% to 0.9%
0.9% to 2.9%
2.9% to 10.8%
©2000 CACI Marketing Systems

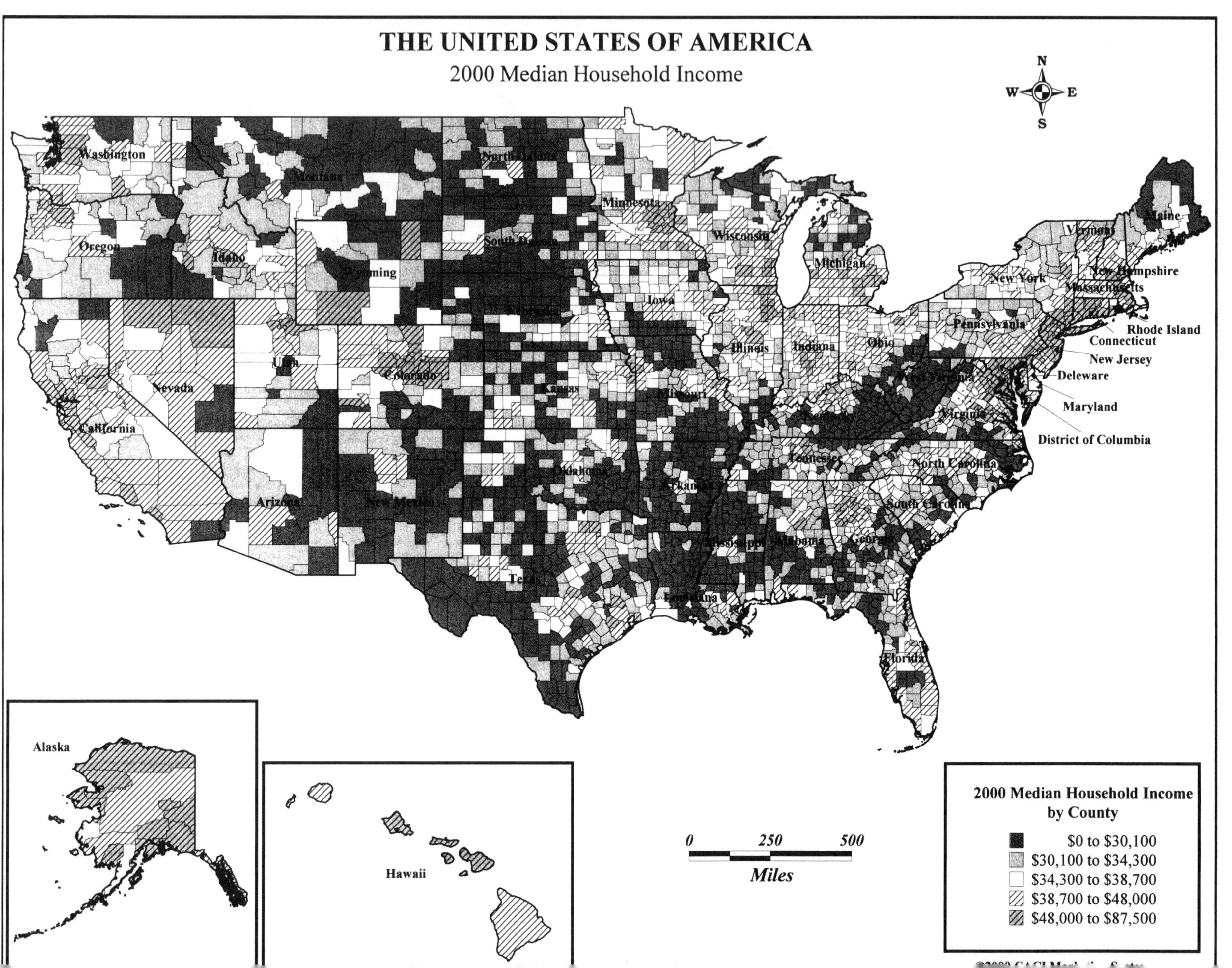
THE UNITED STATES OF AMERICA
2000 Median Household Income
N
W
E
S
Washington
Oregon
California
Idaho
Nevada
Montana
Wyoming
Utah
Arizona
Colorado
New Mexico
North Dakota
South Dakota
Kansas
Oklahoma
Texas
Minnesota
Iowa
Missouri
Arkansas
Louisiana
Wisconsin
Illinois
Mississippi
Michigan
Indiana
Tennessee
Alabama
Ohio
Kentucky
Georgia
Florida
West Virginia
Virginia
North Carolina
South Carolina
Pennsylvania
New York
Vermont
Maine
New Hampshire
Massachusetts
Rhode Island
Connecticut
New Jersey
Deleware
Maryland
District of Columbia
Alaska
Hawaii
0
250
500
Miles
2000 Median Household Income by County
$0 to $30,100
$30,100 to $34,300
$34,300 to $38,700
$38,700 to $48,000
$48,000 to $87,500

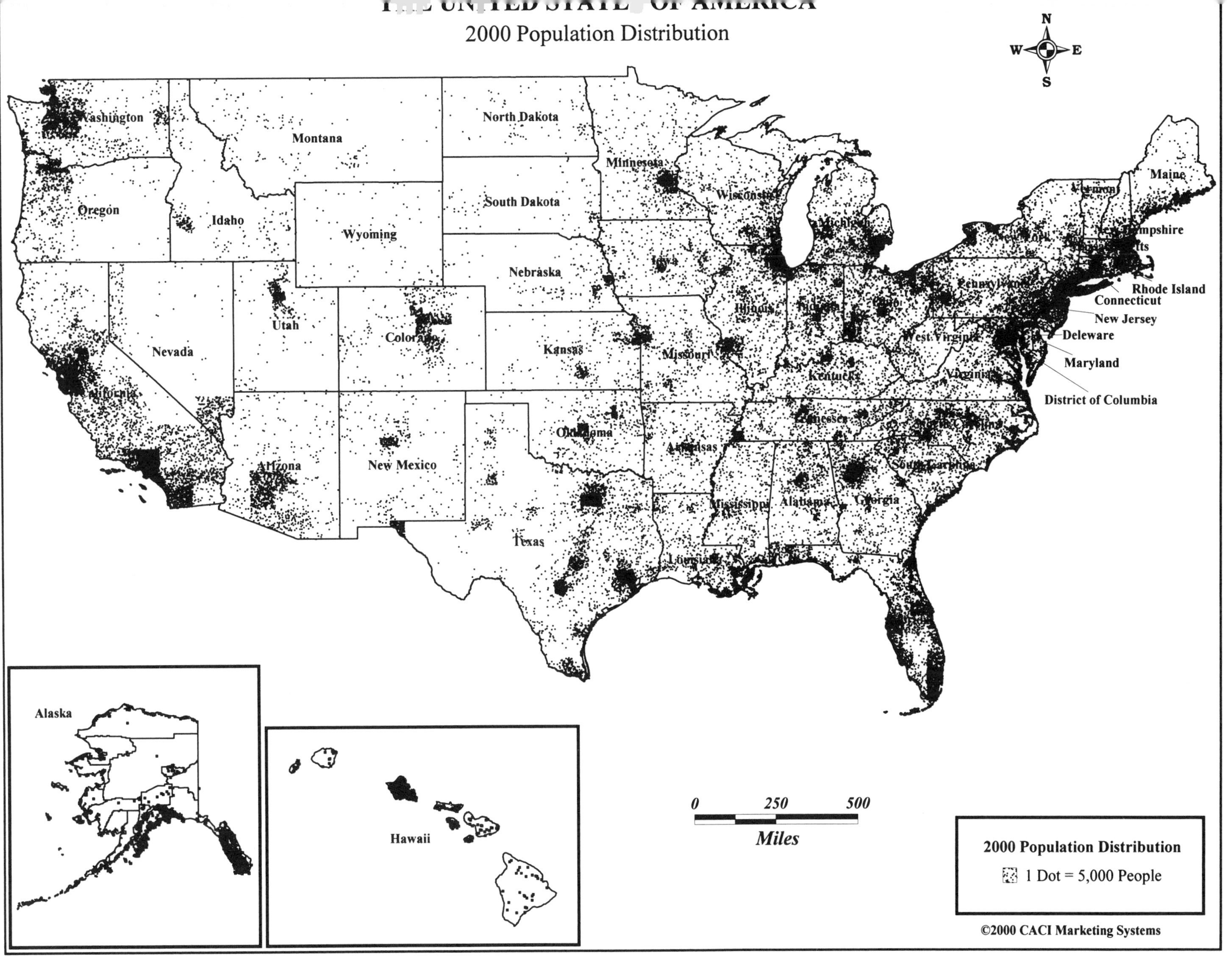
2000 Population Distribution
N
W
E
S
Washington
Oregon
Idaho
Montana
Wyoming
Nevada
Utah
Colorado
Arizona
New Mexico
North Dakota
South Dakota
Nebraska
Kansas
Oklahoma
Texas
Minnesota
Iowa
Missouri
Arkansas
Louisiana
Wisconsin
Illinois
Mississippi
Alabama
Georgia
Kentucky
Tennessee
Ohio
West Virginia
Virginia
Pennsylvania
Maine
Rhode Island
Connecticut
New Jersey
Deleware
Maryland
District of Columbia
Alaska
Hawaii
0
250
500
Miles
2000 Population Distribution
1 Dot = 5,000 People
©2000 CACI Marketing Systems

# COUNTY DEMOGRAPHIC DATA BY STATE

# POPULATION CHANGE

## A

| COUNTY | FIPS Code | MSA Code | DMA Code | POPULATION 1990 | POPULATION 2000 | POPULATION 2005 | 1990-2000 ANNUAL CHANGE % Rate | 1990-2000 ANNUAL CHANGE State Rank | RACE (%) White 1990 | White 2000 | Black 1990 | Black 2000 | Asian/Pacific 1990 | Asian/Pacific 2000 |
|---|---|---|---|---|---|---|---|---|---|---|---|---|---|---|
| AUTAUGA | 001 | 5240 | 698 | 34,222 | 44,099 | 48,897 | 2.5 | 5 | 79.3 | 77.7 | 20.0 | 21.5 | 0.4 | 0.4 |
| BALDWIN | 003 | 5160 | 686 | 98,280 | 139,432 | 157,411 | 3.5 | 2 | 86.0 | 85.2 | 12.9 | 13.6 | 0.2 | 0.3 |
| BARBOUR | 005 | 0000 | 522 | 25,417 | 26,657 | 26,254 | 0.5 | 34 | 55.5 | 52.8 | 44.0 | 46.7 | 0.2 | 0.2 |
| BIBB | 007 | 0000 | 630 | 16,576 | 20,091 | 22,506 | 1.9 | 7 | 78.7 | 77.2 | 21.0 | 22.5 | 0.1 | 0.1 |
| BLOUNT | 009 | 1000 | 630 | 39,248 | 48,759 | 54,851 | 2.1 | 6 | 97.8 | 97.4 | 1.3 | 1.5 | 0.1 | 0.1 |
| BULLOCK | 011 | 0000 | 698 | 11,042 | 11,356 | 11,423 | 0.3 | 39 | 27.5 | 26.0 | 72.3 | 73.8 | 0.1 | 0.1 |
| BUTLER | 013 | 0000 | 698 | 21,892 | 21,424 | 20,939 | -0.2 | 61 | 59.6 | 58.2 | 40.2 | 41.7 | 0.1 | 0.1 |
| CALHOUN | 015 | 0450 | 630 | 116,034 | 116,316 | 115,200 | 0.0 | 53 | 80.0 | 78.9 | 18.6 | 19.4 | 0.7 | 0.9 |
| CHAMBERS | 017 | 0000 | 522 | 36,876 | 36,315 | 35,379 | -0.1 | 57 | 63.9 | 62.0 | 35.9 | 37.8 | 0.0 | 0.0 |
| CHEROKEE | 019 | 0000 | 630 | 19,543 | 22,064 | 22,922 | 1.2 | 14 | 92.9 | 92.2 | 6.6 | 7.2 | 0.1 | 0.1 |
| CHILTON | 021 | 0000 | 630 | 32,458 | 38,267 | 41,578 | 1.6 | 10 | 88.3 | 87.2 | 11.3 | 12.3 | 0.1 | 0.1 |
| CHOCTAW | 023 | 0000 | 711 | 16,018 | 15,337 | 14,465 | -0.4 | 64 | 55.6 | 53.5 | 44.2 | 46.3 | 0.1 | 0.1 |
| CLARKE | 025 | 0000 | 686 | 27,240 | 28,982 | 29,975 | 0.6 | 25 | 57.0 | 55.5 | 42.7 | 44.2 | 0.1 | 0.2 |
| CLAY | 027 | 0000 | 630 | 13,252 | 14,118 | 14,609 | 0.6 | 25 | 83.3 | 82.1 | 16.3 | 17.6 | 0.1 | 0.1 |
| CLEBURNE | 029 | 0000 | 524 | 12,730 | 14,733 | 15,990 | 1.4 | 12 | 94.9 | 94.2 | 4.6 | 5.2 | 0.1 | 0.1 |
| COFFEE | 031 | 0000 | 606 | 40,240 | 42,132 | 42,116 | 0.4 | 36 | 81.3 | 79.9 | 17.2 | 18.3 | 0.8 | 0.9 |
| COLBERT | 033 | 2650 | 691 | 51,666 | 52,398 | 51,635 | 0.1 | 49 | 82.9 | 81.8 | 16.6 | 17.7 | 0.2 | 0.2 |
| CONECUH | 035 | 0000 | 686 | 14,054 | 13,607 | 13,018 | -0.3 | 62 | 57.4 | 56.0 | 42.2 | 43.6 | 0.1 | 0.1 |
| COOSA | 037 | 0000 | 698 | 11,063 | 11,776 | 12,069 | 0.6 | 25 | 65.5 | 63.7 | 34.2 | 36.0 | 0.0 | 0.0 |
| COVINGTON | 039 | 0000 | 698 | 36,478 | 37,662 | 38,082 | 0.3 | 39 | 86.5 | 85.7 | 13.1 | 13.9 | 0.1 | 0.2 |
| CRENSHAW | 041 | 0000 | 698 | 13,635 | 13,615 | 13,593 | 0.0 | 53 | 73.7 | 72.3 | 26.0 | 27.4 | 0.1 | 0.1 |
| CULLMAN | 043 | 0000 | 630 | 67,613 | 76,403 | 80,217 | 1.2 | 14 | 98.7 | 98.6 | 0.8 | 0.9 | 0.2 | 0.2 |
| DALE | 045 | 2180 | 606 | 49,633 | 49,126 | 49,076 | -0.1 | 57 | 79.3 | 77.9 | 17.8 | 18.4 | 1.5 | 1.8 |
| DALLAS | 047 | 0000 | 698 | 48,130 | 46,487 | 45,529 | -0.3 | 62 | 41.8 | 40.5 | 57.8 | 59.1 | 0.3 | 0.3 |
| DEKALB | 049 | 0000 | 691 | 54,651 | 59,510 | 62,291 | 0.8 | 19 | 96.9 | 96.9 | 1.9 | 2.1 | 0.1 | 0.2 |
| ELMORE | 051 | 5240 | 698 | 49,210 | 65,078 | 72,992 | 2.8 | 3 | 76.9 | 75.5 | 22.4 | 23.8 | 0.3 | 0.3 |
| ESCAMBIA | 053 | 0000 | 686 | 35,518 | 36,722 | 36,914 | 0.3 | 39 | 68.5 | 66.9 | 28.3 | 30.3 | 0.2 | 0.2 |
| ETOWAH | 055 | 2880 | 630 | 99,840 | 103,549 | 103,720 | 0.4 | 36 | 85.4 | 84.5 | 13.8 | 14.7 | 0.4 | 0.4 |
| FAYETTE | 057 | 0000 | 630 | 17,962 | 18,115 | 18,167 | 0.1 | 49 | 87.5 | 86.3 | 12.2 | 13.2 | 0.1 | 0.1 |
| FRANKLIN | 059 | 0000 | 691 | 27,814 | 29,803 | 30,247 | 0.7 | 22 | 95.1 | 94.6 | 4.5 | 5.0 | 0.1 | 0.2 |
| GENEVA | 061 | 0000 | 606 | 23,647 | 25,045 | 25,445 | 0.6 | 25 | 87.5 | 86.5 | 11.9 | 12.9 | 0.1 | 0.1 |
| GREENE | 063 | 0000 | 630 | 10,153 | 9,684 | 9,331 | -0.5 | 66 | 19.4 | 18.5 | 80.6 | 81.4 | 0.0 | 0.0 |
| HALE | 065 | 0000 | 630 | 15,498 | 17,033 | 17,845 | 0.9 | 18 | 40.4 | 38.7 | 59.5 | 61.1 | 0.1 | 0.1 |
| HENRY | 067 | 0000 | 606 | 15,374 | 15,839 | 16,039 | 0.3 | 39 | 64.5 | 62.5 | 35.1 | 37.1 | 0.0 | 0.0 |
| HOUSTON | 069 | 2180 | 606 | 81,331 | 86,596 | 89,036 | 0.6 | 25 | 75.6 | 74.0 | 23.3 | 24.7 | 0.6 | 0.7 |
| JACKSON | 071 | 0000 | 691 | 47,796 | 51,804 | 53,310 | 0.8 | 19 | 93.5 | 93.6 | 4.1 | 4.5 | 0.2 | 0.2 |
| JEFFERSON | 073 | 1000 | 630 | 651,525 | 655,820 | 647,940 | 0.1 | 49 | 64.2 | 62.2 | 35.1 | 37.0 | 0.5 | 0.6 |
| LAMAR | 075 | 0000 | 673 | 15,715 | 16,062 | 16,185 | 0.2 | 46 | 87.8 | 87.1 | 11.8 | 12.6 | 0.1 | 0.1 |
| LAUDERDALE | 077 | 2650 | 691 | 79,661 | 84,488 | 85,381 | 0.6 | 25 | 89.8 | 89.0 | 9.7 | 10.4 | 0.2 | 0.3 |
| LAWRENCE | 079 | 2030 | 691 | 31,513 | 34,061 | 35,417 | 0.8 | 19 | 77.9 | 78.8 | 15.2 | 16.8 | 0.1 | 0.1 |
| LEE | 081 | 0580 | 522 | 87,146 | 104,274 | 114,397 | 1.8 | 8 | 74.5 | 72.0 | 23.4 | 25.6 | 1.8 | 2.1 |
| LIMESTONE | 083 | 3440 | 691 | 54,135 | 63,945 | 68,418 | 1.6 | 10 | 86.2 | 84.8 | 13.2 | 14.5 | 0.3 | 0.3 |
| LOWNDES | 085 | 0000 | 698 | 12,658 | 13,088 | 13,371 | 0.3 | 39 | 25.2 | 23.8 | 74.7 | 76.1 | 0.0 | 0.0 |
| MACON | 087 | 0000 | 698 | 24,928 | 22,794 | 21,812 | -0.9 | 67 | 13.8 | 13.2 | 85.6 | 86.2 | 0.4 | 0.5 |
| MADISON | 089 | 3440 | 691 | 238,912 | 283,420 | 298,717 | 1.7 | 9 | 77.1 | 75.7 | 20.1 | 21.2 | 1.8 | 2.1 |
| MARENGO | 091 | 0000 | 698 | 23,084 | 23,026 | 22,376 | 0.0 | 53 | 49.0 | 47.0 | 50.9 | 52.9 | 0.0 | 0.0 |
| MARION | 093 | 0000 | 630 | 29,830 | 30,291 | 29,441 | 0.1 | 49 | 96.4 | 96.0 | 3.2 | 3.7 | 0.1 | 0.2 |
| MARSHALL | 095 | 0000 | 691 | 70,832 | 80,908 | 83,049 | 1.3 | 13 | 97.9 | 97.8 | 1.5 | 1.7 | 0.2 | 0.2 |
| MOBILE | 097 | 5160 | 686 | 378,643 | 400,689 | 405,569 | 0.6 | 25 | 67.3 | 65.4 | 31.1 | 32.8 | 0.9 | 1.1 |
| MONROE | 099 | 0000 | 686 | 23,968 | 23,989 | 23,563 | 0.0 | 53 | 59.7 | 58.1 | 39.1 | 40.8 | 0.2 | 0.3 |
| MONTGOMERY | 101 | 5240 | 698 | 209,085 | 215,031 | 211,162 | 0.3 | 39 | 57.1 | 55.2 | 41.8 | 43.5 | 0.7 | 0.9 |
| MORGAN | 103 | 2030 | 691 | 100,043 | 110,330 | 113,610 | 1.0 | 17 | 89.1 | 88.3 | 10.1 | 10.8 | 0.4 | 0.5 |
| PERRY | 105 | 0000 | 698 | 12,759 | 12,597 | 12,509 | -0.1 | 57 | 35.3 | 33.9 | 64.4 | 65.8 | 0.1 | 0.1 |
| PICKENS | 107 | 0000 | 630 | 20,699 | 21,042 | 21,136 | 0.2 | 46 | 58.0 | 56.6 | 41.8 | 43.1 | 0.1 | 0.2 |
| PIKE | 109 | 0000 | 698 | 27,595 | 28,423 | 28,160 | 0.3 | 39 | 64.6 | 62.3 | 34.6 | 36.9 | 0.2 | 0.3 |
| RANDOLPH | 111 | 0000 | 524 | 19,881 | 20,327 | 20,746 | 0.2 | 46 | 76.1 | 74.8 | 23.6 | 24.9 | 0.1 | 0.1 |
| RUSSELL | 113 | 1800 | 522 | 46,860 | 49,778 | 48,338 | 0.6 | 25 | 60.8 | 58.7 | 38.6 | 40.6 | 0.2 | 0.3 |
| ST. CLAIR | 115 | 1000 | 630 | 50,009 | 65,429 | 73,416 | 2.7 | 4 | 90.3 | 89.4 | 9.1 | 9.8 | 0.2 | 0.2 |
| SHELBY | 117 | 1000 | 630 | 99,358 | 151,856 | 178,965 | 4.2 | 1 | 91.3 | 90.5 | 7.8 | 8.4 | 0.6 | 0.7 |
| SUMTER | 119 | 0000 | 711 | 16,174 | 15,487 | 14,842 | -0.4 | 64 | 29.4 | 27.4 | 70.3 | 72.2 | 0.2 | 0.2 |
| TALLADEGA | 121 | 0000 | 630 | 74,107 | 77,940 | 80,054 | 0.5 | 34 | 68.8 | 67.6 | 30.7 | 32.0 | 0.2 | 0.2 |
| TALLAPOOSA | 123 | 0000 | 698 | 38,826 | 40,390 | 40,682 | 0.4 | 36 | 73.4 | 71.8 | 26.3 | 27.9 | 0.1 | 0.1 |
| TUSCALOOSA | 125 | 8600 | 630 | 150,522 | 162,444 | 167,107 | 0.7 | 22 | 72.7 | 70.7 | 26.2 | 28.0 | 0.8 | 0.9 |
| WALKER | 127 | 0000 | 630 | 67,670 | 71,681 | 73,518 | 0.6 | 25 | 93.2 | 92.5 | 6.5 | 7.1 | 0.2 | 0.2 |
| WASHINGTON | 129 | 0000 | 686 | 16,694 | 17,841 | 18,333 | 0.7 | 22 | 65.8 | 65.2 | 27.7 | 29.7 | 0.1 | 0.1 |
| WILCOX | 131 | 0000 | 698 | 13,568 | 13,374 | 13,174 | -0.1 | 57 | 31.0 | 29.5 | 68.9 | 70.5 | 0.0 | 0.0 |
| WINSTON | 133 | 0000 | 630 | 22,053 | 24,722 | 26,073 | 1.1 | 16 | 99.4 | 99.3 | 0.3 | 0.4 | 0.1 | 0.1 |
| ALABAMA | | | | | | | 0.8 | | 73.7 | 73.1 | 25.3 | 25.8 | 0.5 | 0.7 |
| UNITED STATES | | | | | | | 1.0 | | 80.3 | 77.9 | 12.1 | 12.4 | 2.9 | 3.9 |

| COUNTY | % HISPANIC ORIGIN | | 2000 AGE DISTRIBUTION (%) | | | | | | | | | | MEDIAN AGE | | 2000 Males/ Females (×100) |
|---|---|---|---|---|---|---|---|---|---|---|---|---|---|---|---|
| | 1990 | 2000 | 0-4 | 5-9 | 10-14 | 15-19 | 20-24 | 25-44 | 45-64 | 65-84 | 85+ | 18+ | 1990 | 2000 | |
| AUTAUGA | 0.7 | 1.4 | 7.2 | 7.4 | 7.4 | 7.2 | 6.5 | 30.1 | 23.5 | 9.5 | 1.1 | 73.5 | 31.7 | 35.1 | 94.6 |
| BALDWIN | 1.0 | 2.1 | 6.3 | 6.6 | 6.6 | 6.5 | 5.8 | 27.3 | 24.6 | 14.6 | 1.7 | 76.5 | 35.5 | 39.0 | 93.6 |
| BARBOUR | 0.5 | 1.0 | 6.8 | 7.1 | 6.9 | 7.6 | 7.0 | 29.9 | 21.5 | 11.5 | 1.6 | 74.3 | 32.8 | 35.2 | 96.5 |
| BIBB | 0.2 | 0.7 | 6.7 | 7.0 | 7.1 | 7.8 | 6.9 | 29.0 | 23.5 | 10.4 | 1.6 | 74.4 | 31.9 | 35.5 | 95.5 |
| BLOUNT | 0.7 | 1.6 | 6.3 | 6.3 | 6.5 | 6.7 | 6.2 | 29.5 | 25.8 | 11.3 | 1.4 | 76.9 | 34.5 | 37.8 | 95.2 |
| BULLOCK | 0.6 | 1.0 | 8.2 | 7.9 | 7.4 | 7.6 | 7.9 | 29.3 | 19.2 | 10.7 | 1.8 | 71.6 | 31.7 | 32.2 | 98.0 |
| BUTLER | 0.3 | 0.7 | 7.4 | 7.8 | 7.3 | 8.2 | 6.6 | 26.2 | 21.8 | 12.6 | 2.2 | 72.4 | 33.5 | 35.5 | 88.0 |
| CALHOUN | 1.1 | 2.1 | 5.9 | 6.1 | 6.1 | 7.7 | 8.3 | 29.2 | 23.4 | 11.9 | 1.4 | 78.0 | 32.7 | 36.3 | 93.1 |
| CHAMBERS | 0.3 | 0.8 | 6.3 | 6.4 | 6.4 | 7.2 | 6.8 | 28.1 | 23.2 | 13.6 | 2.0 | 76.5 | 34.8 | 37.5 | 89.8 |
| CHEROKEE | 0.3 | 0.9 | 5.4 | 5.6 | 5.8 | 6.1 | 6.0 | 28.2 | 26.9 | 14.3 | 1.6 | 79.5 | 36.3 | 40.5 | 97.6 |
| CHILTON | 0.4 | 0.9 | 6.4 | 6.6 | 6.7 | 7.0 | 6.4 | 29.0 | 24.7 | 11.6 | 1.6 | 75.9 | 34.0 | 37.3 | 94.1 |
| CHOCTAW | 0.3 | 0.7 | 6.7 | 6.9 | 7.1 | 7.9 | 6.6 | 27.8 | 23.9 | 11.4 | 1.8 | 74.3 | 32.9 | 36.2 | 89.7 |
| CLARKE | 0.4 | 0.7 | 7.1 | 7.1 | 7.0 | 7.8 | 7.0 | 28.7 | 22.7 | 10.9 | 1.6 | 73.9 | 31.7 | 34.9 | 92.6 |
| CLAY | 0.2 | 0.7 | 5.8 | 5.9 | 6.2 | 6.8 | 6.5 | 27.5 | 24.9 | 13.8 | 2.4 | 77.9 | 35.7 | 39.1 | 92.2 |
| CLEBURNE | 0.3 | 0.9 | 6.4 | 6.5 | 6.8 | 6.8 | 5.8 | 29.1 | 25.0 | 12.2 | 1.5 | 76.4 | 34.1 | 37.8 | 97.0 |
| COFFEE | 1.2 | 2.3 | 6.4 | 6.1 | 6.2 | 6.5 | 6.7 | 30.5 | 23.5 | 12.4 | 1.7 | 77.2 | 34.1 | 37.4 | 94.4 |
| COLBERT | 0.4 | 0.9 | 6.0 | 6.1 | 6.1 | 6.3 | 6.2 | 28.6 | 25.6 | 13.6 | 1.6 | 78.1 | 35.7 | 39.2 | 91.8 |
| CONECUH | 0.6 | 1.0 | 6.7 | 7.0 | 6.9 | 7.4 | 6.7 | 26.9 | 22.8 | 13.5 | 2.1 | 74.7 | 34.5 | 37.1 | 91.1 |
| COOSA | 0.2 | 0.5 | 6.5 | 6.5 | 6.3 | 6.9 | 6.6 | 28.3 | 23.8 | 13.4 | 1.7 | 76.6 | 34.0 | 37.4 | 97.4 |
| COVINGTON | 0.4 | 0.9 | 6.1 | 6.2 | 6.4 | 6.8 | 6.1 | 27.1 | 24.5 | 14.6 | 2.1 | 77.2 | 36.2 | 39.2 | 89.5 |
| CRENSHAW | 0.2 | 0.7 | 6.4 | 6.6 | 6.6 | 7.2 | 6.1 | 26.8 | 23.4 | 14.6 | 2.3 | 75.9 | 35.9 | 38.4 | 90.8 |
| CULLMAN | 0.4 | 1.1 | 6.2 | 6.4 | 6.6 | 6.7 | 5.7 | 28.8 | 25.0 | 12.9 | 1.7 | 76.9 | 34.8 | 38.4 | 94.8 |
| DALE | 2.4 | 4.4 | 8.2 | 7.2 | 6.3 | 6.5 | 8.6 | 32.4 | 19.2 | 10.3 | 1.4 | 74.8 | 29.1 | 32.3 | 98.0 |
| DALLAS | 0.3 | 0.5 | 7.7 | 7.8 | 7.6 | 8.5 | 7.4 | 26.9 | 21.1 | 11.2 | 1.8 | 71.8 | 31.1 | 33.5 | 83.6 |
| DEKALB | 0.4 | 1.1 | 5.8 | 6.1 | 6.3 | 6.8 | 6.3 | 29.1 | 25.2 | 12.6 | 1.7 | 77.7 | 34.9 | 38.5 | 93.6 |
| ELMORE | 0.5 | 1.2 | 6.4 | 6.6 | 6.7 | 7.1 | 7.4 | 30.9 | 23.1 | 10.4 | 1.3 | 76.0 | 32.9 | 35.4 | 104.4 |
| ESCAMBIA | 0.5 | 1.0 | 6.1 | 6.3 | 6.5 | 7.3 | 6.9 | 29.5 | 23.9 | 11.9 | 1.8 | 76.9 | 33.9 | 36.9 | 98.7 |
| ETOWAH | 0.3 | 0.9 | 5.6 | 5.8 | 6.0 | 6.6 | 6.3 | 28.1 | 25.3 | 14.2 | 1.9 | 78.6 | 36.0 | 39.5 | 90.7 |
| FAYETTE | 0.4 | 1.1 | 5.8 | 6.0 | 6.1 | 7.0 | 6.2 | 28.3 | 25.4 | 13.0 | 2.1 | 78.1 | 35.6 | 38.7 | 91.8 |
| FRANKLIN | 0.4 | 1.0 | 6.0 | 6.3 | 6.5 | 6.5 | 5.8 | 28.1 | 25.3 | 13.7 | 2.0 | 77.5 | 35.8 | 39.1 | 92.2 |
| GENEVA | 0.5 | 1.2 | 6.1 | 6.1 | 6.3 | 6.9 | 6.1 | 27.3 | 25.2 | 14.0 | 2.0 | 77.4 | 36.4 | 39.2 | 93.1 |
| GREENE | 0.2 | 0.4 | 7.6 | 8.2 | 7.8 | 8.8 | 7.4 | 25.8 | 20.2 | 11.8 | 2.3 | 70.8 | 31.3 | 33.2 | 85.5 |
| HALE | 0.4 | 0.6 | 7.8 | 7.9 | 7.8 | 8.2 | 7.1 | 27.0 | 20.4 | 11.6 | 2.2 | 71.2 | 31.8 | 33.6 | 88.0 |
| HENRY | 0.6 | 1.0 | 6.1 | 6.4 | 6.7 | 7.0 | 6.5 | 27.1 | 24.2 | 14.1 | 1.9 | 76.5 | 35.4 | 38.5 | 88.7 |
| HOUSTON | 0.6 | 1.2 | 7.0 | 7.1 | 7.1 | 7.1 | 6.6 | 29.4 | 23.2 | 11.1 | 1.4 | 74.5 | 33.1 | 36.0 | 91.0 |
| JACKSON | 0.4 | 1.1 | 5.8 | 6.0 | 6.3 | 6.6 | 6.2 | 28.8 | 26.6 | 12.3 | 1.4 | 77.8 | 34.6 | 38.7 | 93.0 |
| JEFFERSON | 0.4 | 0.9 | 6.3 | 6.5 | 6.7 | 7.0 | 6.7 | 29.6 | 23.3 | 12.2 | 1.8 | 76.5 | 34.1 | 37.3 | 88.2 |
| LAMAR | 0.5 | 1.1 | 6.0 | 6.1 | 6.4 | 6.8 | 6.2 | 27.9 | 24.9 | 13.5 | 2.2 | 77.3 | 35.4 | 38.8 | 91.7 |
| LAUDERDALE | 0.4 | 1.0 | 6.0 | 6.0 | 6.0 | 6.8 | 7.0 | 28.8 | 24.7 | 13.1 | 1.7 | 78.3 | 34.7 | 38.3 | 91.2 |
| LAWRENCE | 0.3 | 0.9 | 6.8 | 7.0 | 7.1 | 6.8 | 6.1 | 30.0 | 24.1 | 10.8 | 1.3 | 75.0 | 32.0 | 36.2 | 97.4 |
| LEE | 0.6 | 1.3 | 6.0 | 5.6 | 5.4 | 10.1 | 16.9 | 28.7 | 18.4 | 7.9 | 0.9 | 79.6 | 26.2 | 29.0 | 96.7 |
| LIMESTONE | 0.5 | 1.1 | 6.3 | 6.3 | 6.3 | 6.5 | 6.8 | 32.4 | 23.9 | 10.3 | 1.3 | 77.3 | 32.8 | 36.5 | 100.1 |
| LOWNDES | 0.5 | 0.7 | 8.8 | 8.7 | 8.5 | 9.0 | 8.2 | 27.0 | 19.1 | 9.1 | 1.5 | 68.3 | 28.1 | 29.5 | 85.9 |
| MACON | 0.4 | 0.6 | 6.8 | 6.5 | 6.5 | 11.5 | 10.7 | 25.6 | 18.7 | 11.8 | 1.9 | 75.6 | 28.9 | 31.2 | 84.7 |
| MADISON | 1.2 | 2.4 | 6.8 | 6.5 | 6.1 | 6.6 | 7.1 | 33.5 | 22.9 | 9.5 | 1.0 | 77.0 | 31.9 | 35.6 | 95.3 |
| MARENGO | 0.3 | 0.6 | 7.3 | 7.4 | 7.4 | 7.9 | 7.0 | 27.2 | 22.4 | 11.4 | 1.9 | 72.7 | 32.5 | 35.0 | 89.8 |
| MARION | 0.2 | 0.7 | 5.9 | 6.0 | 6.0 | 6.7 | 6.2 | 28.3 | 25.8 | 13.1 | 2.0 | 78.1 | 35.7 | 39.1 | 96.2 |
| MARSHALL | 0.4 | 1.1 | 6.0 | 6.2 | 6.4 | 6.4 | 5.7 | 28.8 | 25.6 | 13.3 | 1.7 | 77.5 | 35.3 | 39.1 | 92.0 |
| MOBILE | 0.8 | 1.6 | 7.4 | 7.4 | 7.4 | 7.5 | 7.2 | 29.3 | 22.2 | 10.4 | 1.3 | 73.4 | 31.9 | 34.7 | 90.1 |
| MONROE | 0.4 | 0.9 | 7.4 | 7.5 | 7.4 | 8.1 | 7.0 | 28.1 | 21.9 | 10.8 | 1.8 | 72.7 | 31.4 | 34.3 | 93.1 |
| MONTGOMERY | 0.8 | 1.5 | 7.1 | 7.2 | 7.1 | 7.7 | 7.2 | 30.6 | 21.4 | 10.2 | 1.4 | 74.4 | 31.6 | 34.3 | 89.7 |
| MORGAN | 0.6 | 1.4 | 6.4 | 6.7 | 6.7 | 6.7 | 6.0 | 30.5 | 24.5 | 11.1 | 1.3 | 76.1 | 33.6 | 37.2 | 93.7 |
| PERRY | 0.3 | 0.5 | 7.6 | 7.7 | 7.7 | 10.7 | 8.4 | 24.2 | 20.3 | 11.2 | 2.2 | 71.5 | 30.2 | 31.3 | 86.5 |
| PICKENS | 0.2 | 0.6 | 7.0 | 7.2 | 7.2 | 7.3 | 6.6 | 25.9 | 23.3 | 13.2 | 2.2 | 73.9 | 34.3 | 36.8 | 86.8 |
| PIKE | 0.4 | 0.8 | 6.5 | 6.5 | 6.6 | 9.0 | 8.4 | 29.7 | 20.5 | 10.9 | 1.9 | 76.8 | 29.9 | 33.0 | 90.8 |
| RANDOLPH | 0.3 | 0.7 | 6.1 | 6.3 | 6.4 | 7.2 | 6.0 | 28.5 | 23.4 | 13.9 | 2.2 | 76.7 | 34.9 | 38.2 | 94.5 |
| RUSSELL | 0.6 | 1.3 | 7.1 | 6.7 | 6.6 | 6.8 | 6.9 | 29.5 | 23.5 | 11.6 | 1.3 | 75.6 | 33.0 | 36.2 | 91.5 |
| ST. CLAIR | 0.4 | 1.1 | 6.7 | 6.9 | 7.0 | 6.6 | 6.0 | 29.8 | 24.6 | 11.2 | 1.2 | 75.4 | 33.5 | 36.8 | 101.4 |
| SHELBY | 0.5 | 1.3 | 7.4 | 7.5 | 7.0 | 6.6 | 6.3 | 35.4 | 22.1 | 6.9 | 0.8 | 74.2 | 31.5 | 34.7 | 95.1 |
| SUMTER | 0.5 | 0.7 | 7.7 | 7.6 | 7.6 | 9.9 | 9.9 | 26.7 | 18.2 | 10.7 | 1.9 | 72.1 | 28.9 | 30.3 | 85.9 |
| TALLADEGA | 0.7 | 1.2 | 6.6 | 6.7 | 6.8 | 7.7 | 7.0 | 29.1 | 23.4 | 11.6 | 1.3 | 75.5 | 33.0 | 36.2 | 93.3 |
| TALLAPOOSA | 0.2 | 0.5 | 6.0 | 6.3 | 6.5 | 6.4 | 6.0 | 28.0 | 24.8 | 14.1 | 2.0 | 77.3 | 35.5 | 38.8 | 89.5 |
| TUSCALOOSA | 0.6 | 1.3 | 6.1 | 6.1 | 6.0 | 8.4 | 11.0 | 29.9 | 20.8 | 10.4 | 1.3 | 78.2 | 30.6 | 33.3 | 92.4 |
| WALKER | 0.3 | 0.9 | 5.8 | 6.1 | 6.2 | 6.7 | 6.3 | 28.6 | 25.8 | 12.8 | 1.7 | 77.9 | 35.0 | 38.8 | 93.7 |
| WASHINGTON | 0.3 | 0.7 | 7.3 | 7.2 | 7.3 | 8.2 | 6.8 | 28.3 | 23.2 | 10.3 | 1.4 | 73.1 | 31.5 | 34.8 | 96.1 |
| WILCOX | 0.3 | 0.5 | 8.1 | 8.2 | 8.3 | 8.9 | 8.0 | 25.4 | 19.6 | 11.6 | 2.0 | 69.3 | 30.4 | 31.4 | 86.8 |
| WINSTON | 0.3 | 0.9 | 5.9 | 6.0 | 6.2 | 6.5 | 6.0 | 28.6 | 26.3 | 12.9 | 1.6 | 78.0 | 35.5 | 39.2 | 94.6 |
| ALABAMA | 0.6 | 1.3 | 6.6 | 6.6 | 6.6 | 7.2 | 7.2 | 29.6 | 23.2 | 11.5 | 1.5 | 76.0 | 33.0 | 36.2 | 92.2 |
| UNITED STATES | 9.0 | 11.8 | 6.9 | 7.2 | 7.2 | 7.2 | 6.7 | 29.9 | 22.2 | 11.1 | 1.6 | 74.6 | 32.9 | 35.7 | 95.6 |

# HOUSEHOLDS

| COUNTY | HOUSEHOLDS | | | | | FAMILIES | | | MEDIAN HOUSEHOLD INCOME | | | |
|---|---|---|---|---|---|---|---|---|---|---|---|---|
| | 1990 | 2000 | 2005 | % Annual Rate 1990-2000 | 2000 Average HH Size | 1990 | 2000 | % Annual Rate 1990-2000 | 2000 | 2005 | 2000 National Rank | 2000 State Rank |
| AUTAUGA | 11,826 | 15,609 | 17,505 | 3.4 | 2.81 | 9,501 | 12,230 | 3.1 | 41,244 | 45,703 | 565 | 5 |
| BALDWIN | 37,044 | 54,904 | 63,362 | 4.9 | 2.51 | 28,142 | 40,243 | 4.4 | 43,270 | 49,447 | 441 | 3 |
| BARBOUR | 9,218 | 9,711 | 9,751 | 0.6 | 2.58 | 6,687 | 6,810 | 0.2 | 29,206 | 34,375 | 2264 | 48 |
| BIBB | 5,745 | 6,936 | 7,752 | 2.3 | 2.86 | 4,478 | 5,210 | 1.9 | 32,764 | 37,005 | 1578 | 24 |
| BLOUNT | 14,644 | 18,639 | 21,233 | 3.0 | 2.60 | 11,654 | 14,359 | 2.6 | 34,834 | 40,812 | 1277 | 15 |
| BULLOCK | 3,787 | 3,880 | 3,961 | 0.3 | 2.66 | 2,712 | 2,689 | -0.1 | 24,357 | 30,901 | 2877 | 61 |
| BUTLER | 7,935 | 8,007 | 7,947 | 0.1 | 2.65 | 5,825 | 5,672 | -0.3 | 26,456 | 30,528 | 2658 | 58 |
| CALHOUN | 42,983 | 44,935 | 45,257 | 0.5 | 2.49 | 31,718 | 32,221 | 0.2 | 31,771 | 36,580 | 1762 | 30 |
| CHAMBERS | 13,786 | 14,089 | 14,002 | 0.3 | 2.54 | 10,219 | 10,078 | -0.2 | 30,490 | 36,314 | 2040 | 40 |
| CHEROKEE | 7,466 | 8,794 | 9,322 | 2.0 | 2.50 | 5,860 | 6,683 | 1.6 | 31,326 | 38,546 | 1856 | 33 |
| CHILTON | 12,114 | 14,570 | 15,978 | 2.3 | 2.61 | 9,352 | 10,890 | 1.9 | 35,589 | 44,269 | 1157 | 13 |
| CHOCTAW | 5,747 | 5,900 | 5,753 | 0.3 | 2.59 | 4,313 | 4,271 | -0.1 | 26,558 | 29,834 | 2642 | 57 |
| CLARKE | 9,506 | 10,287 | 10,731 | 1.0 | 2.79 | 7,192 | 7,530 | 0.6 | 29,964 | 34,289 | 2162 | 43 |
| CLAY | 5,003 | 5,537 | 5,835 | 1.2 | 2.52 | 3,794 | 4,054 | 0.8 | 30,192 | 35,853 | 2106 | 41 |
| CLEBURNE | 4,776 | 5,749 | 6,361 | 2.3 | 2.55 | 3,748 | 4,345 | 1.8 | 29,567 | 34,335 | 2213 | 46 |
| COFFEE | 15,260 | 16,638 | 16,973 | 1.1 | 2.50 | 11,570 | 12,220 | 0.7 | 32,489 | 35,727 | 1627 | 26 |
| COLBERT | 20,096 | 21,273 | 21,412 | 0.7 | 2.45 | 15,174 | 15,616 | 0.3 | 34,678 | 37,812 | 1294 | 16 |
| CONECUH | 5,259 | 5,352 | 5,244 | 0.2 | 2.52 | 3,898 | 3,824 | -0.2 | 26,602 | 31,487 | 2634 | 56 |
| COOSA | 4,017 | 4,273 | 4,413 | 0.8 | 2.67 | 3,095 | 3,174 | 0.3 | 30,809 | 36,112 | 1968 | 37 |
| COVINGTON | 14,444 | 15,160 | 15,448 | 0.6 | 2.46 | 10,474 | 10,587 | 0.1 | 28,512 | 32,358 | 2363 | 51 |
| CRENSHAW | 5,262 | 5,408 | 5,476 | 0.3 | 2.49 | 3,786 | 3,738 | -0.2 | 26,780 | 30,953 | 2611 | 55 |
| CULLMAN | 25,605 | 29,763 | 31,683 | 1.8 | 2.54 | 19,915 | 22,534 | 1.5 | 33,935 | 38,864 | 1404 | 19 |
| DALE | 17,574 | 17,972 | 18,086 | 0.3 | 2.65 | 13,334 | 13,282 | 0.0 | 33,764 | 40,329 | 1428 | 20 |
| DALLAS | 17,033 | 16,951 | 16,830 | -0.1 | 2.69 | 12,402 | 12,020 | -0.4 | 25,883 | 29,867 | 2724 | 59 |
| DEKALB | 20,968 | 23,320 | 24,668 | 1.3 | 2.53 | 16,094 | 17,359 | 0.9 | 32,391 | 37,318 | 1641 | 27 |
| ELMORE | 16,532 | 22,524 | 25,748 | 3.8 | 2.71 | 13,000 | 17,246 | 3.5 | 41,301 | 48,101 | 562 | 4 |
| ESCAMBIA | 12,899 | 13,652 | 13,950 | 0.7 | 2.56 | 9,507 | 9,743 | 0.3 | 27,665 | 32,463 | 2486 | 53 |
| ETOWAH | 38,675 | 41,461 | 42,206 | 0.8 | 2.47 | 28,585 | 29,852 | 0.5 | 32,308 | 36,650 | 1658 | 28 |
| FAYETTE | 6,859 | 7,101 | 7,213 | 0.4 | 2.53 | 5,165 | 5,176 | 0.0 | 31,405 | 37,956 | 1839 | 32 |
| FRANKLIN | 10,850 | 11,992 | 12,353 | 1.2 | 2.46 | 8,164 | 8,732 | 0.8 | 29,735 | 35,175 | 2196 | 45 |
| GENEVA | 9,231 | 10,101 | 10,427 | 1.1 | 2.47 | 6,870 | 7,233 | 0.6 | 29,182 | 35,003 | 2269 | 49 |
| GREENE | 3,512 | 3,511 | 3,461 | 0.0 | 2.74 | 2,532 | 2,441 | -0.4 | 20,284 | 22,271 | 3093 | 67 |
| HALE | 5,397 | 6,177 | 6,590 | 1.6 | 2.71 | 3,983 | 4,377 | 1.1 | 25,148 | 27,839 | 2798 | 60 |
| HENRY | 5,769 | 6,166 | 6,361 | 0.8 | 2.55 | 4,320 | 4,473 | 0.4 | 31,692 | 37,864 | 1777 | 31 |
| HOUSTON | 30,844 | 33,913 | 35,424 | 1.2 | 2.53 | 22,628 | 24,130 | 0.8 | 35,308 | 39,270 | 1198 | 14 |
| JACKSON | 18,020 | 20,238 | 21,187 | 1.4 | 2.54 | 14,041 | 15,276 | 1.0 | 32,969 | 36,878 | 1544 | 23 |
| JEFFERSON | 251,479 | 260,101 | 260,379 | 0.4 | 2.47 | 176,573 | 177,377 | 0.1 | 40,352 | 43,854 | 642 | 7 |
| LAMAR | 6,005 | 6,182 | 6,257 | 0.4 | 2.56 | 4,512 | 4,471 | -0.1 | 30,654 | 34,560 | 1996 | 39 |
| LAUDERDALE | 30,905 | 33,964 | 34,885 | 1.2 | 2.45 | 22,966 | 24,527 | 0.8 | 36,734 | 40,447 | 1016 | 11 |
| LAWRENCE | 11,410 | 12,636 | 13,291 | 1.2 | 2.68 | 9,032 | 9,723 | 0.9 | 35,999 | 41,674 | 1103 | 12 |
| LEE | 33,097 | 40,935 | 45,632 | 2.6 | 2.44 | 20,115 | 24,420 | 2.4 | 32,662 | 38,081 | 1601 | 25 |
| LIMESTONE | 19,685 | 24,015 | 26,192 | 2.4 | 2.57 | 15,277 | 18,094 | 2.1 | 39,475 | 44,608 | 713 | 8 |
| LOWNDES | 4,056 | 4,336 | 4,504 | 0.8 | 3.01 | 3,143 | 3,275 | 0.5 | 22,435 | 27,161 | 3000 | 64 |
| MACON | 8,483 | 8,128 | 7,913 | -0.5 | 2.55 | 5,535 | 5,112 | -1.0 | 23,689 | 27,210 | 2925 | 62 |
| MADISON | 91,208 | 112,764 | 121,215 | 2.6 | 2.46 | 65,475 | 78,436 | 2.2 | 46,884 | 52,458 | 279 | 2 |
| MARENGO | 8,156 | 8,472 | 8,402 | 0.5 | 2.69 | 6,088 | 6,139 | 0.1 | 30,084 | 35,759 | 2135 | 42 |
| MARION | 11,521 | 12,266 | 12,217 | 0.8 | 2.40 | 8,700 | 8,907 | 0.3 | 29,948 | 33,831 | 2166 | 44 |
| MARSHALL | 27,761 | 32,868 | 34,314 | 2.1 | 2.44 | 20,927 | 23,995 | 1.7 | 33,213 | 37,772 | 1504 | 22 |
| MOBILE | 136,899 | 148,882 | 152,667 | 1.0 | 2.65 | 100,814 | 106,843 | 0.7 | 33,305 | 37,333 | 1490 | 21 |
| MONROE | 8,412 | 8,607 | 8,564 | 0.3 | 2.75 | 6,355 | 6,272 | -0.2 | 34,142 | 40,492 | 1364 | 18 |
| MONTGOMERY | 77,173 | 82,218 | 82,119 | 0.8 | 2.52 | 53,573 | 55,060 | 0.3 | 37,377 | 41,622 | 918 | 10 |
| MORGAN | 37,799 | 43,103 | 45,160 | 1.6 | 2.51 | 28,651 | 31,803 | 1.3 | 41,190 | 45,687 | 570 | 6 |
| PERRY | 4,201 | 4,317 | 4,369 | 0.3 | 2.79 | 3,102 | 3,079 | -0.1 | 22,856 | 26,072 | 2982 | 63 |
| PICKENS | 7,568 | 8,012 | 8,221 | 0.7 | 2.60 | 5,658 | 5,783 | 0.3 | 28,942 | 32,165 | 2305 | 50 |
| PIKE | 10,314 | 11,214 | 11,346 | 1.0 | 2.40 | 6,949 | 7,230 | 0.5 | 27,108 | 30,805 | 2564 | 54 |
| RANDOLPH | 7,553 | 7,747 | 7,927 | 0.3 | 2.59 | 5,640 | 5,552 | -0.2 | 29,420 | 36,045 | 2232 | 47 |
| RUSSELL | 17,499 | 19,264 | 19,034 | 1.2 | 2.55 | 12,736 | 13,514 | 0.7 | 32,073 | 38,042 | 1703 | 29 |
| ST. CLAIR | 17,666 | 23,439 | 26,529 | 3.5 | 2.71 | 14,094 | 18,225 | 3.2 | 39,327 | 46,427 | 725 | 9 |
| SHELBY | 35,985 | 56,553 | 67,422 | 5.6 | 2.66 | 27,767 | 42,377 | 5.3 | 59,845 | 67,885 | 77 | 1 |
| SUMTER | 5,545 | 5,570 | 5,447 | 0.1 | 2.66 | 3,914 | 3,797 | -0.4 | 20,458 | 21,917 | 3088 | 66 |
| TALLADEGA | 26,448 | 28,661 | 29,839 | 1.0 | 2.64 | 20,195 | 21,280 | 0.6 | 31,215 | 36,793 | 1884 | 35 |
| TALLAPOOSA | 14,700 | 16,050 | 16,547 | 1.1 | 2.48 | 10,992 | 11,631 | 0.7 | 31,313 | 35,466 | 1862 | 34 |
| TUSCALOOSA | 55,354 | 62,068 | 64,681 | 1.4 | 2.49 | 37,355 | 40,622 | 1.0 | 34,423 | 40,211 | 1329 | 17 |
| WALKER | 25,554 | 27,877 | 29,009 | 1.1 | 2.54 | 19,534 | 20,674 | 0.7 | 30,837 | 33,896 | 1963 | 36 |
| WASHINGTON | 5,709 | 6,298 | 6,570 | 1.2 | 2.82 | 4,548 | 4,866 | 0.8 | 30,795 | 35,009 | 1970 | 38 |
| WILCOX | 4,415 | 4,511 | 4,520 | 0.3 | 2.91 | 3,289 | 3,255 | -0.1 | 20,461 | 23,234 | 3087 | 65 |
| WINSTON | 8,544 | 9,823 | 10,490 | 1.7 | 2.49 | 6,594 | 7,343 | 1.3 | 28,434 | 31,023 | 2374 | 52 |
| ALABAMA | | | | 1.4 | 2.54 | | | 1.1 | 35,938 | 40,905 | | |
| UNITED STATES | | | | 1.4 | 2.59 | | | 1.1 | 41,914 | 49,127 | | |

| COUNTY | 2000 Per Capita Income | 2000 HH Income Base | 2000 HOUSEHOLD INCOME DISTRIBUTION (%) Less than $15,000 | $15,000 to $24,999 | $25,000 to $49,999 | $50,000 to $99,999 | $100,000 to $149,999 | $150,000 or More | 2000 AVERAGE DISPOSABLE INCOME BY AGE OF HOUSEHOLDER All Ages | <35 | 35-44 | 45-54 | 55-64 | 65+ |
|---|---|---|---|---|---|---|---|---|---|---|---|---|---|---|
| AUTAUGA | 17,477 | 15,609 | 15.3 | 12.0 | 33.8 | 32.0 | 5.6 | 1.4 | 38,100 | 34,464 | 43,301 | 48,266 | 40,130 | 22,400 |
| BALDWIN | 22,046 | 54,904 | 12.2 | 13.2 | 32.7 | 31.1 | 7.9 | 2.9 | 42,347 | 34,994 | 45,656 | 53,310 | 44,853 | 32,569 |
| BARBOUR | 14,322 | 9,711 | 26.9 | 16.3 | 32.7 | 19.4 | 3.7 | 1.1 | 30,096 | 28,212 | 35,825 | 35,768 | 33,099 | 19,373 |
| BIBB | 14,647 | 6,936 | 20.9 | 17.4 | 34.4 | 22.9 | 3.2 | 1.2 | 32,164 | 30,257 | 34,763 | 42,957 | 31,723 | 20,009 |
| BLOUNT | 16,298 | 18,639 | 17.7 | 15.3 | 36.7 | 25.7 | 3.8 | 0.9 | 33,607 | 30,862 | 40,653 | 42,465 | 35,529 | 19,268 |
| BULLOCK | 11,336 | 3,880 | 32.0 | 18.7 | 29.3 | 17.4 | 2.4 | 0.2 | 26,153 | 24,167 | 31,935 | 31,468 | 28,157 | 18,069 |
| BUTLER | 13,511 | 8,007 | 29.0 | 17.9 | 33.9 | 15.2 | 2.8 | 1.2 | 27,916 | 24,404 | 34,078 | 33,480 | 31,161 | 19,518 |
| CALHOUN | 15,324 | 44.927 | 21.3 | 15.7 | 38.1 | 21.7 | 2.6 | 0.7 | 30,825 | 27,200 | 36,693 | 38,369 | 32,060 | 20,683 |
| CHAMBERS | 14,759 | 14,089 | 24.3 | 16.6 | 36.9 | 18.8 | 2.7 | 0.7 | 29,641 | 28,603 | 35,734 | 38,815 | 31,081 | 18,176 |
| CHEROKEE | 15,459 | 8,794 | 21.8 | 16.0 | 36.4 | 22.2 | 2.8 | 0.7 | 30,818 | 31,297 | 35,809 | 39,485 | 31,266 | 19,565 |
| CHILTON | 16,975 | 14,570 | 18.9 | 13.5 | 36.7 | 26.0 | 4.2 | 0.7 | 33,727 | 33,081 | 40,403 | 42,987 | 33,002 | 20,980 |
| CHOCTAW | 15,765 | 5,900 | 34.1 | 13.5 | 26.2 | 21.8 | 3.2 | 1.2 | 29,445 | 28,676 | 34,090 | 38,042 | 29,046 | 17,152 |
| CLARKE | 13,858 | 10,286 | 26.3 | 16.6 | 30.7 | 21.1 | 4.3 | 1.1 | 30,970 | 27,511 | 39,977 | 39,915 | 30,238 | 19,006 |
| CLAY | 15,725 | 5,537 | 22.7 | 16.5 | 36.4 | 20.5 | 2.8 | 1.3 | 31,028 | 29,798 | 38,577 | 40,798 | 31,854 | 17,870 |
| CLEBURNE | 14,384 | 5,749 | 24.4 | 15.5 | 38.0 | 19.5 | 1.9 | 0.7 | 29,113 | 28,506 | 35,378 | 36,060 | 30,068 | 16,841 |
| COFFEE | 16,209 | 16,638 | 20.2 | 17.3 | 34.0 | 23.9 | 3.6 | 1.0 | 32,492 | 28,677 | 38,561 | 42,953 | 35,409 | 19,421 |
| COLBERT | 18,413 | 21,271 | 18.9 | 16.4 | 35.3 | 23.4 | 4.5 | 1.6 | 34,241 | 30,979 | 41,482 | 42,027 | 36,234 | 21,584 |
| CONECUH | 13,468 | 5,352 | 31.1 | 16.6 | 32.6 | 16.4 | 2.7 | 0.6 | 27,092 | 26,748 | 34,355 | 31,759 | 28,261 | 18,156 |
| COOSA | 14,000 | 4,273 | 20.5 | 20.2 | 35.1 | 21.1 | 2.6 | 0.5 | 30,041 | 28,864 | 39,008 | 35,465 | 29,783 | 20,228 |
| COVINGTON | 14,539 | 15,160 | 26.2 | 17.4 | 34.0 | 19.2 | 2.6 | 0.8 | 28,839 | 26,484 | 35,269 | 36,996 | 30,706 | 19,513 |
| CRENSHAW | 14,163 | 5,408 | 29.1 | 17.4 | 32.9 | 16.7 | 3.1 | 1.0 | 28,302 | 27,495 | 36,305 | 34,991 | 29,902 | 17,482 |
| CULLMAN | 16,788 | 29,763 | 18.5 | 17.3 | 35.0 | 23.7 | 4.5 | 1.2 | 33,563 | 30,979 | 39,900 | 43,665 | 35,478 | 19,995 |
| DALE | 15,708 | 17,972 | 17.4 | 16.0 | 38.1 | 24.5 | 3.3 | 0.6 | 32,539 | 28,493 | 36,056 | 44,930 | 36,453 | 21,188 |
| DALLAS | 13,513 | 16,951 | 32.2 | 16.6 | 28.2 | 17.5 | 4.0 | 1.6 | 29,466 | 24,165 | 35,017 | 35,658 | 31,548 | 21,876 |
| DEKALB | 15,361 | 23,320 | 20.8 | 16.0 | 37.0 | 22.2 | 3.4 | 0.6 | 31,404 | 31,889 | 39,732 | 38,343 | 31,674 | 17,536 |
| ELMORE | 17,205 | 22,524 | 14.7 | 12.4 | 34.7 | 31.1 | 5.8 | 1.2 | 38,013 | 34,825 | 42,765 | 50,225 | 38,561 | 23,922 |
| ESCAMBIA | 13,795 | 13,652 | 26.6 | 18.3 | 31.7 | 19.5 | 2.9 | 0.9 | 29,313 | 25,169 | 33,981 | 36,306 | 31,083 | 20,694 |
| ETOWAH | 16,808 | 41,461 | 22.5 | 15.1 | 35.4 | 22.3 | 3.5 | 1.2 | 32,123 | 28,463 | 39,538 | 41,110 | 34,424 | 20,332 |
| FAYETTE | 15,417 | 7,101 | 24.4 | 14.9 | 35.3 | 21.0 | 3.3 | 1.2 | 31,351 | 30,598 | 37,182 | 39,847 | 30,156 | 20,371 |
| FRANKLIN | 15,406 | 11,992 | 23.6 | 17.4 | 35.8 | 19.4 | 3.1 | 0.8 | 29,926 | 29,714 | 37,275 | 39,194 | 28,105 | 18,390 |
| GENEVA | 14,557 | 10,101 | 24.8 | 17.3 | 36.1 | 18.7 | 2.6 | 0.7 | 29,116 | 26,973 | 33,654 | 39,976 | 29,254 | 19,518 |
| GREENE | 10,142 | 3,511 | 41.0 | 17.2 | 27.3 | 12.0 | 1.9 | 0.5 | 23,168 | 18,616 | 29,766 | 29,432 | 24,392 | 15,970 |
| HALE | 16,756 | 6,177 | 32.5 | 17.3 | 28.4 | 16.8 | 3.4 | 1.7 | 28,981 | 26,690 | 30,039 | 41,170 | 29,900 | 17,643 |
| HENRY | 15,367 | 6,166 | 20.6 | 16.2 | 37.8 | 21.2 | 3.4 | 0.8 | 31,143 | 29,647 | 38,382 | 38,125 | 35,436 | 19,350 |
| HOUSTON | 18,802 | 33,913 | 19.3 | 14.6 | 33.9 | 25.6 | 4.8 | 1.9 | 35,582 | 31,201 | 42,206 | 44,765 | 37,408 | 21,661 |
| JACKSON | 15,928 | 20,238 | 19.6 | 16.7 | 36.6 | 23.1 | 3.3 | 0.6 | 31,833 | 29,536 | 40,234 | 39,317 | 31,129 | 19,338 |
| JEFFERSON | 22,330 | 260,101 | 16.7 | 13.0 | 31.3 | 28.6 | 7.2 | 3.3 | 41,025 | 34,557 | 47,254 | 49,967 | 41,945 | 27,783 |
| LAMAR | 14,589 | 6,182 | 24.4 | 17.0 | 36.4 | 19.1 | 2.3 | 0.8 | 29,402 | 26,856 | 35,853 | 38,254 | 30,045 | 18,229 |
| LAUDERDALE | 19,972 | 33,952 | 18.7 | 14.0 | 33.5 | 26.4 | 5.5 | 1.9 | 36,511 | 30,634 | 44,453 | 46,782 | 38,431 | 24,668 |
| LAWRENCE | 17,532 | 12,636 | 19.6 | 13.7 | 35.0 | 26.3 | 4.4 | 1.0 | 34,341 | 32,276 | 43,167 | 44,145 | 32,750 | 19,193 |
| LEE | 19,263 | 40,935 | 26.8 | 12.3 | 29.8 | 22.8 | 5.4 | 2.9 | 35,322 | 23,303 | 46,815 | 50,370 | 41,360 | 26,022 |
| LIMESTONE | 17,923 | 24,015 | 18.2 | 12.0 | 33.5 | 29.3 | 5.5 | 1.5 | 36,855 | 36,161 | 42,494 | 48,134 | 37,375 | 19,744 |
| LOWNDES | 10,232 | 4,336 | 35.9 | 18.2 | 28.0 | 15.4 | 2.0 | 0.6 | 25,111 | 20,804 | 29,073 | 29,691 | 28,304 | 18,505 |
| MACON | 11,640 | 8,128 | 33.5 | 18.5 | 29.7 | 15.5 | 2.2 | 0.7 | 25,935 | 19,819 | 29,351 | 36,430 | 25,823 | 21,158 |
| MADISON | 24,807 | 112,762 | 11.4 | 10.3 | 31.3 | 34.6 | 8.9 | 3.5 | 45,263 | 37,446 | 48,185 | 56,316 | 51,118 | 30,005 |
| MARENGO | 14,247 | 8,472 | 30.1 | 14.1 | 28.0 | 24.4 | 2.9 | 0.6 | 29,931 | 27,230 | 35,574 | 38,005 | 30,662 | 19,432 |
| MARION | 16,044 | 12,266 | 23.1 | 17.6 | 35.8 | 20.2 | 2.6 | 0.8 | 29,938 | 29,017 | 36,892 | 37,468 | 30,948 | 18,282 |
| MARSHALL | 17,233 | 32,868 | 21.0 | 16.5 | 34.1 | 23.4 | 4.0 | 1.2 | 32,795 | 30,702 | 38,588 | 41,703 | 34,459 | 20,524 |
| MOBILE | 16,905 | 148,874 | 21.5 | 15.5 | 32.9 | 24.0 | 4.5 | 1.7 | 34,157 | 28,276 | 39,084 | 41,700 | 35,476 | 24,421 |
| MONROE | 15,202 | 8,607 | 23.3 | 12.9 | 33.8 | 24.4 | 4.2 | 1.4 | 33,339 | 31,645 | 40,328 | 41,208 | 35,589 | 19,987 |
| MONTGOMERY | 19,326 | 82,218 | 18.1 | 14.4 | 32.5 | 27.1 | 5.6 | 2.3 | 37,524 | 31,183 | 42,526 | 46,017 | 39,103 | 27,014 |
| MORGAN | 20,515 | 43,103 | 15.8 | 11.6 | 33.3 | 31.0 | 6.4 | 2.0 | 39,207 | 35,642 | 44,178 | 50,418 | 41,352 | 22,656 |
| PERRY | 11,402 | 4,317 | 34.8 | 19.7 | 27.5 | 14.9 | 2.1 | 1.0 | 25,769 | 22,990 | 31,930 | 29,936 | 26,142 | 19,833 |
| PICKENS | 13,598 | 8,012 | 29.0 | 14.1 | 34.7 | 18.9 | 2.7 | 0.6 | 28,677 | 27,417 | 34,639 | 36,012 | 32,119 | 18,264 |
| PIKE | 15,327 | 11,214 | 30.8 | 16.6 | 29.9 | 17.6 | 4.0 | 1.2 | 29,304 | 25,568 | 35,172 | 36,511 | 33,891 | 20,545 |
| RANDOLPH | 13,618 | 7,747 | 24.2 | 17.7 | 35.3 | 19.8 | 2.6 | 0.5 | 29,143 | 30,201 | 35,944 | 35,019 | 28,616 | 18,415 |
| RUSSELL | 16,110 | 19,253 | 21.1 | 17.2 | 34.2 | 22.9 | 3.9 | 0.7 | 31,918 | 29,684 | 37,333 | 40,307 | 32,202 | 21,471 |
| ST. CLAIR | 17,973 | 23,439 | 14.5 | 13.5 | 36.3 | 28.6 | 5.6 | 1.5 | 37,700 | 33,621 | 44,779 | 46,956 | 38,184 | 24,877 |
| SHELBY | 30,695 | 56,553 | 7.3 | 7.1 | 25.5 | 38.1 | 14.0 | 8.0 | 58,127 | 46,750 | 63,978 | 66,040 | 53,850 | 33,738 |
| SUMTER | 14,009 | 5,568 | 40.1 | 18.9 | 22.7 | 15.0 | 2.1 | 1.2 | 24,951 | 21,332 | 31,491 | 32,354 | 23,231 | 17,259 |
| TALLADEGA | 14,859 | 28,661 | 23.2 | 16.5 | 34.1 | 22.2 | 3.2 | 0.8 | 30,975 | 27,275 | 36,500 | 40,389 | 31,368 | 19,981 |
| TALLAPOOSA | 16,587 | 16,050 | 23.1 | 15.9 | 35.1 | 21.2 | 3.5 | 1.3 | 31,816 | 29,335 | 37,550 | 41,770 | 32,125 | 19,671 |
| TUSCALOOSA | 18,453 | 62,068 | 22.7 | 14.0 | 31.7 | 24.3 | 5.4 | 2.0 | 35,285 | 26,237 | 42,047 | 47,650 | 38,280 | 24,196 |
| WALKER | 16,149 | 27,877 | 22.3 | 18.2 | 34.6 | 20.2 | 3.4 | 1.4 | 31,653 | 29,265 | 37,731 | 40,519 | 31,089 | 20,486 |
| WASHINGTON | 13,383 | 6,298 | 26.2 | 14.7 | 34.6 | 21.3 | 2.8 | 0.4 | 29,682 | 28,808 | 35,064 | 37,371 | 29,055 | 18,629 |
| WILCOX | 10,808 | 4,511 | 38.3 | 20.4 | 24.7 | 12.3 | 2.6 | 1.8 | 25,763 | 22,907 | 30,747 | 32,219 | 25,770 | 17,849 |
| WINSTON | 15,124 | 9,823 | 24.7 | 19.3 | 32.9 | 19.3 | 3.0 | 0.8 | 29,071 | 28,692 | 37,193 | 35,411 | 26,865 | 18,691 |
| ALABAMA | 18,753 | | 19.6 | 14.3 | 32.9 | 25.7 | 5.4 | 2.1 | 36,364 | 31,258 | 42,625 | 45,673 | 37,541 | 23,609 |
| UNITED STATES | 22,162 | | 14.5 | 12.5 | 32.3 | 29.8 | 7.4 | 3.5 | 40,748 | 34,503 | 44,969 | 49,579 | 43,409 | 27,339 |

# ALABAMA

# E

# SPENDING POTENTIAL INDEXES

| COUNTY | FINANCIAL SERVICES | | | | THE HOME | | | | | | ENTERTAINMENT | | | | | | PERSONAL | | | |
|---|---|---|---|---|---|---|---|---|---|---|---|---|---|---|---|---|---|---|---|---|
| | | | | | Home Improvements | | | Furnishings | | | | | | | | | | | | |
| | Auto Loan | Home Loan | Invest-ments | Retire-ment Plans | Home Repair | Lawn & Garden | Remodel-ing | Appli-ances | Elec-tronics | Furni-ture | Restau-rants | Sport-ing Goods | Theater & Concerts | Toys & Hobbies | Travel | Video Rental | Apparel | Auto After-market | Health Insur-ance | Pets & Supplies |
| AUTAUGA | 100 | 87 | 90 | 90 | 97 | 96 | 109 | 98 | 98 | 93 | 95 | 100 | 93 | 101 | 79 | 99 | 94 | 96 | 99 | 101 |
| BALDWIN | 101 | 87 | 95 | 94 | 99 | 100 | 111 | 100 | 97 | 92 | 94 | 100 | 94 | 101 | 82 | 99 | 94 | 96 | 103 | 102 |
| BARBOUR | 97 | 73 | 80 | 80 | 95 | 92 | 111 | 96 | 92 | 83 | 83 | 96 | 84 | 96 | 73 | 96 | 83 | 90 | 99 | 98 |
| BIBB | 97 | 64 | 68 | 74 | 92 | 90 | 112 | 96 | 91 | 75 | 77 | 96 | 79 | 94 | 66 | 95 | 78 | 87 | 102 | 96 |
| BLOUNT | 98 | 70 | 76 | 78 | 94 | 91 | 114 | 96 | 93 | 80 | 82 | 96 | 82 | 97 | 70 | 96 | 82 | 89 | 101 | 98 |
| BULLOCK | 93 | 67 | 68 | 70 | 94 | 88 | 99 | 94 | 88 | 81 | 75 | 89 | 79 | 89 | 71 | 95 | 81 | 87 | 93 | 93 |
| BUTLER | 94 | 67 | 77 | 74 | 95 | 89 | 100 | 95 | 89 | 80 | 76 | 92 | 80 | 91 | 72 | 94 | 80 | 87 | 94 | 94 |
| CALHOUN | 97 | 82 | 89 | 86 | 98 | 94 | 106 | 97 | 93 | 88 | 88 | 96 | 89 | 97 | 78 | 97 | 88 | 92 | 98 | 99 |
| CHAMBERS | 96 | 70 | 78 | 77 | 96 | 92 | 107 | 96 | 91 | 82 | 81 | 94 | 83 | 95 | 72 | 96 | 82 | 89 | 99 | 96 |
| CHEROKEE | 97 | 66 | 73 | 77 | 93 | 91 | 114 | 96 | 92 | 77 | 79 | 95 | 80 | 95 | 69 | 96 | 80 | 88 | 102 | 97 |
| CHILTON | 98 | 70 | 77 | 79 | 94 | 92 | 115 | 97 | 93 | 79 | 82 | 96 | 82 | 97 | 70 | 97 | 82 | 89 | 102 | 99 |
| CHOCTAW | 97 | 63 | 67 | 73 | 92 | 90 | 112 | 96 | 91 | 75 | 77 | 96 | 78 | 94 | 66 | 95 | 78 | 86 | 102 | 96 |
| CLARKE | 98 | 67 | 74 | 77 | 93 | 91 | 112 | 96 | 92 | 78 | 80 | 96 | 81 | 96 | 69 | 96 | 81 | 88 | 101 | 97 |
| CLAY | 97 | 66 | 72 | 75 | 93 | 91 | 111 | 96 | 91 | 77 | 79 | 95 | 80 | 95 | 68 | 96 | 79 | 87 | 102 | 97 |
| CLEBURNE | 98 | 65 | 70 | 75 | 92 | 90 | 113 | 96 | 92 | 77 | 78 | 97 | 80 | 96 | 67 | 96 | 79 | 87 | 102 | 97 |
| COFFEE | 96 | 81 | 86 | 84 | 96 | 93 | 105 | 96 | 94 | 86 | 88 | 95 | 88 | 96 | 77 | 97 | 87 | 92 | 99 | 98 |
| COLBERT | 97 | 78 | 86 | 83 | 97 | 94 | 106 | 97 | 93 | 86 | 86 | 95 | 87 | 97 | 76 | 97 | 86 | 91 | 99 | 98 |
| CONECUH | 96 | 64 | 68 | 72 | 92 | 89 | 108 | 95 | 90 | 76 | 76 | 93 | 78 | 92 | 67 | 95 | 78 | 86 | 99 | 95 |
| COOSA | 97 | 64 | 69 | 74 | 93 | 91 | 113 | 96 | 91 | 76 | 77 | 96 | 79 | 95 | 67 | 95 | 78 | 87 | 102 | 97 |
| COVINGTON | 96 | 68 | 75 | 76 | 94 | 91 | 111 | 95 | 91 | 79 | 80 | 93 | 81 | 94 | 70 | 96 | 80 | 88 | 101 | 96 |
| CRENSHAW | 97 | 63 | 68 | 73 | 92 | 90 | 111 | 95 | 91 | 75 | 77 | 94 | 78 | 94 | 66 | 95 | 78 | 86 | 102 | 96 |
| CULLMAN | 98 | 71 | 79 | 80 | 95 | 92 | 113 | 96 | 92 | 81 | 82 | 96 | 83 | 97 | 72 | 96 | 83 | 89 | 102 | 98 |
| DALE | 96 | 85 | 82 | 84 | 94 | 91 | 103 | 96 | 94 | 88 | 90 | 95 | 88 | 96 | 76 | 97 | 88 | 93 | 96 | 99 |
| DALLAS | 94 | 76 | 85 | 81 | 96 | 90 | 100 | 96 | 90 | 86 | 80 | 93 | 85 | 93 | 76 | 96 | 85 | 90 | 91 | 95 |
| DEKALB | 98 | 68 | 75 | 78 | 93 | 91 | 113 | 96 | 93 | 79 | 80 | 96 | 81 | 96 | 69 | 96 | 81 | 88 | 101 | 97 |
| ELMORE | 100 | 81 | 88 | 88 | 97 | 95 | 113 | 98 | 96 | 88 | 90 | 99 | 90 | 100 | 77 | 98 | 90 | 94 | 102 | 101 |
| ESCAMBIA | 96 | 68 | 76 | 76 | 94 | 90 | 109 | 96 | 91 | 79 | 79 | 94 | 81 | 94 | 70 | 96 | 81 | 88 | 99 | 96 |
| ETOWAH | 97 | 77 | 89 | 84 | 99 | 95 | 107 | 97 | 92 | 86 | 86 | 95 | 87 | 97 | 77 | 96 | 86 | 91 | 100 | 97 |
| FAYETTE | 98 | 67 | 73 | 76 | 93 | 91 | 114 | 96 | 92 | 78 | 80 | 96 | 81 | 96 | 68 | 96 | 80 | 88 | 101 | 97 |
| FRANKLIN | 98 | 68 | 74 | 77 | 94 | 91 | 112 | 96 | 92 | 78 | 80 | 96 | 81 | 96 | 69 | 96 | 80 | 88 | 102 | 97 |
| GENEVA | 97 | 68 | 77 | 77 | 95 | 92 | 111 | 96 | 92 | 79 | 80 | 96 | 82 | 95 | 70 | 96 | 81 | 88 | 102 | 97 |
| GREENE | 92 | 61 | 67 | 69 | 92 | 85 | 96 | 95 | 87 | 77 | 70 | 89 | 75 | 87 | 68 | 95 | 77 | 86 | 89 | 92 |
| HALE | 95 | 63 | 67 | 71 | 93 | 88 | 106 | 95 | 89 | 77 | 74 | 93 | 78 | 91 | 67 | 95 | 78 | 86 | 96 | 95 |
| HENRY | 98 | 67 | 73 | 77 | 93 | 91 | 114 | 96 | 92 | 77 | 79 | 96 | 80 | 96 | 68 | 96 | 80 | 88 | 102 | 98 |
| HOUSTON | 98 | 90 | 93 | 92 | 99 | 97 | 104 | 98 | 96 | 94 | 94 | 99 | 94 | 99 | 82 | 98 | 94 | 96 | 98 | 100 |
| JACKSON | 98 | 73 | 80 | 82 | 94 | 93 | 111 | 97 | 94 | 82 | 83 | 97 | 85 | 97 | 72 | 97 | 84 | 90 | 101 | 98 |
| JEFFERSON | 98 | 96 | 103 | 98 | 103 | 101 | 98 | 99 | 96 | 99 | 96 | 99 | 98 | 99 | 89 | 99 | 99 | 99 | 96 | 99 |
| LAMAR | 97 | 63 | 66 | 73 | 92 | 90 | 112 | 96 | 91 | 75 | 77 | 96 | 78 | 95 | 66 | 95 | 78 | 86 | 102 | 96 |
| LAUDERDALE | 98 | 84 | 93 | 89 | 99 | 97 | 107 | 97 | 94 | 90 | 90 | 97 | 91 | 98 | 81 | 97 | 90 | 93 | 100 | 99 |
| LAWRENCE | 97 | 64 | 68 | 74 | 92 | 90 | 112 | 96 | 91 | 76 | 77 | 96 | 79 | 94 | 67 | 95 | 78 | 87 | 101 | 96 |
| LEE | 95 | 90 | 93 | 90 | 96 | 92 | 104 | 91 | 91 | 85 | 89 | 92 | 86 | 95 | 78 | 94 | 89 | 92 | 95 | 97 |
| LIMESTONE | 98 | 77 | 84 | 84 | 96 | 93 | 112 | 97 | 94 | 85 | 87 | 97 | 87 | 98 | 74 | 97 | 87 | 92 | 101 | 100 |
| LOWNDES | 92 | 63 | 69 | 70 | 92 | 84 | 96 | 96 | 87 | 79 | 71 | 90 | 76 | 88 | 69 | 95 | 78 | 86 | 87 | 93 |
| MACON | 91 | 65 | 65 | 68 | 93 | 83 | 83 | 95 | 86 | 82 | 70 | 85 | 77 | 85 | 71 | 96 | 83 | 88 | 84 | 89 |
| MADISON | 102 | 107 | 103 | 106 | 103 | 105 | 103 | 101 | 103 | 105 | 108 | 105 | 104 | 105 | 93 | 100 | 107 | 104 | 99 | 104 |
| MARENGO | 97 | 72 | 78 | 80 | 94 | 91 | 109 | 96 | 92 | 82 | 82 | 96 | 84 | 96 | 72 | 96 | 83 | 89 | 98 | 98 |
| MARION | 97 | 65 | 70 | 74 | 92 | 91 | 112 | 95 | 91 | 76 | 78 | 95 | 79 | 94 | 67 | 95 | 78 | 87 | 101 | 96 |
| MARSHALL | 98 | 73 | 82 | 81 | 96 | 93 | 112 | 97 | 93 | 82 | 84 | 96 | 85 | 97 | 73 | 97 | 84 | 90 | 102 | 99 |
| MOBILE | 97 | 87 | 92 | 89 | 99 | 95 | 102 | 97 | 94 | 92 | 90 | 96 | 92 | 97 | 82 | 98 | 92 | 95 | 96 | 99 |
| MONROE | 97 | 73 | 82 | 82 | 95 | 93 | 108 | 97 | 93 | 83 | 83 | 96 | 85 | 96 | 74 | 96 | 83 | 90 | 99 | 97 |
| MONTGOMERY | 98 | 97 | 97 | 96 | 101 | 99 | 96 | 99 | 97 | 99 | 98 | 99 | 97 | 99 | 88 | 99 | 99 | 99 | 94 | 100 |
| MORGAN | 99 | 89 | 91 | 91 | 98 | 97 | 106 | 98 | 97 | 94 | 95 | 99 | 94 | 100 | 81 | 99 | 94 | 96 | 99 | 101 |
| PERRY | 94 | 63 | 67 | 70 | 93 | 87 | 101 | 95 | 88 | 77 | 72 | 91 | 77 | 89 | 68 | 94 | 78 | 86 | 92 | 93 |
| PICKENS | 96 | 64 | 68 | 73 | 92 | 89 | 109 | 95 | 91 | 77 | 76 | 94 | 79 | 93 | 67 | 96 | 79 | 87 | 99 | 96 |
| PIKE | 95 | 70 | 76 | 75 | 93 | 89 | 107 | 95 | 90 | 81 | 79 | 92 | 81 | 93 | 71 | 95 | 81 | 88 | 95 | 95 |
| RANDOLPH | 97 | 65 | 69 | 74 | 92 | 90 | 112 | 96 | 92 | 76 | 78 | 96 | 79 | 95 | 67 | 95 | 79 | 87 | 101 | 97 |
| RUSSELL | 96 | 79 | 87 | 82 | 97 | 93 | 103 | 96 | 91 | 87 | 85 | 94 | 87 | 95 | 77 | 97 | 87 | 91 | 96 | 97 |
| ST. CLAIR | 98 | 73 | 78 | 80 | 93 | 91 | 114 | 97 | 93 | 82 | 84 | 97 | 84 | 98 | 71 | 97 | 84 | 90 | 101 | 99 |
| SHELBY | 104 | 106 | 94 | 105 | 99 | 102 | 106 | 103 | 105 | 106 | 109 | 108 | 103 | 106 | 88 | 102 | 108 | 106 | 99 | 106 |
| SUMTER | 93 | 66 | 70 | 71 | 93 | 87 | 99 | 94 | 88 | 79 | 74 | 89 | 78 | 89 | 70 | 94 | 79 | 86 | 92 | 93 |
| TALLADEGA | 96 | 72 | 79 | 78 | 96 | 92 | 107 | 96 | 91 | 82 | 81 | 95 | 84 | 95 | 73 | 96 | 83 | 89 | 99 | 96 |
| TALLAPOOSA | 98 | 71 | 81 | 81 | 95 | 93 | 113 | 97 | 92 | 81 | 82 | 96 | 84 | 97 | 72 | 97 | 83 | 89 | 101 | 98 |
| TUSCALOOSA | 97 | 92 | 97 | 93 | 99 | 96 | 102 | 95 | 94 | 91 | 93 | 95 | 91 | 97 | 83 | 97 | 93 | 95 | 96 | 99 |
| WALKER | 97 | 71 | 79 | 79 | 94 | 92 | 110 | 96 | 92 | 81 | 81 | 96 | 83 | 96 | 71 | 96 | 82 | 89 | 100 | 97 |
| WASHINGTON | 97 | 63 | 66 | 73 | 92 | 90 | 112 | 96 | 91 | 75 | 77 | 96 | 78 | 95 | 66 | 95 | 78 | 86 | 102 | 96 |
| WILCOX | 92 | 62 | 68 | 69 | 92 | 85 | 96 | 95 | 87 | 78 | 70 | 88 | 76 | 87 | 68 | 95 | 78 | 86 | 89 | 92 |
| WINSTON | 97 | 65 | 69 | 74 | 92 | 90 | 113 | 96 | 92 | 76 | 78 | 96 | 79 | 95 | 67 | 96 | 79 | 87 | 102 | 97 |
| ALABAMA | 98 | 85 | 92 | 90 | 98 | 96 | 105 | 98 | 95 | 91 | 90 | 98 | 91 | 98 | 80 | 98 | 91 | 94 | 98 | 99 |
| UNITED STATES | 100 | 100 | 100 | 100 | 100 | 100 | 100 | 100 | 100 | 100 | 100 | 100 | 100 | 100 | 100 | 100 | 100 | 100 | 100 | 100 |

| COUNTY | FIPS Code | MSA Code | DMA Code | POPULATION 1990 | POPULATION 2000 | POPULATION 2005 | 1990-2000 ANNUAL CHANGE % Rate | 1990-2000 ANNUAL CHANGE State Rank | RACE (%) White 1990 | White 2000 | Black 1990 | Black 2000 | Asian/Pacific 1990 | Asian/Pacific 2000 |
|---|---|---|---|---|---|---|---|---|---|---|---|---|---|---|
| ALEUTIANS EAST | 013 | 0000 | 000 | 2,464 | 2,146 | 2,073 | -1.3 | 23 | 33.6 | 29.1 | 0.6 | 0.7 | 18.8 | 18.5 |
| ALEUTIANS WEST | 016 | 0000 | 000 | 9,478 | 3,862 | 3,584 | -8.4 | 25 | 67.1 | 55.0 | 7.0 | 3.9 | 10.3 | 20.3 |
| ANCHORAGE | 020 | 0380 | 743 | 226,338 | 260,161 | 271,496 | 1.4 | 6 | 80.7 | 78.5 | 6.4 | 6.2 | 4.8 | 6.3 |
| BETHEL | 050 | 0000 | 000 | 13,656 | 16,426 | 17,510 | 1.8 | 4 | 15.4 | 13.9 | 0.5 | 0.4 | 0.7 | 0.7 |
| BRISTOL BAY | 060 | 0000 | 000 | 1,410 | 1,059 | 1,042 | -2.8 | 24 | 63.4 | 59.9 | 2.7 | 3.1 | 0.9 | 0.9 |
| DILLINGHAM | 070 | 0000 | 000 | 4,012 | 4,619 | 4,896 | 1.4 | 6 | 25.4 | 23.1 | 0.2 | 0.2 | 0.7 | 0.8 |
| FAIRBANKS NORTH STAR | 090 | 0000 | 745 | 77,720 | 84,733 | 86,449 | 0.8 | 10 | 82.0 | 80.5 | 7.1 | 6.5 | 2.6 | 3.4 |
| HAINES | 100 | 0000 | 000 | 2,117 | 2,281 | 2,245 | 0.7 | 11 | 85.1 | 83.6 | 0.0 | 0.0 | 0.8 | 1.1 |
| JUNEAU | 110 | 0000 | 747 | 26,751 | 30,282 | 30,773 | 1.2 | 8 | 80.6 | 78.2 | 1.1 | 1.1 | 4.3 | 5.5 |
| KENAI PENINSULA | 122 | 0000 | 743 | 40,802 | 49,550 | 52,553 | 1.9 | 3 | 90.9 | 89.8 | 0.5 | 0.5 | 1.0 | 1.3 |
| KETCHIKAN GATEWAY | 130 | 0000 | 000 | 13,828 | 13,941 | 13,157 | 0.1 | 17 | 81.8 | 79.8 | 0.4 | 0.4 | 3.6 | 4.8 |
| KODIAK ISLAND | 150 | 0000 | 000 | 13,309 | 14,256 | 13,744 | 0.7 | 11 | 69.8 | 64.1 | 1.0 | 1.0 | 11.2 | 14.7 |
| LAKE AND PENINSULA | 164 | 0000 | 000 | 1,668 | 1,754 | 1,785 | 0.5 | 14 | 23.3 | 21.1 | 0.0 | 0.0 | 0.7 | 0.6 |
| MATANUSKA-SUSITNA | 170 | 0000 | 743 | 39,683 | 59,949 | 70,016 | 4.1 | 1 | 93.1 | 92.1 | 0.8 | 0.9 | 0.7 | 1.0 |
| NOME | 180 | 0000 | 000 | 8,288 | 8,897 | 8,841 | 0.7 | 11 | 24.4 | 22.2 | 0.1 | 0.1 | 0.7 | 0.7 |
| NORTH SLOPE | 185 | 0000 | 000 | 5,979 | 7,137 | 7,353 | 1.7 | 5 | 21.3 | 19.6 | 0.7 | 0.8 | 4.8 | 5.6 |
| NORTHWEST ARCTIC | 188 | 0000 | 000 | 6,113 | 6,758 | 6,915 | 1.0 | 9 | 13.8 | 12.5 | 0.2 | 0.2 | 0.8 | 1.0 |
| PR OF WALES-OUT KTCH | 201 | 0000 | 000 | 6,278 | 6,632 | 6,301 | 0.5 | 14 | 61.5 | 58.0 | 0.1 | 0.1 | 0.4 | 0.5 |
| SITKA | 220 | 0000 | 000 | 8,588 | 8,087 | 7,575 | -0.6 | 21 | 74.0 | 71.0 | 0.5 | 0.4 | 3.9 | 5.0 |
| SKAGWAY-YAKUTAT-ANGO | 231 | 0000 | 000 | 4,385 | 4,150 | 4,038 | -0.5 | 20 | 60.4 | 57.4 | 0.2 | 0.2 | 0.7 | 0.9 |
| SOUTHEAST FAIRBANKS | 240 | 0000 | 745 | 5,913 | 5,797 | 5,517 | -0.2 | 18 | 79.0 | 77.0 | 4.9 | 4.5 | 1.4 | 1.7 |
| VALDEZ-CORDOVA | 261 | 0000 | 000 | 9,952 | 10,220 | 10,108 | 0.3 | 16 | 82.9 | 81.0 | 0.6 | 0.5 | 3.3 | 4.2 |
| WADE HAMPTON | 270 | 0000 | 000 | 5,791 | 7,067 | 7,575 | 2.0 | 2 | 6.0 | 5.4 | 0.2 | 0.2 | 0.4 | 0.4 |
| WRANGELL-PETERSBURG | 280 | 0000 | 000 | 7,042 | 6,776 | 6,607 | -0.4 | 19 | 78.7 | 76.4 | 0.2 | 0.1 | 1.3 | 1.9 |
| YUKON-KOYUKUK | 290 | 0000 | 000 | 8,478 | 7,983 | 7,527 | -0.6 | 21 | 42.3 | 41.2 | 1.0 | 0.5 | 0.6 | 0.7 |
| ALASKA | | | | | | | 1.2 | | 75.5 | 74.1 | 4.1 | 3.8 | 3.6 | 4.5 |
| UNITED STATES | | | | | | | 1.0 | | 80.3 | 77.9 | 12.1 | 12.4 | 2.9 | 3.9 |

# POPULATION COMPOSITION

| COUNTY | % HISPANIC ORIGIN 1990 | % HISPANIC ORIGIN 2000 | 2000 AGE DISTRIBUTION (%) 0-4 | 5-9 | 10-14 | 15-19 | 20-24 | 25-44 | 45-64 | 65-84 | 85+ | 18+ | MEDIAN AGE 1990 | MEDIAN AGE 2000 | 2000 Males/ Females (×100) |
|---|---|---|---|---|---|---|---|---|---|---|---|---|---|---|---|
| ALEUTIANS EAST | 7.3 | 7.4 | 5.8 | 7.2 | 7.3 | 9.3 | 14.3 | 31.7 | 21.1 | 3.2 | 0.0 | 75.6 | 29.1 | 28.7 | 170.6 |
| ALEUTIANS WEST | 7.8 | 14.5 | 5.0 | 4.5 | 4.3 | 8.9 | 23.1 | 38.1 | 14.0 | 2.1 | 0.0 | 83.9 | 27.0 | 26.7 | 214.8 |
| ANCHORAGE | 4.1 | 5.4 | 7.7 | 8.4 | 8.7 | 8.2 | 7.6 | 30.5 | 23.4 | 5.1 | 0.3 | 70.4 | 29.8 | 32.5 | 105.6 |
| BETHEL | 0.6 | 0.9 | 10.6 | 11.8 | 12.5 | 11.7 | 8.6 | 22.1 | 17.3 | 4.9 | 0.5 | 57.7 | 25.1 | 22.0 | 109.0 |
| BRISTOL BAY | 2.3 | 3.6 | 7.0 | 8.4 | 10.2 | 8.7 | 7.7 | 29.5 | 23.1 | 4.9 | 0.5 | 68.3 | 29.5 | 31.8 | 124.8 |
| DILLINGHAM | 1.2 | 1.3 | 10.8 | 12.0 | 12.1 | 10.4 | 7.4 | 23.1 | 18.7 | 5.0 | 0.4 | 58.6 | 27.1 | 23.2 | 105.4 |
| FAIRBANKS NORTH STAR | 3.7 | 5.1 | 8.1 | 8.6 | 9.0 | 9.8 | 11.4 | 27.5 | 20.8 | 4.4 | 0.4 | 69.0 | 27.6 | 27.5 | 113.1 |
| HAINES | 1.3 | 1.7 | 5.6 | 6.5 | 8.1 | 8.9 | 5.7 | 23.6 | 31.4 | 9.6 | 0.7 | 73.6 | 34.5 | 40.9 | 114.4 |
| JUNEAU | 2.8 | 3.4 | 6.6 | 8.0 | 9.1 | 8.7 | 6.4 | 27.0 | 27.8 | 5.8 | 0.6 | 71.0 | 31.9 | 35.9 | 103.5 |
| KENAI PENINSULA | 1.8 | 2.6 | 6.5 | 8.3 | 9.6 | 10.5 | 6.9 | 24.4 | 26.6 | 6.8 | 0.4 | 68.6 | 31.1 | 34.5 | 113.5 |
| KETCHIKAN GATEWAY | 2.1 | 2.7 | 6.3 | 7.7 | 9.1 | 9.6 | 7.5 | 24.5 | 26.7 | 7.4 | 1.1 | 70.9 | 31.7 | 35.7 | 112.8 |
| KODIAK ISLAND | 5.0 | 5.7 | 8.4 | 8.7 | 9.6 | 9.1 | 9.5 | 29.0 | 21.1 | 4.2 | 0.4 | 67.8 | 28.7 | 29.1 | 122.1 |
| LAKE AND PENINSULA | 1.9 | 1.2 | 10.1 | 11.9 | 12.4 | 9.9 | 6.7 | 22.2 | 20.0 | 6.6 | 0.3 | 59.6 | 27.0 | 24.4 | 118.4 |
| MATANUSKA-SUSITNA | 1.9 | 2.7 | 7.0 | 9.3 | 10.7 | 10.5 | 6.5 | 24.7 | 25.3 | 5.6 | 0.4 | 65.7 | 30.8 | 32.2 | 110.6 |
| NOME | 1.3 | 1.4 | 10.1 | 11.1 | 12.2 | 11.2 | 7.9 | 22.6 | 19.0 | 5.3 | 0.5 | 59.3 | 26.4 | 23.4 | 117.0 |
| NORTH SLOPE | 2.1 | 2.4 | 11.2 | 11.7 | 12.0 | 10.8 | 7.3 | 24.1 | 18.2 | 4.4 | 0.4 | 58.8 | 26.6 | 23.0 | 115.6 |
| NORTHWEST ARCTIC | 0.6 | 0.7 | 13.4 | 13.3 | 13.3 | 11.0 | 7.9 | 22.4 | 13.6 | 4.5 | 0.5 | 52.9 | 22.6 | 19.5 | 107.7 |
| PR OF WALES-OUT KTCH | 1.9 | 2.5 | 7.7 | 8.6 | 9.4 | 9.7 | 7.8 | 24.7 | 26.9 | 5.0 | 0.3 | 68.2 | 30.4 | 32.6 | 125.0 |
| SITKA | 2.4 | 3.0 | 6.7 | 8.1 | 8.9 | 9.5 | 8.1 | 26.6 | 24.7 | 6.6 | 0.9 | 70.6 | 30.4 | 33.7 | 107.8 |
| SKAGWAY-YAKUTAT-ANGO | 1.5 | 1.6 | 6.7 | 8.7 | 9.8 | 10.0 | 6.8 | 24.5 | 24.7 | 8.0 | 0.6 | 67.8 | 31.2 | 33.9 | 120.0 |
| SOUTHEAST FAIRBANKS | 3.0 | 4.0 | 6.9 | 8.8 | 10.2 | 10.9 | 9.0 | 23.1 | 24.6 | 5.8 | 0.6 | 67.2 | 28.8 | 29.8 | 116.5 |
| VALDEZ-CORDOVA | 2.7 | 3.5 | 6.0 | 7.7 | 9.5 | 9.7 | 6.9 | 25.3 | 28.4 | 6.0 | 0.5 | 71.1 | 32.0 | 36.4 | 119.2 |
| WADE HAMPTON | 0.3 | 0.2 | 13.9 | 13.5 | 14.4 | 12.1 | 8.8 | 18.2 | 14.0 | 4.8 | 0.3 | 50.2 | 20.9 | 18.4 | 106.9 |
| WRANGELL-PETERSBURG | 1.7 | 2.4 | 6.7 | 8.2 | 9.5 | 9.5 | 6.7 | 24.1 | 26.2 | 8.0 | 1.0 | 69.1 | 31.7 | 35.8 | 118.1 |
| YUKON-KOYUKUK | 1.0 | 1.2 | 8.3 | 9.5 | 10.5 | 9.6 | 6.8 | 23.8 | 22.4 | 8.4 | 0.7 | 64.5 | 29.4 | 31.2 | 125.1 |
| ALASKA | 3.2 | 4.2 | 7.8 | 8.8 | 9.4 | 9.3 | 8.1 | 27.6 | 23.3 | 5.4 | 0.4 | 68.4 | 29.4 | 31.1 | 110.2 |
| UNITED STATES | 9.0 | 11.8 | 6.9 | 7.2 | 7.2 | 7.2 | 6.7 | 29.9 | 22.2 | 11.1 | 1.6 | 74.6 | 32.9 | 35.7 | 95.6 |

| COUNTY | HOUSEHOLDS 1990 | HOUSEHOLDS 2000 | HOUSEHOLDS 2005 | % Annual Rate 1990-2000 | 2000 Average HH Size | FAMILIES 1990 | FAMILIES 2000 | % Annual Rate 1990-2000 | MEDIAN HOUSEHOLD INCOME 2000 | MEDIAN HOUSEHOLD INCOME 2005 | 2000 National Rank | 2000 State Rank |
|---|---|---|---|---|---|---|---|---|---|---|---|---|
| ALEUTIANS EAST | 533 | 518 | 507 | -0.3 | 2.80 | 377 | 356 | -0.7 | 55,231 | 66,905 | 122 | 14 |
| ALEUTIANS WEST | 1,845 | 673 | 574 | -11.5 | 3.11 | 1,440 | 471 | -12.7 | 48,125 | 61,708 | 234 | 19 |
| ANCHORAGE | 82,702 | 96,171 | 101,012 | 1.8 | 2.65 | 56,503 | 63,052 | 1.3 | 63,105 | 76,082 | 53 | 8 |
| BETHEL | 3,605 | 4,358 | 4,663 | 2.3 | 3.70 | 2,773 | 3,255 | 2.0 | 45,429 | 57,360 | 336 | 20 |
| BRISTOL BAY | 407 | 405 | 413 | -0.1 | 2.61 | 272 | 258 | -0.6 | 66,118 | 73,146 | 29 | 3 |
| DILLINGHAM | 1,215 | 1,425 | 1,523 | 2.0 | 3.24 | 922 | 1,051 | 1.6 | 48,525 | 53,708 | 229 | 18 |
| FAIRBANKS NORTH STAR | 26,693 | 29,857 | 30,678 | 1.4 | 2.72 | 19,032 | 20,431 | 0.9 | 59,329 | 73,340 | 79 | 10 |
| HAINES | 791 | 860 | 849 | 1.0 | 2.57 | 536 | 560 | 0.5 | 39,432 | 44,306 | 719 | 23 |
| JUNEAU | 9,902 | 11,309 | 11,570 | 1.6 | 2.62 | 6,628 | 7,193 | 1.0 | 69,036 | 85,789 | 16 | 2 |
| KENAI PENINSULA | 14,250 | 17,361 | 18,463 | 2.4 | 2.78 | 10,216 | 11,919 | 1.9 | 63,113 | 77,196 | 52 | 7 |
| KETCHIKAN GATEWAY | 5,030 | 4,762 | 4,357 | -0.7 | 2.88 | 3,450 | 3,148 | -1.1 | 65,410 | 75,212 | 33 | 4 |
| KODIAK ISLAND | 4,083 | 4,527 | 4,382 | 1.3 | 2.98 | 2,982 | 3,190 | 0.8 | 57,306 | 73,201 | 99 | 12 |
| LAKE AND PENINSULA | 509 | 520 | 522 | 0.3 | 3.32 | 382 | 378 | -0.1 | 36,833 | 39,063 | 1001 | 25 |
| MATANUSKA-SUSITNA | 13,394 | 20,280 | 23,738 | 5.2 | 2.92 | 10,081 | 14,694 | 4.7 | 64,013 | 79,378 | 43 | 6 |
| NOME | 2,371 | 2,644 | 2,674 | 1.3 | 3.29 | 1,723 | 1,855 | 0.9 | 50,030 | 61,167 | 200 | 17 |
| NORTH SLOPE | 1,673 | 2,052 | 2,122 | 2.5 | 3.42 | 1,209 | 1,425 | 2.0 | 78,494 | 96,557 | 2 | 1 |
| NORTHWEST ARCTIC | 1,526 | 1,746 | 1,816 | 1.6 | 3.83 | 1,190 | 1,336 | 1.4 | 53,038 | 68,814 | 153 | 15 |
| PR OF WALES-OUT KTCH | 2,061 | 2,338 | 2,257 | 1.5 | 2.82 | 1,485 | 1,624 | 1.1 | 57,418 | 70,767 | 96 | 11 |
| SITKA | 2,939 | 2,832 | 2,678 | -0.4 | 2.73 | 2,102 | 1,947 | -0.9 | 60,454 | 65,699 | 70 | 9 |
| SKAGWAY-YAKUTAT-ANGO | 1,422 | 1,510 | 1,533 | 0.7 | 2.68 | 1,010 | 1,029 | 0.2 | 44,484 | 50,193 | 374 | 21 |
| SOUTHEAST FAIRBANKS | 1,909 | 1,880 | 1,783 | -0.2 | 2.96 | 1,473 | 1,408 | -0.5 | 51,460 | 64,131 | 179 | 16 |
| VALDEZ-CORDOVA | 3,425 | 3,666 | 3,643 | 0.8 | 2.71 | 2,312 | 2,384 | 0.4 | 64,513 | 77,726 | 40 | 5 |
| WADE HAMPTON | 1,368 | 1,668 | 1,788 | 2.4 | 4.24 | 1,086 | 1,317 | 2.4 | 37,625 | 46,197 | 887 | 24 |
| WRANGELL-PETERSBURG | 2,514 | 2,408 | 2,336 | -0.5 | 2.75 | 1,788 | 1,642 | -1.0 | 55,281 | 62,663 | 120 | 13 |
| YUKON-KOYUKUK | 2,748 | 2,685 | 2,522 | -0.3 | 2.89 | 1,865 | 1,776 | -0.6 | 41,173 | 51,606 | 572 | 22 |
| ALASKA | | | | 1.8 | 2.78 | | | 1.3 | 61,318 | 74,930 | | |
| UNITED STATES | | | | 1.4 | 2.59 | | | 1.1 | 41,914 | 49,127 | | |

| COUNTY | 2000 Per Capita Income | 2000 HH Income Base | 2000 HOUSEHOLD INCOME DISTRIBUTION (%) | | | | | | 2000 AVERAGE DISPOSABLE INCOME BY AGE OF HOUSEHOLDER | | | | | |
|---|---|---|---|---|---|---|---|---|---|---|---|---|---|---|
| | | | Less than $15,000 | $15,000 to $24,999 | $25,000 to $49,999 | $50,000 to $99,999 | $100,000 to $149,999 | $150,000 or More | All Ages | <35 | 35-44 | 45-54 | 55-64 | 65+ |
| ALEUTIANS EAST | 29,816 | 518 | 6.8 | 5.6 | 29.2 | 32.6 | 14.3 | 11.6 | 65,466 | 51,377 | 59,681 | 68,679 | 60,348 | 47,251 |
| ALEUTIANS WEST | 20,081 | 673 | 5.8 | 13.5 | 32.2 | 36.4 | 8.9 | 3.1 | 46,133 | 35,881 | 52,092 | 54,336 | 44,278 | 30,769 |
| ANCHORAGE | 31,147 | 96,171 | 5.9 | 7.3 | 24.0 | 39.8 | 14.8 | 8.1 | 60,753 | 42,355 | 60,763 | 70,778 | 61,389 | 46,613 |
| BETHEL | 15,687 | 4,358 | 17.8 | 10.4 | 26.1 | 31.6 | 9.9 | 4.2 | 45,052 | 38,904 | 49,084 | 51,811 | 41,932 | 30,919 |
| BRISTOL BAY | 29,220 | 405 | 7.7 | 6.9 | 17.0 | 46.4 | 15.8 | 6.2 | 58,749 | 48,808 | 62,763 | 63,761 | 55,551 | 34,052 |
| DILLINGHAM | 30,726 | 1,425 | 17.6 | 9.4 | 25.1 | 31.9 | 11.8 | 4.2 | 47,020 | 37,100 | 48,034 | 58,226 | 44,846 | 30,050 |
| FAIRBANKS NORTH STAR | 27,525 | 29,856 | 6.7 | 7.9 | 25.6 | 40.8 | 13.1 | 5.8 | 55,236 | 37,687 | 56,958 | 70,063 | 59,144 | 40,798 |
| HAINES | 17,882 | 860 | 16.7 | 12.8 | 31.1 | 32.2 | 5.8 | 1.4 | 38,017 | 28,719 | 38,767 | 45,858 | 37,114 | 26,952 |
| JUNEAU | 30,802 | 11,309 | 4.2 | 6.1 | 20.1 | 44.4 | 18.8 | 6.5 | 61,026 | 44,953 | 61,166 | 74,096 | 63,301 | 38,430 |
| KENAI PENINSULA | 30,420 | 17,361 | 8.2 | 6.9 | 21.0 | 40.8 | 14.3 | 8.8 | 61,206 | 51,119 | 62,844 | 68,689 | 55,037 | 34,247 |
| KETCHIKAN GATEWAY | 29,232 | 4,762 | 4.7 | 5.1 | 23.3 | 44.3 | 15.6 | 7.0 | 61,068 | 45,039 | 61,414 | 69,015 | 61,900 | 41,118 |
| KODIAK ISLAND | 31,016 | 4,527 | 6.2 | 8.4 | 27.8 | 36.2 | 12.0 | 9.5 | 61,741 | 45,884 | 59,592 | 68,011 | 57,072 | 32,701 |
| LAKE AND PENINSULA | 16,789 | 520 | 18.7 | 15.0 | 27.9 | 25.4 | 7.5 | 5.6 | 43,721 | 29,139 | 44,276 | 58,845 | 42,375 | 30,412 |
| MATANUSKA-SUSITNA | 27,952 | 20,280 | 8.4 | 5.6 | 21.7 | 41.6 | 16.1 | 6.7 | 58,512 | 45,908 | 59,629 | 68,472 | 52,916 | 37,956 |
| NOME | 17,397 | 2,644 | 16.0 | 8.6 | 25.4 | 35.6 | 12.2 | 2.2 | 45,235 | 39,139 | 48,671 | 55,695 | 41,086 | 32,170 |
| NORTH SLOPE | 29,607 | 2,052 | 6.1 | 4.9 | 16.4 | 38.3 | 22.1 | 12.3 | 72,885 | 54,432 | 73,282 | 80,686 | 67,452 | 54,087 |
| NORTHWEST ARCTIC | 18,241 | 1,746 | 11.7 | 7.2 | 28.2 | 36.7 | 11.7 | 4.5 | 50,905 | 42,938 | 53,283 | 56,508 | 49,623 | 41,216 |
| PR OF WALES-OUT KTCH | 25,436 | 2,338 | 8.3 | 6.2 | 24.6 | 42.6 | 13.7 | 4.5 | 54,198 | 48,472 | 57,173 | 60,732 | 52,630 | 37,659 |
| SITKA | 25,428 | 2,832 | 5.1 | 6.2 | 25.8 | 47.3 | 12.0 | 3.6 | 53,660 | 42,536 | 53,411 | 63,704 | 54,707 | 41,779 |
| SKAGWAY-YAKUTAT-ANGO | 20,378 | 1,510 | 11.4 | 9.8 | 38.7 | 34.2 | 4.4 | 1.5 | 40,984 | 33,911 | 43,240 | 50,238 | 41,018 | 26,180 |
| SOUTHEAST FAIRBANKS | 21,332 | 1,880 | 8.2 | 11.2 | 28.8 | 37.7 | 10.5 | 3.5 | 48,523 | 39,733 | 48,348 | 56,891 | 53,707 | 33,117 |
| VALDEZ-CORDOVA | 34,618 | 3,666 | 9.7 | 7.4 | 20.4 | 37.2 | 14.3 | 11.0 | 64,650 | 53,658 | 60,938 | 67,994 | 62,896 | 34,121 |
| WADE HAMPTON | 10,905 | 1,668 | 16.5 | 15.6 | 33.5 | 26.2 | 7.3 | 1.0 | 37,327 | 29,769 | 41,297 | 42,936 | 36,712 | 32,698 |
| WRANGELL-PETERSBURG | 27,799 | 2,404 | 8.1 | 5.2 | 30.4 | 38.4 | 12.6 | 5.5 | 54,255 | 46,909 | 55,902 | 59,065 | 53,460 | 36,211 |
| YUKON-KOYUKUK | 17,551 | 2,681 | 22.4 | 9.8 | 27.3 | 31.0 | 7.2 | 2.3 | 39,735 | 32,584 | 42,983 | 46,886 | 36,408 | 28,835 |
| ALASKA | 28,723 | | 7.3 | 7.3 | 24.0 | 39.8 | 14.3 | 7.2 | 58,298 | 42,559 | 59,022 | 68,415 | 57,596 | 40,357 |
| UNITED STATES | 22,162 | | 14.5 | 12.5 | 32.3 | 29.8 | 7.4 | 3.5 | 40,748 | 34,503 | 44,969 | 49,579 | 43,409 | 27,339 |

| COUNTY | FINANCIAL SERVICES | | | | THE HOME | | | | | | ENTERTAINMENT | | | | | | PERSONAL | | | |
|---|---|---|---|---|---|---|---|---|---|---|---|---|---|---|---|---|---|---|---|---|
| | | | | | Home Improvements | | | Furnishings | | | | | | | | | | | | |
| | Auto Loan | Home Loan | Invest-ments | Retire-ment Plans | Home Repair | Lawn & Garden | Remodel-ing | Appli-ances | Elec-tronics | Furni-ture | Restau-rants | Sport-ing Goods | Theater & Concerts | Toys & Hobbies | Travel | Video Rental | Apparel | Auto After-market | Health Insur-ance | Pets & Supplies |
| ALEUTIANS EAST | 100 | 114 | 87 | 97 | 96 | 96 | 93 | 102 | 108 | 103 | 108 | 95 | 95 | 94 | 90 | 98 | 102 | 107 | 94 | 98 |
| ALEUTIANS WEST | 93 | 105 | 82 | 88 | 92 | 91 | 88 | 96 | 100 | 92 | 97 | 88 | 87 | 87 | 84 | 94 | 91 | 98 | 91 | 94 |
| ANCHORAGE | 103 | 114 | 96 | 109 | 102 | 105 | 102 | 105 | 109 | 111 | 112 | 100 | 100 | 99 | 96 | 96 | 110 | 107 | 96 | 99 |
| BETHEL | 98 | 98 | 86 | 91 | 97 | 96 | 98 | 101 | 102 | 100 | 98 | 91 | 90 | 92 | 86 | 94 | 94 | 98 | 95 | 96 |
| BRISTOL BAY | 107 | 112 | 102 | 111 | 105 | 109 | 109 | 108 | 114 | 117 | 118 | 103 | 107 | 105 | 98 | 99 | 119 | 112 | 100 | 102 |
| DILLINGHAM | 98 | 98 | 86 | 91 | 96 | 96 | 98 | 100 | 100 | 99 | 98 | 91 | 89 | 92 | 86 | 94 | 93 | 97 | 95 | 95 |
| FAIRBANKS NORTH STAR | 100 | 106 | 91 | 100 | 99 | 99 | 100 | 101 | 105 | 104 | 105 | 95 | 95 | 95 | 90 | 95 | 103 | 102 | 94 | 97 |
| HAINES | 102 | 78 | 81 | 87 | 97 | 94 | 121 | 102 | 98 | 88 | 88 | 93 | 84 | 96 | 76 | 95 | 90 | 92 | 101 | 97 |
| JUNEAU | 104 | 111 | 98 | 106 | 103 | 106 | 104 | 105 | 108 | 112 | 112 | 100 | 101 | 100 | 96 | 97 | 110 | 107 | 98 | 99 |
| KENAI PENINSULA | 101 | 98 | 86 | 96 | 98 | 97 | 105 | 103 | 105 | 103 | 103 | 95 | 93 | 97 | 86 | 96 | 101 | 101 | 96 | 97 |
| KETCHIKAN GATEWAY | 103 | 110 | 98 | 105 | 103 | 105 | 104 | 104 | 108 | 111 | 111 | 98 | 100 | 100 | 95 | 97 | 110 | 107 | 97 | 99 |
| KODIAK ISLAND | 101 | 113 | 88 | 99 | 98 | 99 | 96 | 103 | 107 | 106 | 108 | 97 | 96 | 95 | 91 | 97 | 104 | 106 | 95 | 99 |
| LAKE AND PENINSULA | 98 | 68 | 73 | 82 | 94 | 93 | 121 | 99 | 94 | 78 | 78 | 89 | 76 | 90 | 73 | 93 | 81 | 88 | 103 | 92 |
| MATANUSKA-SUSITNA | 104 | 105 | 85 | 101 | 98 | 100 | 105 | 105 | 109 | 109 | 110 | 100 | 97 | 100 | 89 | 97 | 108 | 105 | 97 | 99 |
| NOME | 99 | 97 | 88 | 93 | 99 | 98 | 104 | 101 | 101 | 99 | 98 | 92 | 91 | 94 | 86 | 95 | 96 | 98 | 97 | 96 |
| NORTH SLOPE | 100 | 109 | 100 | 100 | 102 | 104 | 97 | 102 | 105 | 104 | 106 | 95 | 97 | 95 | 94 | 96 | 102 | 103 | 98 | 97 |
| NORTHWEST ARCTIC | 96 | 91 | 77 | 85 | 95 | 91 | 95 | 99 | 99 | 97 | 92 | 88 | 86 | 89 | 82 | 94 | 92 | 96 | 91 | 92 |
| PR OF WALES-OUT KTCH | 99 | 81 | 81 | 84 | 94 | 92 | 116 | 100 | 97 | 91 | 90 | 91 | 83 | 93 | 76 | 93 | 88 | 92 | 97 | 94 |
| SITKA | 102 | 103 | 96 | 101 | 101 | 102 | 107 | 104 | 106 | 107 | 107 | 97 | 97 | 99 | 91 | 96 | 106 | 104 | 97 | 98 |
| SKAGWAY-YAKUTAT-ANGO | 99 | 91 | 78 | 87 | 94 | 92 | 105 | 100 | 101 | 97 | 96 | 92 | 87 | 94 | 79 | 95 | 94 | 96 | 94 | 94 |
| SOUTHEAST FAIRBANKS | 100 | 96 | 85 | 94 | 97 | 97 | 106 | 102 | 103 | 100 | 99 | 95 | 91 | 96 | 85 | 96 | 100 | 99 | 96 | 96 |
| VALDEZ-CORDOVA | 103 | 98 | 95 | 103 | 100 | 102 | 113 | 104 | 104 | 102 | 101 | 98 | 95 | 98 | 88 | 96 | 101 | 100 | 100 | 98 |
| WADE HAMPTON | 93 | 85 | 80 | 78 | 94 | 91 | 92 | 98 | 96 | 92 | 84 | 82 | 82 | 85 | 81 | 94 | 86 | 93 | 90 | 92 |
| WRANGELL-PETERSBURG | 102 | 95 | 89 | 96 | 99 | 99 | 109 | 103 | 104 | 100 | 101 | 95 | 93 | 98 | 85 | 96 | 100 | 100 | 98 | 97 |
| YUKON-KOYUKUK | 93 | 85 | 74 | 80 | 94 | 88 | 95 | 96 | 95 | 90 | 85 | 84 | 82 | 86 | 79 | 92 | 88 | 92 | 89 | 90 |
| ALASKA | 102 | 108 | 93 | 103 | 100 | 102 | 103 | 104 | 107 | 107 | 108 | 98 | 97 | 97 | 92 | 96 | 106 | 104 | 96 | 98 |
| UNITED STATES | 100 | 100 | 100 | 100 | 100 | 100 | 100 | 100 | 100 | 100 | 100 | 100 | 100 | 100 | 100 | 100 | 100 | 100 | 100 | 100 |

# POPULATION CHANGE

| COUNTY | FIPS Code | MSA Code | DMA Code | POPULATION 1990 | POPULATION 2000 | POPULATION 2005 | 1990-2000 ANNUAL CHANGE % Rate | 1990-2000 ANNUAL CHANGE State Rank | RACE (%) White 1990 | RACE (%) White 2000 | RACE (%) Black 1990 | RACE (%) Black 2000 | RACE (%) Asian/Pacific 1990 | RACE (%) Asian/Pacific 2000 |
|---|---|---|---|---|---|---|---|---|---|---|---|---|---|---|
| APACHE | 001 | 0000 | 790 | 61,591 | 68,697 | 68,769 | 1.1 | 13 | 20.2 | 20.4 | 0.2 | 0.2 | 0.2 | 0.2 |
| COCHISE | 003 | 0000 | 789 | 97,624 | 113,515 | 117,193 | 1.5 | 12 | 81.7 | 79.1 | 5.2 | 5.2 | 2.3 | 3.0 |
| COCONINO | 005 | 2620 | 753 | 96,591 | 115,214 | 118,913 | 1.7 | 11 | 64.0 | 62.4 | 1.5 | 1.7 | 0.9 | 1.1 |
| GILA | 007 | 0000 | 753 | 40,216 | 49,558 | 52,169 | 2.1 | 8 | 76.5 | 75.0 | 0.2 | 0.2 | 0.3 | 0.5 |
| GRAHAM | 009 | 0000 | 753 | 26,554 | 32,394 | 34,403 | 2.0 | 9 | 77.6 | 76.5 | 1.9 | 1.8 | 0.4 | 0.5 |
| GREENLEE | 011 | 0000 | 753 | 8,008 | 8,881 | 8,764 | 1.0 | 14 | 85.4 | 83.9 | 0.3 | 0.4 | 0.2 | 0.3 |
| LA PAZ | 012 | 0000 | 753 | 13,844 | 15,141 | 15,620 | 0.9 | 15 | 74.7 | 75.8 | 0.9 | 1.0 | 0.7 | 1.0 |
| MARICOPA | 013 | 6200 | 753 | 2,122,101 | 2,942,946 | 3,350,794 | 3.2 | 3 | 84.8 | 81.8 | 3.5 | 3.9 | 1.7 | 2.3 |
| MOHAVE | 015 | 4120 | 753 | 93,497 | 137,212 | 152,864 | 3.8 | 1 | 95.0 | 94.2 | 0.3 | 0.4 | 0.6 | 0.9 |
| NAVAJO | 017 | 0000 | 753 | 77,658 | 100,241 | 109,842 | 2.5 | 7 | 44.0 | 43.7 | 0.9 | 1.0 | 0.3 | 0.4 |
| PIMA | 019 | 8520 | 789 | 666,880 | 816,221 | 880,397 | 2.0 | 9 | 78.7 | 75.3 | 3.1 | 3.5 | 1.8 | 2.3 |
| PINAL | 021 | 6200 | 753 | 116,379 | 156,851 | 179,562 | 3.0 | 4 | 74.9 | 73.3 | 3.1 | 3.2 | 0.4 | 0.6 |
| SANTA CRUZ | 023 | 0000 | 789 | 29,676 | 40,140 | 44,986 | 3.0 | 4 | 74.7 | 73.5 | 0.3 | 0.4 | 0.6 | 0.7 |
| YAVAPAI | 025 | 0000 | 753 | 107,714 | 157,253 | 179,061 | 3.8 | 1 | 95.7 | 95.1 | 0.3 | 0.3 | 0.5 | 0.6 |
| YUMA | 027 | 9360 | 771 | 106,895 | 139,742 | 157,398 | 2.6 | 6 | 75.5 | 72.5 | 2.9 | 2.9 | 1.3 | 1.6 |
| ARIZONA | | | | | | | 2.9 | | 80.9 | 78.6 | 3.0 | 3.4 | 1.5 | 2.0 |
| UNITED STATES | | | | | | | 1.0 | | 80.3 | 77.9 | 12.1 | 12.4 | 2.9 | 3.9 |

| COUNTY | % HISPANIC ORIGIN | | 2000 AGE DISTRIBUTION (%) | | | | | | | | | | MEDIAN AGE | | 2000 Males/ Females (×100) |
|---|---|---|---|---|---|---|---|---|---|---|---|---|---|---|---|
| | 1990 | 2000 | 0-4 | 5-9 | 10-14 | 15-19 | 20-24 | 25-44 | 45-64 | 65-84 | 85+ | 18+ | 1990 | 2000 | |
| APACHE | 4.2 | 5.2 | 11.6 | 12.1 | 12.0 | 10.1 | 7.4 | 23.8 | 16.4 | 6.1 | 0.6 | 57.9 | 23.5 | 22.9 | 96.6 |
| COCHISE | 29.1 | 35.0 | 8.0 | 7.8 | 7.8 | 8.0 | 7.0 | 26.0 | 22.1 | 12.2 | 1.2 | 71.5 | 32.6 | 34.4 | 103.5 |
| COCONINO | 10.0 | 13.0 | 8.4 | 8.6 | 8.5 | 10.6 | 12.0 | 27.9 | 18.0 | 5.5 | 0.5 | 70.7 | 26.2 | 26.5 | 99.6 |
| GILA | 18.6 | 22.9 | 6.9 | 7.1 | 7.2 | 7.2 | 5.7 | 20.0 | 25.1 | 18.9 | 1.9 | 74.0 | 38.8 | 41.6 | 94.9 |
| GRAHAM | 25.2 | 30.1 | 9.2 | 9.6 | 9.5 | 9.4 | 7.2 | 24.3 | 19.2 | 10.4 | 1.2 | 66.4 | 29.4 | 29.2 | 104.7 |
| GREENLEE | 43.2 | 49.2 | 8.0 | 9.2 | 9.6 | 8.9 | 5.9 | 24.6 | 23.2 | 9.7 | 0.9 | 66.8 | 32.1 | 32.7 | 102.0 |
| LA PAZ | 22.7 | 24.5 | 7.5 | 7.3 | 7.5 | 6.5 | 5.2 | 21.2 | 22.3 | 20.8 | 1.7 | 73.6 | 37.3 | 40.6 | 107.4 |
| MARICOPA | 16.3 | 20.7 | 8.2 | 7.9 | 7.6 | 7.1 | 6.6 | 29.4 | 21.1 | 10.8 | 1.4 | 72.3 | 32.0 | 34.6 | 97.4 |
| MOHAVE | 5.3 | 7.0 | 6.1 | 6.3 | 6.5 | 5.9 | 4.7 | 22.0 | 26.6 | 20.5 | 1.5 | 77.4 | 40.7 | 43.9 | 99.6 |
| NAVAJO | 7.3 | 9.2 | 10.5 | 11.0 | 10.9 | 9.4 | 6.7 | 24.1 | 18.9 | 7.8 | 0.7 | 61.4 | 26.5 | 26.3 | 99.0 |
| PIMA | 24.5 | 29.9 | 7.3 | 7.1 | 7.0 | 7.3 | 7.4 | 28.7 | 21.2 | 12.4 | 1.6 | 74.7 | 32.8 | 35.3 | 96.4 |
| PINAL | 29.3 | 34.4 | 8.3 | 8.4 | 8.2 | 8.0 | 6.4 | 24.7 | 21.5 | 13.3 | 1.2 | 70.3 | 32.6 | 34.5 | 106.6 |
| SANTA CRUZ | 78.2 | 81.7 | 10.1 | 9.5 | 9.5 | 9.1 | 7.4 | 24.9 | 19.2 | 9.2 | 0.9 | 65.0 | 29.5 | 28.5 | 92.7 |
| YAVAPAI | 6.4 | 8.4 | 5.6 | 6.0 | 6.2 | 6.7 | 5.1 | 20.7 | 26.2 | 21.4 | 2.1 | 78.2 | 42.4 | 44.7 | 97.1 |
| YUMA | 40.6 | 46.6 | 8.4 | 7.9 | 7.3 | 7.6 | 8.7 | 25.6 | 18.6 | 14.5 | 1.3 | 71.8 | 30.5 | 32.3 | 101.7 |
| ARIZONA | 18.8 | 23.0 | 8.0 | 7.8 | 7.6 | 7.3 | 6.8 | 28.1 | 21.2 | 11.7 | 1.4 | 72.4 | 32.2 | 34.7 | 97.9 |
| UNITED STATES | 9.0 | 11.8 | 6.9 | 7.2 | 7.2 | 7.2 | 6.7 | 29.9 | 22.2 | 11.1 | 1.6 | 74.6 | 32.9 | 35.7 | 95.6 |

# HOUSEHOLDS

| COUNTY | HOUSEHOLDS | | | | | FAMILIES | | | MEDIAN HOUSEHOLD INCOME | | | |
|---|---|---|---|---|---|---|---|---|---|---|---|---|
| | 1990 | 2000 | 2005 | % Annual Rate 1990-2000 | 2000 Average HH Size | 1990 | 2000 | % Annual Rate 1990-2000 | 2000 | 2005 | 2000 National Rank | 2000 State Rank |
| APACHE | 15,981 | 18,181 | 18,241 | 1.6 | 3.72 | 13,014 | 14,641 | 1.4 | 21,621 | 23,787 | 3047 | 15 |
| COCHISE | 34,546 | 41,335 | 43,128 | 2.2 | 2.63 | 25,328 | 29,461 | 1.8 | 29,844 | 34,395 | 2174 | 11 |
| COCONINO | 29,918 | 36,817 | 38,420 | 2.5 | 2.94 | 21,157 | 23,284 | 1.2 | 37,697 | 42,909 | 878 | 3 |
| GILA | 15,438 | 19,946 | 21,461 | 3.2 | 2.45 | 11,204 | 14,016 | 2.8 | 29,832 | 33,750 | 2175 | 12 |
| GRAHAM | 7,930 | 9,892 | 10,673 | 2.7 | 3.03 | 6,153 | 7,497 | 2.4 | 30,116 | 35,986 | 2126 | 9 |
| GREENLEE | 2,809 | 3,337 | 3,401 | 2.1 | 2.66 | 2,110 | 2,441 | 1.8 | 41,541 | 47,819 | 546 | 2 |
| LA PAZ | 5,348 | 5,951 | 6,240 | 1.3 | 2.48 | 3,809 | 4,165 | 1.1 | 22,454 | 25,466 | 2998 | 14 |
| MARICOPA | 807,560 | 1,136,949 | 1,305,782 | 4.2 | 2.55 | 547,211 | 753,871 | 4.0 | 43,214 | 50,870 | 443 | 1 |
| MOHAVE | 36,801 | 54,568 | 60,984 | 4.9 | 2.47 | 26,650 | 38,537 | 4.6 | 32,611 | 39,188 | 1610 | 7 |
| NAVAJO | 22,189 | 29,546 | 32,844 | 3.5 | 3.35 | 17,930 | 23,413 | 3.3 | 29,033 | 34,445 | 2291 | 13 |
| PIMA | 261,792 | 324,895 | 352,631 | 2.7 | 2.46 | 169,666 | 205,449 | 2.3 | 34,130 | 38,841 | 1365 | 5 |
| PINAL | 39,154 | 52,051 | 60,051 | 3.5 | 2.83 | 29,787 | 38,312 | 3.1 | 30,044 | 35,349 | 2145 | 10 |
| SANTA CRUZ | 8,808 | 11,860 | 13,257 | 3.7 | 3.37 | 7,150 | 9,634 | 3.7 | 30,492 | 37,235 | 2038 | 8 |
| YAVAPAI | 44,778 | 66,622 | 76,421 | 4.9 | 2.33 | 31,266 | 45,484 | 4.6 | 33,770 | 39,208 | 1427 | 6 |
| YUMA | 35,791 | 47,750 | 54,062 | 3.6 | 2.86 | 27,671 | 36,669 | 3.5 | 34,377 | 44,755 | 1335 | 4 |
| ARIZONA | | | | 3.8 | 2.58 | | | 3.5 | 39,067 | 45,710 | | |
| UNITED STATES | | | | 1.4 | 2.59 | | | 1.1 | 41,914 | 49,127 | | |

| COUNTY | 2000 Per Capita Income | 2000 HH Income Base | 2000 HOUSEHOLD INCOME DISTRIBUTION (%) | | | | | | 2000 AVERAGE DISPOSABLE INCOME BY AGE OF HOUSEHOLDER | | | | | |
|---|---|---|---|---|---|---|---|---|---|---|---|---|---|---|
| | | | Less than $15,000 | $15,000 to $24,999 | $25,000 to $49,999 | $50,000 to $99,999 | $100,000 to $149,999 | $150,000 or More | All Ages | <35 | 35-44 | 45-54 | 55-64 | 65+ |
| APACHE | 7,822 | 18,176 | 39.4 | 15.7 | 27.9 | 14.9 | 1.9 | 0.3 | 24,241 | 21,420 | 28,817 | 28,075 | 23,957 | 16,163 |
| COCHISE | 14,286 | 41,335 | 24.2 | 17.7 | 35.2 | 19.3 | 2.8 | 0.8 | 29,546 | 24,807 | 33,839 | 37,864 | 32,856 | 21,876 |
| COCONINO | 16,096 | 36,802 | 17.8 | 13.8 | 33.2 | 27.7 | 5.8 | 1.7 | 36,716 | 27,606 | 43,383 | 46,453 | 39,786 | 29,514 |
| GILA | 15,027 | 19,946 | 21.9 | 19.1 | 35.5 | 19.7 | 3.0 | 0.8 | 30,010 | 25,847 | 36,873 | 37,647 | 31,581 | 23,743 |
| GRAHAM | 14,064 | 9,892 | 21.6 | 20.8 | 33.2 | 19.6 | 3.5 | 1.3 | 30,859 | 25,141 | 37,420 | 40,884 | 31,241 | 23,488 |
| GREENLEE | 18,069 | 3,337 | 10.7 | 6.6 | 43.6 | 34.7 | 4.3 | 0.2 | 38,202 | 38,749 | 43,012 | 45,711 | 33,739 | 24,397 |
| LA PAZ | 12,297 | 5,951 | 35.2 | 20.2 | 28.8 | 13.3 | 1.9 | 0.6 | 24,429 | 24,264 | 28,561 | 33,337 | 25,822 | 17,327 |
| MARICOPA | 22,707 | 1,136,943 | 11.7 | 12.9 | 33.3 | 31.5 | 7.6 | 3.1 | 42,402 | 35,954 | 47,073 | 51,724 | 43,771 | 31,331 |
| MOHAVE | 16,580 | 54,545 | 16.7 | 19.0 | 36.9 | 23.1 | 3.4 | 0.9 | 32,421 | 31,574 | 38,954 | 39,829 | 34,345 | 24,727 |
| NAVAJO | 11,083 | 29,536 | 28.0 | 16.0 | 32.5 | 19.7 | 3.0 | 0.9 | 29,293 | 24,809 | 33,530 | 36,915 | 28,164 | 21,934 |
| PIMA | 18,569 | 324,895 | 19.0 | 16.4 | 34.0 | 24.1 | 4.8 | 1.8 | 34,817 | 26,975 | 39,001 | 43,521 | 38,477 | 29,152 |
| PINAL | 12,676 | 52,042 | 22.5 | 18.3 | 36.2 | 20.3 | 2.4 | 0.2 | 29,126 | 26,993 | 34,614 | 36,310 | 29,367 | 21,821 |
| SANTA CRUZ | 12,322 | 11,860 | 23.2 | 18.0 | 34.1 | 20.0 | 3.3 | 1.4 | 31,094 | 27,675 | 34,603 | 34,603 | 35,727 | 22,674 |
| YAVAPAI | 19,212 | 66,622 | 16.8 | 17.9 | 36.5 | 23.3 | 4.2 | 1.3 | 33,821 | 29,303 | 39,743 | 41,719 | 36,801 | 27,914 |
| YUMA | 15,464 | 47,750 | 16.6 | 17.6 | 34.5 | 25.9 | 4.3 | 1.1 | 34,114 | 32,031 | 37,157 | 44,748 | 35,243 | 26,156 |
| ARIZONA | 20,150 | | 14.9 | 14.5 | 33.7 | 28.2 | 6.2 | 2.4 | 38,777 | 32,856 | 43,804 | 47,838 | 40,193 | 29,132 |
| UNITED STATES | 22,162 | | 14.5 | 12.5 | 32.3 | 29.8 | 7.4 | 3.5 | 40,748 | 34,503 | 44,969 | 49,579 | 43,409 | 27,339 |

# SPENDING POTENTIAL INDEXES

| COUNTY | FINANCIAL SERVICES | | | | THE HOME | | | | | | ENTERTAINMENT | | | | | | PERSONAL | | | |
|---|---|---|---|---|---|---|---|---|---|---|---|---|---|---|---|---|---|---|---|---|
| | | | | | Home Improvements | | | Furnishings | | | | | | | | | | | | |
| | Auto Loan | Home Loan | Investments | Retirement Plans | Home Repair | Lawn & Garden | Remodeling | Appliances | Electronics | Furniture | Restaurants | Sporting Goods | Theater & Concerts | Toys & Hobbies | Travel | Video Rental | Apparel | Auto Aftermarket | Health Insurance | Pets & Supplies |
| APACHE | 93 | 82 | 81 | 79 | 94 | 90 | 101 | 97 | 93 | 89 | 82 | 85 | 81 | 85 | 79 | 92 | 85 | 91 | 91 | 90 |
| COCHISE | 97 | 90 | 90 | 91 | 97 | 97 | 103 | 100 | 99 | 94 | 93 | 90 | 87 | 91 | 84 | 93 | 90 | 94 | 98 | 93 |
| COCONINO | 98 | 99 | 90 | 97 | 98 | 97 | 102 | 99 | 99 | 96 | 96 | 91 | 88 | 92 | 87 | 92 | 95 | 97 | 95 | 94 |
| GILA | 98 | 81 | 98 | 90 | 100 | 103 | 110 | 101 | 94 | 88 | 87 | 89 | 85 | 91 | 85 | 92 | 86 | 92 | 103 | 93 |
| GRAHAM | 95 | 76 | 84 | 80 | 95 | 93 | 108 | 97 | 93 | 85 | 82 | 86 | 79 | 88 | 77 | 92 | 82 | 89 | 97 | 90 |
| GREENLEE | 97 | 87 | 80 | 85 | 94 | 92 | 104 | 99 | 99 | 93 | 92 | 89 | 85 | 91 | 79 | 94 | 89 | 94 | 95 | 93 |
| LA PAZ | 96 | 85 | 101 | 85 | 100 | 101 | 101 | 101 | 93 | 88 | 89 | 87 | 86 | 90 | 85 | 91 | 81 | 91 | 103 | 94 |
| MARICOPA | 101 | 106 | 96 | 102 | 102 | 104 | 101 | 103 | 104 | 105 | 105 | 96 | 96 | 96 | 93 | 95 | 102 | 101 | 98 | 97 |
| MOHAVE | 101 | 87 | 106 | 97 | 104 | 109 | 111 | 104 | 96 | 94 | 94 | 92 | 90 | 95 | 91 | 92 | 91 | 94 | 106 | 95 |
| NAVAJO | 96 | 82 | 84 | 83 | 95 | 93 | 108 | 99 | 95 | 89 | 86 | 88 | 82 | 89 | 79 | 92 | 85 | 91 | 96 | 93 |
| PIMA | 99 | 100 | 100 | 98 | 102 | 102 | 101 | 101 | 99 | 99 | 98 | 92 | 92 | 93 | 91 | 93 | 96 | 97 | 98 | 95 |
| PINAL | 97 | 84 | 95 | 85 | 98 | 98 | 106 | 100 | 94 | 90 | 89 | 88 | 85 | 91 | 82 | 92 | 85 | 91 | 100 | 93 |
| SANTA CRUZ | 94 | 92 | 79 | 82 | 92 | 92 | 94 | 98 | 98 | 87 | 89 | 86 | 84 | 87 | 81 | 93 | 84 | 94 | 95 | 95 |
| YAVAPAI | 100 | 88 | 109 | 97 | 105 | 110 | 108 | 104 | 95 | 94 | 94 | 91 | 91 | 94 | 92 | 92 | 90 | 94 | 106 | 95 |
| YUMA | 97 | 94 | 97 | 90 | 99 | 101 | 99 | 101 | 97 | 93 | 94 | 89 | 89 | 91 | 87 | 93 | 88 | 95 | 100 | 95 |
| ARIZONA | 100 | 101 | 97 | 99 | 101 | 103 | 102 | 102 | 101 | 102 | 101 | 94 | 94 | 95 | 91 | 94 | 98 | 99 | 99 | 96 |
| UNITED STATES | 100 | 100 | 100 | 100 | 100 | 100 | 100 | 100 | 100 | 100 | 100 | 100 | 100 | 100 | 100 | 100 | 100 | 100 | 100 | 100 |

| COUNTY | FIPS Code | MSA Code | DMA Code | POPULATION 1990 | POPULATION 2000 | POPULATION 2005 | 1990-2000 ANNUAL CHANGE % Rate | 1990-2000 ANNUAL CHANGE State Rank | RACE (%) White 1990 | White 2000 | Black 1990 | Black 2000 | Asian/Pacific 1990 | Asian/Pacific 2000 |
|---|---|---|---|---|---|---|---|---|---|---|---|---|---|---|
| ARKANSAS | 001 | 0000 | 693 | 21,653 | 20,697 | 20,571 | -0.4 | 58 | 77.7 | 75.3 | 21.9 | 24.1 | 0.2 | 0.2 |
| ASHLEY | 003 | 0000 | 628 | 24,319 | 24,258 | 24,092 | 0.0 | 47 | 72.0 | 68.7 | 27.2 | 29.9 | 0.2 | 0.2 |
| BAXTER | 005 | 0000 | 619 | 31,186 | 36,940 | 38,435 | 1.7 | 13 | 99.3 | 99.1 | 0.0 | 0.0 | 0.2 | 0.3 |
| BENTON | 007 | 2580 | 670 | 97,499 | 142,699 | 164,020 | 3.8 | 1 | 97.4 | 96.5 | 0.1 | 0.2 | 0.5 | 0.7 |
| BOONE | 009 | 0000 | 619 | 28,297 | 31,927 | 32,431 | 1.2 | 23 | 99.1 | 98.9 | 0.0 | 0.1 | 0.2 | 0.2 |
| BRADLEY | 011 | 0000 | 693 | 11,793 | 11,378 | 11,226 | -0.3 | 55 | 67.9 | 64.1 | 30.9 | 33.5 | 0.0 | 0.0 |
| CALHOUN | 013 | 0000 | 693 | 5,826 | 5,638 | 5,533 | -0.3 | 55 | 74.8 | 71.5 | 24.8 | 27.9 | 0.1 | 0.1 |
| CARROLL | 015 | 0000 | 619 | 18,654 | 22,578 | 23,042 | 1.9 | 11 | 98.7 | 98.3 | 0.0 | 0.2 | 0.3 | 0.4 |
| CHICOT | 017 | 0000 | 647 | 15,713 | 14,702 | 13,940 | -0.6 | 63 | 42.6 | 39.1 | 56.4 | 59.1 | 0.4 | 0.4 |
| CLARK | 019 | 0000 | 693 | 21,437 | 21,287 | 20,677 | -0.1 | 53 | 76.2 | 73.4 | 22.9 | 25.5 | 0.4 | 0.4 |
| CLAY | 021 | 0000 | 734 | 18,107 | 16,892 | 16,232 | -0.7 | 65 | 99.6 | 99.4 | 0.0 | 0.1 | 0.1 | 0.1 |
| CLEBURNE | 023 | 0000 | 693 | 19,411 | 23,662 | 25,526 | 2.0 | 8 | 99.4 | 99.2 | 0.0 | 0.1 | 0.1 | 0.2 |
| CLEVELAND | 025 | 0000 | 693 | 7,781 | 8,666 | 9,212 | 1.1 | 29 | 85.9 | 83.7 | 13.6 | 15.6 | 0.2 | 0.2 |
| COLUMBIA | 027 | 0000 | 612 | 25,691 | 24,414 | 23,097 | -0.5 | 61 | 64.5 | 61.0 | 35.0 | 38.4 | 0.2 | 0.3 |
| CONWAY | 029 | 0000 | 693 | 19,151 | 19,898 | 20,049 | 0.4 | 38 | 84.3 | 82.3 | 15.0 | 16.7 | 0.2 | 0.2 |
| CRAIGHEAD | 031 | 3700 | 734 | 68,956 | 78,349 | 81,831 | 1.3 | 22 | 93.5 | 92.3 | 5.5 | 6.2 | 0.6 | 0.7 |
| CRAWFORD | 033 | 2720 | 670 | 42,493 | 52,345 | 57,135 | 2.1 | 6 | 96.4 | 95.6 | 0.9 | 1.1 | 0.9 | 1.3 |
| CRITTENDEN | 035 | 4920 | 640 | 49,939 | 50,431 | 51,755 | 0.1 | 44 | 56.4 | 52.8 | 42.9 | 46.0 | 0.4 | 0.5 |
| CROSS | 037 | 0000 | 640 | 19,225 | 19,279 | 19,145 | 0.0 | 47 | 74.6 | 71.4 | 24.9 | 27.9 | 0.2 | 0.3 |
| DALLAS | 039 | 0000 | 693 | 9,614 | 8,808 | 8,255 | -0.9 | 68 | 61.1 | 58.0 | 38.5 | 41.4 | 0.1 | 0.1 |
| DESHA | 041 | 0000 | 693 | 16,798 | 14,666 | 13,750 | -1.3 | 73 | 56.6 | 52.9 | 42.5 | 45.5 | 0.2 | 0.3 |
| DREW | 043 | 0000 | 693 | 17,369 | 17,549 | 17,328 | 0.1 | 44 | 72.1 | 68.8 | 27.4 | 30.4 | 0.1 | 0.2 |
| FAULKNER | 045 | 4400 | 693 | 60,006 | 81,995 | 91,767 | 3.1 | 2 | 91.1 | 89.8 | 8.0 | 9.0 | 0.4 | 0.5 |
| FRANKLIN | 047 | 0000 | 670 | 14,897 | 16,897 | 17,420 | 1.2 | 23 | 98.3 | 97.9 | 0.7 | 0.8 | 0.2 | 0.2 |
| FULTON | 049 | 0000 | 619 | 10,037 | 11,109 | 11,571 | 1.0 | 30 | 99.3 | 99.3 | 0.1 | 0.1 | 0.1 | 0.1 |
| GARLAND | 051 | 0000 | 693 | 73,397 | 85,387 | 89,932 | 1.5 | 15 | 91.0 | 89.6 | 7.6 | 8.4 | 0.3 | 0.4 |
| GRANT | 053 | 0000 | 693 | 13,948 | 16,179 | 17,136 | 1.5 | 15 | 96.7 | 96.1 | 2.7 | 3.1 | 0.2 | 0.2 |
| GREENE | 055 | 0000 | 734 | 31,804 | 36,852 | 39,129 | 1.4 | 19 | 99.4 | 99.1 | 0.1 | 0.2 | 0.1 | 0.2 |
| HEMPSTEAD | 057 | 0000 | 612 | 21,621 | 22,144 | 22,365 | 0.2 | 42 | 68.9 | 65.0 | 29.9 | 32.9 | 0.2 | 0.3 |
| HOT SPRING | 059 | 0000 | 693 | 26,115 | 29,431 | 30,853 | 1.2 | 23 | 88.3 | 86.7 | 11.0 | 12.4 | 0.1 | 0.2 |
| HOWARD | 061 | 0000 | 612 | 13,569 | 13,667 | 13,573 | 0.1 | 44 | 77.4 | 74.5 | 21.5 | 24.0 | 0.4 | 0.6 |
| INDEPENDENCE | 063 | 0000 | 693 | 31,192 | 33,185 | 33,874 | 0.6 | 35 | 97.3 | 96.5 | 1.9 | 2.3 | 0.4 | 0.6 |
| IZARD | 065 | 0000 | 734 | 11,364 | 13,183 | 13,534 | 1.5 | 15 | 99.1 | 97.7 | 0.1 | 1.5 | 0.2 | 0.2 |
| JACKSON | 067 | 0000 | 693 | 18,944 | 17,306 | 16,283 | -0.9 | 68 | 84.9 | 83.3 | 14.6 | 16.1 | 0.1 | 0.2 |
| JEFFERSON | 069 | 6240 | 693 | 85,487 | 80,092 | 76,719 | -0.6 | 63 | 56.0 | 52.5 | 43.1 | 46.3 | 0.4 | 0.6 |
| JOHNSON | 071 | 0000 | 693 | 18,221 | 21,446 | 21,955 | 1.6 | 14 | 96.8 | 95.7 | 1.7 | 2.0 | 0.4 | 0.5 |
| LAFAYETTE | 073 | 0000 | 612 | 9,643 | 8,754 | 8,302 | -0.9 | 68 | 61.0 | 57.4 | 38.5 | 42.0 | 0.2 | 0.2 |
| LAWRENCE | 075 | 0000 | 734 | 17,457 | 17,375 | 17,516 | 0.0 | 47 | 98.7 | 98.5 | 0.5 | 0.7 | 0.1 | 0.1 |
| LEE | 077 | 0000 | 640 | 13,053 | 12,533 | 11,736 | -0.4 | 58 | 41.7 | 39.1 | 57.4 | 59.2 | 0.4 | 0.5 |
| LINCOLN | 079 | 0000 | 693 | 13,690 | 14,407 | 14,593 | 0.5 | 37 | 62.9 | 60.7 | 36.0 | 37.8 | 0.1 | 0.2 |
| LITTLE RIVER | 081 | 0000 | 612 | 13,966 | 12,987 | 12,596 | -0.7 | 65 | 77.5 | 74.3 | 21.0 | 23.4 | 0.1 | 0.2 |
| LOGAN | 083 | 0000 | 670 | 20,557 | 21,156 | 21,247 | 0.3 | 40 | 97.7 | 97.2 | 1.3 | 1.6 | 0.1 | 0.2 |
| LONOKE | 085 | 4400 | 693 | 39,268 | 52,802 | 59,527 | 2.9 | 3 | 90.1 | 88.5 | 9.0 | 10.3 | 0.3 | 0.4 |
| MADISON | 087 | 0000 | 670 | 11,618 | 13,408 | 13,900 | 1.4 | 19 | 98.4 | 98.0 | 0.0 | 0.0 | 0.1 | 0.2 |
| MARION | 089 | 0000 | 619 | 12,001 | 15,043 | 15,877 | 2.2 | 5 | 99.2 | 99.0 | 0.0 | 0.1 | 0.2 | 0.3 |
| MILLER | 091 | 8360 | 612 | 38,467 | 39,365 | 39,269 | 0.2 | 42 | 76.6 | 73.8 | 22.4 | 24.9 | 0.4 | 0.5 |
| MISSISSIPPI | 093 | 0000 | 640 | 57,525 | 49,615 | 48,068 | -1.4 | 75 | 70.7 | 67.3 | 27.8 | 30.4 | 0.6 | 0.8 |
| MONROE | 095 | 0000 | 693 | 11,333 | 9,860 | 9,228 | -1.3 | 73 | 60.5 | 57.0 | 39.0 | 42.5 | 0.2 | 0.2 |
| MONTGOMERY | 097 | 0000 | 693 | 7,841 | 8,849 | 9,382 | 1.2 | 23 | 98.4 | 98.2 | 0.1 | 0.2 | 0.1 | 0.2 |
| NEVADA | 099 | 0000 | 612 | 10,101 | 10,046 | 10,119 | -0.1 | 53 | 67.9 | 64.2 | 31.6 | 35.1 | 0.0 | 0.1 |
| NEWTON | 101 | 0000 | 619 | 7,666 | 8,292 | 8,576 | 0.8 | 31 | 98.9 | 98.5 | 0.0 | 0.0 | 0.2 | 0.4 |
| OUACHITA | 103 | 0000 | 693 | 30,574 | 27,235 | 25,986 | -1.1 | 72 | 64.4 | 61.3 | 35.1 | 38.1 | 0.2 | 0.3 |
| PERRY | 105 | 0000 | 693 | 7,969 | 9,801 | 10,443 | 2.0 | 8 | 97.6 | 97.2 | 1.5 | 1.7 | 0.2 | 0.3 |
| PHILLIPS | 107 | 0000 | 640 | 28,838 | 26,824 | 25,708 | -0.7 | 65 | 44.8 | 41.9 | 54.6 | 57.2 | 0.2 | 0.4 |
| PIKE | 109 | 0000 | 693 | 10,086 | 10,445 | 10,399 | 0.3 | 40 | 95.4 | 94.4 | 3.7 | 4.3 | 0.1 | 0.1 |
| POINSETT | 111 | 0000 | 640 | 24,664 | 24,702 | 24,740 | 0.0 | 47 | 92.4 | 91.1 | 7.2 | 8.2 | 0.1 | 0.4 |
| POLK | 113 | 0000 | 693 | 17,347 | 19,686 | 20,126 | 1.2 | 23 | 98.2 | 97.4 | 0.0 | 0.0 | 0.2 | 0.3 |
| POPE | 115 | 0000 | 693 | 45,883 | 53,143 | 55,911 | 1.4 | 19 | 96.2 | 95.4 | 2.5 | 2.8 | 0.4 | 0.6 |
| PRAIRIE | 117 | 0000 | 693 | 9,518 | 9,273 | 9,215 | -0.3 | 55 | 85.8 | 84.1 | 13.6 | 15.2 | 0.0 | 0.0 |
| PULASKI | 119 | 4400 | 693 | 349,660 | 349,931 | 349,878 | 0.0 | 47 | 72.2 | 68.6 | 26.4 | 29.3 | 0.8 | 1.1 |
| RANDOLPH | 121 | 0000 | 734 | 16,558 | 18,014 | 18,581 | 0.8 | 31 | 98.6 | 98.3 | 0.9 | 1.0 | 0.1 | 0.1 |
| ST. FRANCIS | 123 | 0000 | 640 | 28,497 | 27,181 | 25,933 | -0.5 | 61 | 51.7 | 48.1 | 47.4 | 50.4 | 0.4 | 0.6 |
| SALINE | 125 | 4400 | 693 | 64,183 | 79,702 | 86,338 | 2.1 | 6 | 96.9 | 96.3 | 2.1 | 2.4 | 0.4 | 0.6 |
| SCOTT | 127 | 0000 | 670 | 10,205 | 10,640 | 10,618 | 0.4 | 38 | 98.3 | 98.1 | 0.0 | 0.0 | 0.5 | 0.7 |
| SEARCY | 129 | 0000 | 693 | 7,841 | 7,836 | 8,027 | 0.0 | 47 | 98.8 | 98.7 | 0.0 | 0.1 | 0.2 | 0.2 |
| SEBASTIAN | 131 | 2720 | 670 | 99,590 | 106,588 | 108,299 | 0.7 | 33 | 89.1 | 86.5 | 5.7 | 6.5 | 3.3 | 4.6 |
| SEVIER | 133 | 0000 | 612 | 13,637 | 14,721 | 14,988 | 0.7 | 33 | 88.6 | 83.2 | 5.8 | 6.3 | 0.1 | 0.1 |
| SHARP | 135 | 0000 | 734 | 14,109 | 17,300 | 18,375 | 2.0 | 8 | 98.6 | 98.3 | 0.5 | 0.6 | 0.1 | 0.2 |
| STONE | 137 | 0000 | 693 | 9,775 | 11,349 | 11,988 | 1.5 | 15 | 99.1 | 99.0 | 0.1 | 0.1 | 0.2 | 0.3 |
| UNION | 139 | 0000 | 628 | 46,719 | 44,756 | 43,681 | -0.4 | 58 | 69.4 | 65.9 | 30.1 | 33.3 | 0.2 | 0.2 |
| VAN BUREN | 141 | 0000 | 693 | 14,008 | 15,822 | 16,522 | 1.2 | 23 | 98.8 | 98.5 | 0.3 | 0.4 | 0.2 | 0.2 |
| WASHINGTON | 143 | 2580 | 670 | 113,409 | 148,267 | 157,052 | 2.6 | 4 | 95.9 | 94.9 | 1.5 | 1.7 | 0.9 | 1.2 |
| WHITE | 145 | 0000 | 693 | 54,676 | 65,880 | 69,980 | 1.8 | 12 | 96.0 | 95.3 | 3.1 | 3.6 | 0.2 | 0.3 |
| WOODRUFF | 147 | 0000 | 693 | 9,520 | 8,596 | 8,043 | -1.0 | 71 | 68.3 | 65.1 | 31.4 | 34.6 | 0.1 | 0.2 |
| YELL | 149 | 0000 | 693 | 17,759 | 18,818 | 18,629 | 0.6 | 35 | 96.7 | 95.9 | 2.1 | 2.4 | 0.6 | 0.7 |
| ARKANSAS | | | | | | | 0.9 | | 82.7 | 82.3 | 15.9 | 15.8 | 0.5 | 0.7 |
| UNITED STATES | | | | | | | 1.0 | | 80.3 | 77.9 | 12.1 | 12.4 | 2.9 | 3.9 |

| COUNTY | % HISPANIC ORIGIN | | 2000 AGE DISTRIBUTION (%) | | | | | | | | | | MEDIAN AGE | | 2000 Males/ Females (×100) |
|---|---|---|---|---|---|---|---|---|---|---|---|---|---|---|---|
| | 1990 | 2000 | 0-4 | 5-9 | 10-14 | 15-19 | 20-24 | 25-44 | 45-64 | 65-84 | 85+ | 18+ | 1990 | 2000 | |
| ARKANSAS | 0.3 | 0.9 | 6.7 | 7.0 | 7.7 | 7.5 | 6.1 | 26.1 | 23.5 | 13.2 | 2.4 | 73.8 | 35.5 | 37.6 | 90.8 |
| ASHLEY | 0.9 | 2.4 | 7.0 | 7.1 | 7.8 | 7.9 | 6.6 | 26.2 | 23.8 | 11.8 | 1.8 | 73.1 | 33.9 | 36.2 | 91.8 |
| BAXTER | 0.5 | 1.7 | 4.7 | 5.1 | 5.6 | 5.6 | 4.5 | 20.9 | 26.3 | 24.2 | 3.2 | 81.1 | 47.1 | 47.9 | 91.5 |
| BENTON | 1.4 | 4.0 | 6.9 | 6.9 | 7.1 | 7.0 | 6.0 | 26.8 | 23.3 | 14.3 | 1.6 | 75.0 | 35.9 | 37.7 | 95.0 |
| BOONE | 0.6 | 1.9 | 6.4 | 6.8 | 7.2 | 6.7 | 5.6 | 26.7 | 23.8 | 14.3 | 2.4 | 75.6 | 36.5 | 38.6 | 91.5 |
| BRADLEY | 1.6 | 4.1 | 6.7 | 6.7 | 7.3 | 7.3 | 6.8 | 24.7 | 23.4 | 14.5 | 2.6 | 74.6 | 36.6 | 37.8 | 91.1 |
| CALHOUN | 0.5 | 1.4 | 7.1 | 7.2 | 7.7 | 8.2 | 5.7 | 26.4 | 23.0 | 12.5 | 2.1 | 73.0 | 34.3 | 36.8 | 93.3 |
| CARROLL | 1.0 | 3.0 | 6.2 | 6.4 | 7.0 | 6.6 | 5.5 | 25.6 | 26.1 | 14.6 | 2.1 | 76.4 | 38.1 | 40.2 | 93.6 |
| CHICOT | 1.0 | 2.4 | 8.0 | 8.2 | 8.4 | 9.3 | 7.6 | 24.1 | 20.4 | 12.0 | 2.1 | 69.4 | 31.9 | 32.1 | 89.9 |
| CLARK | 0.6 | 1.6 | 6.1 | 6.1 | 6.2 | 9.7 | 10.5 | 25.4 | 20.6 | 13.1 | 2.3 | 78.0 | 32.2 | 33.9 | 91.3 |
| CLAY | 0.4 | 1.3 | 5.7 | 5.8 | 6.6 | 6.6 | 5.7 | 24.4 | 25.8 | 16.7 | 2.7 | 77.8 | 39.5 | 41.3 | 92.0 |
| CLEBURNE | 0.5 | 1.7 | 5.1 | 5.5 | 5.8 | 6.2 | 5.0 | 23.4 | 26.6 | 20.1 | 2.3 | 79.6 | 41.7 | 44.3 | 93.6 |
| CLEVELAND | 0.6 | 1.7 | 6.3 | 6.5 | 7.2 | 7.5 | 6.3 | 26.5 | 25.7 | 12.2 | 1.9 | 75.2 | 35.7 | 38.2 | 95.7 |
| COLUMBIA | 0.3 | 0.9 | 7.1 | 7.2 | 7.5 | 8.7 | 7.4 | 25.8 | 21.2 | 12.8 | 2.3 | 73.7 | 33.6 | 35.2 | 89.3 |
| CONWAY | 0.6 | 1.8 | 6.9 | 7.0 | 7.4 | 7.4 | 6.1 | 25.3 | 22.9 | 14.9 | 2.1 | 74.0 | 34.7 | 37.7 | 90.7 |
| CRAIGHEAD | 0.6 | 1.8 | 6.9 | 6.6 | 6.9 | 8.1 | 9.3 | 28.6 | 22.1 | 10.2 | 1.4 | 75.8 | 31.6 | 34.1 | 92.7 |
| CRAWFORD | 1.1 | 3.2 | 7.5 | 7.5 | 8.1 | 7.6 | 6.4 | 28.0 | 23.5 | 10.0 | 1.4 | 72.0 | 32.6 | 35.1 | 95.5 |
| CRITTENDEN | 0.7 | 1.8 | 8.8 | 8.5 | 8.7 | 8.1 | 7.4 | 27.8 | 20.6 | 8.9 | 1.1 | 69.0 | 29.8 | 31.4 | 89.0 |
| CROSS | 0.6 | 1.6 | 7.7 | 7.6 | 7.8 | 8.1 | 7.0 | 26.6 | 22.7 | 10.7 | 1.7 | 71.5 | 32.2 | 34.1 | 94.2 |
| DALLAS | 0.3 | 1.0 | 6.7 | 6.8 | 7.3 | 7.5 | 6.1 | 25.3 | 24.3 | 13.7 | 2.4 | 74.4 | 36.4 | 38.0 | 93.1 |
| DESHA | 0.9 | 2.4 | 8.2 | 8.4 | 8.6 | 8.7 | 6.9 | 25.2 | 20.4 | 11.3 | 2.3 | 69.5 | 31.5 | 32.8 | 86.9 |
| DREW | 0.5 | 1.5 | 7.0 | 7.2 | 7.9 | 8.7 | 8.2 | 26.9 | 22.0 | 10.4 | 1.6 | 73.3 | 31.8 | 33.8 | 93.6 |
| FAULKNER | 0.6 | 1.8 | 7.1 | 7.0 | 7.1 | 9.0 | 9.6 | 29.8 | 20.5 | 8.8 | 1.2 | 74.7 | 29.8 | 32.2 | 93.4 |
| FRANKLIN | 1.2 | 3.0 | 6.4 | 6.8 | 7.3 | 8.3 | 6.0 | 26.1 | 24.3 | 12.6 | 2.2 | 74.4 | 35.4 | 37.4 | 97.9 |
| FULTON | 0.3 | 1.1 | 5.6 | 6.0 | 6.5 | 6.8 | 5.0 | 23.0 | 26.2 | 18.4 | 2.4 | 77.6 | 40.6 | 42.9 | 91.6 |
| GARLAND | 1.1 | 2.9 | 5.6 | 5.8 | 6.3 | 6.1 | 5.3 | 24.0 | 24.6 | 19.7 | 2.7 | 78.6 | 40.8 | 42.8 | 91.1 |
| GRANT | 0.6 | 1.8 | 6.6 | 6.7 | 7.4 | 7.4 | 6.0 | 27.9 | 25.5 | 10.9 | 1.5 | 74.6 | 34.4 | 37.3 | 96.0 |
| GREENE | 0.5 | 1.8 | 6.6 | 6.6 | 7.3 | 7.0 | 6.0 | 26.9 | 25.1 | 12.7 | 1.8 | 75.4 | 35.5 | 38.0 | 94.4 |
| HEMPSTEAD | 1.3 | 3.1 | 7.3 | 7.3 | 7.4 | 7.8 | 6.9 | 26.1 | 22.5 | 12.5 | 2.2 | 73.2 | 34.3 | 36.2 | 92.7 |
| HOT SPRING | 0.4 | 1.4 | 6.3 | 6.7 | 7.1 | 6.9 | 6.3 | 25.4 | 24.9 | 14.4 | 2.0 | 75.7 | 36.4 | 38.8 | 93.8 |
| HOWARD | 0.7 | 1.8 | 7.1 | 7.1 | 7.4 | 7.6 | 6.6 | 26.2 | 22.8 | 12.6 | 2.4 | 73.5 | 34.5 | 36.1 | 94.4 |
| INDEPENDENCE | 0.6 | 1.7 | 6.4 | 6.8 | 7.2 | 7.6 | 6.3 | 27.0 | 24.5 | 12.2 | 1.9 | 74.9 | 34.8 | 37.5 | 94.5 |
| IZARD | 0.6 | 1.8 | 5.5 | 5.8 | 6.1 | 6.4 | 5.0 | 22.5 | 25.7 | 20.0 | 3.0 | 78.5 | 43.9 | 44.0 | 96.1 |
| JACKSON | 0.3 | 1.1 | 6.0 | 6.2 | 7.0 | 7.0 | 5.8 | 25.3 | 24.4 | 15.7 | 2.5 | 76.3 | 36.7 | 40.0 | 91.4 |
| JEFFERSON | 0.5 | 1.3 | 7.2 | 7.2 | 7.5 | 9.1 | 7.9 | 27.0 | 21.6 | 10.9 | 1.6 | 73.0 | 31.9 | 33.4 | 93.5 |
| JOHNSON | 1.2 | 3.2 | 6.4 | 6.5 | 7.0 | 7.6 | 7.2 | 26.1 | 23.8 | 13.1 | 2.3 | 75.8 | 35.3 | 37.3 | 95.4 |
| LAFAYETTE | 0.4 | 1.1 | 6.9 | 7.0 | 7.8 | 7.9 | 6.8 | 24.8 | 23.2 | 13.0 | 2.5 | 73.6 | 35.1 | 36.7 | 92.8 |
| LAWRENCE | 0.3 | 1.2 | 6.2 | 6.5 | 6.9 | 7.5 | 6.0 | 25.7 | 24.0 | 14.6 | 2.7 | 76.1 | 36.7 | 38.8 | 94.0 |
| LEE | 1.3 | 3.2 | 7.6 | 7.8 | 8.2 | 9.4 | 7.8 | 25.3 | 20.1 | 11.8 | 2.0 | 70.0 | 31.9 | 32.1 | 100.8 |
| LINCOLN | 1.1 | 2.3 | 6.1 | 6.0 | 6.5 | 7.1 | 9.2 | 34.2 | 19.8 | 9.3 | 1.6 | 77.0 | 32.2 | 33.0 | 139.2 |
| LITTLE RIVER | 1.1 | 2.8 | 6.7 | 6.9 | 7.6 | 7.9 | 6.8 | 26.6 | 23.6 | 11.9 | 1.9 | 73.7 | 33.8 | 36.3 | 94.2 |
| LOGAN | 0.7 | 1.9 | 6.8 | 7.0 | 7.5 | 8.0 | 5.9 | 25.7 | 23.7 | 13.2 | 2.2 | 73.5 | 35.3 | 37.2 | 97.4 |
| LONOKE | 0.6 | 2.0 | 7.1 | 7.6 | 8.0 | 8.1 | 6.5 | 28.9 | 23.6 | 9.0 | 1.3 | 72.1 | 32.5 | 34.8 | 96.4 |
| MADISON | 1.0 | 2.9 | 6.9 | 7.2 | 7.6 | 7.5 | 5.4 | 25.3 | 25.2 | 13.0 | 1.9 | 73.7 | 36.0 | 38.1 | 97.1 |
| MARION | 0.4 | 1.4 | 5.1 | 5.6 | 6.3 | 6.2 | 5.0 | 22.7 | 27.9 | 19.1 | 2.2 | 79.1 | 42.7 | 44.4 | 95.8 |
| MILLER | 0.8 | 2.2 | 7.4 | 7.3 | 7.7 | 7.7 | 7.2 | 26.9 | 22.6 | 11.5 | 1.7 | 73.0 | 32.7 | 34.9 | 92.7 |
| MISSISSIPPI | 1.3 | 3.3 | 8.8 | 8.3 | 8.6 | 8.0 | 7.7 | 27.7 | 19.6 | 10.0 | 1.3 | 69.5 | 29.4 | 31.3 | 92.6 |
| MONROE | 0.3 | 0.8 | 8.0 | 7.7 | 8.1 | 8.2 | 6.3 | 23.5 | 22.0 | 13.8 | 2.3 | 70.7 | 34.5 | 35.7 | 89.1 |
| MONTGOMERY | 0.7 | 2.2 | 5.6 | 6.0 | 6.2 | 6.2 | 5.1 | 24.1 | 26.4 | 18.0 | 2.3 | 78.3 | 40.1 | 42.5 | 96.4 |
| NEVADA | 0.6 | 1.6 | 6.5 | 6.8 | 6.9 | 7.6 | 6.8 | 26.0 | 23.6 | 13.2 | 2.5 | 74.9 | 35.6 | 36.9 | 91.0 |
| NEWTON | 0.6 | 1.8 | 6.5 | 6.7 | 6.9 | 8.2 | 6.8 | 24.0 | 26.1 | 13.0 | 1.7 | 74.3 | 35.7 | 38.1 | 100.0 |
| OUACHITA | 0.4 | 1.3 | 6.8 | 7.1 | 7.4 | 7.7 | 6.1 | 25.9 | 23.3 | 13.5 | 2.2 | 73.8 | 35.2 | 37.6 | 90.7 |
| PERRY | 0.6 | 1.8 | 6.4 | 6.5 | 6.9 | 7.5 | 5.8 | 26.2 | 25.6 | 13.4 | 1.6 | 75.4 | 36.4 | 38.5 | 96.6 |
| PHILLIPS | 0.8 | 2.1 | 9.3 | 9.0 | 9.2 | 9.1 | 7.4 | 22.9 | 20.2 | 11.0 | 1.9 | 66.5 | 30.8 | 30.0 | 84.7 |
| PIKE | 0.6 | 1.9 | 6.4 | 6.7 | 7.1 | 7.3 | 5.8 | 25.7 | 24.3 | 14.3 | 2.5 | 75.1 | 36.4 | 38.5 | 96.0 |
| POINSETT | 0.5 | 1.7 | 7.0 | 7.0 | 7.6 | 7.2 | 6.0 | 26.5 | 24.4 | 12.5 | 1.8 | 74.1 | 34.6 | 37.2 | 93.9 |
| POLK | 1.7 | 4.6 | 6.5 | 6.8 | 7.2 | 7.3 | 5.5 | 23.8 | 25.1 | 15.4 | 2.3 | 74.8 | 38.0 | 39.6 | 94.3 |
| POPE | 0.9 | 2.7 | 7.2 | 7.0 | 7.3 | 8.2 | 8.0 | 28.4 | 22.5 | 10.0 | 1.5 | 74.1 | 31.8 | 34.3 | 97.5 |
| PRAIRIE | 0.4 | 1.2 | 6.6 | 6.9 | 7.3 | 7.0 | 5.7 | 26.2 | 24.4 | 13.9 | 2.0 | 74.7 | 36.0 | 38.3 | 97.8 |
| PULASKI | 0.9 | 2.5 | 7.3 | 7.0 | 7.2 | 7.1 | 7.2 | 31.2 | 21.7 | 9.9 | 1.4 | 74.3 | 32.4 | 34.8 | 90.4 |
| RANDOLPH | 0.5 | 1.6 | 6.5 | 6.6 | 7.2 | 7.1 | 6.0 | 25.0 | 25.0 | 14.4 | 2.3 | 75.2 | 36.6 | 38.9 | 94.3 |
| ST. FRANCIS | 0.7 | 1.9 | 8.5 | 8.4 | 9.1 | 8.9 | 7.1 | 24.9 | 20.7 | 10.8 | 1.7 | 68.5 | 31.0 | 31.9 | 86.5 |
| SALINE | 0.6 | 1.8 | 6.6 | 6.9 | 7.5 | 7.4 | 6.1 | 29.3 | 24.5 | 10.5 | 1.1 | 74.3 | 33.4 | 36.5 | 97.4 |
| SCOTT | 0.4 | 1.3 | 7.1 | 6.9 | 7.3 | 7.0 | 5.8 | 25.0 | 25.3 | 13.7 | 2.0 | 74.4 | 36.2 | 38.2 | 96.8 |
| SEARCY | 0.4 | 1.3 | 5.8 | 6.2 | 6.5 | 7.0 | 5.9 | 22.8 | 26.0 | 17.0 | 2.7 | 76.8 | 39.7 | 41.6 | 94.0 |
| SEBASTIAN | 1.4 | 3.7 | 7.3 | 7.0 | 7.3 | 7.1 | 6.6 | 28.9 | 22.8 | 11.2 | 1.7 | 74.1 | 33.7 | 35.9 | 93.8 |
| SEVIER | 4.6 | 10.9 | 6.7 | 7.1 | 7.2 | 7.7 | 6.5 | 27.4 | 23.2 | 12.4 | 1.9 | 74.4 | 34.9 | 36.4 | 99.6 |
| SHARP | 0.4 | 1.3 | 5.1 | 5.3 | 6.3 | 6.4 | 5.2 | 21.6 | 25.7 | 21.5 | 2.9 | 79.1 | 44.8 | 45.1 | 91.0 |
| STONE | 0.4 | 1.5 | 5.5 | 5.8 | 6.3 | 7.3 | 5.9 | 23.4 | 27.6 | 16.2 | 2.0 | 77.7 | 39.2 | 42.1 | 95.1 |
| UNION | 0.5 | 1.4 | 7.1 | 7.2 | 7.6 | 7.7 | 6.7 | 26.0 | 22.9 | 12.7 | 2.1 | 73.2 | 34.5 | 36.6 | 91.3 |
| VAN BUREN | 0.7 | 2.1 | 5.3 | 5.5 | 6.3 | 6.3 | 5.1 | 21.4 | 26.0 | 21.9 | 2.2 | 79.0 | 43.2 | 45.1 | 96.9 |
| WASHINGTON | 1.3 | 3.8 | 7.0 | 6.7 | 6.9 | 8.3 | 10.3 | 29.4 | 21.1 | 9.1 | 1.3 | 75.8 | 30.8 | 32.7 | 97.1 |
| WHITE | 0.7 | 1.8 | 6.5 | 6.5 | 7.0 | 8.8 | 8.5 | 26.1 | 23.3 | 11.7 | 1.7 | 75.7 | 33.1 | 35.5 | 94.5 |
| WOODRUFF | 0.2 | 0.7 | 7.4 | 7.4 | 7.7 | 7.7 | 6.8 | 25.0 | 22.8 | 12.9 | 2.4 | 72.8 | 34.3 | 36.1 | 90.3 |
| YELL | 1.0 | 2.7 | 6.9 | 7.1 | 7.6 | 7.0 | 5.4 | 27.2 | 23.7 | 13.2 | 1.9 | 74.0 | 35.6 | 37.3 | 96.3 |
| ARKANSAS | 0.9 | 2.4 | 6.9 | 6.9 | 7.3 | 7.6 | 7.0 | 27.3 | 22.9 | 12.3 | 1.8 | 74.5 | 33.8 | 36.2 | 93.5 |
| UNITED STATES | 9.0 | 11.8 | 6.9 | 7.2 | 7.2 | 7.2 | 6.7 | 29.9 | 22.2 | 11.1 | 1.6 | 74.6 | 32.9 | 35.7 | 95.6 |

| COUNTY | HOUSEHOLDS | | | | | FAMILIES | | | MEDIAN HOUSEHOLD INCOME | | | |
|---|---|---|---|---|---|---|---|---|---|---|---|---|
| | 1990 | 2000 | 2005 | % Annual Rate 1990-2000 | 2000 Average HH Size | 1990 | 2000 | % Annual Rate 1990-2000 | 2000 | 2005 | 2000 National Rank | 2000 State Rank |
| ARKANSAS | 8,389 | 8,105 | 8,098 | -0.4 | 2.51 | 6,051 | 5,646 | -0.8 | 28,601 | 34,973 | 2350 | 25 |
| ASHLEY | 8,890 | 9,066 | 9,092 | 0.2 | 2.64 | 6,817 | 6,735 | -0.1 | 30,542 | 35,455 | 2024 | 15 |
| BAXTER | 13,486 | 16,145 | 16,877 | 2.2 | 2.26 | 9,916 | 11,427 | 1.7 | 26,416 | 29,079 | 2665 | 44 |
| BENTON | 37,555 | 55,463 | 63,991 | 4.8 | 2.54 | 28,999 | 41,615 | 4.5 | 36,132 | 40,890 | 1085 | 5 |
| BOONE | 11,131 | 12,720 | 13,014 | 1.6 | 2.47 | 8,282 | 9,043 | 1.1 | 30,284 | 36,352 | 2088 | 18 |
| BRADLEY | 4,545 | 4,421 | 4,381 | -0.3 | 2.51 | 3,333 | 3,115 | -0.8 | 24,404 | 27,945 | 2870 | 56 |
| CALHOUN | 2,185 | 2,170 | 2,157 | -0.1 | 2.56 | 1,616 | 1,547 | -0.5 | 28,118 | 36,235 | 2424 | 31 |
| CARROLL | 7,550 | 9,273 | 9,523 | 2.5 | 2.42 | 5,436 | 6,361 | 1.9 | 28,048 | 32,684 | 2432 | 32 |
| CHICOT | 5,557 | 5,126 | 4,903 | -1.0 | 2.75 | 3,957 | 3,520 | -1.4 | 20,773 | 24,310 | 3078 | 70 |
| CLARK | 7,907 | 8,145 | 7,974 | 0.4 | 2.36 | 5,476 | 5,448 | -0.1 | 27,481 | 31,992 | 2513 | 37 |
| CLAY | 7,504 | 7,179 | 6,980 | -0.5 | 2.32 | 5,381 | 4,930 | -1.1 | 24,696 | 29,563 | 2838 | 52 |
| CLEBURNE | 7,926 | 9,797 | 10,635 | 2.6 | 2.38 | 6,027 | 7,227 | 2.2 | 27,004 | 30,340 | 2578 | 41 |
| CLEVELAND | 2,868 | 3,211 | 3,422 | 1.4 | 2.68 | 2,267 | 2,455 | 1.0 | 30,295 | 36,278 | 2082 | 17 |
| COLUMBIA | 9,638 | 9,409 | 9,029 | -0.3 | 2.48 | 6,856 | 6,444 | -0.7 | 25,727 | 29,468 | 2739 | 48 |
| CONWAY | 7,179 | 7,586 | 7,687 | 0.7 | 2.57 | 5,358 | 5,451 | 0.2 | 30,455 | 35,782 | 2044 | 16 |
| CRAIGHEAD | 26,285 | 30,773 | 32,638 | 1.9 | 2.46 | 18,877 | 21,493 | 1.6 | 31,414 | 36,363 | 1836 | 11 |
| CRAWFORD | 15,251 | 18,799 | 20,520 | 2.6 | 2.76 | 12,230 | 14,672 | 2.2 | 30,766 | 36,286 | 1977 | 14 |
| CRITTENDEN | 17,120 | 17,451 | 17,982 | 0.2 | 2.86 | 12,985 | 12,900 | -0.1 | 30,874 | 37,264 | 1956 | 12 |
| CROSS | 6,754 | 7,050 | 7,130 | 0.5 | 2.70 | 5,242 | 5,290 | 0.1 | 27,124 | 33,543 | 2561 | 39 |
| DALLAS | 3,600 | 3,385 | 3,210 | -0.7 | 2.54 | 2,624 | 2,372 | -1.2 | 23,495 | 25,646 | 2941 | 62 |
| DESHA | 5,957 | 5,356 | 5,090 | -1.3 | 2.70 | 4,386 | 3,814 | -1.7 | 22,948 | 27,246 | 2976 | 66 |
| DREW | 6,342 | 6,487 | 6,444 | 0.3 | 2.60 | 4,699 | 4,652 | -0.1 | 28,187 | 33,157 | 2417 | 29 |
| FAULKNER | 21,325 | 30,092 | 34,047 | 4.3 | 2.62 | 15,748 | 21,496 | 3.8 | 37,319 | 43,679 | 929 | 3 |
| FRANKLIN | 5,578 | 6,651 | 7,014 | 2.2 | 2.47 | 4,252 | 4,873 | 1.7 | 25,784 | 29,570 | 2735 | 47 |
| FULTON | 4,010 | 4,460 | 4,658 | 1.3 | 2.46 | 3,019 | 3,247 | 0.9 | 21,569 | 25,687 | 3049 | 68 |
| GARLAND | 30,836 | 36,613 | 38,920 | 2.1 | 2.28 | 21,404 | 24,759 | 1.8 | 29,024 | 31,884 | 2292 | 23 |
| GRANT | 5,118 | 6,081 | 6,510 | 2.1 | 2.64 | 4,065 | 4,687 | 1.7 | 34,014 | 41,584 | 1389 | 6 |
| GREENE | 12,325 | 14,638 | 15,724 | 2.1 | 2.49 | 9,339 | 10,724 | 1.7 | 30,838 | 37,355 | 1962 | 13 |
| HEMPSTEAD | 8,212 | 8,510 | 8,643 | 0.4 | 2.55 | 6,001 | 6,022 | 0.0 | 24,747 | 27,537 | 2834 | 51 |
| HOT SPRING | 10,115 | 11,680 | 12,382 | 1.8 | 2.49 | 7,636 | 8,530 | 1.4 | 27,860 | 33,596 | 2461 | 33 |
| HOWARD | 4,975 | 5,061 | 5,047 | 0.2 | 2.62 | 3,738 | 3,673 | -0.2 | 31,539 | 36,812 | 1814 | 10 |
| INDEPENDENCE | 11,846 | 12,738 | 13,065 | 0.9 | 2.55 | 8,898 | 9,239 | 0.5 | 29,384 | 34,718 | 2237 | 21 |
| IZARD | 4,684 | 5,449 | 5,681 | 1.9 | 2.30 | 3,486 | 3,904 | 1.4 | 23,707 | 28,894 | 2922 | 61 |
| JACKSON | 7,361 | 6,916 | 6,595 | -0.8 | 2.47 | 5,370 | 4,869 | -1.2 | 23,149 | 26,425 | 2961 | 65 |
| JEFFERSON | 30,001 | 28,612 | 27,669 | -0.6 | 2.64 | 21,972 | 20,435 | -0.9 | 28,395 | 33,558 | 2379 | 27 |
| JOHNSON | 7,059 | 8,637 | 8,985 | 2.5 | 2.41 | 5,142 | 6,000 | 1.9 | 28,148 | 33,476 | 2421 | 30 |
| LAFAYETTE | 3,584 | 3,314 | 3,168 | -0.9 | 2.61 | 2,586 | 2,306 | -1.4 | 20,236 | 24,490 | 3094 | 71 |
| LAWRENCE | 6,857 | 6,859 | 6,931 | 0.0 | 2.47 | 5,043 | 4,853 | -0.5 | 22,434 | 26,807 | 3001 | 67 |
| LEE | 4,578 | 4,105 | 3,884 | -1.3 | 2.71 | 3,326 | 2,890 | -1.7 | 17,858 | 21,618 | 3131 | 75 |
| LINCOLN | 3,796 | 4,115 | 4,193 | 1.0 | 2.75 | 2,852 | 2,981 | 0.5 | 27,691 | 34,055 | 2477 | 35 |
| LITTLE RIVER | 5,150 | 4,919 | 4,838 | -0.6 | 2.61 | 3,929 | 3,637 | -0.9 | 29,553 | 33,108 | 2214 | 20 |
| LOGAN | 7,628 | 7,951 | 8,023 | 0.5 | 2.58 | 5,717 | 5,726 | 0.0 | 28,529 | 34,739 | 2359 | 26 |
| LONOKE | 13,866 | 18,857 | 21,362 | 3.8 | 2.77 | 11,030 | 14,672 | 3.5 | 37,438 | 45,783 | 904 | 2 |
| MADISON | 4,392 | 5,126 | 5,341 | 1.9 | 2.60 | 3,392 | 3,834 | 1.5 | 27,011 | 32,120 | 2577 | 40 |
| MARION | 4,970 | 6,547 | 7,074 | 3.4 | 2.28 | 3,713 | 4,714 | 2.9 | 24,051 | 28,717 | 2897 | 58 |
| MILLER | 14,273 | 15,093 | 15,288 | 0.7 | 2.56 | 10,560 | 10,815 | 0.3 | 28,233 | 33,927 | 2412 | 28 |
| MISSISSIPPI | 20,420 | 18,380 | 18,092 | -1.3 | 2.67 | 15,370 | 13,440 | -1.6 | 27,152 | 32,767 | 2556 | 38 |
| MONROE | 4,361 | 3,950 | 3,770 | -1.2 | 2.46 | 3,039 | 2,654 | -1.6 | 20,088 | 23,333 | 3097 | 73 |
| MONTGOMERY | 3,062 | 3,530 | 3,775 | 1.7 | 2.42 | 2,296 | 2,549 | 1.3 | 23,990 | 27,304 | 2902 | 59 |
| NEVADA | 3,798 | 3,811 | 3,846 | 0.0 | 2.58 | 2,762 | 2,659 | -0.5 | 26,941 | 35,457 | 2591 | 42 |
| NEWTON | 2,818 | 3,051 | 3,156 | 1.0 | 2.70 | 2,182 | 2,276 | 0.5 | 23,729 | 31,305 | 2921 | 60 |
| OUACHITA | 11,712 | 10,710 | 10,348 | -1.1 | 2.50 | 8,458 | 7,490 | -1.5 | 27,610 | 33,188 | 2496 | 36 |
| PERRY | 3,055 | 3,930 | 4,276 | 3.1 | 2.47 | 2,282 | 2,820 | 2.6 | 24,411 | 26,376 | 2867 | 55 |
| PHILLIPS | 10,183 | 9,723 | 9,436 | -0.6 | 2.72 | 7,275 | 6,756 | -0.9 | 19,276 | 22,337 | 3113 | 74 |
| PIKE | 3,855 | 4,129 | 4,176 | 0.8 | 2.49 | 2,938 | 3,046 | 0.4 | 28,991 | 34,397 | 2297 | 24 |
| POINSETT | 9,368 | 9,592 | 9,729 | 0.3 | 2.54 | 7,064 | 6,992 | -0.1 | 24,556 | 27,540 | 2851 | 53 |
| POLK | 6,827 | 8,015 | 8,325 | 2.0 | 2.43 | 5,076 | 5,683 | 1.4 | 26,091 | 30,356 | 2702 | 46 |
| POPE | 16,828 | 19,832 | 21,008 | 2.0 | 2.59 | 12,681 | 14,569 | 1.7 | 32,209 | 37,295 | 1682 | 9 |
| PRAIRIE | 3,661 | 3,707 | 3,753 | 0.2 | 2.48 | 2,716 | 2,652 | -0.3 | 26,499 | 32,327 | 2655 | 43 |
| PULASKI | 137,209 | 139,533 | 140,617 | 0.2 | 2.46 | 93,512 | 91,716 | -0.2 | 36,602 | 41,003 | 1032 | 4 |
| RANDOLPH | 6,445 | 7,111 | 7,384 | 1.2 | 2.50 | 4,833 | 5,154 | 0.8 | 24,243 | 27,392 | 2885 | 57 |
| ST. FRANCIS | 9,958 | 9,974 | 9,987 | 0.0 | 2.53 | 7,423 | 7,204 | -0.4 | 23,369 | 28,523 | 2951 | 64 |
| SALINE | 23,037 | 29,181 | 31,909 | 2.9 | 2.69 | 18,498 | 22,863 | 2.6 | 41,874 | 48,910 | 523 | 1 |
| SCOTT | 3,957 | 4,187 | 4,206 | 0.7 | 2.51 | 3,030 | 3,089 | 0.2 | 25,050 | 28,711 | 2807 | 50 |
| SEARCY | 3,117 | 3,134 | 3,222 | 0.1 | 2.48 | 2,333 | 2,263 | -0.4 | 20,183 | 23,455 | 3095 | 72 |
| SEBASTIAN | 39,298 | 42,561 | 43,501 | 1.0 | 2.47 | 27,632 | 28,940 | 0.6 | 33,026 | 38,185 | 1534 | 8 |
| SEVIER | 5,118 | 5,564 | 5,679 | 1.0 | 2.60 | 3,825 | 3,989 | 0.5 | 26,364 | 31,137 | 2671 | 45 |
| SHARP | 5,819 | 7,341 | 7,898 | 2.9 | 2.33 | 4,331 | 5,263 | 2.4 | 25,154 | 29,985 | 2797 | 49 |
| STONE | 3,866 | 4,588 | 4,896 | 2.1 | 2.45 | 2,944 | 3,370 | 1.7 | 24,445 | 27,172 | 2861 | 54 |
| UNION | 17,819 | 17,306 | 17,005 | -0.4 | 2.54 | 12,882 | 12,058 | -0.8 | 30,163 | 35,099 | 2118 | 19 |
| VAN BUREN | 5,698 | 6,514 | 6,840 | 1.6 | 2.41 | 4,275 | 4,716 | 1.2 | 23,444 | 25,745 | 2945 | 63 |
| WASHINGTON | 43,372 | 55,463 | 58,409 | 3.0 | 2.56 | 29,963 | 36,685 | 2.5 | 33,684 | 38,240 | 1438 | 7 |
| WHITE | 19,823 | 24,720 | 26,709 | 2.7 | 2.53 | 15,145 | 18,327 | 2.3 | 29,213 | 34,759 | 2263 | 22 |
| WOODRUFF | 3,630 | 3,398 | 3,233 | -0.8 | 2.49 | 2,593 | 2,339 | -1.2 | 20,777 | 25,155 | 3077 | 69 |
| YELL | 6,907 | 7,571 | 7,618 | 1.1 | 2.46 | 5,164 | 5,478 | 0.7 | 27,853 | 33,395 | 2464 | 34 |
| ARKANSAS | | | | 1.3 | 2.53 | | | 0.9 | 30,582 | 35,648 | | |
| UNITED STATES | | | | 1.4 | 2.59 | | | 1.1 | 41,914 | 49,127 | | |

# INCOME

| COUNTY | 2000 Per Capita Income | 2000 HH Income Base | 2000 HOUSEHOLD INCOME DISTRIBUTION (%) Less than $15,000 | $15,000 to $24,999 | $25,000 to $49,999 | $50,000 to $99,999 | $100,000 to $149,999 | $150,000 or More | 2000 AVERAGE DISPOSABLE INCOME BY AGE OF HOUSEHOLDER All Ages | <35 | 35-44 | 45-54 | 55-64 | 65+ |
|---|---|---|---|---|---|---|---|---|---|---|---|---|---|---|
| ARKANSAS | 16,335 | 8,105 | 24.5 | 21.0 | 31.2 | 18.7 | 3.4 | 1.2 | 29,297 | 23,905 | 35,968 | 35,654 | 33,343 | 19,923 |
| ASHLEY | 14,358 | 9,066 | 23.8 | 17.1 | 34.6 | 19.9 | 3.7 | 1.0 | 29,956 | 25,716 | 37,834 | 38,970 | 31,483 | 18,465 |
| BAXTER | 15,318 | 16,145 | 22.0 | 25.2 | 33.7 | 16.4 | 2.0 | 0.8 | 27,017 | 24,642 | 32,924 | 35,633 | 28,682 | 21,546 |
| BENTON | 17,274 | 55,463 | 13.5 | 17.2 | 39.4 | 25.3 | 3.6 | 1.0 | 33,574 | 29,660 | 39,715 | 40,850 | 34,869 | 26,498 |
| BOONE | 15,005 | 12,720 | 20.4 | 20.0 | 37.0 | 19.1 | 2.8 | 0.7 | 29,208 | 27,528 | 37,692 | 35,895 | 31,493 | 19,306 |
| BRADLEY | 11,776 | 4,421 | 32.5 | 18.2 | 31.9 | 15.8 | 1.5 | 0.2 | 24,386 | 21,697 | 32,540 | 31,540 | 27,767 | 15,392 |
| CALHOUN | 13,430 | 2,170 | 22.7 | 20.1 | 37.4 | 17.1 | 2.1 | 0.6 | 27,390 | 27,311 | 33,516 | 33,358 | 29,332 | 16,067 |
| CARROLL | 13,829 | 9,273 | 23.7 | 18.9 | 40.4 | 15.0 | 1.5 | 0.5 | 26,408 | 23,310 | 29,550 | 33,870 | 28,985 | 20,444 |
| CHICOT | 12,905 | 5,125 | 39.2 | 19.6 | 23.4 | 13.1 | 2.6 | 2.0 | 25,665 | 21,465 | 31,966 | 34,724 | 25,306 | 16,672 |
| CLARK | 14,246 | 8,145 | 27.8 | 16.4 | 34.3 | 17.2 | 3.0 | 1.2 | 28,188 | 21,513 | 37,307 | 39,346 | 29,129 | 20,319 |
| CLAY | 13,497 | 7,179 | 28.3 | 22.3 | 33.9 | 13.4 | 1.4 | 0.7 | 24,864 | 24,252 | 30,417 | 34,339 | 26,375 | 16,419 |
| CLEBURNE | 14,240 | 9,797 | 23.6 | 21.0 | 36.7 | 16.6 | 1.6 | 0.5 | 26,676 | 22,803 | 33,593 | 31,514 | 28,739 | 21,320 |
| CLEVELAND | 13,901 | 3,211 | 24.7 | 17.2 | 35.7 | 18.3 | 3.2 | 0.9 | 28,911 | 30,258 | 36,907 | 37,078 | 26,312 | 17,349 |
| COLUMBIA | 13,878 | 9,409 | 28.7 | 20.0 | 30.4 | 16.8 | 2.9 | 1.2 | 27,585 | 23,740 | 35,863 | 35,768 | 29,373 | 18,069 |
| CONWAY | 14,399 | 7,586 | 21.5 | 17.6 | 37.8 | 19.8 | 2.7 | 0.7 | 29,154 | 26,545 | 36,420 | 39,314 | 31,952 | 19,350 |
| CRAIGHEAD | 16,627 | 30,773 | 21.1 | 17.2 | 35.3 | 21.8 | 3.2 | 1.4 | 31,284 | 25,833 | 38,435 | 40,045 | 35,367 | 19,456 |
| CRAWFORD | 14,010 | 18,799 | 19.1 | 19.5 | 37.1 | 20.9 | 2.7 | 0.7 | 29,595 | 26,866 | 36,753 | 34,876 | 30,833 | 18,692 |
| CRITTENDEN | 13,684 | 17,451 | 24.4 | 15.9 | 35.4 | 20.3 | 2.6 | 1.3 | 29,991 | 27,098 | 34,653 | 38,014 | 31,046 | 18,384 |
| CROSS | 13,323 | 7,050 | 26.1 | 20.2 | 32.8 | 17.4 | 2.7 | 0.8 | 27,688 | 23,459 | 35,732 | 32,346 | 27,978 | 19,565 |
| DALLAS | 12,202 | 3,385 | 33.7 | 18.9 | 30.8 | 14.1 | 1.8 | 0.7 | 24,209 | 23,083 | 29,788 | 31,415 | 26,635 | 14,363 |
| DESHA | 12,362 | 5,356 | 35.8 | 17.3 | 27.5 | 14.6 | 3.3 | 1.6 | 26,555 | 21,933 | 33,059 | 33,484 | 26,448 | 19,800 |
| DREW | 14,413 | 6,487 | 23.7 | 21.1 | 33.3 | 17.2 | 3.1 | 1.7 | 29,457 | 24,754 | 37,126 | 34,807 | 32,258 | 19,314 |
| FAULKNER | 16,614 | 30,086 | 14.3 | 15.5 | 37.8 | 27.0 | 4.5 | 0.9 | 34,301 | 28,064 | 42,003 | 45,809 | 36,597 | 23,209 |
| FRANKLIN | 12,661 | 6,651 | 25.5 | 23.1 | 33.7 | 16.0 | 1.7 | 0.1 | 25,543 | 23,470 | 31,459 | 32,643 | 26,177 | 17,169 |
| FULTON | 11,630 | 4,460 | 33.5 | 24.3 | 29.7 | 10.3 | 1.4 | 0.8 | 22,956 | 21,418 | 29,190 | 29,809 | 25,406 | 15,978 |
| GARLAND | 17,291 | 36,613 | 24.8 | 18.2 | 33.7 | 19.0 | 3.1 | 1.2 | 29,237 | 23,276 | 34,728 | 35,654 | 33,924 | 24,359 |
| GRANT | 14,779 | 6,081 | 20.7 | 14.5 | 37.9 | 24.0 | 2.3 | 0.6 | 30,590 | 28,537 | 36,055 | 40,286 | 29,282 | 19,537 |
| GREENE | 15,526 | 14,638 | 20.9 | 18.5 | 36.6 | 20.6 | 2.8 | 0.7 | 29,692 | 27,657 | 36,078 | 37,783 | 31,076 | 18,929 |
| HEMPSTEAD | 11,925 | 8,510 | 29.6 | 20.9 | 33.7 | 13.8 | 1.9 | 0.1 | 24,491 | 22,143 | 32,281 | 30,636 | 24,571 | 16,245 |
| HOT SPRING | 13,290 | 11,680 | 23.7 | 20.9 | 35.3 | 18.4 | 1.7 | 0.1 | 26,708 | 24,313 | 33,724 | 33,239 | 29,384 | 18,412 |
| HOWARD | 15,286 | 5,061 | 19.4 | 16.9 | 38.1 | 20.4 | 4.0 | 1.3 | 31,277 | 27,661 | 40,478 | 42,054 | 34,144 | 19,099 |
| INDEPENDENCE | 15,145 | 12,738 | 23.1 | 19.0 | 35.0 | 18.4 | 3.1 | 1.3 | 29,590 | 27,912 | 36,660 | 37,775 | 29,623 | 17,596 |
| IZARD | 11,706 | 5,449 | 28.5 | 24.5 | 34.8 | 11.7 | 0.6 | 0.0 | 22,678 | 21,232 | 29,713 | 26,484 | 24,251 | 18,120 |
| JACKSON | 12,755 | 6,916 | 32.9 | 20.2 | 30.5 | 13.9 | 2.0 | 0.6 | 24,585 | 22,067 | 33,774 | 29,270 | 23,843 | 18,162 |
| JEFFERSON | 13,555 | 28,611 | 28.0 | 16.5 | 31.9 | 19.8 | 2.9 | 1.0 | 28,584 | 23,908 | 34,740 | 36,768 | 31,263 | 18,998 |
| JOHNSON | 13,918 | 8,637 | 23.5 | 20.0 | 36.3 | 17.5 | 2.4 | 0.2 | 27,138 | 23,963 | 34,244 | 36,795 | 27,115 | 18,545 |
| LAFAYETTE | 10,478 | 3,314 | 39.8 | 19.2 | 26.0 | 13.1 | 1.4 | 0.5 | 22,337 | 21,926 | 27,974 | 27,618 | 23,778 | 15,228 |
| LAWRENCE | 12,521 | 6,859 | 33.3 | 21.8 | 32.1 | 10.5 | 1.8 | 0.5 | 22,969 | 21,742 | 29,548 | 29,338 | 25,266 | 14,918 |
| LEE | 10,799 | 4,105 | 42.8 | 20.7 | 22.9 | 9.5 | 2.3 | 1.9 | 23,626 | 17,791 | 26,774 | 24,719 | 28,827 | 19,563 |
| LINCOLN | 11,493 | 4,115 | 28.1 | 17.0 | 34.4 | 16.9 | 2.5 | 1.1 | 27,654 | 24,903 | 32,803 | 35,160 | 30,694 | 16,698 |
| LITTLE RIVER | 13,238 | 4,919 | 27.4 | 15.1 | 34.8 | 20.3 | 2.1 | 0.3 | 27,654 | 24,109 | 32,652 | 36,989 | 30,441 | 16,403 |
| LOGAN | 12,435 | 7,951 | 22.3 | 20.6 | 38.8 | 17.2 | 1.1 | 0.0 | 26,319 | 24,272 | 32,491 | 32,594 | 29,790 | 17,732 |
| LONOKE | 16,439 | 18,857 | 15.2 | 14.6 | 37.1 | 26.7 | 5.0 | 1.3 | 35,002 | 30,114 | 41,665 | 44,055 | 34,297 | 22,672 |
| MADISON | 12,299 | 5,126 | 23.1 | 23.3 | 36.5 | 15.4 | 1.6 | 0.1 | 25,828 | 25,205 | 28,925 | 33,654 | 25,697 | 18,384 |
| MARION | 13,514 | 6,547 | 26.6 | 25.7 | 33.5 | 12.2 | 1.6 | 0.5 | 24,319 | 22,803 | 30,852 | 27,613 | 26,022 | 19,421 |
| MILLER | 14,012 | 15,093 | 29.1 | 15.5 | 33.2 | 18.0 | 3.1 | 1.1 | 28,234 | 23,957 | 35,155 | 35,463 | 31,307 | 18,416 |
| MISSISSIPPI | 13,227 | 18,380 | 26.3 | 20.1 | 33.1 | 17.3 | 2.5 | 0.7 | 27,243 | 24,308 | 33,230 | 34,488 | 29,146 | 18,071 |
| MONROE | 11,274 | 3,950 | 38.4 | 20.6 | 27.3 | 11.0 | 2.1 | 0.5 | 22,432 | 21,136 | 28,240 | 28,702 | 22,640 | 16,198 |
| MONTGOMERY | 12,580 | 3,530 | 27.4 | 24.9 | 32.2 | 13.0 | 2.0 | 0.5 | 24,542 | 23,016 | 32,183 | 29,131 | 27,362 | 17,435 |
| NEVADA | 15,501 | 3,811 | 24.2 | 22.0 | 30.8 | 17.9 | 3.4 | 1.8 | 29,766 | 25,164 | 40,999 | 36,367 | 29,660 | 20,020 |
| NEWTON | 10,835 | 3,051 | 28.6 | 23.5 | 33.0 | 14.0 | 1.0 | 0.0 | 23,842 | 22,591 | 30,113 | 27,649 | 24,211 | 17,756 |
| OUACHITA | 13,430 | 10,710 | 28.6 | 17.1 | 34.1 | 17.5 | 2.1 | 0.8 | 27,098 | 23,761 | 35,621 | 33,867 | 26,446 | 18,331 |
| PERRY | 11,960 | 3,930 | 30.0 | 21.7 | 33.3 | 13.8 | 1.2 | 0.1 | 23,828 | 22,523 | 28,534 | 29,974 | 25,593 | 15,405 |
| PHILLIPS | 9,928 | 9,723 | 39.8 | 21.0 | 25.8 | 10.9 | 1.8 | 0.6 | 22,173 | 18,652 | 27,391 | 28,794 | 23,122 | 15,907 |
| PIKE | 14,765 | 4,129 | 22.7 | 19.1 | 35.1 | 19.4 | 3.2 | 0.5 | 28,585 | 26,661 | 32,870 | 41,041 | 30,962 | 18,463 |
| POINSETT | 12,670 | 9,592 | 31.2 | 19.6 | 32.6 | 14.2 | 2.0 | 0.5 | 24,864 | 23,577 | 31,541 | 30,086 | 26,516 | 15,864 |
| POLK | 14,987 | 8,015 | 24.4 | 22.7 | 34.8 | 15.0 | 2.6 | 0.5 | 26,322 | 24,838 | 32,668 | 35,231 | 27,175 | 17,948 |
| POPE | 15,509 | 19,832 | 20.3 | 16.4 | 35.7 | 23.1 | 3.6 | 0.9 | 31,318 | 28,775 | 37,559 | 40,419 | 30,854 | 19,620 |
| PRAIRIE | 13,108 | 3,707 | 28.0 | 19.0 | 35.7 | 15.1 | 1.7 | 0.5 | 25,599 | 25,107 | 33,866 | 31,659 | 26,800 | 15,766 |
| PULASKI | 19,688 | 139,531 | 16.9 | 15.6 | 33.8 | 26.3 | 5.3 | 2.1 | 35,842 | 29,101 | 41,981 | 44,417 | 38,965 | 24,242 |
| RANDOLPH | 12,041 | 7,111 | 30.0 | 21.5 | 32.3 | 14.2 | 1.5 | 0.5 | 24,336 | 25,076 | 31,641 | 32,231 | 21,999 | 15,533 |
| ST. FRANCIS | 11,884 | 9,974 | 33.2 | 19.4 | 30.0 | 15.0 | 2.0 | 0.5 | 24,721 | 20,198 | 31,414 | 32,860 | 24,465 | 17,010 |
| SALINE | 17,967 | 29,181 | 11.6 | 11.9 | 38.4 | 32.2 | 5.2 | 0.9 | 36,921 | 32,971 | 42,921 | 46,214 | 37,974 | 24,139 |
| SCOTT | 12,263 | 4,187 | 28.6 | 21.3 | 34.7 | 13.5 | 1.5 | 0.5 | 24,468 | 25,297 | 31,637 | 29,450 | 24,420 | 16,096 |
| SEARCY | 10,293 | 3,134 | 36.7 | 26.4 | 26.9 | 8.4 | 1.2 | 0.5 | 20,527 | 19,256 | 28,672 | 25,524 | 21,443 | 14,396 |
| SEBASTIAN | 17,489 | 42,561 | 18.6 | 17.0 | 36.5 | 22.7 | 3.8 | 1.4 | 32,379 | 27,489 | 38,303 | 40,982 | 35,047 | 22,215 |
| SEVIER | 12,309 | 5,564 | 26.1 | 21.7 | 34.8 | 15.4 | 1.9 | 0.2 | 25,631 | 24,390 | 30,459 | 35,633 | 26,894 | 15,068 |
| SHARP | 12,627 | 7,341 | 27.0 | 22.6 | 35.5 | 14.0 | 0.8 | 0.0 | 24,040 | 22,190 | 30,765 | 29,681 | 23,983 | 20,024 |
| STONE | 11,776 | 4,588 | 28.1 | 23.3 | 34.5 | 13.0 | 1.1 | 0.0 | 23,556 | 22,446 | 26,448 | 27,607 | 26,524 | 18,461 |
| UNION | 15,360 | 17,306 | 25.6 | 16.5 | 34.1 | 19.4 | 3.1 | 1.3 | 29,866 | 24,658 | 36,123 | 39,236 | 32,598 | 19,863 |
| VAN BUREN | 11,912 | 6,514 | 29.1 | 24.4 | 33.3 | 12.2 | 0.9 | 0.1 | 23,193 | 21,096 | 28,388 | 27,317 | 24,953 | 19,450 |
| WASHINGTON | 16,731 | 55,463 | 17.5 | 17.0 | 36.6 | 23.9 | 4.0 | 1.2 | 32,778 | 25,796 | 39,378 | 43,076 | 37,587 | 23,007 |
| WHITE | 15,095 | 24,720 | 24.5 | 18.5 | 34.0 | 19.1 | 2.9 | 1.1 | 29,017 | 25,694 | 36,146 | 38,341 | 30,025 | 17,912 |
| WOODRUFF | 11,748 | 3,398 | 37.0 | 22.3 | 25.8 | 12.0 | 2.3 | 0.6 | 22,978 | 19,316 | 29,448 | 30,218 | 23,992 | 15,707 |
| YELL | 14,312 | 7,571 | 23.3 | 20.1 | 36.4 | 17.2 | 2.2 | 0.8 | 27,626 | 25,473 | 36,519 | 34,466 | 28,996 | 16,803 |
| ARKANSAS | 15,500 | | 22.3 | 18.1 | 34.7 | 20.6 | 3.3 | 1.1 | 30,169 | 26,250 | 36,993 | 38,283 | 31,856 | 20,464 |
| UNITED STATES | 22,162 | | 14.5 | 12.5 | 32.3 | 29.8 | 7.4 | 3.5 | 40,748 | 34,503 | 44,969 | 49,579 | 43,409 | 27,339 |

| COUNTY | FINANCIAL SERVICES | | | | THE HOME | | | | | | ENTERTAINMENT | | | | | | PERSONAL | | | |
|---|---|---|---|---|---|---|---|---|---|---|---|---|---|---|---|---|---|---|---|---|
| | | | | | Home Improvements | | | Furnishings | | | | | | | | | | | | |
| | Auto Loan | Home Loan | Investments | Retirement Plans | Home Repair | Lawn & Garden | Remodeling | Appliances | Electronics | Furniture | Restaurants | Sporting Goods | Theater & Concerts | Toys & Hobbies | Travel | Video Rental | Apparel | Auto Aftermarket | Health Insurance | Pets & Supplies |
| ARKANSAS | 98 | 76 | 85 | 84 | 96 | 93 | 108 | 97 | 93 | 85 | 85 | 97 | 86 | 97 | 75 | 97 | 86 | 91 | 99 | 98 |
| ASHLEY | 97 | 69 | 81 | 81 | 95 | 92 | 110 | 97 | 93 | 80 | 80 | 96 | 83 | 95 | 72 | 96 | 82 | 89 | 99 | 97 |
| BAXTER | 96 | 72 | 101 | 82 | 98 | 100 | 106 | 97 | 89 | 80 | 83 | 93 | 86 | 95 | 78 | 95 | 79 | 89 | 106 | 97 |
| BENTON | 100 | 86 | 95 | 92 | 100 | 100 | 111 | 100 | 96 | 91 | 94 | 98 | 93 | 101 | 82 | 98 | 93 | 95 | 103 | 102 |
| BOONE | 98 | 81 | 94 | 89 | 99 | 97 | 110 | 97 | 94 | 87 | 89 | 96 | 90 | 99 | 79 | 97 | 89 | 93 | 102 | 99 |
| BRADLEY | 95 | 68 | 75 | 75 | 94 | 91 | 110 | 95 | 91 | 79 | 80 | 92 | 81 | 93 | 71 | 95 | 80 | 87 | 100 | 95 |
| CALHOUN | 98 | 68 | 73 | 77 | 93 | 91 | 114 | 96 | 92 | 78 | 80 | 96 | 81 | 96 | 68 | 96 | 81 | 88 | 102 | 98 |
| CARROLL | 98 | 73 | 87 | 84 | 96 | 97 | 112 | 98 | 93 | 82 | 84 | 96 | 85 | 97 | 75 | 97 | 84 | 90 | 104 | 99 |
| CHICOT | 92 | 63 | 70 | 70 | 92 | 85 | 95 | 95 | 88 | 79 | 71 | 87 | 76 | 87 | 69 | 95 | 79 | 86 | 88 | 92 |
| CLARK | 95 | 76 | 83 | 80 | 95 | 92 | 107 | 95 | 92 | 83 | 83 | 92 | 84 | 94 | 75 | 96 | 83 | 89 | 99 | 96 |
| CLAY | 96 | 66 | 74 | 75 | 94 | 91 | 110 | 95 | 91 | 77 | 79 | 94 | 80 | 94 | 69 | 96 | 79 | 87 | 102 | 96 |
| CLEBURNE | 98 | 71 | 90 | 84 | 97 | 99 | 111 | 98 | 92 | 80 | 83 | 95 | 85 | 96 | 76 | 96 | 83 | 90 | 105 | 98 |
| CLEVELAND | 98 | 68 | 73 | 77 | 93 | 91 | 114 | 96 | 92 | 78 | 80 | 96 | 81 | 96 | 68 | 96 | 81 | 88 | 102 | 98 |
| COLUMBIA | 97 | 76 | 89 | 85 | 97 | 95 | 106 | 96 | 93 | 85 | 84 | 95 | 87 | 95 | 77 | 96 | 86 | 91 | 99 | 97 |
| CONWAY | 96 | 70 | 77 | 77 | 95 | 92 | 109 | 95 | 91 | 80 | 81 | 94 | 82 | 95 | 71 | 96 | 81 | 88 | 101 | 96 |
| CRAIGHEAD | 97 | 84 | 91 | 88 | 97 | 95 | 106 | 96 | 94 | 88 | 90 | 95 | 89 | 97 | 79 | 97 | 89 | 93 | 99 | 98 |
| CRAWFORD | 98 | 76 | 81 | 82 | 95 | 92 | 112 | 97 | 94 | 84 | 85 | 96 | 86 | 97 | 73 | 97 | 85 | 91 | 100 | 99 |
| CRITTENDEN | 95 | 84 | 88 | 86 | 97 | 92 | 98 | 96 | 93 | 91 | 87 | 94 | 89 | 95 | 80 | 97 | 90 | 93 | 92 | 97 |
| CROSS | 97 | 74 | 86 | 84 | 96 | 93 | 109 | 97 | 93 | 84 | 83 | 96 | 85 | 96 | 74 | 96 | 85 | 90 | 98 | 98 |
| DALLAS | 97 | 68 | 75 | 76 | 95 | 91 | 109 | 96 | 90 | 80 | 79 | 95 | 82 | 95 | 70 | 96 | 81 | 88 | 99 | 97 |
| DESHA | 94 | 67 | 76 | 76 | 93 | 87 | 103 | 95 | 89 | 79 | 75 | 91 | 79 | 91 | 71 | 96 | 81 | 88 | 91 | 95 |
| DREW | 96 | 70 | 72 | 76 | 92 | 90 | 108 | 95 | 93 | 80 | 81 | 94 | 81 | 94 | 70 | 96 | 82 | 89 | 99 | 96 |
| FAULKNER | 98 | 88 | 88 | 88 | 96 | 93 | 106 | 96 | 95 | 91 | 93 | 97 | 90 | 99 | 78 | 97 | 91 | 94 | 97 | 100 |
| FRANKLIN | 98 | 68 | 74 | 78 | 93 | 91 | 114 | 96 | 93 | 79 | 81 | 96 | 81 | 96 | 69 | 97 | 81 | 88 | 102 | 98 |
| FULTON | 96 | 65 | 77 | 74 | 93 | 92 | 109 | 95 | 91 | 76 | 78 | 92 | 79 | 93 | 69 | 95 | 77 | 87 | 102 | 95 |
| GARLAND | 99 | 84 | 101 | 93 | 101 | 102 | 108 | 99 | 94 | 90 | 91 | 96 | 92 | 98 | 84 | 97 | 91 | 94 | 103 | 100 |
| GRANT | 99 | 75 | 81 | 82 | 94 | 92 | 116 | 97 | 94 | 83 | 86 | 97 | 85 | 99 | 72 | 98 | 86 | 91 | 101 | 100 |
| GREENE | 98 | 68 | 75 | 78 | 93 | 91 | 113 | 96 | 93 | 78 | 81 | 95 | 81 | 96 | 69 | 97 | 81 | 88 | 102 | 98 |
| HEMPSTEAD | 96 | 70 | 75 | 77 | 94 | 91 | 111 | 95 | 91 | 80 | 80 | 94 | 81 | 94 | 71 | 95 | 81 | 88 | 100 | 97 |
| HOT SPRING | 96 | 70 | 77 | 78 | 94 | 91 | 110 | 95 | 92 | 79 | 81 | 93 | 81 | 94 | 71 | 97 | 81 | 88 | 100 | 97 |
| HOWARD | 96 | 71 | 77 | 78 | 94 | 91 | 110 | 95 | 91 | 79 | 81 | 94 | 82 | 95 | 71 | 96 | 82 | 88 | 100 | 97 |
| INDEPENDENCE | 98 | 72 | 79 | 81 | 94 | 92 | 112 | 96 | 94 | 81 | 83 | 96 | 84 | 97 | 71 | 97 | 84 | 90 | 101 | 98 |
| IZARD | 97 | 69 | 89 | 78 | 96 | 96 | 109 | 96 | 90 | 78 | 81 | 94 | 83 | 95 | 73 | 95 | 79 | 88 | 104 | 97 |
| JACKSON | 96 | 69 | 79 | 77 | 95 | 92 | 107 | 96 | 91 | 79 | 79 | 94 | 82 | 94 | 71 | 95 | 80 | 88 | 100 | 96 |
| JEFFERSON | 96 | 80 | 89 | 85 | 98 | 93 | 102 | 96 | 92 | 88 | 85 | 94 | 88 | 95 | 79 | 97 | 88 | 92 | 94 | 97 |
| JOHNSON | 96 | 67 | 73 | 75 | 93 | 91 | 111 | 95 | 92 | 77 | 79 | 93 | 79 | 94 | 69 | 96 | 79 | 87 | 101 | 96 |
| LAFAYETTE | 97 | 66 | 73 | 75 | 93 | 90 | 113 | 96 | 91 | 77 | 78 | 94 | 79 | 94 | 68 | 96 | 79 | 87 | 100 | 96 |
| LAWRENCE | 96 | 64 | 71 | 74 | 92 | 90 | 111 | 95 | 91 | 76 | 78 | 93 | 78 | 93 | 68 | 96 | 78 | 87 | 101 | 95 |
| LEE | 93 | 64 | 71 | 71 | 93 | 86 | 101 | 95 | 89 | 79 | 73 | 91 | 78 | 90 | 69 | 95 | 80 | 87 | 91 | 93 |
| LINCOLN | 96 | 63 | 68 | 72 | 92 | 89 | 108 | 95 | 90 | 76 | 75 | 93 | 78 | 92 | 67 | 95 | 78 | 86 | 97 | 95 |
| LITTLE RIVER | 97 | 72 | 78 | 78 | 93 | 91 | 112 | 95 | 92 | 81 | 83 | 94 | 83 | 96 | 71 | 96 | 82 | 89 | 100 | 97 |
| LOGAN | 97 | 68 | 74 | 77 | 93 | 91 | 112 | 95 | 92 | 78 | 80 | 94 | 80 | 95 | 70 | 96 | 80 | 88 | 101 | 97 |
| LONOKE | 98 | 82 | 86 | 86 | 95 | 93 | 111 | 97 | 96 | 89 | 90 | 97 | 89 | 99 | 76 | 98 | 89 | 93 | 99 | 100 |
| MADISON | 97 | 63 | 69 | 75 | 91 | 90 | 112 | 95 | 91 | 73 | 77 | 96 | 78 | 95 | 67 | 96 | 78 | 87 | 103 | 97 |
| MARION | 97 | 71 | 94 | 80 | 97 | 97 | 108 | 97 | 90 | 79 | 82 | 95 | 84 | 96 | 75 | 95 | 79 | 88 | 104 | 98 |
| MILLER | 94 | 74 | 81 | 77 | 95 | 90 | 103 | 95 | 90 | 83 | 81 | 91 | 83 | 93 | 74 | 95 | 82 | 88 | 95 | 95 |
| MISSISSIPPI | 96 | 77 | 81 | 82 | 95 | 91 | 105 | 96 | 93 | 86 | 84 | 95 | 86 | 95 | 75 | 97 | 86 | 91 | 95 | 97 |
| MONROE | 94 | 65 | 70 | 73 | 92 | 89 | 106 | 94 | 89 | 76 | 75 | 91 | 77 | 91 | 69 | 95 | 78 | 86 | 98 | 93 |
| MONTGOMERY | 97 | 67 | 87 | 79 | 95 | 96 | 109 | 96 | 89 | 75 | 80 | 96 | 82 | 96 | 72 | 95 | 78 | 88 | 105 | 98 |
| NEVADA | 96 | 69 | 74 | 76 | 94 | 91 | 110 | 95 | 91 | 79 | 80 | 93 | 81 | 94 | 71 | 95 | 80 | 88 | 100 | 96 |
| NEWTON | 97 | 65 | 72 | 74 | 92 | 91 | 112 | 95 | 92 | 77 | 78 | 94 | 79 | 94 | 68 | 96 | 79 | 87 | 101 | 96 |
| OUACHITA | 98 | 76 | 87 | 85 | 97 | 94 | 108 | 97 | 93 | 85 | 84 | 96 | 87 | 97 | 76 | 97 | 86 | 91 | 99 | 98 |
| PERRY | 97 | 65 | 70 | 75 | 92 | 90 | 112 | 95 | 91 | 76 | 78 | 96 | 79 | 95 | 67 | 96 | 79 | 87 | 102 | 97 |
| PHILLIPS | 91 | 70 | 75 | 72 | 95 | 87 | 95 | 93 | 87 | 82 | 74 | 86 | 80 | 87 | 74 | 94 | 81 | 87 | 90 | 91 |
| PIKE | 97 | 66 | 72 | 76 | 93 | 91 | 112 | 95 | 92 | 77 | 79 | 94 | 79 | 94 | 68 | 96 | 79 | 87 | 102 | 96 |
| POINSETT | 97 | 65 | 70 | 75 | 93 | 90 | 111 | 96 | 91 | 77 | 77 | 95 | 79 | 94 | 68 | 95 | 79 | 87 | 100 | 97 |
| POLK | 96 | 63 | 70 | 75 | 91 | 90 | 110 | 94 | 91 | 74 | 77 | 93 | 77 | 93 | 67 | 96 | 78 | 87 | 103 | 95 |
| POPE | 99 | 83 | 89 | 88 | 97 | 95 | 110 | 97 | 95 | 88 | 90 | 97 | 90 | 99 | 78 | 98 | 90 | 94 | 100 | 100 |
| PRAIRIE | 97 | 64 | 70 | 74 | 92 | 90 | 113 | 95 | 91 | 76 | 78 | 95 | 79 | 95 | 67 | 95 | 78 | 87 | 102 | 96 |
| PULASKI | 98 | 97 | 99 | 95 | 101 | 99 | 99 | 98 | 97 | 98 | 98 | 98 | 97 | 99 | 87 | 98 | 97 | 98 | 96 | 100 |
| RANDOLPH | 97 | 68 | 73 | 76 | 93 | 91 | 112 | 96 | 92 | 78 | 80 | 95 | 81 | 95 | 69 | 96 | 80 | 88 | 101 | 97 |
| ST. FRANCIS | 94 | 70 | 79 | 76 | 94 | 89 | 102 | 95 | 90 | 82 | 77 | 92 | 82 | 92 | 73 | 96 | 82 | 89 | 92 | 94 |
| SALINE | 99 | 85 | 92 | 90 | 97 | 96 | 112 | 98 | 96 | 91 | 93 | 98 | 91 | 101 | 79 | 99 | 92 | 95 | 101 | 101 |
| SCOTT | 97 | 64 | 70 | 74 | 92 | 90 | 112 | 95 | 92 | 76 | 78 | 94 | 79 | 94 | 67 | 95 | 78 | 87 | 101 | 96 |
| SEARCY | 95 | 63 | 69 | 73 | 92 | 90 | 110 | 94 | 91 | 75 | 77 | 92 | 77 | 92 | 67 | 96 | 77 | 86 | 102 | 95 |
| SEBASTIAN | 98 | 90 | 95 | 92 | 100 | 98 | 104 | 97 | 95 | 93 | 94 | 98 | 94 | 99 | 83 | 97 | 93 | 95 | 99 | 99 |
| SEVIER | 96 | 70 | 76 | 76 | 95 | 91 | 110 | 95 | 91 | 80 | 81 | 93 | 82 | 94 | 71 | 95 | 81 | 88 | 100 | 96 |
| SHARP | 98 | 74 | 97 | 87 | 98 | 101 | 110 | 98 | 92 | 82 | 85 | 94 | 86 | 96 | 79 | 96 | 84 | 90 | 106 | 98 |
| STONE | 97 | 63 | 67 | 73 | 92 | 90 | 112 | 95 | 91 | 75 | 77 | 95 | 78 | 94 | 66 | 95 | 78 | 86 | 102 | 96 |
| UNION | 96 | 78 | 91 | 84 | 99 | 95 | 104 | 96 | 91 | 87 | 86 | 94 | 88 | 95 | 79 | 96 | 86 | 91 | 99 | 97 |
| VAN BUREN | 98 | 72 | 92 | 84 | 97 | 99 | 112 | 98 | 92 | 81 | 84 | 95 | 85 | 97 | 77 | 96 | 83 | 90 | 105 | 98 |
| WASHINGTON | 98 | 89 | 92 | 90 | 98 | 95 | 106 | 95 | 94 | 89 | 93 | 96 | 90 | 98 | 80 | 97 | 91 | 94 | 99 | 99 |
| WHITE | 97 | 72 | 80 | 79 | 94 | 92 | 112 | 96 | 92 | 80 | 82 | 95 | 83 | 96 | 71 | 96 | 82 | 89 | 101 | 97 |
| WOODRUFF | 95 | 64 | 70 | 73 | 92 | 89 | 107 | 95 | 90 | 76 | 75 | 92 | 78 | 92 | 68 | 96 | 78 | 87 | 97 | 95 |
| YELL | 98 | 69 | 74 | 77 | 94 | 91 | 113 | 96 | 92 | 79 | 80 | 96 | 82 | 96 | 69 | 96 | 81 | 88 | 101 | 98 |
| ARKANSAS | 97 | 81 | 89 | 86 | 97 | 95 | 107 | 97 | 94 | 87 | 88 | 96 | 88 | 97 | 78 | 97 | 88 | 92 | 99 | 98 |
| UNITED STATES | 100 | 100 | 100 | 100 | 100 | 100 | 100 | 100 | 100 | 100 | 100 | 100 | 100 | 100 | 100 | 100 | 100 | 100 | 100 | 100 |

## CALIFORNIA

# POPULATION CHANGE

| COUNTY | FIPS Code | MSA Code | DMA Code | POPULATION 1990 | POPULATION 2000 | POPULATION 2005 | 1990-2000 ANNUAL CHANGE % Rate | 1990-2000 ANNUAL CHANGE State Rank | RACE (%) White 1990 | RACE (%) White 2000 | RACE (%) Black 1990 | RACE (%) Black 2000 | RACE (%) Asian/Pacific 1990 | RACE (%) Asian/Pacific 2000 |
|---|---|---|---|---|---|---|---|---|---|---|---|---|---|---|
| ALAMEDA | 001 | 5775 | 807 | 1,279,182 | 1,437,348 | 1,539,662 | 1.1 | 30 | 59.6 | 52.9 | 17.9 | 18.4 | 15.1 | 19.3 |
| ALPINE | 003 | 0000 | 811 | 1,113 | 1,140 | 1,105 | 0.2 | 52 | 72.4 | 72.4 | 0.5 | 0.6 | 0.4 | 0.7 |
| AMADOR | 005 | 0000 | 862 | 30,039 | 34,555 | 36,568 | 1.4 | 20 | 89.5 | 89.3 | 5.6 | 5.1 | 0.7 | 1.0 |
| BUTTE | 007 | 1620 | 868 | 182,120 | 196,641 | 201,336 | 0.8 | 37 | 90.7 | 88.1 | 1.3 | 1.4 | 2.8 | 3.9 |
| CALAVERAS | 009 | 0000 | 862 | 31,998 | 40,546 | 43,068 | 2.3 | 7 | 95.7 | 94.9 | 0.6 | 0.6 | 0.6 | 0.9 |
| COLUSA | 011 | 0000 | 862 | 16,275 | 19,093 | 20,321 | 1.6 | 17 | 76.4 | 71.5 | 0.6 | 0.6 | 2.2 | 2.8 |
| CONTRA COSTA | 013 | 5775 | 807 | 803,732 | 950,545 | 1,034,337 | 1.7 | 14 | 76.0 | 71.2 | 9.3 | 9.5 | 9.6 | 12.9 |
| DEL NORTE | 015 | 0000 | 802 | 23,460 | 26,384 | 25,917 | 1.2 | 27 | 86.1 | 84.3 | 3.7 | 4.7 | 1.9 | 2.6 |
| EL DORADO | 017 | 6920 | 862 | 125,995 | 164,647 | 180,989 | 2.6 | 6 | 94.5 | 92.9 | 0.5 | 0.5 | 1.9 | 2.8 |
| FRESNO | 019 | 2840 | 866 | 667,490 | 769,827 | 803,908 | 1.4 | 20 | 63.3 | 57.3 | 5.0 | 4.8 | 8.6 | 10.2 |
| GLENN | 021 | 0000 | 868 | 24,798 | 26,422 | 26,909 | 0.6 | 42 | 85.4 | 81.9 | 0.6 | 0.6 | 3.3 | 4.2 |
| HUMBOLDT | 023 | 0000 | 802 | 119,118 | 121,008 | 119,039 | 0.2 | 52 | 90.6 | 89.3 | 0.8 | 0.9 | 1.9 | 2.7 |
| IMPERIAL | 025 | 0000 | 771 | 109,303 | 146,764 | 154,379 | 2.9 | 3 | 67.3 | 64.3 | 2.4 | 2.5 | 2.0 | 2.1 |
| INYO | 027 | 0000 | 803 | 18,281 | 17,837 | 17,252 | -0.2 | 56 | 86.3 | 85.1 | 0.4 | 0.4 | 1.0 | 1.4 |
| KERN | 029 | 0680 | 800 | 543,477 | 649,311 | 683,572 | 1.8 | 10 | 69.6 | 62.8 | 5.5 | 5.9 | 3.0 | 3.9 |
| KINGS | 031 | 0000 | 866 | 101,469 | 124,474 | 130,719 | 2.0 | 9 | 64.2 | 58.3 | 8.1 | 7.9 | 3.5 | 4.4 |
| LAKE | 033 | 0000 | 807 | 50,631 | 55,594 | 56,494 | 0.9 | 36 | 91.8 | 89.9 | 1.8 | 2.0 | 0.9 | 1.3 |
| LASSEN | 035 | 0000 | 811 | 27,598 | 32,960 | 32,631 | 1.7 | 14 | 87.7 | 83.2 | 6.2 | 10.1 | 1.1 | 1.5 |
| LOS ANGELES | 037 | 4480 | 803 | 8,863,164 | 9,424,833 | 9,879,261 | 0.6 | 42 | 56.8 | 51.8 | 11.2 | 10.5 | 10.8 | 13.0 |
| MADERA | 039 | 2840 | 866 | 88,090 | 118,307 | 126,149 | 2.9 | 3 | 71.9 | 66.0 | 2.8 | 3.3 | 1.4 | 1.7 |
| MARIN | 041 | 7360 | 807 | 230,096 | 237,832 | 242,391 | 0.3 | 48 | 88.7 | 85.9 | 3.6 | 3.8 | 4.1 | 5.7 |
| MARIPOSA | 043 | 0000 | 866 | 14,302 | 15,560 | 15,322 | 0.8 | 37 | 92.4 | 91.5 | 0.9 | 1.2 | 0.9 | 1.2 |
| MENDOCINO | 045 | 0000 | 807 | 80,345 | 84,446 | 86,302 | 0.5 | 46 | 89.6 | 87.8 | 0.6 | 0.6 | 1.2 | 1.6 |
| MERCED | 047 | 4940 | 866 | 178,403 | 204,109 | 220,046 | 1.3 | 26 | 67.4 | 61.6 | 4.8 | 4.6 | 8.5 | 10.3 |
| MODOC | 049 | 0000 | 813 | 9,678 | 9,083 | 8,464 | -0.6 | 58 | 91.0 | 89.6 | 0.8 | 0.8 | 0.4 | 0.5 |
| MONO | 051 | 0000 | 811 | 9,956 | 10,503 | 10,455 | 0.5 | 46 | 92.7 | 91.7 | 0.4 | 0.4 | 1.3 | 1.8 |
| MONTEREY | 053 | 7120 | 828 | 355,660 | 377,527 | 398,038 | 0.6 | 42 | 63.8 | 57.8 | 6.4 | 6.0 | 7.8 | 9.7 |
| NAPA | 055 | 8720 | 807 | 110,765 | 122,562 | 130,036 | 1.0 | 33 | 88.9 | 85.9 | 1.1 | 1.0 | 3.3 | 4.4 |
| NEVADA | 057 | 0000 | 862 | 78,510 | 93,346 | 98,823 | 1.7 | 14 | 97.3 | 96.6 | 0.2 | 0.2 | 0.8 | 1.2 |
| ORANGE | 059 | 5945 | 803 | 2,410,556 | 2,810,321 | 3,047,014 | 1.5 | 18 | 78.6 | 73.6 | 1.8 | 1.7 | 10.3 | 13.3 |
| PLACER | 061 | 6920 | 862 | 172,796 | 248,590 | 294,086 | 3.6 | 2 | 93.7 | 91.8 | 0.6 | 0.7 | 2.2 | 3.1 |
| PLUMAS | 063 | 0000 | 862 | 19,739 | 20,353 | 20,269 | 0.3 | 48 | 94.2 | 93.3 | 0.8 | 0.8 | 0.6 | 0.8 |
| RIVERSIDE | 065 | 6780 | 804 | 1,170,413 | 1,574,240 | 1,790,181 | 2.9 | 3 | 76.4 | 71.5 | 5.4 | 5.5 | 3.6 | 4.6 |
| SACRAMENTO | 067 | 6920 | 862 | 1,041,219 | 1,200,275 | 1,277,441 | 1.4 | 20 | 75.1 | 70.1 | 9.3 | 9.5 | 9.3 | 12.5 |
| SAN BENITO | 069 | 0000 | 828 | 36,697 | 53,746 | 65,290 | 3.8 | 1 | 69.8 | 64.1 | 0.6 | 0.6 | 2.2 | 2.6 |
| SAN BERNARDINO | 071 | 6780 | 803 | 1,418,380 | 1,697,943 | 1,837,345 | 1.8 | 10 | 73.0 | 68.2 | 8.1 | 7.9 | 4.2 | 5.4 |
| SAN DIEGO | 073 | 7320 | 825 | 2,498,016 | 2,872,950 | 3,125,152 | 1.4 | 20 | 74.9 | 69.9 | 6.4 | 6.0 | 7.9 | 10.5 |
| SAN FRANCISCO | 075 | 7360 | 807 | 723,959 | 750,154 | 765,237 | 0.3 | 48 | 53.6 | 45.8 | 10.9 | 10.4 | 29.1 | 36.2 |
| SAN JOAQUIN | 077 | 8120 | 862 | 480,628 | 574,605 | 631,219 | 1.8 | 10 | 73.5 | 68.6 | 5.6 | 5.6 | 12.4 | 15.6 |
| SAN LUIS OBISPO | 079 | 7460 | 855 | 217,162 | 239,701 | 253,311 | 1.0 | 33 | 89.2 | 86.7 | 2.6 | 2.8 | 2.9 | 3.8 |
| SAN MATEO | 081 | 7360 | 807 | 649,623 | 706,666 | 727,649 | 0.8 | 37 | 71.9 | 66.2 | 5.4 | 5.3 | 16.8 | 21.4 |
| SANTA BARBARA | 083 | 7480 | 855 | 369,608 | 393,737 | 406,078 | 0.6 | 42 | 77.2 | 72.2 | 2.8 | 2.9 | 4.4 | 5.6 |
| SANTA CLARA | 085 | 7400 | 807 | 1,497,577 | 1,662,097 | 1,732,406 | 1.0 | 33 | 68.9 | 62.6 | 3.8 | 3.6 | 17.5 | 21.8 |
| SANTA CRUZ | 087 | 7485 | 828 | 229,734 | 247,902 | 260,754 | 0.7 | 41 | 83.9 | 79.4 | 1.1 | 1.2 | 3.7 | 4.9 |
| SHASTA | 089 | 6690 | 868 | 147,036 | 165,415 | 169,812 | 1.2 | 27 | 93.8 | 92.7 | 0.7 | 0.8 | 1.8 | 2.5 |
| SIERRA | 091 | 0000 | 862 | 3,318 | 3,314 | 3,215 | 0.0 | 54 | 95.7 | 94.9 | 0.2 | 0.2 | 0.4 | 0.4 |
| SISKIYOU | 093 | 0000 | 813 | 43,531 | 43,306 | 42,026 | -0.1 | 55 | 92.1 | 91.2 | 1.6 | 1.7 | 0.9 | 1.2 |
| SOLANO | 095 | 8720 | 862 | 340,421 | 393,002 | 428,349 | 1.4 | 20 | 66.8 | 60.8 | 13.5 | 13.6 | 12.8 | 16.9 |
| SONOMA | 097 | 7500 | 807 | 388,222 | 447,119 | 479,889 | 1.4 | 20 | 90.6 | 87.9 | 1.4 | 1.5 | 2.8 | 3.9 |
| STANISLAUS | 099 | 5170 | 862 | 370,522 | 445,583 | 486,764 | 1.8 | 10 | 80.2 | 75.2 | 1.7 | 1.8 | 5.2 | 6.7 |
| SUTTER | 101 | 9340 | 862 | 64,415 | 79,545 | 85,142 | 2.1 | 8 | 76.9 | 70.9 | 1.6 | 1.7 | 9.4 | 12.4 |
| TEHAMA | 103 | 0000 | 868 | 49,625 | 54,050 | 54,392 | 0.8 | 37 | 91.9 | 89.6 | 0.5 | 0.5 | 0.7 | 1.0 |
| TRINITY | 105 | 0000 | 868 | 13,063 | 12,809 | 12,237 | -0.2 | 56 | 92.9 | 92.0 | 0.4 | 0.4 | 0.8 | 1.0 |
| TULARE | 107 | 8780 | 866 | 311,921 | 362,474 | 381,984 | 1.5 | 18 | 65.7 | 59.1 | 1.5 | 1.4 | 4.3 | 5.2 |
| TUOLUMNE | 109 | 0000 | 862 | 48,456 | 54,257 | 56,687 | 1.1 | 30 | 90.4 | 88.8 | 3.2 | 3.5 | 0.8 | 1.1 |
| VENTURA | 111 | 8735 | 803 | 669,016 | 758,411 | 816,948 | 1.2 | 27 | 79.1 | 74.3 | 2.3 | 2.3 | 5.2 | 6.7 |
| YOLO | 113 | 9270 | 862 | 141,092 | 157,835 | 168,199 | 1.1 | 30 | 75.9 | 70.4 | 2.2 | 2.3 | 8.4 | 10.3 |
| YUBA | 115 | 9340 | 862 | 58,228 | 59,826 | 58,773 | 0.3 | 48 | 78.2 | 73.4 | 4.2 | 4.1 | 8.4 | 11.2 |
| CALIFORNIA | | | | | | | 1.2 | | 69.0 | 64.3 | 7.4 | 7.1 | 9.6 | 11.8 |
| UNITED STATES | | | | | | | 1.0 | | 80.3 | 77.9 | 12.1 | 12.4 | 2.9 | 3.9 |

| COUNTY | % HISPANIC ORIGIN 1990 | % HISPANIC ORIGIN 2000 | 2000 AGE DISTRIBUTION (%) 0-4 | 5-9 | 10-14 | 15-19 | 20-24 | 25-44 | 45-64 | 65-84 | 85+ | 18+ | MEDIAN AGE 1990 | MEDIAN AGE 2000 | 2000 Males/ Females (×100) |
|---|---|---|---|---|---|---|---|---|---|---|---|---|---|---|---|
| ALAMEDA | 14.2 | 18.8 | 6.5 | 7.5 | 6.7 | 6.8 | 6.9 | 33.2 | 21.4 | 9.6 | 1.4 | 75.6 | 32.7 | 35.4 | 96.8 |
| ALPINE | 6.6 | 8.9 | 6.1 | 8.2 | 6.1 | 6.7 | 6.0 | 31.1 | 27.4 | 7.9 | 0.8 | 76.0 | 33.3 | 37.3 | 111.9 |
| AMADOR | 8.4 | 9.8 | 4.2 | 5.7 | 5.3 | 6.7 | 7.2 | 26.6 | 24.7 | 17.6 | 2.0 | 81.4 | 37.9 | 41.2 | 126.3 |
| BUTTE | 7.5 | 10.9 | 6.3 | 7.6 | 6.3 | 7.8 | 9.7 | 25.5 | 19.9 | 14.9 | 2.0 | 76.1 | 33.8 | 35.6 | 97.9 |
| CALAVERAS | 5.4 | 8.0 | 5.4 | 7.4 | 6.8 | 6.2 | 3.9 | 23.6 | 27.2 | 17.7 | 1.7 | 76.0 | 39.5 | 42.9 | 99.9 |
| COLUSA | 33.3 | 41.7 | 7.9 | 8.8 | 7.9 | 8.6 | 6.8 | 25.9 | 20.9 | 11.8 | 1.4 | 70.0 | 32.1 | 33.4 | 104.8 |
| CONTRA COSTA | 11.4 | 15.2 | 6.5 | 7.6 | 7.5 | 6.8 | 5.6 | 29.7 | 24.2 | 10.6 | 1.5 | 74.4 | 34.1 | 37.0 | 95.1 |
| DEL NORTE | 10.3 | 13.5 | 6.7 | 8.5 | 7.1 | 7.2 | 7.5 | 29.7 | 20.1 | 12.0 | 1.2 | 73.3 | 32.3 | 33.7 | 122.1 |
| EL DORADO | 7.0 | 10.0 | 6.3 | 8.3 | 7.3 | 6.8 | 4.7 | 29.2 | 24.1 | 12.1 | 1.2 | 73.8 | 35.3 | 38.1 | 99.9 |
| FRESNO | 35.5 | 43.3 | 8.9 | 10.0 | 8.1 | 8.0 | 7.6 | 29.1 | 17.8 | 9.2 | 1.3 | 68.4 | 29.3 | 30.3 | 99.5 |
| GLENN | 20.0 | 26.5 | 7.9 | 9.7 | 8.1 | 7.9 | 5.8 | 26.2 | 20.3 | 12.2 | 1.8 | 69.1 | 32.6 | 33.9 | 100.9 |
| HUMBOLDT | 4.2 | 6.1 | 6.3 | 8.0 | 6.8 | 7.8 | 7.5 | 29.0 | 21.6 | 11.5 | 1.5 | 74.9 | 33.1 | 35.7 | 99.3 |
| IMPERIAL | 65.8 | 73.8 | 8.3 | 9.8 | 8.3 | 8.8 | 8.3 | 29.2 | 17.0 | 9.4 | 0.9 | 68.0 | 28.8 | 29.2 | 105.6 |
| INYO | 8.4 | 11.9 | 5.6 | 7.5 | 6.7 | 6.3 | 4.4 | 24.5 | 25.3 | 17.1 | 2.6 | 76.0 | 39.0 | 41.9 | 98.1 |
| KERN | 28.0 | 36.1 | 8.8 | 10.1 | 8.1 | 7.7 | 6.9 | 30.3 | 18.1 | 8.9 | 1.0 | 68.4 | 29.7 | 30.7 | 104.6 |
| KINGS | 34.1 | 42.5 | 9.1 | 10.0 | 7.8 | 7.4 | 9.0 | 33.3 | 15.7 | 6.9 | 0.8 | 68.8 | 28.1 | 28.6 | 114.4 |
| LAKE | 7.2 | 10.4 | 5.9 | 7.5 | 6.8 | 6.0 | 4.4 | 23.0 | 24.3 | 20.0 | 2.2 | 76.0 | 40.4 | 42.6 | 98.3 |
| LASSEN | 10.4 | 15.4 | 5.2 | 6.9 | 6.0 | 6.8 | 10.6 | 36.1 | 18.5 | 9.0 | 0.9 | 78.3 | 31.9 | 32.2 | 166.0 |
| LOS ANGELES | 37.8 | 44.5 | 7.8 | 8.1 | 7.3 | 7.1 | 7.6 | 33.0 | 19.4 | 8.6 | 1.2 | 73.0 | 30.7 | 32.6 | 100.2 |
| MADERA | 34.5 | 42.9 | 7.4 | 8.8 | 7.7 | 7.9 | 7.7 | 28.0 | 19.6 | 11.6 | 1.4 | 71.1 | 31.9 | 32.8 | 112.4 |
| MARIN | 7.8 | 10.6 | 4.8 | 5.7 | 5.4 | 5.2 | 5.1 | 31.9 | 27.9 | 12.4 | 1.7 | 81.0 | 38.1 | 41.1 | 98.3 |
| MARIPOSA | 4.9 | 7.1 | 5.2 | 6.9 | 6.2 | 6.3 | 4.9 | 24.1 | 26.6 | 18.0 | 1.7 | 77.9 | 38.9 | 42.7 | 103.2 |
| MENDOCINO | 10.3 | 14.1 | 6.4 | 7.4 | 7.1 | 7.8 | 6.6 | 24.6 | 26.2 | 12.3 | 1.6 | 74.1 | 35.6 | 37.9 | 99.8 |
| MERCED | 32.6 | 40.5 | 9.8 | 11.1 | 8.8 | 8.4 | 7.1 | 28.4 | 17.0 | 8.5 | 1.0 | 65.2 | 27.9 | 28.5 | 101.7 |
| MODOC | 7.2 | 10.1 | 5.6 | 7.9 | 7.5 | 7.4 | 4.6 | 24.0 | 24.2 | 16.5 | 2.2 | 73.8 | 37.2 | 40.5 | 106.5 |
| MONO | 11.3 | 15.3 | 7.0 | 8.2 | 6.4 | 5.9 | 5.9 | 36.0 | 22.7 | 7.3 | 0.5 | 75.0 | 32.3 | 35.2 | 116.5 |
| MONTEREY | 33.6 | 41.3 | 8.1 | 8.8 | 7.2 | 7.3 | 7.9 | 31.9 | 17.8 | 9.7 | 1.3 | 71.9 | 29.6 | 31.7 | 107.2 |
| NAPA | 14.4 | 19.4 | 6.0 | 6.7 | 6.6 | 7.0 | 6.1 | 26.9 | 24.0 | 14.1 | 2.5 | 76.7 | 36.4 | 38.9 | 98.0 |
| NEVADA | 4.2 | 6.3 | 5.1 | 7.2 | 6.7 | 6.3 | 4.2 | 24.9 | 26.0 | 17.6 | 1.9 | 76.8 | 39.3 | 42.5 | 98.5 |
| ORANGE | 23.4 | 29.3 | 7.0 | 7.7 | 6.6 | 6.9 | 7.1 | 33.3 | 20.8 | 9.3 | 1.4 | 74.9 | 31.4 | 34.3 | 100.3 |
| PLACER | 8.0 | 11.6 | 6.4 | 7.8 | 7.3 | 7.1 | 5.4 | 28.4 | 25.0 | 11.1 | 1.4 | 74.2 | 35.1 | 37.3 | 96.3 |
| PLUMAS | 4.6 | 6.9 | 5.4 | 7.4 | 6.9 | 6.4 | 4.2 | 23.4 | 26.8 | 18.0 | 1.7 | 76.0 | 39.0 | 42.7 | 100.6 |
| RIVERSIDE | 26.3 | 34.1 | 8.5 | 9.1 | 7.8 | 7.1 | 6.3 | 29.5 | 18.1 | 12.0 | 1.6 | 70.5 | 31.5 | 33.1 | 99.5 |
| SACRAMENTO | 11.7 | 15.8 | 7.5 | 8.1 | 7.1 | 7.0 | 6.9 | 31.7 | 20.3 | 10.2 | 1.2 | 73.2 | 31.9 | 34.2 | 94.9 |
| SAN BENITO | 45.8 | 55.1 | 8.4 | 9.3 | 8.2 | 7.9 | 6.9 | 29.7 | 19.6 | 9.0 | 1.0 | 69.3 | 30.3 | 31.7 | 99.9 |
| SAN BERNARDINO | 26.7 | 34.4 | 9.1 | 9.7 | 8.3 | 7.8 | 7.1 | 30.7 | 18.2 | 8.1 | 1.0 | 68.3 | 29.3 | 30.6 | 98.9 |
| SAN DIEGO | 20.4 | 26.8 | 7.3 | 7.7 | 6.7 | 6.8 | 7.7 | 33.5 | 19.1 | 9.8 | 1.3 | 74.8 | 30.9 | 33.6 | 101.9 |
| SAN FRANCISCO | 13.9 | 17.1 | 4.4 | 4.8 | 4.5 | 4.9 | 6.6 | 35.9 | 23.7 | 13.0 | 2.1 | 83.6 | 35.8 | 39.1 | 98.7 |
| SAN JOAQUIN | 23.4 | 29.5 | 8.2 | 9.5 | 7.9 | 7.9 | 6.8 | 29.5 | 19.0 | 9.9 | 1.4 | 69.8 | 30.9 | 32.1 | 102.4 |
| SAN LUIS OBISPO | 13.3 | 17.8 | 5.7 | 7.0 | 6.0 | 7.7 | 9.0 | 29.6 | 20.0 | 13.3 | 1.7 | 77.9 | 33.1 | 35.6 | 107.0 |
| SAN MATEO | 17.6 | 22.0 | 6.0 | 6.8 | 6.7 | 6.2 | 5.8 | 31.4 | 24.0 | 11.5 | 1.7 | 76.9 | 34.8 | 37.8 | 97.3 |
| SANTA BARBARA | 26.6 | 33.8 | 6.8 | 7.3 | 6.6 | 7.8 | 8.4 | 31.1 | 19.4 | 10.8 | 1.7 | 75.9 | 31.6 | 33.8 | 100.5 |
| SANTA CLARA | 21.0 | 26.1 | 6.7 | 7.5 | 6.6 | 6.9 | 6.8 | 33.9 | 21.4 | 9.1 | 1.1 | 75.5 | 31.9 | 35.0 | 101.7 |
| SANTA CRUZ | 20.4 | 27.1 | 6.5 | 7.6 | 6.5 | 7.6 | 7.3 | 32.8 | 20.8 | 9.3 | 1.6 | 75.7 | 33.0 | 35.1 | 99.8 |
| SHASTA | 3.8 | 5.8 | 6.8 | 8.4 | 7.4 | 7.3 | 5.5 | 26.4 | 23.2 | 13.5 | 1.6 | 72.9 | 34.9 | 37.3 | 97.1 |
| SIERRA | 5.5 | 8.4 | 5.8 | 8.1 | 6.9 | 6.6 | 3.7 | 23.5 | 27.5 | 15.8 | 2.1 | 74.6 | 38.6 | 42.2 | 104.6 |
| SISKIYOU | 5.9 | 8.4 | 5.8 | 8.0 | 7.3 | 7.2 | 4.9 | 24.3 | 24.6 | 15.9 | 2.0 | 74.4 | 37.3 | 40.4 | 98.3 |
| SOLANO | 13.4 | 17.4 | 7.7 | 9.1 | 7.7 | 7.1 | 6.5 | 32.8 | 19.7 | 8.5 | 0.9 | 71.3 | 30.8 | 33.0 | 102.4 |
| SONOMA | 10.6 | 14.8 | 6.3 | 7.3 | 7.0 | 7.0 | 5.7 | 29.1 | 24.3 | 11.4 | 1.9 | 75.4 | 34.8 | 37.3 | 96.0 |
| STANISLAUS | 21.8 | 28.7 | 8.6 | 9.3 | 8.2 | 7.9 | 6.8 | 29.1 | 19.2 | 9.5 | 1.3 | 69.1 | 30.5 | 31.7 | 96.4 |
| SUTTER | 16.4 | 21.5 | 7.7 | 8.9 | 7.6 | 7.4 | 6.3 | 27.7 | 21.8 | 11.3 | 1.3 | 71.3 | 32.4 | 34.3 | 98.7 |
| TEHAMA | 10.3 | 14.6 | 6.8 | 7.7 | 7.1 | 7.5 | 6.5 | 23.6 | 23.2 | 15.6 | 2.0 | 73.5 | 36.0 | 38.2 | 97.0 |
| TRINITY | 3.3 | 4.9 | 5.4 | 7.4 | 7.2 | 6.7 | 4.6 | 24.3 | 26.7 | 16.3 | 1.5 | 75.4 | 37.8 | 41.6 | 105.8 |
| TULARE | 38.8 | 47.4 | 9.1 | 10.6 | 8.7 | 8.5 | 6.9 | 27.6 | 18.1 | 9.3 | 1.3 | 66.5 | 29.2 | 29.7 | 100.1 |
| TUOLUMNE | 7.7 | 10.1 | 4.8 | 6.5 | 6.1 | 6.1 | 6.3 | 27.7 | 24.0 | 16.9 | 1.6 | 78.8 | 37.2 | 40.2 | 116.2 |
| VENTURA | 26.4 | 33.7 | 7.3 | 8.2 | 7.7 | 7.2 | 6.4 | 31.6 | 21.5 | 8.8 | 1.2 | 72.6 | 31.7 | 34.2 | 101.5 |
| YOLO | 20.0 | 26.4 | 6.9 | 7.3 | 6.4 | 9.0 | 11.0 | 31.5 | 18.1 | 8.7 | 1.1 | 76.0 | 28.9 | 31.2 | 97.5 |
| YUBA | 11.6 | 15.8 | 9.7 | 10.3 | 8.0 | 7.6 | 7.1 | 27.4 | 18.6 | 10.2 | 1.1 | 67.6 | 29.2 | 30.1 | 99.3 |
| CALIFORNIA | 25.8 | 31.7 | 7.4 | 8.1 | 7.2 | 7.1 | 7.1 | 31.9 | 20.2 | 9.7 | 1.3 | 73.3 | 31.5 | 33.7 | 100.0 |
| UNITED STATES | 9.0 | 11.8 | 6.9 | 7.2 | 7.2 | 7.2 | 6.7 | 29.9 | 22.2 | 11.1 | 1.6 | 74.6 | 32.9 | 35.7 | 95.6 |

# HOUSEHOLDS

| COUNTY | HOUSEHOLDS | | | | | FAMILIES | | | MEDIAN HOUSEHOLD INCOME | | | |
|---|---|---|---|---|---|---|---|---|---|---|---|---|
| | 1990 | 2000 | 2005 | % Annual Rate 1990-2000 | 2000 Average HH Size | 1990 | 2000 | % Annual Rate 1990-2000 | 2000 | 2005 | 2000 National Rank | 2000 State Rank |
| ALAMEDA | 479,518 | 550,058 | 594,403 | 1.7 | 2.55 | 308,866 | 346,754 | 1.4 | 56,996 | 70,516 | 101 | 9 |
| ALPINE | 450 | 488 | 486 | 1.0 | 2.33 | 266 | 273 | 0.3 | 35,278 | 40,139 | 1207 | 43 |
| AMADOR | 10,518 | 12,264 | 12,996 | 1.9 | 2.44 | 7,683 | 8,629 | 1.4 | 44,603 | 57,156 | 369 | 20 |
| BUTTE | 71,665 | 78,127 | 80,487 | 1.1 | 2.45 | 46,125 | 48,085 | 0.5 | 34,959 | 42,199 | 1258 | 45 |
| CALAVERAS | 12,649 | 16,467 | 17,713 | 3.2 | 2.44 | 9,416 | 11,858 | 2.8 | 38,934 | 47,903 | 756 | 34 |
| COLUSA | 5,612 | 6,693 | 7,187 | 2.2 | 2.80 | 4,170 | 4,868 | 1.9 | 32,580 | 41,606 | 1614 | 50 |
| CONTRA COSTA | 300,288 | 360,472 | 394,841 | 2.2 | 2.61 | 212,649 | 247,819 | 1.9 | 65,904 | 78,078 | 30 | 2 |
| DEL NORTE | 7,987 | 9,040 | 8,933 | 1.5 | 2.59 | 5,738 | 6,250 | 1.0 | 34,948 | 42,274 | 1261 | 46 |
| EL DORADO | 46,845 | 62,336 | 69,110 | 3.5 | 2.62 | 35,000 | 45,599 | 3.3 | 52,367 | 63,563 | 163 | 12 |
| FRESNO | 220,933 | 255,836 | 268,388 | 1.8 | 2.94 | 161,781 | 183,797 | 1.6 | 37,000 | 43,844 | 979 | 39 |
| GLENN | 8,821 | 9,474 | 9,680 | 0.9 | 2.75 | 6,439 | 6,691 | 0.5 | 31,912 | 40,042 | 1735 | 53 |
| HUMBOLDT | 46,420 | 47,895 | 47,469 | 0.4 | 2.45 | 30,086 | 29,778 | -0.1 | 35,047 | 41,795 | 1246 | 44 |
| IMPERIAL | 32,842 | 42,113 | 44,685 | 3.1 | 3.23 | 26,003 | 33,449 | 3.1 | 27,168 | 31,730 | 2552 | 58 |
| INYO | 7,565 | 7,502 | 7,305 | -0.1 | 2.31 | 5,063 | 4,778 | -0.7 | 35,807 | 43,091 | 1126 | 42 |
| KERN | 181,480 | 213,227 | 225,611 | 2.0 | 2.91 | 135,925 | 156,312 | 1.7 | 38,806 | 48,543 | 771 | 35 |
| KINGS | 29,082 | 34,862 | 37,256 | 2.2 | 3.02 | 22,884 | 26,843 | 2.0 | 34,154 | 43,001 | 1363 | 47 |
| LAKE | 20,805 | 22,969 | 23,399 | 1.2 | 2.37 | 14,257 | 15,080 | 0.7 | 32,814 | 40,935 | 1570 | 49 |
| LASSEN | 8,543 | 9,382 | 9,390 | 1.1 | 2.57 | 6,329 | 6,679 | 0.7 | 40,998 | 50,464 | 589 | 31 |
| LOS ANGELES | 2,989,552 | 3,199,899 | 3,367,195 | 0.8 | 2.89 | 2,013,926 | 2,137,362 | 0.7 | 42,060 | 52,502 | 504 | 28 |
| MADERA | 28,370 | 36,328 | 39,182 | 3.0 | 3.01 | 22,535 | 28,580 | 2.9 | 41,100 | 51,392 | 583 | 30 |
| MARIN | 95,006 | 99,592 | 102,293 | 0.6 | 2.30 | 58,096 | 58,050 | 0.0 | 61,827 | 69,663 | 59 | 4 |
| MARIPOSA | 5,604 | 6,326 | 6,326 | 1.5 | 2.35 | 4,026 | 4,389 | 1.1 | 37,290 | 46,736 | 932 | 38 |
| MENDOCINO | 30,419 | 32,347 | 33,246 | 0.7 | 2.54 | 21,053 | 21,517 | 0.3 | 38,720 | 47,115 | 780 | 36 |
| MERCED | 55,331 | 64,525 | 70,044 | 1.9 | 3.13 | 43,246 | 49,762 | 1.7 | 32,920 | 41,289 | 1550 | 48 |
| MODOC | 3,711 | 3,582 | 3,374 | -0.4 | 2.42 | 2,653 | 2,466 | -0.9 | 29,061 | 36,316 | 2287 | 56 |
| MONO | 3,961 | 4,154 | 4,140 | 0.6 | 2.48 | 2,450 | 2,440 | 0.0 | 41,848 | 52,939 | 525 | 29 |
| MONTEREY | 112,965 | 123,110 | 131,243 | 1.0 | 2.91 | 83,015 | 89,128 | 0.9 | 43,478 | 54,582 | 427 | 25 |
| NAPA | 41,312 | 46,429 | 49,557 | 1.4 | 2.53 | 28,545 | 30,734 | 0.9 | 50,670 | 58,820 | 193 | 14 |
| NEVADA | 30,758 | 37,302 | 39,915 | 2.4 | 2.46 | 22,689 | 26,683 | 2.0 | 47,323 | 58,857 | 262 | 15 |
| ORANGE | 827,066 | 983,013 | 1,075,339 | 2.1 | 2.82 | 583,162 | 676,832 | 1.8 | 61,136 | 74,735 | 65 | 5 |
| PLACER | 64,101 | 92,125 | 108,876 | 4.5 | 2.67 | 47,786 | 66,461 | 4.1 | 58,414 | 69,172 | 84 | 7 |
| PLUMAS | 8,125 | 8,401 | 8,370 | 0.4 | 2.41 | 5,822 | 5,836 | 0.0 | 36,124 | 40,998 | 1088 | 41 |
| RIVERSIDE | 402,067 | 538,585 | 611,949 | 3.6 | 2.87 | 296,028 | 384,683 | 3.2 | 43,898 | 54,441 | 401 | 22 |
| SACRAMENTO | 394,530 | 450,242 | 476,410 | 1.6 | 2.62 | 262,916 | 290,070 | 1.2 | 44,778 | 53,033 | 362 | 19 |
| SAN BENITO | 11,422 | 16,838 | 20,528 | 4.8 | 3.15 | 9,079 | 13,098 | 4.5 | 51,857 | 64,751 | 174 | 13 |
| SAN BERNARDINO | 464,737 | 560,497 | 608,287 | 2.3 | 2.97 | 351,690 | 414,051 | 2.0 | 42,761 | 53,873 | 467 | 26 |
| SAN DIEGO | 887,403 | 1,048,142 | 1,152,222 | 2.0 | 2.65 | 599,428 | 689,842 | 1.7 | 45,892 | 56,513 | 316 | 17 |
| SAN FRANCISCO | 305,584 | 324,039 | 334,016 | 0.7 | 2.24 | 141,906 | 147,778 | 0.5 | 46,285 | 54,590 | 299 | 16 |
| SAN JOAQUIN | 158,156 | 190,570 | 210,297 | 2.3 | 2.93 | 116,878 | 137,595 | 2.0 | 42,117 | 52,807 | 501 | 27 |
| SAN LUIS OBISPO | 80,281 | 89,950 | 95,860 | 1.4 | 2.51 | 52,320 | 56,453 | 0.9 | 45,447 | 56,747 | 334 | 18 |
| SAN MATEO | 241,914 | 269,879 | 281,258 | 1.3 | 2.57 | 162,317 | 176,508 | 1.0 | 62,785 | 72,871 | 54 | 3 |
| SANTA BARBARA | 129,802 | 140,830 | 146,599 | 1.0 | 2.68 | 86,077 | 91,382 | 0.7 | 44,603 | 53,764 | 369 | 20 |
| SANTA CLARA | 520,180 | 594,597 | 628,414 | 1.6 | 2.74 | 359,677 | 401,908 | 1.4 | 68,026 | 81,445 | 20 | 1 |
| SANTA CRUZ | 83,566 | 91,830 | 97,558 | 1.1 | 2.61 | 53,752 | 56,741 | 0.7 | 54,579 | 68,100 | 128 | 10 |
| SHASTA | 55,966 | 64,270 | 66,616 | 1.7 | 2.53 | 40,473 | 44,866 | 1.3 | 36,860 | 42,064 | 998 | 40 |
| SIERRA | 1,336 | 1,368 | 1,359 | 0.3 | 2.39 | 928 | 924 | -0.1 | 37,900 | 44,708 | 857 | 37 |
| SISKIYOU | 17,306 | 17,577 | 17,213 | 0.2 | 2.43 | 12,076 | 11,752 | -0.3 | 31,159 | 35,966 | 1900 | 54 |
| SOLANO | 113,429 | 132,034 | 144,034 | 1.9 | 2.89 | 86,123 | 97,446 | 1.5 | 57,559 | 72,332 | 93 | 8 |
| SONOMA | 149,011 | 173,402 | 187,195 | 1.9 | 2.53 | 99,876 | 111,282 | 1.3 | 52,917 | 65,703 | 154 | 11 |
| STANISLAUS | 125,375 | 150,664 | 164,648 | 2.3 | 2.92 | 94,306 | 110,467 | 1.9 | 43,727 | 54,871 | 414 | 24 |
| SUTTER | 23,111 | 28,484 | 30,460 | 2.6 | 2.76 | 17,032 | 20,490 | 2.3 | 40,071 | 49,489 | 667 | 32 |
| TEHAMA | 18,704 | 20,685 | 20,960 | 1.2 | 2.57 | 13,808 | 14,792 | 0.8 | 32,512 | 40,593 | 1621 | 52 |
| TRINITY | 5,156 | 5,164 | 4,984 | 0.0 | 2.43 | 3,633 | 3,494 | -0.5 | 28,421 | 33,168 | 2377 | 57 |
| TULARE | 97,861 | 115,735 | 122,824 | 2.1 | 3.08 | 76,529 | 88,934 | 1.8 | 32,542 | 41,165 | 1619 | 51 |
| TUOLUMNE | 17,959 | 20,195 | 21,274 | 1.4 | 2.44 | 13,023 | 14,184 | 1.0 | 39,249 | 49,441 | 732 | 33 |
| VENTURA | 217,298 | 248,181 | 268,257 | 1.6 | 3.00 | 164,773 | 183,999 | 1.3 | 59,849 | 74,683 | 76 | 6 |
| YOLO | 50,972 | 58,211 | 62,480 | 1.6 | 2.61 | 32,184 | 35,053 | 1.0 | 43,781 | 54,442 | 410 | 23 |
| YUBA | 19,776 | 20,669 | 20,465 | 0.5 | 2.80 | 14,878 | 15,166 | 0.2 | 31,034 | 38,899 | 1923 | 55 |
| CALIFORNIA | | | | 1.6 | 2.77 | | | 1.4 | 47,551 | 58,616 | | |
| UNITED STATES | | | | 1.4 | 2.59 | | | 1.1 | 41,914 | 49,127 | | |

| COUNTY | 2000 Per Capita Income | 2000 HH Income Base | 2000 HOUSEHOLD INCOME DISTRIBUTION (%) Less than $15,000 | $15,000 to $24,999 | $25,000 to $49,999 | $50,000 to $99,999 | $100,000 to $149,999 | $150,000 or More | 2000 AVERAGE DISPOSABLE INCOME BY AGE OF HOUSEHOLDER All Ages | <35 | 35-44 | 45-54 | 55-64 | 65+ |
|---|---|---|---|---|---|---|---|---|---|---|---|---|---|---|
| ALAMEDA | 29,612 | 550,056 | 9.7 | 7.5 | 25.3 | 38.0 | 12.9 | 6.5 | 51,600 | 44,084 | 54,685 | 59,277 | 53,865 | 35,472 |
| ALPINE | 19,250 | 488 | 14.3 | 23.2 | 29.7 | 27.1 | 4.7 | 1.0 | 32,797 | 30,658 | 31,507 | 37,625 | 36,023 | 27,396 |
| AMADOR | 24,286 | 12,264 | 10.8 | 11.0 | 34.3 | 32.5 | 8.7 | 2.6 | 41,579 | 39,427 | 46,901 | 50,732 | 42,882 | 32,548 |
| BUTTE | 20,434 | 78,127 | 16.2 | 16.8 | 35.4 | 23.1 | 5.3 | 3.2 | 36,436 | 27,997 | 42,539 | 47,862 | 39,719 | 28,342 |
| CALAVERAS | 20,686 | 16,467 | 14.0 | 14.5 | 35.8 | 27.8 | 5.7 | 2.2 | 36,974 | 33,930 | 41,973 | 44,559 | 37,912 | 27,612 |
| COLUSA | 17,165 | 6,693 | 15.5 | 20.9 | 35.9 | 21.7 | 4.0 | 2.0 | 33,372 | 29,015 | 37,149 | 37,376 | 36,442 | 26,565 |
| CONTRA COSTA | 36,040 | 360,472 | 6.7 | 5.2 | 22.0 | 39.2 | 16.2 | 10.7 | 61,389 | 49,603 | 61,540 | 68,915 | 62,948 | 43,955 |
| DEL NORTE | 16,964 | 9,040 | 17.8 | 17.0 | 35.6 | 23.1 | 4.9 | 1.7 | 33,730 | 32,337 | 36,493 | 39,882 | 38,342 | 23,193 |
| EL DORADO | 26,794 | 62,334 | 8.3 | 9.0 | 29.6 | 37.1 | 10.8 | 5.2 | 48,184 | 41,873 | 52,412 | 56,688 | 51,286 | 31,460 |
| FRESNO | 18,436 | 255,836 | 17.0 | 15.0 | 33.2 | 25.4 | 6.1 | 3.5 | 38,028 | 31,033 | 41,802 | 46,172 | 42,321 | 27,923 |
| GLENN | 15,750 | 9,474 | 20.4 | 18.9 | 33.5 | 22.2 | 3.8 | 1.2 | 31,503 | 28,485 | 35,811 | 35,790 | 40,301 | 22,067 |
| HUMBOLDT | 19,576 | 47,895 | 18.9 | 16.0 | 34.9 | 23.3 | 4.7 | 2.2 | 34,326 | 26,811 | 36,955 | 44,168 | 39,609 | 26,419 |
| IMPERIAL | 11,297 | 42,113 | 28.4 | 17.8 | 31.3 | 18.3 | 3.0 | 1.3 | 28,515 | 26,109 | 32,343 | 33,278 | 30,129 | 20,832 |
| INYO | 20,854 | 7,502 | 16.9 | 17.0 | 33.5 | 25.4 | 5.0 | 2.2 | 35,138 | 31,687 | 40,819 | 45,163 | 39,136 | 23,422 |
| KERN | 17,559 | 213,224 | 16.2 | 14.0 | 33.7 | 27.7 | 5.8 | 2.6 | 37,386 | 32,740 | 41,660 | 46,220 | 40,061 | 25,114 |
| KINGS | 13,817 | 34,858 | 17.1 | 17.0 | 37.1 | 23.7 | 3.9 | 1.2 | 32,814 | 28,488 | 37,390 | 39,927 | 35,981 | 23,276 |
| LAKE | 17,598 | 22,969 | 20.6 | 17.5 | 34.2 | 22.6 | 3.8 | 1.3 | 31,738 | 30,400 | 37,733 | 39,100 | 34,629 | 23,641 |
| LASSEN | 20,030 | 9,382 | 14.4 | 12.4 | 35.5 | 30.6 | 5.4 | 1.6 | 37,137 | 32,220 | 45,117 | 44,765 | 39,402 | 25,601 |
| LOS ANGELES | 21,973 | 3,199,884 | 15.0 | 12.5 | 30.7 | 29.1 | 7.6 | 5.1 | 43,185 | 36,409 | 44,111 | 49,754 | 46,185 | 31,679 |
| MADERA | 17,253 | 36,328 | 12.7 | 13.4 | 34.9 | 29.6 | 6.8 | 2.6 | 39,014 | 33,810 | 44,233 | 46,655 | 44,129 | 27,894 |
| MARIN | 42,317 | 99,592 | 6.8 | 7.8 | 24.6 | 34.2 | 13.4 | 13.2 | 63,771 | 49,267 | 58,345 | 67,061 | 65,397 | 46,747 |
| MARIPOSA | 21,163 | 6,326 | 17.4 | 12.6 | 35.9 | 25.3 | 6.3 | 2.6 | 36,632 | 30,884 | 39,338 | 46,580 | 41,738 | 26,382 |
| MENDOCINO | 20,190 | 32,347 | 14.6 | 14.8 | 35.6 | 26.2 | 5.8 | 3.0 | 37,910 | 31,867 | 40,564 | 45,531 | 39,908 | 27,821 |
| MERCED | 14,751 | 64,525 | 18.2 | 18.7 | 35.0 | 22.1 | 4.0 | 2.0 | 33,294 | 28,190 | 37,602 | 40,861 | 37,667 | 23,177 |
| MODOC | 15,677 | 3,582 | 22.6 | 19.4 | 38.0 | 16.2 | 2.7 | 1.1 | 28,810 | 25,062 | 32,761 | 35,653 | 30,956 | 22,704 |
| MONO | 21,783 | 4,154 | 11.1 | 14.1 | 35.3 | 29.8 | 7.5 | 2.2 | 39,186 | 33,970 | 42,245 | 47,929 | 42,631 | 23,253 |
| MONTEREY | 20,548 | 123,109 | 10.0 | 12.8 | 34.8 | 31.7 | 7.3 | 3.5 | 42,071 | 34,741 | 42,895 | 50,601 | 46,296 | 36,985 |
| NAPA | 28,384 | 46,427 | 9.4 | 9.7 | 30.0 | 34.8 | 9.6 | 6.4 | 49,141 | 40,495 | 51,019 | 58,291 | 54,411 | 35,084 |
| NEVADA | 24,678 | 37,302 | 9.2 | 10.7 | 33.1 | 34.8 | 9.0 | 3.2 | 43,456 | 40,143 | 47,439 | 50,381 | 46,410 | 33,454 |
| ORANGE | 31,077 | 983,013 | 6.1 | 6.9 | 25.3 | 38.7 | 14.1 | 8.9 | 57,207 | 48,171 | 58,016 | 64,843 | 60,604 | 39,768 |
| PLACER | 30,567 | 92,125 | 8.1 | 6.5 | 26.5 | 38.2 | 13.4 | 7.3 | 53,640 | 45,647 | 57,322 | 63,235 | 55,036 | 34,407 |
| PLUMAS | 19,533 | 8,401 | 15.9 | 15.8 | 37.3 | 24.3 | 4.7 | 2.0 | 34,591 | 28,822 | 39,450 | 45,458 | 36,865 | 24,728 |
| RIVERSIDE | 20,906 | 538,583 | 13.3 | 11.8 | 32.2 | 31.7 | 7.2 | 3.8 | 42,024 | 38,138 | 45,765 | 49,900 | 45,269 | 30,628 |
| SACRAMENTO | 22,496 | 450,242 | 11.7 | 11.5 | 33.2 | 32.7 | 7.5 | 3.5 | 42,014 | 35,732 | 45,489 | 50,482 | 45,967 | 30,567 |
| SAN BENITO | 22,594 | 16,838 | 6.9 | 10.2 | 30.5 | 37.1 | 10.1 | 5.2 | 48,550 | 41,039 | 50,200 | 56,806 | 54,397 | 34,539 |
| SAN BERNARDINO | 18,245 | 560,493 | 14.0 | 11.5 | 33.2 | 32.4 | 6.5 | 2.4 | 39,363 | 35,572 | 43,697 | 47,900 | 40,523 | 25,170 |
| SAN DIEGO | 24,123 | 1,048,139 | 10.9 | 11.8 | 31.9 | 32.3 | 8.4 | 4.7 | 44,652 | 37,196 | 47,404 | 52,881 | 48,441 | 33,823 |
| SAN FRANCISCO | 31,774 | 324,039 | 13.2 | 10.7 | 29.8 | 30.1 | 9.4 | 6.8 | 47,672 | 43,036 | 49,452 | 50,343 | 49,244 | 35,731 |
| SAN JOAQUIN | 18,885 | 190,564 | 14.5 | 12.2 | 32.9 | 30.7 | 7.0 | 2.8 | 39,504 | 35,669 | 43,775 | 47,051 | 41,875 | 27,844 |
| SAN LUIS OBISPO | 25,660 | 89,950 | 11.0 | 11.7 | 32.6 | 31.3 | 8.8 | 4.7 | 44,593 | 34,942 | 49,058 | 55,306 | 49,268 | 34,770 |
| SAN MATEO | 35,688 | 269,879 | 6.1 | 6.1 | 24.8 | 38.6 | 14.9 | 9.5 | 58,880 | 49,430 | 58,880 | 64,990 | 60,385 | 44,267 |
| SANTA BARBARA | 24,620 | 140,830 | 12.0 | 12.1 | 31.6 | 30.7 | 8.2 | 5.4 | 45,167 | 34,641 | 46,844 | 54,069 | 50,837 | 36,915 |
| SANTA CLARA | 34,200 | 594,597 | 5.9 | 5.0 | 21.1 | 40.9 | 17.3 | 9.8 | 60,801 | 51,345 | 61,221 | 68,586 | 62,903 | 43,312 |
| SANTA CRUZ | 28,851 | 91,829 | 9.1 | 8.6 | 27.3 | 35.9 | 12.2 | 6.9 | 51,214 | 42,716 | 53,355 | 60,834 | 54,069 | 34,161 |
| SHASTA | 19,384 | 64,270 | 16.6 | 14.7 | 36.0 | 25.0 | 5.1 | 2.7 | 36,311 | 31,474 | 40,364 | 46,017 | 38,945 | 24,474 |
| SIERRA | 21,086 | 1,368 | 14.4 | 18.4 | 33.3 | 27.1 | 4.5 | 2.4 | 36,249 | 31,408 | 42,731 | 36,272 | 44,950 | 29,179 |
| SISKIYOU | 17,720 | 17,577 | 19.7 | 19.6 | 35.0 | 19.7 | 4.1 | 1.8 | 31,780 | 27,795 | 35,574 | 40,794 | 36,108 | 21,935 |
| SOLANO | 23,770 | 132,034 | 7.3 | 6.3 | 26.9 | 43.7 | 12.3 | 3.6 | 48,871 | 43,595 | 52,694 | 57,746 | 50,573 | 34,253 |
| SONOMA | 29,200 | 173,402 | 8.1 | 8.4 | 29.6 | 37.2 | 10.9 | 5.7 | 49,452 | 42,946 | 51,513 | 58,303 | 51,761 | 35,822 |
| STANISLAUS | 20,987 | 150,663 | 12.8 | 11.3 | 33.5 | 30.7 | 7.8 | 3.9 | 42,096 | 36,602 | 46,045 | 51,408 | 43,726 | 28,620 |
| SUTTER | 20,187 | 28,484 | 14.8 | 14.1 | 33.2 | 28.0 | 6.3 | 3.6 | 39,289 | 32,794 | 42,621 | 48,056 | 43,830 | 27,793 |
| TEHAMA | 16,943 | 20,685 | 18.3 | 18.1 | 36.4 | 21.9 | 3.9 | 1.5 | 32,324 | 28,746 | 35,515 | 42,019 | 35,261 | 24,115 |
| TRINITY | 14,484 | 5,164 | 25.5 | 18.6 | 33.7 | 18.5 | 2.9 | 0.8 | 28,067 | 25,735 | 31,055 | 32,872 | 30,911 | 21,546 |
| TULARE | 14,944 | 115,735 | 20.0 | 17.3 | 34.0 | 22.2 | 4.2 | 2.4 | 33,783 | 27,705 | 37,054 | 41,857 | 37,016 | 24,897 |
| TUOLUMNE | 20,764 | 20,194 | 12.2 | 15.2 | 35.6 | 27.4 | 6.4 | 3.2 | 39,063 | 33,885 | 44,313 | 48,962 | 41,544 | 28,796 |
| VENTURA | 26,343 | 248,180 | 7.2 | 7.0 | 24.7 | 41.3 | 13.4 | 6.5 | 53,165 | 46,276 | 54,867 | 61,422 | 55,799 | 36,137 |
| YOLO | 23,111 | 58,210 | 13.9 | 12.4 | 30.8 | 30.2 | 8.3 | 4.4 | 42,960 | 32,329 | 48,457 | 55,375 | 49,726 | 33,087 |
| YUBA | 15,225 | 20,669 | 18.9 | 19.9 | 36.7 | 19.9 | 3.3 | 1.3 | 30,726 | 26,098 | 35,478 | 38,084 | 33,683 | 23,932 |
| CALIFORNIA | 24,644 | | 11.9 | 10.8 | 29.7 | 32.6 | 9.5 | 5.5 | 46,445 | 39,081 | 48,623 | 54,321 | 49,552 | 33,400 |
| UNITED STATES | 22,162 | | 14.5 | 12.5 | 32.3 | 29.8 | 7.4 | 3.5 | 40,748 | 34,503 | 44,969 | 49,579 | 43,409 | 27,339 |

# SPENDING POTENTIAL INDEXES

| COUNTY | FINANCIAL SERVICES | | | | THE HOME | | | | | | ENTERTAINMENT | | | | | | PERSONAL | | | |
|---|---|---|---|---|---|---|---|---|---|---|---|---|---|---|---|---|---|---|---|---|
| | | | | | Home Improvements | | | Furnishings | | | | | | | | | | | | |
| | Auto Loan | Home Loan | Invest-ments | Retire-ment Plans | Home Repair | Lawn & Garden | Remodel-ing | Appli-ances | Elec-tronics | Furni-ture | Restau-rants | Sport-ing Goods | Theater & Concerts | Toys & Hobbies | Travel | Video Rental | Apparel | Auto After-market | Health Insur-ance | Pets & Supplies |
| ALAMEDA | 103 | 128 | 113 | 118 | 110 | 114 | 99 | 105 | 112 | 114 | 115 | 101 | 107 | 97 | 108 | 99 | 114 | 113 | 99 | 100 |
| ALPINE | 98 | 78 | 79 | 85 | 96 | 94 | 117 | 99 | 93 | 84 | 84 | 90 | 81 | 92 | 77 | 92 | 85 | 90 | 101 | 93 |
| AMADOR | 102 | 86 | 103 | 98 | 104 | 109 | 113 | 104 | 98 | 94 | 94 | 92 | 91 | 95 | 90 | 93 | 94 | 95 | 106 | 96 |
| BUTTE | 96 | 89 | 99 | 90 | 101 | 100 | 101 | 97 | 93 | 90 | 89 | 86 | 85 | 89 | 86 | 90 | 87 | 91 | 99 | 91 |
| CALAVERAS | 101 | 81 | 92 | 93 | 100 | 101 | 117 | 102 | 98 | 89 | 89 | 93 | 86 | 95 | 83 | 94 | 90 | 93 | 104 | 95 |
| COLUSA | 98 | 80 | 84 | 83 | 96 | 94 | 110 | 100 | 96 | 87 | 86 | 89 | 82 | 91 | 78 | 93 | 84 | 91 | 100 | 94 |
| CONTRA COSTA | 105 | 126 | 114 | 122 | 111 | 117 | 104 | 107 | 114 | 118 | 119 | 104 | 111 | 102 | 109 | 98 | 119 | 114 | 101 | 101 |
| DEL NORTE | 96 | 80 | 90 | 82 | 97 | 96 | 107 | 98 | 94 | 88 | 87 | 87 | 83 | 90 | 79 | 91 | 84 | 90 | 99 | 91 |
| EL DORADO | 103 | 104 | 98 | 105 | 102 | 104 | 107 | 104 | 106 | 106 | 105 | 98 | 98 | 98 | 92 | 96 | 105 | 103 | 100 | 98 |
| FRESNO | 98 | 102 | 94 | 96 | 99 | 99 | 97 | 100 | 101 | 98 | 99 | 91 | 92 | 92 | 90 | 94 | 95 | 98 | 96 | 95 |
| GLENN | 97 | 80 | 82 | 84 | 95 | 93 | 107 | 98 | 96 | 85 | 86 | 87 | 82 | 90 | 77 | 93 | 85 | 90 | 99 | 92 |
| HUMBOLDT | 95 | 87 | 89 | 87 | 99 | 95 | 102 | 97 | 94 | 91 | 89 | 86 | 85 | 90 | 83 | 91 | 88 | 91 | 96 | 91 |
| IMPERIAL | 95 | 98 | 91 | 89 | 96 | 96 | 94 | 100 | 99 | 91 | 93 | 87 | 88 | 88 | 86 | 93 | 87 | 96 | 96 | 96 |
| INYO | 99 | 88 | 104 | 97 | 103 | 104 | 108 | 101 | 99 | 95 | 93 | 91 | 91 | 93 | 89 | 93 | 92 | 95 | 102 | 94 |
| KERN | 98 | 97 | 90 | 92 | 98 | 98 | 99 | 100 | 100 | 97 | 97 | 91 | 90 | 92 | 87 | 94 | 94 | 97 | 96 | 94 |
| KINGS | 96 | 93 | 85 | 88 | 96 | 95 | 99 | 99 | 99 | 94 | 94 | 89 | 87 | 90 | 84 | 93 | 90 | 95 | 95 | 94 |
| LAKE | 99 | 82 | 104 | 91 | 102 | 106 | 108 | 102 | 94 | 89 | 90 | 89 | 87 | 92 | 87 | 92 | 86 | 92 | 105 | 94 |
| LASSEN | 97 | 83 | 81 | 84 | 95 | 93 | 109 | 99 | 97 | 90 | 89 | 89 | 83 | 91 | 78 | 93 | 88 | 92 | 97 | 92 |
| LOS ANGELES | 100 | 125 | 109 | 112 | 107 | 109 | 95 | 103 | 109 | 108 | 110 | 97 | 103 | 93 | 106 | 98 | 107 | 109 | 97 | 99 |
| MADERA | 98 | 91 | 89 | 91 | 98 | 98 | 104 | 101 | 99 | 93 | 93 | 90 | 88 | 92 | 85 | 94 | 91 | 95 | 99 | 95 |
| MARIN | 107 | 138 | 128 | 133 | 119 | 128 | 109 | 109 | 118 | 124 | 127 | 106 | 119 | 104 | 121 | 98 | 129 | 121 | 105 | 103 |
| MARIPOSA | 99 | 81 | 102 | 93 | 102 | 106 | 109 | 102 | 95 | 88 | 88 | 89 | 87 | 92 | 87 | 92 | 87 | 92 | 106 | 93 |
| MENDOCINO | 98 | 88 | 93 | 91 | 101 | 99 | 107 | 100 | 97 | 94 | 92 | 91 | 88 | 93 | 85 | 93 | 91 | 94 | 99 | 93 |
| MERCED | 97 | 96 | 88 | 90 | 96 | 96 | 98 | 100 | 100 | 94 | 95 | 89 | 88 | 90 | 85 | 94 | 90 | 96 | 96 | 95 |
| MODOC | 96 | 64 | 71 | 78 | 92 | 92 | 111 | 97 | 93 | 75 | 77 | 87 | 74 | 88 | 70 | 92 | 78 | 86 | 102 | 89 |
| MONO | 98 | 91 | 76 | 88 | 93 | 92 | 105 | 99 | 99 | 95 | 96 | 92 | 86 | 93 | 80 | 94 | 93 | 95 | 95 | 94 |
| MONTEREY | 101 | 122 | 106 | 110 | 106 | 109 | 97 | 104 | 110 | 107 | 111 | 98 | 103 | 96 | 102 | 97 | 107 | 109 | 99 | 100 |
| NAPA | 102 | 112 | 111 | 109 | 109 | 111 | 102 | 104 | 106 | 109 | 108 | 97 | 102 | 98 | 101 | 95 | 107 | 105 | 101 | 97 |
| NEVADA | 103 | 95 | 101 | 101 | 104 | 108 | 110 | 105 | 102 | 101 | 100 | 95 | 95 | 97 | 92 | 95 | 100 | 99 | 104 | 97 |
| ORANGE | 104 | 129 | 111 | 118 | 109 | 114 | 100 | 106 | 113 | 114 | 118 | 102 | 108 | 99 | 107 | 98 | 115 | 114 | 100 | 102 |
| PLACER | 104 | 105 | 96 | 104 | 103 | 105 | 105 | 105 | 107 | 108 | 108 | 99 | 99 | 99 | 93 | 96 | 106 | 104 | 99 | 98 |
| PLUMAS | 99 | 80 | 89 | 89 | 98 | 100 | 114 | 101 | 97 | 88 | 88 | 90 | 84 | 92 | 81 | 93 | 88 | 92 | 103 | 93 |
| RIVERSIDE | 100 | 101 | 93 | 97 | 100 | 102 | 100 | 103 | 102 | 102 | 102 | 94 | 93 | 95 | 90 | 94 | 98 | 99 | 99 | 96 |
| SACRAMENTO | 99 | 105 | 95 | 99 | 102 | 102 | 97 | 101 | 102 | 103 | 103 | 93 | 94 | 94 | 92 | 94 | 100 | 100 | 96 | 95 |
| SAN BENITO | 101 | 108 | 98 | 103 | 100 | 104 | 101 | 104 | 106 | 104 | 105 | 96 | 97 | 96 | 93 | 96 | 101 | 104 | 99 | 99 |
| SAN BERNARDINO | 99 | 100 | 89 | 95 | 98 | 98 | 100 | 101 | 102 | 100 | 100 | 93 | 92 | 94 | 88 | 94 | 97 | 99 | 96 | 96 |
| SAN DIEGO | 100 | 114 | 102 | 106 | 104 | 106 | 98 | 102 | 106 | 106 | 107 | 96 | 99 | 95 | 98 | 96 | 104 | 105 | 98 | 98 |
| SAN FRANCISCO | 99 | 130 | 110 | 113 | 106 | 108 | 94 | 99 | 111 | 108 | 113 | 95 | 100 | 89 | 108 | 103 | 106 | 108 | 96 | 97 |
| SAN JOAQUIN | 99 | 104 | 95 | 98 | 101 | 101 | 98 | 101 | 103 | 101 | 102 | 93 | 94 | 93 | 91 | 96 | 98 | 100 | 97 | 96 |
| SAN LUIS OBISPO | 100 | 101 | 101 | 100 | 103 | 104 | 104 | 101 | 100 | 100 | 100 | 92 | 93 | 94 | 92 | 93 | 98 | 99 | 100 | 95 |
| SAN MATEO | 105 | 138 | 123 | 127 | 115 | 122 | 103 | 107 | 118 | 119 | 124 | 104 | 115 | 100 | 117 | 101 | 122 | 119 | 102 | 102 |
| SANTA BARBARA | 101 | 119 | 113 | 114 | 109 | 112 | 101 | 103 | 108 | 108 | 110 | 97 | 104 | 97 | 104 | 95 | 108 | 108 | 100 | 99 |
| SANTA CLARA | 105 | 138 | 121 | 127 | 113 | 121 | 103 | 107 | 118 | 118 | 124 | 104 | 114 | 100 | 115 | 100 | 121 | 119 | 102 | 103 |
| SANTA CRUZ | 103 | 122 | 112 | 115 | 109 | 112 | 102 | 105 | 110 | 112 | 113 | 100 | 105 | 99 | 105 | 97 | 111 | 110 | 100 | 100 |
| SHASTA | 97 | 88 | 89 | 89 | 98 | 97 | 105 | 99 | 97 | 93 | 92 | 89 | 87 | 91 | 83 | 93 | 90 | 93 | 98 | 92 |
| SIERRA | 101 | 76 | 87 | 90 | 98 | 99 | 122 | 103 | 97 | 85 | 86 | 92 | 83 | 94 | 80 | 94 | 88 | 92 | 105 | 96 |
| SISKIYOU | 96 | 72 | 80 | 81 | 95 | 94 | 108 | 97 | 94 | 83 | 82 | 86 | 79 | 88 | 76 | 92 | 82 | 88 | 100 | 90 |
| SOLANO | 101 | 110 | 93 | 102 | 100 | 102 | 98 | 103 | 107 | 106 | 108 | 97 | 97 | 96 | 93 | 97 | 104 | 104 | 96 | 97 |
| SONOMA | 102 | 112 | 105 | 108 | 106 | 109 | 103 | 104 | 107 | 110 | 110 | 98 | 101 | 98 | 99 | 96 | 108 | 106 | 100 | 98 |
| STANISLAUS | 99 | 97 | 91 | 94 | 99 | 98 | 101 | 101 | 101 | 99 | 98 | 92 | 91 | 93 | 87 | 94 | 95 | 98 | 97 | 95 |
| SUTTER | 97 | 97 | 91 | 92 | 100 | 98 | 98 | 100 | 99 | 97 | 96 | 90 | 90 | 91 | 88 | 94 | 93 | 97 | 97 | 94 |
| TEHAMA | 97 | 78 | 90 | 85 | 99 | 97 | 108 | 99 | 94 | 87 | 85 | 88 | 83 | 90 | 81 | 91 | 84 | 90 | 100 | 91 |
| TRINITY | 98 | 71 | 85 | 81 | 96 | 96 | 114 | 99 | 93 | 81 | 81 | 89 | 79 | 90 | 76 | 92 | 80 | 88 | 103 | 92 |
| TULARE | 97 | 92 | 88 | 89 | 97 | 96 | 100 | 100 | 99 | 93 | 93 | 89 | 87 | 90 | 84 | 93 | 89 | 95 | 97 | 94 |
| TUOLUMNE | 100 | 85 | 100 | 94 | 102 | 105 | 112 | 103 | 96 | 92 | 92 | 92 | 89 | 94 | 87 | 93 | 90 | 94 | 105 | 95 |
| VENTURA | 106 | 128 | 113 | 122 | 110 | 116 | 104 | 108 | 115 | 118 | 120 | 105 | 111 | 102 | 108 | 98 | 119 | 115 | 102 | 103 |
| YOLO | 97 | 100 | 94 | 95 | 100 | 98 | 98 | 97 | 98 | 95 | 96 | 89 | 88 | 91 | 88 | 92 | 93 | 96 | 96 | 93 |
| YUBA | 94 | 84 | 86 | 83 | 98 | 94 | 101 | 97 | 94 | 90 | 88 | 86 | 83 | 88 | 82 | 91 | 85 | 90 | 96 | 91 |
| CALIFORNIA | 101 | 118 | 106 | 110 | 106 | 109 | 99 | 103 | 108 | 108 | 109 | 97 | 102 | 95 | 102 | 97 | 106 | 107 | 98 | 99 |
| UNITED STATES | 100 | 100 | 100 | 100 | 100 | 100 | 100 | 100 | 100 | 100 | 100 | 100 | 100 | 100 | 100 | 100 | 100 | 100 | 100 | 100 |

| COUNTY | FIPS Code | MSA Code | DMA Code | POPULATION 1990 | POPULATION 2000 | POPULATION 2005 | 1990-2000 ANNUAL CHANGE % Rate | 1990-2000 ANNUAL CHANGE State Rank | RACE (%) White 1990 | White 2000 | Black 1990 | Black 2000 | Asian/Pacific 1990 | Asian/Pacific 2000 |
|---|---|---|---|---|---|---|---|---|---|---|---|---|---|---|
| ADAMS | 001 | 2080 | 751 | 265,038 | 338,422 | 375,483 | 2.4 | 26 | 86.7 | 84.4 | 3.3 | 3.5 | 2.6 | 3.5 |
| ALAMOSA | 003 | 0000 | 751 | 13,617 | 14,699 | 15,168 | 0.7 | 44 | 82.4 | 80.0 | 0.5 | 0.5 | 0.9 | 1.0 |
| ARAPAHOE | 005 | 2080 | 751 | 391,511 | 491,410 | 537,768 | 2.2 | 28 | 89.2 | 87.6 | 5.9 | 6.3 | 2.8 | 3.9 |
| ARCHULETA | 007 | 0000 | 751 | 5,345 | 10,139 | 12,820 | 6.4 | 5 | 87.3 | 84.8 | 0.1 | 0.2 | 0.5 | 0.7 |
| BACA | 009 | 0000 | 752 | 4,556 | 4,298 | 4,197 | -0.6 | 60 | 94.8 | 94.3 | 0.0 | 0.0 | 0.2 | 0.3 |
| BENT | 011 | 0000 | 752 | 5,048 | 5,813 | 5,865 | 1.4 | 37 | 90.9 | 87.5 | 0.7 | 2.4 | 0.6 | 0.7 |
| BOULDER | 013 | 1125 | 751 | 225,339 | 278,798 | 307,073 | 2.1 | 31 | 93.3 | 91.8 | 0.9 | 0.9 | 2.4 | 3.2 |
| CHAFFEE | 015 | 0000 | 751 | 12,684 | 15,913 | 17,517 | 2.2 | 28 | 95.4 | 95.3 | 1.6 | 1.4 | 0.3 | 0.4 |
| CHEYENNE | 017 | 0000 | 752 | 2,397 | 2,193 | 2,101 | -0.9 | 61 | 98.4 | 98.0 | 0.0 | 0.0 | 0.1 | 0.1 |
| CLEAR CREEK | 019 | 0000 | 751 | 7,619 | 9,317 | 10,044 | 2.0 | 33 | 97.7 | 97.3 | 0.3 | 0.3 | 0.5 | 0.7 |
| CONEJOS | 021 | 0000 | 790 | 7,453 | 8,164 | 8,612 | 0.9 | 43 | 85.7 | 84.5 | 0.2 | 0.2 | 0.3 | 0.4 |
| COSTILLA | 023 | 0000 | 790 | 3,190 | 3,572 | 3,558 | 1.1 | 42 | 83.5 | 82.9 | 0.3 | 0.3 | 1.3 | 1.3 |
| CROWLEY | 025 | 0000 | 752 | 3,946 | 4,480 | 4,777 | 1.2 | 40 | 87.7 | 87.3 | 6.6 | 6.1 | 0.8 | 1.1 |
| CUSTER | 027 | 0000 | 751 | 1,926 | 3,773 | 4,654 | 6.8 | 4 | 97.9 | 97.7 | 0.0 | 0.0 | 0.2 | 0.2 |
| DELTA | 029 | 0000 | 751 | 20,980 | 27,711 | 30,404 | 2.8 | 18 | 96.0 | 95.2 | 0.3 | 0.4 | 0.3 | 0.3 |
| DENVER | 031 | 2080 | 751 | 467,610 | 501,126 | 507,765 | 0.7 | 44 | 72.1 | 67.9 | 12.8 | 14.1 | 2.4 | 3.1 |
| DOLORES | 033 | 0000 | 751 | 1,504 | 1,942 | 2,275 | 2.5 | 23 | 96.1 | 95.6 | 0.0 | 0.0 | 0.1 | 0.1 |
| DOUGLAS | 035 | 2080 | 751 | 60,391 | 171,938 | 246,010 | 10.7 | 1 | 97.2 | 96.5 | 0.7 | 0.8 | 0.8 | 1.2 |
| EAGLE | 037 | 0000 | 751 | 21,928 | 36,435 | 43,740 | 5.1 | 7 | 91.6 | 89.6 | 0.2 | 0.2 | 0.5 | 0.6 |
| ELBERT | 039 | 0000 | 751 | 9,646 | 20,931 | 26,853 | 7.9 | 2 | 97.6 | 97.1 | 0.5 | 0.6 | 0.4 | 0.6 |
| EL PASO | 041 | 1720 | 752 | 397,014 | 509,408 | 557,497 | 2.5 | 23 | 86.0 | 83.9 | 7.2 | 7.5 | 2.5 | 3.4 |
| FREMONT | 043 | 0000 | 752 | 32,273 | 45,324 | 48,541 | 3.4 | 13 | 94.7 | 92.7 | 2.6 | 3.9 | 0.3 | 0.4 |
| GARFIELD | 045 | 0000 | 751 | 29,974 | 41,993 | 48,646 | 3.3 | 14 | 97.2 | 96.8 | 0.3 | 0.2 | 0.4 | 0.6 |
| GILPIN | 047 | 0000 | 751 | 3,070 | 4,736 | 6,006 | 4.3 | 11 | 97.5 | 97.1 | 0.5 | 0.7 | 0.4 | 0.6 |
| GRAND | 049 | 0000 | 751 | 7,966 | 10,798 | 12,450 | 3.0 | 16 | 97.4 | 97.0 | 0.2 | 0.2 | 0.5 | 0.6 |
| GUNNISON | 051 | 0000 | 751 | 10,273 | 12,723 | 13,505 | 2.1 | 31 | 97.4 | 97.1 | 0.6 | 0.7 | 0.5 | 0.6 |
| HINSDALE | 053 | 0000 | 751 | 467 | 757 | 846 | 4.8 | 8 | 99.1 | 99.1 | 0.2 | 0.3 | 0.0 | 0.0 |
| HUERFANO | 055 | 0000 | 752 | 6,009 | 6,872 | 7,216 | 1.3 | 38 | 92.7 | 92.1 | 0.4 | 0.7 | 0.2 | 0.2 |
| JACKSON | 057 | 0000 | 751 | 1,605 | 1,557 | 1,616 | -0.3 | 57 | 92.2 | 91.8 | 0.0 | 0.0 | 0.1 | 0.1 |
| JEFFERSON | 059 | 2080 | 751 | 438,430 | 516,073 | 550,749 | 1.6 | 35 | 94.6 | 93.4 | 0.7 | 0.8 | 1.7 | 2.4 |
| KIOWA | 061 | 0000 | 752 | 1,688 | 1,628 | 1,598 | -0.4 | 58 | 97.6 | 97.3 | 0.0 | 0.0 | 0.0 | 0.0 |
| KIT CARSON | 063 | 0000 | 751 | 7,140 | 7,494 | 7,907 | 0.5 | 49 | 95.2 | 94.2 | 0.1 | 0.1 | 0.2 | 0.2 |
| LAKE | 065 | 0000 | 751 | 6,007 | 6,428 | 6,633 | 0.7 | 44 | 91.3 | 90.0 | 0.2 | 0.2 | 0.3 | 0.4 |
| LA PLATA | 067 | 0000 | 790 | 32,284 | 41,741 | 44,844 | 2.5 | 23 | 89.9 | 88.8 | 0.2 | 0.3 | 0.6 | 0.7 |
| LARIMER | 069 | 2670 | 751 | 186,136 | 242,402 | 269,498 | 2.6 | 20 | 94.5 | 93.4 | 0.6 | 0.6 | 1.5 | 1.9 |
| LAS ANIMAS | 071 | 0000 | 752 | 13,765 | 14,844 | 15,514 | 0.7 | 44 | 86.6 | 85.0 | 0.2 | 0.2 | 0.5 | 0.5 |
| LINCOLN | 073 | 0000 | 752 | 4,529 | 5,683 | 5,733 | 2.2 | 28 | 98.1 | 90.7 | 0.1 | 3.4 | 0.3 | 0.3 |
| LOGAN | 075 | 0000 | 751 | 17,567 | 17,924 | 17,873 | 0.2 | 54 | 95.9 | 95.1 | 0.1 | 0.1 | 0.2 | 0.3 |
| MESA | 077 | 2995 | 773 | 93,145 | 117,425 | 128,745 | 2.3 | 27 | 94.7 | 93.7 | 0.4 | 0.4 | 0.7 | 0.9 |
| MINERAL | 079 | 0000 | 751 | 558 | 747 | 855 | 2.9 | 17 | 98.0 | 98.0 | 0.0 | 0.0 | 0.0 | 0.0 |
| MOFFAT | 081 | 0000 | 751 | 11,357 | 12,912 | 13,854 | 1.3 | 38 | 96.2 | 95.5 | 0.1 | 0.1 | 0.4 | 0.5 |
| MONTEZUMA | 083 | 0000 | 790 | 18,672 | 22,925 | 24,264 | 2.0 | 33 | 85.4 | 84.9 | 0.1 | 0.1 | 0.2 | 0.4 |
| MONTROSE | 085 | 0000 | 773 | 24,423 | 32,080 | 35,371 | 2.7 | 19 | 95.8 | 95.0 | 0.3 | 0.3 | 0.3 | 0.4 |
| MORGAN | 087 | 0000 | 751 | 21,939 | 25,668 | 27,044 | 1.5 | 36 | 88.1 | 86.0 | 0.3 | 0.3 | 0.4 | 0.5 |
| OTERO | 089 | 0000 | 752 | 20,185 | 20,561 | 20,306 | 0.2 | 54 | 82.9 | 80.5 | 0.6 | 0.7 | 0.6 | 0.8 |
| OURAY | 091 | 0000 | 773 | 2,295 | 3,602 | 4,252 | 4.5 | 9 | 98.0 | 97.7 | 0.0 | 0.0 | 0.1 | 0.1 |
| PARK | 093 | 0000 | 751 | 7,174 | 15,055 | 19,254 | 7.5 | 3 | 98.0 | 97.8 | 0.6 | 0.6 | 0.2 | 0.3 |
| PHILLIPS | 095 | 0000 | 751 | 4,189 | 4,187 | 4,004 | 0.0 | 56 | 99.6 | 99.6 | 0.0 | 0.0 | 0.2 | 0.3 |
| PITKIN | 097 | 0000 | 751 | 12,661 | 13,290 | 13,084 | 0.5 | 49 | 97.4 | 96.9 | 0.3 | 0.3 | 1.1 | 1.5 |
| PROWERS | 099 | 0000 | 751 | 13,347 | 13,858 | 14,218 | 0.4 | 52 | 85.4 | 83.4 | 0.3 | 0.3 | 0.3 | 0.3 |
| PUEBLO | 101 | 6560 | 752 | 123,051 | 139,071 | 149,424 | 1.2 | 40 | 84.8 | 82.7 | 1.8 | 2.1 | 0.6 | 0.7 |
| RIO BLANCO | 103 | 0000 | 751 | 5,972 | 6,157 | 5,931 | 0.3 | 53 | 97.2 | 96.8 | 0.2 | 0.1 | 0.4 | 0.4 |
| RIO GRANDE | 105 | 0000 | 751 | 10,770 | 11,578 | 11,931 | 0.7 | 44 | 89.8 | 88.6 | 0.1 | 0.1 | 0.1 | 0.2 |
| ROUTT | 107 | 0000 | 751 | 14,088 | 18,281 | 20,030 | 2.6 | 20 | 98.8 | 98.6 | 0.1 | 0.1 | 0.3 | 0.4 |
| SAGUACHE | 109 | 0000 | 751 | 4,619 | 6,319 | 7,059 | 3.1 | 15 | 80.1 | 78.3 | 0.2 | 0.2 | 0.2 | 0.2 |
| SAN JUAN | 111 | 0000 | 751 | 745 | 522 | 522 | -3.4 | 63 | 95.4 | 94.4 | 0.1 | 0.2 | 0.3 | 0.4 |
| SAN MIGUEL | 113 | 0000 | 751 | 3,653 | 5,533 | 5,913 | 4.1 | 12 | 98.8 | 98.7 | 0.1 | 0.1 | 0.3 | 0.3 |
| SEDGWICK | 115 | 0000 | 751 | 2,690 | 2,587 | 2,589 | -0.4 | 58 | 97.2 | 96.9 | 0.4 | 0.5 | 1.2 | 1.2 |
| SUMMIT | 117 | 0000 | 751 | 12,881 | 20,262 | 23,566 | 4.5 | 9 | 97.6 | 97.1 | 0.2 | 0.3 | 0.7 | 1.0 |
| TELLER | 119 | 0000 | 752 | 12,468 | 22,029 | 26,051 | 5.7 | 6 | 97.8 | 97.5 | 0.2 | 0.2 | 0.4 | 0.5 |
| WASHINGTON | 121 | 0000 | 751 | 4,812 | 4,245 | 4,059 | -1.2 | 62 | 98.1 | 98.0 | 0.0 | 0.0 | 0.2 | 0.2 |
| WELD | 123 | 3060 | 751 | 131,821 | 171,203 | 197,136 | 2.6 | 20 | 88.9 | 86.8 | 0.4 | 0.5 | 0.9 | 1.1 |
| YUMA | 125 | 0000 | 751 | 8,954 | 9,471 | 9,662 | 0.5 | 49 | 97.9 | 97.6 | 0.0 | 0.0 | 0.1 | 0.2 |
| COLORADO | | | | | | | 2.3 | | 88.2 | 86.9 | 4.0 | 4.1 | 1.8 | 2.4 |
| UNITED STATES | | | | | | | 1.0 | | 80.3 | 77.9 | 12.1 | 12.4 | 2.9 | 3.9 |

# POPULATION COMPOSITION

## B

| COUNTY | % HISPANIC ORIGIN | | 2000 AGE DISTRIBUTION (%) | | | | | | | | | | MEDIAN AGE | | 2000 Males/ Females (×100) |
|---|---|---|---|---|---|---|---|---|---|---|---|---|---|---|---|
| | 1990 | 2000 | 0-4 | 5-9 | 10-14 | 15-19 | 20-24 | 25-44 | 45-64 | 65-84 | 85+ | 18+ | 1990 | 2000 | |
| ADAMS | 18.6 | 22.7 | 8.1 | 7.9 | 8.1 | 7.7 | 6.3 | 30.9 | 22.2 | 8.0 | 0.8 | 71.3 | 30.7 | 33.8 | 97.4 |
| ALAMOSA | 38.6 | 44.7 | 8.4 | 7.6 | 7.6 | 10.4 | 9.9 | 27.2 | 20.3 | 7.4 | 1.2 | 71.6 | 28.1 | 29.7 | 96.7 |
| ARAPAHOE | 5.6 | 7.2 | 6.9 | 6.9 | 7.6 | 7.4 | 5.9 | 30.5 | 26.0 | 7.9 | 0.8 | 73.9 | 32.4 | 36.5 | 94.6 |
| ARCHULETA | 23.3 | 29.1 | 6.7 | 7.3 | 8.4 | 8.1 | 5.5 | 22.4 | 28.0 | 12.8 | 0.8 | 71.7 | 35.4 | 39.5 | 103.7 |
| BACA | 5.6 | 6.7 | 5.6 | 6.2 | 6.9 | 7.0 | 4.2 | 21.1 | 27.9 | 18.0 | 3.1 | 76.2 | 39.3 | 44.3 | 98.0 |
| BENT | 27.2 | 32.4 | 5.6 | 6.0 | 7.1 | 8.6 | 5.6 | 24.0 | 25.8 | 15.1 | 2.3 | 75.3 | 39.1 | 40.3 | 119.1 |
| BOULDER | 6.7 | 8.7 | 6.1 | 6.5 | 7.0 | 8.1 | 8.6 | 31.1 | 24.7 | 6.9 | 1.0 | 76.7 | 31.6 | 35.4 | 99.3 |
| CHAFFEE | 9.5 | 11.2 | 4.8 | 5.2 | 6.3 | 7.6 | 7.7 | 23.9 | 28.0 | 14.5 | 2.1 | 78.8 | 37.1 | 41.4 | 118.8 |
| CHEYENNE | 3.5 | 4.4 | 8.3 | 8.4 | 8.9 | 7.9 | 5.0 | 24.8 | 22.4 | 11.8 | 2.5 | 68.5 | 32.0 | 35.8 | 106.9 |
| CLEAR CREEK | 3.3 | 4.3 | 5.7 | 6.5 | 7.6 | 7.0 | 4.5 | 29.0 | 32.2 | 6.9 | 0.6 | 75.7 | 35.9 | 40.4 | 109.1 |
| CONEJOS | 59.9 | 65.5 | 8.8 | 8.7 | 9.2 | 9.6 | 6.4 | 21.5 | 22.8 | 11.3 | 1.8 | 66.6 | 31.4 | 32.4 | 100.2 |
| COSTILLA | 76.9 | 80.3 | 7.6 | 7.4 | 7.6 | 8.3 | 6.3 | 21.7 | 25.8 | 13.0 | 2.2 | 72.1 | 35.4 | 37.5 | 99.1 |
| CROWLEY | 23.1 | 27.5 | 5.3 | 5.6 | 5.8 | 7.8 | 9.8 | 32.1 | 21.2 | 10.4 | 2.0 | 78.3 | 34.2 | 34.5 | 176.2 |
| CUSTER | 2.9 | 3.8 | 4.8 | 5.6 | 7.6 | 7.1 | 3.9 | 21.0 | 35.6 | 13.0 | 1.5 | 76.8 | 39.2 | 45.0 | 105.2 |
| DELTA | 9.1 | 11.2 | 5.5 | 6.0 | 7.0 | 7.4 | 4.9 | 20.6 | 28.8 | 16.8 | 2.8 | 76.5 | 40.7 | 43.9 | 98.9 |
| DENVER | 23.0 | 28.1 | 6.8 | 6.5 | 6.9 | 6.4 | 6.2 | 31.5 | 22.8 | 10.9 | 2.0 | 76.3 | 33.9 | 37.2 | 96.4 |
| DOLORES | 3.2 | 4.3 | 6.0 | 6.4 | 8.2 | 7.3 | 5.8 | 22.2 | 29.7 | 12.9 | 1.4 | 74.5 | 36.4 | 41.0 | 102.5 |
| DOUGLAS | 3.2 | 4.4 | 7.8 | 9.1 | 9.7 | 7.4 | 4.7 | 29.9 | 26.5 | 4.7 | 0.3 | 68.5 | 32.3 | 35.8 | 98.7 |
| EAGLE | 13.3 | 17.0 | 8.2 | 7.6 | 7.5 | 6.3 | 6.9 | 39.0 | 21.1 | 3.2 | 0.2 | 72.9 | 30.6 | 33.3 | 109.5 |
| ELBERT | 2.2 | 2.9 | 6.3 | 7.7 | 8.8 | 8.5 | 4.5 | 28.9 | 28.9 | 5.8 | 0.8 | 71.5 | 33.8 | 37.5 | 100.0 |
| EL PASO | 8.7 | 11.3 | 7.9 | 7.2 | 7.4 | 7.9 | 8.4 | 29.7 | 22.9 | 7.7 | 0.9 | 73.1 | 30.2 | 33.1 | 99.1 |
| FREMONT | 8.5 | 12.1 | 4.9 | 5.2 | 6.1 | 7.1 | 7.1 | 28.4 | 25.9 | 13.0 | 2.3 | 79.0 | 37.7 | 39.3 | 122.5 |
| GARFIELD | 5.6 | 7.1 | 7.1 | 7.5 | 8.0 | 8.0 | 5.8 | 28.2 | 25.7 | 8.6 | 1.1 | 72.7 | 32.8 | 36.5 | 104.3 |
| GILPIN | 3.6 | 5.0 | 5.1 | 5.7 | 6.7 | 6.9 | 3.8 | 31.8 | 33.3 | 6.0 | 0.6 | 77.5 | 36.1 | 41.0 | 114.2 |
| GRAND | 3.1 | 4.1 | 5.6 | 6.1 | 7.1 | 7.3 | 6.0 | 31.5 | 27.6 | 8.3 | 0.6 | 76.5 | 33.0 | 37.9 | 112.7 |
| GUNNISON | 3.6 | 4.9 | 6.0 | 5.6 | 5.9 | 11.5 | 12.7 | 29.3 | 22.3 | 6.0 | 0.7 | 79.4 | 28.2 | 31.6 | 110.3 |
| HINSDALE | 0.9 | 1.5 | 2.4 | 4.1 | 4.5 | 5.8 | 3.3 | 27.1 | 36.5 | 15.2 | 1.2 | 85.2 | 39.2 | 46.3 | 114.4 |
| HUERFANO | 40.4 | 44.9 | 5.5 | 5.6 | 6.1 | 7.8 | 6.6 | 20.5 | 27.4 | 17.3 | 3.1 | 77.2 | 39.6 | 43.3 | 96.7 |
| JACKSON | 7.4 | 8.2 | 6.0 | 5.9 | 7.2 | 6.6 | 5.8 | 24.7 | 30.9 | 10.9 | 1.9 | 76.1 | 35.5 | 41.2 | 111.3 |
| JEFFERSON | 7.0 | 8.8 | 6.6 | 6.7 | 7.4 | 7.4 | 5.7 | 29.2 | 27.3 | 8.8 | 1.0 | 74.7 | 33.3 | 37.8 | 97.0 |
| KIOWA | 3.3 | 4.1 | 5.8 | 6.9 | 7.7 | 8.4 | 4.5 | 22.0 | 27.4 | 14.6 | 2.8 | 73.1 | 37.0 | 41.1 | 100.0 |
| KIT CARSON | 6.6 | 8.3 | 7.0 | 7.4 | 8.2 | 7.9 | 4.6 | 22.7 | 26.6 | 13.4 | 2.2 | 72.0 | 34.9 | 39.9 | 100.1 |
| LAKE | 23.9 | 28.3 | 7.7 | 7.4 | 7.6 | 7.8 | 6.4 | 29.9 | 24.2 | 8.1 | 0.9 | 72.8 | 31.2 | 34.7 | 105.4 |
| LA PLATA | 11.1 | 14.1 | 6.3 | 6.4 | 6.7 | 9.7 | 8.8 | 27.0 | 25.3 | 8.9 | 1.0 | 76.1 | 31.9 | 35.1 | 100.7 |
| LARIMER | 6.6 | 8.6 | 6.7 | 6.8 | 7.0 | 8.5 | 9.1 | 29.6 | 23.0 | 8.0 | 1.2 | 75.3 | 31.1 | 34.1 | 98.2 |
| LAS ANIMAS | 44.2 | 50.6 | 6.4 | 6.3 | 7.2 | 8.2 | 6.0 | 21.9 | 26.3 | 14.7 | 2.9 | 75.3 | 37.7 | 40.5 | 97.0 |
| LINCOLN | 1.7 | 8.4 | 5.7 | 6.0 | 6.2 | 7.5 | 7.0 | 28.2 | 24.5 | 12.5 | 2.4 | 76.6 | 36.9 | 37.7 | 132.8 |
| LOGAN | 7.9 | 10.0 | 6.3 | 6.7 | 7.4 | 9.0 | 5.4 | 23.8 | 25.9 | 13.0 | 2.3 | 74.6 | 34.7 | 38.9 | 94.9 |
| MESA | 8.1 | 10.4 | 6.5 | 6.7 | 7.5 | 8.3 | 6.1 | 24.6 | 26.1 | 12.5 | 1.8 | 74.4 | 34.7 | 38.7 | 94.7 |
| MINERAL | 4.8 | 5.8 | 6.7 | 6.0 | 6.6 | 4.7 | 2.5 | 24.2 | 32.4 | 15.5 | 1.3 | 77.9 | 37.5 | 44.5 | 108.1 |
| MOFFAT | 6.1 | 7.9 | 7.7 | 8.1 | 8.9 | 8.4 | 5.9 | 26.4 | 25.5 | 8.1 | 1.0 | 69.6 | 31.8 | 35.2 | 102.4 |
| MONTEZUMA | 8.6 | 11.0 | 7.6 | 7.8 | 8.8 | 8.3 | 5.5 | 23.4 | 25.7 | 11.4 | 1.4 | 70.3 | 33.3 | 36.9 | 96.1 |
| MONTROSE | 11.2 | 14.1 | 6.1 | 6.9 | 7.6 | 7.8 | 5.2 | 22.2 | 28.8 | 13.6 | 1.8 | 74.2 | 37.1 | 41.2 | 96.2 |
| MORGAN | 18.4 | 22.1 | 8.2 | 8.0 | 8.4 | 8.2 | 5.9 | 23.8 | 24.1 | 11.3 | 2.2 | 70.2 | 33.1 | 35.8 | 96.3 |
| OTERO | 35.2 | 40.3 | 7.2 | 7.2 | 8.1 | 8.8 | 6.0 | 21.9 | 25.1 | 13.0 | 2.5 | 71.9 | 34.9 | 37.6 | 95.4 |
| OURAY | 4.5 | 5.7 | 4.8 | 5.5 | 7.4 | 6.0 | 4.0 | 22.4 | 36.6 | 12.0 | 1.2 | 77.9 | 40.1 | 44.9 | 102.7 |
| PARK | 2.9 | 3.8 | 5.4 | 6.5 | 8.0 | 7.1 | 3.9 | 28.5 | 32.9 | 7.3 | 0.4 | 75.2 | 35.6 | 40.9 | 105.4 |
| PHILLIPS | 4.1 | 5.2 | 6.0 | 6.6 | 7.3 | 7.6 | 4.2 | 21.4 | 27.4 | 15.9 | 3.7 | 74.7 | 38.5 | 42.9 | 92.6 |
| PITKIN | 3.8 | 4.6 | 4.5 | 4.5 | 5.1 | 4.6 | 6.2 | 37.6 | 31.2 | 5.8 | 0.4 | 83.0 | 34.8 | 40.0 | 110.0 |
| PROWERS | 23.2 | 27.0 | 7.9 | 8.0 | 8.7 | 9.1 | 6.2 | 23.9 | 23.7 | 10.7 | 1.7 | 69.8 | 32.0 | 34.7 | 95.7 |
| PUEBLO | 35.8 | 41.4 | 6.7 | 6.6 | 7.4 | 8.1 | 6.5 | 24.6 | 25.3 | 12.9 | 1.8 | 74.4 | 34.7 | 38.1 | 94.5 |
| RIO BLANCO | 4.0 | 5.2 | 6.6 | 7.1 | 8.2 | 9.3 | 6.4 | 25.2 | 26.5 | 9.3 | 1.3 | 72.5 | 32.3 | 36.2 | 101.5 |
| RIO GRANDE | 40.3 | 45.5 | 7.6 | 7.7 | 8.3 | 8.5 | 5.6 | 22.7 | 25.6 | 11.9 | 2.0 | 70.8 | 33.7 | 37.3 | 99.0 |
| ROUTT | 2.5 | 3.5 | 6.1 | 6.6 | 7.3 | 7.5 | 7.0 | 34.1 | 25.7 | 5.1 | 0.5 | 75.9 | 32.4 | 36.0 | 113.6 |
| SAGUACHE | 45.6 | 51.5 | 7.8 | 8.1 | 8.8 | 9.1 | 6.3 | 24.6 | 24.8 | 9.2 | 1.3 | 69.4 | 31.8 | 34.6 | 104.9 |
| SAN JUAN | 15.8 | 20.5 | 5.0 | 6.9 | 7.9 | 8.6 | 5.9 | 28.4 | 29.7 | 7.5 | 0.2 | 73.2 | 33.6 | 38.4 | 121.2 |
| SAN MIGUEL | 2.8 | 3.9 | 5.9 | 6.3 | 6.6 | 6.2 | 6.2 | 36.7 | 27.8 | 4.0 | 0.4 | 77.6 | 33.1 | 37.5 | 111.1 |
| SEDGWICK | 8.6 | 10.7 | 4.4 | 5.4 | 6.7 | 7.2 | 4.4 | 21.0 | 29.0 | 18.6 | 3.4 | 78.3 | 40.8 | 45.6 | 96.4 |
| SUMMIT | 2.5 | 3.5 | 6.6 | 5.9 | 6.0 | 5.5 | 8.1 | 42.7 | 21.5 | 3.5 | 0.1 | 78.6 | 30.5 | 34.2 | 115.2 |
| TELLER | 2.6 | 3.4 | 6.2 | 7.0 | 8.3 | 7.4 | 4.2 | 28.7 | 30.1 | 7.5 | 0.5 | 73.3 | 34.6 | 39.3 | 105.2 |
| WASHINGTON | 2.9 | 3.6 | 5.9 | 6.7 | 7.4 | 7.4 | 4.6 | 21.3 | 28.6 | 15.5 | 2.5 | 74.7 | 37.3 | 42.6 | 101.0 |
| WELD | 20.9 | 25.5 | 7.6 | 7.4 | 7.5 | 8.9 | 8.7 | 27.9 | 22.3 | 8.4 | 1.3 | 72.9 | 30.5 | 32.9 | 97.9 |
| YUMA | 3.2 | 4.1 | 6.1 | 6.9 | 8.1 | 8.2 | 4.8 | 22.5 | 27.3 | 13.6 | 2.5 | 73.0 | 35.8 | 40.8 | 97.5 |
| COLORADO | 12.9 | 15.1 | 7.0 | 7.0 | 7.5 | 7.7 | 6.8 | 29.3 | 24.7 | 8.8 | 1.2 | 74.1 | 32.5 | 36.0 | 98.3 |
| UNITED STATES | 9.0 | 11.8 | 6.9 | 7.2 | 7.2 | 7.2 | 6.7 | 29.9 | 22.2 | 11.1 | 1.6 | 74.6 | 32.9 | 35.7 | 95.6 |

| COUNTY | HOUSEHOLDS | | | | | FAMILIES | | | MEDIAN HOUSEHOLD INCOME | | | |
|---|---|---|---|---|---|---|---|---|---|---|---|---|
| | 1990 | 2000 | 2005 | % Annual Rate 1990-2000 | 2000 Average HH Size | 1990 | 2000 | % Annual Rate 1990-2000 | 2000 | 2005 | 2000 National Rank | 2000 State Rank |
| ADAMS | 96,353 | 125,557 | 140,642 | 3.3 | 2.67 | 69,942 | 88,198 | 2.9 | 46,240 | 54,238 | 300 | 17 |
| ALAMOSA | 4,721 | 5,261 | 5,484 | 1.3 | 2.63 | 3,269 | 3,573 | 1.1 | 30,914 | 38,266 | 1945 | 46 |
| ARAPAHOE | 154,710 | 198,908 | 219,974 | 3.1 | 2.46 | 104,529 | 129,906 | 2.7 | 57,392 | 62,810 | 97 | 7 |
| ARCHULETA | 2,010 | 3,995 | 5,166 | 8.7 | 2.54 | 1,547 | 2,992 | 8.3 | 34,064 | 42,267 | 1381 | 35 |
| BACA | 1,872 | 1,822 | 1,807 | -0.3 | 2.32 | 1,310 | 1,230 | -0.8 | 25,491 | 27,348 | 2759 | 58 |
| BENT | 1,865 | 2,015 | 2,079 | 0.9 | 2.40 | 1,286 | 1,332 | 0.4 | 27,413 | 29,550 | 2524 | 55 |
| BOULDER | 88,402 | 111,573 | 123,933 | 2.9 | 2.42 | 54,375 | 66,973 | 2.6 | 55,678 | 63,746 | 114 | 8 |
| CHAFFEE | 4,848 | 6,143 | 6,799 | 2.9 | 2.39 | 3,374 | 4,120 | 2.5 | 34,611 | 42,811 | 1304 | 33 |
| CHEYENNE | 904 | 913 | 917 | 0.1 | 2.35 | 622 | 605 | -0.3 | 37,539 | 46,641 | 893 | 28 |
| CLEAR CREEK | 3,153 | 3,886 | 4,205 | 2.6 | 2.39 | 2,096 | 2,474 | 2.0 | 59,860 | 70,124 | 75 | 5 |
| CONEJOS | 2,492 | 2,782 | 2,961 | 1.3 | 2.92 | 1,920 | 2,113 | 1.2 | 24,366 | 27,121 | 2875 | 59 |
| COSTILLA | 1,192 | 1,442 | 1,488 | 2.3 | 2.48 | 879 | 1,063 | 2.3 | 23,640 | 28,042 | 2927 | 62 |
| CROWLEY | 1,165 | 1,316 | 1,413 | 1.5 | 2.57 | 816 | 881 | 0.9 | 24,088 | 31,149 | 2894 | 61 |
| CUSTER | 770 | 1,568 | 1,972 | 9.0 | 2.41 | 569 | 1,134 | 8.7 | 31,618 | 40,147 | 1797 | 41 |
| DELTA | 8,372 | 11,227 | 12,481 | 3.6 | 2.40 | 6,112 | 7,921 | 3.2 | 31,066 | 37,859 | 1920 | 45 |
| DENVER | 210,952 | 230,146 | 235,021 | 1.1 | 2.13 | 109,037 | 113,492 | 0.5 | 38,599 | 42,767 | 792 | 25 |
| DOLORES | 581 | 783 | 935 | 3.7 | 2.48 | 425 | 551 | 3.2 | 27,475 | 30,787 | 2514 | 54 |
| DOUGLAS | 20,844 | 59,728 | 85,666 | 13.6 | 2.88 | 17,409 | 48,472 | 13.2 | 87,400 | 107,825 | 1 | 1 |
| EAGLE | 8,354 | 14,084 | 17,027 | 6.5 | 2.58 | 5,081 | 8,166 | 5.9 | 60,516 | 73,484 | 69 | 3 |
| ELBERT | 3,377 | 7,518 | 9,756 | 10.2 | 2.78 | 2,763 | 6,055 | 10.0 | 59,943 | 73,764 | 73 | 4 |
| EL PASO | 146,965 | 192,463 | 212,709 | 3.3 | 2.56 | 104,095 | 131,942 | 2.9 | 49,098 | 58,970 | 219 | 15 |
| FREMONT | 11,713 | 15,935 | 17,626 | 3.8 | 2.33 | 8,287 | 10,925 | 3.4 | 32,884 | 39,192 | 1556 | 38 |
| GARFIELD | 11,266 | 16,114 | 18,872 | 4.4 | 2.56 | 7,966 | 11,014 | 4.0 | 45,311 | 53,247 | 341 | 19 |
| GILPIN | 1,308 | 2,000 | 2,525 | 5.3 | 2.37 | 848 | 1,237 | 4.7 | 52,355 | 64,069 | 165 | 11 |
| GRAND | 3,168 | 4,307 | 4,969 | 3.8 | 2.49 | 2,050 | 2,665 | 3.2 | 45,578 | 56,816 | 327 | 18 |
| GUNNISON | 3,855 | 5,019 | 5,425 | 3.2 | 2.32 | 2,218 | 2,811 | 2.9 | 35,674 | 41,518 | 1141 | 32 |
| HINSDALE | 214 | 378 | 440 | 7.1 | 2.00 | 135 | 228 | 6.6 | 36,833 | 40,417 | 1001 | 29 |
| HUERFANO | 2,446 | 2,956 | 3,188 | 2.3 | 2.29 | 1,649 | 1,923 | 1.9 | 24,089 | 27,484 | 2893 | 60 |
| JACKSON | 632 | 623 | 652 | -0.2 | 2.48 | 454 | 432 | -0.6 | 30,871 | 34,128 | 1957 | 47 |
| JEFFERSON | 166,545 | 199,088 | 214,050 | 2.2 | 2.56 | 119,462 | 138,139 | 1.8 | 60,636 | 68,456 | 67 | 2 |
| KIOWA | 657 | 642 | 635 | -0.3 | 2.47 | 473 | 447 | -0.7 | 31,442 | 32,679 | 1834 | 44 |
| KIT CARSON | 2,785 | 2,961 | 3,147 | 0.7 | 2.51 | 2,008 | 2,063 | 0.3 | 31,967 | 34,527 | 1721 | 40 |
| LAKE | 2,382 | 2,650 | 2,790 | 1.3 | 2.42 | 1,562 | 1,659 | 0.7 | 40,281 | 47,865 | 650 | 24 |
| LA PLATA | 11,976 | 15,825 | 17,153 | 3.4 | 2.53 | 8,008 | 10,338 | 3.1 | 42,022 | 47,894 | 510 | 23 |
| LARIMER | 70,472 | 93,407 | 104,606 | 3.5 | 2.53 | 47,247 | 61,031 | 3.2 | 49,808 | 57,664 | 203 | 13 |
| LAS ANIMAS | 5,421 | 5,963 | 6,287 | 1.2 | 2.43 | 3,694 | 3,918 | 0.7 | 26,900 | 31,123 | 2600 | 56 |
| LINCOLN | 1,817 | 1,989 | 2,051 | 1.1 | 2.33 | 1,249 | 1,327 | 0.7 | 33,181 | 40,770 | 1507 | 37 |
| LOGAN | 6,978 | 7,161 | 7,190 | 0.3 | 2.43 | 4,791 | 4,711 | -0.2 | 33,731 | 36,958 | 1432 | 36 |
| MESA | 36,250 | 46,717 | 51,792 | 3.1 | 2.46 | 25,419 | 31,687 | 2.7 | 37,891 | 44,456 | 858 | 27 |
| MINERAL | 247 | 331 | 379 | 3.6 | 2.26 | 159 | 205 | 3.1 | 31,477 | 39,896 | 1821 | 43 |
| MOFFAT | 4,178 | 4,844 | 5,248 | 1.8 | 2.64 | 3,061 | 3,431 | 1.4 | 43,156 | 48,346 | 445 | 22 |
| MONTEZUMA | 6,762 | 8,479 | 9,058 | 2.8 | 2.69 | 5,139 | 6,219 | 2.3 | 36,111 | 42,114 | 1090 | 30 |
| MONTROSE | 9,405 | 12,675 | 14,144 | 3.7 | 2.50 | 6,973 | 9,148 | 3.3 | 35,868 | 39,865 | 1117 | 31 |
| MORGAN | 8,139 | 9,676 | 10,273 | 2.1 | 2.61 | 5,890 | 6,824 | 1.8 | 32,724 | 38,269 | 1589 | 39 |
| OTERO | 7,593 | 7,835 | 7,800 | 0.4 | 2.55 | 5,448 | 5,447 | 0.0 | 28,567 | 32,306 | 2354 | 51 |
| OURAY | 947 | 1,476 | 1,736 | 5.5 | 2.44 | 677 | 1,021 | 5.1 | 44,387 | 57,172 | 380 | 20 |
| PARK | 2,775 | 5,996 | 7,780 | 9.8 | 2.51 | 2,071 | 4,350 | 9.4 | 51,996 | 64,545 | 171 | 12 |
| PHILLIPS | 1,712 | 1,802 | 1,766 | 0.6 | 2.29 | 1,182 | 1,198 | 0.2 | 31,540 | 34,923 | 1812 | 42 |
| PITKIN | 5,877 | 6,297 | 6,264 | 0.8 | 2.09 | 2,687 | 2,790 | 0.5 | 58,449 | 65,658 | 83 | 6 |
| PROWERS | 4,984 | 5,269 | 5,454 | 0.7 | 2.60 | 3,564 | 3,657 | 0.3 | 30,725 | 35,012 | 1982 | 48 |
| PUEBLO | 47,057 | 54,202 | 58,851 | 1.7 | 2.51 | 33,248 | 37,426 | 1.4 | 34,449 | 37,912 | 1321 | 34 |
| RIO BLANCO | 2,181 | 2,306 | 2,256 | 0.7 | 2.58 | 1,609 | 1,642 | 0.2 | 43,533 | 50,739 | 420 | 21 |
| RIO GRANDE | 3,930 | 4,334 | 4,519 | 1.2 | 2.63 | 2,979 | 3,209 | 0.9 | 25,525 | 27,868 | 2753 | 57 |
| ROUTT | 5,483 | 7,136 | 7,842 | 3.2 | 2.53 | 3,451 | 4,279 | 2.6 | 46,982 | 54,272 | 274 | 16 |
| SAGUACHE | 1,643 | 2,342 | 2,667 | 4.4 | 2.66 | 1,214 | 1,694 | 4.1 | 23,432 | 26,935 | 2947 | 63 |
| SAN JUAN | 287 | 207 | 207 | -3.9 | 2.52 | 199 | 138 | -4.3 | 29,375 | 35,893 | 2240 | 50 |
| SAN MIGUEL | 1,489 | 2,383 | 2,612 | 5.9 | 2.30 | 846 | 1,284 | 5.2 | 53,987 | 62,812 | 137 | 9 |
| SEDGWICK | 1,141 | 1,085 | 1,082 | -0.6 | 2.35 | 795 | 727 | -1.1 | 29,628 | 31,765 | 2207 | 49 |
| SUMMIT | 5,295 | 8,193 | 9,452 | 5.4 | 2.47 | 2,847 | 4,079 | 4.5 | 53,375 | 60,699 | 146 | 10 |
| TELLER | 4,720 | 8,685 | 10,467 | 7.7 | 2.53 | 3,602 | 6,414 | 7.2 | 49,286 | 62,395 | 213 | 14 |
| WASHINGTON | 1,915 | 1,832 | 1,823 | -0.5 | 2.30 | 1,374 | 1,274 | -0.9 | 28,372 | 31,239 | 2383 | 52 |
| WELD | 47,470 | 61,534 | 70,806 | 3.2 | 2.71 | 33,763 | 42,693 | 2.9 | 38,270 | 46,189 | 832 | 26 |
| YUMA | 3,472 | 3,745 | 3,848 | 0.9 | 2.50 | 2,460 | 2,546 | 0.4 | 28,331 | 31,667 | 2394 | 53 |
| COLORADO | | | | 3.0 | 2.49 | | | 2.7 | 48,112 | 55,833 | | |
| UNITED STATES | | | | 1.4 | 2.59 | | | 1.1 | 41,914 | 49,127 | | |

# COLORADO

# INCOME

# D

| COUNTY | 2000 Per Capita Income | 2000 HH Income Base | 2000 HOUSEHOLD INCOME DISTRIBUTION (%) | | | | | | 2000 AVERAGE DISPOSABLE INCOME BY AGE OF HOUSEHOLDER | | | | | |
|---|---|---|---|---|---|---|---|---|---|---|---|---|---|---|
| | | | Less than $15,000 | $15,000 to $24,999 | $25,000 to $49,999 | $50,000 to $99,999 | $100,000 to $149,999 | $150,000 or More | All Ages | <35 | 35-44 | 45-54 | 55-64 | 65+ |
| ADAMS | 20,195 | 125,557 | 9.3 | 10.1 | 35.7 | 37.0 | 6.8 | 1.1 | 39,853 | 34,631 | 44,882 | 47,001 | 41,652 | 26,006 |
| ALAMOSA | 14,935 | 5,261 | 22.3 | 16.8 | 34.4 | 21.6 | 3.5 | 1.5 | 30,997 | 23,054 | 34,902 | 39,594 | 33,846 | 21,937 |
| ARAPAHOE | 32,881 | 198,907 | 5.4 | 8.0 | 28.3 | 38.3 | 13.2 | 6.9 | 53,785 | 38,998 | 56,567 | 62,975 | 56,714 | 35,884 |
| ARCHULETA | 20,233 | 3,995 | 13.7 | 14.6 | 41.4 | 21.6 | 5.7 | 3.1 | 36,025 | 25,712 | 45,794 | 36,654 | 38,264 | 28,359 |
| BACA | 13,213 | 1,822 | 28.1 | 20.8 | 35.1 | 14.3 | 1.5 | 0.3 | 24,241 | 22,322 | 28,987 | 29,987 | 25,337 | 18,103 |
| BENT | 13,460 | 2,015 | 28.6 | 18.0 | 37.0 | 14.3 | 2.0 | 0.1 | 24,574 | 20,461 | 28,287 | 30,803 | 28,394 | 16,194 |
| BOULDER | 32,760 | 111,573 | 7.7 | 8.4 | 27.5 | 36.3 | 12.5 | 7.6 | 53,700 | 37,372 | 56,307 | 64,778 | 57,454 | 36,661 |
| CHAFFEE | 18,495 | 6,143 | 14.7 | 18.0 | 37.4 | 23.8 | 4.8 | 1.4 | 33,005 | 25,121 | 38,659 | 41,396 | 35,135 | 24,744 |
| CHEYENNE | 19,452 | 913 | 12.6 | 15.6 | 38.3 | 27.5 | 4.9 | 1.1 | 34,592 | 30,283 | 36,177 | 40,782 | 40,397 | 28,369 |
| CLEAR CREEK | 29,281 | 3,886 | 7.8 | 7.2 | 25.7 | 41.0 | 13.0 | 5.3 | 50,983 | 41,461 | 53,292 | 55,707 | 52,360 | 33,169 |
| CONEJOS | 11,129 | 2,782 | 30.1 | 21.2 | 31.7 | 14.6 | 1.8 | 0.7 | 24,627 | 19,963 | 25,859 | 32,134 | 27,725 | 18,285 |
| COSTILLA | 12,874 | 1,430 | 31.8 | 20.4 | 32.0 | 13.1 | 1.9 | 0.8 | 24,391 | 21,845 | 30,342 | 32,412 | 21,277 | 19,532 |
| CROWLEY | 10,711 | 1,316 | 27.4 | 24.7 | 28.2 | 16.3 | 2.5 | 0.9 | 26,122 | 19,577 | 30,290 | 34,287 | 30,358 | 18,277 |
| CUSTER | 23,011 | 1,568 | 18.1 | 17.7 | 34.0 | 21.3 | 5.1 | 3.8 | 35,634 | 27,502 | 40,929 | 38,274 | 36,782 | 27,352 |
| DELTA | 16,648 | 11,227 | 18.6 | 19.4 | 35.8 | 20.9 | 3.9 | 1.4 | 30,907 | 28,616 | 37,604 | 39,141 | 31,747 | 22,098 |
| DENVER | 27,375 | 230,137 | 15.5 | 14.9 | 32.1 | 25.3 | 7.3 | 4.9 | 41,175 | 31,737 | 44,819 | 47,555 | 43,458 | 31,233 |
| DOLORES | 14,262 | 783 | 24.4 | 19.2 | 34.6 | 18.7 | 2.4 | 0.8 | 27,545 | 25,691 | 32,903 | 31,544 | 28,747 | 20,151 |
| DOUGLAS | 43,515 | 59,728 | 2.6 | 1.9 | 12.7 | 40.1 | 25.9 | 16.7 | 79,690 | 60,443 | 76,700 | 79,242 | 73,404 | 52,417 |
| EAGLE | 31,898 | 14,084 | 4.5 | 5.4 | 28.1 | 41.5 | 14.3 | 6.2 | 55,136 | 45,579 | 58,563 | 59,377 | 50,506 | 35,289 |
| ELBERT | 30,982 | 7,518 | 4.8 | 6.1 | 30.1 | 35.2 | 15.2 | 8.6 | 58,160 | 44,781 | 63,593 | 63,988 | 40,373 | 35,054 |
| EL PASO | 24,165 | 192,463 | 7.7 | 11.4 | 32.0 | 36.1 | 9.7 | 3.3 | 44,537 | 34,631 | 48,930 | 53,319 | 47,404 | 34,620 |
| FREMONT | 17,286 | 15,935 | 18.2 | 18.9 | 35.2 | 21.1 | 4.4 | 2.2 | 33,006 | 25,307 | 40,565 | 43,123 | 31,954 | 23,342 |
| GARFIELD | 22,779 | 16,114 | 8.6 | 9.9 | 38.8 | 30.7 | 8.4 | 3.7 | 42,885 | 33,911 | 47,725 | 50,620 | 45,959 | 26,602 |
| GILPIN | 24,675 | 2,000 | 9.0 | 7.8 | 29.2 | 42.6 | 9.6 | 1.9 | 43,539 | 37,136 | 45,169 | 49,929 | 43,384 | 28,918 |
| GRAND | 20,954 | 4,303 | 7.4 | 11.6 | 36.3 | 36.8 | 7.3 | 0.7 | 39,599 | 35,396 | 43,703 | 44,551 | 41,445 | 26,630 |
| GUNNISON | 18,627 | 5,019 | 17.7 | 17.3 | 34.6 | 23.9 | 5.1 | 1.4 | 33,243 | 23,637 | 36,333 | 43,559 | 41,973 | 28,098 |
| HINSDALE | 20,647 | 378 | 18.0 | 14.8 | 35.2 | 27.8 | 4.0 | 0.3 | 31,462 | 28,466 | 28,696 | 30,996 | 44,529 | 23,824 |
| HUERFANO | 14,212 | 2,956 | 28.7 | 23.1 | 30.8 | 14.1 | 2.8 | 0.6 | 25,090 | 24,191 | 25,253 | 32,872 | 30,569 | 18,252 |
| JACKSON | 14,833 | 623 | 18.3 | 22.3 | 38.7 | 18.1 | 1.8 | 0.8 | 28,281 | 23,657 | 31,010 | 34,607 | 31,371 | 18,188 |
| JEFFERSON | 30,642 | 199,087 | 4.9 | 5.9 | 27.1 | 41.5 | 14.6 | 6.1 | 54,120 | 42,550 | 57,517 | 61,951 | 56,703 | 36,824 |
| KIOWA | 16,271 | 642 | 24.9 | 13.9 | 35.8 | 19.6 | 4.1 | 1.7 | 30,512 | 27,294 | 39,650 | 36,359 | 31,312 | 20,044 |
| KIT CARSON | 16,177 | 2,961 | 21.2 | 15.5 | 38.6 | 20.2 | 3.2 | 1.3 | 30,354 | 25,604 | 35,413 | 37,147 | 30,721 | 23,941 |
| LAKE | 19,067 | 2,650 | 10.0 | 16.5 | 35.2 | 32.5 | 5.4 | 0.4 | 35,438 | 29,793 | 38,788 | 45,035 | 37,616 | 24,854 |
| LA PLATA | 20,809 | 15,825 | 12.1 | 12.4 | 35.4 | 30.5 | 7.4 | 2.1 | 38,967 | 30,455 | 43,804 | 48,466 | 41,092 | 27,008 |
| LARIMER | 26,696 | 93,407 | 10.0 | 10.4 | 29.8 | 34.6 | 10.3 | 5.0 | 46,705 | 35,169 | 52,948 | 57,487 | 49,795 | 31,200 |
| LAS ANIMAS | 14,778 | 5,963 | 27.5 | 20.3 | 29.9 | 18.1 | 3.0 | 1.3 | 27,804 | 21,668 | 32,945 | 34,583 | 31,939 | 20,310 |
| LINCOLN | 14,637 | 1,989 | 15.4 | 19.7 | 38.4 | 23.1 | 3.3 | 0.1 | 30,253 | 26,207 | 38,385 | 33,954 | 32,576 | 23,631 |
| LOGAN | 17,952 | 7,161 | 16.2 | 18.2 | 35.1 | 24.0 | 4.7 | 1.8 | 33,375 | 27,182 | 39,462 | 40,963 | 36,702 | 24,535 |
| MESA | 19,423 | 46,717 | 15.0 | 14.9 | 36.2 | 27.6 | 4.8 | 1.6 | 35,066 | 28,826 | 41,397 | 42,507 | 36,580 | 25,369 |
| MINERAL | 20,267 | 331 | 13.0 | 29.9 | 29.6 | 19.3 | 5.4 | 2.7 | 33,418 | 25,833 | 25,443 | 43,277 | 44,786 | 26,803 |
| MOFFAT | 19,013 | 4,844 | 12.9 | 7.1 | 42.6 | 29.3 | 6.5 | 1.7 | 38,082 | 31,942 | 45,853 | 45,179 | 38,812 | 23,147 |
| MONTEZUMA | 18,298 | 8,479 | 16.6 | 15.1 | 35.6 | 24.4 | 6.0 | 2.2 | 35,197 | 28,465 | 41,361 | 40,022 | 40,235 | 25,047 |
| MONTROSE | 18,949 | 12,675 | 15.4 | 16.6 | 36.2 | 23.8 | 5.7 | 2.4 | 35,226 | 30,305 | 41,374 | 44,318 | 37,906 | 22,033 |
| MORGAN | 16,270 | 9,676 | 17.3 | 17.0 | 38.6 | 21.9 | 3.9 | 1.4 | 31,912 | 27,432 | 38,186 | 38,736 | 34,177 | 21,782 |
| OTERO | 15,496 | 7,835 | 24.3 | 18.7 | 34.0 | 16.6 | 4.5 | 2.0 | 29,964 | 23,242 | 34,738 | 38,810 | 31,712 | 21,093 |
| OURAY | 22,129 | 1,476 | 10.0 | 8.9 | 37.9 | 34.2 | 7.8 | 1.3 | 39,339 | 34,833 | 39,953 | 45,772 | 43,737 | 26,705 |
| PARK | 25,695 | 5,996 | 9.2 | 5.0 | 33.1 | 39.6 | 10.1 | 3.0 | 45,557 | 39,808 | 45,139 | 51,047 | 44,116 | 33,942 |
| PHILLIPS | 16,415 | 1,802 | 15.6 | 22.3 | 37.7 | 21.4 | 2.7 | 0.4 | 29,281 | 25,459 | 32,424 | 37,854 | 31,864 | 22,741 |
| PITKIN | 45,314 | 6,297 | 6.2 | 8.6 | 26.5 | 32.9 | 13.3 | 12.5 | 62,841 | 41,210 | 59,075 | 59,957 | 66,458 | 56,125 |
| PROWERS | 14,496 | 5,269 | 20.6 | 18.4 | 36.9 | 20.1 | 3.5 | 0.5 | 29,079 | 23,031 | 34,337 | 36,033 | 30,450 | 22,282 |
| PUEBLO | 16,686 | 54,190 | 18.7 | 15.8 | 35.4 | 25.2 | 4.0 | 0.9 | 31,920 | 24,977 | 38,901 | 40,529 | 33,566 | 23,153 |
| RIO BLANCO | 22,756 | 2,306 | 9.9 | 9.8 | 40.0 | 29.1 | 7.3 | 3.9 | 42,950 | 34,260 | 44,288 | 52,122 | 42,712 | 31,213 |
| RIO GRANDE | 13,260 | 4,334 | 24.7 | 24.3 | 31.8 | 15.4 | 2.9 | 0.9 | 26,574 | 20,776 | 27,341 | 33,473 | 28,109 | 22,142 |
| ROUTT | 24,994 | 7,136 | 9.5 | 7.9 | 35.6 | 33.9 | 9.5 | 3.6 | 44,103 | 33,722 | 43,683 | 52,501 | 54,415 | 32,116 |
| SAGUACHE | 14,124 | 2,342 | 29.6 | 23.3 | 28.2 | 13.1 | 2.7 | 3.1 | 28,775 | 19,253 | 30,507 | 29,794 | 36,463 | 20,125 |
| SAN JUAN | 12,850 | 207 | 19.3 | 16.9 | 50.7 | 12.1 | 0.0 | 1.0 | 26,863 | 24,786 | 33,663 | 27,727 | 19,840 | 12,857 |
| SAN MIGUEL | 31,358 | 2,383 | 6.2 | 9.5 | 31.0 | 35.6 | 11.2 | 6.6 | 51,323 | 40,154 | 47,846 | 59,286 | 48,861 | 33,370 |
| SEDGWICK | 14,161 | 1,085 | 18.6 | 24.6 | 39.1 | 16.3 | 1.4 | 0.0 | 26,219 | 23,511 | 29,020 | 27,956 | 33,568 | 20,068 |
| SUMMIT | 26,410 | 8,193 | 5.8 | 8.4 | 31.3 | 39.3 | 11.4 | 3.8 | 47,564 | 38,275 | 49,694 | 57,084 | 52,060 | 40,195 |
| TELLER | 25,253 | 8,685 | 8.4 | 8.4 | 34.4 | 35.7 | 9.7 | 3.4 | 45,085 | 39,309 | 50,457 | 52,332 | 39,867 | 28,697 |
| WASHINGTON | 15,645 | 1,832 | 23.7 | 20.7 | 33.8 | 18.3 | 2.8 | 0.6 | 27,754 | 21,444 | 31,041 | 37,159 | 30,386 | 21,184 |
| WELD | 16,985 | 61,534 | 15.4 | 14.2 | 35.9 | 28.1 | 5.1 | 1.4 | 35,012 | 28,287 | 40,967 | 44,568 | 37,091 | 22,954 |
| YUMA | 14,206 | 3,745 | 23.8 | 17.2 | 38.1 | 17.6 | 2.7 | 0.7 | 27,567 | 22,969 | 31,343 | 32,672 | 32,030 | 20,103 |
| COLORADO | 26,360 | | 10.2 | 10.9 | 30.9 | 33.3 | 10.0 | 4.7 | 45,968 | 35,367 | 50,661 | 54,594 | 47,779 | 30,712 |
| UNITED STATES | 22,162 | | 14.5 | 12.5 | 32.3 | 29.8 | 7.4 | 3.5 | 40,748 | 34,503 | 44,969 | 49,579 | 43,409 | 27,339 |

| COUNTY | FINANCIAL SERVICES | | | | THE HOME | | | | | | ENTERTAINMENT | | | | | | PERSONAL | | | |
|---|---|---|---|---|---|---|---|---|---|---|---|---|---|---|---|---|---|---|---|---|
| | | | | | Home Improvements | | | Furnishings | | | | | | | | | | | | |
| | Auto Loan | Home Loan | Invest-ments | Retire-ment Plans | Home Repair | Lawn & Garden | Remodel-ing | Appli-ances | Elec-tronics | Furni-ture | Restau-rants | Sport-ing Goods | Theater & Concerts | Toys & Hobbies | Travel | Video Rental | Apparel | Auto After-market | Health Insur-ance | Pets & Supplies |
| ADAMS | 99 | 99 | 90 | 95 | 100 | 99 | 100 | 101 | 102 | 103 | 102 | 93 | 93 | 95 | 88 | 94 | 99 | 99 | 96 | 95 |
| ALAMOSA | 96 | 89 | 85 | 86 | 95 | 93 | 103 | 98 | 96 | 90 | 90 | 88 | 84 | 90 | 81 | 92 | 87 | 93 | 96 | 93 |
| ARAPAHOE | 104 | 114 | 100 | 111 | 104 | 108 | 103 | 105 | 109 | 113 | 113 | 101 | 102 | 100 | 98 | 96 | 112 | 107 | 98 | 99 |
| ARCHULETA | 101 | 81 | 85 | 91 | 97 | 98 | 120 | 103 | 98 | 90 | 90 | 94 | 85 | 95 | 80 | 94 | 91 | 93 | 103 | 96 |
| BACA | 97 | 63 | 69 | 78 | 92 | 92 | 112 | 97 | 92 | 74 | 76 | 88 | 73 | 88 | 70 | 92 | 78 | 86 | 103 | 90 |
| BENT | 95 | 63 | 70 | 76 | 92 | 92 | 110 | 96 | 93 | 75 | 76 | 84 | 73 | 86 | 70 | 92 | 78 | 86 | 102 | 88 |
| BOULDER | 103 | 113 | 101 | 110 | 104 | 107 | 104 | 104 | 108 | 110 | 110 | 99 | 100 | 99 | 97 | 96 | 110 | 106 | 98 | 98 |
| CHAFFEE | 98 | 75 | 84 | 85 | 97 | 96 | 113 | 99 | 95 | 85 | 84 | 88 | 81 | 91 | 78 | 93 | 85 | 90 | 102 | 92 |
| CHEYENNE | 98 | 73 | 76 | 81 | 92 | 91 | 114 | 98 | 94 | 83 | 83 | 90 | 78 | 91 | 72 | 93 | 83 | 89 | 100 | 92 |
| CLEAR CREEK | 105 | 107 | 98 | 109 | 103 | 106 | 111 | 106 | 109 | 109 | 108 | 101 | 101 | 101 | 94 | 97 | 109 | 106 | 100 | 100 |
| CONEJOS | 97 | 76 | 79 | 80 | 93 | 93 | 109 | 99 | 94 | 84 | 83 | 88 | 80 | 89 | 77 | 92 | 81 | 90 | 100 | 93 |
| COSTILLA | 97 | 83 | 85 | 82 | 99 | 97 | 111 | 99 | 89 | 99 | 86 | 91 | 84 | 85 | 89 | 93 | 87 | 92 | 97 | 88 |
| CROWLEY | 93 | 63 | 71 | 73 | 93 | 91 | 108 | 95 | 94 | 77 | 76 | 81 | 73 | 83 | 71 | 92 | 77 | 85 | 100 | 86 |
| CUSTER | 102 | 72 | 75 | 89 | 95 | 95 | 132 | 103 | 95 | 79 | 81 | 95 | 79 | 96 | 74 | 94 | 85 | 90 | 106 | 97 |
| DELTA | 96 | 69 | 80 | 79 | 95 | 94 | 111 | 98 | 93 | 79 | 80 | 86 | 77 | 88 | 75 | 92 | 80 | 87 | 102 | 90 |
| DENVER | 97 | 103 | 103 | 99 | 104 | 103 | 97 | 100 | 99 | 101 | 98 | 91 | 93 | 91 | 95 | 93 | 97 | 98 | 96 | 93 |
| DOLORES | 99 | 71 | 79 | 83 | 94 | 93 | 119 | 99 | 95 | 80 | 82 | 90 | 78 | 92 | 73 | 93 | 83 | 89 | 102 | 93 |
| DOUGLAS | 110 | 126 | 100 | 121 | 105 | 114 | 107 | 112 | 119 | 126 | 128 | 110 | 112 | 106 | 103 | 100 | 128 | 117 | 100 | 104 |
| EAGLE | 102 | 109 | 85 | 99 | 97 | 99 | 99 | 103 | 107 | 108 | 110 | 98 | 96 | 97 | 90 | 96 | 107 | 104 | 94 | 98 |
| ELBERT | 105 | 101 | 90 | 102 | 100 | 102 | 109 | 105 | 108 | 106 | 107 | 100 | 98 | 100 | 89 | 97 | 107 | 104 | 100 | 100 |
| EL PASO | 100 | 106 | 96 | 102 | 102 | 103 | 100 | 102 | 104 | 106 | 106 | 96 | 96 | 96 | 93 | 95 | 104 | 102 | 96 | 96 |
| FREMONT | 96 | 74 | 85 | 82 | 96 | 95 | 110 | 98 | 95 | 84 | 83 | 86 | 80 | 89 | 77 | 92 | 82 | 89 | 101 | 90 |
| GARFIELD | 100 | 94 | 92 | 94 | 99 | 99 | 107 | 102 | 102 | 100 | 99 | 94 | 92 | 96 | 86 | 95 | 97 | 98 | 98 | 96 |
| GILPIN | 104 | 101 | 100 | 105 | 104 | 105 | 114 | 105 | 105 | 104 | 104 | 99 | 98 | 100 | 93 | 96 | 105 | 103 | 102 | 100 |
| GRAND | 100 | 88 | 83 | 90 | 96 | 96 | 112 | 101 | 99 | 93 | 93 | 93 | 86 | 94 | 81 | 94 | 92 | 95 | 99 | 95 |
| GUNNISON | 98 | 95 | 86 | 92 | 96 | 95 | 104 | 98 | 98 | 94 | 95 | 90 | 86 | 92 | 83 | 92 | 93 | 95 | 95 | 94 |
| HINSDALE | 102 | 72 | 75 | 89 | 95 | 95 | 132 | 103 | 95 | 79 | 81 | 95 | 79 | 96 | 74 | 94 | 85 | 90 | 106 | 97 |
| HUERFANO | 95 | 66 | 78 | 78 | 95 | 94 | 108 | 97 | 92 | 78 | 77 | 85 | 76 | 86 | 74 | 91 | 78 | 86 | 101 | 89 |
| JACKSON | 99 | 74 | 81 | 84 | 95 | 94 | 124 | 100 | 96 | 83 | 83 | 90 | 80 | 92 | 76 | 93 | 85 | 90 | 101 | 94 |
| JEFFERSON | 103 | 110 | 100 | 108 | 104 | 107 | 103 | 105 | 107 | 111 | 111 | 99 | 101 | 99 | 96 | 96 | 110 | 106 | 98 | 98 |
| KIOWA | 97 | 63 | 69 | 78 | 92 | 92 | 112 | 97 | 92 | 74 | 76 | 88 | 73 | 88 | 70 | 92 | 78 | 86 | 103 | 90 |
| KIT CARSON | 97 | 66 | 72 | 79 | 92 | 92 | 112 | 97 | 94 | 77 | 78 | 87 | 75 | 88 | 71 | 93 | 80 | 87 | 102 | 90 |
| LAKE | 96 | 91 | 87 | 87 | 97 | 95 | 103 | 98 | 97 | 95 | 94 | 88 | 87 | 92 | 83 | 93 | 92 | 94 | 95 | 92 |
| LA PLATA | 98 | 91 | 92 | 91 | 99 | 97 | 107 | 99 | 97 | 94 | 93 | 90 | 87 | 92 | 84 | 92 | 92 | 94 | 97 | 94 |
| LARIMER | 102 | 105 | 95 | 103 | 102 | 102 | 104 | 102 | 104 | 104 | 104 | 96 | 95 | 96 | 91 | 94 | 103 | 101 | 97 | 97 |
| LAS ANIMAS | 95 | 73 | 79 | 80 | 97 | 94 | 107 | 97 | 93 | 83 | 80 | 85 | 79 | 86 | 78 | 91 | 81 | 88 | 99 | 89 |
| LINCOLN | 97 | 66 | 71 | 79 | 92 | 91 | 112 | 97 | 93 | 76 | 78 | 89 | 75 | 89 | 70 | 92 | 79 | 87 | 102 | 91 |
| LOGAN | 98 | 84 | 87 | 90 | 98 | 97 | 106 | 99 | 97 | 91 | 90 | 91 | 87 | 93 | 81 | 93 | 90 | 93 | 100 | 93 |
| MESA | 99 | 91 | 95 | 95 | 101 | 100 | 107 | 101 | 100 | 97 | 95 | 92 | 90 | 94 | 87 | 93 | 95 | 96 | 99 | 94 |
| MINERAL | 102 | 72 | 75 | 89 | 95 | 95 | 132 | 103 | 95 | 79 | 81 | 95 | 79 | 96 | 74 | 94 | 85 | 90 | 106 | 97 |
| MOFFAT | 97 | 85 | 78 | 84 | 94 | 92 | 105 | 98 | 97 | 91 | 91 | 89 | 84 | 91 | 78 | 93 | 89 | 93 | 96 | 92 |
| MONTEZUMA | 98 | 77 | 80 | 84 | 96 | 93 | 114 | 99 | 97 | 88 | 86 | 89 | 82 | 92 | 76 | 93 | 87 | 91 | 99 | 93 |
| MONTROSE | 97 | 74 | 79 | 82 | 95 | 93 | 112 | 98 | 95 | 84 | 83 | 88 | 80 | 90 | 75 | 93 | 84 | 89 | 100 | 92 |
| MORGAN | 97 | 75 | 79 | 81 | 94 | 92 | 111 | 98 | 95 | 84 | 84 | 87 | 79 | 90 | 75 | 92 | 83 | 89 | 99 | 92 |
| OTERO | 95 | 74 | 79 | 79 | 94 | 93 | 106 | 97 | 95 | 83 | 82 | 84 | 79 | 87 | 76 | 92 | 81 | 89 | 99 | 90 |
| OURAY | 102 | 70 | 74 | 85 | 93 | 93 | 121 | 101 | 94 | 78 | 81 | 95 | 78 | 95 | 72 | 94 | 84 | 90 | 105 | 96 |
| PARK | 105 | 99 | 94 | 104 | 101 | 103 | 115 | 106 | 107 | 104 | 104 | 100 | 98 | 101 | 90 | 97 | 106 | 104 | 101 | 100 |
| PHILLIPS | 97 | 65 | 72 | 79 | 92 | 92 | 113 | 97 | 93 | 75 | 77 | 88 | 74 | 89 | 70 | 92 | 79 | 87 | 103 | 90 |
| PITKIN | 109 | 140 | 128 | 139 | 119 | 130 | 115 | 111 | 119 | 126 | 130 | 109 | 121 | 106 | 123 | 98 | 133 | 120 | 105 | 103 |
| PROWERS | 97 | 82 | 81 | 84 | 95 | 94 | 105 | 99 | 97 | 88 | 88 | 88 | 83 | 90 | 78 | 93 | 86 | 92 | 99 | 93 |
| PUEBLO | 96 | 88 | 92 | 88 | 101 | 98 | 102 | 99 | 96 | 95 | 91 | 88 | 88 | 91 | 85 | 92 | 90 | 93 | 97 | 92 |
| RIO BLANCO | 99 | 84 | 76 | 86 | 93 | 92 | 106 | 99 | 99 | 91 | 91 | 91 | 84 | 93 | 77 | 94 | 90 | 94 | 97 | 93 |
| RIO GRANDE | 97 | 70 | 75 | 79 | 93 | 92 | 111 | 98 | 94 | 79 | 80 | 87 | 77 | 88 | 73 | 93 | 80 | 88 | 101 | 91 |
| ROUTT | 100 | 98 | 85 | 94 | 97 | 97 | 103 | 101 | 102 | 100 | 101 | 94 | 91 | 95 | 85 | 95 | 99 | 99 | 95 | 96 |
| SAGUACHE | 98 | 77 | 85 | 86 | 95 | 97 | 110 | 100 | 95 | 83 | 84 | 89 | 81 | 90 | 79 | 93 | 83 | 91 | 103 | 94 |
| SAN JUAN | 99 | 80 | 82 | 84 | 95 | 92 | 117 | 100 | 97 | 90 | 89 | 91 | 83 | 94 | 76 | 94 | 88 | 92 | 98 | 95 |
| SAN MIGUEL | 103 | 106 | 95 | 104 | 102 | 104 | 107 | 104 | 106 | 107 | 107 | 100 | 98 | 99 | 92 | 96 | 107 | 104 | 99 | 99 |
| SEDGWICK | 97 | 63 | 69 | 78 | 92 | 92 | 112 | 97 | 92 | 74 | 76 | 88 | 73 | 88 | 70 | 92 | 78 | 86 | 103 | 90 |
| SUMMIT | 100 | 105 | 80 | 94 | 95 | 96 | 95 | 101 | 103 | 104 | 107 | 95 | 92 | 95 | 86 | 95 | 103 | 101 | 92 | 96 |
| TELLER | 104 | 97 | 88 | 100 | 99 | 100 | 113 | 105 | 106 | 102 | 102 | 98 | 95 | 99 | 87 | 97 | 103 | 102 | 100 | 99 |
| WASHINGTON | 97 | 64 | 70 | 78 | 92 | 92 | 111 | 97 | 92 | 74 | 76 | 88 | 74 | 89 | 70 | 92 | 78 | 86 | 103 | 90 |
| WELD | 99 | 91 | 88 | 92 | 97 | 96 | 106 | 100 | 99 | 94 | 94 | 91 | 87 | 93 | 83 | 93 | 93 | 95 | 97 | 95 |
| YUMA | 98 | 65 | 72 | 80 | 92 | 92 | 114 | 98 | 93 | 75 | 78 | 90 | 75 | 90 | 70 | 92 | 80 | 87 | 103 | 92 |
| COLORADO | 101 | 104 | 97 | 103 | 102 | 103 | 103 | 103 | 104 | 105 | 104 | 96 | 96 | 96 | 92 | 95 | 103 | 101 | 98 | 96 |
| UNITED STATES | 100 | 100 | 100 | 100 | 100 | 100 | 100 | 100 | 100 | 100 | 100 | 100 | 100 | 100 | 100 | 100 | 100 | 100 | 100 | 100 |

| COUNTY | FIPS Code | MSA Code | DMA Code | POPULATION 1990 | POPULATION 2000 | POPULATION 2005 | 1990-2000 ANNUAL CHANGE % Rate | 1990-2000 ANNUAL CHANGE State Rank | RACE (%) White 1990 | RACE (%) White 2000 | RACE (%) Black 1990 | RACE (%) Black 2000 | RACE (%) Asian/Pacific 1990 | RACE (%) Asian/Pacific 2000 |
|---|---|---|---|---|---|---|---|---|---|---|---|---|---|---|
| FAIRFIELD | 001 | 5483 | 501 | 827,645 | 845,014 | 862,461 | 0.2 | 5 | 84.6 | 81.7 | 9.8 | 10.6 | 2.1 | 3.4 |
| HARTFORD | 003 | 3283 | 533 | 851,783 | 830,147 | 831,677 | -0.3 | 7 | 83.5 | 80.4 | 10.2 | 11.1 | 1.6 | 2.5 |
| LITCHFIELD | 005 | 0000 | 533 | 174,092 | 183,316 | 187,990 | 0.5 | 2 | 97.9 | 97.1 | 0.9 | 1.1 | 0.8 | 1.4 |
| MIDDLESEX | 007 | 3283 | 533 | 143,196 | 152,818 | 159,253 | 0.6 | 1 | 93.9 | 92.7 | 4.2 | 4.6 | 1.1 | 1.7 |
| NEW HAVEN | 009 | 5483 | 533 | 804,219 | 793,436 | 794,309 | -0.1 | 6 | 85.5 | 82.9 | 10.2 | 11.1 | 1.3 | 2.1 |
| NEW LONDON | 011 | 5523 | 533 | 254,957 | 245,057 | 239,839 | -0.4 | 8 | 91.9 | 90.0 | 4.8 | 5.2 | 1.3 | 2.2 |
| TOLLAND | 013 | 3283 | 533 | 128,699 | 133,789 | 139,160 | 0.4 | 3 | 95.4 | 94.2 | 2.0 | 2.1 | 1.9 | 2.9 |
| WINDHAM | 015 | 0000 | 533 | 102,525 | 105,485 | 106,770 | 0.3 | 4 | 95.9 | 94.6 | 1.1 | 1.2 | 0.7 | 1.2 |
| CONNECTICUT | | | | | | | 0.0 | | 87.0 | 84.6 | 8.3 | 9.0 | 1.5 | 2.5 |
| UNITED STATES | | | | | | | 1.0 | | 80.3 | 77.9 | 12.1 | 12.4 | 2.9 | 3.9 |

| COUNTY | % HISPANIC ORIGIN | | 2000 AGE DISTRIBUTION (%) | | | | | | | | | | MEDIAN AGE | | 2000 Males/ Females (×100) |
|---|---|---|---|---|---|---|---|---|---|---|---|---|---|---|---|
| | 1990 | 2000 | 0-4 | 5-9 | 10-14 | 15-19 | 20-24 | 25-44 | 45-64 | 65-84 | 85+ | 18+ | 1990 | 2000 | |
| FAIRFIELD | 8.6 | 11.3 | 6.4 | 7.0 | 7.8 | 6.1 | 4.8 | 30.0 | 23.8 | 12.2 | 1.9 | 75.2 | 35.5 | 38.1 | 94.0 |
| HARTFORD | 8.4 | 11.1 | 6.5 | 7.2 | 7.4 | 6.3 | 5.3 | 30.3 | 21.9 | 13.0 | 2.1 | 75.5 | 34.5 | 37.3 | 92.7 |
| LITCHFIELD | 1.1 | 1.9 | 6.5 | 7.5 | 7.8 | 6.0 | 4.3 | 30.1 | 23.5 | 12.3 | 2.0 | 74.6 | 35.7 | 38.1 | 96.5 |
| MIDDLESEX | 2.0 | 3.0 | 6.2 | 7.0 | 7.3 | 6.4 | 5.0 | 31.3 | 23.0 | 11.8 | 2.1 | 76.0 | 34.8 | 37.7 | 95.7 |
| NEW HAVEN | 6.3 | 8.6 | 6.7 | 7.3 | 7.5 | 6.4 | 5.6 | 30.2 | 21.1 | 13.0 | 2.2 | 75.1 | 34.2 | 36.8 | 92.7 |
| NEW LONDON | 3.3 | 4.8 | 7.1 | 7.3 | 7.1 | 6.5 | 6.4 | 31.4 | 21.2 | 11.4 | 1.6 | 75.1 | 32.5 | 35.6 | 100.7 |
| TOLLAND | 1.7 | 2.6 | 6.2 | 7.0 | 7.3 | 7.7 | 8.1 | 30.5 | 23.1 | 9.1 | 1.1 | 76.3 | 31.5 | 35.0 | 97.8 |
| WINDHAM | 4.2 | 5.9 | 7.2 | 8.2 | 8.3 | 7.1 | 5.9 | 29.8 | 20.8 | 10.8 | 1.9 | 72.4 | 32.7 | 35.0 | 96.3 |
| CONNECTICUT | 6.5 | 8.7 | 6.6 | 7.2 | 7.5 | 6.4 | 5.4 | 30.3 | 22.3 | 12.4 | 2.0 | 75.2 | 34.4 | 37.2 | 94.3 |
| UNITED STATES | 9.0 | 11.8 | 6.9 | 7.2 | 7.2 | 7.2 | 6.7 | 29.9 | 22.2 | 11.1 | 1.6 | 74.6 | 32.9 | 35.7 | 95.6 |

| COUNTY | HOUSEHOLDS | | | | | FAMILIES | | | MEDIAN HOUSEHOLD INCOME | | | |
|---|---|---|---|---|---|---|---|---|---|---|---|---|
| | 1990 | 2000 | 2005 | % Annual Rate 1990-2000 | 2000 Average HH Size | 1990 | 2000 | % Annual Rate 1990-2000 | 2000 | 2005 | 2000 National Rank | 2000 State Rank |
| FAIRFIELD | 305,011 | 316,165 | 324,996 | 0.4 | 2.63 | 219,031 | 220,335 | 0.1 | 65,240 | 71,702 | 34 | 1 |
| HARTFORD | 324,691 | 319,281 | 321,304 | -0.2 | 2.53 | 224,344 | 212,925 | -0.6 | 49,242 | 56,635 | 215 | 7 |
| LITCHFIELD | 66,371 | 70,675 | 72,890 | 0.8 | 2.56 | 47,776 | 48,846 | 0.3 | 54,068 | 65,258 | 136 | 4 |
| MIDDLESEX | 54,651 | 59,246 | 62,185 | 1.0 | 2.48 | 37,966 | 39,518 | 0.5 | 55,714 | 64,541 | 112 | 3 |
| NEW HAVEN | 304,730 | 304,553 | 306,940 | 0.0 | 2.52 | 209,888 | 202,246 | -0.4 | 49,509 | 58,108 | 211 | 6 |
| NEW LONDON | 93,245 | 92,087 | 90,819 | -0.2 | 2.54 | 66,385 | 63,204 | -0.6 | 51,542 | 61,159 | 178 | 5 |
| TOLLAND | 44,309 | 47,806 | 50,230 | 0.9 | 2.62 | 32,065 | 33,361 | 0.5 | 58,367 | 70,904 | 86 | 2 |
| WINDHAM | 37,471 | 38,985 | 39,700 | 0.5 | 2.63 | 27,038 | 27,134 | 0.0 | 45,219 | 55,272 | 345 | 8 |
| CONNECTICUT | | | | 0.2 | 2.56 | | | -0.2 | 53,506 | 61,897 | | |
| UNITED STATES | | | | 1.4 | 2.59 | | | 1.1 | 41,914 | 49,127 | | |

| COUNTY | 2000 Per Capita Income | 2000 HH Income Base | 2000 HOUSEHOLD INCOME DISTRIBUTION (%) | | | | | | 2000 AVERAGE DISPOSABLE INCOME BY AGE OF HOUSEHOLDER | | | | | |
|---|---|---|---|---|---|---|---|---|---|---|---|---|---|---|
| | | | Less than $15,000 | $15,000 to $24,999 | $25,000 to $49,999 | $50,000 to $99,999 | $100,000 to $149,999 | $150,000 or More | All Ages | <35 | 35-44 | 45-54 | 55-64 | 65+ |
| FAIRFIELD | 42,465 | 316,165 | 7.8 | 6.5 | 21.7 | 34.4 | 14.1 | 15.4 | 67,115 | 51,344 | 61,693 | 71,449 | 67,913 | 43,799 |
| HARTFORD | 25,410 | 319,275 | 11.7 | 9.4 | 29.7 | 36.0 | 8.9 | 4.2 | 43,768 | 37,544 | 46,539 | 54,798 | 48,924 | 27,669 |
| LITCHFIELD | 29,078 | 70,675 | 7.8 | 7.2 | 29.6 | 39.2 | 10.7 | 5.5 | 48,358 | 42,755 | 50,319 | 57,793 | 54,128 | 30,375 |
| MIDDLESEX | 27,952 | 59,246 | 7.3 | 7.3 | 27.8 | 42.9 | 10.4 | 4.3 | 47,166 | 43,995 | 49,786 | 56,541 | 51,279 | 29,696 |
| NEW HAVEN | 25,015 | 304,553 | 12.1 | 8.8 | 29.7 | 36.2 | 9.2 | 4.1 | 43,509 | 38,110 | 46,910 | 54,437 | 48,185 | 27,553 |
| NEW LONDON | 25,527 | 92,087 | 8.4 | 8.1 | 31.4 | 38.5 | 9.9 | 3.7 | 44,614 | 38,793 | 46,634 | 56,089 | 49,422 | 29,559 |
| TOLLAND | 25,891 | 47,806 | 7.3 | 6.1 | 26.1 | 45.4 | 11.9 | 3.4 | 47,337 | 41,700 | 50,601 | 57,349 | 51,220 | 28,767 |
| WINDHAM | 21,207 | 38,985 | 12.1 | 9.6 | 34.6 | 34.8 | 6.8 | 2.1 | 38,804 | 34,888 | 42,180 | 47,685 | 44,960 | 23,596 |
| CONNECTICUT | 29,921 | | 10.0 | 8.1 | 27.7 | 36.6 | 10.6 | 7.0 | 50,081 | 41,488 | 50,857 | 59,429 | 54,470 | 31,943 |
| UNITED STATES | 22,162 | | 14.5 | 12.5 | 32.3 | 29.8 | 7.4 | 3.5 | 40,748 | 34,503 | 44,969 | 49,579 | 43,409 | 27,339 |

# SPENDING POTENTIAL INDEXES

# E

| COUNTY | FINANCIAL SERVICES | | | | THE HOME | | | | | | ENTERTAINMENT | | | | | | PERSONAL | | | |
|---|---|---|---|---|---|---|---|---|---|---|---|---|---|---|---|---|---|---|---|---|
| | | | | | Home Improvements | | | Furnishings | | | | | | | | | | | | |
| | Auto Loan | Home Loan | Investments | Retirement Plans | Home Repair | Lawn & Garden | Remodeling | Appliances | Electronics | Furniture | Restaurants | Sporting Goods | Theater & Concerts | Toys & Hobbies | Travel | Video Rental | Apparel | Auto Aftermarket | Health Insurance | Pets & Supplies |
| FAIRFIELD | 108 | 128 | 126 | 130 | 107 | 115 | 99 | 106 | 112 | 120 | 124 | 115 | 126 | 113 | 123 | 104 | 130 | 117 | 108 | 110 |
| HARTFORD | 101 | 105 | 108 | 104 | 98 | 99 | 91 | 100 | 100 | 107 | 106 | 104 | 107 | 104 | 103 | 101 | 109 | 102 | 102 | 103 |
| LITCHFIELD | 103 | 103 | 105 | 104 | 97 | 98 | 95 | 101 | 102 | 106 | 108 | 105 | 107 | 107 | 100 | 101 | 110 | 103 | 103 | 105 |
| MIDDLESEX | 102 | 102 | 102 | 102 | 95 | 96 | 93 | 100 | 101 | 104 | 106 | 104 | 105 | 106 | 98 | 101 | 108 | 102 | 102 | 105 |
| NEW HAVEN | 100 | 103 | 107 | 103 | 98 | 98 | 91 | 99 | 99 | 105 | 104 | 103 | 105 | 104 | 102 | 100 | 107 | 101 | 102 | 103 |
| NEW LONDON | 100 | 99 | 102 | 99 | 95 | 95 | 92 | 99 | 99 | 101 | 103 | 101 | 102 | 104 | 97 | 100 | 105 | 99 | 102 | 103 |
| TOLLAND | 102 | 103 | 101 | 103 | 95 | 96 | 94 | 100 | 102 | 105 | 108 | 104 | 105 | 107 | 98 | 101 | 110 | 103 | 102 | 105 |
| WINDHAM | 99 | 91 | 93 | 91 | 92 | 90 | 94 | 97 | 95 | 96 | 96 | 98 | 96 | 101 | 90 | 99 | 98 | 95 | 100 | 101 |
| CONNECTICUT | 103 | 110 | 112 | 110 | 100 | 102 | 94 | 101 | 103 | 109 | 110 | 106 | 111 | 106 | 107 | 101 | 113 | 105 | 103 | 105 |
| UNITED STATES | 100 | 100 | 100 | 100 | 100 | 100 | 100 | 100 | 100 | 100 | 100 | 100 | 100 | 100 | 100 | 100 | 100 | 100 | 100 | 100 |

# POPULATION CHANGE

| COUNTY | FIPS Code | MSA Code | DMA Code | POPULATION 1990 | POPULATION 2000 | POPULATION 2005 | 1990-2000 ANNUAL CHANGE % Rate | 1990-2000 ANNUAL CHANGE State Rank | RACE (%) White 1990 | White 2000 | Black 1990 | Black 2000 | Asian/Pacific 1990 | Asian/Pacific 2000 |
|---|---|---|---|---|---|---|---|---|---|---|---|---|---|---|
| KENT | 001 | 2190 | 504 | 110,993 | 127,518 | 134,868 | 1.4 | 2 | 78.7 | 75.1 | 18.6 | 20.9 | 1.3 | 2.1 |
| NEW CASTLE | 003 | 9160 | 504 | 441,946 | 491,415 | 512,681 | 1.0 | 3 | 80.4 | 76.4 | 16.5 | 18.9 | 1.6 | 2.5 |
| SUSSEX | 005 | 0000 | 576 | 113,229 | 143,294 | 158,350 | 2.3 | 1 | 81.6 | 78.9 | 16.8 | 19.0 | 0.5 | 0.8 |
| DELAWARE | | | | | | | 1.3 | | 80.3 | 76.7 | 16.9 | 19.3 | 1.4 | 2.1 |
| UNITED STATES | | | | | | | 1.0 | | 80.3 | 77.9 | 12.1 | 12.4 | 2.9 | 3.9 |

# DELAWARE

# B

# POPULATION COMPOSITION

| COUNTY | % HISPANIC ORIGIN | | 2000 AGE DISTRIBUTION (%) | | | | | | | | | | MEDIAN AGE | | 2000 Males/ Females (×100) |
|---|---|---|---|---|---|---|---|---|---|---|---|---|---|---|---|
| | 1990 | 2000 | 0-4 | 5-9 | 10-14 | 15-19 | 20-24 | 25-44 | 45-64 | 65-84 | 85+ | 18+ | 1990 | 2000 | |
| KENT | 2.3 | 3.8 | 7.5 | 7.3 | 6.9 | 6.9 | 6.6 | 33.1 | 20.5 | 9.9 | 1.2 | 74.5 | 31.1 | 34.0 | 95.5 |
| NEW CASTLE | 2.7 | 4.4 | 6.4 | 6.6 | 6.8 | 6.9 | 6.8 | 32.8 | 21.5 | 10.8 | 1.3 | 76.8 | 32.5 | 35.8 | 94.1 |
| SUSSEX | 1.3 | 2.2 | 6.2 | 6.5 | 6.6 | 6.0 | 4.9 | 28.4 | 23.2 | 16.6 | 1.7 | 77.2 | 36.4 | 39.6 | 95.4 |
| DELAWARE | 2.4 | 3.9 | 6.5 | 6.7 | 6.8 | 6.7 | 6.4 | 32.0 | 21.7 | 11.7 | 1.4 | 76.5 | 32.9 | 36.2 | 94.6 |
| UNITED STATES | 9.0 | 11.8 | 6.9 | 7.2 | 7.2 | 7.2 | 6.7 | 29.9 | 22.2 | 11.1 | 1.6 | 74.6 | 32.9 | 35.7 | 95.6 |

# HOUSEHOLDS

| COUNTY | HOUSEHOLDS | | | | | FAMILIES | | | MEDIAN HOUSEHOLD INCOME | | | |
|---|---|---|---|---|---|---|---|---|---|---|---|---|
| | 1990 | 2000 | 2005 | % Annual Rate 1990-2000 | 2000 Average HH Size | 1990 | 2000 | % Annual Rate 1990-2000 | 2000 | 2005 | 2000 National Rank | 2000 State Rank |
| KENT | 39,655 | 47,211 | 50,723 | 2.1 | 2.62 | 29,343 | 33,796 | 1.7 | 41,669 | 50,793 | 539 | 2 |
| NEW CASTLE | 164,161 | 189,017 | 200,887 | 1.7 | 2.52 | 114,508 | 127,293 | 1.3 | 52,631 | 60,130 | 158 | 1 |
| SUSSEX | 43,681 | 56,969 | 64,017 | 3.3 | 2.47 | 32,016 | 40,127 | 2.8 | 36,442 | 40,574 | 1054 | 3 |
| DELAWARE | | | | 2.1 | 2.53 | | | 1.7 | 47,219 | 54,184 | | |
| UNITED STATES | | | | 1.4 | 2.59 | | | 1.1 | 41,914 | 49,127 | | |

# INCOME

| COUNTY | 2000 Per Capita Income | 2000 HH Income Base | 2000 HOUSEHOLD INCOME DISTRIBUTION (%) Less than $15,000 | $15,000 to $24,999 | $25,000 to $49,999 | $50,000 to $99,999 | $100,000 to $149,999 | $150,000 or More | 2000 AVERAGE DISPOSABLE INCOME BY AGE OF HOUSEHOLDER All Ages | <35 | 35-44 | 45-54 | 55-64 | 65+ |
|---|---|---|---|---|---|---|---|---|---|---|---|---|---|---|
| KENT | 19,567 | 47,211 | 11.7 | 12.5 | 36.6 | 31.2 | 6.1 | 1.9 | 37,892 | 31,426 | 41,892 | 47,592 | 41,616 | 26,807 |
| NEW CASTLE | 27,367 | 189,017 | 8.4 | 8.0 | 30.4 | 38.1 | 10.7 | 4.4 | 47,051 | 39,654 | 50,034 | 57,148 | 50,734 | 33,275 |
| SUSSEX | 18,941 | 56,969 | 15.0 | 16.1 | 36.2 | 25.8 | 5.2 | 1.8 | 34,568 | 31,543 | 41,470 | 41,782 | 36,640 | 24,386 |
| DELAWARE | 24,474 | | 10.2 | 10.3 | 32.5 | 34.6 | 8.9 | 3.5 | 43,151 | 36,896 | 47,294 | 52,745 | 46,227 | 30,023 |
| UNITED STATES | 22,162 | | 14.5 | 12.5 | 32.3 | 29.8 | 7.4 | 3.5 | 40,748 | 34,503 | 44,969 | 49,579 | 43,409 | 27,339 |

| COUNTY | FINANCIAL SERVICES | | | | THE HOME | | | | | | ENTERTAINMENT | | | | | | PERSONAL | | | |
|---|---|---|---|---|---|---|---|---|---|---|---|---|---|---|---|---|---|---|---|---|
| | | | | | Home Improvements | | | Furnishings | | | | | | | | | | | | |
| | Auto Loan | Home Loan | Invest-ments | Retire-ment Plans | Home Repair | Lawn & Garden | Remodel-ing | Appli-ances | Elec-tronics | Furni-ture | Restau-rants | Sport-ing Goods | Theater & Concerts | Toys & Hobbies | Travel | Video Rental | Apparel | Auto After-market | Health Insur-ance | Pets & Supplies |
| KENT | 97 | 89 | 91 | 86 | 97 | 94 | 104 | 96 | 94 | 92 | 94 | 95 | 91 | 98 | 80 | 97 | 91 | 94 | 97 | 99 |
| NEW CASTLE | 100 | 106 | 106 | 103 | 105 | 105 | 99 | 100 | 100 | 104 | 106 | 102 | 103 | 103 | 94 | 99 | 105 | 103 | 99 | 102 |
| SUSSEX | 99 | 81 | 95 | 89 | 99 | 99 | 114 | 99 | 94 | 87 | 90 | 97 | 90 | 100 | 80 | 97 | 89 | 93 | 104 | 101 |
| DELAWARE | 99 | 99 | 102 | 98 | 103 | 102 | 102 | 99 | 98 | 99 | 101 | 100 | 99 | 101 | 89 | 99 | 100 | 100 | 100 | 101 |
| UNITED STATES | 100 | 100 | 100 | 100 | 100 | 100 | 100 | 100 | 100 | 100 | 100 | 100 | 100 | 100 | 100 | 100 | 100 | 100 | 100 | 100 |

| COUNTY | FIPS Code | MSA Code | DMA Code | POPULATION 1990 | POPULATION 2000 | POPULATION 2005 | 1990-2000 ANNUAL CHANGE % Rate | 1990-2000 ANNUAL CHANGE State Rank | RACE (%) White 1990 | White 2000 | Black 1990 | Black 2000 | Asian/Pacific 1990 | Asian/Pacific 2000 |
|---|---|---|---|---|---|---|---|---|---|---|---|---|---|---|
| DISTRICT OF COLUMBIA | 001 | 8840 | 511 | 606,900 | 513,618 | 486,620 | -1.6 | 1 | 29.6 | 31.7 | 65.8 | 61.8 | 1.8 | 3.0 |
| DISTRICT OF COLUMBIA | | | | | | | -1.6 | | 29.6 | 31.7 | 65.8 | 61.8 | 1.9 | 3.0 |
| UNITED STATES | | | | | | | 1.0 | | 80.3 | 77.9 | 12.1 | 12.4 | 2.9 | 3.9 |

| COUNTY | % HISPANIC ORIGIN | | 2000 AGE DISTRIBUTION (%) | | | | | | | | | | MEDIAN AGE | | 2000 Males/ Females (×100) |
|---|---|---|---|---|---|---|---|---|---|---|---|---|---|---|---|
| | 1990 | 2000 | 0-4 | 5-9 | 10-14 | 15-19 | 20-24 | 25-44 | 45-64 | 65-84 | 85+ | 18+ | 1990 | 2000 | |
| DISTRICT OF COLUMBIA | 5.4 | 7.3 | 5.1 | 6.0 | 4.5 | 4.7 | 6.3 | 35.1 | 24.3 | 12.1 | 1.8 | 82.4 | 33.5 | 38.0 | 88.0 |
| DISTRICT OF COLUMBIA | 5.4 | 7.3 | 5.1 | 6.0 | 4.5 | 4.7 | 6.3 | 35.1 | 24.3 | 12.1 | 1.8 | 82.4 | 33.5 | 38.0 | 88.1 |
| UNITED STATES | 9.0 | 11.8 | 6.9 | 7.2 | 7.2 | 7.2 | 6.7 | 29.9 | 22.2 | 11.1 | 1.6 | 74.6 | 32.9 | 35.7 | 95.6 |

| COUNTY | HOUSEHOLDS | | | | | FAMILIES | | | MEDIAN HOUSEHOLD INCOME | | | |
|---|---|---|---|---|---|---|---|---|---|---|---|---|
| | 1990 | 2000 | 2005 | % Annual Rate 1990-2000 | 2000 Average HH Size | 1990 | 2000 | % Annual Rate 1990-2000 | 2000 | 2005 | 2000 National Rank | 2000 State Rank |
| DISTRICT OF COLUMBIA | 249,634 | 224,159 | 218,341 | -1.3 | 2.12 | 122,087 | 106,192 | -1.7 | 40,143 | 45,439 | 660 | 1 |
| DISTRICT OF COLUMBIA | | | | -1.3 | 2.12 | | | -1.7 | 40,143 | 45,439 | | |
| UNITED STATES | | | | 1.4 | 2.59 | | | 1.1 | 41,914 | 49,127 | | |

| COUNTY | 2000 Per Capita Income | 2000 HH Income Base | 2000 HOUSEHOLD INCOME DISTRIBUTION (%) Less than $15,000 | $15,000 to $24,999 | $25,000 to $49,999 | $50,000 to $99,999 | $100,000 to $149,999 | $150,000 or More | 2000 AVERAGE DISPOSABLE INCOME BY AGE OF HOUSEHOLDER All Ages | <35 | 35-44 | 45-54 | 55-64 | 65+ |
|---|---|---|---|---|---|---|---|---|---|---|---|---|---|---|
| DISTRICT OF COLUMBIA | 28,952 | 224,159 | 16.2 | 14.3 | 29.3 | 26.4 | 8.2 | 5.5 | 40,393 | 33,612 | 42,112 | 47,326 | 41,037 | 31,092 |
| DISTRICT OF COLUMBIA | 28,952 | | 16.2 | 14.3 | 29.3 | 26.4 | 8.2 | 5.5 | 40,393 | 33,612 | 42,112 | 47,326 | 41,037 | 31,092 |
| UNITED STATES | 22,162 | | 14.5 | 12.5 | 32.3 | 29.8 | 7.4 | 3.5 | 40,748 | 34,503 | 44,969 | 49,579 | 43,409 | 27,339 |

# DISTRICT OF COLUMBIA SPENDING POTENTIAL INDEXES

# E

| COUNTY | FINANCIAL SERVICES | | | | THE HOME | | | | | | ENTERTAINMENT | | | | | | PERSONAL | | | |
|---|---|---|---|---|---|---|---|---|---|---|---|---|---|---|---|---|---|---|---|---|
| | | | | | Home Improvements | | | Furnishings | | | | | | | | | | | | |
| | Auto Loan | Home Loan | Invest-ments | Retire-ment Plans | Home Repair | Lawn & Garden | Remodel-ing | Appli-ances | Elec-tronics | Furni-ture | Restau-rants | Sport-ing Goods | Theater & Concerts | Toys & Hobbies | Travel | Video Rental | Apparel | Auto After-market | Health Insur-ance | Pets & Supplies |
| DISTRICT OF COLUMBIA | 96 | 106 | 109 | 101 | 106 | 103 | 88 | 99 | 96 | 105 | 95 | 98 | 101 | 94 | 99 | 101 | 105 | 105 | 90 | 98 |
| DISTRICT OF COLUMBIA | 96 | 106 | 109 | 101 | 106 | 103 | 88 | 99 | 96 | 105 | 95 | 98 | 101 | 94 | 99 | 101 | 105 | 105 | 90 | 98 |
| UNITED STATES | 100 | 100 | 100 | 100 | 100 | 100 | 100 | 100 | 100 | 100 | 100 | 100 | 100 | 100 | 100 | 100 | 100 | 100 | 100 | 100 |

# POPULATION CHANGE

| COUNTY | FIPS Code | MSA Code | DMA Code | POPULATION 1990 | POPULATION 2000 | POPULATION 2005 | 1990-2000 ANNUAL CHANGE % Rate | 1990-2000 ANNUAL CHANGE State Rank | RACE (%) White 1990 | White 2000 | Black 1990 | Black 2000 | Asian/Pacific 1990 | Asian/Pacific 2000 |
|---|---|---|---|---|---|---|---|---|---|---|---|---|---|---|
| ALACHUA | 001 | 2900 | 592 | 181,596 | 199,047 | 202,042 | 0.9 | 57 | 77.5 | 72.6 | 19.0 | 22.3 | 2.5 | 3.7 |
| BAKER | 003 | 0000 | 561 | 18,486 | 21,367 | 22,317 | 1.4 | 42 | 84.3 | 81.7 | 15.0 | 17.2 | 0.3 | 0.5 |
| BAY | 005 | 6015 | 656 | 126,994 | 149,113 | 155,109 | 1.6 | 36 | 86.3 | 82.9 | 10.8 | 12.8 | 1.8 | 2.8 |
| BRADFORD | 007 | 0000 | 561 | 22,515 | 25,045 | 25,843 | 1.0 | 53 | 78.6 | 75.1 | 20.2 | 23.3 | 0.4 | 0.7 |
| BREVARD | 009 | 4900 | 534 | 398,978 | 476,045 | 504,234 | 1.7 | 32 | 89.8 | 87.3 | 7.9 | 9.3 | 1.3 | 2.1 |
| BROWARD | 011 | 2680 | 528 | 1,255,488 | 1,565,639 | 1,714,670 | 2.2 | 19 | 81.7 | 77.4 | 15.4 | 18.2 | 1.4 | 2.2 |
| CALHOUN | 013 | 0000 | 656 | 11,011 | 12,475 | 12,670 | 1.2 | 47 | 83.2 | 79.3 | 15.1 | 18.4 | 0.1 | 0.2 |
| CHARLOTTE | 015 | 6580 | 571 | 110,975 | 139,272 | 150,605 | 2.2 | 19 | 95.0 | 93.5 | 3.8 | 4.6 | 0.7 | 1.2 |
| CITRUS | 017 | 0000 | 539 | 93,515 | 118,606 | 130,249 | 2.3 | 17 | 96.7 | 95.6 | 2.4 | 2.9 | 0.4 | 0.7 |
| CLAY | 019 | 3600 | 561 | 105,986 | 145,407 | 165,508 | 3.1 | 11 | 92.2 | 89.7 | 5.2 | 6.2 | 1.7 | 2.8 |
| COLLIER | 021 | 5345 | 571 | 152,099 | 214,106 | 248,907 | 3.4 | 7 | 91.4 | 89.1 | 4.6 | 5.5 | 0.4 | 0.6 |
| COLUMBIA | 023 | 0000 | 561 | 42,613 | 54,740 | 59,770 | 2.5 | 13 | 80.8 | 76.1 | 18.0 | 22.0 | 0.6 | 1.0 |
| DADE | 025 | 5000 | 528 | 1,937,094 | 2,198,826 | 2,318,135 | 1.2 | 47 | 72.9 | 72.3 | 20.5 | 19.9 | 1.4 | 1.8 |
| DE SOTO | 027 | 0000 | 571 | 23,865 | 24,613 | 24,426 | 0.3 | 65 | 80.2 | 76.3 | 15.6 | 17.8 | 0.4 | 0.7 |
| DIXIE | 029 | 0000 | 592 | 10,585 | 13,084 | 13,881 | 2.1 | 23 | 90.6 | 89.7 | 8.7 | 9.4 | 0.2 | 0.3 |
| DUVAL | 031 | 3600 | 561 | 672,971 | 746,815 | 777,244 | 1.0 | 53 | 72.8 | 67.4 | 24.4 | 28.1 | 1.9 | 3.1 |
| ESCAMBIA | 033 | 6080 | 686 | 262,798 | 282,980 | 284,625 | 0.7 | 62 | 76.6 | 71.8 | 20.0 | 23.2 | 1.9 | 3.0 |
| FLAGLER | 035 | 2020 | 534 | 28,701 | 51,440 | 62,321 | 5.9 | 1 | 90.0 | 87.4 | 8.2 | 9.9 | 1.0 | 1.6 |
| FRANKLIN | 037 | 0000 | 656 | 8,967 | 9,933 | 9,713 | 1.0 | 53 | 86.7 | 83.2 | 12.4 | 15.5 | 0.2 | 0.4 |
| GADSDEN | 039 | 8240 | 530 | 41,105 | 44,110 | 44,326 | 0.7 | 62 | 40.6 | 35.4 | 57.7 | 62.2 | 0.2 | 0.4 |
| GILCHRIST | 041 | 0000 | 592 | 9,667 | 14,399 | 16,144 | 4.0 | 3 | 90.6 | 89.7 | 8.5 | 9.3 | 0.2 | 0.3 |
| GLADES | 043 | 0000 | 571 | 7,591 | 8,777 | 9,228 | 1.4 | 42 | 78.9 | 73.2 | 12.1 | 16.4 | 0.2 | 0.2 |
| GULF | 045 | 0000 | 656 | 11,504 | 13,620 | 13,908 | 1.7 | 32 | 80.4 | 72.9 | 18.8 | 26.1 | 0.2 | 0.4 |
| HAMILTON | 047 | 0000 | 530 | 10,930 | 12,895 | 13,500 | 1.6 | 36 | 59.0 | 52.7 | 38.9 | 44.2 | 0.2 | 0.3 |
| HARDEE | 049 | 0000 | 539 | 19,499 | 20,990 | 20,856 | 0.7 | 62 | 84.0 | 78.7 | 5.3 | 7.4 | 0.2 | 0.3 |
| HENDRY | 051 | 0000 | 571 | 25,773 | 29,672 | 30,592 | 1.4 | 42 | 72.1 | 67.7 | 16.7 | 18.2 | 0.4 | 0.5 |
| HERNANDO | 053 | 8280 | 539 | 101,115 | 130,798 | 142,279 | 2.5 | 13 | 95.0 | 93.6 | 3.9 | 4.7 | 0.4 | 0.7 |
| HIGHLANDS | 055 | 0000 | 539 | 68,432 | 74,852 | 75,038 | 0.9 | 57 | 87.3 | 85.0 | 10.0 | 11.2 | 0.6 | 0.9 |
| HILLSBOROUGH | 057 | 8280 | 539 | 834,054 | 957,929 | 1,033,862 | 1.4 | 42 | 82.8 | 79.2 | 13.2 | 15.0 | 1.4 | 2.1 |
| HOLMES | 059 | 0000 | 656 | 15,778 | 18,985 | 20,087 | 1.8 | 30 | 93.4 | 91.5 | 5.0 | 6.2 | 0.3 | 0.5 |
| INDIAN RIVER | 061 | 0000 | 548 | 90,208 | 101,486 | 107,414 | 1.2 | 47 | 90.3 | 88.1 | 8.5 | 10.1 | 0.5 | 0.8 |
| JACKSON | 063 | 0000 | 656 | 41,375 | 44,928 | 45,324 | 0.8 | 59 | 72.7 | 67.8 | 26.2 | 30.8 | 0.2 | 0.3 |
| JEFFERSON | 065 | 0000 | 530 | 11,296 | 13,103 | 13,165 | 1.5 | 40 | 56.1 | 50.3 | 43.4 | 49.0 | 0.2 | 0.3 |
| LAFAYETTE | 067 | 0000 | 530 | 5,578 | 6,561 | 7,001 | 1.6 | 36 | 83.0 | 78.5 | 14.1 | 17.8 | 0.2 | 0.3 |
| LAKE | 069 | 5960 | 534 | 152,104 | 218,088 | 255,917 | 3.6 | 5 | 89.2 | 86.6 | 9.3 | 11.1 | 0.4 | 0.6 |
| LEE | 071 | 2700 | 571 | 335,113 | 407,688 | 443,457 | 1.9 | 28 | 91.4 | 89.2 | 6.6 | 7.8 | 0.6 | 0.9 |
| LEON | 073 | 8240 | 530 | 192,493 | 217,774 | 223,311 | 1.2 | 47 | 73.6 | 68.9 | 24.2 | 27.9 | 1.4 | 2.1 |
| LEVY | 075 | 0000 | 592 | 25,923 | 33,094 | 36,585 | 2.4 | 16 | 86.2 | 83.5 | 12.4 | 14.3 | 0.5 | 0.9 |
| LIBERTY | 077 | 0000 | 656 | 5,569 | 6,732 | 6,841 | 1.9 | 28 | 80.9 | 76.4 | 17.6 | 21.6 | 0.2 | 0.3 |
| MADISON | 079 | 0000 | 530 | 16,569 | 18,063 | 18,801 | 0.8 | 59 | 57.6 | 53.0 | 41.7 | 46.2 | 0.1 | 0.1 |
| MANATEE | 081 | 7510 | 539 | 211,707 | 248,489 | 267,836 | 1.6 | 36 | 89.9 | 87.1 | 7.7 | 9.4 | 0.6 | 0.9 |
| MARION | 083 | 5790 | 534 | 194,833 | 251,138 | 276,818 | 2.5 | 13 | 85.8 | 83.2 | 12.8 | 14.6 | 0.5 | 0.8 |
| MARTIN | 085 | 2710 | 548 | 100,900 | 120,220 | 130,662 | 1.7 | 32 | 91.3 | 89.0 | 6.0 | 6.8 | 0.5 | 0.9 |
| MONROE | 087 | 0000 | 528 | 78,024 | 79,494 | 77,124 | 0.2 | 67 | 92.1 | 90.2 | 5.4 | 6.2 | 0.8 | 1.2 |
| NASSAU | 089 | 3600 | 561 | 43,941 | 58,320 | 65,735 | 2.8 | 12 | 88.9 | 86.4 | 10.3 | 12.5 | 0.3 | 0.5 |
| OKALOOSA | 091 | 2750 | 686 | 143,776 | 171,619 | 179,604 | 1.7 | 32 | 87.1 | 83.8 | 9.0 | 10.3 | 2.5 | 4.0 |
| OKEECHOBEE | 093 | 0000 | 548 | 29,627 | 32,717 | 34,278 | 1.0 | 53 | 84.3 | 79.4 | 6.4 | 8.0 | 0.5 | 0.8 |
| ORANGE | 095 | 5960 | 534 | 677,491 | 833,891 | 914,875 | 2.0 | 26 | 79.6 | 74.7 | 15.2 | 17.5 | 2.1 | 3.2 |
| OSCEOLA | 097 | 5960 | 534 | 107,728 | 155,490 | 179,829 | 3.6 | 5 | 89.3 | 85.7 | 5.5 | 6.5 | 1.5 | 2.4 |
| PALM BEACH | 099 | 8960 | 548 | 863,518 | 1,067,555 | 1,157,553 | 2.1 | 23 | 84.8 | 81.5 | 12.5 | 14.5 | 1.0 | 1.6 |
| PASCO | 101 | 8280 | 539 | 281,131 | 337,270 | 367,817 | 1.8 | 30 | 96.3 | 94.6 | 1.9 | 2.5 | 0.5 | 0.9 |
| PINELLAS | 103 | 8280 | 539 | 851,659 | 881,402 | 894,217 | 0.3 | 65 | 90.5 | 87.6 | 7.7 | 9.5 | 1.1 | 1.9 |
| POLK | 105 | 3980 | 539 | 405,382 | 462,856 | 489,919 | 1.3 | 46 | 84.4 | 81.1 | 13.4 | 15.6 | 0.6 | 1.0 |
| PUTNAM | 107 | 0000 | 561 | 65,070 | 70,313 | 70,912 | 0.8 | 59 | 79.9 | 76.3 | 18.3 | 21.2 | 0.4 | 0.7 |
| ST. JOHNS | 109 | 3600 | 561 | 83,829 | 123,821 | 144,316 | 3.9 | 4 | 90.1 | 87.8 | 8.7 | 10.4 | 0.6 | 1.0 |
| ST. LUCIE | 111 | 2710 | 548 | 150,171 | 184,335 | 196,815 | 2.0 | 26 | 81.3 | 77.7 | 16.4 | 19.0 | 0.7 | 1.1 |
| SANTA ROSA | 113 | 6080 | 686 | 81,608 | 124,879 | 144,228 | 4.2 | 2 | 93.6 | 91.7 | 4.0 | 4.7 | 1.2 | 2.0 |
| SARASOTA | 115 | 7510 | 539 | 277,776 | 309,753 | 325,594 | 1.1 | 51 | 94.6 | 93.2 | 4.3 | 5.3 | 0.5 | 0.9 |
| SEMINOLE | 117 | 5960 | 534 | 287,529 | 364,553 | 399,882 | 2.3 | 17 | 88.2 | 85.0 | 8.5 | 10.0 | 1.7 | 2.7 |
| SUMTER | 119 | 0000 | 534 | 31,577 | 43,953 | 49,852 | 3.3 | 9 | 82.6 | 77.3 | 16.2 | 20.9 | 0.2 | 0.3 |
| SUWANNEE | 121 | 0000 | 530 | 26,780 | 33,593 | 36,673 | 2.2 | 19 | 84.1 | 81.0 | 14.7 | 17.4 | 0.2 | 0.4 |
| TAYLOR | 123 | 0000 | 530 | 17,111 | 19,195 | 19,946 | 1.1 | 51 | 80.6 | 75.0 | 18.0 | 23.1 | 0.2 | 0.3 |
| UNION | 125 | 0000 | 561 | 10,252 | 12,854 | 13,550 | 2.2 | 19 | 75.1 | 70.0 | 23.2 | 27.6 | 0.4 | 0.5 |
| VOLUSIA | 127 | 2020 | 534 | 370,712 | 430,645 | 455,628 | 1.5 | 40 | 88.6 | 85.8 | 9.0 | 10.8 | 0.7 | 1.2 |
| WAKULLA | 129 | 0000 | 530 | 14,202 | 19,754 | 22,036 | 3.3 | 9 | 86.1 | 83.2 | 12.9 | 15.5 | 0.2 | 0.3 |
| WALTON | 131 | 0000 | 656 | 27,760 | 39,049 | 43,556 | 3.4 | 7 | 91.1 | 88.3 | 6.8 | 8.9 | 0.5 | 0.8 |
| WASHINGTON | 133 | 0000 | 656 | 16,919 | 20,930 | 22,441 | 2.1 | 23 | 82.9 | 77.4 | 14.5 | 19.2 | 0.5 | 0.7 |
| FLORIDA | | | | | | | 1.7 | | 83.1 | 80.3 | 13.6 | 15.1 | 1.2 | 1.8 |
| UNITED STATES | | | | | | | 1.0 | | 80.3 | 77.9 | 12.1 | 12.4 | 2.9 | 3.9 |

# POPULATION COMPOSITION

| COUNTY | % HISPANIC ORIGIN | | 2000 AGE DISTRIBUTION (%) | | | | | | | | | | MEDIAN AGE | | 2000 Males/ Females (×100) |
|---|---|---|---|---|---|---|---|---|---|---|---|---|---|---|---|
| | 1990 | 2000 | 0-4 | 5-9 | 10-14 | 15-19 | 20-24 | 25-44 | 45-64 | 65-84 | 85+ | 18+ | 1990 | 2000 | |
| ALACHUA | 3.7 | 5.5 | 6.2 | 6.7 | 6.4 | 10.3 | 14.3 | 29.0 | 17.6 | 8.4 | 1.1 | 77.3 | 28.3 | 29.3 | 95.6 |
| BAKER | 1.1 | 1.9 | 7.4 | 8.7 | 8.9 | 8.6 | 7.5 | 30.4 | 20.1 | 7.6 | 0.8 | 69.5 | 30.2 | 31.0 | 111.1 |
| BAY | 1.8 | 3.0 | 6.7 | 7.4 | 7.6 | 6.8 | 5.9 | 29.0 | 23.1 | 12.5 | 1.1 | 74.4 | 33.2 | 36.7 | 96.9 |
| BRADFORD | 1.9 | 3.0 | 5.8 | 6.8 | 7.2 | 7.1 | 6.9 | 31.8 | 22.0 | 10.9 | 1.3 | 75.8 | 33.6 | 35.3 | 127.2 |
| BREVARD | 3.1 | 5.0 | 6.1 | 6.7 | 6.7 | 6.0 | 5.2 | 27.4 | 23.0 | 17.2 | 1.7 | 77.1 | 36.2 | 39.8 | 97.0 |
| BROWARD | 8.6 | 13.1 | 6.1 | 6.5 | 6.6 | 5.8 | 5.3 | 29.4 | 22.6 | 15.1 | 2.6 | 77.3 | 37.7 | 39.3 | 93.0 |
| CALHOUN | 1.1 | 1.9 | 6.8 | 7.4 | 7.2 | 7.4 | 7.3 | 27.8 | 22.0 | 12.3 | 1.8 | 74.2 | 33.5 | 35.1 | 109.3 |
| CHARLOTTE | 2.5 | 4.3 | 4.2 | 4.8 | 5.1 | 4.5 | 3.5 | 19.3 | 24.7 | 30.7 | 3.3 | 83.3 | 53.6 | 52.7 | 94.0 |
| CITRUS | 1.8 | 3.2 | 4.4 | 4.9 | 5.1 | 4.9 | 4.1 | 19.0 | 24.6 | 29.8 | 3.1 | 82.4 | 50.8 | 51.4 | 93.3 |
| CLAY | 2.6 | 4.5 | 7.1 | 8.2 | 8.6 | 7.5 | 5.8 | 30.7 | 22.7 | 8.3 | 0.9 | 71.3 | 32.0 | 34.5 | 96.7 |
| COLLIER | 13.6 | 18.9 | 5.6 | 6.0 | 6.0 | 5.2 | 4.7 | 24.4 | 23.2 | 22.4 | 2.4 | 79.2 | 40.7 | 43.5 | 96.0 |
| COLUMBIA | 1.5 | 2.4 | 6.8 | 8.0 | 8.3 | 8.0 | 5.9 | 26.5 | 22.6 | 12.7 | 1.2 | 72.1 | 33.6 | 36.0 | 98.8 |
| DADE | 49.2 | 57.9 | 6.9 | 7.1 | 7.3 | 7.0 | 6.5 | 29.4 | 22.2 | 11.8 | 1.8 | 74.6 | 34.2 | 36.2 | 92.4 |
| DE SOTO | 9.6 | 13.3 | 6.6 | 6.9 | 7.4 | 7.0 | 6.3 | 25.3 | 21.4 | 17.4 | 1.8 | 74.9 | 36.6 | 37.9 | 107.8 |
| DIXIE | 0.9 | 1.5 | 6.1 | 7.2 | 7.4 | 6.6 | 5.3 | 24.0 | 25.8 | 16.2 | 1.4 | 75.4 | 36.8 | 40.2 | 105.7 |
| DUVAL | 2.6 | 4.1 | 7.6 | 8.1 | 7.9 | 7.1 | 6.7 | 31.2 | 20.7 | 9.7 | 1.1 | 72.4 | 31.5 | 34.1 | 93.8 |
| ESCAMBIA | 1.9 | 3.2 | 6.8 | 7.4 | 7.6 | 7.7 | 7.3 | 28.2 | 21.9 | 11.8 | 1.3 | 74.3 | 32.4 | 35.3 | 94.5 |
| FLAGLER | 4.4 | 7.0 | 4.7 | 5.4 | 5.9 | 5.0 | 3.7 | 19.8 | 25.5 | 28.5 | 1.6 | 81.0 | 46.4 | 49.6 | 92.5 |
| FRANKLIN | 0.7 | 1.8 | 5.8 | 6.7 | 7.2 | 6.7 | 4.6 | 22.9 | 27.1 | 16.8 | 2.2 | 76.1 | 38.9 | 42.3 | 97.9 |
| GADSDEN | 2.3 | 3.4 | 7.6 | 7.8 | 8.0 | 8.4 | 7.5 | 27.6 | 21.0 | 10.8 | 1.4 | 71.5 | 31.8 | 32.7 | 94.5 |
| GILCHRIST | 1.6 | 2.5 | 6.4 | 7.3 | 7.5 | 9.2 | 8.1 | 24.3 | 23.3 | 12.6 | 1.4 | 74.2 | 33.5 | 35.7 | 110.0 |
| GLADES | 8.0 | 10.6 | 6.0 | 6.8 | 7.0 | 7.0 | 5.5 | 23.1 | 24.7 | 18.4 | 1.5 | 75.7 | 40.0 | 40.7 | 111.3 |
| GULF | 0.7 | 1.6 | 5.5 | 6.4 | 7.1 | 6.9 | 7.0 | 26.8 | 23.7 | 15.1 | 1.6 | 76.7 | 35.7 | 38.1 | 110.8 |
| HAMILTON | 2.7 | 4.2 | 7.0 | 7.5 | 7.6 | 7.8 | 8.9 | 29.6 | 20.7 | 9.7 | 1.2 | 73.1 | 30.9 | 31.7 | 112.9 |
| HARDEE | 23.4 | 30.9 | 8.0 | 8.1 | 8.0 | 8.0 | 7.1 | 26.3 | 20.4 | 12.7 | 1.4 | 71.1 | 32.8 | 33.1 | 106.2 |
| HENDRY | 22.3 | 29.0 | 8.7 | 9.2 | 9.3 | 8.3 | 6.6 | 26.2 | 19.8 | 10.8 | 1.1 | 67.6 | 30.3 | 31.4 | 102.9 |
| HERNANDO | 2.9 | 4.9 | 4.7 | 5.2 | 5.4 | 5.1 | 4.1 | 19.4 | 23.4 | 30.1 | 2.6 | 81.5 | 49.5 | 50.2 | 92.3 |
| HIGHLANDS | 5.1 | 7.6 | 4.9 | 5.6 | 5.8 | 5.2 | 3.8 | 18.1 | 21.8 | 31.2 | 3.6 | 80.4 | 51.5 | 51.4 | 92.0 |
| HILLSBOROUGH | 12.8 | 18.4 | 6.8 | 7.1 | 7.2 | 6.6 | 6.5 | 31.0 | 22.0 | 11.4 | 1.4 | 75.2 | 33.0 | 36.0 | 94.9 |
| HOLMES | 1.1 | 2.2 | 6.0 | 6.6 | 7.0 | 6.9 | 6.5 | 27.0 | 24.4 | 13.8 | 1.8 | 76.2 | 35.6 | 37.9 | 102.3 |
| INDIAN RIVER | 3.0 | 4.6 | 5.1 | 5.8 | 6.0 | 5.5 | 4.2 | 22.0 | 22.8 | 25.8 | 2.9 | 79.8 | 44.0 | 46.2 | 94.0 |
| JACKSON | 2.4 | 4.1 | 5.5 | 6.5 | 7.3 | 9.1 | 7.7 | 27.8 | 22.0 | 12.4 | 1.7 | 75.6 | 34.3 | 35.8 | 109.7 |
| JEFFERSON | 1.2 | 2.4 | 6.6 | 7.0 | 7.2 | 7.8 | 7.5 | 27.4 | 22.6 | 12.3 | 1.7 | 74.4 | 33.8 | 35.3 | 99.4 |
| LAFAYETTE | 4.1 | 5.4 | 5.4 | 6.5 | 7.0 | 7.5 | 8.9 | 33.0 | 20.3 | 10.5 | 1.0 | 76.5 | 32.0 | 33.2 | 148.1 |
| LAKE | 2.8 | 4.6 | 5.3 | 6.0 | 6.3 | 5.6 | 4.3 | 21.4 | 23.3 | 24.6 | 3.1 | 78.9 | 44.7 | 45.9 | 93.8 |
| LEE | 4.5 | 7.0 | 5.5 | 6.0 | 6.1 | 5.2 | 4.2 | 24.1 | 23.1 | 23.2 | 2.7 | 79.3 | 42.0 | 44.2 | 93.9 |
| LEON | 2.4 | 3.6 | 6.0 | 6.8 | 6.9 | 9.6 | 12.5 | 30.7 | 19.0 | 7.6 | 0.9 | 76.6 | 28.8 | 31.0 | 92.1 |
| LEVY | 1.9 | 3.2 | 5.9 | 7.0 | 7.3 | 6.7 | 5.0 | 23.3 | 24.7 | 18.5 | 1.7 | 75.8 | 38.5 | 41.3 | 92.2 |
| LIBERTY | 1.9 | 3.4 | 5.9 | 6.3 | 6.2 | 7.3 | 8.7 | 32.5 | 20.8 | 11.3 | 1.1 | 77.2 | 32.5 | 34.1 | 130.3 |
| MADISON | 1.4 | 2.1 | 7.4 | 7.9 | 8.5 | 8.0 | 7.0 | 27.3 | 20.7 | 11.6 | 1.6 | 71.5 | 32.3 | 33.5 | 107.7 |
| MANATEE | 4.5 | 7.1 | 5.6 | 6.1 | 6.2 | 5.5 | 4.6 | 23.4 | 22.3 | 22.6 | 3.6 | 78.9 | 43.1 | 44.0 | 91.8 |
| MARION | 3.0 | 4.8 | 5.9 | 6.6 | 6.8 | 6.1 | 4.8 | 23.2 | 22.9 | 21.7 | 2.0 | 77.0 | 40.0 | 42.5 | 93.6 |
| MARTIN | 4.7 | 7.2 | 4.8 | 5.4 | 5.5 | 5.0 | 4.1 | 22.9 | 24.2 | 25.4 | 2.9 | 81.5 | 44.5 | 46.9 | 96.9 |
| MONROE | 12.3 | 18.1 | 5.3 | 5.4 | 5.2 | 4.4 | 4.7 | 29.3 | 27.4 | 16.9 | 1.3 | 81.6 | 38.8 | 42.6 | 108.6 |
| NASSAU | 1.1 | 2.0 | 6.7 | 7.2 | 7.5 | 7.1 | 6.2 | 28.2 | 25.0 | 11.2 | 0.9 | 74.2 | 33.4 | 36.8 | 97.5 |
| OKALOOSA | 3.1 | 4.9 | 7.7 | 7.5 | 6.7 | 6.1 | 6.9 | 32.7 | 20.5 | 11.0 | 0.8 | 74.5 | 31.5 | 34.4 | 99.8 |
| OKEECHOBEE | 11.8 | 16.3 | 7.4 | 7.7 | 7.9 | 7.9 | 5.7 | 24.2 | 21.4 | 16.4 | 1.4 | 71.9 | 34.3 | 36.8 | 107.6 |
| ORANGE | 9.6 | 14.3 | 7.1 | 7.5 | 7.4 | 7.0 | 7.3 | 32.4 | 20.3 | 9.8 | 1.2 | 74.1 | 31.5 | 34.2 | 96.6 |
| OSCEOLA | 11.9 | 17.9 | 7.3 | 7.7 | 7.9 | 6.8 | 6.1 | 29.5 | 21.6 | 11.6 | 1.6 | 73.3 | 33.7 | 35.5 | 95.4 |
| PALM BEACH | 7.7 | 11.4 | 5.7 | 6.3 | 6.5 | 5.4 | 4.5 | 26.1 | 22.1 | 19.8 | 3.7 | 78.3 | 39.9 | 42.2 | 91.6 |
| PASCO | 3.3 | 5.7 | 5.2 | 5.8 | 6.0 | 5.3 | 4.2 | 21.7 | 23.3 | 25.3 | 3.2 | 79.9 | 48.0 | 46.5 | 92.4 |
| PINELLAS | 2.4 | 4.0 | 5.0 | 5.5 | 5.8 | 5.3 | 4.7 | 25.9 | 24.1 | 19.9 | 3.8 | 80.7 | 42.1 | 43.7 | 89.3 |
| POLK | 4.1 | 6.3 | 6.6 | 7.2 | 7.4 | 6.9 | 5.5 | 25.0 | 22.4 | 16.9 | 2.0 | 74.7 | 36.5 | 39.0 | 95.0 |
| PUTNAM | 2.6 | 4.2 | 6.5 | 7.4 | 7.8 | 6.9 | 5.3 | 23.5 | 23.4 | 17.7 | 1.6 | 74.1 | 37.3 | 39.8 | 96.3 |
| ST. JOHNS | 2.3 | 3.8 | 5.9 | 6.6 | 7.0 | 6.5 | 5.2 | 26.9 | 24.9 | 15.4 | 1.7 | 76.9 | 37.0 | 40.0 | 94.0 |
| ST. LUCIE | 4.0 | 6.1 | 6.6 | 7.2 | 7.1 | 6.0 | 4.6 | 25.0 | 21.3 | 20.3 | 1.9 | 75.5 | 37.9 | 40.5 | 96.0 |
| SANTA ROSA | 1.5 | 2.7 | 7.3 | 7.8 | 7.8 | 6.9 | 5.9 | 29.9 | 23.3 | 10.2 | 0.8 | 72.9 | 32.5 | 35.8 | 98.7 |
| SARASOTA | 2.1 | 3.6 | 4.2 | 4.8 | 5.1 | 4.6 | 3.7 | 21.7 | 24.7 | 26.9 | 4.3 | 83.2 | 49.0 | 49.4 | 90.0 |
| SEMINOLE | 6.5 | 9.9 | 6.6 | 7.2 | 7.3 | 6.5 | 5.9 | 32.3 | 23.5 | 9.6 | 1.1 | 75.0 | 33.3 | 36.0 | 94.2 |
| SUMTER | 2.4 | 4.0 | 5.6 | 6.4 | 6.6 | 7.2 | 6.8 | 24.0 | 22.5 | 19.0 | 1.7 | 77.2 | 40.1 | 39.7 | 111.7 |
| SUWANNEE | 1.6 | 2.6 | 5.9 | 7.3 | 8.0 | 7.8 | 5.6 | 24.0 | 24.3 | 15.0 | 2.2 | 73.9 | 36.5 | 38.9 | 94.1 |
| TAYLOR | 1.0 | 2.9 | 7.1 | 8.0 | 8.3 | 7.7 | 5.7 | 26.6 | 22.8 | 12.6 | 1.3 | 71.7 | 33.5 | 36.2 | 100.5 |
| UNION | 3.3 | 5.2 | 6.1 | 7.2 | 7.2 | 7.3 | 6.7 | 38.9 | 18.7 | 7.0 | 0.7 | 75.0 | 31.4 | 32.9 | 170.6 |
| VOLUSIA | 4.0 | 5.9 | 5.5 | 5.9 | 6.0 | 6.1 | 5.7 | 25.9 | 22.7 | 19.5 | 2.8 | 79.5 | 39.4 | 41.7 | 95.0 |
| WAKULLA | 0.6 | 1.2 | 6.5 | 7.2 | 7.3 | 7.6 | 6.7 | 26.7 | 25.9 | 10.9 | 1.1 | 74.1 | 34.2 | 36.7 | 94.8 |
| WALTON | 0.9 | 1.7 | 5.4 | 6.4 | 7.1 | 6.4 | 5.1 | 25.6 | 26.4 | 16.1 | 1.5 | 77.1 | 37.8 | 41.1 | 102.7 |
| WASHINGTON | 1.1 | 2.1 | 5.8 | 6.7 | 7.6 | 7.0 | 6.3 | 25.5 | 24.2 | 14.9 | 1.9 | 75.2 | 37.3 | 38.6 | 101.5 |
| FLORIDA | 12.2 | 15.7 | 6.2 | 6.7 | 6.8 | 6.3 | 5.8 | 27.6 | 22.4 | 15.9 | 2.2 | 76.6 | 36.4 | 38.9 | 94.2 |
| UNITED STATES | 9.0 | 11.8 | 6.9 | 7.2 | 7.2 | 7.2 | 6.7 | 29.9 | 22.2 | 11.1 | 1.6 | 74.6 | 32.9 | 35.7 | 95.6 |

| COUNTY | HOUSEHOLDS | | | | | FAMILIES | | | MEDIAN HOUSEHOLD INCOME | | | |
|---|---|---|---|---|---|---|---|---|---|---|---|---|
| | 1990 | 2000 | 2005 | % Annual Rate 1990-2000 | 2000 Average HH Size | 1990 | 2000 | % Annual Rate 1990-2000 | 2000 | 2005 | 2000 National Rank | 2000 State Rank |
| ALACHUA | 71,258 | 77,781 | 78,840 | 1.1 | 2.41 | 41,151 | 43,289 | 0.6 | 30,368 | 33,671 | 2065 | 48 |
| BAKER | 5,554 | 6,478 | 6,798 | 1.9 | 2.99 | 4,511 | 5,136 | 1.6 | 36,760 | 41,729 | 1011 | 27 |
| BAY | 48,938 | 56,923 | 58,898 | 1.8 | 2.57 | 35,608 | 39,787 | 1.4 | 35,659 | 41,782 | 1142 | 30 |
| BRADFORD | 7,193 | 7,874 | 8,159 | 1.1 | 2.69 | 5,470 | 5,777 | 0.7 | 35,794 | 46,581 | 1127 | 29 |
| BREVARD | 161,365 | 191,058 | 201,487 | 2.1 | 2.46 | 113,149 | 128,838 | 1.6 | 39,480 | 45,832 | 712 | 19 |
| BROWARD | 528,442 | 651,888 | 709,903 | 2.6 | 2.38 | 335,022 | 398,711 | 2.1 | 40,269 | 47,132 | 651 | 16 |
| CALHOUN | 3,793 | 4,157 | 4,214 | 1.1 | 2.66 | 2,784 | 2,944 | 0.7 | 28,536 | 32,330 | 2358 | 61 |
| CHARLOTTE | 48,433 | 60,462 | 65,110 | 2.7 | 2.26 | 35,325 | 42,993 | 2.4 | 38,999 | 49,742 | 754 | 21 |
| CITRUS | 40,573 | 51,064 | 55,907 | 2.8 | 2.29 | 29,679 | 36,077 | 2.4 | 31,539 | 35,130 | 1814 | 46 |
| CLAY | 36,663 | 49,995 | 56,715 | 3.8 | 2.88 | 29,643 | 39,621 | 3.6 | 47,802 | 57,428 | 244 | 3 |
| COLLIER | 61,703 | 96,238 | 117,132 | 5.5 | 2.19 | 43,795 | 66,513 | 5.2 | 45,472 | 50,925 | 333 | 4 |
| COLUMBIA | 15,611 | 19,594 | 21,454 | 2.8 | 2.67 | 11,516 | 13,991 | 2.4 | 32,909 | 38,300 | 1552 | 42 |
| DADE | 692,355 | 782,447 | 822,975 | 1.5 | 2.77 | 481,263 | 541,788 | 1.4 | 35,093 | 42,124 | 1240 | 33 |
| DE SOTO | 8,222 | 8,555 | 8,486 | 0.5 | 2.61 | 6,046 | 6,082 | 0.1 | 29,095 | 35,919 | 2284 | 59 |
| DIXIE | 3,916 | 5,014 | 5,392 | 3.0 | 2.50 | 2,894 | 3,568 | 2.6 | 24,375 | 27,525 | 2872 | 67 |
| DUVAL | 257,245 | 287,351 | 298,340 | 1.4 | 2.56 | 175,353 | 188,709 | 0.9 | 40,674 | 47,821 | 612 | 13 |
| ESCAMBIA | 98,608 | 106,397 | 107,501 | 0.9 | 2.55 | 70,068 | 73,052 | 0.5 | 34,585 | 40,185 | 1307 | 36 |
| FLAGLER | 11,880 | 21,458 | 26,122 | 7.4 | 2.38 | 9,168 | 16,318 | 7.2 | 41,203 | 50,602 | 569 | 11 |
| FRANKLIN | 3,628 | 3,987 | 3,901 | 1.2 | 2.41 | 2,586 | 2,740 | 0.7 | 28,610 | 33,143 | 2348 | 60 |
| GADSDEN | 13,405 | 14,041 | 14,001 | 0.6 | 2.93 | 10,139 | 10,423 | 0.3 | 29,486 | 32,297 | 2225 | 55 |
| GILCHRIST | 3,284 | 5,015 | 5,710 | 5.3 | 2.62 | 2,550 | 3,776 | 4.9 | 33,689 | 40,948 | 1437 | 41 |
| GLADES | 2,885 | 2,956 | 3,065 | 0.3 | 2.67 | 2,119 | 2,084 | -0.2 | 31,451 | 40,303 | 1832 | 47 |
| GULF | 4,324 | 4,596 | 4,643 | 0.7 | 2.63 | 3,242 | 3,329 | 0.3 | 35,223 | 40,687 | 1218 | 32 |
| HAMILTON | 3,488 | 3,952 | 4,144 | 1.5 | 2.83 | 2,636 | 2,885 | 1.1 | 25,921 | 31,078 | 2721 | 66 |
| HARDEE | 6,391 | 6,401 | 6,336 | 0.0 | 2.97 | 5,076 | 4,989 | -0.2 | 27,549 | 33,786 | 2504 | 63 |
| HENDRY | 8,402 | 9,612 | 9,891 | 1.6 | 3.01 | 6,533 | 7,280 | 1.3 | 32,001 | 40,029 | 1716 | 44 |
| HERNANDO | 42,300 | 54,814 | 59,664 | 3.2 | 2.37 | 32,567 | 41,005 | 2.8 | 34,817 | 40,579 | 1281 | 34 |
| HIGHLANDS | 29,544 | 32,310 | 32,367 | 1.1 | 2.28 | 21,398 | 22,640 | 0.7 | 29,933 | 35,502 | 2167 | 52 |
| HILLSBOROUGH | 324,872 | 367,736 | 394,122 | 1.5 | 2.55 | 219,585 | 240,606 | 1.1 | 38,893 | 46,349 | 762 | 23 |
| HOLMES | 5,800 | 6,867 | 7,284 | 2.1 | 2.57 | 4,317 | 4,923 | 1.6 | 26,033 | 29,528 | 2710 | 65 |
| INDIAN RIVER | 38,057 | 42,304 | 44,529 | 1.3 | 2.36 | 27,182 | 29,329 | 0.9 | 39,975 | 43,473 | 676 | 17 |
| JACKSON | 14,465 | 15,213 | 15,294 | 0.6 | 2.58 | 10,504 | 10,675 | 0.2 | 27,903 | 32,063 | 2455 | 62 |
| JEFFERSON | 3,982 | 4,396 | 4,446 | 1.2 | 2.75 | 2,980 | 3,170 | 0.8 | 33,875 | 43,488 | 1409 | 38 |
| LAFAYETTE | 1,721 | 1,836 | 1,943 | 0.8 | 2.88 | 1,344 | 1,388 | 0.4 | 29,577 | 35,697 | 2211 | 53 |
| LAKE | 63,616 | 89,906 | 104,974 | 4.3 | 2.38 | 46,258 | 63,258 | 3.9 | 35,372 | 44,035 | 1188 | 31 |
| LEE | 140,124 | 167,954 | 181,376 | 2.2 | 2.40 | 99,698 | 116,156 | 1.9 | 38,522 | 46,997 | 806 | 24 |
| LEON | 74,828 | 84,695 | 86,435 | 1.5 | 2.46 | 45,118 | 49,695 | 1.2 | 40,798 | 47,173 | 604 | 12 |
| LEVY | 10,079 | 12,774 | 14,071 | 2.9 | 2.55 | 7,421 | 9,095 | 2.5 | 29,100 | 33,649 | 2282 | 58 |
| LIBERTY | 1,706 | 1,999 | 2,058 | 1.9 | 2.64 | 1,286 | 1,458 | 1.5 | 33,773 | 43,464 | 1426 | 40 |
| MADISON | 5,522 | 5,790 | 5,976 | 0.6 | 2.83 | 4,103 | 4,162 | 0.2 | 27,512 | 34,032 | 2507 | 64 |
| MANATEE | 91,060 | 105,335 | 112,983 | 1.8 | 2.32 | 61,659 | 68,482 | 1.3 | 39,040 | 48,105 | 748 | 20 |
| MARION | 78,177 | 100,443 | 110,423 | 3.1 | 2.46 | 57,039 | 70,838 | 2.7 | 32,896 | 38,047 | 1554 | 43 |
| MARTIN | 43,022 | 50,650 | 54,704 | 2.0 | 2.32 | 30,060 | 34,285 | 1.6 | 41,915 | 45,960 | 520 | 8 |
| MONROE | 33,583 | 35,125 | 34,303 | 0.5 | 2.21 | 20,598 | 20,705 | 0.1 | 40,674 | 46,382 | 612 | 13 |
| NASSAU | 16,192 | 21,248 | 23,812 | 3.3 | 2.72 | 12,158 | 15,418 | 2.9 | 42,122 | 45,875 | 500 | 6 |
| OKALOOSA | 53,313 | 63,615 | 66,393 | 2.2 | 2.62 | 39,703 | 45,699 | 1.7 | 38,463 | 43,141 | 810 | 25 |
| OKEECHOBEE | 10,214 | 10,638 | 11,063 | 0.5 | 2.81 | 7,695 | 7,759 | 0.1 | 29,568 | 34,898 | 2212 | 54 |
| ORANGE | 254,852 | 315,958 | 347,631 | 2.6 | 2.56 | 171,128 | 205,565 | 2.2 | 41,920 | 50,839 | 519 | 7 |
| OSCEOLA | 39,150 | 56,371 | 65,029 | 4.5 | 2.71 | 29,107 | 40,683 | 4.1 | 38,971 | 49,203 | 755 | 22 |
| PALM BEACH | 365,558 | 449,634 | 486,101 | 2.5 | 2.34 | 242,273 | 288,081 | 2.1 | 41,391 | 45,063 | 558 | 10 |
| PASCO | 121,674 | 145,838 | 159,043 | 2.2 | 2.27 | 85,672 | 98,483 | 1.7 | 33,800 | 39,837 | 1421 | 39 |
| PINELLAS | 380,635 | 391,897 | 396,351 | 0.4 | 2.20 | 236,554 | 231,337 | -0.3 | 35,904 | 42,875 | 1114 | 28 |
| POLK | 155,969 | 176,911 | 186,630 | 1.5 | 2.56 | 114,554 | 126,161 | 1.2 | 36,864 | 45,275 | 997 | 26 |
| PUTNAM | 25,070 | 27,072 | 27,299 | 0.9 | 2.55 | 18,372 | 19,176 | 0.5 | 30,112 | 36,146 | 2128 | 49 |
| ST. JOHNS | 33,426 | 49,774 | 58,161 | 4.9 | 2.44 | 23,260 | 33,701 | 4.6 | 48,962 | 54,409 | 222 | 2 |
| ST. LUCIE | 58,174 | 70,644 | 75,018 | 2.4 | 2.57 | 43,317 | 51,497 | 2.1 | 40,599 | 51,590 | 619 | 15 |
| SANTA ROSA | 29,900 | 45,812 | 52,854 | 5.3 | 2.70 | 23,336 | 34,804 | 5.0 | 42,341 | 49,767 | 484 | 5 |
| SARASOTA | 125,493 | 138,301 | 144,486 | 1.2 | 2.21 | 83,732 | 88,825 | 0.7 | 41,407 | 48,010 | 557 | 9 |
| SEMINOLE | 107,657 | 135,233 | 147,627 | 2.8 | 2.67 | 77,365 | 93,727 | 2.4 | 49,593 | 57,943 | 208 | 1 |
| SUMTER | 12,119 | 15,508 | 17,720 | 3.0 | 2.50 | 8,893 | 10,941 | 2.5 | 29,952 | 34,991 | 2163 | 51 |
| SUWANNEE | 10,034 | 12,766 | 14,027 | 3.0 | 2.59 | 7,429 | 9,199 | 2.6 | 29,420 | 32,756 | 2232 | 56 |
| TAYLOR | 6,401 | 6,636 | 6,848 | 0.4 | 2.72 | 4,838 | 4,856 | 0.0 | 30,078 | 34,459 | 2138 | 50 |
| UNION | 2,658 | 3,021 | 3,223 | 1.6 | 2.97 | 2,106 | 2,331 | 1.2 | 31,560 | 36,595 | 1806 | 45 |
| VOLUSIA | 153,416 | 177,437 | 187,242 | 1.8 | 2.35 | 102,880 | 115,053 | 1.4 | 34,671 | 42,777 | 1296 | 35 |
| WAKULLA | 5,210 | 6,973 | 7,657 | 3.6 | 2.79 | 4,040 | 5,248 | 3.2 | 39,957 | 43,759 | 678 | 18 |
| WALTON | 11,294 | 15,448 | 17,292 | 3.9 | 2.44 | 8,142 | 10,612 | 3.3 | 34,119 | 42,292 | 1369 | 37 |
| WASHINGTON | 6,443 | 7,436 | 7,923 | 1.8 | 2.62 | 4,828 | 5,382 | 1.3 | 29,326 | 34,675 | 2250 | 57 |
| FLORIDA | | | | 2.0 | 2.48 | | | 1.7 | 38,118 | 45,132 | | |
| UNITED STATES | | | | 1.4 | 2.59 | | | 1.1 | 41,914 | 49,127 | | |

# INCOME

| COUNTY | 2000 Per Capita Income | 2000 HH Income Base | 2000 HOUSEHOLD INCOME DISTRIBUTION (%) | | | | | | 2000 AVERAGE DISPOSABLE INCOME BY AGE OF HOUSEHOLDER | | | | | |
|---|---|---|---|---|---|---|---|---|---|---|---|---|---|---|
| | | | Less than $15,000 | $15,000 to $24,999 | $25,000 to $49,999 | $50,000 to $99,999 | $100,000 to $149,999 | $150,000 or More | All Ages | <35 | 35-44 | 45-54 | 55-64 | 65+ |
| ALACHUA | 17,475 | 77,777 | 24.9 | 17.2 | 30.1 | 20.9 | 4.6 | 2.3 | 34,131 | 22,566 | 40,706 | 46,930 | 42,777 | 28,346 |
| BAKER | 13,639 | 6,478 | 16.5 | 13.4 | 39.6 | 25.9 | 3.8 | 0.7 | 34,684 | 29,333 | 40,811 | 42,424 | 35,467 | 21,856 |
| BAY | 17,898 | 56,913 | 16.4 | 15.8 | 36.3 | 26.0 | 4.2 | 1.3 | 35,585 | 30,519 | 38,696 | 43,745 | 38,863 | 27,266 |
| BRADFORD | 15,757 | 7,874 | 16.8 | 13.0 | 37.1 | 27.9 | 4.3 | 0.9 | 35,237 | 33,338 | 39,837 | 44,572 | 37,728 | 23,724 |
| BREVARD | 19,872 | 191,046 | 13.3 | 14.6 | 35.9 | 29.7 | 5.0 | 1.4 | 38,219 | 34,013 | 42,065 | 47,617 | 42,775 | 29,590 |
| BROWARD | 24,450 | 651,888 | 14.1 | 14.5 | 32.9 | 28.0 | 6.7 | 3.8 | 43,079 | 38,441 | 47,454 | 50,510 | 45,330 | 30,528 |
| CALHOUN | 13,126 | 4,157 | 23.7 | 21.0 | 32.4 | 18.8 | 2.9 | 1.2 | 29,806 | 27,948 | 34,893 | 38,307 | 29,919 | 20,342 |
| CHARLOTTE | 21,785 | 60,458 | 9.2 | 17.0 | 38.4 | 28.6 | 5.2 | 1.6 | 39,201 | 38,479 | 45,805 | 47,448 | 41,137 | 33,990 |
| CITRUS | 17,860 | 51,064 | 17.6 | 21.0 | 35.0 | 22.4 | 3.2 | 0.9 | 32,418 | 30,948 | 39,406 | 41,355 | 35,603 | 27,003 |
| CLAY | 19,755 | 49,995 | 7.3 | 10.1 | 35.2 | 38.4 | 7.2 | 1.9 | 44,309 | 37,312 | 46,268 | 55,460 | 46,788 | 30,914 |
| COLLIER | 35,615 | 96,238 | 8.2 | 12.6 | 34.0 | 28.6 | 9.3 | 7.3 | 53,371 | 39,374 | 48,330 | 54,351 | 56,485 | 50,793 |
| COLUMBIA | 14,880 | 19,594 | 19.5 | 17.9 | 36.1 | 22.0 | 3.6 | 0.9 | 32,435 | 28,698 | 37,351 | 40,284 | 32,771 | 24,492 |
| DADE | 19,686 | 782,446 | 20.5 | 15.0 | 31.1 | 23.6 | 5.8 | 3.9 | 39,949 | 34,011 | 41,986 | 44,832 | 41,639 | 29,056 |
| DE SOTO | 14,071 | 8,555 | 20.7 | 21.7 | 34.7 | 19.4 | 2.8 | 0.8 | 30,067 | 28,277 | 36,501 | 36,210 | 31,101 | 23,910 |
| DIXIE | 12,900 | 5,009 | 31.5 | 19.6 | 32.5 | 13.3 | 2.1 | 1.0 | 26,356 | 26,108 | 33,030 | 30,299 | 28,229 | 20,950 |
| DUVAL | 20,568 | 287,346 | 13.7 | 13.3 | 34.8 | 30.1 | 6.1 | 2.1 | 40,062 | 34,598 | 44,449 | 48,527 | 42,861 | 28,160 |
| ESCAMBIA | 16,990 | 106,390 | 18.4 | 16.3 | 35.2 | 24.8 | 4.1 | 1.2 | 34,455 | 28,133 | 37,882 | 42,961 | 37,487 | 27,408 |
| FLAGLER | 23,155 | 21,458 | 9.3 | 14.0 | 38.3 | 29.8 | 6.2 | 2.4 | 41,790 | 36,401 | 42,491 | 47,181 | 46,328 | 38,087 |
| FRANKLIN | 16,686 | 3,987 | 23.9 | 21.8 | 30.0 | 18.7 | 3.9 | 1.7 | 32,060 | 26,929 | 40,036 | 31,210 | 38,837 | 24,717 |
| GADSDEN | 12,004 | 14,041 | 25.5 | 17.9 | 33.8 | 19.2 | 2.9 | 0.8 | 29,410 | 25,163 | 33,199 | 36,371 | 31,362 | 21,353 |
| GILCHRIST | 14,783 | 5,015 | 17.4 | 17.4 | 42.7 | 20.2 | 2.2 | 0.1 | 30,584 | 29,726 | 34,153 | 37,579 | 31,750 | 21,496 |
| GLADES | 17,609 | 2,956 | 15.9 | 22.8 | 34.1 | 23.0 | 3.2 | 1.0 | 32,417 | 31,059 | 40,303 | 40,134 | 29,709 | 26,257 |
| GULF | 13,393 | 4,596 | 17.8 | 18.9 | 35.9 | 24.9 | 2.3 | 0.1 | 31,778 | 32,525 | 36,595 | 39,318 | 35,574 | 20,702 |
| HAMILTON | 11,422 | 3,952 | 33.4 | 14.4 | 35.1 | 14.6 | 1.6 | 1.0 | 26,642 | 24,009 | 26,691 | 34,967 | 28,973 | 17,690 |
| HARDEE | 11,901 | 6,401 | 24.9 | 20.5 | 33.9 | 17.0 | 2.5 | 1.2 | 29,117 | 24,376 | 30,588 | 37,716 | 34,366 | 22,654 |
| HENDRY | 12,878 | 9,612 | 20.5 | 17.1 | 36.0 | 22.4 | 3.3 | 0.6 | 31,581 | 28,650 | 35,875 | 36,499 | 31,220 | 25,729 |
| HERNANDO | 18,036 | 54,814 | 12.1 | 19.4 | 39.6 | 25.0 | 3.3 | 0.7 | 34,329 | 33,106 | 40,254 | 43,257 | 37,103 | 29,637 |
| HIGHLANDS | 17,601 | 32,301 | 18.1 | 21.3 | 37.0 | 19.7 | 2.8 | 1.1 | 31,584 | 29,013 | 38,574 | 40,583 | 34,616 | 27,196 |
| HILLSBOROUGH | 19,743 | 367,723 | 14.8 | 14.5 | 34.4 | 28.3 | 5.8 | 2.1 | 39,066 | 33,936 | 44,475 | 46,917 | 41,122 | 27,372 |
| HOLMES | 13,126 | 6,867 | 27.1 | 21.1 | 32.4 | 15.9 | 2.7 | 0.8 | 27,814 | 23,800 | 34,485 | 33,181 | 32,919 | 18,665 |
| INDIAN RIVER | 26,411 | 42,304 | 12.3 | 15.4 | 33.8 | 26.7 | 7.0 | 4.7 | 44,995 | 35,244 | 46,930 | 50,391 | 47,664 | 40,185 |
| JACKSON | 14,209 | 15,213 | 26.2 | 18.6 | 33.6 | 17.6 | 3.1 | 1.1 | 29,423 | 27,033 | 36,037 | 38,592 | 31,155 | 18,572 |
| JEFFERSON | 15,322 | 4,396 | 19.4 | 16.7 | 33.3 | 23.3 | 5.5 | 1.8 | 35,119 | 30,031 | 39,675 | 42,338 | 39,898 | 26,199 |
| LAFAYETTE | 12,438 | 1,836 | 22.4 | 19.3 | 33.7 | 20.5 | 3.8 | 0.3 | 29,726 | 28,034 | 38,483 | 33,438 | 36,065 | 17,654 |
| LAKE | 18,727 | 89,906 | 13.3 | 18.7 | 37.4 | 25.0 | 4.4 | 1.2 | 35,632 | 35,175 | 42,977 | 45,311 | 37,612 | 28,729 |
| LEE | 21,636 | 167,913 | 11.5 | 16.0 | 37.3 | 27.1 | 5.7 | 2.4 | 39,813 | 36,600 | 44,373 | 46,174 | 44,786 | 33,012 |
| LEON | 22,238 | 84,694 | 16.1 | 13.2 | 30.3 | 29.9 | 7.2 | 3.3 | 42,177 | 28,781 | 49,324 | 54,888 | 51,684 | 32,792 |
| LEVY | 14,264 | 12,774 | 24.0 | 18.9 | 35.5 | 17.6 | 3.3 | 0.7 | 29,430 | 28,452 | 35,449 | 34,899 | 31,501 | 22,605 |
| LIBERTY | 17,143 | 1,989 | 18.8 | 17.6 | 36.0 | 23.9 | 3.0 | 0.9 | 32,395 | 30,680 | 42,766 | 36,916 | 34,236 | 20,640 |
| MADISON | 15,598 | 5,790 | 25.9 | 19.1 | 31.9 | 17.6 | 3.7 | 1.7 | 31,138 | 27,237 | 33,983 | 40,386 | 34,532 | 20,071 |
| MANATEE | 21,940 | 105,332 | 11.6 | 16.0 | 36.8 | 27.8 | 5.9 | 2.0 | 39,467 | 36,123 | 44,414 | 47,543 | 43,857 | 32,897 |
| MARION | 17,276 | 100,442 | 16.4 | 19.2 | 37.2 | 22.5 | 3.6 | 1.2 | 33,700 | 31,776 | 39,634 | 41,741 | 36,395 | 26,388 |
| MARTIN | 29,662 | 50,650 | 12.2 | 13.6 | 33.3 | 27.2 | 8.1 | 5.7 | 48,059 | 39,579 | 49,752 | 54,418 | 51,571 | 40,450 |
| MONROE | 28,887 | 35,124 | 11.7 | 14.7 | 33.9 | 27.3 | 7.7 | 4.8 | 45,445 | 34,570 | 45,120 | 49,908 | 48,546 | 40,748 |
| NASSAU | 20,863 | 21,248 | 12.0 | 12.8 | 34.5 | 30.7 | 6.5 | 3.4 | 43,175 | 36,846 | 45,054 | 52,307 | 48,512 | 29,459 |
| OKALOOSA | 18,353 | 63,614 | 10.7 | 16.8 | 37.6 | 29.2 | 4.4 | 1.4 | 37,941 | 30,369 | 40,099 | 47,722 | 42,511 | 32,613 |
| OKEECHOBEE | 13,271 | 10,638 | 20.8 | 20.4 | 36.1 | 19.5 | 2.2 | 1.0 | 30,243 | 26,986 | 37,117 | 35,728 | 34,873 | 21,244 |
| ORANGE | 21,439 | 315,958 | 10.9 | 13.6 | 35.4 | 31.1 | 6.6 | 2.4 | 41,895 | 36,481 | 45,297 | 49,178 | 45,597 | 30,982 |
| OSCEOLA | 17,605 | 56,371 | 10.8 | 15.5 | 39.7 | 29.2 | 4.0 | 1.0 | 37,141 | 35,722 | 40,765 | 45,395 | 38,549 | 25,922 |
| PALM BEACH | 27,929 | 449,634 | 13.3 | 13.5 | 32.9 | 27.7 | 7.5 | 5.1 | 46,442 | 40,086 | 47,791 | 52,828 | 49,665 | 37,268 |
| PASCO | 18,017 | 145,838 | 15.3 | 18.7 | 38.6 | 24.0 | 2.8 | 0.6 | 33,028 | 33,896 | 40,185 | 41,001 | 34,854 | 26,304 |
| PINELLAS | 23,540 | 391,896 | 15.2 | 17.0 | 35.3 | 24.0 | 5.6 | 3.0 | 39,022 | 34,284 | 43,958 | 48,060 | 42,177 | 29,391 |
| POLK | 18,572 | 176,910 | 14.4 | 15.5 | 36.9 | 26.7 | 5.0 | 1.5 | 37,143 | 33,844 | 43,021 | 45,112 | 40,684 | 28,031 |
| PUTNAM | 14,923 | 27,072 | 23.1 | 18.6 | 34.2 | 20.0 | 3.2 | 1.0 | 30,839 | 29,322 | 36,990 | 39,264 | 33,942 | 21,882 |
| ST. JOHNS | 31,363 | 49,774 | 8.6 | 11.8 | 30.4 | 31.6 | 10.9 | 6.7 | 53,043 | 42,114 | 56,458 | 59,015 | 55,325 | 40,752 |
| ST. LUCIE | 20,133 | 70,644 | 11.7 | 13.4 | 36.8 | 30.2 | 5.9 | 1.9 | 40,006 | 39,030 | 44,223 | 46,081 | 43,246 | 33,557 |
| SANTA ROSA | 20,623 | 45,812 | 11.1 | 12.6 | 35.7 | 31.4 | 7.2 | 2.1 | 41,612 | 34,908 | 44,264 | 50,766 | 45,420 | 31,955 |
| SARASOTA | 27,086 | 138,301 | 10.5 | 14.3 | 35.4 | 28.4 | 7.5 | 4.0 | 44,908 | 37,298 | 48,307 | 51,168 | 49,196 | 39,260 |
| SEMINOLE | 24,603 | 135,233 | 7.9 | 10.0 | 32.6 | 36.2 | 9.7 | 3.7 | 48,435 | 41,546 | 51,895 | 56,366 | 51,217 | 32,838 |
| SUMTER | 13,981 | 15,508 | 22.0 | 18.8 | 36.5 | 19.5 | 2.5 | 0.8 | 30,112 | 27,504 | 40,009 | 35,031 | 31,501 | 23,690 |
| SUWANNEE | 14,589 | 12,766 | 21.7 | 19.8 | 34.8 | 20.0 | 3.0 | 0.8 | 30,464 | 29,560 | 35,827 | 39,550 | 31,474 | 21,398 |
| TAYLOR | 15,509 | 6,636 | 24.0 | 18.0 | 33.5 | 20.1 | 3.3 | 1.1 | 30,999 | 27,521 | 38,457 | 38,363 | 33,856 | 19,784 |
| UNION | 12,685 | 3,021 | 18.9 | 18.8 | 41.6 | 19.4 | 1.2 | 0.1 | 29,063 | 28,403 | 31,781 | 36,984 | 29,152 | 19,582 |
| VOLUSIA | 18,891 | 177,435 | 16.2 | 17.4 | 36.5 | 24.3 | 4.3 | 1.3 | 35,191 | 32,462 | 40,419 | 42,945 | 38,480 | 27,937 |
| WAKULLA | 17,911 | 6,973 | 11.1 | 13.7 | 38.6 | 27.2 | 7.0 | 2.4 | 40,243 | 37,015 | 44,572 | 45,937 | 40,069 | 31,822 |
| WALTON | 17,684 | 15,448 | 18.6 | 16.7 | 34.0 | 24.1 | 5.1 | 1.6 | 35,263 | 27,439 | 37,736 | 41,363 | 40,084 | 29,783 |
| WASHINGTON | 13,189 | 7,436 | 22.9 | 19.3 | 35.4 | 19.7 | 2.1 | 0.7 | 29,271 | 25,640 | 34,898 | 36,222 | 31,978 | 20,375 |
| FLORIDA | 21,473 | | 14.8 | 15.2 | 34.4 | 26.9 | 5.9 | 2.9 | 40,198 | 34,749 | 44,201 | 47,664 | 43,025 | 31,150 |
| UNITED STATES | 22,162 | | 14.5 | 12.5 | 32.3 | 29.8 | 7.4 | 3.5 | 40,748 | 34,503 | 44,969 | 49,579 | 43,409 | 27,339 |

| COUNTY | FINANCIAL SERVICES | | | | THE HOME: Home Improvements | | | THE HOME: Furnishings | | | ENTERTAINMENT | | | | | | PERSONAL | | | |
|---|---|---|---|---|---|---|---|---|---|---|---|---|---|---|---|---|---|---|---|---|
| | Auto Loan | Home Loan | Invest-ments | Retire-ment Plans | Home Repair | Lawn & Garden | Remodel-ing | Appli-ances | Elec-tronics | Furni-ture | Restau-rants | Sport-ing Goods | Theater & Concerts | Toys & Hobbies | Travel | Video Rental | Apparel | Auto After-market | Health Insur-ance | Pets & Supplies |
| ALACHUA | 96 | 98 | 96 | 97 | 98 | 95 | 100 | 93 | 94 | 90 | 94 | 95 | 90 | 96 | 83 | 95 | 93 | 96 | 95 | 98 |
| BAKER | 97 | 83 | 84 | 82 | 92 | 90 | 112 | 96 | 94 | 90 | 92 | 96 | 86 | 98 | 73 | 97 | 88 | 92 | 96 | 99 |
| BAY | 97 | 89 | 95 | 90 | 99 | 98 | 106 | 98 | 94 | 93 | 94 | 96 | 92 | 99 | 83 | 98 | 93 | 95 | 99 | 100 |
| BRADFORD | 96 | 75 | 85 | 81 | 94 | 94 | 110 | 96 | 92 | 83 | 85 | 92 | 84 | 94 | 74 | 97 | 83 | 90 | 101 | 97 |
| BREVARD | 100 | 101 | 104 | 99 | 104 | 105 | 100 | 100 | 98 | 101 | 104 | 101 | 101 | 102 | 91 | 99 | 101 | 100 | 102 | 102 |
| BROWARD | 100 | 104 | 108 | 102 | 105 | 107 | 100 | 100 | 98 | 103 | 104 | 101 | 102 | 102 | 94 | 99 | 101 | 102 | 101 | 102 |
| CALHOUN | 95 | 65 | 70 | 73 | 92 | 90 | 108 | 94 | 91 | 76 | 77 | 91 | 78 | 91 | 69 | 95 | 78 | 86 | 101 | 94 |
| CHARLOTTE | 103 | 93 | 116 | 105 | 108 | 116 | 110 | 105 | 95 | 96 | 100 | 100 | 100 | 104 | 95 | 97 | 97 | 98 | 112 | 104 |
| CITRUS | 99 | 85 | 116 | 96 | 105 | 111 | 107 | 102 | 90 | 89 | 93 | 97 | 95 | 101 | 90 | 95 | 87 | 94 | 110 | 101 |
| CLAY | 102 | 102 | 90 | 97 | 97 | 98 | 103 | 101 | 103 | 103 | 107 | 104 | 99 | 104 | 85 | 101 | 103 | 103 | 98 | 104 |
| COLLIER | 102 | 102 | 110 | 106 | 106 | 113 | 107 | 104 | 99 | 101 | 105 | 102 | 103 | 104 | 95 | 99 | 103 | 102 | 107 | 104 |
| COLUMBIA | 96 | 82 | 89 | 83 | 95 | 93 | 108 | 96 | 93 | 89 | 89 | 94 | 88 | 97 | 76 | 97 | 88 | 92 | 97 | 98 |
| DADE | 97 | 106 | 104 | 98 | 106 | 103 | 99 | 98 | 94 | 109 | 99 | 101 | 100 | 94 | 100 | 100 | 100 | 102 | 95 | 97 |
| DE SOTO | 95 | 76 | 100 | 81 | 98 | 98 | 103 | 97 | 89 | 84 | 84 | 92 | 86 | 95 | 79 | 95 | 81 | 90 | 102 | 97 |
| DIXIE | 97 | 75 | 96 | 82 | 97 | 97 | 109 | 97 | 90 | 82 | 85 | 95 | 86 | 97 | 77 | 96 | 81 | 90 | 104 | 99 |
| DUVAL | 97 | 97 | 94 | 93 | 99 | 97 | 96 | 98 | 96 | 98 | 98 | 98 | 96 | 98 | 86 | 98 | 97 | 98 | 95 | 99 |
| ESCAMBIA | 97 | 94 | 95 | 92 | 100 | 97 | 99 | 97 | 96 | 96 | 96 | 97 | 94 | 98 | 85 | 98 | 96 | 97 | 96 | 99 |
| FLAGLER | 105 | 95 | 115 | 109 | 108 | 119 | 114 | 107 | 97 | 99 | 103 | 102 | 102 | 106 | 97 | 98 | 103 | 101 | 112 | 106 |
| FRANKLIN | 97 | 70 | 92 | 84 | 97 | 98 | 109 | 98 | 91 | 80 | 82 | 95 | 84 | 96 | 77 | 96 | 82 | 89 | 103 | 98 |
| GADSDEN | 92 | 73 | 77 | 74 | 94 | 87 | 96 | 94 | 89 | 87 | 78 | 88 | 82 | 90 | 74 | 97 | 86 | 90 | 89 | 93 |
| GILCHRIST | 96 | 76 | 80 | 79 | 92 | 90 | 112 | 95 | 93 | 85 | 86 | 94 | 84 | 96 | 71 | 97 | 84 | 90 | 98 | 98 |
| GLADES | 97 | 80 | 101 | 84 | 98 | 99 | 110 | 98 | 90 | 85 | 89 | 96 | 88 | 99 | 79 | 96 | 83 | 91 | 104 | 100 |
| GULF | 97 | 73 | 83 | 81 | 96 | 93 | 111 | 97 | 91 | 82 | 83 | 95 | 85 | 97 | 74 | 97 | 84 | 90 | 100 | 98 |
| HAMILTON | 96 | 66 | 70 | 73 | 93 | 89 | 109 | 95 | 91 | 78 | 78 | 95 | 79 | 94 | 68 | 95 | 79 | 87 | 98 | 96 |
| HARDEE | 96 | 80 | 90 | 81 | 95 | 94 | 109 | 96 | 92 | 86 | 88 | 93 | 86 | 96 | 76 | 97 | 84 | 91 | 100 | 99 |
| HENDRY | 96 | 84 | 89 | 83 | 95 | 92 | 107 | 96 | 93 | 90 | 90 | 94 | 88 | 97 | 77 | 97 | 87 | 92 | 96 | 98 |
| HERNANDO | 102 | 89 | 114 | 101 | 106 | 113 | 110 | 104 | 93 | 94 | 97 | 99 | 98 | 103 | 92 | 97 | 94 | 96 | 110 | 103 |
| HIGHLANDS | 97 | 82 | 115 | 90 | 103 | 106 | 102 | 99 | 89 | 86 | 89 | 94 | 92 | 97 | 87 | 95 | 83 | 92 | 107 | 99 |
| HILLSBOROUGH | 98 | 99 | 96 | 95 | 100 | 99 | 99 | 98 | 97 | 99 | 100 | 99 | 97 | 99 | 87 | 99 | 98 | 99 | 97 | 100 |
| HOLMES | 96 | 64 | 69 | 73 | 92 | 90 | 110 | 94 | 91 | 76 | 77 | 93 | 78 | 93 | 67 | 95 | 78 | 86 | 101 | 95 |
| INDIAN RIVER | 102 | 97 | 113 | 104 | 107 | 112 | 107 | 103 | 97 | 99 | 101 | 101 | 102 | 104 | 94 | 98 | 99 | 100 | 107 | 103 |
| JACKSON | 96 | 72 | 79 | 79 | 94 | 91 | 109 | 95 | 92 | 82 | 82 | 92 | 82 | 94 | 72 | 96 | 82 | 89 | 98 | 96 |
| JEFFERSON | 96 | 76 | 83 | 81 | 94 | 91 | 108 | 96 | 93 | 85 | 85 | 94 | 85 | 96 | 74 | 97 | 85 | 90 | 97 | 97 |
| LAFAYETTE | 97 | 70 | 78 | 78 | 93 | 91 | 115 | 96 | 93 | 80 | 82 | 95 | 82 | 96 | 70 | 96 | 82 | 89 | 101 | 98 |
| LAKE | 97 | 83 | 107 | 88 | 101 | 102 | 104 | 98 | 91 | 88 | 90 | 94 | 91 | 98 | 84 | 96 | 85 | 92 | 105 | 99 |
| LEE | 100 | 94 | 107 | 99 | 104 | 108 | 105 | 102 | 96 | 97 | 99 | 100 | 98 | 102 | 91 | 98 | 96 | 98 | 106 | 102 |
| LEON | 99 | 105 | 98 | 102 | 99 | 99 | 101 | 97 | 99 | 99 | 102 | 100 | 97 | 100 | 88 | 98 | 101 | 101 | 96 | 102 |
| LEVY | 96 | 78 | 97 | 82 | 97 | 97 | 107 | 97 | 90 | 85 | 87 | 93 | 87 | 96 | 78 | 96 | 83 | 91 | 102 | 98 |
| LIBERTY | 96 | 74 | 82 | 79 | 93 | 92 | 112 | 96 | 93 | 82 | 84 | 93 | 83 | 96 | 72 | 97 | 83 | 90 | 100 | 97 |
| MADISON | 95 | 69 | 72 | 75 | 93 | 89 | 106 | 95 | 89 | 80 | 78 | 93 | 81 | 93 | 70 | 96 | 82 | 89 | 96 | 95 |
| MANATEE | 99 | 92 | 112 | 97 | 105 | 107 | 103 | 100 | 93 | 94 | 96 | 97 | 97 | 100 | 90 | 97 | 92 | 96 | 105 | 100 |
| MARION | 98 | 86 | 104 | 90 | 101 | 102 | 105 | 99 | 93 | 91 | 93 | 97 | 93 | 99 | 84 | 97 | 88 | 94 | 103 | 100 |
| MARTIN | 103 | 97 | 117 | 107 | 108 | 115 | 110 | 104 | 97 | 98 | 102 | 102 | 102 | 104 | 96 | 98 | 99 | 100 | 110 | 104 |
| MONROE | 100 | 104 | 113 | 104 | 107 | 110 | 106 | 101 | 98 | 101 | 104 | 101 | 102 | 102 | 96 | 99 | 102 | 102 | 105 | 104 |
| NASSAU | 98 | 92 | 99 | 93 | 99 | 99 | 109 | 98 | 96 | 95 | 97 | 98 | 94 | 100 | 83 | 98 | 94 | 96 | 99 | 101 |
| OKALOOSA | 98 | 98 | 96 | 94 | 100 | 99 | 100 | 98 | 98 | 97 | 101 | 99 | 97 | 100 | 86 | 99 | 98 | 99 | 98 | 101 |
| OKEECHOBEE | 97 | 82 | 99 | 85 | 97 | 97 | 108 | 97 | 92 | 88 | 90 | 95 | 89 | 98 | 79 | 96 | 85 | 92 | 101 | 99 |
| ORANGE | 98 | 101 | 93 | 95 | 99 | 98 | 97 | 98 | 98 | 100 | 102 | 99 | 97 | 100 | 87 | 99 | 99 | 99 | 96 | 101 |
| OSCEOLA | 99 | 96 | 87 | 91 | 95 | 95 | 102 | 98 | 98 | 97 | 100 | 99 | 94 | 100 | 82 | 99 | 96 | 97 | 97 | 101 |
| PALM BEACH | 101 | 105 | 110 | 106 | 106 | 110 | 103 | 102 | 99 | 103 | 105 | 103 | 104 | 103 | 96 | 99 | 103 | 102 | 104 | 103 |
| PASCO | 98 | 84 | 111 | 90 | 102 | 105 | 104 | 99 | 90 | 87 | 91 | 95 | 92 | 99 | 86 | 95 | 84 | 92 | 107 | 100 |
| PINELLAS | 98 | 96 | 112 | 98 | 106 | 107 | 100 | 100 | 94 | 98 | 98 | 98 | 99 | 100 | 92 | 97 | 95 | 97 | 104 | 100 |
| POLK | 97 | 86 | 101 | 89 | 100 | 99 | 104 | 98 | 93 | 91 | 92 | 96 | 92 | 98 | 83 | 97 | 89 | 94 | 101 | 99 |
| PUTNAM | 96 | 77 | 95 | 81 | 98 | 96 | 106 | 96 | 90 | 84 | 85 | 93 | 86 | 96 | 78 | 95 | 82 | 90 | 102 | 97 |
| ST. JOHNS | 101 | 100 | 107 | 103 | 103 | 107 | 107 | 102 | 100 | 100 | 103 | 102 | 101 | 103 | 92 | 99 | 102 | 101 | 103 | 103 |
| ST. LUCIE | 101 | 95 | 99 | 97 | 101 | 104 | 104 | 101 | 97 | 98 | 100 | 101 | 97 | 102 | 88 | 99 | 98 | 99 | 102 | 102 |
| SANTA ROSA | 100 | 94 | 92 | 93 | 98 | 97 | 107 | 99 | 99 | 97 | 99 | 100 | 95 | 102 | 82 | 99 | 97 | 98 | 98 | 102 |
| SARASOTA | 101 | 95 | 114 | 102 | 106 | 111 | 105 | 102 | 96 | 97 | 100 | 100 | 100 | 103 | 93 | 98 | 97 | 99 | 108 | 103 |
| SEMINOLE | 102 | 110 | 97 | 104 | 101 | 103 | 100 | 102 | 104 | 107 | 111 | 106 | 104 | 105 | 91 | 101 | 108 | 106 | 98 | 105 |
| SUMTER | 96 | 79 | 101 | 83 | 98 | 98 | 106 | 97 | 90 | 85 | 87 | 94 | 88 | 97 | 79 | 95 | 82 | 90 | 103 | 98 |
| SUWANNEE | 96 | 76 | 88 | 80 | 95 | 93 | 109 | 96 | 92 | 85 | 86 | 94 | 85 | 96 | 75 | 96 | 83 | 90 | 100 | 97 |
| TAYLOR | 97 | 71 | 82 | 78 | 94 | 92 | 110 | 96 | 91 | 81 | 82 | 94 | 83 | 95 | 72 | 96 | 82 | 89 | 99 | 98 |
| UNION | 96 | 76 | 83 | 79 | 92 | 91 | 113 | 95 | 93 | 84 | 86 | 92 | 83 | 95 | 72 | 97 | 84 | 90 | 99 | 97 |
| VOLUSIA | 99 | 92 | 105 | 95 | 103 | 104 | 102 | 99 | 94 | 94 | 96 | 97 | 95 | 99 | 88 | 97 | 93 | 96 | 103 | 100 |
| WAKULLA | 97 | 79 | 83 | 81 | 92 | 90 | 114 | 96 | 93 | 87 | 89 | 95 | 85 | 97 | 72 | 97 | 86 | 91 | 98 | 99 |
| WALTON | 100 | 81 | 102 | 93 | 101 | 105 | 112 | 101 | 94 | 89 | 91 | 97 | 91 | 99 | 84 | 97 | 90 | 93 | 106 | 100 |
| WASHINGTON | 96 | 70 | 86 | 79 | 96 | 94 | 108 | 96 | 92 | 80 | 82 | 93 | 83 | 94 | 73 | 96 | 81 | 88 | 103 | 96 |
| FLORIDA | 99 | 98 | 104 | 98 | 103 | 104 | 102 | 100 | 96 | 99 | 99 | 100 | 98 | 100 | 90 | 98 | 97 | 99 | 101 | 101 |
| UNITED STATES | 100 | 100 | 100 | 100 | 100 | 100 | 100 | 100 | 100 | 100 | 100 | 100 | 100 | 100 | 100 | 100 | 100 | 100 | 100 | 100 |

# POPULATION CHANGE

| COUNTY | FIPS Code | MSA Code | DMA Code | POPULATION 1990 | POPULATION 2000 | POPULATION 2005 | 1990-2000 ANNUAL CHANGE % Rate | 1990-2000 ANNUAL CHANGE State Rank | RACE (%) White 1990 | White 2000 | Black 1990 | Black 2000 | Asian/Pacific 1990 | Asian/Pacific 2000 |
|---|---|---|---|---|---|---|---|---|---|---|---|---|---|---|
| APPLING | 001 | 0000 | 507 | 15,744 | 16,802 | 17,441 | 0.6 | 111 | 78.5 | 73.8 | 20.8 | 24.9 | 0.3 | 0.5 |
| ATKINSON | 003 | 0000 | 525 | 6,213 | 7,413 | 8,003 | 1.7 | 57 | 71.3 | 65.5 | 26.7 | 30.9 | 0.0 | 0.1 |
| BACON | 005 | 0000 | 507 | 9,566 | 10,373 | 10,430 | 0.8 | 97 | 83.9 | 80.5 | 15.5 | 18.5 | 0.2 | 0.4 |
| BAKER | 007 | 0000 | 525 | 3,615 | 3,592 | 3,469 | -0.1 | 150 | 48.3 | 42.5 | 51.5 | 57.3 | 0.1 | 0.1 |
| BALDWIN | 009 | 0000 | 503 | 39,530 | 42,386 | 43,424 | 0.7 | 102 | 56.8 | 51.7 | 42.3 | 46.8 | 0.7 | 1.1 |
| BANKS | 011 | 0000 | 524 | 10,308 | 13,577 | 15,552 | 2.7 | 32 | 95.8 | 94.2 | 3.5 | 4.6 | 0.3 | 0.5 |
| BARROW | 013 | 0520 | 524 | 29,721 | 43,368 | 50,755 | 3.8 | 18 | 87.4 | 83.5 | 11.3 | 14.1 | 0.8 | 1.5 |
| BARTOW | 015 | 0520 | 524 | 55,911 | 77,769 | 91,319 | 3.3 | 24 | 90.2 | 87.4 | 9.0 | 11.2 | 0.3 | 0.5 |
| BEN HILL | 017 | 0000 | 525 | 16,245 | 17,512 | 17,727 | 0.7 | 102 | 68.3 | 62.8 | 31.3 | 36.6 | 0.2 | 0.4 |
| BERRIEN | 019 | 0000 | 525 | 14,153 | 16,784 | 18,077 | 1.7 | 57 | 87.7 | 84.7 | 11.6 | 14.3 | 0.2 | 0.4 |
| BIBB | 021 | 4680 | 503 | 149,967 | 155,360 | 154,954 | 0.3 | 127 | 57.5 | 51.8 | 41.7 | 47.0 | 0.5 | 0.9 |
| BLECKLEY | 023 | 0000 | 503 | 10,430 | 11,459 | 12,139 | 0.9 | 89 | 76.7 | 72.3 | 22.4 | 26.1 | 0.8 | 1.4 |
| BRANTLEY | 025 | 0000 | 561 | 11,077 | 14,234 | 15,909 | 2.5 | 37 | 94.2 | 92.8 | 5.4 | 6.7 | 0.0 | 0.1 |
| BROOKS | 027 | 0000 | 530 | 15,398 | 16,518 | 17,259 | 0.7 | 102 | 57.8 | 52.2 | 41.5 | 46.7 | 0.2 | 0.3 |
| BRYAN | 029 | 7520 | 507 | 15,438 | 25,190 | 29,232 | 4.9 | 7 | 84.3 | 80.4 | 14.9 | 18.2 | 0.5 | 0.9 |
| BULLOCH | 031 | 0000 | 507 | 43,125 | 51,230 | 53,516 | 1.7 | 57 | 73.0 | 67.9 | 26.0 | 30.7 | 0.5 | 0.8 |
| BURKE | 033 | 0000 | 520 | 20,579 | 23,658 | 25,731 | 1.4 | 71 | 47.4 | 41.6 | 52.3 | 58.0 | 0.1 | 0.2 |
| BUTTS | 035 | 0000 | 524 | 15,326 | 18,978 | 21,860 | 2.1 | 41 | 63.7 | 59.7 | 35.5 | 39.1 | 0.3 | 0.6 |
| CALHOUN | 037 | 0000 | 525 | 5,013 | 4,906 | 4,758 | -0.2 | 156 | 40.8 | 35.6 | 58.9 | 64.1 | 0.0 | 0.0 |
| CAMDEN | 039 | 0000 | 561 | 30,167 | 47,859 | 51,731 | 4.6 | 10 | 77.2 | 72.2 | 20.2 | 23.4 | 1.3 | 2.4 |
| CANDLER | 043 | 0000 | 507 | 7,744 | 9,001 | 9,193 | 1.5 | 66 | 67.6 | 62.3 | 31.1 | 35.3 | 0.1 | 0.2 |
| CARROLL | 045 | 0520 | 524 | 71,422 | 86,776 | 95,606 | 1.9 | 48 | 83.5 | 79.7 | 15.7 | 19.1 | 0.3 | 0.6 |
| CATOOSA | 047 | 1560 | 575 | 42,464 | 53,406 | 59,845 | 2.3 | 39 | 98.5 | 97.8 | 0.8 | 1.1 | 0.4 | 0.7 |
| CHARLTON | 049 | 0000 | 561 | 8,496 | 9,516 | 9,818 | 1.1 | 82 | 71.7 | 66.6 | 27.7 | 32.7 | 0.1 | 0.2 |
| CHATHAM | 051 | 7520 | 507 | 216,935 | 227,108 | 228,070 | 0.4 | 126 | 60.2 | 54.3 | 38.1 | 42.9 | 1.1 | 1.9 |
| CHATTAHOOCHEE | 053 | 1800 | 522 | 16,934 | 16,848 | 17,770 | 0.0 | 145 | 59.6 | 54.0 | 30.9 | 30.6 | 2.8 | 4.4 |
| CHATTOOGA | 055 | 0000 | 575 | 22,242 | 22,877 | 23,000 | 0.3 | 127 | 90.9 | 88.4 | 8.7 | 11.1 | 0.1 | 0.2 |
| CHEROKEE | 057 | 0520 | 524 | 90,204 | 148,644 | 183,397 | 5.0 | 6 | 97.2 | 96.1 | 1.9 | 2.4 | 0.3 | 0.6 |
| CLARKE | 059 | 0500 | 524 | 87,594 | 90,769 | 91,374 | 0.3 | 127 | 70.7 | 64.3 | 26.2 | 30.6 | 2.5 | 4.1 |
| CLAY | 061 | 0000 | 522 | 3,364 | 3,563 | 3,738 | 0.6 | 111 | 38.9 | 34.0 | 60.8 | 65.6 | 0.1 | 0.1 |
| CLAYTON | 063 | 0520 | 524 | 182,052 | 217,903 | 238,903 | 1.8 | 51 | 72.4 | 66.7 | 23.8 | 26.8 | 2.8 | 4.8 |
| CLINCH | 065 | 0000 | 530 | 6,160 | 6,712 | 6,905 | 0.8 | 97 | 72.3 | 67.6 | 27.3 | 31.9 | 0.1 | 0.2 |
| COBB | 067 | 0520 | 524 | 447,745 | 599,554 | 679,478 | 2.9 | 25 | 87.5 | 83.9 | 9.9 | 11.6 | 1.8 | 3.2 |
| COFFEE | 069 | 0000 | 525 | 29,592 | 35,610 | 38,817 | 1.8 | 51 | 72.9 | 67.5 | 25.4 | 29.6 | 0.4 | 0.7 |
| COLQUITT | 071 | 0000 | 525 | 36,645 | 41,555 | 44,505 | 1.2 | 78 | 73.8 | 69.3 | 24.2 | 28.3 | 0.1 | 0.2 |
| COLUMBIA | 073 | 0600 | 520 | 66,031 | 95,733 | 107,927 | 3.7 | 19 | 86.0 | 81.6 | 11.0 | 13.1 | 2.3 | 4.3 |
| COOK | 075 | 0000 | 525 | 13,456 | 15,474 | 16,814 | 1.4 | 71 | 69.2 | 64.4 | 30.0 | 34.5 | 0.2 | 0.4 |
| COWETA | 077 | 0520 | 524 | 53,853 | 93,717 | 115,240 | 5.6 | 5 | 76.7 | 71.9 | 22.6 | 27.1 | 0.3 | 0.5 |
| CRAWFORD | 079 | 0000 | 503 | 8,991 | 10,352 | 10,047 | 1.4 | 71 | 67.7 | 62.1 | 30.7 | 35.8 | 0.2 | 0.3 |
| CRISP | 081 | 0000 | 525 | 20,011 | 20,642 | 20,668 | 0.3 | 127 | 58.9 | 53.7 | 40.7 | 45.8 | 0.1 | 0.2 |
| DADE | 083 | 1560 | 575 | 13,147 | 15,633 | 17,124 | 1.7 | 57 | 98.7 | 98.1 | 0.8 | 1.1 | 0.2 | 0.3 |
| DAWSON | 085 | 0000 | 524 | 9,429 | 16,932 | 21,821 | 5.9 | 4 | 98.9 | 98.3 | 0.0 | 0.3 | 0.1 | 0.1 |
| DECATUR | 087 | 0000 | 530 | 25,511 | 27,504 | 28,471 | 0.7 | 102 | 59.7 | 54.3 | 39.5 | 44.6 | 0.2 | 0.3 |
| DEKALB | 089 | 0520 | 524 | 545,837 | 603,600 | 621,075 | 1.0 | 84 | 53.6 | 47.3 | 42.2 | 45.9 | 3.0 | 4.8 |
| DODGE | 091 | 0000 | 503 | 17,607 | 18,182 | 18,380 | 0.3 | 127 | 71.7 | 67.1 | 27.6 | 31.7 | 0.2 | 0.4 |
| DOOLY | 093 | 0000 | 503 | 9,901 | 10,450 | 10,543 | 0.5 | 119 | 50.4 | 44.8 | 49.0 | 54.1 | 0.4 | 0.8 |
| DOUGHERTY | 095 | 0120 | 525 | 96,311 | 94,196 | 90,698 | -0.2 | 156 | 48.8 | 43.7 | 50.2 | 55.0 | 0.5 | 0.8 |
| DOUGLAS | 097 | 0520 | 524 | 71,120 | 93,341 | 104,163 | 2.7 | 32 | 91.0 | 88.5 | 7.9 | 9.6 | 0.5 | 1.0 |
| EARLY | 099 | 0000 | 606 | 11,854 | 12,117 | 12,070 | 0.2 | 137 | 55.5 | 49.9 | 44.1 | 49.6 | 0.1 | 0.2 |
| ECHOLS | 101 | 0000 | 530 | 2,334 | 2,625 | 3,075 | 1.2 | 78 | 86.0 | 82.6 | 11.3 | 14.3 | 0.1 | 0.2 |
| EFFINGHAM | 103 | 7520 | 507 | 25,687 | 40,227 | 48,819 | 4.5 | 11 | 85.3 | 81.8 | 14.1 | 17.3 | 0.2 | 0.4 |
| ELBERT | 105 | 0000 | 567 | 18,949 | 19,409 | 19,667 | 0.2 | 137 | 69.4 | 64.5 | 30.2 | 34.8 | 0.3 | 0.5 |
| EMANUEL | 107 | 0000 | 520 | 20,546 | 21,069 | 21,210 | 0.2 | 137 | 67.0 | 61.9 | 32.5 | 37.3 | 0.2 | 0.4 |
| EVANS | 109 | 0000 | 507 | 8,724 | 10,269 | 11,161 | 1.6 | 63 | 64.8 | 59.8 | 34.0 | 38.3 | 0.2 | 0.4 |
| FANNIN | 111 | 0000 | 575 | 15,992 | 19,338 | 21,282 | 1.9 | 48 | 99.6 | 99.4 | 0.0 | 0.1 | 0.1 | 0.2 |
| FAYETTE | 113 | 0520 | 524 | 62,415 | 95,935 | 113,676 | 4.3 | 13 | 92.5 | 89.5 | 5.4 | 6.7 | 1.7 | 3.1 |
| FLOYD | 115 | 0000 | 524 | 81,251 | 85,915 | 87,951 | 0.5 | 119 | 85.3 | 81.9 | 13.7 | 16.4 | 0.5 | 0.9 |
| FORSYTH | 117 | 0520 | 524 | 44,083 | 106,143 | 152,945 | 9.0 | 1 | 98.8 | 97.9 | 0.0 | 0.0 | 0.2 | 0.4 |
| FRANKLIN | 119 | 0000 | 567 | 16,650 | 19,669 | 21,419 | 1.6 | 63 | 89.5 | 87.1 | 10.1 | 12.3 | 0.2 | 0.3 |
| FULTON | 121 | 0520 | 524 | 648,951 | 754,321 | 802,404 | 1.5 | 66 | 47.8 | 41.7 | 49.9 | 54.6 | 1.3 | 2.1 |
| GILMER | 123 | 0000 | 524 | 13,368 | 20,758 | 25,574 | 4.4 | 12 | 99.2 | 98.8 | 0.3 | 0.2 | 0.1 | 0.3 |
| GLASCOCK | 125 | 0000 | 520 | 2,357 | 2,574 | 2,727 | 0.9 | 89 | 87.2 | 85.1 | 12.6 | 14.7 | 0.0 | 0.0 |
| GLYNN | 127 | 0000 | 561 | 62,496 | 68,657 | 72,164 | 0.9 | 89 | 73.6 | 68.9 | 25.5 | 29.6 | 0.5 | 0.9 |
| GORDON | 129 | 0000 | 524 | 35,072 | 42,981 | 47,438 | 2.0 | 43 | 95.5 | 94.1 | 3.8 | 4.7 | 0.4 | 0.6 |
| GRADY | 131 | 0000 | 530 | 20,279 | 21,681 | 22,144 | 0.7 | 102 | 67.4 | 61.8 | 31.5 | 36.5 | 0.1 | 0.2 |
| GREENE | 133 | 0000 | 524 | 11,793 | 14,469 | 16,306 | 2.0 | 43 | 49.7 | 43.8 | 49.9 | 55.7 | 0.0 | 0.0 |
| GWINNETT | 135 | 0520 | 524 | 352,910 | 569,629 | 683,437 | 4.8 | 8 | 90.9 | 87.0 | 5.2 | 6.0 | 2.9 | 5.2 |
| HABERSHAM | 137 | 0000 | 524 | 27,621 | 33,197 | 36,523 | 1.8 | 51 | 91.7 | 89.6 | 5.6 | 5.8 | 1.9 | 3.3 |
| HALL | 139 | 0000 | 524 | 95,428 | 127,059 | 145,748 | 2.8 | 30 | 87.1 | 82.3 | 8.6 | 10.1 | 0.7 | 1.2 |
| HANCOCK | 141 | 0000 | 503 | 8,908 | 9,036 | 8,985 | 0.1 | 140 | 20.2 | 17.6 | 79.4 | 82.0 | 0.0 | 0.0 |
| HARALSON | 143 | 0000 | 524 | 21,966 | 25,522 | 27,761 | 1.5 | 66 | 93.0 | 91.1 | 6.5 | 8.2 | 0.2 | 0.4 |
| HARRIS | 145 | 1800 | 522 | 17,788 | 23,167 | 25,230 | 2.6 | 34 | 73.7 | 69.0 | 25.7 | 30.0 | 0.2 | 0.4 |
| HART | 147 | 0000 | 567 | 19,712 | 22,482 | 24,203 | 1.3 | 74 | 79.4 | 75.3 | 20.3 | 24.2 | 0.2 | 0.3 |
| HEARD | 149 | 0000 | 524 | 8,628 | 10,763 | 12,134 | 2.2 | 40 | 86.0 | 82.7 | 13.5 | 16.4 | 0.3 | 0.5 |
| HENRY | 151 | 0520 | 524 | 58,741 | 121,383 | 159,878 | 7.3 | 2 | 88.7 | 85.4 | 10.3 | 12.9 | 0.6 | 1.0 |
| HOUSTON | 153 | 4680 | 503 | 89,208 | 109,781 | 120,136 | 2.0 | 43 | 76.3 | 71.5 | 21.7 | 25.2 | 1.2 | 2.0 |
| IRWIN | 155 | 0000 | 525 | 8,649 | 9,312 | 9,939 | 0.7 | 102 | 69.3 | 64.3 | 30.4 | 35.1 | 0.2 | 0.3 |
| GEORGIA | | | | | | | 2.0 | | 71.0 | 68.5 | 27.0 | 28.1 | 1.2 | 2.0 |
| UNITED STATES | | | | | | | 1.0 | | 80.3 | 77.9 | 12.1 | 12.4 | 2.9 | 3.9 |

| COUNTY | % HISPANIC ORIGIN | | 2000 AGE DISTRIBUTION (%) | | | | | | | | | | MEDIAN AGE | | 2000 Males/ Females (×100) |
|---|---|---|---|---|---|---|---|---|---|---|---|---|---|---|---|
| | 1990 | 2000 | 0-4 | 5-9 | 10-14 | 15-19 | 20-24 | 25-44 | 45-64 | 65-84 | 85+ | 18+ | 1990 | 2000 | |
| APPLING | 0.9 | 2.0 | 6.6 | 7.4 | 7.7 | 8.3 | 6.3 | 28.9 | 23.0 | 10.6 | 1.3 | 73.1 | 32.3 | 35.2 | 93.6 |
| ATKINSON | 2.5 | 4.6 | 8.1 | 7.9 | 8.5 | 7.7 | 7.1 | 28.3 | 22.0 | 9.4 | 1.0 | 70.6 | 30.9 | 32.9 | 96.1 |
| BACON | 0.9 | 2.0 | 7.4 | 7.5 | 7.6 | 7.7 | 7.3 | 27.9 | 22.6 | 10.7 | 1.3 | 72.6 | 31.7 | 34.0 | 91.5 |
| BAKER | 0.6 | 0.9 | 7.3 | 7.6 | 8.4 | 8.1 | 6.6 | 27.8 | 21.6 | 11.0 | 1.6 | 72.0 | 31.7 | 34.4 | 86.2 |
| BALDWIN | 0.9 | 1.7 | 5.8 | 5.8 | 6.0 | 8.5 | 8.7 | 33.8 | 20.8 | 9.4 | 1.2 | 77.9 | 31.9 | 33.9 | 109.2 |
| BANKS | 0.5 | 1.4 | 6.5 | 6.7 | 7.1 | 7.4 | 6.4 | 30.3 | 24.5 | 9.9 | 1.1 | 75.1 | 33.1 | 36.2 | 101.0 |
| BARROW | 0.9 | 2.0 | 8.3 | 7.8 | 7.8 | 7.1 | 6.4 | 31.7 | 21.5 | 8.1 | 1.2 | 71.8 | 31.1 | 33.5 | 97.5 |
| BARTOW | 0.9 | 2.2 | 7.8 | 7.5 | 7.5 | 7.1 | 6.5 | 31.5 | 22.5 | 8.6 | 1.0 | 73.0 | 31.5 | 34.2 | 98.2 |
| BEN HILL | 0.5 | 1.1 | 7.8 | 8.0 | 7.9 | 7.9 | 6.9 | 26.7 | 22.0 | 11.1 | 1.8 | 71.2 | 32.4 | 34.2 | 86.2 |
| BERRIEN | 2.0 | 2.9 | 7.4 | 7.3 | 7.5 | 7.6 | 6.3 | 28.1 | 23.6 | 10.7 | 1.5 | 73.3 | 32.9 | 35.4 | 95.0 |
| BIBB | 0.6 | 1.2 | 7.1 | 7.1 | 7.4 | 7.7 | 7.2 | 29.4 | 21.5 | 11.0 | 1.6 | 74.0 | 32.6 | 35.0 | 88.3 |
| BLECKLEY | 0.4 | 1.0 | 6.8 | 6.8 | 7.1 | 9.0 | 6.9 | 27.3 | 22.6 | 11.9 | 1.6 | 74.8 | 32.6 | 35.2 | 95.6 |
| BRANTLEY | 0.3 | 1.1 | 7.4 | 7.4 | 7.5 | 7.8 | 7.1 | 29.7 | 23.4 | 8.9 | 0.9 | 72.9 | 31.1 | 33.7 | 100.1 |
| BROOKS | 1.6 | 2.6 | 8.3 | 8.1 | 8.2 | 8.0 | 6.6 | 26.6 | 20.5 | 11.6 | 2.0 | 70.4 | 32.1 | 33.3 | 91.4 |
| BRYAN | 0.9 | 2.0 | 8.1 | 8.3 | 8.2 | 8.4 | 7.2 | 30.4 | 22.0 | 6.9 | 0.7 | 70.2 | 30.0 | 32.1 | 92.7 |
| BULLOCH | 0.8 | 1.6 | 6.4 | 6.2 | 6.2 | 13.2 | 14.2 | 26.5 | 17.8 | 8.3 | 1.1 | 77.6 | 26.1 | 28.1 | 95.3 |
| BURKE | 0.3 | 0.7 | 9.2 | 9.1 | 9.1 | 8.3 | 6.9 | 27.9 | 19.6 | 8.6 | 1.3 | 67.3 | 29.6 | 30.6 | 90.6 |
| BUTTS | 0.7 | 1.5 | 6.7 | 7.1 | 7.4 | 7.0 | 7.0 | 30.7 | 22.6 | 10.2 | 1.3 | 74.6 | 32.4 | 34.6 | 108.1 |
| CALHOUN | 0.2 | 0.3 | 7.5 | 7.5 | 7.5 | 7.4 | 7.5 | 26.8 | 20.9 | 12.4 | 2.5 | 72.9 | 33.5 | 34.7 | 84.0 |
| CAMDEN | 2.1 | 4.2 | 10.9 | 8.7 | 6.8 | 6.7 | 11.1 | 38.0 | 13.0 | 4.3 | 0.5 | 70.3 | 27.2 | 27.6 | 109.5 |
| CANDLER | 1.8 | 3.7 | 7.2 | 7.2 | 7.4 | 7.8 | 6.2 | 27.2 | 22.9 | 12.2 | 1.8 | 73.3 | 34.6 | 35.8 | 91.6 |
| CARROLL | 0.8 | 2.0 | 7.1 | 7.1 | 7.2 | 8.5 | 8.4 | 30.0 | 21.9 | 8.6 | 1.1 | 74.3 | 30.4 | 33.3 | 94.5 |
| CATOOSA | 0.5 | 1.4 | 6.4 | 6.5 | 7.2 | 6.9 | 5.9 | 30.2 | 25.6 | 10.3 | 1.1 | 75.8 | 33.9 | 37.1 | 93.5 |
| CHARLTON | 0.4 | 1.0 | 8.9 | 8.3 | 8.5 | 7.7 | 6.6 | 28.4 | 21.6 | 8.7 | 1.2 | 69.5 | 30.4 | 32.1 | 94.2 |
| CHATHAM | 1.3 | 2.5 | 7.4 | 7.3 | 7.4 | 7.4 | 7.3 | 29.8 | 21.0 | 11.0 | 1.4 | 73.8 | 32.2 | 34.5 | 93.3 |
| CHATTAHOOCHEE | 10.6 | 18.6 | 8.1 | 8.8 | 8.4 | 9.5 | 24.8 | 34.7 | 4.5 | 1.2 | 0.1 | 71.9 | 22.9 | 23.1 | 190.7 |
| CHATTOOGA | 0.3 | 1.0 | 6.7 | 6.6 | 7.1 | 7.0 | 6.0 | 27.7 | 24.4 | 13.0 | 1.6 | 75.5 | 34.8 | 37.6 | 92.5 |
| CHEROKEE | 1.2 | 2.8 | 8.8 | 8.3 | 7.7 | 6.4 | 5.4 | 36.6 | 20.2 | 5.9 | 0.7 | 71.5 | 31.1 | 33.3 | 101.0 |
| CLARKE | 1.7 | 3.3 | 6.1 | 5.6 | 5.3 | 10.8 | 18.0 | 30.5 | 15.4 | 7.3 | 1.1 | 80.3 | 25.6 | 27.7 | 90.5 |
| CLAY | 0.6 | 1.0 | 7.3 | 7.9 | 8.1 | 7.7 | 6.4 | 25.7 | 20.5 | 14.1 | 2.3 | 72.0 | 34.2 | 35.6 | 81.8 |
| CLAYTON | 2.1 | 4.1 | 8.0 | 7.6 | 7.3 | 7.0 | 7.3 | 35.5 | 20.7 | 6.0 | 0.6 | 73.0 | 29.9 | 32.4 | 94.1 |
| CLINCH | 1.0 | 1.3 | 7.6 | 7.7 | 8.3 | 8.2 | 6.3 | 28.1 | 22.6 | 10.1 | 1.1 | 71.2 | 31.6 | 34.0 | 93.1 |
| COBB | 2.1 | 4.4 | 7.1 | 7.0 | 7.0 | 6.2 | 6.3 | 37.0 | 22.3 | 6.5 | 0.7 | 75.2 | 31.7 | 34.7 | 95.6 |
| COFFEE | 1.9 | 3.4 | 7.9 | 7.9 | 7.9 | 8.0 | 7.1 | 29.6 | 21.6 | 8.9 | 1.2 | 71.6 | 30.5 | 32.8 | 95.3 |
| COLQUITT | 4.3 | 5.4 | 7.4 | 7.6 | 7.6 | 8.2 | 7.2 | 27.3 | 22.1 | 11.1 | 1.6 | 72.4 | 32.6 | 34.2 | 95.4 |
| COLUMBIA | 1.5 | 3.2 | 7.4 | 8.1 | 8.1 | 7.5 | 6.1 | 31.9 | 23.9 | 6.3 | 0.5 | 71.6 | 31.2 | 33.9 | 97.8 |
| COOK | 1.6 | 2.3 | 7.7 | 7.7 | 7.9 | 7.8 | 6.6 | 27.0 | 22.6 | 11.1 | 1.7 | 72.0 | 32.4 | 34.5 | 93.2 |
| COWETA | 0.7 | 1.7 | 8.0 | 8.2 | 8.1 | 6.9 | 5.7 | 31.1 | 22.4 | 8.5 | 1.0 | 71.4 | 32.0 | 34.0 | 93.8 |
| CRAWFORD | 1.7 | 2.5 | 7.5 | 7.4 | 7.8 | 7.3 | 6.6 | 30.9 | 23.0 | 8.4 | 1.1 | 72.8 | 31.7 | 34.3 | 97.8 |
| CRISP | 0.3 | 0.7 | 7.7 | 7.6 | 7.7 | 8.0 | 6.8 | 25.8 | 22.4 | 12.2 | 1.8 | 71.9 | 32.8 | 35.0 | 86.8 |
| DADE | 0.5 | 1.3 | 6.2 | 6.5 | 6.9 | 7.8 | 7.2 | 28.4 | 25.3 | 10.5 | 1.2 | 76.1 | 32.7 | 36.6 | 94.0 |
| DAWSON | 0.4 | 1.3 | 7.5 | 7.4 | 7.7 | 6.9 | 5.9 | 32.1 | 23.6 | 8.2 | 0.8 | 73.2 | 32.0 | 35.0 | 101.2 |
| DECATUR | 1.9 | 2.6 | 7.8 | 7.7 | 7.6 | 8.0 | 7.6 | 28.7 | 20.6 | 10.7 | 1.4 | 72.0 | 31.7 | 33.0 | 91.5 |
| DEKALB | 2.9 | 5.0 | 6.7 | 6.5 | 6.5 | 6.6 | 7.5 | 36.1 | 21.6 | 7.6 | 1.0 | 76.7 | 31.9 | 34.4 | 91.6 |
| DODGE | 0.8 | 1.6 | 6.9 | 6.8 | 7.0 | 7.5 | 6.7 | 28.8 | 22.9 | 11.8 | 1.6 | 74.8 | 33.8 | 35.7 | 97.6 |
| DOOLY | 0.8 | 1.6 | 7.8 | 8.1 | 8.4 | 7.9 | 6.8 | 26.2 | 21.7 | 11.2 | 1.8 | 70.7 | 32.8 | 34.0 | 85.3 |
| DOUGHERTY | 0.8 | 1.6 | 8.0 | 7.9 | 7.9 | 8.9 | 7.7 | 28.4 | 20.3 | 9.6 | 1.2 | 71.2 | 29.9 | 32.1 | 88.8 |
| DOUGLAS | 1.1 | 2.5 | 7.5 | 7.7 | 7.5 | 6.7 | 6.1 | 33.9 | 22.8 | 7.0 | 0.7 | 73.2 | 31.1 | 33.7 | 97.5 |
| EARLY | 0.4 | 0.7 | 7.6 | 7.9 | 8.4 | 8.0 | 6.6 | 25.6 | 21.8 | 11.9 | 2.2 | 70.7 | 33.4 | 34.8 | 85.8 |
| ECHOLS | 1.9 | 3.4 | 7.5 | 7.8 | 8.5 | 7.6 | 7.2 | 29.3 | 22.2 | 8.8 | 1.0 | 71.6 | 30.7 | 33.1 | 106.4 |
| EFFINGHAM | 0.7 | 1.7 | 7.7 | 8.1 | 8.3 | 7.7 | 6.8 | 31.4 | 22.0 | 7.2 | 0.7 | 71.1 | 30.3 | 32.9 | 100.8 |
| ELBERT | 0.7 | 1.7 | 7.1 | 7.3 | 7.5 | 7.1 | 6.2 | 27.1 | 23.4 | 12.4 | 2.1 | 73.9 | 34.4 | 36.8 | 91.4 |
| EMANUEL | 0.4 | 0.9 | 7.8 | 7.7 | 7.9 | 8.1 | 7.0 | 26.7 | 21.8 | 11.3 | 1.7 | 71.3 | 32.3 | 34.1 | 92.8 |
| EVANS | 1.2 | 2.1 | 7.7 | 7.8 | 8.0 | 8.1 | 6.8 | 27.0 | 21.1 | 11.7 | 1.8 | 71.4 | 32.2 | 34.4 | 95.8 |
| FANNIN | 0.4 | 1.3 | 5.6 | 5.8 | 6.4 | 6.2 | 5.1 | 25.5 | 26.6 | 16.7 | 2.2 | 78.3 | 39.0 | 41.9 | 93.1 |
| FAYETTE | 1.6 | 3.7 | 6.6 | 7.4 | 7.8 | 7.3 | 5.1 | 32.2 | 25.6 | 7.2 | 0.8 | 73.5 | 34.1 | 36.4 | 97.4 |
| FLOYD | 1.0 | 2.3 | 6.3 | 6.6 | 6.9 | 7.4 | 6.6 | 28.4 | 23.1 | 12.9 | 1.9 | 76.2 | 34.5 | 37.1 | 92.2 |
| FORSYTH | 1.4 | 3.2 | 7.4 | 7.1 | 7.3 | 6.5 | 5.6 | 33.4 | 24.5 | 7.5 | 0.8 | 74.3 | 32.8 | 35.7 | 100.5 |
| FRANKLIN | 0.5 | 1.3 | 6.1 | 6.3 | 6.7 | 6.9 | 5.6 | 27.7 | 25.0 | 13.8 | 1.8 | 77.0 | 35.9 | 38.6 | 94.8 |
| FULTON | 2.1 | 3.5 | 6.9 | 6.7 | 6.7 | 7.2 | 7.4 | 34.0 | 22.0 | 7.8 | 1.3 | 75.8 | 32.0 | 34.6 | 91.2 |
| GILMER | 0.8 | 2.0 | 6.4 | 6.5 | 6.9 | 6.7 | 5.8 | 27.2 | 25.7 | 13.3 | 1.7 | 76.2 | 35.4 | 38.7 | 96.9 |
| GLASCOCK | 0.3 | 0.8 | 5.3 | 5.6 | 6.0 | 6.8 | 5.6 | 27.4 | 25.3 | 15.2 | 2.8 | 78.7 | 37.0 | 40.5 | 87.9 |
| GLYNN | 0.9 | 2.0 | 6.9 | 7.0 | 7.2 | 7.3 | 6.1 | 28.1 | 23.5 | 12.5 | 1.6 | 74.7 | 34.1 | 36.9 | 90.8 |
| GORDON | 0.6 | 1.5 | 6.9 | 6.9 | 7.3 | 7.2 | 6.3 | 30.4 | 24.1 | 9.6 | 1.2 | 74.4 | 32.4 | 35.8 | 97.3 |
| GRADY | 1.4 | 2.7 | 7.2 | 7.3 | 7.5 | 7.4 | 6.7 | 28.2 | 22.5 | 11.3 | 1.9 | 73.5 | 32.9 | 35.4 | 92.3 |
| GREENE | 0.8 | 1.5 | 7.5 | 8.3 | 8.5 | 7.9 | 6.7 | 26.2 | 22.2 | 11.0 | 1.7 | 70.8 | 32.5 | 34.3 | 88.2 |
| GWINNETT | 2.4 | 5.2 | 8.2 | 8.0 | 7.6 | 6.4 | 6.0 | 38.5 | 20.1 | 4.9 | 0.5 | 72.4 | 30.5 | 33.1 | 97.9 |
| HABERSHAM | 1.2 | 2.7 | 6.1 | 6.2 | 6.4 | 8.6 | 8.1 | 27.4 | 23.2 | 12.4 | 1.7 | 77.3 | 33.3 | 36.4 | 105.5 |
| HALL | 4.8 | 9.0 | 7.4 | 7.1 | 7.2 | 7.0 | 6.5 | 31.8 | 22.7 | 9.3 | 1.1 | 74.5 | 32.3 | 35.0 | 97.8 |
| HANCOCK | 0.7 | 1.1 | 7.8 | 7.7 | 7.8 | 8.4 | 7.2 | 26.9 | 21.2 | 11.3 | 1.8 | 71.3 | 31.0 | 33.6 | 86.4 |
| HARALSON | 0.4 | 1.1 | 7.1 | 7.2 | 7.6 | 7.2 | 5.6 | 28.5 | 23.6 | 11.6 | 1.6 | 73.7 | 33.5 | 36.2 | 94.8 |
| HARRIS | 0.5 | 1.3 | 6.1 | 6.6 | 7.0 | 7.0 | 5.6 | 29.2 | 25.8 | 11.3 | 1.4 | 76.2 | 35.6 | 38.1 | 97.6 |
| HART | 0.4 | 0.9 | 6.4 | 6.8 | 7.0 | 6.2 | 5.6 | 28.2 | 23.8 | 14.0 | 1.9 | 76.0 | 35.7 | 38.1 | 96.0 |
| HEARD | 0.8 | 2.1 | 7.2 | 7.5 | 7.5 | 7.8 | 6.3 | 29.3 | 23.3 | 9.7 | 1.4 | 72.7 | 32.2 | 34.9 | 95.4 |
| HENRY | 0.8 | 2.0 | 7.8 | 7.7 | 7.6 | 6.6 | 5.6 | 33.7 | 22.8 | 7.2 | 0.8 | 72.8 | 31.9 | 34.5 | 97.8 |
| HOUSTON | 1.6 | 3.4 | 7.9 | 7.6 | 7.4 | 6.8 | 6.5 | 32.2 | 22.4 | 8.5 | 0.7 | 73.1 | 31.0 | 34.0 | 94.6 |
| IRWIN | 0.6 | 1.3 | 7.7 | 8.0 | 7.7 | 7.9 | 6.0 | 26.0 | 22.7 | 12.0 | 2.1 | 71.9 | 33.3 | 35.4 | 90.9 |
| GEORGIA | 1.7 | 3.3 | 7.4 | 7.3 | 7.3 | 7.3 | 7.1 | 32.3 | 21.8 | 8.6 | 1.1 | 74.0 | 31.6 | 34.1 | 94.9 |
| UNITED STATES | 9.0 | 11.8 | 6.9 | 7.2 | 7.2 | 7.2 | 6.7 | 29.9 | 22.2 | 11.1 | 1.6 | 74.6 | 32.9 | 35.7 | 95.6 |

# HOUSEHOLDS

| COUNTY | HOUSEHOLDS | | | | | FAMILIES | | | MEDIAN HOUSEHOLD INCOME | | | |
|---|---|---|---|---|---|---|---|---|---|---|---|---|
| | 1990 | 2000 | 2005 | % Annual Rate 1990-2000 | 2000 Average HH Size | 1990 | 2000 | % Annual Rate 1990-2000 | 2000 | 2005 | 2000 National Rank | 2000 State Rank |
| APPLING | 5,834 | 6,382 | 6,705 | 1.1 | 2.61 | 4,275 | 4,512 | 0.7 | 35,279 | 44,868 | 1206 | 59 |
| ATKINSON | 2,210 | 2,670 | 2,901 | 2.3 | 2.77 | 1,647 | 1,918 | 1.9 | 28,614 | 31,471 | 2347 | 128 |
| BACON | 3,442 | 3,849 | 3,927 | 1.4 | 2.66 | 2,645 | 2,871 | 1.0 | 30,247 | 33,495 | 2095 | 116 |
| BAKER | 1,300 | 1,357 | 1,342 | 0.5 | 2.64 | 949 | 951 | 0.0 | 28,929 | 32,147 | 2307 | 126 |
| BALDWIN | 12,165 | 13,505 | 14,044 | 1.3 | 2.60 | 8,735 | 9,465 | 1.0 | 35,165 | 38,100 | 1224 | 62 |
| BANKS | 3,775 | 5,082 | 5,885 | 3.7 | 2.67 | 2,973 | 3,885 | 3.3 | 34,525 | 37,778 | 1315 | 66 |
| BARROW | 10,676 | 15,871 | 18,735 | 4.9 | 2.72 | 8,361 | 12,123 | 4.6 | 43,360 | 52,560 | 435 | 23 |
| BARTOW | 20,091 | 28,447 | 33,801 | 4.3 | 2.70 | 15,665 | 21,711 | 4.0 | 42,888 | 53,652 | 461 | 24 |
| BEN HILL | 5,972 | 6,594 | 6,743 | 1.2 | 2.61 | 4,343 | 4,642 | 0.8 | 30,398 | 35,258 | 2058 | 112 |
| BERRIEN | 5,149 | 6,338 | 6,950 | 2.6 | 2.60 | 3,950 | 4,710 | 2.2 | 30,963 | 34,253 | 1940 | 108 |
| BIBB | 56,307 | 60,315 | 61,112 | 0.8 | 2.50 | 39,301 | 40,877 | 0.5 | 36,779 | 40,336 | 1006 | 52 |
| BLECKLEY | 3,816 | 4,272 | 4,570 | 1.4 | 2.58 | 2,864 | 3,093 | 0.9 | 31,296 | 35,833 | 1865 | 98 |
| BRANTLEY | 3,811 | 4,993 | 5,633 | 3.3 | 2.85 | 3,109 | 3,970 | 3.0 | 34,548 | 41,718 | 1311 | 65 |
| BROOKS | 5,392 | 5,819 | 6,147 | 0.9 | 2.73 | 4,040 | 4,215 | 0.5 | 31,017 | 36,328 | 1930 | 106 |
| BRYAN | 5,070 | 8,306 | 9,649 | 6.2 | 3.02 | 4,226 | 6,784 | 5.9 | 48,120 | 58,786 | 235 | 13 |
| BULLOCH | 14,984 | 18,813 | 20,105 | 2.8 | 2.53 | 9,685 | 11,811 | 2.4 | 31,916 | 36,861 | 1734 | 88 |
| BURKE | 7,037 | 8,273 | 9,101 | 2.0 | 2.83 | 5,288 | 6,043 | 1.6 | 27,628 | 32,445 | 2493 | 133 |
| BUTTS | 4,696 | 6,112 | 7,220 | 3.2 | 2.82 | 3,697 | 4,688 | 2.9 | 37,914 | 48,190 | 854 | 45 |
| CALHOUN | 1,794 | 1,892 | 1,899 | 0.6 | 2.54 | 1,269 | 1,284 | 0.1 | 24,816 | 26,721 | 2822 | 152 |
| CAMDEN | 9,459 | 16,149 | 18,246 | 6.7 | 2.68 | 7,472 | 12,431 | 6.4 | 45,243 | 55,390 | 344 | 19 |
| CANDLER | 2,828 | 3,560 | 3,772 | 2.8 | 2.45 | 2,042 | 2,477 | 2.4 | 28,406 | 33,533 | 2378 | 131 |
| CARROLL | 25,370 | 31,472 | 35,089 | 2.6 | 2.66 | 18,969 | 22,898 | 2.3 | 39,109 | 47,836 | 745 | 37 |
| CATOOSA | 15,745 | 19,998 | 22,512 | 2.9 | 2.65 | 12,366 | 15,360 | 2.7 | 37,726 | 42,677 | 874 | 46 |
| CHARLTON | 2,911 | 3,418 | 3,607 | 2.0 | 2.75 | 2,257 | 2,571 | 1.6 | 35,200 | 44,625 | 1221 | 61 |
| CHATHAM | 81,111 | 86,560 | 87,896 | 0.8 | 2.53 | 56,560 | 58,791 | 0.5 | 38,627 | 44,653 | 788 | 41 |
| CHATTAHOOCHEE | 2,884 | 2,918 | 3,166 | 0.1 | 3.69 | 2,637 | 2,641 | 0.0 | 37,354 | 45,100 | 922 | 49 |
| CHATTOOGA | 8,467 | 8,891 | 9,025 | 0.6 | 2.55 | 6,393 | 6,467 | 0.1 | 31,140 | 36,250 | 1908 | 103 |
| CHEROKEE | 31,309 | 52,546 | 65,369 | 6.5 | 2.81 | 25,760 | 42,137 | 6.1 | 63,495 | 79,025 | 47 | 2 |
| CLARKE | 33,170 | 35,059 | 35,596 | 0.7 | 2.36 | 18,182 | 18,498 | 0.2 | 31,822 | 35,850 | 1754 | 90 |
| CLAY | 1,210 | 1,283 | 1,348 | 0.7 | 2.72 | 874 | 892 | 0.2 | 23,115 | 25,364 | 2963 | 157 |
| CLAYTON | 65,523 | 79,718 | 88,094 | 2.4 | 2.71 | 48,734 | 57,708 | 2.1 | 42,525 | 50,159 | 474 | 26 |
| CLINCH | 2,173 | 2,468 | 2,581 | 1.6 | 2.67 | 1,655 | 1,812 | 1.1 | 30,394 | 35,113 | 2059 | 113 |
| COBB | 171,288 | 232,423 | 265,049 | 3.8 | 2.57 | 120,113 | 159,239 | 3.5 | 58,246 | 66,094 | 87 | 6 |
| COFFEE | 10,541 | 12,935 | 14,238 | 2.5 | 2.71 | 7,981 | 9,527 | 2.2 | 33,523 | 38,079 | 1460 | 76 |
| COLQUITT | 12,980 | 15,070 | 16,378 | 1.8 | 2.63 | 9,736 | 10,997 | 1.5 | 29,541 | 33,493 | 2215 | 122 |
| COLUMBIA | 21,841 | 32,454 | 36,979 | 4.9 | 2.92 | 18,315 | 26,640 | 4.6 | 58,128 | 72,790 | 89 | 7 |
| COOK | 4,825 | 5,788 | 6,419 | 2.2 | 2.62 | 3,607 | 4,214 | 1.9 | 30,577 | 33,863 | 2013 | 110 |
| COWETA | 18,930 | 33,531 | 41,557 | 7.2 | 2.78 | 15,020 | 26,314 | 7.0 | 51,694 | 63,311 | 176 | 11 |
| CRAWFORD | 3,069 | 3,846 | 3,878 | 2.8 | 2.64 | 2,412 | 2,933 | 2.4 | 38,534 | 45,082 | 805 | 42 |
| CRISP | 7,287 | 7,782 | 7,920 | 0.8 | 2.60 | 5,300 | 5,486 | 0.4 | 27,217 | 29,683 | 2546 | 136 |
| DADE | 4,661 | 5,777 | 6,455 | 2.6 | 2.60 | 3,735 | 4,499 | 2.3 | 31,168 | 35,729 | 1895 | 102 |
| DAWSON | 3,360 | 6,016 | 7,736 | 7.3 | 2.81 | 2,734 | 4,792 | 7.0 | 47,309 | 56,946 | 263 | 15 |
| DECATUR | 8,962 | 9,969 | 10,500 | 1.3 | 2.66 | 6,675 | 7,190 | 0.9 | 27,022 | 30,910 | 2574 | 137 |
| DEKALB | 208,690 | 234,816 | 244,300 | 1.4 | 2.51 | 137,603 | 148,959 | 1.0 | 45,712 | 51,829 | 324 | 17 |
| DODGE | 6,387 | 6,806 | 6,979 | 0.8 | 2.53 | 4,687 | 4,794 | 0.3 | 28,783 | 33,824 | 2330 | 127 |
| DOOLY | 3,557 | 3,852 | 3,934 | 1.0 | 2.67 | 2,582 | 2,691 | 0.5 | 23,912 | 26,581 | 2910 | 155 |
| DOUGHERTY | 34,163 | 34,614 | 33,973 | 0.2 | 2.61 | 25,101 | 24,782 | -0.2 | 32,710 | 35,632 | 1592 | 83 |
| DOUGLAS | 24,277 | 33,545 | 38,360 | 4.0 | 2.76 | 19,739 | 26,658 | 3.7 | 54,129 | 64,657 | 135 | 9 |
| EARLY | 4,263 | 4,534 | 4,600 | 0.7 | 2.63 | 3,113 | 3,194 | 0.3 | 23,944 | 26,513 | 2907 | 154 |
| ECHOLS | 816 | 882 | 1,014 | 0.9 | 2.96 | 654 | 689 | 0.6 | 33,011 | 35,688 | 1535 | 80 |
| EFFINGHAM | 8,759 | 13,809 | 16,838 | 5.7 | 2.90 | 7,149 | 11,005 | 5.4 | 46,617 | 58,017 | 288 | 16 |
| ELBERT | 7,115 | 7,487 | 7,692 | 0.6 | 2.55 | 5,314 | 5,417 | 0.2 | 30,847 | 36,714 | 1960 | 109 |
| EMANUEL | 7,420 | 7,795 | 7,937 | 0.6 | 2.66 | 5,501 | 5,593 | 0.2 | 26,937 | 29,604 | 2594 | 140 |
| EVANS | 3,144 | 3,845 | 4,258 | 2.5 | 2.58 | 2,284 | 2,702 | 2.1 | 30,161 | 35,885 | 2120 | 118 |
| FANNIN | 6,334 | 7,878 | 8,778 | 2.7 | 2.44 | 4,844 | 5,848 | 2.3 | 31,932 | 39,440 | 1730 | 87 |
| FAYETTE | 21,054 | 32,876 | 39,247 | 5.6 | 2.91 | 18,018 | 27,427 | 5.2 | 77,986 | 99,148 | 3 | 1 |
| FLOYD | 30,518 | 33,067 | 34,238 | 1.0 | 2.50 | 22,518 | 23,637 | 0.6 | 37,660 | 43,588 | 882 | 47 |
| FORSYTH | 15,938 | 38,254 | 54,981 | 11.2 | 2.77 | 12,787 | 30,031 | 10.9 | 62,194 | 74,701 | 58 | 4 |
| FRANKLIN | 6,365 | 7,857 | 8,743 | 2.6 | 2.46 | 4,787 | 5,737 | 2.2 | 31,678 | 35,028 | 1783 | 92 |
| FULTON | 257,140 | 309,117 | 334,208 | 2.3 | 2.37 | 155,887 | 184,293 | 2.0 | 43,788 | 50,270 | 409 | 21 |
| GILMER | 5,072 | 7,930 | 9,795 | 5.6 | 2.59 | 3,940 | 5,973 | 5.2 | 31,279 | 36,528 | 1873 | 99 |
| GLASCOCK | 867 | 969 | 1,041 | 1.4 | 2.54 | 649 | 696 | 0.9 | 31,179 | 39,787 | 1892 | 101 |
| GLYNN | 23,947 | 26,898 | 28,570 | 1.4 | 2.51 | 17,308 | 18,842 | 1.0 | 41,822 | 48,227 | 529 | 29 |
| GORDON | 12,778 | 15,945 | 17,783 | 2.7 | 2.67 | 9,939 | 12,059 | 2.4 | 38,744 | 45,717 | 778 | 39 |
| GRADY | 7,354 | 8,038 | 8,293 | 1.1 | 2.66 | 5,571 | 5,914 | 0.7 | 28,550 | 33,900 | 2355 | 130 |
| GREENE | 4,083 | 5,024 | 5,669 | 2.5 | 2.85 | 3,012 | 3,615 | 2.2 | 31,255 | 37,205 | 1877 | 100 |
| GWINNETT | 126,971 | 208,805 | 253,018 | 6.2 | 2.72 | 96,396 | 155,486 | 6.0 | 63,185 | 75,393 | 51 | 3 |
| HABERSHAM | 9,966 | 12,327 | 13,739 | 2.6 | 2.55 | 7,672 | 9,214 | 2.2 | 38,925 | 44,488 | 758 | 38 |
| HALL | 34,721 | 46,917 | 54,186 | 3.7 | 2.68 | 26,522 | 35,003 | 3.4 | 45,161 | 53,805 | 351 | 20 |
| HANCOCK | 2,969 | 3,195 | 3,268 | 0.9 | 2.78 | 2,201 | 2,285 | 0.5 | 28,030 | 32,146 | 2436 | 132 |
| HARALSON | 8,248 | 9,802 | 10,775 | 2.1 | 2.58 | 6,252 | 7,208 | 1.7 | 34,649 | 41,350 | 1297 | 64 |
| HARRIS | 6,454 | 8,658 | 9,584 | 3.6 | 2.64 | 5,092 | 6,671 | 3.3 | 45,325 | 53,412 | 339 | 18 |
| HART | 7,459 | 8,814 | 9,652 | 2.0 | 2.51 | 5,679 | 6,513 | 1.7 | 33,918 | 41,916 | 1405 | 71 |
| HEARD | 3,093 | 3,805 | 4,260 | 2.5 | 2.79 | 2,398 | 2,851 | 2.1 | 35,121 | 42,112 | 1231 | 63 |
| HENRY | 20,012 | 41,290 | 54,325 | 9.2 | 2.92 | 16,784 | 33,784 | 8.8 | 58,806 | 74,022 | 82 | 5 |
| HOUSTON | 32,433 | 41,284 | 45,925 | 3.0 | 2.63 | 24,695 | 30,831 | 2.7 | 41,947 | 46,361 | 516 | 28 |
| IRWIN | 3,142 | 3,409 | 3,647 | 1.0 | 2.69 | 2,350 | 2,466 | 0.6 | 31,569 | 34,811 | 1804 | 95 |
| GEORGIA | | | | 2.8 | 2.62 | | | 2.6 | 43,179 | 51,136 | | |
| UNITED STATES | | | | 1.4 | 2.59 | | | 1.1 | 41,914 | 49,127 | | |

 

| COUNTY | 2000 Per Capita Income | 2000 HH Income Base | 2000 HOUSEHOLD INCOME DISTRIBUTION (%) | | | | | | 2000 AVERAGE DISPOSABLE INCOME BY AGE OF HOUSEHOLDER | | | | | |
|---|---|---|---|---|---|---|---|---|---|---|---|---|---|---|
| | | | Less than $15,000 | $15,000 to $24,999 | $25,000 to $49,999 | $50,000 to $99,999 | $100,000 to $149,999 | $150,000 or More | All Ages | <35 | 35-44 | 45-54 | 55-64 | 65+ |
| APPLING | 16,368 | 6,382 | 20.3 | 13.9 | 34.1 | 27.1 | 3.9 | 0.7 | 32,206 | 32,209 | 36,634 | 38,213 | 31,207 | 21,193 |
| ATKINSON | 12,888 | 2,670 | 25.6 | 19.6 | 29.4 | 21.9 | 3.2 | 0.3 | 28,068 | 29,207 | 32,343 | 36,615 | 27,117 | 14,405 |
| BACON | 14,694 | 3,849 | 26.6 | 15.5 | 30.6 | 21.5 | 4.3 | 1.4 | 30,119 | 29,037 | 33,557 | 34,929 | 32,210 | 20,762 |
| BAKER | 13,800 | 1,350 | 22.2 | 20.5 | 36.0 | 17.0 | 3.4 | 0.9 | 28,771 | 25,264 | 33,035 | 35,877 | 27,117 | 22,516 |
| BALDWIN | 15,033 | 13,505 | 19.5 | 15.2 | 34.3 | 24.8 | 4.7 | 1.6 | 33,543 | 27,490 | 37,828 | 41,621 | 36,061 | 23,698 |
| BANKS | 16,009 | 5,082 | 16.5 | 16.3 | 37.5 | 25.1 | 3.6 | 0.9 | 32,413 | 33,705 | 37,094 | 37,721 | 31,400 | 20,105 |
| BARROW | 19,598 | 15,871 | 12.5 | 9.9 | 36.6 | 32.2 | 7.4 | 1.4 | 38,987 | 38,784 | 42,516 | 46,825 | 37,148 | 24,624 |
| BARTOW | 19,696 | 28,442 | 11.0 | 11.9 | 35.8 | 32.4 | 7.1 | 1.8 | 39,259 | 36,625 | 45,533 | 47,184 | 38,482 | 23,881 |
| BEN HILL | 15,149 | 6,594 | 23.3 | 18.5 | 31.3 | 22.5 | 3.3 | 1.0 | 29,977 | 27,392 | 35,682 | 36,246 | 28,778 | 20,748 |
| BERRIEN | 13,859 | 6,338 | 21.6 | 17.7 | 36.0 | 21.7 | 2.8 | 0.2 | 29,028 | 26,920 | 34,896 | 34,115 | 29,851 | 19,744 |
| BIBB | 21,280 | 60,315 | 20.5 | 13.3 | 31.2 | 25.5 | 6.0 | 3.6 | 37,635 | 31,395 | 41,039 | 45,837 | 38,602 | 25,511 |
| BLECKLEY | 15,395 | 4,272 | 21.3 | 18.1 | 32.7 | 22.0 | 4.1 | 1.7 | 31,670 | 28,167 | 36,879 | 39,882 | 36,336 | 18,409 |
| BRANTLEY | 14,603 | 4,993 | 17.6 | 15.7 | 37.8 | 24.7 | 3.3 | 0.8 | 31,906 | 30,420 | 36,516 | 40,064 | 30,802 | 19,020 |
| BROOKS | 13,625 | 5,819 | 22.2 | 16.4 | 38.1 | 20.1 | 2.5 | 0.6 | 28,892 | 30,038 | 31,224 | 33,446 | 29,239 | 21,763 |
| BRYAN | 19,477 | 8,306 | 10.5 | 9.2 | 32.6 | 35.5 | 9.2 | 3.1 | 43,348 | 37,862 | 50,971 | 51,254 | 45,986 | 21,906 |
| BULLOCH | 16,976 | 18,813 | 23.5 | 13.9 | 33.2 | 22.2 | 5.1 | 2.0 | 32,722 | 24,176 | 38,573 | 44,960 | 37,364 | 24,570 |
| BURKE | 13,149 | 8,273 | 28.2 | 16.3 | 30.4 | 20.7 | 3.3 | 1.2 | 28,765 | 24,215 | 30,803 | 38,005 | 31,387 | 18,388 |
| BUTTS | 17,216 | 6,112 | 12.6 | 17.2 | 34.3 | 28.8 | 5.1 | 2.0 | 36,324 | 31,487 | 41,542 | 42,533 | 38,957 | 24,599 |
| CALHOUN | 14,514 | 1,892 | 30.6 | 19.7 | 29.0 | 15.4 | 3.9 | 1.4 | 27,473 | 20,482 | 33,893 | 36,421 | 32,530 | 17,200 |
| CAMDEN | 19,894 | 16,149 | 7.3 | 10.5 | 40.7 | 34.8 | 5.7 | 0.9 | 38,885 | 33,889 | 43,259 | 49,694 | 39,792 | 23,782 |
| CANDLER | 14,611 | 3,560 | 27.4 | 15.5 | 33.2 | 19.5 | 3.7 | 0.9 | 28,778 | 29,435 | 30,501 | 36,551 | 29,653 | 17,063 |
| CARROLL | 18,313 | 31,472 | 14.1 | 13.3 | 36.8 | 29.0 | 5.3 | 1.5 | 36,168 | 31,820 | 41,210 | 44,750 | 36,015 | 23,063 |
| CATOOSA | 16,881 | 19,997 | 14.8 | 14.5 | 36.5 | 29.0 | 4.3 | 1.0 | 34,265 | 32,626 | 39,965 | 41,094 | 35,340 | 19,196 |
| CHARLTON | 14,995 | 3,418 | 18.5 | 14.2 | 37.7 | 25.7 | 3.5 | 0.5 | 31,699 | 29,848 | 34,038 | 40,338 | 31,790 | 20,160 |
| CHATHAM | 20,259 | 86,560 | 17.2 | 13.3 | 33.2 | 27.6 | 6.3 | 2.5 | 37,165 | 31,748 | 40,534 | 44,752 | 40,174 | 27,268 |
| CHATTAHOOCHEE | 12,168 | 2,918 | 6.4 | 20.3 | 42.6 | 29.4 | 1.3 | 0.0 | 33,023 | 31,705 | 34,439 | 39,633 | 31,018 | 19,030 |
| CHATTOOGA | 14,620 | 8,891 | 20.1 | 18.0 | 37.7 | 20.7 | 3.0 | 0.5 | 29,382 | 30,773 | 35,596 | 35,271 | 30,275 | 17,732 |
| CHEROKEE | 27,815 | 52,546 | 6.1 | 4.3 | 23.1 | 46.0 | 16.1 | 4.6 | 53,323 | 52,056 | 57,228 | 58,995 | 51,087 | 28,465 |
| CLARKE | 19,464 | 35,059 | 24.8 | 15.8 | 28.3 | 21.8 | 6.1 | 3.3 | 34,977 | 23,222 | 41,766 | 49,204 | 43,286 | 27,975 |
| CLAY | 12,349 | 1,283 | 36.0 | 17.7 | 27.4 | 14.3 | 3.2 | 1.3 | 26,268 | 20,971 | 31,785 | 34,680 | 28,839 | 17,528 |
| CLAYTON | 18,139 | 79,713 | 9.7 | 12.2 | 39.6 | 33.1 | 4.6 | 0.9 | 36,956 | 32,278 | 38,879 | 44,385 | 39,679 | 24,069 |
| CLINCH | 14,146 | 2,468 | 19.9 | 18.8 | 38.3 | 19.8 | 2.6 | 0.7 | 29,056 | 26,326 | 34,348 | 36,105 | 28,417 | 19,036 |
| COBB | 30,006 | 232,421 | 5.1 | 7.1 | 28.4 | 40.3 | 13.2 | 5.9 | 52,748 | 43,765 | 54,583 | 62,104 | 52,830 | 31,730 |
| COFFEE | 16,786 | 12,935 | 20.9 | 15.6 | 32.7 | 23.3 | 5.3 | 2.2 | 33,807 | 30,742 | 40,441 | 39,285 | 35,092 | 19,787 |
| COLQUITT | 14,654 | 15,070 | 25.5 | 16.8 | 34.0 | 19.7 | 3.2 | 0.9 | 28,835 | 25,197 | 34,418 | 34,576 | 31,987 | 19,075 |
| COLUMBIA | 26,250 | 32,454 | 5.7 | 6.1 | 28.5 | 40.8 | 13.6 | 5.4 | 52,371 | 44,085 | 53,294 | 61,331 | 52,126 | 30,547 |
| COOK | 13,793 | 5,788 | 22.9 | 17.8 | 35.3 | 20.9 | 2.3 | 0.7 | 28,607 | 27,905 | 31,772 | 37,204 | 27,713 | 18,897 |
| COWETA | 26,557 | 33,531 | 9.5 | 8.3 | 30.1 | 35.5 | 10.8 | 5.8 | 48,866 | 43,536 | 52,916 | 58,856 | 45,754 | 29,379 |
| CRAWFORD | 15,913 | 3,846 | 15.7 | 13.1 | 39.3 | 28.5 | 3.2 | 0.2 | 32,741 | 30,732 | 34,535 | 41,387 | 31,809 | 21,780 |
| CRISP | 14,525 | 7,782 | 28.9 | 16.6 | 32.0 | 18.3 | 2.9 | 1.3 | 28,445 | 25,526 | 34,870 | 31,755 | 30,678 | 19,268 |
| DADE | 14,325 | 5,777 | 19.4 | 19.4 | 38.8 | 19.1 | 2.6 | 0.7 | 29,298 | 28,690 | 35,815 | 35,621 | 28,072 | 17,780 |
| DAWSON | 25,079 | 6,016 | 9.5 | 10.1 | 32.9 | 34.7 | 10.0 | 3.0 | 43,408 | 36,345 | 49,011 | 50,169 | 46,714 | 29,008 |
| DECATUR | 12,183 | 9,969 | 27.2 | 18.9 | 34.5 | 17.4 | 2.0 | 0.1 | 25,938 | 23,256 | 29,691 | 32,498 | 27,503 | 18,062 |
| DEKALB | 23,609 | 234,816 | 9.6 | 12.0 | 33.5 | 33.7 | 8.0 | 3.1 | 42,622 | 35,199 | 43,516 | 50,605 | 46,665 | 31,734 |
| DODGE | 13,578 | 6,806 | 28.2 | 15.7 | 33.7 | 18.7 | 3.0 | 0.6 | 27,707 | 26,747 | 31,145 | 37,191 | 26,528 | 17,245 |
| DOOLY | 13,017 | 3,852 | 34.3 | 17.4 | 30.1 | 14.3 | 2.8 | 1.2 | 25,872 | 23,836 | 30,948 | 30,117 | 26,590 | 17,672 |
| DOUGHERTY | 15,953 | 34,614 | 23.0 | 15.9 | 32.2 | 22.8 | 4.4 | 1.6 | 32,141 | 25,610 | 35,897 | 40,985 | 34,844 | 21,989 |
| DOUGLAS | 23,323 | 33,545 | 5.7 | 7.0 | 31.4 | 42.9 | 11.0 | 2.2 | 46,056 | 42,171 | 49,552 | 54,938 | 46,446 | 27,773 |
| EARLY | 12,225 | 4,534 | 33.3 | 18.0 | 28.7 | 16.7 | 2.5 | 0.9 | 25,633 | 23,688 | 33,151 | 27,571 | 29,500 | 16,123 |
| ECHOLS | 13,193 | 882 | 20.9 | 16.9 | 35.9 | 23.2 | 2.5 | 0.6 | 29,490 | 29,039 | 35,853 | 38,592 | 25,308 | 17,012 |
| EFFINGHAM | 18,669 | 13,809 | 10.2 | 8.4 | 35.2 | 37.7 | 7.3 | 1.2 | 40,468 | 37,022 | 44,416 | 48,207 | 42,401 | 26,305 |
| ELBERT | 13,981 | 7,487 | 20.9 | 17.1 | 40.6 | 19.0 | 2.3 | 0.1 | 28,124 | 26,572 | 31,946 | 36,156 | 28,484 | 18,219 |
| EMANUEL | 12,812 | 7,795 | 28.4 | 18.0 | 33.0 | 17.8 | 2.3 | 0.6 | 26,412 | 24,782 | 33,077 | 31,507 | 27,512 | 16,413 |
| EVANS | 15,547 | 3,845 | 24.2 | 15.7 | 37.9 | 19.1 | 2.4 | 0.7 | 28,511 | 29,332 | 32,380 | 34,874 | 27,983 | 19,235 |
| FANNIN | 15,984 | 7,878 | 20.2 | 17.6 | 36.2 | 22.2 | 3.2 | 0.7 | 30,157 | 30,908 | 34,772 | 37,499 | 30,393 | 21,822 |
| FAYETTE | 37,540 | 32,876 | 2.9 | 3.5 | 14.9 | 43.9 | 20.8 | 14.0 | 72,546 | 55,525 | 69,671 | 79,759 | 67,416 | 45,063 |
| FLOYD | 19,760 | 33,065 | 17.5 | 13.8 | 33.9 | 26.4 | 5.9 | 2.5 | 36,451 | 31,712 | 40,156 | 47,588 | 38,818 | 22,565 |
| FORSYTH | 29,635 | 38,254 | 5.3 | 5.1 | 26.4 | 39.6 | 15.8 | 7.7 | 57,159 | 52,113 | 58,922 | 64,209 | 53,307 | 34,729 |
| FRANKLIN | 15,537 | 7,857 | 22.2 | 16.0 | 36.6 | 21.6 | 2.9 | 0.6 | 29,606 | 30,691 | 33,924 | 36,337 | 29,223 | 20,320 |
| FULTON | 31,530 | 309,117 | 16.1 | 12.1 | 27.0 | 26.7 | 9.6 | 8.5 | 49,628 | 37,234 | 49,781 | 57,117 | 48,288 | 32,301 |
| GILMER | 13,962 | 7,929 | 20.0 | 17.7 | 38.7 | 21.0 | 2.4 | 0.2 | 28,718 | 27,636 | 34,113 | 33,532 | 29,886 | 20,746 |
| GLASCOCK | 14,388 | 969 | 21.2 | 16.8 | 36.5 | 22.2 | 3.1 | 0.2 | 29,427 | 30,250 | 33,342 | 35,874 | 30,444 | 18,947 |
| GLYNN | 24,422 | 26,898 | 13.8 | 12.7 | 31.9 | 29.9 | 7.4 | 4.4 | 42,175 | 32,823 | 42,934 | 51,303 | 45,196 | 33,700 |
| GORDON | 17,717 | 15,945 | 13.5 | 13.1 | 39.4 | 27.6 | 4.9 | 1.5 | 35,705 | 34,666 | 40,029 | 42,915 | 35,439 | 21,847 |
| GRADY | 15,210 | 8,038 | 23.3 | 18.6 | 35.3 | 19.0 | 2.9 | 0.9 | 28,797 | 26,940 | 32,685 | 35,425 | 32,039 | 17,794 |
| GREENE | 14,863 | 5,024 | 22.4 | 15.9 | 33.1 | 22.6 | 4.7 | 1.2 | 31,542 | 31,453 | 33,776 | 37,281 | 35,770 | 21,093 |
| GWINNETT | 29,934 | 208,805 | 3.6 | 4.6 | 25.6 | 45.4 | 15.2 | 5.6 | 55,227 | 47,768 | 57,582 | 62,483 | 55,640 | 32,441 |
| HABERSHAM | 18,387 | 12,327 | 13.1 | 15.5 | 36.0 | 28.9 | 5.2 | 1.2 | 35,467 | 34,273 | 41,508 | 41,691 | 36,415 | 24,459 |
| HALL | 21,799 | 46,917 | 10.4 | 10.9 | 34.7 | 32.7 | 8.1 | 3.1 | 42,117 | 37,784 | 47,779 | 49,445 | 41,785 | 26,788 |
| HANCOCK | 11,706 | 3,195 | 28.7 | 15.1 | 37.6 | 16.1 | 2.4 | 0.2 | 26,078 | 25,050 | 32,449 | 29,372 | 26,231 | 17,864 |
| HARALSON | 15,035 | 9,802 | 18.5 | 15.3 | 38.0 | 25.4 | 2.7 | 0.2 | 30,777 | 29,285 | 37,664 | 35,782 | 30,911 | 20,646 |
| HARRIS | 23,999 | 8,658 | 14.2 | 10.5 | 29.0 | 32.3 | 9.8 | 4.4 | 43,640 | 37,462 | 51,109 | 52,683 | 42,318 | 26,180 |
| HART | 17,359 | 8,814 | 18.1 | 13.5 | 38.4 | 24.6 | 4.3 | 1.1 | 32,661 | 31,874 | 37,375 | 39,420 | 35,372 | 22,505 |
| HEARD | 14,648 | 3,805 | 18.3 | 13.3 | 40.2 | 23.5 | 4.1 | 0.6 | 31,933 | 34,259 | 38,131 | 36,811 | 30,075 | 19,076 |
| HENRY | 25,014 | 41,290 | 5.3 | 5.5 | 27.9 | 44.1 | 13.4 | 3.8 | 50,542 | 46,928 | 52,411 | 59,373 | 50,234 | 31,862 |
| HOUSTON | 18,457 | 41,284 | 11.3 | 11.7 | 38.6 | 32.9 | 4.7 | 0.8 | 36,663 | 30,500 | 39,481 | 45,834 | 39,044 | 25,802 |
| IRWIN | 16,370 | 3,409 | 25.6 | 17.3 | 27.3 | 23.2 | 4.3 | 2.2 | 32,039 | 25,416 | 36,519 | 41,431 | 35,344 | 21,724 |
| GEORGIA | 22,304 | | 13.9 | 11.8 | 31.9 | 30.9 | 8.0 | 3.5 | 41,548 | 35,922 | 45,313 | 49,959 | 41,633 | 25,795 |
| UNITED STATES | 22,162 | | 14.5 | 12.5 | 32.3 | 29.8 | 7.4 | 3.5 | 40,748 | 34,503 | 44,969 | 49,579 | 43,409 | 27,339 |

# SPENDING POTENTIAL INDEXES

| COUNTY | FINANCIAL SERVICES | | | | THE HOME | | | | | | ENTERTAINMENT | | | | | | PERSONAL | | | |
|---|---|---|---|---|---|---|---|---|---|---|---|---|---|---|---|---|---|---|---|---|
| | | | | | Home Improvements | | | Furnishings | | | | | | | | | | | | |
| | Auto Loan | Home Loan | Invest-ments | Retire-ment Plans | Home Repair | Lawn & Garden | Remodel-ing | Appli-ances | Elec-tronics | Furni-ture | Restau-rants | Sport-ing Goods | Theater & Concerts | Toys & Hobbies | Travel | Video Rental | Apparel | Auto After-market | Health Insur-ance | Pets & Supplies |
| APPLING | 97 | 68 | 73 | 76 | 93 | 90 | 112 | 96 | 91 | 78 | 80 | 96 | 81 | 95 | 69 | 96 | 80 | 88 | 101 | 97 |
| ATKINSON | 97 | 66 | 72 | 75 | 92 | 91 | 113 | 96 | 92 | 77 | 79 | 95 | 80 | 95 | 68 | 95 | 79 | 87 | 101 | 97 |
| BACON | 96 | 65 | 69 | 73 | 92 | 88 | 108 | 96 | 90 | 77 | 76 | 95 | 78 | 93 | 67 | 95 | 79 | 87 | 97 | 96 |
| BAKER | 97 | 63 | 66 | 73 | 92 | 90 | 112 | 96 | 91 | 75 | 77 | 96 | 78 | 94 | 66 | 95 | 78 | 86 | 101 | 96 |
| BALDWIN | 98 | 88 | 93 | 91 | 99 | 95 | 104 | 98 | 95 | 93 | 91 | 97 | 92 | 98 | 82 | 98 | 94 | 96 | 94 | 100 |
| BANKS | 98 | 70 | 78 | 78 | 93 | 91 | 115 | 96 | 93 | 80 | 82 | 95 | 82 | 96 | 70 | 96 | 82 | 89 | 101 | 98 |
| BARROW | 97 | 77 | 84 | 81 | 96 | 92 | 111 | 96 | 92 | 86 | 87 | 95 | 86 | 97 | 74 | 97 | 85 | 90 | 100 | 98 |
| BARTOW | 98 | 80 | 85 | 84 | 95 | 92 | 112 | 97 | 94 | 87 | 89 | 96 | 87 | 98 | 75 | 97 | 87 | 92 | 99 | 99 |
| BEN HILL | 97 | 74 | 82 | 82 | 95 | 93 | 110 | 96 | 94 | 83 | 84 | 96 | 85 | 96 | 73 | 97 | 84 | 90 | 100 | 98 |
| BERRIEN | 97 | 73 | 80 | 79 | 93 | 91 | 115 | 96 | 93 | 82 | 84 | 95 | 83 | 97 | 71 | 97 | 83 | 90 | 100 | 98 |
| BIBB | 97 | 96 | 100 | 97 | 102 | 99 | 97 | 98 | 96 | 99 | 95 | 99 | 97 | 98 | 89 | 99 | 98 | 99 | 94 | 99 |
| BLECKLEY | 97 | 68 | 76 | 77 | 93 | 91 | 114 | 96 | 93 | 79 | 81 | 94 | 81 | 95 | 70 | 96 | 81 | 88 | 101 | 97 |
| BRANTLEY | 97 | 74 | 78 | 78 | 92 | 90 | 113 | 96 | 93 | 84 | 85 | 96 | 83 | 96 | 70 | 96 | 83 | 89 | 99 | 98 |
| BROOKS | 96 | 68 | 73 | 74 | 93 | 89 | 108 | 95 | 91 | 80 | 78 | 94 | 80 | 93 | 69 | 95 | 80 | 87 | 97 | 96 |
| BRYAN | 100 | 95 | 89 | 93 | 96 | 95 | 106 | 99 | 101 | 97 | 101 | 99 | 95 | 102 | 81 | 100 | 98 | 100 | 97 | 102 |
| BULLOCH | 96 | 84 | 89 | 88 | 95 | 92 | 105 | 93 | 92 | 85 | 86 | 94 | 86 | 95 | 77 | 95 | 87 | 92 | 96 | 97 |
| BURKE | 95 | 75 | 81 | 80 | 95 | 91 | 103 | 96 | 92 | 86 | 81 | 94 | 85 | 94 | 74 | 97 | 85 | 90 | 94 | 96 |
| BUTTS | 98 | 72 | 79 | 79 | 95 | 92 | 112 | 96 | 92 | 82 | 84 | 96 | 84 | 97 | 72 | 96 | 83 | 89 | 101 | 98 |
| CALHOUN | 96 | 65 | 69 | 73 | 93 | 90 | 109 | 95 | 90 | 77 | 77 | 93 | 79 | 93 | 69 | 95 | 78 | 86 | 100 | 95 |
| CAMDEN | 92 | 87 | 78 | 79 | 90 | 86 | 97 | 93 | 93 | 85 | 91 | 91 | 85 | 93 | 74 | 96 | 86 | 92 | 92 | 98 |
| CANDLER | 97 | 72 | 78 | 77 | 94 | 91 | 111 | 96 | 91 | 82 | 83 | 95 | 83 | 96 | 71 | 96 | 82 | 88 | 100 | 97 |
| CARROLL | 97 | 78 | 83 | 82 | 95 | 92 | 111 | 96 | 93 | 85 | 86 | 95 | 85 | 97 | 74 | 97 | 86 | 91 | 99 | 99 |
| CATOOSA | 99 | 82 | 86 | 86 | 96 | 94 | 111 | 97 | 95 | 88 | 91 | 97 | 89 | 100 | 76 | 98 | 90 | 93 | 100 | 100 |
| CHARLTON | 97 | 73 | 77 | 78 | 92 | 90 | 113 | 96 | 92 | 83 | 84 | 96 | 83 | 96 | 70 | 96 | 82 | 89 | 99 | 98 |
| CHATHAM | 97 | 95 | 99 | 94 | 101 | 99 | 97 | 98 | 96 | 98 | 95 | 97 | 96 | 98 | 87 | 99 | 97 | 98 | 94 | 99 |
| CHATTAHOOCHEE | 90 | 87 | 74 | 74 | 87 | 83 | 92 | 91 | 92 | 82 | 89 | 88 | 83 | 89 | 72 | 96 | 83 | 91 | 89 | 97 |
| CHATTOOGA | 97 | 66 | 72 | 75 | 94 | 91 | 111 | 96 | 91 | 78 | 79 | 96 | 81 | 95 | 69 | 95 | 79 | 87 | 101 | 96 |
| CHEROKEE | 103 | 104 | 87 | 98 | 97 | 98 | 104 | 102 | 105 | 105 | 109 | 106 | 101 | 105 | 85 | 102 | 106 | 104 | 98 | 105 |
| CLARKE | 94 | 96 | 94 | 91 | 97 | 92 | 95 | 91 | 92 | 88 | 91 | 91 | 88 | 93 | 82 | 94 | 91 | 94 | 92 | 97 |
| CLAY | 96 | 63 | 68 | 73 | 92 | 90 | 111 | 95 | 91 | 75 | 77 | 93 | 78 | 93 | 67 | 95 | 78 | 86 | 102 | 95 |
| CLAYTON | 98 | 100 | 87 | 92 | 96 | 95 | 97 | 98 | 99 | 99 | 103 | 99 | 96 | 101 | 84 | 99 | 100 | 100 | 95 | 101 |
| CLINCH | 96 | 63 | 66 | 72 | 92 | 89 | 109 | 96 | 90 | 76 | 75 | 95 | 78 | 93 | 66 | 95 | 78 | 86 | 98 | 96 |
| COBB | 104 | 116 | 100 | 110 | 102 | 106 | 102 | 103 | 107 | 111 | 116 | 109 | 108 | 107 | 94 | 102 | 113 | 109 | 99 | 106 |
| COFFEE | 96 | 73 | 78 | 78 | 92 | 89 | 111 | 96 | 92 | 84 | 84 | 95 | 83 | 95 | 70 | 96 | 83 | 89 | 97 | 97 |
| COLQUITT | 96 | 76 | 85 | 81 | 95 | 92 | 111 | 96 | 92 | 85 | 84 | 94 | 85 | 96 | 74 | 96 | 85 | 90 | 98 | 97 |
| COLUMBIA | 104 | 106 | 95 | 103 | 99 | 101 | 106 | 102 | 106 | 107 | 111 | 107 | 104 | 107 | 88 | 102 | 108 | 106 | 99 | 106 |
| COOK | 97 | 69 | 75 | 77 | 93 | 90 | 111 | 96 | 92 | 80 | 80 | 95 | 81 | 95 | 70 | 97 | 82 | 89 | 99 | 97 |
| COWETA | 101 | 94 | 89 | 93 | 98 | 96 | 106 | 99 | 100 | 98 | 99 | 101 | 96 | 102 | 82 | 100 | 99 | 99 | 98 | 103 |
| CRAWFORD | 97 | 76 | 79 | 78 | 92 | 90 | 112 | 96 | 92 | 85 | 86 | 95 | 84 | 96 | 71 | 96 | 83 | 90 | 98 | 98 |
| CRISP | 94 | 69 | 77 | 76 | 93 | 89 | 104 | 95 | 90 | 80 | 77 | 92 | 81 | 92 | 71 | 96 | 81 | 88 | 95 | 95 |
| DADE | 97 | 68 | 75 | 77 | 94 | 91 | 113 | 96 | 92 | 79 | 81 | 96 | 81 | 96 | 69 | 96 | 81 | 88 | 101 | 97 |
| DAWSON | 100 | 80 | 85 | 85 | 95 | 92 | 117 | 98 | 95 | 87 | 90 | 98 | 87 | 101 | 74 | 99 | 89 | 93 | 100 | 102 |
| DECATUR | 96 | 75 | 82 | 81 | 95 | 91 | 108 | 96 | 92 | 83 | 83 | 94 | 84 | 95 | 73 | 96 | 84 | 90 | 97 | 97 |
| DEKALB | 99 | 107 | 100 | 101 | 102 | 102 | 95 | 99 | 100 | 104 | 105 | 102 | 101 | 101 | 92 | 100 | 106 | 104 | 95 | 102 |
| DODGE | 97 | 73 | 83 | 80 | 97 | 93 | 109 | 96 | 92 | 83 | 83 | 94 | 85 | 95 | 74 | 96 | 83 | 89 | 101 | 97 |
| DOOLY | 96 | 65 | 68 | 72 | 93 | 89 | 108 | 95 | 90 | 77 | 76 | 94 | 79 | 92 | 68 | 94 | 78 | 86 | 98 | 95 |
| DOUGHERTY | 95 | 90 | 95 | 91 | 100 | 95 | 95 | 97 | 94 | 95 | 89 | 95 | 93 | 95 | 85 | 98 | 94 | 96 | 91 | 97 |
| DOUGLAS | 101 | 99 | 88 | 94 | 97 | 96 | 102 | 99 | 101 | 100 | 104 | 101 | 97 | 103 | 83 | 100 | 101 | 101 | 97 | 103 |
| EARLY | 96 | 64 | 68 | 73 | 93 | 88 | 106 | 96 | 90 | 78 | 75 | 94 | 79 | 93 | 68 | 96 | 80 | 87 | 96 | 95 |
| ECHOLS | 97 | 73 | 77 | 78 | 92 | 90 | 113 | 96 | 92 | 83 | 84 | 96 | 83 | 96 | 70 | 96 | 82 | 89 | 99 | 98 |
| EFFINGHAM | 98 | 79 | 83 | 82 | 93 | 91 | 115 | 97 | 94 | 87 | 89 | 96 | 86 | 99 | 72 | 97 | 86 | 91 | 99 | 100 |
| ELBERT | 95 | 68 | 73 | 74 | 95 | 91 | 106 | 95 | 90 | 80 | 78 | 93 | 81 | 93 | 71 | 95 | 81 | 87 | 98 | 95 |
| EMANUEL | 97 | 67 | 73 | 76 | 93 | 90 | 110 | 96 | 91 | 78 | 78 | 94 | 80 | 94 | 69 | 96 | 80 | 88 | 99 | 97 |
| EVANS | 96 | 67 | 76 | 77 | 93 | 90 | 111 | 95 | 91 | 78 | 79 | 93 | 80 | 94 | 70 | 96 | 80 | 88 | 99 | 96 |
| FANNIN | 98 | 67 | 73 | 77 | 94 | 91 | 114 | 96 | 91 | 78 | 80 | 96 | 81 | 96 | 69 | 96 | 80 | 88 | 102 | 98 |
| FAYETTE | 109 | 123 | 104 | 119 | 104 | 111 | 107 | 108 | 114 | 120 | 127 | 116 | 116 | 113 | 99 | 104 | 126 | 117 | 102 | 111 |
| FLOYD | 98 | 84 | 95 | 89 | 101 | 97 | 108 | 98 | 94 | 91 | 91 | 97 | 92 | 99 | 82 | 98 | 91 | 94 | 99 | 100 |
| FORSYTH | 103 | 96 | 97 | 99 | 99 | 100 | 113 | 101 | 102 | 99 | 102 | 104 | 99 | 105 | 84 | 101 | 102 | 101 | 101 | 105 |
| FRANKLIN | 98 | 65 | 70 | 75 | 92 | 91 | 115 | 96 | 92 | 76 | 78 | 96 | 79 | 95 | 67 | 96 | 79 | 87 | 102 | 97 |
| FULTON | 100 | 111 | 109 | 110 | 105 | 107 | 98 | 101 | 102 | 107 | 104 | 105 | 106 | 101 | 99 | 101 | 109 | 106 | 94 | 102 |
| GILMER | 98 | 67 | 73 | 77 | 93 | 91 | 115 | 96 | 92 | 78 | 80 | 96 | 81 | 96 | 69 | 96 | 81 | 88 | 102 | 98 |
| GLASCOCK | 97 | 63 | 66 | 73 | 92 | 90 | 112 | 96 | 91 | 75 | 77 | 96 | 78 | 95 | 66 | 95 | 78 | 86 | 102 | 96 |
| GLYNN | 99 | 95 | 105 | 98 | 103 | 103 | 105 | 100 | 97 | 98 | 98 | 99 | 98 | 101 | 89 | 99 | 98 | 99 | 99 | 101 |
| GORDON | 99 | 76 | 83 | 83 | 96 | 93 | 113 | 97 | 94 | 84 | 86 | 97 | 86 | 99 | 74 | 97 | 86 | 91 | 101 | 100 |
| GRADY | 96 | 69 | 75 | 77 | 93 | 89 | 110 | 96 | 92 | 80 | 80 | 94 | 81 | 94 | 69 | 96 | 81 | 88 | 98 | 97 |
| GREENE | 97 | 66 | 72 | 76 | 93 | 90 | 111 | 96 | 92 | 78 | 78 | 96 | 80 | 95 | 68 | 96 | 80 | 88 | 100 | 97 |
| GWINNETT | 104 | 114 | 93 | 106 | 99 | 103 | 101 | 103 | 108 | 111 | 117 | 109 | 106 | 107 | 91 | 102 | 114 | 109 | 98 | 107 |
| HABERSHAM | 100 | 77 | 86 | 85 | 97 | 94 | 116 | 98 | 95 | 85 | 88 | 98 | 87 | 100 | 75 | 98 | 88 | 92 | 102 | 101 |
| HALL | 100 | 91 | 95 | 95 | 99 | 98 | 110 | 99 | 99 | 95 | 97 | 101 | 95 | 102 | 82 | 99 | 96 | 98 | 100 | 102 |
| HANCOCK | 95 | 63 | 66 | 70 | 92 | 87 | 103 | 95 | 89 | 77 | 73 | 93 | 77 | 91 | 67 | 95 | 79 | 86 | 93 | 94 |
| HARALSON | 98 | 70 | 77 | 79 | 94 | 91 | 115 | 97 | 93 | 80 | 82 | 96 | 82 | 97 | 70 | 97 | 83 | 89 | 101 | 99 |
| HARRIS | 99 | 81 | 91 | 87 | 99 | 96 | 112 | 98 | 94 | 88 | 90 | 98 | 90 | 100 | 78 | 98 | 89 | 93 | 102 | 100 |
| HART | 98 | 69 | 75 | 78 | 94 | 92 | 115 | 97 | 92 | 79 | 81 | 97 | 82 | 97 | 69 | 96 | 82 | 89 | 102 | 99 |
| HEARD | 97 | 68 | 72 | 75 | 92 | 90 | 113 | 96 | 92 | 79 | 80 | 96 | 80 | 95 | 68 | 96 | 80 | 88 | 100 | 97 |
| HENRY | 103 | 101 | 91 | 99 | 98 | 99 | 106 | 102 | 104 | 104 | 108 | 105 | 101 | 106 | 85 | 102 | 106 | 104 | 98 | 105 |
| HOUSTON | 98 | 94 | 94 | 92 | 99 | 97 | 102 | 98 | 97 | 97 | 98 | 98 | 96 | 100 | 84 | 99 | 97 | 98 | 97 | 100 |
| IRWIN | 96 | 65 | 70 | 74 | 92 | 89 | 110 | 96 | 91 | 77 | 77 | 94 | 79 | 94 | 67 | 96 | 79 | 87 | 99 | 96 |
| GEORGIA | 99 | 96 | 94 | 96 | 99 | 98 | 103 | 99 | 99 | 98 | 98 | 101 | 97 | 101 | 85 | 99 | 98 | 99 | 97 | 101 |
| UNITED STATES | 100 | 100 | 100 | 100 | 100 | 100 | 100 | 100 | 100 | 100 | 100 | 100 | 100 | 100 | 100 | 100 | 100 | 100 | 100 | 100 |

| COUNTY | FIPS Code | MSA Code | DMA Code | POPULATION 1990 | POPULATION 2000 | POPULATION 2005 | 1990-2000 ANNUAL CHANGE % Rate | 1990-2000 ANNUAL CHANGE State Rank | RACE (%) White 1990 | White 2000 | Black 1990 | Black 2000 | Asian/Pacific 1990 | Asian/Pacific 2000 |
|---|---|---|---|---|---|---|---|---|---|---|---|---|---|---|
| JACKSON | 157 | 0000 | 524 | 30,005 | 40,362 | 46,830 | 2.9 | 25 | 89.8 | 87.1 | 9.7 | 12.1 | 0.2 | 0.3 |
| JASPER | 159 | 0000 | 524 | 8,453 | 10,968 | 12,823 | 2.6 | 34 | 64.8 | 59.7 | 34.8 | 39.8 | 0.1 | 0.2 |
| JEFF DAVIS | 161 | 0000 | 507 | 12,032 | 12,763 | 12,992 | 0.6 | 111 | 83.8 | 79.7 | 15.2 | 18.6 | 0.2 | 0.4 |
| JEFFERSON | 163 | 0000 | 520 | 17,408 | 17,880 | 18,022 | 0.3 | 127 | 44.0 | 38.4 | 55.7 | 61.2 | 0.1 | 0.2 |
| JENKINS | 165 | 0000 | 520 | 8,247 | 8,371 | 8,225 | 0.1 | 140 | 58.3 | 53.0 | 41.4 | 46.6 | 0.2 | 0.4 |
| JOHNSON | 167 | 0000 | 503 | 8,329 | 8,280 | 8,214 | -0.1 | 150 | 65.7 | 60.7 | 34.1 | 39.0 | 0.1 | 0.2 |
| JONES | 169 | 4680 | 503 | 20,739 | 23,650 | 25,334 | 1.3 | 74 | 73.9 | 68.4 | 25.6 | 30.9 | 0.2 | 0.4 |
| LAMAR | 171 | 0000 | 524 | 13,038 | 15,347 | 16,930 | 1.6 | 63 | 65.6 | 60.3 | 34.1 | 39.3 | 0.1 | 0.1 |
| LANIER | 173 | 0000 | 530 | 5,531 | 7,042 | 7,478 | 2.4 | 38 | 71.9 | 66.9 | 26.6 | 31.1 | 0.4 | 0.6 |
| LAURENS | 175 | 0000 | 503 | 39,988 | 44,470 | 46,075 | 1.0 | 84 | 66.2 | 60.8 | 33.3 | 38.4 | 0.3 | 0.6 |
| LEE | 177 | 0120 | 525 | 16,250 | 24,145 | 28,052 | 3.9 | 17 | 80.0 | 76.6 | 19.3 | 22.4 | 0.3 | 0.5 |
| LIBERTY | 179 | 0000 | 507 | 52,745 | 60,022 | 61,509 | 1.3 | 74 | 54.9 | 48.7 | 39.2 | 41.7 | 2.3 | 3.8 |
| LINCOLN | 181 | 0000 | 520 | 7,442 | 8,444 | 8,974 | 1.2 | 78 | 61.8 | 56.5 | 38.0 | 43.1 | 0.1 | 0.3 |
| LONG | 183 | 0000 | 507 | 6,202 | 8,886 | 9,808 | 3.6 | 21 | 75.5 | 70.2 | 21.6 | 25.4 | 0.7 | 1.1 |
| LOWNDES | 185 | 0000 | 530 | 75,981 | 85,889 | 88,336 | 1.2 | 78 | 66.6 | 61.1 | 31.9 | 36.5 | 0.9 | 1.4 |
| LUMPKIN | 187 | 0000 | 524 | 14,573 | 20,589 | 24,569 | 3.4 | 23 | 96.1 | 95.0 | 1.6 | 2.1 | 0.3 | 0.5 |
| MCDUFFIE | 189 | 0600 | 520 | 20,119 | 21,953 | 22,613 | 0.9 | 89 | 63.2 | 57.6 | 36.4 | 41.9 | 0.1 | 0.3 |
| MCINTOSH | 191 | 0000 | 507 | 8,634 | 10,291 | 11,100 | 1.7 | 57 | 56.5 | 49.7 | 43.1 | 49.7 | 0.1 | 0.1 |
| MACON | 193 | 0000 | 503 | 13,114 | 13,087 | 12,897 | 0.0 | 145 | 40.9 | 35.4 | 58.7 | 63.9 | 0.2 | 0.3 |
| MADISON | 195 | 0500 | 567 | 21,050 | 25,732 | 28,416 | 2.0 | 43 | 90.5 | 87.5 | 8.8 | 11.3 | 0.3 | 0.5 |
| MARION | 197 | 0000 | 522 | 5,590 | 6,902 | 7,492 | 2.1 | 41 | 58.1 | 52.1 | 41.3 | 47.1 | 0.2 | 0.3 |
| MERIWETHER | 199 | 0000 | 524 | 22,411 | 23,098 | 23,322 | 0.3 | 127 | 55.1 | 49.0 | 44.6 | 50.6 | 0.1 | 0.1 |
| MILLER | 201 | 0000 | 530 | 6,280 | 6,332 | 6,362 | 0.1 | 140 | 72.3 | 68.2 | 27.5 | 31.5 | 0.1 | 0.1 |
| MITCHELL | 205 | 0000 | 525 | 20,275 | 21,274 | 21,593 | 0.5 | 119 | 51.4 | 45.5 | 47.6 | 53.1 | 0.1 | 0.1 |
| MONROE | 207 | 0000 | 503 | 17,113 | 20,339 | 21,919 | 1.7 | 57 | 67.8 | 62.1 | 31.6 | 37.0 | 0.2 | 0.4 |
| MONTGOMERY | 209 | 0000 | 507 | 7,163 | 7,938 | 8,332 | 1.0 | 84 | 69.8 | 63.3 | 28.3 | 33.5 | 0.2 | 0.3 |
| MORGAN | 211 | 0000 | 524 | 12,883 | 15,842 | 17,819 | 2.0 | 43 | 64.9 | 59.4 | 34.6 | 39.7 | 0.2 | 0.4 |
| MURRAY | 213 | 0000 | 575 | 26,147 | 35,001 | 40,329 | 2.9 | 25 | 99.3 | 98.7 | 0.2 | 0.3 | 0.2 | 0.4 |
| MUSCOGEE | 215 | 1800 | 522 | 179,278 | 181,716 | 179,954 | 0.1 | 140 | 59.0 | 53.1 | 38.0 | 42.0 | 1.4 | 2.4 |
| NEWTON | 217 | 0520 | 524 | 41,808 | 63,220 | 76,294 | 4.1 | 15 | 76.9 | 72.1 | 22.4 | 26.9 | 0.3 | 0.4 |
| OCONEE | 219 | 0500 | 524 | 17,618 | 25,268 | 29,038 | 3.6 | 21 | 91.7 | 89.4 | 7.5 | 9.3 | 0.5 | 0.9 |
| OGLETHORPE | 221 | 0000 | 524 | 9,763 | 11,783 | 12,789 | 1.9 | 48 | 74.7 | 69.6 | 24.8 | 29.7 | 0.1 | 0.1 |
| PAULDING | 223 | 0520 | 524 | 41,611 | 84,917 | 111,325 | 7.2 | 3 | 95.4 | 93.9 | 4.0 | 5.1 | 0.2 | 0.3 |
| PEACH | 225 | 4680 | 503 | 21,189 | 25,517 | 28,106 | 1.8 | 51 | 50.6 | 45.3 | 47.5 | 52.0 | 0.3 | 0.6 |
| PICKENS | 227 | 0520 | 524 | 14,432 | 22,206 | 28,015 | 4.3 | 13 | 97.8 | 97.0 | 1.7 | 2.2 | 0.1 | 0.2 |
| PIERCE | 229 | 0000 | 507 | 13,328 | 15,953 | 16,743 | 1.8 | 51 | 87.7 | 84.6 | 11.8 | 14.4 | 0.1 | 0.2 |
| PIKE | 231 | 0000 | 524 | 10,224 | 13,577 | 15,866 | 2.8 | 30 | 79.4 | 74.5 | 20.1 | 24.8 | 0.2 | 0.4 |
| POLK | 233 | 0000 | 524 | 33,815 | 37,179 | 39,192 | 0.9 | 89 | 84.5 | 80.4 | 14.2 | 17.1 | 0.3 | 0.5 |
| PULASKI | 235 | 0000 | 503 | 8,108 | 8,376 | 8,444 | 0.3 | 127 | 66.6 | 61.3 | 32.5 | 37.0 | 0.2 | 0.4 |
| PUTNAM | 237 | 0000 | 524 | 14,137 | 18,901 | 21,835 | 2.9 | 25 | 65.8 | 61.0 | 33.6 | 38.1 | 0.3 | 0.5 |
| QUITMAN | 239 | 0000 | 522 | 2,209 | 2,443 | 2,414 | 1.0 | 84 | 49.5 | 44.9 | 50.1 | 54.6 | 0.1 | 0.2 |
| RABUN | 241 | 0000 | 524 | 11,648 | 13,924 | 15,149 | 1.8 | 51 | 98.9 | 98.5 | 0.4 | 0.4 | 0.1 | 0.3 |
| RANDOLPH | 243 | 0000 | 522 | 8,023 | 8,041 | 8,171 | 0.0 | 145 | 41.3 | 36.3 | 57.9 | 62.7 | 0.6 | 0.7 |
| RICHMOND | 245 | 0600 | 520 | 189,719 | 189,481 | 185,386 | 0.0 | 145 | 55.1 | 49.0 | 42.0 | 46.2 | 1.7 | 3.0 |
| ROCKDALE | 247 | 0520 | 524 | 54,091 | 70,258 | 75,594 | 2.6 | 34 | 90.4 | 87.6 | 8.1 | 9.8 | 1.0 | 1.8 |
| SCHLEY | 249 | 0000 | 522 | 3,588 | 3,983 | 4,160 | 1.0 | 84 | 64.6 | 58.4 | 34.1 | 38.9 | 0.0 | 0.0 |
| SCREVEN | 251 | 0000 | 507 | 13,842 | 14,528 | 14,820 | 0.5 | 119 | 54.9 | 49.2 | 44.9 | 50.5 | 0.1 | 0.2 |
| SEMINOLE | 253 | 0000 | 606 | 9,010 | 9,907 | 10,403 | 0.9 | 89 | 66.9 | 61.8 | 32.7 | 37.7 | 0.1 | 0.2 |
| SPALDING | 255 | 0520 | 524 | 54,457 | 57,988 | 58,897 | 0.6 | 111 | 70.3 | 65.1 | 29.0 | 33.7 | 0.4 | 0.8 |
| STEPHENS | 257 | 0000 | 567 | 23,257 | 25,359 | 25,565 | 0.8 | 97 | 87.3 | 84.2 | 12.0 | 14.6 | 0.4 | 0.7 |
| STEWART | 259 | 0000 | 522 | 5,654 | 5,346 | 5,211 | -0.5 | 159 | 36.1 | 31.4 | 63.3 | 67.7 | 0.3 | 0.4 |
| SUMTER | 261 | 0000 | 522 | 30,228 | 31,738 | 31,816 | 0.5 | 119 | 52.6 | 46.9 | 46.5 | 51.8 | 0.4 | 0.6 |
| TALBOT | 263 | 0000 | 522 | 6,524 | 7,023 | 7,259 | 0.7 | 102 | 37.3 | 32.2 | 62.3 | 67.3 | 0.0 | 0.1 |
| TALIAFERRO | 265 | 0000 | 520 | 1,915 | 1,937 | 2,012 | 0.1 | 140 | 38.4 | 32.4 | 60.9 | 66.8 | 0.2 | 0.3 |
| TATTNALL | 267 | 0000 | 507 | 17,722 | 19,312 | 19,982 | 0.8 | 97 | 68.2 | 63.5 | 29.2 | 32.4 | 0.3 | 0.5 |
| TAYLOR | 269 | 0000 | 522 | 7,642 | 8,340 | 8,629 | 0.9 | 89 | 56.2 | 50.3 | 43.2 | 48.6 | 0.1 | 0.3 |
| TELFAIR | 271 | 0000 | 503 | 11,000 | 11,352 | 11,086 | 0.3 | 127 | 65.5 | 60.0 | 34.3 | 39.6 | 0.1 | 0.1 |
| TERRELL | 273 | 0000 | 525 | 10,653 | 11,255 | 11,526 | 0.5 | 119 | 39.9 | 34.6 | 59.9 | 65.1 | 0.1 | 0.2 |
| THOMAS | 275 | 0000 | 530 | 38,986 | 43,423 | 44,791 | 1.1 | 82 | 61.5 | 55.9 | 37.9 | 43.1 | 0.2 | 0.3 |
| TIFT | 277 | 0000 | 525 | 34,998 | 37,144 | 38,040 | 0.6 | 111 | 71.3 | 66.3 | 26.8 | 30.6 | 0.5 | 0.9 |
| TOOMBS | 279 | 0000 | 507 | 24,072 | 26,285 | 27,193 | 0.9 | 89 | 73.1 | 67.1 | 23.4 | 26.7 | 0.6 | 1.1 |
| TOWNS | 281 | 0000 | 524 | 6,754 | 9,084 | 10,523 | 2.9 | 25 | 99.7 | 99.7 | 0.0 | 0.0 | 0.1 | 0.0 |
| TREUTLEN | 283 | 0000 | 503 | 5,994 | 5,921 | 5,863 | -0.1 | 150 | 66.8 | 61.6 | 33.1 | 38.2 | 0.0 | 0.0 |
| TROUP | 285 | 0000 | 524 | 55,536 | 59,189 | 60,203 | 0.6 | 111 | 69.2 | 63.9 | 30.1 | 35.0 | 0.5 | 0.9 |
| TURNER | 287 | 0000 | 525 | 8,703 | 9,315 | 9,659 | 0.7 | 102 | 58.9 | 53.8 | 40.6 | 45.4 | 0.2 | 0.4 |
| TWIGGS | 289 | 4680 | 503 | 9,806 | 10,301 | 10,832 | 0.5 | 119 | 53.9 | 48.4 | 45.9 | 51.4 | 0.1 | 0.1 |
| UNION | 291 | 0000 | 524 | 11,993 | 17,985 | 21,672 | 4.0 | 16 | 99.4 | 99.3 | 0.2 | 0.2 | 0.2 | 0.3 |
| UPSON | 293 | 0000 | 524 | 26,300 | 27,130 | 27,350 | 0.3 | 127 | 71.9 | 66.6 | 27.7 | 32.6 | 0.3 | 0.5 |
| WALKER | 295 | 1560 | 575 | 58,340 | 63,455 | 65,829 | 0.8 | 97 | 95.6 | 94.4 | 3.8 | 4.7 | 0.2 | 0.4 |
| WALTON | 297 | 0520 | 524 | 38,586 | 61,766 | 78,120 | 4.7 | 9 | 80.8 | 76.5 | 18.4 | 22.3 | 0.4 | 0.7 |
| WARE | 299 | 0000 | 561 | 35,471 | 35,095 | 34,418 | -0.1 | 150 | 73.3 | 68.6 | 26.0 | 30.3 | 0.3 | 0.6 |
| WARREN | 301 | 0000 | 520 | 6,078 | 6,102 | 6,219 | 0.0 | 145 | 39.7 | 35.0 | 60.2 | 64.8 | 0.1 | 0.2 |
| WASHINGTON | 303 | 0000 | 503 | 19,112 | 20,333 | 20,957 | 0.6 | 111 | 48.1 | 42.6 | 51.7 | 57.1 | 0.1 | 0.2 |
| WAYNE | 305 | 0000 | 507 | 22,356 | 25,914 | 27,403 | 1.5 | 66 | 80.0 | 76.1 | 19.5 | 23.1 | 0.2 | 0.4 |
| WEBSTER | 307 | 0000 | 522 | 2,263 | 2,194 | 2,148 | -0.3 | 158 | 49.8 | 44.7 | 50.0 | 55.2 | 0.0 | 0.0 |
| WHEELER | 309 | 0000 | 503 | 4,903 | 4,840 | 4,722 | -0.1 | 150 | 68.4 | 62.9 | 30.1 | 34.7 | 0.1 | 0.2 |
| WHITE | 311 | 0000 | 524 | 13,006 | 18,900 | 22,395 | 3.7 | 19 | 96.3 | 95.1 | 2.8 | 3.5 | 0.5 | 0.9 |
| GEORGIA | | | | | | | 2.0 | | 71.0 | 68.5 | 27.0 | 28.1 | 1.2 | 2.0 |
| UNITED STATES | | | | | | | 1.0 | | 80.3 | 77.9 | 12.1 | 12.4 | 2.9 | 3.9 |

# POPULATION COMPOSITION

| COUNTY | % HISPANIC ORIGIN | | 2000 AGE DISTRIBUTION (%) | | | | | | | | | | MEDIAN AGE | | 2000 Males/ Females (×100) |
|---|---|---|---|---|---|---|---|---|---|---|---|---|---|---|---|
| | 1990 | 2000 | 0-4 | 5-9 | 10-14 | 15-19 | 20-24 | 25-44 | 45-64 | 65-84 | 85+ | 18+ | 1990 | 2000 | |
| JACKSON | 0.5 | 1.4 | 7.0 | 7.2 | 7.2 | 6.8 | 6.4 | 30.4 | 23.5 | 10.0 | 1.4 | 74.5 | 33.0 | 35.6 | 99.3 |
| JASPER | 0.7 | 1.5 | 7.3 | 7.4 | 7.8 | 7.9 | 5.9 | 27.0 | 23.6 | 11.4 | 1.6 | 72.4 | 33.8 | 36.0 | 94.8 |
| JEFF DAVIS | 1.2 | 2.5 | 7.1 | 7.2 | 7.5 | 7.3 | 6.3 | 29.9 | 23.3 | 10.2 | 1.1 | 73.8 | 31.8 | 34.9 | 97.6 |
| JEFFERSON | 0.2 | 0.5 | 7.9 | 8.0 | 8.2 | 8.4 | 7.0 | 27.4 | 20.3 | 10.7 | 2.1 | 70.8 | 31.4 | 33.0 | 87.2 |
| JENKINS | 0.2 | 0.5 | 7.9 | 7.8 | 8.3 | 7.5 | 6.2 | 26.7 | 22.2 | 11.9 | 1.6 | 71.6 | 32.6 | 35.0 | 89.9 |
| JOHNSON | 0.4 | 1.0 | 7.8 | 7.8 | 8.2 | 7.6 | 6.2 | 26.4 | 21.5 | 12.5 | 2.0 | 71.6 | 32.7 | 34.8 | 88.4 |
| JONES | 0.4 | 0.9 | 7.1 | 7.4 | 7.5 | 7.3 | 6.0 | 31.5 | 23.8 | 8.3 | 1.0 | 73.5 | 32.2 | 35.2 | 94.5 |
| LAMAR | 0.4 | 0.9 | 6.8 | 6.9 | 7.2 | 7.5 | 6.3 | 28.2 | 23.7 | 11.6 | 1.6 | 75.0 | 33.4 | 36.3 | 90.6 |
| LANIER | 1.2 | 2.4 | 7.6 | 7.9 | 8.1 | 7.5 | 6.7 | 29.1 | 22.7 | 9.1 | 1.4 | 71.7 | 31.6 | 34.0 | 95.8 |
| LAURENS | 0.5 | 1.0 | 7.4 | 7.4 | 7.6 | 7.6 | 6.5 | 28.3 | 22.3 | 11.5 | 1.5 | 73.0 | 33.0 | 35.1 | 93.2 |
| LEE | 0.7 | 1.5 | 7.3 | 7.5 | 7.3 | 8.3 | 8.1 | 32.5 | 22.2 | 6.1 | 0.6 | 72.4 | 29.7 | 31.2 | 102.5 |
| LIBERTY | 6.1 | 10.5 | 11.9 | 9.0 | 7.1 | 7.4 | 16.8 | 33.4 | 10.3 | 3.7 | 0.4 | 68.9 | 24.1 | 24.4 | 115.8 |
| LINCOLN | 0.8 | 1.5 | 6.5 | 6.9 | 7.2 | 7.3 | 6.1 | 27.9 | 24.1 | 12.5 | 1.4 | 74.8 | 34.5 | 37.0 | 94.2 |
| LONG | 3.0 | 5.4 | 10.1 | 8.8 | 8.1 | 8.0 | 8.0 | 31.3 | 18.2 | 6.8 | 0.7 | 68.8 | 27.2 | 29.5 | 100.0 |
| LOWNDES | 1.3 | 2.5 | 8.0 | 7.8 | 7.5 | 8.0 | 8.6 | 32.1 | 18.8 | 8.1 | 1.0 | 72.7 | 28.9 | 31.1 | 95.2 |
| LUMPKIN | 1.5 | 3.3 | 6.8 | 6.8 | 6.9 | 9.0 | 8.7 | 29.6 | 22.1 | 8.9 | 1.3 | 76.1 | 30.3 | 33.7 | 98.9 |
| MCDUFFIE | 0.4 | 0.9 | 7.5 | 7.5 | 7.8 | 7.8 | 6.8 | 27.9 | 23.2 | 10.3 | 1.2 | 72.3 | 32.0 | 34.6 | 91.1 |
| MCINTOSH | 0.7 | 1.5 | 7.3 | 7.6 | 7.6 | 7.0 | 6.1 | 28.3 | 23.2 | 11.5 | 1.4 | 73.1 | 33.0 | 35.9 | 94.9 |
| MACON | 0.4 | 0.8 | 8.0 | 7.9 | 8.0 | 8.5 | 7.6 | 26.8 | 21.1 | 10.3 | 1.8 | 70.7 | 31.2 | 32.5 | 87.4 |
| MADISON | 0.9 | 1.9 | 6.9 | 7.0 | 7.3 | 6.9 | 6.2 | 30.8 | 24.1 | 9.4 | 1.2 | 74.5 | 32.8 | 35.9 | 96.1 |
| MARION | 0.4 | 0.9 | 7.6 | 7.9 | 7.7 | 7.7 | 6.3 | 29.2 | 22.8 | 9.5 | 1.3 | 72.0 | 32.1 | 34.4 | 93.8 |
| MERIWETHER | 0.5 | 1.0 | 7.7 | 7.7 | 8.1 | 7.9 | 6.6 | 27.9 | 21.7 | 10.8 | 1.6 | 71.7 | 31.8 | 33.9 | 92.8 |
| MILLER | 0.3 | 0.9 | 6.8 | 7.2 | 7.5 | 7.7 | 6.1 | 25.7 | 23.5 | 13.3 | 2.2 | 73.5 | 34.7 | 36.8 | 90.3 |
| MITCHELL | 1.3 | 2.0 | 7.8 | 8.4 | 8.3 | 8.9 | 7.0 | 26.8 | 20.7 | 10.4 | 1.7 | 69.9 | 30.7 | 32.2 | 88.7 |
| MONROE | 0.6 | 1.1 | 6.7 | 7.0 | 7.1 | 7.5 | 6.6 | 30.3 | 23.6 | 9.8 | 1.5 | 74.8 | 33.0 | 35.3 | 96.6 |
| MONTGOMERY | 2.0 | 3.7 | 6.5 | 6.7 | 7.1 | 9.6 | 8.8 | 29.1 | 21.1 | 9.7 | 1.5 | 75.1 | 30.7 | 32.9 | 99.5 |
| MORGAN | 0.9 | 1.9 | 7.3 | 7.4 | 7.6 | 7.3 | 6.1 | 29.5 | 22.6 | 10.5 | 1.7 | 73.0 | 32.8 | 35.4 | 93.4 |
| MURRAY | 0.5 | 1.5 | 7.6 | 7.5 | 7.7 | 7.4 | 6.5 | 32.1 | 22.7 | 7.6 | 0.9 | 72.9 | 30.4 | 33.7 | 98.8 |
| MUSCOGEE | 3.0 | 5.3 | 8.0 | 7.4 | 7.1 | 7.7 | 7.9 | 30.5 | 19.8 | 10.3 | 1.3 | 73.5 | 30.6 | 32.8 | 94.9 |
| NEWTON | 0.9 | 2.0 | 7.8 | 7.6 | 7.8 | 7.7 | 6.6 | 30.1 | 22.6 | 8.7 | 1.1 | 72.5 | 31.1 | 33.9 | 92.9 |
| OCONEE | 1.0 | 2.3 | 7.4 | 7.8 | 7.9 | 7.1 | 5.8 | 31.7 | 23.3 | 7.6 | 1.4 | 72.5 | 32.5 | 35.3 | 95.6 |
| OGLETHORPE | 0.7 | 1.6 | 7.1 | 7.0 | 7.4 | 7.0 | 6.0 | 30.0 | 24.7 | 9.5 | 1.4 | 74.4 | 33.5 | 36.1 | 94.1 |
| PAULDING | 0.6 | 1.8 | 9.0 | 8.4 | 7.9 | 6.8 | 6.2 | 35.4 | 20.0 | 5.6 | 0.6 | 70.6 | 29.8 | 32.0 | 99.6 |
| PEACH | 1.8 | 2.8 | 6.8 | 7.3 | 7.3 | 9.8 | 8.4 | 28.3 | 21.7 | 9.3 | 1.1 | 74.0 | 30.0 | 32.9 | 91.0 |
| PICKENS | 0.3 | 1.0 | 6.6 | 7.0 | 7.2 | 6.3 | 5.3 | 29.4 | 24.5 | 12.1 | 1.5 | 75.3 | 34.4 | 37.4 | 96.6 |
| PIERCE | 0.8 | 2.0 | 6.5 | 6.8 | 7.6 | 7.7 | 6.3 | 28.7 | 24.7 | 10.5 | 1.2 | 74.4 | 33.3 | 36.3 | 94.0 |
| PIKE | 0.5 | 1.3 | 7.0 | 7.5 | 7.7 | 7.3 | 5.6 | 28.4 | 24.4 | 10.7 | 1.5 | 73.3 | 33.5 | 36.5 | 99.3 |
| POLK | 1.4 | 3.1 | 6.9 | 7.0 | 7.3 | 7.0 | 6.0 | 28.7 | 23.4 | 12.0 | 1.7 | 74.5 | 33.8 | 36.5 | 95.5 |
| PULASKI | 1.0 | 2.0 | 6.9 | 6.8 | 7.0 | 7.7 | 6.2 | 26.2 | 24.0 | 13.3 | 1.9 | 74.6 | 35.3 | 37.3 | 90.5 |
| PUTNAM | 0.7 | 1.4 | 6.5 | 6.9 | 6.7 | 6.9 | 6.0 | 28.3 | 25.1 | 12.2 | 1.3 | 75.6 | 34.2 | 37.4 | 95.6 |
| QUITMAN | 0.0 | 0.4 | 7.6 | 7.6 | 7.0 | 7.0 | 6.2 | 25.3 | 22.8 | 15.1 | 1.4 | 73.1 | 36.0 | 37.0 | 85.4 |
| RABUN | 0.6 | 1.5 | 5.3 | 5.8 | 6.2 | 5.5 | 4.9 | 26.5 | 27.4 | 16.2 | 2.2 | 79.2 | 39.8 | 42.2 | 94.6 |
| RANDOLPH | 0.5 | 0.7 | 7.3 | 7.9 | 8.2 | 9.7 | 7.7 | 24.5 | 19.7 | 12.9 | 2.2 | 71.7 | 32.1 | 33.0 | 84.5 |
| RICHMOND | 2.0 | 3.7 | 7.7 | 7.5 | 7.5 | 8.3 | 7.9 | 30.9 | 19.6 | 9.3 | 1.1 | 73.1 | 30.3 | 32.4 | 95.3 |
| ROCKDALE | 1.1 | 2.5 | 7.1 | 7.3 | 7.5 | 7.1 | 5.8 | 32.1 | 24.2 | 8.0 | 0.9 | 73.7 | 32.1 | 34.9 | 97.5 |
| SCHLEY | 1.5 | 3.4 | 7.8 | 7.5 | 8.2 | 7.5 | 5.8 | 28.7 | 23.3 | 9.7 | 1.5 | 72.1 | 32.3 | 33.9 | 95.9 |
| SCREVEN | 0.4 | 0.8 | 7.6 | 7.9 | 8.3 | 7.5 | 6.4 | 27.5 | 21.4 | 11.4 | 2.0 | 71.5 | 33.0 | 34.8 | 89.6 |
| SEMINOLE | 5.9 | 6.3 | 6.8 | 6.9 | 7.2 | 8.1 | 7.3 | 27.0 | 22.7 | 12.5 | 1.6 | 74.2 | 33.6 | 35.4 | 98.5 |
| SPALDING | 0.6 | 1.4 | 7.6 | 7.6 | 7.8 | 7.2 | 6.7 | 29.7 | 22.4 | 9.9 | 1.3 | 72.6 | 32.1 | 34.3 | 94.0 |
| STEPHENS | 0.6 | 1.5 | 6.3 | 6.3 | 6.6 | 7.2 | 7.0 | 27.6 | 24.1 | 13.2 | 1.6 | 76.9 | 34.8 | 37.5 | 93.8 |
| STEWART | 0.5 | 0.8 | 6.7 | 7.2 | 7.4 | 7.6 | 6.8 | 26.9 | 21.8 | 13.2 | 2.3 | 73.8 | 34.0 | 35.9 | 92.6 |
| SUMTER | 0.6 | 1.3 | 7.8 | 7.7 | 7.6 | 8.2 | 8.0 | 28.9 | 19.8 | 10.0 | 2.0 | 72.2 | 30.4 | 32.3 | 88.8 |
| TALBOT | 0.8 | 1.4 | 6.5 | 6.8 | 7.6 | 7.3 | 6.2 | 29.3 | 23.6 | 11.0 | 1.7 | 74.5 | 33.7 | 36.5 | 90.1 |
| TALIAFERRO | 1.1 | 1.6 | 7.1 | 7.2 | 8.1 | 7.2 | 6.4 | 25.5 | 23.0 | 13.6 | 2.1 | 72.9 | 35.4 | 36.7 | 91.6 |
| TATTNALL | 3.1 | 5.2 | 6.6 | 6.6 | 6.6 | 6.9 | 7.6 | 31.8 | 21.2 | 11.1 | 1.6 | 76.0 | 33.1 | 34.5 | 117.0 |
| TAYLOR | 0.8 | 1.5 | 7.0 | 7.3 | 7.6 | 8.0 | 6.3 | 28.1 | 22.8 | 11.2 | 1.6 | 73.3 | 32.7 | 35.1 | 90.0 |
| TELFAIR | 0.4 | 0.8 | 7.1 | 7.6 | 7.8 | 7.6 | 6.5 | 27.1 | 21.4 | 12.8 | 2.2 | 73.0 | 34.0 | 35.6 | 85.8 |
| TERRELL | 0.4 | 0.7 | 7.7 | 8.0 | 8.2 | 7.8 | 6.9 | 26.1 | 22.1 | 11.4 | 1.9 | 71.0 | 33.1 | 34.3 | 85.6 |
| THOMAS | 0.7 | 1.5 | 7.5 | 7.7 | 7.7 | 7.7 | 6.3 | 27.9 | 22.4 | 11.2 | 1.6 | 72.3 | 33.1 | 35.1 | 88.9 |
| TIFT | 3.5 | 5.6 | 7.9 | 7.6 | 7.9 | 8.6 | 7.8 | 28.9 | 20.6 | 9.4 | 1.3 | 72.1 | 30.7 | 32.3 | 94.3 |
| TOOMBS | 3.4 | 6.6 | 7.7 | 7.8 | 8.0 | 7.7 | 6.5 | 28.4 | 22.1 | 10.2 | 1.5 | 71.5 | 32.0 | 34.2 | 91.2 |
| TOWNS | 0.3 | 0.9 | 4.3 | 4.7 | 4.6 | 7.6 | 4.6 | 22.4 | 26.2 | 22.5 | 3.0 | 83.5 | 43.0 | 46.5 | 95.5 |
| TREUTLEN | 0.3 | 0.7 | 7.4 | 7.6 | 7.8 | 8.0 | 6.5 | 26.9 | 22.3 | 11.8 | 1.8 | 72.4 | 33.2 | 35.0 | 86.3 |
| TROUP | 0.5 | 1.2 | 7.6 | 7.6 | 7.8 | 7.6 | 6.6 | 28.8 | 21.5 | 10.8 | 1.7 | 72.4 | 32.5 | 34.5 | 92.3 |
| TURNER | 0.4 | 0.9 | 8.4 | 8.5 | 8.8 | 8.1 | 6.9 | 25.4 | 20.8 | 11.5 | 1.6 | 69.5 | 31.5 | 32.7 | 88.0 |
| TWIGGS | 0.5 | 1.0 | 8.1 | 7.9 | 7.8 | 8.3 | 6.9 | 28.7 | 21.5 | 9.7 | 1.2 | 71.4 | 30.8 | 33.5 | 89.9 |
| UNION | 0.4 | 1.3 | 5.5 | 5.8 | 6.1 | 6.2 | 5.0 | 25.1 | 26.6 | 17.3 | 2.3 | 78.9 | 39.3 | 42.3 | 98.4 |
| UPSON | 0.4 | 1.0 | 6.6 | 6.8 | 7.1 | 6.7 | 6.0 | 28.4 | 23.2 | 13.1 | 2.1 | 75.4 | 34.8 | 37.4 | 93.3 |
| WALKER | 0.4 | 1.1 | 6.3 | 6.6 | 6.8 | 6.7 | 6.3 | 28.7 | 24.8 | 12.3 | 1.5 | 76.2 | 34.5 | 37.7 | 94.7 |
| WALTON | 0.9 | 2.0 | 7.5 | 7.5 | 7.6 | 7.2 | 6.6 | 30.5 | 22.9 | 9.0 | 1.2 | 73.0 | 31.7 | 34.5 | 93.7 |
| WARE | 0.5 | 1.2 | 6.7 | 6.8 | 7.4 | 7.4 | 6.3 | 27.8 | 22.7 | 12.8 | 2.1 | 74.6 | 34.4 | 36.8 | 94.9 |
| WARREN | 0.0 | 0.3 | 7.7 | 7.8 | 8.2 | 6.9 | 6.5 | 26.7 | 21.2 | 12.6 | 2.4 | 72.1 | 33.4 | 35.5 | 83.8 |
| WASHINGTON | 0.3 | 0.7 | 7.8 | 7.9 | 8.1 | 8.1 | 6.3 | 27.8 | 21.7 | 10.3 | 1.8 | 71.1 | 32.0 | 34.5 | 91.4 |
| WAYNE | 0.8 | 1.7 | 7.4 | 7.6 | 7.7 | 7.4 | 6.8 | 28.0 | 23.1 | 10.7 | 1.3 | 72.7 | 32.6 | 34.8 | 94.3 |
| WEBSTER | 0.0 | 0.3 | 6.7 | 6.9 | 7.2 | 7.4 | 6.3 | 28.9 | 22.7 | 12.4 | 1.5 | 74.6 | 33.5 | 36.3 | 81.8 |
| WHEELER | 2.1 | 3.5 | 7.4 | 7.2 | 8.3 | 7.6 | 6.5 | 26.2 | 22.7 | 12.2 | 1.8 | 72.4 | 34.2 | 35.4 | 95.8 |
| WHITE | 0.8 | 1.9 | 5.6 | 6.0 | 6.2 | 7.2 | 6.0 | 26.6 | 26.5 | 14.3 | 1.7 | 78.3 | 36.8 | 39.7 | 94.9 |
| GEORGIA | 1.7 | 3.3 | 7.4 | 7.3 | 7.3 | 7.3 | 7.1 | 32.3 | 21.8 | 8.6 | 1.1 | 74.0 | 31.6 | 34.1 | 94.9 |
| UNITED STATES | 9.0 | 11.8 | 6.9 | 7.2 | 7.2 | 7.2 | 6.7 | 29.9 | 22.2 | 11.1 | 1.6 | 74.6 | 32.9 | 35.7 | 95.6 |

| COUNTY | HOUSEHOLDS | | | | | FAMILIES | | | MEDIAN HOUSEHOLD INCOME | | | |
|---|---|---|---|---|---|---|---|---|---|---|---|---|
| | 1990 | 2000 | 2005 | % Annual Rate 1990-2000 | 2000 Average HH Size | 1990 | 2000 | % Annual Rate 1990-2000 | 2000 | 2005 | 2000 National Rank | 2000 State Rank |
| JACKSON | 10,721 | 14,704 | 17,215 | 3.9 | 2.70 | 8,353 | 11,144 | 3.6 | 39,216 | 46,814 | 734 | 36 |
| JASPER | 3,036 | 3,960 | 4,640 | 3.3 | 2.75 | 2,307 | 2,911 | 2.9 | 40,298 | 51,378 | 649 | 33 |
| JEFF DAVIS | 4,357 | 4,825 | 5,013 | 1.2 | 2.63 | 3,378 | 3,632 | 0.9 | 30,984 | 36,729 | 1939 | 107 |
| JEFFERSON | 6,093 | 6,389 | 6,505 | 0.6 | 2.73 | 4,489 | 4,544 | 0.1 | 26,889 | 30,810 | 2601 | 141 |
| JENKINS | 2,951 | 3,100 | 3,095 | 0.6 | 2.66 | 2,186 | 2,208 | 0.1 | 25,588 | 30,458 | 2747 | 149 |
| JOHNSON | 3,010 | 3,061 | 3,071 | 0.2 | 2.65 | 2,221 | 2,174 | -0.3 | 26,349 | 32,349 | 2673 | 147 |
| JONES | 7,300 | 8,596 | 9,354 | 2.0 | 2.73 | 5,801 | 6,670 | 1.7 | 42,875 | 50,315 | 462 | 25 |
| LAMAR | 4,669 | 5,632 | 6,304 | 2.3 | 2.68 | 3,568 | 4,191 | 2.0 | 35,872 | 44,310 | 1116 | 54 |
| LANIER | 1,965 | 2,722 | 3,008 | 4.0 | 2.56 | 1,505 | 2,016 | 3.6 | 26,545 | 30,339 | 2647 | 144 |
| LAURENS | 14,514 | 16,729 | 17,608 | 1.7 | 2.59 | 10,822 | 12,105 | 1.4 | 31,566 | 35,515 | 1805 | 96 |
| LEE | 5,199 | 8,157 | 9,700 | 5.6 | 2.88 | 4,293 | 6,576 | 5.3 | 47,622 | 56,370 | 254 | 14 |
| LIBERTY | 15,136 | 17,752 | 18,250 | 2.0 | 2.99 | 12,404 | 14,239 | 1.7 | 34,240 | 42,796 | 1352 | 68 |
| LINCOLN | 2,702 | 3,187 | 3,452 | 2.0 | 2.64 | 2,059 | 2,354 | 1.6 | 30,216 | 33,431 | 2102 | 117 |
| LONG | 2,196 | 3,288 | 3,701 | 5.0 | 2.68 | 1,683 | 2,441 | 4.6 | 29,608 | 38,719 | 2209 | 121 |
| LOWNDES | 26,311 | 30,686 | 32,029 | 1.9 | 2.65 | 19,123 | 21,774 | 1.6 | 35,237 | 41,177 | 1216 | 60 |
| LUMPKIN | 4,976 | 7,370 | 8,973 | 4.9 | 2.62 | 3,872 | 5,589 | 4.5 | 41,061 | 50,536 | 586 | 31 |
| MCDUFFIE | 7,270 | 8,157 | 8,503 | 1.4 | 2.66 | 5,508 | 6,007 | 1.1 | 32,385 | 37,011 | 1643 | 84 |
| MCINTOSH | 3,186 | 3,976 | 4,384 | 2.7 | 2.59 | 2,371 | 2,853 | 2.3 | 30,092 | 35,699 | 2132 | 119 |
| MACON | 4,388 | 4,534 | 4,544 | 0.4 | 2.82 | 3,322 | 3,333 | 0.0 | 26,366 | 29,661 | 2670 | 146 |
| MADISON | 7,740 | 9,325 | 10,222 | 2.3 | 2.74 | 6,061 | 7,105 | 1.9 | 36,875 | 42,302 | 995 | 51 |
| MARION | 1,962 | 2,529 | 2,801 | 3.1 | 2.70 | 1,524 | 1,902 | 2.7 | 27,002 | 31,688 | 2579 | 138 |
| MERIWETHER | 7,637 | 8,114 | 8,313 | 0.7 | 2.78 | 5,800 | 5,972 | 0.4 | 31,599 | 39,155 | 1801 | 93 |
| MILLER | 2,336 | 2,501 | 2,588 | 0.8 | 2.49 | 1,741 | 1,799 | 0.4 | 31,073 | 34,604 | 1919 | 104 |
| MITCHELL | 6,798 | 7,373 | 7,608 | 1.0 | 2.85 | 5,254 | 5,548 | 0.7 | 28,606 | 31,525 | 2349 | 129 |
| MONROE | 5,838 | 7,032 | 7,625 | 2.3 | 2.81 | 4,547 | 5,317 | 1.9 | 40,884 | 49,869 | 599 | 32 |
| MONTGOMERY | 2,493 | 2,711 | 2,864 | 1.0 | 2.68 | 1,842 | 1,930 | 0.6 | 30,323 | 34,830 | 2076 | 114 |
| MORGAN | 4,399 | 5,586 | 6,377 | 2.9 | 2.80 | 3,442 | 4,250 | 2.6 | 40,074 | 50,030 | 666 | 34 |
| MURRAY | 9,363 | 12,657 | 14,655 | 3.7 | 2.75 | 7,499 | 9,868 | 3.4 | 38,356 | 47,268 | 823 | 43 |
| MUSCOGEE | 65,858 | 68,548 | 68,696 | 0.5 | 2.54 | 47,235 | 47,835 | 0.2 | 35,706 | 41,048 | 1135 | 55 |
| NEWTON | 14,401 | 22,293 | 27,187 | 5.4 | 2.80 | 11,337 | 17,253 | 5.2 | 42,465 | 50,924 | 476 | 27 |
| OCONEE | 6,156 | 8,948 | 10,347 | 4.6 | 2.81 | 4,960 | 6,996 | 4.3 | 53,103 | 59,199 | 151 | 10 |
| OGLETHORPE | 3,581 | 4,495 | 4,968 | 2.8 | 2.60 | 2,748 | 3,325 | 2.3 | 35,322 | 40,000 | 1196 | 58 |
| PAULDING | 14,326 | 29,027 | 37,879 | 8.9 | 2.91 | 11,999 | 23,856 | 8.7 | 51,163 | 64,226 | 182 | 12 |
| PEACH | 7,142 | 8,847 | 9,877 | 2.6 | 2.74 | 5,465 | 6,661 | 2.4 | 33,670 | 40,304 | 1440 | 73 |
| PICKENS | 5,386 | 8,270 | 10,419 | 5.3 | 2.66 | 4,239 | 6,317 | 5.0 | 41,132 | 47,436 | 579 | 30 |
| PIERCE | 4,807 | 6,067 | 6,528 | 2.9 | 2.62 | 3,759 | 4,612 | 2.5 | 33,094 | 38,227 | 1521 | 79 |
| PIKE | 3,526 | 4,791 | 5,660 | 3.8 | 2.81 | 2,824 | 3,740 | 3.5 | 38,642 | 47,287 | 783 | 40 |
| POLK | 12,519 | 14,048 | 14,989 | 1.4 | 2.61 | 9,455 | 10,289 | 1.0 | 33,000 | 40,233 | 1539 | 81 |
| PULASKI | 3,098 | 3,363 | 3,471 | 1.0 | 2.45 | 2,185 | 2,309 | 0.7 | 29,831 | 35,223 | 2176 | 120 |
| PUTNAM | 5,229 | 7,141 | 8,365 | 3.8 | 2.59 | 3,938 | 5,238 | 3.5 | 37,183 | 42,193 | 948 | 50 |
| QUITMAN | 857 | 1,024 | 1,050 | 2.2 | 2.38 | 626 | 721 | 1.7 | 24,788 | 27,857 | 2829 | 153 |
| RABUN | 4,630 | 5,630 | 6,175 | 2.4 | 2.44 | 3,477 | 4,091 | 2.0 | 35,641 | 40,969 | 1146 | 56 |
| RANDOLPH | 2,815 | 2,815 | 2,860 | 0.0 | 2.74 | 2,003 | 1,926 | -0.5 | 20,807 | 22,967 | 3076 | 159 |
| RICHMOND | 68,675 | 69,982 | 69,360 | 0.2 | 2.54 | 47,685 | 47,153 | -0.1 | 33,856 | 37,561 | 1413 | 72 |
| ROCKDALE | 18,337 | 24,668 | 27,032 | 3.7 | 2.82 | 15,121 | 20,076 | 3.5 | 56,800 | 66,623 | 105 | 8 |
| SCHLEY | 1,315 | 1,547 | 1,662 | 2.0 | 2.57 | 964 | 1,091 | 1.5 | 31,540 | 39,773 | 1812 | 97 |
| SCREVEN | 5,048 | 5,446 | 5,629 | 0.9 | 2.63 | 3,698 | 3,835 | 0.4 | 31,586 | 41,352 | 1802 | 94 |
| SEMINOLE | 3,137 | 3,656 | 3,946 | 1.9 | 2.55 | 2,336 | 2,639 | 1.5 | 29,110 | 31,872 | 2280 | 124 |
| SPALDING | 19,426 | 21,095 | 21,618 | 1.0 | 2.71 | 14,901 | 15,831 | 0.7 | 38,222 | 47,940 | 838 | 44 |
| STEPHENS | 8,949 | 10,060 | 10,316 | 1.4 | 2.45 | 6,633 | 7,246 | 1.1 | 33,608 | 38,867 | 1450 | 74 |
| STEWART | 1,982 | 1,975 | 1,973 | 0.0 | 2.65 | 1,439 | 1,378 | -0.5 | 25,435 | 30,434 | 2763 | 150 |
| SUMTER | 10,484 | 11,128 | 11,270 | 0.7 | 2.69 | 7,610 | 7,834 | 0.4 | 32,730 | 36,275 | 1587 | 82 |
| TALBOT | 2,345 | 2,631 | 2,774 | 1.4 | 2.67 | 1,765 | 1,908 | 0.9 | 30,547 | 37,750 | 2022 | 111 |
| TALIAFERRO | 727 | 749 | 785 | 0.4 | 2.59 | 492 | 483 | -0.2 | 21,555 | 26,625 | 3050 | 158 |
| TATTNALL | 5,845 | 6,544 | 6,850 | 1.4 | 2.57 | 4,272 | 4,579 | 0.8 | 31,034 | 37,572 | 1923 | 105 |
| TAYLOR | 2,804 | 3,197 | 3,379 | 1.6 | 2.61 | 2,070 | 2,269 | 1.1 | 25,139 | 27,683 | 2799 | 151 |
| TELFAIR | 4,017 | 4,341 | 4,331 | 0.9 | 2.53 | 2,901 | 3,019 | 0.5 | 23,891 | 26,826 | 2912 | 156 |
| TERRELL | 3,738 | 4,049 | 4,200 | 1.0 | 2.74 | 2,772 | 2,906 | 0.6 | 26,674 | 29,077 | 2622 | 142 |
| THOMAS | 14,323 | 16,595 | 17,503 | 1.8 | 2.56 | 10,644 | 11,997 | 1.5 | 32,188 | 35,822 | 1690 | 85 |
| TIFT | 12,184 | 13,149 | 13,566 | 0.9 | 2.71 | 9,101 | 9,597 | 0.6 | 35,338 | 40,347 | 1194 | 57 |
| TOOMBS | 8,804 | 9,839 | 10,312 | 1.4 | 2.62 | 6,386 | 6,916 | 1.0 | 29,298 | 33,466 | 2255 | 123 |
| TOWNS | 2,812 | 3,985 | 4,731 | 4.3 | 2.18 | 2,056 | 2,815 | 3.9 | 32,050 | 37,491 | 1706 | 86 |
| TREUTLEN | 2,158 | 2,222 | 2,244 | 0.4 | 2.63 | 1,607 | 1,595 | -0.1 | 27,500 | 31,935 | 2509 | 134 |
| TROUP | 20,371 | 22,181 | 22,842 | 1.0 | 2.61 | 14,980 | 15,938 | 0.8 | 37,425 | 44,135 | 910 | 48 |
| TURNER | 3,043 | 3,329 | 3,505 | 1.1 | 2.76 | 2,331 | 2,499 | 0.8 | 26,242 | 30,283 | 2684 | 148 |
| TWIGGS | 3,296 | 3,608 | 3,873 | 1.1 | 2.81 | 2,570 | 2,729 | 0.7 | 30,268 | 32,391 | 2091 | 115 |
| UNION | 4,709 | 7,309 | 8,944 | 5.5 | 2.43 | 3,653 | 5,508 | 5.1 | 33,321 | 38,622 | 1487 | 77 |
| UPSON | 9,911 | 10,475 | 10,688 | 0.7 | 2.55 | 7,335 | 7,495 | 0.3 | 34,354 | 40,761 | 1341 | 67 |
| WALKER | 21,697 | 24,642 | 26,109 | 1.6 | 2.54 | 16,887 | 18,598 | 1.2 | 34,110 | 40,192 | 1374 | 70 |
| WALTON | 13,433 | 21,379 | 26,948 | 5.8 | 2.87 | 10,749 | 16,837 | 5.6 | 43,465 | 51,876 | 429 | 22 |
| WARE | 13,046 | 13,320 | 13,253 | 0.3 | 2.51 | 9,416 | 9,328 | -0.1 | 31,854 | 38,018 | 1745 | 89 |
| WARREN | 2,130 | 2,196 | 2,269 | 0.4 | 2.73 | 1,603 | 1,593 | -0.1 | 26,599 | 31,951 | 2635 | 143 |
| WASHINGTON | 6,739 | 7,310 | 7,608 | 1.0 | 2.74 | 4,985 | 5,224 | 0.6 | 33,128 | 40,429 | 1515 | 78 |
| WAYNE | 7,922 | 9,485 | 10,186 | 2.2 | 2.67 | 6,113 | 7,134 | 1.9 | 34,232 | 41,433 | 1353 | 69 |
| WEBSTER | 798 | 785 | 774 | -0.2 | 2.79 | 610 | 579 | -0.6 | 29,077 | 36,103 | 2286 | 125 |
| WHEELER | 1,786 | 1,818 | 1,800 | 0.2 | 2.61 | 1,331 | 1,305 | -0.2 | 26,944 | 30,625 | 2590 | 139 |
| WHITE | 4,907 | 7,353 | 8,827 | 5.0 | 2.50 | 3,798 | 5,571 | 4.8 | 36,276 | 40,125 | 1069 | 53 |
| GEORGIA | | | | 2.8 | 2.62 | | | 2.6 | 43,179 | 51,136 | | |
| UNITED STATES | | | | 1.4 | 2.59 | | | 1.1 | 41,914 | 49,127 | | |

# INCOME

| COUNTY | 2000 Per Capita Income | 2000 HH Income Base | 2000 HOUSEHOLD INCOME DISTRIBUTION (%) Less than $15,000 | $15,000 to $24,999 | $25,000 to $49,999 | $50,000 to $99,999 | $100,000 to $149,999 | $150,000 or More | 2000 AVERAGE DISPOSABLE INCOME BY AGE OF HOUSEHOLDER All Ages | <35 | 35-44 | 45-54 | 55-64 | 65+ |
|---|---|---|---|---|---|---|---|---|---|---|---|---|---|---|
| JACKSON | 17,600 | 14,704 | 13.5 | 13.6 | 37.7 | 29.2 | 5.0 | 1.0 | 35,388 | 34,525 | 40,932 | 40,981 | 35,867 | 22,725 |
| JASPER | 17,481 | 3,960 | 19.5 | 8.3 | 32.5 | 31.8 | 6.6 | 1.3 | 36,369 | 33,356 | 38,135 | 44,541 | 35,790 | 29,426 |
| JEFF DAVIS | 14,577 | 4,825 | 21.4 | 18.0 | 34.7 | 22.0 | 3.3 | 0.7 | 29,686 | 27,768 | 35,109 | 36,909 | 28,447 | 18,494 |
| JEFFERSON | 12,920 | 6,389 | 29.1 | 17.8 | 31.8 | 17.5 | 2.6 | 1.2 | 27,558 | 26,577 | 31,547 | 32,745 | 29,605 | 18,207 |
| JENKINS | 11,873 | 3,100 | 32.9 | 15.8 | 32.3 | 16.4 | 2.3 | 0.3 | 25,445 | 26,499 | 29,290 | 29,101 | 25,539 | 18,241 |
| JOHNSON | 12,358 | 3,061 | 28.0 | 18.4 | 36.3 | 14.7 | 2.4 | 0.3 | 26,052 | 25,651 | 31,572 | 33,031 | 26,065 | 15,579 |
| JONES | 19,936 | 8,596 | 13.9 | 11.9 | 31.9 | 33.1 | 6.7 | 2.5 | 39,341 | 34,287 | 41,438 | 52,265 | 38,189 | 20,805 |
| LAMAR | 16,357 | 5,632 | 17.0 | 15.6 | 36.5 | 26.0 | 4.1 | 0.8 | 33,036 | 31,055 | 39,461 | 40,189 | 31,948 | 22,317 |
| LANIER | 13,533 | 2,722 | 24.1 | 22.6 | 31.2 | 18.1 | 3.6 | 0.4 | 27,577 | 25,547 | 27,575 | 35,467 | 28,515 | 19,452 |
| LAURENS | 16,254 | 16,728 | 22.4 | 16.3 | 34.2 | 20.9 | 4.3 | 1.8 | 31,819 | 28,258 | 36,121 | 39,274 | 31,982 | 21,244 |
| LEE | 18,746 | 8,157 | 10.0 | 9.3 | 33.9 | 37.4 | 8.0 | 1.4 | 40,889 | 37,413 | 45,241 | 46,679 | 41,233 | 25,013 |
| LIBERTY | 13,475 | 17,752 | 11.9 | 21.2 | 40.2 | 23.9 | 2.6 | 0.2 | 31,121 | 27,253 | 34,824 | 41,912 | 32,895 | 22,316 |
| LINCOLN | 14,338 | 3,187 | 24.3 | 16.0 | 35.4 | 20.3 | 3.5 | 0.5 | 28,886 | 29,037 | 33,276 | 36,503 | 29,897 | 18,165 |
| LONG | 13,994 | 3,288 | 21.5 | 20.4 | 34.7 | 20.5 | 2.1 | 0.8 | 29,046 | 26,061 | 35,561 | 38,375 | 30,286 | 15,285 |
| LOWNDES | 17,523 | 30,686 | 18.9 | 15.0 | 33.6 | 25.5 | 5.1 | 2.0 | 34,634 | 28,817 | 39,954 | 42,904 | 36,226 | 23,004 |
| LUMPKIN | 18,171 | 7,370 | 12.5 | 12.1 | 36.2 | 30.5 | 6.6 | 2.1 | 38,175 | 33,518 | 41,485 | 48,132 | 36,654 | 26,794 |
| MCDUFFIE | 15,567 | 8,157 | 23.4 | 16.5 | 34.0 | 21.6 | 3.2 | 1.5 | 30,826 | 27,603 | 34,156 | 38,257 | 31,602 | 20,100 |
| MCINTOSH | 14,471 | 3,976 | 25.1 | 15.5 | 36.5 | 18.6 | 3.5 | 0.9 | 28,808 | 26,162 | 29,882 | 39,286 | 30,326 | 18,015 |
| MACON | 12,138 | 4,534 | 31.9 | 16.1 | 30.4 | 17.7 | 2.8 | 1.1 | 27,072 | 22,216 | 34,196 | 32,965 | 28,798 | 17,520 |
| MADISON | 15,989 | 9,325 | 16.7 | 15.1 | 38.3 | 25.2 | 3.8 | 0.9 | 33,004 | 31,783 | 36,469 | 38,856 | 36,241 | 19,600 |
| MARION | 14,859 | 2,529 | 28.8 | 17.8 | 32.4 | 17.0 | 2.8 | 1.2 | 27,809 | 25,633 | 31,862 | 34,385 | 31,854 | 14,669 |
| MERIWETHER | 14,751 | 8,114 | 21.2 | 17.7 | 34.9 | 20.9 | 4.0 | 1.3 | 30,959 | 28,401 | 34,622 | 40,009 | 33,413 | 18,882 |
| MILLER | 18,489 | 2,501 | 24.4 | 15.2 | 33.8 | 20.5 | 4.2 | 1.8 | 31,166 | 27,771 | 35,894 | 42,818 | 33,326 | 18,535 |
| MITCHELL | 12,963 | 7,373 | 25.2 | 19.1 | 32.9 | 18.8 | 3.2 | 0.9 | 28,392 | 24,685 | 32,522 | 33,541 | 31,328 | 21,154 |
| MONROE | 17,319 | 7,031 | 13.7 | 13.2 | 35.1 | 30.1 | 6.4 | 1.6 | 37,195 | 35,604 | 40,346 | 45,535 | 32,344 | 26,237 |
| MONTGOMERY | 14,016 | 2,711 | 25.7 | 15.2 | 35.5 | 18.1 | 4.0 | 1.6 | 29,788 | 28,705 | 31,873 | 35,924 | 33,675 | 19,585 |
| MORGAN | 18,994 | 5,586 | 15.0 | 11.1 | 33.9 | 29.5 | 7.4 | 3.2 | 39,286 | 33,704 | 42,677 | 46,580 | 39,376 | 30,573 |
| MURRAY | 16,340 | 12,657 | 11.2 | 13.2 | 42.7 | 28.6 | 3.7 | 0.7 | 34,494 | 32,610 | 38,011 | 41,022 | 34,090 | 21,051 |
| MUSCOGEE | 18,620 | 68,543 | 18.6 | 15.3 | 33.7 | 25.2 | 5.2 | 2.0 | 34,742 | 29,043 | 37,774 | 43,362 | 38,321 | 25,021 |
| NEWTON | 18,678 | 22,293 | 12.2 | 11.7 | 35.3 | 32.1 | 6.9 | 1.8 | 38,531 | 36,768 | 41,771 | 46,902 | 37,735 | 24,916 |
| OCONEE | 26,385 | 8,948 | 8.3 | 8.7 | 29.6 | 37.4 | 10.9 | 5.1 | 48,831 | 40,957 | 51,503 | 58,395 | 45,989 | 30,682 |
| OGLETHORPE | 15,588 | 4,495 | 19.2 | 12.0 | 38.2 | 26.9 | 3.5 | 0.2 | 31,768 | 29,908 | 35,236 | 38,542 | 34,754 | 17,794 |
| PAULDING | 20,295 | 29,027 | 7.3 | 5.3 | 35.7 | 41.3 | 9.0 | 1.4 | 43,608 | 43,162 | 45,482 | 50,714 | 42,862 | 26,551 |
| PEACH | 15,695 | 8,847 | 24.2 | 12.9 | 32.2 | 24.7 | 4.2 | 1.8 | 32,794 | 26,958 | 37,744 | 40,140 | 34,473 | 22,049 |
| PICKENS | 19,093 | 8,270 | 13.1 | 12.0 | 37.7 | 27.6 | 7.2 | 2.5 | 38,515 | 35,102 | 42,615 | 47,766 | 39,726 | 26,486 |
| PIERCE | 15,923 | 6,067 | 20.6 | 17.4 | 34.7 | 22.4 | 3.6 | 1.3 | 31,384 | 30,287 | 36,167 | 38,573 | 31,031 | 18,531 |
| PIKE | 16,833 | 4,791 | 14.9 | 14.3 | 37.5 | 26.3 | 5.5 | 1.5 | 35,593 | 32,549 | 40,234 | 42,826 | 35,963 | 23,231 |
| POLK | 15,979 | 14,048 | 20.8 | 15.4 | 35.9 | 22.7 | 4.0 | 1.2 | 31,608 | 29,021 | 36,586 | 40,897 | 33,828 | 18,900 |
| PULASKI | 17,738 | 3,363 | 30.5 | 11.9 | 27.1 | 23.7 | 3.7 | 3.2 | 33,681 | 28,235 | 43,163 | 41,139 | 34,230 | 19,940 |
| PUTNAM | 18,445 | 7,141 | 17.4 | 17.0 | 29.2 | 28.6 | 5.4 | 2.4 | 36,464 | 33,348 | 40,621 | 43,023 | 38,044 | 24,713 |
| QUITMAN | 15,232 | 1,024 | 27.6 | 22.9 | 28.0 | 17.8 | 2.8 | 0.9 | 26,722 | 23,503 | 28,765 | 34,009 | 28,546 | 21,444 |
| RABUN | 18,780 | 5,630 | 15.4 | 17.4 | 35.5 | 24.9 | 5.5 | 1.3 | 34,058 | 32,067 | 37,534 | 39,234 | 37,119 | 27,162 |
| RANDOLPH | 9,880 | 2,815 | 35.2 | 21.9 | 29.7 | 10.7 | 2.0 | 0.5 | 22,515 | 21,652 | 25,303 | 27,977 | 24,115 | 16,329 |
| RICHMOND | 16,896 | 69,981 | 19.6 | 15.8 | 35.1 | 23.9 | 4.3 | 1.5 | 32,840 | 28,183 | 34,861 | 40,176 | 36,821 | 23,438 |
| ROCKDALE | 26,021 | 24,668 | 5.8 | 6.4 | 29.9 | 42.0 | 11.5 | 4.4 | 50,015 | 43,673 | 50,756 | 58,675 | 53,249 | 31,034 |
| SCHLEY | 15,853 | 1,547 | 26.0 | 12.4 | 33.6 | 22.5 | 3.9 | 1.7 | 31,212 | 30,681 | 41,508 | 37,003 | 28,565 | 19,222 |
| SCREVEN | 15,361 | 5,446 | 22.9 | 13.6 | 33.7 | 24.6 | 4.2 | 1.0 | 31,391 | 31,394 | 36,288 | 33,841 | 32,181 | 23,678 |
| SEMINOLE | 15,690 | 3,656 | 26.5 | 17.1 | 31.4 | 20.1 | 3.6 | 1.3 | 29,351 | 26,223 | 37,586 | 41,361 | 26,824 | 18,132 |
| SPALDING | 17,337 | 21,091 | 17.0 | 13.1 | 34.8 | 28.7 | 4.9 | 1.6 | 35,506 | 31,948 | 39,535 | 44,495 | 35,722 | 23,385 |
| STEPHENS | 15,975 | 10,060 | 21.0 | 14.7 | 38.9 | 21.4 | 3.2 | 0.9 | 30,821 | 30,429 | 36,151 | 38,735 | 31,741 | 19,193 |
| STEWART | 12,937 | 1,975 | 29.9 | 19.3 | 31.7 | 15.1 | 3.1 | 0.9 | 25,898 | 25,249 | 27,534 | 32,025 | 26,315 | 19,862 |
| SUMTER | 15,160 | 11,128 | 22.4 | 16.5 | 31.2 | 24.1 | 4.3 | 1.5 | 32,104 | 27,983 | 36,169 | 38,856 | 36,113 | 21,834 |
| TALBOT | 13,598 | 2,631 | 26.4 | 14.7 | 33.0 | 23.6 | 2.2 | 0.2 | 28,432 | 26,479 | 32,296 | 32,929 | 29,515 | 20,546 |
| TALIAFERRO | 10,987 | 749 | 35.8 | 20.3 | 29.2 | 13.1 | 1.5 | 0.1 | 22,470 | 22,256 | 26,578 | 27,872 | 19,896 | 17,284 |
| TATTNALL | 14,914 | 6,543 | 21.5 | 16.3 | 34.9 | 23.4 | 2.9 | 1.0 | 30,482 | 27,561 | 33,958 | 39,255 | 31,473 | 21,784 |
| TAYLOR | 14,277 | 3,197 | 34.2 | 15.6 | 29.2 | 15.9 | 2.8 | 2.2 | 27,907 | 25,810 | 31,347 | 33,239 | 30,483 | 17,081 |
| TELFAIR | 12,932 | 4,341 | 31.7 | 20.1 | 30.3 | 14.3 | 2.2 | 1.3 | 25,925 | 20,932 | 31,990 | 32,311 | 29,939 | 16,937 |
| TERRELL | 12,805 | 4,049 | 28.9 | 18.3 | 34.8 | 14.6 | 2.8 | 0.6 | 26,374 | 23,086 | 31,421 | 31,612 | 28,811 | 18,433 |
| THOMAS | 16,789 | 16,595 | 21.9 | 15.8 | 32.7 | 23.1 | 4.9 | 1.6 | 32,304 | 27,180 | 36,809 | 41,167 | 33,291 | 22,399 |
| TIFT | 17,093 | 13,149 | 20.3 | 14.6 | 32.4 | 25.4 | 5.4 | 1.9 | 34,239 | 30,047 | 39,260 | 42,560 | 34,561 | 23,699 |
| TOOMBS | 14,442 | 9,838 | 26.8 | 17.5 | 29.8 | 20.8 | 3.7 | 1.4 | 29,704 | 27,514 | 35,592 | 36,399 | 28,485 | 18,481 |
| TOWNS | 18,832 | 3,985 | 18.2 | 18.9 | 33.0 | 24.3 | 4.7 | 1.0 | 32,153 | 32,745 | 38,578 | 36,808 | 36,526 | 25,087 |
| TREUTLEN | 12,197 | 2,222 | 25.6 | 19.9 | 36.5 | 16.0 | 1.4 | 0.5 | 25,889 | 24,093 | 31,332 | 32,668 | 27,691 | 15,678 |
| TROUP | 18,543 | 22,181 | 17.7 | 14.0 | 34.4 | 26.4 | 5.4 | 2.2 | 35,746 | 33,105 | 40,910 | 44,353 | 34,957 | 22,415 |
| TURNER | 11,636 | 3,329 | 28.2 | 19.5 | 34.3 | 16.1 | 1.7 | 0.2 | 25,388 | 22,892 | 27,669 | 33,167 | 27,955 | 19,263 |
| TWIGGS | 12,619 | 3,608 | 27.6 | 14.4 | 35.3 | 19.4 | 2.6 | 0.7 | 27,783 | 27,798 | 33,370 | 33,412 | 26,370 | 16,010 |
| UNION | 19,397 | 7,309 | 20.9 | 14.5 | 33.5 | 24.0 | 4.8 | 2.4 | 34,116 | 33,611 | 38,331 | 41,412 | 34,343 | 25,285 |
| UPSON | 17,516 | 10,475 | 17.2 | 16.2 | 38.9 | 21.5 | 4.5 | 1.7 | 32,980 | 29,684 | 35,998 | 43,568 | 34,887 | 21,595 |
| WALKER | 15,962 | 24,632 | 18.6 | 15.1 | 38.9 | 23.6 | 3.1 | 0.7 | 31,254 | 30,415 | 37,939 | 37,577 | 31,295 | 19,635 |
| WALTON | 19,450 | 21,379 | 13.1 | 11.4 | 33.9 | 32.6 | 7.2 | 1.9 | 38,939 | 38,588 | 42,267 | 47,018 | 39,085 | 23,353 |
| WARE | 15,965 | 13,320 | 21.9 | 15.6 | 35.5 | 22.2 | 3.9 | 1.0 | 30,907 | 27,943 | 35,435 | 37,960 | 33,122 | 21,756 |
| WARREN | 11,949 | 2,196 | 28.7 | 17.3 | 33.7 | 18.0 | 1.9 | 0.3 | 26,188 | 23,280 | 29,530 | 33,215 | 28,556 | 17,927 |
| WASHINGTON | 16,052 | 7,310 | 22.3 | 14.9 | 32.1 | 24.2 | 4.9 | 1.6 | 32,848 | 29,483 | 35,720 | 42,279 | 34,520 | 20,022 |
| WAYNE | 14,933 | 9,485 | 21.7 | 14.2 | 35.2 | 24.4 | 3.8 | 0.7 | 31,143 | 28,243 | 36,573 | 38,033 | 34,549 | 18,542 |
| WEBSTER | 14,278 | 785 | 21.9 | 21.2 | 33.5 | 20.0 | 2.2 | 1.3 | 29,373 | 25,854 | 32,629 | 38,508 | 26,731 | 19,791 |
| WHEELER | 14,872 | 1,818 | 28.1 | 18.4 | 35.2 | 15.4 | 2.2 | 0.8 | 25,625 | 24,658 | 30,412 | 31,644 | 26,307 | 15,519 |
| WHITE | 17,651 | 7,353 | 15.8 | 15.3 | 36.1 | 27.3 | 4.4 | 1.2 | 34,013 | 32,038 | 41,959 | 41,535 | 35,565 | 21,765 |
| GEORGIA | 22,304 | | 13.9 | 11.8 | 31.9 | 30.9 | 8.0 | 3.5 | 41,548 | 35,922 | 45,313 | 49,959 | 41,633 | 25,795 |
| UNITED STATES | 22,162 | | 14.5 | 12.5 | 32.3 | 29.8 | 7.4 | 3.5 | 40,748 | 34,503 | 44,969 | 49,579 | 43,409 | 27,339 |

| COUNTY | FINANCIAL SERVICES | | | | THE HOME | | | | | | ENTERTAINMENT | | | | | | PERSONAL | | | |
|---|---|---|---|---|---|---|---|---|---|---|---|---|---|---|---|---|---|---|---|---|
| | | | | | Home Improvements | | | Furnishings | | | | | | | | | | | | |
| | Auto Loan | Home Loan | Investments | Retirement Plans | Home Repair | Lawn & Garden | Remodeling | Appliances | Electronics | Furniture | Restaurants | Sporting Goods | Theater & Concerts | Toys & Hobbies | Travel | Video Rental | Apparel | Auto Aftermarket | Health Insurance | Pets & Supplies |
| JACKSON | 98 | 76 | 81 | 80 | 93 | 91 | 114 | 96 | 93 | 85 | 86 | 96 | 84 | 98 | 71 | 97 | 85 | 90 | 99 | 99 |
| JASPER | 98 | 70 | 76 | 79 | 94 | 91 | 115 | 97 | 93 | 80 | 82 | 96 | 82 | 97 | 70 | 97 | 82 | 89 | 101 | 99 |
| JEFF DAVIS | 97 | 70 | 75 | 77 | 93 | 91 | 113 | 96 | 92 | 80 | 82 | 96 | 82 | 96 | 70 | 96 | 81 | 88 | 100 | 98 |
| JEFFERSON | 95 | 64 | 69 | 72 | 92 | 88 | 106 | 95 | 90 | 78 | 75 | 93 | 78 | 92 | 68 | 95 | 79 | 87 | 95 | 95 |
| JENKINS | 96 | 63 | 67 | 72 | 92 | 89 | 109 | 95 | 91 | 75 | 75 | 94 | 78 | 93 | 66 | 95 | 78 | 86 | 99 | 95 |
| JOHNSON | 97 | 63 | 66 | 73 | 92 | 90 | 112 | 96 | 91 | 75 | 77 | 96 | 78 | 95 | 66 | 95 | 78 | 86 | 102 | 96 |
| JONES | 99 | 82 | 83 | 85 | 94 | 92 | 113 | 98 | 95 | 88 | 91 | 98 | 88 | 100 | 75 | 98 | 89 | 93 | 100 | 101 |
| LAMAR | 97 | 72 | 82 | 79 | 96 | 93 | 109 | 96 | 92 | 82 | 83 | 95 | 84 | 96 | 73 | 96 | 83 | 89 | 101 | 97 |
| LANIER | 98 | 67 | 72 | 76 | 93 | 91 | 114 | 96 | 92 | 78 | 79 | 97 | 81 | 96 | 68 | 96 | 80 | 88 | 102 | 98 |
| LAURENS | 97 | 77 | 85 | 83 | 96 | 92 | 107 | 97 | 93 | 86 | 85 | 96 | 87 | 96 | 75 | 97 | 87 | 92 | 97 | 98 |
| LEE | 99 | 91 | 81 | 87 | 93 | 91 | 105 | 98 | 98 | 95 | 98 | 99 | 91 | 100 | 77 | 99 | 94 | 97 | 96 | 101 |
| LIBERTY | 89 | 87 | 71 | 73 | 86 | 82 | 87 | 90 | 91 | 81 | 89 | 87 | 83 | 88 | 72 | 96 | 83 | 91 | 88 | 96 |
| LINCOLN | 98 | 65 | 70 | 76 | 92 | 91 | 116 | 96 | 91 | 75 | 78 | 96 | 79 | 95 | 67 | 96 | 79 | 87 | 103 | 98 |
| LONG | 97 | 79 | 82 | 80 | 92 | 90 | 113 | 96 | 93 | 88 | 89 | 95 | 85 | 97 | 72 | 97 | 85 | 91 | 97 | 99 |
| LOWNDES | 95 | 89 | 92 | 88 | 97 | 93 | 101 | 95 | 94 | 91 | 91 | 94 | 90 | 96 | 81 | 97 | 91 | 95 | 94 | 98 |
| LUMPKIN | 99 | 78 | 83 | 83 | 94 | 91 | 116 | 97 | 94 | 86 | 88 | 97 | 86 | 99 | 73 | 98 | 87 | 91 | 100 | 100 |
| MCDUFFIE | 96 | 71 | 76 | 76 | 95 | 91 | 107 | 95 | 91 | 82 | 80 | 94 | 82 | 94 | 72 | 96 | 82 | 89 | 98 | 96 |
| MCINTOSH | 97 | 66 | 71 | 76 | 92 | 90 | 114 | 96 | 92 | 77 | 79 | 95 | 80 | 95 | 68 | 96 | 79 | 87 | 102 | 97 |
| MACON | 95 | 65 | 70 | 72 | 93 | 88 | 105 | 95 | 90 | 79 | 75 | 92 | 79 | 92 | 69 | 96 | 81 | 87 | 94 | 94 |
| MADISON | 98 | 72 | 77 | 79 | 93 | 91 | 114 | 96 | 93 | 82 | 83 | 97 | 83 | 97 | 70 | 97 | 83 | 89 | 100 | 99 |
| MARION | 97 | 65 | 70 | 75 | 92 | 90 | 112 | 95 | 92 | 76 | 78 | 95 | 79 | 94 | 67 | 96 | 79 | 87 | 102 | 96 |
| MERIWETHER | 97 | 66 | 72 | 75 | 93 | 91 | 112 | 96 | 91 | 77 | 78 | 95 | 80 | 95 | 68 | 95 | 79 | 87 | 100 | 97 |
| MILLER | 97 | 63 | 67 | 73 | 92 | 90 | 112 | 95 | 91 | 75 | 77 | 95 | 78 | 94 | 66 | 95 | 78 | 86 | 102 | 96 |
| MITCHELL | 94 | 68 | 74 | 74 | 93 | 88 | 104 | 95 | 91 | 82 | 77 | 91 | 80 | 91 | 71 | 97 | 83 | 89 | 94 | 94 |
| MONROE | 99 | 85 | 82 | 87 | 95 | 94 | 104 | 99 | 96 | 93 | 92 | 99 | 91 | 99 | 78 | 99 | 94 | 96 | 97 | 100 |
| MONTGOMERY | 96 | 66 | 72 | 74 | 92 | 90 | 111 | 95 | 92 | 77 | 79 | 93 | 79 | 94 | 68 | 96 | 79 | 87 | 101 | 96 |
| MORGAN | 100 | 74 | 80 | 82 | 95 | 92 | 117 | 98 | 94 | 83 | 85 | 98 | 85 | 99 | 71 | 98 | 86 | 91 | 102 | 101 |
| MURRAY | 98 | 74 | 79 | 80 | 93 | 91 | 115 | 97 | 93 | 83 | 85 | 97 | 84 | 98 | 71 | 97 | 84 | 90 | 100 | 99 |
| MUSCOGEE | 96 | 95 | 101 | 94 | 102 | 99 | 93 | 97 | 95 | 98 | 95 | 96 | 96 | 97 | 89 | 98 | 98 | 99 | 93 | 98 |
| NEWTON | 99 | 80 | 86 | 86 | 96 | 93 | 114 | 98 | 95 | 88 | 90 | 98 | 88 | 100 | 76 | 98 | 89 | 93 | 100 | 101 |
| OCONEE | 103 | 99 | 101 | 101 | 101 | 102 | 109 | 101 | 102 | 100 | 104 | 104 | 101 | 105 | 87 | 101 | 103 | 102 | 102 | 105 |
| OGLETHORPE | 98 | 70 | 75 | 78 | 93 | 90 | 114 | 96 | 93 | 81 | 82 | 96 | 82 | 97 | 69 | 96 | 82 | 89 | 100 | 98 |
| PAULDING | 102 | 93 | 83 | 92 | 95 | 95 | 109 | 100 | 100 | 96 | 100 | 103 | 94 | 103 | 80 | 100 | 98 | 99 | 99 | 104 |
| PEACH | 96 | 77 | 82 | 81 | 95 | 89 | 104 | 97 | 92 | 88 | 83 | 94 | 85 | 95 | 75 | 98 | 88 | 92 | 92 | 98 |
| PICKENS | 99 | 73 | 79 | 82 | 94 | 92 | 117 | 97 | 93 | 81 | 84 | 97 | 84 | 98 | 71 | 98 | 84 | 90 | 102 | 100 |
| PIERCE | 96 | 71 | 77 | 77 | 92 | 90 | 110 | 95 | 92 | 81 | 81 | 94 | 81 | 95 | 70 | 97 | 82 | 89 | 98 | 97 |
| PIKE | 100 | 73 | 79 | 82 | 95 | 92 | 116 | 98 | 94 | 82 | 85 | 98 | 85 | 99 | 71 | 98 | 85 | 91 | 102 | 101 |
| POLK | 97 | 70 | 79 | 78 | 96 | 92 | 109 | 96 | 91 | 81 | 81 | 94 | 83 | 95 | 72 | 96 | 81 | 88 | 100 | 96 |
| PULASKI | 97 | 70 | 78 | 79 | 94 | 90 | 111 | 96 | 92 | 81 | 80 | 94 | 82 | 95 | 71 | 97 | 83 | 89 | 98 | 98 |
| PUTNAM | 98 | 75 | 81 | 82 | 94 | 91 | 117 | 97 | 92 | 83 | 85 | 96 | 84 | 98 | 73 | 97 | 84 | 90 | 100 | 99 |
| QUITMAN | 97 | 63 | 66 | 73 | 92 | 90 | 112 | 96 | 91 | 75 | 77 | 96 | 78 | 95 | 66 | 95 | 78 | 86 | 102 | 96 |
| RABUN | 99 | 71 | 78 | 82 | 94 | 92 | 119 | 97 | 93 | 79 | 82 | 97 | 83 | 98 | 71 | 98 | 83 | 90 | 103 | 100 |
| RANDOLPH | 94 | 65 | 73 | 72 | 93 | 87 | 103 | 96 | 89 | 78 | 74 | 91 | 78 | 90 | 69 | 95 | 79 | 87 | 92 | 94 |
| RICHMOND | 95 | 91 | 93 | 88 | 99 | 95 | 96 | 96 | 93 | 95 | 92 | 94 | 92 | 96 | 84 | 98 | 93 | 96 | 92 | 97 |
| ROCKDALE | 103 | 103 | 95 | 101 | 100 | 101 | 106 | 101 | 104 | 104 | 108 | 105 | 102 | 106 | 88 | 101 | 107 | 105 | 99 | 105 |
| SCHLEY | 98 | 68 | 73 | 77 | 93 | 91 | 114 | 96 | 93 | 78 | 80 | 97 | 81 | 97 | 68 | 96 | 81 | 88 | 102 | 98 |
| SCREVEN | 96 | 66 | 70 | 73 | 94 | 90 | 109 | 95 | 90 | 78 | 77 | 94 | 80 | 93 | 69 | 95 | 79 | 87 | 99 | 96 |
| SEMINOLE | 96 | 71 | 79 | 79 | 95 | 92 | 111 | 97 | 90 | 80 | 81 | 94 | 82 | 95 | 73 | 96 | 82 | 89 | 99 | 97 |
| SPALDING | 97 | 85 | 90 | 87 | 99 | 94 | 105 | 97 | 94 | 92 | 90 | 95 | 90 | 97 | 81 | 97 | 91 | 94 | 96 | 99 |
| STEPHENS | 97 | 73 | 80 | 80 | 96 | 93 | 110 | 96 | 91 | 82 | 83 | 95 | 84 | 96 | 73 | 96 | 83 | 89 | 101 | 97 |
| STEWART | 96 | 62 | 66 | 72 | 92 | 88 | 108 | 96 | 90 | 76 | 74 | 94 | 77 | 92 | 66 | 95 | 78 | 86 | 97 | 95 |
| SUMTER | 95 | 79 | 84 | 82 | 95 | 91 | 102 | 95 | 92 | 87 | 84 | 93 | 86 | 94 | 76 | 97 | 87 | 92 | 94 | 96 |
| TALBOT | 97 | 63 | 66 | 73 | 92 | 90 | 112 | 96 | 91 | 75 | 77 | 96 | 78 | 95 | 66 | 95 | 78 | 86 | 102 | 96 |
| TALIAFERRO | 97 | 63 | 66 | 73 | 92 | 90 | 112 | 96 | 91 | 75 | 77 | 96 | 78 | 95 | 66 | 95 | 78 | 86 | 102 | 96 |
| TATTNALL | 96 | 69 | 78 | 77 | 93 | 91 | 111 | 95 | 92 | 79 | 80 | 93 | 81 | 94 | 70 | 96 | 81 | 88 | 100 | 96 |
| TAYLOR | 97 | 63 | 66 | 73 | 92 | 90 | 112 | 96 | 91 | 75 | 77 | 96 | 78 | 95 | 66 | 95 | 78 | 86 | 102 | 96 |
| TELFAIR | 96 | 63 | 68 | 72 | 92 | 89 | 109 | 95 | 91 | 75 | 75 | 93 | 77 | 92 | 67 | 95 | 78 | 86 | 99 | 95 |
| TERRELL | 93 | 69 | 75 | 73 | 96 | 89 | 100 | 95 | 88 | 82 | 77 | 90 | 81 | 90 | 73 | 95 | 81 | 88 | 93 | 93 |
| THOMAS | 96 | 77 | 85 | 82 | 95 | 91 | 105 | 96 | 92 | 86 | 84 | 94 | 86 | 95 | 75 | 97 | 86 | 91 | 96 | 97 |
| TIFT | 96 | 84 | 91 | 85 | 97 | 94 | 104 | 96 | 93 | 91 | 88 | 94 | 89 | 96 | 80 | 97 | 90 | 93 | 95 | 98 |
| TOOMBS | 96 | 77 | 84 | 81 | 95 | 91 | 106 | 95 | 91 | 85 | 84 | 94 | 85 | 95 | 75 | 96 | 85 | 90 | 97 | 97 |
| TOWNS | 102 | 77 | 95 | 93 | 99 | 103 | 121 | 101 | 94 | 84 | 87 | 100 | 89 | 101 | 81 | 98 | 89 | 93 | 109 | 103 |
| TREUTLEN | 97 | 64 | 69 | 74 | 92 | 89 | 110 | 96 | 91 | 77 | 76 | 95 | 79 | 94 | 67 | 95 | 79 | 87 | 98 | 96 |
| TROUP | 98 | 82 | 89 | 88 | 98 | 94 | 107 | 97 | 95 | 90 | 89 | 97 | 90 | 98 | 79 | 98 | 90 | 93 | 97 | 99 |
| TURNER | 95 | 70 | 74 | 77 | 93 | 89 | 107 | 94 | 89 | 80 | 77 | 93 | 81 | 93 | 71 | 97 | 83 | 89 | 97 | 95 |
| TWIGGS | 97 | 69 | 73 | 76 | 92 | 90 | 112 | 96 | 92 | 80 | 81 | 96 | 81 | 95 | 68 | 96 | 80 | 88 | 100 | 97 |
| UNION | 99 | 69 | 75 | 81 | 93 | 92 | 119 | 97 | 92 | 77 | 80 | 97 | 81 | 97 | 70 | 97 | 82 | 89 | 104 | 99 |
| UPSON | 98 | 74 | 86 | 83 | 98 | 94 | 110 | 97 | 92 | 84 | 84 | 96 | 86 | 97 | 75 | 96 | 85 | 90 | 100 | 98 |
| WALKER | 98 | 75 | 85 | 83 | 97 | 94 | 111 | 97 | 93 | 84 | 85 | 96 | 86 | 98 | 75 | 97 | 85 | 90 | 101 | 99 |
| WALTON | 98 | 78 | 84 | 82 | 96 | 92 | 113 | 97 | 93 | 86 | 88 | 95 | 86 | 98 | 75 | 97 | 86 | 91 | 99 | 99 |
| WARE | 97 | 76 | 86 | 83 | 97 | 93 | 108 | 97 | 93 | 85 | 84 | 95 | 86 | 96 | 76 | 97 | 85 | 91 | 98 | 98 |
| WARREN | 96 | 63 | 66 | 72 | 92 | 89 | 109 | 96 | 90 | 76 | 75 | 95 | 78 | 93 | 66 | 95 | 78 | 86 | 98 | 96 |
| WASHINGTON | 96 | 66 | 70 | 74 | 93 | 89 | 107 | 96 | 90 | 79 | 77 | 94 | 80 | 93 | 68 | 96 | 80 | 87 | 98 | 96 |
| WAYNE | 96 | 73 | 81 | 79 | 94 | 91 | 109 | 96 | 92 | 82 | 83 | 94 | 83 | 95 | 72 | 96 | 83 | 89 | 99 | 97 |
| WEBSTER | 97 | 63 | 66 | 73 | 92 | 90 | 112 | 96 | 91 | 75 | 77 | 96 | 78 | 95 | 66 | 95 | 78 | 86 | 102 | 96 |
| WHEELER | 97 | 63 | 66 | 73 | 92 | 90 | 112 | 96 | 91 | 75 | 77 | 96 | 78 | 95 | 66 | 95 | 78 | 86 | 102 | 96 |
| WHITE | 99 | 78 | 89 | 86 | 97 | 96 | 118 | 98 | 95 | 85 | 88 | 97 | 87 | 100 | 76 | 98 | 88 | 92 | 103 | 101 |
| GEORGIA | 99 | 96 | 94 | 96 | 99 | 98 | 103 | 99 | 99 | 98 | 98 | 101 | 97 | 101 | 85 | 99 | 98 | 99 | 97 | 101 |
| UNITED STATES | 100 | 100 | 100 | 100 | 100 | 100 | 100 | 100 | 100 | 100 | 100 | 100 | 100 | 100 | 100 | 100 | 100 | 100 | 100 | 100 |

# POPULATION CHANGE

| COUNTY | FIPS Code | MSA Code | DMA Code | POPULATION 1990 | POPULATION 2000 | POPULATION 2005 | 1990-2000 ANNUAL CHANGE % Rate | 1990-2000 ANNUAL CHANGE State Rank | RACE (%) White 1990 | White 2000 | Black 1990 | Black 2000 | Asian/Pacific 1990 | Asian/Pacific 2000 |
|---|---|---|---|---|---|---|---|---|---|---|---|---|---|---|
| WHITFIELD | 313 | 0000 | 575 | 72,462 | 84,377 | 90,152 | 1.5 | 66 | 93.2 | 89.9 | 4.0 | 4.9 | 0.4 | 0.8 |
| WILCOX | 315 | 0000 | 503 | 7,008 | 7,477 | 7,764 | 0.6 | 111 | 67.9 | 62.9 | 31.7 | 36.6 | 0.0 | 0.1 |
| WILKES | 317 | 0000 | 520 | 10,597 | 10,532 | 10,411 | -0.1 | 150 | 53.3 | 46.9 | 46.3 | 52.6 | 0.1 | 0.1 |
| WILKINSON | 319 | 0000 | 503 | 10,228 | 10,951 | 11,209 | 0.7 | 102 | 57.8 | 52.1 | 42.1 | 47.7 | 0.1 | 0.1 |
| WORTH | 321 | 0000 | 525 | 19,745 | 22,627 | 23,373 | 1.3 | 74 | 68.6 | 63.5 | 30.6 | 35.4 | 0.2 | 0.4 |
| GEORGIA | | | | | | | 2.0 | | 71.0 | 68.5 | 27.0 | 28.1 | 1.2 | 2.0 |
| UNITED STATES | | | | | | | 1.0 | | 80.3 | 77.9 | 12.1 | 12.4 | 2.9 | 3.9 |

| COUNTY | % HISPANIC ORIGIN | | 2000 AGE DISTRIBUTION (%) | | | | | | | | | | MEDIAN AGE | | 2000 Males/ Females (×100) |
|---|---|---|---|---|---|---|---|---|---|---|---|---|---|---|---|
| | 1990 | 2000 | 0-4 | 5-9 | 10-14 | 15-19 | 20-24 | 25-44 | 45-64 | 65-84 | 85+ | 18+ | 1990 | 2000 | |
| WHITFIELD | 3.2 | 6.6 | 7.0 | 6.8 | 7.2 | 7.1 | 6.6 | 31.2 | 23.8 | 9.2 | 1.1 | 74.8 | 32.2 | 35.3 | 97.3 |
| WILCOX | 0.4 | 1.0 | 7.3 | 7.5 | 8.0 | 7.5 | 6.2 | 25.6 | 22.7 | 13.1 | 2.0 | 72.5 | 34.7 | 36.3 | 90.9 |
| WILKES | 0.4 | 0.8 | 6.6 | 6.6 | 6.9 | 8.0 | 6.4 | 26.3 | 23.8 | 13.2 | 2.2 | 74.8 | 35.4 | 37.8 | 92.5 |
| WILKINSON | 0.3 | 0.7 | 8.0 | 7.8 | 7.8 | 8.1 | 6.6 | 29.5 | 21.1 | 9.7 | 1.3 | 71.5 | 31.2 | 33.4 | 91.0 |
| WORTH | 1.1 | 2.0 | 8.1 | 8.1 | 8.2 | 8.0 | 6.6 | 28.6 | 22.0 | 9.3 | 1.1 | 70.7 | 31.5 | 33.2 | 93.7 |
| GEORGIA | 1.7 | 3.3 | 7.4 | 7.3 | 7.3 | 7.3 | 7.1 | 32.3 | 21.8 | 8.6 | 1.1 | 74.0 | 31.6 | 34.1 | 94.9 |
| UNITED STATES | 9.0 | 11.8 | 6.9 | 7.2 | 7.2 | 7.2 | 6.7 | 29.9 | 22.2 | 11.1 | 1.6 | 74.6 | 32.9 | 35.7 | 95.6 |

# HOUSEHOLDS

| COUNTY | HOUSEHOLDS | | | | | FAMILIES | | | MEDIAN HOUSEHOLD INCOME | | | |
|---|---|---|---|---|---|---|---|---|---|---|---|---|
| | 1990 | 2000 | 2005 | % Annual Rate 1990-2000 | 2000 Average HH Size | 1990 | 2000 | % Annual Rate 1990-2000 | 2000 | 2005 | 2000 National Rank | 2000 State Rank |
| WHITFIELD | 26,859 | 32,014 | 34,604 | 2.2 | 2.62 | 20,506 | 23,874 | 1.9 | 39,597 | 45,654 | 703 | 35 |
| WILCOX | 2,511 | 2,739 | 2,876 | 1.1 | 2.66 | 1,833 | 1,928 | 0.6 | 26,390 | 28,996 | 2667 | 145 |
| WILKES | 4,022 | 4,098 | 4,100 | 0.2 | 2.55 | 2,932 | 2,874 | -0.2 | 27,428 | 31,099 | 2521 | 135 |
| WILKINSON | 3,619 | 3,980 | 4,128 | 1.2 | 2.74 | 2,755 | 2,943 | 0.8 | 33,545 | 38,759 | 1456 | 75 |
| WORTH | 6,895 | 8,260 | 8,718 | 2.2 | 2.72 | 5,428 | 6,341 | 1.9 | 31,762 | 35,056 | 1765 | 91 |
| GEORGIA | | | | 2.8 | 2.62 | | | 2.6 | 43,179 | 51,136 | | |
| UNITED STATES | | | | 1.4 | 2.59 | | | 1.1 | 41,914 | 49,127 | | |

| COUNTY | 2000 Per Capita Income | 2000 HH Income Base | 2000 HOUSEHOLD INCOME DISTRIBUTION (%) Less than $15,000 | $15,000 to $24,999 | $25,000 to $49,999 | $50,000 to $99,999 | $100,000 to $149,999 | $150,000 or More | 2000 AVERAGE DISPOSABLE INCOME BY AGE OF HOUSEHOLDER All Ages | <35 | 35-44 | 45-54 | 55-64 | 65+ |
|---|---|---|---|---|---|---|---|---|---|---|---|---|---|---|
| WHITFIELD | 19,927 | 32,014 | 13.3 | 14.4 | 35.6 | 29.3 | 5.4 | 2.0 | 37,193 | 33,433 | 41,589 | 45,359 | 37,019 | 22,551 |
| WILCOX | 12,687 | 2,739 | 33.3 | 14.9 | 31.4 | 17.2 | 2.2 | 1.0 | 26,621 | 25,353 | 31,241 | 33,430 | 26,612 | 17,996 |
| WILKES | 17,993 | 4,098 | 27.3 | 17.8 | 32.6 | 15.7 | 4.1 | 2.5 | 30,721 | 27,008 | 32,469 | 38,647 | 31,327 | 20,890 |
| WILKINSON | 14,605 | 3,980 | 20.2 | 15.3 | 40.0 | 21.4 | 2.5 | 0.6 | 30,040 | 28,403 | 33,374 | 37,815 | 29,440 | 20,097 |
| WORTH | 14,207 | 8,260 | 25.3 | 14.0 | 35.0 | 21.1 | 3.8 | 0.9 | 29,916 | 24,001 | 33,930 | 39,342 | 32,776 | 19,347 |
| GEORGIA | 22,304 | | 13.9 | 11.8 | 31.9 | 30.9 | 8.0 | 3.5 | 41,548 | 35,922 | 45,313 | 49,959 | 41,633 | 25,795 |
| UNITED STATES | 22,162 | | 14.5 | 12.5 | 32.3 | 29.8 | 7.4 | 3.5 | 40,748 | 34,503 | 44,969 | 49,579 | 43,409 | 27,339 |

# SPENDING POTENTIAL INDEXES

| COUNTY | FINANCIAL SERVICES | | | | THE HOME | | | | | | ENTERTAINMENT | | | | | | PERSONAL | | | |
|---|---|---|---|---|---|---|---|---|---|---|---|---|---|---|---|---|---|---|---|---|
| | | | | | Home Improvements | | | Furnishings | | | | | | | | | | | | |
| | Auto Loan | Home Loan | Invest-ments | Retire-ment Plans | Home Repair | Lawn & Garden | Remodel-ing | Appli-ances | Elec-tronics | Furni-ture | Restau-rants | Sport-ing Goods | Theater & Concerts | Toys & Hobbies | Travel | Video Rental | Apparel | Auto After-market | Health Insur-ance | Pets & Supplies |
| WHITFIELD | 99 | 84 | 91 | 89 | 98 | 96 | 110 | 98 | 96 | 90 | 91 | 98 | 91 | 99 | 79 | 98 | 91 | 94 | 100 | 100 |
| WILCOX | 97 | 67 | 73 | 76 | 93 | 89 | 110 | 96 | 91 | 78 | 78 | 95 | 80 | 94 | 69 | 96 | 80 | 88 | 98 | 97 |
| WILKES | 95 | 66 | 73 | 74 | 94 | 90 | 106 | 95 | 90 | 78 | 77 | 93 | 80 | 93 | 70 | 95 | 79 | 87 | 98 | 95 |
| WILKINSON | 96 | 71 | 76 | 76 | 94 | 90 | 108 | 95 | 91 | 83 | 81 | 94 | 82 | 94 | 71 | 96 | 83 | 89 | 98 | 96 |
| WORTH | 97 | 75 | 80 | 79 | 93 | 90 | 113 | 96 | 93 | 84 | 85 | 95 | 84 | 97 | 71 | 97 | 84 | 90 | 98 | 98 |
| GEORGIA | 99 | 96 | 94 | 96 | 99 | 98 | 103 | 99 | 99 | 98 | 98 | 101 | 97 | 101 | 85 | 99 | 98 | 99 | 97 | 101 |
| UNITED STATES | 100 | 100 | 100 | 100 | 100 | 100 | 100 | 100 | 100 | 100 | 100 | 100 | 100 | 100 | 100 | 100 | 100 | 100 | 100 | 100 |

| COUNTY | FIPS Code | MSA Code | DMA Code | POPULATION 1990 | POPULATION 2000 | POPULATION 2005 | 1990-2000 ANNUAL CHANGE % Rate | 1990-2000 ANNUAL CHANGE State Rank | RACE (%) White 1990 | White 2000 | Black 1990 | Black 2000 | Asian/Pacific 1990 | Asian/Pacific 2000 |
|---|---|---|---|---|---|---|---|---|---|---|---|---|---|---|
| HAWAII | 001 | 0000 | 744 | 120,317 | 143,385 | 148,334 | 1.7 | 2 | 39.7 | 39.0 | 0.5 | 0.9 | 57.1 | 57.2 |
| HONOLULU | 003 | 3320 | 744 | 836,231 | 861,359 | 845,492 | 0.3 | 4 | 31.6 | 29.1 | 3.1 | 3.5 | 63.0 | 64.6 |
| KALAWAO | 005 | 0000 | 744 | 130 | 58 | 58 | -7.6 | 5 | 23.1 | 17.2 | 0.0 | 0.0 | 76.9 | 65.5 |
| KAUAI | 007 | 0000 | 744 | 51,177 | 56,643 | 57,380 | 1.0 | 3 | 34.6 | 33.7 | 0.4 | 0.8 | 62.7 | 63.0 |
| MAUI | 009 | 0000 | 744 | 100,374 | 123,243 | 130,061 | 2.0 | 1 | 39.6 | 38.0 | 0.5 | 0.8 | 57.7 | 58.6 |
| HAWAII | | | | | | | 0.7 | | 33.4 | 31.5 | 2.5 | 2.8 | 61.8 | 63.0 |
| UNITED STATES | | | | | | | 1.0 | | 80.3 | 77.9 | 12.1 | 12.4 | 2.9 | 3.9 |

# POPULATION COMPOSITION

| COUNTY | % HISPANIC ORIGIN | | 2000 AGE DISTRIBUTION (%) | | | | | | | | | | MEDIAN AGE | | 2000 Males/ Females (×100) |
|---|---|---|---|---|---|---|---|---|---|---|---|---|---|---|---|
| | 1990 | 2000 | 0-4 | 5-9 | 10-14 | 15-19 | 20-24 | 25-44 | 45-64 | 65-84 | 85+ | 18+ | 1990 | 2000 | |
| HAWAII | 9.3 | 10.1 | 6.9 | 7.8 | 7.4 | 7.9 | 6.3 | 25.5 | 24.1 | 12.6 | 1.5 | 72.9 | 34.3 | 37.7 | 98.8 |
| HONOLULU | 6.8 | 7.6 | 6.6 | 6.9 | 6.1 | 6.8 | 7.6 | 29.0 | 23.1 | 12.5 | 1.5 | 76.8 | 32.2 | 37.3 | 99.1 |
| KALAWAO | 8.5 | 19.0 | 3.4 | 0.0 | 0.0 | 5.2 | 5.2 | 15.5 | 27.6 | 32.8 | 10.3 | 91.4 | 61.3 | 61.7 | 152.2 |
| KAUAI | 10.9 | 11.6 | 7.0 | 7.8 | 7.2 | 7.6 | 6.0 | 26.2 | 23.7 | 12.7 | 1.8 | 73.3 | 33.9 | 37.8 | 99.9 |
| MAUI | 7.8 | 9.1 | 6.9 | 7.6 | 7.0 | 7.3 | 6.0 | 28.3 | 24.5 | 11.1 | 1.5 | 74.0 | 33.4 | 37.7 | 100.9 |
| HAWAII | 7.3 | 8.3 | 6.6 | 7.1 | 6.4 | 7.0 | 7.2 | 28.4 | 23.4 | 12.4 | 1.5 | 75.8 | 32.6 | 37.4 | 99.3 |
| UNITED STATES | 9.0 | 11.8 | 6.9 | 7.2 | 7.2 | 7.2 | 6.7 | 29.9 | 22.2 | 11.1 | 1.6 | 74.6 | 32.9 | 35.7 | 95.6 |

| COUNTY | HOUSEHOLDS 1990 | HOUSEHOLDS 2000 | HOUSEHOLDS 2005 | HOUSEHOLDS % Annual Rate 1990-2000 | HOUSEHOLDS 2000 Average HH Size | FAMILIES 1990 | FAMILIES 2000 | FAMILIES % Annual Rate 1990-2000 | MEDIAN HOUSEHOLD INCOME 2000 | MEDIAN HOUSEHOLD INCOME 2005 | MEDIAN HOUSEHOLD INCOME 2000 National Rank | MEDIAN HOUSEHOLD INCOME 2000 State Rank |
|---|---|---|---|---|---|---|---|---|---|---|---|---|
| HAWAII | 41,461 | 53,259 | 57,276 | 3.1 | 2.64 | 30,235 | 38,441 | 3.0 | 42,346 | 51,368 | 483 | 4 |
| HONOLULU | 265,304 | 292,879 | 296,902 | 1.2 | 2.82 | 197,294 | 216,777 | 1.1 | 52,209 | 61,436 | 167 | 1 |
| KALAWAO | 62 | 9 | 9 | -20.9 | 1.44 | 23 | 3 | -21.9 | 13,750 | 13,750 | 3141 | 5 |
| KAUAI | 16,295 | 18,870 | 19,556 | 1.8 | 2.96 | 12,367 | 14,255 | 1.7 | 47,751 | 55,674 | 246 | 3 |
| MAUI | 33,145 | 42,699 | 46,225 | 3.1 | 2.84 | 23,537 | 29,809 | 2.9 | 48,518 | 57,215 | 230 | 2 |
| HAWAII | | | | 1.7 | 2.81 | | | 1.6 | 50,350 | 59,490 | | |
| UNITED STATES | | | | 1.4 | 2.59 | | | 1.1 | 41,914 | 49,127 | | |

# INCOME

| COUNTY | 2000 Per Capita Income | 2000 HH Income Base | 2000 HOUSEHOLD INCOME DISTRIBUTION (%) Less than $15,000 | $15,000 to $24,999 | $25,000 to $49,999 | $50,000 to $99,999 | $100,000 to $149,999 | $150,000 or More | 2000 AVERAGE DISPOSABLE INCOME BY AGE OF HOUSEHOLDER All Ages | <35 | 35-44 | 45-54 | 55-64 | 65+ |
|---|---|---|---|---|---|---|---|---|---|---|---|---|---|---|
| HAWAII | 22,460 | 53,259 | 13.9 | 12.7 | 32.1 | 29.8 | 7.6 | 3.9 | 37,388 | 28,994 | 38,594 | 44,132 | 41,817 | 30,742 |
| HONOLULU | 24,093 | 292,876 | 8.2 | 10.4 | 28.7 | 37.3 | 10.6 | 4.8 | 43,380 | 31,931 | 43,018 | 52,950 | 50,711 | 37,873 |
| KALAWAO | 9,884 | 9 | 55.6 | 22.2 | 11.1 | 11.1 | 0.0 | 0.0 | 14,167 | 0 | 20,000 | 42,500 | 0 | 9,286 |
| KAUAI | 20,251 | 18,870 | 9.8 | 11.2 | 32.4 | 35.3 | 8.2 | 3.2 | 38,765 | 34,074 | 38,963 | 47,151 | 46,988 | 28,933 |
| MAUI | 22,388 | 42,699 | 9.4 | 9.9 | 32.5 | 36.1 | 8.8 | 3.4 | 39,951 | 34,510 | 40,771 | 46,375 | 44,296 | 30,625 |
| HAWAII | 23,519 | | 9.1 | 10.7 | 29.7 | 36.1 | 9.9 | 4.4 | 42,024 | 31,905 | 41,983 | 50,720 | 48,703 | 35,728 |
| UNITED STATES | 22,162 | | 14.5 | 12.5 | 32.3 | 29.8 | 7.4 | 3.5 | 40,748 | 34,503 | 44,969 | 49,579 | 43,409 | 27,339 |

# SPENDING POTENTIAL INDEXES

| COUNTY | FINANCIAL SERVICES | | | | THE HOME | | | | | | ENTERTAINMENT | | | | | | PERSONAL | | | |
|---|---|---|---|---|---|---|---|---|---|---|---|---|---|---|---|---|---|---|---|---|
| | | | | | Home Improvements | | | Furnishings | | | | | | | | | | | | |
| | Auto Loan | Home Loan | Invest-ments | Retire-ment Plans | Home Repair | Lawn & Garden | Remodel-ing | Appli-ances | Elec-tronics | Furni-ture | Restau-rants | Sport-ing Goods | Theater & Concerts | Toys & Hobbies | Travel | Video Rental | Apparel | Auto After-market | Health Insur-ance | Pets & Supplies |
| HAWAII | 98 | 130 | 102 | 112 | 93 | 103 | 90 | 96 | 116 | 96 | 115 | 92 | 95 | 86 | 100 | 111 | 98 | 105 | 96 | 97 |
| HONOLULU | 97 | 134 | 105 | 114 | 94 | 104 | 89 | 95 | 117 | 96 | 116 | 91 | 96 | 85 | 102 | 112 | 99 | 107 | 95 | 97 |
| KALAWAO | 97 | 138 | 105 | 115 | 90 | 103 | 85 | 94 | 120 | 93 | 119 | 90 | 94 | 82 | 102 | 117 | 97 | 107 | 95 | 97 |
| KAUAI | 97 | 136 | 105 | 114 | 92 | 103 | 87 | 95 | 119 | 94 | 118 | 91 | 95 | 84 | 102 | 114 | 98 | 107 | 96 | 97 |
| MAUI | 98 | 130 | 102 | 111 | 94 | 104 | 91 | 97 | 116 | 97 | 116 | 92 | 95 | 87 | 100 | 110 | 100 | 106 | 96 | 97 |
| HAWAII | 97 | 133 | 104 | 113 | 94 | 104 | 89 | 96 | 117 | 96 | 116 | 92 | 96 | 85 | 102 | 112 | 99 | 107 | 96 | 97 |
| UNITED STATES | 100 | 100 | 100 | 100 | 100 | 100 | 100 | 100 | 100 | 100 | 100 | 100 | 100 | 100 | 100 | 100 | 100 | 100 | 100 | 100 |

# POPULATION CHANGE

| COUNTY | FIPS Code | MSA Code | DMA Code | POPULATION | | | 1990-2000 ANNUAL CHANGE | | RACE (%) | | | | | |
|---|---|---|---|---|---|---|---|---|---|---|---|---|---|---|
| | | | | | | | | | White | | Black | | Asian/Pacific | |
| | | | | 1990 | 2000 | 2005 | % Rate | State Rank | 1990 | 2000 | 1990 | 2000 | 1990 | 2000 |
| ADA | 001 | 1080 | 757 | 205,775 | 291,195 | 330,591 | 3.4 | 5 | 96.7 | 95.8 | 0.5 | 0.7 | 1.4 | 1.7 |
| ADAMS | 003 | 0000 | 757 | 3,254 | 3,782 | 3,755 | 1.5 | 25 | 98.4 | 98.3 | 0.1 | 0.1 | 0.0 | 0.0 |
| BANNOCK | 005 | 6340 | 758 | 66,026 | 75,394 | 78,057 | 1.3 | 27 | 93.5 | 92.0 | 0.7 | 1.0 | 1.1 | 1.3 |
| BEAR LAKE | 007 | 0000 | 770 | 6,084 | 6,588 | 6,722 | 0.8 | 37 | 98.6 | 98.2 | 0.0 | 0.0 | 0.1 | 0.1 |
| BENEWAH | 009 | 0000 | 881 | 7,937 | 9,095 | 9,279 | 1.3 | 27 | 91.7 | 91.7 | 0.1 | 0.2 | 0.4 | 0.4 |
| BINGHAM | 011 | 0000 | 758 | 37,583 | 42,438 | 44,008 | 1.2 | 30 | 86.3 | 83.7 | 0.1 | 0.3 | 0.7 | 0.9 |
| BLAINE | 013 | 0000 | 760 | 13,552 | 17,454 | 18,176 | 2.5 | 9 | 97.7 | 97.2 | 0.1 | 0.1 | 0.8 | 0.9 |
| BOISE | 015 | 0000 | 757 | 3,509 | 5,461 | 6,238 | 4.4 | 2 | 97.8 | 97.2 | 0.1 | 0.0 | 0.4 | 0.5 |
| BONNER | 017 | 0000 | 881 | 26,622 | 36,782 | 40,445 | 3.2 | 6 | 98.5 | 98.0 | 0.1 | 0.3 | 0.3 | 0.3 |
| BONNEVILLE | 019 | 0000 | 758 | 72,207 | 82,289 | 85,951 | 1.3 | 27 | 95.9 | 94.7 | 0.4 | 0.6 | 1.0 | 1.1 |
| BOUNDARY | 021 | 0000 | 881 | 8,332 | 10,068 | 10,575 | 1.9 | 17 | 95.4 | 95.2 | 0.0 | 0.1 | 0.3 | 0.4 |
| BUTTE | 023 | 0000 | 758 | 2,918 | 2,986 | 2,862 | 0.2 | 42 | 96.9 | 96.1 | 0.0 | 0.0 | 0.2 | 0.2 |
| CAMAS | 025 | 0000 | 757 | 727 | 879 | 947 | 1.9 | 17 | 97.9 | 96.8 | 0.3 | 0.5 | 0.4 | 0.6 |
| CANYON | 027 | 1080 | 757 | 90,076 | 128,486 | 148,431 | 3.5 | 4 | 89.3 | 85.7 | 0.2 | 0.3 | 1.1 | 1.3 |
| CARIBOU | 029 | 0000 | 758 | 6,963 | 7,236 | 7,055 | 0.4 | 39 | 98.0 | 96.4 | 0.1 | 0.7 | 0.2 | 0.2 |
| CASSIA | 031 | 0000 | 760 | 19,532 | 21,870 | 22,540 | 1.1 | 31 | 90.0 | 87.1 | 0.0 | 0.0 | 0.5 | 0.5 |
| CLARK | 033 | 0000 | 758 | 762 | 944 | 1,089 | 2.1 | 13 | 90.3 | 88.1 | 0.0 | 0.0 | 0.0 | 0.0 |
| CLEARWATER | 035 | 0000 | 881 | 8,505 | 9,374 | 9,443 | 1.0 | 33 | 97.1 | 96.7 | 0.1 | 0.2 | 0.2 | 0.4 |
| CUSTER | 037 | 0000 | 758 | 4,133 | 4,054 | 3,882 | -0.2 | 43 | 97.8 | 97.2 | 0.0 | 0.0 | 0.5 | 0.6 |
| ELMORE | 039 | 0000 | 757 | 21,205 | 26,175 | 28,717 | 2.1 | 13 | 89.1 | 86.3 | 3.7 | 4.3 | 2.1 | 2.6 |
| FRANKLIN | 041 | 0000 | 770 | 9,232 | 11,615 | 12,921 | 2.3 | 11 | 98.1 | 97.4 | 0.1 | 0.1 | 0.1 | 0.1 |
| FREMONT | 043 | 0000 | 758 | 10,937 | 11,973 | 12,310 | 0.9 | 34 | 93.9 | 92.1 | 0.1 | 0.1 | 0.3 | 0.4 |
| GEM | 045 | 0000 | 757 | 11,844 | 15,485 | 17,165 | 2.6 | 7 | 95.6 | 94.9 | 0.1 | 0.2 | 0.4 | 0.5 |
| GOODING | 047 | 0000 | 760 | 11,633 | 13,887 | 14,603 | 1.7 | 20 | 93.6 | 91.4 | 0.1 | 0.1 | 0.3 | 0.3 |
| IDAHO | 049 | 0000 | 881 | 13,783 | 15,085 | 15,330 | 0.9 | 34 | 97.1 | 97.0 | 0.0 | 0.0 | 0.2 | 0.2 |
| JEFFERSON | 051 | 0000 | 758 | 16,543 | 20,299 | 22,087 | 2.0 | 15 | 94.5 | 92.1 | 0.0 | 0.2 | 0.2 | 0.3 |
| JEROME | 053 | 0000 | 760 | 15,138 | 18,344 | 19,565 | 1.9 | 17 | 94.5 | 92.9 | 0.1 | 0.1 | 0.4 | 0.4 |
| KOOTENAI | 055 | 0000 | 881 | 69,795 | 108,010 | 124,275 | 4.4 | 2 | 98.1 | 97.8 | 0.1 | 0.2 | 0.5 | 0.6 |
| LATAH | 057 | 0000 | 881 | 30,617 | 32,353 | 31,532 | 0.5 | 38 | 96.0 | 95.2 | 0.6 | 0.8 | 2.3 | 2.7 |
| LEMHI | 059 | 0000 | 758 | 6,899 | 7,970 | 7,930 | 1.4 | 26 | 98.2 | 97.5 | 0.0 | 0.3 | 0.3 | 0.4 |
| LEWIS | 061 | 0000 | 881 | 3,516 | 3,916 | 3,796 | 1.1 | 31 | 94.5 | 94.5 | 0.1 | 0.1 | 0.5 | 0.8 |
| LINCOLN | 063 | 0000 | 760 | 3,308 | 3,875 | 4,065 | 1.6 | 23 | 97.7 | 97.4 | 0.1 | 0.1 | 0.4 | 0.5 |
| MADISON | 065 | 0000 | 758 | 23,674 | 24,728 | 24,349 | 0.4 | 39 | 96.1 | 95.0 | 0.2 | 0.4 | 1.3 | 1.4 |
| MINIDOKA | 067 | 0000 | 760 | 19,361 | 20,245 | 20,053 | 0.4 | 39 | 85.4 | 79.8 | 0.2 | 0.7 | 0.5 | 0.6 |
| NEZ PERCE | 069 | 0000 | 881 | 33,754 | 37,013 | 37,524 | 0.9 | 34 | 93.9 | 93.8 | 0.1 | 0.2 | 0.6 | 0.8 |
| ONEIDA | 071 | 0000 | 770 | 3,492 | 4,116 | 4,377 | 1.6 | 23 | 98.3 | 97.6 | 0.1 | 0.2 | 0.2 | 0.3 |
| OWYHEE | 073 | 0000 | 757 | 8,392 | 10,587 | 11,502 | 2.3 | 11 | 82.6 | 78.6 | 0.3 | 0.2 | 0.9 | 0.9 |
| PAYETTE | 075 | 0000 | 757 | 16,434 | 21,192 | 22,973 | 2.5 | 9 | 92.6 | 90.5 | 0.1 | 0.2 | 1.0 | 1.0 |
| POWER | 077 | 0000 | 758 | 7,086 | 8,463 | 8,771 | 1.7 | 20 | 86.9 | 83.4 | 0.1 | 0.1 | 0.6 | 0.8 |
| SHOSHONE | 079 | 0000 | 881 | 13,931 | 13,528 | 12,917 | -0.3 | 44 | 97.8 | 97.6 | 0.1 | 0.2 | 0.3 | 0.3 |
| TETON | 081 | 0000 | 758 | 3,439 | 5,910 | 6,968 | 5.4 | 1 | 97.7 | 97.0 | 0.1 | 0.0 | 0.0 | 0.1 |
| TWIN FALLS | 083 | 0000 | 760 | 53,580 | 63,800 | 67,940 | 1.7 | 20 | 95.6 | 94.1 | 0.1 | 0.1 | 1.0 | 1.2 |
| VALLEY | 085 | 0000 | 757 | 6,109 | 7,919 | 7,681 | 2.6 | 7 | 98.0 | 97.8 | 0.1 | 0.2 | 0.4 | 0.6 |
| WASHINGTON | 087 | 0000 | 757 | 8,550 | 10,446 | 11,174 | 2.0 | 15 | 89.6 | 86.0 | 0.1 | 0.1 | 1.5 | 1.7 |
| IDAHO | | | | | | | 2.3 | | 94.4 | 93.1 | 0.3 | 0.5 | 0.9 | 1.1 |
| UNITED STATES | | | | | | | 1.0 | | 80.3 | 77.9 | 12.1 | 12.4 | 2.9 | 3.9 |

| COUNTY | % HISPANIC ORIGIN | | 2000 AGE DISTRIBUTION (%) | | | | | | | | | | MEDIAN AGE | | 2000 Males/ Females (×100) |
|---|---|---|---|---|---|---|---|---|---|---|---|---|---|---|---|
| | 1990 | 2000 | 0-4 | 5-9 | 10-14 | 15-19 | 20-24 | 25-44 | 45-64 | 65-84 | 85+ | 18+ | 1990 | 2000 | |
| ADA | 2.7 | 4.4 | 6.9 | 6.9 | 7.3 | 8.1 | 8.3 | 30.5 | 22.5 | 8.2 | 1.2 | 74.0 | 31.9 | 34.2 | 97.5 |
| ADAMS | 1.2 | 2.3 | 6.3 | 6.5 | 7.5 | 7.5 | 5.4 | 24.2 | 27.7 | 13.4 | 1.6 | 74.4 | 36.2 | 40.4 | 109.9 |
| BANNOCK | 4.1 | 6.6 | 8.0 | 7.8 | 7.8 | 9.1 | 9.1 | 28.5 | 20.3 | 8.2 | 1.2 | 70.9 | 29.5 | 30.7 | 99.2 |
| BEAR LAKE | 2.2 | 3.6 | 8.7 | 9.5 | 9.6 | 9.7 | 6.3 | 21.2 | 21.3 | 11.6 | 2.0 | 65.3 | 30.9 | 31.5 | 99.4 |
| BENEWAH | 1.6 | 2.7 | 6.5 | 6.7 | 7.5 | 8.5 | 6.5 | 25.2 | 26.4 | 11.0 | 1.7 | 73.4 | 34.6 | 37.8 | 103.3 |
| BINGHAM | 9.6 | 13.8 | 9.0 | 9.1 | 9.6 | 10.2 | 7.8 | 24.3 | 20.2 | 8.6 | 1.2 | 65.2 | 27.6 | 28.5 | 100.4 |
| BLAINE | 2.9 | 4.4 | 6.5 | 6.5 | 7.2 | 6.7 | 6.6 | 33.9 | 25.3 | 6.6 | 0.7 | 75.4 | 33.3 | 36.8 | 107.8 |
| BOISE | 2.4 | 3.9 | 6.0 | 6.2 | 7.3 | 7.7 | 5.5 | 26.1 | 30.0 | 10.4 | 0.8 | 75.4 | 35.6 | 40.3 | 111.8 |
| BONNER | 1.3 | 2.6 | 6.2 | 6.5 | 7.6 | 7.7 | 6.0 | 25.0 | 27.6 | 11.9 | 1.5 | 74.3 | 36.3 | 39.7 | 99.9 |
| BONNEVILLE | 4.2 | 6.3 | 8.6 | 8.2 | 8.8 | 9.2 | 8.3 | 26.9 | 20.6 | 8.3 | 1.1 | 68.4 | 28.7 | 30.2 | 101.5 |
| BOUNDARY | 3.7 | 4.4 | 6.9 | 7.3 | 7.9 | 10.1 | 6.7 | 24.4 | 24.0 | 11.0 | 1.7 | 71.1 | 32.8 | 35.8 | 104.4 |
| BUTTE | 3.5 | 5.2 | 6.9 | 7.5 | 8.7 | 9.5 | 6.7 | 22.5 | 24.8 | 11.7 | 1.7 | 69.5 | 33.3 | 36.1 | 101.3 |
| CAMAS | 0.6 | 1.7 | 6.6 | 7.1 | 6.9 | 9.0 | 4.8 | 24.8 | 29.0 | 10.6 | 1.3 | 72.1 | 36.8 | 40.0 | 118.7 |
| CANYON | 13.1 | 18.7 | 7.8 | 7.4 | 8.1 | 9.0 | 8.3 | 25.7 | 22.0 | 9.9 | 1.7 | 71.2 | 31.6 | 32.8 | 97.8 |
| CARIBOU | 2.8 | 5.3 | 7.8 | 8.6 | 9.8 | 9.7 | 6.8 | 23.2 | 22.1 | 10.5 | 1.4 | 67.0 | 30.3 | 32.2 | 101.6 |
| CASSIA | 13.4 | 18.4 | 8.8 | 8.8 | 9.3 | 9.7 | 7.5 | 23.7 | 20.3 | 10.4 | 1.4 | 66.4 | 29.2 | 30.0 | 102.7 |
| CLARK | 10.4 | 13.0 | 7.1 | 7.5 | 8.3 | 7.6 | 8.1 | 26.0 | 25.4 | 9.3 | 0.7 | 72.2 | 32.9 | 34.6 | 118.0 |
| CLEARWATER | 1.3 | 2.6 | 4.6 | 5.2 | 6.3 | 7.6 | 6.4 | 25.3 | 29.3 | 13.5 | 1.9 | 78.4 | 37.5 | 41.6 | 110.0 |
| CUSTER | 2.2 | 3.8 | 6.6 | 7.3 | 7.8 | 7.9 | 6.6 | 23.9 | 27.8 | 10.8 | 1.3 | 72.6 | 34.7 | 38.5 | 106.0 |
| ELMORE | 7.5 | 11.2 | 9.8 | 7.8 | 7.0 | 7.1 | 11.0 | 32.0 | 17.5 | 7.0 | 0.8 | 71.2 | 27.7 | 28.7 | 105.8 |
| FRANKLIN | 2.6 | 4.2 | 9.2 | 9.5 | 10.2 | 10.5 | 7.4 | 22.2 | 19.5 | 9.8 | 1.7 | 63.7 | 27.5 | 27.9 | 103.2 |
| FREMONT | 7.0 | 9.8 | 8.3 | 8.6 | 9.2 | 10.9 | 8.0 | 23.2 | 20.6 | 10.0 | 1.3 | 66.4 | 28.1 | 29.3 | 105.5 |
| GEM | 5.2 | 7.2 | 6.7 | 6.8 | 7.1 | 8.6 | 6.4 | 23.6 | 25.4 | 13.5 | 2.0 | 74.0 | 36.0 | 38.3 | 101.0 |
| GOODING | 8.8 | 12.5 | 6.9 | 7.1 | 8.1 | 8.5 | 6.4 | 23.3 | 24.3 | 13.1 | 2.3 | 72.2 | 34.7 | 37.5 | 101.1 |
| IDAHO | 0.9 | 1.7 | 5.9 | 6.4 | 6.9 | 8.2 | 6.6 | 23.3 | 26.6 | 14.0 | 2.1 | 75.1 | 36.5 | 40.3 | 102.2 |
| JEFFERSON | 7.0 | 10.8 | 9.7 | 9.5 | 10.2 | 10.3 | 8.0 | 23.8 | 19.5 | 7.9 | 1.0 | 63.4 | 26.4 | 26.9 | 104.6 |
| JEROME | 6.7 | 9.7 | 7.9 | 8.1 | 8.2 | 9.0 | 7.0 | 24.5 | 22.1 | 11.6 | 1.6 | 69.7 | 32.6 | 34.4 | 100.8 |
| KOOTENAI | 1.5 | 2.7 | 6.3 | 6.4 | 7.0 | 8.0 | 7.0 | 27.0 | 25.9 | 10.9 | 1.4 | 75.5 | 35.0 | 37.6 | 97.7 |
| LATAH | 1.5 | 2.6 | 6.0 | 5.6 | 5.3 | 10.3 | 18.0 | 27.7 | 18.0 | 7.5 | 1.6 | 79.4 | 27.4 | 28.2 | 104.3 |
| LEMHI | 2.0 | 3.7 | 6.1 | 6.9 | 7.3 | 7.7 | 5.9 | 20.6 | 28.1 | 15.4 | 2.1 | 74.2 | 38.1 | 41.8 | 97.3 |
| LEWIS | 1.2 | 2.3 | 5.9 | 6.7 | 7.7 | 8.0 | 5.6 | 22.8 | 25.9 | 15.2 | 2.1 | 74.2 | 36.6 | 40.7 | 109.9 |
| LINCOLN | 5.9 | 8.5 | 6.8 | 7.0 | 8.2 | 8.5 | 7.6 | 23.4 | 24.3 | 12.4 | 1.8 | 72.1 | 33.9 | 36.4 | 107.8 |
| MADISON | 3.2 | 4.8 | 6.8 | 6.4 | 8.1 | 25.3 | 20.1 | 15.0 | 11.9 | 5.5 | 0.9 | 72.5 | 19.9 | 20.9 | 89.3 |
| MINIDOKA | 19.3 | 27.3 | 8.1 | 8.3 | 8.9 | 9.6 | 7.1 | 24.5 | 21.4 | 10.8 | 1.3 | 68.3 | 30.4 | 32.0 | 100.2 |
| NEZ PERCE | 1.2 | 2.1 | 5.7 | 5.8 | 6.3 | 7.6 | 7.6 | 26.3 | 24.7 | 13.7 | 2.4 | 77.7 | 35.6 | 38.9 | 96.4 |
| ONEIDA | 1.6 | 2.8 | 9.2 | 9.0 | 9.8 | 9.4 | 6.5 | 21.2 | 20.1 | 12.3 | 2.4 | 65.0 | 31.4 | 31.3 | 101.2 |
| OWYHEE | 16.8 | 22.6 | 8.1 | 7.7 | 8.4 | 10.6 | 7.7 | 24.0 | 22.1 | 9.8 | 1.6 | 69.1 | 30.4 | 31.5 | 109.7 |
| PAYETTE | 7.3 | 10.5 | 7.4 | 7.4 | 8.0 | 8.7 | 6.8 | 24.0 | 24.2 | 11.6 | 2.0 | 71.7 | 34.1 | 35.9 | 98.6 |
| POWER | 13.2 | 18.4 | 8.3 | 8.2 | 8.7 | 9.8 | 7.0 | 26.3 | 22.2 | 8.5 | 1.0 | 68.0 | 29.8 | 31.1 | 100.9 |
| SHOSHONE | 1.8 | 2.6 | 5.0 | 5.4 | 6.5 | 7.7 | 6.5 | 24.4 | 27.5 | 14.8 | 2.2 | 77.8 | 37.3 | 41.5 | 99.9 |
| TETON | 6.9 | 9.5 | 8.8 | 8.5 | 8.9 | 8.9 | 7.5 | 26.3 | 22.0 | 8.0 | 0.9 | 68.1 | 30.2 | 31.3 | 111.4 |
| TWIN FALLS | 5.8 | 8.7 | 7.1 | 7.1 | 7.7 | 8.8 | 7.2 | 25.4 | 22.9 | 11.7 | 2.0 | 72.5 | 33.3 | 35.5 | 97.0 |
| VALLEY | 1.8 | 3.0 | 5.6 | 6.2 | 7.0 | 7.7 | 5.2 | 25.9 | 29.4 | 11.9 | 1.2 | 76.0 | 37.0 | 40.8 | 107.2 |
| WASHINGTON | 10.7 | 15.6 | 6.8 | 6.9 | 7.6 | 8.2 | 6.4 | 21.8 | 24.4 | 15.2 | 2.6 | 73.1 | 37.3 | 39.0 | 95.1 |
| IDAHO | 5.3 | 7.8 | 7.3 | 7.2 | 7.7 | 9.0 | 8.2 | 26.7 | 22.6 | 9.8 | 1.5 | 72.3 | 31.5 | 33.7 | 99.6 |
| UNITED STATES | 9.0 | 11.8 | 6.9 | 7.2 | 7.2 | 7.2 | 6.7 | 29.9 | 22.2 | 11.1 | 1.6 | 74.6 | 32.9 | 35.7 | 95.6 |

# HOUSEHOLDS

| COUNTY | HOUSEHOLDS 1990 | HOUSEHOLDS 2000 | HOUSEHOLDS 2005 | HOUSEHOLDS % Annual Rate 1990-2000 | HOUSEHOLDS 2000 Average HH Size | FAMILIES 1990 | FAMILIES 2000 | FAMILIES % Annual Rate 1990-2000 | MEDIAN HOUSEHOLD INCOME 2000 | MEDIAN HOUSEHOLD INCOME 2005 | MEDIAN HOUSEHOLD INCOME 2000 National Rank | MEDIAN HOUSEHOLD INCOME 2000 State Rank |
|---|---|---|---|---|---|---|---|---|---|---|---|---|
| ADA | 77,471 | 112,537 | 129,393 | 4.6 | 2.54 | 54,280 | 76,930 | 4.3 | 49,263 | 56,904 | 214 | 2 |
| ADAMS | 1,251 | 1,502 | 1,515 | 2.2 | 2.51 | 956 | 1,114 | 1.9 | 30,609 | 37,224 | 2006 | 33 |
| BANNOCK | 23,412 | 26,990 | 28,122 | 1.7 | 2.75 | 16,794 | 18,729 | 1.3 | 38,805 | 44,668 | 772 | 9 |
| BEAR LAKE | 2,005 | 2,197 | 2,252 | 1.1 | 2.97 | 1,539 | 1,637 | 0.8 | 33,644 | 39,440 | 1445 | 26 |
| BENEWAH | 2,991 | 3,631 | 3,807 | 2.4 | 2.49 | 2,223 | 2,613 | 2.0 | 31,611 | 34,692 | 1798 | 30 |
| BINGHAM | 11,513 | 13,296 | 13,935 | 1.8 | 3.16 | 9,397 | 10,616 | 1.5 | 37,492 | 43,941 | 900 | 15 |
| BLAINE | 5,506 | 7,227 | 7,588 | 3.4 | 2.39 | 3,328 | 4,188 | 2.8 | 50,910 | 61,072 | 185 | 1 |
| BOISE | 1,357 | 2,123 | 2,432 | 5.6 | 2.57 | 985 | 1,489 | 5.1 | 41,526 | 50,155 | 548 | 6 |
| BONNER | 10,269 | 14,530 | 16,167 | 4.3 | 2.52 | 7,493 | 10,309 | 3.9 | 34,968 | 43,429 | 1256 | 19 |
| BONNEVILLE | 24,289 | 28,136 | 29,611 | 1.8 | 2.90 | 18,426 | 20,878 | 1.5 | 43,281 | 50,064 | 440 | 4 |
| BOUNDARY | 2,857 | 3,498 | 3,690 | 2.5 | 2.76 | 2,166 | 2,578 | 2.1 | 33,223 | 43,287 | 1502 | 27 |
| BUTTE | 997 | 1,055 | 1,029 | 0.7 | 2.78 | 762 | 782 | 0.3 | 37,354 | 45,884 | 922 | 17 |
| CAMAS | 275 | 330 | 354 | 2.2 | 2.66 | 209 | 244 | 1.9 | 34,000 | 39,265 | 1393 | 24 |
| CANYON | 31,288 | 45,489 | 53,023 | 4.6 | 2.76 | 23,616 | 33,614 | 4.4 | 37,628 | 45,811 | 886 | 12 |
| CARIBOU | 2,262 | 2,513 | 2,529 | 1.3 | 2.86 | 1,791 | 1,936 | 0.9 | 45,750 | 60,298 | 322 | 3 |
| CASSIA | 6,373 | 7,145 | 7,402 | 1.4 | 3.01 | 4,931 | 5,380 | 1.1 | 31,186 | 35,982 | 1891 | 31 |
| CLARK | 277 | 351 | 410 | 2.9 | 2.62 | 195 | 238 | 2.4 | 27,434 | 30,606 | 2518 | 43 |
| CLEARWATER | 3,213 | 3,654 | 3,746 | 1.6 | 2.41 | 2,392 | 2,627 | 1.1 | 34,122 | 41,796 | 1368 | 22 |
| CUSTER | 1,561 | 1,558 | 1,503 | 0.0 | 2.58 | 1,136 | 1,095 | -0.4 | 39,529 | 48,036 | 708 | 7 |
| ELMORE | 7,136 | 9,196 | 10,309 | 3.1 | 2.71 | 5,596 | 6,932 | 2.6 | 30,577 | 35,262 | 2013 | 35 |
| FRANKLIN | 2,824 | 3,634 | 4,088 | 3.1 | 3.19 | 2,269 | 2,840 | 2.8 | 37,373 | 45,571 | 919 | 16 |
| FREMONT | 3,453 | 3,887 | 4,074 | 1.4 | 3.01 | 2,707 | 2,971 | 1.1 | 32,261 | 41,283 | 1672 | 28 |
| GEM | 4,424 | 5,988 | 6,742 | 3.7 | 2.56 | 3,344 | 4,413 | 3.4 | 34,022 | 41,094 | 1386 | 23 |
| GOODING | 4,320 | 5,366 | 5,750 | 2.7 | 2.53 | 3,128 | 3,764 | 2.3 | 29,851 | 32,735 | 2173 | 39 |
| IDAHO | 5,187 | 5,952 | 6,191 | 1.7 | 2.45 | 3,803 | 4,210 | 1.2 | 30,550 | 36,925 | 2020 | 36 |
| JEFFERSON | 4,871 | 5,836 | 6,280 | 2.2 | 3.47 | 4,034 | 4,737 | 2.0 | 37,500 | 45,815 | 899 | 14 |
| JEROME | 5,325 | 6,731 | 7,320 | 2.9 | 2.69 | 4,083 | 5,019 | 2.5 | 30,203 | 32,835 | 2104 | 38 |
| KOOTENAI | 26,942 | 43,017 | 50,208 | 5.8 | 2.49 | 19,449 | 30,292 | 5.5 | 42,212 | 50,217 | 492 | 5 |
| LATAH | 11,229 | 12,278 | 12,047 | 1.1 | 2.40 | 7,086 | 7,426 | 0.6 | 37,276 | 45,216 | 938 | 18 |
| LEMHI | 2,769 | 3,380 | 3,452 | 2.4 | 2.34 | 1,945 | 2,285 | 2.0 | 30,308 | 35,344 | 2079 | 37 |
| LEWIS | 1,393 | 1,641 | 1,632 | 2.0 | 2.37 | 995 | 1,131 | 1.6 | 28,110 | 30,690 | 2426 | 41 |
| LINCOLN | 1,191 | 1,412 | 1,490 | 2.1 | 2.72 | 865 | 990 | 1.6 | 30,597 | 40,417 | 2010 | 34 |
| MADISON | 5,801 | 5,763 | 5,534 | -0.1 | 4.04 | 4,147 | 3,966 | -0.5 | 37,848 | 49,583 | 863 | 11 |
| MINIDOKA | 6,472 | 6,869 | 6,850 | 0.7 | 2.92 | 5,080 | 5,279 | 0.5 | 33,652 | 38,469 | 1443 | 25 |
| NEZ PERCE | 13,618 | 15,474 | 15,975 | 1.6 | 2.35 | 9,361 | 10,261 | 1.1 | 38,001 | 43,445 | 849 | 10 |
| ONEIDA | 1,159 | 1,400 | 1,504 | 2.3 | 2.91 | 883 | 1,049 | 2.1 | 34,432 | 42,736 | 1325 | 21 |
| OWYHEE | 2,820 | 3,722 | 4,125 | 3.4 | 2.74 | 2,081 | 2,667 | 3.1 | 26,263 | 31,643 | 2683 | 44 |
| PAYETTE | 6,040 | 7,962 | 8,716 | 3.4 | 2.64 | 4,516 | 5,756 | 3.0 | 32,124 | 40,645 | 1697 | 29 |
| POWER | 2,370 | 2,899 | 3,039 | 2.5 | 2.91 | 1,848 | 2,206 | 2.2 | 30,903 | 38,545 | 1947 | 32 |
| SHOSHONE | 5,691 | 5,962 | 5,898 | 0.6 | 2.24 | 3,959 | 3,980 | 0.1 | 27,968 | 31,731 | 2444 | 42 |
| TETON | 1,123 | 1,991 | 2,380 | 7.2 | 2.95 | 834 | 1,440 | 6.8 | 37,522 | 47,373 | 897 | 13 |
| TWIN FALLS | 19,737 | 24,092 | 26,022 | 2.4 | 2.59 | 14,428 | 17,072 | 2.1 | 34,824 | 40,489 | 1278 | 20 |
| VALLEY | 2,404 | 3,280 | 3,275 | 3.8 | 2.36 | 1,767 | 2,325 | 3.4 | 38,870 | 42,183 | 765 | 8 |
| WASHINGTON | 3,257 | 4,149 | 4,519 | 3.0 | 2.49 | 2,367 | 2,917 | 2.6 | 28,369 | 36,953 | 2385 | 40 |
| IDAHO | | | | 3.3 | 2.66 | | | 2.9 | 39,372 | 46,555 | | |
| UNITED STATES | | | | 1.4 | 2.59 | | | 1.1 | 41,914 | 49,127 | | |

| COUNTY | 2000 Per Capita Income | 2000 HH Income Base | 2000 HOUSEHOLD INCOME DISTRIBUTION (%) | | | | | | 2000 AVERAGE DISPOSABLE INCOME BY AGE OF HOUSEHOLDER | | | | | |
|---|---|---|---|---|---|---|---|---|---|---|---|---|---|---|
| | | | Less than $15,000 | $15,000 to $24,999 | $25,000 to $49,999 | $50,000 to $99,999 | $100,000 to $149,999 | $150,000 or More | All Ages | <35 | 35-44 | 45-54 | 55-64 | 65+ |
| ADA | 25,526 | 112,536 | 7.5 | 10.9 | 32.5 | 36.0 | 9.6 | 3.6 | 44,901 | 36,319 | 49,397 | 54,264 | 45,321 | 32,122 |
| ADAMS | 19,328 | 1,502 | 18.0 | 19.3 | 43.5 | 16.2 | 1.5 | 1.6 | 29,457 | 25,375 | 31,231 | 36,765 | 32,362 | 18,693 |
| BANNOCK | 16,777 | 26,981 | 16.2 | 12.4 | 37.1 | 28.3 | 4.9 | 1.2 | 35,014 | 28,160 | 40,982 | 45,139 | 36,159 | 23,763 |
| BEAR LAKE | 13,880 | 2,197 | 18.9 | 17.8 | 39.1 | 20.9 | 2.6 | 0.7 | 30,074 | 26,079 | 35,881 | 37,518 | 34,421 | 18,779 |
| BENEWAH | 15,294 | 3,631 | 19.1 | 18.0 | 39.6 | 20.7 | 2.0 | 0.6 | 29,179 | 28,526 | 33,665 | 32,877 | 30,694 | 19,091 |
| BINGHAM | 14,588 | 13,296 | 12.9 | 15.1 | 39.9 | 27.7 | 3.4 | 1.1 | 34,181 | 28,292 | 37,014 | 43,081 | 37,651 | 24,069 |
| BLAINE | 36,978 | 7,227 | 7.6 | 11.1 | 30.1 | 32.6 | 11.6 | 7.0 | 50,770 | 38,603 | 51,607 | 58,048 | 48,230 | 29,786 |
| BOISE | 23,453 | 2,123 | 11.1 | 9.3 | 41.6 | 26.9 | 8.3 | 2.9 | 39,465 | 35,604 | 44,528 | 40,072 | 40,882 | 33,775 |
| BONNER | 17,736 | 14,530 | 15.1 | 17.6 | 37.2 | 24.8 | 4.1 | 1.3 | 33,199 | 30,506 | 37,126 | 39,941 | 33,216 | 22,189 |
| BONNEVILLE | 19,162 | 28,136 | 10.5 | 13.1 | 34.3 | 33.2 | 6.8 | 2.1 | 39,616 | 32,290 | 45,280 | 49,119 | 44,014 | 26,078 |
| BOUNDARY | 13,862 | 3,498 | 15.8 | 14.4 | 42.9 | 24.6 | 2.2 | 0.1 | 30,601 | 28,315 | 35,931 | 36,079 | 31,173 | 21,308 |
| BUTTE | 16,800 | 1,055 | 12.9 | 10.7 | 42.8 | 26.7 | 6.3 | 0.6 | 34,713 | 33,869 | 37,334 | 42,476 | 33,604 | 24,774 |
| CAMAS | 16,062 | 330 | 9.1 | 23.9 | 37.3 | 23.3 | 6.1 | 0.3 | 33,364 | 31,131 | 31,544 | 38,357 | 34,474 | 28,024 |
| CANYON | 16,616 | 45,478 | 12.4 | 15.7 | 38.2 | 27.7 | 4.9 | 1.1 | 34,981 | 30,641 | 38,812 | 43,877 | 33,808 | 25,500 |
| CARIBOU | 19,605 | 2,513 | 10.4 | 5.9 | 38.9 | 36.1 | 6.7 | 2.0 | 41,381 | 38,380 | 48,505 | 50,399 | 42,135 | 27,251 |
| CASSIA | 13,281 | 7,145 | 18.8 | 19.1 | 38.0 | 20.0 | 2.8 | 1.3 | 30,448 | 25,461 | 36,015 | 38,863 | 31,479 | 20,462 |
| CLARK | 11,953 | 351 | 19.7 | 25.1 | 42.5 | 11.7 | 0.6 | 0.6 | 25,135 | 19,826 | 28,992 | 30,790 | 24,511 | 19,861 |
| CLEARWATER | 16,653 | 3,654 | 14.6 | 19.1 | 39.5 | 23.1 | 2.9 | 0.8 | 31,370 | 27,147 | 35,899 | 38,969 | 32,467 | 20,899 |
| CUSTER | 19,284 | 1,558 | 16.3 | 12.6 | 35.9 | 27.0 | 5.9 | 2.3 | 36,671 | 35,400 | 42,755 | 42,590 | 37,053 | 22,874 |
| ELMORE | 12,578 | 9,196 | 16.3 | 22.6 | 42.8 | 17.4 | 1.0 | 0.0 | 27,524 | 24,560 | 30,773 | 33,986 | 27,311 | 21,019 |
| FRANKLIN | 13,373 | 3,634 | 11.3 | 13.9 | 45.0 | 26.4 | 3.2 | 0.1 | 33,080 | 29,832 | 38,210 | 39,704 | 35,121 | 24,472 |
| FREMONT | 12,108 | 3,887 | 18.3 | 17.0 | 41.7 | 20.6 | 2.3 | 0.1 | 29,253 | 27,036 | 32,462 | 34,359 | 30,457 | 22,264 |
| GEM | 17,068 | 5,988 | 15.7 | 17.1 | 39.3 | 24.2 | 3.1 | 0.7 | 31,635 | 28,725 | 35,566 | 39,144 | 33,229 | 23,027 |
| GOODING | 15,143 | 5,366 | 19.3 | 21.5 | 36.6 | 19.0 | 2.7 | 1.0 | 29,290 | 27,869 | 34,357 | 33,998 | 32,414 | 20,282 |
| IDAHO | 15,207 | 5,952 | 19.3 | 20.3 | 38.1 | 19.3 | 2.4 | 0.7 | 29,135 | 25,419 | 33,807 | 36,796 | 29,690 | 20,448 |
| JEFFERSON | 13,832 | 5,836 | 13.7 | 15.4 | 38.1 | 26.9 | 4.4 | 1.5 | 34,926 | 28,860 | 39,618 | 44,045 | 39,883 | 21,117 |
| JEROME | 14,854 | 6,731 | 18.6 | 21.3 | 36.6 | 19.1 | 3.4 | 0.9 | 29,708 | 27,509 | 33,812 | 35,058 | 33,740 | 19,990 |
| KOOTENAI | 21,743 | 43,017 | 11.1 | 12.7 | 36.1 | 31.2 | 7.0 | 1.9 | 38,845 | 32,840 | 43,349 | 47,747 | 38,100 | 28,240 |
| LATAH | 18,658 | 12,278 | 17.8 | 14.6 | 32.8 | 27.4 | 5.6 | 1.9 | 35,328 | 24,536 | 41,348 | 49,055 | 43,304 | 30,286 |
| LEMHI | 20,484 | 3,380 | 17.3 | 18.5 | 39.3 | 19.9 | 3.5 | 1.6 | 31,074 | 28,777 | 36,762 | 38,315 | 28,947 | 21,741 |
| LEWIS | 13,747 | 1,641 | 22.9 | 20.2 | 39.7 | 14.8 | 2.4 | 0.1 | 26,111 | 24,945 | 29,029 | 28,391 | 30,121 | 20,881 |
| LINCOLN | 13,337 | 1,412 | 17.8 | 21.3 | 40.3 | 18.1 | 2.4 | 0.2 | 28,513 | 24,400 | 32,189 | 34,593 | 30,781 | 19,659 |
| MADISON | 11,712 | 5,763 | 11.3 | 16.9 | 35.6 | 28.6 | 5.7 | 1.9 | 36,683 | 25,879 | 46,554 | 51,137 | 48,598 | 31,035 |
| MINIDOKA | 14,535 | 6,869 | 12.4 | 20.1 | 41.5 | 22.1 | 3.0 | 1.1 | 31,862 | 27,564 | 31,792 | 39,246 | 36,678 | 23,924 |
| NEZ PERCE | 21,033 | 15,474 | 16.1 | 13.1 | 36.7 | 25.9 | 5.9 | 2.2 | 36,204 | 28,874 | 42,903 | 46,136 | 39,099 | 25,675 |
| ONEIDA | 13,419 | 1,400 | 13.9 | 18.5 | 41.7 | 23.3 | 2.4 | 0.1 | 31,002 | 30,465 | 35,045 | 36,548 | 35,649 | 21,953 |
| OWYHEE | 15,540 | 3,722 | 24.3 | 23.2 | 34.3 | 14.4 | 2.0 | 1.9 | 28,266 | 22,875 | 31,744 | 33,977 | 31,297 | 19,244 |
| PAYETTE | 16,000 | 7,962 | 15.3 | 19.4 | 38.8 | 20.6 | 4.5 | 1.5 | 32,161 | 26,463 | 39,047 | 40,236 | 34,389 | 21,277 |
| POWER | 13,217 | 2,899 | 17.0 | 18.5 | 42.0 | 20.2 | 1.4 | 0.9 | 29,806 | 27,266 | 34,121 | 33,794 | 30,310 | 19,456 |
| SHOSHONE | 14,955 | 5,962 | 23.5 | 20.7 | 37.1 | 16.6 | 1.9 | 0.4 | 26,691 | 24,439 | 31,939 | 34,493 | 26,261 | 17,888 |
| TETON | 15,669 | 1,991 | 10.3 | 17.4 | 39.2 | 26.6 | 5.2 | 1.3 | 35,486 | 30,081 | 37,215 | 45,419 | 36,153 | 24,074 |
| TWIN FALLS | 17,006 | 24,091 | 16.2 | 16.7 | 38.0 | 23.9 | 3.8 | 1.5 | 33,041 | 28,015 | 39,204 | 40,862 | 34,167 | 22,639 |
| VALLEY | 24,733 | 3,276 | 10.6 | 16.2 | 39.8 | 23.2 | 7.5 | 2.8 | 37,630 | 27,611 | 37,808 | 48,612 | 40,000 | 28,078 |
| WASHINGTON | 14,812 | 4,149 | 21.3 | 24.5 | 32.4 | 19.0 | 1.9 | 1.0 | 28,341 | 24,523 | 37,665 | 33,462 | 30,857 | 19,849 |
| IDAHO | 19,275 | | 12.8 | 14.6 | 36.3 | 28.4 | 5.9 | 2.0 | 37,085 | 30,971 | 42,209 | 45,831 | 37,897 | 25,545 |
| UNITED STATES | 22,162 | | 14.5 | 12.5 | 32.3 | 29.8 | 7.4 | 3.5 | 40,748 | 34,503 | 44,969 | 49,579 | 43,409 | 27,339 |

# SPENDING POTENTIAL INDEXES

| COUNTY | FINANCIAL SERVICES | | | | THE HOME | | | | | | ENTERTAINMENT | | | | | | PERSONAL | | | |
|---|---|---|---|---|---|---|---|---|---|---|---|---|---|---|---|---|---|---|---|---|
| | | | | | Home Improvements | | | Furnishings | | | | | | | | | | | | |
| | Auto Loan | Home Loan | Investments | Retirement Plans | Home Repair | Lawn & Garden | Remodeling | Appliances | Electronics | Furniture | Restaurants | Sporting Goods | Theater & Concerts | Toys & Hobbies | Travel | Video Rental | Apparel | Auto Aftermarket | Health Insurance | Pets & Supplies |
| ADA | 101 | 101 | 94 | 99 | 101 | 101 | 104 | 102 | 103 | 104 | 103 | 95 | 94 | 96 | 89 | 95 | 101 | 100 | 97 | 96 |
| ADAMS | 101 | 69 | 74 | 83 | 94 | 92 | 117 | 100 | 95 | 79 | 81 | 93 | 78 | 93 | 71 | 93 | 83 | 89 | 103 | 94 |
| BANNOCK | 98 | 93 | 89 | 92 | 98 | 96 | 103 | 99 | 99 | 96 | 95 | 90 | 88 | 92 | 84 | 93 | 94 | 95 | 96 | 93 |
| BEAR LAKE | 99 | 66 | 72 | 80 | 93 | 92 | 116 | 98 | 94 | 77 | 78 | 90 | 76 | 90 | 71 | 93 | 80 | 88 | 103 | 92 |
| BENEWAH | 99 | 71 | 75 | 82 | 95 | 92 | 116 | 99 | 95 | 82 | 82 | 91 | 79 | 92 | 73 | 93 | 83 | 89 | 101 | 93 |
| BINGHAM | 99 | 78 | 82 | 85 | 96 | 93 | 114 | 99 | 96 | 87 | 87 | 90 | 82 | 93 | 77 | 93 | 87 | 91 | 99 | 94 |
| BLAINE | 106 | 119 | 103 | 120 | 105 | 112 | 110 | 108 | 112 | 115 | 116 | 106 | 107 | 102 | 101 | 97 | 117 | 110 | 101 | 101 |
| BOISE | 101 | 70 | 73 | 86 | 94 | 94 | 128 | 102 | 95 | 78 | 80 | 94 | 78 | 94 | 73 | 94 | 83 | 89 | 105 | 96 |
| BONNER | 99 | 76 | 81 | 85 | 96 | 94 | 116 | 100 | 97 | 85 | 85 | 91 | 82 | 93 | 76 | 93 | 86 | 91 | 101 | 94 |
| BONNEVILLE | 100 | 101 | 95 | 99 | 101 | 101 | 103 | 102 | 103 | 103 | 103 | 94 | 95 | 96 | 90 | 95 | 102 | 100 | 97 | 96 |
| BOUNDARY | 97 | 70 | 75 | 79 | 94 | 92 | 114 | 98 | 95 | 81 | 81 | 88 | 77 | 90 | 72 | 93 | 82 | 88 | 100 | 91 |
| BUTTE | 98 | 71 | 80 | 82 | 94 | 93 | 118 | 99 | 95 | 81 | 82 | 89 | 78 | 91 | 74 | 92 | 83 | 89 | 101 | 92 |
| CAMAS | 102 | 78 | 81 | 87 | 97 | 94 | 122 | 102 | 98 | 87 | 88 | 93 | 83 | 96 | 76 | 95 | 89 | 92 | 102 | 97 |
| CANYON | 98 | 83 | 85 | 88 | 97 | 95 | 109 | 99 | 97 | 90 | 89 | 90 | 85 | 92 | 80 | 93 | 89 | 92 | 99 | 93 |
| CARIBOU | 101 | 79 | 79 | 87 | 95 | 94 | 112 | 101 | 97 | 86 | 88 | 94 | 84 | 95 | 76 | 94 | 89 | 93 | 102 | 95 |
| CASSIA | 98 | 76 | 78 | 84 | 95 | 93 | 109 | 99 | 95 | 85 | 85 | 90 | 81 | 91 | 76 | 93 | 85 | 90 | 100 | 93 |
| CLARK | 98 | 80 | 80 | 83 | 93 | 91 | 118 | 99 | 96 | 90 | 88 | 90 | 81 | 92 | 75 | 93 | 86 | 91 | 97 | 93 |
| CLEARWATER | 98 | 71 | 79 | 80 | 95 | 94 | 114 | 99 | 95 | 82 | 82 | 89 | 79 | 90 | 74 | 92 | 82 | 88 | 101 | 92 |
| CUSTER | 99 | 74 | 77 | 83 | 94 | 92 | 118 | 99 | 95 | 83 | 84 | 91 | 80 | 93 | 74 | 93 | 84 | 90 | 101 | 94 |
| ELMORE | 95 | 89 | 82 | 83 | 94 | 92 | 98 | 97 | 97 | 91 | 92 | 87 | 84 | 89 | 80 | 93 | 88 | 93 | 94 | 92 |
| FRANKLIN | 100 | 72 | 78 | 84 | 96 | 94 | 114 | 100 | 93 | 81 | 83 | 93 | 80 | 93 | 75 | 93 | 84 | 89 | 103 | 94 |
| FREMONT | 99 | 76 | 80 | 84 | 95 | 93 | 116 | 99 | 95 | 85 | 85 | 90 | 81 | 92 | 75 | 93 | 86 | 90 | 100 | 93 |
| GEM | 97 | 72 | 77 | 81 | 95 | 92 | 113 | 98 | 94 | 83 | 82 | 88 | 79 | 90 | 75 | 92 | 83 | 88 | 99 | 91 |
| GOODING | 98 | 66 | 71 | 79 | 93 | 92 | 113 | 98 | 93 | 76 | 78 | 89 | 75 | 90 | 71 | 93 | 80 | 87 | 102 | 91 |
| IDAHO | 98 | 68 | 73 | 80 | 93 | 92 | 115 | 99 | 95 | 79 | 80 | 90 | 77 | 90 | 71 | 92 | 81 | 88 | 101 | 92 |
| JEFFERSON | 100 | 82 | 80 | 86 | 95 | 93 | 113 | 100 | 99 | 91 | 91 | 91 | 84 | 94 | 77 | 94 | 90 | 93 | 98 | 95 |
| JEROME | 98 | 73 | 78 | 82 | 95 | 93 | 113 | 98 | 95 | 83 | 83 | 88 | 79 | 91 | 74 | 92 | 84 | 89 | 100 | 92 |
| KOOTENAI | 100 | 90 | 89 | 92 | 99 | 97 | 109 | 101 | 100 | 96 | 95 | 92 | 89 | 95 | 84 | 94 | 95 | 96 | 98 | 95 |
| LATAH | 96 | 90 | 87 | 89 | 96 | 92 | 104 | 94 | 94 | 87 | 89 | 86 | 82 | 89 | 81 | 90 | 88 | 92 | 95 | 92 |
| LEMHI | 97 | 66 | 76 | 79 | 93 | 93 | 112 | 98 | 93 | 76 | 78 | 88 | 75 | 89 | 72 | 92 | 79 | 87 | 103 | 91 |
| LEWIS | 98 | 63 | 69 | 79 | 91 | 92 | 113 | 97 | 92 | 73 | 76 | 90 | 73 | 89 | 69 | 92 | 78 | 87 | 104 | 91 |
| LINCOLN | 96 | 66 | 74 | 78 | 93 | 92 | 113 | 97 | 94 | 78 | 78 | 86 | 75 | 88 | 72 | 92 | 80 | 87 | 101 | 90 |
| MADISON | 95 | 89 | 81 | 87 | 93 | 88 | 103 | 92 | 93 | 84 | 87 | 84 | 79 | 88 | 77 | 89 | 87 | 91 | 93 | 90 |
| MINIDOKA | 99 | 73 | 77 | 83 | 94 | 92 | 114 | 99 | 95 | 82 | 83 | 91 | 79 | 92 | 74 | 93 | 84 | 89 | 101 | 93 |
| NEZ PERCE | 97 | 86 | 91 | 89 | 99 | 97 | 106 | 99 | 97 | 92 | 90 | 89 | 87 | 91 | 83 | 93 | 90 | 93 | 99 | 92 |
| ONEIDA | 98 | 71 | 78 | 82 | 94 | 93 | 116 | 99 | 95 | 81 | 82 | 89 | 78 | 91 | 73 | 93 | 83 | 89 | 101 | 92 |
| OWYHEE | 97 | 73 | 76 | 80 | 93 | 92 | 112 | 98 | 95 | 82 | 82 | 89 | 78 | 90 | 73 | 92 | 82 | 89 | 100 | 92 |
| PAYETTE | 98 | 71 | 77 | 81 | 94 | 92 | 116 | 99 | 95 | 82 | 82 | 89 | 78 | 91 | 73 | 93 | 83 | 89 | 100 | 92 |
| POWER | 99 | 78 | 80 | 83 | 93 | 91 | 116 | 99 | 96 | 88 | 87 | 91 | 81 | 93 | 74 | 93 | 86 | 90 | 98 | 94 |
| SHOSHONE | 95 | 66 | 72 | 76 | 93 | 92 | 110 | 97 | 94 | 79 | 78 | 84 | 75 | 86 | 72 | 92 | 79 | 86 | 100 | 89 |
| TETON | 99 | 68 | 76 | 82 | 93 | 92 | 117 | 99 | 93 | 77 | 80 | 92 | 77 | 92 | 72 | 92 | 82 | 88 | 103 | 93 |
| TWIN FALLS | 98 | 84 | 87 | 89 | 98 | 96 | 108 | 99 | 98 | 91 | 89 | 90 | 86 | 92 | 81 | 93 | 89 | 93 | 99 | 93 |
| VALLEY | 101 | 81 | 77 | 89 | 95 | 94 | 120 | 102 | 98 | 88 | 89 | 94 | 84 | 96 | 77 | 95 | 90 | 94 | 102 | 97 |
| WASHINGTON | 97 | 71 | 80 | 83 | 95 | 94 | 110 | 98 | 93 | 80 | 81 | 89 | 79 | 89 | 75 | 92 | 82 | 88 | 102 | 91 |
| IDAHO | 99 | 89 | 88 | 92 | 98 | 97 | 108 | 100 | 99 | 94 | 93 | 92 | 88 | 93 | 83 | 94 | 93 | 95 | 98 | 94 |
| UNITED STATES | 100 | 100 | 100 | 100 | 100 | 100 | 100 | 100 | 100 | 100 | 100 | 100 | 100 | 100 | 100 | 100 | 100 | 100 | 100 | 100 |

| COUNTY | FIPS Code | MSA Code | DMA Code | POPULATION 1990 | POPULATION 2000 | POPULATION 2005 | 1990-2000 ANNUAL CHANGE % Rate | 1990-2000 ANNUAL CHANGE State Rank | RACE (%) White 1990 | White 2000 | Black 1990 | Black 2000 | Asian/Pacific 1990 | Asian/Pacific 2000 |
|---|---|---|---|---|---|---|---|---|---|---|---|---|---|---|
| ADAMS | 001 | 0000 | 717 | 66,090 | 66,713 | 65,532 | 0.1 | 51 | 96.7 | 96.1 | 2.6 | 3.0 | 0.4 | 0.5 |
| ALEXANDER | 003 | 0000 | 632 | 10,626 | 9,786 | 9,148 | -0.8 | 100 | 66.4 | 62.7 | 32.9 | 36.3 | 0.5 | 0.7 |
| BOND | 005 | 0000 | 609 | 14,991 | 17,095 | 16,798 | 1.3 | 13 | 96.6 | 91.0 | 2.9 | 8.1 | 0.1 | 0.1 |
| BOONE | 007 | 6880 | 610 | 30,806 | 40,371 | 44,505 | 2.7 | 4 | 95.3 | 93.6 | 0.4 | 0.5 | 0.5 | 0.7 |
| BROWN | 009 | 0000 | 717 | 5,836 | 6,944 | 7,080 | 1.7 | 9 | 90.2 | 83.3 | 9.4 | 16.2 | 0.1 | 0.1 |
| BUREAU | 011 | 0000 | 682 | 35,688 | 35,224 | 34,577 | -0.1 | 67 | 98.5 | 97.9 | 0.1 | 0.3 | 0.5 | 0.7 |
| CALHOUN | 013 | 0000 | 609 | 5,322 | 4,817 | 4,597 | -1.0 | 102 | 99.5 | 99.5 | 0.0 | 0.0 | 0.3 | 0.3 |
| CARROLL | 015 | 0000 | 682 | 16,805 | 16,596 | 16,130 | -0.1 | 67 | 98.3 | 97.9 | 0.7 | 0.7 | 0.4 | 0.5 |
| CASS | 017 | 0000 | 717 | 13,437 | 13,249 | 13,212 | -0.1 | 67 | 99.6 | 99.4 | 0.1 | 0.2 | 0.2 | 0.2 |
| CHAMPAIGN | 019 | 1400 | 648 | 173,025 | 170,414 | 171,298 | -0.1 | 67 | 84.7 | 81.9 | 9.6 | 10.6 | 4.6 | 6.3 |
| CHRISTIAN | 021 | 0000 | 648 | 34,418 | 35,787 | 35,740 | 0.4 | 33 | 99.3 | 99.0 | 0.2 | 0.4 | 0.3 | 0.4 |
| CLARK | 023 | 0000 | 581 | 15,921 | 16,610 | 16,909 | 0.4 | 33 | 99.5 | 94.6 | 0.1 | 4.5 | 0.2 | 0.3 |
| CLAY | 025 | 0000 | 581 | 14,460 | 14,254 | 13,953 | -0.1 | 67 | 99.6 | 99.6 | 0.0 | 0.0 | 0.2 | 0.2 |
| CLINTON | 027 | 7040 | 609 | 33,944 | 35,772 | 36,241 | 0.5 | 28 | 96.3 | 95.5 | 3.0 | 3.6 | 0.3 | 0.4 |
| COLES | 029 | 0000 | 648 | 51,644 | 51,681 | 51,056 | 0.0 | 61 | 97.2 | 96.7 | 1.8 | 2.0 | 0.7 | 0.9 |
| COOK | 031 | 1600 | 602 | 5,105,067 | 5,192,969 | 5,196,990 | 0.2 | 45 | 62.8 | 58.6 | 25.8 | 26.4 | 3.7 | 4.9 |
| CRAWFORD | 033 | 0000 | 581 | 19,464 | 20,787 | 20,456 | 0.6 | 24 | 99.2 | 95.4 | 0.3 | 3.8 | 0.2 | 0.3 |
| CUMBERLAND | 035 | 0000 | 648 | 10,670 | 11,099 | 11,083 | 0.4 | 33 | 99.6 | 99.5 | 0.0 | 0.0 | 0.2 | 0.3 |
| DEKALB | 037 | 1600 | 602 | 77,932 | 87,926 | 92,715 | 1.2 | 15 | 93.6 | 92.5 | 2.7 | 2.8 | 2.2 | 2.9 |
| DE WITT | 039 | 0000 | 648 | 16,516 | 16,640 | 16,463 | 0.1 | 51 | 99.2 | 98.9 | 0.2 | 0.3 | 0.3 | 0.4 |
| DOUGLAS | 041 | 0000 | 648 | 19,464 | 19,895 | 19,992 | 0.2 | 45 | 99.1 | 98.7 | 0.1 | 0.2 | 0.2 | 0.3 |
| DUPAGE | 043 | 1600 | 602 | 781,666 | 903,564 | 958,582 | 1.4 | 11 | 91.5 | 88.8 | 2.0 | 2.1 | 5.1 | 7.1 |
| EDGAR | 045 | 0000 | 581 | 19,595 | 19,367 | 18,582 | -0.1 | 67 | 99.4 | 98.6 | 0.3 | 1.1 | 0.1 | 0.1 |
| EDWARDS | 047 | 0000 | 649 | 7,440 | 6,798 | 6,431 | -0.9 | 101 | 99.5 | 99.4 | 0.1 | 0.1 | 0.3 | 0.3 |
| EFFINGHAM | 049 | 0000 | 648 | 31,704 | 33,990 | 35,054 | 0.7 | 19 | 99.4 | 99.2 | 0.0 | 0.1 | 0.3 | 0.4 |
| FAYETTE | 051 | 0000 | 609 | 20,893 | 22,031 | 22,048 | 0.5 | 28 | 96.4 | 94.8 | 2.9 | 4.2 | 0.2 | 0.2 |
| FORD | 053 | 0000 | 648 | 14,275 | 14,022 | 13,909 | -0.2 | 82 | 99.2 | 98.9 | 0.3 | 0.4 | 0.3 | 0.4 |
| FRANKLIN | 055 | 0000 | 632 | 40,319 | 40,273 | 39,818 | 0.0 | 61 | 99.4 | 99.2 | 0.1 | 0.2 | 0.2 | 0.3 |
| FULTON | 057 | 0000 | 675 | 38,080 | 38,618 | 38,310 | 0.1 | 51 | 97.5 | 95.9 | 1.8 | 3.1 | 0.3 | 0.4 |
| GALLATIN | 059 | 0000 | 632 | 6,909 | 6,547 | 6,357 | -0.5 | 94 | 99.0 | 99.0 | 0.6 | 0.6 | 0.2 | 0.2 |
| GREENE | 061 | 0000 | 609 | 15,317 | 15,769 | 15,913 | 0.3 | 38 | 99.4 | 98.6 | 0.1 | 1.0 | 0.1 | 0.1 |
| GRUNDY | 063 | 1600 | 602 | 32,337 | 37,680 | 40,141 | 1.5 | 10 | 98.5 | 97.9 | 0.1 | 0.1 | 0.3 | 0.5 |
| HAMILTON | 065 | 0000 | 632 | 8,499 | 8,578 | 8,553 | 0.1 | 51 | 99.6 | 99.4 | 0.0 | 0.0 | 0.2 | 0.3 |
| HANCOCK | 067 | 0000 | 717 | 21,373 | 20,851 | 20,260 | -0.2 | 82 | 99.5 | 99.4 | 0.1 | 0.2 | 0.2 | 0.2 |
| HARDIN | 069 | 0000 | 632 | 5,189 | 4,866 | 4,667 | -0.6 | 96 | 97.6 | 97.0 | 1.6 | 2.1 | 0.3 | 0.3 |
| HENDERSON | 071 | 0000 | 682 | 8,096 | 8,609 | 8,668 | 0.6 | 24 | 99.3 | 99.2 | 0.1 | 0.1 | 0.1 | 0.2 |
| HENRY | 073 | 1960 | 682 | 51,159 | 51,993 | 52,730 | 0.2 | 45 | 97.7 | 97.1 | 1.3 | 1.5 | 0.3 | 0.3 |
| IROQUOIS | 075 | 0000 | 648 | 30,787 | 31,127 | 30,782 | 0.1 | 51 | 97.9 | 97.3 | 0.5 | 0.6 | 0.2 | 0.3 |
| JACKSON | 077 | 0000 | 632 | 61,067 | 60,463 | 59,458 | -0.1 | 67 | 85.1 | 82.8 | 10.4 | 11.4 | 3.6 | 4.7 |
| JASPER | 079 | 0000 | 581 | 10,609 | 10,541 | 10,393 | -0.1 | 67 | 99.7 | 99.6 | 0.0 | 0.0 | 0.2 | 0.2 |
| JEFFERSON | 081 | 0000 | 632 | 37,020 | 39,261 | 39,643 | 0.6 | 24 | 94.2 | 90.7 | 5.2 | 8.3 | 0.3 | 0.5 |
| JERSEY | 083 | 7040 | 609 | 20,539 | 21,686 | 22,230 | 0.5 | 28 | 99.1 | 99.0 | 0.5 | 0.4 | 0.2 | 0.2 |
| JO DAVIESS | 085 | 0000 | 682 | 21,821 | 21,532 | 21,382 | -0.1 | 67 | 99.6 | 99.5 | 0.1 | 0.1 | 0.1 | 0.1 |
| JOHNSON | 087 | 0000 | 632 | 11,347 | 13,693 | 14,154 | 1.9 | 7 | 90.2 | 88.5 | 9.2 | 10.7 | 0.1 | 0.2 |
| KANE | 089 | 1600 | 602 | 317,471 | 413,257 | 466,211 | 2.6 | 5 | 84.9 | 81.5 | 6.0 | 6.3 | 1.4 | 1.9 |
| KANKAKEE | 091 | 3740 | 602 | 96,255 | 103,121 | 104,996 | 0.7 | 19 | 83.3 | 81.2 | 15.0 | 16.5 | 0.7 | 0.9 |
| KENDALL | 093 | 1600 | 602 | 39,413 | 55,592 | 65,203 | 3.4 | 1 | 96.5 | 95.3 | 0.5 | 0.6 | 0.6 | 0.8 |
| KNOX | 095 | 0000 | 682 | 56,393 | 55,183 | 54,246 | -0.2 | 82 | 92.9 | 91.4 | 5.1 | 5.9 | 0.6 | 0.8 |
| LAKE | 097 | 1600 | 602 | 516,418 | 628,246 | 679,519 | 1.9 | 7 | 87.3 | 84.9 | 6.7 | 7.0 | 2.4 | 3.4 |
| LA SALLE | 099 | 0000 | 602 | 106,913 | 110,366 | 110,989 | 0.3 | 38 | 97.1 | 96.1 | 1.1 | 1.3 | 0.5 | 0.7 |
| LAWRENCE | 101 | 0000 | 581 | 15,972 | 14,977 | 14,146 | -0.6 | 96 | 98.7 | 98.5 | 0.9 | 1.1 | 0.1 | 0.2 |
| LEE | 103 | 0000 | 610 | 34,392 | 35,630 | 35,113 | 0.3 | 38 | 94.6 | 93.0 | 3.6 | 4.5 | 0.5 | 0.7 |
| LIVINGSTON | 105 | 0000 | 675 | 39,301 | 39,638 | 39,571 | 0.1 | 51 | 93.0 | 92.8 | 5.4 | 5.1 | 0.3 | 0.5 |
| LOGAN | 107 | 0000 | 648 | 30,798 | 31,617 | 31,038 | 0.3 | 38 | 94.9 | 93.1 | 4.2 | 5.7 | 0.5 | 0.6 |
| MCDONOUGH | 109 | 0000 | 717 | 35,244 | 35,072 | 34,298 | 0.0 | 61 | 93.6 | 92.9 | 3.6 | 3.5 | 2.3 | 3.0 |
| MCHENRY | 111 | 1600 | 602 | 183,241 | 252,541 | 280,629 | 3.2 | 2 | 97.6 | 96.8 | 0.2 | 0.2 | 0.7 | 1.0 |
| MCLEAN | 113 | 1040 | 675 | 129,180 | 147,251 | 156,125 | 1.3 | 13 | 93.7 | 92.6 | 4.3 | 4.8 | 1.3 | 1.7 |
| MACON | 115 | 2040 | 648 | 117,206 | 112,630 | 109,734 | -0.4 | 91 | 87.2 | 85.9 | 12.1 | 13.1 | 0.4 | 0.6 |
| MACOUPIN | 117 | 0000 | 609 | 47,679 | 49,108 | 49,636 | 0.3 | 38 | 98.7 | 98.5 | 0.8 | 0.9 | 0.2 | 0.3 |
| MADISON | 119 | 7040 | 609 | 249,238 | 259,963 | 262,456 | 0.4 | 33 | 92.4 | 91.3 | 6.5 | 7.2 | 0.6 | 0.8 |
| MARION | 121 | 0000 | 609 | 41,561 | 41,726 | 41,294 | 0.0 | 61 | 95.4 | 94.6 | 3.7 | 4.1 | 0.6 | 0.8 |
| MARSHALL | 123 | 0000 | 675 | 12,846 | 13,040 | 13,351 | 0.1 | 51 | 99.3 | 99.1 | 0.1 | 0.2 | 0.2 | 0.3 |
| MASON | 125 | 0000 | 675 | 16,269 | 16,802 | 16,801 | 0.3 | 38 | 99.5 | 99.3 | 0.0 | 0.0 | 0.2 | 0.3 |
| MASSAC | 127 | 0000 | 632 | 14,752 | 15,398 | 15,318 | 0.4 | 33 | 93.6 | 92.9 | 5.9 | 6.5 | 0.2 | 0.3 |
| MENARD | 129 | 7880 | 648 | 11,164 | 12,874 | 13,647 | 1.4 | 11 | 99.4 | 99.3 | 0.1 | 0.1 | 0.1 | 0.2 |
| MERCER | 131 | 0000 | 682 | 17,290 | 17,682 | 17,863 | 0.2 | 45 | 99.2 | 99.0 | 0.2 | 0.3 | 0.2 | 0.2 |
| MONROE | 133 | 7040 | 609 | 22,422 | 27,926 | 31,131 | 2.2 | 6 | 99.3 | 99.1 | 0.1 | 0.1 | 0.3 | 0.4 |
| MONTGOMERY | 135 | 0000 | 609 | 30,728 | 31,250 | 30,908 | 0.2 | 45 | 97.5 | 96.1 | 1.8 | 2.9 | 0.2 | 0.3 |
| MORGAN | 137 | 0000 | 648 | 36,397 | 34,911 | 33,698 | -0.4 | 91 | 95.0 | 93.8 | 4.1 | 5.0 | 0.4 | 0.5 |
| MOULTRIE | 139 | 0000 | 648 | 13,930 | 14,664 | 15,112 | 0.5 | 28 | 99.7 | 99.6 | 0.1 | 0.1 | 0.1 | 0.2 |
| OGLE | 141 | 6880 | 610 | 45,957 | 51,320 | 53,255 | 1.1 | 16 | 97.7 | 96.9 | 0.1 | 0.2 | 0.3 | 0.4 |
| PEORIA | 143 | 6120 | 675 | 182,827 | 180,694 | 178,408 | -0.1 | 67 | 84.4 | 82.5 | 13.6 | 14.9 | 1.2 | 1.7 |
| PERRY | 145 | 0000 | 632 | 21,412 | 21,333 | 21,355 | 0.0 | 61 | 97.6 | 96.7 | 1.9 | 2.7 | 0.3 | 0.4 |
| PIATT | 147 | 0000 | 648 | 15,548 | 16,756 | 17,399 | 0.7 | 19 | 99.7 | 99.7 | 0.1 | 0.0 | 0.1 | 0.1 |
| PIKE | 149 | 0000 | 717 | 17,577 | 17,185 | 17,011 | -0.2 | 82 | 99.6 | 99.5 | 0.0 | 0.0 | 0.2 | 0.2 |
| POPE | 151 | 0000 | 632 | 4,373 | 4,845 | 5,026 | 1.0 | 17 | 93.1 | 92.3 | 6.1 | 6.7 | 0.1 | 0.1 |
| PULASKI | 153 | 0000 | 632 | 7,523 | 7,315 | 7,368 | -0.3 | 89 | 66.9 | 63.9 | 32.8 | 35.8 | 0.1 | 0.1 |
| ILLINOIS | | | | | | | 0.6 | | 78.3 | 76.1 | 14.8 | 15.0 | 2.5 | 3.4 |
| UNITED STATES | | | | | | | 1.0 | | 80.3 | 77.9 | 12.1 | 12.4 | 2.9 | 3.9 |

# POPULATION COMPOSITION

| COUNTY | % HISPANIC ORIGIN | | 2000 AGE DISTRIBUTION (%) | | | | | | | | | | MEDIAN AGE | | 2000 Males/ Females (×100) |
|---|---|---|---|---|---|---|---|---|---|---|---|---|---|---|---|
| | 1990 | 2000 | 0-4 | 5-9 | 10-14 | 15-19 | 20-24 | 25-44 | 45-64 | 65-84 | 85+ | 18+ | 1990 | 2000 | |
| ADAMS | 0.4 | 1.0 | 6.7 | 7.3 | 7.1 | 7.3 | 5.8 | 26.4 | 22.4 | 14.1 | 2.8 | 74.5 | 35.4 | 37.9 | 92.0 |
| ALEXANDER | 0.5 | 1.2 | 8.1 | 8.5 | 8.0 | 7.2 | 5.8 | 24.7 | 21.5 | 13.9 | 2.4 | 70.7 | 34.8 | 36.0 | 92.4 |
| BOND | 0.5 | 2.2 | 5.6 | 6.3 | 6.2 | 7.8 | 8.4 | 29.1 | 20.8 | 13.4 | 2.5 | 78.1 | 35.0 | 36.3 | 108.5 |
| BOONE | 6.7 | 9.6 | 7.3 | 7.8 | 7.7 | 7.4 | 5.7 | 28.8 | 24.1 | 9.8 | 1.3 | 72.7 | 33.1 | 35.3 | 96.3 |
| BROWN | 1.8 | 3.6 | 4.7 | 5.4 | 5.4 | 7.6 | 11.0 | 35.1 | 17.7 | 10.5 | 2.6 | 80.5 | 33.9 | 33.1 | 167.4 |
| BUREAU | 2.8 | 4.4 | 6.5 | 7.1 | 6.9 | 7.4 | 5.7 | 26.0 | 23.6 | 14.0 | 2.7 | 74.7 | 36.3 | 38.4 | 93.2 |
| CALHOUN | 0.2 | 0.7 | 6.0 | 6.9 | 6.7 | 6.8 | 4.7 | 24.6 | 24.6 | 16.8 | 3.1 | 76.3 | 38.5 | 41.3 | 102.1 |
| CARROLL | 1.8 | 2.9 | 6.3 | 6.9 | 6.7 | 6.7 | 5.2 | 25.2 | 24.5 | 15.8 | 2.7 | 75.8 | 37.5 | 40.2 | 96.0 |
| CASS | 0.4 | 1.0 | 6.4 | 7.0 | 6.8 | 7.1 | 5.6 | 26.8 | 23.6 | 14.0 | 2.7 | 75.4 | 35.8 | 38.6 | 97.5 |
| CHAMPAIGN | 2.0 | 2.8 | 6.2 | 6.4 | 6.2 | 10.7 | 14.7 | 29.2 | 17.5 | 8.0 | 1.2 | 78.2 | 27.8 | 29.1 | 101.2 |
| CHRISTIAN | 0.3 | 0.8 | 6.5 | 7.1 | 7.2 | 6.8 | 5.0 | 26.5 | 23.5 | 14.4 | 2.9 | 75.0 | 36.3 | 39.0 | 91.1 |
| CLARK | 0.3 | 1.7 | 6.0 | 6.8 | 6.7 | 6.8 | 5.4 | 27.6 | 22.8 | 15.0 | 2.9 | 76.3 | 37.0 | 39.0 | 101.3 |
| CLAY | 0.4 | 1.0 | 6.4 | 6.8 | 6.6 | 7.3 | 5.4 | 26.4 | 23.4 | 14.4 | 3.1 | 75.5 | 36.8 | 39.2 | 92.8 |
| CLINTON | 1.0 | 1.8 | 6.6 | 7.5 | 7.4 | 7.2 | 6.6 | 29.8 | 21.0 | 11.8 | 2.0 | 74.0 | 32.8 | 35.3 | 106.9 |
| COLES | 0.8 | 1.4 | 5.3 | 5.9 | 5.9 | 10.7 | 14.1 | 25.2 | 19.5 | 11.3 | 2.1 | 79.9 | 29.8 | 32.3 | 90.6 |
| COOK | 13.6 | 18.1 | 7.4 | 7.4 | 6.9 | 6.7 | 6.6 | 31.3 | 21.5 | 10.7 | 1.5 | 74.4 | 32.6 | 35.1 | 92.9 |
| CRAWFORD | 0.4 | 1.7 | 6.1 | 6.5 | 6.4 | 6.8 | 6.0 | 28.0 | 23.1 | 14.5 | 2.6 | 76.7 | 37.1 | 38.8 | 101.3 |
| CUMBERLAND | 0.4 | 1.0 | 7.6 | 8.0 | 7.6 | 7.7 | 5.5 | 26.9 | 21.7 | 12.8 | 2.2 | 72.1 | 33.9 | 36.1 | 98.5 |
| DEKALB | 3.0 | 4.5 | 6.2 | 6.4 | 5.9 | 10.4 | 15.6 | 26.8 | 18.4 | 8.8 | 1.5 | 78.4 | 27.1 | 29.4 | 97.3 |
| DE WITT | 0.5 | 1.1 | 6.5 | 7.2 | 7.0 | 7.1 | 5.5 | 27.3 | 23.6 | 13.4 | 2.4 | 74.9 | 35.4 | 38.4 | 98.6 |
| DOUGLAS | 1.5 | 2.5 | 7.1 | 8.1 | 7.6 | 7.3 | 5.0 | 26.5 | 22.7 | 13.5 | 2.2 | 72.4 | 34.5 | 37.3 | 95.0 |
| DUPAGE | 4.4 | 6.4 | 7.4 | 7.8 | 7.5 | 6.6 | 5.6 | 33.3 | 22.4 | 8.2 | 1.1 | 73.3 | 32.3 | 35.4 | 97.2 |
| EDGAR | 0.3 | 0.9 | 6.1 | 6.8 | 7.2 | 6.9 | 5.1 | 26.0 | 24.0 | 14.8 | 3.0 | 75.4 | 37.3 | 39.7 | 93.3 |
| EDWARDS | 0.4 | 0.9 | 6.0 | 7.0 | 6.9 | 6.6 | 5.5 | 26.0 | 24.6 | 14.4 | 3.0 | 76.2 | 37.3 | 40.0 | 92.7 |
| EFFINGHAM | 0.4 | 0.9 | 8.4 | 9.0 | 8.4 | 7.4 | 5.3 | 27.8 | 20.5 | 11.3 | 2.0 | 69.7 | 32.0 | 34.5 | 96.6 |
| FAYETTE | 0.7 | 1.5 | 6.2 | 6.9 | 6.8 | 7.3 | 6.6 | 28.3 | 22.1 | 13.2 | 2.5 | 75.6 | 35.3 | 36.8 | 110.4 |
| FORD | 0.6 | 1.2 | 6.6 | 7.3 | 6.8 | 7.1 | 5.6 | 25.0 | 22.7 | 15.5 | 3.3 | 74.6 | 36.9 | 39.8 | 94.2 |
| FRANKLIN | 0.3 | 0.8 | 5.9 | 6.5 | 6.4 | 6.3 | 5.5 | 26.0 | 24.6 | 15.8 | 2.9 | 77.3 | 37.8 | 40.4 | 92.5 |
| FULTON | 0.6 | 1.4 | 5.8 | 6.3 | 6.0 | 6.7 | 7.1 | 26.8 | 23.5 | 15.1 | 2.9 | 77.8 | 36.9 | 39.0 | 98.9 |
| GALLATIN | 0.2 | 0.7 | 5.6 | 6.3 | 6.6 | 6.9 | 5.0 | 24.9 | 26.2 | 15.7 | 3.0 | 77.5 | 39.2 | 41.6 | 93.5 |
| GREENE | 0.3 | 1.0 | 6.9 | 7.6 | 7.2 | 7.2 | 5.6 | 25.4 | 22.3 | 15.0 | 2.9 | 73.9 | 36.0 | 38.3 | 95.1 |
| GRUNDY | 2.3 | 3.7 | 6.9 | 7.4 | 7.3 | 7.2 | 5.9 | 29.8 | 23.3 | 10.5 | 1.7 | 73.8 | 33.3 | 36.3 | 97.5 |
| HAMILTON | 0.3 | 0.9 | 5.8 | 6.9 | 6.7 | 6.8 | 4.7 | 25.0 | 24.1 | 16.7 | 3.4 | 76.4 | 39.1 | 41.1 | 90.3 |
| HANCOCK | 0.3 | 0.8 | 6.3 | 6.9 | 6.7 | 7.3 | 5.6 | 25.1 | 23.9 | 15.5 | 2.8 | 75.5 | 37.3 | 40.0 | 91.1 |
| HARDIN | 0.6 | 1.0 | 5.1 | 6.4 | 6.4 | 6.9 | 5.7 | 26.6 | 24.5 | 15.8 | 2.5 | 78.2 | 37.3 | 40.3 | 103.8 |
| HENDERSON | 0.7 | 1.4 | 6.1 | 7.1 | 7.0 | 7.1 | 4.4 | 25.9 | 26.5 | 13.9 | 2.1 | 75.2 | 37.4 | 40.4 | 97.6 |
| HENRY | 1.6 | 2.7 | 6.5 | 7.0 | 6.9 | 7.2 | 6.1 | 25.8 | 24.5 | 13.5 | 2.4 | 75.0 | 36.0 | 38.3 | 96.8 |
| IROQUOIS | 2.1 | 3.4 | 6.3 | 7.3 | 7.2 | 6.9 | 4.7 | 25.7 | 23.8 | 15.2 | 2.8 | 74.7 | 37.0 | 39.7 | 95.7 |
| JACKSON | 1.8 | 2.7 | 5.4 | 5.2 | 4.9 | 11.6 | 18.1 | 27.8 | 16.7 | 8.8 | 1.5 | 81.8 | 26.5 | 28.4 | 105.8 |
| JASPER | 0.3 | 0.8 | 7.3 | 7.9 | 7.4 | 7.9 | 5.7 | 25.8 | 21.8 | 13.4 | 2.7 | 72.3 | 34.4 | 37.1 | 97.2 |
| JEFFERSON | 0.4 | 1.6 | 6.7 | 7.3 | 7.2 | 7.0 | 6.1 | 28.6 | 21.9 | 13.0 | 2.2 | 74.3 | 34.9 | 36.8 | 101.0 |
| JERSEY | 0.5 | 1.1 | 6.8 | 7.3 | 7.0 | 8.7 | 6.7 | 26.6 | 22.6 | 12.3 | 1.9 | 73.8 | 33.2 | 36.3 | 96.2 |
| JO DAVIESS | 0.4 | 0.9 | 6.1 | 7.2 | 7.1 | 6.9 | 5.0 | 26.2 | 24.2 | 14.8 | 2.4 | 75.0 | 36.2 | 39.4 | 97.8 |
| JOHNSON | 1.7 | 2.6 | 4.5 | 5.1 | 5.3 | 6.4 | 8.7 | 33.9 | 22.6 | 11.7 | 1.9 | 81.5 | 35.9 | 36.7 | 152.5 |
| KANE | 13.7 | 18.8 | 8.5 | 8.8 | 8.3 | 7.6 | 6.1 | 31.4 | 20.6 | 7.4 | 1.2 | 69.9 | 30.9 | 32.8 | 99.1 |
| KANKAKEE | 2.0 | 3.2 | 7.4 | 8.0 | 7.7 | 7.7 | 6.5 | 28.0 | 21.7 | 11.4 | 1.6 | 72.3 | 32.9 | 35.1 | 94.9 |
| KENDALL | 4.6 | 6.7 | 7.2 | 7.8 | 7.8 | 7.6 | 5.5 | 30.1 | 24.8 | 8.3 | 1.0 | 72.6 | 32.0 | 35.2 | 99.4 |
| KNOX | 2.5 | 4.0 | 5.8 | 6.2 | 6.1 | 7.3 | 7.4 | 26.2 | 23.8 | 14.4 | 2.7 | 77.8 | 36.5 | 38.7 | 98.4 |
| LAKE | 7.5 | 10.6 | 7.5 | 8.4 | 8.6 | 7.8 | 5.9 | 30.2 | 22.5 | 8.0 | 1.0 | 71.3 | 31.6 | 34.5 | 100.9 |
| LA SALLE | 3.0 | 4.8 | 6.7 | 7.1 | 6.9 | 7.5 | 6.3 | 26.8 | 22.6 | 13.7 | 2.4 | 74.9 | 35.5 | 37.6 | 97.1 |
| LAWRENCE | 0.4 | 0.9 | 5.9 | 6.8 | 6.8 | 6.6 | 4.9 | 25.9 | 23.3 | 16.0 | 3.6 | 76.5 | 38.0 | 40.4 | 90.9 |
| LEE | 2.1 | 3.5 | 6.8 | 7.3 | 7.2 | 7.0 | 6.2 | 29.2 | 22.3 | 12.0 | 2.1 | 74.5 | 34.2 | 36.5 | 104.5 |
| LIVINGSTON | 2.1 | 3.1 | 6.5 | 7.2 | 6.9 | 7.1 | 6.7 | 29.4 | 21.5 | 12.1 | 2.7 | 75.0 | 34.3 | 36.2 | 103.1 |
| LOGAN | 1.1 | 2.1 | 5.9 | 6.6 | 6.3 | 7.9 | 7.8 | 28.9 | 21.6 | 12.2 | 2.7 | 76.9 | 34.6 | 36.2 | 108.1 |
| MCDONOUGH | 1.0 | 1.6 | 4.8 | 5.3 | 5.1 | 12.7 | 16.2 | 23.5 | 18.5 | 11.3 | 2.4 | 82.2 | 27.3 | 30.1 | 99.5 |
| MCHENRY | 3.3 | 4.9 | 8.0 | 8.6 | 8.3 | 7.0 | 5.1 | 32.3 | 22.1 | 7.6 | 1.1 | 70.7 | 32.2 | 34.8 | 100.7 |
| MCLEAN | 1.3 | 2.2 | 6.4 | 6.6 | 6.3 | 9.9 | 12.7 | 28.6 | 19.2 | 8.9 | 1.5 | 77.1 | 28.8 | 31.5 | 91.7 |
| MACON | 0.5 | 1.0 | 6.5 | 6.9 | 6.9 | 7.4 | 6.8 | 26.8 | 23.8 | 13.0 | 2.0 | 75.4 | 35.0 | 37.5 | 91.9 |
| MACOUPIN | 0.4 | 1.0 | 6.3 | 7.2 | 7.2 | 7.4 | 5.7 | 26.2 | 22.9 | 14.5 | 2.7 | 74.8 | 36.0 | 38.4 | 93.7 |
| MADISON | 1.1 | 1.9 | 6.8 | 7.2 | 7.1 | 7.0 | 6.0 | 29.1 | 22.7 | 12.3 | 1.8 | 74.8 | 33.9 | 36.8 | 93.1 |
| MARION | 0.6 | 1.2 | 6.8 | 7.3 | 7.2 | 7.5 | 5.7 | 26.7 | 23.0 | 13.2 | 2.5 | 74.1 | 35.1 | 37.7 | 93.3 |
| MARSHALL | 0.6 | 1.3 | 5.9 | 6.4 | 6.4 | 6.9 | 5.5 | 25.7 | 24.9 | 15.3 | 3.0 | 77.0 | 37.8 | 40.5 | 92.2 |
| MASON | 0.4 | 0.9 | 6.3 | 7.2 | 7.3 | 7.0 | 5.2 | 26.2 | 24.3 | 14.1 | 2.4 | 74.7 | 36.5 | 39.0 | 95.9 |
| MASSAC | 0.3 | 0.8 | 5.5 | 6.6 | 6.5 | 6.9 | 4.9 | 26.5 | 24.5 | 15.6 | 2.9 | 77.1 | 37.7 | 40.5 | 90.1 |
| MENARD | 0.3 | 0.9 | 6.4 | 7.7 | 7.7 | 7.2 | 4.8 | 27.9 | 24.5 | 11.6 | 2.3 | 73.7 | 35.4 | 38.2 | 94.6 |
| MERCER | 0.6 | 1.3 | 6.4 | 6.9 | 6.8 | 7.3 | 5.5 | 25.7 | 25.5 | 13.5 | 2.5 | 75.3 | 36.0 | 39.2 | 94.8 |
| MONROE | 0.7 | 1.4 | 6.9 | 7.8 | 7.5 | 6.8 | 5.3 | 29.0 | 23.2 | 11.6 | 1.9 | 73.6 | 33.9 | 37.0 | 97.7 |
| MONTGOMERY | 0.8 | 1.7 | 6.5 | 6.9 | 6.6 | 7.7 | 6.7 | 27.4 | 21.4 | 13.9 | 2.9 | 75.1 | 35.3 | 37.3 | 106.6 |
| MORGAN | 0.8 | 1.5 | 5.9 | 6.6 | 6.6 | 8.7 | 7.9 | 27.0 | 21.7 | 13.1 | 2.6 | 76.3 | 34.3 | 36.5 | 96.7 |
| MOULTRIE | 0.3 | 0.8 | 6.5 | 7.4 | 7.4 | 6.9 | 4.7 | 26.1 | 23.3 | 13.8 | 3.9 | 74.0 | 36.7 | 39.2 | 92.8 |
| OGLE | 3.0 | 4.6 | 7.1 | 7.5 | 7.4 | 7.4 | 6.0 | 27.5 | 23.5 | 11.6 | 1.9 | 73.3 | 34.0 | 36.7 | 95.9 |
| PEORIA | 1.4 | 2.4 | 6.7 | 7.2 | 7.1 | 7.7 | 6.9 | 28.0 | 22.4 | 12.1 | 2.0 | 74.8 | 33.8 | 36.3 | 92.9 |
| PERRY | 0.6 | 1.4 | 6.6 | 7.1 | 7.0 | 6.9 | 5.9 | 26.7 | 23.5 | 13.7 | 2.6 | 75.0 | 35.5 | 38.1 | 95.8 |
| PIATT | 0.2 | 0.7 | 6.0 | 6.7 | 6.7 | 7.1 | 5.8 | 26.9 | 24.9 | 13.5 | 2.4 | 76.1 | 36.2 | 39.5 | 96.6 |
| PIKE | 0.4 | 0.9 | 6.2 | 6.9 | 6.8 | 6.9 | 5.1 | 24.8 | 23.8 | 16.2 | 3.3 | 75.9 | 37.9 | 40.5 | 93.6 |
| POPE | 1.3 | 2.1 | 4.7 | 5.7 | 5.8 | 9.8 | 6.7 | 25.9 | 24.0 | 14.6 | 2.7 | 78.6 | 35.8 | 38.8 | 116.0 |
| PULASKI | 0.4 | 0.7 | 7.4 | 8.6 | 7.8 | 7.6 | 5.8 | 24.1 | 21.6 | 14.2 | 2.8 | 71.1 | 34.8 | 36.4 | 88.8 |
| ILLINOIS | 7.9 | 10.7 | 7.2 | 7.5 | 7.2 | 7.2 | 6.6 | 30.2 | 21.9 | 10.7 | 1.6 | 74.1 | 32.8 | 35.4 | 95.3 |
| UNITED STATES | 9.0 | 11.8 | 6.9 | 7.2 | 7.2 | 7.2 | 6.7 | 29.9 | 22.2 | 11.1 | 1.6 | 74.6 | 32.9 | 35.7 | 95.6 |

| COUNTY | HOUSEHOLDS | | | | | FAMILIES | | | MEDIAN HOUSEHOLD INCOME | | | |
|---|---|---|---|---|---|---|---|---|---|---|---|---|
| | 1990 | 2000 | 2005 | % Annual Rate 1990-2000 | 2000 Average HH Size | 1990 | 2000 | % Annual Rate 1990-2000 | 2000 | 2005 | 2000 National Rank | 2000 State Rank |
| ADAMS | 25,515 | 25,989 | 25,674 | 0.2 | 2.47 | 17,682 | 17,335 | -0.2 | 34,378 | 38,029 | 1334 | 61 |
| ALEXANDER | 4,234 | 3,845 | 3,620 | -1.2 | 2.40 | 2,870 | 2,523 | -1.5 | 21,617 | 25,856 | 3048 | 102 |
| BOND | 5,652 | 5,972 | 5,924 | 0.7 | 2.46 | 4,118 | 4,186 | 0.2 | 35,811 | 43,318 | 1125 | 53 |
| BOONE | 10,950 | 14,542 | 16,116 | 3.5 | 2.75 | 8,488 | 11,267 | 3.5 | 53,107 | 61,087 | 150 | 8 |
| BROWN | 1,991 | 2,076 | 2,134 | 0.5 | 2.45 | 1,366 | 1,363 | 0.0 | 32,759 | 41,123 | 1580 | 68 |
| BUREAU | 13,790 | 13,766 | 13,582 | 0.0 | 2.52 | 9,917 | 9,531 | -0.5 | 37,525 | 45,187 | 895 | 39 |
| CALHOUN | 2,048 | 1,926 | 1,872 | -0.7 | 2.46 | 1,511 | 1,371 | -1.2 | 31,936 | 38,430 | 1728 | 74 |
| CARROLL | 6,638 | 6,773 | 6,690 | 0.2 | 2.41 | 4,784 | 4,722 | -0.2 | 33,341 | 38,686 | 1485 | 65 |
| CASS | 5,195 | 5,158 | 5,162 | -0.1 | 2.51 | 3,708 | 3,550 | -0.5 | 32,382 | 37,378 | 1646 | 70 |
| CHAMPAIGN | 63,900 | 63,582 | 64,028 | -0.1 | 2.42 | 38,604 | 36,825 | -0.6 | 36,714 | 41,263 | 1017 | 47 |
| CHRISTIAN | 13,591 | 13,713 | 13,713 | 0.1 | 2.48 | 9,610 | 9,311 | -0.4 | 34,644 | 40,051 | 1298 | 58 |
| CLARK | 6,394 | 6,766 | 6,935 | 0.7 | 2.42 | 4,573 | 4,663 | 0.2 | 34,902 | 41,781 | 1270 | 55 |
| CLAY | 5,708 | 5,789 | 5,744 | 0.2 | 2.40 | 4,116 | 4,013 | -0.3 | 29,467 | 34,578 | 2226 | 90 |
| CLINTON | 11,583 | 12,329 | 12,606 | 0.8 | 2.71 | 8,765 | 9,005 | 0.3 | 40,951 | 48,537 | 591 | 22 |
| COLES | 18,957 | 19,053 | 18,878 | 0.1 | 2.39 | 11,947 | 11,503 | -0.5 | 34,691 | 39,143 | 1292 | 57 |
| COOK | 1,879,488 | 1,922,815 | 1,930,220 | 0.3 | 2.66 | 1,248,468 | 1,244,280 | 0.0 | 45,823 | 51,938 | 320 | 12 |
| CRAWFORD | 7,792 | 7,952 | 7,865 | 0.2 | 2.42 | 5,587 | 5,483 | -0.2 | 31,692 | 36,733 | 1777 | 77 |
| CUMBERLAND | 4,029 | 4,237 | 4,254 | 0.6 | 2.61 | 2,963 | 3,013 | 0.2 | 36,264 | 42,000 | 1072 | 49 |
| DEKALB | 26,413 | 30,368 | 32,312 | 1.7 | 2.56 | 17,035 | 18,948 | 1.3 | 45,561 | 54,292 | 328 | 13 |
| DE WITT | 6,488 | 6,644 | 6,627 | 0.3 | 2.47 | 4,652 | 4,597 | -0.1 | 40,943 | 49,368 | 592 | 23 |
| DOUGLAS | 7,206 | 7,456 | 7,529 | 0.4 | 2.63 | 5,372 | 5,355 | 0.0 | 38,407 | 44,107 | 817 | 35 |
| DUPAGE | 279,344 | 324,637 | 345,339 | 1.8 | 2.75 | 208,804 | 235,178 | 1.5 | 67,836 | 75,595 | 22 | 2 |
| EDGAR | 7,859 | 7,912 | 7,683 | 0.1 | 2.38 | 5,508 | 5,325 | -0.4 | 30,754 | 38,207 | 1979 | 81 |
| EDWARDS | 3,016 | 2,795 | 2,664 | -0.9 | 2.40 | 2,161 | 1,930 | -1.4 | 28,712 | 32,791 | 2335 | 91 |
| EFFINGHAM | 11,465 | 12,349 | 12,767 | 0.9 | 2.72 | 8,482 | 8,861 | 0.5 | 39,094 | 44,278 | 746 | 28 |
| FAYETTE | 7,719 | 8,098 | 8,199 | 0.6 | 2.48 | 5,529 | 5,595 | 0.1 | 33,180 | 40,218 | 1508 | 66 |
| FORD | 5,602 | 5,549 | 5,526 | -0.1 | 2.46 | 3,997 | 3,805 | -0.6 | 37,220 | 43,368 | 946 | 44 |
| FRANKLIN | 16,564 | 16,667 | 16,546 | 0.1 | 2.38 | 11,408 | 11,037 | -0.4 | 26,078 | 31,133 | 2703 | 96 |
| FULTON | 14,893 | 14,896 | 14,838 | 0.0 | 2.43 | 10,528 | 10,122 | -0.5 | 31,708 | 36,686 | 1774 | 76 |
| GALLATIN | 2,784 | 2,677 | 2,622 | -0.5 | 2.38 | 1,972 | 1,826 | -0.9 | 23,606 | 27,478 | 2931 | 101 |
| GREENE | 5,910 | 6,068 | 6,151 | 0.3 | 2.54 | 4,271 | 4,226 | -0.1 | 30,363 | 36,743 | 2066 | 85 |
| GRUNDY | 11,979 | 14,105 | 15,105 | 2.0 | 2.65 | 8,871 | 10,116 | 1.6 | 54,245 | 63,536 | 133 | 7 |
| HAMILTON | 3,476 | 3,562 | 3,578 | 0.3 | 2.38 | 2,468 | 2,416 | -0.3 | 28,028 | 31,140 | 2437 | 92 |
| HANCOCK | 8,409 | 8,326 | 8,141 | -0.1 | 2.46 | 6,061 | 5,786 | -0.6 | 36,232 | 43,418 | 1078 | 50 |
| HARDIN | 2,049 | 1,908 | 1,830 | -0.9 | 2.42 | 1,451 | 1,299 | -1.3 | 23,984 | 26,263 | 2905 | 100 |
| HENDERSON | 3,237 | 3,498 | 3,549 | 0.9 | 2.45 | 2,307 | 2,400 | 0.5 | 34,522 | 40,673 | 1316 | 60 |
| HENRY | 19,514 | 19,847 | 20,136 | 0.2 | 2.59 | 14,374 | 14,136 | -0.2 | 38,718 | 43,790 | 781 | 32 |
| IROQUOIS | 11,788 | 11,997 | 11,901 | 0.2 | 2.54 | 8,643 | 8,458 | -0.3 | 36,901 | 45,430 | 992 | 46 |
| JACKSON | 23,466 | 23,545 | 23,211 | 0.0 | 2.28 | 12,847 | 12,267 | -0.6 | 25,871 | 29,156 | 2725 | 97 |
| JASPER | 3,962 | 4,011 | 3,988 | 0.1 | 2.61 | 2,976 | 2,910 | -0.3 | 35,130 | 43,063 | 1229 | 54 |
| JEFFERSON | 14,606 | 14,873 | 15,059 | 0.2 | 2.49 | 10,387 | 10,221 | -0.2 | 30,735 | 33,760 | 1981 | 82 |
| JERSEY | 7,344 | 7,802 | 8,023 | 0.7 | 2.67 | 5,541 | 5,700 | 0.3 | 40,406 | 45,602 | 635 | 26 |
| JO DAVIESS | 8,371 | 8,241 | 8,173 | -0.2 | 2.59 | 6,106 | 5,832 | -0.6 | 37,282 | 41,760 | 937 | 42 |
| JOHNSON | 3,725 | 4,391 | 4,637 | 2.0 | 2.41 | 2,777 | 3,157 | 1.6 | 32,258 | 41,046 | 1673 | 71 |
| KANE | 107,176 | 139,927 | 158,135 | 3.3 | 2.91 | 81,218 | 103,546 | 3.0 | 58,102 | 70,147 | 90 | 6 |
| KANKAKEE | 34,623 | 37,367 | 38,170 | 0.9 | 2.66 | 24,922 | 26,102 | 0.6 | 41,558 | 48,645 | 544 | 20 |
| KENDALL | 13,301 | 19,050 | 22,499 | 4.5 | 2.90 | 10,753 | 14,916 | 4.0 | 62,211 | 75,778 | 57 | 4 |
| KNOX | 21,909 | 21,411 | 21,150 | -0.3 | 2.39 | 14,957 | 14,071 | -0.7 | 33,826 | 38,098 | 1417 | 64 |
| LAKE | 173,966 | 216,082 | 235,486 | 2.7 | 2.82 | 134,570 | 162,060 | 2.3 | 69,033 | 76,189 | 17 | 1 |
| LA SALLE | 41,284 | 42,880 | 43,345 | 0.5 | 2.51 | 29,312 | 29,296 | 0.0 | 39,192 | 45,726 | 736 | 27 |
| LAWRENCE | 6,320 | 6,028 | 5,741 | -0.6 | 2.38 | 4,449 | 4,097 | -1.0 | 30,652 | 33,081 | 1997 | 83 |
| LEE | 12,475 | 12,980 | 12,896 | 0.5 | 2.54 | 8,936 | 8,977 | 0.1 | 38,924 | 46,132 | 759 | 29 |
| LIVINGSTON | 13,737 | 14,042 | 14,023 | 0.3 | 2.58 | 9,981 | 9,820 | -0.2 | 43,063 | 51,076 | 455 | 17 |
| LOGAN | 11,033 | 10,916 | 10,732 | -0.1 | 2.46 | 7,758 | 7,363 | -0.6 | 37,654 | 44,676 | 883 | 38 |
| MCDONOUGH | 12,255 | 12,325 | 12,082 | 0.1 | 2.31 | 7,587 | 7,363 | -0.4 | 32,004 | 37,796 | 1714 | 73 |
| MCHENRY | 62,940 | 87,179 | 97,107 | 4.0 | 2.88 | 49,778 | 67,248 | 3.7 | 65,507 | 80,008 | 31 | 3 |
| MCLEAN | 46,796 | 53,943 | 57,349 | 1.7 | 2.53 | 30,305 | 33,510 | 1.2 | 49,638 | 58,949 | 207 | 11 |
| MACON | 45,996 | 44,547 | 43,664 | -0.4 | 2.46 | 32,330 | 30,323 | -0.8 | 37,769 | 41,229 | 869 | 37 |
| MACOUPIN | 18,176 | 18,768 | 18,996 | 0.4 | 2.55 | 13,344 | 13,280 | -0.1 | 34,632 | 39,528 | 1302 | 59 |
| MADISON | 94,857 | 100,001 | 101,515 | 0.6 | 2.56 | 68,426 | 69,394 | 0.2 | 40,872 | 46,315 | 600 | 25 |
| MARION | 16,272 | 16,451 | 16,339 | 0.1 | 2.49 | 11,530 | 11,248 | -0.3 | 31,164 | 35,911 | 1896 | 79 |
| MARSHALL | 4,900 | 4,972 | 5,094 | 0.2 | 2.57 | 3,639 | 3,563 | -0.3 | 38,420 | 46,340 | 816 | 34 |
| MASON | 6,342 | 6,642 | 6,682 | 0.6 | 2.50 | 4,643 | 4,703 | 0.2 | 31,863 | 37,229 | 1744 | 75 |
| MASSAC | 5,908 | 6,390 | 6,466 | 1.0 | 2.36 | 4,234 | 4,428 | 0.5 | 29,539 | 32,124 | 2216 | 89 |
| MENARD | 4,199 | 4,800 | 5,065 | 1.6 | 2.64 | 3,193 | 3,581 | 1.4 | 44,729 | 54,352 | 363 | 14 |
| MERCER | 6,572 | 6,815 | 6,927 | 0.4 | 2.56 | 4,930 | 4,935 | 0.0 | 38,754 | 45,614 | 775 | 31 |
| MONROE | 8,189 | 10,261 | 11,466 | 2.8 | 2.69 | 6,242 | 7,499 | 2.2 | 52,378 | 62,924 | 162 | 10 |
| MONTGOMERY | 11,480 | 11,560 | 11,503 | 0.1 | 2.49 | 8,264 | 8,041 | -0.3 | 34,110 | 40,253 | 1374 | 63 |
| MORGAN | 13,678 | 13,211 | 12,797 | -0.4 | 2.41 | 9,283 | 8,607 | -0.9 | 37,502 | 44,833 | 898 | 40 |
| MOULTRIE | 5,122 | 5,374 | 5,530 | 0.6 | 2.62 | 3,862 | 3,929 | 0.2 | 37,907 | 45,488 | 855 | 36 |
| OGLE | 17,132 | 19,277 | 20,086 | 1.4 | 2.63 | 12,774 | 13,972 | 1.1 | 42,815 | 51,631 | 466 | 18 |
| PEORIA | 70,797 | 70,504 | 69,893 | -0.1 | 2.47 | 47,815 | 45,726 | -0.5 | 40,940 | 44,552 | 593 | 24 |
| PERRY | 8,306 | 8,181 | 8,185 | -0.2 | 2.55 | 6,019 | 5,739 | -0.6 | 30,442 | 35,258 | 2048 | 84 |
| PIATT | 5,934 | 6,356 | 6,578 | 0.8 | 2.60 | 4,500 | 4,651 | 0.4 | 41,724 | 47,294 | 534 | 19 |
| PIKE | 7,016 | 6,978 | 6,976 | -0.1 | 2.42 | 4,999 | 4,777 | -0.5 | 29,738 | 37,511 | 2194 | 88 |
| POPE | 1,611 | 1,820 | 1,918 | 1.5 | 2.40 | 1,158 | 1,261 | 1.0 | 26,775 | 32,695 | 2612 | 95 |
| PULASKI | 2,957 | 2,833 | 2,830 | -0.5 | 2.56 | 2,025 | 1,868 | -1.0 | 24,451 | 29,040 | 2858 | 98 |
| ILLINOIS | | | | 0.8 | 2.64 | | | 0.5 | 46,248 | 53,055 | | |
| UNITED STATES | | | | 1.4 | 2.59 | | | 1.1 | 41,914 | 49,127 | | |

| COUNTY | 2000 Per Capita Income | 2000 HH Income Base | 2000 HOUSEHOLD INCOME DISTRIBUTION (%) | | | | | | 2000 AVERAGE DISPOSABLE INCOME BY AGE OF HOUSEHOLDER | | | | | |
|---|---|---|---|---|---|---|---|---|---|---|---|---|---|---|
| | | | Less than $15,000 | $15,000 to $24,999 | $25,000 to $49,999 | $50,000 to $99,999 | $100,000 to $149,999 | $150,000 or More | All Ages | <35 | 35-44 | 45-54 | 55-64 | 65+ |
| ADAMS | 17,119 | 25,989 | 18.3 | 16.3 | 36.9 | 23.3 | 4.0 | 1.1 | 31,827 | 28,460 | 37,153 | 40,597 | 34,350 | 22,086 |
| ALEXANDER | 12,733 | 3,845 | 38.0 | 17.6 | 28.6 | 12.4 | 2.7 | 0.7 | 23,574 | 20,583 | 26,717 | 26,922 | 30,157 | 17,469 |
| BOND | 15,483 | 5,972 | 16.9 | 13.4 | 42.0 | 23.5 | 3.6 | 0.7 | 31,715 | 30,641 | 37,468 | 39,674 | 33,498 | 21,683 |
| BOONE | 24,273 | 14,542 | 6.4 | 6.7 | 32.2 | 39.8 | 11.8 | 3.2 | 47,160 | 40,983 | 49,822 | 59,311 | 51,641 | 28,287 |
| BROWN | 15,151 | 2,076 | 16.9 | 19.5 | 37.3 | 20.7 | 4.3 | 1.3 | 31,161 | 30,507 | 38,216 | 40,525 | 33,549 | 19,868 |
| BUREAU | 17,642 | 13,766 | 15.1 | 13.6 | 38.6 | 27.9 | 4.0 | 0.8 | 33,617 | 31,496 | 40,046 | 42,558 | 36,239 | 22,423 |
| CALHOUN | 15,762 | 1,926 | 22.3 | 14.9 | 36.1 | 23.4 | 2.6 | 0.8 | 29,702 | 29,423 | 37,455 | 42,919 | 30,460 | 18,217 |
| CARROLL | 18,353 | 6,773 | 17.0 | 16.9 | 40.0 | 21.0 | 4.1 | 1.1 | 31,374 | 28,952 | 35,702 | 40,266 | 34,179 | 21,948 |
| CASS | 15,249 | 5,158 | 20.3 | 15.3 | 39.0 | 22.0 | 2.7 | 0.7 | 29,918 | 27,370 | 34,742 | 37,706 | 32,218 | 20,689 |
| CHAMPAIGN | 18,691 | 63,574 | 17.9 | 15.0 | 34.1 | 25.9 | 5.2 | 1.9 | 34,795 | 24,724 | 39,627 | 46,204 | 43,982 | 28,518 |
| CHRISTIAN | 16,820 | 13,713 | 17.6 | 15.7 | 37.0 | 24.6 | 3.8 | 1.3 | 32,208 | 29,686 | 38,058 | 43,362 | 35,407 | 19,714 |
| CLARK | 16,989 | 6,766 | 15.4 | 17.0 | 39.1 | 24.8 | 3.1 | 0.7 | 31,490 | 29,622 | 37,348 | 39,197 | 33,772 | 22,516 |
| CLAY | 14,242 | 5,789 | 21.9 | 20.0 | 39.1 | 16.6 | 2.2 | 0.1 | 26,743 | 26,635 | 32,301 | 33,616 | 27,692 | 17,951 |
| CLINTON | 16,739 | 12,329 | 13.5 | 11.1 | 39.4 | 30.8 | 4.6 | 0.7 | 35,226 | 33,805 | 41,283 | 42,434 | 39,080 | 22,922 |
| COLES | 17,346 | 19,053 | 18.7 | 15.7 | 36.3 | 23.0 | 4.4 | 1.9 | 33,197 | 25,998 | 38,467 | 46,175 | 38,789 | 22,317 |
| COOK | 24,262 | 1,922,799 | 13.2 | 10.7 | 30.7 | 32.0 | 9.0 | 4.5 | 43,648 | 38,450 | 45,406 | 51,853 | 47,752 | 29,603 |
| CRAWFORD | 15,181 | 7,952 | 19.4 | 18.4 | 38.4 | 20.3 | 2.7 | 0.9 | 29,317 | 25,659 | 35,700 | 36,974 | 33,199 | 20,407 |
| CUMBERLAND | 16,124 | 4,237 | 16.4 | 17.4 | 35.8 | 25.8 | 3.8 | 0.8 | 32,157 | 32,231 | 36,510 | 41,343 | 33,614 | 21,192 |
| DEKALB | 20,141 | 30,368 | 11.8 | 9.5 | 34.5 | 33.8 | 7.8 | 2.7 | 40,899 | 31,451 | 45,784 | 54,069 | 48,602 | 29,265 |
| DE WITT | 20,174 | 6,644 | 13.9 | 12.6 | 36.8 | 28.9 | 6.3 | 1.6 | 36,231 | 32,968 | 42,880 | 45,076 | 40,665 | 22,982 |
| DOUGLAS | 16,352 | 7,456 | 14.2 | 14.3 | 40.2 | 27.6 | 3.2 | 0.6 | 32,911 | 30,528 | 37,612 | 41,000 | 37,806 | 22,510 |
| DUPAGE | 33,795 | 324,637 | 3.7 | 4.1 | 22.2 | 44.0 | 17.2 | 8.9 | 60,991 | 50,947 | 60,111 | 70,422 | 65,750 | 38,235 |
| EDGAR | 17,976 | 7,912 | 20.0 | 18.5 | 36.3 | 20.4 | 3.4 | 1.5 | 30,315 | 25,360 | 36,780 | 37,352 | 34,591 | 21,277 |
| EDWARDS | 14,432 | 2,795 | 25.0 | 17.9 | 38.9 | 15.3 | 2.3 | 0.7 | 26,944 | 25,051 | 34,263 | 30,767 | 28,331 | 19,696 |
| EFFINGHAM | 17,546 | 12,349 | 14.5 | 14.0 | 38.1 | 27.7 | 4.2 | 1.5 | 34,947 | 30,822 | 40,058 | 44,637 | 39,582 | 22,306 |
| FAYETTE | 16,424 | 8,098 | 18.5 | 15.6 | 38.8 | 23.0 | 3.5 | 0.6 | 30,715 | 29,627 | 34,500 | 40,555 | 30,408 | 22,015 |
| FORD | 17,268 | 5,549 | 14.1 | 15.1 | 40.3 | 26.8 | 3.1 | 0.8 | 32,754 | 29,199 | 38,674 | 41,899 | 36,457 | 23,188 |
| FRANKLIN | 14,054 | 16,667 | 29.8 | 18.2 | 31.9 | 17.2 | 2.2 | 0.7 | 25,926 | 23,623 | 32,349 | 34,949 | 26,378 | 17,376 |
| FULTON | 15,886 | 14,896 | 19.9 | 18.2 | 36.8 | 21.5 | 3.0 | 0.7 | 29,464 | 25,849 | 36,856 | 37,872 | 30,872 | 21,037 |
| GALLATIN | 13,073 | 2,677 | 32.5 | 20.2 | 32.2 | 12.9 | 1.1 | 1.2 | 24,070 | 24,433 | 28,215 | 29,841 | 23,305 | 16,122 |
| GREENE | 14,490 | 6,068 | 21.5 | 17.7 | 38.7 | 19.1 | 2.4 | 0.6 | 28,069 | 26,466 | 34,291 | 36,456 | 29,338 | 19,342 |
| GRUNDY | 23,754 | 14,105 | 9.0 | 6.2 | 28.3 | 43.4 | 10.7 | 2.4 | 45,296 | 41,870 | 50,791 | 55,660 | 48,656 | 28,194 |
| HAMILTON | 15,740 | 3,562 | 25.9 | 18.0 | 35.4 | 16.1 | 3.3 | 1.2 | 27,724 | 27,110 | 34,111 | 31,991 | 32,197 | 19,730 |
| HANCOCK | 17,288 | 8,326 | 15.7 | 14.6 | 40.3 | 25.4 | 3.2 | 0.8 | 32,083 | 30,638 | 36,584 | 40,778 | 35,040 | 22,728 |
| HARDIN | 12,268 | 1,908 | 32.6 | 18.8 | 31.8 | 14.0 | 2.2 | 0.7 | 24,544 | 22,125 | 29,162 | 32,728 | 25,774 | 16,528 |
| HENDERSON | 16,112 | 3,498 | 18.0 | 17.1 | 37.7 | 23.6 | 2.8 | 0.8 | 30,579 | 27,331 | 35,136 | 43,052 | 29,434 | 20,638 |
| HENRY | 18,631 | 19,847 | 14.0 | 14.3 | 36.6 | 28.9 | 4.8 | 1.4 | 35,082 | 30,484 | 40,487 | 47,150 | 38,434 | 22,345 |
| IROQUOIS | 17,162 | 11,997 | 13.3 | 15.7 | 39.2 | 27.4 | 3.6 | 0.8 | 33,192 | 32,048 | 38,421 | 42,647 | 34,257 | 23,348 |
| JACKSON | 14,832 | 23,545 | 31.6 | 16.9 | 29.0 | 17.7 | 3.4 | 1.4 | 27,797 | 18,764 | 34,025 | 41,348 | 37,530 | 21,540 |
| JASPER | 15,992 | 4,011 | 14.4 | 17.8 | 37.4 | 25.9 | 4.0 | 0.6 | 32,108 | 28,581 | 38,255 | 42,207 | 35,097 | 21,958 |
| JEFFERSON | 15,318 | 14,873 | 24.6 | 16.2 | 35.5 | 19.0 | 3.4 | 1.3 | 29,295 | 25,961 | 37,412 | 36,522 | 28,949 | 18,565 |
| JERSEY | 17,709 | 7,802 | 12.9 | 11.9 | 40.9 | 27.8 | 4.9 | 1.5 | 35,771 | 32,898 | 39,520 | 45,933 | 40,146 | 22,991 |
| JO DAVIESS | 18,143 | 8,241 | 12.7 | 16.2 | 37.9 | 27.5 | 4.5 | 1.3 | 34,353 | 31,650 | 39,845 | 45,337 | 37,562 | 22,874 |
| JOHNSON | 13,846 | 4,391 | 20.7 | 16.0 | 35.5 | 23.8 | 3.0 | 0.9 | 30,364 | 28,672 | 37,490 | 40,905 | 30,221 | 18,724 |
| KANE | 26,505 | 139,926 | 6.5 | 6.5 | 27.5 | 39.9 | 13.6 | 6.0 | 52,482 | 43,536 | 54,560 | 62,678 | 56,202 | 31,809 |
| KANKAKEE | 19,833 | 37,367 | 14.6 | 11.4 | 35.3 | 29.9 | 6.5 | 2.3 | 38,028 | 33,064 | 43,160 | 49,563 | 38,779 | 24,720 |
| KENDALL | 26,245 | 19,050 | 5.3 | 3.0 | 26.0 | 46.8 | 14.3 | 4.5 | 52,746 | 47,451 | 54,894 | 62,623 | 57,155 | 32,620 |
| KNOX | 17,056 | 21,411 | 18.2 | 15.9 | 38.0 | 23.4 | 3.6 | 1.0 | 31,375 | 26,545 | 36,905 | 40,357 | 34,814 | 22,080 |
| LAKE | 39,938 | 216,082 | 5.0 | 4.8 | 22.8 | 35.8 | 16.3 | 15.3 | 70,307 | 51,331 | 66,239 | 74,828 | 70,345 | 44,955 |
| LA SALLE | 18,587 | 42,880 | 15.6 | 12.7 | 36.8 | 28.7 | 5.0 | 1.3 | 34,846 | 32,744 | 40,846 | 44,541 | 37,592 | 22,886 |
| LAWRENCE | 16,467 | 6,028 | 20.9 | 20.2 | 35.8 | 19.6 | 2.7 | 0.9 | 28,663 | 25,706 | 33,537 | 36,912 | 30,819 | 21,113 |
| LEE | 17,026 | 12,980 | 12.4 | 13.6 | 40.1 | 29.1 | 3.9 | 0.9 | 34,212 | 31,543 | 39,451 | 42,797 | 36,629 | 23,619 |
| LIVINGSTON | 19,145 | 14,042 | 10.6 | 10.7 | 38.7 | 32.0 | 6.4 | 1.6 | 38,388 | 33,301 | 44,027 | 46,587 | 42,371 | 28,369 |
| LOGAN | 15,704 | 10,916 | 15.0 | 14.3 | 39.4 | 27.2 | 3.4 | 0.8 | 32,967 | 30,403 | 37,363 | 43,376 | 35,694 | 22,616 |
| MCDONOUGH | 15,037 | 12,325 | 22.8 | 14.6 | 36.5 | 22.3 | 3.0 | 0.9 | 29,999 | 23,289 | 35,735 | 42,230 | 34,971 | 20,930 |
| MCHENRY | 29,566 | 87,179 | 4.6 | 4.0 | 23.0 | 44.2 | 17.1 | 7.1 | 57,674 | 51,129 | 58,403 | 68,067 | 60,503 | 33,402 |
| MCLEAN | 25,661 | 53,941 | 9.9 | 9.5 | 31.0 | 35.0 | 10.1 | 4.5 | 45,788 | 35,878 | 51,076 | 59,244 | 50,031 | 31,432 |
| MACON | 19,703 | 44,547 | 17.4 | 13.7 | 35.2 | 26.7 | 4.9 | 2.2 | 35,281 | 28,424 | 40,850 | 44,633 | 38,871 | 24,442 |
| MACOUPIN | 17,449 | 18,768 | 18.0 | 15.9 | 39.0 | 22.6 | 3.5 | 1.1 | 31,416 | 28,329 | 36,980 | 41,673 | 34,933 | 20,108 |
| MADISON | 19,418 | 99,999 | 15.1 | 12.2 | 35.5 | 29.7 | 5.9 | 1.6 | 36,288 | 31,761 | 41,197 | 47,165 | 40,246 | 22,886 |
| MARION | 17,060 | 16,451 | 22.2 | 17.4 | 36.1 | 19.4 | 3.5 | 1.5 | 30,220 | 26,874 | 35,301 | 39,562 | 31,883 | 19,160 |
| MARSHALL | 17,976 | 4,972 | 14.3 | 15.3 | 36.5 | 28.3 | 4.4 | 1.2 | 33,988 | 31,729 | 40,881 | 44,717 | 36,573 | 22,430 |
| MASON | 16,224 | 6,642 | 18.9 | 19.1 | 37.0 | 21.5 | 2.6 | 0.8 | 29,728 | 24,889 | 35,561 | 37,705 | 32,723 | 20,414 |
| MASSAC | 14,492 | 6,390 | 26.3 | 15.3 | 35.5 | 20.3 | 2.4 | 0.3 | 27,268 | 25,822 | 32,649 | 36,347 | 26,650 | 18,334 |
| MENARD | 20,778 | 4,800 | 11.5 | 10.2 | 35.3 | 33.5 | 7.4 | 2.1 | 39,542 | 36,091 | 43,854 | 47,858 | 41,900 | 27,263 |
| MERCER | 18,302 | 6,815 | 13.3 | 14.6 | 37.2 | 28.6 | 5.0 | 1.3 | 35,064 | 31,904 | 41,011 | 44,524 | 35,804 | 24,198 |
| MONROE | 23,124 | 10,261 | 7.1 | 8.4 | 30.7 | 41.7 | 9.8 | 2.2 | 44,913 | 42,651 | 49,170 | 58,162 | 47,838 | 26,327 |
| MONTGOMERY | 15,532 | 11,560 | 19.7 | 14.2 | 39.3 | 22.9 | 3.2 | 0.8 | 30,608 | 29,585 | 36,495 | 36,876 | 34,568 | 20,935 |
| MORGAN | 18,510 | 13,211 | 14.4 | 14.2 | 37.2 | 27.7 | 5.1 | 1.5 | 34,943 | 30,779 | 41,370 | 44,576 | 38,554 | 24,084 |
| MOULTRIE | 17,458 | 5,374 | 14.6 | 13.5 | 37.9 | 27.5 | 5.0 | 1.5 | 34,744 | 32,769 | 40,738 | 43,979 | 35,303 | 23,157 |
| OGLE | 18,539 | 19,277 | 10.1 | 11.1 | 39.2 | 34.0 | 4.8 | 0.8 | 36,854 | 34,252 | 42,458 | 44,632 | 39,048 | 24,714 |
| PEORIA | 21,328 | 70,500 | 16.1 | 12.9 | 31.9 | 29.5 | 6.9 | 2.6 | 38,111 | 30,677 | 43,292 | 48,829 | 41,813 | 25,729 |
| PERRY | 13,720 | 8,181 | 23.5 | 17.3 | 37.9 | 19.1 | 1.6 | 0.6 | 27,386 | 24,288 | 35,368 | 33,308 | 29,982 | 18,031 |
| PIATT | 19,841 | 6,356 | 8.9 | 12.5 | 41.5 | 29.9 | 5.7 | 1.6 | 37,457 | 31,827 | 42,356 | 48,230 | 42,023 | 26,233 |
| PIKE | 15,120 | 6,978 | 21.9 | 18.4 | 37.7 | 19.2 | 2.2 | 0.7 | 28,137 | 26,262 | 31,794 | 35,497 | 31,859 | 20,509 |
| POPE | 12,053 | 1,820 | 30.3 | 15.8 | 37.4 | 14.8 | 1.7 | 0.1 | 24,691 | 21,716 | 28,180 | 33,580 | 27,833 | 16,255 |
| PULASKI | 12,033 | 2,833 | 34.4 | 16.7 | 32.5 | 13.9 | 1.8 | 0.7 | 24,215 | 23,560 | 30,059 | 31,863 | 25,801 | 15,436 |
| ILLINOIS | 24,170 | | 12.6 | 10.6 | 31.0 | 32.3 | 9.1 | 4.4 | 43,984 | 37,679 | 47,254 | 53,608 | 47,357 | 28,025 |
| UNITED STATES | 22,162 | | 14.5 | 12.5 | 32.3 | 29.8 | 7.4 | 3.5 | 40,748 | 34,503 | 44,969 | 49,579 | 43,409 | 27,339 |

| COUNTY | FINANCIAL SERVICES | | | | THE HOME: Home Improvements | | | THE HOME: Furnishings | | | ENTERTAINMENT | | | | | | PERSONAL | | | |
|---|---|---|---|---|---|---|---|---|---|---|---|---|---|---|---|---|---|---|---|---|
| | Auto Loan | Home Loan | Investments | Retirement Plans | Home Repair | Lawn & Garden | Remodeling | Appliances | Electronics | Furniture | Restaurants | Sporting Goods | Theater & Concerts | Toys & Hobbies | Travel | Video Rental | Apparel | Auto Aftermarket | Health Insurance | Pets & Supplies |
| ADAMS | 97 | 88 | 98 | 93 | 102 | 98 | 104 | 97 | 94 | 92 | 94 | 95 | 97 | 98 | 94 | 100 | 91 | 96 | 102 | 98 |
| ALEXANDER | 91 | 66 | 71 | 71 | 93 | 86 | 96 | 93 | 86 | 79 | 73 | 87 | 80 | 87 | 79 | 98 | 78 | 87 | 93 | 90 |
| BOND | 97 | 74 | 80 | 81 | 94 | 91 | 109 | 96 | 92 | 82 | 85 | 94 | 87 | 96 | 81 | 100 | 83 | 91 | 102 | 97 |
| BOONE | 101 | 98 | 94 | 100 | 99 | 98 | 106 | 100 | 100 | 99 | 103 | 102 | 102 | 103 | 95 | 103 | 99 | 102 | 101 | 103 |
| BROWN | 95 | 66 | 74 | 77 | 91 | 90 | 109 | 94 | 91 | 75 | 79 | 90 | 81 | 92 | 77 | 100 | 78 | 89 | 104 | 94 |
| BUREAU | 97 | 79 | 87 | 86 | 97 | 94 | 107 | 97 | 92 | 86 | 89 | 95 | 91 | 98 | 86 | 101 | 86 | 93 | 103 | 98 |
| CALHOUN | 97 | 64 | 69 | 78 | 91 | 90 | 111 | 96 | 91 | 73 | 78 | 95 | 81 | 95 | 75 | 100 | 77 | 89 | 105 | 96 |
| CARROLL | 97 | 71 | 78 | 82 | 94 | 92 | 108 | 96 | 90 | 79 | 83 | 94 | 86 | 96 | 81 | 100 | 81 | 91 | 104 | 97 |
| CASS | 97 | 74 | 80 | 82 | 95 | 91 | 109 | 96 | 92 | 82 | 85 | 94 | 87 | 96 | 81 | 100 | 83 | 91 | 103 | 97 |
| CHAMPAIGN | 97 | 99 | 98 | 97 | 99 | 97 | 99 | 95 | 96 | 94 | 99 | 96 | 97 | 98 | 96 | 100 | 95 | 99 | 98 | 99 |
| CHRISTIAN | 97 | 78 | 85 | 85 | 96 | 93 | 107 | 96 | 93 | 85 | 88 | 93 | 90 | 96 | 85 | 101 | 85 | 93 | 103 | 97 |
| CLARK | 98 | 72 | 78 | 82 | 94 | 91 | 111 | 96 | 92 | 80 | 84 | 95 | 86 | 97 | 80 | 101 | 82 | 91 | 104 | 98 |
| CLAY | 97 | 71 | 79 | 80 | 94 | 92 | 108 | 96 | 91 | 80 | 83 | 93 | 86 | 95 | 80 | 100 | 81 | 90 | 103 | 96 |
| CLINTON | 99 | 84 | 87 | 88 | 97 | 94 | 108 | 98 | 94 | 89 | 93 | 97 | 94 | 100 | 87 | 101 | 89 | 95 | 102 | 100 |
| COLES | 96 | 86 | 92 | 89 | 98 | 94 | 103 | 94 | 92 | 87 | 91 | 93 | 92 | 96 | 89 | 99 | 87 | 94 | 100 | 97 |
| COOK | 98 | 108 | 107 | 103 | 106 | 104 | 94 | 99 | 99 | 105 | 103 | 100 | 106 | 98 | 108 | 103 | 102 | 105 | 97 | 100 |
| CRAWFORD | 97 | 77 | 83 | 83 | 96 | 93 | 108 | 96 | 92 | 85 | 87 | 94 | 89 | 97 | 84 | 100 | 84 | 92 | 102 | 97 |
| CUMBERLAND | 98 | 74 | 79 | 82 | 93 | 91 | 113 | 96 | 94 | 82 | 86 | 94 | 87 | 97 | 80 | 101 | 83 | 92 | 102 | 98 |
| DEKALB | 97 | 94 | 95 | 94 | 98 | 95 | 102 | 95 | 95 | 92 | 97 | 95 | 95 | 98 | 92 | 99 | 93 | 97 | 99 | 99 |
| DE WITT | 99 | 77 | 83 | 84 | 95 | 92 | 111 | 97 | 93 | 84 | 88 | 96 | 89 | 99 | 82 | 101 | 85 | 93 | 103 | 99 |
| DOUGLAS | 99 | 80 | 85 | 86 | 96 | 93 | 110 | 98 | 94 | 87 | 90 | 96 | 92 | 99 | 85 | 101 | 88 | 94 | 102 | 100 |
| DUPAGE | 105 | 122 | 109 | 118 | 107 | 112 | 103 | 105 | 110 | 115 | 122 | 110 | 118 | 109 | 113 | 106 | 118 | 115 | 103 | 107 |
| EDGAR | 96 | 70 | 77 | 79 | 94 | 91 | 107 | 95 | 91 | 79 | 82 | 92 | 85 | 94 | 80 | 100 | 80 | 90 | 103 | 96 |
| EDWARDS | 98 | 69 | 74 | 80 | 92 | 90 | 113 | 97 | 93 | 78 | 82 | 96 | 84 | 97 | 77 | 100 | 81 | 91 | 104 | 98 |
| EFFINGHAM | 99 | 82 | 85 | 88 | 95 | 93 | 110 | 98 | 96 | 88 | 92 | 96 | 92 | 99 | 85 | 102 | 89 | 95 | 101 | 100 |
| FAYETTE | 95 | 69 | 75 | 78 | 94 | 91 | 107 | 95 | 91 | 79 | 81 | 92 | 84 | 93 | 79 | 99 | 80 | 89 | 103 | 95 |
| FORD | 96 | 76 | 83 | 83 | 95 | 93 | 104 | 95 | 92 | 83 | 86 | 93 | 89 | 96 | 84 | 100 | 84 | 92 | 103 | 96 |
| FRANKLIN | 94 | 69 | 75 | 77 | 93 | 90 | 106 | 94 | 92 | 78 | 81 | 88 | 82 | 91 | 79 | 100 | 79 | 89 | 102 | 94 |
| FULTON | 95 | 76 | 85 | 82 | 97 | 94 | 103 | 95 | 90 | 84 | 86 | 91 | 89 | 94 | 86 | 99 | 83 | 91 | 102 | 95 |
| GALLATIN | 94 | 64 | 71 | 74 | 91 | 89 | 106 | 93 | 91 | 75 | 78 | 87 | 79 | 90 | 76 | 100 | 77 | 88 | 103 | 93 |
| GREENE | 95 | 66 | 73 | 77 | 92 | 90 | 107 | 94 | 91 | 76 | 80 | 91 | 82 | 92 | 78 | 99 | 78 | 89 | 103 | 94 |
| GRUNDY | 100 | 94 | 95 | 96 | 100 | 98 | 106 | 99 | 98 | 98 | 100 | 99 | 100 | 102 | 94 | 102 | 96 | 100 | 101 | 101 |
| HAMILTON | 95 | 66 | 75 | 77 | 92 | 90 | 106 | 94 | 92 | 76 | 79 | 90 | 81 | 91 | 78 | 100 | 78 | 89 | 103 | 94 |
| HANCOCK | 98 | 71 | 78 | 82 | 92 | 90 | 111 | 96 | 92 | 79 | 84 | 95 | 85 | 96 | 79 | 100 | 82 | 91 | 104 | 98 |
| HARDIN | 93 | 64 | 70 | 74 | 91 | 89 | 106 | 93 | 91 | 75 | 78 | 87 | 79 | 89 | 76 | 99 | 76 | 88 | 103 | 92 |
| HENDERSON | 98 | 68 | 74 | 81 | 92 | 90 | 113 | 96 | 92 | 77 | 81 | 95 | 83 | 96 | 77 | 100 | 80 | 90 | 104 | 98 |
| HENRY | 97 | 82 | 86 | 88 | 97 | 94 | 105 | 97 | 94 | 88 | 90 | 95 | 93 | 97 | 87 | 101 | 87 | 94 | 102 | 98 |
| IROQUOIS | 99 | 75 | 82 | 85 | 95 | 92 | 112 | 97 | 93 | 83 | 86 | 96 | 88 | 98 | 82 | 101 | 85 | 92 | 104 | 99 |
| JACKSON | 94 | 90 | 95 | 92 | 97 | 93 | 102 | 91 | 91 | 84 | 89 | 90 | 89 | 93 | 89 | 97 | 87 | 93 | 98 | 96 |
| JASPER | 97 | 69 | 76 | 80 | 92 | 90 | 111 | 95 | 92 | 78 | 82 | 93 | 83 | 95 | 78 | 100 | 80 | 90 | 104 | 97 |
| JEFFERSON | 97 | 80 | 88 | 86 | 97 | 94 | 106 | 97 | 93 | 87 | 88 | 94 | 91 | 96 | 87 | 100 | 86 | 93 | 100 | 97 |
| JERSEY | 97 | 79 | 86 | 86 | 96 | 94 | 108 | 97 | 94 | 86 | 89 | 94 | 91 | 97 | 85 | 101 | 86 | 93 | 103 | 98 |
| JO DAVIESS | 98 | 77 | 84 | 85 | 97 | 94 | 111 | 97 | 91 | 84 | 87 | 96 | 90 | 98 | 85 | 101 | 85 | 92 | 104 | 99 |
| JOHNSON | 97 | 70 | 75 | 81 | 92 | 90 | 114 | 96 | 93 | 78 | 82 | 94 | 84 | 96 | 78 | 101 | 81 | 91 | 104 | 98 |
| KANE | 102 | 112 | 103 | 109 | 103 | 105 | 100 | 102 | 105 | 107 | 112 | 105 | 110 | 105 | 105 | 104 | 107 | 108 | 101 | 104 |
| KANKAKEE | 96 | 90 | 93 | 91 | 99 | 95 | 100 | 97 | 95 | 94 | 94 | 95 | 96 | 97 | 93 | 101 | 92 | 97 | 98 | 98 |
| KENDALL | 103 | 106 | 98 | 105 | 101 | 102 | 104 | 102 | 106 | 107 | 112 | 105 | 109 | 107 | 100 | 105 | 108 | 109 | 101 | 105 |
| KNOX | 96 | 85 | 95 | 89 | 101 | 97 | 103 | 96 | 92 | 90 | 91 | 94 | 95 | 96 | 92 | 99 | 88 | 94 | 101 | 97 |
| LAKE | 106 | 125 | 116 | 125 | 110 | 117 | 107 | 106 | 111 | 116 | 123 | 112 | 122 | 110 | 118 | 106 | 121 | 117 | 105 | 107 |
| LA SALLE | 97 | 85 | 92 | 88 | 100 | 96 | 104 | 97 | 93 | 91 | 93 | 94 | 95 | 98 | 91 | 100 | 89 | 95 | 102 | 98 |
| LAWRENCE | 96 | 71 | 79 | 80 | 94 | 91 | 107 | 95 | 92 | 80 | 83 | 92 | 85 | 94 | 81 | 100 | 81 | 90 | 103 | 96 |
| LEE | 97 | 82 | 87 | 87 | 98 | 94 | 106 | 97 | 93 | 88 | 91 | 95 | 93 | 98 | 87 | 100 | 88 | 94 | 102 | 98 |
| LIVINGSTON | 98 | 80 | 87 | 87 | 97 | 94 | 109 | 97 | 93 | 86 | 89 | 96 | 91 | 98 | 86 | 101 | 87 | 94 | 102 | 99 |
| LOGAN | 96 | 80 | 88 | 85 | 97 | 94 | 105 | 96 | 92 | 86 | 89 | 93 | 91 | 96 | 86 | 100 | 86 | 93 | 102 | 97 |
| MCDONOUGH | 96 | 83 | 91 | 90 | 97 | 94 | 105 | 94 | 92 | 84 | 88 | 93 | 90 | 95 | 87 | 98 | 86 | 93 | 102 | 97 |
| MCHENRY | 104 | 111 | 101 | 109 | 103 | 105 | 104 | 104 | 107 | 110 | 116 | 107 | 112 | 108 | 104 | 105 | 112 | 111 | 102 | 106 |
| MCLEAN | 99 | 98 | 95 | 98 | 99 | 97 | 102 | 97 | 98 | 96 | 100 | 98 | 98 | 100 | 95 | 101 | 96 | 100 | 99 | 100 |
| MACON | 97 | 91 | 95 | 92 | 100 | 97 | 100 | 98 | 95 | 95 | 96 | 96 | 98 | 98 | 94 | 101 | 93 | 98 | 99 | 98 |
| MACOUPIN | 97 | 78 | 86 | 85 | 97 | 94 | 107 | 96 | 92 | 85 | 88 | 93 | 90 | 96 | 86 | 100 | 85 | 92 | 103 | 97 |
| MADISON | 97 | 92 | 98 | 92 | 102 | 98 | 99 | 97 | 94 | 96 | 97 | 95 | 99 | 99 | 96 | 100 | 93 | 97 | 100 | 98 |
| MARION | 97 | 78 | 88 | 87 | 98 | 95 | 107 | 97 | 93 | 86 | 87 | 95 | 91 | 96 | 86 | 100 | 86 | 93 | 102 | 98 |
| MARSHALL | 97 | 75 | 82 | 83 | 97 | 93 | 106 | 96 | 89 | 83 | 86 | 94 | 89 | 97 | 84 | 100 | 83 | 91 | 104 | 97 |
| MASON | 97 | 72 | 77 | 81 | 94 | 91 | 108 | 96 | 92 | 81 | 84 | 94 | 86 | 95 | 80 | 100 | 82 | 91 | 103 | 97 |
| MASSAC | 96 | 74 | 79 | 81 | 94 | 91 | 107 | 95 | 93 | 82 | 84 | 92 | 87 | 95 | 81 | 100 | 82 | 91 | 102 | 96 |
| MENARD | 99 | 84 | 87 | 90 | 96 | 94 | 109 | 98 | 97 | 89 | 93 | 97 | 94 | 100 | 87 | 103 | 90 | 97 | 103 | 100 |
| MERCER | 98 | 75 | 81 | 85 | 94 | 92 | 108 | 96 | 93 | 82 | 86 | 95 | 88 | 97 | 82 | 101 | 84 | 92 | 104 | 98 |
| MONROE | 99 | 92 | 94 | 93 | 99 | 97 | 103 | 98 | 97 | 96 | 99 | 98 | 100 | 102 | 93 | 102 | 96 | 99 | 101 | 100 |
| MONTGOMERY | 96 | 73 | 80 | 81 | 93 | 91 | 106 | 95 | 92 | 80 | 84 | 92 | 86 | 94 | 81 | 100 | 81 | 91 | 103 | 96 |
| MORGAN | 97 | 87 | 93 | 91 | 98 | 96 | 104 | 97 | 95 | 91 | 93 | 95 | 95 | 98 | 90 | 101 | 90 | 96 | 101 | 99 |
| MOULTRIE | 99 | 75 | 80 | 84 | 94 | 91 | 113 | 97 | 93 | 82 | 86 | 96 | 88 | 99 | 81 | 101 | 85 | 93 | 103 | 100 |
| OGLE | 98 | 84 | 88 | 87 | 98 | 94 | 106 | 97 | 93 | 89 | 92 | 95 | 93 | 99 | 88 | 101 | 89 | 94 | 102 | 99 |
| PEORIA | 96 | 94 | 99 | 94 | 102 | 99 | 98 | 97 | 94 | 97 | 97 | 95 | 99 | 98 | 97 | 100 | 94 | 98 | 99 | 98 |
| PERRY | 97 | 72 | 77 | 80 | 93 | 90 | 111 | 96 | 93 | 81 | 83 | 94 | 85 | 95 | 79 | 100 | 82 | 91 | 102 | 97 |
| PIATT | 99 | 87 | 93 | 92 | 99 | 97 | 107 | 99 | 96 | 91 | 95 | 98 | 96 | 101 | 90 | 102 | 91 | 97 | 103 | 100 |
| PIKE | 97 | 68 | 74 | 79 | 92 | 90 | 110 | 95 | 91 | 76 | 81 | 93 | 83 | 95 | 77 | 100 | 79 | 90 | 104 | 96 |
| POPE | 94 | 67 | 74 | 77 | 92 | 90 | 107 | 94 | 92 | 77 | 80 | 88 | 81 | 91 | 78 | 100 | 78 | 89 | 103 | 94 |
| PULASKI | 92 | 67 | 73 | 74 | 92 | 89 | 102 | 93 | 90 | 78 | 78 | 85 | 80 | 88 | 79 | 99 | 77 | 88 | 99 | 92 |
| ILLINOIS | 99 | 103 | 103 | 103 | 103 | 103 | 99 | 100 | 100 | 102 | 103 | 100 | 105 | 100 | 103 | 103 | 101 | 104 | 100 | 101 |
| UNITED STATES | 100 | 100 | 100 | 100 | 100 | 100 | 100 | 100 | 100 | 100 | 100 | 100 | 100 | 100 | 100 | 100 | 100 | 100 | 100 | 100 |

# POPULATION CHANGE

| COUNTY | FIPS Code | MSA Code | DMA Code | POPULATION 1990 | POPULATION 2000 | POPULATION 2005 | 1990-2000 ANNUAL CHANGE % Rate | 1990-2000 ANNUAL CHANGE State Rank | RACE (%) White 1990 | White 2000 | Black 1990 | Black 2000 | Asian/Pacific 1990 | Asian/Pacific 2000 |
|---|---|---|---|---|---|---|---|---|---|---|---|---|---|---|
| PUTNAM | 155 | 0000 | 675 | 5,730 | 5,896 | 6,088 | 0.3 | 38 | 98.0 | 97.3 | 0.2 | 0.2 | 0.1 | 0.2 |
| RANDOLPH | 157 | 0000 | 609 | 34,583 | 33,467 | 32,772 | -0.3 | 89 | 91.2 | 91.0 | 8.2 | 8.3 | 0.2 | 0.3 |
| RICHLAND | 159 | 0000 | 581 | 16,545 | 16,587 | 16,258 | 0.0 | 61 | 99.4 | 99.2 | 0.1 | 0.1 | 0.3 | 0.3 |
| ROCK ISLAND | 161 | 1960 | 682 | 148,723 | 147,176 | 145,463 | -0.1 | 67 | 89.7 | 87.8 | 7.1 | 7.7 | 0.7 | 0.9 |
| ST. CLAIR | 163 | 7040 | 609 | 262,852 | 258,626 | 251,465 | -0.2 | 82 | 71.5 | 68.8 | 27.1 | 29.4 | 0.8 | 1.1 |
| SALINE | 165 | 0000 | 632 | 26,551 | 25,932 | 25,377 | -0.2 | 82 | 95.9 | 95.3 | 3.5 | 4.0 | 0.2 | 0.2 |
| SANGAMON | 167 | 7880 | 648 | 178,386 | 191,665 | 191,918 | 0.7 | 19 | 90.8 | 89.5 | 8.1 | 9.0 | 0.8 | 1.1 |
| SCHUYLER | 169 | 0000 | 717 | 7,498 | 7,437 | 7,148 | -0.1 | 67 | 99.7 | 99.7 | 0.0 | 0.1 | 0.1 | 0.1 |
| SCOTT | 171 | 0000 | 717 | 5,644 | 5,612 | 5,611 | -0.1 | 67 | 99.8 | 99.8 | 0.0 | 0.0 | 0.1 | 0.1 |
| SHELBY | 173 | 0000 | 648 | 22,261 | 22,437 | 22,100 | 0.1 | 51 | 99.7 | 99.7 | 0.1 | 0.1 | 0.1 | 0.2 |
| STARK | 175 | 0000 | 675 | 6,534 | 6,256 | 6,129 | -0.4 | 91 | 99.4 | 99.3 | 0.1 | 0.1 | 0.3 | 0.4 |
| STEPHENSON | 177 | 0000 | 610 | 48,052 | 48,708 | 48,358 | 0.1 | 51 | 92.7 | 91.7 | 6.4 | 7.1 | 0.6 | 0.9 |
| TAZEWELL | 179 | 6120 | 675 | 123,692 | 130,196 | 132,273 | 0.5 | 28 | 99.1 | 98.3 | 0.2 | 0.7 | 0.3 | 0.5 |
| UNION | 181 | 0000 | 632 | 17,619 | 18,038 | 18,048 | 0.2 | 45 | 98.3 | 97.9 | 0.7 | 0.7 | 0.3 | 0.4 |
| VERMILION | 183 | 0000 | 648 | 88,257 | 83,263 | 80,560 | -0.6 | 96 | 89.5 | 87.7 | 8.9 | 10.0 | 0.6 | 0.8 |
| WABASH | 185 | 0000 | 649 | 13,111 | 12,444 | 12,106 | -0.5 | 94 | 98.8 | 98.6 | 0.3 | 0.3 | 0.6 | 0.8 |
| WARREN | 187 | 0000 | 682 | 19,181 | 18,907 | 18,793 | -0.1 | 67 | 97.1 | 96.2 | 1.9 | 2.3 | 0.4 | 0.6 |
| WASHINGTON | 189 | 0000 | 609 | 14,965 | 15,165 | 14,993 | 0.1 | 51 | 99.3 | 99.2 | 0.3 | 0.3 | 0.2 | 0.2 |
| WAYNE | 191 | 0000 | 649 | 17,241 | 16,953 | 16,886 | -0.2 | 82 | 99.4 | 99.2 | 0.1 | 0.1 | 0.3 | 0.3 |
| WHITE | 193 | 0000 | 649 | 16,522 | 15,505 | 15,203 | -0.6 | 96 | 99.2 | 98.9 | 0.2 | 0.5 | 0.2 | 0.3 |
| WHITESIDE | 195 | 0000 | 682 | 60,186 | 59,401 | 58,385 | -0.1 | 67 | 94.9 | 93.1 | 0.7 | 0.8 | 0.3 | 0.4 |
| WILL | 197 | 1600 | 602 | 357,313 | 495,040 | 578,062 | 3.2 | 2 | 84.9 | 82.5 | 10.7 | 11.5 | 1.3 | 1.9 |
| WILLIAMSON | 199 | 0000 | 632 | 57,733 | 61,849 | 63,285 | 0.7 | 19 | 97.2 | 96.3 | 2.0 | 2.6 | 0.4 | 0.6 |
| WINNEBAGO | 201 | 6880 | 610 | 252,913 | 268,731 | 272,036 | 0.6 | 24 | 88.0 | 86.1 | 9.2 | 10.1 | 1.2 | 1.6 |
| WOODFORD | 203 | 6120 | 675 | 32,653 | 35,860 | 37,455 | 0.9 | 18 | 99.2 | 98.9 | 0.2 | 0.4 | 0.3 | 0.4 |
| ILLINOIS | | | | | | | 0.6 | | 78.3 | 76.1 | 14.8 | 15.0 | 2.5 | 3.4 |
| UNITED STATES | | | | | | | 1.0 | | 80.3 | 77.9 | 12.1 | 12.4 | 2.9 | 3.9 |

| COUNTY | % HISPANIC ORIGIN 1990 | % HISPANIC ORIGIN 2000 | 2000 AGE DISTRIBUTION (%) 0-4 | 5-9 | 10-14 | 15-19 | 20-24 | 25-44 | 45-64 | 65-84 | 85+ | 18+ | MEDIAN AGE 1990 | MEDIAN AGE 2000 | 2000 Males/ Females (×100) |
|---|---|---|---|---|---|---|---|---|---|---|---|---|---|---|---|
| PUTNAM | 2.4 | 3.9 | 6.7 | 7.5 | 7.2 | 7.0 | 4.6 | 26.7 | 25.1 | 13.5 | 1.7 | 74.4 | 35.9 | 38.7 | 101.9 |
| RANDOLPH | 1.0 | 1.6 | 5.9 | 6.8 | 6.8 | 6.8 | 7.1 | 30.5 | 21.3 | 12.4 | 2.4 | 76.4 | 34.0 | 36.2 | 116.2 |
| RICHLAND | 0.4 | 1.0 | 6.9 | 7.3 | 7.0 | 7.5 | 5.2 | 26.6 | 22.7 | 14.1 | 2.8 | 74.4 | 35.6 | 38.3 | 93.1 |
| ROCK ISLAND | 5.4 | 8.1 | 6.6 | 7.2 | 7.0 | 7.2 | 6.4 | 27.5 | 23.2 | 12.9 | 2.0 | 75.0 | 34.8 | 37.3 | 93.8 |
| ST. CLAIR | 1.5 | 2.4 | 7.8 | 7.9 | 7.6 | 7.3 | 6.4 | 29.6 | 20.6 | 11.2 | 1.7 | 72.3 | 32.0 | 34.5 | 92.2 |
| SALINE | 0.5 | 1.1 | 6.0 | 6.6 | 6.4 | 7.5 | 5.3 | 24.9 | 23.9 | 16.3 | 3.3 | 76.5 | 38.2 | 40.5 | 92.0 |
| SANGAMON | 0.7 | 1.4 | 6.6 | 7.1 | 7.2 | 6.9 | 6.0 | 29.4 | 23.5 | 11.4 | 1.9 | 74.9 | 34.2 | 37.1 | 90.6 |
| SCHUYLER | 0.1 | 0.5 | 5.6 | 6.6 | 7.0 | 6.8 | 4.9 | 26.4 | 24.1 | 15.4 | 3.1 | 76.3 | 37.4 | 40.4 | 95.8 |
| SCOTT | 0.3 | 0.8 | 6.5 | 7.5 | 7.5 | 6.9 | 4.8 | 26.6 | 23.8 | 13.7 | 2.7 | 74.2 | 35.9 | 38.7 | 94.6 |
| SHELBY | 0.2 | 0.7 | 6.7 | 7.2 | 7.1 | 6.7 | 5.3 | 26.5 | 23.2 | 14.7 | 2.5 | 74.8 | 36.3 | 38.7 | 97.0 |
| STARK | 0.5 | 1.1 | 6.1 | 6.8 | 6.8 | 7.0 | 5.5 | 24.7 | 24.6 | 15.3 | 3.2 | 75.8 | 37.6 | 40.6 | 92.7 |
| STEPHENSON | 0.6 | 1.2 | 6.8 | 7.2 | 7.2 | 7.1 | 5.6 | 27.6 | 23.3 | 13.0 | 2.3 | 74.6 | 35.0 | 37.6 | 94.6 |
| TAZEWELL | 0.7 | 1.5 | 6.3 | 7.0 | 7.1 | 7.0 | 5.7 | 28.5 | 23.9 | 12.6 | 1.9 | 75.2 | 34.8 | 37.8 | 96.4 |
| UNION | 1.0 | 1.8 | 5.7 | 6.4 | 6.5 | 6.5 | 5.3 | 26.2 | 25.4 | 15.1 | 2.8 | 77.3 | 38.0 | 40.5 | 96.2 |
| VERMILION | 1.6 | 2.6 | 6.5 | 6.9 | 6.7 | 7.0 | 6.7 | 27.0 | 23.5 | 13.5 | 2.1 | 75.5 | 35.4 | 37.7 | 97.5 |
| WABASH | 0.6 | 1.1 | 6.3 | 6.9 | 6.8 | 7.5 | 5.7 | 27.5 | 23.1 | 13.9 | 2.3 | 75.7 | 34.9 | 38.3 | 93.3 |
| WARREN | 1.1 | 2.0 | 6.2 | 6.7 | 6.4 | 8.5 | 8.5 | 24.2 | 22.9 | 13.8 | 2.8 | 76.0 | 35.1 | 37.2 | 96.6 |
| WASHINGTON | 0.3 | 0.9 | 6.8 | 7.3 | 7.0 | 7.6 | 5.3 | 26.0 | 23.3 | 14.2 | 2.7 | 74.1 | 35.9 | 38.7 | 95.4 |
| WAYNE | 0.4 | 1.0 | 6.1 | 6.9 | 6.9 | 6.8 | 5.1 | 25.8 | 23.9 | 15.5 | 2.9 | 75.9 | 37.4 | 39.9 | 94.5 |
| WHITE | 0.4 | 0.9 | 6.0 | 6.8 | 6.5 | 6.7 | 5.0 | 24.7 | 23.9 | 17.0 | 3.4 | 76.5 | 38.5 | 41.5 | 92.1 |
| WHITESIDE | 7.4 | 10.9 | 6.7 | 7.2 | 7.0 | 7.1 | 6.2 | 27.0 | 23.6 | 13.1 | 2.0 | 74.6 | 34.7 | 37.3 | 96.1 |
| WILL | 5.6 | 8.1 | 7.6 | 8.3 | 8.2 | 7.6 | 6.2 | 30.6 | 22.6 | 8.0 | 1.0 | 71.3 | 31.1 | 33.8 | 99.2 |
| WILLIAMSON | 0.8 | 1.6 | 6.1 | 6.6 | 6.6 | 6.4 | 5.4 | 28.4 | 24.5 | 13.7 | 2.3 | 76.9 | 36.1 | 39.0 | 95.5 |
| WINNEBAGO | 3.1 | 4.7 | 7.0 | 7.4 | 7.4 | 6.9 | 5.8 | 29.4 | 23.0 | 11.4 | 1.6 | 74.0 | 33.4 | 36.4 | 94.2 |
| WOODFORD | 0.7 | 1.3 | 7.0 | 7.6 | 7.5 | 7.9 | 6.6 | 26.0 | 23.8 | 11.5 | 2.2 | 73.1 | 34.1 | 36.4 | 95.9 |
| ILLINOIS | 7.9 | 10.7 | 7.2 | 7.5 | 7.2 | 7.2 | 6.6 | 30.2 | 21.9 | 10.7 | 1.6 | 74.1 | 32.8 | 35.4 | 95.3 |
| UNITED STATES | 9.0 | 11.8 | 6.9 | 7.2 | 7.2 | 7.2 | 6.7 | 29.9 | 22.2 | 11.1 | 1.6 | 74.6 | 32.9 | 35.7 | 95.6 |

# HOUSEHOLDS

| COUNTY | HOUSEHOLDS | | | | | FAMILIES | | | MEDIAN HOUSEHOLD INCOME | | | |
|---|---|---|---|---|---|---|---|---|---|---|---|---|
| | 1990 | 2000 | 2005 | % Annual Rate 1990-2000 | 2000 Average HH Size | 1990 | 2000 | % Annual Rate 1990-2000 | 2000 | 2005 | 2000 National Rank | 2000 State Rank |
| PUTNAM | 2,204 | 2,290 | 2,372 | 0.5 | 2.57 | 1,657 | 1,670 | 0.1 | 38,713 | 40,840 | 782 | 33 |
| RANDOLPH | 11,949 | 11,627 | 11,385 | -0.3 | 2.55 | 8,651 | 8,108 | -0.8 | 31,393 | 35,940 | 1841 | 78 |
| RICHLAND | 6,503 | 6,627 | 6,542 | 0.2 | 2.45 | 4,674 | 4,575 | -0.3 | 34,857 | 41,726 | 1275 | 56 |
| ROCK ISLAND | 59,317 | 59,117 | 58,675 | 0.0 | 2.42 | 39,934 | 38,050 | -0.6 | 35,946 | 39,195 | 1108 | 52 |
| ST. CLAIR | 95,333 | 95,279 | 93,249 | 0.0 | 2.67 | 68,748 | 66,442 | -0.4 | 37,255 | 42,427 | 941 | 43 |
| SALINE | 10,839 | 10,684 | 10,497 | -0.2 | 2.34 | 7,365 | 6,965 | -0.7 | 24,407 | 28,103 | 2869 | 99 |
| SANGAMON | 72,146 | 78,077 | 78,473 | 1.0 | 2.41 | 47,543 | 49,410 | 0.5 | 41,490 | 46,330 | 553 | 21 |
| SCHUYLER | 3,002 | 3,060 | 2,980 | 0.2 | 2.39 | 2,168 | 2,134 | -0.2 | 30,036 | 37,140 | 2146 | 87 |
| SCOTT | 2,190 | 2,186 | 2,189 | 0.0 | 2.54 | 1,609 | 1,551 | -0.4 | 32,500 | 40,595 | 1624 | 69 |
| SHELBY | 8,563 | 8,851 | 8,840 | 0.4 | 2.51 | 6,435 | 6,453 | 0.0 | 36,035 | 43,768 | 1100 | 51 |
| STARK | 2,512 | 2,420 | 2,376 | -0.5 | 2.54 | 1,831 | 1,697 | -0.9 | 36,447 | 43,659 | 1053 | 48 |
| STEPHENSON | 18,920 | 19,395 | 19,358 | 0.3 | 2.48 | 13,296 | 13,160 | -0.1 | 38,894 | 44,711 | 761 | 30 |
| TAZEWELL | 47,171 | 49,507 | 50,509 | 0.6 | 2.57 | 34,962 | 35,346 | 0.1 | 43,492 | 48,514 | 425 | 16 |
| UNION | 6,838 | 7,105 | 7,145 | 0.5 | 2.41 | 4,854 | 4,884 | 0.1 | 27,618 | 31,027 | 2495 | 94 |
| VERMILION | 34,072 | 32,362 | 31,457 | -0.6 | 2.47 | 23,904 | 21,813 | -1.1 | 32,247 | 36,704 | 1675 | 72 |
| WABASH | 5,032 | 4,844 | 4,736 | -0.5 | 2.52 | 3,602 | 3,351 | -0.9 | 34,329 | 40,383 | 1344 | 62 |
| WARREN | 7,393 | 7,122 | 7,071 | -0.5 | 2.48 | 5,177 | 4,782 | -1.0 | 31,117 | 37,470 | 1911 | 80 |
| WASHINGTON | 5,658 | 5,896 | 5,918 | 0.5 | 2.52 | 4,134 | 4,151 | 0.0 | 37,444 | 46,110 | 903 | 41 |
| WAYNE | 6,935 | 6,862 | 6,858 | -0.1 | 2.45 | 5,061 | 4,848 | -0.5 | 30,169 | 35,287 | 2114 | 86 |
| WHITE | 6,845 | 6,482 | 6,383 | -0.7 | 2.33 | 4,811 | 4,374 | -1.1 | 27,696 | 30,600 | 2476 | 93 |
| WHITESIDE | 22,740 | 22,584 | 22,271 | -0.1 | 2.59 | 16,737 | 16,057 | -0.5 | 37,043 | 40,342 | 970 | 45 |
| WILL | 116,933 | 162,123 | 189,286 | 4.0 | 3.00 | 92,631 | 125,837 | 3.8 | 61,715 | 74,476 | 61 | 5 |
| WILLIAMSON | 23,120 | 24,838 | 25,582 | 0.9 | 2.41 | 16,113 | 16,718 | 0.4 | 32,802 | 37,817 | 1572 | 67 |
| WINNEBAGO | 96,727 | 104,182 | 106,182 | 0.9 | 2.54 | 68,691 | 71,816 | 0.5 | 44,057 | 49,778 | 392 | 15 |
| WOODFORD | 11,395 | 12,575 | 13,172 | 1.2 | 2.77 | 8,951 | 9,602 | 0.9 | 52,502 | 63,776 | 160 | 9 |
| ILLINOIS | | | | 0.8 | 2.64 | | | 0.5 | 46,248 | 53,055 | | |
| UNITED STATES | | | | 1.4 | 2.59 | | | 1.1 | 41,914 | 49,127 | | |

| COUNTY | 2000 Per Capita Income | 2000 HH Income Base | 2000 HOUSEHOLD INCOME DISTRIBUTION (%) | | | | | | 2000 AVERAGE DISPOSABLE INCOME BY AGE OF HOUSEHOLDER | | | | | |
|---|---|---|---|---|---|---|---|---|---|---|---|---|---|---|
| | | | Less than $15,000 | $15,000 to $24,999 | $25,000 to $49,999 | $50,000 to $99,999 | $100,000 to $149,999 | $150,000 or More | All Ages | <35 | 35-44 | 45-54 | 55-64 | 65+ |
| PUTNAM | 20,460 | 2,290 | 10.6 | 13.9 | 40.9 | 27.1 | 4.2 | 3.2 | 38,152 | 29,756 | 45,467 | 47,554 | 36,977 | 26,807 |
| RANDOLPH | 14,302 | 11,627 | 20.8 | 17.1 | 38.6 | 20.8 | 2.2 | 0.6 | 28,767 | 26,949 | 34,645 | 38,937 | 30,267 | 17,480 |
| RICHLAND | 18,458 | 6,627 | 16.8 | 16.9 | 38.3 | 22.7 | 3.8 | 1.4 | 32,334 | 27,014 | 38,430 | 40,804 | 35,598 | 23,518 |
| ROCK ISLAND | 18,377 | 59,117 | 18.0 | 15.3 | 34.8 | 26.1 | 4.4 | 1.4 | 33,227 | 26,882 | 38,318 | 42,920 | 37,212 | 22,817 |
| ST. CLAIR | 17,300 | 95,271 | 18.1 | 14.0 | 34.5 | 26.9 | 5.0 | 1.5 | 34,113 | 29,938 | 38,173 | 43,616 | 37,196 | 22,544 |
| SALINE | 13,117 | 10,684 | 32.4 | 18.6 | 31.2 | 15.0 | 2.2 | 0.6 | 24,773 | 23,584 | 31,458 | 30,891 | 25,923 | 16,922 |
| SANGAMON | 21,645 | 78,077 | 13.2 | 13.2 | 34.5 | 31.2 | 5.9 | 2.0 | 37,619 | 31,560 | 42,048 | 47,272 | 41,593 | 25,154 |
| SCHUYLER | 15,161 | 3,060 | 21.1 | 17.5 | 39.6 | 18.7 | 2.6 | 0.6 | 28,308 | 28,510 | 31,186 | 38,064 | 28,551 | 19,100 |
| SCOTT | 15,343 | 2,186 | 17.2 | 16.2 | 42.5 | 20.2 | 3.2 | 0.7 | 30,099 | 28,047 | 34,570 | 37,874 | 34,110 | 19,850 |
| SHELBY | 17,896 | 8,851 | 16.0 | 13.9 | 40.2 | 23.9 | 4.5 | 1.5 | 33,673 | 31,423 | 38,164 | 41,649 | 39,030 | 23,623 |
| STARK | 16,714 | 2,420 | 14.4 | 16.6 | 36.9 | 27.7 | 3.7 | 0.7 | 32,696 | 28,077 | 37,022 | 42,181 | 35,833 | 24,660 |
| STEPHENSON | 18,897 | 19,395 | 14.1 | 14.0 | 37.9 | 27.8 | 4.6 | 1.5 | 34,990 | 31,313 | 40,061 | 44,038 | 40,030 | 23,254 |
| TAZEWELL | 20,275 | 49,493 | 13.2 | 11.0 | 34.0 | 33.7 | 6.4 | 1.7 | 38,116 | 31,619 | 44,125 | 50,472 | 41,624 | 24,297 |
| UNION | 14,676 | 7,105 | 23.5 | 21.0 | 36.2 | 15.4 | 2.9 | 1.0 | 27,320 | 24,670 | 34,019 | 36,035 | 28,373 | 18,233 |
| VERMILION | 16,559 | 32,362 | 21.1 | 17.2 | 35.8 | 21.1 | 3.4 | 1.4 | 30,773 | 26,334 | 35,681 | 39,780 | 33,767 | 20,307 |
| WABASH | 17,332 | 4,844 | 19.0 | 13.9 | 37.5 | 23.2 | 4.5 | 1.9 | 33,260 | 27,424 | 38,528 | 43,764 | 39,239 | 21,943 |
| WARREN | 14,399 | 7,122 | 18.7 | 19.8 | 38.5 | 20.2 | 2.5 | 0.2 | 28,433 | 25,583 | 33,732 | 34,842 | 31,082 | 21,477 |
| WASHINGTON | 17,364 | 5,896 | 14.6 | 15.9 | 37.3 | 26.7 | 4.6 | 1.0 | 33,252 | 31,945 | 40,510 | 43,654 | 37,193 | 20,033 |
| WAYNE | 14,430 | 6,862 | 21.4 | 18.5 | 38.8 | 18.9 | 2.3 | 0.2 | 27,350 | 26,593 | 31,904 | 34,808 | 29,625 | 19,500 |
| WHITE | 15,316 | 6,482 | 27.8 | 17.1 | 34.5 | 17.5 | 2.1 | 1.0 | 26,813 | 23,825 | 30,803 | 35,327 | 28,496 | 19,772 |
| WHITESIDE | 16,825 | 22,584 | 14.6 | 14.4 | 40.3 | 27.0 | 3.0 | 0.8 | 32,705 | 29,994 | 37,669 | 41,003 | 35,369 | 22,276 |
| WILL | 26,059 | 162,123 | 6.2 | 5.2 | 24.9 | 43.1 | 15.1 | 5.6 | 53,326 | 47,770 | 55,867 | 63,564 | 55,558 | 31,336 |
| WILLIAMSON | 17,533 | 24,832 | 20.7 | 16.3 | 34.8 | 23.1 | 3.7 | 1.5 | 31,579 | 27,033 | 37,051 | 42,464 | 33,861 | 20,492 |
| WINNEBAGO | 22,211 | 104,182 | 12.6 | 11.0 | 34.0 | 32.9 | 7.1 | 2.5 | 39,921 | 34,350 | 44,900 | 50,544 | 43,010 | 25,060 |
| WOODFORD | 23,574 | 12,575 | 6.5 | 8.3 | 31.4 | 39.0 | 10.6 | 4.2 | 47,055 | 40,728 | 52,587 | 58,358 | 48,756 | 31,705 |
| ILLINOIS | 24,170 | | 12.6 | 10.6 | 31.0 | 32.3 | 9.1 | 4.4 | 43,984 | 37,679 | 47,254 | 53,608 | 47,357 | 28,025 |
| UNITED STATES | 22,162 | | 14.5 | 12.5 | 32.3 | 29.8 | 7.4 | 3.5 | 40,748 | 34,503 | 44,969 | 49,579 | 43,409 | 27,339 |

# SPENDING POTENTIAL INDEXES

| COUNTY | FINANCIAL SERVICES | | | | THE HOME | | | | | | ENTERTAINMENT | | | | | | PERSONAL | | | |
|---|---|---|---|---|---|---|---|---|---|---|---|---|---|---|---|---|---|---|---|---|
| | | | | | Home Improvements | | | Furnishings | | | | | | | | | | | | |
| | Auto Loan | Home Loan | Investments | Retirement Plans | Home Repair | Lawn & Garden | Remodeling | Appliances | Electronics | Furniture | Restaurants | Sporting Goods | Theater & Concerts | Toys & Hobbies | Travel | Video Rental | Apparel | Auto Aftermarket | Health Insurance | Pets & Supplies |
| PUTNAM | 100 | 79 | 83 | 87 | 96 | 93 | 116 | 99 | 94 | 86 | 90 | 98 | 91 | 101 | 84 | 102 | 88 | 94 | 103 | 102 |
| RANDOLPH | 98 | 75 | 80 | 82 | 95 | 92 | 110 | 97 | 93 | 83 | 86 | 94 | 88 | 97 | 82 | 100 | 84 | 92 | 102 | 98 |
| RICHLAND | 97 | 75 | 82 | 82 | 95 | 92 | 107 | 96 | 92 | 82 | 85 | 93 | 87 | 96 | 82 | 100 | 83 | 91 | 103 | 97 |
| ROCK ISLAND | 95 | 89 | 97 | 89 | 102 | 97 | 98 | 96 | 92 | 93 | 94 | 93 | 96 | 97 | 94 | 99 | 90 | 95 | 101 | 97 |
| ST. CLAIR | 96 | 90 | 94 | 91 | 99 | 95 | 97 | 97 | 94 | 94 | 93 | 95 | 96 | 96 | 93 | 101 | 92 | 97 | 97 | 97 |
| SALINE | 95 | 70 | 76 | 78 | 92 | 90 | 107 | 94 | 92 | 78 | 81 | 89 | 83 | 92 | 79 | 100 | 79 | 90 | 102 | 95 |
| SANGAMON | 98 | 98 | 100 | 98 | 102 | 100 | 100 | 98 | 98 | 99 | 101 | 98 | 102 | 100 | 99 | 102 | 98 | 101 | 100 | 100 |
| SCHUYLER | 97 | 68 | 75 | 80 | 91 | 90 | 111 | 95 | 91 | 76 | 81 | 93 | 82 | 95 | 77 | 100 | 80 | 90 | 104 | 97 |
| SCOTT | 98 | 68 | 74 | 81 | 91 | 90 | 111 | 96 | 92 | 76 | 81 | 94 | 83 | 96 | 77 | 101 | 80 | 90 | 105 | 97 |
| SHELBY | 98 | 72 | 79 | 83 | 93 | 91 | 111 | 97 | 93 | 80 | 84 | 95 | 86 | 97 | 80 | 101 | 83 | 92 | 104 | 98 |
| STARK | 97 | 71 | 78 | 81 | 94 | 92 | 108 | 96 | 90 | 79 | 83 | 93 | 86 | 95 | 81 | 100 | 81 | 90 | 104 | 96 |
| STEPHENSON | 98 | 88 | 94 | 92 | 100 | 97 | 105 | 97 | 94 | 92 | 94 | 96 | 96 | 99 | 92 | 101 | 91 | 96 | 101 | 99 |
| TAZEWELL | 98 | 92 | 95 | 93 | 101 | 98 | 101 | 98 | 96 | 96 | 98 | 96 | 99 | 100 | 94 | 101 | 94 | 98 | 101 | 99 |
| UNION | 96 | 71 | 77 | 80 | 93 | 91 | 110 | 95 | 93 | 79 | 82 | 92 | 84 | 94 | 79 | 100 | 81 | 90 | 102 | 96 |
| VERMILION | 97 | 84 | 94 | 90 | 101 | 97 | 104 | 97 | 93 | 91 | 91 | 95 | 94 | 97 | 92 | 100 | 88 | 94 | 102 | 97 |
| WABASH | 99 | 84 | 95 | 93 | 99 | 98 | 110 | 98 | 96 | 90 | 92 | 97 | 95 | 99 | 90 | 101 | 91 | 96 | 103 | 99 |
| WARREN | 95 | 73 | 80 | 81 | 94 | 91 | 107 | 95 | 91 | 80 | 83 | 91 | 86 | 94 | 82 | 99 | 81 | 90 | 102 | 96 |
| WASHINGTON | 98 | 71 | 77 | 82 | 93 | 91 | 111 | 96 | 92 | 79 | 83 | 95 | 85 | 96 | 79 | 101 | 82 | 91 | 104 | 98 |
| WAYNE | 97 | 71 | 77 | 81 | 93 | 90 | 112 | 96 | 93 | 80 | 83 | 93 | 85 | 96 | 79 | 100 | 82 | 91 | 103 | 97 |
| WHITE | 95 | 65 | 71 | 76 | 91 | 89 | 107 | 94 | 91 | 74 | 78 | 89 | 80 | 91 | 76 | 100 | 77 | 88 | 104 | 94 |
| WHITESIDE | 97 | 84 | 90 | 87 | 99 | 95 | 105 | 97 | 93 | 90 | 92 | 95 | 94 | 98 | 89 | 100 | 88 | 94 | 102 | 98 |
| WILL | 102 | 109 | 101 | 107 | 103 | 104 | 101 | 102 | 104 | 108 | 111 | 105 | 110 | 105 | 103 | 104 | 108 | 108 | 101 | 104 |
| WILLIAMSON | 97 | 82 | 90 | 89 | 98 | 96 | 106 | 97 | 95 | 88 | 90 | 94 | 93 | 97 | 88 | 101 | 88 | 94 | 103 | 98 |
| WINNEBAGO | 98 | 97 | 97 | 97 | 101 | 99 | 99 | 98 | 97 | 99 | 100 | 98 | 101 | 100 | 97 | 102 | 97 | 100 | 99 | 99 |
| WOODFORD | 100 | 93 | 95 | 96 | 100 | 98 | 107 | 100 | 99 | 96 | 100 | 100 | 101 | 103 | 94 | 103 | 97 | 100 | 102 | 102 |
| ILLINOIS | 99 | 103 | 103 | 103 | 103 | 103 | 99 | 100 | 100 | 102 | 103 | 100 | 105 | 100 | 103 | 103 | 101 | 104 | 100 | 101 |
| UNITED STATES | 100 | 100 | 100 | 100 | 100 | 100 | 100 | 100 | 100 | 100 | 100 | 100 | 100 | 100 | 100 | 100 | 100 | 100 | 100 | 100 |

| COUNTY | FIPS Code | MSA Code | DMA Code | POPULATION | | | 1990-2000 ANNUAL CHANGE | | RACE (%) | | | | | |
|---|---|---|---|---|---|---|---|---|---|---|---|---|---|---|
| | | | | | | | | | White | | Black | | Asian/Pacific | |
| | | | | 1990 | 2000 | 2005 | % Rate | State Rank | 1990 | 2000 | 1990 | 2000 | 1990 | 2000 |
| ADAMS | 001 | 2760 | 509 | 31,095 | 33,333 | 34,223 | 0.7 | 47 | 98.2 | 97.4 | 0.1 | 0.2 | 0.2 | 0.3 |
| ALLEN | 003 | 2760 | 509 | 300,836 | 318,613 | 329,129 | 0.6 | 53 | 87.8 | 85.7 | 10.1 | 11.4 | 0.9 | 1.3 |
| BARTHOLOMEW | 005 | 0000 | 527 | 63,657 | 70,114 | 72,200 | 0.9 | 35 | 97.0 | 96.3 | 1.6 | 1.8 | 1.0 | 1.4 |
| BENTON | 007 | 0000 | 527 | 9,441 | 9,832 | 10,055 | 0.4 | 61 | 99.4 | 99.3 | 0.1 | 0.1 | 0.0 | 0.0 |
| BLACKFORD | 009 | 0000 | 527 | 14,067 | 13,898 | 13,756 | -0.1 | 83 | 99.4 | 99.3 | 0.0 | 0.0 | 0.1 | 0.1 |
| BOONE | 011 | 3480 | 527 | 38,147 | 45,686 | 49,975 | 1.8 | 10 | 99.1 | 98.9 | 0.2 | 0.2 | 0.2 | 0.4 |
| BROWN | 013 | 0000 | 527 | 14,080 | 16,170 | 17,047 | 1.4 | 17 | 99.2 | 99.0 | 0.1 | 0.1 | 0.1 | 0.2 |
| CARROLL | 015 | 0000 | 527 | 18,809 | 20,118 | 20,584 | 0.7 | 47 | 99.5 | 99.4 | 0.1 | 0.1 | 0.0 | 0.0 |
| CASS | 017 | 0000 | 527 | 38,413 | 39,081 | 39,657 | 0.2 | 70 | 98.3 | 98.1 | 0.9 | 0.9 | 0.3 | 0.5 |
| CLARK | 019 | 4520 | 529 | 87,777 | 96,113 | 100,984 | 0.9 | 35 | 93.7 | 92.6 | 5.4 | 6.2 | 0.4 | 0.6 |
| CLAY | 021 | 8320 | 581 | 24,705 | 27,059 | 27,897 | 0.9 | 35 | 99.3 | 99.2 | 0.5 | 0.5 | 0.1 | 0.1 |
| CLINTON | 023 | 3920 | 527 | 30,974 | 32,940 | 32,792 | 0.6 | 53 | 99.0 | 98.5 | 0.1 | 0.3 | 0.2 | 0.2 |
| CRAWFORD | 025 | 0000 | 529 | 9,914 | 10,828 | 11,346 | 0.9 | 35 | 99.5 | 99.5 | 0.1 | 0.1 | 0.1 | 0.1 |
| DAVIESS | 027 | 0000 | 581 | 27,533 | 29,239 | 29,969 | 0.6 | 53 | 99.4 | 99.3 | 0.4 | 0.5 | 0.1 | 0.1 |
| DEARBORN | 029 | 1640 | 515 | 38,835 | 49,029 | 53,482 | 2.3 | 4 | 99.0 | 98.8 | 0.6 | 0.7 | 0.2 | 0.3 |
| DECATUR | 031 | 0000 | 527 | 23,645 | 25,902 | 26,850 | 0.9 | 35 | 99.1 | 99.0 | 0.2 | 0.1 | 0.5 | 0.8 |
| DE KALB | 033 | 2760 | 509 | 35,324 | 40,136 | 42,311 | 1.3 | 21 | 99.1 | 98.8 | 0.1 | 0.1 | 0.2 | 0.4 |
| DELAWARE | 035 | 5280 | 527 | 119,659 | 114,744 | 111,045 | -0.4 | 91 | 93.0 | 91.8 | 6.0 | 6.9 | 0.5 | 0.8 |
| DUBOIS | 037 | 0000 | 649 | 36,616 | 40,496 | 42,580 | 1.0 | 30 | 99.6 | 99.5 | 0.1 | 0.1 | 0.2 | 0.2 |
| ELKHART | 039 | 2330 | 588 | 156,198 | 176,634 | 186,489 | 1.2 | 24 | 93.8 | 92.5 | 4.5 | 5.2 | 0.6 | 0.9 |
| FAYETTE | 041 | 0000 | 527 | 26,015 | 25,748 | 25,176 | -0.1 | 83 | 97.9 | 97.5 | 1.7 | 1.9 | 0.3 | 0.4 |
| FLOYD | 043 | 4520 | 529 | 64,404 | 72,768 | 75,341 | 1.2 | 24 | 95.4 | 94.6 | 4.1 | 4.7 | 0.3 | 0.4 |
| FOUNTAIN | 045 | 0000 | 527 | 17,808 | 18,420 | 18,696 | 0.3 | 64 | 99.5 | 99.3 | 0.0 | 0.0 | 0.2 | 0.3 |
| FRANKLIN | 047 | 0000 | 515 | 19,580 | 22,402 | 23,882 | 1.3 | 21 | 99.6 | 99.5 | 0.1 | 0.1 | 0.1 | 0.2 |
| FULTON | 049 | 0000 | 588 | 18,840 | 21,131 | 22,330 | 1.1 | 29 | 98.5 | 98.2 | 0.8 | 0.9 | 0.2 | 0.3 |
| GIBSON | 051 | 0000 | 649 | 31,913 | 32,290 | 32,604 | 0.1 | 73 | 97.6 | 97.1 | 1.9 | 2.2 | 0.3 | 0.5 |
| GRANT | 053 | 0000 | 527 | 74,169 | 71,608 | 69,294 | -0.3 | 90 | 91.4 | 89.9 | 6.8 | 7.6 | 0.5 | 0.7 |
| GREENE | 055 | 0000 | 581 | 30,410 | 33,190 | 33,370 | 0.9 | 35 | 99.5 | 99.3 | 0.0 | 0.1 | 0.2 | 0.3 |
| HAMILTON | 057 | 3480 | 527 | 108,936 | 180,653 | 222,483 | 5.1 | 1 | 98.0 | 97.3 | 0.6 | 0.7 | 1.1 | 1.7 |
| HANCOCK | 059 | 3480 | 527 | 45,527 | 56,797 | 62,708 | 2.2 | 5 | 99.2 | 98.9 | 0.1 | 0.1 | 0.4 | 0.6 |
| HARRISON | 061 | 4520 | 529 | 29,890 | 36,109 | 39,701 | 1.9 | 7 | 99.2 | 99.0 | 0.4 | 0.5 | 0.1 | 0.2 |
| HENDRICKS | 063 | 3480 | 527 | 75,717 | 101,999 | 117,660 | 2.9 | 2 | 98.4 | 98.4 | 0.9 | 0.7 | 0.4 | 0.6 |
| HENRY | 065 | 0000 | 527 | 48,139 | 48,181 | 47,215 | 0.0 | 79 | 98.6 | 98.3 | 1.0 | 1.1 | 0.2 | 0.2 |
| HOWARD | 067 | 3850 | 527 | 80,827 | 83,784 | 84,195 | 0.4 | 61 | 93.3 | 92.1 | 5.4 | 6.3 | 0.6 | 0.8 |
| HUNTINGTON | 069 | 2760 | 509 | 35,427 | 37,483 | 38,032 | 0.6 | 53 | 98.8 | 98.5 | 0.1 | 0.2 | 0.4 | 0.6 |
| JACKSON | 071 | 0000 | 529 | 37,730 | 41,592 | 42,943 | 1.0 | 30 | 98.8 | 98.5 | 0.4 | 0.4 | 0.5 | 0.7 |
| JASPER | 073 | 0000 | 602 | 24,960 | 29,891 | 32,028 | 1.8 | 10 | 98.8 | 98.7 | 0.4 | 0.4 | 0.2 | 0.2 |
| JAY | 075 | 0000 | 509 | 21,512 | 21,682 | 21,637 | 0.1 | 73 | 99.1 | 98.7 | 0.1 | 0.1 | 0.3 | 0.5 |
| JEFFERSON | 077 | 0000 | 529 | 29,797 | 32,095 | 33,467 | 0.7 | 47 | 97.9 | 97.6 | 1.2 | 1.4 | 0.4 | 0.6 |
| JENNINGS | 079 | 0000 | 529 | 23,661 | 28,571 | 30,899 | 1.9 | 7 | 98.7 | 98.5 | 0.9 | 0.9 | 0.2 | 0.3 |
| JOHNSON | 081 | 3480 | 527 | 88,109 | 115,638 | 130,318 | 2.7 | 3 | 98.1 | 97.8 | 1.0 | 0.9 | 0.6 | 0.9 |
| KNOX | 083 | 0000 | 581 | 39,884 | 38,912 | 38,171 | -0.2 | 86 | 98.1 | 97.8 | 1.2 | 1.3 | 0.4 | 0.6 |
| KOSCIUSKO | 085 | 0000 | 588 | 65,294 | 71,774 | 74,021 | 0.9 | 35 | 98.1 | 97.4 | 0.5 | 0.6 | 0.5 | 0.7 |
| LAGRANGE | 087 | 0000 | 588 | 29,477 | 34,585 | 37,473 | 1.6 | 14 | 98.9 | 98.4 | 0.1 | 0.2 | 0.3 | 0.5 |
| LAKE | 089 | 2960 | 602 | 475,594 | 480,326 | 478,881 | 0.1 | 73 | 70.3 | 66.6 | 24.5 | 26.1 | 0.6 | 0.8 |
| LA PORTE | 091 | 0000 | 602 | 107,066 | 109,993 | 110,326 | 0.3 | 64 | 89.9 | 88.4 | 8.9 | 10.1 | 0.4 | 0.6 |
| LAWRENCE | 093 | 0000 | 527 | 42,836 | 45,896 | 46,638 | 0.7 | 47 | 99.3 | 99.1 | 0.3 | 0.3 | 0.2 | 0.3 |
| MADISON | 095 | 3480 | 527 | 130,669 | 130,629 | 128,835 | 0.0 | 79 | 91.6 | 90.4 | 7.6 | 8.5 | 0.3 | 0.5 |
| MARION | 097 | 3480 | 527 | 797,159 | 809,711 | 803,033 | 0.2 | 70 | 77.2 | 73.9 | 21.3 | 24.0 | 1.0 | 1.4 |
| MARSHALL | 099 | 0000 | 588 | 42,182 | 46,515 | 48,554 | 1.0 | 30 | 98.4 | 97.7 | 0.2 | 0.2 | 0.4 | 0.5 |
| MARTIN | 101 | 0000 | 581 | 10,369 | 10,318 | 10,011 | 0.0 | 79 | 99.5 | 99.4 | 0.1 | 0.1 | 0.1 | 0.2 |
| MIAMI | 103 | 0000 | 527 | 36,897 | 33,908 | 35,180 | -0.8 | 92 | 94.3 | 93.5 | 3.0 | 3.2 | 0.6 | 0.9 |
| MONROE | 105 | 1020 | 527 | 108,978 | 117,343 | 119,507 | 0.7 | 47 | 94.3 | 93.0 | 2.6 | 2.9 | 2.5 | 3.3 |
| MONTGOMERY | 107 | 0000 | 527 | 34,436 | 36,702 | 37,323 | 0.6 | 53 | 98.6 | 98.4 | 0.6 | 0.6 | 0.4 | 0.6 |
| MORGAN | 109 | 3480 | 527 | 55,920 | 68,437 | 74,889 | 2.0 | 6 | 99.5 | 99.4 | 0.0 | 0.0 | 0.2 | 0.3 |
| NEWTON | 111 | 0000 | 602 | 13,551 | 14,927 | 15,356 | 0.9 | 35 | 99.2 | 98.9 | 0.1 | 0.1 | 0.2 | 0.2 |
| NOBLE | 113 | 0000 | 509 | 37,877 | 43,851 | 46,935 | 1.4 | 17 | 98.9 | 98.5 | 0.2 | 0.1 | 0.3 | 0.4 |
| OHIO | 115 | 1640 | 515 | 5,315 | 5,465 | 5,503 | 0.3 | 64 | 98.9 | 98.7 | 0.8 | 0.9 | 0.2 | 0.2 |
| ORANGE | 117 | 0000 | 529 | 18,409 | 20,051 | 21,137 | 0.8 | 46 | 98.9 | 98.9 | 0.7 | 0.7 | 0.1 | 0.2 |
| OWEN | 119 | 0000 | 527 | 17,281 | 20,801 | 21,791 | 1.8 | 10 | 99.3 | 99.2 | 0.3 | 0.3 | 0.1 | 0.2 |
| PARKE | 121 | 0000 | 581 | 15,410 | 17,011 | 17,550 | 1.0 | 30 | 98.8 | 98.2 | 0.8 | 1.3 | 0.1 | 0.1 |
| PERRY | 123 | 0000 | 649 | 19,107 | 19,009 | 18,602 | -0.1 | 83 | 98.5 | 98.2 | 1.1 | 1.3 | 0.2 | 0.2 |
| PIKE | 125 | 0000 | 649 | 12,509 | 13,169 | 13,838 | 0.5 | 58 | 99.7 | 99.6 | 0.0 | 0.0 | 0.2 | 0.2 |
| PORTER | 127 | 2960 | 602 | 128,932 | 149,361 | 157,450 | 1.4 | 17 | 98.0 | 97.2 | 0.4 | 0.4 | 0.7 | 1.1 |
| POSEY | 129 | 2440 | 649 | 25,968 | 26,227 | 25,906 | 0.1 | 73 | 98.5 | 98.2 | 1.1 | 1.3 | 0.1 | 0.2 |
| PULASKI | 131 | 0000 | 588 | 12,643 | 13,623 | 14,073 | 0.7 | 47 | 98.9 | 98.7 | 0.5 | 0.6 | 0.2 | 0.3 |
| PUTNAM | 133 | 0000 | 527 | 30,315 | 35,084 | 36,633 | 1.4 | 17 | 96.3 | 96.1 | 2.7 | 2.6 | 0.5 | 0.7 |
| RANDOLPH | 135 | 0000 | 527 | 27,148 | 27,390 | 27,256 | 0.1 | 73 | 99.3 | 99.1 | 0.2 | 0.2 | 0.1 | 0.2 |
| RIPLEY | 137 | 0000 | 515 | 24,616 | 27,947 | 29,406 | 1.2 | 24 | 99.5 | 99.5 | 0.1 | 0.1 | 0.2 | 0.2 |
| RUSH | 139 | 0000 | 527 | 18,129 | 18,170 | 17,978 | 0.0 | 79 | 98.7 | 98.5 | 0.8 | 0.9 | 0.3 | 0.4 |
| ST. JOSEPH | 141 | 7800 | 588 | 247,052 | 258,862 | 260,685 | 0.5 | 58 | 87.8 | 85.7 | 9.8 | 11.0 | 1.0 | 1.4 |
| SCOTT | 143 | 4520 | 529 | 20,991 | 23,733 | 25,233 | 1.2 | 24 | 99.3 | 99.1 | 0.1 | 0.1 | 0.2 | 0.4 |
| SHELBY | 145 | 3480 | 527 | 40,307 | 44,080 | 45,421 | 0.9 | 35 | 98.6 | 98.3 | 0.8 | 0.9 | 0.4 | 0.5 |
| SPENCER | 147 | 0000 | 649 | 19,490 | 21,391 | 22,408 | 0.9 | 35 | 99.0 | 98.8 | 0.6 | 0.6 | 0.2 | 0.3 |
| STARKE | 149 | 0000 | 588 | 22,747 | 23,597 | 23,597 | 0.4 | 61 | 98.7 | 98.3 | 0.3 | 0.3 | 0.2 | 0.3 |
| STEUBEN | 151 | 0000 | 509 | 27,446 | 32,205 | 33,909 | 1.6 | 14 | 98.9 | 98.7 | 0.2 | 0.2 | 0.5 | 0.6 |
| SULLIVAN | 153 | 0000 | 581 | 18,993 | 21,644 | 22,130 | 1.3 | 21 | 99.5 | 99.5 | 0.1 | 0.1 | 0.1 | 0.1 |
| INDIANA | | | | | | | 0.7 | | 90.6 | 89.6 | 7.8 | 8.2 | 0.7 | 1.0 |
| UNITED STATES | | | | | | | 1.0 | | 80.3 | 77.9 | 12.1 | 12.4 | 2.9 | 3.9 |

# POPULATION COMPOSITION

| COUNTY | % HISPANIC ORIGIN | | 2000 AGE DISTRIBUTION (%) | | | | | | | | | | MEDIAN AGE | | 2000 Males/ Females (×100) |
|---|---|---|---|---|---|---|---|---|---|---|---|---|---|---|---|
| | 1990 | 2000 | 0-4 | 5-9 | 10-14 | 15-19 | 20-24 | 25-44 | 45-64 | 65-84 | 85+ | 18+ | 1990 | 2000 | |
| ADAMS | 2.6 | 4.3 | 8.6 | 8.6 | 8.4 | 8.0 | 6.1 | 27.9 | 20.3 | 10.3 | 1.9 | 69.5 | 30.6 | 32.7 | 96.8 |
| ALLEN | 1.9 | 3.3 | 7.5 | 7.5 | 7.7 | 7.1 | 6.3 | 30.8 | 21.9 | 9.9 | 1.4 | 73.0 | 32.1 | 34.7 | 94.3 |
| BARTHOLOMEW | 0.7 | 1.4 | 6.6 | 6.9 | 7.3 | 6.4 | 5.3 | 29.6 | 25.4 | 11.0 | 1.4 | 75.2 | 34.2 | 37.5 | 95.0 |
| BENTON | 1.1 | 2.1 | 7.3 | 7.8 | 7.6 | 7.5 | 5.6 | 26.2 | 22.4 | 13.4 | 2.3 | 72.4 | 34.7 | 37.0 | 99.6 |
| BLACKFORD | 0.6 | 1.3 | 6.7 | 6.5 | 6.9 | 6.8 | 5.2 | 28.1 | 24.8 | 13.1 | 1.9 | 75.7 | 35.7 | 38.6 | 95.7 |
| BOONE | 0.7 | 1.4 | 7.1 | 7.4 | 7.6 | 6.8 | 4.9 | 30.1 | 24.0 | 10.2 | 2.0 | 73.5 | 34.4 | 37.2 | 94.0 |
| BROWN | 0.7 | 1.4 | 5.8 | 6.2 | 6.7 | 6.4 | 4.9 | 29.2 | 27.7 | 12.0 | 1.2 | 77.3 | 36.5 | 40.1 | 99.8 |
| CARROLL | 0.6 | 1.4 | 6.8 | 6.9 | 7.3 | 6.8 | 5.2 | 28.7 | 24.3 | 12.3 | 1.8 | 74.8 | 35.0 | 37.9 | 96.5 |
| CASS | 0.6 | 1.3 | 6.6 | 6.8 | 6.9 | 6.8 | 6.6 | 27.7 | 23.8 | 13.1 | 1.8 | 75.4 | 35.0 | 37.5 | 93.6 |
| CLARK | 0.6 | 1.3 | 6.3 | 6.5 | 6.9 | 6.8 | 5.9 | 31.1 | 23.8 | 11.2 | 1.5 | 76.3 | 33.8 | 37.1 | 91.7 |
| CLAY | 0.3 | 0.8 | 6.7 | 7.0 | 7.1 | 7.1 | 5.6 | 27.8 | 22.9 | 13.5 | 2.3 | 74.8 | 35.2 | 37.8 | 93.2 |
| CLINTON | 1.5 | 2.5 | 7.2 | 7.4 | 7.5 | 7.1 | 6.1 | 27.6 | 22.5 | 12.3 | 2.3 | 73.3 | 34.1 | 36.6 | 94.0 |
| CRAWFORD | 0.2 | 0.7 | 6.8 | 7.0 | 7.3 | 7.0 | 5.9 | 28.4 | 24.1 | 11.9 | 1.7 | 74.4 | 34.0 | 37.0 | 98.9 |
| DAVIESS | 0.3 | 0.9 | 7.7 | 7.9 | 8.0 | 7.5 | 5.6 | 26.4 | 22.0 | 12.8 | 2.2 | 71.7 | 33.6 | 36.0 | 93.8 |
| DEARBORN | 0.3 | 0.9 | 7.3 | 7.6 | 7.9 | 7.2 | 5.6 | 29.6 | 23.4 | 10.0 | 1.4 | 72.7 | 33.1 | 35.9 | 96.6 |
| DECATUR | 0.4 | 1.0 | 7.3 | 7.5 | 7.5 | 7.2 | 6.2 | 29.3 | 22.2 | 11.1 | 1.8 | 73.2 | 32.6 | 35.7 | 98.7 |
| DE KALB | 0.9 | 1.8 | 7.5 | 7.7 | 7.9 | 7.2 | 5.9 | 30.4 | 21.8 | 10.1 | 1.5 | 72.4 | 31.9 | 35.0 | 96.6 |
| DELAWARE | 0.7 | 1.4 | 5.8 | 5.7 | 5.9 | 9.7 | 11.1 | 26.6 | 22.0 | 11.6 | 1.6 | 79.1 | 31.4 | 34.4 | 90.4 |
| DUBOIS | 0.7 | 1.3 | 7.8 | 7.8 | 7.7 | 6.9 | 5.6 | 30.6 | 21.4 | 10.4 | 1.8 | 72.3 | 32.1 | 35.2 | 96.5 |
| ELKHART | 1.9 | 3.3 | 7.9 | 8.0 | 8.2 | 7.2 | 5.9 | 29.3 | 22.4 | 9.8 | 1.4 | 71.6 | 31.8 | 34.6 | 96.7 |
| FAYETTE | 0.3 | 0.9 | 5.9 | 6.3 | 6.3 | 6.4 | 6.8 | 28.2 | 25.2 | 13.1 | 1.9 | 77.4 | 35.1 | 38.0 | 94.2 |
| FLOYD | 0.4 | 0.9 | 6.7 | 6.9 | 7.1 | 6.9 | 5.9 | 30.4 | 23.8 | 10.9 | 1.5 | 75.1 | 34.0 | 36.9 | 91.9 |
| FOUNTAIN | 0.5 | 1.2 | 6.7 | 6.8 | 7.1 | 6.8 | 5.3 | 27.1 | 24.6 | 13.6 | 2.1 | 75.2 | 35.9 | 38.5 | 94.5 |
| FRANKLIN | 0.3 | 0.8 | 7.2 | 7.4 | 8.1 | 7.5 | 5.7 | 28.8 | 22.8 | 10.7 | 1.7 | 72.5 | 32.7 | 35.6 | 98.7 |
| FULTON | 0.7 | 1.5 | 6.9 | 7.1 | 7.3 | 7.3 | 5.3 | 27.3 | 23.4 | 13.5 | 2.0 | 74.2 | 35.3 | 38.1 | 96.4 |
| GIBSON | 0.4 | 1.0 | 6.5 | 6.7 | 6.9 | 7.3 | 5.6 | 28.3 | 23.4 | 13.1 | 2.2 | 75.5 | 35.1 | 38.1 | 93.2 |
| GRANT | 2.0 | 3.5 | 6.2 | 6.1 | 6.6 | 7.8 | 7.2 | 27.0 | 24.5 | 12.9 | 1.7 | 77.0 | 34.9 | 37.8 | 93.5 |
| GREENE | 0.5 | 1.2 | 6.3 | 6.6 | 6.8 | 6.6 | 5.6 | 27.6 | 24.4 | 13.8 | 2.3 | 76.1 | 35.9 | 38.7 | 95.2 |
| HAMILTON | 0.7 | 1.4 | 7.4 | 8.3 | 8.8 | 7.1 | 4.8 | 31.4 | 23.9 | 7.4 | 0.8 | 70.9 | 32.9 | 35.7 | 95.6 |
| HANCOCK | 0.7 | 1.5 | 6.1 | 6.5 | 7.0 | 7.1 | 5.7 | 29.2 | 26.6 | 10.4 | 1.3 | 75.8 | 34.2 | 37.7 | 97.2 |
| HARRISON | 0.4 | 1.0 | 6.6 | 7.3 | 7.5 | 7.3 | 5.4 | 30.3 | 23.8 | 10.3 | 1.4 | 74.0 | 33.2 | 36.6 | 98.7 |
| HENDRICKS | 0.5 | 1.1 | 6.5 | 7.0 | 7.5 | 7.3 | 5.5 | 31.2 | 24.5 | 9.4 | 1.1 | 74.3 | 33.3 | 36.7 | 100.5 |
| HENRY | 0.4 | 1.0 | 5.8 | 6.1 | 6.4 | 6.2 | 5.9 | 28.7 | 25.8 | 13.3 | 1.8 | 77.8 | 36.1 | 39.1 | 92.7 |
| HOWARD | 1.3 | 2.3 | 6.7 | 6.8 | 7.1 | 6.8 | 5.8 | 29.0 | 25.0 | 11.4 | 1.4 | 75.1 | 34.1 | 37.4 | 91.9 |
| HUNTINGTON | 0.8 | 1.6 | 7.4 | 7.4 | 7.5 | 7.3 | 6.3 | 28.9 | 21.6 | 11.5 | 2.0 | 73.3 | 32.8 | 35.6 | 94.9 |
| JACKSON | 0.3 | 0.9 | 6.8 | 6.9 | 7.4 | 7.0 | 5.9 | 29.5 | 23.3 | 11.4 | 1.8 | 74.4 | 33.6 | 36.6 | 94.5 |
| JASPER | 1.3 | 2.3 | 7.0 | 7.2 | 7.4 | 8.3 | 7.4 | 27.6 | 23.2 | 10.5 | 1.4 | 73.7 | 32.0 | 34.8 | 98.4 |
| JAY | 0.7 | 1.5 | 6.7 | 6.8 | 7.2 | 6.9 | 5.7 | 27.6 | 24.3 | 13.1 | 1.8 | 75.0 | 35.0 | 37.8 | 95.8 |
| JEFFERSON | 0.4 | 1.0 | 6.3 | 6.4 | 6.9 | 7.7 | 7.4 | 28.6 | 23.7 | 11.5 | 1.5 | 76.3 | 33.7 | 36.7 | 95.4 |
| JENNINGS | 0.4 | 1.0 | 6.8 | 7.0 | 7.3 | 6.7 | 5.8 | 30.5 | 24.0 | 10.6 | 1.2 | 74.7 | 33.1 | 36.2 | 98.9 |
| JOHNSON | 0.7 | 1.5 | 6.7 | 6.9 | 7.3 | 7.5 | 6.2 | 31.3 | 23.1 | 9.2 | 1.6 | 74.6 | 32.6 | 35.8 | 94.3 |
| KNOX | 0.5 | 1.1 | 6.0 | 6.2 | 6.3 | 9.8 | 7.3 | 26.9 | 21.7 | 13.4 | 2.4 | 77.9 | 33.5 | 36.2 | 96.1 |
| KOSCIUSKO | 1.9 | 3.4 | 7.7 | 8.0 | 8.1 | 7.6 | 5.7 | 28.5 | 22.5 | 10.5 | 1.4 | 71.7 | 32.2 | 35.3 | 96.3 |
| LAGRANGE | 1.2 | 2.3 | 9.7 | 9.6 | 9.6 | 8.4 | 5.9 | 27.1 | 19.8 | 8.9 | 1.1 | 65.9 | 28.1 | 30.3 | 99.5 |
| LAKE | 9.4 | 13.5 | 7.0 | 7.0 | 7.2 | 7.4 | 6.7 | 29.0 | 22.6 | 11.8 | 1.4 | 74.2 | 33.0 | 35.9 | 91.9 |
| LA PORTE | 1.5 | 2.6 | 6.3 | 6.5 | 6.8 | 6.9 | 6.8 | 30.4 | 23.2 | 11.7 | 1.5 | 76.2 | 34.2 | 36.3 | 106.5 |
| LAWRENCE | 0.3 | 0.9 | 6.2 | 6.6 | 6.8 | 6.5 | 5.6 | 28.7 | 24.9 | 12.8 | 1.9 | 76.4 | 35.3 | 38.2 | 95.4 |
| MADISON | 0.7 | 1.4 | 6.2 | 6.2 | 6.7 | 7.0 | 6.5 | 29.0 | 24.0 | 12.7 | 1.6 | 76.8 | 34.8 | 37.6 | 96.7 |
| MARION | 1.1 | 1.9 | 7.6 | 7.2 | 6.9 | 6.5 | 6.7 | 33.1 | 20.6 | 10.1 | 1.4 | 74.6 | 31.8 | 34.6 | 90.7 |
| MARSHALL | 2.0 | 3.4 | 7.4 | 7.7 | 7.9 | 7.4 | 5.7 | 28.0 | 22.4 | 11.7 | 1.8 | 72.4 | 33.3 | 36.0 | 96.8 |
| MARTIN | 0.1 | 0.6 | 6.6 | 6.8 | 7.2 | 7.0 | 5.6 | 28.7 | 24.0 | 12.5 | 1.4 | 74.9 | 34.1 | 37.3 | 97.2 |
| MIAMI | 1.5 | 2.6 | 7.8 | 7.3 | 7.2 | 6.8 | 6.6 | 30.1 | 21.4 | 11.3 | 1.5 | 73.5 | 31.5 | 34.7 | 96.1 |
| MONROE | 1.3 | 2.2 | 5.2 | 5.1 | 5.1 | 11.9 | 17.4 | 28.8 | 17.4 | 8.0 | 1.0 | 81.9 | 26.4 | 28.6 | 92.5 |
| MONTGOMERY | 0.5 | 1.1 | 6.8 | 7.0 | 7.2 | 7.2 | 6.6 | 28.2 | 22.9 | 12.3 | 1.9 | 75.0 | 34.0 | 36.9 | 100.5 |
| MORGAN | 0.4 | 1.0 | 6.8 | 7.0 | 7.4 | 7.2 | 5.8 | 30.4 | 24.5 | 9.6 | 1.2 | 74.3 | 32.9 | 36.2 | 96.7 |
| NEWTON | 1.3 | 2.4 | 7.1 | 7.6 | 8.0 | 7.5 | 5.5 | 28.5 | 23.6 | 10.6 | 1.7 | 72.7 | 33.6 | 36.2 | 98.0 |
| NOBLE | 1.7 | 2.8 | 7.9 | 8.0 | 7.9 | 7.4 | 5.8 | 29.7 | 21.8 | 10.0 | 1.5 | 71.7 | 31.9 | 34.6 | 97.7 |
| OHIO | 0.1 | 0.7 | 6.6 | 6.8 | 7.4 | 6.6 | 5.6 | 29.5 | 23.8 | 11.7 | 2.1 | 75.4 | 34.1 | 37.4 | 94.0 |
| ORANGE | 0.3 | 0.9 | 6.8 | 6.9 | 7.4 | 7.0 | 5.5 | 28.4 | 23.7 | 12.6 | 1.7 | 74.5 | 34.7 | 37.5 | 95.7 |
| OWEN | 0.3 | 0.9 | 6.7 | 7.1 | 7.3 | 6.8 | 5.6 | 27.9 | 24.6 | 12.5 | 1.6 | 74.7 | 34.7 | 37.7 | 97.5 |
| PARKE | 0.6 | 1.3 | 6.2 | 6.6 | 6.9 | 7.1 | 5.0 | 27.0 | 25.1 | 14.1 | 2.1 | 75.9 | 36.3 | 39.0 | 96.3 |
| PERRY | 0.3 | 0.9 | 6.3 | 6.5 | 6.6 | 7.1 | 7.0 | 30.4 | 22.2 | 12.2 | 1.8 | 76.3 | 33.5 | 36.4 | 103.1 |
| PIKE | 0.3 | 0.9 | 6.0 | 6.5 | 6.5 | 6.7 | 5.2 | 28.3 | 25.6 | 13.3 | 2.0 | 76.8 | 36.3 | 39.3 | 98.8 |
| PORTER | 3.0 | 4.9 | 6.5 | 7.0 | 7.5 | 7.6 | 6.6 | 30.6 | 23.6 | 9.5 | 1.1 | 74.6 | 32.7 | 35.9 | 95.8 |
| POSEY | 0.4 | 1.0 | 7.2 | 7.4 | 7.8 | 6.8 | 5.3 | 30.2 | 23.2 | 10.5 | 1.5 | 73.3 | 33.4 | 36.4 | 98.5 |
| PULASKI | 0.8 | 1.7 | 7.6 | 8.0 | 7.8 | 7.3 | 6.1 | 27.0 | 21.4 | 12.8 | 2.0 | 71.9 | 33.8 | 35.7 | 95.8 |
| PUTNAM | 0.6 | 1.2 | 6.1 | 6.1 | 6.5 | 8.9 | 10.0 | 28.1 | 22.0 | 10.8 | 1.6 | 77.6 | 32.1 | 34.5 | 106.1 |
| RANDOLPH | 0.7 | 1.4 | 6.3 | 6.6 | 6.9 | 6.2 | 6.1 | 28.1 | 24.3 | 13.6 | 2.0 | 76.3 | 35.6 | 38.2 | 94.6 |
| RIPLEY | 0.3 | 0.8 | 7.3 | 7.4 | 7.5 | 7.4 | 5.9 | 28.8 | 22.4 | 11.3 | 1.9 | 73.0 | 33.1 | 35.7 | 97.1 |
| RUSH | 0.3 | 0.8 | 6.7 | 7.1 | 7.6 | 7.5 | 5.6 | 28.5 | 22.6 | 12.5 | 2.0 | 73.8 | 33.6 | 36.6 | 94.3 |
| ST. JOSEPH | 2.1 | 3.5 | 6.8 | 7.0 | 7.2 | 8.1 | 7.8 | 28.1 | 21.5 | 11.8 | 1.8 | 75.0 | 32.8 | 35.2 | 94.3 |
| SCOTT | 0.7 | 1.5 | 7.0 | 7.0 | 7.6 | 7.2 | 6.0 | 29.7 | 24.1 | 10.0 | 1.4 | 73.9 | 32.7 | 36.0 | 94.8 |
| SHELBY | 0.3 | 0.8 | 7.1 | 7.3 | 7.4 | 7.0 | 5.6 | 29.8 | 23.2 | 11.0 | 1.5 | 73.8 | 33.1 | 36.4 | 95.3 |
| SPENCER | 0.5 | 1.1 | 6.9 | 7.2 | 7.5 | 7.0 | 5.5 | 29.7 | 23.6 | 10.9 | 1.7 | 74.0 | 33.7 | 36.6 | 99.6 |
| STARKE | 1.6 | 2.8 | 7.4 | 7.6 | 7.6 | 7.1 | 5.8 | 28.3 | 22.1 | 12.4 | 1.7 | 73.0 | 33.3 | 36.2 | 98.0 |
| STEUBEN | 0.7 | 1.5 | 7.0 | 6.8 | 7.1 | 7.3 | 6.5 | 28.9 | 23.9 | 11.1 | 1.3 | 75.0 | 33.4 | 36.5 | 100.2 |
| SULLIVAN | 0.3 | 0.9 | 6.1 | 6.4 | 7.0 | 6.8 | 5.5 | 27.1 | 24.2 | 14.1 | 2.6 | 76.2 | 36.7 | 39.2 | 93.8 |
| INDIANA | 1.8 | 2.9 | 6.9 | 7.0 | 7.2 | 7.4 | 6.8 | 29.7 | 22.5 | 10.9 | 1.5 | 74.8 | 32.8 | 35.7 | 94.8 |
| UNITED STATES | 9.0 | 11.8 | 6.9 | 7.2 | 7.2 | 7.2 | 6.7 | 29.9 | 22.2 | 11.1 | 1.6 | 74.6 | 32.9 | 35.7 | 95.6 |

 

| COUNTY | HOUSEHOLDS | | | | | FAMILIES | | | MEDIAN HOUSEHOLD INCOME | | | |
|---|---|---|---|---|---|---|---|---|---|---|---|---|
| | 1990 | 2000 | 2005 | % Annual Rate 1990-2000 | 2000 Average HH Size | 1990 | 2000 | % Annual Rate 1990-2000 | 2000 | 2005 | 2000 National Rank | 2000 State Rank |
| ADAMS | 10,470 | 11,469 | 11,919 | 1.1 | 2.86 | 8,075 | 8,592 | 0.8 | 42,009 | 49,745 | 512 | 37 |
| ALLEN | 113,333 | 122,240 | 127,420 | 0.9 | 2.57 | 79,624 | 83,999 | 0.7 | 44,871 | 49,055 | 358 | 23 |
| BARTHOLOMEW | 24,192 | 27,502 | 28,755 | 1.6 | 2.52 | 18,141 | 20,192 | 1.3 | 46,544 | 52,349 | 290 | 17 |
| BENTON | 3,524 | 3,726 | 3,839 | 0.7 | 2.61 | 2,598 | 2,659 | 0.3 | 39,032 | 48,760 | 749 | 56 |
| BLACKFORD | 5,436 | 5,449 | 5,433 | 0.0 | 2.53 | 4,043 | 3,902 | -0.4 | 37,324 | 46,212 | 926 | 65 |
| BOONE | 13,922 | 16,881 | 18,585 | 2.4 | 2.66 | 10,816 | 12,748 | 2.0 | 53,552 | 62,325 | 142 | 5 |
| BROWN | 5,370 | 6,445 | 6,947 | 2.2 | 2.49 | 4,076 | 4,747 | 1.9 | 48,510 | 58,668 | 231 | 9 |
| CARROLL | 7,067 | 7,785 | 8,078 | 1.2 | 2.56 | 5,389 | 5,766 | 0.8 | 43,509 | 53,148 | 421 | 28 |
| CASS | 14,659 | 15,129 | 15,450 | 0.4 | 2.52 | 10,609 | 10,608 | 0.0 | 37,445 | 43,108 | 902 | 62 |
| CLARK | 33,292 | 36,987 | 39,143 | 1.3 | 2.56 | 24,355 | 26,206 | 0.9 | 40,153 | 45,266 | 659 | 45 |
| CLAY | 9,382 | 10,341 | 10,692 | 1.2 | 2.59 | 6,932 | 7,404 | 0.8 | 36,265 | 45,847 | 1071 | 71 |
| CLINTON | 11,450 | 12,558 | 12,691 | 1.1 | 2.57 | 8,610 | 9,167 | 0.8 | 41,453 | 50,964 | 555 | 41 |
| CRAWFORD | 3,660 | 4,025 | 4,246 | 1.2 | 2.67 | 2,754 | 2,944 | 0.8 | 32,829 | 39,963 | 1566 | 90 |
| DAVIESS | 10,012 | 10,805 | 11,164 | 0.9 | 2.66 | 7,404 | 7,750 | 0.6 | 33,794 | 41,354 | 1423 | 86 |
| DEARBORN | 13,642 | 17,493 | 19,243 | 3.1 | 2.77 | 10,692 | 13,508 | 2.9 | 47,692 | 56,603 | 249 | 13 |
| DECATUR | 8,427 | 9,383 | 9,804 | 1.3 | 2.73 | 6,455 | 6,953 | 0.9 | 44,148 | 54,159 | 387 | 24 |
| DE KALB | 12,725 | 14,801 | 15,771 | 1.8 | 2.69 | 9,617 | 10,817 | 1.4 | 45,951 | 54,483 | 313 | 20 |
| DELAWARE | 45,177 | 44,634 | 43,723 | -0.1 | 2.40 | 30,186 | 28,743 | -0.6 | 35,135 | 38,167 | 1228 | 80 |
| DUBOIS | 13,023 | 14,736 | 15,668 | 1.5 | 2.69 | 9,847 | 10,799 | 1.1 | 47,865 | 55,655 | 242 | 11 |
| ELKHART | 56,713 | 65,051 | 69,188 | 1.7 | 2.67 | 41,751 | 46,631 | 1.3 | 45,196 | 54,137 | 348 | 22 |
| FAYETTE | 9,945 | 10,096 | 9,993 | 0.2 | 2.51 | 7,313 | 7,202 | -0.2 | 35,522 | 40,632 | 1166 | 78 |
| FLOYD | 24,085 | 28,028 | 29,409 | 1.9 | 2.56 | 18,058 | 20,530 | 1.6 | 43,324 | 48,736 | 437 | 30 |
| FOUNTAIN | 6,858 | 7,255 | 7,445 | 0.7 | 2.51 | 5,044 | 5,147 | 0.2 | 37,364 | 44,646 | 920 | 63 |
| FRANKLIN | 6,636 | 7,753 | 8,346 | 1.9 | 2.85 | 5,303 | 6,065 | 1.6 | 43,918 | 54,625 | 399 | 25 |
| FULTON | 7,345 | 8,369 | 8,912 | 1.6 | 2.50 | 5,351 | 5,897 | 1.2 | 38,627 | 46,171 | 788 | 57 |
| GIBSON | 12,299 | 12,647 | 12,912 | 0.3 | 2.51 | 9,003 | 8,955 | -0.1 | 36,645 | 41,939 | 1028 | 69 |
| GRANT | 27,701 | 27,354 | 26,862 | -0.2 | 2.47 | 20,196 | 19,324 | -0.5 | 35,794 | 39,032 | 1127 | 74 |
| GREENE | 11,910 | 13,552 | 13,859 | 1.6 | 2.42 | 8,692 | 9,561 | 1.2 | 32,892 | 40,060 | 1555 | 88 |
| HAMILTON | 38,834 | 64,525 | 79,533 | 6.3 | 2.78 | 30,854 | 49,650 | 5.9 | 71,247 | 78,063 | 10 | 1 |
| HANCOCK | 15,959 | 20,500 | 22,955 | 3.1 | 2.74 | 12,886 | 16,124 | 2.8 | 58,977 | 65,999 | 81 | 3 |
| HARRISON | 10,618 | 13,121 | 14,576 | 2.6 | 2.73 | 8,437 | 10,150 | 2.3 | 41,903 | 48,794 | 521 | 39 |
| HENDRICKS | 26,109 | 35,577 | 41,434 | 3.8 | 2.78 | 21,220 | 28,188 | 3.5 | 61,534 | 71,524 | 63 | 2 |
| HENRY | 18,642 | 19,210 | 19,141 | 0.4 | 2.47 | 13,976 | 13,947 | 0.0 | 38,543 | 43,056 | 803 | 58 |
| HOWARD | 31,523 | 33,194 | 33,646 | 0.6 | 2.49 | 22,729 | 23,139 | 0.2 | 46,424 | 51,185 | 295 | 18 |
| HUNTINGTON | 12,830 | 13,780 | 14,123 | 0.9 | 2.63 | 9,643 | 10,100 | 0.6 | 43,416 | 52,479 | 431 | 29 |
| JACKSON | 14,032 | 15,705 | 16,341 | 1.4 | 2.62 | 10,701 | 11,600 | 1.0 | 40,504 | 47,576 | 628 | 43 |
| JASPER | 8,527 | 10,644 | 11,569 | 2.7 | 2.73 | 6,726 | 8,239 | 2.5 | 43,072 | 52,600 | 453 | 32 |
| JAY | 8,161 | 8,422 | 8,491 | 0.4 | 2.55 | 6,035 | 6,006 | -0.1 | 34,865 | 42,279 | 1274 | 81 |
| JEFFERSON | 10,897 | 11,875 | 12,471 | 1.0 | 2.54 | 8,023 | 8,444 | 0.6 | 37,347 | 43,247 | 924 | 64 |
| JENNINGS | 8,351 | 10,662 | 11,774 | 3.0 | 2.63 | 6,430 | 7,970 | 2.6 | 36,552 | 39,673 | 1036 | 70 |
| JOHNSON | 31,354 | 41,936 | 47,710 | 3.6 | 2.68 | 24,260 | 31,490 | 3.2 | 52,636 | 60,622 | 157 | 6 |
| KNOX | 15,145 | 15,268 | 15,133 | 0.1 | 2.39 | 10,248 | 9,919 | -0.4 | 32,837 | 38,404 | 1563 | 89 |
| KOSCIUSKO | 23,449 | 26,445 | 27,618 | 1.5 | 2.67 | 17,924 | 19,626 | 1.1 | 46,751 | 57,817 | 284 | 16 |
| LAGRANGE | 9,209 | 10,868 | 11,813 | 2.0 | 3.14 | 7,402 | 8,558 | 1.8 | 43,179 | 52,354 | 444 | 31 |
| LAKE | 170,748 | 174,787 | 175,522 | 0.3 | 2.72 | 125,761 | 125,118 | -0.1 | 41,149 | 45,788 | 578 | 42 |
| LA PORTE | 38,488 | 39,915 | 40,331 | 0.4 | 2.59 | 27,906 | 27,956 | 0.0 | 42,237 | 50,669 | 487 | 33 |
| LAWRENCE | 16,235 | 17,541 | 17,893 | 0.9 | 2.58 | 12,171 | 12,704 | 0.5 | 39,606 | 46,820 | 700 | 49 |
| MADISON | 49,804 | 50,815 | 50,628 | 0.2 | 2.47 | 35,804 | 35,239 | -0.2 | 39,436 | 43,991 | 717 | 51 |
| MARION | 319,471 | 332,162 | 333,144 | 0.5 | 2.40 | 205,652 | 205,066 | 0.0 | 39,276 | 42,763 | 729 | 54 |
| MARSHALL | 15,146 | 16,713 | 17,442 | 1.2 | 2.74 | 11,508 | 12,255 | 0.8 | 42,124 | 52,957 | 499 | 35 |
| MARTIN | 3,836 | 4,074 | 4,076 | 0.7 | 2.47 | 2,840 | 2,910 | 0.3 | 35,267 | 38,450 | 1209 | 79 |
| MIAMI | 13,484 | 12,975 | 13,661 | -0.5 | 2.59 | 10,284 | 9,615 | -0.8 | 36,126 | 43,026 | 1087 | 73 |
| MONROE | 39,351 | 44,252 | 45,940 | 1.4 | 2.31 | 22,953 | 25,045 | 1.1 | 39,621 | 45,330 | 699 | 48 |
| MONTGOMERY | 13,235 | 14,275 | 14,613 | 0.9 | 2.48 | 9,578 | 9,988 | 0.5 | 41,588 | 48,699 | 542 | 40 |
| MORGAN | 19,600 | 24,128 | 26,507 | 2.6 | 2.81 | 15,885 | 19,092 | 2.3 | 49,730 | 58,552 | 205 | 8 |
| NEWTON | 4,839 | 5,420 | 5,624 | 1.4 | 2.73 | 3,710 | 4,053 | 1.1 | 39,394 | 48,947 | 721 | 52 |
| NOBLE | 13,418 | 15,785 | 17,020 | 2.0 | 2.74 | 10,308 | 11,777 | 1.6 | 46,192 | 57,238 | 302 | 19 |
| OHIO | 1,980 | 2,049 | 2,069 | 0.4 | 2.64 | 1,497 | 1,499 | 0.0 | 43,655 | 51,950 | 417 | 27 |
| ORANGE | 6,950 | 7,648 | 8,104 | 1.2 | 2.59 | 5,169 | 5,507 | 0.8 | 31,468 | 37,480 | 1827 | 92 |
| OWEN | 6,394 | 7,837 | 8,281 | 2.5 | 2.64 | 4,936 | 5,879 | 2.1 | 36,191 | 41,174 | 1079 | 72 |
| PARKE | 5,845 | 6,534 | 6,855 | 1.4 | 2.47 | 4,343 | 4,720 | 1.0 | 36,654 | 45,483 | 1025 | 68 |
| PERRY | 6,845 | 7,048 | 7,041 | 0.4 | 2.56 | 5,137 | 5,120 | 0.0 | 36,853 | 44,713 | 999 | 67 |
| PIKE | 4,925 | 5,260 | 5,566 | 0.8 | 2.48 | 3,658 | 3,762 | 0.3 | 32,100 | 37,279 | 1699 | 91 |
| PORTER | 45,159 | 53,716 | 57,359 | 2.1 | 2.71 | 34,634 | 39,971 | 1.8 | 55,713 | 63,030 | 113 | 4 |
| POSEY | 9,508 | 9,852 | 9,851 | 0.4 | 2.64 | 7,331 | 7,411 | 0.1 | 47,989 | 53,289 | 237 | 10 |
| PULASKI | 4,722 | 5,064 | 5,253 | 0.9 | 2.63 | 3,485 | 3,601 | 0.4 | 38,251 | 46,298 | 834 | 60 |
| PUTNAM | 9,996 | 12,251 | 13,098 | 2.5 | 2.53 | 7,549 | 8,995 | 2.1 | 42,039 | 51,217 | 505 | 36 |
| RANDOLPH | 10,451 | 10,920 | 11,052 | 0.5 | 2.48 | 7,789 | 7,839 | 0.1 | 35,729 | 41,194 | 1132 | 75 |
| RIPLEY | 8,778 | 9,985 | 10,516 | 1.6 | 2.76 | 6,646 | 7,330 | 1.2 | 40,431 | 46,866 | 633 | 44 |
| RUSH | 6,504 | 6,656 | 6,654 | 0.3 | 2.65 | 4,985 | 4,953 | -0.1 | 39,232 | 47,379 | 733 | 55 |
| ST. JOSEPH | 92,365 | 98,506 | 100,129 | 0.8 | 2.50 | 63,629 | 65,732 | 0.4 | 39,722 | 43,494 | 691 | 47 |
| SCOTT | 7,593 | 8,641 | 9,216 | 1.6 | 2.72 | 5,881 | 6,487 | 1.2 | 35,603 | 40,005 | 1153 | 77 |
| SHELBY | 14,761 | 16,299 | 16,907 | 1.2 | 2.66 | 11,169 | 11,989 | 0.9 | 45,292 | 53,656 | 342 | 21 |
| SPENCER | 6,962 | 7,868 | 8,344 | 1.5 | 2.66 | 5,388 | 5,928 | 1.2 | 41,985 | 50,753 | 514 | 38 |
| STARKE | 8,141 | 9,014 | 9,301 | 1.2 | 2.58 | 6,186 | 6,643 | 0.9 | 33,258 | 40,622 | 1499 | 87 |
| STEUBEN | 10,194 | 12,139 | 12,884 | 2.1 | 2.58 | 7,446 | 8,609 | 1.8 | 43,813 | 51,910 | 408 | 26 |
| SULLIVAN | 7,364 | 7,531 | 7,692 | 0.3 | 2.56 | 5,338 | 5,281 | -0.1 | 34,111 | 41,208 | 1373 | 85 |
| INDIANA | | | | 1.1 | 2.56 | | | 0.8 | 42,096 | 48,409 | | |
| UNITED STATES | | | | 1.4 | 2.59 | | | 1.1 | 41,914 | 49,127 | | |

# INCOME

| COUNTY | 2000 Per Capita Income | 2000 HH Income Base | 2000 HOUSEHOLD INCOME DISTRIBUTION (%) Less than $15,000 | $15,000 to $24,999 | $25,000 to $49,999 | $50,000 to $99,999 | $100,000 to $149,999 | $150,000 or More | 2000 AVERAGE DISPOSABLE INCOME BY AGE OF HOUSEHOLDER All Ages | <35 | 35-44 | 45-54 | 55-64 | 65+ |
|---|---|---|---|---|---|---|---|---|---|---|---|---|---|---|
| ADAMS | 18,172 | 11,469 | 10.8 | 11.3 | 38.9 | 32.1 | 5.7 | 1.2 | 38,091 | 32,746 | 41,677 | 50,217 | 41,403 | 25,501 |
| ALLEN | 22,451 | 122,238 | 9.8 | 11.9 | 35.2 | 33.4 | 7.1 | 2.5 | 41,649 | 35,478 | 45,504 | 52,609 | 46,123 | 26,332 |
| BARTHOLOMEW | 23,646 | 27,502 | 9.5 | 10.7 | 34.0 | 34.4 | 8.4 | 3.1 | 43,551 | 35,704 | 46,784 | 55,898 | 46,345 | 29,360 |
| BENTON | 18,148 | 3,726 | 12.3 | 13.7 | 40.0 | 28.6 | 4.1 | 1.4 | 35,888 | 31,572 | 39,408 | 46,098 | 39,942 | 26,268 |
| BLACKFORD | 16,820 | 5,449 | 13.0 | 14.5 | 39.7 | 29.3 | 3.3 | 0.2 | 33,785 | 32,031 | 40,091 | 44,177 | 34,596 | 20,764 |
| BOONE | 33,168 | 16,881 | 6.7 | 8.3 | 30.6 | 33.1 | 11.8 | 9.6 | 57,631 | 43,575 | 59,090 | 67,004 | 59,293 | 34,978 |
| BROWN | 22,852 | 6,445 | 7.6 | 10.0 | 34.5 | 38.5 | 7.7 | 1.9 | 42,826 | 37,158 | 49,434 | 52,159 | 44,447 | 28,550 |
| CARROLL | 19,891 | 7,785 | 9.2 | 11.2 | 39.3 | 33.0 | 6.2 | 1.1 | 39,117 | 35,131 | 45,309 | 48,552 | 41,821 | 26,132 |
| CASS | 17,848 | 15,129 | 14.9 | 14.0 | 39.0 | 26.8 | 4.3 | 1.0 | 34,610 | 29,606 | 37,306 | 45,399 | 39,655 | 23,712 |
| CLARK | 18,714 | 36,987 | 13.5 | 12.6 | 37.5 | 30.3 | 5.1 | 1.1 | 36,612 | 31,693 | 41,160 | 44,237 | 40,920 | 24,493 |
| CLAY | 16,584 | 10,341 | 16.1 | 14.0 | 38.3 | 26.6 | 4.1 | 0.8 | 33,916 | 32,518 | 40,440 | 45,348 | 34,588 | 21,336 |
| CLINTON | 20,014 | 12,558 | 11.1 | 12.8 | 37.8 | 31.0 | 6.0 | 1.4 | 38,157 | 34,199 | 46,392 | 47,999 | 39,244 | 24,495 |
| CRAWFORD | 13,816 | 4,025 | 19.7 | 18.0 | 37.8 | 22.2 | 2.1 | 0.2 | 29,581 | 30,177 | 33,524 | 36,534 | 29,585 | 19,764 |
| DAVIESS | 16,374 | 10,805 | 16.0 | 17.4 | 38.6 | 22.7 | 4.0 | 1.4 | 33,009 | 29,693 | 39,372 | 42,396 | 34,272 | 22,044 |
| DEARBORN | 20,998 | 17,493 | 8.9 | 10.7 | 33.5 | 36.1 | 8.5 | 2.3 | 43,081 | 38,306 | 48,075 | 53,134 | 45,800 | 26,428 |
| DECATUR | 19,369 | 9,383 | 9.3 | 11.4 | 37.6 | 33.6 | 6.5 | 1.6 | 39,979 | 36,056 | 44,351 | 49,617 | 44,684 | 25,912 |
| DE KALB | 20,190 | 14,801 | 7.2 | 10.9 | 37.3 | 36.0 | 7.2 | 1.4 | 41,311 | 36,949 | 47,034 | 50,256 | 43,836 | 27,784 |
| DELAWARE | 19,603 | 44,634 | 20.4 | 14.6 | 33.8 | 24.7 | 4.7 | 1.8 | 34,300 | 26,356 | 39,658 | 46,561 | 38,562 | 22,774 |
| DUBOIS | 21,280 | 14,736 | 8.4 | 8.9 | 35.6 | 36.7 | 8.5 | 1.9 | 42,893 | 41,096 | 48,149 | 53,876 | 43,534 | 27,373 |
| ELKHART | 21,332 | 65,048 | 8.4 | 10.7 | 37.4 | 34.4 | 7.0 | 2.0 | 41,489 | 35,756 | 44,775 | 51,560 | 46,259 | 27,725 |
| FAYETTE | 16,880 | 10,096 | 16.6 | 15.7 | 36.3 | 27.2 | 3.6 | 0.7 | 33,144 | 30,457 | 37,680 | 41,700 | 36,606 | 21,564 |
| FLOYD | 21,358 | 28,027 | 13.4 | 11.5 | 34.3 | 32.3 | 6.4 | 2.1 | 39,563 | 34,254 | 45,282 | 48,654 | 41,340 | 24,610 |
| FOUNTAIN | 17,502 | 7,255 | 13.6 | 15.6 | 40.0 | 26.9 | 3.2 | 0.8 | 33,694 | 30,896 | 38,769 | 42,955 | 35,020 | 23,700 |
| FRANKLIN | 19,228 | 7,753 | 9.5 | 11.5 | 36.0 | 34.0 | 7.3 | 1.8 | 40,464 | 37,166 | 44,392 | 51,509 | 42,234 | 25,705 |
| FULTON | 17,642 | 8,369 | 14.1 | 10.5 | 40.8 | 30.4 | 3.9 | 0.3 | 34,737 | 33,523 | 40,137 | 43,507 | 36,452 | 23,242 |
| GIBSON | 17,271 | 12,647 | 16.0 | 14.6 | 39.2 | 25.3 | 3.8 | 1.2 | 33,797 | 30,030 | 40,014 | 43,527 | 37,054 | 21,410 |
| GRANT | 17,944 | 27,354 | 17.5 | 15.7 | 35.7 | 25.7 | 4.0 | 1.4 | 33,805 | 28,039 | 38,216 | 44,771 | 36,536 | 21,800 |
| GREENE | 16,036 | 13,552 | 19.1 | 16.1 | 38.3 | 23.4 | 2.6 | 0.6 | 30,658 | 28,426 | 35,996 | 40,178 | 31,194 | 20,600 |
| HAMILTON | 40,225 | 64,525 | 3.7 | 5.9 | 19.9 | 38.7 | 17.0 | 14.9 | 72,219 | 55,339 | 71,642 | 77,168 | 67,958 | 40,290 |
| HANCOCK | 28,086 | 20,500 | 6.2 | 5.1 | 27.0 | 43.3 | 13.3 | 5.1 | 53,029 | 45,492 | 59,288 | 65,807 | 55,157 | 31,232 |
| HARRISON | 18,309 | 13,121 | 10.5 | 13.5 | 37.9 | 31.1 | 5.8 | 1.3 | 38,080 | 33,731 | 43,386 | 47,610 | 38,055 | 25,370 |
| HENDRICKS | 27,166 | 35,577 | 5.7 | 4.8 | 23.8 | 46.4 | 14.4 | 4.8 | 53,989 | 47,714 | 59,330 | 65,216 | 56,166 | 32,021 |
| HENRY | 18,781 | 19,210 | 15.0 | 14.5 | 35.9 | 29.1 | 4.4 | 1.1 | 35,253 | 29,468 | 40,829 | 46,732 | 37,128 | 24,111 |
| HOWARD | 24,663 | 33,194 | 11.7 | 9.4 | 33.0 | 35.0 | 8.0 | 2.9 | 42,974 | 34,881 | 47,472 | 55,333 | 48,146 | 26,649 |
| HUNTINGTON | 20,113 | 13,780 | 9.5 | 11.7 | 38.1 | 34.0 | 5.5 | 1.2 | 38,888 | 36,173 | 42,842 | 49,461 | 42,243 | 24,969 |
| JACKSON | 19,632 | 15,705 | 12.3 | 13.4 | 36.8 | 30.8 | 5.6 | 1.2 | 37,192 | 34,056 | 44,155 | 47,667 | 37,275 | 23,801 |
| JASPER | 18,138 | 10,644 | 10.2 | 10.6 | 38.4 | 34.3 | 5.4 | 1.0 | 38,598 | 35,321 | 44,424 | 47,878 | 42,383 | 24,178 |
| JAY | 15,471 | 8,422 | 14.9 | 16.3 | 41.8 | 24.4 | 2.4 | 0.1 | 31,432 | 30,302 | 36,018 | 39,808 | 32,061 | 21,000 |
| JEFFERSON | 17,462 | 11,875 | 12.6 | 17.9 | 38.5 | 25.7 | 3.7 | 1.6 | 34,851 | 29,611 | 39,246 | 41,030 | 37,440 | 26,001 |
| JENNINGS | 16,363 | 10,662 | 14.3 | 16.3 | 39.1 | 25.4 | 3.8 | 1.0 | 33,821 | 30,659 | 41,353 | 41,493 | 35,050 | 21,017 |
| JOHNSON | 25,589 | 41,934 | 7.3 | 8.4 | 30.6 | 38.9 | 10.8 | 4.0 | 48,307 | 40,464 | 54,477 | 58,810 | 50,101 | 29,403 |
| KNOX | 17,755 | 15,268 | 20.7 | 15.5 | 36.1 | 21.9 | 4.5 | 1.3 | 32,342 | 28,178 | 38,660 | 41,581 | 35,778 | 21,679 |
| KOSCIUSKO | 21,098 | 26,445 | 8.0 | 8.9 | 37.2 | 36.7 | 7.7 | 1.6 | 41,939 | 38,233 | 45,287 | 51,809 | 45,905 | 28,566 |
| LAGRANGE | 16,415 | 10,868 | 8.2 | 11.6 | 39.6 | 34.2 | 5.5 | 0.9 | 38,824 | 35,847 | 42,009 | 48,564 | 42,614 | 25,577 |
| LAKE | 18,701 | 174,781 | 15.9 | 11.9 | 33.7 | 30.8 | 5.9 | 1.8 | 37,870 | 32,337 | 42,265 | 47,011 | 41,916 | 25,203 |
| LA PORTE | 20,638 | 39,915 | 12.2 | 12.3 | 35.5 | 31.7 | 6.5 | 1.9 | 39,203 | 34,100 | 44,949 | 49,058 | 43,023 | 25,315 |
| LAWRENCE | 17,856 | 17,541 | 12.9 | 14.6 | 37.4 | 30.4 | 4.0 | 0.9 | 35,478 | 32,288 | 42,505 | 45,474 | 37,245 | 22,194 |
| MADISON | 18,915 | 50,815 | 15.9 | 13.9 | 33.4 | 30.0 | 5.2 | 1.5 | 36,404 | 28,853 | 42,395 | 47,777 | 39,475 | 24,627 |
| MARION | 20,751 | 332,156 | 14.3 | 14.2 | 35.3 | 28.9 | 5.3 | 1.9 | 37,314 | 32,983 | 40,908 | 45,673 | 40,653 | 25,416 |
| MARSHALL | 19,460 | 16,713 | 9.0 | 12.5 | 38.9 | 33.4 | 5.2 | 1.1 | 38,255 | 34,241 | 43,836 | 47,945 | 39,977 | 25,388 |
| MARTIN | 15,660 | 4,074 | 16.1 | 17.3 | 40.2 | 23.8 | 2.4 | 0.3 | 31,295 | 29,271 | 37,496 | 37,220 | 35,426 | 20,482 |
| MIAMI | 16,603 | 12,973 | 13.3 | 17.8 | 38.5 | 26.7 | 3.3 | 0.6 | 33,059 | 28,909 | 38,754 | 41,660 | 37,796 | 21,112 |
| MONROE | 20,923 | 44,252 | 16.7 | 12.7 | 32.8 | 28.0 | 7.2 | 2.6 | 38,687 | 27,717 | 44,210 | 51,704 | 47,341 | 29,625 |
| MONTGOMERY | 19,665 | 14,275 | 12.6 | 12.1 | 37.7 | 31.7 | 5.3 | 0.7 | 36,862 | 34,559 | 41,652 | 46,471 | 38,919 | 25,396 |
| MORGAN | 22,711 | 24,128 | 8.3 | 8.9 | 33.2 | 38.5 | 8.8 | 2.3 | 44,124 | 38,700 | 49,143 | 55,746 | 46,432 | 27,315 |
| NEWTON | 16,995 | 5,420 | 12.6 | 13.9 | 40.0 | 28.6 | 4.1 | 0.9 | 35,316 | 34,578 | 39,786 | 41,581 | 38,235 | 23,501 |
| NOBLE | 19,182 | 15,785 | 8.4 | 8.3 | 38.9 | 36.7 | 6.6 | 1.1 | 40,827 | 37,642 | 46,530 | 51,005 | 43,221 | 25,187 |
| OHIO | 17,389 | 2,049 | 14.1 | 9.1 | 37.7 | 35.4 | 3.5 | 0.1 | 36,286 | 35,096 | 42,986 | 48,412 | 34,688 | 21,517 |
| ORANGE | 13,523 | 7,648 | 18.6 | 18.7 | 42.3 | 18.9 | 1.4 | 0.1 | 28,306 | 27,466 | 33,251 | 34,373 | 29,228 | 18,963 |
| OWEN | 16,999 | 7,837 | 14.0 | 18.2 | 39.0 | 24.1 | 3.6 | 1.1 | 33,346 | 31,389 | 37,712 | 42,679 | 34,670 | 22,076 |
| PARKE | 17,435 | 6,534 | 15.8 | 13.5 | 38.1 | 26.7 | 5.1 | 0.8 | 34,551 | 32,052 | 39,920 | 42,922 | 39,566 | 23,497 |
| PERRY | 17,041 | 7,048 | 15.2 | 13.5 | 41.7 | 26.0 | 2.8 | 0.7 | 33,138 | 31,855 | 37,946 | 42,275 | 34,726 | 21,888 |
| PIKE | 15,272 | 5,260 | 18.8 | 19.8 | 38.2 | 19.7 | 2.9 | 0.6 | 29,782 | 27,559 | 37,312 | 36,756 | 30,322 | 19,471 |
| PORTER | 27,716 | 53,716 | 6.8 | 7.4 | 27.9 | 39.5 | 12.1 | 6.2 | 53,194 | 42,405 | 57,610 | 63,113 | 56,934 | 33,019 |
| POSEY | 22,693 | 9,852 | 9.2 | 8.6 | 34.7 | 36.7 | 8.6 | 2.2 | 43,259 | 40,653 | 48,549 | 53,614 | 42,986 | 29,081 |
| PULASKI | 17,404 | 5,064 | 13.3 | 13.4 | 38.7 | 29.8 | 3.9 | 1.0 | 35,433 | 35,790 | 40,074 | 42,284 | 38,894 | 24,809 |
| PUTNAM | 18,434 | 12,251 | 9.4 | 13.0 | 38.4 | 32.7 | 5.6 | 1.0 | 38,059 | 34,988 | 43,938 | 47,256 | 41,428 | 25,185 |
| RANDOLPH | 16,983 | 10,920 | 15.9 | 14.4 | 40.3 | 26.0 | 2.7 | 0.7 | 32,544 | 29,191 | 37,373 | 40,811 | 36,327 | 22,122 |
| RIPLEY | 18,242 | 9,985 | 13.6 | 12.5 | 38.2 | 28.9 | 5.4 | 1.5 | 36,804 | 34,969 | 42,700 | 48,209 | 36,372 | 22,821 |
| RUSH | 18,102 | 6,656 | 12.4 | 14.7 | 37.4 | 29.1 | 5.2 | 1.2 | 36,360 | 33,129 | 42,108 | 46,298 | 35,684 | 26,699 |
| ST. JOSEPH | 19,451 | 98,506 | 14.0 | 14.1 | 35.9 | 29.0 | 5.3 | 1.7 | 36,952 | 32,187 | 42,223 | 47,977 | 39,942 | 23,303 |
| SCOTT | 15,358 | 8,641 | 16.1 | 17.9 | 39.1 | 22.7 | 3.3 | 0.8 | 32,231 | 29,538 | 35,976 | 38,549 | 33,299 | 23,292 |
| SHELBY | 20,491 | 16,299 | 9.7 | 11.0 | 35.7 | 35.9 | 6.4 | 1.4 | 40,316 | 37,194 | 44,202 | 51,439 | 42,416 | 26,238 |
| SPENCER | 17,567 | 7,868 | 13.1 | 10.8 | 39.6 | 31.3 | 4.6 | 0.6 | 36,491 | 34,820 | 39,393 | 46,177 | 38,318 | 23,649 |
| STARKE | 15,850 | 9,014 | 16.6 | 17.0 | 38.1 | 24.7 | 2.8 | 0.9 | 31,994 | 29,285 | 37,881 | 40,578 | 33,249 | 20,838 |
| STEUBEN | 19,614 | 12,139 | 8.9 | 10.2 | 38.7 | 35.9 | 5.4 | 1.1 | 39,190 | 35,334 | 44,531 | 50,341 | 39,156 | 25,802 |
| SULLIVAN | 15,326 | 7,531 | 18.1 | 16.8 | 36.4 | 24.1 | 3.8 | 0.9 | 32,101 | 31,306 | 39,402 | 41,054 | 32,838 | 19,969 |
| INDIANA | 21,043 | | 12.6 | 12.5 | 34.8 | 31.1 | 6.5 | 2.4 | 39,887 | 33,966 | 44,886 | 50,043 | 42,864 | 25,630 |
| UNITED STATES | 22,162 | | 14.5 | 12.5 | 32.3 | 29.8 | 7.4 | 3.5 | 40,748 | 34,503 | 44,969 | 49,579 | 43,409 | 27,339 |

 

| COUNTY | FINANCIAL SERVICES | | | | THE HOME | | | | | | ENTERTAINMENT | | | | | | PERSONAL | | | |
|---|---|---|---|---|---|---|---|---|---|---|---|---|---|---|---|---|---|---|---|---|
| | | | | | Home Improvements | | | Furnishings | | | | | | | | | | | | |
| | Auto Loan | Home Loan | Investments | Retirement Plans | Home Repair | Lawn & Garden | Remodeling | Appliances | Electronics | Furniture | Restaurants | Sporting Goods | Theater & Concerts | Toys & Hobbies | Travel | Video Rental | Apparel | Auto Aftermarket | Health Insurance | Pets & Supplies |
| ADAMS | 98 | 80 | 85 | 85 | 97 | 93 | 110 | 97 | 93 | 87 | 90 | 95 | 91 | 99 | 85 | 101 | 87 | 94 | 102 | 99 |
| ALLEN | 99 | 99 | 94 | 97 | 100 | 98 | 99 | 99 | 99 | 100 | 102 | 99 | 101 | 101 | 96 | 102 | 98 | 101 | 98 | 100 |
| BARTHOLOMEW | 101 | 95 | 99 | 99 | 101 | 100 | 107 | 100 | 99 | 99 | 101 | 101 | 102 | 103 | 96 | 102 | 98 | 101 | 102 | 102 |
| BENTON | 98 | 73 | 80 | 83 | 94 | 92 | 112 | 97 | 92 | 81 | 85 | 96 | 87 | 98 | 81 | 101 | 83 | 92 | 104 | 99 |
| BLACKFORD | 98 | 76 | 83 | 83 | 96 | 93 | 108 | 97 | 92 | 85 | 87 | 95 | 90 | 97 | 83 | 100 | 84 | 92 | 102 | 98 |
| BOONE | 105 | 110 | 107 | 115 | 104 | 108 | 110 | 104 | 107 | 108 | 112 | 108 | 113 | 108 | 106 | 105 | 110 | 109 | 105 | 105 |
| BROWN | 101 | 82 | 87 | 89 | 97 | 94 | 115 | 99 | 96 | 88 | 93 | 99 | 93 | 102 | 86 | 102 | 90 | 96 | 104 | 102 |
| CARROLL | 100 | 78 | 82 | 86 | 95 | 92 | 116 | 98 | 95 | 85 | 89 | 97 | 90 | 100 | 82 | 102 | 87 | 94 | 103 | 101 |
| CASS | 96 | 81 | 85 | 84 | 98 | 93 | 106 | 96 | 91 | 87 | 89 | 93 | 91 | 96 | 86 | 100 | 86 | 92 | 101 | 97 |
| CLARK | 98 | 91 | 92 | 91 | 99 | 96 | 102 | 98 | 96 | 95 | 97 | 96 | 97 | 99 | 92 | 101 | 93 | 98 | 100 | 99 |
| CLAY | 97 | 76 | 81 | 83 | 96 | 92 | 110 | 97 | 93 | 84 | 86 | 94 | 88 | 97 | 83 | 101 | 84 | 92 | 102 | 98 |
| CLINTON | 98 | 80 | 85 | 85 | 97 | 93 | 109 | 97 | 93 | 87 | 89 | 95 | 91 | 98 | 85 | 100 | 87 | 93 | 101 | 99 |
| CRAWFORD | 98 | 65 | 67 | 75 | 91 | 89 | 112 | 96 | 92 | 76 | 79 | 96 | 82 | 95 | 74 | 99 | 78 | 89 | 102 | 97 |
| DAVIESS | 97 | 73 | 81 | 82 | 95 | 92 | 110 | 96 | 92 | 82 | 85 | 94 | 87 | 96 | 81 | 100 | 83 | 91 | 103 | 98 |
| DEARBORN | 100 | 89 | 91 | 94 | 98 | 96 | 109 | 99 | 98 | 94 | 97 | 99 | 98 | 102 | 90 | 102 | 94 | 99 | 102 | 102 |
| DECATUR | 99 | 78 | 83 | 85 | 95 | 92 | 115 | 98 | 95 | 85 | 89 | 96 | 90 | 99 | 82 | 101 | 87 | 94 | 102 | 100 |
| DE KALB | 99 | 81 | 85 | 86 | 95 | 92 | 112 | 98 | 95 | 88 | 91 | 97 | 92 | 100 | 84 | 101 | 88 | 95 | 102 | 100 |
| DELAWARE | 96 | 91 | 96 | 93 | 101 | 97 | 100 | 96 | 93 | 92 | 94 | 94 | 96 | 97 | 94 | 99 | 91 | 96 | 99 | 98 |
| DUBOIS | 100 | 82 | 83 | 87 | 95 | 92 | 112 | 98 | 96 | 88 | 92 | 98 | 92 | 101 | 84 | 102 | 90 | 96 | 102 | 101 |
| ELKHART | 99 | 89 | 92 | 92 | 98 | 96 | 107 | 98 | 97 | 93 | 96 | 97 | 97 | 100 | 90 | 102 | 93 | 98 | 100 | 100 |
| FAYETTE | 97 | 78 | 83 | 83 | 98 | 93 | 108 | 97 | 92 | 86 | 88 | 94 | 90 | 97 | 85 | 100 | 85 | 92 | 101 | 98 |
| FLOYD | 98 | 92 | 94 | 93 | 100 | 97 | 103 | 98 | 96 | 96 | 97 | 96 | 98 | 99 | 94 | 101 | 93 | 98 | 100 | 99 |
| FOUNTAIN | 98 | 72 | 77 | 81 | 95 | 91 | 111 | 97 | 92 | 82 | 84 | 95 | 87 | 97 | 80 | 100 | 82 | 91 | 103 | 98 |
| FRANKLIN | 99 | 75 | 80 | 83 | 95 | 92 | 112 | 97 | 93 | 83 | 87 | 97 | 88 | 99 | 81 | 101 | 85 | 92 | 103 | 99 |
| FULTON | 99 | 78 | 82 | 87 | 95 | 92 | 112 | 98 | 95 | 85 | 88 | 98 | 90 | 99 | 82 | 101 | 86 | 94 | 103 | 100 |
| GIBSON | 98 | 78 | 83 | 84 | 96 | 92 | 112 | 97 | 93 | 86 | 89 | 95 | 90 | 99 | 84 | 101 | 86 | 93 | 102 | 99 |
| GRANT | 97 | 84 | 91 | 89 | 99 | 96 | 106 | 97 | 93 | 90 | 92 | 95 | 94 | 98 | 90 | 100 | 89 | 95 | 101 | 98 |
| GREENE | 97 | 74 | 79 | 82 | 94 | 91 | 110 | 96 | 93 | 82 | 85 | 93 | 87 | 96 | 81 | 101 | 83 | 91 | 102 | 97 |
| HAMILTON | 107 | 120 | 104 | 120 | 104 | 110 | 107 | 107 | 112 | 117 | 122 | 114 | 118 | 111 | 110 | 107 | 119 | 116 | 103 | 108 |
| HANCOCK | 102 | 101 | 100 | 103 | 102 | 102 | 106 | 101 | 103 | 104 | 108 | 103 | 107 | 106 | 99 | 104 | 105 | 106 | 102 | 104 |
| HARRISON | 100 | 78 | 82 | 86 | 95 | 91 | 116 | 98 | 95 | 85 | 89 | 97 | 90 | 101 | 82 | 102 | 87 | 94 | 103 | 102 |
| HENDRICKS | 103 | 104 | 102 | 106 | 102 | 104 | 106 | 102 | 105 | 106 | 110 | 105 | 109 | 107 | 101 | 105 | 107 | 108 | 102 | 105 |
| HENRY | 97 | 82 | 88 | 86 | 99 | 95 | 106 | 97 | 92 | 89 | 91 | 94 | 93 | 98 | 88 | 100 | 87 | 94 | 102 | 98 |
| HOWARD | 98 | 91 | 96 | 93 | 101 | 98 | 102 | 98 | 95 | 96 | 97 | 96 | 99 | 99 | 94 | 101 | 93 | 98 | 101 | 99 |
| HUNTINGTON | 98 | 82 | 86 | 87 | 96 | 93 | 110 | 97 | 94 | 88 | 91 | 96 | 92 | 99 | 85 | 101 | 88 | 94 | 101 | 100 |
| JACKSON | 98 | 80 | 86 | 86 | 96 | 93 | 110 | 97 | 94 | 87 | 90 | 96 | 91 | 99 | 84 | 101 | 87 | 94 | 102 | 99 |
| JASPER | 100 | 85 | 89 | 90 | 98 | 95 | 111 | 99 | 96 | 90 | 94 | 98 | 95 | 101 | 87 | 102 | 91 | 96 | 103 | 101 |
| JAY | 98 | 75 | 81 | 82 | 96 | 92 | 110 | 97 | 93 | 84 | 86 | 96 | 89 | 97 | 82 | 100 | 84 | 92 | 102 | 98 |
| JEFFERSON | 98 | 81 | 89 | 87 | 98 | 95 | 108 | 98 | 94 | 88 | 91 | 96 | 93 | 99 | 87 | 101 | 88 | 94 | 102 | 99 |
| JENNINGS | 97 | 75 | 80 | 82 | 94 | 91 | 111 | 97 | 93 | 84 | 86 | 95 | 88 | 97 | 81 | 100 | 84 | 92 | 101 | 98 |
| JOHNSON | 101 | 102 | 96 | 102 | 99 | 100 | 103 | 101 | 102 | 102 | 106 | 103 | 104 | 104 | 97 | 103 | 102 | 104 | 101 | 103 |
| KNOX | 95 | 81 | 88 | 86 | 98 | 94 | 103 | 95 | 92 | 87 | 88 | 92 | 91 | 95 | 88 | 99 | 85 | 93 | 101 | 96 |
| KOSCIUSKO | 100 | 83 | 85 | 89 | 95 | 93 | 113 | 99 | 96 | 89 | 93 | 98 | 93 | 101 | 85 | 102 | 90 | 96 | 102 | 102 |
| LAGRANGE | 100 | 75 | 79 | 85 | 94 | 91 | 116 | 98 | 94 | 82 | 87 | 98 | 88 | 100 | 80 | 101 | 85 | 93 | 104 | 101 |
| LAKE | 97 | 93 | 96 | 93 | 101 | 98 | 95 | 98 | 95 | 98 | 96 | 96 | 100 | 98 | 97 | 102 | 96 | 100 | 96 | 98 |
| LA PORTE | 99 | 91 | 98 | 95 | 102 | 99 | 104 | 99 | 96 | 96 | 97 | 97 | 99 | 100 | 95 | 101 | 94 | 98 | 101 | 100 |
| LAWRENCE | 98 | 81 | 88 | 86 | 98 | 94 | 109 | 97 | 93 | 88 | 90 | 95 | 92 | 98 | 87 | 101 | 87 | 94 | 102 | 99 |
| MADISON | 97 | 86 | 93 | 89 | 100 | 96 | 103 | 97 | 93 | 92 | 92 | 94 | 95 | 97 | 92 | 100 | 90 | 95 | 100 | 97 |
| MARION | 97 | 98 | 97 | 96 | 101 | 99 | 94 | 98 | 96 | 99 | 99 | 96 | 100 | 98 | 98 | 101 | 96 | 100 | 97 | 98 |
| MARSHALL | 100 | 84 | 88 | 90 | 96 | 94 | 112 | 99 | 96 | 89 | 93 | 98 | 94 | 101 | 86 | 102 | 91 | 96 | 103 | 101 |
| MARTIN | 98 | 72 | 76 | 80 | 94 | 91 | 112 | 97 | 93 | 81 | 84 | 96 | 86 | 97 | 79 | 100 | 82 | 91 | 102 | 98 |
| MIAMI | 97 | 81 | 84 | 84 | 96 | 92 | 107 | 96 | 92 | 87 | 90 | 94 | 91 | 97 | 85 | 100 | 86 | 93 | 100 | 98 |
| MONROE | 96 | 97 | 97 | 97 | 99 | 95 | 101 | 93 | 94 | 90 | 95 | 94 | 94 | 97 | 93 | 98 | 92 | 97 | 98 | 98 |
| MONTGOMERY | 98 | 81 | 85 | 86 | 97 | 93 | 110 | 97 | 94 | 87 | 90 | 96 | 91 | 99 | 85 | 101 | 87 | 94 | 102 | 100 |
| MORGAN | 99 | 87 | 89 | 90 | 98 | 95 | 108 | 98 | 96 | 92 | 95 | 98 | 96 | 101 | 89 | 102 | 92 | 97 | 101 | 101 |
| NEWTON | 100 | 82 | 85 | 88 | 95 | 93 | 114 | 98 | 97 | 88 | 92 | 97 | 92 | 100 | 84 | 102 | 89 | 95 | 102 | 101 |
| NOBLE | 100 | 78 | 82 | 86 | 95 | 92 | 116 | 98 | 95 | 86 | 90 | 98 | 90 | 101 | 82 | 102 | 87 | 94 | 103 | 102 |
| OHIO | 99 | 78 | 83 | 85 | 97 | 93 | 112 | 98 | 93 | 86 | 89 | 96 | 91 | 99 | 84 | 101 | 86 | 93 | 103 | 100 |
| ORANGE | 97 | 69 | 74 | 78 | 92 | 90 | 112 | 96 | 93 | 79 | 81 | 94 | 84 | 95 | 77 | 100 | 80 | 90 | 102 | 97 |
| OWEN | 99 | 75 | 79 | 83 | 94 | 91 | 114 | 97 | 94 | 83 | 86 | 96 | 88 | 99 | 80 | 101 | 85 | 93 | 103 | 100 |
| PARKE | 98 | 71 | 78 | 82 | 93 | 91 | 112 | 97 | 92 | 79 | 83 | 96 | 85 | 97 | 79 | 100 | 81 | 91 | 104 | 98 |
| PERRY | 98 | 76 | 82 | 84 | 96 | 93 | 111 | 97 | 93 | 85 | 87 | 96 | 90 | 98 | 83 | 100 | 85 | 92 | 102 | 99 |
| PIKE | 97 | 72 | 77 | 80 | 94 | 91 | 110 | 96 | 92 | 81 | 84 | 94 | 86 | 96 | 80 | 100 | 82 | 91 | 103 | 97 |
| PORTER | 102 | 101 | 98 | 101 | 101 | 101 | 106 | 101 | 102 | 103 | 107 | 102 | 105 | 105 | 98 | 104 | 103 | 105 | 101 | 103 |
| POSEY | 100 | 82 | 84 | 88 | 96 | 93 | 112 | 99 | 96 | 89 | 92 | 98 | 93 | 101 | 85 | 102 | 90 | 96 | 102 | 101 |
| PULASKI | 98 | 75 | 82 | 84 | 94 | 92 | 112 | 97 | 94 | 82 | 86 | 96 | 88 | 97 | 81 | 101 | 84 | 92 | 103 | 99 |
| PUTNAM | 97 | 79 | 83 | 84 | 95 | 91 | 110 | 96 | 93 | 85 | 88 | 94 | 89 | 97 | 83 | 100 | 85 | 93 | 101 | 99 |
| RANDOLPH | 97 | 76 | 82 | 83 | 97 | 92 | 110 | 97 | 92 | 85 | 87 | 95 | 89 | 97 | 83 | 100 | 84 | 92 | 102 | 98 |
| RIPLEY | 98 | 77 | 81 | 83 | 95 | 91 | 111 | 97 | 93 | 84 | 87 | 95 | 89 | 98 | 82 | 101 | 85 | 93 | 102 | 99 |
| RUSH | 99 | 76 | 82 | 84 | 95 | 92 | 113 | 97 | 93 | 84 | 88 | 96 | 89 | 99 | 82 | 101 | 86 | 93 | 103 | 100 |
| ST. JOSEPH | 97 | 95 | 98 | 95 | 101 | 99 | 99 | 98 | 96 | 97 | 98 | 97 | 100 | 99 | 97 | 101 | 95 | 99 | 100 | 99 |
| SCOTT | 98 | 71 | 76 | 80 | 94 | 91 | 111 | 97 | 92 | 81 | 83 | 95 | 86 | 96 | 79 | 100 | 82 | 91 | 103 | 98 |
| SHELBY | 99 | 86 | 89 | 90 | 97 | 94 | 110 | 98 | 96 | 91 | 94 | 97 | 95 | 100 | 88 | 102 | 92 | 97 | 101 | 101 |
| SPENCER | 100 | 77 | 81 | 85 | 94 | 91 | 116 | 98 | 95 | 85 | 88 | 97 | 89 | 100 | 81 | 102 | 87 | 94 | 103 | 101 |
| STARKE | 98 | 71 | 75 | 81 | 93 | 90 | 112 | 97 | 93 | 80 | 83 | 95 | 85 | 96 | 78 | 100 | 81 | 91 | 103 | 98 |
| STEUBEN | 99 | 81 | 84 | 88 | 95 | 93 | 116 | 98 | 94 | 85 | 89 | 97 | 90 | 100 | 85 | 101 | 87 | 94 | 104 | 101 |
| SULLIVAN | 97 | 77 | 84 | 83 | 97 | 93 | 108 | 97 | 92 | 85 | 87 | 94 | 89 | 96 | 85 | 100 | 84 | 92 | 102 | 97 |
| INDIANA | 98 | 92 | 94 | 94 | 99 | 97 | 103 | 98 | 96 | 95 | 97 | 98 | 98 | 100 | 93 | 101 | 94 | 98 | 100 | 100 |
| UNITED STATES | 100 | 100 | 100 | 100 | 100 | 100 | 100 | 100 | 100 | 100 | 100 | 100 | 100 | 100 | 100 | 100 | 100 | 100 | 100 | 100 |

# POPULATION CHANGE

| COUNTY | FIPS Code | MSA Code | DMA Code | POPULATION 1990 | POPULATION 2000 | POPULATION 2005 | 1990-2000 ANNUAL CHANGE % Rate | 1990-2000 ANNUAL CHANGE State Rank | RACE (%) White 1990 | White 2000 | Black 1990 | Black 2000 | Asian/Pacific 1990 | Asian/Pacific 2000 |
|---|---|---|---|---|---|---|---|---|---|---|---|---|---|---|
| SWITZERLAND | 155 | 0000 | 515 | 7,738 | 9,139 | 9,971 | 1.6 | 14 | 99.4 | 99.3 | 0.2 | 0.2 | 0.1 | 0.3 |
| TIPPECANOE | 157 | 3920 | 582 | 130,598 | 143,274 | 147,505 | 0.9 | 35 | 93.4 | 91.8 | 2.0 | 2.3 | 3.7 | 4.8 |
| TIPTON | 159 | 3850 | 527 | 16,119 | 16,691 | 16,944 | 0.3 | 64 | 99.2 | 99.0 | 0.1 | 0.1 | 0.3 | 0.4 |
| UNION | 161 | 0000 | 515 | 6,976 | 7,312 | 7,385 | 0.5 | 58 | 99.1 | 98.9 | 0.3 | 0.4 | 0.3 | 0.4 |
| VANDERBURGH | 163 | 2440 | 649 | 165,058 | 167,856 | 167,525 | 0.2 | 70 | 91.6 | 90.4 | 7.5 | 8.5 | 0.6 | 0.8 |
| VERMILLION | 165 | 8320 | 581 | 16,773 | 16,995 | 17,151 | 0.1 | 73 | 99.5 | 99.3 | 0.1 | 0.2 | 0.2 | 0.3 |
| VIGO | 167 | 8320 | 581 | 106,107 | 103,742 | 100,680 | -0.2 | 86 | 92.7 | 91.7 | 5.6 | 6.1 | 1.1 | 1.5 |
| WABASH | 169 | 0000 | 509 | 35,069 | 34,482 | 34,142 | -0.2 | 86 | 98.3 | 97.9 | 0.4 | 0.5 | 0.4 | 0.5 |
| WARREN | 171 | 0000 | 582 | 8,176 | 8,392 | 8,586 | 0.3 | 64 | 99.6 | 99.4 | 0.0 | 0.1 | 0.2 | 0.3 |
| WARRICK | 173 | 2440 | 649 | 44,920 | 53,464 | 57,912 | 1.7 | 13 | 98.6 | 98.2 | 0.8 | 1.0 | 0.3 | 0.5 |
| WASHINGTON | 175 | 0000 | 529 | 23,717 | 28,746 | 31,337 | 1.9 | 7 | 99.6 | 99.5 | 0.1 | 0.1 | 0.1 | 0.1 |
| WAYNE | 177 | 0000 | 542 | 71,951 | 70,840 | 69,393 | -0.2 | 86 | 93.9 | 92.8 | 5.3 | 6.1 | 0.4 | 0.6 |
| WELLS | 179 | 2760 | 509 | 25,948 | 26,862 | 27,089 | 0.3 | 64 | 99.3 | 99.0 | 0.0 | 0.0 | 0.2 | 0.2 |
| WHITE | 181 | 0000 | 527 | 23,265 | 25,693 | 26,650 | 1.0 | 30 | 99.4 | 99.3 | 0.0 | 0.0 | 0.2 | 0.2 |
| WHITLEY | 183 | 2760 | 509 | 27,651 | 31,179 | 33,062 | 1.2 | 24 | 99.4 | 99.3 | 0.1 | 0.1 | 0.1 | 0.2 |
| INDIANA | | | | | | | 0.7 | | 90.6 | 89.6 | 7.8 | 8.2 | 0.7 | 1.0 |
| UNITED STATES | | | | | | | 1.0 | | 80.3 | 77.9 | 12.1 | 12.4 | 2.9 | 3.9 |

| COUNTY | % HISPANIC ORIGIN | | 2000 AGE DISTRIBUTION (%) | | | | | | | | | | MEDIAN AGE | | 2000 Males/ Females (×100) |
|---|---|---|---|---|---|---|---|---|---|---|---|---|---|---|---|
| | 1990 | 2000 | 0-4 | 5-9 | 10-14 | 15-19 | 20-24 | 25-44 | 45-64 | 65-84 | 85+ | 18+ | 1990 | 2000 | |
| SWITZERLAND | 0.3 | 0.9 | 6.7 | 7.0 | 7.0 | 6.9 | 5.9 | 26.9 | 24.4 | 13.2 | 2.0 | 74.9 | 35.2 | 38.0 | 94.0 |
| TIPPECANOE | 1.6 | 2.8 | 6.0 | 5.7 | 5.7 | 11.6 | 16.0 | 28.0 | 17.6 | 8.2 | 1.3 | 79.7 | 26.8 | 28.8 | 102.3 |
| TIPTON | 0.8 | 1.5 | 6.1 | 6.5 | 7.1 | 7.0 | 5.4 | 28.7 | 24.9 | 12.3 | 2.0 | 75.9 | 35.2 | 38.4 | 95.7 |
| UNION | 0.4 | 0.9 | 6.6 | 6.9 | 6.9 | 7.1 | 6.4 | 28.6 | 24.2 | 11.5 | 1.8 | 74.9 | 33.7 | 36.4 | 96.2 |
| VANDERBURGH | 0.5 | 1.2 | 6.5 | 6.7 | 6.9 | 7.0 | 6.2 | 29.4 | 22.0 | 13.2 | 2.1 | 76.2 | 34.5 | 37.3 | 90.9 |
| VERMILLION | 0.4 | 0.9 | 5.9 | 6.3 | 7.0 | 6.8 | 5.5 | 28.1 | 24.8 | 13.3 | 2.3 | 76.8 | 36.5 | 39.2 | 92.3 |
| VIGO | 0.9 | 1.6 | 6.0 | 6.1 | 6.2 | 8.8 | 8.6 | 29.0 | 21.2 | 12.1 | 2.0 | 78.1 | 33.0 | 35.4 | 98.1 |
| WABASH | 0.9 | 1.7 | 6.5 | 6.7 | 7.0 | 8.2 | 6.7 | 27.6 | 22.5 | 12.4 | 2.4 | 75.3 | 33.7 | 36.6 | 94.3 |
| WARREN | 0.3 | 0.8 | 6.9 | 6.9 | 7.5 | 6.6 | 5.1 | 27.5 | 25.7 | 12.1 | 1.7 | 74.6 | 36.0 | 38.3 | 99.6 |
| WARRICK | 0.4 | 1.0 | 6.6 | 7.1 | 7.7 | 7.2 | 5.4 | 31.3 | 24.4 | 9.2 | 1.3 | 74.1 | 33.3 | 36.6 | 97.3 |
| WASHINGTON | 0.5 | 1.1 | 6.7 | 6.9 | 7.7 | 7.1 | 6.0 | 29.8 | 23.6 | 10.7 | 1.6 | 74.4 | 33.3 | 36.4 | 99.3 |
| WAYNE | 0.5 | 1.2 | 6.4 | 6.4 | 6.8 | 7.3 | 6.4 | 27.8 | 23.7 | 13.2 | 2.0 | 76.2 | 34.9 | 37.7 | 92.6 |
| WELLS | 1.0 | 1.9 | 7.6 | 7.7 | 7.7 | 7.6 | 6.1 | 28.2 | 22.2 | 11.0 | 1.9 | 72.4 | 33.1 | 35.9 | 96.5 |
| WHITE | 0.8 | 1.5 | 6.6 | 7.1 | 7.4 | 6.9 | 5.2 | 28.2 | 23.5 | 13.3 | 1.8 | 74.4 | 35.1 | 37.9 | 94.6 |
| WHITLEY | 0.5 | 1.1 | 7.2 | 7.5 | 7.7 | 7.1 | 5.6 | 29.0 | 22.9 | 11.2 | 1.8 | 73.0 | 33.3 | 36.2 | 96.7 |
| INDIANA | 1.8 | 2.9 | 6.9 | 7.0 | 7.2 | 7.4 | 6.8 | 29.7 | 22.5 | 10.9 | 1.5 | 74.8 | 32.8 | 35.7 | 94.8 |
| UNITED STATES | 9.0 | 11.8 | 6.9 | 7.2 | 7.2 | 7.2 | 6.7 | 29.9 | 22.2 | 11.1 | 1.6 | 74.6 | 32.9 | 35.7 | 95.6 |

# HOUSEHOLDS

| COUNTY | HOUSEHOLDS 1990 | HOUSEHOLDS 2000 | HOUSEHOLDS 2005 | % Annual Rate 1990-2000 | 2000 Average HH Size | FAMILIES 1990 | FAMILIES 2000 | % Annual Rate 1990-2000 | MEDIAN HOUSEHOLD INCOME 2000 | MEDIAN HOUSEHOLD INCOME 2005 | 2000 National Rank | 2000 State Rank |
|---|---|---|---|---|---|---|---|---|---|---|---|---|
| SWITZERLAND | 2,839 | 3,487 | 3,876 | 2.5 | 2.59 | 2,099 | 2,488 | 2.1 | 38,462 | 48,583 | 812 | 59 |
| TIPPECANOE | 45,618 | 50,369 | 52,147 | 1.2 | 2.49 | 28,742 | 30,567 | 0.7 | 42,228 | 49,429 | 489 | 34 |
| TIPTON | 6,026 | 6,159 | 6,216 | 0.3 | 2.68 | 4,554 | 4,503 | -0.1 | 47,699 | 56,292 | 248 | 12 |
| UNION | 2,576 | 2,719 | 2,757 | 0.7 | 2.65 | 1,958 | 2,016 | 0.4 | 40,063 | 49,382 | 668 | 46 |
| VANDERBURGH | 66,780 | 68,399 | 68,880 | 0.3 | 2.36 | 44,311 | 43,816 | -0.1 | 37,915 | 41,912 | 852 | 61 |
| VERMILLION | 6,638 | 6,805 | 6,912 | 0.3 | 2.46 | 4,650 | 4,602 | -0.1 | 34,414 | 40,384 | 1331 | 82 |
| VIGO | 39,804 | 39,776 | 38,974 | 0.0 | 2.39 | 26,608 | 25,650 | -0.4 | 34,129 | 38,425 | 1366 | 84 |
| WABASH | 12,630 | 12,669 | 12,656 | 0.0 | 2.57 | 9,450 | 9,200 | -0.3 | 39,528 | 46,596 | 709 | 50 |
| WARREN | 3,015 | 3,164 | 3,273 | 0.6 | 2.62 | 2,378 | 2,426 | 0.2 | 37,016 | 45,145 | 974 | 66 |
| WARRICK | 15,817 | 19,103 | 20,845 | 2.3 | 2.77 | 12,761 | 15,126 | 2.1 | 51,038 | 56,610 | 183 | 7 |
| WASHINGTON | 8,664 | 10,892 | 12,084 | 2.8 | 2.61 | 6,597 | 8,016 | 2.4 | 35,611 | 42,466 | 1151 | 76 |
| WAYNE | 27,587 | 27,709 | 27,411 | 0.1 | 2.46 | 19,766 | 19,175 | -0.4 | 34,176 | 38,232 | 1358 | 83 |
| WELLS | 9,438 | 10,023 | 10,227 | 0.7 | 2.64 | 7,249 | 7,463 | 0.4 | 47,259 | 54,012 | 266 | 14 |
| WHITE | 8,926 | 10,062 | 10,537 | 1.5 | 2.53 | 6,567 | 7,166 | 1.1 | 39,362 | 47,862 | 723 | 53 |
| WHITLEY | 10,010 | 11,491 | 12,286 | 1.7 | 2.67 | 7,677 | 8,553 | 1.3 | 46,904 | 55,206 | 277 | 15 |
| INDIANA | | | | 1.1 | 2.56 | | | 0.8 | 42,096 | 48,409 | | |
| UNITED STATES | | | | 1.4 | 2.59 | | | 1.1 | 41,914 | 49,127 | | |

| COUNTY | 2000 Per Capita Income | 2000 HH Income Base | 2000 HOUSEHOLD INCOME DISTRIBUTION (%) | | | | | | 2000 AVERAGE DISPOSABLE INCOME BY AGE OF HOUSEHOLDER | | | | | |
|---|---|---|---|---|---|---|---|---|---|---|---|---|---|---|
| | | | Less than $15,000 | $15,000 to $24,999 | $25,000 to $49,999 | $50,000 to $99,999 | $100,000 to $149,999 | $150,000 or More | All Ages | <35 | 35-44 | 45-54 | 55-64 | 65+ |
| SWITZERLAND | 17,485 | 3,487 | 15.3 | 12.0 | 39.2 | 28.5 | 4.2 | 0.9 | 34,831 | 35,010 | 39,201 | 42,534 | 36,760 | 23,465 |
| TIPPECANOE | 21,329 | 50,369 | 12.2 | 13.3 | 33.6 | 29.8 | 7.7 | 3.5 | 41,716 | 29,441 | 48,825 | 55,230 | 49,304 | 31,184 |
| TIPTON | 22,281 | 6,159 | 9.8 | 9.7 | 33.5 | 36.5 | 7.8 | 2.8 | 43,242 | 37,390 | 48,896 | 56,384 | 43,532 | 26,571 |
| UNION | 17,189 | 2,719 | 10.5 | 14.4 | 41.1 | 28.8 | 4.6 | 0.6 | 35,826 | 30,995 | 41,194 | 46,128 | 34,194 | 26,577 |
| VANDERBURGH | 20,637 | 68,397 | 16.3 | 14.5 | 34.7 | 26.7 | 5.7 | 2.2 | 36,862 | 31,651 | 42,925 | 46,229 | 40,505 | 24,394 |
| VERMILLION | 17,934 | 6,805 | 19.5 | 15.4 | 35.5 | 24.3 | 3.8 | 1.5 | 32,929 | 30,835 | 43,251 | 39,907 | 33,147 | 19,560 |
| VIGO | 19,526 | 39,770 | 17.5 | 17.0 | 36.3 | 22.4 | 4.7 | 2.2 | 34,475 | 27,659 | 40,170 | 45,533 | 38,320 | 22,805 |
| WABASH | 17,790 | 12,669 | 12.8 | 12.6 | 39.5 | 30.1 | 4.4 | 0.8 | 35,745 | 32,122 | 39,856 | 45,122 | 39,397 | 24,260 |
| WARREN | 16,455 | 3,164 | 12.8 | 15.0 | 40.9 | 27.7 | 3.3 | 0.3 | 33,723 | 29,137 | 42,035 | 41,215 | 34,034 | 22,766 |
| WARRICK | 25,423 | 19,103 | 6.4 | 8.8 | 33.2 | 37.7 | 10.0 | 3.8 | 47,306 | 39,620 | 52,358 | 56,780 | 48,832 | 28,785 |
| WASHINGTON | 15,968 | 10,892 | 15.6 | 17.4 | 38.5 | 24.1 | 3.8 | 0.6 | 32,572 | 30,015 | 37,540 | 39,340 | 33,348 | 22,475 |
| WAYNE | 17,258 | 27,709 | 17.1 | 17.8 | 36.0 | 24.1 | 3.8 | 1.2 | 32,906 | 28,354 | 37,598 | 41,924 | 35,934 | 22,186 |
| WELLS | 20,613 | 10,023 | 8.1 | 9.1 | 37.0 | 37.2 | 7.2 | 1.5 | 42,071 | 36,541 | 48,018 | 50,323 | 46,816 | 29,216 |
| WHITE | 18,450 | 10,062 | 12.0 | 13.9 | 39.3 | 30.1 | 3.8 | 0.9 | 35,371 | 34,509 | 41,039 | 43,943 | 35,404 | 24,738 |
| WHITLEY | 20,291 | 11,491 | 8.8 | 9.6 | 35.2 | 38.3 | 7.0 | 1.2 | 41,080 | 38,113 | 46,548 | 53,168 | 46,119 | 24,746 |
| INDIANA | 21,043 | | 12.6 | 12.5 | 34.8 | 31.1 | 6.5 | 2.4 | 39,887 | 33,966 | 44,886 | 50,043 | 42,864 | 25,630 |
| UNITED STATES | 22,162 | | 14.5 | 12.5 | 32.3 | 29.8 | 7.4 | 3.5 | 40,748 | 34,503 | 44,969 | 49,579 | 43,409 | 27,339 |

# SPENDING POTENTIAL INDEXES

| COUNTY | FINANCIAL SERVICES | | | | THE HOME | | | | | | ENTERTAINMENT | | | | | | PERSONAL | | | |
|---|---|---|---|---|---|---|---|---|---|---|---|---|---|---|---|---|---|---|---|---|
| | | | | | Home Improvements | | | Furnishings | | | | | | | | | | | | |
| | Auto Loan | Home Loan | Invest-ments | Retire-ment Plans | Home Repair | Lawn & Garden | Remodel-ing | Appli-ances | Elec-tronics | Furni-ture | Restau-rants | Sport-ing Goods | Theater & Concerts | Toys & Hobbies | Travel | Video Rental | Apparel | Auto After-market | Health Insur-ance | Pets & Supplies |
| SWITZERLAND | 98 | 72 | 77 | 82 | 93 | 90 | 113 | 97 | 93 | 81 | 84 | 96 | 86 | 97 | 78 | 101 | 82 | 91 | 103 | 99 |
| TIPPECANOE | 98 | 100 | 98 | 98 | 100 | 98 | 99 | 96 | 96 | 95 | 100 | 96 | 98 | 99 | 96 | 100 | 96 | 100 | 99 | 99 |
| TIPTON | 99 | 80 | 85 | 86 | 97 | 93 | 111 | 98 | 94 | 87 | 90 | 96 | 92 | 99 | 85 | 101 | 87 | 94 | 102 | 100 |
| UNION | 97 | 78 | 82 | 84 | 94 | 91 | 109 | 96 | 92 | 83 | 88 | 95 | 88 | 98 | 82 | 100 | 85 | 92 | 102 | 98 |
| VANDERBURGH | 97 | 95 | 99 | 95 | 103 | 99 | 98 | 97 | 95 | 97 | 98 | 96 | 100 | 98 | 98 | 100 | 94 | 98 | 99 | 98 |
| VERMILLION | 97 | 75 | 81 | 82 | 96 | 92 | 110 | 97 | 92 | 84 | 86 | 94 | 88 | 97 | 83 | 100 | 84 | 92 | 103 | 98 |
| VIGO | 97 | 90 | 97 | 93 | 102 | 98 | 103 | 97 | 94 | 93 | 94 | 95 | 97 | 97 | 95 | 100 | 91 | 96 | 100 | 98 |
| WABASH | 98 | 79 | 83 | 85 | 95 | 92 | 110 | 97 | 94 | 86 | 89 | 95 | 90 | 98 | 84 | 101 | 86 | 93 | 102 | 99 |
| WARREN | 100 | 75 | 79 | 84 | 94 | 91 | 115 | 98 | 94 | 83 | 87 | 97 | 88 | 100 | 80 | 102 | 85 | 93 | 103 | 101 |
| WARRICK | 101 | 93 | 90 | 96 | 98 | 96 | 108 | 100 | 101 | 97 | 101 | 101 | 100 | 103 | 91 | 104 | 98 | 102 | 101 | 103 |
| WASHINGTON | 98 | 73 | 78 | 81 | 95 | 92 | 111 | 97 | 92 | 82 | 85 | 96 | 87 | 97 | 80 | 100 | 82 | 91 | 102 | 98 |
| WAYNE | 95 | 83 | 88 | 85 | 99 | 94 | 103 | 96 | 92 | 89 | 90 | 92 | 92 | 96 | 89 | 99 | 86 | 93 | 100 | 97 |
| WELLS | 99 | 83 | 87 | 88 | 97 | 94 | 111 | 98 | 95 | 90 | 92 | 97 | 93 | 99 | 87 | 101 | 89 | 95 | 101 | 100 |
| WHITE | 99 | 76 | 80 | 85 | 95 | 92 | 115 | 98 | 94 | 83 | 87 | 97 | 88 | 99 | 82 | 101 | 85 | 93 | 104 | 100 |
| WHITLEY | 100 | 82 | 84 | 88 | 96 | 92 | 113 | 98 | 95 | 88 | 92 | 98 | 92 | 101 | 84 | 102 | 90 | 95 | 102 | 102 |
| INDIANA | 98 | 92 | 94 | 94 | 99 | 97 | 103 | 98 | 96 | 95 | 97 | 98 | 98 | 100 | 93 | 101 | 94 | 98 | 100 | 100 |
| UNITED STATES | 100 | 100 | 100 | 100 | 100 | 100 | 100 | 100 | 100 | 100 | 100 | 100 | 100 | 100 | 100 | 100 | 100 | 100 | 100 | 100 |

# POPULATION CHANGE

| COUNTY | FIPS Code | MSA Code | DMA Code | POPULATION 1990 | POPULATION 2000 | POPULATION 2005 | 1990-2000 ANNUAL CHANGE % Rate | 1990-2000 ANNUAL CHANGE State Rank | RACE (%) White 1990 | White 2000 | Black 1990 | Black 2000 | Asian/Pacific 1990 | Asian/Pacific 2000 |
|---|---|---|---|---|---|---|---|---|---|---|---|---|---|---|
| ADAIR | 001 | 0000 | 679 | 8,409 | 8,023 | 7,814 | -0.5 | 79 | 99.6 | 99.5 | 0.0 | 0.0 | 0.2 | 0.3 |
| ADAMS | 003 | 0000 | 652 | 4,866 | 4,397 | 4,359 | -1.0 | 98 | 99.6 | 99.5 | 0.1 | 0.1 | 0.1 | 0.1 |
| ALLAMAKEE | 005 | 0000 | 637 | 13,855 | 14,079 | 14,134 | 0.2 | 30 | 99.5 | 99.1 | 0.0 | 0.3 | 0.2 | 0.3 |
| APPANOOSE | 007 | 0000 | 679 | 13,743 | 13,385 | 13,087 | -0.3 | 66 | 98.8 | 98.6 | 0.6 | 0.6 | 0.3 | 0.3 |
| AUDUBON | 009 | 0000 | 679 | 7,334 | 6,785 | 6,701 | -0.8 | 93 | 99.9 | 99.8 | 0.0 | 0.1 | 0.1 | 0.1 |
| BENTON | 011 | 0000 | 637 | 22,429 | 26,170 | 28,071 | 1.5 | 2 | 99.5 | 99.4 | 0.1 | 0.1 | 0.2 | 0.3 |
| BLACK HAWK | 013 | 8920 | 637 | 123,798 | 119,540 | 116,012 | -0.3 | 66 | 91.8 | 90.7 | 6.9 | 7.5 | 0.8 | 1.1 |
| BOONE | 015 | 0000 | 679 | 25,186 | 26,458 | 27,204 | 0.5 | 15 | 99.3 | 99.1 | 0.2 | 0.2 | 0.3 | 0.4 |
| BREMER | 017 | 0000 | 637 | 22,813 | 23,486 | 23,747 | 0.3 | 22 | 99.0 | 98.7 | 0.3 | 0.3 | 0.6 | 0.8 |
| BUCHANAN | 019 | 0000 | 637 | 20,844 | 21,160 | 21,150 | 0.1 | 39 | 99.3 | 99.1 | 0.2 | 0.1 | 0.2 | 0.3 |
| BUENA VISTA | 021 | 0000 | 624 | 19,965 | 19,306 | 18,821 | -0.3 | 66 | 97.5 | 96.6 | 0.3 | 0.3 | 2.0 | 2.7 |
| BUTLER | 023 | 0000 | 637 | 15,731 | 15,411 | 14,978 | -0.2 | 59 | 99.7 | 99.6 | 0.0 | 0.0 | 0.2 | 0.2 |
| CALHOUN | 025 | 0000 | 679 | 11,508 | 11,257 | 10,951 | -0.2 | 59 | 99.3 | 98.7 | 0.3 | 0.8 | 0.2 | 0.2 |
| CARROLL | 027 | 0000 | 679 | 21,423 | 21,475 | 21,259 | 0.0 | 47 | 99.5 | 99.4 | 0.0 | 0.0 | 0.3 | 0.4 |
| CASS | 029 | 0000 | 652 | 15,128 | 14,398 | 13,842 | -0.5 | 79 | 99.6 | 99.6 | 0.1 | 0.1 | 0.1 | 0.1 |
| CEDAR | 031 | 0000 | 682 | 17,381 | 18,153 | 18,598 | 0.4 | 21 | 99.4 | 99.2 | 0.1 | 0.1 | 0.3 | 0.4 |
| CERRO GORDO | 033 | 0000 | 611 | 46,733 | 45,393 | 43,988 | -0.3 | 66 | 97.9 | 97.0 | 0.6 | 0.7 | 0.6 | 0.8 |
| CHEROKEE | 035 | 0000 | 624 | 14,098 | 12,934 | 12,304 | -0.8 | 93 | 99.3 | 99.2 | 0.1 | 0.2 | 0.2 | 0.3 |
| CHICKASAW | 037 | 0000 | 637 | 13,295 | 13,428 | 13,447 | 0.1 | 39 | 99.8 | 99.7 | 0.0 | 0.0 | 0.1 | 0.2 |
| CLARKE | 039 | 0000 | 679 | 8,287 | 8,277 | 8,298 | 0.0 | 47 | 99.6 | 99.5 | 0.0 | 0.0 | 0.3 | 0.3 |
| CLAY | 041 | 0000 | 624 | 17,585 | 17,105 | 16,422 | -0.3 | 66 | 99.2 | 98.9 | 0.0 | 0.0 | 0.5 | 0.7 |
| CLAYTON | 043 | 0000 | 637 | 19,054 | 18,498 | 18,084 | -0.3 | 66 | 99.7 | 99.7 | 0.0 | 0.0 | 0.1 | 0.2 |
| CLINTON | 045 | 0000 | 682 | 51,040 | 49,345 | 48,026 | -0.3 | 66 | 97.7 | 97.2 | 1.4 | 1.6 | 0.4 | 0.6 |
| CRAWFORD | 047 | 0000 | 652 | 16,775 | 16,408 | 16,316 | -0.2 | 59 | 98.8 | 98.4 | 0.4 | 0.4 | 0.5 | 0.7 |
| DALLAS | 049 | 2120 | 679 | 29,755 | 39,486 | 45,723 | 2.8 | 1 | 99.3 | 99.0 | 0.2 | 0.2 | 0.2 | 0.4 |
| DAVIS | 051 | 0000 | 631 | 8,312 | 8,561 | 8,753 | 0.3 | 22 | 99.2 | 99.0 | 0.0 | 0.0 | 0.3 | 0.4 |
| DECATUR | 053 | 0000 | 679 | 8,338 | 8,369 | 8,624 | 0.0 | 47 | 98.3 | 97.8 | 0.4 | 0.5 | 0.9 | 1.2 |
| DELAWARE | 055 | 0000 | 637 | 18,035 | 18,493 | 18,532 | 0.2 | 30 | 99.6 | 99.5 | 0.1 | 0.1 | 0.2 | 0.2 |
| DES MOINES | 057 | 0000 | 682 | 42,614 | 41,839 | 41,267 | -0.2 | 59 | 95.8 | 95.0 | 3.1 | 3.4 | 0.5 | 0.7 |
| DICKINSON | 059 | 0000 | 624 | 14,909 | 16,437 | 17,150 | 1.0 | 7 | 99.5 | 99.4 | 0.1 | 0.1 | 0.2 | 0.3 |
| DUBUQUE | 061 | 2200 | 637 | 86,403 | 88,126 | 88,211 | 0.2 | 30 | 98.8 | 98.5 | 0.4 | 0.4 | 0.5 | 0.7 |
| EMMET | 063 | 0000 | 737 | 11,569 | 10,484 | 9,749 | -1.0 | 98 | 99.3 | 99.0 | 0.2 | 0.2 | 0.3 | 0.3 |
| FAYETTE | 065 | 0000 | 637 | 21,843 | 21,408 | 20,638 | -0.2 | 59 | 99.2 | 98.9 | 0.2 | 0.3 | 0.2 | 0.3 |
| FLOYD | 067 | 0000 | 611 | 17,058 | 16,153 | 15,651 | -0.5 | 79 | 99.4 | 99.1 | 0.0 | 0.0 | 0.3 | 0.3 |
| FRANKLIN | 069 | 0000 | 679 | 11,364 | 10,712 | 10,374 | -0.6 | 85 | 99.0 | 98.5 | 0.1 | 0.1 | 0.1 | 0.2 |
| FREMONT | 071 | 0000 | 652 | 8,226 | 7,641 | 7,322 | -0.7 | 91 | 99.4 | 99.1 | 0.0 | 0.1 | 0.2 | 0.2 |
| GREENE | 073 | 0000 | 679 | 10,045 | 10,001 | 9,891 | 0.0 | 47 | 99.5 | 99.4 | 0.0 | 0.0 | 0.3 | 0.3 |
| GRUNDY | 075 | 0000 | 637 | 12,029 | 12,296 | 12,372 | 0.2 | 30 | 99.6 | 99.6 | 0.1 | 0.1 | 0.2 | 0.2 |
| GUTHRIE | 077 | 0000 | 679 | 10,935 | 11,660 | 12,004 | 0.6 | 12 | 99.5 | 99.4 | 0.1 | 0.1 | 0.1 | 0.2 |
| HAMILTON | 079 | 0000 | 679 | 16,071 | 15,838 | 15,506 | -0.1 | 52 | 98.9 | 98.5 | 0.1 | 0.1 | 0.6 | 0.8 |
| HANCOCK | 081 | 0000 | 611 | 12,638 | 12,026 | 11,969 | -0.5 | 79 | 99.1 | 98.6 | 0.0 | 0.0 | 0.2 | 0.2 |
| HARDIN | 083 | 0000 | 679 | 19,094 | 18,015 | 17,270 | -0.6 | 85 | 98.7 | 98.5 | 0.6 | 0.5 | 0.3 | 0.4 |
| HARRISON | 085 | 0000 | 652 | 14,730 | 15,194 | 15,084 | 0.3 | 22 | 99.5 | 99.3 | 0.1 | 0.1 | 0.3 | 0.5 |
| HENRY | 087 | 0000 | 682 | 19,226 | 20,223 | 20,653 | 0.5 | 15 | 97.3 | 96.6 | 1.1 | 1.3 | 1.1 | 1.5 |
| HOWARD | 089 | 0000 | 611 | 9,809 | 9,509 | 9,193 | -0.3 | 66 | 99.6 | 99.5 | 0.1 | 0.1 | 0.2 | 0.3 |
| HUMBOLDT | 091 | 0000 | 679 | 10,756 | 10,159 | 9,840 | -0.6 | 85 | 99.5 | 99.4 | 0.1 | 0.1 | 0.3 | 0.4 |
| IDA | 093 | 0000 | 624 | 8,365 | 7,893 | 7,712 | -0.6 | 85 | 99.6 | 99.5 | 0.0 | 0.0 | 0.2 | 0.3 |
| IOWA | 095 | 0000 | 637 | 14,630 | 15,782 | 16,383 | 0.7 | 11 | 99.6 | 99.4 | 0.0 | 0.0 | 0.2 | 0.3 |
| JACKSON | 097 | 0000 | 682 | 19,950 | 20,167 | 20,231 | 0.1 | 39 | 99.6 | 99.5 | 0.1 | 0.1 | 0.1 | 0.2 |
| JASPER | 099 | 0000 | 679 | 34,795 | 36,801 | 37,478 | 0.5 | 15 | 99.0 | 98.6 | 0.2 | 0.3 | 0.5 | 0.7 |
| JEFFERSON | 101 | 0000 | 631 | 16,310 | 16,651 | 16,107 | 0.2 | 30 | 98.3 | 97.9 | 0.6 | 0.6 | 0.9 | 1.1 |
| JOHNSON | 103 | 3500 | 637 | 96,119 | 104,754 | 109,439 | 0.8 | 9 | 93.3 | 91.5 | 2.1 | 2.3 | 4.0 | 5.2 |
| JONES | 105 | 0000 | 637 | 19,444 | 20,054 | 19,925 | 0.3 | 22 | 98.0 | 97.7 | 1.5 | 1.8 | 0.1 | 0.1 |
| KEOKUK | 107 | 0000 | 637 | 11,624 | 11,261 | 10,873 | -0.3 | 66 | 99.5 | 99.4 | 0.1 | 0.0 | 0.2 | 0.3 |
| KOSSUTH | 109 | 0000 | 679 | 18,591 | 17,521 | 16,987 | -0.6 | 85 | 99.3 | 99.0 | 0.0 | 0.0 | 0.3 | 0.4 |
| LEE | 111 | 0000 | 717 | 38,687 | 38,151 | 37,383 | -0.1 | 52 | 95.6 | 94.3 | 2.9 | 3.3 | 0.3 | 0.5 |
| LINN | 113 | 1360 | 637 | 168,767 | 186,658 | 195,442 | 1.0 | 7 | 96.7 | 95.9 | 2.0 | 2.2 | 0.8 | 1.1 |
| LOUISA | 115 | 0000 | 682 | 11,592 | 11,948 | 12,006 | 0.3 | 22 | 96.7 | 95.2 | 0.7 | 0.6 | 0.2 | 0.3 |
| LUCAS | 117 | 0000 | 679 | 9,070 | 9,165 | 9,308 | 0.1 | 39 | 99.3 | 99.1 | 0.0 | 0.1 | 0.2 | 0.2 |
| LYON | 119 | 0000 | 725 | 11,952 | 12,053 | 12,165 | 0.1 | 39 | 99.5 | 99.4 | 0.0 | 0.0 | 0.3 | 0.4 |
| MADISON | 121 | 0000 | 679 | 12,483 | 14,283 | 15,200 | 1.3 | 3 | 99.4 | 99.0 | 0.0 | 0.1 | 0.1 | 0.2 |
| MAHASKA | 123 | 0000 | 679 | 21,522 | 22,008 | 22,255 | 0.2 | 30 | 98.8 | 98.4 | 0.2 | 0.2 | 0.8 | 1.2 |
| MARION | 125 | 0000 | 679 | 30,001 | 31,714 | 32,631 | 0.5 | 15 | 98.5 | 98.0 | 0.3 | 0.3 | 0.9 | 1.4 |
| MARSHALL | 127 | 0000 | 679 | 38,276 | 38,816 | 38,980 | 0.1 | 39 | 97.9 | 97.3 | 0.7 | 0.8 | 0.8 | 1.1 |
| MILLS | 129 | 0000 | 652 | 13,202 | 14,946 | 16,090 | 1.2 | 5 | 99.3 | 99.1 | 0.2 | 0.1 | 0.1 | 0.2 |
| MITCHELL | 131 | 0000 | 611 | 10,928 | 11,132 | 11,264 | 0.2 | 30 | 99.7 | 99.6 | 0.0 | 0.0 | 0.2 | 0.2 |
| MONONA | 133 | 0000 | 624 | 10,034 | 10,092 | 10,097 | 0.1 | 39 | 99.5 | 99.4 | 0.0 | 0.0 | 0.1 | 0.2 |
| MONROE | 135 | 0000 | 679 | 8,114 | 7,992 | 7,866 | -0.1 | 52 | 99.1 | 98.8 | 0.2 | 0.3 | 0.4 | 0.6 |
| MONTGOMERY | 137 | 0000 | 652 | 12,076 | 11,628 | 11,241 | -0.4 | 76 | 99.7 | 99.6 | 0.0 | 0.0 | 0.1 | 0.1 |
| MUSCATINE | 139 | 0000 | 682 | 39,907 | 41,306 | 41,871 | 0.3 | 22 | 94.6 | 91.4 | 0.5 | 0.7 | 0.8 | 1.0 |
| O'BRIEN | 141 | 0000 | 624 | 15,444 | 14,445 | 13,600 | -0.7 | 91 | 99.3 | 99.2 | 0.1 | 0.1 | 0.3 | 0.4 |
| OSCEOLA | 143 | 0000 | 725 | 7,267 | 6,865 | 6,627 | -0.6 | 85 | 99.5 | 99.3 | 0.0 | 0.0 | 0.2 | 0.3 |
| PAGE | 145 | 0000 | 652 | 16,870 | 17,045 | 16,582 | 0.1 | 39 | 98.3 | 96.9 | 0.5 | 1.4 | 0.5 | 0.6 |
| PALO ALTO | 147 | 0000 | 624 | 10,669 | 9,827 | 9,390 | -0.8 | 93 | 99.5 | 99.4 | 0.1 | 0.1 | 0.2 | 0.2 |
| PLYMOUTH | 149 | 0000 | 624 | 23,388 | 24,950 | 25,603 | 0.6 | 12 | 99.5 | 99.4 | 0.2 | 0.2 | 0.2 | 0.3 |
| POCAHONTAS | 151 | 0000 | 679 | 9,525 | 8,723 | 8,471 | -0.9 | 97 | 99.6 | 99.5 | 0.0 | 0.0 | 0.2 | 0.2 |
| POLK | 153 | 2120 | 679 | 327,140 | 368,546 | 388,406 | 1.2 | 5 | 92.7 | 90.9 | 4.5 | 5.0 | 1.8 | 2.6 |
| IOWA | | | | | | | 0.3 | | 96.6 | 95.7 | 1.7 | 2.0 | 0.9 | 1.3 |
| UNITED STATES | | | | | | | 1.0 | | 80.3 | 77.9 | 12.1 | 12.4 | 2.9 | 3.9 |

# POPULATION COMPOSITION

| COUNTY | % HISPANIC ORIGIN | | 2000 AGE DISTRIBUTION (%) | | | | | | | | | | MEDIAN AGE | | 2000 Males/ Females (×100) |
|---|---|---|---|---|---|---|---|---|---|---|---|---|---|---|---|
| | 1990 | 2000 | 0-4 | 5-9 | 10-14 | 15-19 | 20-24 | 25-44 | 45-64 | 65-84 | 85+ | 18+ | 1990 | 2000 | |
| ADAIR | 0.4 | 1.1 | 5.9 | 6.3 | 7.6 | 6.7 | 4.5 | 23.4 | 24.2 | 17.3 | 4.1 | 75.7 | 39.3 | 42.0 | 94.5 |
| ADAMS | 0.4 | 1.0 | 6.0 | 6.1 | 7.1 | 6.7 | 3.8 | 23.7 | 25.7 | 17.6 | 3.3 | 76.2 | 40.1 | 42.8 | 99.0 |
| ALLAMAKEE | 0.3 | 0.9 | 6.7 | 7.2 | 7.6 | 7.5 | 5.0 | 23.8 | 23.4 | 15.5 | 3.3 | 73.5 | 36.5 | 39.9 | 97.8 |
| APPANOOSE | 0.5 | 1.3 | 5.8 | 6.2 | 7.3 | 7.5 | 5.0 | 24.9 | 23.9 | 16.3 | 3.2 | 76.0 | 37.9 | 40.7 | 91.7 |
| AUDUBON | 0.3 | 1.0 | 6.1 | 6.6 | 7.1 | 7.0 | 3.9 | 21.8 | 24.6 | 18.7 | 4.2 | 75.3 | 40.3 | 43.2 | 93.0 |
| BENTON | 0.4 | 1.1 | 6.9 | 7.4 | 8.0 | 7.7 | 5.2 | 26.5 | 22.8 | 13.1 | 2.4 | 72.6 | 34.7 | 37.8 | 97.7 |
| BLACK HAWK | 0.7 | 1.6 | 5.9 | 6.2 | 7.1 | 8.7 | 9.1 | 26.9 | 22.5 | 11.9 | 1.8 | 76.6 | 32.8 | 35.9 | 91.6 |
| BOONE | 0.4 | 1.1 | 5.9 | 6.2 | 7.1 | 7.0 | 5.2 | 27.3 | 24.5 | 13.7 | 3.1 | 76.6 | 36.6 | 39.8 | 92.5 |
| BREMER | 0.3 | 0.9 | 5.3 | 5.9 | 6.9 | 9.2 | 8.0 | 24.3 | 24.5 | 13.2 | 2.7 | 77.0 | 35.2 | 38.4 | 95.1 |
| BUCHANAN | 0.5 | 1.3 | 7.3 | 7.8 | 8.4 | 8.3 | 5.5 | 24.9 | 23.2 | 12.5 | 2.0 | 70.9 | 33.4 | 36.5 | 97.3 |
| BUENA VISTA | 0.8 | 1.8 | 6.4 | 6.6 | 7.3 | 8.9 | 8.1 | 24.7 | 20.7 | 14.4 | 2.9 | 75.2 | 33.9 | 36.3 | 95.4 |
| BUTLER | 0.2 | 0.8 | 5.9 | 6.6 | 6.9 | 7.5 | 5.1 | 23.7 | 24.6 | 16.4 | 3.3 | 75.6 | 37.9 | 41.3 | 97.4 |
| CALHOUN | 0.3 | 1.0 | 5.5 | 6.2 | 7.0 | 7.1 | 4.8 | 23.4 | 24.1 | 17.8 | 4.1 | 76.4 | 39.8 | 42.2 | 95.8 |
| CARROLL | 0.3 | 0.8 | 7.2 | 7.7 | 8.4 | 7.8 | 5.1 | 25.0 | 21.5 | 14.4 | 3.0 | 71.6 | 34.2 | 37.1 | 94.6 |
| CASS | 0.3 | 0.9 | 5.8 | 6.5 | 7.3 | 7.2 | 4.2 | 24.5 | 24.5 | 16.5 | 3.4 | 75.6 | 38.3 | 41.4 | 93.1 |
| CEDAR | 0.6 | 1.5 | 6.0 | 6.5 | 7.0 | 7.8 | 5.8 | 25.8 | 24.9 | 13.6 | 2.5 | 75.4 | 36.1 | 39.6 | 95.3 |
| CERRO GORDO | 2.1 | 4.1 | 6.0 | 6.2 | 6.9 | 7.6 | 5.8 | 27.3 | 23.2 | 14.4 | 2.6 | 76.7 | 35.4 | 38.7 | 90.8 |
| CHEROKEE | 0.4 | 0.9 | 6.0 | 6.5 | 7.6 | 7.4 | 4.6 | 24.2 | 24.4 | 16.2 | 3.0 | 74.9 | 37.2 | 40.7 | 94.1 |
| CHICKASAW | 0.3 | 0.9 | 6.4 | 7.0 | 7.5 | 7.8 | 5.2 | 25.1 | 24.0 | 14.1 | 2.9 | 73.8 | 35.7 | 39.6 | 99.7 |
| CLARKE | 0.2 | 0.8 | 6.0 | 6.6 | 7.4 | 7.5 | 4.7 | 25.4 | 24.6 | 14.5 | 3.3 | 75.1 | 36.7 | 40.1 | 92.0 |
| CLAY | 0.3 | 0.8 | 6.4 | 6.8 | 7.9 | 7.3 | 5.4 | 26.7 | 23.0 | 13.8 | 2.6 | 74.5 | 35.1 | 38.4 | 92.0 |
| CLAYTON | 0.3 | 1.0 | 6.5 | 7.1 | 7.5 | 7.7 | 4.8 | 24.7 | 23.7 | 15.1 | 2.9 | 73.6 | 35.9 | 39.7 | 96.8 |
| CLINTON | 0.6 | 1.4 | 6.3 | 6.5 | 7.5 | 7.6 | 5.7 | 26.9 | 24.0 | 13.3 | 2.2 | 75.0 | 35.1 | 38.3 | 93.3 |
| CRAWFORD | 0.6 | 1.3 | 6.3 | 6.6 | 7.7 | 8.4 | 5.1 | 24.8 | 23.8 | 14.4 | 2.8 | 74.0 | 35.4 | 39.0 | 96.5 |
| DALLAS | 0.6 | 1.4 | 6.3 | 6.9 | 7.9 | 7.7 | 5.2 | 28.7 | 24.5 | 10.8 | 1.9 | 73.9 | 34.6 | 37.6 | 97.3 |
| DAVIS | 0.5 | 1.2 | 6.5 | 7.3 | 7.7 | 7.3 | 5.0 | 24.8 | 23.6 | 14.4 | 3.4 | 73.8 | 36.1 | 39.3 | 96.6 |
| DECATUR | 0.5 | 1.3 | 5.7 | 6.0 | 6.7 | 10.5 | 8.2 | 22.8 | 21.6 | 15.1 | 3.5 | 77.5 | 35.5 | 37.7 | 94.9 |
| DELAWARE | 0.4 | 1.1 | 7.4 | 7.8 | 8.0 | 8.7 | 5.3 | 26.2 | 22.1 | 12.4 | 2.0 | 71.0 | 32.7 | 36.5 | 99.5 |
| DES MOINES | 1.2 | 2.4 | 5.9 | 6.2 | 7.1 | 7.5 | 5.9 | 27.0 | 24.6 | 13.5 | 2.4 | 76.4 | 35.9 | 39.0 | 92.1 |
| DICKINSON | 0.3 | 0.9 | 4.8 | 5.5 | 6.7 | 6.5 | 4.4 | 24.5 | 26.9 | 17.9 | 2.8 | 78.7 | 39.7 | 43.4 | 93.0 |
| DUBUQUE | 0.5 | 1.2 | 6.2 | 6.5 | 7.4 | 8.5 | 7.0 | 27.5 | 22.6 | 12.3 | 2.1 | 75.2 | 33.1 | 36.4 | 94.5 |
| EMMET | 0.5 | 1.3 | 5.4 | 6.2 | 7.5 | 9.2 | 5.5 | 24.0 | 23.1 | 16.0 | 3.1 | 76.0 | 36.1 | 39.8 | 94.1 |
| FAYETTE | 0.9 | 2.0 | 6.3 | 6.6 | 7.4 | 8.1 | 5.5 | 24.4 | 23.7 | 15.2 | 2.9 | 74.7 | 36.4 | 39.4 | 96.2 |
| FLOYD | 0.5 | 1.4 | 5.8 | 6.3 | 7.3 | 7.4 | 5.0 | 23.9 | 25.2 | 15.8 | 3.2 | 75.7 | 37.9 | 41.0 | 91.7 |
| FRANKLIN | 1.3 | 2.8 | 6.0 | 6.5 | 7.1 | 7.7 | 4.8 | 23.2 | 25.0 | 16.3 | 3.4 | 75.4 | 38.1 | 41.6 | 95.6 |
| FREMONT | 0.6 | 1.7 | 5.8 | 6.6 | 7.0 | 7.2 | 5.2 | 23.0 | 24.7 | 17.2 | 3.3 | 75.9 | 38.8 | 41.6 | 93.0 |
| GREENE | 0.3 | 0.9 | 5.6 | 6.4 | 7.0 | 7.0 | 4.3 | 23.6 | 24.8 | 17.7 | 3.7 | 76.3 | 39.4 | 42.4 | 93.7 |
| GRUNDY | 0.3 | 0.9 | 5.9 | 6.6 | 7.0 | 7.0 | 5.2 | 22.8 | 25.8 | 16.3 | 3.3 | 75.5 | 38.8 | 42.0 | 94.6 |
| GUTHRIE | 0.3 | 0.9 | 5.3 | 5.7 | 6.4 | 7.7 | 5.1 | 22.8 | 25.2 | 18.4 | 3.4 | 77.3 | 39.9 | 42.9 | 94.3 |
| HAMILTON | 0.7 | 1.7 | 6.1 | 6.6 | 7.1 | 7.0 | 5.3 | 25.3 | 24.3 | 15.7 | 2.7 | 75.7 | 37.1 | 40.3 | 95.2 |
| HANCOCK | 1.0 | 2.3 | 6.4 | 7.1 | 7.7 | 7.9 | 4.7 | 25.7 | 23.0 | 14.6 | 2.9 | 73.4 | 35.4 | 38.9 | 96.2 |
| HARDIN | 0.6 | 1.3 | 5.3 | 5.9 | 6.9 | 9.0 | 4.9 | 23.7 | 23.7 | 16.9 | 3.7 | 76.8 | 37.9 | 41.2 | 95.1 |
| HARRISON | 0.3 | 1.1 | 6.5 | 7.0 | 7.5 | 7.5 | 5.0 | 25.0 | 22.9 | 15.4 | 3.3 | 74.2 | 36.5 | 39.7 | 96.7 |
| HENRY | 0.7 | 1.5 | 5.9 | 6.2 | 7.1 | 7.8 | 6.8 | 28.1 | 23.1 | 12.4 | 2.6 | 76.3 | 34.7 | 37.5 | 101.8 |
| HOWARD | 0.2 | 0.8 | 6.4 | 6.9 | 7.9 | 7.1 | 4.4 | 23.8 | 23.5 | 16.2 | 3.8 | 73.8 | 37.7 | 40.5 | 96.8 |
| HUMBOLDT | 0.3 | 1.0 | 6.0 | 6.6 | 7.2 | 7.1 | 4.1 | 23.9 | 24.5 | 17.6 | 3.0 | 75.5 | 38.6 | 41.8 | 96.5 |
| IDA | 0.3 | 0.9 | 6.5 | 7.3 | 7.7 | 7.6 | 4.2 | 23.8 | 22.4 | 16.9 | 3.7 | 73.3 | 36.9 | 40.5 | 94.8 |
| IOWA | 0.3 | 0.9 | 6.7 | 7.3 | 7.8 | 7.1 | 4.7 | 25.5 | 23.3 | 14.6 | 3.0 | 73.5 | 36.6 | 39.7 | 94.9 |
| JACKSON | 0.5 | 1.2 | 6.4 | 6.9 | 7.9 | 7.8 | 5.1 | 25.6 | 24.2 | 13.9 | 2.3 | 73.9 | 35.0 | 38.5 | 97.5 |
| JASPER | 0.6 | 1.3 | 5.8 | 6.2 | 6.9 | 7.1 | 5.7 | 26.8 | 25.0 | 14.2 | 2.3 | 76.5 | 36.1 | 39.7 | 95.8 |
| JEFFERSON | 0.9 | 1.7 | 5.4 | 6.1 | 6.9 | 7.2 | 4.9 | 30.5 | 25.7 | 11.1 | 2.1 | 77.2 | 36.8 | 39.7 | 96.0 |
| JOHNSON | 1.5 | 3.0 | 5.7 | 5.4 | 5.5 | 10.1 | 16.7 | 32.1 | 17.2 | 6.4 | 1.0 | 80.3 | 27.3 | 29.0 | 96.7 |
| JONES | 0.5 | 1.2 | 5.7 | 6.1 | 7.1 | 7.8 | 7.1 | 27.6 | 23.0 | 13.1 | 2.4 | 76.1 | 34.6 | 37.4 | 111.9 |
| KEOKUK | 0.2 | 0.7 | 6.2 | 6.6 | 7.1 | 8.1 | 4.6 | 24.7 | 23.0 | 16.3 | 3.5 | 75.0 | 37.4 | 40.5 | 97.8 |
| KOSSUTH | 0.5 | 1.3 | 6.3 | 7.0 | 7.7 | 7.8 | 4.4 | 24.2 | 24.1 | 15.4 | 3.1 | 73.5 | 36.7 | 40.2 | 95.9 |
| LEE | 1.9 | 3.7 | 5.9 | 6.3 | 7.3 | 7.3 | 5.9 | 27.4 | 24.1 | 13.5 | 2.3 | 75.8 | 35.8 | 38.6 | 98.5 |
| LINN | 0.9 | 2.1 | 6.3 | 6.5 | 7.2 | 7.4 | 6.6 | 30.3 | 23.5 | 10.6 | 1.6 | 76.0 | 33.1 | 36.4 | 94.9 |
| LOUISA | 3.7 | 6.5 | 6.4 | 6.9 | 7.3 | 7.4 | 6.0 | 27.7 | 23.8 | 12.4 | 2.2 | 74.7 | 34.3 | 37.7 | 103.2 |
| LUCAS | 0.6 | 1.5 | 5.6 | 6.1 | 7.1 | 7.1 | 4.4 | 24.0 | 25.4 | 16.8 | 3.4 | 76.8 | 38.9 | 42.0 | 92.8 |
| LYON | 0.1 | 0.6 | 7.0 | 7.7 | 8.6 | 8.1 | 4.7 | 23.8 | 22.3 | 15.0 | 2.8 | 71.3 | 34.8 | 37.9 | 97.8 |
| MADISON | 0.5 | 1.3 | 6.2 | 6.8 | 7.9 | 8.0 | 5.1 | 26.1 | 24.4 | 12.8 | 2.8 | 74.1 | 36.2 | 38.7 | 96.3 |
| MAHASKA | 0.4 | 1.0 | 6.5 | 6.7 | 7.6 | 7.7 | 6.3 | 26.5 | 22.7 | 13.5 | 2.4 | 74.7 | 34.8 | 37.5 | 96.7 |
| MARION | 0.5 | 1.3 | 6.0 | 6.4 | 7.3 | 8.6 | 7.0 | 26.1 | 23.1 | 13.0 | 2.3 | 75.8 | 34.2 | 37.4 | 99.8 |
| MARSHALL | 0.8 | 1.7 | 5.9 | 6.1 | 6.8 | 7.3 | 5.9 | 26.0 | 25.0 | 14.4 | 2.6 | 76.7 | 36.7 | 39.7 | 96.1 |
| MILLS | 0.5 | 1.4 | 5.6 | 6.3 | 7.9 | 8.1 | 5.4 | 28.8 | 25.1 | 11.1 | 1.8 | 74.9 | 35.1 | 38.0 | 101.3 |
| MITCHELL | 0.4 | 1.2 | 5.9 | 6.4 | 7.2 | 7.5 | 4.4 | 23.3 | 24.1 | 17.0 | 4.1 | 75.4 | 38.3 | 41.6 | 95.5 |
| MONONA | 0.3 | 0.9 | 5.4 | 6.2 | 6.8 | 7.1 | 4.1 | 22.3 | 25.0 | 18.7 | 4.3 | 76.8 | 40.5 | 43.6 | 92.8 |
| MONROE | 0.2 | 0.8 | 5.7 | 6.4 | 7.3 | 7.3 | 5.0 | 24.7 | 24.0 | 16.2 | 3.4 | 75.9 | 37.8 | 40.8 | 94.4 |
| MONTGOMERY | 0.4 | 1.1 | 5.7 | 6.1 | 6.6 | 7.4 | 5.7 | 24.1 | 23.6 | 16.8 | 4.0 | 76.9 | 38.6 | 41.1 | 90.9 |
| MUSCATINE | 7.3 | 12.9 | 6.9 | 7.1 | 7.6 | 7.6 | 6.2 | 28.8 | 23.1 | 10.8 | 1.9 | 73.8 | 33.1 | 36.1 | 97.2 |
| O'BRIEN | 0.3 | 0.8 | 6.0 | 6.7 | 7.4 | 7.5 | 4.9 | 24.2 | 22.6 | 16.9 | 3.7 | 74.9 | 36.9 | 40.3 | 94.5 |
| OSCEOLA | 0.2 | 0.8 | 6.7 | 7.5 | 7.9 | 7.2 | 4.6 | 25.3 | 22.1 | 15.4 | 3.2 | 73.3 | 36.1 | 39.5 | 96.5 |
| PAGE | 1.2 | 2.3 | 5.3 | 5.8 | 6.9 | 7.3 | 6.0 | 25.5 | 23.7 | 16.1 | 3.5 | 77.4 | 38.2 | 40.5 | 100.9 |
| PALO ALTO | 0.2 | 0.8 | 5.8 | 6.5 | 7.4 | 8.1 | 4.8 | 23.1 | 23.3 | 17.0 | 3.9 | 75.6 | 37.5 | 40.9 | 95.1 |
| PLYMOUTH | 0.2 | 0.8 | 6.7 | 7.4 | 8.2 | 8.4 | 5.5 | 25.2 | 22.7 | 13.4 | 2.6 | 72.7 | 34.1 | 37.2 | 96.8 |
| POCAHONTAS | 0.3 | 1.0 | 6.0 | 6.7 | 7.4 | 7.0 | 4.0 | 22.8 | 24.9 | 17.4 | 3.8 | 75.1 | 39.2 | 42.3 | 95.9 |
| POLK | 1.9 | 3.8 | 6.7 | 6.7 | 7.4 | 7.2 | 6.5 | 31.6 | 22.5 | 10.0 | 1.6 | 75.2 | 32.4 | 35.7 | 91.7 |
| IOWA | 1.2 | 2.5 | 6.3 | 6.5 | 7.3 | 7.9 | 6.8 | 27.4 | 22.9 | 12.6 | 2.3 | 75.5 | 34.0 | 37.1 | 95.0 |
| UNITED STATES | 9.0 | 11.8 | 6.9 | 7.2 | 7.2 | 7.2 | 6.7 | 29.9 | 22.2 | 11.1 | 1.6 | 74.6 | 32.9 | 35.7 | 95.6 |

| COUNTY | HOUSEHOLDS | | | | | FAMILIES | | | MEDIAN HOUSEHOLD INCOME | | | |
|---|---|---|---|---|---|---|---|---|---|---|---|---|
| | 1990 | 2000 | 2005 | % Annual Rate 1990-2000 | 2000 Average HH Size | 1990 | 2000 | % Annual Rate 1990-2000 | 2000 | 2005 | 2000 National Rank | 2000 State Rank |
| ADAIR | 3,419 | 3,266 | 3,187 | -0.6 | 2.40 | 2,408 | 2,208 | -1.0 | 29,981 | 36,153 | 2157 | 80 |
| ADAMS | 2,005 | 1,779 | 1,749 | -1.4 | 2.41 | 1,388 | 1,183 | -1.9 | 26,599 | 32,487 | 2635 | 97 |
| ALLAMAKEE | 5,268 | 5,337 | 5,362 | 0.2 | 2.55 | 3,719 | 3,615 | -0.3 | 29,082 | 34,342 | 2285 | 88 |
| APPANOOSE | 5,609 | 5,576 | 5,509 | -0.1 | 2.36 | 3,828 | 3,654 | -0.6 | 26,627 | 32,119 | 2630 | 96 |
| AUDUBON | 2,936 | 2,715 | 2,678 | -0.9 | 2.42 | 2,102 | 1,864 | -1.4 | 29,162 | 32,245 | 2271 | 86 |
| BENTON | 8,518 | 10,005 | 10,765 | 2.0 | 2.58 | 6,270 | 7,126 | 1.6 | 39,668 | 46,162 | 695 | 13 |
| BLACK HAWK | 46,932 | 46,310 | 45,322 | -0.2 | 2.46 | 32,143 | 30,433 | -0.7 | 37,426 | 41,124 | 909 | 26 |
| BOONE | 9,827 | 10,488 | 10,841 | 0.8 | 2.43 | 6,952 | 7,137 | 0.3 | 38,114 | 42,820 | 846 | 23 |
| BREMER | 8,394 | 8,682 | 8,825 | 0.4 | 2.52 | 6,165 | 6,150 | 0.0 | 40,710 | 46,721 | 609 | 9 |
| BUCHANAN | 7,506 | 7,710 | 7,738 | 0.3 | 2.68 | 5,564 | 5,528 | -0.1 | 33,357 | 36,961 | 1481 | 55 |
| BUENA VISTA | 7,515 | 7,171 | 6,968 | -0.6 | 2.49 | 5,217 | 4,781 | -1.1 | 35,498 | 41,917 | 1171 | 41 |
| BUTLER | 6,036 | 6,057 | 5,953 | 0.0 | 2.49 | 4,490 | 4,361 | -0.4 | 34,906 | 39,842 | 1269 | 45 |
| CALHOUN | 4,684 | 4,499 | 4,394 | -0.5 | 2.34 | 3,169 | 2,914 | -1.0 | 32,921 | 39,161 | 1549 | 60 |
| CARROLL | 7,964 | 8,169 | 8,170 | 0.3 | 2.57 | 5,626 | 5,534 | -0.2 | 36,456 | 41,861 | 1050 | 35 |
| CASS | 6,177 | 5,931 | 5,729 | -0.5 | 2.36 | 4,206 | 3,865 | -1.0 | 29,523 | 35,438 | 2219 | 83 |
| CEDAR | 6,684 | 6,991 | 7,179 | 0.5 | 2.56 | 4,909 | 4,960 | 0.1 | 39,188 | 47,200 | 738 | 16 |
| CERRO GORDO | 19,061 | 18,897 | 18,486 | -0.1 | 2.32 | 12,661 | 12,010 | -0.6 | 36,171 | 40,726 | 1082 | 37 |
| CHEROKEE | 5,514 | 5,153 | 4,925 | -0.8 | 2.44 | 3,835 | 3,460 | -1.2 | 31,012 | 33,677 | 1932 | 74 |
| CHICKASAW | 5,040 | 5,154 | 5,185 | 0.3 | 2.56 | 3,657 | 3,585 | -0.2 | 36,637 | 45,808 | 1029 | 33 |
| CLARKE | 3,343 | 3,451 | 3,517 | 0.4 | 2.37 | 2,333 | 2,295 | -0.2 | 29,323 | 36,344 | 2251 | 84 |
| CLAY | 7,074 | 7,086 | 6,898 | 0.0 | 2.38 | 4,836 | 4,654 | -0.5 | 36,774 | 41,968 | 1009 | 31 |
| CLAYTON | 7,218 | 7,119 | 7,013 | -0.2 | 2.55 | 5,209 | 4,960 | -0.6 | 30,625 | 34,345 | 2003 | 76 |
| CLINTON | 19,757 | 19,317 | 18,922 | -0.3 | 2.50 | 14,056 | 13,226 | -0.7 | 35,397 | 39,200 | 1184 | 42 |
| CRAWFORD | 6,397 | 6,314 | 6,316 | -0.2 | 2.51 | 4,486 | 4,249 | -0.7 | 31,470 | 34,602 | 1825 | 69 |
| DALLAS | 11,204 | 14,923 | 17,300 | 3.5 | 2.61 | 8,297 | 10,773 | 3.2 | 43,113 | 48,750 | 448 | 5 |
| DAVIS | 3,093 | 3,135 | 3,183 | 0.2 | 2.67 | 2,319 | 2,256 | -0.3 | 29,747 | 34,389 | 2192 | 82 |
| DECATUR | 3,207 | 3,164 | 3,260 | -0.2 | 2.39 | 2,146 | 2,022 | -0.7 | 22,548 | 27,610 | 2993 | 99 |
| DELAWARE | 6,389 | 6,690 | 6,776 | 0.6 | 2.73 | 4,851 | 4,898 | 0.1 | 33,111 | 37,914 | 1520 | 58 |
| DES MOINES | 16,874 | 16,628 | 16,418 | -0.2 | 2.47 | 11,734 | 11,095 | -0.7 | 37,121 | 42,203 | 957 | 30 |
| DICKINSON | 6,160 | 6,964 | 7,355 | 1.5 | 2.29 | 4,270 | 4,666 | 1.1 | 36,664 | 41,262 | 1023 | 32 |
| DUBUQUE | 30,799 | 31,508 | 31,625 | 0.3 | 2.66 | 22,150 | 21,902 | -0.1 | 39,775 | 43,185 | 688 | 12 |
| EMMET | 4,461 | 4,184 | 3,949 | -0.8 | 2.39 | 3,113 | 2,805 | -1.3 | 32,194 | 37,722 | 1686 | 66 |
| FAYETTE | 8,490 | 8,452 | 8,221 | -0.1 | 2.44 | 5,966 | 5,704 | -0.5 | 28,391 | 31,084 | 2381 | 92 |
| FLOYD | 6,721 | 6,451 | 6,285 | -0.5 | 2.43 | 4,788 | 4,406 | -1.0 | 32,995 | 36,369 | 1541 | 59 |
| FRANKLIN | 4,579 | 4,372 | 4,256 | -0.6 | 2.40 | 3,207 | 2,933 | -1.1 | 33,800 | 39,196 | 1421 | 54 |
| FREMONT | 3,217 | 3,003 | 2,883 | -0.8 | 2.48 | 2,309 | 2,080 | -1.3 | 33,830 | 42,346 | 1416 | 53 |
| GREENE | 4,195 | 4,245 | 4,230 | 0.1 | 2.32 | 2,849 | 2,773 | -0.3 | 33,998 | 40,228 | 1395 | 51 |
| GRUNDY | 4,776 | 4,863 | 4,888 | 0.2 | 2.49 | 3,510 | 3,446 | -0.2 | 40,699 | 46,903 | 611 | 10 |
| GUTHRIE | 4,407 | 4,757 | 4,930 | 0.9 | 2.40 | 3,158 | 3,275 | 0.4 | 32,681 | 39,832 | 1596 | 61 |
| HAMILTON | 6,358 | 6,367 | 6,279 | 0.0 | 2.45 | 4,614 | 4,450 | -0.4 | 37,541 | 43,361 | 892 | 24 |
| HANCOCK | 4,867 | 4,651 | 4,642 | -0.5 | 2.54 | 3,540 | 3,264 | -1.0 | 36,455 | 45,368 | 1051 | 36 |
| HARDIN | 7,611 | 7,414 | 7,196 | -0.3 | 2.31 | 5,280 | 4,923 | -0.8 | 35,524 | 42,052 | 1164 | 39 |
| HARRISON | 5,656 | 5,994 | 6,041 | 0.7 | 2.48 | 4,066 | 4,164 | 0.3 | 34,620 | 43,707 | 1303 | 47 |
| HENRY | 7,089 | 7,413 | 7,596 | 0.5 | 2.50 | 5,075 | 5,110 | 0.1 | 37,438 | 43,375 | 904 | 25 |
| HOWARD | 3,856 | 3,833 | 3,748 | -0.1 | 2.42 | 2,684 | 2,566 | -0.5 | 33,283 | 39,868 | 1496 | 57 |
| HUMBOLDT | 4,339 | 4,179 | 4,083 | -0.5 | 2.39 | 3,101 | 2,872 | -0.9 | 37,287 | 44,175 | 936 | 28 |
| IDA | 3,222 | 3,016 | 2,934 | -0.8 | 2.55 | 2,317 | 2,090 | -1.2 | 31,379 | 38,245 | 1846 | 70 |
| IOWA | 5,713 | 6,208 | 6,467 | 1.0 | 2.50 | 4,126 | 4,319 | 0.6 | 38,125 | 42,274 | 843 | 22 |
| JACKSON | 7,527 | 7,651 | 7,694 | 0.2 | 2.60 | 5,479 | 5,362 | -0.3 | 29,973 | 33,123 | 2158 | 81 |
| JASPER | 13,632 | 14,244 | 14,603 | 0.5 | 2.47 | 10,005 | 10,095 | 0.1 | 42,430 | 50,325 | 477 | 6 |
| JEFFERSON | 6,309 | 6,770 | 6,687 | 0.9 | 2.30 | 4,288 | 4,417 | 0.4 | 32,385 | 36,527 | 1643 | 63 |
| JOHNSON | 36,067 | 39,208 | 40,988 | 1.0 | 2.43 | 20,317 | 21,143 | 0.5 | 40,361 | 46,914 | 641 | 11 |
| JONES | 6,917 | 7,267 | 7,268 | 0.6 | 2.56 | 5,081 | 5,137 | 0.1 | 33,342 | 39,173 | 1484 | 56 |
| KEOKUK | 4,573 | 4,530 | 4,429 | -0.1 | 2.44 | 3,307 | 3,154 | -0.6 | 30,608 | 35,404 | 2007 | 77 |
| KOSSUTH | 7,194 | 6,865 | 6,698 | -0.6 | 2.50 | 5,101 | 4,704 | -1.0 | 30,927 | 34,228 | 1943 | 75 |
| LEE | 14,936 | 14,840 | 14,616 | -0.1 | 2.46 | 10,483 | 10,061 | -0.5 | 35,502 | 40,618 | 1169 | 40 |
| LINN | 65,501 | 72,400 | 75,762 | 1.2 | 2.52 | 45,039 | 48,115 | 0.8 | 44,351 | 49,072 | 381 | 2 |
| LOUISA | 4,296 | 4,474 | 4,515 | 0.5 | 2.62 | 3,194 | 3,208 | 0.1 | 35,050 | 41,955 | 1245 | 44 |
| LUCAS | 3,766 | 3,857 | 3,943 | 0.3 | 2.32 | 2,537 | 2,501 | -0.2 | 29,319 | 35,556 | 2252 | 85 |
| LYON | 4,289 | 4,360 | 4,414 | 0.2 | 2.72 | 3,284 | 3,234 | -0.2 | 31,757 | 37,358 | 1767 | 67 |
| MADISON | 4,715 | 5,375 | 5,710 | 1.6 | 2.61 | 3,492 | 3,801 | 1.0 | 39,540 | 46,953 | 707 | 14 |
| MAHASKA | 8,306 | 8,501 | 8,598 | 0.3 | 2.51 | 6,018 | 5,942 | -0.2 | 34,081 | 40,685 | 1380 | 49 |
| MARION | 10,815 | 11,708 | 12,098 | 1.0 | 2.54 | 7,879 | 8,204 | 0.5 | 41,767 | 51,059 | 533 | 8 |
| MARSHALL | 14,890 | 15,165 | 15,261 | 0.2 | 2.47 | 10,478 | 10,273 | -0.2 | 39,429 | 45,579 | 720 | 15 |
| MILLS | 4,665 | 5,379 | 5,805 | 1.7 | 2.65 | 3,469 | 3,867 | 1.3 | 34,793 | 37,775 | 1284 | 46 |
| MITCHELL | 4,253 | 4,313 | 4,352 | 0.2 | 2.50 | 3,031 | 2,949 | -0.3 | 34,039 | 37,973 | 1385 | 50 |
| MONONA | 4,098 | 4,159 | 4,181 | 0.2 | 2.36 | 2,819 | 2,738 | -0.4 | 28,681 | 32,531 | 2339 | 91 |
| MONROE | 3,196 | 3,171 | 3,129 | -0.1 | 2.46 | 2,238 | 2,126 | -0.6 | 28,178 | 31,742 | 2419 | 93 |
| MONTGOMERY | 4,955 | 4,915 | 4,815 | -0.1 | 2.30 | 3,382 | 3,222 | -0.6 | 31,316 | 36,722 | 1861 | 72 |
| MUSCATINE | 14,806 | 15,382 | 15,622 | 0.5 | 2.64 | 10,891 | 10,980 | 0.1 | 43,816 | 51,779 | 407 | 3 |
| O'BRIEN | 5,980 | 5,765 | 5,500 | -0.4 | 2.41 | 4,236 | 3,904 | -1.0 | 32,283 | 36,485 | 1665 | 64 |
| OSCEOLA | 2,817 | 2,702 | 2,627 | -0.5 | 2.50 | 2,012 | 1,860 | -0.9 | 34,282 | 40,878 | 1349 | 48 |
| PAGE | 6,687 | 6,540 | 6,387 | -0.3 | 2.38 | 4,608 | 4,305 | -0.8 | 31,352 | 36,531 | 1852 | 71 |
| PALO ALTO | 4,183 | 3,929 | 3,789 | -0.8 | 2.42 | 2,806 | 2,520 | -1.3 | 30,086 | 34,045 | 2134 | 79 |
| PLYMOUTH | 8,417 | 9,083 | 9,309 | 0.9 | 2.70 | 6,257 | 6,525 | 0.5 | 38,637 | 45,502 | 786 | 17 |
| POCAHONTAS | 3,820 | 3,507 | 3,410 | -1.0 | 2.43 | 2,680 | 2,365 | -1.5 | 32,557 | 39,979 | 1615 | 62 |
| POLK | 129,237 | 145,560 | 153,377 | 1.5 | 2.47 | 85,847 | 93,594 | 1.1 | 43,301 | 48,983 | 439 | 4 |
| IOWA | | | | 0.5 | 2.50 | | | 0.1 | 37,579 | 43,070 | | |
| UNITED STATES | | | | 1.4 | 2.59 | | | 1.1 | 41,914 | 49,127 | | |

# INCOME

| COUNTY | 2000 Per Capita Income | 2000 HH Income Base | 2000 HOUSEHOLD INCOME DISTRIBUTION (%) | | | | | | 2000 AVERAGE DISPOSABLE INCOME BY AGE OF HOUSEHOLDER | | | | | |
|---|---|---|---|---|---|---|---|---|---|---|---|---|---|---|
| | | | Less than $15,000 | $15,000 to $24,999 | $25,000 to $49,999 | $50,000 to $99,999 | $100,000 to $149,999 | $150,000 or More | All Ages | <35 | 35-44 | 45-54 | 55-64 | 65+ |
| ADAIR | 14,418 | 3,266 | 20.5 | 20.3 | 40.5 | 16.6 | 1.5 | 0.6 | 26,385 | 25,588 | 33,612 | 32,277 | 26,919 | 18,249 |
| ADAMS | 12,777 | 1,779 | 25.4 | 20.0 | 39.8 | 13.3 | 1.5 | 0.0 | 23,807 | 22,016 | 29,875 | 30,178 | 24,686 | 16,597 |
| ALLAMAKEE | 13,733 | 5,337 | 23.1 | 19.8 | 35.7 | 18.3 | 2.9 | 0.3 | 26,605 | 23,700 | 31,684 | 34,395 | 29,837 | 18,295 |
| APPANOOSE | 14,407 | 5,576 | 27.6 | 19.0 | 33.5 | 16.7 | 2.7 | 0.5 | 25,549 | 22,429 | 29,650 | 33,901 | 27,611 | 17,914 |
| AUDUBON | 16,412 | 2,715 | 20.2 | 21.8 | 36.5 | 17.4 | 3.0 | 1.1 | 27,605 | 26,653 | 30,637 | 35,081 | 28,213 | 20,780 |
| BENTON | 17,651 | 10,005 | 14.0 | 13.3 | 38.1 | 29.4 | 4.3 | 1.0 | 33,943 | 29,823 | 39,840 | 41,718 | 36,804 | 23,965 |
| BLACK HAWK | 19,198 | 46,310 | 17.6 | 14.2 | 34.1 | 26.8 | 5.3 | 2.0 | 34,146 | 24,329 | 42,290 | 47,186 | 34,983 | 23,359 |
| BOONE | 18,812 | 10,488 | 14.3 | 13.9 | 39.7 | 25.4 | 5.0 | 1.6 | 33,940 | 27,656 | 39,356 | 43,643 | 37,309 | 23,517 |
| BREMER | 18,420 | 8,682 | 13.5 | 11.1 | 38.3 | 29.4 | 6.0 | 1.7 | 35,715 | 27,424 | 46,059 | 46,240 | 38,601 | 23,262 |
| BUCHANAN | 17,057 | 7,710 | 18.5 | 17.5 | 37.3 | 21.8 | 3.6 | 1.3 | 30,452 | 24,776 | 37,479 | 38,998 | 30,702 | 21,434 |
| BUENA VISTA | 16,285 | 7,171 | 12.9 | 15.9 | 42.9 | 24.3 | 3.3 | 0.7 | 31,553 | 27,563 | 38,688 | 40,352 | 35,887 | 22,991 |
| BUTLER | 16,495 | 6,057 | 15.4 | 16.4 | 39.6 | 25.1 | 3.1 | 0.5 | 30,597 | 27,089 | 38,280 | 39,341 | 32,108 | 21,093 |
| CALHOUN | 17,083 | 4,499 | 16.5 | 17.6 | 38.9 | 22.7 | 3.6 | 0.8 | 30,032 | 26,357 | 34,869 | 38,813 | 35,572 | 21,751 |
| CARROLL | 17,369 | 8,169 | 15.4 | 14.0 | 39.8 | 26.3 | 3.1 | 1.4 | 32,635 | 28,668 | 38,959 | 42,645 | 34,759 | 22,902 |
| CASS | 15,566 | 5,931 | 19.2 | 21.8 | 37.0 | 18.4 | 3.1 | 0.5 | 27,572 | 25,911 | 31,105 | 33,729 | 31,262 | 19,969 |
| CEDAR | 17,409 | 6,991 | 13.6 | 11.9 | 40.5 | 29.3 | 4.1 | 0.7 | 33,463 | 30,731 | 39,642 | 41,436 | 34,339 | 22,888 |
| CERRO GORDO | 18,405 | 18,897 | 14.4 | 16.3 | 38.7 | 25.7 | 4.0 | 1.0 | 32,168 | 28,718 | 38,191 | 40,379 | 34,180 | 23,040 |
| CHEROKEE | 14,734 | 5,153 | 18.6 | 18.8 | 39.1 | 21.0 | 2.5 | 0.1 | 27,807 | 25,380 | 32,986 | 32,862 | 32,159 | 20,313 |
| CHICKASAW | 17,232 | 5,154 | 12.5 | 14.6 | 41.4 | 27.6 | 3.4 | 0.6 | 32,434 | 28,212 | 40,433 | 40,693 | 31,552 | 23,439 |
| CLARKE | 16,389 | 3,451 | 20.6 | 20.9 | 35.4 | 18.4 | 3.4 | 1.3 | 28,411 | 25,166 | 31,543 | 35,828 | 31,961 | 20,548 |
| CLAY | 19,093 | 7,086 | 15.9 | 13.0 | 40.1 | 26.1 | 4.0 | 1.0 | 32,354 | 28,263 | 37,081 | 40,858 | 34,576 | 24,109 |
| CLAYTON | 14,105 | 7,119 | 18.9 | 21.9 | 37.9 | 18.6 | 2.3 | 0.4 | 27,365 | 25,266 | 33,500 | 33,598 | 28,066 | 19,370 |
| CLINTON | 16,464 | 19,317 | 17.2 | 16.2 | 38.5 | 24.6 | 2.8 | 0.8 | 30,562 | 26,856 | 37,424 | 38,410 | 31,145 | 20,200 |
| CRAWFORD | 14,427 | 6,314 | 17.5 | 19.1 | 39.2 | 22.3 | 1.8 | 0.1 | 27,913 | 23,264 | 32,635 | 38,309 | 29,702 | 19,567 |
| DALLAS | 22,807 | 14,923 | 11.2 | 11.9 | 35.5 | 31.5 | 7.2 | 2.8 | 39,004 | 32,611 | 45,405 | 49,655 | 40,363 | 23,266 |
| DAVIS | 14,208 | 3,135 | 18.0 | 22.2 | 38.6 | 19.1 | 1.9 | 0.3 | 26,800 | 22,837 | 31,669 | 34,679 | 29,923 | 17,803 |
| DECATUR | 11,029 | 3,164 | 31.6 | 23.3 | 31.9 | 11.9 | 1.2 | 0.2 | 21,980 | 19,325 | 25,655 | 31,075 | 24,085 | 15,033 |
| DELAWARE | 16,210 | 6,690 | 17.6 | 15.7 | 39.9 | 21.7 | 3.2 | 1.9 | 31,448 | 25,486 | 35,347 | 38,994 | 34,244 | 24,040 |
| DES MOINES | 18,318 | 16,628 | 15.6 | 13.6 | 38.2 | 26.9 | 4.6 | 1.2 | 33,185 | 26,484 | 38,662 | 43,054 | 36,655 | 22,579 |
| DICKINSON | 20,732 | 6,964 | 12.6 | 16.6 | 38.4 | 24.9 | 5.6 | 1.9 | 34,335 | 26,659 | 38,002 | 44,954 | 41,224 | 25,418 |
| DUBUQUE | 18,210 | 31,504 | 13.4 | 13.2 | 37.8 | 28.5 | 5.2 | 1.8 | 35,322 | 28,007 | 41,595 | 46,331 | 37,376 | 24,278 |
| EMMET | 15,359 | 4,184 | 18.1 | 17.6 | 37.9 | 24.0 | 2.3 | 0.1 | 28,663 | 23,056 | 34,314 | 34,630 | 34,198 | 22,856 |
| FAYETTE | 13,712 | 8,452 | 23.7 | 19.3 | 38.3 | 16.1 | 2.1 | 0.6 | 25,897 | 23,583 | 31,023 | 34,348 | 28,575 | 17,176 |
| FLOYD | 17,162 | 6,451 | 18.1 | 16.1 | 39.9 | 21.6 | 3.7 | 0.7 | 29,822 | 22,779 | 37,641 | 37,339 | 32,851 | 23,028 |
| FRANKLIN | 17,489 | 4,372 | 17.8 | 14.8 | 38.6 | 25.5 | 2.7 | 0.7 | 30,527 | 28,653 | 36,656 | 35,932 | 35,843 | 21,673 |
| FREMONT | 15,863 | 3,003 | 17.5 | 15.3 | 42.1 | 22.3 | 2.4 | 0.5 | 29,203 | 27,751 | 34,943 | 34,642 | 31,551 | 21,489 |
| GREENE | 17,948 | 4,245 | 12.6 | 18.5 | 41.2 | 23.1 | 3.9 | 0.7 | 31,068 | 29,965 | 36,283 | 38,013 | 33,052 | 23,126 |
| GRUNDY | 20,744 | 4,863 | 11.3 | 12.4 | 38.8 | 31.6 | 4.8 | 1.1 | 35,309 | 31,615 | 40,655 | 44,209 | 38,876 | 25,886 |
| GUTHRIE | 17,462 | 4,757 | 14.7 | 18.6 | 40.6 | 21.4 | 3.9 | 0.9 | 30,514 | 27,179 | 36,998 | 38,434 | 32,470 | 22,427 |
| HAMILTON | 17,489 | 6,367 | 13.8 | 14.4 | 41.7 | 26.3 | 3.2 | 0.5 | 31,889 | 28,089 | 39,483 | 37,655 | 33,116 | 24,010 |
| HANCOCK | 16,122 | 4,651 | 12.1 | 14.8 | 45.0 | 25.7 | 1.7 | 0.7 | 31,131 | 28,082 | 36,217 | 38,224 | 32,826 | 23,889 |
| HARDIN | 17,926 | 7,414 | 14.3 | 16.2 | 38.6 | 26.7 | 3.3 | 0.8 | 31,618 | 28,862 | 38,109 | 37,903 | 33,630 | 24,360 |
| HARRISON | 16,861 | 5,994 | 17.1 | 15.2 | 38.3 | 25.1 | 3.6 | 0.8 | 31,053 | 28,648 | 37,867 | 41,092 | 33,537 | 19,557 |
| HENRY | 16,621 | 7,413 | 14.0 | 15.4 | 40.2 | 26.2 | 3.6 | 0.7 | 31,967 | 26,984 | 38,628 | 41,188 | 33,384 | 22,231 |
| HOWARD | 15,802 | 3,833 | 16.9 | 16.3 | 41.3 | 22.4 | 3.2 | 0.0 | 29,331 | 26,512 | 34,787 | 35,798 | 31,214 | 22,201 |
| HUMBOLDT | 18,889 | 4,179 | 12.2 | 14.9 | 40.8 | 27.2 | 4.2 | 0.7 | 32,719 | 28,169 | 38,082 | 42,043 | 36,757 | 24,333 |
| IDA | 15,124 | 3,016 | 19.0 | 18.9 | 37.0 | 21.2 | 3.0 | 0.9 | 28,878 | 25,373 | 36,527 | 34,139 | 34,335 | 21,192 |
| IOWA | 18,062 | 6,208 | 12.8 | 13.9 | 41.5 | 27.2 | 3.8 | 0.9 | 33,071 | 32,129 | 39,913 | 40,390 | 34,305 | 21,851 |
| JACKSON | 13,935 | 7,651 | 22.4 | 18.6 | 37.1 | 19.6 | 2.0 | 0.5 | 26,877 | 23,898 | 33,042 | 33,228 | 28,482 | 18,183 |
| JASPER | 19,533 | 14,244 | 11.0 | 10.9 | 38.8 | 33.0 | 5.3 | 1.0 | 36,207 | 33,666 | 43,416 | 44,840 | 36,598 | 24,377 |
| JEFFERSON | 17,488 | 6,770 | 19.2 | 17.0 | 39.7 | 19.9 | 3.3 | 1.0 | 29,202 | 23,820 | 33,594 | 35,060 | 31,526 | 20,375 |
| JOHNSON | 22,010 | 39,207 | 15.1 | 13.5 | 32.0 | 27.4 | 7.5 | 4.5 | 40,007 | 27,167 | 47,050 | 55,462 | 55,386 | 31,478 |
| JONES | 14,308 | 7,267 | 15.9 | 18.1 | 40.7 | 22.8 | 2.5 | 0.1 | 29,184 | 27,615 | 33,166 | 36,905 | 30,990 | 19,437 |
| KEOKUK | 14,184 | 4,530 | 18.9 | 20.3 | 41.0 | 18.0 | 1.4 | 0.5 | 26,790 | 24,822 | 31,227 | 32,515 | 27,724 | 20,554 |
| KOSSUTH | 15,042 | 6,865 | 18.1 | 19.3 | 42.0 | 18.1 | 2.0 | 0.5 | 27,486 | 24,583 | 33,011 | 32,126 | 29,376 | 21,217 |
| LEE | 16,636 | 14,840 | 18.3 | 15.0 | 37.7 | 24.6 | 3.6 | 0.9 | 30,976 | 26,976 | 36,208 | 40,157 | 33,745 | 19,979 |
| LINN | 22,424 | 72,399 | 11.2 | 10.8 | 36.0 | 32.9 | 6.8 | 2.4 | 38,744 | 32,468 | 44,877 | 48,175 | 42,438 | 24,888 |
| LOUISA | 15,611 | 4,474 | 16.7 | 14.7 | 41.0 | 24.4 | 2.6 | 0.7 | 30,415 | 29,027 | 37,110 | 33,769 | 32,743 | 20,322 |
| LUCAS | 14,979 | 3,857 | 24.6 | 17.7 | 37.3 | 17.8 | 2.0 | 0.7 | 26,318 | 24,385 | 30,342 | 32,480 | 31,441 | 18,428 |
| LYON | 14,059 | 4,360 | 16.9 | 17.1 | 41.4 | 22.3 | 1.7 | 0.6 | 28,692 | 27,242 | 33,494 | 35,520 | 32,026 | 20,124 |
| MADISON | 18,373 | 5,375 | 11.8 | 11.4 | 43.0 | 26.9 | 5.1 | 1.8 | 35,156 | 30,502 | 40,964 | 44,386 | 40,097 | 22,686 |
| MAHASKA | 16,176 | 8,501 | 16.7 | 15.9 | 39.6 | 23.6 | 3.2 | 1.0 | 30,898 | 26,654 | 36,676 | 39,240 | 33,062 | 21,791 |
| MARION | 18,822 | 11,708 | 10.5 | 10.7 | 40.4 | 31.7 | 5.6 | 1.1 | 36,261 | 32,143 | 42,846 | 45,401 | 38,504 | 24,852 |
| MARSHALL | 18,989 | 15,165 | 13.4 | 13.8 | 37.7 | 29.3 | 4.6 | 1.2 | 34,367 | 28,254 | 41,089 | 43,778 | 37,417 | 23,355 |
| MILLS | 14,285 | 5,379 | 15.8 | 17.9 | 41.4 | 22.2 | 2.4 | 0.4 | 29,478 | 26,569 | 34,493 | 34,902 | 31,899 | 19,663 |
| MITCHELL | 16,418 | 4,313 | 15.0 | 16.1 | 43.9 | 21.5 | 2.7 | 0.9 | 30,206 | 28,108 | 33,814 | 35,759 | 36,691 | 22,576 |
| MONONA | 14,792 | 4,159 | 22.4 | 20.1 | 38.0 | 16.3 | 2.5 | 0.6 | 26,406 | 23,869 | 31,843 | 32,084 | 30,537 | 19,593 |
| MONROE | 14,269 | 3,171 | 21.8 | 21.3 | 35.1 | 18.3 | 3.1 | 0.3 | 26,538 | 25,821 | 32,111 | 32,812 | 27,792 | 19,050 |
| MONTGOMERY | 15,922 | 4,915 | 20.2 | 17.2 | 41.1 | 19.0 | 1.9 | 0.6 | 27,864 | 25,869 | 33,918 | 33,599 | 28,762 | 20,682 |
| MUSCATINE | 20,327 | 15,382 | 12.1 | 9.9 | 35.9 | 34.7 | 6.3 | 1.1 | 37,284 | 32,233 | 43,159 | 46,915 | 38,253 | 25,803 |
| O'BRIEN | 16,130 | 5,765 | 15.1 | 20.1 | 41.7 | 19.3 | 3.0 | 0.8 | 29,345 | 26,049 | 33,779 | 36,733 | 34,653 | 22,130 |
| OSCEOLA | 17,257 | 2,702 | 16.5 | 18.1 | 37.6 | 23.0 | 3.9 | 1.0 | 30,861 | 28,600 | 33,252 | 42,751 | 33,615 | 21,247 |
| PAGE | 15,405 | 6,540 | 20.7 | 17.8 | 37.1 | 21.1 | 2.5 | 0.8 | 28,337 | 24,752 | 35,949 | 37,134 | 30,546 | 18,746 |
| PALO ALTO | 15,266 | 3,929 | 19.3 | 20.9 | 37.7 | 19.7 | 1.8 | 0.6 | 27,352 | 21,577 | 32,629 | 33,035 | 32,769 | 23,718 |
| PLYMOUTH | 16,888 | 9,083 | 13.3 | 12.6 | 40.2 | 28.7 | 4.3 | 0.9 | 33,613 | 31,028 | 39,549 | 41,734 | 34,654 | 23,550 |
| POCAHONTAS | 16,057 | 3,507 | 17.3 | 17.3 | 41.0 | 21.6 | 2.4 | 0.5 | 29,144 | 26,684 | 34,100 | 36,561 | 29,973 | 22,191 |
| POLK | 22,521 | 145,557 | 11.3 | 11.9 | 35.3 | 32.1 | 6.9 | 2.7 | 38,913 | 32,583 | 44,630 | 48,336 | 40,761 | 26,125 |
| IOWA | 18,653 | | 14.8 | 14.5 | 37.4 | 27.0 | 4.8 | 1.6 | 33,931 | 28,488 | 40,263 | 43,264 | 36,563 | 23,029 |
| UNITED STATES | 22,162 | | 14.5 | 12.5 | 32.3 | 29.8 | 7.4 | 3.5 | 40,748 | 34,503 | 44,969 | 49,579 | 43,409 | 27,339 |

| COUNTY | FINANCIAL SERVICES | | | | THE HOME: Home Improvements | | | THE HOME: Furnishings | | | ENTERTAINMENT | | | | | | PERSONAL | | | |
|---|---|---|---|---|---|---|---|---|---|---|---|---|---|---|---|---|---|---|---|---|
| | Auto Loan | Home Loan | Invest-ments | Retire-ment Plans | Home Repair | Lawn & Garden | Remodel-ing | Appli-ances | Elec-tronics | Furni-ture | Restau-rants | Sport-ing Goods | Theater & Concerts | Toys & Hobbies | Travel | Video Rental | Apparel | Auto After-market | Health Insur-ance | Pets & Supplies |
| ADAIR | 96 | 64 | 70 | 78 | 90 | 89 | 108 | 94 | 90 | 72 | 78 | 92 | 79 | 93 | 75 | 100 | 77 | 89 | 105 | 95 |
| ADAMS | 97 | 66 | 72 | 80 | 91 | 90 | 110 | 95 | 91 | 73 | 79 | 95 | 81 | 95 | 76 | 100 | 79 | 90 | 105 | 97 |
| ALLAMAKEE | 97 | 64 | 70 | 79 | 90 | 90 | 111 | 95 | 90 | 72 | 78 | 94 | 80 | 94 | 75 | 100 | 78 | 89 | 106 | 96 |
| APPANOOSE | 97 | 67 | 74 | 79 | 91 | 90 | 111 | 95 | 92 | 76 | 80 | 93 | 82 | 94 | 77 | 100 | 79 | 90 | 104 | 96 |
| AUDUBON | 97 | 64 | 70 | 79 | 90 | 89 | 109 | 95 | 90 | 72 | 78 | 94 | 79 | 94 | 75 | 100 | 77 | 89 | 106 | 96 |
| BENTON | 99 | 75 | 80 | 85 | 94 | 91 | 113 | 97 | 94 | 82 | 87 | 96 | 88 | 99 | 81 | 102 | 85 | 93 | 104 | 100 |
| BLACK HAWK | 96 | 93 | 99 | 93 | 102 | 98 | 98 | 96 | 94 | 94 | 96 | 94 | 98 | 97 | 96 | 99 | 92 | 97 | 100 | 97 |
| BOONE | 95 | 73 | 80 | 81 | 94 | 91 | 107 | 95 | 92 | 81 | 84 | 90 | 86 | 94 | 82 | 100 | 82 | 91 | 102 | 95 |
| BREMER | 98 | 80 | 84 | 87 | 95 | 93 | 110 | 97 | 94 | 85 | 89 | 95 | 90 | 98 | 84 | 101 | 86 | 94 | 102 | 99 |
| BUCHANAN | 98 | 68 | 73 | 81 | 91 | 90 | 110 | 96 | 90 | 75 | 81 | 96 | 83 | 96 | 77 | 100 | 80 | 90 | 105 | 98 |
| BUENA VISTA | 96 | 81 | 88 | 87 | 95 | 94 | 104 | 95 | 93 | 85 | 89 | 94 | 91 | 96 | 86 | 100 | 86 | 93 | 103 | 97 |
| BUTLER | 97 | 66 | 73 | 80 | 91 | 90 | 110 | 95 | 91 | 74 | 80 | 94 | 81 | 95 | 76 | 100 | 79 | 90 | 105 | 96 |
| CALHOUN | 96 | 68 | 77 | 80 | 92 | 91 | 108 | 95 | 92 | 76 | 81 | 92 | 82 | 93 | 79 | 100 | 79 | 90 | 104 | 95 |
| CARROLL | 98 | 78 | 81 | 86 | 94 | 92 | 106 | 96 | 93 | 83 | 87 | 96 | 90 | 97 | 83 | 101 | 85 | 93 | 103 | 98 |
| CASS | 98 | 71 | 81 | 85 | 93 | 93 | 110 | 96 | 93 | 78 | 83 | 95 | 86 | 96 | 80 | 101 | 82 | 91 | 105 | 98 |
| CEDAR | 99 | 79 | 85 | 86 | 95 | 93 | 111 | 97 | 94 | 85 | 89 | 96 | 90 | 99 | 84 | 101 | 86 | 94 | 103 | 100 |
| CERRO GORDO | 96 | 89 | 95 | 90 | 99 | 97 | 101 | 96 | 94 | 91 | 94 | 94 | 96 | 97 | 92 | 100 | 90 | 96 | 101 | 97 |
| CHEROKEE | 97 | 71 | 80 | 82 | 93 | 92 | 106 | 95 | 91 | 78 | 83 | 94 | 85 | 95 | 81 | 100 | 81 | 91 | 105 | 96 |
| CHICKASAW | 98 | 70 | 76 | 82 | 92 | 90 | 112 | 96 | 92 | 77 | 83 | 96 | 84 | 97 | 78 | 101 | 81 | 91 | 105 | 98 |
| CLARKE | 97 | 70 | 75 | 80 | 92 | 90 | 111 | 96 | 93 | 78 | 82 | 93 | 84 | 95 | 78 | 101 | 81 | 90 | 103 | 97 |
| CLAY | 97 | 81 | 82 | 86 | 93 | 91 | 105 | 96 | 93 | 84 | 89 | 95 | 89 | 97 | 84 | 100 | 86 | 94 | 102 | 98 |
| CLAYTON | 98 | 64 | 69 | 80 | 90 | 90 | 111 | 95 | 90 | 72 | 78 | 96 | 80 | 95 | 75 | 100 | 78 | 89 | 106 | 97 |
| CLINTON | 96 | 85 | 90 | 88 | 99 | 95 | 103 | 96 | 92 | 90 | 92 | 94 | 94 | 97 | 90 | 100 | 88 | 94 | 101 | 98 |
| CRAWFORD | 96 | 69 | 74 | 80 | 91 | 90 | 108 | 95 | 90 | 76 | 81 | 93 | 83 | 94 | 77 | 100 | 79 | 90 | 104 | 96 |
| DALLAS | 99 | 90 | 87 | 93 | 96 | 94 | 106 | 98 | 98 | 92 | 96 | 98 | 96 | 100 | 89 | 102 | 93 | 98 | 101 | 100 |
| DAVIS | 98 | 69 | 75 | 81 | 92 | 90 | 111 | 96 | 92 | 77 | 82 | 95 | 84 | 96 | 78 | 101 | 81 | 91 | 105 | 98 |
| DECATUR | 95 | 66 | 70 | 77 | 90 | 89 | 107 | 94 | 90 | 74 | 78 | 91 | 80 | 92 | 76 | 99 | 77 | 88 | 103 | 95 |
| DELAWARE | 99 | 69 | 74 | 83 | 92 | 90 | 112 | 96 | 91 | 76 | 82 | 97 | 84 | 98 | 78 | 100 | 81 | 91 | 105 | 99 |
| DES MOINES | 96 | 87 | 93 | 89 | 100 | 96 | 103 | 96 | 93 | 92 | 93 | 94 | 95 | 97 | 92 | 100 | 89 | 95 | 100 | 97 |
| DICKINSON | 99 | 78 | 85 | 89 | 95 | 95 | 112 | 98 | 94 | 83 | 88 | 97 | 90 | 99 | 85 | 101 | 86 | 94 | 106 | 100 |
| DUBUQUE | 97 | 89 | 95 | 91 | 100 | 97 | 102 | 97 | 94 | 92 | 95 | 95 | 96 | 98 | 93 | 100 | 91 | 96 | 101 | 98 |
| EMMET | 95 | 70 | 74 | 79 | 92 | 89 | 106 | 94 | 90 | 76 | 81 | 91 | 82 | 93 | 79 | 99 | 79 | 89 | 103 | 95 |
| FAYETTE | 96 | 68 | 74 | 80 | 91 | 90 | 109 | 95 | 91 | 76 | 81 | 93 | 82 | 94 | 78 | 100 | 79 | 90 | 104 | 96 |
| FLOYD | 97 | 75 | 84 | 84 | 95 | 93 | 106 | 96 | 91 | 81 | 86 | 94 | 88 | 96 | 84 | 100 | 83 | 92 | 104 | 97 |
| FRANKLIN | 97 | 65 | 72 | 79 | 90 | 90 | 110 | 95 | 90 | 73 | 79 | 94 | 80 | 95 | 76 | 100 | 78 | 89 | 106 | 96 |
| FREMONT | 98 | 68 | 74 | 82 | 91 | 90 | 112 | 96 | 91 | 75 | 81 | 96 | 83 | 97 | 77 | 101 | 80 | 91 | 105 | 98 |
| GREENE | 97 | 68 | 77 | 81 | 92 | 91 | 108 | 95 | 91 | 76 | 81 | 94 | 83 | 95 | 79 | 100 | 80 | 90 | 105 | 96 |
| GRUNDY | 97 | 67 | 74 | 80 | 91 | 90 | 110 | 95 | 92 | 76 | 81 | 93 | 82 | 94 | 77 | 100 | 79 | 90 | 104 | 96 |
| GUTHRIE | 97 | 72 | 78 | 83 | 92 | 91 | 111 | 96 | 93 | 79 | 83 | 94 | 85 | 96 | 79 | 101 | 82 | 91 | 104 | 97 |
| HAMILTON | 97 | 74 | 82 | 83 | 93 | 92 | 107 | 95 | 91 | 80 | 85 | 94 | 87 | 96 | 82 | 100 | 82 | 91 | 104 | 97 |
| HANCOCK | 98 | 74 | 82 | 84 | 93 | 92 | 109 | 96 | 93 | 80 | 85 | 95 | 87 | 97 | 81 | 101 | 83 | 92 | 104 | 98 |
| HARDIN | 96 | 75 | 84 | 84 | 94 | 93 | 105 | 95 | 93 | 82 | 85 | 92 | 88 | 95 | 83 | 101 | 83 | 92 | 103 | 96 |
| HARRISON | 97 | 67 | 74 | 80 | 91 | 90 | 110 | 95 | 92 | 76 | 81 | 94 | 82 | 95 | 77 | 101 | 80 | 90 | 105 | 97 |
| HENRY | 97 | 76 | 79 | 83 | 93 | 90 | 109 | 96 | 94 | 83 | 87 | 94 | 87 | 96 | 81 | 101 | 84 | 92 | 102 | 98 |
| HOWARD | 98 | 63 | 69 | 80 | 90 | 89 | 110 | 95 | 90 | 71 | 78 | 96 | 80 | 95 | 75 | 100 | 77 | 89 | 107 | 97 |
| HUMBOLDT | 99 | 71 | 80 | 85 | 93 | 92 | 111 | 96 | 93 | 78 | 83 | 97 | 86 | 97 | 80 | 101 | 83 | 92 | 106 | 99 |
| IDA | 96 | 64 | 70 | 78 | 90 | 89 | 108 | 94 | 90 | 72 | 78 | 92 | 79 | 93 | 75 | 100 | 77 | 89 | 105 | 95 |
| IOWA | 98 | 72 | 77 | 83 | 93 | 91 | 113 | 96 | 93 | 80 | 84 | 95 | 86 | 97 | 79 | 101 | 83 | 92 | 104 | 99 |
| JACKSON | 97 | 69 | 74 | 81 | 92 | 90 | 112 | 96 | 92 | 77 | 82 | 95 | 84 | 96 | 78 | 100 | 80 | 90 | 104 | 97 |
| JASPER | 99 | 83 | 90 | 89 | 98 | 95 | 109 | 98 | 94 | 89 | 92 | 97 | 94 | 100 | 88 | 101 | 89 | 95 | 103 | 100 |
| JEFFERSON | 99 | 83 | 88 | 90 | 96 | 95 | 109 | 98 | 95 | 87 | 91 | 98 | 93 | 99 | 87 | 101 | 89 | 96 | 103 | 100 |
| JOHNSON | 96 | 102 | 94 | 97 | 97 | 94 | 97 | 93 | 95 | 91 | 98 | 94 | 94 | 96 | 93 | 98 | 94 | 98 | 96 | 99 |
| JONES | 98 | 74 | 79 | 83 | 93 | 91 | 111 | 97 | 92 | 81 | 85 | 96 | 87 | 98 | 80 | 101 | 83 | 92 | 104 | 99 |
| KEOKUK | 97 | 65 | 71 | 79 | 90 | 90 | 110 | 95 | 90 | 73 | 79 | 94 | 80 | 94 | 76 | 100 | 78 | 89 | 105 | 96 |
| KOSSUTH | 97 | 69 | 74 | 81 | 91 | 90 | 109 | 95 | 90 | 76 | 81 | 95 | 83 | 96 | 78 | 100 | 80 | 90 | 105 | 97 |
| LEE | 97 | 79 | 84 | 84 | 96 | 92 | 107 | 96 | 92 | 85 | 88 | 94 | 90 | 97 | 84 | 100 | 85 | 92 | 101 | 97 |
| LINN | 98 | 98 | 98 | 97 | 101 | 99 | 100 | 98 | 98 | 99 | 102 | 98 | 101 | 100 | 97 | 101 | 97 | 100 | 100 | 100 |
| LOUISA | 98 | 74 | 79 | 83 | 93 | 91 | 113 | 97 | 93 | 81 | 86 | 96 | 87 | 98 | 80 | 101 | 84 | 92 | 103 | 99 |
| LUCAS | 97 | 68 | 74 | 81 | 91 | 90 | 111 | 95 | 92 | 76 | 81 | 94 | 83 | 95 | 77 | 101 | 80 | 90 | 105 | 97 |
| LYON | 97 | 67 | 72 | 80 | 91 | 90 | 109 | 95 | 90 | 74 | 80 | 95 | 82 | 95 | 76 | 100 | 79 | 90 | 105 | 97 |
| MADISON | 98 | 78 | 83 | 85 | 94 | 92 | 110 | 96 | 95 | 84 | 88 | 94 | 89 | 97 | 83 | 101 | 85 | 93 | 102 | 98 |
| MAHASKA | 96 | 76 | 81 | 83 | 94 | 91 | 105 | 95 | 91 | 81 | 85 | 94 | 87 | 95 | 83 | 99 | 82 | 91 | 103 | 97 |
| MARION | 98 | 81 | 86 | 87 | 96 | 93 | 109 | 97 | 95 | 87 | 90 | 96 | 92 | 98 | 85 | 101 | 88 | 94 | 102 | 99 |
| MARSHALL | 97 | 88 | 92 | 90 | 98 | 96 | 102 | 97 | 94 | 91 | 94 | 95 | 95 | 98 | 91 | 100 | 90 | 96 | 101 | 98 |
| MILLS | 99 | 74 | 80 | 85 | 94 | 92 | 113 | 97 | 93 | 81 | 86 | 97 | 87 | 99 | 81 | 101 | 84 | 93 | 105 | 100 |
| MITCHELL | 96 | 65 | 72 | 79 | 91 | 90 | 108 | 95 | 90 | 73 | 79 | 93 | 81 | 94 | 76 | 100 | 78 | 89 | 105 | 95 |
| MONONA | 96 | 64 | 70 | 77 | 90 | 89 | 108 | 94 | 90 | 73 | 78 | 92 | 79 | 93 | 75 | 100 | 77 | 89 | 105 | 95 |
| MONROE | 96 | 67 | 72 | 78 | 91 | 89 | 107 | 94 | 90 | 75 | 80 | 92 | 81 | 93 | 77 | 99 | 78 | 89 | 104 | 95 |
| MONTGOMERY | 96 | 73 | 81 | 81 | 93 | 91 | 107 | 95 | 92 | 80 | 84 | 91 | 85 | 94 | 81 | 100 | 81 | 91 | 102 | 96 |
| MUSCATINE | 98 | 90 | 92 | 92 | 99 | 96 | 106 | 98 | 96 | 93 | 96 | 97 | 97 | 100 | 91 | 101 | 92 | 97 | 101 | 100 |
| O'BRIEN | 97 | 75 | 87 | 87 | 95 | 94 | 106 | 95 | 93 | 81 | 85 | 94 | 88 | 95 | 84 | 100 | 84 | 92 | 104 | 96 |
| OSCEOLA | 99 | 66 | 72 | 81 | 90 | 90 | 111 | 96 | 90 | 73 | 80 | 97 | 82 | 97 | 76 | 101 | 79 | 90 | 106 | 98 |
| PAGE | 95 | 72 | 78 | 80 | 93 | 90 | 106 | 94 | 90 | 79 | 83 | 91 | 85 | 93 | 81 | 99 | 80 | 90 | 102 | 95 |
| PALO ALTO | 95 | 66 | 73 | 78 | 91 | 90 | 107 | 94 | 90 | 75 | 79 | 91 | 81 | 93 | 77 | 100 | 78 | 89 | 104 | 95 |
| PLYMOUTH | 98 | 76 | 81 | 86 | 93 | 92 | 110 | 96 | 94 | 82 | 87 | 96 | 88 | 98 | 82 | 101 | 85 | 93 | 104 | 99 |
| POCAHONTAS | 98 | 69 | 79 | 82 | 92 | 91 | 110 | 96 | 91 | 77 | 82 | 95 | 84 | 96 | 79 | 100 | 81 | 91 | 105 | 97 |
| POLK | 98 | 102 | 97 | 99 | 101 | 99 | 97 | 98 | 98 | 100 | 103 | 99 | 102 | 100 | 99 | 102 | 99 | 102 | 99 | 100 |
| IOWA | 97 | 86 | 90 | 90 | 97 | 95 | 104 | 96 | 94 | 89 | 92 | 96 | 94 | 98 | 89 | 101 | 89 | 95 | 102 | 98 |
| UNITED STATES | 100 | 100 | 100 | 100 | 100 | 100 | 100 | 100 | 100 | 100 | 100 | 100 | 100 | 100 | 100 | 100 | 100 | 100 | 100 | 100 |

# POPULATION CHANGE

| COUNTY | FIPS Code | MSA Code | DMA Code | POPULATION 1990 | POPULATION 2000 | POPULATION 2005 | 1990-2000 ANNUAL CHANGE % Rate | 1990-2000 ANNUAL CHANGE State Rank | RACE (%) White 1990 | White 2000 | Black 1990 | Black 2000 | Asian/Pacific 1990 | Asian/Pacific 2000 |
|---|---|---|---|---|---|---|---|---|---|---|---|---|---|---|
| POTTAWATTAMIE | 155 | 5920 | 652 | 82,628 | 86,886 | 89,199 | 0.5 | 15 | 98.3 | 97.7 | 0.6 | 0.6 | 0.3 | 0.5 |
| POWESHIEK | 157 | 000C | 679 | 19,033 | 18,636 | 18,311 | -0.2 | 59 | 98.3 | 97.8 | 0.5 | 0.5 | 1.0 | 1.3 |
| RINGGOLD | 159 | 0000 | 679 | 5,420 | 5,366 | 5,382 | -0.1 | 52 | 99.4 | 99.3 | 0.0 | 0.0 | 0.3 | 0.4 |
| SAC | 161 | 0000 | 624 | 12,324 | 11,675 | 11,257 | -0.5 | 79 | 99.6 | 99.5 | 0.0 | 0.0 | 0.2 | 0.2 |
| SCOTT | 163 | 1960 | 682 | 150,979 | 160,303 | 164,564 | 0.6 | 12 | 92.3 | 90.6 | 5.3 | 5.8 | 0.9 | 1.3 |
| SHELBY | 165 | 0000 | 652 | 13,230 | 12,670 | 12,131 | -0.4 | 76 | 99.6 | 99.6 | 0.0 | 0.0 | 0.2 | 0.2 |
| SIOUX | 167 | 0000 | 624 | 29,903 | 31,313 | 31,104 | 0.5 | 15 | 99.0 | 98.6 | 0.1 | 0.1 | 0.7 | 1.0 |
| STORY | 169 | 0000 | 679 | 74,252 | 75,700 | 77,240 | 0.2 | 30 | 93.1 | 91.4 | 1.6 | 1.7 | 4.7 | 6.0 |
| TAMA | 171 | 0000 | 637 | 17,419 | 17,828 | 18,009 | 0.2 | 30 | 94.5 | 94.1 | 0.2 | 0.2 | 0.4 | 0.5 |
| TAYLOR | 173 | 0000 | 679 | 7,114 | 6,968 | 6,692 | -0.2 | 59 | 99.4 | 99.1 | 0.0 | 0.0 | 0.3 | 0.4 |
| UNION | 175 | 0000 | 679 | 12,750 | 12,638 | 12,818 | -0.1 | 52 | 99.2 | 99.0 | 0.1 | 0.1 | 0.4 | 0.5 |
| VAN BUREN | 177 | 0000 | 631 | 7,676 | 7,908 | 8,057 | 0.3 | 22 | 99.5 | 99.4 | 0.1 | 0.1 | 0.2 | 0.3 |
| WAPELLO | 179 | 0000 | 631 | 35,687 | 35,439 | 35,350 | -0.1 | 52 | 98.3 | 97.8 | 0.8 | 0.9 | 0.5 | 0.7 |
| WARREN | 181 | 2120 | 679 | 36,033 | 41,006 | 43,006 | 1.3 | 3 | 99.0 | 98.7 | 0.2 | 0.3 | 0.4 | 0.6 |
| WASHINGTON | 183 | 0000 | 637 | 19,612 | 21,319 | 22,162 | 0.8 | 9 | 98.9 | 98.7 | 0.5 | 0.4 | 0.3 | 0.4 |
| WAYNE | 185 | 0000 | 679 | 7,067 | 6,500 | 6,111 | -0.8 | 93 | 99.6 | 99.5 | 0.0 | 0.0 | 0.2 | 0.3 |
| WEBSTER | 187 | 0000 | 679 | 40,342 | 38,678 | 37,922 | -0.4 | 76 | 96.7 | 96.1 | 2.2 | 2.4 | 0.4 | 0.6 |
| WINNEBAGO | 189 | 0000 | 611 | 12,122 | 11,966 | 11,945 | -0.1 | 52 | 98.7 | 98.1 | 0.3 | 0.3 | 0.6 | 1.0 |
| WINNESHIEK | 191 | 0000 | 637 | 20,847 | 20,890 | 20,758 | 0.0 | 47 | 98.7 | 98.3 | 0.2 | 0.2 | 0.9 | 1.2 |
| WOODBURY | 193 | 7720 | 624 | 98,276 | 101,319 | 100,653 | 0.3 | 22 | 93.7 | 92.1 | 1.9 | 2.1 | 1.3 | 1.8 |
| WORTH | 195 | 0000 | 611 | 7,991 | 7,597 | 7,301 | -0.5 | 79 | 99.1 | 98.7 | 0.2 | 0.2 | 0.2 | 0.2 |
| WRIGHT | 197 | 0000 | 679 | 14,269 | 13,777 | 13,217 | -0.3 | 66 | 99.3 | 99.1 | 0.1 | 0.1 | 0.3 | 0.4 |
| IOWA | | | | | | | 0.3 | | 96.6 | 95.7 | 1.7 | 2.0 | 0.9 | 1.3 |
| UNITED STATES | | | | | | | 1.0 | | 80.3 | 77.9 | 12.1 | 12.4 | 2.9 | 3.9 |

# POPULATION COMPOSITION

| COUNTY | % HISPANIC ORIGIN 1990 | % HISPANIC ORIGIN 2000 | 2000 AGE DISTRIBUTION (%) 0-4 | 5-9 | 10-14 | 15-19 | 20-24 | 25-44 | 45-64 | 65-84 | 85+ | 18+ | MEDIAN AGE 1990 | MEDIAN AGE 2000 | 2000 Males/ Females (×100) |
|---|---|---|---|---|---|---|---|---|---|---|---|---|---|---|---|
| POTTAWATTAMIE | 1.8 | 3.6 | 6.7 | 6.7 | 7.6 | 7.8 | 5.8 | 28.0 | 23.6 | 12.1 | 1.7 | 74.4 | 33.5 | 36.9 | 93.0 |
| POWESHIEK | 0.4 | 0.9 | 5.7 | 6.3 | 6.6 | 9.6 | 7.5 | 25.1 | 23.1 | 13.5 | 2.7 | 76.9 | 34.5 | 37.9 | 94.5 |
| RINGGOLD | 0.3 | 0.9 | 5.1 | 6.0 | 6.4 | 7.2 | 4.0 | 22.2 | 25.1 | 20.0 | 4.1 | 77.8 | 42.2 | 44.4 | 93.0 |
| SAC | 0.4 | 1.0 | 6.2 | 6.9 | 7.7 | 7.2 | 4.2 | 23.3 | 23.4 | 17.2 | 3.9 | 74.4 | 38.3 | 41.2 | 98.3 |
| SCOTT | 2.8 | 5.3 | 7.0 | 7.1 | 7.7 | 7.6 | 6.8 | 29.2 | 22.9 | 10.2 | 1.5 | 73.5 | 32.4 | 35.2 | 93.8 |
| SHELBY | 0.3 | 1.0 | 6.0 | 6.7 | 7.6 | 7.6 | 4.3 | 23.9 | 23.7 | 16.6 | 3.5 | 74.6 | 37.3 | 40.7 | 97.8 |
| SIOUX | 0.2 | 0.8 | 7.0 | 7.6 | 8.4 | 10.5 | 8.2 | 23.6 | 20.4 | 12.2 | 2.2 | 72.1 | 30.9 | 33.1 | 95.6 |
| STORY | 1.1 | 2.2 | 5.3 | 4.9 | 5.4 | 11.1 | 19.2 | 26.9 | 17.1 | 8.6 | 1.6 | 81.4 | 25.9 | 27.8 | 106.6 |
| TAMA | 0.7 | 1.6 | 6.0 | 6.4 | 7.5 | 7.4 | 5.1 | 24.3 | 24.6 | 15.5 | 3.3 | 75.3 | 37.4 | 40.5 | 95.6 |
| TAYLOR | 0.6 | 1.5 | 5.9 | 6.4 | 6.6 | 7.6 | 5.2 | 22.2 | 23.8 | 18.0 | 4.4 | 76.0 | 40.0 | 42.3 | 91.5 |
| UNION | 0.3 | 0.9 | 6.0 | 6.3 | 6.6 | 7.4 | 6.2 | 25.8 | 24.1 | 14.4 | 3.2 | 76.8 | 36.5 | 39.1 | 90.0 |
| VAN BUREN | 0.4 | 1.1 | 6.4 | 6.9 | 7.7 | 7.0 | 4.4 | 24.0 | 24.5 | 16.1 | 2.8 | 74.4 | 37.8 | 40.6 | 98.3 |
| WAPELLO | 0.6 | 1.5 | 5.7 | 5.9 | 7.0 | 7.5 | 5.8 | 26.0 | 24.4 | 15.1 | 2.6 | 77.2 | 37.1 | 40.0 | 92.4 |
| WARREN | 0.8 | 1.7 | 6.4 | 6.8 | 7.5 | 8.4 | 6.9 | 27.6 | 25.0 | 9.8 | 1.6 | 74.6 | 32.8 | 36.0 | 95.1 |
| WASHINGTON | 1.0 | 2.1 | 6.7 | 6.8 | 7.7 | 7.2 | 5.4 | 26.3 | 22.9 | 14.1 | 3.0 | 74.1 | 35.7 | 38.5 | 94.5 |
| WAYNE | 0.4 | 1.1 | 5.9 | 6.1 | 7.1 | 6.4 | 4.3 | 22.3 | 24.2 | 19.2 | 4.6 | 76.6 | 42.1 | 43.5 | 91.6 |
| WEBSTER | 1.2 | 2.4 | 6.5 | 6.6 | 7.4 | 7.7 | 5.6 | 25.8 | 23.0 | 14.4 | 2.9 | 75.1 | 35.5 | 38.6 | 92.4 |
| WINNEBAGO | 0.8 | 1.8 | 6.0 | 6.5 | 7.1 | 9.7 | 5.3 | 24.6 | 22.7 | 14.9 | 3.2 | 76.0 | 35.9 | 38.8 | 95.7 |
| WINNESHIEK | 0.3 | 0.9 | 6.0 | 6.2 | 6.8 | 10.7 | 10.2 | 24.5 | 20.7 | 12.5 | 2.4 | 77.1 | 31.7 | 34.4 | 96.3 |
| WOODBURY | 2.8 | 5.0 | 7.0 | 7.0 | 7.9 | 8.2 | 6.9 | 27.8 | 21.6 | 11.6 | 2.0 | 73.4 | 32.9 | 35.2 | 94.6 |
| WORTH | 1.1 | 2.4 | 5.7 | 6.5 | 7.0 | 7.0 | 4.7 | 24.3 | 25.1 | 15.9 | 3.7 | 76.3 | 38.3 | 41.6 | 96.2 |
| WRIGHT | 0.6 | 1.6 | 6.0 | 6.1 | 7.3 | 6.6 | 4.8 | 24.2 | 24.1 | 17.3 | 3.7 | 76.2 | 39.0 | 41.7 | 92.2 |
| IOWA | 1.2 | 2.5 | 6.3 | 6.5 | 7.3 | 7.9 | 6.8 | 27.4 | 22.9 | 12.6 | 2.3 | 75.5 | 34.0 | 37.1 | 95.0 |
| UNITED STATES | 9.0 | 11.8 | 6.9 | 7.2 | 7.2 | 7.2 | 6.7 | 29.9 | 22.2 | 11.1 | 1.6 | 74.6 | 32.9 | 35.7 | 95.6 |

# HOUSEHOLDS

| COUNTY | HOUSEHOLDS | | | | | FAMILIES | | | MEDIAN HOUSEHOLD INCOME | | | |
|---|---|---|---|---|---|---|---|---|---|---|---|---|
| | 1990 | 2000 | 2005 | % Annual Rate 1990-2000 | 2000 Average HH Size | 1990 | 2000 | % Annual Rate 1990-2000 | 2000 | 2005 | 2000 National Rank | 2000 State Rank |
| POTTAWATTAMIE | 31,262 | 33,353 | 34,527 | 0.8 | 2.56 | 22,827 | 23,519 | 0.4 | 38,368 | 46,197 | 822 | 20 |
| POWESHIEK | 7,158 | 7,111 | 7,025 | -0.1 | 2.45 | 5,036 | 4,817 | -0.5 | 37,259 | 43,837 | 940 | 29 |
| RINGGOLD | 2,218 | 2,203 | 2,213 | -0.1 | 2.37 | 1,562 | 1,492 | -0.6 | 26,991 | 33,947 | 2580 | 94 |
| SAC | 4,914 | 4,762 | 4,650 | -0.4 | 2.40 | 3,454 | 3,222 | -0.8 | 30,184 | 36,082 | 2107 | 78 |
| SCOTT | 57,438 | 61,210 | 63,011 | 0.8 | 2.57 | 40,386 | 41,493 | 0.3 | 42,025 | 46,354 | 508 | 7 |
| SHELBY | 5,024 | 4,952 | 4,801 | -0.2 | 2.48 | 3,702 | 3,526 | -0.6 | 32,278 | 37,095 | 1668 | 65 |
| SIOUX | 9,925 | 10,330 | 10,303 | 0.5 | 2.78 | 7,584 | 7,629 | 0.1 | 38,463 | 46,300 | 810 | 19 |
| STORY | 25,941 | 26,890 | 27,548 | 0.4 | 2.44 | 15,884 | 15,734 | -0.1 | 38,261 | 42,333 | 833 | 21 |
| TAMA | 6,768 | 6,976 | 7,065 | 0.4 | 2.50 | 4,878 | 4,822 | -0.1 | 36,005 | 41,662 | 1102 | 38 |
| TAYLOR | 2,859 | 2,890 | 2,813 | 0.1 | 2.35 | 2,013 | 1,950 | -0.4 | 26,660 | 34,743 | 2625 | 95 |
| UNION | 5,173 | 5,124 | 5,194 | -0.1 | 2.42 | 3,502 | 3,333 | -0.6 | 28,837 | 33,663 | 2323 | 89 |
| VAN BUREN | 3,056 | 3,206 | 3,292 | 0.6 | 2.43 | 2,167 | 2,196 | 0.2 | 28,792 | 35,304 | 2328 | 90 |
| WAPELLO | 14,555 | 14,472 | 14,461 | -0.1 | 2.39 | 10,135 | 9,712 | -0.5 | 29,104 | 31,773 | 2281 | 87 |
| WARREN | 12,659 | 14,483 | 15,270 | 1.6 | 2.73 | 9,950 | 11,048 | 1.3 | 47,289 | 55,575 | 265 | 1 |
| WASHINGTON | 7,454 | 8,134 | 8,472 | 1.1 | 2.55 | 5,289 | 5,561 | 0.6 | 38,569 | 47,530 | 798 | 18 |
| WAYNE | 2,953 | 2,759 | 2,612 | -0.8 | 2.31 | 2,062 | 1,854 | -1.3 | 23,769 | 29,318 | 2918 | 98 |
| WEBSTER | 15,963 | 15,296 | 15,067 | -0.5 | 2.41 | 10,928 | 10,080 | -1.0 | 35,094 | 40,573 | 1239 | 43 |
| WINNEBAGO | 4,704 | 4,618 | 4,601 | -0.2 | 2.44 | 3,271 | 3,077 | -0.7 | 31,291 | 35,335 | 1867 | 73 |
| WINNESHIEK | 7,256 | 7,292 | 7,286 | 0.1 | 2.54 | 5,121 | 4,955 | -0.4 | 33,943 | 39,020 | 1403 | 52 |
| WOODBURY | 36,899 | 38,300 | 38,159 | 0.5 | 2.57 | 25,734 | 25,771 | 0.0 | 37,289 | 42,910 | 934 | 27 |
| WORTH | 3,239 | 3,160 | 3,078 | -0.3 | 2.36 | 2,296 | 2,155 | -0.8 | 31,471 | 33,861 | 1824 | 68 |
| WRIGHT | 5,899 | 5,785 | 5,595 | -0.2 | 2.33 | 4,081 | 3,835 | -0.8 | 36,515 | 42,721 | 1040 | 34 |
| IOWA | | | | 0.5 | 2.50 | | | 0.1 | 37,579 | 43,070 | | |
| UNITED STATES | | | | 1.4 | 2.59 | | | 1.1 | 41,914 | 49,127 | | |

| COUNTY | 2000 Per Capita Income | 2000 HH Income Base | 2000 HOUSEHOLD INCOME DISTRIBUTION (%) Less than $15,000 | $15,000 to $24,999 | $25,000 to $49,999 | $50,000 to $99,999 | $100,000 to $149,999 | $150,000 or More | 2000 AVERAGE DISPOSABLE INCOME BY AGE OF HOUSEHOLDER All Ages | <35 | 35-44 | 45-54 | 55-64 | 65+ |
|---|---|---|---|---|---|---|---|---|---|---|---|---|---|---|
| POTTAWATTAMIE | 17,525 | 33,344 | 12.4 | 14.1 | 39.5 | 29.3 | 4.1 | 0.6 | 33,368 | 28,940 | 39,792 | 41,878 | 34,759 | 22,831 |
| POWESHIEK | 17,880 | 7,111 | 14.1 | 13.9 | 40.2 | 26.9 | 3.7 | 1.2 | 32,987 | 27,576 | 40,077 | 40,680 | 37,136 | 23,680 |
| RINGGOLD | 13,432 | 2,203 | 24.4 | 20.5 | 38.9 | 13.5 | 2.5 | 0.2 | 24,717 | 22,272 | 29,316 | 32,304 | 28,633 | 17,430 |
| SAC | 15,312 | 4,762 | 17.7 | 21.0 | 39.1 | 19.6 | 2.0 | 0.6 | 27,767 | 25,087 | 31,884 | 34,965 | 32,251 | 21,078 |
| SCOTT | 21,023 | 61,210 | 13.6 | 12.3 | 33.7 | 31.0 | 6.7 | 2.6 | 37,824 | 29,066 | 44,547 | 48,420 | 40,396 | 25,840 |
| SHELBY | 15,213 | 4,952 | 14.7 | 21.6 | 38.7 | 21.7 | 3.3 | 0.1 | 28,863 | 24,613 | 34,598 | 34,562 | 32,808 | 21,984 |
| SIOUX | 15,925 | 10,330 | 10.4 | 14.1 | 41.0 | 28.6 | 4.8 | 1.1 | 34,411 | 29,006 | 39,889 | 45,344 | 39,085 | 24,137 |
| STORY | 17,909 | 26,889 | 15.8 | 14.0 | 35.0 | 27.1 | 6.0 | 2.1 | 35,194 | 23,942 | 43,149 | 51,657 | 48,471 | 28,489 |
| TAMA | 17,048 | 6,976 | 14.3 | 15.6 | 39.5 | 26.6 | 3.4 | 0.5 | 31,715 | 28,079 | 37,543 | 41,268 | 34,313 | 21,922 |
| TAYLOR | 12,994 | 2,890 | 23.8 | 23.2 | 36.6 | 15.4 | 1.0 | 0.0 | 24,151 | 21,873 | 28,846 | 30,357 | 27,770 | 17,935 |
| UNION | 14,093 | 5,124 | 22.3 | 18.4 | 38.2 | 18.7 | 2.2 | 0.2 | 26,471 | 23,484 | 33,413 | 31,947 | 30,308 | 18,262 |
| VAN BUREN | 14,260 | 3,206 | 19.0 | 22.7 | 38.8 | 17.0 | 2.2 | 0.3 | 26,146 | 25,367 | 27,394 | 33,978 | 29,267 | 19,185 |
| WAPELLO | 15,717 | 14,472 | 22.3 | 20.4 | 35.9 | 17.4 | 2.8 | 1.2 | 27,779 | 22,572 | 32,570 | 38,884 | 30,688 | 18,204 |
| WARREN | 19,785 | 14,483 | 9.3 | 8.3 | 36.3 | 37.3 | 7.7 | 1.1 | 39,261 | 34,615 | 45,524 | 47,870 | 40,537 | 24,577 |
| WASHINGTON | 17,357 | 8,134 | 11.4 | 14.6 | 42.3 | 27.6 | 3.3 | 0.9 | 33,040 | 29,830 | 39,162 | 39,541 | 35,414 | 23,683 |
| WAYNE | 12,427 | 2,759 | 29.4 | 22.9 | 32.4 | 14.1 | 1.1 | 0.0 | 22,679 | 22,250 | 25,945 | 28,063 | 25,225 | 17,271 |
| WEBSTER | 16,957 | 15,296 | 15.8 | 16.0 | 40.3 | 24.6 | 2.6 | 0.7 | 30,629 | 27,254 | 36,609 | 37,939 | 32,302 | 22,428 |
| WINNEBAGO | 14,241 | 4,618 | 18.8 | 19.0 | 41.1 | 18.5 | 2.0 | 0.5 | 27,479 | 23,763 | 33,108 | 33,662 | 31,377 | 19,908 |
| WINNESHIEK | 15,381 | 7,292 | 17.2 | 15.9 | 38.0 | 24.2 | 3.5 | 1.2 | 31,362 | 27,266 | 35,076 | 42,221 | 36,304 | 21,009 |
| WOODBURY | 18,517 | 38,283 | 15.5 | 14.6 | 36.7 | 26.5 | 4.9 | 1.8 | 34,073 | 28,627 | 39,924 | 43,498 | 37,661 | 22,907 |
| WORTH | 16,803 | 3,160 | 15.7 | 22.1 | 39.6 | 18.2 | 3.4 | 1.1 | 29,011 | 26,486 | 33,585 | 35,463 | 31,218 | 21,270 |
| WRIGHT | 18,193 | 5,785 | 15.7 | 13.6 | 40.4 | 25.9 | 3.8 | 0.6 | 31,651 | 28,183 | 36,248 | 38,435 | 35,995 | 24,524 |
| IOWA | 18,653 | | 14.8 | 14.5 | 37.4 | 27.0 | 4.8 | 1.6 | 33,931 | 28,488 | 40,263 | 43,264 | 36,563 | 23,029 |
| UNITED STATES | 22,162 | | 14.5 | 12.5 | 32.3 | 29.8 | 7.4 | 3.5 | 40,748 | 34,503 | 44,969 | 49,579 | 43,409 | 27,339 |

# SPENDING POTENTIAL INDEXES

| COUNTY | FINANCIAL SERVICES | | | | THE HOME | | | | | | ENTERTAINMENT | | | | | | PERSONAL | | | |
|---|---|---|---|---|---|---|---|---|---|---|---|---|---|---|---|---|---|---|---|---|
| | | | | | Home Improvements | | | Furnishings | | | | | | | | | | | | |
| | Auto Loan | Home Loan | Invest-ments | Retire-ment Plans | Home Repair | Lawn & Garden | Remodel-ing | Appli-ances | Elec-tronics | Furni-ture | Restau-rants | Sport-ing Goods | Theater & Concerts | Toys & Hobbies | Travel | Video Rental | Apparel | Auto After-market | Health Insur-ance | Pets & Supplies |
| POTTAWATTAMIE | 96 | 88 | 90 | 89 | 98 | 95 | 101 | 96 | 94 | 91 | 94 | 94 | 95 | 97 | 90 | 100 | 90 | 95 | 100 | 97 |
| POWESHIEK | 98 | 80 | 89 | 90 | 95 | 95 | 108 | 96 | 93 | 83 | 88 | 96 | 90 | 98 | 86 | 100 | 86 | 94 | 104 | 99 |
| RINGGOLD | 98 | 68 | 75 | 82 | 91 | 90 | 114 | 96 | 91 | 75 | 81 | 96 | 83 | 97 | 77 | 100 | 80 | 90 | 105 | 98 |
| SAC | 97 | 64 | 70 | 79 | 90 | 90 | 110 | 95 | 90 | 72 | 78 | 94 | 80 | 94 | 75 | 100 | 77 | 89 | 106 | 96 |
| SCOTT | 98 | 99 | 97 | 97 | 101 | 99 | 99 | 98 | 98 | 98 | 101 | 98 | 101 | 100 | 97 | 101 | 97 | 101 | 99 | 100 |
| SHELBY | 98 | 70 | 79 | 83 | 93 | 92 | 109 | 96 | 91 | 76 | 82 | 96 | 85 | 97 | 79 | 100 | 81 | 91 | 106 | 98 |
| SIOUX | 99 | 73 | 79 | 85 | 93 | 91 | 113 | 97 | 93 | 80 | 85 | 97 | 87 | 98 | 80 | 101 | 84 | 92 | 105 | 100 |
| STORY | 97 | 100 | 98 | 99 | 99 | 96 | 100 | 93 | 95 | 91 | 97 | 95 | 95 | 97 | 95 | 99 | 94 | 98 | 99 | 99 |
| TAMA | 97 | 72 | 80 | 82 | 93 | 92 | 107 | 95 | 91 | 78 | 83 | 94 | 85 | 95 | 81 | 100 | 81 | 91 | 104 | 96 |
| TAYLOR | 97 | 65 | 72 | 79 | 90 | 90 | 110 | 95 | 90 | 73 | 79 | 93 | 80 | 94 | 76 | 100 | 78 | 89 | 105 | 96 |
| UNION | 95 | 74 | 78 | 80 | 93 | 90 | 105 | 94 | 91 | 81 | 84 | 91 | 85 | 94 | 81 | 99 | 81 | 90 | 101 | 95 |
| VAN BUREN | 99 | 65 | 71 | 82 | 90 | 90 | 112 | 96 | 90 | 71 | 79 | 98 | 81 | 97 | 75 | 100 | 79 | 90 | 107 | 98 |
| WAPELLO | 95 | 79 | 88 | 84 | 98 | 94 | 103 | 95 | 91 | 86 | 87 | 91 | 90 | 94 | 87 | 99 | 84 | 91 | 101 | 95 |
| WARREN | 100 | 95 | 94 | 95 | 99 | 97 | 105 | 99 | 99 | 98 | 101 | 100 | 101 | 103 | 94 | 103 | 97 | 101 | 101 | 102 |
| WASHINGTON | 96 | 76 | 82 | 83 | 94 | 91 | 107 | 95 | 92 | 82 | 86 | 93 | 87 | 96 | 82 | 100 | 83 | 92 | 102 | 97 |
| WAYNE | 95 | 64 | 70 | 77 | 90 | 89 | 107 | 94 | 90 | 73 | 78 | 91 | 79 | 92 | 76 | 100 | 77 | 88 | 105 | 94 |
| WEBSTER | 96 | 83 | 89 | 87 | 98 | 95 | 102 | 96 | 92 | 88 | 90 | 94 | 93 | 96 | 89 | 100 | 87 | 94 | 101 | 97 |
| WINNEBAGO | 97 | 75 | 77 | 83 | 92 | 90 | 108 | 96 | 93 | 81 | 86 | 94 | 87 | 96 | 80 | 101 | 83 | 92 | 103 | 98 |
| WINNESHIEK | 97 | 72 | 77 | 82 | 91 | 89 | 109 | 94 | 90 | 75 | 82 | 93 | 83 | 95 | 78 | 98 | 80 | 90 | 103 | 97 |
| WOODBURY | 96 | 93 | 96 | 93 | 100 | 97 | 99 | 96 | 94 | 94 | 95 | 94 | 97 | 97 | 95 | 100 | 91 | 96 | 100 | 97 |
| WORTH | 98 | 66 | 72 | 81 | 91 | 90 | 111 | 95 | 91 | 73 | 80 | 95 | 81 | 96 | 76 | 101 | 79 | 90 | 106 | 97 |
| WRIGHT | 96 | 72 | 77 | 81 | 92 | 91 | 106 | 95 | 92 | 79 | 83 | 93 | 85 | 94 | 80 | 100 | 81 | 91 | 103 | 96 |
| IOWA | 97 | 86 | 90 | 90 | 97 | 95 | 104 | 96 | 94 | 89 | 92 | 96 | 94 | 98 | 89 | 101 | 89 | 95 | 102 | 98 |
| UNITED STATES | 100 | 100 | 100 | 100 | 100 | 100 | 100 | 100 | 100 | 100 | 100 | 100 | 100 | 100 | 100 | 100 | 100 | 100 | 100 | 100 |

| COUNTY | FIPS Code | MSA Code | DMA Code | POPULATION 1990 | POPULATION 2000 | POPULATION 2005 | 1990-2000 ANNUAL CHANGE % Rate | 1990-2000 ANNUAL CHANGE State Rank | RACE (%) White 1990 | White 2000 | Black 1990 | Black 2000 | Asian/Pacific 1990 | Asian/Pacific 2000 |
|---|---|---|---|---|---|---|---|---|---|---|---|---|---|---|
| ALLEN | 001 | 0000 | 603 | 14,638 | 14,376 | 14,088 | -0.2 | 51 | 96.5 | 96.2 | 1.8 | 1.9 | 0.3 | 0.4 |
| ANDERSON | 003 | 0000 | 616 | 7,803 | 8,168 | 8,408 | 0.4 | 26 | 98.3 | 98.2 | 0.5 | 0.5 | 0.1 | 0.2 |
| ATCHISON | 005 | 0000 | 616 | 16,932 | 16,867 | 16,911 | 0.0 | 43 | 92.1 | 90.9 | 5.7 | 6.3 | 0.8 | 1.0 |
| BARBER | 007 | 0000 | 678 | 5,874 | 5,163 | 4,794 | -1.3 | 93 | 98.6 | 98.4 | 0.2 | 0.2 | 0.1 | 0.0 |
| BARTON | 009 | 0000 | 678 | 29,382 | 28,478 | 27,553 | -0.3 | 54 | 96.6 | 95.9 | 1.2 | 1.2 | 0.4 | 0.5 |
| BOURBON | 011 | 0000 | 603 | 14,966 | 14,899 | 14,498 | 0.0 | 43 | 96.5 | 95.8 | 2.8 | 3.3 | 0.1 | 0.2 |
| BROWN | 013 | 0000 | 605 | 11,128 | 10,879 | 10,629 | -0.2 | 51 | 91.6 | 91.4 | 1.2 | 1.3 | 0.1 | 0.2 |
| BUTLER | 015 | 9040 | 678 | 50,580 | 63,758 | 68,799 | 2.3 | 2 | 97.5 | 96.7 | 0.7 | 1.1 | 0.3 | 0.5 |
| CHASE | 017 | 0000 | 678 | 3,021 | 2,820 | 2,651 | -0.7 | 75 | 99.1 | 98.9 | 0.2 | 0.2 | 0.0 | 0.0 |
| CHAUTAUQUA | 019 | 0000 | 671 | 4,407 | 4,230 | 4,024 | -0.4 | 60 | 95.3 | 95.2 | 0.5 | 0.4 | 0.3 | 0.4 |
| CHEROKEE | 021 | 0000 | 603 | 21,374 | 22,371 | 22,220 | 0.4 | 26 | 95.6 | 95.7 | 0.5 | 0.5 | 0.1 | 0.1 |
| CHEYENNE | 023 | 0000 | 678 | 3,243 | 3,239 | 3,323 | 0.0 | 43 | 99.4 | 99.4 | 0.2 | 0.2 | 0.3 | 0.3 |
| CLARK | 025 | 0000 | 678 | 2,418 | 2,324 | 2,235 | -0.4 | 60 | 97.4 | 96.8 | 0.0 | 0.0 | 0.3 | 0.3 |
| CLAY | 027 | 0000 | 605 | 9,158 | 8,982 | 8,542 | -0.2 | 51 | 99.1 | 98.9 | 0.2 | 0.2 | 0.3 | 0.4 |
| CLOUD | 029 | 0000 | 722 | 11,023 | 9,919 | 9,498 | -1.0 | 87 | 99.0 | 98.8 | 0.3 | 0.4 | 0.0 | 0.1 |
| COFFEY | 031 | 0000 | 605 | 8,404 | 8,757 | 8,836 | 0.4 | 26 | 98.9 | 98.8 | 0.1 | 0.1 | 0.2 | 0.3 |
| COMANCHE | 033 | 0000 | 678 | 2,313 | 1,916 | 1,738 | -1.8 | 103 | 99.0 | 98.9 | 0.3 | 0.3 | 0.0 | 0.0 |
| COWLEY | 035 | 0000 | 678 | 36,915 | 36,810 | 36,073 | 0.0 | 43 | 92.9 | 91.9 | 2.9 | 3.1 | 0.9 | 1.1 |
| CRAWFORD | 037 | 0000 | 603 | 35,568 | 36,278 | 35,936 | 0.2 | 35 | 96.3 | 95.8 | 1.3 | 1.4 | 1.2 | 1.5 |
| DECATUR | 039 | 0000 | 678 | 4,021 | 3,309 | 3,023 | -1.9 | 104 | 99.5 | 99.4 | 0.0 | 0.0 | 0.0 | 0.0 |
| DICKINSON | 041 | 0000 | 678 | 18,958 | 19,632 | 19,567 | 0.3 | 32 | 98.1 | 97.7 | 0.6 | 0.6 | 0.3 | 0.4 |
| DONIPHAN | 043 | 0000 | 638 | 8,134 | 8,015 | 8,297 | -0.1 | 47 | 96.4 | 96.0 | 1.9 | 2.2 | 0.2 | 0.3 |
| DOUGLAS | 045 | 4150 | 616 | 81,798 | 100,135 | 108,967 | 2.0 | 3 | 89.1 | 87.9 | 4.1 | 4.3 | 3.2 | 3.9 |
| EDWARDS | 047 | 0000 | 678 | 3,787 | 3,230 | 3,013 | -1.5 | 102 | 96.3 | 94.7 | 0.1 | 0.1 | 0.2 | 0.2 |
| ELK | 049 | 0000 | 678 | 3,327 | 3,396 | 3,446 | 0.2 | 35 | 97.3 | 97.1 | 0.2 | 0.1 | 0.1 | 0.1 |
| ELLIS | 051 | 0000 | 678 | 26,004 | 26,161 | 25,298 | 0.1 | 38 | 98.6 | 98.4 | 0.4 | 0.4 | 0.6 | 0.8 |
| ELLSWORTH | 053 | 0000 | 678 | 6,586 | 6,169 | 5,921 | -0.6 | 66 | 96.4 | 94.9 | 2.0 | 2.9 | 0.2 | 0.2 |
| FINNEY | 055 | 0000 | 678 | 33,070 | 38,080 | 41,405 | 1.4 | 6 | 80.0 | 74.8 | 1.3 | 1.3 | 3.6 | 4.4 |
| FORD | 057 | 0000 | 678 | 27,463 | 29,706 | 30,412 | 0.8 | 15 | 83.3 | 78.2 | 1.7 | 1.7 | 2.4 | 3.1 |
| FRANKLIN | 059 | 0000 | 616 | 21,994 | 25,425 | 26,918 | 1.4 | 6 | 96.4 | 95.4 | 1.3 | 1.4 | 0.5 | 0.8 |
| GEARY | 061 | 0000 | 605 | 30,453 | 24,295 | 21,852 | -2.2 | 105 | 68.8 | 66.5 | 23.6 | 23.0 | 4.0 | 5.8 |
| GOVE | 063 | 0000 | 678 | 3,231 | 3,007 | 2,906 | -0.7 | 75 | 99.6 | 99.7 | 0.1 | 0.1 | 0.1 | 0.0 |
| GRAHAM | 065 | 0000 | 678 | 3,543 | 3,064 | 2,809 | -1.4 | 98 | 96.2 | 95.6 | 2.9 | 3.2 | 0.3 | 0.5 |
| GRANT | 067 | 0000 | 678 | 7,159 | 7,905 | 7,964 | 1.0 | 13 | 84.6 | 79.3 | 0.0 | 0.0 | 0.6 | 0.8 |
| GRAY | 069 | 0000 | 678 | 5,396 | 5,599 | 5,716 | 0.4 | 26 | 95.8 | 94.0 | 0.1 | 0.1 | 0.0 | 0.0 |
| GREELEY | 071 | 0000 | 678 | 1,774 | 1,617 | 1,551 | -0.9 | 83 | 95.1 | 92.4 | 0.6 | 1.2 | 0.1 | 0.1 |
| GREENWOOD | 073 | 0000 | 678 | 7,847 | 7,909 | 7,656 | 0.1 | 38 | 98.4 | 98.1 | 0.1 | 0.1 | 0.0 | 0.0 |
| HAMILTON | 075 | 0000 | 678 | 2,388 | 2,402 | 2,529 | 0.1 | 38 | 94.0 | 91.7 | 0.2 | 0.3 | 1.2 | 1.5 |
| HARPER | 077 | 0000 | 678 | 7,124 | 6,223 | 5,831 | -1.3 | 93 | 98.8 | 98.6 | 0.2 | 0.3 | 0.1 | 0.1 |
| HARVEY | 079 | 9040 | 678 | 31,028 | 34,437 | 35,368 | 1.0 | 13 | 94.4 | 92.8 | 1.8 | 1.9 | 0.7 | 0.9 |
| HASKELL | 081 | 0000 | 678 | 3,886 | 4,091 | 4,303 | 0.5 | 21 | 87.8 | 83.6 | 0.1 | 0.0 | 0.1 | 0.1 |
| HODGEMAN | 083 | 0000 | 678 | 2,177 | 2,243 | 2,281 | 0.3 | 32 | 98.2 | 98.0 | 1.0 | 0.9 | 0.0 | 0.0 |
| JACKSON | 085 | 0000 | 605 | 11,525 | 12,243 | 12,607 | 0.6 | 18 | 92.9 | 93.1 | 0.4 | 0.4 | 0.1 | 0.1 |
| JEFFERSON | 087 | 0000 | 605 | 15,905 | 18,299 | 19,028 | 1.4 | 6 | 98.1 | 98.0 | 0.5 | 0.5 | 0.4 | 0.5 |
| JEWELL | 089 | 0000 | 722 | 4,251 | 3,724 | 3,422 | -1.3 | 93 | 99.6 | 99.6 | 0.0 | 0.0 | 0.1 | 0.1 |
| JOHNSON | 091 | 3760 | 616 | 355,054 | 450,660 | 502,280 | 2.4 | 1 | 95.4 | 94.3 | 1.9 | 2.1 | 1.6 | 2.3 |
| KEARNY | 093 | 0000 | 678 | 4,027 | 4,128 | 4,086 | 0.2 | 35 | 89.4 | 85.6 | 0.1 | 0.1 | 0.1 | 0.1 |
| KINGMAN | 095 | 0000 | 678 | 8,292 | 8,713 | 9,016 | 0.5 | 21 | 99.0 | 98.8 | 0.1 | 0.1 | 0.1 | 0.1 |
| KIOWA | 097 | 0000 | 678 | 3,660 | 3,294 | 3,138 | -1.0 | 87 | 98.4 | 97.8 | 0.2 | 0.5 | 0.3 | 0.3 |
| LABETTE | 099 | 0000 | 603 | 23,693 | 22,862 | 22,415 | -0.3 | 54 | 92.7 | 92.0 | 4.3 | 4.5 | 0.4 | 0.6 |
| LANE | 101 | 0000 | 678 | 2,375 | 2,146 | 2,009 | -1.0 | 87 | 99.1 | 98.7 | 0.0 | 0.1 | 0.0 | 0.0 |
| LEAVENWORTH | 103 | 3760 | 616 | 64,371 | 72,352 | 75,331 | 1.1 | 12 | 85.5 | 84.3 | 11.1 | 11.1 | 1.5 | 2.1 |
| LINCOLN | 105 | 0000 | 678 | 3,653 | 3,327 | 3,272 | -0.9 | 83 | 99.5 | 99.3 | 0.0 | 0.1 | 0.0 | 0.0 |
| LINN | 107 | 0000 | 616 | 8,254 | 9,420 | 10,048 | 1.3 | 9 | 98.8 | 98.6 | 0.4 | 0.5 | 0.1 | 0.1 |
| LOGAN | 109 | 0000 | 678 | 3,081 | 2,894 | 2,685 | -0.6 | 66 | 98.9 | 98.7 | 0.4 | 0.4 | 0.0 | 0.0 |
| LYON | 111 | 0000 | 605 | 34,732 | 33,708 | 33,220 | -0.3 | 54 | 91.6 | 89.2 | 2.1 | 2.1 | 2.0 | 2.6 |
| MCPHERSON | 113 | 0000 | 678 | 27,268 | 28,971 | 29,795 | 0.6 | 18 | 97.8 | 97.3 | 0.8 | 0.8 | 0.5 | 0.6 |
| MARION | 115 | 0000 | 678 | 12,888 | 13,503 | 13,303 | 0.5 | 21 | 98.4 | 98.3 | 0.6 | 0.7 | 0.2 | 0.3 |
| MARSHALL | 117 | 0000 | 605 | 11,705 | 10,815 | 10,361 | -0.8 | 79 | 99.4 | 99.3 | 0.1 | 0.1 | 0.1 | 0.1 |
| MEADE | 119 | 0000 | 678 | 4,247 | 4,408 | 4,413 | 0.4 | 26 | 96.4 | 94.9 | 0.0 | 0.0 | 0.3 | 0.4 |
| MIAMI | 121 | 3760 | 616 | 23,466 | 27,569 | 29,991 | 1.6 | 5 | 96.5 | 96.3 | 2.4 | 2.4 | 0.2 | 0.2 |
| MITCHELL | 123 | 0000 | 678 | 7,203 | 6,937 | 6,837 | -0.4 | 60 | 98.9 | 98.4 | 0.6 | 1.1 | 0.1 | 0.1 |
| MONTGOMERY | 125 | 0000 | 671 | 38,816 | 36,570 | 35,521 | -0.6 | 66 | 90.2 | 89.3 | 6.3 | 6.7 | 0.4 | 0.5 |
| MORRIS | 127 | 0000 | 605 | 6,198 | 6,155 | 6,068 | -0.1 | 47 | 98.4 | 98.1 | 0.3 | 0.3 | 0.2 | 0.2 |
| MORTON | 129 | 0000 | 634 | 3,480 | 3,528 | 3,715 | 0.1 | 38 | 94.7 | 93.1 | 0.1 | 0.1 | 1.1 | 1.4 |
| NEMAHA | 131 | 0000 | 605 | 10,446 | 10,146 | 9,966 | -0.3 | 54 | 99.3 | 99.3 | 0.4 | 0.4 | 0.2 | 0.2 |
| NEOSHO | 133 | 0000 | 603 | 17,035 | 16,572 | 16,232 | -0.3 | 54 | 97.1 | 96.5 | 1.1 | 1.3 | 0.2 | 0.3 |
| NESS | 135 | 0000 | 678 | 4,033 | 3,525 | 3,334 | -1.3 | 93 | 99.6 | 99.5 | 0.0 | 0.0 | 0.1 | 0.1 |
| NORTON | 137 | 0000 | 678 | 5,947 | 5,570 | 5,255 | -0.6 | 66 | 96.3 | 95.1 | 2.3 | 2.9 | 0.3 | 0.5 |
| OSAGE | 139 | 0000 | 605 | 15,248 | 17,313 | 17,881 | 1.2 | 10 | 98.6 | 98.5 | 0.2 | 0.2 | 0.1 | 0.1 |
| OSBORNE | 141 | 0000 | 678 | 4,867 | 4,532 | 4,258 | -0.7 | 75 | 99.3 | 99.3 | 0.1 | 0.1 | 0.1 | 0.2 |
| OTTAWA | 143 | 0000 | 678 | 5,634 | 5,912 | 6,036 | 0.5 | 21 | 99.4 | 99.2 | 0.1 | 0.1 | 0.1 | 0.3 |
| PAWNEE | 145 | 0000 | 678 | 7,555 | 7,156 | 6,910 | -0.5 | 64 | 93.7 | 90.3 | 3.2 | 4.9 | 0.8 | 1.0 |
| PHILLIPS | 147 | 0000 | 722 | 6,590 | 5,889 | 5,556 | -1.1 | 91 | 99.0 | 98.8 | 0.2 | 0.3 | 0.4 | 0.5 |
| POTTAWATOMIE | 149 | 0000 | 605 | 16,128 | 19,269 | 20,895 | 1.8 | 4 | 98.0 | 97.7 | 0.6 | 0.6 | 0.4 | 0.5 |
| PRATT | 151 | 0000 | 678 | 9,702 | 9,443 | 9,075 | -0.3 | 54 | 96.5 | 95.6 | 1.2 | 1.3 | 0.3 | 0.4 |
| RAWLINS | 153 | 0000 | 678 | 3,404 | 2,939 | 2,758 | -1.4 | 98 | 99.4 | 99.3 | 0.1 | 0.1 | 0.2 | 0.3 |
| KANSAS | | | | | | | 0.7 | | 90.1 | 88.9 | 5.8 | 5.7 | 1.3 | 1.8 |
| UNITED STATES | | | | | | | 1.0 | | 80.3 | 77.9 | 12.1 | 12.4 | 2.9 | 3.9 |

# POPULATION COMPOSITION

| COUNTY | % HISPANIC ORIGIN | | 2000 AGE DISTRIBUTION (%) | | | | | | | | | | MEDIAN AGE | | 2000 Males/ Females (×100) |
|---|---|---|---|---|---|---|---|---|---|---|---|---|---|---|---|
| | 1990 | 2000 | 0-4 | 5-9 | 10-14 | 15-19 | 20-24 | 25-44 | 45-64 | 65-84 | 85+ | 18+ | 1990 | 2000 | |
| ALLEN | 1.8 | 3.0 | 6.4 | 6.6 | 7.3 | 8.8 | 6.3 | 24.4 | 22.6 | 14.5 | 3.2 | 74.7 | 35.5 | 38.3 | 94.7 |
| ANDERSON | 0.7 | 1.3 | 6.2 | 6.5 | 7.7 | 8.0 | 4.9 | 23.4 | 23.7 | 16.0 | 3.6 | 74.4 | 38.1 | 40.3 | 94.3 |
| ATCHISON | 2.2 | 3.4 | 6.3 | 6.4 | 7.8 | 10.5 | 7.4 | 24.3 | 21.6 | 13.1 | 2.7 | 73.5 | 33.5 | 35.7 | 97.9 |
| BARBER | 1.2 | 2.2 | 6.0 | 6.9 | 7.6 | 7.7 | 4.4 | 23.9 | 22.7 | 17.7 | 3.2 | 74.4 | 37.5 | 40.8 | 94.2 |
| BARTON | 2.8 | 4.5 | 6.7 | 6.8 | 7.6 | 8.2 | 5.9 | 25.7 | 22.2 | 14.6 | 2.4 | 74.1 | 34.8 | 37.9 | 94.6 |
| BOURBON | 0.5 | 1.2 | 6.4 | 6.6 | 7.6 | 8.8 | 5.6 | 24.3 | 22.5 | 15.0 | 3.2 | 74.7 | 36.8 | 38.6 | 92.5 |
| BROWN | 1.7 | 2.7 | 6.7 | 6.9 | 7.9 | 8.1 | 5.1 | 24.1 | 22.0 | 15.3 | 3.9 | 73.3 | 36.7 | 39.1 | 94.5 |
| BUTLER | 1.5 | 2.6 | 6.9 | 7.0 | 7.7 | 8.3 | 6.6 | 26.8 | 23.3 | 11.5 | 1.8 | 73.2 | 33.8 | 36.4 | 97.3 |
| CHASE | 1.3 | 2.6 | 6.0 | 6.6 | 7.3 | 7.4 | 4.8 | 23.0 | 23.6 | 17.4 | 3.9 | 75.4 | 39.7 | 41.5 | 101.3 |
| CHAUTAUQUA | 1.0 | 1.7 | 5.4 | 5.7 | 6.8 | 7.4 | 4.2 | 21.6 | 25.6 | 19.2 | 4.0 | 77.2 | 43.3 | 44.2 | 95.2 |
| CHEROKEE | 0.8 | 1.6 | 6.3 | 6.4 | 7.0 | 7.7 | 5.9 | 26.3 | 24.2 | 13.7 | 2.6 | 75.5 | 35.8 | 38.3 | 94.9 |
| CHEYENNE | 0.6 | 1.3 | 5.1 | 5.9 | 6.8 | 7.3 | 5.2 | 19.8 | 24.2 | 22.0 | 3.8 | 76.8 | 41.8 | 45.0 | 96.7 |
| CLARK | 1.7 | 2.8 | 4.8 | 6.0 | 7.1 | 7.7 | 4.3 | 22.9 | 24.6 | 17.9 | 4.7 | 76.5 | 41.1 | 43.2 | 95.1 |
| CLAY | 0.4 | 1.0 | 5.8 | 6.1 | 6.7 | 7.7 | 6.4 | 22.9 | 23.1 | 16.9 | 4.5 | 76.1 | 39.2 | 41.2 | 99.4 |
| CLOUD | 0.7 | 1.3 | 5.3 | 5.8 | 6.5 | 8.3 | 5.2 | 23.4 | 22.6 | 17.8 | 5.2 | 78.6 | 39.9 | 41.8 | 91.2 |
| COFFEY | 0.7 | 1.6 | 6.0 | 6.6 | 7.7 | 8.4 | 5.0 | 26.3 | 23.2 | 13.4 | 3.2 | 73.9 | 36.2 | 38.7 | 99.5 |
| COMANCHE | 0.6 | 1.1 | 5.7 | 6.0 | 7.3 | 7.4 | 4.1 | 22.0 | 23.6 | 19.0 | 5.0 | 76.3 | 41.6 | 43.4 | 95.9 |
| COWLEY | 3.0 | 4.8 | 6.4 | 6.5 | 7.6 | 8.2 | 6.3 | 26.3 | 23.1 | 13.1 | 2.6 | 74.8 | 34.7 | 37.6 | 95.2 |
| CRAWFORD | 0.9 | 1.7 | 5.9 | 5.8 | 6.3 | 8.1 | 9.1 | 27.3 | 20.6 | 13.7 | 3.3 | 77.9 | 34.4 | 36.3 | 96.5 |
| DECATUR | 0.3 | 0.9 | 6.1 | 6.5 | 7.7 | 6.6 | 4.0 | 22.0 | 21.8 | 19.7 | 5.6 | 74.7 | 40.2 | 43.1 | 95.9 |
| DICKINSON | 1.8 | 3.1 | 6.1 | 6.2 | 7.7 | 7.6 | 5.1 | 24.8 | 23.9 | 15.1 | 3.4 | 74.9 | 37.3 | 40.1 | 94.6 |
| DONIPHAN | 0.6 | 1.2 | 6.4 | 6.6 | 7.2 | 9.3 | 5.7 | 25.9 | 22.6 | 13.6 | 2.8 | 75.4 | 35.1 | 37.4 | 97.7 |
| DOUGLAS | 2.6 | 4.1 | 5.7 | 5.2 | 5.6 | 11.5 | 18.5 | 29.6 | 16.0 | 6.7 | 1.2 | 80.3 | 25.8 | 27.4 | 98.4 |
| EDWARDS | 5.2 | 8.0 | 5.5 | 6.1 | 6.7 | 8.0 | 5.8 | 22.9 | 23.8 | 17.4 | 3.9 | 76.5 | 39.4 | 41.8 | 93.9 |
| ELK | 1.8 | 3.3 | 5.7 | 5.5 | 6.6 | 6.6 | 4.4 | 20.1 | 25.7 | 20.3 | 5.1 | 77.5 | 47.0 | 45.8 | 97.2 |
| ELLIS | 0.8 | 1.4 | 6.2 | 6.3 | 6.6 | 9.9 | 9.2 | 28.8 | 19.9 | 11.2 | 1.9 | 76.5 | 31.1 | 33.6 | 96.5 |
| ELLSWORTH | 2.8 | 4.8 | 5.2 | 5.5 | 6.1 | 7.7 | 7.4 | 25.8 | 22.4 | 15.7 | 4.2 | 78.0 | 38.0 | 40.1 | 112.7 |
| FINNEY | 25.3 | 33.8 | 10.0 | 9.0 | 9.4 | 9.1 | 7.2 | 31.1 | 16.3 | 6.9 | 1.1 | 66.4 | 27.2 | 28.6 | 102.6 |
| FORD | 14.9 | 20.9 | 8.3 | 7.5 | 8.3 | 8.9 | 7.3 | 28.5 | 19.5 | 10.0 | 1.6 | 71.3 | 30.2 | 32.2 | 102.4 |
| FRANKLIN | 2.1 | 3.7 | 7.3 | 7.0 | 8.1 | 8.3 | 6.7 | 26.7 | 22.1 | 11.4 | 2.4 | 72.5 | 33.3 | 35.6 | 95.5 |
| GEARY | 6.1 | 9.2 | 11.2 | 8.1 | 6.9 | 6.6 | 11.7 | 34.1 | 13.0 | 7.6 | 0.9 | 70.9 | 26.5 | 27.9 | 104.1 |
| GOVE | 0.3 | 0.7 | 5.7 | 6.6 | 7.6 | 7.6 | 4.4 | 22.9 | 24.0 | 17.8 | 3.5 | 74.9 | 38.2 | 41.9 | 103.0 |
| GRAHAM | 0.6 | 1.2 | 5.4 | 5.8 | 6.4 | 8.2 | 5.7 | 22.1 | 24.9 | 17.8 | 3.6 | 76.8 | 39.1 | 42.8 | 97.2 |
| GRANT | 21.6 | 30.1 | 8.2 | 8.5 | 9.4 | 9.4 | 6.1 | 28.4 | 20.3 | 8.7 | 1.1 | 67.7 | 29.2 | 31.6 | 97.8 |
| GRAY | 4.2 | 6.8 | 7.5 | 7.5 | 8.3 | 8.9 | 6.3 | 26.0 | 22.4 | 10.8 | 2.4 | 70.7 | 32.2 | 35.1 | 99.8 |
| GREELEY | 6.0 | 9.8 | 7.4 | 7.7 | 9.0 | 7.9 | 4.8 | 25.7 | 21.2 | 14.0 | 2.4 | 70.4 | 33.2 | 37.2 | 100.4 |
| GREENWOOD | 1.2 | 2.2 | 5.6 | 6.1 | 6.9 | 7.2 | 5.0 | 22.6 | 22.8 | 19.4 | 4.6 | 76.9 | 41.2 | 42.7 | 97.5 |
| HAMILTON | 5.8 | 8.7 | 6.3 | 6.7 | 7.3 | 7.4 | 5.3 | 22.9 | 24.3 | 16.0 | 3.7 | 74.7 | 38.1 | 41.1 | 95.3 |
| HARPER | 1.5 | 2.4 | 5.6 | 6.3 | 7.2 | 7.3 | 4.4 | 23.1 | 23.7 | 17.9 | 4.4 | 75.8 | 39.6 | 42.4 | 96.4 |
| HARVEY | 5.2 | 8.2 | 6.1 | 6.3 | 7.5 | 8.8 | 6.7 | 25.9 | 22.5 | 13.1 | 3.0 | 75.3 | 34.7 | 37.6 | 95.0 |
| HASKELL | 14.3 | 19.9 | 8.0 | 7.9 | 9.4 | 8.7 | 5.4 | 28.2 | 21.7 | 9.5 | 1.3 | 69.0 | 30.5 | 33.8 | 100.0 |
| HODGEMAN | 1.5 | 2.5 | 6.4 | 7.1 | 8.0 | 8.6 | 4.7 | 23.1 | 22.8 | 15.6 | 3.5 | 72.5 | 37.0 | 40.5 | 98.7 |
| JACKSON | 1.1 | 1.8 | 6.5 | 6.9 | 8.3 | 8.3 | 5.3 | 25.7 | 24.0 | 12.5 | 2.5 | 73.1 | 34.9 | 38.0 | 98.6 |
| JEFFERSON | 0.8 | 1.6 | 6.3 | 6.5 | 7.4 | 8.4 | 5.7 | 25.9 | 25.4 | 12.4 | 2.1 | 74.2 | 35.2 | 38.8 | 101.4 |
| JEWELL | 0.2 | 0.5 | 5.0 | 5.6 | 7.1 | 7.2 | 3.8 | 21.4 | 25.6 | 20.2 | 4.1 | 77.1 | 42.7 | 44.9 | 100.2 |
| JOHNSON | 2.0 | 3.4 | 6.5 | 7.1 | 8.1 | 7.2 | 5.5 | 31.3 | 24.1 | 9.0 | 1.1 | 73.7 | 32.8 | 36.5 | 92.8 |
| KEARNY | 16.7 | 23.5 | 8.5 | 8.6 | 9.0 | 8.8 | 6.4 | 26.4 | 21.1 | 9.5 | 1.6 | 68.1 | 30.8 | 32.9 | 104.9 |
| KINGMAN | 0.9 | 1.8 | 6.5 | 7.0 | 7.9 | 8.0 | 5.1 | 23.4 | 23.2 | 15.6 | 3.3 | 73.3 | 36.9 | 40.2 | 96.7 |
| KIOWA | 1.1 | 2.0 | 5.9 | 6.6 | 7.0 | 8.3 | 6.0 | 21.8 | 23.4 | 17.4 | 3.5 | 75.3 | 38.5 | 41.0 | 97.0 |
| LABETTE | 2.2 | 3.7 | 6.3 | 6.5 | 7.4 | 8.6 | 6.1 | 26.1 | 22.2 | 14.0 | 2.8 | 74.8 | 35.0 | 37.6 | 94.7 |
| LANE | 1.9 | 3.2 | 5.8 | 6.6 | 7.8 | 7.7 | 4.8 | 23.0 | 23.8 | 17.0 | 3.5 | 74.0 | 37.9 | 41.0 | 104.8 |
| LEAVENWORTH | 3.4 | 5.3 | 6.3 | 6.7 | 7.5 | 7.2 | 6.3 | 36.2 | 20.5 | 8.1 | 1.1 | 74.9 | 33.1 | 35.2 | 121.0 |
| LINCOLN | 0.4 | 0.9 | 5.0 | 5.4 | 7.5 | 6.9 | 4.0 | 22.2 | 24.5 | 19.1 | 5.7 | 77.2 | 42.4 | 44.5 | 94.1 |
| LINN | 0.4 | 1.0 | 5.8 | 6.1 | 7.4 | 7.9 | 5.0 | 23.1 | 24.9 | 16.5 | 3.4 | 75.6 | 39.3 | 41.3 | 99.0 |
| LOGAN | 0.8 | 1.5 | 6.3 | 6.6 | 7.3 | 8.1 | 5.1 | 22.5 | 23.2 | 17.7 | 3.3 | 74.5 | 38.1 | 41.3 | 97.3 |
| LYON | 6.1 | 9.5 | 7.3 | 6.8 | 7.3 | 9.8 | 11.3 | 28.0 | 17.9 | 9.5 | 2.0 | 74.2 | 29.1 | 30.7 | 95.7 |
| MCPHERSON | 1.2 | 2.2 | 6.4 | 6.6 | 7.3 | 9.2 | 7.4 | 24.6 | 22.4 | 13.1 | 3.1 | 75.0 | 34.7 | 37.5 | 97.2 |
| MARION | 0.9 | 1.6 | 5.4 | 5.7 | 6.4 | 8.7 | 6.1 | 22.5 | 23.3 | 17.6 | 4.4 | 77.8 | 39.4 | 41.9 | 94.3 |
| MARSHALL | 0.4 | 1.0 | 6.3 | 6.8 | 8.0 | 7.3 | 4.6 | 23.0 | 22.7 | 17.2 | 4.1 | 74.1 | 38.4 | 40.9 | 99.8 |
| MEADE | 4.7 | 7.2 | 6.8 | 7.3 | 7.7 | 7.5 | 5.6 | 23.8 | 22.4 | 15.5 | 3.5 | 72.9 | 36.9 | 39.4 | 99.5 |
| MIAMI | 1.2 | 2.1 | 6.6 | 6.8 | 7.6 | 8.1 | 6.0 | 27.3 | 24.2 | 11.4 | 1.9 | 73.8 | 34.3 | 37.2 | 98.5 |
| MITCHELL | 0.4 | 0.9 | 5.9 | 6.3 | 6.9 | 9.7 | 6.1 | 22.4 | 23.2 | 15.0 | 4.5 | 74.8 | 37.7 | 40.0 | 94.8 |
| MONTGOMERY | 1.9 | 3.3 | 6.5 | 6.4 | 7.4 | 8.4 | 5.7 | 24.6 | 23.3 | 14.6 | 3.0 | 75.0 | 36.5 | 38.9 | 91.9 |
| MORRIS | 1.5 | 2.5 | 6.1 | 6.6 | 7.2 | 7.3 | 5.0 | 23.1 | 23.4 | 17.4 | 3.9 | 74.9 | 38.9 | 41.5 | 100.9 |
| MORTON | 10.1 | 14.8 | 6.8 | 7.1 | 8.3 | 8.8 | 5.4 | 26.1 | 22.7 | 12.6 | 2.0 | 71.8 | 33.2 | 36.7 | 99.5 |
| NEMAHA | 0.1 | 0.6 | 7.1 | 7.4 | 8.5 | 8.0 | 4.9 | 23.7 | 21.3 | 15.7 | 3.4 | 71.7 | 35.6 | 38.2 | 98.6 |
| NEOSHO | 2.1 | 3.8 | 6.3 | 6.3 | 7.5 | 8.1 | 5.8 | 25.1 | 23.1 | 14.8 | 3.0 | 75.2 | 36.3 | 39.1 | 93.3 |
| NESS | 0.6 | 1.1 | 5.3 | 5.8 | 6.6 | 8.6 | 6.1 | 23.3 | 23.4 | 17.0 | 4.0 | 76.0 | 38.5 | 41.8 | 98.6 |
| NORTON | 1.4 | 2.4 | 5.1 | 5.3 | 6.1 | 7.6 | 6.8 | 25.9 | 22.9 | 16.1 | 4.3 | 78.9 | 39.0 | 40.3 | 118.0 |
| OSAGE | 1.2 | 2.3 | 6.4 | 6.7 | 7.2 | 7.8 | 6.0 | 25.6 | 23.5 | 14.0 | 2.9 | 74.4 | 36.0 | 39.0 | 95.4 |
| OSBORNE | 0.3 | 0.9 | 6.2 | 6.3 | 7.2 | 7.0 | 4.1 | 21.3 | 23.4 | 19.6 | 5.0 | 75.5 | 42.7 | 43.5 | 94.9 |
| OTTAWA | 0.6 | 1.3 | 5.8 | 6.5 | 7.5 | 7.6 | 4.5 | 24.5 | 25.1 | 15.0 | 3.6 | 75.1 | 38.5 | 40.8 | 95.6 |
| PAWNEE | 3.4 | 6.1 | 5.1 | 5.8 | 6.9 | 8.9 | 5.8 | 24.4 | 24.6 | 15.6 | 2.9 | 76.0 | 37.4 | 40.3 | 104.4 |
| PHILLIPS | 0.5 | 1.0 | 5.8 | 6.3 | 7.4 | 7.3 | 5.0 | 21.8 | 24.9 | 17.3 | 4.3 | 75.5 | 40.4 | 42.6 | 97.2 |
| POTTAWATOMIE | 1.5 | 2.6 | 7.6 | 7.6 | 8.2 | 8.6 | 5.9 | 27.3 | 21.6 | 10.9 | 2.2 | 71.0 | 32.8 | 35.2 | 97.7 |
| PRATT | 1.9 | 3.3 | 5.6 | 6.0 | 7.5 | 8.7 | 5.2 | 24.5 | 24.0 | 15.2 | 3.3 | 75.7 | 36.8 | 40.0 | 96.4 |
| RAWLINS | 0.8 | 1.5 | 5.1 | 6.3 | 7.6 | 7.9 | 3.9 | 22.6 | 24.4 | 18.5 | 3.8 | 75.8 | 38.8 | 42.8 | 99.9 |
| KANSAS | 3.8 | 5.9 | 6.8 | 6.8 | 7.6 | 8.1 | 7.2 | 28.5 | 21.7 | 11.3 | 2.0 | 74.1 | 32.9 | 35.6 | 96.8 |
| UNITED STATES | 9.0 | 11.8 | 6.9 | 7.2 | 7.2 | 7.2 | 6.7 | 29.9 | 22.2 | 11.1 | 1.6 | 74.6 | 32.9 | 35.7 | 95.6 |

| COUNTY | HOUSEHOLDS | | | | | FAMILIES | | | MEDIAN HOUSEHOLD INCOME | | | |
|---|---|---|---|---|---|---|---|---|---|---|---|---|
| | 1990 | 2000 | 2005 | % Annual Rate 1990-2000 | 2000 Average HH Size | 1990 | 2000 | % Annual Rate 1990-2000 | 2000 | 2005 | 2000 National Rank | 2000 State Rank |
| ALLEN | 5,705 | 5,645 | 5,554 | -0.1 | 2.48 | 4,010 | 3,823 | -0.6 | 29,456 | 35,863 | 2229 | 73 |
| ANDERSON | 3,067 | 3,182 | 3,260 | 0.4 | 2.52 | 2,186 | 2,188 | 0.0 | 31,667 | 40,393 | 1785 | 47 |
| ATCHISON | 6,129 | 6,106 | 6,133 | 0.0 | 2.55 | 4,348 | 4,190 | -0.4 | 31,250 | 36,596 | 1879 | 56 |
| BARBER | 2,358 | 2,109 | 1,977 | -1.3 | 2.39 | 1,665 | 1,438 | -1.8 | 29,774 | 35,226 | 2187 | 71 |
| BARTON | 11,561 | 10,717 | 10,131 | -0.9 | 2.59 | 8,144 | 7,269 | -1.4 | 32,724 | 37,643 | 1589 | 38 |
| BOURBON | 5,897 | 5,999 | 5,904 | 0.2 | 2.40 | 4,081 | 4,008 | -0.2 | 27,823 | 33,292 | 2466 | 90 |
| BROWN | 4,347 | 4,337 | 4,279 | 0.0 | 2.45 | 2,991 | 2,870 | -0.5 | 31,940 | 38,118 | 1726 | 44 |
| BUTLER | 18,488 | 23,170 | 25,120 | 2.8 | 2.67 | 14,202 | 17,374 | 2.5 | 47,842 | 58,537 | 243 | 2 |
| CHASE | 1,214 | 1,202 | 1,162 | -0.1 | 2.29 | 873 | 835 | -0.5 | 26,434 | 31,038 | 2662 | 96 |
| CHAUTAUQUA | 1,835 | 1,802 | 1,730 | -0.2 | 2.26 | 1,242 | 1,167 | -0.8 | 21,731 | 24,060 | 3040 | 104 |
| CHEROKEE | 8,396 | 8,879 | 8,865 | 0.7 | 2.49 | 6,007 | 6,121 | 0.2 | 27,061 | 32,013 | 2571 | 94 |
| CHEYENNE | 1,389 | 1,345 | 1,361 | -0.4 | 2.37 | 947 | 880 | -0.9 | 28,180 | 31,109 | 2418 | 84 |
| CLARK | 1,006 | 968 | 932 | -0.5 | 2.34 | 677 | 624 | -1.0 | 34,000 | 38,500 | 1393 | 30 |
| CLAY | 3,641 | 3,599 | 3,456 | -0.1 | 2.40 | 2,595 | 2,466 | -0.6 | 32,511 | 39,748 | 1622 | 41 |
| CLOUD | 4,483 | 3,980 | 3,789 | -1.4 | 2.38 | 2,945 | 2,499 | -2.0 | 31,243 | 38,263 | 1880 | 57 |
| COFFEY | 3,311 | 3,398 | 3,406 | 0.3 | 2.53 | 2,348 | 2,330 | -0.1 | 33,594 | 42,782 | 1452 | 32 |
| COMANCHE | 950 | 804 | 736 | -2.0 | 2.26 | 650 | 528 | -2.5 | 21,170 | 22,885 | 3064 | 105 |
| COWLEY | 14,047 | 13,836 | 13,423 | -0.2 | 2.54 | 10,004 | 9,521 | -0.6 | 33,511 | 40,347 | 1462 | 33 |
| CRAWFORD | 14,606 | 14,708 | 14,529 | 0.1 | 2.35 | 9,145 | 8,807 | -0.5 | 28,896 | 33,582 | 2314 | 78 |
| DECATUR | 1,651 | 1,385 | 1,276 | -2.1 | 2.28 | 1,132 | 914 | -2.6 | 26,221 | 30,242 | 2686 | 97 |
| DICKINSON | 7,542 | 7,813 | 7,787 | 0.4 | 2.46 | 5,323 | 5,322 | 0.0 | 34,393 | 40,755 | 1332 | 29 |
| DONIPHAN | 3,074 | 2,934 | 3,016 | -0.6 | 2.61 | 2,219 | 2,044 | -1.0 | 30,377 | 36,636 | 2062 | 66 |
| DOUGLAS | 30,138 | 36,018 | 38,554 | 2.2 | 2.54 | 17,291 | 19,879 | 1.7 | 37,826 | 45,658 | 867 | 15 |
| EDWARDS | 1,585 | 1,341 | 1,249 | -2.0 | 2.34 | 1,065 | 867 | -2.5 | 27,625 | 31,286 | 2494 | 91 |
| ELK | 1,436 | 1,451 | 1,466 | 0.1 | 2.28 | 966 | 935 | -0.4 | 25,587 | 30,074 | 2748 | 101 |
| ELLIS | 10,096 | 10,134 | 9,857 | 0.0 | 2.43 | 6,546 | 6,341 | -0.4 | 30,996 | 33,487 | 1937 | 60 |
| ELLSWORTH | 2,522 | 2,308 | 2,210 | -1.1 | 2.33 | 1,687 | 1,478 | -1.6 | 31,883 | 37,794 | 1737 | 46 |
| FINNEY | 10,836 | 12,331 | 13,334 | 1.6 | 3.05 | 8,231 | 9,114 | 1.2 | 36,658 | 44,335 | 1024 | 19 |
| FORD | 9,872 | 10,775 | 11,039 | 1.1 | 2.69 | 7,006 | 7,382 | 0.6 | 36,504 | 42,879 | 1041 | 20 |
| FRANKLIN | 8,308 | 9,597 | 10,157 | 1.8 | 2.59 | 6,055 | 6,746 | 1.3 | 37,718 | 45,972 | 876 | 16 |
| GEARY | 10,676 | 8,542 | 7,687 | -2.7 | 2.67 | 8,191 | 6,396 | -3.0 | 30,233 | 35,847 | 2098 | 68 |
| GOVE | 1,284 | 1,195 | 1,155 | -0.9 | 2.48 | 920 | 828 | -1.3 | 26,450 | 27,444 | 2659 | 95 |
| GRAHAM | 1,435 | 1,271 | 1,179 | -1.5 | 2.37 | 999 | 852 | -1.9 | 28,631 | 34,375 | 2344 | 81 |
| GRANT | 2,393 | 2,766 | 2,847 | 1.8 | 2.83 | 1,913 | 2,164 | 1.5 | 45,000 | 54,657 | 355 | 4 |
| GRAY | 1,913 | 2,027 | 2,091 | 0.7 | 2.72 | 1,436 | 1,471 | 0.3 | 39,174 | 46,772 | 739 | 14 |
| GREELEY | 656 | 621 | 607 | -0.7 | 2.55 | 486 | 447 | -1.0 | 30,458 | 32,529 | 2043 | 63 |
| GREENWOOD | 3,285 | 3,438 | 3,398 | 0.6 | 2.24 | 2,198 | 2,210 | 0.1 | 25,731 | 31,388 | 2738 | 100 |
| HAMILTON | 986 | 991 | 1,043 | 0.1 | 2.36 | 647 | 622 | -0.5 | 28,074 | 30,587 | 2429 | 86 |
| HARPER | 3,007 | 2,674 | 2,527 | -1.4 | 2.27 | 2,018 | 1,721 | -1.9 | 25,867 | 30,391 | 2726 | 99 |
| HARVEY | 11,581 | 13,000 | 13,406 | 1.4 | 2.52 | 8,356 | 9,045 | 1.0 | 41,938 | 48,486 | 518 | 7 |
| HASKELL | 1,372 | 1,402 | 1,455 | 0.3 | 2.90 | 1,051 | 1,047 | 0.0 | 31,966 | 35,334 | 1723 | 43 |
| HODGEMAN | 826 | 831 | 837 | 0.1 | 2.65 | 621 | 607 | -0.3 | 32,950 | 36,756 | 1547 | 36 |
| JACKSON | 4,277 | 4,576 | 4,724 | 0.8 | 2.65 | 3,209 | 3,345 | 0.5 | 36,235 | 40,617 | 1076 | 23 |
| JEFFERSON | 5,778 | 6,882 | 7,269 | 2.1 | 2.60 | 4,466 | 5,162 | 1.8 | 41,291 | 48,098 | 563 | 8 |
| JEWELL | 1,806 | 1,610 | 1,491 | -1.4 | 2.29 | 1,265 | 1,083 | -1.9 | 27,957 | 32,261 | 2446 | 87 |
| JOHNSON | 136,433 | 172,225 | 191,342 | 2.9 | 2.60 | 98,151 | 120,268 | 2.5 | 60,086 | 65,871 | 72 | 1 |
| KEARNY | 1,379 | 1,430 | 1,426 | 0.4 | 2.86 | 1,077 | 1,086 | 0.1 | 35,647 | 38,000 | 1144 | 26 |
| KINGMAN | 3,175 | 3,281 | 3,370 | 0.4 | 2.60 | 2,332 | 2,333 | 0.0 | 33,385 | 36,679 | 1479 | 34 |
| KIOWA | 1,466 | 1,369 | 1,328 | -0.8 | 2.29 | 1,013 | 909 | -1.3 | 27,924 | 31,233 | 2449 | 88 |
| LABETTE | 9,377 | 9,056 | 8,874 | -0.4 | 2.44 | 6,393 | 5,953 | -0.9 | 28,429 | 32,685 | 2376 | 82 |
| LANE | 966 | 934 | 903 | -0.4 | 2.24 | 665 | 618 | -0.9 | 26,218 | 31,139 | 2687 | 98 |
| LEAVENWORTH | 19,715 | 22,572 | 23,607 | 1.7 | 2.80 | 15,222 | 17,079 | 1.4 | 47,155 | 58,669 | 270 | 3 |
| LINCOLN | 1,531 | 1,381 | 1,351 | -1.2 | 2.35 | 1,054 | 912 | -1.7 | 27,259 | 32,870 | 2541 | 92 |
| LINN | 3,215 | 3,671 | 3,914 | 1.6 | 2.52 | 2,383 | 2,632 | 1.2 | 30,389 | 37,822 | 2060 | 65 |
| LOGAN | 1,221 | 1,162 | 1,083 | -0.6 | 2.44 | 856 | 784 | -1.1 | 32,155 | 36,776 | 1694 | 42 |
| LYON | 13,059 | 12,735 | 12,543 | -0.3 | 2.51 | 8,476 | 7,952 | -0.8 | 33,292 | 38,852 | 1492 | 35 |
| MCPHERSON | 10,230 | 10,827 | 11,107 | 0.7 | 2.53 | 7,401 | 7,537 | 0.2 | 40,792 | 47,810 | 606 | 9 |
| MARION | 4,975 | 5,229 | 5,146 | 0.6 | 2.42 | 3,578 | 3,617 | 0.1 | 31,529 | 39,322 | 1816 | 50 |
| MARSHALL | 4,689 | 4,341 | 4,164 | -0.9 | 2.42 | 3,219 | 2,869 | -1.4 | 29,148 | 32,395 | 2273 | 74 |
| MEADE | 1,667 | 1,748 | 1,760 | 0.6 | 2.46 | 1,188 | 1,202 | 0.1 | 32,669 | 39,238 | 1599 | 40 |
| MIAMI | 8,402 | 9,928 | 10,806 | 2.0 | 2.69 | 6,370 | 7,361 | 1.8 | 42,929 | 52,260 | 460 | 6 |
| MITCHELL | 2,846 | 2,704 | 2,646 | -0.6 | 2.44 | 1,919 | 1,744 | -1.2 | 36,023 | 42,791 | 1101 | 24 |
| MONTGOMERY | 15,670 | 14,764 | 14,348 | -0.7 | 2.42 | 10,779 | 9,784 | -1.2 | 29,097 | 34,573 | 2283 | 76 |
| MORRIS | 2,528 | 2,487 | 2,440 | -0.2 | 2.44 | 1,821 | 1,724 | -0.7 | 31,382 | 39,393 | 1844 | 53 |
| MORTON | 1,290 | 1,287 | 1,346 | 0.0 | 2.69 | 964 | 931 | -0.4 | 36,386 | 42,598 | 1061 | 21 |
| NEMAHA | 3,996 | 3,820 | 3,720 | -0.5 | 2.63 | 2,823 | 2,591 | -1.0 | 33,640 | 38,176 | 1446 | 31 |
| NEOSHO | 6,748 | 6,527 | 6,374 | -0.4 | 2.46 | 4,734 | 4,405 | -0.9 | 31,001 | 36,806 | 1936 | 59 |
| NESS | 1,670 | 1,472 | 1,399 | -1.5 | 2.35 | 1,143 | 969 | -2.0 | 31,553 | 39,263 | 1808 | 49 |
| NORTON | 2,330 | 2,192 | 2,077 | -0.7 | 2.25 | 1,557 | 1,398 | -1.3 | 31,930 | 39,725 | 1731 | 45 |
| OSAGE | 5,806 | 6,647 | 6,889 | 1.7 | 2.55 | 4,329 | 4,787 | 1.2 | 36,276 | 44,303 | 1069 | 22 |
| OSBORNE | 2,057 | 1,974 | 1,881 | -0.5 | 2.23 | 1,389 | 1,279 | -1.0 | 29,970 | 33,736 | 2159 | 70 |
| OTTAWA | 2,266 | 2,411 | 2,476 | 0.8 | 2.40 | 1,625 | 1,662 | 0.3 | 35,459 | 42,323 | 1177 | 27 |
| PAWNEE | 2,923 | 2,776 | 2,686 | -0.6 | 2.32 | 1,933 | 1,761 | -1.1 | 30,752 | 34,223 | 1980 | 62 |
| PHILLIPS | 2,695 | 2,445 | 2,325 | -1.2 | 2.34 | 1,882 | 1,646 | -1.6 | 31,462 | 36,318 | 1829 | 51 |
| POTTAWATOMIE | 5,938 | 7,181 | 7,838 | 2.3 | 2.64 | 4,390 | 5,146 | 1.9 | 37,409 | 46,396 | 913 | 17 |
| PRATT | 3,937 | 3,932 | 3,827 | 0.0 | 2.33 | 2,698 | 2,595 | -0.5 | 32,681 | 37,728 | 1596 | 39 |
| RAWLINS | 1,361 | 1,223 | 1,169 | -1.3 | 2.36 | 940 | 810 | -1.8 | 28,706 | 33,242 | 2336 | 80 |
| KANSAS | | | | 0.9 | 2.55 | | | 0.5 | 39,174 | 46,093 | | |
| UNITED STATES | | | | 1.4 | 2.59 | | | 1.1 | 41,914 | 49,127 | | |

# INCOME

| COUNTY | 2000 Per Capita Income | 2000 HH Income Base | 2000 HOUSEHOLD INCOME DISTRIBUTION (%) Less than $15,000 | $15,000 to $24,999 | $25,000 to $49,999 | $50,000 to $99,999 | $100,000 to $149,999 | $150,000 or More | 2000 AVERAGE DISPOSABLE INCOME BY AGE OF HOUSEHOLDER All Ages | <35 | 35-44 | 45-54 | 55-64 | 65+ |
|---|---|---|---|---|---|---|---|---|---|---|---|---|---|---|
| ALLEN | 13,965 | 5,645 | 22.6 | 19.0 | 36.4 | 19.3 | 2.6 | 0.2 | 27,747 | 26,232 | 32,293 | 35,816 | 31,694 | 19,116 |
| ANDERSON | 14,996 | 3,182 | 20.5 | 17.0 | 38.6 | 20.8 | 2.2 | 1.0 | 29,578 | 28,377 | 34,112 | 30,670 | 37,355 | 23,479 |
| ATCHISON | 14,451 | 6,106 | 19.0 | 18.6 | 37.7 | 21.3 | 2.7 | 0.8 | 29,823 | 25,609 | 35,309 | 37,192 | 35,586 | 20,511 |
| BARBER | 14,761 | 2,109 | 23.0 | 19.1 | 37.0 | 17.5 | 3.0 | 0.4 | 27,690 | 27,230 | 34,870 | 33,530 | 32,060 | 18,487 |
| BARTON | 15,103 | 10,717 | 17.6 | 19.1 | 39.1 | 21.0 | 2.7 | 0.5 | 29,868 | 26,923 | 33,889 | 37,487 | 34,687 | 21,517 |
| BOURBON | 14,230 | 5,999 | 25.1 | 18.7 | 36.0 | 16.5 | 3.0 | 0.8 | 27,298 | 25,517 | 32,784 | 34,839 | 30,846 | 17,664 |
| BROWN | 16,375 | 4,337 | 17.8 | 19.4 | 36.4 | 22.2 | 3.5 | 0.7 | 30,603 | 25,671 | 34,145 | 39,738 | 35,380 | 23,943 |
| BUTLER | 22,319 | 23,170 | 9.8 | 9.7 | 33.7 | 36.1 | 8.5 | 2.3 | 42,379 | 36,206 | 48,487 | 52,779 | 45,977 | 28,399 |
| CHASE | 14,732 | 1,202 | 25.4 | 21.4 | 36.5 | 13.8 | 2.1 | 0.8 | 26,224 | 31,052 | 28,960 | 27,983 | 26,626 | 20,104 |
| CHAUTAUQUA | 11,367 | 1,602 | 31.9 | 27.3 | 29.9 | 9.7 | 1.1 | 0.2 | 21,099 | 19,129 | 26,279 | 25,722 | 25,173 | 15,512 |
| CHEROKEE | 16,057 | 8,879 | 23.3 | 22.1 | 35.5 | 16.1 | 2.4 | 0.7 | 26,995 | 24,493 | 30,515 | 34,514 | 30,794 | 18,552 |
| CHEYENNE | 14,111 | 1,345 | 24.6 | 19.3 | 37.0 | 17.3 | 1.5 | 0.2 | 26,059 | 24,782 | 30,385 | 29,008 | 26,638 | 23,572 |
| CLARK | 16,196 | 968 | 14.9 | 19.3 | 42.2 | 21.4 | 2.0 | 0.3 | 30,217 | 27,848 | 33,838 | 37,604 | 35,332 | 23,265 |
| CLAY | 19,350 | 3,599 | 14.9 | 18.2 | 37.2 | 22.3 | 5.6 | 1.9 | 33,714 | 31,525 | 37,463 | 41,499 | 37,154 | 25,755 |
| CLOUD | 15,888 | 3,980 | 18.8 | 18.1 | 38.6 | 22.0 | 2.3 | 0.2 | 29,259 | 26,141 | 36,206 | 38,058 | 30,406 | 22,905 |
| COFFEY | 15,797 | 3,398 | 17.6 | 16.4 | 38.1 | 23.9 | 3.2 | 0.7 | 31,168 | 30,021 | 38,209 | 37,917 | 28,987 | 21,177 |
| COMANCHE | 11,908 | 804 | 34.1 | 26.4 | 27.4 | 11.2 | 0.5 | 0.5 | 21,381 | 16,905 | 25,380 | 24,392 | 27,484 | 18,769 |
| COWLEY | 15,370 | 13,836 | 18.7 | 17.1 | 37.8 | 22.7 | 2.6 | 1.0 | 30,879 | 27,753 | 37,736 | 37,117 | 33,922 | 21,167 |
| CRAWFORD | 16,011 | 14,708 | 24.1 | 18.6 | 35.5 | 17.4 | 3.0 | 1.4 | 29,048 | 22,657 | 37,243 | 37,858 | 34,756 | 20,802 |
| DECATUR | 14,290 | 1,385 | 27.4 | 19.6 | 35.5 | 14.3 | 2.5 | 0.7 | 25,661 | 24,845 | 31,946 | 29,250 | 32,685 | 18,470 |
| DICKINSON | 16,769 | 7,813 | 16.7 | 17.7 | 36.9 | 25.0 | 3.0 | 0.6 | 31,396 | 28,300 | 36,715 | 40,639 | 33,387 | 22,347 |
| DONIPHAN | 13,042 | 2,934 | 22.5 | 14.1 | 41.1 | 20.4 | 1.9 | 0.0 | 27,805 | 24,933 | 31,269 | 35,366 | 34,076 | 19,207 |
| DOUGLAS | 18,800 | 36,018 | 18.9 | 12.6 | 33.2 | 25.9 | 6.2 | 3.2 | 37,543 | 25,890 | 44,595 | 54,813 | 48,253 | 31,798 |
| EDWARDS | 15,207 | 1,341 | 19.3 | 25.4 | 36.3 | 16.3 | 1.6 | 1.2 | 27,786 | 22,808 | 31,290 | 37,263 | 29,024 | 21,429 |
| ELK | 14,223 | 1,451 | 32.5 | 16.2 | 36.5 | 11.7 | 1.7 | 1.5 | 25,553 | 25,385 | 34,782 | 25,887 | 31,215 | 19,178 |
| ELLIS | 16,634 | 10,134 | 23.5 | 16.9 | 35.3 | 19.5 | 3.2 | 1.7 | 30,400 | 22,391 | 36,968 | 42,510 | 36,830 | 21,173 |
| ELLSWORTH | 15,630 | 2,308 | 20.2 | 17.2 | 39.0 | 19.6 | 3.2 | 0.9 | 29,859 | 27,045 | 38,989 | 37,894 | 35,776 | 20,177 |
| FINNEY | 14,765 | 12,331 | 11.3 | 17.1 | 41.2 | 25.6 | 3.6 | 1.2 | 34,197 | 28,546 | 38,923 | 39,531 | 38,227 | 28,370 |
| FORD | 15,931 | 10,775 | 13.9 | 18.0 | 37.5 | 25.4 | 4.2 | 1.1 | 33,639 | 28,285 | 37,679 | 41,317 | 39,391 | 25,860 |
| FRANKLIN | 18,526 | 9,597 | 14.3 | 12.8 | 39.9 | 26.0 | 5.3 | 1.7 | 35,660 | 32,075 | 40,906 | 45,154 | 41,758 | 21,965 |
| GEARY | 13,616 | 8,542 | 17.8 | 22.2 | 38.1 | 19.8 | 1.9 | 0.1 | 28,226 | 23,053 | 33,015 | 39,645 | 34,898 | 23,899 |
| GOVE | 12,322 | 1,195 | 23.9 | 22.4 | 39.3 | 13.6 | 0.8 | 0.0 | 24,291 | 24,797 | 28,173 | 30,806 | 28,742 | 16,904 |
| GRAHAM | 17,249 | 1,271 | 22.7 | 17.7 | 36.6 | 18.2 | 3.6 | 1.2 | 28,996 | 25,520 | 33,093 | 36,289 | 33,961 | 22,362 |
| GRANT | 18,025 | 2,766 | 9.4 | 8.2 | 38.8 | 36.3 | 6.9 | 0.4 | 39,331 | 34,009 | 43,992 | 47,406 | 40,731 | 31,709 |
| GRAY | 17,924 | 2,027 | 10.2 | 14.7 | 39.6 | 29.1 | 5.5 | 0.9 | 36,050 | 30,850 | 38,043 | 46,586 | 43,346 | 26,846 |
| GREELEY | 13,987 | 621 | 20.8 | 21.3 | 39.8 | 15.3 | 1.9 | 1.0 | 27,796 | 24,623 | 32,435 | 25,848 | 35,887 | 22,927 |
| GREENWOOD | 15,850 | 3,438 | 25.1 | 23.5 | 33.5 | 14.9 | 2.1 | 1.0 | 26,550 | 23,986 | 30,804 | 30,113 | 37,976 | 19,609 |
| HAMILTON | 15,470 | 991 | 22.4 | 21.6 | 35.2 | 17.2 | 2.3 | 1.3 | 28,246 | 26,061 | 33,970 | 32,672 | 29,507 | 21,472 |
| HARPER | 12,862 | 2,674 | 26.0 | 22.1 | 38.4 | 12.6 | 1.0 | 0.0 | 23,934 | 24,715 | 27,402 | 29,976 | 24,922 | 17,541 |
| HARVEY | 20,020 | 13,000 | 10.6 | 13.0 | 37.6 | 32.1 | 5.2 | 1.5 | 37,746 | 32,767 | 43,288 | 47,290 | 41,439 | 26,750 |
| HASKELL | 12,756 | 1,402 | 13.6 | 22.3 | 41.7 | 20.0 | 1.9 | 0.5 | 29,051 | 25,972 | 34,140 | 32,849 | 30,128 | 22,466 |
| HODGEMAN | 13,698 | 831 | 13.7 | 17.6 | 46.8 | 21.1 | 0.8 | 0.0 | 29,100 | 30,500 | 31,288 | 34,076 | 33,416 | 21,371 |
| JACKSON | 16,531 | 4,576 | 15.9 | 13.9 | 39.9 | 24.4 | 4.4 | 1.6 | 33,772 | 30,222 | 41,703 | 41,932 | 33,872 | 22,672 |
| JEFFERSON | 18,850 | 6,882 | 13.0 | 9.9 | 39.8 | 30.9 | 5.6 | 0.9 | 36,727 | 34,513 | 41,454 | 48,215 | 39,118 | 21,841 |
| JEWELL | 13,990 | 1,610 | 21.2 | 23.7 | 37.4 | 16.8 | 0.9 | 0.0 | 25,826 | 25,467 | 31,403 | 26,884 | 31,127 | 20,552 |
| JOHNSON | 32,202 | 172,225 | 4.4 | 6.9 | 27.0 | 40.2 | 13.6 | 7.8 | 56,907 | 42,975 | 58,614 | 66,616 | 58,831 | 40,115 |
| KEARNY | 15,006 | 1,430 | 13.9 | 15.0 | 44.9 | 21.9 | 3.6 | 0.6 | 32,020 | 27,315 | 31,461 | 36,917 | 41,949 | 26,255 |
| KINGMAN | 15,995 | 3,281 | 17.8 | 18.7 | 35.3 | 23.8 | 3.5 | 0.9 | 31,660 | 32,524 | 36,213 | 41,842 | 32,964 | 21,700 |
| KIOWA | 13,460 | 1,369 | 23.3 | 20.5 | 40.7 | 14.4 | 1.1 | 0.0 | 25,305 | 20,908 | 29,004 | 30,618 | 29,435 | 20,920 |
| LABETTE | 13,804 | 9,056 | 24.2 | 19.5 | 36.5 | 17.5 | 1.7 | 0.6 | 26,864 | 24,491 | 32,616 | 33,695 | 30,531 | 17,649 |
| LANE | 14,603 | 934 | 23.0 | 25.0 | 35.2 | 14.4 | 2.0 | 0.4 | 25,610 | 25,818 | 29,492 | 28,429 | 30,413 | 19,562 |
| LEAVENWORTH | 18,781 | 22,572 | 9.4 | 9.0 | 35.4 | 38.6 | 6.6 | 1.0 | 40,249 | 34,546 | 45,720 | 49,745 | 42,621 | 26,427 |
| LINCOLN | 13,561 | 1,381 | 26.3 | 18.0 | 38.5 | 14.6 | 2.5 | 0.1 | 25,726 | 24,162 | 28,863 | 34,622 | 29,010 | 19,189 |
| LINN | 18,782 | 3,671 | 18.4 | 20.7 | 37.0 | 18.5 | 3.7 | 1.7 | 30,838 | 27,462 | 38,252 | 39,885 | 35,249 | 19,717 |
| LOGAN | 15,726 | 1,162 | 14.2 | 24.4 | 36.2 | 20.9 | 3.7 | 0.6 | 30,586 | 26,221 | 33,702 | 37,914 | 34,540 | 24,706 |
| LYON | 15,638 | 12,735 | 20.1 | 16.0 | 38.8 | 21.2 | 3.0 | 0.9 | 30,629 | 24,325 | 36,798 | 39,415 | 39,448 | 22,123 |
| MCPHERSON | 18,025 | 10,827 | 12.4 | 12.6 | 39.3 | 30.8 | 4.1 | 0.9 | 35,718 | 31,101 | 41,990 | 47,027 | 42,186 | 22,494 |
| MARION | 15,120 | 5,229 | 17.5 | 19.8 | 38.3 | 21.2 | 2.6 | 0.7 | 29,770 | 26,737 | 35,961 | 37,248 | 35,243 | 21,701 |
| MARSHALL | 15,742 | 4,341 | 19.3 | 21.0 | 35.9 | 19.4 | 3.1 | 1.4 | 30,091 | 28,201 | 35,753 | 38,594 | 34,601 | 20,975 |
| MEADE | 14,771 | 1,748 | 15.6 | 19.5 | 43.0 | 19.9 | 2.0 | 0.1 | 29,130 | 26,150 | 32,403 | 36,497 | 32,021 | 23,538 |
| MIAMI | 19,677 | 9,928 | 12.4 | 11.1 | 34.4 | 33.1 | 7.0 | 2.1 | 39,467 | 33,734 | 45,009 | 51,151 | 42,488 | 25,294 |
| MITCHELL | 16,825 | 2,704 | 14.0 | 16.5 | 38.7 | 26.7 | 3.4 | 0.6 | 32,599 | 31,580 | 40,996 | 39,538 | 32,119 | 23,454 |
| MONTGOMERY | 14,568 | 14,764 | 24.7 | 18.6 | 36.1 | 18.0 | 2.0 | 0.7 | 27,484 | 23,349 | 33,655 | 36,222 | 28,473 | 19,730 |
| MORRIS | 15,765 | 2,487 | 20.5 | 19.9 | 33.0 | 22.1 | 3.8 | 0.6 | 30,254 | 27,949 | 35,612 | 37,976 | 36,870 | 20,987 |
| MORTON | 18,373 | 1,287 | 18.5 | 14.4 | 34.4 | 25.6 | 4.4 | 2.7 | 35,563 | 25,408 | 41,067 | 41,523 | 41,429 | 30,895 |
| NEMAHA | 16,678 | 3,820 | 18.5 | 15.0 | 37.9 | 23.5 | 4.2 | 0.9 | 32,225 | 30,127 | 38,528 | 45,700 | 32,823 | 22,172 |
| NEOSHO | 14,400 | 6,527 | 20.5 | 16.9 | 39.0 | 21.2 | 2.2 | 0.2 | 28,684 | 26,151 | 35,044 | 34,215 | 32,385 | 20,499 |
| NESS | 15,514 | 1,472 | 19.4 | 14.4 | 42.3 | 21.5 | 2.3 | 0.0 | 29,083 | 28,596 | 33,881 | 32,125 | 36,349 | 22,167 |
| NORTON | 16,280 | 2,192 | 17.2 | 16.8 | 42.2 | 20.2 | 2.8 | 0.9 | 30,091 | 27,260 | 34,620 | 40,052 | 36,208 | 20,827 |
| OSAGE | 15,637 | 6,647 | 15.9 | 14.1 | 41.8 | 25.8 | 2.3 | 0.1 | 31,471 | 30,487 | 37,291 | 38,718 | 34,175 | 20,725 |
| OSBORNE | 15,607 | 1,974 | 19.8 | 20.9 | 37.9 | 19.0 | 2.3 | 0.2 | 27,881 | 27,638 | 35,296 | 32,003 | 33,482 | 20,933 |
| OTTAWA | 17,070 | 2,411 | 12.7 | 17.0 | 40.4 | 26.2 | 3.6 | 0.2 | 32,280 | 30,771 | 38,174 | 40,104 | 32,815 | 23,480 |
| PAWNEE | 15,816 | 2,776 | 18.8 | 19.3 | 39.7 | 19.7 | 1.7 | 0.8 | 29,079 | 24,074 | 31,873 | 32,967 | 38,042 | 23,089 |
| PHILLIPS | 16,807 | 2,445 | 19.8 | 14.8 | 42.3 | 19.1 | 3.2 | 0.9 | 29,888 | 29,095 | 35,036 | 35,719 | 34,786 | 21,727 |
| POTTAWATOMIE | 17,545 | 7,181 | 12.6 | 15.2 | 39.3 | 26.2 | 5.4 | 1.3 | 35,342 | 29,476 | 42,375 | 45,908 | 38,488 | 24,129 |
| PRATT | 17,509 | 3,932 | 17.9 | 19.5 | 35.2 | 22.3 | 3.6 | 1.5 | 31,826 | 26,530 | 36,603 | 41,172 | 36,634 | 23,311 |
| RAWLINS | 15,517 | 1,223 | 20.9 | 20.0 | 35.8 | 21.2 | 1.5 | 0.7 | 28,037 | 24,413 | 30,660 | 32,757 | 33,478 | 22,915 |
| KANSAS | 20,105 | | 14.5 | 14.0 | 35.0 | 28.1 | 5.9 | 2.4 | 37,751 | 30,612 | 43,142 | 47,811 | 41,695 | 25,693 |
| UNITED STATES | 22,162 | | 14.5 | 12.5 | 32.3 | 29.8 | 7.4 | 3.5 | 40,748 | 34,503 | 44,969 | 49,579 | 43,409 | 27,339 |

| COUNTY | FINANCIAL SERVICES | | | | THE HOME | | | | | | ENTERTAINMENT | | | | | | PERSONAL | | | |
|---|---|---|---|---|---|---|---|---|---|---|---|---|---|---|---|---|---|---|---|---|
| | | | | | Home Improvements | | | Furnishings | | | | | | | | | | | | |
| | Auto Loan | Home Loan | Invest-ments | Retire-ment Plans | Home Repair | Lawn & Garden | Remodel-ing | Appli-ances | Elec-tronics | Furni-ture | Restau-rants | Sport-ing Goods | Theater & Concerts | Toys & Hobbies | Travel | Video Rental | Apparel | Auto After-market | Health Insur-ance | Pets & Supplies |
| ALLEN | 96 | 68 | 75 | 78 | 92 | 90 | 109 | 95 | 92 | 77 | 81 | 91 | 83 | 93 | 78 | 100 | 79 | 89 | 103 | 95 |
| ANDERSON | 97 | 65 | 71 | 79 | 90 | 90 | 109 | 95 | 91 | 73 | 79 | 93 | 81 | 94 | 76 | 100 | 78 | 89 | 105 | 96 |
| ATCHISON | 95 | 75 | 80 | 81 | 93 | 91 | 107 | 94 | 91 | 81 | 84 | 91 | 86 | 94 | 82 | 99 | 82 | 91 | 101 | 96 |
| BARBER | 96 | 64 | 70 | 78 | 90 | 89 | 108 | 94 | 90 | 72 | 78 | 93 | 79 | 93 | 75 | 100 | 77 | 89 | 105 | 95 |
| BARTON | 96 | 83 | 88 | 87 | 96 | 93 | 105 | 96 | 93 | 87 | 90 | 93 | 91 | 96 | 87 | 100 | 87 | 93 | 101 | 97 |
| BOURBON | 96 | 73 | 80 | 81 | 94 | 91 | 108 | 95 | 92 | 81 | 84 | 92 | 86 | 95 | 81 | 100 | 82 | 91 | 103 | 96 |
| BROWN | 95 | 66 | 72 | 78 | 91 | 90 | 107 | 94 | 90 | 75 | 79 | 91 | 81 | 92 | 77 | 100 | 78 | 89 | 104 | 95 |
| BUTLER | 99 | 91 | 95 | 95 | 99 | 97 | 107 | 99 | 97 | 94 | 98 | 98 | 98 | 101 | 92 | 102 | 94 | 99 | 101 | 100 |
| CHASE | 97 | 64 | 70 | 79 | 90 | 89 | 109 | 95 | 90 | 72 | 78 | 94 | 79 | 94 | 75 | 100 | 77 | 89 | 106 | 96 |
| CHAUTAUQUA | 95 | 64 | 70 | 75 | 91 | 89 | 107 | 94 | 91 | 74 | 78 | 90 | 79 | 91 | 75 | 100 | 77 | 88 | 104 | 94 |
| CHEROKEE | 96 | 69 | 74 | 78 | 93 | 90 | 109 | 95 | 92 | 79 | 81 | 92 | 83 | 94 | 78 | 99 | 79 | 89 | 102 | 96 |
| CHEYENNE | 95 | 64 | 70 | 77 | 90 | 89 | 108 | 94 | 90 | 73 | 78 | 91 | 79 | 92 | 76 | 100 | 77 | 88 | 105 | 95 |
| CLARK | 95 | 64 | 70 | 76 | 90 | 89 | 107 | 94 | 91 | 73 | 78 | 90 | 79 | 91 | 76 | 100 | 77 | 88 | 104 | 94 |
| CLAY | 97 | 76 | 90 | 87 | 97 | 96 | 104 | 96 | 92 | 82 | 86 | 94 | 90 | 95 | 86 | 100 | 83 | 92 | 104 | 96 |
| CLOUD | 95 | 68 | 73 | 78 | 91 | 89 | 105 | 94 | 91 | 77 | 80 | 90 | 82 | 92 | 78 | 100 | 78 | 89 | 103 | 94 |
| COFFEY | 98 | 74 | 78 | 83 | 92 | 90 | 111 | 96 | 93 | 81 | 85 | 95 | 86 | 97 | 79 | 101 | 83 | 92 | 103 | 98 |
| COMANCHE | 95 | 65 | 72 | 76 | 91 | 90 | 107 | 94 | 91 | 74 | 78 | 89 | 80 | 91 | 76 | 100 | 77 | 88 | 104 | 94 |
| COWLEY | 97 | 79 | 84 | 85 | 95 | 92 | 107 | 96 | 93 | 85 | 88 | 93 | 90 | 97 | 84 | 101 | 85 | 93 | 102 | 97 |
| CRAWFORD | 96 | 81 | 89 | 88 | 96 | 93 | 105 | 94 | 93 | 84 | 87 | 92 | 89 | 94 | 86 | 99 | 85 | 92 | 101 | 96 |
| DECATUR | 96 | 64 | 70 | 77 | 90 | 89 | 108 | 94 | 90 | 73 | 78 | 92 | 79 | 93 | 75 | 100 | 77 | 88 | 105 | 95 |
| DICKINSON | 97 | 71 | 76 | 81 | 92 | 90 | 110 | 96 | 92 | 79 | 83 | 94 | 85 | 96 | 79 | 100 | 81 | 91 | 103 | 97 |
| DONIPHAN | 98 | 71 | 76 | 81 | 92 | 90 | 112 | 96 | 93 | 79 | 84 | 95 | 85 | 97 | 78 | 101 | 82 | 91 | 103 | 98 |
| DOUGLAS | 95 | 93 | 88 | 90 | 94 | 90 | 99 | 92 | 92 | 86 | 93 | 91 | 89 | 94 | 88 | 97 | 88 | 94 | 96 | 97 |
| EDWARDS | 96 | 66 | 73 | 78 | 91 | 90 | 109 | 94 | 91 | 75 | 79 | 91 | 81 | 93 | 77 | 100 | 78 | 89 | 104 | 95 |
| ELK | 95 | 64 | 70 | 75 | 91 | 89 | 107 | 94 | 91 | 74 | 78 | 89 | 79 | 91 | 76 | 100 | 77 | 88 | 104 | 94 |
| ELLIS | 96 | 88 | 91 | 90 | 96 | 94 | 101 | 95 | 94 | 88 | 92 | 94 | 93 | 96 | 89 | 100 | 88 | 95 | 101 | 97 |
| ELLSWORTH | 95 | 67 | 74 | 78 | 92 | 90 | 109 | 94 | 92 | 77 | 80 | 89 | 81 | 92 | 78 | 100 | 79 | 89 | 103 | 95 |
| FINNEY | 99 | 96 | 85 | 92 | 94 | 93 | 101 | 99 | 99 | 97 | 101 | 99 | 97 | 100 | 90 | 103 | 95 | 100 | 98 | 101 |
| FORD | 98 | 91 | 93 | 93 | 97 | 96 | 104 | 98 | 96 | 94 | 97 | 97 | 96 | 99 | 91 | 101 | 92 | 98 | 100 | 99 |
| FRANKLIN | 97 | 80 | 85 | 85 | 95 | 92 | 109 | 96 | 93 | 86 | 89 | 94 | 90 | 97 | 84 | 100 | 86 | 93 | 101 | 98 |
| GEARY | 93 | 95 | 85 | 86 | 93 | 89 | 93 | 94 | 95 | 89 | 96 | 92 | 93 | 94 | 88 | 100 | 89 | 97 | 94 | 98 |
| GOVE | 97 | 63 | 70 | 79 | 90 | 89 | 109 | 95 | 90 | 72 | 78 | 94 | 80 | 94 | 75 | 100 | 77 | 89 | 106 | 96 |
| GRAHAM | 96 | 64 | 70 | 77 | 90 | 89 | 108 | 94 | 90 | 73 | 78 | 91 | 79 | 92 | 75 | 100 | 77 | 88 | 105 | 95 |
| GRANT | 99 | 83 | 81 | 86 | 93 | 90 | 110 | 98 | 96 | 88 | 92 | 97 | 91 | 100 | 83 | 102 | 88 | 96 | 101 | 101 |
| GRAY | 99 | 83 | 88 | 89 | 95 | 94 | 107 | 98 | 94 | 85 | 91 | 98 | 92 | 100 | 86 | 101 | 88 | 95 | 104 | 100 |
| GREELEY | 98 | 64 | 70 | 80 | 90 | 90 | 110 | 95 | 90 | 71 | 78 | 96 | 80 | 96 | 75 | 100 | 78 | 89 | 106 | 97 |
| GREENWOOD | 95 | 64 | 70 | 76 | 90 | 89 | 107 | 94 | 91 | 73 | 78 | 90 | 79 | 91 | 76 | 100 | 77 | 88 | 104 | 94 |
| HAMILTON | 95 | 64 | 70 | 76 | 90 | 89 | 107 | 94 | 91 | 73 | 78 | 90 | 79 | 91 | 76 | 100 | 77 | 88 | 104 | 94 |
| HARPER | 96 | 65 | 71 | 78 | 90 | 89 | 107 | 94 | 91 | 73 | 78 | 91 | 80 | 93 | 76 | 100 | 77 | 89 | 105 | 95 |
| HARVEY | 97 | 85 | 89 | 87 | 97 | 94 | 106 | 97 | 94 | 89 | 92 | 94 | 93 | 98 | 88 | 101 | 89 | 95 | 101 | 99 |
| HASKELL | 101 | 72 | 77 | 85 | 92 | 91 | 115 | 98 | 93 | 78 | 85 | 100 | 87 | 101 | 78 | 102 | 84 | 93 | 106 | 102 |
| HODGEMAN | 97 | 63 | 70 | 79 | 90 | 89 | 109 | 95 | 90 | 71 | 78 | 94 | 80 | 94 | 75 | 100 | 77 | 89 | 106 | 96 |
| JACKSON | 99 | 73 | 78 | 83 | 93 | 91 | 113 | 97 | 93 | 80 | 85 | 95 | 86 | 98 | 79 | 101 | 83 | 92 | 104 | 99 |
| JEFFERSON | 99 | 76 | 81 | 85 | 94 | 91 | 114 | 97 | 95 | 84 | 88 | 96 | 88 | 99 | 81 | 102 | 86 | 93 | 103 | 100 |
| JEWELL | 97 | 64 | 70 | 79 | 90 | 90 | 110 | 95 | 90 | 72 | 78 | 94 | 80 | 94 | 75 | 100 | 77 | 89 | 106 | 96 |
| JOHNSON | 104 | 115 | 104 | 113 | 104 | 108 | 102 | 103 | 107 | 111 | 117 | 108 | 113 | 107 | 107 | 105 | 113 | 111 | 102 | 105 |
| KEARNY | 98 | 75 | 79 | 83 | 92 | 90 | 112 | 96 | 93 | 83 | 86 | 95 | 87 | 97 | 80 | 101 | 84 | 92 | 102 | 99 |
| KINGMAN | 97 | 67 | 73 | 80 | 91 | 90 | 110 | 95 | 91 | 75 | 80 | 93 | 82 | 95 | 77 | 101 | 79 | 90 | 105 | 97 |
| KIOWA | 94 | 64 | 71 | 76 | 90 | 89 | 107 | 94 | 91 | 74 | 78 | 89 | 79 | 91 | 76 | 100 | 77 | 88 | 104 | 93 |
| LABETTE | 95 | 74 | 78 | 79 | 93 | 90 | 105 | 94 | 91 | 81 | 83 | 90 | 85 | 93 | 81 | 99 | 81 | 90 | 101 | 95 |
| LANE | 96 | 64 | 70 | 78 | 90 | 89 | 108 | 94 | 90 | 72 | 78 | 92 | 79 | 93 | 75 | 100 | 77 | 89 | 105 | 95 |
| LEAVENWORTH | 99 | 97 | 92 | 96 | 98 | 96 | 103 | 98 | 99 | 97 | 101 | 99 | 100 | 101 | 94 | 102 | 97 | 101 | 99 | 101 |
| LINCOLN | 97 | 63 | 70 | 79 | 90 | 89 | 109 | 95 | 90 | 71 | 78 | 94 | 80 | 94 | 75 | 100 | 77 | 89 | 106 | 96 |
| LINN | 97 | 69 | 79 | 81 | 93 | 92 | 112 | 96 | 92 | 77 | 82 | 93 | 84 | 95 | 79 | 100 | 80 | 90 | 105 | 97 |
| LOGAN | 95 | 64 | 70 | 77 | 90 | 89 | 108 | 94 | 90 | 73 | 78 | 91 | 79 | 92 | 76 | 100 | 77 | 88 | 105 | 94 |
| LYON | 96 | 90 | 89 | 89 | 96 | 92 | 100 | 94 | 93 | 88 | 92 | 93 | 91 | 95 | 89 | 99 | 88 | 95 | 98 | 97 |
| MCPHERSON | 98 | 85 | 89 | 91 | 96 | 95 | 107 | 97 | 96 | 89 | 92 | 97 | 94 | 99 | 88 | 102 | 90 | 96 | 103 | 99 |
| MARION | 96 | 66 | 73 | 79 | 91 | 90 | 109 | 95 | 91 | 75 | 80 | 92 | 81 | 94 | 77 | 100 | 79 | 89 | 104 | 96 |
| MARSHALL | 96 | 66 | 73 | 79 | 91 | 90 | 108 | 94 | 91 | 75 | 80 | 92 | 81 | 94 | 77 | 100 | 78 | 89 | 104 | 95 |
| MEADE | 97 | 68 | 74 | 80 | 91 | 90 | 110 | 95 | 92 | 76 | 81 | 93 | 83 | 95 | 77 | 101 | 80 | 90 | 104 | 97 |
| MIAMI | 99 | 84 | 86 | 89 | 96 | 93 | 109 | 97 | 96 | 89 | 92 | 96 | 93 | 99 | 86 | 102 | 89 | 96 | 101 | 100 |
| MITCHELL | 95 | 68 | 74 | 78 | 91 | 90 | 105 | 94 | 90 | 76 | 80 | 90 | 82 | 92 | 78 | 99 | 78 | 89 | 103 | 94 |
| MONTGOMERY | 96 | 75 | 82 | 82 | 96 | 92 | 106 | 96 | 92 | 83 | 85 | 92 | 88 | 94 | 84 | 100 | 83 | 91 | 101 | 96 |
| MORRIS | 96 | 66 | 72 | 79 | 91 | 90 | 110 | 95 | 91 | 75 | 79 | 92 | 81 | 94 | 77 | 100 | 78 | 89 | 105 | 96 |
| MORTON | 96 | 71 | 77 | 80 | 92 | 90 | 110 | 95 | 93 | 79 | 83 | 92 | 84 | 94 | 79 | 100 | 81 | 91 | 103 | 96 |
| NEMAHA | 96 | 64 | 70 | 77 | 90 | 89 | 108 | 94 | 90 | 73 | 78 | 91 | 79 | 92 | 75 | 100 | 77 | 88 | 105 | 95 |
| NEOSHO | 95 | 74 | 83 | 81 | 94 | 92 | 106 | 95 | 92 | 81 | 84 | 91 | 86 | 94 | 82 | 100 | 82 | 91 | 103 | 95 |
| NESS | 98 | 68 | 74 | 82 | 91 | 90 | 111 | 96 | 91 | 75 | 81 | 96 | 83 | 97 | 77 | 101 | 80 | 91 | 105 | 98 |
| NORTON | 95 | 78 | 89 | 84 | 96 | 95 | 101 | 95 | 92 | 83 | 87 | 91 | 90 | 95 | 86 | 100 | 84 | 92 | 104 | 95 |
| OSAGE | 97 | 74 | 77 | 82 | 93 | 90 | 109 | 96 | 93 | 81 | 85 | 94 | 86 | 96 | 80 | 101 | 83 | 92 | 103 | 98 |
| OSBORNE | 95 | 64 | 70 | 76 | 90 | 89 | 107 | 94 | 91 | 73 | 78 | 90 | 79 | 92 | 76 | 100 | 77 | 88 | 104 | 94 |
| OTTAWA | 96 | 69 | 75 | 80 | 92 | 90 | 110 | 95 | 92 | 77 | 81 | 92 | 83 | 94 | 78 | 101 | 80 | 90 | 104 | 96 |
| PAWNEE | 95 | 64 | 71 | 77 | 90 | 89 | 107 | 94 | 91 | 74 | 78 | 90 | 79 | 92 | 76 | 100 | 77 | 88 | 104 | 94 |
| PHILLIPS | 98 | 68 | 74 | 81 | 91 | 90 | 111 | 96 | 92 | 76 | 82 | 95 | 83 | 96 | 77 | 101 | 80 | 91 | 105 | 98 |
| POTTAWATOMIE | 97 | 80 | 78 | 84 | 92 | 90 | 108 | 96 | 95 | 86 | 90 | 95 | 89 | 97 | 82 | 101 | 86 | 94 | 101 | 98 |
| PRATT | 96 | 71 | 81 | 82 | 94 | 92 | 106 | 95 | 91 | 78 | 83 | 93 | 85 | 95 | 81 | 100 | 81 | 91 | 105 | 96 |
| RAWLINS | 97 | 64 | 70 | 79 | 90 | 90 | 110 | 95 | 90 | 72 | 78 | 94 | 80 | 95 | 75 | 100 | 78 | 89 | 106 | 96 |
| KANSAS | 98 | 93 | 93 | 95 | 98 | 97 | 102 | 97 | 97 | 94 | 97 | 97 | 98 | 99 | 93 | 101 | 93 | 98 | 100 | 99 |
| UNITED STATES | 100 | 100 | 100 | 100 | 100 | 100 | 100 | 100 | 100 | 100 | 100 | 100 | 100 | 100 | 100 | 100 | 100 | 100 | 100 | 100 |

| COUNTY | FIPS Code | MSA Code | DMA Code | POPULATION 1990 | POPULATION 2000 | POPULATION 2005 | 1990-2000 ANNUAL CHANGE % Rate | 1990-2000 ANNUAL CHANGE State Rank | RACE (%) White 1990 | White 2000 | Black 1990 | Black 2000 | Asian/Pacific 1990 | Asian/Pacific 2000 |
|---|---|---|---|---|---|---|---|---|---|---|---|---|---|---|
| RENO | 155 | 0000 | 678 | 62,389 | 64,019 | 65,607 | 0.3 | 32 | 93.9 | 92.5 | 2.7 | 2.9 | 0.3 | 0.4 |
| REPUBLIC | 157 | 0000 | 722 | 6,482 | 5,894 | 5,505 | -0.9 | 83 | 99.5 | 99.5 | 0.0 | 0.0 | 0.2 | 0.3 |
| RICE | 159 | 0000 | 678 | 10,610 | 10,127 | 9,612 | -0.5 | 64 | 96.3 | 95.3 | 1.1 | 1.4 | 0.2 | 0.2 |
| RILEY | 161 | 0000 | 605 | 67,139 | 63,114 | 60,173 | -0.6 | 66 | 83.2 | 81.5 | 10.1 | 9.7 | 3.6 | 4.7 |
| ROOKS | 163 | 0000 | 678 | 6,039 | 5,570 | 5,298 | -0.8 | 79 | 98.9 | 98.8 | 0.6 | 0.6 | 0.1 | 0.1 |
| RUSH | 165 | 0000 | 678 | 3,842 | 3,324 | 3,124 | -1.4 | 98 | 99.3 | 99.1 | 0.0 | 0.0 | 0.1 | 0.2 |
| RUSSELL | 167 | 0000 | 678 | 7,835 | 7,388 | 7,046 | -0.6 | 66 | 98.7 | 98.5 | 0.5 | 0.7 | 0.1 | 0.1 |
| SALINE | 169 | 0000 | 678 | 49,301 | 51,323 | 50,973 | 0.4 | 26 | 93.9 | 92.5 | 3.1 | 3.3 | 1.1 | 1.5 |
| SCOTT | 171 | 0000 | 678 | 5,289 | 4,895 | 4,672 | -0.8 | 79 | 97.3 | 95.8 | 0.1 | 0.1 | 0.4 | 0.5 |
| SEDGWICK | 173 | 9040 | 678 | 403,662 | 457,407 | 484,800 | 1.2 | 10 | 85.5 | 83.4 | 8.9 | 9.3 | 2.2 | 2.9 |
| SEWARD | 175 | 0000 | 678 | 18,743 | 20,207 | 20,664 | 0.7 | 16 | 77.3 | 72.4 | 5.9 | 5.6 | 2.4 | 3.0 |
| SHAWNEE | 177 | 8440 | 605 | 160,976 | 171,444 | 174,671 | 0.6 | 18 | 87.7 | 86.0 | 8.3 | 8.7 | 0.7 | 1.1 |
| SHERIDAN | 179 | 0000 | 678 | 3,043 | 2,641 | 2,482 | -1.4 | 98 | 99.2 | 99.0 | 0.0 | 0.0 | 0.2 | 0.3 |
| SHERMAN | 181 | 0000 | 678 | 6,926 | 6,481 | 6,274 | -0.6 | 66 | 94.8 | 92.6 | 0.2 | 0.3 | 0.2 | 0.3 |
| SMITH | 183 | 0000 | 722 | 5,078 | 4,537 | 4,354 | -1.1 | 91 | 99.7 | 99.7 | 0.1 | 0.1 | 0.1 | 0.1 |
| STAFFORD | 185 | 0000 | 678 | 5,365 | 4,950 | 4,729 | -0.8 | 79 | 98.2 | 97.6 | 0.2 | 0.2 | 0.2 | 0.2 |
| STANTON | 187 | 0000 | 678 | 2,333 | 2,203 | 2,094 | -0.6 | 66 | 86.4 | 81.5 | 0.1 | 0.1 | 0.3 | 0.5 |
| STEVENS | 189 | 0000 | 678 | 5,048 | 5,415 | 5,497 | 0.7 | 16 | 90.2 | 86.6 | 0.5 | 0.5 | 0.3 | 0.4 |
| SUMNER | 191 | 0000 | 678 | 25,841 | 27,267 | 27,746 | 0.5 | 21 | 96.2 | 95.2 | 0.5 | 0.6 | 0.3 | 0.4 |
| THOMAS | 193 | 0000 | 678 | 8,258 | 7,885 | 7,498 | -0.4 | 60 | 98.2 | 97.7 | 0.4 | 0.4 | 0.4 | 0.5 |
| TREGO | 195 | 0000 | 678 | 3,694 | 3,220 | 3,024 | -1.3 | 93 | 99.3 | 99.1 | 0.1 | 0.1 | 0.5 | 0.7 |
| WABAUNSEE | 197 | 0000 | 605 | 6,603 | 6,552 | 6,423 | -0.1 | 47 | 98.3 | 97.9 | 0.6 | 0.7 | 0.1 | 0.2 |
| WALLACE | 199 | 0000 | 678 | 1,821 | 1,797 | 1,778 | -0.1 | 47 | 98.0 | 97.4 | 0.3 | 0.3 | 0.2 | 0.3 |
| WASHINGTON | 201 | 0000 | 605 | 7,073 | 6,411 | 6,111 | -1.0 | 87 | 99.7 | 99.6 | 0.1 | 0.0 | 0.0 | 0.0 |
| WICHITA | 203 | 0000 | 678 | 2,758 | 2,525 | 2,435 | -0.9 | 83 | 89.0 | 84.2 | 0.0 | 0.0 | 0.3 | 0.4 |
| WILSON | 205 | 0000 | 603 | 10,289 | 10,360 | 10,482 | 0.1 | 38 | 98.6 | 98.3 | 0.2 | 0.3 | 0.2 | 0.2 |
| WOODSON | 207 | 0000 | 603 | 4,116 | 3,880 | 3,728 | -0.6 | 66 | 98.6 | 98.5 | 0.4 | 0.4 | 0.1 | 0.1 |
| WYANDOTTE | 209 | 3760 | 616 | 161,993 | 150,775 | 146,681 | -0.7 | 75 | 67.1 | 64.5 | 27.5 | 28.1 | 1.2 | 1.6 |
| KANSAS | | | | | | | 0.7 | | 90.1 | 88.9 | 5.8 | 5.7 | 1.3 | 1.8 |
| UNITED STATES | | | | | | | 1.0 | | 80.3 | 77.9 | 12.1 | 12.4 | 2.9 | 3.9 |

| COUNTY | % HISPANIC ORIGIN | | 2000 AGE DISTRIBUTION (%) | | | | | | | | | | MEDIAN AGE | | 2000 Males/ Females (×100) |
|---|---|---|---|---|---|---|---|---|---|---|---|---|---|---|---|
| | 1990 | 2000 | 0-4 | 5-9 | 10-14 | 15-19 | 20-24 | 25-44 | 45-64 | 65-84 | 85+ | 18+ | 1990 | 2000 | |
| RENO | 4.0 | 6.4 | 6.2 | 6.2 | 7.3 | 8.0 | 6.1 | 27.4 | 23.1 | 13.3 | 2.4 | 75.9 | 35.0 | 37.9 | 98.1 |
| REPUBLIC | 0.2 | 0.7 | 5.0 | 5.8 | 6.8 | 6.6 | 4.6 | 20.7 | 24.2 | 20.9 | 5.3 | 77.6 | 44.5 | 45.3 | 93.9 |
| RICE | 2.6 | 4.0 | 6.3 | 6.7 | 7.6 | 8.3 | 7.0 | 22.3 | 22.8 | 15.7 | 3.4 | 74.3 | 37.0 | 39.1 | 93.4 |
| RILEY | 4.2 | 6.5 | 6.6 | 5.4 | 5.4 | 12.1 | 23.9 | 27.9 | 11.4 | 6.2 | 1.0 | 79.9 | 24.0 | 24.3 | 119.8 |
| ROOKS | 0.4 | 0.9 | 6.5 | 6.7 | 8.0 | 7.4 | 4.8 | 23.6 | 22.9 | 16.7 | 3.5 | 73.8 | 37.9 | 40.3 | 94.8 |
| RUSH | 0.9 | 1.6 | 4.8 | 5.2 | 6.9 | 6.6 | 3.7 | 21.5 | 24.7 | 22.3 | 4.2 | 79.0 | 43.1 | 45.9 | 93.9 |
| RUSSELL | 0.6 | 1.2 | 4.9 | 5.6 | 6.5 | 7.1 | 4.3 | 23.5 | 24.8 | 19.6 | 3.6 | 78.4 | 40.9 | 43.7 | 96.6 |
| SALINE | 2.5 | 4.1 | 6.8 | 6.6 | 7.3 | 8.0 | 6.7 | 28.2 | 22.5 | 12.0 | 2.0 | 74.7 | 33.5 | 36.5 | 94.5 |
| SCOTT | 2.6 | 4.5 | 6.8 | 7.1 | 8.4 | 8.7 | 5.0 | 27.1 | 24.2 | 10.4 | 2.3 | 71.7 | 35.0 | 37.0 | 100.9 |
| SEDGWICK | 4.3 | 6.8 | 7.7 | 7.6 | 8.1 | 7.6 | 6.5 | 30.4 | 20.7 | 10.1 | 1.3 | 72.0 | 31.8 | 34.3 | 96.0 |
| SEWARD | 19.5 | 26.5 | 8.9 | 8.3 | 8.7 | 8.8 | 7.6 | 30.0 | 18.1 | 8.3 | 1.2 | 69.2 | 29.0 | 30.4 | 102.9 |
| SHAWNEE | 4.8 | 7.7 | 6.5 | 6.5 | 7.3 | 7.6 | 6.5 | 29.3 | 23.1 | 11.4 | 1.7 | 75.0 | 33.8 | 36.6 | 94.5 |
| SHERIDAN | 0.9 | 1.5 | 6.0 | 6.5 | 8.6 | 7.6 | 4.3 | 22.6 | 24.7 | 16.1 | 3.6 | 73.1 | 37.1 | 41.0 | 103.2 |
| SHERMAN | 6.8 | 10.3 | 6.8 | 6.7 | 7.5 | 8.3 | 5.4 | 24.0 | 24.2 | 14.3 | 2.7 | 74.5 | 35.5 | 38.5 | 95.6 |
| SMITH | 0.1 | 0.5 | 4.8 | 5.3 | 6.6 | 6.7 | 3.7 | 21.1 | 24.6 | 21.2 | 6.0 | 78.5 | 45.1 | 46.4 | 95.6 |
| STAFFORD | 2.1 | 3.7 | 6.2 | 6.6 | 7.9 | 7.4 | 4.4 | 23.8 | 23.4 | 16.8 | 3.5 | 74.5 | 39.0 | 40.8 | 95.6 |
| STANTON | 16.8 | 23.2 | 8.7 | 8.6 | 9.0 | 8.4 | 6.0 | 27.1 | 20.2 | 10.4 | 1.5 | 68.4 | 31.4 | 33.4 | 103.0 |
| STEVENS | 10.9 | 15.9 | 8.2 | 8.1 | 8.4 | 8.1 | 6.1 | 26.3 | 21.2 | 11.6 | 1.8 | 69.5 | 32.7 | 35.0 | 92.6 |
| SUMNER | 3.4 | 5.5 | 7.0 | 7.2 | 8.0 | 8.1 | 5.9 | 25.0 | 22.9 | 13.2 | 2.7 | 72.2 | 34.9 | 37.7 | 98.2 |
| THOMAS | 1.2 | 2.3 | 6.8 | 7.0 | 7.6 | 9.2 | 7.1 | 26.7 | 21.3 | 12.2 | 2.1 | 74.3 | 32.3 | 34.6 | 97.7 |
| TREGO | 0.2 | 0.7 | 5.3 | 5.7 | 6.8 | 8.7 | 5.2 | 21.9 | 23.3 | 18.8 | 4.3 | 75.6 | 39.1 | 42.8 | 100.4 |
| WABAUNSEE | 1.8 | 2.9 | 6.3 | 6.7 | 7.6 | 8.1 | 4.8 | 25.4 | 24.2 | 14.2 | 2.6 | 74.3 | 36.4 | 39.4 | 98.6 |
| WALLACE | 4.3 | 6.6 | 6.7 | 7.1 | 8.0 | 9.1 | 4.8 | 24.8 | 22.2 | 14.4 | 2.9 | 72.7 | 34.6 | 38.1 | 105.1 |
| WASHINGTON | 0.3 | 0.8 | 5.4 | 5.7 | 7.4 | 7.3 | 4.7 | 21.7 | 23.5 | 19.5 | 4.8 | 76.2 | 42.1 | 43.4 | 98.0 |
| WICHITA | 11.8 | 17.6 | 7.1 | 7.8 | 9.0 | 8.6 | 4.6 | 25.0 | 22.9 | 12.4 | 2.7 | 70.3 | 33.6 | 37.0 | 99.6 |
| WILSON | 0.7 | 1.6 | 5.8 | 6.3 | 7.2 | 7.1 | 5.6 | 22.8 | 24.4 | 17.3 | 3.4 | 75.8 | 39.1 | 41.7 | 96.1 |
| WOODSON | 0.6 | 1.3 | 5.4 | 5.7 | 6.6 | 7.2 | 5.5 | 21.6 | 23.5 | 20.3 | 4.3 | 77.3 | 41.4 | 43.6 | 94.1 |
| WYANDOTTE | 6.8 | 10.3 | 7.5 | 7.1 | 7.9 | 8.3 | 7.0 | 29.1 | 20.7 | 10.8 | 1.6 | 72.6 | 31.7 | 34.1 | 91.5 |
| KANSAS | 3.8 | 5.9 | 6.8 | 6.8 | 7.6 | 8.1 | 7.2 | 28.5 | 21.7 | 11.3 | 2.0 | 74.1 | 32.9 | 35.6 | 96.8 |
| UNITED STATES | 9.0 | 11.8 | 6.9 | 7.2 | 7.2 | 7.2 | 6.7 | 29.9 | 22.2 | 11.1 | 1.6 | 74.6 | 32.9 | 35.7 | 95.6 |

# HOUSEHOLDS

| COUNTY | HOUSEHOLDS 1990 | HOUSEHOLDS 2000 | HOUSEHOLDS 2005 | % Annual Rate 1990-2000 | 2000 Average HH Size | FAMILIES 1990 | FAMILIES 2000 | % Annual Rate 1990-2000 | MEDIAN HOUSEHOLD INCOME 2000 | 2005 | 2000 National Rank | 2000 State Rank |
|---|---|---|---|---|---|---|---|---|---|---|---|---|
| RENO | 24,239 | 24,593 | 25,094 | 0.2 | 2.48 | 17,011 | 16,688 | -0.2 | 35,315 | 40,521 | 1197 | 28 |
| REPUBLIC | 2,769 | 2,564 | 2,415 | -0.9 | 2.22 | 1,870 | 1,665 | -1.4 | 31,362 | 34,949 | 1851 | 54 |
| RICE | 4,165 | 3,992 | 3,821 | -0.5 | 2.38 | 2,935 | 2,712 | -1.0 | 27,844 | 30,572 | 2465 | 89 |
| RILEY | 21,280 | 19,889 | 18,769 | -0.8 | 2.57 | 13,450 | 12,087 | -1.3 | 31,052 | 37,729 | 1922 | 58 |
| ROOKS | 2,444 | 2,242 | 2,127 | -1.0 | 2.41 | 1,683 | 1,483 | -1.5 | 30,000 | 34,138 | 2152 | 69 |
| RUSH | 1,642 | 1,428 | 1,345 | -1.7 | 2.27 | 1,123 | 938 | -2.2 | 29,653 | 37,212 | 2206 | 72 |
| RUSSELL | 3,371 | 3,201 | 3,064 | -0.6 | 2.26 | 2,223 | 2,024 | -1.1 | 28,125 | 32,473 | 2423 | 85 |
| SALINE | 19,826 | 20,635 | 20,495 | 0.5 | 2.44 | 13,510 | 13,539 | 0.0 | 35,993 | 39,566 | 1104 | 25 |
| SCOTT | 2,022 | 1,897 | 1,822 | -0.8 | 2.53 | 1,495 | 1,349 | -1.2 | 31,452 | 35,099 | 1831 | 52 |
| SEDGWICK | 156,571 | 179,045 | 190,691 | 1.6 | 2.52 | 107,361 | 119,102 | 1.3 | 40,386 | 46,758 | 639 | 12 |
| SEWARD | 6,614 | 7,147 | 7,321 | 0.9 | 2.79 | 4,926 | 5,186 | 0.6 | 40,531 | 48,303 | 623 | 10 |
| SHAWNEE | 63,768 | 65,544 | 65,467 | 0.3 | 2.56 | 43,046 | 42,942 | 0.0 | 43,973 | 50,468 | 397 | 5 |
| SHERIDAN | 1,171 | 1,040 | 988 | -1.4 | 2.50 | 859 | 737 | -1.8 | 32,833 | 37,267 | 1565 | 37 |
| SHERMAN | 2,733 | 2,516 | 2,419 | -1.0 | 2.51 | 1,920 | 1,703 | -1.4 | 30,427 | 34,695 | 2052 | 64 |
| SMITH | 2,165 | 1,912 | 1,824 | -1.5 | 2.29 | 1,479 | 1,249 | -2.0 | 29,115 | 36,096 | 2279 | 75 |
| STAFFORD | 2,203 | 2,014 | 1,916 | -1.1 | 2.38 | 1,514 | 1,330 | -1.6 | 28,276 | 31,895 | 2403 | 83 |
| STANTON | 831 | 794 | 758 | -0.6 | 2.74 | 640 | 594 | -0.9 | 31,648 | 35,064 | 1793 | 48 |
| STEVENS | 1,885 | 2,026 | 2,056 | 0.9 | 2.64 | 1,397 | 1,455 | 0.5 | 40,398 | 51,003 | 638 | 11 |
| SUMNER | 9,689 | 10,268 | 10,474 | 0.7 | 2.61 | 7,134 | 7,327 | 0.3 | 37,183 | 42,715 | 948 | 18 |
| THOMAS | 3,124 | 2,979 | 2,831 | -0.6 | 2.55 | 2,181 | 1,994 | -1.1 | 31,317 | 35,961 | 1859 | 55 |
| TREGO | 1,464 | 1,267 | 1,186 | -1.7 | 2.47 | 1,048 | 874 | -2.2 | 28,767 | 32,697 | 2331 | 79 |
| WABAUNSEE | 2,482 | 2,490 | 2,457 | 0.0 | 2.59 | 1,868 | 1,824 | -0.3 | 40,302 | 50,409 | 646 | 13 |
| WALLACE | 677 | 667 | 660 | -0.2 | 2.65 | 486 | 461 | -0.6 | 24,659 | 31,719 | 2844 | 102 |
| WASHINGTON | 2,862 | 2,565 | 2,432 | -1.3 | 2.44 | 1,976 | 1,701 | -1.8 | 28,973 | 33,523 | 2302 | 77 |
| WICHITA | 996 | 934 | 910 | -0.8 | 2.66 | 756 | 689 | -1.1 | 30,294 | 31,759 | 2083 | 67 |
| WILSON | 4,194 | 4,123 | 4,125 | -0.2 | 2.47 | 2,912 | 2,756 | -0.7 | 27,149 | 31,466 | 2557 | 93 |
| WOODSON | 1,699 | 1,630 | 1,576 | -0.5 | 2.29 | 1,145 | 1,047 | -1.1 | 23,825 | 27,083 | 2916 | 103 |
| WYANDOTTE | 61,514 | 57,185 | 55,665 | -0.9 | 2.60 | 41,991 | 37,793 | -1.3 | 30,778 | 35,847 | 1975 | 61 |
| KANSAS | | | | 0.9 | 2.55 | | | 0.5 | 39,174 | 46,093 | | |
| UNITED STATES | | | | 1.4 | 2.59 | | | 1.1 | 41,914 | 49,127 | | |

 

| COUNTY | 2000 Per Capita Income | 2000 HH Income Base | 2000 HOUSEHOLD INCOME DISTRIBUTION (%) Less than $15,000 | $15,000 to $24,999 | $25,000 to $49,999 | $50,000 to $99,999 | $100,000 to $149,999 | $150,000 or More | 2000 AVERAGE DISPOSABLE INCOME BY AGE OF HOUSEHOLDER All Ages | <35 | 35-44 | 45-54 | 55-64 | 65+ |
|---|---|---|---|---|---|---|---|---|---|---|---|---|---|---|
| RENO | 17,501 | 24,593 | 15.4 | 16.4 | 39.5 | 23.9 | 3.8 | 1.0 | 32,796 | 27,390 | 38,008 | 42,087 | 37,312 | 22,403 |
| REPUBLIC | 19,287 | 2,564 | 18.2 | 18.8 | 38.7 | 19.1 | 3.9 | 1.3 | 30,329 | 26,670 | 32,037 | 42,503 | 36,172 | 23,081 |
| RICE | 13,307 | 3,992 | 24.7 | 19.2 | 38.7 | 15.9 | 1.3 | 0.2 | 25,737 | 22,840 | 30,355 | 31,591 | 30,749 | 18,748 |
| RILEY | 14,197 | 19,887 | 20.9 | 19.6 | 33.0 | 22.1 | 3.5 | 0.9 | 30,509 | 21,932 | 38,561 | 48,126 | 41,613 | 28,442 |
| ROOKS | 15,978 | 2,242 | 18.5 | 19.9 | 39.6 | 18.1 | 3.0 | 1.0 | 29,201 | 26,981 | 36,527 | 33,647 | 32,699 | 21,507 |
| RUSH | 15,386 | 1,428 | 21.2 | 18.4 | 38.2 | 19.3 | 2.9 | 0.1 | 28,232 | 30,577 | 31,867 | 40,194 | 33,122 | 18,500 |
| RUSSELL | 15,448 | 3,201 | 24.8 | 19.8 | 38.6 | 12.3 | 3.1 | 1.4 | 27,541 | 23,824 | 33,103 | 36,525 | 33,373 | 18,702 |
| SALINE | 19,176 | 20,635 | 15.2 | 15.5 | 37.9 | 25.6 | 4.3 | 1.6 | 34,518 | 27,411 | 40,331 | 42,820 | 40,883 | 24,498 |
| SCOTT | 14,865 | 1,897 | 16.1 | 18.6 | 42.9 | 20.3 | 1.4 | 0.8 | 29,645 | 26,613 | 37,140 | 34,924 | 28,518 | 16,674 |
| SEDGWICK | 20,614 | 179,042 | 13.8 | 13.3 | 35.6 | 29.7 | 5.6 | 2.0 | 37,496 | 30,754 | 41,508 | 46,435 | 42,909 | 26,983 |
| SEWARD | 17,481 | 7,147 | 9.9 | 15.6 | 36.7 | 30.4 | 6.1 | 1.3 | 37,457 | 32,682 | 44,721 | 46,591 | 43,253 | 23,736 |
| SHAWNEE | 20,933 | 65,537 | 10.8 | 12.1 | 34.8 | 33.2 | 7.1 | 2.2 | 40,119 | 31,929 | 44,793 | 50,958 | 44,396 | 29,347 |
| SHERIDAN | 15,574 | 1,040 | 16.4 | 19.9 | 35.8 | 23.9 | 3.9 | 0.2 | 30,909 | 30,707 | 34,034 | 38,791 | 31,578 | 22,738 |
| SHERMAN | 14,906 | 2,516 | 20.1 | 19.8 | 37.8 | 19.0 | 2.5 | 0.9 | 29,203 | 22,209 | 33,728 | 34,963 | 37,581 | 22,149 |
| SMITH | 14,449 | 1,912 | 20.7 | 21.0 | 38.7 | 18.5 | 1.3 | 0.0 | 27,014 | 25,988 | 32,308 | 32,025 | 32,126 | 20,882 |
| STAFFORD | 14,583 | 2,014 | 23.1 | 21.2 | 37.2 | 16.1 | 1.7 | 0.6 | 26,621 | 25,202 | 34,594 | 29,589 | 31,092 | 19,267 |
| STANTON | 14,415 | 794 | 17.6 | 19.4 | 40.4 | 18.6 | 2.5 | 1.4 | 30,156 | 23,299 | 34,180 | 35,751 | 32,450 | 25,816 |
| STEVENS | 17,489 | 2,026 | 13.0 | 11.4 | 38.6 | 30.8 | 5.9 | 0.3 | 35,766 | 31,583 | 42,877 | 43,510 | 35,769 | 26,840 |
| SUMNER | 17,336 | 10,268 | 14.3 | 14.7 | 39.8 | 26.1 | 3.9 | 1.3 | 33,893 | 32,520 | 40,670 | 39,194 | 38,993 | 22,255 |
| THOMAS | 14,857 | 2,979 | 17.4 | 20.8 | 37.3 | 20.5 | 3.0 | 1.0 | 30,021 | 27,185 | 32,947 | 36,062 | 33,236 | 22,909 |
| TREGO | 14,175 | 1,267 | 22.2 | 20.0 | 37.8 | 16.8 | 3.1 | 0.2 | 27,695 | 29,746 | 34,577 | 31,216 | 29,547 | 20,614 |
| WABAUNSEE | 17,140 | 2,490 | 13.2 | 11.0 | 41.2 | 30.8 | 3.6 | 0.2 | 34,375 | 34,420 | 37,239 | 42,946 | 35,636 | 25,663 |
| WALLACE | 10,980 | 667 | 25.3 | 25.3 | 35.1 | 13.2 | 1.1 | 0.0 | 23,666 | 20,306 | 25,748 | 29,055 | 24,066 | 20,833 |
| WASHINGTON | 14,492 | 2,565 | 21.4 | 19.9 | 37.9 | 17.4 | 2.7 | 0.7 | 28,011 | 27,525 | 33,569 | 30,895 | 35,935 | 21,696 |
| WICHITA | 13,300 | 934 | 14.0 | 25.4 | 38.2 | 19.9 | 2.5 | 0.0 | 28,287 | 25,037 | 32,822 | 29,375 | 28,954 | 25,993 |
| WILSON | 13,472 | 4,123 | 25.7 | 21.1 | 33.9 | 16.1 | 2.9 | 0.3 | 26,355 | 26,142 | 31,709 | 33,845 | 25,869 | 19,008 |
| WOODSON | 13,971 | 1,630 | 27.1 | 25.3 | 32.6 | 12.3 | 1.9 | 0.9 | 24,727 | 26,838 | 31,595 | 28,048 | 32,093 | 15,601 |
| WYANDOTTE | 13,666 | 57,167 | 22.2 | 17.6 | 37.6 | 20.5 | 2.0 | 0.2 | 28,008 | 25,037 | 31,738 | 35,535 | 31,457 | 18,536 |
| KANSAS | 20,105 | | 14.5 | 14.0 | 35.0 | 28.1 | 5.9 | 2.4 | 37,751 | 30,612 | 43,142 | 47,811 | 41,695 | 25,693 |
| UNITED STATES | 22,162 | | 14.5 | 12.5 | 32.3 | 29.8 | 7.4 | 3.5 | 40,748 | 34,503 | 44,969 | 49,579 | 43,409 | 27,339 |

# SPENDING POTENTIAL INDEXES

| COUNTY | FINANCIAL SERVICES | | | | THE HOME | | | | | | ENTERTAINMENT | | | | | | PERSONAL | | | |
|---|---|---|---|---|---|---|---|---|---|---|---|---|---|---|---|---|---|---|---|---|
| | | | | | Home Improvements | | | Furnishings | | | | | | | | | | | | |
| | Auto Loan | Home Loan | Investments | Retirement Plans | Home Repair | Lawn & Garden | Remodeling | Appliances | Electronics | Furniture | Restaurants | Sporting Goods | Theater & Concerts | Toys & Hobbies | Travel | Video Rental | Apparel | Auto Aftermarket | Health Insurance | Pets & Supplies |
| RENO | 97 | 89 | 94 | 92 | 100 | 97 | 103 | 97 | 95 | 92 | 94 | 95 | 96 | 98 | 93 | 100 | 91 | 96 | 101 | 98 |
| REPUBLIC | 96 | 64 | 70 | 78 | 90 | 89 | 109 | 95 | 90 | 72 | 78 | 93 | 79 | 94 | 75 | 100 | 77 | 89 | 105 | 96 |
| RICE | 94 | 64 | 71 | 76 | 91 | 89 | 107 | 94 | 91 | 74 | 78 | 89 | 79 | 91 | 76 | 100 | 77 | 88 | 104 | 93 |
| RILEY | 93 | 96 | 88 | 90 | 93 | 89 | 94 | 90 | 92 | 85 | 92 | 90 | 89 | 92 | 88 | 97 | 87 | 94 | 94 | 96 |
| ROOKS | 95 | 65 | 71 | 77 | 90 | 89 | 107 | 94 | 91 | 74 | 78 | 91 | 80 | 92 | 76 | 100 | 77 | 89 | 104 | 94 |
| RUSH | 96 | 64 | 70 | 77 | 90 | 89 | 108 | 94 | 90 | 73 | 78 | 92 | 79 | 93 | 75 | 100 | 77 | 88 | 105 | 95 |
| RUSSELL | 95 | 67 | 74 | 77 | 91 | 90 | 108 | 94 | 92 | 76 | 80 | 89 | 81 | 92 | 77 | 100 | 78 | 89 | 103 | 94 |
| SALINE | 96 | 92 | 96 | 92 | 99 | 97 | 100 | 96 | 94 | 93 | 95 | 94 | 96 | 97 | 93 | 100 | 91 | 96 | 100 | 97 |
| SCOTT | 97 | 75 | 82 | 86 | 93 | 93 | 108 | 96 | 95 | 81 | 85 | 94 | 88 | 96 | 82 | 101 | 84 | 93 | 104 | 97 |
| SEDGWICK | 98 | 98 | 94 | 95 | 99 | 98 | 98 | 98 | 97 | 98 | 101 | 97 | 100 | 99 | 96 | 101 | 96 | 100 | 98 | 99 |
| SEWARD | 97 | 97 | 90 | 93 | 96 | 95 | 98 | 97 | 98 | 96 | 100 | 97 | 98 | 99 | 93 | 102 | 94 | 100 | 98 | 100 |
| SHAWNEE | 98 | 100 | 99 | 98 | 102 | 100 | 99 | 98 | 97 | 100 | 101 | 98 | 102 | 100 | 99 | 101 | 97 | 101 | 99 | 100 |
| SHERIDAN | 97 | 64 | 70 | 79 | 90 | 89 | 109 | 95 | 90 | 72 | 78 | 94 | 79 | 94 | 75 | 100 | 77 | 89 | 106 | 96 |
| SHERMAN | 95 | 66 | 73 | 77 | 91 | 89 | 107 | 94 | 91 | 76 | 80 | 90 | 81 | 92 | 77 | 100 | 78 | 89 | 103 | 94 |
| SMITH | 95 | 64 | 70 | 77 | 90 | 89 | 107 | 94 | 91 | 73 | 78 | 90 | 79 | 92 | 76 | 100 | 77 | 88 | 104 | 94 |
| STAFFORD | 95 | 64 | 70 | 77 | 90 | 89 | 108 | 94 | 90 | 73 | 78 | 91 | 79 | 92 | 76 | 100 | 77 | 88 | 105 | 94 |
| STANTON | 98 | 75 | 77 | 82 | 90 | 89 | 112 | 96 | 92 | 82 | 87 | 97 | 86 | 98 | 78 | 100 | 83 | 92 | 102 | 99 |
| STEVENS | 98 | 77 | 79 | 83 | 92 | 90 | 111 | 97 | 94 | 84 | 88 | 95 | 88 | 97 | 81 | 101 | 85 | 93 | 102 | 99 |
| SUMNER | 98 | 74 | 79 | 83 | 93 | 91 | 112 | 97 | 94 | 82 | 86 | 95 | 87 | 98 | 80 | 101 | 84 | 92 | 103 | 99 |
| THOMAS | 96 | 81 | 82 | 84 | 93 | 91 | 103 | 95 | 93 | 85 | 89 | 93 | 90 | 96 | 84 | 100 | 86 | 93 | 101 | 97 |
| TREGO | 96 | 64 | 71 | 78 | 90 | 89 | 108 | 94 | 91 | 73 | 78 | 92 | 80 | 93 | 76 | 100 | 77 | 89 | 105 | 95 |
| WABAUNSEE | 98 | 74 | 79 | 83 | 93 | 91 | 114 | 97 | 94 | 82 | 85 | 95 | 87 | 97 | 80 | 102 | 84 | 92 | 103 | 99 |
| WALLACE | 96 | 65 | 72 | 78 | 90 | 90 | 109 | 94 | 91 | 74 | 79 | 92 | 80 | 93 | 76 | 100 | 78 | 89 | 105 | 95 |
| WASHINGTON | 96 | 66 | 74 | 79 | 91 | 90 | 107 | 95 | 91 | 74 | 79 | 92 | 81 | 93 | 77 | 100 | 78 | 89 | 105 | 95 |
| WICHITA | 98 | 63 | 69 | 80 | 89 | 89 | 111 | 95 | 89 | 70 | 78 | 97 | 80 | 96 | 75 | 100 | 78 | 89 | 107 | 97 |
| WILSON | 96 | 65 | 74 | 78 | 91 | 90 | 109 | 95 | 91 | 74 | 79 | 92 | 81 | 93 | 77 | 100 | 77 | 89 | 104 | 95 |
| WOODSON | 96 | 66 | 81 | 79 | 93 | 92 | 107 | 95 | 90 | 74 | 80 | 92 | 82 | 94 | 79 | 99 | 77 | 89 | 106 | 96 |
| WYANDOTTE | 93 | 88 | 90 | 85 | 99 | 93 | 92 | 94 | 90 | 92 | 90 | 90 | 93 | 93 | 92 | 99 | 88 | 94 | 95 | 94 |
| KANSAS | 98 | 93 | 93 | 95 | 98 | 97 | 102 | 97 | 97 | 94 | 97 | 97 | 98 | 99 | 93 | 101 | 93 | 98 | 100 | 99 |
| UNITED STATES | 100 | 100 | 100 | 100 | 100 | 100 | 100 | 100 | 100 | 100 | 100 | 100 | 100 | 100 | 100 | 100 | 100 | 100 | 100 | 100 |

| COUNTY | FIPS Code | MSA Code | DMA Code | POPULATION 1990 | POPULATION 2000 | POPULATION 2005 | 1990-2000 ANNUAL CHANGE % Rate | 1990-2000 ANNUAL CHANGE State Rank | RACE (%) White 1990 | White 2000 | Black 1990 | Black 2000 | Asian/Pacific 1990 | Asian/Pacific 2000 |
|---|---|---|---|---|---|---|---|---|---|---|---|---|---|---|
| ADAIR | 001 | 0000 | 736 | 15,360 | 16,477 | 16,592 | 0.7 | 65 | 96.7 | 96.5 | 3.0 | 3.1 | 0.2 | 0.2 |
| ALLEN | 003 | 0000 | 659 | 14,628 | 17,169 | 18,716 | 1.6 | 20 | 98.7 | 98.7 | 1.1 | 1.1 | 0.0 | 0.0 |
| ANDERSON | 005 | 0000 | 541 | 14,571 | 19,151 | 20,933 | 2.7 | 8 | 96.7 | 96.4 | 3.0 | 3.1 | 0.1 | 0.2 |
| BALLARD | 007 | 0000 | 632 | 7,902 | 8,586 | 8,921 | 0.8 | 55 | 96.7 | 96.5 | 3.0 | 3.2 | 0.1 | 0.1 |
| BARREN | 009 | 0000 | 736 | 34,001 | 37,730 | 39,619 | 1.0 | 42 | 94.7 | 94.5 | 4.9 | 5.0 | 0.2 | 0.3 |
| BATH | 011 | 0000 | 541 | 9,692 | 10,931 | 11,828 | 1.2 | 36 | 96.9 | 96.8 | 2.9 | 3.0 | 0.1 | 0.1 |
| BELL | 013 | 0000 | 557 | 31,506 | 28,754 | 27,406 | -0.9 | 119 | 97.0 | 96.8 | 2.6 | 2.7 | 0.3 | 0.4 |
| BOONE | 015 | 1640 | 515 | 57,589 | 86,886 | 104,327 | 4.1 | 2 | 98.5 | 98.1 | 0.6 | 0.7 | 0.6 | 0.9 |
| BOURBON | 017 | 4280 | 541 | 19,236 | 19,406 | 19,580 | 0.1 | 97 | 91.0 | 90.8 | 8.6 | 8.8 | 0.1 | 0.1 |
| BOYD | 019 | 3400 | 564 | 51,150 | 48,387 | 46,179 | -0.5 | 115 | 97.5 | 97.2 | 2.0 | 2.2 | 0.3 | 0.4 |
| BOYLE | 021 | 0000 | 541 | 25,641 | 27,556 | 28,555 | 0.7 | 65 | 90.0 | 89.7 | 9.5 | 9.7 | 0.3 | 0.4 |
| BRACKEN | 023 | 0000 | 515 | 7,766 | 8,549 | 8,897 | 0.9 | 47 | 99.3 | 99.3 | 0.6 | 0.6 | 0.0 | 0.0 |
| BREATHITT | 025 | 0000 | 541 | 15,703 | 15,846 | 16,190 | 0.1 | 97 | 99.6 | 99.5 | 0.2 | 0.2 | 0.1 | 0.2 |
| BRECKINRIDGE | 027 | 0000 | 529 | 16,312 | 17,999 | 19,298 | 1.0 | 42 | 96.1 | 95.9 | 3.6 | 3.7 | 0.1 | 0.2 |
| BULLITT | 029 | 4520 | 529 | 47,567 | 62,325 | 69,333 | 2.7 | 8 | 99.1 | 99.0 | 0.4 | 0.5 | 0.2 | 0.3 |
| BUTLER | 031 | 0000 | 736 | 11,245 | 12,131 | 12,673 | 0.7 | 65 | 99.2 | 99.1 | 0.5 | 0.5 | 0.1 | 0.2 |
| CALDWELL | 033 | 0000 | 632 | 13,232 | 13,402 | 13,565 | 0.1 | 97 | 93.8 | 93.9 | 5.8 | 5.8 | 0.1 | 0.1 |
| CALLOWAY | 035 | 0000 | 632 | 30,735 | 33,434 | 34,049 | 0.8 | 55 | 96.2 | 95.8 | 3.1 | 3.2 | 0.4 | 0.7 |
| CAMPBELL | 037 | 1640 | 515 | 83,866 | 87,339 | 87,344 | 0.4 | 81 | 98.5 | 98.3 | 1.0 | 1.1 | 0.3 | 0.4 |
| CARLISLE | 039 | 0000 | 632 | 5,238 | 5,408 | 5,522 | 0.3 | 87 | 98.6 | 98.4 | 1.1 | 1.1 | 0.1 | 0.1 |
| CARROLL | 041 | 0000 | 529 | 9,292 | 9,885 | 10,387 | 0.6 | 72 | 97.5 | 97.2 | 2.1 | 2.3 | 0.2 | 0.3 |
| CARTER | 043 | 3400 | 564 | 24,340 | 27,372 | 28,701 | 1.2 | 36 | 99.7 | 99.7 | 0.1 | 0.1 | 0.1 | 0.1 |
| CASEY | 045 | 0000 | 541 | 14,211 | 15,044 | 15,723 | 0.6 | 72 | 99.3 | 99.1 | 0.3 | 0.3 | 0.1 | 0.2 |
| CHRISTIAN | 047 | 1660 | 659 | 68,941 | 71,640 | 70,078 | 0.4 | 81 | 71.7 | 70.6 | 24.6 | 24.4 | 1.3 | 1.8 |
| CLARK | 049 | 4280 | 541 | 29,496 | 32,828 | 34,782 | 1.0 | 42 | 94.0 | 93.7 | 5.5 | 5.8 | 0.1 | 0.2 |
| CLAY | 051 | 0000 | 541 | 21,746 | 22,833 | 23,122 | 0.5 | 77 | 98.1 | 97.9 | 1.5 | 1.7 | 0.1 | 0.2 |
| CLINTON | 053 | 0000 | 659 | 9,135 | 9,545 | 9,948 | 0.4 | 81 | 99.8 | 99.7 | 0.1 | 0.2 | 0.1 | 0.2 |
| CRITTENDEN | 055 | 0000 | 632 | 9,196 | 9,583 | 9,724 | 0.4 | 81 | 98.9 | 98.8 | 0.8 | 0.9 | 0.1 | 0.1 |
| CUMBERLAND | 057 | 0000 | 736 | 6,784 | 6,884 | 6,921 | 0.1 | 97 | 95.2 | 95.1 | 4.5 | 4.7 | 0.1 | 0.0 |
| DAVIESS | 059 | 5990 | 649 | 87,189 | 91,353 | 92,296 | 0.5 | 77 | 95.4 | 95.1 | 4.2 | 4.3 | 0.3 | 0.4 |
| EDMONSON | 061 | 0000 | 736 | 10,357 | 11,807 | 12,869 | 1.3 | 31 | 98.1 | 98.3 | 1.6 | 1.5 | 0.1 | 0.1 |
| ELLIOTT | 063 | 0000 | 564 | 6,455 | 6,513 | 6,411 | 0.1 | 97 | 99.9 | 99.9 | 0.0 | 0.0 | 0.0 | 0.0 |
| ESTILL | 065 | 0000 | 541 | 14,614 | 15,508 | 15,516 | 0.6 | 72 | 99.9 | 99.8 | 0.1 | 0.1 | 0.0 | 0.0 |
| FAYETTE | 067 | 4280 | 541 | 225,366 | 245,587 | 254,635 | 0.8 | 55 | 84.5 | 83.2 | 13.4 | 13.9 | 1.6 | 2.4 |
| FLEMING | 069 | 0000 | 541 | 12,292 | 13,757 | 14,536 | 1.1 | 40 | 98.1 | 98.1 | 1.8 | 1.8 | 0.1 | 0.1 |
| FLOYD | 071 | 0000 | 564 | 43,586 | 43,187 | 42,796 | -0.1 | 109 | 99.0 | 98.7 | 0.7 | 0.9 | 0.2 | 0.3 |
| FRANKLIN | 073 | 0000 | 541 | 43,781 | 46,746 | 47,550 | 0.6 | 72 | 91.7 | 90.6 | 7.5 | 8.4 | 0.5 | 0.8 |
| FULTON | 075 | 0000 | 632 | 8,271 | 7,384 | 7,057 | -1.1 | 120 | 81.0 | 80.0 | 18.6 | 19.5 | 0.2 | 0.3 |
| GALLATIN | 077 | 1640 | 515 | 5,393 | 7,753 | 9,285 | 3.6 | 3 | 97.9 | 97.7 | 1.7 | 1.8 | 0.1 | 0.2 |
| GARRARD | 079 | 0000 | 541 | 11,579 | 14,708 | 16,563 | 2.4 | 10 | 95.9 | 95.8 | 3.9 | 3.9 | 0.1 | 0.1 |
| GRANT | 081 | 1640 | 515 | 15,737 | 21,295 | 23,796 | 3.0 | 6 | 99.6 | 99.4 | 0.2 | 0.2 | 0.1 | 0.2 |
| GRAVES | 083 | 0000 | 632 | 33,550 | 36,626 | 37,976 | 0.9 | 47 | 95.2 | 95.0 | 4.5 | 4.7 | 0.1 | 0.2 |
| GRAYSON | 085 | 0000 | 529 | 21,050 | 24,092 | 25,351 | 1.3 | 31 | 99.3 | 99.2 | 0.3 | 0.4 | 0.2 | 0.2 |
| GREEN | 087 | 0000 | 529 | 10,371 | 10,615 | 10,731 | 0.2 | 95 | 96.3 | 96.1 | 3.4 | 3.5 | 0.1 | 0.2 |
| GREENUP | 089 | 3400 | 564 | 36,742 | 36,576 | 35,805 | 0.0 | 105 | 99.1 | 98.9 | 0.4 | 0.4 | 0.3 | 0.4 |
| HANCOCK | 091 | 0000 | 649 | 7,864 | 9,049 | 9,425 | 1.4 | 28 | 98.3 | 98.0 | 1.2 | 1.3 | 0.2 | 0.4 |
| HARDIN | 093 | 0000 | 529 | 89,240 | 92,404 | 96,222 | 0.3 | 87 | 85.1 | 84.7 | 11.1 | 10.3 | 2.1 | 3.1 |
| HARLAN | 095 | 0000 | 557 | 36,574 | 33,834 | 31,723 | -0.8 | 117 | 96.4 | 96.2 | 3.3 | 3.5 | 0.1 | 0.2 |
| HARRISON | 097 | 0000 | 541 | 16,248 | 17,836 | 18,692 | 0.9 | 47 | 96.7 | 96.4 | 2.9 | 3.1 | 0.1 | 0.2 |
| HART | 099 | 0000 | 736 | 14,890 | 17,033 | 17,881 | 1.3 | 31 | 92.6 | 92.0 | 7.2 | 7.6 | 0.1 | 0.1 |
| HENDERSON | 101 | 2440 | 649 | 43,044 | 44,408 | 44,399 | 0.3 | 87 | 92.4 | 92.0 | 7.1 | 7.3 | 0.3 | 0.4 |
| HENRY | 103 | 0000 | 529 | 12,823 | 15,229 | 16,261 | 1.7 | 19 | 95.6 | 95.3 | 4.2 | 4.4 | 0.1 | 0.1 |
| HICKMAN | 105 | 0000 | 632 | 5,566 | 5,101 | 4,881 | -0.8 | 117 | 90.7 | 90.3 | 9.0 | 9.4 | 0.0 | 0.0 |
| HOPKINS | 107 | 0000 | 649 | 46,126 | 46,064 | 45,610 | 0.0 | 105 | 92.9 | 92.4 | 6.6 | 6.9 | 0.3 | 0.4 |
| JACKSON | 109 | 0000 | 541 | 11,955 | 13,143 | 13,662 | 0.9 | 47 | 99.8 | 99.8 | 0.0 | 0.0 | 0.0 | 0.0 |
| JEFFERSON | 111 | 4520 | 529 | 664,937 | 673,747 | 677,741 | 0.1 | 97 | 81.9 | 80.9 | 17.1 | 17.6 | 0.7 | 1.1 |
| JESSAMINE | 113 | 4280 | 541 | 30,508 | 37,990 | 41,445 | 2.2 | 13 | 96.0 | 95.6 | 3.2 | 3.4 | 0.4 | 0.6 |
| JOHNSON | 115 | 0000 | 564 | 23,248 | 24,003 | 24,021 | 0.3 | 87 | 99.4 | 99.3 | 0.1 | 0.1 | 0.3 | 0.5 |
| KENTON | 117 | 1640 | 515 | 142,031 | 147,864 | 150,849 | 0.4 | 81 | 96.4 | 96.0 | 2.9 | 3.0 | 0.4 | 0.7 |
| KNOTT | 119 | 0000 | 541 | 17,906 | 17,881 | 17,633 | 0.0 | 105 | 99.2 | 99.1 | 0.6 | 0.7 | 0.1 | 0.1 |
| KNOX | 121 | 0000 | 541 | 29,676 | 32,146 | 33,032 | 0.8 | 55 | 98.6 | 98.5 | 1.0 | 1.0 | 0.1 | 0.1 |
| LARUE | 123 | 0000 | 529 | 11,679 | 13,272 | 13,894 | 1.3 | 31 | 95.5 | 95.3 | 4.2 | 4.4 | 0.1 | 0.1 |
| LAUREL | 125 | 0000 | 541 | 43,438 | 53,031 | 58,104 | 2.0 | 15 | 98.9 | 98.9 | 0.6 | 0.6 | 0.2 | 0.3 |
| LAWRENCE | 127 | 0000 | 564 | 13,998 | 15,953 | 16,748 | 1.3 | 31 | 99.5 | 99.4 | 0.2 | 0.1 | 0.2 | 0.3 |
| LEE | 129 | 0000 | 541 | 7,422 | 8,015 | 8,094 | 0.8 | 55 | 99.6 | 97.4 | 0.4 | 2.4 | 0.0 | 0.0 |
| LESLIE | 131 | 0000 | 531 | 13,642 | 13,571 | 13,609 | -0.1 | 109 | 99.8 | 99.8 | 0.1 | 0.1 | 0.1 | 0.1 |
| LETCHER | 133 | 0000 | 531 | 27,000 | 25,889 | 25,009 | -0.4 | 113 | 99.0 | 98.9 | 0.7 | 0.8 | 0.1 | 0.2 |
| LEWIS | 135 | 0000 | 564 | 13,029 | 13,464 | 13,432 | 0.3 | 87 | 99.6 | 99.5 | 0.2 | 0.2 | 0.0 | 0.0 |
| LINCOLN | 137 | 0000 | 541 | 20,045 | 22,751 | 23,828 | 1.2 | 36 | 96.5 | 96.3 | 3.1 | 3.2 | 0.1 | 0.1 |
| LIVINGSTON | 139 | 0000 | 632 | 9,062 | 9,565 | 9,916 | 0.5 | 77 | 99.6 | 99.5 | 0.2 | 0.1 | 0.1 | 0.1 |
| LOGAN | 141 | 0000 | 659 | 24,416 | 26,398 | 27,008 | 0.8 | 55 | 91.1 | 90.5 | 8.5 | 9.0 | 0.1 | 0.2 |
| LYON | 143 | 0000 | 632 | 6,624 | 8,111 | 8,397 | 2.0 | 15 | 92.9 | 92.5 | 6.5 | 6.8 | 0.2 | 0.3 |
| MCCRACKEN | 145 | 0000 | 632 | 62,879 | 64,567 | 64,283 | 0.3 | 87 | 89.4 | 88.9 | 10.1 | 10.4 | 0.3 | 0.4 |
| MCCREARY | 147 | 0000 | 557 | 15,603 | 16,841 | 17,277 | 0.7 | 65 | 98.8 | 99.2 | 0.8 | 0.4 | 0.0 | 0.0 |
| MCLEAN | 149 | 0000 | 649 | 9,628 | 9,956 | 10,250 | 0.3 | 87 | 99.4 | 99.4 | 0.5 | 0.5 | 0.0 | 0.0 |
| MADISON | 151 | 4280 | 541 | 57,508 | 69,002 | 74,846 | 1.8 | 18 | 94.1 | 93.7 | 5.1 | 5.2 | 0.6 | 0.8 |
| MAGOFFIN | 153 | 0000 | 564 | 13,077 | 14,166 | 14,775 | 0.8 | 55 | 99.8 | 99.8 | 0.0 | 0.0 | 0.0 | 0.1 |
| KENTUCKY | | | | | | | 0.8 | | 92.0 | 91.8 | 7.1 | 7.2 | 0.5 | 0.7 |
| UNITED STATES | | | | | | | 1.0 | | 80.3 | 77.9 | 12.1 | 12.4 | 2.9 | 3.9 |

# POPULATION COMPOSITION

| COUNTY | % HISPANIC ORIGIN 1990 | % HISPANIC ORIGIN 2000 | 2000 AGE DISTRIBUTION (%) 0-4 | 5-9 | 10-14 | 15-19 | 20-24 | 25-44 | 45-64 | 65-84 | 85+ | 18+ | MEDIAN AGE 1990 | MEDIAN AGE 2000 | 2000 Males/ Females (×100) |
|---|---|---|---|---|---|---|---|---|---|---|---|---|---|---|---|
| ADAIR | 0.6 | 1.3 | 5.6 | 5.9 | 6.1 | 7.4 | 6.9 | 27.8 | 25.3 | 13.0 | 1.9 | 78.3 | 34.9 | 38.4 | 95.4 |
| ALLEN | 0.2 | 0.7 | 6.8 | 6.8 | 6.9 | 7.1 | 6.3 | 26.6 | 25.4 | 12.5 | 1.6 | 75.0 | 35.4 | 38.0 | 94.9 |
| ANDERSON | 0.5 | 1.0 | 6.6 | 6.6 | 7.0 | 6.9 | 6.3 | 30.7 | 24.8 | 9.7 | 1.4 | 75.5 | 33.6 | 36.9 | 96.0 |
| BALLARD | 0.5 | 1.2 | 5.3 | 5.5 | 6.2 | 6.6 | 6.2 | 27.3 | 27.1 | 13.6 | 2.3 | 79.0 | 37.8 | 40.8 | 96.9 |
| BARREN | 0.3 | 0.8 | 6.2 | 6.4 | 6.6 | 6.9 | 5.8 | 27.7 | 25.1 | 13.1 | 2.0 | 76.5 | 35.6 | 39.0 | 91.3 |
| BATH | 0.3 | 0.8 | 6.1 | 6.4 | 6.8 | 6.9 | 5.8 | 28.5 | 25.0 | 12.5 | 2.0 | 76.3 | 35.0 | 38.4 | 94.9 |
| BELL | 0.2 | 0.7 | 6.3 | 6.4 | 6.6 | 7.1 | 6.8 | 29.6 | 24.3 | 11.3 | 1.4 | 76.3 | 33.0 | 36.6 | 93.8 |
| BOONE | 0.6 | 1.2 | 7.5 | 7.7 | 7.8 | 7.6 | 6.6 | 30.6 | 23.2 | 8.0 | 0.9 | 72.4 | 31.4 | 34.4 | 95.6 |
| BOURBON | 0.4 | 1.0 | 6.4 | 6.7 | 7.0 | 6.7 | 6.4 | 28.8 | 25.1 | 11.3 | 1.6 | 75.7 | 34.1 | 37.3 | 94.8 |
| BOYD | 0.9 | 1.5 | 5.3 | 5.6 | 5.9 | 6.8 | 6.7 | 28.5 | 25.7 | 13.7 | 1.7 | 78.9 | 36.5 | 39.8 | 97.7 |
| BOYLE | 0.4 | 1.0 | 5.6 | 6.2 | 6.6 | 7.8 | 6.9 | 27.3 | 25.0 | 12.8 | 1.8 | 77.4 | 34.9 | 38.1 | 96.5 |
| BRACKEN | 0.2 | 0.6 | 6.5 | 6.6 | 6.7 | 6.9 | 6.4 | 28.0 | 23.8 | 13.0 | 2.0 | 75.9 | 34.8 | 37.8 | 92.8 |
| BREATHITT | 0.2 | 0.6 | 6.4 | 6.6 | 7.4 | 8.3 | 7.4 | 29.2 | 24.0 | 9.4 | 1.2 | 74.8 | 31.6 | 35.3 | 98.2 |
| BRECKINRIDGE | 0.3 | 0.8 | 6.2 | 6.5 | 6.7 | 7.3 | 6.3 | 26.5 | 25.9 | 13.0 | 1.6 | 76.1 | 35.4 | 38.7 | 98.7 |
| BULLITT | 0.3 | 0.9 | 6.8 | 7.0 | 7.2 | 7.8 | 6.8 | 32.2 | 24.7 | 7.0 | 0.6 | 74.2 | 30.9 | 34.9 | 99.3 |
| BUTLER | 0.3 | 0.9 | 6.4 | 6.5 | 6.8 | 7.7 | 6.5 | 27.4 | 25.1 | 11.9 | 1.8 | 75.6 | 34.4 | 37.7 | 96.5 |
| CALDWELL | 0.2 | 0.7 | 5.8 | 6.1 | 6.4 | 6.7 | 5.5 | 26.0 | 25.6 | 15.4 | 2.5 | 77.5 | 38.0 | 40.6 | 89.7 |
| CALLOWAY | 0.5 | 1.1 | 5.1 | 5.0 | 5.2 | 9.9 | 12.5 | 25.3 | 22.6 | 12.6 | 1.9 | 81.6 | 32.7 | 35.5 | 93.3 |
| CAMPBELL | 0.4 | 0.9 | 7.3 | 7.3 | 7.4 | 7.2 | 6.7 | 30.0 | 21.6 | 11.1 | 1.4 | 74.0 | 32.4 | 35.4 | 93.5 |
| CARLISLE | 0.4 | 1.0 | 5.7 | 6.0 | 6.2 | 7.0 | 6.1 | 25.6 | 26.5 | 14.6 | 2.1 | 77.7 | 37.9 | 40.5 | 94.7 |
| CARROLL | 0.2 | 0.7 | 6.8 | 6.6 | 7.0 | 7.9 | 6.1 | 27.8 | 24.2 | 12.1 | 1.6 | 74.7 | 33.8 | 37.2 | 93.9 |
| CARTER | 0.2 | 0.8 | 6.0 | 6.3 | 6.7 | 8.0 | 7.5 | 28.1 | 25.3 | 10.7 | 1.3 | 76.3 | 33.0 | 36.7 | 96.2 |
| CASEY | 0.3 | 0.9 | 6.2 | 6.3 | 6.8 | 7.1 | 6.2 | 27.2 | 25.3 | 13.0 | 1.8 | 76.0 | 35.1 | 38.3 | 93.1 |
| CHRISTIAN | 3.4 | 5.1 | 8.8 | 7.0 | 5.9 | 7.4 | 13.5 | 30.2 | 17.2 | 8.6 | 1.3 | 75.0 | 27.7 | 28.8 | 111.9 |
| CLARK | 0.3 | 0.9 | 6.2 | 6.4 | 6.8 | 7.0 | 5.9 | 29.2 | 26.2 | 10.9 | 1.4 | 76.3 | 34.2 | 38.0 | 94.8 |
| CLAY | 0.2 | 0.6 | 7.2 | 7.4 | 7.7 | 8.1 | 7.5 | 29.6 | 22.5 | 8.9 | 1.2 | 72.7 | 30.3 | 33.8 | 96.0 |
| CLINTON | 0.4 | 1.0 | 5.9 | 6.0 | 6.4 | 6.6 | 6.1 | 28.6 | 25.9 | 12.8 | 1.8 | 77.5 | 35.5 | 39.3 | 91.9 |
| CRITTENDEN | 0.3 | 0.8 | 6.1 | 6.4 | 6.8 | 7.0 | 5.4 | 26.3 | 25.8 | 13.7 | 2.5 | 76.5 | 36.7 | 39.8 | 95.1 |
| CUMBERLAND | 0.3 | 0.9 | 6.2 | 6.4 | 6.1 | 6.6 | 5.9 | 26.4 | 25.5 | 15.0 | 2.0 | 77.3 | 37.3 | 40.0 | 91.1 |
| DAVIESS | 0.4 | 0.9 | 7.0 | 7.0 | 6.8 | 7.4 | 6.7 | 28.5 | 23.5 | 11.6 | 1.5 | 74.8 | 33.2 | 36.4 | 92.1 |
| EDMONSON | 0.2 | 0.8 | 6.0 | 6.0 | 6.7 | 8.0 | 6.7 | 26.3 | 26.9 | 12.2 | 1.3 | 76.5 | 34.8 | 38.5 | 97.6 |
| ELLIOTT | 0.2 | 0.8 | 7.0 | 7.2 | 7.1 | 7.6 | 7.2 | 28.4 | 24.2 | 9.9 | 1.3 | 73.9 | 32.0 | 35.4 | 94.9 |
| ESTILL | 0.3 | 0.9 | 6.1 | 6.1 | 6.5 | 7.2 | 6.5 | 29.6 | 25.1 | 11.1 | 1.8 | 77.0 | 33.4 | 37.2 | 93.3 |
| FAYETTE | 1.1 | 1.9 | 6.4 | 5.9 | 5.8 | 7.3 | 9.9 | 33.9 | 21.0 | 8.7 | 1.2 | 78.7 | 31.3 | 34.2 | 91.8 |
| FLEMING | 0.5 | 1.1 | 6.1 | 6.3 | 6.5 | 7.1 | 6.4 | 28.3 | 25.0 | 12.3 | 1.9 | 76.6 | 34.7 | 38.2 | 96.3 |
| FLOYD | 0.3 | 0.8 | 6.7 | 6.8 | 7.3 | 7.9 | 7.2 | 29.2 | 23.7 | 10.0 | 1.2 | 74.1 | 32.1 | 35.6 | 95.4 |
| FRANKLIN | 0.4 | 0.9 | 5.7 | 6.0 | 6.3 | 7.0 | 6.6 | 30.2 | 25.5 | 11.2 | 1.4 | 78.0 | 34.5 | 37.7 | 93.2 |
| FULTON | 0.3 | 0.7 | 6.2 | 6.4 | 6.6 | 7.4 | 6.5 | 26.1 | 23.1 | 14.8 | 3.0 | 76.4 | 36.9 | 38.8 | 88.6 |
| GALLATIN | 0.1 | 0.6 | 7.1 | 7.4 | 7.8 | 6.7 | 6.6 | 28.3 | 24.5 | 10.2 | 1.4 | 73.6 | 32.9 | 35.8 | 95.8 |
| GARRARD | 0.3 | 0.8 | 5.8 | 6.0 | 6.2 | 6.7 | 5.9 | 28.6 | 26.5 | 12.6 | 1.7 | 77.8 | 35.8 | 39.4 | 94.7 |
| GRANT | 0.2 | 0.7 | 7.1 | 7.3 | 7.4 | 7.3 | 6.7 | 29.1 | 24.5 | 9.6 | 1.1 | 73.6 | 32.2 | 35.6 | 97.6 |
| GRAVES | 0.3 | 0.8 | 6.0 | 6.3 | 6.5 | 6.9 | 5.7 | 27.1 | 25.6 | 13.5 | 2.3 | 76.8 | 37.0 | 39.4 | 93.8 |
| GRAYSON | 0.4 | 1.0 | 6.1 | 6.3 | 6.7 | 7.2 | 6.4 | 27.7 | 25.8 | 12.3 | 1.4 | 76.6 | 34.8 | 38.3 | 95.1 |
| GREEN | 0.6 | 1.2 | 5.2 | 5.7 | 6.0 | 6.4 | 5.6 | 27.2 | 26.4 | 15.2 | 2.3 | 79.2 | 37.5 | 41.2 | 95.3 |
| GREENUP | 0.2 | 0.7 | 5.3 | 5.6 | 6.1 | 6.8 | 6.3 | 27.8 | 28.0 | 12.8 | 1.3 | 78.8 | 35.6 | 40.2 | 92.5 |
| HANCOCK | 0.4 | 1.1 | 6.8 | 6.8 | 7.5 | 7.7 | 6.4 | 29.9 | 25.2 | 8.8 | 1.0 | 73.9 | 32.6 | 36.2 | 100.3 |
| HARDIN | 2.8 | 3.7 | 8.4 | 7.5 | 6.9 | 8.0 | 9.5 | 31.4 | 19.5 | 7.8 | 0.9 | 73.4 | 27.8 | 31.0 | 101.6 |
| HARLAN | 0.3 | 0.8 | 6.7 | 6.9 | 7.2 | 7.9 | 6.9 | 28.5 | 23.4 | 11.1 | 1.4 | 74.2 | 32.6 | 36.1 | 94.2 |
| HARRISON | 0.3 | 0.8 | 6.3 | 6.7 | 6.8 | 7.2 | 6.3 | 28.1 | 24.6 | 12.0 | 1.9 | 75.5 | 34.7 | 37.7 | 93.9 |
| HART | 0.4 | 1.1 | 6.2 | 6.5 | 6.7 | 6.9 | 6.4 | 28.0 | 24.9 | 12.9 | 1.5 | 76.1 | 34.9 | 38.0 | 93.8 |
| HENDERSON | 0.4 | 0.9 | 6.6 | 6.8 | 6.9 | 7.4 | 6.2 | 29.5 | 24.2 | 10.9 | 1.5 | 75.2 | 33.5 | 37.1 | 93.4 |
| HENRY | 0.2 | 0.7 | 6.5 | 6.4 | 6.7 | 6.8 | 6.1 | 28.7 | 26.2 | 11.1 | 1.4 | 76.2 | 34.9 | 38.1 | 97.1 |
| HICKMAN | 0.3 | 0.9 | 6.1 | 5.9 | 6.4 | 6.1 | 5.6 | 26.1 | 25.4 | 15.1 | 3.3 | 77.7 | 38.9 | 41.0 | 89.3 |
| HOPKINS | 0.4 | 1.0 | 6.2 | 6.7 | 6.9 | 6.7 | 6.3 | 28.1 | 25.0 | 12.1 | 1.9 | 75.9 | 34.7 | 38.2 | 92.7 |
| JACKSON | 0.3 | 0.8 | 6.9 | 7.0 | 7.4 | 7.9 | 6.9 | 28.8 | 23.4 | 10.2 | 1.5 | 73.9 | 32.5 | 35.5 | 97.7 |
| JEFFERSON | 0.7 | 1.3 | 6.2 | 6.4 | 6.8 | 6.7 | 6.5 | 29.8 | 23.7 | 12.2 | 1.7 | 76.7 | 34.1 | 37.7 | 90.2 |
| JESSAMINE | 0.6 | 1.2 | 6.9 | 6.9 | 7.0 | 7.6 | 8.2 | 31.7 | 22.5 | 8.1 | 1.0 | 74.8 | 30.7 | 34.2 | 96.2 |
| JOHNSON | 0.2 | 0.6 | 5.9 | 6.3 | 6.8 | 7.8 | 7.0 | 29.3 | 25.2 | 10.5 | 1.1 | 76.2 | 33.2 | 37.0 | 95.7 |
| KENTON | 0.5 | 1.1 | 7.6 | 7.2 | 7.2 | 7.0 | 7.2 | 31.0 | 21.9 | 9.7 | 1.3 | 73.8 | 31.8 | 34.7 | 93.7 |
| KNOTT | 0.2 | 0.7 | 6.5 | 7.0 | 7.2 | 8.9 | 8.0 | 29.6 | 22.7 | 9.0 | 1.0 | 74.1 | 30.7 | 34.2 | 96.6 |
| KNOX | 0.3 | 0.8 | 6.9 | 6.9 | 7.3 | 8.2 | 7.5 | 28.2 | 23.7 | 9.9 | 1.5 | 74.2 | 31.9 | 35.1 | 93.8 |
| LARUE | 0.5 | 1.2 | 6.0 | 6.2 | 6.4 | 7.3 | 6.0 | 27.5 | 25.5 | 13.3 | 2.0 | 76.9 | 36.1 | 39.2 | 97.2 |
| LAUREL | 0.4 | 1.0 | 6.5 | 6.7 | 7.0 | 7.6 | 6.9 | 30.0 | 24.3 | 9.8 | 1.3 | 75.2 | 32.5 | 36.2 | 96.0 |
| LAWRENCE | 0.2 | 0.7 | 6.4 | 6.6 | 7.3 | 7.7 | 6.8 | 28.1 | 24.8 | 10.9 | 1.3 | 74.8 | 33.1 | 36.6 | 97.6 |
| LEE | 0.1 | 1.4 | 7.1 | 7.1 | 7.1 | 7.8 | 6.4 | 26.9 | 23.3 | 12.2 | 2.1 | 74.1 | 33.5 | 36.5 | 92.6 |
| LESLIE | 0.3 | 0.9 | 7.3 | 7.2 | 8.0 | 7.6 | 7.6 | 30.1 | 22.7 | 8.6 | 1.0 | 72.8 | 30.4 | 34.0 | 97.8 |
| LETCHER | 0.2 | 0.7 | 6.2 | 6.6 | 7.3 | 7.8 | 7.2 | 29.4 | 24.2 | 10.2 | 1.2 | 75.0 | 32.4 | 36.1 | 94.8 |
| LEWIS | 0.2 | 0.6 | 6.1 | 6.4 | 7.1 | 7.7 | 6.9 | 28.8 | 24.6 | 11.0 | 1.4 | 75.5 | 33.1 | 36.7 | 98.8 |
| LINCOLN | 0.2 | 0.7 | 6.5 | 6.7 | 7.1 | 6.9 | 6.3 | 28.5 | 24.4 | 12.1 | 1.5 | 75.4 | 33.7 | 37.3 | 98.7 |
| LIVINGSTON | 0.3 | 0.9 | 5.2 | 5.6 | 6.0 | 5.8 | 5.7 | 28.5 | 27.6 | 13.7 | 1.7 | 79.7 | 36.9 | 40.8 | 96.5 |
| LOGAN | 0.3 | 0.8 | 6.2 | 6.4 | 6.7 | 7.3 | 6.0 | 27.7 | 25.2 | 12.5 | 1.8 | 76.1 | 34.8 | 38.4 | 94.0 |
| LYON | 0.4 | 1.0 | 3.7 | 3.8 | 4.3 | 4.8 | 6.8 | 32.0 | 26.8 | 15.6 | 2.3 | 85.3 | 38.4 | 41.6 | 126.4 |
| MCCRACKEN | 0.5 | 1.1 | 5.8 | 6.1 | 6.4 | 6.9 | 6.1 | 27.8 | 25.2 | 13.5 | 2.2 | 77.5 | 36.2 | 39.5 | 90.3 |
| MCCREARY | 0.2 | 0.6 | 7.0 | 7.2 | 7.4 | 8.4 | 7.4 | 28.1 | 23.9 | 9.5 | 1.0 | 73.2 | 30.8 | 34.0 | 97.3 |
| MCLEAN | 0.2 | 0.6 | 5.7 | 6.1 | 6.4 | 7.1 | 6.2 | 27.5 | 26.8 | 12.4 | 1.7 | 77.5 | 36.0 | 39.3 | 97.8 |
| MADISON | 0.3 | 0.8 | 5.8 | 5.6 | 5.7 | 9.8 | 13.2 | 28.6 | 21.1 | 9.0 | 1.2 | 79.5 | 28.8 | 32.2 | 91.1 |
| MAGOFFIN | 0.1 | 0.6 | 6.9 | 7.5 | 7.7 | 8.5 | 7.7 | 30.1 | 22.2 | 8.4 | 1.0 | 72.5 | 29.6 | 33.3 | 96.8 |
| KENTUCKY | 0.6 | 1.2 | 6.5 | 6.5 | 6.7 | 7.4 | 7.3 | 29.5 | 23.7 | 10.9 | 1.5 | 76.1 | 33.0 | 36.4 | 94.4 |
| UNITED STATES | 9.0 | 11.8 | 6.9 | 7.2 | 7.2 | 7.2 | 6.7 | 29.9 | 22.2 | 11.1 | 1.6 | 74.6 | 32.9 | 35.7 | 95.6 |

| COUNTY | HOUSEHOLDS | | | | | FAMILIES | | | MEDIAN HOUSEHOLD INCOME | | | |
|---|---|---|---|---|---|---|---|---|---|---|---|---|
| | 1990 | 2000 | 2005 | % Annual Rate 1990-2000 | 2000 Average HH Size | 1990 | 2000 | % Annual Rate 1990-2000 | 2000 | 2005 | 2000 National Rank | 2000 State Rank |
| ADAIR | 5,800 | 6,344 | 6,438 | 1.1 | 2.53 | 4,414 | 4,665 | 0.7 | 25,000 | 28,816 | 2811 | 96 |
| ALLEN | 5,595 | 6,655 | 7,299 | 2.1 | 2.56 | 4,270 | 4,906 | 1.7 | 29,808 | 37,336 | 2182 | 62 |
| ANDERSON | 5,438 | 7,401 | 8,221 | 3.8 | 2.57 | 4,229 | 5,596 | 3.5 | 43,489 | 50,579 | 426 | 6 |
| BALLARD | 3,191 | 3,574 | 3,768 | 1.4 | 2.37 | 2,324 | 2,505 | 0.9 | 29,787 | 32,986 | 2185 | 63 |
| BARREN | 13,136 | 14,820 | 15,684 | 1.5 | 2.50 | 9,901 | 10,835 | 1.1 | 30,635 | 33,642 | 1999 | 57 |
| BATH | 3,659 | 4,212 | 4,604 | 1.7 | 2.56 | 2,791 | 3,103 | 1.3 | 25,505 | 29,835 | 2755 | 90 |
| BELL | 11,512 | 10,675 | 10,258 | -0.9 | 2.65 | 8,796 | 7,921 | -1.3 | 21,549 | 23,612 | 3051 | 110 |
| BOONE | 20,127 | 30,718 | 37,076 | 5.3 | 2.82 | 15,722 | 23,790 | 5.1 | 50,285 | 59,134 | 198 | 2 |
| BOURBON | 7,250 | 7,450 | 7,581 | 0.3 | 2.58 | 5,497 | 5,477 | 0.0 | 34,610 | 42,555 | 1305 | 27 |
| BOYD | 19,876 | 19,403 | 18,821 | -0.3 | 2.41 | 14,736 | 13,936 | -0.7 | 33,422 | 36,247 | 1471 | 33 |
| BOYLE | 9,483 | 10,392 | 10,869 | 1.1 | 2.46 | 6,974 | 7,317 | 0.6 | 36,060 | 41,450 | 1094 | 23 |
| BRACKEN | 2,872 | 3,248 | 3,424 | 1.5 | 2.61 | 2,179 | 2,371 | 1.0 | 31,621 | 36,595 | 1795 | 47 |
| BREATHITT | 5,555 | 5,721 | 5,909 | 0.4 | 2.72 | 4,385 | 4,375 | 0.0 | 20,531 | 22,476 | 3083 | 115 |
| BRECKINRIDGE | 6,159 | 6,907 | 7,463 | 1.4 | 2.59 | 4,660 | 5,032 | 0.9 | 27,400 | 31,906 | 2526 | 73 |
| BULLITT | 15,965 | 21,143 | 23,638 | 3.5 | 2.94 | 13,453 | 17,416 | 3.2 | 46,015 | 53,941 | 308 | 4 |
| BUTLER | 4,180 | 4,592 | 4,841 | 1.1 | 2.59 | 3,206 | 3,375 | 0.6 | 27,857 | 33,639 | 2463 | 71 |
| CALDWELL | 5,274 | 5,395 | 5,490 | 0.3 | 2.44 | 3,843 | 3,801 | -0.1 | 28,276 | 31,614 | 2403 | 69 |
| CALLOWAY | 11,607 | 13,268 | 13,790 | 1.6 | 2.25 | 7,936 | 8,653 | 1.1 | 31,290 | 34,106 | 1868 | 52 |
| CAMPBELL | 31,169 | 33,054 | 33,383 | 0.7 | 2.61 | 22,237 | 22,844 | 0.3 | 42,642 | 49,515 | 470 | 7 |
| CARLISLE | 2,106 | 2,166 | 2,207 | 0.3 | 2.50 | 1,546 | 1,529 | -0.1 | 29,360 | 31,331 | 2243 | 64 |
| CARROLL | 3,505 | 3,667 | 3,827 | 0.5 | 2.66 | 2,537 | 2,566 | 0.1 | 31,851 | 36,394 | 1746 | 45 |
| CARTER | 8,679 | 9,980 | 10,574 | 1.7 | 2.69 | 6,884 | 7,678 | 1.3 | 26,978 | 31,678 | 2583 | 77 |
| CASEY | 5,436 | 5,869 | 6,196 | 0.9 | 2.54 | 4,172 | 4,303 | 0.4 | 24,245 | 30,200 | 2884 | 100 |
| CHRISTIAN | 21,636 | 23,829 | 23,568 | 1.2 | 2.66 | 16,651 | 17,812 | 0.8 | 31,150 | 39,511 | 1905 | 53 |
| CLARK | 10,973 | 12,324 | 13,117 | 1.4 | 2.64 | 8,496 | 9,359 | 1.2 | 37,317 | 41,714 | 930 | 18 |
| CLAY | 7,367 | 7,979 | 8,197 | 1.0 | 2.84 | 6,101 | 6,403 | 0.6 | 21,750 | 26,096 | 3038 | 107 |
| CLINTON | 3,591 | 3,786 | 3,965 | 0.6 | 2.50 | 2,673 | 2,715 | 0.2 | 18,726 | 20,561 | 3125 | 119 |
| CRITTENDEN | 3,646 | 3,912 | 4,021 | 0.9 | 2.41 | 2,657 | 2,742 | 0.4 | 29,116 | 33,996 | 2278 | 67 |
| CUMBERLAND | 2,714 | 2,772 | 2,797 | 0.3 | 2.45 | 2,013 | 1,984 | -0.2 | 21,917 | 24,014 | 3030 | 106 |
| DAVIESS | 33,036 | 35,236 | 35,908 | 0.8 | 2.53 | 23,980 | 24,828 | 0.4 | 36,247 | 41,168 | 1074 | 22 |
| EDMONSON | 3,843 | 4,437 | 4,869 | 1.8 | 2.62 | 3,089 | 3,469 | 1.4 | 25,503 | 29,012 | 2756 | 91 |
| ELLIOTT | 2,324 | 2,444 | 2,454 | 0.6 | 2.66 | 1,839 | 1,874 | 0.2 | 20,963 | 24,475 | 3067 | 112 |
| ESTILL | 5,357 | 5,854 | 5,939 | 1.1 | 2.63 | 4,185 | 4,436 | 0.7 | 26,669 | 30,860 | 2624 | 82 |
| FAYETTE | 89,529 | 99,322 | 103,841 | 1.3 | 2.35 | 56,412 | 60,295 | 0.8 | 41,533 | 45,285 | 547 | 10 |
| FLEMING | 4,626 | 5,274 | 5,617 | 1.6 | 2.58 | 3,510 | 3,853 | 1.1 | 27,241 | 31,241 | 2545 | 74 |
| FLOYD | 15,664 | 15,789 | 15,801 | 0.1 | 2.70 | 12,408 | 12,158 | -0.2 | 24,209 | 26,379 | 2887 | 101 |
| FRANKLIN | 17,385 | 18,714 | 19,182 | 0.9 | 2.40 | 12,087 | 12,474 | 0.4 | 41,007 | 46,227 | 588 | 11 |
| FULTON | 3,378 | 3,120 | 3,031 | -1.0 | 2.33 | 2,316 | 2,054 | -1.4 | 25,752 | 28,403 | 2737 | 87 |
| GALLATIN | 1,941 | 2,890 | 3,520 | 4.9 | 2.67 | 1,493 | 2,152 | 4.5 | 33,478 | 41,542 | 1467 | 32 |
| GARRARD | 4,435 | 5,654 | 6,377 | 3.0 | 2.58 | 3,458 | 4,276 | 2.6 | 31,478 | 38,430 | 1820 | 48 |
| GRANT | 5,585 | 7,733 | 8,732 | 4.0 | 2.73 | 4,395 | 5,930 | 3.7 | 37,077 | 44,377 | 964 | 19 |
| GRAVES | 13,377 | 14,684 | 15,297 | 1.1 | 2.45 | 9,851 | 10,475 | 0.7 | 31,322 | 34,491 | 1858 | 51 |
| GRAYSON | 7,991 | 9,499 | 10,176 | 2.1 | 2.51 | 6,114 | 7,030 | 1.7 | 26,787 | 31,057 | 2610 | 81 |
| GREEN | 4,089 | 4,322 | 4,435 | 0.7 | 2.42 | 3,124 | 3,183 | 0.2 | 26,845 | 33,410 | 2606 | 79 |
| GREENUP | 13,414 | 13,709 | 13,584 | 0.3 | 2.64 | 10,808 | 10,741 | -0.1 | 32,775 | 35,951 | 1575 | 40 |
| HANCOCK | 2,795 | 3,321 | 3,514 | 2.1 | 2.70 | 2,267 | 2,636 | 1.8 | 40,232 | 46,920 | 655 | 12 |
| HARDIN | 29,358 | 30,926 | 32,356 | 0.6 | 2.77 | 23,141 | 23,745 | 0.3 | 37,670 | 44,921 | 881 | 17 |
| HARLAN | 13,269 | 12,804 | 12,255 | -0.4 | 2.62 | 10,197 | 9,536 | -0.8 | 21,699 | 24,960 | 3043 | 109 |
| HARRISON | 6,086 | 6,835 | 7,245 | 1.4 | 2.56 | 4,574 | 5,002 | 1.1 | 33,349 | 39,583 | 1482 | 34 |
| HART | 5,740 | 6,717 | 7,131 | 1.9 | 2.53 | 4,334 | 4,917 | 1.5 | 25,554 | 31,036 | 2750 | 89 |
| HENDERSON | 16,558 | 17,381 | 17,529 | 0.6 | 2.52 | 12,208 | 12,449 | 0.2 | 38,634 | 45,792 | 787 | 16 |
| HENRY | 4,896 | 5,834 | 6,242 | 2.1 | 2.60 | 3,702 | 4,277 | 1.8 | 34,285 | 43,454 | 1348 | 29 |
| HICKMAN | 2,188 | 2,085 | 2,035 | -0.6 | 2.37 | 1,629 | 1,498 | -1.0 | 30,376 | 34,010 | 2063 | 59 |
| HOPKINS | 17,760 | 18,134 | 18,154 | 0.3 | 2.50 | 13,336 | 13,190 | -0.1 | 30,547 | 34,485 | 2022 | 58 |
| JACKSON | 4,381 | 4,879 | 5,105 | 1.3 | 2.68 | 3,457 | 3,727 | 0.9 | 20,948 | 23,793 | 3069 | 113 |
| JEFFERSON | 264,138 | 271,735 | 275,490 | 0.3 | 2.44 | 179,671 | 178,803 | -0.1 | 40,183 | 43,727 | 657 | 13 |
| JESSAMINE | 10,601 | 13,426 | 14,754 | 2.9 | 2.74 | 8,474 | 10,477 | 2.6 | 40,132 | 47,379 | 662 | 14 |
| JOHNSON | 8,469 | 8,901 | 8,987 | 0.6 | 2.66 | 6,629 | 6,765 | 0.2 | 25,235 | 29,543 | 2786 | 94 |
| KENTON | 52,690 | 55,577 | 57,070 | 0.6 | 2.63 | 37,424 | 38,541 | 0.4 | 44,143 | 50,358 | 388 | 5 |
| KNOTT | 6,086 | 6,187 | 6,215 | 0.2 | 2.81 | 4,905 | 4,882 | -0.1 | 23,757 | 26,423 | 2920 | 102 |
| KNOX | 10,718 | 11,943 | 12,439 | 1.3 | 2.65 | 8,330 | 9,003 | 0.9 | 20,621 | 22,456 | 3080 | 114 |
| LARUE | 4,503 | 5,253 | 5,569 | 1.9 | 2.50 | 3,424 | 3,855 | 1.4 | 32,384 | 40,942 | 1645 | 43 |
| LAUREL | 15,585 | 19,159 | 21,051 | 2.5 | 2.74 | 12,567 | 15,024 | 2.2 | 29,249 | 33,042 | 2259 | 65 |
| LAWRENCE | 5,007 | 5,789 | 6,122 | 1.8 | 2.74 | 3,937 | 4,417 | 1.4 | 25,311 | 29,565 | 2779 | 93 |
| LEE | 2,760 | 2,911 | 2,988 | 0.6 | 2.56 | 2,128 | 2,169 | 0.2 | 19,197 | 20,649 | 3116 | 116 |
| LESLIE | 4,711 | 4,816 | 4,895 | 0.3 | 2.80 | 3,892 | 3,873 | -0.1 | 24,631 | 30,246 | 2847 | 98 |
| LETCHER | 9,731 | 9,542 | 9,319 | -0.2 | 2.70 | 7,701 | 7,328 | -0.6 | 23,171 | 25,956 | 2959 | 103 |
| LEWIS | 4,713 | 5,061 | 5,095 | 0.9 | 2.64 | 3,690 | 3,844 | 0.5 | 25,713 | 32,131 | 2740 | 88 |
| LINCOLN | 7,431 | 8,672 | 9,203 | 1.9 | 2.60 | 5,786 | 6,545 | 1.5 | 29,158 | 32,703 | 2272 | 66 |
| LIVINGSTON | 3,593 | 3,849 | 4,016 | 0.8 | 2.46 | 2,711 | 2,803 | 0.4 | 33,090 | 37,071 | 1524 | 35 |
| LOGAN | 9,302 | 10,232 | 10,551 | 1.2 | 2.56 | 6,992 | 7,427 | 0.7 | 33,718 | 40,501 | 1433 | 30 |
| LYON | 2,355 | 2,980 | 3,160 | 2.9 | 2.23 | 1,682 | 2,038 | 2.4 | 32,824 | 38,448 | 1567 | 37 |
| MCCRACKEN | 25,625 | 26,632 | 26,698 | 0.5 | 2.38 | 18,088 | 18,303 | 0.1 | 36,042 | 39,294 | 1098 | 24 |
| MCCREARY | 5,479 | 6,012 | 6,212 | 1.1 | 2.76 | 4,305 | 4,581 | 0.8 | 18,909 | 21,128 | 3123 | 118 |
| MCLEAN | 3,672 | 3,851 | 3,994 | 0.6 | 2.55 | 2,802 | 2,840 | 0.2 | 30,240 | 35,014 | 2097 | 60 |
| MADISON | 20,012 | 24,766 | 27,245 | 2.6 | 2.53 | 14,569 | 17,260 | 2.1 | 33,085 | 38,527 | 1525 | 36 |
| MAGOFFIN | 4,440 | 4,828 | 5,044 | 1.0 | 2.89 | 3,651 | 3,864 | 0.7 | 21,212 | 25,661 | 3062 | 111 |
| KENTUCKY | | | | 1.2 | 2.56 | | | 0.8 | 34,473 | 39,332 | | |
| UNITED STATES | | | | 1.4 | 2.59 | | | 1.1 | 41,914 | 49,127 | | |

# INCOME

| COUNTY | 2000 Per Capita Income | 2000 HH Income Base | 2000 HOUSEHOLD INCOME DISTRIBUTION (%) | | | | | | 2000 AVERAGE DISPOSABLE INCOME BY AGE OF HOUSEHOLDER | | | | | |
|---|---|---|---|---|---|---|---|---|---|---|---|---|---|---|
| | | | Less than $15,000 | $15,000 to $24,999 | $25,000 to $49,999 | $50,000 to $99,999 | $100,000 to $149,999 | $150,000 or More | All Ages | <35 | 35-44 | 45-54 | 55-64 | 65+ |
| ADAIR | 13,008 | 6,344 | 31.8 | 18.3 | 32.9 | 14.0 | 2.2 | 0.8 | 25,423 | 25,866 | 34,318 | 28,461 | 24,914 | 15,798 |
| ALLEN | 14,163 | 6,655 | 20.6 | 20.4 | 36.4 | 18.6 | 3.6 | 0.4 | 28,967 | 28,121 | 34,921 | 36,892 | 27,601 | 18,958 |
| ANDERSON | 20,064 | 7,401 | 11.9 | 10.3 | 37.6 | 32.4 | 6.0 | 1.9 | 39,109 | 33,244 | 45,061 | 48,737 | 40,946 | 23,046 |
| BALLARD | 16,530 | 3,574 | 25.9 | 15.1 | 35.5 | 18.7 | 3.2 | 1.7 | 30,109 | 29,173 | 35,757 | 38,087 | 29,516 | 16,751 |
| BARREN | 17,158 | 14,820 | 23.1 | 17.2 | 33.8 | 20.3 | 3.9 | 1.7 | 31,212 | 28,630 | 40,427 | 39,539 | 27,584 | 19,079 |
| BATH | 12,040 | 4,212 | 31.9 | 17.1 | 33.5 | 15.1 | 2.1 | 0.3 | 24,882 | 24,199 | 32,302 | 29,097 | 23,481 | 15,323 |
| BELL | 10,976 | 10,675 | 37.3 | 18.8 | 28.1 | 13.1 | 2.2 | 0.6 | 23,517 | 22,090 | 28,056 | 25,764 | 22,941 | 18,759 |
| BOONE | 22,243 | 30,718 | 8.4 | 7.4 | 33.8 | 37.6 | 9.8 | 3.0 | 45,910 | 40,331 | 51,818 | 55,679 | 44,540 | 24,353 |
| BOURBON | 17,234 | 7,450 | 20.7 | 15.4 | 33.2 | 24.2 | 5.1 | 1.4 | 33,298 | 29,072 | 37,423 | 44,783 | 33,729 | 20,094 |
| BOYD | 18,198 | 19,403 | 22.4 | 15.0 | 32.6 | 23.7 | 4.5 | 1.9 | 33,180 | 26,856 | 40,712 | 42,917 | 34,197 | 20,719 |
| BOYLE | 17,694 | 10,392 | 19.2 | 13.9 | 34.9 | 25.7 | 4.8 | 1.4 | 34,230 | 29,472 | 40,852 | 42,135 | 33,242 | 23,994 |
| BRACKEN | 15,091 | 3,248 | 23.3 | 16.1 | 35.8 | 21.0 | 3.2 | 0.6 | 29,676 | 30,280 | 37,607 | 36,709 | 28,444 | 19,015 |
| BREATHITT | 11,473 | 5,721 | 40.3 | 16.6 | 28.6 | 12.1 | 1.8 | 0.6 | 23,151 | 20,417 | 30,376 | 26,352 | 19,783 | 16,180 |
| BRECKINRIDGE | 14,404 | 6,907 | 28.2 | 16.8 | 33.5 | 17.3 | 3.3 | 1.0 | 27,811 | 25,634 | 35,222 | 32,124 | 27,880 | 18,953 |
| BULLITT | 17,619 | 21,143 | 9.9 | 8.9 | 36.6 | 37.9 | 5.9 | 0.9 | 39,464 | 34,416 | 43,739 | 48,478 | 37,813 | 24,323 |
| BUTLER | 13,173 | 4,592 | 23.8 | 19.9 | 37.0 | 17.1 | 1.6 | 0.6 | 27,061 | 25,934 | 30,922 | 32,175 | 28,312 | 17,508 |
| CALDWELL | 14,002 | 5,395 | 27.4 | 16.3 | 36.2 | 17.4 | 2.5 | 0.3 | 26,759 | 25,303 | 36,651 | 30,726 | 26,045 | 18,688 |
| CALLOWAY | 18,687 | 13,268 | 22.9 | 17.7 | 32.2 | 20.2 | 4.3 | 2.7 | 33,120 | 26,251 | 40,830 | 42,932 | 35,580 | 21,309 |
| CAMPBELL | 20,243 | 33,054 | 13.6 | 11.2 | 34.5 | 31.6 | 7.2 | 1.9 | 39,274 | 34,935 | 44,575 | 50,412 | 40,933 | 24,557 |
| CARLISLE | 14,240 | 2,166 | 23.8 | 20.7 | 33.2 | 19.3 | 2.6 | 0.4 | 28,079 | 27,901 | 35,360 | 34,797 | 30,192 | 17,560 |
| CARROLL | 15,568 | 3,667 | 21.7 | 18.2 | 30.5 | 23.8 | 4.5 | 1.3 | 31,903 | 27,135 | 36,097 | 42,337 | 32,773 | 21,079 |
| CARTER | 12,046 | 9,980 | 29.0 | 17.6 | 36.1 | 14.6 | 2.1 | 0.6 | 25,905 | 23,907 | 32,788 | 30,628 | 25,056 | 16,278 |
| CASEY | 13,650 | 5,869 | 29.4 | 22.2 | 30.3 | 15.1 | 2.2 | 0.8 | 25,751 | 26,680 | 32,553 | 30,023 | 23,415 | 17,363 |
| CHRISTIAN | 14,170 | 23,829 | 16.8 | 21.7 | 37.5 | 21.1 | 2.7 | 0.2 | 29,433 | 24,956 | 36,267 | 37,880 | 31,255 | 20,864 |
| CLARK | 17,847 | 12,324 | 17.8 | 14.2 | 35.3 | 25.7 | 5.2 | 1.9 | 35,336 | 29,037 | 41,207 | 44,703 | 33,344 | 22,875 |
| CLAY | 10,313 | 7,979 | 36.0 | 19.4 | 28.4 | 13.7 | 1.9 | 0.5 | 23,642 | 23,237 | 29,021 | 23,747 | 22,637 | 18,559 |
| CLINTON | 12,464 | 3,786 | 40.8 | 22.1 | 22.6 | 10.3 | 2.7 | 1.5 | 23,399 | 20,474 | 30,442 | 29,157 | 20,037 | 16,733 |
| CRITTENDEN | 16,586 | 3,912 | 27.4 | 15.3 | 36.1 | 17.4 | 2.8 | 0.9 | 28,186 | 26,043 | 34,928 | 36,703 | 30,161 | 16,392 |
| CUMBERLAND | 10,995 | 2,772 | 35.0 | 23.7 | 28.0 | 12.5 | 0.8 | 0.0 | 21,770 | 21,761 | 29,115 | 23,583 | 21,897 | 16,164 |
| DAVIESS | 17,628 | 35,233 | 17.9 | 14.1 | 36.4 | 25.9 | 4.5 | 1.3 | 33,970 | 28,672 | 39,961 | 43,211 | 35,294 | 21,937 |
| EDMONSON | 11,695 | 4,437 | 27.4 | 21.6 | 34.5 | 14.7 | 1.7 | 0.2 | 24,704 | 23,738 | 31,490 | 29,640 | 23,552 | 16,017 |
| ELLIOTT | 9,621 | 2,444 | 39.4 | 18.4 | 31.0 | 9.9 | 1.3 | 0.0 | 21,097 | 20,475 | 27,677 | 23,031 | 19,843 | 13,891 |
| ESTILL | 12,152 | 5,854 | 28.7 | 17.1 | 35.3 | 16.6 | 2.0 | 0.2 | 25,788 | 23,919 | 29,603 | 32,138 | 22,351 | 20,400 |
| FAYETTE | 25,343 | 99,321 | 14.3 | 12.9 | 32.1 | 28.0 | 7.9 | 4.7 | 43,248 | 32,000 | 48,438 | 52,370 | 46,454 | 29,745 |
| FLEMING | 12,965 | 5,274 | 29.6 | 16.9 | 33.9 | 15.9 | 3.1 | 0.6 | 26,718 | 25,600 | 31,353 | 34,552 | 23,799 | 17,979 |
| FLOYD | 12,205 | 15,789 | 32.6 | 18.7 | 30.1 | 15.7 | 2.1 | 0.8 | 25,568 | 23,851 | 31,402 | 29,214 | 23,681 | 17,974 |
| FRANKLIN | 20,392 | 18,714 | 12.4 | 13.7 | 35.7 | 31.3 | 5.4 | 1.6 | 37,486 | 29,819 | 43,092 | 46,711 | 39,930 | 25,765 |
| FULTON | 14,548 | 3,120 | 33.1 | 15.4 | 30.1 | 17.2 | 3.1 | 1.2 | 26,858 | 22,560 | 35,074 | 36,454 | 25,979 | 18,527 |
| GALLATIN | 15,166 | 2,890 | 18.7 | 16.3 | 39.4 | 21.3 | 3.6 | 0.7 | 31,135 | 28,111 | 35,610 | 40,311 | 31,575 | 18,709 |
| GARRARD | 14,972 | 5,654 | 22.2 | 16.8 | 36.7 | 19.5 | 3.6 | 1.2 | 30,401 | 28,584 | 36,662 | 34,981 | 28,779 | 22,201 |
| GRANT | 16,599 | 7,733 | 16.3 | 13.4 | 38.4 | 26.4 | 4.4 | 1.2 | 34,361 | 28,925 | 40,389 | 43,246 | 36,022 | 21,000 |
| GRAVES | 17,060 | 14,684 | 23.4 | 15.8 | 34.4 | 21.0 | 3.6 | 1.7 | 31,356 | 28,206 | 37,554 | 42,339 | 29,553 | 19,888 |
| GRAYSON | 13,755 | 9,499 | 27.8 | 18.5 | 35.4 | 15.9 | 1.8 | 0.6 | 26,231 | 24,316 | 33,497 | 30,892 | 25,733 | 16,475 |
| GREEN | 13,849 | 4,322 | 28.0 | 17.7 | 33.6 | 17.7 | 2.4 | 0.6 | 26,731 | 26,790 | 35,251 | 31,163 | 26,236 | 17,812 |
| GREENUP | 15,493 | 13,709 | 23.3 | 14.9 | 35.4 | 22.0 | 3.2 | 1.2 | 31,090 | 26,805 | 36,545 | 37,332 | 33,226 | 20,155 |
| HANCOCK | 17,782 | 3,321 | 17.2 | 11.6 | 33.6 | 30.1 | 6.4 | 1.2 | 36,441 | 31,683 | 42,881 | 46,995 | 30,954 | 21,590 |
| HARDIN | 16,523 | 30,926 | 12.4 | 16.3 | 38.7 | 26.9 | 4.4 | 1.3 | 35,091 | 28,805 | 39,564 | 43,839 | 36,100 | 25,760 |
| HARLAN | 11,021 | 12,804 | 36.9 | 19.1 | 29.1 | 12.6 | 1.9 | 0.5 | 23,339 | 21,512 | 30,305 | 26,453 | 20,637 | 17,006 |
| HARRISON | 15,539 | 6,835 | 20.0 | 15.4 | 36.1 | 24.2 | 3.6 | 0.6 | 31,394 | 28,920 | 39,394 | 35,930 | 33,115 | 19,754 |
| HART | 13,112 | 6,717 | 29.7 | 19.3 | 32.7 | 15.7 | 2.1 | 0.5 | 25,769 | 24,307 | 33,303 | 31,277 | 23,760 | 18,307 |
| HENDERSON | 21,688 | 17,381 | 15.7 | 12.1 | 37.6 | 26.0 | 5.8 | 2.9 | 37,953 | 32,038 | 44,868 | 45,469 | 39,105 | 22,727 |
| HENRY | 16,232 | 5,834 | 19.5 | 13.7 | 36.4 | 25.9 | 3.6 | 0.9 | 32,371 | 30,312 | 38,957 | 37,515 | 31,969 | 21,908 |
| HICKMAN | 14,554 | 2,085 | 26.7 | 16.0 | 33.6 | 21.3 | 2.2 | 0.2 | 27,884 | 23,809 | 35,595 | 34,525 | 28,883 | 18,785 |
| HOPKINS | 15,288 | 18,134 | 24.1 | 16.8 | 35.6 | 19.3 | 3.0 | 1.3 | 29,894 | 26,131 | 36,885 | 36,061 | 30,256 | 19,510 |
| JACKSON | 17,117 | 4,879 | 37.1 | 21.5 | 26.8 | 10.1 | 2.5 | 2.0 | 24,973 | 22,064 | 34,471 | 25,286 | 26,218 | 14,113 |
| JEFFERSON | 22,283 | 271,732 | 15.3 | 13.3 | 33.0 | 28.9 | 6.8 | 2.8 | 39,351 | 31,932 | 44,557 | 48,313 | 40,260 | 27,236 |
| JESSAMINE | 20,674 | 13,426 | 12.7 | 12.8 | 36.2 | 28.4 | 6.9 | 2.9 | 39,807 | 31,672 | 45,290 | 46,927 | 39,552 | 26,862 |
| JOHNSON | 13,375 | 8,901 | 32.3 | 17.4 | 30.6 | 16.2 | 2.3 | 1.3 | 26,875 | 25,176 | 33,770 | 30,091 | 24,111 | 19,015 |
| KENTON | 21,030 | 55,577 | 12.3 | 11.4 | 33.7 | 32.9 | 7.4 | 2.3 | 40,698 | 36,225 | 46,177 | 50,078 | 41,501 | 24,713 |
| KNOTT | 10,919 | 6,187 | 36.7 | 14.8 | 30.3 | 15.4 | 2.3 | 0.6 | 24,899 | 23,723 | 31,796 | 27,010 | 21,386 | 17,525 |
| KNOX | 14,303 | 11,943 | 37.2 | 21.5 | 24.6 | 11.3 | 2.8 | 2.5 | 26,598 | 20,368 | 33,124 | 30,550 | 25,333 | 17,071 |
| LARUE | 15,825 | 5,253 | 22.5 | 12.9 | 38.1 | 23.0 | 2.6 | 0.9 | 30,607 | 29,450 | 34,677 | 33,359 | 32,153 | 23,386 |
| LAUREL | 14,284 | 19,159 | 24.6 | 18.8 | 32.8 | 19.5 | 3.2 | 1.2 | 29,596 | 27,026 | 34,855 | 37,046 | 26,876 | 17,830 |
| LAWRENCE | 12,590 | 5,789 | 31.5 | 18.0 | 30.5 | 15.8 | 3.0 | 1.3 | 27,130 | 25,044 | 35,051 | 31,107 | 24,573 | 18,293 |
| LEE | 10,712 | 2,911 | 38.9 | 22.4 | 24.2 | 11.8 | 1.8 | 0.9 | 22,873 | 19,222 | 29,062 | 21,993 | 25,895 | 18,642 |
| LESLIE | 11,665 | 4,816 | 36.0 | 14.5 | 32.3 | 14.5 | 2.2 | 0.5 | 24,823 | 26,592 | 27,526 | 28,203 | 21,468 | 16,842 |
| LETCHER | 11,139 | 9,542 | 34.4 | 18.0 | 32.1 | 13.1 | 1.8 | 0.5 | 24,225 | 23,712 | 30,247 | 26,491 | 20,917 | 18,399 |
| LEWIS | 12,422 | 5,061 | 29.8 | 19.0 | 33.6 | 14.6 | 2.3 | 0.8 | 26,052 | 25,245 | 29,841 | 32,264 | 23,263 | 18,770 |
| LINCOLN | 13,901 | 8,672 | 25.0 | 18.4 | 37.2 | 15.7 | 2.7 | 1.1 | 27,903 | 26,137 | 36,007 | 33,338 | 25,631 | 19,228 |
| LIVINGSTON | 15,717 | 3,849 | 21.3 | 15.0 | 39.2 | 20.8 | 3.0 | 0.8 | 30,400 | 29,337 | 35,681 | 36,371 | 31,631 | 19,938 |
| LOGAN | 16,851 | 10,232 | 18.5 | 15.6 | 37.7 | 22.3 | 4.6 | 1.4 | 32,787 | 31,218 | 41,741 | 40,619 | 30,758 | 20,156 |
| LYON | 16,578 | 2,980 | 21.6 | 17.6 | 32.1 | 23.7 | 3.8 | 1.3 | 31,924 | 32,955 | 39,124 | 44,373 | 29,227 | 20,212 |
| MCCRACKEN | 22,369 | 26,632 | 18.3 | 15.1 | 33.8 | 24.2 | 5.5 | 3.2 | 37,257 | 30,775 | 42,551 | 48,347 | 36,846 | 22,709 |
| MCCREARY | 8,840 | 6,012 | 40.7 | 21.7 | 27.0 | 9.8 | 0.8 | 0.1 | 20,063 | 18,189 | 21,935 | 23,715 | 20,136 | 15,073 |
| MCLEAN | 13,766 | 3,851 | 22.7 | 18.9 | 36.8 | 19.2 | 2.0 | 0.4 | 27,795 | 26,581 | 35,442 | 32,807 | 26,378 | 18,746 |
| MADISON | 16,756 | 24,766 | 22.0 | 14.6 | 34.2 | 22.8 | 4.7 | 1.8 | 33,103 | 26,414 | 39,030 | 42,388 | 35,644 | 21,592 |
| MAGOFFIN | 10,593 | 4,828 | 36.7 | 19.4 | 29.6 | 12.1 | 1.7 | 0.5 | 22,887 | 20,981 | 28,846 | 25,551 | 19,866 | 16,491 |
| KENTUCKY | 17,910 | | 20.3 | 15.1 | 33.7 | 24.1 | 4.9 | 1.9 | 34,208 | 29,344 | 40,489 | 41,778 | 33,655 | 22,337 |
| UNITED STATES | 22,162 | | 14.5 | 12.5 | 32.3 | 29.8 | 7.4 | 3.5 | 40,748 | 34,503 | 44,969 | 49,579 | 43,409 | 27,339 |

| COUNTY | FINANCIAL SERVICES | | | | THE HOME | | | | | | ENTERTAINMENT | | | | | | PERSONAL | | | |
|---|---|---|---|---|---|---|---|---|---|---|---|---|---|---|---|---|---|---|---|---|
| | | | | | Home Improvements | | | Furnishings | | | | | | | | | | | | |
| | Auto Loan | Home Loan | Investments | Retirement Plans | Home Repair | Lawn & Garden | Remodeling | Appliances | Electronics | Furniture | Restaurants | Sporting Goods | Theater & Concerts | Toys & Hobbies | Travel | Video Rental | Apparel | Auto Aftermarket | Health Insurance | Pets & Supplies |
| ADAIR | 97 | 63 | 68 | 73 | 92 | 90 | 111 | 95 | 91 | 75 | 77 | 94 | 78 | 93 | 66 | 95 | 78 | 86 | 102 | 96 |
| ALLEN | 98 | 65 | 69 | 74 | 92 | 90 | 113 | 96 | 92 | 76 | 78 | 96 | 79 | 95 | 67 | 96 | 79 | 87 | 102 | 97 |
| ANDERSON | 100 | 81 | 88 | 86 | 97 | 94 | 114 | 98 | 95 | 88 | 91 | 98 | 89 | 102 | 76 | 99 | 90 | 93 | 102 | 102 |
| BALLARD | 97 | 68 | 75 | 77 | 93 | 91 | 113 | 96 | 92 | 78 | 80 | 95 | 81 | 96 | 69 | 96 | 81 | 88 | 101 | 97 |
| BARREN | 97 | 72 | 79 | 80 | 96 | 92 | 110 | 96 | 91 | 81 | 82 | 95 | 84 | 96 | 73 | 96 | 83 | 89 | 101 | 97 |
| BATH | 97 | 63 | 67 | 73 | 92 | 90 | 112 | 95 | 91 | 75 | 77 | 95 | 78 | 94 | 66 | 95 | 78 | 86 | 102 | 96 |
| BELL | 95 | 67 | 71 | 73 | 94 | 90 | 107 | 94 | 90 | 78 | 78 | 92 | 79 | 92 | 70 | 95 | 79 | 87 | 100 | 94 |
| BOONE | 101 | 98 | 93 | 96 | 98 | 98 | 105 | 100 | 101 | 99 | 103 | 101 | 98 | 103 | 84 | 100 | 101 | 101 | 99 | 103 |
| BOURBON | 98 | 75 | 82 | 82 | 96 | 92 | 112 | 97 | 92 | 84 | 85 | 95 | 85 | 98 | 74 | 97 | 86 | 91 | 99 | 99 |
| BOYD | 97 | 80 | 93 | 85 | 100 | 97 | 106 | 97 | 92 | 88 | 88 | 94 | 89 | 97 | 80 | 97 | 88 | 91 | 101 | 97 |
| BOYLE | 98 | 77 | 87 | 85 | 97 | 95 | 109 | 97 | 94 | 85 | 86 | 96 | 88 | 97 | 76 | 97 | 86 | 91 | 101 | 98 |
| BRACKEN | 97 | 67 | 77 | 77 | 93 | 92 | 110 | 96 | 92 | 78 | 79 | 95 | 81 | 95 | 70 | 96 | 80 | 88 | 102 | 96 |
| BREATHITT | 97 | 66 | 73 | 75 | 93 | 91 | 111 | 95 | 91 | 78 | 79 | 94 | 80 | 94 | 68 | 96 | 79 | 87 | 101 | 96 |
| BRECKINRIDGE | 98 | 66 | 72 | 77 | 93 | 91 | 114 | 96 | 92 | 77 | 79 | 96 | 80 | 96 | 68 | 96 | 80 | 88 | 102 | 98 |
| BULLITT | 100 | 87 | 91 | 91 | 97 | 96 | 112 | 99 | 90 | 93 | 96 | 100 | 93 | 102 | 79 | 99 | 94 | 97 | 100 | 102 |
| BUTLER | 97 | 64 | 69 | 74 | 92 | 90 | 113 | 96 | 92 | 76 | 78 | 96 | 79 | 95 | 67 | 95 | 78 | 87 | 101 | 97 |
| CALDWELL | 97 | 69 | 76 | 78 | 93 | 91 | 111 | 95 | 92 | 79 | 80 | 93 | 81 | 95 | 70 | 97 | 81 | 88 | 101 | 97 |
| CALLOWAY | 97 | 81 | 91 | 87 | 97 | 95 | 109 | 96 | 93 | 86 | 87 | 95 | 88 | 97 | 78 | 96 | 87 | 92 | 100 | 98 |
| CAMPBELL | 98 | 95 | 103 | 94 | 104 | 101 | 102 | 98 | 95 | 97 | 98 | 97 | 97 | 100 | 88 | 98 | 97 | 97 | 100 | 100 |
| CARLISLE | 97 | 63 | 68 | 73 | 92 | 90 | 111 | 95 | 91 | 75 | 77 | 94 | 78 | 94 | 66 | 95 | 78 | 86 | 102 | 96 |
| CARROLL | 96 | 68 | 75 | 76 | 95 | 92 | 109 | 95 | 91 | 79 | 80 | 94 | 81 | 94 | 71 | 95 | 80 | 87 | 101 | 96 |
| CARTER | 97 | 64 | 68 | 74 | 92 | 90 | 113 | 96 | 91 | 75 | 77 | 96 | 79 | 95 | 66 | 95 | 78 | 87 | 102 | 97 |
| CASEY | 97 | 64 | 69 | 74 | 92 | 90 | 113 | 96 | 92 | 76 | 77 | 95 | 79 | 94 | 67 | 95 | 78 | 87 | 101 | 96 |
| CHRISTIAN | 94 | 84 | 85 | 82 | 96 | 91 | 99 | 94 | 92 | 87 | 88 | 92 | 87 | 94 | 78 | 96 | 87 | 92 | 94 | 97 |
| CLARK | 99 | 84 | 91 | 89 | 98 | 96 | 111 | 98 | 95 | 90 | 91 | 98 | 91 | 100 | 79 | 98 | 91 | 94 | 100 | 101 |
| CLAY | 96 | 67 | 72 | 75 | 93 | 91 | 110 | 95 | 91 | 77 | 79 | 94 | 80 | 94 | 69 | 95 | 79 | 87 | 101 | 96 |
| CLINTON | 97 | 63 | 66 | 73 | 92 | 90 | 112 | 96 | 91 | 75 | 77 | 96 | 78 | 95 | 66 | 95 | 78 | 86 | 102 | 96 |
| CRITTENDEN | 97 | 63 | 69 | 74 | 92 | 90 | 111 | 95 | 91 | 74 | 77 | 94 | 78 | 94 | 67 | 96 | 78 | 87 | 102 | 96 |
| CUMBERLAND | 97 | 65 | 67 | 73 | 93 | 90 | 111 | 95 | 91 | 77 | 77 | 95 | 79 | 94 | 67 | 95 | 78 | 86 | 101 | 96 |
| DAVIESS | 97 | 89 | 97 | 90 | 101 | 98 | 103 | 97 | 95 | 93 | 94 | 96 | 94 | 99 | 84 | 97 | 93 | 95 | 99 | 99 |
| EDMONSON | 98 | 64 | 68 | 74 | 92 | 90 | 114 | 96 | 91 | 75 | 77 | 97 | 79 | 95 | 66 | 95 | 78 | 87 | 102 | 97 |
| ELLIOTT | 97 | 63 | 66 | 73 | 92 | 90 | 112 | 96 | 91 | 75 | 77 | 96 | 78 | 95 | 66 | 95 | 78 | 86 | 102 | 96 |
| ESTILL | 97 | 64 | 69 | 73 | 93 | 91 | 111 | 95 | 91 | 76 | 77 | 95 | 79 | 94 | 67 | 95 | 78 | 87 | 101 | 96 |
| FAYETTE | 99 | 105 | 102 | 101 | 102 | 102 | 98 | 98 | 99 | 101 | 103 | 100 | 100 | 100 | 91 | 98 | 102 | 101 | 97 | 101 |
| FLEMING | 97 | 63 | 68 | 74 | 92 | 90 | 112 | 95 | 91 | 74 | 77 | 96 | 78 | 95 | 66 | 96 | 78 | 87 | 103 | 97 |
| FLOYD | 96 | 67 | 73 | 75 | 92 | 90 | 111 | 95 | 92 | 78 | 79 | 93 | 80 | 94 | 69 | 96 | 79 | 87 | 101 | 96 |
| FRANKLIN | 99 | 96 | 102 | 96 | 103 | 102 | 103 | 99 | 98 | 98 | 100 | 99 | 98 | 101 | 88 | 98 | 98 | 98 | 101 | 101 |
| FULTON | 95 | 67 | 76 | 75 | 94 | 90 | 106 | 95 | 90 | 79 | 78 | 91 | 80 | 92 | 71 | 96 | 80 | 87 | 97 | 95 |
| GALLATIN | 98 | 72 | 77 | 79 | 93 | 91 | 114 | 97 | 93 | 81 | 83 | 97 | 83 | 97 | 70 | 97 | 83 | 89 | 101 | 99 |
| GARRARD | 98 | 67 | 74 | 77 | 93 | 91 | 113 | 96 | 92 | 77 | 80 | 95 | 81 | 96 | 69 | 96 | 81 | 88 | 102 | 97 |
| GRANT | 98 | 72 | 78 | 80 | 94 | 91 | 116 | 97 | 93 | 81 | 84 | 97 | 83 | 98 | 71 | 97 | 84 | 90 | 101 | 99 |
| GRAVES | 97 | 70 | 77 | 78 | 95 | 92 | 111 | 96 | 92 | 80 | 81 | 94 | 82 | 95 | 71 | 96 | 82 | 88 | 101 | 97 |
| GRAYSON | 97 | 66 | 71 | 76 | 93 | 91 | 114 | 96 | 92 | 77 | 78 | 95 | 80 | 95 | 68 | 96 | 79 | 87 | 102 | 97 |
| GREEN | 97 | 63 | 68 | 74 | 92 | 90 | 112 | 95 | 91 | 74 | 77 | 95 | 78 | 94 | 66 | 96 | 78 | 87 | 103 | 96 |
| GREENUP | 99 | 78 | 87 | 86 | 97 | 95 | 113 | 98 | 95 | 86 | 88 | 98 | 88 | 99 | 76 | 98 | 88 | 92 | 102 | 100 |
| HANCOCK | 99 | 71 | 77 | 80 | 94 | 91 | 116 | 97 | 93 | 81 | 83 | 98 | 83 | 98 | 70 | 97 | 84 | 90 | 102 | 100 |
| HARDIN | 96 | 87 | 88 | 86 | 95 | 93 | 104 | 96 | 95 | 89 | 93 | 95 | 89 | 97 | 78 | 98 | 90 | 94 | 97 | 100 |
| HARLAN | 95 | 65 | 70 | 73 | 93 | 90 | 108 | 95 | 90 | 77 | 77 | 92 | 79 | 92 | 68 | 95 | 78 | 86 | 100 | 95 |
| HARRISON | 98 | 74 | 80 | 81 | 95 | 92 | 114 | 96 | 93 | 82 | 84 | 95 | 84 | 98 | 72 | 97 | 85 | 90 | 101 | 99 |
| HART | 97 | 65 | 70 | 74 | 93 | 90 | 112 | 95 | 91 | 77 | 78 | 95 | 79 | 94 | 68 | 95 | 79 | 87 | 101 | 96 |
| HENDERSON | 98 | 81 | 85 | 86 | 97 | 93 | 109 | 97 | 95 | 88 | 89 | 95 | 88 | 98 | 77 | 98 | 88 | 93 | 100 | 99 |
| HENRY | 98 | 74 | 81 | 82 | 95 | 92 | 114 | 97 | 93 | 83 | 85 | 96 | 85 | 98 | 73 | 98 | 85 | 90 | 102 | 99 |
| HICKMAN | 97 | 63 | 66 | 73 | 92 | 90 | 112 | 96 | 91 | 75 | 77 | 96 | 78 | 95 | 66 | 95 | 78 | 86 | 102 | 96 |
| HOPKINS | 97 | 76 | 83 | 83 | 96 | 93 | 110 | 96 | 94 | 84 | 86 | 95 | 86 | 97 | 74 | 97 | 86 | 91 | 101 | 98 |
| JACKSON | 97 | 63 | 66 | 73 | 92 | 90 | 112 | 96 | 91 | 75 | 77 | 96 | 78 | 95 | 66 | 95 | 78 | 86 | 102 | 96 |
| JEFFERSON | 98 | 99 | 106 | 99 | 105 | 103 | 98 | 99 | 96 | 100 | 99 | 99 | 100 | 100 | 92 | 98 | 100 | 99 | 98 | 99 |
| JESSAMINE | 100 | 94 | 94 | 96 | 98 | 97 | 110 | 99 | 98 | 95 | 98 | 101 | 95 | 102 | 82 | 99 | 97 | 98 | 100 | 102 |
| JOHNSON | 97 | 66 | 72 | 75 | 93 | 91 | 112 | 95 | 92 | 77 | 78 | 95 | 80 | 94 | 68 | 96 | 79 | 87 | 101 | 96 |
| KENTON | 98 | 97 | 100 | 95 | 103 | 100 | 101 | 98 | 96 | 98 | 99 | 98 | 98 | 100 | 88 | 98 | 97 | 98 | 99 | 100 |
| KNOTT | 97 | 66 | 74 | 75 | 93 | 91 | 113 | 95 | 92 | 77 | 79 | 94 | 80 | 94 | 68 | 96 | 80 | 87 | 101 | 96 |
| KNOX | 96 | 65 | 71 | 74 | 93 | 91 | 110 | 95 | 91 | 76 | 78 | 93 | 79 | 93 | 68 | 95 | 78 | 87 | 101 | 95 |
| LARUE | 98 | 73 | 82 | 81 | 96 | 93 | 111 | 96 | 93 | 82 | 84 | 95 | 85 | 97 | 73 | 97 | 84 | 90 | 101 | 98 |
| LAUREL | 98 | 71 | 77 | 80 | 93 | 92 | 111 | 96 | 94 | 81 | 83 | 96 | 83 | 96 | 71 | 97 | 83 | 90 | 101 | 98 |
| LAWRENCE | 97 | 65 | 70 | 74 | 92 | 90 | 112 | 95 | 92 | 76 | 78 | 95 | 79 | 94 | 67 | 96 | 79 | 87 | 102 | 96 |
| LEE | 97 | 63 | 67 | 73 | 92 | 90 | 111 | 95 | 91 | 75 | 77 | 95 | 78 | 94 | 66 | 95 | 78 | 86 | 102 | 96 |
| LESLIE | 97 | 63 | 66 | 73 | 92 | 90 | 112 | 96 | 91 | 75 | 77 | 96 | 78 | 95 | 66 | 95 | 78 | 86 | 102 | 96 |
| LETCHER | 97 | 65 | 70 | 73 | 93 | 91 | 111 | 95 | 91 | 77 | 78 | 95 | 79 | 94 | 68 | 95 | 78 | 87 | 101 | 96 |
| LEWIS | 98 | 65 | 70 | 76 | 92 | 91 | 113 | 96 | 92 | 76 | 78 | 97 | 80 | 96 | 67 | 96 | 79 | 87 | 102 | 98 |
| LINCOLN | 97 | 64 | 68 | 74 | 92 | 90 | 112 | 96 | 92 | 76 | 77 | 96 | 79 | 95 | 67 | 95 | 78 | 87 | 102 | 97 |
| LIVINGSTON | 98 | 68 | 74 | 78 | 93 | 91 | 114 | 96 | 93 | 79 | 81 | 97 | 82 | 97 | 69 | 97 | 81 | 88 | 102 | 98 |
| LOGAN | 98 | 68 | 74 | 78 | 94 | 91 | 113 | 96 | 92 | 78 | 81 | 96 | 82 | 97 | 69 | 96 | 81 | 88 | 102 | 98 |
| LYON | 97 | 69 | 83 | 80 | 94 | 94 | 112 | 96 | 91 | 78 | 81 | 93 | 82 | 95 | 72 | 97 | 80 | 89 | 104 | 97 |
| MCCRACKEN | 99 | 87 | 98 | 93 | 101 | 98 | 106 | 98 | 96 | 93 | 92 | 98 | 94 | 99 | 83 | 98 | 93 | 95 | 99 | 100 |
| MCCREARY | 96 | 65 | 68 | 73 | 93 | 90 | 110 | 95 | 91 | 76 | 77 | 94 | 79 | 93 | 68 | 95 | 78 | 86 | 101 | 96 |
| MCLEAN | 98 | 65 | 71 | 75 | 93 | 91 | 113 | 96 | 92 | 77 | 78 | 96 | 80 | 95 | 67 | 96 | 79 | 87 | 102 | 97 |
| MADISON | 97 | 86 | 91 | 88 | 97 | 94 | 106 | 95 | 94 | 88 | 90 | 95 | 89 | 97 | 79 | 96 | 89 | 93 | 98 | 99 |
| MAGOFFIN | 97 | 63 | 67 | 73 | 92 | 90 | 112 | 95 | 91 | 75 | 77 | 95 | 78 | 94 | 66 | 95 | 78 | 86 | 102 | 96 |
| KENTUCKY | 98 | 84 | 91 | 89 | 98 | 96 | 106 | 97 | 95 | 89 | 90 | 97 | 91 | 98 | 80 | 97 | 90 | 93 | 100 | 99 |
| UNITED STATES | 100 | 100 | 100 | 100 | 100 | 100 | 100 | 100 | 100 | 100 | 100 | 100 | 100 | 100 | 100 | 100 | 100 | 100 | 100 | 100 |

# POPULATION CHANGE

| COUNTY | FIPS Code | MSA Code | DMA Code | POPULATION 1990 | POPULATION 2000 | POPULATION 2005 | 1990-2000 ANNUAL CHANGE % Rate | 1990-2000 ANNUAL CHANGE State Rank | RACE (%) White 1990 | RACE (%) White 2000 | RACE (%) Black 1990 | RACE (%) Black 2000 | RACE (%) Asian/Pacific 1990 | RACE (%) Asian/Pacific 2000 |
|---|---|---|---|---|---|---|---|---|---|---|---|---|---|---|
| MARION | 155 | 0000 | 529 | 16,499 | 17,189 | 17,525 | 0.4 | 81 | 90.8 | 90.4 | 8.9 | 9.3 | 0.1 | 0.2 |
| MARSHALL | 157 | 0000 | 632 | 27,205 | 30,416 | 31,317 | 1.1 | 40 | 99.6 | 99.5 | 0.0 | 0.0 | 0.1 | 0.2 |
| MARTIN | 159 | 0000 | 564 | 12,526 | 11,723 | 10,872 | -0.6 | 116 | 99.8 | 99.8 | 0.1 | 0.0 | 0.1 | 0.1 |
| MASON | 161 | 0000 | 515 | 16,666 | 16,765 | 16,469 | 0.1 | 97 | 92.1 | 91.6 | 7.6 | 8.1 | 0.1 | 0.2 |
| MEADE | 163 | 0000 | 529 | 24,170 | 29,732 | 32,413 | 2.0 | 15 | 87.5 | 86.9 | 9.9 | 9.5 | 1.1 | 1.6 |
| MENIFEE | 165 | 0000 | 541 | 5,092 | 5,983 | 6,550 | 1.6 | 20 | 97.9 | 98.1 | 1.7 | 1.5 | 0.1 | 0.1 |
| MERCER | 167 | 0000 | 541 | 19,148 | 20,972 | 21,822 | 0.9 | 47 | 95.1 | 94.8 | 4.3 | 4.4 | 0.4 | 0.6 |
| METCALFE | 169 | 0000 | 736 | 8,963 | 9,662 | 9,968 | 0.7 | 65 | 97.2 | 97.0 | 2.5 | 2.5 | 0.1 | 0.2 |
| MONROE | 171 | 0000 | 659 | 11,401 | 11,110 | 10,878 | -0.3 | 112 | 96.7 | 96.2 | 3.1 | 3.5 | 0.1 | 0.1 |
| MONTGOMERY | 173 | 0000 | 541 | 19,561 | 22,074 | 24,244 | 1.2 | 36 | 95.5 | 95.2 | 4.2 | 4.5 | 0.1 | 0.1 |
| MORGAN | 175 | 0000 | 541 | 11,648 | 13,750 | 14,184 | 1.6 | 20 | 99.0 | 97.5 | 0.9 | 2.4 | 0.1 | 0.1 |
| MUHLENBERG | 177 | 0000 | 649 | 31,318 | 31,982 | 32,075 | 0.2 | 95 | 95.6 | 95.5 | 4.1 | 4.2 | 0.1 | 0.2 |
| NELSON | 179 | 0000 | 529 | 29,710 | 37,922 | 42,624 | 2.4 | 10 | 93.5 | 93.0 | 6.1 | 6.5 | 0.2 | 0.3 |
| NICHOLAS | 181 | 0000 | 541 | 6,725 | 7,196 | 7,535 | 0.7 | 65 | 98.3 | 98.0 | 1.3 | 1.4 | 0.3 | 0.4 |
| OHIO | 183 | 0000 | 649 | 21,105 | 22,255 | 22,870 | 0.5 | 77 | 98.8 | 98.7 | 0.8 | 0.9 | 0.1 | 0.2 |
| OLDHAM | 185 | 4520 | 529 | 33,263 | 47,093 | 53,491 | 3.5 | 4 | 95.7 | 95.6 | 3.6 | 3.4 | 0.4 | 0.6 |
| OWEN | 187 | 0000 | 515 | 9,035 | 10,582 | 11,372 | 1.6 | 20 | 98.0 | 98.0 | 1.7 | 1.8 | 0.1 | 0.1 |
| OWSLEY | 189 | 0000 | 541 | 5,036 | 5,370 | 5,343 | 0.6 | 72 | 99.6 | 99.6 | 0.3 | 0.4 | 0.0 | 0.0 |
| PENDLETON | 191 | 1640 | 515 | 12,036 | 14,075 | 14,698 | 1.5 | 24 | 99.3 | 99.3 | 0.4 | 0.3 | 0.1 | 0.1 |
| PERRY | 193 | 0000 | 541 | 30,283 | 30,685 | 30,089 | 0.1 | 97 | 97.9 | 97.7 | 1.7 | 1.9 | 0.2 | 0.3 |
| PIKE | 195 | 0000 | 564 | 72,583 | 71,226 | 69,055 | -0.2 | 111 | 99.3 | 99.1 | 0.4 | 0.4 | 0.2 | 0.3 |
| POWELL | 197 | 0000 | 541 | 11,686 | 13,568 | 15,044 | 1.5 | 24 | 99.0 | 98.9 | 0.7 | 0.8 | 0.1 | 0.1 |
| PULASKI | 199 | 0000 | 541 | 49,489 | 57,823 | 61,434 | 1.5 | 24 | 98.3 | 98.3 | 1.2 | 1.2 | 0.2 | 0.3 |
| ROBERTSON | 201 | 0000 | 515 | 2,124 | 2,300 | 2,472 | 0.8 | 55 | 99.8 | 99.8 | 0.2 | 0.2 | 0.0 | 0.0 |
| ROCKCASTLE | 203 | 0000 | 541 | 14,803 | 16,083 | 16,639 | 0.8 | 55 | 99.7 | 99.6 | 0.0 | 0.0 | 0.1 | 0.1 |
| ROWAN | 205 | 0000 | 541 | 20,353 | 22,313 | 23,002 | 0.9 | 47 | 97.7 | 97.4 | 1.5 | 1.6 | 0.5 | 0.7 |
| RUSSELL | 207 | 0000 | 541 | 14,716 | 16,193 | 16,243 | 0.9 | 47 | 99.2 | 99.3 | 0.6 | 0.6 | 0.0 | 0.0 |
| SCOTT | 209 | 4280 | 541 | 23,867 | 33,574 | 40,101 | 3.4 | 5 | 93.0 | 92.5 | 6.3 | 6.6 | 0.4 | 0.7 |
| SHELBY | 211 | 0000 | 529 | 24,824 | 31,376 | 35,453 | 2.3 | 12 | 89.5 | 89.2 | 9.9 | 10.0 | 0.4 | 0.5 |
| SIMPSON | 213 | 0000 | 659 | 15,145 | 16,741 | 17,540 | 1.0 | 42 | 88.6 | 88.0 | 11.0 | 11.4 | 0.2 | 0.3 |
| SPENCER | 215 | 0000 | 529 | 6,801 | 11,083 | 14,271 | 4.9 | 1 | 98.1 | 98.1 | 1.7 | 1.6 | 0.2 | 0.2 |
| TAYLOR | 217 | 0000 | 529 | 21,146 | 22,990 | 23,244 | 0.8 | 55 | 94.7 | 94.4 | 5.1 | 5.3 | 0.1 | 0.2 |
| TODD | 219 | 0000 | 659 | 10,940 | 11,320 | 11,479 | 0.3 | 87 | 88.6 | 88.2 | 11.0 | 11.3 | 0.1 | 0.1 |
| TRIGG | 221 | 0000 | 659 | 10,361 | 12,823 | 13,982 | 2.1 | 14 | 87.8 | 87.1 | 11.8 | 12.4 | 0.1 | 0.2 |
| TRIMBLE | 223 | 0000 | 529 | 6,090 | 8,159 | 9,376 | 2.9 | 7 | 99.6 | 99.6 | 0.0 | 0.0 | 0.0 | 0.0 |
| UNION | 225 | 0000 | 649 | 16,557 | 16,493 | 16,439 | 0.0 | 105 | 84.0 | 84.5 | 15.4 | 14.8 | 0.3 | 0.3 |
| WARREN | 227 | 0000 | 736 | 76,673 | 88,329 | 91,648 | 1.4 | 28 | 90.7 | 90.0 | 8.2 | 8.5 | 0.8 | 1.2 |
| WASHINGTON | 229 | 0000 | 529 | 10,441 | 11,164 | 11,747 | 0.7 | 65 | 90.8 | 90.4 | 8.7 | 9.2 | 0.2 | 0.1 |
| WAYNE | 231 | 0000 | 541 | 17,468 | 19,372 | 20,293 | 1.0 | 42 | 97.9 | 97.8 | 1.8 | 1.9 | 0.0 | 0.0 |
| WEBSTER | 233 | 0000 | 649 | 13,955 | 13,425 | 13,249 | -0.4 | 113 | 93.9 | 93.5 | 5.6 | 5.8 | 0.2 | 0.3 |
| WHITLEY | 235 | 0000 | 541 | 33,326 | 36,379 | 37,672 | 0.9 | 47 | 99.0 | 98.9 | 0.6 | 0.7 | 0.2 | 0.2 |
| WOLFE | 237 | 0000 | 541 | 6,503 | 7,588 | 8,037 | 1.5 | 24 | 99.7 | 99.6 | 0.1 | 0.2 | 0.0 | 0.1 |
| WOODFORD | 239 | 4280 | 541 | 19,955 | 22,966 | 23,967 | 1.4 | 28 | 93.0 | 92.6 | 6.5 | 6.7 | 0.1 | 0.2 |
| KENTUCKY | | | | | | | 0.8 | | 92.0 | 91.8 | 7.1 | 7.2 | 0.5 | 0.7 |
| UNITED STATES | | | | | | | 1.0 | | 80.3 | 77.9 | 12.1 | 12.4 | 2.9 | 3.9 |

| COUNTY | % HISPANIC ORIGIN 1990 | % HISPANIC ORIGIN 2000 | 2000 AGE DISTRIBUTION (%) 0-4 | 5-9 | 10-14 | 15-19 | 20-24 | 25-44 | 45-64 | 65-84 | 85+ | 18+ | MEDIAN AGE 1990 | MEDIAN AGE 2000 | 2000 Males/ Females (×100) |
|---|---|---|---|---|---|---|---|---|---|---|---|---|---|---|---|
| MARION | 0.3 | 0.7 | 6.3 | 6.8 | 7.1 | 7.2 | 7.5 | 29.8 | 22.7 | 11.0 | 1.6 | 75.4 | 32.3 | 35.8 | 99.5 |
| MARSHALL | 0.4 | 1.0 | 5.6 | 6.0 | 6.3 | 6.3 | 5.3 | 26.3 | 26.5 | 15.4 | 2.2 | 78.2 | 38.2 | 41.3 | 95.8 |
| MARTIN | 0.2 | 0.6 | 7.4 | 7.5 | 8.0 | 8.4 | 7.7 | 30.1 | 22.0 | 8.1 | 0.9 | 72.1 | 29.5 | 32.9 | 96.3 |
| MASON | 0.5 | 1.0 | 6.4 | 6.7 | 6.8 | 6.9 | 6.4 | 28.0 | 23.6 | 13.4 | 1.8 | 75.8 | 35.0 | 37.8 | 94.3 |
| MEADE | 2.4 | 3.9 | 10.1 | 9.1 | 7.1 | 6.6 | 7.4 | 34.2 | 18.1 | 6.7 | 0.7 | 69.6 | 28.1 | 29.9 | 97.6 |
| MENIFEE | 0.5 | 1.1 | 6.4 | 6.5 | 7.0 | 9.1 | 7.0 | 27.9 | 24.5 | 10.4 | 1.2 | 75.0 | 32.4 | 36.0 | 99.6 |
| MERCER | 0.5 | 1.1 | 5.9 | 6.2 | 6.3 | 6.6 | 6.4 | 27.9 | 25.7 | 13.1 | 1.9 | 77.6 | 35.9 | 39.1 | 92.7 |
| METCALFE | 0.3 | 0.9 | 6.1 | 6.4 | 6.6 | 6.6 | 5.6 | 28.2 | 24.9 | 13.7 | 1.9 | 76.7 | 35.5 | 39.0 | 91.5 |
| MONROE | 0.6 | 1.1 | 6.0 | 6.1 | 6.4 | 6.7 | 6.2 | 27.5 | 25.9 | 13.2 | 1.9 | 77.2 | 35.9 | 39.2 | 92.7 |
| MONTGOMERY | 0.3 | 0.8 | 5.9 | 6.2 | 6.5 | 6.7 | 6.5 | 28.8 | 26.0 | 11.7 | 1.5 | 77.1 | 34.1 | 38.0 | 93.0 |
| MORGAN | 0.4 | 0.9 | 6.0 | 6.2 | 6.4 | 7.3 | 7.3 | 31.9 | 22.9 | 10.5 | 1.4 | 76.7 | 32.9 | 35.9 | 114.2 |
| MUHLENBERG | 0.3 | 0.7 | 5.8 | 6.0 | 6.3 | 7.5 | 6.9 | 27.4 | 25.7 | 12.6 | 1.9 | 77.4 | 34.8 | 38.5 | 93.3 |
| NELSON | 0.4 | 1.0 | 7.1 | 7.4 | 7.4 | 7.6 | 7.0 | 30.2 | 22.8 | 9.2 | 1.1 | 73.3 | 31.6 | 34.9 | 95.7 |
| NICHOLAS | 0.2 | 0.7 | 5.6 | 6.0 | 6.4 | 7.1 | 6.4 | 27.5 | 26.2 | 12.9 | 1.8 | 77.4 | 35.9 | 39.2 | 95.4 |
| OHIO | 0.4 | 1.0 | 6.5 | 6.7 | 6.9 | 7.2 | 6.4 | 26.6 | 25.3 | 12.4 | 2.0 | 75.3 | 35.0 | 38.2 | 92.5 |
| OLDHAM | 0.6 | 1.3 | 5.9 | 6.3 | 6.8 | 8.0 | 7.6 | 30.4 | 27.4 | 6.9 | 0.7 | 75.9 | 33.0 | 35.9 | 105.8 |
| OWEN | 0.2 | 0.6 | 6.3 | 6.6 | 7.0 | 7.0 | 6.1 | 27.6 | 25.7 | 11.7 | 1.9 | 75.6 | 35.0 | 38.2 | 101.2 |
| OWSLEY | 0.3 | 0.7 | 6.3 | 6.4 | 6.9 | 7.4 | 7.4 | 27.2 | 24.6 | 12.0 | 1.8 | 75.6 | 34.3 | 37.2 | 102.9 |
| PENDLETON | 0.2 | 0.8 | 7.8 | 7.5 | 7.7 | 7.4 | 6.8 | 29.1 | 22.9 | 9.7 | 1.3 | 72.4 | 31.6 | 34.6 | 96.1 |
| PERRY | 0.2 | 0.6 | 6.2 | 6.5 | 7.3 | 7.9 | 7.6 | 30.3 | 23.8 | 9.3 | 1.2 | 75.2 | 31.7 | 35.5 | 96.0 |
| PIKE | 0.3 | 0.8 | 5.9 | 6.3 | 7.0 | 7.7 | 7.2 | 30.1 | 24.6 | 10.1 | 1.0 | 76.0 | 32.4 | 36.5 | 96.3 |
| POWELL | 0.4 | 0.9 | 7.1 | 7.3 | 7.6 | 8.0 | 7.0 | 29.3 | 24.4 | 8.3 | 1.0 | 73.0 | 31.3 | 34.7 | 96.4 |
| PULASKI | 0.4 | 1.0 | 5.8 | 6.2 | 6.5 | 6.6 | 6.0 | 28.5 | 25.7 | 13.1 | 1.7 | 77.6 | 35.2 | 38.9 | 94.7 |
| ROBERTSON | 0.2 | 0.6 | 5.8 | 6.2 | 6.3 | 7.0 | 6.4 | 26.7 | 25.9 | 13.7 | 2.0 | 77.7 | 36.5 | 39.3 | 95.9 |
| ROCKCASTLE | 0.4 | 1.0 | 6.5 | 6.6 | 7.0 | 7.0 | 6.1 | 29.6 | 24.5 | 11.2 | 1.6 | 75.7 | 33.0 | 36.7 | 97.1 |
| ROWAN | 0.4 | 0.9 | 5.5 | 5.1 | 5.2 | 13.3 | 15.8 | 25.8 | 19.7 | 8.4 | 1.1 | 80.8 | 26.0 | 29.1 | 93.0 |
| RUSSELL | 0.3 | 0.8 | 5.8 | 6.0 | 6.3 | 6.6 | 5.4 | 28.8 | 25.6 | 13.7 | 1.8 | 77.9 | 36.1 | 39.5 | 93.7 |
| SCOTT | 0.4 | 1.0 | 6.5 | 6.8 | 7.0 | 8.3 | 7.8 | 30.2 | 23.6 | 8.6 | 1.2 | 75.4 | 31.8 | 35.2 | 95.4 |
| SHELBY | 0.4 | 0.9 | 6.1 | 6.4 | 6.8 | 7.3 | 6.0 | 28.5 | 26.1 | 11.2 | 1.6 | 76.3 | 34.9 | 37.9 | 91.9 |
| SIMPSON | 0.3 | 0.8 | 6.7 | 7.0 | 7.3 | 6.9 | 6.3 | 28.4 | 24.5 | 11.2 | 1.8 | 74.8 | 33.8 | 36.9 | 97.1 |
| SPENCER | 0.1 | 0.5 | 6.4 | 6.8 | 7.0 | 7.1 | 6.2 | 30.2 | 25.3 | 9.8 | 1.2 | 75.4 | 33.3 | 37.0 | 101.5 |
| TAYLOR | 0.2 | 0.7 | 6.0 | 6.1 | 6.4 | 7.8 | 6.6 | 27.8 | 25.1 | 12.7 | 1.6 | 77.1 | 34.5 | 38.3 | 93.1 |
| TODD | 0.5 | 1.1 | 6.7 | 6.9 | 7.1 | 7.1 | 6.0 | 28.6 | 23.2 | 12.6 | 1.8 | 75.0 | 34.1 | 37.2 | 95.5 |
| TRIGG | 0.3 | 0.7 | 5.3 | 5.3 | 6.0 | 6.2 | 5.7 | 25.1 | 28.2 | 16.3 | 1.9 | 79.5 | 39.7 | 42.5 | 95.8 |
| TRIMBLE | 0.5 | 1.1 | 6.7 | 6.7 | 6.8 | 7.2 | 6.0 | 28.7 | 26.1 | 10.5 | 1.4 | 75.2 | 34.6 | 37.9 | 96.4 |
| UNION | 0.7 | 1.2 | 5.8 | 6.3 | 6.5 | 13.3 | 8.9 | 25.9 | 21.3 | 10.6 | 1.4 | 74.3 | 30.1 | 33.0 | 105.2 |
| WARREN | 0.6 | 1.2 | 6.0 | 6.1 | 6.3 | 8.9 | 9.3 | 29.9 | 22.6 | 9.6 | 1.3 | 77.8 | 31.2 | 34.4 | 92.0 |
| WASHINGTON | 0.5 | 1.2 | 6.8 | 7.2 | 7.1 | 7.1 | 6.6 | 27.6 | 23.0 | 12.5 | 2.0 | 74.5 | 33.7 | 36.9 | 91.3 |
| WAYNE | 0.3 | 0.8 | 6.3 | 6.5 | 6.8 | 7.4 | 6.4 | 28.1 | 25.0 | 12.1 | 1.4 | 75.9 | 34.0 | 37.5 | 97.2 |
| WEBSTER | 0.2 | 0.7 | 6.1 | 6.5 | 6.8 | 7.2 | 6.4 | 27.2 | 24.7 | 12.7 | 2.4 | 76.1 | 35.3 | 38.2 | 93.6 |
| WHITLEY | 0.3 | 0.8 | 6.6 | 6.7 | 6.9 | 8.2 | 8.0 | 27.4 | 24.1 | 10.6 | 1.4 | 75.3 | 32.4 | 35.5 | 92.3 |
| WOLFE | 0.1 | 0.5 | 6.4 | 6.9 | 7.4 | 8.0 | 6.7 | 29.2 | 24.6 | 9.7 | 1.1 | 74.1 | 32.5 | 36.0 | 98.6 |
| WOODFORD | 0.5 | 1.1 | 6.5 | 7.2 | 7.7 | 7.1 | 5.3 | 29.7 | 26.0 | 9.2 | 1.3 | 74.4 | 33.7 | 37.4 | 91.4 |
| KENTUCKY | 0.6 | 1.2 | 6.5 | 6.5 | 6.7 | 7.4 | 7.3 | 29.5 | 23.7 | 10.9 | 1.5 | 76.1 | 33.0 | 36.4 | 94.4 |
| UNITED STATES | 9.0 | 11.8 | 6.9 | 7.2 | 7.2 | 7.2 | 6.7 | 29.9 | 22.2 | 11.1 | 1.6 | 74.6 | 32.9 | 35.7 | 95.6 |

# HOUSEHOLDS

| COUNTY | HOUSEHOLDS 1990 | HOUSEHOLDS 2000 | HOUSEHOLDS 2005 | % Annual Rate 1990-2000 | 2000 Average HH Size | FAMILIES 1990 | FAMILIES 2000 | % Annual Rate 1990-2000 | MEDIAN HOUSEHOLD INCOME 2000 | 2005 | 2000 National Rank | 2000 State Rank |
|---|---|---|---|---|---|---|---|---|---|---|---|---|
| MARION | 5,688 | 6,048 | 6,238 | 0.7 | 2.72 | 4,356 | 4,488 | 0.4 | 27,579 | 30,246 | 2498 | 72 |
| MARSHALL | 10,789 | 12,530 | 13,135 | 1.8 | 2.39 | 8,297 | 9,304 | 1.4 | 35,083 | 37,998 | 1243 | 26 |
| MARTIN | 4,300 | 4,205 | 3,984 | -0.3 | 2.79 | 3,539 | 3,377 | -0.6 | 24,629 | 27,248 | 2848 | 99 |
| MASON | 6,537 | 6,815 | 6,812 | 0.5 | 2.43 | 4,746 | 4,745 | 0.0 | 31,009 | 35,952 | 1934 | 54 |
| MEADE | 8,080 | 10,191 | 11,244 | 2.9 | 2.91 | 6,736 | 8,304 | 2.6 | 35,511 | 42,641 | 1168 | 25 |
| MENIFEE | 1,842 | 2,215 | 2,453 | 2.3 | 2.63 | 1,448 | 1,686 | 1.9 | 24,917 | 28,513 | 2814 | 97 |
| MERCER | 7,413 | 8,321 | 8,759 | 1.4 | 2.50 | 5,625 | 6,104 | 1.0 | 34,365 | 40,096 | 1336 | 28 |
| METCALFE | 3,433 | 3,811 | 3,986 | 1.3 | 2.50 | 2,627 | 2,809 | 0.8 | 25,972 | 30,413 | 2716 | 84 |
| MONROE | 4,505 | 4,480 | 4,426 | -0.1 | 2.45 | 3,368 | 3,221 | -0.5 | 26,341 | 30,641 | 2674 | 83 |
| MONTGOMERY | 7,312 | 8,120 | 8,852 | 1.3 | 2.69 | 5,639 | 6,074 | 0.9 | 31,472 | 36,315 | 1822 | 49 |
| MORGAN | 4,089 | 4,565 | 4,751 | 1.3 | 2.71 | 3,240 | 3,499 | 0.9 | 22,097 | 27,276 | 3023 | 105 |
| MUHLENBERG | 11,683 | 12,326 | 12,553 | 0.7 | 2.54 | 8,983 | 9,192 | 0.3 | 27,168 | 30,323 | 2552 | 75 |
| NELSON | 10,417 | 13,465 | 15,224 | 3.2 | 2.77 | 8,103 | 10,147 | 2.8 | 39,333 | 45,667 | 724 | 15 |
| NICHOLAS | 2,621 | 2,768 | 2,878 | 0.7 | 2.58 | 1,945 | 1,969 | 0.1 | 25,802 | 30,705 | 2733 | 86 |
| OHIO | 7,816 | 8,369 | 8,666 | 0.8 | 2.62 | 6,087 | 6,328 | 0.5 | 28,107 | 32,231 | 2427 | 70 |
| OLDHAM | 10,673 | 15,451 | 17,690 | 4.6 | 2.91 | 8,948 | 12,643 | 4.3 | 56,572 | 62,077 | 107 | 1 |
| OWEN | 3,412 | 4,102 | 4,465 | 2.3 | 2.55 | 2,585 | 3,014 | 1.9 | 33,487 | 42,511 | 1465 | 31 |
| OWSLEY | 1,848 | 2,036 | 2,056 | 1.2 | 2.58 | 1,455 | 1,558 | 0.8 | 17,371 | 19,091 | 3136 | 120 |
| PENDLETON | 4,332 | 5,021 | 5,221 | 1.8 | 2.79 | 3,358 | 3,768 | 1.4 | 37,004 | 45,836 | 977 | 21 |
| PERRY | 10,598 | 11,089 | 11,043 | 0.6 | 2.75 | 8,446 | 8,593 | 0.2 | 26,818 | 32,181 | 2608 | 80 |
| PIKE | 26,148 | 26,403 | 25,964 | 0.1 | 2.66 | 20,960 | 20,550 | -0.2 | 26,959 | 29,800 | 2588 | 78 |
| POWELL | 4,057 | 4,762 | 5,310 | 2.0 | 2.83 | 3,251 | 3,713 | 1.6 | 27,131 | 32,028 | 2559 | 76 |
| PULASKI | 18,866 | 22,376 | 23,926 | 2.1 | 2.54 | 14,413 | 16,564 | 1.7 | 28,952 | 34,223 | 2304 | 68 |
| ROBERTSON | 820 | 873 | 931 | 0.8 | 2.62 | 575 | 585 | 0.2 | 31,335 | 35,653 | 1855 | 50 |
| ROCKCASTLE | 5,464 | 6,142 | 6,460 | 1.4 | 2.59 | 4,256 | 4,631 | 1.0 | 25,113 | 30,169 | 2803 | 95 |
| ROWAN | 6,755 | 7,819 | 8,276 | 1.8 | 2.40 | 4,770 | 5,323 | 1.3 | 25,847 | 28,701 | 2729 | 85 |
| RUSSELL | 5,896 | 6,671 | 6,783 | 1.5 | 2.41 | 4,414 | 4,819 | 1.1 | 25,389 | 30,722 | 2767 | 92 |
| SCOTT | 8,501 | 11,986 | 14,327 | 4.3 | 2.72 | 6,597 | 9,062 | 3.9 | 42,026 | 47,497 | 507 | 9 |
| SHELBY | 9,048 | 11,553 | 13,108 | 3.0 | 2.64 | 7,033 | 8,773 | 2.7 | 42,428 | 49,623 | 478 | 8 |
| SIMPSON | 5,767 | 6,476 | 6,839 | 1.4 | 2.56 | 4,344 | 4,735 | 1.1 | 32,138 | 36,878 | 1696 | 44 |
| SPENCER | 2,451 | 3,901 | 4,966 | 5.8 | 2.83 | 1,947 | 3,030 | 5.5 | 32,662 | 37,843 | 1601 | 41 |
| TAYLOR | 8,216 | 9,132 | 9,338 | 1.3 | 2.46 | 6,224 | 6,696 | 0.9 | 30,096 | 33,129 | 2131 | 61 |
| TODD | 4,104 | 4,294 | 4,381 | 0.6 | 2.62 | 3,106 | 3,145 | 0.2 | 32,801 | 40,731 | 1573 | 38 |
| TRIGG | 4,104 | 5,258 | 5,824 | 3.0 | 2.41 | 3,106 | 3,861 | 2.7 | 30,661 | 37,333 | 1994 | 56 |
| TRIMBLE | 2,246 | 3,043 | 3,514 | 3.7 | 2.66 | 1,795 | 2,356 | 3.4 | 32,493 | 39,752 | 1626 | 42 |
| UNION | 5,580 | 5,758 | 5,798 | 0.4 | 2.58 | 4,186 | 4,178 | 0.0 | 31,813 | 35,182 | 1756 | 46 |
| WARREN | 28,819 | 33,831 | 35,580 | 2.0 | 2.46 | 20,014 | 22,937 | 1.7 | 37,055 | 41,490 | 967 | 20 |
| WASHINGTON | 3,709 | 4,014 | 4,252 | 1.0 | 2.72 | 2,907 | 3,042 | 0.6 | 32,801 | 40,970 | 1573 | 38 |
| WAYNE | 6,517 | 7,452 | 7,919 | 1.6 | 2.58 | 5,131 | 5,665 | 1.2 | 21,703 | 23,960 | 3042 | 108 |
| WEBSTER | 5,372 | 5,248 | 5,219 | -0.3 | 2.52 | 4,028 | 3,798 | -0.7 | 30,852 | 38,114 | 1959 | 55 |
| WHITLEY | 12,153 | 13,551 | 14,183 | 1.3 | 2.60 | 9,286 | 10,048 | 1.0 | 23,058 | 26,760 | 2967 | 104 |
| WOLFE | 2,451 | 2,871 | 3,047 | 1.9 | 2.62 | 1,859 | 2,105 | 1.5 | 19,175 | 22,509 | 3118 | 117 |
| WOODFORD | 7,223 | 8,729 | 9,320 | 2.3 | 2.59 | 5,710 | 6,699 | 2.0 | 46,121 | 49,685 | 303 | 3 |
| KENTUCKY | | | | 1.2 | 2.56 | | | 0.8 | 34,473 | 39,332 | | |
| UNITED STATES | | | | 1.4 | 2.59 | | | 1.1 | 41,914 | 49,127 | | |

| COUNTY | 2000 Per Capita Income | 2000 HH Income Base | 2000 HOUSEHOLD INCOME DISTRIBUTION (%) Less than $15,000 | $15,000 to $24,999 | $25,000 to $49,999 | $50,000 to $99,999 | $100,000 to $149,999 | $150,000 or More | 2000 AVERAGE DISPOSABLE INCOME BY AGE OF HOUSEHOLDER All Ages | <35 | 35-44 | 45-54 | 55-64 | 65+ |
|---|---|---|---|---|---|---|---|---|---|---|---|---|---|---|
| MARION | 14,039 | 6,048 | 27.2 | 17.2 | 35.4 | 17.2 | 2.1 | 0.8 | 27,335 | 23,545 | 33,124 | 32,922 | 25,841 | 18,987 |
| MARSHALL | 18,427 | 12,530 | 19.0 | 16.1 | 35.5 | 24.3 | 3.9 | 1.3 | 32,875 | 31,383 | 42,628 | 43,122 | 31,666 | 19,208 |
| MARTIN | 13,266 | 4,205 | 34.7 | 15.8 | 26.5 | 19.5 | 2.4 | 1.2 | 27,356 | 23,195 | 33,901 | 31,898 | 23,165 | 19,192 |
| MASON | 15,604 | 6,815 | 24.7 | 15.4 | 34.0 | 22.0 | 3.0 | 0.8 | 29,671 | 26,521 | 38,189 | 36,122 | 26,508 | 21,016 |
| MEADE | 14,040 | 10,191 | 10.7 | 19.6 | 40.4 | 26.7 | 2.5 | 0.2 | 32,227 | 29,020 | 36,987 | 39,866 | 30,706 | 23,464 |
| MENIFEE | 10,774 | 2,215 | 28.8 | 21.4 | 36.6 | 12.4 | 0.8 | 0.1 | 23,341 | 21,794 | 27,993 | 26,464 | 24,283 | 16,018 |
| MERCER | 17,562 | 8,321 | 18.3 | 14.3 | 38.9 | 22.4 | 4.7 | 1.4 | 33,107 | 29,346 | 39,313 | 42,429 | 32,707 | 21,971 |
| METCALFE | 12,566 | 3,811 | 30.1 | 17.9 | 34.4 | 15.1 | 2.1 | 0.5 | 25,412 | 24,119 | 30,250 | 29,532 | 26,220 | 18,481 |
| MONROE | 13,757 | 4,480 | 29.9 | 17.8 | 34.2 | 15.3 | 1.8 | 0.9 | 26,411 | 28,744 | 34,486 | 29,997 | 25,925 | 15,173 |
| MONTGOMERY | 14,516 | 8,120 | 22.5 | 17.3 | 34.9 | 20.9 | 3.6 | 0.9 | 30,174 | 29,139 | 36,346 | 35,532 | 29,373 | 19,638 |
| MORGAN | 10,665 | 4,565 | 35.7 | 19.5 | 27.9 | 13.1 | 2.6 | 1.2 | 24,895 | 24,081 | 31,956 | 27,461 | 24,310 | 16,419 |
| MUHLENBERG | 15,416 | 12,326 | 27.2 | 18.6 | 33.0 | 16.8 | 3.0 | 1.3 | 28,366 | 24,725 | 36,362 | 33,921 | 27,444 | 19,123 |
| NELSON | 17,109 | 13,465 | 14.2 | 13.1 | 36.9 | 28.8 | 5.8 | 1.2 | 36,299 | 32,257 | 40,403 | 45,202 | 34,275 | 24,844 |
| NICHOLAS | 11,852 | 2,768 | 29.5 | 19.0 | 35.2 | 14.6 | 1.6 | 0.1 | 24,956 | 23,407 | 32,693 | 29,168 | 25,413 | 15,453 |
| OHIO | 12,404 | 8,369 | 25.3 | 19.8 | 35.0 | 18.0 | 1.9 | 0.1 | 26,285 | 24,751 | 32,088 | 30,880 | 26,733 | 17,467 |
| OLDHAM | 26,182 | 15,451 | 7.4 | 9.0 | 25.9 | 38.6 | 12.9 | 6.3 | 53,384 | 40,991 | 58,686 | 61,480 | 49,724 | 28,100 |
| OWEN | 14,991 | 4,102 | 20.6 | 15.6 | 35.8 | 25.0 | 2.9 | 0.1 | 30,499 | 29,801 | 34,503 | 37,176 | 30,424 | 20,472 |
| OWSLEY | 10,077 | 2,036 | 43.7 | 20.4 | 22.7 | 10.9 | 1.6 | 0.7 | 21,321 | 16,422 | 21,904 | 25,124 | 21,371 | 20,698 |
| PENDLETON | 15,441 | 5,021 | 16.2 | 13.5 | 39.1 | 26.5 | 4.2 | 0.5 | 33,429 | 30,666 | 39,926 | 40,725 | 31,449 | 21,630 |
| PERRY | 12,668 | 11,089 | 30.9 | 16.6 | 33.4 | 15.2 | 2.8 | 1.0 | 27,030 | 24,843 | 35,322 | 28,111 | 23,754 | 21,246 |
| PIKE | 13,445 | 26,403 | 28.2 | 18.3 | 32.1 | 17.7 | 2.9 | 0.9 | 27,655 | 25,743 | 34,815 | 30,780 | 24,983 | 18,925 |
| POWELL | 11,497 | 4,762 | 26.3 | 19.2 | 35.8 | 16.8 | 1.8 | 0.1 | 25,951 | 22,575 | 33,070 | 28,120 | 25,983 | 17,093 |
| PULASKI | 14,568 | 22,376 | 24.1 | 19.3 | 33.4 | 19.1 | 3.2 | 0.9 | 28,877 | 27,840 | 35,485 | 35,007 | 27,974 | 19,153 |
| ROBERTSON | 13,695 | 873 | 23.0 | 14.3 | 39.9 | 20.6 | 2.1 | 0.1 | 28,491 | 29,802 | 33,690 | 32,126 | 29,167 | 20,844 |
| ROCKCASTLE | 12,305 | 6,142 | 29.5 | 20.3 | 33.7 | 14.7 | 1.6 | 0.2 | 24,704 | 24,399 | 30,982 | 28,718 | 21,958 | 17,605 |
| ROWAN | 12,627 | 7,819 | 30.2 | 18.1 | 31.5 | 16.1 | 2.8 | 1.3 | 27,326 | 21,778 | 34,695 | 32,051 | 28,375 | 19,151 |
| RUSSELL | 13,599 | 6,671 | 29.7 | 19.6 | 31.3 | 16.1 | 2.7 | 0.6 | 26,116 | 26,066 | 33,787 | 31,319 | 24,053 | 16,613 |
| SCOTT | 22,399 | 11,986 | 14.4 | 10.4 | 33.5 | 30.3 | 7.3 | 4.1 | 42,467 | 33,257 | 48,595 | 50,715 | 43,677 | 24,119 |
| SHELBY | 23,554 | 11,553 | 13.4 | 10.9 | 35.0 | 29.9 | 6.9 | 4.0 | 42,443 | 33,014 | 48,437 | 49,674 | 42,051 | 29,409 |
| SIMPSON | 15,797 | 6,476 | 18.9 | 19.3 | 35.1 | 23.2 | 2.8 | 0.7 | 30,726 | 27,293 | 37,626 | 37,855 | 32,840 | 18,912 |
| SPENCER | 15,959 | 3,901 | 18.3 | 18.2 | 34.3 | 23.0 | 4.4 | 1.8 | 33,270 | 25,672 | 38,784 | 42,442 | 33,504 | 20,432 |
| TAYLOR | 13,842 | 9,132 | 25.3 | 15.7 | 38.8 | 17.6 | 2.1 | 0.6 | 27,638 | 27,274 | 33,996 | 30,982 | 28,370 | 18,436 |
| TODD | 15,098 | 4,294 | 20.6 | 16.6 | 35.8 | 22.9 | 3.4 | 0.8 | 30,772 | 31,116 | 36,191 | 37,036 | 30,615 | 21,027 |
| TRIGG | 16,106 | 5,258 | 22.9 | 16.9 | 33.1 | 22.5 | 3.8 | 0.9 | 30,258 | 25,956 | 38,767 | 41,401 | 30,405 | 19,822 |
| TRIMBLE | 14,648 | 3,043 | 19.4 | 16.3 | 37.7 | 23.3 | 2.9 | 0.4 | 30,430 | 28,155 | 35,446 | 38,471 | 30,255 | 17,540 |
| UNION | 15,837 | 5,758 | 22.3 | 18.5 | 33.3 | 19.9 | 4.1 | 1.9 | 32,015 | 26,611 | 36,968 | 39,758 | 30,439 | 23,271 |
| WARREN | 19,671 | 33,831 | 19.2 | 12.4 | 34.6 | 26.3 | 5.4 | 2.1 | 35,837 | 29,168 | 42,164 | 45,935 | 34,470 | 23,498 |
| WASHINGTON | 16,339 | 4,014 | 20.5 | 16.5 | 35.4 | 23.3 | 3.4 | 0.9 | 31,111 | 27,638 | 35,136 | 37,824 | 33,963 | 23,033 |
| WAYNE | 10,569 | 7,452 | 34.4 | 23.8 | 28.1 | 12.4 | 1.2 | 0.1 | 22,302 | 20,796 | 29,576 | 25,315 | 20,315 | 16,575 |
| WEBSTER | 14,450 | 5,248 | 25.1 | 17.1 | 32.1 | 22.1 | 3.2 | 0.3 | 28,965 | 25,891 | 37,352 | 36,503 | 29,170 | 17,417 |
| WHITLEY | 12,329 | 13,551 | 34.6 | 18.1 | 29.2 | 14.9 | 2.3 | 1.0 | 25,339 | 24,340 | 31,842 | 27,635 | 24,458 | 17,643 |
| WOLFE | 9,423 | 2,871 | 40.7 | 19.6 | 29.5 | 9.4 | 0.8 | 0.1 | 20,635 | 20,262 | 22,573 | 22,627 | 21,406 | 15,626 |
| WOODFORD | 22,055 | 8,729 | 10.6 | 11.9 | 33.2 | 34.6 | 7.2 | 2.6 | 42,149 | 35,655 | 45,896 | 54,092 | 37,625 | 24,700 |
| KENTUCKY | 17,910 | | 20.3 | 15.1 | 33.7 | 24.1 | 4.9 | 1.9 | 34,208 | 29,344 | 40,489 | 41,778 | 33,655 | 22,337 |
| UNITED STATES | 22,162 | | 14.5 | 12.5 | 32.3 | 29.8 | 7.4 | 3.5 | 40,748 | 34,503 | 44,969 | 49,579 | 43,409 | 27,339 |

# SPENDING POTENTIAL INDEXES

| COUNTY | FINANCIAL SERVICES | | | | THE HOME | | | | | | ENTERTAINMENT | | | | | | PERSONAL | | | |
|---|---|---|---|---|---|---|---|---|---|---|---|---|---|---|---|---|---|---|---|---|
| | | | | | Home Improvements | | | Furnishings | | | | | | | | | | | | |
| | Auto Loan | Home Loan | Investments | Retirement Plans | Home Repair | Lawn & Garden | Remodeling | Appliances | Electronics | Furniture | Restaurants | Sporting Goods | Theater & Concerts | Toys & Hobbies | Travel | Video Rental | Apparel | Auto Aftermarket | Health Insurance | Pets & Supplies |
| MARION | 98 | 67 | 71 | 76 | 93 | 91 | 113 | 96 | 92 | 77 | 79 | 97 | 80 | 96 | 68 | 96 | 80 | 88 | 102 | 98 |
| MARSHALL | 98 | 73 | 81 | 82 | 95 | 92 | 115 | 97 | 93 | 81 | 84 | 96 | 84 | 98 | 72 | 98 | 85 | 90 | 103 | 99 |
| MARTIN | 96 | 66 | 68 | 73 | 94 | 90 | 109 | 95 | 90 | 78 | 77 | 94 | 79 | 93 | 69 | 94 | 78 | 86 | 100 | 96 |
| MASON | 96 | 77 | 84 | 82 | 97 | 93 | 108 | 96 | 92 | 84 | 85 | 94 | 86 | 96 | 76 | 96 | 85 | 90 | 101 | 97 |
| MEADE | 96 | 80 | 80 | 81 | 93 | 89 | 109 | 95 | 93 | 83 | 88 | 94 | 85 | 96 | 73 | 97 | 86 | 91 | 98 | 99 |
| MENIFEE | 97 | 63 | 66 | 73 | 92 | 90 | 112 | 96 | 91 | 75 | 77 | 96 | 78 | 95 | 66 | 95 | 78 | 86 | 102 | 96 |
| MERCER | 97 | 76 | 85 | 82 | 96 | 93 | 112 | 97 | 93 | 85 | 85 | 94 | 86 | 97 | 75 | 97 | 86 | 91 | 99 | 99 |
| METCALFE | 97 | 63 | 68 | 75 | 92 | 90 | 112 | 95 | 91 | 74 | 77 | 96 | 78 | 95 | 66 | 96 | 78 | 87 | 103 | 97 |
| MONROE | 97 | 63 | 67 | 73 | 92 | 90 | 112 | 95 | 91 | 75 | 77 | 95 | 78 | 94 | 66 | 95 | 78 | 86 | 102 | 96 |
| MONTGOMERY | 97 | 70 | 76 | 79 | 94 | 91 | 112 | 96 | 92 | 80 | 81 | 95 | 82 | 96 | 71 | 96 | 82 | 89 | 101 | 98 |
| MORGAN | 96 | 63 | 68 | 73 | 92 | 90 | 111 | 95 | 91 | 75 | 77 | 94 | 78 | 93 | 67 | 95 | 78 | 86 | 102 | 95 |
| MUHLENBERG | 97 | 69 | 78 | 78 | 94 | 92 | 111 | 96 | 92 | 79 | 80 | 95 | 82 | 95 | 71 | 96 | 81 | 88 | 101 | 97 |
| NELSON | 98 | 74 | 81 | 81 | 95 | 92 | 114 | 97 | 93 | 83 | 85 | 96 | 84 | 97 | 72 | 97 | 84 | 90 | 101 | 99 |
| NICHOLAS | 96 | 63 | 68 | 73 | 92 | 90 | 111 | 95 | 91 | 75 | 77 | 94 | 78 | 93 | 66 | 95 | 78 | 86 | 102 | 96 |
| OHIO | 97 | 64 | 69 | 74 | 92 | 90 | 111 | 95 | 91 | 75 | 77 | 94 | 78 | 94 | 67 | 96 | 78 | 87 | 102 | 96 |
| OLDHAM | 105 | 111 | 103 | 110 | 102 | 106 | 107 | 104 | 108 | 110 | 114 | 108 | 108 | 108 | 93 | 102 | 113 | 109 | 100 | 106 |
| OWEN | 99 | 68 | 74 | 80 | 93 | 91 | 117 | 97 | 92 | 77 | 80 | 97 | 81 | 97 | 69 | 97 | 81 | 89 | 104 | 99 |
| OWSLEY | 93 | 62 | 68 | 70 | 92 | 87 | 101 | 95 | 89 | 76 | 72 | 90 | 76 | 89 | 68 | 95 | 77 | 86 | 93 | 93 |
| PENDLETON | 99 | 70 | 77 | 80 | 94 | 91 | 115 | 97 | 93 | 80 | 83 | 97 | 83 | 98 | 70 | 97 | 83 | 90 | 102 | 100 |
| PERRY | 97 | 67 | 73 | 75 | 93 | 91 | 112 | 95 | 92 | 78 | 79 | 95 | 80 | 95 | 69 | 95 | 80 | 87 | 101 | 97 |
| PIKE | 97 | 67 | 72 | 75 | 93 | 91 | 111 | 96 | 91 | 78 | 79 | 96 | 80 | 95 | 68 | 95 | 79 | 87 | 101 | 97 |
| POWELL | 97 | 63 | 66 | 73 | 92 | 90 | 112 | 96 | 91 | 75 | 77 | 96 | 78 | 95 | 66 | 95 | 78 | 86 | 102 | 96 |
| PULASKI | 97 | 69 | 76 | 78 | 94 | 91 | 112 | 96 | 92 | 79 | 81 | 94 | 81 | 95 | 70 | 96 | 81 | 88 | 101 | 97 |
| ROBERTSON | 97 | 63 | 66 | 73 | 92 | 90 | 112 | 96 | 91 | 75 | 77 | 96 | 78 | 95 | 66 | 95 | 78 | 86 | 102 | 96 |
| ROCKCASTLE | 97 | 63 | 66 | 73 | 92 | 90 | 112 | 96 | 91 | 75 | 77 | 96 | 78 | 95 | 66 | 95 | 78 | 86 | 102 | 96 |
| ROWAN | 96 | 79 | 84 | 84 | 95 | 91 | 108 | 93 | 91 | 81 | 85 | 93 | 83 | 95 | 74 | 94 | 84 | 90 | 99 | 97 |
| RUSSELL | 98 | 63 | 67 | 73 | 92 | 90 | 113 | 96 | 91 | 75 | 77 | 96 | 78 | 95 | 66 | 95 | 78 | 87 | 102 | 97 |
| SCOTT | 99 | 83 | 84 | 86 | 95 | 93 | 109 | 97 | 96 | 88 | 91 | 97 | 89 | 99 | 76 | 98 | 90 | 94 | 100 | 100 |
| SHELBY | 100 | 88 | 92 | 92 | 99 | 97 | 111 | 99 | 97 | 93 | 95 | 99 | 94 | 102 | 81 | 99 | 95 | 97 | 101 | 102 |
| SIMPSON | 97 | 71 | 77 | 78 | 94 | 91 | 111 | 96 | 91 | 81 | 81 | 95 | 82 | 95 | 71 | 96 | 82 | 89 | 99 | 97 |
| SPENCER | 100 | 72 | 79 | 82 | 94 | 92 | 116 | 97 | 93 | 80 | 84 | 99 | 84 | 100 | 71 | 98 | 85 | 91 | 103 | 101 |
| TAYLOR | 97 | 73 | 81 | 79 | 96 | 92 | 112 | 96 | 91 | 82 | 83 | 94 | 84 | 96 | 73 | 96 | 83 | 89 | 100 | 97 |
| TODD | 97 | 66 | 72 | 76 | 93 | 91 | 112 | 96 | 91 | 78 | 79 | 96 | 80 | 95 | 68 | 96 | 80 | 87 | 102 | 97 |
| TRIGG | 98 | 70 | 84 | 82 | 95 | 96 | 114 | 97 | 92 | 79 | 82 | 96 | 83 | 97 | 73 | 96 | 82 | 89 | 104 | 98 |
| TRIMBLE | 99 | 68 | 74 | 78 | 93 | 91 | 114 | 97 | 93 | 79 | 81 | 97 | 82 | 97 | 69 | 96 | 81 | 89 | 102 | 99 |
| UNION | 97 | 75 | 84 | 81 | 95 | 93 | 109 | 96 | 93 | 83 | 85 | 95 | 85 | 97 | 74 | 97 | 85 | 90 | 101 | 98 |
| WARREN | 99 | 91 | 94 | 92 | 99 | 97 | 105 | 97 | 96 | 93 | 95 | 98 | 93 | 100 | 82 | 98 | 94 | 96 | 98 | 100 |
| WASHINGTON | 96 | 68 | 77 | 77 | 94 | 92 | 111 | 95 | 91 | 78 | 80 | 94 | 81 | 95 | 71 | 96 | 80 | 88 | 102 | 96 |
| WAYNE | 98 | 64 | 68 | 74 | 92 | 91 | 113 | 96 | 91 | 75 | 77 | 96 | 79 | 95 | 67 | 95 | 78 | 87 | 102 | 97 |
| WEBSTER | 97 | 65 | 71 | 75 | 93 | 90 | 111 | 95 | 91 | 77 | 78 | 94 | 79 | 94 | 68 | 96 | 79 | 87 | 101 | 96 |
| WHITLEY | 96 | 68 | 75 | 76 | 94 | 91 | 109 | 95 | 91 | 78 | 79 | 94 | 81 | 94 | 70 | 96 | 80 | 88 | 100 | 96 |
| WOLFE | 97 | 63 | 66 | 73 | 92 | 90 | 112 | 96 | 91 | 75 | 77 | 96 | 78 | 95 | 66 | 95 | 78 | 86 | 102 | 96 |
| WOODFORD | 104 | 95 | 96 | 99 | 100 | 100 | 113 | 102 | 103 | 99 | 103 | 104 | 100 | 107 | 84 | 101 | 103 | 102 | 102 | 106 |
| KENTUCKY | 98 | 84 | 91 | 89 | 98 | 96 | 106 | 97 | 95 | 89 | 90 | 97 | 91 | 98 | 80 | 97 | 90 | 93 | 100 | 99 |
| UNITED STATES | 100 | 100 | 100 | 100 | 100 | 100 | 100 | 100 | 100 | 100 | 100 | 100 | 100 | 100 | 100 | 100 | 100 | 100 | 100 | 100 |

| COUNTY | FIPS Code | MSA Code | DMA Code | POPULATION 1990 | POPULATION 2000 | POPULATION 2005 | 1990-2000 ANNUAL CHANGE % Rate | 1990-2000 ANNUAL CHANGE State Rank | RACE (%) White 1990 | White 2000 | Black 1990 | Black 2000 | Asian/Pacific 1990 | Asian/Pacific 2000 |
|---|---|---|---|---|---|---|---|---|---|---|---|---|---|---|
| ACADIA | 001 | 3880 | 642 | 55,882 | 58,093 | 58,900 | 0.4 | 26 | 81.5 | 79.5 | 18.2 | 20.2 | 0.1 | 0.2 |
| ALLEN | 003 | 0000 | 643 | 21,226 | 24,244 | 24,439 | 1.3 | 7 | 76.8 | 72.3 | 21.2 | 25.5 | 0.2 | 0.3 |
| ASCENSION | 005 | 0760 | 716 | 58,214 | 76,244 | 87,052 | 2.7 | 3 | 76.4 | 73.8 | 22.8 | 25.2 | 0.3 | 0.4 |
| ASSUMPTION | 007 | 0000 | 716 | 22,753 | 23,436 | 24,357 | 0.3 | 30 | 67.1 | 63.8 | 32.3 | 35.5 | 0.3 | 0.4 |
| AVOYELLES | 009 | 0000 | 644 | 39,159 | 40,739 | 40,903 | 0.4 | 26 | 72.3 | 68.8 | 27.0 | 30.4 | 0.1 | 0.2 |
| BEAUREGARD | 011 | 0000 | 643 | 30,083 | 32,497 | 33,637 | 0.8 | 13 | 83.9 | 82.3 | 14.9 | 16.3 | 0.5 | 0.6 |
| BIENVILLE | 013 | 0000 | 612 | 15,979 | 15,677 | 15,377 | -0.2 | 48 | 56.2 | 52.6 | 43.5 | 47.1 | 0.1 | 0.1 |
| BOSSIER | 015 | 7680 | 612 | 86,088 | 94,269 | 97,987 | 0.9 | 10 | 77.9 | 75.5 | 20.2 | 21.9 | 1.1 | 1.5 |
| CADDO | 017 | 7680 | 612 | 248,253 | 241,554 | 236,533 | -0.3 | 55 | 59.0 | 56.2 | 40.1 | 42.7 | 0.4 | 0.6 |
| CALCASIEU | 019 | 3960 | 643 | 168,134 | 181,361 | 185,326 | 0.7 | 17 | 76.2 | 73.9 | 22.9 | 25.0 | 0.4 | 0.5 |
| CALDWELL | 021 | 0000 | 628 | 9,810 | 10,562 | 10,992 | 0.7 | 17 | 81.2 | 79.2 | 17.9 | 19.9 | 0.1 | 0.2 |
| CAMERON | 023 | 0000 | 643 | 9,260 | 9,014 | 9,149 | -0.3 | 55 | 93.8 | 92.7 | 5.4 | 6.3 | 0.3 | 0.4 |
| CATAHOULA | 025 | 0000 | 628 | 11,065 | 10,827 | 10,447 | -0.2 | 48 | 73.5 | 71.4 | 26.0 | 28.1 | 0.0 | 0.1 |
| CLAIBORNE | 027 | 0000 | 612 | 17,405 | 16,680 | 15,964 | -0.4 | 60 | 53.5 | 50.6 | 46.2 | 49.1 | 0.1 | 0.1 |
| CONCORDIA | 029 | 0000 | 628 | 20,828 | 20,482 | 20,038 | -0.2 | 48 | 63.2 | 60.7 | 36.5 | 38.9 | 0.1 | 0.2 |
| DE SOTO | 031 | 0000 | 612 | 25,346 | 25,278 | 25,832 | 0.0 | 42 | 55.2 | 51.8 | 44.0 | 47.3 | 0.0 | 0.0 |
| EAST BATON ROUGE | 033 | 0760 | 716 | 380,105 | 392,877 | 390,812 | 0.3 | 30 | 63.3 | 60.2 | 34.8 | 37.4 | 1.4 | 1.8 |
| EAST CARROLL | 035 | 0000 | 628 | 9,709 | 8,588 | 7,963 | -1.2 | 63 | 34.6 | 32.3 | 64.8 | 67.0 | 0.2 | 0.3 |
| EAST FELICIANA | 037 | 0000 | 716 | 19,211 | 21,207 | 21,725 | 1.0 | 8 | 52.2 | 48.7 | 47.3 | 50.7 | 0.1 | 0.1 |
| EVANGELINE | 039 | 0000 | 642 | 33,274 | 34,424 | 34,948 | 0.3 | 30 | 73.3 | 70.7 | 26.1 | 28.8 | 0.1 | 0.1 |
| FRANKLIN | 041 | 0000 | 628 | 22,387 | 22,127 | 21,839 | -0.1 | 47 | 68.2 | 65.9 | 31.4 | 33.8 | 0.1 | 0.2 |
| GRANT | 043 | 0000 | 644 | 17,526 | 19,433 | 20,630 | 1.0 | 8 | 84.8 | 83.1 | 14.5 | 16.2 | 0.2 | 0.2 |
| IBERIA | 045 | 0000 | 642 | 68,297 | 74,021 | 76,940 | 0.8 | 13 | 68.7 | 65.7 | 29.5 | 32.1 | 1.2 | 1.6 |
| IBERVILLE | 047 | 0000 | 716 | 31,049 | 31,300 | 31,019 | 0.1 | 40 | 53.2 | 49.8 | 46.3 | 49.6 | 0.2 | 0.2 |
| JACKSON | 049 | 0000 | 628 | 15,705 | 15,398 | 15,148 | -0.2 | 48 | 70.5 | 67.3 | 29.2 | 32.3 | 0.1 | 0.1 |
| JEFFERSON | 051 | 5560 | 622 | 448,306 | 446,086 | 437,685 | 0.0 | 42 | 78.3 | 76.1 | 17.6 | 18.7 | 2.2 | 3.0 |
| JEFFERSON DAVIS | 053 | 0000 | 642 | 30,722 | 31,345 | 30,958 | 0.2 | 34 | 80.5 | 78.4 | 19.0 | 21.0 | 0.1 | 0.2 |
| LAFAYETTE | 055 | 3880 | 642 | 164,762 | 189,184 | 198,045 | 1.4 | 6 | 76.1 | 73.5 | 22.4 | 24.6 | 1.0 | 1.2 |
| LAFOURCHE | 057 | 3350 | 622 | 85,860 | 90,072 | 92,970 | 0.5 | 21 | 84.3 | 82.8 | 12.5 | 13.8 | 0.8 | 1.1 |
| LA SALLE | 059 | 0000 | 628 | 13,662 | 13,695 | 13,643 | 0.0 | 42 | 89.8 | 88.5 | 9.2 | 10.4 | 0.3 | 0.4 |
| LINCOLN | 061 | 0000 | 628 | 41,745 | 41,095 | 40,849 | -0.2 | 48 | 59.0 | 56.4 | 39.7 | 42.1 | 0.8 | 1.1 |
| LIVINGSTON | 063 | 0760 | 716 | 70,526 | 94,044 | 108,173 | 2.8 | 2 | 94.0 | 93.1 | 5.6 | 6.3 | 0.2 | 0.2 |
| MADISON | 065 | 0000 | 628 | 12,463 | 12,962 | 12,842 | 0.4 | 26 | 39.8 | 36.6 | 59.5 | 62.6 | 0.1 | 0.1 |
| MOREHOUSE | 067 | 0000 | 628 | 31,938 | 31,049 | 30,105 | -0.3 | 55 | 58.2 | 55.4 | 41.5 | 44.3 | 0.1 | 0.2 |
| NATCHITOCHES | 069 | 0000 | 612 | 36,689 | 37,285 | 37,729 | 0.2 | 34 | 60.9 | 57.4 | 37.6 | 40.9 | 0.4 | 0.5 |
| ORLEANS | 071 | 5560 | 622 | 496,938 | 456,811 | 436,865 | -0.8 | 61 | 34.9 | 32.5 | 61.9 | 63.7 | 1.9 | 2.5 |
| OUACHITA | 073 | 5200 | 628 | 142,191 | 146,669 | 146,646 | 0.3 | 30 | 68.1 | 65.5 | 31.0 | 33.4 | 0.5 | 0.7 |
| PLAQUEMINES | 075 | 5560 | 622 | 25,575 | 26,158 | 26,412 | 0.2 | 34 | 72.4 | 69.8 | 23.2 | 25.1 | 2.0 | 2.7 |
| POINTE COUPEE | 077 | 0000 | 716 | 22,540 | 23,501 | 23,675 | 0.4 | 26 | 58.5 | 55.5 | 41.1 | 44.1 | 0.1 | 0.1 |
| RAPIDES | 079 | 0220 | 644 | 131,556 | 127,051 | 128,153 | -0.3 | 55 | 70.7 | 68.1 | 28.0 | 30.2 | 0.7 | 0.9 |
| RED RIVER | 081 | 0000 | 612 | 9,387 | 9,421 | 9,090 | 0.0 | 42 | 61.3 | 57.2 | 38.2 | 42.3 | 0.1 | 0.1 |
| RICHLAND | 083 | 0000 | 628 | 20,629 | 21,156 | 21,524 | 0.2 | 34 | 63.1 | 60.7 | 36.5 | 38.9 | 0.1 | 0.1 |
| SABINE | 085 | 0000 | 612 | 22,646 | 23,853 | 24,077 | 0.5 | 21 | 79.2 | 77.6 | 17.6 | 19.0 | 0.1 | 0.1 |
| ST. BERNARD | 087 | 5560 | 622 | 66,631 | 65,385 | 63,560 | -0.2 | 48 | 93.3 | 92.3 | 4.7 | 5.1 | 0.9 | 1.4 |
| ST. CHARLES | 089 | 5560 | 622 | 42,437 | 49,190 | 51,943 | 1.5 | 4 | 74.6 | 71.8 | 24.2 | 26.6 | 0.4 | 0.6 |
| ST. HELENA | 091 | 0000 | 716 | 9,874 | 9,582 | 9,461 | -0.3 | 55 | 47.9 | 44.6 | 51.9 | 55.2 | 0.0 | 0.0 |
| ST. JAMES | 093 | 5560 | 622 | 20,879 | 21,312 | 21,889 | 0.2 | 34 | 50.2 | 46.9 | 49.6 | 52.9 | 0.1 | 0.1 |
| ST. JOHN THE BAPTIST | 095 | 5560 | 622 | 39,996 | 42,697 | 43,802 | 0.6 | 19 | 62.6 | 59.1 | 36.1 | 39.2 | 0.4 | 0.5 |
| ST. LANDRY | 097 | 3880 | 642 | 80,331 | 84,720 | 87,077 | 0.5 | 21 | 59.2 | 56.1 | 40.3 | 43.4 | 0.2 | 0.3 |
| ST. MARTIN | 099 | 3880 | 642 | 43,978 | 48,070 | 50,086 | 0.9 | 10 | 65.5 | 62.5 | 33.0 | 35.8 | 0.7 | 1.0 |
| ST. MARY | 101 | 0000 | 716 | 58,086 | 56,626 | 55,786 | -0.2 | 48 | 64.9 | 62.0 | 31.6 | 34.0 | 1.7 | 2.2 |
| ST. TAMMANY | 103 | 5560 | 622 | 144,508 | 197,614 | 220,842 | 3.1 | 1 | 87.8 | 86.2 | 11.0 | 12.2 | 0.5 | 0.7 |
| TANGIPAHOA | 105 | 0000 | 622 | 85,709 | 99,741 | 106,906 | 1.5 | 4 | 70.7 | 68.0 | 28.6 | 31.2 | 0.3 | 0.4 |
| TENSAS | 107 | 0000 | 628 | 7,103 | 6,467 | 6,118 | -0.9 | 62 | 46.3 | 43.8 | 53.3 | 55.9 | 0.1 | 0.0 |
| TERREBONNE | 109 | 3350 | 622 | 96,982 | 106,618 | 111,130 | 0.9 | 10 | 77.4 | 75.5 | 16.5 | 18.3 | 0.7 | 1.0 |
| UNION | 111 | 0000 | 628 | 20,690 | 22,345 | 23,197 | 0.8 | 13 | 71.8 | 69.0 | 27.9 | 30.5 | 0.1 | 0.2 |
| VERMILION | 113 | 0000 | 642 | 50,055 | 52,757 | 54,389 | 0.5 | 21 | 84.4 | 82.5 | 13.9 | 15.4 | 1.4 | 1.8 |
| VERNON | 115 | 0000 | 644 | 61,961 | 51,146 | 49,104 | -1.9 | 64 | 74.0 | 71.7 | 20.8 | 21.5 | 2.4 | 3.3 |
| WASHINGTON | 117 | 0000 | 622 | 43,185 | 43,173 | 43,237 | 0.0 | 42 | 68.7 | 66.1 | 31.0 | 33.5 | 0.1 | 0.2 |
| WEBSTER | 119 | 7680 | 612 | 41,989 | 42,896 | 43,404 | 0.2 | 34 | 68.0 | 65.5 | 31.6 | 34.1 | 0.1 | 0.2 |
| WEST BATON ROUGE | 121 | 0760 | 716 | 19,419 | 20,396 | 20,269 | 0.5 | 21 | 63.5 | 60.1 | 36.0 | 39.3 | 0.1 | 0.2 |
| WEST CARROLL | 123 | 0000 | 628 | 12,093 | 12,176 | 12,220 | 0.1 | 40 | 82.7 | 80.6 | 16.7 | 18.7 | 0.0 | 0.1 |
| WEST FELICIANA | 125 | 0000 | 716 | 12,915 | 13,988 | 14,757 | 0.8 | 13 | 43.9 | 41.7 | 55.4 | 57.6 | 0.1 | 0.1 |
| WINN | 127 | 0000 | 628 | 16,269 | 17,365 | 16,722 | 0.6 | 19 | 69.7 | 64.2 | 29.5 | 34.9 | 0.1 | 0.2 |
| LOUISIANA | | | | | | | 0.4 | | 67.3 | 65.7 | 30.8 | 32.1 | 1.0 | 1.3 |
| UNITED STATES | | | | | | | 1.0 | | 80.3 | 77.9 | 12.1 | 12.4 | 2.9 | 3.9 |

# POPULATION COMPOSITION



| COUNTY | % HISPANIC ORIGIN | | 2000 AGE DISTRIBUTION (%) | | | | | | | | | | MEDIAN AGE | | 2000 Males/ Females (×100) |
|---|---|---|---|---|---|---|---|---|---|---|---|---|---|---|---|
| | 1990 | 2000 | 0-4 | 5-9 | 10-14 | 15-19 | 20-24 | 25-44 | 45-64 | 65-84 | 85+ | 18+ | 1990 | 2000 | |
| ACADIA | 0.7 | 1.2 | 7.7 | 7.9 | 8.3 | 8.8 | 7.1 | 25.7 | 22.6 | 10.6 | 1.4 | 70.6 | 30.5 | 33.9 | 90.8 |
| ALLEN | 3.2 | 5.9 | 6.4 | 6.5 | 7.1 | 7.8 | 7.1 | 30.0 | 23.0 | 10.6 | 1.5 | 75.1 | 32.5 | 35.7 | 113.9 |
| ASCENSION | 1.6 | 2.3 | 7.5 | 7.9 | 8.4 | 8.8 | 7.5 | 29.8 | 22.2 | 7.1 | 0.8 | 70.8 | 29.4 | 32.4 | 95.8 |
| ASSUMPTION | 1.3 | 1.8 | 7.3 | 7.7 | 8.4 | 8.7 | 7.6 | 27.3 | 22.4 | 9.4 | 1.2 | 71.3 | 29.7 | 33.4 | 93.4 |
| AVOYELLES | 1.6 | 2.3 | 6.8 | 7.2 | 7.4 | 8.5 | 7.2 | 25.6 | 22.9 | 12.5 | 1.9 | 73.3 | 32.7 | 35.9 | 94.7 |
| BEAUREGARD | 1.4 | 2.0 | 6.9 | 7.0 | 7.6 | 8.1 | 7.4 | 28.2 | 23.4 | 10.3 | 1.2 | 73.5 | 31.6 | 35.0 | 99.9 |
| BIENVILLE | 0.5 | 0.8 | 6.8 | 7.1 | 7.4 | 8.5 | 6.6 | 23.3 | 23.3 | 14.0 | 2.8 | 73.4 | 34.6 | 37.5 | 91.2 |
| BOSSIER | 2.1 | 3.0 | 7.3 | 7.2 | 7.3 | 8.0 | 7.8 | 29.0 | 22.7 | 9.6 | 1.1 | 73.4 | 30.6 | 34.2 | 93.0 |
| CADDO | 1.0 | 1.5 | 6.8 | 6.9 | 7.4 | 8.2 | 7.3 | 26.6 | 23.2 | 11.7 | 1.8 | 73.8 | 32.7 | 36.1 | 87.3 |
| CALCASIEU | 1.1 | 1.7 | 6.8 | 7.2 | 7.6 | 8.4 | 7.3 | 27.6 | 23.6 | 10.5 | 1.1 | 73.5 | 31.6 | 35.3 | 93.9 |
| CALDWELL | 1.6 | 2.2 | 6.5 | 6.6 | 7.9 | 8.2 | 6.6 | 25.0 | 24.7 | 12.5 | 2.0 | 73.6 | 33.5 | 37.3 | 95.9 |
| CAMERON | 1.5 | 2.3 | 7.9 | 8.1 | 8.3 | 8.2 | 5.8 | 28.6 | 21.7 | 10.3 | 1.1 | 70.7 | 30.7 | 35.1 | 96.9 |
| CATAHOULA | 0.6 | 1.0 | 7.0 | 7.4 | 8.1 | 8.4 | 6.8 | 24.6 | 24.0 | 12.1 | 1.6 | 72.3 | 32.3 | 36.2 | 93.2 |
| CLAIBORNE | 0.2 | 0.4 | 5.9 | 6.2 | 6.6 | 8.0 | 8.5 | 26.1 | 22.4 | 13.7 | 2.7 | 76.6 | 34.7 | 36.8 | 108.4 |
| CONCORDIA | 0.6 | 1.0 | 6.7 | 7.2 | 7.9 | 8.6 | 7.0 | 24.6 | 24.3 | 12.1 | 1.5 | 72.7 | 32.3 | 36.2 | 89.2 |
| DE SOTO | 1.5 | 1.9 | 7.1 | 7.3 | 7.8 | 8.6 | 7.0 | 25.4 | 23.0 | 11.9 | 1.9 | 72.5 | 32.4 | 35.7 | 90.0 |
| EAST BATON ROUGE | 1.5 | 2.1 | 6.8 | 7.1 | 7.4 | 8.9 | 8.7 | 29.6 | 21.6 | 8.8 | 1.1 | 74.2 | 29.9 | 33.0 | 91.1 |
| EAST CARROLL | 1.2 | 1.5 | 8.9 | 8.7 | 9.3 | 9.7 | 8.3 | 22.4 | 19.8 | 11.2 | 1.8 | 66.8 | 28.1 | 29.3 | 88.3 |
| EAST FELICIANA | 1.0 | 1.2 | 7.0 | 7.2 | 7.5 | 8.7 | 8.7 | 29.4 | 21.4 | 8.7 | 1.4 | 72.9 | 31.1 | 32.6 | 112.9 |
| EVANGELINE | 0.8 | 1.3 | 7.7 | 7.8 | 8.3 | 8.7 | 7.1 | 24.7 | 22.5 | 11.7 | 1.6 | 70.7 | 31.1 | 34.3 | 91.6 |
| FRANKLIN | 0.5 | 0.9 | 6.8 | 7.1 | 8.0 | 8.8 | 7.2 | 24.0 | 23.0 | 12.8 | 2.2 | 72.3 | 32.4 | 35.9 | 89.9 |
| GRANT | 0.9 | 1.4 | 7.0 | 7.4 | 7.8 | 8.5 | 6.7 | 26.2 | 23.8 | 11.0 | 1.6 | 72.6 | 31.9 | 35.7 | 93.5 |
| IBERIA | 1.9 | 2.7 | 7.9 | 8.0 | 8.4 | 8.7 | 7.5 | 27.1 | 21.6 | 9.6 | 1.2 | 70.4 | 29.8 | 32.7 | 92.4 |
| IBERVILLE | 1.9 | 2.5 | 7.2 | 7.3 | 7.6 | 8.7 | 8.4 | 28.9 | 21.4 | 9.4 | 1.1 | 72.8 | 30.5 | 32.7 | 95.9 |
| JACKSON | 0.3 | 0.6 | 5.9 | 6.6 | 7.5 | 8.4 | 6.9 | 24.1 | 24.8 | 13.8 | 2.1 | 74.9 | 34.5 | 38.3 | 91.7 |
| JEFFERSON | 5.9 | 7.7 | 6.4 | 6.4 | 6.9 | 7.5 | 7.1 | 30.0 | 23.9 | 10.6 | 1.1 | 75.7 | 32.3 | 36.4 | 91.1 |
| JEFFERSON DAVIS | 0.7 | 1.1 | 7.2 | 7.5 | 8.1 | 8.6 | 6.7 | 25.3 | 23.3 | 11.7 | 1.5 | 71.8 | 31.5 | 35.5 | 92.5 |
| LAFAYETTE | 1.6 | 2.3 | 7.5 | 7.5 | 7.5 | 8.5 | 8.4 | 30.5 | 20.9 | 8.2 | 1.0 | 73.0 | 29.8 | 32.6 | 92.6 |
| LAFOURCHE | 1.5 | 2.2 | 7.5 | 7.7 | 7.9 | 8.6 | 6.9 | 29.4 | 21.9 | 9.2 | 1.0 | 72.1 | 29.4 | 33.7 | 95.5 |
| LA SALLE | 0.3 | 0.7 | 6.1 | 6.4 | 6.8 | 8.2 | 6.5 | 25.4 | 24.7 | 13.6 | 2.2 | 75.4 | 34.8 | 38.5 | 90.1 |
| LINCOLN | 0.9 | 1.3 | 5.4 | 5.6 | 5.9 | 13.9 | 17.1 | 22.0 | 19.0 | 9.5 | 1.5 | 78.8 | 24.8 | 26.8 | 92.7 |
| LIVINGSTON | 0.9 | 1.6 | 7.2 | 7.6 | 7.8 | 8.4 | 7.1 | 29.2 | 23.7 | 8.2 | 0.8 | 72.2 | 30.2 | 33.8 | 98.1 |
| MADISON | 1.0 | 1.5 | 7.8 | 7.8 | 8.8 | 9.9 | 8.0 | 24.6 | 20.8 | 10.5 | 1.8 | 68.9 | 29.9 | 31.5 | 91.1 |
| MOREHOUSE | 0.4 | 0.7 | 6.9 | 7.4 | 8.0 | 8.9 | 7.2 | 24.5 | 22.2 | 13.0 | 1.8 | 72.1 | 32.0 | 35.4 | 89.0 |
| NATCHITOCHES | 1.3 | 1.8 | 7.0 | 7.2 | 7.5 | 11.6 | 9.5 | 24.0 | 20.9 | 10.8 | 1.5 | 72.5 | 29.2 | 31.5 | 90.1 |
| ORLEANS | 3.5 | 4.3 | 7.0 | 6.9 | 7.4 | 8.4 | 7.9 | 28.7 | 21.2 | 10.9 | 1.7 | 74.0 | 31.6 | 34.4 | 87.4 |
| OUACHITA | 0.8 | 1.3 | 7.1 | 7.1 | 7.6 | 9.2 | 8.9 | 26.8 | 21.9 | 10.1 | 1.4 | 73.1 | 30.2 | 33.2 | 88.5 |
| PLAQUEMINES | 2.3 | 3.2 | 7.8 | 7.9 | 7.9 | 8.3 | 7.6 | 30.0 | 20.8 | 9.0 | 0.7 | 71.3 | 29.4 | 32.6 | 101.1 |
| POINTE COUPEE | 0.7 | 1.2 | 7.1 | 7.3 | 7.6 | 9.0 | 7.0 | 26.1 | 23.0 | 11.3 | 1.6 | 72.4 | 31.6 | 35.5 | 93.1 |
| RAPIDES | 1.2 | 1.7 | 6.9 | 7.1 | 7.5 | 8.3 | 7.5 | 27.2 | 22.8 | 11.2 | 1.5 | 73.5 | 31.4 | 35.2 | 90.6 |
| RED RIVER | 0.6 | 0.8 | 7.7 | 8.0 | 8.0 | 9.0 | 6.9 | 23.8 | 22.0 | 12.9 | 1.8 | 70.6 | 31.8 | 34.7 | 89.1 |
| RICHLAND | 1.0 | 1.3 | 7.0 | 7.5 | 8.2 | 8.8 | 7.1 | 24.5 | 22.4 | 12.5 | 2.2 | 71.9 | 32.2 | 35.3 | 88.8 |
| SABINE | 4.6 | 6.2 | 6.9 | 7.0 | 7.5 | 8.0 | 6.4 | 23.5 | 24.8 | 14.1 | 1.9 | 73.6 | 34.5 | 38.0 | 94.8 |
| ST. BERNARD | 6.3 | 8.5 | 6.4 | 6.4 | 7.0 | 7.5 | 6.9 | 28.2 | 23.8 | 12.7 | 1.1 | 75.7 | 32.6 | 37.1 | 91.6 |
| ST. CHARLES | 2.5 | 3.5 | 8.1 | 8.7 | 8.7 | 8.2 | 6.2 | 30.0 | 21.4 | 8.1 | 0.8 | 69.4 | 30.3 | 33.6 | 94.4 |
| ST. HELENA | 0.5 | 0.7 | 7.7 | 7.9 | 8.4 | 8.7 | 7.5 | 25.4 | 22.6 | 10.5 | 1.4 | 70.7 | 30.6 | 33.6 | 91.5 |
| ST. JAMES | 0.5 | 0.8 | 7.9 | 8.1 | 8.5 | 8.9 | 6.9 | 27.9 | 21.6 | 9.0 | 1.1 | 70.2 | 29.4 | 32.8 | 90.8 |
| ST. JOHN THE BAPTIST | 2.4 | 3.3 | 8.4 | 9.0 | 8.7 | 8.6 | 6.7 | 30.2 | 20.3 | 7.2 | 0.8 | 68.6 | 28.7 | 31.5 | 94.5 |
| ST. LANDRY | 0.8 | 1.3 | 7.6 | 7.9 | 8.3 | 8.9 | 7.2 | 24.8 | 22.9 | 11.1 | 1.4 | 70.8 | 30.9 | 34.0 | 90.9 |
| ST. MARTIN | 1.1 | 1.7 | 8.2 | 8.3 | 8.6 | 8.8 | 6.9 | 28.2 | 21.5 | 8.6 | 0.9 | 69.5 | 29.2 | 32.4 | 94.9 |
| ST. MARY | 1.9 | 2.7 | 8.2 | 8.1 | 8.5 | 8.9 | 7.0 | 27.7 | 21.6 | 9.0 | 1.0 | 69.8 | 29.6 | 32.6 | 94.2 |
| ST. TAMMANY | 2.2 | 3.1 | 6.9 | 7.4 | 8.0 | 8.1 | 5.9 | 29.2 | 24.7 | 8.9 | 0.9 | 72.5 | 32.4 | 36.1 | 96.4 |
| TANGIPAHOA | 1.1 | 1.6 | 7.0 | 7.4 | 8.0 | 9.6 | 8.6 | 26.5 | 22.2 | 9.5 | 1.2 | 72.4 | 30.1 | 32.9 | 91.4 |
| TENSAS | 0.6 | 0.9 | 7.5 | 7.8 | 8.4 | 9.3 | 6.9 | 23.7 | 21.5 | 13.1 | 1.9 | 70.0 | 32.5 | 34.6 | 85.8 |
| TERREBONNE | 1.4 | 2.2 | 8.1 | 8.2 | 8.3 | 8.7 | 7.1 | 28.9 | 21.6 | 8.3 | 0.8 | 70.0 | 29.3 | 32.4 | 96.4 |
| UNION | 0.6 | 1.1 | 6.5 | 6.9 | 7.5 | 7.9 | 6.6 | 24.8 | 25.1 | 12.8 | 1.9 | 74.2 | 34.4 | 37.9 | 92.4 |
| VERMILION | 1.2 | 1.8 | 7.2 | 7.7 | 8.0 | 8.5 | 6.7 | 26.1 | 22.7 | 11.4 | 1.7 | 71.8 | 31.5 | 35.3 | 94.6 |
| VERNON | 5.5 | 7.4 | 8.6 | 6.2 | 5.9 | 9.1 | 19.8 | 28.3 | 14.2 | 7.0 | 0.9 | 75.6 | 24.7 | 25.1 | 128.8 |
| WASHINGTON | 0.6 | 0.9 | 6.2 | 6.7 | 7.4 | 8.4 | 6.9 | 25.7 | 24.2 | 12.9 | 1.6 | 74.3 | 33.3 | 37.2 | 92.9 |
| WEBSTER | 0.5 | 0.9 | 6.4 | 6.6 | 7.2 | 7.9 | 6.6 | 24.7 | 24.9 | 13.7 | 2.1 | 75.0 | 34.7 | 38.5 | 89.6 |
| WEST BATON ROUGE | 1.1 | 1.6 | 7.5 | 7.6 | 8.0 | 8.3 | 6.8 | 29.7 | 22.4 | 8.8 | 0.9 | 72.2 | 30.5 | 33.7 | 94.9 |
| WEST CARROLL | 1.0 | 1.3 | 6.5 | 7.0 | 7.5 | 8.4 | 6.5 | 24.0 | 24.9 | 13.3 | 1.8 | 73.6 | 34.1 | 37.9 | 92.3 |
| WEST FELICIANA | 1.6 | 1.5 | 4.8 | 5.0 | 5.2 | 6.5 | 9.2 | 43.4 | 19.0 | 6.1 | 0.9 | 80.9 | 33.1 | 33.8 | 203.4 |
| WINN | 0.9 | 1.2 | 6.1 | 6.4 | 7.2 | 7.8 | 8.1 | 26.4 | 23.3 | 12.8 | 1.9 | 75.6 | 33.5 | 36.3 | 103.3 |
| LOUISIANA | 2.2 | 2.9 | 7.1 | 7.2 | 7.6 | 8.5 | 7.7 | 28.0 | 22.4 | 10.2 | 1.3 | 73.2 | 31.0 | 34.4 | 92.7 |
| UNITED STATES | 9.0 | 11.8 | 6.9 | 7.2 | 7.2 | 7.2 | 6.7 | 29.9 | 22.2 | 11.1 | 1.6 | 74.6 | 32.9 | 35.7 | 95.6 |

| COUNTY | HOUSEHOLDS | | | | | FAMILIES | | | MEDIAN HOUSEHOLD INCOME | | | |
|---|---|---|---|---|---|---|---|---|---|---|---|---|
| | 1990 | 2000 | 2005 | % Annual Rate 1990-2000 | 2000 Average HH Size | 1990 | 2000 | % Annual Rate 1990-2000 | 2000 | 2005 | 2000 National Rank | 2000 State Rank |
| ACADIA | 19,285 | 20,882 | 21,594 | 1.0 | 2.75 | 14,827 | 15,594 | 0.6 | 23,908 | 26,183 | 2911 | 52 |
| ALLEN | 7,080 | 7,522 | 7,697 | 0.7 | 2.71 | 5,470 | 5,636 | 0.4 | 26,306 | 30,681 | 2676 | 37 |
| ASCENSION | 19,337 | 26,122 | 30,282 | 3.7 | 2.90 | 15,590 | 20,640 | 3.5 | 42,077 | 46,024 | 503 | 3 |
| ASSUMPTION | 7,397 | 7,981 | 8,479 | 0.9 | 2.92 | 5,899 | 6,173 | 0.6 | 30,307 | 35,376 | 2080 | 23 |
| AVOYELLES | 13,480 | 14,485 | 14,931 | 0.9 | 2.62 | 10,219 | 10,669 | 0.5 | 22,663 | 24,964 | 2987 | 58 |
| BEAUREGARD | 10,362 | 11,622 | 12,252 | 1.4 | 2.69 | 8,024 | 8,781 | 1.1 | 32,289 | 36,730 | 1663 | 17 |
| BIENVILLE | 5,852 | 5,939 | 5,928 | 0.2 | 2.54 | 4,219 | 4,116 | -0.3 | 24,207 | 27,899 | 2888 | 50 |
| BOSSIER | 30,718 | 34,981 | 37,024 | 1.6 | 2.64 | 23,334 | 25,842 | 1.2 | 37,041 | 41,953 | 971 | 8 |
| CADDO | 93,248 | 93,789 | 93,544 | 0.1 | 2.51 | 65,122 | 63,362 | -0.3 | 31,284 | 34,338 | 1871 | 19 |
| CALCASIEU | 60,328 | 68,024 | 71,059 | 1.5 | 2.62 | 45,035 | 49,591 | 1.2 | 35,254 | 38,450 | 1211 | 10 |
| CALDWELL | 3,575 | 3,903 | 4,089 | 1.1 | 2.65 | 2,709 | 2,838 | 0.6 | 25,210 | 29,676 | 2791 | 47 |
| CAMERON | 3,153 | 3,275 | 3,429 | 0.5 | 2.74 | 2,540 | 2,574 | 0.2 | 35,257 | 43,734 | 1210 | 9 |
| CATAHOULA | 3,927 | 4,089 | 4,064 | 0.5 | 2.61 | 2,977 | 3,002 | 0.1 | 22,891 | 26,380 | 2978 | 57 |
| CLAIBORNE | 6,065 | 6,003 | 5,856 | -0.1 | 2.51 | 4,314 | 4,102 | -0.6 | 23,295 | 26,692 | 2954 | 53 |
| CONCORDIA | 7,341 | 7,637 | 7,680 | 0.5 | 2.64 | 5,585 | 5,651 | 0.1 | 26,420 | 31,703 | 2664 | 36 |
| DE SOTO | 9,129 | 9,217 | 9,488 | 0.1 | 2.71 | 6,819 | 6,670 | -0.3 | 25,220 | 29,842 | 2790 | 46 |
| EAST BATON ROUGE | 138,620 | 149,839 | 152,257 | 0.9 | 2.54 | 95,915 | 101,153 | 0.6 | 37,046 | 40,814 | 969 | 7 |
| EAST CARROLL | 3,129 | 2,943 | 2,806 | -0.7 | 2.81 | 2,289 | 2,112 | -1.0 | 15,163 | 16,486 | 3140 | 64 |
| EAST FELICIANA | 5,589 | 6,259 | 6,537 | 1.4 | 2.94 | 4,407 | 4,828 | 1.1 | 29,452 | 31,968 | 2230 | 26 |
| EVANGELINE | 11,795 | 12,560 | 12,935 | 0.8 | 2.70 | 8,861 | 9,188 | 0.4 | 23,144 | 26,709 | 2962 | 55 |
| FRANKLIN | 7,776 | 7,947 | 8,004 | 0.3 | 2.70 | 5,862 | 5,798 | -0.1 | 22,959 | 26,264 | 2975 | 56 |
| GRANT | 6,261 | 7,171 | 7,733 | 1.7 | 2.68 | 4,810 | 5,338 | 1.3 | 26,444 | 31,425 | 2660 | 35 |
| IBERIA | 22,847 | 26,000 | 27,674 | 1.6 | 2.82 | 17,807 | 19,733 | 1.3 | 28,368 | 31,024 | 2386 | 29 |
| IBERVILLE | 9,875 | 10,254 | 10,416 | 0.5 | 2.81 | 7,604 | 7,677 | 0.1 | 30,333 | 33,497 | 2073 | 22 |
| JACKSON | 5,817 | 5,937 | 5,968 | 0.2 | 2.54 | 4,265 | 4,223 | -0.1 | 27,509 | 33,259 | 2508 | 31 |
| JEFFERSON | 166,398 | 174,880 | 176,233 | 0.6 | 2.53 | 118,308 | 119,658 | 0.1 | 38,572 | 41,942 | 797 | 5 |
| JEFFERSON DAVIS | 10,669 | 11,469 | 11,607 | 0.9 | 2.70 | 8,231 | 8,601 | 0.5 | 26,163 | 28,801 | 2694 | 39 |
| LAFAYETTE | 60,411 | 73,697 | 79,375 | 2.4 | 2.51 | 42,206 | 49,937 | 2.1 | 34,358 | 37,406 | 1339 | 12 |
| LAFOURCHE | 28,835 | 31,878 | 33,773 | 1.2 | 2.78 | 22,860 | 24,598 | 0.9 | 32,621 | 36,728 | 1607 | 14 |
| LA SALLE | 5,086 | 5,234 | 5,296 | 0.3 | 2.57 | 3,781 | 3,756 | -0.1 | 27,296 | 31,483 | 2536 | 33 |
| LINCOLN | 13,669 | 14,533 | 14,675 | 0.7 | 2.48 | 9,019 | 9,267 | 0.3 | 29,534 | 31,952 | 2218 | 25 |
| LIVINGSTON | 23,814 | 32,716 | 38,174 | 3.9 | 2.86 | 19,301 | 25,906 | 3.6 | 38,624 | 44,785 | 790 | 4 |
| MADISON | 4,252 | 4,295 | 4,292 | 0.1 | 2.81 | 3,059 | 3,003 | -0.2 | 22,255 | 26,107 | 3013 | 60 |
| MOREHOUSE | 10,961 | 11,064 | 10,914 | 0.1 | 2.74 | 8,321 | 8,153 | -0.2 | 26,284 | 32,367 | 2680 | 38 |
| NATCHITOCHES | 12,644 | 13,473 | 13,790 | 0.8 | 2.64 | 9,095 | 9,354 | 0.3 | 23,170 | 25,805 | 2960 | 54 |
| ORLEANS | 188,235 | 179,069 | 173,996 | -0.6 | 2.46 | 118,026 | 107,911 | -1.1 | 24,808 | 27,534 | 2825 | 49 |
| OUACHITA | 50,518 | 54,045 | 54,955 | 0.8 | 2.62 | 36,482 | 38,111 | 0.5 | 30,718 | 33,584 | 1984 | 21 |
| PLAQUEMINES | 8,213 | 8,904 | 9,244 | 1.0 | 2.87 | 6,574 | 6,936 | 0.7 | 31,274 | 34,937 | 1874 | 20 |
| POINTE COUPEE | 7,736 | 8,533 | 8,832 | 1.2 | 2.72 | 5,923 | 6,343 | 0.8 | 28,372 | 33,232 | 2383 | 28 |
| RAPIDES | 45,941 | 46,149 | 47,287 | 0.1 | 2.65 | 34,195 | 33,441 | -0.3 | 28,028 | 30,772 | 2437 | 30 |
| RED RIVER | 3,321 | 3,493 | 3,454 | 0.6 | 2.63 | 2,505 | 2,555 | 0.2 | 22,151 | 24,831 | 3019 | 61 |
| RICHLAND | 7,079 | 7,531 | 7,793 | 0.8 | 2.74 | 5,370 | 5,542 | 0.4 | 22,293 | 26,907 | 3009 | 59 |
| SABINE | 8,361 | 9,187 | 9,468 | 1.1 | 2.54 | 6,225 | 6,629 | 0.8 | 24,971 | 27,149 | 2813 | 48 |
| ST. BERNARD | 23,156 | 23,975 | 23,967 | 0.4 | 2.69 | 18,291 | 18,293 | 0.0 | 34,158 | 37,561 | 1361 | 13 |
| ST. CHARLES | 14,333 | 17,584 | 19,083 | 2.5 | 2.78 | 11,422 | 13,636 | 2.2 | 44,095 | 49,444 | 389 | 2 |
| ST. HELENA | 3,328 | 3,354 | 3,373 | 0.1 | 2.83 | 2,497 | 2,435 | -0.3 | 25,365 | 30,328 | 2770 | 44 |
| ST. JAMES | 6,432 | 6,903 | 7,263 | 0.9 | 3.06 | 5,363 | 5,643 | 0.6 | 32,369 | 35,963 | 1649 | 16 |
| ST. JOHN THE BAPTIST | 12,710 | 14,165 | 14,831 | 1.3 | 3.00 | 10,326 | 11,216 | 1.0 | 37,321 | 41,427 | 928 | 6 |
| ST. LANDRY | 27,477 | 30,219 | 31,709 | 1.2 | 2.76 | 20,993 | 22,472 | 0.8 | 22,057 | 24,392 | 3025 | 62 |
| ST. MARTIN | 14,634 | 17,063 | 18,361 | 1.9 | 2.79 | 11,560 | 13,124 | 1.5 | 27,317 | 31,845 | 2533 | 32 |
| ST. MARY | 19,456 | 20,030 | 20,257 | 0.4 | 2.79 | 14,887 | 14,866 | 0.0 | 29,772 | 32,257 | 2188 | 24 |
| ST. TAMMANY | 50,346 | 72,636 | 83,206 | 4.5 | 2.70 | 39,359 | 55,074 | 4.2 | 45,280 | 50,696 | 343 | 1 |
| TANGIPAHOA | 29,663 | 36,211 | 39,664 | 2.4 | 2.68 | 21,680 | 25,720 | 2.1 | 25,864 | 29,233 | 2727 | 42 |
| TENSAS | 2,515 | 2,390 | 2,309 | -0.6 | 2.65 | 1,831 | 1,687 | -1.0 | 17,912 | 20,456 | 3129 | 63 |
| TERREBONNE | 31,837 | 36,477 | 38,912 | 1.7 | 2.89 | 25,250 | 28,247 | 1.4 | 31,317 | 34,899 | 1859 | 18 |
| UNION | 7,528 | 8,402 | 8,884 | 1.3 | 2.61 | 5,811 | 6,265 | 0.9 | 28,450 | 32,954 | 2372 | 27 |
| VERMILION | 17,762 | 19,530 | 20,576 | 1.2 | 2.67 | 13,429 | 14,335 | 0.8 | 26,162 | 29,455 | 2695 | 40 |
| VERNON | 19,111 | 15,073 | 14,490 | -2.8 | 2.81 | 15,323 | 11,842 | -3.1 | 26,960 | 32,710 | 2587 | 34 |
| WASHINGTON | 15,475 | 15,948 | 16,220 | 0.4 | 2.61 | 11,516 | 11,498 | 0.0 | 25,290 | 28,989 | 2781 | 45 |
| WEBSTER | 15,849 | 16,718 | 17,174 | 0.6 | 2.52 | 11,556 | 11,819 | 0.3 | 25,828 | 29,444 | 2732 | 43 |
| WEST BATON ROUGE | 6,606 | 7,549 | 7,824 | 1.6 | 2.68 | 5,156 | 5,743 | 1.3 | 34,925 | 37,666 | 1265 | 11 |
| WEST CARROLL | 4,394 | 4,607 | 4,703 | 0.6 | 2.61 | 3,303 | 3,343 | 0.1 | 24,054 | 30,853 | 2896 | 51 |
| WEST FELICIANA | 2,741 | 3,264 | 3,622 | 2.1 | 2.74 | 2,080 | 2,403 | 1.8 | 32,461 | 41,482 | 1630 | 15 |
| WINN | 5,787 | 6,085 | 5,977 | 0.6 | 2.56 | 4,265 | 4,331 | 0.2 | 25,958 | 30,773 | 2717 | 41 |
| LOUISIANA | | | | 1.0 | 2.63 | | | 0.6 | 31,622 | 35,502 | | |
| UNITED STATES | | | | 1.4 | 2.59 | | | 1.1 | 41,914 | 49,127 | | |

# INCOME

| COUNTY | 2000 Per Capita Income | 2000 HH Income Base | 2000 HOUSEHOLD INCOME DISTRIBUTION (%) | | | | | | 2000 AVERAGE DISPOSABLE INCOME BY AGE OF HOUSEHOLDER | | | | | |
|---|---|---|---|---|---|---|---|---|---|---|---|---|---|---|
| | | | Less than $15,000 | $15,000 to $24,999 | $25,000 to $49,999 | $50,000 to $99,999 | $100,000 to $149,999 | $150,000 or More | All Ages | <35 | 35-44 | 45-54 | 55-64 | 65+ |
| ACADIA | 12,071 | 20,882 | 33.4 | 18.3 | 29.8 | 14.8 | 2.6 | 1.1 | 27,212 | 23,870 | 31,148 | 33,190 | 26,939 | 19,021 |
| ALLEN | 11,755 | 7,522 | 28.9 | 18.9 | 32.9 | 16.6 | 2.0 | 0.6 | 27,683 | 26,135 | 32,171 | 33,119 | 29,104 | 18,455 |
| ASCENSION | 17,549 | 26,122 | 16.6 | 9.4 | 34.2 | 31.3 | 6.7 | 1.7 | 39,997 | 35,725 | 46,699 | 46,547 | 39,145 | 23,045 |
| ASSUMPTION | 12,985 | 7,981 | 23.8 | 16.9 | 34.4 | 20.6 | 3.6 | 0.7 | 31,150 | 27,997 | 35,747 | 37,507 | 31,726 | 21,246 |
| AVOYELLES | 11,385 | 14,485 | 35.0 | 19.2 | 29.1 | 13.2 | 2.5 | 1.1 | 26,105 | 24,340 | 33,371 | 31,104 | 24,274 | 17,159 |
| BEAUREGARD | 15,572 | 11,622 | 22.2 | 16.5 | 33.1 | 23.0 | 3.9 | 1.3 | 33,057 | 29,345 | 40,509 | 41,224 | 29,482 | 21,634 |
| BIENVILLE | 12,560 | 5,939 | 32.7 | 18.8 | 28.6 | 17.0 | 2.1 | 0.8 | 27,193 | 24,488 | 30,530 | 35,649 | 27,931 | 19,348 |
| BOSSIER | 16,848 | 34,971 | 16.6 | 14.6 | 36.2 | 27.4 | 4.1 | 1.1 | 35,860 | 30,204 | 41,926 | 44,707 | 38,579 | 22,452 |
| CADDO | 17,351 | 93,787 | 24.5 | 15.8 | 31.9 | 21.4 | 4.4 | 2.0 | 34,002 | 26,830 | 39,681 | 41,467 | 35,274 | 24,205 |
| CALCASIEU | 17,125 | 68,024 | 21.5 | 14.3 | 33.3 | 24.5 | 4.7 | 1.7 | 35,300 | 28,803 | 40,850 | 44,517 | 35,953 | 23,676 |
| CALDWELL | 13,587 | 3,903 | 29.1 | 20.6 | 28.4 | 16.9 | 3.5 | 1.6 | 29,686 | 25,938 | 40,127 | 33,949 | 31,028 | 16,326 |
| CAMERON | 15,811 | 3,275 | 19.1 | 15.7 | 33.5 | 26.3 | 4.3 | 1.2 | 34,933 | 35,412 | 37,657 | 40,956 | 34,308 | 24,495 |
| CATAHOULA | 12,218 | 4,089 | 34.8 | 19.5 | 28.4 | 13.8 | 2.5 | 0.9 | 26,217 | 22,378 | 29,595 | 31,811 | 28,476 | 18,934 |
| CLAIBORNE | 11,896 | 6,003 | 34.3 | 18.6 | 30.1 | 14.4 | 1.8 | 0.9 | 26,129 | 24,775 | 29,639 | 36,354 | 26,254 | 17,563 |
| CONCORDIA | 13,188 | 7,637 | 31.3 | 16.4 | 31.9 | 16.8 | 2.6 | 1.1 | 28,329 | 23,455 | 33,848 | 34,889 | 29,602 | 19,300 |
| DE SOTO | 12,708 | 9,217 | 32.5 | 17.2 | 29.1 | 17.6 | 2.7 | 1.0 | 28,219 | 24,182 | 36,085 | 34,218 | 28,295 | 18,193 |
| EAST BATON ROUGE | 19,847 | 149,839 | 20.6 | 13.4 | 30.6 | 26.6 | 5.9 | 3.0 | 38,901 | 28,727 | 43,954 | 48,128 | 41,747 | 28,682 |
| EAST CARROLL | 10,435 | 2,943 | 49.6 | 20.6 | 17.4 | 9.3 | 1.9 | 1.2 | 21,721 | 16,433 | 26,201 | 24,874 | 25,160 | 17,623 |
| EAST FELICIANA | 11,471 | 6,259 | 23.8 | 19.8 | 31.4 | 21.0 | 3.3 | 0.7 | 30,569 | 27,292 | 34,402 | 35,871 | 31,959 | 21,117 |
| EVANGELINE | 12,355 | 12,560 | 34.2 | 18.9 | 30.5 | 12.7 | 2.6 | 1.1 | 26,532 | 26,027 | 30,983 | 30,658 | 27,328 | 17,454 |
| FRANKLIN | 11,568 | 7,947 | 34.4 | 18.5 | 29.6 | 13.8 | 2.7 | 1.0 | 26,487 | 25,154 | 30,345 | 34,345 | 25,393 | 17,978 |
| GRANT | 12,889 | 7,171 | 27.3 | 19.7 | 32.7 | 17.2 | 2.5 | 0.7 | 28,273 | 27,361 | 31,021 | 37,506 | 26,933 | 17,334 |
| IBERIA | 13,562 | 26,000 | 27.8 | 16.1 | 34.0 | 18.1 | 2.9 | 1.1 | 29,951 | 26,360 | 33,968 | 35,433 | 31,717 | 20,574 |
| IBERVILLE | 14,870 | 10,254 | 27.0 | 14.7 | 31.7 | 20.7 | 4.1 | 1.8 | 32,366 | 29,330 | 39,063 | 38,189 | 31,998 | 20,472 |
| JACKSON | 17,501 | 5,937 | 27.0 | 17.9 | 32.1 | 18.4 | 3.2 | 1.4 | 30,668 | 26,080 | 34,105 | 42,082 | 32,775 | 19,413 |
| JEFFERSON | 19,098 | 174,879 | 15.5 | 13.9 | 35.1 | 28.4 | 5.3 | 1.7 | 38,034 | 32,329 | 42,407 | 45,723 | 40,002 | 26,287 |
| JEFFERSON DAVIS | 12,893 | 11,469 | 28.4 | 19.5 | 30.7 | 18.3 | 2.4 | 0.7 | 28,436 | 26,384 | 34,345 | 33,330 | 29,042 | 19,654 |
| LAFAYETTE | 18,757 | 73,697 | 22.4 | 14.5 | 31.6 | 23.4 | 5.4 | 2.7 | 36,748 | 28,845 | 42,709 | 44,055 | 37,524 | 25,938 |
| LAFOURCHE | 15,478 | 31,872 | 21.6 | 15.5 | 34.6 | 23.3 | 3.9 | 1.1 | 33,332 | 28,447 | 39,752 | 41,038 | 32,011 | 22,504 |
| LA SALLE | 13,413 | 5,234 | 25.3 | 20.2 | 36.7 | 15.4 | 1.6 | 0.9 | 28,305 | 27,692 | 35,403 | 34,479 | 26,568 | 18,067 |
| LINCOLN | 15,657 | 14,533 | 28.7 | 14.6 | 31.0 | 18.9 | 4.5 | 2.4 | 33,010 | 21,069 | 42,428 | 45,339 | 37,570 | 23,824 |
| LIVINGSTON | 16,293 | 32,716 | 13.3 | 14.2 | 38.8 | 27.5 | 5.0 | 1.3 | 37,522 | 33,735 | 43,516 | 46,314 | 35,036 | 21,202 |
| MADISON | 10,819 | 4,295 | 36.1 | 18.8 | 27.3 | 14.3 | 2.7 | 0.6 | 25,862 | 22,588 | 32,193 | 30,497 | 26,590 | 18,208 |
| MOREHOUSE | 13,599 | 11,064 | 31.3 | 16.9 | 29.9 | 17.2 | 3.5 | 1.3 | 29,332 | 23,423 | 34,262 | 40,052 | 29,837 | 19,047 |
| NATCHITOCHES | 12,402 | 13,473 | 34.9 | 17.7 | 28.3 | 14.8 | 2.8 | 1.4 | 27,453 | 22,930 | 33,448 | 34,077 | 29,033 | 17,899 |
| ORLEANS | 17,313 | 179,067 | 33.1 | 17.2 | 26.7 | 16.1 | 3.9 | 3.1 | 32,091 | 24,728 | 35,286 | 37,331 | 32,326 | 24,420 |
| OUACHITA | 16,082 | 54,045 | 25.3 | 16.4 | 31.2 | 21.2 | 4.1 | 1.8 | 33,054 | 25,775 | 38,403 | 42,386 | 35,457 | 22,247 |
| PLAQUEMINES | 13,613 | 8,902 | 22.8 | 16.0 | 36.5 | 21.7 | 2.4 | 0.6 | 31,053 | 28,477 | 35,756 | 36,896 | 31,261 | 20,284 |
| POINTE COUPEE | 13,635 | 8,520 | 30.0 | 15.0 | 31.8 | 19.1 | 3.2 | 0.9 | 29,827 | 27,595 | 37,784 | 33,976 | 26,378 | 21,566 |
| RAPIDES | 14,162 | 46,147 | 26.3 | 18.1 | 32.6 | 18.8 | 2.9 | 1.3 | 30,417 | 25,044 | 35,573 | 36,582 | 33,532 | 21,249 |
| RED RIVER | 10,949 | 3,493 | 35.9 | 18.6 | 30.9 | 12.5 | 1.7 | 0.5 | 24,729 | 21,834 | 29,367 | 30,590 | 27,901 | 16,201 |
| RICHLAND | 12,044 | 7,531 | 36.1 | 18.0 | 28.1 | 15.3 | 1.8 | 0.7 | 25,606 | 23,081 | 33,716 | 30,341 | 25,576 | 16,855 |
| SABINE | 12,740 | 9,187 | 31.2 | 18.8 | 31.8 | 15.5 | 2.0 | 0.7 | 26,858 | 24,296 | 32,704 | 34,782 | 26,403 | 18,174 |
| ST. BERNARD | 15,071 | 23,975 | 18.3 | 16.2 | 38.4 | 23.6 | 3.0 | 0.5 | 32,776 | 30,656 | 37,628 | 38,832 | 33,543 | 22,607 |
| ST. CHARLES | 18,777 | 17,584 | 13.5 | 10.2 | 34.8 | 33.0 | 6.7 | 1.8 | 41,256 | 37,358 | 47,831 | 47,784 | 39,749 | 23,380 |
| ST. HELENA | 12,069 | 3,354 | 30.6 | 18.7 | 31.2 | 16.9 | 2.1 | 0.6 | 27,339 | 24,926 | 32,305 | 31,709 | 28,782 | 18,258 |
| ST. JAMES | 12,495 | 6,903 | 26.1 | 15.1 | 32.0 | 23.7 | 2.5 | 0.6 | 31,273 | 29,909 | 35,555 | 37,614 | 30,504 | 19,781 |
| ST. JOHN THE BAPTIST | 14,999 | 14,165 | 18.2 | 12.8 | 36.0 | 28.1 | 4.0 | 1.0 | 35,650 | 32,467 | 41,767 | 43,053 | 31,789 | 19,549 |
| ST. LANDRY | 11,531 | 30,219 | 37.4 | 17.0 | 29.1 | 13.3 | 2.1 | 1.1 | 25,839 | 23,067 | 29,622 | 31,787 | 24,510 | 18,015 |
| ST. MARTIN | 12,169 | 17,053 | 26.8 | 18.3 | 36.2 | 15.8 | 2.3 | 0.6 | 28,246 | 26,572 | 33,054 | 32,210 | 28,392 | 17,567 |
| ST. MARY | 13,023 | 20,026 | 24.5 | 17.7 | 35.2 | 19.1 | 2.8 | 0.7 | 29,986 | 26,508 | 34,145 | 35,861 | 30,030 | 21,086 |
| ST. TAMMANY | 23,661 | 72,636 | 12.7 | 11.2 | 31.1 | 30.8 | 8.9 | 5.4 | 47,587 | 36,612 | 52,725 | 55,919 | 45,632 | 28,298 |
| TANGIPAHOA | 12,667 | 36,211 | 31.4 | 17.2 | 30.4 | 17.1 | 3.0 | 0.9 | 28,358 | 23,815 | 34,695 | 34,421 | 28,437 | 19,136 |
| TENSAS | 13,390 | 2,390 | 43.5 | 16.6 | 23.7 | 11.3 | 2.4 | 2.6 | 26,483 | 21,136 | 27,951 | 26,536 | 29,091 | 24,977 |
| TERREBONNE | 14,728 | 36,477 | 22.7 | 17.0 | 33.7 | 21.7 | 3.7 | 1.3 | 32,505 | 28,006 | 36,663 | 40,534 | 31,893 | 21,278 |
| UNION | 14,041 | 8,402 | 27.3 | 16.2 | 32.4 | 19.7 | 3.3 | 1.1 | 30,309 | 26,703 | 37,578 | 38,657 | 29,432 | 18,963 |
| VERMILION | 12,969 | 19,530 | 30.4 | 17.6 | 31.5 | 16.8 | 2.6 | 1.1 | 28,442 | 24,425 | 35,126 | 33,702 | 28,568 | 19,716 |
| VERNON | 11,586 | 15,073 | 21.0 | 25.2 | 38.0 | 14.9 | 1.0 | 0.0 | 26,774 | 23,535 | 33,358 | 35,447 | 27,134 | 17,780 |
| WASHINGTON | 13,113 | 15,948 | 31.0 | 18.6 | 29.6 | 16.9 | 2.7 | 1.2 | 28,495 | 24,434 | 31,432 | 36,521 | 30,190 | 20,105 |
| WEBSTER | 12,899 | 16,718 | 30.4 | 18.0 | 32.9 | 16.2 | 1.9 | 0.6 | 27,034 | 23,622 | 32,718 | 34,600 | 27,816 | 17,999 |
| WEST BATON ROUGE | 16,008 | 7,549 | 20.7 | 14.7 | 35.8 | 23.7 | 4.1 | 1.1 | 33,943 | 31,757 | 39,655 | 40,862 | 30,693 | 21,728 |
| WEST CARROLL | 12,300 | 4,607 | 32.5 | 18.7 | 30.8 | 14.7 | 2.2 | 1.0 | 26,956 | 22,533 | 32,974 | 36,262 | 27,065 | 17,851 |
| WEST FELICIANA | 10,827 | 3,264 | 25.9 | 13.8 | 29.7 | 26.7 | 3.5 | 0.4 | 32,248 | 28,524 | 36,808 | 38,789 | 28,652 | 25,529 |
| WINN | 15,049 | 6,085 | 29.3 | 18.6 | 31.1 | 16.1 | 3.4 | 1.6 | 29,342 | 26,705 | 36,064 | 39,151 | 28,978 | 16,878 |
| LOUISIANA | 16,391 | | 24.2 | 15.7 | 32.0 | 21.9 | 4.3 | 1.9 | 33,918 | 28,008 | 39,291 | 41,400 | 34,336 | 22,821 |
| UNITED STATES | 22,162 | | 14.5 | 12.5 | 32.3 | 29.8 | 7.4 | 3.5 | 40,748 | 34,503 | 44,969 | 49,579 | 43,409 | 27,339 |

| COUNTY | FINANCIAL SERVICES | | | | THE HOME | | | | | | ENTERTAINMENT | | | | | | PERSONAL | | | |
|---|---|---|---|---|---|---|---|---|---|---|---|---|---|---|---|---|---|---|---|---|
| | | | | | Home Improvements | | | Furnishings | | | | | | | | | | | | |
| | Auto Loan | Home Loan | Invest-ments | Retire-ment Plans | Home Repair | Lawn & Garden | Remodel-ing | Appli-ances | Elec-tronics | Furni-ture | Restau-rants | Sport-ing Goods | Theater & Concerts | Toys & Hobbies | Travel | Video Rental | Apparel | Auto After-market | Health Insur-ance | Pets & Supplies |
| ACADIA | 95 | 70 | 78 | 78 | 94 | 91 | 107 | 95 | 91 | 80 | 79 | 92 | 81 | 93 | 72 | 96 | 81 | 88 | 97 | 95 |
| ALLEN | 95 | 68 | 73 | 75 | 94 | 89 | 106 | 95 | 90 | 79 | 77 | 92 | 80 | 92 | 71 | 95 | 80 | 87 | 96 | 95 |
| ASCENSION | 98 | 82 | 82 | 84 | 94 | 91 | 109 | 97 | 95 | 89 | 90 | 97 | 88 | 99 | 75 | 98 | 89 | 93 | 97 | 100 |
| ASSUMPTION | 98 | 68 | 72 | 77 | 93 | 91 | 113 | 96 | 92 | 78 | 80 | 97 | 81 | 96 | 68 | 96 | 80 | 88 | 101 | 98 |
| AVOYELLES | 94 | 64 | 71 | 73 | 92 | 88 | 104 | 94 | 89 | 77 | 75 | 90 | 77 | 90 | 69 | 95 | 78 | 86 | 96 | 94 |
| BEAUREGARD | 96 | 77 | 81 | 81 | 94 | 90 | 111 | 96 | 92 | 84 | 85 | 95 | 85 | 96 | 73 | 97 | 85 | 91 | 98 | 99 |
| BIENVILLE | 95 | 67 | 76 | 75 | 95 | 91 | 105 | 95 | 90 | 80 | 78 | 93 | 81 | 92 | 71 | 95 | 80 | 87 | 97 | 95 |
| BOSSIER | 97 | 92 | 89 | 89 | 97 | 94 | 101 | 97 | 96 | 94 | 95 | 97 | 92 | 98 | 81 | 98 | 93 | 96 | 95 | 99 |
| CADDO | 96 | 91 | 98 | 92 | 100 | 97 | 96 | 97 | 94 | 95 | 91 | 96 | 93 | 96 | 85 | 98 | 94 | 96 | 93 | 98 |
| CALCASIEU | 97 | 85 | 92 | 88 | 98 | 95 | 103 | 97 | 94 | 92 | 90 | 96 | 91 | 97 | 81 | 98 | 91 | 94 | 96 | 98 |
| CALDWELL | 96 | 64 | 69 | 74 | 92 | 88 | 108 | 96 | 90 | 76 | 75 | 95 | 78 | 93 | 67 | 96 | 79 | 87 | 97 | 96 |
| CAMERON | 100 | 74 | 80 | 84 | 95 | 92 | 118 | 98 | 94 | 82 | 85 | 99 | 85 | 100 | 72 | 98 | 86 | 91 | 103 | 102 |
| CATAHOULA | 94 | 62 | 68 | 72 | 92 | 87 | 104 | 96 | 89 | 76 | 72 | 92 | 76 | 91 | 68 | 95 | 78 | 86 | 94 | 94 |
| CLAIBORNE | 95 | 69 | 84 | 77 | 96 | 93 | 104 | 96 | 90 | 80 | 79 | 93 | 82 | 93 | 73 | 95 | 80 | 88 | 98 | 96 |
| CONCORDIA | 95 | 70 | 78 | 79 | 94 | 89 | 105 | 96 | 90 | 81 | 78 | 93 | 81 | 93 | 72 | 96 | 82 | 89 | 94 | 96 |
| DE SOTO | 96 | 70 | 76 | 76 | 93 | 90 | 110 | 95 | 91 | 80 | 79 | 93 | 81 | 93 | 70 | 96 | 81 | 88 | 98 | 96 |
| EAST BATON ROUGE | 99 | 101 | 99 | 99 | 101 | 99 | 98 | 98 | 99 | 100 | 99 | 100 | 98 | 100 | 89 | 99 | 101 | 101 | 94 | 101 |
| EAST CARROLL | 91 | 74 | 87 | 77 | 97 | 90 | 98 | 92 | 85 | 82 | 74 | 89 | 82 | 88 | 77 | 95 | 83 | 88 | 92 | 89 |
| EAST FELICIANA | 94 | 72 | 74 | 74 | 93 | 86 | 100 | 95 | 90 | 86 | 78 | 91 | 82 | 91 | 72 | 98 | 86 | 90 | 90 | 95 |
| EVANGELINE | 95 | 68 | 75 | 76 | 94 | 89 | 106 | 95 | 90 | 79 | 77 | 92 | 80 | 92 | 71 | 96 | 80 | 88 | 96 | 95 |
| FRANKLIN | 95 | 64 | 69 | 72 | 93 | 88 | 105 | 95 | 89 | 77 | 75 | 93 | 78 | 92 | 68 | 95 | 78 | 86 | 96 | 95 |
| GRANT | 97 | 68 | 74 | 77 | 93 | 90 | 111 | 96 | 92 | 79 | 80 | 95 | 81 | 95 | 69 | 96 | 81 | 88 | 99 | 97 |
| IBERIA | 96 | 78 | 84 | 82 | 96 | 92 | 107 | 96 | 93 | 86 | 84 | 95 | 86 | 95 | 75 | 97 | 86 | 91 | 96 | 97 |
| IBERVILLE | 94 | 71 | 76 | 74 | 96 | 90 | 102 | 95 | 89 | 84 | 79 | 92 | 83 | 92 | 73 | 96 | 83 | 89 | 96 | 94 |
| JACKSON | 96 | 68 | 75 | 77 | 93 | 89 | 109 | 96 | 91 | 79 | 78 | 94 | 80 | 94 | 70 | 96 | 81 | 88 | 96 | 97 |
| JEFFERSON | 98 | 101 | 101 | 97 | 103 | 101 | 97 | 99 | 98 | 102 | 102 | 99 | 100 | 101 | 90 | 99 | 101 | 100 | 97 | 100 |
| JEFFERSON DAVIS | 95 | 67 | 74 | 75 | 93 | 90 | 108 | 95 | 91 | 78 | 78 | 92 | 79 | 93 | 70 | 96 | 80 | 87 | 98 | 96 |
| LAFAYETTE | 98 | 98 | 92 | 95 | 98 | 96 | 100 | 98 | 98 | 98 | 98 | 99 | 95 | 99 | 85 | 99 | 97 | 99 | 94 | 100 |
| LAFOURCHE | 97 | 75 | 80 | 81 | 94 | 92 | 110 | 96 | 93 | 83 | 84 | 96 | 84 | 96 | 73 | 97 | 84 | 90 | 99 | 98 |
| LA SALLE | 97 | 69 | 76 | 78 | 93 | 91 | 110 | 96 | 93 | 79 | 80 | 95 | 82 | 95 | 70 | 96 | 81 | 88 | 99 | 97 |
| LINCOLN | 96 | 86 | 95 | 88 | 98 | 94 | 101 | 95 | 92 | 89 | 87 | 93 | 88 | 94 | 81 | 96 | 90 | 93 | 94 | 97 |
| LIVINGSTON | 98 | 80 | 82 | 83 | 94 | 91 | 111 | 97 | 94 | 88 | 89 | 97 | 87 | 99 | 74 | 98 | 87 | 92 | 98 | 100 |
| MADISON | 92 | 67 | 76 | 74 | 93 | 85 | 99 | 94 | 87 | 80 | 72 | 89 | 78 | 88 | 72 | 95 | 81 | 87 | 88 | 92 |
| MOREHOUSE | 95 | 69 | 78 | 77 | 94 | 90 | 104 | 96 | 90 | 80 | 77 | 93 | 81 | 92 | 72 | 96 | 82 | 88 | 95 | 95 |
| NATCHITOCHES | 94 | 72 | 80 | 78 | 94 | 89 | 103 | 94 | 90 | 81 | 78 | 91 | 81 | 91 | 73 | 95 | 83 | 88 | 94 | 94 |
| ORLEANS | 94 | 94 | 104 | 95 | 102 | 97 | 89 | 97 | 93 | 96 | 88 | 94 | 94 | 92 | 90 | 98 | 95 | 97 | 88 | 95 |
| OUACHITA | 97 | 88 | 95 | 90 | 99 | 95 | 101 | 97 | 94 | 92 | 90 | 96 | 91 | 97 | 82 | 98 | 92 | 95 | 95 | 98 |
| PLAQUEMINES | 96 | 80 | 84 | 82 | 94 | 91 | 106 | 96 | 93 | 87 | 87 | 95 | 87 | 97 | 75 | 97 | 87 | 92 | 95 | 98 |
| POINTE COUPEE | 96 | 69 | 77 | 78 | 93 | 89 | 110 | 96 | 91 | 80 | 78 | 93 | 80 | 94 | 71 | 96 | 82 | 88 | 96 | 97 |
| RAPIDES | 96 | 83 | 89 | 86 | 97 | 93 | 101 | 96 | 93 | 89 | 87 | 94 | 89 | 95 | 79 | 97 | 89 | 93 | 95 | 97 |
| RED RIVER | 93 | 63 | 68 | 71 | 92 | 87 | 103 | 94 | 88 | 76 | 73 | 90 | 77 | 89 | 68 | 95 | 78 | 86 | 94 | 92 |
| RICHLAND | 95 | 64 | 70 | 73 | 93 | 89 | 106 | 95 | 89 | 77 | 75 | 92 | 78 | 92 | 68 | 95 | 79 | 86 | 97 | 94 |
| SABINE | 97 | 70 | 83 | 80 | 96 | 94 | 111 | 97 | 91 | 80 | 81 | 96 | 83 | 96 | 73 | 96 | 81 | 89 | 101 | 98 |
| ST. BERNARD | 98 | 91 | 95 | 90 | 101 | 99 | 100 | 98 | 96 | 96 | 97 | 97 | 95 | 100 | 84 | 98 | 95 | 96 | 100 | 99 |
| ST. CHARLES | 102 | 100 | 92 | 101 | 99 | 100 | 104 | 102 | 102 | 102 | 102 | 106 | 100 | 103 | 86 | 101 | 103 | 102 | 97 | 104 |
| ST. HELENA | 95 | 64 | 66 | 71 | 92 | 88 | 105 | 95 | 90 | 78 | 74 | 93 | 78 | 92 | 67 | 96 | 79 | 87 | 96 | 94 |
| ST. JAMES | 96 | 71 | 75 | 78 | 94 | 88 | 106 | 96 | 91 | 82 | 79 | 95 | 82 | 94 | 71 | 97 | 84 | 90 | 94 | 97 |
| ST. JOHN THE BAPTIST | 99 | 92 | 84 | 91 | 96 | 95 | 101 | 99 | 100 | 97 | 96 | 101 | 95 | 100 | 81 | 100 | 97 | 98 | 95 | 101 |
| ST. LANDRY | 94 | 69 | 76 | 76 | 94 | 89 | 102 | 95 | 90 | 81 | 77 | 92 | 81 | 91 | 72 | 95 | 81 | 88 | 94 | 95 |
| ST. MARTIN | 96 | 69 | 72 | 75 | 93 | 89 | 109 | 95 | 91 | 80 | 79 | 94 | 81 | 94 | 69 | 96 | 82 | 88 | 98 | 96 |
| ST. MARY | 96 | 74 | 79 | 79 | 94 | 90 | 105 | 96 | 92 | 84 | 81 | 94 | 84 | 94 | 73 | 97 | 84 | 90 | 96 | 96 |
| ST. TAMMANY | 103 | 101 | 96 | 102 | 100 | 101 | 108 | 102 | 103 | 103 | 105 | 105 | 101 | 105 | 87 | 101 | 104 | 103 | 99 | 104 |
| TANGIPAHOA | 95 | 72 | 79 | 77 | 94 | 89 | 105 | 94 | 90 | 82 | 80 | 92 | 82 | 92 | 72 | 96 | 82 | 89 | 95 | 95 |
| TENSAS | 92 | 64 | 70 | 72 | 93 | 85 | 98 | 95 | 87 | 78 | 71 | 90 | 77 | 88 | 70 | 95 | 79 | 86 | 90 | 93 |
| TERREBONNE | 97 | 82 | 84 | 84 | 96 | 92 | 105 | 97 | 94 | 89 | 88 | 96 | 88 | 97 | 77 | 97 | 88 | 93 | 97 | 98 |
| UNION | 97 | 68 | 73 | 78 | 93 | 90 | 113 | 96 | 91 | 78 | 79 | 96 | 81 | 95 | 69 | 96 | 81 | 88 | 100 | 98 |
| VERMILION | 97 | 70 | 77 | 78 | 93 | 90 | 111 | 95 | 91 | 80 | 81 | 94 | 81 | 95 | 71 | 96 | 82 | 89 | 100 | 97 |
| VERNON | 92 | 82 | 75 | 76 | 89 | 85 | 98 | 92 | 92 | 82 | 87 | 90 | 83 | 91 | 72 | 96 | 83 | 90 | 93 | 97 |
| WASHINGTON | 95 | 68 | 78 | 76 | 94 | 90 | 104 | 96 | 90 | 80 | 77 | 92 | 81 | 92 | 72 | 96 | 81 | 88 | 96 | 95 |
| WEBSTER | 95 | 74 | 86 | 80 | 97 | 92 | 104 | 96 | 91 | 84 | 81 | 93 | 85 | 94 | 75 | 96 | 84 | 89 | 96 | 96 |
| WEST BATON ROUGE | 96 | 80 | 80 | 80 | 95 | 90 | 103 | 96 | 93 | 89 | 86 | 94 | 86 | 95 | 75 | 98 | 89 | 92 | 94 | 97 |
| WEST CARROLL | 96 | 64 | 70 | 73 | 92 | 90 | 111 | 95 | 91 | 76 | 77 | 94 | 78 | 93 | 67 | 95 | 78 | 87 | 100 | 96 |
| WEST FELICIANA | 94 | 79 | 84 | 80 | 94 | 89 | 103 | 95 | 90 | 87 | 85 | 92 | 85 | 94 | 75 | 96 | 85 | 90 | 92 | 96 |
| WINN | 95 | 65 | 73 | 74 | 93 | 89 | 106 | 95 | 90 | 78 | 76 | 92 | 79 | 92 | 69 | 96 | 79 | 87 | 97 | 95 |
| LOUISIANA | 97 | 87 | 92 | 90 | 98 | 95 | 101 | 97 | 95 | 92 | 90 | 97 | 92 | 97 | 82 | 98 | 92 | 95 | 95 | 98 |
| UNITED STATES | 100 | 100 | 100 | 100 | 100 | 100 | 100 | 100 | 100 | 100 | 100 | 100 | 100 | 100 | 100 | 100 | 100 | 100 | 100 | 100 |

# POPULATION CHANGE

| COUNTY | FIPS Code | MSA Code | DMA Code | POPULATION 1990 | POPULATION 2000 | POPULATION 2005 | 1990-2000 ANNUAL CHANGE % Rate | 1990-2000 ANNUAL CHANGE State Rank | RACE (%) White 1990 | RACE (%) White 2000 | RACE (%) Black 1990 | RACE (%) Black 2000 | RACE (%) Asian/Pacific 1990 | RACE (%) Asian/Pacific 2000 |
|---|---|---|---|---|---|---|---|---|---|---|---|---|---|---|
| ANDROSCOGGIN | 001 | 4243 | 500 | 105,259 | 101,289 | 100,909 | -0.4 | 14 | 98.5 | 98.2 | 0.5 | 0.6 | 0.5 | 0.7 |
| AROOSTOOK | 003 | 0000 | 552 | 86,936 | 74,909 | 70,448 | -1.4 | 16 | 97.3 | 97.1 | 1.1 | 1.2 | 0.5 | 0.6 |
| CUMBERLAND | 005 | 6403 | 500 | 243,135 | 258,514 | 268,517 | 0.6 | 4 | 98.1 | 97.7 | 0.6 | 0.8 | 0.9 | 1.1 |
| FRANKLIN | 007 | 0000 | 500 | 29,008 | 28,749 | 28,483 | -0.1 | 11 | 99.2 | 99.1 | 0.1 | 0.1 | 0.3 | 0.3 |
| HANCOCK | 009 | 0000 | 537 | 46,948 | 49,744 | 50,042 | 0.6 | 4 | 99.0 | 98.9 | 0.2 | 0.2 | 0.3 | 0.4 |
| KENNEBEC | 011 | 0000 | 500 | 115,904 | 115,134 | 114,543 | -0.1 | 11 | 98.9 | 98.7 | 0.2 | 0.3 | 0.4 | 0.6 |
| KNOX | 013 | 0000 | 500 | 36,310 | 38,363 | 39,243 | 0.5 | 7 | 99.3 | 99.2 | 0.2 | 0.2 | 0.2 | 0.3 |
| LINCOLN | 015 | 0000 | 500 | 30,357 | 32,108 | 32,913 | 0.5 | 7 | 99.4 | 99.4 | 0.1 | 0.1 | 0.1 | 0.2 |
| OXFORD | 017 | 0000 | 500 | 52,602 | 54,551 | 55,953 | 0.4 | 9 | 99.4 | 99.3 | 0.1 | 0.2 | 0.3 | 0.3 |
| PENOBSCOT | 019 | 0733 | 537 | 146,601 | 144,122 | 142,526 | -0.2 | 13 | 98.0 | 97.8 | 0.4 | 0.5 | 0.6 | 0.8 |
| PISCATAQUIS | 021 | 0000 | 537 | 18,653 | 17,965 | 17,415 | -0.4 | 14 | 99.1 | 99.0 | 0.1 | 0.1 | 0.3 | 0.4 |
| SAGADAHOC | 023 | 0000 | 500 | 33,535 | 36,776 | 39,182 | 0.9 | 2 | 97.8 | 97.3 | 1.0 | 1.1 | 0.7 | 1.1 |
| SOMERSET | 025 | 0000 | 537 | 49,767 | 52,749 | 53,507 | 0.6 | 4 | 99.2 | 99.1 | 0.1 | 0.1 | 0.2 | 0.3 |
| WALDO | 027 | 0000 | 537 | 33,018 | 37,358 | 39,362 | 1.2 | 1 | 99.3 | 99.3 | 0.1 | 0.2 | 0.2 | 0.3 |
| WASHINGTON | 029 | 0000 | 537 | 35,308 | 35,139 | 34,096 | 0.0 | 10 | 95.5 | 95.9 | 0.2 | 0.2 | 0.2 | 0.3 |
| YORK | 031 | 0000 | 500 | 164,587 | 179,749 | 190,412 | 0.9 | 2 | 98.7 | 98.4 | 0.3 | 0.4 | 0.7 | 0.9 |
| MAINE | | | | | | | 0.2 | | 98.4 | 98.2 | 0.4 | 0.5 | 0.5 | 0.7 |
| UNITED STATES | | | | | | | 1.0 | | 80.3 | 77.9 | 12.1 | 12.4 | 2.9 | 3.9 |

| COUNTY | % HISPANIC ORIGIN | | 2000 AGE DISTRIBUTION (%) | | | | | | | | | | MEDIAN AGE | | 2000 Males/ Females (×100) |
|---|---|---|---|---|---|---|---|---|---|---|---|---|---|---|---|
| | 1990 | 2000 | 0-4 | 5-9 | 10-14 | 15-19 | 20-24 | 25-44 | 45-64 | 65-84 | 85+ | 18+ | 1990 | 2000 | |
| ANDROSCOGGIN | 0.7 | 1.3 | 5.4 | 6.2 | 7.4 | 7.5 | 6.6 | 30.4 | 22.6 | 12.0 | 1.9 | 76.7 | 32.8 | 37.0 | 94.5 |
| AROOSTOOK | 0.6 | 1.1 | 5.0 | 5.7 | 7.1 | 6.9 | 6.7 | 29.8 | 23.2 | 13.6 | 1.9 | 78.1 | 33.3 | 38.1 | 100.5 |
| CUMBERLAND | 0.6 | 1.2 | 5.0 | 5.6 | 6.8 | 6.8 | 6.4 | 32.8 | 23.2 | 11.6 | 1.8 | 78.9 | 33.7 | 37.7 | 92.9 |
| FRANKLIN | 0.4 | 0.8 | 5.0 | 6.1 | 7.6 | 8.2 | 6.7 | 29.1 | 23.8 | 11.9 | 1.7 | 77.2 | 32.9 | 37.6 | 94.4 |
| HANCOCK | 0.6 | 1.1 | 5.2 | 6.1 | 7.0 | 7.0 | 5.2 | 28.1 | 26.1 | 13.2 | 2.1 | 77.5 | 35.8 | 39.9 | 98.4 |
| KENNEBEC | 0.4 | 1.0 | 4.8 | 5.9 | 7.2 | 7.6 | 6.2 | 30.0 | 24.2 | 12.3 | 1.8 | 77.8 | 34.2 | 38.4 | 93.7 |
| KNOX | 0.4 | 0.8 | 5.3 | 6.2 | 7.1 | 6.9 | 5.3 | 26.7 | 26.3 | 14.0 | 2.2 | 77.1 | 37.0 | 40.6 | 96.3 |
| LINCOLN | 0.4 | 0.9 | 4.6 | 5.8 | 7.3 | 6.6 | 4.3 | 27.5 | 26.2 | 15.4 | 2.3 | 78.1 | 37.4 | 41.5 | 95.7 |
| OXFORD | 0.4 | 0.9 | 5.2 | 6.2 | 7.7 | 6.8 | 5.0 | 28.9 | 24.6 | 13.6 | 2.0 | 76.5 | 35.0 | 39.3 | 96.0 |
| PENOBSCOT | 0.5 | 1.0 | 4.8 | 5.6 | 6.9 | 8.2 | 7.7 | 30.7 | 23.2 | 11.4 | 1.5 | 78.9 | 32.5 | 37.1 | 95.7 |
| PISCATAQUIS | 0.4 | 0.8 | 4.5 | 5.7 | 7.5 | 7.0 | 5.0 | 27.2 | 25.9 | 15.0 | 2.3 | 77.7 | 36.5 | 41.0 | 96.1 |
| SAGADAHOC | 1.0 | 1.8 | 5.7 | 6.5 | 7.7 | 6.7 | 5.7 | 32.5 | 23.5 | 10.2 | 1.5 | 76.0 | 32.7 | 37.0 | 97.4 |
| SOMERSET | 0.3 | 0.8 | 5.6 | 6.4 | 7.3 | 7.2 | 5.9 | 29.0 | 24.6 | 12.2 | 1.8 | 76.0 | 33.8 | 38.1 | 96.9 |
| WALDO | 0.5 | 1.0 | 5.5 | 6.5 | 7.6 | 7.4 | 5.8 | 27.1 | 26.1 | 12.4 | 1.6 | 75.8 | 34.7 | 39.0 | 96.4 |
| WASHINGTON | 0.4 | 1.0 | 4.6 | 5.7 | 7.5 | 7.3 | 5.7 | 27.5 | 24.8 | 14.5 | 2.3 | 77.8 | 35.7 | 40.0 | 96.6 |
| YORK | 0.6 | 1.2 | 5.8 | 6.6 | 7.6 | 6.8 | 5.4 | 30.6 | 24.1 | 11.4 | 1.6 | 75.7 | 33.7 | 37.8 | 95.2 |
| MAINE | 0.6 | 1.1 | 5.2 | 6.0 | 7.2 | 7.2 | 6.2 | 30.3 | 24.0 | 12.2 | 1.8 | 77.5 | 33.9 | 38.1 | 95.3 |
| UNITED STATES | 9.0 | 11.8 | 6.9 | 7.2 | 7.2 | 7.2 | 6.7 | 29.9 | 22.2 | 11.1 | 1.6 | 74.6 | 32.9 | 35.7 | 95.6 |

# HOUSEHOLDS

| COUNTY | HOUSEHOLDS 1990 | HOUSEHOLDS 2000 | HOUSEHOLDS 2005 | HOUSEHOLDS % Annual Rate 1990-2000 | HOUSEHOLDS 2000 Average HH Size | FAMILIES 1990 | FAMILIES 2000 | FAMILIES % Annual Rate 1990-2000 | MEDIAN HOUSEHOLD INCOME 2000 | MEDIAN HOUSEHOLD INCOME 2005 | MEDIAN HOUSEHOLD INCOME 2000 National Rank | MEDIAN HOUSEHOLD INCOME 2000 State Rank |
|---|---|---|---|---|---|---|---|---|---|---|---|---|
| ANDROSCOGGIN | 40,017 | 40,537 | 41,324 | 0.2 | 2.42 | 28,047 | 27,613 | -0.2 | 37,357 | 45,181 | 921 | 5 |
| AROOSTOOK | 31,366 | 29,124 | 28,417 | -0.9 | 2.41 | 23,439 | 21,188 | -1.2 | 28,285 | 32,861 | 2402 | 16 |
| CUMBERLAND | 94,512 | 105,909 | 112,640 | 1.4 | 2.38 | 63,087 | 68,566 | 1.0 | 43,509 | 50,063 | 421 | 1 |
| FRANKLIN | 10,778 | 11,397 | 11,585 | 0.7 | 2.46 | 7,599 | 7,737 | 0.2 | 32,026 | 37,256 | 1709 | 11 |
| HANCOCK | 18,342 | 20,745 | 21,506 | 1.5 | 2.32 | 12,836 | 13,986 | 1.0 | 35,679 | 40,701 | 1139 | 8 |
| KENNEBEC | 43,889 | 45,669 | 46,440 | 0.5 | 2.44 | 30,869 | 31,168 | 0.1 | 37,142 | 43,301 | 953 | 6 |
| KNOX | 14,344 | 15,846 | 16,610 | 1.2 | 2.33 | 9,849 | 10,494 | 0.8 | 36,889 | 44,028 | 993 | 7 |
| LINCOLN | 11,968 | 13,251 | 13,932 | 1.2 | 2.40 | 8,585 | 9,190 | 0.8 | 38,345 | 45,687 | 826 | 4 |
| OXFORD | 20,064 | 21,653 | 22,645 | 0.9 | 2.48 | 14,573 | 15,213 | 0.5 | 33,659 | 41,180 | 1441 | 10 |
| PENOBSCOT | 54,063 | 55,813 | 56,522 | 0.4 | 2.45 | 38,125 | 38,206 | 0.0 | 34,565 | 39,967 | 1308 | 9 |
| PISCATAQUIS | 7,194 | 7,372 | 7,389 | 0.3 | 2.41 | 5,210 | 5,156 | -0.1 | 30,172 | 37,174 | 2112 | 13 |
| SAGADAHOC | 12,581 | 14,576 | 15,968 | 1.8 | 2.48 | 9,141 | 10,241 | 1.4 | 40,870 | 49,220 | 601 | 3 |
| SOMERSET | 18,513 | 20,825 | 21,713 | 1.4 | 2.50 | 13,511 | 14,644 | 1.0 | 29,250 | 33,642 | 2258 | 14 |
| WALDO | 12,415 | 14,756 | 15,925 | 2.1 | 2.50 | 9,045 | 10,395 | 1.7 | 31,842 | 38,235 | 1751 | 12 |
| WASHINGTON | 13,418 | 14,171 | 14,147 | 0.7 | 2.40 | 9,666 | 9,846 | 0.2 | 28,303 | 32,833 | 2397 | 15 |
| YORK | 61,848 | 70,328 | 75,945 | 1.6 | 2.53 | 45,103 | 49,562 | 1.1 | 42,533 | 50,128 | 473 | 2 |
| MAINE | | | | 0.9 | 2.43 | | | 0.5 | 37,175 | 43,579 | | |
| UNITED STATES | | | | 1.4 | 2.59 | | | 1.1 | 41,914 | 49,127 | | |

| COUNTY | 2000 Per Capita Income | 2000 HH Income Base | 2000 HOUSEHOLD INCOME DISTRIBUTION (%) Less than $15,000 | $15,000 to $24,999 | $25,000 to $49,999 | $50,000 to $99,999 | $100,000 to $149,999 | $150,000 or More | 2000 AVERAGE DISPOSABLE INCOME BY AGE OF HOUSEHOLDER All Ages | <35 | 35-44 | 45-54 | 55-64 | 65+ |
|---|---|---|---|---|---|---|---|---|---|---|---|---|---|---|
| ANDROSCOGGIN | 18,817 | 40,537 | 15.3 | 13.5 | 38.3 | 26.9 | 4.6 | 1.3 | 33,592 | 31,150 | 40,342 | 41,152 | 35,430 | 20,207 |
| AROOSTOOK | 14,224 | 29,121 | 23.7 | 20.2 | 38.2 | 16.0 | 1.5 | 0.5 | 25,601 | 24,109 | 31,502 | 32,515 | 26,619 | 15,249 |
| CUMBERLAND | 23,546 | 105,906 | 11.5 | 11.5 | 35.0 | 32.0 | 7.4 | 2.7 | 39,207 | 35,359 | 45,031 | 46,938 | 41,914 | 25,501 |
| FRANKLIN | 15,237 | 11,397 | 19.7 | 18.2 | 38.4 | 20.5 | 2.4 | 0.8 | 28,572 | 24,763 | 32,953 | 35,276 | 31,874 | 18,450 |
| HANCOCK | 19,912 | 20,745 | 14.7 | 16.7 | 38.2 | 23.9 | 4.6 | 1.9 | 33,260 | 28,779 | 38,226 | 40,688 | 36,144 | 22,475 |
| KENNEBEC | 18,285 | 45,669 | 15.6 | 14.2 | 37.9 | 27.0 | 4.0 | 1.3 | 33,083 | 29,626 | 38,519 | 41,207 | 34,450 | 20,859 |
| KNOX | 20,216 | 15,846 | 14.2 | 16.5 | 36.9 | 26.6 | 4.3 | 1.6 | 33,354 | 29,332 | 38,150 | 39,657 | 34,191 | 26,186 |
| LINCOLN | 19,993 | 13,251 | 13.3 | 14.9 | 38.5 | 26.8 | 4.8 | 1.8 | 34,360 | 31,059 | 38,495 | 39,026 | 36,211 | 27,682 |
| OXFORD | 16,516 | 21,653 | 17.6 | 16.9 | 38.5 | 23.0 | 3.1 | 0.9 | 30,240 | 29,087 | 34,864 | 36,849 | 33,361 | 18,966 |
| PENOBSCOT | 16,830 | 55,811 | 17.8 | 16.6 | 37.2 | 23.8 | 3.4 | 1.2 | 31,077 | 27,628 | 36,675 | 38,439 | 32,893 | 19,470 |
| PISCATAQUIS | 14,043 | 7,372 | 21.7 | 18.5 | 40.4 | 17.6 | 1.7 | 0.1 | 26,247 | 25,496 | 32,022 | 30,397 | 27,166 | 17,504 |
| SAGADAHOC | 19,159 | 14,576 | 11.3 | 11.9 | 40.3 | 31.0 | 4.5 | 0.9 | 35,029 | 32,282 | 39,474 | 42,456 | 35,862 | 23,107 |
| SOMERSET | 14,334 | 20,822 | 22.9 | 19.8 | 36.8 | 17.6 | 2.2 | 0.7 | 26,679 | 25,962 | 33,322 | 31,882 | 26,633 | 15,874 |
| WALDO | 17,775 | 14,756 | 20.4 | 16.0 | 36.9 | 20.8 | 4.2 | 1.6 | 30,562 | 27,056 | 34,509 | 37,376 | 30,800 | 22,050 |
| WASHINGTON | 14,468 | 14,171 | 24.2 | 19.7 | 36.2 | 17.1 | 2.3 | 0.6 | 26,270 | 23,975 | 31,742 | 32,724 | 28,687 | 17,321 |
| YORK | 20,003 | 70,328 | 10.9 | 11.8 | 38.4 | 32.4 | 5.2 | 1.3 | 36,503 | 34,532 | 41,915 | 42,854 | 37,169 | 24,204 |
| MAINE | 18,925 | | 15.4 | 14.7 | 37.4 | 26.5 | 4.6 | 1.5 | 33,487 | 30,671 | 39,210 | 40,548 | 34,953 | 21,724 |
| UNITED STATES | 22,162 | | 14.5 | 12.5 | 32.3 | 29.8 | 7.4 | 3.5 | 40,748 | 34,503 | 44,969 | 49,579 | 43,409 | 27,339 |

# SPENDING POTENTIAL INDEXES

| COUNTY | FINANCIAL SERVICES | | | | THE HOME | | | | | | ENTERTAINMENT | | | | | | PERSONAL | | | |
|---|---|---|---|---|---|---|---|---|---|---|---|---|---|---|---|---|---|---|---|---|
| | | | | | Home Improvements | | | Furnishings | | | | | | | | | | | | |
| | Auto Loan | Home Loan | Invest-ments | Retire-ment Plans | Home Repair | Lawn & Garden | Remodel-ing | Appli-ances | Elec-tronics | Furni-ture | Restau-rants | Sport-ing Goods | Theater & Concerts | Toys & Hobbies | Travel | Video Rental | Apparel | Auto After-market | Health Insur-ance | Pets & Supplies |
| ANDROSCOGGIN | 98 | 84 | 89 | 87 | 90 | 88 | 96 | 96 | 93 | 90 | 91 | 96 | 92 | 99 | 86 | 98 | 93 | 91 | 101 | 100 |
| AROOSTOOK | 97 | 73 | 78 | 80 | 86 | 84 | 100 | 95 | 92 | 82 | 84 | 95 | 85 | 97 | 78 | 98 | 86 | 88 | 102 | 99 |
| CUMBERLAND | 101 | 98 | 102 | 100 | 95 | 95 | 95 | 99 | 98 | 100 | 101 | 102 | 101 | 104 | 96 | 100 | 104 | 99 | 102 | 104 |
| FRANKLIN | 100 | 77 | 82 | 85 | 88 | 85 | 105 | 97 | 93 | 85 | 87 | 98 | 88 | 101 | 80 | 99 | 90 | 90 | 103 | 102 |
| HANCOCK | 101 | 77 | 84 | 88 | 88 | 88 | 108 | 98 | 93 | 84 | 87 | 100 | 89 | 102 | 81 | 99 | 90 | 91 | 106 | 103 |
| KENNEBEC | 99 | 85 | 90 | 89 | 91 | 88 | 99 | 97 | 94 | 91 | 92 | 98 | 93 | 101 | 86 | 99 | 94 | 93 | 102 | 102 |
| KNOX | 100 | 80 | 89 | 89 | 90 | 90 | 105 | 98 | 93 | 87 | 89 | 99 | 91 | 102 | 85 | 99 | 93 | 92 | 105 | 103 |
| LINCOLN | 101 | 74 | 81 | 86 | 87 | 86 | 110 | 98 | 94 | 83 | 86 | 100 | 87 | 102 | 79 | 100 | 90 | 91 | 106 | 104 |
| OXFORD | 99 | 74 | 80 | 83 | 88 | 86 | 105 | 97 | 92 | 83 | 85 | 97 | 87 | 100 | 79 | 98 | 88 | 89 | 104 | 101 |
| PENOBSCOT | 98 | 84 | 89 | 87 | 89 | 87 | 98 | 96 | 93 | 89 | 91 | 97 | 91 | 100 | 85 | 98 | 92 | 92 | 101 | 101 |
| PISCATAQUIS | 99 | 69 | 74 | 80 | 85 | 84 | 108 | 97 | 92 | 79 | 81 | 98 | 83 | 99 | 75 | 98 | 85 | 88 | 104 | 101 |
| SAGADAHOC | 100 | 85 | 87 | 88 | 89 | 87 | 99 | 97 | 95 | 92 | 94 | 99 | 93 | 102 | 85 | 99 | 95 | 93 | 101 | 102 |
| SOMERSET | 98 | 72 | 77 | 80 | 86 | 84 | 103 | 96 | 92 | 82 | 84 | 97 | 85 | 99 | 77 | 98 | 86 | 88 | 103 | 100 |
| WALDO | 99 | 71 | 75 | 81 | 86 | 84 | 106 | 96 | 93 | 81 | 83 | 97 | 85 | 99 | 76 | 99 | 87 | 89 | 104 | 101 |
| WASHINGTON | 98 | 68 | 74 | 79 | 85 | 84 | 104 | 95 | 91 | 78 | 80 | 95 | 82 | 97 | 75 | 98 | 84 | 87 | 104 | 99 |
| YORK | 101 | 90 | 92 | 94 | 91 | 91 | 100 | 99 | 97 | 95 | 97 | 101 | 96 | 104 | 89 | 100 | 99 | 96 | 102 | 104 |
| MAINE | 100 | 85 | 90 | 90 | 90 | 89 | 100 | 97 | 95 | 91 | 92 | 99 | 93 | 101 | 86 | 99 | 95 | 93 | 102 | 102 |
| UNITED STATES | 100 | 100 | 100 | 100 | 100 | 100 | 100 | 100 | 100 | 100 | 100 | 100 | 100 | 100 | 100 | 100 | 100 | 100 | 100 | 100 |

| COUNTY | FIPS Code | MSA Code | DMA Code | POPULATION 1990 | POPULATION 2000 | POPULATION 2005 | 1990-2000 ANNUAL CHANGE % Rate | 1990-2000 ANNUAL CHANGE State Rank | RACE (%) White 1990 | RACE (%) White 2000 | RACE (%) Black 1990 | RACE (%) Black 2000 | RACE (%) Asian/Pacific 1990 | RACE (%) Asian/Pacific 2000 |
|---|---|---|---|---|---|---|---|---|---|---|---|---|---|---|
| ALLEGANY | 001 | 1900 | 511 | 74,946 | 70,432 | 66,827 | -0.6 | 23 | 97.3 | 96.4 | 2.0 | 2.7 | 0.4 | 0.6 |
| ANNE ARUNDEL | 003 | 0720 | 512 | 427,239 | 486,186 | 514,536 | 1.3 | 11 | 85.7 | 80.9 | 11.8 | 15.5 | 1.8 | 2.6 |
| BALTIMORE | 005 | 0720 | 512 | 692,134 | 726,226 | 737,938 | 0.5 | 18 | 84.9 | 79.9 | 12.3 | 16.2 | 2.2 | 3.2 |
| CALVERT | 009 | 8840 | 511 | 51,372 | 75,999 | 87,199 | 3.9 | 1 | 83.4 | 77.8 | 15.7 | 20.8 | 0.6 | 0.8 |
| CAROLINE | 011 | 0000 | 512 | 27,035 | 29,907 | 30,871 | 1.0 | 14 | 82.7 | 76.8 | 16.5 | 22.1 | 0.3 | 0.4 |
| CARROLL | 013 | 0720 | 512 | 123,372 | 155,415 | 170,091 | 2.3 | 5 | 96.7 | 95.6 | 2.4 | 3.1 | 0.6 | 0.9 |
| CECIL | 015 | 9160 | 512 | 71,347 | 86,002 | 94,635 | 1.8 | 9 | 94.5 | 92.8 | 4.5 | 5.8 | 0.4 | 0.7 |
| CHARLES | 017 | 8840 | 511 | 101,154 | 124,145 | 137,531 | 2.0 | 6 | 79.3 | 73.1 | 18.2 | 23.7 | 1.3 | 1.9 |
| DORCHESTER | 019 | 0000 | 512 | 30,236 | 29,930 | 29,843 | -0.1 | 22 | 71.3 | 63.7 | 27.9 | 35.2 | 0.5 | 0.6 |
| FREDERICK | 021 | 8840 | 511 | 150,208 | 194,852 | 214,783 | 2.6 | 3 | 93.1 | 90.5 | 5.3 | 7.3 | 1.0 | 1.5 |
| GARRETT | 023 | 0000 | 508 | 28,138 | 29,425 | 29,600 | 0.4 | 20 | 99.4 | 99.2 | 0.4 | 0.5 | 0.1 | 0.2 |
| HARFORD | 025 | 0720 | 512 | 182,132 | 221,395 | 238,815 | 1.9 | 8 | 89.3 | 85.7 | 8.5 | 11.1 | 1.4 | 2.0 |
| HOWARD | 027 | 0720 | 512 | 187,328 | 249,998 | 284,542 | 2.9 | 2 | 83.2 | 77.3 | 11.8 | 15.6 | 4.3 | 6.2 |
| KENT | 029 | 0000 | 512 | 17,842 | 19,154 | 19,476 | 0.7 | 15 | 78.9 | 73.2 | 19.8 | 25.2 | 0.4 | 0.5 |
| MONTGOMERY | 031 | 8840 | 511 | 757,027 | 863,876 | 921,711 | 1.3 | 11 | 76.7 | 69.6 | 12.2 | 15.1 | 8.2 | 11.2 |
| PRINCE GEORGE'S | 033 | 8840 | 511 | 729,268 | 786,864 | 812,773 | 0.7 | 15 | 43.1 | 35.2 | 50.7 | 57.3 | 3.9 | 4.7 |
| QUEEN ANNE'S | 035 | 0720 | 512 | 33,953 | 41,602 | 46,173 | 2.0 | 6 | 88.1 | 83.7 | 11.3 | 15.5 | 0.4 | 0.5 |
| ST. MARY'S | 037 | 0000 | 511 | 75,974 | 90,604 | 99,264 | 1.7 | 10 | 84.4 | 79.3 | 13.5 | 17.8 | 1.2 | 1.8 |
| SOMERSET | 039 | 0000 | 576 | 23,440 | 24,176 | 23,879 | 0.3 | 21 | 60.9 | 51.6 | 38.2 | 47.3 | 0.4 | 0.5 |
| TALBOT | 041 | 0000 | 512 | 30,549 | 34,073 | 35,952 | 1.1 | 13 | 81.3 | 75.0 | 18.0 | 24.1 | 0.3 | 0.5 |
| WASHINGTON | 043 | 3180 | 511 | 121,393 | 128,198 | 130,136 | 0.5 | 18 | 92.9 | 91.4 | 6.0 | 7.0 | 0.7 | 1.0 |
| WICOMICO | 045 | 0000 | 576 | 74,339 | 79,743 | 80,705 | 0.7 | 15 | 76.3 | 69.4 | 22.3 | 28.8 | 0.9 | 1.3 |
| WORCESTER | 047 | 0000 | 576 | 35,028 | 44,545 | 48,899 | 2.4 | 4 | 77.8 | 70.9 | 21.3 | 28.1 | 0.5 | 0.6 |
| BALTIMORE CITY | 510 | 0720 | 512 | 736,014 | 620,155 | 563,090 | -1.7 | 24 | 39.1 | 31.1 | 59.2 | 66.9 | 1.1 | 1.3 |
| MARYLAND | | | | | | | 0.8 | | 71.0 | 66.9 | 24.9 | 27.5 | 2.9 | 4.1 |
| UNITED STATES | | | | | | | 1.0 | | 80.3 | 77.9 | 12.1 | 12.4 | 2.9 | 3.9 |

# POPULATION COMPOSITION

## B

| COUNTY | % HISPANIC ORIGIN | | 2000 AGE DISTRIBUTION (%) | | | | | | | | | | MEDIAN AGE | | 2000 Males/ Females (×100) |
|---|---|---|---|---|---|---|---|---|---|---|---|---|---|---|---|
| | 1990 | 2000 | 0-4 | 5-9 | 10-14 | 15-19 | 20-24 | 25-44 | 45-64 | 65-84 | 85+ | 18+ | 1990 | 2000 | |
| ALLEGANY | 0.4 | 1.1 | 5.2 | 6.1 | 6.6 | 7.9 | 6.7 | 25.2 | 23.4 | 16.4 | 2.5 | 78.2 | 37.5 | 39.6 | 91.2 |
| ANNE ARUNDEL | 1.6 | 2.7 | 6.4 | 7.2 | 7.4 | 6.8 | 6.0 | 32.9 | 22.9 | 9.5 | 1.0 | 75.2 | 32.7 | 35.9 | 101.0 |
| BALTIMORE | 1.2 | 2.1 | 5.9 | 6.5 | 6.9 | 6.3 | 5.5 | 30.3 | 23.2 | 13.6 | 1.9 | 77.2 | 35.2 | 38.4 | 91.0 |
| CALVERT | 1.0 | 1.8 | 7.1 | 8.1 | 8.3 | 7.2 | 5.1 | 31.4 | 23.6 | 8.4 | 0.9 | 72.0 | 32.6 | 35.5 | 97.6 |
| CAROLINE | 0.9 | 1.6 | 6.8 | 7.8 | 8.1 | 7.1 | 5.1 | 28.4 | 22.6 | 12.3 | 1.8 | 73.1 | 34.3 | 36.8 | 95.0 |
| CARROLL | 0.7 | 1.6 | 6.7 | 7.7 | 8.0 | 7.2 | 5.2 | 30.5 | 24.0 | 9.2 | 1.4 | 73.4 | 33.3 | 36.2 | 97.1 |
| CECIL | 0.9 | 1.8 | 7.1 | 7.7 | 7.8 | 7.3 | 5.7 | 30.2 | 23.0 | 10.1 | 1.1 | 73.0 | 32.6 | 35.3 | 99.6 |
| CHARLES | 1.7 | 2.9 | 7.6 | 8.6 | 8.5 | 7.4 | 5.7 | 33.9 | 20.8 | 6.9 | 0.7 | 70.9 | 30.2 | 33.1 | 98.5 |
| DORCHESTER | 0.6 | 1.1 | 6.0 | 6.6 | 6.9 | 6.5 | 5.4 | 27.3 | 23.7 | 15.4 | 2.1 | 76.7 | 37.0 | 39.6 | 93.2 |
| FREDERICK | 1.1 | 2.2 | 6.8 | 7.9 | 8.0 | 7.2 | 6.0 | 32.5 | 21.7 | 8.6 | 1.2 | 73.2 | 32.3 | 35.0 | 97.6 |
| GARRETT | 0.4 | 1.0 | 6.0 | 7.5 | 7.9 | 7.8 | 5.2 | 27.9 | 23.1 | 12.7 | 1.8 | 73.8 | 33.7 | 37.1 | 96.7 |
| HARFORD | 1.5 | 2.6 | 7.2 | 7.9 | 7.9 | 6.8 | 5.2 | 32.1 | 22.9 | 9.1 | 0.8 | 73.0 | 32.1 | 35.3 | 98.0 |
| HOWARD | 2.0 | 3.3 | 6.7 | 7.8 | 7.9 | 6.3 | 4.9 | 36.1 | 22.9 | 6.7 | 0.8 | 73.6 | 32.2 | 35.6 | 98.7 |
| KENT | 2.6 | 3.6 | 5.5 | 6.2 | 6.4 | 8.0 | 6.9 | 25.6 | 23.1 | 16.0 | 2.2 | 78.3 | 36.6 | 39.0 | 93.5 |
| MONTGOMERY | 7.4 | 10.9 | 6.4 | 7.1 | 7.3 | 6.0 | 5.2 | 33.9 | 22.7 | 10.0 | 1.4 | 75.5 | 33.9 | 36.8 | 93.1 |
| PRINCE GEORGE'S | 4.1 | 5.3 | 6.7 | 7.0 | 7.2 | 7.1 | 7.2 | 35.1 | 21.3 | 7.6 | 0.8 | 75.4 | 30.9 | 34.2 | 93.3 |
| QUEEN ANNE'S | 0.6 | 1.2 | 6.5 | 7.3 | 7.8 | 6.8 | 4.7 | 28.9 | 24.0 | 12.6 | 1.4 | 74.4 | 35.5 | 38.3 | 97.8 |
| ST. MARY'S | 1.6 | 2.8 | 8.8 | 8.6 | 7.8 | 6.7 | 6.7 | 34.5 | 18.7 | 7.5 | 0.9 | 71.1 | 29.5 | 32.0 | 101.5 |
| SOMERSET | 1.0 | 1.6 | 5.1 | 5.4 | 5.4 | 8.1 | 9.5 | 32.4 | 19.6 | 12.9 | 1.7 | 81.0 | 33.8 | 34.4 | 122.2 |
| TALBOT | 0.5 | 1.1 | 5.5 | 6.4 | 6.5 | 5.7 | 4.5 | 26.6 | 24.5 | 17.8 | 2.7 | 78.2 | 39.6 | 41.7 | 91.9 |
| WASHINGTON | 0.7 | 1.5 | 6.1 | 6.5 | 6.7 | 6.4 | 6.4 | 30.9 | 22.4 | 12.9 | 1.8 | 77.1 | 34.4 | 36.9 | 102.7 |
| WICOMICO | 0.8 | 1.5 | 6.4 | 6.9 | 7.1 | 7.8 | 7.2 | 29.2 | 22.1 | 11.7 | 1.6 | 75.7 | 33.2 | 35.7 | 93.4 |
| WORCESTER | 0.8 | 1.3 | 5.5 | 6.2 | 6.4 | 5.5 | 4.5 | 28.2 | 23.8 | 17.9 | 2.1 | 78.7 | 37.5 | 41.0 | 94.0 |
| BALTIMORE CITY | 1.0 | 1.4 | 7.1 | 7.3 | 7.4 | 7.3 | 6.6 | 31.0 | 20.1 | 11.6 | 1.7 | 74.5 | 32.6 | 35.1 | 88.3 |
| MARYLAND | 2.6 | 4.1 | 6.6 | 7.2 | 7.4 | 6.7 | 5.9 | 32.4 | 22.2 | 10.3 | 1.3 | 75.1 | 33.0 | 36.0 | 94.5 |
| UNITED STATES | 9.0 | 11.8 | 6.9 | 7.2 | 7.2 | 7.2 | 6.7 | 29.9 | 22.2 | 11.1 | 1.6 | 74.6 | 32.9 | 35.7 | 95.6 |

| COUNTY | HOUSEHOLDS | | | | | FAMILIES | | | MEDIAN HOUSEHOLD INCOME | | | |
|---|---|---|---|---|---|---|---|---|---|---|---|---|
| | 1990 | 2000 | 2005 | % Annual Rate 1990-2000 | 2000 Average HH Size | 1990 | 2000 | % Annual Rate 1990-2000 | 2000 | 2005 | 2000 National Rank | 2000 State Rank |
| ALLEGANY | 29,634 | 28,616 | 27,447 | -0.4 | 2.36 | 20,403 | 18,798 | -1.0 | 30,266 | 33,604 | 2092 | 24 |
| ANNE ARUNDEL | 149,114 | 173,885 | 186,128 | 1.9 | 2.71 | 113,425 | 127,644 | 1.4 | 64,669 | 77,447 | 38 | 5 |
| BALTIMORE | 268,280 | 287,924 | 295,854 | 0.9 | 2.47 | 189,835 | 195,276 | 0.3 | 48,536 | 54,630 | 228 | 13 |
| CALVERT | 16,986 | 25,992 | 30,299 | 5.3 | 2.91 | 13,882 | 20,653 | 4.9 | 64,683 | 76,788 | 37 | 4 |
| CAROLINE | 9,983 | 11,205 | 11,648 | 1.4 | 2.63 | 7,412 | 8,038 | 1.0 | 37,103 | 46,044 | 959 | 18 |
| CARROLL | 42,248 | 54,671 | 60,562 | 3.2 | 2.79 | 33,909 | 42,629 | 2.8 | 62,510 | 75,795 | 55 | 6 |
| CECIL | 24,725 | 30,556 | 33,977 | 2.6 | 2.76 | 19,267 | 23,184 | 2.3 | 50,842 | 61,520 | 188 | 11 |
| CHARLES | 32,950 | 41,203 | 46,164 | 2.7 | 2.97 | 26,767 | 32,501 | 2.4 | 77,360 | 89,612 | 6 | 2 |
| DORCHESTER | 12,117 | 12,059 | 12,078 | -0.1 | 2.43 | 8,490 | 8,130 | -0.5 | 32,399 | 38,329 | 1639 | 21 |
| FREDERICK | 52,570 | 69,315 | 77,201 | 3.4 | 2.74 | 40,216 | 51,643 | 3.1 | 61,792 | 73,684 | 60 | 7 |
| GARRETT | 10,110 | 10,733 | 10,862 | 0.7 | 2.70 | 7,781 | 8,013 | 0.4 | 32,335 | 40,609 | 1654 | 22 |
| HARFORD | 63,193 | 80,065 | 87,452 | 2.9 | 2.76 | 50,158 | 61,744 | 2.6 | 57,510 | 68,977 | 95 | 8 |
| HOWARD | 68,337 | 92,672 | 106,207 | 3.8 | 2.68 | 50,691 | 66,513 | 3.3 | 77,952 | 89,748 | 4 | 1 |
| KENT | 6,702 | 7,203 | 7,349 | 0.9 | 2.48 | 4,689 | 4,778 | 0.2 | 41,518 | 48,240 | 549 | 15 |
| MONTGOMERY | 282,228 | 327,346 | 352,006 | 1.8 | 2.62 | 198,232 | 222,570 | 1.4 | 70,896 | 77,543 | 11 | 3 |
| PRINCE GEORGE'S | 258,011 | 284,519 | 297,273 | 1.2 | 2.70 | 182,447 | 195,150 | 0.8 | 55,607 | 64,665 | 115 | 9 |
| QUEEN ANNE'S | 12,489 | 15,537 | 17,366 | 2.7 | 2.66 | 9,731 | 11,731 | 2.3 | 55,462 | 69,113 | 118 | 10 |
| ST. MARY'S | 25,500 | 31,949 | 35,783 | 2.8 | 2.76 | 19,521 | 23,700 | 2.4 | 50,509 | 58,951 | 195 | 12 |
| SOMERSET | 7,977 | 8,058 | 8,052 | 0.1 | 2.41 | 5,580 | 5,415 | -0.4 | 32,034 | 39,816 | 1707 | 23 |
| TALBOT | 12,677 | 14,250 | 15,123 | 1.4 | 2.35 | 8,877 | 9,560 | 0.9 | 44,186 | 50,823 | 386 | 14 |
| WASHINGTON | 44,762 | 48,208 | 49,432 | 0.9 | 2.49 | 32,349 | 33,780 | 0.5 | 41,059 | 49,074 | 587 | 16 |
| WICOMICO | 27,772 | 30,438 | 31,114 | 1.1 | 2.52 | 19,513 | 20,822 | 0.8 | 38,741 | 43,154 | 779 | 17 |
| WORCESTER | 14,142 | 18,437 | 20,462 | 3.3 | 2.39 | 9,797 | 11,653 | 2.1 | 35,396 | 38,364 | 1185 | 19 |
| BALTIMORE CITY | 276,484 | 241,138 | 222,393 | -1.6 | 2.48 | 172,842 | 144,982 | -2.1 | 33,416 | 39,081 | 1474 | 20 |
| MARYLAND | | | | 1.3 | 2.62 | | | 1.0 | 54,427 | 63,444 | | |
| UNITED STATES | | | | 1.4 | 2.59 | | | 1.1 | 41,914 | 49,127 | | |

| COUNTY | 2000 Per Capita Income | 2000 HH Income Base | 2000 HOUSEHOLD INCOME DISTRIBUTION (%) | | | | | | 2000 AVERAGE DISPOSABLE INCOME BY AGE OF HOUSEHOLDER | | | | | |
|---|---|---|---|---|---|---|---|---|---|---|---|---|---|---|
| | | | Less than $15,000 | $15,000 to $24,999 | $25,000 to $49,999 | $50,000 to $99,999 | $100,000 to $149,999 | $150,000 or More | All Ages | <35 | 35-44 | 45-54 | 55-64 | 65+ |
| ALLEGANY | 17,508 | 28,616 | 21.8 | 19.3 | 34.8 | 19.1 | 3.3 | 1.8 | 29,374 | 25,543 | 36,203 | 38,464 | 31,121 | 19,677 |
| ANNE ARUNDEL | 31,081 | 173,885 | 4.3 | 5.4 | 23.9 | 42.9 | 16.0 | 7.6 | 56,036 | 46,415 | 57,466 | 65,024 | 57,974 | 38,450 |
| BALTIMORE | 25,896 | 287,924 | 8.3 | 9.9 | 33.6 | 35.7 | 8.6 | 3.9 | 43,621 | 38,155 | 46,615 | 52,254 | 46,305 | 31,080 |
| CALVERT | 27,516 | 25,992 | 5.9 | 3.6 | 23.3 | 46.2 | 15.4 | 5.7 | 53,347 | 45,103 | 54,371 | 63,883 | 52,851 | 34,846 |
| CAROLINE | 16,519 | 11,205 | 16.8 | 14.0 | 37.6 | 26.6 | 4.2 | 0.8 | 31,997 | 31,086 | 38,406 | 37,931 | 32,741 | 20,874 |
| CARROLL | 27,365 | 54,671 | 5.6 | 3.8 | 24.6 | 46.2 | 14.8 | 4.9 | 51,903 | 46,647 | 55,225 | 61,487 | 51,807 | 33,981 |
| CECIL | 22,869 | 30,556 | 8.2 | 8.7 | 31.8 | 38.9 | 9.6 | 2.7 | 42,841 | 37,543 | 46,769 | 53,467 | 42,766 | 28,691 |
| CHARLES | 30,831 | 41,203 | 4.1 | 2.9 | 16.0 | 45.9 | 23.2 | 7.9 | 60,979 | 53,525 | 62,823 | 70,953 | 58,571 | 41,010 |
| DORCHESTER | 17,665 | 12,059 | 18.7 | 16.4 | 37.0 | 22.3 | 4.1 | 1.6 | 31,024 | 28,209 | 37,179 | 37,639 | 33,831 | 22,271 |
| FREDERICK | 27,528 | 69,315 | 5.7 | 4.5 | 26.0 | 44.0 | 14.7 | 5.1 | 51,495 | 46,422 | 54,081 | 60,867 | 50,894 | 34,495 |
| GARRETT | 14,990 | 10,733 | 19.1 | 17.1 | 35.4 | 24.3 | 3.0 | 1.0 | 29,899 | 26,919 | 35,190 | 37,603 | 30,642 | 19,467 |
| HARFORD | 26,416 | 80,065 | 5.6 | 6.4 | 28.3 | 43.1 | 12.2 | 4.4 | 48,646 | 42,856 | 51,309 | 57,640 | 50,194 | 31,897 |
| HOWARD | 37,666 | 92,672 | 3.4 | 3.3 | 16.2 | 44.9 | 21.7 | 10.5 | 64,934 | 53,633 | 64,209 | 73,465 | 65,657 | 39,811 |
| KENT | 23,884 | 7,203 | 15.3 | 11.6 | 33.1 | 28.2 | 7.5 | 4.3 | 40,018 | 32,006 | 40,262 | 50,140 | 43,647 | 30,344 |
| MONTGOMERY | 38,882 | 327,346 | 3.7 | 4.8 | 21.2 | 40.7 | 17.7 | 12.0 | 64,685 | 48,997 | 60,331 | 69,868 | 67,466 | 53,432 |
| PRINCE GEORGE'S | 24,220 | 284,513 | 4.9 | 7.6 | 30.2 | 43.9 | 10.9 | 2.5 | 45,528 | 39,257 | 46,075 | 52,825 | 49,878 | 35,644 |
| QUEEN ANNE'S | 29,057 | 15,537 | 8.1 | 7.0 | 28.5 | 38.9 | 12.2 | 5.4 | 49,047 | 43,325 | 49,713 | 60,553 | 52,682 | 32,045 |
| ST. MARY'S | 21,156 | 31,949 | 6.5 | 10.1 | 32.7 | 40.6 | 8.2 | 2.0 | 41,756 | 37,330 | 44,240 | 51,988 | 41,802 | 29,760 |
| SOMERSET | 14,586 | 8,058 | 21.1 | 15.6 | 37.8 | 22.2 | 2.6 | 0.8 | 28,663 | 28,077 | 35,822 | 33,510 | 29,191 | 20,214 |
| TALBOT | 29,474 | 14,250 | 11.5 | 12.8 | 30.7 | 29.8 | 9.4 | 5.8 | 44,761 | 35,835 | 46,463 | 52,554 | 48,834 | 35,286 |
| WASHINGTON | 19,415 | 48,206 | 13.3 | 11.4 | 37.7 | 30.7 | 5.6 | 1.4 | 35,663 | 32,899 | 41,347 | 44,617 | 37,204 | 24,084 |
| WICOMICO | 19,219 | 30,438 | 14.6 | 13.4 | 36.9 | 28.1 | 5.3 | 1.8 | 34,705 | 31,766 | 39,284 | 43,770 | 36,412 | 21,850 |
| WORCESTER | 19,078 | 18,423 | 18.3 | 15.0 | 37.4 | 23.5 | 4.4 | 1.4 | 31,823 | 28,367 | 38,920 | 37,471 | 35,915 | 23,777 |
| BALTIMORE CITY | 17,905 | 241,122 | 22.2 | 15.0 | 32.9 | 23.9 | 4.4 | 1.6 | 31,328 | 27,626 | 35,129 | 37,270 | 33,386 | 23,267 |
| MARYLAND | 27,573 | | 8.5 | 8.3 | 28.1 | 37.8 | 11.9 | 5.4 | 48,317 | 40,836 | 50,237 | 56,712 | 50,186 | 34,105 |
| UNITED STATES | 22,162 | | 14.5 | 12.5 | 32.3 | 29.8 | 7.4 | 3.5 | 40,748 | 34,503 | 44,969 | 49,579 | 43,409 | 27,339 |

| COUNTY | FINANCIAL SERVICES | | | | THE HOME | | | | | | ENTERTAINMENT | | | | | | PERSONAL | | | |
|---|---|---|---|---|---|---|---|---|---|---|---|---|---|---|---|---|---|---|---|---|
| | | | | | Home Improvements | | | Furnishings | | | | | | | | | | | | |
| | Auto Loan | Home Loan | Investments | Retirement Plans | Home Repair | Lawn & Garden | Remodeling | Appliances | Electronics | Furniture | Restaurants | Sporting Goods | Theater & Concerts | Toys & Hobbies | Travel | Video Rental | Apparel | Auto Aftermarket | Health Insurance | Pets & Supplies |
| ALLEGANY | 94 | 83 | 98 | 85 | 104 | 99 | 99 | 95 | 89 | 90 | 89 | 91 | 91 | 95 | 85 | 95 | 87 | 91 | 101 | 95 |
| ANNE ARUNDEL | 104 | 113 | 109 | 111 | 106 | 109 | 103 | 103 | 106 | 111 | 115 | 107 | 110 | 108 | 97 | 101 | 114 | 109 | 101 | 106 |
| BALTIMORE | 99 | 105 | 108 | 102 | 106 | 106 | 98 | 100 | 99 | 104 | 106 | 101 | 103 | 102 | 94 | 99 | 104 | 102 | 100 | 101 |
| CALVERT | 105 | 109 | 101 | 107 | 102 | 105 | 107 | 104 | 108 | 110 | 115 | 108 | 108 | 109 | 92 | 103 | 114 | 110 | 100 | 107 |
| CAROLINE | 98 | 76 | 85 | 83 | 97 | 94 | 111 | 97 | 92 | 85 | 86 | 95 | 87 | 98 | 75 | 97 | 86 | 91 | 102 | 99 |
| CARROLL | 104 | 108 | 103 | 106 | 103 | 105 | 105 | 103 | 106 | 108 | 113 | 106 | 107 | 108 | 92 | 102 | 111 | 108 | 101 | 106 |
| CECIL | 100 | 95 | 95 | 96 | 100 | 99 | 107 | 100 | 99 | 98 | 100 | 101 | 97 | 103 | 84 | 99 | 99 | 99 | 100 | 102 |
| CHARLES | 103 | 107 | 95 | 102 | 101 | 102 | 102 | 102 | 105 | 108 | 112 | 106 | 105 | 106 | 90 | 102 | 110 | 107 | 98 | 105 |
| DORCHESTER | 96 | 78 | 93 | 83 | 100 | 96 | 104 | 96 | 90 | 87 | 85 | 93 | 88 | 95 | 80 | 96 | 86 | 90 | 99 | 96 |
| FREDERICK | 102 | 104 | 99 | 101 | 102 | 103 | 104 | 101 | 103 | 104 | 108 | 104 | 103 | 105 | 90 | 101 | 106 | 104 | 100 | 104 |
| GARRETT | 98 | 70 | 77 | 80 | 93 | 92 | 115 | 96 | 92 | 79 | 81 | 95 | 82 | 97 | 70 | 97 | 82 | 89 | 102 | 98 |
| HARFORD | 102 | 105 | 98 | 101 | 102 | 102 | 102 | 101 | 103 | 106 | 109 | 104 | 103 | 105 | 90 | 101 | 107 | 105 | 99 | 104 |
| HOWARD | 108 | 125 | 108 | 121 | 106 | 114 | 106 | 107 | 113 | 120 | 126 | 115 | 116 | 112 | 102 | 104 | 125 | 116 | 102 | 110 |
| KENT | 97 | 85 | 100 | 89 | 103 | 100 | 103 | 97 | 92 | 90 | 92 | 95 | 93 | 99 | 84 | 97 | 90 | 93 | 103 | 98 |
| MONTGOMERY | 107 | 134 | 123 | 128 | 114 | 122 | 107 | 107 | 114 | 120 | 128 | 115 | 122 | 111 | 113 | 104 | 127 | 120 | 105 | 109 |
| PRINCE GEORGE'S | 99 | 106 | 101 | 101 | 103 | 102 | 94 | 100 | 100 | 105 | 104 | 101 | 102 | 101 | 93 | 101 | 107 | 106 | 94 | 102 |
| QUEEN ANNE'S | 103 | 100 | 103 | 104 | 102 | 104 | 109 | 101 | 103 | 102 | 105 | 105 | 103 | 106 | 89 | 101 | 105 | 103 | 102 | 105 |
| ST. MARY'S | 100 | 99 | 93 | 96 | 99 | 98 | 104 | 99 | 101 | 99 | 103 | 101 | 98 | 103 | 85 | 100 | 100 | 101 | 99 | 104 |
| SOMERSET | 94 | 73 | 80 | 77 | 97 | 92 | 104 | 95 | 89 | 83 | 82 | 91 | 83 | 93 | 75 | 95 | 82 | 88 | 98 | 95 |
| TALBOT | 101 | 97 | 113 | 105 | 107 | 110 | 111 | 101 | 98 | 99 | 101 | 102 | 102 | 103 | 94 | 98 | 101 | 99 | 105 | 103 |
| WASHINGTON | 97 | 87 | 96 | 88 | 101 | 97 | 105 | 97 | 93 | 91 | 92 | 95 | 92 | 98 | 82 | 97 | 91 | 94 | 100 | 99 |
| WICOMICO | 97 | 90 | 95 | 91 | 99 | 97 | 103 | 97 | 95 | 94 | 94 | 96 | 93 | 99 | 83 | 98 | 94 | 96 | 97 | 99 |
| WORCESTER | 99 | 79 | 94 | 90 | 99 | 100 | 114 | 100 | 93 | 85 | 88 | 98 | 89 | 99 | 81 | 97 | 89 | 93 | 104 | 101 |
| BALTIMORE CITY | 91 | 84 | 92 | 82 | 101 | 93 | 82 | 95 | 87 | 93 | 81 | 87 | 89 | 88 | 85 | 97 | 92 | 94 | 87 | 91 |
| MARYLAND | 101 | 109 | 107 | 107 | 105 | 107 | 101 | 101 | 103 | 107 | 108 | 105 | 106 | 104 | 96 | 101 | 108 | 106 | 99 | 103 |
| UNITED STATES | 100 | 100 | 100 | 100 | 100 | 100 | 100 | 100 | 100 | 100 | 100 | 100 | 100 | 100 | 100 | 100 | 100 | 100 | 100 | 100 |

# POPULATION CHANGE

| COUNTY | FIPS Code | MSA Code | DMA Code | POPULATION 1990 | POPULATION 2000 | POPULATION 2005 | 1990-2000 ANNUAL CHANGE % Rate | 1990-2000 ANNUAL CHANGE State Rank | RACE (%) White 1990 | White 2000 | Black 1990 | Black 2000 | Asian/Pacific 1990 | Asian/Pacific 2000 |
|---|---|---|---|---|---|---|---|---|---|---|---|---|---|---|
| BARNSTABLE | 001 | 0743 | 506 | 186,605 | 216,032 | 233,725 | 1.4 | 3 | 96.2 | 95.3 | 1.5 | 1.9 | 0.5 | 0.8 |
| BERKSHIRE | 003 | 6323 | 532 | 139,352 | 131,557 | 128,088 | -0.6 | 14 | 97.0 | 96.0 | 1.8 | 2.3 | 0.7 | 1.1 |
| BRISTOL | 005 | 1123 | 521 | 506,325 | 522,848 | 535,762 | 0.3 | 8 | 95.3 | 93.8 | 1.6 | 2.1 | 0.9 | 1.5 |
| DUKES | 007 | 0000 | 506 | 11,639 | 14,294 | 15,541 | 2.0 | 2 | 94.3 | 93.2 | 2.9 | 3.6 | 0.4 | 0.6 |
| ESSEX | 009 | 1123 | 506 | 670,080 | 709,300 | 733,449 | 0.6 | 5 | 92.0 | 88.9 | 2.4 | 3.1 | 1.5 | 2.4 |
| FRANKLIN | 011 | 0000 | 543 | 70,092 | 70,825 | 70,909 | 0.1 | 11 | 97.9 | 97.1 | 0.7 | 0.9 | 0.7 | 1.1 |
| HAMPDEN | 013 | 8003 | 543 | 456,310 | 438,272 | 432,355 | -0.4 | 13 | 85.0 | 80.9 | 7.5 | 9.2 | 0.9 | 1.3 |
| HAMPSHIRE | 015 | 8003 | 543 | 146,568 | 151,242 | 153,021 | 0.3 | 8 | 93.8 | 91.6 | 1.7 | 2.1 | 3.1 | 4.5 |
| MIDDLESEX | 017 | 1123 | 506 | 1,398,468 | 1,432,041 | 1,458,163 | 0.2 | 10 | 92.1 | 88.9 | 2.9 | 3.5 | 3.7 | 5.8 |
| NANTUCKET | 019 | 0000 | 506 | 6,012 | 8,510 | 10,051 | 3.4 | 1 | 96.3 | 95.5 | 2.5 | 3.0 | 0.3 | 0.4 |
| NORFOLK | 021 | 1123 | 506 | 616,087 | 645,585 | 655,897 | 0.5 | 6 | 94.6 | 92.2 | 2.0 | 2.5 | 2.9 | 4.7 |
| PLYMOUTH | 023 | 1123 | 506 | 435,276 | 478,784 | 506,997 | 0.9 | 4 | 93.4 | 91.6 | 3.8 | 4.8 | 0.8 | 1.3 |
| SUFFOLK | 025 | 1123 | 506 | 663,906 | 641,524 | 640,673 | -0.3 | 12 | 66.1 | 58.5 | 22.5 | 26.2 | 5.0 | 7.4 |
| WORCESTER | 027 | 1123 | 506 | 709,705 | 745,668 | 779,846 | 0.5 | 6 | 93.8 | 91.5 | 2.1 | 2.6 | 1.6 | 2.6 |
| MASSACHUSETTS | | | | | | | 0.3 | | 89.8 | 87.0 | 5.0 | 5.8 | 2.4 | 3.7 |
| UNITED STATES | | | | | | | 1.0 | | 80.3 | 77.9 | 12.1 | 12.4 | 2.9 | 3.9 |

| COUNTY | % HISPANIC ORIGIN 1990 | % HISPANIC ORIGIN 2000 | 2000 AGE DISTRIBUTION (%) 0-4 | 5-9 | 10-14 | 15-19 | 20-24 | 25-44 | 45-64 | 65-84 | 85+ | 18+ | MEDIAN AGE 1990 | MEDIAN AGE 2000 | 2000 Males/ Females (×100) |
|---|---|---|---|---|---|---|---|---|---|---|---|---|---|---|---|
| BARNSTABLE | 1.2 | 2.0 | 5.6 | 6.4 | 6.6 | 5.3 | 4.1 | 26.3 | 24.6 | 18.2 | 2.9 | 78.3 | 39.5 | 42.2 | 91.4 |
| BERKSHIRE | 1.0 | 1.8 | 5.5 | 6.5 | 6.8 | 6.6 | 5.2 | 28.4 | 23.0 | 15.3 | 2.5 | 77.7 | 35.9 | 39.2 | 93.1 |
| BRISTOL | 2.7 | 4.1 | 6.4 | 7.1 | 7.4 | 6.1 | 5.2 | 31.0 | 22.0 | 12.8 | 1.9 | 75.6 | 33.8 | 36.8 | 92.6 |
| DUKES | 1.0 | 1.7 | 5.7 | 6.9 | 7.0 | 5.1 | 3.2 | 31.3 | 25.1 | 13.7 | 2.0 | 76.8 | 37.1 | 40.4 | 96.5 |
| ESSEX | 7.2 | 10.3 | 6.5 | 7.1 | 7.4 | 6.1 | 5.2 | 30.4 | 23.0 | 12.3 | 2.0 | 75.5 | 34.5 | 37.4 | 92.6 |
| FRANKLIN | 1.2 | 2.0 | 6.4 | 6.9 | 7.1 | 6.3 | 5.9 | 29.3 | 24.3 | 11.9 | 2.0 | 75.8 | 34.9 | 37.6 | 94.4 |
| HAMPDEN | 10.0 | 13.4 | 6.8 | 7.1 | 7.2 | 6.9 | 6.0 | 29.4 | 21.4 | 13.1 | 2.1 | 75.2 | 33.4 | 36.4 | 92.1 |
| HAMPSHIRE | 2.7 | 3.9 | 4.9 | 5.8 | 5.8 | 10.0 | 10.6 | 30.7 | 19.8 | 10.7 | 1.5 | 81.0 | 30.3 | 34.0 | 90.1 |
| MIDDLESEX | 3.4 | 4.9 | 5.8 | 6.3 | 6.7 | 5.9 | 5.5 | 34.0 | 22.6 | 11.3 | 1.8 | 78.2 | 33.6 | 37.3 | 93.7 |
| NANTUCKET | 0.8 | 1.6 | 6.0 | 6.8 | 6.5 | 4.3 | 3.5 | 36.6 | 23.7 | 11.0 | 1.7 | 77.7 | 35.5 | 38.3 | 102.5 |
| NORFOLK | 1.4 | 2.2 | 5.7 | 6.3 | 6.7 | 5.3 | 4.8 | 32.8 | 23.6 | 12.8 | 2.1 | 78.5 | 35.1 | 38.5 | 91.2 |
| PLYMOUTH | 2.2 | 3.4 | 6.8 | 7.5 | 7.7 | 6.4 | 5.2 | 30.7 | 23.6 | 10.6 | 1.6 | 74.3 | 33.1 | 36.1 | 95.5 |
| SUFFOLK | 11.0 | 14.2 | 6.5 | 6.5 | 5.9 | 6.4 | 8.0 | 36.4 | 18.5 | 10.1 | 1.7 | 78.8 | 30.8 | 33.7 | 92.7 |
| WORCESTER | 4.6 | 6.7 | 6.9 | 7.4 | 7.4 | 6.6 | 5.8 | 30.8 | 21.6 | 11.6 | 1.9 | 74.8 | 33.1 | 36.1 | 95.5 |
| MASSACHUSETTS | 4.8 | 6.6 | 6.3 | 6.8 | 6.9 | 6.2 | 5.7 | 32.0 | 22.2 | 12.0 | 1.9 | 76.9 | 33.6 | 36.8 | 93.2 |
| UNITED STATES | 9.0 | 11.8 | 6.9 | 7.2 | 7.2 | 7.2 | 6.7 | 29.9 | 22.2 | 11.1 | 1.6 | 74.6 | 32.9 | 35.7 | 95.6 |

| COUNTY | HOUSEHOLDS | | | | | FAMILIES | | | MEDIAN HOUSEHOLD INCOME | | | |
|---|---|---|---|---|---|---|---|---|---|---|---|---|
| | 1990 | 2000 | 2005 | % Annual Rate 1990-2000 | 2000 Average HH Size | 1990 | 2000 | % Annual Rate 1990-2000 | 2000 | 2005 | 2000 National Rank | 2000 State Rank |
| BARNSTABLE | 77,586 | 91,913 | 100,741 | 2.1 | 2.30 | 52,006 | 59,059 | 1.6 | 43,269 | 50,276 | 442 | 9 |
| BERKSHIRE | 54,315 | 53,511 | 53,160 | -0.2 | 2.35 | 36,622 | 34,538 | -0.7 | 38,834 | 44,374 | 769 | 13 |
| BRISTOL | 187,668 | 198,763 | 206,313 | 0.7 | 2.57 | 135,656 | 139,138 | 0.3 | 41,720 | 51,479 | 535 | 10 |
| DUKES | 5,003 | 6,315 | 6,969 | 2.9 | 2.25 | 3,026 | 3,651 | 2.3 | 45,194 | 54,817 | 349 | 7 |
| ESSEX | 251,285 | 273,462 | 287,261 | 1.0 | 2.53 | 175,332 | 184,317 | 0.6 | 47,975 | 56,548 | 238 | 5 |
| FRANKLIN | 27,640 | 28,425 | 28,830 | 0.3 | 2.43 | 18,351 | 18,092 | -0.2 | 39,159 | 47,252 | 742 | 12 |
| HAMPDEN | 169,906 | 167,424 | 167,527 | -0.2 | 2.52 | 118,753 | 112,793 | -0.6 | 37,461 | 44,249 | 901 | 14 |
| HAMPSHIRE | 50,052 | 53,043 | 54,363 | 0.7 | 2.49 | 32,327 | 32,900 | 0.2 | 45,996 | 56,130 | 310 | 6 |
| MIDDLESEX | 519,527 | 552,767 | 573,711 | 0.8 | 2.49 | 347,305 | 357,622 | 0.4 | 56,950 | 63,419 | 103 | 2 |
| NANTUCKET | 2,597 | 3,707 | 4,393 | 4.4 | 2.28 | 1,488 | 2,004 | 3.7 | 50,061 | 53,519 | 199 | 4 |
| NORFOLK | 227,798 | 248,767 | 258,048 | 1.1 | 2.52 | 158,381 | 166,991 | 0.6 | 62,429 | 70,370 | 56 | 1 |
| PLYMOUTH | 149,519 | 169,537 | 182,321 | 1.5 | 2.76 | 112,853 | 123,842 | 1.1 | 55,993 | 66,432 | 111 | 3 |
| SUFFOLK | 264,061 | 257,766 | 259,341 | -0.3 | 2.35 | 138,177 | 130,138 | -0.7 | 41,311 | 48,856 | 561 | 11 |
| WORCESTER | 260,153 | 281,001 | 297,807 | 0.9 | 2.56 | 184,469 | 192,406 | 0.5 | 44,453 | 53,912 | 376 | 8 |
| MASSACHUSETTS | | | | 0.7 | 2.51 | | | 0.3 | 48,636 | 56,863 | | |
| UNITED STATES | | | | 1.4 | 2.59 | | | 1.1 | 41,914 | 49,127 | | |

| COUNTY | 2000 Per Capita Income | 2000 HH Income Base | 2000 HOUSEHOLD INCOME DISTRIBUTION (%) Less than $15,000 | $15,000 to $24,999 | $25,000 to $49,999 | $50,000 to $99,999 | $100,000 to $149,999 | $150,000 or More | 2000 AVERAGE DISPOSABLE INCOME BY AGE OF HOUSEHOLDER All Ages | <35 | 35-44 | 45-54 | 55-64 | 65+ |
|---|---|---|---|---|---|---|---|---|---|---|---|---|---|---|
| BARNSTABLE | 24,369 | 91,913 | 12.8 | 12.0 | 33.3 | 31.6 | 7.4 | 3.0 | 38,289 | 35,878 | 43,015 | 48,384 | 42,910 | 27,021 |
| BERKSHIRE | 20,792 | 53,511 | 17.0 | 13.1 | 34.2 | 28.2 | 5.2 | 2.4 | 34,681 | 31,354 | 38,516 | 45,412 | 39,901 | 22,602 |
| BRISTOL | 19,663 | 198,762 | 17.3 | 10.3 | 32.7 | 31.7 | 6.0 | 2.0 | 35,633 | 34,895 | 40,950 | 45,521 | 39,986 | 20,090 |
| DUKES | 27,392 | 6,315 | 10.6 | 9.3 | 35.3 | 29.7 | 9.9 | 5.2 | 43,068 | 36,769 | 44,697 | 45,562 | 48,210 | 35,762 |
| ESSEX | 25,033 | 273,461 | 14.9 | 9.2 | 28.0 | 34.2 | 9.3 | 4.4 | 42,389 | 38,286 | 46,530 | 52,792 | 47,796 | 24,391 |
| FRANKLIN | 18,962 | 28,425 | 15.5 | 12.9 | 37.1 | 28.8 | 4.7 | 1.1 | 33,022 | 29,695 | 36,450 | 41,755 | 37,622 | 21,485 |
| HAMPDEN | 18,446 | 167,416 | 19.5 | 12.5 | 34.4 | 27.3 | 4.7 | 1.7 | 32,878 | 29,563 | 36,966 | 42,643 | 38,006 | 20,801 |
| HAMPSHIRE | 21,498 | 53,043 | 12.4 | 10.4 | 32.1 | 33.5 | 8.1 | 3.4 | 40,255 | 33,475 | 43,832 | 51,657 | 48,486 | 25,726 |
| MIDDLESEX | 30,592 | 552,767 | 9.9 | 7.1 | 25.4 | 38.0 | 12.6 | 7.0 | 50,177 | 43,650 | 51,799 | 59,856 | 55,644 | 31,893 |
| NANTUCKET | 27,463 | 3,707 | 12.7 | 8.4 | 28.9 | 36.9 | 9.5 | 3.6 | 41,682 | 34,717 | 43,732 | 49,648 | 46,020 | 31,996 |
| NORFOLK | 34,215 | 248,767 | 8.2 | 5.8 | 23.1 | 39.0 | 14.5 | 9.5 | 56,173 | 49,077 | 57,445 | 65,519 | 61,343 | 35,405 |
| PLYMOUTH | 25,668 | 169,537 | 10.3 | 6.8 | 25.9 | 40.1 | 12.0 | 5.0 | 46,969 | 42,202 | 50,330 | 57,177 | 51,235 | 27,842 |
| SUFFOLK | 24,068 | 257,763 | 18.1 | 11.2 | 29.7 | 29.4 | 7.8 | 3.8 | 38,370 | 36,395 | 40,863 | 45,277 | 41,682 | 24,914 |
| WORCESTER | 20,702 | 280,994 | 15.0 | 10.2 | 31.8 | 34.0 | 6.9 | 2.2 | 37,476 | 35,272 | 42,503 | 48,106 | 42,045 | 20,984 |
| MASSACHUSETTS | 25,526 | | 13.5 | 9.1 | 28.8 | 34.4 | 9.5 | 4.7 | 43,224 | 38,730 | 46,636 | 53,180 | 48,358 | 26,556 |
| UNITED STATES | 22,162 | | 14.5 | 12.5 | 32.3 | 29.8 | 7.4 | 3.5 | 40,748 | 34,503 | 44,969 | 49,579 | 43,409 | 27,339 |

| COUNTY | FINANCIAL SERVICES | | | | THE HOME | | | | | | ENTERTAINMENT | | | | | | PERSONAL | | | |
|---|---|---|---|---|---|---|---|---|---|---|---|---|---|---|---|---|---|---|---|---|
| | | | | | Home Improvements | | | Furnishings | | | | | | | | | | | | |
| | Auto Loan | Home Loan | Invest-ments | Retire-ment Plans | Home Repair | Lawn & Garden | Remodel-ing | Appli-ances | Elec-tronics | Furni-ture | Restau-rants | Sport-ing Goods | Theater & Concerts | Toys & Hobbies | Travel | Video Rental | Apparel | Auto After-market | Health Insur-ance | Pets & Supplies |
| BARNSTABLE | 103 | 92 | 103 | 101 | 95 | 100 | 101 | 102 | 97 | 97 | 100 | 103 | 101 | 105 | 97 | 100 | 102 | 98 | 109 | 105 |
| BERKSHIRE | 98 | 90 | 100 | 93 | 95 | 93 | 93 | 97 | 93 | 96 | 95 | 97 | 97 | 101 | 94 | 98 | 97 | 94 | 102 | 100 |
| BRISTOL | 98 | 96 | 98 | 96 | 95 | 93 | 91 | 97 | 96 | 99 | 99 | 99 | 100 | 101 | 96 | 99 | 100 | 97 | 100 | 101 |
| DUKES | 102 | 85 | 91 | 95 | 90 | 92 | 106 | 99 | 95 | 89 | 92 | 102 | 94 | 103 | 87 | 100 | 96 | 94 | 107 | 104 |
| ESSEX | 102 | 108 | 111 | 108 | 100 | 101 | 93 | 100 | 101 | 108 | 108 | 105 | 109 | 105 | 106 | 101 | 111 | 104 | 103 | 104 |
| FRANKLIN | 98 | 91 | 96 | 91 | 93 | 91 | 94 | 96 | 94 | 94 | 95 | 97 | 96 | 100 | 91 | 98 | 96 | 94 | 101 | 101 |
| HAMPDEN | 97 | 93 | 102 | 94 | 96 | 94 | 90 | 97 | 93 | 99 | 97 | 97 | 99 | 100 | 97 | 98 | 99 | 95 | 100 | 99 |
| HAMPSHIRE | 99 | 98 | 101 | 97 | 94 | 93 | 91 | 97 | 96 | 98 | 100 | 99 | 99 | 102 | 95 | 98 | 101 | 97 | 101 | 102 |
| MIDDLESEX | 104 | 118 | 117 | 116 | 103 | 106 | 95 | 102 | 106 | 113 | 116 | 109 | 115 | 108 | 113 | 102 | 119 | 110 | 104 | 107 |
| NANTUCKET | 105 | 102 | 96 | 104 | 93 | 98 | 101 | 103 | 103 | 103 | 107 | 108 | 104 | 108 | 97 | 102 | 109 | 103 | 106 | 108 |
| NORFOLK | 105 | 118 | 119 | 118 | 103 | 108 | 95 | 103 | 107 | 114 | 118 | 110 | 117 | 110 | 113 | 103 | 121 | 110 | 106 | 108 |
| PLYMOUTH | 102 | 103 | 104 | 104 | 96 | 98 | 94 | 100 | 102 | 105 | 107 | 105 | 107 | 106 | 100 | 101 | 110 | 103 | 102 | 105 |
| SUFFOLK | 97 | 105 | 105 | 97 | 98 | 94 | 85 | 95 | 94 | 102 | 97 | 98 | 99 | 96 | 103 | 100 | 102 | 98 | 97 | 100 |
| WORCESTER | 100 | 98 | 101 | 98 | 95 | 94 | 92 | 98 | 97 | 101 | 102 | 101 | 102 | 103 | 97 | 99 | 103 | 98 | 101 | 102 |
| MASSACHUSETTS | 101 | 107 | 109 | 106 | 99 | 100 | 93 | 100 | 101 | 106 | 106 | 104 | 107 | 104 | 104 | 101 | 109 | 103 | 103 | 104 |
| UNITED STATES | 100 | 100 | 100 | 100 | 100 | 100 | 100 | 100 | 100 | 100 | 100 | 100 | 100 | 100 | 100 | 100 | 100 | 100 | 100 | 100 |

| COUNTY | FIPS Code | MSA Code | DMA Code | POPULATION 1990 | POPULATION 2000 | POPULATION 2005 | 1990-2000 ANNUAL CHANGE % Rate | 1990-2000 ANNUAL CHANGE State Rank | RACE (%) White 1990 | White 2000 | Black 1990 | Black 2000 | Asian/Pacific 1990 | Asian/Pacific 2000 |
|---|---|---|---|---|---|---|---|---|---|---|---|---|---|---|
| ALCONA | 001 | 0000 | 583 | 10,145 | 11,252 | 11,816 | 1.0 | 35 | 98.8 | 98.6 | 0.3 | 0.4 | 0.3 | 0.4 |
| ALGER | 003 | 0000 | 553 | 8,972 | 10,112 | 10,262 | 1.2 | 27 | 93.9 | 91.8 | 2.4 | 4.5 | 0.3 | 0.4 |
| ALLEGAN | 005 | 3000 | 563 | 90,509 | 104,972 | 112,706 | 1.5 | 23 | 95.9 | 95.4 | 1.6 | 1.5 | 0.5 | 0.7 |
| ALPENA | 007 | 0000 | 583 | 30,605 | 30,635 | 30,757 | 0.0 | 71 | 99.2 | 99.1 | 0.1 | 0.2 | 0.3 | 0.4 |
| ANTRIM | 009 | 0000 | 540 | 18,185 | 22,410 | 24,721 | 2.1 | 7 | 98.4 | 98.2 | 0.1 | 0.2 | 0.1 | 0.2 |
| ARENAC | 011 | 0000 | 513 | 14,931 | 16,632 | 17,119 | 1.1 | 31 | 98.4 | 97.9 | 0.1 | 0.6 | 0.3 | 0.3 |
| BARAGA | 013 | 0000 | 553 | 7,954 | 8,704 | 8,866 | 0.9 | 41 | 87.6 | 86.1 | 0.6 | 2.6 | 0.1 | 0.2 |
| BARRY | 015 | 0000 | 563 | 50,057 | 54,902 | 56,273 | 0.9 | 41 | 98.7 | 98.5 | 0.2 | 0.3 | 0.3 | 0.4 |
| BAY | 017 | 6960 | 513 | 111,723 | 109,091 | 107,003 | -0.2 | 76 | 96.4 | 95.8 | 1.1 | 1.2 | 0.4 | 0.5 |
| BENZIE | 019 | 0000 | 540 | 12,200 | 15,706 | 17,936 | 2.5 | 2 | 97.2 | 97.0 | 0.2 | 0.3 | 0.3 | 0.4 |
| BERRIEN | 021 | 0870 | 588 | 161,378 | 159,495 | 158,243 | -0.1 | 74 | 82.6 | 81.0 | 15.4 | 16.5 | 0.9 | 1.3 |
| BRANCH | 023 | 0000 | 563 | 41,502 | 43,884 | 44,214 | 0.5 | 57 | 97.1 | 95.9 | 1.7 | 2.6 | 0.4 | 0.5 |
| CALHOUN | 025 | 3720 | 563 | 135,982 | 142,237 | 146,131 | 0.4 | 60 | 87.3 | 85.9 | 10.6 | 11.5 | 0.8 | 1.2 |
| CASS | 027 | 0000 | 588 | 49,477 | 50,374 | 51,042 | 0.2 | 67 | 90.6 | 89.6 | 7.5 | 8.3 | 0.4 | 0.5 |
| CHARLEVOIX | 029 | 0000 | 540 | 21,468 | 25,496 | 27,786 | 1.7 | 12 | 97.8 | 97.7 | 0.1 | 0.1 | 0.2 | 0.3 |
| CHEBOYGAN | 031 | 0000 | 540 | 21,398 | 24,516 | 26,301 | 1.3 | 24 | 97.4 | 97.1 | 0.1 | 0.1 | 0.3 | 0.4 |
| CHIPPEWA | 033 | 0000 | 540 | 34,604 | 38,031 | 38,653 | 0.9 | 41 | 81.9 | 82.0 | 6.3 | 6.5 | 0.4 | 0.6 |
| CLARE | 035 | 0000 | 540 | 24,952 | 30,409 | 32,731 | 1.9 | 9 | 98.8 | 98.7 | 0.2 | 0.2 | 0.2 | 0.3 |
| CLINTON | 037 | 4040 | 551 | 57,883 | 64,851 | 67,960 | 1.1 | 31 | 97.9 | 97.3 | 0.4 | 0.4 | 0.3 | 0.5 |
| CRAWFORD | 039 | 0000 | 540 | 12,260 | 14,445 | 15,317 | 1.6 | 18 | 96.3 | 96.6 | 2.2 | 1.8 | 0.3 | 0.5 |
| DELTA | 041 | 0000 | 553 | 37,780 | 38,832 | 38,754 | 0.3 | 64 | 97.5 | 97.4 | 0.0 | 0.1 | 0.3 | 0.4 |
| DICKINSON | 043 | 0000 | 553 | 26,831 | 26,868 | 26,490 | 0.0 | 71 | 98.9 | 98.6 | 0.1 | 0.2 | 0.4 | 0.6 |
| EATON | 045 | 4040 | 551 | 92,879 | 102,471 | 105,735 | 1.0 | 35 | 94.3 | 93.5 | 3.6 | 3.8 | 0.6 | 0.9 |
| EMMET | 047 | 0000 | 540 | 25,040 | 29,371 | 31,225 | 1.6 | 18 | 96.3 | 96.1 | 0.5 | 0.6 | 0.3 | 0.4 |
| GENESEE | 049 | 2640 | 513 | 430,459 | 438,296 | 443,303 | 0.2 | 67 | 78.2 | 76.4 | 19.6 | 20.9 | 0.7 | 1.0 |
| GLADWIN | 051 | 0000 | 513 | 21,896 | 26,062 | 27,920 | 1.7 | 12 | 99.1 | 98.9 | 0.1 | 0.2 | 0.2 | 0.2 |
| GOGEBIC | 053 | 0000 | 676 | 18,052 | 16,817 | 15,731 | -0.7 | 80 | 96.9 | 96.9 | 1.3 | 1.2 | 0.1 | 0.2 |
| GRAND TRAVERSE | 055 | 0000 | 540 | 64,273 | 76,504 | 82,266 | 1.7 | 12 | 98.0 | 97.9 | 0.4 | 0.4 | 0.5 | 0.7 |
| GRATIOT | 057 | 0000 | 513 | 38,982 | 40,033 | 40,036 | 0.3 | 64 | 97.0 | 96.4 | 0.8 | 0.9 | 0.3 | 0.3 |
| HILLSDALE | 059 | 0000 | 551 | 43,431 | 47,456 | 49,489 | 0.9 | 41 | 98.8 | 98.6 | 0.3 | 0.3 | 0.3 | 0.4 |
| HOUGHTON | 061 | 0000 | 553 | 35,446 | 35,321 | 34,625 | 0.0 | 71 | 97.2 | 96.1 | 0.4 | 0.9 | 1.7 | 2.4 |
| HURON | 063 | 0000 | 513 | 34,951 | 35,299 | 35,364 | 0.1 | 69 | 99.1 | 98.9 | 0.1 | 0.1 | 0.2 | 0.2 |
| INGHAM | 065 | 4040 | 551 | 281,912 | 284,599 | 281,710 | 0.1 | 69 | 84.1 | 81.7 | 9.9 | 10.6 | 2.7 | 3.8 |
| IONIA | 067 | 0000 | 563 | 57,024 | 67,652 | 70,256 | 1.7 | 12 | 93.2 | 93.1 | 5.3 | 5.0 | 0.2 | 0.3 |
| IOSCO | 069 | 0000 | 513 | 30,209 | 26,118 | 26,983 | -1.4 | 82 | 95.9 | 95.8 | 2.1 | 1.9 | 0.9 | 1.2 |
| IRON | 071 | 0000 | 553 | 13,175 | 12,745 | 12,393 | -0.3 | 79 | 98.9 | 97.6 | 0.0 | 1.3 | 0.2 | 0.3 |
| ISABELLA | 073 | 0000 | 513 | 54,624 | 59,702 | 62,541 | 0.9 | 41 | 95.6 | 95.0 | 1.2 | 1.3 | 0.8 | 1.2 |
| JACKSON | 075 | 3520 | 551 | 149,756 | 158,219 | 162,835 | 0.5 | 57 | 90.5 | 89.9 | 8.0 | 8.2 | 0.4 | 0.6 |
| KALAMAZOO | 077 | 3720 | 563 | 223,411 | 230,183 | 231,658 | 0.3 | 64 | 88.4 | 86.9 | 8.9 | 9.6 | 1.4 | 2.0 |
| KALKASKA | 079 | 0000 | 540 | 13,497 | 15,979 | 16,943 | 1.7 | 12 | 98.7 | 98.5 | 0.1 | 0.2 | 0.2 | 0.2 |
| KENT | 081 | 3000 | 563 | 500,631 | 555,157 | 579,294 | 1.0 | 35 | 88.7 | 87.1 | 8.1 | 8.8 | 1.1 | 1.6 |
| KEWEENAW | 083 | 0000 | 553 | 1,701 | 2,190 | 2,428 | 2.5 | 2 | 99.2 | 99.2 | 0.1 | 0.0 | 0.4 | 0.5 |
| LAKE | 085 | 0000 | 540 | 8,583 | 10,880 | 12,092 | 2.3 | 5 | 85.5 | 84.3 | 13.4 | 14.4 | 0.1 | 0.2 |
| LAPEER | 087 | 2160 | 505 | 74,768 | 90,622 | 96,959 | 1.9 | 9 | 97.7 | 97.2 | 0.6 | 0.7 | 0.4 | 0.5 |
| LEELANAU | 089 | 0000 | 540 | 16,527 | 19,671 | 21,118 | 1.7 | 12 | 96.6 | 96.4 | 0.1 | 0.2 | 0.3 | 0.4 |
| LENAWEE | 091 | 0440 | 547 | 91,476 | 100,720 | 105,392 | 0.9 | 41 | 94.4 | 92.7 | 1.6 | 2.1 | 0.5 | 0.8 |
| LIVINGSTON | 093 | 0440 | 505 | 115,645 | 156,246 | 179,994 | 3.0 | 1 | 98.2 | 98.0 | 0.6 | 0.6 | 0.4 | 0.6 |
| LUCE | 095 | 0000 | 540 | 5,763 | 6,769 | 6,821 | 1.6 | 18 | 94.0 | 87.3 | 0.0 | 6.4 | 0.1 | 0.3 |
| MACKINAC | 097 | 0000 | 540 | 10,674 | 11,121 | 11,237 | 0.4 | 60 | 83.9 | 84.0 | 0.0 | 0.4 | 0.1 | 0.2 |
| MACOMB | 099 | 2160 | 505 | 717,400 | 796,719 | 821,923 | 1.0 | 35 | 96.7 | 95.9 | 1.4 | 1.6 | 1.3 | 1.9 |
| MANISTEE | 101 | 0000 | 540 | 21,265 | 23,852 | 24,787 | 1.1 | 31 | 98.1 | 96.3 | 0.3 | 1.6 | 0.3 | 0.4 |
| MARQUETTE | 103 | 0000 | 553 | 70,887 | 62,445 | 60,912 | -1.2 | 81 | 96.0 | 95.5 | 1.7 | 1.8 | 0.8 | 1.1 |
| MASON | 105 | 0000 | 540 | 25,537 | 28,062 | 28,592 | 0.9 | 41 | 97.7 | 97.2 | 0.6 | 0.8 | 0.3 | 0.5 |
| MECOSTA | 107 | 0000 | 540 | 37,308 | 41,329 | 44,352 | 1.0 | 35 | 95.8 | 95.7 | 2.6 | 2.5 | 0.5 | 0.6 |
| MENOMINEE | 109 | 0000 | 658 | 24,920 | 24,449 | 24,451 | -0.2 | 76 | 98.2 | 98.1 | 0.0 | 0.0 | 0.2 | 0.3 |
| MIDLAND | 111 | 6960 | 513 | 75,651 | 82,444 | 84,757 | 0.8 | 52 | 97.1 | 96.4 | 1.0 | 1.0 | 1.1 | 1.6 |
| MISSAUKEE | 113 | 0000 | 540 | 12,147 | 14,356 | 15,425 | 1.6 | 18 | 98.9 | 98.7 | 0.0 | 0.0 | 0.2 | 0.4 |
| MONROE | 115 | 2160 | 505 | 133,600 | 146,417 | 153,875 | 0.9 | 41 | 96.9 | 96.3 | 1.8 | 1.9 | 0.4 | 0.6 |
| MONTCALM | 117 | 0000 | 563 | 53,059 | 62,207 | 66,241 | 1.6 | 18 | 96.5 | 95.9 | 1.8 | 2.1 | 0.3 | 0.4 |
| MONTMORENCY | 119 | 0000 | 540 | 8,936 | 10,054 | 10,265 | 1.2 | 27 | 99.2 | 99.2 | 0.0 | 0.0 | 0.1 | 0.1 |
| MUSKEGON | 121 | 3000 | 563 | 158,983 | 169,116 | 174,439 | 0.6 | 54 | 84.2 | 82.6 | 13.6 | 14.8 | 0.3 | 0.5 |
| NEWAYGO | 123 | 0000 | 563 | 38,202 | 47,021 | 50,390 | 2.0 | 8 | 96.2 | 95.5 | 1.2 | 1.4 | 0.3 | 0.4 |
| OAKLAND | 125 | 2160 | 505 | 1,083,592 | 1,185,990 | 1,216,462 | 0.9 | 41 | 89.6 | 87.7 | 7.2 | 7.8 | 2.3 | 3.4 |
| OCEANA | 127 | 0000 | 563 | 22,454 | 25,094 | 26,052 | 1.1 | 31 | 94.5 | 93.4 | 0.3 | 0.3 | 0.2 | 0.3 |
| OGEMAW | 129 | 0000 | 513 | 18,681 | 21,329 | 22,012 | 1.3 | 24 | 99.0 | 98.9 | 0.1 | 0.2 | 0.1 | 0.2 |
| ONTONAGON | 131 | 0000 | 553 | 8,854 | 7,476 | 6,802 | -1.6 | 83 | 98.5 | 98.4 | 0.0 | 0.2 | 0.2 | 0.2 |
| OSCEOLA | 133 | 0000 | 540 | 20,146 | 22,291 | 22,741 | 1.0 | 35 | 98.8 | 98.5 | 0.3 | 0.4 | 0.2 | 0.3 |
| OSCODA | 135 | 0000 | 540 | 7,842 | 8,941 | 9,157 | 1.3 | 24 | 99.2 | 99.2 | 0.0 | 0.0 | 0.1 | 0.1 |
| OTSEGO | 137 | 0000 | 540 | 17,957 | 23,204 | 25,640 | 2.5 | 2 | 98.8 | 98.3 | 0.1 | 0.3 | 0.5 | 0.7 |
| OTTAWA | 139 | 3000 | 563 | 187,768 | 235,015 | 258,785 | 2.2 | 6 | 95.7 | 94.5 | 0.5 | 0.6 | 1.3 | 1.9 |
| PRESQUE ISLE | 141 | 0000 | 540 | 13,743 | 14,662 | 15,036 | 0.6 | 54 | 99.3 | 99.1 | 0.1 | 0.2 | 0.2 | 0.3 |
| ROSCOMMON | 143 | 0000 | 540 | 19,776 | 23,797 | 25,007 | 1.8 | 11 | 99.1 | 99.0 | 0.2 | 0.2 | 0.1 | 0.2 |
| SAGINAW | 145 | 6960 | 513 | 211,946 | 208,508 | 204,890 | -0.2 | 76 | 78.1 | 75.8 | 17.4 | 18.5 | 0.6 | 0.9 |
| ST. CLAIR | 147 | 2160 | 505 | 145,607 | 163,870 | 174,326 | 1.2 | 27 | 96.4 | 95.8 | 2.1 | 2.3 | 0.3 | 0.5 |
| ST. JOSEPH | 149 | 0000 | 563 | 58,913 | 61,666 | 62,814 | 0.4 | 60 | 96.2 | 95.6 | 2.7 | 3.0 | 0.4 | 0.7 |
| SANILAC | 151 | 0000 | 505 | 39,928 | 43,809 | 45,638 | 0.9 | 41 | 98.3 | 97.9 | 0.1 | 0.2 | 0.2 | 0.3 |
| SCHOOLCRAFT | 153 | 0000 | 553 | 8,302 | 8,824 | 8,998 | 0.6 | 54 | 93.4 | 91.9 | 0.1 | 1.9 | 0.2 | 0.2 |
| MICHIGAN | | | | | | | 0.6 | | 83.4 | 82.6 | 13.9 | 14.0 | 1.1 | 1.6 |
| UNITED STATES | | | | | | | 1.0 | | 80.3 | 77.9 | 12.1 | 12.4 | 2.9 | 3.9 |

# POPULATION COMPOSITION

| COUNTY | % HISPANIC ORIGIN | | 2000 AGE DISTRIBUTION (%) | | | | | | | | | | MEDIAN AGE | | 2000 Males/ Females (×100) |
|---|---|---|---|---|---|---|---|---|---|---|---|---|---|---|---|
| | 1990 | 2000 | 0-4 | 5-9 | 10-14 | 15-19 | 20-24 | 25-44 | 45-64 | 65-84 | 85+ | 18+ | 1990 | 2000 | |
| ALCONA | 0.5 | 1.1 | 4.4 | 5.4 | 6.1 | 5.9 | 3.9 | 22.6 | 27.3 | 21.6 | 2.7 | 80.1 | 44.8 | 46.1 | 100.8 |
| ALGER | 0.5 | 1.0 | 5.1 | 6.3 | 7.1 | 7.3 | 6.0 | 27.3 | 24.2 | 14.6 | 2.2 | 76.9 | 36.7 | 39.2 | 109.9 |
| ALLEGAN | 3.2 | 4.5 | 7.4 | 8.2 | 8.4 | 7.8 | 5.8 | 29.2 | 22.0 | 9.8 | 1.4 | 71.1 | 31.9 | 34.9 | 98.9 |
| ALPENA | 0.5 | 1.0 | 6.0 | 6.7 | 6.8 | 7.4 | 6.0 | 27.2 | 23.9 | 13.9 | 2.1 | 75.9 | 35.3 | 38.8 | 94.4 |
| ANTRIM | 0.5 | 1.0 | 6.3 | 7.1 | 7.3 | 6.8 | 5.0 | 25.8 | 24.4 | 15.4 | 2.0 | 74.9 | 36.8 | 39.9 | 95.9 |
| ARENAC | 1.1 | 1.6 | 6.2 | 6.8 | 7.1 | 7.3 | 5.8 | 26.3 | 23.7 | 15.2 | 1.9 | 75.4 | 35.7 | 39.1 | 96.2 |
| BARAGA | 0.4 | 0.8 | 5.9 | 6.9 | 6.9 | 7.0 | 6.8 | 25.9 | 23.9 | 14.0 | 2.8 | 76.0 | 36.7 | 37.9 | 109.9 |
| BARRY | 1.0 | 1.7 | 6.5 | 7.4 | 7.8 | 7.5 | 5.7 | 27.8 | 25.0 | 11.0 | 1.4 | 73.8 | 33.8 | 37.2 | 99.1 |
| BAY | 3.1 | 4.4 | 6.3 | 6.9 | 7.2 | 7.0 | 6.3 | 28.9 | 23.9 | 11.9 | 1.6 | 75.4 | 33.9 | 37.0 | 94.7 |
| BENZIE | 1.1 | 1.7 | 6.0 | 6.8 | 7.2 | 6.5 | 4.6 | 25.6 | 25.3 | 16.0 | 2.1 | 75.9 | 37.5 | 40.7 | 97.6 |
| BERRIEN | 1.7 | 2.4 | 6.3 | 7.2 | 7.7 | 7.4 | 6.1 | 28.2 | 22.8 | 12.5 | 1.8 | 74.4 | 33.6 | 36.7 | 92.4 |
| BRANCH | 1.1 | 1.8 | 6.5 | 7.5 | 7.7 | 7.5 | 5.7 | 29.3 | 22.6 | 11.5 | 1.6 | 73.6 | 33.4 | 36.1 | 97.6 |
| CALHOUN | 1.9 | 2.8 | 6.5 | 7.0 | 7.4 | 7.8 | 6.8 | 27.5 | 23.3 | 12.2 | 1.7 | 74.6 | 33.9 | 36.5 | 94.6 |
| CASS | 1.3 | 2.0 | 6.3 | 7.0 | 7.4 | 7.2 | 5.8 | 27.7 | 24.8 | 12.3 | 1.5 | 75.0 | 34.4 | 37.6 | 97.1 |
| CHARLEVOIX | 0.5 | 1.0 | 6.3 | 7.3 | 7.8 | 6.9 | 5.0 | 28.3 | 24.0 | 12.7 | 1.8 | 74.2 | 34.7 | 38.0 | 97.0 |
| CHEBOYGAN | 0.4 | 0.8 | 6.2 | 6.9 | 7.1 | 7.3 | 5.3 | 24.8 | 25.0 | 15.3 | 2.0 | 75.1 | 37.1 | 40.0 | 94.7 |
| CHIPPEWA | 0.8 | 1.3 | 5.3 | 6.2 | 6.5 | 8.1 | 9.4 | 32.0 | 20.1 | 11.0 | 1.5 | 78.1 | 32.2 | 34.3 | 126.8 |
| CLARE | 0.5 | 1.0 | 6.5 | 7.3 | 7.8 | 6.8 | 4.9 | 25.6 | 23.9 | 15.4 | 1.8 | 74.0 | 36.2 | 38.8 | 94.5 |
| CLINTON | 2.2 | 3.2 | 6.5 | 7.3 | 7.8 | 7.4 | 5.9 | 30.2 | 24.5 | 9.3 | 1.2 | 73.8 | 32.3 | 35.9 | 99.3 |
| CRAWFORD | 0.6 | 1.2 | 6.2 | 7.1 | 7.4 | 7.5 | 5.0 | 27.4 | 23.4 | 14.1 | 1.8 | 74.6 | 34.7 | 38.3 | 106.9 |
| DELTA | 0.4 | 0.8 | 5.8 | 6.8 | 7.7 | 7.5 | 5.6 | 27.4 | 23.6 | 13.6 | 2.1 | 75.0 | 35.2 | 38.2 | 95.8 |
| DICKINSON | 0.4 | 0.9 | 6.2 | 7.0 | 7.2 | 7.4 | 5.6 | 26.2 | 23.7 | 14.2 | 2.5 | 74.6 | 36.3 | 39.0 | 99.9 |
| EATON | 2.4 | 3.4 | 6.0 | 7.1 | 7.8 | 7.5 | 6.2 | 30.9 | 23.7 | 9.4 | 1.4 | 74.6 | 32.9 | 36.0 | 93.9 |
| EMMET | 0.5 | 0.9 | 6.4 | 7.4 | 7.8 | 7.2 | 5.5 | 27.8 | 24.4 | 11.6 | 1.9 | 73.9 | 34.5 | 37.6 | 97.3 |
| GENESEE | 2.1 | 2.9 | 6.8 | 7.2 | 7.6 | 7.4 | 6.5 | 29.9 | 22.9 | 10.4 | 1.2 | 73.9 | 32.0 | 35.4 | 91.8 |
| GLADWIN | 0.6 | 1.2 | 6.1 | 6.9 | 7.7 | 6.9 | 4.9 | 24.6 | 24.5 | 16.5 | 1.9 | 74.9 | 36.9 | 39.8 | 97.9 |
| GOGEBIC | 0.4 | 0.8 | 5.0 | 6.0 | 6.4 | 7.1 | 5.2 | 24.2 | 22.9 | 19.6 | 3.6 | 78.7 | 40.2 | 42.2 | 97.6 |
| GRAND TRAVERSE | 0.8 | 1.4 | 6.4 | 7.3 | 7.7 | 7.6 | 6.1 | 29.4 | 23.5 | 10.3 | 1.6 | 74.2 | 33.2 | 36.4 | 96.1 |
| GRATIOT | 3.8 | 5.3 | 6.1 | 7.1 | 7.8 | 8.5 | 7.2 | 27.7 | 21.8 | 11.5 | 2.4 | 74.5 | 32.7 | 35.6 | 95.7 |
| HILLSDALE | 0.9 | 1.6 | 6.7 | 7.5 | 8.3 | 8.2 | 6.3 | 27.5 | 22.3 | 11.4 | 1.7 | 72.9 | 32.6 | 35.6 | 97.2 |
| HOUGHTON | 0.5 | 1.0 | 5.5 | 6.1 | 6.5 | 10.6 | 11.7 | 24.3 | 19.6 | 13.5 | 2.4 | 78.2 | 31.7 | 33.7 | 113.0 |
| HURON | 1.1 | 1.8 | 6.1 | 7.2 | 7.8 | 7.2 | 5.1 | 26.1 | 22.4 | 15.7 | 2.4 | 74.2 | 35.8 | 38.5 | 97.2 |
| INGHAM | 4.8 | 6.5 | 6.4 | 6.7 | 6.9 | 9.7 | 11.5 | 30.7 | 19.3 | 7.7 | 1.1 | 76.3 | 28.4 | 31.3 | 91.9 |
| IONIA | 2.1 | 3.0 | 6.5 | 7.4 | 7.8 | 9.0 | 9.3 | 31.0 | 19.4 | 8.3 | 1.3 | 73.7 | 29.9 | 31.7 | 120.6 |
| IOSCO | 1.2 | 1.7 | 7.1 | 7.3 | 6.7 | 6.1 | 6.0 | 27.5 | 20.2 | 16.8 | 2.3 | 75.3 | 32.6 | 37.2 | 97.4 |
| IRON | 0.5 | 1.1 | 4.9 | 5.7 | 6.0 | 6.8 | 5.1 | 21.2 | 24.1 | 22.1 | 4.3 | 78.8 | 43.6 | 45.3 | 93.0 |
| ISABELLA | 1.3 | 2.1 | 5.8 | 6.3 | 6.6 | 12.5 | 17.7 | 25.9 | 16.3 | 7.8 | 1.1 | 77.9 | 24.6 | 25.9 | 91.3 |
| JACKSON | 1.5 | 2.3 | 6.4 | 7.0 | 7.3 | 7.0 | 6.4 | 30.5 | 22.6 | 11.3 | 1.6 | 75.2 | 33.4 | 36.2 | 103.6 |
| KALAMAZOO | 1.8 | 2.6 | 6.3 | 6.7 | 7.0 | 8.6 | 9.6 | 29.1 | 21.4 | 9.8 | 1.5 | 76.1 | 31.0 | 33.8 | 92.7 |
| KALKASKA | 0.6 | 1.2 | 6.7 | 7.8 | 8.6 | 7.4 | 5.3 | 28.2 | 22.6 | 12.1 | 1.3 | 72.1 | 33.1 | 36.3 | 101.9 |
| KENT | 2.9 | 4.2 | 7.6 | 8.1 | 8.3 | 7.9 | 6.3 | 30.9 | 20.2 | 9.3 | 1.5 | 71.6 | 30.7 | 33.7 | 94.0 |
| KEWEENAW | 0.4 | 1.0 | 4.4 | 5.2 | 6.8 | 5.8 | 3.8 | 23.1 | 27.5 | 20.0 | 3.5 | 80.0 | 46.4 | 45.7 | 100.7 |
| LAKE | 0.7 | 1.2 | 6.0 | 7.1 | 7.5 | 6.5 | 4.6 | 22.6 | 25.9 | 17.6 | 2.2 | 75.1 | 40.9 | 41.8 | 95.5 |
| LAPEER | 2.0 | 3.0 | 6.5 | 7.3 | 7.5 | 7.7 | 6.4 | 30.5 | 24.4 | 8.7 | 1.0 | 74.0 | 31.8 | 35.0 | 99.9 |
| LEELANAU | 1.1 | 1.8 | 6.1 | 7.1 | 7.7 | 6.6 | 4.1 | 27.9 | 24.8 | 13.9 | 1.8 | 75.0 | 36.5 | 39.6 | 99.6 |
| LENAWEE | 6.0 | 8.0 | 6.4 | 7.1 | 7.5 | 8.2 | 6.9 | 28.3 | 23.1 | 10.9 | 1.5 | 74.0 | 32.6 | 35.4 | 97.3 |
| LIVINGSTON | 0.8 | 1.5 | 6.3 | 7.5 | 8.1 | 7.4 | 5.2 | 30.6 | 25.8 | 8.3 | 0.9 | 73.5 | 32.9 | 36.3 | 100.5 |
| LUCE | 0.5 | 1.6 | 5.2 | 6.1 | 7.0 | 7.1 | 6.4 | 29.3 | 23.1 | 13.8 | 2.0 | 77.1 | 37.1 | 38.0 | 118.4 |
| MACKINAC | 0.3 | 0.7 | 6.1 | 6.8 | 7.1 | 6.5 | 5.5 | 25.0 | 25.0 | 15.9 | 2.0 | 75.4 | 37.1 | 40.3 | 99.4 |
| MACOMB | 1.1 | 1.8 | 5.8 | 6.4 | 6.9 | 6.5 | 5.7 | 31.6 | 23.3 | 12.4 | 1.5 | 77.1 | 33.9 | 37.5 | 94.5 |
| MANISTEE | 1.5 | 2.6 | 5.2 | 6.2 | 6.8 | 6.7 | 4.9 | 26.8 | 25.4 | 15.6 | 2.3 | 77.5 | 38.1 | 40.9 | 96.9 |
| MARQUETTE | 0.8 | 1.3 | 6.1 | 6.6 | 6.8 | 8.6 | 8.9 | 30.7 | 19.8 | 10.9 | 1.5 | 76.7 | 30.7 | 33.9 | 102.9 |
| MASON | 1.6 | 2.4 | 6.3 | 7.1 | 7.4 | 7.3 | 5.7 | 25.1 | 24.3 | 14.4 | 2.3 | 74.7 | 36.2 | 39.1 | 95.1 |
| MECOSTA | 1.0 | 1.6 | 5.8 | 6.3 | 6.8 | 10.7 | 13.3 | 25.3 | 19.4 | 11.0 | 1.4 | 77.7 | 25.6 | 31.1 | 103.6 |
| MENOMINEE | 0.2 | 0.6 | 5.9 | 6.7 | 6.9 | 7.5 | 6.0 | 26.6 | 24.0 | 13.8 | 2.5 | 75.6 | 35.8 | 39.0 | 98.4 |
| MIDLAND | 1.4 | 2.2 | 6.3 | 7.2 | 7.8 | 7.5 | 6.1 | 30.5 | 23.0 | 10.2 | 1.3 | 74.3 | 32.5 | 36.1 | 97.3 |
| MISSAUKEE | 0.6 | 1.1 | 7.2 | 8.0 | 7.9 | 8.4 | 5.6 | 26.0 | 22.3 | 12.8 | 1.7 | 71.3 | 33.5 | 36.4 | 98.5 |
| MONROE | 1.6 | 2.4 | 6.8 | 7.5 | 7.8 | 7.3 | 6.0 | 29.9 | 23.2 | 10.1 | 1.3 | 73.5 | 32.2 | 35.5 | 98.0 |
| MONTCALM | 1.7 | 2.6 | 6.7 | 7.6 | 8.1 | 7.9 | 6.3 | 29.7 | 21.6 | 10.6 | 1.4 | 72.6 | 32.3 | 34.7 | 105.6 |
| MONTMORENCY | 0.7 | 1.2 | 5.0 | 6.3 | 7.1 | 6.4 | 4.0 | 22.7 | 25.4 | 20.4 | 2.7 | 77.5 | 41.6 | 43.9 | 97.3 |
| MUSKEGON | 2.3 | 3.2 | 6.9 | 7.7 | 8.0 | 7.5 | 6.1 | 29.2 | 21.5 | 11.5 | 1.6 | 72.9 | 32.7 | 35.3 | 97.0 |
| NEWAYGO | 2.5 | 3.6 | 7.5 | 8.3 | 8.5 | 7.9 | 5.6 | 26.2 | 22.6 | 11.9 | 1.6 | 70.6 | 33.3 | 35.8 | 97.2 |
| OAKLAND | 1.8 | 2.7 | 6.0 | 6.7 | 7.4 | 6.6 | 5.3 | 32.6 | 23.9 | 10.1 | 1.4 | 76.0 | 33.8 | 37.3 | 94.6 |
| OCEANA | 6.2 | 8.1 | 7.0 | 7.9 | 8.5 | 7.6 | 5.3 | 26.7 | 23.2 | 12.2 | 1.6 | 71.5 | 33.5 | 36.4 | 97.7 |
| OGEMAW | 0.6 | 1.1 | 6.2 | 6.9 | 7.2 | 7.1 | 5.1 | 25.0 | 23.4 | 17.1 | 2.1 | 75.2 | 37.0 | 39.9 | 98.9 |
| ONTONAGON | 0.4 | 0.9 | 5.2 | 5.8 | 6.9 | 6.4 | 4.4 | 24.5 | 26.5 | 17.9 | 2.5 | 77.7 | 40.2 | 43.0 | 103.8 |
| OSCEOLA | 0.7 | 1.3 | 6.6 | 7.7 | 8.4 | 8.1 | 5.4 | 26.4 | 23.5 | 12.3 | 1.5 | 71.9 | 33.5 | 36.6 | 99.2 |
| OSCODA | 0.6 | 1.1 | 5.8 | 6.9 | 7.0 | 6.1 | 4.0 | 23.4 | 25.3 | 18.9 | 2.4 | 76.4 | 40.0 | 42.5 | 98.3 |
| OTSEGO | 0.4 | 0.8 | 6.9 | 7.6 | 7.8 | 7.7 | 5.6 | 27.5 | 23.1 | 12.3 | 1.5 | 72.8 | 33.7 | 36.7 | 97.6 |
| OTTAWA | 4.2 | 5.8 | 7.6 | 8.2 | 8.3 | 8.5 | 7.0 | 30.1 | 20.4 | 8.5 | 1.3 | 71.4 | 30.3 | 32.7 | 96.9 |
| PRESQUE ISLE | 0.3 | 0.7 | 5.3 | 6.6 | 7.2 | 6.9 | 4.8 | 23.8 | 24.0 | 19.1 | 2.4 | 76.3 | 38.5 | 41.7 | 98.5 |
| ROSCOMMON | 0.5 | 1.0 | 4.9 | 5.8 | 6.3 | 5.8 | 3.9 | 22.4 | 25.9 | 22.9 | 2.1 | 79.3 | 44.9 | 45.8 | 97.2 |
| SAGINAW | 6.2 | 8.1 | 6.5 | 7.3 | 7.9 | 7.7 | 6.2 | 28.8 | 22.7 | 11.2 | 1.7 | 73.6 | 32.7 | 35.8 | 91.7 |
| ST. CLAIR | 1.8 | 2.7 | 6.7 | 7.3 | 7.7 | 7.3 | 5.9 | 29.4 | 23.3 | 11.0 | 1.5 | 73.9 | 32.9 | 36.1 | 95.3 |
| ST. JOSEPH | 0.9 | 1.6 | 6.9 | 7.8 | 8.3 | 7.6 | 5.7 | 28.5 | 22.1 | 11.5 | 1.8 | 72.4 | 32.8 | 35.8 | 96.3 |
| SANILAC | 2.3 | 3.3 | 6.9 | 7.6 | 7.7 | 7.4 | 5.9 | 26.9 | 22.4 | 13.2 | 1.9 | 72.9 | 34.1 | 36.8 | 96.9 |
| SCHOOLCRAFT | 0.4 | 0.8 | 5.1 | 6.4 | 7.1 | 7.1 | 4.8 | 26.6 | 25.0 | 15.5 | 2.4 | 76.7 | 37.5 | 40.4 | 98.6 |
| MICHIGAN | 2.2 | 3.1 | 6.5 | 7.2 | 7.6 | 7.4 | 6.6 | 30.0 | 22.4 | 10.9 | 1.5 | 74.5 | 32.6 | 35.8 | 94.8 |
| UNITED STATES | 9.0 | 11.8 | 6.9 | 7.2 | 7.2 | 7.2 | 6.7 | 29.9 | 22.2 | 11.1 | 1.6 | 74.6 | 32.9 | 35.7 | 95.6 |

| COUNTY | HOUSEHOLDS | | | | | FAMILIES | | | MEDIAN HOUSEHOLD INCOME | | | |
|---|---|---|---|---|---|---|---|---|---|---|---|---|
| | 1990 | 2000 | 2005 | % Annual Rate 1990-2000 | 2000 Average HH Size | 1990 | 2000 | % Annual Rate 1990-2000 | 2000 | 2005 | 2000 National Rank | 2000 State Rank |
| ALCONA | 4,261 | 5,004 | 5,398 | 2.0 | 2.23 | 3,087 | 3,509 | 1.6 | 27,924 | 32,035 | 2449 | 74 |
| ALGER | 3,337 | 3,642 | 3,739 | 1.1 | 2.49 | 2,435 | 2,569 | 0.7 | 32,183 | 35,232 | 1691 | 56 |
| ALLEGAN | 31,709 | 37,668 | 40,820 | 2.1 | 2.76 | 24,347 | 28,223 | 1.8 | 45,897 | 53,920 | 315 | 11 |
| ALPENA | 11,838 | 12,176 | 12,385 | 0.3 | 2.49 | 8,562 | 8,485 | -0.1 | 32,014 | 34,776 | 1713 | 57 |
| ANTRIM | 6,980 | 8,909 | 9,993 | 3.0 | 2.49 | 5,202 | 6,423 | 2.6 | 35,431 | 39,952 | 1182 | 42 |
| ARENAC | 5,642 | 6,434 | 6,712 | 1.6 | 2.54 | 4,175 | 4,605 | 1.2 | 27,642 | 31,649 | 2491 | 77 |
| BARAGA | 3,065 | 3,240 | 3,343 | 0.7 | 2.45 | 2,102 | 2,133 | 0.2 | 31,290 | 37,732 | 1868 | 60 |
| BARRY | 17,763 | 20,165 | 21,019 | 1.5 | 2.69 | 13,969 | 15,477 | 1.3 | 42,228 | 50,420 | 489 | 18 |
| BAY | 42,188 | 42,795 | 42,794 | 0.2 | 2.52 | 30,544 | 29,968 | -0.2 | 39,366 | 42,470 | 722 | 30 |
| BENZIE | 4,772 | 6,230 | 7,160 | 3.3 | 2.50 | 3,505 | 4,425 | 2.9 | 31,610 | 35,328 | 1799 | 58 |
| BERRIEN | 61,025 | 62,290 | 62,642 | 0.2 | 2.52 | 43,845 | 43,271 | -0.2 | 39,136 | 43,816 | 744 | 31 |
| BRANCH | 14,921 | 15,920 | 16,242 | 0.8 | 2.60 | 11,011 | 11,409 | 0.4 | 35,682 | 42,979 | 1138 | 41 |
| CALHOUN | 51,812 | 55,960 | 58,316 | 0.9 | 2.47 | 36,394 | 37,897 | 0.5 | 41,167 | 45,598 | 573 | 22 |
| CASS | 18,239 | 18,776 | 19,152 | 0.4 | 2.66 | 13,848 | 13,871 | 0.0 | 40,401 | 49,074 | 636 | 26 |
| CHARLEVOIX | 8,243 | 9,948 | 10,923 | 2.3 | 2.55 | 5,994 | 7,002 | 1.9 | 39,948 | 46,071 | 680 | 28 |
| CHEBOYGAN | 8,201 | 9,681 | 10,540 | 2.0 | 2.51 | 6,123 | 7,017 | 1.7 | 31,377 | 34,770 | 1847 | 59 |
| CHIPPEWA | 11,541 | 13,262 | 13,805 | 1.7 | 2.45 | 8,006 | 8,917 | 1.3 | 33,292 | 41,126 | 1492 | 51 |
| CLARE | 9,698 | 12,271 | 13,441 | 2.9 | 2.45 | 7,113 | 8,701 | 2.5 | 27,017 | 31,005 | 2575 | 79 |
| CLINTON | 20,212 | 23,334 | 24,850 | 1.8 | 2.76 | 15,917 | 17,829 | 1.4 | 53,429 | 63,037 | 145 | 5 |
| CRAWFORD | 4,441 | 5,496 | 5,942 | 2.6 | 2.53 | 3,330 | 4,005 | 2.3 | 33,792 | 41,780 | 1424 | 48 |
| DELTA | 14,531 | 15,567 | 15,843 | 0.8 | 2.47 | 10,307 | 10,702 | 0.5 | 34,379 | 37,490 | 1333 | 46 |
| DICKINSON | 10,633 | 10,978 | 10,982 | 0.4 | 2.42 | 7,496 | 7,439 | -0.1 | 38,590 | 45,252 | 793 | 32 |
| EATON | 34,027 | 38,764 | 40,624 | 1.6 | 2.61 | 25,272 | 27,792 | 1.2 | 47,211 | 54,352 | 268 | 10 |
| EMMET | 9,516 | 11,549 | 12,468 | 2.4 | 2.50 | 6,789 | 7,922 | 1.9 | 37,007 | 40,416 | 975 | 35 |
| GENESEE | 161,296 | 169,438 | 174,036 | 0.6 | 2.56 | 115,849 | 118,061 | 0.2 | 45,205 | 50,531 | 347 | 13 |
| GLADWIN | 8,357 | 10,268 | 11,167 | 2.5 | 2.52 | 6,277 | 7,466 | 2.1 | 30,497 | 35,179 | 2035 | 64 |
| GOGEBIC | 7,449 | 7,167 | 6,813 | -0.5 | 2.23 | 4,875 | 4,480 | -1.0 | 28,263 | 31,467 | 2406 | 73 |
| GRAND TRAVERSE | 23,965 | 29,379 | 31,988 | 2.5 | 2.56 | 17,066 | 20,386 | 2.2 | 43,020 | 49,313 | 457 | 17 |
| GRATIOT | 13,659 | 14,538 | 14,794 | 0.8 | 2.58 | 10,274 | 10,584 | 0.4 | 35,955 | 41,659 | 1106 | 39 |
| HILLSDALE | 15,637 | 17,485 | 18,466 | 1.4 | 2.64 | 11,759 | 12,802 | 1.0 | 38,279 | 47,201 | 829 | 33 |
| HOUGHTON | 13,172 | 13,745 | 13,738 | 0.5 | 2.34 | 8,095 | 8,031 | -0.1 | 27,654 | 30,374 | 2488 | 76 |
| HURON | 13,268 | 13,837 | 14,074 | 0.5 | 2.51 | 9,679 | 9,740 | 0.1 | 33,322 | 37,388 | 1486 | 50 |
| INGHAM | 102,648 | 106,626 | 106,597 | 0.5 | 2.49 | 64,864 | 65,087 | 0.0 | 41,252 | 47,365 | 564 | 21 |
| IONIA | 18,447 | 21,068 | 22,368 | 1.6 | 2.72 | 13,970 | 15,509 | 1.3 | 41,339 | 50,292 | 560 | 20 |
| IOSCO | 11,588 | 10,286 | 10,805 | -1.4 | 2.45 | 8,471 | 7,285 | -1.8 | 27,703 | 32,342 | 2475 | 75 |
| IRON | 5,655 | 5,543 | 5,466 | -0.2 | 2.20 | 3,757 | 3,524 | -0.8 | 25,662 | 28,390 | 2742 | 81 |
| ISABELLA | 17,591 | 19,731 | 20,942 | 1.4 | 2.70 | 11,528 | 12,489 | 1.0 | 32,222 | 36,291 | 1680 | 55 |
| JACKSON | 53,660 | 58,578 | 61,241 | 1.1 | 2.55 | 38,878 | 41,255 | 0.7 | 40,997 | 47,499 | 590 | 24 |
| KALAMAZOO | 83,702 | 88,752 | 90,449 | 0.7 | 2.48 | 55,406 | 57,110 | 0.4 | 40,184 | 43,377 | 656 | 27 |
| KALKASKA | 4,934 | 5,971 | 6,395 | 2.3 | 2.65 | 3,729 | 4,390 | 2.0 | 35,338 | 41,809 | 1194 | 43 |
| KENT | 181,740 | 205,427 | 216,418 | 1.5 | 2.64 | 129,053 | 142,060 | 1.2 | 44,656 | 50,729 | 368 | 15 |
| KEWEENAW | 777 | 1,013 | 1,128 | 3.3 | 2.16 | 477 | 590 | 2.6 | 22,270 | 24,773 | 3012 | 83 |
| LAKE | 3,536 | 4,700 | 5,343 | 3.5 | 2.29 | 2,414 | 3,091 | 3.0 | 24,303 | 26,875 | 2881 | 82 |
| LAPEER | 24,659 | 31,125 | 34,000 | 2.9 | 2.86 | 20,004 | 24,730 | 2.6 | 51,862 | 62,437 | 173 | 7 |
| LEELANAU | 6,274 | 7,708 | 8,407 | 2.5 | 2.54 | 4,767 | 5,692 | 2.2 | 45,431 | 51,714 | 335 | 12 |
| LENAWEE | 31,635 | 35,080 | 37,059 | 1.3 | 2.73 | 24,160 | 26,102 | 0.9 | 44,581 | 52,695 | 371 | 16 |
| LIVINGSTON | 38,887 | 53,659 | 62,416 | 4.0 | 2.89 | 31,533 | 42,537 | 3.7 | 66,995 | 78,795 | 25 | 1 |
| LUCE | 2,154 | 2,356 | 2,444 | 1.1 | 2.43 | 1,536 | 1,615 | 0.6 | 28,706 | 31,260 | 2336 | 72 |
| MACKINAC | 4,240 | 4,579 | 4,704 | 0.9 | 2.40 | 3,005 | 3,140 | 0.5 | 31,196 | 33,781 | 1888 | 61 |
| MACOMB | 264,991 | 306,885 | 323,260 | 1.8 | 2.57 | 195,549 | 219,422 | 1.4 | 51,698 | 56,405 | 175 | 8 |
| MANISTEE | 8,580 | 9,654 | 10,209 | 1.4 | 2.37 | 6,064 | 6,620 | 1.1 | 30,047 | 32,432 | 2144 | 69 |
| MARQUETTE | 25,435 | 22,591 | 22,228 | -1.4 | 2.56 | 18,054 | 15,582 | -1.8 | 36,046 | 39,591 | 1097 | 38 |
| MASON | 9,984 | 11,311 | 11,722 | 1.5 | 2.43 | 7,189 | 7,908 | 1.2 | 32,545 | 35,721 | 1617 | 53 |
| MECOSTA | 12,260 | 15,070 | 16,564 | 2.5 | 2.56 | 8,298 | 10,044 | 2.3 | 31,011 | 34,073 | 1933 | 63 |
| MENOMINEE | 9,766 | 9,945 | 10,101 | 0.2 | 2.42 | 6,854 | 6,720 | -0.2 | 32,419 | 35,546 | 1636 | 54 |
| MIDLAND | 27,791 | 31,710 | 33,337 | 1.6 | 2.56 | 20,881 | 23,155 | 1.3 | 48,670 | 52,901 | 226 | 9 |
| MISSAUKEE | 4,389 | 5,282 | 5,725 | 2.3 | 2.69 | 3,397 | 3,963 | 1.9 | 30,467 | 36,284 | 2042 | 65 |
| MONROE | 46,508 | 52,687 | 56,288 | 1.5 | 2.75 | 36,204 | 39,889 | 1.2 | 53,598 | 61,305 | 140 | 4 |
| MONTCALM | 18,563 | 22,153 | 23,930 | 2.2 | 2.68 | 14,145 | 16,393 | 1.8 | 34,275 | 41,119 | 1350 | 47 |
| MONTMORENCY | 3,600 | 4,234 | 4,412 | 2.0 | 2.35 | 2,635 | 2,997 | 1.6 | 29,725 | 35,329 | 2197 | 70 |
| MUSKEGON | 57,798 | 62,836 | 65,666 | 1.0 | 2.60 | 42,199 | 44,661 | 0.7 | 36,951 | 42,278 | 985 | 36 |
| NEWAYGO | 13,776 | 17,464 | 18,985 | 2.9 | 2.67 | 10,656 | 13,131 | 2.6 | 35,084 | 40,938 | 1242 | 45 |
| OAKLAND | 410,488 | 466,087 | 486,354 | 1.6 | 2.52 | 291,645 | 320,946 | 1.2 | 63,246 | 68,853 | 50 | 2 |
| OCEANA | 8,071 | 9,378 | 9,918 | 1.8 | 2.65 | 6,223 | 7,038 | 1.5 | 32,863 | 37,560 | 1561 | 52 |
| OGEMAW | 7,190 | 8,551 | 8,992 | 2.1 | 2.47 | 5,346 | 6,165 | 1.7 | 27,573 | 33,222 | 2501 | 78 |
| ONTONAGON | 3,641 | 3,294 | 3,096 | -1.2 | 2.23 | 2,514 | 2,173 | -1.8 | 30,081 | 32,860 | 2136 | 67 |
| OSCEOLA | 7,347 | 8,339 | 8,607 | 1.5 | 2.64 | 5,542 | 6,112 | 1.2 | 31,151 | 34,937 | 1904 | 62 |
| OSCODA | 3,160 | 3,757 | 3,928 | 2.1 | 2.35 | 2,281 | 2,624 | 1.7 | 30,292 | 36,385 | 2085 | 66 |
| OTSEGO | 6,522 | 8,657 | 9,688 | 3.5 | 2.65 | 4,988 | 6,446 | 3.2 | 41,518 | 49,299 | 549 | 19 |
| OTTAWA | 62,664 | 80,050 | 89,222 | 3.0 | 2.85 | 49,476 | 61,753 | 2.7 | 56,631 | 65,663 | 106 | 3 |
| PRESQUE ISLE | 5,376 | 5,897 | 6,128 | 1.1 | 2.47 | 3,925 | 4,171 | 0.7 | 28,865 | 33,561 | 2320 | 71 |
| ROSCOMMON | 8,516 | 10,721 | 11,511 | 2.8 | 2.21 | 6,038 | 7,364 | 2.4 | 26,480 | 29,197 | 2657 | 80 |
| SAGINAW | 78,256 | 79,687 | 79,874 | 0.2 | 2.56 | 57,294 | 56,625 | -0.1 | 37,137 | 40,979 | 954 | 34 |
| ST. CLAIR | 52,882 | 61,164 | 65,946 | 1.8 | 2.66 | 39,649 | 44,746 | 1.5 | 44,922 | 51,814 | 356 | 14 |
| ST. JOSEPH | 21,579 | 23,060 | 23,728 | 0.8 | 2.64 | 16,070 | 16,666 | 0.4 | 40,521 | 47,564 | 625 | 25 |
| SANILAC | 14,658 | 16,449 | 17,320 | 1.4 | 2.64 | 10,961 | 11,883 | 1.0 | 35,145 | 42,467 | 1226 | 44 |
| SCHOOLCRAFT | 3,294 | 3,581 | 3,729 | 1.0 | 2.39 | 2,374 | 2,504 | 0.6 | 30,053 | 32,964 | 2143 | 68 |
| MICHIGAN | | | | 1.1 | 2.58 | | | 0.8 | 43,403 | 49,028 | | |
| UNITED STATES | | | | 1.4 | 2.59 | | | 1.1 | 41,914 | 49,127 | | |

# INCOME

| COUNTY | 2000 Per Capita Income | 2000 HH Income Base | 2000 HOUSEHOLD INCOME DISTRIBUTION (%) | | | | | | 2000 AVERAGE DISPOSABLE INCOME BY AGE OF HOUSEHOLDER | | | | | |
|---|---|---|---|---|---|---|---|---|---|---|---|---|---|---|
| | | | Less than $15,000 | $15,000 to $24,999 | $25,000 to $49,999 | $50,000 to $99,999 | $100,000 to $149,999 | $150,000 or More | All Ages | <35 | 35-44 | 45-54 | 55-64 | 65+ |
| ALCONA | 15,361 | 5,004 | 20.7 | 23.5 | 37.5 | 15.4 | 2.4 | 0.6 | 26,217 | 26,337 | 30,137 | 34,623 | 30,569 | 18,380 |
| ALGER | 13,570 | 3,642 | 19.5 | 16.0 | 42.1 | 20.7 | 1.6 | 0.1 | 27,779 | 27,264 | 32,927 | 36,868 | 30,475 | 16,765 |
| ALLEGAN | 20,245 | 37,668 | 9.1 | 10.3 | 36.2 | 35.5 | 7.3 | 1.6 | 39,621 | 35,669 | 44,446 | 50,865 | 42,603 | 23,712 |
| ALPENA | 16,584 | 12,176 | 19.7 | 17.2 | 37.7 | 20.5 | 3.3 | 1.5 | 30,500 | 26,857 | 35,579 | 42,314 | 34,396 | 18,148 |
| ANTRIM | 18,044 | 8,909 | 13.7 | 18.7 | 38.4 | 23.3 | 4.6 | 1.3 | 32,645 | 28,414 | 38,597 | 40,933 | 36,783 | 23,542 |
| ARENAC | 14,502 | 6,434 | 24.6 | 20.4 | 33.3 | 17.8 | 2.8 | 1.1 | 27,468 | 24,439 | 32,553 | 40,125 | 30,259 | 16,931 |
| BARAGA | 14,180 | 3,240 | 21.3 | 16.8 | 38.1 | 20.6 | 2.9 | 0.3 | 28,111 | 26,590 | 34,594 | 37,339 | 31,957 | 16,920 |
| BARRY | 18,453 | 20,165 | 11.4 | 11.4 | 37.1 | 34.1 | 5.1 | 0.9 | 36,300 | 32,372 | 42,113 | 46,603 | 38,951 | 22,115 |
| BAY | 19,240 | 42,795 | 18.3 | 12.1 | 34.0 | 28.5 | 5.4 | 1.8 | 35,035 | 27,866 | 41,569 | 48,607 | 39,074 | 20,865 |
| BENZIE | 16,542 | 6,230 | 15.7 | 20.1 | 40.2 | 19.5 | 3.3 | 1.3 | 30,296 | 26,666 | 33,163 | 41,640 | 33,717 | 21,081 |
| BERRIEN | 20,284 | 62,289 | 15.7 | 12.7 | 35.6 | 27.2 | 6.1 | 2.6 | 36,633 | 30,551 | 41,380 | 48,550 | 42,728 | 23,284 |
| BRANCH | 16,180 | 15,920 | 15.7 | 15.7 | 38.1 | 25.6 | 3.9 | 1.0 | 32,278 | 27,819 | 38,248 | 42,589 | 35,923 | 20,435 |
| CALHOUN | 20,649 | 55,958 | 14.8 | 12.2 | 34.1 | 30.5 | 6.2 | 2.2 | 37,061 | 31,188 | 42,518 | 48,800 | 41,698 | 23,940 |
| CASS | 19,195 | 18,776 | 13.0 | 12.7 | 37.1 | 30.3 | 5.5 | 1.5 | 35,911 | 31,365 | 41,469 | 45,445 | 41,702 | 22,636 |
| CHARLEVOIX | 19,829 | 9,948 | 13.7 | 12.7 | 36.9 | 29.8 | 5.5 | 1.4 | 35,522 | 32,951 | 41,497 | 47,109 | 38,658 | 20,817 |
| CHEBOYGAN | 15,344 | 9,681 | 16.7 | 19.5 | 41.0 | 19.0 | 3.0 | 0.8 | 28,945 | 25,358 | 35,462 | 37,594 | 33,503 | 19,714 |
| CHIPPEWA | 15,184 | 13,262 | 17.8 | 16.9 | 38.4 | 22.8 | 3.3 | 0.8 | 30,220 | 27,512 | 36,890 | 38,071 | 35,494 | 18,823 |
| CLARE | 14,440 | 12,271 | 26.4 | 20.1 | 33.2 | 16.6 | 2.7 | 1.1 | 26,758 | 24,209 | 34,835 | 33,589 | 30,228 | 16,908 |
| CLINTON | 23,288 | 23,334 | 7.2 | 7.7 | 30.3 | 42.6 | 9.8 | 2.4 | 44,666 | 39,348 | 49,988 | 57,462 | 45,975 | 26,172 |
| CRAWFORD | 15,651 | 5,496 | 14.4 | 20.1 | 38.6 | 23.5 | 3.1 | 0.5 | 30,242 | 27,257 | 35,340 | 40,086 | 31,906 | 20,284 |
| DELTA | 17,917 | 15,567 | 18.5 | 15.6 | 37.7 | 23.1 | 3.9 | 1.3 | 31,467 | 28,695 | 37,531 | 42,930 | 36,612 | 18,240 |
| DICKINSON | 22,877 | 10,978 | 14.3 | 14.0 | 37.5 | 26.5 | 5.8 | 2.0 | 35,382 | 32,343 | 44,077 | 46,244 | 39,500 | 20,819 |
| EATON | 21,666 | 38,764 | 8.7 | 11.1 | 33.5 | 37.7 | 7.1 | 2.0 | 40,605 | 33,827 | 45,517 | 51,180 | 46,250 | 24,872 |
| EMMET | 19,115 | 11,549 | 13.6 | 15.7 | 37.7 | 25.9 | 5.2 | 2.0 | 34,866 | 29,185 | 41,396 | 43,130 | 37,842 | 22,118 |
| GENESEE | 21,520 | 169,425 | 16.6 | 9.8 | 29.4 | 34.4 | 7.5 | 2.2 | 39,077 | 30,852 | 44,905 | 52,374 | 42,707 | 24,694 |
| GLADWIN | 15,786 | 10,268 | 22.8 | 17.9 | 35.1 | 19.6 | 3.3 | 1.2 | 29,053 | 26,438 | 35,133 | 41,324 | 31,234 | 18,458 |
| GOGEBIC | 15,776 | 7,167 | 22.8 | 20.2 | 37.0 | 16.3 | 2.8 | 1.0 | 27,079 | 25,975 | 36,262 | 38,302 | 30,831 | 17,350 |
| GRAND TRAVERSE | 20,733 | 29,379 | 10.0 | 12.0 | 36.3 | 32.4 | 7.2 | 2.2 | 39,016 | 32,846 | 44,649 | 49,082 | 42,156 | 24,541 |
| GRATIOT | 16,587 | 14,538 | 16.1 | 16.6 | 37.7 | 24.4 | 3.9 | 1.4 | 32,443 | 27,877 | 38,255 | 42,816 | 35,747 | 20,371 |
| HILLSDALE | 19,370 | 17,485 | 13.1 | 13.0 | 40.3 | 27.2 | 4.9 | 1.6 | 35,020 | 31,610 | 40,943 | 45,998 | 37,944 | 21,040 |
| HOUGHTON | 14,264 | 13,745 | 26.2 | 18.7 | 34.4 | 17.1 | 2.9 | 0.7 | 26,587 | 22,684 | 32,860 | 37,916 | 32,475 | 16,886 |
| HURON | 16,605 | 13,837 | 16.9 | 17.2 | 38.4 | 22.2 | 4.1 | 1.1 | 31,052 | 29,467 | 38,395 | 41,453 | 35,088 | 19,969 |
| INGHAM | 20,904 | 106,626 | 15.2 | 12.1 | 33.2 | 29.5 | 7.0 | 3.0 | 38,728 | 28,666 | 43,385 | 51,667 | 47,337 | 25,929 |
| IONIA | 15,792 | 21,068 | 13.9 | 11.4 | 36.9 | 31.4 | 5.3 | 1.0 | 35,479 | 31,906 | 41,145 | 46,669 | 38,001 | 19,861 |
| IOSCO | 13,699 | 10,286 | 20.4 | 23.6 | 37.3 | 16.5 | 1.9 | 0.3 | 25,957 | 24,061 | 33,631 | 35,154 | 30,616 | 16,648 |
| IRON | 14,153 | 5,543 | 26.5 | 22.2 | 35.7 | 13.4 | 1.7 | 0.5 | 24,253 | 23,187 | 34,506 | 35,411 | 27,733 | 15,325 |
| ISABELLA | 14,729 | 19,731 | 21.4 | 17.6 | 33.4 | 22.2 | 4.0 | 1.4 | 30,775 | 23,342 | 37,369 | 43,507 | 39,273 | 19,682 |
| JACKSON | 19,654 | 58,578 | 14.1 | 12.2 | 35.0 | 30.2 | 6.4 | 2.2 | 37,208 | 31,551 | 42,819 | 49,009 | 41,624 | 23,168 |
| KALAMAZOO | 20,784 | 88,752 | 16.0 | 12.7 | 33.6 | 28.4 | 6.2 | 3.1 | 38,035 | 28,257 | 43,450 | 51,059 | 44,595 | 23,354 |
| KALKASKA | 15,299 | 5,971 | 14.1 | 16.6 | 40.4 | 26.0 | 2.7 | 0.2 | 30,775 | 29,261 | 37,662 | 39,467 | 30,987 | 19,133 |
| KENT | 21,662 | 205,425 | 10.6 | 10.9 | 35.6 | 32.8 | 7.4 | 2.7 | 40,457 | 34,794 | 44,982 | 51,477 | 45,196 | 24,043 |
| KEWEENAW | 14,621 | 1,013 | 29.6 | 25.9 | 29.3 | 11.9 | 2.3 | 1.0 | 23,400 | 25,331 | 33,182 | 28,616 | 26,973 | 13,627 |
| LAKE | 14,203 | 4,700 | 29.5 | 21.8 | 31.1 | 14.7 | 2.4 | 0.7 | 24,619 | 24,233 | 28,025 | 31,226 | 26,222 | 18,377 |
| LAPEER | 22,203 | 31,125 | 9.9 | 8.8 | 28.6 | 40.6 | 9.5 | 2.6 | 43,694 | 36,625 | 50,633 | 56,136 | 44,936 | 25,078 |
| LEELANAU | 22,520 | 7,708 | 9.8 | 12.1 | 33.6 | 34.3 | 7.6 | 2.6 | 40,401 | 33,235 | 44,612 | 51,842 | 44,952 | 27,539 |
| LENAWEE | 20,042 | 35,080 | 11.7 | 11.0 | 34.4 | 34.1 | 6.9 | 1.9 | 38,962 | 34,484 | 43,907 | 51,447 | 43,024 | 22,704 |
| LIVINGSTON | 29,712 | 53,659 | 5.1 | 4.4 | 20.3 | 46.7 | 17.0 | 6.6 | 56,947 | 47,673 | 59,598 | 68,106 | 60,428 | 32,223 |
| LUCE | 12,987 | 2,356 | 22.5 | 19.2 | 40.3 | 16.8 | 1.2 | 0.0 | 25,514 | 22,924 | 28,470 | 35,784 | 28,992 | 17,171 |
| MACKINAC | 16,012 | 4,579 | 18.8 | 18.8 | 38.1 | 21.0 | 2.6 | 0.7 | 28,758 | 24,498 | 35,405 | 40,210 | 31,800 | 18,871 |
| MACOMB | 24,198 | 306,883 | 9.0 | 8.6 | 30.0 | 40.7 | 9.3 | 2.4 | 43,521 | 39,785 | 47,787 | 56,273 | 50,053 | 25,921 |
| MANISTEE | 15,045 | 9,654 | 24.5 | 16.8 | 36.4 | 19.0 | 2.7 | 0.7 | 27,439 | 24,152 | 33,299 | 36,817 | 32,110 | 17,031 |
| MARQUETTE | 16,952 | 22,590 | 16.6 | 14.9 | 38.1 | 24.5 | 4.5 | 1.5 | 32,991 | 26,669 | 40,513 | 45,167 | 38,851 | 19,152 |
| MASON | 17,456 | 11,311 | 18.3 | 18.5 | 37.7 | 20.3 | 4.0 | 1.3 | 30,491 | 25,767 | 38,391 | 40,402 | 34,749 | 18,589 |
| MECOSTA | 14,937 | 15,070 | 22.6 | 17.2 | 34.9 | 21.0 | 3.2 | 1.1 | 29,288 | 23,319 | 36,090 | 41,504 | 33,265 | 19,358 |
| MENOMINEE | 16,006 | 9,945 | 19.7 | 16.7 | 38.0 | 22.2 | 2.6 | 0.7 | 29,274 | 28,018 | 36,427 | 37,225 | 32,660 | 17,227 |
| MIDLAND | 25,793 | 31,710 | 11.6 | 10.3 | 29.6 | 33.8 | 10.2 | 4.6 | 45,061 | 35,603 | 48,927 | 59,438 | 50,372 | 26,074 |
| MISSAUKEE | 13,285 | 5,282 | 20.1 | 18.6 | 39.1 | 19.8 | 2.2 | 0.2 | 27,411 | 25,595 | 33,857 | 35,481 | 29,597 | 16,989 |
| MONROE | 23,577 | 52,687 | 10.0 | 7.0 | 28.1 | 40.8 | 10.7 | 3.4 | 45,510 | 39,754 | 51,015 | 59,716 | 48,888 | 26,610 |
| MONTCALM | 15,234 | 22,153 | 16.7 | 16.6 | 39.0 | 23.3 | 3.5 | 0.9 | 30,923 | 28,716 | 35,707 | 41,734 | 33,969 | 17,235 |
| MONTMORENCY | 15,461 | 4,234 | 19.5 | 21.4 | 37.8 | 18.5 | 2.2 | 0.6 | 27,093 | 27,610 | 34,389 | 33,992 | 31,118 | 19,052 |
| MUSKEGON | 17,955 | 62,836 | 16.4 | 14.1 | 37.0 | 25.9 | 5.0 | 1.6 | 33,935 | 29,013 | 39,292 | 44,887 | 38,972 | 21,003 |
| NEWAYGO | 16,587 | 17,464 | 16.9 | 15.6 | 37.9 | 24.3 | 4.2 | 1.3 | 32,283 | 29,321 | 38,344 | 42,363 | 34,743 | 19,155 |
| OAKLAND | 38,144 | 466,087 | 6.3 | 5.7 | 24.5 | 37.6 | 14.6 | 11.2 | 61,626 | 46,862 | 60,964 | 72,408 | 65,584 | 38,181 |
| OCEANA | 14,980 | 9,378 | 18.5 | 16.6 | 39.3 | 21.3 | 3.5 | 0.9 | 30,046 | 27,063 | 35,905 | 39,996 | 32,879 | 18,167 |
| OGEMAW | 14,860 | 8,551 | 23.5 | 20.7 | 36.3 | 15.8 | 2.7 | 1.0 | 26,774 | 25,338 | 35,947 | 35,086 | 27,167 | 17,258 |
| ONTONAGON | 17,394 | 3,294 | 22.8 | 17.9 | 38.6 | 17.0 | 2.9 | 0.8 | 27,582 | 25,843 | 32,850 | 40,588 | 31,026 | 15,791 |
| OSCEOLA | 14,774 | 8,339 | 19.8 | 17.0 | 40.8 | 18.8 | 2.9 | 0.7 | 28,471 | 26,438 | 35,125 | 37,366 | 31,144 | 16,896 |
| OSCODA | 16,271 | 3,757 | 17.8 | 23.0 | 38.5 | 16.7 | 3.0 | 1.0 | 28,087 | 26,281 | 37,720 | 37,704 | 29,878 | 18,719 |
| OTSEGO | 18,571 | 8,657 | 12.7 | 11.4 | 37.1 | 32.0 | 5.6 | 1.2 | 36,376 | 32,974 | 41,354 | 51,021 | 36,745 | 22,292 |
| OTTAWA | 25,433 | 80,050 | 5.7 | 5.0 | 30.7 | 41.4 | 13.0 | 4.2 | 49,755 | 42,702 | 54,048 | 63,065 | 54,967 | 29,487 |
| PRESQUE ISLE | 13,900 | 5,897 | 22.6 | 18.9 | 38.6 | 17.8 | 1.8 | 0.3 | 26,212 | 24,522 | 32,378 | 37,427 | 31,345 | 16,766 |
| ROSCOMMON | 15,418 | 10,721 | 24.0 | 23.3 | 32.9 | 16.7 | 2.5 | 0.7 | 25,931 | 26,176 | 33,794 | 31,832 | 31,105 | 17,861 |
| SAGINAW | 17,519 | 79,687 | 20.5 | 13.1 | 32.6 | 27.9 | 4.5 | 1.4 | 33,210 | 26,084 | 37,968 | 44,828 | 38,564 | 21,202 |
| ST. CLAIR | 21,343 | 61,164 | 13.0 | 10.2 | 33.1 | 33.0 | 7.9 | 2.8 | 40,253 | 33,946 | 44,826 | 53,937 | 44,630 | 24,289 |
| ST. JOSEPH | 18,868 | 23,060 | 12.9 | 12.6 | 37.6 | 29.5 | 5.8 | 1.7 | 36,224 | 30,999 | 41,862 | 48,131 | 40,400 | 23,473 |
| SANILAC | 16,135 | 16,449 | 16.3 | 16.7 | 37.6 | 25.2 | 3.5 | 0.7 | 31,302 | 29,243 | 37,937 | 41,319 | 35,173 | 18,783 |
| SCHOOLCRAFT | 14,831 | 3,581 | 21.8 | 20.4 | 35.8 | 19.1 | 2.4 | 0.5 | 27,507 | 24,521 | 35,000 | 36,776 | 29,767 | 17,486 |
| MICHIGAN | 22,281 | | 14.8 | 11.2 | 31.6 | 31.5 | 7.6 | 3.4 | 40,429 | 33,253 | 45,056 | 52,082 | 45,156 | 24,635 |
| UNITED STATES | 22,162 | | 14.5 | 12.5 | 32.3 | 29.8 | 7.4 | 3.5 | 40,748 | 34,503 | 44,969 | 49,579 | 43,409 | 27,339 |

| COUNTY | FINANCIAL SERVICES | | | | THE HOME | | | | | | ENTERTAINMENT | | | | | | PERSONAL | | | |
|---|---|---|---|---|---|---|---|---|---|---|---|---|---|---|---|---|---|---|---|---|
| | | | | | Home Improvements | | | Furnishings | | | | | | | | | | | | |
| | Auto Loan | Home Loan | Invest-ments | Retire-ment Plans | Home Repair | Lawn & Garden | Remodel-ing | Appli-ances | Elec-tronics | Furni-ture | Restau-rants | Sport-ing Goods | Theater & Concerts | Toys & Hobbies | Travel | Video Rental | Apparel | Auto After-market | Health Insur-ance | Pets & Supplies |
| ALCONA | 100 | 71 | 77 | 87 | 93 | 93 | 123 | 99 | 92 | 77 | 82 | 98 | 85 | 99 | 80 | 102 | 83 | 92 | 108 | 101 |
| ALGER | 98 | 71 | 76 | 83 | 94 | 92 | 117 | 97 | 91 | 78 | 82 | 96 | 85 | 97 | 80 | 100 | 81 | 91 | 105 | 99 |
| ALLEGAN | 99 | 83 | 84 | 87 | 95 | 92 | 111 | 98 | 96 | 88 | 92 | 97 | 92 | 100 | 84 | 102 | 89 | 95 | 101 | 101 |
| ALPENA | 97 | 79 | 85 | 85 | 97 | 94 | 108 | 96 | 93 | 86 | 88 | 94 | 90 | 96 | 86 | 100 | 85 | 93 | 102 | 97 |
| ANTRIM | 99 | 73 | 80 | 86 | 94 | 94 | 119 | 98 | 93 | 80 | 84 | 97 | 87 | 99 | 82 | 101 | 84 | 92 | 106 | 100 |
| ARENAC | 97 | 68 | 71 | 79 | 93 | 90 | 114 | 97 | 91 | 77 | 80 | 95 | 83 | 95 | 78 | 99 | 79 | 89 | 104 | 97 |
| BARAGA | 94 | 65 | 72 | 76 | 91 | 90 | 108 | 94 | 91 | 75 | 78 | 88 | 80 | 90 | 77 | 100 | 77 | 88 | 104 | 93 |
| BARRY | 100 | 80 | 82 | 87 | 95 | 92 | 114 | 98 | 95 | 86 | 90 | 98 | 91 | 100 | 83 | 102 | 88 | 95 | 102 | 101 |
| BAY | 96 | 87 | 93 | 88 | 100 | 96 | 101 | 96 | 93 | 92 | 93 | 94 | 95 | 97 | 91 | 100 | 89 | 95 | 100 | 97 |
| BENZIE | 99 | 74 | 78 | 84 | 93 | 92 | 114 | 98 | 94 | 81 | 85 | 96 | 87 | 98 | 81 | 101 | 84 | 92 | 104 | 99 |
| BERRIEN | 96 | 88 | 95 | 90 | 100 | 96 | 103 | 97 | 93 | 92 | 93 | 95 | 96 | 97 | 93 | 100 | 90 | 96 | 100 | 97 |
| BRANCH | 98 | 78 | 82 | 84 | 95 | 92 | 111 | 97 | 92 | 85 | 88 | 95 | 89 | 98 | 83 | 100 | 85 | 93 | 102 | 99 |
| CALHOUN | 96 | 90 | 96 | 92 | 101 | 97 | 100 | 97 | 94 | 94 | 94 | 95 | 97 | 98 | 94 | 100 | 92 | 97 | 99 | 98 |
| CASS | 99 | 79 | 83 | 86 | 96 | 92 | 112 | 98 | 94 | 86 | 89 | 96 | 90 | 99 | 84 | 101 | 87 | 94 | 102 | 100 |
| CHARLEVOIX | 99 | 78 | 84 | 86 | 95 | 93 | 115 | 98 | 93 | 83 | 87 | 97 | 89 | 99 | 83 | 101 | 85 | 93 | 104 | 100 |
| CHEBOYGAN | 98 | 73 | 76 | 84 | 93 | 91 | 118 | 97 | 92 | 79 | 83 | 96 | 86 | 98 | 80 | 101 | 82 | 92 | 105 | 99 |
| CHIPPEWA | 96 | 81 | 82 | 85 | 95 | 91 | 109 | 96 | 92 | 84 | 87 | 94 | 89 | 96 | 85 | 100 | 85 | 93 | 101 | 98 |
| CLARE | 99 | 70 | 75 | 84 | 93 | 91 | 120 | 98 | 92 | 77 | 82 | 97 | 85 | 98 | 79 | 101 | 82 | 91 | 106 | 100 |
| CLINTON | 100 | 95 | 94 | 96 | 99 | 97 | 105 | 99 | 99 | 99 | 102 | 100 | 101 | 103 | 94 | 103 | 98 | 101 | 101 | 102 |
| CRAWFORD | 100 | 73 | 76 | 86 | 93 | 92 | 122 | 98 | 93 | 79 | 84 | 98 | 86 | 99 | 80 | 102 | 83 | 92 | 106 | 101 |
| DELTA | 97 | 81 | 86 | 85 | 98 | 94 | 107 | 97 | 92 | 87 | 89 | 94 | 91 | 97 | 87 | 100 | 86 | 93 | 101 | 98 |
| DICKINSON | 97 | 82 | 88 | 88 | 98 | 95 | 106 | 97 | 93 | 87 | 90 | 94 | 93 | 97 | 88 | 100 | 87 | 94 | 103 | 98 |
| EATON | 99 | 96 | 91 | 94 | 98 | 96 | 103 | 99 | 99 | 97 | 102 | 99 | 99 | 101 | 93 | 103 | 97 | 101 | 99 | 101 |
| EMMET | 100 | 87 | 91 | 92 | 98 | 96 | 111 | 99 | 95 | 91 | 94 | 98 | 95 | 101 | 89 | 102 | 91 | 97 | 103 | 101 |
| GENESEE | 96 | 94 | 97 | 94 | 101 | 98 | 97 | 97 | 95 | 98 | 96 | 96 | 99 | 98 | 97 | 101 | 95 | 99 | 97 | 98 |
| GLADWIN | 98 | 69 | 75 | 82 | 93 | 91 | 116 | 97 | 92 | 77 | 81 | 96 | 84 | 96 | 78 | 100 | 80 | 90 | 105 | 99 |
| GOGEBIC | 94 | 70 | 79 | 79 | 95 | 92 | 106 | 95 | 90 | 79 | 81 | 89 | 84 | 92 | 82 | 100 | 79 | 89 | 103 | 94 |
| GRAND TRAVERSE | 100 | 96 | 96 | 97 | 99 | 99 | 104 | 99 | 99 | 98 | 101 | 99 | 100 | 102 | 95 | 102 | 97 | 101 | 101 | 101 |
| GRATIOT | 97 | 80 | 84 | 85 | 95 | 92 | 108 | 96 | 93 | 86 | 89 | 94 | 90 | 97 | 84 | 100 | 86 | 93 | 101 | 98 |
| HILLSDALE | 99 | 80 | 84 | 87 | 95 | 92 | 112 | 98 | 94 | 86 | 89 | 97 | 91 | 99 | 84 | 101 | 87 | 94 | 102 | 100 |
| HOUGHTON | 92 | 73 | 79 | 78 | 93 | 89 | 102 | 91 | 88 | 77 | 81 | 86 | 82 | 89 | 81 | 97 | 78 | 88 | 100 | 92 |
| HURON | 97 | 71 | 76 | 81 | 94 | 91 | 112 | 96 | 91 | 79 | 83 | 95 | 85 | 96 | 80 | 100 | 81 | 90 | 104 | 97 |
| INGHAM | 96 | 99 | 96 | 96 | 99 | 96 | 97 | 96 | 95 | 95 | 98 | 95 | 98 | 97 | 96 | 100 | 95 | 99 | 97 | 98 |
| IONIA | 99 | 81 | 84 | 86 | 95 | 92 | 111 | 97 | 94 | 87 | 90 | 96 | 91 | 99 | 84 | 101 | 88 | 94 | 102 | 100 |
| IOSCO | 97 | 74 | 76 | 82 | 92 | 90 | 113 | 96 | 92 | 79 | 84 | 94 | 85 | 96 | 80 | 101 | 82 | 92 | 103 | 99 |
| IRON | 96 | 67 | 72 | 79 | 91 | 90 | 113 | 95 | 92 | 75 | 79 | 91 | 81 | 93 | 78 | 100 | 78 | 89 | 105 | 95 |
| ISABELLA | 96 | 86 | 87 | 88 | 95 | 90 | 105 | 93 | 91 | 84 | 89 | 92 | 88 | 95 | 85 | 98 | 86 | 93 | 98 | 97 |
| JACKSON | 98 | 89 | 95 | 92 | 100 | 97 | 104 | 98 | 95 | 94 | 95 | 96 | 97 | 99 | 93 | 101 | 92 | 97 | 100 | 99 |
| KALAMAZOO | 98 | 100 | 99 | 99 | 101 | 99 | 99 | 97 | 97 | 98 | 101 | 97 | 100 | 100 | 98 | 101 | 97 | 100 | 99 | 100 |
| KALKASKA | 100 | 77 | 80 | 86 | 93 | 91 | 119 | 98 | 94 | 83 | 88 | 98 | 88 | 100 | 81 | 102 | 86 | 94 | 104 | 101 |
| KENT | 98 | 97 | 94 | 95 | 99 | 97 | 100 | 97 | 97 | 97 | 100 | 97 | 99 | 99 | 95 | 101 | 95 | 99 | 98 | 99 |
| KEWEENAW | 94 | 66 | 74 | 76 | 92 | 90 | 108 | 94 | 91 | 75 | 79 | 88 | 80 | 91 | 78 | 100 | 77 | 88 | 104 | 94 |
| LAKE | 99 | 71 | 78 | 86 | 94 | 92 | 120 | 99 | 91 | 78 | 81 | 98 | 85 | 98 | 81 | 101 | 82 | 92 | 104 | 101 |
| LAPEER | 100 | 91 | 90 | 93 | 97 | 95 | 108 | 99 | 98 | 94 | 98 | 99 | 98 | 102 | 90 | 103 | 95 | 99 | 101 | 102 |
| LEELANAU | 102 | 85 | 88 | 94 | 96 | 96 | 117 | 101 | 98 | 90 | 94 | 101 | 96 | 103 | 88 | 103 | 93 | 98 | 105 | 104 |
| LENAWEE | 99 | 86 | 90 | 91 | 97 | 95 | 110 | 98 | 96 | 91 | 94 | 97 | 95 | 100 | 88 | 102 | 91 | 97 | 102 | 101 |
| LIVINGSTON | 105 | 111 | 102 | 110 | 103 | 106 | 106 | 104 | 108 | 111 | 116 | 108 | 112 | 109 | 104 | 106 | 112 | 112 | 102 | 107 |
| LUCE | 95 | 67 | 72 | 79 | 91 | 90 | 112 | 95 | 92 | 75 | 79 | 91 | 81 | 93 | 78 | 100 | 78 | 89 | 104 | 95 |
| MACKINAC | 98 | 73 | 77 | 84 | 93 | 91 | 117 | 97 | 92 | 79 | 83 | 95 | 85 | 97 | 81 | 101 | 82 | 92 | 105 | 99 |
| MACOMB | 99 | 102 | 102 | 100 | 103 | 103 | 98 | 100 | 99 | 103 | 106 | 100 | 105 | 102 | 101 | 102 | 101 | 103 | 101 | 101 |
| MANISTEE | 97 | 73 | 79 | 82 | 95 | 92 | 112 | 96 | 91 | 81 | 84 | 94 | 87 | 96 | 82 | 100 | 82 | 91 | 103 | 97 |
| MARQUETTE | 97 | 88 | 90 | 90 | 97 | 94 | 104 | 96 | 94 | 90 | 93 | 95 | 94 | 97 | 90 | 100 | 89 | 96 | 100 | 99 |
| MASON | 98 | 78 | 85 | 87 | 96 | 94 | 112 | 97 | 93 | 84 | 87 | 95 | 90 | 98 | 85 | 101 | 85 | 93 | 104 | 99 |
| MECOSTA | 97 | 83 | 87 | 89 | 95 | 93 | 109 | 95 | 93 | 84 | 89 | 94 | 89 | 96 | 86 | 99 | 86 | 94 | 101 | 98 |
| MENOMINEE | 97 | 74 | 80 | 82 | 95 | 92 | 110 | 96 | 92 | 83 | 85 | 94 | 88 | 96 | 82 | 100 | 83 | 91 | 103 | 97 |
| MIDLAND | 102 | 101 | 100 | 104 | 101 | 102 | 107 | 101 | 101 | 102 | 105 | 103 | 105 | 104 | 99 | 103 | 101 | 103 | 102 | 103 |
| MISSAUKEE | 99 | 71 | 75 | 83 | 93 | 91 | 118 | 97 | 93 | 78 | 82 | 96 | 85 | 97 | 79 | 101 | 82 | 91 | 105 | 99 |
| MONROE | 99 | 91 | 93 | 93 | 99 | 97 | 106 | 99 | 97 | 95 | 98 | 98 | 98 | 101 | 92 | 102 | 94 | 98 | 101 | 101 |
| MONTCALM | 98 | 76 | 80 | 83 | 94 | 91 | 112 | 97 | 94 | 83 | 86 | 95 | 88 | 97 | 81 | 100 | 84 | 92 | 102 | 99 |
| MONTMORENCY | 101 | 73 | 78 | 90 | 94 | 94 | 126 | 100 | 93 | 78 | 83 | 101 | 87 | 101 | 82 | 102 | 84 | 93 | 109 | 103 |
| MUSKEGON | 96 | 87 | 95 | 89 | 100 | 96 | 102 | 97 | 93 | 93 | 93 | 95 | 96 | 97 | 93 | 100 | 90 | 95 | 99 | 98 |
| NEWAYGO | 99 | 74 | 78 | 83 | 93 | 91 | 115 | 97 | 94 | 82 | 85 | 97 | 87 | 98 | 80 | 101 | 83 | 92 | 103 | 99 |
| OAKLAND | 104 | 118 | 113 | 118 | 108 | 112 | 104 | 104 | 107 | 113 | 117 | 108 | 117 | 107 | 113 | 104 | 114 | 112 | 103 | 105 |
| OCEANA | 98 | 74 | 77 | 83 | 93 | 91 | 115 | 97 | 93 | 82 | 84 | 96 | 86 | 97 | 80 | 100 | 83 | 92 | 103 | 99 |
| OGEMAW | 99 | 71 | 76 | 85 | 93 | 92 | 120 | 98 | 93 | 78 | 82 | 97 | 85 | 98 | 79 | 101 | 82 | 92 | 106 | 100 |
| ONTONAGON | 95 | 74 | 81 | 81 | 95 | 93 | 105 | 95 | 92 | 82 | 85 | 91 | 88 | 94 | 83 | 100 | 82 | 91 | 103 | 95 |
| OSCEOLA | 98 | 71 | 75 | 81 | 93 | 91 | 115 | 97 | 92 | 79 | 82 | 95 | 85 | 96 | 79 | 100 | 81 | 91 | 103 | 98 |
| OSCODA | 100 | 71 | 74 | 86 | 92 | 92 | 125 | 99 | 92 | 76 | 82 | 99 | 85 | 99 | 79 | 102 | 82 | 92 | 108 | 101 |
| OTSEGO | 99 | 79 | 79 | 87 | 93 | 92 | 115 | 98 | 94 | 84 | 88 | 97 | 89 | 99 | 82 | 102 | 86 | 94 | 104 | 100 |
| OTTAWA | 100 | 98 | 93 | 97 | 98 | 98 | 104 | 99 | 100 | 99 | 103 | 100 | 101 | 103 | 94 | 103 | 99 | 102 | 100 | 102 |
| PRESQUE ISLE | 97 | 70 | 75 | 81 | 93 | 91 | 115 | 96 | 92 | 78 | 81 | 94 | 84 | 95 | 79 | 100 | 80 | 90 | 104 | 97 |
| ROSCOMMON | 101 | 76 | 87 | 91 | 96 | 97 | 122 | 101 | 93 | 81 | 86 | 99 | 89 | 101 | 86 | 102 | 85 | 94 | 109 | 102 |
| SAGINAW | 96 | 89 | 96 | 90 | 101 | 96 | 99 | 97 | 93 | 94 | 93 | 94 | 97 | 97 | 94 | 100 | 92 | 96 | 98 | 97 |
| ST. CLAIR | 98 | 89 | 93 | 92 | 99 | 96 | 106 | 98 | 95 | 93 | 95 | 97 | 97 | 100 | 92 | 101 | 92 | 97 | 101 | 100 |
| ST. JOSEPH | 97 | 80 | 84 | 85 | 96 | 92 | 109 | 97 | 93 | 86 | 89 | 95 | 90 | 98 | 85 | 100 | 86 | 93 | 101 | 99 |
| SANILAC | 98 | 73 | 79 | 82 | 94 | 91 | 112 | 97 | 92 | 80 | 84 | 96 | 86 | 97 | 80 | 100 | 82 | 91 | 103 | 98 |
| SCHOOLCRAFT | 98 | 70 | 75 | 83 | 94 | 92 | 117 | 97 | 91 | 78 | 82 | 95 | 84 | 96 | 80 | 101 | 81 | 91 | 106 | 98 |
| MICHIGAN | 98 | 96 | 98 | 98 | 101 | 99 | 102 | 99 | 97 | 97 | 98 | 98 | 101 | 100 | 97 | 102 | 96 | 100 | 99 | 100 |
| UNITED STATES | 100 | 100 | 100 | 100 | 100 | 100 | 100 | 100 | 100 | 100 | 100 | 100 | 100 | 100 | 100 | 100 | 100 | 100 | 100 | 100 |

# POPULATION CHANGE

| COUNTY | FIPS Code | MSA Code | DMA Code | POPULATION 1990 | POPULATION 2000 | POPULATION 2005 | 1990-2000 ANNUAL CHANGE % Rate | 1990-2000 ANNUAL CHANGE State Rank | RACE (%) White 1990 | RACE (%) White 2000 | RACE (%) Black 1990 | RACE (%) Black 2000 | RACE (%) Asian/Pacific 1990 | RACE (%) Asian/Pacific 2000 |
|---|---|---|---|---|---|---|---|---|---|---|---|---|---|---|
| SHIAWASSEE | 155 | 0000 | 513 | 69,770 | 72,369 | 72,484 | 0.4 | 60 | 98.4 | 98.2 | 0.1 | 0.1 | 0.3 | 0.5 |
| TUSCOLA | 157 | 0000 | 513 | 55,498 | 58,371 | 59,236 | 0.5 | 57 | 97.4 | 97.1 | 0.9 | 0.8 | 0.4 | 0.5 |
| VAN BUREN | 159 | 3720 | 563 | 70,060 | 76,183 | 77,675 | 0.8 | 52 | 90.2 | 88.9 | 6.7 | 7.4 | 0.3 | 0.5 |
| WASHTENAW | 161 | 0440 | 505 | 282,937 | 309,690 | 327,190 | 0.9 | 41 | 83.5 | 80.9 | 11.2 | 12.0 | 4.1 | 5.8 |
| WAYNE | 163 | 2160 | 505 | 2,111,687 | 2,098,033 | 2,056,271 | -0.1 | 74 | 57.4 | 54.8 | 40.2 | 42.2 | 1.0 | 1.5 |
| WEXFORD | 165 | 0000 | 540 | 26,360 | 29,880 | 31,450 | 1.2 | 27 | 98.8 | 98.5 | 0.1 | 0.2 | 0.3 | 0.5 |
| MICHIGAN | | | | | | | 0.6 | | 83.4 | 82.6 | 13.9 | 14.0 | 1.1 | 1.6 |
| UNITED STATES | | | | | | | 1.0 | | 80.3 | 77.9 | 12.1 | 12.4 | 2.9 | 3.9 |

| COUNTY | % HISPANIC ORIGIN | | 2000 AGE DISTRIBUTION (%) | | | | | | | | | | MEDIAN AGE | | 2000 Males/ Females (×100) |
|---|---|---|---|---|---|---|---|---|---|---|---|---|---|---|---|
| | 1990 | 2000 | 0-4 | 5-9 | 10-14 | 15-19 | 20-24 | 25-44 | 45-64 | 65-84 | 85+ | 18+ | 1990 | 2000 | |
| SHIAWASSEE | 1.5 | 2.3 | 6.5 | 7.1 | 7.4 | 7.5 | 6.4 | 29.5 | 24.0 | 10.2 | 1.3 | 74.4 | 32.5 | 35.9 | 95.5 |
| TUSCOLA | 2.1 | 3.0 | 6.4 | 7.2 | 7.5 | 7.5 | 6.1 | 29.0 | 24.2 | 10.6 | 1.5 | 74.3 | 33.0 | 36.3 | 99.1 |
| VAN BUREN | 3.2 | 4.4 | 7.0 | 7.7 | 7.9 | 7.8 | 6.4 | 27.4 | 23.4 | 10.9 | 1.7 | 72.6 | 33.3 | 35.6 | 96.9 |
| WASHTENAW | 2.0 | 2.8 | 5.6 | 6.1 | 6.3 | 8.8 | 11.9 | 33.3 | 19.8 | 7.2 | 1.1 | 78.7 | 29.2 | 32.3 | 96.9 |
| WAYNE | 2.4 | 3.2 | 7.0 | 7.5 | 8.1 | 6.9 | 6.1 | 29.8 | 21.7 | 11.5 | 1.5 | 73.4 | 32.5 | 35.5 | 90.3 |
| WEXFORD | 0.6 | 1.1 | 7.1 | 7.6 | 7.9 | 8.0 | 6.0 | 27.3 | 22.4 | 12.0 | 1.7 | 72.3 | 33.2 | 36.0 | 95.5 |
| MICHIGAN | 2.2 | 3.1 | 6.5 | 7.2 | 7.6 | 7.4 | 6.6 | 30.0 | 22.4 | 10.9 | 1.5 | 74.5 | 32.6 | 35.8 | 94.8 |
| UNITED STATES | 9.0 | 11.8 | 6.9 | 7.2 | 7.2 | 7.2 | 6.7 | 29.9 | 22.2 | 11.1 | 1.6 | 74.6 | 32.9 | 35.7 | 95.6 |

# HOUSEHOLDS

| COUNTY | HOUSEHOLDS | | | | | FAMILIES | | | MEDIAN HOUSEHOLD INCOME | | | |
|---|---|---|---|---|---|---|---|---|---|---|---|---|
| | 1990 | 2000 | 2005 | % Annual Rate 1990-2000 | 2000 Average HH Size | 1990 | 2000 | % Annual Rate 1990-2000 | 2000 | 2005 | 2000 National Rank | 2000 State Rank |
| SHIAWASSEE | 24,864 | 26,849 | 27,395 | 0.9 | 2.67 | 19,130 | 20,129 | 0.6 | 41,107 | 48,026 | 582 | 23 |
| TUSCOLA | 19,469 | 21,346 | 22,103 | 1.1 | 2.69 | 15,131 | 16,148 | 0.8 | 39,519 | 45,750 | 710 | 29 |
| VAN BUREN | 25,402 | 28,365 | 29,290 | 1.3 | 2.66 | 19,032 | 20,643 | 1.0 | 36,451 | 43,188 | 1052 | 37 |
| WASHTENAW | 104,528 | 118,947 | 127,679 | 1.6 | 2.44 | 63,807 | 71,088 | 1.3 | 52,852 | 59,175 | 155 | 6 |
| WAYNE | 780,535 | 797,187 | 792,310 | 0.3 | 2.60 | 537,548 | 532,524 | -0.1 | 35,868 | 39,424 | 1117 | 40 |
| WEXFORD | 9,923 | 11,390 | 12,062 | 1.7 | 2.60 | 7,273 | 8,077 | 1.3 | 33,414 | 37,300 | 1475 | 49 |
| MICHIGAN | | | | 1.1 | 2.58 | | | 0.8 | 43,403 | 49,028 | | |
| UNITED STATES | | | | 1.4 | 2.59 | | | 1.1 | 41,914 | 49,127 | | |

| COUNTY | 2000 Per Capita Income | 2000 HH Income Base | 2000 HOUSEHOLD INCOME DISTRIBUTION (%) Less than $15,000 | $15,000 to $24,999 | $25,000 to $49,999 | $50,000 to $99,999 | $100,000 to $149,999 | $150,000 or More | 2000 AVERAGE DISPOSABLE INCOME BY AGE OF HOUSEHOLDER All Ages | <35 | 35-44 | 45-54 | 55-64 | 65+ |
|---|---|---|---|---|---|---|---|---|---|---|---|---|---|---|
| SHIAWASSEE | 18,605 | 26,849 | 14.0 | 11.5 | 37.4 | 30.3 | 5.2 | 1.5 | 35,963 | 30,159 | 40,835 | 48,436 | 39,611 | 21,314 |
| TUSCOLA | 17,597 | 21,346 | 15.0 | 13.5 | 36.3 | 29.4 | 4.5 | 1.3 | 34,455 | 28,930 | 39,682 | 45,943 | 37,444 | 21,230 |
| VAN BUREN | 17,115 | 28,365 | 16.8 | 14.2 | 37.6 | 26.0 | 4.4 | 1.1 | 32,811 | 29,320 | 38,469 | 41,598 | 36,227 | 20,346 |
| WASHTENAW | 28,586 | 118,947 | 9.9 | 9.2 | 27.5 | 35.7 | 11.3 | 6.5 | 49,688 | 34,786 | 52,989 | 64,318 | 59,292 | 36,328 |
| WAYNE | 17,644 | 797,165 | 23.3 | 12.6 | 30.7 | 26.8 | 4.9 | 1.7 | 33,123 | 27,610 | 36,997 | 42,733 | 38,109 | 21,715 |
| WEXFORD | 17,252 | 11,390 | 18.2 | 16.4 | 38.5 | 21.6 | 3.7 | 1.6 | 31,704 | 27,334 | 38,649 | 41,735 | 34,868 | 19,120 |
| MICHIGAN | 22,281 | | 14.8 | 11.2 | 31.6 | 31.5 | 7.6 | 3.4 | 40,429 | 33,253 | 45,056 | 52,082 | 45,156 | 24,635 |
| UNITED STATES | 22,162 | | 14.5 | 12.5 | 32.3 | 29.8 | 7.4 | 3.5 | 40,748 | 34,503 | 44,969 | 49,579 | 43,409 | 27,339 |

# SPENDING POTENTIAL INDEXES

| COUNTY | FINANCIAL SERVICES | | | | THE HOME | | | | | | ENTERTAINMENT | | | | | | PERSONAL | | | |
|---|---|---|---|---|---|---|---|---|---|---|---|---|---|---|---|---|---|---|---|---|
| | | | | | Home Improvements | | | Furnishings | | | | | | | | | | | | |
| | Auto Loan | Home Loan | Invest-ments | Retire-ment Plans | Home Repair | Lawn & Garden | Remodel-ing | Appli-ances | Elec-tronics | Furni-ture | Restau-rants | Sport-ing Goods | Theater & Concerts | Toys & Hobbies | Travel | Video Rental | Apparel | Auto After-market | Health Insur-ance | Pets & Supplies |
| SHIAWASSEE | 98 | 84 | 87 | 87 | 97 | 93 | 108 | 98 | 94 | 90 | 92 | 96 | 93 | 99 | 87 | 101 | 89 | 95 | 101 | 100 |
| TUSCOLA | 98 | 77 | 81 | 84 | 95 | 91 | 112 | 97 | 93 | 84 | 88 | 96 | 89 | 98 | 82 | 101 | 85 | 93 | 102 | 99 |
| VAN BUREN | 97 | 78 | 78 | 82 | 93 | 90 | 107 | 96 | 93 | 85 | 87 | 94 | 88 | 96 | 82 | 100 | 84 | 93 | 100 | 97 |
| WASHTENAW | 101 | 114 | 107 | 111 | 104 | 106 | 102 | 99 | 103 | 104 | 110 | 103 | 108 | 103 | 107 | 102 | 106 | 107 | 100 | 103 |
| WAYNE | 95 | 92 | 98 | 93 | 102 | 97 | 91 | 97 | 93 | 97 | 91 | 94 | 98 | 95 | 98 | 101 | 94 | 98 | 93 | 95 |
| WEXFORD | 97 | 78 | 82 | 83 | 95 | 92 | 108 | 96 | 92 | 84 | 87 | 94 | 89 | 97 | 83 | 100 | 85 | 92 | 102 | 98 |
| MICHIGAN | 98 | 96 | 98 | 98 | 101 | 99 | 102 | 99 | 97 | 97 | 98 | 98 | 101 | 100 | 97 | 102 | 96 | 100 | 99 | 100 |
| UNITED STATES | 100 | 100 | 100 | 100 | 100 | 100 | 100 | 100 | 100 | 100 | 100 | 100 | 100 | 100 | 100 | 100 | 100 | 100 | 100 | 100 |

| COUNTY | FIPS Code | MSA Code | DMA Code | POPULATION 1990 | POPULATION 2000 | POPULATION 2005 | 1990-2000 ANNUAL CHANGE % Rate | 1990-2000 ANNUAL CHANGE State Rank | RACE (%) White 1990 | White 2000 | Black 1990 | Black 2000 | Asian/Pacific 1990 | Asian/Pacific 2000 |
|---|---|---|---|---|---|---|---|---|---|---|---|---|---|---|
| AITKIN | 001 | 0000 | 676 | 12,425 | 14,469 | 15,381 | 1.5 | 15 | 98.1 | 97.8 | 0.1 | 0.1 | 0.2 | 0.4 |
| ANOKA | 003 | 5120 | 613 | 243,641 | 304,930 | 335,045 | 2.2 | 9 | 97.2 | 96.0 | 0.5 | 0.8 | 1.2 | 2.0 |
| BECKER | 005 | 0000 | 724 | 27,881 | 29,990 | 31,131 | 0.7 | 32 | 92.7 | 91.8 | 0.1 | 0.1 | 0.4 | 0.6 |
| BELTRAMI | 007 | 0000 | 613 | 34,384 | 39,655 | 41,823 | 1.4 | 17 | 82.6 | 81.0 | 0.3 | 0.4 | 0.6 | 0.8 |
| BENTON | 009 | 6980 | 613 | 30,185 | 35,415 | 38,299 | 1.6 | 13 | 98.8 | 98.4 | 0.2 | 0.3 | 0.4 | 0.7 |
| BIG STONE | 011 | 0000 | 613 | 6,285 | 5,499 | 5,151 | -1.3 | 86 | 99.2 | 99.0 | 0.1 | 0.1 | 0.2 | 0.4 |
| BLUE EARTH | 013 | 0000 | 737 | 54,044 | 53,903 | 54,051 | 0.0 | 52 | 97.4 | 96.3 | 0.5 | 0.6 | 1.5 | 2.3 |
| BROWN | 015 | 0000 | 737 | 26,984 | 26,766 | 26,098 | -0.1 | 55 | 99.3 | 98.9 | 0.0 | 0.0 | 0.4 | 0.6 |
| CARLTON | 017 | 0000 | 676 | 29,259 | 31,643 | 32,403 | 0.8 | 28 | 95.1 | 94.2 | 0.1 | 0.4 | 0.3 | 0.4 |
| CARVER | 019 | 5120 | 613 | 47,915 | 68,940 | 78,780 | 3.6 | 3 | 98.4 | 97.6 | 0.2 | 0.3 | 0.9 | 1.5 |
| CASS | 021 | 0000 | 613 | 21,791 | 27,698 | 30,928 | 2.4 | 8 | 88.6 | 87.6 | 0.2 | 0.2 | 0.2 | 0.4 |
| CHIPPEWA | 023 | 0000 | 613 | 13,228 | 13,010 | 12,922 | -0.2 | 59 | 99.1 | 98.6 | 0.0 | 0.1 | 0.3 | 0.6 |
| CHISAGO | 025 | 5120 | 613 | 30,521 | 43,684 | 50,553 | 3.6 | 3 | 98.9 | 98.5 | 0.2 | 0.3 | 0.3 | 0.5 |
| CLAY | 027 | 2520 | 724 | 50,422 | 51,787 | 52,092 | 0.3 | 43 | 96.3 | 95.0 | 0.3 | 0.5 | 0.8 | 1.2 |
| CLEARWATER | 029 | 0000 | 724 | 8,309 | 8,090 | 7,817 | -0.3 | 61 | 92.2 | 91.4 | 0.0 | 0.0 | 0.1 | 0.2 |
| COOK | 031 | 0000 | 676 | 3,868 | 4,812 | 5,017 | 2.2 | 9 | 92.3 | 91.5 | 0.1 | 0.2 | 0.5 | 0.8 |
| COTTONWOOD | 033 | 0000 | 613 | 12,694 | 11,793 | 11,236 | -0.7 | 77 | 99.0 | 98.5 | 0.1 | 0.1 | 0.7 | 1.0 |
| CROW WING | 035 | 0000 | 613 | 44,249 | 53,347 | 57,131 | 1.8 | 12 | 98.6 | 98.2 | 0.2 | 0.4 | 0.3 | 0.5 |
| DAKOTA | 037 | 5120 | 613 | 275,227 | 356,327 | 392,573 | 2.6 | 7 | 96.2 | 94.2 | 1.2 | 1.9 | 1.7 | 2.7 |
| DODGE | 039 | 0000 | 611 | 15,731 | 17,601 | 18,590 | 1.1 | 23 | 98.7 | 98.1 | 0.1 | 0.1 | 0.4 | 0.6 |
| DOUGLAS | 041 | 0000 | 613 | 28,674 | 31,521 | 32,781 | 0.9 | 27 | 99.3 | 99.0 | 0.0 | 0.1 | 0.3 | 0.6 |
| FARIBAULT | 043 | 0000 | 613 | 16,937 | 16,199 | 15,963 | -0.4 | 67 | 98.4 | 97.5 | 0.1 | 0.1 | 0.3 | 0.6 |
| FILLMORE | 045 | 0000 | 611 | 20,777 | 20,659 | 20,517 | -0.1 | 55 | 99.4 | 99.2 | 0.0 | 0.0 | 0.2 | 0.4 |
| FREEBORN | 047 | 0000 | 611 | 33,060 | 31,416 | 30,982 | -0.5 | 70 | 97.5 | 96.1 | 0.0 | 0.0 | 0.4 | 0.6 |
| GOODHUE | 049 | 0000 | 613 | 40,690 | 43,685 | 45,212 | 0.7 | 32 | 98.6 | 98.2 | 0.2 | 0.2 | 0.4 | 0.7 |
| GRANT | 051 | 0000 | 613 | 6,246 | 6,047 | 5,897 | -0.3 | 61 | 99.5 | 99.3 | 0.0 | 0.1 | 0.2 | 0.4 |
| HENNEPIN | 053 | 5120 | 613 | 1,032,431 | 1,068,727 | 1,089,943 | 0.3 | 43 | 89.3 | 84.9 | 5.8 | 8.3 | 2.9 | 4.5 |
| HOUSTON | 055 | 3870 | 702 | 18,497 | 19,618 | 20,280 | 0.6 | 35 | 99.3 | 99.0 | 0.1 | 0.2 | 0.3 | 0.4 |
| HUBBARD | 057 | 0000 | 613 | 14,939 | 17,222 | 18,167 | 1.4 | 17 | 98.0 | 97.9 | 0.0 | 0.0 | 0.1 | 0.2 |
| ISANTI | 059 | 5120 | 613 | 25,921 | 31,598 | 35,144 | 2.0 | 11 | 98.7 | 98.2 | 0.3 | 0.4 | 0.4 | 0.7 |
| ITASCA | 061 | 0000 | 676 | 40,863 | 44,445 | 45,890 | 0.8 | 28 | 96.3 | 95.9 | 0.1 | 0.2 | 0.2 | 0.3 |
| JACKSON | 063 | 0000 | 613 | 11,677 | 11,272 | 10,759 | -0.3 | 61 | 97.7 | 96.5 | 0.0 | 0.0 | 1.4 | 2.3 |
| KANABEC | 065 | 0000 | 613 | 12,802 | 14,666 | 15,832 | 1.3 | 19 | 98.9 | 98.5 | 0.2 | 0.2 | 0.4 | 0.6 |
| KANDIYOHI | 067 | 0000 | 613 | 38,761 | 40,832 | 40,813 | 0.5 | 36 | 97.6 | 96.4 | 0.2 | 0.3 | 0.3 | 0.5 |
| KITTSON | 069 | 0000 | 724 | 5,767 | 5,088 | 4,774 | -1.2 | 85 | 99.4 | 99.1 | 0.0 | 0.0 | 0.2 | 0.3 |
| KOOCHICHING | 071 | 0000 | 676 | 16,299 | 14,760 | 14,078 | -1.0 | 83 | 95.9 | 95.3 | 0.3 | 0.4 | 0.3 | 0.5 |
| LAC QUI PARLE | 073 | 0000 | 613 | 8,924 | 7,668 | 7,068 | -1.5 | 87 | 99.4 | 99.2 | 0.1 | 0.1 | 0.3 | 0.5 |
| LAKE | 075 | 0000 | 676 | 10,415 | 10,817 | 11,088 | 0.4 | 40 | 99.2 | 99.0 | 0.0 | 0.0 | 0.2 | 0.3 |
| LAKE OF THE WOODS | 077 | 0000 | 724 | 4,076 | 4,651 | 4,842 | 1.3 | 19 | 99.2 | 98.8 | 0.0 | 0.0 | 0.2 | 0.5 |
| LE SUEUR | 079 | 0000 | 613 | 23,239 | 25,702 | 26,853 | 1.0 | 24 | 99.3 | 99.0 | 0.1 | 0.1 | 0.3 | 0.4 |
| LINCOLN | 081 | 0000 | 725 | 6,890 | 6,351 | 5,999 | -0.8 | 80 | 99.5 | 99.4 | 0.0 | 0.0 | 0.1 | 0.1 |
| LYON | 083 | 0000 | 613 | 24,789 | 24,141 | 23,530 | -0.3 | 61 | 98.5 | 97.9 | 0.3 | 0.4 | 0.5 | 0.7 |
| MCLEOD | 085 | 0000 | 613 | 32,030 | 34,902 | 36,704 | 0.8 | 28 | 98.9 | 98.4 | 0.1 | 0.1 | 0.4 | 0.7 |
| MAHNOMEN | 087 | 0000 | 724 | 5,044 | 5,093 | 5,105 | 0.1 | 49 | 76.0 | 74.2 | 0.0 | 0.0 | 0.1 | 0.2 |
| MARSHALL | 089 | 0000 | 724 | 10,993 | 9,937 | 9,458 | -1.0 | 83 | 99.1 | 98.8 | 0.0 | 0.0 | 0.1 | 0.2 |
| MARTIN | 091 | 0000 | 737 | 22,914 | 21,617 | 20,762 | -0.6 | 73 | 99.1 | 98.8 | 0.0 | 0.0 | 0.4 | 0.5 |
| MEEKER | 093 | 0000 | 613 | 20,846 | 21,843 | 22,281 | 0.5 | 36 | 98.7 | 98.1 | 0.1 | 0.2 | 0.4 | 0.7 |
| MILLE LACS | 095 | 0000 | 613 | 18,670 | 21,690 | 23,351 | 1.5 | 15 | 96.2 | 95.7 | 0.1 | 0.2 | 0.2 | 0.3 |
| MORRISON | 097 | 0000 | 613 | 29,604 | 30,543 | 30,697 | 0.3 | 43 | 99.3 | 99.1 | 0.1 | 0.2 | 0.2 | 0.3 |
| MOWER | 099 | 0000 | 611 | 37,385 | 37,170 | 37,242 | -0.1 | 55 | 98.7 | 98.0 | 0.2 | 0.2 | 0.8 | 1.3 |
| MURRAY | 101 | 0000 | 725 | 9,660 | 9,504 | 9,431 | -0.2 | 59 | 99.7 | 99.5 | 0.0 | 0.0 | 0.2 | 0.3 |
| NICOLLET | 103 | 0000 | 613 | 28,076 | 29,148 | 28,514 | 0.4 | 40 | 98.4 | 97.8 | 0.3 | 0.4 | 0.7 | 1.2 |
| NOBLES | 105 | 0000 | 725 | 20,098 | 18,882 | 17,772 | -0.6 | 73 | 96.6 | 94.9 | 0.2 | 0.3 | 2.0 | 3.2 |
| NORMAN | 107 | 0000 | 724 | 7,975 | 7,468 | 7,227 | -0.6 | 73 | 98.6 | 98.3 | 0.1 | 0.1 | 0.2 | 0.3 |
| OLMSTED | 109 | 6820 | 611 | 106,470 | 121,226 | 131,096 | 1.3 | 19 | 95.7 | 93.5 | 0.7 | 1.0 | 3.0 | 4.9 |
| OTTER TAIL | 111 | 0000 | 724 | 50,714 | 56,238 | 59,525 | 1.0 | 24 | 99.0 | 98.7 | 0.1 | 0.1 | 0.4 | 0.6 |
| PENNINGTON | 113 | 0000 | 724 | 13,306 | 13,569 | 13,618 | 0.2 | 48 | 98.5 | 98.0 | 0.1 | 0.1 | 0.4 | 0.6 |
| PINE | 115 | 0000 | 613 | 21,264 | 25,059 | 27,268 | 1.6 | 13 | 95.8 | 95.8 | 1.7 | 1.3 | 0.4 | 0.6 |
| PIPESTONE | 117 | 0000 | 725 | 10,491 | 9,933 | 9,638 | -0.5 | 70 | 97.7 | 96.9 | 0.1 | 0.1 | 0.7 | 1.3 |
| POLK | 119 | 2985 | 724 | 32,498 | 30,353 | 28,277 | -0.7 | 77 | 96.9 | 95.8 | 0.2 | 0.3 | 0.3 | 0.5 |
| POPE | 121 | 0000 | 613 | 10,745 | 10,865 | 10,761 | 0.1 | 49 | 99.6 | 99.4 | 0.0 | 0.1 | 0.1 | 0.2 |
| RAMSEY | 123 | 5120 | 613 | 485,765 | 487,061 | 490,533 | 0.0 | 52 | 88.0 | 82.9 | 4.7 | 6.6 | 5.1 | 7.7 |
| RED LAKE | 125 | 0000 | 724 | 4,525 | 4,155 | 3,927 | -0.8 | 80 | 98.9 | 98.4 | 0.0 | 0.0 | 0.1 | 0.1 |
| REDWOOD | 127 | 0000 | 613 | 17,254 | 16,313 | 15,786 | -0.5 | 70 | 97.8 | 97.4 | 0.2 | 0.2 | 0.2 | 0.3 |
| RENVILLE | 129 | 0000 | 613 | 17,673 | 16,701 | 16,178 | -0.6 | 73 | 98.6 | 97.9 | 0.0 | 0.0 | 0.3 | 0.4 |
| RICE | 131 | 0000 | 613 | 49,183 | 55,745 | 59,442 | 1.2 | 22 | 97.8 | 96.6 | 0.4 | 0.7 | 1.2 | 1.8 |
| ROCK | 133 | 0000 | 725 | 9,806 | 9,529 | 9,094 | -0.3 | 61 | 99.2 | 99.0 | 0.1 | 0.2 | 0.2 | 0.3 |
| ROSEAU | 135 | 0000 | 724 | 15,026 | 16,076 | 16,042 | 0.7 | 32 | 98.3 | 97.7 | 0.0 | 0.0 | 0.6 | 1.1 |
| ST. LOUIS | 137 | 2240 | 676 | 198,213 | 193,111 | 191,175 | -0.3 | 61 | 96.9 | 96.2 | 0.6 | 0.8 | 0.5 | 0.9 |
| SCOTT | 139 | 5120 | 613 | 57,846 | 86,521 | 103,835 | 4.0 | 2 | 97.8 | 96.9 | 0.5 | 0.6 | 0.9 | 1.5 |
| SHERBURNE | 141 | 5120 | 613 | 41,945 | 66,155 | 80,010 | 4.5 | 1 | 98.2 | 97.8 | 0.6 | 0.6 | 0.5 | 0.8 |
| SIBLEY | 143 | 0000 | 613 | 14,366 | 14,846 | 15,216 | 0.3 | 43 | 99.3 | 98.9 | 0.0 | 0.0 | 0.2 | 0.3 |
| STEARNS | 145 | 6980 | 613 | 118,791 | 131,176 | 136,624 | 1.0 | 24 | 98.5 | 97.9 | 0.3 | 0.5 | 0.7 | 1.1 |
| STEELE | 147 | 0000 | 613 | 30,729 | 32,344 | 33,683 | 0.5 | 36 | 98.5 | 97.7 | 0.2 | 0.2 | 0.5 | 0.8 |
| STEVENS | 149 | 0000 | 613 | 10,634 | 9,923 | 9,659 | -0.7 | 77 | 97.5 | 96.6 | 0.5 | 0.7 | 1.1 | 1.7 |
| SWIFT | 151 | 0000 | 613 | 10,724 | 11,253 | 10,813 | 0.5 | 36 | 99.1 | 96.6 | 0.0 | 1.5 | 0.4 | 0.5 |
| TODD | 153 | 0000 | 613 | 23,363 | 24,362 | 24,992 | 0.4 | 40 | 99.4 | 99.3 | 0.0 | 0.0 | 0.2 | 0.4 |
| MINNESOTA | | | | | | | 0.9 | | 94.4 | 92.5 | 2.2 | 2.9 | 1.8 | 2.7 |
| UNITED STATES | | | | | | | 1.0 | | 80.3 | 77.9 | 12.1 | 12.4 | 2.9 | 3.9 |

# MINNESOTA POPULATION COMPOSITION

# B

| COUNTY | % HISPANIC ORIGIN | | 2000 AGE DISTRIBUTION (%) | | | | | | | | | | MEDIAN AGE | | |
|---|---|---|---|---|---|---|---|---|---|---|---|---|---|---|---|
| | 1990 | 2000 | 0-4 | 5-9 | 10-14 | 15-19 | 20-24 | 25-44 | 45-64 | 65-84 | 85+ | 18+ | 1990 | 2000 | 2000 Males/ Females (×100) |
| AITKIN | 0.3 | 0.7 | 4.9 | 5.4 | 6.2 | 7.7 | 5.0 | 20.4 | 27.0 | 20.3 | 3.2 | 78.5 | 42.8 | 45.3 | 99.7 |
| ANOKA | 0.9 | 1.9 | 7.2 | 7.5 | 8.9 | 8.2 | 6.1 | 32.7 | 21.8 | 7.0 | 0.6 | 71.3 | 29.9 | 33.5 | 100.0 |
| BECKER | 0.4 | 1.0 | 6.7 | 7.2 | 8.0 | 8.2 | 5.5 | 24.2 | 24.1 | 13.6 | 2.5 | 72.7 | 35.0 | 38.2 | 99.0 |
| BELTRAMI | 0.4 | 1.0 | 7.0 | 7.7 | 9.0 | 10.1 | 8.6 | 26.6 | 19.7 | 9.7 | 1.6 | 71.1 | 29.2 | 31.5 | 99.3 |
| BENTON | 0.5 | 1.2 | 7.6 | 7.8 | 8.8 | 8.5 | 7.7 | 30.1 | 18.8 | 8.7 | 2.0 | 70.7 | 29.2 | 32.1 | 98.5 |
| BIG STONE | 0.4 | 0.9 | 5.9 | 6.5 | 7.7 | 7.4 | 3.9 | 20.9 | 24.1 | 18.6 | 4.9 | 74.7 | 40.4 | 43.3 | 92.9 |
| BLUE EARTH | 0.9 | 1.8 | 5.4 | 5.7 | 6.8 | 11.0 | 15.4 | 25.4 | 17.9 | 10.3 | 2.0 | 78.5 | 27.6 | 30.0 | 98.8 |
| BROWN | 0.6 | 1.3 | 6.2 | 6.9 | 8.1 | 8.7 | 6.1 | 24.7 | 22.1 | 14.4 | 2.8 | 73.6 | 34.5 | 37.8 | 94.5 |
| CARLTON | 0.3 | 0.9 | 6.3 | 6.8 | 7.6 | 8.0 | 6.1 | 25.7 | 24.0 | 13.5 | 2.1 | 74.0 | 34.9 | 38.3 | 99.0 |
| CARVER | 0.5 | 1.2 | 8.2 | 8.8 | 9.4 | 7.6 | 5.6 | 31.9 | 20.3 | 7.0 | 1.1 | 68.8 | 30.6 | 33.3 | 102.0 |
| CASS | 0.4 | 0.9 | 6.2 | 6.6 | 7.6 | 7.8 | 5.6 | 21.7 | 25.1 | 17.2 | 2.3 | 74.4 | 38.3 | 41.1 | 102.0 |
| CHIPPEWA | 0.7 | 1.6 | 5.7 | 6.7 | 8.1 | 7.9 | 4.7 | 23.7 | 23.4 | 16.1 | 3.7 | 74.2 | 37.5 | 40.4 | 93.8 |
| CHISAGO | 0.4 | 1.1 | 7.0 | 7.7 | 9.5 | 8.6 | 5.4 | 28.6 | 22.6 | 9.1 | 1.6 | 70.4 | 32.2 | 35.1 | 102.2 |
| CLAY | 2.3 | 4.0 | 6.0 | 6.4 | 7.3 | 11.3 | 11.8 | 25.4 | 19.5 | 10.4 | 1.9 | 76.3 | 28.9 | 31.6 | 93.6 |
| CLEARWATER | 0.2 | 0.7 | 6.1 | 7.1 | 8.9 | 8.6 | 4.8 | 23.2 | 23.9 | 14.0 | 3.4 | 72.3 | 36.5 | 39.1 | 101.0 |
| COOK | 0.4 | 0.7 | 5.0 | 5.9 | 7.2 | 6.6 | 3.6 | 26.4 | 28.5 | 14.9 | 2.0 | 77.4 | 38.3 | 42.5 | 101.0 |
| COTTONWOOD | 0.5 | 1.2 | 5.4 | 6.0 | 8.0 | 7.4 | 4.6 | 22.3 | 24.1 | 17.8 | 4.3 | 75.4 | 39.2 | 42.3 | 96.0 |
| CROW WING | 0.4 | 0.9 | 6.0 | 6.6 | 8.1 | 8.0 | 5.3 | 25.1 | 24.4 | 14.4 | 2.2 | 74.4 | 35.8 | 39.1 | 95.3 |
| DAKOTA | 1.5 | 2.8 | 8.0 | 8.5 | 9.1 | 7.3 | 5.6 | 34.0 | 20.7 | 6.1 | 0.7 | 69.9 | 30.2 | 33.2 | 97.0 |
| DODGE | 1.0 | 2.1 | 7.3 | 8.1 | 9.4 | 8.8 | 5.4 | 27.6 | 21.3 | 10.2 | 2.0 | 69.5 | 31.6 | 34.6 | 99.0 |
| DOUGLAS | 0.3 | 0.8 | 5.9 | 6.7 | 8.2 | 8.2 | 5.3 | 25.0 | 23.1 | 14.6 | 2.9 | 74.5 | 35.2 | 38.7 | 98.1 |
| FARIBAULT | 1.9 | 3.4 | 5.3 | 6.4 | 7.8 | 7.7 | 4.6 | 22.2 | 24.2 | 18.1 | 3.8 | 75.1 | 38.9 | 42.3 | 94.1 |
| FILLMORE | 0.3 | 0.9 | 6.0 | 6.9 | 8.2 | 8.2 | 4.6 | 23.5 | 22.9 | 16.0 | 3.7 | 73.5 | 36.4 | 40.0 | 98.5 |
| FREEBORN | 3.3 | 5.6 | 5.8 | 6.3 | 7.7 | 7.5 | 5.1 | 24.6 | 24.4 | 15.9 | 2.8 | 75.4 | 37.1 | 40.5 | 97.1 |
| GOODHUE | 0.4 | 1.1 | 6.2 | 7.1 | 8.4 | 8.3 | 5.1 | 26.8 | 22.9 | 12.4 | 2.8 | 72.8 | 34.2 | 37.7 | 98.4 |
| GRANT | 0.1 | 0.6 | 5.3 | 6.4 | 7.8 | 7.5 | 3.9 | 21.7 | 24.5 | 18.6 | 4.3 | 75.0 | 40.7 | 43.2 | 96.1 |
| HENNEPIN | 1.4 | 2.4 | 6.1 | 6.2 | 7.1 | 6.9 | 6.9 | 33.3 | 22.1 | 9.7 | 1.7 | 76.7 | 32.7 | 36.3 | 94.5 |
| HOUSTON | 0.2 | 0.7 | 6.6 | 7.2 | 8.7 | 7.9 | 5.0 | 26.5 | 22.4 | 13.0 | 2.7 | 72.3 | 34.2 | 37.6 | 99.1 |
| HUBBARD | 0.2 | 0.8 | 5.6 | 6.4 | 8.2 | 7.8 | 4.6 | 23.5 | 26.1 | 15.4 | 2.3 | 74.4 | 37.7 | 41.1 | 98.4 |
| ISANTI | 0.5 | 1.1 | 6.7 | 7.5 | 9.3 | 9.0 | 5.6 | 28.3 | 22.9 | 9.0 | 1.8 | 70.7 | 32.0 | 35.2 | 100.2 |
| ITASCA | 0.3 | 0.9 | 5.8 | 6.3 | 7.3 | 8.3 | 6.2 | 23.9 | 26.0 | 14.2 | 2.2 | 75.1 | 35.9 | 39.9 | 99.0 |
| JACKSON | 1.0 | 1.8 | 6.3 | 6.8 | 7.5 | 8.0 | 5.2 | 23.7 | 22.8 | 16.3 | 3.4 | 74.2 | 36.9 | 40.4 | 101.6 |
| KANABEC | 0.5 | 1.2 | 6.7 | 7.5 | 8.9 | 8.8 | 5.2 | 26.0 | 23.0 | 12.0 | 1.9 | 71.1 | 33.5 | 36.4 | 98.7 |
| KANDIYOHI | 3.5 | 6.3 | 7.1 | 7.3 | 7.7 | 8.1 | 6.2 | 27.5 | 22.0 | 12.0 | 2.2 | 73.4 | 33.0 | 36.0 | 98.5 |
| KITTSON | 0.8 | 1.7 | 5.8 | 6.6 | 7.9 | 7.4 | 4.0 | 22.9 | 23.9 | 17.7 | 4.0 | 74.9 | 38.6 | 42.1 | 99.0 |
| KOOCHICHING | 1.1 | 2.0 | 5.3 | 5.8 | 7.3 | 8.2 | 5.5 | 27.2 | 25.1 | 13.9 | 1.9 | 76.7 | 35.6 | 39.4 | 108.4 |
| LAC QUI PARLE | 0.3 | 0.7 | 5.5 | 6.4 | 8.0 | 7.3 | 3.8 | 21.6 | 23.9 | 19.1 | 4.2 | 74.7 | 39.4 | 43.1 | 98.9 |
| LAKE | 0.3 | 0.9 | 4.8 | 5.5 | 7.2 | 7.1 | 4.3 | 23.5 | 27.8 | 17.7 | 2.1 | 77.8 | 39.2 | 43.4 | 100.0 |
| LAKE OF THE WOODS | 0.6 | 1.5 | 6.8 | 7.5 | 8.6 | 8.0 | 4.8 | 24.6 | 24.2 | 13.4 | 2.1 | 71.6 | 35.5 | 38.5 | 98.0 |
| LE SUEUR | 0.5 | 1.3 | 6.6 | 7.3 | 8.9 | 8.4 | 5.4 | 26.2 | 22.8 | 12.3 | 2.2 | 71.8 | 33.5 | 36.8 | 99.8 |
| LINCOLN | 0.4 | 0.9 | 5.1 | 5.7 | 6.2 | 8.2 | 5.4 | 20.6 | 23.9 | 19.9 | 5.1 | 77.3 | 41.4 | 44.1 | 95.4 |
| LYON | 0.9 | 1.8 | 6.1 | 6.8 | 8.1 | 9.7 | 8.2 | 25.4 | 20.4 | 12.7 | 2.6 | 74.6 | 31.6 | 35.1 | 97.0 |
| MCLEOD | 0.9 | 1.9 | 6.9 | 7.3 | 8.9 | 8.2 | 5.7 | 27.3 | 21.9 | 11.6 | 2.2 | 71.8 | 32.9 | 36.0 | 100.1 |
| MAHNOMEN | 0.5 | 1.0 | 6.6 | 7.2 | 7.5 | 8.8 | 6.4 | 22.5 | 23.0 | 15.1 | 2.9 | 72.6 | 35.0 | 38.2 | 101.9 |
| MARSHALL | 1.0 | 2.0 | 5.8 | 6.8 | 7.2 | 8.0 | 6.1 | 23.1 | 24.9 | 15.5 | 2.6 | 74.5 | 36.5 | 40.4 | 102.6 |
| MARTIN | 0.6 | 1.3 | 5.8 | 6.6 | 8.1 | 7.7 | 4.6 | 24.2 | 23.6 | 16.0 | 3.3 | 74.4 | 37.0 | 40.5 | 97.3 |
| MEEKER | 1.1 | 2.2 | 6.5 | 7.3 | 8.8 | 8.3 | 5.0 | 24.6 | 23.1 | 13.7 | 2.5 | 71.7 | 34.9 | 37.8 | 98.7 |
| MILLE LACS | 0.5 | 1.1 | 6.5 | 7.3 | 8.8 | 8.2 | 5.1 | 24.4 | 23.1 | 13.9 | 2.7 | 72.1 | 34.8 | 38.0 | 98.3 |
| MORRISON | 0.3 | 0.9 | 6.8 | 7.8 | 9.3 | 8.8 | 5.2 | 24.8 | 21.9 | 13.1 | 2.2 | 70.3 | 32.7 | 36.2 | 101.4 |
| MOWER | 0.7 | 1.5 | 5.6 | 6.3 | 7.7 | 7.8 | 5.1 | 24.0 | 23.3 | 17.1 | 3.1 | 75.6 | 37.4 | 40.5 | 95.6 |
| MURRAY | 0.2 | 0.8 | 5.4 | 6.4 | 8.5 | 7.7 | 4.5 | 22.2 | 24.5 | 17.7 | 3.1 | 74.4 | 38.3 | 41.6 | 98.9 |
| NICOLLET | 0.7 | 1.6 | 6.6 | 6.9 | 7.4 | 9.8 | 10.3 | 28.1 | 20.1 | 9.3 | 1.6 | 74.9 | 30.1 | 32.4 | 98.6 |
| NOBLES | 1.3 | 2.4 | 5.8 | 6.5 | 7.9 | 8.0 | 5.4 | 24.6 | 23.3 | 15.4 | 3.0 | 74.9 | 35.8 | 39.3 | 97.8 |
| NORMAN | 0.9 | 1.7 | 5.8 | 6.7 | 7.0 | 7.8 | 5.3 | 21.7 | 23.3 | 18.1 | 4.3 | 75.1 | 39.0 | 42.1 | 100.5 |
| OLMSTED | 0.9 | 1.8 | 7.2 | 7.7 | 8.6 | 7.5 | 5.7 | 31.7 | 21.3 | 8.7 | 1.6 | 72.1 | 31.6 | 35.2 | 94.7 |
| OTTER TAIL | 0.4 | 1.0 | 5.8 | 6.5 | 8.0 | 7.8 | 4.8 | 23.9 | 24.4 | 15.7 | 3.1 | 74.9 | 37.3 | 40.5 | 99.9 |
| PENNINGTON | 0.8 | 1.7 | 5.9 | 6.3 | 8.2 | 8.6 | 6.1 | 26.6 | 22.5 | 12.7 | 3.0 | 74.8 | 34.1 | 37.2 | 99.5 |
| PINE | 1.6 | 2.3 | 5.9 | 6.8 | 8.6 | 8.4 | 5.3 | 25.8 | 23.7 | 13.3 | 2.2 | 73.1 | 34.5 | 37.8 | 108.8 |
| PIPESTONE | 0.4 | 1.1 | 6.4 | 7.2 | 8.5 | 8.3 | 4.6 | 23.2 | 21.6 | 16.5 | 3.7 | 72.7 | 36.0 | 39.1 | 94.7 |
| POLK | 3.5 | 6.1 | 6.3 | 7.1 | 8.3 | 8.9 | 5.8 | 24.5 | 22.4 | 13.9 | 2.9 | 73.2 | 34.8 | 37.5 | 98.5 |
| POPE | 0.1 | 0.5 | 5.9 | 7.0 | 8.3 | 7.8 | 4.2 | 21.9 | 23.8 | 17.5 | 3.7 | 73.2 | 38.5 | 41.5 | 99.7 |
| RAMSEY | 2.9 | 4.8 | 6.8 | 6.8 | 7.7 | 7.5 | 6.8 | 31.4 | 20.9 | 10.3 | 1.8 | 74.7 | 32.0 | 35.3 | 92.6 |
| RED LAKE | 1.0 | 1.9 | 6.7 | 7.1 | 7.8 | 9.0 | 5.1 | 23.7 | 22.9 | 14.9 | 2.7 | 72.0 | 35.5 | 38.7 | 102.8 |
| REDWOOD | 0.5 | 1.2 | 6.3 | 7.1 | 8.5 | 7.9 | 4.5 | 23.3 | 23.0 | 15.8 | 3.6 | 72.5 | 36.7 | 39.8 | 97.7 |
| RENVILLE | 1.2 | 2.4 | 6.2 | 7.1 | 8.5 | 7.8 | 4.5 | 23.1 | 22.9 | 16.5 | 3.4 | 73.0 | 36.7 | 40.2 | 98.9 |
| RICE | 1.1 | 2.1 | 6.0 | 6.5 | 7.8 | 11.1 | 10.1 | 26.5 | 20.7 | 9.4 | 1.9 | 75.1 | 30.2 | 32.8 | 99.0 |
| ROCK | 0.3 | 0.8 | 5.8 | 6.8 | 8.4 | 8.3 | 4.6 | 23.4 | 23.0 | 16.4 | 3.3 | 73.4 | 36.6 | 40.1 | 96.1 |
| ROSEAU | 0.2 | 0.7 | 8.5 | 8.9 | 9.4 | 7.9 | 5.4 | 27.9 | 20.0 | 10.1 | 2.0 | 67.7 | 30.6 | 33.9 | 104.9 |
| ST. LOUIS | 0.5 | 1.1 | 5.4 | 5.7 | 6.5 | 7.9 | 7.1 | 26.4 | 24.2 | 14.3 | 2.5 | 78.1 | 35.7 | 39.1 | 96.1 |
| SCOTT | 0.7 | 1.5 | 7.9 | 8.2 | 9.3 | 8.1 | 5.5 | 33.1 | 20.9 | 6.0 | 0.9 | 69.4 | 30.2 | 33.1 | 103.7 |
| SHERBURNE | 0.6 | 1.3 | 7.5 | 8.0 | 9.4 | 9.0 | 8.2 | 31.2 | 19.8 | 5.9 | 0.9 | 69.5 | 28.6 | 30.8 | 103.9 |
| SIBLEY | 0.9 | 1.9 | 6.4 | 7.0 | 8.9 | 7.8 | 4.8 | 24.1 | 23.6 | 14.5 | 2.8 | 72.5 | 35.5 | 38.8 | 100.8 |
| STEARNS | 0.4 | 1.1 | 7.0 | 7.1 | 7.5 | 10.4 | 10.6 | 28.6 | 18.3 | 9.1 | 1.4 | 73.7 | 27.9 | 30.6 | 100.4 |
| STEELE | 1.8 | 3.2 | 6.7 | 7.2 | 8.6 | 8.3 | 6.0 | 27.4 | 22.2 | 11.6 | 2.1 | 72.3 | 32.7 | 36.1 | 96.8 |
| STEVENS | 0.5 | 1.2 | 5.1 | 5.8 | 7.0 | 12.8 | 11.8 | 21.9 | 19.2 | 13.7 | 2.8 | 78.2 | 30.5 | 33.1 | 94.0 |
| SWIFT | 0.7 | 2.2 | 5.0 | 6.0 | 7.8 | 7.5 | 5.4 | 25.1 | 22.6 | 17.0 | 3.5 | 75.6 | 38.0 | 40.6 | 108.8 |
| TODD | 0.2 | 0.8 | 6.7 | 7.0 | 7.5 | 8.9 | 6.2 | 23.6 | 23.4 | 14.1 | 2.5 | 72.8 | 34.6 | 37.8 | 98.0 |
| MINNESOTA | 1.2 | 2.3 | 6.6 | 7.0 | 8.0 | 8.0 | 6.6 | 29.7 | 22.0 | 10.4 | 1.8 | 73.8 | 32.5 | 35.7 | 97.2 |
| UNITED STATES | 9.0 | 11.8 | 6.9 | 7.2 | 7.2 | 7.2 | 6.7 | 29.9 | 22.2 | 11.1 | 1.6 | 74.6 | 32.9 | 35.7 | 95.6 |

| COUNTY | HOUSEHOLDS | | | | | FAMILIES | | | MEDIAN HOUSEHOLD INCOME | | | |
|---|---|---|---|---|---|---|---|---|---|---|---|---|
| | 1990 | 2000 | 2005 | % Annual Rate 1990-2000 | 2000 Average HH Size | 1990 | 2000 | % Annual Rate 1990-2000 | 2000 | 2005 | 2000 National Rank | 2000 State Rank |
| AITKIN | 5,126 | 6,169 | 6,656 | 2.3 | 2.32 | 3,620 | 4,141 | 1.6 | 29,332 | 33,405 | 2249 | 82 |
| ANOKA | 82,437 | 104,381 | 115,453 | 2.9 | 2.89 | 65,136 | 81,099 | 2.7 | 58,996 | 68,672 | 80 | 5 |
| BECKER | 10,477 | 11,337 | 11,802 | 1.0 | 2.61 | 7,555 | 7,903 | 0.5 | 33,064 | 36,687 | 1527 | 64 |
| BELTRAMI | 11,870 | 13,900 | 14,688 | 1.9 | 2.74 | 8,390 | 9,478 | 1.5 | 33,628 | 38,569 | 1448 | 62 |
| BENTON | 10,935 | 12,935 | 14,042 | 2.1 | 2.69 | 7,562 | 8,613 | 1.6 | 42,038 | 50,399 | 506 | 21 |
| BIG STONE | 2,463 | 2,203 | 2,085 | -1.3 | 2.36 | 1,727 | 1,490 | -1.8 | 29,260 | 32,305 | 2257 | 83 |
| BLUE EARTH | 19,277 | 19,515 | 19,635 | 0.1 | 2.57 | 11,993 | 11,600 | -0.4 | 40,586 | 46,442 | 622 | 26 |
| BROWN | 10,321 | 10,333 | 10,189 | 0.0 | 2.49 | 7,167 | 6,872 | -0.5 | 40,511 | 46,005 | 627 | 27 |
| CARLTON | 10,842 | 11,729 | 12,141 | 1.0 | 2.57 | 7,856 | 8,244 | 0.6 | 41,155 | 45,536 | 576 | 22 |
| CARVER | 16,601 | 24,097 | 27,623 | 4.6 | 2.83 | 12,864 | 18,092 | 4.2 | 63,691 | 77,271 | 46 | 3 |
| CASS | 8,302 | 10,781 | 12,131 | 3.2 | 2.52 | 6,097 | 7,647 | 2.8 | 31,287 | 36,187 | 1870 | 77 |
| CHIPPEWA | 5,245 | 5,245 | 5,251 | 0.0 | 2.44 | 3,684 | 3,522 | -0.5 | 36,499 | 42,439 | 1042 | 45 |
| CHISAGO | 10,551 | 15,337 | 17,865 | 4.6 | 2.81 | 8,183 | 11,597 | 4.3 | 50,874 | 61,592 | 187 | 10 |
| CLAY | 17,490 | 18,355 | 18,536 | 0.6 | 2.62 | 11,921 | 12,035 | 0.1 | 41,088 | 47,546 | 584 | 23 |
| CLEARWATER | 3,064 | 3,109 | 3,063 | 0.2 | 2.54 | 2,240 | 2,181 | -0.3 | 29,990 | 35,350 | 2156 | 81 |
| COOK | 1,632 | 2,126 | 2,262 | 3.3 | 2.23 | 1,072 | 1,345 | 2.8 | 37,005 | 39,899 | 976 | 41 |
| COTTONWOOD | 5,060 | 4,824 | 4,651 | -0.6 | 2.38 | 3,585 | 3,290 | -1.0 | 32,190 | 37,565 | 1689 | 72 |
| CROW WING | 17,204 | 21,031 | 22,651 | 2.5 | 2.49 | 12,161 | 14,527 | 2.2 | 36,653 | 41,710 | 1026 | 43 |
| DAKOTA | 98,293 | 130,188 | 144,996 | 3.5 | 2.72 | 73,632 | 94,866 | 3.1 | 63,302 | 73,976 | 49 | 4 |
| DODGE | 5,538 | 6,272 | 6,662 | 1.5 | 2.78 | 4,277 | 4,691 | 1.1 | 45,021 | 54,601 | 353 | 17 |
| DOUGLAS | 10,988 | 12,331 | 12,959 | 1.4 | 2.51 | 7,781 | 8,494 | 1.1 | 36,907 | 42,118 | 989 | 42 |
| FARIBAULT | 6,772 | 6,546 | 6,482 | -0.4 | 2.42 | 4,710 | 4,368 | -0.9 | 32,618 | 38,298 | 1609 | 67 |
| FILLMORE | 7,822 | 7,956 | 7,988 | 0.2 | 2.53 | 5,654 | 5,542 | -0.2 | 32,488 | 37,879 | 1628 | 68 |
| FREEBORN | 13,029 | 12,570 | 12,495 | -0.4 | 2.45 | 9,287 | 8,639 | -0.9 | 35,143 | 41,276 | 1227 | 52 |
| GOODHUE | 15,198 | 16,652 | 17,408 | 1.1 | 2.55 | 10,903 | 11,545 | 0.7 | 46,117 | 53,466 | 304 | 16 |
| GRANT | 2,454 | 2,461 | 2,441 | 0.0 | 2.38 | 1,737 | 1,681 | -0.4 | 32,997 | 38,544 | 1540 | 66 |
| HENNEPIN | 419,060 | 438,305 | 449,093 | 0.5 | 2.38 | 257,347 | 261,175 | 0.2 | 53,173 | 58,839 | 149 | 8 |
| HOUSTON | 6,844 | 7,283 | 7,539 | 0.8 | 2.65 | 5,053 | 5,192 | 0.3 | 40,452 | 46,315 | 632 | 29 |
| HUBBARD | 5,781 | 6,881 | 7,362 | 2.1 | 2.48 | 4,274 | 4,897 | 1.7 | 31,877 | 37,809 | 1739 | 74 |
| ISANTI | 8,810 | 10,932 | 12,210 | 2.7 | 2.85 | 6,815 | 8,231 | 2.3 | 49,231 | 59,968 | 216 | 11 |
| ITASCA | 15,461 | 17,126 | 17,842 | 1.2 | 2.56 | 11,424 | 12,267 | 0.9 | 36,481 | 39,958 | 1047 | 46 |
| JACKSON | 4,560 | 4,527 | 4,385 | -0.1 | 2.44 | 3,272 | 3,125 | -0.6 | 34,365 | 40,898 | 1336 | 59 |
| KANABEC | 4,753 | 5,481 | 5,939 | 1.7 | 2.66 | 3,485 | 3,876 | 1.3 | 34,746 | 42,137 | 1289 | 57 |
| KANDIYOHI | 14,298 | 15,396 | 15,504 | 0.9 | 2.60 | 10,145 | 10,558 | 0.5 | 40,496 | 47,546 | 629 | 28 |
| KITTSON | 2,274 | 2,103 | 2,017 | -0.9 | 2.34 | 1,586 | 1,412 | -1.4 | 30,920 | 35,359 | 1944 | 78 |
| KOOCHICHING | 6,025 | 5,774 | 5,579 | -0.5 | 2.51 | 4,278 | 3,953 | -1.0 | 38,276 | 41,586 | 830 | 38 |
| LAC QUI PARLE | 3,505 | 3,142 | 2,950 | -1.3 | 2.36 | 2,487 | 2,141 | -1.8 | 33,046 | 40,619 | 1530 | 65 |
| LAKE | 4,242 | 4,375 | 4,471 | 0.4 | 2.44 | 3,019 | 3,007 | 0.0 | 38,930 | 41,661 | 757 | 35 |
| LAKE OF THE WOODS | 1,576 | 1,810 | 1,892 | 1.7 | 2.54 | 1,169 | 1,300 | 1.3 | 37,245 | 45,479 | 942 | 39 |
| LE SUEUR | 8,468 | 9,621 | 10,182 | 1.6 | 2.64 | 6,247 | 6,869 | 1.2 | 44,239 | 53,412 | 383 | 19 |
| LINCOLN | 2,704 | 2,530 | 2,406 | -0.8 | 2.43 | 1,904 | 1,707 | -1.3 | 28,333 | 35,952 | 2392 | 87 |
| LYON | 9,073 | 9,162 | 9,012 | 0.1 | 2.50 | 6,251 | 6,015 | -0.5 | 40,006 | 47,580 | 674 | 30 |
| MCLEOD | 11,815 | 12,952 | 13,661 | 1.1 | 2.66 | 8,611 | 9,095 | 0.7 | 46,870 | 57,198 | 281 | 14 |
| MAHNOMEN | 1,805 | 1,839 | 1,849 | 0.2 | 2.72 | 1,339 | 1,311 | -0.3 | 28,504 | 32,213 | 2365 | 86 |
| MARSHALL | 4,194 | 3,954 | 3,838 | -0.7 | 2.48 | 3,017 | 2,741 | -1.2 | 34,643 | 41,714 | 1299 | 58 |
| MARTIN | 9,129 | 8,801 | 8,537 | -0.4 | 2.40 | 6,378 | 5,911 | -0.9 | 37,240 | 43,776 | 944 | 40 |
| MEEKER | 7,651 | 8,223 | 8,492 | 0.9 | 2.61 | 5,628 | 5,859 | 0.5 | 39,776 | 48,862 | 687 | 32 |
| MILLE LACS | 6,911 | 8,201 | 8,922 | 2.1 | 2.60 | 5,031 | 5,752 | 1.6 | 35,015 | 41,712 | 1249 | 55 |
| MORRISON | 10,399 | 10,971 | 11,135 | 0.7 | 2.73 | 7,715 | 7,880 | 0.3 | 34,318 | 42,027 | 1345 | 61 |
| MOWER | 15,028 | 15,082 | 15,181 | 0.0 | 2.42 | 10,373 | 10,034 | -0.4 | 38,351 | 41,627 | 824 | 36 |
| MURRAY | 3,758 | 3,754 | 3,748 | 0.0 | 2.49 | 2,715 | 2,612 | -0.5 | 32,177 | 40,944 | 1693 | 73 |
| NICOLLET | 9,478 | 10,227 | 10,120 | 0.9 | 2.63 | 6,786 | 7,068 | 0.5 | 47,662 | 58,025 | 250 | 13 |
| NOBLES | 7,683 | 7,365 | 6,989 | -0.5 | 2.50 | 5,525 | 5,110 | -0.9 | 32,421 | 38,052 | 1635 | 70 |
| NORMAN | 3,118 | 2,948 | 2,866 | -0.7 | 2.46 | 2,155 | 1,961 | -1.1 | 30,636 | 35,346 | 1998 | 79 |
| OLMSTED | 40,058 | 45,925 | 49,878 | 1.7 | 2.58 | 27,737 | 30,628 | 1.2 | 52,841 | 60,388 | 156 | 9 |
| OTTER TAIL | 19,510 | 22,007 | 23,456 | 1.5 | 2.50 | 13,939 | 15,046 | 0.9 | 34,939 | 40,061 | 1264 | 56 |
| PENNINGTON | 5,173 | 5,380 | 5,459 | 0.5 | 2.46 | 3,463 | 3,423 | -0.1 | 35,252 | 38,919 | 1212 | 51 |
| PINE | 7,577 | 9,033 | 9,883 | 2.2 | 2.63 | 5,514 | 6,290 | 1.6 | 34,347 | 40,932 | 1342 | 60 |
| PIPESTONE | 4,078 | 3,948 | 3,866 | -0.4 | 2.45 | 2,821 | 2,617 | -0.9 | 32,379 | 40,319 | 1647 | 71 |
| POLK | 11,984 | 11,283 | 10,549 | -0.7 | 2.57 | 8,506 | 7,712 | -1.2 | 35,121 | 40,990 | 1231 | 53 |
| POPE | 4,135 | 4,228 | 4,214 | 0.3 | 2.51 | 2,986 | 2,956 | -0.1 | 32,460 | 39,521 | 1631 | 69 |
| RAMSEY | 190,500 | 193,855 | 196,851 | 0.2 | 2.43 | 120,206 | 117,745 | -0.3 | 44,444 | 49,536 | 377 | 18 |
| RED LAKE | 1,730 | 1,645 | 1,581 | -0.6 | 2.49 | 1,171 | 1,070 | -1.1 | 31,726 | 37,282 | 1772 | 76 |
| REDWOOD | 6,554 | 6,287 | 6,119 | -0.5 | 2.52 | 4,643 | 4,275 | -1.0 | 36,411 | 42,364 | 1059 | 48 |
| RENVILLE | 6,790 | 6,550 | 6,406 | -0.4 | 2.49 | 4,848 | 4,510 | -0.9 | 36,439 | 41,433 | 1055 | 47 |
| RICE | 16,347 | 18,870 | 20,344 | 1.8 | 2.64 | 11,644 | 13,027 | 1.4 | 46,532 | 54,986 | 291 | 15 |
| ROCK | 3,754 | 3,751 | 3,631 | 0.0 | 2.50 | 2,733 | 2,640 | -0.4 | 35,047 | 41,875 | 1246 | 54 |
| ROSEAU | 5,415 | 5,894 | 5,924 | 1.0 | 2.69 | 4,016 | 4,192 | 0.5 | 39,966 | 45,956 | 677 | 31 |
| ST. LOUIS | 78,901 | 78,383 | 78,135 | -0.1 | 2.40 | 51,903 | 49,616 | -0.5 | 39,204 | 42,427 | 735 | 33 |
| SCOTT | 19,367 | 29,046 | 34,915 | 5.0 | 2.95 | 15,438 | 22,627 | 4.7 | 65,451 | 79,312 | 32 | 2 |
| SHERBURNE | 13,643 | 21,832 | 26,528 | 5.9 | 2.97 | 10,715 | 16,757 | 5.6 | 57,224 | 70,522 | 100 | 6 |
| SIBLEY | 5,323 | 5,472 | 5,594 | 0.3 | 2.68 | 3,942 | 3,927 | 0.0 | 36,059 | 43,975 | 1095 | 49 |
| STEARNS | 39,776 | 44,794 | 47,083 | 1.5 | 2.78 | 27,766 | 30,352 | 1.1 | 42,964 | 50,031 | 459 | 20 |
| STEELE | 11,342 | 12,081 | 12,621 | 0.8 | 2.63 | 8,328 | 8,558 | 0.3 | 48,644 | 59,654 | 227 | 12 |
| STEVENS | 3,823 | 3,688 | 3,632 | -0.4 | 2.49 | 2,478 | 2,279 | -1.0 | 36,546 | 42,003 | 1037 | 44 |
| SWIFT | 4,268 | 4,118 | 4,005 | -0.4 | 2.38 | 2,950 | 2,705 | -1.0 | 30,167 | 33,046 | 2116 | 80 |
| TODD | 8,589 | 8,999 | 9,257 | 0.6 | 2.68 | 6,209 | 6,296 | 0.2 | 29,227 | 34,012 | 2261 | 84 |
| MINNESOTA | | | | 1.3 | 2.57 | | | 1.0 | 47,612 | 54,787 | | |
| UNITED STATES | | | | 1.4 | 2.59 | | | 1.1 | 41,914 | 49,127 | | |

| COUNTY | 2000 Per Capita Income | 2000 HH Income Base | 2000 HOUSEHOLD INCOME DISTRIBUTION (%) Less than $15,000 | $15,000 to $24,999 | $25,000 to $49,999 | $50,000 to $99,999 | $100,000 to $149,999 | $150,000 or More | 2000 AVERAGE DISPOSABLE INCOME BY AGE OF HOUSEHOLDER All Ages | <35 | 35-44 | 45-54 | 55-64 | 65+ |
|---|---|---|---|---|---|---|---|---|---|---|---|---|---|---|
| AITKIN | 16,506 | 6,169 | 19.1 | 22.0 | 35.6 | 18.5 | 3.4 | 1.4 | 29,078 | 26,435 | 34,157 | 41,160 | 32,747 | 19,722 |
| ANOKA | 24,227 | 104,381 | 4.7 | 4.2 | 29.1 | 45.4 | 13.3 | 3.3 | 48,784 | 43,077 | 51,371 | 59,119 | 51,538 | 30,049 |
| BECKER | 17,227 | 11,337 | 16.9 | 17.9 | 38.2 | 21.1 | 4.4 | 1.6 | 31,307 | 26,465 | 36,920 | 38,554 | 36,099 | 21,748 |
| BELTRAMI | 14,928 | 13,900 | 18.4 | 15.6 | 36.9 | 23.8 | 4.1 | 1.1 | 31,110 | 25,056 | 35,597 | 39,906 | 35,750 | 22,279 |
| BENTON | 18,922 | 12,935 | 11.5 | 11.0 | 38.5 | 31.0 | 6.4 | 1.6 | 36,916 | 33,159 | 41,823 | 48,213 | 42,524 | 21,765 |
| BIG STONE | 15,353 | 2,203 | 19.2 | 21.0 | 40.0 | 16.3 | 2.9 | 0.7 | 27,130 | 24,279 | 30,684 | 35,370 | 32,142 | 20,270 |
| BLUE EARTH | 19,119 | 19,515 | 13.2 | 12.9 | 36.7 | 28.4 | 6.5 | 2.4 | 36,713 | 28,464 | 41,908 | 50,801 | 44,124 | 27,846 |
| BROWN | 18,555 | 10,333 | 11.6 | 13.5 | 39.0 | 30.2 | 4.9 | 0.8 | 34,554 | 32,383 | 40,623 | 45,181 | 36,558 | 24,230 |
| CARLTON | 18,581 | 11,729 | 15.2 | 10.9 | 36.4 | 30.2 | 5.7 | 1.6 | 35,502 | 33,023 | 43,717 | 44,704 | 38,336 | 20,873 |
| CARVER | 31,250 | 24,097 | 5.1 | 4.0 | 26.1 | 40.0 | 16.1 | 8.8 | 57,718 | 49,821 | 60,278 | 65,788 | 59,413 | 31,861 |
| CASS | 16,132 | 10,781 | 18.4 | 19.9 | 35.7 | 20.9 | 3.9 | 1.3 | 29,970 | 26,572 | 34,900 | 38,915 | 33,198 | 21,470 |
| CHIPPEWA | 18,481 | 5,245 | 16.2 | 14.3 | 38.2 | 25.6 | 4.3 | 1.3 | 32,785 | 29,388 | 38,755 | 43,868 | 37,389 | 22,711 |
| CHISAGO | 21,697 | 15,337 | 9.9 | 6.6 | 32.3 | 39.4 | 9.9 | 2.0 | 42,137 | 38,790 | 47,607 | 51,291 | 45,289 | 24,831 |
| CLAY | 18,515 | 18,353 | 15.1 | 11.0 | 36.6 | 29.1 | 6.2 | 2.0 | 36,054 | 27,257 | 41,962 | 48,084 | 43,350 | 26,199 |
| CLEARWATER | 14,151 | 3,109 | 21.6 | 18.9 | 36.7 | 19.8 | 2.5 | 0.5 | 27,307 | 25,399 | 33,760 | 35,546 | 31,185 | 17,130 |
| COOK | 21,540 | 2,126 | 10.7 | 15.5 | 42.1 | 24.9 | 4.8 | 2.0 | 34,539 | 28,267 | 33,979 | 42,444 | 39,469 | 27,449 |
| COTTONWOOD | 15,110 | 4,824 | 17.9 | 18.7 | 40.9 | 20.5 | 2.0 | 0.0 | 27,950 | 25,782 | 33,242 | 32,834 | 32,999 | 21,601 |
| CROW WING | 19,406 | 21,031 | 15.2 | 15.8 | 36.4 | 25.7 | 5.0 | 2.0 | 33,994 | 29,130 | 39,826 | 44,941 | 38,074 | 22,303 |
| DAKOTA | 29,967 | 130,188 | 3.8 | 4.2 | 25.3 | 44.9 | 15.8 | 6.0 | 54,077 | 45,695 | 55,869 | 64,429 | 56,955 | 33,490 |
| DODGE | 19,678 | 6,272 | 10.3 | 9.8 | 37.4 | 34.6 | 6.4 | 1.6 | 38,240 | 35,493 | 43,349 | 48,098 | 42,097 | 23,227 |
| DOUGLAS | 17,551 | 12,331 | 15.7 | 14.0 | 38.3 | 26.6 | 4.6 | 0.9 | 32,696 | 29,341 | 38,853 | 43,325 | 36,095 | 21,832 |
| FARIBAULT | 16,672 | 6,546 | 16.7 | 18.7 | 39.0 | 21.8 | 2.9 | 0.8 | 29,610 | 24,984 | 33,676 | 38,087 | 35,093 | 23,237 |
| FILLMORE | 15,244 | 7,956 | 19.1 | 16.2 | 39.7 | 21.3 | 3.0 | 0.7 | 29,165 | 27,785 | 34,191 | 38,342 | 33,590 | 20,245 |
| FREEBORN | 16,702 | 12,570 | 15.1 | 15.7 | 39.9 | 25.9 | 2.8 | 0.6 | 30,838 | 28,599 | 35,761 | 38,920 | 35,613 | 21,529 |
| GOODHUE | 23,415 | 16,652 | 11.3 | 9.2 | 33.9 | 32.9 | 8.8 | 4.0 | 42,334 | 36,903 | 47,577 | 55,534 | 47,203 | 26,302 |
| GRANT | 16,672 | 2,461 | 17.9 | 17.8 | 35.8 | 24.1 | 3.7 | 0.7 | 30,273 | 28,754 | 36,217 | 38,922 | 35,142 | 21,584 |
| HENNEPIN | 32,993 | 438,305 | 8.4 | 8.7 | 29.1 | 34.3 | 11.6 | 7.8 | 51,201 | 39,788 | 53,419 | 61,641 | 55,494 | 32,845 |
| HOUSTON | 18,968 | 7,283 | 12.5 | 13.4 | 37.8 | 29.3 | 5.9 | 1.3 | 35,199 | 33,191 | 39,849 | 46,499 | 39,208 | 22,346 |
| HUBBARD | 15,961 | 6,881 | 17.9 | 17.9 | 38.2 | 21.6 | 3.7 | 0.7 | 29,443 | 26,305 | 35,854 | 39,639 | 31,877 | 19,339 |
| ISANTI | 19,873 | 10,932 | 8.7 | 7.8 | 34.7 | 38.9 | 8.4 | 1.6 | 40,740 | 36,100 | 45,076 | 51,718 | 44,422 | 26,038 |
| ITASCA | 17,585 | 17,126 | 17.3 | 14.5 | 37.6 | 25.0 | 4.2 | 1.3 | 32,350 | 27,787 | 38,711 | 42,710 | 34,710 | 20,729 |
| JACKSON | 16,888 | 4,527 | 17.0 | 17.7 | 40.3 | 21.2 | 3.2 | 0.8 | 30,113 | 26,103 | 34,648 | 38,265 | 34,275 | 23,383 |
| KANABEC | 15,370 | 5,481 | 18.5 | 14.4 | 39.4 | 23.9 | 3.2 | 0.6 | 30,205 | 28,587 | 34,723 | 39,240 | 34,580 | 18,100 |
| KANDIYOHI | 19,749 | 15,396 | 14.6 | 10.9 | 37.0 | 29.2 | 6.5 | 1.8 | 36,204 | 30,443 | 42,620 | 47,435 | 40,881 | 24,170 |
| KITTSON | 15,865 | 2,103 | 20.9 | 17.0 | 38.4 | 20.0 | 2.9 | 0.9 | 28,562 | 23,956 | 35,361 | 37,775 | 32,661 | 20,089 |
| KOOCHICHING | 20,298 | 5,774 | 16.6 | 13.9 | 32.7 | 29.9 | 4.9 | 2.0 | 34,835 | 32,927 | 41,197 | 46,496 | 34,607 | 21,345 |
| LAC QUI PARLE | 16,121 | 3,142 | 17.4 | 18.0 | 39.0 | 23.0 | 2.5 | 0.1 | 28,849 | 27,627 | 32,677 | 34,610 | 33,814 | 22,800 |
| LAKE | 20,159 | 4,375 | 11.0 | 14.5 | 40.5 | 28.2 | 4.7 | 1.2 | 34,528 | 31,112 | 40,370 | 44,744 | 38,952 | 23,330 |
| LAKE OF THE WOODS | 16,563 | 1,810 | 14.4 | 13.2 | 41.4 | 27.9 | 3.0 | 0.2 | 31,892 | 29,886 | 37,269 | 38,913 | 35,783 | 20,118 |
| LE SUEUR | 20,327 | 9,621 | 10.9 | 10.5 | 36.6 | 32.4 | 7.7 | 1.8 | 38,374 | 35,842 | 43,434 | 50,871 | 42,297 | 24,186 |
| LINCOLN | 14,484 | 2,530 | 23.0 | 20.6 | 35.6 | 17.6 | 2.5 | 0.8 | 26,906 | 25,000 | 32,674 | 36,988 | 32,276 | 19,085 |
| LYON | 19,146 | 9,162 | 14.4 | 12.0 | 36.5 | 29.2 | 6.1 | 1.9 | 35,914 | 31,441 | 41,261 | 47,383 | 40,909 | 23,778 |
| MCLEOD | 21,582 | 12,952 | 10.2 | 8.4 | 35.4 | 36.4 | 7.9 | 1.7 | 39,832 | 36,306 | 45,834 | 53,577 | 42,106 | 25,305 |
| MAHNOMEN | 12,809 | 1,839 | 24.5 | 19.6 | 34.4 | 18.6 | 2.4 | 0.5 | 26,498 | 22,569 | 32,804 | 34,871 | 29,531 | 19,621 |
| MARSHALL | 16,090 | 3,954 | 17.1 | 16.3 | 39.3 | 24.0 | 3.0 | 0.3 | 30,078 | 28,555 | 36,554 | 37,346 | 34,182 | 20,770 |
| MARTIN | 18,146 | 8,801 | 13.8 | 13.4 | 41.9 | 26.0 | 4.1 | 0.9 | 32,760 | 28,740 | 36,873 | 41,670 | 39,201 | 23,942 |
| MEEKER | 18,435 | 8,223 | 13.8 | 12.7 | 37.4 | 28.9 | 5.8 | 1.5 | 34,955 | 31,545 | 42,199 | 45,612 | 39,390 | 22,083 |
| MILLE LACS | 16,573 | 8,201 | 16.8 | 15.2 | 39.4 | 22.3 | 4.7 | 1.7 | 32,222 | 30,612 | 38,777 | 43,132 | 34,231 | 19,252 |
| MORRISON | 15,544 | 10,971 | 18.5 | 15.3 | 37.4 | 24.2 | 3.6 | 1.1 | 30,857 | 28,371 | 36,373 | 40,772 | 34,442 | 18,814 |
| MOWER | 18,988 | 15,082 | 14.1 | 14.0 | 38.0 | 28.0 | 4.8 | 1.1 | 33,812 | 32,111 | 40,796 | 44,716 | 36,103 | 23,629 |
| MURRAY | 15,703 | 3,754 | 18.7 | 16.5 | 39.9 | 21.9 | 2.5 | 0.5 | 28,755 | 25,605 | 33,611 | 35,469 | 33,838 | 22,485 |
| NICOLLET | 21,452 | 10,227 | 8.3 | 8.7 | 35.7 | 36.0 | 8.7 | 2.7 | 41,793 | 34,828 | 47,537 | 51,910 | 47,235 | 28,860 |
| NOBLES | 16,081 | 7,365 | 16.9 | 17.8 | 40.0 | 20.7 | 3.6 | 1.0 | 30,087 | 26,803 | 35,194 | 38,235 | 31,860 | 22,545 |
| NORMAN | 14,315 | 2,948 | 20.8 | 18.7 | 38.2 | 19.8 | 2.3 | 0.2 | 27,328 | 26,766 | 31,254 | 35,501 | 31,527 | 20,280 |
| OLMSTED | 25,888 | 45,925 | 8.3 | 7.6 | 30.1 | 37.6 | 11.4 | 4.9 | 47,003 | 38,549 | 50,750 | 59,701 | 51,224 | 29,793 |
| OTTER TAIL | 18,301 | 22,007 | 15.5 | 16.6 | 38.3 | 23.4 | 4.5 | 1.7 | 32,640 | 28,849 | 37,832 | 44,143 | 36,692 | 21,770 |
| PENNINGTON | 18,630 | 5,380 | 17.1 | 14.8 | 38.3 | 23.0 | 4.9 | 1.9 | 32,743 | 26,373 | 39,804 | 45,569 | 33,564 | 21,710 |
| PINE | 16,089 | 9,033 | 16.7 | 15.1 | 40.3 | 22.0 | 4.6 | 1.4 | 31,695 | 30,047 | 38,108 | 41,705 | 34,763 | 19,268 |
| PIPESTONE | 16,240 | 3,948 | 18.8 | 16.2 | 38.8 | 21.9 | 3.6 | 0.7 | 29,638 | 26,552 | 33,482 | 40,667 | 34,572 | 22,543 |
| POLK | 15,914 | 11,283 | 16.9 | 16.1 | 38.3 | 24.2 | 3.8 | 0.6 | 30,798 | 26,835 | 36,230 | 39,560 | 33,667 | 22,123 |
| POPE | 16,623 | 4,228 | 15.6 | 19.2 | 38.5 | 21.3 | 4.0 | 1.5 | 31,184 | 30,691 | 37,741 | 40,355 | 35,660 | 21,238 |
| RAMSEY | 24,097 | 193,854 | 11.9 | 11.8 | 33.2 | 31.8 | 7.6 | 3.8 | 40,781 | 33,310 | 43,900 | 52,211 | 46,040 | 26,923 |
| RED LAKE | 14,814 | 1,645 | 19.6 | 18.3 | 38.0 | 20.9 | 3.0 | 0.2 | 28,179 | 26,349 | 33,979 | 34,346 | 31,891 | 19,652 |
| REDWOOD | 17,089 | 6,287 | 14.8 | 15.1 | 39.2 | 25.7 | 4.5 | 0.8 | 32,341 | 30,681 | 37,534 | 40,871 | 36,300 | 23,776 |
| RENVILLE | 17,246 | 6,550 | 14.5 | 14.8 | 40.2 | 26.2 | 3.7 | 0.6 | 31,989 | 29,716 | 35,844 | 41,496 | 38,718 | 23,034 |
| RICE | 21,304 | 18,870 | 10.6 | 10.8 | 32.9 | 33.4 | 8.9 | 3.3 | 41,493 | 35,251 | 48,059 | 52,393 | 45,488 | 24,557 |
| ROCK | 17,472 | 3,751 | 17.1 | 13.8 | 40.1 | 23.6 | 4.3 | 1.2 | 31,648 | 31,069 | 36,497 | 41,328 | 36,556 | 22,431 |
| ROSEAU | 16,340 | 5,894 | 12.4 | 11.5 | 42.4 | 29.7 | 3.8 | 0.2 | 33,252 | 32,061 | 37,413 | 42,661 | 36,725 | 20,277 |
| ST. LOUIS | 20,451 | 78,383 | 16.1 | 12.1 | 36.0 | 27.7 | 5.9 | 2.1 | 35,436 | 29,687 | 42,801 | 46,940 | 38,434 | 23,558 |
| SCOTT | 28,514 | 29,046 | 5.3 | 3.8 | 23.3 | 43.5 | 17.4 | 6.8 | 55,727 | 50,411 | 58,651 | 65,296 | 54,256 | 29,613 |
| SHERBURNE | 22,812 | 21,832 | 5.6 | 5.5 | 29.3 | 43.6 | 12.8 | 3.2 | 47,355 | 40,642 | 51,953 | 56,831 | 50,782 | 28,751 |
| SIBLEY | 15,933 | 5,472 | 15.0 | 14.6 | 40.0 | 26.3 | 3.5 | 0.6 | 31,581 | 29,737 | 36,407 | 41,206 | 35,894 | 21,800 |
| STEARNS | 19,447 | 44,794 | 10.3 | 11.8 | 37.1 | 31.3 | 7.3 | 2.2 | 38,368 | 33,258 | 44,694 | 48,964 | 42,762 | 24,805 |
| STEELE | 21,743 | 12,081 | 8.4 | 8.6 | 35.0 | 37.7 | 8.5 | 1.9 | 40,884 | 37,242 | 46,848 | 51,073 | 45,963 | 26,990 |
| STEVENS | 17,195 | 3,688 | 16.7 | 14.6 | 38.6 | 24.7 | 4.4 | 1.0 | 32,066 | 27,272 | 39,080 | 44,172 | 36,475 | 23,528 |
| SWIFT | 14,690 | 4,118 | 18.8 | 18.9 | 41.5 | 17.7 | 2.6 | 0.6 | 27,397 | 26,737 | 33,226 | 37,452 | 30,029 | 19,437 |
| TODD | 13,127 | 8,999 | 22.7 | 18.4 | 37.6 | 18.2 | 2.5 | 0.5 | 26,676 | 25,446 | 33,493 | 35,651 | 29,274 | 16,569 |
| MINNESOTA | 24,804 | | 10.5 | 10.0 | 32.2 | 33.5 | 9.5 | 4.3 | 43,593 | 36,990 | 48,415 | 54,568 | 46,928 | 26,595 |
| UNITED STATES | 22,162 | | 14.5 | 12.5 | 32.3 | 29.8 | 7.4 | 3.5 | 40,748 | 34,503 | 44,969 | 49,579 | 43,409 | 27,339 |

| COUNTY | FINANCIAL SERVICES | | | | THE HOME | | | | | | ENTERTAINMENT | | | | | | PERSONAL | | | |
|---|---|---|---|---|---|---|---|---|---|---|---|---|---|---|---|---|---|---|---|---|
| | | | | | Home Improvements | | | Furnishings | | | | | | | | | | | | |
| | Auto Loan | Home Loan | Invest-ments | Retire-ment Plans | Home Repair | Lawn & Garden | Remodel-ing | Appli-ances | Elec-tronics | Furni-ture | Restau-rants | Sport-ing Goods | Theater & Concerts | Toys & Hobbies | Travel | Video Rental | Apparel | Auto After-market | Health Insur-ance | Pets & Supplies |
| AITKIN | 99 | 70 | 77 | 85 | 93 | 92 | 120 | 98 | 92 | 77 | 82 | 96 | 84 | 97 | 80 | 101 | 81 | 91 | 106 | 99 |
| ANOKA | 101 | 104 | 91 | 98 | 98 | 98 | 98 | 100 | 103 | 104 | 109 | 102 | 104 | 103 | 97 | 104 | 103 | 105 | 98 | 103 |
| BECKER | 98 | 72 | 78 | 85 | 93 | 92 | 114 | 97 | 93 | 79 | 84 | 96 | 86 | 97 | 81 | 101 | 82 | 92 | 105 | 99 |
| BELTRAMI | 97 | 87 | 85 | 89 | 96 | 92 | 102 | 96 | 94 | 89 | 91 | 95 | 92 | 97 | 88 | 100 | 89 | 96 | 99 | 98 |
| BENTON | 96 | 86 | 86 | 87 | 94 | 93 | 103 | 96 | 94 | 88 | 93 | 94 | 92 | 97 | 87 | 100 | 88 | 95 | 99 | 98 |
| BIG STONE | 96 | 64 | 71 | 78 | 90 | 90 | 109 | 94 | 91 | 73 | 78 | 92 | 80 | 93 | 76 | 100 | 77 | 89 | 105 | 95 |
| BLUE EARTH | 96 | 88 | 91 | 91 | 96 | 93 | 102 | 93 | 92 | 86 | 91 | 93 | 90 | 96 | 88 | 98 | 88 | 94 | 100 | 97 |
| BROWN | 97 | 79 | 88 | 88 | 96 | 94 | 106 | 96 | 93 | 85 | 88 | 95 | 91 | 97 | 86 | 101 | 86 | 93 | 104 | 98 |
| CARLTON | 99 | 76 | 82 | 85 | 95 | 92 | 112 | 97 | 94 | 84 | 88 | 95 | 89 | 98 | 82 | 101 | 85 | 93 | 103 | 99 |
| CARVER | 102 | 102 | 87 | 98 | 96 | 97 | 103 | 101 | 103 | 102 | 108 | 104 | 103 | 104 | 94 | 104 | 103 | 105 | 99 | 104 |
| CASS | 99 | 71 | 75 | 84 | 93 | 91 | 119 | 97 | 92 | 77 | 82 | 97 | 84 | 97 | 80 | 101 | 81 | 91 | 106 | 100 |
| CHIPPEWA | 97 | 72 | 81 | 83 | 93 | 92 | 107 | 95 | 92 | 78 | 84 | 94 | 86 | 95 | 81 | 100 | 81 | 91 | 104 | 97 |
| CHISAGO | 100 | 88 | 85 | 91 | 95 | 93 | 109 | 99 | 99 | 93 | 97 | 99 | 96 | 102 | 87 | 103 | 94 | 99 | 101 | 102 |
| CLAY | 97 | 92 | 89 | 92 | 97 | 94 | 100 | 95 | 95 | 91 | 95 | 95 | 94 | 97 | 91 | 100 | 91 | 97 | 99 | 99 |
| CLEARWATER | 97 | 67 | 73 | 80 | 91 | 90 | 111 | 95 | 92 | 76 | 81 | 94 | 82 | 95 | 77 | 100 | 79 | 90 | 104 | 97 |
| COOK | 100 | 72 | 76 | 87 | 93 | 92 | 123 | 99 | 93 | 78 | 83 | 99 | 86 | 100 | 80 | 102 | 83 | 93 | 107 | 102 |
| COTTONWOOD | 97 | 71 | 83 | 84 | 94 | 94 | 106 | 96 | 91 | 78 | 83 | 95 | 86 | 95 | 82 | 100 | 81 | 91 | 106 | 96 |
| CROW WING | 99 | 82 | 87 | 91 | 96 | 95 | 113 | 98 | 95 | 86 | 90 | 98 | 92 | 99 | 87 | 102 | 88 | 95 | 104 | 100 |
| DAKOTA | 103 | 110 | 91 | 103 | 98 | 100 | 99 | 102 | 105 | 108 | 114 | 106 | 107 | 105 | 99 | 105 | 108 | 108 | 98 | 104 |
| DODGE | 100 | 86 | 85 | 91 | 95 | 93 | 108 | 98 | 97 | 90 | 94 | 98 | 94 | 100 | 86 | 103 | 91 | 97 | 102 | 101 |
| DOUGLAS | 98 | 78 | 82 | 87 | 94 | 93 | 110 | 97 | 94 | 84 | 87 | 96 | 90 | 97 | 84 | 101 | 85 | 94 | 103 | 99 |
| FARIBAULT | 96 | 64 | 71 | 78 | 90 | 89 | 108 | 94 | 91 | 73 | 78 | 91 | 80 | 93 | 76 | 100 | 77 | 89 | 105 | 95 |
| FILLMORE | 97 | 64 | 70 | 79 | 90 | 90 | 109 | 95 | 90 | 72 | 78 | 94 | 80 | 94 | 75 | 100 | 78 | 89 | 106 | 96 |
| FREEBORN | 98 | 81 | 89 | 88 | 99 | 95 | 106 | 97 | 92 | 87 | 90 | 96 | 93 | 98 | 88 | 100 | 87 | 94 | 103 | 98 |
| GOODHUE | 99 | 80 | 85 | 88 | 95 | 93 | 110 | 97 | 95 | 86 | 90 | 97 | 91 | 99 | 85 | 101 | 87 | 95 | 103 | 100 |
| GRANT | 97 | 65 | 71 | 80 | 90 | 90 | 111 | 95 | 90 | 73 | 78 | 94 | 80 | 95 | 76 | 100 | 78 | 89 | 106 | 96 |
| HENNEPIN | 100 | 111 | 105 | 107 | 104 | 105 | 99 | 100 | 102 | 106 | 109 | 103 | 108 | 103 | 106 | 103 | 105 | 106 | 100 | 102 |
| HOUSTON | 99 | 82 | 84 | 88 | 94 | 93 | 107 | 97 | 96 | 86 | 91 | 97 | 92 | 99 | 85 | 102 | 88 | 95 | 103 | 99 |
| HUBBARD | 99 | 75 | 79 | 85 | 95 | 92 | 117 | 98 | 93 | 81 | 85 | 96 | 88 | 98 | 82 | 101 | 84 | 92 | 104 | 100 |
| ISANTI | 99 | 87 | 86 | 89 | 95 | 93 | 107 | 98 | 97 | 90 | 95 | 97 | 94 | 100 | 86 | 103 | 91 | 97 | 101 | 101 |
| ITASCA | 98 | 75 | 81 | 85 | 94 | 92 | 113 | 97 | 94 | 82 | 86 | 95 | 88 | 97 | 82 | 101 | 84 | 93 | 104 | 99 |
| JACKSON | 97 | 65 | 71 | 79 | 90 | 90 | 109 | 95 | 90 | 73 | 79 | 93 | 80 | 94 | 76 | 100 | 78 | 89 | 105 | 96 |
| KANABEC | 99 | 78 | 84 | 86 | 94 | 92 | 115 | 98 | 95 | 85 | 89 | 97 | 90 | 99 | 82 | 101 | 86 | 94 | 103 | 100 |
| KANDIYOHI | 98 | 81 | 86 | 88 | 95 | 93 | 108 | 96 | 93 | 85 | 89 | 95 | 90 | 97 | 85 | 100 | 86 | 94 | 103 | 99 |
| KITTSON | 97 | 64 | 71 | 80 | 90 | 90 | 110 | 95 | 90 | 72 | 79 | 95 | 80 | 95 | 75 | 100 | 78 | 89 | 106 | 97 |
| KOOCHICHING | 97 | 79 | 85 | 85 | 96 | 93 | 112 | 97 | 92 | 85 | 88 | 95 | 90 | 98 | 85 | 100 | 85 | 93 | 103 | 99 |
| LAC QUI PARLE | 97 | 64 | 70 | 79 | 90 | 89 | 109 | 95 | 90 | 72 | 78 | 94 | 79 | 94 | 75 | 100 | 77 | 89 | 106 | 96 |
| LAKE | 99 | 81 | 93 | 90 | 99 | 97 | 110 | 99 | 93 | 87 | 91 | 96 | 94 | 99 | 89 | 101 | 88 | 94 | 106 | 99 |
| LAKE OF THE WOODS | 98 | 70 | 75 | 82 | 93 | 91 | 115 | 97 | 93 | 78 | 82 | 95 | 84 | 96 | 78 | 101 | 81 | 91 | 104 | 98 |
| LE SUEUR | 99 | 81 | 83 | 88 | 95 | 92 | 112 | 98 | 96 | 87 | 90 | 97 | 91 | 100 | 84 | 102 | 88 | 95 | 102 | 101 |
| LINCOLN | 97 | 64 | 70 | 79 | 90 | 89 | 109 | 95 | 90 | 72 | 78 | 94 | 79 | 94 | 75 | 100 | 77 | 89 | 106 | 96 |
| LYON | 98 | 79 | 83 | 87 | 94 | 92 | 109 | 95 | 93 | 82 | 87 | 95 | 88 | 97 | 83 | 100 | 85 | 93 | 103 | 98 |
| MCLEOD | 98 | 83 | 85 | 87 | 95 | 93 | 109 | 97 | 95 | 88 | 92 | 96 | 92 | 99 | 85 | 101 | 89 | 95 | 101 | 99 |
| MAHNOMEN | 97 | 65 | 71 | 80 | 91 | 90 | 112 | 95 | 91 | 73 | 79 | 93 | 80 | 94 | 76 | 100 | 78 | 89 | 105 | 96 |
| MARSHALL | 98 | 64 | 70 | 80 | 90 | 90 | 111 | 95 | 90 | 72 | 79 | 96 | 80 | 96 | 75 | 100 | 78 | 89 | 106 | 97 |
| MARTIN | 98 | 74 | 83 | 84 | 95 | 93 | 107 | 96 | 91 | 81 | 85 | 95 | 88 | 97 | 83 | 100 | 83 | 92 | 104 | 97 |
| MEEKER | 98 | 74 | 80 | 84 | 93 | 91 | 112 | 97 | 94 | 81 | 86 | 96 | 87 | 98 | 80 | 101 | 84 | 92 | 104 | 99 |
| MILLE LACS | 98 | 72 | 78 | 83 | 93 | 91 | 115 | 97 | 93 | 80 | 84 | 95 | 86 | 97 | 80 | 101 | 83 | 92 | 104 | 99 |
| MORRISON | 98 | 69 | 75 | 82 | 92 | 90 | 112 | 96 | 91 | 76 | 82 | 96 | 84 | 97 | 78 | 100 | 81 | 91 | 105 | 98 |
| MOWER | 97 | 82 | 93 | 88 | 99 | 97 | 103 | 97 | 92 | 88 | 90 | 94 | 93 | 97 | 90 | 100 | 87 | 94 | 103 | 97 |
| MURRAY | 98 | 64 | 70 | 80 | 90 | 90 | 111 | 95 | 90 | 71 | 78 | 96 | 80 | 95 | 75 | 100 | 78 | 89 | 106 | 97 |
| NICOLLET | 99 | 93 | 90 | 93 | 97 | 95 | 105 | 97 | 98 | 94 | 98 | 98 | 97 | 100 | 91 | 101 | 94 | 99 | 100 | 101 |
| NOBLES | 97 | 78 | 88 | 88 | 96 | 94 | 106 | 96 | 92 | 83 | 87 | 95 | 90 | 97 | 86 | 100 | 85 | 93 | 104 | 97 |
| NORMAN | 97 | 64 | 70 | 79 | 90 | 89 | 109 | 95 | 90 | 72 | 78 | 94 | 79 | 94 | 75 | 100 | 77 | 89 | 106 | 96 |
| OLMSTED | 101 | 106 | 101 | 104 | 102 | 103 | 102 | 101 | 102 | 104 | 108 | 103 | 106 | 104 | 102 | 103 | 104 | 105 | 101 | 103 |
| OTTER TAIL | 98 | 76 | 82 | 87 | 94 | 93 | 111 | 97 | 93 | 81 | 86 | 96 | 88 | 97 | 83 | 101 | 84 | 93 | 104 | 99 |
| PENNINGTON | 96 | 76 | 81 | 82 | 94 | 91 | 107 | 95 | 92 | 83 | 86 | 92 | 87 | 95 | 82 | 100 | 83 | 91 | 102 | 96 |
| PINE | 98 | 70 | 75 | 82 | 92 | 91 | 115 | 97 | 92 | 78 | 82 | 95 | 84 | 96 | 79 | 101 | 81 | 91 | 105 | 98 |
| PIPESTONE | 97 | 65 | 71 | 79 | 90 | 90 | 110 | 95 | 91 | 73 | 79 | 94 | 81 | 94 | 76 | 100 | 78 | 89 | 105 | 96 |
| POLK | 96 | 77 | 82 | 83 | 94 | 91 | 105 | 95 | 91 | 82 | 86 | 93 | 88 | 95 | 82 | 100 | 83 | 91 | 102 | 96 |
| POPE | 98 | 66 | 72 | 81 | 91 | 90 | 113 | 96 | 91 | 73 | 79 | 95 | 81 | 95 | 76 | 101 | 79 | 90 | 106 | 97 |
| RAMSEY | 98 | 104 | 101 | 100 | 102 | 101 | 97 | 98 | 98 | 101 | 103 | 98 | 103 | 99 | 101 | 102 | 99 | 102 | 99 | 100 |
| RED LAKE | 98 | 67 | 73 | 82 | 91 | 90 | 112 | 96 | 91 | 74 | 81 | 96 | 82 | 97 | 76 | 101 | 80 | 90 | 106 | 98 |
| REDWOOD | 98 | 68 | 74 | 81 | 91 | 90 | 110 | 96 | 91 | 75 | 81 | 96 | 83 | 96 | 77 | 101 | 80 | 90 | 105 | 98 |
| RENVILLE | 97 | 66 | 72 | 80 | 90 | 90 | 109 | 95 | 90 | 73 | 79 | 95 | 81 | 95 | 76 | 100 | 78 | 89 | 105 | 97 |
| RICE | 99 | 90 | 91 | 94 | 97 | 95 | 107 | 98 | 97 | 92 | 96 | 97 | 96 | 100 | 90 | 102 | 93 | 98 | 101 | 100 |
| ROCK | 99 | 75 | 85 | 86 | 96 | 94 | 109 | 97 | 92 | 81 | 86 | 97 | 89 | 98 | 84 | 101 | 84 | 92 | 105 | 99 |
| ROSEAU | 99 | 76 | 80 | 84 | 94 | 91 | 114 | 98 | 94 | 83 | 88 | 97 | 88 | 99 | 80 | 102 | 85 | 93 | 103 | 100 |
| ST. LOUIS | 96 | 86 | 93 | 89 | 99 | 96 | 102 | 96 | 93 | 90 | 92 | 93 | 94 | 97 | 91 | 100 | 88 | 95 | 101 | 97 |
| SCOTT | 103 | 106 | 92 | 103 | 99 | 100 | 103 | 102 | 105 | 106 | 111 | 105 | 107 | 106 | 98 | 105 | 107 | 108 | 100 | 105 |
| SHERBURNE | 101 | 100 | 84 | 95 | 95 | 94 | 101 | 99 | 102 | 100 | 106 | 101 | 100 | 103 | 92 | 104 | 100 | 104 | 98 | 103 |
| SIBLEY | 98 | 69 | 75 | 82 | 91 | 90 | 112 | 96 | 92 | 76 | 82 | 96 | 83 | 97 | 77 | 101 | 81 | 91 | 105 | 98 |
| STEARNS | 98 | 91 | 86 | 91 | 95 | 93 | 101 | 96 | 95 | 90 | 95 | 96 | 94 | 98 | 88 | 101 | 91 | 97 | 100 | 99 |
| STEELE | 98 | 87 | 89 | 89 | 97 | 94 | 105 | 97 | 96 | 91 | 95 | 96 | 95 | 99 | 89 | 101 | 91 | 96 | 101 | 99 |
| STEVENS | 96 | 69 | 74 | 80 | 90 | 88 | 108 | 93 | 89 | 73 | 80 | 92 | 80 | 93 | 77 | 98 | 78 | 89 | 103 | 95 |
| SWIFT | 96 | 64 | 70 | 78 | 90 | 89 | 108 | 94 | 90 | 72 | 78 | 93 | 79 | 93 | 75 | 100 | 77 | 89 | 105 | 95 |
| TODD | 98 | 68 | 75 | 82 | 91 | 91 | 112 | 96 | 91 | 75 | 81 | 95 | 83 | 96 | 78 | 101 | 80 | 90 | 106 | 97 |
| MINNESOTA | 100 | 98 | 94 | 98 | 99 | 99 | 102 | 99 | 99 | 97 | 101 | 100 | 101 | 101 | 96 | 102 | 97 | 101 | 101 | 101 |
| UNITED STATES | 100 | 100 | 100 | 100 | 100 | 100 | 100 | 100 | 100 | 100 | 100 | 100 | 100 | 100 | 100 | 100 | 100 | 100 | 100 | 100 |

# POPULATION CHANGE

| COUNTY | FIPS Code | MSA Code | DMA Code | POPULATION 1990 | POPULATION 2000 | POPULATION 2005 | 1990-2000 ANNUAL CHANGE % Rate | 1990-2000 ANNUAL CHANGE State Rank | RACE (%) White 1990 | White 2000 | Black 1990 | Black 2000 | Asian/Pacific 1990 | Asian/Pacific 2000 |
|---|---|---|---|---|---|---|---|---|---|---|---|---|---|---|
| TRAVERSE | 155 | 0000 | 613 | 4,463 | 4,121 | 3,895 | -0.8 | 80 | 96.8 | 96.5 | 0.0 | 0.0 | 0.4 | 0.5 |
| WABASHA | 157 | 0000 | 613 | 19,744 | 21,322 | 22,268 | 0.8 | 28 | 99.2 | 98.8 | 0.1 | 0.1 | 0.5 | 0.7 |
| WADENA | 159 | 0000 | 613 | 13,154 | 13,297 | 13,647 | 0.1 | 49 | 99.0 | 98.8 | 0.1 | 0.1 | 0.3 | 0.4 |
| WASECA | 161 | 0000 | 613 | 18,079 | 18,614 | 18,848 | 0.3 | 43 | 98.9 | 98.3 | 0.1 | 0.3 | 0.4 | 0.7 |
| WASHINGTON | 163 | 5120 | 613 | 145,896 | 208,217 | 235,619 | 3.5 | 5 | 96.8 | 95.6 | 1.1 | 1.4 | 1.1 | 1.8 |
| WATONWAN | 165 | 0000 | 737 | 11,682 | 11,540 | 11,502 | -0.1 | 55 | 95.2 | 92.7 | 0.1 | 0.1 | 0.5 | 0.7 |
| WILKIN | 167 | 0000 | 724 | 7,516 | 7,242 | 7,022 | -0.4 | 67 | 98.8 | 98.3 | 0.0 | 0.0 | 0.3 | 0.6 |
| WINONA | 169 | 0000 | 702 | 47,828 | 47,608 | 46,689 | 0.0 | 52 | 98.0 | 97.2 | 0.4 | 0.6 | 1.1 | 1.7 |
| WRIGHT | 171 | 5120 | 613 | 68,710 | 90,323 | 102,634 | 2.7 | 6 | 99.0 | 98.6 | 0.1 | 0.2 | 0.4 | 0.6 |
| YELLOW MEDICINE | 173 | 0000 | 613 | 11,684 | 11,211 | 10,730 | -0.4 | 67 | 98.4 | 97.9 | 0.0 | 0.0 | 0.2 | 0.3 |
| MINNESOTA | | | | | | | 0.9 | | 94.4 | 92.5 | 2.2 | 2.9 | 1.8 | 2.7 |
| UNITED STATES | | | | | | | 1.0 | | 80.3 | 77.9 | 12.1 | 12.4 | 2.9 | 3.9 |

| COUNTY | % HISPANIC ORIGIN 1990 | % HISPANIC ORIGIN 2000 | 2000 AGE DISTRIBUTION (%) 0-4 | 5-9 | 10-14 | 15-19 | 20-24 | 25-44 | 45-64 | 65-84 | 85+ | 18+ | MEDIAN AGE 1990 | MEDIAN AGE 2000 | 2000 Males/ Females (×100) |
|---|---|---|---|---|---|---|---|---|---|---|---|---|---|---|---|
| TRAVERSE | 0.2 | 0.6 | 5.7 | 6.6 | 7.9 | 7.2 | 3.8 | 19.8 | 23.6 | 20.7 | 4.6 | 74.5 | 41.3 | 44.2 | 96.1 |
| WABASHA | 0.4 | 1.1 | 6.9 | 7.4 | 8.3 | 8.2 | 5.4 | 25.1 | 23.7 | 12.7 | 2.3 | 72.2 | 34.2 | 37.6 | 98.4 |
| WADENA | 0.4 | 0.9 | 6.2 | 7.0 | 8.5 | 8.2 | 4.9 | 22.8 | 23.2 | 16.0 | 3.2 | 73.1 | 36.0 | 39.4 | 97.8 |
| WASECA | 0.7 | 1.5 | 6.3 | 7.0 | 8.7 | 8.5 | 6.0 | 26.8 | 21.5 | 12.7 | 2.4 | 73.0 | 33.2 | 36.6 | 100.9 |
| WASHINGTON | 1.3 | 2.5 | 6.9 | 7.7 | 8.8 | 8.0 | 5.6 | 31.1 | 24.3 | 6.8 | 0.8 | 71.3 | 31.5 | 34.9 | 98.9 |
| WATONWAN | 5.1 | 8.3 | 6.6 | 7.2 | 8.4 | 7.9 | 5.0 | 23.6 | 22.8 | 15.5 | 3.0 | 72.7 | 35.7 | 38.9 | 98.1 |
| WILKIN | 0.6 | 1.3 | 6.9 | 7.6 | 8.1 | 8.1 | 5.4 | 24.9 | 21.6 | 14.3 | 3.0 | 72.0 | 34.4 | 37.9 | 99.7 |
| WINONA | 0.7 | 1.5 | 5.6 | 6.1 | 7.3 | 11.3 | 10.7 | 25.8 | 20.1 | 11.0 | 2.1 | 76.7 | 30.2 | 33.1 | 96.4 |
| WRIGHT | 0.4 | 1.0 | 7.7 | 8.3 | 9.7 | 8.8 | 6.0 | 29.7 | 20.9 | 7.8 | 1.2 | 68.7 | 30.0 | 32.7 | 102.1 |
| YELLOW MEDICINE | 0.7 | 1.5 | 5.9 | 6.8 | 8.2 | 8.1 | 4.3 | 22.7 | 23.7 | 16.5 | 3.8 | 74.0 | 37.6 | 40.8 | 100.6 |
| MINNESOTA | 1.2 | 2.3 | 6.6 | 7.0 | 8.0 | 8.0 | 6.6 | 29.7 | 22.0 | 10.4 | 1.8 | 73.8 | 32.5 | 35.7 | 97.2 |
| UNITED STATES | 9.0 | 11.8 | 6.9 | 7.2 | 7.2 | 7.2 | 6.7 | 29.9 | 22.2 | 11.1 | 1.6 | 74.6 | 32.9 | 35.7 | 95.6 |

# HOUSEHOLDS

| COUNTY | HOUSEHOLDS | | | | | FAMILIES | | | MEDIAN HOUSEHOLD INCOME | | | |
|---|---|---|---|---|---|---|---|---|---|---|---|---|
| | 1990 | 2000 | 2005 | % Annual Rate 1990-2000 | 2000 Average HH Size | 1990 | 2000 | % Annual Rate 1990-2000 | 2000 | 2005 | 2000 National Rank | 2000 State Rank |
| TRAVERSE | 1,778 | 1,710 | 1,645 | -0.5 | 2.34 | 1,253 | 1,157 | -1.0 | 31,820 | 34,869 | 1755 | 75 |
| WABASHA | 7,286 | 7,961 | 8,366 | 1.1 | 2.64 | 5,387 | 5,681 | 0.6 | 40,857 | 48,440 | 602 | 24 |
| WADENA | 4,978 | 5,107 | 5,280 | 0.3 | 2.52 | 3,468 | 3,423 | -0.2 | 29,052 | 32,697 | 2290 | 85 |
| WASECA | 6,649 | 6,854 | 6,970 | 0.4 | 2.62 | 4,756 | 4,736 | -0.1 | 40,797 | 49,539 | 605 | 25 |
| WASHINGTON | 49,246 | 71,222 | 81,065 | 4.6 | 2.88 | 39,277 | 55,493 | 4.3 | 69,183 | 78,722 | 15 | 1 |
| WATONWAN | 4,530 | 4,465 | 4,453 | -0.2 | 2.54 | 3,133 | 2,961 | -0.7 | 33,115 | 40,683 | 1519 | 63 |
| WILKIN | 2,805 | 2,751 | 2,691 | -0.2 | 2.59 | 2,022 | 1,918 | -0.6 | 38,346 | 42,992 | 825 | 37 |
| WINONA | 16,930 | 17,244 | 17,053 | 0.2 | 2.55 | 11,329 | 11,170 | -0.2 | 39,061 | 44,707 | 747 | 34 |
| WRIGHT | 23,013 | 30,497 | 34,786 | 3.5 | 2.94 | 18,071 | 23,267 | 3.1 | 53,224 | 65,470 | 148 | 7 |
| YELLOW MEDICINE | 4,607 | 4,525 | 4,379 | -0.2 | 2.42 | 3,208 | 3,011 | -0.8 | 35,625 | 42,446 | 1149 | 50 |
| MINNESOTA | | | | 1.3 | 2.57 | | | 1.0 | 47,612 | 54,787 | | |
| UNITED STATES | | | | 1.4 | 2.59 | | | 1.1 | 41,914 | 49,127 | | |

| COUNTY | 2000 Per Capita Income | 2000 HH Income Base | 2000 HOUSEHOLD INCOME DISTRIBUTION (%) Less than $15,000 | $15,000 to $24,999 | $25,000 to $49,999 | $50,000 to $99,999 | $100,000 to $149,999 | $150,000 or More | 2000 AVERAGE DISPOSABLE INCOME BY AGE OF HOUSEHOLDER All Ages | <35 | 35-44 | 45-54 | 55-64 | 65+ |
|---|---|---|---|---|---|---|---|---|---|---|---|---|---|---|
| TRAVERSE | 15,552 | 1,710 | 18.4 | 18.3 | 39.1 | 22.1 | 2.1 | 0.1 | 28,077 | 26,418 | 31,773 | 34,549 | 32,758 | 22,899 |
| WABASHA | 18,968 | 7,961 | 12.6 | 11.5 | 38.6 | 30.0 | 6.0 | 1.5 | 35,975 | 32,737 | 41,802 | 46,419 | 38,569 | 23,540 |
| WADENA | 14,079 | 5,107 | 24.3 | 17.8 | 35.7 | 18.4 | 3.1 | 0.7 | 27,165 | 25,418 | 34,897 | 34,802 | 30,434 | 18,017 |
| WASECA | 17,642 | 6,854 | 14.2 | 11.3 | 37.6 | 31.5 | 4.5 | 0.9 | 34,380 | 30,734 | 39,726 | 45,059 | 36,116 | 23,625 |
| WASHINGTON | 33,676 | 71,222 | 4.6 | 3.7 | 20.7 | 43.3 | 19.3 | 8.3 | 58,930 | 48,256 | 60,702 | 67,799 | 61,352 | 35,947 |
| WATONWAN | 15,532 | 4,465 | 17.1 | 17.4 | 40.7 | 21.7 | 2.4 | 0.8 | 29,214 | 26,146 | 34,949 | 37,295 | 32,629 | 21,399 |
| WILKIN | 17,448 | 2,751 | 14.5 | 12.3 | 39.8 | 27.7 | 4.8 | 0.9 | 33,573 | 32,185 | 39,383 | 41,361 | 37,575 | 24,229 |
| WINONA | 18,691 | 17,244 | 13.7 | 13.2 | 37.9 | 27.2 | 5.8 | 2.2 | 35,586 | 28,408 | 40,549 | 48,593 | 42,118 | 23,633 |
| WRIGHT | 22,063 | 30,497 | 7.7 | 6.0 | 32.3 | 39.8 | 11.3 | 2.9 | 44,851 | 40,661 | 49,234 | 55,957 | 47,130 | 26,040 |
| YELLOW MEDICINE | 17,871 | 4,525 | 15.5 | 15.9 | 38.2 | 25.1 | 4.4 | 0.9 | 31,749 | 27,697 | 37,523 | 41,750 | 36,915 | 23,240 |
| MINNESOTA | 24,804 | | 10.5 | 10.0 | 32.2 | 33.5 | 9.5 | 4.3 | 43,593 | 36,990 | 48,415 | 54,568 | 46,928 | 26,595 |
| UNITED STATES | 22,162 | | 14.5 | 12.5 | 32.3 | 29.8 | 7.4 | 3.5 | 40,748 | 34,503 | 44,969 | 49,579 | 43,409 | 27,339 |

# SPENDING POTENTIAL INDEXES

| COUNTY | FINANCIAL SERVICES | | | | THE HOME: Home Improvements | | | THE HOME: Furnishings | | | ENTERTAINMENT | | | | | | PERSONAL | | | |
|---|---|---|---|---|---|---|---|---|---|---|---|---|---|---|---|---|---|---|---|---|
| | Auto Loan | Home Loan | Investments | Retirement Plans | Home Repair | Lawn & Garden | Remodeling | Appliances | Electronics | Furniture | Restaurants | Sporting Goods | Theater & Concerts | Toys & Hobbies | Travel | Video Rental | Apparel | Auto Aftermarket | Health Insurance | Pets & Supplies |
| TRAVERSE | 96 | 64 | 70 | 78 | 90 | 89 | 108 | 94 | 90 | 72 | 78 | 92 | 79 | 93 | 75 | 100 | 77 | 89 | 105 | 95 |
| WABASHA | 99 | 75 | 82 | 86 | 94 | 92 | 114 | 98 | 94 | 82 | 87 | 97 | 88 | 99 | 82 | 101 | 85 | 93 | 105 | 100 |
| WADENA | 96 | 67 | 73 | 79 | 91 | 90 | 108 | 94 | 91 | 75 | 80 | 92 | 81 | 93 | 77 | 100 | 78 | 89 | 104 | 95 |
| WASECA | 98 | 78 | 82 | 85 | 94 | 92 | 110 | 97 | 94 | 84 | 88 | 96 | 89 | 98 | 83 | 101 | 86 | 94 | 102 | 99 |
| WASHINGTON | 105 | 114 | 99 | 111 | 102 | 105 | 103 | 104 | 109 | 112 | 118 | 109 | 113 | 108 | 104 | 106 | 113 | 112 | 101 | 106 |
| WATONWAN | 97 | 69 | 76 | 81 | 92 | 90 | 111 | 95 | 91 | 77 | 81 | 94 | 83 | 96 | 78 | 100 | 80 | 90 | 104 | 97 |
| WILKIN | 97 | 69 | 76 | 81 | 91 | 90 | 112 | 96 | 92 | 76 | 82 | 95 | 83 | 96 | 78 | 100 | 80 | 90 | 104 | 97 |
| WINONA | 96 | 86 | 89 | 88 | 97 | 93 | 105 | 95 | 92 | 88 | 91 | 94 | 92 | 97 | 88 | 100 | 88 | 94 | 100 | 98 |
| WRIGHT | 100 | 92 | 85 | 92 | 95 | 94 | 106 | 99 | 99 | 95 | 99 | 99 | 97 | 101 | 89 | 103 | 95 | 100 | 99 | 101 |
| YELLOW MEDICINE | 97 | 66 | 73 | 81 | 91 | 90 | 109 | 95 | 90 | 74 | 80 | 95 | 82 | 96 | 77 | 100 | 79 | 90 | 106 | 97 |
| MINNESOTA | 100 | 98 | 94 | 98 | 99 | 99 | 102 | 99 | 99 | 97 | 101 | 100 | 101 | 101 | 96 | 102 | 97 | 101 | 101 | 101 |
| UNITED STATES | 100 | 100 | 100 | 100 | 100 | 100 | 100 | 100 | 100 | 100 | 100 | 100 | 100 | 100 | 100 | 100 | 100 | 100 | 100 | 100 |

| COUNTY | FIPS Code | MSA Code | DMA Code | POPULATION 1990 | 2000 | 2005 | 1990-2000 ANNUAL CHANGE % Rate | State Rank | RACE (%) White 1990 | White 2000 | Black 1990 | Black 2000 | Asian/Pacific 1990 | Asian/Pacific 2000 |
|---|---|---|---|---|---|---|---|---|---|---|---|---|---|---|
| ADAMS | 001 | 0000 | 718 | 35,356 | 33,324 | 31,698 | -0.6 | 75 | 51.0 | 48.8 | 48.7 | 50.8 | 0.2 | 0.2 |
| ALCORN | 003 | 0000 | 640 | 31,722 | 33,286 | 34,229 | 0.5 | 35 | 88.5 | 87.3 | 11.2 | 12.4 | 0.2 | 0.2 |
| AMITE | 005 | 0000 | 716 | 13,328 | 14,012 | 14,516 | 0.5 | 35 | 54.6 | 51.3 | 45.3 | 48.5 | 0.0 | 0.1 |
| ATTALA | 007 | 0000 | 718 | 18,481 | 18,319 | 18,219 | -0.1 | 63 | 60.1 | 57.8 | 39.5 | 41.8 | 0.2 | 0.2 |
| BENTON | 009 | 0000 | 640 | 8,046 | 8,114 | 8,224 | 0.1 | 53 | 60.5 | 58.7 | 39.4 | 41.2 | 0.0 | 0.1 |
| BOLIVAR | 011 | 0000 | 647 | 41,875 | 39,493 | 37,873 | -0.6 | 75 | 36.4 | 34.2 | 62.9 | 64.8 | 0.3 | 0.5 |
| CALHOUN | 013 | 0000 | 673 | 14,908 | 14,879 | 14,820 | 0.0 | 56 | 72.6 | 70.5 | 27.0 | 29.1 | 0.0 | 0.0 |
| CARROLL | 015 | 0000 | 647 | 9,237 | 9,963 | 9,957 | 0.7 | 23 | 60.2 | 57.3 | 39.6 | 42.4 | 0.1 | 0.2 |
| CHICKASAW | 017 | 0000 | 673 | 18,085 | 18,114 | 18,080 | 0.0 | 56 | 61.2 | 58.9 | 38.6 | 40.8 | 0.1 | 0.1 |
| CHOCTAW | 019 | 0000 | 673 | 9,071 | 9,373 | 9,446 | 0.3 | 46 | 69.7 | 67.6 | 30.1 | 32.1 | 0.1 | 0.2 |
| CLAIBORNE | 021 | 0000 | 718 | 11,370 | 11,658 | 11,946 | 0.2 | 51 | 17.5 | 16.8 | 82.1 | 82.9 | 0.1 | 0.2 |
| CLARKE | 023 | 0000 | 711 | 17,313 | 18,644 | 19,618 | 0.7 | 23 | 65.3 | 63.2 | 34.5 | 36.6 | 0.0 | 0.1 |
| CLAY | 025 | 0000 | 673 | 21,120 | 21,674 | 21,789 | 0.3 | 46 | 46.3 | 44.3 | 53.3 | 55.3 | 0.2 | 0.2 |
| COAHOMA | 027 | 0000 | 640 | 31,665 | 30,945 | 30,207 | -0.2 | 66 | 34.7 | 33.1 | 64.6 | 66.1 | 0.4 | 0.5 |
| COPIAH | 029 | 0000 | 718 | 27,592 | 28,998 | 29,485 | 0.5 | 35 | 49.3 | 46.8 | 50.4 | 52.9 | 0.1 | 0.1 |
| COVINGTON | 031 | 0000 | 710 | 16,527 | 18,059 | 18,928 | 0.9 | 20 | 64.7 | 61.7 | 35.1 | 38.1 | 0.1 | 0.2 |
| DESOTO | 033 | 4920 | 640 | 67,910 | 106,961 | 130,886 | 4.5 | 1 | 86.7 | 85.1 | 12.8 | 14.2 | 0.2 | 0.3 |
| FORREST | 035 | 3285 | 710 | 68,314 | 75,479 | 78,336 | 1.0 | 17 | 68.3 | 65.5 | 30.7 | 33.3 | 0.7 | 0.9 |
| FRANKLIN | 037 | 0000 | 718 | 8,377 | 8,107 | 7,848 | -0.3 | 70 | 63.1 | 61.2 | 36.8 | 38.7 | 0.0 | 0.1 |
| GEORGE | 039 | 0000 | 686 | 16,673 | 20,754 | 23,548 | 2.2 | 8 | 90.1 | 89.1 | 9.5 | 10.4 | 0.1 | 0.2 |
| GREENE | 041 | 0000 | 686 | 10,220 | 12,568 | 12,265 | 2.0 | 9 | 78.3 | 75.5 | 21.5 | 24.2 | 0.1 | 0.1 |
| GRENADA | 043 | 0000 | 647 | 21,555 | 22,501 | 22,741 | 0.4 | 42 | 58.3 | 55.3 | 41.4 | 44.2 | 0.1 | 0.2 |
| HANCOCK | 045 | 0920 | 622 | 31,760 | 42,618 | 48,145 | 2.9 | 3 | 90.1 | 88.9 | 8.7 | 9.6 | 0.5 | 0.7 |
| HARRISON | 047 | 0920 | 746 | 165,365 | 180,411 | 186,142 | 0.9 | 20 | 77.2 | 74.4 | 19.5 | 20.9 | 2.6 | 3.8 |
| HINDS | 049 | 3560 | 718 | 254,441 | 244,562 | 238,656 | -0.4 | 72 | 48.4 | 46.0 | 50.9 | 53.1 | 0.5 | 0.7 |
| HOLMES | 051 | 0000 | 718 | 21,604 | 21,629 | 21,949 | 0.0 | 56 | 24.0 | 22.9 | 75.8 | 76.8 | 0.1 | 0.2 |
| HUMPHREYS | 053 | 0000 | 718 | 12,134 | 11,139 | 10,768 | -0.8 | 79 | 31.8 | 29.9 | 67.8 | 69.5 | 0.4 | 0.5 |
| ISSAQUENA | 055 | 0000 | 718 | 1,909 | 1,630 | 1,603 | -1.5 | 82 | 43.6 | 40.7 | 56.2 | 59.0 | 0.2 | 0.2 |
| ITAWAMBA | 057 | 0000 | 673 | 20,017 | 21,087 | 21,161 | 0.5 | 35 | 92.9 | 91.9 | 6.8 | 7.7 | 0.2 | 0.2 |
| JACKSON | 059 | 0920 | 746 | 115,243 | 134,832 | 143,640 | 1.5 | 11 | 78.2 | 75.9 | 20.5 | 22.3 | 1.0 | 1.4 |
| JASPER | 061 | 0000 | 710 | 17,114 | 18,396 | 19,787 | 0.7 | 23 | 49.1 | 46.7 | 50.8 | 53.2 | 0.0 | 0.1 |
| JEFFERSON | 063 | 0000 | 718 | 8,653 | 8,343 | 8,139 | -0.4 | 72 | 13.7 | 13.0 | 86.2 | 86.9 | 0.0 | 0.1 |
| JEFFERSON DAVIS | 065 | 0000 | 718 | 14,051 | 13,719 | 13,468 | -0.2 | 66 | 45.1 | 43.0 | 54.6 | 56.6 | 0.2 | 0.3 |
| JONES | 067 | 0000 | 710 | 62,031 | 62,873 | 61,978 | 0.1 | 53 | 74.5 | 72.6 | 25.0 | 26.8 | 0.2 | 0.2 |
| KEMPER | 069 | 0000 | 711 | 10,356 | 10,473 | 10,401 | 0.1 | 53 | 42.6 | 40.0 | 55.4 | 57.7 | 0.1 | 0.1 |
| LAFAYETTE | 071 | 0000 | 640 | 31,826 | 35,190 | 36,547 | 1.0 | 17 | 72.7 | 69.5 | 25.1 | 27.6 | 2.0 | 2.8 |
| LAMAR | 073 | 3285 | 710 | 30,424 | 39,250 | 44,809 | 2.5 | 5 | 87.4 | 85.9 | 12.0 | 13.2 | 0.4 | 0.5 |
| LAUDERDALE | 075 | 0000 | 711 | 75,555 | 75,767 | 74,736 | 0.0 | 56 | 64.5 | 61.8 | 34.8 | 37.2 | 0.5 | 0.7 |
| LAWRENCE | 077 | 0000 | 718 | 12,458 | 13,136 | 13,499 | 0.5 | 35 | 66.6 | 64.4 | 33.2 | 35.4 | 0.1 | 0.2 |
| LEAKE | 079 | 0000 | 718 | 18,436 | 19,715 | 20,319 | 0.7 | 23 | 60.1 | 57.3 | 35.6 | 37.9 | 0.0 | 0.1 |
| LEE | 081 | 0000 | 673 | 65,581 | 75,893 | 79,447 | 1.4 | 13 | 78.2 | 76.0 | 21.4 | 23.4 | 0.2 | 0.3 |
| LEFLORE | 083 | 0000 | 647 | 37,341 | 36,499 | 34,960 | -0.2 | 66 | 38.9 | 36.2 | 60.6 | 63.1 | 0.3 | 0.5 |
| LINCOLN | 085 | 0000 | 718 | 30,278 | 32,333 | 33,448 | 0.6 | 29 | 69.9 | 67.6 | 29.9 | 32.1 | 0.2 | 0.2 |
| LOWNDES | 087 | 0000 | 673 | 59,308 | 60,294 | 59,121 | 0.2 | 51 | 61.9 | 59.1 | 37.2 | 39.7 | 0.5 | 0.7 |
| MADISON | 089 | 3560 | 718 | 53,794 | 76,539 | 86,348 | 3.5 | 2 | 55.4 | 52.3 | 44.1 | 47.1 | 0.4 | 0.5 |
| MARION | 091 | 0000 | 710 | 25,544 | 26,686 | 27,391 | 0.4 | 42 | 69.4 | 66.7 | 30.2 | 32.9 | 0.2 | 0.2 |
| MARSHALL | 093 | 0000 | 640 | 30,361 | 32,424 | 32,998 | 0.6 | 29 | 48.9 | 46.5 | 50.7 | 52.9 | 0.1 | 0.2 |
| MONROE | 095 | 0000 | 673 | 36,582 | 38,377 | 39,087 | 0.5 | 35 | 69.4 | 67.2 | 30.3 | 32.5 | 0.1 | 0.1 |
| MONTGOMERY | 097 | 0000 | 673 | 12,388 | 12,389 | 12,359 | 0.0 | 56 | 55.8 | 53.5 | 43.9 | 46.1 | 0.1 | 0.2 |
| NESHOBA | 099 | 0000 | 711 | 24,800 | 27,834 | 28,872 | 1.1 | 15 | 68.3 | 65.9 | 18.6 | 20.2 | 0.1 | 0.3 |
| NEWTON | 101 | 0000 | 711 | 20,291 | 21,851 | 22,433 | 0.7 | 23 | 67.5 | 65.1 | 28.7 | 31.0 | 0.0 | 0.0 |
| NOXUBEE | 103 | 0000 | 673 | 12,604 | 12,543 | 12,761 | 0.0 | 56 | 31.4 | 29.7 | 68.1 | 69.9 | 0.1 | 0.1 |
| OKTIBBEHA | 105 | 0000 | 673 | 38,375 | 39,877 | 40,430 | 0.4 | 42 | 62.7 | 59.0 | 34.3 | 37.0 | 2.7 | 3.6 |
| PANOLA | 107 | 0000 | 640 | 29,996 | 34,529 | 36,971 | 1.4 | 13 | 51.3 | 49.1 | 48.4 | 50.5 | 0.1 | 0.2 |
| PEARL RIVER | 109 | 0000 | 622 | 38,714 | 49,160 | 55,046 | 2.4 | 6 | 85.0 | 83.3 | 14.3 | 15.8 | 0.2 | 0.3 |
| PERRY | 111 | 0000 | 710 | 10,865 | 12,156 | 12,754 | 1.1 | 15 | 76.7 | 74.4 | 22.5 | 24.8 | 0.0 | 0.0 |
| PIKE | 113 | 0000 | 718 | 36,882 | 38,107 | 38,356 | 0.3 | 46 | 54.0 | 51.4 | 45.7 | 48.3 | 0.1 | 0.2 |
| PONTOTOC | 115 | 0000 | 673 | 22,237 | 26,094 | 28,141 | 1.6 | 10 | 85.1 | 82.8 | 14.6 | 16.7 | 0.1 | 0.2 |
| PRENTISS | 117 | 0000 | 673 | 23,278 | 24,658 | 25,428 | 0.6 | 29 | 88.0 | 86.5 | 11.8 | 13.3 | 0.1 | 0.1 |
| QUITMAN | 119 | 0000 | 640 | 10,490 | 9,733 | 9,499 | -0.7 | 78 | 40.5 | 38.3 | 59.0 | 61.2 | 0.2 | 0.3 |
| RANKIN | 121 | 3560 | 718 | 87,161 | 115,145 | 129,051 | 2.8 | 4 | 82.6 | 80.2 | 16.8 | 19.0 | 0.4 | 0.5 |
| SCOTT | 123 | 0000 | 718 | 24,137 | 24,854 | 24,573 | 0.3 | 46 | 61.4 | 59.2 | 38.0 | 40.1 | 0.1 | 0.1 |
| SHARKEY | 125 | 0000 | 718 | 7,066 | 6,485 | 6,198 | -0.8 | 79 | 33.1 | 30.7 | 66.3 | 68.6 | 0.3 | 0.4 |
| SIMPSON | 127 | 0000 | 718 | 23,953 | 25,427 | 25,780 | 0.6 | 29 | 67.3 | 64.5 | 32.3 | 35.0 | 0.1 | 0.1 |
| SMITH | 129 | 0000 | 718 | 14,798 | 15,569 | 16,230 | 0.5 | 35 | 77.8 | 75.9 | 21.9 | 23.8 | 0.0 | 0.1 |
| STONE | 131 | 0000 | 746 | 10,750 | 13,753 | 15,114 | 2.4 | 6 | 77.8 | 75.4 | 21.8 | 24.2 | 0.1 | 0.1 |
| SUNFLOWER | 133 | 0000 | 647 | 32,867 | 32,969 | 31,573 | 0.0 | 56 | 35.3 | 32.5 | 64.2 | 66.7 | 0.3 | 0.4 |
| TALLAHATCHIE | 135 | 0000 | 647 | 15,210 | 14,466 | 13,860 | -0.5 | 74 | 41.1 | 38.5 | 58.4 | 60.9 | 0.3 | 0.5 |
| TATE | 137 | 0000 | 640 | 21,432 | 24,879 | 27,100 | 1.5 | 11 | 65.1 | 62.4 | 34.6 | 37.2 | 0.1 | 0.2 |
| TIPPAH | 139 | 0000 | 640 | 19,523 | 21,180 | 21,712 | 0.8 | 22 | 83.2 | 82.0 | 16.6 | 17.8 | 0.1 | 0.1 |
| TISHOMINGO | 141 | 0000 | 673 | 17,683 | 18,842 | 19,334 | 0.6 | 29 | 96.2 | 95.7 | 3.6 | 4.1 | 0.1 | 0.1 |
| TUNICA | 143 | 0000 | 640 | 8,164 | 7,877 | 7,595 | -0.3 | 70 | 24.4 | 22.9 | 75.3 | 76.8 | 0.1 | 0.1 |
| UNION | 145 | 0000 | 673 | 22,085 | 24,435 | 25,934 | 1.0 | 17 | 85.1 | 83.2 | 14.5 | 16.4 | 0.1 | 0.1 |
| WALTHALL | 147 | 0000 | 718 | 14,352 | 14,143 | 13,810 | -0.1 | 63 | 57.5 | 55.3 | 42.2 | 44.3 | 0.2 | 0.3 |
| WARREN | 149 | 0000 | 718 | 47,880 | 49,130 | 49,042 | 0.3 | 46 | 60.3 | 57.7 | 39.0 | 41.4 | 0.5 | 0.7 |
| WASHINGTON | 151 | 0000 | 647 | 67,935 | 63,653 | 60,653 | -0.6 | 75 | 41.7 | 39.2 | 57.7 | 60.0 | 0.4 | 0.5 |
| WAYNE | 153 | 0000 | 710 | 19,517 | 20,903 | 22,199 | 0.7 | 23 | 64.1 | 61.1 | 35.6 | 38.5 | 0.2 | 0.2 |
| MISSISSIPPI | | | | | | | 0.8 | | 63.5 | 62.5 | 35.6 | 36.3 | 0.5 | 0.7 |
| UNITED STATES | | | | | | | 1.0 | | 80.3 | 77.9 | 12.1 | 12.4 | 2.9 | 3.9 |

# POPULATION COMPOSITION

| COUNTY | % HISPANIC ORIGIN | | 2000 AGE DISTRIBUTION (%) | | | | | | | | | | MEDIAN AGE | | 2000 Males/ Females (×100) |
|---|---|---|---|---|---|---|---|---|---|---|---|---|---|---|---|
| | 1990 | 2000 | 0-4 | 5-9 | 10-14 | 15-19 | 20-24 | 25-44 | 45-64 | 65-84 | 85+ | 18+ | 1990 | 2000 | |
| ADAMS | 0.4 | 0.7 | 7.0 | 7.2 | 7.3 | 7.7 | 6.4 | 26.6 | 22.9 | 13.1 | 1.8 | 73.7 | 33.7 | 37.0 | 84.4 |
| ALCORN | 0.4 | 0.9 | 5.8 | 6.1 | 6.7 | 6.9 | 6.3 | 28.0 | 25.2 | 12.9 | 2.0 | 77.2 | 35.5 | 38.9 | 92.0 |
| AMITE | 0.2 | 0.5 | 7.0 | 7.3 | 7.7 | 7.8 | 6.9 | 26.5 | 22.7 | 12.5 | 1.7 | 73.1 | 33.2 | 35.8 | 93.0 |
| ATTALA | 0.3 | 0.6 | 6.6 | 6.9 | 7.0 | 7.8 | 6.8 | 25.6 | 22.6 | 14.3 | 2.4 | 74.7 | 35.1 | 37.2 | 88.1 |
| BENTON | 0.5 | 0.8 | 7.2 | 7.5 | 7.8 | 7.8 | 7.3 | 26.7 | 21.3 | 12.8 | 1.6 | 72.6 | 31.7 | 34.7 | 93.4 |
| BOLIVAR | 0.9 | 1.2 | 8.8 | 8.3 | 8.4 | 10.2 | 10.1 | 25.7 | 18.0 | 8.9 | 1.6 | 68.9 | 26.4 | 27.8 | 85.7 |
| CALHOUN | 0.5 | 1.0 | 6.5 | 6.6 | 6.8 | 7.4 | 6.9 | 26.7 | 23.3 | 13.4 | 2.3 | 75.6 | 34.8 | 37.3 | 92.3 |
| CARROLL | 0.5 | 0.6 | 7.0 | 7.1 | 7.5 | 7.5 | 6.8 | 26.2 | 24.0 | 12.3 | 1.6 | 73.8 | 33.9 | 36.5 | 91.4 |
| CHICKASAW | 0.5 | 0.8 | 7.8 | 8.1 | 8.3 | 7.8 | 6.4 | 27.8 | 21.3 | 10.6 | 1.8 | 71.1 | 31.4 | 34.0 | 93.7 |
| CHOCTAW | 0.3 | 0.7 | 6.8 | 7.3 | 8.1 | 8.6 | 6.7 | 26.0 | 22.9 | 11.6 | 2.0 | 72.2 | 32.7 | 35.4 | 89.4 |
| CLAIBORNE | 0.5 | 0.6 | 7.0 | 7.1 | 7.3 | 15.4 | 14.0 | 23.1 | 16.1 | 8.6 | 1.4 | 73.6 | 24.1 | 24.7 | 85.6 |
| CLARKE | 0.4 | 0.7 | 6.9 | 7.2 | 7.4 | 7.7 | 7.0 | 27.2 | 22.4 | 12.1 | 2.1 | 73.8 | 33.1 | 35.9 | 88.8 |
| CLAY | 0.4 | 0.6 | 7.5 | 7.7 | 7.8 | 9.1 | 8.1 | 27.1 | 20.3 | 10.7 | 1.8 | 71.9 | 30.7 | 32.7 | 89.7 |
| COAHOMA | 0.9 | 1.0 | 8.8 | 8.6 | 8.7 | 9.2 | 8.2 | 25.2 | 19.0 | 10.4 | 1.9 | 68.3 | 29.0 | 29.8 | 83.4 |
| COPIAH | 0.4 | 0.6 | 7.3 | 7.3 | 7.5 | 10.5 | 7.7 | 26.3 | 20.7 | 11.0 | 1.7 | 72.6 | 30.3 | 32.8 | 90.9 |
| COVINGTON | 0.3 | 0.6 | 7.9 | 7.9 | 8.1 | 7.9 | 6.8 | 27.5 | 22.0 | 10.3 | 1.5 | 71.1 | 31.2 | 33.6 | 93.8 |
| DESOTO | 0.5 | 1.0 | 7.4 | 7.7 | 7.7 | 6.9 | 5.9 | 31.3 | 23.7 | 8.5 | 0.8 | 73.0 | 31.5 | 34.7 | 95.5 |
| FORREST | 0.7 | 1.3 | 7.0 | 6.7 | 6.4 | 9.3 | 12.4 | 28.0 | 19.0 | 9.8 | 1.4 | 75.7 | 28.8 | 30.5 | 86.9 |
| FRANKLIN | 0.3 | 0.6 | 7.4 | 7.8 | 7.5 | 8.1 | 6.0 | 26.0 | 21.9 | 13.1 | 2.1 | 72.3 | 33.6 | 36.1 | 91.2 |
| GEORGE | 0.3 | 0.8 | 7.0 | 7.3 | 7.7 | 8.3 | 7.0 | 28.3 | 23.2 | 9.9 | 1.3 | 72.8 | 30.9 | 34.4 | 96.6 |
| GREENE | 0.6 | 1.2 | 6.7 | 6.8 | 6.9 | 7.5 | 8.0 | 31.4 | 21.6 | 9.8 | 1.2 | 75.0 | 31.0 | 33.5 | 113.8 |
| GRENADA | 0.4 | 0.7 | 7.2 | 7.5 | 7.7 | 7.5 | 6.8 | 27.3 | 22.7 | 11.6 | 1.7 | 73.0 | 32.5 | 35.4 | 87.1 |
| HANCOCK | 1.7 | 2.8 | 6.7 | 6.7 | 7.3 | 7.1 | 5.9 | 26.2 | 24.8 | 14.1 | 1.2 | 75.0 | 34.5 | 38.5 | 98.2 |
| HARRISON | 1.8 | 2.8 | 7.7 | 7.4 | 7.1 | 7.6 | 7.8 | 30.5 | 20.4 | 10.3 | 1.1 | 73.6 | 30.7 | 33.2 | 98.4 |
| HINDS | 0.5 | 0.7 | 7.2 | 7.3 | 7.5 | 8.7 | 7.7 | 29.6 | 20.8 | 9.8 | 1.4 | 73.5 | 30.8 | 33.6 | 87.6 |
| HOLMES | 0.3 | 0.4 | 8.8 | 8.8 | 8.7 | 10.5 | 8.6 | 24.6 | 17.9 | 10.3 | 1.9 | 67.6 | 27.6 | 28.4 | 86.5 |
| HUMPHREYS | 0.6 | 0.6 | 9.1 | 9.3 | 8.6 | 9.5 | 8.2 | 25.7 | 18.4 | 9.5 | 1.7 | 66.8 | 27.6 | 28.8 | 87.3 |
| ISSAQUENA | 0.3 | 0.4 | 9.2 | 8.5 | 8.6 | 8.0 | 7.5 | 25.9 | 21.9 | 8.9 | 1.5 | 68.1 | 30.3 | 31.4 | 90.0 |
| ITAWAMBA | 0.5 | 1.1 | 5.8 | 6.1 | 6.6 | 7.9 | 6.1 | 27.7 | 24.9 | 13.0 | 2.0 | 77.6 | 35.1 | 38.0 | 96.7 |
| JACKSON | 0.9 | 1.7 | 7.0 | 7.3 | 7.5 | 7.5 | 7.3 | 29.3 | 23.4 | 9.8 | 1.0 | 73.6 | 31.7 | 34.8 | 97.4 |
| JASPER | 0.2 | 0.5 | 7.1 | 7.3 | 7.3 | 8.2 | 7.2 | 28.0 | 21.8 | 11.2 | 1.9 | 73.0 | 31.8 | 34.5 | 91.2 |
| JEFFERSON | 0.5 | 0.5 | 8.3 | 8.5 | 8.7 | 9.6 | 8.4 | 26.1 | 19.4 | 9.5 | 1.5 | 68.4 | 28.0 | 29.8 | 88.0 |
| JEFFERSON DAVIS | 0.3 | 0.4 | 7.2 | 7.5 | 7.9 | 8.5 | 7.5 | 26.7 | 21.3 | 11.6 | 1.7 | 72.1 | 31.2 | 33.8 | 88.9 |
| JONES | 0.3 | 0.7 | 6.5 | 6.8 | 7.1 | 8.2 | 6.6 | 27.4 | 22.9 | 12.5 | 1.9 | 74.9 | 33.6 | 36.6 | 92.0 |
| KEMPER | 0.3 | 0.4 | 7.1 | 7.3 | 7.4 | 10.0 | 7.9 | 25.7 | 20.6 | 11.8 | 2.3 | 72.7 | 31.9 | 33.3 | 92.3 |
| LAFAYETTE | 0.6 | 1.1 | 5.5 | 5.3 | 5.1 | 11.3 | 17.2 | 28.4 | 17.6 | 8.2 | 1.3 | 80.9 | 25.8 | 28.7 | 94.1 |
| LAMAR | 0.6 | 1.2 | 7.5 | 7.7 | 7.7 | 7.6 | 7.2 | 31.6 | 21.4 | 8.3 | 1.1 | 72.4 | 30.4 | 33.3 | 94.5 |
| LAUDERDALE | 0.7 | 1.1 | 7.1 | 7.1 | 7.0 | 7.9 | 7.6 | 28.6 | 21.5 | 11.4 | 1.8 | 74.3 | 32.1 | 34.8 | 89.9 |
| LAWRENCE | 0.4 | 0.7 | 7.1 | 7.2 | 7.3 | 8.4 | 6.9 | 27.3 | 22.4 | 11.8 | 1.6 | 73.1 | 32.3 | 35.3 | 92.7 |
| LEAKE | 0.3 | 0.5 | 6.8 | 7.1 | 7.4 | 7.9 | 6.7 | 26.4 | 22.6 | 12.9 | 2.3 | 73.9 | 33.7 | 36.4 | 92.0 |
| LEE | 0.5 | 1.0 | 7.4 | 7.3 | 7.3 | 7.1 | 6.6 | 30.4 | 22.4 | 9.9 | 1.4 | 73.6 | 31.9 | 35.1 | 90.8 |
| LEFLORE | 0.4 | 0.5 | 8.0 | 8.0 | 8.0 | 9.3 | 9.4 | 26.1 | 18.8 | 10.4 | 1.9 | 70.8 | 29.2 | 30.4 | 88.2 |
| LINCOLN | 0.2 | 0.5 | 6.3 | 6.5 | 6.8 | 7.7 | 6.9 | 27.5 | 23.6 | 12.6 | 2.0 | 75.5 | 33.7 | 37.1 | 90.9 |
| LOWNDES | 0.8 | 1.4 | 7.9 | 7.5 | 7.5 | 7.8 | 8.5 | 30.6 | 20.1 | 8.8 | 1.3 | 72.5 | 29.5 | 32.1 | 90.4 |
| MADISON | 0.5 | 0.9 | 8.2 | 8.0 | 7.7 | 7.4 | 7.5 | 33.2 | 19.1 | 7.6 | 1.4 | 71.8 | 29.6 | 32.3 | 89.3 |
| MARION | 0.5 | 0.9 | 7.0 | 7.2 | 7.7 | 8.7 | 6.7 | 27.1 | 21.7 | 12.1 | 1.7 | 72.5 | 32.0 | 35.2 | 94.3 |
| MARSHALL | 0.4 | 0.6 | 7.8 | 7.8 | 8.1 | 8.5 | 8.1 | 27.5 | 21.1 | 10.0 | 1.3 | 71.8 | 30.1 | 32.6 | 90.2 |
| MONROE | 0.5 | 0.8 | 7.0 | 7.2 | 7.6 | 7.7 | 6.3 | 27.9 | 22.9 | 11.5 | 1.8 | 73.5 | 32.8 | 35.6 | 89.9 |
| MONTGOMERY | 0.4 | 0.5 | 6.7 | 7.2 | 7.1 | 8.2 | 7.0 | 25.7 | 22.7 | 13.3 | 2.3 | 74.0 | 33.8 | 36.3 | 87.3 |
| NESHOBA | 0.4 | 1.0 | 7.1 | 7.4 | 7.5 | 8.0 | 7.1 | 26.8 | 22.5 | 11.8 | 1.8 | 73.0 | 32.6 | 34.9 | 92.3 |
| NEWTON | 0.4 | 1.0 | 6.8 | 7.1 | 7.2 | 8.6 | 6.9 | 26.7 | 22.0 | 12.5 | 2.1 | 74.4 | 33.1 | 35.5 | 92.4 |
| NOXUBEE | 0.2 | 0.3 | 9.1 | 8.9 | 8.6 | 8.8 | 7.7 | 26.4 | 18.7 | 10.0 | 1.8 | 68.1 | 29.0 | 29.9 | 89.8 |
| OKTIBBEHA | 0.9 | 1.4 | 6.3 | 5.9 | 5.5 | 11.7 | 18.1 | 28.6 | 15.4 | 7.3 | 1.1 | 78.9 | 24.7 | 26.5 | 98.2 |
| PANOLA | 0.5 | 0.8 | 8.1 | 8.0 | 8.0 | 9.1 | 7.3 | 26.9 | 20.2 | 10.7 | 1.6 | 70.4 | 30.0 | 32.3 | 90.9 |
| PEARL RIVER | 0.8 | 1.5 | 6.8 | 7.2 | 7.4 | 8.2 | 6.6 | 26.9 | 24.0 | 11.6 | 1.2 | 73.9 | 32.5 | 35.7 | 92.9 |
| PERRY | 0.4 | 0.9 | 7.5 | 7.6 | 7.7 | 8.0 | 7.2 | 28.7 | 22.2 | 9.8 | 1.3 | 72.4 | 30.5 | 33.7 | 93.7 |
| PIKE | 0.5 | 0.8 | 6.8 | 7.3 | 7.6 | 8.7 | 7.4 | 26.8 | 21.7 | 11.9 | 1.8 | 73.3 | 32.2 | 34.8 | 87.9 |
| PONTOTOC | 0.3 | 0.7 | 6.7 | 6.7 | 7.3 | 7.3 | 6.8 | 29.0 | 23.3 | 11.3 | 1.7 | 74.9 | 33.1 | 36.2 | 94.3 |
| PRENTISS | 0.4 | 0.9 | 6.4 | 6.3 | 6.8 | 8.5 | 7.4 | 27.2 | 23.4 | 12.6 | 1.6 | 76.7 | 33.1 | 36.5 | 92.5 |
| QUITMAN | 0.5 | 0.7 | 8.5 | 8.1 | 8.6 | 9.1 | 7.7 | 25.8 | 19.1 | 11.3 | 1.9 | 69.1 | 29.9 | 31.0 | 87.4 |
| RANKIN | 0.6 | 1.2 | 6.3 | 6.6 | 6.9 | 7.3 | 6.8 | 31.0 | 24.6 | 9.4 | 1.0 | 75.7 | 32.7 | 36.1 | 93.8 |
| SCOTT | 0.6 | 1.0 | 7.7 | 7.6 | 7.9 | 7.8 | 6.9 | 27.5 | 21.4 | 11.4 | 1.8 | 72.0 | 31.6 | 34.4 | 92.0 |
| SHARKEY | 0.7 | 0.7 | 9.1 | 9.2 | 9.0 | 9.1 | 8.3 | 26.4 | 18.4 | 9.0 | 1.6 | 67.2 | 26.7 | 28.5 | 85.1 |
| SIMPSON | 0.3 | 0.6 | 7.2 | 7.5 | 7.7 | 7.9 | 6.9 | 27.7 | 22.4 | 11.0 | 1.7 | 72.6 | 32.2 | 35.1 | 95.2 |
| SMITH | 0.5 | 1.0 | 6.9 | 7.1 | 7.5 | 7.6 | 6.2 | 27.6 | 23.2 | 12.0 | 1.9 | 73.9 | 33.1 | 36.2 | 96.4 |
| STONE | 0.5 | 0.9 | 7.0 | 7.6 | 7.7 | 9.4 | 7.4 | 26.5 | 22.1 | 11.0 | 1.3 | 73.6 | 30.9 | 33.7 | 95.9 |
| SUNFLOWER | 0.6 | 1.0 | 7.1 | 7.2 | 7.3 | 9.6 | 10.4 | 31.3 | 17.1 | 8.5 | 1.6 | 73.2 | 28.6 | 29.8 | 119.9 |
| TALLAHATCHIE | 0.5 | 0.7 | 8.5 | 8.3 | 8.5 | 8.9 | 8.0 | 25.8 | 19.6 | 10.5 | 1.8 | 69.2 | 29.5 | 30.7 | 89.2 |
| TATE | 0.6 | 1.0 | 7.2 | 7.4 | 7.7 | 9.1 | 7.7 | 27.6 | 22.2 | 9.7 | 1.5 | 73.2 | 30.6 | 33.3 | 91.8 |
| TIPPAH | 0.3 | 0.8 | 6.7 | 6.9 | 7.3 | 7.2 | 6.4 | 28.4 | 23.1 | 11.8 | 2.1 | 74.7 | 33.4 | 36.4 | 90.8 |
| TISHOMINGO | 0.3 | 0.9 | 5.9 | 5.9 | 6.4 | 6.4 | 6.0 | 27.0 | 25.7 | 14.6 | 2.0 | 78.1 | 36.9 | 39.9 | 91.0 |
| TUNICA | 1.0 | 0.9 | 9.7 | 9.4 | 9.5 | 10.0 | 8.7 | 25.0 | 17.2 | 9.0 | 1.4 | 65.1 | 25.6 | 26.9 | 85.4 |
| UNION | 0.5 | 0.9 | 6.3 | 6.6 | 7.0 | 6.8 | 6.5 | 28.3 | 24.1 | 12.3 | 2.0 | 75.9 | 34.4 | 37.2 | 93.9 |
| WALTHALL | 0.3 | 0.6 | 7.4 | 7.9 | 8.1 | 8.6 | 7.1 | 26.0 | 21.4 | 11.7 | 1.7 | 71.5 | 31.3 | 33.8 | 94.0 |
| WARREN | 0.5 | 0.9 | 7.0 | 7.2 | 7.4 | 7.9 | 7.2 | 28.4 | 22.8 | 10.5 | 1.7 | 73.4 | 32.4 | 35.2 | 90.5 |
| WASHINGTON | 0.6 | 0.9 | 8.4 | 8.5 | 8.5 | 9.0 | 7.8 | 27.3 | 19.4 | 9.6 | 1.5 | 69.1 | 29.1 | 30.6 | 87.6 |
| WAYNE | 0.4 | 0.7 | 7.4 | 7.9 | 7.7 | 8.6 | 7.0 | 28.5 | 21.8 | 9.6 | 1.4 | 71.6 | 30.9 | 33.5 | 91.4 |
| MISSISSIPPI | 0.6 | 1.1 | 7.2 | 7.3 | 7.4 | 8.2 | 7.7 | 28.5 | 21.5 | 10.5 | 1.5 | 73.4 | 31.2 | 33.9 | 92.0 |
| UNITED STATES | 9.0 | 11.8 | 6.9 | 7.2 | 7.2 | 7.2 | 6.7 | 29.9 | 22.2 | 11.1 | 1.6 | 74.6 | 32.9 | 35.7 | 95.6 |

| COUNTY | HOUSEHOLDS 1990 | HOUSEHOLDS 2000 | HOUSEHOLDS 2005 | HOUSEHOLDS % Annual Rate 1990-2000 | HOUSEHOLDS 2000 Average HH Size | FAMILIES 1990 | FAMILIES 2000 | FAMILIES % Annual Rate 1990-2000 | MEDIAN HOUSEHOLD INCOME 2000 | MEDIAN HOUSEHOLD INCOME 2005 | MEDIAN HOUSEHOLD INCOME 2000 National Rank | MEDIAN HOUSEHOLD INCOME 2000 State Rank |
|---|---|---|---|---|---|---|---|---|---|---|---|---|
| ADAMS | 13,262 | 13,248 | 12,952 | 0.0 | 2.49 | 9,690 | 9,352 | -0.4 | 26,869 | 31,676 | 2603 | 46 |
| ALCORN | 12,449 | 13,222 | 13,681 | 0.7 | 2.49 | 9,150 | 9,357 | 0.3 | 29,692 | 32,983 | 2203 | 26 |
| AMITE | 4,830 | 5,215 | 5,473 | 0.9 | 2.68 | 3,594 | 3,745 | 0.5 | 26,050 | 31,785 | 2709 | 53 |
| ATTALA | 6,945 | 7,114 | 7,209 | 0.3 | 2.55 | 5,027 | 4,992 | -0.1 | 24,810 | 28,619 | 2824 | 59 |
| BENTON | 2,842 | 3,005 | 3,129 | 0.7 | 2.68 | 2,192 | 2,240 | 0.3 | 24,441 | 29,106 | 2862 | 61 |
| BOLIVAR | 13,292 | 13,036 | 12,736 | -0.2 | 2.89 | 9,692 | 9,227 | -0.6 | 23,558 | 26,363 | 2934 | 63 |
| CALHOUN | 5,662 | 5,782 | 5,847 | 0.3 | 2.54 | 4,187 | 4,133 | -0.2 | 28,718 | 34,573 | 2334 | 31 |
| CARROLL | 3,352 | 3,765 | 3,836 | 1.4 | 2.64 | 2,556 | 2,781 | 1.0 | 26,442 | 31,604 | 2661 | 51 |
| CHICKASAW | 6,480 | 6,619 | 6,664 | 0.3 | 2.72 | 4,902 | 4,812 | -0.2 | 27,120 | 30,910 | 2562 | 43 |
| CHOCTAW | 3,217 | 3,475 | 3,575 | 0.9 | 2.64 | 2,436 | 2,529 | 0.5 | 26,652 | 33,598 | 2626 | 49 |
| CLAIBORNE | 3,342 | 3,544 | 3,656 | 0.7 | 2.80 | 2,359 | 2,430 | 0.4 | 20,129 | 24,211 | 3096 | 76 |
| CLARKE | 6,334 | 7,000 | 7,463 | 1.2 | 2.64 | 4,780 | 5,093 | 0.8 | 27,175 | 32,300 | 2551 | 41 |
| CLAY | 7,251 | 7,658 | 7,800 | 0.7 | 2.75 | 5,451 | 5,603 | 0.3 | 26,684 | 29,114 | 2619 | 47 |
| COAHOMA | 10,530 | 10,567 | 10,453 | 0.0 | 2.85 | 7,538 | 7,334 | -0.3 | 22,351 | 24,975 | 3006 | 69 |
| COPIAH | 9,304 | 10,131 | 10,473 | 1.0 | 2.73 | 6,993 | 7,358 | 0.6 | 26,682 | 33,189 | 2620 | 48 |
| COVINGTON | 5,786 | 6,565 | 7,005 | 1.5 | 2.74 | 4,441 | 4,857 | 1.1 | 28,032 | 34,926 | 2434 | 33 |
| DESOTO | 23,273 | 37,792 | 46,944 | 6.1 | 2.82 | 19,340 | 30,567 | 5.7 | 45,316 | 51,960 | 340 | 2 |
| FORREST | 25,150 | 28,475 | 29,967 | 1.5 | 2.48 | 16,726 | 18,387 | 1.2 | 28,877 | 32,104 | 2319 | 29 |
| FRANKLIN | 3,086 | 3,151 | 3,128 | 0.3 | 2.55 | 2,284 | 2,238 | -0.2 | 23,362 | 29,589 | 2952 | 64 |
| GEORGE | 5,779 | 7,429 | 8,556 | 3.1 | 2.78 | 4,610 | 5,769 | 2.8 | 30,632 | 34,050 | 2001 | 20 |
| GREENE | 3,327 | 3,820 | 3,819 | 1.7 | 2.72 | 2,635 | 2,938 | 1.3 | 29,404 | 36,898 | 2234 | 27 |
| GRENADA | 7,701 | 8,256 | 8,451 | 0.8 | 2.68 | 5,738 | 5,992 | 0.5 | 27,718 | 30,569 | 2473 | 37 |
| HANCOCK | 11,817 | 16,354 | 18,747 | 4.0 | 2.57 | 8,717 | 11,664 | 3.6 | 30,432 | 33,882 | 2050 | 21 |
| HARRISON | 59,557 | 67,497 | 70,728 | 1.5 | 2.58 | 42,921 | 47,482 | 1.2 | 34,877 | 40,850 | 1273 | 8 |
| HINDS | 91,023 | 90,094 | 89,161 | -0.1 | 2.62 | 64,032 | 61,636 | -0.5 | 34,917 | 40,127 | 1266 | 7 |
| HOLMES | 7,139 | 7,287 | 7,486 | 0.2 | 2.90 | 5,207 | 5,163 | -0.1 | 17,775 | 19,390 | 3132 | 80 |
| HUMPHREYS | 3,926 | 3,749 | 3,694 | -0.6 | 2.95 | 2,878 | 2,676 | -0.9 | 18,598 | 20,391 | 3126 | 79 |
| ISSAQUENA | 633 | 552 | 549 | -1.6 | 2.95 | 476 | 400 | -2.1 | 17,734 | 19,395 | 3134 | 82 |
| ITAWAMBA | 7,497 | 8,169 | 8,348 | 1.0 | 2.49 | 5,790 | 6,088 | 0.6 | 31,303 | 35,363 | 1863 | 15 |
| JACKSON | 40,454 | 47,940 | 51,652 | 2.1 | 2.76 | 31,583 | 36,576 | 1.8 | 37,871 | 42,877 | 861 | 4 |
| JASPER | 5,956 | 6,384 | 6,862 | 0.8 | 2.86 | 4,606 | 4,773 | 0.4 | 26,982 | 31,711 | 2581 | 45 |
| JEFFERSON | 2,814 | 2,795 | 2,773 | -0.1 | 2.96 | 2,114 | 2,047 | -0.4 | 17,759 | 21,903 | 3133 | 81 |
| JEFFERSON DAVIS | 4,787 | 4,849 | 4,846 | 0.2 | 2.80 | 3,674 | 3,601 | -0.2 | 22,786 | 25,426 | 2984 | 67 |
| JONES | 22,506 | 23,548 | 23,563 | 0.6 | 2.60 | 16,976 | 17,325 | 0.2 | 29,365 | 34,275 | 2242 | 28 |
| KEMPER | 3,626 | 3,864 | 3,960 | 0.8 | 2.59 | 2,642 | 2,689 | 0.2 | 23,054 | 26,383 | 2968 | 65 |
| LAFAYETTE | 11,090 | 13,046 | 13,888 | 2.0 | 2.37 | 6,968 | 7,765 | 1.3 | 28,526 | 32,612 | 2360 | 32 |
| LAMAR | 10,883 | 14,379 | 16,614 | 3.4 | 2.72 | 8,497 | 10,902 | 3.1 | 34,800 | 41,082 | 1283 | 9 |
| LAUDERDALE | 28,232 | 29,066 | 29,035 | 0.4 | 2.52 | 20,032 | 20,016 | 0.0 | 31,206 | 35,816 | 1886 | 16 |
| LAWRENCE | 4,506 | 4,950 | 5,186 | 1.1 | 2.63 | 3,416 | 3,608 | 0.7 | 26,069 | 28,214 | 2704 | 52 |
| LEAKE | 6,788 | 7,376 | 7,668 | 1.0 | 2.65 | 5,054 | 5,292 | 0.6 | 25,325 | 30,481 | 2777 | 56 |
| LEE | 24,450 | 29,197 | 31,036 | 2.2 | 2.57 | 18,116 | 20,971 | 1.8 | 36,472 | 42,164 | 1048 | 5 |
| LEFLORE | 12,749 | 12,708 | 12,415 | 0.0 | 2.69 | 8,977 | 8,717 | -0.4 | 22,235 | 24,516 | 3015 | 70 |
| LINCOLN | 11,089 | 12,105 | 12,676 | 1.1 | 2.62 | 8,318 | 8,823 | 0.7 | 27,433 | 30,794 | 2519 | 39 |
| LOWNDES | 21,402 | 22,845 | 22,925 | 0.8 | 2.58 | 15,698 | 16,325 | 0.5 | 33,004 | 38,859 | 1537 | 11 |
| MADISON | 19,276 | 29,123 | 33,793 | 5.1 | 2.59 | 13,638 | 19,914 | 4.7 | 41,718 | 49,393 | 536 | 3 |
| MARION | 9,110 | 9,731 | 10,105 | 0.8 | 2.69 | 6,897 | 7,148 | 0.4 | 24,328 | 27,335 | 2879 | 62 |
| MARSHALL | 10,077 | 11,263 | 11,688 | 1.4 | 2.82 | 7,790 | 8,433 | 1.0 | 30,201 | 36,250 | 2105 | 24 |
| MONROE | 13,348 | 14,513 | 15,041 | 1.0 | 2.62 | 10,077 | 10,599 | 0.6 | 30,219 | 35,722 | 2101 | 23 |
| MONTGOMERY | 4,532 | 4,681 | 4,737 | 0.4 | 2.62 | 3,349 | 3,341 | 0.0 | 25,468 | 28,784 | 2760 | 54 |
| NESHOBA | 8,848 | 10,354 | 10,958 | 1.9 | 2.65 | 6,754 | 7,605 | 1.4 | 30,878 | 35,120 | 1953 | 19 |
| NEWTON | 7,358 | 8,011 | 8,298 | 1.0 | 2.64 | 5,579 | 5,883 | 0.6 | 30,287 | 36,573 | 2086 | 22 |
| NOXUBEE | 4,140 | 4,156 | 4,253 | 0.0 | 3.00 | 3,092 | 2,995 | -0.4 | 22,976 | 27,642 | 2974 | 66 |
| OKTIBBEHA | 12,916 | 13,977 | 14,416 | 1.0 | 2.50 | 8,261 | 8,471 | 0.3 | 27,161 | 31,991 | 2554 | 42 |
| PANOLA | 10,130 | 11,923 | 12,936 | 2.0 | 2.84 | 7,652 | 8,689 | 1.6 | 27,415 | 33,947 | 2523 | 40 |
| PEARL RIVER | 13,760 | 18,076 | 20,583 | 3.4 | 2.69 | 10,699 | 13,708 | 3.0 | 31,372 | 39,091 | 1848 | 14 |
| PERRY | 3,802 | 4,272 | 4,503 | 1.4 | 2.82 | 2,951 | 3,219 | 1.1 | 27,081 | 33,385 | 2568 | 44 |
| PIKE | 13,408 | 14,174 | 14,431 | 0.7 | 2.64 | 9,709 | 9,928 | 0.3 | 24,664 | 27,179 | 2843 | 60 |
| PONTOTOC | 8,346 | 10,114 | 11,104 | 2.4 | 2.56 | 6,379 | 7,407 | 1.8 | 31,427 | 38,327 | 1835 | 13 |
| PRENTISS | 8,647 | 9,355 | 9,782 | 1.0 | 2.56 | 6,570 | 6,880 | 0.6 | 27,766 | 32,042 | 2471 | 36 |
| QUITMAN | 3,521 | 3,425 | 3,421 | -0.3 | 2.82 | 2,569 | 2,409 | -0.8 | 20,962 | 25,223 | 3068 | 73 |
| RANKIN | 29,858 | 40,432 | 46,224 | 3.7 | 2.73 | 23,888 | 31,338 | 3.3 | 46,872 | 54,075 | 280 | 1 |
| SCOTT | 8,511 | 9,066 | 9,115 | 0.8 | 2.72 | 6,480 | 6,677 | 0.4 | 25,467 | 27,410 | 2761 | 55 |
| SHARKEY | 2,084 | 1,991 | 1,941 | -0.6 | 3.23 | 1,601 | 1,484 | -0.9 | 19,037 | 22,017 | 3122 | 78 |
| SIMPSON | 8,357 | 9,135 | 9,419 | 1.1 | 2.69 | 6,347 | 6,708 | 0.7 | 30,928 | 34,945 | 1942 | 18 |
| SMITH | 5,276 | 5,687 | 5,999 | 0.9 | 2.72 | 4,105 | 4,277 | 0.5 | 31,017 | 36,001 | 1930 | 17 |
| STONE | 3,685 | 4,898 | 5,485 | 3.5 | 2.68 | 2,796 | 3,606 | 3.1 | 30,063 | 35,102 | 2140 | 25 |
| SUNFLOWER | 9,650 | 9,384 | 9,085 | -0.3 | 2.93 | 7,039 | 6,615 | -0.8 | 21,129 | 24,183 | 3065 | 72 |
| TALLAHATCHIE | 5,034 | 5,064 | 4,976 | 0.1 | 2.85 | 3,717 | 3,612 | -0.3 | 21,908 | 27,304 | 3031 | 71 |
| TATE | 7,024 | 8,347 | 9,227 | 2.1 | 2.86 | 5,576 | 6,449 | 1.8 | 35,247 | 42,705 | 1214 | 6 |
| TIPPAH | 7,158 | 8,025 | 8,359 | 1.4 | 2.60 | 5,487 | 5,940 | 1.0 | 27,908 | 31,819 | 2454 | 35 |
| TISHOMINGO | 7,059 | 7,802 | 8,149 | 1.2 | 2.39 | 5,314 | 5,667 | 0.8 | 28,834 | 32,414 | 2324 | 30 |
| TUNICA | 2,526 | 2,547 | 2,508 | 0.1 | 3.08 | 1,876 | 1,841 | -0.2 | 20,327 | 23,621 | 3092 | 75 |
| UNION | 8,367 | 9,488 | 10,192 | 1.5 | 2.56 | 6,339 | 6,910 | 1.1 | 32,019 | 37,636 | 1711 | 12 |
| WALTHALL | 4,929 | 5,092 | 5,088 | 0.4 | 2.74 | 3,771 | 3,766 | 0.0 | 22,590 | 25,669 | 2989 | 68 |
| WARREN | 17,407 | 18,595 | 18,933 | 0.8 | 2.61 | 12,671 | 13,186 | 0.5 | 33,864 | 36,760 | 1411 | 10 |
| WASHINGTON | 22,593 | 22,087 | 21,478 | -0.3 | 2.85 | 16,764 | 15,978 | -0.6 | 27,643 | 32,102 | 2490 | 38 |
| WAYNE | 6,858 | 7,515 | 8,077 | 1.1 | 2.77 | 5,336 | 5,682 | 0.8 | 26,546 | 29,272 | 2646 | 50 |
| MISSISSIPPI | | | | 1.4 | 2.66 | | | 1.0 | 31,144 | 36,358 | | |
| UNITED STATES | | | | 1.4 | 2.59 | | | 1.1 | 41,914 | 49,127 | | |

# INCOME

| COUNTY | 2000 Per Capita Income | 2000 HH Income Base | 2000 HOUSEHOLD INCOME DISTRIBUTION (%) | | | | | | 2000 AVERAGE DISPOSABLE INCOME BY AGE OF HOUSEHOLDER | | | | | |
|---|---|---|---|---|---|---|---|---|---|---|---|---|---|---|
| | | | Less than $15,000 | $15,000 to $24,999 | $25,000 to $49,999 | $50,000 to $99,999 | $100,000 to $149,999 | $150,000 or More | All Ages | <35 | 35-44 | 45-54 | 55-64 | 65+ |
| ADAMS | 16,229 | 13,248 | 29.7 | 16.9 | 29.0 | 18.2 | 3.9 | 2.4 | 31,163 | 26,126 | 35,943 | 36,905 | 31,749 | 22,354 |
| ALCORN | 14,264 | 13,222 | 25.6 | 16.4 | 36.1 | 19.0 | 2.4 | 0.6 | 28,852 | 29,434 | 34,639 | 36,092 | 27,688 | 17,656 |
| AMITE | 13,818 | 5,215 | 29.9 | 18.4 | 31.3 | 17.1 | 2.4 | 0.9 | 27,438 | 26,082 | 33,859 | 34,313 | 26,882 | 17,333 |
| ATTALA | 12,681 | 7,114 | 29.5 | 20.9 | 30.4 | 16.5 | 2.3 | 0.5 | 26,468 | 26,554 | 29,329 | 36,551 | 24,993 | 18,614 |
| BENTON | 10,895 | 3,005 | 29.8 | 21.5 | 32.8 | 14.6 | 1.2 | 0.1 | 24,682 | 26,123 | 26,517 | 31,189 | 25,472 | 17,103 |
| BOLIVAR | 11,537 | 13,036 | 36.1 | 16.3 | 26.5 | 16.6 | 3.4 | 1.1 | 27,025 | 23,564 | 31,536 | 32,229 | 29,548 | 18,215 |
| CALHOUN | 13,772 | 5,782 | 24.4 | 17.7 | 37.7 | 18.2 | 1.9 | 0.1 | 27,839 | 28,605 | 32,599 | 36,510 | 26,593 | 17,515 |
| CARROLL | 13,314 | 3,765 | 29.8 | 16.7 | 31.1 | 18.0 | 3.4 | 1.0 | 28,451 | 26,551 | 35,430 | 33,714 | 30,338 | 17,074 |
| CHICKASAW | 12,477 | 6,619 | 26.1 | 19.9 | 37.4 | 14.2 | 1.6 | 0.9 | 26,959 | 25,106 | 32,594 | 33,143 | 24,699 | 17,736 |
| CHOCTAW | 13,168 | 3,475 | 26.6 | 19.7 | 34.6 | 16.8 | 1.8 | 0.5 | 27,036 | 25,999 | 33,675 | 31,650 | 27,824 | 16,758 |
| CLAIBORNE | 8,429 | 3,544 | 39.8 | 18.0 | 26.1 | 15.7 | 0.5 | 0.0 | 22,839 | 22,602 | 26,662 | 26,616 | 21,831 | 15,701 |
| CLARKE | 12,500 | 7,000 | 27.0 | 18.9 | 36.3 | 15.4 | 2.0 | 0.2 | 26,836 | 26,979 | 30,345 | 31,216 | 30,098 | 17,675 |
| CLAY | 13,263 | 7,658 | 28.4 | 18.7 | 32.8 | 16.6 | 2.2 | 1.4 | 28,456 | 24,954 | 34,362 | 33,360 | 28,253 | 18,653 |
| COAHOMA | 12,155 | 10,567 | 36.5 | 17.2 | 28.6 | 13.4 | 3.0 | 1.4 | 26,702 | 23,313 | 29,535 | 33,185 | 27,922 | 19,517 |
| COPIAH | 12,927 | 10,131 | 29.4 | 18.2 | 30.4 | 18.2 | 3.0 | 0.8 | 28,226 | 26,643 | 31,495 | 34,545 | 28,751 | 19,693 |
| COVINGTON | 13,467 | 6,565 | 25.5 | 18.5 | 31.7 | 20.8 | 2.8 | 0.8 | 29,408 | 27,938 | 35,240 | 35,546 | 28,547 | 19,343 |
| DESOTO | 20,029 | 37,792 | 11.0 | 10.4 | 35.0 | 34.8 | 6.9 | 1.9 | 41,403 | 38,725 | 45,161 | 48,659 | 42,814 | 23,579 |
| FORREST | 17,785 | 28,473 | 25.5 | 17.8 | 29.9 | 19.6 | 4.5 | 2.6 | 33,285 | 26,139 | 37,961 | 41,289 | 36,511 | 23,531 |
| FRANKLIN | 12,313 | 3,151 | 33.4 | 19.4 | 30.8 | 13.1 | 2.2 | 1.1 | 26,006 | 20,677 | 32,406 | 32,708 | 27,562 | 18,047 |
| GEORGE | 12,990 | 7,429 | 23.3 | 17.0 | 36.6 | 20.0 | 2.8 | 0.3 | 29,324 | 28,216 | 34,864 | 35,649 | 28,236 | 18,272 |
| GREENE | 10,634 | 3,820 | 23.4 | 17.6 | 37.5 | 19.4 | 2.0 | 0.2 | 28,548 | 26,250 | 33,055 | 34,815 | 29,186 | 19,299 |
| GRENADA | 12,839 | 8,256 | 26.4 | 18.3 | 33.7 | 18.4 | 2.6 | 0.7 | 28,523 | 27,420 | 34,936 | 34,811 | 27,303 | 17,963 |
| HANCOCK | 15,847 | 16,354 | 26.2 | 14.4 | 32.8 | 20.7 | 4.2 | 1.6 | 31,711 | 27,233 | 36,219 | 39,006 | 32,340 | 23,619 |
| HARRISON | 16,870 | 67,497 | 17.3 | 16.4 | 35.2 | 25.7 | 4.4 | 1.1 | 34,250 | 29,560 | 39,250 | 40,349 | 36,253 | 25,269 |
| HINDS | 18,599 | 90,093 | 20.9 | 15.1 | 31.8 | 24.4 | 5.2 | 2.7 | 36,426 | 29,324 | 39,584 | 44,339 | 37,715 | 24,973 |
| HOLMES | 10,994 | 7,287 | 44.6 | 17.2 | 22.5 | 11.2 | 2.4 | 2.1 | 25,063 | 19,370 | 26,217 | 33,324 | 25,721 | 18,997 |
| HUMPHREYS | 11,954 | 3,749 | 41.0 | 20.6 | 22.5 | 11.6 | 1.9 | 2.4 | 25,767 | 22,703 | 30,814 | 32,638 | 22,591 | 15,344 |
| ISSAQUENA | 7,904 | 552 | 45.3 | 16.7 | 28.3 | 9.1 | 0.7 | 0.0 | 20,190 | 18,333 | 25,641 | 22,860 | 21,397 | 12,009 |
| ITAWAMBA | 16,190 | 8,169 | 19.2 | 17.9 | 41.1 | 18.8 | 2.3 | 0.6 | 30,202 | 29,462 | 36,933 | 39,442 | 29,697 | 17,259 |
| JACKSON | 17,009 | 47,940 | 17.2 | 12.9 | 36.1 | 28.1 | 4.5 | 1.3 | 35,731 | 31,115 | 39,539 | 43,152 | 37,692 | 23,510 |
| JASPER | 12,592 | 6,384 | 28.5 | 17.8 | 33.1 | 17.2 | 2.7 | 0.8 | 27,967 | 26,456 | 34,521 | 32,224 | 27,853 | 18,781 |
| JEFFERSON | 8,538 | 2,795 | 43.7 | 19.6 | 24.3 | 11.1 | 1.1 | 0.3 | 21,133 | 18,029 | 25,377 | 25,308 | 18,865 | 15,501 |
| JEFFERSON DAVIS | 10,778 | 4,849 | 34.4 | 20.7 | 27.0 | 15.5 | 1.8 | 0.7 | 25,260 | 22,751 | 28,678 | 32,890 | 25,717 | 16,369 |
| JONES | 15,519 | 23,548 | 24.6 | 18.8 | 31.7 | 20.3 | 3.6 | 1.0 | 30,384 | 26,639 | 36,083 | 38,157 | 31,889 | 19,172 |
| KEMPER | 20,416 | 3,864 | 33.4 | 19.6 | 29.4 | 12.3 | 3.1 | 2.2 | 27,749 | 24,007 | 31,659 | 35,256 | 27,759 | 18,385 |
| LAFAYETTE | 16,320 | 13,046 | 26.6 | 17.8 | 29.7 | 19.5 | 4.3 | 2.2 | 32,062 | 24,184 | 36,735 | 45,881 | 34,729 | 21,412 |
| LAMAR | 16,944 | 14,379 | 21.4 | 14.4 | 32.1 | 24.4 | 5.3 | 2.4 | 35,797 | 29,487 | 40,865 | 45,637 | 34,622 | 19,829 |
| LAUDERDALE | 16,858 | 29,066 | 24.2 | 16.6 | 32.1 | 20.9 | 4.4 | 1.8 | 32,719 | 29,311 | 39,404 | 39,096 | 32,078 | 21,132 |
| LAWRENCE | 12,752 | 4,950 | 28.7 | 18.9 | 32.8 | 17.1 | 2.1 | 0.5 | 26,903 | 24,965 | 30,048 | 34,809 | 29,362 | 17,035 |
| LEAKE | 11,565 | 7,376 | 29.0 | 20.4 | 33.7 | 15.1 | 1.7 | 0.2 | 25,591 | 27,812 | 31,635 | 28,758 | 24,346 | 17,738 |
| LEE | 18,302 | 29,197 | 18.0 | 13.2 | 35.6 | 26.7 | 4.6 | 2.0 | 36,245 | 34,059 | 40,040 | 45,193 | 34,491 | 21,211 |
| LEFLORE | 14,536 | 12,708 | 36.9 | 17.5 | 27.3 | 13.5 | 2.4 | 2.4 | 27,797 | 22,522 | 31,176 | 32,247 | 28,718 | 19,173 |
| LINCOLN | 14,598 | 12,105 | 26.0 | 19.6 | 30.8 | 18.8 | 3.3 | 1.5 | 30,177 | 27,394 | 36,706 | 37,415 | 26,379 | 21,234 |
| LOWNDES | 17,554 | 22,842 | 22.6 | 14.8 | 33.2 | 23.9 | 4.2 | 1.3 | 33,255 | 29,153 | 38,992 | 39,441 | 34,815 | 20,388 |
| MADISON | 21,829 | 29,123 | 16.3 | 12.8 | 30.7 | 28.4 | 8.0 | 3.7 | 41,755 | 39,649 | 47,300 | 47,041 | 36,642 | 24,437 |
| MARION | 13,306 | 9,731 | 29.8 | 21.5 | 30.6 | 14.7 | 2.5 | 0.9 | 26,656 | 24,584 | 31,280 | 34,204 | 23,897 | 18,759 |
| MARSHALL | 12,833 | 11,263 | 24.8 | 16.1 | 34.3 | 21.4 | 2.8 | 0.7 | 29,993 | 31,263 | 32,653 | 38,100 | 28,068 | 18,782 |
| MONROE | 13,692 | 14,513 | 24.2 | 17.3 | 36.7 | 18.4 | 2.9 | 0.6 | 29,322 | 28,372 | 33,347 | 37,078 | 28,618 | 19,622 |
| MONTGOMERY | 11,650 | 4,681 | 31.6 | 17.4 | 34.7 | 14.5 | 1.6 | 0.2 | 25,307 | 25,500 | 29,422 | 30,828 | 24,119 | 18,309 |
| NESHOBA | 14,199 | 10,354 | 21.9 | 17.8 | 36.3 | 20.8 | 2.6 | 0.7 | 30,356 | 28,411 | 38,443 | 36,450 | 28,113 | 20,056 |
| NEWTON | 13,990 | 8,011 | 22.4 | 18.0 | 34.6 | 21.4 | 2.7 | 1.0 | 30,583 | 29,549 | 35,763 | 37,994 | 30,556 | 20,174 |
| NOXUBEE | 10,976 | 4,156 | 32.5 | 20.8 | 28.8 | 15.6 | 1.8 | 0.6 | 25,307 | 22,984 | 28,550 | 31,460 | 24,386 | 18,400 |
| OKTIBBEHA | 13,132 | 13,977 | 32.9 | 14.1 | 28.5 | 20.1 | 3.2 | 1.2 | 29,301 | 20,153 | 35,736 | 39,431 | 37,487 | 22,676 |
| PANOLA | 11,913 | 11,923 | 26.7 | 17.9 | 34.4 | 18.0 | 2.5 | 0.6 | 28,099 | 27,353 | 32,066 | 34,953 | 27,428 | 18,225 |
| PEARL RIVER | 15,331 | 18,076 | 23.0 | 17.2 | 33.7 | 19.9 | 4.4 | 1.7 | 32,364 | 29,002 | 37,859 | 38,044 | 34,003 | 20,981 |
| PERRY | 11,975 | 4,272 | 27.7 | 18.5 | 33.9 | 16.9 | 2.4 | 0.7 | 27,760 | 24,981 | 33,163 | 34,783 | 28,412 | 16,003 |
| PIKE | 13,134 | 14,174 | 33.0 | 17.4 | 29.0 | 15.8 | 3.2 | 1.5 | 27,893 | 24,291 | 31,480 | 34,626 | 29,231 | 19,290 |
| PONTOTOC | 14,249 | 10,114 | 22.5 | 16.2 | 37.7 | 21.2 | 2.3 | 0.2 | 29,623 | 30,397 | 35,356 | 37,548 | 29,185 | 15,899 |
| PRENTISS | 13,942 | 9,355 | 26.1 | 17.7 | 35.3 | 17.6 | 2.4 | 0.9 | 28,519 | 27,308 | 36,903 | 33,047 | 28,863 | 17,524 |
| QUITMAN | 10,052 | 3,425 | 37.2 | 20.5 | 27.4 | 12.9 | 1.6 | 0.5 | 23,587 | 23,030 | 25,531 | 31,194 | 23,761 | 16,578 |
| RANKIN | 20,571 | 40,432 | 11.3 | 9.8 | 33.0 | 35.4 | 8.3 | 2.4 | 42,926 | 37,888 | 47,858 | 51,782 | 43,059 | 25,815 |
| SCOTT | 12,258 | 9,066 | 31.1 | 18.0 | 32.2 | 14.9 | 2.8 | 1.1 | 27,208 | 25,694 | 31,308 | 35,271 | 25,658 | 16,527 |
| SHARKEY | 8,459 | 1,991 | 41.4 | 18.6 | 26.2 | 11.5 | 1.5 | 0.8 | 22,651 | 19,220 | 27,102 | 27,583 | 21,047 | 16,019 |
| SIMPSON | 13,724 | 9,135 | 22.1 | 17.6 | 35.2 | 22.0 | 2.6 | 0.5 | 30,321 | 28,433 | 35,055 | 35,795 | 32,104 | 19,865 |
| SMITH | 15,141 | 5,687 | 22.0 | 16.9 | 34.5 | 22.3 | 3.4 | 0.8 | 31,143 | 30,014 | 36,792 | 41,351 | 29,539 | 19,508 |
| STONE | 13,426 | 4,898 | 23.5 | 18.3 | 35.6 | 18.4 | 3.2 | 0.9 | 30,062 | 27,764 | 33,253 | 37,672 | 29,590 | 21,717 |
| SUNFLOWER | 10,535 | 9,384 | 38.3 | 17.5 | 27.0 | 13.5 | 2.4 | 1.3 | 25,518 | 21,816 | 28,214 | 32,646 | 28,963 | 15,410 |
| TALLAHATCHIE | 9,890 | 5,064 | 35.9 | 20.4 | 30.6 | 11.2 | 1.2 | 0.6 | 23,513 | 22,013 | 27,948 | 28,391 | 22,047 | 17,180 |
| TATE | 14,590 | 8,347 | 19.0 | 15.2 | 36.3 | 23.2 | 5.0 | 1.3 | 34,067 | 30,862 | 39,507 | 43,500 | 32,971 | 20,862 |
| TIPPAH | 13,072 | 8,025 | 24.4 | 18.1 | 37.3 | 18.1 | 2.0 | 0.2 | 27,874 | 28,608 | 34,147 | 34,952 | 25,401 | 16,713 |
| TISHOMINGO | 14,432 | 7,802 | 23.8 | 17.9 | 37.3 | 18.5 | 2.3 | 0.2 | 28,238 | 28,517 | 35,435 | 36,419 | 26,041 | 17,883 |
| TUNICA | 13,340 | 2,547 | 38.9 | 17.1 | 24.4 | 12.4 | 3.5 | 3.9 | 30,395 | 21,638 | 27,714 | 38,382 | 34,370 | 22,127 |
| UNION | 15,382 | 9,488 | 19.3 | 16.4 | 39.5 | 21.3 | 2.8 | 0.7 | 31,204 | 30,502 | 37,701 | 39,904 | 31,394 | 17,853 |
| WALTHALL | 11,668 | 5,092 | 34.4 | 20.3 | 27.6 | 14.8 | 2.0 | 1.0 | 25,692 | 22,592 | 30,287 | 30,749 | 25,584 | 18,458 |
| WARREN | 16,528 | 18,595 | 23.3 | 15.4 | 31.2 | 24.4 | 4.0 | 1.7 | 33,460 | 28,897 | 38,965 | 41,204 | 31,688 | 21,705 |
| WASHINGTON | 15,358 | 22,087 | 29.5 | 16.0 | 30.5 | 17.7 | 4.2 | 2.3 | 31,289 | 24,685 | 37,014 | 38,686 | 31,276 | 20,126 |
| WAYNE | 12,105 | 7,515 | 28.7 | 18.3 | 34.0 | 16.3 | 2.2 | 0.6 | 27,044 | 25,331 | 30,760 | 32,854 | 26,875 | 18,332 |
| MISSISSIPPI | 15,620 | | 24.1 | 16.2 | 32.7 | 21.6 | 4.0 | 1.5 | 32,177 | 28,646 | 37,129 | 39,522 | 32,438 | 20,720 |
| UNITED STATES | 22,162 | | 14.5 | 12.5 | 32.3 | 29.8 | 7.4 | 3.5 | 40,748 | 34,503 | 44,969 | 49,579 | 43,409 | 27,339 |

# SPENDING POTENTIAL INDEXES

| COUNTY | FINANCIAL SERVICES | | | | THE HOME | | | | | | ENTERTAINMENT | | | | | | PERSONAL | | | |
|---|---|---|---|---|---|---|---|---|---|---|---|---|---|---|---|---|---|---|---|---|
| | | | | | Home Improvements | | | Furnishings | | | | | | | | | | | | |
| | Auto Loan | Home Loan | Investments | Retirement Plans | Home Repair | Lawn & Garden | Remodeling | Appliances | Electronics | Furniture | Restaurants | Sporting Goods | Theater & Concerts | Toys & Hobbies | Travel | Video Rental | Apparel | Auto Aftermarket | Health Insurance | Pets & Supplies |
| ADAMS | 95 | 76 | 90 | 82 | 98 | 94 | 100 | 96 | 91 | 86 | 82 | 93 | 86 | 93 | 78 | 96 | 85 | 90 | 95 | 95 |
| ALCORN | 97 | 72 | 81 | 80 | 96 | 92 | 109 | 96 | 92 | 82 | 82 | 95 | 84 | 95 | 73 | 96 | 83 | 89 | 100 | 97 |
| AMITE | 96 | 63 | 67 | 73 | 92 | 90 | 110 | 95 | 91 | 75 | 76 | 94 | 78 | 93 | 66 | 95 | 78 | 86 | 100 | 96 |
| ATTALA | 96 | 71 | 81 | 79 | 95 | 92 | 108 | 96 | 92 | 82 | 80 | 93 | 83 | 94 | 73 | 95 | 82 | 89 | 97 | 96 |
| BENTON | 97 | 63 | 66 | 73 | 92 | 90 | 112 | 96 | 91 | 75 | 77 | 96 | 78 | 95 | 66 | 95 | 78 | 86 | 102 | 96 |
| BOLIVAR | 92 | 78 | 89 | 82 | 98 | 89 | 89 | 96 | 90 | 89 | 78 | 90 | 86 | 90 | 80 | 96 | 87 | 91 | 86 | 93 |
| CALHOUN | 97 | 67 | 72 | 75 | 94 | 91 | 111 | 95 | 91 | 78 | 79 | 95 | 80 | 94 | 69 | 95 | 79 | 87 | 101 | 96 |
| CARROLL | 97 | 71 | 79 | 79 | 94 | 90 | 113 | 96 | 92 | 81 | 81 | 95 | 82 | 96 | 71 | 97 | 83 | 89 | 98 | 98 |
| CHICKASAW | 97 | 64 | 67 | 73 | 92 | 90 | 112 | 96 | 91 | 76 | 77 | 96 | 79 | 95 | 66 | 95 | 78 | 87 | 101 | 97 |
| CHOCTAW | 96 | 65 | 68 | 73 | 93 | 90 | 110 | 95 | 91 | 76 | 77 | 94 | 79 | 93 | 68 | 95 | 78 | 86 | 101 | 95 |
| CLAIBORNE | 89 | 69 | 71 | 68 | 93 | 82 | 83 | 93 | 85 | 81 | 71 | 83 | 77 | 83 | 73 | 93 | 80 | 86 | 83 | 90 |
| CLARKE | 97 | 67 | 72 | 76 | 93 | 91 | 111 | 95 | 91 | 78 | 79 | 95 | 81 | 95 | 69 | 96 | 80 | 87 | 101 | 97 |
| CLAY | 95 | 75 | 88 | 82 | 97 | 93 | 105 | 96 | 91 | 84 | 81 | 93 | 85 | 94 | 76 | 95 | 84 | 89 | 96 | 96 |
| COAHOMA | 91 | 77 | 89 | 80 | 98 | 90 | 91 | 94 | 88 | 87 | 77 | 89 | 85 | 89 | 79 | 95 | 85 | 90 | 88 | 91 |
| COPIAH | 96 | 66 | 72 | 74 | 93 | 90 | 108 | 95 | 90 | 78 | 77 | 93 | 79 | 93 | 69 | 95 | 79 | 87 | 98 | 95 |
| COVINGTON | 97 | 66 | 74 | 76 | 94 | 91 | 110 | 96 | 91 | 78 | 78 | 96 | 81 | 95 | 69 | 95 | 80 | 87 | 100 | 97 |
| DESOTO | 100 | 90 | 85 | 90 | 96 | 95 | 107 | 99 | 99 | 95 | 98 | 101 | 94 | 102 | 79 | 100 | 96 | 98 | 99 | 102 |
| FORREST | 94 | 85 | 93 | 86 | 98 | 93 | 99 | 94 | 91 | 87 | 86 | 92 | 87 | 94 | 80 | 95 | 88 | 92 | 94 | 96 |
| FRANKLIN | 95 | 63 | 68 | 72 | 92 | 89 | 107 | 95 | 90 | 75 | 75 | 92 | 77 | 92 | 67 | 95 | 77 | 86 | 98 | 94 |
| GEORGE | 97 | 63 | 67 | 73 | 92 | 90 | 112 | 95 | 91 | 75 | 77 | 95 | 78 | 94 | 66 | 95 | 78 | 86 | 102 | 96 |
| GREENE | 97 | 63 | 67 | 73 | 92 | 90 | 112 | 95 | 91 | 75 | 77 | 95 | 78 | 94 | 66 | 95 | 78 | 86 | 102 | 96 |
| GRENADA | 96 | 70 | 76 | 77 | 95 | 89 | 107 | 96 | 91 | 82 | 79 | 94 | 82 | 94 | 71 | 97 | 83 | 89 | 95 | 97 |
| HANCOCK | 98 | 74 | 88 | 86 | 97 | 97 | 113 | 98 | 93 | 82 | 84 | 96 | 86 | 97 | 77 | 97 | 85 | 91 | 103 | 99 |
| HARRISON | 96 | 91 | 95 | 90 | 99 | 96 | 100 | 97 | 95 | 93 | 94 | 95 | 92 | 97 | 83 | 98 | 93 | 96 | 96 | 99 |
| HINDS | 97 | 95 | 98 | 95 | 101 | 98 | 96 | 98 | 96 | 98 | 95 | 98 | 96 | 98 | 87 | 99 | 98 | 99 | 93 | 99 |
| HOLMES | 90 | 63 | 67 | 67 | 93 | 83 | 90 | 94 | 85 | 79 | 68 | 86 | 75 | 85 | 70 | 94 | 78 | 85 | 85 | 90 |
| HUMPHREYS | 92 | 64 | 67 | 69 | 93 | 86 | 97 | 94 | 87 | 79 | 72 | 88 | 77 | 87 | 70 | 95 | 79 | 86 | 90 | 91 |
| ISSAQUENA | 97 | 63 | 66 | 73 | 92 | 90 | 112 | 96 | 91 | 75 | 77 | 96 | 78 | 95 | 66 | 95 | 78 | 86 | 102 | 96 |
| ITAWAMBA | 98 | 65 | 70 | 75 | 93 | 91 | 112 | 96 | 91 | 77 | 78 | 96 | 80 | 95 | 67 | 95 | 79 | 87 | 102 | 97 |
| JACKSON | 99 | 90 | 93 | 92 | 100 | 97 | 104 | 98 | 97 | 95 | 95 | 99 | 95 | 100 | 83 | 99 | 96 | 97 | 98 | 101 |
| JASPER | 97 | 64 | 68 | 74 | 92 | 90 | 112 | 96 | 92 | 76 | 77 | 96 | 79 | 95 | 66 | 95 | 78 | 87 | 102 | 97 |
| JEFFERSON | 87 | 61 | 63 | 63 | 93 | 78 | 71 | 95 | 83 | 82 | 64 | 79 | 74 | 79 | 71 | 95 | 80 | 86 | 77 | 86 |
| JEFFERSON DAVIS | 97 | 64 | 69 | 74 | 92 | 90 | 112 | 95 | 92 | 76 | 78 | 95 | 79 | 94 | 67 | 95 | 78 | 87 | 101 | 96 |
| JONES | 97 | 75 | 85 | 83 | 96 | 93 | 109 | 97 | 93 | 84 | 84 | 95 | 86 | 96 | 75 | 97 | 86 | 91 | 98 | 98 |
| KEMPER | 95 | 67 | 69 | 73 | 94 | 90 | 108 | 94 | 90 | 78 | 78 | 93 | 80 | 92 | 70 | 94 | 78 | 86 | 100 | 95 |
| LAFAYETTE | 95 | 86 | 89 | 85 | 95 | 91 | 104 | 93 | 92 | 85 | 88 | 92 | 86 | 94 | 78 | 95 | 86 | 92 | 97 | 97 |
| LAMAR | 100 | 89 | 90 | 92 | 97 | 97 | 107 | 99 | 99 | 93 | 96 | 100 | 94 | 101 | 80 | 99 | 94 | 97 | 100 | 102 |
| LAUDERDALE | 96 | 85 | 95 | 87 | 99 | 95 | 104 | 97 | 93 | 90 | 89 | 95 | 90 | 97 | 81 | 97 | 90 | 93 | 96 | 98 |
| LAWRENCE | 97 | 65 | 71 | 74 | 92 | 90 | 113 | 95 | 92 | 76 | 78 | 95 | 79 | 94 | 67 | 95 | 79 | 87 | 101 | 96 |
| LEAKE | 96 | 63 | 68 | 73 | 92 | 90 | 110 | 95 | 91 | 75 | 76 | 94 | 78 | 93 | 67 | 95 | 78 | 86 | 101 | 95 |
| LEE | 99 | 87 | 90 | 91 | 98 | 96 | 107 | 98 | 97 | 93 | 94 | 99 | 93 | 100 | 80 | 98 | 94 | 96 | 99 | 101 |
| LEFLORE | 94 | 81 | 93 | 86 | 98 | 92 | 96 | 96 | 92 | 89 | 81 | 93 | 87 | 92 | 81 | 97 | 88 | 92 | 90 | 95 |
| LINCOLN | 98 | 75 | 88 | 85 | 96 | 94 | 109 | 97 | 94 | 84 | 83 | 96 | 86 | 96 | 75 | 97 | 86 | 91 | 98 | 98 |
| LOWNDES | 98 | 89 | 93 | 92 | 98 | 96 | 104 | 98 | 96 | 93 | 92 | 99 | 93 | 99 | 82 | 98 | 93 | 96 | 96 | 100 |
| MADISON | 100 | 100 | 93 | 98 | 99 | 99 | 98 | 99 | 100 | 100 | 101 | 102 | 98 | 101 | 86 | 99 | 100 | 100 | 95 | 101 |
| MARION | 97 | 67 | 74 | 77 | 93 | 91 | 109 | 96 | 92 | 78 | 78 | 94 | 81 | 94 | 69 | 96 | 80 | 88 | 100 | 96 |
| MARSHALL | 96 | 67 | 71 | 74 | 93 | 89 | 110 | 95 | 91 | 79 | 78 | 94 | 80 | 94 | 68 | 96 | 81 | 88 | 98 | 96 |
| MONROE | 97 | 69 | 76 | 77 | 94 | 91 | 111 | 96 | 91 | 79 | 80 | 95 | 82 | 95 | 70 | 96 | 81 | 88 | 100 | 97 |
| MONTGOMERY | 94 | 64 | 68 | 72 | 93 | 88 | 105 | 95 | 89 | 77 | 75 | 92 | 78 | 91 | 68 | 95 | 78 | 86 | 96 | 94 |
| NESHOBA | 96 | 69 | 75 | 76 | 94 | 91 | 109 | 96 | 91 | 79 | 80 | 94 | 81 | 94 | 71 | 95 | 80 | 88 | 99 | 97 |
| NEWTON | 97 | 65 | 71 | 75 | 93 | 91 | 112 | 96 | 92 | 77 | 78 | 96 | 80 | 95 | 68 | 96 | 79 | 87 | 102 | 97 |
| NOXUBEE | 93 | 65 | 68 | 70 | 94 | 87 | 101 | 95 | 88 | 79 | 74 | 91 | 78 | 90 | 70 | 94 | 78 | 86 | 93 | 93 |
| OKTIBBEHA | 94 | 84 | 88 | 85 | 95 | 91 | 100 | 91 | 90 | 83 | 85 | 90 | 84 | 92 | 77 | 93 | 86 | 90 | 95 | 96 |
| PANOLA | 96 | 70 | 81 | 80 | 96 | 92 | 108 | 96 | 91 | 81 | 80 | 95 | 83 | 94 | 73 | 95 | 82 | 88 | 98 | 96 |
| PEARL RIVER | 98 | 73 | 79 | 80 | 94 | 91 | 113 | 96 | 93 | 82 | 83 | 96 | 84 | 97 | 71 | 97 | 84 | 90 | 101 | 99 |
| PERRY | 97 | 68 | 74 | 76 | 93 | 91 | 112 | 95 | 92 | 79 | 80 | 94 | 81 | 95 | 70 | 96 | 80 | 88 | 101 | 97 |
| PIKE | 95 | 71 | 81 | 77 | 96 | 91 | 104 | 95 | 90 | 82 | 79 | 92 | 82 | 92 | 73 | 96 | 82 | 88 | 96 | 95 |
| PONTOTOC | 97 | 66 | 72 | 75 | 93 | 91 | 112 | 96 | 92 | 77 | 79 | 95 | 80 | 95 | 68 | 96 | 80 | 87 | 101 | 97 |
| PRENTISS | 97 | 68 | 75 | 76 | 94 | 92 | 109 | 96 | 92 | 79 | 80 | 95 | 82 | 95 | 70 | 95 | 80 | 88 | 101 | 96 |
| QUITMAN | 93 | 62 | 67 | 70 | 92 | 86 | 100 | 95 | 88 | 77 | 71 | 91 | 76 | 89 | 67 | 95 | 78 | 86 | 92 | 93 |
| RANKIN | 101 | 97 | 95 | 97 | 98 | 99 | 107 | 99 | 100 | 100 | 102 | 102 | 98 | 103 | 85 | 100 | 100 | 100 | 99 | 103 |
| SCOTT | 97 | 69 | 79 | 79 | 95 | 92 | 110 | 96 | 92 | 80 | 80 | 96 | 83 | 95 | 71 | 96 | 82 | 89 | 100 | 97 |
| SHARKEY | 95 | 62 | 67 | 71 | 92 | 88 | 106 | 95 | 90 | 76 | 74 | 92 | 77 | 91 | 67 | 95 | 78 | 86 | 96 | 94 |
| SIMPSON | 97 | 66 | 72 | 75 | 93 | 90 | 112 | 95 | 92 | 78 | 79 | 94 | 80 | 94 | 68 | 96 | 80 | 87 | 101 | 97 |
| SMITH | 97 | 64 | 68 | 74 | 92 | 90 | 113 | 96 | 91 | 75 | 77 | 96 | 79 | 95 | 66 | 95 | 78 | 87 | 102 | 97 |
| STONE | 97 | 72 | 80 | 79 | 93 | 91 | 114 | 96 | 93 | 81 | 83 | 93 | 82 | 96 | 71 | 97 | 83 | 89 | 101 | 97 |
| SUNFLOWER | 93 | 71 | 86 | 79 | 97 | 89 | 94 | 96 | 89 | 85 | 75 | 90 | 83 | 89 | 77 | 96 | 84 | 89 | 88 | 93 |
| TALLAHATCHIE | 94 | 65 | 68 | 71 | 94 | 87 | 101 | 95 | 88 | 78 | 74 | 91 | 78 | 90 | 69 | 94 | 78 | 86 | 93 | 94 |
| TATE | 98 | 75 | 83 | 83 | 95 | 93 | 110 | 97 | 94 | 84 | 84 | 97 | 86 | 97 | 73 | 97 | 85 | 91 | 100 | 99 |
| TIPPAH | 98 | 65 | 69 | 74 | 92 | 90 | 113 | 96 | 92 | 76 | 78 | 96 | 79 | 95 | 67 | 95 | 79 | 87 | 101 | 97 |
| TISHOMINGO | 98 | 65 | 70 | 75 | 93 | 91 | 113 | 96 | 92 | 76 | 78 | 96 | 80 | 95 | 68 | 96 | 79 | 87 | 102 | 97 |
| TUNICA | 88 | 65 | 77 | 70 | 94 | 82 | 78 | 96 | 85 | 82 | 68 | 83 | 77 | 83 | 74 | 94 | 80 | 87 | 80 | 89 |
| UNION | 97 | 68 | 75 | 77 | 94 | 91 | 113 | 96 | 92 | 79 | 80 | 95 | 82 | 96 | 70 | 96 | 81 | 88 | 101 | 97 |
| WALTHALL | 97 | 63 | 67 | 73 | 92 | 90 | 111 | 95 | 91 | 75 | 76 | 95 | 78 | 94 | 66 | 95 | 78 | 86 | 100 | 96 |
| WARREN | 98 | 92 | 98 | 95 | 101 | 98 | 101 | 99 | 97 | 97 | 95 | 99 | 96 | 100 | 85 | 99 | 96 | 98 | 95 | 100 |
| WASHINGTON | 94 | 82 | 93 | 86 | 99 | 93 | 94 | 97 | 92 | 91 | 83 | 93 | 89 | 93 | 82 | 97 | 90 | 93 | 90 | 95 |
| WAYNE | 96 | 66 | 70 | 74 | 93 | 89 | 108 | 95 | 91 | 78 | 77 | 94 | 79 | 93 | 68 | 95 | 79 | 87 | 98 | 96 |
| MISSISSIPPI | 97 | 81 | 87 | 86 | 97 | 94 | 105 | 97 | 94 | 88 | 87 | 96 | 88 | 96 | 78 | 97 | 88 | 93 | 97 | 98 |
| UNITED STATES | 100 | 100 | 100 | 100 | 100 | 100 | 100 | 100 | 100 | 100 | 100 | 100 | 100 | 100 | 100 | 100 | 100 | 100 | 100 | 100 |

# POPULATION CHANGE

| COUNTY | FIPS Code | MSA Code | DMA Code | POPULATION 1990 | POPULATION 2000 | POPULATION 2005 | 1990-2000 ANNUAL CHANGE % Rate | 1990-2000 ANNUAL CHANGE State Rank | RACE (%) White 1990 | RACE (%) White 2000 | RACE (%) Black 1990 | RACE (%) Black 2000 | RACE (%) Asian/Pacific 1990 | RACE (%) Asian/Pacific 2000 |
|---|---|---|---|---|---|---|---|---|---|---|---|---|---|---|
| WEBSTER | 155 | 0000 | 673 | 10,222 | 10,695 | 11,006 | 0.4 | 42 | 77.8 | 76.2 | 22.1 | 23.6 | 0.1 | 0.1 |
| WILKINSON | 157 | 0000 | 716 | 9,678 | 8,948 | 8,495 | -0.8 | 79 | 32.3 | 30.4 | 67.5 | 69.3 | 0.0 | 0.0 |
| WINSTON | 159 | 0000 | 673 | 19,433 | 19,207 | 18,973 | -0.1 | 63 | 57.4 | 55.0 | 41.7 | 43.9 | 0.1 | 0.1 |
| YALOBUSHA | 161 | 0000 | 673 | 12,033 | 12,775 | 13,500 | 0.6 | 29 | 62.2 | 59.8 | 37.6 | 40.0 | 0.1 | 0.1 |
| YAZOO | 163 | 0000 | 718 | 25,506 | 25,109 | 24,604 | -0.2 | 66 | 46.9 | 44.6 | 52.7 | 54.9 | 0.2 | 0.3 |
| MISSISSIPPI | | | | | | | 0.8 | | 63.5 | 62.5 | 35.6 | 36.3 | 0.5 | 0.7 |
| UNITED STATES | | | | | | | 1.0 | | 80.3 | 77.9 | 12.1 | 12.4 | 2.9 | 3.9 |

| COUNTY | % HISPANIC ORIGIN | | 2000 AGE DISTRIBUTION (%) | | | | | | | | | | MEDIAN AGE | | 2000 Males/ Females (×100) |
|---|---|---|---|---|---|---|---|---|---|---|---|---|---|---|---|
| | 1990 | 2000 | 0-4 | 5-9 | 10-14 | 15-19 | 20-24 | 25-44 | 45-64 | 65-84 | 85+ | 18+ | 1990 | 2000 | |
| WEBSTER | 0.6 | 1.1 | 6.3 | 6.5 | 6.8 | 8.3 | 6.7 | 26.4 | 23.2 | 13.3 | 2.4 | 75.5 | 34.8 | 37.2 | 94.4 |
| WILKINSON | 0.5 | 0.6 | 7.7 | 8.0 | 7.7 | 8.3 | 7.0 | 26.7 | 20.8 | 11.6 | 2.1 | 71.6 | 31.4 | 34.1 | 88.1 |
| WINSTON | 0.4 | 0.6 | 6.7 | 7.1 | 7.4 | 8.1 | 6.6 | 26.3 | 22.7 | 12.9 | 2.2 | 73.5 | 33.9 | 36.5 | 89.4 |
| YALOBUSHA | 0.4 | 0.7 | 6.8 | 6.9 | 7.3 | 7.8 | 6.4 | 26.6 | 22.6 | 13.7 | 2.1 | 74.2 | 34.8 | 36.9 | 88.3 |
| YAZOO | 0.4 | 0.6 | 8.2 | 8.3 | 8.3 | 8.4 | 7.4 | 25.6 | 20.5 | 11.2 | 2.0 | 69.9 | 31.1 | 32.6 | 87.7 |
| MISSISSIPPI | 0.6 | 1.1 | 7.2 | 7.3 | 7.4 | 8.2 | 7.7 | 28.5 | 21.5 | 10.5 | 1.5 | 73.4 | 31.2 | 33.9 | 92.0 |
| UNITED STATES | 9.0 | 11.8 | 6.9 | 7.2 | 7.2 | 7.2 | 6.7 | 29.9 | 22.2 | 11.1 | 1.6 | 74.6 | 32.9 | 35.7 | 95.6 |

# HOUSEHOLDS

| COUNTY | HOUSEHOLDS | | | | | FAMILIES | | | MEDIAN HOUSEHOLD INCOME | | | |
|---|---|---|---|---|---|---|---|---|---|---|---|---|
| | 1990 | 2000 | 2005 | % Annual Rate 1990-2000 | 2000 Average HH Size | 1990 | 2000 | % Annual Rate 1990-2000 | 2000 | 2005 | 2000 National Rank | 2000 State Rank |
| WEBSTER | 3,826 | 4,083 | 4,252 | 0.8 | 2.57 | 2,814 | 2,896 | 0.3 | 25,174 | 29,188 | 2794 | 57 |
| WILKINSON | 3,347 | 3,244 | 3,151 | -0.4 | 2.71 | 2,520 | 2,367 | -0.8 | 20,014 | 22,434 | 3099 | 77 |
| WINSTON | 7,061 | 7,221 | 7,285 | 0.3 | 2.63 | 5,251 | 5,194 | -0.1 | 27,933 | 31,620 | 2448 | 34 |
| YALOBUSHA | 4,614 | 4,931 | 5,227 | 0.8 | 2.57 | 3,244 | 3,320 | 0.3 | 24,890 | 26,869 | 2816 | 58 |
| YAZOO | 8,813 | 9,114 | 9,137 | 0.4 | 2.72 | 6,463 | 6,485 | 0.0 | 20,867 | 22,697 | 3074 | 74 |
| MISSISSIPPI | | | | 1.4 | 2.66 | | | 1.0 | 31,144 | 36,358 | | |
| UNITED STATES | | | | 1.4 | 2.59 | | | 1.1 | 41,914 | 49,127 | | |

| COUNTY | 2000 Per Capita Income | 2000 HH Income Base | 2000 HOUSEHOLD INCOME DISTRIBUTION (%) Less than $15,000 | $15,000 to $24,999 | $25,000 to $49,999 | $50,000 to $99,999 | $100,000 to $149,999 | $150,000 or More | 2000 AVERAGE DISPOSABLE INCOME BY AGE OF HOUSEHOLDER All Ages | <35 | 35-44 | 45-54 | 55-64 | 65+ |
|---|---|---|---|---|---|---|---|---|---|---|---|---|---|---|
| WEBSTER | 12,000 | 4,083 | 31.1 | 18.5 | 32.2 | 16.0 | 1.6 | 0.6 | 25,854 | 25,272 | 31,805 | 31,721 | 26,737 | 17,192 |
| WILKINSON | 11,383 | 3,244 | 39.6 | 20.8 | 26.1 | 11.5 | 1.5 | 0.5 | 22,505 | 23,040 | 25,482 | 25,925 | 22,851 | 16,289 |
| WINSTON | 13,743 | 7,221 | 27.4 | 17.3 | 34.5 | 17.0 | 3.1 | 0.7 | 28,375 | 24,199 | 33,058 | 36,837 | 30,073 | 19,035 |
| YALOBUSHA | 11,748 | 4,931 | 30.6 | 19.6 | 34.0 | 13.8 | 1.9 | 0.2 | 25,019 | 25,253 | 31,706 | 29,626 | 25,016 | 16,860 |
| YAZOO | 12,038 | 9,114 | 38.9 | 18.1 | 27.3 | 11.7 | 2.6 | 1.5 | 25,496 | 21,787 | 29,579 | 30,571 | 26,843 | 17,577 |
| MISSISSIPPI | 15,620 | | 24.1 | 16.2 | 32.7 | 21.6 | 4.0 | 1.5 | 32,177 | 28,646 | 37,129 | 39,522 | 32,438 | 20,720 |
| UNITED STATES | 22,162 | | 14.5 | 12.5 | 32.3 | 29.8 | 7.4 | 3.5 | 40,748 | 34,503 | 44,969 | 49,579 | 43,409 | 27,339 |

# SPENDING POTENTIAL INDEXES

| COUNTY | FINANCIAL SERVICES | | | | THE HOME | | | | | | ENTERTAINMENT | | | | | | PERSONAL | | | |
|---|---|---|---|---|---|---|---|---|---|---|---|---|---|---|---|---|---|---|---|---|
| | | | | | Home Improvements | | | Furnishings | | | | | | | | | | | | |
| | Auto Loan | Home Loan | Invest-ments | Retire-ment Plans | Home Repair | Lawn & Garden | Remodel-ing | Appli-ances | Elec-tronics | Furni-ture | Restau-rants | Sport-ing Goods | Theater & Concerts | Toys & Hobbies | Travel | Video Rental | Apparel | Auto After-market | Health Insur-ance | Pets & Supplies |
| WEBSTER | 96 | 65 | 71 | 74 | 92 | 90 | 111 | 95 | 91 | 77 | 77 | 94 | 79 | 93 | 68 | 95 | 79 | 87 | 100 | 96 |
| WILKINSON | 93 | 61 | 67 | 69 | 92 | 85 | 97 | 95 | 88 | 77 | 70 | 89 | 75 | 88 | 68 | 95 | 77 | 86 | 90 | 92 |
| WINSTON | 97 | 66 | 72 | 75 | 93 | 91 | 111 | 96 | 91 | 77 | 78 | 95 | 80 | 95 | 68 | 96 | 79 | 87 | 101 | 97 |
| YALOBUSHA | 96 | 65 | 69 | 73 | 93 | 90 | 109 | 95 | 91 | 77 | 77 | 93 | 79 | 93 | 68 | 95 | 78 | 86 | 101 | 95 |
| YAZOO | 95 | 71 | 84 | 80 | 96 | 91 | 102 | 96 | 90 | 83 | 78 | 93 | 83 | 92 | 74 | 96 | 83 | 89 | 94 | 95 |
| MISSISSIPPI | 97 | 81 | 87 | 86 | 97 | 94 | 105 | 97 | 94 | 88 | 87 | 96 | 88 | 96 | 78 | 97 | 88 | 93 | 97 | 98 |
| UNITED STATES | 100 | 100 | 100 | 100 | 100 | 100 | 100 | 100 | 100 | 100 | 100 | 100 | 100 | 100 | 100 | 100 | 100 | 100 | 100 | 100 |

| COUNTY | FIPS Code | MSA Code | DMA Code | POPULATION 1990 | POPULATION 2000 | POPULATION 2005 | 1990-2000 ANNUAL CHANGE % Rate | 1990-2000 ANNUAL CHANGE State Rank | RACE (%) White 1990 | RACE (%) White 2000 | RACE (%) Black 1990 | RACE (%) Black 2000 | RACE (%) Asian/Pacific 1990 | RACE (%) Asian/Pacific 2000 |
|---|---|---|---|---|---|---|---|---|---|---|---|---|---|---|
| ADAIR | 001 | 0000 | 631 | 24,577 | 24,135 | 23,811 | -0.2 | 94 | 97.8 | 97.1 | 0.9 | 1.1 | 0.9 | 1.2 |
| ANDREW | 003 | 7000 | 638 | 14,632 | 15,682 | 16,144 | 0.7 | 55 | 99.2 | 99.1 | 0.2 | 0.2 | 0.2 | 0.2 |
| ATCHISON | 005 | 0000 | 652 | 7,457 | 6,983 | 6,797 | -0.6 | 106 | 97.6 | 97.2 | 1.1 | 1.3 | 0.2 | 0.2 |
| AUDRAIN | 007 | 0000 | 604 | 23,599 | 23,418 | 23,271 | -0.1 | 91 | 93.4 | 91.7 | 6.0 | 7.5 | 0.4 | 0.6 |
| BARRY | 009 | 0000 | 619 | 27,547 | 33,410 | 34,676 | 1.9 | 14 | 98.5 | 98.4 | 0.1 | 0.1 | 0.3 | 0.4 |
| BARTON | 011 | 0000 | 603 | 11,312 | 12,210 | 12,618 | 0.7 | 55 | 98.6 | 98.5 | 0.1 | 0.1 | 0.2 | 0.3 |
| BATES | 013 | 0000 | 616 | 15,025 | 16,211 | 16,990 | 0.7 | 55 | 98.6 | 98.4 | 0.7 | 0.8 | 0.1 | 0.1 |
| BENTON | 015 | 0000 | 619 | 13,859 | 17,735 | 19,716 | 2.4 | 10 | 99.1 | 99.1 | 0.1 | 0.1 | 0.1 | 0.2 |
| BOLLINGER | 017 | 0000 | 632 | 10,619 | 12,014 | 12,956 | 1.2 | 35 | 99.3 | 99.1 | 0.1 | 0.2 | 0.3 | 0.4 |
| BOONE | 019 | 1740 | 604 | 112,379 | 131,788 | 138,949 | 1.6 | 21 | 89.0 | 86.4 | 7.5 | 8.9 | 2.8 | 3.9 |
| BUCHANAN | 021 | 7000 | 638 | 83,083 | 81,530 | 80,896 | -0.2 | 94 | 95.5 | 94.6 | 3.2 | 3.7 | 0.3 | 0.5 |
| BUTLER | 023 | 0000 | 632 | 38,765 | 40,380 | 40,425 | 0.4 | 70 | 94.1 | 93.0 | 5.1 | 6.1 | 0.3 | 0.5 |
| CALDWELL | 025 | 0000 | 616 | 8,380 | 9,038 | 9,567 | 0.7 | 55 | 99.5 | 99.4 | 0.2 | 0.2 | 0.0 | 0.0 |
| CALLAWAY | 027 | 0000 | 604 | 32,809 | 38,400 | 40,903 | 1.5 | 27 | 94.3 | 92.8 | 4.8 | 6.1 | 0.4 | 0.5 |
| CAMDEN | 029 | 0000 | 619 | 27,495 | 35,262 | 38,693 | 2.5 | 8 | 99.1 | 99.1 | 0.2 | 0.2 | 0.2 | 0.2 |
| CAPE GIRARDEAU | 031 | 0000 | 632 | 61,633 | 67,811 | 70,976 | 0.9 | 43 | 94.0 | 92.9 | 4.8 | 5.7 | 0.8 | 1.0 |
| CARROLL | 033 | 0000 | 616 | 10,748 | 10,043 | 9,727 | -0.7 | 110 | 97.6 | 97.0 | 2.0 | 2.6 | 0.1 | 0.2 |
| CARTER | 035 | 0000 | 632 | 5,515 | 6,300 | 6,334 | 1.3 | 32 | 99.1 | 99.0 | 0.0 | 0.0 | 0.1 | 0.1 |
| CASS | 037 | 3760 | 616 | 63,808 | 85,572 | 97,823 | 2.9 | 5 | 97.5 | 97.0 | 1.1 | 1.3 | 0.4 | 0.6 |
| CEDAR | 039 | 0000 | 619 | 12,093 | 13,549 | 14,347 | 1.1 | 38 | 99.0 | 98.9 | 0.0 | 0.0 | 0.2 | 0.2 |
| CHARITON | 041 | 0000 | 604 | 9,202 | 8,470 | 8,048 | -0.8 | 112 | 96.0 | 95.3 | 3.7 | 4.4 | 0.1 | 0.1 |
| CHRISTIAN | 043 | 7920 | 619 | 32,644 | 53,556 | 64,587 | 4.9 | 1 | 98.9 | 98.6 | 0.1 | 0.2 | 0.2 | 0.4 |
| CLARK | 045 | 0000 | 717 | 7,547 | 7,315 | 7,061 | -0.3 | 98 | 99.7 | 99.6 | 0.0 | 0.1 | 0.1 | 0.1 |
| CLAY | 047 | 3760 | 616 | 153,411 | 183,443 | 199,908 | 1.8 | 16 | 96.3 | 95.4 | 1.8 | 2.0 | 0.7 | 1.1 |
| CLINTON | 049 | 3760 | 616 | 16,595 | 19,985 | 22,226 | 1.8 | 16 | 97.1 | 96.6 | 2.0 | 2.5 | 0.1 | 0.2 |
| COLE | 051 | 0000 | 604 | 63,579 | 69,912 | 71,874 | 0.9 | 43 | 91.4 | 90.4 | 7.6 | 8.4 | 0.4 | 0.6 |
| COOPER | 053 | 0000 | 604 | 14,835 | 16,215 | 16,545 | 0.9 | 43 | 91.4 | 89.1 | 7.7 | 9.9 | 0.3 | 0.4 |
| CRAWFORD | 055 | 0000 | 609 | 19,173 | 22,636 | 23,738 | 1.6 | 21 | 99.6 | 99.5 | 0.0 | 0.1 | 0.2 | 0.2 |
| DADE | 057 | 0000 | 619 | 7,449 | 7,976 | 8,166 | 0.7 | 55 | 98.5 | 98.3 | 0.3 | 0.3 | 0.2 | 0.3 |
| DALLAS | 059 | 0000 | 619 | 12,646 | 15,836 | 17,159 | 2.2 | 12 | 99.0 | 98.9 | 0.1 | 0.2 | 0.1 | 0.2 |
| DAVIESS | 061 | 0000 | 616 | 7,865 | 8,146 | 8,631 | 0.3 | 75 | 99.3 | 99.2 | 0.0 | 0.0 | 0.2 | 0.3 |
| DE KALB | 063 | 0000 | 638 | 9,967 | 11,368 | 11,788 | 1.3 | 32 | 90.4 | 88.0 | 7.4 | 9.0 | 0.3 | 0.5 |
| DENT | 065 | 0000 | 619 | 13,702 | 14,337 | 14,744 | 0.4 | 70 | 99.0 | 98.8 | 0.1 | 0.1 | 0.2 | 0.3 |
| DOUGLAS | 067 | 0000 | 619 | 11,876 | 12,458 | 12,654 | 0.5 | 66 | 99.0 | 98.9 | 0.0 | 0.0 | 0.1 | 0.2 |
| DUNKLIN | 069 | 0000 | 632 | 33,112 | 32,390 | 31,721 | -0.2 | 94 | 91.4 | 89.9 | 7.9 | 9.4 | 0.2 | 0.3 |
| FRANKLIN | 071 | 7040 | 609 | 80,603 | 94,373 | 100,705 | 1.6 | 21 | 98.5 | 98.2 | 0.9 | 1.1 | 0.2 | 0.4 |
| GASCONADE | 073 | 0000 | 609 | 14,006 | 15,102 | 15,689 | 0.7 | 55 | 99.6 | 99.6 | 0.1 | 0.0 | 0.1 | 0.2 |
| GENTRY | 075 | 0000 | 616 | 6,848 | 6,859 | 6,795 | 0.0 | 85 | 99.3 | 99.3 | 0.1 | 0.1 | 0.1 | 0.1 |
| GREENE | 077 | 7920 | 619 | 207,949 | 227,798 | 231,812 | 0.9 | 43 | 96.6 | 96.0 | 1.8 | 2.1 | 0.7 | 1.1 |
| GRUNDY | 079 | 0000 | 616 | 10,536 | 10,085 | 9,842 | -0.4 | 100 | 99.2 | 99.0 | 0.1 | 0.1 | 0.2 | 0.4 |
| HARRISON | 081 | 0000 | 616 | 8,469 | 8,420 | 8,425 | -0.1 | 91 | 99.2 | 99.0 | 0.1 | 0.1 | 0.3 | 0.4 |
| HENRY | 083 | 0000 | 616 | 20,044 | 21,344 | 21,682 | 0.6 | 62 | 98.1 | 97.6 | 1.1 | 1.4 | 0.2 | 0.4 |
| HICKORY | 085 | 0000 | 619 | 7,335 | 8,818 | 9,302 | 1.8 | 16 | 99.0 | 99.0 | 0.1 | 0.1 | 0.1 | 0.1 |
| HOLT | 087 | 0000 | 638 | 6,034 | 5,540 | 5,433 | -0.8 | 112 | 99.3 | 99.3 | 0.1 | 0.1 | 0.1 | 0.1 |
| HOWARD | 089 | 0000 | 604 | 9,631 | 9,628 | 9,467 | 0.0 | 85 | 91.8 | 90.3 | 7.6 | 9.0 | 0.2 | 0.2 |
| HOWELL | 091 | 0000 | 619 | 31,447 | 36,389 | 38,058 | 1.4 | 30 | 98.9 | 98.8 | 0.2 | 0.3 | 0.2 | 0.4 |
| IRON | 093 | 0000 | 609 | 10,726 | 10,945 | 10,993 | 0.2 | 82 | 99.1 | 98.8 | 0.5 | 0.7 | 0.1 | 0.2 |
| JACKSON | 095 | 3760 | 616 | 633,232 | 655,259 | 659,409 | 0.3 | 75 | 75.6 | 71.5 | 21.4 | 24.7 | 1.0 | 1.4 |
| JASPER | 097 | 3710 | 603 | 90,465 | 101,193 | 105,143 | 1.1 | 38 | 96.3 | 95.9 | 1.3 | 1.6 | 0.6 | 0.7 |
| JEFFERSON | 099 | 7040 | 609 | 171,380 | 201,136 | 215,448 | 1.6 | 21 | 98.6 | 98.3 | 0.7 | 0.9 | 0.3 | 0.5 |
| JOHNSON | 101 | 0000 | 616 | 42,514 | 48,520 | 50,745 | 1.3 | 32 | 91.7 | 90.1 | 5.8 | 6.6 | 1.4 | 2.1 |
| KNOX | 103 | 0000 | 717 | 4,482 | 4,290 | 4,185 | -0.4 | 100 | 99.5 | 99.3 | 0.1 | 0.3 | 0.1 | 0.1 |
| LACLEDE | 105 | 0000 | 619 | 27,158 | 31,930 | 34,463 | 1.6 | 21 | 98.7 | 98.5 | 0.4 | 0.4 | 0.3 | 0.4 |
| LAFAYETTE | 107 | 3760 | 616 | 31,107 | 32,996 | 33,870 | 0.6 | 62 | 96.4 | 95.7 | 2.8 | 3.4 | 0.2 | 0.3 |
| LAWRENCE | 109 | 0000 | 619 | 30,236 | 33,872 | 35,750 | 1.1 | 38 | 98.6 | 98.5 | 0.1 | 0.1 | 0.2 | 0.3 |
| LEWIS | 111 | 0000 | 717 | 10,233 | 10,258 | 10,400 | 0.0 | 85 | 96.2 | 95.6 | 3.3 | 3.9 | 0.2 | 0.2 |
| LINCOLN | 113 | 7040 | 609 | 28,892 | 38,912 | 44,801 | 2.9 | 5 | 97.2 | 96.6 | 2.0 | 2.5 | 0.2 | 0.3 |
| LINN | 115 | 0000 | 616 | 13,885 | 13,866 | 13,861 | 0.0 | 85 | 98.8 | 98.6 | 0.8 | 0.9 | 0.1 | 0.1 |
| LIVINGSTON | 117 | 0000 | 616 | 14,592 | 13,922 | 13,426 | -0.5 | 103 | 97.3 | 96.3 | 2.2 | 3.0 | 0.2 | 0.2 |
| MCDONALD | 119 | 0000 | 603 | 16,938 | 20,457 | 21,905 | 1.9 | 14 | 96.3 | 96.4 | 0.0 | 0.0 | 0.2 | 0.4 |
| MACON | 121 | 0000 | 631 | 15,345 | 15,543 | 15,988 | 0.1 | 83 | 97.1 | 96.6 | 2.4 | 2.9 | 0.1 | 0.2 |
| MADISON | 123 | 0000 | 632 | 11,127 | 11,731 | 12,150 | 0.5 | 66 | 99.2 | 99.0 | 0.1 | 0.1 | 0.3 | 0.4 |
| MARIES | 125 | 0000 | 604 | 7,976 | 8,462 | 8,645 | 0.6 | 62 | 99.2 | 99.1 | 0.3 | 0.3 | 0.1 | 0.2 |
| MARION | 127 | 0000 | 717 | 27,682 | 27,660 | 27,367 | 0.0 | 85 | 94.7 | 93.6 | 4.5 | 5.4 | 0.4 | 0.6 |
| MERCER | 129 | 0000 | 679 | 3,723 | 3,939 | 3,855 | 0.6 | 62 | 99.7 | 99.7 | 0.1 | 0.1 | 0.0 | 0.1 |
| MILLER | 131 | 0000 | 604 | 20,700 | 22,748 | 23,378 | 0.9 | 43 | 99.3 | 99.2 | 0.1 | 0.2 | 0.1 | 0.2 |
| MISSISSIPPI | 133 | 0000 | 632 | 14,442 | 13,235 | 12,728 | -0.8 | 112 | 80.3 | 76.5 | 19.4 | 23.1 | 0.1 | 0.1 |
| MONITEAU | 135 | 0000 | 604 | 12,298 | 13,398 | 13,798 | 0.8 | 53 | 97.9 | 97.8 | 1.3 | 1.4 | 0.3 | 0.4 |
| MONROE | 137 | 0000 | 717 | 9,104 | 9,209 | 9,562 | 0.1 | 83 | 95.7 | 94.9 | 3.9 | 4.7 | 0.2 | 0.2 |
| MONTGOMERY | 139 | 0000 | 604 | 11,355 | 12,199 | 12,684 | 0.7 | 55 | 97.0 | 96.5 | 2.5 | 2.9 | 0.2 | 0.3 |
| MORGAN | 141 | 0000 | 604 | 15,574 | 19,350 | 21,556 | 2.1 | 13 | 98.7 | 98.5 | 0.6 | 0.7 | 0.2 | 0.2 |
| NEW MADRID | 143 | 0000 | 632 | 20,928 | 19,673 | 18,425 | -0.6 | 106 | 83.9 | 81.0 | 15.7 | 18.5 | 0.2 | 0.2 |
| NEWTON | 145 | 3710 | 603 | 44,445 | 50,323 | 53,333 | 1.2 | 35 | 96.7 | 96.6 | 0.4 | 0.5 | 0.5 | 0.8 |
| NODAWAY | 147 | 0000 | 638 | 21,709 | 20,372 | 19,598 | -0.6 | 106 | 98.0 | 97.6 | 0.8 | 0.9 | 0.8 | 0.9 |
| OREGON | 149 | 0000 | 619 | 9,470 | 10,380 | 10,860 | 0.9 | 43 | 99.3 | 99.2 | 0.0 | 0.0 | 0.1 | 0.2 |
| OSAGE | 151 | 0000 | 604 | 12,018 | 12,561 | 12,756 | 0.4 | 70 | 99.4 | 99.3 | 0.3 | 0.3 | 0.0 | 0.0 |
| OZARK | 153 | 0000 | 619 | 8,598 | 10,070 | 10,622 | 1.6 | 21 | 99.2 | 99.0 | 0.0 | 0.1 | 0.1 | 0.2 |
| MISSOURI | | | | | | | 0.7 | | 87.7 | 87.0 | 10.7 | 11.0 | 0.8 | 1.1 |
| UNITED STATES | | | | | | | 1.0 | | 80.3 | 77.9 | 12.1 | 12.4 | 2.9 | 3.9 |

# POPULATION COMPOSITION

| COUNTY | % HISPANIC ORIGIN | | 2000 AGE DISTRIBUTION (%) | | | | | | | | | | MEDIAN AGE | | 2000 Males/ Females (×100) |
|---|---|---|---|---|---|---|---|---|---|---|---|---|---|---|---|
| | 1990 | 2000 | 0-4 | 5-9 | 10-14 | 15-19 | 20-24 | 25-44 | 45-64 | 65-84 | 85+ | 18+ | 1990 | 2000 | |
| ADAIR | 0.7 | 1.5 | 5.1 | 5.2 | 5.8 | 14.1 | 15.7 | 25.0 | 17.2 | 10.0 | 1.8 | 80.7 | 27.4 | 28.8 | 87.9 |
| ANDREW | 0.7 | 1.4 | 6.0 | 6.8 | 8.0 | 7.4 | 5.8 | 27.6 | 23.3 | 12.6 | 2.4 | 74.5 | 35.2 | 37.9 | 95.0 |
| ATCHISON | 1.4 | 2.1 | 4.7 | 5.6 | 6.4 | 8.9 | 7.4 | 24.1 | 22.6 | 16.7 | 3.5 | 78.9 | 38.0 | 40.3 | 98.5 |
| AUDRAIN | 0.3 | 0.8 | 6.3 | 6.8 | 7.2 | 7.4 | 6.0 | 24.7 | 23.2 | 15.7 | 2.8 | 74.8 | 37.0 | 39.2 | 94.3 |
| BARRY | 0.6 | 1.1 | 6.0 | 6.5 | 7.5 | 7.2 | 5.5 | 25.4 | 24.7 | 15.0 | 2.1 | 75.4 | 37.3 | 39.4 | 97.1 |
| BARTON | 0.5 | 1.1 | 6.4 | 7.3 | 8.0 | 7.2 | 5.3 | 26.5 | 22.2 | 14.4 | 2.7 | 73.7 | 36.2 | 38.1 | 95.6 |
| BATES | 0.5 | 1.1 | 6.3 | 6.9 | 7.2 | 7.7 | 5.5 | 24.0 | 23.1 | 16.1 | 3.1 | 74.7 | 37.5 | 39.7 | 94.6 |
| BENTON | 0.6 | 1.2 | 4.6 | 5.2 | 6.1 | 6.4 | 4.4 | 21.9 | 28.3 | 20.5 | 2.6 | 79.9 | 44.7 | 46.0 | 96.2 |
| BOLLINGER | 0.7 | 1.3 | 6.7 | 7.1 | 7.6 | 7.2 | 5.8 | 25.9 | 23.5 | 14.1 | 2.1 | 74.2 | 35.9 | 37.9 | 95.6 |
| BOONE | 1.1 | 1.8 | 6.4 | 6.4 | 6.4 | 10.0 | 13.8 | 31.8 | 17.0 | 7.1 | 1.1 | 77.5 | 27.7 | 29.8 | 93.7 |
| BUCHANAN | 2.1 | 3.3 | 6.7 | 7.0 | 7.4 | 7.6 | 6.6 | 28.1 | 21.5 | 12.7 | 2.3 | 74.5 | 34.1 | 36.3 | 91.9 |
| BUTLER | 0.6 | 1.2 | 6.1 | 6.4 | 6.9 | 7.4 | 6.2 | 26.6 | 23.4 | 14.9 | 2.0 | 76.0 | 35.9 | 38.5 | 91.9 |
| CALDWELL | 0.6 | 1.2 | 6.9 | 7.3 | 7.6 | 6.9 | 5.7 | 23.9 | 22.8 | 15.4 | 3.5 | 73.7 | 37.6 | 39.0 | 91.4 |
| CALLAWAY | 0.5 | 1.1 | 6.6 | 7.1 | 7.4 | 8.6 | 7.8 | 28.0 | 22.0 | 10.7 | 1.7 | 74.4 | 32.6 | 35.1 | 94.5 |
| CAMDEN | 0.6 | 1.2 | 4.9 | 5.5 | 6.2 | 5.9 | 4.3 | 24.0 | 29.0 | 18.7 | 1.4 | 79.5 | 41.7 | 44.4 | 101.0 |
| CAPE GIRARDEAU | 0.5 | 1.0 | 6.1 | 6.6 | 7.0 | 8.4 | 8.4 | 28.8 | 21.6 | 11.3 | 1.9 | 76.5 | 32.2 | 35.3 | 93.5 |
| CARROLL | 0.4 | 0.9 | 6.1 | 6.7 | 7.0 | 7.3 | 5.8 | 24.0 | 23.6 | 16.1 | 3.3 | 75.2 | 38.2 | 40.1 | 92.3 |
| CARTER | 0.6 | 1.2 | 6.6 | 6.9 | 8.2 | 7.7 | 6.0 | 25.0 | 24.4 | 13.3 | 1.8 | 73.4 | 35.7 | 37.8 | 98.1 |
| CASS | 1.3 | 2.3 | 7.2 | 7.6 | 8.0 | 7.5 | 6.0 | 29.3 | 23.1 | 9.7 | 1.6 | 72.5 | 32.3 | 35.6 | 95.1 |
| CEDAR | 0.5 | 1.1 | 5.5 | 5.9 | 7.1 | 6.7 | 5.2 | 22.4 | 24.7 | 19.4 | 3.2 | 77.2 | 42.4 | 43.0 | 90.8 |
| CHARITON | 0.2 | 0.6 | 6.1 | 7.0 | 7.6 | 7.1 | 4.9 | 23.9 | 23.3 | 16.9 | 3.3 | 74.4 | 38.7 | 40.5 | 93.1 |
| CHRISTIAN | 0.7 | 1.3 | 6.6 | 7.3 | 8.3 | 7.8 | 5.8 | 30.8 | 22.5 | 9.7 | 1.2 | 72.9 | 32.6 | 35.7 | 96.6 |
| CLARK | 0.3 | 0.9 | 6.3 | 7.0 | 7.2 | 7.6 | 5.9 | 25.5 | 24.2 | 13.8 | 2.6 | 74.8 | 35.9 | 38.5 | 99.9 |
| CLAY | 2.3 | 3.7 | 6.5 | 6.8 | 7.3 | 7.3 | 6.4 | 31.8 | 22.9 | 10.0 | 1.1 | 75.1 | 32.8 | 36.1 | 93.6 |
| CLINTON | 0.8 | 1.5 | 6.8 | 7.3 | 7.6 | 7.6 | 5.9 | 26.0 | 24.3 | 12.1 | 2.4 | 73.3 | 35.1 | 37.6 | 95.4 |
| COLE | 0.7 | 1.4 | 6.2 | 6.5 | 6.9 | 7.3 | 7.4 | 32.8 | 21.2 | 9.9 | 1.7 | 76.0 | 32.8 | 34.9 | 107.7 |
| COOPER | 0.6 | 1.2 | 5.7 | 6.5 | 7.1 | 10.0 | 9.7 | 24.5 | 20.8 | 13.3 | 2.4 | 76.3 | 34.1 | 35.5 | 112.5 |
| CRAWFORD | 0.6 | 1.2 | 6.3 | 7.0 | 7.8 | 7.7 | 5.6 | 26.5 | 23.8 | 13.3 | 2.0 | 74.1 | 35.6 | 37.9 | 95.7 |
| DADE | 1.0 | 1.8 | 6.6 | 7.3 | 7.5 | 7.1 | 4.5 | 23.6 | 22.2 | 17.3 | 3.8 | 73.8 | 38.9 | 40.4 | 95.7 |
| DALLAS | 0.5 | 1.0 | 6.4 | 7.0 | 8.2 | 7.5 | 5.3 | 25.6 | 24.0 | 14.0 | 2.1 | 73.5 | 36.6 | 38.4 | 96.9 |
| DAVIESS | 0.6 | 1.2 | 6.7 | 7.4 | 7.6 | 7.3 | 4.9 | 23.9 | 22.8 | 16.2 | 3.2 | 73.4 | 38.0 | 39.5 | 92.4 |
| DE KALB | 2.0 | 3.1 | 4.8 | 5.3 | 5.8 | 7.4 | 10.6 | 34.3 | 18.3 | 11.0 | 2.6 | 79.7 | 33.7 | 33.6 | 163.0 |
| DENT | 0.6 | 1.2 | 6.0 | 6.5 | 6.9 | 7.5 | 6.4 | 24.8 | 23.8 | 15.5 | 2.7 | 75.6 | 37.3 | 39.5 | 93.4 |
| DOUGLAS | 0.8 | 1.5 | 6.4 | 6.9 | 7.7 | 7.5 | 5.0 | 24.4 | 25.0 | 14.6 | 2.4 | 74.1 | 37.0 | 39.5 | 95.3 |
| DUNKLIN | 0.5 | 1.0 | 6.4 | 6.7 | 7.0 | 7.1 | 6.3 | 25.8 | 23.6 | 14.6 | 2.5 | 75.4 | 36.1 | 38.4 | 88.9 |
| FRANKLIN | 0.5 | 1.1 | 7.2 | 7.5 | 8.0 | 7.8 | 5.9 | 29.1 | 22.6 | 10.5 | 1.4 | 72.5 | 32.2 | 35.4 | 97.7 |
| GASCONADE | 0.2 | 0.7 | 6.3 | 6.8 | 7.4 | 6.8 | 5.1 | 25.8 | 22.3 | 16.6 | 2.9 | 75.1 | 37.6 | 39.5 | 93.8 |
| GENTRY | 0.4 | 0.9 | 5.9 | 6.8 | 7.3 | 7.0 | 4.9 | 23.2 | 22.6 | 17.8 | 4.6 | 75.6 | 40.2 | 41.2 | 92.7 |
| GREENE | 0.9 | 1.6 | 5.9 | 6.1 | 6.6 | 8.2 | 8.3 | 30.3 | 21.9 | 11.0 | 1.7 | 77.8 | 32.5 | 35.5 | 92.8 |
| GRUNDY | 0.7 | 1.4 | 5.4 | 6.2 | 6.9 | 7.2 | 4.5 | 24.6 | 24.7 | 16.9 | 3.6 | 77.1 | 39.7 | 41.8 | 89.2 |
| HARRISON | 0.4 | 1.0 | 5.3 | 6.2 | 6.6 | 6.7 | 4.8 | 23.9 | 23.5 | 18.8 | 4.2 | 77.7 | 41.4 | 42.8 | 97.3 |
| HENRY | 0.7 | 1.4 | 5.9 | 6.6 | 7.1 | 6.8 | 5.6 | 24.9 | 24.0 | 16.1 | 3.1 | 76.2 | 38.3 | 40.3 | 92.5 |
| HICKORY | 0.4 | 0.9 | 4.1 | 4.9 | 5.4 | 6.0 | 4.1 | 19.4 | 27.5 | 26.0 | 2.8 | 81.7 | 50.3 | 50.2 | 96.3 |
| HOLT | 0.3 | 0.7 | 6.1 | 7.0 | 7.4 | 7.2 | 5.5 | 24.0 | 22.7 | 16.1 | 4.1 | 74.6 | 38.5 | 40.0 | 95.9 |
| HOWARD | 0.5 | 0.9 | 6.2 | 6.5 | 7.0 | 9.7 | 7.9 | 24.1 | 21.4 | 14.3 | 2.9 | 75.6 | 34.9 | 37.1 | 94.4 |
| HOWELL | 0.5 | 1.1 | 6.2 | 6.7 | 7.6 | 7.5 | 5.7 | 25.8 | 23.9 | 14.4 | 2.2 | 74.8 | 36.4 | 38.6 | 94.1 |
| IRON | 0.4 | 0.9 | 5.8 | 6.5 | 7.7 | 8.0 | 5.6 | 25.0 | 24.0 | 14.5 | 2.9 | 74.9 | 37.1 | 39.1 | 90.4 |
| JACKSON | 3.0 | 4.3 | 6.8 | 6.9 | 7.3 | 7.0 | 6.5 | 31.3 | 21.3 | 11.1 | 1.7 | 74.8 | 33.1 | 35.8 | 91.3 |
| JASPER | 0.9 | 1.6 | 6.3 | 6.7 | 7.1 | 7.7 | 6.7 | 28.4 | 22.5 | 12.6 | 2.0 | 75.6 | 34.1 | 36.8 | 93.1 |
| JEFFERSON | 0.7 | 1.4 | 7.4 | 7.8 | 8.4 | 7.8 | 6.1 | 31.9 | 21.6 | 8.1 | 0.9 | 71.6 | 30.7 | 33.9 | 98.8 |
| JOHNSON | 1.7 | 2.7 | 7.2 | 6.6 | 6.4 | 11.0 | 14.7 | 28.5 | 16.5 | 7.8 | 1.3 | 76.5 | 26.2 | 27.6 | 101.7 |
| KNOX | 0.2 | 0.6 | 5.6 | 5.9 | 7.1 | 6.7 | 4.9 | 24.1 | 24.8 | 17.5 | 3.4 | 77.0 | 40.4 | 42.1 | 94.0 |
| LACLEDE | 0.5 | 1.1 | 6.8 | 7.2 | 7.7 | 7.5 | 5.9 | 27.7 | 22.7 | 12.5 | 2.0 | 73.8 | 34.2 | 36.8 | 95.8 |
| LAFAYETTE | 0.7 | 1.3 | 6.6 | 7.1 | 7.5 | 7.7 | 6.0 | 26.6 | 23.0 | 12.9 | 2.6 | 74.2 | 35.3 | 37.2 | 97.5 |
| LAWRENCE | 0.7 | 1.3 | 6.7 | 7.1 | 7.5 | 7.4 | 5.9 | 26.2 | 22.9 | 13.8 | 2.5 | 73.9 | 35.6 | 37.6 | 95.7 |
| LEWIS | 0.3 | 0.7 | 5.6 | 6.1 | 6.4 | 10.4 | 8.0 | 24.5 | 21.8 | 14.1 | 3.1 | 78.1 | 34.1 | 36.9 | 93.8 |
| LINCOLN | 0.8 | 1.4 | 7.6 | 8.1 | 8.6 | 7.8 | 5.8 | 29.2 | 22.0 | 9.5 | 1.4 | 70.7 | 31.9 | 34.7 | 100.4 |
| LINN | 0.7 | 1.3 | 6.3 | 6.6 | 7.0 | 7.7 | 5.4 | 23.6 | 22.2 | 17.4 | 3.9 | 75.1 | 39.4 | 40.5 | 90.0 |
| LIVINGSTON | 0.4 | 0.9 | 5.9 | 6.5 | 7.2 | 7.2 | 6.1 | 26.3 | 22.5 | 15.1 | 3.2 | 75.9 | 37.0 | 38.9 | 85.4 |
| MCDONALD | 0.7 | 1.3 | 7.3 | 7.6 | 8.1 | 7.5 | 6.0 | 26.5 | 22.9 | 12.5 | 1.6 | 72.4 | 34.1 | 36.4 | 100.3 |
| MACON | 0.4 | 0.9 | 5.4 | 6.1 | 7.4 | 7.2 | 5.5 | 25.7 | 23.6 | 15.8 | 3.3 | 76.5 | 38.5 | 40.4 | 92.8 |
| MADISON | 0.6 | 1.0 | 6.2 | 6.7 | 7.2 | 7.2 | 6.0 | 25.9 | 22.5 | 15.5 | 2.8 | 75.4 | 36.6 | 38.8 | 92.9 |
| MARIES | 0.5 | 1.1 | 6.3 | 6.6 | 7.6 | 7.4 | 5.4 | 25.5 | 24.9 | 14.4 | 2.0 | 74.7 | 36.6 | 38.9 | 97.1 |
| MARION | 0.4 | 1.0 | 6.8 | 7.1 | 7.4 | 8.4 | 6.7 | 25.8 | 22.0 | 13.0 | 2.8 | 73.5 | 34.7 | 36.8 | 91.8 |
| MERCER | 0.2 | 0.6 | 4.5 | 5.8 | 6.6 | 7.0 | 4.2 | 22.8 | 25.3 | 19.9 | 3.9 | 78.5 | 43.3 | 44.3 | 97.6 |
| MILLER | 0.5 | 1.1 | 7.0 | 7.3 | 7.8 | 7.9 | 5.7 | 26.6 | 22.7 | 13.0 | 2.1 | 72.9 | 34.0 | 36.9 | 96.5 |
| MISSISSIPPI | 0.3 | 0.7 | 7.1 | 7.2 | 7.7 | 7.8 | 6.7 | 25.7 | 22.6 | 13.1 | 2.1 | 73.1 | 33.9 | 36.3 | 89.5 |
| MONITEAU | 0.4 | 0.9 | 6.2 | 7.1 | 7.8 | 7.9 | 6.0 | 27.7 | 21.7 | 13.2 | 2.4 | 73.8 | 34.2 | 36.9 | 98.0 |
| MONROE | 0.5 | 1.1 | 6.6 | 7.4 | 8.0 | 7.6 | 5.3 | 25.1 | 22.8 | 14.1 | 3.0 | 73.0 | 36.1 | 38.3 | 97.6 |
| MONTGOMERY | 0.4 | 1.0 | 6.8 | 7.3 | 7.5 | 7.2 | 5.7 | 25.0 | 22.9 | 14.6 | 3.1 | 73.7 | 37.1 | 38.7 | 94.9 |
| MORGAN | 0.4 | 1.0 | 5.9 | 6.1 | 7.0 | 6.3 | 4.7 | 22.7 | 26.6 | 18.3 | 2.5 | 77.2 | 41.6 | 43.0 | 97.0 |
| NEW MADRID | 0.4 | 0.9 | 7.0 | 7.2 | 7.7 | 8.0 | 6.6 | 26.6 | 22.6 | 12.5 | 1.8 | 73.0 | 33.2 | 35.9 | 93.9 |
| NEWTON | 0.8 | 1.5 | 6.7 | 7.1 | 7.6 | 7.4 | 5.9 | 27.3 | 23.8 | 12.5 | 1.8 | 74.3 | 34.6 | 37.0 | 95.2 |
| NODAWAY | 0.6 | 1.2 | 5.3 | 6.0 | 6.4 | 13.0 | 14.5 | 23.8 | 17.2 | 11.4 | 2.3 | 78.7 | 28.2 | 29.5 | 93.9 |
| OREGON | 0.3 | 0.8 | 5.1 | 5.6 | 7.2 | 7.2 | 5.2 | 24.6 | 26.5 | 16.4 | 2.3 | 77.7 | 40.2 | 41.9 | 93.8 |
| OSAGE | 0.5 | 1.0 | 6.9 | 7.2 | 7.6 | 7.7 | 5.8 | 29.3 | 21.4 | 12.2 | 1.8 | 74.0 | 32.5 | 35.4 | 107.2 |
| OZARK | 0.7 | 1.3 | 4.5 | 5.5 | 6.6 | 6.9 | 4.7 | 23.3 | 27.3 | 18.9 | 2.3 | 78.8 | 42.0 | 44.0 | 98.5 |
| MISSOURI | 1.2 | 2.0 | 6.5 | 6.9 | 7.4 | 7.6 | 6.7 | 29.1 | 22.3 | 11.7 | 1.8 | 74.8 | 33.6 | 36.3 | 94.0 |
| UNITED STATES | 9.0 | 11.8 | 6.9 | 7.2 | 7.2 | 7.2 | 6.7 | 29.9 | 22.2 | 11.1 | 1.6 | 74.6 | 32.9 | 35.7 | 95.6 |

| COUNTY | HOUSEHOLDS | | | | | FAMILIES | | | MEDIAN HOUSEHOLD INCOME | | | |
|---|---|---|---|---|---|---|---|---|---|---|---|---|
| | 1990 | 2000 | 2005 | % Annual Rate 1990-2000 | 2000 Average HH Size | 1990 | 2000 | % Annual Rate 1990-2000 | 2000 | 2005 | 2000 National Rank | 2000 State Rank |
| ADAIR | 9,060 | 8,947 | 8,852 | -0.2 | 2.33 | 5,408 | 5,075 | -0.8 | 27,681 | 31,640 | 2481 | 78 |
| ANDREW | 5,429 | 5,923 | 6,149 | 1.1 | 2.60 | 4,185 | 4,419 | 0.7 | 39,160 | 46,544 | 741 | 17 |
| ATCHISON | 2,961 | 2,751 | 2,666 | -0.9 | 2.36 | 2,033 | 1,803 | -1.4 | 31,323 | 35,662 | 1857 | 48 |
| AUDRAIN | 9,205 | 9,292 | 9,308 | 0.1 | 2.46 | 6,667 | 6,468 | -0.4 | 34,022 | 38,456 | 1386 | 30 |
| BARRY | 10,858 | 13,535 | 14,224 | 2.7 | 2.44 | 8,046 | 9,649 | 2.2 | 30,165 | 35,890 | 2117 | 57 |
| BARTON | 4,524 | 4,942 | 5,138 | 1.1 | 2.44 | 3,188 | 3,360 | 0.6 | 28,975 | 35,105 | 2300 | 63 |
| BATES | 5,918 | 6,283 | 6,534 | 0.7 | 2.53 | 4,303 | 4,392 | 0.2 | 29,628 | 36,551 | 2207 | 61 |
| BENTON | 5,764 | 7,544 | 8,472 | 3.3 | 2.32 | 4,212 | 5,258 | 2.7 | 26,638 | 30,950 | 2628 | 91 |
| BOLLINGER | 3,946 | 4,370 | 4,658 | 1.2 | 2.71 | 3,057 | 3,247 | 0.7 | 30,985 | 39,267 | 1938 | 51 |
| BOONE | 41,937 | 50,457 | 53,762 | 2.3 | 2.40 | 25,573 | 29,666 | 1.8 | 40,163 | 45,121 | 658 | 13 |
| BUCHANAN | 32,486 | 32,167 | 32,022 | -0.1 | 2.46 | 22,319 | 21,214 | -0.6 | 32,501 | 36,930 | 1623 | 39 |
| BUTLER | 15,334 | 16,272 | 16,429 | 0.7 | 2.43 | 10,970 | 11,210 | 0.3 | 26,338 | 30,064 | 2675 | 93 |
| CALDWELL | 3,222 | 3,496 | 3,712 | 1.0 | 2.53 | 2,369 | 2,480 | 0.6 | 29,880 | 37,962 | 2170 | 60 |
| CALLAWAY | 11,552 | 13,657 | 14,699 | 2.0 | 2.60 | 8,639 | 9,854 | 1.6 | 37,435 | 44,083 | 907 | 20 |
| CAMDEN | 11,305 | 14,673 | 16,181 | 3.2 | 2.38 | 8,596 | 10,792 | 2.8 | 35,816 | 43,218 | 1122 | 23 |
| CAPE GIRARDEAU | 23,390 | 25,654 | 26,835 | 1.1 | 2.51 | 16,158 | 17,273 | 0.8 | 38,191 | 43,737 | 840 | 18 |
| CARROLL | 4,332 | 4,123 | 4,026 | -0.6 | 2.39 | 3,016 | 2,773 | -1.0 | 28,025 | 34,940 | 2439 | 74 |
| CARTER | 2,128 | 2,568 | 2,636 | 2.3 | 2.43 | 1,520 | 1,759 | 1.8 | 24,602 | 26,676 | 2849 | 101 |
| CASS | 22,892 | 30,812 | 35,274 | 3.7 | 2.75 | 17,839 | 23,317 | 3.3 | 46,660 | 54,750 | 286 | 6 |
| CEDAR | 5,003 | 5,598 | 5,924 | 1.4 | 2.37 | 3,525 | 3,763 | 0.8 | 25,567 | 30,333 | 2749 | 97 |
| CHARITON | 3,661 | 3,405 | 3,250 | -0.9 | 2.44 | 2,597 | 2,318 | -1.4 | 28,659 | 35,147 | 2341 | 65 |
| CHRISTIAN | 11,937 | 19,581 | 23,594 | 6.2 | 2.72 | 9,510 | 15,119 | 5.8 | 41,680 | 50,832 | 538 | 11 |
| CLARK | 2,859 | 2,833 | 2,765 | -0.1 | 2.55 | 2,108 | 2,000 | -0.6 | 30,347 | 36,781 | 2068 | 54 |
| CLAY | 58,915 | 70,316 | 76,535 | 2.2 | 2.57 | 42,458 | 49,050 | 1.8 | 48,708 | 55,078 | 224 | 3 |
| CLINTON | 6,112 | 7,399 | 8,245 | 2.3 | 2.65 | 4,639 | 5,446 | 2.0 | 40,085 | 46,723 | 665 | 14 |
| COLE | 22,976 | 25,540 | 26,477 | 1.3 | 2.50 | 15,887 | 17,294 | 1.0 | 45,384 | 51,174 | 337 | 7 |
| COOPER | 5,359 | 5,671 | 5,784 | 0.7 | 2.55 | 3,903 | 4,018 | 0.4 | 33,625 | 39,159 | 1449 | 31 |
| CRAWFORD | 7,299 | 8,693 | 9,150 | 2.1 | 2.57 | 5,455 | 6,256 | 1.7 | 30,131 | 36,520 | 2125 | 58 |
| DADE | 2,976 | 3,166 | 3,228 | 0.8 | 2.45 | 2,098 | 2,141 | 0.2 | 26,916 | 31,113 | 2597 | 88 |
| DALLAS | 4,899 | 6,119 | 6,612 | 2.7 | 2.57 | 3,648 | 4,377 | 2.2 | 27,586 | 33,513 | 2497 | 80 |
| DAVIESS | 3,040 | 3,051 | 3,183 | 0.0 | 2.64 | 2,211 | 2,130 | -0.5 | 28,225 | 34,078 | 2413 | 70 |
| DE KALB | 3,054 | 3,299 | 3,439 | 0.9 | 2.59 | 2,246 | 2,319 | 0.4 | 34,083 | 41,380 | 1378 | 29 |
| DENT | 5,327 | 5,530 | 5,663 | 0.5 | 2.56 | 3,938 | 3,919 | -0.1 | 26,000 | 30,411 | 2712 | 95 |
| DOUGLAS | 4,587 | 4,902 | 5,023 | 0.8 | 2.52 | 3,409 | 3,515 | 0.4 | 24,227 | 30,245 | 2886 | 103 |
| DUNKLIN | 13,128 | 13,031 | 12,843 | -0.1 | 2.44 | 9,292 | 8,870 | -0.6 | 24,147 | 26,396 | 2891 | 104 |
| FRANKLIN | 28,856 | 34,009 | 36,412 | 2.0 | 2.75 | 22,246 | 25,561 | 1.7 | 43,416 | 51,639 | 431 | 8 |
| GASCONADE | 5,543 | 6,021 | 6,275 | 1.0 | 2.46 | 3,959 | 4,126 | 0.5 | 34,716 | 42,444 | 1290 | 25 |
| GENTRY | 2,756 | 2,832 | 2,841 | 0.3 | 2.34 | 1,909 | 1,886 | -0.1 | 28,214 | 31,780 | 2414 | 71 |
| GREENE | 81,463 | 90,450 | 92,537 | 1.3 | 2.40 | 54,525 | 59,322 | 1.0 | 37,290 | 41,568 | 932 | 22 |
| GRUNDY | 4,346 | 4,174 | 4,081 | -0.5 | 2.35 | 2,994 | 2,765 | -1.0 | 27,668 | 31,643 | 2485 | 79 |
| HARRISON | 3,574 | 3,675 | 3,715 | 0.3 | 2.24 | 2,460 | 2,428 | -0.2 | 26,507 | 31,067 | 2653 | 92 |
| HENRY | 8,189 | 8,803 | 8,981 | 0.9 | 2.39 | 5,689 | 5,882 | 0.4 | 28,525 | 33,409 | 2361 | 66 |
| HICKORY | 3,183 | 3,842 | 4,059 | 2.3 | 2.27 | 2,349 | 2,730 | 1.8 | 24,858 | 29,184 | 2817 | 99 |
| HOLT | 2,440 | 2,224 | 2,173 | -1.1 | 2.43 | 1,689 | 1,477 | -1.6 | 27,344 | 32,677 | 2531 | 83 |
| HOWARD | 3,571 | 3,633 | 3,597 | 0.2 | 2.45 | 2,518 | 2,465 | -0.3 | 31,460 | 36,611 | 1830 | 46 |
| HOWELL | 12,283 | 14,397 | 15,146 | 1.9 | 2.49 | 9,027 | 10,123 | 1.4 | 26,157 | 30,663 | 2697 | 94 |
| IRON | 3,995 | 4,076 | 4,094 | 0.2 | 2.58 | 2,970 | 2,921 | -0.2 | 27,063 | 32,536 | 2570 | 86 |
| JACKSON | 252,582 | 263,095 | 265,661 | 0.5 | 2.45 | 164,361 | 165,633 | 0.1 | 40,250 | 45,174 | 653 | 12 |
| JASPER | 36,134 | 40,783 | 42,588 | 1.5 | 2.42 | 24,890 | 27,122 | 1.0 | 32,462 | 36,606 | 1629 | 40 |
| JEFFERSON | 59,199 | 70,365 | 75,868 | 2.1 | 2.83 | 47,211 | 54,683 | 1.8 | 47,235 | 56,393 | 267 | 5 |
| JOHNSON | 14,579 | 16,991 | 17,909 | 1.9 | 2.58 | 10,213 | 11,401 | 1.3 | 34,883 | 41,194 | 1272 | 24 |
| KNOX | 1,819 | 1,781 | 1,755 | -0.3 | 2.34 | 1,273 | 1,193 | -0.8 | 24,411 | 26,543 | 2867 | 102 |
| LACLEDE | 10,420 | 12,469 | 13,572 | 2.2 | 2.52 | 7,749 | 8,881 | 1.7 | 31,512 | 38,475 | 1817 | 44 |
| LAFAYETTE | 11,732 | 12,538 | 12,915 | 0.8 | 2.56 | 8,570 | 8,853 | 0.4 | 34,678 | 40,178 | 1294 | 26 |
| LAWRENCE | 11,724 | 13,246 | 14,038 | 1.5 | 2.51 | 8,487 | 9,189 | 1.0 | 31,191 | 38,168 | 1889 | 50 |
| LEWIS | 3,745 | 3,771 | 3,834 | 0.1 | 2.48 | 2,655 | 2,562 | -0.4 | 31,651 | 36,000 | 1791 | 43 |
| LINCOLN | 10,316 | 14,030 | 16,221 | 3.8 | 2.75 | 7,913 | 10,410 | 3.4 | 41,823 | 53,366 | 528 | 10 |
| LINN | 5,704 | 5,659 | 5,642 | -0.1 | 2.39 | 3,837 | 3,670 | -0.5 | 27,192 | 31,279 | 2547 | 85 |
| LIVINGSTON | 5,645 | 5,413 | 5,249 | -0.5 | 2.41 | 3,910 | 3,608 | -1.0 | 33,195 | 38,713 | 1506 | 33 |
| MCDONALD | 6,386 | 7,832 | 8,444 | 2.5 | 2.58 | 4,784 | 5,653 | 2.0 | 27,493 | 32,045 | 2510 | 81 |
| MACON | 6,160 | 6,179 | 6,330 | 0.0 | 2.46 | 4,376 | 4,224 | -0.4 | 28,389 | 32,740 | 2382 | 68 |
| MADISON | 4,344 | 4,544 | 4,687 | 0.5 | 2.55 | 3,205 | 3,216 | 0.0 | 27,397 | 32,840 | 2528 | 82 |
| MARIES | 3,028 | 3,316 | 3,440 | 1.1 | 2.52 | 2,271 | 2,408 | 0.7 | 28,199 | 31,281 | 2415 | 72 |
| MARION | 10,728 | 10,807 | 10,731 | 0.1 | 2.48 | 7,412 | 7,241 | -0.3 | 33,041 | 38,478 | 1531 | 34 |
| MERCER | 1,577 | 1,708 | 1,688 | 1.0 | 2.27 | 1,079 | 1,107 | 0.3 | 27,802 | 34,821 | 2470 | 75 |
| MILLER | 7,977 | 8,754 | 8,988 | 1.1 | 2.57 | 5,740 | 6,057 | 0.7 | 29,333 | 32,941 | 2248 | 62 |
| MISSISSIPPI | 5,411 | 5,007 | 4,842 | -0.9 | 2.60 | 3,968 | 3,517 | -1.5 | 22,175 | 26,076 | 3018 | 114 |
| MONITEAU | 4,583 | 5,055 | 5,229 | 1.2 | 2.57 | 3,328 | 3,518 | 0.7 | 32,975 | 40,096 | 1543 | 35 |
| MONROE | 3,471 | 3,479 | 3,603 | 0.0 | 2.59 | 2,466 | 2,368 | -0.5 | 29,991 | 32,560 | 2155 | 59 |
| MONTGOMERY | 4,341 | 4,778 | 5,027 | 1.2 | 2.49 | 3,114 | 3,290 | 0.7 | 32,769 | 40,638 | 1577 | 37 |
| MORGAN | 6,269 | 7,822 | 8,734 | 2.7 | 2.44 | 4,629 | 5,573 | 2.3 | 30,306 | 35,071 | 2081 | 55 |
| NEW MADRID | 7,795 | 7,605 | 7,248 | -0.3 | 2.55 | 5,726 | 5,392 | -0.7 | 26,699 | 32,027 | 2617 | 90 |
| NEWTON | 16,886 | 19,307 | 20,563 | 1.6 | 2.57 | 12,678 | 14,057 | 1.3 | 34,161 | 39,375 | 1360 | 28 |
| NODAWAY | 7,620 | 7,237 | 6,985 | -0.6 | 2.43 | 4,996 | 4,553 | -1.1 | 30,900 | 35,882 | 1948 | 52 |
| OREGON | 3,851 | 4,229 | 4,430 | 1.1 | 2.43 | 2,820 | 2,984 | 0.7 | 23,049 | 27,632 | 2970 | 110 |
| OSAGE | 4,262 | 4,444 | 4,507 | 0.5 | 2.79 | 3,181 | 3,192 | 0.0 | 38,121 | 43,425 | 845 | 19 |
| OZARK | 3,486 | 4,185 | 4,466 | 2.2 | 2.38 | 2,616 | 3,033 | 1.8 | 25,122 | 29,473 | 2801 | 98 |
| MISSOURI | | | | 1.0 | 2.52 | | | 0.6 | 38,422 | 44,218 | | |
| UNITED STATES | | | | 1.4 | 2.59 | | | 1.1 | 41,914 | 49,127 | | |

# INCOME

| COUNTY | 2000 Per Capita Income | 2000 HH Income Base | 2000 HOUSEHOLD INCOME DISTRIBUTION (%) | | | | | | 2000 AVERAGE DISPOSABLE INCOME BY AGE OF HOUSEHOLDER | | | | | |
|---|---|---|---|---|---|---|---|---|---|---|---|---|---|---|
| | | | Less than $15,000 | $15,000 to $24,999 | $25,000 to $49,999 | $50,000 to $99,999 | $100,000 to $149,999 | $150,000 or More | All Ages | <35 | 35-44 | 45-54 | 55-64 | 65+ |
| ADAIR | 15,505 | 8,947 | 27.2 | 17.8 | 32.1 | 17.4 | 3.6 | 1.9 | 29,748 | 21,289 | 37,632 | 40,988 | 33,761 | 22,788 |
| ANDREW | 17,309 | 5,923 | 16.2 | 10.5 | 38.5 | 28.8 | 5.3 | 0.7 | 35,061 | 33,010 | 40,967 | 43,664 | 34,845 | 22,217 |
| ATCHISON | 15,439 | 2,751 | 19.2 | 19.1 | 37.1 | 20.8 | 3.0 | 0.9 | 29,836 | 24,963 | 35,690 | 35,728 | 35,769 | 22,629 |
| AUDRAIN | 17,081 | 9,292 | 18.0 | 15.8 | 39.0 | 22.9 | 3.5 | 0.9 | 31,821 | 28,067 | 36,946 | 41,007 | 36,319 | 22,644 |
| BARRY | 14,740 | 13,535 | 19.3 | 20.7 | 38.5 | 19.0 | 2.0 | 0.5 | 28,340 | 28,451 | 34,033 | 33,651 | 27,817 | 20,741 |
| BARTON | 14,792 | 4,942 | 20.7 | 21.8 | 37.5 | 16.7 | 2.8 | 0.7 | 28,277 | 25,578 | 37,104 | 34,170 | 30,013 | 18,569 |
| BATES | 13,842 | 6,283 | 23.0 | 17.9 | 38.9 | 17.5 | 2.4 | 0.4 | 27,795 | 25,839 | 33,954 | 35,657 | 30,140 | 18,543 |
| BENTON | 15,274 | 7,544 | 24.1 | 23.1 | 34.0 | 15.9 | 2.3 | 0.6 | 26,605 | 25,860 | 34,669 | 32,359 | 28,335 | 19,357 |
| BOLLINGER | 14,080 | 4,370 | 20.2 | 18.6 | 37.4 | 20.6 | 2.7 | 0.6 | 29,662 | 29,754 | 33,932 | 39,194 | 28,406 | 19,783 |
| BOONE | 20,734 | 50,457 | 15.9 | 13.5 | 31.9 | 29.5 | 6.7 | 2.5 | 38,629 | 28,249 | 45,059 | 50,274 | 47,814 | 30,281 |
| BUCHANAN | 16,032 | 32,149 | 20.9 | 15.7 | 37.0 | 22.2 | 3.3 | 1.0 | 31,180 | 27,014 | 36,844 | 39,145 | 34,681 | 21,181 |
| BUTLER | 15,235 | 16,272 | 27.4 | 20.2 | 31.6 | 15.8 | 3.4 | 1.7 | 28,655 | 26,182 | 34,994 | 36,228 | 30,437 | 18,438 |
| CALDWELL | 14,463 | 3,496 | 23.6 | 18.2 | 35.4 | 19.7 | 2.5 | 0.6 | 28,487 | 26,594 | 34,789 | 39,004 | 27,888 | 19,121 |
| CALLAWAY | 15,655 | 13,657 | 13.4 | 14.4 | 39.8 | 28.6 | 3.5 | 0.2 | 33,682 | 31,076 | 39,445 | 41,655 | 36,462 | 20,657 |
| CAMDEN | 19,908 | 14,673 | 13.3 | 19.5 | 35.4 | 24.6 | 5.3 | 1.9 | 35,479 | 29,134 | 42,671 | 43,514 | 36,953 | 26,694 |
| CAPE GIRARDEAU | 18,570 | 25,654 | 16.5 | 13.3 | 35.6 | 27.8 | 5.1 | 1.7 | 36,015 | 29,180 | 43,131 | 44,905 | 40,406 | 24,825 |
| CARROLL | 15,261 | 4,123 | 23.3 | 21.7 | 34.0 | 16.8 | 3.3 | 1.0 | 28,506 | 27,242 | 34,059 | 33,932 | 31,666 | 20,900 |
| CARTER | 12,770 | 2,568 | 28.0 | 22.7 | 32.1 | 14.8 | 2.2 | 0.2 | 24,910 | 23,015 | 27,729 | 31,663 | 27,248 | 17,076 |
| CASS | 20,406 | 30,812 | 9.4 | 9.8 | 35.5 | 36.6 | 7.1 | 1.6 | 41,355 | 36,862 | 46,397 | 51,222 | 43,979 | 25,239 |
| CEDAR | 12,886 | 5,598 | 27.2 | 21.4 | 35.5 | 14.2 | 1.6 | 0.1 | 24,722 | 23,108 | 29,614 | 31,718 | 28,559 | 17,236 |
| CHARITON | 14,366 | 3,405 | 23.2 | 18.9 | 37.2 | 18.3 | 2.3 | 0.2 | 27,571 | 24,569 | 32,196 | 36,156 | 32,337 | 19,245 |
| CHRISTIAN | 18,130 | 19,581 | 10.5 | 11.5 | 38.9 | 33.0 | 5.1 | 1.0 | 37,877 | 35,041 | 43,464 | 44,433 | 40,167 | 22,971 |
| CLARK | 13,874 | 2,833 | 22.9 | 15.6 | 38.5 | 20.7 | 2.2 | 0.1 | 28,433 | 26,296 | 35,363 | 35,348 | 30,719 | 18,323 |
| CLAY | 22,878 | 70,315 | 7.5 | 9.9 | 34.2 | 38.6 | 7.8 | 2.0 | 43,253 | 37,310 | 47,798 | 53,580 | 45,859 | 27,467 |
| CLINTON | 18,442 | 7,399 | 14.4 | 12.8 | 37.4 | 28.1 | 5.7 | 1.6 | 36,634 | 32,779 | 40,261 | 48,398 | 37,580 | 23,090 |
| COLE | 22,552 | 25,540 | 10.2 | 11.3 | 34.4 | 34.4 | 7.4 | 2.5 | 41,883 | 35,347 | 45,780 | 52,186 | 45,791 | 27,677 |
| COOPER | 14,135 | 5,671 | 17.9 | 16.2 | 40.9 | 21.2 | 3.5 | 0.3 | 30,682 | 27,794 | 34,283 | 41,299 | 31,097 | 22,051 |
| CRAWFORD | 14,347 | 8,693 | 21.8 | 18.1 | 37.9 | 19.4 | 2.3 | 0.5 | 28,512 | 29,679 | 31,079 | 36,462 | 28,479 | 18,736 |
| DADE | 13,502 | 3,166 | 25.4 | 19.5 | 37.9 | 14.8 | 2.0 | 0.5 | 26,297 | 26,096 | 30,744 | 32,204 | 29,206 | 19,003 |
| DALLAS | 13,334 | 6,119 | 25.7 | 19.6 | 34.5 | 16.7 | 3.4 | 0.2 | 27,134 | 26,456 | 34,799 | 32,240 | 29,825 | 16,633 |
| DAVIESS | 14,096 | 3,051 | 20.4 | 21.8 | 38.2 | 16.2 | 2.6 | 0.9 | 28,686 | 24,029 | 34,319 | 38,894 | 31,438 | 20,482 |
| DE KALB | 13,763 | 3,299 | 18.1 | 14.9 | 38.6 | 22.6 | 4.7 | 1.2 | 32,674 | 30,718 | 39,993 | 43,198 | 35,250 | 19,214 |
| DENT | 14,309 | 5,530 | 27.3 | 20.6 | 30.7 | 16.3 | 3.3 | 1.7 | 28,550 | 25,337 | 33,003 | 38,224 | 29,791 | 19,199 |
| DOUGLAS | 13,070 | 4,902 | 29.2 | 22.7 | 33.1 | 13.3 | 0.9 | 0.9 | 24,542 | 22,517 | 31,786 | 26,585 | 26,854 | 17,808 |
| DUNKLIN | 14,887 | 13,031 | 31.3 | 20.1 | 30.6 | 13.8 | 2.7 | 1.5 | 26,558 | 24,067 | 32,458 | 32,534 | 28,906 | 17,518 |
| FRANKLIN | 18,602 | 34,009 | 10.8 | 11.3 | 36.9 | 34.3 | 5.7 | 0.9 | 38,467 | 35,335 | 44,620 | 48,110 | 40,325 | 22,881 |
| GASCONADE | 17,429 | 6,021 | 16.4 | 15.9 | 40.0 | 22.6 | 4.0 | 1.2 | 32,702 | 30,803 | 40,355 | 41,472 | 35,839 | 21,456 |
| GENTRY | 17,654 | 2,832 | 21.7 | 21.9 | 35.7 | 15.5 | 3.5 | 1.8 | 29,641 | 27,313 | 32,291 | 43,317 | 31,365 | 20,124 |
| GREENE | 19,613 | 90,450 | 15.6 | 14.7 | 35.5 | 27.0 | 5.3 | 1.9 | 36,233 | 29,569 | 42,243 | 45,118 | 40,201 | 24,967 |
| GRUNDY | 15,159 | 4,174 | 25.9 | 19.5 | 33.3 | 17.2 | 3.3 | 0.8 | 28,146 | 23,209 | 33,146 | 39,381 | 31,695 | 18,934 |
| HARRISON | 15,397 | 3,675 | 26.7 | 20.4 | 35.2 | 15.2 | 2.0 | 0.5 | 25,862 | 26,584 | 33,496 | 33,108 | 25,600 | 18,081 |
| HENRY | 15,481 | 8,803 | 22.6 | 19.6 | 35.7 | 18.5 | 2.8 | 0.8 | 28,854 | 27,584 | 35,248 | 38,447 | 30,145 | 19,009 |
| HICKORY | 12,928 | 3,842 | 25.5 | 24.9 | 34.9 | 14.1 | 0.7 | 0.0 | 24,053 | 24,459 | 29,153 | 26,708 | 29,129 | 18,868 |
| HOLT | 13,999 | 2,224 | 23.1 | 21.5 | 36.2 | 16.2 | 2.4 | 0.5 | 27,168 | 26,832 | 31,645 | 31,681 | 27,987 | 21,363 |
| HOWARD | 14,011 | 3,633 | 21.0 | 18.5 | 38.0 | 20.0 | 2.3 | 0.2 | 28,615 | 26,217 | 33,754 | 34,109 | 34,211 | 20,343 |
| HOWELL | 13,639 | 14,397 | 27.5 | 20.2 | 33.4 | 15.7 | 2.6 | 0.7 | 26,666 | 24,371 | 33,498 | 31,548 | 29,225 | 17,723 |
| IRON | 13,164 | 4,076 | 24.6 | 21.6 | 33.5 | 17.5 | 2.2 | 0.6 | 27,319 | 24,491 | 33,050 | 35,598 | 26,104 | 19,916 |
| JACKSON | 20,447 | 263,074 | 14.9 | 13.0 | 34.3 | 30.1 | 5.9 | 1.7 | 37,467 | 33,010 | 42,362 | 46,330 | 39,761 | 25,366 |
| JASPER | 16,512 | 40,783 | 19.1 | 17.4 | 36.9 | 22.5 | 3.3 | 0.8 | 31,155 | 28,458 | 36,431 | 39,761 | 32,290 | 20,613 |
| JEFFERSON | 19,126 | 70,365 | 8.3 | 7.9 | 37.7 | 38.3 | 6.8 | 1.1 | 41,261 | 37,558 | 45,741 | 50,308 | 41,248 | 24,890 |
| JOHNSON | 15,718 | 16,991 | 16.1 | 16.9 | 37.7 | 25.0 | 3.4 | 1.0 | 32,943 | 25,782 | 39,892 | 43,946 | 38,398 | 23,535 |
| KNOX | 13,139 | 1,781 | 29.3 | 21.7 | 31.4 | 16.1 | 1.0 | 0.6 | 24,912 | 24,419 | 28,930 | 27,086 | 28,498 | 19,555 |
| LACLEDE | 14,514 | 12,469 | 18.3 | 18.9 | 39.1 | 21.6 | 2.1 | 0.1 | 29,293 | 29,056 | 33,115 | 35,793 | 30,462 | 19,582 |
| LAFAYETTE | 16,087 | 12,538 | 16.2 | 17.1 | 38.9 | 24.0 | 3.1 | 0.7 | 31,955 | 29,613 | 36,590 | 40,664 | 34,574 | 21,666 |
| LAWRENCE | 14,739 | 13,246 | 19.9 | 18.4 | 38.3 | 20.6 | 2.3 | 0.6 | 29,404 | 27,498 | 35,484 | 36,619 | 32,223 | 19,597 |
| LEWIS | 14,362 | 3,771 | 21.2 | 15.8 | 38.4 | 21.6 | 2.6 | 0.5 | 29,878 | 26,613 | 36,461 | 39,468 | 31,802 | 20,552 |
| LINCOLN | 17,628 | 14,030 | 12.5 | 11.4 | 37.1 | 32.7 | 5.2 | 1.1 | 37,550 | 34,409 | 42,080 | 46,595 | 39,510 | 22,757 |
| LINN | 13,868 | 5,659 | 26.2 | 20.5 | 34.0 | 16.8 | 2.1 | 0.4 | 26,477 | 27,170 | 35,010 | 32,236 | 27,953 | 17,455 |
| LIVINGSTON | 17,354 | 5,413 | 19.2 | 17.2 | 35.5 | 23.3 | 3.9 | 1.0 | 31,797 | 29,242 | 37,464 | 39,049 | 33,663 | 23,720 |
| MCDONALD | 13,105 | 7,832 | 23.4 | 22.1 | 36.0 | 16.3 | 1.7 | 0.6 | 26,738 | 24,848 | 31,191 | 33,291 | 27,931 | 18,704 |
| MACON | 14,139 | 6,179 | 23.1 | 20.5 | 35.4 | 17.7 | 2.7 | 0.6 | 27,920 | 24,102 | 34,631 | 35,348 | 32,071 | 19,060 |
| MADISON | 13,937 | 4,544 | 24.8 | 20.1 | 35.6 | 15.2 | 2.8 | 1.5 | 28,000 | 23,208 | 32,745 | 40,541 | 27,235 | 18,372 |
| MARIES | 14,054 | 3,316 | 24.6 | 19.2 | 36.7 | 17.0 | 1.8 | 0.7 | 27,190 | 26,707 | 33,191 | 34,287 | 28,571 | 16,529 |
| MARION | 15,902 | 10,807 | 19.4 | 15.4 | 38.3 | 22.7 | 3.5 | 0.7 | 31,196 | 28,007 | 38,059 | 37,050 | 33,424 | 22,381 |
| MERCER | 14,638 | 1,708 | 25.6 | 19.5 | 33.9 | 18.6 | 2.3 | 0.1 | 26,950 | 28,510 | 36,119 | 32,497 | 26,608 | 19,105 |
| MILLER | 14,269 | 8,754 | 20.8 | 19.2 | 39.1 | 18.4 | 1.9 | 0.6 | 28,191 | 27,052 | 32,877 | 34,407 | 29,192 | 18,902 |
| MISSISSIPPI | 12,791 | 5,007 | 35.4 | 18.5 | 28.9 | 13.8 | 2.4 | 1.0 | 25,027 | 22,511 | 27,746 | 33,014 | 27,284 | 16,023 |
| MONITEAU | 15,047 | 5,055 | 17.9 | 19.5 | 37.1 | 21.4 | 3.3 | 0.8 | 30,868 | 27,103 | 35,108 | 42,183 | 35,678 | 18,893 |
| MONROE | 13,587 | 3,479 | 22.0 | 19.3 | 37.5 | 18.6 | 2.4 | 0.2 | 27,808 | 28,629 | 29,340 | 35,153 | 29,695 | 19,172 |
| MONTGOMERY | 15,565 | 4,778 | 19.1 | 16.2 | 41.0 | 20.7 | 2.4 | 0.7 | 30,018 | 28,352 | 37,517 | 35,533 | 33,201 | 20,660 |
| MORGAN | 15,512 | 7,822 | 20.5 | 20.2 | 35.1 | 20.5 | 2.9 | 0.9 | 29,707 | 25,630 | 36,127 | 36,969 | 33,344 | 21,328 |
| NEW MADRID | 13,501 | 7,605 | 30.0 | 17.3 | 33.2 | 16.0 | 2.8 | 0.7 | 26,643 | 24,192 | 31,392 | 34,198 | 27,175 | 17,849 |
| NEWTON | 17,205 | 19,307 | 16.2 | 18.0 | 36.7 | 24.2 | 3.5 | 1.5 | 33,301 | 29,006 | 38,976 | 42,900 | 35,082 | 21,101 |
| NODAWAY | 14,325 | 7,237 | 23.4 | 15.3 | 35.9 | 20.7 | 3.9 | 0.9 | 30,254 | 23,705 | 35,625 | 43,164 | 35,914 | 22,076 |
| OREGON | 12,895 | 4,229 | 32.4 | 21.3 | 28.3 | 15.3 | 2.2 | 0.6 | 25,163 | 24,608 | 30,898 | 31,453 | 25,218 | 16,887 |
| OSAGE | 15,727 | 4,441 | 11.9 | 13.9 | 43.7 | 25.8 | 4.0 | 0.7 | 34,652 | 33,098 | 39,309 | 45,091 | 39,737 | 21,096 |
| OZARK | 12,871 | 4,185 | 26.7 | 23.1 | 32.6 | 16.1 | 1.5 | 0.1 | 24,686 | 23,452 | 28,402 | 30,602 | 25,666 | 18,940 |
| MISSOURI | 19,444 | | 15.8 | 14.1 | 34.4 | 28.2 | 5.6 | 1.9 | 36,824 | 32,026 | 42,273 | 46,089 | 39,038 | 23,886 |
| UNITED STATES | 22,162 | | 14.5 | 12.5 | 32.3 | 29.8 | 7.4 | 3.5 | 40,748 | 34,503 | 44,969 | 49,579 | 43,409 | 27,339 |

| COUNTY | FINANCIAL SERVICES | | | | THE HOME | | | | | | ENTERTAINMENT | | | | | | PERSONAL | | | |
|---|---|---|---|---|---|---|---|---|---|---|---|---|---|---|---|---|---|---|---|---|
| | | | | | Home Improvements | | | Furnishings | | | | | | | | | | | | |
| | Auto Loan | Home Loan | Invest-ments | Retire-ment Plans | Home Repair | Lawn & Garden | Remodel-ing | Appli-ances | Elec-tronics | Furni-ture | Restau-rants | Sport-ing Goods | Theater & Concerts | Toys & Hobbies | Travel | Video Rental | Apparel | Auto After-market | Health Insur-ance | Pets & Supplies |
| ADAIR | 95 | 86 | 86 | 86 | 95 | 90 | 102 | 93 | 92 | 85 | 89 | 91 | 89 | 94 | 86 | 98 | 86 | 93 | 98 | 97 |
| ANDREW | 98 | 77 | 83 | 85 | 94 | 92 | 111 | 97 | 94 | 84 | 88 | 95 | 89 | 98 | 83 | 101 | 85 | 93 | 103 | 99 |
| ATCHISON | 95 | 64 | 70 | 77 | 90 | 89 | 107 | 94 | 90 | 73 | 78 | 91 | 79 | 92 | 76 | 100 | 77 | 88 | 105 | 94 |
| AUDRAIN | 96 | 72 | 78 | 80 | 93 | 91 | 109 | 95 | 92 | 80 | 83 | 92 | 85 | 94 | 80 | 100 | 81 | 90 | 102 | 96 |
| BARRY | 97 | 69 | 81 | 80 | 94 | 93 | 109 | 97 | 92 | 79 | 82 | 94 | 85 | 95 | 80 | 99 | 79 | 90 | 104 | 97 |
| BARTON | 97 | 66 | 72 | 79 | 91 | 90 | 111 | 96 | 91 | 75 | 80 | 95 | 82 | 95 | 76 | 100 | 79 | 90 | 104 | 97 |
| BATES | 96 | 65 | 72 | 78 | 91 | 89 | 108 | 95 | 91 | 74 | 79 | 93 | 81 | 93 | 76 | 100 | 78 | 89 | 104 | 96 |
| BENTON | 98 | 68 | 78 | 83 | 93 | 92 | 115 | 97 | 91 | 76 | 81 | 95 | 84 | 96 | 79 | 100 | 80 | 90 | 106 | 98 |
| BOLLINGER | 97 | 63 | 66 | 75 | 91 | 89 | 110 | 96 | 91 | 75 | 77 | 95 | 81 | 94 | 73 | 99 | 77 | 88 | 103 | 96 |
| BOONE | 99 | 100 | 92 | 98 | 97 | 96 | 101 | 97 | 98 | 96 | 101 | 98 | 98 | 99 | 94 | 101 | 97 | 101 | 98 | 100 |
| BUCHANAN | 96 | 86 | 91 | 88 | 100 | 95 | 101 | 96 | 93 | 91 | 91 | 93 | 94 | 96 | 91 | 99 | 88 | 94 | 100 | 96 |
| BUTLER | 96 | 75 | 81 | 82 | 95 | 92 | 106 | 96 | 92 | 83 | 84 | 93 | 88 | 94 | 83 | 99 | 82 | 91 | 101 | 96 |
| CALDWELL | 97 | 69 | 75 | 80 | 92 | 90 | 111 | 95 | 92 | 77 | 82 | 93 | 83 | 95 | 78 | 101 | 80 | 90 | 104 | 97 |
| CALLAWAY | 98 | 84 | 84 | 86 | 95 | 93 | 106 | 97 | 95 | 89 | 92 | 95 | 92 | 98 | 86 | 101 | 88 | 95 | 100 | 99 |
| CAMDEN | 101 | 77 | 88 | 92 | 96 | 98 | 120 | 101 | 94 | 82 | 87 | 99 | 90 | 100 | 87 | 101 | 87 | 94 | 108 | 102 |
| CAPE GIRARDEAU | 99 | 92 | 99 | 96 | 101 | 99 | 105 | 98 | 97 | 94 | 98 | 98 | 98 | 100 | 94 | 101 | 94 | 98 | 102 | 101 |
| CARROLL | 95 | 65 | 70 | 77 | 91 | 89 | 107 | 94 | 90 | 73 | 78 | 91 | 80 | 92 | 76 | 100 | 77 | 88 | 104 | 95 |
| CARTER | 97 | 66 | 71 | 76 | 92 | 90 | 112 | 96 | 92 | 77 | 79 | 95 | 82 | 94 | 75 | 99 | 78 | 89 | 102 | 96 |
| CASS | 100 | 93 | 91 | 95 | 97 | 96 | 105 | 99 | 100 | 95 | 100 | 99 | 99 | 102 | 91 | 103 | 96 | 101 | 101 | 102 |
| CEDAR | 95 | 69 | 79 | 79 | 93 | 92 | 108 | 95 | 92 | 79 | 81 | 90 | 83 | 92 | 80 | 99 | 79 | 89 | 103 | 94 |
| CHARITON | 98 | 68 | 74 | 81 | 91 | 90 | 111 | 96 | 92 | 76 | 81 | 95 | 83 | 96 | 77 | 101 | 80 | 90 | 105 | 98 |
| CHRISTIAN | 100 | 84 | 83 | 88 | 95 | 92 | 112 | 98 | 96 | 89 | 93 | 98 | 93 | 101 | 84 | 102 | 90 | 96 | 101 | 102 |
| CLARK | 97 | 65 | 70 | 78 | 91 | 90 | 110 | 95 | 91 | 74 | 79 | 94 | 81 | 95 | 75 | 100 | 78 | 89 | 105 | 96 |
| CLAY | 100 | 103 | 98 | 100 | 101 | 100 | 100 | 99 | 101 | 103 | 107 | 100 | 104 | 103 | 99 | 103 | 102 | 104 | 100 | 101 |
| CLINTON | 98 | 76 | 80 | 84 | 94 | 91 | 112 | 97 | 94 | 83 | 87 | 95 | 88 | 98 | 81 | 101 | 85 | 93 | 103 | 99 |
| COLE | 101 | 103 | 101 | 103 | 102 | 102 | 103 | 101 | 102 | 103 | 107 | 102 | 106 | 104 | 101 | 103 | 103 | 105 | 101 | 103 |
| COOPER | 98 | 71 | 76 | 82 | 92 | 90 | 112 | 96 | 92 | 79 | 83 | 96 | 85 | 97 | 79 | 101 | 82 | 91 | 104 | 99 |
| CRAWFORD | 98 | 69 | 73 | 79 | 92 | 90 | 114 | 97 | 93 | 79 | 81 | 96 | 84 | 96 | 77 | 100 | 80 | 90 | 103 | 98 |
| DADE | 97 | 63 | 69 | 79 | 90 | 89 | 110 | 95 | 90 | 72 | 78 | 95 | 80 | 95 | 75 | 100 | 77 | 89 | 106 | 96 |
| DALLAS | 97 | 67 | 72 | 79 | 91 | 90 | 111 | 96 | 92 | 75 | 80 | 95 | 82 | 95 | 76 | 100 | 79 | 90 | 104 | 97 |
| DAVIESS | 97 | 65 | 71 | 80 | 90 | 90 | 110 | 95 | 91 | 73 | 79 | 95 | 81 | 95 | 76 | 100 | 78 | 90 | 106 | 97 |
| DE KALB | 97 | 69 | 76 | 80 | 92 | 90 | 111 | 95 | 92 | 77 | 82 | 93 | 83 | 95 | 78 | 101 | 80 | 90 | 104 | 97 |
| DENT | 95 | 65 | 71 | 75 | 92 | 90 | 107 | 94 | 91 | 76 | 78 | 91 | 81 | 92 | 77 | 99 | 77 | 88 | 102 | 94 |
| DOUGLAS | 98 | 64 | 67 | 77 | 91 | 89 | 111 | 96 | 91 | 74 | 78 | 96 | 81 | 95 | 74 | 99 | 77 | 89 | 104 | 97 |
| DUNKLIN | 95 | 70 | 77 | 79 | 94 | 91 | 107 | 95 | 92 | 80 | 81 | 92 | 84 | 93 | 80 | 99 | 80 | 90 | 101 | 95 |
| FRANKLIN | 99 | 79 | 83 | 85 | 95 | 92 | 112 | 97 | 94 | 86 | 89 | 96 | 90 | 99 | 83 | 101 | 87 | 94 | 102 | 100 |
| GASCONADE | 98 | 70 | 75 | 80 | 92 | 90 | 113 | 96 | 93 | 79 | 82 | 95 | 84 | 96 | 78 | 100 | 81 | 91 | 103 | 98 |
| GENTRY | 96 | 64 | 70 | 77 | 90 | 89 | 108 | 94 | 90 | 73 | 78 | 91 | 79 | 92 | 75 | 100 | 77 | 88 | 105 | 95 |
| GREENE | 99 | 96 | 95 | 97 | 99 | 97 | 103 | 98 | 97 | 96 | 99 | 98 | 98 | 100 | 94 | 101 | 95 | 99 | 100 | 100 |
| GRUNDY | 97 | 70 | 76 | 83 | 92 | 91 | 108 | 95 | 93 | 77 | 82 | 94 | 84 | 95 | 79 | 101 | 81 | 91 | 104 | 96 |
| HARRISON | 97 | 64 | 70 | 78 | 90 | 89 | 109 | 95 | 90 | 72 | 78 | 93 | 79 | 94 | 75 | 100 | 77 | 89 | 106 | 96 |
| HENRY | 95 | 68 | 76 | 79 | 93 | 91 | 107 | 95 | 92 | 78 | 80 | 91 | 83 | 92 | 79 | 100 | 79 | 89 | 103 | 95 |
| HICKORY | 95 | 71 | 96 | 80 | 97 | 97 | 103 | 96 | 89 | 78 | 83 | 90 | 87 | 93 | 86 | 98 | 77 | 90 | 106 | 95 |
| HOLT | 96 | 67 | 73 | 79 | 91 | 90 | 110 | 95 | 91 | 75 | 80 | 92 | 81 | 94 | 77 | 100 | 79 | 89 | 104 | 96 |
| HOWARD | 96 | 69 | 76 | 80 | 92 | 90 | 111 | 95 | 92 | 78 | 82 | 92 | 83 | 94 | 78 | 100 | 80 | 90 | 103 | 96 |
| HOWELL | 97 | 72 | 78 | 80 | 94 | 91 | 109 | 96 | 92 | 81 | 83 | 93 | 86 | 95 | 80 | 100 | 81 | 90 | 102 | 97 |
| IRON | 96 | 64 | 67 | 74 | 91 | 89 | 109 | 95 | 92 | 75 | 78 | 93 | 81 | 93 | 74 | 99 | 77 | 88 | 103 | 95 |
| JACKSON | 97 | 99 | 97 | 96 | 101 | 98 | 95 | 98 | 96 | 99 | 99 | 97 | 101 | 98 | 98 | 101 | 97 | 101 | 97 | 99 |
| JASPER | 96 | 81 | 87 | 85 | 97 | 93 | 105 | 96 | 93 | 87 | 89 | 93 | 91 | 96 | 87 | 100 | 86 | 93 | 101 | 97 |
| JEFFERSON | 99 | 87 | 84 | 88 | 95 | 92 | 107 | 98 | 97 | 92 | 95 | 97 | 94 | 100 | 86 | 102 | 91 | 97 | 100 | 100 |
| JOHNSON | 95 | 89 | 86 | 87 | 93 | 90 | 99 | 93 | 93 | 85 | 91 | 91 | 89 | 94 | 86 | 99 | 86 | 94 | 97 | 97 |
| KNOX | 95 | 64 | 70 | 76 | 90 | 89 | 107 | 94 | 91 | 73 | 78 | 90 | 79 | 91 | 76 | 100 | 77 | 88 | 104 | 94 |
| LACLEDE | 97 | 71 | 75 | 79 | 93 | 90 | 110 | 96 | 92 | 80 | 82 | 94 | 85 | 95 | 79 | 99 | 81 | 90 | 102 | 97 |
| LAFAYETTE | 97 | 75 | 80 | 82 | 94 | 91 | 109 | 96 | 93 | 83 | 86 | 94 | 87 | 96 | 82 | 100 | 83 | 92 | 102 | 98 |
| LAWRENCE | 97 | 71 | 77 | 81 | 93 | 90 | 112 | 96 | 93 | 80 | 83 | 94 | 85 | 96 | 79 | 100 | 82 | 91 | 103 | 97 |
| LEWIS | 96 | 69 | 76 | 80 | 93 | 90 | 109 | 95 | 92 | 78 | 82 | 93 | 84 | 95 | 79 | 100 | 80 | 90 | 103 | 96 |
| LINCOLN | 98 | 78 | 83 | 84 | 94 | 92 | 111 | 97 | 94 | 85 | 89 | 96 | 89 | 98 | 82 | 101 | 86 | 93 | 102 | 99 |
| LINN | 96 | 67 | 74 | 78 | 92 | 90 | 109 | 95 | 91 | 77 | 80 | 92 | 82 | 93 | 78 | 100 | 79 | 89 | 104 | 95 |
| LIVINGSTON | 97 | 80 | 88 | 86 | 96 | 94 | 106 | 96 | 93 | 85 | 88 | 93 | 90 | 96 | 86 | 100 | 85 | 93 | 102 | 97 |
| MCDONALD | 97 | 65 | 69 | 75 | 91 | 89 | 111 | 96 | 92 | 76 | 79 | 94 | 82 | 94 | 75 | 99 | 78 | 88 | 102 | 96 |
| MACON | 97 | 70 | 77 | 81 | 92 | 91 | 109 | 96 | 93 | 78 | 82 | 94 | 84 | 95 | 79 | 100 | 80 | 90 | 104 | 96 |
| MADISON | 96 | 65 | 71 | 75 | 92 | 90 | 108 | 95 | 92 | 76 | 79 | 92 | 81 | 92 | 76 | 99 | 77 | 88 | 103 | 94 |
| MARIES | 98 | 70 | 75 | 80 | 92 | 90 | 112 | 96 | 93 | 79 | 82 | 95 | 85 | 96 | 77 | 100 | 81 | 91 | 103 | 98 |
| MARION | 96 | 77 | 84 | 83 | 96 | 92 | 107 | 96 | 92 | 84 | 86 | 92 | 89 | 95 | 85 | 99 | 84 | 92 | 101 | 96 |
| MERCER | 97 | 63 | 69 | 78 | 90 | 89 | 109 | 95 | 90 | 72 | 78 | 94 | 80 | 94 | 75 | 100 | 77 | 89 | 105 | 96 |
| MILLER | 97 | 70 | 75 | 80 | 92 | 90 | 112 | 96 | 92 | 79 | 82 | 95 | 84 | 96 | 78 | 100 | 80 | 90 | 103 | 97 |
| MISSISSIPPI | 95 | 67 | 74 | 76 | 93 | 89 | 105 | 96 | 90 | 79 | 78 | 93 | 83 | 92 | 78 | 98 | 79 | 89 | 98 | 95 |
| MONITEAU | 97 | 71 | 77 | 80 | 93 | 91 | 109 | 96 | 92 | 79 | 83 | 93 | 85 | 95 | 79 | 100 | 81 | 90 | 103 | 97 |
| MONROE | 97 | 66 | 72 | 78 | 91 | 90 | 110 | 95 | 92 | 76 | 80 | 93 | 82 | 94 | 76 | 100 | 79 | 89 | 104 | 96 |
| MONTGOMERY | 97 | 67 | 72 | 79 | 92 | 90 | 111 | 96 | 92 | 77 | 80 | 94 | 83 | 95 | 76 | 100 | 79 | 90 | 103 | 97 |
| MORGAN | 99 | 70 | 77 | 84 | 93 | 92 | 117 | 98 | 93 | 78 | 82 | 96 | 85 | 97 | 80 | 101 | 82 | 91 | 105 | 99 |
| NEW MADRID | 97 | 67 | 70 | 76 | 92 | 89 | 109 | 96 | 92 | 78 | 79 | 95 | 83 | 94 | 76 | 99 | 79 | 89 | 100 | 96 |
| NEWTON | 99 | 82 | 88 | 88 | 97 | 94 | 110 | 98 | 95 | 88 | 91 | 97 | 92 | 99 | 86 | 101 | 88 | 95 | 102 | 100 |
| NODAWAY | 97 | 82 | 84 | 88 | 93 | 91 | 105 | 95 | 92 | 83 | 88 | 95 | 89 | 97 | 85 | 99 | 86 | 94 | 102 | 98 |
| OREGON | 96 | 63 | 68 | 75 | 91 | 89 | 109 | 95 | 91 | 74 | 78 | 93 | 80 | 93 | 74 | 99 | 77 | 88 | 104 | 95 |
| OSAGE | 99 | 72 | 77 | 83 | 93 | 91 | 114 | 97 | 93 | 80 | 84 | 97 | 86 | 98 | 79 | 101 | 83 | 92 | 104 | 99 |
| OZARK | 97 | 65 | 76 | 78 | 92 | 92 | 109 | 96 | 90 | 74 | 79 | 95 | 82 | 95 | 77 | 99 | 77 | 89 | 105 | 97 |
| MISSOURI | 98 | 92 | 94 | 95 | 99 | 97 | 102 | 98 | 97 | 94 | 96 | 98 | 98 | 99 | 93 | 101 | 94 | 98 | 100 | 99 |
| UNITED STATES | 100 | 100 | 100 | 100 | 100 | 100 | 100 | 100 | 100 | 100 | 100 | 100 | 100 | 100 | 100 | 100 | 100 | 100 | 100 | 100 |

# POPULATION CHANGE

**A**

| COUNTY | FIPS Code | MSA Code | DMA Code | POPULATION 1990 | POPULATION 2000 | POPULATION 2005 | 1990-2000 ANNUAL CHANGE % Rate | 1990-2000 ANNUAL CHANGE State Rank | RACE (%) White 1990 | White 2000 | Black 1990 | Black 2000 | Asian/Pacific 1990 | Asian/Pacific 2000 |
|---|---|---|---|---|---|---|---|---|---|---|---|---|---|---|
| PEMISCOT | 155 | 0000 | 640 | 21,921 | 20,969 | 20,090 | -0.4 | 100 | 74.0 | 70.1 | 25.5 | 29.3 | 0.2 | 0.3 |
| PERRY | 157 | 0000 | 632 | 16,648 | 17,416 | 17,344 | 0.4 | 70 | 99.3 | 99.0 | 0.1 | 0.1 | 0.4 | 0.6 |
| PETTIS | 159 | 0000 | 616 | 35,437 | 37,212 | 37,713 | 0.5 | 66 | 95.8 | 94.9 | 3.3 | 4.0 | 0.3 | 0.5 |
| PHELPS | 161 | 0000 | 619 | 35,248 | 39,337 | 41,244 | 1.1 | 38 | 95.9 | 94.9 | 1.1 | 1.2 | 2.2 | 3.1 |
| PIKE | 163 | 0000 | 609 | 15,969 | 16,486 | 16,887 | 0.3 | 75 | 94.1 | 93.0 | 5.3 | 6.4 | 0.2 | 0.2 |
| PLATTE | 165 | 3760 | 616 | 57,867 | 73,208 | 80,733 | 2.3 | 11 | 95.3 | 94.0 | 2.1 | 2.5 | 1.4 | 2.0 |
| POLK | 167 | 0000 | 619 | 21,826 | 25,928 | 27,003 | 1.7 | 20 | 98.5 | 98.3 | 0.3 | 0.4 | 0.3 | 0.5 |
| PULASKI | 169 | 0000 | 619 | 41,307 | 38,279 | 38,246 | -0.7 | 110 | 80.2 | 77.7 | 13.6 | 14.0 | 2.9 | 4.3 |
| PUTNAM | 171 | 0000 | 631 | 5,079 | 4,834 | 4,649 | -0.5 | 103 | 99.6 | 99.2 | 0.0 | 0.4 | 0.1 | 0.1 |
| RALLS | 173 | 0000 | 717 | 8,476 | 9,336 | 10,193 | 0.9 | 43 | 98.1 | 97.6 | 1.6 | 2.1 | 0.1 | 0.1 |
| RANDOLPH | 175 | 0000 | 604 | 24,370 | 23,799 | 23,485 | -0.2 | 94 | 91.6 | 89.9 | 7.5 | 9.1 | 0.3 | 0.5 |
| RAY | 177 | 3760 | 616 | 21,971 | 24,041 | 25,357 | 0.9 | 43 | 97.8 | 97.3 | 1.4 | 1.7 | 0.2 | 0.2 |
| REYNOLDS | 179 | 0000 | 632 | 6,661 | 6,611 | 6,530 | -0.1 | 91 | 99.6 | 99.4 | 0.0 | 0.2 | 0.1 | 0.1 |
| RIPLEY | 181 | 0000 | 734 | 12,303 | 14,331 | 15,121 | 1.5 | 27 | 99.3 | 99.1 | 0.0 | 0.1 | 0.2 | 0.2 |
| ST. CHARLES | 183 | 7040 | 609 | 212,907 | 288,746 | 330,023 | 3.0 | 4 | 96.5 | 95.6 | 2.3 | 2.8 | 0.7 | 1.0 |
| ST. CLAIR | 185 | 0000 | 619 | 8,457 | 9,373 | 9,902 | 1.0 | 42 | 99.1 | 99.1 | 0.3 | 0.2 | 0.1 | 0.2 |
| STE. GENEVIEVE | 186 | 0000 | 609 | 16,037 | 17,637 | 18,485 | 0.9 | 43 | 99.3 | 99.2 | 0.3 | 0.3 | 0.1 | 0.2 |
| ST. FRANCOIS | 187 | 0000 | 609 | 48,904 | 56,358 | 59,210 | 1.4 | 30 | 97.4 | 96.7 | 2.0 | 2.5 | 0.3 | 0.4 |
| ST. LOUIS | 189 | 7040 | 609 | 993,529 | 994,475 | 985,552 | 0.0 | 85 | 84.2 | 81.1 | 14.0 | 16.4 | 1.4 | 2.0 |
| SALINE | 195 | 0000 | 616 | 23,523 | 22,792 | 22,797 | -0.3 | 98 | 93.4 | 92.0 | 5.7 | 7.0 | 0.3 | 0.3 |
| SCHUYLER | 197 | 0000 | 631 | 4,236 | 4,416 | 4,418 | 0.4 | 70 | 99.6 | 99.5 | 0.0 | 0.0 | 0.1 | 0.1 |
| SCOTLAND | 199 | 0000 | 717 | 4,822 | 4,968 | 5,199 | 0.3 | 75 | 99.7 | 99.7 | 0.1 | 0.1 | 0.0 | 0.0 |
| SCOTT | 201 | 0000 | 632 | 39,376 | 40,731 | 41,532 | 0.3 | 75 | 90.6 | 88.8 | 8.9 | 10.5 | 0.2 | 0.2 |
| SHANNON | 203 | 0000 | 619 | 7,613 | 8,373 | 8,707 | 0.9 | 43 | 99.5 | 99.5 | 0.0 | 0.0 | 0.1 | 0.0 |
| SHELBY | 205 | 0000 | 717 | 6,942 | 6,597 | 6,292 | -0.5 | 103 | 98.8 | 98.5 | 0.8 | 1.1 | 0.0 | 0.1 |
| STODDARD | 207 | 0000 | 632 | 28,895 | 29,657 | 29,774 | 0.3 | 75 | 98.1 | 97.7 | 1.4 | 1.7 | 0.2 | 0.2 |
| STONE | 209 | 0000 | 619 | 19,078 | 28,032 | 30,879 | 3.8 | 2 | 99.0 | 98.9 | 0.0 | 0.1 | 0.2 | 0.3 |
| SULLIVAN | 211 | 0000 | 631 | 6,326 | 6,884 | 6,991 | 0.8 | 53 | 99.7 | 99.4 | 0.0 | 0.2 | 0.0 | 0.0 |
| TANEY | 213 | 0000 | 619 | 25,561 | 36,297 | 40,477 | 3.5 | 3 | 98.8 | 98.6 | 0.1 | 0.1 | 0.3 | 0.5 |
| TEXAS | 215 | 0000 | 619 | 21,476 | 22,521 | 22,826 | 0.5 | 66 | 99.2 | 99.0 | 0.1 | 0.1 | 0.3 | 0.4 |
| VERNON | 217 | 0000 | 603 | 19,041 | 19,562 | 19,892 | 0.3 | 75 | 98.7 | 98.5 | 0.3 | 0.3 | 0.3 | 0.5 |
| WARREN | 219 | 7040 | 609 | 19,534 | 26,294 | 30,518 | 2.9 | 5 | 96.8 | 96.1 | 2.6 | 3.2 | 0.2 | 0.2 |
| WASHINGTON | 221 | 0000 | 609 | 20,380 | 23,703 | 25,397 | 1.5 | 27 | 97.7 | 96.7 | 1.9 | 2.9 | 0.1 | 0.2 |
| WAYNE | 223 | 0000 | 632 | 11,543 | 13,102 | 13,417 | 1.2 | 35 | 99.4 | 99.2 | 0.1 | 0.3 | 0.1 | 0.1 |
| WEBSTER | 225 | 7920 | 619 | 23,753 | 30,741 | 34,575 | 2.5 | 8 | 98.2 | 98.1 | 0.8 | 0.8 | 0.2 | 0.2 |
| WORTH | 227 | 0000 | 638 | 2,440 | 2,285 | 2,237 | -0.6 | 106 | 99.4 | 99.3 | 0.0 | 0.0 | 0.2 | 0.2 |
| WRIGHT | 229 | 0000 | 619 | 16,758 | 20,190 | 21,604 | 1.8 | 16 | 98.9 | 98.9 | 0.2 | 0.3 | 0.1 | 0.1 |
| ST. LOUIS CITY | 510 | 7040 | 609 | 396,685 | 328,443 | 302,281 | -1.8 | 115 | 50.9 | 45.4 | 47.5 | 52.7 | 0.9 | 1.3 |
| MISSOURI | | | | | | | 0.7 | | 87.7 | 87.0 | 10.7 | 11.0 | 0.8 | 1.1 |
| UNITED STATES | | | | | | | 1.0 | | 80.3 | 77.9 | 12.1 | 12.4 | 2.9 | 3.9 |

| COUNTY | % HISPANIC ORIGIN 1990 | % HISPANIC ORIGIN 2000 | 2000 AGE DISTRIBUTION (%) 0-4 | 5-9 | 10-14 | 15-19 | 20-24 | 25-44 | 45-64 | 65-84 | 85+ | 18+ | MEDIAN AGE 1990 | MEDIAN AGE 2000 | 2000 Males/ Females (×100) |
|---|---|---|---|---|---|---|---|---|---|---|---|---|---|---|---|
| PEMISCOT | 0.4 | 0.8 | 7.9 | 8.1 | 9.1 | 8.7 | 6.7 | 24.8 | 20.4 | 12.5 | 1.9 | 69.5 | 32.6 | 33.4 | 89.5 |
| PERRY | 0.4 | 1.0 | 6.9 | 7.3 | 7.6 | 7.7 | 6.4 | 27.0 | 21.7 | 13.0 | 2.5 | 73.3 | 34.4 | 36.4 | 100.2 |
| PETTIS | 0.8 | 1.4 | 6.6 | 7.0 | 7.4 | 7.3 | 5.9 | 27.8 | 22.2 | 13.6 | 2.1 | 74.5 | 34.6 | 37.4 | 94.2 |
| PHELPS | 0.9 | 1.6 | 5.9 | 6.1 | 6.8 | 9.1 | 10.3 | 27.0 | 21.4 | 11.9 | 1.6 | 77.2 | 31.9 | 34.5 | 105.6 |
| PIKE | 0.7 | 1.4 | 6.7 | 7.2 | 7.5 | 7.5 | 5.8 | 24.8 | 23.2 | 14.8 | 2.5 | 73.8 | 36.0 | 38.5 | 95.1 |
| PLATTE | 2.0 | 3.2 | 6.5 | 6.9 | 7.4 | 6.8 | 6.0 | 32.4 | 24.9 | 8.2 | 1.0 | 75.2 | 32.7 | 36.1 | 96.4 |
| POLK | 0.8 | 1.4 | 6.2 | 6.5 | 6.8 | 9.0 | 8.1 | 26.0 | 21.0 | 13.9 | 2.4 | 76.5 | 33.3 | 35.8 | 95.9 |
| PULASKI | 4.7 | 6.8 | 8.7 | 7.7 | 6.3 | 9.3 | 11.0 | 35.0 | 14.3 | 6.8 | 0.9 | 73.5 | 26.8 | 28.4 | 122.2 |
| PUTNAM | 0.5 | 1.0 | 5.5 | 6.0 | 6.5 | 6.5 | 4.6 | 23.5 | 23.7 | 19.7 | 4.1 | 78.0 | 42.2 | 43.2 | 96.7 |
| RALLS | 0.2 | 0.7 | 5.6 | 6.5 | 7.9 | 7.5 | 5.4 | 27.3 | 24.8 | 12.9 | 2.0 | 74.9 | 36.5 | 38.8 | 95.4 |
| RANDOLPH | 0.7 | 1.4 | 5.9 | 6.3 | 7.2 | 7.6 | 7.9 | 29.9 | 20.7 | 12.1 | 2.5 | 76.3 | 34.4 | 35.7 | 109.6 |
| RAY | 0.5 | 1.1 | 6.6 | 7.2 | 8.3 | 7.8 | 5.5 | 27.5 | 24.5 | 11.0 | 1.7 | 72.9 | 34.1 | 37.1 | 96.9 |
| REYNOLDS | 0.4 | 1.0 | 5.7 | 6.3 | 7.6 | 7.8 | 5.2 | 25.2 | 26.0 | 14.1 | 2.0 | 75.2 | 36.8 | 39.8 | 97.6 |
| RIPLEY | 0.6 | 1.3 | 6.3 | 6.7 | 7.9 | 7.7 | 5.8 | 24.4 | 24.3 | 14.9 | 2.0 | 74.1 | 37.1 | 38.7 | 89.7 |
| ST. CHARLES | 1.1 | 1.9 | 7.9 | 8.4 | 8.6 | 7.4 | 5.8 | 33.0 | 21.2 | 6.8 | 0.7 | 70.4 | 30.7 | 33.4 | 97.0 |
| ST. CLAIR | 0.4 | 1.0 | 5.4 | 6.1 | 6.8 | 7.1 | 4.5 | 22.7 | 25.0 | 19.0 | 3.4 | 77.1 | 42.2 | 43.1 | 92.7 |
| STE. GENEVIEVE | 0.3 | 0.8 | 6.8 | 7.3 | 7.6 | 7.5 | 6.1 | 27.5 | 22.8 | 12.5 | 1.9 | 73.5 | 33.9 | 37.0 | 97.6 |
| ST. FRANCOIS | 0.5 | 1.1 | 6.0 | 6.3 | 6.8 | 7.8 | 7.4 | 28.7 | 22.0 | 13.2 | 2.0 | 76.3 | 34.4 | 36.6 | 104.5 |
| ST. LOUIS | 1.0 | 1.7 | 6.0 | 6.6 | 7.5 | 7.1 | 5.8 | 29.5 | 23.6 | 12.2 | 1.8 | 75.7 | 34.6 | 37.8 | 91.1 |
| SALINE | 0.9 | 1.5 | 6.0 | 6.4 | 6.7 | 8.5 | 7.9 | 25.5 | 22.3 | 13.9 | 2.7 | 76.2 | 35.2 | 37.3 | 94.2 |
| SCHUYLER | 0.4 | 0.9 | 6.4 | 7.4 | 7.8 | 6.9 | 4.3 | 24.3 | 23.2 | 15.9 | 3.8 | 74.1 | 39.1 | 40.3 | 97.6 |
| SCOTLAND | 0.2 | 0.7 | 6.7 | 7.4 | 8.1 | 7.1 | 4.3 | 23.7 | 22.2 | 16.8 | 3.8 | 73.1 | 38.6 | 40.0 | 97.6 |
| SCOTT | 0.5 | 1.0 | 7.0 | 7.4 | 8.0 | 7.3 | 6.2 | 28.0 | 23.1 | 11.3 | 1.7 | 73.1 | 33.1 | 35.9 | 91.6 |
| SHANNON | 0.3 | 0.8 | 6.8 | 6.9 | 7.8 | 7.4 | 5.5 | 25.9 | 24.1 | 13.7 | 1.9 | 73.7 | 35.6 | 38.1 | 94.5 |
| SHELBY | 0.3 | 0.9 | 6.3 | 7.2 | 7.5 | 7.6 | 5.1 | 23.6 | 22.5 | 15.8 | 4.6 | 73.7 | 38.6 | 40.0 | 90.0 |
| STODDARD | 0.5 | 1.0 | 5.8 | 6.2 | 6.8 | 7.5 | 5.9 | 26.3 | 24.8 | 14.3 | 2.4 | 76.7 | 36.7 | 39.3 | 93.3 |
| STONE | 0.6 | 1.2 | 4.8 | 5.3 | 6.2 | 6.3 | 4.6 | 23.2 | 28.7 | 19.3 | 1.7 | 79.8 | 42.9 | 44.8 | 96.2 |
| SULLIVAN | 0.4 | 1.1 | 5.1 | 5.6 | 6.8 | 6.7 | 5.4 | 24.2 | 25.5 | 17.0 | 3.5 | 78.2 | 42.3 | 42.4 | 94.5 |
| TANEY | 0.8 | 1.5 | 4.9 | 5.5 | 6.2 | 7.1 | 6.1 | 24.5 | 26.3 | 17.4 | 2.1 | 79.7 | 40.2 | 42.0 | 95.0 |
| TEXAS | 0.5 | 1.1 | 6.2 | 6.9 | 7.3 | 7.2 | 6.0 | 24.8 | 24.3 | 15.0 | 2.3 | 74.9 | 36.5 | 39.1 | 94.8 |
| VERNON | 0.5 | 1.1 | 6.2 | 6.8 | 7.2 | 8.8 | 6.4 | 24.9 | 23.2 | 14.3 | 2.2 | 75.0 | 35.6 | 37.8 | 91.1 |
| WARREN | 0.8 | 1.5 | 7.6 | 8.0 | 8.4 | 7.5 | 5.6 | 27.2 | 22.7 | 11.5 | 1.5 | 71.4 | 33.6 | 36.2 | 97.9 |
| WASHINGTON | 0.4 | 0.9 | 6.7 | 7.2 | 8.4 | 8.5 | 6.6 | 29.0 | 22.3 | 10.2 | 1.2 | 72.5 | 31.6 | 34.4 | 106.1 |
| WAYNE | 0.4 | 0.9 | 5.6 | 6.1 | 7.0 | 7.2 | 5.2 | 23.7 | 25.9 | 17.2 | 2.2 | 76.9 | 39.8 | 41.5 | 96.0 |
| WEBSTER | 0.6 | 1.2 | 6.9 | 7.4 | 7.9 | 7.5 | 6.4 | 27.9 | 23.2 | 11.0 | 1.8 | 73.1 | 32.7 | 35.7 | 100.8 |
| WORTH | 0.4 | 0.8 | 5.6 | 6.5 | 7.3 | 6.7 | 4.6 | 21.2 | 24.8 | 18.6 | 4.8 | 76.1 | 42.4 | 43.5 | 93.6 |
| WRIGHT | 0.4 | 0.9 | 7.1 | 7.5 | 7.7 | 8.0 | 5.9 | 25.2 | 22.4 | 14.0 | 2.2 | 72.5 | 35.1 | 37.2 | 95.1 |
| ST. LOUIS CITY | 1.3 | 1.9 | 7.3 | 7.3 | 7.4 | 7.4 | 7.3 | 29.9 | 19.1 | 12.0 | 2.3 | 73.8 | 32.8 | 34.6 | 85.6 |
| MISSOURI | 1.2 | 2.0 | 6.5 | 6.9 | 7.4 | 7.6 | 6.7 | 29.1 | 22.3 | 11.7 | 1.8 | 74.8 | 33.6 | 36.3 | 94.0 |
| UNITED STATES | 9.0 | 11.8 | 6.9 | 7.2 | 7.2 | 7.2 | 6.7 | 29.9 | 22.2 | 11.1 | 1.6 | 74.6 | 32.9 | 35.7 | 95.6 |

# HOUSEHOLDS

| COUNTY | HOUSEHOLDS | | | | | FAMILIES | | | MEDIAN HOUSEHOLD INCOME | | | |
|---|---|---|---|---|---|---|---|---|---|---|---|---|
| | 1990 | 2000 | 2005 | % Annual Rate 1990-2000 | 2000 Average HH Size | 1990 | 2000 | % Annual Rate 1990-2000 | 2000 | 2005 | 2000 National Rank | 2000 State Rank |
| PEMISCOT | 8,210 | 8,098 | 7,874 | -0.2 | 2.54 | 5,757 | 5,490 | -0.6 | 22,369 | 24,763 | 3005 | 113 |
| PERRY | 6,111 | 6,438 | 6,432 | 0.6 | 2.65 | 4,537 | 4,621 | 0.2 | 37,403 | 47,238 | 915 | 21 |
| PETTIS | 14,056 | 14,876 | 15,136 | 0.7 | 2.48 | 9,947 | 10,141 | 0.2 | 32,823 | 37,888 | 1568 | 36 |
| PHELPS | 13,277 | 15,065 | 15,918 | 1.5 | 2.44 | 9,125 | 9,926 | 1.0 | 30,270 | 33,733 | 2090 | 56 |
| PIKE | 6,083 | 6,362 | 6,559 | 0.5 | 2.54 | 4,380 | 4,386 | 0.0 | 31,217 | 38,291 | 1883 | 49 |
| PLATTE | 22,142 | 28,089 | 31,002 | 2.9 | 2.58 | 16,077 | 19,661 | 2.5 | 55,191 | 61,596 | 124 | 2 |
| POLK | 8,031 | 9,722 | 10,187 | 2.3 | 2.53 | 5,899 | 6,857 | 1.8 | 28,899 | 35,021 | 2313 | 64 |
| PULASKI | 12,397 | 12,049 | 12,110 | -0.3 | 2.81 | 9,882 | 9,336 | -0.7 | 30,496 | 35,333 | 2036 | 53 |
| PUTNAM | 2,166 | 2,093 | 2,028 | -0.4 | 2.27 | 1,472 | 1,365 | -0.9 | 23,232 | 27,122 | 2956 | 109 |
| RALLS | 3,226 | 3,391 | 3,622 | 0.6 | 2.73 | 2,474 | 2,519 | 0.2 | 33,220 | 36,769 | 1503 | 32 |
| RANDOLPH | 8,943 | 8,718 | 8,647 | -0.3 | 2.47 | 6,235 | 5,842 | -0.8 | 28,032 | 30,871 | 2434 | 73 |
| RAY | 8,020 | 9,038 | 9,667 | 1.5 | 2.64 | 6,215 | 6,784 | 1.1 | 39,707 | 49,930 | 692 | 15 |
| REYNOLDS | 2,542 | 2,532 | 2,506 | 0.0 | 2.57 | 1,950 | 1,881 | -0.4 | 28,301 | 35,530 | 2398 | 69 |
| RIPLEY | 4,788 | 5,667 | 6,022 | 2.1 | 2.51 | 3,522 | 4,013 | 1.6 | 23,259 | 27,573 | 2955 | 108 |
| ST. CHARLES | 74,331 | 101,912 | 117,059 | 3.9 | 2.81 | 57,815 | 77,429 | 3.6 | 57,999 | 68,365 | 92 | 1 |
| ST. CLAIR | 3,499 | 3,809 | 3,987 | 1.0 | 2.41 | 2,441 | 2,543 | 0.5 | 25,897 | 31,974 | 2722 | 96 |
| STE. GENEVIEVE | 5,707 | 6,515 | 6,953 | 1.6 | 2.67 | 4,416 | 4,903 | 1.3 | 39,678 | 48,484 | 693 | 16 |
| ST. FRANCOIS | 17,670 | 20,623 | 21,941 | 1.9 | 2.54 | 13,101 | 14,788 | 1.5 | 32,313 | 40,982 | 1657 | 41 |
| ST. LOUIS | 380,110 | 384,786 | 383,442 | 0.1 | 2.54 | 270,421 | 263,161 | -0.3 | 47,926 | 52,309 | 240 | 4 |
| SALINE | 8,903 | 8,586 | 8,570 | -0.4 | 2.47 | 6,121 | 5,671 | -0.9 | 31,383 | 37,594 | 1843 | 47 |
| SCHUYLER | 1,729 | 1,847 | 1,855 | 0.8 | 2.36 | 1,234 | 1,271 | 0.4 | 23,762 | 28,170 | 2919 | 107 |
| SCOTLAND | 1,956 | 1,964 | 2,029 | 0.0 | 2.47 | 1,325 | 1,279 | -0.4 | 23,804 | 27,979 | 2917 | 106 |
| SCOTT | 14,761 | 15,203 | 15,475 | 0.4 | 2.65 | 10,950 | 10,914 | 0.0 | 31,502 | 36,078 | 1818 | 45 |
| SHANNON | 2,917 | 3,259 | 3,415 | 1.4 | 2.54 | 2,199 | 2,372 | 0.9 | 24,015 | 29,264 | 2900 | 105 |
| SHELBY | 2,809 | 2,755 | 2,666 | -0.2 | 2.32 | 1,919 | 1,814 | -0.7 | 26,941 | 29,489 | 2591 | 87 |
| STODDARD | 11,383 | 11,788 | 11,906 | 0.4 | 2.46 | 8,366 | 8,380 | 0.0 | 27,684 | 32,506 | 2480 | 77 |
| STONE | 7,885 | 11,560 | 12,703 | 4.7 | 2.41 | 5,975 | 8,495 | 4.4 | 34,305 | 39,727 | 1347 | 27 |
| SULLIVAN | 2,615 | 3,113 | 3,298 | 2.1 | 2.14 | 1,809 | 2,075 | 1.7 | 26,702 | 33,563 | 2616 | 89 |
| TANEY | 10,321 | 14,703 | 16,364 | 4.4 | 2.39 | 7,497 | 10,413 | 4.1 | 32,689 | 36,992 | 1594 | 38 |
| TEXAS | 8,441 | 8,860 | 8,985 | 0.6 | 2.52 | 6,195 | 6,276 | 0.2 | 24,658 | 29,308 | 2845 | 100 |
| VERNON | 7,301 | 7,668 | 7,838 | 0.6 | 2.44 | 5,085 | 5,138 | 0.1 | 27,689 | 33,027 | 2478 | 76 |
| WARREN | 7,070 | 9,540 | 11,085 | 3.7 | 2.73 | 5,423 | 7,111 | 3.3 | 42,128 | 51,250 | 498 | 9 |
| WASHINGTON | 6,982 | 8,017 | 8,624 | 1.7 | 2.82 | 5,420 | 6,025 | 1.3 | 27,313 | 33,225 | 2535 | 84 |
| WAYNE | 4,607 | 5,373 | 5,570 | 1.9 | 2.41 | 3,417 | 3,835 | 1.4 | 21,508 | 24,253 | 3054 | 115 |
| WEBSTER | 8,391 | 10,911 | 12,299 | 3.2 | 2.74 | 6,569 | 8,175 | 2.7 | 32,096 | 38,468 | 1701 | 42 |
| WORTH | 1,037 | 970 | 950 | -0.8 | 2.28 | 679 | 610 | -1.3 | 22,925 | 25,096 | 2977 | 112 |
| WRIGHT | 6,510 | 7,840 | 8,385 | 2.3 | 2.55 | 4,725 | 5,478 | 1.8 | 23,037 | 27,412 | 2971 | 111 |
| ST. LOUIS CITY | 164,931 | 138,661 | 128,478 | -2.1 | 2.29 | 90,945 | 72,739 | -2.7 | 28,511 | 32,062 | 2364 | 67 |
| MISSOURI | | | | 1.0 | 2.52 | | | 0.6 | 38,422 | 44,218 | | |
| UNITED STATES | | | | 1.4 | 2.59 | | | 1.1 | 41,914 | 49,127 | | |

| COUNTY | 2000 Per Capita Income | 2000 HH Income Base | 2000 HOUSEHOLD INCOME DISTRIBUTION (%) | | | | | | 2000 AVERAGE DISPOSABLE INCOME BY AGE OF HOUSEHOLDER | | | | | |
|---|---|---|---|---|---|---|---|---|---|---|---|---|---|---|
| | | | Less than $15,000 | $15,000 to $24,999 | $25,000 to $49,999 | $50,000 to $99,999 | $100,000 to $149,999 | $150,000 or More | All Ages | <35 | 35-44 | 45-54 | 55-64 | 65+ |
| PEMISCOT | 12,384 | 8,098 | 35.8 | 19.1 | 28.7 | 13.4 | 2.2 | 0.8 | 24,263 | 22,442 | 28,847 | 29,487 | 26,262 | 16,860 |
| PERRY | 17,165 | 6,438 | 16.0 | 12.8 | 38.1 | 28.1 | 4.2 | 0.8 | 34,299 | 32,025 | 40,513 | 46,186 | 32,598 | 21,966 |
| PETTIS | 16,279 | 14,876 | 19.5 | 16.1 | 38.0 | 22.2 | 3.2 | 0.9 | 31,070 | 28,340 | 37,231 | 38,422 | 34,368 | 20,498 |
| PHELPS | 16,145 | 15,065 | 22.8 | 17.7 | 33.8 | 20.4 | 3.6 | 1.7 | 31,222 | 22,358 | 37,987 | 44,678 | 32,392 | 20,801 |
| PIKE | 14,591 | 6,362 | 21.2 | 18.0 | 36.6 | 21.1 | 2.6 | 0.5 | 29,353 | 27,973 | 33,158 | 38,346 | 31,443 | 19,965 |
| PLATTE | 25,654 | 28,089 | 5.8 | 7.7 | 29.7 | 42.1 | 11.7 | 3.2 | 48,621 | 40,860 | 51,141 | 58,643 | 52,644 | 30,877 |
| POLK | 13,817 | 9,722 | 22.5 | 19.7 | 35.6 | 18.6 | 2.8 | 0.7 | 28,700 | 25,540 | 34,171 | 39,634 | 29,621 | 19,979 |
| PULASKI | 12,732 | 12,049 | 14.5 | 23.2 | 40.5 | 20.2 | 1.4 | 0.1 | 28,731 | 26,528 | 31,332 | 38,219 | 29,737 | 19,309 |
| PUTNAM | 12,915 | 2,093 | 32.5 | 21.3 | 31.5 | 12.1 | 2.0 | 0.7 | 23,896 | 24,054 | 31,327 | 30,554 | 24,796 | 16,531 |
| RALLS | 14,873 | 3,391 | 17.3 | 18.2 | 38.7 | 21.9 | 2.8 | 1.1 | 31,764 | 28,897 | 35,821 | 37,531 | 34,529 | 22,355 |
| RANDOLPH | 15,085 | 8,718 | 23.4 | 20.3 | 37.3 | 16.3 | 2.1 | 0.7 | 27,386 | 24,914 | 33,976 | 32,201 | 30,153 | 18,708 |
| RAY | 17,285 | 9,038 | 14.0 | 11.9 | 38.7 | 29.9 | 4.7 | 0.8 | 35,613 | 33,197 | 40,804 | 45,970 | 33,843 | 22,555 |
| REYNOLDS | 13,903 | 2,532 | 22.3 | 22.4 | 34.8 | 16.6 | 3.2 | 0.8 | 28,119 | 25,000 | 37,318 | 34,322 | 27,161 | 18,477 |
| RIPLEY | 11,972 | 5,667 | 32.8 | 20.6 | 31.0 | 13.2 | 1.9 | 0.5 | 24,123 | 23,158 | 27,861 | 30,464 | 23,602 | 17,947 |
| ST. CHARLES | 24,370 | 101,912 | 4.7 | 5.7 | 28.1 | 46.1 | 12.5 | 2.9 | 50,055 | 44,042 | 53,356 | 59,667 | 53,209 | 30,657 |
| ST. CLAIR | 12,939 | 3,809 | 27.6 | 20.5 | 34.4 | 15.9 | 1.4 | 0.2 | 25,336 | 23,125 | 31,280 | 34,628 | 26,087 | 18,026 |
| STE. GENEVIEVE | 17,146 | 6,515 | 14.6 | 11.0 | 41.0 | 28.3 | 4.1 | 1.0 | 35,459 | 32,971 | 40,451 | 46,220 | 39,228 | 20,849 |
| ST. FRANCOIS | 15,263 | 20,623 | 19.8 | 17.3 | 36.4 | 22.8 | 3.1 | 0.6 | 30,787 | 28,634 | 37,366 | 38,876 | 30,749 | 20,582 |
| ST. LOUIS | 25,430 | 384,785 | 9.3 | 10.5 | 32.5 | 34.9 | 8.5 | 4.3 | 46,005 | 37,774 | 49,278 | 55,544 | 48,925 | 30,722 |
| SALINE | 15,451 | 8,586 | 18.6 | 20.2 | 36.3 | 21.2 | 2.9 | 0.8 | 30,279 | 25,733 | 36,259 | 39,570 | 33,122 | 20,581 |
| SCHUYLER | 13,114 | 1,847 | 29.6 | 23.2 | 31.0 | 13.6 | 2.0 | 0.7 | 24,769 | 22,909 | 29,280 | 33,242 | 27,026 | 16,191 |
| SCOTLAND | 11,629 | 1,964 | 31.8 | 20.5 | 33.6 | 13.0 | 1.1 | 0.1 | 23,150 | 21,546 | 25,807 | 31,138 | 25,311 | 16,498 |
| SCOTT | 14,654 | 15,203 | 24.2 | 16.2 | 34.3 | 21.1 | 3.2 | 1.1 | 30,192 | 27,797 | 36,694 | 38,482 | 29,576 | 17,605 |
| SHANNON | 12,090 | 3,259 | 29.7 | 22.5 | 30.9 | 14.6 | 2.1 | 0.2 | 24,534 | 23,944 | 31,664 | 28,252 | 24,578 | 17,223 |
| SHELBY | 13,848 | 2,755 | 24.0 | 22.1 | 35.8 | 15.9 | 2.2 | 0.1 | 26,123 | 25,300 | 30,711 | 31,694 | 26,892 | 19,909 |
| STODDARD | 14,626 | 11,788 | 26.5 | 18.0 | 35.0 | 16.9 | 3.0 | 0.6 | 27,561 | 27,642 | 35,299 | 32,769 | 28,229 | 17,250 |
| STONE | 18,515 | 11,560 | 14.5 | 19.5 | 35.5 | 25.2 | 4.4 | 1.1 | 33,307 | 29,517 | 37,965 | 43,608 | 33,050 | 26,688 |
| SULLIVAN | 16,022 | 3,113 | 25.2 | 22.6 | 33.9 | 16.6 | 1.2 | 0.6 | 26,044 | 26,072 | 29,470 | 35,799 | 27,281 | 17,249 |
| TANEY | 18,194 | 14,703 | 16.1 | 20.0 | 35.7 | 22.9 | 3.7 | 1.7 | 33,003 | 28,276 | 39,040 | 42,523 | 33,533 | 24,341 |
| TEXAS | 12,118 | 8,860 | 28.5 | 22.3 | 32.8 | 14.3 | 2.1 | 0.1 | 24,491 | 23,408 | 27,965 | 30,655 | 26,663 | 16,697 |
| VERNON | 13,736 | 7,668 | 22.2 | 22.3 | 34.9 | 18.0 | 2.2 | 0.5 | 27,431 | 24,980 | 34,149 | 33,774 | 30,088 | 18,346 |
| WARREN | 18,744 | 9,540 | 12.9 | 9.3 | 38.6 | 31.1 | 6.4 | 1.8 | 38,700 | 34,561 | 44,059 | 48,795 | 42,098 | 24,323 |
| WASHINGTON | 11,788 | 8,017 | 27.3 | 18.0 | 34.5 | 17.6 | 2.3 | 0.3 | 26,848 | 24,339 | 34,192 | 32,982 | 25,729 | 16,894 |
| WAYNE | 15,823 | 5,373 | 34.8 | 22.8 | 27.7 | 10.7 | 2.1 | 1.9 | 25,316 | 20,977 | 33,960 | 31,170 | 27,617 | 14,961 |
| WEBSTER | 13,866 | 10,911 | 19.3 | 17.4 | 39.1 | 20.9 | 2.8 | 0.6 | 30,261 | 27,620 | 35,725 | 36,853 | 33,443 | 19,166 |
| WORTH | 12,224 | 970 | 32.4 | 22.2 | 31.9 | 12.7 | 0.9 | 0.0 | 22,536 | 22,929 | 29,765 | 29,413 | 24,936 | 13,998 |
| WRIGHT | 10,749 | 7,840 | 32.2 | 21.6 | 33.9 | 11.4 | 0.9 | 0.0 | 22,560 | 21,847 | 26,810 | 28,207 | 23,470 | 15,665 |
| ST. LOUIS CITY | 16,907 | 138,632 | 25.4 | 18.5 | 32.4 | 19.0 | 3.4 | 1.4 | 29,513 | 26,899 | 33,647 | 36,358 | 31,973 | 20,889 |
| MISSOURI | 19,444 | | 15.8 | 14.1 | 34.4 | 28.2 | 5.6 | 1.9 | 36,824 | 32,026 | 42,273 | 46,089 | 39,038 | 23,886 |
| UNITED STATES | 22,162 | | 14.5 | 12.5 | 32.3 | 29.8 | 7.4 | 3.5 | 40,748 | 34,503 | 44,969 | 49,579 | 43,409 | 27,339 |

# SPENDING POTENTIAL INDEXES

| COUNTY | FINANCIAL SERVICES | | | | THE HOME | | | | | | ENTERTAINMENT | | | | | | PERSONAL | | | |
|---|---|---|---|---|---|---|---|---|---|---|---|---|---|---|---|---|---|---|---|---|
| | | | | | Home Improvements | | | Furnishings | | | | | | | | | | | | |
| | Auto Loan | Home Loan | Investments | Retirement Plans | Home Repair | Lawn & Garden | Remodeling | Appliances | Electronics | Furniture | Restaurants | Sporting Goods | Theater & Concerts | Toys & Hobbies | Travel | Video Rental | Apparel | Auto Aftermarket | Health Insurance | Pets & Supplies |
| PEMISCOT | 94 | 68 | 74 | 77 | 94 | 89 | 103 | 95 | 90 | 80 | 77 | 92 | 83 | 91 | 80 | 98 | 79 | 89 | 97 | 94 |
| PERRY | 98 | 76 | 82 | 83 | 96 | 92 | 111 | 97 | 93 | 84 | 87 | 95 | 89 | 98 | 83 | 101 | 85 | 92 | 103 | 99 |
| PETTIS | 97 | 82 | 91 | 88 | 98 | 95 | 107 | 97 | 93 | 88 | 90 | 94 | 93 | 97 | 89 | 100 | 88 | 94 | 102 | 98 |
| PHELPS | 97 | 87 | 92 | 90 | 97 | 95 | 104 | 95 | 94 | 88 | 92 | 94 | 93 | 96 | 89 | 100 | 88 | 95 | 101 | 98 |
| PIKE | 97 | 67 | 72 | 78 | 92 | 90 | 110 | 95 | 92 | 76 | 80 | 93 | 82 | 94 | 76 | 100 | 79 | 89 | 103 | 96 |
| PLATTE | 103 | 111 | 97 | 107 | 100 | 103 | 102 | 102 | 106 | 108 | 114 | 106 | 109 | 106 | 102 | 105 | 109 | 109 | 100 | 105 |
| POLK | 96 | 73 | 79 | 82 | 93 | 91 | 108 | 95 | 92 | 79 | 83 | 92 | 85 | 94 | 80 | 100 | 81 | 91 | 103 | 96 |
| PULASKI | 93 | 84 | 76 | 80 | 90 | 87 | 100 | 94 | 94 | 84 | 90 | 91 | 88 | 93 | 82 | 100 | 84 | 93 | 96 | 97 |
| PUTNAM | 96 | 64 | 70 | 78 | 90 | 89 | 108 | 94 | 90 | 72 | 78 | 93 | 79 | 93 | 75 | 100 | 77 | 89 | 105 | 95 |
| RALLS | 99 | 73 | 77 | 83 | 93 | 91 | 114 | 98 | 94 | 81 | 85 | 97 | 87 | 99 | 79 | 101 | 84 | 92 | 103 | 100 |
| RANDOLPH | 96 | 81 | 84 | 84 | 96 | 92 | 106 | 96 | 93 | 87 | 88 | 93 | 90 | 96 | 85 | 100 | 85 | 93 | 100 | 97 |
| RAY | 98 | 75 | 81 | 83 | 95 | 92 | 111 | 97 | 93 | 83 | 86 | 95 | 88 | 98 | 82 | 101 | 84 | 92 | 103 | 99 |
| REYNOLDS | 97 | 66 | 69 | 77 | 92 | 90 | 113 | 96 | 92 | 76 | 79 | 95 | 82 | 95 | 75 | 99 | 78 | 89 | 103 | 97 |
| RIPLEY | 96 | 63 | 66 | 74 | 91 | 89 | 109 | 95 | 91 | 75 | 77 | 93 | 80 | 93 | 74 | 99 | 76 | 88 | 103 | 95 |
| ST. CHARLES | 102 | 107 | 90 | 101 | 98 | 99 | 100 | 102 | 105 | 106 | 112 | 105 | 106 | 105 | 97 | 105 | 106 | 107 | 99 | 104 |
| ST. CLAIR | 96 | 65 | 70 | 78 | 91 | 90 | 111 | 95 | 91 | 74 | 78 | 93 | 80 | 93 | 76 | 100 | 78 | 89 | 104 | 96 |
| STE. GENEVIEVE | 99 | 78 | 83 | 86 | 95 | 92 | 113 | 98 | 95 | 86 | 89 | 97 | 90 | 99 | 83 | 101 | 87 | 94 | 102 | 100 |
| ST. FRANCOIS | 97 | 73 | 80 | 82 | 95 | 92 | 110 | 96 | 93 | 82 | 85 | 94 | 87 | 96 | 82 | 100 | 83 | 91 | 103 | 97 |
| ST. LOUIS | 101 | 110 | 109 | 109 | 106 | 108 | 99 | 102 | 103 | 108 | 111 | 104 | 111 | 104 | 108 | 104 | 108 | 108 | 101 | 102 |
| SALINE | 95 | 71 | 77 | 79 | 93 | 90 | 107 | 94 | 91 | 79 | 82 | 91 | 84 | 93 | 80 | 99 | 80 | 90 | 102 | 95 |
| SCHUYLER | 97 | 64 | 70 | 79 | 90 | 89 | 109 | 95 | 90 | 72 | 78 | 94 | 79 | 94 | 75 | 100 | 77 | 89 | 106 | 96 |
| SCOTLAND | 97 | 64 | 70 | 79 | 90 | 89 | 109 | 95 | 90 | 72 | 78 | 94 | 79 | 94 | 75 | 100 | 77 | 89 | 106 | 96 |
| SCOTT | 98 | 80 | 86 | 88 | 97 | 94 | 109 | 98 | 95 | 88 | 89 | 97 | 92 | 98 | 86 | 101 | 87 | 94 | 101 | 99 |
| SHANNON | 97 | 63 | 66 | 74 | 91 | 89 | 110 | 96 | 92 | 75 | 77 | 95 | 81 | 93 | 73 | 98 | 77 | 88 | 102 | 96 |
| SHELBY | 97 | 65 | 71 | 79 | 91 | 90 | 109 | 95 | 90 | 74 | 79 | 93 | 81 | 94 | 76 | 100 | 78 | 89 | 105 | 96 |
| STODDARD | 97 | 71 | 76 | 80 | 93 | 91 | 110 | 96 | 93 | 80 | 82 | 95 | 86 | 95 | 79 | 100 | 81 | 91 | 102 | 97 |
| STONE | 101 | 80 | 99 | 95 | 100 | 105 | 113 | 102 | 94 | 86 | 91 | 99 | 94 | 100 | 93 | 100 | 89 | 95 | 109 | 101 |
| SULLIVAN | 96 | 64 | 70 | 77 | 90 | 89 | 108 | 94 | 90 | 73 | 78 | 92 | 79 | 93 | 75 | 100 | 77 | 88 | 105 | 95 |
| TANEY | 99 | 80 | 96 | 92 | 98 | 100 | 111 | 99 | 94 | 87 | 91 | 96 | 93 | 99 | 90 | 101 | 87 | 95 | 106 | 100 |
| TEXAS | 97 | 64 | 69 | 77 | 91 | 89 | 110 | 95 | 91 | 74 | 78 | 95 | 81 | 94 | 75 | 99 | 77 | 89 | 104 | 96 |
| VERNON | 96 | 69 | 75 | 79 | 92 | 90 | 109 | 95 | 92 | 78 | 81 | 92 | 83 | 93 | 78 | 100 | 79 | 90 | 103 | 96 |
| WARREN | 99 | 79 | 85 | 85 | 95 | 92 | 114 | 98 | 94 | 85 | 89 | 97 | 90 | 100 | 83 | 101 | 86 | 94 | 103 | 101 |
| WASHINGTON | 96 | 64 | 67 | 74 | 91 | 89 | 109 | 95 | 91 | 76 | 78 | 93 | 81 | 93 | 75 | 98 | 77 | 88 | 102 | 95 |
| WAYNE | 97 | 64 | 67 | 76 | 91 | 89 | 113 | 96 | 92 | 75 | 78 | 96 | 81 | 95 | 74 | 99 | 77 | 89 | 103 | 97 |
| WEBSTER | 98 | 71 | 75 | 81 | 93 | 90 | 113 | 97 | 93 | 80 | 83 | 96 | 86 | 97 | 78 | 100 | 82 | 91 | 103 | 99 |
| WORTH | 96 | 64 | 70 | 78 | 90 | 89 | 108 | 94 | 90 | 72 | 78 | 92 | 79 | 93 | 75 | 100 | 77 | 89 | 105 | 95 |
| WRIGHT | 97 | 65 | 69 | 77 | 91 | 89 | 109 | 95 | 90 | 75 | 78 | 95 | 81 | 94 | 76 | 99 | 78 | 89 | 104 | 96 |
| ST. LOUIS CITY | 90 | 84 | 93 | 82 | 101 | 92 | 86 | 94 | 87 | 91 | 83 | 87 | 91 | 88 | 94 | 98 | 86 | 93 | 91 | 91 |
| MISSOURI | 98 | 92 | 94 | 95 | 99 | 97 | 102 | 98 | 97 | 94 | 96 | 98 | 98 | 99 | 93 | 101 | 94 | 98 | 100 | 99 |
| UNITED STATES | 100 | 100 | 100 | 100 | 100 | 100 | 100 | 100 | 100 | 100 | 100 | 100 | 100 | 100 | 100 | 100 | 100 | 100 | 100 | 100 |

| COUNTY | FIPS Code | MSA Code | DMA Code | POPULATION 1990 | POPULATION 2000 | POPULATION 2005 | 1990-2000 ANNUAL CHANGE % Rate | 1990-2000 ANNUAL CHANGE State Rank | RACE (%) White 1990 | White 2000 | Black 1990 | Black 2000 | Asian/Pacific 1990 | Asian/Pacific 2000 |
|---|---|---|---|---|---|---|---|---|---|---|---|---|---|---|
| BEAVERHEAD | 001 | 0000 | 754 | 8,424 | 8,742 | 8,507 | 0.4 | 24 | 97.3 | 97.2 | 0.1 | 0.1 | 0.3 | 0.3 |
| BIG HORN | 003 | 0000 | 756 | 11,337 | 12,620 | 12,834 | 1.1 | 17 | 43.4 | 38.9 | 0.2 | 0.2 | 0.4 | 0.5 |
| BLAINE | 005 | 0000 | 755 | 6,728 | 7,065 | 7,020 | 0.5 | 21 | 60.0 | 57.4 | 0.1 | 0.1 | 0.1 | 0.1 |
| BROADWATER | 007 | 0000 | 754 | 3,318 | 4,218 | 4,489 | 2.4 | 5 | 98.1 | 97.9 | 0.0 | 0.0 | 0.2 | 0.2 |
| CARBON | 009 | 0000 | 756 | 8,080 | 9,658 | 10,225 | 1.8 | 8 | 98.7 | 98.5 | 0.0 | 0.1 | 0.2 | 0.2 |
| CARTER | 011 | 0000 | 764 | 1,503 | 1,429 | 1,409 | -0.5 | 43 | 98.9 | 98.7 | 0.0 | 0.0 | 0.1 | 0.1 |
| CASCADE | 013 | 3040 | 755 | 77,691 | 77,903 | 75,961 | 0.0 | 28 | 93.1 | 92.2 | 1.4 | 1.6 | 1.0 | 1.1 |
| CHOUTEAU | 015 | 0000 | 755 | 5,452 | 4,978 | 4,766 | -0.9 | 48 | 95.8 | 95.5 | 0.1 | 0.1 | 0.2 | 0.2 |
| CUSTER | 017 | 0000 | 756 | 11,697 | 11,717 | 11,134 | 0.0 | 28 | 97.4 | 97.0 | 0.1 | 0.1 | 0.2 | 0.2 |
| DANIELS | 019 | 0000 | 687 | 2,266 | 1,925 | 1,769 | -1.6 | 54 | 98.9 | 98.6 | 0.0 | 0.0 | 0.8 | 1.1 |
| DAWSON | 021 | 0000 | 798 | 9,505 | 8,548 | 7,964 | -1.0 | 50 | 98.6 | 98.4 | 0.0 | 0.0 | 0.3 | 0.4 |
| DEER LODGE | 023 | 0000 | 754 | 10,278 | 9,584 | 8,918 | -0.7 | 44 | 96.4 | 95.7 | 0.3 | 0.4 | 0.2 | 0.2 |
| FALLON | 025 | 0000 | 687 | 3,103 | 2,842 | 2,636 | -0.9 | 48 | 99.2 | 99.0 | 0.0 | 0.0 | 0.4 | 0.6 |
| FERGUS | 027 | 0000 | 755 | 12,083 | 12,069 | 11,530 | 0.0 | 28 | 98.7 | 98.5 | 0.1 | 0.1 | 0.1 | 0.1 |
| FLATHEAD | 029 | 0000 | 762 | 59,218 | 73,438 | 77,097 | 2.1 | 7 | 97.8 | 97.4 | 0.1 | 0.1 | 0.4 | 0.4 |
| GALLATIN | 031 | 0000 | 754 | 50,463 | 65,139 | 71,505 | 2.5 | 4 | 97.5 | 97.2 | 0.2 | 0.2 | 0.9 | 0.9 |
| GARFIELD | 033 | 0000 | 756 | 1,589 | 1,419 | 1,416 | -1.1 | 52 | 99.6 | 99.5 | 0.0 | 0.0 | 0.1 | 0.2 |
| GLACIER | 035 | 0000 | 755 | 12,121 | 12,626 | 12,742 | 0.4 | 24 | 43.4 | 42.3 | 0.1 | 0.2 | 0.1 | 0.1 |
| GOLDEN VALLEY | 037 | 0000 | 756 | 912 | 1,067 | 1,147 | 1.5 | 11 | 98.1 | 97.7 | 0.0 | 0.0 | 0.4 | 0.4 |
| GRANITE | 039 | 0000 | 762 | 2,548 | 2,672 | 2,717 | 0.5 | 21 | 98.9 | 98.7 | 0.0 | 0.0 | 0.2 | 0.3 |
| HILL | 041 | 0000 | 755 | 17,654 | 16,862 | 15,914 | -0.4 | 41 | 83.4 | 81.6 | 0.1 | 0.1 | 0.5 | 0.6 |
| JEFFERSON | 043 | 0000 | 754 | 7,939 | 10,607 | 11,856 | 2.9 | 2 | 98.0 | 97.6 | 0.1 | 0.1 | 0.2 | 0.2 |
| JUDITH BASIN | 045 | 0000 | 755 | 2,282 | 2,281 | 2,262 | 0.0 | 28 | 99.4 | 99.3 | 0.0 | 0.0 | 0.3 | 0.3 |
| LAKE | 047 | 0000 | 762 | 21,041 | 26,197 | 27,813 | 2.2 | 6 | 78.0 | 75.5 | 0.1 | 0.1 | 0.2 | 0.1 |
| LEWIS AND CLARK | 049 | 0000 | 766 | 47,495 | 54,400 | 56,268 | 1.3 | 14 | 96.8 | 96.4 | 0.1 | 0.2 | 0.5 | 0.6 |
| LIBERTY | 051 | 0000 | 755 | 2,295 | 2,222 | 2,203 | -0.3 | 38 | 99.3 | 99.2 | 0.1 | 0.1 | 0.1 | 0.1 |
| LINCOLN | 053 | 0000 | 881 | 17,481 | 18,859 | 19,122 | 0.7 | 20 | 97.8 | 97.6 | 0.1 | 0.1 | 0.3 | 0.4 |
| MCCONE | 055 | 0000 | 687 | 2,276 | 1,884 | 1,694 | -1.8 | 56 | 99.1 | 98.9 | 0.0 | 0.1 | 0.1 | 0.1 |
| MADISON | 057 | 0000 | 754 | 5,989 | 6,978 | 7,232 | 1.5 | 11 | 98.6 | 98.5 | 0.0 | 0.0 | 0.2 | 0.2 |
| MEAGHER | 059 | 0000 | 756 | 1,819 | 1,767 | 1,721 | -0.3 | 38 | 98.1 | 97.9 | 0.0 | 0.0 | 0.1 | 0.1 |
| MINERAL | 061 | 0000 | 762 | 3,315 | 3,925 | 4,231 | 1.7 | 9 | 96.7 | 96.6 | 0.1 | 0.1 | 0.7 | 0.7 |
| MISSOULA | 063 | 5140 | 762 | 78,687 | 89,724 | 91,829 | 1.3 | 14 | 96.1 | 95.6 | 0.2 | 0.3 | 1.1 | 1.2 |
| MUSSELSHELL | 065 | 0000 | 756 | 4,106 | 4,546 | 4,518 | 1.0 | 18 | 98.8 | 98.5 | 0.0 | 0.0 | 0.2 | 0.2 |
| PARK | 067 | 0000 | 756 | 14,562 | 16,010 | 16,188 | 0.9 | 19 | 97.7 | 97.3 | 0.5 | 0.6 | 0.5 | 0.6 |
| PETROLEUM | 069 | 0000 | 756 | 519 | 501 | 501 | -0.3 | 38 | 99.4 | 99.4 | 0.0 | 0.0 | 0.0 | 0.0 |
| PHILLIPS | 071 | 0000 | 755 | 5,163 | 4,598 | 4,343 | -1.1 | 52 | 91.8 | 90.3 | 0.0 | 0.0 | 0.3 | 0.4 |
| PONDERA | 073 | 0000 | 755 | 6,433 | 6,191 | 5,934 | -0.4 | 41 | 88.5 | 87.2 | 0.1 | 0.1 | 0.3 | 0.3 |
| POWDER RIVER | 075 | 0000 | 756 | 2,090 | 1,734 | 1,569 | -1.8 | 56 | 97.8 | 97.6 | 0.0 | 0.0 | 0.1 | 0.2 |
| POWELL | 077 | 0000 | 754 | 6,620 | 6,918 | 6,786 | 0.4 | 24 | 94.7 | 93.3 | 0.3 | 0.4 | 0.4 | 0.3 |
| PRAIRIE | 079 | 0000 | 798 | 1,383 | 1,367 | 1,404 | -0.1 | 33 | 98.4 | 98.2 | 0.0 | 0.0 | 0.3 | 0.4 |
| RAVALLI | 081 | 0000 | 762 | 25,010 | 36,542 | 40,350 | 3.8 | 1 | 98.1 | 97.8 | 0.1 | 0.2 | 0.3 | 0.3 |
| RICHLAND | 083 | 0000 | 687 | 10,716 | 9,978 | 9,614 | -0.7 | 44 | 97.5 | 97.2 | 0.0 | 0.0 | 0.2 | 0.3 |
| ROOSEVELT | 085 | 0000 | 687 | 10,999 | 10,847 | 10,527 | -0.1 | 33 | 50.6 | 47.0 | 0.2 | 0.1 | 0.4 | 0.4 |
| ROSEBUD | 087 | 0000 | 756 | 10,505 | 9,709 | 9,365 | -0.8 | 47 | 71.8 | 69.2 | 0.3 | 0.3 | 0.5 | 0.5 |
| SANDERS | 089 | 0000 | 762 | 8,669 | 10,265 | 10,469 | 1.7 | 9 | 93.8 | 93.0 | 0.1 | 0.1 | 0.4 | 0.5 |
| SHERIDAN | 091 | 0000 | 687 | 4,732 | 4,006 | 3,677 | -1.6 | 54 | 98.3 | 98.0 | 0.0 | 0.0 | 0.3 | 0.3 |
| SILVER BOW | 093 | 0000 | 754 | 33,941 | 33,684 | 32,377 | -0.1 | 33 | 97.3 | 96.8 | 0.1 | 0.1 | 0.4 | 0.5 |
| STILLWATER | 095 | 0000 | 756 | 6,536 | 8,570 | 9,759 | 2.7 | 3 | 98.4 | 98.3 | 0.1 | 0.1 | 0.2 | 0.1 |
| SWEET GRASS | 097 | 0000 | 756 | 3,154 | 3,674 | 4,153 | 1.5 | 11 | 99.1 | 99.0 | 0.1 | 0.1 | 0.2 | 0.1 |
| TETON | 099 | 0000 | 755 | 6,271 | 6,476 | 6,692 | 0.3 | 27 | 98.1 | 97.9 | 0.0 | 0.0 | 0.1 | 0.1 |
| TOOLE | 101 | 0000 | 755 | 5,046 | 4,556 | 4,356 | -1.0 | 50 | 97.1 | 96.6 | 0.1 | 0.2 | 0.3 | 0.4 |
| TREASURE | 103 | 0000 | 756 | 874 | 859 | 853 | -0.2 | 36 | 97.7 | 96.9 | 0.0 | 0.0 | 0.2 | 0.2 |
| VALLEY | 105 | 0000 | 755 | 8,239 | 8,061 | 7,716 | -0.2 | 36 | 90.1 | 89.3 | 0.1 | 0.1 | 0.2 | 0.3 |
| WHEATLAND | 107 | 0000 | 756 | 2,246 | 2,238 | 2,254 | 0.0 | 28 | 98.1 | 97.9 | 0.0 | 0.0 | 0.4 | 0.4 |
| WIBAUX | 109 | 0000 | 687 | 1,191 | 1,106 | 1,054 | -0.7 | 44 | 99.7 | 99.6 | 0.0 | 0.0 | 0.2 | 0.2 |
| YELLOWSTONE | 111 | 0880 | 756 | 113,419 | 127,939 | 131,708 | 1.2 | 16 | 95.2 | 94.4 | 0.5 | 0.5 | 0.5 | 0.6 |
| YELLOWSTONE NTL PARK | 113 | 0000 | 756 | 52 | 55 | 55 | 0.5 | 21 | 100.0 | 76.4 | 0.0 | 0.0 | 0.0 | 0.0 |
| MONTANA | | | | | | | 1.0 | | 92.8 | 92.2 | 0.3 | 0.3 | 0.5 | 0.6 |
| UNITED STATES | | | | | | | 1.0 | | 80.3 | 77.9 | 12.1 | 12.4 | 2.9 | 3.9 |

# POPULATION COMPOSITION

| COUNTY | % HISPANIC ORIGIN 1990 | % HISPANIC ORIGIN 2000 | 2000 AGE DISTRIBUTION (%) 0-4 | 5-9 | 10-14 | 15-19 | 20-24 | 25-44 | 45-64 | 65-84 | 85+ | 18+ | MEDIAN AGE 1990 | MEDIAN AGE 2000 | 2000 Males/ Females (×100) |
|---|---|---|---|---|---|---|---|---|---|---|---|---|---|---|---|
| BEAVERHEAD | 1.6 | 2.0 | 5.7 | 6.5 | 7.6 | 9.2 | 8.1 | 24.8 | 25.7 | 10.4 | 1.9 | 75.5 | 32.5 | 37.1 | 103.5 |
| BIG HORN | 2.6 | 3.1 | 9.3 | 9.7 | 10.5 | 9.5 | 6.8 | 23.5 | 21.5 | 8.0 | 1.2 | 64.2 | 28.0 | 28.9 | 97.5 |
| BLAINE | 0.8 | 1.0 | 7.6 | 8.0 | 9.4 | 9.1 | 6.3 | 23.0 | 23.5 | 11.3 | 1.8 | 68.9 | 31.6 | 34.9 | 99.9 |
| BROADWATER | 1.0 | 1.4 | 5.4 | 6.3 | 7.9 | 8.3 | 5.0 | 22.4 | 28.6 | 14.4 | 1.8 | 74.5 | 36.4 | 41.7 | 103.1 |
| CARBON | 1.1 | 1.7 | 4.5 | 5.8 | 7.5 | 8.0 | 4.6 | 22.3 | 29.4 | 15.4 | 2.6 | 76.5 | 38.5 | 43.5 | 95.9 |
| CARTER | 0.8 | 1.3 | 5.5 | 5.9 | 7.3 | 7.4 | 4.3 | 21.8 | 29.9 | 15.2 | 2.7 | 76.0 | 38.1 | 43.3 | 106.2 |
| CASCADE | 1.8 | 2.5 | 6.5 | 6.5 | 7.4 | 7.7 | 7.3 | 26.1 | 25.2 | 11.4 | 1.8 | 74.9 | 32.7 | 37.3 | 97.0 |
| CHOUTEAU | 0.5 | 0.7 | 5.2 | 6.2 | 7.7 | 7.9 | 4.6 | 22.4 | 27.4 | 16.0 | 2.5 | 75.0 | 36.8 | 42.4 | 106.1 |
| CUSTER | 1.4 | 2.0 | 5.0 | 5.8 | 7.4 | 9.6 | 5.9 | 23.6 | 25.7 | 14.3 | 2.7 | 75.9 | 35.5 | 40.5 | 95.3 |
| DANIELS | 0.5 | 1.2 | 4.2 | 4.8 | 5.7 | 7.5 | 5.7 | 20.2 | 28.7 | 20.0 | 3.2 | 79.6 | 41.6 | 46.2 | 94.2 |
| DAWSON | 0.7 | 1.2 | 5.2 | 6.0 | 7.6 | 8.5 | 5.6 | 23.7 | 26.6 | 14.2 | 2.5 | 76.0 | 35.5 | 40.8 | 99.3 |
| DEER LODGE | 1.5 | 2.3 | 4.3 | 4.7 | 6.2 | 8.9 | 6.6 | 22.8 | 27.5 | 16.7 | 2.3 | 79.2 | 38.3 | 42.7 | 98.5 |
| FALLON | 0.2 | 0.6 | 6.2 | 7.1 | 8.3 | 8.4 | 4.5 | 22.0 | 27.0 | 14.4 | 2.1 | 71.9 | 35.2 | 40.9 | 101.7 |
| FERGUS | 0.6 | 1.1 | 5.1 | 6.0 | 7.4 | 7.8 | 5.2 | 22.0 | 27.4 | 15.8 | 3.3 | 76.3 | 38.0 | 42.7 | 97.5 |
| FLATHEAD | 1.0 | 1.7 | 5.5 | 6.3 | 7.8 | 8.1 | 5.8 | 25.5 | 28.1 | 11.2 | 1.7 | 75.0 | 35.3 | 40.0 | 98.9 |
| GALLATIN | 1.2 | 1.8 | 5.6 | 5.9 | 6.5 | 9.8 | 13.0 | 29.2 | 21.4 | 7.6 | 1.0 | 78.1 | 29.8 | 32.5 | 104.9 |
| GARFIELD | 0.0 | 0.4 | 5.4 | 6.5 | 8.8 | 8.2 | 5.5 | 22.6 | 26.9 | 13.5 | 2.6 | 73.2 | 35.5 | 40.4 | 105.1 |
| GLACIER | 0.6 | 0.9 | 9.1 | 9.5 | 10.6 | 9.7 | 7.0 | 24.1 | 20.7 | 8.1 | 1.1 | 64.2 | 28.2 | 28.7 | 97.8 |
| GOLDEN VALLEY | 0.9 | 1.2 | 5.3 | 6.3 | 8.0 | 7.9 | 5.2 | 21.1 | 28.3 | 15.1 | 2.8 | 74.4 | 37.5 | 42.4 | 106.0 |
| GRANITE | 0.4 | 0.9 | 5.0 | 5.9 | 7.3 | 8.2 | 5.0 | 22.2 | 29.8 | 14.4 | 2.3 | 76.5 | 38.5 | 42.8 | 110.1 |
| HILL | 1.0 | 1.4 | 6.7 | 7.3 | 8.6 | 9.1 | 7.2 | 25.5 | 23.2 | 10.6 | 1.8 | 72.0 | 31.7 | 35.3 | 99.0 |
| JEFFERSON | 1.0 | 1.8 | 5.4 | 6.3 | 7.6 | 8.7 | 6.4 | 24.2 | 30.3 | 9.7 | 1.3 | 74.3 | 35.1 | 40.0 | 101.6 |
| JUDITH BASIN | 0.4 | 1.0 | 4.5 | 5.4 | 7.2 | 8.0 | 4.3 | 22.8 | 30.1 | 15.7 | 1.9 | 77.4 | 38.2 | 43.6 | 104.0 |
| LAKE | 1.9 | 2.3 | 6.4 | 7.1 | 8.6 | 8.9 | 6.0 | 22.1 | 26.4 | 12.6 | 2.0 | 72.1 | 34.7 | 38.7 | 100.2 |
| LEWIS AND CLARK | 1.2 | 1.8 | 5.6 | 6.3 | 7.5 | 8.6 | 6.6 | 26.7 | 27.1 | 10.0 | 1.5 | 75.4 | 34.1 | 38.5 | 96.1 |
| LIBERTY | 0.2 | 0.5 | 6.1 | 7.3 | 7.5 | 8.0 | 4.2 | 22.0 | 24.0 | 18.0 | 2.9 | 73.1 | 34.0 | 41.6 | 95.6 |
| LINCOLN | 1.1 | 1.6 | 5.7 | 6.5 | 8.2 | 8.3 | 5.7 | 23.4 | 28.6 | 12.1 | 1.4 | 73.8 | 34.7 | 40.2 | 102.0 |
| MCCONE | 0.4 | 0.8 | 4.9 | 5.6 | 6.7 | 8.2 | 5.9 | 23.0 | 27.2 | 16.6 | 2.0 | 77.5 | 36.0 | 42.4 | 100.9 |
| MADISON | 1.5 | 2.2 | 4.9 | 5.9 | 6.8 | 7.4 | 5.4 | 22.7 | 29.3 | 15.0 | 2.5 | 77.3 | 37.8 | 43.0 | 107.8 |
| MEAGHER | 1.4 | 2.0 | 5.1 | 5.7 | 7.2 | 7.6 | 4.4 | 23.5 | 28.4 | 16.0 | 2.2 | 76.9 | 37.7 | 42.9 | 108.9 |
| MINERAL | 1.2 | 1.8 | 5.5 | 6.3 | 8.2 | 8.1 | 5.4 | 23.1 | 29.4 | 12.8 | 1.3 | 74.5 | 35.4 | 41.2 | 103.4 |
| MISSOULA | 1.2 | 1.9 | 5.7 | 6.0 | 7.0 | 8.8 | 9.6 | 28.9 | 23.7 | 8.9 | 1.4 | 76.9 | 31.6 | 35.6 | 97.3 |
| MUSSELSHELL | 0.9 | 1.5 | 3.5 | 4.9 | 6.9 | 8.2 | 5.1 | 22.4 | 29.8 | 16.7 | 2.6 | 78.8 | 39.8 | 44.4 | 101.2 |
| PARK | 1.6 | 2.3 | 5.5 | 6.4 | 7.4 | 7.6 | 5.3 | 24.2 | 28.4 | 13.1 | 2.0 | 75.7 | 37.0 | 41.4 | 97.5 |
| PETROLEUM | 0.0 | 0.4 | 6.0 | 7.0 | 7.8 | 6.4 | 3.6 | 25.5 | 28.1 | 14.2 | 1.4 | 74.9 | 35.8 | 41.1 | 120.7 |
| PHILLIPS | 0.9 | 1.2 | 5.9 | 6.8 | 8.4 | 8.6 | 5.7 | 23.3 | 25.4 | 13.4 | 2.4 | 72.4 | 34.0 | 39.1 | 97.7 |
| PONDERA | 0.5 | 0.9 | 6.6 | 7.1 | 8.5 | 8.1 | 5.7 | 22.5 | 24.6 | 14.1 | 2.8 | 72.0 | 34.2 | 39.3 | 99.0 |
| POWDER RIVER | 1.0 | 1.4 | 5.2 | 6.1 | 7.3 | 8.0 | 4.2 | 22.0 | 27.7 | 16.7 | 2.9 | 75.8 | 36.7 | 43.3 | 104.2 |
| POWELL | 1.2 | 1.8 | 4.4 | 4.8 | 5.9 | 7.4 | 8.0 | 30.4 | 26.0 | 11.2 | 1.9 | 80.0 | 35.9 | 38.7 | 153.9 |
| PRAIRIE | 1.2 | 1.8 | 4.1 | 4.3 | 7.2 | 7.2 | 4.3 | 20.5 | 29.7 | 19.2 | 3.4 | 79.2 | 43.4 | 46.4 | 106.5 |
| RAVALLI | 1.5 | 2.1 | 5.1 | 6.0 | 7.6 | 8.3 | 5.3 | 22.1 | 30.2 | 13.3 | 2.1 | 75.5 | 37.8 | 42.3 | 97.4 |
| RICHLAND | 2.2 | 3.0 | 6.4 | 7.1 | 8.6 | 8.8 | 5.7 | 24.4 | 24.9 | 12.1 | 1.8 | 71.6 | 33.0 | 38.0 | 98.8 |
| ROOSEVELT | 0.9 | 1.2 | 9.0 | 9.1 | 10.1 | 9.3 | 6.4 | 24.0 | 21.5 | 9.2 | 1.4 | 65.6 | 29.8 | 30.8 | 96.0 |
| ROSEBUD | 2.1 | 2.5 | 7.5 | 8.1 | 10.2 | 9.8 | 6.9 | 26.4 | 23.3 | 6.9 | 0.9 | 67.4 | 29.4 | 31.8 | 104.5 |
| SANDERS | 1.2 | 1.7 | 5.3 | 6.2 | 7.9 | 8.5 | 5.4 | 22.0 | 28.9 | 13.8 | 2.1 | 74.9 | 37.0 | 41.8 | 102.8 |
| SHERIDAN | 0.8 | 1.4 | 4.7 | 5.6 | 7.4 | 7.2 | 4.4 | 21.1 | 27.6 | 18.4 | 3.6 | 77.1 | 39.6 | 44.8 | 97.3 |
| SILVER BOW | 2.4 | 3.5 | 5.4 | 5.7 | 7.0 | 8.1 | 6.7 | 24.7 | 26.6 | 13.7 | 2.2 | 77.2 | 35.9 | 40.3 | 97.7 |
| STILLWATER | 1.4 | 1.9 | 6.0 | 6.9 | 8.0 | 7.7 | 5.5 | 22.6 | 27.6 | 13.4 | 2.3 | 73.7 | 36.5 | 40.9 | 100.0 |
| SWEET GRASS | 0.2 | 0.6 | 5.4 | 6.3 | 7.5 | 7.5 | 5.0 | 20.1 | 28.4 | 16.2 | 3.4 | 75.4 | 39.2 | 43.7 | 96.7 |
| TETON | 0.6 | 1.1 | 5.4 | 6.4 | 8.0 | 8.6 | 5.3 | 21.8 | 27.6 | 14.1 | 2.8 | 74.2 | 36.5 | 41.4 | 98.7 |
| TOOLE | 0.7 | 1.3 | 6.0 | 6.8 | 8.2 | 8.5 | 5.1 | 24.2 | 27.8 | 11.6 | 1.8 | 73.0 | 35.3 | 39.6 | 98.7 |
| TREASURE | 3.0 | 5.2 | 5.0 | 5.8 | 7.6 | 8.3 | 4.9 | 23.1 | 28.8 | 14.6 | 2.1 | 75.2 | 36.3 | 42.3 | 99.8 |
| VALLEY | 0.8 | 1.2 | 5.2 | 6.0 | 7.4 | 8.2 | 4.9 | 22.7 | 27.8 | 15.1 | 2.7 | 75.6 | 36.9 | 42.2 | 100.3 |
| WHEATLAND | 1.0 | 1.5 | 5.4 | 5.5 | 7.7 | 7.4 | 5.5 | 21.0 | 27.1 | 17.2 | 3.4 | 76.3 | 38.5 | 43.5 | 103.3 |
| WIBAUX | 0.2 | 0.5 | 4.7 | 5.6 | 7.6 | 8.0 | 5.2 | 22.1 | 26.9 | 16.9 | 3.2 | 76.2 | 37.4 | 42.8 | 102.6 |
| YELLOWSTONE | 2.8 | 3.8 | 5.8 | 6.2 | 7.5 | 8.2 | 7.0 | 26.8 | 25.6 | 11.1 | 1.7 | 75.5 | 33.5 | 37.9 | 94.8 |
| YELLOWSTONE NTL PARK | 0.0 | 18.2 | 5.5 | 5.5 | 5.5 | 3.6 | 3.6 | 16.4 | 21.8 | 38.2 | 0.0 | 80.0 | 39.2 | 52.5 | 120.0 |
| MONTANA | 1.5 | 2.2 | 5.8 | 6.4 | 7.6 | 8.5 | 7.1 | 25.5 | 25.9 | 11.4 | 1.8 | 75.0 | 33.8 | 38.2 | 98.8 |
| UNITED STATES | 9.0 | 11.8 | 6.9 | 7.2 | 7.2 | 7.2 | 6.7 | 29.9 | 22.2 | 11.1 | 1.6 | 74.6 | 32.9 | 35.7 | 95.6 |

| COUNTY | HOUSEHOLDS 1990 | HOUSEHOLDS 2000 | HOUSEHOLDS 2005 | % Annual Rate 1990-2000 | 2000 Average HH Size | FAMILIES 1990 | FAMILIES 2000 | % Annual Rate 1990-2000 | MEDIAN HOUSEHOLD INCOME 2000 | MEDIAN HOUSEHOLD INCOME 2005 | 2000 National Rank | 2000 State Rank |
|---|---|---|---|---|---|---|---|---|---|---|---|---|
| BEAVERHEAD | 3,211 | 3,470 | 3,440 | 0.9 | 2.41 | 2,156 | 2,265 | 0.6 | 31,655 | 36,513 | 1789 | 18 |
| BIG HORN | 3,448 | 4,005 | 4,155 | 1.8 | 3.12 | 2,739 | 3,091 | 1.5 | 26,299 | 32,966 | 2677 | 40 |
| BLAINE | 2,379 | 2,668 | 2,734 | 1.4 | 2.59 | 1,702 | 1,840 | 0.9 | 22,579 | 24,960 | 2991 | 53 |
| BROADWATER | 1,280 | 1,735 | 1,904 | 3.8 | 2.41 | 921 | 1,207 | 3.3 | 30,091 | 32,444 | 2133 | 26 |
| CARBON | 3,269 | 4,034 | 4,338 | 2.6 | 2.37 | 2,288 | 2,717 | 2.1 | 27,868 | 31,189 | 2460 | 36 |
| CARTER | 589 | 644 | 679 | 1.1 | 2.19 | 409 | 444 | 1.0 | 20,944 | 22,650 | 3071 | 56 |
| CASCADE | 30,133 | 31,554 | 31,352 | 0.6 | 2.41 | 21,037 | 21,238 | 0.1 | 31,811 | 35,503 | 1757 | 17 |
| CHOUTEAU | 2,064 | 2,007 | 1,979 | -0.3 | 2.41 | 1,518 | 1,427 | -0.7 | 28,549 | 31,155 | 2356 | 33 |
| CUSTER | 4,631 | 4,928 | 4,809 | 0.8 | 2.30 | 3,095 | 3,132 | 0.1 | 31,026 | 36,981 | 1925 | 22 |
| DANIELS | 919 | 830 | 785 | -1.2 | 2.27 | 635 | 550 | -1.7 | 33,143 | 37,621 | 1513 | 12 |
| DAWSON | 3,691 | 3,552 | 3,416 | -0.5 | 2.37 | 2,617 | 2,417 | -1.0 | 34,022 | 39,105 | 1386 | 11 |
| DEER LODGE | 4,060 | 4,142 | 4,022 | 0.2 | 2.11 | 2,654 | 2,628 | -0.1 | 29,815 | 31,977 | 2179 | 29 |
| FALLON | 1,166 | 1,139 | 1,088 | -0.3 | 2.47 | 864 | 818 | -0.7 | 30,434 | 36,383 | 2049 | 23 |
| FERGUS | 4,603 | 4,787 | 4,648 | 0.5 | 2.39 | 3,211 | 3,215 | 0.0 | 29,764 | 35,705 | 2190 | 30 |
| FLATHEAD | 22,834 | 29,185 | 31,051 | 3.0 | 2.49 | 16,386 | 20,138 | 2.5 | 35,104 | 39,359 | 1237 | 8 |
| GALLATIN | 19,015 | 25,336 | 28,250 | 3.5 | 2.45 | 12,332 | 15,936 | 3.2 | 34,845 | 38,328 | 1276 | 9 |
| GARFIELD | 577 | 510 | 506 | -1.5 | 2.75 | 434 | 371 | -1.9 | 23,636 | 28,250 | 2929 | 51 |
| GLACIER | 3,816 | 4,015 | 4,073 | 0.6 | 3.01 | 2,886 | 2,961 | 0.3 | 23,990 | 31,041 | 2902 | 49 |
| GOLDEN VALLEY | 330 | 421 | 471 | 3.0 | 2.29 | 230 | 283 | 2.5 | 20,380 | 25,129 | 3089 | 57 |
| GRANITE | 1,051 | 1,175 | 1,232 | 1.4 | 2.26 | 708 | 758 | 0.8 | 23,640 | 27,825 | 2927 | 50 |
| HILL | 6,426 | 6,498 | 6,288 | 0.1 | 2.49 | 4,490 | 4,385 | -0.3 | 32,748 | 37,447 | 1583 | 14 |
| JEFFERSON | 2,867 | 3,985 | 4,534 | 4.1 | 2.60 | 2,168 | 2,929 | 3.7 | 43,152 | 51,202 | 446 | 2 |
| JUDITH BASIN | 908 | 953 | 987 | 0.6 | 2.32 | 657 | 670 | 0.2 | 25,995 | 28,365 | 2713 | 43 |
| LAKE | 7,814 | 10,198 | 11,059 | 3.3 | 2.51 | 5,686 | 7,154 | 2.8 | 30,180 | 33,378 | 2109 | 25 |
| LEWIS AND CLARK | 18,649 | 21,949 | 23,014 | 2.0 | 2.41 | 12,610 | 14,289 | 1.5 | 37,169 | 42,641 | 950 | 4 |
| LIBERTY | 788 | 831 | 857 | 0.6 | 2.36 | 558 | 568 | 0.2 | 30,225 | 32,702 | 2099 | 24 |
| LINCOLN | 6,668 | 7,502 | 7,757 | 1.4 | 2.50 | 4,905 | 5,330 | 1.0 | 26,195 | 29,234 | 2689 | 42 |
| MCCONE | 844 | 748 | 695 | -1.5 | 2.47 | 644 | 553 | -1.8 | 28,243 | 35,433 | 2411 | 34 |
| MADISON | 2,387 | 2,877 | 3,026 | 2.3 | 2.36 | 1,641 | 1,901 | 1.8 | 31,402 | 39,231 | 1840 | 20 |
| MEAGHER | 709 | 741 | 744 | 0.5 | 2.22 | 478 | 484 | 0.2 | 24,375 | 26,667 | 2872 | 47 |
| MINERAL | 1,282 | 1,532 | 1,659 | 2.2 | 2.53 | 903 | 1,039 | 1.7 | 27,544 | 31,680 | 2505 | 37 |
| MISSOULA | 30,782 | 36,319 | 37,786 | 2.0 | 2.39 | 19,847 | 22,577 | 1.6 | 32,986 | 36,078 | 1542 | 13 |
| MUSSELSHELL | 1,661 | 1,949 | 1,990 | 2.0 | 2.28 | 1,110 | 1,250 | 1.5 | 24,786 | 31,485 | 2830 | 45 |
| PARK | 5,619 | 6,290 | 6,393 | 1.4 | 2.44 | 3,761 | 4,092 | 1.0 | 35,129 | 42,131 | 1230 | 7 |
| PETROLEUM | 209 | 208 | 208 | -0.1 | 2.41 | 155 | 150 | -0.4 | 23,500 | 24,500 | 2940 | 52 |
| PHILLIPS | 1,931 | 1,830 | 1,780 | -0.6 | 2.43 | 1,354 | 1,236 | -1.1 | 26,875 | 34,038 | 2602 | 39 |
| PONDERA | 2,246 | 2,343 | 2,326 | 0.5 | 2.42 | 1,632 | 1,643 | 0.1 | 29,342 | 31,875 | 2247 | 31 |
| POWDER RIVER | 805 | 713 | 666 | -1.5 | 2.38 | 586 | 502 | -1.9 | 29,950 | 36,786 | 2165 | 28 |
| POWELL | 2,234 | 2,423 | 2,436 | 1.0 | 2.30 | 1,527 | 1,581 | 0.4 | 26,288 | 29,559 | 2679 | 41 |
| PRAIRIE | 568 | 576 | 599 | 0.2 | 2.34 | 409 | 401 | -0.2 | 22,121 | 27,009 | 3021 | 54 |
| RAVALLI | 9,698 | 14,969 | 16,941 | 5.4 | 2.41 | 7,045 | 10,472 | 4.9 | 31,576 | 35,840 | 1803 | 19 |
| RICHLAND | 3,956 | 3,827 | 3,757 | -0.4 | 2.57 | 2,909 | 2,718 | -0.8 | 27,917 | 32,018 | 2452 | 35 |
| ROOSEVELT | 3,694 | 3,760 | 3,723 | 0.2 | 2.84 | 2,774 | 2,755 | -0.1 | 25,617 | 29,090 | 2744 | 44 |
| ROSEBUD | 3,479 | 3,344 | 3,288 | -0.5 | 2.86 | 2,629 | 2,461 | -0.8 | 34,812 | 39,694 | 1282 | 10 |
| SANDERS | 3,397 | 4,145 | 4,286 | 2.4 | 2.46 | 2,377 | 2,787 | 1.9 | 27,381 | 32,372 | 2529 | 38 |
| SHERIDAN | 1,899 | 1,758 | 1,683 | -0.9 | 2.22 | 1,339 | 1,193 | -1.4 | 31,828 | 35,536 | 1753 | 16 |
| SILVER BOW | 13,899 | 14,700 | 14,556 | 0.7 | 2.24 | 9,025 | 9,114 | 0.1 | 31,188 | 34,049 | 1890 | 21 |
| STILLWATER | 2,523 | 3,374 | 3,882 | 3.6 | 2.51 | 1,854 | 2,393 | 3.1 | 35,478 | 44,264 | 1175 | 5 |
| SWEET GRASS | 1,281 | 1,440 | 1,601 | 1.4 | 2.52 | 872 | 941 | 0.9 | 32,204 | 39,935 | 1685 | 15 |
| TETON | 2,329 | 2,452 | 2,561 | 0.6 | 2.50 | 1,665 | 1,682 | 0.1 | 28,640 | 31,241 | 2343 | 32 |
| TOOLE | 1,922 | 1,843 | 1,811 | -0.5 | 2.30 | 1,315 | 1,211 | -1.0 | 35,244 | 41,212 | 1215 | 6 |
| TREASURE | 339 | 357 | 366 | 0.6 | 2.41 | 256 | 261 | 0.2 | 24,438 | 26,696 | 2863 | 46 |
| VALLEY | 3,268 | 3,376 | 3,318 | 0.4 | 2.35 | 2,281 | 2,270 | -0.1 | 30,008 | 32,303 | 2151 | 27 |
| WHEATLAND | 849 | 933 | 1,018 | 1.2 | 2.11 | 550 | 582 | 0.7 | 21,961 | 25,240 | 3028 | 55 |
| WIBAUX | 454 | 463 | 461 | 0.2 | 2.30 | 316 | 310 | -0.2 | 24,330 | 29,635 | 2878 | 48 |
| YELLOWSTONE | 44,689 | 51,830 | 54,089 | 1.8 | 2.43 | 30,500 | 34,097 | 1.4 | 37,406 | 42,224 | 914 | 3 |
| YELLOWSTONE NTL PARK | 24 | 26 | 26 | 1.0 | 2.12 | 16 | 16 | 0.0 | 43,750 | 56,579 | 413 | 1 |
| MONTANA | | | | 1.8 | 2.44 | | | 1.3 | 32,474 | 36,874 | | |
| UNITED STATES | | | | 1.4 | 2.59 | | | 1.1 | 41,914 | 49,127 | | |

# INCOME

| COUNTY | 2000 Per Capita Income | 2000 HH Income Base | 2000 HOUSEHOLD INCOME DISTRIBUTION (%) | | | | | | 2000 AVERAGE DISPOSABLE INCOME BY AGE OF HOUSEHOLDER | | | | | |
|---|---|---|---|---|---|---|---|---|---|---|---|---|---|---|
| | | | Less than $15,000 | $15,000 to $24,999 | $25,000 to $49,999 | $50,000 to $99,999 | $100,000 to $149,999 | $150,000 or More | All Ages | <35 | 35-44 | 45-54 | 55-64 | 65+ |
| BEAVERHEAD | 17,481 | 3,470 | 22.1 | 16.3 | 37.1 | 20.7 | 3.2 | 0.6 | 29,059 | 22,851 | 37,302 | 34,248 | 32,617 | 19,289 |
| BIG HORN | 10,354 | 4,005 | 30.5 | 17.5 | 31.7 | 18.1 | 2.1 | 0.1 | 24,778 | 20,524 | 28,670 | 28,636 | 26,509 | 18,140 |
| BLAINE | 10,900 | 2,668 | 31.3 | 23.4 | 31.8 | 12.3 | 1.4 | 0.0 | 22,285 | 16,698 | 27,903 | 25,252 | 24,129 | 18,172 |
| BROADWATER | 15,191 | 1,735 | 18.7 | 23.1 | 36.5 | 18.7 | 2.3 | 0.8 | 27,563 | 25,761 | 33,913 | 29,584 | 27,362 | 21,651 |
| CARBON | 16,425 | 4,034 | 25.1 | 19.6 | 33.1 | 17.6 | 2.9 | 1.8 | 28,602 | 27,861 | 33,420 | 33,885 | 26,962 | 19,814 |
| CARTER | 18,021 | 644 | 34.0 | 23.9 | 25.6 | 10.6 | 3.7 | 2.2 | 25,992 | 17,528 | 28,784 | 35,573 | 25,740 | 20,051 |
| CASCADE | 16,912 | 31,549 | 18.7 | 19.3 | 36.8 | 20.9 | 3.3 | 1.1 | 30,142 | 23,316 | 35,527 | 36,251 | 32,478 | 23,702 |
| CHOUTEAU | 14,900 | 2,007 | 19.3 | 24.6 | 33.0 | 19.0 | 3.7 | 0.4 | 27,763 | 23,156 | 31,515 | 27,187 | 33,168 | 25,326 |
| CUSTER | 15,896 | 4,928 | 20.9 | 18.0 | 38.0 | 19.9 | 2.5 | 0.6 | 28,482 | 22,053 | 31,337 | 36,609 | 32,958 | 21,898 |
| DANIELS | 15,941 | 830 | 16.8 | 21.1 | 40.8 | 19.4 | 1.9 | 0.0 | 27,843 | 23,855 | 33,201 | 31,541 | 29,406 | 23,154 |
| DAWSON | 16,088 | 3,552 | 18.5 | 16.2 | 39.8 | 22.2 | 2.9 | 0.4 | 29,481 | 24,763 | 35,230 | 35,616 | 33,854 | 20,057 |
| DEER LODGE | 14,410 | 4,142 | 22.0 | 17.7 | 43.5 | 16.2 | 0.7 | 0.0 | 25,371 | 23,584 | 27,729 | 31,117 | 26,805 | 19,784 |
| FALLON | 14,141 | 1,139 | 15.2 | 22.9 | 44.7 | 15.6 | 0.9 | 0.7 | 26,518 | 25,156 | 28,296 | 33,189 | 27,972 | 20,140 |
| FERGUS | 15,570 | 4,787 | 20.4 | 21.4 | 37.9 | 16.5 | 2.7 | 1.1 | 27,902 | 23,619 | 32,811 | 33,094 | 31,144 | 20,261 |
| FLATHEAD | 17,889 | 29,176 | 18.0 | 15.1 | 37.2 | 24.9 | 3.8 | 1.1 | 31,841 | 25,276 | 36,590 | 38,370 | 33,581 | 22,463 |
| GALLATIN | 22,357 | 25,336 | 17.0 | 15.6 | 35.8 | 23.4 | 5.3 | 3.0 | 35,624 | 23,067 | 39,480 | 47,342 | 45,201 | 29,512 |
| GARFIELD | 14,267 | 510 | 28.2 | 24.1 | 30.4 | 11.6 | 2.9 | 2.8 | 28,515 | 17,388 | 29,885 | 32,340 | 33,636 | 19,566 |
| GLACIER | 9,509 | 4,015 | 33.3 | 18.4 | 33.2 | 14.0 | 1.1 | 0.1 | 22,727 | 19,433 | 25,161 | 26,071 | 24,642 | 17,785 |
| GOLDEN VALLEY | 10,602 | 421 | 38.0 | 20.0 | 35.2 | 6.2 | 0.2 | 0.5 | 19,782 | 19,875 | 24,113 | 27,878 | 16,955 | 13,926 |
| GRANITE | 13,959 | 1,175 | 31.6 | 22.6 | 31.8 | 10.0 | 3.5 | 0.5 | 23,292 | 21,676 | 23,000 | 28,708 | 18,431 | 22,508 |
| HILL | 16,128 | 6,498 | 19.7 | 15.7 | 36.6 | 23.0 | 3.9 | 1.1 | 30,733 | 22,749 | 38,709 | 35,669 | 37,648 | 21,612 |
| JEFFERSON | 20,980 | 3,985 | 13.4 | 9.9 | 36.4 | 29.2 | 7.1 | 4.1 | 40,987 | 32,185 | 48,589 | 45,909 | 40,263 | 24,152 |
| JUDITH BASIN | 14,527 | 953 | 23.4 | 24.3 | 35.6 | 13.2 | 2.3 | 1.2 | 26,021 | 20,317 | 26,820 | 31,757 | 30,020 | 20,070 |
| LAKE | 14,987 | 10,198 | 21.0 | 19.3 | 36.9 | 18.0 | 3.5 | 1.2 | 28,926 | 24,319 | 30,022 | 36,786 | 31,055 | 22,948 |
| LEWIS AND CLARK | 17,877 | 21,949 | 15.5 | 14.5 | 37.8 | 27.6 | 3.8 | 0.9 | 32,863 | 24,921 | 36,785 | 41,276 | 34,711 | 24,822 |
| LIBERTY | 14,402 | 831 | 17.5 | 21.1 | 38.8 | 18.7 | 3.6 | 0.5 | 28,509 | 21,935 | 30,901 | 34,671 | 30,007 | 25,722 |
| LINCOLN | 13,085 | 7,502 | 26.9 | 20.2 | 37.7 | 12.8 | 1.8 | 0.7 | 24,553 | 22,294 | 30,089 | 29,644 | 24,270 | 14,803 |
| MCCONE | 14,945 | 748 | 17.5 | 22.9 | 38.2 | 17.7 | 3.1 | 0.7 | 28,270 | 21,880 | 28,401 | 37,509 | 30,657 | 23,364 |
| MADISON | 15,514 | 2,877 | 21.5 | 16.7 | 36.6 | 22.6 | 2.1 | 0.5 | 28,188 | 25,563 | 29,141 | 32,319 | 33,180 | 22,247 |
| MEAGHER | 12,195 | 741 | 28.3 | 22.4 | 37.4 | 10.9 | 0.8 | 0.1 | 22,571 | 16,802 | 28,041 | 26,760 | 22,865 | 19,058 |
| MINERAL | 12,610 | 1,532 | 22.2 | 21.2 | 39.1 | 16.1 | 1.4 | 0.1 | 25,147 | 20,413 | 31,617 | 29,890 | 25,687 | 18,329 |
| MISSOULA | 18,412 | 36,319 | 20.1 | 16.6 | 35.1 | 22.1 | 4.3 | 1.8 | 32,025 | 22,517 | 37,111 | 41,423 | 35,158 | 24,102 |
| MUSSELSHELL | 13,613 | 1,949 | 27.8 | 22.6 | 32.0 | 15.2 | 2.3 | 0.2 | 24,441 | 27,882 | 32,467 | 26,940 | 22,043 | 16,631 |
| PARK | 17,581 | 6,290 | 16.5 | 16.4 | 37.9 | 25.2 | 3.2 | 0.8 | 31,403 | 27,126 | 35,846 | 34,695 | 32,997 | 26,396 |
| PETROLEUM | 12,557 | 208 | 30.3 | 24.0 | 32.7 | 10.6 | 1.0 | 1.4 | 23,777 | 19,667 | 24,800 | 26,886 | 32,845 | 15,500 |
| PHILLIPS | 13,983 | 1,830 | 25.0 | 20.3 | 36.8 | 15.1 | 2.5 | 0.4 | 25,712 | 22,720 | 30,423 | 30,016 | 29,999 | 17,706 |
| PONDERA | 14,384 | 2,343 | 23.9 | 16.4 | 39.2 | 17.5 | 2.4 | 0.7 | 27,624 | 21,442 | 29,740 | 33,895 | 32,133 | 22,054 |
| POWDER RIVER | 18,564 | 713 | 21.2 | 20.6 | 34.6 | 17.4 | 2.8 | 3.4 | 32,467 | 22,136 | 32,601 | 36,336 | 39,795 | 22,962 |
| POWELL | 12,837 | 2,423 | 26.2 | 20.4 | 39.0 | 13.5 | 0.5 | 0.6 | 23,910 | 19,477 | 29,051 | 29,825 | 24,660 | 16,037 |
| PRAIRIE | 11,490 | 576 | 31.9 | 24.1 | 31.9 | 10.8 | 1.2 | 0.0 | 21,124 | 20,906 | 25,250 | 25,268 | 24,381 | 14,186 |
| RAVALLI | 16,681 | 14,969 | 18.5 | 19.2 | 38.0 | 19.4 | 3.6 | 1.3 | 29,969 | 24,029 | 34,748 | 37,359 | 31,341 | 21,082 |
| RICHLAND | 12,341 | 3,827 | 22.2 | 22.3 | 38.2 | 16.0 | 1.3 | 0.0 | 24,948 | 22,213 | 29,387 | 27,650 | 27,451 | 18,498 |
| ROOSEVELT | 10,389 | 3,760 | 28.7 | 20.2 | 36.0 | 13.9 | 1.1 | 0.0 | 23,293 | 19,201 | 25,877 | 26,772 | 23,670 | 20,323 |
| ROSEBUD | 13,043 | 3,344 | 20.0 | 14.5 | 39.6 | 24.2 | 1.5 | 0.1 | 28,878 | 23,534 | 35,609 | 32,909 | 26,478 | 18,531 |
| SANDERS | 13,994 | 4,145 | 19.9 | 25.0 | 38.3 | 15.2 | 0.8 | 0.8 | 25,655 | 25,257 | 32,265 | 28,997 | 24,152 | 17,137 |
| SHERIDAN | 16,637 | 1,758 | 18.8 | 18.2 | 39.4 | 21.3 | 2.3 | 0.1 | 28,305 | 23,803 | 31,472 | 33,298 | 33,053 | 23,213 |
| SILVER BOW | 17,964 | 14,695 | 23.0 | 17.6 | 32.3 | 21.8 | 3.8 | 1.5 | 30,416 | 23,846 | 36,410 | 39,849 | 31,663 | 20,581 |
| STILLWATER | 16,516 | 3,374 | 15.2 | 15.9 | 39.7 | 24.6 | 3.9 | 0.7 | 31,522 | 30,275 | 36,241 | 37,998 | 34,561 | 20,145 |
| SWEET GRASS | 15,985 | 1,440 | 15.7 | 21.9 | 37.2 | 20.3 | 4.0 | 1.0 | 30,496 | 24,933 | 33,536 | 38,786 | 33,377 | 22,341 |
| TETON | 14,098 | 2,452 | 24.0 | 19.8 | 34.4 | 18.0 | 3.0 | 0.9 | 27,681 | 23,274 | 31,066 | 31,432 | 31,279 | 23,001 |
| TOOLE | 18,033 | 1,843 | 19.4 | 12.8 | 39.8 | 23.0 | 3.3 | 1.8 | 32,402 | 27,069 | 37,245 | 36,322 | 32,562 | 26,762 |
| TREASURE | 14,735 | 357 | 27.7 | 23.5 | 31.9 | 10.9 | 3.9 | 2.0 | 26,980 | 14,423 | 23,713 | 39,376 | 27,776 | 24,361 |
| VALLEY | 15,437 | 3,375 | 22.5 | 18.9 | 37.6 | 18.0 | 2.5 | 0.5 | 27,463 | 22,717 | 33,825 | 31,790 | 29,716 | 21,467 |
| WHEATLAND | 12,443 | 933 | 28.8 | 25.7 | 35.2 | 8.9 | 1.2 | 0.2 | 21,648 | 19,864 | 24,951 | 26,759 | 20,822 | 17,710 |
| WIBAUX | 12,091 | 463 | 25.5 | 26.1 | 37.6 | 10.2 | 0.7 | 0.0 | 22,003 | 19,829 | 28,250 | 22,276 | 22,917 | 18,370 |
| YELLOWSTONE | 18,702 | 51,830 | 15.6 | 14.3 | 36.7 | 27.1 | 5.0 | 1.4 | 34,238 | 27,405 | 39,120 | 41,767 | 37,057 | 25,273 |
| YELLOWSTONE NTL PARK | 20,682 | 26 | 0.0 | 0.0 | 100.0 | 0.0 | 0.0 | 0.0 | 32,885 | 33,125 | 33,125 | 31,786 | 33,125 | 33,571 |
| MONTANA | 16,982 | | 19.5 | 17.2 | 36.6 | 21.9 | 3.6 | 1.2 | 30,753 | 24,090 | 35,624 | 37,665 | 32,967 | 22,582 |
| UNITED STATES | 22,162 | | 14.5 | 12.5 | 32.3 | 29.8 | 7.4 | 3.5 | 40,748 | 34,503 | 44,969 | 49,579 | 43,409 | 27,339 |

| COUNTY | FINANCIAL SERVICES | | | | THE HOME | | | | | | ENTERTAINMENT | | | | | | PERSONAL | | | |
|---|---|---|---|---|---|---|---|---|---|---|---|---|---|---|---|---|---|---|---|---|
| | | | | | Home Improvements | | | Furnishings | | | | | | | | | | | | |
| | Auto Loan | Home Loan | Invest-ments | Retire-ment Plans | Home Repair | Lawn & Garden | Remodel-ing | Appli-ances | Elec-tronics | Furni-ture | Restau-rants | Sport-ing Goods | Theater & Concerts | Toys & Hobbies | Travel | Video Rental | Apparel | Auto After-market | Health Insur-ance | Pets & Supplies |
| BEAVERHEAD | 96 | 76 | 77 | 81 | 93 | 91 | 112 | 97 | 94 | 84 | 83 | 87 | 79 | 89 | 75 | 92 | 83 | 89 | 98 | 91 |
| BIG HORN | 94 | 70 | 75 | 77 | 93 | 91 | 107 | 96 | 92 | 80 | 77 | 84 | 76 | 85 | 74 | 92 | 80 | 87 | 98 | 89 |
| BLAINE | 96 | 72 | 80 | 82 | 95 | 94 | 107 | 97 | 93 | 80 | 80 | 87 | 78 | 88 | 76 | 91 | 81 | 88 | 101 | 90 |
| BROADWATER | 98 | 68 | 74 | 80 | 94 | 92 | 113 | 98 | 95 | 79 | 80 | 88 | 77 | 90 | 72 | 93 | 81 | 88 | 102 | 91 |
| CARBON | 97 | 64 | 72 | 79 | 92 | 93 | 113 | 97 | 93 | 75 | 77 | 88 | 74 | 88 | 71 | 92 | 79 | 87 | 103 | 90 |
| CARTER | 99 | 63 | 69 | 80 | 91 | 92 | 113 | 98 | 92 | 72 | 76 | 91 | 74 | 90 | 69 | 92 | 78 | 87 | 104 | 92 |
| CASCADE | 97 | 90 | 93 | 91 | 101 | 98 | 102 | 99 | 97 | 95 | 93 | 89 | 89 | 92 | 86 | 92 | 92 | 94 | 97 | 92 |
| CHOUTEAU | 98 | 64 | 70 | 79 | 92 | 92 | 113 | 97 | 92 | 74 | 77 | 89 | 74 | 89 | 70 | 92 | 79 | 87 | 103 | 91 |
| CUSTER | 98 | 82 | 91 | 89 | 98 | 98 | 108 | 99 | 98 | 89 | 88 | 89 | 85 | 91 | 81 | 93 | 88 | 92 | 101 | 92 |
| DANIELS | 97 | 63 | 69 | 78 | 92 | 92 | 112 | 97 | 92 | 74 | 76 | 88 | 73 | 88 | 70 | 92 | 78 | 86 | 103 | 90 |
| DAWSON | 98 | 82 | 90 | 88 | 98 | 97 | 107 | 99 | 97 | 89 | 89 | 90 | 86 | 92 | 81 | 93 | 88 | 92 | 101 | 92 |
| DEER LODGE | 95 | 71 | 83 | 80 | 97 | 95 | 107 | 97 | 94 | 82 | 80 | 84 | 79 | 86 | 77 | 92 | 81 | 87 | 100 | 88 |
| FALLON | 99 | 71 | 78 | 83 | 94 | 93 | 117 | 99 | 95 | 81 | 82 | 91 | 79 | 92 | 73 | 93 | 84 | 89 | 102 | 93 |
| FERGUS | 97 | 69 | 74 | 80 | 94 | 92 | 111 | 97 | 93 | 78 | 79 | 88 | 77 | 89 | 73 | 92 | 80 | 87 | 101 | 91 |
| FLATHEAD | 99 | 83 | 84 | 87 | 97 | 95 | 111 | 100 | 97 | 91 | 90 | 90 | 85 | 93 | 79 | 93 | 89 | 92 | 99 | 94 |
| GALLATIN | 97 | 94 | 88 | 92 | 97 | 94 | 104 | 97 | 97 | 92 | 93 | 89 | 85 | 91 | 83 | 91 | 92 | 94 | 95 | 93 |
| GARFIELD | 98 | 63 | 69 | 79 | 91 | 92 | 113 | 98 | 92 | 73 | 76 | 90 | 73 | 90 | 69 | 92 | 78 | 87 | 104 | 91 |
| GLACIER | 94 | 77 | 79 | 79 | 95 | 91 | 104 | 96 | 92 | 87 | 80 | 85 | 79 | 86 | 78 | 92 | 85 | 89 | 94 | 88 |
| GOLDEN VALLEY | 101 | 63 | 68 | 83 | 91 | 92 | 116 | 99 | 91 | 70 | 76 | 96 | 74 | 93 | 68 | 93 | 79 | 88 | 107 | 94 |
| GRANITE | 97 | 69 | 77 | 80 | 93 | 93 | 116 | 98 | 95 | 80 | 80 | 87 | 77 | 89 | 73 | 92 | 81 | 88 | 101 | 91 |
| HILL | 97 | 88 | 86 | 88 | 98 | 95 | 102 | 99 | 97 | 94 | 92 | 90 | 87 | 92 | 83 | 93 | 92 | 94 | 96 | 92 |
| JEFFERSON | 101 | 90 | 91 | 96 | 99 | 99 | 111 | 101 | 103 | 97 | 96 | 93 | 91 | 95 | 84 | 95 | 96 | 97 | 99 | 95 |
| JUDITH BASIN | 100 | 63 | 68 | 81 | 91 | 92 | 114 | 98 | 92 | 72 | 76 | 92 | 74 | 91 | 69 | 93 | 79 | 87 | 105 | 92 |
| LAKE | 98 | 70 | 76 | 82 | 94 | 93 | 116 | 99 | 94 | 81 | 81 | 89 | 78 | 90 | 74 | 93 | 82 | 89 | 102 | 92 |
| LEWIS AND CLARK | 99 | 94 | 94 | 94 | 101 | 99 | 105 | 100 | 99 | 99 | 97 | 92 | 91 | 94 | 87 | 94 | 96 | 96 | 98 | 94 |
| LIBERTY | 98 | 63 | 69 | 79 | 92 | 92 | 112 | 97 | 92 | 73 | 76 | 89 | 73 | 89 | 70 | 92 | 78 | 86 | 103 | 91 |
| LINCOLN | 98 | 69 | 74 | 78 | 94 | 92 | 114 | 98 | 95 | 81 | 80 | 88 | 77 | 90 | 72 | 92 | 81 | 88 | 100 | 91 |
| MCCONE | 98 | 63 | 69 | 80 | 91 | 92 | 113 | 98 | 92 | 73 | 76 | 90 | 73 | 90 | 69 | 92 | 78 | 87 | 104 | 91 |
| MADISON | 98 | 64 | 70 | 80 | 92 | 92 | 116 | 98 | 93 | 74 | 77 | 90 | 74 | 90 | 70 | 93 | 79 | 87 | 104 | 92 |
| MEAGHER | 97 | 65 | 71 | 79 | 93 | 92 | 115 | 98 | 93 | 76 | 77 | 88 | 74 | 89 | 71 | 93 | 79 | 87 | 103 | 91 |
| MINERAL | 97 | 69 | 75 | 80 | 94 | 92 | 114 | 98 | 95 | 81 | 80 | 86 | 77 | 89 | 73 | 93 | 82 | 88 | 101 | 91 |
| MISSOULA | 97 | 93 | 92 | 92 | 100 | 97 | 103 | 98 | 97 | 95 | 93 | 89 | 87 | 91 | 85 | 92 | 92 | 94 | 96 | 93 |
| MUSSELSHELL | 97 | 63 | 69 | 78 | 92 | 92 | 112 | 97 | 92 | 74 | 76 | 89 | 73 | 89 | 70 | 92 | 78 | 86 | 103 | 90 |
| PARK | 97 | 72 | 76 | 81 | 94 | 92 | 114 | 98 | 94 | 83 | 82 | 88 | 78 | 90 | 74 | 92 | 83 | 89 | 100 | 92 |
| PETROLEUM | 101 | 63 | 68 | 83 | 91 | 92 | 116 | 99 | 91 | 70 | 76 | 96 | 74 | 93 | 68 | 93 | 79 | 88 | 107 | 94 |
| PHILLIPS | 96 | 66 | 73 | 78 | 92 | 91 | 111 | 97 | 93 | 78 | 78 | 86 | 75 | 87 | 71 | 92 | 79 | 87 | 101 | 90 |
| PONDERA | 96 | 70 | 74 | 79 | 93 | 91 | 108 | 96 | 92 | 80 | 79 | 87 | 77 | 88 | 73 | 92 | 81 | 87 | 100 | 89 |
| POWDER RIVER | 98 | 63 | 69 | 80 | 91 | 92 | 113 | 98 | 92 | 73 | 76 | 90 | 73 | 90 | 69 | 92 | 78 | 87 | 104 | 91 |
| POWELL | 97 | 70 | 82 | 82 | 96 | 96 | 108 | 98 | 94 | 80 | 81 | 88 | 79 | 89 | 76 | 92 | 82 | 88 | 103 | 90 |
| PRAIRIE | 97 | 63 | 69 | 78 | 92 | 92 | 112 | 97 | 92 | 74 | 76 | 88 | 73 | 88 | 70 | 92 | 78 | 86 | 103 | 90 |
| RAVALLI | 99 | 73 | 78 | 83 | 95 | 93 | 115 | 99 | 96 | 83 | 84 | 89 | 80 | 92 | 74 | 93 | 85 | 90 | 101 | 93 |
| RICHLAND | 97 | 70 | 74 | 80 | 92 | 92 | 110 | 97 | 95 | 81 | 81 | 87 | 77 | 89 | 72 | 93 | 81 | 88 | 100 | 90 |
| ROOSEVELT | 94 | 72 | 75 | 77 | 95 | 91 | 105 | 95 | 90 | 82 | 78 | 85 | 77 | 86 | 75 | 90 | 81 | 87 | 97 | 88 |
| ROSEBUD | 97 | 81 | 80 | 85 | 95 | 92 | 107 | 99 | 97 | 92 | 87 | 90 | 83 | 90 | 78 | 94 | 89 | 92 | 95 | 92 |
| SANDERS | 96 | 68 | 75 | 78 | 94 | 92 | 113 | 97 | 95 | 81 | 80 | 86 | 77 | 88 | 72 | 92 | 81 | 87 | 100 | 90 |
| SHERIDAN | 97 | 64 | 71 | 78 | 92 | 92 | 112 | 97 | 93 | 75 | 77 | 87 | 74 | 88 | 70 | 92 | 79 | 87 | 102 | 90 |
| SILVER BOW | 97 | 85 | 95 | 91 | 102 | 100 | 105 | 99 | 96 | 92 | 89 | 88 | 87 | 90 | 85 | 92 | 89 | 92 | 99 | 91 |
| STILLWATER | 98 | 70 | 75 | 81 | 94 | 92 | 114 | 98 | 95 | 80 | 81 | 89 | 78 | 91 | 72 | 93 | 82 | 89 | 102 | 92 |
| SWEET GRASS | 97 | 63 | 69 | 78 | 92 | 92 | 112 | 97 | 92 | 74 | 76 | 88 | 73 | 88 | 70 | 92 | 78 | 86 | 103 | 90 |
| TETON | 99 | 73 | 84 | 86 | 95 | 96 | 109 | 99 | 94 | 79 | 82 | 91 | 80 | 91 | 76 | 93 | 83 | 89 | 103 | 92 |
| TOOLE | 97 | 67 | 72 | 79 | 93 | 92 | 112 | 97 | 93 | 77 | 79 | 88 | 76 | 89 | 71 | 92 | 80 | 87 | 102 | 91 |
| TREASURE | 101 | 63 | 68 | 83 | 91 | 92 | 116 | 99 | 91 | 70 | 76 | 96 | 74 | 93 | 68 | 93 | 79 | 88 | 107 | 94 |
| VALLEY | 99 | 77 | 88 | 87 | 98 | 97 | 110 | 100 | 95 | 85 | 86 | 91 | 83 | 92 | 79 | 93 | 86 | 91 | 103 | 93 |
| WHEATLAND | 97 | 63 | 69 | 78 | 92 | 92 | 111 | 97 | 92 | 74 | 76 | 87 | 73 | 88 | 70 | 92 | 78 | 86 | 103 | 90 |
| WIBAUX | 97 | 63 | 69 | 78 | 92 | 92 | 111 | 97 | 92 | 74 | 76 | 87 | 73 | 88 | 70 | 92 | 78 | 86 | 103 | 90 |
| YELLOWSTONE | 99 | 95 | 96 | 95 | 101 | 100 | 103 | 100 | 100 | 99 | 97 | 92 | 91 | 94 | 88 | 93 | 96 | 96 | 98 | 94 |
| YELLOWSTONE NTL PARK | 100 | 98 | 77 | 90 | 94 | 92 | 98 | 101 | 104 | 102 | 103 | 93 | 90 | 95 | 82 | 96 | 100 | 101 | 92 | 95 |
| MONTANA | 98 | 84 | 87 | 89 | 98 | 96 | 107 | 99 | 97 | 90 | 89 | 89 | 85 | 91 | 81 | 93 | 89 | 92 | 99 | 92 |
| UNITED STATES | 100 | 100 | 100 | 100 | 100 | 100 | 100 | 100 | 100 | 100 | 100 | 100 | 100 | 100 | 100 | 100 | 100 | 100 | 100 | 100 |

# POPULATION CHANGE

| COUNTY | FIPS Code | MSA Code | DMA Code | POPULATION 1990 | POPULATION 2000 | POPULATION 2005 | 1990-2000 ANNUAL CHANGE % Rate | 1990-2000 ANNUAL CHANGE State Rank | RACE (%) White 1990 | White 2000 | Black 1990 | Black 2000 | Asian/Pacific 1990 | Asian/Pacific 2000 |
|---|---|---|---|---|---|---|---|---|---|---|---|---|---|---|
| ADAMS | 001 | 0000 | 722 | 29,625 | 29,161 | 28,532 | -0.2 | 40 | 98.2 | 97.3 | 0.6 | 0.7 | 0.4 | 0.6 |
| ANTELOPE | 003 | 0000 | 722 | 7,965 | 7,188 | 6,917 | -1.0 | 80 | 99.6 | 99.5 | 0.0 | 0.0 | 0.1 | 0.2 |
| ARTHUR | 005 | 0000 | 740 | 462 | 405 | 405 | -1.3 | 83 | 99.4 | 99.3 | 0.0 | 0.0 | 0.0 | 0.0 |
| BANNER | 007 | 0000 | 764 | 852 | 816 | 799 | -0.4 | 54 | 97.7 | 95.6 | 0.1 | 0.1 | 0.0 | 0.0 |
| BLAINE | 009 | 0000 | 740 | 675 | 559 | 559 | -1.8 | 90 | 99.4 | 99.3 | 0.1 | 0.2 | 0.0 | 0.0 |
| BOONE | 011 | 0000 | 722 | 6,667 | 6,321 | 6,155 | -0.5 | 57 | 99.7 | 99.7 | 0.0 | 0.0 | 0.0 | 0.0 |
| BOX BUTTE | 013 | 0000 | 751 | 13,130 | 12,581 | 12,124 | -0.4 | 54 | 95.2 | 93.2 | 0.4 | 0.4 | 0.4 | 0.7 |
| BOYD | 015 | 0000 | 722 | 2,835 | 2,468 | 2,295 | -1.3 | 83 | 99.1 | 98.9 | 0.0 | 0.0 | 0.0 | 0.0 |
| BROWN | 017 | 0000 | 722 | 3,657 | 3,463 | 3,291 | -0.5 | 57 | 99.4 | 99.2 | 0.0 | 0.0 | 0.2 | 0.3 |
| BUFFALO | 019 | 0000 | 722 | 37,447 | 40,323 | 40,771 | 0.7 | 11 | 97.3 | 95.5 | 0.4 | 0.5 | 0.4 | 0.7 |
| BURT | 021 | 0000 | 652 | 7,868 | 7,899 | 7,861 | 0.0 | 30 | 98.5 | 98.0 | 0.1 | 0.1 | 0.2 | 0.3 |
| BUTLER | 023 | 0000 | 652 | 8,601 | 8,588 | 8,493 | 0.0 | 30 | 99.5 | 99.4 | 0.1 | 0.1 | 0.2 | 0.3 |
| CASS | 025 | 5920 | 652 | 21,318 | 25,267 | 27,411 | 1.7 | 2 | 98.7 | 98.0 | 0.2 | 0.2 | 0.3 | 0.6 |
| CEDAR | 027 | 0000 | 624 | 10,131 | 9,541 | 9,192 | -0.6 | 63 | 99.7 | 99.6 | 0.1 | 0.1 | 0.1 | 0.1 |
| CHASE | 029 | 0000 | 722 | 4,381 | 4,251 | 4,244 | -0.3 | 45 | 99.3 | 98.8 | 0.0 | 0.0 | 0.0 | 0.0 |
| CHERRY | 031 | 0000 | 725 | 6,307 | 6,312 | 6,245 | 0.0 | 30 | 96.8 | 96.2 | 0.0 | 0.0 | 0.2 | 0.3 |
| CHEYENNE | 033 | 0000 | 751 | 9,494 | 9,381 | 9,148 | -0.1 | 35 | 97.4 | 95.7 | 0.1 | 0.1 | 0.2 | 0.2 |
| CLAY | 035 | 0000 | 722 | 7,123 | 7,066 | 6,929 | -0.1 | 35 | 99.2 | 98.8 | 0.0 | 0.0 | 0.2 | 0.2 |
| COLFAX | 037 | 0000 | 652 | 9,139 | 10,753 | 11,129 | 1.6 | 3 | 98.5 | 97.7 | 0.0 | 0.0 | 0.1 | 0.1 |
| CUMING | 039 | 0000 | 652 | 10,117 | 9,961 | 9,861 | -0.2 | 40 | 99.6 | 99.4 | 0.1 | 0.1 | 0.2 | 0.3 |
| CUSTER | 041 | 0000 | 722 | 12,270 | 11,706 | 11,127 | -0.5 | 57 | 99.0 | 98.7 | 0.0 | 0.0 | 0.1 | 0.2 |
| DAKOTA | 043 | 7720 | 624 | 16,742 | 19,408 | 20,766 | 1.5 | 5 | 92.5 | 88.6 | 0.5 | 0.5 | 2.1 | 3.5 |
| DAWES | 045 | 0000 | 751 | 9,021 | 8,794 | 8,609 | -0.2 | 40 | 94.1 | 93.0 | 0.6 | 0.7 | 0.8 | 1.3 |
| DAWSON | 047 | 0000 | 722 | 19,940 | 23,350 | 23,741 | 1.6 | 3 | 97.9 | 96.4 | 0.1 | 0.1 | 0.2 | 0.3 |
| DEUEL | 049 | 0000 | 751 | 2,237 | 1,962 | 1,840 | -1.3 | 83 | 97.7 | 96.3 | 0.0 | 0.1 | 0.3 | 0.4 |
| DIXON | 051 | 0000 | 624 | 6,143 | 6,379 | 6,483 | 0.4 | 18 | 99.7 | 99.7 | 0.1 | 0.1 | 0.0 | 0.1 |
| DODGE | 053 | 0000 | 652 | 34,500 | 35,230 | 35,382 | 0.2 | 23 | 98.9 | 98.4 | 0.2 | 0.3 | 0.3 | 0.6 |
| DOUGLAS | 055 | 5920 | 652 | 416,444 | 449,099 | 463,399 | 0.7 | 11 | 86.3 | 83.9 | 10.9 | 11.6 | 1.0 | 1.6 |
| DUNDY | 057 | 0000 | 678 | 2,582 | 2,111 | 1,889 | -1.9 | 91 | 99.5 | 99.1 | 0.0 | 0.0 | 0.2 | 0.2 |
| FILLMORE | 059 | 0000 | 722 | 7,103 | 6,895 | 6,816 | -0.3 | 45 | 99.1 | 99.0 | 0.2 | 0.3 | 0.1 | 0.1 |
| FRANKLIN | 061 | 0000 | 722 | 3,938 | 3,633 | 3,419 | -0.8 | 73 | 99.4 | 99.3 | 0.2 | 0.1 | 0.2 | 0.2 |
| FRONTIER | 063 | 0000 | 722 | 3,101 | 3,169 | 3,226 | 0.2 | 23 | 99.1 | 98.8 | 0.0 | 0.0 | 0.3 | 0.4 |
| FURNAS | 065 | 0000 | 722 | 5,553 | 5,383 | 5,244 | -0.3 | 45 | 99.3 | 99.0 | 0.1 | 0.1 | 0.1 | 0.2 |
| GAGE | 067 | 0000 | 722 | 22,794 | 22,663 | 22,429 | -0.1 | 35 | 98.8 | 98.4 | 0.2 | 0.2 | 0.3 | 0.6 |
| GARDEN | 069 | 0000 | 751 | 2,460 | 2,022 | 1,815 | -1.9 | 91 | 99.8 | 99.7 | 0.0 | 0.0 | 0.0 | 0.0 |
| GARFIELD | 071 | 0000 | 722 | 2,141 | 1,994 | 1,893 | -0.7 | 69 | 99.6 | 99.5 | 0.0 | 0.0 | 0.2 | 0.4 |
| GOSPER | 073 | 0000 | 722 | 1,928 | 2,250 | 2,218 | 1.5 | 5 | 99.9 | 100.0 | 0.0 | 0.0 | 0.1 | 0.0 |
| GRANT | 075 | 0000 | 764 | 769 | 698 | 698 | -0.9 | 77 | 98.8 | 98.6 | 0.0 | 0.0 | 0.4 | 0.6 |
| GREELEY | 077 | 0000 | 722 | 3,006 | 2,769 | 2,663 | -0.8 | 73 | 99.8 | 99.7 | 0.0 | 0.0 | 0.1 | 0.1 |
| HALL | 079 | 0000 | 722 | 48,925 | 51,872 | 52,489 | 0.6 | 13 | 96.6 | 94.2 | 0.3 | 0.3 | 1.1 | 1.8 |
| HAMILTON | 081 | 0000 | 722 | 8,862 | 9,669 | 10,152 | 0.9 | 9 | 99.4 | 99.2 | 0.1 | 0.1 | 0.3 | 0.4 |
| HARLAN | 083 | 0000 | 722 | 3,810 | 3,642 | 3,501 | -0.4 | 54 | 99.8 | 99.8 | 0.1 | 0.1 | 0.0 | 0.0 |
| HAYES | 085 | 0000 | 722 | 1,222 | 1,057 | 1,015 | -1.4 | 87 | 99.7 | 99.5 | 0.0 | 0.0 | 0.2 | 0.3 |
| HITCHCOCK | 087 | 0000 | 722 | 3,750 | 3,333 | 3,174 | -1.1 | 81 | 99.5 | 99.4 | 0.0 | 0.0 | 0.1 | 0.1 |
| HOLT | 089 | 0000 | 722 | 12,599 | 11,768 | 11,208 | -0.7 | 69 | 99.5 | 99.4 | 0.0 | 0.0 | 0.1 | 0.2 |
| HOOKER | 091 | 0000 | 740 | 793 | 681 | 681 | -1.5 | 88 | 99.9 | 99.7 | 0.0 | 0.0 | 0.0 | 0.0 |
| HOWARD | 093 | 0000 | 722 | 6,055 | 6,583 | 6,807 | 0.8 | 10 | 99.4 | 99.1 | 0.0 | 0.0 | 0.0 | 0.1 |
| JEFFERSON | 095 | 0000 | 722 | 8,759 | 8,234 | 7,968 | -0.6 | 63 | 99.4 | 99.3 | 0.0 | 0.1 | 0.1 | 0.1 |
| JOHNSON | 097 | 0000 | 652 | 4,673 | 4,529 | 4,434 | -0.3 | 45 | 97.2 | 94.9 | 0.0 | 0.0 | 2.3 | 4.1 |
| KEARNEY | 099 | 0000 | 722 | 6,629 | 6,917 | 7,189 | 0.4 | 18 | 99.2 | 98.6 | 0.0 | 0.0 | 0.1 | 0.1 |
| KEITH | 101 | 0000 | 751 | 8,584 | 9,001 | 9,611 | 0.5 | 15 | 97.9 | 96.7 | 0.1 | 0.1 | 0.2 | 0.3 |
| KEYA PAHA | 103 | 0000 | 722 | 1,029 | 938 | 938 | -0.9 | 77 | 99.9 | 99.9 | 0.0 | 0.0 | 0.0 | 0.0 |
| KIMBALL | 105 | 0000 | 751 | 4,108 | 4,009 | 3,920 | -0.2 | 40 | 99.2 | 98.8 | 0.0 | 0.0 | 0.1 | 0.2 |
| KNOX | 107 | 0000 | 624 | 9,534 | 8,931 | 8,370 | -0.6 | 63 | 94.7 | 93.9 | 0.0 | 0.0 | 0.2 | 0.3 |
| LANCASTER | 109 | 4360 | 722 | 213,641 | 239,742 | 250,114 | 1.1 | 8 | 94.9 | 92.9 | 2.2 | 2.4 | 1.6 | 2.5 |
| LINCOLN | 111 | 0000 | 740 | 32,508 | 34,050 | 35,017 | 0.5 | 15 | 96.5 | 93.8 | 0.3 | 0.3 | 0.4 | 0.6 |
| LOGAN | 113 | 0000 | 740 | 878 | 899 | 919 | 0.2 | 23 | 99.4 | 99.2 | 0.3 | 0.3 | 0.0 | 0.0 |
| LOUP | 115 | 0000 | 722 | 683 | 643 | 643 | -0.6 | 63 | 99.9 | 99.8 | 0.0 | 0.0 | 0.1 | 0.2 |
| MCPHERSON | 117 | 0000 | 740 | 546 | 542 | 542 | -0.1 | 35 | 99.8 | 99.6 | 0.2 | 0.4 | 0.0 | 0.0 |
| MADISON | 119 | 0000 | 624 | 32,655 | 34,005 | 33,123 | 0.4 | 18 | 97.2 | 95.9 | 0.7 | 0.7 | 0.3 | 0.5 |
| MERRICK | 121 | 0000 | 722 | 8,042 | 8,023 | 7,882 | 0.0 | 30 | 99.4 | 99.1 | 0.0 | 0.0 | 0.3 | 0.5 |
| MORRILL | 123 | 0000 | 764 | 5,423 | 5,239 | 4,970 | -0.3 | 45 | 95.9 | 93.2 | 0.0 | 0.0 | 0.1 | 0.2 |
| NANCE | 125 | 0000 | 722 | 4,275 | 4,004 | 3,752 | -0.6 | 63 | 99.4 | 99.0 | 0.0 | 0.0 | 0.2 | 0.3 |
| NEMAHA | 127 | 0000 | 652 | 7,980 | 7,559 | 7,262 | -0.5 | 57 | 98.7 | 98.7 | 0.9 | 0.8 | 0.2 | 0.2 |
| NUCKOLLS | 129 | 0000 | 722 | 5,786 | 5,035 | 4,678 | -1.3 | 83 | 99.8 | 99.8 | 0.0 | 0.0 | 0.0 | 0.0 |
| OTOE | 131 | 0000 | 652 | 14,252 | 14,901 | 15,405 | 0.4 | 18 | 99.2 | 98.9 | 0.2 | 0.2 | 0.2 | 0.3 |
| PAWNEE | 133 | 0000 | 652 | 3,317 | 3,046 | 2,852 | -0.8 | 73 | 99.6 | 99.5 | 0.1 | 0.1 | 0.1 | 0.2 |
| PERKINS | 135 | 0000 | 722 | 3,367 | 3,198 | 3,163 | -0.5 | 57 | 98.6 | 97.7 | 0.0 | 0.0 | 0.2 | 0.3 |
| PHELPS | 137 | 0000 | 722 | 9,715 | 9,785 | 9,560 | 0.1 | 27 | 99.4 | 99.0 | 0.1 | 0.1 | 0.2 | 0.3 |
| PIERCE | 139 | 0000 | 624 | 7,827 | 7,955 | 8,000 | 0.2 | 23 | 99.4 | 99.2 | 0.0 | 0.0 | 0.1 | 0.2 |
| PLATTE | 141 | 0000 | 652 | 29,820 | 30,255 | 29,648 | 0.1 | 27 | 99.0 | 98.4 | 0.2 | 0.2 | 0.2 | 0.5 |
| POLK | 143 | 0000 | 722 | 5,675 | 5,475 | 5,266 | -0.3 | 45 | 99.2 | 98.7 | 0.0 | 0.0 | 0.2 | 0.3 |
| RED WILLOW | 145 | 0000 | 722 | 11,705 | 11,298 | 11,268 | -0.3 | 45 | 98.8 | 98.2 | 0.1 | 0.1 | 0.2 | 0.3 |
| RICHARDSON | 147 | 0000 | 652 | 9,937 | 9,244 | 8,828 | -0.7 | 69 | 98.0 | 97.6 | 0.1 | 0.1 | 0.1 | 0.2 |
| ROCK | 149 | 0000 | 722 | 2,019 | 1,654 | 1,485 | -1.9 | 91 | 99.9 | 99.8 | 0.0 | 0.0 | 0.0 | 0.0 |
| SALINE | 151 | 0000 | 722 | 12,715 | 13,177 | 13,508 | 0.3 | 22 | 98.6 | 98.0 | 0.1 | 0.1 | 0.9 | 1.3 |
| SARPY | 153 | 5920 | 652 | 102,583 | 124,827 | 136,513 | 1.9 | 1 | 91.4 | 88.9 | 5.2 | 5.4 | 1.9 | 3.1 |
| NEBRASKA | | | | | | | 0.6 | | 93.8 | 92.0 | 3.6 | 4.0 | 0.8 | 1.3 |
| UNITED STATES | | | | | | | 1.0 | | 80.3 | 77.9 | 12.1 | 12.4 | 2.9 | 3.9 |

| COUNTY | % HISPANIC ORIGIN 1990 | % HISPANIC ORIGIN 2000 | 2000 AGE DISTRIBUTION (%) 0-4 | 5-9 | 10-14 | 15-19 | 20-24 | 25-44 | 45-64 | 65-84 | 85+ | 18+ | MEDIAN AGE 1990 | MEDIAN AGE 2000 | 2000 Males/ Females (×100) |
|---|---|---|---|---|---|---|---|---|---|---|---|---|---|---|---|
| ADAMS | 1.0 | 2.4 | 6.2 | 6.2 | 7.3 | 8.7 | 7.5 | 26.1 | 22.1 | 13.1 | 2.8 | 75.9 | 34.3 | 37.2 | 95.3 |
| ANTELOPE | 0.1 | 0.5 | 7.1 | 7.6 | 9.0 | 8.4 | 4.7 | 22.5 | 22.5 | 15.2 | 3.1 | 70.1 | 35.5 | 38.5 | 98.1 |
| ARTHUR | 0.0 | 0.5 | 5.9 | 5.9 | 7.7 | 6.4 | 3.7 | 22.7 | 27.7 | 17.5 | 2.5 | 75.6 | 37.8 | 43.1 | 99.5 |
| BANNER | 2.2 | 5.0 | 6.1 | 6.6 | 8.7 | 8.6 | 4.0 | 23.7 | 27.6 | 13.8 | 0.9 | 72.2 | 36.3 | 40.3 | 100.5 |
| BLAINE | 0.0 | 0.4 | 5.7 | 5.7 | 8.2 | 9.5 | 5.0 | 22.9 | 27.4 | 13.1 | 2.5 | 73.2 | 37.2 | 39.5 | 93.4 |
| BOONE | 0.3 | 0.8 | 7.0 | 7.4 | 8.9 | 7.5 | 4.7 | 22.4 | 22.7 | 16.3 | 3.2 | 71.3 | 36.2 | 39.4 | 102.1 |
| BOX BUTTE | 5.5 | 10.6 | 7.3 | 7.6 | 8.1 | 9.5 | 7.4 | 25.1 | 22.6 | 10.2 | 2.2 | 70.1 | 32.8 | 35.2 | 99.1 |
| BOYD | 0.2 | 0.8 | 5.3 | 6.2 | 8.3 | 7.4 | 4.1 | 20.3 | 24.8 | 19.0 | 4.6 | 74.2 | 41.1 | 43.9 | 99.2 |
| BROWN | 0.6 | 1.6 | 5.7 | 5.9 | 7.9 | 7.5 | 4.7 | 21.9 | 25.2 | 17.6 | 3.4 | 74.9 | 39.0 | 42.4 | 95.0 |
| BUFFALO | 2.7 | 5.6 | 6.4 | 6.2 | 7.2 | 11.5 | 12.8 | 26.4 | 18.2 | 9.3 | 1.9 | 75.6 | 28.6 | 30.0 | 95.9 |
| BURT | 0.9 | 2.1 | 5.6 | 6.2 | 7.8 | 7.9 | 4.8 | 21.7 | 24.6 | 17.5 | 3.8 | 74.8 | 38.8 | 42.2 | 95.7 |
| BUTLER | 0.2 | 0.9 | 6.0 | 6.9 | 8.2 | 8.3 | 5.0 | 23.2 | 23.9 | 15.1 | 3.4 | 73.2 | 37.0 | 39.9 | 100.6 |
| CASS | 0.9 | 2.3 | 7.2 | 7.3 | 8.2 | 7.8 | 5.9 | 27.5 | 23.2 | 11.3 | 1.7 | 72.2 | 33.4 | 36.4 | 101.0 |
| CEDAR | 0.2 | 0.7 | 7.3 | 7.6 | 9.1 | 8.4 | 5.2 | 22.1 | 21.6 | 15.2 | 3.5 | 70.1 | 34.5 | 37.8 | 100.1 |
| CHASE | 2.0 | 4.3 | 7.1 | 7.5 | 8.0 | 8.6 | 5.7 | 21.3 | 23.7 | 15.0 | 3.2 | 71.0 | 36.8 | 40.1 | 92.4 |
| CHERRY | 0.4 | 1.1 | 6.7 | 6.9 | 8.4 | 7.5 | 4.6 | 23.5 | 25.5 | 14.3 | 2.7 | 72.8 | 36.1 | 40.2 | 99.4 |
| CHEYENNE | 3.3 | 7.1 | 6.6 | 6.9 | 7.8 | 8.3 | 6.0 | 23.4 | 23.0 | 15.1 | 2.8 | 73.3 | 35.9 | 38.9 | 95.4 |
| CLAY | 0.6 | 1.6 | 6.0 | 6.6 | 7.2 | 8.2 | 5.9 | 22.9 | 24.4 | 15.4 | 3.4 | 74.6 | 37.3 | 40.7 | 92.6 |
| COLFAX | 2.5 | 4.6 | 6.8 | 7.1 | 7.9 | 7.5 | 5.7 | 22.9 | 21.0 | 17.4 | 3.7 | 73.2 | 35.3 | 39.2 | 100.2 |
| CUMING | 0.1 | 0.7 | 6.5 | 6.8 | 8.1 | 8.1 | 5.1 | 22.7 | 23.5 | 15.9 | 3.4 | 72.8 | 36.8 | 39.8 | 99.1 |
| CUSTER | 0.7 | 1.8 | 5.9 | 6.6 | 7.6 | 7.6 | 5.9 | 20.9 | 24.6 | 17.0 | 4.0 | 74.6 | 39.1 | 41.8 | 95.2 |
| DAKOTA | 6.1 | 11.5 | 7.9 | 7.6 | 8.7 | 8.5 | 7.2 | 27.6 | 21.5 | 9.4 | 1.6 | 70.4 | 31.2 | 33.2 | 98.2 |
| DAWES | 1.6 | 3.2 | 5.8 | 5.8 | 6.6 | 13.4 | 12.8 | 22.2 | 19.2 | 11.6 | 2.5 | 76.6 | 30.6 | 30.9 | 98.6 |
| DAWSON | 3.3 | 6.9 | 6.7 | 6.9 | 7.8 | 7.9 | 6.4 | 23.9 | 24.3 | 13.6 | 2.6 | 73.4 | 36.1 | 38.4 | 95.7 |
| DEUEL | 4.6 | 8.7 | 6.0 | 6.4 | 7.6 | 7.6 | 4.8 | 22.1 | 23.2 | 18.2 | 3.9 | 74.7 | 38.9 | 41.8 | 98.4 |
| DIXON | 0.1 | 0.5 | 6.5 | 7.4 | 8.6 | 7.5 | 5.1 | 23.2 | 23.6 | 14.7 | 3.4 | 72.3 | 36.9 | 39.6 | 101.1 |
| DODGE | 0.6 | 1.7 | 6.1 | 6.3 | 7.5 | 8.5 | 6.6 | 24.5 | 23.5 | 14.1 | 2.9 | 75.2 | 35.5 | 38.5 | 92.4 |
| DOUGLAS | 2.7 | 5.8 | 7.0 | 7.1 | 8.0 | 7.8 | 7.0 | 30.2 | 21.4 | 10.1 | 1.5 | 73.4 | 31.8 | 34.9 | 93.3 |
| DUNDY | 0.6 | 1.7 | 4.6 | 5.9 | 7.2 | 7.6 | 4.9 | 23.4 | 23.5 | 18.6 | 4.2 | 76.9 | 39.0 | 42.5 | 95.3 |
| FILLMORE | 0.5 | 1.3 | 5.8 | 6.4 | 7.7 | 8.6 | 4.9 | 22.1 | 24.0 | 16.6 | 3.9 | 73.7 | 38.3 | 41.3 | 97.7 |
| FRANKLIN | 0.2 | 0.7 | 5.6 | 5.5 | 7.3 | 6.9 | 4.0 | 21.2 | 25.5 | 19.3 | 4.7 | 76.7 | 42.6 | 44.6 | 95.3 |
| FRONTIER | 0.6 | 1.6 | 5.7 | 6.8 | 8.1 | 8.6 | 4.5 | 22.9 | 26.9 | 13.4 | 2.9 | 73.7 | 37.3 | 40.6 | 101.8 |
| FURNAS | 0.7 | 1.7 | 4.6 | 5.5 | 7.2 | 7.3 | 4.5 | 21.6 | 24.5 | 19.0 | 5.7 | 77.7 | 42.4 | 44.5 | 94.5 |
| GAGE | 0.5 | 1.3 | 5.9 | 6.2 | 7.1 | 7.6 | 5.3 | 25.4 | 24.0 | 15.3 | 3.4 | 76.3 | 37.2 | 40.2 | 93.7 |
| GARDEN | 0.6 | 1.6 | 5.2 | 5.9 | 6.7 | 6.8 | 4.0 | 21.0 | 25.9 | 20.0 | 4.5 | 77.5 | 41.9 | 45.2 | 94.4 |
| GARFIELD | 0.1 | 0.6 | 5.8 | 6.0 | 7.3 | 7.8 | 4.2 | 20.3 | 25.9 | 18.4 | 4.4 | 74.9 | 41.4 | 43.9 | 94.5 |
| GOSPER | 0.5 | 1.2 | 4.6 | 5.1 | 7.4 | 7.3 | 4.0 | 21.6 | 29.4 | 17.5 | 3.2 | 77.9 | 40.7 | 45.0 | 106.6 |
| GRANT | 0.3 | 0.9 | 6.3 | 7.4 | 8.5 | 7.4 | 4.0 | 24.9 | 26.2 | 13.5 | 1.7 | 71.9 | 35.1 | 39.3 | 98.3 |
| GREELEY | 0.1 | 0.5 | 6.3 | 7.2 | 8.8 | 8.5 | 5.2 | 21.0 | 22.9 | 16.3 | 3.8 | 71.3 | 36.6 | 39.8 | 97.8 |
| HALL | 4.3 | 8.8 | 7.2 | 7.1 | 7.8 | 7.9 | 7.3 | 26.8 | 22.3 | 11.6 | 2.0 | 72.9 | 33.2 | 35.6 | 94.4 |
| HAMILTON | 0.6 | 1.6 | 6.6 | 7.3 | 8.2 | 8.5 | 5.5 | 23.8 | 24.1 | 13.0 | 3.0 | 71.7 | 35.2 | 38.7 | 97.6 |
| HARLAN | 0.1 | 0.5 | 5.1 | 6.0 | 7.1 | 7.4 | 3.8 | 21.7 | 26.0 | 19.4 | 3.5 | 76.4 | 41.1 | 44.3 | 94.6 |
| HAYES | 0.5 | 1.6 | 5.4 | 6.1 | 7.9 | 7.9 | 4.4 | 23.1 | 27.4 | 15.9 | 2.0 | 74.7 | 38.2 | 42.0 | 107.7 |
| HITCHCOCK | 0.6 | 1.6 | 5.1 | 6.3 | 7.6 | 9.2 | 6.5 | 21.0 | 24.2 | 16.3 | 3.8 | 74.2 | 37.5 | 41.3 | 95.1 |
| HOLT | 0.2 | 0.8 | 7.2 | 7.4 | 9.1 | 7.9 | 5.1 | 23.5 | 22.2 | 14.7 | 2.9 | 70.8 | 34.4 | 38.1 | 99.5 |
| HOOKER | 1.8 | 4.7 | 5.3 | 6.2 | 7.0 | 7.2 | 5.4 | 18.9 | 24.5 | 20.1 | 5.3 | 75.9 | 42.3 | 44.9 | 98.0 |
| HOWARD | 0.7 | 1.7 | 6.3 | 6.7 | 8.5 | 8.3 | 4.8 | 22.7 | 24.8 | 15.0 | 2.9 | 72.7 | 37.2 | 40.3 | 97.5 |
| JEFFERSON | 0.9 | 2.2 | 5.8 | 6.1 | 7.5 | 7.2 | 4.7 | 22.7 | 24.2 | 18.1 | 3.7 | 75.8 | 39.9 | 42.4 | 96.0 |
| JOHNSON | 1.0 | 2.5 | 5.3 | 6.1 | 7.3 | 7.4 | 4.2 | 22.5 | 25.1 | 18.1 | 4.0 | 76.3 | 40.5 | 43.2 | 94.0 |
| KEARNEY | 1.7 | 3.8 | 6.6 | 7.1 | 8.1 | 7.7 | 5.1 | 25.0 | 23.6 | 13.6 | 3.2 | 73.1 | 35.7 | 39.0 | 99.6 |
| KEITH | 3.9 | 7.5 | 6.3 | 6.5 | 7.6 | 8.4 | 5.9 | 22.9 | 24.4 | 15.9 | 2.2 | 74.1 | 36.6 | 40.4 | 96.4 |
| KEYA PAHA | 0.1 | 0.7 | 4.6 | 5.7 | 7.2 | 7.8 | 4.1 | 24.1 | 26.1 | 18.3 | 2.1 | 76.3 | 39.1 | 42.8 | 108.4 |
| KIMBALL | 3.6 | 7.1 | 6.1 | 6.5 | 7.9 | 7.1 | 4.6 | 22.9 | 25.3 | 16.8 | 2.7 | 74.4 | 38.2 | 41.6 | 96.7 |
| KNOX | 0.1 | 0.6 | 5.5 | 6.0 | 7.8 | 7.4 | 4.4 | 21.0 | 24.5 | 19.1 | 4.2 | 75.3 | 40.6 | 43.6 | 95.8 |
| LANCASTER | 1.8 | 4.1 | 6.4 | 6.3 | 6.8 | 8.7 | 10.0 | 30.8 | 20.3 | 9.3 | 1.5 | 76.7 | 30.7 | 33.2 | 95.6 |
| LINCOLN | 5.0 | 10.1 | 6.6 | 6.9 | 8.2 | 8.7 | 6.1 | 25.1 | 23.6 | 12.7 | 2.0 | 72.8 | 34.6 | 37.4 | 95.7 |
| LOGAN | 0.3 | 1.1 | 6.6 | 7.2 | 10.1 | 9.5 | 4.2 | 23.6 | 23.6 | 13.5 | 1.8 | 68.6 | 33.7 | 37.8 | 100.7 |
| LOUP | 0.1 | 0.6 | 5.8 | 6.2 | 7.9 | 7.8 | 4.7 | 23.6 | 26.1 | 15.6 | 2.3 | 74.2 | 38.9 | 41.7 | 94.8 |
| MCPHERSON | 0.0 | 0.4 | 5.9 | 7.6 | 7.6 | 8.5 | 3.3 | 22.5 | 25.1 | 17.2 | 2.4 | 71.4 | 36.8 | 41.1 | 104.5 |
| MADISON | 1.7 | 3.8 | 7.6 | 7.6 | 8.3 | 8.8 | 6.6 | 27.7 | 20.3 | 10.8 | 2.3 | 71.5 | 32.2 | 34.4 | 97.0 |
| MERRICK | 0.9 | 2.2 | 6.5 | 7.2 | 7.9 | 7.5 | 5.3 | 23.4 | 24.4 | 14.6 | 3.1 | 73.2 | 36.2 | 39.7 | 101.0 |
| MORRILL | 8.0 | 14.9 | 6.6 | 6.8 | 8.4 | 8.0 | 4.8 | 22.6 | 25.3 | 14.4 | 3.2 | 72.5 | 37.4 | 40.2 | 99.7 |
| NANCE | 0.9 | 2.2 | 6.8 | 7.2 | 8.8 | 7.5 | 4.7 | 22.6 | 23.2 | 16.1 | 3.1 | 71.9 | 36.3 | 39.8 | 99.9 |
| NEMAHA | 0.3 | 0.8 | 5.8 | 6.0 | 7.0 | 9.7 | 8.2 | 23.4 | 23.0 | 14.0 | 2.9 | 76.5 | 35.1 | 38.2 | 99.7 |
| NUCKOLLS | 0.3 | 0.9 | 5.0 | 5.9 | 7.5 | 7.4 | 4.4 | 21.0 | 24.6 | 19.9 | 4.3 | 76.3 | 40.3 | 44.1 | 92.0 |
| OTOE | 0.7 | 1.9 | 6.1 | 6.5 | 7.4 | 7.8 | 5.4 | 23.1 | 24.3 | 15.8 | 3.7 | 75.0 | 38.2 | 41.0 | 95.6 |
| PAWNEE | 0.5 | 1.4 | 5.5 | 5.7 | 7.4 | 6.6 | 4.4 | 20.3 | 24.1 | 21.3 | 4.7 | 76.7 | 44.1 | 45.1 | 93.6 |
| PERKINS | 1.6 | 3.3 | 5.9 | 6.6 | 8.9 | 8.3 | 4.6 | 21.9 | 24.9 | 15.5 | 3.4 | 72.5 | 37.7 | 41.1 | 100.9 |
| PHELPS | 0.9 | 2.2 | 6.3 | 6.6 | 8.1 | 7.8 | 5.0 | 24.9 | 24.1 | 13.8 | 3.4 | 73.8 | 36.0 | 39.4 | 94.3 |
| PIERCE | 0.2 | 0.8 | 7.1 | 7.7 | 8.7 | 8.3 | 5.2 | 23.3 | 22.8 | 14.0 | 2.9 | 71.1 | 35.4 | 37.8 | 97.1 |
| PLATTE | 0.9 | 2.1 | 7.9 | 8.0 | 8.8 | 8.9 | 6.4 | 25.9 | 21.5 | 10.9 | 1.7 | 69.4 | 32.1 | 34.5 | 96.8 |
| POLK | 0.5 | 1.4 | 5.4 | 6.3 | 7.9 | 7.9 | 4.7 | 22.1 | 24.7 | 16.9 | 4.1 | 74.8 | 39.4 | 42.1 | 98.0 |
| RED WILLOW | 1.8 | 3.7 | 6.3 | 6.7 | 7.8 | 8.6 | 5.8 | 24.4 | 22.9 | 14.9 | 2.6 | 74.5 | 35.0 | 38.4 | 92.5 |
| RICHARDSON | 0.4 | 1.3 | 6.1 | 6.4 | 7.4 | 7.5 | 4.6 | 22.3 | 24.2 | 17.4 | 4.3 | 75.1 | 39.7 | 42.1 | 94.6 |
| ROCK | 0.3 | 1.1 | 5.8 | 6.5 | 8.0 | 8.5 | 4.2 | 23.3 | 23.9 | 16.7 | 3.1 | 73.7 | 36.8 | 40.8 | 97.8 |
| SALINE | 0.6 | 1.5 | 5.9 | 6.0 | 7.1 | 10.0 | 7.5 | 23.0 | 22.3 | 14.5 | 3.7 | 76.1 | 35.7 | 38.4 | 96.8 |
| SARPY | 3.3 | 6.9 | 8.6 | 8.3 | 8.1 | 7.2 | 7.4 | 34.2 | 20.0 | 5.8 | 0.5 | 70.5 | 28.6 | 31.1 | 98.6 |
| NEBRASKA | 2.3 | 5.0 | 6.8 | 6.9 | 7.8 | 8.3 | 7.2 | 27.6 | 21.9 | 11.5 | 2.1 | 73.7 | 33.0 | 35.7 | 95.7 |
| UNITED STATES | 9.0 | 11.8 | 6.9 | 7.2 | 7.2 | 7.2 | 6.7 | 29.9 | 22.2 | 11.1 | 1.6 | 74.6 | 32.9 | 35.7 | 95.6 |

# HOUSEHOLDS

| COUNTY | HOUSEHOLDS | | | | | FAMILIES | | | MEDIAN HOUSEHOLD INCOME | | | |
|---|---|---|---|---|---|---|---|---|---|---|---|---|
| | 1990 | 2000 | 2005 | % Annual Rate 1990-2000 | 2000 Average HH Size | 1990 | 2000 | % Annual Rate 1990-2000 | 2000 | 2005 | 2000 National Rank | 2000 State Rank |
| ADAMS | 11,593 | 11,462 | 11,247 | -0.1 | 2.39 | 7,781 | 7,467 | -0.5 | 35,347 | 40,589 | 1191 | 21 |
| ANTELOPE | 3,045 | 2,701 | 2,580 | -1.4 | 2.63 | 2,189 | 1,875 | -1.9 | 26,580 | 29,580 | 2640 | 60 |
| ARTHUR | 187 | 175 | 175 | -0.8 | 2.31 | 139 | 126 | -1.2 | 19,896 | 21,827 | 3100 | 91 |
| BANNER | 305 | 324 | 333 | 0.7 | 2.52 | 262 | 273 | 0.5 | 24,853 | 29,013 | 2818 | 73 |
| BLAINE | 268 | 220 | 220 | -2.4 | 2.54 | 188 | 149 | -2.8 | 22,500 | 27,500 | 2996 | 87 |
| BOONE | 2,560 | 2,439 | 2,382 | -0.6 | 2.54 | 1,802 | 1,661 | -1.0 | 29,769 | 32,000 | 2189 | 44 |
| BOX BUTTE | 4,898 | 4,761 | 4,619 | -0.3 | 2.60 | 3,491 | 3,291 | -0.7 | 36,707 | 43,020 | 1019 | 11 |
| BOYD | 1,148 | 1,015 | 951 | -1.5 | 2.37 | 785 | 668 | -1.9 | 24,429 | 29,327 | 2865 | 78 |
| BROWN | 1,499 | 1,451 | 1,391 | -0.4 | 2.35 | 1,034 | 961 | -0.9 | 24,523 | 30,236 | 2853 | 77 |
| BUFFALO | 13,736 | 15,124 | 15,433 | 1.2 | 2.49 | 8,922 | 9,346 | 0.6 | 35,816 | 41,188 | 1122 | 18 |
| BURT | 3,139 | 3,220 | 3,235 | 0.3 | 2.39 | 2,180 | 2,145 | -0.2 | 31,558 | 38,329 | 1807 | 31 |
| BUTLER | 3,253 | 3,307 | 3,297 | 0.2 | 2.55 | 2,301 | 2,246 | -0.3 | 34,981 | 43,798 | 1255 | 22 |
| CASS | 7,797 | 9,353 | 10,209 | 2.2 | 2.67 | 5,908 | 6,899 | 1.9 | 45,488 | 54,141 | 331 | 2 |
| CEDAR | 3,652 | 3,451 | 3,331 | -0.7 | 2.70 | 2,652 | 2,427 | -1.1 | 32,345 | 38,151 | 1652 | 27 |
| CHASE | 1,704 | 1,652 | 1,652 | -0.4 | 2.52 | 1,223 | 1,145 | -0.8 | 29,000 | 32,470 | 2294 | 48 |
| CHERRY | 2,438 | 2,434 | 2,406 | 0.0 | 2.57 | 1,760 | 1,693 | -0.5 | 24,717 | 29,167 | 2837 | 76 |
| CHEYENNE | 3,851 | 3,833 | 3,752 | -0.1 | 2.42 | 2,660 | 2,542 | -0.5 | 33,119 | 36,367 | 1517 | 25 |
| CLAY | 2,741 | 2,750 | 2,714 | 0.0 | 2.51 | 2,009 | 1,949 | -0.4 | 31,801 | 34,953 | 1760 | 30 |
| COLFAX | 3,562 | 4,315 | 4,526 | 2.4 | 2.45 | 2,449 | 2,853 | 1.9 | 30,662 | 34,755 | 1993 | 38 |
| CUMING | 3,851 | 3,813 | 3,787 | -0.1 | 2.55 | 2,741 | 2,622 | -0.5 | 29,721 | 32,538 | 2199 | 45 |
| CUSTER | 4,953 | 4,839 | 4,650 | -0.3 | 2.37 | 3,452 | 3,251 | -0.7 | 27,677 | 32,627 | 2483 | 56 |
| DAKOTA | 6,035 | 6,922 | 7,365 | 1.7 | 2.77 | 4,417 | 4,875 | 1.2 | 39,280 | 47,052 | 728 | 6 |
| DAWES | 3,327 | 3,172 | 3,109 | -0.6 | 2.41 | 2,168 | 1,977 | -1.1 | 28,861 | 32,447 | 2321 | 51 |
| DAWSON | 7,829 | 9,143 | 9,295 | 1.9 | 2.51 | 5,626 | 6,291 | 1.4 | 31,298 | 34,042 | 1864 | 33 |
| DEUEL | 915 | 824 | 783 | -1.3 | 2.34 | 633 | 547 | -1.8 | 28,977 | 32,006 | 2299 | 49 |
| DIXON | 2,338 | 2,404 | 2,433 | 0.3 | 2.61 | 1,685 | 1,679 | 0.0 | 29,802 | 32,274 | 2183 | 43 |
| DODGE | 13,445 | 13,943 | 14,114 | 0.4 | 2.44 | 9,388 | 9,379 | 0.0 | 36,327 | 43,489 | 1065 | 16 |
| DOUGLAS | 161,113 | 174,438 | 180,424 | 1.0 | 2.52 | 106,414 | 111,533 | 0.6 | 43,838 | 48,353 | 406 | 4 |
| DUNDY | 1,085 | 954 | 884 | -1.5 | 2.15 | 726 | 614 | -2.0 | 25,325 | 29,031 | 2777 | 67 |
| FILLMORE | 2,829 | 2,748 | 2,729 | -0.4 | 2.39 | 1,951 | 1,829 | -0.8 | 30,790 | 33,191 | 1972 | 36 |
| FRANKLIN | 1,655 | 1,553 | 1,474 | -0.8 | 2.27 | 1,139 | 1,027 | -1.2 | 27,574 | 33,900 | 2500 | 57 |
| FRONTIER | 1,206 | 1,188 | 1,188 | -0.2 | 2.62 | 863 | 822 | -0.6 | 28,929 | 33,784 | 2307 | 50 |
| FURNAS | 2,334 | 2,237 | 2,168 | -0.5 | 2.31 | 1,512 | 1,387 | -1.0 | 24,740 | 27,398 | 2835 | 75 |
| GAGE | 9,019 | 8,962 | 8,864 | -0.1 | 2.40 | 6,194 | 5,927 | -0.5 | 31,906 | 35,989 | 1736 | 29 |
| GARDEN | 1,040 | 884 | 807 | -2.0 | 2.21 | 705 | 576 | -2.4 | 25,538 | 31,473 | 2751 | 65 |
| GARFIELD | 864 | 818 | 782 | -0.7 | 2.35 | 601 | 547 | -1.1 | 22,857 | 25,773 | 2981 | 86 |
| GOSPER | 764 | 973 | 999 | 3.0 | 2.26 | 592 | 734 | 2.6 | 32,154 | 38,594 | 1695 | 28 |
| GRANT | 303 | 304 | 304 | 0.0 | 2.30 | 227 | 221 | -0.3 | 23,529 | 29,000 | 2936 | 85 |
| GREELEY | 1,133 | 1,061 | 1,029 | -0.8 | 2.54 | 781 | 704 | -1.3 | 23,932 | 26,504 | 2908 | 83 |
| HALL | 18,678 | 20,015 | 20,360 | 0.8 | 2.53 | 13,052 | 13,531 | 0.4 | 36,387 | 40,990 | 1060 | 13 |
| HAMILTON | 3,235 | 3,522 | 3,692 | 1.0 | 2.68 | 2,466 | 2,606 | 0.7 | 32,545 | 35,780 | 1617 | 26 |
| HARLAN | 1,585 | 1,564 | 1,526 | -0.2 | 2.29 | 1,100 | 1,050 | -0.6 | 24,826 | 26,316 | 2821 | 74 |
| HAYES | 480 | 416 | 400 | -1.7 | 2.54 | 366 | 309 | -2.0 | 24,028 | 28,000 | 2899 | 82 |
| HITCHCOCK | 1,467 | 1,353 | 1,313 | -1.0 | 2.39 | 1,021 | 907 | -1.4 | 26,225 | 29,877 | 2685 | 63 |
| HOLT | 4,744 | 4,517 | 4,342 | -0.6 | 2.56 | 3,356 | 3,085 | -1.0 | 29,310 | 31,585 | 2254 | 46 |
| HOOKER | 332 | 291 | 291 | -1.6 | 2.23 | 219 | 183 | -2.2 | 24,191 | 27,417 | 2890 | 81 |
| HOWARD | 2,309 | 2,495 | 2,570 | 0.9 | 2.61 | 1,690 | 1,757 | 0.5 | 29,134 | 32,292 | 2275 | 47 |
| JEFFERSON | 3,634 | 3,462 | 3,373 | -0.6 | 2.34 | 2,500 | 2,303 | -1.0 | 28,682 | 33,789 | 2338 | 52 |
| JOHNSON | 1,940 | 1,897 | 1,864 | -0.3 | 2.34 | 1,321 | 1,244 | -0.7 | 27,953 | 34,201 | 2447 | 55 |
| KEARNEY | 2,523 | 2,693 | 2,830 | 0.8 | 2.48 | 1,844 | 1,900 | 0.4 | 35,647 | 39,188 | 1144 | 19 |
| KEITH | 3,430 | 3,497 | 3,687 | 0.2 | 2.55 | 2,426 | 2,391 | -0.2 | 31,147 | 37,684 | 1907 | 34 |
| KEYA PAHA | 419 | 394 | 394 | -0.7 | 2.38 | 312 | 285 | -1.1 | 19,271 | 23,971 | 3114 | 93 |
| KIMBALL | 1,650 | 1,655 | 1,640 | 0.0 | 2.38 | 1,170 | 1,134 | -0.4 | 30,152 | 36,297 | 2123 | 41 |
| KNOX | 3,817 | 3,673 | 3,486 | -0.5 | 2.37 | 2,636 | 2,445 | -0.9 | 25,227 | 27,435 | 2788 | 69 |
| LANCASTER | 82,759 | 93,055 | 97,307 | 1.4 | 2.44 | 52,985 | 57,730 | 1.0 | 43,777 | 50,536 | 411 | 5 |
| LINCOLN | 12,676 | 13,157 | 13,477 | 0.5 | 2.55 | 8,903 | 8,937 | 0.0 | 36,378 | 39,377 | 1062 | 14 |
| LOGAN | 320 | 319 | 322 | 0.0 | 2.82 | 248 | 240 | -0.4 | 25,417 | 31,250 | 2764 | 66 |
| LOUP | 276 | 268 | 268 | -0.4 | 2.40 | 198 | 186 | -0.8 | 21,944 | 27,065 | 3029 | 89 |
| MCPHERSON | 212 | 219 | 219 | 0.4 | 2.47 | 159 | 159 | 0.0 | 22,321 | 25,795 | 3007 | 88 |
| MADISON | 12,283 | 13,035 | 12,805 | 0.7 | 2.52 | 8,427 | 8,613 | 0.3 | 36,575 | 42,341 | 1034 | 12 |
| MERRICK | 3,061 | 3,069 | 3,020 | 0.0 | 2.55 | 2,228 | 2,155 | -0.4 | 28,251 | 30,492 | 2410 | 54 |
| MORRILL | 2,083 | 2,117 | 2,057 | 0.2 | 2.42 | 1,507 | 1,479 | -0.2 | 27,400 | 34,460 | 2526 | 58 |
| NANCE | 1,585 | 1,495 | 1,404 | -0.7 | 2.55 | 1,137 | 1,038 | -1.1 | 30,683 | 38,618 | 1989 | 37 |
| NEMAHA | 3,079 | 2,983 | 2,871 | -0.4 | 2.40 | 2,097 | 1,958 | -0.8 | 34,542 | 39,416 | 1313 | 24 |
| NUCKOLLS | 2,359 | 2,097 | 1,970 | -1.4 | 2.34 | 1,637 | 1,402 | -1.9 | 25,198 | 27,180 | 2792 | 70 |
| OTOE | 5,657 | 6,001 | 6,250 | 0.7 | 2.43 | 3,932 | 4,010 | 0.2 | 34,634 | 40,315 | 1300 | 23 |
| PAWNEE | 1,408 | 1,315 | 1,241 | -0.8 | 2.27 | 947 | 854 | -1.2 | 24,198 | 30,392 | 2889 | 80 |
| PERKINS | 1,283 | 1,195 | 1,170 | -0.9 | 2.63 | 939 | 845 | -1.3 | 27,061 | 32,447 | 2571 | 59 |
| PHELPS | 3,769 | 3,843 | 3,772 | 0.2 | 2.48 | 2,694 | 2,639 | -0.2 | 35,953 | 40,973 | 1107 | 17 |
| PIERCE | 2,929 | 2,969 | 2,985 | 0.2 | 2.63 | 2,144 | 2,108 | -0.2 | 30,452 | 34,458 | 2045 | 39 |
| PLATTE | 10,954 | 11,372 | 11,262 | 0.5 | 2.63 | 7,918 | 7,951 | 0.1 | 36,365 | 41,938 | 1063 | 15 |
| POLK | 2,223 | 2,207 | 2,151 | -0.1 | 2.41 | 1,590 | 1,522 | -0.5 | 39,026 | 49,759 | 750 | 7 |
| RED WILLOW | 4,723 | 4,525 | 4,500 | -0.5 | 2.45 | 3,205 | 2,960 | -1.0 | 31,472 | 36,845 | 1822 | 32 |
| RICHARDSON | 4,120 | 3,882 | 3,725 | -0.7 | 2.32 | 2,747 | 2,471 | -1.3 | 28,594 | 34,974 | 2351 | 53 |
| ROCK | 798 | 680 | 623 | -1.9 | 2.42 | 570 | 470 | -2.3 | 25,058 | 28,125 | 2805 | 71 |
| SALINE | 4,829 | 4,912 | 5,003 | 0.2 | 2.49 | 3,310 | 3,233 | -0.3 | 35,439 | 43,021 | 1180 | 20 |
| SARPY | 33,960 | 41,888 | 46,036 | 2.6 | 2.95 | 27,532 | 33,146 | 2.3 | 47,748 | 57,307 | 247 | 1 |
| NEBRASKA | | | | 0.8 | 2.53 | | | 0.4 | 37,925 | 43,544 | | |
| UNITED STATES | | | | 1.4 | 2.59 | | | 1.1 | 41,914 | 49,127 | | |

| COUNTY | 2000 Per Capita Income | 2000 HH Income Base | 2000 HOUSEHOLD INCOME DISTRIBUTION (%) | | | | | | 2000 AVERAGE DISPOSABLE INCOME BY AGE OF HOUSEHOLDER | | | | | |
|---|---|---|---|---|---|---|---|---|---|---|---|---|---|---|
| | | | Less than $15,000 | $15,000 to $24,999 | $25,000 to $49,999 | $50,000 to $99,999 | $100,000 to $149,999 | $150,000 or More | All Ages | <35 | 35-44 | 45-54 | 55-64 | 65+ |
| ADAMS | 19,038 | 11,462 | 15.1 | 16.3 | 38.5 | 24.6 | 4.1 | 1.4 | 33,321 | 27,684 | 39,159 | 41,767 | 38,538 | 23,523 |
| ANTELOPE | 13,052 | 2,701 | 24.0 | 22.7 | 35.8 | 15.4 | 1.4 | 0.7 | 25,648 | 25,385 | 30,079 | 32,270 | 28,121 | 18,388 |
| ARTHUR | 10,355 | 175 | 34.3 | 32.6 | 26.9 | 6.3 | 0.0 | 0.0 | 18,814 | 15,833 | 24,432 | 20,000 | 9,919 | 20,200 |
| BANNER | 11,193 | 324 | 29.3 | 21.0 | 37.0 | 11.7 | 0.9 | 0.0 | 23,002 | 17,202 | 26,706 | 28,829 | 20,049 | 19,635 |
| BLAINE | 10,809 | 220 | 30.5 | 24.6 | 35.0 | 8.2 | 1.8 | 0.0 | 21,568 | 16,337 | 23,148 | 30,625 | 24,063 | 16,667 |
| BOONE | 13,953 | 2,439 | 21.5 | 19.0 | 38.5 | 18.2 | 2.1 | 0.7 | 27,588 | 23,946 | 35,126 | 34,396 | 30,265 | 19,699 |
| BOX BUTTE | 17,589 | 4,761 | 14.4 | 15.3 | 37.8 | 27.2 | 4.0 | 1.3 | 34,003 | 27,551 | 41,898 | 41,394 | 36,448 | 21,466 |
| BOYD | 13,864 | 1,015 | 28.2 | 22.9 | 33.1 | 12.8 | 1.8 | 1.3 | 25,893 | 23,397 | 33,333 | 30,435 | 26,358 | 19,624 |
| BROWN | 13,314 | 1,451 | 27.4 | 23.3 | 31.7 | 15.6 | 1.5 | 0.5 | 24,446 | 21,372 | 31,002 | 27,449 | 32,308 | 17,664 |
| BUFFALO | 17,285 | 15,124 | 16.6 | 14.5 | 37.5 | 25.8 | 4.4 | 1.4 | 33,668 | 26,415 | 42,188 | 44,305 | 40,566 | 22,726 |
| BURT | 15,883 | 3,220 | 17.7 | 19.4 | 38.8 | 20.1 | 3.3 | 0.8 | 29,514 | 27,679 | 35,295 | 32,411 | 35,507 | 23,445 |
| BUTLER | 17,958 | 3,307 | 14.9 | 16.2 | 40.6 | 24.9 | 2.7 | 0.8 | 31,739 | 30,108 | 37,367 | 38,902 | 34,135 | 23,365 |
| CASS | 19,764 | 9,353 | 9.7 | 8.9 | 37.7 | 35.8 | 6.8 | 1.2 | 39,174 | 33,339 | 45,972 | 47,930 | 40,450 | 27,732 |
| CEDAR | 14,495 | 3,451 | 16.2 | 17.0 | 41.4 | 22.5 | 2.3 | 0.6 | 30,288 | 29,167 | 38,502 | 35,723 | 32,619 | 21,939 |
| CHASE | 13,639 | 1,652 | 18.2 | 23.9 | 37.9 | 18.3 | 1.1 | 0.7 | 27,405 | 24,646 | 31,299 | 33,848 | 28,611 | 21,410 |
| CHERRY | 15,853 | 2,434 | 24.0 | 26.7 | 30.1 | 13.5 | 3.7 | 2.0 | 27,869 | 22,023 | 29,681 | 31,236 | 31,982 | 23,800 |
| CHEYENNE | 16,655 | 3,833 | 17.1 | 19.4 | 37.1 | 22.6 | 2.8 | 1.0 | 30,617 | 24,245 | 37,970 | 39,897 | 35,344 | 22,737 |
| CLAY | 14,476 | 2,750 | 16.3 | 19.8 | 41.5 | 19.9 | 2.6 | 0.0 | 28,810 | 24,843 | 32,886 | 34,333 | 32,078 | 22,979 |
| COLFAX | 14,706 | 4,315 | 16.8 | 20.7 | 42.6 | 17.9 | 1.4 | 0.6 | 28,104 | 26,874 | 34,948 | 36,210 | 32,268 | 19,584 |
| CUMING | 14,402 | 3,813 | 16.6 | 22.6 | 39.3 | 18.4 | 2.8 | 0.4 | 28,295 | 26,070 | 33,091 | 37,592 | 29,003 | 21,231 |
| CUSTER | 15,185 | 4,839 | 21.4 | 22.4 | 36.6 | 16.2 | 2.7 | 0.7 | 27,365 | 23,304 | 32,594 | 32,150 | 35,306 | 20,988 |
| DAKOTA | 16,487 | 6,922 | 13.7 | 13.1 | 38.4 | 30.6 | 3.6 | 0.6 | 34,124 | 30,462 | 41,780 | 41,248 | 35,254 | 20,676 |
| DAWES | 13,810 | 3,172 | 26.6 | 18.5 | 33.8 | 17.1 | 2.9 | 1.1 | 27,479 | 19,103 | 38,866 | 34,985 | 34,188 | 19,550 |
| DAWSON | 14,914 | 9,143 | 17.4 | 21.0 | 39.5 | 19.2 | 2.2 | 0.7 | 28,883 | 23,936 | 34,290 | 35,544 | 31,651 | 22,157 |
| DEUEL | 15,981 | 824 | 19.7 | 21.7 | 38.4 | 16.5 | 2.9 | 0.9 | 27,773 | 26,100 | 31,107 | 36,231 | 31,463 | 22,713 |
| DIXON | 12,936 | 2,404 | 20.1 | 18.9 | 42.4 | 17.5 | 1.1 | 0.0 | 26,658 | 26,449 | 30,667 | 31,729 | 28,844 | 19,517 |
| DODGE | 17,542 | 13,943 | 15.2 | 14.2 | 41.4 | 25.4 | 3.1 | 0.7 | 32,159 | 28,027 | 38,820 | 40,650 | 33,740 | 23,262 |
| DOUGLAS | 24,668 | 174,438 | 11.7 | 12.4 | 33.3 | 29.8 | 8.3 | 4.6 | 42,875 | 32,327 | 48,410 | 52,965 | 45,492 | 29,137 |
| DUNDY | 14,151 | 954 | 27.8 | 21.2 | 38.3 | 11.5 | 0.3 | 0.9 | 23,960 | 23,459 | 27,210 | 27,465 | 26,499 | 18,944 |
| FILLMORE | 15,953 | 2,748 | 18.2 | 21.0 | 37.6 | 20.2 | 2.3 | 0.8 | 29,010 | 27,164 | 35,046 | 30,165 | 34,366 | 22,785 |
| FRANKLIN | 13,946 | 1,553 | 22.2 | 21.5 | 38.0 | 17.3 | 1.0 | 0.0 | 25,554 | 27,587 | 29,520 | 30,443 | 26,911 | 19,643 |
| FRONTIER | 13,282 | 1,188 | 22.6 | 19.9 | 35.6 | 19.4 | 2.1 | 0.4 | 27,275 | 21,881 | 33,376 | 29,694 | 35,062 | 20,179 |
| FURNAS | 13,766 | 2,227 | 23.2 | 27.4 | 32.9 | 14.3 | 1.9 | 0.4 | 24,779 | 24,751 | 28,707 | 33,255 | 25,731 | 19,087 |
| GAGE | 15,069 | 8,962 | 20.2 | 16.6 | 41.0 | 19.6 | 2.5 | 0.2 | 28,482 | 25,254 | 33,399 | 36,171 | 32,787 | 20,390 |
| GARDEN | 13,931 | 884 | 23.0 | 25.5 | 33.5 | 16.7 | 1.2 | 0.1 | 24,992 | 21,649 | 30,417 | 32,339 | 26,679 | 19,302 |
| GARFIELD | 11,889 | 818 | 30.2 | 24.9 | 33.7 | 10.3 | 0.7 | 0.1 | 21,696 | 20,273 | 23,130 | 30,385 | 23,559 | 16,258 |
| GOSPER | 16,483 | 973 | 14.7 | 20.6 | 40.3 | 22.2 | 1.5 | 0.7 | 29,453 | 21,765 | 34,316 | 34,420 | 34,890 | 23,368 |
| GRANT | 13,551 | 304 | 26.0 | 27.3 | 31.6 | 11.5 | 3.6 | 0.0 | 23,923 | 19,118 | 23,897 | 28,692 | 27,000 | 21,233 |
| GREELEY | 11,381 | 1,061 | 24.0 | 28.2 | 34.0 | 13.2 | 0.6 | 0.0 | 23,077 | 19,167 | 30,427 | 28,629 | 20,537 | 19,037 |
| HALL | 16,752 | 20,015 | 15.1 | 14.5 | 40.2 | 26.2 | 3.3 | 0.8 | 32,578 | 27,772 | 39,344 | 40,824 | 33,912 | 22,344 |
| HAMILTON | 14,750 | 3,522 | 14.9 | 18.5 | 41.5 | 21.8 | 2.6 | 0.8 | 30,330 | 25,370 | 35,207 | 38,644 | 32,256 | 22,050 |
| HARLAN | 12,988 | 1,564 | 25.7 | 24.7 | 36.6 | 11.1 | 1.5 | 0.5 | 23,336 | 20,393 | 29,751 | 28,310 | 26,846 | 17,171 |
| HAYES | 20,538 | 416 | 28.9 | 22.8 | 22.6 | 18.5 | 2.6 | 4.6 | 32,833 | 21,937 | 32,583 | 32,518 | 51,750 | 19,542 |
| HITCHCOCK | 16,896 | 1,353 | 20.6 | 25.7 | 34.3 | 15.7 | 2.5 | 1.1 | 27,056 | 24,943 | 30,148 | 36,246 | 29,693 | 19,340 |
| HOLT | 14,762 | 4,517 | 21.5 | 19.5 | 36.8 | 18.0 | 3.0 | 1.2 | 28,737 | 24,638 | 30,905 | 38,285 | 35,221 | 19,856 |
| HOOKER | 12,343 | 291 | 25.4 | 26.5 | 36.1 | 11.7 | 0.3 | 0.0 | 22,302 | 20,795 | 29,013 | 25,699 | 28,041 | 16,226 |
| HOWARD | 12,435 | 2,495 | 20.0 | 20.6 | 42.2 | 16.3 | 0.9 | 0.0 | 26,053 | 23,464 | 32,444 | 32,563 | 27,790 | 18,554 |
| JEFFERSON | 14,459 | 3,462 | 24.0 | 19.3 | 40.3 | 14.6 | 1.0 | 0.8 | 25,989 | 25,791 | 31,241 | 31,356 | 27,283 | 19,557 |
| JOHNSON | 15,556 | 1,897 | 22.6 | 20.9 | 39.2 | 15.4 | 1.0 | 0.8 | 26,460 | 25,623 | 33,723 | 30,308 | 31,123 | 18,898 |
| KEARNEY | 17,232 | 2,693 | 12.2 | 14.6 | 43.9 | 24.8 | 3.5 | 0.9 | 33,210 | 26,741 | 37,235 | 39,223 | 38,392 | 28,002 |
| KEITH | 14,540 | 3,497 | 15.4 | 21.3 | 41.0 | 20.4 | 1.3 | 0.6 | 28,888 | 24,209 | 35,136 | 35,417 | 28,929 | 22,883 |
| KEYA PAHA | 9,531 | 394 | 40.9 | 23.1 | 27.2 | 8.6 | 0.3 | 0.0 | 18,839 | 13,520 | 19,474 | 24,479 | 19,417 | 17,172 |
| KIMBALL | 15,067 | 1,655 | 22.7 | 16.7 | 36.6 | 22.2 | 1.7 | 0.1 | 28,184 | 23,038 | 29,357 | 31,961 | 35,823 | 23,725 |
| KNOX | 14,469 | 3,673 | 26.7 | 22.8 | 32.8 | 15.0 | 1.7 | 1.0 | 25,727 | 25,026 | 30,584 | 34,369 | 27,690 | 18,377 |
| LANCASTER | 22,285 | 93,055 | 11.5 | 11.7 | 35.0 | 32.3 | 7.3 | 2.2 | 39,610 | 30,370 | 46,683 | 50,157 | 45,750 | 28,675 |
| LINCOLN | 18,044 | 13,157 | 18.7 | 12.4 | 37.5 | 25.9 | 4.2 | 1.3 | 33,165 | 26,104 | 40,590 | 41,442 | 37,539 | 22,731 |
| LOGAN | 11,016 | 319 | 23.8 | 25.4 | 36.7 | 12.2 | 1.3 | 0.6 | 23,096 | 17,361 | 24,816 | 24,588 | 19,375 | 24,574 |
| LOUP | 11,965 | 268 | 28.0 | 26.5 | 30.6 | 13.4 | 1.5 | 0.0 | 23,088 | 25,313 | 25,854 | 23,427 | 18,382 | 23,667 |
| MCPHERSON | 13,758 | 219 | 33.8 | 22.4 | 26.5 | 13.2 | 2.3 | 1.8 | 26,296 | 21,532 | 23,871 | 32,613 | 39,405 | 17,336 |
| MADISON | 16,946 | 13,035 | 13.9 | 15.9 | 39.9 | 26.4 | 3.2 | 0.7 | 32,753 | 29,174 | 39,274 | 39,665 | 36,238 | 21,521 |
| MERRICK | 13,475 | 3,069 | 18.3 | 22.9 | 39.5 | 16.8 | 2.1 | 0.5 | 26,952 | 25,421 | 32,387 | 32,512 | 27,928 | 20,321 |
| MORRILL | 15,832 | 2,117 | 22.4 | 22.5 | 34.3 | 17.3 | 2.7 | 0.8 | 27,499 | 22,056 | 32,136 | 34,045 | 33,079 | 19,254 |
| NANCE | 12,942 | 1,495 | 17.7 | 18.8 | 44.2 | 18.5 | 0.7 | 0.0 | 27,201 | 27,287 | 33,156 | 31,820 | 27,511 | 20,039 |
| NEMAHA | 17,048 | 2,983 | 20.2 | 15.6 | 34.7 | 24.1 | 4.1 | 1.4 | 31,891 | 26,115 | 41,395 | 38,844 | 33,352 | 22,575 |
| NUCKOLLS | 12,256 | 2,097 | 25.3 | 24.1 | 37.3 | 12.3 | 1.0 | 0.0 | 23,170 | 22,412 | 28,868 | 29,904 | 23,759 | 17,285 |
| OTOE | 16,622 | 6,001 | 17.5 | 14.5 | 41.1 | 23.9 | 2.5 | 0.5 | 30,715 | 28,095 | 39,128 | 37,425 | 33,116 | 21,374 |
| PAWNEE | 12,117 | 1,315 | 29.2 | 22.4 | 36.4 | 11.6 | 0.5 | 0.0 | 22,510 | 20,692 | 28,956 | 26,694 | 22,676 | 18,397 |
| PERKINS | 12,117 | 1,195 | 20.3 | 23.3 | 41.5 | 13.6 | 1.3 | 0.1 | 25,140 | 20,843 | 32,146 | 30,889 | 30,173 | 16,420 |
| PHELPS | 17,676 | 3,843 | 12.1 | 15.1 | 42.9 | 24.9 | 3.9 | 1.1 | 33,175 | 27,816 | 36,230 | 40,538 | 36,649 | 26,270 |
| PIERCE | 13,813 | 2,969 | 19.1 | 20.8 | 37.5 | 19.7 | 2.5 | 0.5 | 28,281 | 26,557 | 36,513 | 36,430 | 29,166 | 18,053 |
| PLATTE | 16,442 | 11,372 | 11.9 | 17.7 | 40.0 | 26.0 | 3.5 | 0.9 | 33,086 | 27,997 | 39,138 | 40,880 | 36,030 | 23,760 |
| POLK | 18,313 | 2,207 | 12.6 | 11.5 | 42.6 | 28.9 | 4.0 | 0.3 | 34,024 | 33,393 | 40,351 | 36,800 | 37,856 | 27,455 |
| RED WILLOW | 16,024 | 4,525 | 18.2 | 20.0 | 37.0 | 21.8 | 2.3 | 0.7 | 29,607 | 24,069 | 35,225 | 36,740 | 31,362 | 23,564 |
| RICHARDSON | 14,549 | 3,882 | 23.6 | 20.1 | 35.9 | 18.8 | 1.6 | 0.1 | 26,279 | 25,574 | 33,286 | 32,913 | 25,375 | 19,471 |
| ROCK | 12,606 | 680 | 25.9 | 24.0 | 35.6 | 13.4 | 1.2 | 0.0 | 23,724 | 20,556 | 30,805 | 29,051 | 21,960 | 18,954 |
| SALINE | 14,860 | 4,912 | 15.9 | 16.1 | 41.2 | 24.6 | 2.1 | 0.1 | 30,579 | 29,405 | 35,034 | 39,709 | 31,082 | 21,656 |
| SARPY | 18,548 | 41,888 | 4.6 | 10.4 | 38.1 | 40.6 | 5.7 | 0.7 | 40,462 | 33,032 | 43,728 | 50,007 | 44,006 | 29,423 |
| NEBRASKA | 19,393 | | 14.3 | 14.9 | 36.6 | 27.0 | 5.2 | 2.0 | 35,837 | 29,458 | 42,366 | 44,678 | 38,685 | 24,332 |
| UNITED STATES | 22,162 | | 14.5 | 12.5 | 32.3 | 29.8 | 7.4 | 3.5 | 40,748 | 34,503 | 44,969 | 49,579 | 43,409 | 27,339 |

# SPENDING POTENTIAL INDEXES

| COUNTY | FINANCIAL SERVICES | | | | THE HOME | | | | | | ENTERTAINMENT | | | | | | PERSONAL | | | |
|---|---|---|---|---|---|---|---|---|---|---|---|---|---|---|---|---|---|---|---|---|
| | | | | | Home Improvements | | | Furnishings | | | | | | | | | | | | |
| | Auto Loan | Home Loan | Investments | Retirement Plans | Home Repair | Lawn & Garden | Remodeling | Appliances | Electronics | Furniture | Restaurants | Sporting Goods | Theater & Concerts | Toys & Hobbies | Travel | Video Rental | Apparel | Auto Aftermarket | Health Insurance | Pets & Supplies |
| ADAMS | 97 | 91 | 95 | 92 | 99 | 97 | 101 | 97 | 94 | 93 | 95 | 96 | 97 | 98 | 93 | 100 | 91 | 97 | 101 | 98 |
| ANTELOPE | 96 | 64 | 70 | 78 | 90 | 89 | 108 | 94 | 90 | 72 | 78 | 93 | 79 | 93 | 75 | 100 | 77 | 89 | 105 | 95 |
| ARTHUR | 101 | 63 | 68 | 83 | 89 | 90 | 113 | 97 | 89 | 68 | 78 | 101 | 80 | 99 | 74 | 101 | 78 | 90 | 109 | 100 |
| BANNER | 101 | 63 | 68 | 83 | 89 | 90 | 113 | 97 | 89 | 68 | 78 | 101 | 80 | 99 | 74 | 101 | 78 | 90 | 109 | 100 |
| BLAINE | 98 | 71 | 80 | 82 | 92 | 91 | 115 | 96 | 92 | 79 | 84 | 95 | 85 | 97 | 79 | 100 | 82 | 91 | 104 | 98 |
| BOONE | 97 | 63 | 70 | 79 | 90 | 89 | 110 | 95 | 90 | 71 | 78 | 95 | 80 | 95 | 75 | 100 | 77 | 89 | 106 | 96 |
| BOX BUTTE | 97 | 79 | 78 | 83 | 92 | 90 | 107 | 96 | 95 | 85 | 89 | 94 | 88 | 96 | 81 | 101 | 85 | 93 | 101 | 98 |
| BOYD | 97 | 63 | 70 | 80 | 90 | 89 | 110 | 95 | 90 | 71 | 78 | 95 | 80 | 95 | 75 | 100 | 77 | 89 | 106 | 97 |
| BROWN | 95 | 64 | 70 | 76 | 90 | 89 | 107 | 94 | 91 | 73 | 78 | 90 | 79 | 91 | 76 | 100 | 77 | 88 | 104 | 94 |
| BUFFALO | 96 | 89 | 87 | 90 | 95 | 92 | 101 | 95 | 94 | 89 | 93 | 94 | 92 | 96 | 88 | 100 | 89 | 95 | 99 | 98 |
| BURT | 95 | 65 | 71 | 77 | 91 | 89 | 108 | 94 | 91 | 74 | 78 | 91 | 80 | 92 | 76 | 100 | 77 | 89 | 104 | 95 |
| BUTLER | 98 | 66 | 72 | 81 | 91 | 90 | 111 | 96 | 91 | 73 | 80 | 96 | 82 | 96 | 76 | 101 | 79 | 90 | 106 | 98 |
| CASS | 99 | 85 | 83 | 89 | 94 | 92 | 110 | 98 | 97 | 89 | 94 | 98 | 93 | 100 | 85 | 102 | 90 | 97 | 101 | 101 |
| CEDAR | 97 | 64 | 70 | 79 | 90 | 89 | 109 | 95 | 90 | 72 | 78 | 94 | 79 | 94 | 75 | 100 | 77 | 89 | 106 | 96 |
| CHASE | 98 | 68 | 74 | 81 | 91 | 90 | 111 | 96 | 92 | 76 | 81 | 95 | 83 | 96 | 77 | 101 | 80 | 90 | 105 | 98 |
| CHERRY | 97 | 64 | 70 | 79 | 90 | 89 | 109 | 95 | 90 | 72 | 78 | 94 | 79 | 94 | 75 | 100 | 77 | 89 | 106 | 96 |
| CHEYENNE | 95 | 72 | 78 | 81 | 93 | 91 | 104 | 95 | 91 | 79 | 83 | 92 | 85 | 94 | 81 | 100 | 81 | 90 | 103 | 95 |
| CLAY | 97 | 68 | 74 | 80 | 91 | 90 | 110 | 95 | 92 | 76 | 81 | 92 | 82 | 94 | 77 | 101 | 79 | 90 | 104 | 96 |
| COLFAX | 96 | 67 | 75 | 79 | 91 | 90 | 111 | 95 | 91 | 76 | 80 | 92 | 82 | 94 | 77 | 100 | 79 | 90 | 104 | 96 |
| CUMING | 97 | 68 | 74 | 80 | 91 | 90 | 110 | 95 | 92 | 76 | 81 | 94 | 83 | 95 | 77 | 101 | 80 | 90 | 104 | 97 |
| CUSTER | 96 | 64 | 71 | 78 | 90 | 90 | 109 | 94 | 91 | 73 | 78 | 92 | 80 | 93 | 76 | 100 | 77 | 89 | 105 | 95 |
| DAKOTA | 97 | 85 | 88 | 88 | 96 | 93 | 108 | 97 | 95 | 90 | 93 | 95 | 93 | 98 | 87 | 101 | 89 | 95 | 99 | 99 |
| DAWES | 95 | 78 | 81 | 84 | 93 | 90 | 103 | 92 | 91 | 79 | 84 | 90 | 85 | 92 | 82 | 98 | 82 | 91 | 101 | 95 |
| DAWSON | 97 | 75 | 79 | 83 | 93 | 91 | 108 | 96 | 93 | 82 | 86 | 94 | 87 | 96 | 81 | 101 | 83 | 92 | 103 | 98 |
| DEUEL | 95 | 64 | 71 | 76 | 90 | 89 | 107 | 94 | 91 | 73 | 78 | 89 | 79 | 91 | 76 | 100 | 77 | 88 | 104 | 94 |
| DIXON | 99 | 68 | 73 | 83 | 91 | 90 | 113 | 97 | 91 | 74 | 81 | 98 | 83 | 98 | 76 | 101 | 81 | 91 | 107 | 99 |
| DODGE | 97 | 86 | 93 | 91 | 99 | 97 | 103 | 97 | 95 | 91 | 93 | 95 | 95 | 97 | 91 | 101 | 90 | 96 | 102 | 98 |
| DOUGLAS | 99 | 105 | 102 | 104 | 103 | 102 | 98 | 99 | 99 | 103 | 105 | 100 | 105 | 101 | 103 | 102 | 101 | 103 | 99 | 101 |
| DUNDY | 97 | 64 | 70 | 79 | 90 | 89 | 109 | 95 | 90 | 72 | 78 | 94 | 79 | 94 | 75 | 100 | 77 | 89 | 106 | 96 |
| FILLMORE | 97 | 66 | 72 | 80 | 90 | 90 | 110 | 95 | 91 | 73 | 79 | 95 | 81 | 95 | 76 | 100 | 79 | 90 | 106 | 97 |
| FRANKLIN | 96 | 64 | 70 | 78 | 90 | 89 | 108 | 94 | 90 | 72 | 78 | 93 | 79 | 93 | 75 | 100 | 77 | 89 | 105 | 95 |
| FRONTIER | 98 | 64 | 70 | 81 | 90 | 90 | 112 | 96 | 90 | 71 | 78 | 97 | 80 | 96 | 75 | 100 | 78 | 90 | 107 | 98 |
| FURNAS | 96 | 64 | 70 | 77 | 90 | 89 | 108 | 94 | 90 | 73 | 78 | 91 | 79 | 92 | 75 | 100 | 77 | 88 | 105 | 95 |
| GAGE | 96 | 71 | 78 | 81 | 93 | 91 | 107 | 95 | 91 | 78 | 83 | 93 | 84 | 94 | 80 | 100 | 81 | 90 | 103 | 96 |
| GARDEN | 95 | 64 | 70 | 77 | 90 | 89 | 108 | 94 | 90 | 73 | 78 | 91 | 79 | 92 | 76 | 100 | 77 | 88 | 105 | 94 |
| GARFIELD | 95 | 64 | 70 | 77 | 90 | 89 | 108 | 94 | 90 | 73 | 78 | 91 | 79 | 92 | 76 | 100 | 77 | 88 | 105 | 94 |
| GOSPER | 97 | 65 | 71 | 80 | 90 | 90 | 112 | 95 | 90 | 73 | 79 | 95 | 80 | 95 | 76 | 100 | 78 | 89 | 106 | 97 |
| GRANT | 101 | 63 | 68 | 83 | 89 | 90 | 113 | 97 | 89 | 68 | 78 | 101 | 80 | 99 | 74 | 101 | 78 | 90 | 109 | 100 |
| GREELEY | 97 | 63 | 70 | 79 | 90 | 89 | 110 | 95 | 90 | 71 | 78 | 95 | 80 | 95 | 75 | 100 | 77 | 89 | 106 | 96 |
| HALL | 97 | 92 | 95 | 92 | 99 | 96 | 101 | 97 | 95 | 94 | 96 | 95 | 97 | 98 | 93 | 100 | 92 | 97 | 100 | 98 |
| HAMILTON | 99 | 73 | 78 | 84 | 93 | 91 | 114 | 97 | 94 | 81 | 86 | 97 | 87 | 99 | 79 | 102 | 84 | 93 | 104 | 100 |
| HARLAN | 97 | 65 | 71 | 80 | 90 | 90 | 112 | 95 | 91 | 73 | 79 | 94 | 81 | 95 | 76 | 100 | 78 | 89 | 106 | 97 |
| HAYES | 99 | 63 | 69 | 81 | 89 | 89 | 111 | 96 | 89 | 70 | 78 | 98 | 80 | 97 | 74 | 100 | 78 | 89 | 107 | 98 |
| HITCHCOCK | 95 | 64 | 70 | 76 | 90 | 89 | 107 | 94 | 91 | 73 | 78 | 90 | 79 | 92 | 76 | 100 | 77 | 88 | 104 | 94 |
| HOLT | 98 | 64 | 71 | 80 | 90 | 90 | 111 | 95 | 90 | 72 | 79 | 96 | 80 | 96 | 75 | 100 | 78 | 89 | 106 | 97 |
| HOOKER | 93 | 64 | 71 | 74 | 91 | 89 | 105 | 93 | 91 | 75 | 78 | 86 | 79 | 89 | 76 | 100 | 76 | 88 | 103 | 92 |
| HOWARD | 98 | 65 | 71 | 80 | 90 | 90 | 110 | 95 | 90 | 73 | 79 | 95 | 81 | 95 | 76 | 100 | 78 | 90 | 106 | 97 |
| JEFFERSON | 97 | 67 | 74 | 80 | 91 | 90 | 111 | 95 | 91 | 75 | 80 | 94 | 82 | 95 | 77 | 100 | 79 | 90 | 105 | 97 |
| JOHNSON | 98 | 63 | 69 | 80 | 90 | 89 | 110 | 95 | 90 | 71 | 78 | 96 | 80 | 95 | 75 | 100 | 77 | 89 | 106 | 97 |
| KEARNEY | 98 | 73 | 76 | 83 | 92 | 90 | 111 | 96 | 93 | 80 | 85 | 95 | 86 | 97 | 79 | 101 | 83 | 92 | 104 | 98 |
| KEITH | 98 | 73 | 78 | 83 | 92 | 91 | 113 | 96 | 92 | 79 | 84 | 95 | 85 | 97 | 80 | 101 | 82 | 91 | 104 | 98 |
| KEYA PAHA | 101 | 63 | 68 | 83 | 89 | 90 | 113 | 97 | 89 | 68 | 78 | 101 | 80 | 99 | 74 | 101 | 78 | 90 | 109 | 100 |
| KIMBALL | 98 | 74 | 78 | 83 | 93 | 90 | 110 | 96 | 91 | 79 | 85 | 96 | 86 | 98 | 80 | 101 | 83 | 92 | 104 | 99 |
| KNOX | 97 | 64 | 70 | 79 | 90 | 90 | 109 | 95 | 90 | 72 | 78 | 93 | 80 | 94 | 75 | 100 | 77 | 89 | 106 | 96 |
| LANCASTER | 98 | 101 | 97 | 97 | 100 | 98 | 97 | 97 | 97 | 97 | 101 | 97 | 99 | 99 | 97 | 101 | 97 | 100 | 98 | 100 |
| LINCOLN | 97 | 83 | 87 | 88 | 96 | 93 | 105 | 96 | 94 | 88 | 91 | 95 | 92 | 97 | 87 | 100 | 87 | 94 | 101 | 98 |
| LOGAN | 101 | 63 | 68 | 83 | 89 | 90 | 113 | 97 | 89 | 68 | 78 | 101 | 80 | 99 | 74 | 101 | 78 | 90 | 109 | 100 |
| LOUP | 101 | 63 | 68 | 83 | 89 | 90 | 113 | 97 | 89 | 68 | 78 | 101 | 80 | 99 | 74 | 101 | 78 | 90 | 109 | 100 |
| MCPHERSON | 101 | 63 | 68 | 83 | 89 | 90 | 113 | 97 | 89 | 68 | 78 | 101 | 80 | 99 | 74 | 101 | 78 | 90 | 109 | 100 |
| MADISON | 97 | 87 | 88 | 88 | 96 | 93 | 104 | 96 | 94 | 90 | 93 | 95 | 93 | 98 | 88 | 101 | 89 | 95 | 100 | 98 |
| MERRICK | 97 | 65 | 71 | 80 | 90 | 90 | 110 | 95 | 91 | 73 | 79 | 95 | 81 | 95 | 76 | 100 | 78 | 90 | 106 | 97 |
| MORRILL | 96 | 64 | 70 | 78 | 90 | 89 | 108 | 94 | 90 | 72 | 78 | 92 | 79 | 93 | 75 | 100 | 77 | 89 | 105 | 95 |
| NANCE | 97 | 63 | 70 | 79 | 90 | 89 | 110 | 95 | 90 | 71 | 78 | 95 | 80 | 95 | 75 | 100 | 77 | 89 | 106 | 96 |
| NEMAHA | 95 | 70 | 74 | 78 | 91 | 89 | 104 | 93 | 89 | 76 | 80 | 90 | 82 | 92 | 78 | 99 | 78 | 89 | 103 | 94 |
| NUCKOLLS | 96 | 64 | 70 | 78 | 90 | 89 | 108 | 94 | 90 | 72 | 78 | 92 | 79 | 93 | 75 | 100 | 77 | 89 | 105 | 95 |
| OTOE | 97 | 68 | 74 | 80 | 92 | 91 | 109 | 95 | 90 | 76 | 80 | 95 | 83 | 95 | 78 | 100 | 79 | 90 | 105 | 97 |
| PAWNEE | 98 | 65 | 71 | 81 | 90 | 90 | 111 | 95 | 90 | 72 | 79 | 96 | 81 | 96 | 75 | 100 | 78 | 90 | 106 | 97 |
| PERKINS | 97 | 63 | 70 | 79 | 90 | 89 | 110 | 95 | 90 | 71 | 78 | 95 | 80 | 95 | 75 | 100 | 77 | 89 | 106 | 96 |
| PHELPS | 99 | 78 | 83 | 87 | 95 | 93 | 111 | 98 | 95 | 84 | 89 | 98 | 91 | 100 | 83 | 102 | 87 | 94 | 104 | 100 |
| PIERCE | 97 | 68 | 74 | 80 | 91 | 90 | 110 | 95 | 92 | 76 | 81 | 93 | 82 | 95 | 77 | 100 | 79 | 90 | 104 | 96 |
| PLATTE | 99 | 86 | 87 | 90 | 96 | 94 | 106 | 98 | 96 | 90 | 94 | 97 | 94 | 100 | 88 | 102 | 90 | 96 | 102 | 100 |
| POLK | 96 | 64 | 70 | 78 | 90 | 89 | 109 | 95 | 90 | 72 | 78 | 93 | 79 | 94 | 75 | 100 | 77 | 89 | 105 | 96 |
| RED WILLOW | 97 | 80 | 88 | 88 | 96 | 94 | 105 | 96 | 93 | 85 | 88 | 94 | 91 | 97 | 86 | 100 | 86 | 93 | 103 | 97 |
| RICHARDSON | 96 | 65 | 71 | 77 | 91 | 90 | 109 | 94 | 91 | 74 | 79 | 92 | 80 | 93 | 76 | 100 | 77 | 89 | 104 | 95 |
| ROCK | 97 | 64 | 70 | 79 | 90 | 89 | 109 | 95 | 90 | 72 | 78 | 94 | 79 | 94 | 75 | 100 | 77 | 89 | 106 | 96 |
| SALINE | 97 | 69 | 76 | 81 | 92 | 90 | 112 | 96 | 92 | 77 | 82 | 94 | 83 | 96 | 78 | 100 | 81 | 90 | 104 | 97 |
| SARPY | 99 | 103 | 87 | 95 | 96 | 95 | 96 | 99 | 101 | 101 | 107 | 100 | 101 | 101 | 94 | 103 | 100 | 104 | 97 | 102 |
| NEBRASKA | 98 | 91 | 92 | 94 | 97 | 96 | 102 | 97 | 96 | 92 | 95 | 97 | 96 | 98 | 92 | 101 | 92 | 97 | 101 | 99 |
| UNITED STATES | 100 | 100 | 100 | 100 | 100 | 100 | 100 | 100 | 100 | 100 | 100 | 100 | 100 | 100 | 100 | 100 | 100 | 100 | 100 | 100 |

| COUNTY | FIPS Code | MSA Code | DMA Code | POPULATION 1990 | POPULATION 2000 | POPULATION 2005 | 1990-2000 ANNUAL CHANGE % Rate | 1990-2000 ANNUAL CHANGE State Rank | RACE (%) White 1990 | White 2000 | Black 1990 | Black 2000 | Asian/Pacific 1990 | Asian/Pacific 2000 |
|---|---|---|---|---|---|---|---|---|---|---|---|---|---|---|
| SAUNDERS | 155 | 0000 | 652 | 18,285 | 19,311 | 19,580 | 0.5 | 15 | 99.3 | 99.0 | 0.1 | 0.1 | 0.2 | 0.3 |
| SCOTTS BLUFF | 157 | 0000 | 759 | 36,025 | 36,007 | 35,652 | 0.0 | 30 | 91.1 | 86.1 | 0.2 | 0.3 | 0.5 | 0.8 |
| SEWARD | 159 | 0000 | 722 | 15,450 | 16,467 | 16,691 | 0.6 | 13 | 99.2 | 98.9 | 0.1 | 0.1 | 0.2 | 0.4 |
| SHERIDAN | 161 | 0000 | 764 | 6,750 | 6,372 | 6,122 | -0.6 | 63 | 91.9 | 90.2 | 0.0 | 0.1 | 0.2 | 0.5 |
| SHERMAN | 163 | 0000 | 722 | 3,718 | 3,451 | 3,355 | -0.7 | 69 | 99.5 | 99.1 | 0.0 | 0.0 | 0.3 | 0.6 |
| SIOUX | 165 | 0000 | 764 | 1,549 | 1,389 | 1,241 | -1.1 | 81 | 97.5 | 95.0 | 0.0 | 0.0 | 0.1 | 0.2 |
| STANTON | 167 | 0000 | 624 | 6,244 | 6,047 | 5,789 | -0.3 | 45 | 98.8 | 98.6 | 0.4 | 0.4 | 0.1 | 0.1 |
| THAYER | 169 | 0000 | 722 | 6,635 | 6,102 | 5,775 | -0.8 | 73 | 99.4 | 99.2 | 0.1 | 0.1 | 0.1 | 0.1 |
| THOMAS | 171 | 0000 | 740 | 851 | 809 | 811 | -0.5 | 57 | 99.5 | 99.5 | 0.0 | 0.0 | 0.0 | 0.0 |
| THURSTON | 173 | 0000 | 624 | 6,936 | 6,988 | 6,667 | 0.1 | 27 | 55.7 | 53.3 | 0.1 | 0.2 | 0.1 | 0.2 |
| VALLEY | 175 | 0000 | 722 | 5,169 | 4,434 | 4,080 | -1.5 | 88 | 99.2 | 98.7 | 0.1 | 0.1 | 0.2 | 0.3 |
| WASHINGTON | 177 | 5920 | 652 | 16,607 | 19,070 | 20,254 | 1.4 | 7 | 98.8 | 98.2 | 0.5 | 0.6 | 0.2 | 0.3 |
| WAYNE | 179 | 0000 | 624 | 9,364 | 9,131 | 8,788 | -0.2 | 40 | 98.9 | 98.7 | 0.4 | 0.4 | 0.4 | 0.6 |
| WEBSTER | 181 | 0000 | 722 | 4,279 | 3,881 | 3,632 | -0.9 | 77 | 99.5 | 99.2 | 0.0 | 0.0 | 0.3 | 0.6 |
| WHEELER | 183 | 0000 | 722 | 948 | 916 | 879 | -0.3 | 45 | 99.7 | 99.6 | 0.0 | 0.0 | 0.3 | 0.4 |
| YORK | 185 | 0000 | 722 | 14,428 | 14,285 | 13,764 | -0.1 | 35 | 98.5 | 98.1 | 0.6 | 0.6 | 0.3 | 0.5 |
| NEBRASKA | | | | | | | 0.6 | | 93.8 | 92.0 | 3.6 | 4.0 | 0.8 | 1.3 |
| UNITED STATES | | | | | | | 1.0 | | 80.3 | 77.9 | 12.1 | 12.4 | 2.9 | 3.9 |

# POPULATION COMPOSITION



| COUNTY | % HISPANIC ORIGIN | | 2000 AGE DISTRIBUTION (%) | | | | | | | | | | MEDIAN AGE | | 2000 Males/ Females (×100) |
|---|---|---|---|---|---|---|---|---|---|---|---|---|---|---|---|
| | 1990 | 2000 | 0-4 | 5-9 | 10-14 | 15-19 | 20-24 | 25-44 | 45-64 | 65-84 | 85+ | 18+ | 1990 | 2000 | |
| SAUNDERS | 0.6 | 1.5 | 6.6 | 6.9 | 8.4 | 8.0 | 5.3 | 25.0 | 24.3 | 13.1 | 2.5 | 72.6 | 35.1 | 38.4 | 100.2 |
| SCOTTS BLUFF | 14.5 | 25.4 | 6.4 | 6.7 | 7.4 | 8.3 | 7.1 | 24.6 | 23.3 | 13.9 | 2.4 | 74.3 | 35.1 | 37.6 | 93.3 |
| SEWARD | 0.5 | 1.4 | 6.0 | 6.4 | 7.7 | 10.6 | 8.6 | 23.8 | 22.1 | 12.3 | 2.5 | 75.1 | 33.1 | 35.5 | 100.9 |
| SHERIDAN | 1.0 | 2.4 | 5.5 | 6.5 | 8.0 | 8.3 | 5.3 | 22.0 | 24.0 | 16.9 | 3.4 | 74.0 | 38.1 | 41.2 | 97.3 |
| SHERMAN | 0.2 | 0.9 | 5.8 | 6.2 | 8.3 | 8.4 | 5.0 | 20.8 | 24.5 | 17.8 | 3.1 | 74.0 | 38.6 | 41.5 | 101.5 |
| SIOUX | 2.8 | 6.2 | 5.0 | 5.8 | 8.4 | 7.2 | 4.2 | 22.2 | 30.5 | 14.9 | 1.9 | 75.7 | 38.5 | 43.2 | 102.8 |
| STANTON | 0.4 | 1.1 | 8.0 | 8.2 | 9.1 | 8.6 | 6.4 | 25.1 | 21.6 | 11.0 | 2.0 | 68.9 | 31.6 | 34.6 | 100.4 |
| THAYER | 0.9 | 2.1 | 5.1 | 5.8 | 6.9 | 7.9 | 4.9 | 21.3 | 24.6 | 18.8 | 4.8 | 76.6 | 41.8 | 43.8 | 96.5 |
| THOMAS | 1.3 | 2.6 | 5.1 | 6.9 | 8.8 | 9.6 | 4.7 | 23.4 | 27.7 | 12.5 | 1.4 | 72.4 | 35.8 | 39.5 | 93.1 |
| THURSTON | 0.9 | 1.8 | 10.0 | 9.7 | 10.1 | 8.7 | 6.9 | 21.8 | 19.7 | 11.2 | 2.0 | 64.7 | 29.9 | 29.6 | 97.5 |
| VALLEY | 0.3 | 1.1 | 5.4 | 6.3 | 7.2 | 7.8 | 4.6 | 21.7 | 24.7 | 18.3 | 3.9 | 75.6 | 39.7 | 42.9 | 93.5 |
| WASHINGTON | 0.6 | 1.5 | 5.6 | 6.3 | 7.9 | 9.0 | 6.6 | 26.1 | 25.5 | 11.1 | 2.0 | 74.8 | 34.8 | 38.1 | 96.8 |
| WAYNE | 0.2 | 0.7 | 6.2 | 6.1 | 6.4 | 14.2 | 11.7 | 23.7 | 18.0 | 11.7 | 2.1 | 76.7 | 28.6 | 30.7 | 94.2 |
| WEBSTER | 0.3 | 0.8 | 5.3 | 5.8 | 7.3 | 7.0 | 4.1 | 20.6 | 25.3 | 19.5 | 4.9 | 76.5 | 43.8 | 44.8 | 93.7 |
| WHEELER | 0.0 | 0.4 | 8.2 | 8.7 | 10.0 | 8.0 | 5.0 | 23.4 | 21.7 | 13.2 | 1.7 | 66.6 | 33.0 | 36.5 | 100.9 |
| YORK | 0.8 | 1.9 | 6.7 | 6.8 | 8.1 | 8.9 | 6.0 | 24.3 | 22.9 | 13.6 | 2.7 | 73.2 | 34.8 | 37.7 | 95.1 |
| NEBRASKA | 2.3 | 5.0 | 6.8 | 6.9 | 7.8 | 8.3 | 7.2 | 27.6 | 21.9 | 11.5 | 2.1 | 73.7 | 33.0 | 35.7 | 95.7 |
| UNITED STATES | 9.0 | 11.8 | 6.9 | 7.2 | 7.2 | 7.2 | 6.7 | 29.9 | 22.2 | 11.1 | 1.6 | 74.6 | 32.9 | 35.7 | 95.6 |

| COUNTY | HOUSEHOLDS | | | | | FAMILIES | | | MEDIAN HOUSEHOLD INCOME | | | |
|---|---|---|---|---|---|---|---|---|---|---|---|---|
| | 1990 | 2000 | 2005 | % Annual Rate 1990-2000 | 2000 Average HH Size | 1990 | 2000 | % Annual Rate 1990-2000 | 2000 | 2005 | 2000 National Rank | 2000 State Rank |
| SAUNDERS | 6,809 | 7,238 | 7,358 | 0.7 | 2.63 | 5,028 | 5,163 | 0.3 | 36,792 | 45,355 | 1004 | 10 |
| SCOTTS BLUFF | 14,056 | 14,105 | 13,990 | 0.0 | 2.51 | 9,882 | 9,569 | -0.4 | 30,416 | 33,836 | 2055 | 40 |
| SEWARD | 5,432 | 5,745 | 5,827 | 0.7 | 2.63 | 3,997 | 4,077 | 0.2 | 37,890 | 42,671 | 859 | 8 |
| SHERIDAN | 2,618 | 2,477 | 2,379 | -0.7 | 2.51 | 1,831 | 1,666 | -1.1 | 24,417 | 28,589 | 2866 | 79 |
| SHERMAN | 1,431 | 1,298 | 1,249 | -1.2 | 2.61 | 1,013 | 886 | -1.6 | 19,282 | 23,513 | 3112 | 92 |
| SIOUX | 612 | 585 | 539 | -0.5 | 2.37 | 465 | 432 | -0.9 | 21,734 | 27,125 | 3039 | 90 |
| STANTON | 2,167 | 2,167 | 2,107 | 0.0 | 2.76 | 1,692 | 1,646 | -0.3 | 29,965 | 32,409 | 2161 | 42 |
| THAYER | 2,669 | 2,509 | 2,400 | -0.7 | 2.34 | 1,884 | 1,713 | -1.1 | 24,906 | 27,515 | 2815 | 72 |
| THOMAS | 316 | 292 | 289 | -1.0 | 2.77 | 249 | 225 | -1.2 | 25,694 | 31,477 | 2741 | 64 |
| THURSTON | 2,288 | 2,358 | 2,287 | 0.4 | 2.92 | 1,715 | 1,728 | 0.1 | 26,528 | 28,903 | 2648 | 61 |
| VALLEY | 2,141 | 1,869 | 1,734 | -1.6 | 2.32 | 1,434 | 1,203 | -2.1 | 26,369 | 29,367 | 2669 | 62 |
| WASHINGTON | 6,017 | 6,969 | 7,439 | 1.8 | 2.66 | 4,563 | 5,117 | 1.4 | 45,067 | 50,440 | 352 | 3 |
| WAYNE | 3,232 | 3,252 | 3,167 | 0.1 | 2.44 | 2,211 | 2,127 | -0.5 | 30,891 | 36,795 | 1950 | 35 |
| WEBSTER | 1,755 | 1,639 | 1,556 | -0.8 | 2.27 | 1,203 | 1,081 | -1.3 | 23,705 | 26,092 | 2923 | 84 |
| WHEELER | 350 | 339 | 326 | -0.4 | 2.70 | 262 | 247 | -0.7 | 25,234 | 28,393 | 2787 | 68 |
| YORK | 5,467 | 5,486 | 5,325 | 0.0 | 2.48 | 3,915 | 3,794 | -0.4 | 37,738 | 43,388 | 873 | 9 |
| NEBRASKA | | | | 0.8 | 2.53 | | | 0.4 | 37,925 | 43,544 | | |
| UNITED STATES | | | | 1.4 | 2.59 | | | 1.1 | 41,914 | 49,127 | | |

| COUNTY | 2000 Per Capita Income | 2000 HH Income Base | 2000 HOUSEHOLD INCOME DISTRIBUTION (%) Less than $15,000 | $15,000 to $24,999 | $25,000 to $49,999 | $50,000 to $99,999 | $100,000 to $149,999 | $150,000 or More | 2000 AVERAGE DISPOSABLE INCOME BY AGE OF HOUSEHOLDER All Ages | <35 | 35-44 | 45-54 | 55-64 | 65+ |
|---|---|---|---|---|---|---|---|---|---|---|---|---|---|---|
| SAUNDERS | 16,271 | 7,238 | 12.1 | 15.1 | 42.7 | 26.5 | 3.2 | 0.5 | 32,806 | 30,400 | 36,298 | 40,400 | 35,579 | 23,651 |
| SCOTTS BLUFF | 15,062 | 14,105 | 21.2 | 18.4 | 37.3 | 19.8 | 2.5 | 0.9 | 28,804 | 24,517 | 35,003 | 35,800 | 31,848 | 20,111 |
| SEWARD | 15,648 | 5,745 | 12.6 | 14.5 | 42.3 | 27.0 | 3.0 | 0.5 | 32,953 | 28,364 | 37,798 | 42,748 | 35,950 | 23,736 |
| SHERIDAN | 15,258 | 2,477 | 30.1 | 20.9 | 32.6 | 11.8 | 3.4 | 1.3 | 25,431 | 20,634 | 31,472 | 31,869 | 27,307 | 19,208 |
| SHERMAN | 9,163 | 1,298 | 38.0 | 24.4 | 28.8 | 8.1 | 0.7 | 0.0 | 19,607 | 18,763 | 24,914 | 24,339 | 22,032 | 13,983 |
| SIOUX | 13,751 | 585 | 29.2 | 27.2 | 30.3 | 10.9 | 2.1 | 0.3 | 22,778 | 16,250 | 23,239 | 28,549 | 27,508 | 18,656 |
| STANTON | 12,139 | 2,167 | 19.3 | 21.4 | 39.9 | 18.4 | 1.1 | 0.0 | 26,742 | 22,966 | 32,447 | 33,279 | 26,698 | 18,177 |
| THAYER | 11,700 | 2,509 | 26.0 | 24.2 | 38.7 | 10.1 | 1.1 | 0.0 | 22,639 | 19,973 | 27,259 | 28,855 | 24,807 | 17,461 |
| THOMAS | 11,610 | 292 | 17.1 | 31.2 | 32.9 | 17.5 | 1.4 | 0.0 | 25,377 | 18,963 | 25,605 | 31,962 | 28,269 | 20,799 |
| THURSTON | 12,807 | 2,358 | 25.5 | 21.2 | 35.3 | 14.2 | 3.0 | 0.8 | 26,270 | 22,517 | 28,409 | 32,366 | 30,620 | 20,607 |
| VALLEY | 12,872 | 1,869 | 25.0 | 21.9 | 38.0 | 14.2 | 0.8 | 0.0 | 24,191 | 22,170 | 30,247 | 28,717 | 28,927 | 17,597 |
| WASHINGTON | 21,253 | 6,969 | 8.1 | 15.1 | 33.4 | 33.6 | 7.3 | 2.6 | 40,960 | 34,087 | 48,397 | 49,889 | 44,820 | 24,142 |
| WAYNE | 13,508 | 3,252 | 18.6 | 20.2 | 38.3 | 20.7 | 2.1 | 0.1 | 28,321 | 22,223 | 37,589 | 34,991 | 31,839 | 22,467 |
| WEBSTER | 12,121 | 1,639 | 29.7 | 23.0 | 33.4 | 12.8 | 0.7 | 0.4 | 22,786 | 20,509 | 29,925 | 28,204 | 25,836 | 16,265 |
| WHEELER | 11,256 | 339 | 25.4 | 24.2 | 39.2 | 10.3 | 0.6 | 0.3 | 23,119 | 15,833 | 27,487 | 29,113 | 22,895 | 20,201 |
| YORK | 17,235 | 5,486 | 10.5 | 16.2 | 43.1 | 25.5 | 4.0 | 0.8 | 33,487 | 29,088 | 37,538 | 40,688 | 39,334 | 25,305 |
| NEBRASKA | 19,393 | | 14.3 | 14.9 | 36.6 | 27.0 | 5.2 | 2.0 | 35,837 | 29,458 | 42,366 | 44,678 | 38,685 | 24,332 |
| UNITED STATES | 22,162 | | 14.5 | 12.5 | 32.3 | 29.8 | 7.4 | 3.5 | 40,748 | 34,503 | 44,969 | 49,579 | 43,409 | 27,339 |

| COUNTY | FINANCIAL SERVICES | | | | THE HOME | | | | | | ENTERTAINMENT | | | | | | PERSONAL | | | |
|---|---|---|---|---|---|---|---|---|---|---|---|---|---|---|---|---|---|---|---|---|
| | | | | | Home Improvements | | | Furnishings | | | | | | | | | | | | |
| | Auto Loan | Home Loan | Invest-ments | Retire-ment Plans | Home Repair | Lawn & Garden | Remodel-ing | Appli-ances | Elec-tronics | Furni-ture | Restau-rants | Sport-ing Goods | Theater & Concerts | Toys & Hobbies | Travel | Video Rental | Apparel | Auto After-market | Health Insur-ance | Pets & Supplies |
| SAUNDERS | 99 | 76 | 80 | 86 | 93 | 91 | 111 | 97 | 94 | 82 | 87 | 97 | 88 | 99 | 81 | 102 | 85 | 94 | 104 | 99 |
| SCOTTS BLUFF | 97 | 86 | 94 | 90 | 98 | 96 | 102 | 97 | 95 | 90 | 92 | 94 | 94 | 97 | 90 | 101 | 88 | 95 | 102 | 98 |
| SEWARD | 98 | 85 | 91 | 91 | 97 | 95 | 107 | 97 | 95 | 89 | 93 | 97 | 94 | 99 | 88 | 101 | 90 | 96 | 103 | 99 |
| SHERIDAN | 96 | 64 | 70 | 78 | 90 | 89 | 108 | 94 | 90 | 72 | 78 | 92 | 79 | 93 | 75 | 100 | 77 | 89 | 105 | 95 |
| SHERMAN | 97 | 63 | 70 | 79 | 90 | 89 | 109 | 95 | 90 | 71 | 78 | 94 | 80 | 94 | 75 | 100 | 77 | 89 | 106 | 96 |
| SIOUX | 101 | 63 | 68 | 83 | 89 | 90 | 113 | 97 | 89 | 68 | 78 | 101 | 80 | 99 | 74 | 101 | 78 | 90 | 109 | 100 |
| STANTON | 98 | 77 | 75 | 84 | 91 | 90 | 106 | 96 | 94 | 82 | 87 | 96 | 87 | 97 | 80 | 101 | 84 | 94 | 103 | 98 |
| THAYER | 98 | 63 | 69 | 80 | 90 | 89 | 110 | 95 | 90 | 71 | 78 | 96 | 80 | 95 | 75 | 100 | 77 | 89 | 107 | 97 |
| THOMAS | 101 | 63 | 68 | 83 | 89 | 90 | 113 | 97 | 89 | 68 | 78 | 101 | 80 | 99 | 74 | 101 | 78 | 90 | 109 | 100 |
| THURSTON | 93 | 68 | 71 | 76 | 92 | 88 | 103 | 93 | 87 | 76 | 76 | 90 | 81 | 90 | 79 | 98 | 78 | 88 | 100 | 92 |
| VALLEY | 96 | 64 | 70 | 78 | 90 | 89 | 108 | 94 | 90 | 72 | 78 | 92 | 79 | 93 | 75 | 100 | 77 | 89 | 105 | 95 |
| WASHINGTON | 101 | 86 | 88 | 93 | 96 | 95 | 111 | 99 | 98 | 90 | 95 | 99 | 96 | 102 | 88 | 103 | 92 | 98 | 103 | 102 |
| WAYNE | 95 | 70 | 75 | 81 | 91 | 88 | 108 | 92 | 89 | 74 | 81 | 91 | 81 | 93 | 77 | 98 | 79 | 89 | 103 | 95 |
| WEBSTER | 95 | 64 | 70 | 77 | 90 | 89 | 107 | 94 | 90 | 73 | 78 | 91 | 79 | 92 | 76 | 100 | 77 | 88 | 104 | 94 |
| WHEELER | 101 | 63 | 68 | 83 | 89 | 90 | 113 | 97 | 89 | 68 | 78 | 101 | 80 | 99 | 74 | 101 | 78 | 90 | 109 | 100 |
| YORK | 97 | 76 | 81 | 85 | 93 | 92 | 107 | 96 | 93 | 82 | 86 | 95 | 88 | 96 | 82 | 101 | 84 | 92 | 103 | 97 |
| NEBRASKA | 98 | 91 | 92 | 94 | 97 | 96 | 102 | 97 | 96 | 92 | 95 | 97 | 96 | 98 | 92 | 101 | 92 | 97 | 101 | 99 |
| UNITED STATES | 100 | 100 | 100 | 100 | 100 | 100 | 100 | 100 | 100 | 100 | 100 | 100 | 100 | 100 | 100 | 100 | 100 | 100 | 100 | 100 |

# POPULATION CHANGE

| COUNTY | FIPS Code | MSA Code | DMA Code | POPULATION 1990 | POPULATION 2000 | POPULATION 2005 | 1990-2000 ANNUAL CHANGE % Rate | 1990-2000 ANNUAL CHANGE State Rank | RACE (%) White 1990 | White 2000 | Black 1990 | Black 2000 | Asian/Pacific 1990 | Asian/Pacific 2000 |
|---|---|---|---|---|---|---|---|---|---|---|---|---|---|---|
| CHURCHILL | 001 | 0000 | 811 | 17,938 | 23,889 | 26,235 | 2.8 | 7 | 89.4 | 86.0 | 1.1 | 1.2 | 2.6 | 4.0 |
| CLARK | 003 | 4120 | 839 | 741,459 | 1,274,502 | 1,558,093 | 5.4 | 2 | 81.3 | 76.1 | 9.5 | 10.1 | 3.5 | 5.1 |
| DOUGLAS | 005 | 0000 | 811 | 27,637 | 38,350 | 42,184 | 3.2 | 5 | 94.5 | 92.5 | 0.3 | 0.4 | 1.3 | 1.9 |
| ELKO | 007 | 0000 | 770 | 33,530 | 45,981 | 47,783 | 3.1 | 6 | 86.4 | 82.1 | 0.8 | 0.7 | 0.8 | 1.2 |
| ESMERALDA | 009 | 0000 | 811 | 1,344 | 1,104 | 1,024 | -1.9 | 16 | 87.1 | 82.7 | 0.5 | 0.7 | 0.6 | 0.9 |
| EUREKA | 011 | 0000 | 751 | 1,547 | 1,896 | 2,028 | 2.0 | 10 | 93.2 | 90.7 | 0.3 | 0.5 | 0.7 | 1.0 |
| HUMBOLDT | 013 | 0000 | 811 | 12,844 | 18,179 | 19,567 | 3.4 | 4 | 83.8 | 78.0 | 0.6 | 0.7 | 0.5 | 0.7 |
| LANDER | 015 | 0000 | 811 | 6,266 | 6,603 | 6,215 | 0.5 | 14 | 90.4 | 87.0 | 0.1 | 0.1 | 0.3 | 0.3 |
| LINCOLN | 017 | 0000 | 839 | 3,775 | 4,280 | 4,541 | 1.2 | 12 | 94.2 | 91.0 | 2.1 | 3.5 | 0.4 | 0.5 |
| LYON | 019 | 0000 | 811 | 20,001 | 32,838 | 39,674 | 5.0 | 3 | 91.9 | 88.6 | 0.3 | 0.4 | 0.8 | 1.2 |
| MINERAL | 021 | 0000 | 811 | 6,475 | 5,003 | 4,302 | -2.5 | 17 | 79.4 | 74.8 | 5.4 | 7.3 | 1.1 | 1.5 |
| NYE | 023 | 4120 | 839 | 17,781 | 31,182 | 38,340 | 5.6 | 1 | 92.2 | 90.0 | 1.6 | 1.7 | 0.9 | 1.3 |
| PERSHING | 027 | 0000 | 811 | 4,336 | 4,822 | 4,936 | 1.0 | 13 | 86.8 | 79.0 | 0.3 | 4.1 | 0.6 | 0.8 |
| STOREY | 029 | 0000 | 811 | 2,526 | 3,035 | 3,271 | 1.8 | 11 | 94.6 | 92.4 | 0.3 | 0.5 | 1.1 | 1.6 |
| WASHOE | 031 | 6720 | 811 | 254,667 | 326,967 | 362,512 | 2.5 | 8 | 88.4 | 83.9 | 2.2 | 2.5 | 3.9 | 5.7 |
| WHITE PINE | 033 | 0000 | 770 | 9,264 | 9,735 | 9,213 | 0.5 | 14 | 91.3 | 87.1 | 2.0 | 3.8 | 0.4 | 0.6 |
| CARSON CITY | 510 | 0000 | 811 | 40,443 | 50,838 | 54,851 | 2.3 | 9 | 90.7 | 87.5 | 1.7 | 2.0 | 1.4 | 2.1 |
| NEVADA | | | | | | | 4.5 | | 84.3 | 79.0 | 6.6 | 7.5 | 3.2 | 4.7 |
| UNITED STATES | | | | | | | 1.0 | | 80.3 | 77.9 | 12.1 | 12.4 | 2.9 | 3.9 |

| COUNTY | % HISPANIC ORIGIN | | 2000 AGE DISTRIBUTION (%) | | | | | | | | | | MEDIAN AGE | | 2000 Males/ Females (×100) |
|---|---|---|---|---|---|---|---|---|---|---|---|---|---|---|---|
| | 1990 | 2000 | 0-4 | 5-9 | 10-14 | 15-19 | 20-24 | 25-44 | 45-64 | 65-84 | 85+ | 18+ | 1990 | 2000 | |
| CHURCHILL | 5.6 | 9.4 | 8.4 | 8.0 | 7.9 | 7.8 | 6.7 | 25.1 | 23.3 | 11.4 | 1.5 | 70.9 | 33.0 | 34.9 | 102.2 |
| CLARK | 11.2 | 18.5 | 7.9 | 7.7 | 7.5 | 6.6 | 6.1 | 30.3 | 22.6 | 10.4 | 0.9 | 73.0 | 33.1 | 35.1 | 102.1 |
| DOUGLAS | 6.0 | 10.3 | 7.1 | 7.5 | 8.1 | 6.5 | 4.5 | 25.8 | 25.9 | 13.5 | 1.1 | 73.0 | 36.2 | 39.4 | 103.3 |
| ELKO | 12.9 | 21.0 | 10.1 | 9.9 | 9.7 | 8.5 | 6.3 | 28.9 | 20.5 | 5.5 | 0.7 | 64.8 | 29.4 | 29.6 | 114.0 |
| ESMERALDA | 9.3 | 13.8 | 6.3 | 6.8 | 7.4 | 7.2 | 5.3 | 26.4 | 27.6 | 12.2 | 0.9 | 75.4 | 35.8 | 39.5 | 124.4 |
| EUREKA | 8.9 | 14.3 | 8.1 | 8.4 | 8.9 | 6.4 | 6.6 | 24.8 | 26.3 | 9.9 | 0.6 | 70.8 | 33.3 | 36.2 | 117.4 |
| HUMBOLDT | 18.2 | 28.7 | 9.1 | 9.3 | 9.3 | 8.3 | 6.6 | 28.1 | 21.7 | 7.1 | 0.6 | 67.1 | 30.6 | 31.3 | 115.2 |
| LANDER | 12.6 | 20.6 | 10.1 | 10.2 | 10.4 | 8.5 | 6.5 | 27.0 | 21.0 | 5.7 | 0.7 | 63.5 | 28.7 | 28.9 | 108.6 |
| LINCOLN | 4.1 | 7.9 | 7.8 | 7.9 | 9.3 | 12.9 | 5.3 | 18.3 | 20.8 | 15.8 | 1.9 | 64.8 | 33.4 | 33.0 | 113.9 |
| LYON | 7.6 | 12.8 | 7.6 | 7.8 | 8.1 | 7.8 | 5.8 | 21.5 | 25.1 | 15.0 | 1.4 | 71.3 | 36.4 | 38.9 | 104.8 |
| MINERAL | 8.4 | 12.6 | 8.0 | 7.8 | 8.3 | 9.3 | 5.0 | 21.4 | 22.3 | 16.2 | 1.7 | 69.7 | 33.9 | 37.3 | 108.6 |
| NYE | 7.0 | 11.3 | 6.7 | 6.6 | 7.0 | 6.0 | 4.5 | 21.9 | 26.5 | 19.7 | 1.0 | 75.7 | 36.5 | 42.9 | 115.0 |
| PERSHING | 15.3 | 22.8 | 9.7 | 9.1 | 9.0 | 7.7 | 6.3 | 25.9 | 21.6 | 9.5 | 1.3 | 67.4 | 31.7 | 32.1 | 116.2 |
| STOREY | 3.8 | 6.4 | 6.1 | 6.6 | 7.6 | 5.9 | 5.3 | 26.3 | 30.8 | 10.1 | 1.1 | 76.0 | 37.6 | 40.6 | 99.1 |
| WASHOE | 9.0 | 14.9 | 7.6 | 7.1 | 7.0 | 7.0 | 6.6 | 29.6 | 23.9 | 10.1 | 1.1 | 74.5 | 33.6 | 36.2 | 104.8 |
| WHITE PINE | 9.2 | 15.0 | 7.5 | 7.7 | 8.1 | 7.6 | 7.1 | 26.4 | 23.4 | 11.1 | 1.2 | 72.0 | 33.8 | 35.3 | 133.8 |
| CARSON CITY | 7.7 | 12.5 | 6.8 | 6.6 | 6.8 | 6.5 | 5.7 | 26.6 | 24.9 | 14.5 | 1.6 | 76.0 | 36.6 | 39.1 | 106.7 |
| NEVADA | 10.4 | 17.3 | 7.9 | 7.6 | 7.5 | 6.8 | 6.1 | 29.5 | 23.1 | 10.6 | 0.9 | 73.0 | 33.3 | 35.5 | 103.7 |
| UNITED STATES | 9.0 | 11.8 | 6.9 | 7.2 | 7.2 | 7.2 | 6.7 | 29.9 | 22.2 | 11.1 | 1.6 | 74.6 | 32.9 | 35.7 | 95.6 |

# HOUSEHOLDS

| COUNTY | HOUSEHOLDS 1990 | HOUSEHOLDS 2000 | HOUSEHOLDS 2005 | % Annual Rate 1990-2000 | 2000 Average HH Size | FAMILIES 1990 | FAMILIES 2000 | % Annual Rate 1990-2000 | MEDIAN HOUSEHOLD INCOME 2000 | 2005 | 2000 National Rank | 2000 State Rank |
|---|---|---|---|---|---|---|---|---|---|---|---|---|
| CHURCHILL | 6,666 | 9,103 | 10,109 | 3.8 | 2.57 | 4,791 | 6,317 | 3.4 | 43,883 | 55,767 | 403 | 8 |
| CLARK | 287,025 | 493,026 | 601,411 | 6.8 | 2.56 | 188,729 | 323,104 | 6.7 | 46,375 | 55,553 | 296 | 5 |
| DOUGLAS | 10,571 | 14,663 | 16,101 | 4.0 | 2.60 | 7,860 | 10,650 | 3.8 | 47,975 | 55,839 | 238 | 4 |
| ELKO | 11,777 | 16,990 | 18,057 | 4.5 | 2.67 | 8,486 | 11,900 | 4.2 | 53,669 | 65,801 | 139 | 2 |
| ESMERALDA | 588 | 486 | 452 | -2.3 | 2.26 | 348 | 273 | -2.9 | 34,565 | 41,522 | 1308 | 16 |
| EUREKA | 617 | 942 | 1,112 | 5.3 | 2.00 | 386 | 563 | 4.7 | 39,500 | 43,314 | 711 | 11 |
| HUMBOLDT | 4,538 | 6,966 | 7,777 | 5.3 | 2.57 | 3,224 | 4,787 | 4.9 | 50,742 | 65,069 | 192 | 3 |
| LANDER | 2,212 | 2,475 | 2,429 | 1.4 | 2.66 | 1,619 | 1,755 | 1.0 | 41,163 | 46,720 | 574 | 10 |
| LINCOLN | 1,325 | 1,517 | 1,632 | 1.7 | 2.59 | 907 | 995 | 1.1 | 24,483 | 27,697 | 2855 | 17 |
| LYON | 7,680 | 12,522 | 15,111 | 6.1 | 2.60 | 5,633 | 8,883 | 5.7 | 37,958 | 45,780 | 850 | 13 |
| MINERAL | 2,529 | 2,024 | 1,770 | -2.7 | 2.41 | 1,723 | 1,318 | -3.2 | 37,630 | 43,176 | 885 | 14 |
| NYE | 6,664 | 12,368 | 15,516 | 7.8 | 2.43 | 4,648 | 8,319 | 7.3 | 43,128 | 51,340 | 447 | 9 |
| PERSHING | 1,614 | 1,844 | 1,915 | 1.6 | 2.58 | 1,137 | 1,257 | 1.2 | 36,310 | 41,635 | 1066 | 15 |
| STOREY | 1,006 | 1,240 | 1,341 | 2.6 | 2.42 | 691 | 812 | 2.0 | 54,735 | 64,984 | 126 | 1 |
| WASHOE | 102,294 | 131,530 | 145,812 | 3.1 | 2.44 | 64,311 | 80,073 | 2.7 | 45,888 | 52,482 | 317 | 6 |
| WHITE PINE | 3,296 | 3,414 | 3,268 | 0.4 | 2.49 | 2,287 | 2,286 | 0.0 | 39,265 | 47,978 | 731 | 12 |
| CARSON CITY | 15,895 | 19,793 | 21,371 | 2.7 | 2.41 | 10,620 | 12,608 | 2.1 | 45,214 | 53,568 | 346 | 7 |
| NEVADA | | | | 5.6 | 2.54 | | | 5.4 | 46,090 | 54,726 | | |
| UNITED STATES | | | | 1.4 | 2.59 | | | 1.1 | 41,914 | 49,127 | | |

| COUNTY | 2000 Per Capita Income | 2000 HH Income Base | 2000 HOUSEHOLD INCOME DISTRIBUTION (%) Less than $15,000 | $15,000 to $24,999 | $25,000 to $49,999 | $50,000 to $99,999 | $100,000 to $149,999 | $150,000 or More | 2000 AVERAGE DISPOSABLE INCOME BY AGE OF HOUSEHOLDER All Ages | <35 | 35-44 | 45-54 | 55-64 | 65+ |
|---|---|---|---|---|---|---|---|---|---|---|---|---|---|---|
| CHURCHILL | 20,661 | 9,097 | 11.3 | 10.2 | 35.8 | 32.9 | 8.0 | 1.7 | 42,221 | 37,566 | 48,037 | 53,437 | 45,547 | 29,796 |
| CLARK | 24,150 | 493,026 | 9.6 | 11.5 | 33.2 | 34.0 | 8.5 | 3.2 | 45,910 | 40,272 | 49,704 | 54,174 | 47,219 | 32,761 |
| DOUGLAS | 27,221 | 14,663 | 7.1 | 11.4 | 33.7 | 34.1 | 9.5 | 4.3 | 49,194 | 42,277 | 49,508 | 56,740 | 52,888 | 36,139 |
| ELKO | 27,693 | 16,990 | 7.8 | 6.5 | 30.8 | 37.7 | 12.1 | 5.2 | 53,064 | 44,967 | 53,951 | 61,378 | 56,482 | 39,014 |
| ESMERALDA | 18,042 | 486 | 20.2 | 12.8 | 36.8 | 25.7 | 4.1 | 0.4 | 33,323 | 35,153 | 36,713 | 38,114 | 36,959 | 19,034 |
| EUREKA | 23,900 | 942 | 12.9 | 13.9 | 39.3 | 26.8 | 5.1 | 2.1 | 38,052 | 32,794 | 39,945 | 45,196 | 40,376 | 26,441 |
| HUMBOLDT | 24,197 | 6,966 | 9.4 | 5.7 | 34.0 | 39.0 | 9.8 | 2.1 | 46,608 | 42,366 | 50,326 | 56,125 | 46,443 | 33,239 |
| LANDER | 18,388 | 2,475 | 13.8 | 10.6 | 40.0 | 28.7 | 5.3 | 1.7 | 38,916 | 35,809 | 43,906 | 42,990 | 42,953 | 24,530 |
| LINCOLN | 10,554 | 1,516 | 32.2 | 19.0 | 35.0 | 12.4 | 0.9 | 0.5 | 24,797 | 26,744 | 26,422 | 37,680 | 28,840 | 15,218 |
| LYON | 17,843 | 12,522 | 13.9 | 15.7 | 36.3 | 28.6 | 4.3 | 1.3 | 36,986 | 36,531 | 41,276 | 44,737 | 41,786 | 24,689 |
| MINERAL | 16,051 | 2,024 | 21.3 | 10.6 | 39.9 | 26.5 | 1.6 | 0.1 | 32,284 | 31,850 | 41,757 | 38,409 | 37,510 | 21,853 |
| NYE | 24,390 | 12,368 | 12.0 | 12.0 | 37.2 | 29.0 | 6.9 | 3.0 | 42,783 | 42,779 | 48,376 | 56,595 | 45,975 | 26,711 |
| PERSHING | 16,347 | 1,836 | 16.6 | 10.7 | 43.3 | 24.7 | 3.8 | 1.0 | 34,760 | 33,192 | 39,578 | 44,351 | 35,262 | 21,333 |
| STOREY | 29,954 | 1,240 | 11.6 | 8.4 | 25.2 | 39.0 | 11.1 | 4.7 | 51,525 | 47,576 | 50,983 | 61,385 | 54,741 | 29,120 |
| WASHOE | 24,884 | 131,530 | 9.7 | 11.9 | 33.5 | 33.1 | 8.4 | 3.5 | 45,730 | 38,238 | 49,048 | 54,482 | 48,102 | 32,922 |
| WHITE PINE | 17,817 | 3,414 | 16.4 | 11.3 | 35.5 | 29.4 | 6.0 | 1.5 | 37,994 | 36,205 | 46,337 | 47,747 | 40,392 | 22,477 |
| CARSON CITY | 23,099 | 19,790 | 10.6 | 10.0 | 35.3 | 33.9 | 7.5 | 2.7 | 44,271 | 38,574 | 48,777 | 54,031 | 48,155 | 31,706 |
| NEVADA | 24,115 | | 9.8 | 11.4 | 33.5 | 33.7 | 8.4 | 3.2 | 45,641 | 39,906 | 49,413 | 54,160 | 47,414 | 32,251 |
| UNITED STATES | 22,162 | | 14.5 | 12.5 | 32.3 | 29.8 | 7.4 | 3.5 | 40,748 | 34,503 | 44,969 | 49,579 | 43,409 | 27,339 |

# SPENDING POTENTIAL INDEXES

| COUNTY | FINANCIAL SERVICES | | | | THE HOME | | | | | | ENTERTAINMENT | | | | | | PERSONAL | | | |
|---|---|---|---|---|---|---|---|---|---|---|---|---|---|---|---|---|---|---|---|---|
| | | | | | Home Improvements | | | Furnishings | | | | | | | | | | | | |
| | Auto Loan | Home Loan | Investments | Retirement Plans | Home Repair | Lawn & Garden | Remodeling | Appliances | Electronics | Furniture | Restaurants | Sporting Goods | Theater & Concerts | Toys & Hobbies | Travel | Video Rental | Apparel | Auto Aftermarket | Health Insurance | Pets & Supplies |
| CHURCHILL | 98 | 81 | 82 | 83 | 95 | 92 | 114 | 99 | 96 | 90 | 89 | 89 | 82 | 92 | 76 | 93 | 87 | 91 | 97 | 93 |
| CLARK | 101 | 105 | 91 | 99 | 101 | 101 | 99 | 102 | 104 | 106 | 105 | 96 | 95 | 95 | 91 | 95 | 102 | 101 | 95 | 96 |
| DOUGLAS | 103 | 107 | 98 | 105 | 104 | 106 | 105 | 105 | 107 | 109 | 109 | 98 | 99 | 99 | 95 | 96 | 108 | 105 | 99 | 98 |
| ELKO | 100 | 98 | 86 | 94 | 98 | 97 | 105 | 101 | 102 | 102 | 101 | 95 | 91 | 95 | 86 | 94 | 98 | 98 | 96 | 96 |
| ESMERALDA | 97 | 81 | 81 | 82 | 93 | 91 | 115 | 99 | 96 | 92 | 90 | 89 | 82 | 92 | 75 | 93 | 87 | 91 | 95 | 93 |
| EUREKA | 97 | 81 | 82 | 82 | 93 | 91 | 115 | 99 | 96 | 92 | 90 | 90 | 82 | 92 | 75 | 93 | 87 | 91 | 95 | 93 |
| HUMBOLDT | 97 | 87 | 86 | 86 | 96 | 94 | 109 | 99 | 97 | 95 | 93 | 90 | 85 | 92 | 80 | 93 | 90 | 93 | 96 | 93 |
| LANDER | 97 | 81 | 81 | 82 | 93 | 91 | 115 | 99 | 96 | 92 | 90 | 89 | 82 | 92 | 75 | 93 | 87 | 91 | 95 | 93 |
| LINCOLN | 95 | 71 | 81 | 78 | 94 | 93 | 109 | 97 | 94 | 82 | 81 | 84 | 77 | 87 | 74 | 92 | 80 | 87 | 100 | 89 |
| LYON | 97 | 80 | 84 | 83 | 95 | 94 | 110 | 99 | 96 | 89 | 88 | 89 | 82 | 91 | 77 | 93 | 85 | 91 | 99 | 92 |
| MINERAL | 96 | 86 | 89 | 85 | 99 | 96 | 103 | 98 | 95 | 94 | 91 | 87 | 86 | 91 | 83 | 92 | 88 | 92 | 97 | 91 |
| NYE | 98 | 85 | 102 | 87 | 101 | 102 | 104 | 101 | 93 | 91 | 91 | 90 | 87 | 92 | 85 | 91 | 84 | 91 | 103 | 93 |
| PERSHING | 96 | 85 | 86 | 84 | 95 | 93 | 108 | 98 | 95 | 92 | 91 | 88 | 83 | 91 | 79 | 92 | 87 | 91 | 95 | 92 |
| STOREY | 99 | 94 | 78 | 88 | 94 | 92 | 102 | 101 | 102 | 99 | 100 | 92 | 88 | 95 | 81 | 95 | 96 | 98 | 93 | 95 |
| WASHOE | 100 | 106 | 98 | 102 | 103 | 103 | 101 | 101 | 103 | 104 | 104 | 95 | 95 | 95 | 93 | 94 | 102 | 101 | 97 | 96 |
| WHITE PINE | 95 | 79 | 79 | 80 | 94 | 91 | 105 | 96 | 94 | 87 | 85 | 85 | 81 | 88 | 77 | 91 | 84 | 89 | 96 | 89 |
| CARSON CITY | 100 | 102 | 99 | 99 | 103 | 103 | 101 | 102 | 101 | 103 | 102 | 94 | 95 | 95 | 91 | 94 | 99 | 99 | 99 | 95 |
| NEVADA | 100 | 104 | 92 | 99 | 101 | 101 | 100 | 102 | 103 | 104 | 103 | 95 | 94 | 95 | 91 | 95 | 101 | 100 | 96 | 96 |
| UNITED STATES | 100 | 100 | 100 | 100 | 100 | 100 | 100 | 100 | 100 | 100 | 100 | 100 | 100 | 100 | 100 | 100 | 100 | 100 | 100 | 100 |

| COUNTY | FIPS Code | MSA Code | DMA Code | POPULATION 1990 | POPULATION 2000 | POPULATION 2005 | 1990-2000 ANNUAL CHANGE % Rate | 1990-2000 ANNUAL CHANGE State Rank | RACE (%) White 1990 | White 2000 | Black 1990 | Black 2000 | Asian/Pacific 1990 | Asian/Pacific 2000 |
|---|---|---|---|---|---|---|---|---|---|---|---|---|---|---|
| BELKNAP | 001 | 0000 | 506 | 49,216 | 54,353 | 57,727 | 1.0 | 3 | 99.1 | 98.9 | 0.1 | 0.2 | 0.4 | 0.6 |
| CARROLL | 003 | 0000 | 500 | 35,410 | 40,882 | 44,371 | 1.4 | 1 | 99.3 | 99.2 | 0.2 | 0.2 | 0.3 | 0.4 |
| CHESHIRE | 005 | 0000 | 506 | 70,121 | 72,673 | 74,078 | 0.3 | 9 | 99.0 | 98.7 | 0.3 | 0.3 | 0.4 | 0.6 |
| COOS | 007 | 0000 | 500 | 34,828 | 32,531 | 31,578 | -0.7 | 10 | 99.2 | 99.0 | 0.1 | 0.1 | 0.4 | 0.5 |
| GRAFTON | 009 | 0000 | 523 | 74,929 | 78,860 | 80,356 | 0.5 | 7 | 98.0 | 97.6 | 0.5 | 0.6 | 1.1 | 1.4 |
| HILLSBOROUGH | 011 | 1123 | 506 | 336,073 | 372,124 | 395,841 | 1.0 | 3 | 97.2 | 96.4 | 0.9 | 1.0 | 1.1 | 1.6 |
| MERRIMACK | 013 | 0000 | 506 | 120,005 | 131,524 | 139,577 | 0.9 | 5 | 98.8 | 98.4 | 0.4 | 0.5 | 0.5 | 0.7 |
| ROCKINGHAM | 015 | 1123 | 506 | 245,845 | 279,954 | 302,296 | 1.3 | 2 | 97.7 | 97.1 | 0.9 | 0.9 | 0.9 | 1.4 |
| STRAFFORD | 017 | 1123 | 506 | 104,233 | 111,668 | 116,575 | 0.7 | 6 | 98.2 | 97.7 | 0.6 | 0.5 | 0.9 | 1.3 |
| SULLIVAN | 019 | 0000 | 523 | 38,592 | 40,531 | 41,914 | 0.5 | 7 | 99.0 | 98.8 | 0.2 | 0.2 | 0.4 | 0.6 |
| NEW HAMPSHIRE | | | | | | | 0.9 | | 98.0 | 97.5 | 0.7 | 0.7 | 0.8 | 1.2 |
| UNITED STATES | | | | | | | 1.0 | | 80.3 | 77.9 | 12.1 | 12.4 | 2.9 | 3.9 |

# POPULATION COMPOSITION



| COUNTY | % HISPANIC ORIGIN | | 2000 AGE DISTRIBUTION (%) | | | | | | | | | | MEDIAN AGE | | 2000 Males/ Females (×100) |
|---|---|---|---|---|---|---|---|---|---|---|---|---|---|---|---|
| | 1990 | 2000 | 0-4 | 5-9 | 10-14 | 15-19 | 20-24 | 25-44 | 45-64 | 65-84 | 85+ | 18+ | 1990 | 2000 | |
| BELKNAP | 0.5 | 1.2 | 5.7 | 6.4 | 7.5 | 6.5 | 5.3 | 30.0 | 23.9 | 12.9 | 1.7 | 76.2 | 35.0 | 38.2 | 96.8 |
| CARROLL | 0.4 | 0.9 | 4.8 | 6.2 | 7.6 | 6.0 | 3.7 | 30.1 | 23.9 | 15.6 | 2.1 | 77.5 | 36.9 | 40.3 | 97.6 |
| CHESHIRE | 0.5 | 1.1 | 5.3 | 6.4 | 7.8 | 8.3 | 6.6 | 30.3 | 21.2 | 12.2 | 1.8 | 76.7 | 33.4 | 36.4 | 95.1 |
| COOS | 0.4 | 1.1 | 5.4 | 6.2 | 7.1 | 6.5 | 5.2 | 28.5 | 23.2 | 15.5 | 2.4 | 77.1 | 36.3 | 39.4 | 95.8 |
| GRAFTON | 0.8 | 1.6 | 5.2 | 6.1 | 7.0 | 9.3 | 8.5 | 28.9 | 21.9 | 11.5 | 1.7 | 78.1 | 32.2 | 35.7 | 98.3 |
| HILLSBOROUGH | 1.7 | 3.0 | 6.4 | 7.2 | 8.2 | 6.7 | 5.2 | 34.1 | 21.1 | 9.6 | 1.4 | 74.4 | 32.2 | 35.6 | 96.2 |
| MERRIMACK | 0.6 | 1.4 | 5.6 | 6.7 | 8.2 | 6.8 | 5.1 | 33.9 | 21.1 | 10.9 | 1.9 | 75.7 | 33.5 | 36.4 | 98.1 |
| ROCKINGHAM | 1.0 | 1.8 | 6.3 | 7.2 | 8.2 | 6.1 | 4.8 | 34.8 | 22.2 | 9.1 | 1.2 | 74.4 | 32.6 | 36.1 | 98.0 |
| STRAFFORD | 0.8 | 1.6 | 6.0 | 6.7 | 7.4 | 8.9 | 7.5 | 33.2 | 19.0 | 10.0 | 1.3 | 76.5 | 30.5 | 34.1 | 95.0 |
| SULLIVAN | 0.4 | 1.0 | 5.8 | 6.7 | 7.8 | 6.7 | 5.0 | 29.0 | 23.7 | 13.4 | 1.8 | 75.5 | 35.3 | 38.2 | 98.4 |
| NEW HAMPSHIRE | 1.0 | 1.9 | 6.0 | 6.9 | 8.0 | 7.0 | 5.6 | 33.0 | 21.6 | 10.6 | 1.5 | 75.4 | 32.8 | 36.1 | 96.9 |
| UNITED STATES | 9.0 | 11.8 | 6.9 | 7.2 | 7.2 | 7.2 | 6.7 | 29.9 | 22.2 | 11.1 | 1.6 | 74.6 | 32.9 | 35.7 | 95.6 |

| COUNTY | HOUSEHOLDS | | | | | FAMILIES | | | MEDIAN HOUSEHOLD INCOME | | | |
|---|---|---|---|---|---|---|---|---|---|---|---|---|
| | 1990 | 2000 | 2005 | % Annual Rate 1990-2000 | 2000 Average HH Size | 1990 | 2000 | % Annual Rate 1990-2000 | 2000 | 2005 | 2000 National Rank | 2000 State Rank |
| BELKNAP | 18,839 | 21,046 | 22,669 | 1.4 | 2.51 | 13,334 | 14,393 | 0.9 | 41,665 | 50,297 | 540 | 5 |
| CARROLL | 14,253 | 16,692 | 18,264 | 1.9 | 2.42 | 9,866 | 11,135 | 1.5 | 35,701 | 40,658 | 1137 | 9 |
| CHESHIRE | 25,856 | 27,637 | 28,652 | 0.8 | 2.49 | 18,155 | 18,716 | 0.4 | 41,355 | 50,007 | 559 | 6 |
| COOS | 13,799 | 13,430 | 13,302 | -0.3 | 2.38 | 9,608 | 8,985 | -0.8 | 33,993 | 40,275 | 1396 | 10 |
| GRAFTON | 27,542 | 29,815 | 30,827 | 1.0 | 2.45 | 18,544 | 19,283 | 0.5 | 40,301 | 45,551 | 647 | 8 |
| HILLSBOROUGH | 124,567 | 143,799 | 156,035 | 1.8 | 2.55 | 88,473 | 99,041 | 1.4 | 48,279 | 57,926 | 233 | 2 |
| MERRIMACK | 44,595 | 49,832 | 53,669 | 1.4 | 2.53 | 31,801 | 34,322 | 0.9 | 45,804 | 54,613 | 321 | 3 |
| ROCKINGHAM | 89,118 | 104,827 | 114,899 | 2.0 | 2.65 | 65,939 | 75,000 | 1.6 | 56,962 | 66,846 | 102 | 1 |
| STRAFFORD | 37,744 | 41,812 | 44,374 | 1.2 | 2.52 | 26,231 | 27,939 | 0.8 | 44,308 | 53,708 | 382 | 4 |
| SULLIVAN | 14,873 | 16,109 | 16,889 | 1.0 | 2.49 | 10,650 | 11,172 | 0.6 | 40,338 | 49,459 | 643 | 7 |
| NEW HAMPSHIRE | | | | 1.5 | 2.54 | | | 1.1 | 46,866 | 55,884 | | |
| UNITED STATES | | | | 1.4 | 2.59 | | | 1.1 | 41,914 | 49,127 | | |

| COUNTY | 2000 Per Capita Income | 2000 HH Income Base | 2000 HOUSEHOLD INCOME DISTRIBUTION (%) Less than $15,000 | $15,000 to $24,999 | $25,000 to $49,999 | $50,000 to $99,999 | $100,000 to $149,999 | $150,000 or More | 2000 AVERAGE DISPOSABLE INCOME BY AGE OF HOUSEHOLDER All Ages | <35 | 35-44 | 45-54 | 55-64 | 65+ |
|---|---|---|---|---|---|---|---|---|---|---|---|---|---|---|
| BELKNAP | 20,442 | 21,046 | 10.9 | 13.4 | 36.8 | 31.0 | 6.0 | 1.9 | 38,307 | 37,339 | 42,828 | 45,076 | 42,782 | 24,796 |
| CARROLL | 18,679 | 16,692 | 14.8 | 16.5 | 37.0 | 26.1 | 4.1 | 1.5 | 33,881 | 33,193 | 37,282 | 38,912 | 39,182 | 24,883 |
| CHESHIRE | 20,003 | 27,637 | 11.8 | 11.8 | 37.4 | 31.0 | 6.0 | 2.0 | 38,192 | 36,901 | 42,850 | 47,239 | 43,638 | 24,419 |
| COOS | 16,667 | 13,430 | 19.6 | 15.2 | 39.6 | 21.4 | 3.3 | 1.0 | 30,831 | 32,197 | 38,662 | 37,092 | 35,845 | 17,803 |
| GRAFTON | 20,555 | 29,815 | 13.5 | 12.7 | 36.8 | 27.7 | 6.7 | 2.6 | 38,587 | 36,280 | 42,733 | 46,407 | 44,104 | 24,830 |
| HILLSBOROUGH | 23,250 | 143,799 | 10.3 | 9.1 | 32.8 | 37.1 | 8.1 | 2.7 | 43,359 | 41,260 | 47,060 | 52,891 | 46,188 | 25,018 |
| MERRIMACK | 23,132 | 49,832 | 9.5 | 10.7 | 35.2 | 34.4 | 7.6 | 2.6 | 42,013 | 40,317 | 47,106 | 48,673 | 46,174 | 26,365 |
| ROCKINGHAM | 27,832 | 104,827 | 6.2 | 6.5 | 28.5 | 41.5 | 12.4 | 4.9 | 51,548 | 48,258 | 54,850 | 60,804 | 52,452 | 30,840 |
| STRAFFORD | 20,351 | 41,812 | 10.3 | 10.7 | 36.9 | 34.5 | 6.1 | 1.5 | 39,323 | 38,406 | 43,258 | 48,033 | 43,510 | 24,154 |
| SULLIVAN | 19,254 | 16,109 | 13.6 | 11.2 | 39.6 | 30.2 | 4.6 | 0.8 | 35,410 | 35,691 | 40,994 | 43,554 | 37,855 | 22,962 |
| NEW HAMPSHIRE | 23,086 | | 10.2 | 9.9 | 33.7 | 35.2 | 8.1 | 2.8 | 42,879 | 41,111 | 47,248 | 51,660 | 46,004 | 25,721 |
| UNITED STATES | 22,162 | | 14.5 | 12.5 | 32.3 | 29.8 | 7.4 | 3.5 | 40,748 | 34,503 | 44,969 | 49,579 | 43,409 | 27,339 |

| COUNTY | FINANCIAL SERVICES | | | | THE HOME | | | | | | ENTERTAINMENT | | | | | | PERSONAL | | | |
|---|---|---|---|---|---|---|---|---|---|---|---|---|---|---|---|---|---|---|---|---|
| | | | | | Home Improvements | | | Furnishings | | | | | | | | | | | | |
| | Auto Loan | Home Loan | Invest-ments | Retire-ment Plans | Home Repair | Lawn & Garden | Remodel-ing | Appli-ances | Elec-tronics | Furni-ture | Restau-rants | Sport-ing Goods | Theater & Concerts | Toys & Hobbies | Travel | Video Rental | Apparel | Auto After-market | Health Insur-ance | Pets & Supplies |
| BELKNAP | 100 | 86 | 87 | 91 | 89 | 88 | 102 | 98 | 96 | 91 | 94 | 100 | 93 | 103 | 86 | 100 | 96 | 94 | 103 | 103 |
| CARROLL | 102 | 76 | 82 | 89 | 87 | 88 | 112 | 99 | 93 | 83 | 86 | 102 | 88 | 103 | 81 | 100 | 91 | 91 | 107 | 104 |
| CHESHIRE | 100 | 88 | 93 | 91 | 91 | 89 | 99 | 97 | 95 | 93 | 95 | 99 | 95 | 102 | 88 | 99 | 97 | 94 | 102 | 103 |
| COOS | 97 | 75 | 82 | 82 | 90 | 87 | 100 | 96 | 90 | 84 | 85 | 95 | 87 | 98 | 82 | 97 | 87 | 88 | 103 | 99 |
| GRAFTON | 100 | 86 | 91 | 92 | 90 | 89 | 102 | 97 | 95 | 90 | 93 | 99 | 93 | 102 | 87 | 99 | 95 | 94 | 103 | 103 |
| HILLSBOROUGH | 102 | 103 | 96 | 102 | 93 | 94 | 93 | 100 | 102 | 104 | 107 | 105 | 104 | 105 | 96 | 101 | 108 | 102 | 100 | 105 |
| MERRIMACK | 101 | 97 | 95 | 98 | 92 | 93 | 96 | 99 | 100 | 99 | 102 | 102 | 100 | 105 | 93 | 101 | 104 | 99 | 102 | 104 |
| ROCKINGHAM | 104 | 106 | 97 | 104 | 93 | 96 | 94 | 102 | 104 | 107 | 111 | 107 | 106 | 108 | 97 | 102 | 112 | 105 | 101 | 107 |
| STRAFFORD | 98 | 91 | 89 | 90 | 89 | 88 | 93 | 96 | 95 | 93 | 96 | 98 | 94 | 100 | 87 | 98 | 96 | 94 | 99 | 101 |
| SULLIVAN | 100 | 80 | 86 | 88 | 89 | 88 | 103 | 97 | 94 | 88 | 90 | 98 | 91 | 101 | 83 | 99 | 92 | 92 | 103 | 102 |
| NEW HAMPSHIRE | 102 | 97 | 94 | 98 | 92 | 92 | 96 | 99 | 100 | 100 | 102 | 103 | 100 | 105 | 93 | 101 | 104 | 99 | 101 | 104 |
| UNITED STATES | 100 | 100 | 100 | 100 | 100 | 100 | 100 | 100 | 100 | 100 | 100 | 100 | 100 | 100 | 100 | 100 | 100 | 100 | 100 | 100 |

# POPULATION CHANGE

| COUNTY | FIPS Code | MSA Code | DMA Code | POPULATION 1990 | POPULATION 2000 | POPULATION 2005 | 1990-2000 ANNUAL CHANGE % Rate | 1990-2000 ANNUAL CHANGE State Rank | RACE (%) White 1990 | White 2000 | Black 1990 | Black 2000 | Asian/Pacific 1990 | Asian/Pacific 2000 |
|---|---|---|---|---|---|---|---|---|---|---|---|---|---|---|
| ATLANTIC | 001 | 0560 | 504 | 224,327 | 241,221 | 249,284 | 0.7 | 10 | 76.7 | 71.7 | 17.4 | 19.5 | 2.1 | 3.6 |
| BERGEN | 003 | 0875 | 501 | 825,380 | 860,210 | 875,706 | 0.4 | 13 | 87.0 | 81.5 | 4.9 | 5.4 | 6.6 | 11.0 |
| BURLINGTON | 005 | 6160 | 504 | 395,066 | 427,078 | 440,301 | 0.8 | 9 | 82.2 | 78.3 | 14.3 | 16.2 | 2.1 | 3.5 |
| CAMDEN | 007 | 6160 | 504 | 502,824 | 502,318 | 498,403 | 0.0 | 18 | 76.6 | 71.1 | 16.2 | 18.2 | 2.3 | 3.9 |
| CAPE MAY | 009 | 0560 | 504 | 95,089 | 98,054 | 98,255 | 0.3 | 14 | 92.6 | 90.7 | 5.6 | 6.6 | 0.6 | 1.1 |
| CUMBERLAND | 011 | 8760 | 504 | 138,053 | 139,808 | 138,286 | 0.1 | 16 | 73.5 | 68.2 | 16.9 | 18.5 | 0.8 | 1.4 |
| ESSEX | 013 | 5640 | 501 | 778,206 | 745,190 | 734,462 | -0.4 | 21 | 51.1 | 46.4 | 40.6 | 42.2 | 2.7 | 4.3 |
| GLOUCESTER | 015 | 6160 | 504 | 230,082 | 252,760 | 264,006 | 0.9 | 8 | 89.3 | 86.5 | 8.7 | 10.2 | 1.2 | 2.2 |
| HUDSON | 017 | 3640 | 501 | 553,099 | 554,254 | 554,446 | 0.0 | 18 | 68.8 | 63.3 | 14.4 | 14.4 | 6.6 | 9.7 |
| HUNTERDON | 019 | 5015 | 501 | 107,776 | 126,538 | 136,523 | 1.6 | 2 | 96.3 | 95.0 | 2.1 | 2.2 | 1.3 | 2.3 |
| MERCER | 021 | 8480 | 504 | 325,824 | 335,522 | 343,737 | 0.3 | 14 | 75.1 | 70.1 | 18.9 | 20.8 | 3.1 | 5.0 |
| MIDDLESEX | 023 | 5015 | 501 | 671,780 | 723,375 | 750,040 | 0.7 | 10 | 81.9 | 75.8 | 8.0 | 8.7 | 6.7 | 10.8 |
| MONMOUTH | 025 | 5190 | 501 | 553,124 | 619,804 | 657,283 | 1.1 | 4 | 87.4 | 83.8 | 8.5 | 9.6 | 2.8 | 4.7 |
| MORRIS | 027 | 5640 | 501 | 421,353 | 468,445 | 492,507 | 1.0 | 6 | 91.8 | 88.1 | 3.0 | 3.3 | 4.0 | 6.8 |
| OCEAN | 029 | 5190 | 501 | 433,203 | 504,961 | 542,320 | 1.5 | 3 | 95.3 | 93.6 | 2.8 | 3.3 | 0.9 | 1.6 |
| PASSAIC | 031 | 0875 | 501 | 453,060 | 486,831 | 495,368 | 0.7 | 10 | 71.9 | 64.0 | 14.6 | 17.1 | 2.6 | 4.0 |
| SALEM | 033 | 6160 | 504 | 65,294 | 64,680 | 63,345 | -0.1 | 20 | 83.3 | 80.0 | 14.7 | 17.0 | 0.6 | 1.0 |
| SOMERSET | 035 | 5015 | 501 | 240,279 | 294,732 | 325,580 | 2.0 | 1 | 88.0 | 83.5 | 6.2 | 7.0 | 4.4 | 7.5 |
| SUSSEX | 037 | 5640 | 501 | 130,943 | 146,083 | 153,053 | 1.1 | 4 | 97.6 | 96.6 | 0.9 | 1.1 | 0.9 | 1.6 |
| UNION | 039 | 5640 | 501 | 493,819 | 499,102 | 500,981 | 0.1 | 16 | 74.4 | 69.8 | 18.8 | 20.2 | 2.8 | 4.5 |
| WARREN | 041 | 5640 | 501 | 91,607 | 101,420 | 107,042 | 1.0 | 6 | 97.2 | 96.1 | 1.4 | 1.7 | 0.8 | 1.4 |
| NEW JERSEY | | | | | | | 0.6 | | 79.3 | 75.3 | 13.4 | 14.1 | 3.5 | 5.7 |
| UNITED STATES | | | | | | | 1.0 | | 80.3 | 77.9 | 12.1 | 12.4 | 2.9 | 3.9 |

| COUNTY | % HISPANIC ORIGIN | | 2000 AGE DISTRIBUTION (%) | | | | | | | | | | MEDIAN AGE | | 2000 Males/ Females (×100) |
|---|---|---|---|---|---|---|---|---|---|---|---|---|---|---|---|
| | 1990 | 2000 | 0-4 | 5-9 | 10-14 | 15-19 | 20-24 | 25-44 | 45-64 | 65-84 | 85+ | 18+ | 1990 | 2000 | |
| ATLANTIC | 7.2 | 10.5 | 7.1 | 7.3 | 6.8 | 6.3 | 6.0 | 31.0 | 21.5 | 12.3 | 1.9 | 75.4 | 34.0 | 36.6 | 93.0 |
| BERGEN | 6.0 | 8.8 | 5.5 | 6.1 | 6.6 | 5.7 | 5.1 | 29.6 | 25.5 | 13.9 | 2.0 | 78.3 | 37.6 | 40.1 | 93.2 |
| BURLINGTON | 3.2 | 4.9 | 6.8 | 7.7 | 7.0 | 6.6 | 6.0 | 31.1 | 22.2 | 11.1 | 1.4 | 74.9 | 33.0 | 36.1 | 97.3 |
| CAMDEN | 7.2 | 10.5 | 7.5 | 7.9 | 7.6 | 6.8 | 6.0 | 30.3 | 21.4 | 11.0 | 1.4 | 72.9 | 32.8 | 35.3 | 92.9 |
| CAPE MAY | 2.0 | 3.3 | 6.4 | 7.0 | 6.7 | 5.9 | 4.6 | 27.2 | 23.1 | 16.7 | 2.5 | 76.5 | 37.7 | 39.9 | 94.0 |
| CUMBERLAND | 13.3 | 18.6 | 7.3 | 8.0 | 7.5 | 6.9 | 6.1 | 29.5 | 21.3 | 11.7 | 1.6 | 73.1 | 33.3 | 35.3 | 97.0 |
| ESSEX | 12.6 | 16.8 | 6.9 | 7.4 | 7.2 | 6.8 | 6.4 | 30.9 | 22.1 | 10.7 | 1.6 | 74.7 | 33.4 | 35.9 | 90.1 |
| GLOUCESTER | 1.8 | 3.0 | 7.2 | 7.9 | 7.5 | 7.1 | 6.2 | 30.3 | 22.1 | 10.4 | 1.2 | 73.3 | 32.5 | 35.4 | 94.4 |
| HUDSON | 33.2 | 41.6 | 6.8 | 6.5 | 6.3 | 6.0 | 7.1 | 34.7 | 20.9 | 10.3 | 1.4 | 77.0 | 33.1 | 35.4 | 96.4 |
| HUNTERDON | 1.6 | 2.7 | 6.1 | 7.4 | 7.8 | 6.2 | 4.8 | 30.0 | 27.3 | 9.2 | 1.2 | 74.9 | 35.2 | 38.2 | 98.0 |
| MERCER | 6.0 | 8.6 | 6.4 | 7.1 | 6.7 | 7.1 | 6.7 | 30.3 | 22.5 | 11.5 | 1.6 | 76.2 | 34.1 | 36.7 | 94.0 |
| MIDDLESEX | 8.9 | 12.5 | 6.5 | 6.8 | 6.4 | 6.5 | 6.6 | 32.3 | 22.0 | 11.7 | 1.3 | 77.1 | 33.4 | 36.6 | 96.2 |
| MONMOUTH | 4.1 | 6.2 | 6.6 | 7.6 | 7.4 | 6.3 | 5.1 | 30.3 | 23.9 | 11.1 | 1.7 | 74.6 | 35.0 | 37.7 | 94.3 |
| MORRIS | 4.7 | 6.9 | 5.9 | 6.8 | 7.2 | 6.1 | 4.9 | 30.9 | 26.3 | 10.5 | 1.4 | 76.4 | 35.3 | 38.4 | 95.2 |
| OCEAN | 3.2 | 5.2 | 6.4 | 7.1 | 6.7 | 5.7 | 4.6 | 26.1 | 20.6 | 19.4 | 3.4 | 76.3 | 38.5 | 40.7 | 90.4 |
| PASSAIC | 21.7 | 30.0 | 7.3 | 7.5 | 7.1 | 6.7 | 6.5 | 30.9 | 21.5 | 10.8 | 1.6 | 74.3 | 33.4 | 35.6 | 93.6 |
| SALEM | 2.2 | 3.5 | 6.4 | 6.9 | 6.8 | 6.9 | 6.3 | 27.7 | 24.3 | 12.8 | 1.9 | 75.7 | 35.1 | 37.8 | 93.6 |
| SOMERSET | 4.2 | 6.3 | 6.5 | 7.1 | 6.9 | 5.5 | 4.6 | 33.3 | 24.5 | 10.2 | 1.4 | 76.1 | 34.8 | 38.0 | 96.4 |
| SUSSEX | 2.2 | 3.7 | 7.6 | 8.8 | 8.4 | 6.6 | 4.7 | 32.2 | 22.9 | 7.6 | 1.2 | 71.1 | 32.9 | 35.7 | 98.9 |
| UNION | 13.7 | 19.0 | 6.2 | 6.6 | 6.9 | 6.1 | 5.6 | 30.0 | 23.5 | 13.2 | 1.9 | 76.7 | 35.8 | 38.4 | 92.9 |
| WARREN | 1.9 | 3.3 | 7.0 | 7.7 | 7.6 | 6.6 | 5.3 | 29.3 | 23.7 | 11.2 | 1.7 | 73.7 | 34.4 | 37.2 | 93.4 |
| NEW JERSEY | 9.6 | 12.9 | 6.6 | 7.1 | 7.0 | 6.3 | 5.8 | 30.7 | 22.9 | 11.9 | 1.7 | 75.7 | 34.5 | 37.2 | 94.1 |
| UNITED STATES | 9.0 | 11.8 | 6.9 | 7.2 | 7.2 | 7.2 | 6.7 | 29.9 | 22.2 | 11.1 | 1.6 | 74.6 | 32.9 | 35.7 | 95.6 |

| COUNTY | HOUSEHOLDS | | | | | FAMILIES | | | MEDIAN HOUSEHOLD INCOME | | | |
|---|---|---|---|---|---|---|---|---|---|---|---|---|
| | 1990 | 2000 | 2005 | % Annual Rate 1990-2000 | 2000 Average HH Size | 1990 | 2000 | % Annual Rate 1990-2000 | 2000 | 2005 | 2000 National Rank | 2000 State Rank |
| ATLANTIC | 85,123 | 92,100 | 95,447 | 1.0 | 2.55 | 56,576 | 58,479 | 0.4 | 43,911 | 52,059 | 400 | 18 |
| BERGEN | 308,880 | 327,873 | 336,901 | 0.7 | 2.60 | 225,188 | 231,501 | 0.3 | 64,460 | 71,123 | 41 | 5 |
| BURLINGTON | 136,554 | 147,770 | 153,168 | 1.0 | 2.77 | 104,190 | 108,769 | 0.5 | 58,129 | 68,085 | 88 | 8 |
| CAMDEN | 178,758 | 181,029 | 180,839 | 0.2 | 2.73 | 129,568 | 126,588 | -0.3 | 45,962 | 54,129 | 311 | 15 |
| CAPE MAY | 37,856 | 39,316 | 39,480 | 0.5 | 2.43 | 25,667 | 25,430 | -0.1 | 42,372 | 53,243 | 479 | 19 |
| CUMBERLAND | 47,118 | 48,019 | 47,708 | 0.2 | 2.76 | 34,966 | 34,646 | -0.1 | 40,597 | 48,628 | 620 | 21 |
| ESSEX | 278,752 | 268,713 | 265,970 | -0.4 | 2.70 | 191,363 | 179,984 | -0.7 | 44,727 | 51,811 | 364 | 16 |
| GLOUCESTER | 78,845 | 86,960 | 91,058 | 1.2 | 2.86 | 60,808 | 64,994 | 0.8 | 56,010 | 67,525 | 110 | 10 |
| HUDSON | 208,739 | 212,031 | 213,634 | 0.2 | 2.57 | 136,143 | 137,005 | 0.1 | 40,632 | 49,862 | 617 | 20 |
| HUNTERDON | 37,906 | 45,098 | 49,028 | 2.1 | 2.73 | 29,295 | 33,775 | 1.7 | 77,246 | 88,878 | 7 | 2 |
| MERCER | 116,941 | 120,657 | 123,765 | 0.4 | 2.65 | 82,447 | 81,968 | -0.1 | 57,353 | 66,076 | 98 | 9 |
| MIDDLESEX | 238,833 | 263,286 | 276,026 | 1.2 | 2.66 | 175,451 | 187,295 | 0.8 | 59,439 | 70,334 | 78 | 7 |
| MONMOUTH | 197,570 | 223,169 | 237,497 | 1.5 | 2.73 | 145,892 | 159,991 | 1.1 | 63,727 | 75,443 | 45 | 6 |
| MORRIS | 148,751 | 168,827 | 179,194 | 1.5 | 2.73 | 113,074 | 125,088 | 1.2 | 71,310 | 78,558 | 9 | 3 |
| OCEAN | 168,147 | 197,670 | 213,113 | 2.0 | 2.52 | 120,783 | 136,245 | 1.5 | 49,782 | 58,311 | 204 | 13 |
| PASSAIC | 155,269 | 168,437 | 172,030 | 1.0 | 2.83 | 115,135 | 122,189 | 0.7 | 48,795 | 61,002 | 223 | 14 |
| SALEM | 23,794 | 23,894 | 23,632 | 0.1 | 2.63 | 17,645 | 17,140 | -0.4 | 44,454 | 50,016 | 375 | 17 |
| SOMERSET | 88,346 | 110,797 | 123,600 | 2.8 | 2.62 | 65,368 | 79,496 | 2.4 | 77,881 | 86,718 | 5 | 1 |
| SUSSEX | 44,456 | 49,793 | 52,276 | 1.4 | 2.90 | 35,516 | 38,675 | 1.0 | 67,517 | 83,928 | 24 | 4 |
| UNION | 180,076 | 184,306 | 186,210 | 0.3 | 2.67 | 131,260 | 130,638 | -0.1 | 54,277 | 61,655 | 132 | 12 |
| WARREN | 33,997 | 37,473 | 39,471 | 1.2 | 2.68 | 25,011 | 26,552 | 0.7 | 55,521 | 68,045 | 117 | 11 |
| NEW JERSEY | | | | 0.9 | 2.67 | | | 0.5 | 55,149 | 64,448 | | |
| UNITED STATES | | | | 1.4 | 2.59 | | | 1.1 | 41,914 | 49,127 | | |

| COUNTY | 2000 Per Capita Income | 2000 HH Income Base | 2000 HOUSEHOLD INCOME DISTRIBUTION (%) | | | | | | 2000 AVERAGE DISPOSABLE INCOME BY AGE OF HOUSEHOLDER | | | | | |
|---|---|---|---|---|---|---|---|---|---|---|---|---|---|---|
| | | | Less than $15,000 | $15,000 to $24,999 | $25,000 to $49,999 | $50,000 to $99,999 | $100,000 to $149,999 | $150,000 or More | All Ages | <35 | 35-44 | 45-54 | 55-64 | 65+ |
| ATLANTIC | 23,175 | 92,100 | 13.1 | 11.1 | 32.8 | 31.9 | 7.4 | 3.7 | 39,084 | 37,268 | 43,020 | 46,785 | 44,130 | 23,828 |
| BERGEN | 38,272 | 327,873 | 7.3 | 6.1 | 22.5 | 37.3 | 14.9 | 11.8 | 59,315 | 51,444 | 58,588 | 65,815 | 64,006 | 38,135 |
| BURLINGTON | 27,277 | 147,770 | 5.3 | 6.6 | 28.4 | 41.8 | 12.6 | 5.4 | 48,668 | 44,335 | 51,560 | 56,856 | 53,439 | 31,539 |
| CAMDEN | 22,499 | 181,027 | 12.7 | 10.1 | 32.1 | 33.1 | 8.3 | 3.8 | 40,377 | 37,410 | 43,881 | 47,804 | 44,907 | 24,858 |
| CAPE MAY | 24,522 | 39,316 | 12.3 | 12.4 | 33.6 | 29.8 | 7.9 | 4.1 | 39,334 | 38,040 | 45,306 | 50,610 | 43,838 | 24,503 |
| CUMBERLAND | 18,416 | 48,019 | 16.3 | 11.4 | 34.4 | 30.2 | 5.9 | 1.9 | 34,529 | 32,797 | 39,167 | 42,556 | 37,576 | 22,275 |
| ESSEX | 25,882 | 268,709 | 16.6 | 11.1 | 27.5 | 28.9 | 9.2 | 6.7 | 43,762 | 36,236 | 45,286 | 48,679 | 47,881 | 30,302 |
| GLOUCESTER | 24,187 | 86,960 | 7.8 | 7.0 | 27.5 | 42.5 | 11.7 | 3.5 | 44,795 | 43,895 | 48,755 | 52,850 | 47,920 | 26,773 |
| HUDSON | 20,807 | 212,030 | 17.0 | 11.8 | 32.2 | 29.3 | 7.1 | 2.7 | 36,115 | 37,215 | 38,510 | 40,693 | 40,037 | 22,770 |
| HUNTERDON | 38,628 | 45,098 | 3.9 | 3.4 | 17.4 | 41.3 | 20.3 | 13.6 | 66,383 | 56,917 | 65,585 | 73,568 | 64,443 | 38,265 |
| MERCER | 30,226 | 120,657 | 8.7 | 8.1 | 25.9 | 36.7 | 12.7 | 8.0 | 51,142 | 44,893 | 53,475 | 59,467 | 54,620 | 32,462 |
| MIDDLESEX | 26,997 | 263,285 | 7.4 | 6.1 | 25.4 | 42.9 | 13.5 | 4.7 | 47,946 | 46,537 | 50,739 | 56,312 | 53,782 | 29,995 |
| MONMOUTH | 33,538 | 223,169 | 7.5 | 5.8 | 22.8 | 38.9 | 14.9 | 10.2 | 56,549 | 49,597 | 58,049 | 64,648 | 60,404 | 32,234 |
| MORRIS | 38,500 | 168,827 | 4.4 | 4.1 | 20.3 | 41.1 | 17.2 | 12.9 | 63,862 | 53,199 | 61,140 | 68,682 | 67,678 | 40,753 |
| OCEAN | 25,501 | 197,669 | 10.4 | 10.0 | 29.9 | 36.9 | 9.1 | 3.8 | 41,537 | 44,957 | 49,812 | 53,328 | 47,149 | 26,044 |
| PASSAIC | 22,981 | 168,434 | 12.7 | 9.6 | 29.0 | 34.9 | 9.7 | 4.2 | 42,108 | 40,149 | 44,093 | 48,870 | 48,411 | 26,552 |
| SALEM | 20,449 | 23,894 | 14.0 | 10.3 | 33.4 | 34.2 | 6.3 | 1.9 | 36,413 | 35,638 | 43,314 | 43,118 | 39,541 | 22,106 |
| SOMERSET | 43,347 | 110,797 | 3.7 | 3.3 | 17.2 | 40.2 | 20.6 | 15.0 | 69,039 | 59,909 | 66,809 | 72,074 | 69,669 | 42,805 |
| SUSSEX | 29,350 | 49,793 | 5.5 | 3.3 | 19.7 | 47.9 | 16.9 | 6.7 | 54,196 | 52,329 | 54,620 | 60,874 | 57,137 | 31,225 |
| UNION | 29,511 | 184,305 | 10.3 | 8.1 | 26.8 | 35.6 | 12.1 | 7.2 | 48,698 | 44,511 | 50,637 | 54,985 | 55,954 | 31,485 |
| WARREN | 25,819 | 37,473 | 9.9 | 6.0 | 26.7 | 41.5 | 11.8 | 4.1 | 45,097 | 44,342 | 50,468 | 52,844 | 49,372 | 25,905 |
| NEW JERSEY | 28,926 | | 9.9 | 7.9 | 26.5 | 36.6 | 12.1 | 7.0 | 48,859 | 44,187 | 51,112 | 56,303 | 53,799 | 30,415 |
| UNITED STATES | 22,162 | | 14.5 | 12.5 | 32.3 | 29.8 | 7.4 | 3.5 | 40,748 | 34,503 | 44,969 | 49,579 | 43,409 | 27,339 |

# SPENDING POTENTIAL INDEXES

| COUNTY | FINANCIAL SERVICES | | | | THE HOME | | | | | | ENTERTAINMENT | | | | | | PERSONAL | | | |
|---|---|---|---|---|---|---|---|---|---|---|---|---|---|---|---|---|---|---|---|---|
| | | | | | Home Improvements | | | Furnishings | | | | | | | | | | | | |
| | Auto Loan | Home Loan | Invest-ments | Retire-ment Plans | Home Repair | Lawn & Garden | Remodel-ing | Appli-ances | Elec-tronics | Furni-ture | Restau-rants | Sport-ing Goods | Theater & Concerts | Toys & Hobbies | Travel | Video Rental | Apparel | Auto After-market | Health Insur-ance | Pets & Supplies |
| ATLANTIC | 98 | 94 | 96 | 93 | 94 | 92 | 89 | 98 | 95 | 99 | 98 | 99 | 98 | 100 | 94 | 100 | 101 | 97 | 99 | 101 |
| BERGEN | 106 | 129 | 127 | 127 | 108 | 114 | 96 | 105 | 112 | 119 | 123 | 113 | 124 | 111 | 123 | 105 | 128 | 117 | 108 | 110 |
| BURLINGTON | 102 | 104 | 100 | 103 | 95 | 97 | 92 | 101 | 102 | 106 | 109 | 105 | 106 | 106 | 99 | 101 | 111 | 103 | 102 | 105 |
| CAMDEN | 100 | 101 | 101 | 100 | 96 | 96 | 90 | 99 | 99 | 104 | 103 | 102 | 104 | 103 | 99 | 100 | 106 | 101 | 100 | 102 |
| CAPE MAY | 102 | 84 | 95 | 95 | 92 | 95 | 105 | 101 | 95 | 91 | 93 | 102 | 95 | 104 | 90 | 100 | 96 | 94 | 108 | 104 |
| CUMBERLAND | 96 | 86 | 91 | 86 | 93 | 89 | 93 | 96 | 91 | 95 | 92 | 95 | 94 | 98 | 90 | 98 | 94 | 92 | 100 | 98 |
| ESSEX | 100 | 108 | 116 | 109 | 102 | 102 | 89 | 100 | 100 | 109 | 101 | 104 | 109 | 100 | 112 | 102 | 111 | 105 | 98 | 101 |
| GLOUCESTER | 102 | 99 | 96 | 99 | 93 | 94 | 93 | 100 | 100 | 103 | 105 | 104 | 103 | 105 | 95 | 101 | 107 | 100 | 101 | 104 |
| HUDSON | 96 | 102 | 96 | 90 | 100 | 93 | 85 | 95 | 91 | 108 | 96 | 98 | 100 | 91 | 107 | 102 | 101 | 98 | 96 | 97 |
| HUNTERDON | 110 | 123 | 113 | 125 | 101 | 109 | 100 | 108 | 115 | 121 | 127 | 117 | 123 | 116 | 114 | 105 | 133 | 117 | 107 | 113 |
| MERCER | 103 | 109 | 111 | 111 | 100 | 102 | 92 | 102 | 103 | 109 | 109 | 107 | 111 | 106 | 107 | 102 | 113 | 105 | 102 | 105 |
| MIDDLESEX | 103 | 111 | 107 | 108 | 98 | 100 | 91 | 101 | 104 | 109 | 112 | 107 | 109 | 106 | 105 | 102 | 113 | 106 | 103 | 106 |
| MONMOUTH | 106 | 117 | 115 | 118 | 101 | 107 | 96 | 104 | 108 | 114 | 117 | 112 | 117 | 110 | 111 | 103 | 121 | 110 | 105 | 108 |
| MORRIS | 109 | 131 | 123 | 130 | 106 | 114 | 99 | 107 | 116 | 123 | 130 | 117 | 127 | 115 | 122 | 106 | 135 | 121 | 108 | 113 |
| OCEAN | 102 | 95 | 103 | 99 | 95 | 97 | 95 | 101 | 98 | 99 | 101 | 102 | 102 | 105 | 96 | 100 | 102 | 98 | 106 | 104 |
| PASSAIC | 101 | 109 | 112 | 106 | 101 | 101 | 92 | 100 | 100 | 111 | 106 | 105 | 109 | 102 | 109 | 102 | 110 | 105 | 101 | 103 |
| SALEM | 98 | 86 | 94 | 90 | 93 | 90 | 95 | 97 | 94 | 94 | 93 | 97 | 95 | 101 | 90 | 98 | 96 | 93 | 101 | 100 |
| SOMERSET | 109 | 127 | 117 | 126 | 104 | 112 | 98 | 107 | 114 | 120 | 127 | 116 | 124 | 114 | 118 | 105 | 132 | 118 | 107 | 111 |
| SUSSEX | 107 | 111 | 104 | 112 | 96 | 100 | 97 | 104 | 108 | 113 | 117 | 111 | 113 | 111 | 103 | 104 | 120 | 110 | 103 | 109 |
| UNION | 102 | 113 | 118 | 112 | 103 | 105 | 91 | 101 | 103 | 112 | 110 | 106 | 113 | 104 | 113 | 103 | 115 | 108 | 103 | 104 |
| WARREN | 101 | 98 | 98 | 99 | 94 | 94 | 94 | 100 | 100 | 102 | 104 | 103 | 103 | 105 | 96 | 100 | 106 | 100 | 102 | 104 |
| NEW JERSEY | 103 | 111 | 111 | 111 | 100 | 103 | 93 | 102 | 104 | 110 | 110 | 107 | 111 | 106 | 109 | 102 | 114 | 107 | 103 | 105 |
| UNITED STATES | 100 | 100 | 100 | 100 | 100 | 100 | 100 | 100 | 100 | 100 | 100 | 100 | 100 | 100 | 100 | 100 | 100 | 100 | 100 | 100 |

| COUNTY | FIPS Code | MSA Code | DMA Code | POPULATION 1990 | POPULATION 2000 | POPULATION 2005 | 1990-2000 ANNUAL CHANGE % Rate | 1990-2000 ANNUAL CHANGE State Rank | RACE (%) White 1990 | White 2000 | Black 1990 | Black 2000 | Asian/Pacific 1990 | Asian/Pacific 2000 |
|---|---|---|---|---|---|---|---|---|---|---|---|---|---|---|
| BERNALILLO | 001 | 0200 | 790 | 480,577 | 523,500 | 523,518 | 0.8 | 20 | 76.9 | 74.2 | 2.7 | 3.4 | 1.5 | 2.3 |
| CATRON | 003 | 0000 | 790 | 2,563 | 2,924 | 3,205 | 1.3 | 11 | 97.9 | 97.9 | 0.3 | 0.3 | 0.1 | 0.1 |
| CHAVES | 005 | 0000 | 790 | 57,849 | 62,400 | 62,422 | 0.7 | 21 | 82.6 | 80.7 | 2.1 | 2.6 | 0.5 | 0.7 |
| CIBOLA | 006 | 0000 | 790 | 23,794 | 27,272 | 29,170 | 1.3 | 11 | 58.4 | 57.7 | 0.8 | 0.8 | 0.3 | 0.5 |
| COLFAX | 007 | 0000 | 790 | 12,925 | 13,683 | 13,728 | 0.6 | 22 | 82.8 | 81.6 | 0.3 | 0.5 | 0.2 | 0.2 |
| CURRY | 009 | 0000 | 634 | 42,207 | 42,501 | 40,576 | 0.1 | 26 | 75.6 | 71.8 | 6.9 | 7.7 | 1.9 | 2.9 |
| DE BACA | 011 | 0000 | 790 | 2,252 | 2,364 | 2,387 | 0.5 | 23 | 93.6 | 93.5 | 0.1 | 0.0 | 0.0 | 0.0 |
| DONA ANA | 013 | 4100 | 765 | 135,510 | 172,519 | 183,394 | 2.4 | 6 | 91.1 | 90.2 | 1.6 | 1.8 | 0.9 | 1.3 |
| EDDY | 015 | 0000 | 790 | 48,605 | 53,089 | 52,922 | 0.9 | 18 | 81.5 | 79.4 | 1.7 | 2.2 | 0.4 | 0.7 |
| GRANT | 017 | 0000 | 790 | 27,676 | 31,409 | 31,767 | 1.2 | 13 | 93.0 | 92.4 | 0.5 | 0.6 | 0.2 | 0.4 |
| GUADALUPE | 019 | 0000 | 790 | 4,156 | 3,995 | 3,857 | -0.4 | 30 | 74.0 | 73.2 | 0.3 | 0.5 | 0.7 | 0.9 |
| HARDING | 021 | 0000 | 790 | 987 | 827 | 754 | -1.7 | 33 | 79.7 | 78.2 | 0.2 | 0.2 | 0.1 | 0.1 |
| HIDALGO | 023 | 0000 | 790 | 5,958 | 5,939 | 5,517 | 0.0 | 28 | 91.6 | 90.8 | 0.2 | 0.2 | 0.6 | 1.0 |
| LEA | 025 | 0000 | 790 | 55,765 | 54,383 | 51,092 | -0.2 | 29 | 82.2 | 80.6 | 4.7 | 5.2 | 0.4 | 0.5 |
| LINCOLN | 027 | 0000 | 790 | 12,219 | 17,194 | 19,294 | 3.4 | 4 | 91.5 | 90.9 | 0.5 | 0.6 | 0.2 | 0.3 |
| LOS ALAMOS | 028 | 7490 | 790 | 18,115 | 18,300 | 18,349 | 0.1 | 26 | 94.2 | 93.0 | 0.5 | 0.6 | 2.4 | 3.3 |
| LUNA | 029 | 0000 | 790 | 18,110 | 24,801 | 27,037 | 3.1 | 5 | 90.0 | 88.9 | 1.4 | 1.9 | 0.3 | 0.4 |
| MCKINLEY | 031 | 0000 | 790 | 60,686 | 66,853 | 66,503 | 0.9 | 18 | 21.9 | 21.1 | 0.5 | 0.6 | 0.4 | 0.6 |
| MORA | 033 | 0000 | 790 | 4,264 | 5,015 | 5,405 | 1.6 | 10 | 56.8 | 56.2 | 0.0 | 0.0 | 0.1 | 0.1 |
| OTERO | 035 | 0000 | 790 | 51,928 | 53,976 | 52,892 | 0.4 | 24 | 79.6 | 77.4 | 5.3 | 5.5 | 1.9 | 2.7 |
| QUAY | 037 | 0000 | 634 | 10,823 | 9,753 | 9,177 | -1.0 | 32 | 74.2 | 71.9 | 1.4 | 2.0 | 0.4 | 0.5 |
| RIO ARRIBA | 039 | 0000 | 790 | 34,365 | 38,442 | 39,921 | 1.1 | 15 | 70.8 | 70.2 | 0.4 | 0.5 | 0.2 | 0.3 |
| ROOSEVELT | 041 | 0000 | 634 | 16,702 | 17,140 | 16,609 | 0.3 | 25 | 79.7 | 77.4 | 1.3 | 1.4 | 0.6 | 0.8 |
| SANDOVAL | 043 | 0200 | 790 | 63,319 | 92,589 | 104,489 | 3.8 | 3 | 68.6 | 65.7 | 1.5 | 1.9 | 0.8 | 1.2 |
| SAN JUAN | 045 | 0000 | 790 | 91,605 | 112,771 | 127,304 | 2.0 | 8 | 56.6 | 54.2 | 0.5 | 0.6 | 0.2 | 0.4 |
| SAN MIGUEL | 047 | 0000 | 790 | 25,743 | 28,414 | 28,045 | 1.0 | 17 | 63.7 | 62.4 | 0.7 | 0.9 | 0.6 | 0.9 |
| SANTA FE | 049 | 7490 | 790 | 98,928 | 126,029 | 135,058 | 2.4 | 6 | 80.3 | 78.8 | 0.6 | 0.9 | 0.5 | 0.8 |
| SIERRA | 051 | 0000 | 790 | 9,912 | 11,042 | 11,260 | 1.1 | 15 | 93.4 | 92.6 | 0.4 | 0.6 | 0.1 | 0.2 |
| SOCORRO | 053 | 0000 | 790 | 14,764 | 16,609 | 17,232 | 1.2 | 13 | 77.4 | 75.8 | 0.8 | 0.8 | 1.4 | 2.0 |
| TAOS | 055 | 0000 | 790 | 23,118 | 27,510 | 29,424 | 1.7 | 9 | 73.0 | 72.0 | 0.3 | 0.4 | 0.4 | 0.5 |
| TORRANCE | 057 | 0000 | 790 | 10,285 | 17,024 | 20,040 | 5.0 | 1 | 87.0 | 85.6 | 0.4 | 0.6 | 0.2 | 0.3 |
| UNION | 059 | 0000 | 634 | 4,124 | 3,840 | 3,726 | -0.7 | 31 | 96.2 | 95.9 | 0.0 | 0.0 | 0.1 | 0.1 |
| VALENCIA | 061 | 0200 | 790 | 45,235 | 66,814 | 75,460 | 3.9 | 2 | 77.5 | 75.7 | 1.1 | 1.3 | 0.4 | 0.7 |
| NEW MEXICO | | | | | | | 1.4 | | 75.6 | 73.8 | 2.0 | 2.3 | 0.9 | 1.3 |
| UNITED STATES | | | | | | | 1.0 | | 80.3 | 77.9 | 12.1 | 12.4 | 2.9 | 3.9 |

# POPULATION COMPOSITION

## B

| COUNTY | % HISPANIC ORIGIN | | 2000 AGE DISTRIBUTION (%) | | | | | | | | | | MEDIAN AGE | | 2000 Males/ Females (×100) |
|---|---|---|---|---|---|---|---|---|---|---|---|---|---|---|---|
| | 1990 | 2000 | 0-4 | 5-9 | 10-14 | 15-19 | 20-24 | 25-44 | 45-64 | 65-84 | 85+ | 18+ | 1990 | 2000 | |
| BERNALILLO | 37.1 | 40.3 | 6.7 | 6.9 | 7.1 | 7.5 | 7.1 | 29.9 | 23.1 | 10.3 | 1.3 | 74.9 | 32.2 | 36.2 | 95.0 |
| CATRON | 28.4 | 30.5 | 5.2 | 6.1 | 7.2 | 7.3 | 4.4 | 21.8 | 28.9 | 17.4 | 1.8 | 76.4 | 37.8 | 43.8 | 113.7 |
| CHAVES | 36.8 | 39.9 | 7.4 | 7.9 | 8.2 | 9.8 | 6.7 | 23.9 | 21.7 | 12.5 | 1.9 | 70.7 | 31.8 | 35.0 | 97.9 |
| CIBOLA | 34.1 | 34.4 | 7.8 | 8.4 | 9.0 | 8.8 | 7.1 | 26.0 | 21.3 | 10.5 | 1.1 | 69.2 | 29.4 | 32.5 | 95.4 |
| COLFAX | 47.9 | 50.8 | 6.1 | 6.6 | 7.6 | 9.2 | 5.3 | 23.2 | 25.2 | 14.4 | 2.4 | 73.5 | 35.5 | 39.7 | 100.1 |
| CURRY | 23.7 | 27.5 | 8.2 | 8.3 | 8.2 | 8.6 | 7.8 | 27.9 | 19.9 | 9.5 | 1.6 | 70.2 | 29.0 | 31.8 | 95.6 |
| DE BACA | 32.7 | 35.2 | 5.2 | 6.6 | 6.7 | 7.4 | 4.1 | 20.4 | 26.6 | 19.0 | 4.1 | 76.4 | 40.8 | 44.7 | 96.2 |
| DONA ANA | 56.4 | 59.2 | 8.1 | 7.9 | 8.0 | 9.4 | 9.7 | 27.1 | 19.8 | 8.8 | 1.0 | 71.0 | 27.9 | 30.5 | 98.8 |
| EDDY | 35.3 | 38.3 | 7.0 | 7.8 | 8.3 | 8.6 | 6.2 | 24.3 | 22.9 | 12.8 | 2.1 | 71.3 | 33.4 | 36.6 | 97.1 |
| GRANT | 50.8 | 53.5 | 6.9 | 7.5 | 8.2 | 8.9 | 6.8 | 23.0 | 23.6 | 13.3 | 1.7 | 72.0 | 33.2 | 36.6 | 97.5 |
| GUADALUPE | 84.3 | 85.7 | 7.4 | 7.6 | 8.1 | 8.6 | 6.8 | 25.1 | 22.4 | 12.3 | 1.8 | 71.1 | 32.3 | 35.6 | 99.1 |
| HARDING | 46.7 | 50.1 | 5.6 | 5.7 | 7.7 | 7.7 | 4.7 | 20.0 | 25.9 | 19.7 | 3.0 | 75.5 | 38.3 | 44.0 | 103.7 |
| HIDALGO | 50.1 | 52.3 | 7.7 | 8.0 | 9.0 | 9.0 | 7.0 | 25.2 | 21.7 | 10.7 | 1.6 | 69.1 | 30.7 | 33.2 | 101.0 |
| LEA | 29.8 | 32.2 | 7.8 | 8.5 | 9.0 | 9.2 | 6.7 | 25.3 | 21.5 | 10.6 | 1.4 | 68.9 | 30.2 | 33.1 | 98.0 |
| LINCOLN | 28.0 | 30.1 | 5.5 | 6.4 | 6.9 | 7.0 | 5.1 | 23.6 | 28.9 | 15.0 | 1.6 | 76.8 | 37.1 | 42.1 | 99.4 |
| LOS ALAMOS | 11.1 | 12.4 | 4.8 | 5.7 | 7.1 | 7.1 | 4.3 | 24.4 | 33.2 | 12.4 | 0.9 | 77.3 | 37.8 | 43.1 | 101.4 |
| LUNA | 47.6 | 51.2 | 7.1 | 7.4 | 8.2 | 8.3 | 6.0 | 20.7 | 23.6 | 16.6 | 2.0 | 71.7 | 36.7 | 38.7 | 93.1 |
| MCKINLEY | 12.8 | 13.4 | 10.2 | 10.7 | 10.8 | 9.6 | 7.2 | 26.8 | 17.8 | 6.2 | 0.8 | 62.2 | 25.4 | 26.2 | 93.2 |
| MORA | 85.0 | 86.0 | 6.9 | 7.5 | 7.4 | 9.2 | 6.6 | 24.4 | 23.2 | 13.1 | 1.9 | 72.5 | 33.8 | 36.6 | 101.2 |
| OTERO | 23.8 | 26.8 | 8.5 | 8.0 | 7.9 | 7.7 | 7.8 | 27.8 | 20.6 | 10.6 | 1.0 | 71.0 | 29.0 | 32.6 | 101.1 |
| QUAY | 37.5 | 40.1 | 5.9 | 6.6 | 7.3 | 7.8 | 5.1 | 22.7 | 26.7 | 15.4 | 2.5 | 75.0 | 37.0 | 41.3 | 95.1 |
| RIO ARRIBA | 72.6 | 73.5 | 8.6 | 8.3 | 8.7 | 9.0 | 7.1 | 27.0 | 21.5 | 8.7 | 1.2 | 68.7 | 29.9 | 32.1 | 98.3 |
| ROOSEVELT | 27.2 | 30.5 | 7.2 | 7.2 | 7.4 | 10.8 | 8.6 | 26.7 | 19.3 | 11.2 | 1.6 | 73.7 | 28.8 | 32.0 | 97.2 |
| SANDOVAL | 27.4 | 29.8 | 8.5 | 9.1 | 8.9 | 7.7 | 5.5 | 29.7 | 20.3 | 9.3 | 1.0 | 68.5 | 30.8 | 33.6 | 96.4 |
| SAN JUAN | 13.1 | 14.2 | 8.6 | 9.6 | 9.9 | 9.2 | 6.8 | 26.6 | 20.4 | 8.0 | 0.9 | 65.9 | 28.1 | 30.2 | 96.4 |
| SAN MIGUEL | 79.6 | 80.9 | 7.8 | 7.6 | 7.9 | 10.3 | 8.2 | 26.3 | 21.1 | 9.4 | 1.4 | 71.0 | 30.5 | 32.3 | 99.8 |
| SANTA FE | 49.5 | 52.2 | 6.3 | 6.5 | 7.1 | 7.5 | 6.5 | 28.9 | 26.3 | 9.8 | 1.2 | 75.6 | 34.3 | 38.0 | 96.0 |
| SIERRA | 24.0 | 26.3 | 5.0 | 5.3 | 5.4 | 5.6 | 4.1 | 16.8 | 26.4 | 27.4 | 3.9 | 80.6 | 51.0 | 51.5 | 98.5 |
| SOCORRO | 47.8 | 50.1 | 7.4 | 7.7 | 8.3 | 9.4 | 8.0 | 26.5 | 21.7 | 9.8 | 1.2 | 71.2 | 30.0 | 33.0 | 103.0 |
| TAOS | 64.9 | 66.8 | 6.8 | 7.2 | 7.7 | 8.4 | 6.2 | 26.3 | 25.6 | 10.3 | 1.3 | 73.0 | 33.9 | 37.2 | 97.0 |
| TORRANCE | 37.8 | 41.0 | 7.0 | 7.9 | 8.7 | 8.7 | 5.9 | 26.1 | 24.9 | 9.6 | 1.2 | 70.3 | 32.7 | 36.2 | 103.0 |
| UNION | 33.7 | 36.3 | 6.6 | 7.3 | 7.6 | 8.0 | 4.3 | 21.6 | 25.9 | 16.0 | 2.6 | 73.1 | 37.0 | 41.2 | 96.5 |
| VALENCIA | 50.3 | 53.6 | 7.7 | 8.1 | 8.5 | 8.3 | 6.3 | 27.4 | 23.3 | 9.4 | 1.0 | 70.3 | 31.5 | 34.9 | 100.0 |
| NEW MEXICO | 38.2 | 41.2 | 7.4 | 7.7 | 8.0 | 8.3 | 7.1 | 27.5 | 22.4 | 10.3 | 1.3 | 71.9 | 31.3 | 34.8 | 96.8 |
| UNITED STATES | 9.0 | 11.8 | 6.9 | 7.2 | 7.2 | 7.2 | 6.7 | 29.9 | 22.2 | 11.1 | 1.6 | 74.6 | 32.9 | 35.7 | 95.6 |

| COUNTY | HOUSEHOLDS | | | | | FAMILIES | | | MEDIAN HOUSEHOLD INCOME | | | |
|---|---|---|---|---|---|---|---|---|---|---|---|---|
| | 1990 | 2000 | 2005 | % Annual Rate 1990-2000 | 2000 Average HH Size | 1990 | 2000 | % Annual Rate 1990-2000 | 2000 | 2005 | 2000 National Rank | 2000 State Rank |
| BERNALILLO | 185,582 | 208,729 | 211,901 | 1.4 | 2.47 | 124,794 | 136,418 | 1.1 | 40,521 | 45,975 | 625 | 4 |
| CATRON | 1,010 | 1,204 | 1,347 | 2.2 | 2.43 | 722 | 829 | 1.7 | 26,552 | 31,403 | 2645 | 22 |
| CHAVES | 20,589 | 22,400 | 22,579 | 1.0 | 2.70 | 15,165 | 16,082 | 0.7 | 28,504 | 34,126 | 2365 | 18 |
| CIBOLA | 7,292 | 8,439 | 9,119 | 1.8 | 3.11 | 5,796 | 6,592 | 1.6 | 25,245 | 27,157 | 2784 | 25 |
| COLFAX | 4,959 | 5,336 | 5,385 | 0.9 | 2.50 | 3,558 | 3,723 | 0.6 | 31,803 | 39,537 | 1759 | 10 |
| CURRY | 15,113 | 16,157 | 15,841 | 0.8 | 2.58 | 11,466 | 12,005 | 0.6 | 31,019 | 36,879 | 1928 | 13 |
| DE BACA | 913 | 990 | 1,014 | 1.0 | 2.34 | 643 | 672 | 0.5 | 24,667 | 30,042 | 2842 | 28 |
| DONA ANA | 45,029 | 59,353 | 64,098 | 3.4 | 2.83 | 33,228 | 43,154 | 3.2 | 29,240 | 34,541 | 2260 | 17 |
| EDDY | 17,472 | 19,598 | 19,766 | 1.4 | 2.68 | 13,272 | 14,596 | 1.2 | 32,630 | 38,154 | 1606 | 9 |
| GRANT | 9,773 | 11,598 | 12,034 | 2.1 | 2.63 | 7,428 | 8,665 | 1.9 | 31,127 | 36,231 | 1910 | 12 |
| GUADALUPE | 1,520 | 1,509 | 1,484 | -0.1 | 2.63 | 1,136 | 1,136 | 0.0 | 21,307 | 26,765 | 3058 | 33 |
| HARDING | 396 | 365 | 349 | -1.0 | 2.27 | 273 | 242 | -1.5 | 26,696 | 33,173 | 2618 | 21 |
| HIDALGO | 2,004 | 2,131 | 2,040 | 0.7 | 2.73 | 1,545 | 1,614 | 0.5 | 35,815 | 42,721 | 1124 | 6 |
| LEA | 19,306 | 19,647 | 18,877 | 0.2 | 2.72 | 14,933 | 14,897 | 0.0 | 31,412 | 35,744 | 1837 | 11 |
| LINCOLN | 4,789 | 6,974 | 7,960 | 4.7 | 2.41 | 3,441 | 4,861 | 4.3 | 27,654 | 30,548 | 2488 | 19 |
| LOS ALAMOS | 7,213 | 7,562 | 7,718 | 0.6 | 2.41 | 5,318 | 5,395 | 0.2 | 70,764 | 78,660 | 12 | 1 |
| LUNA | 6,797 | 9,568 | 10,563 | 4.2 | 2.57 | 4,895 | 6,740 | 4.0 | 22,291 | 27,184 | 3010 | 30 |
| MCKINLEY | 16,588 | 18,830 | 19,002 | 1.5 | 3.51 | 13,364 | 14,990 | 1.4 | 25,362 | 31,576 | 2772 | 24 |
| MORA | 1,519 | 1,818 | 1,977 | 2.2 | 2.75 | 1,127 | 1,360 | 2.3 | 21,759 | 25,805 | 3037 | 32 |
| OTERO | 18,155 | 19,479 | 19,286 | 0.9 | 2.71 | 13,948 | 14,530 | 0.5 | 30,577 | 36,918 | 2013 | 14 |
| QUAY | 4,238 | 3,956 | 3,790 | -0.8 | 2.44 | 3,061 | 2,798 | -1.1 | 22,075 | 24,167 | 3024 | 31 |
| RIO ARRIBA | 11,461 | 13,008 | 13,604 | 1.5 | 2.93 | 8,835 | 10,114 | 1.7 | 30,430 | 38,403 | 2051 | 15 |
| ROOSEVELT | 5,991 | 6,642 | 6,582 | 1.3 | 2.45 | 4,156 | 4,495 | 1.0 | 25,933 | 31,905 | 2718 | 23 |
| SANDOVAL | 20,867 | 31,336 | 35,807 | 5.1 | 2.95 | 16,614 | 24,193 | 4.7 | 46,559 | 55,521 | 289 | 2 |
| SAN JUAN | 28,740 | 34,771 | 38,906 | 2.3 | 3.22 | 22,726 | 26,781 | 2.0 | 33,060 | 38,219 | 1528 | 8 |
| SAN MIGUEL | 8,701 | 9,797 | 9,820 | 1.4 | 2.71 | 6,405 | 7,252 | 1.5 | 29,378 | 37,209 | 2239 | 16 |
| SANTA FE | 37,840 | 49,825 | 54,229 | 3.4 | 2.47 | 25,041 | 32,206 | 3.1 | 44,836 | 51,080 | 359 | 3 |
| SIERRA | 4,428 | 5,077 | 5,245 | 1.7 | 2.11 | 2,834 | 3,094 | 1.1 | 25,006 | 29,395 | 2810 | 27 |
| SOCORRO | 5,217 | 5,962 | 6,247 | 1.6 | 2.70 | 3,705 | 4,145 | 1.4 | 26,868 | 31,811 | 2604 | 20 |
| TAOS | 8,752 | 10,773 | 11,711 | 2.6 | 2.55 | 6,131 | 7,511 | 2.5 | 25,182 | 29,151 | 2793 | 26 |
| TORRANCE | 3,670 | 6,033 | 7,307 | 6.2 | 2.68 | 2,785 | 4,466 | 5.9 | 33,091 | 41,735 | 1523 | 7 |
| UNION | 1,615 | 1,574 | 1,562 | -0.3 | 2.40 | 1,150 | 1,084 | -0.7 | 23,700 | 31,639 | 2924 | 29 |
| VALENCIA | 15,170 | 23,574 | 27,238 | 5.5 | 2.77 | 11,992 | 18,274 | 5.2 | 37,929 | 47,865 | 851 | 5 |
| NEW MEXICO | | | | 2.1 | 2.67 | | | 1.8 | 35,131 | 41,077 | | |
| UNITED STATES | | | | 1.4 | 2.59 | | | 1.1 | 41,914 | 49,127 | | |

| COUNTY | 2000 Per Capita Income | 2000 HH Income Base | 2000 HOUSEHOLD INCOME DISTRIBUTION (%) | | | | | | 2000 AVERAGE DISPOSABLE INCOME BY AGE OF HOUSEHOLDER | | | | | |
|---|---|---|---|---|---|---|---|---|---|---|---|---|---|---|
| | | | Less than $15,000 | $15,000 to $24,999 | $25,000 to $49,999 | $50,000 to $99,999 | $100,000 to $149,999 | $150,000 or More | All Ages | <35 | 35-44 | 45-54 | 55-64 | 65+ |
| BERNALILLO | 21,629 | 208,727 | 14.0 | 14.0 | 32.9 | 29.5 | 7.1 | 2.5 | 39,324 | 30,633 | 42,979 | 48,660 | 44,896 | 30,769 |
| CATRON | 12,317 | 1,204 | 24.6 | 19.4 | 40.4 | 15.0 | 0.7 | 0.0 | 24,938 | 23,107 | 27,831 | 31,744 | 29,616 | 16,795 |
| CHAVES | 14,264 | 22,400 | 24.9 | 19.2 | 33.5 | 18.1 | 3.0 | 1.3 | 29,635 | 23,155 | 34,546 | 36,002 | 34,833 | 23,532 |
| CIBOLA | 9,908 | 8,439 | 30.2 | 19.3 | 33.5 | 14.8 | 2.1 | 0.2 | 25,348 | 22,262 | 29,430 | 29,783 | 26,158 | 20,531 |
| COLFAX | 17,032 | 5,336 | 19.6 | 17.0 | 36.7 | 21.4 | 4.0 | 1.2 | 31,985 | 27,328 | 36,417 | 38,896 | 37,910 | 23,424 |
| CURRY | 14,835 | 16,157 | 18.1 | 21.6 | 35.7 | 20.9 | 3.1 | 0.6 | 30,550 | 25,484 | 36,453 | 37,122 | 35,662 | 23,591 |
| DE BACA | 13,386 | 990 | 30.1 | 20.5 | 33.3 | 13.8 | 1.6 | 0.6 | 25,212 | 22,143 | 26,623 | 35,455 | 31,380 | 19,144 |
| DONA ANA | 13,354 | 59,353 | 24.6 | 17.8 | 34.0 | 19.6 | 3.0 | 1.1 | 29,862 | 23,026 | 33,637 | 38,165 | 35,022 | 24,779 |
| EDDY | 15,134 | 19,598 | 21.0 | 16.4 | 36.1 | 21.3 | 4.2 | 1.1 | 31,808 | 28,226 | 37,614 | 37,682 | 34,612 | 24,365 |
| GRANT | 14,023 | 11,598 | 20.6 | 18.3 | 36.1 | 21.2 | 3.2 | 0.6 | 30,213 | 25,383 | 35,285 | 40,623 | 32,566 | 22,072 |
| GUADALUPE | 10,001 | 1,509 | 35.9 | 20.1 | 32.3 | 10.3 | 1.3 | 0.1 | 22,409 | 20,618 | 25,932 | 27,634 | 23,987 | 16,764 |
| HARDING | 16,075 | 365 | 21.9 | 25.5 | 30.4 | 17.8 | 3.8 | 0.6 | 28,692 | 24,315 | 38,447 | 33,382 | 38,810 | 20,057 |
| HIDALGO | 16,401 | 2,131 | 20.2 | 11.5 | 39.6 | 23.8 | 4.0 | 0.8 | 33,198 | 30,152 | 38,532 | 39,747 | 36,855 | 22,924 |
| LEA | 14,200 | 19,647 | 22.6 | 16.3 | 35.7 | 21.4 | 3.2 | 0.8 | 30,623 | 25,494 | 36,450 | 37,274 | 32,721 | 24,113 |
| LINCOLN | 16,715 | 6,974 | 25.5 | 18.9 | 33.2 | 17.9 | 3.2 | 1.4 | 29,412 | 25,465 | 33,893 | 34,305 | 30,350 | 23,514 |
| LOS ALAMOS | 32,565 | 7,562 | 6.1 | 4.4 | 16.8 | 48.0 | 19.7 | 5.0 | 56,694 | 36,333 | 57,875 | 67,004 | 66,059 | 47,204 |
| LUNA | 11,887 | 9,566 | 32.0 | 22.6 | 29.5 | 13.4 | 2.1 | 0.4 | 24,490 | 19,513 | 28,087 | 30,616 | 26,931 | 21,599 |
| MCKINLEY | 9,820 | 18,821 | 31.8 | 17.6 | 30.6 | 16.7 | 2.7 | 0.6 | 26,791 | 23,448 | 29,456 | 31,744 | 28,517 | 19,978 |
| MORA | 11,707 | 1,818 | 33.6 | 23.8 | 25.2 | 14.6 | 1.9 | 0.9 | 25,133 | 22,199 | 27,835 | 34,350 | 30,462 | 17,045 |
| OTERO | 13,896 | 19,476 | 16.9 | 22.3 | 36.8 | 21.3 | 2.2 | 0.6 | 30,177 | 25,300 | 35,184 | 36,655 | 34,074 | 24,121 |
| QUAY | 11,478 | 3,956 | 34.5 | 22.1 | 29.5 | 12.1 | 1.7 | 0.3 | 23,326 | 18,808 | 29,074 | 29,126 | 25,661 | 17,745 |
| RIO ARRIBA | 12,753 | 13,008 | 23.4 | 17.8 | 33.6 | 21.6 | 3.0 | 0.5 | 29,741 | 26,919 | 34,846 | 35,430 | 30,665 | 20,102 |
| ROOSEVELT | 14,429 | 6,642 | 27.7 | 21.5 | 31.2 | 15.2 | 3.1 | 1.3 | 28,246 | 22,020 | 31,738 | 38,406 | 32,701 | 23,304 |
| SANDOVAL | 18,581 | 31,336 | 9.2 | 8.9 | 36.5 | 36.7 | 7.5 | 1.2 | 41,226 | 38,888 | 45,542 | 46,641 | 42,590 | 30,765 |
| SAN JUAN | 12,732 | 34,771 | 22.7 | 15.2 | 34.4 | 23.1 | 3.7 | 1.1 | 31,873 | 26,845 | 37,307 | 39,449 | 31,979 | 22,239 |
| SAN MIGUEL | 13,854 | 9,795 | 24.0 | 17.2 | 34.9 | 19.8 | 2.9 | 1.2 | 29,872 | 24,997 | 34,577 | 35,133 | 31,710 | 23,192 |
| SANTA FE | 26,088 | 49,825 | 10.8 | 13.0 | 31.7 | 31.2 | 8.6 | 4.8 | 45,058 | 33,276 | 45,775 | 52,051 | 48,788 | 37,016 |
| SIERRA | 19,597 | 5,077 | 27.7 | 22.3 | 29.4 | 14.2 | 3.7 | 2.8 | 29,792 | 28,560 | 35,585 | 37,800 | 33,786 | 23,395 |
| SOCORRO | 12,660 | 5,947 | 31.1 | 15.4 | 32.0 | 17.8 | 2.6 | 1.1 | 27,755 | 21,732 | 33,197 | 36,894 | 28,528 | 21,157 |
| TAOS | 13,765 | 10,772 | 29.5 | 20.2 | 30.3 | 16.6 | 2.6 | 0.8 | 27,125 | 22,555 | 31,501 | 32,131 | 28,859 | 19,204 |
| TORRANCE | 17,989 | 6,033 | 19.1 | 17.0 | 36.4 | 23.0 | 3.7 | 1.0 | 32,082 | 28,663 | 38,339 | 36,747 | 33,168 | 22,270 |
| UNION | 14,215 | 1,574 | 32.7 | 18.1 | 30.6 | 15.5 | 2.5 | 0.6 | 25,808 | 22,876 | 30,730 | 33,631 | 29,170 | 17,778 |
| VALENCIA | 17,237 | 23,574 | 15.4 | 13.6 | 37.0 | 27.9 | 4.9 | 1.3 | 35,819 | 29,723 | 40,982 | 43,757 | 36,194 | 26,572 |
| NEW MEXICO | 17,428 | | 18.7 | 15.7 | 33.5 | 25.1 | 5.3 | 1.8 | 35,040 | 28,013 | 39,399 | 43,150 | 38,690 | 26,905 |
| UNITED STATES | 22,162 | | 14.5 | 12.5 | 32.3 | 29.8 | 7.4 | 3.5 | 40,748 | 34,503 | 44,969 | 49,579 | 43,409 | 27,339 |

| COUNTY | FINANCIAL SERVICES | | | | THE HOME | | | | | | ENTERTAINMENT | | | | | | PERSONAL | | | |
|---|---|---|---|---|---|---|---|---|---|---|---|---|---|---|---|---|---|---|---|---|
| | | | | | Home Improvements | | | Furnishings | | | | | | | | | | | | |
| | Auto Loan | Home Loan | Investments | Retirement Plans | Home Repair | Lawn & Garden | Remodeling | Appliances | Electronics | Furniture | Restaurants | Sporting Goods | Theater & Concerts | Toys & Hobbies | Travel | Video Rental | Apparel | Auto Aftermarket | Health Insurance | Pets & Supplies |
| BERNALILLO | 99 | 103 | 98 | 99 | 102 | 102 | 100 | 101 | 101 | 103 | 101 | 93 | 94 | 94 | 92 | 94 | 99 | 99 | 97 | 95 |
| CATRON | 97 | 63 | 69 | 77 | 92 | 92 | 111 | 97 | 93 | 74 | 76 | 87 | 73 | 88 | 70 | 92 | 78 | 86 | 103 | 90 |
| CHAVES | 97 | 89 | 96 | 91 | 100 | 99 | 104 | 100 | 98 | 94 | 91 | 88 | 88 | 90 | 86 | 92 | 89 | 94 | 99 | 93 |
| CIBOLA | 94 | 81 | 79 | 79 | 96 | 92 | 105 | 97 | 93 | 90 | 84 | 85 | 81 | 86 | 80 | 91 | 84 | 90 | 94 | 89 |
| COLFAX | 95 | 75 | 80 | 80 | 95 | 93 | 109 | 97 | 93 | 84 | 82 | 85 | 79 | 88 | 77 | 92 | 82 | 89 | 100 | 90 |
| CURRY | 97 | 90 | 90 | 90 | 98 | 96 | 103 | 99 | 98 | 94 | 92 | 89 | 87 | 91 | 84 | 93 | 91 | 94 | 96 | 93 |
| DE BACA | 97 | 64 | 70 | 79 | 92 | 92 | 113 | 97 | 93 | 74 | 76 | 88 | 74 | 88 | 70 | 92 | 78 | 87 | 103 | 90 |
| DONA ANA | 96 | 93 | 90 | 88 | 96 | 95 | 100 | 98 | 97 | 92 | 92 | 87 | 86 | 89 | 84 | 92 | 88 | 94 | 96 | 94 |
| EDDY | 97 | 86 | 92 | 87 | 98 | 97 | 105 | 100 | 97 | 93 | 91 | 88 | 86 | 90 | 83 | 93 | 88 | 93 | 98 | 93 |
| GRANT | 96 | 81 | 80 | 82 | 93 | 93 | 105 | 99 | 96 | 87 | 87 | 87 | 81 | 89 | 78 | 93 | 84 | 91 | 98 | 93 |
| GUADALUPE | 95 | 88 | 85 | 80 | 100 | 96 | 107 | 99 | 88 | 106 | 87 | 89 | 85 | 82 | 94 | 93 | 89 | 93 | 93 | 86 |
| HARDING | 97 | 63 | 69 | 78 | 92 | 92 | 111 | 97 | 92 | 74 | 76 | 88 | 73 | 88 | 70 | 92 | 78 | 86 | 103 | 90 |
| HIDALGO | 96 | 88 | 82 | 83 | 93 | 92 | 103 | 100 | 98 | 93 | 91 | 87 | 84 | 90 | 80 | 93 | 87 | 94 | 95 | 94 |
| LEA | 98 | 92 | 90 | 90 | 98 | 97 | 102 | 100 | 99 | 96 | 94 | 90 | 88 | 91 | 85 | 93 | 91 | 95 | 97 | 94 |
| LINCOLN | 100 | 74 | 78 | 86 | 94 | 94 | 123 | 101 | 95 | 82 | 83 | 92 | 80 | 93 | 75 | 93 | 84 | 90 | 103 | 95 |
| LOS ALAMOS | 109 | 123 | 121 | 127 | 115 | 122 | 110 | 110 | 114 | 124 | 122 | 106 | 113 | 105 | 111 | 98 | 125 | 114 | 105 | 103 |
| LUNA | 95 | 79 | 88 | 79 | 95 | 95 | 103 | 99 | 95 | 85 | 84 | 84 | 81 | 87 | 79 | 92 | 80 | 90 | 100 | 92 |
| MCKINLEY | 95 | 86 | 87 | 85 | 95 | 94 | 102 | 99 | 96 | 91 | 87 | 87 | 84 | 88 | 82 | 93 | 87 | 93 | 95 | 93 |
| MORA | 94 | 90 | 86 | 79 | 99 | 96 | 104 | 99 | 90 | 104 | 88 | 87 | 85 | 82 | 92 | 93 | 88 | 93 | 93 | 87 |
| OTERO | 96 | 90 | 88 | 88 | 97 | 95 | 103 | 99 | 97 | 94 | 93 | 89 | 87 | 91 | 83 | 93 | 91 | 94 | 95 | 93 |
| QUAY | 97 | 77 | 83 | 83 | 95 | 95 | 109 | 99 | 95 | 86 | 85 | 88 | 82 | 90 | 78 | 93 | 84 | 90 | 100 | 92 |
| RIO ARRIBA | 94 | 89 | 84 | 79 | 101 | 96 | 108 | 98 | 88 | 109 | 87 | 89 | 86 | 82 | 95 | 93 | 90 | 93 | 91 | 85 |
| ROOSEVELT | 96 | 80 | 85 | 83 | 97 | 94 | 106 | 97 | 93 | 86 | 85 | 86 | 81 | 88 | 80 | 91 | 84 | 89 | 98 | 91 |
| SANDOVAL | 103 | 105 | 89 | 100 | 100 | 102 | 103 | 105 | 106 | 108 | 107 | 98 | 96 | 97 | 91 | 96 | 104 | 103 | 98 | 98 |
| SAN JUAN | 97 | 88 | 87 | 88 | 96 | 94 | 107 | 100 | 98 | 95 | 92 | 90 | 86 | 92 | 81 | 93 | 90 | 94 | 95 | 93 |
| SAN MIGUEL | 95 | 93 | 91 | 83 | 104 | 99 | 107 | 98 | 88 | 112 | 90 | 90 | 88 | 82 | 100 | 93 | 92 | 94 | 93 | 85 |
| SANTA FE | 101 | 110 | 101 | 103 | 104 | 105 | 103 | 103 | 105 | 109 | 106 | 97 | 98 | 95 | 97 | 96 | 104 | 104 | 97 | 97 |
| SIERRA | 95 | 78 | 108 | 83 | 102 | 104 | 101 | 100 | 90 | 84 | 84 | 85 | 84 | 88 | 86 | 89 | 78 | 88 | 104 | 91 |
| SOCORRO | 95 | 84 | 85 | 82 | 95 | 93 | 105 | 97 | 94 | 89 | 87 | 86 | 82 | 87 | 81 | 91 | 84 | 91 | 95 | 91 |
| TAOS | 95 | 91 | 92 | 85 | 101 | 98 | 105 | 99 | 92 | 103 | 90 | 89 | 87 | 85 | 92 | 93 | 90 | 94 | 95 | 89 |
| TORRANCE | 97 | 77 | 78 | 81 | 93 | 91 | 113 | 98 | 94 | 87 | 85 | 89 | 80 | 90 | 75 | 92 | 84 | 89 | 98 | 92 |
| UNION | 96 | 65 | 70 | 77 | 93 | 92 | 110 | 97 | 92 | 76 | 77 | 86 | 74 | 87 | 71 | 92 | 78 | 86 | 102 | 89 |
| VALENCIA | 97 | 83 | 85 | 84 | 94 | 94 | 111 | 99 | 97 | 91 | 89 | 89 | 83 | 91 | 78 | 93 | 86 | 92 | 97 | 93 |
| NEW MEXICO | 98 | 96 | 94 | 94 | 100 | 99 | 103 | 101 | 99 | 99 | 96 | 91 | 90 | 92 | 88 | 94 | 94 | 97 | 97 | 94 |
| UNITED STATES | 100 | 100 | 100 | 100 | 100 | 100 | 100 | 100 | 100 | 100 | 100 | 100 | 100 | 100 | 100 | 100 | 100 | 100 | 100 | 100 |

# POPULATION CHANGE



| COUNTY | FIPS Code | MSA Code | DMA Code | POPULATION 1990 | POPULATION 2000 | POPULATION 2005 | 1990-2000 ANNUAL CHANGE % Rate | 1990-2000 ANNUAL CHANGE State Rank | RACE (%) White 1990 | RACE (%) White 2000 | RACE (%) Black 1990 | RACE (%) Black 2000 | RACE (%) Asian/Pacific 1990 | RACE (%) Asian/Pacific 2000 |
|---|---|---|---|---|---|---|---|---|---|---|---|---|---|---|
| ALBANY | 001 | 0160 | 532 | 292,594 | 290,833 | 284,704 | -0.1 | 38 | 89.1 | 86.9 | 8.4 | 9.5 | 1.7 | 2.6 |
| ALLEGANY | 003 | 0000 | 514 | 50,470 | 50,482 | 50,083 | 0.0 | 29 | 98.4 | 98.0 | 0.6 | 0.7 | 0.6 | 0.9 |
| BRONX | 005 | 5600 | 501 | 1,203,789 | 1,195,696 | 1,202,731 | -0.1 | 38 | 35.7 | 33.0 | 37.3 | 36.4 | 3.0 | 3.8 |
| BROOME | 007 | 0960 | 502 | 212,160 | 193,485 | 184,940 | -0.9 | 61 | 95.7 | 94.4 | 2.0 | 2.3 | 1.7 | 2.6 |
| CATTARAUGUS | 009 | 0000 | 514 | 84,234 | 84,202 | 82,721 | 0.0 | 29 | 96.3 | 95.6 | 0.9 | 1.0 | 0.4 | 0.6 |
| CAYUGA | 011 | 8160 | 555 | 82,313 | 81,294 | 79,284 | -0.1 | 38 | 95.1 | 94.6 | 3.6 | 3.8 | 0.4 | 0.6 |
| CHAUTAUQUA | 013 | 3610 | 514 | 141,895 | 136,435 | 131,542 | -0.4 | 53 | 96.1 | 94.9 | 1.7 | 2.1 | 0.4 | 0.6 |
| CHEMUNG | 015 | 2335 | 565 | 95,195 | 91,248 | 88,856 | -0.4 | 53 | 92.8 | 91.7 | 5.5 | 6.1 | 0.7 | 1.1 |
| CHENANGO | 017 | 0000 | 502 | 51,768 | 50,370 | 48,713 | -0.3 | 49 | 98.5 | 98.1 | 0.7 | 0.8 | 0.3 | 0.5 |
| CLINTON | 019 | 0000 | 523 | 85,969 | 79,363 | 77,608 | -0.8 | 60 | 93.7 | 92.7 | 4.4 | 4.7 | 0.8 | 1.2 |
| COLUMBIA | 021 | 0000 | 532 | 62,982 | 62,892 | 62,328 | 0.0 | 29 | 95.1 | 94.0 | 3.9 | 4.6 | 0.4 | 0.6 |
| CORTLAND | 023 | 0000 | 555 | 48,963 | 47,790 | 46,677 | -0.2 | 43 | 98.3 | 97.9 | 0.7 | 0.8 | 0.5 | 0.7 |
| DELAWARE | 025 | 0000 | 502 | 47,225 | 46,149 | 45,105 | -0.2 | 43 | 98.1 | 97.6 | 1.0 | 1.2 | 0.4 | 0.6 |
| DUTCHESS | 027 | 2281 | 501 | 259,462 | 270,448 | 281,033 | 0.4 | 14 | 88.3 | 86.1 | 8.4 | 9.1 | 2.2 | 3.5 |
| ERIE | 029 | 1280 | 514 | 968,532 | 918,095 | 879,341 | -0.5 | 57 | 85.9 | 83.5 | 11.3 | 12.8 | 1.1 | 1.6 |
| ESSEX | 031 | 0000 | 523 | 37,152 | 37,420 | 36,991 | 0.1 | 25 | 96.0 | 95.5 | 2.8 | 3.1 | 0.4 | 0.6 |
| FRANKLIN | 033 | 0000 | 523 | 46,540 | 48,302 | 47,274 | 0.4 | 14 | 90.0 | 87.2 | 3.7 | 5.3 | 0.3 | 0.4 |
| FULTON | 035 | 0000 | 532 | 54,191 | 52,562 | 51,146 | -0.3 | 49 | 98.0 | 97.2 | 1.2 | 1.7 | 0.4 | 0.7 |
| GENESEE | 037 | 6840 | 514 | 60,060 | 60,273 | 59,305 | 0.0 | 29 | 96.5 | 95.7 | 1.8 | 2.0 | 0.4 | 0.6 |
| GREENE | 039 | 0000 | 532 | 44,739 | 48,579 | 49,696 | 0.8 | 5 | 93.0 | 91.5 | 4.9 | 5.6 | 0.4 | 0.6 |
| HAMILTON | 041 | 0000 | 532 | 5,279 | 5,185 | 5,160 | -0.2 | 43 | 99.4 | 99.4 | 0.2 | 0.2 | 0.1 | 0.1 |
| HERKIMER | 043 | 8680 | 526 | 65,797 | 62,664 | 59,325 | -0.5 | 57 | 99.2 | 99.0 | 0.3 | 0.4 | 0.2 | 0.4 |
| JEFFERSON | 045 | 0000 | 549 | 110,943 | 108,825 | 103,527 | -0.2 | 43 | 91.2 | 89.1 | 5.9 | 6.6 | 0.9 | 1.4 |
| KINGS | 047 | 5600 | 501 | 2,300,664 | 2,269,132 | 2,271,693 | -0.1 | 38 | 46.9 | 42.6 | 37.9 | 38.6 | 4.8 | 6.7 |
| LEWIS | 049 | 0000 | 549 | 26,796 | 27,186 | 26,674 | 0.1 | 25 | 98.8 | 98.4 | 0.4 | 0.5 | 0.3 | 0.6 |
| LIVINGSTON | 051 | 6840 | 538 | 62,372 | 66,027 | 66,891 | 0.6 | 10 | 96.2 | 94.6 | 2.4 | 3.4 | 0.5 | 0.8 |
| MADISON | 053 | 8160 | 555 | 69,120 | 71,236 | 71,697 | 0.3 | 20 | 97.6 | 97.2 | 1.1 | 1.2 | 0.6 | 0.8 |
| MONROE | 055 | 6840 | 538 | 713,968 | 710,260 | 698,986 | -0.1 | 38 | 84.1 | 81.3 | 11.9 | 13.1 | 1.8 | 2.7 |
| MONTGOMERY | 057 | 0160 | 532 | 51,981 | 49,980 | 48,082 | -0.4 | 53 | 96.5 | 95.4 | 0.9 | 1.1 | 0.4 | 0.7 |
| NASSAU | 059 | 5380 | 501 | 1,287,348 | 1,307,462 | 1,319,920 | 0.2 | 23 | 86.6 | 83.6 | 8.6 | 9.6 | 3.1 | 4.8 |
| NEW YORK | 061 | 5600 | 501 | 1,487,536 | 1,558,193 | 1,590,561 | 0.5 | 11 | 58.3 | 52.3 | 22.0 | 22.9 | 7.4 | 10.3 |
| NIAGARA | 063 | 1280 | 514 | 220,756 | 214,763 | 207,896 | -0.3 | 49 | 93.0 | 91.9 | 5.5 | 6.2 | 0.4 | 0.6 |
| ONEIDA | 065 | 8680 | 526 | 250,836 | 227,790 | 218,422 | -0.9 | 61 | 92.7 | 91.0 | 5.4 | 6.4 | 0.9 | 1.3 |
| ONONDAGA | 067 | 8160 | 555 | 468,973 | 453,894 | 442,203 | -0.3 | 49 | 89.2 | 87.4 | 8.0 | 9.0 | 1.5 | 2.2 |
| ONTARIO | 069 | 6840 | 538 | 95,101 | 100,032 | 101,214 | 0.5 | 11 | 97.0 | 96.2 | 1.8 | 2.2 | 0.5 | 0.8 |
| ORANGE | 071 | 5660 | 501 | 307,647 | 337,929 | 356,066 | 0.9 | 4 | 88.9 | 86.9 | 7.2 | 7.9 | 1.2 | 1.8 |
| ORLEANS | 073 | 6840 | 514 | 41,846 | 45,046 | 45,166 | 0.7 | 8 | 91.5 | 89.1 | 6.6 | 8.3 | 0.4 | 0.5 |
| OSWEGO | 075 | 8160 | 555 | 121,771 | 123,810 | 122,604 | 0.2 | 23 | 98.5 | 98.1 | 0.5 | 0.5 | 0.4 | 0.6 |
| OTSEGO | 077 | 0000 | 526 | 60,517 | 60,574 | 60,236 | 0.0 | 29 | 97.7 | 97.2 | 1.3 | 1.5 | 0.5 | 0.8 |
| PUTNAM | 079 | 5600 | 501 | 83,941 | 96,224 | 102,987 | 1.3 | 1 | 97.5 | 96.7 | 1.0 | 1.1 | 0.9 | 1.4 |
| QUEENS | 081 | 5600 | 501 | 1,951,598 | 2,010,078 | 2,054,865 | 0.3 | 20 | 57.9 | 52.0 | 21.7 | 21.8 | 12.2 | 16.7 |
| RENSSELAER | 083 | 0160 | 532 | 154,429 | 150,830 | 146,504 | -0.2 | 43 | 94.7 | 93.5 | 3.3 | 3.8 | 1.4 | 2.0 |
| RICHMOND | 085 | 5600 | 501 | 378,977 | 418,589 | 444,750 | 1.0 | 2 | 85.0 | 81.3 | 8.1 | 8.7 | 4.5 | 6.9 |
| ROCKLAND | 087 | 5600 | 501 | 265,475 | 286,713 | 299,830 | 0.8 | 5 | 83.9 | 80.5 | 10.0 | 10.8 | 4.1 | 6.2 |
| ST. LAWRENCE | 089 | 0000 | 549 | 111,974 | 112,440 | 110,427 | 0.0 | 29 | 96.7 | 94.8 | 1.4 | 2.6 | 0.7 | 1.0 |
| SARATOGA | 091 | 0160 | 532 | 181,276 | 201,596 | 210,937 | 1.0 | 2 | 97.6 | 96.9 | 1.3 | 1.4 | 0.8 | 1.2 |
| SCHENECTADY | 093 | 0160 | 532 | 149,285 | 142,791 | 137,360 | -0.4 | 53 | 93.7 | 92.2 | 4.3 | 4.8 | 1.2 | 2.0 |
| SCHOHARIE | 095 | 0160 | 532 | 31,859 | 31,973 | 31,555 | 0.0 | 29 | 97.6 | 97.1 | 1.3 | 1.5 | 0.3 | 0.5 |
| SCHUYLER | 097 | 0000 | 565 | 18,662 | 19,264 | 19,458 | 0.3 | 20 | 98.3 | 97.7 | 0.8 | 1.2 | 0.2 | 0.3 |
| SENECA | 099 | 0000 | 555 | 33,683 | 31,845 | 31,361 | -0.5 | 57 | 97.2 | 96.8 | 1.6 | 1.6 | 0.6 | 1.0 |
| STEUBEN | 101 | 0000 | 565 | 99,088 | 97,421 | 95,912 | -0.2 | 43 | 97.9 | 97.3 | 1.2 | 1.3 | 0.6 | 0.9 |
| SUFFOLK | 103 | 5380 | 501 | 1,321,864 | 1,395,062 | 1,449,294 | 0.5 | 11 | 90.0 | 87.9 | 6.3 | 7.0 | 1.7 | 2.7 |
| SULLIVAN | 105 | 0000 | 501 | 69,277 | 69,183 | 68,420 | 0.0 | 29 | 88.4 | 86.8 | 8.5 | 9.1 | 0.8 | 1.3 |
| TIOGA | 107 | 0960 | 502 | 52,337 | 52,082 | 51,417 | 0.0 | 29 | 98.4 | 97.9 | 0.6 | 0.7 | 0.6 | 1.0 |
| TOMPKINS | 109 | 0000 | 555 | 94,097 | 97,874 | 98,953 | 0.4 | 14 | 90.2 | 87.6 | 3.3 | 3.7 | 5.5 | 7.5 |
| ULSTER | 111 | 0000 | 501 | 165,304 | 167,442 | 168,144 | 0.1 | 25 | 92.6 | 91.0 | 4.9 | 5.6 | 1.2 | 1.8 |
| WARREN | 113 | 2975 | 532 | 59,209 | 61,517 | 61,936 | 0.4 | 14 | 98.7 | 98.3 | 0.5 | 0.6 | 0.5 | 0.8 |
| WASHINGTON | 115 | 2975 | 532 | 59,330 | 60,081 | 59,708 | 0.1 | 25 | 95.6 | 95.4 | 3.5 | 3.4 | 0.2 | 0.3 |
| WAYNE | 117 | 6840 | 538 | 89,123 | 95,957 | 98,237 | 0.7 | 8 | 95.4 | 94.3 | 3.1 | 3.7 | 0.4 | 0.6 |
| WESTCHESTER | 119 | 5600 | 501 | 874,866 | 909,719 | 930,050 | 0.4 | 14 | 79.4 | 75.6 | 13.7 | 14.9 | 3.7 | 5.6 |
| WYOMING | 121 | 0000 | 514 | 42,507 | 44,200 | 44,254 | 0.4 | 14 | 93.5 | 92.3 | 4.9 | 5.5 | 0.3 | 0.5 |
| YATES | 123 | 0000 | 555 | 22,810 | 24,732 | 25,662 | 0.8 | 5 | 98.6 | 98.1 | 0.6 | 0.9 | 0.3 | 0.5 |
| NEW YORK | | | | | | | 0.1 | | 74.4 | 71.3 | 15.9 | 16.4 | 3.9 | 5.5 |
| UNITED STATES | | | | | | | 1.0 | | 80.3 | 77.9 | 12.1 | 12.4 | 2.9 | 3.9 |

| COUNTY | % HISPANIC ORIGIN 1990 | % HISPANIC ORIGIN 2000 | 2000 AGE DISTRIBUTION (%) 0-4 | 5-9 | 10-14 | 15-19 | 20-24 | 25-44 | 45-64 | 65-84 | 85+ | 18+ | MEDIAN AGE 1990 | MEDIAN AGE 2000 | 2000 Males/ Females (×100) |
|---|---|---|---|---|---|---|---|---|---|---|---|---|---|---|---|
| ALBANY | 1.8 | 2.7 | 5.7 | 6.3 | 6.3 | 7.2 | 7.5 | 29.8 | 22.5 | 12.6 | 2.2 | 78.4 | 33.9 | 37.1 | 90.8 |
| ALLEGANY | 0.6 | 1.2 | 6.5 | 7.7 | 7.2 | 10.9 | 8.2 | 24.3 | 21.3 | 12.0 | 1.9 | 74.5 | 31.1 | 33.7 | 99.4 |
| BRONX | 43.5 | 48.8 | 8.6 | 8.6 | 7.5 | 7.1 | 7.3 | 30.5 | 19.6 | 9.2 | 1.7 | 71.4 | 30.9 | 32.2 | 87.5 |
| BROOME | 1.2 | 1.9 | 6.3 | 7.1 | 6.4 | 6.9 | 6.5 | 28.8 | 22.1 | 13.8 | 2.2 | 76.9 | 34.1 | 37.4 | 94.3 |
| CATTARAUGUS | 0.6 | 1.2 | 6.9 | 8.5 | 7.7 | 7.8 | 6.0 | 26.6 | 22.2 | 12.4 | 1.9 | 72.6 | 33.2 | 35.9 | 95.6 |
| CAYUGA | 1.5 | 2.1 | 7.0 | 7.6 | 7.1 | 7.3 | 6.3 | 29.4 | 21.7 | 11.8 | 1.9 | 74.1 | 33.1 | 35.6 | 102.8 |
| CHAUTAUQUA | 2.9 | 4.3 | 6.4 | 7.7 | 7.0 | 7.4 | 6.4 | 26.8 | 22.3 | 13.6 | 2.3 | 75.0 | 34.3 | 37.0 | 95.3 |
| CHEMUNG | 1.5 | 2.2 | 6.6 | 7.7 | 7.0 | 6.9 | 6.3 | 27.7 | 22.4 | 13.3 | 2.1 | 74.8 | 34.2 | 36.9 | 96.1 |
| CHENANGO | 0.9 | 1.6 | 7.0 | 8.4 | 7.8 | 6.5 | 5.1 | 27.9 | 22.9 | 12.3 | 2.0 | 72.6 | 33.9 | 36.9 | 97.2 |
| CLINTON | 2.4 | 3.5 | 7.0 | 7.7 | 6.6 | 7.3 | 8.7 | 32.0 | 19.5 | 9.9 | 1.4 | 75.4 | 29.9 | 33.0 | 106.0 |
| COLUMBIA | 1.6 | 2.5 | 6.3 | 7.2 | 7.1 | 6.8 | 5.1 | 26.4 | 25.2 | 13.6 | 2.4 | 75.1 | 36.5 | 39.1 | 98.0 |
| CORTLAND | 0.9 | 1.6 | 6.6 | 7.6 | 6.9 | 9.1 | 9.2 | 27.6 | 20.6 | 10.8 | 1.7 | 75.3 | 30.3 | 33.5 | 92.6 |
| DELAWARE | 1.1 | 1.8 | 6.1 | 7.6 | 6.9 | 8.1 | 5.1 | 24.9 | 23.8 | 15.2 | 2.4 | 75.6 | 35.6 | 39.0 | 98.7 |
| DUTCHESS | 3.8 | 5.0 | 6.4 | 7.2 | 7.1 | 7.0 | 6.1 | 30.7 | 23.3 | 10.6 | 1.6 | 75.6 | 33.4 | 36.5 | 100.8 |
| ERIE | 2.3 | 3.4 | 6.3 | 6.9 | 6.8 | 6.6 | 6.0 | 28.9 | 22.5 | 14.0 | 2.0 | 76.4 | 34.7 | 37.8 | 92.0 |
| ESSEX | 2.0 | 2.7 | 6.2 | 7.2 | 6.7 | 6.1 | 5.6 | 29.4 | 23.2 | 13.3 | 2.3 | 76.2 | 35.0 | 37.9 | 109.2 |
| FRANKLIN | 2.4 | 4.2 | 6.2 | 7.6 | 6.8 | 7.4 | 7.0 | 31.5 | 21.2 | 10.8 | 1.6 | 75.3 | 32.8 | 34.7 | 115.0 |
| FULTON | 0.8 | 1.5 | 6.4 | 6.9 | 6.7 | 7.4 | 5.9 | 27.2 | 24.2 | 13.1 | 2.1 | 75.3 | 35.2 | 37.8 | 94.5 |
| GENESEE | 0.8 | 1.4 | 7.0 | 7.8 | 7.4 | 7.4 | 5.4 | 28.6 | 22.7 | 11.9 | 1.8 | 73.6 | 33.3 | 36.5 | 95.4 |
| GREENE | 3.4 | 4.8 | 5.9 | 6.8 | 6.5 | 6.3 | 6.7 | 28.0 | 24.1 | 13.4 | 2.2 | 77.0 | 35.5 | 38.0 | 105.9 |
| HAMILTON | 0.6 | 1.0 | 4.2 | 6.1 | 5.8 | 5.4 | 3.9 | 25.7 | 29.4 | 17.6 | 1.9 | 80.7 | 40.2 | 44.3 | 102.3 |
| HERKIMER | 0.6 | 1.1 | 6.4 | 7.9 | 7.1 | 6.8 | 5.0 | 27.3 | 23.2 | 14.1 | 2.2 | 74.8 | 35.3 | 38.1 | 95.0 |
| JEFFERSON | 2.8 | 4.5 | 8.6 | 7.9 | 6.4 | 7.0 | 9.6 | 31.4 | 18.3 | 9.3 | 1.5 | 73.5 | 29.2 | 31.1 | 106.8 |
| KINGS | 20.1 | 23.9 | 7.7 | 7.9 | 7.1 | 6.6 | 7.0 | 31.1 | 20.7 | 10.3 | 1.5 | 73.4 | 32.3 | 33.8 | 88.5 |
| LEWIS | 0.5 | 1.0 | 7.9 | 8.8 | 8.0 | 7.5 | 5.6 | 27.8 | 21.8 | 11.0 | 1.5 | 70.4 | 31.5 | 35.1 | 100.2 |
| LIVINGSTON | 1.6 | 2.8 | 6.2 | 7.0 | 6.6 | 9.5 | 9.1 | 28.6 | 21.4 | 10.1 | 1.5 | 76.4 | 31.2 | 33.9 | 93.7 |
| MADISON | 0.8 | 1.4 | 6.5 | 7.9 | 7.0 | 9.9 | 7.5 | 27.6 | 21.6 | 10.5 | 1.5 | 75.0 | 31.0 | 34.2 | 97.1 |
| MONROE | 3.7 | 5.2 | 6.7 | 7.4 | 7.3 | 7.0 | 6.5 | 29.4 | 22.7 | 11.2 | 1.8 | 74.9 | 33.0 | 36.2 | 92.6 |
| MONTGOMERY | 5.2 | 7.4 | 6.7 | 7.8 | 6.9 | 6.3 | 5.1 | 26.7 | 22.1 | 15.9 | 2.7 | 74.7 | 36.6 | 38.8 | 93.1 |
| NASSAU | 6.0 | 8.0 | 5.6 | 6.5 | 6.9 | 5.9 | 4.9 | 29.4 | 24.6 | 14.5 | 1.8 | 77.6 | 36.6 | 39.7 | 93.4 |
| NEW YORK | 26.0 | 30.9 | 5.2 | 5.2 | 4.7 | 4.9 | 6.4 | 35.6 | 25.3 | 10.9 | 1.8 | 82.3 | 35.9 | 38.6 | 89.7 |
| NIAGARA | 1.0 | 1.6 | 6.6 | 7.3 | 7.0 | 6.8 | 5.7 | 28.0 | 22.9 | 13.6 | 1.9 | 75.1 | 34.6 | 37.6 | 92.7 |
| ONEIDA | 2.3 | 3.6 | 6.4 | 7.4 | 6.6 | 6.8 | 6.5 | 28.8 | 21.4 | 13.9 | 2.2 | 76.0 | 33.8 | 36.8 | 99.9 |
| ONONDAGA | 1.5 | 2.4 | 6.8 | 7.4 | 7.1 | 7.6 | 6.8 | 28.9 | 21.7 | 11.9 | 1.8 | 75.0 | 32.8 | 35.9 | 92.1 |
| ONTARIO | 1.3 | 2.2 | 6.4 | 7.3 | 7.1 | 7.1 | 5.9 | 28.3 | 24.6 | 11.5 | 1.6 | 75.3 | 34.1 | 37.4 | 96.4 |
| ORANGE | 7.0 | 9.3 | 7.7 | 8.4 | 7.9 | 7.3 | 6.4 | 29.7 | 22.1 | 9.1 | 1.3 | 71.8 | 31.9 | 34.2 | 100.6 |
| ORLEANS | 2.5 | 4.0 | 7.0 | 7.6 | 7.1 | 7.5 | 6.5 | 29.8 | 22.2 | 10.7 | 1.6 | 73.9 | 32.5 | 35.0 | 100.7 |
| OSWEGO | 1.0 | 1.7 | 7.4 | 8.0 | 7.4 | 8.3 | 7.6 | 28.8 | 21.6 | 9.6 | 1.3 | 73.0 | 30.5 | 33.6 | 97.7 |
| OTSEGO | 1.2 | 1.9 | 5.9 | 7.2 | 6.5 | 9.5 | 8.4 | 25.1 | 22.1 | 13.0 | 2.1 | 76.8 | 33.1 | 36.2 | 93.0 |
| PUTNAM | 2.7 | 3.9 | 6.7 | 8.1 | 8.1 | 6.1 | 4.2 | 31.3 | 25.7 | 8.6 | 1.2 | 73.3 | 33.7 | 37.0 | 98.8 |
| QUEENS | 19.5 | 22.8 | 6.1 | 6.2 | 6.0 | 5.6 | 6.2 | 32.8 | 22.9 | 12.2 | 1.9 | 78.5 | 35.2 | 37.5 | 92.7 |
| RENSSELAER | 1.2 | 1.9 | 6.5 | 7.0 | 6.7 | 7.4 | 7.3 | 29.4 | 22.2 | 11.7 | 1.8 | 76.2 | 32.8 | 36.0 | 97.2 |
| RICHMOND | 8.0 | 10.5 | 7.0 | 7.6 | 7.3 | 5.9 | 5.4 | 32.0 | 23.0 | 10.4 | 1.4 | 74.7 | 33.3 | 36.0 | 93.9 |
| ROCKLAND | 6.7 | 8.7 | 6.7 | 7.6 | 7.4 | 6.4 | 5.4 | 29.3 | 25.2 | 10.6 | 1.6 | 74.5 | 34.1 | 37.3 | 94.2 |
| ST. LAWRENCE | 1.1 | 2.5 | 6.2 | 7.5 | 6.8 | 9.5 | 9.3 | 27.0 | 20.9 | 11.2 | 1.6 | 75.9 | 30.8 | 33.5 | 103.7 |
| SARATOGA | 1.1 | 1.8 | 6.7 | 7.6 | 7.2 | 6.6 | 5.7 | 31.5 | 23.7 | 9.7 | 1.2 | 74.7 | 32.8 | 36.1 | 96.5 |
| SCHENECTADY | 1.7 | 2.6 | 6.3 | 7.0 | 7.0 | 6.5 | 5.8 | 27.9 | 23.1 | 14.0 | 2.3 | 76.0 | 35.6 | 38.4 | 92.7 |
| SCHOHARIE | 1.7 | 2.6 | 6.0 | 6.8 | 6.4 | 9.5 | 6.4 | 26.2 | 24.2 | 12.7 | 1.8 | 77.0 | 33.5 | 37.1 | 96.1 |
| SCHUYLER | 0.9 | 1.6 | 6.6 | 7.7 | 7.2 | 7.1 | 5.9 | 25.9 | 25.0 | 12.5 | 2.0 | 74.1 | 34.7 | 38.0 | 99.6 |
| SENECA | 1.1 | 1.7 | 6.8 | 7.6 | 7.2 | 6.7 | 5.6 | 27.2 | 23.7 | 13.2 | 2.0 | 74.4 | 34.7 | 37.8 | 97.2 |
| STEUBEN | 0.5 | 1.1 | 7.0 | 7.7 | 7.2 | 7.0 | 5.8 | 26.5 | 23.7 | 13.2 | 1.9 | 73.7 | 34.4 | 37.4 | 97.8 |
| SUFFOLK | 6.6 | 8.9 | 6.4 | 7.3 | 7.2 | 6.0 | 5.1 | 31.2 | 24.2 | 11.1 | 1.5 | 75.5 | 33.5 | 37.3 | 95.3 |
| SULLIVAN | 6.9 | 9.1 | 6.7 | 7.8 | 6.9 | 6.6 | 5.4 | 29.5 | 22.9 | 12.5 | 1.7 | 74.9 | 34.8 | 37.0 | 107.5 |
| TIOGA | 0.7 | 1.3 | 7.3 | 8.2 | 7.7 | 7.1 | 5.6 | 28.3 | 23.5 | 10.8 | 1.3 | 72.2 | 33.0 | 36.3 | 97.2 |
| TOMPKINS | 2.2 | 3.2 | 5.3 | 6.1 | 5.3 | 12.4 | 14.7 | 29.3 | 17.6 | 8.0 | 1.3 | 80.7 | 27.2 | 29.5 | 98.1 |
| ULSTER | 4.1 | 5.8 | 6.1 | 6.9 | 6.9 | 6.8 | 6.1 | 29.5 | 24.2 | 11.7 | 1.7 | 76.4 | 34.4 | 37.6 | 98.7 |
| WARREN | 0.8 | 1.5 | 6.3 | 7.2 | 6.7 | 6.6 | 5.6 | 28.9 | 24.6 | 12.2 | 1.9 | 76.0 | 34.4 | 37.7 | 94.6 |
| WASHINGTON | 2.2 | 3.0 | 6.7 | 7.8 | 7.2 | 6.5 | 6.1 | 30.1 | 22.1 | 11.8 | 1.8 | 74.4 | 33.0 | 35.8 | 107.3 |
| WAYNE | 1.7 | 2.7 | 7.4 | 8.2 | 7.8 | 7.2 | 5.6 | 28.6 | 23.6 | 10.1 | 1.4 | 72.1 | 32.9 | 35.9 | 97.6 |
| WESTCHESTER | 9.9 | 12.4 | 6.1 | 6.7 | 6.5 | 5.8 | 5.5 | 30.1 | 24.6 | 12.6 | 2.1 | 77.3 | 36.2 | 38.7 | 91.4 |
| WYOMING | 2.4 | 3.4 | 6.4 | 8.0 | 7.2 | 6.7 | 6.4 | 32.3 | 21.1 | 10.3 | 1.6 | 74.4 | 32.4 | 34.8 | 118.5 |
| YATES | 1.0 | 1.7 | 6.9 | 7.9 | 7.5 | 7.7 | 5.5 | 25.4 | 24.2 | 12.9 | 2.0 | 73.3 | 34.8 | 37.6 | 96.3 |
| NEW YORK | 12.3 | 14.9 | 6.6 | 7.1 | 6.7 | 6.5 | 6.3 | 30.6 | 22.8 | 11.6 | 1.7 | 76.0 | 33.9 | 36.6 | 93.1 |
| UNITED STATES | 9.0 | 11.8 | 6.9 | 7.2 | 7.2 | 7.2 | 6.7 | 29.9 | 22.2 | 11.1 | 1.6 | 74.6 | 32.9 | 35.7 | 95.6 |

# HOUSEHOLDS

| COUNTY | HOUSEHOLDS | | | | | FAMILIES | | | MEDIAN HOUSEHOLD INCOME | | | |
|---|---|---|---|---|---|---|---|---|---|---|---|---|
| | 1990 | 2000 | 2005 | % Annual Rate 1990-2000 | 2000 Average HH Size | 1990 | 2000 | % Annual Rate 1990-2000 | 2000 | 2005 | 2000 National Rank | 2000 State Rank |
| ALBANY | 115,824 | 118,443 | 117,370 | 0.3 | 2.34 | 71,455 | 70,096 | -0.2 | 43,643 | 49,519 | 418 | 12 |
| ALLEGANY | 17,011 | 17,604 | 17,639 | 0.4 | 2.62 | 12,318 | 12,286 | 0.0 | 32,735 | 39,092 | 1585 | 52 |
| BRONX | 424,112 | 420,601 | 423,037 | -0.1 | 2.75 | 288,609 | 285,219 | -0.1 | 27,117 | 34,692 | 2563 | 62 |
| BROOME | 81,843 | 76,659 | 74,328 | -0.8 | 2.42 | 54,819 | 49,471 | -1.2 | 35,607 | 40,153 | 1152 | 40 |
| CATTARAUGUS | 30,456 | 31,488 | 31,398 | 0.4 | 2.57 | 21,657 | 21,603 | 0.0 | 31,967 | 36,442 | 1721 | 55 |
| CAYUGA | 29,075 | 29,271 | 28,947 | 0.1 | 2.60 | 20,927 | 20,417 | -0.3 | 37,267 | 42,803 | 939 | 33 |
| CHAUTAUQUA | 53,696 | 52,768 | 51,527 | -0.2 | 2.47 | 37,203 | 35,191 | -0.7 | 32,870 | 37,549 | 1559 | 51 |
| CHEMUNG | 35,275 | 34,675 | 34,211 | -0.2 | 2.49 | 24,808 | 23,529 | -0.6 | 35,495 | 40,813 | 1173 | 41 |
| CHENANGO | 19,141 | 19,292 | 18,965 | 0.1 | 2.57 | 13,821 | 13,485 | -0.3 | 33,507 | 38,935 | 1464 | 49 |
| CLINTON | 29,123 | 27,879 | 27,666 | -0.5 | 2.59 | 20,839 | 19,381 | -0.9 | 37,150 | 42,372 | 952 | 34 |
| COLUMBIA | 23,696 | 24,167 | 24,214 | 0.2 | 2.51 | 16,882 | 16,595 | -0.2 | 40,134 | 47,403 | 661 | 21 |
| CORTLAND | 17,247 | 17,244 | 17,029 | 0.0 | 2.58 | 11,799 | 11,459 | -0.4 | 35,344 | 41,105 | 1193 | 43 |
| DELAWARE | 17,646 | 17,503 | 17,245 | -0.1 | 2.52 | 12,374 | 11,844 | -0.5 | 31,469 | 35,513 | 1826 | 57 |
| DUTCHESS | 89,567 | 95,192 | 99,803 | 0.7 | 2.66 | 64,757 | 66,536 | 0.3 | 49,921 | 59,550 | 202 | 8 |
| ERIE | 376,994 | 371,395 | 362,203 | -0.2 | 2.41 | 254,472 | 241,704 | -0.6 | 38,638 | 42,188 | 785 | 26 |
| ESSEX | 13,721 | 14,211 | 14,273 | 0.4 | 2.45 | 9,498 | 9,438 | -0.1 | 34,114 | 38,353 | 1371 | 47 |
| FRANKLIN | 16,284 | 17,010 | 16,928 | 0.5 | 2.51 | 11,265 | 11,346 | 0.1 | 31,076 | 35,931 | 1916 | 60 |
| FULTON | 20,995 | 20,710 | 20,411 | -0.2 | 2.47 | 14,602 | 13,875 | -0.6 | 31,624 | 36,552 | 1794 | 56 |
| GENESEE | 21,614 | 22,297 | 22,231 | 0.4 | 2.65 | 16,050 | 16,029 | 0.0 | 40,108 | 47,071 | 664 | 22 |
| GREENE | 16,596 | 18,105 | 18,733 | 1.1 | 2.49 | 11,642 | 12,215 | 0.6 | 38,382 | 45,993 | 821 | 28 |
| HAMILTON | 2,153 | 2,172 | 2,188 | 0.1 | 2.35 | 1,508 | 1,470 | -0.3 | 32,020 | 36,563 | 1710 | 54 |
| HERKIMER | 24,936 | 24,612 | 23,699 | -0.2 | 2.50 | 17,576 | 16,743 | -0.6 | 31,231 | 35,558 | 1881 | 59 |
| JEFFERSON | 37,851 | 37,185 | 35,675 | -0.2 | 2.67 | 28,163 | 26,971 | -0.5 | 33,791 | 40,632 | 1425 | 48 |
| KINGS | 828,199 | 813,480 | 813,788 | -0.2 | 2.75 | 555,284 | 540,307 | -0.3 | 30,105 | 37,813 | 2130 | 61 |
| LEWIS | 9,253 | 9,742 | 9,728 | 0.6 | 2.76 | 7,056 | 7,223 | 0.3 | 32,387 | 37,487 | 1642 | 53 |
| LIVINGSTON | 21,197 | 22,852 | 23,455 | 0.9 | 2.61 | 15,178 | 15,808 | 0.5 | 41,478 | 48,616 | 554 | 18 |
| MADISON | 23,567 | 25,014 | 25,415 | 0.7 | 2.66 | 17,162 | 17,585 | 0.3 | 39,723 | 45,091 | 690 | 24 |
| MONROE | 271,944 | 278,536 | 277,840 | 0.3 | 2.47 | 182,813 | 181,179 | -0.1 | 46,017 | 50,775 | 307 | 10 |
| MONTGOMERY | 20,185 | 19,938 | 19,427 | -0.1 | 2.46 | 14,028 | 13,309 | -0.6 | 33,165 | 37,782 | 1510 | 50 |
| NASSAU | 431,515 | 446,232 | 454,366 | 0.4 | 2.88 | 344,502 | 346,025 | 0.1 | 69,798 | 80,511 | 14 | 2 |
| NEW YORK | 716,422 | 756,559 | 775,380 | 0.7 | 1.98 | 301,041 | 313,029 | 0.5 | 43,440 | 48,626 | 430 | 13 |
| NIAGARA | 84,809 | 85,881 | 84,740 | 0.2 | 2.46 | 59,732 | 58,543 | -0.2 | 37,577 | 41,581 | 891 | 31 |
| ONEIDA | 92,562 | 85,848 | 83,221 | -0.9 | 2.48 | 63,735 | 57,050 | -1.3 | 37,065 | 41,788 | 966 | 35 |
| ONONDAGA | 177,898 | 176,921 | 174,560 | -0.1 | 2.48 | 118,575 | 113,743 | -0.5 | 40,665 | 45,526 | 614 | 20 |
| ONTARIO | 34,929 | 37,861 | 38,784 | 1.0 | 2.57 | 25,143 | 26,369 | 0.6 | 43,096 | 48,797 | 452 | 14 |
| ORANGE | 101,506 | 112,311 | 118,685 | 1.2 | 2.89 | 77,111 | 82,850 | 0.9 | 52,462 | 65,354 | 161 | 7 |
| ORLEANS | 14,428 | 15,315 | 15,463 | 0.7 | 2.70 | 10,685 | 10,955 | 0.3 | 37,653 | 44,438 | 884 | 30 |
| OSWEGO | 42,434 | 44,207 | 44,231 | 0.5 | 2.70 | 30,905 | 31,197 | 0.1 | 37,431 | 42,303 | 908 | 32 |
| OTSEGO | 21,725 | 22,191 | 22,260 | 0.3 | 2.52 | 14,768 | 14,541 | -0.2 | 34,564 | 40,607 | 1310 | 46 |
| PUTNAM | 28,094 | 32,829 | 35,460 | 1.9 | 2.90 | 22,549 | 25,531 | 1.5 | 70,139 | 86,502 | 13 | 1 |
| QUEENS | 720,149 | 747,704 | 767,192 | 0.5 | 2.65 | 490,915 | 501,546 | 0.3 | 41,232 | 50,384 | 567 | 19 |
| RENSSELAER | 57,612 | 58,128 | 57,364 | 0.1 | 2.49 | 39,356 | 38,212 | -0.4 | 42,505 | 49,683 | 475 | 16 |
| RICHMOND | 130,519 | 146,235 | 156,526 | 1.4 | 2.81 | 99,059 | 107,496 | 1.0 | 57,540 | 67,741 | 94 | 6 |
| ROCKLAND | 84,874 | 93,858 | 99,047 | 1.2 | 2.98 | 66,583 | 71,830 | 0.9 | 67,826 | 79,125 | 23 | 3 |
| ST. LAWRENCE | 37,964 | 39,193 | 39,126 | 0.4 | 2.57 | 26,784 | 26,772 | 0.0 | 31,280 | 35,460 | 1872 | 58 |
| SARATOGA | 66,425 | 75,981 | 80,544 | 1.6 | 2.60 | 48,363 | 53,508 | 1.2 | 49,306 | 55,944 | 212 | 9 |
| SCHENECTADY | 59,181 | 58,726 | 57,467 | -0.1 | 2.36 | 39,702 | 37,877 | -0.6 | 42,977 | 48,316 | 458 | 15 |
| SCHOHARIE | 11,257 | 11,731 | 11,708 | 0.5 | 2.58 | 8,127 | 8,212 | 0.1 | 36,881 | 44,793 | 994 | 36 |
| SCHUYLER | 6,818 | 7,162 | 7,311 | 0.6 | 2.61 | 5,025 | 5,127 | 0.2 | 34,818 | 41,811 | 1280 | 45 |
| SENECA | 12,285 | 12,019 | 11,930 | -0.3 | 2.60 | 8,998 | 8,491 | -0.7 | 36,492 | 41,671 | 1044 | 38 |
| STEUBEN | 37,299 | 37,751 | 37,637 | 0.1 | 2.54 | 26,447 | 25,882 | -0.3 | 35,160 | 38,233 | 1225 | 44 |
| SUFFOLK | 424,719 | 458,800 | 481,274 | 0.9 | 2.99 | 340,593 | 356,241 | 0.5 | 63,448 | 75,437 | 48 | 5 |
| SULLIVAN | 24,576 | 24,645 | 24,422 | 0.0 | 2.59 | 17,090 | 16,580 | -0.4 | 38,439 | 46,750 | 815 | 27 |
| TIOGA | 18,838 | 19,448 | 19,544 | 0.4 | 2.66 | 14,470 | 14,503 | 0.0 | 38,847 | 43,823 | 766 | 25 |
| TOMPKINS | 33,338 | 34,659 | 35,256 | 0.5 | 2.44 | 19,049 | 19,149 | 0.1 | 36,526 | 40,011 | 1039 | 37 |
| ULSTER | 60,807 | 62,279 | 63,015 | 0.3 | 2.54 | 42,213 | 41,514 | -0.2 | 42,364 | 52,628 | 480 | 17 |
| WARREN | 22,559 | 24,007 | 24,435 | 0.8 | 2.52 | 15,788 | 16,244 | 0.3 | 40,057 | 45,923 | 669 | 23 |
| WASHINGTON | 20,256 | 21,232 | 21,394 | 0.6 | 2.67 | 15,023 | 15,203 | 0.1 | 37,699 | 45,450 | 877 | 29 |
| WAYNE | 31,977 | 35,091 | 36,302 | 1.1 | 2.69 | 23,961 | 25,550 | 0.8 | 43,851 | 51,264 | 405 | 11 |
| WESTCHESTER | 320,030 | 336,555 | 346,045 | 0.6 | 2.62 | 227,827 | 233,209 | 0.3 | 64,957 | 73,128 | 35 | 4 |
| WYOMING | 13,897 | 14,575 | 14,762 | 0.6 | 2.73 | 10,528 | 10,732 | 0.2 | 36,164 | 43,046 | 1084 | 39 |
| YATES | 8,419 | 9,111 | 9,448 | 1.0 | 2.64 | 6,100 | 6,411 | 0.6 | 35,457 | 43,648 | 1178 | 42 |
| NEW YORK | | | | 0.3 | 2.59 | | | 0.0 | 42,807 | 50,643 | | |
| UNITED STATES | | | | 1.4 | 2.59 | | | 1.1 | 41,914 | 49,127 | | |

| COUNTY | 2000 Per Capita Income | 2000 HH Income Base | 2000 HOUSEHOLD INCOME DISTRIBUTION (%) Less than $15,000 | $15,000 to $24,999 | $25,000 to $49,999 | $50,000 to $99,999 | $100,000 to $149,999 | $150,000 or More | 2000 AVERAGE DISPOSABLE INCOME BY AGE OF HOUSEHOLDER All Ages | <35 | 35-44 | 45-54 | 55-64 | 65+ |
|---|---|---|---|---|---|---|---|---|---|---|---|---|---|---|
| ALBANY | 24,137 | 118,441 | 12.8 | 11.8 | 32.9 | 31.4 | 7.7 | 3.4 | 39,027 | 32,882 | 43,801 | 49,355 | 43,466 | 25,845 |
| ALLEGANY | 14,666 | 17,603 | 17.4 | 16.5 | 39.3 | 22.2 | 3.6 | 1.0 | 29,517 | 26,273 | 34,429 | 37,741 | 32,141 | 19,909 |
| BRONX | 13,330 | 420,564 | 30.8 | 15.8 | 29.5 | 19.7 | 3.2 | 1.0 | 26,604 | 24,388 | 28,341 | 31,140 | 29,756 | 19,680 |
| BROOME | 17,834 | 76,659 | 18.3 | 15.0 | 35.6 | 25.8 | 3.9 | 1.4 | 31,299 | 28,157 | 36,595 | 41,047 | 35,188 | 19,677 |
| CATTARAUGUS | 15,914 | 31,488 | 17.2 | 19.4 | 38.2 | 20.4 | 3.5 | 1.3 | 29,196 | 25,704 | 34,077 | 37,666 | 32,449 | 18,567 |
| CAYUGA | 17,153 | 29,271 | 16.0 | 14.5 | 37.5 | 26.6 | 4.3 | 1.3 | 32,080 | 29,731 | 37,179 | 41,455 | 35,393 | 19,199 |
| CHAUTAUQUA | 16,417 | 52,768 | 19.7 | 16.6 | 37.8 | 21.4 | 3.4 | 1.1 | 29,164 | 25,571 | 34,671 | 37,941 | 32,080 | 19,135 |
| CHEMUNG | 17,597 | 34,674 | 16.9 | 15.8 | 37.6 | 23.9 | 4.2 | 1.6 | 31,416 | 28,238 | 37,520 | 40,215 | 33,439 | 19,959 |
| CHENANGO | 16,575 | 19,292 | 16.2 | 18.7 | 38.3 | 22.5 | 3.4 | 1.0 | 29,816 | 27,145 | 35,998 | 36,723 | 32,017 | 18,762 |
| CLINTON | 17,179 | 27,879 | 15.5 | 14.9 | 36.3 | 26.9 | 5.1 | 1.4 | 32,733 | 28,721 | 38,557 | 41,241 | 37,311 | 20,925 |
| COLUMBIA | 21,439 | 24,167 | 13.9 | 13.1 | 35.9 | 27.4 | 6.4 | 3.4 | 36,859 | 32,065 | 43,084 | 44,147 | 41,726 | 22,804 |
| CORTLAND | 15,269 | 17,244 | 17.2 | 15.3 | 39.1 | 24.2 | 3.5 | 0.8 | 30,129 | 26,862 | 36,520 | 38,286 | 33,006 | 18,149 |
| DELAWARE | 14,895 | 17,503 | 18.8 | 19.1 | 37.3 | 21.0 | 3.1 | 0.6 | 28,049 | 26,224 | 32,693 | 34,375 | 31,713 | 19,566 |
| DUTCHESS | 21,988 | 95,192 | 10.6 | 9.4 | 30.1 | 39.6 | 7.9 | 2.4 | 40,060 | 37,661 | 43,845 | 48,995 | 44,867 | 23,749 |
| ERIE | 20,820 | 371,387 | 17.2 | 13.2 | 33.8 | 27.4 | 5.9 | 2.5 | 34,566 | 30,288 | 40,110 | 44,390 | 39,020 | 22,109 |
| ESSEX | 16,380 | 14,211 | 18.4 | 15.5 | 37.0 | 24.8 | 3.4 | 0.9 | 29,742 | 28,631 | 35,638 | 37,937 | 31,099 | 18,972 |
| FRANKLIN | 14,314 | 17,010 | 20.8 | 18.1 | 37.4 | 20.1 | 2.7 | 0.9 | 27,837 | 26,446 | 35,626 | 34,715 | 27,796 | 15,044 |
| FULTON | 16,150 | 20,710 | 20.3 | 17.5 | 38.6 | 19.8 | 2.9 | 1.0 | 28,200 | 25,160 | 33,266 | 36,303 | 31,152 | 18,125 |
| GENESEE | 18,014 | 22,297 | 13.2 | 13.0 | 37.9 | 30.3 | 4.4 | 1.2 | 33,476 | 31,624 | 38,492 | 42,388 | 36,309 | 20,206 |
| GREENE | 19,031 | 18,104 | 15.2 | 12.8 | 37.8 | 26.4 | 5.5 | 2.3 | 34,143 | 33,292 | 38,575 | 43,099 | 36,034 | 21,688 |
| HAMILTON | 15,797 | 2,172 | 14.7 | 23.2 | 38.8 | 20.4 | 2.8 | 0.1 | 27,452 | 26,636 | 32,836 | 33,227 | 30,720 | 19,071 |
| HERKIMER | 14,820 | 24,612 | 20.8 | 17.8 | 38.4 | 19.7 | 2.5 | 0.8 | 27,458 | 26,942 | 33,344 | 35,331 | 30,207 | 16,000 |
| JEFFERSON | 15,195 | 37,185 | 17.0 | 17.0 | 38.0 | 23.9 | 3.3 | 0.8 | 29,778 | 27,145 | 35,586 | 37,228 | 32,523 | 18,976 |
| KINGS | 15,077 | 813,463 | 27.4 | 15.2 | 30.2 | 21.5 | 4.1 | 1.6 | 29,034 | 27,856 | 31,318 | 33,865 | 32,049 | 19,898 |
| LEWIS | 13,843 | 9,742 | 19.6 | 16.3 | 40.9 | 20.8 | 1.7 | 0.7 | 27,648 | 26,592 | 32,539 | 35,442 | 29,165 | 16,272 |
| LIVINGSTON | 17,913 | 22,852 | 11.6 | 12.8 | 37.0 | 31.6 | 5.5 | 1.5 | 35,005 | 31,530 | 39,266 | 45,407 | 37,396 | 22,081 |
| MADISON | 17,834 | 25,014 | 12.9 | 13.6 | 36.7 | 29.9 | 5.3 | 1.6 | 34,469 | 31,550 | 40,040 | 42,614 | 37,888 | 21,227 |
| MONROE | 23,096 | 278,531 | 13.2 | 10.4 | 31.1 | 34.2 | 8.1 | 3.1 | 39,203 | 33,693 | 43,395 | 49,867 | 43,474 | 24,870 |
| MONTGOMERY | 16,689 | 19,938 | 18.3 | 17.3 | 37.9 | 22.7 | 2.9 | 0.9 | 28,957 | 28,184 | 35,039 | 36,997 | 32,827 | 18,282 |
| NASSAU | 36,517 | 446,232 | 6.1 | 5.2 | 19.5 | 39.4 | 16.8 | 13.0 | 62,807 | 53,506 | 59,865 | 68,562 | 67,448 | 43,829 |
| NEW YORK | 45,174 | 756,559 | 17.9 | 11.0 | 26.4 | 23.6 | 9.3 | 11.8 | 52,597 | 44,032 | 49,778 | 50,343 | 48,751 | 37,994 |
| NIAGARA | 18,627 | 85,881 | 15.9 | 13.4 | 38.0 | 27.3 | 4.2 | 1.3 | 32,307 | 29,174 | 37,657 | 42,273 | 35,393 | 20,339 |
| ONEIDA | 17,746 | 85,838 | 16.4 | 14.8 | 35.8 | 27.3 | 4.5 | 1.3 | 32,159 | 29,289 | 37,218 | 41,461 | 36,766 | 21,228 |
| ONONDAGA | 20,471 | 176,920 | 15.1 | 12.5 | 34.2 | 30.0 | 6.0 | 2.2 | 35,317 | 31,256 | 40,518 | 44,336 | 39,295 | 22,399 |
| ONTARIO | 20,902 | 37,861 | 11.2 | 11.7 | 36.8 | 32.4 | 6.2 | 1.7 | 36,169 | 32,936 | 40,438 | 45,431 | 38,619 | 22,622 |
| ORANGE | 22,112 | 112,310 | 10.8 | 7.8 | 28.1 | 39.3 | 10.4 | 3.6 | 42,847 | 39,845 | 46,427 | 51,887 | 46,396 | 24,685 |
| ORLEANS | 15,799 | 15,315 | 12.8 | 15.1 | 40.6 | 27.5 | 3.1 | 0.8 | 31,538 | 30,155 | 36,799 | 40,723 | 33,237 | 18,845 |
| OSWEGO | 16,060 | 44,207 | 17.1 | 13.8 | 36.3 | 27.9 | 4.0 | 1.0 | 31,664 | 29,822 | 37,448 | 39,720 | 32,505 | 17,662 |
| OTSEGO | 16,774 | 22,187 | 16.9 | 16.8 | 36.3 | 24.7 | 4.1 | 1.3 | 30,814 | 26,753 | 36,370 | 40,210 | 34,524 | 20,515 |
| PUTNAM | 31,126 | 32,829 | 5.7 | 3.5 | 19.4 | 44.4 | 18.9 | 8.1 | 56,473 | 52,245 | 56,041 | 64,206 | 60,193 | 32,661 |
| QUEENS | 19,603 | 747,679 | 15.6 | 12.0 | 32.7 | 31.0 | 6.6 | 2.1 | 35,671 | 35,505 | 37,479 | 41,666 | 40,576 | 24,644 |
| RENSSELAER | 20,060 | 58,128 | 13.2 | 12.3 | 34.4 | 32.3 | 6.3 | 1.6 | 35,481 | 32,930 | 40,560 | 44,007 | 39,475 | 22,987 |
| RICHMOND | 25,572 | 146,234 | 11.0 | 6.5 | 24.1 | 40.1 | 13.0 | 5.2 | 46,983 | 43,816 | 48,847 | 55,748 | 52,113 | 28,081 |
| ROCKLAND | 29,954 | 93,858 | 7.3 | 5.3 | 19.9 | 40.2 | 17.3 | 10.0 | 57,667 | 47,263 | 56,159 | 66,071 | 65,763 | 34,912 |
| ST. LAWRENCE | 14,169 | 39,192 | 22.4 | 17.0 | 36.0 | 20.9 | 2.9 | 0.8 | 27,793 | 24,986 | 33,482 | 35,282 | 30,844 | 17,118 |
| SARATOGA | 23,153 | 75,978 | 9.1 | 9.2 | 32.5 | 37.6 | 8.7 | 2.8 | 40,892 | 37,986 | 45,375 | 50,654 | 42,500 | 23,795 |
| SCHENECTADY | 23,240 | 58,726 | 12.2 | 12.5 | 33.8 | 31.5 | 7.2 | 2.9 | 37,716 | 33,031 | 42,205 | 49,119 | 42,252 | 24,591 |
| SCHOHARIE | 17,523 | 11,722 | 14.3 | 15.3 | 37.6 | 26.8 | 4.7 | 1.5 | 32,486 | 30,329 | 37,162 | 40,700 | 35,939 | 20,658 |
| SCHUYLER | 15,038 | 7,162 | 13.9 | 16.8 | 42.2 | 24.3 | 2.7 | 0.1 | 29,222 | 27,015 | 33,846 | 35,797 | 32,221 | 19,046 |
| SENECA | 16,569 | 12,019 | 15.5 | 14.9 | 39.2 | 26.2 | 3.2 | 1.0 | 31,105 | 27,057 | 36,016 | 40,246 | 34,377 | 19,978 |
| STEUBEN | 17,834 | 37,751 | 16.5 | 16.8 | 36.6 | 24.4 | 4.2 | 1.5 | 31,340 | 28,162 | 37,153 | 40,680 | 33,800 | 19,662 |
| SUFFOLK | 27,935 | 458,799 | 6.9 | 5.5 | 22.3 | 42.3 | 15.5 | 7.5 | 53,049 | 47,301 | 53,370 | 62,216 | 58,878 | 32,769 |
| SULLIVAN | 18,544 | 24,645 | 16.1 | 13.9 | 34.9 | 27.2 | 5.5 | 2.3 | 33,967 | 31,309 | 39,771 | 40,844 | 37,231 | 21,727 |
| TIOGA | 17,264 | 19,448 | 14.8 | 14.0 | 36.2 | 29.6 | 4.6 | 0.7 | 32,553 | 29,638 | 36,527 | 43,149 | 34,536 | 18,465 |
| TOMPKINS | 18,112 | 34,659 | 18.9 | 15.0 | 32.5 | 24.5 | 6.2 | 3.0 | 34,644 | 24,646 | 38,799 | 45,829 | 44,207 | 26,985 |
| ULSTER | 19,674 | 62,279 | 13.4 | 11.7 | 35.0 | 32.2 | 5.9 | 1.9 | 35,658 | 33,532 | 38,949 | 44,581 | 38,557 | 22,465 |
| WARREN | 21,876 | 24,007 | 13.3 | 12.9 | 36.6 | 28.1 | 6.1 | 3.0 | 36,775 | 32,610 | 42,662 | 44,867 | 38,124 | 24,264 |
| WASHINGTON | 16,838 | 21,232 | 14.8 | 13.6 | 39.9 | 27.8 | 3.2 | 0.7 | 31,320 | 30,110 | 36,472 | 38,795 | 34,135 | 19,916 |
| WAYNE | 19,021 | 35,091 | 12.9 | 10.8 | 35.3 | 33.4 | 6.1 | 1.5 | 35,974 | 33,825 | 41,003 | 45,966 | 36,536 | 20,248 |
| WESTCHESTER | 41,579 | 336,555 | 8.8 | 6.6 | 21.8 | 32.8 | 14.6 | 15.4 | 64,747 | 50,855 | 61,161 | 67,292 | 66,236 | 43,909 |
| WYOMING | 14,075 | 14,575 | 13.3 | 16.5 | 42.4 | 24.6 | 2.7 | 0.5 | 30,066 | 28,887 | 34,577 | 36,853 | 32,493 | 18,784 |
| YATES | 16,236 | 9,111 | 15.6 | 15.8 | 38.1 | 25.3 | 4.4 | 0.9 | 30,941 | 28,188 | 35,523 | 38,984 | 35,613 | 20,187 |
| NEW YORK | 24,235 | | 16.2 | 11.5 | 29.7 | 29.5 | 8.1 | 5.0 | 40,926 | 35,448 | 42,934 | 47,623 | 44,515 | 27,215 |
| UNITED STATES | 22,162 | | 14.5 | 12.5 | 32.3 | 29.8 | 7.4 | 3.5 | 40,748 | 34,503 | 44,969 | 49,579 | 43,409 | 27,339 |

# SPENDING POTENTIAL INDEXES

| COUNTY | FINANCIAL SERVICES | | | | THE HOME | | | | | | ENTERTAINMENT | | | | | | PERSONAL | | | |
|---|---|---|---|---|---|---|---|---|---|---|---|---|---|---|---|---|---|---|---|---|
| | | | | | Home Improvements | | | Furnishings | | | | | | | | | | | | |
| | Auto Loan | Home Loan | Invest-ments | Retire-ment Plans | Home Repair | Lawn & Garden | Remodel-ing | Appli-ances | Elec-tronics | Furni-ture | Restau-rants | Sport-ing Goods | Theater & Concerts | Toys & Hobbies | Travel | Video Rental | Apparel | Auto After-market | Health Insur-ance | Pets & Supplies |
| ALBANY | 100 | 99 | 105 | 101 | 97 | 96 | 91 | 98 | 97 | 101 | 101 | 100 | 102 | 102 | 99 | 99 | 104 | 98 | 101 | 102 |
| ALLEGANY | 97 | 73 | 79 | 81 | 87 | 84 | 100 | 94 | 91 | 81 | 83 | 94 | 85 | 97 | 78 | 97 | 86 | 88 | 102 | 98 |
| BRONX | 96 | 98 | 95 | 88 | 100 | 93 | 88 | 95 | 88 | 109 | 94 | 98 | 98 | 90 | 107 | 101 | 99 | 97 | 95 | 94 |
| BROOME | 98 | 90 | 98 | 92 | 94 | 92 | 93 | 97 | 93 | 95 | 95 | 97 | 96 | 100 | 92 | 98 | 97 | 94 | 101 | 100 |
| CATTARAUGUS | 98 | 76 | 83 | 83 | 89 | 86 | 101 | 96 | 91 | 85 | 86 | 95 | 88 | 98 | 81 | 98 | 88 | 89 | 103 | 99 |
| CAYUGA | 98 | 82 | 90 | 86 | 92 | 89 | 98 | 96 | 92 | 90 | 90 | 96 | 92 | 99 | 86 | 98 | 92 | 91 | 102 | 100 |
| CHAUTAUQUA | 96 | 79 | 88 | 83 | 91 | 88 | 95 | 95 | 90 | 88 | 88 | 94 | 90 | 97 | 85 | 97 | 89 | 89 | 102 | 98 |
| CHEMUNG | 97 | 87 | 96 | 90 | 94 | 91 | 92 | 96 | 92 | 94 | 93 | 96 | 95 | 99 | 91 | 97 | 94 | 92 | 101 | 99 |
| CHENANGO | 99 | 75 | 81 | 83 | 88 | 85 | 103 | 97 | 93 | 85 | 87 | 97 | 87 | 100 | 79 | 99 | 89 | 90 | 102 | 101 |
| CLINTON | 98 | 85 | 91 | 89 | 90 | 88 | 98 | 96 | 94 | 90 | 92 | 97 | 92 | 99 | 86 | 98 | 93 | 92 | 101 | 101 |
| COLUMBIA | 100 | 86 | 94 | 92 | 92 | 91 | 100 | 98 | 95 | 92 | 93 | 99 | 95 | 102 | 88 | 99 | 96 | 94 | 103 | 102 |
| CORTLAND | 97 | 83 | 89 | 87 | 90 | 87 | 97 | 95 | 92 | 88 | 90 | 95 | 90 | 99 | 85 | 97 | 92 | 91 | 101 | 100 |
| DELAWARE | 99 | 72 | 79 | 84 | 87 | 86 | 107 | 97 | 92 | 81 | 84 | 98 | 86 | 100 | 79 | 99 | 87 | 89 | 105 | 101 |
| DUTCHESS | 102 | 105 | 105 | 105 | 97 | 98 | 94 | 100 | 102 | 106 | 108 | 105 | 107 | 106 | 101 | 101 | 110 | 103 | 102 | 106 |
| ERIE | 97 | 92 | 101 | 94 | 96 | 93 | 88 | 97 | 93 | 98 | 95 | 97 | 98 | 99 | 95 | 98 | 98 | 95 | 100 | 99 |
| ESSEX | 98 | 76 | 83 | 83 | 89 | 87 | 102 | 96 | 90 | 84 | 85 | 96 | 88 | 98 | 82 | 98 | 88 | 89 | 104 | 99 |
| FRANKLIN | 98 | 73 | 80 | 81 | 87 | 85 | 101 | 95 | 91 | 82 | 83 | 95 | 85 | 97 | 79 | 97 | 86 | 88 | 103 | 99 |
| FULTON | 97 | 78 | 84 | 83 | 91 | 87 | 99 | 96 | 90 | 87 | 86 | 95 | 89 | 98 | 84 | 97 | 88 | 89 | 102 | 99 |
| GENESEE | 99 | 83 | 89 | 87 | 91 | 88 | 99 | 97 | 93 | 90 | 92 | 97 | 92 | 101 | 85 | 99 | 94 | 92 | 102 | 101 |
| GREENE | 99 | 75 | 82 | 84 | 88 | 86 | 104 | 96 | 92 | 83 | 86 | 96 | 87 | 100 | 81 | 98 | 89 | 89 | 104 | 101 |
| HAMILTON | 103 | 70 | 74 | 88 | 85 | 86 | 120 | 100 | 92 | 76 | 82 | 103 | 84 | 104 | 77 | 100 | 87 | 90 | 110 | 106 |
| HERKIMER | 97 | 78 | 87 | 84 | 91 | 88 | 98 | 96 | 90 | 88 | 88 | 96 | 90 | 99 | 85 | 97 | 89 | 89 | 103 | 99 |
| JEFFERSON | 96 | 80 | 82 | 82 | 87 | 84 | 97 | 95 | 91 | 85 | 88 | 94 | 87 | 97 | 81 | 98 | 89 | 90 | 100 | 100 |
| KINGS | 96 | 102 | 97 | 91 | 101 | 93 | 84 | 95 | 91 | 108 | 95 | 98 | 100 | 91 | 108 | 102 | 101 | 98 | 95 | 97 |
| LEWIS | 100 | 72 | 78 | 82 | 87 | 85 | 107 | 97 | 92 | 82 | 84 | 99 | 86 | 100 | 77 | 99 | 88 | 89 | 104 | 102 |
| LIVINGSTON | 98 | 82 | 85 | 85 | 88 | 85 | 99 | 96 | 93 | 88 | 91 | 96 | 90 | 100 | 82 | 98 | 92 | 91 | 101 | 101 |
| MADISON | 98 | 83 | 88 | 87 | 90 | 87 | 98 | 96 | 93 | 90 | 91 | 97 | 92 | 100 | 85 | 98 | 93 | 92 | 101 | 101 |
| MONROE | 99 | 98 | 102 | 99 | 95 | 95 | 90 | 98 | 97 | 101 | 100 | 100 | 101 | 102 | 97 | 99 | 104 | 98 | 100 | 102 |
| MONTGOMERY | 95 | 79 | 88 | 82 | 93 | 89 | 93 | 95 | 88 | 89 | 88 | 93 | 91 | 97 | 87 | 96 | 89 | 88 | 102 | 97 |
| NASSAU | 108 | 127 | 129 | 129 | 108 | 116 | 97 | 106 | 113 | 120 | 126 | 114 | 127 | 114 | 124 | 105 | 132 | 118 | 109 | 110 |
| NEW YORK | 100 | 119 | 111 | 108 | 101 | 100 | 90 | 99 | 100 | 112 | 107 | 105 | 108 | 98 | 114 | 102 | 111 | 105 | 98 | 103 |
| NIAGARA | 97 | 88 | 95 | 89 | 94 | 91 | 92 | 96 | 92 | 95 | 94 | 96 | 96 | 100 | 91 | 98 | 95 | 93 | 101 | 99 |
| ONEIDA | 97 | 89 | 98 | 91 | 94 | 91 | 92 | 96 | 93 | 95 | 94 | 96 | 96 | 99 | 92 | 98 | 96 | 93 | 101 | 100 |
| ONONDAGA | 99 | 96 | 99 | 96 | 95 | 93 | 90 | 97 | 96 | 99 | 99 | 99 | 99 | 101 | 95 | 99 | 101 | 97 | 100 | 101 |
| ONTARIO | 100 | 88 | 93 | 92 | 92 | 90 | 98 | 98 | 96 | 94 | 95 | 100 | 96 | 102 | 89 | 99 | 97 | 95 | 102 | 102 |
| ORANGE | 102 | 101 | 100 | 102 | 95 | 95 | 94 | 100 | 101 | 104 | 106 | 104 | 104 | 105 | 98 | 101 | 108 | 102 | 101 | 105 |
| ORLEANS | 98 | 77 | 83 | 82 | 89 | 86 | 100 | 96 | 91 | 86 | 87 | 95 | 88 | 99 | 82 | 98 | 89 | 89 | 102 | 100 |
| OSWEGO | 98 | 80 | 85 | 84 | 89 | 86 | 100 | 96 | 92 | 88 | 89 | 96 | 89 | 99 | 82 | 98 | 91 | 90 | 101 | 100 |
| OTSEGO | 99 | 79 | 88 | 86 | 89 | 87 | 100 | 96 | 93 | 86 | 88 | 96 | 89 | 99 | 83 | 98 | 91 | 91 | 103 | 101 |
| PUTNAM | 107 | 113 | 109 | 114 | 99 | 103 | 97 | 105 | 110 | 115 | 120 | 111 | 116 | 113 | 107 | 104 | 124 | 112 | 104 | 110 |
| QUEENS | 98 | 109 | 103 | 98 | 101 | 96 | 83 | 97 | 97 | 108 | 101 | 101 | 104 | 94 | 110 | 104 | 106 | 103 | 97 | 101 |
| RENSSELAER | 98 | 92 | 98 | 92 | 94 | 92 | 91 | 97 | 94 | 96 | 97 | 97 | 97 | 101 | 93 | 98 | 98 | 95 | 101 | 101 |
| RICHMOND | 103 | 108 | 105 | 106 | 98 | 99 | 92 | 101 | 103 | 108 | 109 | 106 | 108 | 106 | 103 | 102 | 113 | 105 | 101 | 106 |
| ROCKLAND | 107 | 126 | 120 | 123 | 104 | 110 | 96 | 105 | 112 | 119 | 123 | 114 | 122 | 112 | 118 | 105 | 127 | 117 | 106 | 111 |
| ST. LAWRENCE | 97 | 78 | 84 | 83 | 89 | 86 | 99 | 95 | 91 | 85 | 86 | 95 | 88 | 97 | 82 | 97 | 88 | 89 | 101 | 99 |
| SARATOGA | 102 | 97 | 93 | 98 | 91 | 92 | 96 | 99 | 100 | 101 | 103 | 104 | 100 | 105 | 92 | 101 | 104 | 99 | 101 | 104 |
| SCHENECTADY | 99 | 97 | 105 | 98 | 97 | 96 | 90 | 98 | 96 | 101 | 100 | 99 | 102 | 102 | 98 | 99 | 102 | 97 | 102 | 101 |
| SCHOHARIE | 99 | 78 | 84 | 85 | 88 | 87 | 104 | 97 | 93 | 85 | 87 | 97 | 88 | 100 | 81 | 99 | 90 | 90 | 103 | 101 |
| SCHUYLER | 100 | 73 | 80 | 83 | 88 | 85 | 105 | 97 | 93 | 84 | 86 | 98 | 87 | 100 | 78 | 99 | 89 | 89 | 104 | 101 |
| SENECA | 98 | 78 | 85 | 84 | 89 | 87 | 100 | 96 | 92 | 87 | 89 | 96 | 90 | 100 | 82 | 98 | 90 | 90 | 103 | 100 |
| STEUBEN | 98 | 78 | 87 | 85 | 89 | 88 | 100 | 96 | 92 | 87 | 88 | 96 | 90 | 99 | 83 | 98 | 90 | 90 | 103 | 100 |
| SUFFOLK | 104 | 113 | 113 | 112 | 100 | 104 | 94 | 103 | 107 | 111 | 115 | 108 | 115 | 110 | 108 | 103 | 119 | 110 | 105 | 107 |
| SULLIVAN | 99 | 80 | 86 | 88 | 89 | 88 | 104 | 97 | 93 | 86 | 88 | 98 | 90 | 100 | 84 | 99 | 91 | 91 | 104 | 102 |
| TIOGA | 100 | 85 | 89 | 89 | 90 | 88 | 100 | 98 | 95 | 92 | 94 | 99 | 94 | 102 | 85 | 99 | 96 | 93 | 102 | 102 |
| TOMPKINS | 99 | 101 | 101 | 99 | 93 | 92 | 94 | 95 | 96 | 95 | 99 | 99 | 97 | 100 | 95 | 98 | 101 | 97 | 99 | 103 |
| ULSTER | 100 | 93 | 100 | 96 | 94 | 93 | 96 | 98 | 96 | 97 | 99 | 100 | 99 | 103 | 93 | 100 | 101 | 97 | 103 | 103 |
| WARREN | 100 | 87 | 92 | 92 | 91 | 90 | 100 | 97 | 95 | 92 | 93 | 100 | 95 | 102 | 88 | 99 | 96 | 94 | 103 | 102 |
| WASHINGTON | 98 | 78 | 83 | 83 | 90 | 86 | 100 | 96 | 91 | 86 | 87 | 96 | 89 | 99 | 82 | 98 | 90 | 89 | 102 | 100 |
| WAYNE | 99 | 85 | 86 | 88 | 89 | 87 | 99 | 97 | 95 | 91 | 93 | 99 | 93 | 101 | 84 | 99 | 95 | 93 | 101 | 102 |
| WESTCHESTER | 107 | 129 | 128 | 130 | 109 | 116 | 99 | 105 | 111 | 120 | 123 | 115 | 125 | 111 | 125 | 104 | 129 | 116 | 107 | 109 |
| WYOMING | 100 | 77 | 82 | 84 | 88 | 85 | 103 | 97 | 93 | 86 | 88 | 98 | 89 | 101 | 80 | 99 | 91 | 91 | 103 | 102 |
| YATES | 100 | 74 | 81 | 84 | 87 | 86 | 106 | 97 | 92 | 83 | 85 | 98 | 87 | 101 | 79 | 99 | 89 | 90 | 104 | 102 |
| NEW YORK | 100 | 105 | 107 | 103 | 99 | 98 | 92 | 99 | 99 | 106 | 103 | 103 | 105 | 101 | 105 | 101 | 107 | 102 | 101 | 102 |
| UNITED STATES | 100 | 100 | 100 | 100 | 100 | 100 | 100 | 100 | 100 | 100 | 100 | 100 | 100 | 100 | 100 | 100 | 100 | 100 | 100 | 100 |

| COUNTY | FIPS Code | MSA Code | DMA Code | POPULATION 1990 | POPULATION 2000 | POPULATION 2005 | 1990-2000 ANNUAL CHANGE % Rate | 1990-2000 ANNUAL CHANGE State Rank | RACE (%) White 1990 | White 2000 | Black 1990 | Black 2000 | Asian/Pacific 1990 | Asian/Pacific 2000 |
|---|---|---|---|---|---|---|---|---|---|---|---|---|---|---|
| ALAMANCE | 001 | 3120 | 518 | 108,213 | 122,629 | 130,205 | 1.2 | 45 | 79.8 | 78.8 | 19.2 | 19.7 | 0.5 | 0.8 |
| ALEXANDER | 003 | 3290 | 517 | 27,544 | 32,633 | 35,807 | 1.7 | 27 | 93.2 | 92.5 | 6.1 | 6.2 | 0.2 | 0.3 |
| ALLEGHANY | 005 | 0000 | 518 | 9,590 | 9,887 | 10,065 | 0.3 | 86 | 97.4 | 96.7 | 1.8 | 2.1 | 0.1 | 0.1 |
| ANSON | 007 | 0000 | 517 | 23,474 | 24,186 | 23,923 | 0.3 | 86 | 52.2 | 50.2 | 47.3 | 49.2 | 0.1 | 0.2 |
| ASHE | 009 | 0000 | 517 | 22,209 | 24,491 | 25,553 | 1.0 | 55 | 98.9 | 98.7 | 0.6 | 0.7 | 0.1 | 0.2 |
| AVERY | 011 | 0000 | 517 | 14,867 | 15,955 | 16,492 | 0.7 | 73 | 98.2 | 98.1 | 1.1 | 0.9 | 0.2 | 0.2 |
| BEAUFORT | 013 | 0000 | 545 | 42,283 | 45,600 | 47,824 | 0.7 | 73 | 68.5 | 67.8 | 31.2 | 31.6 | 0.1 | 0.2 |
| BERTIE | 015 | 0000 | 545 | 20,388 | 20,350 | 20,143 | 0.0 | 94 | 38.2 | 38.2 | 61.5 | 61.4 | 0.1 | 0.1 |
| BLADEN | 017 | 0000 | 550 | 28,663 | 31,139 | 32,148 | 0.8 | 69 | 59.1 | 57.9 | 39.1 | 39.9 | 0.1 | 0.2 |
| BRUNSWICK | 019 | 9200 | 550 | 50,985 | 73,958 | 87,500 | 3.7 | 1 | 81.1 | 80.4 | 18.1 | 18.4 | 0.2 | 0.2 |
| BUNCOMBE | 021 | 0480 | 567 | 174,821 | 198,061 | 207,230 | 1.2 | 45 | 90.9 | 90.1 | 8.2 | 8.5 | 0.4 | 0.8 |
| BURKE | 023 | 3290 | 517 | 75,744 | 83,894 | 87,756 | 1.0 | 55 | 91.8 | 90.0 | 6.8 | 7.6 | 1.0 | 1.9 |
| CABARRUS | 025 | 1520 | 517 | 98,935 | 128,900 | 149,042 | 2.6 | 9 | 86.2 | 85.4 | 13.0 | 13.3 | 0.4 | 0.7 |
| CALDWELL | 027 | 3290 | 517 | 70,709 | 77,016 | 79,901 | 0.8 | 69 | 94.1 | 93.6 | 5.5 | 5.7 | 0.2 | 0.3 |
| CAMDEN | 029 | 0000 | 544 | 5,904 | 6,968 | 7,450 | 1.6 | 30 | 74.3 | 73.8 | 25.1 | 25.4 | 0.2 | 0.3 |
| CARTERET | 031 | 0000 | 545 | 52,556 | 60,508 | 62,903 | 1.4 | 35 | 90.3 | 89.4 | 8.3 | 8.5 | 0.6 | 1.0 |
| CASWELL | 033 | 0000 | 518 | 20,693 | 22,594 | 23,344 | 0.9 | 63 | 58.7 | 56.4 | 40.8 | 42.8 | 0.1 | 0.2 |
| CATAWBA | 035 | 3290 | 517 | 118,412 | 136,233 | 145,874 | 1.4 | 35 | 89.8 | 88.8 | 9.0 | 9.2 | 0.7 | 1.2 |
| CHATHAM | 037 | 6640 | 560 | 38,759 | 47,370 | 51,695 | 2.0 | 18 | 75.9 | 74.4 | 22.8 | 23.4 | 0.2 | 0.3 |
| CHEROKEE | 039 | 0000 | 575 | 20,170 | 23,617 | 25,793 | 1.6 | 30 | 95.8 | 94.7 | 1.8 | 2.2 | 0.2 | 0.4 |
| CHOWAN | 041 | 0000 | 544 | 13,506 | 14,379 | 14,759 | 0.6 | 78 | 61.8 | 61.0 | 37.7 | 38.2 | 0.2 | 0.4 |
| CLAY | 043 | 0000 | 524 | 7,155 | 8,958 | 9,988 | 2.2 | 17 | 98.7 | 98.0 | 0.6 | 1.1 | 0.1 | 0.2 |
| CLEVELAND | 045 | 0000 | 517 | 84,714 | 94,983 | 99,843 | 1.1 | 51 | 78.3 | 77.5 | 20.9 | 21.3 | 0.5 | 0.8 |
| COLUMBUS | 047 | 0000 | 550 | 49,587 | 53,253 | 54,746 | 0.7 | 73 | 66.3 | 64.9 | 30.6 | 31.4 | 0.1 | 0.2 |
| CRAVEN | 049 | 0000 | 545 | 81,613 | 90,038 | 93,273 | 1.0 | 55 | 71.9 | 70.2 | 25.9 | 26.1 | 0.9 | 1.5 |
| CUMBERLAND | 051 | 2560 | 560 | 274,566 | 283,175 | 280,616 | 0.3 | 86 | 61.9 | 59.2 | 31.9 | 30.9 | 2.1 | 3.5 |
| CURRITUCK | 053 | 5720 | 544 | 13,736 | 18,837 | 21,476 | 3.1 | 7 | 87.7 | 87.4 | 11.2 | 11.1 | 0.4 | 0.7 |
| DARE | 055 | 0000 | 544 | 22,746 | 30,687 | 35,162 | 3.0 | 8 | 95.7 | 95.1 | 3.6 | 3.7 | 0.3 | 0.6 |
| DAVIDSON | 057 | 3120 | 518 | 126,677 | 144,701 | 153,914 | 1.3 | 39 | 89.4 | 88.7 | 9.7 | 10.0 | 0.4 | 0.6 |
| DAVIE | 059 | 3120 | 518 | 27,859 | 33,500 | 37,387 | 1.8 | 22 | 90.4 | 89.6 | 8.9 | 9.4 | 0.2 | 0.3 |
| DUPLIN | 061 | 0000 | 545 | 39,995 | 43,653 | 45,064 | 0.9 | 63 | 64.8 | 63.0 | 33.2 | 33.3 | 0.1 | 0.2 |
| DURHAM | 063 | 6640 | 560 | 181,835 | 206,411 | 217,549 | 1.2 | 45 | 60.4 | 58.8 | 37.2 | 37.4 | 1.8 | 2.9 |
| EDGECOMBE | 065 | 6895 | 560 | 56,558 | 54,286 | 52,459 | -0.4 | 98 | 43.6 | 42.8 | 56.0 | 56.6 | 0.1 | 0.2 |
| FORSYTH | 067 | 3120 | 518 | 265,878 | 290,346 | 298,080 | 0.9 | 63 | 74.1 | 73.0 | 24.9 | 25.2 | 0.6 | 1.1 |
| FRANKLIN | 069 | 6640 | 560 | 36,414 | 46,609 | 51,687 | 2.4 | 12 | 64.0 | 62.2 | 35.3 | 36.6 | 0.2 | 0.3 |
| GASTON | 071 | 1520 | 517 | 175,093 | 186,328 | 192,087 | 0.6 | 78 | 86.2 | 85.3 | 13.0 | 13.3 | 0.5 | 0.9 |
| GATES | 073 | 0000 | 544 | 9,305 | 10,259 | 10,661 | 1.0 | 55 | 54.8 | 53.8 | 44.9 | 45.8 | 0.1 | 0.2 |
| GRAHAM | 075 | 0000 | 567 | 7,196 | 7,613 | 7,639 | 0.6 | 78 | 93.5 | 91.8 | 0.0 | 0.4 | 0.1 | 0.2 |
| GRANVILLE | 077 | 0000 | 560 | 38,345 | 45,304 | 49,101 | 1.6 | 30 | 60.2 | 59.1 | 38.9 | 39.5 | 0.3 | 0.5 |
| GREENE | 079 | 0000 | 545 | 15,384 | 18,808 | 20,118 | 2.0 | 18 | 56.9 | 55.8 | 42.4 | 42.9 | 0.0 | 0.0 |
| GUILFORD | 081 | 3120 | 518 | 347,420 | 395,483 | 416,370 | 1.3 | 39 | 71.8 | 70.6 | 26.4 | 26.6 | 1.1 | 1.8 |
| HALIFAX | 083 | 0000 | 560 | 55,516 | 55,506 | 53,902 | 0.0 | 94 | 46.8 | 45.9 | 49.7 | 50.1 | 0.3 | 0.5 |
| HARNETT | 085 | 0000 | 560 | 67,822 | 86,423 | 96,189 | 2.4 | 12 | 75.4 | 73.9 | 22.6 | 22.9 | 0.4 | 0.8 |
| HAYWOOD | 087 | 0000 | 567 | 46,942 | 52,552 | 55,263 | 1.1 | 51 | 98.0 | 97.8 | 1.4 | 1.5 | 0.1 | 0.2 |
| HENDERSON | 089 | 0000 | 567 | 69,285 | 83,524 | 89,692 | 1.8 | 22 | 95.5 | 94.6 | 3.4 | 3.5 | 0.4 | 0.7 |
| HERTFORD | 091 | 0000 | 544 | 22,523 | 21,886 | 21,586 | -0.3 | 97 | 40.9 | 40.3 | 57.6 | 57.9 | 0.4 | 0.6 |
| HOKE | 093 | 0000 | 560 | 22,856 | 32,269 | 37,045 | 3.4 | 5 | 42.2 | 40.3 | 43.2 | 43.0 | 0.4 | 0.6 |
| HYDE | 095 | 0000 | 545 | 5,411 | 5,801 | 5,666 | 0.7 | 73 | 66.5 | 62.2 | 32.9 | 36.5 | 0.1 | 0.1 |
| IREDELL | 097 | 0000 | 517 | 92,931 | 121,361 | 140,397 | 2.6 | 9 | 83.1 | 82.0 | 16.0 | 16.4 | 0.4 | 0.7 |
| JACKSON | 099 | 0000 | 567 | 26,846 | 30,608 | 32,360 | 1.3 | 39 | 87.9 | 86.2 | 1.6 | 1.6 | 0.4 | 0.6 |
| JOHNSTON | 101 | 6640 | 560 | 81,306 | 115,045 | 135,897 | 3.4 | 5 | 80.9 | 79.1 | 17.7 | 18.3 | 0.2 | 0.3 |
| JONES | 103 | 0000 | 545 | 9,414 | 9,275 | 9,052 | -0.1 | 96 | 60.4 | 59.6 | 39.1 | 39.5 | 0.2 | 0.3 |
| LEE | 105 | 0000 | 560 | 41,374 | 50,090 | 53,256 | 1.9 | 21 | 75.4 | 73.8 | 22.7 | 23.0 | 0.5 | 0.8 |
| LENOIR | 107 | 0000 | 545 | 57,274 | 58,851 | 58,801 | 0.3 | 86 | 59.9 | 58.9 | 39.4 | 39.9 | 0.3 | 0.5 |
| LINCOLN | 109 | 1520 | 517 | 50,319 | 59,764 | 64,055 | 1.7 | 27 | 90.8 | 89.9 | 8.2 | 8.4 | 0.3 | 0.6 |
| MCDOWELL | 111 | 0000 | 567 | 35,681 | 41,096 | 43,721 | 1.4 | 35 | 95.0 | 94.0 | 4.1 | 4.7 | 0.6 | 1.0 |
| MACON | 113 | 0000 | 567 | 23,499 | 29,532 | 32,667 | 2.3 | 15 | 97.5 | 97.2 | 1.6 | 1.5 | 0.3 | 0.4 |
| MADISON | 115 | 0480 | 567 | 16,953 | 19,109 | 20,111 | 1.2 | 45 | 98.8 | 98.4 | 0.8 | 0.9 | 0.2 | 0.3 |
| MARTIN | 117 | 0000 | 545 | 25,078 | 26,107 | 25,956 | 0.4 | 85 | 55.0 | 54.5 | 44.6 | 44.8 | 0.2 | 0.3 |
| MECKLENBURG | 119 | 1520 | 517 | 511,433 | 665,804 | 751,884 | 2.6 | 9 | 71.3 | 69.5 | 26.3 | 26.5 | 1.7 | 2.9 |
| MITCHELL | 121 | 0000 | 567 | 14,433 | 14,765 | 14,772 | 0.2 | 90 | 99.5 | 98.9 | 0.2 | 0.5 | 0.1 | 0.2 |
| MONTGOMERY | 123 | 0000 | 518 | 23,346 | 24,486 | 25,304 | 0.5 | 82 | 71.8 | 70.4 | 25.7 | 25.3 | 0.6 | 1.1 |
| MOORE | 125 | 0000 | 560 | 59,013 | 74,358 | 81,726 | 2.3 | 15 | 80.4 | 79.6 | 18.4 | 18.6 | 0.3 | 0.4 |
| NASH | 127 | 6895 | 560 | 76,677 | 93,889 | 101,391 | 2.0 | 18 | 67.7 | 66.7 | 31.5 | 31.9 | 0.3 | 0.5 |
| NEW HANOVER | 129 | 9200 | 550 | 120,284 | 152,931 | 163,315 | 2.4 | 12 | 78.9 | 77.7 | 20.0 | 20.6 | 0.5 | 0.9 |
| NORTHAMPTON | 131 | 0000 | 560 | 20,798 | 21,215 | 21,104 | 0.2 | 90 | 40.4 | 40.0 | 59.3 | 59.6 | 0.1 | 0.1 |
| ONSLOW | 133 | 3605 | 545 | 149,838 | 142,291 | 141,253 | -0.5 | 99 | 74.7 | 72.3 | 19.9 | 18.6 | 2.0 | 3.4 |
| ORANGE | 135 | 6640 | 560 | 93,851 | 113,164 | 121,254 | 1.8 | 22 | 80.8 | 78.3 | 15.9 | 16.3 | 2.5 | 4.2 |
| PAMLICO | 137 | 0000 | 545 | 11,372 | 12,358 | 12,601 | 0.8 | 69 | 73.5 | 72.8 | 25.9 | 26.5 | 0.2 | 0.3 |
| PASQUOTANK | 139 | 0000 | 544 | 31,298 | 35,753 | 36,429 | 1.3 | 39 | 62.0 | 59.6 | 37.0 | 38.8 | 0.6 | 1.0 |
| PENDER | 141 | 0000 | 550 | 28,855 | 41,481 | 47,338 | 3.6 | 2 | 68.7 | 66.7 | 30.4 | 31.8 | 0.2 | 0.2 |
| PERQUIMANS | 143 | 0000 | 544 | 10,447 | 11,405 | 11,958 | 0.9 | 63 | 66.8 | 66.4 | 32.8 | 33.0 | 0.2 | 0.4 |
| PERSON | 145 | 0000 | 560 | 30,180 | 34,355 | 36,167 | 1.3 | 39 | 68.7 | 67.8 | 30.2 | 30.6 | 0.0 | 0.1 |
| PITT | 147 | 3150 | 545 | 107,924 | 129,773 | 138,769 | 1.8 | 22 | 65.5 | 63.6 | 33.3 | 34.2 | 0.7 | 1.1 |
| POLK | 149 | 0000 | 567 | 14,416 | 17,072 | 17,953 | 1.7 | 27 | 92.1 | 91.4 | 7.3 | 7.6 | 0.2 | 0.3 |
| RANDOLPH | 151 | 3120 | 518 | 106,546 | 125,478 | 135,753 | 1.6 | 30 | 93.0 | 92.1 | 6.0 | 6.1 | 0.3 | 0.6 |
| RICHMOND | 153 | 0000 | 517 | 44,518 | 45,652 | 45,327 | 0.2 | 90 | 69.2 | 67.9 | 28.9 | 29.5 | 0.4 | 0.7 |
| NORTH CAROLINA | | | | | | | 1.6 | | 75.6 | 74.5 | 22.0 | 22.0 | 0.8 | 1.4 |
| UNITED STATES | | | | | | | 1.0 | | 80.3 | 77.9 | 12.1 | 12.4 | 2.9 | 3.9 |

# B

| COUNTY | % HISPANIC ORIGIN 1990 | % HISPANIC ORIGIN 2000 | 2000 AGE DISTRIBUTION (%) 0-4 | 5-9 | 10-14 | 15-19 | 20-24 | 25-44 | 45-64 | 65-84 | 85+ | 18+ | MEDIAN AGE 1990 | MEDIAN AGE 2000 | 2000 Males/ Females (×100) |
|---|---|---|---|---|---|---|---|---|---|---|---|---|---|---|---|
| ALAMANCE | 0.7 | 1.8 | 6.0 | 6.5 | 6.9 | 6.6 | 5.6 | 28.7 | 24.4 | 13.6 | 1.7 | 77.3 | 35.6 | 38.5 | 90.9 |
| ALEXANDER | 0.7 | 1.8 | 6.3 | 7.0 | 7.4 | 6.5 | 5.3 | 30.0 | 25.5 | 10.8 | 1.3 | 75.5 | 33.8 | 37.4 | 98.6 |
| ALLEGHANY | 0.9 | 1.9 | 4.9 | 5.8 | 6.3 | 5.8 | 4.6 | 25.7 | 26.6 | 17.5 | 2.8 | 79.2 | 39.6 | 42.8 | 92.8 |
| ANSON | 0.3 | 0.7 | 6.5 | 7.4 | 7.8 | 6.9 | 5.9 | 28.8 | 22.0 | 12.6 | 2.0 | 73.8 | 34.2 | 36.3 | 93.3 |
| ASHE | 0.5 | 1.1 | 5.0 | 5.9 | 6.5 | 5.9 | 4.9 | 27.0 | 26.9 | 15.4 | 2.4 | 78.9 | 38.6 | 41.6 | 93.6 |
| AVERY | 0.8 | 1.5 | 5.6 | 6.1 | 6.5 | 8.2 | 5.7 | 27.0 | 25.9 | 13.3 | 1.8 | 78.2 | 35.0 | 38.5 | 101.3 |
| BEAUFORT | 0.5 | 1.2 | 6.5 | 7.2 | 7.8 | 6.6 | 5.2 | 26.8 | 24.4 | 13.7 | 1.9 | 74.4 | 35.7 | 38.4 | 90.4 |
| BERTIE | 0.2 | 0.4 | 7.5 | 7.8 | 7.9 | 7.6 | 6.0 | 26.8 | 21.8 | 12.9 | 1.6 | 71.8 | 33.4 | 35.8 | 87.7 |
| BLADEN | 0.5 | 1.2 | 6.3 | 7.4 | 7.8 | 7.0 | 5.4 | 27.3 | 24.3 | 12.8 | 1.6 | 74.1 | 34.9 | 37.5 | 89.3 |
| BRUNSWICK | 0.7 | 1.8 | 6.3 | 6.7 | 6.9 | 5.7 | 4.6 | 26.1 | 26.0 | 16.4 | 1.2 | 76.5 | 37.1 | 40.6 | 95.8 |
| BUNCOMBE | 0.7 | 1.8 | 6.2 | 6.5 | 6.9 | 6.2 | 5.3 | 28.4 | 24.5 | 13.8 | 2.1 | 76.8 | 36.8 | 39.0 | 91.3 |
| BURKE | 0.5 | 1.3 | 6.4 | 6.6 | 7.1 | 7.1 | 5.2 | 28.9 | 25.1 | 12.2 | 1.4 | 75.7 | 35.1 | 37.8 | 97.9 |
| CABARRUS | 0.5 | 1.4 | 6.9 | 7.3 | 7.4 | 6.3 | 5.2 | 29.8 | 24.2 | 11.4 | 1.4 | 74.6 | 34.6 | 37.0 | 94.1 |
| CALDWELL | 0.4 | 1.3 | 6.4 | 6.7 | 7.2 | 6.1 | 5.2 | 29.8 | 25.3 | 11.9 | 1.4 | 76.1 | 34.6 | 37.9 | 96.2 |
| CAMDEN | 0.4 | 1.1 | 6.4 | 6.9 | 7.3 | 6.2 | 5.1 | 28.2 | 25.6 | 12.9 | 1.4 | 75.6 | 35.8 | 38.7 | 99.4 |
| CARTERET | 0.9 | 2.1 | 6.3 | 6.6 | 6.6 | 5.6 | 5.0 | 29.2 | 24.4 | 14.7 | 1.5 | 77.2 | 35.9 | 39.0 | 97.4 |
| CASWELL | 0.7 | 1.4 | 5.9 | 6.6 | 6.9 | 6.5 | 5.6 | 28.9 | 25.2 | 12.8 | 1.6 | 76.7 | 35.8 | 38.6 | 99.1 |
| CATAWBA | 0.8 | 2.0 | 6.5 | 6.9 | 7.3 | 6.4 | 5.5 | 30.1 | 24.5 | 11.5 | 1.3 | 75.7 | 34.3 | 37.3 | 94.4 |
| CHATHAM | 1.5 | 3.2 | 6.6 | 6.9 | 6.9 | 5.7 | 4.5 | 29.8 | 24.1 | 13.5 | 1.9 | 76.3 | 36.1 | 38.8 | 94.7 |
| CHEROKEE | 0.6 | 1.8 | 5.4 | 5.8 | 6.1 | 6.1 | 5.4 | 25.9 | 26.3 | 16.6 | 2.3 | 78.9 | 39.3 | 41.6 | 92.5 |
| CHOWAN | 0.7 | 1.6 | 7.0 | 7.9 | 7.7 | 6.6 | 4.8 | 25.5 | 23.0 | 15.1 | 2.3 | 73.2 | 36.4 | 38.3 | 86.8 |
| CLAY | 0.6 | 1.6 | 4.8 | 6.1 | 6.6 | 6.6 | 4.3 | 24.7 | 26.1 | 18.6 | 2.3 | 78.3 | 40.2 | 43.0 | 94.8 |
| CLEVELAND | 0.4 | 1.2 | 6.7 | 7.1 | 7.5 | 6.6 | 5.6 | 28.4 | 24.3 | 12.1 | 1.5 | 74.8 | 34.7 | 37.2 | 93.2 |
| COLUMBUS | 0.5 | 1.1 | 6.8 | 7.7 | 8.0 | 7.1 | 5.4 | 27.3 | 24.0 | 12.3 | 1.4 | 73.1 | 34.3 | 36.8 | 91.1 |
| CRAVEN | 2.2 | 4.5 | 8.7 | 7.7 | 6.7 | 6.2 | 9.1 | 30.0 | 19.2 | 11.4 | 1.1 | 73.5 | 30.2 | 32.4 | 97.5 |
| CUMBERLAND | 4.8 | 9.4 | 9.7 | 8.3 | 7.0 | 7.0 | 10.6 | 34.4 | 15.8 | 6.7 | 0.6 | 71.7 | 27.3 | 28.7 | 104.1 |
| CURRITUCK | 0.8 | 2.1 | 7.4 | 7.9 | 7.8 | 6.2 | 4.7 | 29.3 | 24.1 | 11.4 | 1.2 | 73.0 | 34.3 | 36.8 | 101.5 |
| DARE | 0.9 | 2.2 | 6.7 | 7.1 | 6.6 | 5.3 | 4.5 | 31.9 | 24.0 | 12.8 | 1.2 | 76.4 | 35.2 | 38.2 | 98.5 |
| DAVIDSON | 0.5 | 1.3 | 6.5 | 6.9 | 7.3 | 6.2 | 5.2 | 30.1 | 25.0 | 11.5 | 1.3 | 75.5 | 34.5 | 37.5 | 96.2 |
| DAVIE | 0.5 | 1.3 | 5.7 | 6.5 | 7.2 | 6.2 | 4.8 | 28.9 | 25.9 | 13.0 | 1.7 | 76.8 | 36.3 | 39.3 | 96.4 |
| DUPLIN | 2.5 | 5.1 | 7.0 | 7.6 | 7.8 | 6.9 | 5.5 | 27.9 | 23.4 | 12.4 | 1.5 | 73.3 | 34.3 | 36.6 | 93.3 |
| DURHAM | 1.1 | 2.4 | 7.0 | 7.1 | 7.0 | 7.1 | 7.5 | 33.5 | 20.4 | 9.2 | 1.4 | 75.7 | 31.7 | 34.3 | 89.6 |
| EDGECOMBE | 0.5 | 0.9 | 7.4 | 8.2 | 8.5 | 7.0 | 5.9 | 29.1 | 22.0 | 10.4 | 1.5 | 71.6 | 32.6 | 34.6 | 84.6 |
| FORSYTH | 0.8 | 1.9 | 6.6 | 6.8 | 6.8 | 6.4 | 6.1 | 30.9 | 23.1 | 11.5 | 1.7 | 76.4 | 33.9 | 36.8 | 89.4 |
| FRANKLIN | 0.8 | 1.7 | 6.7 | 7.3 | 7.5 | 7.0 | 5.6 | 30.0 | 23.5 | 10.9 | 1.6 | 75.0 | 33.7 | 36.4 | 93.3 |
| GASTON | 0.5 | 1.3 | 7.1 | 7.4 | 7.5 | 6.6 | 5.5 | 29.8 | 23.3 | 11.4 | 1.4 | 74.0 | 33.5 | 36.2 | 92.8 |
| GATES | 0.2 | 0.6 | 7.1 | 7.9 | 7.7 | 6.7 | 4.9 | 28.3 | 23.1 | 12.8 | 1.5 | 73.2 | 34.2 | 36.8 | 97.4 |
| GRAHAM | 0.4 | 1.3 | 5.8 | 6.2 | 6.6 | 6.0 | 5.4 | 27.6 | 26.5 | 14.2 | 1.7 | 77.9 | 37.0 | 39.4 | 97.9 |
| GRANVILLE | 0.9 | 1.9 | 6.7 | 7.0 | 7.5 | 6.3 | 5.6 | 31.0 | 23.6 | 10.9 | 1.5 | 74.9 | 34.1 | 36.6 | 97.0 |
| GREENE | 1.1 | 2.4 | 6.5 | 7.5 | 7.5 | 6.7 | 5.9 | 30.7 | 22.6 | 11.3 | 1.3 | 74.3 | 33.5 | 35.9 | 103.3 |
| GUILFORD | 0.8 | 1.9 | 6.5 | 6.7 | 6.8 | 6.9 | 6.8 | 30.9 | 22.9 | 11.0 | 1.6 | 76.7 | 33.4 | 36.2 | 89.6 |
| HALIFAX | 0.4 | 0.9 | 7.2 | 7.4 | 7.6 | 7.4 | 6.3 | 27.6 | 22.2 | 12.7 | 1.6 | 73.1 | 33.6 | 35.6 | 92.5 |
| HARNETT | 1.7 | 3.8 | 8.2 | 7.6 | 7.4 | 7.1 | 7.6 | 29.5 | 21.3 | 10.1 | 1.2 | 73.0 | 31.3 | 33.2 | 94.3 |
| HAYWOOD | 0.5 | 1.5 | 5.6 | 5.9 | 6.3 | 5.6 | 4.6 | 26.0 | 26.9 | 16.7 | 2.4 | 78.8 | 39.9 | 42.3 | 91.2 |
| HENDERSON | 1.2 | 3.1 | 5.6 | 6.2 | 6.4 | 5.5 | 4.3 | 25.2 | 24.9 | 19.1 | 2.8 | 78.4 | 40.7 | 42.8 | 91.9 |
| HERTFORD | 0.4 | 0.8 | 7.0 | 8.0 | 7.8 | 8.3 | 5.9 | 25.6 | 22.5 | 12.9 | 1.9 | 72.8 | 33.6 | 36.0 | 86.8 |
| HOKE | 1.0 | 1.9 | 8.7 | 9.2 | 9.1 | 8.0 | 6.6 | 30.0 | 19.8 | 7.6 | 0.9 | 68.3 | 29.6 | 30.7 | 98.9 |
| HYDE | 0.8 | 1.7 | 6.1 | 6.8 | 8.1 | 7.6 | 5.3 | 26.9 | 22.7 | 14.4 | 2.1 | 74.3 | 35.8 | 37.5 | 103.8 |
| IREDELL | 0.7 | 1.9 | 6.8 | 7.1 | 7.3 | 6.3 | 5.1 | 29.3 | 24.7 | 11.9 | 1.4 | 75.1 | 34.8 | 37.5 | 94.1 |
| JACKSON | 0.6 | 1.5 | 5.2 | 5.8 | 6.0 | 10.1 | 9.4 | 25.7 | 23.6 | 12.4 | 1.8 | 79.7 | 33.0 | 36.2 | 93.2 |
| JOHNSTON | 1.6 | 3.5 | 7.1 | 7.4 | 7.6 | 6.3 | 5.3 | 30.4 | 24.3 | 10.4 | 1.2 | 74.1 | 34.3 | 36.4 | 95.2 |
| JONES | 0.6 | 1.3 | 7.5 | 7.8 | 8.0 | 6.6 | 4.7 | 26.9 | 22.9 | 14.2 | 1.4 | 72.6 | 34.2 | 37.3 | 88.9 |
| LEE | 1.9 | 4.0 | 7.3 | 7.8 | 7.7 | 6.5 | 5.3 | 28.5 | 23.2 | 12.3 | 1.4 | 73.2 | 34.2 | 36.5 | 93.3 |
| LENOIR | 0.8 | 1.7 | 6.3 | 6.7 | 7.2 | 6.9 | 5.9 | 28.5 | 24.0 | 12.9 | 1.6 | 75.4 | 34.7 | 37.4 | 88.9 |
| LINCOLN | 1.1 | 2.9 | 7.0 | 7.3 | 7.5 | 6.3 | 5.2 | 29.9 | 24.2 | 11.4 | 1.3 | 74.5 | 33.9 | 36.8 | 96.7 |
| MCDOWELL | 0.3 | 1.0 | 6.2 | 6.6 | 7.2 | 6.3 | 5.1 | 29.0 | 24.9 | 12.9 | 1.8 | 76.2 | 35.7 | 38.3 | 97.4 |
| MACON | 0.7 | 1.8 | 5.1 | 5.8 | 6.1 | 5.6 | 3.9 | 23.7 | 27.4 | 19.5 | 2.8 | 79.7 | 42.7 | 44.8 | 92.3 |
| MADISON | 0.5 | 1.5 | 5.6 | 6.1 | 6.8 | 7.5 | 6.4 | 26.1 | 25.3 | 14.0 | 2.1 | 77.6 | 36.8 | 39.2 | 98.1 |
| MARTIN | 0.4 | 0.8 | 6.8 | 7.3 | 7.5 | 6.8 | 5.6 | 27.1 | 24.0 | 13.1 | 1.6 | 74.0 | 34.7 | 37.2 | 91.2 |
| MECKLENBURG | 1.3 | 3.0 | 7.5 | 7.6 | 7.3 | 6.4 | 6.2 | 33.9 | 21.5 | 8.5 | 1.1 | 74.2 | 32.0 | 34.5 | 92.3 |
| MITCHELL | 0.3 | 1.2 | 5.5 | 6.1 | 6.4 | 6.1 | 4.6 | 26.5 | 26.6 | 15.8 | 2.4 | 78.2 | 39.0 | 41.6 | 93.1 |
| MONTGOMERY | 2.4 | 5.1 | 6.5 | 6.9 | 7.4 | 7.0 | 6.9 | 28.7 | 23.3 | 11.8 | 1.5 | 75.0 | 33.7 | 35.9 | 106.2 |
| MOORE | 0.8 | 1.9 | 5.9 | 6.4 | 6.7 | 6.1 | 4.8 | 25.5 | 22.5 | 19.5 | 2.5 | 77.3 | 38.6 | 41.2 | 91.4 |
| NASH | 0.8 | 1.7 | 6.6 | 7.2 | 7.3 | 6.5 | 5.8 | 29.8 | 23.9 | 11.4 | 1.4 | 75.0 | 33.8 | 36.7 | 91.8 |
| NEW HANOVER | 0.8 | 1.9 | 6.0 | 6.4 | 6.6 | 7.0 | 6.8 | 30.3 | 23.8 | 11.6 | 1.4 | 77.6 | 33.9 | 36.8 | 89.7 |
| NORTHAMPTON | 0.6 | 1.0 | 6.3 | 7.4 | 7.4 | 6.6 | 5.2 | 26.5 | 23.7 | 15.0 | 1.9 | 74.9 | 36.3 | 38.5 | 93.6 |
| ONSLOW | 5.4 | 9.9 | 10.3 | 8.3 | 6.6 | 7.3 | 17.3 | 31.3 | 12.3 | 6.0 | 0.6 | 72.4 | 24.6 | 25.1 | 132.2 |
| ORANGE | 1.4 | 3.2 | 5.9 | 5.9 | 5.7 | 8.7 | 13.0 | 32.6 | 18.9 | 8.1 | 1.2 | 79.8 | 28.9 | 31.6 | 90.5 |
| PAMLICO | 0.5 | 1.5 | 6.1 | 6.9 | 7.2 | 5.9 | 4.4 | 24.9 | 25.7 | 16.7 | 2.2 | 76.2 | 38.3 | 41.4 | 92.6 |
| PASQUOTANK | 0.8 | 2.0 | 7.9 | 8.1 | 8.1 | 8.6 | 7.8 | 26.2 | 20.4 | 11.4 | 1.7 | 71.6 | 32.2 | 33.4 | 89.5 |
| PENDER | 0.9 | 2.1 | 6.6 | 7.1 | 7.2 | 6.1 | 5.1 | 28.2 | 25.2 | 13.2 | 1.3 | 75.3 | 35.9 | 38.4 | 97.1 |
| PERQUIMANS | 0.3 | 0.8 | 6.5 | 7.5 | 7.4 | 6.1 | 4.6 | 24.7 | 23.9 | 17.2 | 2.2 | 74.9 | 37.6 | 40.2 | 92.4 |
| PERSON | 0.8 | 1.8 | 6.9 | 7.2 | 7.6 | 6.2 | 5.1 | 29.5 | 24.0 | 12.0 | 1.6 | 74.6 | 34.8 | 37.4 | 93.4 |
| PITT | 0.9 | 2.0 | 6.9 | 7.1 | 7.0 | 8.6 | 10.6 | 30.4 | 19.5 | 8.8 | 1.0 | 75.3 | 29.5 | 31.6 | 91.3 |
| POLK | 0.8 | 2.1 | 5.0 | 5.5 | 5.9 | 5.4 | 4.4 | 23.4 | 25.2 | 21.0 | 4.1 | 80.2 | 43.3 | 45.2 | 86.2 |
| RANDOLPH | 0.7 | 1.8 | 6.9 | 7.1 | 7.3 | 6.1 | 5.2 | 30.0 | 24.4 | 11.6 | 1.3 | 75.0 | 34.3 | 37.2 | 95.9 |
| RICHMOND | 0.7 | 1.4 | 6.9 | 7.4 | 8.1 | 7.3 | 6.1 | 27.0 | 23.1 | 12.6 | 1.5 | 73.1 | 34.0 | 36.1 | 92.1 |
| NORTH CAROLINA | 1.2 | 2.5 | 6.9 | 7.2 | 7.2 | 6.7 | 6.6 | 30.3 | 22.6 | 11.1 | 1.4 | 75.1 | 33.1 | 35.7 | 94.1 |
| UNITED STATES | 9.0 | 11.8 | 6.9 | 7.2 | 7.2 | 7.2 | 6.7 | 29.9 | 22.2 | 11.1 | 1.6 | 74.6 | 32.9 | 35.7 | 95.6 |

| COUNTY | HOUSEHOLDS | | | | | FAMILIES | | | MEDIAN HOUSEHOLD INCOME | | | |
|---|---|---|---|---|---|---|---|---|---|---|---|---|
| | 1990 | 2000 | 2005 | % Annual Rate 1990-2000 | 2000 Average HH Size | 1990 | 2000 | % Annual Rate 1990-2000 | 2000 | 2005 | 2000 National Rank | 2000 State Rank |
| ALAMANCE | 42,652 | 48,324 | 51,354 | 1.5 | 2.47 | 30,745 | 33,789 | 1.2 | 36,412 | 40,984 | 1058 | 36 |
| ALEXANDER | 10,331 | 12,168 | 13,314 | 2.0 | 2.66 | 8,049 | 9,201 | 1.6 | 36,610 | 41,063 | 1030 | 35 |
| ALLEGHANY | 3,894 | 4,027 | 4,105 | 0.4 | 2.40 | 2,829 | 2,801 | -0.1 | 28,325 | 31,819 | 2395 | 87 |
| ANSON | 8,531 | 8,522 | 8,483 | 0.0 | 2.67 | 6,359 | 6,132 | -0.4 | 29,705 | 32,923 | 2200 | 80 |
| ASHE | 8,848 | 9,764 | 10,187 | 1.2 | 2.48 | 6,748 | 7,191 | 0.8 | 28,593 | 31,101 | 2352 | 83 |
| AVERY | 5,520 | 6,107 | 6,340 | 1.2 | 2.51 | 4,162 | 4,428 | 0.8 | 31,019 | 34,178 | 1928 | 63 |
| BEAUFORT | 16,157 | 17,198 | 17,928 | 0.8 | 2.61 | 11,840 | 12,174 | 0.3 | 29,815 | 34,984 | 2179 | 77 |
| BERTIE | 7,412 | 7,382 | 7,329 | 0.0 | 2.73 | 5,501 | 5,277 | -0.5 | 25,931 | 31,714 | 2719 | 95 |
| BLADEN | 10,760 | 11,719 | 12,132 | 1.0 | 2.61 | 8,017 | 8,438 | 0.6 | 30,628 | 33,481 | 2002 | 68 |
| BRUNSWICK | 20,069 | 29,165 | 34,543 | 4.6 | 2.52 | 15,291 | 21,584 | 4.3 | 36,131 | 41,708 | 1086 | 38 |
| BUNCOMBE | 70,802 | 80,364 | 84,379 | 1.5 | 2.39 | 49,335 | 54,244 | 1.2 | 37,739 | 42,735 | 872 | 27 |
| BURKE | 29,184 | 32,298 | 33,917 | 1.2 | 2.50 | 21,711 | 23,236 | 0.8 | 35,707 | 40,479 | 1134 | 40 |
| CABARRUS | 37,515 | 48,207 | 55,407 | 3.1 | 2.64 | 28,367 | 35,535 | 2.8 | 46,103 | 52,954 | 305 | 3 |
| CALDWELL | 27,172 | 29,904 | 31,203 | 1.2 | 2.55 | 20,656 | 22,054 | 0.8 | 34,915 | 40,163 | 1267 | 44 |
| CAMDEN | 2,180 | 2,672 | 2,910 | 2.5 | 2.60 | 1,692 | 2,008 | 2.1 | 39,636 | 46,426 | 698 | 18 |
| CARTERET | 21,238 | 24,903 | 26,121 | 1.9 | 2.39 | 15,276 | 17,350 | 1.6 | 38,561 | 45,219 | 799 | 24 |
| CASWELL | 7,468 | 7,918 | 8,222 | 0.7 | 2.67 | 5,781 | 5,918 | 0.3 | 33,317 | 40,193 | 1488 | 50 |
| CATAWBA | 45,700 | 52,960 | 56,886 | 1.8 | 2.54 | 33,773 | 37,971 | 1.4 | 40,035 | 43,938 | 671 | 16 |
| CHATHAM | 15,293 | 18,578 | 20,260 | 2.4 | 2.52 | 11,227 | 13,140 | 1.9 | 41,785 | 47,645 | 532 | 8 |
| CHEROKEE | 7,966 | 9,324 | 10,195 | 1.9 | 2.50 | 6,069 | 6,861 | 1.5 | 29,459 | 36,587 | 2227 | 81 |
| CHOWAN | 5,113 | 5,433 | 5,568 | 0.7 | 2.60 | 3,775 | 3,863 | 0.3 | 29,741 | 32,815 | 2193 | 79 |
| CLAY | 2,928 | 3,658 | 4,103 | 2.7 | 2.42 | 2,177 | 2,595 | 2.2 | 28,482 | 32,292 | 2370 | 86 |
| CLEVELAND | 32,037 | 35,900 | 37,784 | 1.4 | 2.59 | 24,282 | 26,490 | 1.1 | 36,190 | 41,618 | 1080 | 37 |
| COLUMBUS | 18,459 | 19,656 | 20,246 | 0.8 | 2.65 | 13,754 | 14,154 | 0.3 | 28,255 | 31,506 | 2409 | 88 |
| CRAVEN | 29,542 | 32,252 | 33,441 | 1.1 | 2.65 | 22,481 | 23,768 | 0.7 | 36,672 | 42,545 | 1022 | 34 |
| CUMBERLAND | 91,500 | 95,949 | 95,284 | 0.6 | 2.75 | 69,966 | 71,580 | 0.3 | 37,288 | 44,881 | 935 | 30 |
| CURRITUCK | 5,038 | 6,977 | 7,980 | 4.0 | 2.67 | 3,854 | 5,182 | 3.7 | 42,149 | 52,791 | 497 | 6 |
| DARE | 9,349 | 12,697 | 14,630 | 3.8 | 2.39 | 6,425 | 8,383 | 3.3 | 39,936 | 45,832 | 681 | 17 |
| DAVIDSON | 48,944 | 56,184 | 59,980 | 1.7 | 2.55 | 37,176 | 41,430 | 1.3 | 37,411 | 43,958 | 912 | 28 |
| DAVIE | 10,785 | 13,092 | 14,697 | 2.4 | 2.53 | 8,270 | 9,723 | 2.0 | 41,240 | 45,897 | 566 | 10 |
| DUPLIN | 14,925 | 16,242 | 16,750 | 1.0 | 2.64 | 11,036 | 11,538 | 0.5 | 31,006 | 33,796 | 1935 | 64 |
| DURHAM | 72,297 | 82,895 | 87,827 | 1.7 | 2.38 | 45,985 | 50,828 | 1.2 | 43,067 | 49,647 | 454 | 4 |
| EDGECOMBE | 20,319 | 19,568 | 19,010 | -0.5 | 2.71 | 15,085 | 14,111 | -0.8 | 29,813 | 34,299 | 2181 | 78 |
| FORSYTH | 107,419 | 118,117 | 121,795 | 1.2 | 2.38 | 72,621 | 77,409 | 0.8 | 40,458 | 44,368 | 631 | 15 |
| FRANKLIN | 13,503 | 17,519 | 19,558 | 3.2 | 2.59 | 10,047 | 12,650 | 2.8 | 37,904 | 47,228 | 856 | 26 |
| GASTON | 65,347 | 69,435 | 71,609 | 0.7 | 2.65 | 49,754 | 51,228 | 0.4 | 40,746 | 46,377 | 608 | 11 |
| GATES | 3,352 | 3,687 | 3,840 | 1.2 | 2.74 | 2,593 | 2,758 | 0.8 | 32,665 | 39,142 | 1600 | 53 |
| GRAHAM | 2,772 | 2,942 | 2,971 | 0.7 | 2.55 | 2,166 | 2,212 | 0.3 | 28,931 | 32,882 | 2306 | 82 |
| GRANVILLE | 13,134 | 15,540 | 16,957 | 2.1 | 2.68 | 9,883 | 11,311 | 1.6 | 40,461 | 49,677 | 630 | 14 |
| GREENE | 5,395 | 6,594 | 7,165 | 2.5 | 2.66 | 4,066 | 4,807 | 2.0 | 30,620 | 32,809 | 2005 | 69 |
| GUILFORD | 137,706 | 158,028 | 167,093 | 1.7 | 2.42 | 92,891 | 103,207 | 1.3 | 41,568 | 46,435 | 543 | 9 |
| HALIFAX | 20,335 | 20,581 | 20,136 | 0.1 | 2.62 | 14,874 | 14,616 | -0.2 | 27,483 | 32,325 | 2511 | 91 |
| HARNETT | 25,150 | 32,137 | 35,910 | 3.0 | 2.60 | 18,529 | 22,912 | 2.6 | 32,448 | 37,741 | 1634 | 55 |
| HAYWOOD | 19,211 | 21,587 | 22,778 | 1.4 | 2.39 | 14,120 | 15,328 | 1.0 | 31,161 | 34,965 | 1897 | 60 |
| HENDERSON | 28,709 | 34,770 | 37,415 | 2.3 | 2.37 | 21,169 | 24,769 | 1.9 | 39,452 | 44,940 | 716 | 21 |
| HERTFORD | 8,150 | 8,143 | 8,092 | 0.0 | 2.61 | 5,921 | 5,711 | -0.4 | 26,586 | 30,727 | 2637 | 93 |
| HOKE | 7,405 | 10,603 | 12,251 | 4.4 | 2.92 | 5,794 | 8,052 | 4.1 | 30,314 | 35,749 | 2077 | 72 |
| HYDE | 2,094 | 2,060 | 2,031 | -0.2 | 2.50 | 1,533 | 1,451 | -0.7 | 22,544 | 24,583 | 2994 | 99 |
| IREDELL | 35,573 | 46,190 | 53,285 | 3.2 | 2.61 | 26,869 | 34,067 | 2.9 | 42,850 | 50,517 | 464 | 5 |
| JACKSON | 9,683 | 11,408 | 12,209 | 2.0 | 2.43 | 6,970 | 7,919 | 1.6 | 31,344 | 36,330 | 1854 | 59 |
| JOHNSTON | 31,566 | 44,529 | 52,657 | 4.3 | 2.55 | 23,217 | 31,883 | 3.9 | 40,704 | 48,689 | 610 | 12 |
| JONES | 3,492 | 3,484 | 3,438 | 0.0 | 2.64 | 2,639 | 2,544 | -0.4 | 28,021 | 29,915 | 2441 | 90 |
| LEE | 15,689 | 19,574 | 21,121 | 2.7 | 2.52 | 11,739 | 14,254 | 2.4 | 39,459 | 45,689 | 714 | 19 |
| LENOIR | 21,938 | 22,782 | 22,852 | 0.5 | 2.52 | 15,611 | 15,725 | 0.1 | 30,157 | 33,743 | 2121 | 75 |
| LINCOLN | 18,764 | 22,302 | 23,926 | 2.1 | 2.65 | 14,661 | 16,934 | 1.8 | 38,332 | 45,216 | 828 | 25 |
| MCDOWELL | 13,680 | 15,507 | 16,588 | 1.5 | 2.55 | 10,366 | 11,384 | 1.1 | 33,418 | 38,183 | 1472 | 49 |
| MACON | 9,834 | 12,485 | 13,880 | 2.9 | 2.32 | 7,235 | 8,861 | 2.5 | 31,831 | 35,703 | 1752 | 57 |
| MADISON | 6,488 | 7,483 | 7,952 | 1.7 | 2.45 | 4,806 | 5,357 | 1.3 | 30,505 | 37,065 | 2030 | 71 |
| MARTIN | 9,317 | 9,762 | 9,730 | 0.6 | 2.65 | 6,900 | 6,994 | 0.2 | 25,174 | 29,291 | 2794 | 97 |
| MECKLENBURG | 200,219 | 261,316 | 295,514 | 3.3 | 2.50 | 134,361 | 170,925 | 3.0 | 49,077 | 54,412 | 220 | 2 |
| MITCHELL | 5,779 | 5,946 | 5,976 | 0.3 | 2.45 | 4,420 | 4,384 | -0.1 | 30,533 | 35,299 | 2026 | 70 |
| MONTGOMERY | 8,290 | 8,632 | 8,908 | 0.5 | 2.70 | 6,274 | 6,324 | 0.1 | 30,780 | 36,468 | 1974 | 66 |
| MOORE | 23,827 | 30,017 | 33,008 | 2.8 | 2.44 | 17,483 | 21,220 | 2.4 | 39,456 | 43,150 | 715 | 20 |
| NASH | 29,041 | 35,436 | 38,390 | 2.4 | 2.59 | 21,224 | 25,073 | 2.0 | 37,111 | 42,709 | 958 | 31 |
| NEW HANOVER | 48,139 | 62,860 | 68,048 | 3.3 | 2.37 | 32,400 | 41,222 | 3.0 | 38,844 | 42,230 | 768 | 22 |
| NORTHAMPTON | 7,591 | 7,849 | 7,847 | 0.4 | 2.61 | 5,644 | 5,625 | 0.0 | 26,603 | 30,626 | 2633 | 92 |
| ONSLOW | 40,658 | 41,002 | 40,950 | 0.1 | 2.79 | 32,971 | 32,616 | -0.1 | 32,286 | 40,783 | 1664 | 56 |
| ORANGE | 36,104 | 44,390 | 47,792 | 2.5 | 2.35 | 21,123 | 25,081 | 2.1 | 41,943 | 46,581 | 517 | 7 |
| PAMLICO | 4,523 | 5,036 | 5,192 | 1.3 | 2.43 | 3,382 | 3,639 | 0.9 | 30,273 | 35,067 | 2089 | 73 |
| PASQUOTANK | 11,384 | 12,642 | 12,945 | 1.3 | 2.61 | 8,326 | 9,087 | 1.1 | 31,076 | 36,365 | 1916 | 62 |
| PENDER | 11,112 | 16,249 | 18,861 | 4.7 | 2.49 | 8,420 | 11,982 | 4.4 | 35,496 | 40,851 | 1172 | 42 |
| PERQUIMANS | 3,988 | 4,461 | 4,733 | 1.4 | 2.53 | 3,038 | 3,253 | 0.8 | 28,072 | 35,807 | 2430 | 89 |
| PERSON | 11,423 | 13,180 | 13,977 | 1.7 | 2.58 | 8,570 | 9,664 | 1.5 | 38,604 | 44,931 | 791 | 23 |
| PITT | 40,491 | 49,511 | 53,340 | 2.5 | 2.50 | 26,434 | 30,942 | 1.9 | 35,552 | 39,873 | 1161 | 41 |
| POLK | 6,110 | 7,356 | 7,816 | 2.3 | 2.28 | 4,346 | 5,001 | 1.7 | 36,928 | 41,851 | 988 | 32 |
| RANDOLPH | 41,096 | 48,395 | 52,408 | 2.0 | 2.57 | 31,363 | 35,851 | 1.6 | 36,907 | 43,142 | 989 | 33 |
| RICHMOND | 16,793 | 17,433 | 17,450 | 0.5 | 2.55 | 12,270 | 12,261 | 0.0 | 28,493 | 32,031 | 2367 | 85 |
| NORTH CAROLINA | | | | 2.0 | 2.53 | | | 1.6 | 38,498 | 44,239 | | |
| UNITED STATES | | | | 1.4 | 2.59 | | | 1.1 | 41,914 | 49,127 | | |

# INCOME

| COUNTY | 2000 Per Capita Income | 2000 HH Income Base | 2000 HOUSEHOLD INCOME DISTRIBUTION (%): Less than $15,000 | $15,000 to $24,999 | $25,000 to $49,999 | $50,000 to $99,999 | $100,000 to $149,999 | $150,000 or More | 2000 AVERAGE DISPOSABLE INCOME BY AGE OF HOUSEHOLDER: All Ages | <35 | 35-44 | 45-54 | 55-64 | 65+ |
|---|---|---|---|---|---|---|---|---|---|---|---|---|---|---|
| ALAMANCE | 18,271 | 48,324 | 15.9 | 15.3 | 37.3 | 26.3 | 4.1 | 1.3 | 33,687 | 30,714 | 38,621 | 41,768 | 37,835 | 21,498 |
| ALEXANDER | 16,103 | 12,168 | 16.0 | 14.5 | 38.8 | 26.4 | 3.5 | 0.9 | 32,868 | 30,698 | 38,467 | 41,466 | 34,846 | 19,110 |
| ALLEGHANY | 15,829 | 4,027 | 23.3 | 19.8 | 34.6 | 17.5 | 3.3 | 1.5 | 29,352 | 28,284 | 39,130 | 30,742 | 31,232 | 21,435 |
| ANSON | 13,021 | 8,522 | 23.4 | 17.3 | 37.0 | 20.0 | 2.2 | 0.2 | 27,635 | 26,890 | 31,893 | 35,403 | 29,127 | 17,041 |
| ASHE | 14,028 | 9,764 | 23.0 | 20.4 | 35.0 | 18.6 | 2.3 | 0.6 | 27,385 | 25,814 | 33,482 | 33,072 | 28,536 | 19,471 |
| AVERY | 15,471 | 6,107 | 20.3 | 18.7 | 34.1 | 22.0 | 3.8 | 1.1 | 30,644 | 28,302 | 36,810 | 36,306 | 35,561 | 19,672 |
| BEAUFORT | 14,891 | 17,198 | 24.7 | 17.5 | 33.2 | 20.2 | 3.4 | 1.1 | 29,279 | 26,036 | 34,500 | 37,444 | 31,834 | 19,210 |
| BERTIE | 11,925 | 7,382 | 27.8 | 20.1 | 32.8 | 16.9 | 2.2 | 0.2 | 25,702 | 24,259 | 30,789 | 32,114 | 25,381 | 18,202 |
| BLADEN | 15,642 | 11,719 | 23.3 | 16.8 | 35.0 | 20.9 | 3.0 | 1.0 | 29,279 | 26,248 | 37,433 | 36,454 | 26,968 | 19,732 |
| BRUNSWICK | 18,350 | 29,165 | 16.9 | 16.1 | 34.7 | 25.9 | 4.9 | 1.5 | 34,015 | 30,617 | 38,667 | 41,120 | 35,755 | 25,649 |
| BUNCOMBE | 20,071 | 80,364 | 15.3 | 13.9 | 36.6 | 27.4 | 5.1 | 1.6 | 35,262 | 31,090 | 40,417 | 43,354 | 37,137 | 25,644 |
| BURKE | 16,049 | 32,298 | 15.4 | 15.5 | 40.3 | 25.6 | 2.7 | 0.6 | 31,958 | 29,378 | 37,229 | 40,051 | 34,693 | 20,118 |
| CABARRUS | 23,106 | 48,207 | 9.5 | 10.7 | 34.6 | 33.0 | 8.5 | 3.8 | 43,152 | 37,926 | 49,603 | 54,330 | 43,148 | 25,830 |
| CALDWELL | 16,109 | 29,904 | 17.0 | 14.6 | 40.7 | 24.3 | 2.8 | 0.6 | 31,322 | 29,116 | 36,671 | 39,005 | 32,197 | 20,026 |
| CAMDEN | 15,747 | 2,672 | 17.2 | 10.7 | 41.9 | 28.1 | 2.1 | 0.0 | 32,260 | 31,882 | 35,210 | 40,145 | 31,964 | 24,580 |
| CARTERET | 21,115 | 24,903 | 14.0 | 13.7 | 36.7 | 28.3 | 5.6 | 1.7 | 35,981 | 28,873 | 40,115 | 45,242 | 38,566 | 29,877 |
| CASWELL | 14,686 | 7,918 | 20.9 | 13.7 | 38.5 | 23.2 | 3.3 | 0.5 | 30,406 | 31,749 | 35,797 | 37,159 | 31,606 | 17,495 |
| CATAWBA | 19,487 | 52,960 | 11.8 | 12.8 | 38.8 | 30.4 | 4.7 | 1.5 | 36,406 | 32,576 | 41,160 | 45,097 | 38,443 | 24,132 |
| CHATHAM | 20,874 | 18,578 | 13.3 | 11.1 | 36.3 | 30.8 | 6.6 | 1.9 | 38,063 | 33,377 | 42,415 | 44,949 | 41,522 | 28,659 |
| CHEROKEE | 13,844 | 9,324 | 23.8 | 18.3 | 36.1 | 19.5 | 2.2 | 0.1 | 27,353 | 25,923 | 32,831 | 32,715 | 29,577 | 19,300 |
| CHOWAN | 14,527 | 5,433 | 23.8 | 19.5 | 35.5 | 17.3 | 3.2 | 0.7 | 28,084 | 24,846 | 31,934 | 35,279 | 29,384 | 20,829 |
| CLAY | 15,638 | 3,658 | 25.2 | 16.8 | 38.6 | 17.0 | 2.3 | 0.1 | 26,616 | 24,382 | 34,031 | 31,543 | 32,058 | 18,019 |
| CLEVELAND | 16,650 | 35,899 | 17.1 | 14.6 | 37.9 | 25.4 | 3.8 | 1.1 | 32,833 | 29,602 | 37,458 | 41,807 | 35,052 | 20,706 |
| COLUMBUS | 13,856 | 19,656 | 26.8 | 17.9 | 31.8 | 19.6 | 3.0 | 0.9 | 28,207 | 26,209 | 36,324 | 35,073 | 27,093 | 17,287 |
| CRAVEN | 16,987 | 32,252 | 15.9 | 15.1 | 37.6 | 26.1 | 4.2 | 1.2 | 33,759 | 28,239 | 38,775 | 44,241 | 36,835 | 25,528 |
| CUMBERLAND | 16,561 | 95,949 | 12.9 | 16.7 | 37.2 | 27.7 | 4.4 | 1.2 | 34,680 | 29,525 | 39,742 | 43,472 | 37,356 | 25,701 |
| CURRITUCK | 19,448 | 6,977 | 10.8 | 10.7 | 38.2 | 34.3 | 5.0 | 1.0 | 37,210 | 36,347 | 41,726 | 44,623 | 35,972 | 25,928 |
| DARE | 21,316 | 12,697 | 11.8 | 15.3 | 37.1 | 27.8 | 6.1 | 2.0 | 36,956 | 31,166 | 40,777 | 44,175 | 40,061 | 28,361 |
| DAVIDSON | 17,849 | 56,184 | 15.2 | 13.6 | 38.9 | 26.8 | 4.4 | 1.1 | 34,076 | 31,105 | 39,915 | 41,892 | 34,854 | 21,403 |
| DAVIE | 21,209 | 13,092 | 13.7 | 13.3 | 34.3 | 29.9 | 6.2 | 2.5 | 38,241 | 32,412 | 43,540 | 49,383 | 39,893 | 24,011 |
| DUPLIN | 14,491 | 16,242 | 21.9 | 17.0 | 37.7 | 20.4 | 2.4 | 0.6 | 28,873 | 27,745 | 34,676 | 35,497 | 28,573 | 19,153 |
| DURHAM | 22,505 | 82,893 | 13.4 | 12.1 | 32.5 | 32.1 | 7.1 | 2.9 | 40,055 | 33,253 | 44,543 | 49,382 | 42,283 | 27,893 |
| EDGECOMBE | 13,126 | 19,568 | 24.3 | 17.3 | 34.9 | 20.7 | 2.5 | 0.4 | 28,213 | 26,048 | 33,155 | 34,660 | 28,339 | 17,955 |
| FORSYTH | 23,094 | 118,116 | 14.4 | 14.2 | 32.9 | 28.8 | 6.6 | 3.2 | 39,056 | 31,697 | 43,574 | 49,272 | 40,984 | 26,790 |
| FRANKLIN | 17,311 | 17,519 | 17.4 | 12.3 | 36.6 | 28.1 | 4.4 | 1.2 | 34,299 | 33,317 | 39,091 | 41,706 | 34,862 | 21,357 |
| GASTON | 18,913 | 69,435 | 13.1 | 13.0 | 36.2 | 30.8 | 5.5 | 1.4 | 36,412 | 33,827 | 42,174 | 46,108 | 36,890 | 22,802 |
| GATES | 15,547 | 3,687 | 22.6 | 15.9 | 37.2 | 20.4 | 2.6 | 1.4 | 30,022 | 28,313 | 34,614 | 40,780 | 30,335 | 17,970 |
| GRAHAM | 15,226 | 2,942 | 25.9 | 18.1 | 33.6 | 17.5 | 3.7 | 1.2 | 28,453 | 25,887 | 29,858 | 38,798 | 29,846 | 19,090 |
| GRANVILLE | 17,327 | 15,540 | 15.5 | 11.0 | 37.2 | 30.0 | 5.4 | 0.9 | 35,426 | 34,450 | 39,564 | 44,183 | 36,151 | 21,610 |
| GREENE | 12,651 | 6,594 | 23.3 | 18.0 | 37.1 | 19.4 | 1.8 | 0.5 | 27,787 | 27,280 | 32,754 | 34,768 | 28,278 | 16,488 |
| GUILFORD | 23,924 | 158,028 | 12.8 | 13.3 | 33.8 | 28.7 | 7.5 | 3.9 | 41,025 | 33,596 | 45,900 | 50,716 | 43,631 | 27,568 |
| HALIFAX | 13,147 | 20,581 | 27.0 | 18.2 | 33.3 | 18.2 | 2.6 | 0.6 | 27,280 | 25,703 | 32,838 | 32,341 | 28,525 | 19,129 |
| HARNETT | 15,088 | 32,137 | 19.6 | 17.2 | 36.7 | 22.6 | 3.1 | 0.9 | 30,603 | 27,544 | 36,769 | 38,286 | 31,542 | 19,811 |
| HAYWOOD | 16,182 | 21,587 | 20.6 | 18.6 | 36.1 | 21.0 | 2.7 | 1.0 | 29,765 | 26,483 | 35,748 | 37,996 | 32,639 | 20,357 |
| HENDERSON | 20,733 | 34,770 | 13.0 | 13.6 | 37.1 | 29.3 | 5.7 | 1.4 | 36,367 | 31,228 | 40,586 | 43,634 | 40,510 | 30,487 |
| HERTFORD | 13,339 | 8,143 | 27.0 | 20.3 | 31.4 | 18.5 | 2.3 | 0.6 | 26,605 | 23,579 | 31,734 | 32,975 | 27,015 | 19,251 |
| HOKE | 11,949 | 10,603 | 23.0 | 16.5 | 37.9 | 20.5 | 2.0 | 0.2 | 28,028 | 25,312 | 31,844 | 34,431 | 29,325 | 17,051 |
| HYDE | 12,816 | 2,060 | 28.9 | 26.5 | 29.3 | 12.2 | 2.0 | 1.0 | 24,455 | 21,972 | 27,197 | 32,821 | 25,201 | 18,275 |
| IREDELL | 20,674 | 46,190 | 12.6 | 11.5 | 35.6 | 31.7 | 6.7 | 1.9 | 38,471 | 34,427 | 44,127 | 49,235 | 40,382 | 23,621 |
| JACKSON | 15,073 | 11,408 | 22.8 | 16.6 | 35.5 | 21.4 | 2.9 | 0.9 | 29,458 | 24,584 | 35,270 | 37,857 | 30,428 | 21,250 |
| JOHNSTON | 20,769 | 44,529 | 16.3 | 10.3 | 35.5 | 30.0 | 6.5 | 1.5 | 36,612 | 35,634 | 43,018 | 45,894 | 34,602 | 20,721 |
| JONES | 16,910 | 3,484 | 26.3 | 17.4 | 37.7 | 17.2 | 1.4 | 0.1 | 25,779 | 25,197 | 30,884 | 30,797 | 26,365 | 18,098 |
| LEE | 18,785 | 19,574 | 14.5 | 13.7 | 36.6 | 28.8 | 4.9 | 1.5 | 35,685 | 30,780 | 40,603 | 42,280 | 38,868 | 26,843 |
| LENOIR | 15,298 | 22,782 | 25.2 | 16.1 | 34.9 | 19.8 | 2.9 | 1.1 | 29,208 | 26,952 | 33,918 | 35,979 | 30,325 | 20,019 |
| LINCOLN | 17,628 | 22,302 | 13.9 | 13.8 | 38.2 | 28.4 | 4.5 | 1.2 | 34,888 | 32,115 | 40,078 | 43,921 | 35,411 | 21,630 |
| MCDOWELL | 15,404 | 15,507 | 17.7 | 17.0 | 39.8 | 21.9 | 3.0 | 0.6 | 30,517 | 29,743 | 36,480 | 39,027 | 30,000 | 18,727 |
| MACON | 16,958 | 12,485 | 20.6 | 16.7 | 37.8 | 21.3 | 2.7 | 1.0 | 29,836 | 27,696 | 34,115 | 39,060 | 30,362 | 22,871 |
| MADISON | 14,590 | 7,483 | 23.3 | 17.1 | 36.0 | 20.2 | 2.9 | 0.6 | 28,696 | 29,131 | 33,880 | 37,140 | 28,175 | 18,929 |
| MARTIN | 11,565 | 9,762 | 30.7 | 19.0 | 32.6 | 16.0 | 1.5 | 0.2 | 24,651 | 23,179 | 30,157 | 30,345 | 25,367 | 16,760 |
| MECKLENBURG | 26,229 | 261,313 | 9.3 | 10.9 | 30.8 | 35.4 | 9.6 | 4.1 | 44,990 | 38,400 | 48,832 | 53,640 | 47,498 | 30,003 |
| MITCHELL | 15,363 | 5,946 | 19.4 | 19.9 | 38.0 | 19.6 | 2.5 | 0.6 | 28,913 | 29,051 | 33,445 | 35,018 | 31,834 | 19,500 |
| MONTGOMERY | 14,913 | 8,632 | 21.3 | 16.4 | 37.7 | 20.9 | 2.6 | 1.0 | 29,717 | 27,762 | 34,828 | 36,961 | 31,908 | 18,452 |
| MOORE | 22,257 | 30,015 | 14.1 | 13.7 | 35.4 | 27.9 | 6.1 | 2.7 | 38,128 | 30,432 | 39,859 | 44,464 | 40,760 | 35,177 |
| NASH | 18,556 | 35,436 | 16.4 | 15.2 | 35.0 | 26.8 | 5.0 | 1.6 | 34,778 | 31,540 | 39,380 | 43,645 | 36,452 | 21,505 |
| NEW HANOVER | 22,557 | 62,860 | 15.8 | 13.6 | 34.3 | 27.1 | 6.1 | 3.1 | 37,825 | 29,749 | 42,541 | 48,113 | 40,564 | 26,614 |
| NORTHAMPTON | 11,830 | 7,849 | 26.8 | 19.5 | 36.0 | 15.8 | 1.8 | 0.1 | 25,153 | 24,137 | 28,678 | 30,607 | 26,892 | 18,408 |
| ONSLOW | 14,852 | 41,002 | 12.4 | 22.2 | 40.8 | 22.2 | 2.0 | 0.5 | 30,428 | 25,937 | 35,985 | 38,813 | 35,674 | 23,625 |
| ORANGE | 24,355 | 44,390 | 14.1 | 14.0 | 30.5 | 27.7 | 8.9 | 4.8 | 42,638 | 28,892 | 48,358 | 55,776 | 49,395 | 36,614 |
| PAMLICO | 15,831 | 5,036 | 22.3 | 17.0 | 36.3 | 20.1 | 3.2 | 1.1 | 29,684 | 24,720 | 35,497 | 39,319 | 33,410 | 20,123 |
| PASQUOTANK | 15,162 | 12,642 | 22.1 | 17.1 | 36.1 | 19.7 | 3.8 | 1.2 | 30,390 | 25,623 | 34,584 | 41,266 | 31,440 | 20,106 |
| PENDER | 18,411 | 16,249 | 18.0 | 15.7 | 34.5 | 25.5 | 4.7 | 1.6 | 33,730 | 29,064 | 38,874 | 41,506 | 35,076 | 24,257 |
| PERQUIMANS | 14,710 | 4,461 | 24.7 | 19.2 | 31.4 | 20.6 | 3.3 | 0.9 | 28,971 | 25,689 | 33,686 | 39,245 | 33,550 | 19,337 |
| PERSON | 17,083 | 13,180 | 15.6 | 13.8 | 37.4 | 28.4 | 4.2 | 0.7 | 33,823 | 34,498 | 38,972 | 39,684 | 35,386 | 21,277 |
| PITT | 18,477 | 49,511 | 21.0 | 14.8 | 31.7 | 24.9 | 5.2 | 2.4 | 34,623 | 28,141 | 40,004 | 45,876 | 36,459 | 21,973 |
| POLK | 20,859 | 7,356 | 16.4 | 14.0 | 37.8 | 24.6 | 5.8 | 1.4 | 34,747 | 30,644 | 36,803 | 39,501 | 40,400 | 30,680 |
| RANDOLPH | 16,898 | 48,395 | 13.8 | 14.1 | 41.2 | 26.7 | 3.5 | 0.7 | 33,233 | 31,019 | 38,857 | 40,333 | 34,711 | 20,442 |
| RICHMOND | 12,757 | 17,433 | 25.3 | 17.7 | 38.3 | 16.8 | 1.7 | 0.1 | 26,169 | 25,254 | 31,868 | 32,727 | 27,432 | 16,101 |
| NORTH CAROLINA | 19,736 | | 15.4 | 14.1 | 34.9 | 27.7 | 5.8 | 2.1 | 36,471 | 31,935 | 41,916 | 45,251 | 37,794 | 23,975 |
| UNITED STATES | 22,162 | | 14.5 | 12.5 | 32.3 | 29.8 | 7.4 | 3.5 | 40,748 | 34,503 | 44,969 | 49,579 | 43,409 | 27,339 |

| COUNTY | FINANCIAL SERVICES | | | | THE HOME | | | | | | ENTERTAINMENT | | | | | | PERSONAL | | | |
|---|---|---|---|---|---|---|---|---|---|---|---|---|---|---|---|---|---|---|---|---|
| | | | | | Home Improvements | | | Furnishings | | | | | | | | | | | | |
| | Auto Loan | Home Loan | Invest-ments | Retire-ment Plans | Home Repair | Lawn & Garden | Remodel-ing | Appli-ances | Elec-tronics | Furni-ture | Restau-rants | Sport-ing Goods | Theater & Concerts | Toys & Hobbies | Travel | Video Rental | Apparel | Auto After-market | Health Insur-ance | Pets & Supplies |
| ALAMANCE | 98 | 84 | 92 | 88 | 99 | 96 | 108 | 97 | 94 | 90 | 91 | 96 | 91 | 99 | 80 | 97 | 90 | 93 | 100 | 99 |
| ALEXANDER | 98 | 68 | 74 | 78 | 93 | 91 | 114 | 96 | 93 | 79 | 81 | 97 | 81 | 97 | 69 | 96 | 81 | 88 | 102 | 98 |
| ALLEGHANY | 97 | 65 | 71 | 75 | 92 | 91 | 113 | 95 | 92 | 76 | 78 | 94 | 79 | 94 | 68 | 96 | 79 | 87 | 102 | 96 |
| ANSON | 97 | 66 | 73 | 75 | 93 | 91 | 112 | 96 | 92 | 77 | 78 | 96 | 80 | 95 | 68 | 95 | 79 | 87 | 101 | 97 |
| ASHE | 97 | 67 | 74 | 76 | 93 | 91 | 114 | 96 | 92 | 78 | 80 | 95 | 80 | 95 | 68 | 96 | 80 | 88 | 101 | 97 |
| AVERY | 99 | 72 | 82 | 84 | 95 | 95 | 117 | 98 | 93 | 80 | 83 | 97 | 84 | 98 | 73 | 97 | 84 | 90 | 104 | 100 |
| BEAUFORT | 97 | 74 | 82 | 81 | 95 | 92 | 110 | 96 | 92 | 83 | 84 | 95 | 85 | 96 | 74 | 97 | 84 | 90 | 99 | 98 |
| BERTIE | 97 | 64 | 68 | 73 | 92 | 90 | 112 | 95 | 91 | 76 | 77 | 96 | 78 | 94 | 66 | 95 | 78 | 87 | 101 | 96 |
| BLADEN | 97 | 67 | 74 | 77 | 93 | 91 | 113 | 96 | 92 | 78 | 80 | 96 | 81 | 96 | 69 | 96 | 81 | 88 | 101 | 97 |
| BRUNSWICK | 100 | 79 | 91 | 88 | 97 | 98 | 117 | 99 | 93 | 86 | 89 | 98 | 88 | 100 | 78 | 98 | 88 | 93 | 104 | 101 |
| BUNCOMBE | 98 | 87 | 98 | 91 | 101 | 99 | 107 | 98 | 95 | 92 | 93 | 97 | 93 | 100 | 83 | 98 | 92 | 95 | 100 | 100 |
| BURKE | 98 | 75 | 83 | 82 | 96 | 93 | 113 | 97 | 93 | 84 | 86 | 96 | 86 | 98 | 74 | 97 | 86 | 91 | 101 | 99 |
| CABARRUS | 99 | 89 | 94 | 92 | 100 | 97 | 108 | 99 | 97 | 94 | 96 | 99 | 94 | 101 | 82 | 99 | 95 | 97 | 100 | 101 |
| CALDWELL | 99 | 73 | 80 | 81 | 95 | 92 | 114 | 97 | 93 | 82 | 84 | 97 | 85 | 98 | 72 | 97 | 84 | 90 | 101 | 99 |
| CAMDEN | 96 | 75 | 85 | 80 | 97 | 94 | 112 | 96 | 92 | 84 | 85 | 94 | 85 | 96 | 75 | 96 | 85 | 90 | 101 | 97 |
| CARTERET | 99 | 87 | 95 | 92 | 98 | 99 | 111 | 99 | 96 | 91 | 94 | 98 | 92 | 100 | 82 | 98 | 93 | 95 | 102 | 101 |
| CASWELL | 97 | 65 | 69 | 74 | 92 | 90 | 113 | 96 | 92 | 76 | 78 | 96 | 79 | 95 | 67 | 96 | 79 | 87 | 102 | 97 |
| CATAWBA | 99 | 84 | 92 | 89 | 98 | 96 | 111 | 98 | 95 | 89 | 91 | 98 | 91 | 100 | 79 | 98 | 91 | 94 | 101 | 101 |
| CHATHAM | 99 | 82 | 88 | 87 | 96 | 95 | 111 | 98 | 95 | 88 | 91 | 97 | 89 | 99 | 77 | 98 | 89 | 93 | 101 | 100 |
| CHEROKEE | 97 | 68 | 77 | 77 | 94 | 92 | 112 | 96 | 92 | 78 | 80 | 95 | 81 | 95 | 70 | 96 | 80 | 88 | 102 | 97 |
| CHOWAN | 97 | 70 | 75 | 77 | 94 | 90 | 111 | 96 | 92 | 80 | 81 | 95 | 82 | 95 | 70 | 96 | 81 | 88 | 100 | 97 |
| CLAY | 98 | 65 | 70 | 77 | 92 | 91 | 117 | 97 | 92 | 75 | 78 | 97 | 79 | 96 | 68 | 96 | 79 | 88 | 103 | 98 |
| CLEVELAND | 98 | 76 | 84 | 83 | 97 | 93 | 112 | 97 | 93 | 85 | 86 | 97 | 87 | 98 | 75 | 97 | 86 | 91 | 101 | 99 |
| COLUMBUS | 97 | 69 | 78 | 78 | 94 | 92 | 111 | 96 | 92 | 80 | 81 | 95 | 82 | 95 | 71 | 96 | 81 | 88 | 101 | 97 |
| CRAVEN | 97 | 88 | 95 | 90 | 98 | 97 | 103 | 97 | 95 | 91 | 93 | 96 | 92 | 97 | 82 | 98 | 92 | 95 | 98 | 99 |
| CUMBERLAND | 94 | 91 | 86 | 85 | 94 | 91 | 95 | 94 | 94 | 89 | 93 | 93 | 89 | 94 | 79 | 97 | 90 | 95 | 93 | 98 |
| CURRITUCK | 100 | 85 | 94 | 91 | 98 | 97 | 115 | 99 | 96 | 91 | 94 | 99 | 92 | 102 | 79 | 99 | 93 | 95 | 102 | 102 |
| DARE | 101 | 92 | 93 | 94 | 99 | 100 | 112 | 101 | 98 | 95 | 98 | 101 | 95 | 103 | 83 | 99 | 97 | 98 | 103 | 103 |
| DAVIDSON | 99 | 78 | 85 | 84 | 96 | 93 | 112 | 97 | 94 | 86 | 88 | 97 | 87 | 99 | 75 | 97 | 87 | 92 | 101 | 100 |
| DAVIE | 101 | 83 | 93 | 91 | 99 | 97 | 115 | 99 | 97 | 90 | 92 | 100 | 92 | 102 | 79 | 99 | 92 | 95 | 102 | 102 |
| DUPLIN | 97 | 67 | 74 | 75 | 93 | 91 | 112 | 95 | 91 | 78 | 79 | 94 | 80 | 95 | 69 | 96 | 80 | 87 | 101 | 96 |
| DURHAM | 99 | 103 | 99 | 99 | 101 | 100 | 97 | 99 | 99 | 102 | 102 | 101 | 100 | 100 | 90 | 100 | 103 | 102 | 94 | 101 |
| EDGECOMBE | 96 | 76 | 82 | 80 | 95 | 91 | 103 | 96 | 92 | 86 | 83 | 94 | 85 | 94 | 74 | 97 | 86 | 91 | 95 | 96 |
| FORSYTH | 99 | 98 | 101 | 98 | 102 | 101 | 101 | 99 | 98 | 99 | 99 | 99 | 98 | 101 | 88 | 99 | 100 | 100 | 97 | 101 |
| FRANKLIN | 97 | 72 | 77 | 78 | 93 | 90 | 112 | 96 | 92 | 82 | 83 | 95 | 83 | 96 | 70 | 96 | 82 | 89 | 99 | 98 |
| GASTON | 98 | 85 | 91 | 89 | 99 | 96 | 107 | 98 | 95 | 91 | 92 | 98 | 92 | 99 | 80 | 98 | 91 | 94 | 100 | 100 |
| GATES | 97 | 64 | 70 | 74 | 92 | 90 | 112 | 95 | 92 | 76 | 78 | 95 | 79 | 94 | 67 | 95 | 78 | 87 | 101 | 96 |
| GRAHAM | 98 | 63 | 67 | 74 | 92 | 90 | 113 | 96 | 91 | 75 | 77 | 97 | 79 | 95 | 66 | 95 | 78 | 87 | 102 | 97 |
| GRANVILLE | 97 | 77 | 86 | 81 | 95 | 92 | 110 | 96 | 93 | 86 | 86 | 94 | 86 | 97 | 75 | 97 | 86 | 91 | 98 | 98 |
| GREENE | 97 | 73 | 82 | 80 | 95 | 92 | 114 | 96 | 93 | 82 | 84 | 94 | 84 | 97 | 73 | 97 | 84 | 90 | 101 | 98 |
| GUILFORD | 99 | 100 | 101 | 100 | 102 | 102 | 101 | 99 | 99 | 100 | 101 | 101 | 99 | 101 | 89 | 99 | 101 | 100 | 98 | 101 |
| HALIFAX | 96 | 76 | 87 | 82 | 98 | 94 | 105 | 96 | 91 | 85 | 83 | 94 | 86 | 95 | 77 | 96 | 85 | 90 | 98 | 96 |
| HARNETT | 95 | 76 | 81 | 79 | 94 | 91 | 108 | 95 | 92 | 83 | 85 | 93 | 84 | 95 | 73 | 96 | 83 | 90 | 98 | 97 |
| HAYWOOD | 97 | 77 | 88 | 84 | 99 | 96 | 110 | 97 | 91 | 86 | 87 | 95 | 88 | 98 | 78 | 97 | 86 | 91 | 102 | 98 |
| HENDERSON | 100 | 85 | 101 | 93 | 102 | 103 | 111 | 100 | 95 | 91 | 94 | 98 | 94 | 101 | 84 | 98 | 93 | 95 | 105 | 101 |
| HERTFORD | 96 | 73 | 83 | 79 | 96 | 92 | 106 | 96 | 91 | 82 | 81 | 94 | 84 | 94 | 74 | 95 | 82 | 89 | 98 | 96 |
| HOKE | 97 | 72 | 78 | 78 | 94 | 91 | 112 | 96 | 92 | 83 | 84 | 95 | 83 | 96 | 71 | 96 | 82 | 89 | 100 | 97 |
| HYDE | 98 | 64 | 68 | 76 | 92 | 91 | 116 | 96 | 91 | 75 | 77 | 97 | 79 | 96 | 67 | 96 | 79 | 87 | 103 | 98 |
| IREDELL | 100 | 85 | 93 | 90 | 99 | 97 | 112 | 98 | 96 | 91 | 92 | 99 | 92 | 101 | 80 | 98 | 92 | 95 | 101 | 101 |
| JACKSON | 97 | 78 | 87 | 85 | 96 | 94 | 113 | 96 | 93 | 84 | 86 | 95 | 86 | 97 | 76 | 97 | 86 | 91 | 102 | 99 |
| JOHNSTON | 98 | 78 | 84 | 82 | 95 | 92 | 111 | 97 | 93 | 86 | 87 | 96 | 86 | 98 | 74 | 97 | 86 | 91 | 100 | 99 |
| JONES | 98 | 67 | 73 | 77 | 93 | 91 | 114 | 96 | 92 | 78 | 80 | 96 | 81 | 96 | 68 | 96 | 81 | 88 | 101 | 98 |
| LEE | 99 | 87 | 97 | 92 | 100 | 99 | 110 | 99 | 96 | 93 | 93 | 98 | 93 | 100 | 83 | 98 | 93 | 95 | 100 | 100 |
| LENOIR | 97 | 82 | 92 | 87 | 99 | 95 | 104 | 98 | 94 | 91 | 88 | 96 | 90 | 97 | 80 | 98 | 91 | 94 | 96 | 98 |
| LINCOLN | 99 | 82 | 88 | 88 | 97 | 95 | 113 | 98 | 95 | 89 | 91 | 98 | 90 | 100 | 77 | 98 | 90 | 93 | 101 | 101 |
| MCDOWELL | 98 | 70 | 77 | 79 | 94 | 92 | 114 | 97 | 93 | 80 | 82 | 96 | 83 | 97 | 70 | 97 | 83 | 89 | 102 | 99 |
| MACON | 99 | 72 | 81 | 84 | 95 | 94 | 119 | 97 | 92 | 79 | 83 | 97 | 83 | 98 | 73 | 98 | 84 | 90 | 105 | 100 |
| MADISON | 98 | 68 | 75 | 78 | 93 | 91 | 114 | 96 | 92 | 78 | 80 | 96 | 81 | 96 | 69 | 96 | 81 | 88 | 102 | 98 |
| MARTIN | 97 | 70 | 77 | 78 | 95 | 92 | 111 | 96 | 92 | 80 | 81 | 94 | 82 | 95 | 71 | 96 | 82 | 88 | 101 | 97 |
| MECKLENBURG | 100 | 106 | 98 | 101 | 101 | 102 | 99 | 100 | 101 | 103 | 105 | 103 | 101 | 102 | 90 | 100 | 105 | 103 | 96 | 102 |
| MITCHELL | 98 | 69 | 75 | 78 | 94 | 91 | 114 | 96 | 92 | 79 | 81 | 96 | 82 | 97 | 69 | 96 | 81 | 88 | 102 | 98 |
| MONTGOMERY | 98 | 68 | 75 | 78 | 93 | 91 | 116 | 96 | 92 | 78 | 80 | 96 | 81 | 96 | 69 | 96 | 81 | 88 | 102 | 98 |
| MOORE | 100 | 86 | 103 | 95 | 102 | 104 | 111 | 100 | 95 | 92 | 93 | 99 | 94 | 100 | 85 | 98 | 93 | 95 | 104 | 101 |
| NASH | 99 | 85 | 88 | 89 | 97 | 96 | 107 | 98 | 96 | 91 | 92 | 98 | 91 | 99 | 79 | 98 | 91 | 94 | 99 | 100 |
| NEW HANOVER | 99 | 98 | 100 | 97 | 102 | 100 | 102 | 98 | 98 | 98 | 99 | 99 | 97 | 100 | 88 | 99 | 99 | 99 | 97 | 101 |
| NORTHAMPTON | 96 | 64 | 70 | 73 | 93 | 89 | 108 | 96 | 90 | 77 | 76 | 94 | 79 | 93 | 68 | 95 | 78 | 87 | 98 | 95 |
| ONSLOW | 91 | 87 | 77 | 77 | 89 | 85 | 94 | 92 | 92 | 84 | 90 | 89 | 84 | 91 | 74 | 96 | 85 | 92 | 91 | 97 |
| ORANGE | 97 | 98 | 98 | 95 | 99 | 97 | 102 | 94 | 95 | 92 | 97 | 96 | 92 | 98 | 84 | 96 | 95 | 97 | 97 | 100 |
| PAMLICO | 99 | 73 | 85 | 85 | 95 | 96 | 117 | 98 | 93 | 82 | 85 | 98 | 85 | 99 | 74 | 97 | 85 | 91 | 104 | 100 |
| PASQUOTANK | 95 | 77 | 80 | 80 | 94 | 90 | 104 | 96 | 91 | 86 | 83 | 93 | 85 | 95 | 74 | 97 | 86 | 91 | 94 | 97 |
| PENDER | 100 | 80 | 94 | 90 | 98 | 100 | 115 | 100 | 95 | 88 | 90 | 98 | 90 | 100 | 79 | 97 | 89 | 93 | 104 | 101 |
| PERQUIMANS | 97 | 69 | 76 | 77 | 92 | 91 | 112 | 95 | 92 | 78 | 81 | 93 | 80 | 95 | 69 | 97 | 81 | 88 | 102 | 97 |
| PERSON | 98 | 77 | 85 | 83 | 97 | 93 | 113 | 97 | 93 | 86 | 87 | 96 | 87 | 99 | 75 | 97 | 87 | 91 | 101 | 100 |
| PITT | 95 | 89 | 85 | 86 | 95 | 91 | 99 | 94 | 93 | 89 | 91 | 94 | 88 | 95 | 78 | 96 | 90 | 94 | 93 | 98 |
| POLK | 98 | 83 | 100 | 90 | 102 | 102 | 108 | 99 | 93 | 89 | 91 | 97 | 92 | 99 | 83 | 97 | 90 | 93 | 104 | 99 |
| RANDOLPH | 98 | 76 | 82 | 81 | 95 | 92 | 113 | 96 | 93 | 85 | 86 | 96 | 85 | 98 | 73 | 97 | 85 | 91 | 100 | 99 |
| RICHMOND | 96 | 72 | 83 | 79 | 97 | 94 | 108 | 96 | 91 | 82 | 82 | 95 | 84 | 95 | 74 | 95 | 82 | 89 | 100 | 96 |
| NORTH CAROLINA | 98 | 88 | 92 | 91 | 98 | 97 | 106 | 98 | 96 | 92 | 93 | 98 | 92 | 99 | 81 | 98 | 93 | 95 | 99 | 100 |
| UNITED STATES | 100 | 100 | 100 | 100 | 100 | 100 | 100 | 100 | 100 | 100 | 100 | 100 | 100 | 100 | 100 | 100 | 100 | 100 | 100 | 100 |

| COUNTY | FIPS Code | MSA Code | DMA Code | POPULATION 1990 | POPULATION 2000 | POPULATION 2005 | 1990-2000 ANNUAL CHANGE % Rate | 1990-2000 ANNUAL CHANGE State Rank | RACE (%) White 1990 | White 2000 | Black 1990 | Black 2000 | Asian/Pacific 1990 | Asian/Pacific 2000 |
|---|---|---|---|---|---|---|---|---|---|---|---|---|---|---|
| ROBESON | 155 | 0000 | 570 | 105,179 | 117,679 | 123,023 | 1.1 | 51 | 36.1 | 33.8 | 24.9 | 24.2 | 0.2 | 0.4 |
| ROCKINGHAM | 157 | 0000 | 518 | 86,064 | 90,658 | 92,447 | 0.5 | 82 | 78.9 | 78.0 | 20.4 | 20.7 | 0.2 | 0.4 |
| ROWAN | 159 | 1520 | 517 | 110,605 | 128,190 | 136,275 | 1.4 | 35 | 83.0 | 81.9 | 16.1 | 16.6 | 0.4 | 0.7 |
| RUTHERFORD | 161 | 0000 | 567 | 56,918 | 62,107 | 65,025 | 0.9 | 63 | 88.1 | 87.6 | 11.4 | 11.7 | 0.2 | 0.3 |
| SAMPSON | 163 | 0000 | 560 | 47,297 | 53,430 | 56,371 | 1.2 | 45 | 64.0 | 62.5 | 33.2 | 33.5 | 0.2 | 0.3 |
| SCOTLAND | 165 | 0000 | 570 | 33,754 | 36,153 | 36,975 | 0.7 | 73 | 56.4 | 55.0 | 36.1 | 36.4 | 0.2 | 0.4 |
| STANLY | 167 | 0000 | 517 | 51,765 | 57,206 | 60,361 | 1.0 | 55 | 87.5 | 86.6 | 11.5 | 11.8 | 0.5 | 0.8 |
| STOKES | 169 | 3120 | 518 | 37,223 | 44,547 | 47,864 | 1.8 | 22 | 93.8 | 92.9 | 5.6 | 6.0 | 0.2 | 0.3 |
| SURRY | 171 | 0000 | 518 | 61,704 | 68,704 | 72,442 | 1.1 | 51 | 94.6 | 93.6 | 4.5 | 4.7 | 0.1 | 0.2 |
| SWAIN | 173 | 0000 | 567 | 11,268 | 12,435 | 12,898 | 1.0 | 55 | 70.6 | 66.9 | 1.7 | 1.8 | 0.3 | 0.6 |
| TRANSYLVANIA | 175 | 0000 | 567 | 25,520 | 29,279 | 31,399 | 1.3 | 39 | 94.5 | 94.2 | 4.7 | 4.7 | 0.4 | 0.6 |
| TYRRELL | 177 | 0000 | 545 | 3,856 | 3,896 | 3,686 | 0.1 | 93 | 59.6 | 58.8 | 40.0 | 40.5 | 0.1 | 0.3 |
| UNION | 179 | 1520 | 517 | 84,211 | 119,842 | 142,131 | 3.5 | 3 | 83.2 | 82.3 | 15.9 | 16.2 | 0.3 | 0.5 |
| VANCE | 181 | 0000 | 560 | 38,892 | 42,977 | 45,279 | 1.0 | 55 | 54.4 | 53.5 | 45.0 | 45.5 | 0.2 | 0.2 |
| WAKE | 183 | 6640 | 560 | 423,380 | 604,719 | 693,649 | 3.5 | 3 | 76.5 | 74.6 | 20.8 | 20.8 | 1.9 | 3.4 |
| WARREN | 185 | 0000 | 560 | 17,265 | 18,974 | 19,596 | 0.9 | 63 | 38.2 | 37.5 | 57.0 | 56.9 | 0.1 | 0.1 |
| WASHINGTON | 187 | 0000 | 545 | 13,997 | 13,334 | 12,789 | -0.5 | 99 | 54.0 | 53.6 | 45.5 | 45.6 | 0.3 | 0.5 |
| WATAUGA | 189 | 0000 | 517 | 36,952 | 41,813 | 43,795 | 1.2 | 45 | 97.2 | 96.8 | 2.1 | 2.2 | 0.4 | 0.7 |
| WAYNE | 191 | 2980 | 560 | 104,666 | 111,718 | 111,994 | 0.6 | 78 | 66.1 | 64.5 | 32.3 | 32.8 | 0.8 | 1.4 |
| WILKES | 193 | 0000 | 518 | 59,393 | 64,307 | 67,668 | 0.8 | 69 | 94.7 | 94.0 | 4.8 | 5.1 | 0.2 | 0.3 |
| WILSON | 195 | 0000 | 560 | 66,061 | 69,500 | 71,734 | 0.5 | 82 | 61.5 | 60.5 | 37.7 | 38.1 | 0.3 | 0.4 |
| YADKIN | 197 | 3120 | 518 | 30,488 | 35,642 | 37,683 | 1.5 | 34 | 94.7 | 93.5 | 4.2 | 4.4 | 0.1 | 0.1 |
| YANCEY | 199 | 0000 | 567 | 15,419 | 17,080 | 18,149 | 1.0 | 55 | 98.7 | 98.5 | 1.0 | 1.0 | 0.1 | 0.1 |
| NORTH CAROLINA | | | | | | | 1.6 | | 75.6 | 74.5 | 22.0 | 22.0 | 0.8 | 1.4 |
| UNITED STATES | | | | | | | 1.0 | | 80.3 | 77.9 | 12.1 | 12.4 | 2.9 | 3.9 |

| COUNTY | % HISPANIC ORIGIN 1990 | % HISPANIC ORIGIN 2000 | 2000 AGE DISTRIBUTION (%) 0-4 | 5-9 | 10-14 | 15-19 | 20-24 | 25-44 | 45-64 | 65-84 | 85+ | 18+ | MEDIAN AGE 1990 | MEDIAN AGE 2000 | 2000 Males/ Females (×100) |
|---|---|---|---|---|---|---|---|---|---|---|---|---|---|---|---|
| ROBESON | 0.7 | 1.2 | 8.2 | 8.7 | 8.9 | 7.9 | 6.6 | 28.6 | 20.6 | 9.4 | 1.1 | 69.4 | 30.3 | 31.9 | 91.1 |
| ROCKINGHAM | 0.7 | 1.8 | 6.6 | 6.9 | 7.2 | 6.2 | 5.2 | 28.8 | 24.7 | 12.8 | 1.7 | 75.6 | 35.5 | 38.2 | 91.3 |
| ROWAN | 0.6 | 1.6 | 6.9 | 7.3 | 7.4 | 6.5 | 5.5 | 28.5 | 23.4 | 12.9 | 1.8 | 74.9 | 35.2 | 37.3 | 95.1 |
| RUTHERFORD | 0.6 | 1.6 | 6.4 | 6.9 | 7.2 | 6.2 | 5.3 | 28.3 | 24.3 | 13.5 | 1.9 | 75.8 | 35.6 | 37.9 | 93.7 |
| SAMPSON | 1.5 | 3.3 | 6.6 | 7.4 | 7.9 | 6.9 | 5.5 | 27.7 | 23.8 | 12.6 | 1.5 | 73.8 | 34.7 | 37.0 | 91.9 |
| SCOTLAND | 0.9 | 2.0 | 7.2 | 7.6 | 7.7 | 8.0 | 7.9 | 27.4 | 23.1 | 9.9 | 1.3 | 72.8 | 31.5 | 33.3 | 89.4 |
| STANLY | 0.6 | 1.6 | 6.9 | 7.3 | 7.6 | 6.7 | 5.4 | 27.8 | 23.6 | 13.0 | 1.7 | 74.5 | 34.8 | 37.0 | 93.8 |
| STOKES | 0.7 | 1.9 | 6.3 | 6.9 | 7.3 | 6.5 | 5.1 | 30.3 | 25.1 | 11.0 | 1.5 | 75.6 | 34.3 | 37.5 | 96.7 |
| SURRY | 1.0 | 2.5 | 6.1 | 6.5 | 7.0 | 6.1 | 5.2 | 28.3 | 25.5 | 13.6 | 1.9 | 76.8 | 36.3 | 39.1 | 92.6 |
| SWAIN | 0.7 | 1.5 | 6.7 | 7.2 | 7.5 | 7.4 | 5.3 | 26.3 | 23.9 | 13.7 | 2.0 | 74.4 | 35.3 | 37.8 | 100.5 |
| TRANSYLVANIA | 0.6 | 1.6 | 5.3 | 5.9 | 6.3 | 7.6 | 5.5 | 24.6 | 24.3 | 18.1 | 2.3 | 78.6 | 38.0 | 41.2 | 94.3 |
| TYRRELL | 0.3 | 0.8 | 7.2 | 7.5 | 7.7 | 8.1 | 6.6 | 24.8 | 22.4 | 13.5 | 2.2 | 72.4 | 35.4 | 36.6 | 93.9 |
| UNION | 0.8 | 2.0 | 7.8 | 8.2 | 8.3 | 7.1 | 5.7 | 30.0 | 23.3 | 8.8 | 1.0 | 71.7 | 32.0 | 34.6 | 96.9 |
| VANCE | 0.7 | 1.5 | 7.3 | 7.7 | 8.0 | 7.1 | 6.0 | 28.8 | 22.3 | 11.2 | 1.5 | 72.7 | 33.0 | 35.2 | 90.4 |
| WAKE | 1.3 | 2.9 | 7.2 | 7.3 | 7.1 | 6.6 | 7.3 | 35.4 | 21.1 | 7.1 | 0.9 | 75.1 | 31.4 | 33.8 | 95.3 |
| WARREN | 0.6 | 1.2 | 6.7 | 7.3 | 7.4 | 6.4 | 5.8 | 24.8 | 23.4 | 16.1 | 2.1 | 74.7 | 37.1 | 38.9 | 94.0 |
| WASHINGTON | 0.5 | 1.1 | 7.1 | 7.9 | 8.3 | 7.0 | 5.6 | 26.5 | 23.1 | 12.9 | 1.6 | 72.4 | 34.0 | 36.5 | 90.8 |
| WATAUGA | 0.7 | 1.9 | 4.5 | 4.8 | 4.7 | 11.9 | 17.8 | 25.8 | 20.0 | 9.3 | 1.1 | 83.3 | 27.8 | 30.6 | 94.7 |
| WAYNE | 1.3 | 2.8 | 7.4 | 7.3 | 7.1 | 6.5 | 7.2 | 31.8 | 21.1 | 10.4 | 1.1 | 74.2 | 31.8 | 33.8 | 101.0 |
| WILKES | 0.6 | 1.6 | 5.9 | 6.5 | 7.1 | 6.3 | 5.1 | 29.5 | 25.7 | 12.3 | 1.5 | 76.7 | 35.2 | 38.5 | 95.9 |
| WILSON | 0.8 | 1.8 | 6.6 | 7.5 | 7.7 | 7.2 | 5.9 | 28.4 | 23.3 | 11.9 | 1.4 | 73.9 | 33.8 | 36.4 | 88.7 |
| YADKIN | 1.3 | 3.1 | 6.2 | 6.5 | 6.9 | 5.9 | 4.9 | 28.6 | 25.7 | 13.4 | 1.8 | 76.8 | 36.6 | 39.2 | 94.8 |
| YANCEY | 0.3 | 1.0 | 5.9 | 6.2 | 6.9 | 5.9 | 4.9 | 26.9 | 25.8 | 15.3 | 2.2 | 77.4 | 38.0 | 40.7 | 93.9 |
| NORTH CAROLINA | 1.2 | 2.5 | 6.9 | 7.2 | 7.2 | 6.7 | 6.6 | 30.3 | 22.6 | 11.1 | 1.4 | 75.1 | 33.1 | 35.7 | 94.1 |
| UNITED STATES | 9.0 | 11.8 | 6.9 | 7.2 | 7.2 | 7.2 | 6.7 | 29.9 | 22.2 | 11.1 | 1.6 | 74.6 | 32.9 | 35.7 | 95.6 |

| COUNTY | HOUSEHOLDS | | | | | FAMILIES | | | MEDIAN HOUSEHOLD INCOME | | | |
|---|---|---|---|---|---|---|---|---|---|---|---|---|
| | 1990 | 2000 | 2005 | % Annual Rate 1990-2000 | 2000 Average HH Size | 1990 | 2000 | % Annual Rate 1990-2000 | 2000 | 2005 | 2000 National Rank | 2000 State Rank |
| ROBESON | 36,154 | 40,495 | 42,479 | 1.4 | 2.84 | 27,429 | 29,801 | 1.0 | 30,697 | 34,571 | 1987 | 67 |
| ROCKINGHAM | 33,446 | 35,444 | 36,235 | 0.7 | 2.54 | 24,671 | 25,285 | 0.3 | 33,542 | 39,974 | 1458 | 47 |
| ROWAN | 42,512 | 49,670 | 53,075 | 1.9 | 2.50 | 31,055 | 35,157 | 1.5 | 37,398 | 43,807 | 916 | 29 |
| RUTHERFORD | 22,198 | 24,232 | 25,409 | 1.1 | 2.53 | 16,480 | 17,402 | 0.7 | 33,860 | 40,173 | 1412 | 46 |
| SAMPSON | 17,526 | 19,828 | 21,051 | 1.5 | 2.64 | 13,191 | 14,449 | 1.1 | 29,902 | 32,402 | 2168 | 76 |
| SCOTLAND | 11,837 | 12,856 | 13,228 | 1.0 | 2.73 | 8,971 | 9,461 | 0.6 | 32,659 | 37,582 | 1603 | 54 |
| STANLY | 19,747 | 21,859 | 23,085 | 1.2 | 2.57 | 14,967 | 16,061 | 0.9 | 34,156 | 39,463 | 1362 | 45 |
| STOKES | 14,123 | 16,977 | 18,319 | 2.3 | 2.59 | 11,022 | 12,832 | 1.9 | 36,048 | 41,223 | 1096 | 39 |
| SURRY | 24,252 | 26,896 | 28,349 | 1.3 | 2.52 | 18,252 | 19,645 | 0.9 | 31,666 | 36,322 | 1786 | 58 |
| SWAIN | 4,173 | 4,695 | 4,921 | 1.4 | 2.51 | 3,083 | 3,342 | 1.0 | 24,286 | 28,243 | 2883 | 98 |
| TRANSYLVANIA | 9,924 | 11,602 | 12,544 | 1.9 | 2.42 | 7,496 | 8,480 | 1.5 | 33,290 | 36,248 | 1494 | 51 |
| TYRRELL | 1,471 | 1,418 | 1,352 | -0.4 | 2.56 | 1,078 | 1,001 | -0.9 | 19,838 | 21,618 | 3102 | 100 |
| UNION | 29,307 | 41,248 | 48,612 | 4.2 | 2.87 | 23,530 | 32,480 | 4.0 | 40,658 | 47,164 | 615 | 13 |
| VANCE | 14,166 | 15,827 | 16,740 | 1.4 | 2.67 | 10,502 | 11,435 | 1.0 | 30,870 | 36,479 | 1958 | 65 |
| WAKE | 165,743 | 239,415 | 276,378 | 4.6 | 2.45 | 109,543 | 155,778 | 4.4 | 54,542 | 61,188 | 129 | 1 |
| WARREN | 6,305 | 6,822 | 7,085 | 1.0 | 2.66 | 4,762 | 4,975 | 0.5 | 25,527 | 29,757 | 2752 | 96 |
| WASHINGTON | 5,052 | 4,924 | 4,761 | -0.3 | 2.67 | 3,839 | 3,623 | -0.7 | 28,514 | 32,026 | 2362 | 84 |
| WATAUGA | 13,693 | 15,401 | 16,166 | 1.4 | 2.39 | 8,415 | 9,069 | 0.9 | 31,095 | 35,087 | 1915 | 61 |
| WAYNE | 36,889 | 39,598 | 39,918 | 0.9 | 2.62 | 27,577 | 28,747 | 0.5 | 34,948 | 41,246 | 1261 | 43 |
| WILKES | 23,021 | 24,746 | 26,008 | 0.9 | 2.56 | 17,586 | 18,270 | 0.5 | 30,171 | 32,538 | 2113 | 74 |
| WILSON | 25,093 | 26,210 | 27,038 | 0.5 | 2.58 | 18,031 | 18,194 | 0.1 | 32,726 | 37,241 | 1588 | 52 |
| YADKIN | 12,068 | 14,256 | 15,160 | 2.0 | 2.47 | 9,173 | 10,484 | 1.6 | 33,527 | 39,311 | 1459 | 48 |
| YANCEY | 6,124 | 6,738 | 7,135 | 1.2 | 2.51 | 4,683 | 4,962 | 0.7 | 26,513 | 29,563 | 2651 | 94 |
| NORTH CAROLINA | | | | 2.0 | 2.53 | | | 1.6 | 38,498 | 44,239 | | |
| UNITED STATES | | | | 1.4 | 2.59 | | | 1.1 | 41,914 | 49,127 | | |

| COUNTY | 2000 Per Capita Income | 2000 HH Income Base | 2000 HOUSEHOLD INCOME DISTRIBUTION (%) Less than $15,000 | $15,000 to $24,999 | $25,000 to $49,999 | $50,000 to $99,999 | $100,000 to $149,999 | $150,000 or More | 2000 AVERAGE DISPOSABLE INCOME BY AGE OF HOUSEHOLDER All Ages | <35 | 35-44 | 45-54 | 55-64 | 65+ |
|---|---|---|---|---|---|---|---|---|---|---|---|---|---|---|
| ROBESON | 13,808 | 40,495 | 23.8 | 17.3 | 34.9 | 19.6 | 3.4 | 1.1 | 29,489 | 25,038 | 34,672 | 37,039 | 30,603 | 19,166 |
| ROCKINGHAM | 15,593 | 35,444 | 19.5 | 15.8 | 37.4 | 23.9 | 2.8 | 0.6 | 30,627 | 28,754 | 36,586 | 38,397 | 31,309 | 19,408 |
| ROWAN | 17,860 | 49,670 | 15.3 | 13.8 | 38.2 | 27.4 | 4.3 | 1.0 | 33,945 | 31,769 | 39,604 | 42,966 | 35,177 | 21,205 |
| RUTHERFORD | 16,567 | 24,232 | 18.7 | 14.8 | 39.9 | 22.8 | 3.0 | 0.9 | 31,095 | 29,880 | 36,638 | 37,933 | 32,919 | 20,672 |
| SAMPSON | 14,395 | 19,828 | 23.7 | 17.3 | 34.3 | 20.7 | 3.5 | 0.7 | 29,073 | 28,214 | 36,324 | 33,940 | 29,719 | 18,940 |
| SCOTLAND | 14,644 | 12,856 | 20.4 | 16.5 | 36.2 | 22.4 | 3.8 | 0.8 | 30,786 | 27,285 | 36,483 | 38,129 | 33,052 | 19,026 |
| STANLY | 15,725 | 21,859 | 17.7 | 14.9 | 39.6 | 24.0 | 3.3 | 0.6 | 31,178 | 30,126 | 36,122 | 39,507 | 32,488 | 19,615 |
| STOKES | 16,133 | 16,977 | 16.7 | 15.2 | 38.9 | 25.1 | 3.3 | 0.8 | 32,205 | 31,505 | 39,919 | 39,797 | 31,236 | 16,798 |
| SURRY | 15,623 | 26,896 | 20.7 | 16.3 | 37.5 | 21.7 | 3.1 | 0.8 | 30,081 | 29,168 | 36,095 | 38,348 | 30,135 | 18,199 |
| SWAIN | 12,787 | 4,695 | 29.7 | 21.7 | 33.0 | 13.9 | 0.9 | 0.8 | 24,362 | 23,156 | 27,685 | 30,001 | 26,441 | 16,082 |
| TRANSYLVANIA | 16,939 | 11,602 | 19.6 | 18.6 | 34.4 | 22.7 | 3.6 | 1.2 | 31,362 | 25,953 | 36,436 | 39,385 | 36,611 | 24,198 |
| TYRRELL | 14,761 | 1,418 | 35.5 | 26.0 | 27.5 | 10.8 | 0.3 | 0.0 | 20,353 | 23,145 | 22,286 | 25,830 | 19,624 | 13,380 |
| UNION | 17,767 | 41,245 | 13.3 | 13.5 | 35.4 | 30.2 | 5.7 | 1.9 | 37,354 | 33,029 | 42,969 | 46,148 | 38,336 | 20,729 |
| VANCE | 15,182 | 15,827 | 23.0 | 17.7 | 34.5 | 19.8 | 3.5 | 1.4 | 30,247 | 26,512 | 35,213 | 38,383 | 30,493 | 19,453 |
| WAKE | 28,673 | 239,414 | 7.5 | 8.6 | 28.4 | 38.3 | 12.2 | 5.0 | 49,126 | 39,964 | 52,927 | 60,098 | 51,756 | 32,875 |
| WARREN | 12,594 | 6,822 | 29.5 | 19.5 | 30.8 | 17.2 | 2.2 | 0.7 | 25,884 | 24,806 | 29,898 | 32,405 | 27,655 | 18,587 |
| WASHINGTON | 13,444 | 4,924 | 27.0 | 15.7 | 34.2 | 19.7 | 2.7 | 0.7 | 28,226 | 23,025 | 32,761 | 37,006 | 34,951 | 17,988 |
| WATAUGA | 16,557 | 15,401 | 23.7 | 17.0 | 30.4 | 21.8 | 5.2 | 1.9 | 31,991 | 21,841 | 40,248 | 45,925 | 36,983 | 24,885 |
| WAYNE | 16,288 | 39,598 | 17.2 | 16.2 | 37.4 | 24.8 | 3.6 | 0.9 | 32,136 | 28,299 | 38,143 | 40,303 | 34,017 | 20,846 |
| WILKES | 14,658 | 24,746 | 21.5 | 17.9 | 38.9 | 18.2 | 2.6 | 0.9 | 28,701 | 26,880 | 34,355 | 35,019 | 29,461 | 17,874 |
| WILSON | 16,201 | 26,210 | 23.2 | 14.8 | 34.4 | 22.6 | 3.9 | 1.2 | 31,092 | 27,557 | 36,198 | 38,009 | 32,881 | 20,591 |
| YADKIN | 16,341 | 14,256 | 20.3 | 15.7 | 36.1 | 23.3 | 3.7 | 1.0 | 31,088 | 30,646 | 37,398 | 39,888 | 32,380 | 17,151 |
| YANCEY | 12,544 | 6,738 | 26.2 | 20.7 | 35.8 | 15.6 | 1.6 | 0.1 | 25,096 | 24,052 | 30,495 | 32,052 | 25,288 | 17,095 |
| NORTH CAROLINA | 19,736 | | 15.4 | 14.1 | 34.9 | 27.7 | 5.8 | 2.1 | 36,471 | 31,935 | 41,916 | 45,251 | 37,794 | 23,975 |
| UNITED STATES | 22,162 | | 14.5 | 12.5 | 32.3 | 29.8 | 7.4 | 3.5 | 40,748 | 34,503 | 44,969 | 49,579 | 43,409 | 27,339 |

| COUNTY | FINANCIAL SERVICES | | | | THE HOME | | | | | | ENTERTAINMENT | | | | | | PERSONAL | | | |
|---|---|---|---|---|---|---|---|---|---|---|---|---|---|---|---|---|---|---|---|---|
| | | | | | Home Improvements | | | Furnishings | | | | | | | | | | | | |
| | Auto Loan | Home Loan | Invest-ments | Retire-ment Plans | Home Repair | Lawn & Garden | Remodel-ing | Appli-ances | Elec-tronics | Furni-ture | Restau-rants | Sport-ing Goods | Theater & Concerts | Toys & Hobbies | Travel | Video Rental | Apparel | Auto After-market | Health Insur-ance | Pets & Supplies |
| ROBESON | 96 | 72 | 80 | 78 | 95 | 92 | 108 | 96 | 91 | 82 | 82 | 95 | 83 | 94 | 73 | 95 | 82 | 89 | 99 | 96 |
| ROCKINGHAM | 97 | 76 | 87 | 82 | 98 | 94 | 109 | 96 | 91 | 85 | 86 | 95 | 87 | 97 | 76 | 96 | 85 | 90 | 101 | 97 |
| ROWAN | 98 | 80 | 87 | 84 | 98 | 94 | 110 | 97 | 93 | 88 | 89 | 96 | 88 | 99 | 77 | 97 | 88 | 92 | 100 | 99 |
| RUTHERFORD | 98 | 74 | 81 | 82 | 96 | 93 | 113 | 97 | 93 | 83 | 85 | 96 | 85 | 98 | 73 | 97 | 85 | 90 | 101 | 99 |
| SAMPSON | 97 | 70 | 77 | 78 | 94 | 91 | 112 | 96 | 92 | 80 | 82 | 96 | 83 | 96 | 71 | 96 | 82 | 89 | 101 | 98 |
| SCOTLAND | 97 | 80 | 90 | 86 | 97 | 95 | 107 | 97 | 94 | 88 | 87 | 96 | 89 | 96 | 78 | 97 | 88 | 92 | 98 | 98 |
| STANLY | 98 | 77 | 84 | 83 | 96 | 93 | 114 | 97 | 93 | 85 | 87 | 96 | 86 | 98 | 75 | 97 | 87 | 91 | 101 | 99 |
| STOKES | 99 | 74 | 79 | 81 | 94 | 91 | 114 | 97 | 94 | 83 | 85 | 97 | 85 | 98 | 71 | 97 | 85 | 91 | 101 | 100 |
| SURRY | 98 | 75 | 84 | 82 | 97 | 94 | 111 | 97 | 93 | 84 | 85 | 96 | 86 | 97 | 74 | 97 | 85 | 90 | 101 | 98 |
| SWAIN | 96 | 65 | 71 | 75 | 92 | 91 | 112 | 95 | 91 | 76 | 78 | 93 | 78 | 93 | 68 | 96 | 78 | 87 | 102 | 96 |
| TRANSYLVANIA | 100 | 80 | 96 | 90 | 100 | 101 | 113 | 99 | 95 | 87 | 90 | 98 | 91 | 100 | 80 | 98 | 90 | 93 | 105 | 101 |
| TYRRELL | 95 | 67 | 75 | 75 | 93 | 88 | 107 | 96 | 90 | 79 | 76 | 93 | 79 | 93 | 70 | 96 | 80 | 88 | 94 | 96 |
| UNION | 100 | 88 | 91 | 93 | 98 | 96 | 113 | 99 | 98 | 92 | 94 | 100 | 93 | 102 | 80 | 99 | 94 | 96 | 100 | 102 |
| VANCE | 96 | 80 | 87 | 83 | 97 | 93 | 105 | 96 | 93 | 88 | 86 | 95 | 87 | 96 | 77 | 97 | 87 | 91 | 96 | 97 |
| WAKE | 102 | 109 | 98 | 105 | 101 | 103 | 101 | 101 | 103 | 105 | 109 | 105 | 102 | 104 | 91 | 100 | 107 | 105 | 97 | 104 |
| WARREN | 98 | 65 | 70 | 75 | 92 | 91 | 115 | 96 | 92 | 76 | 78 | 96 | 79 | 95 | 67 | 96 | 79 | 87 | 102 | 97 |
| WASHINGTON | 96 | 65 | 69 | 74 | 93 | 89 | 109 | 96 | 90 | 77 | 77 | 95 | 79 | 94 | 68 | 95 | 79 | 87 | 99 | 96 |
| WATAUGA | 96 | 85 | 87 | 86 | 95 | 91 | 109 | 93 | 91 | 82 | 87 | 92 | 84 | 95 | 77 | 94 | 86 | 91 | 98 | 98 |
| WAYNE | 96 | 83 | 86 | 84 | 96 | 93 | 104 | 96 | 93 | 89 | 89 | 95 | 88 | 97 | 77 | 97 | 89 | 93 | 96 | 98 |
| WILKES | 98 | 69 | 76 | 78 | 94 | 91 | 113 | 96 | 92 | 80 | 81 | 96 | 82 | 96 | 70 | 96 | 82 | 89 | 101 | 98 |
| WILSON | 97 | 84 | 93 | 90 | 99 | 96 | 104 | 97 | 95 | 91 | 89 | 97 | 91 | 98 | 81 | 97 | 91 | 94 | 97 | 99 |
| YADKIN | 98 | 71 | 78 | 80 | 94 | 91 | 115 | 97 | 93 | 81 | 83 | 97 | 83 | 98 | 71 | 97 | 83 | 89 | 101 | 99 |
| YANCEY | 97 | 63 | 68 | 74 | 92 | 90 | 113 | 95 | 91 | 75 | 77 | 95 | 78 | 94 | 66 | 95 | 78 | 87 | 102 | 96 |
| NORTH CAROLINA | 98 | 88 | 92 | 91 | 98 | 97 | 106 | 98 | 96 | 92 | 93 | 98 | 92 | 99 | 81 | 98 | 93 | 95 | 99 | 100 |
| UNITED STATES | 100 | 100 | 100 | 100 | 100 | 100 | 100 | 100 | 100 | 100 | 100 | 100 | 100 | 100 | 100 | 100 | 100 | 100 | 100 | 100 |

| COUNTY | FIPS Code | MSA Code | DMA Code | POPULATION 1990 | POPULATION 2000 | POPULATION 2005 | 1990-2000 ANNUAL CHANGE % Rate | 1990-2000 ANNUAL CHANGE State Rank | White 1990 | White 2000 | Black 1990 | Black 2000 | Asian/Pacific 1990 | Asian/Pacific 2000 |
|---|---|---|---|---|---|---|---|---|---|---|---|---|---|---|
| ADAMS | 001 | 0000 | 687 | 3,174 | 2,592 | 2,350 | -2.0 | 44 | 99.6 | 99.4 | 0.1 | 0.2 | 0.0 | 0.0 |
| BARNES | 003 | 0000 | 724 | 12,545 | 11,788 | 11,416 | -0.6 | 15 | 98.9 | 98.7 | 0.2 | 0.3 | 0.3 | 0.4 |
| BENSON | 005 | 0000 | 724 | 7,198 | 6,743 | 6,555 | -0.6 | 15 | 61.4 | 56.7 | 0.0 | 0.0 | 0.0 | 0.0 |
| BILLINGS | 007 | 0000 | 687 | 1,108 | 1,052 | 984 | -0.5 | 12 | 99.7 | 99.7 | 0.0 | 0.0 | 0.0 | 0.0 |
| BOTTINEAU | 009 | 0000 | 687 | 8,011 | 7,172 | 6,821 | -1.1 | 29 | 99.0 | 98.9 | 0.1 | 0.1 | 0.2 | 0.2 |
| BOWMAN | 011 | 0000 | 687 | 3,596 | 3,254 | 3,179 | -1.0 | 26 | 99.7 | 99.7 | 0.0 | 0.0 | 0.1 | 0.2 |
| BURKE | 013 | 0000 | 687 | 3,002 | 2,116 | 1,788 | -3.4 | 53 | 99.3 | 99.0 | 0.0 | 0.0 | 0.2 | 0.3 |
| BURLEIGH | 015 | 1010 | 687 | 60,131 | 67,930 | 70,729 | 1.2 | 2 | 96.6 | 95.8 | 0.1 | 0.1 | 0.4 | 0.6 |
| CASS | 017 | 2520 | 724 | 102,874 | 120,073 | 128,359 | 1.5 | 1 | 97.6 | 96.7 | 0.3 | 0.3 | 1.0 | 1.4 |
| CAVALIER | 019 | 0000 | 724 | 6,064 | 4,673 | 3,997 | -2.5 | 49 | 99.1 | 98.9 | 0.1 | 0.1 | 0.1 | 0.1 |
| DICKEY | 021 | 0000 | 724 | 6,107 | 5,657 | 5,630 | -0.7 | 19 | 99.1 | 99.0 | 0.1 | 0.1 | 0.2 | 0.3 |
| DIVIDE | 023 | 0000 | 687 | 2,899 | 2,230 | 1,970 | -2.5 | 49 | 99.3 | 99.2 | 0.0 | 0.0 | 0.2 | 0.3 |
| DUNN | 025 | 0000 | 687 | 4,005 | 3,379 | 3,091 | -1.6 | 39 | 90.0 | 87.6 | 0.0 | 0.0 | 0.1 | 0.3 |
| EDDY | 027 | 0000 | 724 | 2,951 | 2,767 | 2,629 | -0.6 | 15 | 98.3 | 98.1 | 0.0 | 0.0 | 0.0 | 0.0 |
| EMMONS | 029 | 0000 | 687 | 4,830 | 4,263 | 4,073 | -1.2 | 33 | 99.8 | 99.8 | 0.0 | 0.0 | 0.1 | 0.1 |
| FOSTER | 031 | 0000 | 724 | 3,983 | 3,775 | 3,718 | -0.5 | 12 | 99.3 | 99.3 | 0.0 | 0.0 | 0.1 | 0.0 |
| GOLDEN VALLEY | 033 | 0000 | 687 | 2,108 | 1,734 | 1,558 | -1.9 | 41 | 99.0 | 97.6 | 0.0 | 0.0 | 0.4 | 0.6 |
| GRAND FORKS | 035 | 2985 | 724 | 70,683 | 62,916 | 59,805 | -1.1 | 29 | 94.5 | 93.1 | 2.0 | 2.3 | 1.2 | 1.8 |
| GRANT | 037 | 0000 | 687 | 3,549 | 2,768 | 2,394 | -2.4 | 48 | 98.9 | 98.7 | 0.0 | 0.0 | 0.1 | 0.2 |
| GRIGGS | 039 | 0000 | 724 | 3,303 | 2,724 | 2,468 | -1.9 | 41 | 99.6 | 99.4 | 0.0 | 0.0 | 0.2 | 0.2 |
| HETTINGER | 041 | 0000 | 687 | 3,445 | 2,785 | 2,531 | -2.1 | 46 | 99.6 | 99.5 | 0.0 | 0.0 | 0.2 | 0.3 |
| KIDDER | 043 | 0000 | 687 | 3,332 | 2,733 | 2,442 | -1.9 | 41 | 99.9 | 99.9 | 0.0 | 0.0 | 0.1 | 0.1 |
| LAMOURE | 045 | 0000 | 724 | 5,383 | 4,621 | 4,256 | -1.5 | 36 | 99.8 | 99.8 | 0.0 | 0.0 | 0.0 | 0.0 |
| LOGAN | 047 | 0000 | 687 | 2,847 | 2,207 | 1,924 | -2.5 | 49 | 99.7 | 99.6 | 0.0 | 0.0 | 0.0 | 0.0 |
| MCHENRY | 049 | 0000 | 687 | 6,528 | 5,881 | 5,494 | -1.0 | 26 | 99.5 | 99.5 | 0.1 | 0.1 | 0.2 | 0.2 |
| MCINTOSH | 051 | 0000 | 687 | 4,021 | 3,326 | 2,992 | -1.8 | 40 | 99.7 | 99.6 | 0.0 | 0.0 | 0.1 | 0.2 |
| MCKENZIE | 053 | 0000 | 687 | 6,383 | 5,446 | 5,002 | -1.5 | 36 | 85.3 | 82.5 | 0.0 | 0.1 | 0.0 | 0.1 |
| MCLEAN | 055 | 0000 | 687 | 10,457 | 9,523 | 9,134 | -0.9 | 25 | 94.4 | 93.2 | 0.0 | 0.0 | 0.1 | 0.1 |
| MERCER | 057 | 0000 | 687 | 9,808 | 9,097 | 8,552 | -0.7 | 19 | 97.1 | 96.3 | 0.1 | 0.2 | 0.4 | 0.7 |
| MORTON | 059 | 1010 | 687 | 23,700 | 24,607 | 24,835 | 0.4 | 5 | 97.9 | 97.6 | 0.1 | 0.1 | 0.2 | 0.3 |
| MOUNTRAIL | 061 | 0000 | 687 | 7,021 | 6,449 | 6,126 | -0.8 | 23 | 79.8 | 76.0 | 0.1 | 0.0 | 0.2 | 0.3 |
| NELSON | 063 | 0000 | 724 | 4,410 | 3,578 | 3,218 | -2.0 | 44 | 99.7 | 99.7 | 0.0 | 0.1 | 0.1 | 0.1 |
| OLIVER | 065 | 0000 | 687 | 2,381 | 2,132 | 2,005 | -1.1 | 29 | 98.3 | 98.1 | 0.0 | 0.0 | 0.0 | 0.0 |
| PEMBINA | 067 | 0000 | 724 | 9,238 | 8,233 | 7,669 | -1.1 | 29 | 97.4 | 96.8 | 0.2 | 0.2 | 0.1 | 0.1 |
| PIERCE | 069 | 0000 | 687 | 5,052 | 4,560 | 4,392 | -1.0 | 26 | 99.2 | 99.0 | 0.0 | 0.0 | 0.3 | 0.4 |
| RAMSEY | 071 | 0000 | 724 | 12,681 | 11,785 | 11,024 | -0.7 | 19 | 94.8 | 93.8 | 0.2 | 0.2 | 0.2 | 0.4 |
| RANSOM | 073 | 0000 | 724 | 5,921 | 5,696 | 5,524 | -0.4 | 11 | 99.5 | 99.3 | 0.1 | 0.1 | 0.1 | 0.2 |
| RENVILLE | 075 | 0000 | 687 | 3,160 | 2,781 | 2,690 | -1.2 | 33 | 98.3 | 98.1 | 0.4 | 0.4 | 0.3 | 0.6 |
| RICHLAND | 077 | 0000 | 724 | 18,148 | 17,825 | 17,341 | -0.2 | 8 | 97.1 | 96.6 | 0.1 | 0.1 | 0.5 | 0.7 |
| ROLETTE | 079 | 0000 | 687 | 12,772 | 14,322 | 14,795 | 1.1 | 3 | 33.0 | 29.1 | 0.2 | 0.3 | 0.1 | 0.2 |
| SARGENT | 081 | 0000 | 724 | 4,549 | 4,215 | 4,077 | -0.7 | 19 | 99.5 | 99.5 | 0.0 | 0.0 | 0.1 | 0.1 |
| SHERIDAN | 083 | 0000 | 687 | 2,148 | 1,619 | 1,414 | -2.7 | 52 | 99.5 | 99.4 | 0.0 | 0.0 | 0.0 | 0.0 |
| SIOUX | 085 | 0000 | 687 | 3,761 | 4,174 | 4,280 | 1.0 | 4 | 24.1 | 20.8 | 0.1 | 0.1 | 0.3 | 0.5 |
| SLOPE | 087 | 0000 | 687 | 907 | 904 | 978 | 0.0 | 6 | 99.6 | 99.6 | 0.0 | 0.0 | 0.0 | 0.0 |
| STARK | 089 | 0000 | 687 | 22,832 | 22,394 | 21,921 | -0.2 | 8 | 98.8 | 98.5 | 0.1 | 0.1 | 0.3 | 0.6 |
| STEELE | 091 | 0000 | 724 | 2,420 | 2,149 | 1,991 | -1.2 | 33 | 99.8 | 99.7 | 0.0 | 0.0 | 0.1 | 0.1 |
| STUTSMAN | 093 | 0000 | 724 | 22,241 | 20,980 | 20,436 | -0.6 | 15 | 98.6 | 98.2 | 0.2 | 0.3 | 0.4 | 0.6 |
| TOWNER | 095 | 0000 | 724 | 3,627 | 2,893 | 2,603 | -2.2 | 47 | 98.3 | 98.0 | 0.1 | 0.0 | 0.1 | 0.2 |
| TRAILL | 097 | 0000 | 724 | 8,752 | 8,552 | 8,520 | -0.2 | 8 | 98.5 | 98.0 | 0.1 | 0.1 | 0.3 | 0.4 |
| WALSH | 099 | 0000 | 724 | 13,840 | 13,213 | 12,496 | -0.5 | 12 | 97.2 | 96.0 | 0.1 | 0.1 | 0.4 | 0.7 |
| WARD | 101 | 0000 | 687 | 57,921 | 58,210 | 57,402 | 0.0 | 6 | 94.2 | 92.8 | 2.4 | 2.5 | 1.0 | 1.6 |
| WELLS | 103 | 0000 | 687 | 5,864 | 5,021 | 4,673 | -1.5 | 36 | 99.7 | 99.7 | 0.0 | 0.0 | 0.1 | 0.1 |
| WILLIAMS | 105 | 0000 | 687 | 21,129 | 19,515 | 18,321 | -0.8 | 23 | 94.8 | 93.7 | 0.1 | 0.1 | 0.2 | 0.3 |
| NORTH DAKOTA | | | | | | | -0.1 | | 94.6 | 93.4 | 0.6 | 0.6 | 0.5 | 0.8 |
| UNITED STATES | | | | | | | 1.0 | | 80.3 | 77.9 | 12.1 | 12.4 | 2.9 | 3.9 |

# B

| COUNTY | % HISPANIC ORIGIN | | 2000 AGE DISTRIBUTION (%) | | | | | | | | | | MEDIAN AGE | | 2000 Males/ Females (×100) |
|---|---|---|---|---|---|---|---|---|---|---|---|---|---|---|---|
| | 1990 | 2000 | 0-4 | 5-9 | 10-14 | 15-19 | 20-24 | 25-44 | 45-64 | 65-84 | 85+ | 18+ | 1990 | 2000 | |
| ADAMS | 0.0 | 0.6 | 4.9 | 5.6 | 7.2 | 7.3 | 4.4 | 22.6 | 26.1 | 17.9 | 4.1 | 77.1 | 39.3 | 43.8 | 98.5 |
| BARNES | 0.3 | 0.7 | 5.0 | 5.5 | 7.1 | 8.6 | 7.2 | 23.1 | 23.7 | 15.9 | 3.8 | 77.9 | 36.6 | 40.8 | 95.8 |
| BENSON | 0.3 | 0.5 | 8.6 | 8.8 | 9.8 | 9.2 | 5.9 | 21.8 | 21.1 | 12.5 | 2.4 | 67.0 | 31.0 | 32.9 | 100.8 |
| BILLINGS | 0.0 | 0.5 | 5.6 | 6.8 | 9.3 | 9.2 | 4.6 | 25.0 | 26.9 | 11.5 | 1.0 | 71.0 | 33.2 | 39.0 | 105.9 |
| BOTTINEAU | 0.2 | 0.6 | 4.6 | 5.3 | 7.2 | 9.0 | 4.9 | 22.4 | 25.3 | 17.3 | 4.1 | 77.5 | 37.9 | 42.9 | 102.0 |
| BOWMAN | 0.2 | 0.6 | 4.8 | 5.8 | 7.8 | 7.8 | 4.2 | 22.5 | 26.3 | 17.4 | 3.5 | 75.8 | 37.2 | 43.2 | 95.4 |
| BURKE | 0.5 | 0.9 | 3.5 | 4.8 | 6.7 | 7.2 | 4.0 | 20.5 | 27.6 | 21.6 | 4.0 | 79.7 | 42.7 | 47.3 | 100.2 |
| BURLEIGH | 0.6 | 1.3 | 5.9 | 6.4 | 7.6 | 8.4 | 6.6 | 29.4 | 23.6 | 10.4 | 1.7 | 75.3 | 32.0 | 36.7 | 93.8 |
| CASS | 0.7 | 1.6 | 6.0 | 5.9 | 6.9 | 8.2 | 10.4 | 31.7 | 20.8 | 8.5 | 1.7 | 77.3 | 30.0 | 33.7 | 98.5 |
| CAVALIER | 0.1 | 0.4 | 5.2 | 5.7 | 7.7 | 7.4 | 3.8 | 21.5 | 27.1 | 17.8 | 3.7 | 76.5 | 38.9 | 44.1 | 99.4 |
| DICKEY | 0.5 | 1.1 | 4.5 | 5.5 | 6.8 | 8.9 | 6.7 | 21.8 | 24.6 | 16.6 | 4.7 | 78.3 | 37.4 | 42.3 | 98.6 |
| DIVIDE | 0.2 | 0.5 | 4.6 | 5.0 | 7.1 | 5.9 | 3.8 | 20.3 | 26.2 | 22.1 | 5.0 | 78.9 | 43.9 | 47.3 | 101.1 |
| DUNN | 0.6 | 1.2 | 6.0 | 7.1 | 8.7 | 8.2 | 4.3 | 22.9 | 25.2 | 15.5 | 2.2 | 72.8 | 35.1 | 40.4 | 103.2 |
| EDDY | 0.1 | 0.5 | 4.7 | 5.5 | 6.6 | 7.4 | 5.9 | 20.7 | 23.6 | 20.6 | 4.9 | 77.8 | 40.5 | 44.4 | 99.2 |
| EMMONS | 0.1 | 0.5 | 5.0 | 5.5 | 7.3 | 7.3 | 4.1 | 20.1 | 26.6 | 20.3 | 3.8 | 77.2 | 40.4 | 45.5 | 103.3 |
| FOSTER | 0.3 | 0.7 | 5.4 | 6.3 | 7.5 | 7.9 | 4.0 | 22.4 | 25.4 | 16.8 | 4.3 | 75.4 | 37.6 | 42.8 | 95.5 |
| GOLDEN VALLEY | 0.0 | 0.6 | 5.2 | 6.5 | 8.7 | 9.3 | 4.7 | 21.0 | 22.9 | 17.9 | 3.7 | 72.5 | 36.0 | 41.1 | 103.3 |
| GRAND FORKS | 1.5 | 2.6 | 6.9 | 6.2 | 6.6 | 9.5 | 13.0 | 31.2 | 17.3 | 7.6 | 1.5 | 76.6 | 27.3 | 29.7 | 103.5 |
| GRANT | 0.3 | 0.7 | 4.5 | 5.6 | 7.1 | 7.7 | 3.9 | 20.4 | 27.5 | 20.1 | 3.3 | 77.5 | 39.9 | 45.5 | 104.7 |
| GRIGGS | 0.1 | 0.5 | 4.8 | 5.8 | 7.1 | 7.8 | 5.2 | 19.8 | 25.8 | 19.3 | 4.5 | 76.9 | 41.0 | 44.7 | 99.3 |
| HETTINGER | 0.1 | 0.4 | 4.9 | 5.6 | 7.4 | 7.1 | 3.9 | 20.8 | 26.2 | 21.0 | 3.2 | 77.1 | 40.5 | 45.3 | 96.3 |
| KIDDER | 0.2 | 0.6 | 4.4 | 5.4 | 8.0 | 7.8 | 4.0 | 21.0 | 26.9 | 19.6 | 3.0 | 76.5 | 38.6 | 44.6 | 105.3 |
| LAMOURE | 0.1 | 0.8 | 4.8 | 5.7 | 7.6 | 7.5 | 4.2 | 21.6 | 25.9 | 19.1 | 3.8 | 76.5 | 39.3 | 44.2 | 101.9 |
| LOGAN | 0.3 | 0.8 | 4.7 | 5.5 | 6.9 | 6.8 | 3.6 | 20.6 | 27.6 | 20.9 | 3.4 | 77.7 | 42.4 | 46.4 | 103.4 |
| MCHENRY | 0.2 | 0.5 | 4.5 | 5.4 | 7.5 | 7.6 | 4.3 | 21.2 | 27.6 | 18.4 | 3.4 | 76.8 | 39.3 | 44.6 | 103.5 |
| MCINTOSH | 0.1 | 0.6 | 3.9 | 4.9 | 5.7 | 6.1 | 3.1 | 17.5 | 25.5 | 26.9 | 6.3 | 81.0 | 48.7 | 52.1 | 91.4 |
| MCKENZIE | 0.8 | 1.5 | 7.2 | 7.9 | 9.4 | 8.6 | 4.6 | 24.4 | 23.9 | 12.0 | 1.9 | 69.4 | 33.0 | 37.2 | 102.5 |
| MCLEAN | 0.4 | 0.7 | 5.0 | 6.0 | 8.0 | 7.9 | 4.6 | 22.7 | 26.0 | 17.0 | 2.9 | 75.1 | 37.3 | 42.5 | 101.0 |
| MERCER | 0.4 | 0.9 | 7.0 | 7.8 | 9.1 | 8.0 | 4.3 | 28.7 | 22.2 | 11.0 | 1.9 | 70.3 | 32.4 | 36.7 | 101.9 |
| MORTON | 0.3 | 0.7 | 5.6 | 6.5 | 8.1 | 8.8 | 5.5 | 26.3 | 24.1 | 12.9 | 2.2 | 73.8 | 33.1 | 38.3 | 97.5 |
| MOUNTRAIL | 0.4 | 0.8 | 6.2 | 6.7 | 7.9 | 8.2 | 5.7 | 21.6 | 25.1 | 15.5 | 3.2 | 73.6 | 35.9 | 40.6 | 98.6 |
| NELSON | 0.2 | 0.4 | 4.0 | 4.8 | 6.7 | 6.5 | 3.4 | 19.3 | 27.0 | 22.3 | 6.0 | 79.9 | 44.3 | 48.6 | 96.3 |
| OLIVER | 0.2 | 0.7 | 5.4 | 7.0 | 8.3 | 9.5 | 6.0 | 23.4 | 27.8 | 11.3 | 1.4 | 72.3 | 33.3 | 39.5 | 107.2 |
| PEMBINA | 0.9 | 1.8 | 5.3 | 6.2 | 7.9 | 8.0 | 4.3 | 23.9 | 25.5 | 15.4 | 3.6 | 75.1 | 36.7 | 41.7 | 98.2 |
| PIERCE | 0.0 | 0.4 | 4.4 | 5.2 | 7.1 | 7.3 | 4.5 | 21.2 | 25.2 | 19.5 | 5.5 | 77.8 | 40.2 | 45.2 | 98.4 |
| RAMSEY | 0.4 | 0.8 | 5.6 | 6.2 | 7.5 | 8.2 | 5.7 | 24.7 | 23.8 | 14.7 | 3.5 | 76.2 | 35.1 | 40.0 | 96.7 |
| RANSOM | 0.4 | 0.9 | 4.8 | 5.8 | 6.9 | 7.6 | 4.8 | 22.5 | 25.4 | 18.0 | 4.1 | 76.8 | 38.6 | 43.4 | 110.9 |
| RENVILLE | 0.2 | 0.7 | 4.6 | 5.9 | 7.4 | 8.3 | 4.2 | 23.3 | 26.8 | 16.1 | 3.5 | 76.1 | 37.2 | 42.7 | 97.1 |
| RICHLAND | 0.3 | 0.6 | 5.6 | 6.1 | 8.1 | 11.0 | 7.9 | 24.6 | 21.4 | 12.4 | 2.9 | 75.6 | 32.4 | 35.5 | 107.6 |
| ROLETTE | 0.5 | 0.8 | 9.7 | 9.7 | 11.1 | 9.5 | 7.5 | 24.3 | 18.5 | 8.4 | 1.3 | 63.5 | 26.7 | 27.0 | 96.9 |
| SARGENT | 0.2 | 0.6 | 4.8 | 5.6 | 7.8 | 7.7 | 4.4 | 24.0 | 28.0 | 15.3 | 2.4 | 76.5 | 37.6 | 42.6 | 106.2 |
| SHERIDAN | 0.0 | 0.2 | 4.6 | 5.1 | 6.7 | 6.6 | 3.3 | 20.3 | 28.2 | 21.9 | 3.3 | 78.4 | 43.0 | 47.2 | 109.2 |
| SIOUX | 0.8 | 0.9 | 11.5 | 10.5 | 10.8 | 11.1 | 8.6 | 22.9 | 17.7 | 6.7 | 0.3 | 59.8 | 22.9 | 23.6 | 106.6 |
| SLOPE | 0.1 | 0.9 | 4.1 | 6.1 | 8.2 | 8.4 | 4.4 | 23.7 | 28.9 | 15.3 | 1.0 | 75.7 | 34.7 | 42.3 | 112.2 |
| STARK | 0.6 | 1.2 | 6.2 | 6.9 | 8.0 | 9.0 | 6.4 | 27.4 | 21.7 | 12.3 | 2.0 | 73.4 | 31.7 | 36.1 | 96.3 |
| STEELE | 0.2 | 0.6 | 5.1 | 5.5 | 7.4 | 7.2 | 3.5 | 21.3 | 29.1 | 18.5 | 2.4 | 76.5 | 39.8 | 45.0 | 102.9 |
| STUTSMAN | 0.4 | 1.0 | 5.1 | 5.7 | 7.2 | 8.4 | 6.5 | 25.3 | 24.2 | 14.9 | 2.8 | 77.1 | 35.0 | 40.2 | 94.8 |
| TOWNER | 0.1 | 0.4 | 5.6 | 6.2 | 8.1 | 7.2 | 4.0 | 22.3 | 23.6 | 18.7 | 4.4 | 75.7 | 38.0 | 43.0 | 99.7 |
| TRAILL | 1.2 | 2.1 | 5.0 | 5.8 | 7.2 | 9.1 | 6.8 | 22.9 | 23.9 | 15.2 | 4.2 | 76.9 | 35.7 | 40.6 | 98.0 |
| WALSH | 3.2 | 5.2 | 5.7 | 6.4 | 8.0 | 7.7 | 5.0 | 24.3 | 24.4 | 15.2 | 3.3 | 74.9 | 36.1 | 40.6 | 100.0 |
| WARD | 1.5 | 2.6 | 7.1 | 6.5 | 7.4 | 8.1 | 9.2 | 29.5 | 19.9 | 10.4 | 1.9 | 74.8 | 29.3 | 33.0 | 98.0 |
| WELLS | 0.1 | 0.7 | 4.7 | 5.4 | 6.7 | 7.1 | 3.6 | 20.5 | 26.9 | 20.1 | 4.9 | 77.9 | 42.1 | 46.3 | 93.2 |
| WILLIAMS | 0.5 | 1.1 | 5.9 | 6.9 | 7.9 | 8.6 | 5.3 | 26.0 | 23.8 | 13.3 | 2.2 | 73.8 | 33.4 | 38.5 | 96.5 |
| NORTH DAKOTA | 0.7 | 1.5 | 6.0 | 6.3 | 7.5 | 8.5 | 7.6 | 27.2 | 22.4 | 12.2 | 2.4 | 75.4 | 32.4 | 36.5 | 98.8 |
| UNITED STATES | 9.0 | 11.8 | 6.9 | 7.2 | 7.2 | 7.2 | 6.7 | 29.9 | 22.2 | 11.1 | 1.6 | 74.6 | 32.9 | 35.7 | 95.6 |

| COUNTY | HOUSEHOLDS | | | | | FAMILIES | | | MEDIAN HOUSEHOLD INCOME | | | |
|---|---|---|---|---|---|---|---|---|---|---|---|---|
| | 1990 | 2000 | 2005 | % Annual Rate 1990-2000 | 2000 Average HH Size | 1990 | 2000 | % Annual Rate 1990-2000 | 2000 | 2005 | 2000 National Rank | 2000 State Rank |
| ADAMS | 1,266 | 1,098 | 1,022 | -1.7 | 2.28 | 868 | 721 | -2.2 | 26,582 | 30,707 | 2639 | 37 |
| BARNES | 4,975 | 4,855 | 4,796 | -0.3 | 2.30 | 3,341 | 3,125 | -0.8 | 28,350 | 31,965 | 2389 | 28 |
| BENSON | 2,415 | 2,366 | 2,351 | -0.2 | 2.84 | 1,827 | 1,745 | -0.6 | 22,403 | 26,472 | 3003 | 48 |
| BILLINGS | 387 | 372 | 350 | -0.5 | 2.83 | 305 | 286 | -0.8 | 29,352 | 33,594 | 2245 | 25 |
| BOTTINEAU | 3,105 | 2,884 | 2,780 | -0.9 | 2.38 | 2,173 | 1,938 | -1.4 | 30,556 | 34,602 | 2016 | 17 |
| BOWMAN | 1,420 | 1,377 | 1,392 | -0.4 | 2.31 | 989 | 928 | -0.8 | 27,278 | 30,893 | 2538 | 33 |
| BURKE | 1,252 | 949 | 832 | -3.3 | 2.21 | 863 | 632 | -3.7 | 29,056 | 34,250 | 2288 | 26 |
| BURLEIGH | 22,684 | 26,442 | 27,984 | 1.9 | 2.49 | 15,809 | 17,856 | 1.5 | 39,435 | 44,605 | 718 | 2 |
| CASS | 40,281 | 48,331 | 52,381 | 2.2 | 2.39 | 25,219 | 28,785 | 1.6 | 37,238 | 42,092 | 945 | 3 |
| CAVALIER | 2,375 | 1,993 | 1,767 | -2.1 | 2.30 | 1,673 | 1,346 | -2.6 | 30,423 | 33,715 | 2054 | 20 |
| DICKEY | 2,299 | 2,191 | 2,213 | -0.6 | 2.38 | 1,618 | 1,483 | -1.1 | 27,578 | 32,060 | 2499 | 31 |
| DIVIDE | 1,193 | 979 | 889 | -2.4 | 2.17 | 832 | 658 | -2.8 | 33,030 | 40,925 | 1532 | 10 |
| DUNN | 1,433 | 1,293 | 1,222 | -1.2 | 2.58 | 1,074 | 940 | -1.6 | 27,317 | 35,333 | 2533 | 32 |
| EDDY | 1,194 | 1,191 | 1,166 | 0.0 | 2.25 | 801 | 767 | -0.5 | 25,098 | 31,131 | 2804 | 39 |
| EMMONS | 1,849 | 1,719 | 1,686 | -0.9 | 2.44 | 1,377 | 1,243 | -1.2 | 21,679 | 26,206 | 3044 | 50 |
| FOSTER | 1,541 | 1,528 | 1,537 | -0.1 | 2.41 | 1,102 | 1,054 | -0.5 | 27,246 | 33,455 | 2544 | 35 |
| GOLDEN VALLEY | 811 | 736 | 692 | -1.2 | 2.25 | 547 | 476 | -1.7 | 23,974 | 30,517 | 2906 | 43 |
| GRAND FORKS | 25,340 | 23,986 | 23,418 | -0.7 | 2.40 | 16,858 | 15,258 | -1.2 | 34,271 | 39,888 | 1351 | 6 |
| GRANT | 1,374 | 1,167 | 1,051 | -2.0 | 2.34 | 1,000 | 828 | -2.3 | 22,017 | 27,442 | 3027 | 49 |
| GRIGGS | 1,294 | 1,122 | 1,039 | -1.7 | 2.38 | 951 | 796 | -2.1 | 24,688 | 27,431 | 2840 | 41 |
| HETTINGER | 1,341 | 1,169 | 1,097 | -1.7 | 2.33 | 983 | 835 | -2.0 | 30,208 | 36,298 | 2103 | 21 |
| KIDDER | 1,247 | 1,087 | 1,000 | -1.7 | 2.48 | 956 | 812 | -2.0 | 21,472 | 27,500 | 3055 | 51 |
| LAMOURE | 2,075 | 1,852 | 1,737 | -1.4 | 2.44 | 1,483 | 1,279 | -1.8 | 28,167 | 32,646 | 2420 | 29 |
| LOGAN | 1,096 | 927 | 842 | -2.0 | 2.30 | 819 | 684 | -2.2 | 25,128 | 30,833 | 2800 | 38 |
| MCHENRY | 2,551 | 2,439 | 2,345 | -0.5 | 2.39 | 1,837 | 1,703 | -0.9 | 24,462 | 32,205 | 2857 | 42 |
| MCINTOSH | 1,687 | 1,452 | 1,331 | -1.8 | 2.19 | 1,196 | 995 | -2.2 | 22,697 | 27,195 | 2986 | 46 |
| MCKENZIE | 2,301 | 2,094 | 1,985 | -1.1 | 2.58 | 1,684 | 1,486 | -1.5 | 31,651 | 38,978 | 1791 | 13 |
| MCLEAN | 3,933 | 3,750 | 3,676 | -0.6 | 2.48 | 2,889 | 2,666 | -1.0 | 30,549 | 36,067 | 2021 | 18 |
| MERCER | 3,560 | 3,483 | 3,357 | -0.3 | 2.58 | 2,707 | 2,556 | -0.7 | 48,687 | 57,357 | 225 | 1 |
| MORTON | 8,677 | 9,353 | 9,595 | 0.9 | 2.59 | 6,369 | 6,653 | 0.5 | 34,909 | 39,859 | 1268 | 4 |
| MOUNTRAIL | 2,587 | 2,494 | 2,425 | -0.4 | 2.51 | 1,851 | 1,722 | -0.9 | 26,979 | 30,763 | 2582 | 36 |
| NELSON | 1,831 | 1,554 | 1,427 | -2.0 | 2.19 | 1,230 | 1,002 | -2.5 | 24,830 | 29,688 | 2820 | 40 |
| OLIVER | 809 | 774 | 752 | -0.5 | 2.75 | 644 | 602 | -0.8 | 28,915 | 39,000 | 2311 | 27 |
| PEMBINA | 3,555 | 3,319 | 3,159 | -0.8 | 2.42 | 2,515 | 2,260 | -1.3 | 32,879 | 36,366 | 1557 | 11 |
| PIERCE | 1,974 | 1,890 | 1,872 | -0.5 | 2.30 | 1,363 | 1,253 | -1.0 | 27,258 | 30,636 | 2542 | 34 |
| RAMSEY | 4,977 | 4,879 | 4,682 | -0.2 | 2.30 | 3,355 | 3,163 | -0.7 | 29,390 | 31,816 | 2236 | 24 |
| RANSOM | 2,284 | 2,294 | 2,271 | 0.1 | 2.37 | 1,607 | 1,556 | -0.4 | 33,306 | 37,796 | 1489 | 8 |
| RENVILLE | 1,209 | 1,098 | 1,078 | -1.2 | 2.48 | 887 | 777 | -1.6 | 34,125 | 43,676 | 1367 | 7 |
| RICHLAND | 6,518 | 6,551 | 6,474 | 0.1 | 2.45 | 4,508 | 4,333 | -0.5 | 33,274 | 37,422 | 1497 | 9 |
| ROLETTE | 4,150 | 4,914 | 5,211 | 2.1 | 2.88 | 3,121 | 3,607 | 1.8 | 22,877 | 26,850 | 2980 | 45 |
| SARGENT | 1,763 | 1,790 | 1,809 | 0.2 | 2.32 | 1,268 | 1,242 | -0.3 | 31,464 | 34,030 | 1828 | 14 |
| SHERIDAN | 858 | 677 | 605 | -2.8 | 2.35 | 648 | 499 | -3.1 | 22,426 | 30,657 | 3002 | 47 |
| SIOUX | 1,022 | 1,192 | 1,252 | 1.9 | 3.50 | 828 | 954 | 1.7 | 19,698 | 25,000 | 3105 | 53 |
| SLOPE | 333 | 335 | 374 | 0.1 | 2.70 | 249 | 248 | 0.0 | 19,831 | 27,375 | 3104 | 52 |
| STARK | 8,479 | 8,825 | 8,906 | 0.5 | 2.46 | 5,977 | 5,981 | 0.0 | 30,184 | 35,409 | 2107 | 22 |
| STEELE | 991 | 962 | 932 | -0.4 | 2.23 | 701 | 658 | -0.8 | 34,516 | 37,875 | 1317 | 5 |
| STUTSMAN | 8,661 | 8,365 | 8,291 | -0.4 | 2.34 | 5,826 | 5,410 | -0.9 | 30,821 | 33,940 | 1965 | 15 |
| TOWNER | 1,433 | 1,198 | 1,101 | -2.1 | 2.34 | 971 | 780 | -2.6 | 23,615 | 27,127 | 2930 | 44 |
| TRAILL | 3,327 | 3,316 | 3,343 | 0.0 | 2.45 | 2,310 | 2,222 | -0.5 | 32,596 | 35,753 | 1611 | 12 |
| WALSH | 5,229 | 5,238 | 5,056 | 0.0 | 2.44 | 3,680 | 3,539 | -0.5 | 30,018 | 35,230 | 2150 | 23 |
| WARD | 21,485 | 22,549 | 22,650 | 0.6 | 2.49 | 15,259 | 15,403 | 0.1 | 30,499 | 34,975 | 2034 | 19 |
| WELLS | 2,406 | 2,211 | 2,127 | -1.0 | 2.22 | 1,680 | 1,484 | -1.5 | 28,080 | 31,042 | 2428 | 30 |
| WILLIAMS | 8,041 | 7,852 | 7,576 | -0.3 | 2.44 | 5,642 | 5,300 | -0.8 | 30,669 | 36,445 | 1992 | 16 |
| NORTH DAKOTA | | | | 0.4 | 2.44 | | | -0.1 | 32,300 | 37,344 | | |
| UNITED STATES | | | | 1.4 | 2.59 | | | 1.1 | 41,914 | 49,127 | | |

| COUNTY | 2000 Per Capita Income | 2000 HH Income Base | 2000 HOUSEHOLD INCOME DISTRIBUTION (%) Less than $15,000 | $15,000 to $24,999 | $25,000 to $49,999 | $50,000 to $99,999 | $100,000 to $149,999 | $150,000 or More | 2000 AVERAGE DISPOSABLE INCOME BY AGE OF HOUSEHOLDER All Ages | <35 | 35-44 | 45-54 | 55-64 | 65+ |
|---|---|---|---|---|---|---|---|---|---|---|---|---|---|---|
| ADAMS | 13,729 | 1,098 | 28.8 | 18.4 | 36.6 | 13.6 | 2.1 | 0.6 | 25,666 | 19,773 | 36,088 | 33,699 | 24,218 | 16,995 |
| BARNES | 14,833 | 4,855 | 22.0 | 21.4 | 35.8 | 17.7 | 2.4 | 0.7 | 28,288 | 23,325 | 33,242 | 37,435 | 29,604 | 22,168 |
| BENSON | 9,696 | 2,366 | 30.5 | 25.7 | 30.5 | 12.6 | 0.9 | 0.0 | 22,873 | 19,763 | 26,903 | 26,260 | 24,704 | 19,484 |
| BILLINGS | 11,021 | 372 | 31.5 | 12.4 | 37.6 | 17.7 | 0.5 | 0.3 | 25,948 | 26,148 | 29,717 | 30,489 | 20,890 | 21,067 |
| BOTTINEAU | 15,131 | 2,884 | 19.9 | 19.9 | 37.6 | 19.2 | 3.1 | 0.4 | 29,312 | 24,252 | 36,453 | 32,912 | 35,106 | 22,900 |
| BOWMAN | 13,653 | 1,377 | 24.3 | 21.6 | 35.7 | 17.3 | 1.1 | 0.1 | 26,275 | 24,643 | 32,431 | 29,389 | 28,605 | 20,174 |
| BURKE | 15,327 | 949 | 20.0 | 21.6 | 37.8 | 18.7 | 1.9 | 0.0 | 27,853 | 30,371 | 36,841 | 35,449 | 29,007 | 19,874 |
| BURLEIGH | 19,043 | 26,442 | 13.1 | 15.0 | 36.8 | 28.4 | 5.1 | 1.6 | 37,053 | 30,448 | 42,392 | 47,103 | 40,273 | 24,000 |
| CASS | 19,276 | 48,329 | 15.7 | 14.3 | 36.8 | 26.7 | 4.9 | 1.7 | 36,159 | 28,087 | 42,677 | 46,554 | 39,866 | 27,260 |
| CAVALIER | 15,907 | 1,993 | 20.8 | 20.6 | 36.8 | 18.5 | 2.5 | 0.8 | 29,153 | 27,459 | 37,192 | 34,363 | 32,101 | 22,012 |
| DICKEY | 13,012 | 2,191 | 25.0 | 20.8 | 36.9 | 14.9 | 2.2 | 0.3 | 26,404 | 22,234 | 32,747 | 31,515 | 30,561 | 20,239 |
| DIVIDE | 16,958 | 979 | 15.3 | 19.9 | 41.1 | 21.1 | 2.5 | 0.1 | 30,220 | 27,172 | 37,461 | 33,723 | 33,322 | 25,555 |
| DUNN | 13,427 | 1,293 | 25.8 | 17.9 | 36.7 | 16.4 | 2.6 | 0.6 | 27,944 | 22,500 | 33,850 | 29,667 | 28,306 | 24,702 |
| EDDY | 12,574 | 1,191 | 23.1 | 26.7 | 38.5 | 11.2 | 0.5 | 0.0 | 23,759 | 26,691 | 27,819 | 26,748 | 27,156 | 18,453 |
| EMMONS | 11,648 | 1,719 | 32.6 | 24.8 | 28.0 | 13.0 | 1.3 | 0.2 | 23,064 | 21,766 | 28,187 | 27,031 | 24,466 | 18,342 |
| FOSTER | 13,519 | 1,528 | 20.0 | 23.1 | 38.0 | 17.7 | 1.2 | 0.0 | 26,836 | 27,175 | 31,483 | 34,789 | 27,534 | 19,678 |
| GOLDEN VALLEY | 12,019 | 736 | 28.9 | 23.2 | 35.1 | 12.2 | 0.5 | 0.0 | 23,339 | 20,330 | 29,212 | 27,259 | 23,956 | 19,460 |
| GRAND FORKS | 16,998 | 23,983 | 16.8 | 16.1 | 38.7 | 23.8 | 3.6 | 0.9 | 32,937 | 25,935 | 39,612 | 43,988 | 41,436 | 24,307 |
| GRANT | 11,189 | 1,167 | 35.7 | 20.3 | 32.5 | 10.7 | 0.9 | 0.0 | 21,842 | 22,004 | 30,156 | 25,691 | 19,923 | 17,042 |
| GRIGGS | 11,746 | 1,122 | 25.6 | 25.2 | 37.8 | 10.6 | 0.8 | 0.0 | 23,084 | 19,044 | 28,436 | 29,052 | 26,944 | 18,263 |
| HETTINGER | 16,061 | 1,169 | 21.6 | 19.6 | 32.0 | 22.3 | 3.9 | 0.7 | 30,467 | 33,093 | 34,908 | 36,423 | 33,343 | 22,913 |
| KIDDER | 10,955 | 1,087 | 32.5 | 24.8 | 30.5 | 11.0 | 1.1 | 0.1 | 22,424 | 21,592 | 27,299 | 26,576 | 24,371 | 17,654 |
| LAMOURE | 13,429 | 1,852 | 21.0 | 23.5 | 36.2 | 18.1 | 1.2 | 0.0 | 27,018 | 27,212 | 31,144 | 34,806 | 30,149 | 19,742 |
| LOGAN | 14,190 | 927 | 27.4 | 22.3 | 38.0 | 10.1 | 1.4 | 0.8 | 24,645 | 24,799 | 28,333 | 32,951 | 30,400 | 17,104 |
| MCHENRY | 12,488 | 2,439 | 26.4 | 24.9 | 34.2 | 13.6 | 0.9 | 0.0 | 24,194 | 25,626 | 33,294 | 27,290 | 21,756 | 18,711 |
| MCINTOSH | 12,027 | 1,452 | 31.5 | 23.3 | 33.8 | 10.9 | 0.6 | 0.0 | 22,076 | 23,289 | 30,628 | 28,605 | 23,529 | 16,746 |
| MCKENZIE | 13,560 | 2,094 | 22.5 | 15.0 | 41.9 | 18.5 | 2.0 | 0.1 | 28,684 | 26,089 | 32,713 | 34,567 | 26,413 | 22,381 |
| MCLEAN | 14,086 | 3,750 | 22.9 | 17.5 | 36.8 | 20.7 | 2.0 | 0.2 | 28,631 | 29,523 | 36,597 | 35,117 | 27,887 | 19,177 |
| MERCER | 20,434 | 3,483 | 11.8 | 7.5 | 33.1 | 39.5 | 7.1 | 1.0 | 41,639 | 43,365 | 49,220 | 50,287 | 35,998 | 25,438 |
| MORTON | 15,943 | 9,353 | 17.3 | 17.1 | 38.1 | 23.0 | 3.6 | 0.9 | 32,450 | 27,996 | 39,333 | 43,022 | 34,198 | 20,795 |
| MOUNTRAIL | 13,556 | 2,494 | 25.5 | 19.4 | 39.6 | 13.7 | 1.2 | 0.6 | 26,247 | 22,036 | 31,782 | 34,372 | 25,900 | 19,383 |
| NELSON | 13,015 | 1,554 | 25.9 | 24.5 | 35.7 | 13.2 | 0.7 | 0.0 | 23,975 | 22,737 | 30,711 | 30,159 | 24,790 | 18,641 |
| OLIVER | 12,257 | 774 | 22.0 | 20.5 | 36.4 | 19.9 | 1.2 | 0.0 | 27,949 | 24,390 | 34,870 | 36,333 | 23,193 | 15,932 |
| PEMBINA | 16,648 | 3,319 | 16.1 | 19.8 | 37.8 | 22.4 | 3.2 | 0.6 | 31,403 | 28,466 | 39,361 | 37,357 | 34,241 | 22,136 |
| PIERCE | 12,786 | 1,890 | 25.8 | 18.3 | 40.2 | 15.0 | 0.7 | 0.0 | 25,020 | 27,011 | 29,223 | 30,282 | 25,211 | 18,746 |
| RAMSEY | 16,197 | 4,879 | 20.7 | 21.6 | 36.4 | 17.5 | 2.3 | 1.4 | 29,540 | 23,957 | 33,011 | 36,061 | 39,090 | 21,217 |
| RANSOM | 16,941 | 2,294 | 18.9 | 14.3 | 42.0 | 21.2 | 2.6 | 1.0 | 31,279 | 27,884 | 43,158 | 39,846 | 29,443 | 20,741 |
| RENVILLE | 16,567 | 1,098 | 12.2 | 17.9 | 41.5 | 24.8 | 3.5 | 0.1 | 32,543 | 30,817 | 34,603 | 39,725 | 37,967 | 23,758 |
| RICHLAND | 15,404 | 6,551 | 19.2 | 14.5 | 39.3 | 22.5 | 3.6 | 0.9 | 31,871 | 24,963 | 39,593 | 39,448 | 38,066 | 23,132 |
| ROLETTE | 9,938 | 4,914 | 35.1 | 18.0 | 32.5 | 12.5 | 1.7 | 0.2 | 23,620 | 17,401 | 28,719 | 29,584 | 26,042 | 20,444 |
| SARGENT | 15,682 | 1,790 | 20.1 | 17.0 | 40.2 | 20.5 | 2.0 | 0.2 | 28,939 | 29,480 | 38,439 | 32,025 | 33,180 | 18,707 |
| SHERIDAN | 11,110 | 677 | 29.5 | 23.8 | 37.4 | 9.2 | 0.2 | 0.0 | 21,728 | 19,221 | 29,263 | 24,153 | 23,479 | 16,402 |
| SIOUX | 7,132 | 1,192 | 39.6 | 18.8 | 30.1 | 10.3 | 1.1 | 0.1 | 21,091 | 17,909 | 23,160 | 23,526 | 20,833 | 20,526 |
| SLOPE | 9,486 | 335 | 32.2 | 26.0 | 32.8 | 8.4 | 0.6 | 0.0 | 21,321 | 18,111 | 18,551 | 25,187 | 26,071 | 18,874 |
| STARK | 14,756 | 8,825 | 21.8 | 19.6 | 35.7 | 20.2 | 2.4 | 0.4 | 28,995 | 24,898 | 36,673 | 35,831 | 29,479 | 19,706 |
| STEELE | 18,068 | 962 | 13.2 | 20.8 | 38.8 | 23.6 | 2.8 | 0.8 | 32,629 | 31,982 | 36,440 | 38,808 | 41,111 | 22,583 |
| STUTSMAN | 15,836 | 8,365 | 21.1 | 18.4 | 36.2 | 20.5 | 2.8 | 1.0 | 30,277 | 25,544 | 36,664 | 36,658 | 35,364 | 21,379 |
| TOWNER | 12,595 | 1,198 | 28.3 | 25.1 | 32.4 | 12.9 | 1.3 | 0.0 | 23,794 | 23,094 | 27,326 | 28,157 | 30,991 | 17,669 |
| TRAILL | 15,482 | 3,316 | 17.5 | 18.8 | 39.0 | 21.6 | 2.7 | 0.5 | 30,489 | 26,549 | 38,830 | 37,475 | 32,857 | 22,767 |
| WALSH | 14,927 | 5,238 | 20.8 | 20.3 | 39.4 | 16.8 | 2.0 | 0.7 | 28,400 | 24,213 | 33,906 | 36,447 | 33,619 | 19,161 |
| WARD | 14,770 | 22,549 | 19.6 | 19.8 | 37.6 | 20.0 | 2.3 | 0.7 | 29,689 | 25,112 | 35,895 | 38,598 | 32,737 | 20,827 |
| WELLS | 15,958 | 2,211 | 24.9 | 18.9 | 33.9 | 19.2 | 2.3 | 0.9 | 28,413 | 28,474 | 36,845 | 33,545 | 33,592 | 20,055 |
| WILLIAMS | 15,369 | 7,852 | 19.7 | 20.4 | 37.9 | 19.0 | 2.4 | 0.6 | 29,334 | 26,158 | 36,855 | 33,083 | 29,316 | 22,153 |
| NORTH DAKOTA | 16,189 | | 19.3 | 17.7 | 37.0 | 21.9 | 3.3 | 0.9 | 31,496 | 26,663 | 38,247 | 39,642 | 34,148 | 22,008 |
| UNITED STATES | 22,162 | | 14.5 | 12.5 | 32.3 | 29.8 | 7.4 | 3.5 | 40,748 | 34,503 | 44,969 | 49,579 | 43,409 | 27,339 |

| COUNTY | FINANCIAL SERVICES | | | | THE HOME | | | | | | ENTERTAINMENT | | | | | | PERSONAL | | | |
|---|---|---|---|---|---|---|---|---|---|---|---|---|---|---|---|---|---|---|---|---|
| | | | | | Home Improvements | | | Furnishings | | | | | | | | | | | | |
| | Auto Loan | Home Loan | Invest-ments | Retire-ment Plans | Home Repair | Lawn & Garden | Remodel-ing | Appli-ances | Elec-tronics | Furni-ture | Restau-rants | Sport-ing Goods | Theater & Concerts | Toys & Hobbies | Travel | Video Rental | Apparel | Auto After-market | Health Insur-ance | Pets & Supplies |
| ADAMS | 96 | 67 | 71 | 78 | 90 | 89 | 106 | 94 | 91 | 75 | 80 | 91 | 81 | 93 | 77 | 100 | 78 | 89 | 104 | 95 |
| BARNES | 96 | 76 | 87 | 84 | 96 | 93 | 104 | 95 | 90 | 81 | 85 | 93 | 88 | 95 | 85 | 99 | 82 | 91 | 103 | 96 |
| BENSON | 94 | 67 | 70 | 76 | 92 | 88 | 105 | 93 | 88 | 76 | 77 | 90 | 80 | 90 | 78 | 99 | 78 | 88 | 101 | 93 |
| BILLINGS | 101 | 65 | 70 | 85 | 90 | 90 | 117 | 97 | 90 | 70 | 79 | 101 | 82 | 100 | 75 | 101 | 80 | 91 | 109 | 101 |
| BOTTINEAU | 96 | 67 | 73 | 80 | 91 | 90 | 110 | 95 | 91 | 75 | 80 | 93 | 82 | 94 | 77 | 100 | 79 | 90 | 105 | 96 |
| BOWMAN | 96 | 64 | 70 | 78 | 90 | 89 | 109 | 95 | 90 | 72 | 78 | 93 | 79 | 94 | 75 | 100 | 77 | 89 | 105 | 96 |
| BURKE | 96 | 64 | 71 | 78 | 90 | 89 | 108 | 94 | 90 | 73 | 78 | 92 | 80 | 93 | 76 | 100 | 77 | 89 | 105 | 95 |
| BURLEIGH | 98 | 97 | 94 | 95 | 99 | 97 | 100 | 98 | 98 | 98 | 101 | 98 | 100 | 100 | 95 | 102 | 96 | 100 | 99 | 100 |
| CASS | 97 | 101 | 91 | 95 | 98 | 96 | 95 | 96 | 96 | 96 | 101 | 97 | 98 | 98 | 95 | 100 | 95 | 99 | 97 | 99 |
| CAVALIER | 99 | 68 | 73 | 82 | 91 | 90 | 112 | 96 | 91 | 75 | 81 | 97 | 83 | 97 | 76 | 101 | 80 | 91 | 106 | 99 |
| DICKEY | 96 | 65 | 71 | 78 | 90 | 89 | 107 | 94 | 90 | 73 | 78 | 92 | 80 | 93 | 76 | 99 | 77 | 89 | 104 | 95 |
| DIVIDE | 96 | 64 | 70 | 77 | 90 | 89 | 108 | 94 | 90 | 73 | 78 | 92 | 79 | 93 | 75 | 100 | 77 | 88 | 105 | 95 |
| DUNN | 99 | 65 | 70 | 81 | 90 | 90 | 112 | 96 | 90 | 71 | 79 | 98 | 81 | 97 | 75 | 100 | 78 | 90 | 107 | 98 |
| EDDY | 95 | 64 | 70 | 77 | 90 | 89 | 107 | 94 | 91 | 73 | 78 | 90 | 79 | 92 | 76 | 100 | 77 | 88 | 104 | 94 |
| EMMONS | 95 | 64 | 70 | 76 | 90 | 89 | 108 | 94 | 91 | 73 | 78 | 91 | 79 | 92 | 75 | 100 | 77 | 88 | 104 | 94 |
| FOSTER | 96 | 65 | 71 | 78 | 90 | 90 | 109 | 94 | 91 | 73 | 79 | 92 | 80 | 93 | 76 | 100 | 78 | 89 | 105 | 95 |
| GOLDEN VALLEY | 97 | 67 | 75 | 80 | 91 | 90 | 111 | 95 | 91 | 75 | 80 | 94 | 82 | 95 | 77 | 100 | 79 | 90 | 105 | 96 |
| GRAND FORKS | 95 | 95 | 88 | 90 | 95 | 92 | 95 | 94 | 94 | 90 | 96 | 93 | 93 | 95 | 90 | 99 | 90 | 96 | 96 | 97 |
| GRANT | 97 | 64 | 70 | 79 | 90 | 89 | 109 | 95 | 90 | 72 | 78 | 94 | 79 | 94 | 75 | 100 | 77 | 89 | 106 | 96 |
| GRIGGS | 98 | 65 | 71 | 80 | 90 | 90 | 110 | 95 | 90 | 72 | 79 | 95 | 81 | 95 | 75 | 100 | 78 | 89 | 106 | 97 |
| HETTINGER | 97 | 66 | 74 | 80 | 91 | 91 | 108 | 95 | 91 | 74 | 80 | 93 | 82 | 94 | 77 | 100 | 79 | 90 | 105 | 96 |
| KIDDER | 99 | 64 | 70 | 82 | 90 | 90 | 112 | 96 | 90 | 70 | 78 | 98 | 80 | 97 | 75 | 100 | 78 | 90 | 107 | 98 |
| LAMOURE | 97 | 64 | 70 | 78 | 90 | 89 | 109 | 95 | 90 | 72 | 78 | 93 | 79 | 94 | 75 | 100 | 77 | 89 | 106 | 96 |
| LOGAN | 98 | 63 | 69 | 80 | 90 | 89 | 110 | 95 | 90 | 71 | 78 | 95 | 80 | 95 | 75 | 100 | 77 | 89 | 106 | 97 |
| MCHENRY | 97 | 65 | 71 | 79 | 90 | 90 | 109 | 95 | 91 | 73 | 79 | 93 | 80 | 94 | 76 | 100 | 78 | 89 | 105 | 96 |
| MCINTOSH | 96 | 64 | 70 | 78 | 90 | 89 | 108 | 94 | 90 | 72 | 78 | 93 | 79 | 93 | 75 | 100 | 77 | 89 | 105 | 95 |
| MCKENZIE | 98 | 70 | 73 | 82 | 91 | 89 | 109 | 96 | 91 | 76 | 81 | 96 | 83 | 96 | 78 | 100 | 81 | 91 | 104 | 97 |
| MCLEAN | 97 | 72 | 74 | 82 | 91 | 90 | 107 | 96 | 93 | 79 | 83 | 94 | 85 | 95 | 79 | 101 | 82 | 92 | 103 | 97 |
| MERCER | 101 | 91 | 78 | 92 | 93 | 93 | 104 | 99 | 100 | 94 | 99 | 102 | 96 | 101 | 87 | 104 | 94 | 100 | 101 | 102 |
| MORTON | 97 | 82 | 80 | 85 | 93 | 91 | 103 | 96 | 94 | 87 | 91 | 94 | 90 | 97 | 84 | 101 | 87 | 94 | 101 | 97 |
| MOUNTRAIL | 96 | 65 | 71 | 79 | 90 | 90 | 109 | 95 | 90 | 73 | 79 | 93 | 80 | 94 | 76 | 100 | 78 | 89 | 105 | 96 |
| NELSON | 97 | 63 | 69 | 79 | 90 | 89 | 110 | 95 | 90 | 71 | 78 | 95 | 80 | 95 | 75 | 100 | 77 | 89 | 106 | 96 |
| OLIVER | 101 | 72 | 77 | 85 | 92 | 91 | 115 | 98 | 92 | 78 | 85 | 100 | 86 | 101 | 78 | 102 | 84 | 93 | 106 | 101 |
| PEMBINA | 97 | 66 | 72 | 80 | 90 | 90 | 110 | 95 | 90 | 73 | 79 | 95 | 81 | 95 | 76 | 100 | 78 | 90 | 106 | 97 |
| PIERCE | 97 | 67 | 73 | 79 | 91 | 90 | 110 | 95 | 91 | 75 | 80 | 93 | 82 | 94 | 77 | 100 | 79 | 90 | 105 | 96 |
| RAMSEY | 97 | 81 | 86 | 87 | 95 | 93 | 105 | 96 | 93 | 86 | 89 | 94 | 91 | 96 | 86 | 101 | 86 | 94 | 102 | 97 |
| RANSOM | 96 | 64 | 70 | 78 | 90 | 89 | 109 | 94 | 90 | 72 | 78 | 93 | 79 | 93 | 75 | 100 | 77 | 89 | 105 | 95 |
| RENVILLE | 98 | 67 | 73 | 81 | 91 | 90 | 111 | 95 | 91 | 75 | 80 | 95 | 82 | 96 | 77 | 101 | 79 | 90 | 105 | 97 |
| RICHLAND | 96 | 77 | 76 | 83 | 91 | 89 | 103 | 94 | 92 | 81 | 86 | 93 | 86 | 95 | 81 | 100 | 83 | 92 | 101 | 97 |
| ROLETTE | 91 | 74 | 75 | 75 | 94 | 87 | 99 | 93 | 88 | 84 | 79 | 87 | 84 | 88 | 83 | 98 | 81 | 89 | 94 | 92 |
| SARGENT | 98 | 66 | 72 | 81 | 91 | 90 | 111 | 96 | 91 | 74 | 80 | 96 | 82 | 96 | 76 | 100 | 79 | 90 | 106 | 98 |
| SHERIDAN | 97 | 65 | 72 | 80 | 90 | 90 | 111 | 95 | 90 | 73 | 79 | 95 | 81 | 95 | 76 | 100 | 78 | 89 | 106 | 97 |
| SIOUX | 90 | 74 | 73 | 75 | 94 | 85 | 96 | 90 | 83 | 80 | 74 | 88 | 83 | 87 | 84 | 97 | 81 | 88 | 92 | 89 |
| SLOPE | 99 | 63 | 69 | 82 | 89 | 89 | 112 | 96 | 89 | 70 | 78 | 99 | 80 | 97 | 74 | 100 | 78 | 90 | 108 | 98 |
| STARK | 97 | 86 | 81 | 88 | 93 | 92 | 102 | 96 | 96 | 89 | 93 | 96 | 92 | 97 | 85 | 102 | 89 | 96 | 100 | 98 |
| STEELE | 99 | 64 | 70 | 82 | 90 | 90 | 113 | 96 | 90 | 71 | 78 | 98 | 80 | 97 | 75 | 101 | 78 | 90 | 108 | 98 |
| STUTSMAN | 96 | 82 | 81 | 86 | 94 | 91 | 103 | 95 | 94 | 85 | 89 | 93 | 90 | 96 | 84 | 100 | 86 | 94 | 100 | 97 |
| TOWNER | 97 | 64 | 70 | 78 | 90 | 89 | 109 | 95 | 90 | 72 | 78 | 94 | 79 | 94 | 75 | 100 | 77 | 89 | 106 | 96 |
| TRAILL | 95 | 66 | 73 | 78 | 91 | 89 | 108 | 94 | 90 | 74 | 79 | 91 | 80 | 93 | 77 | 99 | 78 | 89 | 104 | 95 |
| WALSH | 96 | 71 | 80 | 83 | 93 | 92 | 107 | 95 | 91 | 77 | 82 | 93 | 85 | 94 | 80 | 100 | 81 | 90 | 105 | 96 |
| WARD | 96 | 91 | 87 | 88 | 95 | 93 | 98 | 95 | 95 | 91 | 95 | 94 | 94 | 96 | 89 | 100 | 90 | 96 | 98 | 98 |
| WELLS | 96 | 64 | 70 | 77 | 90 | 89 | 108 | 94 | 90 | 73 | 78 | 91 | 79 | 92 | 75 | 100 | 77 | 88 | 105 | 95 |
| WILLIAMS | 97 | 82 | 80 | 85 | 93 | 91 | 103 | 96 | 94 | 86 | 90 | 94 | 90 | 96 | 84 | 101 | 86 | 94 | 101 | 97 |
| NORTH DAKOTA | 97 | 86 | 85 | 88 | 94 | 93 | 101 | 95 | 94 | 87 | 91 | 95 | 92 | 96 | 87 | 100 | 88 | 95 | 100 | 98 |
| UNITED STATES | 100 | 100 | 100 | 100 | 100 | 100 | 100 | 100 | 100 | 100 | 100 | 100 | 100 | 100 | 100 | 100 | 100 | 100 | 100 | 100 |

# POPULATION CHANGE

| COUNTY | FIPS Code | MSA Code | DMA Code | POPULATION 1990 | POPULATION 2000 | POPULATION 2005 | 1990-2000 ANNUAL CHANGE % Rate | 1990-2000 ANNUAL CHANGE State Rank | RACE (%) White 1990 | White 2000 | Black 1990 | Black 2000 | Asian/Pacific 1990 | Asian/Pacific 2000 |
|---|---|---|---|---|---|---|---|---|---|---|---|---|---|---|
| ADAMS | 001 | 0000 | 515 | 25,371 | 28,867 | 29,821 | 1.3 | 17 | 99.4 | 99.2 | 0.2 | 0.2 | 0.1 | 0.2 |
| ALLEN | 003 | 4320 | 558 | 109,755 | 106,435 | 104,159 | -0.3 | 83 | 87.6 | 85.7 | 11.2 | 12.8 | 0.5 | 0.7 |
| ASHLAND | 005 | 0000 | 510 | 47,507 | 52,321 | 54,120 | 0.9 | 26 | 98.3 | 97.8 | 1.0 | 1.2 | 0.6 | 0.8 |
| ASHTABULA | 007 | 1680 | 510 | 99,821 | 103,602 | 104,820 | 0.4 | 46 | 95.6 | 94.9 | 3.1 | 3.6 | 0.4 | 0.5 |
| ATHENS | 009 | 0000 | 564 | 59,549 | 61,677 | 62,056 | 0.3 | 56 | 94.3 | 93.3 | 2.8 | 3.1 | 2.3 | 3.0 |
| AUGLAIZE | 011 | 4320 | 542 | 44,585 | 47,253 | 47,784 | 0.6 | 40 | 99.2 | 99.0 | 0.1 | 0.2 | 0.4 | 0.6 |
| BELMONT | 013 | 9000 | 554 | 71,074 | 70,816 | 68,650 | 0.0 | 70 | 97.8 | 97.3 | 1.8 | 2.2 | 0.2 | 0.3 |
| BROWN | 015 | 1640 | 515 | 34,966 | 42,314 | 45,987 | 1.9 | 7 | 98.6 | 98.3 | 1.2 | 1.4 | 0.1 | 0.1 |
| BUTLER | 017 | 3200 | 515 | 291,479 | 336,522 | 351,724 | 1.4 | 14 | 94.3 | 93.3 | 4.5 | 5.2 | 0.9 | 1.3 |
| CARROLL | 019 | 1320 | 510 | 26,521 | 29,544 | 30,809 | 1.1 | 19 | 99.0 | 98.9 | 0.5 | 0.6 | 0.1 | 0.2 |
| CHAMPAIGN | 021 | 0000 | 542 | 36,019 | 38,774 | 39,836 | 0.7 | 34 | 96.3 | 95.7 | 2.8 | 3.2 | 0.3 | 0.5 |
| CLARK | 023 | 2000 | 542 | 147,548 | 144,545 | 142,318 | -0.2 | 79 | 90.3 | 88.9 | 8.8 | 10.0 | 0.4 | 0.6 |
| CLERMONT | 025 | 1640 | 515 | 150,187 | 181,796 | 196,914 | 1.9 | 7 | 98.6 | 98.3 | 0.9 | 1.0 | 0.3 | 0.4 |
| CLINTON | 027 | 0000 | 515 | 35,415 | 41,297 | 44,239 | 1.5 | 11 | 97.3 | 96.8 | 2.0 | 2.4 | 0.4 | 0.5 |
| COLUMBIANA | 029 | 9320 | 536 | 108,276 | 111,290 | 111,240 | 0.3 | 56 | 98.2 | 97.9 | 1.3 | 1.5 | 0.2 | 0.3 |
| COSHOCTON | 031 | 0000 | 535 | 35,427 | 36,258 | 36,524 | 0.2 | 63 | 98.3 | 97.9 | 1.2 | 1.4 | 0.3 | 0.5 |
| CRAWFORD | 033 | 4800 | 535 | 47,870 | 46,894 | 46,317 | -0.2 | 79 | 98.9 | 98.7 | 0.5 | 0.6 | 0.2 | 0.4 |
| CUYAHOGA | 035 | 1680 | 510 | 1,412,140 | 1,363,264 | 1,321,845 | -0.3 | 83 | 72.6 | 69.4 | 24.8 | 27.2 | 1.3 | 1.8 |
| DARKE | 037 | 0000 | 542 | 53,619 | 54,017 | 53,790 | 0.1 | 66 | 99.0 | 98.8 | 0.3 | 0.4 | 0.2 | 0.3 |
| DEFIANCE | 039 | 0000 | 547 | 39,350 | 39,506 | 38,796 | 0.0 | 70 | 93.9 | 92.3 | 1.3 | 1.5 | 0.3 | 0.4 |
| DELAWARE | 041 | 1840 | 535 | 66,929 | 109,125 | 135,991 | 4.9 | 1 | 97.0 | 96.5 | 2.1 | 2.4 | 0.6 | 0.7 |
| ERIE | 043 | 0000 | 510 | 76,779 | 77,653 | 76,463 | 0.1 | 66 | 90.7 | 89.5 | 8.2 | 9.2 | 0.3 | 0.5 |
| FAIRFIELD | 045 | 1840 | 535 | 103,461 | 129,277 | 142,088 | 2.2 | 5 | 98.2 | 98.0 | 1.1 | 1.2 | 0.4 | 0.5 |
| FAYETTE | 047 | 0000 | 535 | 27,466 | 28,369 | 28,218 | 0.3 | 56 | 96.8 | 96.2 | 2.4 | 2.8 | 0.4 | 0.5 |
| FRANKLIN | 049 | 1840 | 535 | 961,437 | 1,033,293 | 1,060,487 | 0.7 | 34 | 81.5 | 78.7 | 15.9 | 17.8 | 2.0 | 2.8 |
| FULTON | 051 | 8400 | 547 | 38,498 | 42,585 | 44,533 | 1.0 | 24 | 96.4 | 95.2 | 0.2 | 0.3 | 0.4 | 0.5 |
| GALLIA | 053 | 0000 | 564 | 30,954 | 33,404 | 34,130 | 0.7 | 34 | 96.4 | 95.7 | 2.8 | 3.3 | 0.4 | 0.6 |
| GEAUGA | 055 | 1680 | 510 | 81,129 | 90,752 | 96,435 | 1.1 | 19 | 98.2 | 97.7 | 1.3 | 1.5 | 0.4 | 0.6 |
| GREENE | 057 | 2000 | 542 | 136,731 | 150,396 | 156,497 | 0.9 | 26 | 90.7 | 89.2 | 7.0 | 7.8 | 1.6 | 2.2 |
| GUERNSEY | 059 | 0000 | 554 | 39,024 | 41,089 | 41,772 | 0.5 | 44 | 97.8 | 97.4 | 1.6 | 1.8 | 0.4 | 0.5 |
| HAMILTON | 061 | 1640 | 515 | 866,228 | 835,058 | 808,202 | -0.4 | 85 | 77.7 | 74.9 | 20.9 | 23.3 | 1.1 | 1.5 |
| HANCOCK | 063 | 0000 | 547 | 65,536 | 69,723 | 71,412 | 0.6 | 40 | 97.0 | 96.2 | 0.9 | 1.0 | 0.6 | 0.9 |
| HARDIN | 065 | 0000 | 535 | 31,111 | 31,663 | 31,694 | 0.2 | 63 | 98.6 | 98.3 | 0.8 | 0.8 | 0.4 | 0.5 |
| HARRISON | 067 | 0000 | 554 | 16,085 | 16,057 | 15,994 | 0.0 | 70 | 97.3 | 96.9 | 2.4 | 2.8 | 0.1 | 0.1 |
| HENRY | 069 | 0000 | 547 | 29,108 | 29,883 | 29,938 | 0.3 | 56 | 96.0 | 95.1 | 0.5 | 0.5 | 0.3 | 0.5 |
| HIGHLAND | 071 | 0000 | 515 | 35,728 | 41,654 | 44,577 | 1.5 | 11 | 97.6 | 97.2 | 1.9 | 2.3 | 0.2 | 0.3 |
| HOCKING | 073 | 0000 | 535 | 25,533 | 29,407 | 30,665 | 1.4 | 14 | 98.7 | 98.5 | 0.9 | 1.1 | 0.1 | 0.1 |
| HOLMES | 075 | 0000 | 510 | 32,849 | 38,786 | 41,303 | 1.6 | 9 | 99.6 | 99.5 | 0.2 | 0.2 | 0.1 | 0.2 |
| HURON | 077 | 0000 | 510 | 56,240 | 60,853 | 62,594 | 0.8 | 30 | 97.8 | 97.2 | 1.1 | 1.2 | 0.3 | 0.4 |
| JACKSON | 079 | 0000 | 564 | 30,230 | 32,779 | 33,408 | 0.8 | 30 | 98.9 | 98.7 | 0.7 | 0.8 | 0.1 | 0.2 |
| JEFFERSON | 081 | 8080 | 554 | 80,298 | 72,629 | 67,680 | -1.0 | 88 | 93.7 | 92.8 | 5.6 | 6.3 | 0.3 | 0.5 |
| KNOX | 083 | 0000 | 535 | 47,473 | 54,541 | 57,724 | 1.4 | 14 | 98.5 | 98.2 | 0.8 | 0.9 | 0.4 | 0.6 |
| LAKE | 085 | 1680 | 510 | 215,499 | 227,950 | 230,511 | 0.5 | 44 | 97.4 | 96.8 | 1.6 | 1.9 | 0.7 | 1.0 |
| LAWRENCE | 087 | 3400 | 564 | 61,834 | 64,384 | 64,566 | 0.4 | 46 | 97.2 | 96.8 | 2.5 | 2.9 | 0.1 | 0.2 |
| LICKING | 089 | 1840 | 535 | 128,300 | 138,595 | 148,456 | 0.8 | 30 | 97.6 | 97.2 | 1.7 | 2.0 | 0.4 | 0.5 |
| LOGAN | 091 | 0000 | 542 | 42,310 | 47,287 | 49,624 | 1.1 | 19 | 97.3 | 96.6 | 1.9 | 2.3 | 0.6 | 0.8 |
| LORAIN | 093 | 1680 | 510 | 271,126 | 282,468 | 284,216 | 0.4 | 46 | 89.1 | 87.1 | 7.8 | 9.0 | 0.5 | 0.7 |
| LUCAS | 095 | 8400 | 547 | 462,361 | 444,512 | 434,787 | -0.4 | 85 | 82.2 | 79.7 | 14.8 | 16.5 | 1.1 | 1.5 |
| MADISON | 097 | 1840 | 535 | 37,068 | 41,589 | 42,821 | 1.1 | 19 | 91.6 | 90.2 | 7.5 | 8.6 | 0.4 | 0.6 |
| MAHONING | 099 | 9320 | 536 | 264,806 | 250,259 | 238,687 | -0.5 | 87 | 83.5 | 81.3 | 15.0 | 16.7 | 0.4 | 0.5 |
| MARION | 101 | 0000 | 535 | 64,274 | 66,647 | 65,545 | 0.4 | 46 | 94.8 | 93.9 | 4.2 | 4.8 | 0.4 | 0.7 |
| MEDINA | 103 | 1680 | 510 | 122,354 | 150,244 | 165,109 | 2.0 | 6 | 98.5 | 98.1 | 0.7 | 0.8 | 0.6 | 0.8 |
| MEIGS | 105 | 0000 | 564 | 22,987 | 24,047 | 24,227 | 0.4 | 46 | 98.9 | 98.7 | 0.8 | 0.9 | 0.1 | 0.1 |
| MERCER | 107 | 0000 | 542 | 39,443 | 41,040 | 41,181 | 0.4 | 46 | 99.2 | 99.0 | 0.0 | 0.0 | 0.3 | 0.4 |
| MIAMI | 109 | 2000 | 542 | 93,182 | 99,287 | 102,025 | 0.6 | 40 | 97.1 | 96.6 | 1.9 | 2.2 | 0.7 | 0.9 |
| MONROE | 111 | 0000 | 554 | 15,497 | 15,509 | 15,793 | 0.0 | 70 | 99.6 | 99.6 | 0.1 | 0.1 | 0.1 | 0.1 |
| MONTGOMERY | 113 | 2000 | 542 | 573,809 | 562,841 | 547,652 | -0.2 | 79 | 80.8 | 78.4 | 17.7 | 19.7 | 1.0 | 1.4 |
| MORGAN | 115 | 0000 | 535 | 14,194 | 14,525 | 14,527 | 0.2 | 63 | 95.3 | 94.5 | 4.0 | 4.7 | 0.1 | 0.1 |
| MORROW | 117 | 0000 | 535 | 27,749 | 32,738 | 35,662 | 1.6 | 9 | 99.4 | 99.2 | 0.2 | 0.3 | 0.1 | 0.2 |
| MUSKINGUM | 119 | 0000 | 596 | 82,068 | 84,960 | 85,773 | 0.3 | 56 | 95.2 | 94.4 | 4.2 | 4.9 | 0.2 | 0.3 |
| NOBLE | 121 | 0000 | 554 | 11,336 | 14,916 | 15,393 | 2.7 | 3 | 99.7 | 99.6 | 0.1 | 0.1 | 0.1 | 0.1 |
| OTTAWA | 123 | 0000 | 547 | 40,029 | 41,542 | 42,793 | 0.4 | 46 | 97.5 | 97.0 | 0.7 | 0.8 | 0.2 | 0.3 |
| PAULDING | 125 | 0000 | 509 | 20,488 | 20,037 | 19,857 | -0.2 | 79 | 97.2 | 96.5 | 1.2 | 1.4 | 0.1 | 0.1 |
| PERRY | 127 | 0000 | 535 | 31,557 | 34,374 | 34,949 | 0.8 | 30 | 99.5 | 99.5 | 0.2 | 0.2 | 0.1 | 0.1 |
| PICKAWAY | 129 | 1840 | 535 | 48,255 | 53,731 | 55,252 | 1.1 | 19 | 93.0 | 92.2 | 6.3 | 6.9 | 0.2 | 0.3 |
| PIKE | 131 | 0000 | 535 | 24,249 | 28,294 | 29,799 | 1.5 | 11 | 98.2 | 97.9 | 1.3 | 1.6 | 0.2 | 0.3 |
| PORTAGE | 133 | 0080 | 510 | 142,585 | 152,552 | 156,583 | 0.7 | 34 | 96.1 | 95.5 | 2.7 | 3.0 | 0.8 | 1.1 |
| PREBLE | 135 | 0000 | 542 | 40,113 | 43,782 | 45,369 | 0.9 | 26 | 99.3 | 99.2 | 0.4 | 0.4 | 0.2 | 0.2 |
| PUTNAM | 137 | 0000 | 547 | 33,819 | 35,226 | 35,388 | 0.4 | 46 | 98.2 | 97.7 | 0.1 | 0.1 | 0.1 | 0.1 |
| RICHLAND | 139 | 4800 | 510 | 126,137 | 129,830 | 131,028 | 0.3 | 56 | 91.2 | 89.6 | 7.9 | 9.4 | 0.5 | 0.6 |
| ROSS | 141 | 0000 | 535 | 69,330 | 76,176 | 78,375 | 0.9 | 26 | 92.8 | 91.6 | 6.4 | 7.5 | 0.4 | 0.6 |
| SANDUSKY | 143 | 0000 | 547 | 61,963 | 61,573 | 60,399 | -0.1 | 76 | 94.1 | 92.8 | 2.5 | 2.9 | 0.2 | 0.3 |
| SCIOTO | 145 | 0000 | 564 | 80,327 | 80,018 | 78,281 | 0.0 | 70 | 96.2 | 96.5 | 3.1 | 2.6 | 0.2 | 0.3 |
| SENECA | 147 | 0000 | 547 | 59,733 | 59,618 | 58,855 | 0.0 | 70 | 96.2 | 95.5 | 2.0 | 2.2 | 0.4 | 0.5 |
| SHELBY | 149 | 0000 | 542 | 44,915 | 48,308 | 50,052 | 0.7 | 34 | 97.5 | 96.9 | 1.4 | 1.6 | 0.9 | 1.2 |
| STARK | 151 | 1320 | 510 | 367,585 | 373,023 | 372,256 | 0.1 | 66 | 92.3 | 91.2 | 6.8 | 7.7 | 0.4 | 0.6 |
| SUMMIT | 153 | 0080 | 510 | 514,990 | 539,243 | 544,095 | 0.4 | 46 | 86.8 | 84.8 | 11.9 | 13.4 | 1.0 | 1.3 |
| OHIO | | | | | | | 0.4 | | 87.8 | 86.6 | 10.7 | 11.4 | 0.8 | 1.2 |
| UNITED STATES | | | | | | | 1.0 | | 80.3 | 77.9 | 12.1 | 12.4 | 2.9 | 3.9 |

| COUNTY | % HISPANIC ORIGIN 1990 | % HISPANIC ORIGIN 2000 | 2000 AGE DISTRIBUTION (%) 0-4 | 5-9 | 10-14 | 15-19 | 20-24 | 25-44 | 45-64 | 65-84 | 85+ | 18+ | MEDIAN AGE 1990 | MEDIAN AGE 2000 | 2000 Males/ Females (×100) |
|---|---|---|---|---|---|---|---|---|---|---|---|---|---|---|---|
| ADAMS | 0.4 | 0.9 | 6.8 | 7.2 | 7.4 | 7.4 | 6.3 | 27.9 | 23.4 | 12.0 | 1.6 | 73.8 | 32.9 | 36.2 | 96.6 |
| ALLEN | 1.1 | 1.8 | 6.7 | 7.1 | 7.6 | 7.7 | 6.7 | 29.2 | 21.3 | 11.9 | 1.8 | 74.3 | 33.0 | 35.3 | 100.2 |
| ASHLAND | 0.4 | 0.9 | 6.6 | 7.0 | 7.3 | 8.5 | 7.0 | 26.9 | 22.8 | 12.0 | 1.8 | 74.3 | 33.3 | 36.0 | 96.7 |
| ASHTABULA | 1.5 | 2.4 | 6.6 | 7.0 | 7.6 | 7.3 | 5.9 | 27.9 | 23.1 | 12.8 | 1.7 | 74.1 | 34.4 | 37.0 | 94.2 |
| ATHENS | 0.7 | 1.3 | 5.0 | 5.4 | 5.7 | 12.8 | 17.7 | 26.3 | 17.8 | 8.3 | 1.2 | 80.9 | 25.4 | 27.8 | 96.1 |
| AUGLAIZE | 0.5 | 1.1 | 7.1 | 7.8 | 8.2 | 7.5 | 5.6 | 28.5 | 21.4 | 12.2 | 1.9 | 72.2 | 32.8 | 35.8 | 95.5 |
| BELMONT | 0.3 | 0.8 | 5.2 | 5.8 | 6.6 | 6.8 | 5.7 | 27.7 | 24.0 | 16.0 | 2.3 | 78.2 | 37.9 | 40.3 | 93.1 |
| BROWN | 0.1 | 0.6 | 6.7 | 7.4 | 8.2 | 7.6 | 5.7 | 29.2 | 22.8 | 10.8 | 1.7 | 73.0 | 32.7 | 35.8 | 97.1 |
| BUTLER | 0.5 | 1.0 | 6.6 | 7.1 | 7.4 | 8.3 | 8.0 | 29.5 | 21.9 | 10.1 | 1.2 | 74.7 | 31.5 | 34.7 | 93.6 |
| CARROLL | 0.4 | 0.9 | 6.1 | 6.9 | 7.8 | 7.4 | 5.3 | 28.6 | 24.1 | 12.2 | 1.6 | 74.5 | 34.3 | 37.7 | 96.9 |
| CHAMPAIGN | 0.7 | 1.2 | 6.3 | 6.8 | 7.3 | 7.1 | 5.7 | 28.7 | 25.3 | 11.2 | 1.7 | 75.4 | 34.3 | 37.3 | 97.5 |
| CLARK | 0.7 | 1.2 | 6.1 | 6.6 | 7.1 | 7.6 | 6.6 | 27.7 | 23.9 | 12.6 | 1.8 | 76.0 | 34.3 | 37.5 | 92.6 |
| CLERMONT | 0.5 | 1.0 | 7.2 | 7.8 | 8.2 | 7.4 | 6.0 | 32.5 | 21.9 | 8.0 | 1.0 | 72.3 | 31.2 | 34.1 | 96.0 |
| CLINTON | 0.3 | 0.8 | 6.6 | 7.1 | 7.3 | 7.9 | 6.9 | 28.6 | 22.9 | 11.2 | 1.5 | 74.5 | 32.7 | 35.9 | 95.2 |
| COLUMBIANA | 0.4 | 0.8 | 6.4 | 6.9 | 7.2 | 7.0 | 6.2 | 27.3 | 24.1 | 13.3 | 1.7 | 75.2 | 35.0 | 37.9 | 93.4 |
| COSHOCTON | 0.3 | 0.8 | 6.4 | 7.2 | 7.6 | 7.3 | 5.4 | 27.5 | 23.8 | 13.0 | 1.8 | 74.3 | 34.7 | 37.8 | 93.9 |
| CRAWFORD | 0.5 | 1.0 | 6.3 | 6.8 | 7.5 | 7.2 | 5.6 | 27.9 | 23.9 | 12.9 | 1.9 | 75.0 | 34.5 | 37.8 | 93.9 |
| CUYAHOGA | 2.2 | 3.1 | 6.3 | 6.7 | 7.3 | 6.8 | 5.9 | 28.8 | 22.5 | 13.8 | 2.0 | 75.8 | 34.9 | 37.9 | 89.3 |
| DARKE | 0.6 | 1.2 | 6.7 | 7.2 | 7.4 | 7.2 | 5.8 | 28.1 | 23.1 | 12.2 | 2.1 | 74.1 | 33.9 | 36.9 | 94.8 |
| DEFIANCE | 6.8 | 9.2 | 6.8 | 7.2 | 7.4 | 7.6 | 6.7 | 28.6 | 23.6 | 10.6 | 1.5 | 73.9 | 32.6 | 35.5 | 97.6 |
| DELAWARE | 0.5 | 1.0 | 6.3 | 7.3 | 8.0 | 7.9 | 5.6 | 30.4 | 25.0 | 8.4 | 1.0 | 73.7 | 33.4 | 36.6 | 98.4 |
| ERIE | 1.5 | 2.3 | 6.3 | 6.7 | 7.1 | 6.9 | 6.1 | 27.4 | 24.7 | 13.1 | 1.5 | 75.6 | 34.9 | 38.2 | 94.8 |
| FAIRFIELD | 0.5 | 1.0 | 6.1 | 6.8 | 7.3 | 7.5 | 6.5 | 28.8 | 25.2 | 10.5 | 1.4 | 75.4 | 33.6 | 36.9 | 97.8 |
| FAYETTE | 0.3 | 0.8 | 6.4 | 6.9 | 7.2 | 6.8 | 6.1 | 27.7 | 24.1 | 12.7 | 1.9 | 75.3 | 34.8 | 37.6 | 94.7 |
| FRANKLIN | 1.0 | 1.5 | 6.8 | 6.8 | 6.9 | 7.3 | 8.4 | 33.5 | 20.1 | 9.0 | 1.2 | 75.8 | 30.8 | 33.7 | 92.4 |
| FULTON | 4.8 | 6.7 | 7.1 | 7.7 | 7.9 | 7.6 | 5.7 | 29.1 | 22.8 | 10.4 | 1.7 | 72.4 | 32.5 | 35.7 | 95.1 |
| GALLIA | 0.5 | 1.0 | 6.2 | 7.0 | 7.5 | 7.9 | 6.1 | 28.5 | 23.6 | 11.7 | 1.6 | 74.8 | 33.5 | 36.8 | 96.2 |
| GEAUGA | 0.4 | 0.8 | 6.6 | 7.3 | 8.2 | 7.2 | 4.9 | 27.9 | 25.2 | 11.5 | 1.3 | 73.4 | 34.5 | 38.1 | 97.2 |
| GREENE | 1.0 | 1.6 | 5.9 | 6.4 | 6.8 | 8.5 | 7.6 | 29.0 | 23.7 | 10.8 | 1.2 | 76.7 | 32.4 | 35.7 | 94.7 |
| GUERNSEY | 0.3 | 0.8 | 6.6 | 6.9 | 7.2 | 7.5 | 6.1 | 27.5 | 23.8 | 12.8 | 1.8 | 74.8 | 34.7 | 37.3 | 92.5 |
| HAMILTON | 0.6 | 1.0 | 7.0 | 7.2 | 7.7 | 7.5 | 6.7 | 29.5 | 21.0 | 11.7 | 1.8 | 73.9 | 32.8 | 35.5 | 90.8 |
| HANCOCK | 2.6 | 3.8 | 6.7 | 7.1 | 7.4 | 7.5 | 6.4 | 29.3 | 22.4 | 11.3 | 1.7 | 74.3 | 33.0 | 36.1 | 94.1 |
| HARDIN | 0.5 | 1.0 | 6.2 | 6.7 | 6.9 | 8.8 | 9.0 | 27.6 | 21.7 | 11.3 | 1.8 | 76.0 | 31.6 | 34.4 | 97.9 |
| HARRISON | 0.3 | 0.7 | 5.2 | 6.0 | 7.1 | 7.2 | 5.4 | 27.1 | 24.5 | 15.3 | 2.3 | 77.1 | 36.8 | 40.0 | 93.4 |
| HENRY | 4.6 | 6.1 | 7.3 | 7.8 | 8.2 | 8.0 | 5.5 | 28.1 | 21.7 | 11.5 | 1.9 | 71.6 | 33.0 | 35.6 | 98.5 |
| HIGHLAND | 0.3 | 0.8 | 6.7 | 7.1 | 7.5 | 7.3 | 5.8 | 27.5 | 23.3 | 12.9 | 1.8 | 74.1 | 34.2 | 37.0 | 95.4 |
| HOCKING | 0.4 | 0.9 | 6.4 | 6.9 | 7.4 | 7.1 | 5.5 | 28.3 | 25.1 | 11.8 | 1.5 | 75.1 | 34.3 | 37.7 | 101.1 |
| HOLMES | 0.4 | 0.9 | 10.0 | 10.5 | 10.3 | 8.1 | 5.4 | 26.6 | 18.6 | 9.2 | 1.4 | 64.2 | 27.7 | 29.8 | 97.9 |
| HURON | 1.8 | 2.7 | 7.4 | 7.8 | 8.0 | 7.3 | 6.1 | 29.1 | 22.3 | 10.6 | 1.4 | 72.2 | 32.1 | 34.9 | 95.9 |
| JACKSON | 0.3 | 0.8 | 6.3 | 6.9 | 7.9 | 7.5 | 6.0 | 28.5 | 23.3 | 12.0 | 1.7 | 74.2 | 33.9 | 36.8 | 92.3 |
| JEFFERSON | 0.5 | 1.0 | 5.3 | 5.7 | 6.1 | 6.9 | 6.6 | 26.0 | 25.4 | 16.0 | 2.0 | 78.9 | 37.6 | 40.7 | 90.2 |
| KNOX | 0.4 | 0.8 | 5.7 | 6.4 | 7.1 | 8.5 | 7.4 | 27.3 | 23.3 | 12.6 | 1.8 | 76.5 | 34.2 | 37.2 | 93.6 |
| LAKE | 0.7 | 1.3 | 6.0 | 6.5 | 7.1 | 6.6 | 5.6 | 30.2 | 24.5 | 12.1 | 1.4 | 76.4 | 34.3 | 38.2 | 94.1 |
| LAWRENCE | 0.2 | 0.6 | 6.2 | 6.5 | 6.9 | 7.2 | 6.2 | 28.1 | 24.4 | 12.9 | 1.5 | 75.9 | 34.2 | 37.4 | 90.7 |
| LICKING | 0.5 | 1.0 | 6.4 | 6.8 | 7.2 | 7.7 | 6.4 | 28.4 | 23.9 | 11.5 | 1.5 | 75.2 | 33.5 | 36.9 | 93.0 |
| LOGAN | 0.4 | 0.8 | 6.9 | 7.3 | 7.4 | 7.2 | 5.9 | 28.1 | 22.7 | 12.8 | 1.7 | 73.9 | 33.7 | 36.5 | 95.2 |
| LORAIN | 5.6 | 7.6 | 6.6 | 7.0 | 7.3 | 7.4 | 6.9 | 29.5 | 22.9 | 11.2 | 1.4 | 74.8 | 32.8 | 35.7 | 95.4 |
| LUCAS | 3.4 | 4.6 | 7.0 | 7.2 | 7.6 | 7.4 | 6.8 | 29.7 | 21.3 | 11.4 | 1.7 | 74.1 | 32.5 | 35.1 | 91.3 |
| MADISON | 0.6 | 1.1 | 6.0 | 6.3 | 6.8 | 6.8 | 7.6 | 35.0 | 21.2 | 9.3 | 1.0 | 76.9 | 32.3 | 34.4 | 122.2 |
| MAHONING | 2.2 | 3.3 | 5.9 | 6.3 | 6.7 | 6.8 | 6.2 | 27.3 | 23.3 | 15.5 | 2.0 | 76.9 | 36.3 | 39.0 | 90.7 |
| MARION | 0.8 | 1.4 | 6.4 | 6.7 | 7.3 | 7.0 | 6.2 | 31.0 | 22.4 | 11.5 | 1.5 | 75.2 | 33.6 | 36.2 | 103.1 |
| MEDINA | 0.6 | 1.1 | 6.3 | 7.1 | 7.6 | 7.4 | 5.6 | 29.5 | 25.6 | 9.7 | 1.2 | 74.3 | 33.3 | 36.7 | 95.9 |
| MEIGS | 0.3 | 0.7 | 5.9 | 6.7 | 7.6 | 7.4 | 5.8 | 27.4 | 24.5 | 12.8 | 1.9 | 75.1 | 35.1 | 38.0 | 94.3 |
| MERCER | 0.7 | 1.3 | 7.8 | 8.3 | 8.7 | 7.7 | 5.6 | 27.7 | 20.3 | 12.2 | 1.7 | 70.2 | 31.8 | 34.5 | 100.1 |
| MIAMI | 0.4 | 0.9 | 6.4 | 6.8 | 7.2 | 7.2 | 5.9 | 28.4 | 24.8 | 11.8 | 1.5 | 75.2 | 34.3 | 37.3 | 94.7 |
| MONROE | 0.2 | 0.6 | 5.7 | 6.2 | 6.6 | 7.0 | 6.0 | 26.4 | 26.4 | 13.6 | 2.0 | 77.0 | 36.5 | 39.9 | 95.8 |
| MONTGOMERY | 0.8 | 1.3 | 6.5 | 6.7 | 7.2 | 7.0 | 6.4 | 29.9 | 22.5 | 12.1 | 1.6 | 75.6 | 33.3 | 36.6 | 92.1 |
| MORGAN | 0.3 | 0.7 | 6.9 | 7.3 | 7.5 | 7.8 | 6.3 | 25.9 | 23.2 | 13.2 | 2.0 | 73.3 | 34.1 | 37.1 | 93.2 |
| MORROW | 0.3 | 0.8 | 6.4 | 7.2 | 8.4 | 7.6 | 5.7 | 29.2 | 24.4 | 9.8 | 1.3 | 73.3 | 33.0 | 36.2 | 98.6 |
| MUSKINGUM | 0.3 | 0.7 | 6.6 | 6.9 | 7.2 | 7.7 | 6.6 | 28.2 | 22.8 | 12.3 | 1.8 | 74.9 | 33.5 | 36.4 | 91.8 |
| NOBLE | 0.2 | 0.7 | 6.4 | 7.2 | 7.8 | 7.3 | 6.3 | 30.0 | 21.7 | 11.5 | 1.9 | 74.4 | 33.6 | 35.4 | 108.4 |
| OTTAWA | 3.7 | 5.0 | 5.3 | 6.2 | 6.8 | 6.8 | 5.0 | 28.1 | 25.1 | 15.0 | 1.8 | 77.6 | 36.4 | 40.3 | 96.2 |
| PAULDING | 3.1 | 4.5 | 7.2 | 7.7 | 8.0 | 7.8 | 5.9 | 28.6 | 23.2 | 10.4 | 1.4 | 72.2 | 32.1 | 35.3 | 96.6 |
| PERRY | 0.3 | 0.7 | 6.7 | 7.5 | 8.2 | 7.8 | 5.8 | 29.2 | 22.3 | 10.9 | 1.6 | 72.7 | 32.4 | 35.5 | 96.3 |
| PICKAWAY | 0.7 | 1.2 | 5.8 | 6.1 | 6.8 | 6.7 | 7.2 | 33.9 | 22.9 | 9.5 | 1.1 | 77.4 | 33.0 | 35.6 | 122.7 |
| PIKE | 0.3 | 0.8 | 6.5 | 7.2 | 8.0 | 7.9 | 6.0 | 28.5 | 22.7 | 11.4 | 1.8 | 73.3 | 32.9 | 35.9 | 95.3 |
| PORTAGE | 0.6 | 1.1 | 6.0 | 6.4 | 6.7 | 9.0 | 9.7 | 29.6 | 21.9 | 9.9 | 1.0 | 77.1 | 30.0 | 34.0 | 94.4 |
| PREBLE | 0.3 | 0.7 | 6.5 | 7.1 | 7.5 | 7.4 | 5.6 | 28.6 | 24.5 | 11.6 | 1.3 | 74.4 | 33.7 | 37.2 | 97.0 |
| PUTNAM | 4.2 | 5.8 | 8.3 | 8.8 | 8.7 | 8.1 | 5.8 | 28.6 | 19.8 | 10.2 | 1.6 | 69.2 | 30.8 | 33.2 | 99.3 |
| RICHLAND | 0.7 | 1.3 | 6.3 | 6.6 | 7.0 | 7.0 | 7.0 | 27.9 | 24.1 | 12.5 | 1.5 | 75.8 | 34.3 | 37.1 | 96.8 |
| ROSS | 0.5 | 1.0 | 5.7 | 6.1 | 6.4 | 7.5 | 7.4 | 31.3 | 23.0 | 11.2 | 1.4 | 77.2 | 33.8 | 36.3 | 114.8 |
| SANDUSKY | 5.7 | 7.7 | 6.8 | 7.2 | 7.4 | 7.4 | 6.4 | 28.8 | 22.4 | 12.0 | 1.7 | 74.1 | 33.2 | 36.2 | 96.5 |
| SCIOTO | 0.3 | 0.8 | 6.1 | 6.7 | 7.5 | 7.6 | 6.2 | 28.0 | 22.9 | 13.0 | 2.1 | 75.0 | 34.2 | 36.9 | 94.0 |
| SENECA | 2.8 | 4.0 | 6.8 | 7.1 | 7.3 | 8.5 | 7.3 | 27.7 | 22.0 | 11.7 | 1.8 | 74.0 | 32.5 | 35.3 | 95.5 |
| SHELBY | 0.4 | 0.9 | 7.4 | 7.8 | 8.0 | 7.8 | 5.9 | 29.4 | 21.7 | 10.4 | 1.6 | 71.8 | 31.6 | 34.9 | 100.1 |
| STARK | 0.7 | 1.3 | 6.1 | 6.5 | 7.0 | 7.1 | 6.1 | 28.2 | 24.1 | 13.1 | 1.8 | 76.2 | 35.0 | 38.1 | 92.1 |
| SUMMIT | 0.6 | 1.1 | 6.1 | 6.5 | 7.0 | 6.9 | 6.3 | 30.0 | 22.9 | 12.6 | 1.7 | 76.4 | 34.3 | 37.4 | 92.0 |
| OHIO | 1.3 | 2.0 | 6.5 | 6.9 | 7.3 | 7.4 | 6.7 | 29.5 | 22.6 | 11.8 | 1.6 | 75.2 | 33.3 | 36.3 | 93.6 |
| UNITED STATES | 9.0 | 11.8 | 6.9 | 7.2 | 7.2 | 7.2 | 6.7 | 29.9 | 22.2 | 11.1 | 1.6 | 74.6 | 32.9 | 35.7 | 95.6 |

# HOUSEHOLDS

| COUNTY | HOUSEHOLDS | | | | | FAMILIES | | | MEDIAN HOUSEHOLD INCOME | | | |
|---|---|---|---|---|---|---|---|---|---|---|---|---|
| | 1990 | 2000 | 2005 | % Annual Rate 1990-2000 | 2000 Average HH Size | 1990 | 2000 | % Annual Rate 1990-2000 | 2000 | 2005 | 2000 National Rank | 2000 State Rank |
| ADAMS | 9,192 | 10,828 | 11,372 | 2.0 | 2.63 | 7,056 | 8,038 | 1.6 | 24,432 | 28,134 | 2864 | 87 |
| ALLEN | 39,408 | 38,587 | 38,084 | -0.3 | 2.61 | 28,973 | 27,432 | -0.7 | 35,593 | 40,162 | 1154 | 55 |
| ASHLAND | 17,101 | 19,241 | 20,125 | 1.4 | 2.61 | 12,719 | 13,873 | 1.1 | 37,066 | 44,015 | 965 | 44 |
| ASHTABULA | 36,760 | 39,219 | 40,213 | 0.8 | 2.59 | 27,137 | 28,002 | 0.4 | 32,234 | 36,014 | 1677 | 67 |
| ATHENS | 20,139 | 21,498 | 21,930 | 0.8 | 2.47 | 12,508 | 12,797 | 0.3 | 27,962 | 32,826 | 2445 | 80 |
| AUGLAIZE | 15,976 | 17,295 | 17,676 | 1.0 | 2.70 | 12,260 | 12,890 | 0.6 | 40,922 | 46,820 | 597 | 27 |
| BELMONT | 28,161 | 27,928 | 27,490 | -0.1 | 2.40 | 20,219 | 19,256 | -0.6 | 28,306 | 31,073 | 2396 | 78 |
| BROWN | 12,379 | 15,261 | 16,737 | 2.6 | 2.74 | 9,755 | 11,711 | 2.2 | 35,234 | 41,659 | 1217 | 57 |
| BUTLER | 104,535 | 124,647 | 132,094 | 2.2 | 2.61 | 77,931 | 90,946 | 1.9 | 45,953 | 52,437 | 312 | 6 |
| CARROLL | 9,667 | 11,124 | 11,780 | 1.7 | 2.61 | 7,432 | 8,288 | 1.3 | 36,362 | 45,271 | 1064 | 51 |
| CHAMPAIGN | 13,253 | 14,440 | 14,940 | 1.0 | 2.64 | 10,026 | 10,617 | 0.7 | 41,598 | 49,380 | 541 | 23 |
| CLARK | 55,198 | 55,201 | 54,841 | 0.0 | 2.55 | 40,419 | 39,159 | -0.4 | 37,588 | 42,566 | 889 | 41 |
| CLERMONT | 52,726 | 65,533 | 71,908 | 2.7 | 2.75 | 41,347 | 49,981 | 2.3 | 45,364 | 52,236 | 338 | 8 |
| CLINTON | 13,038 | 15,553 | 16,885 | 2.2 | 2.59 | 9,759 | 11,352 | 1.8 | 41,154 | 50,298 | 577 | 25 |
| COLUMBIANA | 40,775 | 42,974 | 43,524 | 0.6 | 2.56 | 30,445 | 31,069 | 0.2 | 33,006 | 37,576 | 1536 | 65 |
| COSHOCTON | 13,433 | 13,947 | 14,144 | 0.5 | 2.56 | 9,900 | 9,924 | 0.0 | 32,123 | 36,967 | 1698 | 68 |
| CRAWFORD | 18,383 | 18,456 | 18,443 | 0.0 | 2.51 | 13,472 | 13,038 | -0.4 | 33,873 | 39,864 | 1410 | 63 |
| CUYAHOGA | 563,243 | 557,576 | 547,534 | -0.1 | 2.40 | 370,083 | 352,630 | -0.6 | 36,673 | 40,132 | 1021 | 46 |
| DARKE | 19,459 | 20,047 | 20,164 | 0.4 | 2.65 | 14,895 | 14,884 | 0.0 | 38,561 | 45,711 | 799 | 38 |
| DEFIANCE | 14,070 | 14,533 | 14,474 | 0.4 | 2.66 | 10,634 | 10,636 | 0.0 | 41,502 | 45,847 | 552 | 24 |
| DELAWARE | 23,116 | 36,103 | 43,960 | 5.6 | 2.94 | 18,376 | 28,473 | 5.5 | 54,149 | 60,480 | 134 | 4 |
| ERIE | 28,932 | 30,096 | 30,050 | 0.5 | 2.54 | 20,959 | 21,185 | 0.1 | 40,399 | 44,665 | 637 | 30 |
| FAIRFIELD | 36,813 | 46,866 | 51,993 | 3.0 | 2.70 | 28,791 | 35,829 | 2.7 | 45,737 | 52,338 | 323 | 7 |
| FAYETTE | 10,221 | 10,852 | 10,927 | 0.7 | 2.57 | 7,682 | 7,903 | 0.3 | 35,591 | 42,358 | 1156 | 56 |
| FRANKLIN | 378,723 | 414,319 | 428,934 | 1.1 | 2.43 | 241,881 | 255,173 | 0.7 | 40,608 | 45,516 | 618 | 29 |
| FULTON | 13,504 | 15,324 | 16,212 | 1.5 | 2.75 | 10,559 | 11,639 | 1.2 | 42,348 | 49,665 | 482 | 19 |
| GALLIA | 11,367 | 12,819 | 13,355 | 1.5 | 2.53 | 8,543 | 9,332 | 1.1 | 30,287 | 33,011 | 2086 | 73 |
| GEAUGA | 26,906 | 31,115 | 33,608 | 1.8 | 2.89 | 22,164 | 24,971 | 1.5 | 56,294 | 64,106 | 109 | 1 |
| GREENE | 48,351 | 53,056 | 55,059 | 1.1 | 2.72 | 36,723 | 39,236 | 0.8 | 47,209 | 53,860 | 269 | 5 |
| GUERNSEY | 14,894 | 16,217 | 16,738 | 1.0 | 2.49 | 10,790 | 11,345 | 0.6 | 28,481 | 33,068 | 2371 | 77 |
| HAMILTON | 338,881 | 336,281 | 329,978 | -0.1 | 2.42 | 221,348 | 213,398 | -0.4 | 36,498 | 39,903 | 1043 | 50 |
| HANCOCK | 24,642 | 26,614 | 27,478 | 0.9 | 2.57 | 18,035 | 18,793 | 0.5 | 41,788 | 49,492 | 531 | 22 |
| HARDIN | 11,250 | 11,780 | 11,934 | 0.6 | 2.53 | 8,063 | 8,117 | 0.1 | 32,869 | 38,129 | 1560 | 66 |
| HARRISON | 6,111 | 6,300 | 6,371 | 0.4 | 2.51 | 4,564 | 4,538 | -0.1 | 26,857 | 32,454 | 2605 | 83 |
| HENRY | 10,401 | 10,917 | 11,056 | 0.6 | 2.69 | 7,904 | 8,035 | 0.2 | 42,875 | 50,712 | 462 | 16 |
| HIGHLAND | 13,230 | 15,605 | 16,786 | 2.0 | 2.64 | 9,986 | 11,405 | 1.6 | 30,887 | 37,613 | 1951 | 72 |
| HOCKING | 9,351 | 11,052 | 11,674 | 2.0 | 2.59 | 7,108 | 8,156 | 1.7 | 31,665 | 36,542 | 1787 | 70 |
| HOLMES | 9,315 | 11,237 | 12,087 | 2.3 | 3.37 | 7,693 | 9,058 | 2.0 | 36,559 | 45,758 | 1035 | 49 |
| HURON | 20,239 | 22,447 | 23,371 | 1.3 | 2.69 | 15,368 | 16,552 | 0.9 | 36,652 | 41,657 | 1027 | 47 |
| JACKSON | 11,260 | 12,532 | 12,938 | 1.3 | 2.59 | 8,491 | 9,164 | 0.9 | 26,554 | 30,132 | 2643 | 84 |
| JEFFERSON | 31,311 | 29,323 | 27,817 | -0.8 | 2.41 | 22,603 | 20,375 | -1.2 | 28,880 | 31,293 | 2318 | 76 |
| KNOX | 17,230 | 20,474 | 22,065 | 2.1 | 2.50 | 12,781 | 14,803 | 1.8 | 36,122 | 42,235 | 1089 | 52 |
| LAKE | 80,421 | 86,202 | 87,761 | 0.8 | 2.61 | 59,629 | 61,571 | 0.4 | 44,402 | 50,239 | 379 | 9 |
| LAWRENCE | 22,899 | 24,519 | 24,922 | 0.8 | 2.60 | 17,574 | 18,296 | 0.5 | 25,980 | 28,764 | 2715 | 86 |
| LICKING | 47,254 | 52,624 | 57,247 | 1.3 | 2.57 | 35,574 | 38,191 | 0.9 | 43,658 | 50,133 | 416 | 13 |
| LOGAN | 15,952 | 18,021 | 19,008 | 1.5 | 2.59 | 11,753 | 12,890 | 1.1 | 41,075 | 50,253 | 585 | 26 |
| LORAIN | 96,064 | 102,312 | 104,274 | 0.8 | 2.69 | 72,947 | 75,433 | 0.4 | 42,735 | 47,767 | 469 | 18 |
| LUCAS | 177,500 | 174,300 | 172,410 | -0.2 | 2.50 | 119,709 | 113,319 | -0.7 | 35,865 | 39,755 | 1119 | 54 |
| MADISON | 11,990 | 13,691 | 14,300 | 1.6 | 2.68 | 9,259 | 10,264 | 1.3 | 43,306 | 52,843 | 438 | 14 |
| MAHONING | 101,136 | 98,730 | 95,803 | -0.3 | 2.48 | 72,646 | 68,481 | -0.7 | 31,150 | 34,163 | 1905 | 71 |
| MARION | 23,484 | 23,904 | 23,737 | 0.2 | 2.57 | 17,354 | 17,102 | -0.2 | 36,096 | 41,537 | 1092 | 53 |
| MEDINA | 41,792 | 52,243 | 57,931 | 2.7 | 2.85 | 33,827 | 41,288 | 2.4 | 54,589 | 62,298 | 127 | 3 |
| MEIGS | 8,662 | 9,255 | 9,416 | 0.8 | 2.57 | 6,485 | 6,698 | 0.4 | 24,288 | 29,864 | 2882 | 88 |
| MERCER | 13,398 | 14,439 | 14,724 | 0.9 | 2.81 | 10,430 | 10,928 | 0.6 | 37,125 | 41,337 | 955 | 43 |
| MIAMI | 34,559 | 37,473 | 38,830 | 1.0 | 2.63 | 26,437 | 27,755 | 0.6 | 44,055 | 52,127 | 393 | 11 |
| MONROE | 5,754 | 5,868 | 6,033 | 0.2 | 2.61 | 4,423 | 4,369 | -0.1 | 28,191 | 32,327 | 2416 | 79 |
| MONTGOMERY | 226,192 | 223,230 | 217,864 | -0.2 | 2.47 | 154,383 | 146,716 | -0.6 | 38,761 | 43,654 | 774 | 36 |
| MORGAN | 5,170 | 5,390 | 5,441 | 0.5 | 2.65 | 3,904 | 3,935 | 0.1 | 27,550 | 31,514 | 2503 | 81 |
| MORROW | 9,656 | 11,484 | 12,567 | 2.1 | 2.83 | 7,792 | 9,060 | 1.8 | 39,001 | 46,516 | 753 | 34 |
| MUSKINGUM | 30,753 | 32,449 | 33,077 | 0.7 | 2.56 | 22,494 | 22,970 | 0.3 | 33,118 | 38,815 | 1518 | 64 |
| NOBLE | 4,137 | 4,662 | 4,889 | 1.5 | 2.65 | 3,136 | 3,418 | 1.0 | 30,000 | 35,631 | 2152 | 74 |
| OTTAWA | 15,170 | 16,044 | 16,680 | 0.7 | 2.55 | 11,375 | 11,600 | 0.2 | 41,864 | 46,339 | 524 | 21 |
| PAULDING | 7,252 | 7,231 | 7,236 | 0.0 | 2.75 | 5,651 | 5,476 | -0.4 | 36,598 | 42,311 | 1033 | 48 |
| PERRY | 11,264 | 12,659 | 13,056 | 1.4 | 2.69 | 8,669 | 9,426 | 1.0 | 29,656 | 35,556 | 2204 | 75 |
| PICKAWAY | 15,602 | 18,006 | 18,932 | 1.8 | 2.62 | 12,243 | 13,782 | 1.4 | 39,668 | 47,750 | 695 | 31 |
| PIKE | 8,805 | 10,590 | 11,313 | 2.3 | 2.63 | 6,742 | 7,877 | 1.9 | 31,729 | 37,353 | 1769 | 69 |
| PORTAGE | 49,229 | 55,025 | 57,251 | 1.4 | 2.65 | 35,760 | 39,013 | 1.1 | 42,310 | 49,676 | 486 | 20 |
| PREBLE | 14,347 | 15,978 | 16,714 | 1.3 | 2.72 | 11,449 | 12,410 | 1.0 | 39,294 | 46,507 | 727 | 32 |
| PUTNAM | 11,082 | 11,886 | 12,107 | 0.9 | 2.93 | 8,900 | 9,298 | 0.5 | 43,108 | 50,166 | 450 | 15 |
| RICHLAND | 47,573 | 48,465 | 48,803 | 0.2 | 2.59 | 34,632 | 34,121 | -0.2 | 34,959 | 40,200 | 1258 | 59 |
| ROSS | 24,325 | 27,335 | 28,586 | 1.4 | 2.54 | 18,057 | 19,633 | 1.0 | 34,213 | 39,547 | 1354 | 61 |
| SANDUSKY | 22,464 | 22,992 | 22,878 | 0.3 | 2.63 | 16,869 | 16,743 | -0.1 | 37,535 | 43,744 | 894 | 42 |
| SCIOTO | 29,786 | 30,775 | 30,541 | 0.4 | 2.51 | 21,676 | 21,696 | 0.0 | 26,381 | 29,120 | 2668 | 85 |
| SENECA | 21,277 | 21,798 | 21,795 | 0.3 | 2.64 | 15,776 | 15,644 | -0.1 | 34,991 | 39,224 | 1252 | 58 |
| SHELBY | 15,626 | 17,012 | 17,726 | 1.0 | 2.80 | 12,136 | 12,837 | 0.7 | 43,920 | 52,993 | 398 | 12 |
| STARK | 139,573 | 144,586 | 145,805 | 0.4 | 2.52 | 101,539 | 101,639 | 0.0 | 38,640 | 43,154 | 784 | 37 |
| SUMMIT | 199,998 | 215,014 | 219,743 | 0.9 | 2.47 | 139,236 | 144,707 | 0.5 | 40,806 | 44,933 | 603 | 28 |
| OHIO | | | | 0.7 | 2.54 | | | 0.4 | 38,607 | 43,591 | | |
| UNITED STATES | | | | 1.4 | 2.59 | | | 1.1 | 41,914 | 49,127 | | |

| COUNTY | 2000 Per Capita Income | 2000 HH Income Base | 2000 HOUSEHOLD INCOME DISTRIBUTION (%) | | | | | | 2000 AVERAGE DISPOSABLE INCOME BY AGE OF HOUSEHOLDER | | | | | |
|---|---|---|---|---|---|---|---|---|---|---|---|---|---|---|
| | | | Less than $15,000 | $15,000 to $24,999 | $25,000 to $49,999 | $50,000 to $99,999 | $100,000 to $149,999 | $150,000 or More | All Ages | <35 | 35-44 | 45-54 | 55-64 | 65+ |
| ADAMS | 12,797 | 10,828 | 33.3 | 17.8 | 32.5 | 13.4 | 2.1 | 0.9 | 24,899 | 22,156 | 30,765 | 31,026 | 25,785 | 15,623 |
| ALLEN | 15,902 | 38,586 | 17.9 | 15.4 | 37.4 | 24.9 | 3.5 | 1.0 | 32,195 | 27,135 | 38,075 | 41,668 | 35,601 | 21,150 |
| ASHLAND | 16,610 | 19,241 | 15.0 | 16.1 | 37.7 | 26.2 | 3.9 | 1.1 | 33,312 | 29,688 | 38,617 | 43,325 | 36,277 | 21,683 |
| ASHTABULA | 14,698 | 39,219 | 20.3 | 17.0 | 38.1 | 21.5 | 2.5 | 0.7 | 29,506 | 25,771 | 34,819 | 37,154 | 33,201 | 19,166 |
| ATHENS | 14,168 | 21,498 | 27.5 | 17.5 | 31.7 | 18.4 | 3.5 | 1.4 | 28,733 | 21,070 | 34,104 | 42,308 | 32,857 | 19,947 |
| AUGLAIZE | 17,119 | 17,295 | 11.0 | 13.0 | 41.1 | 30.0 | 4.3 | 0.7 | 35,156 | 32,869 | 39,830 | 46,597 | 37,533 | 22,509 |
| BELMONT | 13,999 | 27,928 | 24.6 | 19.5 | 35.9 | 17.5 | 2.2 | 0.4 | 26,657 | 23,807 | 32,336 | 34,481 | 28,607 | 18,747 |
| BROWN | 15,853 | 15,261 | 15.9 | 15.0 | 38.1 | 25.6 | 4.3 | 1.1 | 32,985 | 29,686 | 38,362 | 43,292 | 32,973 | 21,248 |
| BUTLER | 22,050 | 124,646 | 11.8 | 10.9 | 32.0 | 34.3 | 8.0 | 3.1 | 41,952 | 34,559 | 47,326 | 53,313 | 45,004 | 26,354 |
| CARROLL | 15,864 | 11,124 | 15.7 | 13.3 | 40.8 | 26.9 | 3.1 | 0.2 | 32,006 | 29,711 | 36,461 | 40,377 | 33,631 | 21,641 |
| CHAMPAIGN | 17,834 | 14,440 | 13.3 | 11.0 | 37.9 | 32.4 | 4.5 | 0.8 | 35,980 | 34,098 | 40,416 | 45,055 | 37,423 | 23,166 |
| CLARK | 17,753 | 55,196 | 16.4 | 13.6 | 36.6 | 28.1 | 4.2 | 1.2 | 34,053 | 28,924 | 38,584 | 44,850 | 35,725 | 23,334 |
| CLERMONT | 19,911 | 65,533 | 9.7 | 11.0 | 35.1 | 35.5 | 7.0 | 1.8 | 40,009 | 35,004 | 45,384 | 49,204 | 41,532 | 23,809 |
| CLINTON | 19,427 | 15,553 | 13.6 | 11.3 | 37.1 | 30.5 | 6.0 | 1.5 | 36,927 | 32,548 | 42,122 | 47,810 | 38,770 | 24,495 |
| COLUMBIANA | 15,482 | 42,974 | 19.2 | 16.2 | 38.1 | 22.9 | 3.0 | 0.7 | 30,373 | 26,840 | 35,893 | 38,382 | 33,632 | 20,009 |
| COSHOCTON | 14,762 | 13,947 | 20.1 | 16.9 | 39.2 | 20.5 | 2.8 | 0.6 | 29,438 | 27,802 | 34,896 | 38,223 | 30,789 | 18,618 |
| CRAWFORD | 16,138 | 18,456 | 16.9 | 16.3 | 40.1 | 23.7 | 2.5 | 0.5 | 30,571 | 26,857 | 34,731 | 39,595 | 33,265 | 21,075 |
| CUYAHOGA | 20,678 | 557,568 | 19.1 | 14.0 | 33.0 | 26.1 | 5.4 | 2.4 | 35,567 | 30,219 | 39,990 | 44,746 | 39,828 | 24,503 |
| DARKE | 16,946 | 20,047 | 13.1 | 14.0 | 39.3 | 29.1 | 3.8 | 0.7 | 33,923 | 31,907 | 39,297 | 44,005 | 35,583 | 21,557 |
| DEFIANCE | 17,534 | 14,533 | 11.6 | 12.7 | 37.4 | 33.1 | 4.7 | 0.6 | 35,988 | 32,034 | 40,939 | 46,333 | 38,652 | 23,243 |
| DELAWARE | 26,827 | 36,103 | 7.4 | 8.2 | 30.3 | 34.9 | 12.0 | 7.2 | 52,446 | 41,130 | 57,656 | 61,289 | 50,880 | 28,425 |
| ERIE | 19,168 | 30,096 | 14.4 | 14.5 | 34.5 | 30.0 | 4.9 | 1.7 | 36,059 | 29,940 | 41,988 | 47,615 | 39,711 | 23,352 |
| FAIRFIELD | 22,227 | 46,866 | 10.7 | 11.7 | 32.7 | 33.3 | 8.0 | 3.6 | 42,343 | 36,888 | 47,959 | 53,680 | 42,671 | 24,831 |
| FAYETTE | 16,202 | 10,852 | 16.5 | 16.5 | 37.2 | 25.4 | 3.7 | 0.7 | 32,238 | 28,975 | 37,749 | 40,086 | 34,680 | 22,456 |
| FRANKLIN | 20,973 | 414,313 | 14.0 | 13.4 | 34.4 | 30.1 | 6.0 | 2.1 | 37,475 | 31,419 | 42,752 | 47,146 | 40,919 | 25,891 |
| FULTON | 17,966 | 15,324 | 9.4 | 11.2 | 40.9 | 32.8 | 4.7 | 1.0 | 37,129 | 33,829 | 41,519 | 46,112 | 39,764 | 24,939 |
| GALLIA | 14,323 | 12,819 | 25.5 | 16.7 | 35.6 | 18.8 | 2.8 | 0.7 | 28,057 | 24,401 | 34,048 | 35,097 | 29,625 | 18,265 |
| GEAUGA | 27,543 | 31,115 | 6.1 | 6.8 | 29.8 | 37.2 | 12.6 | 7.6 | 54,074 | 41,774 | 55,835 | 64,328 | 60,885 | 31,947 |
| GREENE | 21,207 | 53,056 | 10.6 | 9.4 | 33.1 | 36.1 | 8.3 | 2.5 | 42,212 | 33,618 | 45,722 | 54,435 | 47,120 | 29,628 |
| GUERNSEY | 13,485 | 16,217 | 24.8 | 18.8 | 36.1 | 18.3 | 1.8 | 0.2 | 26,502 | 23,652 | 31,292 | 32,997 | 29,709 | 17,694 |
| HAMILTON | 20,852 | 336,277 | 19.2 | 14.4 | 32.7 | 25.5 | 5.3 | 2.9 | 36,253 | 28,902 | 41,350 | 45,911 | 39,651 | 24,673 |
| HANCOCK | 20,144 | 26,614 | 11.8 | 12.1 | 38.0 | 31.0 | 5.3 | 1.9 | 37,690 | 32,031 | 42,467 | 49,306 | 43,161 | 23,371 |
| HARDIN | 15,428 | 11,780 | 20.8 | 15.5 | 37.9 | 22.4 | 2.7 | 0.7 | 30,061 | 25,809 | 35,613 | 39,934 | 34,137 | 19,768 |
| HARRISON | 12,396 | 6,300 | 26.8 | 19.1 | 37.6 | 15.2 | 1.3 | 0.1 | 24,734 | 24,709 | 26,961 | 31,444 | 26,862 | 17,970 |
| HENRY | 17,864 | 10,917 | 10.1 | 10.7 | 40.5 | 33.0 | 4.9 | 0.7 | 36,762 | 35,085 | 42,164 | 45,803 | 42,179 | 22,713 |
| HIGHLAND | 14,145 | 15,605 | 22.1 | 16.7 | 37.7 | 20.0 | 3.0 | 0.6 | 28,832 | 27,361 | 32,977 | 37,691 | 30,147 | 19,254 |
| HOCKING | 14,492 | 11,052 | 19.7 | 18.8 | 38.3 | 20.2 | 2.3 | 0.7 | 29,158 | 25,346 | 34,034 | 36,961 | 31,949 | 18,468 |
| HOLMES | 13,713 | 11,237 | 13.4 | 16.2 | 38.2 | 26.4 | 4.1 | 1.6 | 34,497 | 29,384 | 37,846 | 42,673 | 39,626 | 23,529 |
| HURON | 15,662 | 22,447 | 13.7 | 15.9 | 40.4 | 26.3 | 3.1 | 0.6 | 32,468 | 29,252 | 36,803 | 40,673 | 35,366 | 20,723 |
| JACKSON | 13,936 | 12,532 | 28.5 | 18.5 | 33.8 | 15.9 | 2.2 | 1.1 | 26,763 | 23,236 | 32,943 | 32,891 | 28,141 | 17,208 |
| JEFFERSON | 14,950 | 29,323 | 25.9 | 17.5 | 35.2 | 18.6 | 2.3 | 0.6 | 27,194 | 24,116 | 32,986 | 35,277 | 30,691 | 17,968 |
| KNOX | 15,692 | 20,474 | 14.9 | 16.1 | 39.2 | 26.6 | 3.1 | 0.2 | 31,776 | 28,691 | 36,295 | 40,114 | 34,544 | 21,607 |
| LAKE | 20,463 | 86,202 | 9.6 | 11.3 | 36.6 | 35.3 | 5.7 | 1.5 | 39,061 | 35,818 | 43,236 | 48,913 | 42,969 | 24,518 |
| LAWRENCE | 12,540 | 24,519 | 30.3 | 18.1 | 31.6 | 17.6 | 2.0 | 0.4 | 25,623 | 21,906 | 30,338 | 33,596 | 28,641 | 16,610 |
| LICKING | 20,959 | 52,624 | 12.1 | 11.7 | 34.5 | 32.6 | 7.1 | 1.9 | 38,994 | 33,476 | 44,915 | 50,470 | 42,102 | 24,759 |
| LOGAN | 18,672 | 18,021 | 13.8 | 11.8 | 36.3 | 31.4 | 5.6 | 1.2 | 36,311 | 34,515 | 44,440 | 46,418 | 36,524 | 22,367 |
| LORAIN | 18,983 | 102,312 | 12.9 | 11.4 | 35.1 | 33.1 | 6.1 | 1.4 | 37,796 | 32,233 | 42,808 | 48,270 | 41,470 | 24,634 |
| LUCAS | 18,525 | 174,296 | 20.1 | 14.4 | 33.5 | 25.5 | 4.6 | 2.0 | 34,076 | 28,115 | 39,197 | 44,780 | 38,118 | 21,771 |
| MADISON | 18,730 | 13,691 | 9.9 | 12.9 | 35.8 | 33.9 | 5.9 | 1.5 | 38,367 | 35,431 | 41,883 | 48,894 | 42,850 | 24,290 |
| MAHONING | 15,904 | 98,730 | 22.7 | 17.4 | 34.9 | 20.9 | 3.1 | 1.0 | 29,713 | 25,368 | 35,230 | 39,087 | 32,421 | 20,026 |
| MARION | 16,561 | 23,904 | 16.0 | 14.4 | 38.7 | 26.1 | 3.6 | 1.3 | 33,245 | 29,597 | 38,361 | 42,964 | 34,216 | 22,406 |
| MEDINA | 23,495 | 52,243 | 7.4 | 6.4 | 30.0 | 42.3 | 10.7 | 3.2 | 46,829 | 40,698 | 51,239 | 56,911 | 50,641 | 28,440 |
| MEIGS | 11,533 | 9,255 | 31.1 | 20.3 | 32.5 | 14.4 | 1.5 | 0.2 | 23,916 | 20,790 | 28,842 | 29,153 | 26,262 | 16,430 |
| MERCER | 15,485 | 14,439 | 13.7 | 14.6 | 42.7 | 25.4 | 2.7 | 1.0 | 32,810 | 30,976 | 38,820 | 40,505 | 34,898 | 21,816 |
| MIAMI | 21,561 | 37,473 | 10.3 | 11.9 | 35.3 | 33.3 | 7.0 | 2.3 | 40,105 | 34,141 | 47,080 | 52,088 | 43,219 | 24,725 |
| MONROE | 12,080 | 5,868 | 27.5 | 17.7 | 37.8 | 15.5 | 1.4 | 0.1 | 25,262 | 22,618 | 27,941 | 35,168 | 28,021 | 16,364 |
| MONTGOMERY | 19,488 | 223,226 | 16.2 | 13.7 | 34.9 | 28.6 | 5.0 | 1.7 | 35,534 | 30,518 | 40,137 | 45,681 | 38,751 | 24,054 |
| MORGAN | 11,793 | 5,389 | 27.4 | 17.4 | 38.5 | 15.5 | 1.1 | 0.1 | 24,887 | 22,373 | 29,373 | 31,975 | 26,141 | 16,849 |
| MORROW | 15,143 | 11,484 | 11.6 | 14.3 | 43.1 | 27.5 | 3.3 | 0.2 | 33,184 | 29,633 | 37,554 | 42,150 | 33,021 | 21,610 |
| MUSKINGUM | 15,186 | 32,449 | 20.6 | 15.5 | 38.1 | 22.1 | 2.9 | 0.8 | 30,146 | 27,193 | 35,319 | 38,540 | 31,779 | 20,259 |
| NOBLE | 11,252 | 4,662 | 20.8 | 18.4 | 42.5 | 17.2 | 1.1 | 0.0 | 26,661 | 25,232 | 31,510 | 32,831 | 29,812 | 17,275 |
| OTTAWA | 19,955 | 16,044 | 12.6 | 12.4 | 37.0 | 31.4 | 5.2 | 1.5 | 36,912 | 33,593 | 43,516 | 47,436 | 40,008 | 23,879 |
| PAULDING | 15,033 | 7,231 | 14.3 | 13.8 | 41.6 | 27.5 | 2.7 | 0.2 | 32,014 | 28,731 | 37,979 | 40,831 | 32,316 | 21,136 |
| PERRY | 12,751 | 12,659 | 22.7 | 19.3 | 37.2 | 18.7 | 2.0 | 0.1 | 26,988 | 24,653 | 31,269 | 34,393 | 28,349 | 16,903 |
| PICKAWAY | 17,026 | 18,006 | 13.3 | 13.6 | 37.8 | 30.1 | 4.4 | 0.8 | 34,857 | 30,541 | 40,820 | 43,776 | 36,016 | 23,539 |
| PIKE | 13,813 | 10,590 | 25.8 | 14.3 | 34.2 | 23.0 | 2.5 | 0.1 | 28,485 | 25,497 | 35,161 | 34,091 | 29,391 | 20,270 |
| PORTAGE | 18,987 | 55,025 | 12.7 | 12.0 | 35.6 | 31.3 | 6.7 | 1.7 | 37,986 | 30,134 | 41,445 | 49,134 | 44,897 | 27,059 |
| PREBLE | 16,334 | 15,978 | 12.2 | 14.4 | 39.7 | 29.4 | 3.7 | 0.5 | 34,020 | 31,277 | 39,306 | 43,168 | 36,654 | 21,846 |
| PUTNAM | 17,770 | 11,886 | 10.2 | 9.2 | 41.8 | 33.3 | 4.7 | 0.8 | 37,269 | 33,955 | 43,727 | 45,510 | 42,856 | 23,410 |
| RICHLAND | 16,047 | 48,465 | 17.5 | 16.4 | 37.5 | 24.6 | 3.0 | 1.1 | 31,875 | 27,930 | 36,858 | 41,541 | 35,349 | 19,803 |
| ROSS | 15,764 | 27,335 | 20.5 | 14.9 | 35.2 | 24.3 | 4.1 | 1.1 | 31,904 | 27,395 | 37,788 | 38,811 | 35,567 | 21,525 |
| SANDUSKY | 16,627 | 22,992 | 14.8 | 13.3 | 40.4 | 27.3 | 3.5 | 0.8 | 33,218 | 29,942 | 38,448 | 42,354 | 36,872 | 21,083 |
| SCIOTO | 14,130 | 30,775 | 29.2 | 18.3 | 32.2 | 16.1 | 2.9 | 1.2 | 27,078 | 22,649 | 32,374 | 34,832 | 29,280 | 18,981 |
| SENECA | 15,025 | 21,798 | 17.3 | 15.7 | 40.3 | 23.3 | 2.7 | 0.7 | 30,979 | 27,554 | 36,111 | 40,508 | 32,017 | 20,900 |
| SHELBY | 19,571 | 17,012 | 9.8 | 11.8 | 37.8 | 33.1 | 5.8 | 1.7 | 38,858 | 34,694 | 43,531 | 48,188 | 44,333 | 25,093 |
| STARK | 19,351 | 144,586 | 14.5 | 13.3 | 37.4 | 28.2 | 5.0 | 1.6 | 35,615 | 31,116 | 40,288 | 45,173 | 39,226 | 23,906 |
| SUMMIT | 22,200 | 215,013 | 14.8 | 12.9 | 33.2 | 29.6 | 6.9 | 2.7 | 38,617 | 32,489 | 43,462 | 50,148 | 43,370 | 24,842 |
| OHIO | 19,315 | | 16.1 | 13.6 | 34.9 | 28.0 | 5.4 | 2.0 | 35,978 | 30,645 | 41,145 | 45,889 | 39,280 | 23,523 |
| UNITED STATES | 22,162 | | 14.5 | 12.5 | 32.3 | 29.8 | 7.4 | 3.5 | 40,748 | 34,503 | 44,969 | 49,579 | 43,409 | 27,339 |

# SPENDING POTENTIAL INDEXES

| COUNTY | FINANCIAL SERVICES | | | | THE HOME | | | | | | ENTERTAINMENT | | | | | | PERSONAL | | | |
|---|---|---|---|---|---|---|---|---|---|---|---|---|---|---|---|---|---|---|---|---|
| | | | | | Home Improvements | | | Furnishings | | | | | | | | | | | | |
| | Auto Loan | Home Loan | Invest-ments | Retire-ment Plans | Home Repair | Lawn & Garden | Remodel-ing | Appli-ances | Elec-tronics | Furni-ture | Restau-rants | Sport-ing Goods | Theater & Concerts | Toys & Hobbies | Travel | Video Rental | Apparel | Auto After-market | Health Insur-ance | Pets & Supplies |
| ADAMS | 97 | 63 | 66 | 74 | 91 | 89 | 110 | 95 | 91 | 75 | 77 | 94 | 80 | 93 | 74 | 98 | 76 | 88 | 103 | 95 |
| ALLEN | 96 | 90 | 95 | 91 | 100 | 96 | 101 | 97 | 94 | 93 | 94 | 95 | 96 | 98 | 93 | 100 | 91 | 96 | 100 | 98 |
| ASHLAND | 98 | 81 | 87 | 87 | 97 | 94 | 110 | 98 | 95 | 88 | 91 | 96 | 92 | 99 | 86 | 101 | 88 | 95 | 102 | 100 |
| ASHTABULA | 95 | 80 | 86 | 83 | 99 | 94 | 104 | 96 | 90 | 88 | 88 | 93 | 91 | 95 | 88 | 99 | 85 | 92 | 101 | 96 |
| ATHENS | 95 | 85 | 91 | 88 | 96 | 93 | 104 | 93 | 92 | 85 | 88 | 91 | 89 | 94 | 87 | 97 | 86 | 93 | 99 | 96 |
| AUGLAIZE | 98 | 81 | 84 | 86 | 96 | 93 | 110 | 98 | 94 | 87 | 90 | 96 | 91 | 99 | 85 | 101 | 87 | 94 | 102 | 100 |
| BELMONT | 94 | 77 | 86 | 81 | 100 | 94 | 101 | 95 | 89 | 86 | 86 | 91 | 90 | 94 | 88 | 98 | 83 | 91 | 101 | 94 |
| BROWN | 99 | 74 | 80 | 83 | 94 | 92 | 113 | 97 | 94 | 83 | 86 | 96 | 88 | 98 | 80 | 101 | 84 | 92 | 103 | 99 |
| BUTLER | 100 | 102 | 98 | 102 | 101 | 101 | 101 | 100 | 100 | 101 | 104 | 101 | 104 | 102 | 99 | 102 | 100 | 103 | 100 | 101 |
| CARROLL | 98 | 73 | 78 | 82 | 94 | 91 | 113 | 97 | 93 | 82 | 85 | 96 | 87 | 97 | 80 | 100 | 83 | 91 | 103 | 99 |
| CHAMPAIGN | 99 | 85 | 89 | 90 | 98 | 95 | 110 | 98 | 95 | 90 | 94 | 98 | 95 | 101 | 88 | 102 | 91 | 96 | 102 | 101 |
| CLARK | 96 | 89 | 96 | 90 | 101 | 97 | 99 | 97 | 93 | 94 | 94 | 94 | 97 | 97 | 94 | 100 | 91 | 96 | 100 | 97 |
| CLERMONT | 100 | 97 | 93 | 96 | 98 | 97 | 105 | 99 | 100 | 98 | 102 | 100 | 100 | 102 | 93 | 103 | 98 | 101 | 100 | 102 |
| CLINTON | 97 | 79 | 84 | 84 | 96 | 92 | 109 | 97 | 93 | 86 | 89 | 95 | 90 | 98 | 84 | 100 | 86 | 93 | 101 | 98 |
| COLUMBIANA | 96 | 78 | 84 | 82 | 98 | 93 | 106 | 96 | 91 | 86 | 87 | 93 | 90 | 96 | 86 | 99 | 84 | 92 | 101 | 97 |
| COSHOCTON | 97 | 78 | 87 | 85 | 99 | 95 | 106 | 97 | 92 | 87 | 88 | 95 | 91 | 96 | 87 | 99 | 85 | 92 | 102 | 97 |
| CRAWFORD | 97 | 80 | 87 | 85 | 98 | 94 | 106 | 97 | 92 | 88 | 89 | 94 | 92 | 97 | 87 | 100 | 86 | 93 | 101 | 97 |
| CUYAHOGA | 97 | 100 | 109 | 101 | 106 | 104 | 95 | 99 | 96 | 101 | 99 | 97 | 104 | 98 | 105 | 101 | 98 | 101 | 98 | 98 |
| DARKE | 98 | 79 | 84 | 86 | 96 | 93 | 111 | 97 | 94 | 86 | 89 | 96 | 91 | 99 | 84 | 101 | 87 | 94 | 102 | 100 |
| DEFIANCE | 98 | 82 | 84 | 85 | 96 | 92 | 109 | 97 | 94 | 88 | 91 | 96 | 92 | 99 | 85 | 101 | 88 | 94 | 101 | 99 |
| DELAWARE | 105 | 110 | 104 | 112 | 103 | 106 | 109 | 104 | 107 | 108 | 113 | 108 | 112 | 108 | 104 | 105 | 110 | 110 | 103 | 106 |
| ERIE | 98 | 91 | 98 | 93 | 102 | 98 | 103 | 98 | 94 | 95 | 96 | 96 | 98 | 99 | 95 | 101 | 93 | 97 | 101 | 99 |
| FAIRFIELD | 101 | 101 | 100 | 104 | 102 | 102 | 105 | 101 | 101 | 102 | 104 | 102 | 105 | 103 | 99 | 103 | 101 | 103 | 102 | 102 |
| FAYETTE | 96 | 76 | 81 | 82 | 96 | 92 | 109 | 96 | 92 | 85 | 86 | 93 | 88 | 96 | 83 | 99 | 84 | 91 | 101 | 97 |
| FRANKLIN | 98 | 103 | 98 | 100 | 101 | 100 | 95 | 98 | 98 | 101 | 102 | 99 | 102 | 99 | 100 | 101 | 99 | 102 | 97 | 100 |
| FULTON | 100 | 82 | 85 | 87 | 96 | 93 | 112 | 98 | 95 | 88 | 92 | 97 | 92 | 101 | 84 | 102 | 89 | 95 | 102 | 101 |
| GALLIA | 97 | 72 | 77 | 80 | 93 | 91 | 110 | 96 | 93 | 80 | 83 | 94 | 85 | 95 | 79 | 100 | 81 | 91 | 102 | 97 |
| GEAUGA | 105 | 108 | 112 | 115 | 107 | 110 | 108 | 104 | 107 | 110 | 114 | 108 | 114 | 109 | 108 | 105 | 112 | 110 | 105 | 106 |
| GREENE | 100 | 103 | 104 | 104 | 104 | 103 | 101 | 100 | 101 | 103 | 106 | 101 | 106 | 103 | 102 | 102 | 103 | 104 | 101 | 102 |
| GUERNSEY | 96 | 75 | 80 | 80 | 95 | 91 | 106 | 95 | 91 | 83 | 85 | 92 | 87 | 95 | 82 | 99 | 82 | 91 | 101 | 96 |
| HAMILTON | 97 | 101 | 105 | 101 | 104 | 102 | 97 | 98 | 97 | 101 | 100 | 98 | 103 | 99 | 102 | 101 | 98 | 101 | 98 | 99 |
| HANCOCK | 99 | 91 | 96 | 93 | 99 | 97 | 105 | 98 | 96 | 93 | 97 | 97 | 97 | 100 | 92 | 101 | 93 | 98 | 101 | 100 |
| HARDIN | 97 | 75 | 80 | 82 | 94 | 91 | 110 | 95 | 92 | 81 | 85 | 94 | 86 | 96 | 81 | 99 | 83 | 91 | 102 | 98 |
| HARRISON | 95 | 67 | 73 | 75 | 93 | 90 | 106 | 94 | 91 | 77 | 80 | 90 | 82 | 92 | 78 | 99 | 78 | 88 | 103 | 94 |
| HENRY | 99 | 81 | 86 | 87 | 96 | 93 | 112 | 98 | 95 | 87 | 91 | 97 | 92 | 100 | 85 | 101 | 89 | 95 | 102 | 101 |
| HIGHLAND | 97 | 72 | 79 | 80 | 95 | 92 | 109 | 96 | 92 | 81 | 83 | 94 | 86 | 95 | 81 | 99 | 81 | 90 | 102 | 97 |
| HOCKING | 98 | 72 | 76 | 80 | 94 | 91 | 111 | 97 | 92 | 82 | 84 | 95 | 86 | 96 | 80 | 100 | 82 | 91 | 102 | 98 |
| HOLMES | 99 | 72 | 76 | 83 | 92 | 90 | 114 | 97 | 93 | 80 | 84 | 98 | 86 | 99 | 78 | 101 | 83 | 92 | 104 | 100 |
| HURON | 98 | 80 | 84 | 85 | 96 | 92 | 110 | 97 | 93 | 87 | 89 | 95 | 90 | 98 | 84 | 100 | 86 | 93 | 101 | 99 |
| JACKSON | 95 | 68 | 71 | 75 | 94 | 90 | 107 | 95 | 90 | 79 | 80 | 93 | 83 | 93 | 78 | 98 | 78 | 89 | 101 | 95 |
| JEFFERSON | 95 | 81 | 92 | 85 | 101 | 96 | 100 | 96 | 90 | 90 | 89 | 92 | 93 | 95 | 91 | 99 | 86 | 92 | 100 | 95 |
| KNOX | 98 | 82 | 90 | 88 | 98 | 95 | 108 | 98 | 93 | 88 | 91 | 95 | 93 | 98 | 88 | 101 | 88 | 94 | 103 | 99 |
| LAKE | 99 | 100 | 103 | 99 | 103 | 102 | 99 | 99 | 98 | 102 | 105 | 99 | 105 | 102 | 100 | 102 | 100 | 102 | 101 | 100 |
| LAWRENCE | 96 | 74 | 79 | 80 | 96 | 92 | 106 | 96 | 91 | 83 | 84 | 93 | 87 | 94 | 83 | 99 | 81 | 90 | 101 | 96 |
| LICKING | 99 | 94 | 99 | 96 | 101 | 99 | 104 | 99 | 97 | 97 | 99 | 98 | 100 | 101 | 96 | 101 | 95 | 99 | 101 | 100 |
| LOGAN | 98 | 78 | 83 | 85 | 95 | 92 | 113 | 97 | 93 | 85 | 88 | 95 | 89 | 98 | 83 | 101 | 85 | 93 | 102 | 99 |
| LORAIN | 97 | 95 | 98 | 94 | 102 | 99 | 99 | 98 | 96 | 98 | 99 | 96 | 100 | 99 | 97 | 101 | 95 | 99 | 100 | 98 |
| LUCAS | 96 | 96 | 100 | 96 | 102 | 99 | 97 | 97 | 95 | 97 | 97 | 96 | 100 | 97 | 98 | 100 | 95 | 98 | 98 | 98 |
| MADISON | 97 | 85 | 88 | 87 | 97 | 93 | 107 | 97 | 94 | 90 | 93 | 95 | 93 | 98 | 88 | 101 | 89 | 95 | 100 | 98 |
| MAHONING | 95 | 89 | 100 | 91 | 103 | 98 | 97 | 97 | 92 | 95 | 93 | 94 | 98 | 96 | 96 | 100 | 91 | 96 | 99 | 96 |
| MARION | 97 | 86 | 91 | 89 | 100 | 96 | 104 | 97 | 93 | 91 | 92 | 95 | 94 | 97 | 91 | 100 | 89 | 95 | 101 | 98 |
| MEDINA | 102 | 102 | 98 | 102 | 101 | 101 | 104 | 101 | 103 | 104 | 108 | 103 | 106 | 105 | 99 | 104 | 104 | 106 | 101 | 103 |
| MEIGS | 95 | 68 | 71 | 75 | 93 | 90 | 107 | 95 | 91 | 78 | 80 | 92 | 83 | 93 | 78 | 98 | 78 | 89 | 102 | 95 |
| MERCER | 100 | 81 | 85 | 88 | 96 | 93 | 114 | 98 | 95 | 88 | 91 | 97 | 92 | 100 | 85 | 102 | 89 | 95 | 102 | 101 |
| MIAMI | 99 | 92 | 95 | 95 | 101 | 98 | 104 | 99 | 96 | 96 | 98 | 98 | 99 | 100 | 94 | 101 | 94 | 98 | 101 | 100 |
| MONROE | 96 | 66 | 70 | 75 | 93 | 90 | 108 | 95 | 91 | 78 | 79 | 94 | 83 | 93 | 77 | 98 | 78 | 88 | 102 | 95 |
| MONTGOMERY | 97 | 98 | 100 | 97 | 102 | 100 | 96 | 98 | 96 | 99 | 99 | 97 | 101 | 98 | 99 | 101 | 96 | 100 | 98 | 98 |
| MORGAN | 97 | 67 | 73 | 77 | 92 | 90 | 110 | 96 | 92 | 77 | 80 | 94 | 83 | 94 | 76 | 99 | 78 | 89 | 103 | 96 |
| MORROW | 100 | 77 | 80 | 85 | 94 | 91 | 115 | 98 | 95 | 84 | 88 | 97 | 89 | 100 | 81 | 102 | 86 | 93 | 103 | 101 |
| MUSKINGUM | 97 | 82 | 88 | 86 | 99 | 95 | 105 | 97 | 92 | 89 | 89 | 94 | 92 | 96 | 88 | 100 | 86 | 93 | 101 | 97 |
| NOBLE | 97 | 66 | 69 | 77 | 91 | 90 | 112 | 96 | 92 | 76 | 79 | 95 | 82 | 95 | 75 | 99 | 78 | 89 | 103 | 97 |
| OTTAWA | 100 | 83 | 91 | 92 | 99 | 97 | 113 | 99 | 94 | 89 | 92 | 98 | 94 | 101 | 89 | 101 | 90 | 96 | 104 | 101 |
| PAULDING | 99 | 74 | 78 | 82 | 95 | 91 | 113 | 97 | 93 | 83 | 86 | 97 | 88 | 98 | 80 | 101 | 84 | 92 | 102 | 99 |
| PERRY | 98 | 70 | 75 | 80 | 93 | 90 | 113 | 97 | 93 | 80 | 83 | 96 | 85 | 97 | 77 | 100 | 81 | 91 | 103 | 98 |
| PICKAWAY | 98 | 82 | 87 | 86 | 96 | 93 | 109 | 97 | 93 | 88 | 91 | 95 | 92 | 98 | 86 | 100 | 88 | 94 | 101 | 99 |
| PIKE | 96 | 71 | 78 | 78 | 94 | 92 | 107 | 96 | 91 | 81 | 83 | 94 | 86 | 95 | 80 | 98 | 80 | 90 | 102 | 96 |
| PORTAGE | 98 | 91 | 93 | 93 | 98 | 95 | 105 | 97 | 95 | 92 | 96 | 96 | 96 | 99 | 91 | 100 | 92 | 97 | 100 | 100 |
| PREBLE | 99 | 78 | 82 | 85 | 95 | 92 | 114 | 98 | 94 | 85 | 89 | 97 | 90 | 100 | 82 | 101 | 87 | 94 | 102 | 100 |
| PUTNAM | 100 | 80 | 84 | 87 | 96 | 92 | 115 | 99 | 95 | 87 | 91 | 98 | 91 | 101 | 83 | 102 | 88 | 95 | 103 | 102 |
| RICHLAND | 97 | 86 | 93 | 89 | 100 | 96 | 104 | 97 | 93 | 91 | 92 | 95 | 95 | 98 | 91 | 100 | 89 | 95 | 101 | 98 |
| ROSS | 97 | 80 | 89 | 86 | 98 | 95 | 106 | 97 | 93 | 87 | 89 | 95 | 92 | 97 | 87 | 100 | 86 | 93 | 102 | 97 |
| SANDUSKY | 97 | 82 | 86 | 85 | 97 | 93 | 106 | 97 | 92 | 88 | 91 | 94 | 92 | 98 | 87 | 100 | 87 | 93 | 101 | 98 |
| SCIOTO | 95 | 75 | 84 | 81 | 97 | 93 | 103 | 95 | 91 | 84 | 84 | 91 | 88 | 93 | 85 | 99 | 82 | 91 | 101 | 95 |
| SENECA | 97 | 82 | 88 | 86 | 99 | 94 | 107 | 97 | 93 | 88 | 90 | 95 | 92 | 98 | 88 | 100 | 87 | 94 | 102 | 98 |
| SHELBY | 100 | 86 | 90 | 92 | 97 | 95 | 112 | 99 | 97 | 91 | 94 | 99 | 95 | 101 | 88 | 102 | 91 | 97 | 102 | 101 |
| STARK | 97 | 92 | 98 | 93 | 102 | 99 | 100 | 98 | 94 | 96 | 96 | 96 | 99 | 98 | 96 | 100 | 93 | 97 | 100 | 98 |
| SUMMIT | 98 | 100 | 105 | 100 | 105 | 103 | 97 | 99 | 96 | 101 | 101 | 98 | 104 | 100 | 102 | 101 | 98 | 101 | 100 | 99 |
| OHIO | 98 | 94 | 98 | 96 | 101 | 99 | 101 | 98 | 96 | 96 | 97 | 97 | 100 | 99 | 96 | 101 | 95 | 99 | 100 | 99 |
| UNITED STATES | 100 | 100 | 100 | 100 | 100 | 100 | 100 | 100 | 100 | 100 | 100 | 100 | 100 | 100 | 100 | 100 | 100 | 100 | 100 | 100 |

# POPULATION CHANGE

| COUNTY | FIPS Code | MSA Code | DMA Code | POPULATION 1990 | POPULATION 2000 | POPULATION 2005 | 1990-2000 ANNUAL CHANGE % Rate | 1990-2000 ANNUAL CHANGE State Rank | RACE (%) White 1990 | White 2000 | Black 1990 | Black 2000 | Asian/Pacific 1990 | Asian/Pacific 2000 |
|---|---|---|---|---|---|---|---|---|---|---|---|---|---|---|
| TRUMBULL | 155 | 9320 | 536 | 227,813 | 224,421 | 219,891 | -0.1 | 76 | 92.6 | 91.5 | 6.7 | 7.6 | 0.4 | 0.6 |
| TUSCARAWAS | 157 | 0000 | 510 | 84,090 | 89,186 | 90,834 | 0.6 | 40 | 98.8 | 98.6 | 0.7 | 0.9 | 0.2 | 0.3 |
| UNION | 159 | 0000 | 535 | 31,969 | 41,745 | 46,543 | 2.6 | 4 | 95.6 | 95.7 | 3.7 | 3.4 | 0.4 | 0.6 |
| VAN WERT | 161 | 0000 | 509 | 30,464 | 30,033 | 29,737 | -0.1 | 76 | 98.1 | 97.7 | 0.6 | 0.7 | 0.3 | 0.4 |
| VINTON | 163 | 0000 | 564 | 11,098 | 12,482 | 13,151 | 1.2 | 18 | 99.8 | 99.8 | 0.0 | 0.0 | 0.0 | 0.0 |
| WARREN | 165 | 1640 | 515 | 113,909 | 159,689 | 191,271 | 3.4 | 2 | 97.0 | 96.6 | 2.1 | 2.2 | 0.6 | 0.8 |
| WASHINGTON | 167 | 6020 | 597 | 62,254 | 62,808 | 61,724 | 0.1 | 66 | 98.2 | 97.8 | 1.2 | 1.5 | 0.3 | 0.5 |
| WAYNE | 169 | 0000 | 510 | 101,461 | 111,895 | 116,170 | 1.0 | 24 | 97.7 | 97.3 | 1.5 | 1.7 | 0.5 | 0.7 |
| WILLIAMS | 171 | 0000 | 547 | 36,956 | 38,347 | 38,096 | 0.4 | 46 | 98.4 | 98.0 | 0.1 | 0.1 | 0.3 | 0.5 |
| WOOD | 173 | 8400 | 547 | 113,269 | 121,154 | 125,273 | 0.7 | 34 | 96.5 | 95.7 | 1.0 | 1.1 | 0.9 | 1.2 |
| WYANDOT | 175 | 0000 | 547 | 22,254 | 22,998 | 23,431 | 0.3 | 56 | 99.2 | 99.1 | 0.1 | 0.1 | 0.3 | 0.4 |
| OHIO | | | | | | | 0.4 | | 87.8 | 86.6 | 10.7 | 11.4 | 0.8 | 1.2 |
| UNITED STATES | | | | | | | 1.0 | | 80.3 | 77.9 | 12.1 | 12.4 | 2.9 | 3.9 |

# POPULATION COMPOSITION

| COUNTY | % HISPANIC ORIGIN 1990 | % HISPANIC ORIGIN 2000 | 2000 AGE DISTRIBUTION (%) 0-4 | 5-9 | 10-14 | 15-19 | 20-24 | 25-44 | 45-64 | 65-84 | 85+ | 18+ | MEDIAN AGE 1990 | MEDIAN AGE 2000 | 2000 Males/ Females (×100) |
|---|---|---|---|---|---|---|---|---|---|---|---|---|---|---|---|
| TRUMBULL | 0.6 | 1.2 | 5.9 | 6.3 | 7.0 | 6.9 | 5.7 | 28.4 | 24.4 | 13.9 | 1.5 | 76.6 | 35.6 | 38.8 | 92.6 |
| TUSCARAWAS | 0.3 | 0.7 | 6.4 | 6.9 | 7.3 | 7.2 | 5.7 | 27.8 | 23.8 | 13.0 | 1.9 | 74.9 | 35.0 | 38.0 | 92.7 |
| UNION | 0.5 | 1.0 | 6.5 | 6.9 | 7.3 | 7.8 | 7.0 | 31.5 | 22.1 | 9.6 | 1.3 | 74.5 | 32.9 | 35.0 | 93.4 |
| VAN WERT | 1.6 | 2.5 | 6.8 | 7.2 | 7.6 | 7.5 | 5.9 | 28.0 | 22.7 | 12.3 | 2.0 | 73.6 | 34.0 | 36.8 | 95.0 |
| VINTON | 0.3 | 0.8 | 6.3 | 6.8 | 8.0 | 7.8 | 5.9 | 28.6 | 23.7 | 11.4 | 1.5 | 73.9 | 33.6 | 36.5 | 97.9 |
| WARREN | 0.5 | 1.0 | 6.6 | 7.2 | 7.6 | 6.9 | 5.5 | 32.9 | 23.2 | 9.0 | 1.1 | 74.4 | 32.7 | 35.9 | 100.9 |
| WASHINGTON | 0.4 | 0.8 | 5.9 | 6.4 | 6.8 | 7.4 | 6.4 | 27.9 | 24.6 | 12.8 | 1.8 | 76.5 | 34.6 | 38.2 | 93.4 |
| WAYNE | 0.4 | 0.9 | 7.1 | 7.5 | 7.9 | 8.0 | 6.3 | 28.5 | 22.6 | 10.5 | 1.5 | 72.9 | 32.2 | 35.2 | 97.0 |
| WILLIAMS | 2.2 | 3.2 | 6.9 | 7.4 | 7.6 | 7.5 | 6.0 | 29.4 | 22.4 | 11.0 | 1.8 | 73.3 | 33.2 | 36.0 | 99.4 |
| WOOD | 2.5 | 3.7 | 5.7 | 6.4 | 6.8 | 9.7 | 11.7 | 28.5 | 20.3 | 9.5 | 1.3 | 77.1 | 29.3 | 32.5 | 92.3 |
| WYANDOT | 0.7 | 1.3 | 6.9 | 7.2 | 7.4 | 7.5 | 5.7 | 27.9 | 22.4 | 12.7 | 2.2 | 73.8 | 34.1 | 36.9 | 92.3 |
| OHIO | 1.3 | 2.0 | 6.5 | 6.9 | 7.3 | 7.4 | 6.7 | 29.5 | 22.6 | 11.8 | 1.6 | 75.2 | 33.3 | 36.3 | 93.6 |
| UNITED STATES | 9.0 | 11.8 | 6.9 | 7.2 | 7.2 | 7.2 | 6.7 | 29.9 | 22.2 | 11.1 | 1.6 | 74.6 | 32.9 | 35.7 | 95.6 |

| COUNTY | HOUSEHOLDS | | | | | FAMILIES | | | MEDIAN HOUSEHOLD INCOME | | | |
|---|---|---|---|---|---|---|---|---|---|---|---|---|
| | 1990 | 2000 | 2005 | % Annual Rate 1990-2000 | 2000 Average HH Size | 1990 | 2000 | % Annual Rate 1990-2000 | 2000 | 2005 | 2000 National Rank | 2000 State Rank |
| TRUMBULL | 86,056 | 86,724 | 86,213 | 0.1 | 2.54 | 63,512 | 61,796 | -0.3 | 36,757 | 40,329 | 1013 | 45 |
| TUSCARAWAS | 31,971 | 34,704 | 35,801 | 1.0 | 2.54 | 23,634 | 24,709 | 0.5 | 34,535 | 40,786 | 1314 | 60 |
| UNION | 11,037 | 14,730 | 16,689 | 3.6 | 2.67 | 8,578 | 11,096 | 3.2 | 44,239 | 51,610 | 383 | 10 |
| VAN WERT | 11,266 | 11,290 | 11,270 | 0.0 | 2.62 | 8,565 | 8,313 | -0.4 | 37,850 | 44,634 | 862 | 39 |
| VINTON | 4,069 | 4,617 | 4,886 | 1.5 | 2.68 | 3,117 | 3,414 | 1.1 | 27,031 | 32,401 | 2573 | 82 |
| WARREN | 39,150 | 55,466 | 66,900 | 4.3 | 2.79 | 31,663 | 43,565 | 3.9 | 55,143 | 64,638 | 125 | 2 |
| WASHINGTON | 23,636 | 24,654 | 24,619 | 0.5 | 2.48 | 17,421 | 17,565 | 0.1 | 34,009 | 37,853 | 1390 | 62 |
| WAYNE | 35,619 | 40,214 | 42,191 | 1.5 | 2.71 | 26,949 | 29,547 | 1.1 | 38,897 | 46,245 | 760 | 35 |
| WILLIAMS | 13,807 | 14,527 | 14,647 | 0.6 | 2.57 | 10,320 | 10,516 | 0.2 | 39,003 | 45,230 | 752 | 33 |
| WOOD | 39,677 | 44,004 | 46,098 | 1.3 | 2.59 | 27,486 | 29,495 | 0.9 | 42,742 | 48,661 | 468 | 17 |
| WYANDOT | 8,168 | 8,608 | 8,853 | 0.6 | 2.62 | 6,130 | 6,230 | 0.2 | 37,841 | 47,366 | 865 | 40 |
| OHIO | | | | 0.7 | 2.54 | | | 0.4 | 38,607 | 43,591 | | |
| UNITED STATES | | | | 1.4 | 2.59 | | | 1.1 | 41,914 | 49,127 | | |

# INCOME

| COUNTY | 2000 Per Capita Income | 2000 HH Income Base | 2000 HOUSEHOLD INCOME DISTRIBUTION (%) Less than $15,000 | $15,000 to $24,999 | $25,000 to $49,999 | $50,000 to $99,999 | $100,000 to $149,999 | $150,000 or More | 2000 AVERAGE DISPOSABLE INCOME BY AGE OF HOUSEHOLDER All Ages | <35 | 35-44 | 45-54 | 55-64 | 65+ |
|---|---|---|---|---|---|---|---|---|---|---|---|---|---|---|
| TRUMBULL | 17,957 | 86,718 | 16.5 | 14.8 | 36.4 | 27.0 | 4.0 | 1.2 | 33,574 | 27,834 | 38,235 | 44,697 | 37,056 | 22,159 |
| TUSCARAWAS | 15,829 | 34,704 | 16.8 | 16.2 | 40.4 | 23.4 | 2.5 | 0.7 | 30,919 | 27,863 | 36,572 | 39,936 | 32,738 | 19,794 |
| UNION | 20,371 | 14,730 | 12.0 | 10.2 | 35.6 | 33.5 | 7.0 | 1.8 | 39,226 | 35,850 | 45,187 | 49,544 | 40,193 | 24,294 |
| VAN WERT | 16,404 | 11,290 | 10.9 | 14.6 | 44.1 | 26.6 | 3.4 | 0.5 | 33,318 | 29,848 | 37,798 | 42,829 | 35,964 | 22,758 |
| VINTON | 12,507 | 4,617 | 26.5 | 19.2 | 34.8 | 17.1 | 1.8 | 0.7 | 26,450 | 23,661 | 30,400 | 30,935 | 29,615 | 18,902 |
| WARREN | 24,939 | 55,464 | 6.5 | 7.7 | 29.3 | 40.0 | 12.1 | 4.4 | 48,851 | 43,704 | 53,699 | 58,137 | 49,940 | 29,450 |
| WASHINGTON | 16,233 | 24,654 | 19.6 | 16.3 | 36.8 | 23.2 | 3.4 | 0.8 | 30,925 | 27,948 | 35,708 | 40,128 | 33,982 | 19,553 |
| WAYNE | 17,241 | 40,214 | 12.2 | 13.7 | 39.6 | 29.0 | 4.4 | 1.1 | 35,131 | 29,495 | 38,635 | 43,370 | 40,473 | 25,130 |
| WILLIAMS | 17,870 | 14,527 | 11.9 | 13.0 | 42.5 | 27.5 | 4.0 | 1.0 | 34,670 | 31,404 | 40,524 | 42,180 | 38,684 | 22,059 |
| WOOD | 21,970 | 44,004 | 12.3 | 12.0 | 34.5 | 29.6 | 7.8 | 3.9 | 41,577 | 31,403 | 48,398 | 54,316 | 46,380 | 26,952 |
| WYANDOT | 16,452 | 8,608 | 12.8 | 13.6 | 42.6 | 27.1 | 3.5 | 0.5 | 33,286 | 30,824 | 39,802 | 40,142 | 36,573 | 22,658 |
| OHIO | 19,315 | | 16.1 | 13.6 | 34.9 | 28.0 | 5.4 | 2.0 | 35,978 | 30,645 | 41,145 | 45,889 | 39,280 | 23,523 |
| UNITED STATES | 22,162 | | 14.5 | 12.5 | 32.3 | 29.8 | 7.4 | 3.5 | 40,748 | 34,503 | 44,969 | 49,579 | 43,409 | 27,339 |

| COUNTY | FINANCIAL SERVICES | | | | THE HOME | | | | | | ENTERTAINMENT | | | | | | PERSONAL | | | |
|---|---|---|---|---|---|---|---|---|---|---|---|---|---|---|---|---|---|---|---|---|
| | | | | | Home Improvements | | | Furnishings | | | | | | | | | | | | |
| | Auto Loan | Home Loan | Invest-ments | Retire-ment Plans | Home Repair | Lawn & Garden | Remodel-ing | Appli-ances | Elec-tronics | Furni-ture | Restau-rants | Sport-ing Goods | Theater & Concerts | Toys & Hobbies | Travel | Video Rental | Apparel | Auto After-market | Health Insur-ance | Pets & Supplies |
| TRUMBULL | 96 | 87 | 94 | 89 | 102 | 97 | 101 | 97 | 92 | 93 | 93 | 94 | 96 | 97 | 93 | 100 | 90 | 95 | 101 | 97 |
| TUSCARAWAS | 97 | 81 | 87 | 86 | 98 | 94 | 106 | 97 | 93 | 88 | 90 | 95 | 92 | 98 | 87 | 100 | 87 | 93 | 102 | 98 |
| UNION | 99 | 86 | 89 | 90 | 96 | 94 | 111 | 98 | 97 | 91 | 95 | 98 | 95 | 101 | 87 | 102 | 91 | 97 | 101 | 101 |
| VAN WERT | 98 | 80 | 86 | 85 | 98 | 93 | 109 | 97 | 93 | 87 | 90 | 95 | 92 | 99 | 86 | 101 | 87 | 93 | 102 | 99 |
| VINTON | 97 | 63 | 65 | 74 | 91 | 89 | 111 | 96 | 92 | 75 | 77 | 96 | 81 | 94 | 73 | 98 | 77 | 88 | 102 | 96 |
| WARREN | 101 | 98 | 93 | 98 | 99 | 98 | 103 | 100 | 101 | 100 | 104 | 101 | 103 | 103 | 95 | 103 | 100 | 103 | 100 | 102 |
| WASHINGTON | 98 | 81 | 86 | 86 | 96 | 94 | 108 | 97 | 94 | 87 | 90 | 95 | 92 | 98 | 85 | 101 | 87 | 94 | 102 | 99 |
| WAYNE | 99 | 86 | 89 | 89 | 97 | 94 | 109 | 98 | 95 | 90 | 93 | 97 | 94 | 100 | 88 | 101 | 90 | 96 | 101 | 100 |
| WILLIAMS | 99 | 81 | 85 | 86 | 96 | 93 | 111 | 98 | 94 | 88 | 91 | 96 | 92 | 99 | 85 | 101 | 88 | 94 | 102 | 100 |
| WOOD | 100 | 99 | 100 | 102 | 101 | 100 | 106 | 98 | 98 | 97 | 101 | 100 | 101 | 101 | 97 | 101 | 97 | 101 | 101 | 101 |
| WYANDOT | 98 | 79 | 85 | 85 | 97 | 93 | 110 | 97 | 93 | 87 | 90 | 95 | 91 | 98 | 85 | 101 | 87 | 93 | 102 | 99 |
| OHIO | 98 | 94 | 98 | 96 | 101 | 99 | 101 | 98 | 96 | 96 | 97 | 97 | 100 | 99 | 96 | 101 | 95 | 99 | 100 | 99 |
| UNITED STATES | 100 | 100 | 100 | 100 | 100 | 100 | 100 | 100 | 100 | 100 | 100 | 100 | 100 | 100 | 100 | 100 | 100 | 100 | 100 | 100 |

# OKLAHOMA

# POPULATION CHANGE

| COUNTY | FIPS Code | MSA Code | DMA Code | POPULATION 1990 | POPULATION 2000 | POPULATION 2005 | 1990-2000 ANNUAL CHANGE % Rate | 1990-2000 ANNUAL CHANGE State Rank | RACE (%) White 1990 | White 2000 | Black 1990 | Black 2000 | Asian/Pacific 1990 | Asian/Pacific 2000 |
|---|---|---|---|---|---|---|---|---|---|---|---|---|---|---|
| ADAIR | 001 | 0000 | 671 | 18,421 | 20,732 | 21,675 | 1.2 | 11 | 55.6 | 55.8 | 0.0 | 0.0 | 0.1 | 0.1 |
| ALFALFA | 003 | 0000 | 650 | 6,416 | 5,801 | 5,529 | -1.0 | 69 | 93.1 | 92.3 | 3.2 | 3.4 | 0.1 | 0.1 |
| ATOKA | 005 | 0000 | 657 | 12,778 | 13,439 | 13,703 | 0.5 | 29 | 81.1 | 81.1 | 5.9 | 6.1 | 0.1 | 0.2 |
| BEAVER | 007 | 0000 | 634 | 6,023 | 6,032 | 6,115 | 0.0 | 49 | 95.3 | 93.7 | 0.0 | 0.0 | 0.0 | 0.0 |
| BECKHAM | 009 | 0000 | 650 | 18,812 | 19,805 | 19,842 | 0.5 | 29 | 93.4 | 91.9 | 2.0 | 2.2 | 0.2 | 0.3 |
| BLAINE | 011 | 0000 | 650 | 11,470 | 10,141 | 9,458 | -1.2 | 72 | 85.2 | 84.6 | 4.4 | 4.7 | 0.2 | 0.2 |
| BRYAN | 013 | 0000 | 657 | 32,089 | 35,271 | 36,874 | 0.9 | 17 | 83.5 | 83.6 | 1.3 | 1.4 | 0.4 | 0.5 |
| CADDO | 015 | 0000 | 650 | 29,550 | 30,584 | 30,187 | 0.3 | 38 | 72.0 | 71.2 | 2.5 | 3.3 | 0.2 | 0.3 |
| CANADIAN | 017 | 5880 | 650 | 74,409 | 87,602 | 93,237 | 1.6 | 6 | 90.7 | 90.0 | 2.4 | 2.5 | 1.6 | 2.1 |
| CARTER | 019 | 0000 | 657 | 42,919 | 44,807 | 45,575 | 0.4 | 35 | 82.0 | 81.5 | 8.3 | 8.8 | 0.4 | 0.5 |
| CHEROKEE | 021 | 0000 | 671 | 34,049 | 40,089 | 42,932 | 1.6 | 6 | 64.8 | 65.4 | 1.1 | 1.1 | 0.2 | 0.2 |
| CHOCTAW | 023 | 0000 | 657 | 15,302 | 14,957 | 14,621 | -0.2 | 54 | 71.4 | 71.2 | 12.8 | 13.4 | 0.2 | 0.2 |
| CIMARRON | 025 | 0000 | 634 | 3,301 | 2,871 | 2,628 | -1.4 | 74 | 92.6 | 90.0 | 0.0 | 0.0 | 0.4 | 0.4 |
| CLEVELAND | 027 | 5880 | 650 | 174,253 | 206,353 | 220,684 | 1.7 | 3 | 88.5 | 87.8 | 3.0 | 3.1 | 2.3 | 2.7 |
| COAL | 029 | 0000 | 657 | 5,780 | 6,156 | 6,325 | 0.6 | 26 | 82.3 | 82.9 | 0.8 | 0.9 | 0.0 | 0.0 |
| COMANCHE | 031 | 4200 | 627 | 111,486 | 105,572 | 100,338 | -0.5 | 62 | 71.5 | 69.5 | 17.9 | 17.8 | 2.7 | 3.5 |
| COTTON | 033 | 0000 | 627 | 6,651 | 6,567 | 6,363 | -0.1 | 52 | 87.4 | 86.8 | 2.1 | 2.3 | 0.1 | 0.1 |
| CRAIG | 035 | 0000 | 671 | 14,104 | 14,888 | 15,012 | 0.5 | 29 | 77.0 | 77.0 | 3.4 | 3.6 | 0.2 | 0.3 |
| CREEK | 037 | 8560 | 671 | 60,915 | 69,172 | 74,104 | 1.2 | 11 | 87.9 | 87.9 | 3.1 | 3.4 | 0.2 | 0.3 |
| CUSTER | 039 | 0000 | 650 | 26,897 | 25,524 | 25,199 | -0.5 | 62 | 85.1 | 83.0 | 3.5 | 3.5 | 0.6 | 0.7 |
| DELAWARE | 041 | 0000 | 671 | 28,070 | 35,609 | 38,855 | 2.3 | 2 | 74.3 | 74.2 | 0.1 | 0.1 | 0.2 | 0.2 |
| DEWEY | 043 | 0000 | 650 | 5,551 | 4,794 | 4,481 | -1.4 | 74 | 93.4 | 93.1 | 0.1 | 0.1 | 0.1 | 0.1 |
| ELLIS | 045 | 0000 | 650 | 4,497 | 4,175 | 4,081 | -0.7 | 65 | 96.8 | 96.0 | 0.1 | 0.1 | 0.2 | 0.3 |
| GARFIELD | 047 | 2340 | 650 | 56,735 | 56,993 | 57,122 | 0.0 | 49 | 92.4 | 91.7 | 3.6 | 3.7 | 1.0 | 1.3 |
| GARVIN | 049 | 0000 | 650 | 26,605 | 26,714 | 26,639 | 0.0 | 49 | 89.4 | 89.0 | 2.7 | 3.0 | 0.2 | 0.3 |
| GRADY | 051 | 0000 | 650 | 41,747 | 46,461 | 48,433 | 1.0 | 15 | 90.1 | 89.5 | 3.7 | 3.9 | 0.3 | 0.4 |
| GRANT | 053 | 0000 | 650 | 5,689 | 5,157 | 4,776 | -1.0 | 69 | 97.8 | 97.3 | 0.1 | 0.0 | 0.2 | 0.3 |
| GREER | 055 | 0000 | 650 | 6,559 | 6,364 | 6,252 | -0.3 | 58 | 87.1 | 84.8 | 6.9 | 7.6 | 0.2 | 0.3 |
| HARMON | 057 | 0000 | 650 | 3,793 | 3,250 | 3,006 | -1.5 | 77 | 75.2 | 67.7 | 7.6 | 7.3 | 0.2 | 0.2 |
| HARPER | 059 | 0000 | 650 | 4,063 | 3,546 | 3,383 | -1.3 | 73 | 97.8 | 97.1 | 0.1 | 0.1 | 0.1 | 0.1 |
| HASKELL | 061 | 0000 | 671 | 10,940 | 11,478 | 11,758 | 0.5 | 29 | 84.2 | 84.6 | 0.9 | 1.0 | 0.1 | 0.1 |
| HUGHES | 063 | 0000 | 650 | 13,023 | 14,074 | 14,119 | 0.8 | 19 | 79.5 | 77.8 | 2.9 | 5.7 | 0.1 | 0.2 |
| JACKSON | 065 | 0000 | 627 | 28,764 | 28,248 | 27,497 | -0.2 | 54 | 80.2 | 76.3 | 9.4 | 9.4 | 1.4 | 1.7 |
| JEFFERSON | 067 | 0000 | 627 | 7,010 | 6,452 | 6,133 | -0.8 | 66 | 90.4 | 88.8 | 0.6 | 0.8 | 0.3 | 0.3 |
| JOHNSTON | 069 | 0000 | 657 | 10,032 | 10,342 | 10,457 | 0.3 | 38 | 81.5 | 81.4 | 2.1 | 2.2 | 0.1 | 0.2 |
| KAY | 071 | 0000 | 650 | 48,056 | 46,263 | 45,293 | -0.4 | 60 | 89.4 | 89.3 | 1.8 | 1.9 | 0.5 | 0.6 |
| KINGFISHER | 073 | 0000 | 650 | 13,212 | 13,511 | 13,613 | 0.2 | 43 | 92.3 | 91.3 | 2.3 | 2.3 | 0.1 | 0.1 |
| KIOWA | 075 | 0000 | 650 | 11,347 | 10,358 | 9,687 | -0.9 | 68 | 84.0 | 82.2 | 5.4 | 5.7 | 0.3 | 0.4 |
| LATIMER | 077 | 0000 | 671 | 10,333 | 10,169 | 9,984 | -0.2 | 54 | 82.5 | 82.2 | 1.5 | 1.4 | 0.2 | 0.3 |
| LE FLORE | 079 | 0000 | 670 | 43,270 | 47,012 | 48,201 | 0.8 | 19 | 85.3 | 85.3 | 2.4 | 2.6 | 0.2 | 0.3 |
| LINCOLN | 081 | 0000 | 650 | 29,216 | 32,164 | 33,991 | 0.9 | 17 | 90.3 | 90.1 | 2.7 | 2.9 | 0.2 | 0.2 |
| LOGAN | 083 | 5880 | 650 | 29,011 | 30,742 | 32,160 | 0.6 | 26 | 81.5 | 79.2 | 13.9 | 15.7 | 0.3 | 0.4 |
| LOVE | 085 | 0000 | 657 | 8,157 | 8,616 | 8,774 | 0.5 | 29 | 85.7 | 86.2 | 4.4 | 3.3 | 0.1 | 0.2 |
| MCCLAIN | 087 | 5880 | 650 | 22,795 | 27,150 | 29,381 | 1.7 | 3 | 91.1 | 90.7 | 1.0 | 1.1 | 0.2 | 0.2 |
| MCCURTAIN | 089 | 0000 | 612 | 33,433 | 34,844 | 35,190 | 0.4 | 35 | 74.2 | 74.0 | 10.3 | 10.9 | 0.3 | 0.4 |
| MCINTOSH | 091 | 0000 | 671 | 16,779 | 19,526 | 20,792 | 1.5 | 8 | 76.0 | 76.6 | 5.3 | 5.5 | 0.2 | 0.2 |
| MAJOR | 093 | 0000 | 650 | 8,055 | 7,602 | 7,325 | -0.6 | 64 | 97.3 | 96.8 | 0.0 | 0.0 | 0.1 | 0.2 |
| MARSHALL | 095 | 0000 | 657 | 10,829 | 12,534 | 13,307 | 1.4 | 10 | 86.9 | 86.6 | 1.7 | 2.1 | 0.1 | 0.2 |
| MAYES | 097 | 0000 | 671 | 33,366 | 38,876 | 41,898 | 1.5 | 8 | 81.3 | 81.7 | 0.2 | 0.2 | 0.2 | 0.3 |
| MURRAY | 099 | 0000 | 650 | 12,042 | 12,523 | 12,828 | 0.4 | 35 | 86.5 | 86.6 | 1.7 | 1.9 | 0.1 | 0.2 |
| MUSKOGEE | 101 | 0000 | 671 | 68,078 | 70,175 | 70,635 | 0.3 | 38 | 71.8 | 71.2 | 14.0 | 14.8 | 0.4 | 0.5 |
| NOBLE | 103 | 0000 | 650 | 11,045 | 11,360 | 11,462 | 0.3 | 38 | 89.0 | 88.9 | 1.8 | 2.0 | 0.2 | 0.2 |
| NOWATA | 105 | 0000 | 671 | 9,992 | 10,163 | 10,570 | 0.2 | 43 | 79.8 | 80.2 | 3.6 | 4.0 | 0.1 | 0.1 |
| OKFUSKEE | 107 | 0000 | 671 | 11,551 | 11,189 | 10,928 | -0.3 | 58 | 67.8 | 67.9 | 11.5 | 12.4 | 0.1 | 0.2 |
| OKLAHOMA | 109 | 5880 | 650 | 599,611 | 641,471 | 658,565 | 0.7 | 21 | 77.0 | 75.2 | 14.7 | 15.3 | 2.0 | 2.5 |
| OKMULGEE | 111 | 0000 | 671 | 36,490 | 39,050 | 40,265 | 0.7 | 21 | 75.0 | 74.5 | 12.1 | 12.9 | 0.2 | 0.3 |
| OSAGE | 113 | 8560 | 671 | 41,645 | 43,145 | 43,985 | 0.3 | 38 | 74.4 | 73.8 | 10.1 | 11.3 | 0.2 | 0.2 |
| OTTAWA | 115 | 0000 | 603 | 30,561 | 30,981 | 31,376 | 0.1 | 47 | 80.2 | 80.6 | 0.6 | 0.3 | 0.3 | 0.4 |
| PAWNEE | 117 | 0000 | 671 | 15,575 | 16,716 | 17,541 | 0.7 | 21 | 88.4 | 88.7 | 0.8 | 0.9 | 0.2 | 0.2 |
| PAYNE | 119 | 0000 | 650 | 61,507 | 65,611 | 66,547 | 0.6 | 26 | 89.4 | 88.7 | 2.9 | 3.3 | 2.8 | 3.0 |
| PITTSBURG | 121 | 0000 | 671 | 40,581 | 43,720 | 44,945 | 0.7 | 21 | 83.2 | 82.3 | 3.7 | 4.6 | 0.3 | 0.3 |
| PONTOTOC | 123 | 0000 | 657 | 34,119 | 34,735 | 34,913 | 0.2 | 43 | 82.8 | 82.9 | 2.5 | 2.7 | 0.3 | 0.4 |
| POTTAWATOMIE | 125 | 5880 | 650 | 58,760 | 63,013 | 64,966 | 0.7 | 21 | 85.0 | 85.1 | 2.3 | 2.4 | 0.6 | 0.7 |
| PUSHMATAHA | 127 | 0000 | 657 | 10,997 | 11,573 | 11,725 | 0.5 | 29 | 83.3 | 83.8 | 1.0 | 1.1 | 0.1 | 0.1 |
| ROGER MILLS | 129 | 0000 | 650 | 4,147 | 3,575 | 3,487 | -1.4 | 74 | 95.2 | 95.2 | 0.1 | 0.1 | 0.1 | 0.1 |
| ROGERS | 131 | 8560 | 671 | 55,170 | 72,953 | 84,697 | 2.8 | 1 | 85.6 | 85.9 | 0.8 | 0.9 | 0.3 | 0.4 |
| SEMINOLE | 133 | 0000 | 650 | 25,412 | 24,394 | 23,648 | -0.4 | 60 | 74.9 | 75.0 | 7.6 | 8.2 | 0.2 | 0.2 |
| SEQUOYAH | 135 | 2720 | 670 | 33,828 | 38,308 | 40,469 | 1.2 | 11 | 76.5 | 76.9 | 2.3 | 2.5 | 0.2 | 0.3 |
| STEPHENS | 137 | 0000 | 627 | 42,299 | 42,940 | 42,269 | 0.1 | 47 | 91.8 | 90.8 | 2.2 | 2.4 | 0.4 | 0.5 |
| TEXAS | 139 | 0000 | 634 | 16,419 | 18,540 | 19,503 | 1.2 | 11 | 92.2 | 89.3 | 0.4 | 0.4 | 0.2 | 0.3 |
| TILLMAN | 141 | 0000 | 627 | 10,384 | 9,333 | 8,914 | -1.0 | 69 | 75.7 | 71.0 | 10.0 | 9.9 | 0.3 | 0.3 |
| TULSA | 143 | 8560 | 671 | 503,341 | 554,828 | 583,166 | 1.0 | 15 | 83.0 | 81.9 | 9.9 | 10.4 | 1.2 | 1.5 |
| WAGONER | 145 | 8560 | 671 | 47,883 | 57,054 | 61,777 | 1.7 | 3 | 85.9 | 85.7 | 4.1 | 4.4 | 0.4 | 0.5 |
| WASHINGTON | 147 | 0000 | 671 | 48,066 | 47,780 | 48,261 | -0.1 | 52 | 88.1 | 87.7 | 2.7 | 2.8 | 0.9 | 1.1 |
| WASHITA | 149 | 0000 | 650 | 11,441 | 11,673 | 11,579 | 0.2 | 43 | 95.7 | 95.1 | 0.2 | 0.2 | 0.2 | 0.2 |
| WOODS | 151 | 0000 | 650 | 9,103 | 8,406 | 7,982 | -0.8 | 66 | 96.8 | 96.1 | 0.5 | 0.5 | 0.3 | 0.4 |
| WOODWARD | 153 | 0000 | 650 | 18,976 | 18,562 | 18,430 | -0.2 | 54 | 94.8 | 93.9 | 0.7 | 0.8 | 0.4 | 0.6 |
| OKLAHOMA | | | | | | | 0.7 | | 82.1 | 81.3 | 7.4 | 7.7 | 1.1 | 1.3 |
| UNITED STATES | | | | | | | 1.0 | | 80.3 | 77.9 | 12.1 | 12.4 | 2.9 | 3.9 |

| COUNTY | % HISPANIC ORIGIN | | 2000 AGE DISTRIBUTION (%) | | | | | | | | | | MEDIAN AGE | | 2000 Males/ Females (×100) |
|---|---|---|---|---|---|---|---|---|---|---|---|---|---|---|---|
| | 1990 | 2000 | 0-4 | 5-9 | 10-14 | 15-19 | 20-24 | 25-44 | 45-64 | 65-84 | 85+ | 18+ | 1990 | 2000 | |
| ADAIR | 1.3 | 2.0 | 7.9 | 7.7 | 8.2 | 8.4 | 7.0 | 25.9 | 22.5 | 10.9 | 1.5 | 71.0 | 31.6 | 33.7 | 95.9 |
| ALFALFA | 1.6 | 2.8 | 5.0 | 5.3 | 6.2 | 6.6 | 6.2 | 24.6 | 25.2 | 17.4 | 3.4 | 79.0 | 40.0 | 42.0 | 111.9 |
| ATOKA | 0.9 | 1.6 | 6.0 | 6.2 | 7.5 | 8.0 | 6.6 | 26.3 | 24.5 | 13.1 | 1.9 | 75.4 | 34.8 | 37.7 | 110.6 |
| BEAVER | 5.0 | 7.8 | 6.0 | 6.6 | 7.9 | 7.7 | 5.4 | 24.0 | 25.8 | 14.5 | 2.0 | 74.0 | 36.6 | 39.9 | 99.9 |
| BECKHAM | 4.2 | 7.1 | 7.2 | 7.5 | 8.2 | 8.2 | 5.9 | 24.8 | 22.7 | 12.9 | 2.7 | 72.0 | 34.5 | 36.9 | 94.1 |
| BLAINE | 2.5 | 4.1 | 7.1 | 7.4 | 8.0 | 8.2 | 5.4 | 23.1 | 23.2 | 14.4 | 3.3 | 72.3 | 35.8 | 38.4 | 93.2 |
| BRYAN | 1.4 | 2.4 | 6.4 | 6.3 | 7.2 | 8.3 | 8.0 | 24.4 | 23.8 | 13.4 | 2.1 | 75.6 | 34.6 | 37.1 | 93.2 |
| CADDO | 4.8 | 6.1 | 7.4 | 7.5 | 8.0 | 8.1 | 6.2 | 24.2 | 23.0 | 13.2 | 2.5 | 72.1 | 34.3 | 36.7 | 97.0 |
| CANADIAN | 2.6 | 4.2 | 7.2 | 7.4 | 7.9 | 8.0 | 6.8 | 29.2 | 24.3 | 8.0 | 1.1 | 72.4 | 32.0 | 34.8 | 99.3 |
| CARTER | 1.8 | 3.0 | 6.7 | 6.8 | 7.9 | 7.8 | 5.9 | 24.7 | 24.0 | 13.9 | 2.4 | 73.5 | 35.3 | 38.3 | 93.7 |
| CHEROKEE | 1.4 | 2.1 | 7.3 | 7.1 | 7.4 | 8.5 | 8.0 | 26.7 | 21.7 | 11.6 | 1.6 | 73.6 | 31.9 | 34.3 | 94.2 |
| CHOCTAW | 1.3 | 2.2 | 7.0 | 7.0 | 8.2 | 8.1 | 6.1 | 22.3 | 24.0 | 14.9 | 2.4 | 72.5 | 35.9 | 38.2 | 91.5 |
| CIMARRON | 12.5 | 18.0 | 6.0 | 6.8 | 7.5 | 7.9 | 5.9 | 22.4 | 25.1 | 15.8 | 2.7 | 74.2 | 37.2 | 40.5 | 101.6 |
| CLEVELAND | 2.7 | 4.5 | 6.8 | 6.7 | 7.2 | 8.9 | 10.4 | 31.2 | 21.1 | 7.0 | 0.8 | 74.9 | 29.7 | 31.7 | 100.6 |
| COAL | 0.7 | 1.1 | 6.3 | 6.6 | 7.0 | 7.4 | 6.6 | 24.5 | 24.1 | 14.8 | 2.7 | 75.5 | 36.4 | 39.2 | 94.7 |
| COMANCHE | 6.2 | 9.6 | 8.3 | 7.5 | 7.5 | 8.7 | 11.0 | 28.9 | 18.5 | 8.5 | 0.9 | 72.2 | 28.2 | 29.4 | 105.9 |
| COTTON | 3.5 | 5.0 | 6.5 | 6.7 | 7.1 | 7.4 | 5.7 | 24.6 | 23.8 | 15.1 | 3.0 | 75.0 | 37.1 | 39.4 | 92.1 |
| CRAIG | 0.7 | 1.4 | 5.7 | 5.7 | 6.8 | 7.0 | 5.8 | 25.6 | 26.7 | 14.3 | 2.3 | 77.5 | 37.9 | 40.6 | 96.8 |
| CREEK | 1.1 | 1.9 | 6.7 | 6.8 | 7.9 | 8.0 | 6.0 | 25.2 | 25.5 | 12.2 | 1.7 | 73.5 | 34.2 | 37.9 | 95.0 |
| CUSTER | 6.0 | 9.6 | 7.2 | 7.1 | 7.1 | 10.0 | 9.9 | 26.6 | 19.7 | 10.3 | 2.0 | 74.3 | 29.7 | 31.9 | 96.6 |
| DELAWARE | 0.8 | 1.5 | 6.0 | 6.1 | 6.7 | 6.7 | 5.0 | 21.9 | 25.9 | 19.3 | 2.2 | 77.0 | 39.9 | 42.9 | 94.1 |
| DEWEY | 1.3 | 2.3 | 6.4 | 6.4 | 6.8 | 7.4 | 6.5 | 22.5 | 24.7 | 15.4 | 3.9 | 75.3 | 38.2 | 41.1 | 96.5 |
| ELLIS | 3.1 | 5.0 | 4.9 | 5.8 | 7.4 | 7.7 | 4.8 | 22.1 | 26.2 | 18.0 | 3.0 | 76.1 | 39.9 | 43.0 | 96.1 |
| GARFIELD | 1.9 | 3.3 | 6.7 | 6.8 | 7.4 | 7.5 | 6.9 | 25.9 | 23.7 | 13.0 | 2.2 | 74.5 | 34.2 | 37.4 | 92.7 |
| GARVIN | 1.2 | 2.2 | 6.0 | 6.3 | 6.8 | 7.9 | 6.1 | 24.3 | 23.6 | 15.9 | 3.2 | 76.1 | 37.0 | 40.0 | 91.9 |
| GRADY | 1.7 | 3.0 | 6.9 | 7.0 | 7.4 | 8.1 | 6.7 | 26.2 | 24.3 | 11.3 | 2.0 | 73.7 | 33.4 | 36.6 | 93.5 |
| GRANT | 1.0 | 2.0 | 6.4 | 6.7 | 7.5 | 6.9 | 4.7 | 22.2 | 24.5 | 17.4 | 3.6 | 74.6 | 39.5 | 41.8 | 91.9 |
| GREER | 5.1 | 7.9 | 4.8 | 5.1 | 6.0 | 6.7 | 7.0 | 25.6 | 23.5 | 17.3 | 4.0 | 80.2 | 39.9 | 41.0 | 114.9 |
| HARMON | 17.3 | 25.9 | 7.4 | 7.1 | 8.7 | 8.2 | 6.2 | 21.0 | 20.9 | 16.6 | 3.9 | 71.4 | 37.7 | 37.6 | 92.6 |
| HARPER | 1.8 | 3.1 | 5.3 | 5.8 | 6.2 | 7.6 | 6.1 | 22.1 | 25.9 | 17.5 | 3.4 | 77.2 | 39.2 | 43.0 | 98.2 |
| HASKELL | 0.7 | 1.4 | 6.0 | 6.3 | 7.3 | 7.9 | 5.7 | 22.7 | 25.8 | 15.8 | 2.5 | 75.3 | 38.0 | 40.9 | 94.6 |
| HUGHES | 1.0 | 2.3 | 5.2 | 5.5 | 6.9 | 7.5 | 6.0 | 22.8 | 25.4 | 17.2 | 3.5 | 77.5 | 40.5 | 42.2 | 94.9 |
| JACKSON | 11.6 | 17.7 | 9.2 | 8.1 | 8.1 | 7.8 | 8.4 | 28.5 | 18.7 | 9.5 | 1.6 | 70.2 | 29.7 | 30.7 | 97.8 |
| JEFFERSON | 4.4 | 6.9 | 5.7 | 6.0 | 6.4 | 7.2 | 5.7 | 23.4 | 24.4 | 17.3 | 4.0 | 77.2 | 38.7 | 41.8 | 91.6 |
| JOHNSTON | 1.2 | 2.0 | 6.1 | 6.4 | 7.2 | 8.9 | 6.5 | 24.4 | 24.2 | 13.7 | 2.4 | 75.5 | 35.3 | 37.8 | 94.5 |
| KAY | 1.8 | 3.0 | 6.7 | 6.9 | 7.6 | 7.8 | 6.1 | 24.2 | 23.7 | 14.3 | 2.6 | 74.1 | 35.6 | 38.6 | 94.3 |
| KINGFISHER | 3.1 | 5.0 | 6.7 | 7.4 | 8.1 | 8.1 | 5.4 | 24.9 | 23.7 | 13.3 | 2.5 | 72.5 | 34.1 | 37.9 | 95.8 |
| KIOWA | 5.3 | 8.5 | 6.8 | 7.0 | 7.6 | 8.0 | 5.7 | 22.3 | 23.0 | 16.1 | 3.5 | 73.1 | 37.8 | 39.3 | 92.6 |
| LATIMER | 1.1 | 1.9 | 6.6 | 6.7 | 7.8 | 9.9 | 7.2 | 22.8 | 22.9 | 14.0 | 2.0 | 74.3 | 33.8 | 36.3 | 99.4 |
| LE FLORE | 1.0 | 1.8 | 6.8 | 7.0 | 7.6 | 7.5 | 6.5 | 25.5 | 24.6 | 12.3 | 2.1 | 73.9 | 34.3 | 37.1 | 96.4 |
| LINCOLN | 1.1 | 2.0 | 6.5 | 6.8 | 7.5 | 8.1 | 6.3 | 24.8 | 25.1 | 12.9 | 2.0 | 74.0 | 34.8 | 38.0 | 96.4 |
| LOGAN | 1.9 | 3.3 | 6.4 | 6.7 | 7.5 | 10.5 | 8.6 | 24.3 | 23.1 | 10.7 | 2.1 | 73.8 | 32.6 | 35.1 | 96.6 |
| LOVE | 4.1 | 6.2 | 5.7 | 6.3 | 6.8 | 7.3 | 6.6 | 25.4 | 25.8 | 13.8 | 2.3 | 76.5 | 36.1 | 38.9 | 100.8 |
| MCCLAIN | 2.5 | 4.0 | 6.0 | 6.6 | 7.6 | 8.4 | 5.9 | 25.8 | 26.7 | 11.4 | 1.5 | 74.5 | 34.3 | 38.2 | 99.8 |
| MCCURTAIN | 1.4 | 2.1 | 7.4 | 7.3 | 8.5 | 8.4 | 6.7 | 24.2 | 24.2 | 11.6 | 1.7 | 71.4 | 33.0 | 35.7 | 92.9 |
| MCINTOSH | 0.9 | 1.5 | 5.3 | 5.6 | 6.7 | 7.0 | 5.0 | 20.4 | 28.0 | 19.6 | 2.4 | 77.9 | 42.3 | 45.0 | 92.5 |
| MAJOR | 1.6 | 2.8 | 6.3 | 6.9 | 7.2 | 8.1 | 6.0 | 22.5 | 25.1 | 14.8 | 3.3 | 74.7 | 37.3 | 40.7 | 96.7 |
| MARSHALL | 2.5 | 3.9 | 5.6 | 5.7 | 6.6 | 7.4 | 5.1 | 22.4 | 26.4 | 18.2 | 2.6 | 77.6 | 41.0 | 43.0 | 94.7 |
| MAYES | 0.9 | 1.6 | 6.6 | 6.8 | 7.7 | 7.8 | 5.8 | 23.6 | 25.6 | 14.4 | 1.8 | 74.1 | 35.6 | 39.1 | 96.6 |
| MURRAY | 1.4 | 2.5 | 5.7 | 6.0 | 6.6 | 7.7 | 6.0 | 23.0 | 25.7 | 16.3 | 2.9 | 76.8 | 38.2 | 41.2 | 97.7 |
| MUSKOGEE | 1.3 | 2.2 | 6.6 | 6.9 | 7.8 | 8.4 | 6.7 | 25.4 | 23.3 | 12.8 | 2.0 | 73.7 | 34.3 | 36.8 | 93.4 |
| NOBLE | 1.1 | 1.9 | 6.8 | 7.0 | 7.4 | 7.9 | 5.8 | 25.4 | 24.4 | 12.7 | 2.6 | 73.8 | 35.1 | 38.5 | 96.1 |
| NOWATA | 0.7 | 1.5 | 5.9 | 6.1 | 7.4 | 7.4 | 5.5 | 22.9 | 26.3 | 15.7 | 2.6 | 75.9 | 38.4 | 41.2 | 96.1 |
| OKFUSKEE | 1.2 | 2.1 | 6.3 | 6.4 | 7.2 | 8.3 | 6.7 | 24.3 | 24.6 | 13.7 | 2.4 | 74.8 | 36.1 | 37.9 | 105.7 |
| OKLAHOMA | 4.2 | 6.7 | 7.2 | 7.1 | 7.5 | 7.5 | 6.9 | 29.6 | 22.0 | 10.7 | 1.4 | 73.9 | 32.5 | 35.3 | 93.2 |
| OKMULGEE | 1.3 | 2.2 | 6.8 | 6.9 | 7.5 | 8.4 | 6.3 | 23.6 | 24.1 | 13.9 | 2.5 | 74.0 | 35.5 | 37.9 | 94.8 |
| OSAGE | 1.6 | 2.7 | 6.5 | 6.9 | 7.6 | 7.7 | 6.4 | 25.1 | 25.7 | 12.4 | 1.7 | 74.1 | 34.9 | 38.0 | 98.9 |
| OTTAWA | 1.2 | 2.1 | 6.0 | 6.0 | 7.0 | 8.7 | 6.1 | 22.6 | 25.4 | 16.0 | 2.2 | 76.8 | 37.0 | 40.3 | 90.4 |
| PAWNEE | 0.7 | 1.4 | 6.5 | 6.9 | 7.5 | 7.4 | 6.1 | 23.9 | 26.1 | 13.6 | 2.0 | 74.3 | 36.2 | 39.6 | 99.5 |
| PAYNE | 1.5 | 2.7 | 5.7 | 5.6 | 5.8 | 11.5 | 17.4 | 26.2 | 17.6 | 8.8 | 1.6 | 79.7 | 26.9 | 28.0 | 99.5 |
| PITTSBURG | 1.2 | 2.1 | 5.6 | 6.0 | 6.6 | 7.2 | 6.4 | 24.9 | 25.0 | 15.7 | 2.5 | 77.2 | 37.5 | 40.1 | 100.9 |
| PONTOTOC | 1.2 | 2.1 | 6.2 | 6.3 | 7.2 | 8.8 | 8.3 | 24.9 | 23.2 | 12.9 | 2.3 | 75.8 | 34.2 | 36.6 | 90.8 |
| POTTAWATOMIE | 1.7 | 2.6 | 6.5 | 6.6 | 7.0 | 9.0 | 7.6 | 25.6 | 23.8 | 12.0 | 2.0 | 75.1 | 33.4 | 36.2 | 92.6 |
| PUSHMATAHA | 1.2 | 2.2 | 6.0 | 6.4 | 7.2 | 7.6 | 5.6 | 21.8 | 26.9 | 16.1 | 2.5 | 75.4 | 38.6 | 41.5 | 96.9 |
| ROGER MILLS | 1.8 | 2.9 | 6.2 | 6.8 | 8.0 | 8.1 | 5.1 | 23.6 | 24.9 | 15.0 | 2.2 | 73.5 | 36.1 | 39.6 | 98.7 |
| ROGERS | 1.1 | 2.0 | 6.7 | 7.0 | 8.0 | 8.0 | 5.8 | 26.1 | 26.3 | 10.9 | 1.2 | 73.4 | 33.9 | 37.6 | 96.6 |
| SEMINOLE | 1.3 | 2.3 | 6.3 | 6.7 | 7.5 | 8.1 | 6.1 | 23.4 | 24.8 | 14.8 | 2.5 | 74.6 | 36.3 | 39.2 | 92.1 |
| SEQUOYAH | 0.9 | 1.6 | 6.9 | 6.7 | 8.1 | 8.1 | 6.8 | 25.1 | 25.3 | 11.3 | 1.6 | 73.1 | 33.4 | 36.5 | 96.3 |
| STEPHENS | 2.2 | 3.9 | 6.0 | 6.5 | 7.1 | 7.5 | 6.3 | 24.1 | 24.3 | 15.5 | 2.7 | 75.5 | 37.0 | 40.2 | 92.5 |
| TEXAS | 10.0 | 15.5 | 6.7 | 7.2 | 7.9 | 9.2 | 7.4 | 25.3 | 24.2 | 10.6 | 1.4 | 72.6 | 32.8 | 35.5 | 100.5 |
| TILLMAN | 14.1 | 21.1 | 7.0 | 7.4 | 8.0 | 8.7 | 6.4 | 21.9 | 22.9 | 14.6 | 3.1 | 71.9 | 36.0 | 37.3 | 95.3 |
| TULSA | 2.4 | 4.0 | 7.2 | 7.2 | 7.7 | 7.5 | 7.0 | 29.2 | 22.6 | 10.3 | 1.4 | 73.6 | 32.7 | 35.5 | 93.4 |
| WAGONER | 1.3 | 2.5 | 6.7 | 7.1 | 8.3 | 8.6 | 6.2 | 27.2 | 26.1 | 8.8 | 1.0 | 72.3 | 32.9 | 36.1 | 97.7 |
| WASHINGTON | 1.6 | 2.8 | 6.2 | 6.5 | 7.5 | 7.9 | 6.1 | 23.7 | 25.5 | 14.5 | 2.2 | 74.8 | 36.7 | 40.2 | 91.9 |
| WASHITA | 3.5 | 5.7 | 6.3 | 6.7 | 7.2 | 8.3 | 5.5 | 23.4 | 23.3 | 16.1 | 3.3 | 74.0 | 36.8 | 39.7 | 93.6 |
| WOODS | 1.5 | 2.8 | 5.2 | 5.4 | 6.2 | 8.7 | 8.7 | 22.1 | 22.7 | 17.0 | 3.9 | 79.4 | 37.5 | 40.0 | 95.9 |
| WOODWARD | 3.0 | 4.9 | 6.8 | 6.8 | 7.3 | 8.5 | 6.9 | 26.7 | 23.3 | 11.8 | 1.8 | 73.8 | 33.3 | 36.6 | 100.3 |
| OKLAHOMA | 2.7 | 4.4 | 6.9 | 6.9 | 7.5 | 8.0 | 7.3 | 27.1 | 23.2 | 11.6 | 1.7 | 74.2 | 33.2 | 36.0 | 95.4 |
| UNITED STATES | 9.0 | 11.8 | 6.9 | 7.2 | 7.2 | 7.2 | 6.7 | 29.9 | 22.2 | 11.1 | 1.6 | 74.6 | 32.9 | 35.7 | 95.6 |

# HOUSEHOLDS

| COUNTY | HOUSEHOLDS | | | | | FAMILIES | | | MEDIAN HOUSEHOLD INCOME | | | |
|---|---|---|---|---|---|---|---|---|---|---|---|---|
| | 1990 | 2000 | 2005 | % Annual Rate 1990-2000 | 2000 Average HH Size | 1990 | 2000 | % Annual Rate 1990-2000 | 2000 | 2005 | 2000 National Rank | 2000 State Rank |
| ADAIR | 6,386 | 7,219 | 7,561 | 1.5 | 2.84 | 4,938 | 5,390 | 1.1 | 26,670 | 31,536 | 2623 | 45 |
| ALFALFA | 2,469 | 2,301 | 2,225 | -0.9 | 2.23 | 1,741 | 1,565 | -1.3 | 21,728 | 24,205 | 3041 | 73 |
| ATOKA | 4,495 | 4,695 | 4,763 | 0.5 | 2.63 | 3,362 | 3,385 | 0.1 | 22,513 | 24,987 | 2995 | 70 |
| BEAVER | 2,327 | 2,393 | 2,460 | 0.3 | 2.49 | 1,768 | 1,768 | 0.0 | 36,998 | 45,714 | 980 | 8 |
| BECKHAM | 7,351 | 7,713 | 7,778 | 0.6 | 2.48 | 5,206 | 5,266 | 0.1 | 28,624 | 33,571 | 2345 | 35 |
| BLAINE | 4,418 | 4,004 | 3,779 | -1.2 | 2.46 | 3,130 | 2,730 | -1.6 | 25,338 | 28,398 | 2775 | 58 |
| BRYAN | 12,524 | 13,815 | 14,473 | 1.2 | 2.49 | 8,887 | 9,501 | 0.8 | 26,609 | 32,384 | 2632 | 46 |
| CADDO | 10,879 | 11,142 | 11,085 | 0.3 | 2.62 | 8,092 | 8,028 | -0.1 | 23,527 | 26,185 | 2937 | 66 |
| CANADIAN | 25,597 | 30,466 | 32,583 | 2.1 | 2.80 | 20,384 | 23,703 | 1.8 | 47,646 | 58,326 | 252 | 1 |
| CARTER | 16,601 | 17,371 | 17,709 | 0.6 | 2.51 | 12,089 | 12,203 | 0.1 | 30,163 | 34,152 | 2118 | 30 |
| CHEROKEE | 12,657 | 15,263 | 16,463 | 2.3 | 2.56 | 9,193 | 10,682 | 1.8 | 26,104 | 28,479 | 2700 | 51 |
| CHOCTAW | 5,952 | 5,881 | 5,778 | -0.1 | 2.50 | 4,251 | 4,042 | -0.6 | 19,834 | 21,711 | 3103 | 76 |
| CIMARRON | 1,300 | 1,150 | 1,061 | -1.5 | 2.47 | 937 | 799 | -1.9 | 22,560 | 25,201 | 2992 | 69 |
| CLEVELAND | 63,991 | 76,700 | 82,582 | 2.2 | 2.58 | 45,073 | 51,996 | 1.7 | 42,233 | 51,910 | 488 | 3 |
| COAL | 2,279 | 2,380 | 2,415 | 0.5 | 2.56 | 1,593 | 1,610 | 0.1 | 21,228 | 24,441 | 3061 | 75 |
| COMANCHE | 37,569 | 38,016 | 36,536 | 0.1 | 2.65 | 28,724 | 28,381 | -0.1 | 32,960 | 38,916 | 1546 | 16 |
| COTTON | 2,609 | 2,626 | 2,571 | 0.1 | 2.46 | 1,919 | 1,871 | -0.3 | 25,057 | 29,134 | 2806 | 59 |
| CRAIG | 5,272 | 5,518 | 5,611 | 0.6 | 2.41 | 3,719 | 3,742 | 0.1 | 28,484 | 33,308 | 2369 | 36 |
| CREEK | 22,470 | 25,483 | 27,274 | 1.5 | 2.69 | 17,336 | 19,033 | 1.1 | 31,919 | 39,195 | 1732 | 20 |
| CUSTER | 9,918 | 9,457 | 9,330 | -0.6 | 2.56 | 6,851 | 6,332 | -1.0 | 30,138 | 34,928 | 2124 | 31 |
| DELAWARE | 11,003 | 13,925 | 15,170 | 2.9 | 2.53 | 8,306 | 10,057 | 2.3 | 30,063 | 33,633 | 2140 | 32 |
| DEWEY | 2,221 | 1,949 | 1,836 | -1.6 | 2.41 | 1,582 | 1,336 | -2.0 | 23,990 | 26,196 | 2902 | 63 |
| ELLIS | 1,826 | 1,768 | 1,765 | -0.4 | 2.32 | 1,307 | 1,220 | -0.8 | 25,495 | 27,917 | 2758 | 54 |
| GARFIELD | 22,460 | 22,766 | 22,877 | 0.2 | 2.44 | 15,738 | 15,327 | -0.3 | 33,003 | 36,923 | 1538 | 15 |
| GARVIN | 10,417 | 10,654 | 10,697 | 0.3 | 2.44 | 7,547 | 7,478 | -0.1 | 27,015 | 30,826 | 2576 | 42 |
| GRADY | 15,544 | 17,525 | 18,394 | 1.5 | 2.61 | 11,828 | 12,937 | 1.1 | 32,332 | 40,835 | 1656 | 17 |
| GRANT | 2,327 | 2,158 | 2,019 | -0.9 | 2.34 | 1,660 | 1,487 | -1.3 | 25,400 | 27,926 | 2765 | 56 |
| GREER | 2,551 | 2,404 | 2,341 | -0.7 | 2.26 | 1,665 | 1,521 | -1.1 | 26,563 | 31,525 | 2641 | 47 |
| HARMON | 1,486 | 1,342 | 1,273 | -1.2 | 2.30 | 1,009 | 877 | -1.7 | 19,500 | 21,343 | 3107 | 77 |
| HARPER | 1,645 | 1,431 | 1,364 | -1.7 | 2.42 | 1,173 | 982 | -2.1 | 31,621 | 34,405 | 1795 | 24 |
| HASKELL | 4,319 | 4,531 | 4,641 | 0.6 | 2.51 | 3,155 | 3,188 | 0.1 | 23,648 | 28,618 | 2926 | 64 |
| HUGHES | 5,224 | 5,302 | 5,339 | 0.2 | 2.41 | 3,746 | 3,648 | -0.3 | 23,514 | 28,530 | 2939 | 67 |
| JACKSON | 10,455 | 10,505 | 10,291 | 0.1 | 2.62 | 7,879 | 7,706 | -0.3 | 30,551 | 37,157 | 2019 | 27 |
| JEFFERSON | 2,843 | 2,644 | 2,538 | -0.9 | 2.37 | 1,960 | 1,760 | -1.3 | 22,994 | 25,114 | 2973 | 68 |
| JOHNSTON | 3,783 | 3,955 | 4,018 | 0.5 | 2.53 | 2,774 | 2,796 | 0.1 | 25,368 | 30,866 | 2769 | 57 |
| KAY | 19,083 | 18,501 | 18,173 | -0.4 | 2.44 | 13,421 | 12,493 | -0.9 | 32,262 | 37,530 | 1671 | 18 |
| KINGFISHER | 4,932 | 5,085 | 5,141 | 0.4 | 2.62 | 3,689 | 3,689 | 0.0 | 35,499 | 42,457 | 1170 | 9 |
| KIOWA | 4,551 | 4,202 | 3,951 | -1.0 | 2.39 | 3,175 | 2,826 | -1.4 | 21,538 | 25,060 | 3052 | 74 |
| LATIMER | 3,693 | 3,712 | 3,675 | 0.1 | 2.58 | 2,795 | 2,717 | -0.3 | 28,354 | 35,230 | 2387 | 37 |
| LE FLORE | 15,938 | 17,404 | 17,878 | 1.1 | 2.64 | 12,072 | 12,740 | 0.7 | 28,996 | 34,425 | 2296 | 34 |
| LINCOLN | 10,839 | 11,823 | 12,435 | 1.1 | 2.70 | 8,345 | 8,834 | 0.7 | 31,874 | 38,621 | 1742 | 22 |
| LOGAN | 10,180 | 10,842 | 11,314 | 0.8 | 2.68 | 7,604 | 7,852 | 0.4 | 38,875 | 47,548 | 763 | 5 |
| LOVE | 2,992 | 3,301 | 3,358 | 1.2 | 2.58 | 2,239 | 2,378 | 0.7 | 27,686 | 31,614 | 2479 | 40 |
| MCCLAIN | 8,332 | 9,888 | 10,680 | 2.1 | 2.72 | 6,646 | 7,643 | 1.7 | 35,407 | 40,787 | 1183 | 10 |
| MCCURTAIN | 12,234 | 12,905 | 13,108 | 0.6 | 2.66 | 9,199 | 9,392 | 0.3 | 26,554 | 30,095 | 2643 | 48 |
| MCINTOSH | 6,786 | 7,926 | 8,451 | 1.9 | 2.42 | 4,991 | 5,564 | 1.3 | 26,676 | 32,462 | 2621 | 44 |
| MAJOR | 3,121 | 3,068 | 3,015 | -0.2 | 2.44 | 2,341 | 2,227 | -0.6 | 30,945 | 34,840 | 1941 | 26 |
| MARSHALL | 4,350 | 5,132 | 5,498 | 2.0 | 2.38 | 3,179 | 3,637 | 1.6 | 26,168 | 30,235 | 2693 | 49 |
| MAYES | 12,672 | 14,753 | 15,897 | 1.9 | 2.61 | 9,654 | 10,878 | 1.5 | 31,763 | 37,742 | 1764 | 23 |
| MURRAY | 4,651 | 4,791 | 4,892 | 0.4 | 2.52 | 3,342 | 3,329 | 0.0 | 26,904 | 30,405 | 2599 | 43 |
| MUSKOGEE | 25,174 | 26,043 | 26,252 | 0.4 | 2.59 | 18,194 | 18,282 | 0.1 | 30,385 | 36,693 | 2061 | 28 |
| NOBLE | 4,225 | 4,426 | 4,502 | 0.6 | 2.50 | 3,033 | 3,063 | 0.1 | 31,943 | 39,551 | 1725 | 19 |
| NOWATA | 3,994 | 4,043 | 4,196 | 0.1 | 2.46 | 2,866 | 2,787 | -0.3 | 24,811 | 30,644 | 2823 | 60 |
| OKFUSKEE | 4,164 | 4,131 | 4,075 | -0.1 | 2.52 | 3,016 | 2,875 | -0.6 | 23,584 | 28,516 | 2932 | 65 |
| OKLAHOMA | 237,879 | 253,488 | 259,968 | 0.8 | 2.47 | 158,862 | 163,563 | 0.4 | 35,193 | 40,515 | 1222 | 11 |
| OKMULGEE | 14,044 | 15,203 | 15,760 | 1.0 | 2.49 | 10,023 | 10,427 | 0.5 | 26,058 | 31,032 | 2706 | 52 |
| OSAGE | 15,383 | 15,965 | 16,298 | 0.5 | 2.63 | 11,503 | 11,603 | 0.1 | 34,311 | 43,148 | 1346 | 13 |
| OTTAWA | 12,124 | 12,589 | 12,810 | 0.5 | 2.40 | 8,546 | 8,560 | 0.0 | 25,856 | 28,471 | 2728 | 53 |
| PAWNEE | 6,006 | 6,491 | 6,836 | 0.9 | 2.56 | 4,524 | 4,777 | 0.7 | 30,358 | 37,127 | 2067 | 29 |
| PAYNE | 23,834 | 25,292 | 25,709 | 0.7 | 2.34 | 14,201 | 14,512 | 0.3 | 29,952 | 34,036 | 2163 | 33 |
| PITTSBURG | 15,911 | 16,496 | 16,868 | 0.4 | 2.48 | 11,427 | 11,430 | 0.0 | 27,889 | 31,702 | 2456 | 38 |
| PONTOTOC | 13,310 | 13,587 | 13,662 | 0.2 | 2.46 | 9,320 | 9,268 | -0.1 | 26,158 | 30,092 | 2696 | 50 |
| POTTAWATOMIE | 21,796 | 23,389 | 24,167 | 0.9 | 2.60 | 16,013 | 16,718 | 0.5 | 31,879 | 39,768 | 1738 | 21 |
| PUSHMATAHA | 4,370 | 4,671 | 4,770 | 0.8 | 2.44 | 3,145 | 3,224 | 0.3 | 22,119 | 25,160 | 3022 | 72 |
| ROGER MILLS | 1,586 | 1,353 | 1,314 | -1.9 | 2.62 | 1,194 | 988 | -2.3 | 24,696 | 27,029 | 2838 | 61 |
| ROGERS | 19,866 | 26,282 | 30,514 | 3.5 | 2.75 | 15,928 | 20,309 | 3.0 | 43,680 | 52,969 | 415 | 2 |
| SEMINOLE | 9,665 | 9,408 | 9,183 | -0.3 | 2.53 | 7,005 | 6,604 | -0.7 | 25,436 | 30,817 | 2762 | 55 |
| SEQUOYAH | 12,335 | 14,165 | 15,062 | 1.7 | 2.67 | 9,551 | 10,637 | 1.3 | 27,803 | 32,010 | 2469 | 39 |
| STEPHENS | 16,764 | 17,353 | 17,239 | 0.4 | 2.44 | 12,397 | 12,384 | 0.0 | 31,255 | 38,134 | 1877 | 25 |
| TEXAS | 6,214 | 7,540 | 8,182 | 2.4 | 2.42 | 4,608 | 5,420 | 2.0 | 34,684 | 38,591 | 1293 | 12 |
| TILLMAN | 3,933 | 3,554 | 3,407 | -1.2 | 2.55 | 2,847 | 2,490 | -1.6 | 22,238 | 27,608 | 3014 | 71 |
| TULSA | 202,537 | 225,018 | 237,419 | 1.3 | 2.42 | 135,243 | 146,117 | 0.9 | 37,242 | 42,184 | 943 | 7 |
| WAGONER | 16,946 | 20,409 | 22,215 | 2.3 | 2.78 | 13,697 | 16,152 | 2.0 | 39,874 | 49,618 | 684 | 4 |
| WASHINGTON | 19,242 | 19,086 | 19,264 | -0.1 | 2.47 | 14,035 | 13,427 | -0.5 | 38,387 | 44,555 | 820 | 6 |
| WASHITA | 4,421 | 4,622 | 4,629 | 0.5 | 2.47 | 3,291 | 3,323 | 0.1 | 24,131 | 26,868 | 2892 | 62 |
| WOODS | 3,803 | 3,488 | 3,353 | -1.0 | 2.18 | 2,429 | 2,123 | -1.6 | 27,432 | 30,102 | 2520 | 41 |
| WOODWARD | 7,087 | 6,965 | 6,928 | -0.2 | 2.55 | 5,209 | 4,922 | -0.7 | 33,298 | 39,054 | 1491 | 14 |
| OKLAHOMA | | | | 1.0 | 2.52 | | | 0.6 | 33,255 | 39,070 | | |
| UNITED STATES | | | | 1.4 | 2.59 | | | 1.1 | 41,914 | 49,127 | | |

| COUNTY | 2000 Per Capita Income | 2000 HH Income Base | 2000 HOUSEHOLD INCOME DISTRIBUTION (%) | | | | | | 2000 AVERAGE DISPOSABLE INCOME BY AGE OF HOUSEHOLDER | | | | | |
|---|---|---|---|---|---|---|---|---|---|---|---|---|---|---|
| | | | Less than $15,000 | $15,000 to $24,999 | $25,000 to $49,999 | $50,000 to $99,999 | $100,000 to $149,999 | $150,000 or More | All Ages | <35 | 35-44 | 45-54 | 55-64 | 65+ |
| ADAIR | 11,937 | 7,219 | 24.9 | 21.7 | 33.7 | 16.7 | 2.5 | 0.6 | 27,064 | 24,477 | 33,477 | 34,371 | 27,019 | 18,309 |
| ALFALFA | 12,070 | 2,301 | 32.7 | 23.0 | 30.8 | 11.0 | 2.0 | 0.5 | 23,063 | 22,150 | 27,923 | 27,858 | 25,441 | 17,595 |
| ATOKA | 11,898 | 4,695 | 34.9 | 21.2 | 29.9 | 11.6 | 1.8 | 0.6 | 23,337 | 21,068 | 24,806 | 32,170 | 23,953 | 17,496 |
| BEAVER | 16,879 | 2,393 | 13.3 | 15.0 | 40.7 | 27.5 | 3.1 | 0.4 | 33,108 | 28,111 | 40,919 | 39,027 | 35,734 | 25,056 |
| BECKHAM | 16,035 | 7,713 | 25.4 | 19.2 | 30.8 | 18.4 | 4.2 | 1.9 | 30,384 | 23,832 | 38,188 | 37,770 | 31,192 | 22,820 |
| BLAINE | 12,456 | 4,004 | 29.5 | 19.8 | 35.3 | 13.6 | 1.4 | 0.5 | 24,574 | 22,297 | 31,411 | 26,445 | 28,262 | 18,461 |
| BRYAN | 14,455 | 13,815 | 28.8 | 18.2 | 32.1 | 16.9 | 2.8 | 1.3 | 27,768 | 21,866 | 35,151 | 37,542 | 30,889 | 19,024 |
| CADDO | 11,967 | 11,142 | 31.0 | 22.0 | 30.6 | 13.3 | 2.4 | 0.7 | 24,932 | 21,888 | 28,815 | 31,789 | 28,456 | 17,952 |
| CANADIAN | 20,373 | 30,466 | 9.6 | 8.7 | 34.8 | 37.1 | 8.0 | 1.8 | 41,826 | 34,619 | 47,830 | 49,488 | 45,993 | 28,270 |
| CARTER | 16,919 | 17,371 | 24.4 | 16.5 | 35.3 | 18.5 | 3.8 | 1.6 | 30,588 | 27,509 | 34,554 | 36,659 | 33,010 | 22,564 |
| CHEROKEE | 14,977 | 15,263 | 28.0 | 20.1 | 31.4 | 15.9 | 2.6 | 2.0 | 28,604 | 20,967 | 36,069 | 33,295 | 31,372 | 23,136 |
| CHOCTAW | 10,882 | 5,881 | 39.7 | 19.4 | 27.6 | 11.5 | 1.4 | 0.5 | 22,151 | 19,019 | 29,079 | 28,368 | 22,362 | 16,076 |
| CIMARRON | 12,313 | 1,150 | 33.3 | 20.3 | 33.1 | 10.4 | 2.1 | 0.9 | 23,805 | 19,989 | 29,974 | 30,552 | 21,386 | 20,665 |
| CLEVELAND | 20,135 | 76,695 | 13.2 | 12.0 | 34.4 | 32.1 | 6.6 | 1.8 | 38,738 | 28,554 | 44,358 | 49,816 | 45,879 | 30,820 |
| COAL | 11,149 | 2,380 | 35.6 | 22.7 | 30.1 | 9.2 | 1.6 | 0.8 | 22,884 | 22,987 | 27,165 | 26,972 | 27,003 | 15,039 |
| COMANCHE | 15,157 | 38,003 | 16.2 | 18.8 | 38.4 | 22.7 | 3.0 | 0.8 | 31,328 | 25,597 | 34,624 | 38,847 | 35,654 | 26,884 |
| COTTON | 12,002 | 2,626 | 31.7 | 18.2 | 36.4 | 12.2 | 1.3 | 0.3 | 24,078 | 23,551 | 30,084 | 30,250 | 25,098 | 16,357 |
| CRAIG | 14,088 | 5,518 | 23.5 | 19.6 | 36.3 | 17.8 | 2.2 | 0.7 | 27,608 | 24,494 | 33,573 | 33,642 | 30,749 | 20,019 |
| CREEK | 14,597 | 25,483 | 20.5 | 16.6 | 36.8 | 22.6 | 2.8 | 0.6 | 30,217 | 27,373 | 35,612 | 37,131 | 32,288 | 20,655 |
| CUSTER | 13,988 | 9,457 | 24.3 | 17.1 | 34.5 | 20.8 | 2.7 | 0.7 | 29,047 | 21,954 | 36,390 | 36,405 | 33,905 | 24,044 |
| DELAWARE | 15,102 | 13,925 | 19.9 | 20.8 | 35.6 | 19.1 | 3.6 | 1.0 | 29,940 | 28,769 | 34,682 | 37,792 | 32,619 | 23,153 |
| DEWEY | 12,099 | 1,949 | 32.0 | 19.6 | 32.7 | 14.1 | 1.5 | 0.1 | 23,560 | 22,561 | 28,503 | 27,596 | 25,237 | 17,344 |
| ELLIS | 13,280 | 1,768 | 24.7 | 24.1 | 34.7 | 15.0 | 1.5 | 0.1 | 25,004 | 26,193 | 30,035 | 29,272 | 25,637 | 18,502 |
| GARFIELD | 16,644 | 22,766 | 17.9 | 16.9 | 38.2 | 22.2 | 3.8 | 1.0 | 31,738 | 27,199 | 36,651 | 39,416 | 34,279 | 24,575 |
| GARVIN | 13,862 | 10,654 | 26.3 | 19.7 | 35.2 | 15.0 | 2.8 | 1.0 | 27,161 | 24,323 | 33,680 | 32,632 | 28,680 | 21,072 |
| GRADY | 15,923 | 17,525 | 21.1 | 16.4 | 34.9 | 23.0 | 3.6 | 1.2 | 31,462 | 26,503 | 37,136 | 39,023 | 34,495 | 21,779 |
| GRANT | 13,347 | 2,158 | 27.9 | 21.4 | 33.8 | 14.2 | 2.3 | 0.4 | 25,248 | 22,793 | 27,470 | 31,092 | 29,942 | 20,223 |
| GREER | 13,765 | 2,404 | 25.2 | 21.7 | 32.5 | 16.1 | 3.4 | 1.1 | 28,006 | 27,073 | 36,162 | 35,229 | 33,146 | 19,622 |
| HARMON | 11,103 | 1,342 | 39.7 | 22.3 | 24.4 | 11.6 | 1.3 | 0.7 | 21,730 | 23,364 | 24,611 | 25,852 | 22,988 | 16,404 |
| HARPER | 15,425 | 1,431 | 17.7 | 21.4 | 39.4 | 18.2 | 2.6 | 0.8 | 29,473 | 25,963 | 37,619 | 31,718 | 36,081 | 21,725 |
| HASKELL | 12,281 | 4,531 | 30.7 | 22.1 | 31.1 | 13.6 | 2.4 | 0.2 | 24,428 | 22,391 | 32,180 | 29,852 | 23,575 | 18,792 |
| HUGHES | 13,553 | 5,302 | 31.5 | 21.4 | 33.5 | 11.0 | 1.7 | 0.9 | 24,119 | 22,439 | 27,813 | 30,424 | 24,207 | 19,180 |
| JACKSON | 14,627 | 10,505 | 19.7 | 20.0 | 35.1 | 21.5 | 3.1 | 0.7 | 29,742 | 25,716 | 34,069 | 39,681 | 33,571 | 21,350 |
| JEFFERSON | 12,413 | 2,644 | 31.3 | 23.5 | 30.9 | 12.0 | 1.8 | 0.5 | 23,812 | 23,726 | 25,399 | 30,800 | 27,134 | 17,556 |
| JOHNSTON | 12,439 | 3,955 | 30.1 | 19.0 | 33.2 | 14.5 | 2.7 | 0.5 | 25,336 | 21,739 | 34,944 | 31,323 | 24,408 | 18,089 |
| KAY | 17,635 | 18,501 | 21.1 | 16.5 | 35.3 | 21.7 | 3.8 | 1.6 | 32,119 | 26,276 | 39,789 | 38,196 | 37,864 | 23,159 |
| KINGFISHER | 16,223 | 5,085 | 15.0 | 16.2 | 37.9 | 26.5 | 3.8 | 0.7 | 32,990 | 29,978 | 36,002 | 41,148 | 35,208 | 25,893 |
| KIOWA | 12,629 | 4,202 | 34.3 | 22.0 | 29.5 | 11.4 | 1.5 | 1.3 | 24,322 | 22,118 | 27,518 | 29,219 | 29,309 | 18,383 |
| LATIMER | 16,153 | 3,712 | 20.2 | 23.4 | 33.4 | 19.0 | 2.8 | 1.2 | 29,246 | 26,446 | 33,521 | 34,819 | 32,872 | 20,995 |
| LE FLORE | 13,328 | 17,404 | 23.9 | 19.4 | 35.0 | 18.7 | 2.5 | 0.5 | 27,771 | 24,947 | 34,448 | 34,447 | 28,568 | 19,415 |
| LINCOLN | 14,972 | 11,823 | 22.9 | 15.6 | 36.0 | 21.3 | 3.4 | 0.8 | 29,953 | 26,981 | 36,135 | 37,872 | 31,239 | 20,232 |
| LOGAN | 19,624 | 10,842 | 15.8 | 14.0 | 33.1 | 27.7 | 6.2 | 3.2 | 38,888 | 30,962 | 47,878 | 46,946 | 40,231 | 24,301 |
| LOVE | 13,067 | 3,301 | 26.3 | 18.6 | 37.7 | 14.5 | 1.8 | 1.1 | 26,807 | 23,768 | 30,454 | 32,522 | 30,648 | 19,250 |
| MCCLAIN | 15,891 | 9,888 | 18.9 | 14.6 | 36.6 | 24.0 | 5.0 | 1.1 | 32,964 | 29,100 | 37,631 | 41,680 | 37,524 | 20,246 |
| MCCURTAIN | 14,128 | 12,905 | 27.3 | 19.7 | 31.7 | 17.1 | 3.1 | 1.2 | 27,916 | 24,143 | 33,876 | 35,164 | 27,863 | 19,885 |
| MCINTOSH | 15,489 | 7,926 | 23.5 | 22.6 | 34.0 | 16.2 | 2.6 | 1.1 | 27,724 | 23,709 | 31,206 | 33,656 | 30,645 | 23,337 |
| MAJOR | 14,908 | 3,068 | 22.2 | 15.4 | 40.9 | 18.5 | 2.4 | 0.6 | 28,597 | 26,230 | 34,122 | 36,934 | 26,611 | 22,145 |
| MARSHALL | 16,818 | 5,132 | 27.0 | 20.5 | 32.0 | 14.4 | 3.6 | 2.5 | 29,668 | 27,408 | 38,154 | 37,130 | 28,747 | 19,926 |
| MAYES | 15,903 | 14,753 | 19.0 | 18.6 | 36.9 | 19.4 | 4.1 | 2.0 | 32,206 | 27,108 | 34,481 | 44,405 | 33,461 | 23,092 |
| MURRAY | 14,079 | 4,791 | 28.3 | 18.6 | 37.8 | 12.4 | 2.0 | 0.8 | 25,726 | 21,984 | 27,723 | 32,938 | 29,448 | 19,000 |
| MUSKOGEE | 14,964 | 26,042 | 25.4 | 16.0 | 32.8 | 21.2 | 3.4 | 1.1 | 29,934 | 25,004 | 35,303 | 38,049 | 31,894 | 22,558 |
| NOBLE | 15,876 | 4,426 | 19.6 | 17.2 | 37.5 | 20.5 | 3.7 | 1.5 | 31,263 | 28,411 | 39,483 | 37,984 | 33,090 | 20,279 |
| NOWATA | 12,688 | 4,043 | 27.8 | 22.6 | 33.3 | 14.4 | 1.7 | 0.3 | 24,962 | 23,070 | 28,007 | 31,948 | 29,346 | 17,664 |
| OKFUSKEE | 15,700 | 4,131 | 31.0 | 21.5 | 28.7 | 12.4 | 3.3 | 3.1 | 29,307 | 21,418 | 25,685 | 39,395 | 35,121 | 22,689 |
| OKLAHOMA | 19,089 | 253,479 | 17.0 | 16.5 | 34.7 | 25.3 | 4.6 | 2.0 | 34,719 | 27,492 | 39,073 | 43,161 | 39,773 | 26,014 |
| OKMULGEE | 12,948 | 15,203 | 29.6 | 18.7 | 34.8 | 14.1 | 2.2 | 0.7 | 25,756 | 21,871 | 31,389 | 32,483 | 27,493 | 19,355 |
| OSAGE | 16,613 | 15,965 | 19.5 | 14.0 | 35.7 | 25.8 | 3.7 | 1.3 | 33,022 | 28,307 | 36,930 | 41,259 | 39,725 | 20,579 |
| OTTAWA | 13,237 | 12,589 | 27.4 | 20.7 | 34.6 | 15.0 | 1.7 | 0.6 | 25,604 | 22,816 | 29,200 | 33,742 | 28,706 | 18,424 |
| PAWNEE | 14,971 | 6,491 | 22.9 | 17.5 | 35.8 | 20.2 | 2.7 | 0.8 | 29,320 | 25,917 | 32,660 | 37,112 | 33,557 | 20,624 |
| PAYNE | 17,083 | 25,292 | 26.1 | 16.3 | 31.8 | 20.2 | 4.1 | 1.6 | 30,672 | 21,127 | 39,913 | 44,961 | 39,077 | 25,955 |
| PITTSBURG | 14,582 | 16,496 | 24.2 | 19.9 | 35.2 | 16.4 | 2.7 | 1.6 | 28,772 | 25,011 | 34,093 | 35,657 | 31,195 | 21,203 |
| PONTOTOC | 14,459 | 13,587 | 29.7 | 18.4 | 31.2 | 16.3 | 3.2 | 1.1 | 27,393 | 22,467 | 32,833 | 35,314 | 32,840 | 18,611 |
| POTTAWATOMIE | 15,332 | 23,389 | 21.8 | 16.1 | 35.0 | 22.8 | 3.2 | 1.1 | 30,950 | 26,419 | 36,815 | 41,745 | 32,091 | 20,925 |
| PUSHMATAHA | 13,035 | 4,671 | 31.0 | 25.4 | 27.4 | 13.1 | 2.2 | 0.9 | 24,615 | 21,846 | 28,879 | 28,855 | 29,297 | 17,655 |
| ROGER MILLS | 12,931 | 1,353 | 25.9 | 24.8 | 30.5 | 15.4 | 2.1 | 1.3 | 27,049 | 25,947 | 26,891 | 28,555 | 35,673 | 22,389 |
| ROGERS | 18,891 | 26,282 | 12.0 | 11.8 | 34.2 | 33.6 | 6.7 | 1.7 | 39,107 | 34,052 | 44,193 | 47,783 | 42,288 | 24,902 |
| SEMINOLE | 14,407 | 9,408 | 30.3 | 18.9 | 34.0 | 13.5 | 2.5 | 0.9 | 25,754 | 22,796 | 28,998 | 33,179 | 27,556 | 20,067 |
| SEQUOYAH | 14,057 | 14,165 | 25.8 | 18.4 | 34.8 | 17.9 | 2.3 | 0.7 | 27,742 | 24,967 | 33,232 | 34,419 | 28,406 | 18,860 |
| STEPHENS | 15,845 | 17,353 | 24.1 | 14.6 | 35.4 | 21.5 | 3.5 | 1.0 | 30,301 | 26,063 | 36,301 | 38,679 | 33,976 | 22,296 |
| TEXAS | 17,346 | 7,540 | 16.1 | 17.9 | 36.7 | 24.9 | 3.7 | 0.7 | 32,411 | 26,467 | 36,728 | 40,061 | 37,361 | 22,702 |
| TILLMAN | 10,565 | 3,554 | 35.1 | 20.8 | 33.8 | 9.0 | 0.5 | 0.8 | 22,105 | 19,349 | 27,723 | 29,063 | 21,635 | 16,372 |
| TULSA | 21,491 | 225,015 | 16.3 | 15.1 | 33.5 | 26.3 | 5.9 | 2.9 | 37,658 | 29,287 | 42,133 | 45,822 | 42,114 | 27,402 |
| WAGONER | 17,648 | 20,409 | 15.0 | 13.9 | 34.6 | 30.0 | 4.9 | 1.7 | 36,476 | 31,085 | 42,195 | 45,250 | 38,349 | 20,311 |
| WASHINGTON | 21,368 | 19,086 | 15.9 | 15.2 | 31.5 | 28.5 | 6.4 | 2.5 | 37,594 | 28,115 | 43,330 | 47,927 | 41,290 | 29,905 |
| WASHITA | 12,756 | 4,622 | 29.3 | 21.8 | 30.8 | 14.8 | 3.1 | 0.3 | 25,295 | 22,146 | 30,713 | 30,395 | 29,572 | 19,059 |
| WOODS | 18,280 | 3,488 | 27.0 | 18.9 | 30.7 | 17.1 | 3.3 | 3.1 | 31,446 | 22,949 | 37,848 | 35,405 | 37,920 | 26,147 |
| WOODWARD | 15,545 | 6,965 | 16.5 | 17.9 | 38.7 | 22.2 | 3.7 | 0.9 | 31,740 | 26,203 | 34,888 | 39,078 | 38,558 | 24,308 |
| OKLAHOMA | 17,482 | | 19.8 | 16.6 | 34.3 | 23.3 | 4.3 | 1.7 | 33,043 | 26,989 | 38,466 | 41,397 | 36,423 | 23,614 |
| UNITED STATES | 22,162 | | 14.5 | 12.5 | 32.3 | 29.8 | 7.4 | 3.5 | 40,748 | 34,503 | 44,969 | 49,579 | 43,409 | 27,339 |

| COUNTY | FINANCIAL SERVICES | | | | THE HOME | | | | | | ENTERTAINMENT | | | | | | PERSONAL | | | |
|---|---|---|---|---|---|---|---|---|---|---|---|---|---|---|---|---|---|---|---|---|
| | | | | | Home Improvements | | | Furnishings | | | | | | | | | | | | |
| | Auto Loan | Home Loan | Investments | Retirement Plans | Home Repair | Lawn & Garden | Remodeling | Appliances | Electronics | Furniture | Restaurants | Sporting Goods | Theater & Concerts | Toys & Hobbies | Travel | Video Rental | Apparel | Auto Aftermarket | Health Insurance | Pets & Supplies |
| ADAIR | 96 | 67 | 70 | 74 | 94 | 90 | 109 | 95 | 90 | 78 | 78 | 94 | 80 | 93 | 69 | 95 | 79 | 87 | 100 | 96 |
| ALFALFA | 97 | 65 | 73 | 78 | 91 | 91 | 112 | 95 | 90 | 73 | 78 | 94 | 78 | 95 | 69 | 97 | 79 | 88 | 104 | 96 |
| ATOKA | 96 | 66 | 73 | 75 | 93 | 90 | 109 | 95 | 91 | 77 | 78 | 92 | 79 | 93 | 69 | 96 | 79 | 87 | 99 | 96 |
| BEAVER | 97 | 70 | 78 | 80 | 92 | 91 | 113 | 95 | 92 | 78 | 82 | 95 | 81 | 96 | 70 | 97 | 82 | 89 | 102 | 98 |
| BECKHAM | 96 | 71 | 78 | 79 | 92 | 91 | 111 | 95 | 92 | 79 | 82 | 92 | 81 | 95 | 71 | 97 | 82 | 89 | 101 | 97 |
| BLAINE | 97 | 65 | 73 | 77 | 92 | 91 | 112 | 95 | 91 | 74 | 78 | 94 | 78 | 94 | 68 | 97 | 79 | 88 | 103 | 96 |
| BRYAN | 96 | 74 | 81 | 80 | 94 | 91 | 108 | 95 | 92 | 81 | 83 | 92 | 83 | 95 | 73 | 96 | 82 | 89 | 100 | 97 |
| CADDO | 95 | 67 | 75 | 77 | 92 | 90 | 109 | 95 | 91 | 77 | 78 | 91 | 79 | 93 | 70 | 97 | 80 | 88 | 100 | 95 |
| CANADIAN | 100 | 99 | 92 | 96 | 98 | 98 | 102 | 99 | 101 | 100 | 103 | 101 | 98 | 102 | 85 | 100 | 101 | 101 | 98 | 102 |
| CARTER | 97 | 81 | 93 | 88 | 98 | 96 | 108 | 96 | 95 | 88 | 88 | 95 | 89 | 97 | 79 | 97 | 89 | 93 | 100 | 98 |
| CHEROKEE | 96 | 75 | 78 | 79 | 93 | 90 | 109 | 94 | 91 | 80 | 83 | 92 | 82 | 94 | 72 | 95 | 82 | 89 | 100 | 97 |
| CHOCTAW | 95 | 63 | 70 | 73 | 92 | 89 | 107 | 94 | 90 | 75 | 76 | 91 | 77 | 91 | 68 | 96 | 78 | 86 | 100 | 94 |
| CIMARRON | 96 | 66 | 76 | 78 | 92 | 91 | 112 | 95 | 91 | 75 | 79 | 93 | 79 | 94 | 69 | 97 | 80 | 88 | 103 | 96 |
| CLEVELAND | 99 | 101 | 91 | 95 | 97 | 96 | 99 | 97 | 99 | 98 | 102 | 99 | 95 | 100 | 84 | 98 | 99 | 99 | 96 | 101 |
| COAL | 96 | 67 | 74 | 76 | 93 | 91 | 110 | 94 | 90 | 76 | 79 | 92 | 79 | 93 | 70 | 96 | 79 | 87 | 102 | 95 |
| COMANCHE | 95 | 92 | 87 | 87 | 96 | 93 | 96 | 95 | 95 | 91 | 94 | 94 | 91 | 95 | 81 | 97 | 91 | 95 | 95 | 98 |
| COTTON | 96 | 66 | 74 | 76 | 92 | 91 | 110 | 94 | 92 | 76 | 79 | 91 | 79 | 93 | 69 | 97 | 79 | 87 | 102 | 95 |
| CRAIG | 96 | 68 | 76 | 78 | 93 | 91 | 110 | 94 | 91 | 77 | 80 | 92 | 80 | 94 | 70 | 97 | 80 | 88 | 102 | 96 |
| CREEK | 98 | 75 | 82 | 82 | 95 | 92 | 113 | 96 | 93 | 83 | 85 | 95 | 85 | 97 | 73 | 97 | 85 | 91 | 101 | 99 |
| CUSTER | 96 | 82 | 83 | 84 | 94 | 91 | 105 | 94 | 93 | 84 | 87 | 93 | 85 | 95 | 75 | 96 | 86 | 91 | 98 | 97 |
| DELAWARE | 98 | 73 | 96 | 86 | 98 | 101 | 111 | 98 | 91 | 81 | 84 | 96 | 86 | 97 | 78 | 96 | 83 | 90 | 107 | 99 |
| DEWEY | 96 | 63 | 72 | 76 | 91 | 91 | 109 | 94 | 90 | 73 | 77 | 92 | 77 | 93 | 68 | 97 | 78 | 87 | 103 | 95 |
| ELLIS | 97 | 67 | 76 | 79 | 92 | 91 | 112 | 95 | 91 | 76 | 80 | 93 | 80 | 95 | 70 | 97 | 81 | 88 | 103 | 97 |
| GARFIELD | 97 | 85 | 91 | 88 | 98 | 96 | 103 | 96 | 94 | 89 | 91 | 94 | 90 | 97 | 81 | 97 | 89 | 93 | 100 | 98 |
| GARVIN | 95 | 68 | 76 | 77 | 93 | 91 | 109 | 94 | 92 | 78 | 80 | 90 | 80 | 93 | 70 | 97 | 80 | 88 | 102 | 95 |
| GRADY | 97 | 79 | 83 | 84 | 95 | 92 | 108 | 96 | 95 | 86 | 87 | 94 | 87 | 97 | 75 | 98 | 87 | 92 | 99 | 98 |
| GRANT | 96 | 67 | 76 | 78 | 92 | 91 | 110 | 94 | 91 | 75 | 79 | 92 | 79 | 93 | 70 | 97 | 80 | 88 | 103 | 96 |
| GREER | 94 | 64 | 73 | 74 | 92 | 91 | 107 | 93 | 91 | 74 | 77 | 87 | 76 | 90 | 69 | 96 | 77 | 86 | 102 | 93 |
| HARMON | 93 | 71 | 75 | 75 | 95 | 91 | 103 | 93 | 88 | 79 | 79 | 89 | 80 | 90 | 74 | 94 | 79 | 87 | 99 | 94 |
| HARPER | 95 | 65 | 74 | 76 | 92 | 91 | 109 | 94 | 91 | 75 | 78 | 90 | 78 | 92 | 69 | 97 | 79 | 87 | 103 | 95 |
| HASKELL | 96 | 65 | 73 | 75 | 92 | 91 | 111 | 94 | 92 | 76 | 78 | 92 | 78 | 93 | 68 | 96 | 79 | 87 | 102 | 95 |
| HUGHES | 93 | 63 | 72 | 73 | 92 | 90 | 106 | 93 | 91 | 75 | 76 | 87 | 76 | 90 | 69 | 96 | 77 | 86 | 101 | 93 |
| JACKSON | 94 | 88 | 86 | 85 | 95 | 92 | 99 | 94 | 94 | 87 | 91 | 93 | 88 | 94 | 79 | 97 | 88 | 93 | 96 | 98 |
| JEFFERSON | 94 | 64 | 73 | 74 | 92 | 91 | 108 | 93 | 91 | 75 | 77 | 88 | 77 | 91 | 69 | 97 | 78 | 86 | 102 | 93 |
| JOHNSTON | 96 | 64 | 70 | 74 | 92 | 90 | 109 | 94 | 91 | 75 | 77 | 93 | 78 | 93 | 68 | 95 | 78 | 86 | 102 | 95 |
| KAY | 96 | 84 | 93 | 87 | 99 | 97 | 103 | 96 | 94 | 89 | 90 | 94 | 90 | 97 | 81 | 97 | 89 | 93 | 101 | 97 |
| KINGFISHER | 98 | 74 | 82 | 82 | 94 | 92 | 112 | 96 | 93 | 81 | 85 | 95 | 84 | 98 | 72 | 98 | 84 | 90 | 102 | 99 |
| KIOWA | 93 | 68 | 75 | 76 | 93 | 91 | 106 | 93 | 90 | 77 | 79 | 88 | 79 | 91 | 71 | 96 | 79 | 87 | 101 | 94 |
| LATIMER | 95 | 71 | 78 | 77 | 94 | 91 | 110 | 94 | 92 | 80 | 81 | 90 | 81 | 93 | 72 | 96 | 81 | 88 | 100 | 95 |
| LE FLORE | 97 | 70 | 76 | 78 | 93 | 91 | 111 | 95 | 93 | 79 | 81 | 94 | 82 | 95 | 70 | 96 | 81 | 88 | 101 | 97 |
| LINCOLN | 97 | 71 | 78 | 79 | 93 | 91 | 112 | 95 | 93 | 80 | 83 | 93 | 82 | 95 | 71 | 97 | 82 | 89 | 101 | 97 |
| LOGAN | 98 | 85 | 86 | 88 | 95 | 93 | 107 | 96 | 97 | 89 | 91 | 96 | 89 | 98 | 77 | 98 | 90 | 95 | 99 | 99 |
| LOVE | 96 | 68 | 76 | 77 | 93 | 91 | 112 | 95 | 92 | 78 | 80 | 92 | 80 | 94 | 70 | 97 | 81 | 88 | 101 | 96 |
| MCCLAIN | 98 | 77 | 85 | 84 | 95 | 93 | 113 | 97 | 95 | 85 | 87 | 95 | 86 | 98 | 74 | 98 | 87 | 92 | 101 | 99 |
| MCCURTAIN | 96 | 68 | 73 | 75 | 94 | 90 | 109 | 95 | 91 | 79 | 78 | 93 | 80 | 93 | 70 | 95 | 80 | 87 | 99 | 96 |
| MCINTOSH | 97 | 69 | 82 | 80 | 94 | 94 | 113 | 96 | 91 | 77 | 80 | 93 | 81 | 95 | 72 | 97 | 80 | 88 | 104 | 97 |
| MAJOR | 97 | 65 | 74 | 78 | 92 | 91 | 111 | 95 | 91 | 74 | 79 | 94 | 78 | 95 | 69 | 97 | 79 | 88 | 104 | 96 |
| MARSHALL | 97 | 66 | 72 | 78 | 92 | 91 | 115 | 96 | 91 | 75 | 78 | 94 | 79 | 95 | 69 | 97 | 79 | 88 | 103 | 97 |
| MAYES | 98 | 72 | 82 | 81 | 95 | 93 | 113 | 97 | 93 | 81 | 83 | 96 | 84 | 97 | 72 | 97 | 83 | 90 | 102 | 99 |
| MURRAY | 96 | 71 | 79 | 80 | 94 | 91 | 112 | 95 | 92 | 80 | 82 | 92 | 82 | 95 | 72 | 97 | 83 | 89 | 101 | 97 |
| MUSKOGEE | 97 | 81 | 88 | 86 | 97 | 94 | 106 | 96 | 94 | 87 | 88 | 95 | 88 | 97 | 78 | 97 | 88 | 92 | 99 | 98 |
| NOBLE | 98 | 73 | 80 | 81 | 94 | 92 | 114 | 96 | 93 | 81 | 84 | 95 | 83 | 97 | 72 | 98 | 84 | 90 | 102 | 99 |
| NOWATA | 95 | 65 | 72 | 74 | 92 | 91 | 110 | 94 | 91 | 76 | 78 | 91 | 78 | 92 | 68 | 96 | 78 | 87 | 102 | 95 |
| OKFUSKEE | 93 | 67 | 71 | 72 | 94 | 90 | 105 | 94 | 90 | 78 | 77 | 89 | 79 | 90 | 71 | 94 | 78 | 86 | 99 | 93 |
| OKLAHOMA | 97 | 98 | 99 | 96 | 102 | 100 | 98 | 97 | 96 | 98 | 99 | 98 | 97 | 99 | 88 | 98 | 97 | 98 | 97 | 99 |
| OKMULGEE | 95 | 70 | 78 | 78 | 94 | 91 | 109 | 94 | 91 | 79 | 80 | 91 | 81 | 93 | 72 | 96 | 81 | 88 | 100 | 95 |
| OSAGE | 98 | 79 | 86 | 86 | 95 | 94 | 111 | 97 | 95 | 86 | 87 | 96 | 87 | 98 | 75 | 98 | 88 | 92 | 101 | 99 |
| OTTAWA | 97 | 78 | 93 | 87 | 98 | 97 | 108 | 96 | 93 | 85 | 86 | 94 | 88 | 96 | 78 | 97 | 86 | 91 | 102 | 97 |
| PAWNEE | 97 | 71 | 78 | 80 | 93 | 91 | 112 | 95 | 93 | 80 | 83 | 94 | 82 | 96 | 71 | 97 | 83 | 89 | 102 | 98 |
| PAYNE | 96 | 89 | 92 | 89 | 96 | 93 | 104 | 93 | 92 | 85 | 90 | 92 | 87 | 95 | 79 | 95 | 88 | 92 | 98 | 97 |
| PITTSBURG | 97 | 75 | 89 | 84 | 96 | 95 | 110 | 96 | 93 | 83 | 85 | 93 | 86 | 96 | 76 | 97 | 85 | 90 | 102 | 98 |
| PONTOTOC | 97 | 81 | 88 | 86 | 97 | 94 | 108 | 96 | 93 | 86 | 87 | 95 | 87 | 97 | 78 | 96 | 87 | 92 | 99 | 99 |
| POTTAWATOMIE | 96 | 80 | 86 | 84 | 97 | 93 | 108 | 96 | 93 | 86 | 87 | 94 | 87 | 96 | 77 | 97 | 87 | 91 | 99 | 98 |
| PUSHMATAHA | 94 | 66 | 73 | 75 | 92 | 91 | 108 | 94 | 91 | 76 | 78 | 90 | 78 | 92 | 69 | 96 | 78 | 87 | 102 | 94 |
| ROGER MILLS | 98 | 64 | 72 | 79 | 91 | 91 | 112 | 95 | 90 | 71 | 78 | 96 | 78 | 96 | 68 | 97 | 79 | 88 | 105 | 98 |
| ROGERS | 100 | 89 | 91 | 92 | 98 | 96 | 110 | 99 | 99 | 93 | 96 | 100 | 94 | 102 | 80 | 100 | 95 | 97 | 100 | 102 |
| SEMINOLE | 95 | 68 | 77 | 77 | 93 | 91 | 109 | 94 | 91 | 78 | 80 | 91 | 80 | 93 | 71 | 96 | 80 | 88 | 101 | 95 |
| SEQUOYAH | 97 | 72 | 78 | 79 | 95 | 92 | 111 | 96 | 92 | 82 | 82 | 95 | 83 | 96 | 72 | 96 | 82 | 89 | 100 | 98 |
| STEPHENS | 98 | 81 | 93 | 88 | 98 | 97 | 107 | 97 | 95 | 87 | 89 | 95 | 90 | 98 | 79 | 98 | 89 | 93 | 102 | 98 |
| TEXAS | 98 | 79 | 85 | 85 | 94 | 92 | 111 | 95 | 93 | 83 | 87 | 96 | 86 | 98 | 74 | 97 | 86 | 92 | 101 | 99 |
| TILLMAN | 93 | 67 | 74 | 73 | 94 | 90 | 104 | 93 | 89 | 78 | 78 | 87 | 79 | 89 | 72 | 95 | 78 | 86 | 100 | 93 |
| TULSA | 99 | 101 | 100 | 98 | 102 | 101 | 99 | 98 | 98 | 99 | 101 | 99 | 98 | 100 | 89 | 98 | 100 | 100 | 98 | 100 |
| WAGONER | 100 | 88 | 90 | 92 | 97 | 96 | 110 | 99 | 98 | 93 | 95 | 100 | 93 | 101 | 80 | 99 | 94 | 97 | 100 | 102 |
| WASHINGTON | 101 | 95 | 107 | 101 | 104 | 104 | 109 | 100 | 100 | 98 | 99 | 100 | 100 | 102 | 89 | 99 | 100 | 99 | 102 | 102 |
| WASHITA | 97 | 70 | 80 | 81 | 93 | 93 | 109 | 95 | 92 | 78 | 82 | 94 | 82 | 95 | 72 | 97 | 82 | 89 | 103 | 97 |
| WOODS | 97 | 80 | 95 | 90 | 97 | 97 | 105 | 95 | 93 | 84 | 87 | 95 | 88 | 96 | 79 | 97 | 87 | 92 | 103 | 97 |
| WOODWARD | 97 | 82 | 86 | 85 | 95 | 94 | 106 | 96 | 95 | 87 | 89 | 95 | 88 | 97 | 77 | 98 | 88 | 93 | 101 | 99 |
| OKLAHOMA | 97 | 88 | 92 | 90 | 98 | 96 | 104 | 97 | 95 | 91 | 93 | 96 | 92 | 98 | 81 | 98 | 92 | 95 | 99 | 99 |
| UNITED STATES | 100 | 100 | 100 | 100 | 100 | 100 | 100 | 100 | 100 | 100 | 100 | 100 | 100 | 100 | 100 | 100 | 100 | 100 | 100 | 100 |

| COUNTY | FIPS Code | MSA Code | DMA Code | POPULATION 1990 | POPULATION 2000 | POPULATION 2005 | 1990-2000 ANNUAL CHANGE % Rate | 1990-2000 ANNUAL CHANGE State Rank | RACE (%) White 1990 | White 2000 | Black 1990 | Black 2000 | Asian/Pacific 1990 | Asian/Pacific 2000 |
|---|---|---|---|---|---|---|---|---|---|---|---|---|---|---|
| BAKER | 001 | 0000 | 820 | 15,317 | 16,206 | 15,945 | 0.6 | 28 | 98.1 | 97.8 | 0.2 | 0.2 | 0.3 | 0.4 |
| BENTON | 003 | 1890 | 801 | 70,811 | 77,187 | 77,073 | 0.8 | 25 | 92.0 | 90.1 | 0.9 | 1.0 | 5.5 | 6.7 |
| CLACKAMAS | 005 | 6440 | 820 | 278,850 | 342,786 | 365,541 | 2.0 | 10 | 96.3 | 95.1 | 0.4 | 0.4 | 1.7 | 2.4 |
| CLATSOP | 007 | 0000 | 820 | 33,301 | 35,357 | 35,466 | 0.6 | 28 | 96.4 | 95.4 | 0.3 | 0.4 | 1.3 | 1.9 |
| COLUMBIA | 009 | 6440 | 820 | 37,557 | 46,248 | 50,685 | 2.1 | 8 | 97.3 | 96.6 | 0.1 | 0.1 | 0.8 | 1.1 |
| COOS | 011 | 0000 | 801 | 60,273 | 61,331 | 59,662 | 0.2 | 33 | 95.9 | 95.2 | 0.2 | 0.3 | 1.0 | 1.3 |
| CROOK | 013 | 0000 | 820 | 14,111 | 18,047 | 19,862 | 2.4 | 6 | 96.6 | 95.7 | 0.1 | 0.1 | 0.3 | 0.5 |
| CURRY | 015 | 0000 | 813 | 19,327 | 21,229 | 21,565 | 0.9 | 22 | 96.4 | 96.1 | 0.2 | 0.2 | 0.6 | 0.8 |
| DESCHUTES | 017 | 0000 | 821 | 74,958 | 115,342 | 137,164 | 4.3 | 1 | 97.8 | 97.2 | 0.1 | 0.1 | 0.6 | 0.8 |
| DOUGLAS | 019 | 0000 | 801 | 94,649 | 102,070 | 103,460 | 0.7 | 27 | 96.9 | 96.3 | 0.2 | 0.2 | 0.7 | 1.0 |
| GILLIAM | 021 | 0000 | 820 | 1,717 | 2,118 | 2,349 | 2.1 | 8 | 98.6 | 98.2 | 0.0 | 0.0 | 0.5 | 0.8 |
| GRANT | 023 | 0000 | 757 | 7,853 | 7,781 | 7,422 | -0.1 | 35 | 97.9 | 97.6 | 0.1 | 0.1 | 0.2 | 0.2 |
| HARNEY | 025 | 0000 | 820 | 7,060 | 7,383 | 7,822 | 0.4 | 31 | 94.8 | 94.5 | 0.0 | 0.0 | 0.6 | 0.7 |
| HOOD RIVER | 027 | 0000 | 820 | 16,903 | 20,202 | 21,705 | 1.8 | 14 | 90.8 | 87.3 | 0.3 | 0.4 | 1.8 | 2.4 |
| JACKSON | 029 | 4890 | 813 | 146,389 | 178,400 | 191,404 | 1.9 | 11 | 95.8 | 94.4 | 0.2 | 0.3 | 1.0 | 1.3 |
| JEFFERSON | 031 | 0000 | 820 | 13,676 | 17,064 | 18,057 | 2.2 | 7 | 74.2 | 73.6 | 0.2 | 0.2 | 0.5 | 0.6 |
| JOSEPHINE | 033 | 0000 | 813 | 62,649 | 75,811 | 80,367 | 1.9 | 11 | 97.0 | 96.3 | 0.2 | 0.2 | 0.7 | 1.0 |
| KLAMATH | 035 | 0000 | 813 | 57,702 | 63,869 | 65,959 | 1.0 | 20 | 92.2 | 90.7 | 0.7 | 0.8 | 0.8 | 1.0 |
| LAKE | 037 | 0000 | 813 | 7,186 | 7,151 | 7,043 | 0.0 | 34 | 95.0 | 94.0 | 0.1 | 0.1 | 0.6 | 0.8 |
| LANE | 039 | 2400 | 801 | 282,912 | 317,460 | 329,798 | 1.1 | 19 | 95.4 | 94.3 | 0.7 | 0.8 | 2.0 | 2.5 |
| LINCOLN | 041 | 0000 | 820 | 38,889 | 45,092 | 45,097 | 1.5 | 15 | 96.1 | 95.6 | 0.2 | 0.2 | 0.9 | 1.2 |
| LINN | 043 | 0000 | 820 | 91,227 | 106,417 | 111,884 | 1.5 | 15 | 96.9 | 95.9 | 0.2 | 0.2 | 0.9 | 1.3 |
| MALHEUR | 045 | 0000 | 757 | 26,038 | 28,480 | 28,703 | 0.9 | 22 | 81.6 | 74.6 | 0.2 | 0.4 | 3.1 | 4.0 |
| MARION | 047 | 7080 | 820 | 228,483 | 276,902 | 297,356 | 1.9 | 11 | 91.5 | 88.3 | 0.9 | 1.0 | 1.8 | 2.4 |
| MORROW | 049 | 0000 | 810 | 7,625 | 10,987 | 13,310 | 3.6 | 2 | 89.6 | 85.1 | 0.1 | 0.1 | 0.4 | 0.6 |
| MULTNOMAH | 051 | 6440 | 820 | 583,887 | 636,907 | 653,234 | 0.9 | 22 | 87.0 | 83.6 | 6.0 | 6.9 | 4.7 | 6.4 |
| POLK | 053 | 7080 | 820 | 49,541 | 63,684 | 69,978 | 2.5 | 5 | 93.3 | 91.2 | 0.4 | 0.4 | 1.4 | 1.7 |
| SHERMAN | 055 | 0000 | 820 | 1,918 | 1,773 | 1,709 | -0.8 | 36 | 97.2 | 96.3 | 0.0 | 0.0 | 0.7 | 0.8 |
| TILLAMOOK | 057 | 0000 | 820 | 21,570 | 24,551 | 25,209 | 1.3 | 17 | 97.4 | 96.9 | 0.2 | 0.2 | 0.8 | 1.0 |
| UMATILLA | 059 | 0000 | 810 | 59,249 | 67,750 | 72,629 | 1.3 | 17 | 89.0 | 85.3 | 0.6 | 0.7 | 0.9 | 1.2 |
| UNION | 061 | 0000 | 820 | 23,598 | 24,755 | 24,470 | 0.5 | 30 | 96.7 | 96.2 | 0.4 | 0.4 | 1.2 | 1.5 |
| WALLOWA | 063 | 0000 | 881 | 6,911 | 7,189 | 6,856 | 0.4 | 31 | 98.8 | 98.6 | 0.1 | 0.1 | 0.4 | 0.4 |
| WASCO | 065 | 0000 | 820 | 21,683 | 23,505 | 24,301 | 0.8 | 25 | 91.8 | 90.0 | 0.3 | 0.4 | 1.1 | 1.5 |
| WASHINGTON | 067 | 6440 | 820 | 311,554 | 418,377 | 464,060 | 2.9 | 3 | 91.9 | 88.9 | 0.7 | 0.7 | 4.3 | 5.9 |
| WHEELER | 069 | 0000 | 820 | 1,396 | 1,547 | 1,487 | 1.0 | 20 | 99.0 | 99.0 | 0.1 | 0.1 | 0.1 | 0.1 |
| YAMHILL | 071 | 6440 | 820 | 65,551 | 85,150 | 93,883 | 2.6 | 4 | 94.8 | 93.4 | 0.6 | 0.5 | 1.2 | 1.5 |
| OREGON | | | | | | | 1.6 | | 92.8 | 90.8 | 1.6 | 1.8 | 2.4 | 3.3 |
| UNITED STATES | | | | | | | 1.0 | | 80.3 | 77.9 | 12.1 | 12.4 | 2.9 | 3.9 |

# POPULATION COMPOSITION

| COUNTY | % HISPANIC ORIGIN | | 2000 AGE DISTRIBUTION (%) | | | | | | | | | | MEDIAN AGE | | 2000 Males/ Females (×100) |
|---|---|---|---|---|---|---|---|---|---|---|---|---|---|---|---|
| | 1990 | 2000 | 0-4 | 5-9 | 10-14 | 15-19 | 20-24 | 25-44 | 45-64 | 65-84 | 85+ | 18+ | 1990 | 2000 | |
| BAKER | 1.8 | 3.3 | 6.0 | 6.6 | 7.4 | 7.1 | 4.9 | 22.7 | 27.0 | 15.4 | 2.8 | 75.3 | 37.9 | 41.6 | 100.7 |
| BENTON | 2.5 | 4.2 | 5.6 | 5.7 | 6.0 | 10.2 | 13.8 | 27.9 | 21.0 | 8.6 | 1.2 | 79.0 | 29.3 | 31.6 | 102.5 |
| CLACKAMAS | 2.6 | 4.5 | 6.1 | 6.6 | 7.4 | 7.2 | 5.9 | 27.4 | 27.4 | 10.4 | 1.6 | 75.3 | 35.1 | 38.3 | 96.3 |
| CLATSOP | 1.9 | 3.7 | 6.3 | 6.6 | 7.1 | 7.9 | 6.6 | 24.7 | 25.9 | 13.0 | 2.0 | 75.1 | 35.9 | 38.9 | 100.8 |
| COLUMBIA | 1.8 | 3.4 | 6.8 | 7.3 | 7.8 | 7.5 | 6.4 | 25.4 | 26.8 | 10.7 | 1.4 | 73.2 | 34.8 | 37.4 | 100.0 |
| COOS | 2.2 | 4.0 | 5.8 | 6.2 | 6.9 | 7.0 | 5.3 | 24.2 | 26.8 | 15.6 | 2.1 | 76.5 | 37.6 | 41.2 | 99.0 |
| CROOK | 2.7 | 4.9 | 6.6 | 6.9 | 7.7 | 7.6 | 5.5 | 24.8 | 25.8 | 13.4 | 1.6 | 73.7 | 35.8 | 38.8 | 102.8 |
| CURRY | 1.8 | 3.2 | 5.0 | 5.2 | 6.0 | 5.5 | 4.1 | 20.3 | 28.1 | 23.6 | 2.4 | 80.2 | 44.0 | 47.7 | 99.3 |
| DESCHUTES | 2.0 | 3.8 | 6.2 | 6.5 | 7.4 | 7.1 | 5.5 | 27.6 | 26.8 | 11.6 | 1.3 | 75.5 | 35.9 | 38.9 | 100.2 |
| DOUGLAS | 2.4 | 4.1 | 6.4 | 6.6 | 7.4 | 7.5 | 5.6 | 24.4 | 26.0 | 14.2 | 1.9 | 74.8 | 36.0 | 39.6 | 99.2 |
| GILLIAM | 1.7 | 3.4 | 5.4 | 6.3 | 7.2 | 8.8 | 5.3 | 22.9 | 25.3 | 16.5 | 2.3 | 75.9 | 37.8 | 41.9 | 99.8 |
| GRANT | 1.9 | 3.4 | 6.2 | 6.7 | 7.6 | 7.4 | 4.8 | 24.6 | 27.6 | 13.2 | 2.1 | 74.6 | 36.4 | 40.4 | 102.4 |
| HARNEY | 3.1 | 5.5 | 6.6 | 6.9 | 7.8 | 7.3 | 4.9 | 24.7 | 27.2 | 12.6 | 1.8 | 73.5 | 35.7 | 39.5 | 102.8 |
| HOOD RIVER | 16.3 | 24.6 | 7.5 | 7.2 | 7.8 | 7.6 | 5.9 | 27.5 | 23.7 | 10.9 | 1.8 | 72.6 | 34.1 | 36.1 | 105.5 |
| JACKSON | 4.1 | 6.9 | 6.2 | 6.4 | 7.1 | 7.3 | 6.0 | 25.8 | 25.9 | 13.6 | 1.9 | 76.0 | 36.7 | 39.5 | 96.3 |
| JEFFERSON | 10.6 | 15.5 | 9.0 | 8.2 | 8.5 | 7.5 | 6.1 | 25.0 | 21.8 | 12.7 | 1.3 | 69.4 | 31.4 | 34.1 | 100.9 |
| JOSEPHINE | 2.8 | 5.0 | 5.8 | 6.1 | 6.9 | 6.9 | 5.0 | 23.0 | 27.5 | 16.5 | 2.3 | 76.7 | 39.9 | 42.5 | 96.3 |
| KLAMATH | 5.2 | 8.7 | 6.5 | 6.7 | 7.5 | 7.8 | 6.2 | 25.8 | 25.4 | 12.4 | 1.6 | 74.6 | 34.9 | 37.7 | 101.9 |
| LAKE | 3.8 | 6.3 | 6.7 | 6.9 | 8.1 | 7.1 | 4.8 | 23.6 | 27.0 | 13.9 | 1.9 | 73.0 | 36.3 | 40.2 | 101.3 |
| LANE | 2.4 | 4.3 | 6.1 | 6.2 | 6.6 | 7.8 | 8.3 | 28.1 | 24.2 | 11.1 | 1.7 | 77.0 | 33.9 | 36.6 | 95.2 |
| LINCOLN | 1.5 | 2.9 | 5.4 | 5.9 | 6.5 | 6.3 | 4.7 | 23.8 | 27.9 | 17.3 | 2.0 | 77.9 | 39.6 | 43.2 | 94.7 |
| LINN | 2.4 | 4.3 | 6.7 | 6.8 | 7.5 | 7.6 | 6.0 | 26.4 | 25.2 | 12.0 | 1.7 | 74.4 | 34.8 | 37.6 | 98.2 |
| MALHEUR | 19.8 | 28.6 | 8.1 | 8.0 | 8.5 | 8.7 | 5.9 | 23.4 | 23.1 | 12.4 | 1.9 | 70.1 | 33.7 | 34.8 | 98.0 |
| MARION | 8.0 | 13.0 | 7.0 | 7.1 | 7.4 | 7.7 | 6.8 | 28.2 | 22.5 | 11.3 | 2.0 | 73.9 | 33.7 | 35.6 | 99.5 |
| MORROW | 10.8 | 16.5 | 7.4 | 7.6 | 7.8 | 8.2 | 6.4 | 25.6 | 24.4 | 11.2 | 1.4 | 71.8 | 33.6 | 36.0 | 101.7 |
| MULTNOMAH | 3.1 | 5.8 | 6.5 | 6.2 | 6.6 | 6.8 | 7.1 | 31.6 | 23.5 | 10.0 | 1.8 | 76.9 | 34.2 | 36.5 | 96.6 |
| POLK | 5.7 | 9.0 | 6.3 | 6.6 | 7.4 | 8.3 | 8.0 | 24.6 | 23.5 | 13.3 | 2.1 | 75.3 | 34.2 | 37.0 | 94.7 |
| SHERMAN | 1.5 | 2.8 | 6.5 | 7.0 | 8.1 | 7.0 | 3.7 | 23.6 | 26.0 | 16.4 | 1.8 | 73.1 | 37.6 | 41.6 | 105.2 |
| TILLAMOOK | 1.7 | 3.1 | 5.5 | 5.9 | 6.8 | 6.4 | 4.5 | 22.3 | 27.7 | 18.7 | 2.2 | 77.5 | 40.4 | 44.0 | 98.9 |
| UMATILLA | 9.0 | 14.3 | 7.2 | 7.2 | 7.8 | 8.1 | 7.0 | 26.8 | 23.3 | 11.0 | 1.6 | 72.9 | 33.2 | 35.0 | 104.0 |
| UNION | 1.6 | 2.9 | 6.5 | 6.8 | 7.6 | 8.5 | 7.3 | 25.6 | 24.2 | 11.6 | 2.0 | 74.3 | 34.0 | 36.5 | 98.8 |
| WALLOWA | 1.6 | 3.2 | 5.6 | 6.7 | 7.3 | 7.6 | 5.4 | 21.6 | 27.9 | 15.6 | 2.3 | 75.1 | 37.8 | 42.2 | 99.0 |
| WASCO | 4.9 | 8.1 | 6.6 | 6.7 | 7.6 | 7.4 | 5.6 | 24.2 | 25.6 | 13.9 | 2.3 | 74.2 | 36.9 | 39.6 | 95.5 |
| WASHINGTON | 4.6 | 7.6 | 7.2 | 7.1 | 7.6 | 7.1 | 6.2 | 31.7 | 23.4 | 8.3 | 1.4 | 73.8 | 32.7 | 35.3 | 96.3 |
| WHEELER | 0.9 | 2.1 | 5.2 | 5.6 | 6.3 | 6.2 | 4.3 | 19.3 | 29.5 | 20.9 | 2.7 | 78.7 | 44.1 | 47.0 | 96.1 |
| YAMHILL | 6.3 | 10.1 | 7.3 | 7.5 | 7.8 | 8.7 | 7.1 | 27.1 | 22.5 | 10.3 | 1.7 | 72.5 | 32.8 | 34.6 | 100.0 |
| OREGON | 4.0 | 6.8 | 6.5 | 6.6 | 7.2 | 7.4 | 6.7 | 28.1 | 24.6 | 11.3 | 1.7 | 75.4 | 34.5 | 37.1 | 97.6 |
| UNITED STATES | 9.0 | 11.8 | 6.9 | 7.2 | 7.2 | 7.2 | 6.7 | 29.9 | 22.2 | 11.1 | 1.6 | 74.6 | 32.9 | 35.7 | 95.6 |

| COUNTY | HOUSEHOLDS 1990 | HOUSEHOLDS 2000 | HOUSEHOLDS 2005 | HOUSEHOLDS % Annual Rate 1990-2000 | HOUSEHOLDS 2000 Average HH Size | FAMILIES 1990 | FAMILIES 2000 | FAMILIES % Annual Rate 1990-2000 | MEDIAN HOUSEHOLD INCOME 2000 | MEDIAN HOUSEHOLD INCOME 2005 | MEDIAN HOUSEHOLD INCOME 2000 National Rank | MEDIAN HOUSEHOLD INCOME 2000 State Rank |
|---|---|---|---|---|---|---|---|---|---|---|---|---|
| BAKER | 6,118 | 6,681 | 6,658 | 1.1 | 2.38 | 4,307 | 4,564 | 0.7 | 32,003 | 39,200 | 1715 | 25 |
| BENTON | 26,126 | 29,859 | 30,242 | 1.6 | 2.40 | 16,353 | 18,001 | 1.2 | 42,211 | 48,684 | 493 | 5 |
| CLACKAMAS | 103,530 | 130,328 | 140,532 | 2.8 | 2.61 | 76,704 | 92,831 | 2.3 | 51,223 | 58,755 | 181 | 2 |
| CLATSOP | 13,374 | 14,321 | 14,415 | 0.8 | 2.41 | 8,918 | 9,162 | 0.3 | 35,115 | 40,962 | 1235 | 17 |
| COLUMBIA | 13,910 | 17,289 | 19,028 | 2.7 | 2.66 | 10,387 | 12,515 | 2.3 | 44,043 | 51,110 | 394 | 3 |
| COOS | 24,134 | 25,306 | 24,970 | 0.6 | 2.38 | 17,011 | 17,143 | 0.1 | 29,883 | 32,260 | 2169 | 31 |
| CROOK | 5,455 | 6,962 | 7,656 | 3.0 | 2.57 | 4,017 | 5,002 | 2.7 | 36,991 | 46,820 | 981 | 11 |
| CURRY | 8,311 | 9,311 | 9,547 | 1.4 | 2.26 | 5,892 | 6,361 | 0.9 | 30,885 | 33,936 | 1952 | 29 |
| DESCHUTES | 29,217 | 44,750 | 53,119 | 5.3 | 2.56 | 21,202 | 31,346 | 4.9 | 41,120 | 46,905 | 580 | 6 |
| DOUGLAS | 35,872 | 39,651 | 40,663 | 1.2 | 2.54 | 26,620 | 28,456 | 0.8 | 31,990 | 36,047 | 1717 | 26 |
| GILLIAM | 696 | 868 | 968 | 2.7 | 2.44 | 499 | 602 | 2.3 | 35,305 | 43,158 | 1200 | 15 |
| GRANT | 3,092 | 3,271 | 3,217 | 0.7 | 2.35 | 2,210 | 2,256 | 0.3 | 34,755 | 41,467 | 1287 | 18 |
| HARNEY | 2,760 | 2,946 | 3,151 | 0.8 | 2.49 | 1,990 | 2,042 | 0.3 | 26,278 | 30,330 | 2681 | 35 |
| HOOD RIVER | 6,425 | 7,690 | 8,268 | 2.2 | 2.59 | 4,592 | 5,280 | 1.7 | 36,419 | 44,455 | 1057 | 13 |
| JACKSON | 57,238 | 70,839 | 76,500 | 2.6 | 2.47 | 40,141 | 47,909 | 2.2 | 35,300 | 39,401 | 1201 | 16 |
| JEFFERSON | 4,744 | 5,957 | 6,314 | 2.8 | 2.83 | 3,659 | 4,481 | 2.5 | 34,428 | 41,814 | 1327 | 19 |
| JOSEPHINE | 25,081 | 31,275 | 33,625 | 2.7 | 2.39 | 17,880 | 21,563 | 2.3 | 29,380 | 32,811 | 2238 | 32 |
| KLAMATH | 22,341 | 25,296 | 26,408 | 1.5 | 2.49 | 15,777 | 17,354 | 1.2 | 33,417 | 39,157 | 1473 | 22 |
| LAKE | 2,765 | 2,761 | 2,725 | 0.0 | 2.56 | 2,063 | 1,994 | -0.4 | 31,727 | 36,920 | 1771 | 28 |
| LANE | 110,799 | 127,342 | 133,810 | 1.7 | 2.43 | 73,498 | 81,206 | 1.2 | 35,516 | 40,344 | 1167 | 14 |
| LINCOLN | 16,455 | 19,536 | 19,767 | 2.1 | 2.28 | 11,078 | 12,556 | 1.5 | 33,671 | 39,145 | 1439 | 21 |
| LINN | 34,716 | 41,213 | 43,682 | 2.1 | 2.56 | 25,345 | 28,996 | 1.6 | 37,437 | 42,703 | 906 | 10 |
| MALHEUR | 9,457 | 10,551 | 10,774 | 1.3 | 2.64 | 6,902 | 7,471 | 1.0 | 29,218 | 34,359 | 2262 | 33 |
| MARION | 83,494 | 102,674 | 110,720 | 2.5 | 2.59 | 58,409 | 69,560 | 2.1 | 40,370 | 47,941 | 640 | 7 |
| MORROW | 2,803 | 3,990 | 4,805 | 4.4 | 2.75 | 2,107 | 2,908 | 4.0 | 34,046 | 43,710 | 1383 | 20 |
| MULTNOMAH | 242,140 | 266,112 | 273,958 | 1.2 | 2.34 | 143,137 | 151,760 | 0.7 | 39,601 | 45,601 | 702 | 8 |
| POLK | 18,167 | 24,008 | 26,682 | 3.4 | 2.59 | 12,970 | 16,650 | 3.1 | 38,750 | 45,732 | 776 | 9 |
| SHERMAN | 784 | 738 | 717 | -0.7 | 2.40 | 561 | 510 | -1.1 | 30,153 | 36,042 | 2122 | 30 |
| TILLAMOOK | 8,846 | 10,257 | 10,622 | 1.8 | 2.35 | 6,144 | 6,861 | 1.3 | 33,349 | 40,236 | 1482 | 23 |
| UMATILLA | 22,020 | 25,192 | 27,014 | 1.6 | 2.61 | 15,598 | 17,251 | 1.2 | 32,410 | 37,902 | 1638 | 24 |
| UNION | 9,035 | 9,644 | 9,604 | 0.8 | 2.51 | 6,347 | 6,534 | 0.4 | 31,867 | 36,518 | 1743 | 27 |
| WALLOWA | 2,796 | 3,006 | 2,910 | 0.9 | 2.37 | 1,980 | 2,052 | 0.4 | 29,175 | 34,040 | 2270 | 34 |
| WASCO | 8,607 | 9,310 | 9,611 | 1.0 | 2.49 | 6,016 | 6,253 | 0.5 | 36,797 | 44,399 | 1003 | 12 |
| WASHINGTON | 118,997 | 161,438 | 179,839 | 3.8 | 2.57 | 83,098 | 108,636 | 3.3 | 52,008 | 60,415 | 170 | 1 |
| WHEELER | 584 | 665 | 647 | 1.6 | 2.31 | 416 | 457 | 1.1 | 21,893 | 28,355 | 3032 | 36 |
| YAMHILL | 22,424 | 29,919 | 33,363 | 3.6 | 2.73 | 17,016 | 22,047 | 3.2 | 43,891 | 53,399 | 402 | 4 |
| OREGON | | | | 2.2 | 2.49 | | | 1.8 | 39,843 | 46,114 | | |
| UNITED STATES | | | | 1.4 | 2.59 | | | 1.1 | 41,914 | 49,127 | | |

# INCOME

| COUNTY | 2000 Per Capita Income | 2000 HH Income Base | 2000 HOUSEHOLD INCOME DISTRIBUTION (%) Less than $15,000 | $15,000 to $24,999 | $25,000 to $49,999 | $50,000 to $99,999 | $100,000 to $149,999 | $150,000 or More | 2000 AVERAGE DISPOSABLE INCOME BY AGE OF HOUSEHOLDER All Ages | <35 | 35-44 | 45-54 | 55-64 | 65+ |
|---|---|---|---|---|---|---|---|---|---|---|---|---|---|---|
| BAKER | 16,191 | 6,681 | 19.0 | 17.5 | 39.4 | 20.2 | 3.3 | 0.7 | 28,113 | 25,430 | 32,167 | 36,725 | 28,262 | 20,533 |
| BENTON | 22,396 | 29,859 | 14.7 | 12.4 | 31.6 | 29.4 | 8.1 | 3.9 | 39,086 | 26,802 | 43,114 | 52,860 | 47,409 | 32,302 |
| CLACKAMAS | 26,262 | 130,328 | 7.5 | 9.3 | 31.7 | 36.5 | 10.3 | 4.8 | 45,093 | 37,220 | 49,137 | 54,410 | 47,879 | 29,080 |
| CLATSOP | 17,907 | 14,321 | 18.7 | 15.4 | 36.1 | 24.2 | 3.8 | 1.8 | 31,297 | 26,799 | 35,041 | 38,542 | 33,537 | 22,492 |
| COLUMBIA | 20,934 | 17,289 | 11.6 | 12.6 | 33.9 | 32.7 | 7.0 | 2.4 | 37,447 | 31,622 | 42,369 | 47,526 | 39,781 | 23,715 |
| COOS | 15,741 | 25,306 | 22.3 | 18.4 | 38.1 | 17.2 | 3.0 | 1.1 | 27,031 | 23,928 | 32,319 | 34,998 | 29,012 | 18,062 |
| CROOK | 16,476 | 6,962 | 13.2 | 15.7 | 39.6 | 27.6 | 3.7 | 0.2 | 31,135 | 31,996 | 37,302 | 36,136 | 31,349 | 20,777 |
| CURRY | 18,386 | 9,311 | 20.2 | 17.5 | 37.6 | 18.7 | 4.2 | 1.7 | 29,213 | 27,451 | 35,025 | 37,674 | 31,474 | 21,925 |
| DESCHUTES | 20,511 | 44,750 | 10.6 | 13.5 | 37.2 | 30.0 | 6.7 | 2.1 | 36,410 | 31,201 | 40,357 | 45,160 | 39,344 | 23,862 |
| DOUGLAS | 14,960 | 39,643 | 18.3 | 18.2 | 39.8 | 21.2 | 2.1 | 0.5 | 27,735 | 25,306 | 31,233 | 35,436 | 30,499 | 18,988 |
| GILLIAM | 17,600 | 868 | 14.8 | 17.7 | 40.7 | 22.1 | 3.1 | 1.6 | 30,653 | 28,887 | 34,379 | 36,168 | 36,433 | 22,883 |
| GRANT | 16,525 | 3,271 | 16.1 | 15.9 | 41.7 | 23.4 | 2.8 | 0.1 | 28,928 | 27,397 | 32,560 | 35,471 | 31,615 | 18,827 |
| HARNEY | 13,055 | 2,946 | 23.0 | 24.7 | 36.7 | 13.8 | 1.2 | 0.7 | 24,128 | 21,159 | 28,065 | 29,562 | 23,496 | 17,811 |
| HOOD RIVER | 17,094 | 7,689 | 14.8 | 15.3 | 37.8 | 26.1 | 5.0 | 1.1 | 32,011 | 26,660 | 37,975 | 39,659 | 33,985 | 22,997 |
| JACKSON | 18,135 | 70,839 | 17.7 | 15.2 | 37.4 | 24.4 | 4.0 | 1.2 | 31,022 | 26,296 | 35,632 | 39,169 | 33,419 | 21,998 |
| JEFFERSON | 14,644 | 5,957 | 16.3 | 16.8 | 38.4 | 23.7 | 4.1 | 0.8 | 30,216 | 27,325 | 33,666 | 38,935 | 31,854 | 22,943 |
| JOSEPHINE | 16,186 | 31,275 | 23.1 | 18.0 | 36.6 | 17.8 | 3.3 | 1.2 | 27,354 | 24,304 | 31,613 | 36,157 | 28,323 | 19,130 |
| KLAMATH | 16,421 | 25,296 | 19.0 | 16.3 | 37.9 | 22.6 | 3.3 | 0.9 | 29,400 | 25,256 | 33,876 | 38,012 | 31,578 | 20,043 |
| LAKE | 15,416 | 2,761 | 20.5 | 15.6 | 38.9 | 19.7 | 4.1 | 1.2 | 28,937 | 26,715 | 29,603 | 38,470 | 32,179 | 19,566 |
| LANE | 18,245 | 127,331 | 17.3 | 15.6 | 35.9 | 25.3 | 4.4 | 1.4 | 31,669 | 25,212 | 36,517 | 41,602 | 35,215 | 21,753 |
| LINCOLN | 18,919 | 19,536 | 16.4 | 18.0 | 37.2 | 22.6 | 4.2 | 1.6 | 30,602 | 28,107 | 34,983 | 38,132 | 32,159 | 22,480 |
| LINN | 17,687 | 41,213 | 14.7 | 14.3 | 38.4 | 27.3 | 4.4 | 1.0 | 32,147 | 28,401 | 37,426 | 41,145 | 34,682 | 20,877 |
| MALHEUR | 14,376 | 10,551 | 22.7 | 19.5 | 35.6 | 18.3 | 2.9 | 1.0 | 27,146 | 23,705 | 32,481 | 33,209 | 31,226 | 18,750 |
| MARION | 19,190 | 102,665 | 12.0 | 14.0 | 37.1 | 29.5 | 5.8 | 1.6 | 34,963 | 29,973 | 40,005 | 44,148 | 37,969 | 24,688 |
| MORROW | 14,458 | 3,990 | 16.8 | 15.3 | 40.2 | 24.9 | 2.7 | 0.2 | 29,165 | 26,214 | 32,500 | 35,915 | 31,190 | 20,852 |
| MULTNOMAH | 21,951 | 266,104 | 14.0 | 14.1 | 35.1 | 28.8 | 5.9 | 2.1 | 35,148 | 30,215 | 39,325 | 43,126 | 38,054 | 24,107 |
| POLK | 19,346 | 24,008 | 14.1 | 15.5 | 35.0 | 28.4 | 5.5 | 1.6 | 33,897 | 25,911 | 38,958 | 45,444 | 38,720 | 23,851 |
| SHERMAN | 17,184 | 738 | 24.1 | 17.2 | 36.9 | 16.3 | 3.9 | 1.6 | 27,597 | 22,969 | 30,683 | 33,966 | 31,258 | 22,080 |
| TILLAMOOK | 18,011 | 10,257 | 17.1 | 17.8 | 37.2 | 23.1 | 3.6 | 1.1 | 29,930 | 26,657 | 34,338 | 40,155 | 29,778 | 22,861 |
| UMATILLA | 15,695 | 25,192 | 18.3 | 18.3 | 37.5 | 22.0 | 3.1 | 0.8 | 28,861 | 25,066 | 33,974 | 36,292 | 30,915 | 19,782 |
| UNION | 15,073 | 9,644 | 21.1 | 16.6 | 38.0 | 20.7 | 2.9 | 0.7 | 27,990 | 22,750 | 33,585 | 36,976 | 32,294 | 17,882 |
| WALLOWA | 14,445 | 3,006 | 22.6 | 19.3 | 38.8 | 17.3 | 1.8 | 0.2 | 25,234 | 25,136 | 26,368 | 33,119 | 26,923 | 18,274 |
| WASCO | 18,948 | 9,310 | 16.6 | 14.2 | 35.7 | 27.3 | 4.6 | 1.6 | 32,590 | 25,537 | 37,280 | 42,925 | 37,023 | 23,428 |
| WASHINGTON | 26,115 | 161,438 | 6.3 | 9.0 | 32.1 | 38.3 | 10.5 | 3.9 | 44,419 | 37,680 | 48,124 | 54,069 | 47,601 | 28,741 |
| WHEELER | 13,639 | 665 | 34.1 | 22.0 | 29.9 | 11.3 | 2.0 | 0.8 | 22,102 | 19,441 | 24,857 | 29,586 | 22,964 | 17,333 |
| YAMHILL | 22,612 | 29,919 | 11.1 | 11.6 | 34.7 | 32.5 | 7.7 | 2.3 | 38,254 | 31,719 | 43,619 | 48,275 | 42,206 | 25,152 |
| OREGON | 20,754 | | 13.7 | 13.8 | 35.4 | 28.8 | 6.2 | 2.2 | 35,484 | 30,078 | 40,209 | 44,693 | 38,211 | 23,703 |
| UNITED STATES | 22,162 | | 14.5 | 12.5 | 32.3 | 29.8 | 7.4 | 3.5 | 40,748 | 34,503 | 44,969 | 49,579 | 43,409 | 27,339 |

| COUNTY | FINANCIAL SERVICES | | | | THE HOME | | | | | | ENTERTAINMENT | | | | | | PERSONAL | | | |
|---|---|---|---|---|---|---|---|---|---|---|---|---|---|---|---|---|---|---|---|---|
| | | | | | Home Improvements | | | Furnishings | | | | | | | | | | | | |
| | Auto Loan | Home Loan | Invest-ments | Retire-ment Plans | Home Repair | Lawn & Garden | Remodel-ing | Appli-ances | Elec-tronics | Furni-ture | Restau-rants | Sport-ing Goods | Theater & Concerts | Toys & Hobbies | Travel | Video Rental | Apparel | Auto After-market | Health Insur-ance | Pets & Supplies |
| BAKER | 97 | 70 | 78 | 81 | 94 | 93 | 111 | 98 | 94 | 80 | 81 | 88 | 78 | 89 | 74 | 92 | 81 | 88 | 102 | 91 |
| BENTON | 99 | 103 | 101 | 103 | 103 | 102 | 103 | 99 | 100 | 99 | 99 | 92 | 92 | 94 | 91 | 92 | 99 | 99 | 97 | 95 |
| CLACKAMAS | 102 | 104 | 102 | 105 | 104 | 106 | 107 | 104 | 105 | 106 | 106 | 97 | 99 | 98 | 94 | 95 | 105 | 102 | 100 | 97 |
| CLATSOP | 98 | 80 | 86 | 85 | 99 | 96 | 111 | 99 | 94 | 88 | 87 | 88 | 83 | 91 | 80 | 92 | 87 | 90 | 100 | 92 |
| COLUMBIA | 100 | 82 | 84 | 87 | 98 | 94 | 116 | 101 | 98 | 91 | 90 | 91 | 85 | 94 | 79 | 94 | 90 | 93 | 99 | 95 |
| COOS | 97 | 78 | 85 | 84 | 97 | 95 | 109 | 99 | 96 | 87 | 86 | 88 | 83 | 90 | 78 | 92 | 86 | 90 | 99 | 92 |
| CROOK | 99 | 74 | 78 | 83 | 94 | 92 | 116 | 99 | 96 | 85 | 85 | 91 | 80 | 92 | 74 | 93 | 85 | 90 | 100 | 94 |
| CURRY | 97 | 76 | 96 | 85 | 99 | 100 | 107 | 99 | 93 | 85 | 85 | 86 | 83 | 90 | 82 | 91 | 83 | 89 | 103 | 91 |
| DESCHUTES | 100 | 91 | 92 | 93 | 99 | 99 | 110 | 101 | 100 | 96 | 95 | 92 | 89 | 95 | 85 | 94 | 94 | 96 | 99 | 95 |
| DOUGLAS | 98 | 78 | 84 | 84 | 97 | 95 | 111 | 99 | 96 | 87 | 86 | 89 | 82 | 91 | 78 | 92 | 86 | 90 | 99 | 92 |
| GILLIAM | 101 | 70 | 75 | 85 | 93 | 93 | 118 | 100 | 94 | 78 | 82 | 95 | 79 | 95 | 72 | 94 | 84 | 90 | 104 | 95 |
| GRANT | 100 | 74 | 80 | 84 | 95 | 93 | 117 | 100 | 96 | 84 | 85 | 91 | 81 | 93 | 74 | 93 | 86 | 90 | 101 | 94 |
| HARNEY | 98 | 74 | 79 | 82 | 96 | 93 | 113 | 99 | 94 | 85 | 84 | 90 | 80 | 91 | 75 | 92 | 84 | 89 | 100 | 92 |
| HOOD RIVER | 97 | 81 | 85 | 84 | 96 | 94 | 110 | 99 | 96 | 88 | 88 | 88 | 83 | 91 | 78 | 92 | 86 | 91 | 98 | 92 |
| JACKSON | 99 | 89 | 94 | 92 | 101 | 99 | 107 | 100 | 98 | 94 | 93 | 91 | 88 | 93 | 85 | 93 | 92 | 94 | 99 | 94 |
| JEFFERSON | 97 | 81 | 89 | 84 | 97 | 96 | 109 | 99 | 95 | 90 | 87 | 89 | 83 | 91 | 80 | 92 | 86 | 91 | 98 | 92 |
| JOSEPHINE | 97 | 76 | 85 | 82 | 97 | 95 | 109 | 98 | 94 | 85 | 84 | 87 | 81 | 90 | 78 | 92 | 83 | 89 | 100 | 91 |
| KLAMATH | 98 | 83 | 86 | 89 | 98 | 96 | 110 | 100 | 97 | 91 | 89 | 91 | 86 | 92 | 81 | 93 | 89 | 92 | 98 | 93 |
| LAKE | 99 | 74 | 81 | 85 | 95 | 94 | 112 | 99 | 95 | 84 | 84 | 92 | 82 | 93 | 75 | 93 | 85 | 90 | 102 | 93 |
| LANE | 98 | 94 | 95 | 94 | 101 | 99 | 103 | 99 | 98 | 96 | 95 | 90 | 89 | 93 | 87 | 92 | 94 | 95 | 97 | 93 |
| LINCOLN | 99 | 83 | 95 | 91 | 100 | 102 | 112 | 101 | 96 | 90 | 90 | 91 | 86 | 93 | 84 | 93 | 89 | 92 | 103 | 94 |
| LINN | 98 | 82 | 87 | 86 | 98 | 95 | 109 | 99 | 96 | 89 | 88 | 89 | 84 | 92 | 80 | 92 | 88 | 91 | 99 | 93 |
| MALHEUR | 97 | 75 | 80 | 82 | 95 | 93 | 109 | 98 | 93 | 83 | 83 | 89 | 80 | 90 | 76 | 92 | 83 | 89 | 100 | 92 |
| MARION | 98 | 94 | 94 | 94 | 101 | 99 | 103 | 100 | 99 | 97 | 96 | 91 | 91 | 93 | 87 | 93 | 95 | 96 | 97 | 94 |
| MORROW | 98 | 76 | 77 | 83 | 93 | 92 | 115 | 99 | 95 | 85 | 86 | 91 | 80 | 92 | 74 | 93 | 85 | 90 | 99 | 93 |
| MULTNOMAH | 97 | 100 | 100 | 97 | 103 | 101 | 99 | 99 | 98 | 100 | 97 | 90 | 92 | 92 | 92 | 92 | 97 | 97 | 96 | 93 |
| POLK | 98 | 90 | 93 | 93 | 100 | 98 | 105 | 99 | 98 | 93 | 93 | 90 | 88 | 92 | 85 | 92 | 92 | 95 | 98 | 93 |
| SHERMAN | 100 | 66 | 73 | 83 | 92 | 92 | 117 | 99 | 92 | 74 | 78 | 93 | 76 | 93 | 70 | 93 | 81 | 88 | 104 | 93 |
| TILLAMOOK | 100 | 75 | 87 | 87 | 98 | 98 | 117 | 101 | 95 | 84 | 85 | 91 | 82 | 93 | 79 | 93 | 86 | 91 | 104 | 94 |
| UMATILLA | 97 | 84 | 86 | 86 | 97 | 94 | 108 | 98 | 96 | 90 | 89 | 88 | 84 | 91 | 80 | 92 | 88 | 91 | 97 | 92 |
| UNION | 98 | 84 | 87 | 87 | 97 | 95 | 109 | 98 | 96 | 90 | 89 | 89 | 84 | 91 | 81 | 92 | 89 | 92 | 98 | 93 |
| WALLOWA | 98 | 67 | 72 | 81 | 93 | 92 | 116 | 98 | 94 | 77 | 79 | 89 | 76 | 90 | 71 | 93 | 81 | 88 | 103 | 92 |
| WASCO | 96 | 83 | 89 | 86 | 99 | 96 | 105 | 98 | 95 | 90 | 88 | 88 | 85 | 90 | 81 | 92 | 87 | 91 | 98 | 91 |
| WASHINGTON | 102 | 107 | 94 | 103 | 101 | 103 | 102 | 104 | 106 | 107 | 108 | 98 | 97 | 98 | 92 | 96 | 106 | 103 | 97 | 98 |
| WHEELER | 98 | 63 | 69 | 80 | 91 | 92 | 113 | 98 | 92 | 73 | 76 | 90 | 73 | 90 | 69 | 92 | 78 | 87 | 104 | 91 |
| YAMHILL | 99 | 87 | 86 | 89 | 97 | 95 | 110 | 100 | 99 | 94 | 93 | 91 | 87 | 94 | 81 | 94 | 92 | 94 | 97 | 94 |
| OREGON | 99 | 94 | 95 | 95 | 101 | 100 | 105 | 100 | 99 | 97 | 96 | 92 | 91 | 94 | 87 | 93 | 95 | 96 | 98 | 94 |
| UNITED STATES | 100 | 100 | 100 | 100 | 100 | 100 | 100 | 100 | 100 | 100 | 100 | 100 | 100 | 100 | 100 | 100 | 100 | 100 | 100 | 100 |

# POPULATION CHANGE

| COUNTY | FIPS Code | MSA Code | DMA Code | POPULATION 1990 | POPULATION 2000 | POPULATION 2005 | 1990-2000 ANNUAL CHANGE % Rate | 1990-2000 ANNUAL CHANGE State Rank | RACE (%) White 1990 | RACE (%) White 2000 | RACE (%) Black 1990 | RACE (%) Black 2000 | RACE (%) Asian/Pacific 1990 | RACE (%) Asian/Pacific 2000 |
|---|---|---|---|---|---|---|---|---|---|---|---|---|---|---|
| ADAMS | 001 | 0000 | 566 | 78,274 | 88,782 | 94,009 | 1.2 | 6 | 97.5 | 96.8 | 1.2 | 1.4 | 0.5 | 0.7 |
| ALLEGHENY | 003 | 6280 | 508 | 1,336,449 | 1,246,467 | 1,190,187 | -0.7 | 63 | 87.5 | 85.2 | 11.2 | 13.0 | 1.0 | 1.5 |
| ARMSTRONG | 005 | 0000 | 508 | 73,478 | 72,758 | 71,518 | -0.1 | 45 | 99.0 | 98.7 | 0.8 | 1.0 | 0.1 | 0.2 |
| BEAVER | 007 | 6280 | 508 | 186,093 | 181,366 | 174,916 | -0.3 | 55 | 93.9 | 92.8 | 5.6 | 6.6 | 0.2 | 0.3 |
| BEDFORD | 009 | 0000 | 574 | 47,919 | 49,893 | 50,894 | 0.4 | 22 | 99.3 | 99.1 | 0.3 | 0.4 | 0.2 | 0.3 |
| BERKS | 011 | 6680 | 504 | 336,523 | 360,479 | 371,653 | 0.7 | 14 | 93.5 | 91.5 | 3.0 | 3.4 | 0.8 | 1.2 |
| BLAIR | 013 | 0280 | 574 | 130,542 | 129,421 | 126,866 | -0.1 | 45 | 98.7 | 98.4 | 0.8 | 1.0 | 0.3 | 0.4 |
| BRADFORD | 015 | 0000 | 577 | 60,967 | 62,174 | 61,793 | 0.2 | 32 | 99.1 | 98.8 | 0.2 | 0.3 | 0.4 | 0.6 |
| BUCKS | 017 | 6160 | 504 | 541,174 | 599,363 | 626,651 | 1.0 | 9 | 95.0 | 93.6 | 2.8 | 3.3 | 1.6 | 2.4 |
| BUTLER | 019 | 6280 | 508 | 152,013 | 174,253 | 183,103 | 1.3 | 5 | 98.9 | 98.7 | 0.5 | 0.6 | 0.4 | 0.6 |
| CAMBRIA | 021 | 3680 | 574 | 163,029 | 152,137 | 144,256 | -0.7 | 63 | 97.3 | 96.5 | 2.3 | 2.9 | 0.2 | 0.3 |
| CAMERON | 023 | 0000 | 574 | 5,913 | 5,526 | 5,307 | -0.7 | 63 | 99.4 | 99.4 | 0.1 | 0.1 | 0.1 | 0.1 |
| CARBON | 025 | 0240 | 577 | 56,846 | 58,956 | 59,201 | 0.4 | 22 | 99.2 | 98.9 | 0.2 | 0.2 | 0.3 | 0.5 |
| CENTRE | 027 | 8050 | 574 | 123,786 | 132,407 | 133,604 | 0.7 | 14 | 94.2 | 92.3 | 2.3 | 2.6 | 3.1 | 4.5 |
| CHESTER | 029 | 6160 | 504 | 376,396 | 437,220 | 473,029 | 1.5 | 3 | 91.6 | 89.9 | 6.4 | 7.3 | 1.1 | 1.6 |
| CLARION | 031 | 0000 | 508 | 41,699 | 41,572 | 41,157 | 0.0 | 38 | 98.8 | 98.5 | 0.5 | 0.5 | 0.5 | 0.7 |
| CLEARFIELD | 033 | 0000 | 574 | 78,097 | 80,659 | 80,298 | 0.3 | 26 | 99.4 | 99.0 | 0.2 | 0.4 | 0.2 | 0.4 |
| CLINTON | 035 | 0000 | 577 | 37,182 | 36,659 | 36,065 | -0.1 | 45 | 99.1 | 98.9 | 0.4 | 0.5 | 0.3 | 0.4 |
| COLUMBIA | 037 | 7560 | 577 | 63,202 | 63,476 | 62,491 | 0.0 | 38 | 99.0 | 98.7 | 0.4 | 0.5 | 0.4 | 0.5 |
| CRAWFORD | 039 | 0000 | 516 | 86,169 | 89,072 | 88,898 | 0.3 | 26 | 98.2 | 97.7 | 1.2 | 1.6 | 0.3 | 0.5 |
| CUMBERLAND | 041 | 3240 | 566 | 195,257 | 211,638 | 216,739 | 0.8 | 11 | 96.8 | 95.6 | 1.6 | 2.0 | 1.3 | 1.9 |
| DAUPHIN | 043 | 3240 | 566 | 237,813 | 245,728 | 246,269 | 0.3 | 26 | 82.4 | 79.2 | 15.0 | 17.1 | 1.2 | 1.7 |
| DELAWARE | 045 | 6160 | 504 | 547,651 | 540,164 | 533,528 | -0.1 | 45 | 86.5 | 83.9 | 11.2 | 12.8 | 1.8 | 2.7 |
| ELK | 047 | 0000 | 574 | 34,878 | 34,125 | 33,052 | -0.2 | 52 | 99.5 | 99.2 | 0.0 | 0.1 | 0.3 | 0.5 |
| ERIE | 049 | 2360 | 516 | 275,572 | 275,921 | 270,638 | 0.0 | 38 | 93.6 | 92.1 | 5.2 | 6.2 | 0.5 | 0.7 |
| FAYETTE | 051 | 6280 | 508 | 145,351 | 143,222 | 140,487 | -0.1 | 45 | 96.2 | 95.4 | 3.5 | 4.2 | 0.2 | 0.2 |
| FOREST | 053 | 0000 | 574 | 4,802 | 4,939 | 4,927 | 0.3 | 26 | 98.5 | 97.2 | 0.9 | 2.0 | 0.1 | 0.1 |
| FRANKLIN | 055 | 0000 | 511 | 121,082 | 129,493 | 132,741 | 0.7 | 14 | 96.7 | 95.9 | 2.3 | 2.7 | 0.5 | 0.8 |
| FULTON | 057 | 0000 | 511 | 13,837 | 14,702 | 15,092 | 0.6 | 18 | 98.8 | 98.6 | 0.9 | 1.0 | 0.1 | 0.2 |
| GREENE | 059 | 0000 | 508 | 39,550 | 42,008 | 41,688 | 0.6 | 18 | 98.5 | 96.2 | 1.0 | 3.0 | 0.3 | 0.4 |
| HUNTINGDON | 061 | 0000 | 574 | 44,164 | 44,747 | 44,714 | 0.1 | 35 | 95.1 | 94.1 | 4.5 | 5.4 | 0.2 | 0.3 |
| INDIANA | 063 | 0000 | 508 | 89,994 | 87,274 | 84,464 | -0.3 | 55 | 97.8 | 97.3 | 1.3 | 1.5 | 0.6 | 0.9 |
| JEFFERSON | 065 | 0000 | 574 | 46,083 | 45,954 | 45,302 | 0.0 | 38 | 99.6 | 99.4 | 0.1 | 0.1 | 0.2 | 0.3 |
| JUNIATA | 067 | 0000 | 566 | 20,625 | 22,334 | 22,987 | 0.8 | 11 | 99.5 | 99.3 | 0.1 | 0.2 | 0.2 | 0.3 |
| LACKAWANNA | 069 | 7560 | 577 | 219,039 | 204,747 | 195,872 | -0.7 | 63 | 98.4 | 98.0 | 0.7 | 0.8 | 0.6 | 0.9 |
| LANCASTER | 071 | 4000 | 566 | 422,822 | 463,301 | 479,792 | 0.9 | 10 | 94.1 | 92.2 | 2.4 | 2.7 | 1.1 | 1.6 |
| LAWRENCE | 073 | 0000 | 508 | 96,246 | 94,161 | 92,358 | -0.2 | 52 | 96.5 | 95.9 | 3.0 | 3.5 | 0.3 | 0.4 |
| LEBANON | 075 | 3240 | 566 | 113,744 | 118,173 | 119,708 | 0.4 | 22 | 97.5 | 96.6 | 0.6 | 0.7 | 0.8 | 1.2 |
| LEHIGH | 077 | 0240 | 504 | 291,130 | 300,816 | 305,232 | 0.3 | 26 | 93.3 | 91.2 | 2.3 | 2.6 | 1.3 | 1.9 |
| LUZERNE | 079 | 7560 | 577 | 328,149 | 309,365 | 296,322 | -0.6 | 62 | 98.1 | 97.7 | 1.2 | 1.3 | 0.5 | 0.7 |
| LYCOMING | 081 | 9140 | 577 | 118,710 | 116,016 | 112,610 | -0.2 | 52 | 96.9 | 96.3 | 2.4 | 2.7 | 0.4 | 0.6 |
| MCKEAN | 083 | 0000 | 514 | 47,131 | 45,667 | 44,109 | -0.3 | 55 | 97.9 | 97.0 | 1.1 | 1.6 | 0.3 | 0.5 |
| MERCER | 085 | 7610 | 536 | 121,003 | 121,201 | 119,922 | 0.0 | 38 | 94.6 | 93.5 | 4.9 | 5.8 | 0.3 | 0.5 |
| MIFFLIN | 087 | 0000 | 566 | 46,197 | 46,726 | 46,391 | 0.1 | 35 | 99.4 | 99.2 | 0.2 | 0.3 | 0.2 | 0.3 |
| MONROE | 089 | 0000 | 577 | 95,709 | 131,622 | 147,128 | 3.2 | 2 | 96.9 | 96.1 | 1.8 | 2.1 | 0.7 | 1.1 |
| MONTGOMERY | 091 | 6160 | 504 | 678,111 | 728,573 | 751,391 | 0.7 | 14 | 91.4 | 89.3 | 5.8 | 6.6 | 2.4 | 3.6 |
| MONTOUR | 093 | 0000 | 577 | 17,735 | 17,513 | 17,209 | -0.1 | 45 | 98.5 | 97.9 | 0.4 | 0.6 | 0.8 | 1.2 |
| NORTHAMPTON | 095 | 0240 | 504 | 247,105 | 260,757 | 265,891 | 0.5 | 20 | 94.2 | 92.4 | 2.1 | 2.5 | 1.1 | 1.6 |
| NORTHUMBERLAND | 097 | 0000 | 577 | 96,771 | 92,308 | 88,160 | -0.5 | 61 | 99.2 | 98.9 | 0.3 | 0.5 | 0.2 | 0.3 |
| PERRY | 099 | 3240 | 566 | 41,172 | 44,558 | 45,268 | 0.8 | 11 | 99.4 | 99.3 | 0.2 | 0.3 | 0.2 | 0.2 |
| PHILADELPHIA | 101 | 6160 | 504 | 1,585,577 | 1,400,293 | 1,315,216 | -1.2 | 67 | 53.5 | 48.3 | 39.9 | 42.8 | 2.7 | 3.8 |
| PIKE | 103 | 5660 | 501 | 27,966 | 42,507 | 48,294 | 4.2 | 1 | 98.0 | 97.5 | 0.9 | 1.1 | 0.5 | 0.7 |
| POTTER | 105 | 0000 | 514 | 16,717 | 17,112 | 17,099 | 0.2 | 32 | 99.5 | 99.2 | 0.1 | 0.3 | 0.2 | 0.3 |
| SCHUYLKILL | 107 | 0000 | 577 | 152,585 | 147,610 | 141,859 | -0.3 | 55 | 99.0 | 97.5 | 0.6 | 1.7 | 0.3 | 0.5 |
| SNYDER | 109 | 0000 | 577 | 36,680 | 37,834 | 37,637 | 0.3 | 26 | 99.1 | 98.8 | 0.4 | 0.5 | 0.3 | 0.4 |
| SOMERSET | 111 | 3680 | 574 | 78,218 | 79,827 | 78,814 | 0.2 | 32 | 99.6 | 99.4 | 0.1 | 0.2 | 0.2 | 0.2 |
| SULLIVAN | 113 | 0000 | 577 | 6,104 | 6,013 | 5,892 | -0.1 | 45 | 98.3 | 98.1 | 1.0 | 1.1 | 0.1 | 0.2 |
| SUSQUEHANNA | 115 | 0000 | 577 | 40,380 | 42,360 | 42,772 | 0.5 | 20 | 99.3 | 99.0 | 0.2 | 0.3 | 0.2 | 0.3 |
| TIOGA | 117 | 0000 | 565 | 41,126 | 41,734 | 42,083 | 0.1 | 35 | 98.8 | 98.7 | 0.6 | 0.6 | 0.3 | 0.4 |
| UNION | 119 | 0000 | 577 | 36,176 | 40,685 | 41,437 | 1.2 | 6 | 96.2 | 91.3 | 2.7 | 7.0 | 0.7 | 0.9 |
| VENANGO | 121 | 0000 | 508 | 59,381 | 57,391 | 56,137 | -0.3 | 55 | 98.7 | 98.4 | 0.8 | 1.0 | 0.2 | 0.3 |
| WARREN | 123 | 0000 | 516 | 45,050 | 43,291 | 41,941 | -0.4 | 60 | 99.4 | 99.3 | 0.1 | 0.1 | 0.2 | 0.4 |
| WASHINGTON | 125 | 6280 | 508 | 204,584 | 204,546 | 202,591 | 0.0 | 38 | 96.2 | 95.5 | 3.3 | 3.9 | 0.3 | 0.4 |
| WAYNE | 127 | 0000 | 577 | 39,944 | 46,550 | 48,951 | 1.5 | 3 | 98.8 | 98.0 | 0.7 | 1.3 | 0.2 | 0.4 |
| WESTMORELAND | 129 | 6280 | 508 | 370,321 | 369,264 | 362,365 | 0.0 | 38 | 97.5 | 96.9 | 1.9 | 2.2 | 0.4 | 0.6 |
| WYOMING | 131 | 7560 | 577 | 28,076 | 29,298 | 29,299 | 0.4 | 22 | 99.0 | 98.6 | 0.5 | 0.7 | 0.3 | 0.4 |
| YORK | 133 | 9280 | 566 | 339,574 | 379,431 | 393,835 | 1.1 | 8 | 95.2 | 94.0 | 3.2 | 3.8 | 0.6 | 0.9 |
| PENNSYLVANIA | | | | | | | 0.1 | | 88.5 | 87.4 | 9.2 | 9.5 | 1.2 | 1.7 |
| UNITED STATES | | | | | | | 1.0 | | 80.3 | 77.9 | 12.1 | 12.4 | 2.9 | 3.9 |

| COUNTY | % HISPANIC ORIGIN | | 2000 AGE DISTRIBUTION (%) | | | | | | | | | | MEDIAN AGE | | 2000 Males/ Females (×100) |
|---|---|---|---|---|---|---|---|---|---|---|---|---|---|---|---|
| | 1990 | 2000 | 0-4 | 5-9 | 10-14 | 15-19 | 20-24 | 25-44 | 45-64 | 65-84 | 85+ | 18+ | 1990 | 2000 | |
| ADAMS | 1.6 | 2.6 | 6.2 | 7.1 | 7.5 | 7.5 | 5.8 | 28.9 | 23.1 | 12.1 | 1.9 | 75.3 | 33.5 | 37.1 | 95.2 |
| ALLEGHENY | 0.7 | 1.3 | 5.3 | 6.1 | 6.7 | 6.4 | 5.5 | 28.8 | 23.2 | 15.7 | 2.2 | 78.4 | 36.7 | 39.9 | 89.2 |
| ARMSTRONG | 0.2 | 0.7 | 5.5 | 6.2 | 6.6 | 6.9 | 5.3 | 27.8 | 24.2 | 15.4 | 2.2 | 77.7 | 36.6 | 40.1 | 92.2 |
| BEAVER | 0.6 | 1.2 | 5.6 | 6.3 | 6.7 | 6.6 | 5.5 | 27.0 | 23.8 | 16.4 | 2.0 | 77.5 | 37.0 | 40.3 | 91.2 |
| BEDFORD | 0.2 | 0.7 | 5.8 | 6.6 | 7.0 | 6.4 | 5.1 | 28.1 | 24.6 | 14.6 | 1.8 | 76.8 | 35.7 | 39.4 | 96.2 |
| BERKS | 5.1 | 7.5 | 5.8 | 6.5 | 7.1 | 6.9 | 5.6 | 28.5 | 23.5 | 14.0 | 2.1 | 76.7 | 35.4 | 38.6 | 93.9 |
| BLAIR | 0.3 | 0.8 | 5.6 | 6.2 | 6.6 | 7.1 | 6.0 | 27.2 | 23.9 | 15.2 | 2.3 | 77.6 | 36.2 | 39.3 | 90.1 |
| BRADFORD | 0.4 | 0.9 | 6.2 | 7.3 | 8.0 | 6.9 | 4.9 | 27.9 | 23.6 | 13.1 | 2.0 | 74.1 | 34.6 | 37.9 | 95.3 |
| BUCKS | 1.6 | 2.7 | 6.2 | 7.1 | 7.8 | 6.6 | 5.1 | 30.7 | 23.8 | 11.3 | 1.4 | 74.8 | 33.7 | 37.3 | 95.8 |
| BUTLER | 0.4 | 0.9 | 5.9 | 6.7 | 7.1 | 7.4 | 6.1 | 28.9 | 23.8 | 12.3 | 1.8 | 76.4 | 34.0 | 37.6 | 94.9 |
| CAMBRIA | 0.6 | 1.3 | 5.1 | 5.8 | 6.1 | 7.0 | 6.6 | 26.7 | 23.5 | 16.8 | 2.5 | 79.0 | 37.4 | 40.3 | 92.7 |
| CAMERON | 0.1 | 0.5 | 6.0 | 7.1 | 7.2 | 6.7 | 4.3 | 26.1 | 23.1 | 17.2 | 2.2 | 75.3 | 37.3 | 40.3 | 96.8 |
| CARBON | 0.9 | 1.7 | 5.3 | 6.2 | 6.9 | 6.1 | 4.9 | 28.0 | 23.9 | 16.6 | 2.1 | 77.8 | 37.5 | 40.5 | 93.9 |
| CENTRE | 1.1 | 1.9 | 4.8 | 5.2 | 5.3 | 9.9 | 18.1 | 28.8 | 17.8 | 8.9 | 1.2 | 82.0 | 27.0 | 29.6 | 105.4 |
| CHESTER | 2.3 | 3.4 | 6.1 | 7.3 | 8.2 | 7.0 | 5.3 | 30.0 | 24.1 | 10.6 | 1.4 | 74.4 | 33.8 | 37.2 | 95.3 |
| CLARION | 0.3 | 0.8 | 5.3 | 6.0 | 6.1 | 9.7 | 9.7 | 26.6 | 22.0 | 12.7 | 1.9 | 78.9 | 32.2 | 35.5 | 93.4 |
| CLEARFIELD | 0.3 | 0.8 | 5.9 | 6.7 | 7.0 | 6.5 | 5.5 | 27.9 | 23.6 | 14.7 | 2.1 | 76.5 | 35.6 | 38.9 | 94.1 |
| CLINTON | 0.2 | 0.7 | 5.1 | 6.1 | 6.9 | 8.6 | 7.1 | 26.4 | 23.1 | 14.8 | 2.0 | 78.0 | 34.8 | 38.3 | 92.7 |
| COLUMBIA | 0.5 | 1.2 | 5.1 | 5.9 | 6.5 | 9.2 | 8.2 | 26.8 | 22.2 | 14.1 | 2.0 | 79.0 | 34.1 | 37.2 | 89.9 |
| CRAWFORD | 0.4 | 0.9 | 6.0 | 6.7 | 7.1 | 8.0 | 6.5 | 26.5 | 23.6 | 13.6 | 2.1 | 76.0 | 34.6 | 37.7 | 94.1 |
| CUMBERLAND | 0.7 | 1.4 | 5.1 | 5.9 | 6.5 | 7.6 | 7.1 | 29.1 | 24.0 | 13.0 | 1.8 | 79.0 | 34.6 | 38.1 | 93.3 |
| DAUPHIN | 2.5 | 3.8 | 5.9 | 6.7 | 7.1 | 6.0 | 5.3 | 31.3 | 23.0 | 13.0 | 1.8 | 76.9 | 35.0 | 38.1 | 91.5 |
| DELAWARE | 1.1 | 1.9 | 6.1 | 6.7 | 7.4 | 7.3 | 5.7 | 29.1 | 21.6 | 14.0 | 2.0 | 76.1 | 34.6 | 37.7 | 91.0 |
| ELK | 0.2 | 0.7 | 5.9 | 7.0 | 7.5 | 6.7 | 4.9 | 27.8 | 23.3 | 15.1 | 1.9 | 75.3 | 35.4 | 38.8 | 96.7 |
| ERIE | 1.2 | 2.1 | 6.3 | 7.0 | 7.3 | 8.1 | 7.1 | 28.0 | 21.9 | 12.6 | 1.7 | 75.3 | 32.9 | 35.8 | 93.7 |
| FAYETTE | 0.3 | 0.8 | 5.5 | 6.1 | 6.5 | 6.4 | 5.8 | 27.2 | 24.4 | 16.0 | 2.1 | 78.0 | 36.9 | 40.2 | 91.8 |
| FOREST | 0.5 | 1.2 | 4.6 | 5.4 | 5.7 | 9.3 | 3.7 | 23.3 | 27.5 | 18.2 | 2.3 | 77.6 | 40.7 | 43.5 | 111.5 |
| FRANKLIN | 0.9 | 1.6 | 5.8 | 6.6 | 7.0 | 6.6 | 5.1 | 29.1 | 24.3 | 13.5 | 1.9 | 76.7 | 35.0 | 38.6 | 93.9 |
| FULTON | 0.2 | 0.7 | 6.3 | 7.1 | 7.6 | 6.7 | 5.1 | 28.5 | 24.2 | 12.9 | 1.5 | 74.8 | 34.1 | 37.9 | 98.3 |
| GREENE | 0.5 | 1.3 | 5.3 | 6.4 | 7.5 | 7.6 | 6.2 | 29.0 | 22.2 | 13.6 | 2.1 | 76.7 | 35.2 | 37.6 | 89.3 |
| HUNTINGDON | 0.4 | 0.9 | 5.3 | 6.1 | 7.0 | 7.5 | 7.0 | 29.8 | 22.7 | 12.8 | 1.8 | 77.6 | 34.3 | 37.1 | 109.1 |
| INDIANA | 0.4 | 0.9 | 5.1 | 6.3 | 7.0 | 9.5 | 9.5 | 27.1 | 21.3 | 12.6 | 1.7 | 78.0 | 31.8 | 35.3 | 92.9 |
| JEFFERSON | 0.2 | 0.7 | 5.9 | 6.7 | 6.9 | 7.2 | 5.5 | 27.2 | 23.4 | 14.8 | 2.4 | 76.2 | 35.8 | 39.2 | 94.1 |
| JUNIATA | 0.2 | 0.7 | 6.1 | 6.8 | 7.1 | 6.7 | 5.3 | 28.8 | 23.8 | 13.3 | 2.0 | 75.9 | 34.6 | 38.3 | 96.6 |
| LACKAWANNA | 0.5 | 1.1 | 5.2 | 6.0 | 6.7 | 6.6 | 5.6 | 27.2 | 23.1 | 17.0 | 2.5 | 78.5 | 37.7 | 40.3 | 88.8 |
| LANCASTER | 3.7 | 5.6 | 6.9 | 7.6 | 7.9 | 7.3 | 5.9 | 29.1 | 21.7 | 11.7 | 1.9 | 73.5 | 32.8 | 35.9 | 94.2 |
| LAWRENCE | 0.4 | 0.9 | 5.6 | 6.2 | 6.6 | 7.1 | 6.0 | 25.7 | 23.7 | 16.7 | 2.4 | 77.5 | 37.3 | 40.3 | 90.7 |
| LEBANON | 2.3 | 3.8 | 5.8 | 6.6 | 7.1 | 6.6 | 5.5 | 28.8 | 23.9 | 13.6 | 2.1 | 76.6 | 35.2 | 38.6 | 95.8 |
| LEHIGH | 5.2 | 7.6 | 5.7 | 6.4 | 7.0 | 6.4 | 5.4 | 29.3 | 23.7 | 14.0 | 2.1 | 77.3 | 35.7 | 39.1 | 93.2 |
| LUZERNE | 0.6 | 1.2 | 5.0 | 5.8 | 6.4 | 6.3 | 5.3 | 27.6 | 23.5 | 17.4 | 2.5 | 79.2 | 38.2 | 40.9 | 90.8 |
| LYCOMING | 0.5 | 1.1 | 6.1 | 6.6 | 7.1 | 7.1 | 6.1 | 28.1 | 23.3 | 13.6 | 2.0 | 76.2 | 34.8 | 37.9 | 93.8 |
| MCKEAN | 1.1 | 2.0 | 5.6 | 6.6 | 7.3 | 7.1 | 5.4 | 28.1 | 23.2 | 14.2 | 2.4 | 76.2 | 35.9 | 38.6 | 99.0 |
| MERCER | 0.4 | 0.9 | 5.3 | 6.3 | 7.0 | 7.3 | 6.1 | 26.6 | 23.4 | 15.8 | 2.4 | 77.5 | 36.4 | 39.6 | 94.2 |
| MIFFLIN | 0.3 | 0.8 | 6.0 | 6.8 | 7.4 | 6.6 | 5.0 | 27.8 | 24.2 | 14.4 | 2.0 | 75.8 | 35.7 | 38.9 | 92.5 |
| MONROE | 2.1 | 3.6 | 6.3 | 7.3 | 7.8 | 6.9 | 5.4 | 30.7 | 22.7 | 11.6 | 1.4 | 74.9 | 34.0 | 37.0 | 97.1 |
| MONTGOMERY | 1.2 | 2.1 | 5.6 | 6.4 | 7.0 | 5.9 | 4.9 | 30.6 | 23.4 | 14.0 | 2.2 | 77.5 | 35.8 | 39.2 | 91.8 |
| MONTOUR | 0.7 | 1.2 | 6.1 | 6.9 | 7.5 | 7.2 | 4.9 | 27.9 | 23.1 | 14.0 | 2.3 | 75.0 | 35.2 | 38.8 | 89.5 |
| NORTHAMPTON | 4.7 | 7.0 | 5.8 | 6.5 | 7.0 | 7.2 | 6.4 | 28.1 | 23.4 | 13.7 | 1.8 | 77.0 | 34.9 | 38.3 | 94.9 |
| NORTHUMBERLAND | 0.5 | 1.2 | 5.6 | 6.2 | 6.5 | 6.3 | 5.6 | 26.9 | 24.0 | 16.2 | 2.6 | 77.7 | 37.8 | 40.3 | 92.0 |
| PERRY | 0.5 | 1.1 | 6.0 | 7.1 | 8.1 | 6.9 | 5.0 | 31.1 | 23.6 | 11.0 | 1.3 | 74.5 | 33.4 | 37.1 | 98.9 |
| PHILADELPHIA | 5.6 | 7.7 | 6.7 | 6.9 | 7.4 | 6.7 | 6.7 | 30.3 | 20.6 | 12.8 | 2.0 | 75.5 | 33.2 | 35.8 | 87.6 |
| PIKE | 2.3 | 3.7 | 6.5 | 7.6 | 7.8 | 5.8 | 3.8 | 28.8 | 24.1 | 14.1 | 1.5 | 74.4 | 35.9 | 39.1 | 98.5 |
| POTTER | 0.4 | 1.0 | 6.4 | 7.1 | 7.4 | 7.3 | 5.7 | 25.3 | 24.1 | 14.6 | 2.1 | 74.2 | 35.7 | 38.6 | 95.6 |
| SCHUYLKILL | 0.4 | 1.3 | 4.9 | 5.8 | 6.5 | 6.1 | 5.1 | 28.0 | 23.5 | 17.7 | 2.4 | 79.0 | 38.5 | 41.0 | 96.4 |
| SNYDER | 0.4 | 0.9 | 6.6 | 7.1 | 7.3 | 8.0 | 7.1 | 29.0 | 21.8 | 11.7 | 1.5 | 75.0 | 32.6 | 35.8 | 95.0 |
| SOMERSET | 0.3 | 0.8 | 5.8 | 6.5 | 6.8 | 6.5 | 5.5 | 27.3 | 24.2 | 15.3 | 2.2 | 76.9 | 36.3 | 39.8 | 93.6 |
| SULLIVAN | 0.4 | 0.9 | 5.1 | 5.7 | 6.0 | 8.6 | 5.0 | 25.0 | 23.7 | 17.7 | 3.3 | 78.3 | 38.2 | 41.5 | 100.8 |
| SUSQUEHANNA | 0.4 | 1.0 | 6.5 | 7.4 | 7.6 | 7.1 | 5.2 | 27.5 | 23.8 | 12.9 | 2.0 | 74.0 | 34.9 | 38.0 | 98.0 |
| TIOGA | 0.3 | 0.9 | 5.6 | 6.8 | 7.5 | 8.2 | 6.1 | 26.4 | 23.6 | 13.7 | 2.1 | 75.9 | 34.2 | 37.9 | 95.1 |
| UNION | 1.8 | 4.4 | 5.1 | 5.9 | 6.4 | 9.5 | 9.6 | 29.8 | 20.9 | 10.8 | 1.9 | 79.3 | 32.5 | 35.1 | 120.0 |
| VENANGO | 0.3 | 0.9 | 5.9 | 6.7 | 7.0 | 7.1 | 5.7 | 26.9 | 24.5 | 14.5 | 1.9 | 75.9 | 35.8 | 39.4 | 94.4 |
| WARREN | 0.3 | 0.8 | 5.7 | 6.8 | 7.5 | 6.5 | 4.8 | 27.5 | 24.6 | 14.5 | 2.2 | 76.0 | 36.3 | 39.8 | 94.5 |
| WASHINGTON | 0.6 | 1.2 | 5.1 | 5.9 | 6.4 | 6.7 | 5.8 | 27.0 | 25.1 | 15.9 | 2.1 | 78.8 | 37.5 | 40.8 | 92.1 |
| WAYNE | 0.9 | 1.9 | 6.0 | 6.9 | 7.3 | 6.5 | 5.1 | 27.1 | 24.5 | 14.4 | 2.2 | 75.8 | 36.3 | 39.3 | 98.9 |
| WESTMORELAND | 0.4 | 0.9 | 5.2 | 5.9 | 6.5 | 6.2 | 5.3 | 27.4 | 25.2 | 16.2 | 2.1 | 78.7 | 37.7 | 41.1 | 92.1 |
| WYOMING | 0.5 | 1.0 | 6.3 | 7.3 | 8.0 | 7.9 | 5.3 | 28.1 | 24.1 | 11.2 | 1.6 | 74.1 | 33.1 | 36.5 | 97.8 |
| YORK | 1.5 | 2.5 | 5.8 | 6.7 | 7.3 | 6.4 | 5.0 | 31.1 | 23.9 | 12.1 | 1.7 | 76.4 | 34.5 | 38.1 | 95.9 |
| PENNSYLVANIA | 2.0 | 3.0 | 5.8 | 6.6 | 7.1 | 6.8 | 5.9 | 28.9 | 23.0 | 13.9 | 2.0 | 76.8 | 35.0 | 38.2 | 92.6 |
| UNITED STATES | 9.0 | 11.8 | 6.9 | 7.2 | 7.2 | 7.2 | 6.7 | 29.9 | 22.2 | 11.1 | 1.6 | 74.6 | 32.9 | 35.7 | 95.6 |

| COUNTY | HOUSEHOLDS 1990 | HOUSEHOLDS 2000 | HOUSEHOLDS 2005 | HOUSEHOLDS % Annual Rate 1990-2000 | HOUSEHOLDS 2000 Average HH Size | FAMILIES 1990 | FAMILIES 2000 | FAMILIES % Annual Rate 1990-2000 | MEDIAN HOUSEHOLD INCOME 2000 | MEDIAN HOUSEHOLD INCOME 2005 | MEDIAN HOUSEHOLD INCOME 2000 National Rank | MEDIAN HOUSEHOLD INCOME 2000 State Rank |
|---|---|---|---|---|---|---|---|---|---|---|---|---|
| ADAMS | 28,067 | 32,483 | 34,704 | 1.8 | 2.65 | 21,192 | 23,839 | 1.4 | 41,896 | 50,136 | 522 | 15 |
| ALLEGHENY | 541,261 | 518,734 | 502,202 | -0.5 | 2.33 | 358,317 | 329,417 | -1.0 | 38,520 | 41,789 | 807 | 18 |
| ARMSTRONG | 28,309 | 28,618 | 28,420 | 0.1 | 2.51 | 20,853 | 20,377 | -0.3 | 31,497 | 36,099 | 1819 | 49 |
| BEAVER | 71,939 | 72,447 | 70,986 | 0.1 | 2.46 | 52,698 | 51,186 | -0.4 | 35,542 | 38,801 | 1163 | 27 |
| BEDFORD | 18,038 | 19,014 | 19,506 | 0.6 | 2.61 | 13,748 | 14,022 | 0.2 | 32,281 | 38,787 | 1666 | 46 |
| BERKS | 127,649 | 138,397 | 143,495 | 1.0 | 2.54 | 91,268 | 96,092 | 0.6 | 45,547 | 53,660 | 329 | 9 |
| BLAIR | 50,332 | 50,979 | 50,585 | 0.2 | 2.47 | 35,787 | 34,963 | -0.3 | 31,380 | 35,053 | 1845 | 51 |
| BRADFORD | 22,492 | 23,592 | 23,787 | 0.6 | 2.59 | 16,691 | 16,979 | 0.2 | 32,547 | 37,616 | 1616 | 44 |
| BUCKS | 190,507 | 214,858 | 226,514 | 1.5 | 2.75 | 145,924 | 159,366 | 1.1 | 59,903 | 69,224 | 74 | 3 |
| BUTLER | 55,325 | 65,193 | 69,397 | 2.0 | 2.59 | 41,054 | 47,012 | 1.7 | 41,542 | 46,999 | 545 | 16 |
| CAMBRIA | 62,004 | 59,590 | 57,491 | -0.5 | 2.43 | 44,179 | 40,727 | -1.0 | 30,332 | 32,995 | 2075 | 59 |
| CAMERON | 2,395 | 2,292 | 2,227 | -0.5 | 2.39 | 1,630 | 1,489 | -1.1 | 28,664 | 31,475 | 2340 | 64 |
| CARBON | 21,989 | 23,178 | 23,494 | 0.6 | 2.51 | 15,977 | 16,234 | 0.2 | 36,433 | 45,256 | 1056 | 22 |
| CENTRE | 42,683 | 46,525 | 47,530 | 1.1 | 2.49 | 26,359 | 27,741 | 0.6 | 37,017 | 41,171 | 973 | 21 |
| CHESTER | 133,257 | 156,691 | 170,501 | 2.0 | 2.71 | 99,324 | 113,719 | 1.7 | 67,962 | 77,367 | 21 | 1 |
| CLARION | 14,990 | 15,279 | 15,292 | 0.2 | 2.53 | 10,575 | 10,378 | -0.2 | 30,686 | 33,628 | 1988 | 55 |
| CLEARFIELD | 29,808 | 30,719 | 30,924 | 0.4 | 2.53 | 21,798 | 21,680 | -0.1 | 30,808 | 34,141 | 1969 | 53 |
| CLINTON | 13,844 | 14,057 | 13,999 | 0.2 | 2.47 | 9,876 | 9,678 | -0.2 | 30,591 | 35,668 | 2012 | 56 |
| COLUMBIA | 23,478 | 23,976 | 23,886 | 0.3 | 2.47 | 16,604 | 16,382 | -0.2 | 33,972 | 41,433 | 1398 | 36 |
| CRAWFORD | 32,185 | 33,806 | 34,107 | 0.6 | 2.54 | 23,036 | 23,413 | 0.2 | 31,728 | 35,379 | 1770 | 48 |
| CUMBERLAND | 73,452 | 80,630 | 83,407 | 1.1 | 2.46 | 51,978 | 55,362 | 0.8 | 46,479 | 50,710 | 292 | 8 |
| DAUPHIN | 95,264 | 100,020 | 100,962 | 0.6 | 2.42 | 63,156 | 63,839 | 0.1 | 42,609 | 48,197 | 472 | 13 |
| DELAWARE | 201,374 | 201,684 | 200,999 | 0.0 | 2.58 | 142,587 | 137,203 | -0.5 | 47,610 | 53,834 | 256 | 5 |
| ELK | 13,131 | 13,235 | 13,012 | 0.1 | 2.55 | 9,686 | 9,427 | -0.3 | 36,283 | 39,544 | 1068 | 24 |
| ERIE | 101,564 | 103,566 | 102,708 | 0.2 | 2.55 | 71,125 | 70,295 | -0.1 | 38,400 | 43,045 | 819 | 20 |
| FAYETTE | 56,110 | 56,967 | 56,708 | 0.2 | 2.48 | 40,941 | 40,048 | -0.3 | 25,995 | 28,423 | 2713 | 67 |
| FOREST | 1,908 | 1,987 | 2,024 | 0.5 | 2.29 | 1,336 | 1,336 | 0.0 | 30,244 | 35,086 | 2096 | 61 |
| FRANKLIN | 45,675 | 49,667 | 51,321 | 1.0 | 2.56 | 34,199 | 36,009 | 0.6 | 38,467 | 45,428 | 809 | 19 |
| FULTON | 5,139 | 5,506 | 5,672 | 0.8 | 2.66 | 3,926 | 4,057 | 0.4 | 34,507 | 43,946 | 1318 | 33 |
| GREENE | 14,624 | 15,273 | 15,329 | 0.5 | 2.55 | 10,691 | 10,738 | 0.1 | 28,392 | 31,754 | 2380 | 65 |
| HUNTINGDON | 15,527 | 15,916 | 16,011 | 0.3 | 2.54 | 11,297 | 11,170 | -0.1 | 33,404 | 40,619 | 1476 | 40 |
| INDIANA | 31,710 | 31,650 | 30,990 | 0.0 | 2.57 | 22,508 | 21,676 | -0.5 | 30,555 | 33,527 | 2017 | 57 |
| JEFFERSON | 17,608 | 17,930 | 17,852 | 0.2 | 2.52 | 12,918 | 12,669 | -0.2 | 30,116 | 33,622 | 2126 | 62 |
| JUNIATA | 7,598 | 8,407 | 8,737 | 1.2 | 2.61 | 5,804 | 6,192 | 0.8 | 33,815 | 41,570 | 1419 | 37 |
| LACKAWANNA | 84,528 | 81,120 | 78,534 | -0.5 | 2.44 | 58,387 | 53,836 | -1.0 | 33,392 | 39,218 | 1477 | 41 |
| LANCASTER | 150,956 | 167,716 | 174,854 | 1.3 | 2.68 | 112,106 | 121,388 | 1.0 | 47,611 | 57,863 | 255 | 4 |
| LAWRENCE | 36,350 | 36,411 | 36,132 | 0.0 | 2.51 | 26,779 | 25,879 | -0.4 | 30,249 | 32,451 | 2094 | 60 |
| LEBANON | 42,688 | 45,308 | 46,384 | 0.7 | 2.53 | 31,163 | 32,031 | 0.3 | 40,015 | 44,897 | 673 | 17 |
| LEHIGH | 112,887 | 118,342 | 120,968 | 0.6 | 2.48 | 79,183 | 80,498 | 0.2 | 43,985 | 50,750 | 396 | 11 |
| LUZERNE | 128,483 | 124,179 | 120,394 | -0.4 | 2.41 | 88,412 | 82,031 | -0.9 | 34,006 | 38,613 | 1392 | 35 |
| LYCOMING | 44,949 | 44,838 | 43,999 | 0.0 | 2.50 | 32,165 | 31,023 | -0.4 | 34,420 | 41,945 | 1330 | 34 |
| MCKEAN | 17,837 | 17,653 | 17,272 | -0.1 | 2.44 | 12,590 | 11,927 | -0.7 | 34,765 | 40,214 | 1286 | 32 |
| MERCER | 45,591 | 46,706 | 46,783 | 0.3 | 2.47 | 33,275 | 32,921 | -0.1 | 33,653 | 38,536 | 1442 | 39 |
| MIFFLIN | 17,697 | 18,307 | 18,389 | 0.4 | 2.52 | 12,842 | 12,872 | 0.0 | 31,096 | 35,162 | 1914 | 52 |
| MONROE | 34,206 | 47,818 | 53,792 | 4.1 | 2.67 | 25,751 | 35,086 | 3.8 | 47,067 | 59,503 | 273 | 7 |
| MONTGOMERY | 254,995 | 280,580 | 292,707 | 1.2 | 2.53 | 181,075 | 192,203 | 0.7 | 60,375 | 66,234 | 71 | 2 |
| MONTOUR | 6,543 | 6,720 | 6,682 | 0.3 | 2.46 | 4,606 | 4,613 | 0.0 | 35,985 | 39,286 | 1105 | 25 |
| NORTHAMPTON | 90,955 | 97,347 | 99,993 | 0.8 | 2.59 | 67,185 | 69,987 | 0.5 | 47,492 | 57,468 | 258 | 6 |
| NORTHUMBERLAND | 38,736 | 37,156 | 35,890 | -0.5 | 2.39 | 26,998 | 24,988 | -0.9 | 30,333 | 35,907 | 2073 | 58 |
| PERRY | 14,949 | 16,569 | 17,057 | 1.3 | 2.66 | 11,627 | 12,543 | 0.9 | 42,017 | 51,245 | 511 | 14 |
| PHILADELPHIA | 603,075 | 548,085 | 520,497 | -1.2 | 2.49 | 378,045 | 329,523 | -1.7 | 31,987 | 37,598 | 1718 | 47 |
| PIKE | 10,536 | 16,087 | 18,304 | 5.3 | 2.62 | 8,004 | 11,926 | 5.0 | 43,109 | 52,715 | 449 | 12 |
| POTTER | 6,246 | 6,553 | 6,629 | 0.6 | 2.57 | 4,600 | 4,670 | 0.2 | 31,443 | 35,668 | 1833 | 50 |
| SCHUYLKILL | 60,773 | 59,059 | 57,448 | -0.3 | 2.41 | 42,278 | 39,286 | -0.9 | 32,670 | 38,796 | 1598 | 43 |
| SNYDER | 12,764 | 13,543 | 13,652 | 0.7 | 2.63 | 9,697 | 9,995 | 0.4 | 35,294 | 40,431 | 1203 | 29 |
| SOMERSET | 29,574 | 30,158 | 30,090 | 0.2 | 2.55 | 22,057 | 21,791 | -0.1 | 29,654 | 33,320 | 2205 | 63 |
| SULLIVAN | 2,280 | 2,330 | 2,322 | 0.3 | 2.39 | 1,601 | 1,581 | -0.2 | 26,637 | 30,099 | 2629 | 66 |
| SUSQUEHANNA | 14,898 | 15,908 | 16,215 | 0.8 | 2.63 | 11,238 | 11,590 | 0.4 | 32,458 | 37,585 | 1632 | 45 |
| TIOGA | 14,974 | 15,663 | 15,959 | 0.5 | 2.56 | 11,103 | 11,196 | 0.1 | 33,803 | 39,989 | 1420 | 38 |
| UNION | 11,689 | 12,375 | 12,682 | 0.7 | 2.63 | 8,637 | 8,920 | 0.4 | 35,923 | 40,854 | 1111 | 26 |
| VENANGO | 22,408 | 22,110 | 21,827 | -0.2 | 2.53 | 16,470 | 15,750 | -0.5 | 30,757 | 33,286 | 1978 | 54 |
| WARREN | 17,244 | 17,139 | 16,839 | -0.1 | 2.47 | 12,519 | 12,018 | -0.5 | 35,270 | 39,577 | 1208 | 30 |
| WASHINGTON | 78,533 | 80,553 | 80,659 | 0.3 | 2.48 | 57,237 | 56,859 | -0.1 | 34,952 | 37,937 | 1260 | 31 |
| WAYNE | 14,638 | 16,856 | 17,758 | 1.7 | 2.65 | 10,903 | 12,238 | 1.4 | 33,174 | 40,474 | 1509 | 42 |
| WESTMORELAND | 144,080 | 146,978 | 146,013 | 0.2 | 2.46 | 106,031 | 104,432 | -0.2 | 35,491 | 38,593 | 1174 | 28 |
| WYOMING | 10,002 | 10,463 | 10,520 | 0.5 | 2.69 | 7,464 | 7,571 | 0.2 | 36,294 | 43,089 | 1067 | 23 |
| YORK | 128,666 | 145,890 | 152,634 | 1.5 | 2.56 | 94,919 | 104,825 | 1.2 | 44,823 | 51,586 | 360 | 10 |
| PENNSYLVANIA | | | | 0.3 | 2.52 | | | -0.1 | 40,344 | 46,169 | | |
| UNITED STATES | | | | 1.4 | 2.59 | | | 1.1 | 41,914 | 49,127 | | |

| COUNTY | 2000 Per Capita Income | 2000 HH Income Base | 2000 HOUSEHOLD INCOME DISTRIBUTION (%) | | | | | | 2000 AVERAGE DISPOSABLE INCOME BY AGE OF HOUSEHOLDER | | | | | |
|---|---|---|---|---|---|---|---|---|---|---|---|---|---|---|
| | | | Less than $15,000 | $15,000 to $24,999 | $25,000 to $49,999 | $50,000 to $99,999 | $100,000 to $149,999 | $150,000 or More | All Ages | <35 | 35-44 | 45-54 | 55-64 | 65+ |
| ADAMS | 19,054 | 32,483 | 9.4 | 11.8 | 40.9 | 31.6 | 5.0 | 1.3 | 37,097 | 33,364 | 41,324 | 46,601 | 40,740 | 24,501 |
| ALLEGHENY | 23,931 | 518,730 | 16.7 | 13.7 | 33.0 | 26.3 | 6.5 | 3.9 | 39,113 | 33,612 | 44,050 | 49,335 | 43,178 | 25,244 |
| ARMSTRONG | 14,790 | 28,618 | 19.6 | 18.7 | 39.5 | 19.6 | 2.0 | 0.6 | 28,087 | 27,311 | 33,528 | 35,658 | 30,406 | 18,561 |
| BEAVER | 17,813 | 72,447 | 17.4 | 16.1 | 36.1 | 25.6 | 3.9 | 1.0 | 32,104 | 30,444 | 37,708 | 41,575 | 34,971 | 21,322 |
| BEDFORD | 14,411 | 19,014 | 17.7 | 18.2 | 40.0 | 21.7 | 2.4 | 0.1 | 28,653 | 27,602 | 34,254 | 36,432 | 30,616 | 19,133 |
| BERKS | 22,412 | 138,397 | 10.9 | 10.5 | 34.9 | 33.5 | 7.7 | 2.6 | 40,894 | 38,356 | 46,503 | 52,441 | 44,604 | 25,407 |
| BLAIR | 15,719 | 50,973 | 20.6 | 17.4 | 38.2 | 20.7 | 2.5 | 0.7 | 28,867 | 26,564 | 34,500 | 36,017 | 32,913 | 18,900 |
| BRADFORD | 15,414 | 23,592 | 19.1 | 16.8 | 37.9 | 22.2 | 3.1 | 0.9 | 30,162 | 28,296 | 36,222 | 39,031 | 33,509 | 17,236 |
| BUCKS | 29,230 | 214,857 | 5.4 | 6.2 | 27.0 | 41.3 | 13.9 | 6.4 | 54,450 | 47,717 | 56,366 | 65,360 | 57,730 | 33,490 |
| BUTLER | 19,662 | 65,193 | 13.4 | 12.4 | 35.8 | 30.9 | 5.8 | 1.7 | 37,072 | 33,722 | 40,722 | 47,721 | 39,708 | 23,525 |
| CAMBRIA | 15,202 | 59,588 | 21.2 | 18.8 | 37.0 | 19.8 | 2.4 | 0.7 | 28,195 | 26,287 | 34,433 | 36,637 | 30,650 | 19,314 |
| CAMERON | 14,336 | 2,292 | 18.5 | 23.6 | 38.7 | 16.6 | 2.6 | 0.0 | 26,278 | 28,655 | 32,236 | 31,108 | 31,679 | 16,100 |
| CARBON | 17,843 | 23,178 | 15.0 | 14.4 | 39.4 | 26.2 | 4.2 | 0.9 | 32,846 | 33,087 | 39,389 | 41,582 | 36,923 | 20,709 |
| CENTRE | 18,387 | 46,523 | 16.5 | 15.0 | 33.6 | 26.2 | 6.0 | 2.7 | 36,578 | 25,962 | 42,403 | 51,732 | 46,434 | 26,138 |
| CHESTER | 37,382 | 156,691 | 4.6 | 5.3 | 22.3 | 39.1 | 16.8 | 11.9 | 65,825 | 52,581 | 64,088 | 74,047 | 67,955 | 41,467 |
| CLARION | 14,002 | 15,279 | 21.5 | 17.8 | 38.0 | 19.8 | 2.4 | 0.6 | 28,119 | 24,412 | 33,067 | 37,423 | 30,909 | 18,998 |
| CLEARFIELD | 14,891 | 30,712 | 21.3 | 18.2 | 37.5 | 19.9 | 2.3 | 0.9 | 28,408 | 27,042 | 35,154 | 35,974 | 30,702 | 18,028 |
| CLINTON | 14,744 | 14,057 | 20.2 | 18.6 | 38.6 | 19.4 | 2.5 | 0.7 | 28,371 | 26,029 | 33,977 | 37,681 | 31,112 | 18,362 |
| COLUMBIA | 16,967 | 23,976 | 14.7 | 17.8 | 39.2 | 23.0 | 4.0 | 1.3 | 32,160 | 29,334 | 40,245 | 40,798 | 34,603 | 20,443 |
| CRAWFORD | 14,968 | 33,806 | 20.1 | 18.2 | 38.3 | 20.0 | 2.8 | 0.8 | 28,972 | 25,766 | 33,843 | 37,994 | 31,380 | 18,832 |
| CUMBERLAND | 22,390 | 80,630 | 7.8 | 11.4 | 35.7 | 35.9 | 7.2 | 2.1 | 41,060 | 35,398 | 45,360 | 52,033 | 46,075 | 27,708 |
| DAUPHIN | 22,191 | 100,019 | 11.8 | 12.0 | 35.8 | 31.8 | 6.6 | 2.1 | 38,702 | 34,738 | 43,429 | 48,526 | 42,235 | 25,156 |
| DELAWARE | 24,816 | 201,684 | 10.6 | 10.2 | 31.8 | 33.7 | 8.8 | 4.9 | 45,629 | 40,228 | 47,925 | 56,522 | 52,225 | 29,720 |
| ELK | 15,878 | 13,235 | 16.7 | 14.0 | 41.3 | 25.2 | 2.7 | 0.2 | 30,755 | 32,117 | 36,103 | 39,076 | 34,387 | 18,976 |
| ERIE | 18,894 | 103,566 | 15.2 | 13.2 | 37.3 | 27.7 | 5.1 | 1.6 | 35,189 | 30,211 | 39,791 | 46,292 | 40,073 | 22,594 |
| FAYETTE | 14,243 | 56,967 | 27.4 | 20.6 | 33.8 | 15.2 | 2.1 | 1.0 | 25,738 | 23,068 | 30,892 | 31,732 | 28,447 | 18,295 |
| FOREST | 14,216 | 1,987 | 18.7 | 22.4 | 39.7 | 17.4 | 1.8 | 0.1 | 26,420 | 28,292 | 31,385 | 33,551 | 25,507 | 18,969 |
| FRANKLIN | 18,288 | 49,667 | 11.8 | 15.1 | 39.9 | 28.0 | 4.0 | 1.2 | 34,518 | 31,634 | 39,583 | 42,990 | 36,864 | 23,172 |
| FULTON | 15,308 | 5,506 | 15.4 | 16.2 | 41.0 | 24.4 | 2.4 | 0.6 | 30,789 | 30,131 | 36,707 | 38,618 | 31,258 | 20,519 |
| GREENE | 14,901 | 15,273 | 24.7 | 18.8 | 35.3 | 17.8 | 2.6 | 0.8 | 27,162 | 24,385 | 33,327 | 33,876 | 28,304 | 18,678 |
| HUNTINGDON | 15,725 | 15,916 | 18.0 | 15.6 | 39.7 | 22.7 | 3.1 | 0.8 | 30,531 | 28,296 | 35,967 | 40,290 | 33,983 | 18,773 |
| INDIANA | 14,082 | 31,650 | 22.6 | 17.4 | 36.6 | 20.2 | 2.6 | 0.7 | 28,318 | 23,716 | 34,442 | 36,583 | 31,331 | 19,334 |
| JEFFERSON | 14,951 | 17,930 | 21.1 | 18.8 | 37.9 | 19.1 | 2.3 | 0.7 | 27,896 | 25,984 | 32,257 | 35,053 | 31,980 | 18,968 |
| JUNIATA | 14,714 | 8,407 | 13.9 | 18.1 | 42.2 | 23.6 | 2.1 | 0.1 | 29,726 | 29,530 | 34,785 | 36,064 | 32,259 | 19,151 |
| LACKAWANNA | 18,453 | 81,115 | 20.6 | 15.1 | 35.5 | 22.4 | 4.3 | 2.1 | 32,785 | 30,742 | 38,109 | 43,760 | 37,256 | 20,385 |
| LANCASTER | 21,665 | 167,709 | 8.2 | 9.3 | 35.6 | 36.7 | 8.1 | 2.2 | 42,070 | 38,520 | 45,800 | 52,956 | 46,023 | 27,886 |
| LAWRENCE | 15,647 | 36,411 | 21.0 | 18.9 | 37.0 | 18.9 | 2.9 | 1.2 | 29,138 | 25,481 | 33,935 | 38,358 | 33,859 | 19,293 |
| LEBANON | 18,671 | 45,308 | 12.3 | 12.7 | 39.5 | 30.0 | 4.5 | 1.1 | 35,255 | 33,630 | 40,627 | 45,135 | 37,559 | 21,646 |
| LEHIGH | 22,462 | 118,338 | 11.1 | 11.9 | 35.0 | 32.7 | 6.9 | 2.4 | 39,858 | 36,223 | 45,171 | 51,117 | 43,159 | 25,207 |
| LUZERNE | 19,135 | 124,178 | 19.0 | 15.8 | 37.1 | 22.0 | 4.2 | 2.0 | 32,655 | 30,925 | 38,952 | 43,757 | 36,702 | 20,332 |
| LYCOMING | 16,121 | 44,838 | 16.8 | 16.4 | 40.0 | 23.4 | 2.9 | 0.7 | 30,682 | 27,731 | 35,823 | 38,884 | 34,425 | 20,340 |
| MCKEAN | 17,213 | 17,653 | 18.0 | 15.2 | 38.4 | 22.9 | 4.3 | 1.3 | 31,955 | 29,271 | 37,454 | 41,339 | 35,956 | 20,634 |
| MERCER | 16,338 | 46,706 | 17.3 | 16.5 | 38.7 | 23.3 | 3.4 | 0.8 | 30,982 | 27,956 | 35,324 | 40,078 | 36,275 | 20,932 |
| MIFFLIN | 14,327 | 18,307 | 19.2 | 19.4 | 39.7 | 19.3 | 2.3 | 0.2 | 27,727 | 26,996 | 32,676 | 35,383 | 30,536 | 17,245 |
| MONROE | 21,574 | 47,818 | 8.9 | 10.0 | 34.7 | 35.5 | 8.4 | 2.4 | 41,989 | 40,796 | 46,226 | 52,550 | 43,517 | 25,002 |
| MONTGOMERY | 36,073 | 280,580 | 5.5 | 6.9 | 26.6 | 37.2 | 13.8 | 10.0 | 59,991 | 49,182 | 59,569 | 69,207 | 63,721 | 41,038 |
| MONTOUR | 21,870 | 6,720 | 15.0 | 15.7 | 37.5 | 23.5 | 5.6 | 2.6 | 35,941 | 31,711 | 42,110 | 43,658 | 36,881 | 21,299 |
| NORTHAMPTON | 23,319 | 97,347 | 9.8 | 9.6 | 33.7 | 35.4 | 8.6 | 2.9 | 42,780 | 39,679 | 47,449 | 55,849 | 44,803 | 26,257 |
| NORTHUMBERLAND | 14,735 | 37,156 | 22.1 | 18.3 | 38.9 | 18.1 | 2.0 | 0.6 | 27,380 | 27,583 | 34,442 | 34,971 | 28,919 | 17,067 |
| PERRY | 18,032 | 16,569 | 9.3 | 11.8 | 41.1 | 32.7 | 4.5 | 0.6 | 35,921 | 34,514 | 40,704 | 44,393 | 36,531 | 22,264 |
| PHILADELPHIA | 17,080 | 548,039 | 23.9 | 15.2 | 33.0 | 22.5 | 3.9 | 1.5 | 31,005 | 28,622 | 34,336 | 38,241 | 34,887 | 21,488 |
| PIKE | 21,692 | 16,087 | 10.1 | 13.4 | 36.2 | 30.2 | 7.0 | 3.1 | 40,476 | 40,377 | 46,389 | 49,768 | 44,688 | 22,387 |
| POTTER | 14,915 | 6,553 | 18.8 | 18.5 | 39.3 | 20.2 | 2.6 | 0.7 | 28,869 | 26,774 | 33,125 | 39,887 | 32,459 | 17,337 |
| SCHUYLKILL | 16,194 | 59,059 | 21.0 | 15.4 | 38.3 | 21.8 | 2.7 | 0.7 | 29,452 | 31,170 | 36,244 | 39,944 | 31,762 | 17,887 |
| SNYDER | 15,479 | 13,543 | 15.0 | 15.7 | 41.2 | 24.1 | 3.2 | 0.9 | 31,777 | 28,823 | 36,325 | 41,424 | 35,402 | 19,380 |
| SOMERSET | 14,564 | 30,155 | 20.7 | 20.0 | 37.6 | 18.6 | 2.3 | 0.9 | 27,869 | 26,297 | 32,846 | 35,667 | 29,882 | 18,766 |
| SULLIVAN | 14,292 | 2,330 | 25.5 | 21.4 | 37.1 | 13.4 | 2.0 | 0.6 | 24,846 | 25,384 | 30,797 | 33,580 | 27,422 | 13,923 |
| SUSQUEHANNA | 15,444 | 15,908 | 18.9 | 17.0 | 39.0 | 21.1 | 3.1 | 1.0 | 30,176 | 28,005 | 35,753 | 39,356 | 31,827 | 18,151 |
| TIOGA | 15,750 | 15,663 | 16.5 | 18.2 | 37.8 | 23.3 | 3.4 | 0.9 | 30,946 | 27,162 | 36,869 | 40,472 | 35,102 | 19,988 |
| UNION | 15,117 | 12,375 | 13.7 | 16.7 | 39.4 | 25.1 | 3.5 | 1.6 | 33,529 | 28,514 | 38,919 | 43,273 | 36,830 | 20,456 |
| VENANGO | 14,531 | 22,110 | 19.6 | 20.2 | 37.6 | 19.7 | 2.3 | 0.6 | 28,048 | 24,390 | 32,538 | 36,562 | 31,144 | 19,028 |
| WARREN | 17,191 | 17,139 | 14.9 | 16.5 | 40.5 | 24.1 | 2.9 | 1.1 | 31,881 | 27,878 | 36,095 | 40,749 | 37,460 | 20,801 |
| WASHINGTON | 19,296 | 80,550 | 18.9 | 15.4 | 34.8 | 24.0 | 4.7 | 2.2 | 33,972 | 30,253 | 39,403 | 44,972 | 37,514 | 21,139 |
| WAYNE | 16,453 | 16,856 | 16.2 | 17.2 | 39.2 | 21.6 | 3.9 | 1.9 | 32,433 | 30,802 | 38,475 | 42,026 | 33,262 | 19,909 |
| WESTMORELAND | 18,841 | 146,978 | 17.6 | 16.0 | 35.2 | 24.9 | 4.5 | 1.8 | 33,540 | 30,229 | 39,467 | 44,565 | 37,084 | 20,682 |
| WYOMING | 16,230 | 10,463 | 15.7 | 14.9 | 38.3 | 26.2 | 4.0 | 0.9 | 32,816 | 30,814 | 37,615 | 43,683 | 32,257 | 19,532 |
| YORK | 21,008 | 145,889 | 9.6 | 10.6 | 37.6 | 34.5 | 6.1 | 1.6 | 39,071 | 36,305 | 43,873 | 49,124 | 42,619 | 23,962 |
| PENNSYLVANIA | 21,645 | | 14.8 | 13.1 | 34.1 | 28.4 | 6.5 | 3.1 | 38,768 | 34,429 | 43,367 | 48,861 | 42,361 | 24,642 |
| UNITED STATES | 22,162 | | 14.5 | 12.5 | 32.3 | 29.8 | 7.4 | 3.5 | 40,748 | 34,503 | 44,969 | 49,579 | 43,409 | 27,339 |

| COUNTY | FINANCIAL SERVICES | | | | THE HOME | | | | | | ENTERTAINMENT | | | | | | PERSONAL | | | |
|---|---|---|---|---|---|---|---|---|---|---|---|---|---|---|---|---|---|---|---|---|
| | | | | | Home Improvements | | | Furnishings | | | | | | | | | | | | |
| | Auto Loan | Home Loan | Invest-ments | Retire-ment Plans | Home Repair | Lawn & Garden | Remodel-ing | Appli-ances | Elec-tronics | Furni-ture | Restau-rants | Sport-ing Goods | Theater & Concerts | Toys & Hobbies | Travel | Video Rental | Apparel | Auto After-market | Health Insur-ance | Pets & Supplies |
| ADAMS | 101 | 79 | 86 | 87 | 89 | 87 | 105 | 98 | 95 | 88 | 90 | 99 | 90 | 102 | 82 | 99 | 93 | 92 | 103 | 103 |
| ALLEGHENY | 99 | 97 | 108 | 101 | 98 | 97 | 90 | 99 | 95 | 101 | 99 | 100 | 103 | 102 | 100 | 99 | 103 | 97 | 102 | 101 |
| ARMSTRONG | 97 | 74 | 83 | 81 | 90 | 87 | 99 | 96 | 90 | 85 | 85 | 95 | 88 | 98 | 82 | 97 | 87 | 88 | 103 | 98 |
| BEAVER | 97 | 84 | 95 | 87 | 95 | 91 | 92 | 97 | 91 | 93 | 91 | 95 | 95 | 99 | 90 | 97 | 93 | 91 | 102 | 98 |
| BEDFORD | 99 | 67 | 73 | 78 | 85 | 84 | 104 | 96 | 92 | 79 | 80 | 97 | 83 | 98 | 74 | 98 | 84 | 87 | 104 | 99 |
| BERKS | 100 | 89 | 98 | 93 | 95 | 93 | 97 | 98 | 95 | 96 | 96 | 99 | 97 | 102 | 92 | 99 | 98 | 95 | 103 | 102 |
| BLAIR | 96 | 80 | 89 | 84 | 92 | 89 | 95 | 96 | 90 | 89 | 88 | 95 | 91 | 97 | 87 | 97 | 90 | 90 | 102 | 98 |
| BRADFORD | 99 | 73 | 81 | 82 | 87 | 86 | 104 | 96 | 93 | 83 | 85 | 97 | 87 | 99 | 79 | 98 | 88 | 89 | 103 | 101 |
| BUCKS | 104 | 107 | 106 | 109 | 97 | 100 | 95 | 102 | 104 | 108 | 111 | 108 | 110 | 109 | 102 | 102 | 114 | 105 | 103 | 106 |
| BUTLER | 99 | 85 | 90 | 89 | 91 | 89 | 98 | 97 | 95 | 92 | 94 | 99 | 94 | 102 | 87 | 99 | 95 | 93 | 102 | 102 |
| CAMBRIA | 96 | 81 | 95 | 86 | 95 | 91 | 92 | 96 | 89 | 91 | 89 | 94 | 93 | 97 | 90 | 97 | 91 | 90 | 103 | 97 |
| CAMERON | 98 | 74 | 83 | 82 | 91 | 88 | 100 | 96 | 89 | 85 | 86 | 96 | 88 | 99 | 83 | 97 | 88 | 88 | 104 | 99 |
| CARBON | 96 | 77 | 85 | 81 | 93 | 88 | 97 | 96 | 88 | 87 | 87 | 94 | 89 | 97 | 85 | 97 | 88 | 88 | 103 | 98 |
| CENTRE | 99 | 95 | 97 | 99 | 92 | 91 | 96 | 95 | 95 | 92 | 96 | 99 | 94 | 101 | 91 | 97 | 99 | 96 | 101 | 102 |
| CHESTER | 107 | 115 | 111 | 118 | 99 | 105 | 99 | 105 | 109 | 113 | 117 | 113 | 115 | 111 | 108 | 103 | 122 | 110 | 105 | 109 |
| CLARION | 98 | 73 | 79 | 81 | 86 | 84 | 103 | 94 | 91 | 81 | 83 | 95 | 84 | 97 | 78 | 97 | 86 | 88 | 103 | 99 |
| CLEARFIELD | 97 | 72 | 80 | 80 | 88 | 86 | 99 | 95 | 91 | 83 | 83 | 95 | 86 | 97 | 80 | 97 | 86 | 88 | 103 | 98 |
| CLINTON | 98 | 76 | 85 | 84 | 90 | 87 | 101 | 96 | 91 | 86 | 86 | 97 | 89 | 99 | 83 | 98 | 89 | 89 | 103 | 100 |
| COLUMBIA | 98 | 79 | 88 | 85 | 91 | 88 | 100 | 96 | 91 | 87 | 89 | 96 | 90 | 99 | 84 | 98 | 91 | 90 | 103 | 100 |
| CRAWFORD | 98 | 74 | 83 | 83 | 89 | 87 | 101 | 96 | 92 | 84 | 85 | 97 | 87 | 98 | 81 | 98 | 88 | 89 | 103 | 100 |
| CUMBERLAND | 102 | 97 | 103 | 101 | 95 | 96 | 97 | 99 | 99 | 100 | 102 | 103 | 102 | 105 | 96 | 100 | 105 | 99 | 103 | 104 |
| DAUPHIN | 99 | 94 | 100 | 95 | 95 | 93 | 91 | 98 | 95 | 99 | 97 | 99 | 99 | 101 | 95 | 99 | 101 | 97 | 100 | 101 |
| DELAWARE | 101 | 105 | 113 | 108 | 100 | 102 | 92 | 100 | 100 | 106 | 106 | 104 | 108 | 105 | 105 | 100 | 110 | 102 | 103 | 103 |
| ELK | 98 | 75 | 83 | 82 | 90 | 87 | 100 | 96 | 91 | 86 | 86 | 96 | 89 | 99 | 82 | 97 | 88 | 89 | 103 | 99 |
| ERIE | 98 | 87 | 94 | 91 | 93 | 90 | 95 | 97 | 93 | 93 | 93 | 97 | 95 | 100 | 90 | 98 | 95 | 93 | 101 | 100 |
| FAYETTE | 95 | 74 | 85 | 80 | 91 | 88 | 94 | 95 | 88 | 85 | 84 | 93 | 88 | 95 | 84 | 96 | 86 | 87 | 102 | 96 |
| FOREST | 101 | 69 | 74 | 86 | 85 | 85 | 117 | 99 | 92 | 76 | 81 | 101 | 83 | 102 | 76 | 100 | 86 | 89 | 109 | 104 |
| FRANKLIN | 100 | 81 | 91 | 88 | 91 | 89 | 101 | 98 | 94 | 90 | 91 | 98 | 93 | 101 | 85 | 99 | 93 | 92 | 103 | 102 |
| FULTON | 99 | 66 | 71 | 77 | 85 | 83 | 105 | 96 | 92 | 78 | 80 | 98 | 82 | 98 | 73 | 98 | 83 | 87 | 103 | 100 |
| GREENE | 96 | 69 | 77 | 77 | 88 | 85 | 98 | 95 | 90 | 81 | 82 | 93 | 84 | 95 | 78 | 96 | 84 | 86 | 103 | 97 |
| HUNTINGDON | 99 | 72 | 80 | 81 | 88 | 86 | 102 | 96 | 92 | 83 | 84 | 97 | 86 | 98 | 79 | 98 | 87 | 88 | 103 | 100 |
| INDIANA | 98 | 78 | 85 | 85 | 89 | 87 | 99 | 95 | 91 | 85 | 87 | 96 | 88 | 98 | 82 | 97 | 89 | 89 | 102 | 99 |
| JEFFERSON | 97 | 70 | 78 | 79 | 88 | 86 | 100 | 95 | 90 | 81 | 82 | 94 | 85 | 97 | 78 | 97 | 85 | 87 | 103 | 98 |
| JUNIATA | 99 | 72 | 79 | 81 | 88 | 86 | 103 | 96 | 92 | 83 | 84 | 97 | 86 | 99 | 78 | 98 | 87 | 88 | 103 | 100 |
| LACKAWANNA | 96 | 85 | 96 | 88 | 96 | 92 | 93 | 96 | 90 | 93 | 92 | 95 | 95 | 99 | 92 | 97 | 93 | 91 | 102 | 98 |
| LANCASTER | 100 | 89 | 93 | 93 | 91 | 90 | 99 | 98 | 96 | 94 | 96 | 100 | 96 | 103 | 89 | 99 | 98 | 95 | 102 | 103 |
| LAWRENCE | 96 | 81 | 94 | 86 | 94 | 91 | 93 | 96 | 90 | 91 | 89 | 95 | 93 | 98 | 89 | 97 | 91 | 90 | 103 | 98 |
| LEBANON | 99 | 84 | 91 | 88 | 92 | 89 | 99 | 97 | 93 | 91 | 92 | 98 | 93 | 101 | 87 | 98 | 94 | 92 | 102 | 101 |
| LEHIGH | 100 | 97 | 103 | 100 | 96 | 96 | 94 | 99 | 97 | 101 | 101 | 102 | 102 | 103 | 97 | 99 | 103 | 98 | 103 | 102 |
| LUZERNE | 96 | 83 | 95 | 87 | 95 | 91 | 93 | 96 | 90 | 92 | 91 | 94 | 94 | 98 | 91 | 97 | 92 | 90 | 102 | 98 |
| LYCOMING | 98 | 81 | 91 | 86 | 92 | 89 | 96 | 96 | 91 | 89 | 89 | 96 | 91 | 99 | 86 | 97 | 91 | 90 | 102 | 99 |
| MCKEAN | 96 | 75 | 85 | 81 | 91 | 88 | 96 | 95 | 89 | 85 | 85 | 94 | 88 | 96 | 83 | 96 | 87 | 88 | 103 | 97 |
| MERCER | 97 | 80 | 92 | 84 | 93 | 90 | 94 | 96 | 90 | 89 | 88 | 95 | 91 | 98 | 87 | 97 | 90 | 90 | 102 | 98 |
| MIFFLIN | 97 | 72 | 81 | 79 | 89 | 87 | 98 | 96 | 90 | 83 | 83 | 95 | 86 | 97 | 80 | 96 | 85 | 87 | 103 | 98 |
| MONROE | 104 | 93 | 94 | 99 | 92 | 93 | 103 | 101 | 100 | 97 | 100 | 105 | 100 | 106 | 91 | 101 | 104 | 99 | 104 | 106 |
| MONTGOMERY | 105 | 114 | 116 | 117 | 102 | 107 | 97 | 103 | 106 | 112 | 116 | 110 | 116 | 110 | 111 | 102 | 120 | 108 | 106 | 107 |
| MONTOUR | 101 | 87 | 100 | 96 | 94 | 93 | 101 | 99 | 96 | 94 | 95 | 101 | 97 | 103 | 91 | 99 | 98 | 95 | 104 | 103 |
| NORTHAMPTON | 101 | 94 | 101 | 98 | 96 | 95 | 96 | 99 | 96 | 99 | 99 | 101 | 101 | 103 | 95 | 99 | 102 | 97 | 103 | 102 |
| NORTHUMBERLAND | 96 | 78 | 87 | 82 | 92 | 88 | 95 | 95 | 89 | 88 | 87 | 93 | 90 | 97 | 86 | 97 | 89 | 89 | 102 | 97 |
| PERRY | 100 | 79 | 84 | 86 | 89 | 87 | 103 | 97 | 94 | 88 | 90 | 99 | 90 | 102 | 82 | 99 | 93 | 92 | 103 | 102 |
| PHILADELPHIA | 93 | 86 | 95 | 85 | 94 | 89 | 81 | 95 | 88 | 95 | 86 | 92 | 93 | 93 | 94 | 98 | 94 | 93 | 93 | 95 |
| PIKE | 102 | 75 | 82 | 89 | 88 | 88 | 114 | 99 | 93 | 82 | 86 | 102 | 88 | 104 | 81 | 100 | 90 | 91 | 108 | 105 |
| POTTER | 98 | 68 | 75 | 79 | 86 | 85 | 106 | 96 | 91 | 79 | 80 | 96 | 83 | 97 | 76 | 97 | 84 | 87 | 104 | 99 |
| SCHUYLKILL | 96 | 79 | 89 | 83 | 94 | 89 | 94 | 96 | 88 | 89 | 88 | 94 | 91 | 97 | 88 | 97 | 89 | 89 | 102 | 97 |
| SNYDER | 98 | 75 | 83 | 83 | 88 | 86 | 102 | 96 | 93 | 84 | 86 | 96 | 87 | 99 | 80 | 98 | 88 | 89 | 102 | 100 |
| SOMERSET | 97 | 71 | 79 | 79 | 88 | 86 | 101 | 96 | 91 | 82 | 83 | 95 | 85 | 97 | 79 | 97 | 86 | 88 | 103 | 98 |
| SULLIVAN | 101 | 67 | 72 | 84 | 85 | 85 | 115 | 98 | 92 | 76 | 80 | 101 | 82 | 101 | 75 | 99 | 85 | 88 | 108 | 103 |
| SUSQUEHANNA | 100 | 74 | 81 | 84 | 88 | 86 | 106 | 97 | 93 | 84 | 86 | 98 | 87 | 101 | 79 | 99 | 89 | 90 | 104 | 102 |
| TIOGA | 100 | 73 | 82 | 84 | 87 | 86 | 105 | 96 | 93 | 83 | 85 | 98 | 86 | 100 | 79 | 98 | 88 | 89 | 104 | 101 |
| UNION | 102 | 86 | 96 | 94 | 93 | 92 | 103 | 99 | 96 | 92 | 95 | 101 | 96 | 104 | 88 | 100 | 98 | 95 | 105 | 104 |
| VENANGO | 98 | 74 | 82 | 82 | 89 | 86 | 101 | 96 | 91 | 84 | 85 | 95 | 87 | 98 | 81 | 98 | 87 | 89 | 103 | 99 |
| WARREN | 98 | 77 | 85 | 83 | 90 | 87 | 100 | 96 | 91 | 86 | 87 | 96 | 89 | 99 | 83 | 98 | 89 | 89 | 103 | 100 |
| WASHINGTON | 98 | 85 | 96 | 91 | 94 | 92 | 95 | 97 | 92 | 93 | 93 | 97 | 96 | 100 | 91 | 98 | 95 | 92 | 103 | 99 |
| WAYNE | 100 | 73 | 79 | 85 | 87 | 86 | 109 | 98 | 93 | 82 | 85 | 99 | 86 | 101 | 79 | 99 | 89 | 90 | 105 | 103 |
| WESTMORELAND | 98 | 86 | 98 | 91 | 95 | 93 | 94 | 98 | 93 | 94 | 94 | 98 | 97 | 101 | 92 | 98 | 96 | 93 | 103 | 100 |
| WYOMING | 101 | 74 | 79 | 84 | 87 | 85 | 108 | 98 | 94 | 83 | 86 | 99 | 87 | 102 | 77 | 100 | 90 | 90 | 104 | 103 |
| YORK | 100 | 88 | 93 | 92 | 92 | 90 | 98 | 98 | 96 | 94 | 96 | 100 | 96 | 103 | 89 | 99 | 98 | 95 | 102 | 102 |
| PENNSYLVANIA | 99 | 92 | 100 | 96 | 95 | 94 | 94 | 98 | 95 | 97 | 96 | 100 | 99 | 101 | 94 | 99 | 100 | 96 | 102 | 101 |
| UNITED STATES | 100 | 100 | 100 | 100 | 100 | 100 | 100 | 100 | 100 | 100 | 100 | 100 | 100 | 100 | 100 | 100 | 100 | 100 | 100 | 100 |

| COUNTY | FIPS Code | MSA Code | DMA Code | POPULATION 1990 | POPULATION 2000 | POPULATION 2005 | 1990-2000 ANNUAL CHANGE % Rate | 1990-2000 ANNUAL CHANGE State Rank | RACE (%) White 1990 | White 2000 | Black 1990 | Black 2000 | Asian/Pacific 1990 | Asian/Pacific 2000 |
|---|---|---|---|---|---|---|---|---|---|---|---|---|---|---|
| BRISTOL | 001 | 6483 | 521 | 48,859 | 49,067 | 48,892 | 0.0 | 3 | 98.8 | 98.4 | 0.4 | 0.4 | 0.6 | 0.8 |
| KENT | 003 | 6483 | 521 | 161,135 | 162,410 | 163,904 | 0.1 | 2 | 98.1 | 97.6 | 0.7 | 0.8 | 0.8 | 1.1 |
| NEWPORT | 005 | 0000 | 521 | 87,194 | 83,212 | 83,912 | -0.5 | 5 | 93.9 | 92.9 | 3.9 | 4.2 | 1.2 | 1.6 |
| PROVIDENCE | 007 | 6483 | 521 | 596,270 | 573,303 | 569,347 | -0.4 | 4 | 87.7 | 84.4 | 5.6 | 6.6 | 2.4 | 3.0 |
| WASHINGTON | 009 | 6483 | 521 | 110,006 | 124,019 | 131,668 | 1.2 | 1 | 96.6 | 95.7 | 1.0 | 1.1 | 1.3 | 1.7 |
| RHODE ISLAND | | | | | | | -0.1 | | 91.4 | 89.4 | 3.9 | 4.5 | 1.8 | 2.3 |
| UNITED STATES | | | | | | | 1.0 | | 80.3 | 77.9 | 12.1 | 12.4 | 2.9 | 3.9 |

| COUNTY | % HISPANIC ORIGIN 1990 | % HISPANIC ORIGIN 2000 | 2000 AGE DISTRIBUTION (%) 0-4 | 5-9 | 10-14 | 15-19 | 20-24 | 25-44 | 45-64 | 65-84 | 85+ | 18+ | MEDIAN AGE 1990 | MEDIAN AGE 2000 | 2000 Males/ Females (×100) |
|---|---|---|---|---|---|---|---|---|---|---|---|---|---|---|---|
| BRISTOL | 1.4 | 2.6 | 5.7 | 7.0 | 7.4 | 6.6 | 5.1 | 28.3 | 22.0 | 15.7 | 2.3 | 77.0 | 35.8 | 38.8 | 93.8 |
| KENT | 1.1 | 2.2 | 5.6 | 7.0 | 7.5 | 5.4 | 4.3 | 31.0 | 22.5 | 14.5 | 2.2 | 76.7 | 35.8 | 38.8 | 91.6 |
| NEWPORT | 2.0 | 3.2 | 6.2 | 7.2 | 7.2 | 5.6 | 5.4 | 32.8 | 20.9 | 12.7 | 2.0 | 76.5 | 33.7 | 36.8 | 95.0 |
| PROVIDENCE | 6.8 | 10.6 | 6.4 | 7.0 | 7.0 | 6.7 | 6.4 | 30.6 | 20.1 | 13.5 | 2.3 | 76.3 | 33.6 | 36.3 | 91.9 |
| WASHINGTON | 1.0 | 1.9 | 5.9 | 7.1 | 7.3 | 7.8 | 6.0 | 30.8 | 22.2 | 11.4 | 1.7 | 76.6 | 32.7 | 35.9 | 94.9 |
| RHODE ISLAND | 4.6 | 7.1 | 6.2 | 7.0 | 7.2 | 6.5 | 5.8 | 30.8 | 20.9 | 13.4 | 2.2 | 76.5 | 34.0 | 36.8 | 92.6 |
| UNITED STATES | 9.0 | 11.8 | 6.9 | 7.2 | 7.2 | 7.2 | 6.7 | 29.9 | 22.2 | 11.1 | 1.6 | 74.6 | 32.9 | 35.7 | 95.6 |

| COUNTY | HOUSEHOLDS | | | | | FAMILIES | | | MEDIAN HOUSEHOLD INCOME | | | |
|---|---|---|---|---|---|---|---|---|---|---|---|---|
| | 1990 | 2000 | 2005 | % Annual Rate 1990-2000 | 2000 Average HH Size | 1990 | 2000 | % Annual Rate 1990-2000 | 2000 | 2005 | 2000 National Rank | 2000 State Rank |
| BRISTOL | 17,559 | 18,059 | 18,235 | 0.3 | 2.57 | 13,086 | 12,978 | -0.1 | 51,891 | 60,195 | 172 | 2 |
| KENT | 62,058 | 63,561 | 64,657 | 0.3 | 2.52 | 43,723 | 42,865 | -0.2 | 49,208 | 57,932 | 217 | 3 |
| NEWPORT | 32,687 | 32,256 | 32,683 | -0.2 | 2.51 | 22,334 | 21,314 | -0.6 | 47,353 | 55,659 | 261 | 4 |
| PROVIDENCE | 226,362 | 218,796 | 218,179 | -0.4 | 2.51 | 151,706 | 141,624 | -0.8 | 37,721 | 45,000 | 875 | 5 |
| WASHINGTON | 39,311 | 45,417 | 48,650 | 1.8 | 2.61 | 28,037 | 31,096 | 1.3 | 52,545 | 62,194 | 159 | 1 |
| RHODE ISLAND | | | | 0.0 | 2.53 | | | -0.4 | 42,500 | 50,661 | | |
| UNITED STATES | | | | 1.4 | 2.59 | | | 1.1 | 41,914 | 49,127 | | |

| COUNTY | 2000 Per Capita Income | 2000 HH Income Base | 2000 HOUSEHOLD INCOME DISTRIBUTION (%) Less than $15,000 | $15,000 to $24,999 | $25,000 to $49,999 | $50,000 to $99,999 | $100,000 to $149,999 | $150,000 or More | 2000 AVERAGE DISPOSABLE INCOME BY AGE OF HOUSEHOLDER All Ages | <35 | 35-44 | 45-54 | 55-64 | 65+ |
|---|---|---|---|---|---|---|---|---|---|---|---|---|---|---|
| BRISTOL | 27,795 | 18,059 | 9.0 | 9.0 | 30.0 | 34.6 | 10.7 | 6.7 | 49,186 | 44,145 | 52,927 | 59,331 | 55,751 | 31,808 |
| KENT | 25,258 | 63,561 | 10.8 | 8.7 | 31.4 | 35.6 | 9.4 | 4.1 | 44,036 | 41,852 | 49,619 | 55,288 | 49,052 | 26,092 |
| NEWPORT | 24,546 | 32,256 | 10.9 | 10.5 | 31.3 | 34.6 | 8.7 | 4.0 | 43,120 | 36,729 | 48,573 | 52,913 | 48,682 | 28,765 |
| PROVIDENCE | 18,883 | 218,796 | 19.0 | 12.9 | 33.9 | 27.0 | 5.2 | 2.0 | 34,244 | 32,113 | 39,754 | 42,783 | 38,855 | 21,542 |
| WASHINGTON | 26,970 | 45,417 | 7.3 | 7.1 | 32.1 | 36.9 | 10.7 | 6.0 | 48,824 | 40,621 | 51,856 | 59,749 | 53,587 | 32,573 |
| RHODE ISLAND | 21,898 | | 15.1 | 11.1 | 32.9 | 30.7 | 7.1 | 3.2 | 39,112 | 35,424 | 44,276 | 48,870 | 44,309 | 24,614 |
| UNITED STATES | 22,162 | | 14.5 | 12.5 | 32.3 | 29.8 | 7.4 | 3.5 | 40,748 | 34,503 | 44,969 | 49,579 | 43,409 | 27,339 |

| COUNTY | FINANCIAL SERVICES | | | | THE HOME | | | | | | ENTERTAINMENT | | | | | | PERSONAL | | | |
|---|---|---|---|---|---|---|---|---|---|---|---|---|---|---|---|---|---|---|---|---|
| | | | | | Home Improvements | | | Furnishings | | | | | | | | | | | | |
| | Auto Loan | Home Loan | Invest-ments | Retire-ment Plans | Home Repair | Lawn & Garden | Remodel-ing | Appli-ances | Elec-tronics | Furni-ture | Restau-rants | Sport-ing Goods | Theater & Concerts | Toys & Hobbies | Travel | Video Rental | Apparel | Auto After-market | Health Insur-ance | Pets & Supplies |
| BRISTOL | 104 | 109 | 119 | 116 | 103 | 107 | 97 | 103 | 103 | 111 | 112 | 108 | 114 | 109 | 111 | 101 | 117 | 105 | 106 | 105 |
| KENT | 101 | 101 | 107 | 102 | 98 | 98 | 92 | 100 | 99 | 104 | 105 | 103 | 106 | 105 | 100 | 100 | 107 | 100 | 104 | 103 |
| NEWPORT | 101 | 104 | 106 | 103 | 96 | 97 | 93 | 99 | 100 | 103 | 105 | 103 | 104 | 105 | 100 | 100 | 107 | 101 | 103 | 105 |
| PROVIDENCE | 97 | 94 | 101 | 93 | 96 | 93 | 89 | 96 | 93 | 98 | 96 | 97 | 98 | 98 | 97 | 98 | 98 | 95 | 100 | 99 |
| WASHINGTON | 103 | 100 | 101 | 102 | 95 | 96 | 97 | 101 | 101 | 103 | 105 | 104 | 104 | 106 | 97 | 101 | 108 | 101 | 104 | 106 |
| RHODE ISLAND | 99 | 98 | 104 | 98 | 97 | 96 | 92 | 98 | 96 | 101 | 100 | 100 | 102 | 102 | 99 | 99 | 102 | 98 | 102 | 101 |
| UNITED STATES | 100 | 100 | 100 | 100 | 100 | 100 | 100 | 100 | 100 | 100 | 100 | 100 | 100 | 100 | 100 | 100 | 100 | 100 | 100 | 100 |

| COUNTY | FIPS Code | MSA Code | DMA Code | POPULATION 1990 | POPULATION 2000 | POPULATION 2005 | 1990-2000 ANNUAL CHANGE % Rate | 1990-2000 ANNUAL CHANGE State Rank | RACE (%) White 1990 | White 2000 | Black 1990 | Black 2000 | Asian/Pacific 1990 | Asian/Pacific 2000 |
|---|---|---|---|---|---|---|---|---|---|---|---|---|---|---|
| ABBEVILLE | 001 | 0000 | 567 | 23,862 | 24,783 | 25,270 | 0.4 | 35 | 68.1 | 66.8 | 31.6 | 32.7 | 0.2 | 0.4 |
| AIKEN | 003 | 0600 | 520 | 120,940 | 136,518 | 141,975 | 1.2 | 13 | 75.0 | 74.2 | 24.2 | 24.7 | 0.5 | 0.6 |
| ALLENDALE | 005 | 0000 | 520 | 11,722 | 11,224 | 10,730 | -0.4 | 45 | 31.1 | 30.7 | 68.0 | 68.2 | 0.1 | 0.1 |
| ANDERSON | 007 | 3160 | 567 | 145,196 | 164,918 | 175,487 | 1.3 | 8 | 82.9 | 82.2 | 16.6 | 17.2 | 0.2 | 0.3 |
| BAMBERG | 009 | 0000 | 520 | 16,902 | 16,157 | 15,519 | -0.4 | 45 | 38.3 | 37.7 | 61.4 | 61.9 | 0.1 | 0.2 |
| BARNWELL | 011 | 0000 | 520 | 20,293 | 21,845 | 22,095 | 0.7 | 32 | 56.7 | 56.1 | 42.8 | 43.4 | 0.1 | 0.1 |
| BEAUFORT | 013 | 0000 | 507 | 86,425 | 115,637 | 129,282 | 2.9 | 1 | 69.2 | 69.1 | 28.4 | 27.9 | 0.9 | 1.3 |
| BERKELEY | 015 | 1440 | 519 | 128,776 | 145,717 | 162,710 | 1.2 | 13 | 72.9 | 71.2 | 24.2 | 24.6 | 2.0 | 3.0 |
| CALHOUN | 017 | 0000 | 546 | 12,753 | 14,453 | 15,489 | 1.2 | 13 | 48.2 | 47.3 | 51.6 | 52.4 | 0.1 | 0.1 |
| CHARLESTON | 019 | 1440 | 519 | 295,039 | 324,185 | 342,987 | 0.9 | 22 | 63.6 | 62.1 | 34.9 | 35.9 | 0.9 | 1.3 |
| CHEROKEE | 021 | 3160 | 567 | 44,506 | 50,828 | 54,584 | 1.3 | 8 | 78.6 | 77.8 | 20.6 | 21.1 | 0.4 | 0.6 |
| CHESTER | 023 | 0000 | 517 | 32,170 | 35,452 | 38,029 | 1.0 | 17 | 59.6 | 59.0 | 40.0 | 40.5 | 0.1 | 0.2 |
| CHESTERFIELD | 025 | 0000 | 517 | 38,577 | 41,957 | 44,045 | 0.8 | 28 | 66.2 | 65.5 | 33.4 | 34.2 | 0.1 | 0.1 |
| CLARENDON | 027 | 0000 | 546 | 28,450 | 31,068 | 31,798 | 0.9 | 22 | 43.1 | 42.2 | 56.5 | 57.4 | 0.1 | 0.1 |
| COLLETON | 029 | 0000 | 519 | 34,377 | 37,964 | 39,462 | 1.0 | 17 | 54.3 | 53.7 | 45.0 | 45.6 | 0.1 | 0.1 |
| DARLINGTON | 031 | 0000 | 570 | 61,851 | 66,830 | 68,520 | 0.8 | 28 | 59.6 | 59.0 | 40.1 | 40.6 | 0.1 | 0.1 |
| DILLON | 033 | 0000 | 570 | 29,114 | 29,770 | 30,023 | 0.2 | 39 | 54.5 | 54.1 | 43.7 | 44.1 | 0.2 | 0.3 |
| DORCHESTER | 035 | 1440 | 519 | 83,060 | 92,811 | 103,182 | 1.1 | 16 | 75.0 | 73.7 | 23.0 | 23.8 | 0.9 | 1.4 |
| EDGEFIELD | 037 | 0600 | 520 | 18,375 | 20,089 | 20,522 | 0.9 | 22 | 53.3 | 52.1 | 46.3 | 47.5 | 0.2 | 0.2 |
| FAIRFIELD | 039 | 0000 | 546 | 22,295 | 22,690 | 23,238 | 0.2 | 39 | 41.5 | 41.5 | 58.3 | 58.2 | 0.1 | 0.2 |
| FLORENCE | 041 | 2655 | 570 | 114,344 | 125,880 | 129,114 | 0.9 | 22 | 60.8 | 60.2 | 38.7 | 39.2 | 0.3 | 0.4 |
| GEORGETOWN | 043 | 0000 | 519 | 46,302 | 56,281 | 62,044 | 1.9 | 5 | 56.5 | 56.9 | 43.2 | 42.6 | 0.1 | 0.2 |
| GREENVILLE | 045 | 3160 | 567 | 320,167 | 363,766 | 387,945 | 1.3 | 8 | 80.9 | 80.1 | 18.0 | 18.5 | 0.7 | 1.0 |
| GREENWOOD | 047 | 0000 | 567 | 59,567 | 63,909 | 65,011 | 0.7 | 32 | 69.2 | 68.2 | 30.2 | 30.9 | 0.4 | 0.6 |
| HAMPTON | 049 | 0000 | 507 | 18,191 | 19,119 | 19,182 | 0.5 | 34 | 45.5 | 45.4 | 54.3 | 54.4 | 0.1 | 0.1 |
| HORRY | 051 | 5330 | 570 | 144,053 | 183,239 | 206,483 | 2.4 | 2 | 81.3 | 80.8 | 17.5 | 17.5 | 0.8 | 1.1 |
| JASPER | 053 | 0000 | 507 | 15,487 | 18,170 | 19,011 | 1.6 | 6 | 42.2 | 41.1 | 57.4 | 58.4 | 0.2 | 0.3 |
| KERSHAW | 055 | 0000 | 546 | 43,599 | 50,009 | 53,525 | 1.3 | 8 | 71.2 | 70.4 | 28.3 | 28.9 | 0.2 | 0.3 |
| LANCASTER | 057 | 0000 | 517 | 54,516 | 60,424 | 64,523 | 1.0 | 17 | 74.4 | 74.1 | 25.4 | 25.6 | 0.1 | 0.2 |
| LAURENS | 059 | 0000 | 567 | 58,092 | 63,892 | 66,456 | 0.9 | 22 | 71.4 | 70.3 | 28.2 | 29.2 | 0.2 | 0.2 |
| LEE | 061 | 0000 | 546 | 18,437 | 20,402 | 20,728 | 1.0 | 17 | 37.2 | 36.6 | 62.5 | 62.8 | 0.2 | 0.2 |
| LEXINGTON | 063 | 1760 | 546 | 167,611 | 213,356 | 235,039 | 2.4 | 2 | 87.9 | 87.4 | 11.0 | 11.2 | 0.6 | 0.9 |
| MCCORMICK | 065 | 0000 | 520 | 8,868 | 9,660 | 9,943 | 0.8 | 28 | 41.1 | 40.7 | 58.5 | 58.9 | 0.1 | 0.1 |
| MARION | 067 | 0000 | 570 | 33,899 | 34,377 | 33,889 | 0.1 | 41 | 44.7 | 44.0 | 54.6 | 55.2 | 0.4 | 0.5 |
| MARLBORO | 069 | 0000 | 570 | 29,361 | 29,380 | 28,824 | 0.0 | 42 | 48.7 | 47.4 | 48.5 | 49.8 | 0.1 | 0.1 |
| NEWBERRY | 071 | 0000 | 546 | 33,172 | 34,439 | 34,708 | 0.4 | 35 | 64.8 | 63.6 | 34.7 | 35.7 | 0.3 | 0.4 |
| OCONEE | 073 | 0000 | 567 | 57,494 | 65,954 | 70,357 | 1.3 | 8 | 90.5 | 90.0 | 8.8 | 9.0 | 0.3 | 0.4 |
| ORANGEBURG | 075 | 0000 | 546 | 84,803 | 87,487 | 87,334 | 0.3 | 38 | 41.2 | 40.6 | 58.1 | 58.6 | 0.4 | 0.5 |
| PICKENS | 077 | 3160 | 567 | 93,894 | 109,617 | 116,946 | 1.5 | 7 | 91.6 | 90.9 | 7.3 | 7.6 | 0.8 | 1.2 |
| RICHLAND | 079 | 1760 | 546 | 285,720 | 309,635 | 321,729 | 0.8 | 28 | 56.0 | 54.9 | 41.8 | 42.0 | 1.3 | 1.9 |
| SALUDA | 081 | 0000 | 520 | 16,357 | 16,990 | 17,024 | 0.4 | 35 | 66.5 | 66.0 | 33.1 | 33.5 | 0.1 | 0.1 |
| SPARTANBURG | 083 | 3160 | 567 | 226,800 | 251,945 | 263,659 | 1.0 | 17 | 78.2 | 77.2 | 20.7 | 21.2 | 0.8 | 1.1 |
| SUMTER | 085 | 8140 | 546 | 102,637 | 112,842 | 115,172 | 0.9 | 22 | 55.3 | 54.2 | 43.2 | 43.9 | 0.9 | 1.2 |
| UNION | 087 | 0000 | 567 | 30,337 | 30,255 | 29,754 | 0.0 | 42 | 69.8 | 69.2 | 29.9 | 30.5 | 0.1 | 0.2 |
| WILLIAMSBURG | 089 | 0000 | 519 | 36,815 | 36,722 | 36,139 | 0.0 | 42 | 35.6 | 35.1 | 64.2 | 64.7 | 0.1 | 0.1 |
| YORK | 091 | 1520 | 517 | 131,497 | 162,477 | 181,720 | 2.1 | 4 | 78.7 | 77.9 | 20.0 | 20.6 | 0.5 | 0.8 |
| SOUTH CAROLINA | | | | | | | 1.2 | | 69.0 | 68.7 | 29.8 | 29.7 | 0.6 | 0.9 |
| UNITED STATES | | | | | | | 1.0 | | 80.3 | 77.9 | 12.1 | 12.4 | 2.9 | 3.9 |

| COUNTY | % HISPANIC ORIGIN | | 2000 AGE DISTRIBUTION (%) | | | | | | | | | | MEDIAN AGE | | 2000 Males/ Females (×100) |
|---|---|---|---|---|---|---|---|---|---|---|---|---|---|---|---|
| | 1990 | 2000 | 0-4 | 5-9 | 10-14 | 15-19 | 20-24 | 25-44 | 45-64 | 65-84 | 85+ | 18+ | 1990 | 2000 | |
| ABBEVILLE | 0.4 | 0.8 | 6.0 | 6.5 | 6.8 | 7.5 | 7.1 | 27.0 | 24.3 | 12.9 | 1.8 | 76.6 | 34.2 | 37.6 | 89.7 |
| AIKEN | 0.7 | 1.5 | 6.5 | 7.0 | 7.1 | 7.0 | 6.4 | 29.8 | 23.6 | 11.5 | 1.1 | 75.2 | 32.7 | 36.6 | 93.2 |
| ALLENDALE | 1.4 | 1.6 | 6.5 | 7.1 | 7.2 | 8.8 | 10.1 | 29.2 | 19.7 | 9.9 | 1.6 | 74.2 | 30.0 | 31.4 | 109.3 |
| ANDERSON | 0.4 | 1.0 | 5.8 | 6.3 | 6.6 | 6.7 | 5.9 | 28.8 | 25.8 | 12.6 | 1.5 | 77.4 | 34.8 | 38.8 | 92.3 |
| BAMBERG | 0.4 | 0.8 | 6.3 | 7.0 | 7.1 | 10.5 | 9.1 | 25.9 | 21.1 | 11.6 | 1.4 | 74.0 | 29.6 | 33.1 | 87.4 |
| BARNWELL | 0.7 | 1.1 | 7.1 | 7.7 | 7.9 | 7.6 | 6.8 | 28.5 | 22.3 | 10.6 | 1.5 | 72.5 | 31.6 | 34.9 | 92.3 |
| BEAUFORT | 2.5 | 3.8 | 7.5 | 6.9 | 6.1 | 7.0 | 8.9 | 29.1 | 19.3 | 14.0 | 1.2 | 76.7 | 30.1 | 34.1 | 99.1 |
| BERKELEY | 2.0 | 3.5 | 8.7 | 8.7 | 8.0 | 7.0 | 7.4 | 33.9 | 19.0 | 6.7 | 0.6 | 70.3 | 28.2 | 30.9 | 99.3 |
| CALHOUN | 0.3 | 0.6 | 6.3 | 7.0 | 7.2 | 7.3 | 6.0 | 28.6 | 24.6 | 11.6 | 1.5 | 75.2 | 34.2 | 37.3 | 89.0 |
| CHARLESTON | 1.3 | 2.1 | 7.1 | 7.0 | 6.5 | 6.6 | 8.0 | 32.2 | 20.8 | 10.6 | 1.2 | 76.1 | 30.1 | 34.3 | 92.5 |
| CHEROKEE | 0.6 | 1.2 | 6.0 | 6.4 | 6.9 | 7.1 | 6.5 | 28.9 | 25.1 | 11.7 | 1.5 | 76.3 | 33.6 | 37.5 | 92.2 |
| CHESTER | 0.2 | 0.6 | 6.4 | 7.0 | 7.2 | 7.3 | 6.4 | 28.5 | 24.3 | 11.4 | 1.5 | 74.9 | 33.1 | 36.7 | 89.9 |
| CHESTERFIELD | 0.4 | 0.8 | 6.4 | 6.9 | 7.2 | 7.1 | 6.4 | 28.1 | 24.9 | 11.7 | 1.3 | 75.2 | 33.3 | 36.9 | 91.8 |
| CLARENDON | 0.5 | 0.8 | 6.4 | 7.2 | 7.4 | 7.4 | 6.8 | 28.2 | 23.4 | 11.9 | 1.3 | 74.4 | 32.7 | 36.1 | 96.4 |
| COLLETON | 0.5 | 1.0 | 6.6 | 7.4 | 7.5 | 7.5 | 6.3 | 27.7 | 24.2 | 11.5 | 1.3 | 73.7 | 32.8 | 36.4 | 90.9 |
| DARLINGTON | 0.3 | 0.7 | 6.1 | 6.8 | 7.1 | 7.1 | 6.6 | 28.5 | 25.2 | 11.2 | 1.4 | 75.5 | 33.0 | 36.8 | 90.4 |
| DILLON | 0.3 | 0.6 | 7.2 | 7.7 | 8.2 | 7.9 | 7.0 | 27.7 | 22.3 | 10.7 | 1.3 | 71.8 | 30.9 | 34.1 | 87.4 |
| DORCHESTER | 1.3 | 2.3 | 7.8 | 7.9 | 7.3 | 6.7 | 7.1 | 34.5 | 20.4 | 7.6 | 0.9 | 73.0 | 29.7 | 32.8 | 97.6 |
| EDGEFIELD | 0.4 | 0.8 | 6.6 | 7.2 | 7.3 | 7.1 | 6.5 | 30.7 | 22.8 | 10.5 | 1.3 | 74.3 | 32.6 | 35.7 | 97.2 |
| FAIRFIELD | 0.5 | 0.8 | 6.3 | 6.9 | 7.3 | 7.7 | 6.6 | 28.5 | 23.0 | 12.1 | 1.7 | 74.9 | 32.4 | 36.4 | 92.4 |
| FLORENCE | 0.4 | 0.9 | 6.3 | 6.9 | 7.4 | 7.6 | 7.1 | 29.5 | 23.6 | 10.4 | 1.1 | 74.9 | 32.2 | 35.8 | 88.3 |
| GEORGETOWN | 0.4 | 0.8 | 6.3 | 7.1 | 7.4 | 7.2 | 6.2 | 27.0 | 23.2 | 14.4 | 1.2 | 74.6 | 32.7 | 37.6 | 90.5 |
| GREENVILLE | 0.9 | 1.9 | 6.0 | 6.6 | 7.0 | 7.1 | 6.4 | 30.1 | 24.3 | 11.2 | 1.4 | 76.5 | 33.4 | 37.2 | 92.6 |
| GREENWOOD | 0.4 | 0.9 | 5.9 | 6.4 | 6.6 | 7.3 | 6.9 | 28.5 | 24.1 | 12.5 | 1.6 | 77.0 | 33.7 | 37.5 | 88.6 |
| HAMPTON | 0.4 | 0.7 | 7.4 | 8.1 | 8.1 | 8.1 | 6.7 | 26.7 | 22.3 | 11.2 | 1.4 | 71.4 | 31.1 | 34.4 | 87.5 |
| HORRY | 0.9 | 1.6 | 5.9 | 6.2 | 6.2 | 5.9 | 6.1 | 30.2 | 24.1 | 14.2 | 1.1 | 78.2 | 33.8 | 38.4 | 93.7 |
| JASPER | 0.4 | 0.8 | 7.3 | 7.9 | 8.1 | 7.5 | 7.2 | 28.6 | 21.6 | 10.5 | 1.3 | 71.9 | 30.7 | 33.6 | 97.4 |
| KERSHAW | 0.6 | 1.2 | 5.8 | 6.6 | 6.9 | 7.3 | 5.9 | 29.5 | 25.3 | 11.5 | 1.2 | 76.1 | 34.0 | 37.9 | 92.3 |
| LANCASTER | 0.4 | 0.9 | 6.3 | 6.8 | 7.1 | 6.9 | 6.1 | 29.2 | 25.1 | 11.3 | 1.3 | 75.7 | 33.4 | 37.3 | 91.5 |
| LAURENS | 0.4 | 0.9 | 5.9 | 6.3 | 6.6 | 7.4 | 6.8 | 28.3 | 25.1 | 11.8 | 1.7 | 77.0 | 34.0 | 37.6 | 91.8 |
| LEE | 0.4 | 0.8 | 6.1 | 7.0 | 7.3 | 7.8 | 7.6 | 31.2 | 20.8 | 10.8 | 1.3 | 74.5 | 31.0 | 34.5 | 98.5 |
| LEXINGTON | 0.8 | 1.7 | 6.2 | 6.8 | 7.1 | 6.7 | 6.0 | 31.5 | 25.5 | 9.3 | 0.9 | 75.8 | 32.6 | 36.7 | 94.1 |
| MCCORMICK | 0.3 | 0.5 | 4.3 | 5.1 | 6.1 | 8.1 | 9.8 | 31.2 | 20.9 | 12.5 | 2.0 | 79.6 | 32.5 | 35.3 | 120.7 |
| MARION | 0.3 | 0.6 | 6.5 | 7.4 | 8.1 | 7.9 | 6.8 | 27.4 | 23.3 | 11.3 | 1.3 | 72.8 | 32.0 | 35.7 | 83.0 |
| MARLBORO | 0.3 | 0.6 | 6.5 | 7.0 | 7.2 | 7.1 | 7.1 | 29.1 | 23.4 | 11.2 | 1.3 | 74.8 | 31.8 | 35.5 | 90.5 |
| NEWBERRY | 0.4 | 0.9 | 5.8 | 6.4 | 6.6 | 7.4 | 6.6 | 28.0 | 24.4 | 13.0 | 1.9 | 77.1 | 34.2 | 38.0 | 92.4 |
| OCONEE | 0.9 | 1.9 | 5.4 | 6.0 | 6.4 | 6.3 | 5.7 | 28.3 | 26.3 | 14.1 | 1.5 | 78.3 | 35.5 | 40.0 | 95.7 |
| ORANGEBURG | 0.4 | 0.7 | 6.3 | 7.1 | 7.2 | 8.9 | 8.2 | 27.3 | 22.4 | 11.3 | 1.4 | 75.0 | 31.1 | 34.9 | 86.6 |
| PICKENS | 0.6 | 1.3 | 5.3 | 5.6 | 5.9 | 9.4 | 11.3 | 27.6 | 22.8 | 10.6 | 1.3 | 79.6 | 30.4 | 34.8 | 97.6 |
| RICHLAND | 1.6 | 2.7 | 5.8 | 6.1 | 6.1 | 8.2 | 9.7 | 33.5 | 20.5 | 8.9 | 1.1 | 78.0 | 30.4 | 33.6 | 93.5 |
| SALUDA | 0.5 | 0.9 | 5.7 | 6.6 | 6.7 | 7.1 | 6.0 | 27.8 | 25.3 | 13.1 | 1.8 | 76.8 | 34.6 | 38.7 | 94.0 |
| SPARTANBURG | 0.7 | 1.4 | 5.8 | 6.4 | 6.8 | 6.8 | 6.0 | 29.8 | 25.2 | 11.8 | 1.5 | 77.1 | 34.0 | 37.7 | 93.1 |
| SUMTER | 1.2 | 1.9 | 7.4 | 7.4 | 7.0 | 7.0 | 8.4 | 32.9 | 19.8 | 9.0 | 1.1 | 74.2 | 29.6 | 32.3 | 98.0 |
| UNION | 0.2 | 0.6 | 5.6 | 6.0 | 6.4 | 6.5 | 6.0 | 28.4 | 25.9 | 13.5 | 1.8 | 78.1 | 35.3 | 39.5 | 88.0 |
| WILLIAMSBURG | 0.4 | 0.5 | 6.8 | 7.7 | 8.4 | 8.4 | 7.2 | 27.2 | 22.1 | 10.9 | 1.3 | 71.9 | 30.6 | 34.1 | 87.2 |
| YORK | 0.6 | 1.2 | 6.4 | 6.9 | 7.2 | 7.1 | 6.6 | 30.2 | 24.0 | 10.6 | 1.1 | 75.7 | 32.2 | 36.1 | 93.2 |
| SOUTH CAROLINA | 0.9 | 1.6 | 6.4 | 6.8 | 6.9 | 7.2 | 7.2 | 30.2 | 23.1 | 11.0 | 1.3 | 75.9 | 32.0 | 35.9 | 93.1 |
| UNITED STATES | 9.0 | 11.8 | 6.9 | 7.2 | 7.2 | 7.2 | 6.7 | 29.9 | 22.2 | 11.1 | 1.6 | 74.6 | 32.9 | 35.7 | 95.6 |

| COUNTY | HOUSEHOLDS | | | | | FAMILIES | | | MEDIAN HOUSEHOLD INCOME | | | |
|---|---|---|---|---|---|---|---|---|---|---|---|---|
| | 1990 | 2000 | 2005 | % Annual Rate 1990-2000 | 2000 Average HH Size | 1990 | 2000 | % Annual Rate 1990-2000 | 2000 | 2005 | 2000 National Rank | 2000 State Rank |
| ABBEVILLE | 8,780 | 9,552 | 9,975 | 1.0 | 2.52 | 6,560 | 6,914 | 0.6 | 33,028 | 37,604 | 1533 | 26 |
| AIKEN | 44,883 | 52,575 | 55,600 | 1.9 | 2.57 | 33,450 | 38,022 | 1.6 | 41,510 | 46,131 | 551 | 6 |
| ALLENDALE | 3,791 | 3,727 | 3,643 | -0.2 | 2.64 | 2,720 | 2,585 | -0.6 | 25,342 | 30,053 | 2774 | 45 |
| ANDERSON | 55,481 | 65,960 | 71,742 | 2.1 | 2.48 | 41,495 | 48,140 | 1.8 | 37,053 | 41,179 | 968 | 15 |
| BAMBERG | 5,587 | 5,618 | 5,528 | 0.1 | 2.69 | 4,118 | 3,994 | -0.4 | 26,188 | 29,468 | 2691 | 40 |
| BARNWELL | 7,100 | 8,018 | 8,287 | 1.5 | 2.69 | 5,369 | 5,888 | 1.1 | 33,966 | 37,149 | 1399 | 22 |
| BEAUFORT | 30,712 | 43,613 | 50,291 | 4.3 | 2.47 | 22,854 | 31,829 | 4.1 | 42,005 | 47,080 | 513 | 5 |
| BERKELEY | 42,386 | 48,436 | 54,688 | 1.6 | 2.96 | 34,083 | 38,024 | 1.3 | 38,401 | 46,642 | 818 | 11 |
| CALHOUN | 4,487 | 5,368 | 5,903 | 2.2 | 2.67 | 3,396 | 3,924 | 1.8 | 32,062 | 37,560 | 1704 | 29 |
| CHARLESTON | 107,069 | 127,186 | 137,700 | 2.1 | 2.49 | 73,392 | 84,400 | 1.7 | 40,781 | 46,630 | 607 | 8 |
| CHEROKEE | 16,456 | 19,617 | 21,514 | 2.2 | 2.57 | 12,353 | 14,319 | 1.8 | 34,440 | 41,342 | 1323 | 21 |
| CHESTER | 11,448 | 13,122 | 14,340 | 1.7 | 2.69 | 8,658 | 9,629 | 1.3 | 33,272 | 40,085 | 1498 | 24 |
| CHESTERFIELD | 14,047 | 15,929 | 17,064 | 1.5 | 2.61 | 10,571 | 11,599 | 1.1 | 31,104 | 36,371 | 1913 | 33 |
| CLARENDON | 9,544 | 10,560 | 11,078 | 1.2 | 2.81 | 7,414 | 7,974 | 0.9 | 26,053 | 29,397 | 2708 | 42 |
| COLLETON | 12,040 | 13,820 | 14,674 | 1.7 | 2.73 | 9,220 | 10,298 | 1.3 | 29,820 | 34,230 | 2178 | 36 |
| DARLINGTON | 21,999 | 25,264 | 26,687 | 1.7 | 2.60 | 16,684 | 18,644 | 1.4 | 32,819 | 36,755 | 1569 | 27 |
| DILLON | 9,887 | 10,728 | 11,156 | 1.0 | 2.75 | 7,423 | 7,805 | 0.6 | 27,364 | 31,747 | 2530 | 39 |
| DORCHESTER | 28,213 | 32,562 | 36,785 | 1.8 | 2.79 | 22,317 | 25,010 | 1.4 | 40,925 | 48,820 | 595 | 7 |
| EDGEFIELD | 6,424 | 7,291 | 7,692 | 1.5 | 2.64 | 4,904 | 5,442 | 1.3 | 32,334 | 40,159 | 1655 | 28 |
| FAIRFIELD | 7,467 | 7,878 | 8,212 | 0.7 | 2.83 | 5,698 | 5,821 | 0.3 | 31,688 | 37,299 | 1780 | 31 |
| FLORENCE | 40,217 | 46,683 | 49,086 | 1.8 | 2.64 | 30,175 | 34,095 | 1.5 | 35,524 | 39,585 | 1164 | 16 |
| GEORGETOWN | 16,275 | 20,720 | 23,401 | 3.0 | 2.70 | 12,536 | 15,438 | 2.6 | 35,435 | 38,780 | 1181 | 17 |
| GREENVILLE | 122,878 | 145,957 | 159,121 | 2.1 | 2.44 | 87,897 | 101,443 | 1.8 | 42,198 | 46,954 | 495 | 3 |
| GREENWOOD | 22,730 | 25,574 | 26,712 | 1.4 | 2.42 | 16,300 | 17,730 | 1.0 | 35,090 | 38,764 | 1241 | 19 |
| HAMPTON | 6,322 | 6,978 | 7,166 | 1.2 | 2.73 | 4,766 | 5,088 | 0.8 | 28,292 | 33,171 | 2399 | 38 |
| HORRY | 55,764 | 76,909 | 89,939 | 4.0 | 2.34 | 40,450 | 54,153 | 3.6 | 37,298 | 42,832 | 931 | 14 |
| JASPER | 5,298 | 6,052 | 6,476 | 1.6 | 2.77 | 4,033 | 4,467 | 1.2 | 29,016 | 35,140 | 2293 | 37 |
| KERSHAW | 15,810 | 18,968 | 20,745 | 2.2 | 2.61 | 12,214 | 14,400 | 2.0 | 39,303 | 47,774 | 726 | 9 |
| LANCASTER | 19,778 | 23,022 | 25,177 | 1.9 | 2.61 | 15,313 | 17,365 | 1.5 | 35,021 | 39,610 | 1248 | 20 |
| LAURENS | 20,660 | 24,256 | 26,019 | 2.0 | 2.53 | 15,584 | 17,781 | 1.6 | 35,203 | 39,995 | 1220 | 18 |
| LEE | 6,054 | 6,644 | 6,956 | 1.1 | 2.82 | 4,683 | 4,962 | 0.7 | 24,527 | 27,417 | 2852 | 46 |
| LEXINGTON | 61,633 | 82,537 | 93,135 | 3.6 | 2.57 | 47,274 | 61,662 | 3.3 | 46,960 | 52,062 | 276 | 1 |
| MCCORMICK | 2,731 | 3,201 | 3,410 | 1.9 | 2.58 | 2,054 | 2,327 | 1.5 | 31,765 | 37,846 | 1763 | 30 |
| MARION | 11,766 | 12,564 | 12,701 | 0.8 | 2.72 | 8,899 | 9,208 | 0.4 | 26,063 | 29,517 | 2705 | 41 |
| MARLBORO | 10,163 | 10,535 | 10,630 | 0.4 | 2.66 | 7,513 | 7,562 | 0.1 | 25,887 | 28,934 | 2723 | 43 |
| NEWBERRY | 12,314 | 13,465 | 13,885 | 1.1 | 2.51 | 9,005 | 9,498 | 0.6 | 33,757 | 40,574 | 1429 | 23 |
| OCONEE | 22,358 | 26,686 | 29,066 | 2.2 | 2.45 | 16,875 | 19,549 | 1.8 | 37,424 | 41,921 | 911 | 13 |
| ORANGEBURG | 28,909 | 31,500 | 32,286 | 1.0 | 2.66 | 21,565 | 22,834 | 0.7 | 30,342 | 34,289 | 2069 | 35 |
| PICKENS | 33,422 | 41,924 | 46,122 | 2.8 | 2.45 | 24,159 | 29,493 | 2.4 | 38,124 | 43,548 | 844 | 12 |
| RICHLAND | 101,590 | 116,117 | 123,745 | 1.6 | 2.44 | 67,604 | 74,485 | 1.2 | 42,198 | 48,418 | 495 | 3 |
| SALUDA | 5,824 | 6,425 | 6,629 | 1.2 | 2.60 | 4,485 | 4,754 | 0.7 | 31,348 | 37,218 | 1853 | 32 |
| SPARTANBURG | 84,503 | 98,202 | 105,093 | 1.8 | 2.50 | 62,663 | 70,873 | 1.5 | 38,458 | 44,766 | 813 | 10 |
| SUMTER | 32,723 | 35,807 | 36,365 | 1.1 | 2.95 | 25,673 | 27,456 | 0.8 | 33,160 | 40,565 | 1511 | 25 |
| UNION | 11,407 | 11,990 | 12,085 | 0.6 | 2.50 | 8,519 | 8,670 | 0.2 | 30,553 | 35,107 | 2018 | 34 |
| WILLIAMSBURG | 12,108 | 12,830 | 13,007 | 0.7 | 2.85 | 9,380 | 9,645 | 0.3 | 25,846 | 28,731 | 2730 | 44 |
| YORK | 47,006 | 61,061 | 69,933 | 3.2 | 2.60 | 35,908 | 45,355 | 2.9 | 45,489 | 52,324 | 330 | 2 |
| SOUTH CAROLINA | | | | 2.1 | 2.56 | | | 1.7 | 37,975 | 43,472 | | |
| UNITED STATES | | | | 1.4 | 2.59 | | | 1.1 | 41,914 | 49,127 | | |

| COUNTY | 2000 Per Capita Income | 2000 HH Income Base | 2000 HOUSEHOLD INCOME DISTRIBUTION (%) Less than $15,000 | $15,000 to $24,999 | $25,000 to $49,999 | $50,000 to $99,999 | $100,000 to $149,999 | $150,000 or More | 2000 AVERAGE DISPOSABLE INCOME BY AGE OF HOUSEHOLDER All Ages | <35 | 35-44 | 45-54 | 55-64 | 65+ |
|---|---|---|---|---|---|---|---|---|---|---|---|---|---|---|
| ABBEVILLE | 16,161 | 9,552 | 20.4 | 15.0 | 38.4 | 23.0 | 2.9 | 0.4 | 30,149 | 29,235 | 36,777 | 37,459 | 28,756 | 19,334 |
| AIKEN | 20,035 | 52,575 | 15.7 | 11.9 | 33.2 | 30.4 | 6.9 | 2.0 | 37,813 | 34,747 | 43,678 | 44,924 | 38,806 | 24,729 |
| ALLENDALE | 12,642 | 3,727 | 31.6 | 17.8 | 28.6 | 16.9 | 3.1 | 1.9 | 27,933 | 24,681 | 34,218 | 33,455 | 26,373 | 16,832 |
| ANDERSON | 19,353 | 65,960 | 16.8 | 14.4 | 36.3 | 25.8 | 5.0 | 1.7 | 34,644 | 32,795 | 40,115 | 43,098 | 35,862 | 20,536 |
| BAMBERG | 12,940 | 5,618 | 30.1 | 17.5 | 31.0 | 17.0 | 3.1 | 1.3 | 27,550 | 23,073 | 30,498 | 35,597 | 28,265 | 19,327 |
| BARNWELL | 16,954 | 8,011 | 23.9 | 13.5 | 34.3 | 22.9 | 4.4 | 1.1 | 31,527 | 29,120 | 33,945 | 39,015 | 34,866 | 20,008 |
| BEAUFORT | 23,547 | 43,613 | 13.2 | 13.1 | 32.5 | 29.1 | 8.0 | 4.2 | 42,045 | 33,030 | 41,276 | 46,831 | 49,265 | 41,413 |
| BERKELEY | 15,239 | 48,426 | 11.5 | 14.3 | 40.9 | 29.6 | 3.4 | 0.3 | 33,940 | 30,594 | 36,883 | 41,463 | 34,665 | 22,672 |
| CALHOUN | 15,052 | 5,368 | 23.0 | 13.8 | 38.4 | 20.5 | 3.3 | 1.0 | 30,112 | 28,144 | 33,136 | 36,123 | 33,284 | 19,598 |
| CHARLESTON | 22,035 | 127,186 | 14.2 | 13.7 | 32.7 | 29.3 | 7.0 | 3.1 | 39,390 | 32,964 | 42,308 | 48,097 | 43,292 | 29,511 |
| CHEROKEE | 15,819 | 19,617 | 18.5 | 13.9 | 39.0 | 24.7 | 3.4 | 0.6 | 31,535 | 29,126 | 35,845 | 38,606 | 34,325 | 19,859 |
| CHESTER | 15,329 | 13,122 | 19.0 | 16.2 | 37.7 | 23.2 | 3.3 | 0.6 | 30,943 | 28,690 | 36,006 | 39,790 | 29,163 | 20,113 |
| CHESTERFIELD | 14,581 | 15,929 | 22.8 | 17.3 | 34.9 | 21.1 | 3.1 | 0.7 | 29,453 | 27,383 | 33,967 | 36,531 | 29,913 | 18,225 |
| CLARENDON | 12,910 | 10,560 | 29.1 | 19.0 | 31.7 | 17.0 | 2.4 | 0.8 | 26,497 | 25,971 | 28,907 | 31,713 | 27,667 | 17,952 |
| COLLETON | 13,406 | 13,815 | 26.3 | 14.9 | 36.6 | 18.1 | 3.2 | 1.0 | 28,546 | 27,653 | 30,845 | 35,990 | 28,443 | 18,840 |
| DARLINGTON | 16,404 | 25,264 | 21.8 | 15.7 | 32.8 | 24.0 | 4.4 | 1.3 | 32,025 | 29,385 | 36,478 | 38,744 | 31,808 | 21,272 |
| DILLON | 12,610 | 10,728 | 26.6 | 19.4 | 33.4 | 17.7 | 2.4 | 0.6 | 26,919 | 24,718 | 31,091 | 32,540 | 28,155 | 17,377 |
| DORCHESTER | 17,066 | 32,562 | 13.0 | 11.8 | 37.4 | 31.9 | 5.0 | 1.0 | 36,347 | 32,221 | 41,313 | 43,683 | 38,746 | 22,739 |
| EDGEFIELD | 17,446 | 7,291 | 23.1 | 15.7 | 32.3 | 24.6 | 3.6 | 0.8 | 30,718 | 28,522 | 36,325 | 37,309 | 31,525 | 18,563 |
| FAIRFIELD | 13,652 | 7,878 | 22.8 | 15.9 | 35.8 | 21.6 | 3.1 | 0.8 | 29,801 | 27,374 | 35,684 | 36,527 | 29,401 | 19,897 |
| FLORENCE | 17,461 | 46,683 | 20.5 | 14.1 | 33.9 | 24.7 | 4.8 | 2.0 | 33,960 | 30,447 | 37,035 | 42,684 | 33,322 | 21,543 |
| GEORGETOWN | 17,603 | 20,720 | 19.9 | 14.6 | 33.5 | 24.6 | 5.4 | 2.0 | 34,426 | 28,549 | 36,533 | 42,849 | 39,420 | 26,543 |
| GREENVILLE | 23,423 | 145,956 | 13.2 | 12.5 | 33.5 | 29.9 | 7.5 | 3.5 | 40,868 | 35,054 | 45,203 | 50,474 | 42,037 | 25,514 |
| GREENWOOD | 18,386 | 25,574 | 20.1 | 14.4 | 34.2 | 25.3 | 4.3 | 1.7 | 33,461 | 29,375 | 38,985 | 43,049 | 33,818 | 21,373 |
| HAMPTON | 12,789 | 6,978 | 28.1 | 17.2 | 34.1 | 17.7 | 2.3 | 0.7 | 27,080 | 25,415 | 28,824 | 34,937 | 29,406 | 17,090 |
| HORRY | 20,509 | 76,909 | 14.2 | 15.2 | 36.7 | 27.2 | 5.2 | 1.6 | 35,431 | 30,705 | 39,647 | 41,367 | 37,299 | 29,457 |
| JASPER | 11,842 | 6,052 | 26.6 | 15.1 | 38.3 | 18.1 | 1.7 | 0.1 | 26,416 | 27,276 | 28,956 | 31,025 | 25,380 | 17,282 |
| KERSHAW | 18,307 | 18,968 | 13.9 | 12.5 | 37.4 | 29.8 | 5.5 | 1.0 | 35,704 | 31,675 | 38,997 | 42,728 | 37,970 | 25,089 |
| LANCASTER | 16,248 | 23,022 | 18.9 | 15.0 | 36.8 | 24.8 | 3.7 | 0.8 | 31,978 | 29,348 | 36,142 | 40,439 | 34,177 | 18,862 |
| LAURENS | 16,555 | 24,256 | 17.4 | 14.2 | 38.7 | 25.3 | 3.6 | 0.8 | 32,371 | 30,165 | 37,939 | 39,835 | 32,729 | 20,251 |
| LEE | 11,533 | 6,644 | 31.6 | 19.5 | 31.4 | 15.9 | 1.5 | 0.1 | 24,438 | 22,395 | 27,970 | 30,218 | 23,363 | 17,274 |
| LEXINGTON | 23,026 | 82,534 | 9.2 | 9.8 | 34.7 | 35.8 | 8.2 | 2.3 | 41,876 | 35,937 | 45,159 | 52,348 | 42,181 | 27,004 |
| MCCORMICK | 14,456 | 3,201 | 22.5 | 16.1 | 36.4 | 19.1 | 4.0 | 2.0 | 31,550 | 31,243 | 37,080 | 35,653 | 33,858 | 21,338 |
| MARION | 12,679 | 12,564 | 29.4 | 18.6 | 32.3 | 16.6 | 2.5 | 0.5 | 26,117 | 23,769 | 29,982 | 30,985 | 25,787 | 19,383 |
| MARLBORO | 11,682 | 10,535 | 29.3 | 18.9 | 33.3 | 16.4 | 1.9 | 0.2 | 25,246 | 24,657 | 29,828 | 30,060 | 23,945 | 16,647 |
| NEWBERRY | 16,154 | 13,465 | 19.0 | 15.0 | 38.2 | 23.4 | 3.7 | 0.8 | 31,442 | 27,863 | 35,916 | 40,746 | 33,357 | 20,850 |
| OCONEE | 19,435 | 26,686 | 15.3 | 15.7 | 35.7 | 26.5 | 5.1 | 1.8 | 35,232 | 30,625 | 41,522 | 42,566 | 37,975 | 24,690 |
| ORANGEBURG | 13,956 | 31,500 | 26.1 | 15.7 | 32.8 | 21.0 | 3.6 | 0.8 | 29,285 | 26,431 | 33,396 | 35,358 | 30,633 | 20,260 |
| PICKENS | 18,713 | 41,924 | 16.4 | 13.2 | 36.1 | 27.3 | 5.3 | 1.7 | 35,423 | 29,672 | 42,048 | 45,137 | 37,789 | 23,104 |
| RICHLAND | 20,936 | 116,117 | 12.7 | 12.8 | 33.3 | 31.8 | 7.1 | 2.2 | 39,078 | 32,677 | 42,408 | 47,116 | 43,121 | 29,798 |
| SALUDA | 14,557 | 6,425 | 22.2 | 16.7 | 35.4 | 22.6 | 2.6 | 0.6 | 29,477 | 28,497 | 32,274 | 35,768 | 32,076 | 19,645 |
| SPARTANBURG | 18,989 | 98,201 | 15.4 | 13.3 | 36.1 | 28.6 | 5.2 | 1.4 | 35,511 | 33,096 | 40,716 | 43,472 | 35,850 | 22,505 |
| SUMTER | 14,395 | 35,804 | 18.6 | 17.4 | 35.7 | 24.0 | 3.5 | 0.9 | 31,460 | 27,641 | 34,810 | 39,066 | 33,543 | 21,635 |
| UNION | 14,297 | 11,990 | 24.2 | 16.4 | 37.7 | 19.4 | 2.1 | 0.2 | 27,770 | 26,720 | 32,719 | 34,127 | 29,039 | 17,054 |
| WILLIAMSBURG | 11,379 | 12,830 | 29.2 | 19.0 | 32.8 | 16.1 | 2.5 | 0.4 | 25,753 | 24,762 | 29,085 | 31,184 | 26,512 | 17,636 |
| YORK | 22,063 | 61,061 | 11.8 | 11.0 | 32.4 | 33.8 | 8.1 | 2.9 | 41,686 | 36,515 | 46,413 | 50,567 | 44,160 | 26,389 |
| SOUTH CAROLINA | 18,998 | | 16.3 | 13.8 | 34.8 | 27.6 | 5.6 | 1.9 | 35,928 | 31,758 | 40,040 | 43,833 | 37,442 | 24,491 |
| UNITED STATES | 22,162 | | 14.5 | 12.5 | 32.3 | 29.8 | 7.4 | 3.5 | 40,748 | 34,503 | 44,969 | 49,579 | 43,409 | 27,339 |

| COUNTY | FINANCIAL SERVICES | | | | THE HOME | | | | | | ENTERTAINMENT | | | | | | PERSONAL | | | |
|---|---|---|---|---|---|---|---|---|---|---|---|---|---|---|---|---|---|---|---|---|
| | | | | | Home Improvements | | | Furnishings | | | | | | | | | | | | |
| | Auto Loan | Home Loan | Invest-ments | Retire-ment Plans | Home Repair | Lawn & Garden | Remodel-ing | Appli-ances | Elec-tronics | Furni-ture | Restau-rants | Sport-ing Goods | Theater & Concerts | Toys & Hobbies | Travel | Video Rental | Apparel | Auto After-market | Health Insur-ance | Pets & Supplies |
| ABBEVILLE | 97 | 70 | 76 | 78 | 95 | 92 | 113 | 96 | 92 | 80 | 81 | 95 | 82 | 96 | 71 | 96 | 81 | 88 | 101 | 98 |
| AIKEN | 99 | 90 | 96 | 93 | 99 | 98 | 105 | 98 | 97 | 95 | 95 | 99 | 95 | 100 | 83 | 98 | 94 | 96 | 99 | 100 |
| ALLENDALE | 91 | 69 | 76 | 72 | 96 | 87 | 92 | 95 | 87 | 83 | 74 | 88 | 80 | 88 | 74 | 95 | 81 | 88 | 89 | 92 |
| ANDERSON | 98 | 79 | 87 | 85 | 97 | 94 | 109 | 97 | 94 | 87 | 88 | 97 | 88 | 98 | 77 | 97 | 88 | 92 | 100 | 99 |
| BAMBERG | 95 | 67 | 77 | 75 | 94 | 89 | 101 | 96 | 90 | 81 | 76 | 92 | 80 | 91 | 71 | 96 | 81 | 88 | 94 | 95 |
| BARNWELL | 96 | 72 | 76 | 77 | 94 | 90 | 108 | 96 | 91 | 82 | 81 | 94 | 83 | 95 | 71 | 96 | 83 | 89 | 98 | 97 |
| BEAUFORT | 100 | 99 | 103 | 101 | 102 | 105 | 107 | 101 | 98 | 97 | 101 | 100 | 98 | 101 | 90 | 98 | 99 | 99 | 102 | 102 |
| BERKELEY | 97 | 90 | 83 | 86 | 94 | 92 | 102 | 97 | 97 | 92 | 96 | 97 | 91 | 98 | 78 | 98 | 92 | 96 | 96 | 100 |
| CALHOUN | 96 | 71 | 77 | 78 | 93 | 89 | 109 | 96 | 92 | 82 | 80 | 94 | 82 | 95 | 70 | 96 | 82 | 89 | 96 | 97 |
| CHARLESTON | 98 | 98 | 97 | 95 | 100 | 99 | 97 | 98 | 97 | 98 | 98 | 99 | 97 | 99 | 87 | 99 | 99 | 99 | 95 | 100 |
| CHEROKEE | 98 | 75 | 84 | 82 | 96 | 94 | 109 | 97 | 93 | 84 | 84 | 96 | 86 | 97 | 74 | 96 | 85 | 90 | 100 | 98 |
| CHESTER | 97 | 72 | 80 | 79 | 96 | 92 | 109 | 96 | 91 | 82 | 82 | 95 | 84 | 96 | 73 | 96 | 83 | 89 | 100 | 97 |
| CHESTERFIELD | 96 | 68 | 72 | 75 | 94 | 91 | 109 | 95 | 91 | 79 | 79 | 95 | 81 | 94 | 69 | 95 | 80 | 88 | 100 | 96 |
| CLARENDON | 96 | 68 | 78 | 76 | 95 | 92 | 109 | 96 | 90 | 79 | 79 | 95 | 81 | 94 | 71 | 95 | 80 | 88 | 99 | 97 |
| COLLETON | 97 | 73 | 81 | 79 | 95 | 92 | 110 | 96 | 92 | 83 | 83 | 95 | 84 | 95 | 73 | 96 | 83 | 89 | 99 | 97 |
| DARLINGTON | 98 | 77 | 87 | 85 | 97 | 94 | 109 | 97 | 94 | 86 | 86 | 97 | 88 | 97 | 76 | 97 | 86 | 91 | 99 | 99 |
| DILLON | 95 | 70 | 74 | 76 | 95 | 91 | 106 | 95 | 91 | 81 | 80 | 93 | 82 | 93 | 71 | 95 | 82 | 88 | 98 | 96 |
| DORCHESTER | 99 | 96 | 87 | 93 | 96 | 95 | 102 | 98 | 100 | 96 | 100 | 101 | 95 | 101 | 81 | 100 | 97 | 99 | 97 | 102 |
| EDGEFIELD | 99 | 74 | 77 | 81 | 94 | 92 | 112 | 97 | 94 | 83 | 85 | 98 | 85 | 98 | 71 | 97 | 84 | 90 | 101 | 99 |
| FAIRFIELD | 97 | 67 | 71 | 75 | 94 | 91 | 111 | 96 | 91 | 78 | 79 | 95 | 80 | 94 | 69 | 95 | 79 | 87 | 101 | 96 |
| FLORENCE | 98 | 85 | 92 | 89 | 98 | 95 | 104 | 97 | 95 | 91 | 90 | 97 | 91 | 98 | 80 | 98 | 91 | 94 | 97 | 99 |
| GEORGETOWN | 98 | 82 | 100 | 91 | 101 | 102 | 108 | 99 | 94 | 89 | 89 | 97 | 91 | 98 | 83 | 97 | 90 | 94 | 102 | 100 |
| GREENVILLE | 100 | 97 | 100 | 100 | 102 | 101 | 105 | 100 | 99 | 99 | 100 | 102 | 99 | 102 | 88 | 99 | 99 | 100 | 99 | 102 |
| GREENWOOD | 97 | 83 | 94 | 89 | 100 | 96 | 107 | 97 | 94 | 90 | 89 | 96 | 91 | 98 | 81 | 97 | 90 | 93 | 99 | 99 |
| HAMPTON | 95 | 70 | 77 | 76 | 95 | 91 | 107 | 95 | 90 | 81 | 80 | 93 | 82 | 93 | 72 | 95 | 81 | 88 | 98 | 96 |
| HORRY | 99 | 88 | 98 | 93 | 100 | 101 | 110 | 100 | 95 | 92 | 94 | 98 | 93 | 100 | 84 | 98 | 93 | 95 | 102 | 101 |
| JASPER | 96 | 66 | 69 | 73 | 93 | 90 | 108 | 95 | 91 | 79 | 77 | 93 | 80 | 93 | 69 | 96 | 80 | 88 | 99 | 95 |
| KERSHAW | 98 | 82 | 89 | 86 | 97 | 95 | 109 | 97 | 94 | 90 | 90 | 97 | 90 | 99 | 78 | 98 | 89 | 93 | 99 | 99 |
| LANCASTER | 98 | 76 | 84 | 84 | 97 | 94 | 112 | 97 | 93 | 85 | 85 | 97 | 87 | 98 | 75 | 97 | 86 | 91 | 101 | 99 |
| LAURENS | 97 | 75 | 83 | 81 | 96 | 93 | 108 | 96 | 92 | 84 | 84 | 95 | 85 | 96 | 74 | 96 | 85 | 90 | 99 | 97 |
| LEE | 96 | 63 | 66 | 72 | 92 | 89 | 109 | 96 | 90 | 76 | 75 | 95 | 78 | 93 | 66 | 95 | 78 | 86 | 98 | 96 |
| LEXINGTON | 101 | 99 | 98 | 99 | 100 | 101 | 106 | 100 | 101 | 101 | 103 | 103 | 99 | 103 | 87 | 100 | 101 | 101 | 99 | 103 |
| MCCORMICK | 97 | 64 | 69 | 73 | 92 | 90 | 111 | 96 | 91 | 76 | 76 | 95 | 78 | 94 | 67 | 95 | 78 | 87 | 99 | 96 |
| MARION | 96 | 68 | 78 | 77 | 95 | 91 | 107 | 96 | 91 | 80 | 78 | 95 | 82 | 94 | 71 | 95 | 81 | 88 | 97 | 96 |
| MARLBORO | 97 | 67 | 73 | 76 | 94 | 90 | 110 | 96 | 91 | 79 | 79 | 95 | 81 | 95 | 69 | 96 | 80 | 88 | 99 | 97 |
| NEWBERRY | 97 | 73 | 80 | 80 | 96 | 93 | 111 | 96 | 91 | 82 | 83 | 95 | 84 | 96 | 73 | 96 | 83 | 89 | 101 | 97 |
| OCONEE | 99 | 76 | 85 | 84 | 96 | 94 | 115 | 98 | 94 | 84 | 86 | 97 | 86 | 99 | 74 | 97 | 86 | 91 | 102 | 100 |
| ORANGEBURG | 96 | 74 | 82 | 82 | 95 | 92 | 105 | 97 | 93 | 85 | 82 | 95 | 85 | 95 | 74 | 97 | 85 | 91 | 96 | 97 |
| PICKENS | 98 | 81 | 89 | 86 | 96 | 93 | 110 | 95 | 93 | 85 | 88 | 95 | 87 | 97 | 76 | 96 | 87 | 92 | 100 | 99 |
| RICHLAND | 99 | 101 | 98 | 98 | 101 | 100 | 97 | 99 | 98 | 101 | 101 | 100 | 99 | 100 | 89 | 99 | 102 | 102 | 95 | 101 |
| SALUDA | 97 | 68 | 74 | 76 | 95 | 92 | 110 | 96 | 91 | 79 | 80 | 95 | 82 | 95 | 70 | 95 | 80 | 87 | 101 | 96 |
| SPARTANBURG | 98 | 83 | 90 | 88 | 98 | 96 | 108 | 98 | 95 | 90 | 90 | 98 | 91 | 99 | 79 | 98 | 91 | 94 | 99 | 100 |
| SUMTER | 96 | 86 | 89 | 87 | 96 | 94 | 101 | 97 | 95 | 91 | 91 | 96 | 90 | 96 | 79 | 97 | 91 | 94 | 95 | 99 |
| UNION | 97 | 67 | 74 | 75 | 95 | 92 | 110 | 96 | 90 | 79 | 79 | 95 | 81 | 95 | 70 | 95 | 80 | 87 | 101 | 96 |
| WILLIAMSBURG | 96 | 65 | 71 | 74 | 93 | 90 | 110 | 96 | 91 | 78 | 78 | 95 | 80 | 94 | 68 | 95 | 79 | 87 | 99 | 96 |
| YORK | 99 | 90 | 95 | 93 | 99 | 97 | 108 | 98 | 97 | 94 | 95 | 99 | 94 | 101 | 82 | 99 | 95 | 97 | 99 | 101 |
| SOUTH CAROLINA | 98 | 88 | 93 | 91 | 98 | 97 | 105 | 98 | 96 | 92 | 93 | 98 | 93 | 99 | 81 | 98 | 93 | 95 | 99 | 100 |
| UNITED STATES | 100 | 100 | 100 | 100 | 100 | 100 | 100 | 100 | 100 | 100 | 100 | 100 | 100 | 100 | 100 | 100 | 100 | 100 | 100 | 100 |

| COUNTY | FIPS Code | MSA Code | DMA Code | POPULATION 1990 | POPULATION 2000 | POPULATION 2005 | 1990-2000 ANNUAL CHANGE % Rate | 1990-2000 ANNUAL CHANGE State Rank | RACE (%) White 1990 | White 2000 | Black 1990 | Black 2000 | Asian/Pacific 1990 | Asian/Pacific 2000 |
|---|---|---|---|---|---|---|---|---|---|---|---|---|---|---|
| AURORA | 003 | 0000 | 725 | 3,135 | 2,995 | 2,946 | -0.4 | 39 | 98.4 | 98.7 | 0.0 | 0.0 | 0.1 | 0.1 |
| BEADLE | 005 | 0000 | 725 | 18,253 | 16,194 | 15,246 | -1.2 | 58 | 98.3 | 97.9 | 0.4 | 0.5 | 0.3 | 0.4 |
| BENNETT | 007 | 0000 | 764 | 3,206 | 3,293 | 3,206 | 0.3 | 16 | 53.3 | 50.4 | 0.2 | 0.4 | 0.1 | 0.1 |
| BON HOMME | 009 | 0000 | 725 | 7,089 | 7,121 | 6,805 | 0.0 | 25 | 97.3 | 93.7 | 0.3 | 0.7 | 0.1 | 0.1 |
| BROOKINGS | 011 | 0000 | 725 | 25,207 | 25,888 | 25,630 | 0.3 | 16 | 97.8 | 97.1 | 0.3 | 0.4 | 1.2 | 1.7 |
| BROWN | 013 | 0000 | 725 | 35,580 | 35,072 | 34,288 | -0.1 | 28 | 96.6 | 95.8 | 0.1 | 0.2 | 0.4 | 0.6 |
| BRULE | 015 | 0000 | 725 | 5,485 | 5,484 | 5,392 | 0.0 | 25 | 92.6 | 92.1 | 0.1 | 0.2 | 0.2 | 0.3 |
| BUFFALO | 017 | 0000 | 725 | 1,759 | 1,776 | 1,788 | 0.1 | 22 | 22.3 | 20.8 | 0.0 | 0.0 | 0.0 | 0.0 |
| BUTTE | 019 | 0000 | 764 | 7,914 | 8,686 | 8,312 | 0.9 | 11 | 96.4 | 95.4 | 0.3 | 0.4 | 0.2 | 0.3 |
| CAMPBELL | 021 | 0000 | 687 | 1,965 | 1,820 | 1,693 | -0.7 | 46 | 99.7 | 99.8 | 0.1 | 0.0 | 0.0 | 0.0 |
| CHARLES MIX | 023 | 0000 | 725 | 9,131 | 9,108 | 8,702 | 0.0 | 25 | 78.0 | 75.0 | 0.0 | 0.0 | 0.0 | 0.0 |
| CLARK | 025 | 0000 | 725 | 4,403 | 4,261 | 4,116 | -0.3 | 34 | 99.4 | 99.3 | 0.1 | 0.3 | 0.2 | 0.1 |
| CLAY | 027 | 0000 | 725 | 13,186 | 13,067 | 12,825 | -0.1 | 28 | 95.2 | 94.3 | 0.4 | 0.7 | 1.1 | 1.3 |
| CODINGTON | 029 | 0000 | 725 | 22,698 | 25,396 | 25,605 | 1.1 | 8 | 98.4 | 98.0 | 0.1 | 0.1 | 0.3 | 0.4 |
| CORSON | 031 | 0000 | 687 | 4,195 | 4,046 | 3,770 | -0.4 | 39 | 51.3 | 49.7 | 0.0 | 0.0 | 0.1 | 0.1 |
| CUSTER | 033 | 0000 | 764 | 6,179 | 7,096 | 7,452 | 1.4 | 6 | 97.1 | 96.6 | 0.1 | 0.3 | 0.2 | 0.2 |
| DAVISON | 035 | 0000 | 725 | 17,503 | 17,920 | 18,207 | 0.2 | 19 | 98.1 | 97.4 | 0.1 | 0.2 | 0.4 | 0.5 |
| DAY | 037 | 0000 | 725 | 6,978 | 6,027 | 5,586 | -1.4 | 61 | 93.1 | 91.8 | 0.0 | 0.0 | 0.1 | 0.1 |
| DEUEL | 039 | 0000 | 725 | 4,522 | 4,421 | 4,274 | -0.2 | 31 | 99.5 | 99.4 | 0.0 | 0.0 | 0.2 | 0.2 |
| DEWEY | 041 | 0000 | 687 | 5,523 | 6,112 | 6,658 | 1.0 | 9 | 33.0 | 29.4 | 0.2 | 0.3 | 0.1 | 0.3 |
| DOUGLAS | 043 | 0000 | 725 | 3,746 | 3,487 | 3,391 | -0.7 | 46 | 99.3 | 99.3 | 0.0 | 0.0 | 0.1 | 0.1 |
| EDMUNDS | 045 | 0000 | 725 | 4,356 | 4,161 | 4,015 | -0.4 | 39 | 99.4 | 99.3 | 0.0 | 0.0 | 0.1 | 0.1 |
| FALL RIVER | 047 | 0000 | 764 | 7,353 | 6,788 | 6,599 | -0.8 | 50 | 92.6 | 91.0 | 0.4 | 0.4 | 0.4 | 0.6 |
| FAULK | 049 | 0000 | 725 | 2,744 | 2,479 | 2,374 | -1.0 | 55 | 99.7 | 99.7 | 0.0 | 0.0 | 0.0 | 0.0 |
| GRANT | 051 | 0000 | 725 | 8,372 | 7,887 | 7,568 | -0.6 | 44 | 99.3 | 99.0 | 0.0 | 0.0 | 0.2 | 0.3 |
| GREGORY | 053 | 0000 | 725 | 5,359 | 4,859 | 4,617 | -1.0 | 55 | 94.5 | 93.6 | 0.0 | 0.0 | 0.1 | 0.1 |
| HAAKON | 055 | 0000 | 764 | 2,624 | 2,262 | 2,101 | -1.4 | 61 | 97.9 | 96.9 | 0.2 | 0.4 | 0.5 | 0.9 |
| HAMLIN | 057 | 0000 | 725 | 4,974 | 5,454 | 5,664 | 0.9 | 11 | 99.4 | 99.2 | 0.1 | 0.1 | 0.1 | 0.2 |
| HAND | 059 | 0000 | 725 | 4,272 | 4,125 | 4,047 | -0.3 | 34 | 99.5 | 99.4 | 0.1 | 0.0 | 0.3 | 0.4 |
| HANSON | 061 | 0000 | 725 | 2,994 | 3,050 | 3,233 | 0.2 | 19 | 99.8 | 99.7 | 0.0 | 0.0 | 0.0 | 0.0 |
| HARDING | 063 | 0000 | 764 | 1,669 | 1,424 | 1,302 | -1.5 | 63 | 98.6 | 97.1 | 0.3 | 0.1 | 0.0 | 0.0 |
| HUGHES | 065 | 0000 | 725 | 14,817 | 15,471 | 15,610 | 0.4 | 15 | 92.6 | 91.4 | 0.1 | 0.2 | 0.3 | 0.4 |
| HUTCHINSON | 067 | 0000 | 725 | 8,262 | 8,061 | 8,042 | -0.2 | 31 | 99.5 | 99.4 | 0.0 | 0.0 | 0.1 | 0.1 |
| HYDE | 069 | 0000 | 725 | 1,696 | 1,563 | 1,456 | -0.8 | 50 | 96.5 | 96.0 | 0.1 | 0.1 | 0.1 | 0.2 |
| JACKSON | 071 | 0000 | 764 | 2,811 | 2,969 | 3,095 | 0.5 | 14 | 57.2 | 52.6 | 0.1 | 0.2 | 0.2 | 0.3 |
| JERAULD | 073 | 0000 | 725 | 2,425 | 2,067 | 1,905 | -1.5 | 63 | 99.5 | 99.5 | 0.0 | 0.0 | 0.3 | 0.3 |
| JONES | 075 | 0000 | 725 | 1,324 | 1,182 | 1,113 | -1.1 | 57 | 99.4 | 99.3 | 0.0 | 0.0 | 0.1 | 0.1 |
| KINGSBURY | 077 | 0000 | 725 | 5,925 | 5,705 | 5,557 | -0.4 | 39 | 99.7 | 99.6 | 0.0 | 0.0 | 0.1 | 0.1 |
| LAKE | 079 | 0000 | 725 | 10,550 | 10,680 | 10,661 | 0.1 | 22 | 99.2 | 98.9 | 0.1 | 0.1 | 0.2 | 0.4 |
| LAWRENCE | 081 | 0000 | 764 | 20,655 | 21,034 | 21,380 | 0.2 | 19 | 96.6 | 95.8 | 0.1 | 0.2 | 0.3 | 0.4 |
| LINCOLN | 083 | 7760 | 725 | 15,427 | 22,794 | 28,301 | 3.9 | 1 | 99.1 | 98.6 | 0.1 | 0.2 | 0.3 | 0.4 |
| LYMAN | 085 | 0000 | 725 | 3,638 | 3,770 | 3,706 | 0.3 | 16 | 70.9 | 67.0 | 0.1 | 0.1 | 0.1 | 0.1 |
| MCCOOK | 087 | 0000 | 725 | 5,688 | 5,506 | 5,260 | -0.3 | 34 | 99.4 | 99.3 | 0.0 | 0.0 | 0.1 | 0.1 |
| MCPHERSON | 089 | 0000 | 725 | 3,228 | 2,638 | 2,380 | -1.9 | 65 | 99.8 | 99.8 | 0.0 | 0.0 | 0.1 | 0.1 |
| MARSHALL | 091 | 0000 | 725 | 4,844 | 4,478 | 4,266 | -0.8 | 50 | 94.3 | 93.5 | 0.0 | 0.0 | 0.0 | 0.1 |
| MEADE | 093 | 0000 | 764 | 21,878 | 21,185 | 20,090 | -0.3 | 34 | 94.4 | 92.7 | 2.4 | 2.8 | 0.8 | 1.1 |
| MELLETTE | 095 | 0000 | 725 | 2,137 | 2,051 | 2,093 | -0.4 | 39 | 53.0 | 49.3 | 0.0 | 0.0 | 0.1 | 0.1 |
| MINER | 097 | 0000 | 725 | 3,272 | 2,589 | 2,263 | -2.3 | 66 | 99.8 | 99.8 | 0.0 | 0.0 | 0.0 | 0.0 |
| MINNEHAHA | 099 | 7760 | 725 | 123,809 | 144,713 | 154,365 | 1.5 | 5 | 97.3 | 96.1 | 0.6 | 0.9 | 0.6 | 0.9 |
| MOODY | 101 | 0000 | 725 | 6,507 | 6,384 | 6,152 | -0.2 | 31 | 91.5 | 89.7 | 0.2 | 0.2 | 0.2 | 0.3 |
| PENNINGTON | 103 | 6660 | 764 | 81,343 | 88,677 | 91,380 | 0.8 | 13 | 89.5 | 87.0 | 1.6 | 2.3 | 1.1 | 1.5 |
| PERKINS | 105 | 0000 | 687 | 3,932 | 3,424 | 3,223 | -1.3 | 59 | 98.1 | 97.9 | 0.2 | 0.1 | 0.1 | 0.1 |
| POTTER | 107 | 0000 | 725 | 3,190 | 2,799 | 2,613 | -1.3 | 59 | 99.0 | 98.8 | 0.0 | 0.0 | 0.1 | 0.1 |
| ROBERTS | 109 | 0000 | 725 | 9,914 | 9,765 | 9,574 | -0.1 | 28 | 76.8 | 73.3 | 0.0 | 0.0 | 0.1 | 0.1 |
| SANBORN | 111 | 0000 | 725 | 2,833 | 2,649 | 2,500 | -0.7 | 46 | 99.9 | 99.9 | 0.0 | 0.0 | 0.1 | 0.1 |
| SHANNON | 113 | 0000 | 764 | 9,902 | 12,715 | 13,931 | 2.5 | 2 | 5.0 | 4.9 | 0.1 | 0.2 | 0.1 | 0.1 |
| SPINK | 115 | 0000 | 725 | 7,981 | 7,346 | 6,915 | -0.8 | 50 | 99.1 | 99.0 | 0.0 | 0.0 | 0.0 | 0.0 |
| STANLEY | 117 | 0000 | 725 | 2,453 | 2,894 | 2,890 | 1.6 | 4 | 93.5 | 92.4 | 0.0 | 0.0 | 0.0 | 0.0 |
| SULLY | 119 | 0000 | 725 | 1,589 | 1,471 | 1,400 | -0.7 | 46 | 98.9 | 99.0 | 0.1 | 0.0 | 0.0 | 0.0 |
| TODD | 121 | 0000 | 725 | 8,352 | 9,611 | 10,218 | 1.4 | 6 | 17.1 | 14.7 | 0.1 | 0.1 | 0.1 | 0.1 |
| TRIPP | 123 | 0000 | 725 | 6,924 | 6,539 | 6,142 | -0.6 | 44 | 90.2 | 88.6 | 0.0 | 0.0 | 0.1 | 0.1 |
| TURNER | 125 | 0000 | 725 | 8,576 | 8,679 | 8,776 | 0.1 | 22 | 99.6 | 99.6 | 0.0 | 0.0 | 0.0 | 0.0 |
| UNION | 127 | 0000 | 624 | 10,189 | 12,732 | 14,048 | 2.2 | 3 | 99.0 | 98.6 | 0.2 | 0.3 | 0.3 | 0.4 |
| WALWORTH | 129 | 0000 | 725 | 6,087 | 5,589 | 5,465 | -0.8 | 50 | 92.1 | 90.2 | 0.0 | 0.0 | 0.2 | 0.3 |
| YANKTON | 135 | 0000 | 725 | 19,252 | 21,353 | 22,191 | 1.0 | 9 | 96.9 | 96.2 | 0.6 | 0.9 | 0.3 | 0.5 |
| ZIEBACH | 137 | 0000 | 764 | 2,220 | 2,151 | 2,085 | -0.3 | 34 | 35.6 | 32.1 | 0.1 | 0.1 | 0.2 | 0.2 |
| SOUTH DAKOTA | | | | | | | 0.5 | | 91.6 | 90.1 | 0.5 | 0.7 | 0.5 | 0.6 |
| UNITED STATES | | | | | | | 1.0 | | 80.3 | 77.9 | 12.1 | 12.4 | 2.9 | 3.9 |

# POPULATION COMPOSITION

| COUNTY | % HISPANIC ORIGIN | | 2000 AGE DISTRIBUTION (%) | | | | | | | | | | MEDIAN AGE | | 2000 Males/ Females (×100) |
|---|---|---|---|---|---|---|---|---|---|---|---|---|---|---|---|
| | 1990 | 2000 | 0-4 | 5-9 | 10-14 | 15-19 | 20-24 | 25-44 | 45-64 | 65-84 | 85+ | 18+ | 1990 | 2000 | |
| AURORA | 0.2 | 0.7 | 5.1 | 5.7 | 7.6 | 10.3 | 4.4 | 21.0 | 23.5 | 17.5 | 4.9 | 73.8 | 38.6 | 42.1 | 103.3 |
| BEADLE | 0.4 | 1.0 | 6.0 | 6.3 | 7.6 | 7.8 | 6.1 | 24.9 | 23.2 | 15.3 | 3.0 | 75.2 | 35.5 | 39.5 | 95.3 |
| BENNETT | 1.1 | 1.7 | 8.4 | 9.4 | 10.1 | 9.9 | 6.3 | 24.0 | 20.0 | 10.2 | 1.6 | 65.4 | 29.2 | 30.1 | 95.1 |
| BON HOMME | 0.5 | 1.3 | 5.3 | 5.7 | 6.7 | 8.3 | 6.7 | 26.1 | 21.2 | 16.2 | 3.8 | 76.6 | 37.6 | 39.0 | 112.3 |
| BROOKINGS | 0.3 | 0.9 | 5.5 | 5.4 | 5.6 | 12.2 | 17.4 | 26.7 | 16.2 | 9.3 | 1.7 | 79.9 | 26.3 | 28.2 | 103.5 |
| BROWN | 0.3 | 1.0 | 5.6 | 6.0 | 7.1 | 9.1 | 8.0 | 27.1 | 21.9 | 13.0 | 2.4 | 76.8 | 33.0 | 36.9 | 92.3 |
| BRULE | 0.6 | 1.2 | 6.3 | 7.8 | 10.5 | 8.9 | 5.1 | 23.4 | 21.6 | 13.7 | 2.7 | 68.7 | 32.6 | 36.6 | 99.5 |
| BUFFALO | 0.2 | 0.1 | 13.0 | 11.1 | 11.9 | 10.5 | 9.0 | 21.8 | 15.7 | 6.5 | 0.5 | 57.0 | 21.8 | 21.9 | 106.8 |
| BUTTE | 2.8 | 4.8 | 6.7 | 7.0 | 8.4 | 7.8 | 5.4 | 25.5 | 23.6 | 13.6 | 2.0 | 72.4 | 34.4 | 38.4 | 99.9 |
| CAMPBELL | 0.0 | 0.3 | 4.9 | 6.2 | 6.5 | 6.8 | 3.6 | 21.2 | 25.1 | 22.8 | 3.1 | 77.4 | 39.2 | 45.7 | 100.4 |
| CHARLES MIX | 0.4 | 0.7 | 7.1 | 7.7 | 9.3 | 9.0 | 5.5 | 21.8 | 22.6 | 13.9 | 3.2 | 69.7 | 33.9 | 37.1 | 96.5 |
| CLARK | 0.3 | 0.7 | 5.7 | 6.5 | 7.9 | 8.2 | 4.3 | 21.8 | 24.7 | 17.6 | 3.2 | 74.0 | 38.8 | 42.0 | 101.8 |
| CLAY | 0.8 | 1.5 | 4.0 | 3.8 | 5.2 | 20.1 | 25.1 | 19.4 | 14.1 | 6.8 | 1.5 | 82.0 | 24.3 | 23.4 | 93.5 |
| CODINGTON | 0.2 | 0.8 | 6.4 | 6.9 | 7.8 | 8.6 | 7.0 | 27.3 | 21.4 | 12.3 | 2.4 | 73.8 | 32.9 | 36.0 | 94.8 |
| CORSON | 1.1 | 1.0 | 9.8 | 9.2 | 10.3 | 9.2 | 6.9 | 21.1 | 19.4 | 13.0 | 1.1 | 64.2 | 27.9 | 29.0 | 100.0 |
| CUSTER | 0.7 | 1.6 | 5.3 | 6.3 | 6.7 | 8.4 | 7.0 | 22.9 | 27.2 | 14.2 | 2.0 | 75.9 | 36.7 | 41.0 | 99.9 |
| DAVISON | 0.2 | 0.8 | 6.2 | 6.6 | 7.5 | 8.8 | 7.9 | 25.3 | 21.4 | 13.2 | 3.1 | 74.7 | 33.6 | 36.6 | 92.8 |
| DAY | 0.2 | 0.6 | 5.9 | 6.4 | 7.8 | 7.6 | 4.9 | 22.1 | 23.4 | 17.6 | 4.2 | 74.5 | 38.7 | 41.8 | 96.1 |
| DEUEL | 0.3 | 0.9 | 5.4 | 6.3 | 7.4 | 7.9 | 4.2 | 22.5 | 25.8 | 17.4 | 3.1 | 75.4 | 38.9 | 42.6 | 106.6 |
| DEWEY | 0.8 | 0.7 | 11.2 | 10.9 | 11.1 | 9.7 | 7.1 | 24.5 | 16.9 | 7.8 | 0.9 | 60.0 | 25.8 | 25.0 | 92.9 |
| DOUGLAS | 0.1 | 0.5 | 6.4 | 7.1 | 8.3 | 8.3 | 4.4 | 21.1 | 23.1 | 17.3 | 4.0 | 72.1 | 36.8 | 41.0 | 97.8 |
| EDMUNDS | 0.1 | 0.6 | 5.6 | 6.1 | 7.4 | 7.4 | 4.3 | 21.1 | 24.5 | 19.1 | 4.4 | 75.1 | 40.1 | 43.5 | 99.0 |
| FALL RIVER | 1.6 | 3.0 | 4.0 | 5.1 | 6.3 | 7.7 | 4.9 | 22.4 | 28.0 | 18.7 | 3.0 | 79.1 | 40.9 | 44.8 | 107.7 |
| FAULK | 0.1 | 0.5 | 5.7 | 6.3 | 7.5 | 7.2 | 4.4 | 20.3 | 25.7 | 19.4 | 3.6 | 75.8 | 39.5 | 44.0 | 100.7 |
| GRANT | 0.1 | 0.6 | 5.7 | 6.7 | 8.1 | 8.7 | 5.0 | 25.4 | 22.9 | 14.7 | 2.8 | 73.1 | 34.9 | 39.3 | 98.7 |
| GREGORY | 0.5 | 1.1 | 5.8 | 6.8 | 8.1 | 7.8 | 4.3 | 21.4 | 23.2 | 18.7 | 3.9 | 73.5 | 38.1 | 42.1 | 94.4 |
| HAAKON | 0.4 | 1.2 | 6.2 | 8.0 | 9.6 | 9.6 | 5.6 | 24.8 | 21.4 | 12.4 | 2.4 | 69.2 | 31.9 | 36.2 | 95.2 |
| HAMLIN | 0.3 | 1.0 | 5.8 | 6.9 | 8.1 | 8.6 | 4.7 | 21.7 | 23.1 | 17.4 | 3.7 | 73.3 | 37.7 | 40.9 | 98.3 |
| HAND | 0.3 | 0.8 | 5.2 | 5.9 | 7.7 | 8.3 | 4.6 | 21.9 | 25.3 | 17.6 | 3.5 | 74.9 | 38.1 | 42.4 | 96.7 |
| HANSON | 0.1 | 0.6 | 5.9 | 6.5 | 9.0 | 8.7 | 5.5 | 23.3 | 25.0 | 13.9 | 2.2 | 72.4 | 34.6 | 38.6 | 103.1 |
| HARDING | 0.2 | 0.8 | 7.3 | 8.2 | 9.6 | 10.8 | 4.4 | 23.7 | 23.5 | 11.2 | 1.4 | 66.4 | 32.2 | 36.2 | 105.2 |
| HUGHES | 0.8 | 1.4 | 6.3 | 6.7 | 8.1 | 8.1 | 6.1 | 28.2 | 23.8 | 10.8 | 2.0 | 73.3 | 33.3 | 37.4 | 90.5 |
| HUTCHINSON | 0.2 | 0.7 | 5.0 | 5.7 | 7.2 | 7.6 | 4.2 | 20.4 | 24.5 | 20.5 | 4.9 | 76.9 | 41.7 | 45.0 | 97.8 |
| HYDE | 0.4 | 1.2 | 5.1 | 6.5 | 7.6 | 7.1 | 4.2 | 21.9 | 24.3 | 18.5 | 4.8 | 75.5 | 39.4 | 43.3 | 91.8 |
| JACKSON | 0.5 | 0.5 | 8.9 | 8.9 | 9.9 | 10.0 | 6.3 | 23.0 | 21.1 | 10.4 | 1.6 | 65.5 | 30.0 | 30.6 | 99.3 |
| JERAULD | 0.0 | 0.6 | 4.4 | 5.4 | 6.9 | 7.7 | 4.7 | 21.0 | 25.8 | 19.7 | 4.3 | 77.7 | 40.4 | 44.8 | 99.1 |
| JONES | 0.1 | 0.7 | 6.5 | 6.9 | 8.3 | 8.1 | 4.8 | 23.5 | 24.9 | 15.2 | 1.8 | 72.2 | 36.4 | 39.7 | 108.8 |
| KINGSBURY | 0.1 | 0.6 | 5.2 | 5.9 | 7.7 | 7.4 | 4.4 | 21.9 | 24.2 | 18.7 | 4.5 | 75.9 | 39.7 | 43.3 | 94.4 |
| LAKE | 0.3 | 0.9 | 5.5 | 6.2 | 7.2 | 10.7 | 7.8 | 24.9 | 21.4 | 13.6 | 2.8 | 75.6 | 33.8 | 36.8 | 95.1 |
| LAWRENCE | 1.6 | 3.0 | 5.9 | 6.2 | 7.1 | 10.5 | 9.1 | 27.1 | 20.6 | 11.7 | 1.9 | 75.5 | 32.4 | 34.8 | 97.2 |
| LINCOLN | 0.1 | 0.6 | 6.7 | 7.7 | 8.6 | 8.4 | 6.3 | 26.2 | 23.3 | 10.6 | 2.2 | 71.2 | 33.2 | 36.5 | 99.6 |
| LYMAN | 0.5 | 0.7 | 8.4 | 8.5 | 9.2 | 8.6 | 6.5 | 23.3 | 21.2 | 12.7 | 1.6 | 68.4 | 31.4 | 34.4 | 104.4 |
| MCCOOK | 0.1 | 0.5 | 6.0 | 6.5 | 8.0 | 8.0 | 4.7 | 22.3 | 23.4 | 17.1 | 4.0 | 73.8 | 38.3 | 41.3 | 99.3 |
| MCPHERSON | 0.0 | 0.3 | 4.7 | 5.1 | 6.8 | 6.7 | 4.0 | 19.6 | 26.9 | 21.4 | 4.7 | 78.4 | 47.0 | 47.2 | 92.7 |
| MARSHALL | 0.3 | 0.6 | 5.5 | 6.3 | 7.3 | 7.6 | 4.6 | 22.3 | 24.8 | 17.8 | 3.9 | 75.4 | 38.9 | 42.7 | 99.1 |
| MEADE | 1.8 | 3.5 | 7.2 | 7.7 | 8.6 | 8.8 | 7.1 | 29.8 | 19.4 | 10.1 | 1.3 | 71.2 | 29.8 | 33.0 | 105.4 |
| MELLETTE | 0.7 | 1.0 | 8.9 | 9.1 | 9.9 | 9.6 | 7.0 | 22.9 | 19.5 | 10.8 | 2.3 | 65.2 | 30.3 | 30.0 | 97.6 |
| MINER | 0.2 | 0.5 | 5.7 | 6.5 | 8.2 | 7.3 | 4.8 | 21.2 | 22.7 | 18.8 | 4.7 | 74.4 | 38.9 | 42.1 | 100.5 |
| MINNEHAHA | 0.5 | 1.4 | 6.8 | 7.2 | 7.9 | 7.8 | 6.9 | 31.0 | 21.0 | 9.9 | 1.6 | 73.7 | 31.4 | 35.0 | 92.4 |
| MOODY | 0.2 | 0.7 | 6.7 | 7.5 | 8.6 | 8.5 | 5.8 | 23.6 | 23.2 | 13.6 | 2.5 | 71.2 | 34.1 | 37.6 | 102.0 |
| PENNINGTON | 2.2 | 3.8 | 7.6 | 7.0 | 7.7 | 7.9 | 8.5 | 30.0 | 20.4 | 9.6 | 1.3 | 73.1 | 30.1 | 33.3 | 97.4 |
| PERKINS | 0.4 | 1.1 | 4.7 | 5.8 | 7.1 | 7.2 | 4.5 | 24.2 | 24.8 | 18.5 | 3.1 | 76.7 | 38.6 | 42.9 | 100.7 |
| POTTER | 0.2 | 0.5 | 4.8 | 5.6 | 7.5 | 7.6 | 4.9 | 21.6 | 24.8 | 19.0 | 4.3 | 76.3 | 38.9 | 43.7 | 94.5 |
| ROBERTS | 0.3 | 0.6 | 6.9 | 7.3 | 8.6 | 8.5 | 5.7 | 22.5 | 23.0 | 14.2 | 3.3 | 71.3 | 35.5 | 37.9 | 101.7 |
| SANBORN | 0.5 | 1.5 | 5.8 | 6.8 | 7.8 | 7.9 | 4.5 | 22.9 | 24.2 | 16.9 | 3.2 | 74.3 | 36.0 | 41.4 | 103.8 |
| SHANNON | 1.8 | 1.4 | 12.8 | 12.1 | 12.7 | 11.5 | 8.6 | 22.7 | 14.3 | 4.8 | 0.4 | 55.4 | 20.6 | 20.5 | 98.7 |
| SPINK | 0.2 | 0.6 | 5.7 | 6.2 | 7.7 | 7.8 | 4.9 | 24.6 | 24.1 | 15.7 | 3.2 | 75.1 | 36.2 | 40.6 | 95.0 |
| STANLEY | 0.4 | 1.0 | 6.6 | 7.0 | 8.6 | 8.8 | 6.0 | 26.4 | 25.5 | 9.9 | 1.0 | 71.7 | 32.6 | 36.3 | 99.0 |
| SULLY | 0.2 | 0.7 | 4.5 | 6.3 | 7.3 | 8.4 | 4.6 | 25.2 | 27.8 | 14.4 | 1.6 | 76.2 | 35.6 | 41.0 | 104.3 |
| TODD | 1.5 | 1.4 | 12.5 | 11.9 | 12.8 | 11.0 | 8.3 | 23.2 | 14.4 | 5.4 | 0.5 | 55.7 | 21.0 | 21.0 | 95.6 |
| TRIPP | 0.1 | 0.6 | 6.7 | 7.1 | 8.5 | 8.5 | 5.2 | 23.6 | 23.1 | 15.0 | 2.3 | 71.9 | 34.5 | 38.4 | 100.0 |
| TURNER | 0.2 | 0.7 | 5.1 | 6.1 | 7.6 | 7.8 | 4.5 | 22.6 | 24.6 | 17.7 | 4.1 | 75.9 | 39.0 | 42.8 | 95.8 |
| UNION | 0.7 | 1.6 | 6.3 | 7.1 | 7.7 | 8.4 | 5.9 | 24.7 | 23.8 | 13.6 | 2.4 | 73.2 | 35.0 | 38.4 | 97.6 |
| WALWORTH | 0.4 | 1.0 | 5.7 | 6.2 | 7.0 | 7.9 | 5.7 | 20.6 | 24.7 | 18.4 | 3.9 | 75.8 | 39.7 | 42.8 | 94.5 |
| YANKTON | 0.5 | 1.1 | 6.0 | 6.5 | 7.4 | 8.2 | 7.0 | 27.8 | 22.7 | 12.1 | 2.3 | 75.4 | 33.5 | 37.1 | 96.1 |
| ZIEBACH | 1.3 | 1.1 | 12.5 | 11.2 | 11.1 | 10.3 | 6.8 | 23.1 | 16.1 | 8.3 | 0.6 | 58.2 | 24.4 | 23.6 | 95.5 |
| SOUTH DAKOTA | 0.8 | 1.6 | 6.6 | 7.0 | 7.9 | 8.8 | 7.4 | 26.6 | 21.5 | 12.1 | 2.2 | 73.3 | 32.5 | 35.7 | 96.7 |
| UNITED STATES | 9.0 | 11.8 | 6.9 | 7.2 | 7.2 | 7.2 | 6.7 | 29.9 | 22.2 | 11.1 | 1.6 | 74.6 | 32.9 | 35.7 | 95.6 |

| COUNTY | HOUSEHOLDS | | | | | FAMILIES | | | MEDIAN HOUSEHOLD INCOME | | | |
|---|---|---|---|---|---|---|---|---|---|---|---|---|
| | 1990 | 2000 | 2005 | % Annual Rate 1990-2000 | 2000 Average HH Size | 1990 | 2000 | % Annual Rate 1990-2000 | 2000 | 2005 | 2000 National Rank | 2000 State Rank |
| AURORA | 1,146 | 1,092 | 1,075 | -0.6 | 2.53 | 815 | 752 | -1.0 | 23,836 | 26,190 | 2915 | 53 |
| BEADLE | 7,341 | 6,839 | 6,587 | -0.9 | 2.30 | 4,940 | 4,409 | -1.4 | 32,621 | 38,694 | 1607 | 17 |
| BENNETT | 1,030 | 1,115 | 1,113 | 1.0 | 2.91 | 749 | 780 | 0.5 | 22,878 | 28,197 | 2979 | 54 |
| BON HOMME | 2,647 | 2,581 | 2,481 | -0.3 | 2.38 | 1,852 | 1,740 | -0.8 | 26,149 | 32,158 | 2698 | 44 |
| BROOKINGS | 8,910 | 9,405 | 9,381 | 0.7 | 2.44 | 5,601 | 5,564 | -0.1 | 33,555 | 38,355 | 1455 | 12 |
| BROWN | 13,867 | 13,989 | 13,825 | 0.1 | 2.40 | 9,324 | 9,064 | -0.3 | 34,820 | 39,053 | 1279 | 9 |
| BRULE | 1,996 | 2,049 | 2,045 | 0.3 | 2.51 | 1,354 | 1,339 | -0.1 | 32,396 | 41,764 | 1640 | 18 |
| BUFFALO | 446 | 440 | 438 | -0.2 | 3.97 | 387 | 379 | -0.3 | 20,521 | 24,200 | 3085 | 61 |
| BUTTE | 3,033 | 3,532 | 3,474 | 1.9 | 2.42 | 2,141 | 2,409 | 1.4 | 31,160 | 37,247 | 1899 | 22 |
| CAMPBELL | 767 | 760 | 730 | -0.1 | 2.37 | 573 | 551 | -0.5 | 21,174 | 26,548 | 3063 | 59 |
| CHARLES MIX | 3,232 | 3,329 | 3,242 | 0.4 | 2.66 | 2,294 | 2,288 | 0.0 | 26,267 | 30,380 | 2682 | 43 |
| CLARK | 1,700 | 1,682 | 1,640 | -0.1 | 2.51 | 1,218 | 1,164 | -0.5 | 25,241 | 29,542 | 2785 | 50 |
| CLAY | 4,433 | 4,618 | 4,564 | 0.5 | 2.35 | 2,606 | 2,533 | -0.3 | 29,853 | 35,738 | 2172 | 26 |
| CODINGTON | 8,739 | 9,992 | 10,172 | 1.6 | 2.50 | 5,954 | 6,531 | 1.1 | 34,633 | 37,778 | 1301 | 10 |
| CORSON | 1,303 | 1,316 | 1,254 | 0.1 | 3.07 | 1,004 | 989 | -0.2 | 19,224 | 22,885 | 3115 | 65 |
| CUSTER | 2,352 | 2,716 | 2,855 | 1.8 | 2.52 | 1,723 | 1,913 | 1.3 | 31,972 | 36,834 | 1719 | 20 |
| DAVISON | 6,948 | 7,156 | 7,288 | 0.4 | 2.43 | 4,464 | 4,384 | -0.2 | 33,431 | 38,146 | 1470 | 13 |
| DAY | 2,732 | 2,516 | 2,401 | -1.0 | 2.34 | 1,907 | 1,687 | -1.5 | 26,737 | 31,286 | 2614 | 40 |
| DEUEL | 1,767 | 1,802 | 1,778 | 0.2 | 2.42 | 1,304 | 1,290 | -0.1 | 27,328 | 34,885 | 2532 | 38 |
| DEWEY | 1,721 | 1,874 | 2,025 | 1.0 | 3.26 | 1,301 | 1,380 | 0.7 | 20,366 | 23,962 | 3090 | 62 |
| DOUGLAS | 1,352 | 1,297 | 1,280 | -0.5 | 2.61 | 995 | 923 | -0.9 | 27,095 | 32,644 | 2567 | 39 |
| EDMUNDS | 1,669 | 1,644 | 1,607 | -0.2 | 2.45 | 1,216 | 1,156 | -0.6 | 29,120 | 34,825 | 2276 | 32 |
| FALL RIVER | 2,864 | 2,841 | 2,791 | -0.1 | 2.29 | 1,886 | 1,771 | -0.8 | 29,724 | 34,402 | 2198 | 27 |
| FAULK | 1,057 | 976 | 945 | -1.0 | 2.49 | 752 | 674 | -1.3 | 26,649 | 33,268 | 2627 | 41 |
| GRANT | 3,154 | 3,074 | 2,999 | -0.3 | 2.51 | 2,264 | 2,141 | -0.7 | 32,761 | 38,337 | 1579 | 15 |
| GREGORY | 2,139 | 1,983 | 1,906 | -0.9 | 2.42 | 1,422 | 1,266 | -1.4 | 24,984 | 31,688 | 2812 | 51 |
| HAAKON | 926 | 811 | 759 | -1.6 | 2.74 | 654 | 553 | -2.0 | 30,427 | 34,957 | 2052 | 24 |
| HAMLIN | 1,854 | 2,015 | 2,083 | 1.0 | 2.63 | 1,321 | 1,386 | 0.6 | 29,608 | 36,981 | 2209 | 28 |
| HAND | 1,625 | 1,601 | 1,583 | -0.2 | 2.49 | 1,189 | 1,127 | -0.6 | 25,617 | 30,206 | 2744 | 47 |
| HANSON | 1,072 | 1,079 | 1,123 | 0.1 | 2.83 | 812 | 807 | -0.1 | 32,750 | 39,632 | 1582 | 16 |
| HARDING | 592 | 520 | 482 | -1.6 | 2.66 | 439 | 374 | -1.9 | 25,929 | 34,125 | 2720 | 46 |
| HUGHES | 5,780 | 6,084 | 6,160 | 0.6 | 2.50 | 3,941 | 3,978 | 0.1 | 42,023 | 46,532 | 509 | 2 |
| HUTCHINSON | 3,221 | 3,175 | 3,180 | -0.2 | 2.44 | 2,282 | 2,173 | -0.6 | 27,871 | 33,223 | 2458 | 36 |
| HYDE | 680 | 653 | 620 | -0.5 | 2.32 | 458 | 423 | -1.0 | 27,472 | 32,431 | 2515 | 37 |
| JACKSON | 903 | 957 | 1,000 | 0.7 | 3.08 | 680 | 702 | 0.4 | 21,525 | 23,793 | 3053 | 57 |
| JERAULD | 966 | 884 | 846 | -1.1 | 2.29 | 683 | 612 | -1.3 | 23,868 | 25,707 | 2913 | 52 |
| JONES | 519 | 472 | 448 | -1.1 | 2.50 | 382 | 335 | -1.6 | 28,889 | 32,500 | 2317 | 33 |
| KINGSBURY | 2,357 | 2,279 | 2,223 | -0.4 | 2.42 | 1,629 | 1,517 | -0.9 | 28,434 | 35,055 | 2374 | 34 |
| LAKE | 4,030 | 4,115 | 4,133 | 0.3 | 2.47 | 2,740 | 2,689 | -0.2 | 35,943 | 45,590 | 1109 | 8 |
| LAWRENCE | 7,926 | 8,460 | 8,825 | 0.8 | 2.36 | 5,286 | 5,392 | 0.2 | 37,083 | 46,326 | 962 | 6 |
| LINCOLN | 5,461 | 7,964 | 9,820 | 4.7 | 2.82 | 4,231 | 6,084 | 4.5 | 45,657 | 58,374 | 325 | 1 |
| LYMAN | 1,268 | 1,321 | 1,304 | 0.5 | 2.85 | 940 | 953 | 0.2 | 29,191 | 33,550 | 2267 | 31 |
| MCCOOK | 2,145 | 2,127 | 2,056 | -0.1 | 2.50 | 1,544 | 1,480 | -0.5 | 30,634 | 39,292 | 2000 | 23 |
| MCPHERSON | 1,332 | 1,117 | 1,020 | -2.1 | 2.31 | 973 | 790 | -2.5 | 18,862 | 22,331 | 3124 | 66 |
| MARSHALL | 1,919 | 1,820 | 1,756 | -0.6 | 2.43 | 1,339 | 1,224 | -1.1 | 22,854 | 25,298 | 2983 | 55 |
| MEADE | 7,084 | 7,220 | 6,935 | 0.2 | 2.82 | 5,580 | 5,582 | 0.0 | 36,777 | 42,388 | 1007 | 7 |
| MELLETTE | 681 | 656 | 672 | -0.5 | 3.05 | 507 | 477 | -0.7 | 19,545 | 22,632 | 3106 | 63 |
| MINER | 1,276 | 1,067 | 958 | -2.1 | 2.34 | 888 | 717 | -2.6 | 26,054 | 32,647 | 2707 | 45 |
| MINNEHAHA | 47,681 | 55,720 | 59,376 | 1.9 | 2.52 | 31,928 | 35,929 | 1.4 | 41,805 | 48,194 | 530 | 3 |
| MOODY | 2,398 | 2,411 | 2,347 | 0.1 | 2.61 | 1,755 | 1,701 | -0.4 | 33,973 | 40,257 | 1397 | 11 |
| PENNINGTON | 30,553 | 33,449 | 34,532 | 1.1 | 2.61 | 21,762 | 23,109 | 0.7 | 39,015 | 47,044 | 751 | 4 |
| PERKINS | 1,586 | 1,418 | 1,353 | -1.3 | 2.37 | 1,112 | 959 | -1.8 | 22,049 | 23,940 | 3026 | 56 |
| POTTER | 1,249 | 1,115 | 1,050 | -1.4 | 2.45 | 875 | 756 | -1.8 | 31,369 | 37,969 | 1849 | 21 |
| ROBERTS | 3,619 | 3,610 | 3,564 | 0.0 | 2.64 | 2,576 | 2,492 | -0.4 | 25,276 | 29,525 | 2782 | 49 |
| SANBORN | 1,059 | 1,031 | 991 | -0.3 | 2.52 | 775 | 728 | -0.8 | 29,518 | 37,865 | 2220 | 29 |
| SHANNON | 2,205 | 2,836 | 3,107 | 3.1 | 4.45 | 1,883 | 2,410 | 3.0 | 20,647 | 22,109 | 3079 | 60 |
| SPINK | 3,022 | 2,898 | 2,771 | -0.5 | 2.42 | 2,088 | 1,931 | -0.9 | 25,369 | 27,046 | 2768 | 48 |
| STANLEY | 921 | 1,134 | 1,157 | 2.6 | 2.55 | 669 | 797 | 2.1 | 33,289 | 39,475 | 1495 | 14 |
| SULLY | 621 | 576 | 549 | -0.9 | 2.55 | 462 | 417 | -1.2 | 30,250 | 34,904 | 2093 | 25 |
| TODD | 2,210 | 2,483 | 2,609 | 1.4 | 3.84 | 1,776 | 1,978 | 1.3 | 21,339 | 25,186 | 3056 | 58 |
| TRIPP | 2,573 | 2,516 | 2,403 | -0.3 | 2.55 | 1,864 | 1,761 | -0.7 | 28,333 | 35,781 | 2392 | 35 |
| TURNER | 3,332 | 3,390 | 3,439 | 0.2 | 2.50 | 2,411 | 2,380 | -0.2 | 29,359 | 35,698 | 2244 | 30 |
| UNION | 3,859 | 4,899 | 5,447 | 2.9 | 2.57 | 2,789 | 3,426 | 2.5 | 37,332 | 43,801 | 925 | 5 |
| WALWORTH | 2,447 | 2,256 | 2,212 | -1.0 | 2.40 | 1,720 | 1,529 | -1.4 | 26,492 | 29,457 | 2656 | 42 |
| YANKTON | 7,107 | 7,928 | 8,252 | 1.3 | 2.51 | 4,825 | 5,163 | 0.8 | 32,061 | 35,795 | 1705 | 19 |
| ZIEBACH | 630 | 622 | 608 | -0.2 | 3.45 | 492 | 476 | -0.4 | 19,286 | 24,808 | 3111 | 64 |
| SOUTH DAKOTA | | | | 0.8 | 2.56 | | | 0.4 | 34,164 | 40,407 | | |
| UNITED STATES | | | | 1.4 | 2.59 | | | 1.1 | 41,914 | 49,127 | | |

| COUNTY | 2000 Per Capita Income | 2000 HH Income Base | 2000 HOUSEHOLD INCOME DISTRIBUTION (%) | | | | | | 2000 AVERAGE DISPOSABLE INCOME BY AGE OF HOUSEHOLDER | | | | | |
|---|---|---|---|---|---|---|---|---|---|---|---|---|---|---|
| | | | Less than $15,000 | $15,000 to $24,999 | $25,000 to $49,999 | $50,000 to $99,999 | $100,000 to $149,999 | $150,000 or More | All Ages | <35 | 35-44 | 45-54 | 55-64 | 65+ |
| AURORA | 11,295 | 1,092 | 29.5 | 23.0 | 33.9 | 12.0 | 0.9 | 0.7 | 23,396 | 22,097 | 32,423 | 30,044 | 22,238 | 15,262 |
| BEADLE | 15,708 | 6,839 | 18.2 | 16.5 | 41.5 | 22.0 | 1.8 | 0.1 | 28,871 | 25,477 | 33,852 | 36,653 | 32,799 | 20,803 |
| BENNETT | 10,836 | 1,115 | 29.5 | 23.8 | 30.0 | 13.5 | 2.2 | 1.0 | 24,936 | 18,286 | 22,885 | 29,923 | 36,821 | 20,961 |
| BON HOMME | 11,624 | 2,581 | 24.1 | 23.5 | 37.2 | 14.0 | 1.2 | 0.0 | 24,365 | 25,563 | 29,024 | 31,192 | 26,229 | 17,315 |
| BROOKINGS | 15,407 | 9,405 | 18.3 | 18.1 | 36.5 | 22.5 | 3.8 | 0.9 | 31,576 | 23,751 | 40,014 | 46,402 | 40,939 | 24,043 |
| BROWN | 18,060 | 13,989 | 17.4 | 16.1 | 36.8 | 24.7 | 3.8 | 1.2 | 32,869 | 26,893 | 38,552 | 44,208 | 35,216 | 23,251 |
| BRULE | 15,300 | 2,049 | 16.4 | 18.5 | 39.7 | 21.6 | 3.4 | 0.5 | 30,605 | 25,678 | 35,991 | 39,648 | 33,598 | 22,383 |
| BUFFALO | 6,554 | 440 | 37.1 | 22.7 | 30.2 | 8.6 | 1.4 | 0.0 | 20,386 | 17,893 | 23,424 | 20,665 | 27,022 | 14,750 |
| BUTTE | 15,558 | 3,532 | 21.2 | 18.2 | 38.1 | 19.2 | 2.5 | 0.8 | 28,680 | 21,575 | 32,166 | 39,732 | 34,080 | 19,885 |
| CAMPBELL | 11,445 | 760 | 33.2 | 25.3 | 28.2 | 12.0 | 0.9 | 0.5 | 22,446 | 22,000 | 31,055 | 29,312 | 22,237 | 15,742 |
| CHARLES MIX | 11,553 | 3,329 | 26.2 | 21.5 | 35.4 | 15.4 | 1.4 | 0.1 | 24,766 | 23,493 | 27,377 | 31,444 | 27,651 | 17,973 |
| CLARK | 12,163 | 1,682 | 26.9 | 22.7 | 35.6 | 13.5 | 1.3 | 0.1 | 23,980 | 26,010 | 26,591 | 29,797 | 25,666 | 17,965 |
| CLAY | 14,346 | 4,618 | 25.2 | 16.0 | 34.1 | 20.9 | 3.0 | 0.8 | 29,309 | 20,021 | 35,232 | 47,805 | 44,147 | 28,034 |
| CODINGTON | 16,391 | 9,992 | 17.2 | 18.0 | 36.7 | 23.5 | 3.8 | 0.9 | 31,979 | 25,982 | 38,707 | 44,055 | 39,433 | 19,819 |
| CORSON | 8,512 | 1,316 | 41.5 | 17.9 | 27.3 | 11.9 | 1.3 | 0.2 | 20,940 | 19,201 | 22,847 | 22,274 | 22,293 | 19,115 |
| CUSTER | 15,604 | 2,716 | 19.1 | 17.6 | 37.5 | 22.0 | 2.8 | 0.9 | 30,067 | 22,003 | 36,536 | 37,305 | 34,550 | 21,829 |
| DAVISON | 16,164 | 7,156 | 15.8 | 18.8 | 39.8 | 22.5 | 2.3 | 0.7 | 30,839 | 27,048 | 37,333 | 39,503 | 34,205 | 21,753 |
| DAY | 13,518 | 2,516 | 25.0 | 21.3 | 35.2 | 16.4 | 1.9 | 0.1 | 25,199 | 25,011 | 29,339 | 33,131 | 27,231 | 18,010 |
| DEUEL | 15,069 | 1,802 | 22.3 | 23.2 | 31.4 | 18.8 | 3.9 | 0.4 | 27,784 | 25,919 | 37,026 | 38,340 | 29,084 | 17,100 |
| DEWEY | 8,391 | 1,874 | 40.0 | 19.9 | 28.1 | 9.5 | 1.8 | 0.9 | 21,484 | 19,202 | 22,751 | 26,077 | 25,134 | 14,045 |
| DOUGLAS | 12,541 | 1,297 | 19.5 | 23.5 | 37.5 | 17.2 | 2.2 | 0.1 | 26,559 | 27,336 | 34,439 | 31,135 | 27,375 | 18,099 |
| EDMUNDS | 13,748 | 1,644 | 23.5 | 16.4 | 40.2 | 17.5 | 2.3 | 0.2 | 26,995 | 26,469 | 34,293 | 30,376 | 30,628 | 20,169 |
| FALL RIVER | 16,616 | 2,841 | 21.8 | 19.0 | 36.4 | 18.7 | 3.4 | 0.6 | 28,365 | 25,083 | 34,531 | 37,918 | 31,286 | 19,057 |
| FAULK | 12,801 | 976 | 22.6 | 24.2 | 34.9 | 16.8 | 1.4 | 0.0 | 25,279 | 23,897 | 29,272 | 28,682 | 30,000 | 20,390 |
| GRANT | 15,008 | 3,074 | 18.7 | 16.3 | 41.1 | 21.0 | 2.4 | 0.4 | 29,660 | 27,109 | 32,839 | 38,783 | 34,647 | 19,350 |
| GREGORY | 13,094 | 1,983 | 28.6 | 21.4 | 32.2 | 15.4 | 1.8 | 0.6 | 24,817 | 21,960 | 30,354 | 34,265 | 26,919 | 18,323 |
| HAAKON | 14,340 | 811 | 16.4 | 24.3 | 37.2 | 17.6 | 2.6 | 1.9 | 30,275 | 25,353 | 31,957 | 42,898 | 36,400 | 19,409 |
| HAMLIN | 12,896 | 2,015 | 23.5 | 17.1 | 40.9 | 16.0 | 2.2 | 0.2 | 26,801 | 25,681 | 28,933 | 34,077 | 33,232 | 18,646 |
| HAND | 12,961 | 1,601 | 25.7 | 23.1 | 31.9 | 17.5 | 1.3 | 0.5 | 25,535 | 23,127 | 30,802 | 28,385 | 31,717 | 19,406 |
| HANSON | 14,563 | 1,079 | 17.5 | 16.8 | 39.0 | 22.6 | 3.1 | 1.0 | 31,271 | 31,791 | 31,417 | 36,834 | 38,550 | 21,797 |
| HARDING | 11,489 | 520 | 23.7 | 23.9 | 36.4 | 15.0 | 1.2 | 0.0 | 24,938 | 21,720 | 28,288 | 26,014 | 32,014 | 18,550 |
| HUGHES | 20,179 | 6,084 | 11.4 | 12.3 | 37.8 | 31.1 | 5.7 | 1.7 | 38,118 | 31,723 | 42,280 | 48,188 | 42,216 | 27,810 |
| HUTCHINSON | 14,267 | 3,175 | 23.2 | 19.8 | 37.6 | 16.9 | 1.9 | 0.7 | 26,877 | 26,727 | 31,893 | 31,619 | 31,907 | 20,398 |
| HYDE | 14,328 | 653 | 26.0 | 17.2 | 38.1 | 16.4 | 1.7 | 0.6 | 26,226 | 25,898 | 28,527 | 30,419 | 34,186 | 20,191 |
| JACKSON | 8,887 | 957 | 32.5 | 24.0 | 31.9 | 9.8 | 1.7 | 0.1 | 21,881 | 16,667 | 23,992 | 27,182 | 24,297 | 20,731 |
| JERAULD | 13,398 | 884 | 27.4 | 25.3 | 30.9 | 14.7 | 1.1 | 0.6 | 24,093 | 28,920 | 29,435 | 25,528 | 27,649 | 17,320 |
| JONES | 14,187 | 472 | 17.6 | 23.3 | 37.9 | 18.4 | 2.5 | 0.2 | 27,844 | 23,524 | 28,652 | 36,286 | 33,144 | 20,814 |
| KINGSBURY | 13,614 | 2,279 | 22.8 | 19.7 | 39.7 | 15.8 | 1.9 | 0.1 | 26,274 | 24,265 | 30,603 | 33,472 | 35,348 | 16,971 |
| LAKE | 17,822 | 4,115 | 14.5 | 13.5 | 42.3 | 25.6 | 3.2 | 0.9 | 33,289 | 28,225 | 36,282 | 42,331 | 45,680 | 23,152 |
| LAWRENCE | 18,096 | 8,460 | 16.8 | 13.3 | 37.5 | 27.0 | 4.3 | 1.1 | 33,762 | 25,911 | 41,064 | 46,525 | 40,144 | 22,813 |
| LINCOLN | 19,628 | 7,964 | 9.1 | 9.6 | 37.2 | 34.2 | 7.8 | 2.0 | 41,669 | 38,140 | 47,020 | 51,434 | 43,020 | 24,882 |
| LYMAN | 13,016 | 1,321 | 22.4 | 19.8 | 35.3 | 17.9 | 3.8 | 0.8 | 28,663 | 22,855 | 27,653 | 36,294 | 38,590 | 22,268 |
| MCCOOK | 14,551 | 2,127 | 18.3 | 19.0 | 38.9 | 21.1 | 2.2 | 0.5 | 28,887 | 28,155 | 32,434 | 36,465 | 33,667 | 20,394 |
| MCPHERSON | 10,690 | 1,117 | 40.4 | 22.7 | 27.2 | 7.7 | 2.0 | 0.1 | 19,644 | 16,815 | 25,963 | 22,426 | 28,139 | 12,928 |
| MARSHALL | 11,105 | 1,820 | 27.5 | 27.9 | 34.9 | 9.1 | 0.7 | 0.0 | 21,521 | 20,983 | 25,448 | 25,564 | 23,880 | 16,696 |
| MEADE | 14,638 | 7,220 | 11.5 | 18.2 | 40.9 | 26.3 | 2.8 | 0.3 | 32,360 | 29,170 | 36,379 | 39,679 | 36,437 | 21,810 |
| MELLETTE | 9,395 | 656 | 41.9 | 20.7 | 27.9 | 5.6 | 2.4 | 1.4 | 22,085 | 18,087 | 20,534 | 24,425 | 34,334 | 16,472 |
| MINER | 15,070 | 1,067 | 23.9 | 24.1 | 32.5 | 14.9 | 2.5 | 2.1 | 28,040 | 27,467 | 34,727 | 35,146 | 38,595 | 17,700 |
| MINNEHAHA | 20,292 | 55,720 | 10.8 | 12.6 | 37.6 | 31.8 | 5.6 | 1.7 | 38,419 | 32,738 | 43,317 | 48,558 | 42,464 | 25,365 |
| MOODY | 14,985 | 2,411 | 16.3 | 15.8 | 41.4 | 23.4 | 2.5 | 0.5 | 30,756 | 27,996 | 36,341 | 40,178 | 35,265 | 20,582 |
| PENNINGTON | 18,969 | 33,449 | 11.0 | 16.0 | 37.7 | 28.1 | 5.5 | 1.7 | 36,889 | 29,991 | 41,679 | 47,181 | 43,110 | 25,967 |
| PERKINS | 12,557 | 1,418 | 32.4 | 24.3 | 30.4 | 10.9 | 1.3 | 0.7 | 22,766 | 19,367 | 25,043 | 24,377 | 25,893 | 20,386 |
| POTTER | 15,983 | 1,115 | 18.4 | 19.5 | 36.1 | 21.9 | 3.6 | 0.6 | 29,904 | 26,009 | 35,875 | 35,523 | 35,466 | 23,440 |
| ROBERTS | 10,700 | 3,610 | 29.5 | 19.9 | 38.2 | 11.7 | 0.8 | 0.0 | 22,720 | 22,230 | 25,227 | 26,509 | 26,032 | 16,263 |
| SANBORN | 14,271 | 1,031 | 20.3 | 18.3 | 38.2 | 20.6 | 2.5 | 0.1 | 27,990 | 26,863 | 31,284 | 36,676 | 32,921 | 19,686 |
| SHANNON | 5,602 | 2,836 | 37.1 | 23.3 | 29.3 | 9.6 | 0.6 | 0.1 | 20,275 | 16,969 | 20,249 | 26,137 | 21,723 | 17,983 |
| SPINK | 13,070 | 2,898 | 27.4 | 21.7 | 33.7 | 14.6 | 1.7 | 0.9 | 25,206 | 21,176 | 31,143 | 29,719 | 30,477 | 18,915 |
| STANLEY | 19,201 | 1,134 | 15.3 | 17.9 | 39.1 | 19.6 | 5.9 | 2.2 | 34,621 | 26,748 | 35,440 | 41,764 | 35,626 | 29,496 |
| SULLY | 16,046 | 576 | 17.4 | 20.5 | 38.7 | 16.3 | 5.2 | 1.9 | 31,670 | 22,991 | 29,236 | 39,531 | 43,517 | 26,177 |
| TODD | 6,921 | 2,483 | 39.5 | 18.8 | 29.2 | 11.2 | 1.3 | 0.1 | 21,113 | 16,998 | 24,873 | 24,374 | 27,894 | 14,804 |
| TRIPP | 16,939 | 2,516 | 20.8 | 22.2 | 35.7 | 15.9 | 3.1 | 2.3 | 30,680 | 21,532 | 36,760 | 41,560 | 35,480 | 21,547 |
| TURNER | 14,073 | 3,390 | 20.7 | 19.8 | 39.7 | 17.0 | 2.5 | 0.5 | 27,500 | 26,646 | 31,459 | 34,717 | 32,592 | 19,707 |
| UNION | 16,872 | 4,899 | 14.4 | 14.1 | 39.3 | 28.2 | 3.5 | 0.6 | 33,306 | 33,092 | 37,883 | 38,855 | 35,868 | 24,440 |
| WALWORTH | 14,807 | 2,256 | 26.1 | 20.7 | 36.6 | 12.2 | 3.1 | 1.3 | 26,598 | 24,299 | 35,264 | 32,748 | 30,038 | 17,295 |
| YANKTON | 14,910 | 7,928 | 17.9 | 18.6 | 40.5 | 19.7 | 2.6 | 0.7 | 29,692 | 26,478 | 35,022 | 37,874 | 31,687 | 19,249 |
| ZIEBACH | 8,803 | 622 | 39.2 | 20.7 | 24.8 | 11.3 | 2.4 | 1.6 | 24,280 | 18,769 | 24,789 | 34,665 | 27,144 | 18,177 |
| SOUTH DAKOTA | 16,386 | | 17.4 | 16.7 | 37.2 | 23.8 | 3.8 | 1.1 | 32,328 | 27,818 | 37,662 | 41,463 | 36,537 | 21,847 |
| UNITED STATES | 22,162 | | 14.5 | 12.5 | 32.3 | 29.8 | 7.4 | 3.5 | 40,748 | 34,503 | 44,969 | 49,579 | 43,409 | 27,339 |

| COUNTY | FINANCIAL SERVICES | | | | THE HOME | | | | | | ENTERTAINMENT | | | | | | PERSONAL | | | |
|---|---|---|---|---|---|---|---|---|---|---|---|---|---|---|---|---|---|---|---|---|
| | | | | | Home Improvements | | | Furnishings | | | | | | | | | | | | |
| | Auto Loan | Home Loan | Invest-ments | Retire-ment Plans | Home Repair | Lawn & Garden | Remodel-ing | Appli-ances | Elec-tronics | Furni-ture | Restau-rants | Sport-ing Goods | Theater & Concerts | Toys & Hobbies | Travel | Video Rental | Apparel | Auto After-market | Health Insur-ance | Pets & Supplies |
| AURORA | 96 | 64 | 70 | 77 | 90 | 89 | 108 | 94 | 90 | 73 | 78 | 91 | 79 | 92 | 75 | 100 | 77 | 88 | 105 | 95 |
| BEADLE | 96 | 79 | 89 | 85 | 96 | 94 | 103 | 95 | 91 | 83 | 87 | 93 | 90 | 95 | 86 | 100 | 84 | 92 | 103 | 96 |
| BENNETT | 96 | 64 | 69 | 76 | 91 | 89 | 108 | 94 | 91 | 74 | 78 | 92 | 80 | 92 | 75 | 99 | 77 | 88 | 104 | 95 |
| BON HOMME | 96 | 64 | 70 | 77 | 90 | 89 | 108 | 94 | 90 | 73 | 78 | 92 | 79 | 93 | 75 | 100 | 77 | 88 | 105 | 95 |
| BROOKINGS | 94 | 88 | 86 | 88 | 94 | 90 | 99 | 91 | 90 | 83 | 89 | 90 | 87 | 93 | 86 | 97 | 85 | 92 | 98 | 96 |
| BROWN | 97 | 90 | 93 | 92 | 98 | 96 | 102 | 96 | 94 | 91 | 94 | 96 | 95 | 98 | 92 | 100 | 90 | 96 | 101 | 99 |
| BRULE | 98 | 70 | 75 | 82 | 91 | 90 | 111 | 96 | 92 | 78 | 83 | 95 | 84 | 97 | 78 | 101 | 81 | 91 | 104 | 98 |
| BUFFALO | 89 | 70 | 65 | 71 | 92 | 81 | 92 | 89 | 82 | 80 | 68 | 87 | 80 | 83 | 81 | 98 | 82 | 89 | 86 | 85 |
| BUTTE | 98 | 71 | 76 | 82 | 93 | 90 | 112 | 96 | 92 | 79 | 83 | 95 | 85 | 97 | 79 | 100 | 82 | 91 | 103 | 98 |
| CAMPBELL | 99 | 63 | 69 | 81 | 89 | 89 | 111 | 96 | 89 | 70 | 78 | 97 | 80 | 96 | 74 | 100 | 78 | 89 | 107 | 98 |
| CHARLES MIX | 95 | 65 | 70 | 78 | 91 | 89 | 107 | 94 | 90 | 74 | 78 | 92 | 80 | 92 | 77 | 99 | 77 | 89 | 104 | 95 |
| CLARK | 98 | 63 | 69 | 80 | 90 | 89 | 110 | 95 | 90 | 71 | 78 | 96 | 80 | 96 | 75 | 100 | 77 | 89 | 107 | 97 |
| CLAY | 94 | 89 | 94 | 93 | 95 | 91 | 100 | 89 | 88 | 79 | 87 | 90 | 86 | 92 | 88 | 95 | 84 | 91 | 98 | 95 |
| CODINGTON | 97 | 88 | 93 | 91 | 98 | 96 | 100 | 96 | 93 | 90 | 93 | 95 | 94 | 97 | 91 | 100 | 89 | 95 | 100 | 97 |
| CORSON | 93 | 72 | 72 | 77 | 95 | 89 | 102 | 93 | 86 | 80 | 79 | 91 | 83 | 91 | 83 | 97 | 79 | 89 | 99 | 94 |
| CUSTER | 98 | 73 | 78 | 82 | 92 | 90 | 113 | 96 | 93 | 80 | 85 | 95 | 85 | 97 | 79 | 101 | 83 | 92 | 103 | 98 |
| DAVISON | 93 | 79 | 83 | 81 | 94 | 91 | 99 | 93 | 90 | 83 | 86 | 89 | 87 | 93 | 84 | 99 | 82 | 91 | 100 | 94 |
| DAY | 97 | 67 | 73 | 81 | 91 | 90 | 112 | 95 | 91 | 74 | 80 | 94 | 82 | 95 | 77 | 100 | 79 | 90 | 105 | 97 |
| DEUEL | 97 | 63 | 70 | 80 | 90 | 89 | 110 | 95 | 90 | 71 | 78 | 95 | 80 | 95 | 75 | 100 | 77 | 89 | 106 | 97 |
| DEWEY | 95 | 71 | 75 | 79 | 91 | 88 | 109 | 94 | 89 | 79 | 79 | 93 | 83 | 93 | 79 | 99 | 81 | 90 | 99 | 94 |
| DOUGLAS | 98 | 63 | 69 | 80 | 90 | 89 | 110 | 95 | 90 | 71 | 78 | 96 | 80 | 96 | 75 | 100 | 77 | 89 | 107 | 97 |
| EDMUNDS | 98 | 67 | 73 | 81 | 91 | 90 | 111 | 95 | 91 | 74 | 80 | 95 | 82 | 96 | 76 | 101 | 79 | 90 | 105 | 97 |
| FALL RIVER | 95 | 65 | 72 | 77 | 91 | 90 | 107 | 94 | 91 | 74 | 79 | 90 | 80 | 92 | 76 | 100 | 77 | 89 | 104 | 94 |
| FAULK | 97 | 63 | 69 | 79 | 90 | 89 | 110 | 95 | 90 | 72 | 78 | 95 | 80 | 94 | 75 | 100 | 77 | 89 | 106 | 96 |
| GRANT | 99 | 71 | 77 | 83 | 92 | 90 | 113 | 97 | 93 | 79 | 84 | 97 | 86 | 98 | 78 | 101 | 83 | 92 | 105 | 100 |
| GREGORY | 97 | 64 | 70 | 79 | 90 | 89 | 109 | 95 | 90 | 72 | 78 | 94 | 79 | 94 | 75 | 100 | 77 | 89 | 106 | 96 |
| HAAKON | 99 | 69 | 74 | 83 | 91 | 90 | 113 | 96 | 92 | 76 | 82 | 97 | 84 | 98 | 77 | 101 | 81 | 91 | 106 | 99 |
| HAMLIN | 98 | 64 | 70 | 81 | 90 | 90 | 112 | 96 | 90 | 72 | 78 | 96 | 80 | 96 | 75 | 100 | 78 | 89 | 107 | 97 |
| HAND | 97 | 64 | 70 | 78 | 90 | 89 | 109 | 95 | 90 | 72 | 78 | 93 | 79 | 94 | 75 | 100 | 77 | 89 | 106 | 96 |
| HANSON | 98 | 71 | 77 | 85 | 92 | 92 | 109 | 96 | 93 | 77 | 83 | 96 | 85 | 96 | 79 | 101 | 82 | 92 | 105 | 98 |
| HARDING | 101 | 63 | 68 | 83 | 89 | 90 | 113 | 97 | 89 | 68 | 78 | 101 | 80 | 99 | 74 | 101 | 78 | 90 | 109 | 100 |
| HUGHES | 99 | 99 | 98 | 97 | 100 | 99 | 100 | 98 | 98 | 98 | 101 | 99 | 101 | 101 | 97 | 102 | 96 | 101 | 100 | 100 |
| HUTCHINSON | 96 | 64 | 70 | 78 | 90 | 89 | 108 | 94 | 90 | 72 | 78 | 92 | 79 | 93 | 75 | 100 | 77 | 89 | 105 | 95 |
| HYDE | 96 | 64 | 70 | 78 | 90 | 89 | 108 | 94 | 90 | 72 | 78 | 93 | 79 | 93 | 75 | 100 | 77 | 89 | 105 | 95 |
| JACKSON | 93 | 65 | 69 | 75 | 91 | 87 | 105 | 93 | 87 | 75 | 74 | 90 | 79 | 89 | 77 | 99 | 78 | 88 | 99 | 92 |
| JERAULD | 98 | 67 | 74 | 81 | 90 | 90 | 112 | 96 | 91 | 74 | 80 | 96 | 82 | 96 | 77 | 100 | 80 | 90 | 106 | 98 |
| JONES | 96 | 64 | 70 | 77 | 90 | 89 | 108 | 94 | 90 | 73 | 78 | 92 | 79 | 93 | 75 | 100 | 77 | 89 | 105 | 95 |
| KINGSBURY | 97 | 63 | 70 | 80 | 90 | 89 | 110 | 95 | 90 | 71 | 78 | 95 | 80 | 95 | 75 | 100 | 77 | 89 | 106 | 97 |
| LAKE | 98 | 74 | 83 | 85 | 95 | 93 | 110 | 96 | 92 | 80 | 85 | 95 | 87 | 97 | 83 | 101 | 83 | 92 | 105 | 98 |
| LAWRENCE | 95 | 86 | 83 | 84 | 95 | 90 | 102 | 95 | 92 | 87 | 89 | 92 | 90 | 95 | 86 | 99 | 85 | 93 | 97 | 97 |
| LINCOLN | 100 | 87 | 85 | 92 | 95 | 94 | 106 | 98 | 98 | 91 | 95 | 99 | 95 | 101 | 87 | 103 | 92 | 98 | 102 | 101 |
| LYMAN | 97 | 65 | 68 | 78 | 90 | 88 | 105 | 95 | 89 | 75 | 76 | 95 | 81 | 94 | 76 | 101 | 81 | 90 | 102 | 96 |
| MCCOOK | 98 | 68 | 74 | 81 | 91 | 90 | 111 | 96 | 92 | 76 | 81 | 95 | 83 | 96 | 77 | 101 | 80 | 90 | 105 | 98 |
| MCPHERSON | 96 | 65 | 72 | 78 | 92 | 90 | 107 | 94 | 89 | 74 | 78 | 93 | 81 | 93 | 78 | 100 | 77 | 89 | 104 | 95 |
| MARSHALL | 97 | 65 | 71 | 80 | 91 | 90 | 112 | 95 | 91 | 73 | 79 | 94 | 80 | 94 | 76 | 100 | 78 | 89 | 106 | 96 |
| MEADE | 97 | 84 | 76 | 85 | 91 | 89 | 102 | 96 | 96 | 86 | 92 | 95 | 90 | 97 | 82 | 102 | 87 | 96 | 99 | 99 |
| MELLETTE | 93 | 73 | 73 | 78 | 96 | 89 | 101 | 94 | 87 | 80 | 80 | 91 | 84 | 91 | 84 | 96 | 79 | 89 | 100 | 94 |
| MINER | 97 | 63 | 70 | 79 | 90 | 89 | 109 | 95 | 90 | 71 | 78 | 94 | 80 | 94 | 75 | 100 | 77 | 89 | 106 | 96 |
| MINNEHAHA | 98 | 99 | 93 | 96 | 99 | 97 | 99 | 98 | 98 | 98 | 102 | 98 | 100 | 100 | 95 | 102 | 96 | 100 | 99 | 100 |
| MOODY | 97 | 66 | 72 | 80 | 91 | 90 | 110 | 95 | 91 | 74 | 80 | 95 | 81 | 95 | 76 | 100 | 79 | 90 | 105 | 97 |
| PENNINGTON | 98 | 97 | 93 | 95 | 98 | 96 | 101 | 97 | 98 | 96 | 100 | 97 | 98 | 99 | 94 | 101 | 95 | 100 | 98 | 100 |
| PERKINS | 97 | 63 | 70 | 80 | 90 | 89 | 110 | 95 | 90 | 71 | 78 | 95 | 80 | 95 | 75 | 100 | 77 | 89 | 106 | 97 |
| POTTER | 98 | 67 | 74 | 81 | 91 | 90 | 113 | 96 | 91 | 74 | 80 | 95 | 82 | 96 | 77 | 100 | 79 | 90 | 106 | 97 |
| ROBERTS | 96 | 66 | 71 | 78 | 91 | 90 | 109 | 95 | 90 | 75 | 79 | 92 | 81 | 93 | 78 | 99 | 78 | 89 | 104 | 95 |
| SANBORN | 98 | 63 | 69 | 80 | 90 | 89 | 110 | 95 | 90 | 71 | 78 | 96 | 80 | 95 | 75 | 100 | 77 | 89 | 106 | 97 |
| SHANNON | 85 | 74 | 69 | 67 | 95 | 81 | 88 | 86 | 79 | 81 | 68 | 82 | 81 | 80 | 86 | 96 | 81 | 87 | 83 | 81 |
| SPINK | 96 | 64 | 70 | 79 | 90 | 90 | 109 | 95 | 90 | 72 | 78 | 93 | 80 | 94 | 75 | 100 | 77 | 89 | 105 | 96 |
| STANLEY | 97 | 78 | 80 | 82 | 90 | 89 | 112 | 96 | 93 | 86 | 89 | 96 | 87 | 98 | 79 | 100 | 84 | 93 | 100 | 99 |
| SULLY | 101 | 63 | 68 | 83 | 89 | 90 | 113 | 97 | 89 | 68 | 78 | 101 | 80 | 99 | 74 | 101 | 78 | 90 | 109 | 100 |
| TODD | 87 | 76 | 74 | 72 | 93 | 82 | 91 | 87 | 81 | 81 | 70 | 85 | 82 | 83 | 84 | 97 | 82 | 88 | 86 | 84 |
| TRIPP | 97 | 68 | 75 | 80 | 91 | 90 | 111 | 95 | 91 | 76 | 81 | 94 | 82 | 95 | 77 | 100 | 80 | 90 | 104 | 97 |
| TURNER | 97 | 63 | 70 | 79 | 90 | 89 | 109 | 95 | 90 | 71 | 78 | 95 | 80 | 95 | 75 | 100 | 77 | 89 | 106 | 96 |
| UNION | 99 | 72 | 77 | 83 | 93 | 91 | 113 | 97 | 93 | 79 | 84 | 96 | 86 | 98 | 79 | 101 | 83 | 92 | 104 | 99 |
| WALWORTH | 95 | 66 | 73 | 77 | 91 | 90 | 108 | 94 | 91 | 75 | 79 | 90 | 80 | 92 | 77 | 100 | 78 | 89 | 104 | 94 |
| YANKTON | 99 | 84 | 89 | 90 | 96 | 95 | 108 | 97 | 96 | 88 | 92 | 96 | 93 | 99 | 87 | 102 | 89 | 96 | 102 | 99 |
| ZIEBACH | 96 | 65 | 68 | 80 | 90 | 87 | 108 | 94 | 86 | 72 | 74 | 98 | 80 | 94 | 76 | 99 | 79 | 89 | 101 | 95 |
| SOUTH DAKOTA | 97 | 85 | 86 | 89 | 95 | 93 | 104 | 96 | 94 | 87 | 91 | 95 | 92 | 97 | 87 | 100 | 88 | 95 | 101 | 98 |
| UNITED STATES | 100 | 100 | 100 | 100 | 100 | 100 | 100 | 100 | 100 | 100 | 100 | 100 | 100 | 100 | 100 | 100 | 100 | 100 | 100 | 100 |

# POPULATION CHANGE

| COUNTY | FIPS Code | MSA Code | DMA Code | POPULATION 1990 | POPULATION 2000 | POPULATION 2005 | 1990-2000 ANNUAL CHANGE % Rate | 1990-2000 ANNUAL CHANGE State Rank | RACE (%) White 1990 | White 2000 | Black 1990 | Black 2000 | Asian/Pacific 1990 | Asian/Pacific 2000 |
|---|---|---|---|---|---|---|---|---|---|---|---|---|---|---|
| ANDERSON | 001 | 3840 | 557 | 68,250 | 71,173 | 70,976 | 0.4 | 81 | 94.7 | 93.6 | 4.0 | 4.5 | 0.8 | 1.3 |
| BEDFORD | 003 | 0000 | 659 | 30,411 | 35,265 | 37,155 | 1.5 | 34 | 89.1 | 87.6 | 10.1 | 11.1 | 0.5 | 0.8 |
| BENTON | 005 | 0000 | 659 | 14,524 | 16,664 | 17,517 | 1.3 | 43 | 97.1 | 96.6 | 2.4 | 2.7 | 0.2 | 0.4 |
| BLEDSOE | 007 | 0000 | 575 | 9,669 | 11,141 | 12,092 | 1.4 | 37 | 95.6 | 95.6 | 3.9 | 3.8 | 0.0 | 0.0 |
| BLOUNT | 009 | 3840 | 557 | 85,969 | 104,319 | 112,109 | 1.9 | 24 | 96.0 | 95.3 | 3.2 | 3.6 | 0.5 | 0.7 |
| BRADLEY | 011 | 0000 | 575 | 73,712 | 84,999 | 89,451 | 1.4 | 37 | 95.1 | 94.2 | 3.9 | 4.4 | 0.3 | 0.5 |
| CAMPBELL | 013 | 0000 | 557 | 35,079 | 38,863 | 40,745 | 1.0 | 60 | 99.0 | 98.9 | 0.4 | 0.4 | 0.1 | 0.2 |
| CANNON | 015 | 0000 | 659 | 10,467 | 12,404 | 13,175 | 1.7 | 28 | 97.8 | 97.3 | 1.8 | 2.0 | 0.1 | 0.2 |
| CARROLL | 017 | 0000 | 639 | 27,514 | 29,713 | 31,007 | 0.8 | 67 | 88.3 | 87.2 | 11.4 | 12.5 | 0.0 | 0.1 |
| CARTER | 019 | 3660 | 531 | 51,505 | 53,405 | 53,886 | 0.4 | 81 | 98.6 | 98.2 | 0.9 | 1.0 | 0.3 | 0.4 |
| CHEATHAM | 021 | 5360 | 659 | 27,140 | 37,103 | 41,909 | 3.1 | 4 | 97.5 | 97.1 | 2.0 | 2.2 | 0.1 | 0.2 |
| CHESTER | 023 | 3580 | 640 | 12,819 | 15,084 | 16,207 | 1.6 | 31 | 88.6 | 87.6 | 11.0 | 12.0 | 0.2 | 0.2 |
| CLAIBORNE | 025 | 0000 | 557 | 26,137 | 30,059 | 31,675 | 1.4 | 37 | 98.3 | 97.9 | 1.0 | 1.1 | 0.4 | 0.6 |
| CLAY | 027 | 0000 | 659 | 7,238 | 7,266 | 7,254 | 0.0 | 93 | 98.1 | 97.9 | 1.6 | 1.7 | 0.0 | 0.1 |
| COCKE | 029 | 0000 | 557 | 29,141 | 32,629 | 34,316 | 1.1 | 54 | 97.5 | 97.2 | 2.1 | 2.3 | 0.1 | 0.1 |
| COFFEE | 031 | 0000 | 659 | 40,339 | 46,887 | 49,635 | 1.5 | 34 | 95.3 | 94.5 | 3.7 | 4.1 | 0.6 | 1.0 |
| CROCKETT | 033 | 0000 | 640 | 13,378 | 14,194 | 14,748 | 0.6 | 73 | 82.9 | 81.2 | 16.8 | 18.5 | 0.1 | 0.1 |
| CUMBERLAND | 035 | 0000 | 557 | 34,736 | 46,472 | 52,221 | 2.9 | 6 | 99.2 | 99.1 | 0.1 | 0.1 | 0.1 | 0.2 |
| DAVIDSON | 037 | 5360 | 659 | 510,784 | 528,378 | 520,100 | 0.3 | 86 | 74.7 | 72.1 | 23.4 | 25.1 | 1.4 | 2.1 |
| DECATUR | 039 | 0000 | 659 | 10,472 | 10,811 | 10,926 | 0.3 | 86 | 95.5 | 94.9 | 4.0 | 4.4 | 0.2 | 0.3 |
| DEKALB | 041 | 0000 | 659 | 14,360 | 16,398 | 17,489 | 1.3 | 43 | 98.0 | 97.6 | 1.5 | 1.6 | 0.1 | 0.1 |
| DICKSON | 043 | 5360 | 659 | 35,061 | 44,020 | 48,950 | 2.2 | 18 | 94.5 | 93.9 | 5.0 | 5.5 | 0.2 | 0.3 |
| DYER | 045 | 0000 | 640 | 34,854 | 36,914 | 37,861 | 0.6 | 73 | 87.6 | 86.2 | 11.9 | 13.1 | 0.2 | 0.3 |
| FAYETTE | 047 | 4920 | 640 | 25,559 | 32,495 | 37,680 | 2.4 | 15 | 55.6 | 53.4 | 44.2 | 46.3 | 0.1 | 0.1 |
| FENTRESS | 049 | 0000 | 557 | 14,669 | 16,562 | 17,601 | 1.2 | 46 | 99.8 | 99.7 | 0.0 | 0.0 | 0.1 | 0.2 |
| FRANKLIN | 051 | 0000 | 659 | 34,725 | 38,095 | 39,442 | 0.9 | 62 | 93.4 | 92.5 | 6.0 | 6.6 | 0.3 | 0.4 |
| GIBSON | 053 | 0000 | 640 | 46,315 | 48,093 | 48,423 | 0.4 | 81 | 80.4 | 78.6 | 19.3 | 21.0 | 0.1 | 0.2 |
| GILES | 055 | 0000 | 659 | 25,741 | 29,211 | 30,188 | 1.2 | 46 | 86.2 | 84.7 | 13.2 | 14.5 | 0.2 | 0.3 |
| GRAINGER | 057 | 0000 | 557 | 17,095 | 20,618 | 22,609 | 1.8 | 26 | 99.1 | 98.9 | 0.6 | 0.7 | 0.0 | 0.1 |
| GREENE | 059 | 0000 | 531 | 55,853 | 61,698 | 65,546 | 1.0 | 60 | 97.5 | 97.1 | 2.2 | 2.4 | 0.1 | 0.2 |
| GRUNDY | 061 | 0000 | 575 | 13,362 | 14,098 | 14,347 | 0.5 | 77 | 99.5 | 99.3 | 0.1 | 0.1 | 0.0 | 0.1 |
| HAMBLEN | 063 | 0000 | 557 | 50,480 | 54,503 | 56,010 | 0.8 | 67 | 94.9 | 94.4 | 4.6 | 4.9 | 0.3 | 0.4 |
| HAMILTON | 065 | 1560 | 575 | 285,536 | 294,848 | 295,705 | 0.3 | 86 | 79.6 | 77.6 | 19.1 | 20.6 | 0.9 | 1.3 |
| HANCOCK | 067 | 0000 | 557 | 6,739 | 6,743 | 6,627 | 0.0 | 93 | 97.9 | 97.9 | 1.8 | 1.8 | 0.0 | 0.0 |
| HARDEMAN | 069 | 0000 | 640 | 23,377 | 24,608 | 25,362 | 0.5 | 77 | 62.2 | 60.0 | 37.4 | 39.5 | 0.3 | 0.4 |
| HARDIN | 071 | 0000 | 639 | 22,633 | 25,503 | 26,787 | 1.2 | 46 | 95.2 | 94.6 | 4.4 | 4.9 | 0.2 | 0.3 |
| HAWKINS | 073 | 3660 | 531 | 44,565 | 50,724 | 53,822 | 1.3 | 43 | 98.0 | 97.6 | 1.7 | 1.9 | 0.1 | 0.2 |
| HAYWOOD | 075 | 0000 | 640 | 19,437 | 19,329 | 18,900 | -0.1 | 95 | 49.8 | 47.5 | 49.7 | 51.6 | 0.1 | 0.1 |
| HENDERSON | 077 | 0000 | 639 | 21,844 | 25,181 | 27,186 | 1.4 | 37 | 91.5 | 90.5 | 8.3 | 9.2 | 0.1 | 0.1 |
| HENRY | 079 | 0000 | 659 | 27,888 | 30,255 | 31,073 | 0.8 | 67 | 89.5 | 88.5 | 10.1 | 10.9 | 0.2 | 0.3 |
| HICKMAN | 081 | 0000 | 659 | 16,754 | 21,897 | 24,909 | 2.6 | 11 | 94.5 | 93.7 | 5.1 | 5.8 | 0.0 | 0.1 |
| HOUSTON | 083 | 0000 | 659 | 7,018 | 7,941 | 8,227 | 1.2 | 46 | 95.8 | 95.2 | 3.8 | 4.2 | 0.1 | 0.1 |
| HUMPHREYS | 085 | 0000 | 659 | 15,795 | 17,356 | 18,207 | 0.9 | 62 | 96.1 | 95.5 | 3.5 | 3.9 | 0.2 | 0.3 |
| JACKSON | 087 | 0000 | 659 | 9,297 | 9,707 | 10,008 | 0.4 | 81 | 99.5 | 99.3 | 0.1 | 0.1 | 0.2 | 0.3 |
| JEFFERSON | 089 | 0000 | 557 | 33,016 | 46,659 | 54,347 | 3.4 | 3 | 96.7 | 96.3 | 2.8 | 3.1 | 0.1 | 0.2 |
| JOHNSON | 091 | 0000 | 531 | 13,766 | 16,819 | 17,233 | 2.0 | 22 | 99.3 | 94.8 | 0.4 | 4.5 | 0.1 | 0.2 |
| KNOX | 093 | 3840 | 557 | 335,749 | 377,863 | 387,259 | 1.2 | 46 | 89.8 | 88.3 | 8.8 | 9.6 | 1.0 | 1.5 |
| LAKE | 095 | 0000 | 632 | 7,129 | 8,054 | 7,683 | 1.2 | 46 | 76.0 | 68.9 | 23.9 | 30.9 | 0.0 | 0.0 |
| LAUDERDALE | 097 | 0000 | 640 | 23,491 | 24,296 | 24,602 | 0.3 | 86 | 68.1 | 65.9 | 31.1 | 33.1 | 0.1 | 0.1 |
| LAWRENCE | 099 | 0000 | 659 | 35,303 | 39,950 | 41,571 | 1.2 | 46 | 98.2 | 97.8 | 1.4 | 1.6 | 0.2 | 0.3 |
| LEWIS | 101 | 0000 | 659 | 9,247 | 11,336 | 12,367 | 2.0 | 22 | 98.2 | 98.0 | 1.3 | 1.4 | 0.1 | 0.1 |
| LINCOLN | 103 | 0000 | 691 | 28,157 | 30,155 | 31,383 | 0.7 | 72 | 90.9 | 89.7 | 8.6 | 9.5 | 0.2 | 0.4 |
| LOUDON | 105 | 3840 | 557 | 31,255 | 40,774 | 45,216 | 2.6 | 11 | 98.3 | 98.1 | 1.3 | 1.4 | 0.2 | 0.3 |
| MCMINN | 107 | 0000 | 575 | 42,383 | 46,679 | 48,086 | 0.9 | 62 | 94.6 | 93.8 | 4.8 | 5.4 | 0.3 | 0.4 |
| MCNAIRY | 109 | 0000 | 640 | 22,422 | 24,567 | 25,898 | 0.9 | 62 | 93.3 | 92.3 | 6.4 | 7.2 | 0.2 | 0.3 |
| MACON | 111 | 0000 | 659 | 15,906 | 18,949 | 20,958 | 1.7 | 28 | 99.4 | 99.2 | 0.3 | 0.4 | 0.1 | 0.1 |
| MADISON | 113 | 3580 | 639 | 77,982 | 87,646 | 92,170 | 1.1 | 54 | 68.5 | 66.1 | 31.0 | 33.2 | 0.3 | 0.5 |
| MARION | 115 | 1560 | 575 | 24,860 | 27,135 | 28,251 | 0.9 | 62 | 95.5 | 95.0 | 4.2 | 4.6 | 0.1 | 0.2 |
| MARSHALL | 117 | 0000 | 659 | 21,539 | 26,785 | 28,586 | 2.1 | 19 | 90.7 | 89.3 | 8.9 | 10.0 | 0.2 | 0.5 |
| MAURY | 119 | 0000 | 659 | 54,812 | 71,597 | 77,433 | 2.6 | 11 | 83.7 | 82.0 | 15.7 | 17.1 | 0.3 | 0.5 |
| MEIGS | 121 | 0000 | 575 | 8,033 | 10,388 | 11,588 | 2.5 | 14 | 98.1 | 98.0 | 1.5 | 1.6 | 0.0 | 0.0 |
| MONROE | 123 | 0000 | 557 | 30,541 | 36,347 | 40,115 | 1.7 | 28 | 96.8 | 96.4 | 2.7 | 3.0 | 0.2 | 0.3 |
| MONTGOMERY | 125 | 1660 | 659 | 100,498 | 132,090 | 145,867 | 2.7 | 8 | 78.7 | 76.1 | 17.8 | 18.5 | 1.8 | 2.8 |
| MOORE | 127 | 0000 | 659 | 4,721 | 5,135 | 5,111 | 0.8 | 67 | 96.1 | 95.7 | 3.7 | 4.0 | 0.0 | 0.0 |
| MORGAN | 129 | 0000 | 557 | 17,300 | 18,759 | 19,137 | 0.8 | 67 | 98.0 | 97.6 | 1.5 | 1.8 | 0.1 | 0.2 |
| OBION | 131 | 0000 | 632 | 31,717 | 32,310 | 32,641 | 0.2 | 92 | 89.3 | 88.2 | 10.3 | 11.3 | 0.2 | 0.2 |
| OVERTON | 133 | 0000 | 659 | 17,636 | 19,943 | 21,303 | 1.2 | 46 | 99.7 | 99.5 | 0.2 | 0.3 | 0.0 | 0.0 |
| PERRY | 135 | 0000 | 659 | 6,612 | 7,657 | 8,101 | 1.4 | 37 | 97.9 | 97.4 | 1.8 | 2.1 | 0.1 | 0.1 |
| PICKETT | 137 | 0000 | 659 | 4,548 | 4,751 | 4,957 | 0.4 | 81 | 99.9 | 99.9 | 0.0 | 0.0 | 0.0 | 0.1 |
| POLK | 139 | 0000 | 575 | 13,643 | 15,322 | 16,389 | 1.1 | 54 | 99.5 | 99.0 | 0.0 | 0.0 | 0.3 | 0.5 |
| PUTNAM | 141 | 0000 | 659 | 51,373 | 60,665 | 64,493 | 1.6 | 31 | 97.1 | 96.4 | 1.7 | 1.8 | 0.9 | 1.3 |
| RHEA | 143 | 0000 | 575 | 24,344 | 28,419 | 29,929 | 1.5 | 34 | 96.8 | 96.2 | 2.4 | 2.6 | 0.2 | 0.4 |
| ROANE | 145 | 0000 | 557 | 47,227 | 50,122 | 50,767 | 0.6 | 73 | 96.2 | 95.6 | 3.1 | 3.5 | 0.4 | 0.7 |
| ROBERTSON | 147 | 5360 | 659 | 41,494 | 56,588 | 65,126 | 3.1 | 4 | 88.7 | 87.3 | 11.0 | 12.2 | 0.1 | 0.2 |
| RUTHERFORD | 149 | 5360 | 659 | 118,570 | 177,120 | 205,795 | 4.0 | 2 | 89.2 | 87.5 | 9.0 | 9.8 | 1.4 | 2.2 |
| SCOTT | 151 | 0000 | 557 | 18,358 | 20,447 | 21,463 | 1.1 | 54 | 99.5 | 99.3 | 0.0 | 0.1 | 0.1 | 0.1 |
| SEQUATCHIE | 153 | 0000 | 575 | 8,863 | 11,165 | 12,780 | 2.3 | 16 | 99.9 | 99.8 | 0.0 | 0.1 | 0.1 | 0.1 |
| TENNESSEE | | | | | | | 1.3 | | 83.0 | 82.1 | 16.0 | 16.4 | 0.7 | 1.0 |
| UNITED STATES | | | | | | | 1.0 | | 80.3 | 77.9 | 12.1 | 12.4 | 2.9 | 3.9 |

| COUNTY | % HISPANIC ORIGIN | | 2000 AGE DISTRIBUTION (%) | | | | | | | | | | MEDIAN AGE | | 2000 Males/ Females (×100) |
|---|---|---|---|---|---|---|---|---|---|---|---|---|---|---|---|
| | 1990 | 2000 | 0-4 | 5-9 | 10-14 | 15-19 | 20-24 | 25-44 | 45-64 | 65-84 | 85+ | 18+ | 1990 | 2000 | |
| ANDERSON | 0.6 | 1.4 | 5.8 | 6.2 | 6.5 | 6.6 | 6.0 | 27.9 | 25.5 | 13.9 | 1.8 | 77.6 | 36.5 | 39.5 | 92.0 |
| BEDFORD | 0.6 | 1.4 | 6.5 | 6.7 | 6.9 | 6.7 | 6.3 | 28.3 | 24.2 | 12.6 | 1.8 | 75.8 | 34.9 | 37.5 | 94.0 |
| BENTON | 0.5 | 1.3 | 5.6 | 5.8 | 6.1 | 6.3 | 5.2 | 26.6 | 26.4 | 15.7 | 2.3 | 78.5 | 38.6 | 41.1 | 90.7 |
| BLEDSOE | 0.4 | 1.1 | 5.7 | 5.9 | 6.5 | 7.7 | 6.5 | 31.3 | 24.6 | 10.5 | 1.4 | 77.2 | 34.0 | 37.0 | 117.9 |
| BLOUNT | 0.4 | 1.2 | 5.9 | 6.1 | 6.3 | 6.3 | 5.7 | 29.8 | 26.1 | 12.2 | 1.6 | 78.0 | 36.1 | 39.0 | 92.4 |
| BRADLEY | 1.0 | 2.2 | 6.3 | 6.3 | 6.6 | 7.5 | 7.3 | 30.3 | 24.2 | 10.4 | 1.2 | 76.9 | 33.2 | 36.1 | 92.4 |
| CAMPBELL | 0.3 | 1.0 | 6.2 | 6.4 | 6.5 | 6.5 | 6.2 | 28.5 | 25.3 | 12.6 | 1.7 | 76.9 | 35.0 | 37.9 | 92.2 |
| CANNON | 0.4 | 1.0 | 6.3 | 6.5 | 6.7 | 7.1 | 5.6 | 28.0 | 24.7 | 13.1 | 1.9 | 76.1 | 35.4 | 38.3 | 95.2 |
| CARROLL | 0.5 | 1.1 | 6.1 | 6.3 | 6.6 | 6.8 | 6.0 | 26.4 | 25.4 | 14.2 | 2.2 | 77.1 | 37.3 | 39.5 | 92.6 |
| CARTER | 0.4 | 1.1 | 5.3 | 5.6 | 5.9 | 6.3 | 5.9 | 29.3 | 26.6 | 13.3 | 1.8 | 79.7 | 36.2 | 39.6 | 94.7 |
| CHEATHAM | 0.5 | 1.3 | 7.5 | 7.6 | 7.6 | 6.7 | 5.6 | 32.7 | 23.8 | 7.6 | 0.9 | 73.0 | 32.1 | 35.2 | 100.4 |
| CHESTER | 0.4 | 0.8 | 6.2 | 6.6 | 6.7 | 8.6 | 8.4 | 26.4 | 22.8 | 12.4 | 1.9 | 76.9 | 32.8 | 35.8 | 92.5 |
| CLAIBORNE | 0.3 | 1.0 | 6.0 | 6.4 | 6.7 | 7.5 | 6.6 | 29.0 | 25.0 | 11.4 | 1.4 | 76.4 | 34.0 | 37.4 | 94.3 |
| CLAY | 0.4 | 1.1 | 5.4 | 5.8 | 6.4 | 6.4 | 6.0 | 28.0 | 27.2 | 13.0 | 1.9 | 78.6 | 37.1 | 39.8 | 95.1 |
| COCKE | 0.5 | 1.3 | 5.7 | 5.9 | 6.4 | 6.6 | 6.1 | 29.4 | 26.5 | 12.0 | 1.5 | 78.0 | 35.2 | 38.8 | 92.3 |
| COFFEE | 0.6 | 1.5 | 6.7 | 6.9 | 7.1 | 7.0 | 6.0 | 27.7 | 24.2 | 13.0 | 1.6 | 75.2 | 35.0 | 37.7 | 93.9 |
| CROCKETT | 0.4 | 0.9 | 6.3 | 6.7 | 6.7 | 6.8 | 5.6 | 27.9 | 24.1 | 13.6 | 2.3 | 76.1 | 36.3 | 38.5 | 92.3 |
| CUMBERLAND | 0.4 | 1.0 | 5.9 | 6.1 | 6.2 | 6.3 | 5.3 | 26.5 | 24.9 | 17.0 | 1.9 | 78.0 | 37.5 | 40.7 | 93.3 |
| DAVIDSON | 0.9 | 1.9 | 6.8 | 6.4 | 6.2 | 6.8 | 7.6 | 33.3 | 21.6 | 9.9 | 1.4 | 77.1 | 32.6 | 35.3 | 90.3 |
| DECATUR | 0.5 | 1.2 | 5.4 | 5.5 | 5.7 | 6.4 | 6.0 | 26.8 | 26.4 | 15.3 | 2.4 | 79.4 | 38.6 | 41.0 | 92.8 |
| DEKALB | 0.4 | 1.3 | 5.9 | 6.2 | 6.4 | 6.4 | 6.1 | 27.4 | 26.0 | 13.7 | 1.9 | 77.5 | 36.5 | 39.1 | 91.8 |
| DICKSON | 0.5 | 1.3 | 7.3 | 7.3 | 7.5 | 7.0 | 6.1 | 29.4 | 23.8 | 10.2 | 1.4 | 73.6 | 33.0 | 35.8 | 94.3 |
| DYER | 0.4 | 1.1 | 6.6 | 6.9 | 6.9 | 7.0 | 6.2 | 29.0 | 24.1 | 11.5 | 1.7 | 75.5 | 34.4 | 37.0 | 90.9 |
| FAYETTE | 0.5 | 0.9 | 7.7 | 8.1 | 8.3 | 7.9 | 6.1 | 28.0 | 22.6 | 10.0 | 1.4 | 71.0 | 32.3 | 34.4 | 94.7 |
| FENTRESS | 0.3 | 0.9 | 6.1 | 6.5 | 6.8 | 7.3 | 6.2 | 28.4 | 25.8 | 11.5 | 1.4 | 76.2 | 34.6 | 37.7 | 96.5 |
| FRANKLIN | 0.5 | 1.3 | 6.0 | 6.4 | 6.6 | 7.6 | 7.2 | 27.0 | 24.8 | 12.9 | 1.7 | 76.9 | 35.1 | 38.1 | 96.6 |
| GIBSON | 0.4 | 1.0 | 6.1 | 6.4 | 6.6 | 6.6 | 5.8 | 27.0 | 24.7 | 14.6 | 2.2 | 77.0 | 37.1 | 39.3 | 89.6 |
| GILES | 0.4 | 1.1 | 6.6 | 6.8 | 7.1 | 7.0 | 5.9 | 27.2 | 24.9 | 12.5 | 1.9 | 75.5 | 35.6 | 37.7 | 93.8 |
| GRAINGER | 0.2 | 0.8 | 5.9 | 6.1 | 6.6 | 6.7 | 6.1 | 29.4 | 26.4 | 11.3 | 1.5 | 77.4 | 34.7 | 38.3 | 98.3 |
| GREENE | 0.3 | 0.9 | 5.4 | 5.7 | 6.2 | 6.3 | 5.4 | 29.0 | 27.0 | 13.3 | 1.6 | 79.0 | 36.4 | 39.9 | 94.1 |
| GRUNDY | 0.5 | 1.4 | 6.6 | 6.7 | 6.8 | 7.1 | 6.7 | 28.0 | 24.9 | 11.5 | 1.7 | 75.5 | 33.7 | 36.8 | 93.2 |
| HAMBLEN | 0.3 | 1.0 | 5.8 | 6.1 | 6.5 | 6.3 | 5.5 | 29.7 | 26.8 | 12.1 | 1.2 | 78.0 | 35.1 | 38.7 | 93.6 |
| HAMILTON | 0.7 | 1.5 | 6.2 | 6.5 | 6.8 | 6.7 | 6.4 | 29.1 | 24.5 | 12.1 | 1.7 | 76.7 | 34.7 | 37.8 | 90.3 |
| HANCOCK | 0.5 | 1.4 | 6.3 | 6.4 | 6.6 | 7.0 | 6.2 | 28.1 | 24.2 | 13.4 | 1.7 | 76.2 | 35.1 | 37.8 | 97.6 |
| HARDEMAN | 0.7 | 1.7 | 7.5 | 7.7 | 7.8 | 7.4 | 6.6 | 27.7 | 22.1 | 11.5 | 1.7 | 72.5 | 32.9 | 35.2 | 93.9 |
| HARDIN | 0.4 | 1.1 | 6.1 | 6.5 | 6.7 | 6.5 | 5.9 | 26.9 | 26.0 | 13.5 | 1.9 | 76.7 | 36.3 | 39.0 | 94.4 |
| HAWKINS | 0.3 | 0.9 | 5.8 | 6.0 | 6.3 | 6.6 | 5.8 | 29.7 | 26.6 | 11.9 | 1.5 | 78.0 | 35.4 | 38.9 | 95.9 |
| HAYWOOD | 0.8 | 1.6 | 7.3 | 7.4 | 7.4 | 7.8 | 7.4 | 27.6 | 21.9 | 11.1 | 2.0 | 73.0 | 32.8 | 34.9 | 88.2 |
| HENDERSON | 0.5 | 1.1 | 6.1 | 6.4 | 6.7 | 6.7 | 5.8 | 27.9 | 25.2 | 13.3 | 1.8 | 76.8 | 35.6 | 38.7 | 93.5 |
| HENRY | 0.4 | 1.1 | 5.6 | 5.9 | 6.2 | 6.3 | 5.5 | 25.6 | 25.5 | 16.9 | 2.6 | 78.6 | 39.2 | 41.6 | 93.6 |
| HICKMAN | 0.4 | 1.1 | 6.3 | 6.3 | 6.7 | 6.4 | 5.9 | 31.0 | 24.7 | 11.5 | 1.3 | 76.9 | 35.0 | 37.4 | 106.7 |
| HOUSTON | 0.6 | 1.5 | 5.7 | 6.1 | 6.3 | 6.2 | 5.8 | 26.2 | 25.8 | 15.6 | 2.3 | 77.8 | 37.7 | 40.4 | 93.7 |
| HUMPHREYS | 0.4 | 1.1 | 5.9 | 6.4 | 6.5 | 6.6 | 5.8 | 27.3 | 26.0 | 13.8 | 1.6 | 76.9 | 36.4 | 39.5 | 98.3 |
| JACKSON | 0.4 | 1.1 | 5.5 | 5.7 | 6.4 | 6.0 | 5.8 | 27.6 | 26.6 | 14.3 | 2.1 | 78.6 | 37.7 | 40.5 | 95.0 |
| JEFFERSON | 0.3 | 0.9 | 5.3 | 5.5 | 5.8 | 7.4 | 7.0 | 28.2 | 27.2 | 12.2 | 1.4 | 79.6 | 35.4 | 39.2 | 95.1 |
| JOHNSON | 0.2 | 1.3 | 5.3 | 5.3 | 6.1 | 6.2 | 6.2 | 28.9 | 26.8 | 13.2 | 2.1 | 79.5 | 37.6 | 40.0 | 105.7 |
| KNOX | 0.6 | 1.5 | 6.2 | 6.2 | 6.1 | 6.9 | 7.7 | 31.0 | 23.4 | 11.0 | 1.5 | 78.0 | 33.7 | 36.6 | 91.4 |
| LAKE | 0.4 | 0.9 | 4.6 | 4.5 | 5.0 | 6.8 | 12.7 | 35.0 | 19.7 | 10.1 | 1.7 | 82.7 | 34.1 | 33.5 | 160.9 |
| LAUDERDALE | 0.8 | 1.6 | 7.1 | 7.6 | 7.5 | 7.1 | 6.7 | 29.6 | 21.7 | 10.8 | 1.8 | 73.5 | 32.8 | 34.9 | 96.0 |
| LAWRENCE | 0.4 | 1.1 | 7.2 | 7.1 | 7.2 | 6.8 | 6.0 | 27.8 | 24.2 | 12.2 | 1.7 | 74.5 | 34.2 | 37.0 | 93.1 |
| LEWIS | 0.6 | 1.5 | 6.5 | 7.1 | 7.2 | 7.3 | 5.9 | 27.6 | 24.4 | 12.3 | 1.7 | 74.7 | 34.6 | 37.4 | 96.7 |
| LINCOLN | 0.5 | 1.2 | 6.4 | 6.6 | 6.9 | 6.8 | 5.6 | 28.4 | 24.4 | 13.1 | 1.8 | 76.0 | 35.5 | 38.3 | 94.8 |
| LOUDON | 0.3 | 0.9 | 5.9 | 6.0 | 6.3 | 6.2 | 5.5 | 28.5 | 26.3 | 13.8 | 1.6 | 78.1 | 36.4 | 40.0 | 93.5 |
| MCMINN | 0.4 | 1.1 | 6.0 | 6.3 | 6.6 | 6.8 | 6.1 | 28.3 | 25.7 | 12.4 | 1.7 | 77.0 | 35.3 | 38.6 | 91.7 |
| MCNAIRY | 0.4 | 1.1 | 5.8 | 6.1 | 6.4 | 6.4 | 6.1 | 26.7 | 26.8 | 13.6 | 2.1 | 77.6 | 37.2 | 40.0 | 94.5 |
| MACON | 0.2 | 0.8 | 6.7 | 6.8 | 7.0 | 6.7 | 6.1 | 28.9 | 24.6 | 11.7 | 1.5 | 75.5 | 34.5 | 37.2 | 94.9 |
| MADISON | 0.5 | 1.0 | 6.9 | 7.2 | 7.1 | 7.6 | 7.2 | 29.6 | 21.9 | 10.7 | 1.7 | 74.7 | 33.0 | 35.2 | 90.0 |
| MARION | 0.3 | 1.0 | 6.4 | 6.6 | 7.0 | 7.0 | 6.0 | 28.8 | 25.8 | 11.0 | 1.4 | 75.7 | 34.1 | 37.5 | 96.1 |
| MARSHALL | 0.4 | 1.1 | 6.4 | 6.8 | 7.0 | 6.8 | 6.1 | 29.5 | 24.5 | 11.4 | 1.6 | 75.9 | 34.9 | 37.3 | 94.4 |
| MAURY | 0.6 | 1.5 | 6.9 | 7.1 | 7.3 | 6.7 | 6.0 | 29.9 | 24.0 | 10.7 | 1.4 | 74.8 | 34.0 | 36.7 | 92.4 |
| MEIGS | 0.2 | 0.8 | 5.5 | 6.0 | 6.7 | 6.8 | 6.2 | 29.3 | 27.1 | 11.0 | 1.3 | 77.6 | 35.0 | 38.7 | 100.3 |
| MONROE | 0.4 | 1.1 | 6.2 | 6.6 | 6.9 | 6.7 | 6.1 | 28.1 | 25.9 | 12.0 | 1.5 | 76.5 | 34.6 | 38.0 | 95.1 |
| MONTGOMERY | 3.2 | 5.8 | 9.2 | 7.6 | 6.6 | 6.8 | 10.0 | 33.8 | 18.5 | 6.8 | 0.8 | 73.1 | 28.5 | 30.4 | 100.2 |
| MOORE | 0.4 | 1.1 | 5.7 | 6.2 | 6.4 | 6.4 | 6.1 | 28.6 | 26.6 | 12.5 | 1.5 | 77.7 | 35.9 | 38.7 | 95.7 |
| MORGAN | 0.3 | 1.0 | 6.0 | 6.3 | 6.8 | 7.1 | 6.7 | 32.1 | 23.8 | 9.9 | 1.3 | 76.4 | 33.2 | 35.9 | 113.5 |
| OBION | 0.4 | 1.1 | 5.8 | 6.1 | 6.3 | 6.4 | 6.1 | 28.3 | 26.3 | 12.7 | 2.0 | 77.8 | 36.1 | 39.0 | 92.4 |
| OVERTON | 0.4 | 1.2 | 5.6 | 6.0 | 6.4 | 6.8 | 6.0 | 27.9 | 26.8 | 12.8 | 1.8 | 77.9 | 36.6 | 39.6 | 96.3 |
| PERRY | 0.5 | 1.4 | 6.8 | 6.6 | 7.1 | 6.5 | 5.1 | 25.4 | 26.4 | 14.2 | 1.9 | 75.4 | 37.8 | 40.1 | 95.8 |
| PICKETT | 0.3 | 1.0 | 6.3 | 6.4 | 6.9 | 6.4 | 5.6 | 25.8 | 26.6 | 13.7 | 2.3 | 76.3 | 37.7 | 39.9 | 95.4 |
| POLK | 0.3 | 0.9 | 5.5 | 5.9 | 6.2 | 5.6 | 6.1 | 28.9 | 27.2 | 13.0 | 1.7 | 79.0 | 36.3 | 39.4 | 99.0 |
| PUTNAM | 0.6 | 1.4 | 5.8 | 5.9 | 6.1 | 7.9 | 8.3 | 29.7 | 23.2 | 11.5 | 1.6 | 78.8 | 32.3 | 35.9 | 96.5 |
| RHEA | 0.5 | 1.4 | 6.1 | 6.4 | 6.7 | 7.6 | 6.3 | 28.0 | 25.2 | 12.1 | 1.6 | 76.5 | 34.6 | 37.9 | 93.2 |
| ROANE | 0.4 | 1.2 | 5.4 | 5.9 | 6.1 | 6.2 | 5.8 | 27.3 | 26.9 | 14.7 | 1.7 | 78.9 | 37.4 | 40.6 | 92.8 |
| ROBERTSON | 0.4 | 1.1 | 7.5 | 7.7 | 7.5 | 6.9 | 5.7 | 30.2 | 23.4 | 9.8 | 1.4 | 73.1 | 33.1 | 35.8 | 96.5 |
| RUTHERFORD | 0.8 | 1.8 | 7.7 | 7.6 | 7.1 | 7.5 | 8.6 | 33.5 | 20.2 | 6.9 | 0.8 | 73.6 | 29.8 | 32.2 | 96.1 |
| SCOTT | 0.2 | 0.8 | 7.0 | 7.3 | 8.0 | 7.4 | 6.8 | 28.6 | 23.5 | 9.9 | 1.4 | 72.9 | 31.8 | 35.0 | 95.1 |
| SEQUATCHIE | 0.3 | 0.9 | 6.3 | 6.4 | 7.2 | 6.9 | 6.3 | 29.9 | 25.5 | 10.2 | 1.4 | 76.1 | 33.9 | 37.1 | 98.0 |
| TENNESSEE | 0.7 | 1.5 | 6.6 | 6.7 | 6.8 | 7.0 | 6.7 | 30.2 | 23.7 | 10.9 | 1.5 | 76.0 | 33.6 | 36.4 | 93.3 |
| UNITED STATES | 9.0 | 11.8 | 6.9 | 7.2 | 7.2 | 7.2 | 6.7 | 29.9 | 22.2 | 11.1 | 1.6 | 74.6 | 32.9 | 35.7 | 95.6 |

# HOUSEHOLDS

| COUNTY | HOUSEHOLDS | | | | | FAMILIES | | | MEDIAN HOUSEHOLD INCOME | | | |
|---|---|---|---|---|---|---|---|---|---|---|---|---|
| | 1990 | 2000 | 2005 | % Annual Rate 1990-2000 | 2000 Average HH Size | 1990 | 2000 | % Annual Rate 1990-2000 | 2000 | 2005 | 2000 National Rank | 2000 State Rank |
| ANDERSON | 27,384 | 29,259 | 29,571 | 0.8 | 2.40 | 19,846 | 20,494 | 0.4 | 39,191 | 43,726 | 737 | 12 |
| BEDFORD | 11,608 | 13,794 | 14,712 | 2.1 | 2.53 | 8,768 | 10,116 | 1.7 | 34,357 | 39,671 | 1340 | 32 |
| BENTON | 5,784 | 6,781 | 7,200 | 1.9 | 2.42 | 4,333 | 4,917 | 1.5 | 30,623 | 35,890 | 2004 | 65 |
| BLEDSOE | 3,261 | 3,897 | 4,331 | 2.2 | 2.56 | 2,522 | 2,916 | 1.8 | 27,675 | 31,926 | 2484 | 83 |
| BLOUNT | 33,624 | 42,097 | 45,843 | 2.8 | 2.45 | 25,344 | 30,782 | 2.4 | 40,046 | 45,322 | 670 | 10 |
| BRADLEY | 27,604 | 32,322 | 34,583 | 1.9 | 2.53 | 21,157 | 24,188 | 1.6 | 36,789 | 40,504 | 1005 | 21 |
| CAMPBELL | 13,150 | 15,028 | 15,995 | 1.6 | 2.57 | 10,158 | 11,268 | 1.3 | 27,636 | 32,590 | 2492 | 85 |
| CANNON | 3,980 | 4,880 | 5,271 | 2.5 | 2.52 | 3,035 | 3,620 | 2.2 | 35,101 | 43,851 | 1238 | 27 |
| CARROLL | 10,727 | 11,803 | 12,428 | 1.2 | 2.46 | 8,013 | 8,510 | 0.7 | 33,450 | 40,197 | 1469 | 39 |
| CARTER | 20,189 | 21,688 | 22,257 | 0.9 | 2.40 | 14,979 | 15,541 | 0.4 | 29,348 | 33,586 | 2246 | 74 |
| CHEATHAM | 9,515 | 13,485 | 15,492 | 4.3 | 2.73 | 7,748 | 10,736 | 4.0 | 49,013 | 60,906 | 221 | 4 |
| CHESTER | 4,558 | 5,608 | 6,158 | 2.5 | 2.50 | 3,505 | 4,178 | 2.2 | 32,281 | 38,163 | 1666 | 47 |
| CLAIBORNE | 9,629 | 11,496 | 12,333 | 2.2 | 2.56 | 7,579 | 8,780 | 1.8 | 27,656 | 36,200 | 2487 | 84 |
| CLAY | 2,855 | 2,942 | 2,975 | 0.4 | 2.44 | 2,144 | 2,132 | -0.1 | 26,964 | 32,737 | 2586 | 88 |
| COCKE | 11,191 | 12,863 | 13,704 | 1.7 | 2.51 | 8,483 | 9,445 | 1.3 | 27,069 | 31,214 | 2569 | 87 |
| COFFEE | 15,500 | 18,451 | 19,760 | 2.1 | 2.51 | 11,727 | 13,498 | 1.7 | 35,248 | 38,964 | 1213 | 26 |
| CROCKETT | 5,183 | 5,646 | 5,941 | 1.0 | 2.47 | 3,856 | 4,054 | 0.6 | 30,704 | 34,165 | 1986 | 63 |
| CUMBERLAND | 13,426 | 18,692 | 21,398 | 4.1 | 2.46 | 10,451 | 14,062 | 3.7 | 31,222 | 36,444 | 1882 | 56 |
| DAVIDSON | 207,530 | 222,388 | 222,803 | 0.8 | 2.27 | 131,395 | 135,125 | 0.3 | 42,200 | 46,267 | 494 | 8 |
| DECATUR | 4,216 | 4,483 | 4,592 | 0.7 | 2.38 | 3,109 | 3,167 | 0.2 | 28,894 | 33,954 | 2315 | 79 |
| DEKALB | 5,696 | 6,669 | 7,199 | 1.9 | 2.44 | 4,316 | 4,882 | 1.5 | 30,501 | 34,926 | 2031 | 68 |
| DICKSON | 13,019 | 17,025 | 19,307 | 3.3 | 2.55 | 10,099 | 12,877 | 3.0 | 37,097 | 43,298 | 961 | 19 |
| DYER | 13,617 | 14,961 | 15,626 | 1.1 | 2.43 | 9,923 | 10,570 | 0.8 | 32,748 | 37,500 | 1583 | 45 |
| FAYETTE | 8,453 | 11,200 | 13,254 | 3.5 | 2.86 | 6,717 | 8,693 | 3.2 | 36,904 | 42,606 | 991 | 20 |
| FENTRESS | 5,511 | 6,433 | 6,947 | 1.9 | 2.56 | 4,258 | 4,801 | 1.5 | 23,530 | 26,329 | 2935 | 93 |
| FRANKLIN | 12,660 | 14,271 | 14,987 | 1.5 | 2.57 | 9,883 | 10,845 | 1.1 | 34,986 | 39,634 | 1254 | 28 |
| GIBSON | 18,361 | 19,719 | 20,172 | 0.9 | 2.40 | 13,472 | 13,991 | 0.5 | 32,209 | 36,086 | 1682 | 48 |
| GILES | 9,832 | 11,498 | 12,057 | 1.9 | 2.51 | 7,454 | 8,448 | 1.5 | 34,944 | 40,423 | 1263 | 29 |
| GRAINGER | 6,394 | 7,947 | 8,838 | 2.7 | 2.57 | 5,076 | 6,124 | 2.3 | 30,537 | 35,758 | 2025 | 67 |
| GREENE | 21,482 | 24,599 | 26,614 | 1.7 | 2.44 | 16,280 | 18,070 | 1.3 | 31,135 | 35,862 | 1909 | 58 |
| GRUNDY | 4,784 | 5,314 | 5,540 | 1.3 | 2.61 | 3,743 | 4,031 | 0.9 | 26,361 | 31,679 | 2672 | 89 |
| HAMBLEN | 19,429 | 21,792 | 22,766 | 1.4 | 2.47 | 14,795 | 16,176 | 1.1 | 35,911 | 40,890 | 1113 | 23 |
| HAMILTON | 111,799 | 118,453 | 120,285 | 0.7 | 2.43 | 78,964 | 81,480 | 0.4 | 37,676 | 41,146 | 880 | 17 |
| HANCOCK | 2,484 | 2,562 | 2,555 | 0.4 | 2.57 | 1,924 | 1,920 | 0.0 | 20,533 | 24,267 | 3082 | 95 |
| HARDEMAN | 8,276 | 9,034 | 9,438 | 1.1 | 2.66 | 6,190 | 6,508 | 0.6 | 29,736 | 33,903 | 2195 | 72 |
| HARDIN | 8,726 | 10,030 | 10,637 | 1.7 | 2.51 | 6,633 | 7,399 | 1.3 | 29,793 | 33,067 | 2184 | 71 |
| HAWKINS | 17,167 | 20,293 | 21,931 | 2.0 | 2.48 | 13,223 | 15,156 | 1.7 | 32,873 | 36,653 | 1558 | 42 |
| HAYWOOD | 7,014 | 7,245 | 7,241 | 0.4 | 2.64 | 5,150 | 5,147 | 0.0 | 27,291 | 30,859 | 2537 | 86 |
| HENDERSON | 8,527 | 10,128 | 11,091 | 2.1 | 2.47 | 6,466 | 7,418 | 1.7 | 33,392 | 39,351 | 1477 | 40 |
| HENRY | 11,362 | 12,736 | 13,260 | 1.4 | 2.34 | 8,216 | 8,886 | 1.0 | 30,670 | 35,799 | 1991 | 64 |
| HICKMAN | 5,976 | 7,842 | 9,027 | 3.3 | 2.61 | 4,608 | 5,873 | 3.0 | 33,125 | 40,303 | 1516 | 41 |
| HOUSTON | 2,683 | 3,153 | 3,324 | 2.0 | 2.46 | 2,039 | 2,316 | 1.6 | 30,914 | 36,097 | 1945 | 60 |
| HUMPHREYS | 6,063 | 6,883 | 7,336 | 1.5 | 2.48 | 4,593 | 5,037 | 1.1 | 33,713 | 37,769 | 1436 | 35 |
| JACKSON | 3,642 | 3,953 | 4,154 | 1.0 | 2.42 | 2,782 | 2,922 | 0.6 | 29,119 | 33,732 | 2277 | 77 |
| JEFFERSON | 12,329 | 18,245 | 21,678 | 4.9 | 2.47 | 9,510 | 13,638 | 4.5 | 32,804 | 38,393 | 1571 | 43 |
| JOHNSON | 5,406 | 6,377 | 6,696 | 2.0 | 2.40 | 4,081 | 4,647 | 1.6 | 25,365 | 29,336 | 2770 | 90 |
| KNOX | 133,639 | 151,470 | 155,399 | 1.5 | 2.42 | 90,561 | 100,341 | 1.3 | 38,041 | 41,778 | 848 | 14 |
| LAKE | 2,418 | 2,300 | 2,184 | -0.6 | 2.42 | 1,735 | 1,588 | -1.1 | 24,682 | 29,742 | 2841 | 92 |
| LAUDERDALE | 8,423 | 8,823 | 9,036 | 0.6 | 2.62 | 6,351 | 6,432 | 0.2 | 28,286 | 32,194 | 2400 | 81 |
| LAWRENCE | 13,338 | 15,496 | 16,340 | 1.8 | 2.56 | 10,265 | 11,618 | 1.5 | 33,466 | 39,755 | 1468 | 38 |
| LEWIS | 3,533 | 4,406 | 4,847 | 2.7 | 2.54 | 2,606 | 3,125 | 2.2 | 28,893 | 31,658 | 2316 | 80 |
| LINCOLN | 10,881 | 12,072 | 12,803 | 1.3 | 2.47 | 8,230 | 8,795 | 0.8 | 31,652 | 37,245 | 1790 | 54 |
| LOUDON | 12,155 | 16,328 | 18,357 | 3.6 | 2.48 | 9,289 | 12,160 | 3.3 | 37,763 | 41,904 | 871 | 16 |
| MCMINN | 16,351 | 18,681 | 19,580 | 1.6 | 2.46 | 12,458 | 13,776 | 1.2 | 31,210 | 34,649 | 1885 | 57 |
| MCNAIRY | 8,834 | 9,912 | 10,574 | 1.4 | 2.45 | 6,678 | 7,237 | 1.0 | 29,144 | 32,046 | 2274 | 76 |
| MACON | 6,159 | 7,505 | 8,399 | 2.4 | 2.51 | 4,711 | 5,545 | 2.0 | 29,487 | 33,060 | 2224 | 73 |
| MADISON | 29,609 | 33,990 | 36,150 | 1.7 | 2.50 | 21,301 | 23,858 | 1.4 | 37,100 | 41,863 | 960 | 18 |
| MARION | 9,215 | 10,352 | 10,939 | 1.4 | 2.60 | 7,171 | 7,833 | 1.1 | 30,795 | 35,052 | 1970 | 61 |
| MARSHALL | 8,268 | 10,748 | 11,720 | 3.2 | 2.47 | 6,120 | 7,751 | 2.9 | 36,546 | 42,187 | 1037 | 22 |
| MAURY | 20,608 | 27,935 | 30,738 | 3.8 | 2.54 | 15,552 | 20,652 | 3.5 | 43,374 | 50,059 | 434 | 7 |
| MEIGS | 2,996 | 4,053 | 4,619 | 3.7 | 2.54 | 2,333 | 3,052 | 3.3 | 29,055 | 34,232 | 2289 | 78 |
| MONROE | 11,363 | 14,012 | 15,703 | 2.6 | 2.56 | 8,781 | 10,492 | 2.2 | 31,775 | 37,399 | 1761 | 52 |
| MONTGOMERY | 34,345 | 48,723 | 54,888 | 4.3 | 2.63 | 26,914 | 37,476 | 4.1 | 39,902 | 49,853 | 682 | 11 |
| MOORE | 1,734 | 1,962 | 1,988 | 1.5 | 2.61 | 1,391 | 1,534 | 1.2 | 41,111 | 48,527 | 581 | 9 |
| MORGAN | 5,841 | 6,555 | 6,855 | 1.4 | 2.61 | 4,621 | 5,031 | 1.0 | 30,342 | 37,979 | 2069 | 70 |
| OBION | 12,412 | 12,933 | 13,210 | 0.5 | 2.47 | 9,219 | 9,290 | 0.1 | 33,517 | 36,478 | 1461 | 36 |
| OVERTON | 6,734 | 8,019 | 8,779 | 2.1 | 2.46 | 5,266 | 6,061 | 1.7 | 28,260 | 32,082 | 2407 | 82 |
| PERRY | 2,512 | 3,009 | 3,236 | 2.2 | 2.49 | 1,905 | 2,195 | 1.7 | 31,935 | 36,924 | 1729 | 49 |
| PICKETT | 1,786 | 1,883 | 1,974 | 0.6 | 2.49 | 1,330 | 1,349 | 0.2 | 21,883 | 24,030 | 3033 | 94 |
| POLK | 5,092 | 5,882 | 6,375 | 1.8 | 2.59 | 4,010 | 4,490 | 1.4 | 33,716 | 42,551 | 1434 | 34 |
| PUTNAM | 19,753 | 24,647 | 26,655 | 2.7 | 2.38 | 13,994 | 16,832 | 2.3 | 32,733 | 36,114 | 1586 | 46 |
| RHEA | 9,185 | 11,065 | 11,833 | 2.3 | 2.50 | 6,985 | 8,132 | 1.9 | 30,602 | 36,516 | 2009 | 66 |
| ROANE | 18,453 | 20,351 | 20,983 | 1.2 | 2.44 | 13,967 | 14,863 | 0.8 | 35,300 | 40,109 | 1201 | 25 |
| ROBERTSON | 14,801 | 20,565 | 23,881 | 4.1 | 2.73 | 11,886 | 16,245 | 3.9 | 44,692 | 55,150 | 366 | 6 |
| RUTHERFORD | 42,118 | 65,598 | 77,475 | 5.5 | 2.62 | 31,225 | 47,741 | 5.3 | 48,326 | 55,931 | 232 | 5 |
| SCOTT | 6,534 | 7,514 | 8,006 | 1.7 | 2.70 | 5,128 | 5,711 | 1.3 | 25,348 | 29,077 | 2773 | 91 |
| SEQUATCHIE | 3,287 | 4,128 | 4,718 | 2.8 | 2.68 | 2,555 | 3,095 | 2.4 | 31,410 | 37,601 | 1838 | 55 |
| TENNESSEE | | | | 1.9 | 2.50 | | | 1.6 | 37,221 | 42,289 | | |
| UNITED STATES | | | | 1.4 | 2.59 | | | 1.1 | 41,914 | 49,127 | | |

| COUNTY | 2000 Per Capita Income | 2000 HH Income Base | 2000 HOUSEHOLD INCOME DISTRIBUTION (%) | | | | | | 2000 AVERAGE DISPOSABLE INCOME BY AGE OF HOUSEHOLDER | | | | | |
|---|---|---|---|---|---|---|---|---|---|---|---|---|---|---|
| | | | Less than $15,000 | $15,000 to $24,999 | $25,000 to $49,999 | $50,000 to $99,999 | $100,000 to $149,999 | $150,000 or More | All Ages | <35 | 35-44 | 45-54 | 55-64 | 65+ |
| ANDERSON | 21,250 | 29,259 | 16.7 | 12.5 | 33.5 | 29.5 | 6.0 | 1.8 | 39,109 | 33,666 | 43,278 | 50,972 | 43,834 | 27,090 |
| BEDFORD | 16,752 | 13,794 | 19.3 | 15.5 | 36.5 | 23.7 | 4.0 | 1.1 | 34,236 | 32,738 | 40,333 | 41,190 | 35,993 | 22,325 |
| BENTON | 15,923 | 6,781 | 21.5 | 18.3 | 36.6 | 18.9 | 3.5 | 1.2 | 31,834 | 30,668 | 37,884 | 40,003 | 33,843 | 21,405 |
| BLEDSOE | 11,848 | 3,897 | 24.0 | 20.8 | 37.8 | 15.7 | 1.6 | 0.1 | 27,431 | 27,774 | 35,165 | 29,400 | 26,442 | 18,256 |
| BLOUNT | 20,820 | 42,097 | 14.9 | 13.5 | 34.7 | 29.5 | 5.6 | 1.8 | 39,371 | 34,009 | 45,859 | 48,138 | 42,111 | 25,224 |
| BRADLEY | 17,402 | 32,322 | 17.4 | 14.1 | 37.0 | 26.1 | 4.1 | 1.4 | 36,253 | 33,156 | 41,455 | 45,352 | 38,040 | 21,537 |
| CAMPBELL | 13,442 | 15,028 | 26.6 | 18.7 | 34.8 | 16.9 | 2.6 | 0.5 | 28,485 | 26,951 | 33,441 | 32,051 | 31,702 | 20,625 |
| CANNON | 15,695 | 4,880 | 17.9 | 14.8 | 38.6 | 25.8 | 2.8 | 0.2 | 33,264 | 33,685 | 37,967 | 39,444 | 35,362 | 22,206 |
| CARROLL | 16,885 | 11,803 | 19.0 | 15.8 | 38.1 | 22.9 | 3.7 | 0.6 | 33,150 | 33,385 | 39,551 | 40,787 | 33,936 | 20,938 |
| CARTER | 15,459 | 21,688 | 23.6 | 18.4 | 35.4 | 19.6 | 2.5 | 0.6 | 30,114 | 28,102 | 35,983 | 38,771 | 31,638 | 18,416 |
| CHEATHAM | 20,994 | 13,485 | 9.9 | 8.4 | 32.8 | 39.5 | 8.1 | 1.3 | 44,693 | 42,932 | 50,331 | 53,323 | 42,837 | 26,872 |
| CHESTER | 13,952 | 5,608 | 21.1 | 13.7 | 40.3 | 22.6 | 2.2 | 0.1 | 31,005 | 30,647 | 38,301 | 36,504 | 30,418 | 20,367 |
| CLAIBORNE | 14,239 | 11,496 | 24.6 | 20.8 | 31.8 | 19.4 | 2.6 | 0.9 | 29,981 | 29,360 | 36,120 | 34,555 | 29,393 | 19,973 |
| CLAY | 13,585 | 2,942 | 25.3 | 19.9 | 34.9 | 17.3 | 2.0 | 0.6 | 28,174 | 28,773 | 33,126 | 35,023 | 28,789 | 15,970 |
| COCKE | 13,900 | 12,863 | 25.8 | 19.4 | 36.2 | 15.5 | 2.3 | 0.9 | 28,438 | 24,723 | 32,289 | 37,835 | 29,778 | 17,437 |
| COFFEE | 17,100 | 18,451 | 20.0 | 13.8 | 34.6 | 26.0 | 4.4 | 1.2 | 35,364 | 32,050 | 40,435 | 48,576 | 37,301 | 21,190 |
| CROCKETT | 16,441 | 5,646 | 23.4 | 16.7 | 36.2 | 19.9 | 2.8 | 1.0 | 31,236 | 31,156 | 36,515 | 38,911 | 31,769 | 19,560 |
| CUMBERLAND | 15,953 | 18,692 | 18.2 | 18.3 | 36.7 | 23.2 | 3.0 | 0.6 | 32,269 | 27,295 | 36,785 | 39,215 | 36,828 | 25,547 |
| DAVIDSON | 25,391 | 222,386 | 12.6 | 13.0 | 33.5 | 29.7 | 7.6 | 3.7 | 44,508 | 36,538 | 49,023 | 53,278 | 49,307 | 31,000 |
| DECATUR | 19,215 | 4,483 | 21.6 | 20.5 | 34.7 | 18.9 | 3.3 | 1.1 | 31,132 | 28,966 | 38,514 | 40,039 | 31,911 | 19,876 |
| DEKALB | 15,313 | 6,669 | 21.2 | 19.8 | 35.4 | 19.4 | 3.4 | 0.8 | 31,363 | 27,727 | 37,614 | 40,518 | 33,104 | 20,586 |
| DICKSON | 18,122 | 17,025 | 17.3 | 13.5 | 35.2 | 28.1 | 4.5 | 1.4 | 37,028 | 32,893 | 43,572 | 47,284 | 37,807 | 22,028 |
| DYER | 17,039 | 14,961 | 22.3 | 15.6 | 35.0 | 21.5 | 4.2 | 1.4 | 33,629 | 31,622 | 39,116 | 41,464 | 35,639 | 19,365 |
| FAYETTE | 19,075 | 11,200 | 17.8 | 12.3 | 36.8 | 24.4 | 5.7 | 3.0 | 39,188 | 35,342 | 42,512 | 50,838 | 38,113 | 23,703 |
| FENTRESS | 12,571 | 6,433 | 28.9 | 24.3 | 31.3 | 13.0 | 1.9 | 0.8 | 26,146 | 25,417 | 30,926 | 31,208 | 24,244 | 17,150 |
| FRANKLIN | 16,088 | 14,258 | 17.9 | 15.6 | 36.9 | 25.1 | 3.7 | 0.9 | 34,554 | 30,627 | 41,442 | 43,359 | 35,783 | 22,905 |
| GIBSON | 16,098 | 19,719 | 21.4 | 16.9 | 36.1 | 22.3 | 2.6 | 0.7 | 31,814 | 32,038 | 36,562 | 42,077 | 32,000 | 20,151 |
| GILES | 19,306 | 11,498 | 19.2 | 15.3 | 35.1 | 23.7 | 4.2 | 2.5 | 36,910 | 32,750 | 41,447 | 48,027 | 38,616 | 22,292 |
| GRAINGER | 13,617 | 7,947 | 19.9 | 19.9 | 39.2 | 19.0 | 2.0 | 0.1 | 29,700 | 29,933 | 33,555 | 33,800 | 30,808 | 19,554 |
| GREENE | 14,853 | 24,599 | 19.7 | 19.6 | 38.4 | 19.4 | 2.5 | 0.5 | 30,768 | 29,816 | 34,515 | 38,918 | 31,185 | 20,382 |
| GRUNDY | 11,789 | 5,314 | 24.7 | 22.3 | 36.5 | 15.9 | 0.6 | 0.0 | 26,215 | 26,068 | 29,557 | 33,155 | 25,007 | 17,471 |
| HAMBLEN | 17,579 | 21,792 | 16.5 | 15.7 | 36.2 | 26.4 | 4.2 | 1.1 | 35,639 | 31,383 | 41,105 | 45,514 | 37,297 | 23,172 |
| HAMILTON | 22,006 | 118,452 | 16.7 | 14.3 | 33.1 | 25.9 | 6.3 | 3.7 | 41,521 | 34,313 | 47,324 | 52,167 | 43,619 | 25,292 |
| HANCOCK | 10,009 | 2,562 | 38.3 | 21.2 | 28.7 | 10.5 | 1.3 | 0.0 | 22,544 | 22,268 | 26,444 | 26,826 | 22,879 | 16,435 |
| HARDEMAN | 13,825 | 9,034 | 22.8 | 19.2 | 34.9 | 20.1 | 2.6 | 0.5 | 30,188 | 29,334 | 33,056 | 29,981 | 29,931 | 20,971 |
| HARDIN | 17,929 | 10,030 | 23.1 | 18.6 | 33.2 | 18.7 | 4.1 | 2.3 | 33,692 | 31,308 | 39,780 | 45,672 | 31,329 | 19,320 |
| HAWKINS | 16,048 | 20,293 | 20.8 | 16.5 | 36.6 | 22.2 | 3.2 | 0.7 | 32,345 | 29,380 | 39,712 | 40,405 | 33,135 | 18,959 |
| HAYWOOD | 13,721 | 7,245 | 28.0 | 18.5 | 32.3 | 16.6 | 3.1 | 1.6 | 29,976 | 24,975 | 38,133 | 37,116 | 32,207 | 18,412 |
| HENDERSON | 15,876 | 10,128 | 17.4 | 15.9 | 40.0 | 23.3 | 3.2 | 0.3 | 32,724 | 32,473 | 38,254 | 43,078 | 31,822 | 19,905 |
| HENRY | 17,107 | 12,736 | 22.0 | 17.7 | 35.7 | 20.7 | 2.9 | 1.1 | 31,783 | 29,342 | 40,187 | 40,242 | 31,056 | 22,469 |
| HICKMAN | 15,469 | 7,842 | 17.7 | 15.3 | 38.3 | 23.8 | 4.3 | 0.7 | 34,006 | 34,868 | 40,338 | 39,722 | 31,866 | 23,449 |
| HOUSTON | 15,039 | 3,153 | 21.1 | 18.7 | 36.5 | 20.2 | 3.0 | 0.5 | 30,703 | 29,526 | 35,801 | 39,381 | 32,411 | 19,891 |
| HUMPHREYS | 16,255 | 6,883 | 18.7 | 17.1 | 35.2 | 24.7 | 3.7 | 0.6 | 33,361 | 31,968 | 39,912 | 42,511 | 32,355 | 22,219 |
| JACKSON | 15,593 | 3,953 | 23.7 | 18.3 | 33.4 | 20.2 | 2.7 | 1.7 | 31,510 | 30,991 | 42,044 | 34,170 | 32,734 | 20,291 |
| JEFFERSON | 16,290 | 18,245 | 18.6 | 17.6 | 36.8 | 22.5 | 3.2 | 1.3 | 33,521 | 28,736 | 40,079 | 41,384 | 35,325 | 21,663 |
| JOHNSON | 11,171 | 6,377 | 28.3 | 21.0 | 36.3 | 13.3 | 1.2 | 0.1 | 25,138 | 25,220 | 28,738 | 30,144 | 24,278 | 17,508 |
| KNOX | 23,136 | 151,470 | 17.5 | 13.9 | 31.6 | 26.4 | 6.5 | 4.1 | 42,623 | 33,436 | 48,011 | 53,079 | 44,543 | 27,034 |
| LAKE | 11,564 | 2,300 | 29.3 | 21.6 | 34.2 | 13.0 | 1.3 | 0.6 | 25,295 | 22,523 | 27,913 | 30,972 | 24,294 | 21,300 |
| LAUDERDALE | 12,568 | 8,823 | 25.6 | 18.3 | 36.4 | 17.3 | 1.8 | 0.6 | 28,476 | 28,514 | 31,955 | 36,152 | 28,903 | 16,447 |
| LAWRENCE | 17,075 | 15,496 | 17.9 | 16.5 | 38.4 | 23.3 | 3.1 | 0.8 | 33,372 | 32,189 | 40,066 | 43,276 | 33,121 | 19,484 |
| LEWIS | 13,666 | 4,406 | 20.7 | 21.3 | 38.0 | 18.0 | 1.6 | 0.5 | 29,144 | 30,357 | 33,344 | 35,672 | 27,515 | 18,878 |
| LINCOLN | 15,940 | 12,072 | 21.9 | 17.0 | 36.5 | 20.4 | 3.4 | 0.7 | 31,684 | 30,528 | 39,197 | 41,328 | 31,379 | 18,867 |
| LOUDON | 20,243 | 16,326 | 15.7 | 15.3 | 34.4 | 26.6 | 5.7 | 2.3 | 38,792 | 32,497 | 45,281 | 47,505 | 45,175 | 25,712 |
| MCMINN | 15,625 | 18,681 | 23.6 | 16.4 | 34.1 | 21.7 | 3.4 | 0.7 | 31,697 | 28,442 | 36,898 | 41,913 | 32,995 | 18,345 |
| MCNAIRY | 13,953 | 9,912 | 25.3 | 17.2 | 37.1 | 18.0 | 2.3 | 0.2 | 28,597 | 28,002 | 32,926 | 39,063 | 27,468 | 17,369 |
| MACON | 15,500 | 7,503 | 25.1 | 18.2 | 36.4 | 17.4 | 2.1 | 0.9 | 29,397 | 30,787 | 35,830 | 36,358 | 27,551 | 16,869 |
| MADISON | 19,103 | 33,990 | 16.8 | 14.9 | 33.9 | 26.4 | 5.9 | 2.2 | 38,490 | 33,811 | 44,007 | 49,818 | 40,623 | 23,890 |
| MARION | 14,433 | 10,352 | 20.9 | 18.1 | 36.4 | 20.9 | 2.9 | 0.7 | 31,288 | 28,993 | 36,665 | 39,832 | 32,576 | 19,124 |
| MARSHALL | 17,963 | 10,748 | 16.9 | 15.1 | 37.2 | 26.0 | 3.8 | 1.1 | 35,539 | 31,782 | 41,394 | 45,332 | 38,528 | 20,680 |
| MAURY | 21,101 | 27,935 | 14.7 | 9.9 | 34.2 | 32.3 | 6.9 | 2.0 | 41,831 | 38,676 | 49,093 | 51,297 | 41,779 | 26,395 |
| MEIGS | 13,854 | 4,053 | 25.5 | 16.7 | 36.1 | 19.1 | 1.9 | 0.7 | 29,604 | 26,729 | 33,915 | 37,505 | 28,715 | 18,028 |
| MONROE | 14,935 | 14,012 | 18.8 | 19.3 | 37.0 | 21.7 | 2.7 | 0.6 | 31,799 | 29,882 | 37,881 | 38,739 | 32,121 | 21,067 |
| MONTGOMERY | 17,941 | 48,718 | 10.6 | 14.2 | 38.7 | 31.3 | 4.3 | 0.9 | 38,449 | 33,957 | 42,803 | 48,110 | 41,026 | 26,534 |
| MOORE | 18,585 | 1,962 | 10.6 | 11.5 | 40.8 | 29.7 | 6.7 | 0.8 | 39,525 | 37,965 | 39,127 | 54,435 | 44,853 | 23,027 |
| MORGAN | 12,628 | 6,555 | 21.4 | 18.6 | 38.2 | 20.1 | 1.7 | 0.1 | 29,493 | 28,866 | 33,814 | 35,896 | 30,551 | 17,785 |
| OBION | 17,731 | 12,933 | 20.4 | 16.4 | 35.3 | 22.4 | 4.0 | 1.5 | 34,351 | 32,724 | 39,760 | 44,759 | 34,827 | 20,469 |
| OVERTON | 13,710 | 8,019 | 22.2 | 20.7 | 38.0 | 17.0 | 2.0 | 0.1 | 28,363 | 28,276 | 36,159 | 32,591 | 30,427 | 16,883 |
| PERRY | 15,868 | 3,009 | 17.7 | 21.4 | 33.9 | 23.0 | 3.4 | 0.7 | 32,245 | 34,628 | 36,647 | 39,919 | 32,732 | 20,850 |
| PICKETT | 19,110 | 1,883 | 31.7 | 23.8 | 28.3 | 11.3 | 3.0 | 2.0 | 28,685 | 22,877 | 28,962 | 38,612 | 30,173 | 16,758 |
| POLK | 15,503 | 5,882 | 18.4 | 15.9 | 37.5 | 24.4 | 3.3 | 0.5 | 33,122 | 34,847 | 35,970 | 41,690 | 32,688 | 21,669 |
| PUTNAM | 17,526 | 24,644 | 19.9 | 17.6 | 34.4 | 22.5 | 4.0 | 1.5 | 34,230 | 28,433 | 44,027 | 43,003 | 36,573 | 21,947 |
| RHEA | 14,750 | 11,065 | 22.6 | 17.8 | 34.5 | 21.5 | 2.9 | 0.7 | 31,112 | 30,413 | 38,719 | 36,976 | 29,691 | 20,065 |
| ROANE | 19,262 | 20,351 | 17.9 | 15.6 | 34.3 | 24.6 | 5.3 | 2.3 | 37,375 | 30,860 | 42,325 | 49,229 | 43,000 | 25,289 |
| ROBERTSON | 21,191 | 20,565 | 11.2 | 10.4 | 34.6 | 33.0 | 8.3 | 2.4 | 44,460 | 41,082 | 51,080 | 54,816 | 43,733 | 26,758 |
| RUTHERFORD | 22,327 | 65,598 | 9.8 | 8.5 | 33.7 | 36.8 | 8.9 | 2.2 | 46,004 | 40,114 | 52,944 | 56,864 | 46,069 | 29,489 |
| SCOTT | 12,083 | 7,514 | 29.4 | 19.9 | 34.6 | 14.1 | 1.4 | 0.6 | 26,199 | 24,888 | 29,297 | 33,079 | 23,829 | 18,659 |
| SEQUATCHIE | 14,701 | 4,128 | 23.3 | 16.1 | 36.4 | 19.5 | 3.5 | 1.2 | 32,412 | 33,913 | 33,926 | 40,773 | 31,125 | 18,346 |
| TENNESSEE | 19,874 | | 17.1 | 14.4 | 34.0 | 26.4 | 5.7 | 2.4 | 39,053 | 34,053 | 44,876 | 48,417 | 39,984 | 24,353 |
| UNITED STATES | 22,162 | | 14.5 | 12.5 | 32.3 | 29.8 | 7.4 | 3.5 | 40,748 | 34,503 | 44,969 | 49,579 | 43,409 | 27,339 |

# SPENDING POTENTIAL INDEXES

| COUNTY | FINANCIAL SERVICES | | | | THE HOME | | | | | | ENTERTAINMENT | | | | | | PERSONAL | | | |
|---|---|---|---|---|---|---|---|---|---|---|---|---|---|---|---|---|---|---|---|---|
| | | | | | Home Improvements | | | Furnishings | | | | | | | | | | | | |
| | Auto Loan | Home Loan | Invest-ments | Retire-ment Plans | Home Repair | Lawn & Garden | Remodel-ing | Appli-ances | Elec-tronics | Furni-ture | Restau-rants | Sport-ing Goods | Theater & Concerts | Toys & Hobbies | Travel | Video Rental | Apparel | Auto After-market | Health Insur-ance | Pets & Supplies |
| ANDERSON | 98 | 89 | 100 | 92 | 102 | 100 | 105 | 98 | 95 | 94 | 95 | 98 | 95 | 100 | 84 | 97 | 93 | 95 | 101 | 99 |
| BEDFORD | 97 | 74 | 83 | 81 | 96 | 93 | 111 | 96 | 92 | 83 | 84 | 95 | 85 | 96 | 74 | 96 | 84 | 90 | 100 | 98 |
| BENTON | 97 | 65 | 71 | 76 | 92 | 91 | 114 | 96 | 92 | 76 | 78 | 96 | 79 | 95 | 68 | 96 | 79 | 87 | 102 | 97 |
| BLEDSOE | 96 | 63 | 68 | 73 | 92 | 90 | 111 | 95 | 91 | 75 | 77 | 94 | 78 | 93 | 67 | 95 | 78 | 86 | 102 | 95 |
| BLOUNT | 99 | 85 | 94 | 90 | 100 | 98 | 109 | 98 | 95 | 91 | 93 | 98 | 93 | 100 | 81 | 98 | 92 | 95 | 101 | 100 |
| BRADLEY | 99 | 85 | 87 | 87 | 97 | 94 | 108 | 97 | 95 | 90 | 92 | 97 | 91 | 99 | 78 | 98 | 91 | 94 | 100 | 100 |
| CAMPBELL | 96 | 69 | 76 | 76 | 95 | 92 | 110 | 95 | 91 | 79 | 80 | 94 | 82 | 94 | 71 | 95 | 80 | 88 | 101 | 96 |
| CANNON | 98 | 67 | 73 | 77 | 93 | 91 | 113 | 96 | 92 | 78 | 80 | 96 | 81 | 96 | 68 | 96 | 80 | 88 | 102 | 98 |
| CARROLL | 97 | 66 | 72 | 75 | 94 | 91 | 111 | 96 | 91 | 78 | 79 | 95 | 81 | 95 | 69 | 95 | 79 | 87 | 101 | 96 |
| CARTER | 96 | 74 | 82 | 80 | 97 | 93 | 108 | 96 | 91 | 83 | 84 | 94 | 85 | 96 | 75 | 96 | 83 | 89 | 100 | 97 |
| CHEATHAM | 100 | 84 | 82 | 87 | 95 | 92 | 113 | 99 | 97 | 90 | 93 | 99 | 90 | 102 | 75 | 99 | 92 | 95 | 100 | 102 |
| CHESTER | 97 | 69 | 77 | 78 | 93 | 91 | 113 | 96 | 93 | 79 | 81 | 95 | 82 | 96 | 70 | 97 | 82 | 89 | 102 | 98 |
| CLAIBORNE | 97 | 67 | 72 | 75 | 92 | 91 | 113 | 96 | 92 | 78 | 79 | 96 | 80 | 95 | 68 | 96 | 80 | 88 | 101 | 97 |
| CLAY | 97 | 63 | 67 | 73 | 92 | 90 | 112 | 96 | 91 | 75 | 77 | 96 | 78 | 94 | 66 | 95 | 78 | 86 | 102 | 96 |
| COCKE | 96 | 68 | 72 | 75 | 94 | 91 | 110 | 95 | 90 | 79 | 79 | 94 | 81 | 94 | 70 | 95 | 79 | 87 | 100 | 96 |
| COFFEE | 98 | 84 | 98 | 91 | 102 | 99 | 107 | 98 | 95 | 92 | 92 | 98 | 93 | 99 | 83 | 97 | 91 | 94 | 102 | 99 |
| CROCKETT | 97 | 68 | 74 | 76 | 94 | 91 | 111 | 96 | 91 | 78 | 80 | 94 | 81 | 95 | 70 | 96 | 80 | 88 | 102 | 97 |
| CUMBERLAND | 98 | 74 | 86 | 84 | 97 | 96 | 113 | 98 | 92 | 83 | 84 | 96 | 86 | 97 | 76 | 96 | 85 | 90 | 103 | 99 |
| DAVIDSON | 97 | 101 | 100 | 97 | 102 | 101 | 96 | 98 | 97 | 100 | 100 | 98 | 98 | 99 | 90 | 98 | 100 | 100 | 95 | 99 |
| DECATUR | 97 | 66 | 73 | 76 | 93 | 91 | 115 | 96 | 92 | 77 | 79 | 96 | 80 | 95 | 68 | 96 | 80 | 87 | 102 | 97 |
| DEKALB | 97 | 67 | 75 | 76 | 93 | 91 | 115 | 96 | 92 | 78 | 80 | 95 | 80 | 95 | 69 | 96 | 80 | 88 | 101 | 97 |
| DICKSON | 98 | 73 | 79 | 80 | 95 | 92 | 113 | 96 | 93 | 82 | 83 | 95 | 84 | 97 | 72 | 97 | 83 | 90 | 101 | 99 |
| DYER | 96 | 73 | 80 | 79 | 95 | 91 | 110 | 96 | 91 | 82 | 82 | 93 | 83 | 95 | 73 | 96 | 83 | 89 | 98 | 97 |
| FAYETTE | 98 | 72 | 77 | 80 | 94 | 92 | 113 | 96 | 93 | 81 | 83 | 97 | 83 | 97 | 71 | 97 | 83 | 89 | 101 | 98 |
| FENTRESS | 97 | 65 | 70 | 74 | 93 | 90 | 112 | 95 | 91 | 77 | 78 | 95 | 79 | 94 | 68 | 95 | 79 | 87 | 101 | 96 |
| FRANKLIN | 98 | 75 | 83 | 82 | 96 | 93 | 113 | 97 | 93 | 83 | 85 | 96 | 85 | 98 | 73 | 97 | 85 | 90 | 101 | 99 |
| GIBSON | 96 | 70 | 77 | 77 | 95 | 91 | 107 | 96 | 90 | 81 | 80 | 94 | 83 | 94 | 72 | 95 | 81 | 88 | 99 | 96 |
| GILES | 97 | 70 | 77 | 77 | 95 | 92 | 111 | 96 | 91 | 80 | 81 | 95 | 83 | 96 | 71 | 96 | 81 | 88 | 101 | 97 |
| GRAINGER | 97 | 65 | 70 | 75 | 92 | 90 | 113 | 96 | 92 | 76 | 78 | 96 | 79 | 95 | 67 | 95 | 79 | 87 | 101 | 97 |
| GREENE | 98 | 72 | 79 | 80 | 95 | 93 | 111 | 96 | 93 | 82 | 83 | 96 | 84 | 97 | 72 | 96 | 83 | 90 | 101 | 98 |
| GRUNDY | 97 | 63 | 67 | 73 | 92 | 90 | 112 | 95 | 91 | 75 | 77 | 96 | 78 | 94 | 66 | 95 | 78 | 86 | 102 | 96 |
| HAMBLEN | 98 | 80 | 87 | 86 | 98 | 95 | 110 | 97 | 94 | 87 | 88 | 97 | 89 | 99 | 77 | 97 | 88 | 92 | 101 | 99 |
| HAMILTON | 98 | 96 | 101 | 97 | 102 | 100 | 101 | 98 | 97 | 98 | 97 | 99 | 98 | 100 | 88 | 98 | 98 | 98 | 97 | 100 |
| HANCOCK | 97 | 63 | 66 | 73 | 92 | 90 | 112 | 96 | 91 | 75 | 77 | 96 | 78 | 95 | 66 | 95 | 78 | 86 | 102 | 96 |
| HARDEMAN | 96 | 66 | 72 | 74 | 94 | 91 | 108 | 96 | 90 | 78 | 78 | 94 | 80 | 94 | 69 | 95 | 79 | 87 | 99 | 96 |
| HARDIN | 97 | 67 | 72 | 76 | 93 | 91 | 113 | 96 | 92 | 78 | 79 | 96 | 80 | 95 | 68 | 96 | 80 | 88 | 101 | 97 |
| HAWKINS | 97 | 71 | 77 | 79 | 94 | 91 | 112 | 96 | 92 | 80 | 82 | 95 | 83 | 96 | 71 | 96 | 82 | 89 | 101 | 98 |
| HAYWOOD | 96 | 69 | 73 | 76 | 94 | 90 | 110 | 96 | 91 | 80 | 79 | 95 | 81 | 94 | 70 | 95 | 81 | 88 | 99 | 97 |
| HENDERSON | 98 | 67 | 72 | 77 | 93 | 91 | 114 | 96 | 92 | 78 | 80 | 97 | 81 | 96 | 68 | 96 | 80 | 88 | 102 | 98 |
| HENRY | 97 | 70 | 82 | 79 | 95 | 93 | 110 | 96 | 91 | 79 | 81 | 94 | 82 | 95 | 73 | 96 | 81 | 88 | 101 | 97 |
| HICKMAN | 98 | 69 | 76 | 78 | 93 | 91 | 114 | 96 | 93 | 79 | 81 | 96 | 82 | 96 | 70 | 97 | 82 | 89 | 102 | 98 |
| HOUSTON | 97 | 63 | 67 | 73 | 92 | 90 | 112 | 95 | 91 | 75 | 77 | 95 | 78 | 94 | 66 | 95 | 78 | 86 | 102 | 96 |
| HUMPHREYS | 99 | 73 | 80 | 81 | 95 | 92 | 115 | 97 | 93 | 82 | 84 | 97 | 84 | 98 | 72 | 97 | 84 | 90 | 102 | 100 |
| JACKSON | 96 | 63 | 68 | 73 | 92 | 90 | 111 | 95 | 91 | 75 | 77 | 94 | 78 | 93 | 67 | 95 | 78 | 86 | 102 | 95 |
| JEFFERSON | 99 | 75 | 80 | 83 | 94 | 92 | 114 | 97 | 94 | 82 | 85 | 97 | 85 | 98 | 72 | 97 | 85 | 91 | 102 | 100 |
| JOHNSON | 97 | 63 | 66 | 73 | 92 | 90 | 112 | 96 | 91 | 75 | 77 | 96 | 78 | 95 | 66 | 95 | 78 | 86 | 102 | 96 |
| KNOX | 99 | 97 | 99 | 97 | 102 | 100 | 102 | 98 | 97 | 97 | 98 | 99 | 97 | 100 | 87 | 98 | 98 | 98 | 99 | 100 |
| LAKE | 95 | 66 | 69 | 73 | 93 | 90 | 108 | 94 | 90 | 77 | 77 | 92 | 79 | 92 | 69 | 95 | 78 | 86 | 100 | 95 |
| LAUDERDALE | 97 | 66 | 71 | 74 | 93 | 91 | 111 | 95 | 91 | 77 | 78 | 95 | 80 | 94 | 68 | 95 | 79 | 87 | 101 | 96 |
| LAWRENCE | 97 | 70 | 76 | 78 | 95 | 91 | 112 | 96 | 92 | 80 | 81 | 95 | 82 | 96 | 71 | 96 | 82 | 88 | 101 | 98 |
| LEWIS | 96 | 63 | 69 | 73 | 92 | 90 | 110 | 94 | 91 | 75 | 77 | 92 | 77 | 93 | 67 | 96 | 77 | 86 | 102 | 95 |
| LINCOLN | 97 | 72 | 79 | 80 | 96 | 92 | 111 | 96 | 91 | 81 | 83 | 95 | 84 | 97 | 72 | 96 | 83 | 89 | 101 | 98 |
| LOUDON | 99 | 80 | 90 | 88 | 99 | 97 | 112 | 98 | 94 | 88 | 89 | 98 | 90 | 99 | 79 | 98 | 89 | 93 | 102 | 100 |
| MCMINN | 97 | 70 | 77 | 78 | 95 | 92 | 112 | 96 | 92 | 80 | 82 | 95 | 82 | 96 | 71 | 96 | 82 | 88 | 101 | 97 |
| MCNAIRY | 97 | 63 | 67 | 73 | 92 | 90 | 112 | 96 | 91 | 75 | 77 | 96 | 78 | 94 | 66 | 95 | 78 | 86 | 102 | 96 |
| MACON | 98 | 68 | 74 | 77 | 94 | 91 | 113 | 96 | 92 | 79 | 80 | 96 | 82 | 96 | 69 | 96 | 81 | 88 | 102 | 98 |
| MADISON | 98 | 91 | 92 | 93 | 99 | 97 | 101 | 98 | 96 | 95 | 94 | 99 | 94 | 98 | 83 | 98 | 95 | 96 | 96 | 99 |
| MARION | 96 | 67 | 73 | 75 | 94 | 91 | 110 | 95 | 91 | 78 | 79 | 94 | 81 | 94 | 69 | 95 | 79 | 87 | 101 | 96 |
| MARSHALL | 98 | 75 | 81 | 82 | 96 | 92 | 114 | 97 | 93 | 84 | 85 | 96 | 85 | 98 | 73 | 97 | 86 | 91 | 101 | 100 |
| MAURY | 99 | 84 | 92 | 89 | 99 | 96 | 109 | 98 | 95 | 90 | 91 | 97 | 92 | 100 | 80 | 98 | 91 | 94 | 100 | 100 |
| MEIGS | 97 | 63 | 66 | 73 | 92 | 90 | 112 | 96 | 91 | 75 | 77 | 96 | 78 | 95 | 66 | 95 | 78 | 86 | 102 | 96 |
| MONROE | 98 | 65 | 70 | 75 | 93 | 91 | 113 | 96 | 92 | 77 | 78 | 96 | 80 | 95 | 67 | 96 | 79 | 87 | 102 | 97 |
| MONTGOMERY | 94 | 89 | 83 | 83 | 94 | 90 | 99 | 94 | 94 | 87 | 92 | 93 | 88 | 95 | 77 | 97 | 89 | 94 | 94 | 99 |
| MOORE | 100 | 80 | 86 | 86 | 98 | 94 | 115 | 98 | 94 | 87 | 90 | 98 | 89 | 101 | 76 | 99 | 90 | 93 | 102 | 102 |
| MORGAN | 98 | 67 | 72 | 77 | 93 | 91 | 114 | 96 | 92 | 78 | 80 | 97 | 81 | 96 | 68 | 96 | 80 | 88 | 102 | 98 |
| OBION | 98 | 76 | 87 | 84 | 98 | 95 | 110 | 97 | 93 | 85 | 85 | 97 | 87 | 97 | 76 | 96 | 86 | 91 | 101 | 98 |
| OVERTON | 97 | 64 | 69 | 73 | 93 | 91 | 111 | 96 | 91 | 76 | 78 | 96 | 79 | 94 | 67 | 95 | 78 | 87 | 101 | 96 |
| PERRY | 97 | 63 | 66 | 73 | 92 | 90 | 112 | 96 | 91 | 75 | 77 | 96 | 78 | 95 | 66 | 95 | 78 | 86 | 102 | 96 |
| PICKETT | 97 | 63 | 66 | 73 | 92 | 90 | 112 | 96 | 91 | 75 | 77 | 96 | 78 | 95 | 66 | 95 | 78 | 86 | 102 | 96 |
| POLK | 97 | 67 | 74 | 76 | 94 | 92 | 111 | 96 | 91 | 79 | 80 | 96 | 82 | 95 | 70 | 96 | 80 | 88 | 101 | 97 |
| PUTNAM | 98 | 81 | 90 | 86 | 97 | 94 | 110 | 96 | 94 | 86 | 88 | 95 | 88 | 98 | 77 | 97 | 88 | 92 | 100 | 99 |
| RHEA | 98 | 67 | 73 | 76 | 93 | 91 | 113 | 96 | 92 | 78 | 79 | 96 | 81 | 96 | 68 | 96 | 80 | 88 | 101 | 97 |
| ROANE | 99 | 84 | 94 | 91 | 100 | 98 | 109 | 98 | 96 | 90 | 91 | 99 | 92 | 100 | 81 | 98 | 91 | 94 | 102 | 100 |
| ROBERTSON | 99 | 79 | 84 | 85 | 96 | 92 | 114 | 98 | 94 | 86 | 89 | 97 | 87 | 100 | 75 | 98 | 89 | 93 | 101 | 101 |
| RUTHERFORD | 101 | 98 | 89 | 95 | 97 | 96 | 105 | 99 | 100 | 97 | 101 | 101 | 96 | 102 | 83 | 100 | 98 | 99 | 98 | 103 |
| SCOTT | 97 | 64 | 68 | 73 | 92 | 90 | 112 | 95 | 91 | 76 | 77 | 95 | 78 | 94 | 66 | 95 | 78 | 87 | 101 | 96 |
| SEQUATCHIE | 97 | 66 | 70 | 74 | 92 | 90 | 113 | 96 | 92 | 77 | 79 | 96 | 80 | 95 | 67 | 95 | 79 | 87 | 101 | 97 |
| TENNESSEE | 98 | 88 | 92 | 91 | 99 | 97 | 105 | 98 | 96 | 92 | 92 | 98 | 93 | 99 | 82 | 98 | 93 | 95 | 99 | 100 |
| UNITED STATES | 100 | 100 | 100 | 100 | 100 | 100 | 100 | 100 | 100 | 100 | 100 | 100 | 100 | 100 | 100 | 100 | 100 | 100 | 100 | 100 |

| COUNTY | FIPS Code | MSA Code | DMA Code | POPULATION 1990 | POPULATION 2000 | POPULATION 2005 | 1990-2000 ANNUAL CHANGE % Rate | 1990-2000 ANNUAL CHANGE State Rank | RACE (%) White 1990 | White 2000 | Black 1990 | Black 2000 | Asian/Pacific 1990 | Asian/Pacific 2000 |
|---|---|---|---|---|---|---|---|---|---|---|---|---|---|---|
| SEVIER | 155 | 3840 | 557 | 51,043 | 67,430 | 74,807 | 2.8 | 7 | 98.9 | 98.5 | 0.4 | 0.4 | 0.4 | 0.6 |
| SHELBY | 157 | 4920 | 640 | 826,330 | 876,612 | 895,677 | 0.6 | 73 | 55.1 | 52.2 | 43.6 | 45.9 | 0.9 | 1.4 |
| SMITH | 159 | 0000 | 659 | 14,143 | 17,151 | 19,052 | 1.9 | 24 | 96.3 | 95.8 | 3.2 | 3.7 | 0.1 | 0.1 |
| STEWART | 161 | 0000 | 659 | 9,479 | 12,016 | 13,308 | 2.3 | 16 | 98.0 | 97.8 | 1.0 | 1.0 | 0.3 | 0.5 |
| SULLIVAN | 163 | 3660 | 531 | 143,596 | 150,424 | 151,416 | 0.5 | 77 | 97.5 | 97.1 | 1.8 | 2.0 | 0.3 | 0.5 |
| SUMNER | 165 | 5360 | 659 | 103,281 | 128,179 | 139,170 | 2.1 | 19 | 94.0 | 93.1 | 5.4 | 6.0 | 0.3 | 0.5 |
| TIPTON | 167 | 4920 | 640 | 37,568 | 49,482 | 55,231 | 2.7 | 8 | 75.7 | 73.8 | 23.6 | 25.2 | 0.3 | 0.4 |
| TROUSDALE | 169 | 0000 | 659 | 5,920 | 7,089 | 7,686 | 1.8 | 26 | 85.1 | 83.4 | 14.4 | 16.1 | 0.1 | 0.2 |
| UNICOI | 171 | 3660 | 531 | 16,549 | 17,372 | 17,726 | 0.5 | 77 | 99.6 | 99.3 | 0.0 | 0.2 | 0.1 | 0.1 |
| UNION | 173 | 3840 | 557 | 13,694 | 16,947 | 18,752 | 2.1 | 19 | 99.7 | 99.5 | 0.0 | 0.2 | 0.0 | 0.1 |
| VAN BUREN | 175 | 0000 | 659 | 4,846 | 4,995 | 4,933 | 0.3 | 86 | 99.5 | 99.4 | 0.1 | 0.2 | 0.0 | 0.0 |
| WARREN | 177 | 0000 | 659 | 32,992 | 36,772 | 38,486 | 1.1 | 54 | 95.5 | 94.4 | 3.4 | 3.9 | 0.4 | 0.6 |
| WASHINGTON | 179 | 3660 | 531 | 92,315 | 103,693 | 107,980 | 1.1 | 54 | 95.8 | 95.2 | 3.5 | 3.9 | 0.4 | 0.6 |
| WAYNE | 181 | 0000 | 659 | 13,935 | 16,421 | 16,469 | 1.6 | 31 | 98.8 | 93.7 | 1.0 | 5.5 | 0.1 | 0.1 |
| WEAKLEY | 183 | 0000 | 632 | 31,972 | 33,083 | 33,661 | 0.3 | 86 | 91.9 | 90.8 | 6.9 | 7.6 | 0.9 | 1.1 |
| WHITE | 185 | 0000 | 659 | 20,090 | 23,158 | 24,645 | 1.4 | 37 | 97.8 | 97.4 | 1.9 | 2.2 | 0.1 | 0.2 |
| WILLIAMSON | 187 | 5360 | 659 | 81,021 | 129,687 | 158,943 | 4.7 | 1 | 92.4 | 91.4 | 6.7 | 7.3 | 0.6 | 0.9 |
| WILSON | 189 | 5360 | 659 | 67,675 | 88,948 | 101,163 | 2.7 | 8 | 92.4 | 91.4 | 6.8 | 7.6 | 0.4 | 0.6 |
| TENNESSEE | | | | | | | 1.3 | | 83.0 | 82.1 | 16.0 | 16.4 | 0.7 | 1.0 |
| UNITED STATES | | | | | | | 1.0 | | 80.3 | 77.9 | 12.1 | 12.4 | 2.9 | 3.9 |

# POPULATION COMPOSITION

| COUNTY | % HISPANIC ORIGIN | | 2000 AGE DISTRIBUTION (%) | | | | | | | | | | MEDIAN AGE | | 2000 Males/ Females (×100) |
|---|---|---|---|---|---|---|---|---|---|---|---|---|---|---|---|
| | 1990 | 2000 | 0-4 | 5-9 | 10-14 | 15-19 | 20-24 | 25-44 | 45-64 | 65-84 | 85+ | 18+ | 1990 | 2000 | |
| SEVIER | 0.5 | 1.2 | 5.8 | 6.1 | 6.4 | 6.4 | 5.5 | 29.8 | 26.6 | 12.0 | 1.4 | 77.8 | 35.4 | 39.0 | 94.6 |
| SHELBY | 0.9 | 1.6 | 7.7 | 7.7 | 7.4 | 7.4 | 7.1 | 31.6 | 21.0 | 8.8 | 1.2 | 73.1 | 31.3 | 33.6 | 90.6 |
| SMITH | 0.3 | 1.0 | 6.8 | 6.9 | 6.9 | 6.6 | 5.7 | 28.7 | 24.5 | 12.3 | 1.8 | 75.4 | 35.2 | 37.8 | 94.1 |
| STEWART | 0.5 | 1.3 | 5.1 | 5.6 | 6.1 | 6.2 | 5.5 | 27.2 | 27.7 | 14.7 | 1.8 | 79.4 | 38.7 | 41.3 | 96.6 |
| SULLIVAN | 0.4 | 1.0 | 5.5 | 5.8 | 6.2 | 6.0 | 5.4 | 28.7 | 27.1 | 13.8 | 1.6 | 78.9 | 36.9 | 40.3 | 92.7 |
| SUMNER | 0.5 | 1.4 | 6.7 | 7.0 | 7.2 | 7.1 | 6.0 | 29.8 | 25.5 | 9.6 | 1.2 | 74.7 | 33.2 | 36.4 | 95.8 |
| TIPTON | 0.7 | 1.5 | 8.3 | 8.4 | 8.2 | 7.7 | 6.7 | 28.6 | 22.0 | 8.9 | 1.2 | 70.3 | 30.9 | 33.4 | 95.5 |
| TROUSDALE | 0.5 | 1.2 | 5.8 | 6.5 | 6.7 | 6.7 | 5.8 | 28.8 | 25.4 | 12.3 | 1.9 | 77.1 | 36.3 | 38.8 | 93.9 |
| UNICOI | 0.6 | 1.4 | 5.1 | 5.4 | 5.7 | 5.9 | 5.2 | 28.6 | 26.8 | 15.0 | 2.2 | 80.1 | 37.9 | 41.3 | 93.9 |
| UNION | 0.3 | 0.9 | 6.8 | 7.0 | 7.3 | 6.8 | 6.4 | 30.3 | 24.7 | 9.4 | 1.2 | 74.8 | 32.5 | 36.1 | 97.6 |
| VAN BUREN | 0.2 | 0.9 | 6.5 | 6.8 | 7.2 | 6.7 | 6.1 | 29.0 | 24.9 | 11.4 | 1.3 | 75.6 | 33.8 | 37.4 | 98.8 |
| WARREN | 0.8 | 2.0 | 6.2 | 6.5 | 6.7 | 6.8 | 5.9 | 28.4 | 25.0 | 12.6 | 1.8 | 76.4 | 35.0 | 38.2 | 92.8 |
| WASHINGTON | 0.5 | 1.3 | 5.7 | 5.8 | 5.9 | 6.9 | 7.4 | 30.1 | 24.5 | 12.0 | 1.8 | 79.2 | 34.7 | 37.8 | 93.9 |
| WAYNE | 0.4 | 1.6 | 5.9 | 6.0 | 6.4 | 6.6 | 7.1 | 30.8 | 24.0 | 11.5 | 1.6 | 77.4 | 34.8 | 36.9 | 111.8 |
| WEAKLEY | 0.4 | 1.0 | 5.9 | 5.9 | 5.9 | 9.3 | 9.4 | 27.4 | 21.5 | 12.5 | 2.2 | 78.8 | 33.0 | 35.5 | 93.4 |
| WHITE | 0.4 | 1.1 | 5.9 | 6.3 | 6.6 | 6.3 | 5.5 | 27.6 | 25.8 | 13.9 | 2.0 | 77.3 | 36.7 | 39.5 | 93.2 |
| WILLIAMSON | 0.6 | 1.6 | 6.6 | 7.6 | 8.2 | 7.5 | 5.4 | 29.0 | 27.0 | 7.8 | 0.9 | 72.7 | 34.1 | 36.5 | 95.2 |
| WILSON | 0.6 | 1.5 | 6.9 | 7.3 | 7.4 | 6.9 | 5.6 | 31.3 | 25.1 | 8.5 | 1.0 | 74.2 | 33.4 | 36.4 | 97.8 |
| TENNESSEE | 0.7 | 1.5 | 6.6 | 6.7 | 6.8 | 7.0 | 6.7 | 30.2 | 23.7 | 10.9 | 1.5 | 76.0 | 33.6 | 36.4 | 93.3 |
| UNITED STATES | 9.0 | 11.8 | 6.9 | 7.2 | 7.2 | 7.2 | 6.7 | 29.9 | 22.2 | 11.1 | 1.6 | 74.6 | 32.9 | 35.7 | 95.6 |

| COUNTY | HOUSEHOLDS | | | | | FAMILIES | | | MEDIAN HOUSEHOLD INCOME | | | |
|---|---|---|---|---|---|---|---|---|---|---|---|---|
| | 1990 | 2000 | 2005 | % Annual Rate 1990-2000 | 2000 Average HH Size | 1990 | 2000 | % Annual Rate 1990-2000 | 2000 | 2005 | 2000 National Rank | 2000 State Rank |
| SEVIER | 19,520 | 26,617 | 30,024 | 3.8 | 2.50 | 15,091 | 19,988 | 3.5 | 34,446 | 39,174 | 1322 | 31 |
| SHELBY | 303,571 | 328,065 | 338,145 | 0.9 | 2.60 | 212,076 | 224,104 | 0.7 | 38,874 | 43,452 | 764 | 13 |
| SMITH | 5,358 | 6,591 | 7,378 | 2.5 | 2.58 | 4,151 | 4,969 | 2.2 | 33,902 | 39,453 | 1407 | 33 |
| STEWART | 3,678 | 4,857 | 5,485 | 3.4 | 2.44 | 2,812 | 3,613 | 3.1 | 31,023 | 35,735 | 1926 | 59 |
| SULLIVAN | 56,729 | 61,630 | 63,105 | 1.0 | 2.41 | 42,516 | 44,783 | 0.6 | 34,707 | 37,497 | 1291 | 30 |
| SUMNER | 36,850 | 47,112 | 51,878 | 3.0 | 2.69 | 29,511 | 36,691 | 2.7 | 49,592 | 57,766 | 209 | 3 |
| TIPTON | 13,033 | 17,688 | 20,027 | 3.8 | 2.78 | 10,345 | 13,773 | 3.5 | 37,886 | 45,068 | 860 | 15 |
| TROUSDALE | 2,261 | 2,771 | 3,037 | 2.5 | 2.51 | 1,715 | 2,041 | 2.1 | 31,849 | 39,071 | 1747 | 50 |
| UNICOI | 6,621 | 7,141 | 7,385 | 0.9 | 2.40 | 4,938 | 5,145 | 0.5 | 30,370 | 32,554 | 2064 | 69 |
| UNION | 4,932 | 6,255 | 7,001 | 2.9 | 2.69 | 3,992 | 4,913 | 2.5 | 31,743 | 39,798 | 1768 | 53 |
| VAN BUREN | 1,799 | 1,948 | 1,968 | 1.0 | 2.56 | 1,451 | 1,526 | 0.6 | 31,809 | 37,957 | 1758 | 51 |
| WARREN | 12,681 | 14,489 | 15,350 | 1.6 | 2.51 | 9,601 | 10,628 | 1.2 | 33,511 | 39,232 | 1462 | 37 |
| WASHINGTON | 35,823 | 42,156 | 44,731 | 2.0 | 2.37 | 25,375 | 28,920 | 1.6 | 35,614 | 39,207 | 1150 | 24 |
| WAYNE | 5,174 | 5,729 | 5,853 | 1.2 | 2.55 | 4,079 | 4,371 | 0.8 | 29,206 | 34,995 | 2264 | 75 |
| WEAKLEY | 11,992 | 12,806 | 13,217 | 0.8 | 2.40 | 8,589 | 8,863 | 0.4 | 32,755 | 39,264 | 1581 | 44 |
| WHITE | 7,722 | 9,308 | 10,124 | 2.3 | 2.47 | 5,986 | 6,899 | 1.7 | 30,711 | 38,143 | 1985 | 62 |
| WILLIAMSON | 27,928 | 45,405 | 56,047 | 6.1 | 2.84 | 23,096 | 36,517 | 5.7 | 66,420 | 74,352 | 27 | 1 |
| WILSON | 24,070 | 32,130 | 36,829 | 3.6 | 2.75 | 19,610 | 25,704 | 3.3 | 50,825 | 59,333 | 189 | 2 |
| TENNESSEE | | | | 1.9 | 2.50 | | | 1.6 | 37,221 | 42,289 | | |
| UNITED STATES | | | | 1.4 | 2.59 | | | 1.1 | 41,914 | 49,127 | | |

| COUNTY | 2000 Per Capita Income | 2000 HH Income Base | 2000 HOUSEHOLD INCOME DISTRIBUTION (%) Less than $15,000 | $15,000 to $24,999 | $25,000 to $49,999 | $50,000 to $99,999 | $100,000 to $149,999 | $150,000 or More | 2000 AVERAGE DISPOSABLE INCOME BY AGE OF HOUSEHOLDER All Ages | <35 | 35-44 | 45-54 | 55-64 | 65+ |
|---|---|---|---|---|---|---|---|---|---|---|---|---|---|---|
| SEVIER | 16,961 | 26,617 | 15.8 | 17.3 | 38.4 | 23.9 | 3.7 | 0.9 | 34,390 | 30,911 | 39,257 | 40,863 | 37,461 | 23,526 |
| SHELBY | 20,197 | 328,059 | 17.7 | 13.6 | 31.4 | 27.7 | 6.7 | 3.0 | 40,897 | 34,518 | 45,918 | 50,604 | 41,296 | 25,554 |
| SMITH | 16,519 | 6,591 | 18.9 | 16.0 | 37.8 | 22.8 | 3.4 | 1.1 | 33,613 | 32,116 | 38,463 | 43,649 | 35,385 | 19,568 |
| STEWART | 16,004 | 4,857 | 20.8 | 16.6 | 39.8 | 20.1 | 2.6 | 0.3 | 30,767 | 30,225 | 33,942 | 40,482 | 32,517 | 19,775 |
| SULLIVAN | 19,493 | 61,630 | 18.9 | 15.9 | 34.6 | 23.7 | 4.7 | 2.2 | 36,576 | 31,983 | 41,916 | 46,877 | 37,536 | 23,507 |
| SUMNER | 23,231 | 47,112 | 9.3 | 9.3 | 31.9 | 36.2 | 9.8 | 3.6 | 48,679 | 42,135 | 53,944 | 59,633 | 50,504 | 28,993 |
| TIPTON | 16,441 | 17,688 | 15.9 | 13.1 | 38.2 | 27.5 | 4.3 | 1.0 | 36,674 | 34,090 | 39,783 | 47,203 | 37,901 | 21,077 |
| TROUSDALE | 15,160 | 2,770 | 20.0 | 19.4 | 34.4 | 22.1 | 3.5 | 0.7 | 32,176 | 32,078 | 37,311 | 42,325 | 29,647 | 19,286 |
| UNICOI | 16,283 | 7,141 | 26.0 | 15.6 | 34.7 | 19.0 | 3.5 | 1.2 | 31,402 | 29,687 | 39,522 | 42,012 | 30,118 | 18,189 |
| UNION | 13,288 | 6,255 | 19.8 | 17.6 | 39.5 | 21.3 | 1.8 | 0.1 | 30,466 | 28,681 | 36,060 | 33,865 | 32,650 | 19,217 |
| VAN BUREN | 13,792 | 1,948 | 19.7 | 15.4 | 42.1 | 21.7 | 1.1 | 0.0 | 30,059 | 31,659 | 36,289 | 31,227 | 31,941 | 18,977 |
| WARREN | 17,013 | 14,489 | 20.3 | 14.4 | 37.2 | 23.3 | 3.8 | 1.2 | 34,152 | 32,142 | 40,026 | 42,686 | 35,438 | 21,083 |
| WASHINGTON | 19,097 | 42,150 | 18.9 | 14.9 | 33.9 | 25.5 | 5.1 | 1.7 | 36,655 | 31,198 | 42,955 | 44,589 | 39,540 | 25,193 |
| WAYNE | 12,823 | 5,729 | 21.4 | 20.6 | 38.6 | 17.1 | 2.2 | 0.2 | 28,657 | 27,971 | 34,646 | 35,626 | 27,285 | 18,084 |
| WEAKLEY | 15,814 | 12,806 | 21.3 | 16.2 | 35.9 | 22.5 | 3.4 | 0.8 | 32,673 | 29,558 | 40,663 | 42,624 | 34,125 | 20,046 |
| WHITE | 14,739 | 9,308 | 21.4 | 17.8 | 37.4 | 20.8 | 2.5 | 0.2 | 30,317 | 29,902 | 37,195 | 38,086 | 31,334 | 19,123 |
| WILLIAMSON | 35,717 | 45,405 | 5.4 | 6.3 | 23.2 | 37.2 | 15.3 | 12.7 | 70,778 | 51,842 | 73,798 | 77,127 | 65,892 | 40,402 |
| WILSON | 23,609 | 32,130 | 8.2 | 8.6 | 32.1 | 37.6 | 10.0 | 3.4 | 49,175 | 44,263 | 54,735 | 57,738 | 47,266 | 30,558 |
| TENNESSEE | 19,874 | | 17.1 | 14.4 | 34.0 | 26.4 | 5.7 | 2.4 | 39,053 | 34,053 | 44,876 | 48,417 | 39,984 | 24,353 |
| UNITED STATES | 22,162 | | 14.5 | 12.5 | 32.3 | 29.8 | 7.4 | 3.5 | 40,748 | 34,503 | 44,969 | 49,579 | 43,409 | 27,339 |

| COUNTY | FINANCIAL SERVICES | | | | THE HOME | | | | | | ENTERTAINMENT | | | | | | PERSONAL | | | |
|---|---|---|---|---|---|---|---|---|---|---|---|---|---|---|---|---|---|---|---|---|
| | | | | | Home Improvements | | | Furnishings | | | | | | | | | | | | |
| | Auto Loan | Home Loan | Invest-ments | Retire-ment Plans | Home Repair | Lawn & Garden | Remodel-ing | Appli-ances | Elec-tronics | Furni-ture | Restau-rants | Sport-ing Goods | Theater & Concerts | Toys & Hobbies | Travel | Video Rental | Apparel | Auto After-market | Health Insur-ance | Pets & Supplies |
| SEVIER | 99 | 77 | 85 | 84 | 96 | 94 | 115 | 98 | 94 | 85 | 88 | 97 | 87 | 99 | 75 | 98 | 87 | 92 | 102 | 100 |
| SHELBY | 98 | 100 | 98 | 99 | 101 | 100 | 95 | 99 | 98 | 102 | 98 | 100 | 99 | 99 | 90 | 100 | 102 | 101 | 93 | 100 |
| SMITH | 98 | 69 | 75 | 77 | 94 | 91 | 113 | 96 | 92 | 79 | 81 | 96 | 82 | 96 | 70 | 96 | 81 | 88 | 101 | 98 |
| STEWART | 97 | 65 | 70 | 75 | 92 | 91 | 113 | 96 | 92 | 77 | 78 | 96 | 80 | 95 | 67 | 96 | 79 | 87 | 102 | 97 |
| SULLIVAN | 98 | 84 | 94 | 89 | 100 | 97 | 108 | 98 | 94 | 91 | 92 | 97 | 92 | 99 | 81 | 98 | 91 | 94 | 101 | 100 |
| SUMNER | 101 | 96 | 97 | 98 | 100 | 100 | 108 | 100 | 100 | 99 | 101 | 102 | 99 | 103 | 85 | 100 | 100 | 100 | 100 | 103 |
| TIPTON | 98 | 77 | 83 | 82 | 95 | 91 | 114 | 96 | 93 | 85 | 86 | 95 | 85 | 98 | 74 | 97 | 86 | 91 | 99 | 99 |
| TROUSDALE | 98 | 67 | 72 | 76 | 93 | 91 | 114 | 96 | 92 | 78 | 79 | 97 | 81 | 96 | 68 | 96 | 80 | 88 | 102 | 98 |
| UNICOI | 97 | 69 | 76 | 77 | 96 | 92 | 109 | 96 | 90 | 80 | 81 | 95 | 82 | 95 | 71 | 96 | 81 | 88 | 101 | 96 |
| UNION | 98 | 65 | 69 | 74 | 92 | 90 | 113 | 96 | 92 | 76 | 78 | 96 | 79 | 95 | 67 | 95 | 79 | 87 | 101 | 97 |
| VAN BUREN | 97 | 63 | 66 | 73 | 92 | 90 | 112 | 96 | 91 | 75 | 77 | 96 | 78 | 95 | 66 | 95 | 78 | 86 | 102 | 96 |
| WARREN | 97 | 71 | 79 | 79 | 94 | 92 | 111 | 96 | 92 | 81 | 82 | 94 | 83 | 96 | 72 | 96 | 82 | 89 | 101 | 97 |
| WASHINGTON | 98 | 86 | 93 | 88 | 99 | 96 | 108 | 97 | 94 | 90 | 91 | 96 | 91 | 99 | 80 | 97 | 90 | 94 | 100 | 100 |
| WAYNE | 97 | 63 | 66 | 73 | 92 | 90 | 112 | 96 | 91 | 75 | 77 | 96 | 78 | 95 | 66 | 95 | 78 | 86 | 102 | 96 |
| WEAKLEY | 97 | 74 | 82 | 82 | 95 | 92 | 111 | 95 | 92 | 81 | 84 | 95 | 84 | 96 | 73 | 96 | 84 | 90 | 101 | 98 |
| WHITE | 97 | 66 | 71 | 75 | 93 | 91 | 112 | 96 | 91 | 77 | 79 | 96 | 80 | 95 | 68 | 95 | 79 | 87 | 101 | 97 |
| WILLIAMSON | 108 | 119 | 106 | 119 | 105 | 112 | 110 | 107 | 112 | 116 | 121 | 115 | 115 | 112 | 99 | 104 | 121 | 114 | 103 | 110 |
| WILSON | 102 | 97 | 96 | 98 | 100 | 100 | 108 | 100 | 102 | 100 | 102 | 103 | 100 | 104 | 85 | 100 | 102 | 101 | 100 | 104 |
| TENNESSEE | 98 | 88 | 92 | 91 | 99 | 97 | 105 | 98 | 96 | 92 | 92 | 98 | 93 | 99 | 82 | 98 | 93 | 95 | 99 | 100 |
| UNITED STATES | 100 | 100 | 100 | 100 | 100 | 100 | 100 | 100 | 100 | 100 | 100 | 100 | 100 | 100 | 100 | 100 | 100 | 100 | 100 | 100 |

# POPULATION CHANGE

| COUNTY | FIPS Code | MSA Code | DMA Code | POPULATION 1990 | POPULATION 2000 | POPULATION 2005 | 1990-2000 ANNUAL CHANGE % Rate | 1990-2000 ANNUAL CHANGE State Rank | RACE (%) White 1990 | White 2000 | Black 1990 | Black 2000 | Asian/Pacific 1990 | Asian/Pacific 2000 |
|---|---|---|---|---|---|---|---|---|---|---|---|---|---|---|
| ANDERSON | 001 | 0000 | 623 | 48,024 | 52,351 | 53,043 | 0.8 | 111 | 69.5 | 66.0 | 23.2 | 24.6 | 0.3 | 0.4 |
| ANDREWS | 003 | 0000 | 633 | 14,338 | 13,607 | 12,959 | -0.5 | 211 | 75.6 | 70.6 | 1.9 | 2.1 | 1.1 | 1.5 |
| ANGELINA | 005 | 0000 | 709 | 69,884 | 78,214 | 81,290 | 1.1 | 86 | 78.3 | 75.2 | 15.4 | 16.6 | 0.4 | 0.6 |
| ARANSAS | 007 | 0000 | 600 | 17,892 | 23,553 | 25,640 | 2.7 | 30 | 85.4 | 82.0 | 1.8 | 2.0 | 3.3 | 4.6 |
| ARCHER | 009 | 9080 | 627 | 7,973 | 8,258 | 8,304 | 0.3 | 155 | 97.7 | 96.9 | 0.1 | 0.2 | 0.1 | 0.1 |
| ARMSTRONG | 011 | 0000 | 634 | 2,021 | 2,219 | 2,333 | 0.9 | 104 | 97.8 | 96.9 | 0.0 | 0.0 | 0.3 | 0.6 |
| ATASCOSA | 013 | 0000 | 641 | 30,533 | 38,402 | 43,242 | 2.3 | 43 | 81.9 | 79.7 | 0.5 | 0.6 | 0.2 | 0.3 |
| AUSTIN | 015 | 0000 | 618 | 19,832 | 24,262 | 26,368 | 2.0 | 51 | 81.9 | 79.8 | 13.2 | 13.8 | 0.1 | 0.2 |
| BAILEY | 017 | 0000 | 651 | 7,064 | 6,671 | 6,448 | -0.6 | 216 | 92.5 | 91.6 | 1.8 | 1.8 | 0.2 | 0.2 |
| BANDERA | 019 | 0000 | 641 | 10,562 | 17,400 | 21,356 | 5.0 | 5 | 94.9 | 93.6 | 0.2 | 0.3 | 0.2 | 0.4 |
| BASTROP | 021 | 0640 | 635 | 38,263 | 54,707 | 64,520 | 3.5 | 20 | 77.4 | 74.1 | 11.8 | 12.2 | 0.3 | 0.5 |
| BAYLOR | 023 | 0000 | 627 | 4,385 | 4,050 | 3,858 | -0.8 | 221 | 90.4 | 88.2 | 4.1 | 4.3 | 0.3 | 0.5 |
| BEE | 025 | 0000 | 600 | 25,135 | 30,052 | 30,294 | 1.8 | 60 | 77.4 | 74.2 | 2.9 | 3.0 | 0.9 | 1.1 |
| BELL | 027 | 3810 | 625 | 191,088 | 223,071 | 225,923 | 1.5 | 71 | 71.2 | 67.5 | 18.9 | 18.9 | 2.9 | 4.5 |
| BEXAR | 029 | 7240 | 641 | 1,185,394 | 1,390,711 | 1,480,902 | 1.6 | 68 | 74.1 | 71.5 | 7.1 | 6.7 | 1.3 | 1.8 |
| BLANCO | 031 | 0000 | 635 | 5,972 | 8,726 | 9,788 | 3.8 | 15 | 93.7 | 92.8 | 0.9 | 1.0 | 0.4 | 0.5 |
| BORDEN | 033 | 0000 | 651 | 799 | 771 | 780 | -0.3 | 194 | 96.2 | 95.5 | 0.3 | 0.5 | 0.0 | 0.0 |
| BOSQUE | 035 | 0000 | 623 | 15,125 | 16,750 | 17,070 | 1.0 | 98 | 93.7 | 92.1 | 2.1 | 2.3 | 0.3 | 0.5 |
| BOWIE | 037 | 8360 | 612 | 81,665 | 84,152 | 84,290 | 0.3 | 155 | 77.0 | 75.1 | 21.8 | 23.4 | 0.3 | 0.5 |
| BRAZORIA | 039 | 1145 | 618 | 191,707 | 239,649 | 266,040 | 2.2 | 45 | 80.8 | 77.6 | 8.3 | 8.5 | 1.0 | 1.6 |
| BRAZOS | 041 | 1260 | 625 | 121,862 | 135,403 | 141,106 | 1.0 | 98 | 77.8 | 73.7 | 11.2 | 12.0 | 3.5 | 4.9 |
| BREWSTER | 043 | 0000 | 633 | 8,681 | 8,779 | 8,701 | 0.1 | 173 | 95.6 | 95.1 | 1.0 | 0.8 | 0.6 | 0.8 |
| BRISCOE | 045 | 0000 | 634 | 1,971 | 1,790 | 1,721 | -0.9 | 224 | 79.1 | 74.3 | 3.5 | 3.7 | 0.0 | 0.0 |
| BROOKS | 047 | 0000 | 600 | 8,204 | 8,422 | 8,455 | 0.3 | 155 | 82.3 | 81.8 | 0.0 | 0.1 | 0.1 | 0.1 |
| BROWN | 049 | 0000 | 662 | 34,371 | 36,916 | 37,318 | 0.7 | 118 | 88.1 | 85.0 | 4.5 | 5.3 | 0.3 | 0.4 |
| BURLESON | 051 | 0000 | 625 | 13,625 | 15,740 | 16,377 | 1.4 | 74 | 74.7 | 71.6 | 17.8 | 18.7 | 0.1 | 0.2 |
| BURNET | 053 | 0000 | 635 | 22,677 | 35,717 | 43,791 | 4.5 | 9 | 91.7 | 87.9 | 1.2 | 2.1 | 0.3 | 0.4 |
| CALDWELL | 055 | 0640 | 635 | 26,392 | 33,612 | 37,552 | 2.4 | 40 | 71.7 | 68.4 | 10.7 | 10.8 | 0.3 | 0.4 |
| CALHOUN | 057 | 0000 | 618 | 19,053 | 20,353 | 19,992 | 0.6 | 126 | 77.8 | 74.2 | 2.9 | 3.0 | 2.9 | 3.8 |
| CALLAHAN | 059 | 0000 | 662 | 11,859 | 13,036 | 13,624 | 0.9 | 104 | 96.8 | 95.8 | 0.0 | 0.0 | 0.3 | 0.6 |
| CAMERON | 061 | 1240 | 636 | 260,120 | 334,853 | 363,711 | 2.5 | 38 | 82.4 | 81.6 | 0.3 | 0.3 | 0.3 | 0.4 |
| CAMP | 063 | 0000 | 612 | 9,904 | 11,007 | 11,278 | 1.0 | 98 | 72.0 | 69.2 | 23.8 | 25.2 | 0.1 | 0.1 |
| CARSON | 065 | 0000 | 634 | 6,576 | 6,792 | 6,969 | 0.3 | 155 | 96.0 | 94.9 | 0.2 | 0.3 | 0.1 | 0.2 |
| CASS | 067 | 0000 | 612 | 29,982 | 30,606 | 30,519 | 0.2 | 164 | 78.9 | 77.1 | 20.2 | 21.8 | 0.1 | 0.1 |
| CASTRO | 069 | 0000 | 634 | 9,070 | 8,226 | 8,023 | -0.9 | 224 | 60.9 | 56.1 | 2.9 | 2.6 | 0.2 | 0.2 |
| CHAMBERS | 071 | 3360 | 618 | 20,088 | 24,389 | 26,342 | 1.9 | 54 | 83.3 | 80.7 | 12.7 | 14.0 | 0.6 | 0.9 |
| CHEROKEE | 073 | 0000 | 709 | 41,049 | 44,049 | 46,003 | 0.7 | 118 | 78.1 | 74.8 | 16.9 | 18.5 | 0.5 | 0.7 |
| CHILDRESS | 075 | 0000 | 634 | 5,953 | 7,490 | 7,231 | 2.3 | 43 | 83.5 | 71.1 | 5.4 | 11.9 | 0.3 | 0.3 |
| CLAY | 077 | 0000 | 627 | 10,024 | 10,536 | 10,693 | 0.5 | 133 | 97.3 | 96.4 | 0.3 | 0.3 | 0.2 | 0.4 |
| COCHRAN | 079 | 0000 | 651 | 4,377 | 3,694 | 3,366 | -1.6 | 245 | 68.5 | 65.1 | 5.3 | 5.4 | 0.0 | 0.0 |
| COKE | 081 | 0000 | 661 | 3,424 | 3,343 | 3,286 | -0.2 | 189 | 94.1 | 92.4 | 0.2 | 0.3 | 0.1 | 0.1 |
| COLEMAN | 083 | 0000 | 662 | 9,710 | 9,377 | 9,029 | -0.3 | 194 | 92.6 | 90.8 | 2.5 | 3.0 | 0.1 | 0.1 |
| COLLIN | 085 | 1920 | 623 | 264,036 | 485,328 | 624,066 | 6.1 | 1 | 89.1 | 86.1 | 4.1 | 4.4 | 2.8 | 4.4 |
| COLLINGSWORTH | 087 | 0000 | 634 | 3,573 | 3,111 | 2,898 | -1.3 | 235 | 83.3 | 80.3 | 6.4 | 6.6 | 0.1 | 0.1 |
| COLORADO | 089 | 0000 | 618 | 18,383 | 19,212 | 19,913 | 0.4 | 143 | 72.6 | 69.2 | 17.0 | 17.5 | 0.1 | 0.1 |
| COMAL | 091 | 7240 | 641 | 51,832 | 79,884 | 95,560 | 4.3 | 11 | 90.3 | 87.9 | 0.9 | 0.9 | 0.3 | 0.5 |
| COMANCHE | 093 | 0000 | 623 | 13,381 | 13,625 | 13,803 | 0.2 | 164 | 91.9 | 89.6 | 0.1 | 0.3 | 0.1 | 0.1 |
| CONCHO | 095 | 0000 | 661 | 3,044 | 2,961 | 2,919 | -0.3 | 194 | 89.3 | 88.3 | 0.5 | 0.5 | 0.2 | 0.2 |
| COOKE | 097 | 0000 | 623 | 30,777 | 33,820 | 35,878 | 0.9 | 104 | 92.2 | 90.6 | 3.8 | 4.1 | 0.4 | 0.7 |
| CORYELL | 099 | 3810 | 625 | 64,213 | 73,770 | 74,408 | 1.4 | 74 | 70.2 | 66.4 | 21.2 | 21.5 | 2.6 | 3.9 |
| COTTLE | 101 | 0000 | 634 | 2,247 | 1,862 | 1,731 | -1.8 | 247 | 82.5 | 80.2 | 8.9 | 9.2 | 0.1 | 0.3 |
| CRANE | 103 | 0000 | 633 | 4,652 | 4,211 | 4,011 | -1.0 | 228 | 66.6 | 60.9 | 2.8 | 3.3 | 0.2 | 0.3 |
| CROCKETT | 105 | 0000 | 661 | 4,078 | 4,370 | 4,245 | 0.7 | 118 | 98.5 | 96.8 | 1.0 | 2.7 | 0.1 | 0.1 |
| CROSBY | 107 | 0000 | 651 | 7,304 | 6,957 | 6,812 | -0.5 | 211 | 79.2 | 76.2 | 4.4 | 4.8 | 0.1 | 0.1 |
| CULBERSON | 109 | 0000 | 765 | 3,407 | 2,989 | 2,848 | -1.3 | 235 | 70.4 | 68.4 | 0.1 | 0.2 | 0.8 | 0.9 |
| DALLAM | 111 | 0000 | 634 | 5,461 | 6,736 | 7,283 | 2.1 | 46 | 84.2 | 80.1 | 2.1 | 2.4 | 0.3 | 0.5 |
| DALLAS | 113 | 1920 | 623 | 1,852,810 | 2,085,177 | 2,198,108 | 1.2 | 82 | 67.0 | 62.8 | 19.9 | 20.4 | 2.8 | 4.1 |
| DAWSON | 115 | 0000 | 651 | 14,349 | 14,267 | 13,425 | -0.1 | 183 | 68.2 | 61.6 | 4.3 | 7.4 | 0.1 | 0.1 |
| DEAF SMITH | 117 | 0000 | 634 | 19,153 | 18,645 | 17,877 | -0.3 | 194 | 75.8 | 72.8 | 1.6 | 1.6 | 0.2 | 0.2 |
| DELTA | 119 | 0000 | 623 | 4,857 | 4,999 | 5,125 | 0.3 | 155 | 90.3 | 89.1 | 8.3 | 9.2 | 0.1 | 0.3 |
| DENTON | 121 | 1920 | 623 | 273,525 | 423,358 | 518,814 | 4.4 | 10 | 88.5 | 85.6 | 5.0 | 5.2 | 2.5 | 3.9 |
| DEWITT | 123 | 0000 | 641 | 18,840 | 19,107 | 18,295 | 0.1 | 173 | 76.2 | 70.3 | 11.2 | 13.8 | 0.1 | 0.1 |
| DICKENS | 125 | 0000 | 651 | 2,571 | 2,131 | 1,934 | -1.8 | 247 | 85.3 | 82.4 | 4.4 | 4.9 | 0.0 | 0.0 |
| DIMMIT | 127 | 0000 | 641 | 10,433 | 10,313 | 10,138 | -0.1 | 183 | 72.8 | 71.7 | 0.6 | 0.7 | 0.1 | 0.1 |
| DONLEY | 129 | 0000 | 634 | 3,696 | 3,834 | 3,862 | 0.4 | 143 | 95.3 | 94.4 | 3.4 | 4.0 | 0.1 | 0.1 |
| DUVAL | 131 | 0000 | 600 | 12,918 | 13,719 | 14,032 | 0.6 | 126 | 78.8 | 77.1 | 0.1 | 1.6 | 0.1 | 0.1 |
| EASTLAND | 133 | 0000 | 662 | 18,488 | 17,395 | 16,882 | -0.6 | 216 | 94.5 | 92.9 | 2.1 | 2.9 | 0.2 | 0.3 |
| ECTOR | 135 | 5800 | 633 | 118,934 | 124,524 | 125,005 | 0.4 | 143 | 76.8 | 72.8 | 4.7 | 4.8 | 0.6 | 0.8 |
| EDWARDS | 137 | 0000 | 641 | 2,266 | 3,714 | 3,988 | 4.9 | 6 | 93.3 | 94.5 | 0.0 | 0.0 | 0.2 | 0.1 |
| ELLIS | 139 | 1920 | 623 | 85,167 | 111,126 | 128,594 | 2.6 | 34 | 81.1 | 78.1 | 10.0 | 10.4 | 0.3 | 0.4 |
| EL PASO | 141 | 2320 | 765 | 591,610 | 710,795 | 754,282 | 1.8 | 60 | 76.5 | 75.1 | 3.7 | 3.3 | 1.1 | 1.4 |
| ERATH | 143 | 0000 | 623 | 27,991 | 31,632 | 32,477 | 1.2 | 82 | 94.4 | 92.6 | 0.7 | 0.9 | 0.4 | 0.6 |
| FALLS | 145 | 0000 | 625 | 17,712 | 17,083 | 16,215 | -0.4 | 205 | 64.3 | 60.0 | 27.2 | 28.4 | 0.1 | 0.2 |
| FANNIN | 147 | 0000 | 623 | 24,804 | 29,046 | 31,027 | 1.6 | 68 | 91.6 | 88.8 | 6.6 | 8.3 | 0.2 | 0.4 |
| FAYETTE | 149 | 0000 | 635 | 20,095 | 21,530 | 22,207 | 0.7 | 118 | 86.2 | 83.8 | 8.4 | 9.2 | 0.1 | 0.1 |
| FISHER | 151 | 0000 | 662 | 4,842 | 4,119 | 3,784 | -1.6 | 245 | 91.8 | 90.2 | 3.9 | 4.2 | 0.0 | 0.0 |
| FLOYD | 153 | 0000 | 651 | 8,497 | 8,071 | 7,852 | -0.5 | 211 | 65.0 | 59.2 | 3.8 | 3.9 | 0.2 | 0.2 |
| TEXAS | | | | | | | 1.8 | | 75.2 | 72.3 | 11.9 | 11.9 | 1.9 | 2.8 |
| UNITED STATES | | | | | | | 1.0 | | 80.3 | 77.9 | 12.1 | 12.4 | 2.9 | 3.9 |

| COUNTY | % HISPANIC ORIGIN 1990 | % HISPANIC ORIGIN 2000 | 2000 AGE DISTRIBUTION (%) 0-4 | 5-9 | 10-14 | 15-19 | 20-24 | 25-44 | 45-64 | 65-84 | 85+ | 18+ | MEDIAN AGE 1990 | MEDIAN AGE 2000 | 2000 Males/ Females (×100) |
|---|---|---|---|---|---|---|---|---|---|---|---|---|---|---|---|
| ANDERSON | 8.2 | 10.9 | 6.0 | 6.2 | 6.3 | 7.4 | 9.7 | 33.4 | 19.4 | 9.8 | 1.7 | 77.3 | 31.4 | 32.5 | 143.6 |
| ANDREWS | 31.7 | 38.6 | 9.5 | 9.2 | 9.1 | 8.8 | 6.8 | 25.4 | 20.5 | 9.6 | 1.1 | 66.2 | 29.4 | 30.7 | 97.4 |
| ANGELINA | 8.7 | 11.7 | 7.4 | 7.5 | 7.8 | 8.1 | 6.7 | 26.7 | 23.3 | 10.9 | 1.6 | 72.4 | 32.3 | 35.4 | 95.7 |
| ARANSAS | 20.1 | 24.6 | 6.8 | 6.7 | 6.9 | 6.7 | 5.2 | 22.3 | 25.8 | 17.9 | 1.7 | 75.5 | 38.1 | 41.7 | 98.6 |
| ARCHER | 2.4 | 3.7 | 6.7 | 7.4 | 7.7 | 7.4 | 5.5 | 25.4 | 25.0 | 13.2 | 1.7 | 73.5 | 34.7 | 38.7 | 101.5 |
| ARMSTRONG | 2.7 | 4.2 | 5.9 | 6.5 | 6.8 | 8.9 | 5.5 | 21.2 | 24.0 | 17.4 | 3.7 | 74.5 | 38.4 | 41.8 | 92.3 |
| ATASCOSA | 52.6 | 59.1 | 9.0 | 8.8 | 8.8 | 9.0 | 6.8 | 25.2 | 21.3 | 9.6 | 1.5 | 67.8 | 30.4 | 31.5 | 98.0 |
| AUSTIN | 10.5 | 14.0 | 6.9 | 7.1 | 7.3 | 7.8 | 5.9 | 24.9 | 24.3 | 13.2 | 2.6 | 73.9 | 35.7 | 38.1 | 97.7 |
| BAILEY | 38.8 | 45.5 | 8.3 | 8.6 | 8.4 | 8.4 | 6.0 | 23.5 | 22.1 | 12.9 | 1.7 | 69.0 | 32.1 | 34.8 | 98.7 |
| BANDERA | 11.1 | 14.3 | 5.7 | 5.9 | 6.6 | 6.5 | 4.0 | 22.8 | 30.7 | 16.1 | 1.7 | 77.3 | 40.3 | 44.1 | 100.0 |
| BASTROP | 18.1 | 23.5 | 8.0 | 8.0 | 8.0 | 7.6 | 5.8 | 27.9 | 23.5 | 9.8 | 1.5 | 71.0 | 33.4 | 35.7 | 102.1 |
| BAYLOR | 7.6 | 10.5 | 6.1 | 6.4 | 6.6 | 6.1 | 4.7 | 20.9 | 25.5 | 19.7 | 4.0 | 77.1 | 42.9 | 44.4 | 90.5 |
| BEE | 51.4 | 59.8 | 8.1 | 7.4 | 7.2 | 7.9 | 9.7 | 30.8 | 18.5 | 9.0 | 1.3 | 72.3 | 29.6 | 30.6 | 122.3 |
| BELL | 13.1 | 17.7 | 10.2 | 8.1 | 6.7 | 7.1 | 10.5 | 32.3 | 16.6 | 7.4 | 1.1 | 71.4 | 27.8 | 29.0 | 101.2 |
| BEXAR | 49.7 | 57.3 | 8.2 | 8.1 | 7.9 | 8.0 | 7.3 | 30.2 | 20.2 | 9.0 | 1.1 | 71.3 | 30.0 | 32.3 | 94.7 |
| BLANCO | 14.1 | 16.7 | 6.4 | 6.6 | 6.9 | 6.4 | 4.2 | 21.6 | 24.5 | 20.6 | 2.9 | 76.1 | 38.8 | 43.6 | 92.4 |
| BORDEN | 15.0 | 18.9 | 6.6 | 7.7 | 7.3 | 7.7 | 3.6 | 22.2 | 29.3 | 14.5 | 1.2 | 73.0 | 36.3 | 41.6 | 104.0 |
| BOSQUE | 9.5 | 13.0 | 6.2 | 6.5 | 6.8 | 6.8 | 5.0 | 22.0 | 25.4 | 17.7 | 3.5 | 76.2 | 41.0 | 42.6 | 95.8 |
| BOWIE | 1.6 | 2.4 | 6.7 | 7.0 | 7.6 | 7.6 | 6.2 | 26.9 | 24.0 | 12.2 | 1.8 | 74.0 | 34.0 | 37.3 | 94.9 |
| BRAZORIA | 17.6 | 22.6 | 7.9 | 7.9 | 7.8 | 7.7 | 6.8 | 30.9 | 22.1 | 8.1 | 0.8 | 71.7 | 31.1 | 33.6 | 105.7 |
| BRAZOS | 13.7 | 18.1 | 7.0 | 6.3 | 5.7 | 12.4 | 21.2 | 25.0 | 15.2 | 6.3 | 0.9 | 78.0 | 24.2 | 24.4 | 104.4 |
| BREWSTER | 42.6 | 51.2 | 6.9 | 6.5 | 6.2 | 8.6 | 9.0 | 25.6 | 22.5 | 13.0 | 1.7 | 76.6 | 32.4 | 35.8 | 101.6 |
| BRISCOE | 18.6 | 23.7 | 7.0 | 6.9 | 8.2 | 7.2 | 5.0 | 20.6 | 27.3 | 15.6 | 2.3 | 72.9 | 39.3 | 41.6 | 102.7 |
| BROOKS | 89.4 | 91.7 | 9.7 | 9.1 | 8.5 | 8.9 | 6.9 | 23.6 | 20.6 | 11.2 | 1.5 | 67.0 | 30.2 | 31.1 | 94.9 |
| BROWN | 11.1 | 14.9 | 6.9 | 7.0 | 7.4 | 8.7 | 6.4 | 24.0 | 23.6 | 13.5 | 2.5 | 73.5 | 35.0 | 37.7 | 96.5 |
| BURLESON | 11.9 | 16.1 | 7.1 | 7.5 | 7.6 | 7.5 | 5.6 | 24.1 | 24.3 | 14.3 | 2.1 | 73.0 | 35.4 | 38.6 | 97.3 |
| BURNET | 10.8 | 15.7 | 6.6 | 6.8 | 7.1 | 7.1 | 4.9 | 23.2 | 26.3 | 15.7 | 2.3 | 74.9 | 40.0 | 41.1 | 95.9 |
| CALDWELL | 37.8 | 45.3 | 8.0 | 8.0 | 7.8 | 10.6 | 7.6 | 25.3 | 20.7 | 10.0 | 1.9 | 70.0 | 30.7 | 32.0 | 102.9 |
| CALHOUN | 36.2 | 42.2 | 7.9 | 7.8 | 7.8 | 8.0 | 6.3 | 25.3 | 24.1 | 11.7 | 1.2 | 71.5 | 32.7 | 35.9 | 97.9 |
| CALLAHAN | 4.1 | 5.9 | 6.6 | 7.5 | 7.3 | 7.7 | 5.0 | 23.1 | 26.0 | 14.2 | 2.5 | 73.4 | 36.7 | 40.1 | 94.5 |
| CAMERON | 81.9 | 85.8 | 9.6 | 9.0 | 9.1 | 9.7 | 8.5 | 25.7 | 18.6 | 8.9 | 1.1 | 66.2 | 27.4 | 28.0 | 92.3 |
| CAMP | 5.1 | 7.1 | 6.6 | 6.8 | 7.6 | 7.4 | 5.9 | 24.1 | 24.8 | 14.5 | 2.2 | 74.6 | 36.1 | 39.3 | 94.1 |
| CARSON | 5.4 | 7.2 | 7.3 | 7.7 | 7.5 | 8.1 | 6.6 | 24.0 | 23.5 | 13.4 | 2.1 | 72.2 | 34.5 | 38.0 | 91.3 |
| CASS | 1.2 | 2.0 | 6.4 | 7.0 | 7.5 | 7.8 | 5.7 | 24.0 | 25.3 | 14.2 | 2.3 | 74.2 | 35.7 | 39.5 | 93.1 |
| CASTRO | 46.2 | 52.9 | 10.0 | 9.8 | 9.3 | 9.5 | 6.4 | 23.3 | 20.5 | 9.9 | 1.2 | 64.5 | 28.4 | 29.5 | 98.1 |
| CHAMBERS | 5.9 | 8.1 | 6.6 | 6.9 | 7.1 | 8.1 | 6.8 | 27.7 | 26.5 | 9.4 | 0.9 | 74.4 | 32.7 | 36.4 | 98.3 |
| CHEROKEE | 6.6 | 9.1 | 7.0 | 7.0 | 7.3 | 7.8 | 6.5 | 25.3 | 23.6 | 13.1 | 2.4 | 74.2 | 35.0 | 37.3 | 101.2 |
| CHILDRESS | 14.3 | 22.8 | 5.5 | 6.2 | 6.5 | 7.7 | 6.4 | 25.0 | 24.2 | 14.9 | 3.6 | 76.6 | 39.5 | 39.8 | 106.5 |
| CLAY | 2.4 | 3.8 | 6.3 | 6.5 | 6.8 | 7.7 | 5.2 | 23.5 | 26.3 | 15.2 | 2.4 | 75.5 | 37.3 | 41.2 | 96.3 |
| COCHRAN | 42.4 | 48.2 | 9.3 | 9.0 | 9.1 | 9.7 | 6.4 | 23.1 | 20.8 | 11.0 | 1.5 | 66.2 | 30.1 | 30.8 | 100.5 |
| COKE | 12.3 | 16.4 | 5.7 | 6.2 | 6.5 | 6.5 | 4.5 | 20.2 | 26.4 | 19.7 | 4.4 | 76.7 | 44.0 | 45.3 | 92.3 |
| COLEMAN | 11.7 | 15.5 | 6.9 | 6.7 | 7.2 | 6.5 | 4.9 | 20.5 | 24.3 | 19.0 | 4.2 | 75.0 | 41.6 | 43.0 | 92.6 |
| COLLIN | 6.9 | 9.5 | 8.1 | 8.1 | 8.2 | 7.5 | 5.7 | 33.6 | 23.5 | 4.7 | 0.5 | 70.9 | 30.9 | 34.2 | 99.0 |
| COLLINGSWORTH | 15.7 | 20.6 | 6.8 | 6.9 | 6.9 | 8.4 | 5.8 | 22.1 | 21.4 | 17.6 | 4.1 | 73.4 | 38.4 | 40.3 | 96.0 |
| COLORADO | 15.4 | 20.1 | 6.9 | 7.4 | 7.3 | 7.4 | 5.2 | 22.5 | 24.1 | 16.2 | 3.0 | 73.6 | 37.4 | 40.2 | 92.7 |
| COMAL | 22.9 | 29.2 | 6.4 | 6.8 | 7.2 | 7.0 | 5.3 | 24.5 | 26.4 | 14.6 | 1.8 | 75.3 | 36.7 | 40.2 | 96.3 |
| COMANCHE | 16.5 | 21.3 | 6.8 | 6.6 | 6.8 | 6.7 | 4.8 | 21.7 | 25.7 | 17.3 | 3.7 | 75.6 | 41.4 | 42.4 | 98.2 |
| CONCHO | 39.2 | 43.2 | 5.7 | 5.9 | 6.1 | 7.0 | 7.3 | 28.1 | 22.8 | 14.2 | 2.9 | 77.7 | 35.9 | 37.6 | 119.2 |
| COOKE | 4.6 | 6.4 | 7.4 | 7.5 | 7.7 | 8.3 | 5.5 | 24.6 | 23.6 | 13.5 | 1.9 | 72.1 | 34.2 | 37.5 | 96.2 |
| CORYELL | 9.7 | 14.1 | 9.6 | 8.0 | 5.9 | 8.7 | 16.1 | 34.5 | 11.8 | 4.7 | 0.7 | 73.3 | 25.4 | 25.8 | 126.3 |
| COTTLE | 16.3 | 20.0 | 6.0 | 6.8 | 6.9 | 7.1 | 4.5 | 20.1 | 24.5 | 20.4 | 3.7 | 75.1 | 41.2 | 43.8 | 95.4 |
| CRANE | 33.9 | 39.9 | 8.5 | 9.1 | 9.1 | 9.7 | 6.3 | 26.0 | 20.8 | 9.2 | 1.3 | 66.7 | 29.8 | 31.3 | 99.7 |
| CROCKETT | 49.6 | 53.0 | 7.7 | 7.9 | 8.3 | 8.4 | 7.0 | 24.0 | 23.7 | 11.6 | 1.4 | 70.5 | 33.1 | 35.5 | 104.0 |
| CROSBY | 42.6 | 49.7 | 8.6 | 8.7 | 8.4 | 8.5 | 6.4 | 22.3 | 22.2 | 12.7 | 2.2 | 68.8 | 32.6 | 34.0 | 96.0 |
| CULBERSON | 71.0 | 75.4 | 9.7 | 9.3 | 8.4 | 9.8 | 6.6 | 24.5 | 21.5 | 9.4 | 0.8 | 66.4 | 28.9 | 29.9 | 103.3 |
| DALLAM | 21.1 | 27.2 | 8.6 | 8.5 | 8.3 | 8.4 | 5.9 | 25.0 | 21.7 | 11.7 | 1.8 | 69.1 | 32.6 | 35.2 | 98.9 |
| DALLAS | 17.0 | 21.7 | 8.2 | 7.6 | 7.3 | 7.2 | 7.0 | 32.6 | 21.4 | 7.7 | 1.0 | 72.8 | 30.6 | 33.7 | 96.3 |
| DAWSON | 42.7 | 48.6 | 7.9 | 7.9 | 7.8 | 8.5 | 7.1 | 26.3 | 20.9 | 11.7 | 1.9 | 70.7 | 32.7 | 33.6 | 108.9 |
| DEAF SMITH | 48.8 | 55.8 | 10.1 | 9.7 | 9.4 | 9.0 | 7.3 | 24.3 | 19.5 | 9.2 | 1.5 | 65.0 | 28.3 | 28.9 | 98.7 |
| DELTA | 1.4 | 2.3 | 6.3 | 6.8 | 6.9 | 7.6 | 5.2 | 22.8 | 24.9 | 15.9 | 3.6 | 75.3 | 39.7 | 40.8 | 93.4 |
| DENTON | 7.0 | 9.8 | 8.3 | 8.0 | 7.6 | 7.6 | 8.4 | 35.0 | 20.0 | 4.5 | 0.6 | 72.1 | 29.0 | 31.7 | 97.6 |
| DEWITT | 24.2 | 31.2 | 7.1 | 7.2 | 7.1 | 7.9 | 6.2 | 22.3 | 22.0 | 16.2 | 4.0 | 73.4 | 37.3 | 39.2 | 90.9 |
| DICKENS | 18.6 | 23.4 | 5.6 | 6.0 | 6.1 | 6.3 | 6.0 | 21.8 | 24.7 | 19.0 | 4.4 | 78.3 | 42.3 | 43.5 | 93.4 |
| DIMMIT | 83.3 | 86.7 | 9.5 | 9.1 | 9.3 | 9.8 | 7.9 | 23.9 | 19.3 | 9.8 | 1.4 | 65.8 | 27.8 | 28.5 | 96.1 |
| DONLEY | 3.8 | 5.5 | 5.2 | 5.7 | 6.1 | 9.7 | 5.3 | 20.2 | 25.5 | 18.5 | 3.8 | 78.7 | 42.0 | 43.4 | 92.4 |
| DUVAL | 87.2 | 88.4 | 9.2 | 8.4 | 8.4 | 9.0 | 7.5 | 25.3 | 20.5 | 10.3 | 1.5 | 68.4 | 30.0 | 30.8 | 98.6 |
| EASTLAND | 7.6 | 10.1 | 5.6 | 6.3 | 6.3 | 9.0 | 5.9 | 21.5 | 24.2 | 17.5 | 3.5 | 77.2 | 39.0 | 41.5 | 94.9 |
| ECTOR | 31.4 | 38.0 | 9.2 | 8.9 | 8.4 | 8.5 | 6.6 | 27.2 | 21.0 | 9.3 | 1.0 | 68.4 | 30.2 | 32.0 | 96.4 |
| EDWARDS | 52.2 | 43.0 | 6.5 | 6.5 | 6.4 | 6.5 | 5.1 | 17.4 | 18.6 | 28.8 | 4.3 | 76.1 | 32.0 | 46.4 | 100.6 |
| ELLIS | 13.2 | 17.5 | 8.3 | 8.2 | 8.2 | 8.2 | 6.4 | 28.5 | 22.6 | 8.3 | 1.3 | 70.1 | 31.0 | 33.4 | 97.8 |
| EL PASO | 69.6 | 75.4 | 9.4 | 8.6 | 8.2 | 9.0 | 8.4 | 28.4 | 19.1 | 8.0 | 0.9 | 68.4 | 27.9 | 29.3 | 93.7 |
| ERATH | 8.8 | 12.1 | 7.3 | 6.9 | 6.7 | 9.4 | 10.3 | 25.5 | 20.1 | 11.5 | 2.3 | 75.2 | 30.7 | 33.1 | 98.3 |
| FALLS | 11.7 | 16.3 | 7.1 | 7.1 | 7.4 | 8.2 | 6.9 | 24.7 | 21.5 | 14.3 | 2.9 | 73.6 | 35.1 | 36.2 | 107.1 |
| FANNIN | 2.0 | 4.2 | 6.3 | 6.4 | 6.8 | 6.9 | 5.7 | 23.9 | 24.2 | 16.3 | 3.4 | 76.2 | 38.8 | 40.7 | 93.3 |
| FAYETTE | 8.5 | 11.5 | 6.1 | 6.6 | 6.8 | 6.9 | 5.0 | 23.0 | 24.4 | 17.9 | 3.4 | 76.1 | 39.3 | 42.0 | 97.0 |
| FISHER | 20.6 | 26.4 | 6.5 | 6.7 | 6.6 | 7.3 | 5.6 | 21.6 | 24.8 | 17.1 | 4.0 | 75.3 | 39.3 | 42.1 | 98.3 |
| FLOYD | 39.8 | 47.2 | 9.4 | 9.0 | 8.7 | 8.3 | 6.3 | 22.3 | 21.2 | 12.7 | 2.1 | 67.6 | 32.5 | 33.2 | 96.8 |
| TEXAS | 25.6 | 30.4 | 8.1 | 7.8 | 7.7 | 8.0 | 7.4 | 29.6 | 21.4 | 8.8 | 1.2 | 71.8 | 30.8 | 33.2 | 97.3 |
| UNITED STATES | 9.0 | 11.8 | 6.9 | 7.2 | 7.2 | 7.2 | 6.7 | 29.9 | 22.2 | 11.1 | 1.6 | 74.6 | 32.9 | 35.7 | 95.6 |

# HOUSEHOLDS

| COUNTY | HOUSEHOLDS | | | | | FAMILIES | | | MEDIAN HOUSEHOLD INCOME | | | |
|---|---|---|---|---|---|---|---|---|---|---|---|---|
| | 1990 | 2000 | 2005 | % Annual Rate 1990-2000 | 2000 Average HH Size | 1990 | 2000 | % Annual Rate 1990-2000 | 2000 | 2005 | 2000 National Rank | 2000 State Rank |
| ANDERSON | 14,223 | 15,207 | 15,499 | 0.8 | 2.66 | 10,745 | 11,206 | 0.5 | 33,639 | 41,922 | 1447 | 78 |
| ANDREWS | 4,758 | 4,672 | 4,517 | -0.2 | 2.90 | 3,830 | 3,693 | -0.4 | 37,122 | 46,576 | 956 | 37 |
| ANGELINA | 25,004 | 28,445 | 29,921 | 1.6 | 2.68 | 18,908 | 20,908 | 1.2 | 32,371 | 37,754 | 1648 | 93 |
| ARANSAS | 6,938 | 9,496 | 10,525 | 3.9 | 2.46 | 5,114 | 6,783 | 3.5 | 31,846 | 37,464 | 1749 | 109 |
| ARCHER | 2,957 | 3,133 | 3,185 | 0.7 | 2.61 | 2,305 | 2,376 | 0.4 | 36,491 | 44,503 | 1045 | 46 |
| ARMSTRONG | 768 | 835 | 874 | 1.0 | 2.59 | 572 | 600 | 0.6 | 35,353 | 43,462 | 1189 | 58 |
| ATASCOSA | 9,940 | 12,504 | 14,076 | 2.8 | 3.04 | 7,887 | 9,790 | 2.7 | 29,872 | 36,759 | 2171 | 146 |
| AUSTIN | 7,478 | 9,252 | 10,104 | 2.6 | 2.60 | 5,418 | 6,474 | 2.2 | 37,581 | 45,994 | 890 | 35 |
| BAILEY | 2,454 | 2,471 | 2,445 | 0.1 | 2.68 | 1,916 | 1,891 | -0.2 | 25,270 | 28,584 | 2783 | 205 |
| BANDERA | 4,180 | 6,901 | 8,458 | 6.3 | 2.48 | 3,078 | 4,917 | 5.8 | 37,210 | 47,763 | 947 | 36 |
| BASTROP | 13,379 | 19,157 | 22,622 | 4.4 | 2.78 | 10,098 | 14,109 | 4.1 | 38,445 | 47,874 | 814 | 32 |
| BAYLOR | 1,906 | 1,831 | 1,778 | -0.5 | 2.17 | 1,269 | 1,169 | -1.0 | 25,158 | 29,487 | 2796 | 206 |
| BEE | 8,592 | 8,742 | 8,929 | 0.2 | 2.79 | 6,447 | 6,431 | 0.0 | 29,271 | 35,304 | 2256 | 154 |
| BELL | 67,240 | 80,915 | 82,885 | 2.3 | 2.64 | 50,394 | 59,077 | 1.9 | 35,652 | 43,336 | 1143 | 54 |
| BEXAR | 409,043 | 487,183 | 523,474 | 2.1 | 2.78 | 297,145 | 345,471 | 1.8 | 36,963 | 42,028 | 984 | 41 |
| BLANCO | 2,338 | 3,554 | 4,058 | 5.2 | 2.40 | 1,692 | 2,469 | 4.7 | 34,430 | 40,441 | 1326 | 66 |
| BORDEN | 294 | 283 | 286 | -0.5 | 2.72 | 242 | 228 | -0.7 | 34,196 | 43,125 | 1357 | 69 |
| BOSQUE | 5,990 | 6,558 | 6,636 | 1.1 | 2.50 | 4,345 | 4,587 | 0.7 | 32,654 | 41,200 | 1604 | 89 |
| BOWIE | 30,595 | 31,655 | 31,881 | 0.4 | 2.56 | 22,319 | 22,433 | 0.1 | 36,168 | 42,172 | 1083 | 50 |
| BRAZORIA | 64,019 | 81,241 | 90,946 | 2.9 | 2.83 | 50,044 | 61,841 | 2.6 | 46,891 | 54,833 | 278 | 10 |
| BRAZOS | 43,725 | 49,463 | 51,923 | 1.5 | 2.49 | 24,903 | 26,837 | 0.9 | 32,909 | 40,140 | 1552 | 84 |
| BREWSTER | 3,350 | 3,590 | 3,624 | 0.8 | 2.34 | 2,162 | 2,247 | 0.5 | 27,880 | 35,286 | 2457 | 173 |
| BRISCOE | 789 | 766 | 761 | -0.4 | 2.33 | 567 | 530 | -0.8 | 21,855 | 25,709 | 3036 | 235 |
| BROOKS | 2,673 | 2,837 | 2,895 | 0.7 | 2.94 | 2,079 | 2,204 | 0.7 | 19,416 | 21,073 | 3109 | 247 |
| BROWN | 13,097 | 14,143 | 14,424 | 0.9 | 2.47 | 9,388 | 9,832 | 0.6 | 27,534 | 32,235 | 2506 | 176 |
| BURLESON | 5,176 | 6,222 | 6,587 | 2.3 | 2.49 | 3,685 | 4,264 | 1.8 | 28,649 | 34,775 | 2342 | 164 |
| BURNET | 9,055 | 13,903 | 16,978 | 5.3 | 2.51 | 6,661 | 9,860 | 4.9 | 33,232 | 40,214 | 1501 | 80 |
| CALDWELL | 8,745 | 11,230 | 12,713 | 3.1 | 2.79 | 6,549 | 8,274 | 2.9 | 31,689 | 38,388 | 1779 | 113 |
| CALHOUN | 6,777 | 7,497 | 7,482 | 1.2 | 2.69 | 5,138 | 5,554 | 0.9 | 31,260 | 34,118 | 1876 | 121 |
| CALLAHAN | 4,565 | 5,059 | 5,306 | 1.3 | 2.55 | 3,433 | 3,691 | 0.9 | 29,509 | 35,656 | 2221 | 149 |
| CAMERON | 73,278 | 97,214 | 107,026 | 3.5 | 3.39 | 60,178 | 79,515 | 3.4 | 26,185 | 30,126 | 2692 | 197 |
| CAMP | 3,773 | 4,314 | 4,473 | 1.6 | 2.52 | 2,757 | 3,029 | 1.1 | 26,509 | 28,910 | 2652 | 193 |
| CARSON | 2,402 | 2,470 | 2,528 | 0.3 | 2.71 | 1,876 | 1,870 | 0.0 | 40,321 | 51,104 | 645 | 27 |
| CASS | 11,320 | 11,941 | 12,099 | 0.6 | 2.53 | 8,447 | 8,637 | 0.3 | 30,079 | 35,483 | 2137 | 141 |
| CASTRO | 2,877 | 2,696 | 2,672 | -0.8 | 3.03 | 2,293 | 2,122 | -0.9 | 26,503 | 28,318 | 2654 | 194 |
| CHAMBERS | 6,930 | 8,649 | 9,459 | 2.7 | 2.81 | 5,481 | 6,667 | 2.4 | 50,388 | 59,517 | 196 | 6 |
| CHEROKEE | 14,981 | 15,998 | 16,825 | 0.8 | 2.58 | 10,888 | 11,222 | 0.4 | 29,969 | 34,896 | 2160 | 145 |
| CHILDRESS | 2,435 | 2,498 | 2,391 | 0.3 | 2.39 | 1,678 | 1,700 | 0.2 | 26,102 | 31,215 | 2701 | 198 |
| CLAY | 3,808 | 4,128 | 4,249 | 1.0 | 2.52 | 2,916 | 3,053 | 0.6 | 32,723 | 41,144 | 1591 | 87 |
| COCHRAN | 1,430 | 1,296 | 1,221 | -1.2 | 2.76 | 1,133 | 1,014 | -1.3 | 28,929 | 31,477 | 2307 | 159 |
| COKE | 1,374 | 1,379 | 1,370 | 0.0 | 2.37 | 994 | 965 | -0.4 | 26,583 | 31,486 | 2638 | 192 |
| COLEMAN | 4,026 | 3,965 | 3,861 | -0.2 | 2.31 | 2,745 | 2,605 | -0.6 | 22,736 | 27,083 | 2985 | 226 |
| COLLIN | 95,805 | 180,539 | 234,950 | 8.0 | 2.67 | 71,903 | 135,325 | 8.0 | 66,563 | 74,125 | 26 | 1 |
| COLLINGSWORTH | 1,447 | 1,338 | 1,284 | -0.9 | 2.27 | 994 | 880 | -1.5 | 20,814 | 23,500 | 3075 | 241 |
| COLORADO | 7,024 | 7,428 | 7,735 | 0.7 | 2.54 | 5,023 | 5,140 | 0.3 | 31,849 | 40,369 | 1747 | 108 |
| COMAL | 19,315 | 30,147 | 36,246 | 5.5 | 2.62 | 14,659 | 22,411 | 5.3 | 46,195 | 55,229 | 301 | 11 |
| COMANCHE | 5,318 | 5,467 | 5,553 | 0.3 | 2.44 | 3,826 | 3,798 | -0.1 | 25,756 | 28,696 | 2736 | 200 |
| CONCHO | 1,063 | 1,115 | 1,140 | 0.6 | 2.32 | 755 | 768 | 0.2 | 20,599 | 22,240 | 3081 | 242 |
| COOKE | 11,545 | 12,634 | 13,380 | 1.1 | 2.62 | 8,515 | 9,078 | 0.8 | 36,243 | 43,940 | 1075 | 48 |
| CORYELL | 16,687 | 20,435 | 20,901 | 2.5 | 2.88 | 13,589 | 16,319 | 2.2 | 35,902 | 45,002 | 1115 | 51 |
| COTTLE | 915 | 783 | 738 | -1.9 | 2.34 | 623 | 512 | -2.4 | 19,479 | 23,966 | 3108 | 246 |
| CRANE | 1,537 | 1,479 | 1,453 | -0.5 | 2.81 | 1,232 | 1,161 | -0.7 | 42,312 | 50,745 | 485 | 20 |
| CROCKETT | 1,449 | 1,670 | 1,679 | 1.7 | 2.57 | 1,091 | 1,233 | 1.5 | 27,183 | 30,461 | 2549 | 181 |
| CROSBY | 2,516 | 2,508 | 2,509 | 0.0 | 2.73 | 1,913 | 1,880 | -0.2 | 22,595 | 26,305 | 2988 | 227 |
| CULBERSON | 1,076 | 963 | 926 | -1.3 | 3.09 | 862 | 770 | -1.4 | 21,857 | 26,588 | 3035 | 234 |
| DALLAM | 2,122 | 2,714 | 2,988 | 3.0 | 2.47 | 1,505 | 1,861 | 2.6 | 30,896 | 32,683 | 1949 | 127 |
| DALLAS | 701,686 | 803,787 | 854,904 | 1.7 | 2.56 | 463,127 | 516,085 | 1.3 | 44,898 | 50,208 | 357 | 13 |
| DAWSON | 5,084 | 4,765 | 4,538 | -0.8 | 2.70 | 3,818 | 3,541 | -0.9 | 24,589 | 27,086 | 2850 | 214 |
| DEAF SMITH | 6,182 | 6,271 | 6,119 | 0.2 | 2.95 | 4,919 | 4,924 | 0.0 | 26,929 | 30,046 | 2596 | 188 |
| DELTA | 1,901 | 1,975 | 2,030 | 0.5 | 2.47 | 1,364 | 1,361 | 0.0 | 31,368 | 40,804 | 1850 | 119 |
| DENTON | 101,984 | 159,844 | 196,705 | 5.6 | 2.60 | 69,607 | 108,223 | 5.5 | 54,447 | 65,967 | 130 | 5 |
| DEWITT | 7,195 | 7,080 | 6,887 | -0.2 | 2.45 | 5,061 | 4,824 | -0.6 | 27,125 | 32,460 | 2560 | 183 |
| DICKENS | 1,073 | 943 | 879 | -1.6 | 2.22 | 707 | 595 | -2.1 | 22,390 | 27,933 | 3004 | 231 |
| DIMMIT | 3,072 | 3,087 | 3,063 | 0.1 | 3.32 | 2,548 | 2,552 | 0.0 | 17,183 | 18,902 | 3137 | 253 |
| DONLEY | 1,515 | 1,577 | 1,603 | 0.5 | 2.30 | 1,066 | 1,080 | 0.2 | 25,517 | 27,967 | 2754 | 202 |
| DUVAL | 4,159 | 4,364 | 4,520 | 0.6 | 3.02 | 3,274 | 3,422 | 0.5 | 20,328 | 23,427 | 3091 | 243 |
| EASTLAND | 7,354 | 7,056 | 6,880 | -0.5 | 2.36 | 5,054 | 4,682 | -0.9 | 23,444 | 28,358 | 2945 | 222 |
| ECTOR | 42,322 | 45,525 | 46,446 | 0.9 | 2.70 | 31,551 | 33,087 | 0.6 | 32,277 | 39,759 | 1670 | 101 |
| EDWARDS | 795 | 1,464 | 1,662 | 7.7 | 2.53 | 594 | 1,076 | 7.5 | 19,046 | 22,278 | 3121 | 249 |
| ELLIS | 28,588 | 36,913 | 42,582 | 3.1 | 2.97 | 22,949 | 28,976 | 2.9 | 46,007 | 56,431 | 309 | 12 |
| EL PASO | 178,366 | 220,611 | 236,814 | 2.6 | 3.18 | 142,854 | 175,636 | 2.5 | 30,494 | 35,140 | 2037 | 133 |
| ERATH | 10,877 | 12,561 | 13,031 | 1.8 | 2.39 | 7,014 | 7,812 | 1.3 | 28,257 | 33,556 | 2408 | 169 |
| FALLS | 6,492 | 6,123 | 5,822 | -0.7 | 2.49 | 4,477 | 4,060 | -1.2 | 28,725 | 36,061 | 2333 | 163 |
| FANNIN | 9,691 | 11,321 | 12,271 | 1.9 | 2.42 | 6,977 | 7,864 | 1.5 | 30,514 | 36,759 | 2029 | 132 |
| FAYETTE | 8,101 | 8,819 | 9,154 | 1.0 | 2.40 | 5,645 | 5,913 | 0.6 | 32,098 | 40,488 | 1700 | 105 |
| FISHER | 1,892 | 1,659 | 1,547 | -1.6 | 2.44 | 1,383 | 1,173 | -2.0 | 27,482 | 30,770 | 2512 | 177 |
| FLOYD | 2,982 | 2,922 | 2,884 | -0.2 | 2.73 | 2,280 | 2,204 | -0.4 | 24,806 | 27,000 | 2826 | 209 |
| TEXAS | | | | 2.4 | 2.71 | | | 2.1 | 39,535 | 46,148 | | |
| UNITED STATES | | | | 1.4 | 2.59 | | | 1.1 | 41,914 | 49,127 | | |

| COUNTY | 2000 Per Capita Income | 2000 HH Income Base | 2000 HOUSEHOLD INCOME DISTRIBUTION (%) Less than $15,000 | $15,000 to $24,999 | $25,000 to $49,999 | $50,000 to $99,999 | $100,000 to $149,999 | $150,000 or More | 2000 AVERAGE DISPOSABLE INCOME BY AGE OF HOUSEHOLDER All Ages | <35 | 35-44 | 45-54 | 55-64 | 65+ |
|---|---|---|---|---|---|---|---|---|---|---|---|---|---|---|
| ANDERSON | 14,237 | 15,207 | 19.5 | 15.3 | 36.7 | 22.6 | 4.4 | 1.4 | 34,024 | 30,871 | 39,625 | 44,174 | 37,656 | 21,842 |
| ANDREWS | 15,694 | 4,672 | 14.0 | 16.0 | 36.6 | 28.2 | 4.1 | 1.1 | 36,153 | 31,169 | 40,116 | 42,410 | 40,403 | 26,457 |
| ANGELINA | 17,054 | 28,445 | 20.8 | 16.3 | 35.1 | 22.3 | 3.9 | 1.6 | 33,732 | 28,950 | 39,065 | 43,333 | 34,572 | 21,594 |
| ARANSAS | 19,489 | 9,496 | 19.3 | 18.0 | 34.7 | 19.7 | 5.1 | 3.2 | 36,726 | 27,617 | 37,240 | 42,918 | 40,016 | 32,362 |
| ARCHER | 17,399 | 3,133 | 16.3 | 16.2 | 36.1 | 25.1 | 4.8 | 1.6 | 36,088 | 33,483 | 45,284 | 43,182 | 37,505 | 22,093 |
| ARMSTRONG | 16,803 | 835 | 18.7 | 16.1 | 33.2 | 25.6 | 4.9 | 1.6 | 35,312 | 30,223 | 45,496 | 48,688 | 41,615 | 22,217 |
| ATASCOSA | 12,780 | 12,504 | 24.4 | 18.2 | 32.2 | 20.1 | 3.6 | 1.4 | 31,401 | 27,688 | 36,135 | 38,939 | 31,020 | 22,286 |
| AUSTIN | 20,594 | 9,252 | 18.6 | 12.9 | 33.8 | 26.0 | 6.0 | 2.7 | 38,578 | 32,415 | 42,300 | 52,461 | 41,722 | 24,623 |
| BAILEY | 13,832 | 2,471 | 23.2 | 26.4 | 30.4 | 13.8 | 4.9 | 1.3 | 29,752 | 22,446 | 35,046 | 35,363 | 35,826 | 21,516 |
| BANDERA | 19,941 | 6,901 | 16.8 | 13.8 | 34.2 | 27.3 | 4.9 | 3.0 | 39,466 | 33,178 | 43,279 | 43,684 | 40,564 | 31,780 |
| BASTROP | 16,485 | 19,157 | 15.6 | 15.0 | 34.9 | 28.2 | 5.2 | 1.1 | 36,575 | 33,835 | 41,611 | 42,957 | 38,856 | 24,751 |
| BAYLOR | 15,743 | 1,831 | 33.2 | 16.5 | 30.3 | 16.1 | 2.5 | 1.5 | 27,863 | 28,845 | 32,919 | 38,641 | 32,214 | 18,037 |
| BEE | 13,087 | 8,742 | 25.4 | 18.5 | 33.7 | 19.0 | 2.7 | 0.6 | 29,414 | 27,992 | 31,643 | 36,380 | 33,469 | 20,849 |
| BELL | 16,738 | 80,915 | 14.5 | 17.8 | 36.3 | 25.8 | 4.4 | 1.3 | 35,644 | 29,481 | 41,071 | 46,322 | 42,181 | 26,708 |
| BEXAR | 17,863 | 487,179 | 16.6 | 15.4 | 33.6 | 26.6 | 5.7 | 2.2 | 38,119 | 30,664 | 41,460 | 45,927 | 41,461 | 30,210 |
| BLANCO | 23,514 | 3,554 | 18.5 | 14.0 | 36.8 | 21.9 | 5.3 | 3.5 | 38,745 | 34,927 | 44,201 | 49,279 | 39,492 | 26,931 |
| BORDEN | 26,691 | 283 | 15.9 | 13.1 | 35.0 | 17.0 | 8.8 | 10.3 | 52,270 | 40,428 | 33,499 | 63,540 | 56,366 | 30,465 |
| BOSQUE | 17,815 | 6,558 | 20.1 | 16.7 | 33.6 | 22.5 | 5.2 | 1.9 | 34,680 | 30,170 | 43,933 | 45,482 | 37,558 | 23,069 |
| BOWIE | 18,027 | 31,655 | 18.7 | 15.2 | 33.4 | 25.9 | 4.9 | 1.9 | 36,375 | 31,127 | 42,395 | 45,363 | 36,333 | 25,365 |
| BRAZORIA | 19,618 | 81,241 | 10.8 | 10.8 | 32.3 | 36.6 | 7.5 | 2.1 | 43,294 | 37,140 | 48,062 | 52,500 | 44,471 | 29,469 |
| BRAZOS | 19,707 | 49,463 | 24.5 | 14.2 | 29.5 | 22.8 | 5.6 | 3.4 | 37,408 | 24,753 | 47,844 | 52,998 | 53,621 | 32,314 |
| BREWSTER | 18,989 | 3,590 | 26.1 | 18.5 | 28.2 | 19.1 | 5.0 | 3.1 | 34,359 | 21,893 | 40,319 | 42,722 | 44,798 | 26,466 |
| BRISCOE | 13,808 | 766 | 33.3 | 20.6 | 30.8 | 12.0 | 2.2 | 1.0 | 25,389 | 25,894 | 24,558 | 31,587 | 30,376 | 17,206 |
| BROOKS | 9,511 | 2,837 | 41.3 | 18.8 | 26.8 | 10.1 | 2.5 | 0.6 | 23,000 | 17,474 | 29,587 | 30,692 | 21,969 | 18,042 |
| BROWN | 14,013 | 14,143 | 26.3 | 18.6 | 33.0 | 18.3 | 3.0 | 0.9 | 29,352 | 25,187 | 36,259 | 38,117 | 29,875 | 20,639 |
| BURLESON | 14,610 | 6,222 | 25.6 | 17.4 | 35.0 | 18.2 | 3.0 | 0.9 | 29,504 | 26,989 | 35,655 | 36,045 | 29,663 | 22,098 |
| BURNET | 20,681 | 13,903 | 18.0 | 17.4 | 34.7 | 22.2 | 5.0 | 2.9 | 36,769 | 28,258 | 39,717 | 43,254 | 41,651 | 30,533 |
| CALDWELL | 14,768 | 11,230 | 21.9 | 18.1 | 33.7 | 20.8 | 4.0 | 1.4 | 32,703 | 27,158 | 38,919 | 37,600 | 36,371 | 23,428 |
| CALHOUN | 14,409 | 7,497 | 23.8 | 17.2 | 33.4 | 21.9 | 2.6 | 1.1 | 31,210 | 27,463 | 35,148 | 40,475 | 30,894 | 21,871 |
| CALLAHAN | 15,376 | 5,059 | 23.6 | 18.8 | 34.5 | 19.6 | 2.6 | 1.0 | 30,244 | 26,961 | 35,478 | 39,937 | 30,936 | 20,032 |
| CAMERON | 11,074 | 97,214 | 29.6 | 18.4 | 29.8 | 18.0 | 3.1 | 1.2 | 29,258 | 25,006 | 31,594 | 33,534 | 31,153 | 24,430 |
| CAMP | 13,489 | 4,314 | 31.2 | 15.6 | 34.2 | 16.2 | 2.3 | 0.5 | 27,254 | 25,111 | 32,993 | 32,980 | 28,342 | 19,030 |
| CARSON | 19,536 | 2,470 | 11.5 | 12.8 | 37.0 | 30.7 | 6.4 | 1.6 | 39,831 | 38,420 | 45,525 | 49,328 | 41,799 | 26,647 |
| CASS | 14,570 | 11,941 | 25.2 | 15.4 | 34.9 | 20.9 | 2.8 | 0.9 | 30,492 | 27,198 | 37,990 | 36,123 | 33,579 | 20,870 |
| CASTRO | 11,535 | 2,696 | 26.0 | 20.5 | 32.0 | 18.3 | 2.5 | 0.7 | 28,652 | 24,686 | 34,280 | 33,698 | 31,094 | 20,185 |
| CHAMBERS | 21,015 | 8,649 | 12.3 | 7.3 | 29.8 | 37.4 | 10.2 | 3.0 | 46,053 | 41,638 | 53,728 | 54,671 | 46,791 | 28,767 |
| CHEROKEE | 14,150 | 15,998 | 23.9 | 16.7 | 36.2 | 18.8 | 3.3 | 1.2 | 30,784 | 27,615 | 38,496 | 36,336 | 35,216 | 20,474 |
| CHILDRESS | 12,288 | 2,498 | 29.4 | 18.5 | 31.1 | 16.2 | 3.4 | 1.4 | 29,515 | 25,237 | 35,728 | 32,066 | 36,173 | 21,355 |
| CLAY | 15,855 | 4,128 | 18.9 | 16.5 | 39.8 | 21.2 | 2.8 | 0.8 | 32,082 | 30,715 | 37,046 | 39,072 | 36,637 | 20,746 |
| COCHRAN | 14,411 | 1,296 | 24.3 | 18.4 | 34.2 | 17.9 | 3.6 | 1.7 | 31,741 | 27,173 | 32,926 | 37,687 | 36,250 | 25,731 |
| COKE | 15,041 | 1,379 | 26.3 | 20.2 | 30.0 | 19.4 | 3.5 | 0.7 | 29,335 | 27,758 | 37,268 | 32,950 | 35,015 | 22,267 |
| COLEMAN | 13,050 | 3,965 | 34.3 | 19.7 | 30.3 | 12.9 | 2.2 | 0.5 | 25,120 | 22,037 | 31,054 | 34,880 | 30,806 | 18,176 |
| COLLIN | 34,342 | 180,539 | 4.5 | 6.1 | 22.4 | 40.0 | 16.8 | 10.3 | 66,619 | 49,514 | 67,836 | 74,443 | 64,600 | 36,577 |
| COLLINGSWORTH | 13,747 | 1,338 | 37.5 | 20.0 | 24.9 | 14.2 | 2.7 | 0.8 | 25,252 | 18,875 | 31,476 | 38,766 | 26,079 | 18,082 |
| COLORADO | 16,286 | 7,428 | 22.1 | 16.2 | 32.8 | 23.0 | 4.6 | 1.4 | 33,381 | 30,236 | 41,614 | 42,833 | 35,529 | 24,048 |
| COMAL | 24,081 | 30,147 | 10.7 | 10.8 | 32.7 | 32.4 | 9.2 | 4.3 | 46,729 | 37,691 | 50,218 | 56,045 | 49,161 | 36,905 |
| COMANCHE | 14,879 | 5,467 | 27.4 | 20.9 | 32.5 | 14.5 | 2.9 | 1.8 | 29,169 | 28,740 | 33,933 | 39,651 | 32,293 | 18,826 |
| CONCHO | 11,332 | 1,115 | 37.5 | 21.2 | 29.2 | 10.4 | 1.2 | 0.5 | 22,711 | 20,387 | 25,063 | 32,089 | 25,795 | 15,875 |
| COOKE | 19,400 | 12,634 | 17.6 | 13.8 | 36.7 | 24.0 | 5.2 | 2.7 | 37,930 | 30,816 | 40,820 | 47,636 | 42,730 | 27,865 |
| CORYELL | 13,487 | 20,435 | 9.3 | 19.9 | 42.3 | 25.7 | 2.6 | 0.2 | 33,902 | 29,678 | 37,749 | 43,118 | 38,742 | 26,182 |
| COTTLE | 12,992 | 783 | 43.2 | 16.9 | 27.6 | 9.7 | 1.3 | 1.4 | 24,084 | 18,000 | 25,695 | 26,133 | 32,000 | 18,837 |
| CRANE | 17,154 | 1,479 | 13.0 | 10.7 | 36.0 | 32.3 | 7.4 | 0.6 | 39,420 | 36,697 | 46,375 | 45,714 | 44,461 | 24,779 |
| CROCKETT | 15,344 | 1,670 | 29.9 | 16.8 | 29.0 | 19.2 | 3.3 | 1.9 | 30,662 | 26,328 | 30,324 | 38,627 | 31,182 | 23,166 |
| CROSBY | 12,856 | 2,508 | 30.9 | 23.2 | 29.2 | 13.6 | 1.9 | 1.3 | 26,614 | 23,478 | 27,493 | 33,894 | 28,540 | 20,753 |
| CULBERSON | 9,901 | 963 | 32.1 | 23.2 | 29.5 | 11.9 | 3.0 | 0.3 | 25,249 | 22,181 | 34,731 | 22,981 | 26,965 | 20,314 |
| DALLAM | 15,267 | 2,714 | 18.1 | 16.3 | 41.4 | 20.9 | 3.1 | 0.3 | 31,127 | 29,055 | 36,485 | 35,901 | 31,131 | 24,303 |
| DALLAS | 25,437 | 803,784 | 10.7 | 12.7 | 32.2 | 31.1 | 8.6 | 4.6 | 47,033 | 37,473 | 49,010 | 54,835 | 50,508 | 35,286 |
| DAWSON | 15,369 | 4,765 | 31.0 | 19.7 | 29.3 | 16.1 | 2.7 | 1.2 | 27,995 | 21,996 | 34,799 | 31,337 | 33,893 | 21,174 |
| DEAF SMITH | 12,709 | 6,271 | 26.4 | 19.2 | 31.1 | 18.2 | 4.0 | 1.1 | 30,404 | 23,354 | 32,841 | 37,847 | 37,807 | 23,442 |
| DELTA | 14,556 | 1,975 | 27.1 | 10.9 | 34.8 | 23.8 | 3.1 | 0.2 | 30,432 | 31,788 | 31,456 | 45,645 | 31,831 | 19,600 |
| DENTON | 26,013 | 159,844 | 7.9 | 7.9 | 28.7 | 39.6 | 11.5 | 4.5 | 51,539 | 39,606 | 57,271 | 62,802 | 54,267 | 32,786 |
| DEWITT | 14,424 | 7,080 | 29.5 | 16.3 | 32.3 | 18.3 | 3.0 | 0.7 | 28,823 | 27,855 | 34,039 | 37,070 | 32,620 | 19,628 |
| DICKENS | 13,639 | 943 | 33.7 | 19.6 | 30.3 | 13.7 | 2.0 | 0.6 | 25,380 | 25,686 | 28,666 | 36,220 | 29,491 | 17,529 |
| DIMMIT | 7,483 | 3,087 | 43.6 | 21.1 | 22.8 | 11.0 | 1.3 | 0.2 | 21,179 | 20,913 | 27,323 | 23,312 | 19,699 | 15,392 |
| DONLEY | 13,985 | 1,577 | 30.7 | 18.3 | 34.0 | 13.7 | 2.5 | 0.8 | 26,772 | 21,987 | 33,280 | 37,478 | 32,048 | 19,079 |
| DUVAL | 11,884 | 4,364 | 38.9 | 20.5 | 25.4 | 12.9 | 1.5 | 0.8 | 23,835 | 20,482 | 28,184 | 30,138 | 25,594 | 16,589 |
| EASTLAND | 13,388 | 7,056 | 31.0 | 21.7 | 29.4 | 15.0 | 2.2 | 0.7 | 26,075 | 24,962 | 32,979 | 34,767 | 28,427 | 17,531 |
| ECTOR | 15,878 | 45,525 | 20.6 | 16.8 | 34.6 | 22.7 | 3.8 | 1.5 | 33,600 | 27,372 | 37,682 | 40,207 | 36,763 | 25,831 |
| EDWARDS | 11,073 | 1,464 | 39.0 | 21.5 | 27.5 | 9.3 | 1.6 | 1.1 | 23,278 | 22,149 | 26,788 | 24,777 | 30,669 | 20,277 |
| ELLIS | 20,510 | 36,913 | 10.9 | 10.8 | 32.6 | 33.0 | 8.7 | 4.1 | 46,676 | 40,265 | 49,478 | 57,549 | 49,695 | 26,472 |
| EL PASO | 12,891 | 220,608 | 22.1 | 18.5 | 33.2 | 21.2 | 3.6 | 1.3 | 32,323 | 26,167 | 33,819 | 38,646 | 36,678 | 26,283 |
| ERATH | 16,027 | 12,561 | 26.5 | 17.7 | 31.6 | 19.1 | 3.5 | 1.5 | 31,204 | 25,076 | 37,857 | 45,627 | 35,376 | 19,971 |
| FALLS | 13,689 | 6,123 | 26.8 | 17.8 | 31.0 | 19.7 | 3.6 | 1.2 | 30,305 | 28,819 | 35,822 | 36,571 | 32,257 | 23,829 |
| FANNIN | 15,350 | 11,321 | 24.2 | 16.2 | 35.5 | 20.2 | 3.1 | 0.9 | 30,766 | 30,140 | 37,245 | 42,091 | 31,295 | 20,009 |
| FAYETTE | 17,508 | 8,819 | 21.8 | 17.8 | 32.5 | 22.4 | 4.2 | 1.3 | 32,940 | 33,440 | 39,514 | 40,917 | 34,281 | 23,300 |
| FISHER | 14,378 | 1,659 | 26.5 | 19.5 | 33.2 | 16.2 | 3.6 | 1.2 | 29,287 | 26,693 | 36,264 | 35,932 | 38,050 | 18,912 |
| FLOYD | 12,198 | 2,922 | 30.8 | 19.5 | 29.9 | 16.4 | 2.7 | 0.8 | 27,251 | 24,463 | 27,859 | 29,089 | 29,333 | 26,429 |
| TEXAS | 20,236 | | 16.2 | 13.9 | 31.8 | 28.0 | 6.9 | 3.2 | 41,217 | 33,340 | 45,769 | 49,732 | 43,451 | 28,369 |
| UNITED STATES | 22,162 | | 14.5 | 12.5 | 32.3 | 29.8 | 7.4 | 3.5 | 40,748 | 34,503 | 44,969 | 49,579 | 43,409 | 27,339 |

| COUNTY | FINANCIAL SERVICES | | | | THE HOME | | | | | | ENTERTAINMENT | | | | | | PERSONAL | | | |
|---|---|---|---|---|---|---|---|---|---|---|---|---|---|---|---|---|---|---|---|---|
| | | | | | Home Improvements | | | Furnishings | | | | | | | | | | | | |
| | Auto Loan | Home Loan | Invest-ments | Retire-ment Plans | Home Repair | Lawn & Garden | Remodel-ing | Appli-ances | Elec-tronics | Furni-ture | Restau-rants | Sport-ing Goods | Theater & Concerts | Toys & Hobbies | Travel | Video Rental | Apparel | Auto After-market | Health Insur-ance | Pets & Supplies |
| ANDERSON | 96 | 78 | 84 | 82 | 95 | 92 | 108 | 96 | 93 | 85 | 87 | 93 | 86 | 96 | 75 | 97 | 86 | 91 | 99 | 98 |
| ANDREWS | 98 | 90 | 98 | 91 | 98 | 97 | 106 | 98 | 96 | 93 | 95 | 96 | 93 | 99 | 82 | 98 | 92 | 96 | 100 | 101 |
| ANGELINA | 97 | 80 | 87 | 84 | 97 | 93 | 107 | 96 | 93 | 87 | 87 | 95 | 88 | 97 | 77 | 97 | 87 | 92 | 99 | 98 |
| ARANSAS | 99 | 85 | 102 | 92 | 100 | 103 | 110 | 100 | 93 | 90 | 92 | 96 | 91 | 99 | 84 | 97 | 90 | 94 | 105 | 101 |
| ARCHER | 100 | 82 | 88 | 92 | 96 | 96 | 112 | 98 | 97 | 86 | 90 | 100 | 91 | 100 | 78 | 99 | 91 | 95 | 104 | 101 |
| ARMSTRONG | 96 | 63 | 72 | 77 | 91 | 91 | 110 | 94 | 90 | 72 | 77 | 93 | 77 | 94 | 68 | 97 | 78 | 87 | 104 | 96 |
| ATASCOSA | 96 | 84 | 87 | 81 | 93 | 92 | 106 | 97 | 94 | 86 | 89 | 92 | 86 | 95 | 77 | 97 | 84 | 93 | 99 | 101 |
| AUSTIN | 97 | 72 | 79 | 80 | 93 | 91 | 113 | 96 | 93 | 80 | 83 | 94 | 83 | 96 | 71 | 97 | 83 | 90 | 102 | 98 |
| BAILEY | 95 | 74 | 79 | 79 | 91 | 91 | 105 | 95 | 92 | 78 | 82 | 92 | 82 | 94 | 72 | 97 | 80 | 90 | 102 | 98 |
| BANDERA | 99 | 75 | 83 | 85 | 95 | 94 | 120 | 98 | 93 | 82 | 85 | 97 | 85 | 99 | 74 | 98 | 86 | 91 | 104 | 101 |
| BASTROP | 97 | 82 | 83 | 83 | 93 | 91 | 108 | 96 | 94 | 89 | 90 | 95 | 87 | 97 | 75 | 98 | 87 | 92 | 97 | 99 |
| BAYLOR | 94 | 64 | 73 | 74 | 92 | 91 | 107 | 93 | 91 | 74 | 77 | 87 | 76 | 90 | 69 | 97 | 77 | 86 | 102 | 93 |
| BEE | 95 | 89 | 90 | 86 | 94 | 94 | 99 | 96 | 95 | 89 | 92 | 92 | 89 | 94 | 80 | 97 | 87 | 94 | 98 | 100 |
| BELL | 95 | 94 | 89 | 88 | 96 | 93 | 97 | 95 | 96 | 91 | 96 | 95 | 91 | 96 | 81 | 98 | 92 | 96 | 95 | 99 |
| BEXAR | 98 | 102 | 96 | 97 | 98 | 99 | 98 | 99 | 99 | 99 | 102 | 99 | 97 | 99 | 87 | 99 | 97 | 100 | 97 | 102 |
| BLANCO | 97 | 66 | 74 | 79 | 92 | 91 | 112 | 95 | 91 | 74 | 79 | 95 | 79 | 96 | 69 | 97 | 80 | 88 | 104 | 97 |
| BORDEN | 101 | 63 | 70 | 82 | 90 | 91 | 115 | 96 | 88 | 68 | 77 | 102 | 78 | 100 | 66 | 97 | 79 | 88 | 108 | 100 |
| BOSQUE | 97 | 73 | 88 | 83 | 96 | 96 | 112 | 97 | 93 | 81 | 84 | 93 | 84 | 96 | 75 | 97 | 84 | 90 | 104 | 98 |
| BOWIE | 97 | 85 | 91 | 89 | 98 | 95 | 105 | 97 | 95 | 91 | 90 | 96 | 91 | 97 | 80 | 98 | 90 | 94 | 97 | 99 |
| BRAZORIA | 100 | 97 | 92 | 95 | 97 | 97 | 105 | 99 | 100 | 98 | 101 | 101 | 96 | 102 | 83 | 100 | 99 | 100 | 98 | 102 |
| BRAZOS | 95 | 101 | 95 | 96 | 96 | 93 | 97 | 90 | 92 | 86 | 93 | 92 | 87 | 94 | 82 | 94 | 91 | 94 | 94 | 97 |
| BREWSTER | 95 | 87 | 91 | 85 | 95 | 94 | 104 | 95 | 93 | 87 | 90 | 92 | 87 | 95 | 79 | 97 | 86 | 93 | 99 | 99 |
| BRISCOE | 96 | 63 | 72 | 76 | 91 | 91 | 109 | 94 | 90 | 72 | 77 | 92 | 77 | 93 | 68 | 97 | 78 | 87 | 104 | 95 |
| BROOKS | 93 | 88 | 89 | 79 | 92 | 92 | 97 | 96 | 94 | 86 | 89 | 89 | 86 | 92 | 79 | 97 | 81 | 93 | 98 | 101 |
| BROWN | 97 | 76 | 82 | 83 | 96 | 92 | 112 | 96 | 92 | 83 | 84 | 95 | 85 | 96 | 75 | 97 | 85 | 91 | 100 | 98 |
| BURLESON | 96 | 66 | 72 | 76 | 93 | 91 | 112 | 95 | 91 | 76 | 78 | 93 | 79 | 94 | 69 | 96 | 79 | 87 | 102 | 96 |
| BURNET | 99 | 80 | 101 | 91 | 101 | 103 | 111 | 99 | 92 | 86 | 89 | 96 | 90 | 99 | 83 | 97 | 88 | 93 | 107 | 100 |
| CALDWELL | 95 | 82 | 84 | 80 | 92 | 91 | 105 | 96 | 94 | 86 | 88 | 92 | 86 | 95 | 75 | 97 | 84 | 92 | 98 | 99 |
| CALHOUN | 97 | 86 | 93 | 87 | 96 | 96 | 107 | 97 | 95 | 88 | 91 | 95 | 90 | 97 | 80 | 98 | 88 | 94 | 101 | 101 |
| CALLAHAN | 95 | 72 | 79 | 78 | 92 | 91 | 110 | 94 | 92 | 81 | 83 | 91 | 81 | 94 | 71 | 97 | 82 | 89 | 100 | 96 |
| CAMERON | 94 | 93 | 95 | 85 | 95 | 96 | 96 | 97 | 95 | 88 | 92 | 91 | 90 | 93 | 82 | 97 | 85 | 95 | 99 | 102 |
| CAMP | 96 | 71 | 80 | 80 | 94 | 91 | 114 | 96 | 92 | 80 | 81 | 93 | 82 | 95 | 72 | 97 | 83 | 89 | 100 | 97 |
| CARSON | 99 | 81 | 88 | 87 | 97 | 95 | 110 | 98 | 95 | 87 | 91 | 98 | 90 | 101 | 77 | 98 | 90 | 94 | 102 | 101 |
| CASS | 96 | 68 | 75 | 77 | 93 | 91 | 111 | 95 | 92 | 79 | 80 | 93 | 81 | 94 | 70 | 96 | 81 | 88 | 101 | 96 |
| CASTRO | 95 | 77 | 82 | 79 | 91 | 91 | 103 | 96 | 92 | 80 | 84 | 92 | 83 | 94 | 74 | 97 | 80 | 91 | 101 | 99 |
| CHAMBERS | 99 | 81 | 82 | 85 | 94 | 92 | 112 | 98 | 96 | 87 | 90 | 98 | 88 | 100 | 74 | 99 | 89 | 93 | 99 | 101 |
| CHEROKEE | 96 | 76 | 84 | 83 | 95 | 93 | 110 | 96 | 94 | 84 | 84 | 94 | 85 | 95 | 74 | 97 | 85 | 91 | 99 | 97 |
| CHILDRESS | 95 | 65 | 73 | 75 | 91 | 90 | 106 | 94 | 90 | 74 | 77 | 90 | 77 | 91 | 69 | 97 | 78 | 87 | 101 | 95 |
| CLAY | 98 | 68 | 76 | 81 | 92 | 91 | 115 | 96 | 92 | 76 | 80 | 96 | 80 | 97 | 70 | 97 | 81 | 89 | 104 | 98 |
| COCHRAN | 95 | 79 | 83 | 79 | 91 | 92 | 102 | 96 | 92 | 81 | 85 | 91 | 83 | 93 | 75 | 97 | 80 | 91 | 101 | 99 |
| COKE | 97 | 66 | 74 | 79 | 92 | 91 | 116 | 95 | 91 | 75 | 79 | 93 | 79 | 95 | 70 | 97 | 80 | 88 | 104 | 97 |
| COLEMAN | 95 | 66 | 77 | 78 | 92 | 92 | 108 | 94 | 91 | 75 | 79 | 91 | 79 | 93 | 70 | 97 | 79 | 87 | 103 | 95 |
| COLLIN | 105 | 117 | 100 | 113 | 102 | 107 | 105 | 104 | 109 | 112 | 118 | 111 | 110 | 108 | 95 | 102 | 116 | 111 | 100 | 107 |
| COLLINGSWORTH | 94 | 64 | 72 | 75 | 91 | 91 | 108 | 93 | 91 | 74 | 77 | 89 | 76 | 91 | 68 | 97 | 78 | 86 | 103 | 94 |
| COLORADO | 97 | 74 | 83 | 81 | 94 | 93 | 111 | 96 | 93 | 81 | 84 | 93 | 84 | 96 | 73 | 97 | 83 | 90 | 102 | 98 |
| COMAL | 102 | 97 | 106 | 102 | 103 | 106 | 109 | 102 | 100 | 99 | 102 | 101 | 100 | 103 | 90 | 99 | 100 | 101 | 104 | 104 |
| COMANCHE | 96 | 68 | 75 | 78 | 92 | 91 | 110 | 95 | 91 | 76 | 79 | 92 | 79 | 94 | 70 | 97 | 80 | 88 | 103 | 96 |
| CONCHO | 97 | 66 | 73 | 78 | 91 | 91 | 109 | 95 | 90 | 73 | 78 | 94 | 78 | 94 | 69 | 97 | 79 | 88 | 104 | 97 |
| COOKE | 98 | 83 | 94 | 90 | 99 | 98 | 111 | 98 | 94 | 89 | 90 | 96 | 90 | 98 | 81 | 97 | 90 | 93 | 101 | 100 |
| CORYELL | 93 | 88 | 78 | 81 | 90 | 87 | 96 | 93 | 94 | 84 | 91 | 91 | 86 | 93 | 75 | 97 | 87 | 93 | 93 | 98 |
| COTTLE | 95 | 63 | 72 | 76 | 91 | 91 | 109 | 94 | 90 | 73 | 77 | 91 | 77 | 92 | 68 | 97 | 78 | 87 | 103 | 95 |
| CRANE | 99 | 91 | 93 | 90 | 97 | 96 | 107 | 98 | 97 | 94 | 96 | 98 | 94 | 101 | 81 | 99 | 93 | 97 | 99 | 102 |
| CROCKETT | 95 | 77 | 83 | 79 | 92 | 92 | 107 | 96 | 93 | 81 | 84 | 91 | 83 | 94 | 74 | 97 | 82 | 91 | 101 | 98 |
| CROSBY | 94 | 79 | 83 | 79 | 92 | 92 | 102 | 96 | 93 | 81 | 85 | 90 | 84 | 92 | 75 | 97 | 80 | 91 | 100 | 99 |
| CULBERSON | 93 | 88 | 89 | 79 | 92 | 92 | 97 | 96 | 94 | 86 | 89 | 89 | 86 | 92 | 79 | 97 | 81 | 93 | 98 | 101 |
| DALLAM | 97 | 74 | 80 | 81 | 93 | 91 | 112 | 96 | 93 | 80 | 84 | 94 | 83 | 97 | 72 | 98 | 83 | 90 | 102 | 99 |
| DALLAS | 100 | 110 | 102 | 104 | 102 | 103 | 97 | 100 | 102 | 104 | 107 | 103 | 103 | 102 | 93 | 100 | 105 | 104 | 97 | 103 |
| DAWSON | 95 | 81 | 87 | 81 | 93 | 93 | 102 | 96 | 93 | 83 | 86 | 92 | 85 | 94 | 77 | 97 | 82 | 92 | 101 | 100 |
| DEAF SMITH | 95 | 85 | 87 | 83 | 93 | 93 | 102 | 97 | 95 | 86 | 89 | 92 | 87 | 94 | 77 | 97 | 84 | 93 | 99 | 100 |
| DELTA | 97 | 68 | 77 | 80 | 93 | 91 | 112 | 95 | 92 | 77 | 81 | 94 | 80 | 96 | 70 | 98 | 81 | 89 | 103 | 98 |
| DENTON | 102 | 109 | 92 | 102 | 98 | 99 | 101 | 100 | 104 | 104 | 110 | 105 | 101 | 104 | 88 | 100 | 107 | 105 | 97 | 104 |
| DEWITT | 94 | 68 | 75 | 75 | 92 | 90 | 106 | 94 | 91 | 77 | 79 | 90 | 79 | 92 | 71 | 96 | 79 | 88 | 100 | 95 |
| DICKENS | 94 | 64 | 72 | 74 | 91 | 91 | 108 | 93 | 91 | 74 | 77 | 88 | 76 | 91 | 69 | 97 | 77 | 86 | 103 | 93 |
| DIMMIT | 93 | 88 | 89 | 79 | 92 | 92 | 97 | 96 | 94 | 86 | 89 | 89 | 86 | 92 | 79 | 97 | 81 | 93 | 98 | 101 |
| DONLEY | 96 | 65 | 77 | 77 | 92 | 92 | 109 | 94 | 90 | 73 | 78 | 92 | 78 | 93 | 70 | 97 | 78 | 87 | 104 | 95 |
| DUVAL | 93 | 88 | 89 | 79 | 92 | 92 | 97 | 96 | 94 | 86 | 89 | 89 | 86 | 92 | 79 | 97 | 81 | 93 | 98 | 101 |
| EASTLAND | 94 | 65 | 74 | 75 | 92 | 91 | 108 | 93 | 91 | 75 | 78 | 89 | 78 | 91 | 69 | 96 | 78 | 87 | 102 | 94 |
| ECTOR | 97 | 94 | 95 | 91 | 98 | 97 | 100 | 98 | 96 | 95 | 97 | 96 | 94 | 98 | 84 | 98 | 93 | 97 | 98 | 100 |
| EDWARDS | 97 | 80 | 83 | 84 | 93 | 93 | 114 | 98 | 93 | 82 | 86 | 95 | 85 | 97 | 76 | 98 | 83 | 92 | 103 | 102 |
| ELLIS | 100 | 93 | 90 | 93 | 97 | 96 | 107 | 99 | 99 | 96 | 98 | 101 | 95 | 102 | 82 | 100 | 97 | 98 | 99 | 102 |
| EL PASO | 96 | 101 | 92 | 91 | 96 | 96 | 93 | 98 | 98 | 93 | 98 | 96 | 94 | 96 | 85 | 99 | 92 | 99 | 97 | 102 |
| ERATH | 96 | 81 | 88 | 84 | 96 | 93 | 107 | 93 | 91 | 83 | 86 | 93 | 85 | 95 | 76 | 95 | 85 | 90 | 100 | 97 |
| FALLS | 95 | 69 | 80 | 78 | 95 | 91 | 103 | 95 | 90 | 79 | 78 | 91 | 81 | 92 | 73 | 96 | 81 | 88 | 97 | 95 |
| FANNIN | 96 | 73 | 83 | 80 | 95 | 93 | 108 | 95 | 93 | 82 | 83 | 93 | 84 | 95 | 74 | 96 | 83 | 89 | 101 | 96 |
| FAYETTE | 96 | 69 | 78 | 78 | 93 | 92 | 109 | 95 | 92 | 78 | 81 | 92 | 81 | 94 | 71 | 97 | 81 | 88 | 102 | 96 |
| FISHER | 96 | 63 | 72 | 77 | 91 | 91 | 110 | 94 | 90 | 72 | 77 | 93 | 77 | 93 | 68 | 97 | 78 | 87 | 104 | 95 |
| FLOYD | 96 | 77 | 81 | 80 | 91 | 91 | 104 | 96 | 92 | 79 | 84 | 93 | 83 | 94 | 74 | 97 | 80 | 91 | 102 | 100 |
| TEXAS | 99 | 100 | 96 | 98 | 99 | 99 | 101 | 99 | 99 | 98 | 100 | 100 | 97 | 100 | 87 | 99 | 98 | 100 | 98 | 102 |
| UNITED STATES | 100 | 100 | 100 | 100 | 100 | 100 | 100 | 100 | 100 | 100 | 100 | 100 | 100 | 100 | 100 | 100 | 100 | 100 | 100 | 100 |

| COUNTY | FIPS Code | MSA Code | DMA Code | POPULATION 1990 | POPULATION 2000 | POPULATION 2005 | 1990-2000 ANNUAL CHANGE % Rate | 1990-2000 ANNUAL CHANGE State Rank | RACE (%) White 1990 | RACE (%) White 2000 | RACE (%) Black 1990 | RACE (%) Black 2000 | RACE (%) Asian/Pacific 1990 | RACE (%) Asian/Pacific 2000 |
|---|---|---|---|---|---|---|---|---|---|---|---|---|---|---|
| FOARD | 155 | 0000 | 627 | 1,794 | 1,603 | 1,519 | -1.1 | 231 | 86.5 | 82.7 | 4.9 | 6.0 | 0.2 | 0.3 |
| FORT BEND | 157 | 3360 | 618 | 225,421 | 369,826 | 450,208 | 4.9 | 6 | 62.6 | 57.7 | 20.7 | 20.6 | 6.4 | 9.2 |
| FRANKLIN | 159 | 0000 | 709 | 7,802 | 10,157 | 11,234 | 2.6 | 34 | 91.5 | 89.9 | 4.5 | 4.7 | 0.2 | 0.4 |
| FREESTONE | 161 | 0000 | 623 | 15,818 | 17,698 | 17,972 | 1.1 | 86 | 78.3 | 73.7 | 19.0 | 21.5 | 0.2 | 0.4 |
| FRIO | 163 | 0000 | 641 | 13,472 | 15,974 | 16,270 | 1.7 | 65 | 67.7 | 60.6 | 1.4 | 8.3 | 0.3 | 0.3 |
| GAINES | 165 | 0000 | 651 | 14,123 | 14,775 | 14,824 | 0.4 | 143 | 73.5 | 68.2 | 2.4 | 2.4 | 0.1 | 0.1 |
| GALVESTON | 167 | 2920 | 618 | 217,399 | 251,546 | 267,018 | 1.4 | 74 | 75.5 | 72.5 | 17.6 | 18.3 | 1.6 | 2.5 |
| GARZA | 169 | 0000 | 651 | 5,143 | 4,450 | 4,132 | -1.4 | 238 | 89.2 | 88.0 | 6.4 | 6.7 | 0.4 | 0.5 |
| GILLESPIE | 171 | 0000 | 641 | 17,204 | 20,731 | 22,402 | 1.8 | 60 | 94.9 | 93.4 | 0.2 | 0.4 | 0.2 | 0.2 |
| GLASSCOCK | 173 | 0000 | 633 | 1,447 | 1,470 | 1,591 | 0.2 | 164 | 79.9 | 75.3 | 0.0 | 0.0 | 0.0 | 0.0 |
| GOLIAD | 175 | 0000 | 641 | 5,980 | 7,310 | 8,194 | 2.0 | 51 | 82.8 | 80.6 | 6.8 | 6.9 | 0.1 | 0.2 |
| GONZALES | 177 | 0000 | 641 | 17,205 | 17,616 | 17,852 | 0.2 | 164 | 75.7 | 72.8 | 10.0 | 10.1 | 0.1 | 0.2 |
| GRAY | 179 | 0000 | 634 | 23,967 | 23,093 | 22,094 | -0.4 | 205 | 90.0 | 85.8 | 3.8 | 5.7 | 0.5 | 0.7 |
| GRAYSON | 181 | 7640 | 657 | 95,021 | 105,315 | 113,115 | 1.0 | 98 | 90.0 | 88.5 | 6.9 | 7.6 | 0.4 | 0.7 |
| GREGG | 183 | 4420 | 709 | 104,948 | 113,679 | 116,193 | 0.8 | 111 | 78.0 | 75.8 | 19.0 | 20.3 | 0.5 | 0.7 |
| GRIMES | 185 | 0000 | 618 | 18,828 | 24,698 | 27,943 | 2.7 | 30 | 68.4 | 65.9 | 24.5 | 25.0 | 0.2 | 0.3 |
| GUADALUPE | 187 | 7240 | 641 | 64,873 | 85,380 | 98,024 | 2.7 | 30 | 81.6 | 78.5 | 5.6 | 5.9 | 0.7 | 1.1 |
| HALE | 189 | 0000 | 651 | 34,671 | 36,462 | 36,315 | 0.5 | 133 | 68.7 | 64.3 | 5.3 | 5.4 | 0.4 | 0.6 |
| HALL | 191 | 0000 | 634 | 3,905 | 3,557 | 3,378 | -0.9 | 224 | 74.5 | 69.9 | 7.8 | 8.1 | 0.2 | 0.2 |
| HAMILTON | 193 | 0000 | 623 | 7,733 | 7,619 | 7,629 | -0.1 | 183 | 95.6 | 93.7 | 0.0 | 0.1 | 0.3 | 0.5 |
| HANSFORD | 195 | 0000 | 634 | 5,848 | 5,442 | 5,618 | -0.7 | 219 | 82.4 | 78.4 | 0.0 | 0.0 | 0.2 | 0.4 |
| HARDEMAN | 197 | 0000 | 627 | 5,283 | 4,263 | 3,805 | -2.1 | 253 | 83.8 | 79.8 | 6.1 | 6.6 | 0.3 | 0.4 |
| HARDIN | 199 | 0840 | 692 | 41,320 | 50,266 | 53,229 | 1.9 | 54 | 90.7 | 89.5 | 8.4 | 9.3 | 0.1 | 0.2 |
| HARRIS | 201 | 3360 | 618 | 2,818,199 | 3,302,269 | 3,543,295 | 1.6 | 68 | 64.7 | 60.4 | 19.2 | 19.2 | 3.9 | 5.7 |
| HARRISON | 203 | 4420 | 612 | 57,483 | 59,966 | 60,845 | 0.4 | 143 | 70.3 | 67.6 | 27.9 | 30.0 | 0.3 | 0.4 |
| HARTLEY | 205 | 0000 | 634 | 3,634 | 5,313 | 5,565 | 3.8 | 15 | 96.6 | 82.2 | 0.2 | 10.7 | 0.2 | 0.2 |
| HASKELL | 207 | 0000 | 662 | 6,820 | 5,877 | 5,422 | -1.4 | 238 | 80.4 | 75.5 | 3.6 | 3.9 | 0.2 | 0.4 |
| HAYS | 209 | 0640 | 635 | 65,614 | 96,330 | 114,064 | 3.8 | 15 | 84.4 | 80.9 | 3.4 | 3.6 | 0.7 | 0.9 |
| HEMPHILL | 211 | 0000 | 634 | 3,720 | 3,433 | 3,247 | -0.8 | 221 | 94.2 | 93.2 | 0.2 | 0.4 | 0.1 | 0.1 |
| HENDERSON | 213 | 1920 | 623 | 58,543 | 72,666 | 81,307 | 2.1 | 46 | 89.2 | 87.6 | 8.1 | 8.8 | 0.2 | 0.4 |
| HIDALGO | 215 | 4880 | 636 | 383,545 | 549,938 | 625,504 | 3.6 | 19 | 74.8 | 73.8 | 0.2 | 0.2 | 0.3 | 0.4 |
| HILL | 217 | 0000 | 623 | 27,146 | 31,578 | 34,152 | 1.5 | 71 | 87.2 | 85.1 | 9.3 | 10.1 | 0.1 | 0.2 |
| HOCKLEY | 219 | 0000 | 651 | 24,199 | 23,151 | 22,069 | -0.4 | 205 | 78.3 | 74.9 | 4.2 | 4.6 | 0.1 | 0.2 |
| HOOD | 221 | 2800 | 623 | 28,981 | 40,091 | 46,844 | 3.2 | 26 | 96.8 | 95.9 | 0.2 | 0.3 | 0.6 | 1.0 |
| HOPKINS | 223 | 0000 | 623 | 28,833 | 30,831 | 31,943 | 0.7 | 118 | 88.0 | 86.3 | 8.6 | 9.3 | 0.2 | 0.4 |
| HOUSTON | 225 | 0000 | 709 | 21,375 | 22,386 | 23,166 | 0.5 | 133 | 67.2 | 65.0 | 29.6 | 30.8 | 0.2 | 0.3 |
| HOWARD | 227 | 0000 | 633 | 32,343 | 31,495 | 30,494 | -0.3 | 194 | 78.2 | 74.1 | 3.8 | 4.0 | 0.5 | 0.7 |
| HUDSPETH | 229 | 0000 | 765 | 2,915 | 3,271 | 3,445 | 1.1 | 86 | 80.4 | 78.9 | 0.5 | 0.6 | 0.1 | 0.1 |
| HUNT | 231 | 1920 | 623 | 64,343 | 73,096 | 79,932 | 1.3 | 78 | 86.6 | 84.3 | 10.6 | 11.7 | 0.5 | 1.0 |
| HUTCHINSON | 233 | 0000 | 634 | 25,689 | 23,510 | 22,509 | -0.9 | 224 | 88.2 | 85.2 | 2.6 | 3.0 | 0.4 | 0.6 |
| IRION | 235 | 0000 | 661 | 1,629 | 1,688 | 1,661 | 0.3 | 155 | 98.8 | 98.6 | 0.1 | 0.1 | 0.0 | 0.0 |
| JACK | 237 | 0000 | 623 | 6,981 | 7,563 | 7,972 | 0.8 | 111 | 96.7 | 95.7 | 0.7 | 0.9 | 0.1 | 0.2 |
| JACKSON | 239 | 0000 | 618 | 13,039 | 13,649 | 13,656 | 0.4 | 143 | 83.3 | 81.1 | 9.3 | 9.6 | 0.1 | 0.1 |
| JASPER | 241 | 0000 | 692 | 31,102 | 33,658 | 34,455 | 0.8 | 111 | 79.6 | 77.8 | 18.9 | 20.2 | 0.1 | 0.2 |
| JEFF DAVIS | 243 | 0000 | 633 | 1,946 | 2,491 | 2,866 | 2.4 | 40 | 85.9 | 83.5 | 0.4 | 0.6 | 0.2 | 0.2 |
| JEFFERSON | 245 | 0840 | 692 | 239,397 | 241,017 | 239,451 | 0.1 | 173 | 64.4 | 60.7 | 31.1 | 33.2 | 2.1 | 3.1 |
| JIM HOGG | 247 | 0000 | 600 | 5,109 | 4,964 | 4,921 | -0.3 | 194 | 85.6 | 85.4 | 0.1 | 0.1 | 0.1 | 0.1 |
| JIM WELLS | 249 | 0000 | 600 | 37,679 | 40,402 | 41,376 | 0.7 | 118 | 75.6 | 73.8 | 0.6 | 0.6 | 0.3 | 0.4 |
| JOHNSON | 251 | 2800 | 623 | 97,165 | 126,763 | 147,269 | 2.6 | 34 | 93.0 | 90.9 | 2.6 | 3.1 | 0.5 | 0.8 |
| JONES | 253 | 0000 | 662 | 16,490 | 18,915 | 19,304 | 1.3 | 78 | 83.6 | 72.9 | 4.0 | 9.2 | 0.2 | 0.3 |
| KARNES | 255 | 0000 | 641 | 12,455 | 15,060 | 14,802 | 1.9 | 54 | 76.7 | 67.7 | 2.9 | 10.4 | 0.1 | 0.2 |
| KAUFMAN | 257 | 1920 | 623 | 52,220 | 70,317 | 81,457 | 2.9 | 29 | 82.0 | 79.9 | 14.0 | 14.8 | 0.4 | 0.7 |
| KENDALL | 259 | 0000 | 641 | 14,589 | 22,568 | 26,093 | 4.3 | 11 | 93.8 | 92.5 | 0.4 | 0.6 | 0.3 | 0.4 |
| KENEDY | 261 | 0000 | 600 | 460 | 433 | 433 | -0.6 | 216 | 82.2 | 81.5 | 0.0 | 0.0 | 0.0 | 0.0 |
| KENT | 263 | 0000 | 651 | 1,010 | 841 | 841 | -1.8 | 247 | 89.3 | 86.7 | 0.6 | 1.0 | 0.0 | 0.0 |
| KERR | 265 | 0000 | 641 | 36,304 | 43,884 | 47,147 | 1.9 | 54 | 90.5 | 88.0 | 2.2 | 2.7 | 0.4 | 0.6 |
| KIMBLE | 267 | 0000 | 661 | 4,122 | 4,275 | 4,473 | 0.4 | 143 | 88.6 | 85.5 | 0.0 | 0.1 | 0.2 | 0.4 |
| KING | 269 | 0000 | 627 | 354 | 306 | 306 | -1.4 | 238 | 89.5 | 88.9 | 0.0 | 0.0 | 0.0 | 0.0 |
| KINNEY | 271 | 0000 | 641 | 3,119 | 3,481 | 3,587 | 1.1 | 86 | 88.0 | 86.2 | 1.8 | 2.2 | 0.3 | 0.4 |
| KLEBERG | 273 | 0000 | 600 | 30,274 | 29,429 | 28,201 | -0.3 | 194 | 68.2 | 65.3 | 3.3 | 3.0 | 1.4 | 1.6 |
| KNOX | 275 | 0000 | 662 | 4,837 | 4,002 | 3,634 | -1.8 | 247 | 77.8 | 73.8 | 7.0 | 7.0 | 0.1 | 0.1 |
| LAMAR | 277 | 0000 | 623 | 43,949 | 46,272 | 47,359 | 0.5 | 133 | 83.8 | 82.1 | 14.6 | 15.8 | 0.3 | 0.5 |
| LAMB | 279 | 0000 | 651 | 15,072 | 14,750 | 14,672 | -0.2 | 189 | 86.5 | 85.0 | 5.5 | 5.4 | 0.2 | 0.2 |
| LAMPASAS | 281 | 0000 | 625 | 13,521 | 17,841 | 18,684 | 2.7 | 30 | 90.0 | 86.9 | 2.0 | 2.3 | 1.0 | 1.7 |
| LA SALLE | 283 | 0000 | 641 | 5,254 | 5,981 | 5,924 | 1.3 | 78 | 67.9 | 61.0 | 1.0 | 8.3 | 0.2 | 0.5 |
| LAVACA | 285 | 0000 | 641 | 18,690 | 18,976 | 19,305 | 0.1 | 173 | 88.5 | 86.3 | 7.2 | 7.9 | 0.1 | 0.1 |
| LEE | 287 | 0000 | 635 | 12,854 | 14,985 | 15,559 | 1.5 | 71 | 78.2 | 75.0 | 13.8 | 14.9 | 0.1 | 0.2 |
| LEON | 289 | 0000 | 625 | 12,665 | 15,163 | 16,601 | 1.8 | 60 | 84.7 | 82.9 | 12.8 | 13.8 | 0.1 | 0.1 |
| LIBERTY | 291 | 3360 | 618 | 52,726 | 68,681 | 76,251 | 2.6 | 34 | 83.5 | 79.5 | 13.1 | 15.5 | 0.2 | 0.3 |
| LIMESTONE | 293 | 0000 | 625 | 20,946 | 21,425 | 21,209 | 0.2 | 164 | 74.9 | 71.7 | 19.8 | 21.1 | 0.2 | 0.3 |
| LIPSCOMB | 295 | 0000 | 634 | 3,143 | 3,041 | 3,131 | -0.3 | 194 | 98.4 | 98.1 | 0.0 | 0.0 | 0.4 | 0.5 |
| LIVE OAK | 297 | 0000 | 600 | 9,556 | 10,093 | 10,026 | 0.5 | 133 | 87.0 | 84.4 | 0.1 | 0.2 | 0.3 | 0.5 |
| LLANO | 299 | 0000 | 635 | 11,631 | 14,160 | 15,750 | 1.9 | 54 | 97.9 | 97.3 | 0.2 | 0.5 | 0.2 | 0.3 |
| LOVING | 301 | 0000 | 633 | 107 | 113 | 113 | 0.5 | 133 | 86.9 | 85.0 | 0.0 | 0.0 | 0.0 | 0.0 |
| LUBBOCK | 303 | 4600 | 651 | 222,636 | 227,339 | 224,460 | 0.2 | 164 | 79.1 | 75.4 | 7.7 | 8.0 | 1.2 | 1.7 |
| LYNN | 305 | 0000 | 651 | 6,758 | 6,665 | 6,699 | -0.1 | 183 | 77.2 | 74.0 | 3.3 | 3.3 | 0.2 | 0.2 |
| MCCULLOCH | 307 | 0000 | 661 | 8,778 | 8,851 | 9,107 | 0.1 | 173 | 89.5 | 86.9 | 1.9 | 2.4 | 0.1 | 0.1 |
| TEXAS | | | | | | | 1.8 | | 75.2 | 72.3 | 11.9 | 11.9 | 1.9 | 2.8 |
| UNITED STATES | | | | | | | 1.0 | | 80.3 | 77.9 | 12.1 | 12.4 | 2.9 | 3.9 |

# POPULATION COMPOSITION

| COUNTY | % HISPANIC ORIGIN 1990 | % HISPANIC ORIGIN 2000 | 2000 AGE DISTRIBUTION (%) 0-4 | 5-9 | 10-14 | 15-19 | 20-24 | 25-44 | 45-64 | 65-84 | 85+ | 18+ | MEDIAN AGE 1990 | MEDIAN AGE 2000 | 2000 Males/ Females (×100) |
|---|---|---|---|---|---|---|---|---|---|---|---|---|---|---|---|
| FOARD | 13.0 | 18.0 | 6.7 | 7.1 | 6.9 | 6.8 | 4.9 | 21.2 | 23.8 | 18.3 | 4.4 | 75.2 | 40.9 | 42.4 | 88.1 |
| FORT BEND | 19.5 | 24.1 | 8.7 | 9.2 | 9.0 | 8.2 | 5.6 | 32.2 | 21.3 | 5.3 | 0.5 | 67.9 | 30.5 | 32.5 | 100.3 |
| FRANKLIN | 4.6 | 6.5 | 6.5 | 6.9 | 7.1 | 7.0 | 4.9 | 23.0 | 26.8 | 15.4 | 2.4 | 74.8 | 37.8 | 41.1 | 96.8 |
| FREESTONE | 3.9 | 7.8 | 6.8 | 6.8 | 7.0 | 7.6 | 6.8 | 23.8 | 23.4 | 14.7 | 3.3 | 74.3 | 36.6 | 38.9 | 94.2 |
| FRIO | 72.4 | 73.3 | 9.0 | 8.4 | 8.5 | 8.6 | 8.1 | 28.7 | 18.7 | 8.8 | 1.3 | 68.4 | 28.5 | 30.3 | 112.9 |
| GAINES | 32.6 | 40.0 | 10.5 | 10.0 | 9.6 | 9.1 | 7.1 | 24.6 | 19.7 | 8.4 | 1.0 | 63.7 | 27.8 | 28.1 | 101.8 |
| GALVESTON | 14.2 | 18.7 | 7.3 | 7.4 | 7.4 | 7.5 | 6.7 | 28.7 | 23.6 | 10.4 | 1.1 | 73.3 | 32.6 | 35.9 | 96.2 |
| GARZA | 28.3 | 35.1 | 8.5 | 8.5 | 8.7 | 8.2 | 6.0 | 22.5 | 22.5 | 12.9 | 2.2 | 68.8 | 32.9 | 35.3 | 93.4 |
| GILLESPIE | 14.1 | 18.0 | 6.2 | 6.6 | 6.7 | 6.5 | 4.3 | 21.1 | 24.8 | 20.3 | 3.7 | 76.2 | 42.1 | 44.1 | 93.4 |
| GLASSCOCK | 29.3 | 36.3 | 9.9 | 10.8 | 8.6 | 9.0 | 4.9 | 25.8 | 23.8 | 6.6 | 0.6 | 64.6 | 28.2 | 31.2 | 103.0 |
| GOLIAD | 35.9 | 43.6 | 7.1 | 7.5 | 7.4 | 7.8 | 5.1 | 24.5 | 24.8 | 13.6 | 2.2 | 72.7 | 35.9 | 38.7 | 93.6 |
| GONZALES | 35.7 | 43.0 | 8.2 | 8.1 | 7.9 | 8.0 | 6.1 | 23.3 | 21.8 | 14.0 | 2.6 | 70.9 | 34.0 | 36.1 | 96.0 |
| GRAY | 7.9 | 11.5 | 6.5 | 7.0 | 7.0 | 7.4 | 5.5 | 24.8 | 24.5 | 14.8 | 2.4 | 74.6 | 36.1 | 39.5 | 96.6 |
| GRAYSON | 2.9 | 4.4 | 6.6 | 6.8 | 7.1 | 7.6 | 6.1 | 25.6 | 24.7 | 13.3 | 2.2 | 75.1 | 35.0 | 38.6 | 92.3 |
| GREGG | 3.6 | 5.1 | 7.3 | 7.4 | 7.5 | 8.0 | 6.6 | 26.8 | 23.1 | 11.3 | 1.8 | 73.2 | 32.8 | 36.0 | 93.0 |
| GRIMES | 14.1 | 18.3 | 7.0 | 7.3 | 7.2 | 8.9 | 8.7 | 27.9 | 21.1 | 10.3 | 1.6 | 73.6 | 32.5 | 33.3 | 122.6 |
| GUADALUPE | 29.7 | 36.4 | 7.8 | 7.7 | 7.8 | 8.0 | 6.7 | 27.4 | 22.8 | 10.6 | 1.3 | 72.0 | 32.4 | 35.0 | 97.3 |
| HALE | 41.6 | 48.8 | 9.4 | 8.9 | 8.4 | 8.8 | 7.7 | 25.0 | 19.9 | 10.3 | 1.6 | 68.0 | 29.6 | 30.5 | 98.1 |
| HALL | 18.6 | 23.4 | 6.1 | 6.3 | 6.8 | 7.2 | 4.8 | 20.3 | 24.7 | 19.7 | 4.2 | 76.3 | 42.9 | 43.8 | 90.7 |
| HAMILTON | 5.2 | 7.8 | 5.9 | 6.3 | 6.5 | 6.8 | 4.9 | 21.7 | 23.0 | 19.5 | 5.4 | 77.1 | 43.5 | 43.5 | 95.7 |
| HANSFORD | 20.1 | 24.9 | 7.8 | 8.5 | 8.2 | 8.1 | 5.3 | 23.8 | 24.0 | 12.4 | 1.9 | 70.0 | 32.9 | 36.7 | 99.3 |
| HARDEMAN | 11.1 | 15.5 | 7.0 | 7.1 | 7.6 | 7.6 | 5.5 | 20.9 | 23.9 | 16.7 | 3.8 | 73.7 | 38.9 | 40.7 | 92.0 |
| HARDIN | 1.6 | 2.8 | 6.9 | 7.6 | 8.0 | 8.3 | 5.8 | 26.1 | 25.3 | 10.7 | 1.3 | 72.4 | 33.1 | 36.8 | 97.2 |
| HARRIS | 22.9 | 28.3 | 8.4 | 7.9 | 7.7 | 7.5 | 7.1 | 32.1 | 21.5 | 6.9 | 0.8 | 71.5 | 30.3 | 32.9 | 97.9 |
| HARRISON | 2.2 | 3.3 | 6.8 | 7.5 | 7.8 | 8.9 | 6.8 | 25.8 | 23.7 | 10.9 | 1.8 | 72.7 | 32.9 | 35.9 | 93.4 |
| HARTLEY | 5.5 | 15.0 | 5.4 | 6.1 | 6.9 | 7.5 | 6.3 | 28.1 | 26.2 | 11.3 | 2.3 | 76.2 | 37.4 | 38.8 | 119.0 |
| HASKELL | 19.2 | 24.9 | 6.6 | 6.8 | 7.2 | 6.7 | 4.8 | 21.2 | 23.5 | 19.4 | 3.8 | 75.1 | 40.4 | 42.5 | 97.0 |
| HAYS | 27.8 | 35.4 | 6.8 | 6.8 | 6.8 | 10.9 | 14.5 | 27.6 | 18.9 | 6.8 | 0.9 | 75.5 | 26.6 | 28.4 | 100.8 |
| HEMPHILL | 11.1 | 13.3 | 7.3 | 8.0 | 8.6 | 7.9 | 5.2 | 25.0 | 24.8 | 11.1 | 2.0 | 70.7 | 33.7 | 37.2 | 97.9 |
| HENDERSON | 4.0 | 5.8 | 6.0 | 6.3 | 6.7 | 7.0 | 5.3 | 22.3 | 27.2 | 17.5 | 1.7 | 76.9 | 38.9 | 42.3 | 95.2 |
| HIDALGO | 85.2 | 88.6 | 9.7 | 9.4 | 8.8 | 9.4 | 9.4 | 26.8 | 17.1 | 8.4 | 1.1 | 66.2 | 26.1 | 27.0 | 95.2 |
| HILL | 8.2 | 11.5 | 6.6 | 6.9 | 7.1 | 8.0 | 5.7 | 22.8 | 24.5 | 15.5 | 2.8 | 74.5 | 37.9 | 39.9 | 93.6 |
| HOCKLEY | 31.6 | 37.4 | 8.8 | 8.9 | 8.5 | 10.5 | 7.5 | 25.1 | 20.0 | 9.6 | 1.2 | 68.5 | 29.1 | 30.1 | 97.6 |
| HOOD | 4.7 | 6.2 | 6.4 | 6.9 | 6.8 | 6.7 | 4.6 | 24.0 | 26.4 | 16.6 | 1.5 | 75.6 | 37.0 | 41.5 | 98.5 |
| HOPKINS | 4.9 | 6.6 | 7.0 | 7.2 | 7.5 | 7.5 | 5.7 | 25.8 | 24.3 | 12.9 | 2.2 | 73.8 | 34.4 | 38.0 | 97.6 |
| HOUSTON | 4.5 | 6.3 | 6.2 | 6.7 | 6.8 | 7.9 | 6.0 | 26.6 | 22.4 | 14.8 | 2.6 | 75.3 | 36.0 | 37.8 | 106.5 |
| HOWARD | 26.6 | 32.6 | 7.6 | 7.4 | 7.4 | 7.9 | 6.0 | 25.5 | 23.2 | 13.1 | 1.8 | 73.0 | 34.0 | 36.8 | 102.2 |
| HUDSPETH | 66.4 | 71.9 | 8.7 | 8.5 | 8.2 | 9.1 | 7.4 | 25.6 | 21.7 | 9.5 | 1.4 | 68.9 | 29.7 | 31.2 | 106.2 |
| HUNT | 4.5 | 6.5 | 7.1 | 7.1 | 7.3 | 8.1 | 7.1 | 25.4 | 24.5 | 11.6 | 1.7 | 73.7 | 33.7 | 36.6 | 96.4 |
| HUTCHINSON | 9.8 | 13.1 | 7.1 | 7.7 | 8.0 | 8.4 | 5.7 | 24.4 | 23.2 | 13.9 | 1.6 | 72.0 | 34.1 | 37.2 | 98.4 |
| IRION | 23.6 | 29.3 | 8.1 | 7.6 | 7.8 | 7.4 | 5.0 | 24.4 | 26.1 | 12.3 | 1.4 | 71.7 | 34.1 | 37.6 | 99.5 |
| JACK | 3.3 | 4.9 | 7.0 | 7.4 | 7.6 | 7.2 | 4.7 | 23.1 | 25.6 | 14.6 | 2.7 | 73.2 | 37.1 | 40.2 | 95.6 |
| JACKSON | 21.3 | 27.0 | 7.0 | 7.7 | 7.5 | 8.1 | 5.1 | 23.4 | 24.4 | 14.7 | 2.1 | 72.7 | 35.7 | 38.9 | 93.8 |
| JASPER | 1.9 | 2.9 | 6.6 | 7.3 | 7.7 | 8.2 | 5.7 | 23.7 | 25.1 | 13.8 | 2.0 | 73.1 | 35.0 | 38.7 | 92.6 |
| JEFF DAVIS | 39.6 | 46.3 | 5.9 | 5.7 | 7.7 | 7.6 | 5.5 | 22.0 | 28.3 | 15.1 | 2.0 | 75.0 | 38.6 | 41.6 | 107.2 |
| JEFFERSON | 5.3 | 7.3 | 7.0 | 7.2 | 7.4 | 7.6 | 6.7 | 27.1 | 23.0 | 12.3 | 1.7 | 74.0 | 33.4 | 36.6 | 94.4 |
| JIM HOGG | 91.2 | 93.0 | 10.1 | 9.1 | 8.7 | 8.5 | 6.9 | 23.8 | 20.8 | 10.6 | 1.6 | 67.2 | 30.6 | 30.9 | 95.9 |
| JIM WELLS | 72.2 | 77.7 | 8.9 | 8.6 | 8.4 | 8.9 | 6.9 | 25.0 | 21.4 | 10.4 | 1.5 | 68.6 | 30.6 | 32.2 | 97.3 |
| JOHNSON | 7.7 | 10.7 | 7.5 | 7.7 | 7.9 | 8.0 | 6.3 | 28.1 | 24.2 | 9.0 | 1.3 | 72.0 | 32.1 | 35.4 | 99.7 |
| JONES | 16.9 | 24.5 | 6.3 | 6.7 | 6.8 | 7.8 | 6.3 | 25.7 | 23.4 | 14.0 | 3.0 | 75.1 | 36.5 | 38.5 | 104.6 |
| KARNES | 47.5 | 50.2 | 7.8 | 7.8 | 7.2 | 8.3 | 6.9 | 25.9 | 19.6 | 13.8 | 2.7 | 72.0 | 33.6 | 34.9 | 110.6 |
| KAUFMAN | 6.4 | 8.7 | 7.4 | 7.8 | 8.0 | 8.1 | 5.9 | 26.6 | 24.7 | 10.0 | 1.5 | 71.6 | 32.9 | 36.1 | 96.3 |
| KENDALL | 16.4 | 19.8 | 6.9 | 7.1 | 7.3 | 7.3 | 5.0 | 25.2 | 26.2 | 12.7 | 2.2 | 73.9 | 36.8 | 39.6 | 96.1 |
| KENEDY | 78.7 | 82.9 | 7.9 | 7.9 | 8.8 | 8.8 | 7.6 | 25.4 | 20.8 | 12.2 | 0.7 | 70.7 | 32.3 | 34.1 | 92.4 |
| KENT | 11.9 | 14.9 | 5.7 | 6.9 | 6.9 | 7.5 | 3.7 | 19.7 | 25.3 | 20.8 | 3.4 | 75.4 | 40.4 | 44.7 | 97.0 |
| KERR | 16.5 | 21.2 | 6.3 | 6.3 | 6.7 | 7.1 | 5.2 | 21.5 | 23.6 | 20.2 | 3.1 | 76.3 | 40.5 | 42.6 | 91.5 |
| KIMBLE | 18.7 | 24.1 | 5.9 | 6.2 | 6.9 | 7.5 | 5.1 | 19.9 | 27.2 | 18.2 | 3.2 | 75.9 | 41.0 | 43.8 | 98.0 |
| KING | 15.0 | 16.3 | 6.9 | 6.9 | 6.2 | 7.5 | 7.2 | 29.4 | 27.1 | 8.8 | 0.0 | 73.5 | 32.5 | 35.5 | 100.0 |
| KINNEY | 50.3 | 56.6 | 6.8 | 6.5 | 6.7 | 6.5 | 5.6 | 21.4 | 23.1 | 21.6 | 1.8 | 75.6 | 39.8 | 42.2 | 105.4 |
| KLEBERG | 61.2 | 68.3 | 8.7 | 8.1 | 8.0 | 9.3 | 9.2 | 29.3 | 17.8 | 8.6 | 1.1 | 70.8 | 27.7 | 29.4 | 99.8 |
| KNOX | 22.5 | 28.6 | 7.5 | 7.7 | 7.7 | 7.4 | 4.9 | 21.3 | 22.6 | 17.1 | 3.7 | 72.0 | 37.7 | 40.0 | 96.7 |
| LAMAR | 1.1 | 2.1 | 6.9 | 7.0 | 7.5 | 7.8 | 5.9 | 24.8 | 24.4 | 13.3 | 2.3 | 74.1 | 35.1 | 38.3 | 91.4 |
| LAMB | 36.6 | 43.7 | 8.1 | 8.5 | 8.0 | 8.2 | 6.0 | 22.3 | 22.2 | 14.3 | 2.4 | 70.2 | 34.1 | 36.1 | 94.6 |
| LAMPASAS | 13.0 | 17.5 | 7.7 | 7.4 | 7.7 | 7.5 | 5.4 | 24.0 | 25.5 | 12.5 | 2.2 | 72.4 | 35.4 | 38.1 | 95.7 |
| LA SALLE | 77.4 | 75.8 | 8.8 | 8.7 | 8.2 | 8.9 | 8.2 | 26.4 | 19.4 | 10.1 | 1.3 | 68.5 | 30.2 | 30.4 | 107.0 |
| LAVACA | 8.5 | 12.1 | 6.3 | 6.8 | 7.1 | 7.1 | 5.0 | 22.4 | 24.2 | 17.5 | 3.5 | 75.2 | 39.3 | 41.6 | 94.8 |
| LEE | 11.0 | 14.4 | 7.4 | 7.5 | 7.8 | 9.6 | 5.4 | 24.4 | 22.8 | 12.8 | 2.3 | 70.7 | 33.6 | 36.5 | 102.0 |
| LEON | 4.0 | 5.7 | 6.7 | 7.0 | 7.1 | 7.2 | 5.0 | 22.4 | 25.0 | 17.2 | 2.4 | 74.7 | 37.6 | 41.1 | 95.5 |
| LIBERTY | 5.5 | 8.5 | 7.1 | 7.4 | 7.8 | 8.1 | 6.6 | 27.6 | 24.0 | 10.2 | 1.2 | 72.7 | 32.5 | 35.6 | 105.2 |
| LIMESTONE | 7.0 | 10.1 | 6.9 | 7.0 | 7.5 | 7.3 | 5.7 | 25.8 | 23.4 | 13.8 | 2.6 | 73.9 | 36.2 | 38.2 | 94.7 |
| LIPSCOMB | 12.1 | 14.8 | 6.8 | 7.5 | 7.6 | 7.6 | 4.2 | 23.5 | 25.9 | 15.1 | 1.9 | 72.5 | 35.8 | 40.3 | 101.7 |
| LIVE OAK | 34.8 | 42.1 | 7.0 | 7.2 | 7.6 | 7.3 | 5.4 | 23.0 | 26.1 | 14.5 | 1.9 | 73.5 | 36.4 | 39.7 | 94.7 |
| LLANO | 3.9 | 5.2 | 4.2 | 4.6 | 4.9 | 4.7 | 3.9 | 16.6 | 25.0 | 31.8 | 4.4 | 83.2 | 55.4 | 54.3 | 90.1 |
| LOVING | 13.1 | 15.0 | 4.4 | 7.1 | 5.3 | 7.1 | 4.4 | 25.7 | 29.2 | 16.8 | 0.0 | 78.8 | 35.4 | 41.8 | 130.6 |
| LUBBOCK | 22.9 | 28.9 | 7.6 | 7.3 | 7.0 | 8.8 | 9.7 | 30.3 | 19.1 | 9.0 | 1.2 | 74.1 | 28.8 | 31.7 | 96.8 |
| LYNN | 41.7 | 48.8 | 8.8 | 8.7 | 8.5 | 7.8 | 6.1 | 23.2 | 22.7 | 12.3 | 1.8 | 68.7 | 32.5 | 34.4 | 96.7 |
| MCCULLOCH | 26.4 | 33.5 | 7.4 | 7.3 | 7.8 | 7.9 | 5.6 | 22.2 | 22.9 | 15.4 | 3.5 | 72.4 | 38.1 | 38.9 | 93.3 |
| TEXAS | 25.6 | 30.4 | 8.1 | 7.8 | 7.7 | 8.0 | 7.4 | 29.6 | 21.4 | 8.8 | 1.2 | 71.8 | 30.8 | 33.2 | 97.3 |
| UNITED STATES | 9.0 | 11.8 | 6.9 | 7.2 | 7.2 | 7.2 | 6.7 | 29.9 | 22.2 | 11.1 | 1.6 | 74.6 | 32.9 | 35.7 | 95.6 |

| COUNTY | HOUSEHOLDS 1990 | HOUSEHOLDS 2000 | HOUSEHOLDS 2005 | % Annual Rate 1990-2000 | 2000 Average HH Size | FAMILIES 1990 | FAMILIES 2000 | % Annual Rate 1990-2000 | MEDIAN HOUSEHOLD INCOME 2000 | 2005 | 2000 National Rank | 2000 State Rank |
|---|---|---|---|---|---|---|---|---|---|---|---|---|
| FOARD | 739 | 705 | 690 | -0.6 | 2.22 | 499 | 456 | -1.1 | 23,849 | 28,882 | 2914 | 219 |
| FORT BEND | 70,424 | 116,367 | 141,993 | 6.3 | 3.14 | 58,921 | 95,341 | 6.0 | 61,441 | 76,674 | 64 | 3 |
| FRANKLIN | 3,017 | 3,953 | 4,370 | 3.3 | 2.55 | 2,250 | 2,836 | 2.8 | 32,494 | 38,795 | 1625 | 91 |
| FREESTONE | 6,063 | 6,417 | 6,582 | 0.7 | 2.50 | 4,337 | 4,433 | 0.3 | 32,835 | 41,222 | 1564 | 86 |
| FRIO | 4,129 | 4,508 | 4,600 | 1.1 | 3.19 | 3,300 | 3,580 | 1.0 | 16,941 | 18,595 | 3138 | 254 |
| GAINES | 4,502 | 4,879 | 4,987 | 1.0 | 3.01 | 3,616 | 3,877 | 0.8 | 27,815 | 31,694 | 2467 | 174 |
| GALVESTON | 81,451 | 95,461 | 101,997 | 1.9 | 2.61 | 58,178 | 66,337 | 1.6 | 43,390 | 49,326 | 433 | 18 |
| GARZA | 1,822 | 1,636 | 1,545 | -1.3 | 2.69 | 1,387 | 1,223 | -1.5 | 30,294 | 36,505 | 2083 | 139 |
| GILLESPIE | 6,711 | 8,049 | 8,689 | 2.2 | 2.48 | 4,964 | 5,693 | 1.7 | 37,001 | 46,634 | 978 | 40 |
| GLASSCOCK | 456 | 443 | 469 | -0.3 | 3.31 | 378 | 360 | -0.6 | 36,490 | 43,580 | 1046 | 47 |
| GOLIAD | 2,208 | 2,806 | 3,202 | 2.9 | 2.59 | 1,664 | 2,070 | 2.7 | 32,033 | 41,075 | 1708 | 106 |
| GONZALES | 6,231 | 6,443 | 6,552 | 0.4 | 2.69 | 4,484 | 4,531 | 0.1 | 26,189 | 31,872 | 2690 | 196 |
| GRAY | 9,548 | 9,039 | 8,754 | -0.7 | 2.41 | 6,932 | 6,340 | -1.1 | 32,631 | 37,381 | 1605 | 90 |
| GRAYSON | 36,847 | 41,261 | 44,360 | 1.4 | 2.51 | 26,534 | 28,691 | 1.0 | 33,854 | 39,585 | 1414 | 74 |
| GREGG | 40,027 | 44,555 | 46,105 | 1.3 | 2.50 | 28,307 | 30,503 | 0.9 | 35,552 | 40,471 | 1161 | 57 |
| GRIMES | 6,040 | 7,974 | 9,117 | 3.4 | 2.74 | 4,464 | 5,706 | 3.0 | 32,841 | 41,709 | 1562 | 85 |
| GUADALUPE | 22,663 | 30,303 | 35,079 | 3.6 | 2.77 | 17,681 | 23,162 | 3.3 | 38,249 | 46,730 | 835 | 33 |
| HALE | 11,703 | 12,342 | 12,410 | 0.6 | 2.85 | 8,917 | 9,254 | 0.5 | 30,410 | 35,011 | 2056 | 137 |
| HALL | 1,669 | 1,577 | 1,527 | -0.7 | 2.22 | 1,084 | 986 | -1.1 | 18,402 | 21,570 | 3127 | 250 |
| HAMILTON | 3,250 | 3,269 | 3,290 | 0.1 | 2.27 | 2,212 | 2,126 | -0.5 | 27,427 | 33,062 | 2522 | 178 |
| HANSFORD | 2,112 | 1,950 | 2,007 | -1.0 | 2.76 | 1,626 | 1,464 | -1.3 | 28,790 | 31,415 | 2329 | 161 |
| HARDEMAN | 2,101 | 1,813 | 1,668 | -1.8 | 2.28 | 1,438 | 1,192 | -2.2 | 26,789 | 31,125 | 2609 | 190 |
| HARDIN | 14,693 | 17,931 | 19,137 | 2.4 | 2.75 | 11,631 | 13,844 | 2.1 | 36,756 | 41,642 | 1014 | 42 |
| HARRIS | 1,026,448 | 1,209,283 | 1,301,502 | 2.0 | 2.70 | 701,439 | 810,398 | 1.8 | 41,429 | 46,675 | 556 | 24 |
| HARRISON | 20,705 | 21,776 | 22,267 | 0.6 | 2.67 | 15,537 | 15,880 | 0.3 | 32,698 | 39,392 | 1593 | 88 |
| HARTLEY | 1,332 | 1,400 | 1,460 | 0.6 | 2.77 | 1,031 | 1,067 | 0.4 | 35,000 | 40,030 | 1250 | 64 |
| HASKELL | 2,753 | 2,528 | 2,394 | -1.0 | 2.29 | 1,961 | 1,741 | -1.4 | 24,759 | 30,781 | 2832 | 211 |
| HAYS | 22,218 | 33,880 | 40,905 | 5.2 | 2.64 | 14,479 | 21,636 | 5.0 | 41,968 | 52,186 | 515 | 22 |
| HEMPHILL | 1,348 | 1,290 | 1,241 | -0.5 | 2.62 | 1,034 | 962 | -0.9 | 35,293 | 36,889 | 1204 | 59 |
| HENDERSON | 22,947 | 28,436 | 31,851 | 2.6 | 2.51 | 17,215 | 20,677 | 2.2 | 30,447 | 35,629 | 2047 | 136 |
| HIDALGO | 103,479 | 150,047 | 171,679 | 4.6 | 3.63 | 87,912 | 126,800 | 4.5 | 23,020 | 26,332 | 2972 | 225 |
| HILL | 10,268 | 11,960 | 12,944 | 1.9 | 2.56 | 7,432 | 8,294 | 1.3 | 31,022 | 39,234 | 1927 | 126 |
| HOCKLEY | 7,988 | 7,871 | 7,611 | -0.2 | 2.87 | 6,322 | 6,113 | -0.4 | 33,567 | 41,200 | 1454 | 79 |
| HOOD | 11,137 | 15,311 | 17,823 | 3.9 | 2.60 | 8,709 | 11,671 | 3.6 | 47,794 | 58,073 | 245 | 8 |
| HOPKINS | 10,965 | 11,832 | 12,299 | 0.9 | 2.58 | 8,041 | 8,395 | 0.5 | 27,924 | 34,120 | 2449 | 172 |
| HOUSTON | 7,792 | 8,006 | 8,254 | 0.3 | 2.54 | 5,600 | 5,539 | -0.1 | 26,948 | 32,245 | 2589 | 186 |
| HOWARD | 11,477 | 11,466 | 11,211 | 0.0 | 2.56 | 8,491 | 8,185 | -0.4 | 32,191 | 40,853 | 1687 | 104 |
| HUDSPETH | 946 | 1,117 | 1,204 | 2.0 | 2.83 | 717 | 845 | 2.0 | 21,327 | 29,524 | 3057 | 237 |
| HUNT | 24,075 | 27,337 | 29,891 | 1.6 | 2.62 | 17,608 | 19,332 | 1.1 | 35,079 | 43,311 | 1244 | 63 |
| HUTCHINSON | 9,642 | 9,054 | 8,777 | -0.8 | 2.56 | 7,282 | 6,636 | -1.1 | 37,035 | 41,733 | 972 | 39 |
| IRION | 601 | 665 | 675 | 1.2 | 2.54 | 478 | 516 | 0.9 | 36,750 | 46,188 | 1015 | 43 |
| JACK | 2,725 | 3,021 | 3,221 | 1.3 | 2.47 | 1,970 | 2,086 | 0.7 | 31,293 | 39,109 | 1866 | 120 |
| JACKSON | 4,833 | 5,149 | 5,203 | 0.8 | 2.61 | 3,606 | 3,717 | 0.4 | 32,257 | 39,154 | 1674 | 102 |
| JASPER | 11,427 | 12,659 | 13,106 | 1.2 | 2.63 | 8,749 | 9,362 | 0.8 | 31,550 | 35,785 | 1810 | 117 |
| JEFF DAVIS | 779 | 1,062 | 1,259 | 3.8 | 2.29 | 541 | 714 | 3.4 | 28,548 | 36,505 | 2357 | 166 |
| JEFFERSON | 90,520 | 91,049 | 91,223 | 0.1 | 2.55 | 64,130 | 62,617 | -0.3 | 34,343 | 37,562 | 1343 | 68 |
| JIM HOGG | 1,675 | 1,685 | 1,698 | 0.1 | 2.94 | 1,317 | 1,322 | 0.0 | 22,491 | 26,208 | 2997 | 229 |
| JIM WELLS | 11,979 | 13,014 | 13,404 | 1.0 | 3.07 | 9,590 | 10,353 | 0.9 | 28,062 | 33,676 | 2431 | 171 |
| JOHNSON | 33,462 | 43,254 | 50,288 | 3.2 | 2.86 | 26,849 | 33,868 | 2.9 | 43,777 | 55,119 | 411 | 17 |
| JONES | 6,180 | 5,972 | 6,095 | -0.4 | 2.63 | 4,578 | 4,326 | -0.7 | 27,184 | 33,959 | 2548 | 180 |
| KARNES | 4,337 | 4,371 | 4,325 | 0.1 | 2.75 | 3,259 | 3,235 | -0.1 | 25,009 | 29,898 | 2808 | 207 |
| KAUFMAN | 17,827 | 23,977 | 27,684 | 3.7 | 2.89 | 13,969 | 18,380 | 3.4 | 42,085 | 51,868 | 502 | 21 |
| KENDALL | 5,342 | 8,430 | 9,820 | 5.7 | 2.63 | 4,146 | 6,381 | 5.4 | 42,351 | 47,563 | 481 | 19 |
| KENEDY | 145 | 141 | 141 | -0.3 | 2.99 | 117 | 113 | -0.4 | 19,861 | 21,827 | 3101 | 245 |
| KENT | 399 | 344 | 353 | -1.8 | 2.34 | 287 | 238 | -2.2 | 32,292 | 37,656 | 1661 | 99 |
| KERR | 14,384 | 17,962 | 19,542 | 2.7 | 2.34 | 10,045 | 12,099 | 2.3 | 34,118 | 37,898 | 1370 | 70 |
| KIMBLE | 1,624 | 1,640 | 1,693 | 0.1 | 2.57 | 1,191 | 1,162 | -0.3 | 24,833 | 28,231 | 2819 | 208 |
| KING | 124 | 135 | 135 | 1.0 | 2.27 | 103 | 110 | 0.8 | 34,044 | 38,750 | 1384 | 71 |
| KINNEY | 1,187 | 1,411 | 1,498 | 2.1 | 2.44 | 843 | 977 | 1.8 | 22,453 | 27,283 | 2999 | 230 |
| KLEBERG | 10,058 | 10,151 | 9,893 | 0.1 | 2.78 | 7,343 | 7,254 | -0.1 | 31,174 | 39,751 | 1893 | 123 |
| KNOX | 1,887 | 1,634 | 1,517 | -1.7 | 2.38 | 1,324 | 1,103 | -2.2 | 23,188 | 26,769 | 2958 | 224 |
| LAMAR | 16,798 | 18,045 | 18,636 | 0.9 | 2.52 | 12,209 | 12,735 | 0.5 | 32,304 | 38,902 | 1659 | 97 |
| LAMB | 5,488 | 5,454 | 5,461 | -0.1 | 2.68 | 4,106 | 3,992 | -0.3 | 28,352 | 32,096 | 2388 | 167 |
| LAMPASAS | 5,058 | 6,978 | 7,461 | 4.0 | 2.53 | 3,785 | 5,054 | 3.6 | 31,676 | 37,044 | 1784 | 115 |
| LA SALLE | 1,701 | 1,795 | 1,798 | 0.7 | 2.97 | 1,302 | 1,362 | 0.5 | 20,947 | 23,991 | 3070 | 238 |
| LAVACA | 7,349 | 7,489 | 7,644 | 0.2 | 2.48 | 5,229 | 5,132 | -0.2 | 28,970 | 34,468 | 2303 | 158 |
| LEE | 4,706 | 5,707 | 6,052 | 2.4 | 2.52 | 3,479 | 4,071 | 1.9 | 35,177 | 43,028 | 1223 | 61 |
| LEON | 5,006 | 5,870 | 6,360 | 1.9 | 2.57 | 3,613 | 4,083 | 1.5 | 32,343 | 41,386 | 1653 | 96 |
| LIBERTY | 18,538 | 22,607 | 25,041 | 2.4 | 2.84 | 14,179 | 16,845 | 2.1 | 33,744 | 40,266 | 1430 | 76 |
| LIMESTONE | 7,722 | 7,694 | 7,617 | 0.0 | 2.53 | 5,460 | 5,231 | -0.5 | 29,775 | 37,190 | 2186 | 147 |
| LIPSCOMB | 1,230 | 1,175 | 1,201 | -0.6 | 2.58 | 906 | 839 | -0.9 | 34,007 | 38,910 | 1391 | 72 |
| LIVE OAK | 3,550 | 3,858 | 3,883 | 1.0 | 2.60 | 2,683 | 2,852 | 0.7 | 32,230 | 41,250 | 1679 | 103 |
| LLANO | 5,278 | 6,445 | 7,166 | 2.5 | 2.16 | 3,696 | 4,316 | 1.9 | 29,995 | 33,708 | 2154 | 144 |
| LOVING | 42 | 45 | 45 | 0.8 | 2.51 | 28 | 28 | 0.0 | 31,875 | 38,125 | 1740 | 107 |
| LUBBOCK | 81,534 | 85,237 | 84,983 | 0.5 | 2.56 | 55,462 | 56,304 | 0.2 | 35,679 | 40,299 | 1139 | 53 |
| LYNN | 2,383 | 2,454 | 2,519 | 0.4 | 2.70 | 1,843 | 1,867 | 0.2 | 22,586 | 25,502 | 2990 | 228 |
| MCCULLOCH | 3,409 | 3,436 | 3,537 | 0.1 | 2.52 | 2,400 | 2,350 | -0.3 | 25,785 | 30,767 | 2734 | 199 |
| TEXAS | | | | 2.4 | 2.71 | | | 2.1 | 39,535 | 46,148 | | |
| UNITED STATES | | | | 1.4 | 2.59 | | | 1.1 | 41,914 | 49,127 | | |

# INCOME

| COUNTY | 2000 Per Capita Income | 2000 HH Income Base | 2000 HOUSEHOLD INCOME DISTRIBUTION (%) Less than $15,000 | $15,000 to $24,999 | $25,000 to $49,999 | $50,000 to $99,999 | $100,000 to $149,999 | $150,000 or More | 2000 AVERAGE DISPOSABLE INCOME BY AGE OF HOUSEHOLDER All Ages | <35 | 35-44 | 45-54 | 55-64 | 65+ |
|---|---|---|---|---|---|---|---|---|---|---|---|---|---|---|
| FOARD | 13,418 | 705 | 25.0 | 27.5 | 30.9 | 14.9 | 1.7 | 0.0 | 25,067 | 22,019 | 28,256 | 31,058 | 31,116 | 19,553 |
| FORT BEND | 26,675 | 116,367 | 6.0 | 5.0 | 25.6 | 41.3 | 14.7 | 7.5 | 60,202 | 49,750 | 61,241 | 65,697 | 57,975 | 39,123 |
| FRANKLIN | 18,622 | 3,953 | 22.3 | 16.8 | 34.4 | 18.5 | 4.6 | 3.5 | 36,560 | 30,874 | 35,839 | 47,626 | 40,950 | 25,176 |
| FREESTONE | 15,411 | 6,417 | 24.4 | 14.3 | 31.4 | 25.1 | 3.8 | 1.0 | 32,764 | 33,760 | 42,058 | 39,893 | 32,114 | 21,115 |
| FRIO | 8,021 | 4,508 | 43.8 | 19.3 | 24.1 | 10.3 | 1.5 | 1.1 | 22,702 | 20,415 | 22,304 | 27,325 | 27,196 | 17,071 |
| GAINES | 12,418 | 4,879 | 25.0 | 19.6 | 33.7 | 17.5 | 2.8 | 1.3 | 29,981 | 26,810 | 33,515 | 36,892 | 31,700 | 21,817 |
| GALVESTON | 22,788 | 95,461 | 15.4 | 11.5 | 30.6 | 30.9 | 7.7 | 3.9 | 44,001 | 35,093 | 47,972 | 54,283 | 46,712 | 28,925 |
| GARZA | 15,142 | 1,636 | 25.1 | 17.0 | 33.3 | 18.0 | 4.7 | 1.9 | 32,224 | 29,684 | 33,310 | 38,663 | 43,411 | 19,900 |
| GILLESPIE | 18,906 | 8,049 | 16.6 | 13.1 | 36.7 | 26.8 | 5.1 | 1.6 | 36,888 | 33,218 | 39,705 | 44,482 | 40,905 | 31,397 |
| GLASSCOCK | 23,918 | 443 | 19.2 | 12.4 | 37.9 | 17.6 | 7.0 | 5.9 | 43,322 | 29,064 | 39,562 | 45,634 | 53,549 | 30,000 |
| GOLIAD | 17,418 | 2,806 | 21.5 | 18.1 | 31.9 | 22.5 | 4.6 | 1.4 | 33,323 | 31,381 | 44,257 | 35,566 | 34,454 | 23,520 |
| GONZALES | 13,748 | 6,443 | 29.6 | 18.5 | 31.8 | 16.6 | 2.5 | 1.2 | 28,454 | 23,615 | 34,892 | 34,141 | 31,956 | 21,226 |
| GRAY | 18,380 | 9,039 | 22.2 | 15.4 | 34.7 | 22.7 | 3.5 | 1.5 | 33,508 | 29,646 | 37,383 | 41,577 | 36,014 | 25,618 |
| GRAYSON | 18,052 | 41,261 | 18.7 | 15.6 | 36.3 | 22.9 | 4.5 | 2.0 | 35,340 | 29,954 | 41,982 | 43,985 | 37,801 | 23,648 |
| GREGG | 18,241 | 44,555 | 20.1 | 14.5 | 33.7 | 24.8 | 5.0 | 1.9 | 36,093 | 29,852 | 41,410 | 44,297 | 38,277 | 25,856 |
| GRIMES | 14,837 | 7,974 | 21.9 | 14.9 | 33.4 | 23.1 | 5.1 | 1.6 | 34,436 | 32,014 | 38,417 | 43,802 | 36,001 | 24,070 |
| GUADALUPE | 16,579 | 30,303 | 16.3 | 14.4 | 35.2 | 28.3 | 4.8 | 1.1 | 36,237 | 31,202 | 39,406 | 44,794 | 39,816 | 26,566 |
| HALE | 14,372 | 12,342 | 20.6 | 20.0 | 34.1 | 20.8 | 3.4 | 1.1 | 31,827 | 26,405 | 36,450 | 37,478 | 35,391 | 25,675 |
| HALL | 12,917 | 1,577 | 41.8 | 20.9 | 25.1 | 10.3 | 1.8 | 0.2 | 21,715 | 21,250 | 25,130 | 29,848 | 24,435 | 16,159 |
| HAMILTON | 19,571 | 3,269 | 25.2 | 20.2 | 29.9 | 18.5 | 4.5 | 1.8 | 31,604 | 31,481 | 35,234 | 38,992 | 46,016 | 21,138 |
| HANSFORD | 14,040 | 1,950 | 23.2 | 19.7 | 36.8 | 16.1 | 2.7 | 1.5 | 30,815 | 23,803 | 36,888 | 33,079 | 38,346 | 23,018 |
| HARDEMAN | 16,455 | 1,813 | 25.9 | 21.8 | 29.2 | 15.4 | 5.7 | 1.9 | 31,461 | 26,973 | 45,270 | 42,602 | 26,696 | 22,403 |
| HARDIN | 17,608 | 17,930 | 17.2 | 14.5 | 35.4 | 27.0 | 4.4 | 1.6 | 36,109 | 32,265 | 42,211 | 44,308 | 37,424 | 22,721 |
| HARRIS | 22,047 | 1,209,279 | 14.4 | 13.6 | 31.3 | 29.3 | 7.6 | 3.9 | 43,646 | 33,916 | 46,465 | 50,465 | 47,209 | 31,750 |
| HARRISON | 15,179 | 21,776 | 22.6 | 15.4 | 33.9 | 23.2 | 3.9 | 1.0 | 32,726 | 28,862 | 37,591 | 40,004 | 35,804 | 22,591 |
| HARTLEY | 14,986 | 1,400 | 16.1 | 11.1 | 43.1 | 23.1 | 3.6 | 2.9 | 38,075 | 26,489 | 40,848 | 43,914 | 36,164 | 33,708 |
| HASKELL | 13,982 | 2,528 | 30.3 | 20.3 | 31.8 | 14.6 | 2.5 | 0.7 | 26,684 | 27,236 | 35,400 | 31,598 | 33,079 | 18,660 |
| HAYS | 20,916 | 33,880 | 17.9 | 11.3 | 29.7 | 30.3 | 7.4 | 3.4 | 42,143 | 27,828 | 50,350 | 54,957 | 47,216 | 36,703 |
| HEMPHILL | 21,350 | 1,290 | 16.9 | 15.4 | 38.6 | 20.9 | 5.7 | 2.6 | 37,527 | 31,453 | 39,665 | 35,927 | 42,369 | 29,971 |
| HENDERSON | 15,750 | 28,436 | 23.1 | 17.8 | 33.9 | 21.0 | 3.1 | 1.1 | 31,377 | 28,174 | 36,311 | 40,347 | 33,085 | 22,018 |
| HIDALGO | 9,342 | 150,047 | 33.5 | 19.7 | 28.2 | 15.1 | 2.5 | 1.1 | 26,855 | 22,906 | 29,616 | 30,692 | 28,851 | 22,096 |
| HILL | 17,162 | 11,960 | 24.2 | 15.8 | 33.4 | 21.7 | 3.9 | 1.0 | 31,937 | 29,107 | 36,820 | 43,173 | 34,527 | 20,643 |
| HOCKLEY | 16,092 | 7,871 | 20.2 | 16.2 | 33.7 | 24.0 | 4.2 | 1.8 | 34,781 | 27,941 | 43,359 | 43,039 | 36,760 | 22,935 |
| HOOD | 22,752 | 15,311 | 11.3 | 12.1 | 28.7 | 34.5 | 9.2 | 4.2 | 46,685 | 42,054 | 58,051 | 53,235 | 50,821 | 31,870 |
| HOPKINS | 15,671 | 11,832 | 25.6 | 19.0 | 31.6 | 18.8 | 3.2 | 1.7 | 31,170 | 27,818 | 36,388 | 40,598 | 32,143 | 18,851 |
| HOUSTON | 14,418 | 8,006 | 30.7 | 15.9 | 31.2 | 17.3 | 3.7 | 1.2 | 29,386 | 25,527 | 36,168 | 38,256 | 31,510 | 20,963 |
| HOWARD | 16,060 | 11,466 | 21.7 | 14.9 | 35.1 | 23.6 | 3.7 | 1.0 | 33,029 | 26,871 | 38,257 | 38,310 | 39,328 | 26,030 |
| HUDSPETH | 11,615 | 1,117 | 32.8 | 23.2 | 25.2 | 12.9 | 5.3 | 0.7 | 27,653 | 16,934 | 29,632 | 30,836 | 47,971 | 22,304 |
| HUNT | 17,350 | 27,337 | 20.1 | 14.4 | 33.6 | 25.8 | 4.3 | 1.8 | 35,518 | 29,404 | 40,857 | 46,475 | 37,711 | 22,971 |
| HUTCHINSON | 17,051 | 9,051 | 17.1 | 13.8 | 37.7 | 25.7 | 4.5 | 1.2 | 35,616 | 30,457 | 45,436 | 42,080 | 39,362 | 24,292 |
| IRION | 20,376 | 665 | 13.5 | 17.1 | 35.2 | 25.9 | 5.6 | 2.7 | 39,480 | 33,709 | 45,725 | 46,990 | 38,905 | 28,145 |
| JACK | 15,999 | 3,021 | 23.0 | 17.7 | 32.3 | 21.5 | 4.1 | 1.4 | 32,557 | 26,014 | 40,525 | 41,709 | 38,497 | 21,001 |
| JACKSON | 16,277 | 5,149 | 22.3 | 16.0 | 32.2 | 22.4 | 5.2 | 1.9 | 34,259 | 32,072 | 40,489 | 46,989 | 32,430 | 24,777 |
| JASPER | 15,684 | 12,659 | 20.9 | 18.0 | 34.0 | 22.6 | 3.5 | 1.0 | 32,194 | 28,109 | 37,732 | 40,376 | 35,354 | 22,325 |
| JEFF DAVIS | 16,143 | 1,062 | 22.4 | 18.4 | 35.1 | 20.4 | 2.8 | 0.9 | 30,201 | 24,970 | 36,100 | 32,403 | 35,491 | 25,200 |
| JEFFERSON | 17,929 | 91,044 | 21.9 | 14.8 | 33.0 | 23.6 | 4.5 | 2.2 | 35,621 | 29,422 | 41,242 | 43,242 | 37,582 | 25,596 |
| JIM HOGG | 11,766 | 1,685 | 33.0 | 21.1 | 26.5 | 15.6 | 2.8 | 1.0 | 26,857 | 19,044 | 32,176 | 30,180 | 36,883 | 21,418 |
| JIM WELLS | 12,600 | 13,014 | 26.9 | 18.5 | 30.5 | 19.4 | 3.3 | 1.5 | 30,662 | 27,145 | 36,939 | 37,971 | 29,460 | 20,415 |
| JOHNSON | 19,130 | 43,254 | 12.0 | 11.0 | 34.6 | 32.2 | 7.8 | 2.5 | 42,744 | 36,444 | 47,226 | 51,795 | 46,578 | 26,831 |
| JONES | 14,240 | 5,972 | 26.3 | 19.5 | 33.6 | 16.3 | 2.8 | 1.5 | 29,572 | 25,692 | 35,106 | 35,352 | 30,674 | 21,941 |
| KARNES | 11,807 | 4,371 | 32.4 | 17.6 | 31.1 | 15.2 | 2.6 | 1.1 | 27,657 | 25,696 | 30,177 | 35,208 | 29,466 | 21,391 |
| KAUFMAN | 19,589 | 23,977 | 14.5 | 11.8 | 33.2 | 29.9 | 7.3 | 3.3 | 42,523 | 35,756 | 49,280 | 51,268 | 41,900 | 27,515 |
| KENDALL | 21,929 | 8,430 | 14.9 | 12.6 | 32.5 | 30.3 | 6.5 | 3.2 | 42,111 | 33,264 | 43,197 | 52,235 | 45,286 | 29,945 |
| KENEDY | 13,132 | 141 | 34.0 | 29.8 | 21.3 | 7.8 | 2.8 | 4.3 | 29,770 | 28,906 | 42,747 | 19,352 | 20,104 | 18,750 |
| KENT | 16,667 | 344 | 22.1 | 15.7 | 35.8 | 21.5 | 3.8 | 1.2 | 32,357 | 31,875 | 33,317 | 46,559 | 40,620 | 21,345 |
| KERR | 19,993 | 17,962 | 16.9 | 17.9 | 34.1 | 23.4 | 5.6 | 2.2 | 36,745 | 27,684 | 38,400 | 44,038 | 43,031 | 32,551 |
| KIMBLE | 16,161 | 1,640 | 25.9 | 24.4 | 26.9 | 15.6 | 4.0 | 3.3 | 32,291 | 22,770 | 40,860 | 45,404 | 29,784 | 22,786 |
| KING | 21,180 | 135 | 10.4 | 17.8 | 46.7 | 20.0 | 3.0 | 2.2 | 37,644 | 29,833 | 33,162 | 45,055 | 39,515 | 27,250 |
| KINNEY | 12,221 | 1,411 | 30.1 | 25.2 | 29.5 | 12.8 | 2.2 | 0.2 | 25,028 | 22,741 | 33,816 | 27,054 | 24,953 | 21,930 |
| KLEBERG | 15,383 | 10,150 | 26.3 | 14.4 | 28.4 | 24.7 | 4.8 | 1.5 | 33,303 | 27,177 | 37,425 | 43,002 | 36,979 | 26,254 |
| KNOX | 12,759 | 1,634 | 32.6 | 20.4 | 31.0 | 13.7 | 1.6 | 0.7 | 25,451 | 23,209 | 30,592 | 35,931 | 26,679 | 17,062 |
| LAMAR | 16,393 | 18,045 | 23.1 | 14.6 | 34.3 | 22.6 | 4.3 | 1.2 | 33,115 | 30,211 | 38,793 | 41,704 | 35,022 | 21,557 |
| LAMB | 14,168 | 5,454 | 25.0 | 20.1 | 29.8 | 20.1 | 3.8 | 1.1 | 30,553 | 26,561 | 35,778 | 37,917 | 37,412 | 22,576 |
| LAMPASAS | 15,537 | 6,978 | 23.7 | 16.4 | 34.7 | 20.3 | 3.7 | 1.2 | 31,642 | 24,986 | 36,282 | 37,442 | 35,776 | 25,419 |
| LA SALLE | 10,068 | 1,795 | 37.6 | 20.2 | 25.6 | 13.5 | 1.8 | 1.3 | 25,505 | 22,024 | 28,036 | 31,147 | 27,141 | 16,377 |
| LAVACA | 14,981 | 7,489 | 26.4 | 17.1 | 32.6 | 20.2 | 2.5 | 1.2 | 30,234 | 26,277 | 36,129 | 43,847 | 32,338 | 20,799 |
| LEE | 17,291 | 5,707 | 19.2 | 14.5 | 34.4 | 25.5 | 4.7 | 1.6 | 35,478 | 34,194 | 41,857 | 44,804 | 35,090 | 23,674 |
| LEON | 16,617 | 5,870 | 22.3 | 14.6 | 34.9 | 22.6 | 4.3 | 1.3 | 33,199 | 35,273 | 39,185 | 41,304 | 33,427 | 23,866 |
| LIBERTY | 14,016 | 22,607 | 21.6 | 14.8 | 34.6 | 23.9 | 4.0 | 1.1 | 33,347 | 30,492 | 39,778 | 41,853 | 32,016 | 20,993 |
| LIMESTONE | 14,629 | 7,694 | 25.6 | 17.0 | 33.3 | 19.5 | 3.4 | 1.2 | 30,864 | 30,011 | 34,783 | 38,890 | 31,974 | 21,934 |
| LIPSCOMB | 16,551 | 1,175 | 18.2 | 16.7 | 38.0 | 21.9 | 3.5 | 1.7 | 33,858 | 29,614 | 39,497 | 41,951 | 40,510 | 23,094 |
| LIVE OAK | 15,885 | 3,858 | 19.3 | 21.2 | 31.6 | 22.6 | 3.9 | 1.4 | 33,134 | 30,744 | 38,849 | 41,752 | 31,530 | 25,675 |
| LLANO | 20,980 | 6,445 | 22.4 | 20.6 | 33.4 | 16.7 | 3.8 | 3.0 | 33,964 | 30,106 | 32,414 | 43,096 | 40,913 | 28,188 |
| LOVING | 14,392 | 45 | 11.1 | 24.4 | 40.0 | 24.4 | 0.0 | 0.0 | 31,444 | 31,944 | 26,364 | 26,000 | 55,833 | 34,167 |
| LUBBOCK | 18,563 | 85,237 | 19.2 | 14.9 | 32.8 | 25.6 | 5.4 | 2.1 | 37,085 | 27,694 | 43,286 | 48,288 | 41,425 | 29,897 |
| LYNN | 13,578 | 2,454 | 36.8 | 16.6 | 28.8 | 12.6 | 3.9 | 1.3 | 26,869 | 19,090 | 31,745 | 35,132 | 34,825 | 17,605 |
| MCCULLOCH | 13,802 | 3,436 | 30.3 | 18.0 | 31.1 | 15.9 | 3.6 | 1.1 | 28,501 | 25,569 | 32,776 | 37,530 | 32,516 | 21,159 |
| TEXAS | 20,236 | | 16.2 | 13.9 | 31.8 | 28.0 | 6.9 | 3.2 | 41,217 | 33,340 | 45,769 | 49,732 | 43,451 | 28,369 |
| UNITED STATES | 22,162 | | 14.5 | 12.5 | 32.3 | 29.8 | 7.4 | 3.5 | 40,748 | 34,503 | 44,969 | 49,579 | 43,409 | 27,339 |

| COUNTY | FINANCIAL SERVICES | | | | THE HOME | | | | | | ENTERTAINMENT | | | | | | PERSONAL | | | |
|---|---|---|---|---|---|---|---|---|---|---|---|---|---|---|---|---|---|---|---|---|
| | | | | | Home Improvements | | | Furnishings | | | | | | | | | | | | |
| | Auto Loan | Home Loan | Invest-ments | Retire-ment Plans | Home Repair | Lawn & Garden | Remodel-ing | Appli-ances | Elec-tronics | Furni-ture | Restau-rants | Sport-ing Goods | Theater & Concerts | Toys & Hobbies | Travel | Video Rental | Apparel | Auto After-market | Health Insur-ance | Pets & Supplies |
| FOARD | 96 | 63 | 72 | 77 | 91 | 91 | 109 | 94 | 90 | 72 | 77 | 92 | 77 | 93 | 68 | 97 | 78 | 87 | 104 | 95 |
| FORT BEND | 106 | 118 | 100 | 114 | 102 | 108 | 105 | 105 | 110 | 114 | 119 | 112 | 111 | 109 | 96 | 103 | 117 | 112 | 100 | 108 |
| FRANKLIN | 98 | 70 | 77 | 82 | 93 | 92 | 118 | 96 | 92 | 77 | 81 | 95 | 81 | 97 | 71 | 98 | 82 | 89 | 104 | 99 |
| FREESTONE | 95 | 73 | 81 | 79 | 93 | 91 | 108 | 95 | 92 | 82 | 82 | 92 | 82 | 94 | 72 | 97 | 83 | 89 | 99 | 96 |
| FRIO | 93 | 85 | 87 | 79 | 92 | 92 | 98 | 96 | 93 | 84 | 87 | 89 | 85 | 92 | 78 | 97 | 81 | 93 | 99 | 100 |
| GAINES | 95 | 87 | 90 | 83 | 94 | 93 | 101 | 97 | 94 | 88 | 90 | 92 | 88 | 95 | 79 | 97 | 85 | 94 | 99 | 101 |
| GALVESTON | 98 | 96 | 96 | 95 | 100 | 98 | 100 | 98 | 97 | 98 | 98 | 99 | 96 | 99 | 86 | 99 | 97 | 99 | 96 | 100 |
| GARZA | 95 | 73 | 79 | 78 | 91 | 91 | 105 | 95 | 92 | 78 | 82 | 91 | 81 | 93 | 72 | 97 | 79 | 90 | 102 | 98 |
| GILLESPIE | 98 | 79 | 94 | 88 | 99 | 98 | 108 | 97 | 94 | 85 | 88 | 95 | 89 | 98 | 79 | 98 | 88 | 92 | 105 | 99 |
| GLASSCOCK | 101 | 63 | 70 | 82 | 90 | 91 | 115 | 96 | 88 | 68 | 77 | 102 | 78 | 100 | 66 | 97 | 79 | 88 | 108 | 100 |
| GOLIAD | 98 | 77 | 82 | 83 | 93 | 92 | 111 | 97 | 93 | 82 | 86 | 96 | 85 | 98 | 73 | 98 | 84 | 92 | 102 | 101 |
| GONZALES | 95 | 77 | 82 | 79 | 92 | 91 | 107 | 96 | 93 | 82 | 85 | 91 | 83 | 94 | 74 | 97 | 82 | 91 | 100 | 98 |
| GRAY | 97 | 84 | 95 | 90 | 99 | 98 | 103 | 97 | 95 | 89 | 90 | 95 | 92 | 97 | 82 | 98 | 90 | 94 | 101 | 98 |
| GRAYSON | 97 | 83 | 91 | 87 | 98 | 96 | 107 | 96 | 94 | 88 | 90 | 95 | 90 | 97 | 79 | 97 | 89 | 93 | 100 | 98 |
| GREGG | 97 | 91 | 94 | 91 | 99 | 97 | 101 | 97 | 95 | 94 | 94 | 96 | 93 | 98 | 83 | 98 | 93 | 96 | 97 | 99 |
| GRIMES | 95 | 74 | 82 | 80 | 95 | 92 | 107 | 95 | 91 | 82 | 82 | 93 | 83 | 94 | 74 | 96 | 83 | 89 | 98 | 97 |
| GUADALUPE | 98 | 88 | 89 | 88 | 96 | 94 | 108 | 98 | 96 | 91 | 94 | 97 | 91 | 99 | 79 | 98 | 91 | 95 | 99 | 101 |
| HALE | 96 | 91 | 97 | 90 | 97 | 97 | 99 | 97 | 95 | 90 | 94 | 94 | 92 | 97 | 83 | 97 | 89 | 96 | 100 | 101 |
| HALL | 95 | 66 | 74 | 76 | 91 | 91 | 108 | 94 | 91 | 74 | 78 | 91 | 78 | 92 | 69 | 97 | 78 | 88 | 103 | 95 |
| HAMILTON | 96 | 67 | 78 | 79 | 92 | 92 | 109 | 94 | 91 | 75 | 80 | 92 | 80 | 94 | 70 | 97 | 80 | 88 | 103 | 96 |
| HANSFORD | 98 | 72 | 79 | 82 | 93 | 92 | 113 | 96 | 92 | 78 | 83 | 96 | 83 | 98 | 71 | 98 | 83 | 90 | 103 | 100 |
| HARDEMAN | 92 | 66 | 73 | 73 | 93 | 90 | 103 | 93 | 89 | 77 | 77 | 86 | 78 | 89 | 71 | 95 | 78 | 86 | 99 | 92 |
| HARDIN | 98 | 79 | 83 | 84 | 95 | 92 | 109 | 97 | 95 | 87 | 88 | 96 | 87 | 98 | 75 | 98 | 87 | 92 | 99 | 99 |
| HARRIS | 100 | 109 | 99 | 103 | 101 | 102 | 98 | 100 | 102 | 103 | 106 | 103 | 102 | 101 | 92 | 100 | 104 | 104 | 96 | 103 |
| HARRISON | 97 | 78 | 85 | 83 | 95 | 92 | 108 | 97 | 94 | 87 | 86 | 95 | 87 | 96 | 75 | 97 | 87 | 92 | 97 | 98 |
| HARTLEY | 100 | 72 | 79 | 84 | 93 | 92 | 116 | 97 | 92 | 78 | 84 | 100 | 84 | 101 | 71 | 98 | 85 | 91 | 105 | 102 |
| HASKELL | 96 | 67 | 74 | 78 | 91 | 91 | 110 | 95 | 91 | 74 | 79 | 93 | 79 | 94 | 70 | 97 | 79 | 88 | 104 | 97 |
| HAYS | 98 | 100 | 96 | 98 | 97 | 98 | 103 | 96 | 96 | 93 | 98 | 97 | 92 | 98 | 85 | 96 | 95 | 98 | 98 | 101 |
| HEMPHILL | 99 | 75 | 78 | 83 | 93 | 91 | 111 | 96 | 93 | 81 | 86 | 97 | 84 | 98 | 72 | 98 | 85 | 91 | 102 | 99 |
| HENDERSON | 98 | 79 | 99 | 87 | 99 | 99 | 110 | 98 | 92 | 85 | 88 | 95 | 89 | 98 | 80 | 96 | 85 | 92 | 104 | 99 |
| HIDALGO | 94 | 92 | 92 | 84 | 94 | 94 | 96 | 97 | 95 | 88 | 91 | 91 | 89 | 93 | 81 | 97 | 84 | 95 | 98 | 102 |
| HILL | 97 | 73 | 83 | 81 | 95 | 93 | 110 | 96 | 92 | 81 | 83 | 94 | 84 | 96 | 73 | 97 | 83 | 90 | 101 | 98 |
| HOCKLEY | 97 | 90 | 95 | 90 | 97 | 96 | 104 | 97 | 96 | 91 | 94 | 95 | 91 | 98 | 82 | 98 | 90 | 96 | 100 | 101 |
| HOOD | 101 | 89 | 102 | 96 | 101 | 104 | 113 | 101 | 96 | 95 | 97 | 99 | 95 | 102 | 85 | 98 | 96 | 97 | 104 | 102 |
| HOPKINS | 97 | 72 | 79 | 81 | 94 | 91 | 112 | 96 | 92 | 80 | 82 | 95 | 82 | 97 | 71 | 97 | 83 | 89 | 101 | 98 |
| HOUSTON | 95 | 70 | 78 | 77 | 93 | 89 | 108 | 95 | 90 | 80 | 78 | 92 | 81 | 93 | 71 | 96 | 82 | 88 | 97 | 95 |
| HOWARD | 98 | 89 | 98 | 92 | 100 | 99 | 104 | 98 | 97 | 93 | 94 | 96 | 94 | 99 | 84 | 98 | 93 | 96 | 101 | 100 |
| HUDSPETH | 93 | 88 | 89 | 79 | 92 | 92 | 97 | 96 | 94 | 86 | 89 | 89 | 86 | 92 | 79 | 97 | 81 | 93 | 98 | 101 |
| HUNT | 97 | 81 | 90 | 86 | 97 | 94 | 108 | 96 | 93 | 87 | 88 | 95 | 88 | 97 | 78 | 96 | 87 | 92 | 99 | 98 |
| HUTCHINSON | 98 | 85 | 94 | 90 | 99 | 97 | 107 | 97 | 96 | 90 | 92 | 96 | 92 | 99 | 81 | 98 | 91 | 94 | 101 | 100 |
| IRION | 101 | 79 | 85 | 86 | 96 | 93 | 119 | 99 | 96 | 86 | 90 | 99 | 88 | 103 | 74 | 99 | 91 | 94 | 102 | 103 |
| JACK | 97 | 69 | 77 | 80 | 93 | 91 | 113 | 96 | 92 | 78 | 81 | 94 | 81 | 96 | 70 | 97 | 82 | 89 | 103 | 98 |
| JACKSON | 94 | 68 | 76 | 76 | 93 | 91 | 106 | 94 | 90 | 77 | 78 | 90 | 79 | 92 | 71 | 96 | 79 | 88 | 100 | 95 |
| JASPER | 97 | 68 | 76 | 77 | 94 | 92 | 112 | 95 | 92 | 78 | 80 | 94 | 81 | 95 | 70 | 96 | 81 | 88 | 101 | 96 |
| JEFF DAVIS | 96 | 71 | 77 | 80 | 92 | 92 | 115 | 96 | 92 | 77 | 81 | 93 | 81 | 95 | 72 | 98 | 81 | 89 | 104 | 98 |
| JEFFERSON | 96 | 91 | 97 | 91 | 101 | 97 | 97 | 97 | 94 | 94 | 92 | 95 | 93 | 96 | 85 | 97 | 93 | 96 | 95 | 97 |
| JIM HOGG | 93 | 88 | 89 | 79 | 92 | 92 | 97 | 96 | 94 | 86 | 89 | 89 | 86 | 92 | 79 | 97 | 81 | 93 | 98 | 101 |
| JIM WELLS | 95 | 91 | 95 | 85 | 94 | 95 | 99 | 97 | 95 | 89 | 92 | 91 | 89 | 94 | 81 | 97 | 85 | 95 | 99 | 101 |
| JOHNSON | 99 | 90 | 91 | 91 | 97 | 96 | 108 | 98 | 98 | 95 | 97 | 99 | 94 | 101 | 81 | 99 | 95 | 97 | 98 | 101 |
| JONES | 95 | 73 | 80 | 78 | 93 | 90 | 108 | 95 | 92 | 81 | 82 | 91 | 82 | 93 | 72 | 97 | 82 | 89 | 99 | 96 |
| KARNES | 94 | 81 | 85 | 79 | 92 | 92 | 102 | 96 | 93 | 84 | 86 | 90 | 85 | 93 | 76 | 97 | 81 | 92 | 99 | 99 |
| KAUFMAN | 98 | 84 | 88 | 87 | 96 | 94 | 109 | 97 | 96 | 90 | 91 | 97 | 90 | 99 | 78 | 98 | 91 | 94 | 98 | 100 |
| KENDALL | 101 | 98 | 98 | 99 | 99 | 100 | 107 | 100 | 101 | 99 | 102 | 102 | 99 | 104 | 86 | 100 | 101 | 102 | 100 | 104 |
| KENEDY | 93 | 88 | 89 | 79 | 92 | 92 | 97 | 96 | 94 | 86 | 89 | 89 | 86 | 92 | 79 | 97 | 81 | 93 | 98 | 101 |
| KENT | 97 | 63 | 71 | 78 | 91 | 91 | 111 | 94 | 90 | 72 | 77 | 94 | 77 | 94 | 68 | 97 | 78 | 87 | 105 | 96 |
| KERR | 98 | 84 | 101 | 90 | 100 | 101 | 107 | 98 | 93 | 89 | 91 | 94 | 91 | 98 | 83 | 97 | 89 | 93 | 104 | 99 |
| KIMBLE | 97 | 65 | 73 | 79 | 92 | 91 | 114 | 95 | 90 | 73 | 78 | 94 | 78 | 95 | 69 | 97 | 79 | 88 | 105 | 97 |
| KING | 97 | 82 | 84 | 81 | 92 | 90 | 113 | 96 | 93 | 89 | 91 | 95 | 86 | 98 | 73 | 97 | 87 | 92 | 97 | 99 |
| KINNEY | 94 | 85 | 109 | 83 | 99 | 101 | 98 | 98 | 90 | 85 | 89 | 91 | 89 | 95 | 84 | 95 | 80 | 92 | 104 | 100 |
| KLEBERG | 95 | 94 | 93 | 88 | 95 | 94 | 96 | 96 | 95 | 91 | 94 | 92 | 90 | 95 | 82 | 97 | 89 | 96 | 96 | 100 |
| KNOX | 94 | 64 | 72 | 74 | 91 | 91 | 108 | 93 | 91 | 74 | 77 | 89 | 76 | 91 | 69 | 97 | 77 | 86 | 103 | 93 |
| LAMAR | 97 | 78 | 87 | 85 | 97 | 94 | 110 | 97 | 93 | 86 | 86 | 95 | 87 | 97 | 77 | 97 | 87 | 92 | 99 | 98 |
| LAMB | 96 | 75 | 82 | 80 | 92 | 92 | 105 | 96 | 92 | 80 | 83 | 92 | 83 | 94 | 73 | 97 | 81 | 90 | 101 | 98 |
| LAMPASAS | 96 | 78 | 83 | 83 | 95 | 93 | 104 | 95 | 93 | 84 | 87 | 93 | 86 | 95 | 75 | 97 | 85 | 91 | 101 | 97 |
| LA SALLE | 94 | 84 | 86 | 80 | 92 | 92 | 100 | 97 | 93 | 84 | 87 | 91 | 85 | 93 | 77 | 97 | 81 | 93 | 99 | 101 |
| LAVACA | 96 | 67 | 74 | 78 | 93 | 91 | 111 | 95 | 91 | 76 | 79 | 93 | 80 | 94 | 70 | 97 | 80 | 88 | 103 | 96 |
| LEE | 97 | 74 | 81 | 81 | 94 | 91 | 114 | 96 | 93 | 82 | 84 | 95 | 83 | 97 | 72 | 97 | 84 | 90 | 101 | 98 |
| LEON | 97 | 71 | 88 | 82 | 95 | 96 | 111 | 96 | 92 | 80 | 83 | 93 | 83 | 95 | 75 | 96 | 82 | 89 | 104 | 97 |
| LIBERTY | 96 | 73 | 80 | 79 | 94 | 91 | 111 | 96 | 92 | 82 | 83 | 94 | 83 | 95 | 72 | 96 | 82 | 89 | 99 | 97 |
| LIMESTONE | 95 | 71 | 79 | 79 | 94 | 91 | 109 | 95 | 91 | 80 | 81 | 91 | 82 | 94 | 72 | 97 | 82 | 89 | 101 | 96 |
| LIPSCOMB | 99 | 69 | 77 | 82 | 93 | 91 | 114 | 96 | 92 | 76 | 82 | 98 | 82 | 99 | 70 | 98 | 83 | 90 | 105 | 100 |
| LIVE OAK | 99 | 78 | 85 | 85 | 94 | 94 | 115 | 98 | 94 | 83 | 87 | 97 | 86 | 99 | 75 | 98 | 86 | 92 | 103 | 102 |
| LLANO | 100 | 83 | 110 | 96 | 103 | 109 | 111 | 101 | 92 | 88 | 92 | 96 | 93 | 100 | 88 | 96 | 89 | 94 | 109 | 101 |
| LOVING | 100 | 107 | 116 | 104 | 105 | 109 | 96 | 100 | 99 | 98 | 105 | 100 | 103 | 102 | 94 | 98 | 99 | 100 | 104 | 100 |
| LUBBOCK | 97 | 97 | 96 | 93 | 99 | 97 | 99 | 96 | 96 | 95 | 97 | 96 | 94 | 98 | 85 | 97 | 95 | 97 | 97 | 100 |
| LYNN | 97 | 74 | 79 | 81 | 91 | 91 | 106 | 96 | 91 | 77 | 82 | 96 | 82 | 96 | 72 | 97 | 80 | 91 | 103 | 100 |
| MCCULLOCH | 97 | 78 | 89 | 83 | 95 | 95 | 105 | 96 | 92 | 82 | 86 | 94 | 86 | 96 | 76 | 97 | 84 | 91 | 103 | 99 |
| TEXAS | 99 | 100 | 96 | 98 | 99 | 99 | 101 | 99 | 99 | 98 | 100 | 100 | 97 | 100 | 87 | 99 | 98 | 100 | 98 | 102 |
| UNITED STATES | 100 | 100 | 100 | 100 | 100 | 100 | 100 | 100 | 100 | 100 | 100 | 100 | 100 | 100 | 100 | 100 | 100 | 100 | 100 | 100 |

# POPULATION CHANGE

| COUNTY | FIPS Code | MSA Code | DMA Code | POPULATION 1990 | POPULATION 2000 | POPULATION 2005 | 1990-2000 ANNUAL CHANGE % Rate | 1990-2000 ANNUAL CHANGE State Rank | RACE (%) White 1990 | White 2000 | Black 1990 | Black 2000 | Asian/Pacific 1990 | Asian/Pacific 2000 |
|---|---|---|---|---|---|---|---|---|---|---|---|---|---|---|
| MCLENNAN | 309 | 8800 | 625 | 189,123 | 205,331 | 210,795 | 0.8 | 111 | 77.3 | 74.3 | 15.6 | 16.4 | 0.7 | 1.1 |
| MCMULLEN | 311 | 0000 | 641 | 817 | 804 | 817 | -0.2 | 189 | 87.3 | 85.4 | 0.0 | 0.0 | 0.0 | 0.0 |
| MADISON | 313 | 0000 | 625 | 10,931 | 11,940 | 12,263 | 0.9 | 104 | 73.0 | 71.9 | 23.6 | 24.2 | 0.1 | 0.2 |
| MARION | 315 | 0000 | 612 | 9,984 | 11,172 | 12,016 | 1.1 | 86 | 68.0 | 66.3 | 31.0 | 32.7 | 0.1 | 0.1 |
| MARTIN | 317 | 0000 | 633 | 4,956 | 5,008 | 5,056 | 0.1 | 173 | 63.7 | 57.8 | 1.8 | 1.7 | 0.2 | 0.2 |
| MASON | 319 | 0000 | 635 | 3,423 | 3,652 | 3,673 | 0.6 | 126 | 90.1 | 87.5 | 0.2 | 0.2 | 0.1 | 0.2 |
| MATAGORDA | 321 | 0000 | 618 | 36,928 | 37,766 | 37,442 | 0.2 | 164 | 72.1 | 68.6 | 13.8 | 13.8 | 2.3 | 3.2 |
| MAVERICK | 323 | 0000 | 641 | 36,378 | 49,625 | 54,634 | 3.1 | 27 | 65.3 | 65.1 | 0.1 | 0.1 | 0.2 | 0.2 |
| MEDINA | 325 | 0000 | 641 | 27,312 | 39,502 | 44,313 | 3.7 | 18 | 86.4 | 82.0 | 0.3 | 2.9 | 0.2 | 0.4 |
| MENARD | 327 | 0000 | 661 | 2,252 | 2,229 | 2,247 | -0.1 | 183 | 92.2 | 90.6 | 0.3 | 0.4 | 0.0 | 0.0 |
| MIDLAND | 329 | 5800 | 633 | 106,611 | 119,204 | 122,270 | 1.1 | 86 | 81.6 | 78.5 | 7.8 | 8.2 | 0.8 | 1.2 |
| MILAM | 331 | 0000 | 625 | 22,946 | 24,449 | 25,155 | 0.6 | 126 | 81.1 | 78.8 | 12.8 | 13.3 | 0.2 | 0.2 |
| MILLS | 333 | 0000 | 625 | 4,531 | 4,731 | 4,742 | 0.4 | 143 | 93.5 | 91.5 | 0.2 | 0.3 | 0.0 | 0.0 |
| MITCHELL | 335 | 0000 | 662 | 8,016 | 8,754 | 8,611 | 0.9 | 104 | 78.8 | 66.1 | 4.5 | 14.1 | 0.1 | 0.1 |
| MONTAGUE | 337 | 0000 | 627 | 17,274 | 18,987 | 20,084 | 0.9 | 104 | 97.5 | 96.9 | 0.0 | 0.1 | 0.1 | 0.1 |
| MONTGOMERY | 339 | 3360 | 618 | 182,201 | 302,368 | 374,731 | 5.1 | 4 | 91.2 | 89.3 | 4.3 | 4.6 | 0.7 | 1.1 |
| MOORE | 341 | 0000 | 634 | 17,865 | 19,936 | 20,921 | 1.1 | 86 | 71.6 | 65.9 | 0.5 | 0.7 | 1.6 | 2.2 |
| MORRIS | 343 | 0000 | 612 | 13,200 | 13,056 | 12,650 | -0.1 | 183 | 74.0 | 72.2 | 24.4 | 25.8 | 0.1 | 0.2 |
| MOTLEY | 345 | 0000 | 651 | 1,532 | 1,313 | 1,291 | -1.5 | 243 | 88.9 | 86.5 | 4.4 | 5.1 | 0.3 | 0.5 |
| NACOGDOCHES | 347 | 0000 | 709 | 54,753 | 56,437 | 56,325 | 0.3 | 155 | 79.9 | 77.1 | 16.5 | 18.1 | 0.6 | 0.8 |
| NAVARRO | 349 | 0000 | 623 | 39,926 | 42,138 | 43,544 | 0.5 | 133 | 75.9 | 73.5 | 19.0 | 19.8 | 0.7 | 1.0 |
| NEWTON | 351 | 0000 | 692 | 13,569 | 14,392 | 14,599 | 0.6 | 126 | 76.7 | 74.6 | 22.4 | 24.3 | 0.1 | 0.1 |
| NOLAN | 353 | 0000 | 662 | 16,594 | 16,180 | 15,808 | -0.2 | 189 | 78.0 | 73.7 | 4.7 | 4.8 | 0.1 | 0.1 |
| NUECES | 355 | 1880 | 600 | 291,145 | 315,888 | 318,184 | 0.8 | 111 | 75.6 | 72.8 | 4.4 | 4.2 | 0.9 | 1.2 |
| OCHILTREE | 357 | 0000 | 634 | 9,128 | 8,647 | 8,468 | -0.5 | 211 | 87.9 | 85.3 | 0.0 | 0.1 | 0.1 | 0.1 |
| OLDHAM | 359 | 0000 | 634 | 2,278 | 2,219 | 2,264 | -0.3 | 194 | 92.7 | 91.5 | 0.4 | 0.6 | 0.8 | 0.7 |
| ORANGE | 361 | 0840 | 692 | 80,509 | 85,659 | 87,639 | 0.6 | 126 | 90.2 | 89.0 | 8.4 | 9.1 | 0.6 | 0.9 |
| PALO PINTO | 363 | 0000 | 623 | 25,055 | 26,441 | 27,817 | 0.5 | 133 | 91.0 | 89.1 | 3.2 | 3.3 | 0.7 | 1.1 |
| PANOLA | 365 | 0000 | 612 | 22,035 | 23,027 | 23,198 | 0.4 | 143 | 80.3 | 78.4 | 18.4 | 20.1 | 0.1 | 0.2 |
| PARKER | 367 | 2800 | 623 | 64,785 | 88,600 | 104,229 | 3.1 | 27 | 96.1 | 95.0 | 0.9 | 1.0 | 0.4 | 0.6 |
| PARMER | 369 | 0000 | 634 | 9,863 | 10,374 | 10,504 | 0.5 | 133 | 91.0 | 89.6 | 1.2 | 1.4 | 0.2 | 0.3 |
| PECOS | 371 | 0000 | 633 | 14,675 | 16,019 | 15,785 | 0.9 | 104 | 64.4 | 57.5 | 0.4 | 5.0 | 0.2 | 0.2 |
| POLK | 373 | 0000 | 618 | 30,687 | 55,025 | 67,399 | 5.9 | 3 | 81.8 | 78.0 | 12.7 | 14.4 | 0.3 | 0.4 |
| POTTER | 375 | 0320 | 634 | 97,874 | 109,578 | 112,231 | 1.1 | 86 | 75.5 | 71.1 | 8.9 | 9.4 | 2.6 | 3.7 |
| PRESIDIO | 377 | 0000 | 633 | 6,637 | 9,291 | 10,972 | 3.3 | 24 | 84.7 | 83.9 | 0.1 | 0.3 | 0.2 | 0.4 |
| RAINS | 379 | 0000 | 623 | 6,715 | 9,322 | 11,101 | 3.3 | 24 | 94.0 | 92.8 | 4.3 | 4.9 | 0.1 | 0.2 |
| RANDALL | 381 | 0320 | 634 | 89,673 | 100,579 | 105,485 | 1.1 | 86 | 94.4 | 92.7 | 1.2 | 1.4 | 0.7 | 1.1 |
| REAGAN | 383 | 0000 | 633 | 4,514 | 3,700 | 3,361 | -1.9 | 252 | 78.6 | 74.9 | 2.8 | 3.1 | 0.0 | 0.0 |
| REAL | 385 | 0000 | 641 | 2,412 | 2,744 | 2,859 | 1.3 | 78 | 85.6 | 83.3 | 0.0 | 0.0 | 0.0 | 0.0 |
| RED RIVER | 387 | 0000 | 612 | 14,317 | 13,639 | 13,390 | -0.5 | 211 | 78.2 | 76.4 | 20.1 | 21.4 | 0.1 | 0.1 |
| REEVES | 389 | 0000 | 633 | 15,852 | 13,764 | 12,785 | -1.4 | 238 | 96.5 | 96.3 | 2.2 | 2.3 | 0.2 | 0.3 |
| REFUGIO | 391 | 0000 | 600 | 7,976 | 7,668 | 7,334 | -0.4 | 205 | 77.7 | 75.2 | 8.1 | 8.2 | 0.1 | 0.1 |
| ROBERTS | 393 | 0000 | 634 | 1,025 | 907 | 907 | -1.2 | 234 | 97.8 | 97.1 | 0.0 | 0.0 | 0.2 | 0.3 |
| ROBERTSON | 395 | 0000 | 625 | 15,511 | 15,893 | 16,508 | 0.2 | 164 | 64.8 | 61.7 | 27.5 | 28.2 | 0.1 | 0.1 |
| ROCKWALL | 397 | 1920 | 623 | 25,604 | 41,405 | 50,944 | 4.8 | 8 | 93.7 | 92.4 | 3.3 | 3.7 | 0.6 | 1.0 |
| RUNNELS | 399 | 0000 | 662 | 11,294 | 11,300 | 11,091 | 0.0 | 182 | 92.4 | 91.0 | 1.6 | 1.7 | 0.1 | 0.2 |
| RUSK | 401 | 0000 | 709 | 43,735 | 45,976 | 46,780 | 0.5 | 133 | 77.1 | 74.6 | 20.5 | 22.1 | 0.1 | 0.2 |
| SABINE | 403 | 0000 | 612 | 9,586 | 10,585 | 10,766 | 1.0 | 98 | 87.6 | 86.5 | 11.7 | 12.4 | 0.1 | 0.2 |
| SAN AUGUSTINE | 405 | 0000 | 709 | 7,999 | 8,099 | 8,146 | 0.1 | 173 | 70.8 | 69.4 | 28.1 | 29.1 | 0.1 | 0.1 |
| SAN JACINTO | 407 | 0000 | 618 | 16,372 | 23,384 | 27,470 | 3.5 | 20 | 82.6 | 80.9 | 15.5 | 16.7 | 0.1 | 0.1 |
| SAN PATRICIO | 409 | 1880 | 600 | 58,749 | 72,870 | 78,819 | 2.1 | 46 | 76.3 | 72.8 | 1.6 | 2.5 | 0.3 | 0.5 |
| SAN SABA | 411 | 0000 | 625 | 5,401 | 5,801 | 5,745 | 0.7 | 118 | 91.5 | 88.8 | 0.3 | 1.4 | 0.0 | 0.0 |
| SCHLEICHER | 413 | 0000 | 661 | 2,990 | 2,906 | 2,749 | -0.3 | 194 | 69.5 | 63.7 | 0.9 | 1.0 | 0.0 | 0.1 |
| SCURRY | 415 | 0000 | 651 | 18,634 | 17,422 | 16,337 | -0.7 | 219 | 75.7 | 70.5 | 4.7 | 5.4 | 0.2 | 0.3 |
| SHACKELFORD | 417 | 0000 | 662 | 3,316 | 3,190 | 3,036 | -0.4 | 205 | 94.2 | 92.4 | 0.4 | 0.4 | 0.1 | 0.1 |
| SHELBY | 419 | 0000 | 612 | 22,034 | 22,682 | 22,666 | 0.3 | 155 | 77.4 | 75.7 | 21.5 | 22.8 | 0.1 | 0.2 |
| SHERMAN | 421 | 0000 | 634 | 2,858 | 2,927 | 3,044 | 0.2 | 164 | 98.5 | 98.4 | 0.1 | 0.1 | 0.2 | 0.2 |
| SMITH | 423 | 8640 | 709 | 151,309 | 171,832 | 181,486 | 1.2 | 82 | 75.1 | 72.6 | 20.9 | 22.2 | 0.4 | 0.6 |
| SOMERVELL | 425 | 0000 | 623 | 5,360 | 6,826 | 7,862 | 2.4 | 40 | 90.5 | 88.6 | 0.2 | 0.2 | 0.4 | 0.5 |
| STARR | 427 | 0000 | 636 | 40,518 | 57,727 | 63,654 | 3.5 | 20 | 61.9 | 61.6 | 0.1 | 0.1 | 0.1 | 0.1 |
| STEPHENS | 429 | 0000 | 662 | 9,010 | 9,727 | 9,680 | 0.7 | 118 | 90.9 | 85.7 | 2.8 | 5.3 | 0.3 | 0.4 |
| STERLING | 431 | 0000 | 661 | 1,438 | 1,296 | 1,238 | -1.0 | 228 | 86.5 | 83.2 | 0.0 | 0.0 | 0.0 | 0.0 |
| STONEWALL | 433 | 0000 | 662 | 2,013 | 1,669 | 1,531 | -1.8 | 247 | 94.3 | 93.9 | 4.4 | 4.6 | 0.3 | 0.4 |
| SUTTON | 435 | 0000 | 661 | 4,135 | 4,255 | 3,979 | 0.3 | 155 | 75.6 | 71.7 | 0.0 | 0.0 | 0.1 | 0.2 |
| SWISHER | 437 | 0000 | 634 | 8,133 | 8,218 | 8,008 | 0.1 | 173 | 70.1 | 63.3 | 4.2 | 6.7 | 0.2 | 0.2 |
| TARRANT | 439 | 2800 | 623 | 1,170,103 | 1,410,661 | 1,549,645 | 1.8 | 60 | 78.4 | 74.7 | 12.0 | 12.6 | 2.5 | 3.8 |
| TAYLOR | 441 | 0040 | 662 | 119,655 | 124,780 | 126,362 | 0.4 | 143 | 83.8 | 80.8 | 6.3 | 6.5 | 1.2 | 1.9 |
| TERRELL | 443 | 0000 | 633 | 1,410 | 1,202 | 1,202 | -1.5 | 243 | 84.3 | 82.5 | 0.1 | 0.1 | 0.1 | 0.2 |
| TERRY | 445 | 0000 | 651 | 13,218 | 12,695 | 12,257 | -0.4 | 205 | 77.2 | 73.0 | 3.4 | 4.6 | 0.2 | 0.2 |
| THROCKMORTON | 447 | 0000 | 627 | 1,880 | 1,681 | 1,607 | -1.1 | 231 | 94.6 | 92.9 | 0.0 | 0.0 | 0.4 | 0.7 |
| TITUS | 449 | 0000 | 612 | 24,009 | 25,482 | 26,072 | 0.6 | 126 | 77.7 | 74.3 | 13.4 | 14.3 | 0.1 | 0.2 |
| TOM GREEN | 451 | 7200 | 661 | 98,458 | 102,330 | 102,375 | 0.4 | 143 | 80.8 | 76.9 | 4.2 | 4.3 | 1.0 | 1.4 |
| TRAVIS | 453 | 0640 | 635 | 576,407 | 743,348 | 825,921 | 2.5 | 38 | 73.3 | 68.5 | 11.0 | 11.4 | 2.9 | 4.0 |
| TRINITY | 455 | 0000 | 709 | 11,445 | 12,836 | 13,435 | 1.1 | 86 | 84.0 | 82.5 | 14.4 | 15.5 | 0.2 | 0.2 |
| TYLER | 457 | 0000 | 692 | 16,646 | 20,615 | 21,271 | 2.1 | 46 | 87.4 | 82.4 | 12.0 | 15.8 | 0.1 | 0.1 |
| UPSHUR | 459 | 4420 | 709 | 31,370 | 37,173 | 40,269 | 1.7 | 65 | 86.3 | 84.6 | 12.4 | 13.7 | 0.1 | 0.2 |
| UPTON | 461 | 0000 | 633 | 4,447 | 3,433 | 2,972 | -2.5 | 254 | 78.4 | 74.9 | 2.1 | 2.3 | 0.0 | 0.1 |
| TEXAS | | | | | | | 1.8 | | 75.2 | 72.3 | 11.9 | 11.9 | 1.9 | 2.8 |
| UNITED STATES | | | | | | | 1.0 | | 80.3 | 77.9 | 12.1 | 12.4 | 2.9 | 3.9 |

# POPULATION COMPOSITION

| COUNTY | % HISPANIC ORIGIN | | 2000 AGE DISTRIBUTION (%) | | | | | | | | | | MEDIAN AGE | | 2000 Males/ Females (×100) |
|---|---|---|---|---|---|---|---|---|---|---|---|---|---|---|---|
| | 1990 | 2000 | 0-4 | 5-9 | 10-14 | 15-19 | 20-24 | 25-44 | 45-64 | 65-84 | 85+ | 18+ | 1990 | 2000 | |
| MCLENNAN | 12.5 | 16.6 | 7.5 | 7.2 | 7.2 | 9.0 | 9.5 | 25.6 | 21.3 | 11.0 | 1.7 | 73.8 | 31.1 | 33.4 | 94.2 |
| MCMULLEN | 39.2 | 45.3 | 6.8 | 7.0 | 7.0 | 6.6 | 4.0 | 23.4 | 27.6 | 15.8 | 1.9 | 75.0 | 37.9 | 42.0 | 107.2 |
| MADISON | 10.8 | 12.9 | 5.8 | 5.9 | 5.9 | 9.0 | 14.2 | 26.0 | 19.4 | 11.5 | 2.4 | 78.3 | 29.9 | 30.2 | 146.2 |
| MARION | 1.5 | 2.2 | 6.0 | 6.3 | 7.1 | 6.9 | 4.9 | 22.2 | 27.8 | 16.8 | 2.1 | 76.1 | 39.8 | 42.7 | 98.6 |
| MARTIN | 39.5 | 46.8 | 9.5 | 9.3 | 9.1 | 8.8 | 6.3 | 23.4 | 21.7 | 10.1 | 1.6 | 66.1 | 30.7 | 31.6 | 97.6 |
| MASON | 19.6 | 25.1 | 6.2 | 6.2 | 6.5 | 6.9 | 4.4 | 21.2 | 26.5 | 18.1 | 3.9 | 76.4 | 42.4 | 44.0 | 94.5 |
| MATAGORDA | 24.6 | 30.3 | 8.8 | 8.6 | 8.5 | 7.9 | 6.2 | 26.1 | 21.9 | 10.5 | 1.5 | 69.1 | 31.4 | 33.8 | 98.0 |
| MAVERICK | 93.5 | 95.0 | 10.1 | 9.6 | 9.5 | 10.1 | 8.1 | 24.8 | 18.8 | 8.0 | 0.8 | 64.1 | 25.6 | 26.8 | 90.1 |
| MEDINA | 44.4 | 50.7 | 7.6 | 7.5 | 7.9 | 8.6 | 6.8 | 26.2 | 22.3 | 11.4 | 1.6 | 71.6 | 33.1 | 34.7 | 107.5 |
| MENARD | 32.2 | 39.1 | 6.9 | 7.3 | 6.6 | 7.1 | 4.3 | 21.5 | 24.5 | 18.0 | 3.7 | 74.6 | 41.7 | 42.5 | 103.4 |
| MIDLAND | 21.4 | 26.9 | 9.1 | 8.9 | 8.5 | 7.8 | 6.1 | 28.2 | 21.0 | 9.2 | 1.1 | 68.6 | 31.0 | 33.0 | 93.9 |
| MILAM | 15.1 | 19.7 | 7.1 | 7.6 | 7.9 | 8.0 | 5.5 | 22.9 | 23.8 | 14.5 | 2.8 | 72.4 | 35.8 | 38.5 | 95.2 |
| MILLS | 10.7 | 14.5 | 6.1 | 6.2 | 7.3 | 6.6 | 4.5 | 20.9 | 25.2 | 19.2 | 4.2 | 75.9 | 42.8 | 44.0 | 96.4 |
| MITCHELL | 29.8 | 35.9 | 6.1 | 6.5 | 6.7 | 7.7 | 7.2 | 26.6 | 21.5 | 14.8 | 2.9 | 75.7 | 37.3 | 37.6 | 112.8 |
| MONTAGUE | 3.2 | 4.3 | 6.4 | 6.7 | 7.0 | 7.1 | 4.8 | 22.2 | 25.8 | 16.7 | 3.3 | 75.4 | 39.6 | 42.1 | 93.1 |
| MONTGOMERY | 7.3 | 9.9 | 7.6 | 7.9 | 8.0 | 7.9 | 6.0 | 28.6 | 25.0 | 8.3 | 0.8 | 71.6 | 32.1 | 35.5 | 99.1 |
| MOORE | 31.9 | 38.1 | 9.6 | 9.1 | 8.7 | 8.7 | 7.1 | 26.7 | 19.5 | 9.5 | 1.0 | 66.9 | 29.3 | 30.5 | 99.8 |
| MORRIS | 1.8 | 2.8 | 6.4 | 7.2 | 7.5 | 7.6 | 5.2 | 23.9 | 25.0 | 14.8 | 2.4 | 74.1 | 35.7 | 39.8 | 95.0 |
| MOTLEY | 8.9 | 11.3 | 5.4 | 5.6 | 6.9 | 6.7 | 4.6 | 20.4 | 25.7 | 20.6 | 4.0 | 77.6 | 43.4 | 45.2 | 98.0 |
| NACOGDOCHES | 5.1 | 7.2 | 6.4 | 6.5 | 6.5 | 10.3 | 14.4 | 24.9 | 19.5 | 9.9 | 1.6 | 76.8 | 27.6 | 30.3 | 95.0 |
| NAVARRO | 7.2 | 9.9 | 7.4 | 7.4 | 7.6 | 8.3 | 6.1 | 24.7 | 23.2 | 12.7 | 2.5 | 72.9 | 34.2 | 36.8 | 93.9 |
| NEWTON | 1.1 | 1.7 | 7.0 | 7.7 | 8.0 | 8.3 | 5.8 | 24.1 | 25.2 | 12.5 | 1.5 | 72.3 | 33.5 | 37.4 | 95.1 |
| NOLAN | 25.6 | 32.2 | 7.6 | 7.6 | 7.7 | 8.1 | 6.3 | 24.2 | 23.2 | 13.0 | 2.4 | 72.3 | 34.4 | 36.8 | 95.5 |
| NUECES | 52.2 | 59.8 | 8.5 | 8.2 | 8.0 | 8.2 | 7.1 | 28.6 | 21.0 | 9.3 | 1.1 | 70.3 | 30.5 | 32.6 | 95.0 |
| OCHILTREE | 18.0 | 22.3 | 8.4 | 8.5 | 8.3 | 8.0 | 5.7 | 26.7 | 22.3 | 10.8 | 1.2 | 69.6 | 31.5 | 35.0 | 101.0 |
| OLDHAM | 8.8 | 10.4 | 5.7 | 6.8 | 14.1 | 15.4 | 4.1 | 20.5 | 21.4 | 11.0 | 1.0 | 60.9 | 27.8 | 29.5 | 137.8 |
| ORANGE | 2.4 | 3.6 | 6.9 | 7.3 | 7.8 | 7.9 | 5.9 | 26.4 | 25.6 | 11.1 | 1.1 | 73.2 | 32.9 | 37.1 | 96.0 |
| PALO PINTO | 9.2 | 12.2 | 7.4 | 7.1 | 7.4 | 7.3 | 5.7 | 24.2 | 24.8 | 14.1 | 2.2 | 73.6 | 35.6 | 38.8 | 94.3 |
| PANOLA | 2.2 | 3.2 | 6.6 | 7.3 | 7.8 | 8.4 | 6.1 | 24.4 | 24.5 | 12.9 | 2.0 | 73.5 | 34.6 | 37.7 | 94.2 |
| PARKER | 4.2 | 5.9 | 7.0 | 7.4 | 7.7 | 7.7 | 5.6 | 27.1 | 26.0 | 10.1 | 1.2 | 73.1 | 33.6 | 37.4 | 100.6 |
| PARMER | 41.5 | 48.7 | 9.3 | 9.2 | 8.7 | 8.9 | 6.2 | 24.5 | 21.4 | 10.1 | 1.8 | 66.8 | 30.4 | 32.0 | 103.9 |
| PECOS | 56.8 | 60.2 | 8.5 | 8.4 | 8.1 | 9.0 | 7.8 | 26.3 | 21.2 | 9.5 | 1.2 | 68.9 | 29.6 | 31.3 | 106.5 |
| POLK | 5.2 | 8.9 | 6.1 | 6.3 | 6.7 | 6.8 | 5.4 | 22.6 | 25.3 | 18.7 | 2.1 | 76.7 | 39.8 | 42.1 | 101.8 |
| POTTER | 19.7 | 24.5 | 8.9 | 8.0 | 7.7 | 7.7 | 7.0 | 27.0 | 20.4 | 11.5 | 1.8 | 71.1 | 31.3 | 33.6 | 94.6 |
| PRESIDIO | 81.6 | 85.1 | 8.7 | 8.4 | 8.3 | 9.4 | 7.1 | 23.3 | 21.7 | 11.5 | 1.7 | 68.4 | 31.5 | 31.8 | 93.3 |
| RAINS | 2.4 | 3.5 | 5.9 | 6.6 | 7.0 | 7.3 | 4.8 | 23.4 | 27.3 | 15.8 | 1.9 | 76.3 | 38.2 | 41.9 | 97.2 |
| RANDALL | 6.9 | 9.7 | 7.2 | 7.5 | 7.8 | 8.1 | 7.2 | 28.9 | 24.3 | 8.1 | 0.9 | 73.0 | 32.3 | 35.1 | 93.1 |
| REAGAN | 43.0 | 51.1 | 9.9 | 9.7 | 9.3 | 10.2 | 8.2 | 25.5 | 19.1 | 7.1 | 1.1 | 64.5 | 26.9 | 27.1 | 101.7 |
| REAL | 23.8 | 27.7 | 6.2 | 5.9 | 6.6 | 7.1 | 5.1 | 20.3 | 27.3 | 18.9 | 2.6 | 77.3 | 41.6 | 44.0 | 95.0 |
| RED RIVER | 1.9 | 3.0 | 5.7 | 6.2 | 6.7 | 7.3 | 5.6 | 22.8 | 25.7 | 16.5 | 3.5 | 77.0 | 39.0 | 41.8 | 90.3 |
| REEVES | 72.8 | 77.5 | 9.3 | 9.1 | 8.6 | 9.1 | 7.7 | 25.3 | 19.6 | 10.0 | 1.2 | 67.2 | 29.1 | 29.7 | 108.0 |
| REFUGIO | 39.7 | 47.1 | 6.7 | 7.1 | 7.3 | 8.0 | 6.0 | 24.2 | 24.4 | 14.3 | 2.1 | 74.1 | 35.1 | 38.6 | 92.7 |
| ROBERTS | 3.3 | 4.5 | 6.4 | 7.3 | 8.3 | 8.3 | 3.6 | 24.1 | 29.1 | 11.8 | 1.1 | 72.1 | 35.2 | 40.2 | 97.2 |
| ROBERTSON | 12.3 | 16.5 | 8.1 | 8.0 | 8.0 | 7.7 | 6.0 | 23.4 | 22.3 | 14.0 | 2.5 | 71.1 | 34.2 | 36.5 | 93.0 |
| ROCKWALL | 5.9 | 8.0 | 7.1 | 7.7 | 8.2 | 7.4 | 5.0 | 28.9 | 26.2 | 8.5 | 1.0 | 72.2 | 33.1 | 37.2 | 98.9 |
| RUNNELS | 24.3 | 30.3 | 7.2 | 7.5 | 7.5 | 7.8 | 5.4 | 22.5 | 23.6 | 15.3 | 3.3 | 72.7 | 37.0 | 39.1 | 98.0 |
| RUSK | 4.0 | 6.0 | 6.8 | 7.3 | 7.7 | 7.9 | 5.6 | 25.0 | 24.1 | 13.1 | 2.4 | 73.3 | 35.0 | 38.2 | 94.7 |
| SABINE | 1.2 | 2.1 | 5.3 | 5.4 | 5.9 | 5.9 | 4.3 | 18.3 | 28.0 | 24.3 | 2.5 | 79.5 | 46.8 | 48.9 | 93.9 |
| SAN AUGUSTINE | 1.7 | 2.6 | 6.3 | 6.7 | 6.9 | 6.9 | 5.1 | 21.1 | 25.2 | 18.6 | 3.2 | 75.8 | 40.4 | 42.6 | 90.6 |
| SAN JACINTO | 2.6 | 3.9 | 6.1 | 6.7 | 7.0 | 7.5 | 5.0 | 22.7 | 28.4 | 15.1 | 1.5 | 75.4 | 37.5 | 41.6 | 101.5 |
| SAN PATRICIO | 50.7 | 56.7 | 8.2 | 8.1 | 7.9 | 8.7 | 7.6 | 27.1 | 21.5 | 9.6 | 1.2 | 70.3 | 30.6 | 31.5 | 101.9 |
| SAN SABA | 18.5 | 22.6 | 6.9 | 7.3 | 7.6 | 8.3 | 5.0 | 20.7 | 23.8 | 16.7 | 3.9 | 72.8 | 39.1 | 40.4 | 96.2 |
| SCHLEICHER | 35.5 | 42.6 | 8.2 | 8.7 | 8.9 | 8.2 | 5.5 | 22.8 | 22.2 | 13.2 | 2.3 | 68.4 | 33.4 | 36.1 | 96.9 |
| SCURRY | 23.9 | 29.7 | 7.3 | 7.6 | 7.4 | 8.6 | 6.8 | 27.7 | 21.1 | 11.7 | 1.8 | 72.8 | 32.6 | 34.7 | 111.1 |
| SHACKELFORD | 8.2 | 11.3 | 6.7 | 6.8 | 7.0 | 8.3 | 5.6 | 22.9 | 23.6 | 15.5 | 3.6 | 73.7 | 37.3 | 40.5 | 100.6 |
| SHELBY | 2.4 | 3.5 | 7.0 | 7.0 | 7.5 | 7.4 | 5.7 | 23.2 | 24.8 | 15.0 | 2.6 | 73.9 | 36.5 | 39.4 | 91.8 |
| SHERMAN | 18.8 | 22.6 | 6.9 | 7.7 | 7.7 | 7.8 | 4.4 | 23.7 | 26.0 | 14.1 | 1.8 | 72.5 | 34.4 | 39.3 | 98.8 |
| SMITH | 5.9 | 8.0 | 7.2 | 7.2 | 7.4 | 7.8 | 6.5 | 27.0 | 23.4 | 11.9 | 1.7 | 73.9 | 33.2 | 36.5 | 93.2 |
| SOMERVELL | 14.0 | 17.4 | 8.1 | 8.3 | 9.1 | 8.2 | 6.1 | 26.2 | 22.4 | 9.6 | 2.0 | 69.2 | 31.7 | 34.3 | 106.5 |
| STARR | 97.2 | 97.9 | 10.7 | 10.0 | 9.8 | 10.4 | 8.7 | 25.3 | 17.8 | 6.4 | 0.8 | 62.8 | 23.9 | 25.2 | 97.3 |
| STEPHENS | 8.5 | 12.9 | 7.0 | 7.1 | 7.1 | 8.3 | 5.7 | 22.4 | 23.9 | 15.8 | 2.6 | 73.2 | 37.1 | 39.2 | 94.3 |
| STERLING | 25.5 | 31.3 | 9.4 | 9.6 | 8.8 | 8.2 | 5.2 | 26.6 | 19.7 | 10.4 | 2.0 | 66.8 | 30.3 | 32.9 | 97.0 |
| STONEWALL | 11.8 | 14.7 | 6.6 | 7.1 | 6.8 | 7.2 | 4.5 | 22.0 | 24.4 | 17.9 | 3.5 | 74.8 | 38.0 | 41.9 | 94.3 |
| SUTTON | 45.1 | 52.7 | 7.6 | 7.8 | 8.2 | 8.6 | 6.3 | 26.2 | 24.1 | 9.9 | 1.3 | 70.7 | 32.4 | 35.3 | 91.9 |
| SWISHER | 30.7 | 36.2 | 8.1 | 8.1 | 8.0 | 7.9 | 6.2 | 23.0 | 22.4 | 14.3 | 2.1 | 71.0 | 34.2 | 36.1 | 102.2 |
| TARRANT | 12.0 | 15.9 | 8.3 | 7.8 | 7.4 | 7.2 | 6.9 | 32.2 | 21.6 | 7.6 | 1.0 | 72.3 | 30.5 | 33.6 | 97.2 |
| TAYLOR | 14.6 | 18.7 | 8.1 | 7.5 | 7.0 | 9.1 | 9.5 | 27.1 | 19.7 | 10.3 | 1.7 | 72.8 | 30.2 | 31.8 | 96.0 |
| TERRELL | 53.3 | 60.1 | 6.8 | 6.8 | 7.8 | 7.5 | 5.7 | 22.4 | 27.7 | 13.3 | 2.0 | 73.2 | 36.2 | 40.2 | 113.1 |
| TERRY | 39.3 | 45.9 | 8.8 | 8.9 | 8.6 | 8.8 | 6.2 | 23.7 | 20.9 | 12.3 | 1.8 | 68.2 | 31.3 | 33.1 | 98.6 |
| THROCKMORTON | 7.2 | 9.7 | 6.2 | 6.3 | 7.1 | 6.2 | 4.5 | 21.7 | 26.9 | 17.0 | 4.2 | 76.5 | 40.4 | 43.6 | 96.6 |
| TITUS | 10.6 | 14.3 | 8.3 | 8.0 | 8.0 | 7.9 | 6.4 | 26.3 | 22.0 | 11.1 | 1.9 | 71.1 | 32.7 | 34.8 | 96.6 |
| TOM GREEN | 25.9 | 32.5 | 7.9 | 7.7 | 7.3 | 8.6 | 7.9 | 26.9 | 21.0 | 11.0 | 1.7 | 73.0 | 31.2 | 33.7 | 94.3 |
| TRAVIS | 21.1 | 27.2 | 7.7 | 7.0 | 6.5 | 7.9 | 10.2 | 33.9 | 19.4 | 6.6 | 0.9 | 75.1 | 29.5 | 31.9 | 98.6 |
| TRINITY | 2.4 | 3.4 | 5.8 | 6.1 | 6.4 | 6.6 | 4.9 | 20.8 | 26.4 | 20.5 | 2.5 | 77.6 | 41.2 | 44.5 | 94.0 |
| TYLER | 1.1 | 5.5 | 5.6 | 6.1 | 6.6 | 7.1 | 6.0 | 23.8 | 26.1 | 16.3 | 2.3 | 77.1 | 39.8 | 41.3 | 103.5 |
| UPSHUR | 2.0 | 3.0 | 6.9 | 7.3 | 7.8 | 8.0 | 6.2 | 24.4 | 25.2 | 12.3 | 1.9 | 73.4 | 34.2 | 37.8 | 94.8 |
| UPTON | 37.5 | 44.4 | 8.8 | 9.4 | 9.2 | 9.1 | 6.1 | 24.9 | 21.8 | 9.5 | 1.3 | 66.7 | 29.8 | 32.1 | 96.8 |
| TEXAS | 25.6 | 30.4 | 8.1 | 7.8 | 7.7 | 8.0 | 7.4 | 29.6 | 21.4 | 8.8 | 1.2 | 71.8 | 30.8 | 33.2 | 97.3 |
| UNITED STATES | 9.0 | 11.8 | 6.9 | 7.2 | 7.2 | 7.2 | 6.7 | 29.9 | 22.2 | 11.1 | 1.6 | 74.6 | 32.9 | 35.7 | 95.6 |

# HOUSEHOLDS

| COUNTY | HOUSEHOLDS | | | | | FAMILIES | | | MEDIAN HOUSEHOLD INCOME | | | |
|---|---|---|---|---|---|---|---|---|---|---|---|---|
| | 1990 | 2000 | 2005 | % Annual Rate 1990-2000 | 2000 Average HH Size | 1990 | 2000 | % Annual Rate 1990-2000 | 2000 | 2005 | 2000 National Rank | 2000 State Rank |
| MCLENNAN | 70,208 | 77,235 | 79,748 | 1.2 | 2.56 | 47,862 | 51,370 | 0.9 | 36,607 | 43,878 | 1031 | 45 |
| MCMULLEN | 319 | 312 | 316 | -0.3 | 2.56 | 234 | 222 | -0.6 | 33,833 | 36,786 | 1415 | 75 |
| MADISON | 3,349 | 3,790 | 3,968 | 1.5 | 2.49 | 2,397 | 2,605 | 1.0 | 26,424 | 31,061 | 2663 | 195 |
| MARION | 4,048 | 4,655 | 5,070 | 1.7 | 2.39 | 2,841 | 3,133 | 1.2 | 23,461 | 26,410 | 2944 | 221 |
| MARTIN | 1,632 | 1,693 | 1,729 | 0.4 | 2.94 | 1,306 | 1,342 | 0.3 | 27,106 | 30,767 | 2565 | 184 |
| MASON | 1,435 | 1,608 | 1,652 | 1.4 | 2.24 | 1,004 | 1,086 | 1.0 | 20,872 | 22,252 | 3073 | 240 |
| MATAGORDA | 13,164 | 13,688 | 13,675 | 0.5 | 2.74 | 9,761 | 9,872 | 0.1 | 33,092 | 37,244 | 1522 | 82 |
| MAVERICK | 9,756 | 13,849 | 15,539 | 4.3 | 3.57 | 8,214 | 11,673 | 4.4 | 19,196 | 21,473 | 3117 | 248 |
| MEDINA | 9,109 | 12,611 | 14,434 | 4.0 | 2.87 | 7,246 | 9,904 | 3.9 | 35,280 | 43,767 | 1205 | 60 |
| MENARD | 937 | 980 | 1,016 | 0.5 | 2.24 | 624 | 631 | 0.1 | 21,636 | 24,363 | 3046 | 236 |
| MIDLAND | 38,920 | 45,156 | 47,143 | 1.8 | 2.62 | 28,571 | 32,013 | 1.4 | 44,567 | 50,777 | 372 | 15 |
| MILAM | 8,686 | 9,396 | 9,740 | 1.0 | 2.57 | 6,191 | 6,459 | 0.5 | 27,406 | 32,766 | 2525 | 179 |
| MILLS | 1,782 | 1,902 | 1,913 | 0.8 | 2.36 | 1,264 | 1,301 | 0.4 | 24,655 | 31,214 | 2846 | 213 |
| MITCHELL | 3,054 | 2,917 | 2,899 | -0.6 | 2.50 | 2,183 | 2,015 | -1.0 | 24,503 | 29,424 | 2854 | 215 |
| MONTAGUE | 6,858 | 7,618 | 8,106 | 1.3 | 2.43 | 4,950 | 5,300 | 0.8 | 28,998 | 35,621 | 2295 | 156 |
| MONTGOMERY | 63,563 | 106,205 | 132,005 | 6.4 | 2.83 | 50,077 | 81,968 | 6.2 | 49,928 | 57,842 | 201 | 7 |
| MOORE | 6,101 | 6,909 | 7,302 | 1.5 | 2.86 | 4,793 | 5,346 | 1.3 | 36,674 | 42,814 | 1020 | 44 |
| MORRIS | 4,988 | 5,161 | 5,111 | 0.4 | 2.48 | 3,751 | 3,758 | 0.0 | 30,683 | 33,948 | 1989 | 130 |
| MOTLEY | 647 | 553 | 543 | -1.9 | 2.37 | 444 | 365 | -2.3 | 22,201 | 28,036 | 3016 | 233 |
| NACOGDOCHES | 20,124 | 21,339 | 21,436 | 0.7 | 2.46 | 12,786 | 13,180 | 0.4 | 27,564 | 32,212 | 2502 | 175 |
| NAVARRO | 14,874 | 15,906 | 16,570 | 0.8 | 2.57 | 10,757 | 11,161 | 0.4 | 32,362 | 41,139 | 1650 | 94 |
| NEWTON | 4,910 | 5,243 | 5,335 | 0.8 | 2.73 | 3,767 | 3,889 | 0.4 | 28,127 | 32,636 | 2422 | 170 |
| NOLAN | 6,183 | 6,214 | 6,155 | 0.1 | 2.51 | 4,509 | 4,380 | -0.4 | 29,318 | 35,750 | 2253 | 153 |
| NUECES | 99,740 | 110,547 | 112,480 | 1.3 | 2.81 | 74,048 | 80,265 | 1.0 | 35,113 | 40,520 | 1236 | 62 |
| OCHILTREE | 3,328 | 3,276 | 3,269 | -0.2 | 2.62 | 2,590 | 2,494 | -0.5 | 35,702 | 39,607 | 1136 | 52 |
| OLDHAM | 681 | 625 | 624 | -1.0 | 2.92 | 537 | 482 | -1.3 | 33,950 | 36,389 | 1402 | 73 |
| ORANGE | 29,025 | 31,428 | 32,427 | 1.0 | 2.71 | 22,738 | 24,043 | 0.7 | 39,986 | 43,248 | 675 | 29 |
| PALO PINTO | 9,531 | 10,061 | 10,585 | 0.7 | 2.58 | 6,951 | 7,104 | 0.3 | 28,819 | 35,697 | 2325 | 160 |
| PANOLA | 8,241 | 8,811 | 8,968 | 0.8 | 2.58 | 6,100 | 6,271 | 0.3 | 30,515 | 35,057 | 2028 | 131 |
| PARKER | 23,048 | 31,592 | 37,220 | 3.9 | 2.77 | 18,349 | 24,598 | 3.6 | 44,426 | 55,826 | 378 | 16 |
| PARMER | 3,241 | 3,432 | 3,487 | 0.7 | 2.98 | 2,576 | 2,696 | 0.6 | 24,805 | 27,020 | 2827 | 210 |
| PECOS | 4,712 | 4,571 | 4,531 | -0.4 | 3.02 | 3,772 | 3,625 | -0.5 | 29,693 | 37,714 | 2202 | 148 |
| POLK | 11,855 | 20,805 | 26,123 | 7.1 | 2.48 | 8,799 | 14,912 | 6.6 | 29,493 | 34,759 | 2223 | 150 |
| POTTER | 37,344 | 41,263 | 42,371 | 1.2 | 2.56 | 25,301 | 27,181 | 0.9 | 31,387 | 35,124 | 1842 | 118 |
| PRESIDIO | 2,255 | 3,202 | 3,806 | 4.3 | 2.88 | 1,684 | 2,392 | 4.3 | 20,889 | 25,196 | 3072 | 239 |
| RAINS | 2,609 | 3,642 | 4,346 | 4.1 | 2.53 | 1,942 | 2,602 | 3.6 | 30,876 | 39,643 | 1955 | 128 |
| RANDALL | 34,553 | 39,535 | 41,866 | 1.6 | 2.50 | 25,086 | 27,946 | 1.3 | 41,190 | 47,472 | 570 | 25 |
| REAGAN | 1,358 | 1,260 | 1,214 | -0.9 | 2.91 | 1,128 | 1,034 | -1.0 | 39,167 | 49,766 | 740 | 30 |
| REAL | 924 | 1,057 | 1,110 | 1.6 | 2.52 | 691 | 771 | 1.3 | 28,750 | 32,756 | 2332 | 162 |
| RED RIVER | 5,688 | 5,545 | 5,498 | -0.3 | 2.41 | 4,021 | 3,784 | -0.7 | 24,082 | 28,667 | 2895 | 217 |
| REEVES | 4,838 | 4,360 | 4,122 | -1.3 | 3.00 | 3,862 | 3,454 | -1.3 | 24,752 | 31,250 | 2833 | 212 |
| REFUGIO | 2,937 | 2,995 | 2,946 | 0.2 | 2.54 | 2,190 | 2,187 | 0.0 | 30,057 | 32,780 | 2142 | 142 |
| ROBERTS | 391 | 356 | 356 | -1.1 | 2.55 | 303 | 269 | -1.4 | 38,750 | 45,588 | 776 | 31 |
| ROBERTSON | 5,793 | 5,820 | 5,981 | 0.1 | 2.69 | 4,122 | 4,001 | -0.4 | 27,144 | 33,791 | 2558 | 182 |
| ROCKWALL | 8,838 | 13,956 | 16,970 | 5.7 | 2.95 | 7,234 | 11,163 | 5.4 | 64,020 | 78,365 | 42 | 2 |
| RUNNELS | 4,346 | 4,529 | 4,528 | 0.5 | 2.46 | 3,130 | 3,161 | 0.1 | 28,340 | 35,095 | 2391 | 168 |
| RUSK | 16,327 | 17,275 | 17,712 | 0.7 | 2.60 | 12,122 | 12,415 | 0.3 | 31,155 | 36,490 | 1903 | 124 |
| SABINE | 3,985 | 4,498 | 4,629 | 1.5 | 2.31 | 2,946 | 3,197 | 1.0 | 28,617 | 34,723 | 2346 | 165 |
| SAN AUGUSTINE | 3,073 | 3,194 | 3,248 | 0.5 | 2.47 | 2,264 | 2,273 | 0.0 | 23,996 | 27,350 | 2901 | 218 |
| SAN JACINTO | 6,247 | 9,118 | 10,823 | 4.7 | 2.56 | 4,742 | 6,677 | 4.2 | 31,702 | 38,348 | 1775 | 112 |
| SAN PATRICIO | 18,776 | 23,056 | 25,281 | 2.5 | 3.03 | 15,096 | 18,205 | 2.3 | 32,419 | 39,099 | 1636 | 92 |
| SAN SABA | 2,122 | 2,156 | 2,139 | 0.2 | 2.44 | 1,503 | 1,468 | -0.3 | 20,037 | 23,308 | 3098 | 244 |
| SCHLEICHER | 1,051 | 1,045 | 999 | -0.1 | 2.74 | 814 | 796 | -0.3 | 32,278 | 41,326 | 1668 | 100 |
| SCURRY | 6,368 | 6,056 | 5,767 | -0.6 | 2.61 | 4,854 | 4,522 | -0.9 | 33,202 | 41,172 | 1505 | 81 |
| SHACKELFORD | 1,336 | 1,364 | 1,333 | 0.3 | 2.29 | 920 | 903 | -0.2 | 26,625 | 29,806 | 2631 | 191 |
| SHELBY | 8,476 | 8,925 | 9,019 | 0.6 | 2.49 | 6,166 | 6,243 | 0.2 | 26,933 | 30,689 | 2595 | 187 |
| SHERMAN | 1,053 | 1,060 | 1,095 | 0.1 | 2.73 | 810 | 794 | -0.2 | 28,974 | 31,614 | 2301 | 157 |
| SMITH | 56,800 | 65,751 | 70,108 | 1.8 | 2.57 | 41,184 | 46,194 | 1.4 | 37,080 | 42,971 | 963 | 38 |
| SOMERVELL | 1,902 | 2,399 | 2,755 | 2.9 | 2.78 | 1,436 | 1,765 | 2.5 | 41,702 | 51,917 | 537 | 23 |
| STARR | 10,331 | 15,082 | 16,817 | 4.7 | 3.82 | 9,192 | 13,411 | 4.7 | 17,877 | 20,729 | 3130 | 251 |
| STEPHENS | 3,556 | 3,670 | 3,667 | 0.4 | 2.47 | 2,526 | 2,514 | -0.1 | 30,309 | 37,058 | 2078 | 138 |
| STERLING | 494 | 460 | 448 | -0.9 | 2.75 | 396 | 360 | -1.1 | 40,300 | 52,073 | 648 | 28 |
| STONEWALL | 806 | 713 | 675 | -1.5 | 2.29 | 567 | 482 | -1.9 | 30,026 | 37,650 | 2149 | 143 |
| SUTTON | 1,466 | 1,618 | 1,582 | 1.2 | 2.60 | 1,115 | 1,216 | 1.1 | 29,200 | 31,636 | 2266 | 155 |
| SWISHER | 2,993 | 2,895 | 2,850 | -0.4 | 2.63 | 2,218 | 2,092 | -0.7 | 26,972 | 29,770 | 2584 | 185 |
| TARRANT | 438,634 | 535,714 | 592,124 | 2.5 | 2.60 | 306,547 | 363,366 | 2.1 | 47,594 | 56,718 | 257 | 9 |
| TAYLOR | 43,301 | 44,683 | 45,382 | 0.4 | 2.60 | 31,027 | 30,968 | 0.0 | 34,425 | 41,260 | 1328 | 67 |
| TERRELL | 524 | 436 | 436 | -2.2 | 2.76 | 377 | 305 | -2.5 | 23,571 | 27,222 | 2933 | 220 |
| TERRY | 4,478 | 4,224 | 4,113 | -0.7 | 2.87 | 3,553 | 3,294 | -0.9 | 31,551 | 35,655 | 1809 | 116 |
| THROCKMORTON | 790 | 731 | 709 | -0.9 | 2.26 | 532 | 472 | -1.4 | 23,220 | 26,289 | 2957 | 223 |
| TITUS | 8,508 | 9,272 | 9,582 | 1.0 | 2.69 | 6,442 | 6,793 | 0.6 | 31,680 | 36,237 | 1782 | 114 |
| TOM GREEN | 35,408 | 37,564 | 37,859 | 0.7 | 2.59 | 25,212 | 25,991 | 0.4 | 35,592 | 42,775 | 1155 | 55 |
| TRAVIS | 232,861 | 305,911 | 342,341 | 3.4 | 2.37 | 135,428 | 174,951 | 3.2 | 44,662 | 51,151 | 367 | 14 |
| TRINITY | 4,647 | 5,288 | 5,564 | 1.6 | 2.40 | 3,347 | 3,668 | 1.1 | 26,907 | 33,005 | 2598 | 189 |
| TYLER | 6,459 | 7,335 | 7,680 | 1.6 | 2.49 | 4,864 | 5,328 | 1.1 | 32,355 | 42,146 | 1651 | 95 |
| UPSHUR | 11,360 | 13,555 | 14,725 | 2.2 | 2.69 | 8,749 | 10,136 | 1.8 | 31,064 | 35,441 | 1921 | 125 |
| UPTON | 1,472 | 1,227 | 1,099 | -2.2 | 2.77 | 1,154 | 947 | -2.4 | 33,734 | 42,946 | 1431 | 77 |
| TEXAS | | | | 2.4 | 2.71 | | | 2.1 | 39,535 | 46,148 | | |
| UNITED STATES | | | | 1.4 | 2.59 | | | 1.1 | 41,914 | 49,127 | | |

| COUNTY | 2000 Per Capita Income | 2000 HH Income Base | 2000 HOUSEHOLD INCOME DISTRIBUTION (%) | | | | | | 2000 AVERAGE DISPOSABLE INCOME BY AGE OF HOUSEHOLDER | | | | | |
|---|---|---|---|---|---|---|---|---|---|---|---|---|---|---|
| | | | Less than $15,000 | $15,000 to $24,999 | $25,000 to $49,999 | $50,000 to $99,999 | $100,000 to $149,999 | $150,000 or More | All Ages | <35 | 35-44 | 45-54 | 55-64 | 65+ |
| MCLENNAN | 18,696 | 77,231 | 19.6 | 13.6 | 32.7 | 26.6 | 5.6 | 2.0 | 37,161 | 28,274 | 43,724 | 48,472 | 41,683 | 27,797 |
| MCMULLEN | 19,302 | 312 | 20.2 | 13.1 | 37.5 | 19.6 | 6.1 | 3.5 | 37,951 | 27,443 | 35,311 | 44,585 | 47,859 | 29,635 |
| MADISON | 13,313 | 3,790 | 29.1 | 18.4 | 30.5 | 17.9 | 2.7 | 1.4 | 29,713 | 30,068 | 34,111 | 37,556 | 28,843 | 19,615 |
| MARION | 14,990 | 4,655 | 34.1 | 18.6 | 29.8 | 13.9 | 2.3 | 1.4 | 26,801 | 26,517 | 30,371 | 37,629 | 25,915 | 17,955 |
| MARTIN | 13,735 | 1,693 | 25.3 | 20.1 | 30.2 | 18.0 | 3.4 | 2.9 | 32,659 | 25,989 | 35,817 | 37,014 | 40,819 | 19,830 |
| MASON | 11,796 | 1,608 | 38.2 | 19.8 | 28.9 | 11.4 | 1.5 | 0.2 | 22,564 | 20,403 | 29,703 | 25,870 | 29,733 | 14,803 |
| MATAGORDA | 15,371 | 13,687 | 23.3 | 14.6 | 32.3 | 24.2 | 4.1 | 1.5 | 33,713 | 30,534 | 39,284 | 41,446 | 35,190 | 21,495 |
| MAVERICK | 9,787 | 13,849 | 38.9 | 22.2 | 22.7 | 11.5 | 2.7 | 2.1 | 26,269 | 20,330 | 30,585 | 28,969 | 29,252 | 18,022 |
| MEDINA | 15,346 | 12,611 | 19.2 | 15.4 | 35.2 | 24.2 | 4.7 | 1.3 | 34,948 | 31,631 | 40,145 | 40,528 | 36,420 | 25,834 |
| MENARD | 15,894 | 980 | 34.2 | 22.4 | 25.0 | 13.6 | 2.8 | 2.1 | 27,567 | 24,640 | 26,787 | 37,799 | 31,558 | 19,889 |
| MIDLAND | 26,817 | 45,156 | 13.0 | 13.0 | 30.0 | 29.9 | 8.3 | 5.8 | 48,474 | 35,753 | 51,346 | 55,177 | 50,539 | 38,149 |
| MILAM | 15,717 | 9,396 | 30.8 | 15.1 | 30.1 | 19.9 | 2.8 | 1.3 | 29,658 | 28,316 | 38,085 | 37,290 | 30,022 | 18,854 |
| MILLS | 16,033 | 1,902 | 28.8 | 22.0 | 28.8 | 15.2 | 2.8 | 2.4 | 30,353 | 26,211 | 34,096 | 44,013 | 32,470 | 19,668 |
| MITCHELL | 12,778 | 2,917 | 30.3 | 20.3 | 30.5 | 14.8 | 2.6 | 1.4 | 27,790 | 25,682 | 31,122 | 31,936 | 34,759 | 20,468 |
| MONTAGUE | 17,353 | 7,618 | 23.9 | 19.5 | 31.5 | 18.7 | 4.3 | 2.2 | 32,339 | 30,767 | 40,694 | 37,779 | 38,645 | 20,310 |
| MONTGOMERY | 24,843 | 106,205 | 10.7 | 9.6 | 29.8 | 33.5 | 10.5 | 5.9 | 51,182 | 41,040 | 55,701 | 59,838 | 49,726 | 31,082 |
| MOORE | 16,011 | 6,909 | 13.6 | 14.1 | 39.9 | 27.7 | 3.9 | 0.8 | 35,886 | 31,716 | 39,778 | 44,532 | 40,479 | 25,222 |
| MORRIS | 16,717 | 5,161 | 23.6 | 16.6 | 35.9 | 19.8 | 3.2 | 0.9 | 30,579 | 27,421 | 35,043 | 38,168 | 35,657 | 21,274 |
| MOTLEY | 12,270 | 553 | 33.6 | 21.0 | 30.4 | 13.4 | 1.5 | 0.2 | 24,091 | 24,467 | 22,880 | 27,936 | 29,924 | 20,859 |
| NACOGDOCHES | 15,019 | 21,339 | 28.5 | 16.5 | 32.1 | 17.5 | 3.8 | 1.6 | 30,634 | 21,071 | 36,786 | 44,204 | 34,687 | 23,201 |
| NAVARRO | 16,133 | 15,906 | 21.9 | 16.6 | 33.2 | 22.3 | 4.5 | 1.5 | 33,618 | 30,809 | 40,491 | 42,241 | 32,001 | 24,519 |
| NEWTON | 12,927 | 5,243 | 24.8 | 19.6 | 35.7 | 17.1 | 2.2 | 0.6 | 28,282 | 29,640 | 35,459 | 30,378 | 29,887 | 18,761 |
| NOLAN | 13,983 | 6,214 | 23.5 | 19.3 | 35.9 | 18.3 | 2.4 | 0.7 | 29,368 | 24,006 | 34,649 | 35,803 | 32,352 | 22,345 |
| NUECES | 16,788 | 110,545 | 20.3 | 14.8 | 33.7 | 24.7 | 4.6 | 1.9 | 35,768 | 30,274 | 39,121 | 42,624 | 38,424 | 26,049 |
| OCHILTREE | 19,270 | 3,276 | 14.6 | 15.8 | 38.4 | 25.0 | 4.6 | 1.7 | 36,641 | 30,290 | 38,692 | 43,116 | 38,028 | 31,498 |
| OLDHAM | 12,681 | 625 | 15.0 | 18.6 | 41.4 | 20.0 | 2.4 | 2.6 | 34,955 | 26,239 | 40,330 | 41,263 | 42,928 | 23,016 |
| ORANGE | 18,020 | 31,419 | 16.5 | 13.4 | 34.0 | 29.1 | 5.4 | 1.6 | 37,645 | 31,379 | 44,310 | 47,221 | 38,691 | 25,642 |
| PALO PINTO | 14,118 | 10,061 | 22.0 | 21.2 | 35.1 | 18.3 | 2.4 | 1.2 | 29,944 | 26,146 | 35,243 | 39,222 | 31,633 | 20,246 |
| PANOLA | 15,103 | 8,811 | 27.2 | 14.8 | 32.7 | 20.0 | 3.7 | 1.7 | 31,698 | 28,052 | 38,550 | 40,190 | 32,177 | 20,675 |
| PARKER | 21,075 | 31,592 | 12.0 | 10.5 | 34.3 | 32.7 | 7.7 | 2.9 | 43,621 | 37,578 | 47,180 | 53,290 | 47,042 | 26,879 |
| PARMER | 11,577 | 3,432 | 25.3 | 25.1 | 32.1 | 15.2 | 1.8 | 0.6 | 26,745 | 23,959 | 28,914 | 31,009 | 28,349 | 21,215 |
| PECOS | 13,545 | 4,571 | 26.0 | 17.3 | 31.5 | 20.9 | 3.5 | 0.9 | 30,700 | 28,538 | 35,758 | 35,520 | 35,487 | 19,720 |
| POLK | 16,744 | 20,805 | 23.8 | 18.8 | 32.7 | 18.2 | 4.1 | 2.4 | 33,224 | 31,011 | 40,510 | 39,762 | 35,730 | 22,948 |
| POTTER | 15,490 | 41,263 | 21.3 | 17.3 | 35.4 | 21.5 | 3.4 | 1.1 | 32,160 | 27,271 | 36,939 | 38,227 | 35,890 | 25,398 |
| PRESIDIO | 10,156 | 3,202 | 36.4 | 23.4 | 24.2 | 13.2 | 2.0 | 0.8 | 24,306 | 25,657 | 30,148 | 27,842 | 24,103 | 16,269 |
| RAINS | 15,600 | 3,642 | 19.9 | 20.2 | 35.1 | 20.6 | 3.4 | 0.9 | 31,489 | 27,505 | 36,221 | 42,378 | 35,640 | 20,967 |
| RANDALL | 21,476 | 39,535 | 12.5 | 13.1 | 35.8 | 30.7 | 5.5 | 2.5 | 40,727 | 30,838 | 45,125 | 48,374 | 44,408 | 30,413 |
| REAGAN | 18,465 | 1,260 | 8.4 | 17.0 | 37.5 | 28.0 | 5.7 | 3.3 | 41,495 | 32,022 | 43,113 | 50,412 | 43,885 | 31,765 |
| REAL | 13,089 | 1,057 | 24.1 | 18.6 | 40.5 | 15.0 | 1.6 | 0.1 | 27,351 | 21,467 | 29,295 | 32,403 | 31,910 | 23,602 |
| RED RIVER | 12,614 | 5,545 | 33.4 | 18.1 | 30.8 | 15.2 | 2.2 | 0.3 | 25,877 | 24,211 | 32,056 | 33,328 | 27,539 | 17,967 |
| REEVES | 10,245 | 4,360 | 32.9 | 17.4 | 34.1 | 14.4 | 1.2 | 0.0 | 24,608 | 24,456 | 28,521 | 30,047 | 26,724 | 15,817 |
| REFUGIO | 16,824 | 2,995 | 24.2 | 18.1 | 29.5 | 20.8 | 5.2 | 2.2 | 34,056 | 22,770 | 36,777 | 44,425 | 37,488 | 26,386 |
| ROBERTS | 23,814 | 356 | 12.4 | 11.5 | 46.9 | 22.5 | 4.2 | 2.5 | 39,618 | 28,049 | 41,906 | 44,590 | 41,458 | 31,377 |
| ROBERTSON | 13,660 | 5,820 | 32.4 | 14.3 | 32.3 | 16.8 | 3.0 | 1.1 | 28,661 | 28,049 | 34,207 | 37,178 | 30,345 | 18,974 |
| ROCKWALL | 32,183 | 13,956 | 6.1 | 4.3 | 24.6 | 39.2 | 14.8 | 11.1 | 66,501 | 49,279 | 66,975 | 73,221 | 62,477 | 44,391 |
| RUNNELS | 15,945 | 4,529 | 22.8 | 20.1 | 33.3 | 18.4 | 4.0 | 1.4 | 31,159 | 27,842 | 37,994 | 40,965 | 33,559 | 22,006 |
| RUSK | 14,212 | 17,275 | 23.5 | 16.5 | 35.6 | 20.8 | 2.9 | 0.7 | 30,739 | 29,792 | 35,717 | 37,021 | 31,213 | 21,667 |
| SABINE | 17,668 | 4,498 | 24.3 | 19.1 | 30.7 | 21.5 | 3.3 | 1.2 | 31,021 | 30,717 | 37,667 | 37,909 | 34,558 | 24,632 |
| SAN AUGUSTINE | 13,069 | 3,194 | 32.0 | 19.7 | 29.5 | 14.9 | 3.0 | 1.0 | 27,165 | 25,676 | 34,876 | 32,938 | 31,346 | 19,100 |
| SAN JACINTO | 17,454 | 9,118 | 24.0 | 14.7 | 34.6 | 19.2 | 5.4 | 2.2 | 34,060 | 31,820 | 43,118 | 39,362 | 32,522 | 26,170 |
| SAN PATRICIO | 13,860 | 23,053 | 21.8 | 16.3 | 33.7 | 22.4 | 4.2 | 1.6 | 33,859 | 28,457 | 37,764 | 41,590 | 35,192 | 25,753 |
| SAN SABA | 18,503 | 2,156 | 39.1 | 17.7 | 29.4 | 10.1 | 2.6 | 1.2 | 24,827 | 20,373 | 35,236 | 30,547 | 27,308 | 17,067 |
| SCHLEICHER | 16,111 | 1,045 | 20.6 | 16.0 | 33.7 | 22.6 | 5.4 | 1.8 | 34,880 | 29,752 | 40,655 | 41,977 | 32,750 | 30,184 |
| SCURRY | 14,770 | 6,056 | 20.1 | 15.8 | 37.1 | 22.9 | 3.2 | 0.9 | 32,727 | 28,135 | 39,785 | 39,928 | 35,709 | 22,946 |
| SHACKELFORD | 18,758 | 1,364 | 27.0 | 20.2 | 30.9 | 17.7 | 3.2 | 1.1 | 29,849 | 26,924 | 36,926 | 33,432 | 35,536 | 20,573 |
| SHELBY | 14,639 | 8,925 | 28.2 | 17.9 | 31.3 | 18.2 | 3.1 | 1.3 | 29,418 | 25,157 | 36,232 | 37,230 | 32,017 | 19,177 |
| SHERMAN | 12,802 | 1,060 | 24.0 | 18.9 | 36.5 | 17.7 | 2.5 | 0.5 | 28,739 | 25,861 | 30,790 | 35,369 | 34,543 | 20,128 |
| SMITH | 19,538 | 65,749 | 17.3 | 14.7 | 33.3 | 26.5 | 5.8 | 2.4 | 38,295 | 31,594 | 43,079 | 47,303 | 41,379 | 27,487 |
| SOMERVELL | 17,385 | 2,399 | 17.1 | 11.3 | 30.1 | 34.1 | 6.3 | 1.3 | 38,777 | 33,698 | 49,073 | 44,453 | 46,862 | 22,751 |
| STARR | 8,774 | 15,082 | 44.1 | 18.8 | 22.5 | 11.8 | 2.1 | 0.7 | 22,767 | 18,750 | 24,916 | 24,699 | 25,102 | 21,555 |
| STEPHENS | 16,914 | 3,670 | 23.5 | 19.5 | 31.4 | 18.6 | 4.9 | 2.1 | 32,984 | 25,671 | 35,896 | 46,296 | 35,919 | 24,791 |
| STERLING | 23,113 | 460 | 13.7 | 12.4 | 36.5 | 28.0 | 6.5 | 2.8 | 41,973 | 34,250 | 45,890 | 49,064 | 44,605 | 30,590 |
| STONEWALL | 15,474 | 713 | 21.3 | 19.4 | 37.3 | 19.1 | 3.0 | 0.0 | 29,765 | 28,083 | 37,435 | 36,158 | 36,206 | 19,636 |
| SUTTON | 15,893 | 1,618 | 26.2 | 19.8 | 27.1 | 18.5 | 5.0 | 3.5 | 34,542 | 24,490 | 42,953 | 43,320 | 35,039 | 22,563 |
| SWISHER | 13,251 | 2,895 | 24.8 | 21.6 | 32.8 | 16.4 | 3.6 | 0.9 | 29,393 | 25,989 | 37,804 | 32,271 | 35,915 | 22,181 |
| TARRANT | 24,017 | 535,713 | 9.9 | 11.2 | 31.6 | 34.8 | 9.1 | 3.6 | 46,629 | 37,823 | 50,585 | 56,498 | 49,688 | 32,241 |
| TAYLOR | 16,691 | 44,679 | 17.7 | 16.5 | 35.6 | 25.1 | 3.8 | 1.4 | 34,967 | 28,084 | 41,285 | 42,781 | 40,803 | 25,608 |
| TERRELL | 10,777 | 436 | 35.1 | 16.7 | 30.3 | 16.7 | 1.2 | 0.0 | 25,275 | 18,619 | 26,382 | 37,311 | 28,205 | 18,156 |
| TERRY | 16,620 | 4,224 | 22.3 | 17.5 | 31.7 | 21.1 | 3.8 | 3.6 | 36,237 | 29,555 | 37,055 | 45,554 | 40,330 | 26,426 |
| THROCKMORTON | 14,375 | 731 | 31.7 | 21.5 | 28.9 | 14.5 | 2.5 | 1.0 | 26,793 | 23,575 | 28,217 | 29,675 | 37,651 | 21,174 |
| TITUS | 17,298 | 9,272 | 23.4 | 16.0 | 31.6 | 23.0 | 4.1 | 2.0 | 34,228 | 30,281 | 40,315 | 44,743 | 34,350 | 20,092 |
| TOM GREEN | 17,071 | 37,564 | 17.0 | 16.0 | 35.6 | 25.7 | 4.4 | 1.4 | 35,598 | 29,300 | 41,117 | 44,355 | 38,959 | 26,110 |
| TRAVIS | 26,979 | 305,908 | 12.5 | 12.6 | 30.3 | 30.5 | 9.4 | 4.8 | 47,147 | 33,371 | 51,531 | 58,280 | 53,756 | 41,530 |
| TRINITY | 14,545 | 5,288 | 28.8 | 18.1 | 31.5 | 17.7 | 2.9 | 1.0 | 28,821 | 27,595 | 36,042 | 36,128 | 31,848 | 21,204 |
| TYLER | 14,662 | 7,335 | 21.6 | 15.1 | 35.1 | 24.7 | 3.0 | 0.6 | 32,052 | 30,581 | 36,803 | 41,047 | 33,780 | 23,370 |
| UPSHUR | 14,417 | 13,555 | 23.2 | 16.6 | 36.8 | 19.7 | 2.8 | 0.9 | 30,695 | 29,363 | 35,357 | 38,039 | 31,602 | 20,742 |
| UPTON | 14,556 | 1,227 | 18.5 | 16.2 | 37.5 | 24.4 | 2.8 | 0.7 | 32,895 | 29,665 | 40,760 | 34,728 | 36,226 | 20,826 |
| TEXAS | 20,236 | | 16.2 | 13.9 | 31.8 | 28.0 | 6.9 | 3.2 | 41,217 | 33,340 | 45,769 | 49,732 | 43,451 | 28,369 |
| UNITED STATES | 22,162 | | 14.5 | 12.5 | 32.3 | 29.8 | 7.4 | 3.5 | 40,748 | 34,503 | 44,969 | 49,579 | 43,409 | 27,339 |

# SPENDING POTENTIAL INDEXES

| COUNTY | FINANCIAL SERVICES | | | | THE HOME | | | | | | ENTERTAINMENT | | | | | | PERSONAL | | | |
|---|---|---|---|---|---|---|---|---|---|---|---|---|---|---|---|---|---|---|---|---|
| | | | | | Home Improvements | | | Furnishings | | | | | | | | | | | | |
| | Auto Loan | Home Loan | Investments | Retirement Plans | Home Repair | Lawn & Garden | Remodeling | Appliances | Electronics | Furniture | Restaurants | Sporting Goods | Theater & Concerts | Toys & Hobbies | Travel | Video Rental | Apparel | Auto Aftermarket | Health Insurance | Pets & Supplies |
| MCLENNAN | 96 | 92 | 97 | 92 | 100 | 97 | 101 | 96 | 94 | 92 | 93 | 95 | 92 | 97 | 84 | 97 | 93 | 95 | 97 | 98 |
| MCMULLEN | 101 | 63 | 70 | 82 | 90 | 91 | 115 | 96 | 88 | 68 | 77 | 102 | 78 | 100 | 66 | 97 | 79 | 88 | 108 | 100 |
| MADISON | 93 | 70 | 75 | 75 | 94 | 91 | 106 | 93 | 90 | 79 | 80 | 88 | 80 | 90 | 72 | 95 | 79 | 87 | 100 | 94 |
| MARION | 96 | 66 | 80 | 76 | 94 | 92 | 109 | 96 | 90 | 77 | 77 | 94 | 80 | 94 | 71 | 95 | 78 | 87 | 101 | 96 |
| MARTIN | 96 | 80 | 84 | 80 | 91 | 92 | 104 | 96 | 92 | 81 | 85 | 93 | 84 | 94 | 75 | 97 | 81 | 92 | 101 | 100 |
| MASON | 96 | 67 | 75 | 79 | 91 | 91 | 110 | 95 | 91 | 74 | 79 | 93 | 79 | 94 | 70 | 97 | 79 | 88 | 104 | 97 |
| MATAGORDA | 97 | 85 | 86 | 86 | 95 | 93 | 105 | 97 | 95 | 89 | 91 | 95 | 89 | 98 | 78 | 98 | 89 | 94 | 98 | 100 |
| MAVERICK | 93 | 88 | 89 | 79 | 92 | 92 | 97 | 96 | 94 | 86 | 89 | 89 | 86 | 92 | 79 | 97 | 81 | 93 | 98 | 101 |
| MEDINA | 96 | 82 | 87 | 81 | 93 | 92 | 105 | 97 | 94 | 85 | 88 | 93 | 86 | 95 | 76 | 97 | 83 | 92 | 100 | 100 |
| MENARD | 95 | 71 | 78 | 78 | 92 | 91 | 109 | 95 | 92 | 77 | 81 | 91 | 81 | 93 | 72 | 97 | 80 | 89 | 102 | 97 |
| MIDLAND | 101 | 105 | 101 | 102 | 101 | 103 | 101 | 100 | 102 | 103 | 106 | 103 | 101 | 103 | 90 | 100 | 104 | 103 | 98 | 103 |
| MILAM | 96 | 67 | 75 | 77 | 93 | 91 | 109 | 95 | 92 | 77 | 79 | 92 | 79 | 93 | 70 | 97 | 80 | 88 | 101 | 96 |
| MILLS | 95 | 63 | 72 | 75 | 91 | 91 | 108 | 93 | 90 | 73 | 77 | 90 | 76 | 91 | 68 | 97 | 78 | 87 | 103 | 94 |
| MITCHELL | 95 | 70 | 78 | 77 | 92 | 91 | 109 | 95 | 92 | 77 | 81 | 90 | 80 | 92 | 71 | 97 | 80 | 88 | 102 | 96 |
| MONTAGUE | 95 | 68 | 75 | 77 | 93 | 91 | 111 | 95 | 91 | 77 | 79 | 91 | 80 | 93 | 70 | 96 | 80 | 88 | 102 | 95 |
| MONTGOMERY | 101 | 96 | 94 | 96 | 98 | 99 | 108 | 100 | 100 | 98 | 101 | 102 | 97 | 103 | 84 | 100 | 99 | 100 | 99 | 103 |
| MOORE | 98 | 91 | 93 | 90 | 97 | 96 | 104 | 98 | 96 | 90 | 94 | 97 | 93 | 99 | 81 | 98 | 91 | 96 | 100 | 102 |
| MORRIS | 97 | 70 | 77 | 78 | 94 | 91 | 111 | 95 | 92 | 79 | 81 | 93 | 81 | 95 | 71 | 97 | 82 | 89 | 101 | 97 |
| MOTLEY | 94 | 63 | 72 | 75 | 91 | 91 | 108 | 93 | 90 | 73 | 77 | 89 | 76 | 91 | 68 | 97 | 78 | 87 | 103 | 94 |
| NACOGDOCHES | 95 | 83 | 89 | 86 | 95 | 91 | 104 | 92 | 91 | 83 | 85 | 91 | 84 | 93 | 77 | 94 | 85 | 90 | 96 | 96 |
| NAVARRO | 96 | 80 | 86 | 84 | 95 | 93 | 107 | 96 | 94 | 86 | 87 | 94 | 87 | 96 | 76 | 98 | 87 | 92 | 98 | 98 |
| NEWTON | 98 | 68 | 78 | 79 | 94 | 93 | 113 | 97 | 92 | 79 | 80 | 96 | 82 | 96 | 71 | 96 | 81 | 88 | 102 | 98 |
| NOLAN | 97 | 81 | 92 | 86 | 98 | 96 | 104 | 97 | 94 | 87 | 88 | 94 | 89 | 96 | 79 | 97 | 87 | 93 | 101 | 98 |
| NUECES | 98 | 99 | 94 | 93 | 97 | 97 | 98 | 98 | 98 | 97 | 100 | 98 | 96 | 99 | 85 | 99 | 96 | 99 | 97 | 102 |
| OCHILTREE | 97 | 75 | 82 | 81 | 93 | 91 | 111 | 96 | 93 | 81 | 85 | 94 | 84 | 97 | 73 | 97 | 83 | 91 | 102 | 99 |
| OLDHAM | 101 | 76 | 79 | 85 | 93 | 92 | 114 | 98 | 94 | 81 | 87 | 100 | 86 | 101 | 72 | 99 | 87 | 92 | 104 | 102 |
| ORANGE | 98 | 81 | 87 | 86 | 97 | 93 | 110 | 97 | 94 | 88 | 89 | 97 | 89 | 99 | 77 | 98 | 89 | 93 | 99 | 100 |
| PALO PINTO | 96 | 78 | 86 | 83 | 97 | 94 | 107 | 96 | 92 | 85 | 86 | 94 | 87 | 96 | 77 | 96 | 86 | 91 | 101 | 97 |
| PANOLA | 97 | 73 | 84 | 80 | 95 | 92 | 109 | 96 | 92 | 82 | 84 | 94 | 84 | 96 | 73 | 96 | 83 | 89 | 100 | 97 |
| PARKER | 100 | 87 | 91 | 91 | 97 | 95 | 112 | 98 | 98 | 92 | 95 | 99 | 93 | 101 | 79 | 99 | 94 | 96 | 100 | 102 |
| PARMER | 96 | 78 | 82 | 80 | 91 | 92 | 104 | 96 | 92 | 80 | 84 | 93 | 83 | 94 | 74 | 97 | 80 | 91 | 102 | 100 |
| PECOS | 95 | 88 | 89 | 82 | 94 | 92 | 100 | 96 | 94 | 88 | 91 | 91 | 88 | 95 | 79 | 97 | 85 | 94 | 98 | 100 |
| POLK | 98 | 73 | 89 | 83 | 97 | 96 | 112 | 97 | 91 | 81 | 83 | 95 | 85 | 97 | 76 | 96 | 83 | 90 | 103 | 98 |
| POTTER | 94 | 92 | 96 | 88 | 99 | 96 | 97 | 95 | 93 | 92 | 92 | 92 | 91 | 95 | 84 | 96 | 89 | 94 | 96 | 98 |
| PRESIDIO | 94 | 87 | 89 | 80 | 92 | 92 | 99 | 97 | 94 | 86 | 89 | 90 | 86 | 93 | 78 | 97 | 82 | 93 | 98 | 101 |
| RAINS | 97 | 67 | 74 | 79 | 92 | 91 | 115 | 96 | 91 | 75 | 79 | 95 | 79 | 96 | 69 | 97 | 80 | 88 | 104 | 98 |
| RANDALL | 99 | 102 | 98 | 98 | 101 | 100 | 101 | 99 | 99 | 100 | 104 | 100 | 99 | 102 | 88 | 99 | 101 | 100 | 98 | 101 |
| REAGAN | 96 | 84 | 86 | 82 | 93 | 92 | 107 | 97 | 94 | 87 | 90 | 93 | 87 | 96 | 76 | 98 | 85 | 93 | 99 | 101 |
| REAL | 98 | 74 | 79 | 84 | 93 | 93 | 120 | 98 | 92 | 78 | 83 | 96 | 83 | 98 | 73 | 98 | 83 | 91 | 105 | 101 |
| RED RIVER | 94 | 67 | 74 | 74 | 93 | 90 | 108 | 94 | 91 | 78 | 78 | 90 | 79 | 91 | 70 | 95 | 79 | 87 | 99 | 94 |
| REEVES | 94 | 89 | 87 | 81 | 92 | 92 | 97 | 97 | 95 | 88 | 91 | 91 | 88 | 93 | 79 | 97 | 84 | 95 | 97 | 101 |
| REFUGIO | 96 | 82 | 93 | 84 | 96 | 95 | 103 | 97 | 93 | 85 | 89 | 93 | 88 | 96 | 79 | 97 | 85 | 93 | 102 | 100 |
| ROBERTS | 101 | 63 | 70 | 82 | 90 | 91 | 115 | 96 | 88 | 68 | 77 | 102 | 78 | 100 | 66 | 97 | 79 | 88 | 108 | 100 |
| ROBERTSON | 93 | 66 | 73 | 73 | 92 | 88 | 104 | 94 | 90 | 78 | 76 | 89 | 78 | 90 | 70 | 96 | 79 | 87 | 96 | 93 |
| ROCKWALL | 109 | 122 | 109 | 123 | 105 | 113 | 111 | 108 | 113 | 119 | 123 | 116 | 116 | 113 | 100 | 104 | 123 | 116 | 103 | 110 |
| RUNNELS | 95 | 69 | 76 | 77 | 92 | 91 | 108 | 94 | 92 | 76 | 80 | 91 | 80 | 93 | 70 | 97 | 79 | 88 | 102 | 96 |
| RUSK | 97 | 73 | 82 | 81 | 95 | 92 | 109 | 96 | 93 | 82 | 83 | 95 | 84 | 96 | 73 | 97 | 84 | 90 | 100 | 98 |
| SABINE | 97 | 71 | 97 | 81 | 98 | 99 | 107 | 97 | 90 | 79 | 83 | 94 | 85 | 95 | 77 | 95 | 79 | 89 | 106 | 97 |
| SAN AUGUSTINE | 95 | 64 | 73 | 75 | 92 | 90 | 109 | 95 | 90 | 75 | 76 | 92 | 78 | 93 | 69 | 96 | 78 | 87 | 100 | 95 |
| SAN JACINTO | 97 | 69 | 88 | 80 | 96 | 96 | 110 | 97 | 91 | 78 | 80 | 95 | 83 | 95 | 74 | 95 | 80 | 88 | 103 | 97 |
| SAN PATRICIO | 96 | 90 | 89 | 87 | 94 | 94 | 101 | 97 | 96 | 91 | 93 | 95 | 91 | 97 | 80 | 98 | 89 | 96 | 99 | 100 |
| SAN SABA | 95 | 69 | 76 | 77 | 93 | 91 | 109 | 94 | 90 | 77 | 79 | 91 | 80 | 93 | 72 | 96 | 80 | 88 | 101 | 95 |
| SCHLEICHER | 98 | 79 | 83 | 83 | 93 | 92 | 110 | 97 | 93 | 82 | 87 | 96 | 85 | 98 | 74 | 98 | 84 | 92 | 102 | 102 |
| SCURRY | 97 | 87 | 92 | 88 | 97 | 96 | 104 | 97 | 95 | 89 | 92 | 95 | 91 | 98 | 80 | 98 | 89 | 94 | 100 | 100 |
| SHACKELFORD | 95 | 68 | 76 | 77 | 93 | 91 | 109 | 94 | 92 | 77 | 80 | 89 | 79 | 92 | 70 | 97 | 80 | 88 | 102 | 95 |
| SHELBY | 95 | 65 | 74 | 74 | 93 | 91 | 108 | 95 | 90 | 76 | 77 | 92 | 79 | 93 | 69 | 95 | 78 | 87 | 100 | 95 |
| SHERMAN | 100 | 63 | 70 | 82 | 90 | 91 | 114 | 96 | 89 | 69 | 77 | 101 | 78 | 99 | 67 | 97 | 79 | 88 | 108 | 100 |
| SMITH | 99 | 91 | 95 | 93 | 99 | 98 | 104 | 98 | 96 | 94 | 95 | 98 | 94 | 99 | 83 | 98 | 95 | 97 | 98 | 100 |
| SOMERVELL | 98 | 87 | 90 | 88 | 95 | 94 | 109 | 97 | 97 | 91 | 93 | 96 | 90 | 98 | 78 | 98 | 90 | 95 | 99 | 100 |
| STARR | 93 | 88 | 89 | 79 | 92 | 92 | 97 | 96 | 94 | 86 | 89 | 89 | 86 | 92 | 79 | 97 | 81 | 93 | 98 | 101 |
| STEPHENS | 96 | 71 | 80 | 80 | 95 | 93 | 112 | 96 | 91 | 80 | 81 | 94 | 82 | 95 | 73 | 96 | 81 | 89 | 102 | 98 |
| STERLING | 101 | 76 | 82 | 86 | 95 | 92 | 118 | 98 | 94 | 83 | 88 | 100 | 86 | 102 | 73 | 99 | 88 | 92 | 103 | 103 |
| STONEWALL | 94 | 63 | 72 | 75 | 91 | 91 | 108 | 93 | 91 | 73 | 77 | 89 | 76 | 91 | 68 | 97 | 78 | 87 | 103 | 94 |
| SUTTON | 97 | 83 | 86 | 83 | 93 | 93 | 106 | 97 | 94 | 85 | 88 | 94 | 87 | 96 | 77 | 98 | 84 | 93 | 100 | 102 |
| SWISHER | 95 | 74 | 81 | 79 | 92 | 92 | 104 | 95 | 92 | 79 | 83 | 91 | 82 | 93 | 73 | 97 | 81 | 90 | 101 | 97 |
| TARRANT | 101 | 108 | 98 | 103 | 101 | 102 | 99 | 100 | 102 | 104 | 108 | 104 | 102 | 103 | 90 | 100 | 105 | 104 | 97 | 103 |
| TAYLOR | 97 | 96 | 96 | 94 | 100 | 98 | 99 | 97 | 96 | 94 | 97 | 96 | 94 | 98 | 85 | 97 | 94 | 97 | 98 | 100 |
| TERRELL | 95 | 72 | 78 | 77 | 91 | 91 | 105 | 95 | 91 | 77 | 81 | 91 | 81 | 93 | 72 | 97 | 79 | 89 | 102 | 97 |
| TERRY | 98 | 89 | 100 | 94 | 99 | 100 | 104 | 98 | 97 | 91 | 94 | 97 | 93 | 99 | 84 | 98 | 91 | 96 | 102 | 102 |
| THROCKMORTON | 95 | 63 | 72 | 75 | 91 | 91 | 109 | 94 | 90 | 73 | 77 | 90 | 77 | 92 | 68 | 97 | 78 | 87 | 103 | 94 |
| TITUS | 97 | 82 | 88 | 87 | 98 | 95 | 108 | 96 | 95 | 89 | 89 | 95 | 89 | 97 | 79 | 97 | 88 | 93 | 99 | 99 |
| TOM GREEN | 97 | 95 | 94 | 92 | 98 | 97 | 100 | 97 | 97 | 95 | 97 | 97 | 94 | 99 | 84 | 98 | 94 | 97 | 98 | 101 |
| TRAVIS | 99 | 109 | 98 | 103 | 100 | 100 | 98 | 98 | 100 | 100 | 105 | 101 | 98 | 101 | 90 | 98 | 102 | 102 | 96 | 102 |
| TRINITY | 94 | 71 | 97 | 78 | 98 | 97 | 102 | 96 | 88 | 81 | 80 | 91 | 84 | 93 | 77 | 95 | 79 | 88 | 100 | 96 |
| TYLER | 97 | 73 | 85 | 82 | 96 | 94 | 113 | 96 | 92 | 81 | 83 | 95 | 84 | 96 | 74 | 96 | 83 | 90 | 102 | 98 |
| UPSHUR | 97 | 73 | 81 | 80 | 94 | 92 | 113 | 96 | 93 | 82 | 84 | 95 | 84 | 97 | 72 | 97 | 84 | 90 | 101 | 98 |
| UPTON | 99 | 80 | 84 | 84 | 94 | 92 | 112 | 98 | 94 | 84 | 88 | 97 | 87 | 99 | 75 | 98 | 86 | 93 | 102 | 102 |
| TEXAS | 99 | 100 | 96 | 98 | 99 | 99 | 101 | 99 | 99 | 98 | 100 | 100 | 97 | 100 | 87 | 99 | 98 | 100 | 98 | 102 |
| UNITED STATES | 100 | 100 | 100 | 100 | 100 | 100 | 100 | 100 | 100 | 100 | 100 | 100 | 100 | 100 | 100 | 100 | 100 | 100 | 100 | 100 |

| COUNTY | FIPS Code | MSA Code | DMA Code | POPULATION 1990 | POPULATION 2000 | POPULATION 2005 | 1990-2000 ANNUAL CHANGE % Rate | 1990-2000 ANNUAL CHANGE State Rank | RACE (%) White 1990 | White 2000 | Black 1990 | Black 2000 | Asian/Pacific 1990 | Asian/Pacific 2000 |
|---|---|---|---|---|---|---|---|---|---|---|---|---|---|---|
| UVALDE | 463 | 0000 | 641 | 23,340 | 26,367 | 28,154 | 1.2 | 82 | 64.6 | 60.9 | 0.2 | 0.3 | 0.3 | 0.4 |
| VAL VERDE | 465 | 0000 | 641 | 38,721 | 44,729 | 47,497 | 1.4 | 74 | 68.9 | 66.2 | 2.0 | 1.9 | 0.6 | 0.8 |
| VAN ZANDT | 467 | 0000 | 623 | 37,944 | 45,884 | 50,169 | 1.9 | 54 | 93.2 | 92.0 | 3.8 | 4.1 | 0.1 | 0.2 |
| VICTORIA | 469 | 8750 | 626 | 74,361 | 82,629 | 85,479 | 1.0 | 98 | 79.7 | 76.5 | 6.6 | 7.0 | 0.3 | 0.5 |
| WALKER | 471 | 0000 | 618 | 50,917 | 55,224 | 56,472 | 0.8 | 111 | 68.6 | 65.8 | 24.2 | 25.0 | 0.6 | 1.0 |
| WALLER | 473 | 3360 | 618 | 23,390 | 28,724 | 31,984 | 2.0 | 51 | 55.5 | 54.0 | 37.6 | 37.0 | 0.3 | 0.4 |
| WARD | 475 | 0000 | 633 | 13,115 | 11,329 | 10,519 | -1.4 | 238 | 75.5 | 71.4 | 3.5 | 3.5 | 0.2 | 0.2 |
| WASHINGTON | 477 | 0000 | 618 | 26,154 | 29,264 | 30,128 | 1.1 | 86 | 75.6 | 73.5 | 20.9 | 22.0 | 0.7 | 1.0 |
| WEBB | 479 | 4080 | 749 | 133,239 | 199,480 | 230,933 | 4.0 | 13 | 70.3 | 69.8 | 0.1 | 0.1 | 0.4 | 0.5 |
| WHARTON | 481 | 0000 | 618 | 39,955 | 40,431 | 41,094 | 0.1 | 173 | 72.9 | 70.1 | 15.8 | 15.9 | 0.3 | 0.4 |
| WHEELER | 483 | 0000 | 634 | 5,879 | 5,321 | 5,314 | -1.0 | 228 | 92.3 | 90.1 | 2.6 | 3.0 | 0.4 | 0.6 |
| WICHITA | 485 | 9080 | 627 | 122,378 | 128,133 | 127,521 | 0.4 | 143 | 83.7 | 80.0 | 9.2 | 10.4 | 1.5 | 2.3 |
| WILBARGER | 487 | 0000 | 627 | 15,121 | 13,972 | 13,635 | -0.8 | 221 | 79.4 | 76.0 | 8.9 | 9.2 | 0.5 | 0.8 |
| WILLACY | 489 | 0000 | 636 | 17,705 | 19,745 | 20,228 | 1.1 | 86 | 78.1 | 77.4 | 0.4 | 0.4 | 0.1 | 0.1 |
| WILLIAMSON | 491 | 0640 | 635 | 139,551 | 255,951 | 331,186 | 6.1 | 1 | 87.4 | 84.4 | 4.9 | 5.3 | 1.3 | 2.0 |
| WILSON | 493 | 7240 | 641 | 22,650 | 33,727 | 39,808 | 4.0 | 13 | 86.8 | 84.1 | 1.1 | 1.2 | 0.1 | 0.1 |
| WINKLER | 495 | 0000 | 633 | 8,626 | 7,663 | 7,220 | -1.1 | 231 | 71.7 | 66.3 | 1.9 | 2.1 | 0.1 | 0.1 |
| WISE | 497 | 0000 | 623 | 34,679 | 48,911 | 59,618 | 3.4 | 23 | 93.9 | 92.1 | 1.1 | 1.4 | 0.2 | 0.4 |
| WOOD | 499 | 0000 | 709 | 29,380 | 34,755 | 36,325 | 1.7 | 65 | 89.7 | 86.8 | 8.2 | 10.2 | 0.1 | 0.2 |
| YOAKUM | 501 | 0000 | 651 | 8,786 | 7,690 | 7,121 | -1.3 | 235 | 71.7 | 67.8 | 1.0 | 1.0 | 0.1 | 0.2 |
| YOUNG | 503 | 0000 | 627 | 18,126 | 17,573 | 17,590 | -0.3 | 194 | 93.9 | 92.4 | 1.5 | 1.6 | 0.3 | 0.4 |
| ZAPATA | 505 | 0000 | 749 | 9,279 | 11,532 | 12,054 | 2.1 | 46 | 72.0 | 70.4 | 0.0 | 0.0 | 0.1 | 0.1 |
| ZAVALA | 507 | 0000 | 641 | 12,162 | 11,865 | 11,746 | -0.2 | 189 | 53.0 | 52.1 | 2.4 | 2.5 | 0.0 | 0.0 |
| TEXAS | | | | | | | 1.8 | | 75.2 | 72.3 | 11.9 | 11.9 | 1.9 | 2.8 |
| UNITED STATES | | | | | | | 1.0 | | 80.3 | 77.9 | 12.1 | 12.4 | 2.9 | 3.9 |

# POPULATION COMPOSITION

| COUNTY | % HISPANIC ORIGIN | | 2000 AGE DISTRIBUTION (%) | | | | | | | | | | MEDIAN AGE | | 2000 Males/ Females (×100) |
|---|---|---|---|---|---|---|---|---|---|---|---|---|---|---|---|
| | 1990 | 2000 | 0-4 | 5-9 | 10-14 | 15-19 | 20-24 | 25-44 | 45-64 | 65-84 | 85+ | 18+ | 1990 | 2000 | |
| UVALDE | 60.4 | 66.8 | 9.1 | 8.4 | 8.5 | 9.2 | 7.3 | 24.3 | 21.0 | 10.4 | 1.7 | 68.6 | 29.9 | 31.2 | 93.6 |
| VAL VERDE | 70.5 | 77.2 | 9.3 | 8.6 | 8.3 | 8.4 | 8.7 | 28.1 | 18.7 | 8.9 | 1.0 | 68.6 | 27.8 | 28.8 | 99.9 |
| VAN ZANDT | 4.0 | 5.6 | 6.1 | 6.6 | 7.0 | 7.3 | 5.1 | 23.1 | 26.9 | 15.6 | 2.2 | 75.5 | 37.9 | 41.4 | 96.2 |
| VICTORIA | 34.1 | 41.5 | 8.3 | 8.3 | 8.3 | 8.2 | 6.4 | 27.5 | 21.8 | 10.0 | 1.2 | 70.1 | 31.6 | 33.9 | 95.6 |
| WALKER | 10.8 | 14.0 | 5.3 | 5.0 | 4.9 | 9.5 | 13.9 | 33.9 | 18.7 | 7.7 | 1.1 | 81.3 | 30.3 | 31.9 | 150.9 |
| WALLER | 11.1 | 14.7 | 7.1 | 6.8 | 6.8 | 11.8 | 11.1 | 24.6 | 21.1 | 9.5 | 1.3 | 75.1 | 28.2 | 30.5 | 97.6 |
| WARD | 36.8 | 44.6 | 8.0 | 8.4 | 8.4 | 10.2 | 6.5 | 25.2 | 21.2 | 10.9 | 1.4 | 68.2 | 30.5 | 32.6 | 100.4 |
| WASHINGTON | 4.4 | 6.2 | 7.0 | 7.1 | 7.2 | 9.1 | 6.9 | 25.1 | 21.5 | 13.5 | 2.6 | 74.6 | 34.2 | 36.4 | 95.5 |
| WEBB | 93.9 | 95.4 | 10.4 | 10.1 | 9.6 | 9.4 | 8.7 | 28.1 | 16.5 | 6.4 | 0.8 | 64.1 | 25.5 | 26.1 | 95.4 |
| WHARTON | 25.3 | 31.6 | 8.0 | 8.3 | 8.1 | 8.3 | 6.0 | 25.1 | 22.5 | 11.7 | 2.0 | 70.6 | 32.6 | 35.4 | 96.5 |
| WHEELER | 6.4 | 9.2 | 6.1 | 7.1 | 7.5 | 7.2 | 5.1 | 21.1 | 25.4 | 16.4 | 4.1 | 74.2 | 38.6 | 42.0 | 93.1 |
| WICHITA | 8.6 | 11.8 | 7.4 | 7.2 | 6.8 | 8.9 | 8.0 | 27.4 | 21.5 | 11.1 | 1.8 | 74.7 | 31.7 | 34.2 | 98.3 |
| WILBARGER | 14.5 | 18.8 | 7.2 | 7.2 | 7.2 | 8.6 | 5.8 | 24.3 | 22.8 | 14.1 | 2.8 | 73.0 | 35.2 | 37.7 | 99.6 |
| WILLACY | 84.4 | 87.2 | 9.6 | 9.2 | 9.4 | 9.8 | 7.9 | 24.1 | 18.7 | 9.9 | 1.3 | 65.3 | 27.5 | 28.1 | 94.6 |
| WILLIAMSON | 14.3 | 19.2 | 8.7 | 8.8 | 8.5 | 8.0 | 6.3 | 32.4 | 20.6 | 5.9 | 0.9 | 69.1 | 30.1 | 32.1 | 96.9 |
| WILSON | 35.6 | 43.3 | 8.2 | 8.4 | 8.2 | 8.5 | 6.5 | 25.9 | 22.8 | 10.1 | 1.5 | 69.6 | 32.0 | 34.1 | 99.2 |
| WINKLER | 36.8 | 44.4 | 8.7 | 8.9 | 8.9 | 8.9 | 6.3 | 24.7 | 20.9 | 11.4 | 1.4 | 67.5 | 31.1 | 32.5 | 97.9 |
| WISE | 7.7 | 10.5 | 7.4 | 7.6 | 7.8 | 7.6 | 5.6 | 26.8 | 25.3 | 10.4 | 1.5 | 72.3 | 33.5 | 36.8 | 103.4 |
| WOOD | 2.7 | 4.3 | 5.6 | 6.2 | 6.6 | 7.5 | 5.8 | 22.1 | 26.1 | 17.4 | 2.7 | 77.0 | 39.6 | 42.3 | 95.1 |
| YOAKUM | 36.6 | 42.0 | 8.9 | 9.3 | 8.9 | 9.0 | 6.4 | 26.6 | 20.6 | 9.2 | 1.1 | 66.8 | 29.0 | 31.2 | 101.7 |
| YOUNG | 6.4 | 8.7 | 7.1 | 7.3 | 7.5 | 7.1 | 4.9 | 23.7 | 24.3 | 15.2 | 2.9 | 73.5 | 36.4 | 40.0 | 92.6 |
| ZAPATA | 81.0 | 85.8 | 10.4 | 9.4 | 9.1 | 9.0 | 7.3 | 23.7 | 18.9 | 11.0 | 1.2 | 65.2 | 29.0 | 28.9 | 95.5 |
| ZAVALA | 89.4 | 91.3 | 10.2 | 9.2 | 9.2 | 9.7 | 8.1 | 25.5 | 18.0 | 9.0 | 1.0 | 65.4 | 26.8 | 27.4 | 101.1 |
| TEXAS | 25.6 | 30.4 | 8.1 | 7.8 | 7.7 | 8.0 | 7.4 | 29.6 | 21.4 | 8.8 | 1.2 | 71.8 | 30.8 | 33.2 | 97.3 |
| UNITED STATES | 9.0 | 11.8 | 6.9 | 7.2 | 7.2 | 7.2 | 6.7 | 29.9 | 22.2 | 11.1 | 1.6 | 74.6 | 32.9 | 35.7 | 95.6 |

| COUNTY | HOUSEHOLDS | | | | | FAMILIES | | | MEDIAN HOUSEHOLD INCOME | | | |
|---|---|---|---|---|---|---|---|---|---|---|---|---|
| | 1990 | 2000 | 2005 | % Annual Rate 1990-2000 | 2000 Average HH Size | 1990 | 2000 | % Annual Rate 1990-2000 | 2000 | 2005 | 2000 National Rank | 2000 State Rank |
| UVALDE | 7,553 | 8,527 | 9,090 | 1.5 | 3.05 | 5,949 | 6,637 | 1.3 | 25,293 | 30,269 | 2780 | 204 |
| VAL VERDE | 11,840 | 13,981 | 14,988 | 2.0 | 3.15 | 9,633 | 11,275 | 1.9 | 25,390 | 30,480 | 2766 | 203 |
| VAN ZANDT | 14,349 | 17,468 | 19,184 | 2.4 | 2.58 | 10,968 | 12,871 | 2.0 | 31,761 | 39,981 | 1766 | 111 |
| VICTORIA | 26,228 | 29,728 | 31,057 | 1.5 | 2.75 | 19,820 | 21,940 | 1.2 | 40,338 | 45,999 | 643 | 26 |
| WALKER | 14,918 | 16,573 | 17,157 | 1.3 | 2.47 | 9,521 | 10,201 | 0.8 | 30,492 | 37,437 | 2038 | 134 |
| WALLER | 7,402 | 9,258 | 10,381 | 2.7 | 2.79 | 5,360 | 6,490 | 2.3 | 29,401 | 33,272 | 2235 | 151 |
| WARD | 4,444 | 3,977 | 3,761 | -1.3 | 2.75 | 3,437 | 3,004 | -1.6 | 24,482 | 30,688 | 2856 | 216 |
| WASHINGTON | 9,619 | 11,075 | 11,594 | 1.7 | 2.50 | 6,821 | 7,647 | 1.4 | 32,918 | 38,698 | 1551 | 83 |
| WEBB | 34,438 | 52,067 | 60,521 | 5.1 | 3.79 | 29,469 | 44,833 | 5.2 | 30,477 | 37,879 | 2041 | 135 |
| WHARTON | 14,210 | 14,467 | 14,745 | 0.2 | 2.76 | 10,523 | 10,440 | -0.1 | 31,845 | 36,619 | 1750 | 110 |
| WHEELER | 2,350 | 2,141 | 2,142 | -1.1 | 2.43 | 1,653 | 1,448 | -1.6 | 29,367 | 31,921 | 2241 | 152 |
| WICHITA | 45,271 | 47,013 | 47,140 | 0.5 | 2.52 | 32,241 | 32,446 | 0.1 | 34,990 | 42,374 | 1253 | 65 |
| WILBARGER | 5,741 | 5,405 | 5,302 | -0.7 | 2.47 | 3,999 | 3,627 | -1.2 | 30,819 | 38,674 | 1966 | 129 |
| WILLACY | 5,049 | 5,751 | 5,952 | 1.6 | 3.40 | 4,153 | 4,713 | 1.5 | 22,288 | 25,657 | 3011 | 232 |
| WILLIAMSON | 48,792 | 89,115 | 114,965 | 7.6 | 2.84 | 37,440 | 66,977 | 7.3 | 55,423 | 68,752 | 119 | 4 |
| WILSON | 7,481 | 11,286 | 13,418 | 5.1 | 2.96 | 6,132 | 9,121 | 4.9 | 36,233 | 44,242 | 1077 | 49 |
| WINKLER | 2,941 | 2,745 | 2,645 | -0.8 | 2.77 | 2,326 | 2,130 | -1.1 | 32,300 | 38,105 | 1660 | 98 |
| WISE | 12,175 | 16,764 | 20,330 | 4.0 | 2.83 | 9,581 | 12,833 | 3.6 | 38,167 | 46,457 | 841 | 34 |
| WOOD | 11,426 | 13,764 | 14,577 | 2.3 | 2.43 | 8,443 | 9,803 | 1.8 | 31,199 | 37,743 | 1887 | 122 |
| YOAKUM | 2,839 | 2,573 | 2,424 | -1.2 | 2.97 | 2,362 | 2,102 | -1.4 | 35,585 | 42,418 | 1159 | 56 |
| YOUNG | 7,101 | 7,019 | 7,081 | -0.1 | 2.47 | 5,200 | 4,973 | -0.5 | 30,174 | 35,870 | 2111 | 140 |
| ZAPATA | 2,862 | 3,688 | 3,922 | 3.1 | 3.12 | 2,368 | 3,013 | 3.0 | 25,592 | 31,517 | 2746 | 201 |
| ZAVALA | 3,356 | 3,344 | 3,344 | 0.0 | 3.47 | 2,783 | 2,765 | -0.1 | 17,514 | 20,621 | 3135 | 252 |
| TEXAS | | | | 2.4 | 2.71 | | | 2.1 | 39,535 | 46,148 | | |
| UNITED STATES | | | | 1.4 | 2.59 | | | 1.1 | 41,914 | 49,127 | | |

| COUNTY | 2000 Per Capita Income | 2000 HH Income Base | 2000 HOUSEHOLD INCOME DISTRIBUTION (%) Less than $15,000 | $15,000 to $24,999 | $25,000 to $49,999 | $50,000 to $99,999 | $100,000 to $149,999 | $150,000 or More | 2000 AVERAGE DISPOSABLE INCOME BY AGE OF HOUSEHOLDER All Ages | <35 | 35-44 | 45-54 | 55-64 | 65+ |
|---|---|---|---|---|---|---|---|---|---|---|---|---|---|---|
| UVALDE | 12,969 | 8,527 | 29.0 | 20.6 | 29.0 | 15.9 | 3.4 | 2.2 | 30,453 | 24,770 | 32,694 | 35,535 | 35,149 | 24,386 |
| VAL VERDE | 10,942 | 13,981 | 30.6 | 18.7 | 31.4 | 15.9 | 2.7 | 0.7 | 27,419 | 24,600 | 31,745 | 33,262 | 29,637 | 19,859 |
| VAN ZANDT | 15,919 | 17,468 | 20.5 | 18.2 | 33.0 | 23.1 | 3.7 | 1.4 | 33,257 | 32,231 | 38,931 | 41,594 | 35,226 | 22,864 |
| VICTORIA | 19,911 | 29,728 | 17.2 | 12.5 | 32.4 | 28.3 | 6.5 | 3.0 | 40,842 | 32,534 | 45,799 | 50,240 | 41,123 | 28,040 |
| WALKER | 14,424 | 16,573 | 25.5 | 17.0 | 31.4 | 20.4 | 4.3 | 1.5 | 32,230 | 23,960 | 39,785 | 43,049 | 38,654 | 26,352 |
| WALLER | 14,153 | 9,258 | 26.9 | 17.5 | 30.3 | 20.5 | 3.3 | 1.5 | 31,534 | 24,702 | 37,347 | 39,642 | 33,585 | 21,342 |
| WARD | 11,689 | 3,977 | 30.5 | 20.4 | 32.4 | 14.5 | 1.3 | 0.8 | 26,213 | 23,868 | 30,741 | 30,644 | 28,380 | 17,438 |
| WASHINGTON | 16,759 | 11,075 | 21.6 | 14.9 | 34.0 | 23.1 | 4.5 | 1.9 | 34,667 | 28,558 | 39,964 | 45,138 | 42,583 | 23,259 |
| WEBB | 11,462 | 52,067 | 24.9 | 16.8 | 31.4 | 20.3 | 4.7 | 2.0 | 33,408 | 30,468 | 35,833 | 38,652 | 34,146 | 23,838 |
| WHARTON | 14,813 | 14,467 | 24.0 | 15.3 | 33.2 | 22.1 | 4.2 | 1.3 | 32,687 | 29,000 | 37,099 | 39,858 | 35,469 | 23,849 |
| WHEELER | 14,740 | 2,141 | 25.1 | 18.1 | 34.4 | 18.6 | 3.0 | 0.7 | 29,464 | 26,156 | 34,950 | 41,595 | 31,239 | 19,279 |
| WICHITA | 17,255 | 46,999 | 18.2 | 15.7 | 35.2 | 25.1 | 4.4 | 1.4 | 35,115 | 29,663 | 39,498 | 44,096 | 38,383 | 26,315 |
| WILBARGER | 14,562 | 5,405 | 22.5 | 16.9 | 36.1 | 21.0 | 3.2 | 0.3 | 30,544 | 28,534 | 37,929 | 38,391 | 33,399 | 22,020 |
| WILLACY | 9,430 | 5,751 | 34.7 | 19.3 | 28.9 | 13.9 | 2.1 | 1.1 | 25,977 | 21,384 | 25,791 | 34,605 | 29,526 | 20,387 |
| WILLIAMSON | 24,739 | 89,115 | 7.4 | 7.5 | 28.4 | 40.0 | 12.5 | 4.2 | 51,558 | 44,332 | 55,739 | 63,440 | 49,338 | 30,513 |
| WILSON | 15,361 | 11,286 | 16.7 | 15.9 | 35.0 | 25.7 | 4.9 | 1.8 | 36,351 | 32,480 | 41,461 | 44,777 | 36,800 | 23,621 |
| WINKLER | 14,422 | 2,745 | 20.0 | 18.6 | 38.2 | 19.2 | 3.0 | 1.0 | 31,272 | 28,137 | 36,152 | 39,389 | 33,087 | 23,359 |
| WISE | 18,166 | 16,764 | 14.9 | 13.6 | 36.1 | 26.5 | 6.2 | 2.7 | 39,660 | 32,765 | 45,811 | 49,128 | 39,430 | 26,502 |
| WOOD | 16,650 | 13,764 | 22.0 | 18.2 | 33.6 | 20.9 | 4.0 | 1.3 | 32,189 | 29,254 | 38,407 | 42,235 | 35,126 | 22,189 |
| YOAKUM | 15,528 | 2,573 | 19.2 | 14.9 | 34.4 | 23.6 | 5.7 | 2.3 | 36,692 | 31,650 | 39,375 | 46,946 | 34,868 | 27,125 |
| YOUNG | 17,223 | 7,019 | 24.0 | 16.5 | 36.0 | 17.0 | 3.8 | 2.7 | 33,547 | 28,110 | 40,041 | 43,499 | 35,437 | 22,168 |
| ZAPATA | 11,131 | 3,688 | 30.6 | 18.3 | 30.9 | 16.1 | 3.3 | 0.9 | 27,947 | 23,279 | 30,651 | 33,892 | 32,708 | 22,364 |
| ZAVALA | 7,512 | 3,344 | 42.8 | 21.6 | 22.7 | 10.1 | 1.8 | 1.0 | 22,324 | 18,781 | 26,050 | 24,576 | 27,761 | 16,965 |
| TEXAS | 20,236 | | 16.2 | 13.9 | 31.8 | 28.0 | 6.9 | 3.2 | 41,217 | 33,340 | 45,769 | 49,732 | 43,451 | 28,369 |
| UNITED STATES | 22,162 | | 14.5 | 12.5 | 32.3 | 29.8 | 7.4 | 3.5 | 40,748 | 34,503 | 44,969 | 49,579 | 43,409 | 27,339 |

| COUNTY | FINANCIAL SERVICES | | | | THE HOME | | | | | | ENTERTAINMENT | | | | | | PERSONAL | | | |
|---|---|---|---|---|---|---|---|---|---|---|---|---|---|---|---|---|---|---|---|---|
| | | | | | Home Improvements | | | Furnishings | | | | | | | | | | | | |
| | Auto Loan | Home Loan | Investments | Retirement Plans | Home Repair | Lawn & Garden | Remodeling | Appliances | Electronics | Furniture | Restaurants | Sporting Goods | Theater & Concerts | Toys & Hobbies | Travel | Video Rental | Apparel | Auto Aftermarket | Health Insurance | Pets & Supplies |
| UVALDE | 95 | 84 | 88 | 82 | 93 | 93 | 105 | 97 | 94 | 85 | 88 | 92 | 86 | 95 | 78 | 97 | 83 | 93 | 100 | 101 |
| VAL VERDE | 95 | 91 | 87 | 83 | 92 | 92 | 98 | 97 | 96 | 89 | 92 | 92 | 89 | 94 | 79 | 98 | 86 | 95 | 97 | 101 |
| VAN ZANDT | 97 | 71 | 81 | 80 | 94 | 92 | 112 | 95 | 93 | 80 | 82 | 93 | 82 | 95 | 72 | 97 | 82 | 89 | 102 | 97 |
| VICTORIA | 99 | 100 | 98 | 99 | 99 | 99 | 102 | 99 | 100 | 98 | 100 | 100 | 97 | 101 | 86 | 99 | 97 | 100 | 99 | 103 |
| WALKER | 96 | 89 | 91 | 90 | 95 | 93 | 106 | 94 | 92 | 87 | 91 | 94 | 87 | 96 | 79 | 95 | 89 | 93 | 97 | 98 |
| WALLER | 95 | 81 | 85 | 83 | 96 | 91 | 106 | 95 | 92 | 86 | 86 | 92 | 86 | 95 | 77 | 96 | 86 | 91 | 96 | 98 |
| WARD | 96 | 89 | 92 | 87 | 96 | 95 | 103 | 97 | 95 | 92 | 93 | 95 | 91 | 98 | 80 | 97 | 90 | 95 | 98 | 100 |
| WASHINGTON | 96 | 76 | 84 | 82 | 95 | 93 | 108 | 95 | 92 | 83 | 84 | 93 | 85 | 95 | 75 | 97 | 84 | 90 | 100 | 97 |
| WEBB | 95 | 93 | 89 | 85 | 93 | 93 | 97 | 97 | 96 | 89 | 92 | 92 | 89 | 94 | 81 | 98 | 85 | 96 | 98 | 102 |
| WHARTON | 98 | 79 | 89 | 86 | 96 | 95 | 109 | 97 | 94 | 85 | 87 | 96 | 87 | 97 | 77 | 98 | 86 | 92 | 101 | 100 |
| WHEELER | 94 | 64 | 74 | 75 | 92 | 91 | 109 | 93 | 91 | 74 | 78 | 89 | 77 | 91 | 69 | 97 | 78 | 87 | 103 | 94 |
| WICHITA | 97 | 91 | 96 | 92 | 100 | 97 | 101 | 97 | 95 | 93 | 94 | 96 | 94 | 98 | 84 | 97 | 93 | 96 | 98 | 98 |
| WILBARGER | 96 | 70 | 82 | 80 | 95 | 93 | 108 | 95 | 91 | 79 | 81 | 93 | 82 | 95 | 73 | 97 | 82 | 89 | 102 | 97 |
| WILLACY | 93 | 89 | 92 | 81 | 93 | 93 | 97 | 97 | 94 | 87 | 90 | 89 | 87 | 92 | 80 | 97 | 82 | 94 | 98 | 101 |
| WILLIAMSON | 103 | 107 | 90 | 101 | 98 | 100 | 101 | 101 | 104 | 105 | 110 | 106 | 102 | 105 | 87 | 101 | 107 | 105 | 98 | 105 |
| WILSON | 96 | 81 | 84 | 80 | 92 | 91 | 107 | 96 | 93 | 85 | 87 | 93 | 85 | 95 | 74 | 97 | 83 | 92 | 99 | 99 |
| WINKLER | 97 | 86 | 90 | 85 | 95 | 94 | 105 | 97 | 95 | 89 | 91 | 94 | 89 | 98 | 79 | 98 | 88 | 94 | 100 | 101 |
| WISE | 99 | 77 | 84 | 84 | 95 | 93 | 116 | 98 | 94 | 85 | 88 | 97 | 86 | 100 | 74 | 98 | 87 | 92 | 102 | 101 |
| WOOD | 97 | 69 | 79 | 80 | 94 | 92 | 112 | 96 | 92 | 78 | 81 | 93 | 81 | 95 | 71 | 97 | 82 | 89 | 102 | 97 |
| YOAKUM | 97 | 88 | 88 | 86 | 95 | 93 | 104 | 97 | 96 | 90 | 93 | 96 | 90 | 99 | 78 | 98 | 89 | 95 | 99 | 101 |
| YOUNG | 97 | 72 | 80 | 80 | 94 | 91 | 112 | 95 | 92 | 80 | 83 | 93 | 82 | 96 | 72 | 97 | 83 | 89 | 102 | 97 |
| ZAPATA | 94 | 86 | 103 | 82 | 97 | 98 | 98 | 97 | 91 | 85 | 89 | 90 | 88 | 93 | 82 | 96 | 80 | 92 | 102 | 100 |
| ZAVALA | 93 | 88 | 89 | 79 | 92 | 92 | 97 | 96 | 94 | 86 | 89 | 89 | 86 | 92 | 79 | 97 | 81 | 93 | 98 | 101 |
| TEXAS | 99 | 100 | 96 | 98 | 99 | 99 | 101 | 99 | 99 | 98 | 100 | 100 | 97 | 100 | 87 | 99 | 98 | 100 | 98 | 102 |
| UNITED STATES | 100 | 100 | 100 | 100 | 100 | 100 | 100 | 100 | 100 | 100 | 100 | 100 | 100 | 100 | 100 | 100 | 100 | 100 | 100 | 100 |

# POPULATION CHANGE

| COUNTY | FIPS Code | MSA Code | DMA Code | POPULATION 1990 | POPULATION 2000 | POPULATION 2005 | 1990-2000 ANNUAL CHANGE % Rate | 1990-2000 ANNUAL CHANGE State Rank | RACE (%) White 1990 | White 2000 | Black 1990 | Black 2000 | Asian/Pacific 1990 | Asian/Pacific 2000 |
|---|---|---|---|---|---|---|---|---|---|---|---|---|---|---|
| BEAVER | 001 | 0000 | 770 | 4,765 | 6,110 | 6,650 | 2.5 | 11 | 97.5 | 96.9 | 0.1 | 0.1 | 0.4 | 0.6 |
| BOX ELDER | 003 | 0000 | 770 | 36,485 | 43,671 | 48,018 | 1.8 | 15 | 95.2 | 93.6 | 0.1 | 0.1 | 1.1 | 1.6 |
| CACHE | 005 | 0000 | 770 | 70,183 | 88,098 | 92,221 | 2.2 | 12 | 94.8 | 93.2 | 0.3 | 0.3 | 2.7 | 3.6 |
| CARBON | 007 | 0000 | 770 | 20,228 | 20,899 | 20,897 | 0.3 | 28 | 94.2 | 91.9 | 0.3 | 0.4 | 0.6 | 0.8 |
| DAGGETT | 009 | 0000 | 770 | 690 | 709 | 709 | 0.3 | 28 | 97.7 | 97.3 | 0.0 | 0.0 | 0.7 | 1.0 |
| DAVIS | 011 | 7160 | 770 | 187,941 | 245,599 | 275,312 | 2.6 | 10 | 94.9 | 93.5 | 1.3 | 1.4 | 1.7 | 2.4 |
| DUCHESNE | 013 | 0000 | 770 | 12,645 | 15,009 | 16,245 | 1.7 | 16 | 93.4 | 92.4 | 0.1 | 0.2 | 0.3 | 0.4 |
| EMERY | 015 | 0000 | 770 | 10,332 | 11,162 | 11,659 | 0.8 | 25 | 98.0 | 97.3 | 0.0 | 0.0 | 0.3 | 0.5 |
| GARFIELD | 017 | 0000 | 770 | 3,980 | 4,318 | 4,473 | 0.8 | 25 | 97.7 | 97.7 | 0.0 | 0.0 | 0.2 | 0.3 |
| GRAND | 019 | 0000 | 770 | 6,620 | 8,263 | 8,660 | 2.2 | 12 | 95.8 | 95.4 | 0.1 | 0.4 | 0.4 | 0.5 |
| IRON | 021 | 0000 | 770 | 20,789 | 30,239 | 34,273 | 3.7 | 3 | 95.8 | 95.6 | 0.2 | 0.3 | 0.5 | 0.7 |
| JUAB | 023 | 0000 | 770 | 5,817 | 8,030 | 9,237 | 3.2 | 7 | 97.6 | 97.3 | 0.0 | 0.0 | 0.2 | 0.2 |
| KANE | 025 | 2620 | 770 | 5,169 | 6,173 | 6,285 | 1.7 | 16 | 97.3 | 96.9 | 0.1 | 0.1 | 0.5 | 0.6 |
| MILLARD | 027 | 0000 | 770 | 11,333 | 12,516 | 13,001 | 1.0 | 23 | 95.3 | 93.9 | 0.0 | 0.0 | 0.9 | 1.3 |
| MORGAN | 029 | 0000 | 770 | 5,528 | 7,348 | 8,106 | 2.8 | 9 | 98.8 | 98.4 | 0.1 | 0.2 | 0.3 | 0.4 |
| PIUTE | 031 | 0000 | 770 | 1,277 | 1,517 | 1,695 | 1.7 | 16 | 99.2 | 99.2 | 0.0 | 0.0 | 0.1 | 0.1 |
| RICH | 033 | 0000 | 770 | 1,725 | 1,950 | 2,126 | 1.2 | 22 | 98.8 | 98.3 | 0.1 | 0.1 | 0.3 | 0.4 |
| SALT LAKE | 035 | 7160 | 770 | 725,956 | 856,773 | 889,624 | 1.6 | 21 | 93.0 | 90.6 | 0.8 | 1.0 | 2.8 | 3.7 |
| SAN JUAN | 037 | 0000 | 770 | 12,621 | 13,615 | 13,670 | 0.7 | 27 | 43.6 | 44.2 | 0.1 | 0.2 | 0.3 | 0.5 |
| SANPETE | 039 | 0000 | 770 | 16,259 | 22,631 | 25,499 | 3.3 | 6 | 95.6 | 93.7 | 0.1 | 0.2 | 1.5 | 1.7 |
| SEVIER | 041 | 0000 | 770 | 15,431 | 18,968 | 20,541 | 2.0 | 14 | 97.1 | 96.6 | 0.0 | 0.1 | 0.2 | 0.3 |
| SUMMIT | 043 | 0000 | 770 | 15,518 | 28,715 | 33,915 | 6.2 | 1 | 98.6 | 98.2 | 0.1 | 0.1 | 0.5 | 0.7 |
| TOOELE | 045 | 0000 | 770 | 26,601 | 37,811 | 47,618 | 3.5 | 4 | 91.5 | 88.9 | 0.9 | 0.9 | 0.8 | 1.1 |
| UINTAH | 047 | 0000 | 770 | 22,211 | 26,298 | 27,911 | 1.7 | 16 | 88.0 | 87.1 | 0.0 | 0.0 | 0.4 | 0.6 |
| UTAH | 049 | 6520 | 770 | 263,590 | 355,170 | 396,568 | 3.0 | 8 | 96.2 | 95.0 | 0.1 | 0.2 | 1.5 | 2.0 |
| WASATCH | 051 | 0000 | 770 | 10,089 | 14,262 | 16,719 | 3.4 | 5 | 98.5 | 98.1 | 0.0 | 0.0 | 0.2 | 0.3 |
| WASHINGTON | 053 | 0000 | 770 | 48,560 | 88,560 | 104,800 | 6.0 | 2 | 97.2 | 96.8 | 0.1 | 0.1 | 0.6 | 0.8 |
| WAYNE | 055 | 0000 | 770 | 2,177 | 2,397 | 2,456 | 0.9 | 24 | 97.5 | 96.6 | 0.0 | 0.0 | 0.1 | 0.1 |
| WEBER | 057 | 7160 | 770 | 158,330 | 187,364 | 197,053 | 1.7 | 16 | 92.6 | 89.9 | 1.5 | 1.9 | 1.5 | 1.9 |
| UTAH | | | | | | | 2.2 | | 93.8 | 92.2 | 0.7 | 0.8 | 1.9 | 2.6 |
| UNITED STATES | | | | | | | 1.0 | | 80.3 | 77.9 | 12.1 | 12.4 | 2.9 | 3.9 |

| COUNTY | % HISPANIC ORIGIN | | 2000 AGE DISTRIBUTION (%) | | | | | | | | | | MEDIAN AGE | | 2000 Males/ Females (×100) |
|---|---|---|---|---|---|---|---|---|---|---|---|---|---|---|---|
| | 1990 | 2000 | 0-4 | 5-9 | 10-14 | 15-19 | 20-24 | 25-44 | 45-64 | 65-84 | 85+ | 18+ | 1990 | 2000 | |
| BEAVER | 2.5 | 4.1 | 8.3 | 8.2 | 8.5 | 10.2 | 6.9 | 21.2 | 21.4 | 13.3 | 2.1 | 68.1 | 31.9 | 33.2 | 97.0 |
| BOX ELDER | 4.4 | 6.8 | 10.6 | 9.7 | 9.4 | 10.1 | 7.7 | 23.6 | 18.9 | 8.9 | 1.3 | 63.4 | 26.7 | 27.0 | 99.7 |
| CACHE | 2.5 | 4.3 | 11.2 | 9.3 | 8.5 | 10.2 | 12.6 | 27.7 | 13.6 | 5.8 | 1.1 | 65.9 | 23.7 | 24.3 | 100.1 |
| CARBON | 11.1 | 17.0 | 8.0 | 7.5 | 8.1 | 10.2 | 8.2 | 24.4 | 20.0 | 11.8 | 1.7 | 70.0 | 30.8 | 31.7 | 95.7 |
| DAGGETT | 2.2 | 3.8 | 9.4 | 7.6 | 8.2 | 8.0 | 6.3 | 23.1 | 25.1 | 10.7 | 1.4 | 68.7 | 32.1 | 35.3 | 100.3 |
| DAVIS | 3.9 | 6.2 | 10.6 | 9.1 | 9.2 | 10.3 | 9.5 | 26.6 | 17.6 | 6.5 | 0.7 | 64.5 | 24.7 | 25.9 | 100.4 |
| DUCHESNE | 2.8 | 4.9 | 10.7 | 9.7 | 9.8 | 10.8 | 8.1 | 23.5 | 18.9 | 7.6 | 0.9 | 62.2 | 25.0 | 25.7 | 103.0 |
| EMERY | 2.1 | 3.5 | 9.8 | 9.5 | 9.8 | 10.9 | 8.0 | 24.2 | 19.0 | 7.8 | 1.1 | 63.3 | 25.4 | 26.6 | 103.9 |
| GARFIELD | 0.9 | 1.7 | 8.8 | 8.3 | 8.3 | 9.4 | 6.9 | 20.9 | 21.9 | 13.8 | 1.7 | 68.5 | 31.3 | 33.5 | 102.6 |
| GRAND | 4.4 | 7.5 | 7.4 | 7.0 | 7.6 | 8.5 | 7.1 | 24.8 | 24.5 | 11.9 | 1.2 | 71.9 | 34.0 | 36.4 | 94.1 |
| IRON | 1.8 | 2.9 | 9.2 | 7.9 | 8.1 | 11.0 | 13.0 | 24.0 | 17.2 | 8.4 | 1.0 | 68.9 | 24.5 | 25.5 | 99.0 |
| JUAB | 1.3 | 2.2 | 9.4 | 8.7 | 9.4 | 10.6 | 7.7 | 22.4 | 20.1 | 10.0 | 1.7 | 64.9 | 28.9 | 28.5 | 98.9 |
| KANE | 2.0 | 3.3 | 8.7 | 8.1 | 8.6 | 9.5 | 7.6 | 21.4 | 21.9 | 12.5 | 1.7 | 68.2 | 30.8 | 32.3 | 103.3 |
| MILLARD | 3.5 | 5.6 | 11.2 | 10.0 | 9.8 | 10.7 | 7.1 | 21.9 | 18.0 | 9.8 | 1.6 | 61.2 | 26.2 | 26.0 | 101.5 |
| MORGAN | 1.4 | 2.4 | 9.2 | 9.1 | 9.5 | 11.1 | 7.5 | 23.0 | 22.1 | 7.5 | 1.0 | 64.6 | 26.5 | 28.1 | 103.3 |
| PIUTE | 1.2 | 2.3 | 6.4 | 6.7 | 7.2 | 9.3 | 6.9 | 17.3 | 26.6 | 17.6 | 2.0 | 72.4 | 38.5 | 41.3 | 108.7 |
| RICH | 1.2 | 2.3 | 10.5 | 9.6 | 10.1 | 10.8 | 6.4 | 22.7 | 18.9 | 9.7 | 1.3 | 61.2 | 26.8 | 27.4 | 105.7 |
| SALT LAKE | 6.0 | 9.4 | 9.5 | 8.6 | 8.5 | 9.0 | 8.8 | 29.1 | 18.2 | 7.3 | 1.0 | 67.8 | 27.8 | 28.7 | 99.0 |
| SAN JUAN | 3.5 | 5.2 | 11.3 | 10.2 | 10.6 | 10.2 | 8.9 | 24.0 | 17.1 | 6.6 | 1.2 | 61.1 | 22.7 | 24.4 | 99.7 |
| SANPETE | 3.4 | 6.0 | 8.6 | 8.7 | 8.9 | 13.6 | 9.9 | 21.7 | 17.8 | 9.4 | 1.5 | 67.4 | 24.4 | 25.4 | 101.7 |
| SEVIER | 1.9 | 3.2 | 9.3 | 8.7 | 9.2 | 10.5 | 7.7 | 21.3 | 20.0 | 11.6 | 1.8 | 65.3 | 29.0 | 29.1 | 99.2 |
| SUMMIT | 2.1 | 3.5 | 8.6 | 8.0 | 8.2 | 8.4 | 7.8 | 32.4 | 21.1 | 4.9 | 0.5 | 69.5 | 30.2 | 31.2 | 104.4 |
| TOOELE | 11.1 | 16.1 | 8.9 | 7.9 | 8.3 | 9.9 | 8.7 | 26.1 | 21.0 | 8.3 | 0.9 | 68.3 | 28.3 | 29.2 | 102.2 |
| UINTAH | 3.1 | 4.8 | 10.2 | 9.4 | 9.5 | 10.4 | 8.1 | 24.4 | 19.0 | 8.1 | 0.9 | 63.7 | 26.1 | 26.9 | 98.2 |
| UTAH | 3.2 | 5.2 | 10.3 | 7.7 | 8.2 | 12.5 | 18.1 | 22.3 | 13.9 | 6.2 | 0.9 | 67.2 | 22.5 | 23.1 | 96.8 |
| WASATCH | 2.5 | 3.9 | 9.9 | 8.8 | 9.3 | 10.0 | 8.6 | 25.0 | 19.5 | 7.7 | 1.1 | 65.1 | 27.2 | 27.6 | 101.8 |
| WASHINGTON | 1.8 | 3.0 | 9.7 | 8.5 | 8.4 | 10.9 | 8.7 | 21.5 | 17.4 | 13.3 | 1.7 | 66.9 | 28.4 | 28.1 | 97.3 |
| WAYNE | 1.1 | 3.3 | 8.6 | 8.5 | 9.2 | 10.6 | 6.1 | 22.3 | 20.4 | 12.7 | 1.7 | 66.2 | 30.6 | 31.9 | 108.4 |
| WEBER | 7.0 | 10.9 | 9.3 | 8.3 | 8.3 | 8.8 | 8.3 | 27.6 | 18.6 | 9.6 | 1.3 | 68.7 | 28.8 | 29.7 | 96.6 |
| UTAH | 4.9 | 7.5 | 9.8 | 8.5 | 8.6 | 10.0 | 10.5 | 26.5 | 17.5 | 7.7 | 1.0 | 67.0 | 26.2 | 26.8 | 98.8 |
| UNITED STATES | 9.0 | 11.8 | 6.9 | 7.2 | 7.2 | 7.2 | 6.7 | 29.9 | 22.2 | 11.1 | 1.6 | 74.6 | 32.9 | 35.7 | 95.6 |

# HOUSEHOLDS

| COUNTY | HOUSEHOLDS 1990 | HOUSEHOLDS 2000 | HOUSEHOLDS 2005 | HOUSEHOLDS % Annual Rate 1990-2000 | HOUSEHOLDS 2000 Average HH Size | FAMILIES 1990 | FAMILIES 2000 | FAMILIES % Annual Rate 1990-2000 | MEDIAN HOUSEHOLD INCOME 2000 | MEDIAN HOUSEHOLD INCOME 2005 | 2000 National Rank | 2000 State Rank |
|---|---|---|---|---|---|---|---|---|---|---|---|---|
| BEAVER | 1,594 | 2,187 | 2,458 | 3.9 | 2.77 | 1,228 | 1,637 | 3.5 | 30,111 | 36,942 | 2129 | 26 |
| BOX ELDER | 10,954 | 13,283 | 14,698 | 2.4 | 3.27 | 8,979 | 10,656 | 2.1 | 43,497 | 53,481 | 424 | 9 |
| CACHE | 21,021 | 25,772 | 26,677 | 2.5 | 3.37 | 15,898 | 18,960 | 2.2 | 37,693 | 46,508 | 879 | 12 |
| CARBON | 6,907 | 7,785 | 8,142 | 1.5 | 2.62 | 5,280 | 5,804 | 1.2 | 34,603 | 39,279 | 1306 | 18 |
| DAGGETT | 253 | 326 | 326 | 3.1 | 2.17 | 184 | 237 | 3.1 | 36,071 | 42,353 | 1093 | 16 |
| DAVIS | 53,598 | 74,718 | 86,395 | 4.1 | 3.24 | 45,352 | 62,081 | 3.9 | 50,608 | 58,807 | 194 | 2 |
| DUCHESNE | 3,707 | 4,750 | 5,328 | 3.1 | 3.15 | 3,056 | 3,821 | 2.7 | 30,844 | 35,536 | 1961 | 24 |
| EMERY | 2,998 | 3,386 | 3,614 | 1.5 | 3.28 | 2,494 | 2,756 | 1.2 | 40,905 | 49,386 | 598 | 10 |
| GARFIELD | 1,321 | 1,482 | 1,559 | 1.4 | 2.90 | 1,050 | 1,144 | 1.0 | 31,169 | 38,631 | 1894 | 23 |
| GRAND | 2,489 | 3,654 | 4,129 | 4.8 | 2.24 | 1,734 | 2,480 | 4.4 | 34,436 | 41,687 | 1324 | 19 |
| IRON | 6,269 | 9,664 | 11,244 | 5.4 | 3.06 | 4,878 | 7,315 | 5.0 | 38,578 | 48,066 | 795 | 11 |
| JUAB | 1,801 | 2,603 | 3,061 | 4.6 | 3.05 | 1,407 | 1,988 | 4.3 | 36,188 | 42,198 | 1081 | 15 |
| KANE | 1,724 | 2,303 | 2,471 | 3.6 | 2.67 | 1,329 | 1,728 | 3.2 | 31,956 | 37,514 | 1724 | 22 |
| MILLARD | 3,349 | 3,565 | 3,636 | 0.8 | 3.49 | 2,683 | 2,782 | 0.4 | 36,760 | 43,664 | 1011 | 14 |
| MORGAN | 1,555 | 2,139 | 2,397 | 3.9 | 3.43 | 1,357 | 1,840 | 3.8 | 48,011 | 59,444 | 236 | 3 |
| PIUTE | 449 | 549 | 623 | 2.5 | 2.76 | 350 | 418 | 2.2 | 26,292 | 34,010 | 2678 | 28 |
| RICH | 521 | 552 | 583 | 0.7 | 3.49 | 420 | 434 | 0.4 | 30,221 | 33,795 | 2100 | 25 |
| SALT LAKE | 240,680 | 300,330 | 320,341 | 2.7 | 2.82 | 175,036 | 215,191 | 2.5 | 45,474 | 52,464 | 332 | 7 |
| SAN JUAN | 3,375 | 4,218 | 4,538 | 2.7 | 3.20 | 2,773 | 3,406 | 2.5 | 25,226 | 28,439 | 2789 | 29 |
| SANPETE | 4,859 | 6,609 | 7,474 | 3.8 | 3.26 | 3,708 | 4,890 | 3.4 | 29,757 | 36,907 | 2191 | 27 |
| SEVIER | 4,877 | 6,335 | 7,051 | 3.2 | 2.96 | 3,883 | 4,897 | 2.9 | 32,191 | 38,301 | 1687 | 21 |
| SUMMIT | 5,271 | 10,528 | 12,876 | 8.7 | 2.71 | 3,776 | 7,361 | 8.4 | 63,934 | 74,283 | 44 | 1 |
| TOOELE | 8,581 | 12,841 | 16,561 | 5.0 | 2.92 | 6,783 | 9,985 | 4.8 | 37,322 | 42,258 | 927 | 13 |
| UINTAH | 6,670 | 8,394 | 9,171 | 2.8 | 3.12 | 5,478 | 6,739 | 2.5 | 34,896 | 42,875 | 1271 | 17 |
| UTAH | 70,168 | 93,210 | 103,185 | 3.5 | 3.71 | 56,511 | 74,013 | 3.3 | 45,839 | 55,045 | 319 | 6 |
| WASATCH | 3,074 | 4,428 | 5,240 | 4.5 | 3.20 | 2,478 | 3,476 | 4.2 | 47,072 | 58,689 | 272 | 4 |
| WASHINGTON | 15,256 | 30,068 | 36,928 | 8.6 | 2.91 | 12,112 | 23,461 | 8.3 | 44,011 | 54,995 | 395 | 8 |
| WAYNE | 699 | 793 | 825 | 1.5 | 2.98 | 554 | 613 | 1.2 | 32,946 | 41,318 | 1548 | 20 |
| WEBER | 53,253 | 66,335 | 71,501 | 2.7 | 2.79 | 40,091 | 49,038 | 2.5 | 46,824 | 56,450 | 283 | 5 |
| UTAH | | | | 3.3 | 3.03 | | | 3.1 | 44,395 | 52,426 | | |
| UNITED STATES | | | | 1.4 | 2.59 | | | 1.1 | 41,914 | 49,127 | | |

| COUNTY | 2000 Per Capita Income | 2000 HH Income Base | 2000 HOUSEHOLD INCOME DISTRIBUTION (%) Less than $15,000 | $15,000 to $24,999 | $25,000 to $49,999 | $50,000 to $99,999 | $100,000 to $149,999 | $150,000 or More | 2000 AVERAGE DISPOSABLE INCOME BY AGE OF HOUSEHOLDER All Ages | <35 | 35-44 | 45-54 | 55-64 | 65+ |
|---|---|---|---|---|---|---|---|---|---|---|---|---|---|---|
| BEAVER | 12,534 | 2,187 | 19.6 | 21.5 | 37.4 | 19.7 | 1.7 | 0.1 | 27,254 | 25,128 | 33,953 | 35,040 | 32,045 | 17,418 |
| BOX ELDER | 16,096 | 13,283 | 9.3 | 8.1 | 41.3 | 34.7 | 5.6 | 1.0 | 38,361 | 32,967 | 42,000 | 48,983 | 45,355 | 26,426 |
| CACHE | 13,380 | 25,768 | 14.5 | 14.4 | 38.3 | 27.6 | 4.3 | 0.9 | 33,837 | 26,767 | 38,672 | 46,800 | 43,210 | 25,139 |
| CARBON | 15,199 | 7,782 | 20.7 | 14.9 | 36.4 | 24.1 | 3.1 | 0.9 | 30,700 | 26,309 | 40,553 | 37,229 | 31,708 | 20,151 |
| DAGGETT | 17,870 | 326 | 12.6 | 21.2 | 39.3 | 25.2 | 1.8 | 0.0 | 30,314 | 29,648 | 36,268 | 38,571 | 31,167 | 15,476 |
| DAVIS | 18,827 | 74,718 | 5.8 | 7.8 | 35.4 | 40.2 | 8.7 | 2.1 | 43,402 | 34,252 | 46,461 | 55,697 | 50,891 | 30,865 |
| DUCHESNE | 11,517 | 4,740 | 21.1 | 16.8 | 41.7 | 18.5 | 1.2 | 0.8 | 27,818 | 24,754 | 30,427 | 34,472 | 29,672 | 19,095 |
| EMERY | 13,073 | 3,386 | 14.0 | 11.1 | 41.6 | 30.9 | 2.4 | 0.2 | 33,313 | 31,357 | 40,014 | 40,448 | 34,984 | 19,085 |
| GARFIELD | 13,207 | 1,482 | 16.0 | 21.5 | 39.6 | 18.8 | 3.4 | 0.8 | 29,091 | 26,467 | 32,307 | 37,236 | 35,110 | 20,891 |
| GRAND | 18,870 | 3,654 | 16.2 | 13.4 | 41.5 | 23.7 | 4.1 | 1.2 | 32,249 | 27,657 | 36,522 | 42,015 | 33,148 | 22,666 |
| IRON | 15,075 | 9,664 | 11.9 | 15.9 | 37.5 | 28.1 | 5.1 | 1.6 | 35,270 | 26,790 | 41,520 | 49,918 | 42,976 | 26,920 |
| JUAB | 12,469 | 2,603 | 16.7 | 14.4 | 42.6 | 25.2 | 1.1 | 0.0 | 29,954 | 28,503 | 35,844 | 37,609 | 28,346 | 19,867 |
| KANE | 14,680 | 2,303 | 17.9 | 19.0 | 37.1 | 22.5 | 2.7 | 0.8 | 29,989 | 26,773 | 32,109 | 41,227 | 35,912 | 18,406 |
| MILLARD | 11,184 | 3,565 | 15.7 | 13.4 | 44.0 | 25.3 | 1.6 | 0.1 | 30,636 | 30,056 | 36,519 | 37,009 | 32,389 | 20,638 |
| MORGAN | 16,370 | 2,139 | 7.0 | 8.5 | 37.2 | 37.5 | 8.4 | 1.5 | 41,303 | 34,191 | 45,223 | 51,918 | 47,749 | 25,213 |
| PIUTE | 10,993 | 549 | 23.7 | 23.5 | 38.8 | 13.1 | 0.9 | 0.0 | 24,007 | 21,875 | 29,375 | 29,554 | 26,890 | 17,895 |
| RICH | 9,327 | 552 | 21.7 | 19.2 | 41.7 | 16.5 | 0.9 | 0.0 | 25,643 | 21,538 | 32,402 | 30,777 | 21,250 | 20,000 |
| SALT LAKE | 20,728 | 300,330 | 9.4 | 11.4 | 34.8 | 33.5 | 8.2 | 2.7 | 41,173 | 33,483 | 45,778 | 51,362 | 46,519 | 28,837 |
| SAN JUAN | 9,360 | 4,218 | 33.2 | 16.2 | 32.6 | 15.5 | 2.4 | 0.2 | 24,074 | 22,859 | 26,311 | 27,284 | 26,426 | 16,510 |
| SANPETE | 10,654 | 6,609 | 22.0 | 19.4 | 37.7 | 18.3 | 2.0 | 0.6 | 27,488 | 25,129 | 31,295 | 35,183 | 31,655 | 18,573 |
| SEVIER | 12,378 | 6,335 | 19.3 | 16.9 | 40.4 | 21.3 | 1.9 | 0.2 | 28,537 | 26,922 | 35,024 | 37,887 | 31,006 | 16,793 |
| SUMMIT | 38,953 | 10,528 | 3.7 | 7.1 | 26.6 | 34.9 | 14.5 | 13.1 | 64,106 | 46,564 | 64,266 | 74,332 | 55,334 | 31,044 |
| TOOELE | 13,943 | 12,841 | 14.9 | 12.5 | 42.1 | 28.5 | 1.8 | 0.1 | 31,724 | 26,588 | 35,848 | 40,913 | 34,111 | 20,835 |
| UINTAH | 12,898 | 8,394 | 18.0 | 15.5 | 40.2 | 22.8 | 2.9 | 0.6 | 30,579 | 26,492 | 36,188 | 36,333 | 31,097 | 21,762 |
| UTAH | 15,807 | 93,210 | 9.4 | 10.5 | 35.4 | 34.2 | 8.1 | 2.5 | 41,187 | 32,408 | 47,764 | 54,899 | 50,463 | 30,527 |
| WASATCH | 18,009 | 4,427 | 10.3 | 8.6 | 34.7 | 35.2 | 8.8 | 2.4 | 41,292 | 37,050 | 47,411 | 50,044 | 42,904 | 25,827 |
| WASHINGTON | 18,184 | 30,068 | 7.9 | 13.7 | 35.6 | 34.3 | 7.1 | 1.4 | 38,911 | 35,410 | 45,583 | 47,867 | 43,862 | 30,652 |
| WAYNE | 12,779 | 793 | 14.6 | 22.1 | 38.0 | 22.6 | 2.7 | 0.1 | 29,436 | 25,216 | 34,686 | 39,247 | 31,796 | 19,232 |
| WEBER | 19,972 | 66,334 | 9.0 | 9.5 | 35.2 | 37.7 | 7.2 | 1.4 | 40,227 | 34,433 | 44,723 | 51,063 | 46,321 | 28,428 |
| UTAH | 18,462 | | 10.0 | 11.3 | 35.7 | 33.4 | 7.4 | 2.2 | 39,988 | 32,718 | 44,911 | 50,872 | 45,507 | 27,888 |
| UNITED STATES | 22,162 | | 14.5 | 12.5 | 32.3 | 29.8 | 7.4 | 3.5 | 40,748 | 34,503 | 44,969 | 49,579 | 43,409 | 27,339 |

# SPENDING POTENTIAL INDEXES

| COUNTY | FINANCIAL SERVICES | | | | THE HOME | | | | | | ENTERTAINMENT | | | | | | PERSONAL | | | |
|---|---|---|---|---|---|---|---|---|---|---|---|---|---|---|---|---|---|---|---|---|
| | | | | | Home Improvements | | | Furnishings | | | | | | | | | | | | |
| | Auto Loan | Home Loan | Invest-ments | Retire-ment Plans | Home Repair | Lawn & Garden | Remodel-ing | Appli-ances | Elec-tronics | Furni-ture | Restau-rants | Sport-ing Goods | Theater & Concerts | Toys & Hobbies | Travel | Video Rental | Apparel | Auto After-market | Health Insur-ance | Pets & Supplies |
| BEAVER | 96 | 64 | 71 | 78 | 92 | 92 | 112 | 97 | 93 | 76 | 77 | 86 | 74 | 87 | 71 | 92 | 78 | 86 | 102 | 89 |
| BOX ELDER | 100 | 86 | 84 | 89 | 98 | 95 | 111 | 101 | 99 | 93 | 93 | 92 | 87 | 95 | 80 | 94 | 93 | 94 | 98 | 95 |
| CACHE | 99 | 98 | 90 | 96 | 99 | 97 | 103 | 99 | 100 | 97 | 98 | 92 | 89 | 94 | 86 | 93 | 97 | 97 | 96 | 94 |
| CARBON | 97 | 79 | 80 | 83 | 96 | 93 | 108 | 98 | 97 | 89 | 87 | 87 | 82 | 90 | 77 | 93 | 86 | 91 | 98 | 91 |
| DAGGETT | 101 | 79 | 76 | 89 | 95 | 94 | 123 | 102 | 98 | 86 | 87 | 95 | 83 | 96 | 77 | 95 | 89 | 93 | 103 | 97 |
| DAVIS | 101 | 104 | 90 | 99 | 100 | 100 | 101 | 103 | 105 | 107 | 107 | 96 | 96 | 97 | 90 | 96 | 105 | 103 | 96 | 97 |
| DUCHESNE | 98 | 83 | 79 | 85 | 93 | 92 | 111 | 100 | 98 | 91 | 90 | 91 | 83 | 93 | 76 | 94 | 89 | 93 | 97 | 93 |
| EMERY | 100 | 85 | 80 | 87 | 95 | 93 | 112 | 101 | 99 | 93 | 93 | 92 | 85 | 94 | 78 | 94 | 92 | 94 | 97 | 95 |
| GARFIELD | 97 | 68 | 74 | 79 | 94 | 92 | 114 | 98 | 95 | 80 | 79 | 87 | 77 | 89 | 72 | 92 | 81 | 87 | 100 | 91 |
| GRAND | 98 | 80 | 82 | 83 | 95 | 92 | 114 | 99 | 96 | 89 | 88 | 89 | 82 | 92 | 76 | 93 | 87 | 91 | 97 | 93 |
| IRON | 96 | 89 | 82 | 86 | 95 | 92 | 102 | 97 | 97 | 92 | 92 | 88 | 85 | 91 | 80 | 92 | 90 | 93 | 95 | 92 |
| JUAB | 101 | 77 | 81 | 86 | 97 | 94 | 119 | 101 | 98 | 87 | 88 | 92 | 83 | 95 | 76 | 94 | 89 | 92 | 101 | 96 |
| KANE | 97 | 72 | 76 | 79 | 92 | 91 | 113 | 98 | 94 | 83 | 83 | 87 | 78 | 89 | 73 | 92 | 82 | 88 | 99 | 91 |
| MILLARD | 99 | 82 | 77 | 86 | 94 | 92 | 108 | 100 | 99 | 89 | 90 | 91 | 84 | 93 | 77 | 94 | 89 | 93 | 98 | 93 |
| MORGAN | 104 | 93 | 92 | 98 | 100 | 100 | 115 | 104 | 105 | 100 | 100 | 97 | 94 | 99 | 86 | 96 | 101 | 100 | 100 | 99 |
| PIUTE | 99 | 63 | 69 | 80 | 91 | 92 | 113 | 98 | 92 | 73 | 76 | 91 | 74 | 90 | 69 | 92 | 78 | 87 | 104 | 92 |
| RICH | 100 | 70 | 76 | 85 | 94 | 93 | 123 | 100 | 94 | 79 | 81 | 93 | 78 | 93 | 73 | 93 | 83 | 89 | 104 | 94 |
| SALT LAKE | 100 | 104 | 95 | 100 | 102 | 102 | 100 | 102 | 103 | 105 | 104 | 95 | 95 | 96 | 92 | 94 | 103 | 101 | 96 | 96 |
| SAN JUAN | 96 | 89 | 81 | 85 | 94 | 92 | 103 | 99 | 98 | 94 | 90 | 88 | 84 | 90 | 80 | 93 | 89 | 94 | 93 | 93 |
| SANPETE | 97 | 69 | 75 | 80 | 93 | 92 | 114 | 97 | 93 | 78 | 80 | 88 | 76 | 89 | 72 | 92 | 81 | 87 | 101 | 91 |
| SEVIER | 98 | 76 | 81 | 84 | 95 | 94 | 113 | 99 | 97 | 86 | 85 | 88 | 81 | 91 | 76 | 93 | 86 | 90 | 100 | 92 |
| SUMMIT | 105 | 108 | 86 | 104 | 98 | 102 | 105 | 106 | 109 | 109 | 110 | 102 | 98 | 99 | 90 | 97 | 109 | 105 | 97 | 100 |
| TOOELE | 97 | 88 | 87 | 88 | 99 | 96 | 105 | 100 | 97 | 95 | 93 | 89 | 87 | 92 | 83 | 93 | 91 | 94 | 97 | 93 |
| UINTAH | 98 | 81 | 80 | 84 | 95 | 92 | 111 | 99 | 97 | 90 | 88 | 89 | 83 | 91 | 77 | 93 | 88 | 92 | 97 | 93 |
| UTAH | 99 | 97 | 88 | 94 | 98 | 96 | 102 | 99 | 100 | 97 | 98 | 91 | 89 | 94 | 85 | 93 | 97 | 98 | 95 | 94 |
| WASATCH | 99 | 87 | 78 | 87 | 94 | 92 | 107 | 100 | 100 | 94 | 93 | 91 | 86 | 93 | 78 | 95 | 92 | 95 | 96 | 94 |
| WASHINGTON | 99 | 86 | 85 | 90 | 96 | 96 | 110 | 101 | 99 | 93 | 92 | 92 | 86 | 93 | 81 | 94 | 91 | 94 | 99 | 94 |
| WAYNE | 101 | 65 | 70 | 83 | 91 | 91 | 116 | 99 | 92 | 73 | 78 | 95 | 75 | 93 | 69 | 93 | 80 | 88 | 105 | 94 |
| WEBER | 99 | 98 | 93 | 95 | 101 | 100 | 101 | 101 | 101 | 102 | 100 | 92 | 93 | 94 | 89 | 94 | 98 | 98 | 97 | 94 |
| UTAH | 100 | 99 | 91 | 97 | 100 | 99 | 102 | 101 | 102 | 101 | 101 | 93 | 92 | 95 | 88 | 94 | 99 | 99 | 96 | 95 |
| UNITED STATES | 100 | 100 | 100 | 100 | 100 | 100 | 100 | 100 | 100 | 100 | 100 | 100 | 100 | 100 | 100 | 100 | 100 | 100 | 100 | 100 |

| COUNTY | FIPS Code | MSA Code | DMA Code | POPULATION 1990 | POPULATION 2000 | POPULATION 2005 | 1990-2000 ANNUAL CHANGE % Rate | 1990-2000 ANNUAL CHANGE State Rank | RACE (%) White 1990 | White 2000 | Black 1990 | Black 2000 | Asian/Pacific 1990 | Asian/Pacific 2000 |
|---|---|---|---|---|---|---|---|---|---|---|---|---|---|---|
| ADDISON | 001 | 0000 | 523 | 32,953 | 35,700 | 37,027 | 0.8 | 5 | 98.6 | 98.3 | 0.4 | 0.5 | 0.6 | 0.8 |
| BENNINGTON | 003 | 0000 | 532 | 35,845 | 35,958 | 35,861 | 0.0 | 13 | 98.9 | 98.7 | 0.3 | 0.4 | 0.5 | 0.7 |
| CALEDONIA | 005 | 0000 | 523 | 27,846 | 28,916 | 29,434 | 0.4 | 8 | 99.1 | 99.0 | 0.2 | 0.2 | 0.3 | 0.4 |
| CHITTENDEN | 007 | 1303 | 523 | 131,761 | 145,221 | 151,643 | 1.0 | 4 | 97.8 | 96.9 | 0.6 | 1.0 | 1.1 | 1.6 |
| ESSEX | 009 | 0000 | 523 | 6,405 | 6,700 | 6,970 | 0.4 | 8 | 99.2 | 99.1 | 0.2 | 0.4 | 0.2 | 0.2 |
| FRANKLIN | 011 | 1303 | 523 | 39,980 | 44,830 | 46,880 | 1.1 | 2 | 98.1 | 98.2 | 0.1 | 0.2 | 0.2 | 0.4 |
| GRAND ISLE | 013 | 1303 | 523 | 5,318 | 6,499 | 7,134 | 2.0 | 1 | 99.1 | 99.0 | 0.3 | 0.4 | 0.2 | 0.4 |
| LAMOILLE | 015 | 0000 | 523 | 19,735 | 22,165 | 23,343 | 1.1 | 2 | 99.1 | 99.0 | 0.1 | 0.2 | 0.4 | 0.5 |
| ORANGE | 017 | 0000 | 523 | 26,149 | 27,967 | 28,406 | 0.7 | 6 | 99.2 | 99.0 | 0.2 | 0.3 | 0.3 | 0.4 |
| ORLEANS | 019 | 0000 | 523 | 24,053 | 25,827 | 26,470 | 0.7 | 6 | 99.3 | 99.0 | 0.2 | 0.3 | 0.2 | 0.3 |
| RUTLAND | 021 | 0000 | 523 | 62,142 | 62,365 | 62,068 | 0.0 | 13 | 99.2 | 98.9 | 0.2 | 0.4 | 0.3 | 0.5 |
| WASHINGTON | 023 | 0000 | 523 | 54,928 | 56,359 | 56,635 | 0.3 | 10 | 98.9 | 98.7 | 0.3 | 0.4 | 0.4 | 0.6 |
| WINDHAM | 025 | 0000 | 506 | 41,588 | 42,639 | 42,486 | 0.2 | 12 | 98.6 | 98.0 | 0.4 | 0.6 | 0.6 | 1.0 |
| WINDSOR | 027 | 0000 | 523 | 54,055 | 55,568 | 56,177 | 0.3 | 10 | 98.9 | 98.5 | 0.2 | 0.4 | 0.5 | 0.8 |
| VERMONT | | | | | | | 0.6 | | 98.6 | 98.2 | 0.4 | 0.5 | 0.6 | 0.8 |
| UNITED STATES | | | | | | | 1.0 | | 80.3 | 77.9 | 12.1 | 12.4 | 2.9 | 3.9 |

# POPULATION COMPOSITION

| COUNTY | % HISPANIC ORIGIN | | 2000 AGE DISTRIBUTION (%) | | | | | | | | | | MEDIAN AGE | | |
|---|---|---|---|---|---|---|---|---|---|---|---|---|---|---|---|
| | 1990 | 2000 | 0-4 | 5-9 | 10-14 | 15-19 | 20-24 | 25-44 | 45-64 | 65-84 | 85+ | 18+ | 1990 | 2000 | 2000 Males/ Females (×100) |
| ADDISON | 0.6 | 1.2 | 5.2 | 6.3 | 7.5 | 8.9 | 7.4 | 30.1 | 23.9 | 9.5 | 1.3 | 76.9 | 31.6 | 36.3 | 100.2 |
| BENNINGTON | 0.6 | 1.2 | 5.2 | 6.2 | 7.2 | 6.7 | 5.3 | 28.5 | 25.4 | 13.1 | 2.4 | 77.7 | 34.9 | 39.6 | 94.8 |
| CALEDONIA | 0.3 | 0.8 | 5.3 | 6.5 | 7.9 | 7.7 | 5.5 | 28.9 | 24.6 | 11.8 | 1.8 | 75.9 | 33.5 | 38.0 | 96.9 |
| CHITTENDEN | 0.9 | 1.6 | 5.1 | 5.7 | 6.7 | 8.2 | 8.4 | 34.3 | 22.2 | 8.1 | 1.2 | 79.1 | 30.3 | 34.9 | 94.6 |
| ESSEX | 0.5 | 0.9 | 4.9 | 6.0 | 7.9 | 6.5 | 4.1 | 27.6 | 27.6 | 13.7 | 1.6 | 77.2 | 36.0 | 41.0 | 96.9 |
| FRANKLIN | 0.3 | 0.9 | 6.1 | 7.2 | 8.5 | 7.0 | 4.8 | 32.0 | 23.4 | 9.5 | 1.5 | 73.8 | 31.7 | 36.1 | 98.9 |
| GRAND ISLE | 0.4 | 1.0 | 5.2 | 6.4 | 7.8 | 6.0 | 3.9 | 31.0 | 27.8 | 10.9 | 1.0 | 76.8 | 34.4 | 39.6 | 102.9 |
| LAMOILLE | 0.5 | 0.9 | 5.3 | 6.3 | 7.6 | 7.6 | 5.9 | 32.0 | 24.1 | 9.7 | 1.5 | 77.2 | 32.1 | 36.9 | 101.1 |
| ORANGE | 0.4 | 0.9 | 5.5 | 6.6 | 8.1 | 7.5 | 4.9 | 30.1 | 24.8 | 10.9 | 1.6 | 75.6 | 33.1 | 37.9 | 101.2 |
| ORLEANS | 0.4 | 1.0 | 5.1 | 6.6 | 8.1 | 7.0 | 4.7 | 28.3 | 25.8 | 12.4 | 1.8 | 75.6 | 34.2 | 39.1 | 99.9 |
| RUTLAND | 0.4 | 1.0 | 4.9 | 5.8 | 6.9 | 7.0 | 5.5 | 30.4 | 25.2 | 12.3 | 2.0 | 78.6 | 34.3 | 39.1 | 95.3 |
| WASHINGTON | 1.2 | 1.9 | 5.0 | 6.1 | 7.2 | 7.1 | 6.0 | 30.3 | 25.5 | 10.8 | 2.0 | 77.7 | 34.2 | 38.5 | 96.9 |
| WINDHAM | 0.7 | 1.3 | 5.1 | 6.1 | 7.2 | 6.4 | 5.0 | 31.4 | 25.4 | 11.3 | 2.0 | 77.7 | 34.5 | 39.0 | 97.2 |
| WINDSOR | 0.5 | 1.0 | 4.8 | 5.9 | 7.1 | 6.0 | 4.4 | 29.9 | 26.8 | 13.0 | 1.9 | 78.3 | 36.0 | 40.5 | 96.7 |
| VERMONT | 0.7 | 1.3 | 5.2 | 6.1 | 7.3 | 7.3 | 6.1 | 31.2 | 24.5 | 10.6 | 1.7 | 77.6 | 33.0 | 37.5 | 96.9 |
| UNITED STATES | 9.0 | 11.8 | 6.9 | 7.2 | 7.2 | 7.2 | 6.7 | 29.9 | 22.2 | 11.1 | 1.6 | 74.6 | 32.9 | 35.7 | 95.6 |

| COUNTY | HOUSEHOLDS | | | | | FAMILIES | | | MEDIAN HOUSEHOLD INCOME | | | |
|---|---|---|---|---|---|---|---|---|---|---|---|---|
| | 1990 | 2000 | 2005 | % Annual Rate 1990-2000 | 2000 Average HH Size | 1990 | 2000 | % Annual Rate 1990-2000 | 2000 | 2005 | 2000 National Rank | 2000 State Rank |
| ADDISON | 11,410 | 13,267 | 14,234 | 1.8 | 2.51 | 8,322 | 9,369 | 1.4 | 39,877 | 47,070 | 683 | 5 |
| BENNINGTON | 13,595 | 14,445 | 14,786 | 0.7 | 2.41 | 9,527 | 9,769 | 0.3 | 39,764 | 48,266 | 689 | 7 |
| CALEDONIA | 10,368 | 11,103 | 11,485 | 0.8 | 2.52 | 7,323 | 7,582 | 0.4 | 34,176 | 40,432 | 1358 | 12 |
| CHITTENDEN | 48,439 | 57,365 | 61,965 | 2.1 | 2.40 | 31,336 | 35,961 | 1.7 | 50,748 | 58,121 | 191 | 1 |
| ESSEX | 2,344 | 2,586 | 2,763 | 1.2 | 2.48 | 1,738 | 1,854 | 0.8 | 30,342 | 37,490 | 2069 | 14 |
| FRANKLIN | 14,326 | 17,041 | 18,346 | 2.1 | 2.60 | 10,705 | 12,382 | 1.8 | 39,870 | 49,732 | 686 | 6 |
| GRAND ISLE | 2,018 | 2,623 | 2,965 | 3.2 | 2.48 | 1,484 | 1,866 | 2.8 | 41,161 | 48,032 | 575 | 2 |
| LAMOILLE | 7,397 | 8,766 | 9,449 | 2.1 | 2.45 | 4,941 | 5,611 | 1.6 | 38,192 | 46,258 | 839 | 9 |
| ORANGE | 9,455 | 10,836 | 11,359 | 1.7 | 2.52 | 6,996 | 7,765 | 1.3 | 40,658 | 50,414 | 615 | 3 |
| ORLEANS | 8,873 | 9,956 | 10,464 | 1.4 | 2.53 | 6,514 | 7,078 | 1.0 | 31,699 | 35,959 | 1776 | 13 |
| RUTLAND | 23,690 | 25,387 | 26,038 | 0.8 | 2.37 | 16,307 | 16,853 | 0.4 | 37,915 | 44,497 | 852 | 11 |
| WASHINGTON | 20,948 | 22,806 | 23,562 | 1.0 | 2.36 | 14,111 | 14,833 | 0.6 | 39,957 | 46,338 | 678 | 4 |
| WINDHAM | 16,264 | 17,353 | 17,675 | 0.8 | 2.38 | 10,867 | 11,171 | 0.3 | 38,074 | 46,818 | 847 | 10 |
| WINDSOR | 21,523 | 23,488 | 24,463 | 1.1 | 2.33 | 14,724 | 15,440 | 0.6 | 38,845 | 45,615 | 767 | 8 |
| VERMONT | | | | 1.4 | 2.43 | | | 1.0 | 40,913 | 48,538 | | |
| UNITED STATES | | | | 1.4 | 2.59 | | | 1.1 | 41,914 | 49,127 | | |

# INCOME

| COUNTY | 2000 Per Capita Income | 2000 HH Income Base | 2000 HOUSEHOLD INCOME DISTRIBUTION (%) Less than $15,000 | $15,000 to $24,999 | $25,000 to $49,999 | $50,000 to $99,999 | $100,000 to $149,999 | $150,000 or More | 2000 AVERAGE DISPOSABLE INCOME BY AGE OF HOUSEHOLDER All Ages | <35 | 35-44 | 45-54 | 55-64 | 65+ |
|---|---|---|---|---|---|---|---|---|---|---|---|---|---|---|
| ADDISON | 18,528 | 13,267 | 12.8 | 13.4 | 38.3 | 29.1 | 5.1 | 1.4 | 35,243 | 31,665 | 39,639 | 42,042 | 39,612 | 22,938 |
| BENNINGTON | 22,104 | 14,445 | 14.5 | 12.7 | 36.8 | 26.5 | 6.4 | 3.1 | 37,526 | 31,003 | 41,733 | 49,017 | 40,777 | 24,775 |
| CALEDONIA | 15,952 | 11,103 | 16.9 | 16.2 | 40.0 | 23.4 | 2.8 | 0.6 | 30,216 | 27,752 | 36,149 | 37,581 | 31,611 | 19,686 |
| CHITTENDEN | 26,120 | 57,365 | 9.6 | 8.7 | 30.6 | 37.5 | 9.7 | 4.0 | 44,752 | 38,492 | 48,486 | 54,969 | 49,168 | 27,495 |
| ESSEX | 14,204 | 2,586 | 18.3 | 19.8 | 42.4 | 17.6 | 1.6 | 0.3 | 26,947 | 28,242 | 31,804 | 33,419 | 29,004 | 16,950 |
| FRANKLIN | 18,567 | 17,041 | 12.8 | 12.4 | 39.2 | 28.8 | 5.5 | 1.3 | 35,288 | 32,819 | 41,301 | 43,424 | 36,933 | 20,148 |
| GRAND ISLE | 22,656 | 2,623 | 12.0 | 13.0 | 36.9 | 28.5 | 6.5 | 3.1 | 38,469 | 35,055 | 42,285 | 48,371 | 38,309 | 22,931 |
| LAMOILLE | 19,235 | 8,766 | 14.2 | 13.8 | 37.6 | 27.8 | 4.9 | 1.6 | 34,580 | 29,619 | 39,135 | 43,410 | 39,186 | 20,811 |
| ORANGE | 20,079 | 10,836 | 9.9 | 12.3 | 41.2 | 28.6 | 6.1 | 1.9 | 36,825 | 33,499 | 39,781 | 44,282 | 38,850 | 26,950 |
| ORLEANS | 15,404 | 9,956 | 19.1 | 17.6 | 39.4 | 20.1 | 2.8 | 1.0 | 29,351 | 26,966 | 34,781 | 36,612 | 31,395 | 18,954 |
| RUTLAND | 19,195 | 25,387 | 14.2 | 13.7 | 38.9 | 27.1 | 4.5 | 1.6 | 34,252 | 31,165 | 38,570 | 42,330 | 38,718 | 22,234 |
| WASHINGTON | 20,829 | 22,806 | 13.4 | 12.4 | 38.1 | 28.3 | 5.7 | 2.1 | 36,263 | 32,768 | 40,955 | 45,476 | 39,887 | 21,575 |
| WINDHAM | 19,274 | 17,353 | 13.6 | 13.4 | 40.0 | 27.9 | 4.1 | 1.1 | 33,739 | 32,001 | 36,874 | 42,505 | 36,673 | 21,071 |
| WINDSOR | 21,561 | 23,488 | 13.0 | 15.5 | 36.6 | 26.8 | 5.8 | 2.3 | 35,899 | 31,712 | 40,403 | 43,474 | 41,682 | 22,466 |
| VERMONT | 21,048 | | 12.8 | 12.6 | 36.7 | 29.5 | 6.1 | 2.3 | 37,144 | 33,498 | 41,652 | 45,856 | 40,530 | 22,952 |
| UNITED STATES | 22,162 | | 14.5 | 12.5 | 32.3 | 29.8 | 7.4 | 3.5 | 40,748 | 34,503 | 44,969 | 49,579 | 43,409 | 27,339 |

| COUNTY | FINANCIAL SERVICES | | | | THE HOME | | | | | | ENTERTAINMENT | | | | | | PERSONAL | | | |
|---|---|---|---|---|---|---|---|---|---|---|---|---|---|---|---|---|---|---|---|---|
| | | | | | Home Improvements | | | Furnishings | | | | | | | | | | | | |
| | Auto Loan | Home Loan | Invest-ments | Retire-ment Plans | Home Repair | Lawn & Garden | Remodel-ing | Appli-ances | Elec-tronics | Furni-ture | Restau-rants | Sport-ing Goods | Theater & Concerts | Toys & Hobbies | Travel | Video Rental | Apparel | Auto After-market | Health Insur-ance | Pets & Supplies |
| ADDISON | 100 | 82 | 85 | 88 | 88 | 87 | 102 | 97 | 94 | 88 | 91 | 99 | 91 | 102 | 83 | 99 | 94 | 93 | 103 | 103 |
| BENNINGTON | 99 | 85 | 92 | 89 | 91 | 89 | 100 | 97 | 94 | 90 | 92 | 98 | 93 | 101 | 87 | 99 | 94 | 93 | 103 | 102 |
| CALEDONIA | 99 | 76 | 81 | 83 | 88 | 85 | 104 | 96 | 92 | 84 | 86 | 97 | 87 | 100 | 80 | 98 | 89 | 89 | 103 | 101 |
| CHITTENDEN | 101 | 103 | 95 | 101 | 92 | 92 | 92 | 98 | 100 | 101 | 105 | 102 | 101 | 104 | 95 | 100 | 106 | 101 | 99 | 104 |
| ESSEX | 101 | 68 | 73 | 83 | 85 | 85 | 112 | 98 | 92 | 78 | 81 | 101 | 83 | 101 | 75 | 99 | 86 | 88 | 106 | 103 |
| FRANKLIN | 99 | 79 | 79 | 84 | 87 | 85 | 99 | 96 | 93 | 86 | 89 | 98 | 89 | 100 | 80 | 99 | 91 | 91 | 102 | 101 |
| GRAND ISLE | 102 | 70 | 75 | 85 | 86 | 85 | 116 | 99 | 93 | 78 | 82 | 102 | 84 | 103 | 76 | 100 | 87 | 89 | 108 | 104 |
| LAMOILLE | 99 | 83 | 85 | 87 | 88 | 86 | 101 | 97 | 94 | 89 | 91 | 98 | 91 | 101 | 83 | 99 | 93 | 92 | 102 | 102 |
| ORANGE | 101 | 81 | 85 | 88 | 88 | 87 | 105 | 98 | 95 | 88 | 91 | 100 | 91 | 103 | 82 | 100 | 94 | 92 | 103 | 103 |
| ORLEANS | 99 | 70 | 75 | 81 | 86 | 84 | 104 | 96 | 91 | 79 | 82 | 97 | 84 | 99 | 77 | 98 | 85 | 88 | 105 | 100 |
| RUTLAND | 98 | 83 | 88 | 88 | 90 | 88 | 99 | 96 | 93 | 89 | 91 | 97 | 92 | 100 | 85 | 98 | 93 | 92 | 102 | 101 |
| WASHINGTON | 99 | 91 | 93 | 93 | 92 | 90 | 96 | 97 | 96 | 95 | 96 | 99 | 96 | 102 | 90 | 99 | 98 | 95 | 101 | 102 |
| WINDHAM | 100 | 85 | 89 | 90 | 90 | 88 | 102 | 97 | 94 | 89 | 92 | 99 | 92 | 101 | 86 | 99 | 94 | 93 | 103 | 102 |
| WINDSOR | 99 | 84 | 90 | 89 | 90 | 89 | 101 | 97 | 93 | 89 | 91 | 98 | 92 | 101 | 86 | 99 | 94 | 92 | 103 | 102 |
| VERMONT | 100 | 88 | 89 | 92 | 90 | 89 | 99 | 97 | 95 | 92 | 94 | 99 | 94 | 102 | 87 | 99 | 96 | 94 | 102 | 102 |
| UNITED STATES | 100 | 100 | 100 | 100 | 100 | 100 | 100 | 100 | 100 | 100 | 100 | 100 | 100 | 100 | 100 | 100 | 100 | 100 | 100 | 100 |

# POPULATION CHANGE

| COUNTY | FIPS Code | MSA Code | DMA Code | POPULATION 1990 | POPULATION 2000 | POPULATION 2005 | 1990-2000 ANNUAL CHANGE % Rate | 1990-2000 ANNUAL CHANGE State Rank | RACE (%) White 1990 | White 2000 | Black 1990 | Black 2000 | Asian/Pacific 1990 | Asian/Pacific 2000 |
|---|---|---|---|---|---|---|---|---|---|---|---|---|---|---|
| ACCOMACK | 001 | 0000 | 544 | 31,703 | 32,095 | 31,958 | 0.1 | 96 | 64.7 | 61.7 | 34.5 | 37.2 | 0.2 | 0.3 |
| ALBEMARLE | 003 | 1540 | 584 | 68,040 | 81,066 | 86,037 | 1.7 | 32 | 87.1 | 84.4 | 10.0 | 11.6 | 2.4 | 3.4 |
| ALLEGHANY | 005 | 0000 | 573 | 13,176 | 12,117 | 11,941 | -0.8 | 129 | 97.1 | 96.9 | 2.5 | 2.6 | 0.3 | 0.4 |
| AMELIA | 007 | 0000 | 556 | 8,787 | 10,830 | 11,931 | 2.1 | 20 | 67.5 | 63.2 | 32.1 | 36.4 | 0.1 | 0.2 |
| AMHERST | 009 | 4640 | 573 | 28,578 | 30,616 | 31,954 | 0.7 | 60 | 79.0 | 76.3 | 20.1 | 22.8 | 0.3 | 0.4 |
| APPOMATTOX | 011 | 0000 | 573 | 12,298 | 13,480 | 14,281 | 0.9 | 56 | 76.9 | 74.2 | 22.9 | 25.6 | 0.0 | 0.1 |
| ARLINGTON | 013 | 8840 | 511 | 170,936 | 175,361 | 177,561 | 0.2 | 90 | 76.6 | 70.9 | 10.5 | 11.0 | 6.8 | 9.5 |
| AUGUSTA | 015 | 0000 | 569 | 54,677 | 61,921 | 65,695 | 1.2 | 45 | 95.9 | 95.3 | 3.7 | 4.1 | 0.2 | 0.4 |
| BATH | 017 | 0000 | 573 | 4,799 | 4,944 | 5,023 | 0.3 | 87 | 94.5 | 93.4 | 5.2 | 6.1 | 0.2 | 0.3 |
| BEDFORD | 019 | 4640 | 573 | 45,656 | 58,483 | 62,976 | 2.4 | 15 | 91.7 | 90.0 | 7.9 | 9.4 | 0.2 | 0.4 |
| BLAND | 021 | 0000 | 559 | 6,514 | 6,795 | 6,792 | 0.4 | 81 | 96.1 | 95.3 | 3.5 | 4.1 | 0.1 | 0.1 |
| BOTETOURT | 023 | 6800 | 573 | 24,992 | 29,668 | 32,093 | 1.7 | 32 | 95.0 | 94.0 | 4.5 | 5.3 | 0.3 | 0.4 |
| BRUNSWICK | 025 | 0000 | 556 | 15,987 | 18,442 | 18,939 | 1.4 | 39 | 41.3 | 37.8 | 58.5 | 62.0 | 0.1 | 0.1 |
| BUCHANAN | 027 | 0000 | 531 | 31,333 | 28,014 | 25,816 | -1.1 | 132 | 99.3 | 96.9 | 0.2 | 2.4 | 0.2 | 0.2 |
| BUCKINGHAM | 029 | 0000 | 556 | 12,873 | 14,884 | 15,500 | 1.4 | 39 | 58.8 | 53.8 | 40.9 | 45.9 | 0.2 | 0.2 |
| CAMPBELL | 031 | 4640 | 573 | 47,572 | 50,591 | 51,769 | 0.6 | 66 | 85.0 | 82.5 | 14.5 | 16.6 | 0.4 | 0.5 |
| CAROLINE | 033 | 0000 | 556 | 19,217 | 22,269 | 23,248 | 1.4 | 39 | 60.8 | 56.1 | 37.7 | 42.1 | 0.3 | 0.4 |
| CARROLL | 035 | 0000 | 573 | 26,594 | 27,835 | 27,980 | 0.4 | 81 | 99.2 | 98.8 | 0.4 | 0.6 | 0.1 | 0.2 |
| CHARLES CITY | 036 | 6760 | 556 | 6,282 | 7,359 | 7,953 | 1.6 | 35 | 28.7 | 25.2 | 63.2 | 66.8 | 0.2 | 0.2 |
| CHARLOTTE | 037 | 0000 | 573 | 11,688 | 12,505 | 12,955 | 0.7 | 60 | 63.2 | 59.6 | 36.5 | 40.1 | 0.0 | 0.0 |
| CHESTERFIELD | 041 | 6760 | 556 | 209,274 | 256,665 | 273,406 | 2.0 | 22 | 84.6 | 81.2 | 13.0 | 15.4 | 1.8 | 2.6 |
| CLARKE | 043 | 8840 | 511 | 12,101 | 13,026 | 13,907 | 0.7 | 60 | 90.8 | 89.0 | 8.7 | 10.2 | 0.2 | 0.4 |
| CRAIG | 045 | 0000 | 573 | 4,372 | 4,986 | 5,216 | 1.3 | 43 | 99.6 | 99.6 | 0.2 | 0.2 | 0.1 | 0.1 |
| CULPEPER | 047 | 8840 | 511 | 27,791 | 34,073 | 36,635 | 2.0 | 22 | 81.2 | 76.5 | 17.2 | 21.3 | 1.1 | 1.6 |
| CUMBERLAND | 049 | 0000 | 556 | 7,825 | 7,892 | 7,999 | 0.1 | 96 | 60.9 | 57.0 | 38.7 | 42.6 | 0.2 | 0.2 |
| DICKENSON | 051 | 0000 | 531 | 17,620 | 16,535 | 15,658 | -0.6 | 123 | 99.4 | 99.0 | 0.4 | 0.7 | 0.1 | 0.2 |
| DINWIDDIE | 053 | 6760 | 556 | 20,960 | 25,886 | 27,213 | 2.1 | 20 | 63.7 | 58.3 | 35.6 | 40.8 | 0.3 | 0.4 |
| ESSEX | 057 | 0000 | 556 | 8,689 | 9,112 | 9,069 | 0.5 | 74 | 61.3 | 57.2 | 37.6 | 41.5 | 0.5 | 0.6 |
| FAIRFAX | 059 | 8840 | 511 | 818,584 | 961,877 | 1,041,485 | 1.6 | 35 | 81.3 | 76.3 | 7.7 | 8.2 | 8.5 | 12.0 |
| FAUQUIER | 061 | 8840 | 511 | 48,741 | 56,435 | 62,280 | 1.4 | 39 | 87.5 | 85.3 | 11.2 | 12.9 | 0.6 | 0.9 |
| FLOYD | 063 | 0000 | 573 | 12,005 | 13,415 | 14,185 | 1.1 | 49 | 97.2 | 96.5 | 2.4 | 2.9 | 0.2 | 0.3 |
| FLUVANNA | 065 | 1540 | 556 | 12,429 | 20,401 | 24,252 | 5.0 | 2 | 76.6 | 73.8 | 22.9 | 25.5 | 0.1 | 0.2 |
| FRANKLIN | 067 | 0000 | 573 | 39,549 | 45,868 | 49,026 | 1.5 | 37 | 88.9 | 87.0 | 10.7 | 12.5 | 0.2 | 0.2 |
| FREDERICK | 069 | 0000 | 511 | 45,723 | 57,678 | 62,441 | 2.3 | 17 | 97.4 | 96.6 | 1.8 | 2.3 | 0.5 | 0.7 |
| GILES | 071 | 0000 | 573 | 16,366 | 16,346 | 16,525 | 0.0 | 106 | 98.0 | 97.5 | 1.7 | 2.2 | 0.1 | 0.2 |
| GLOUCESTER | 073 | 5720 | 544 | 30,131 | 36,051 | 38,919 | 1.8 | 28 | 87.8 | 85.4 | 11.1 | 13.1 | 0.6 | 1.0 |
| GOOCHLAND | 075 | 6760 | 556 | 14,163 | 17,952 | 19,432 | 2.3 | 17 | 69.9 | 63.6 | 29.7 | 35.9 | 0.2 | 0.3 |
| GRAYSON | 077 | 0000 | 518 | 16,278 | 16,489 | 16,689 | 0.1 | 96 | 96.6 | 95.9 | 3.0 | 3.5 | 0.1 | 0.1 |
| GREENE | 079 | 1540 | 584 | 10,297 | 15,277 | 18,202 | 3.9 | 6 | 93.0 | 91.6 | 6.4 | 7.7 | 0.3 | 0.4 |
| GREENSVILLE | 081 | 0000 | 556 | 8,853 | 11,308 | 11,190 | 2.4 | 15 | 44.1 | 36.2 | 55.5 | 63.1 | 0.3 | 0.4 |
| HALIFAX | 083 | 0000 | 573 | 29,033 | 29,883 | 30,012 | 0.3 | 87 | 60.3 | 57.6 | 39.2 | 41.9 | 0.1 | 0.1 |
| HANOVER | 085 | 6760 | 556 | 63,306 | 88,325 | 102,865 | 3.3 | 7 | 89.2 | 87.1 | 10.1 | 11.9 | 0.4 | 0.6 |
| HENRICO | 087 | 6760 | 556 | 217,881 | 246,589 | 256,947 | 1.2 | 45 | 77.3 | 73.4 | 20.1 | 22.9 | 2.0 | 2.9 |
| HENRY | 089 | 0000 | 573 | 56,942 | 55,424 | 54,387 | -0.3 | 114 | 76.4 | 73.3 | 23.1 | 26.2 | 0.2 | 0.2 |
| HIGHLAND | 091 | 0000 | 573 | 2,635 | 2,462 | 2,372 | -0.7 | 127 | 99.8 | 99.8 | 0.1 | 0.1 | 0.1 | 0.1 |
| ISLE OF WIGHT | 093 | 5720 | 544 | 25,053 | 30,091 | 32,440 | 1.8 | 28 | 67.8 | 64.2 | 31.6 | 35.0 | 0.3 | 0.4 |
| JAMES CITY | 095 | 5720 | 544 | 34,859 | 47,293 | 54,083 | 3.0 | 9 | 79.8 | 77.9 | 18.5 | 19.6 | 1.3 | 2.0 |
| KING AND QUEEN | 097 | 0000 | 556 | 6,289 | 6,590 | 6,808 | 0.5 | 74 | 56.8 | 53.0 | 41.9 | 45.6 | 0.2 | 0.2 |
| KING GEORGE | 099 | 8840 | 511 | 13,527 | 18,143 | 20,368 | 2.9 | 11 | 78.3 | 74.9 | 20.2 | 23.0 | 0.9 | 1.4 |
| KING WILLIAM | 101 | 0000 | 556 | 10,913 | 13,290 | 14,507 | 1.9 | 26 | 67.4 | 63.5 | 30.3 | 33.9 | 0.2 | 0.4 |
| LANCASTER | 103 | 0000 | 556 | 10,896 | 11,361 | 11,459 | 0.4 | 81 | 69.4 | 66.8 | 30.2 | 32.7 | 0.1 | 0.1 |
| LEE | 105 | 0000 | 531 | 24,496 | 23,732 | 23,270 | -0.3 | 114 | 99.4 | 99.0 | 0.4 | 0.8 | 0.1 | 0.1 |
| LOUDOUN | 107 | 8840 | 511 | 86,129 | 167,265 | 221,380 | 6.7 | 1 | 89.5 | 86.8 | 7.2 | 8.3 | 2.4 | 3.7 |
| LOUISA | 109 | 0000 | 556 | 20,325 | 25,578 | 28,298 | 2.3 | 17 | 73.7 | 69.9 | 25.7 | 29.4 | 0.2 | 0.3 |
| LUNENBURG | 111 | 0000 | 556 | 11,419 | 11,637 | 10,911 | 0.2 | 90 | 62.0 | 56.2 | 37.6 | 43.3 | 0.2 | 0.2 |
| MADISON | 113 | 0000 | 584 | 11,949 | 12,695 | 13,004 | 0.6 | 66 | 85.2 | 82.5 | 14.2 | 16.8 | 0.2 | 0.2 |
| MATHEWS | 115 | 5720 | 544 | 8,348 | 9,350 | 9,850 | 1.1 | 49 | 85.5 | 83.4 | 14.1 | 16.0 | 0.2 | 0.3 |
| MECKLENBURG | 117 | 0000 | 560 | 29,241 | 31,016 | 31,161 | 0.6 | 66 | 61.3 | 57.4 | 38.4 | 42.3 | 0.2 | 0.2 |
| MIDDLESEX | 119 | 0000 | 556 | 8,653 | 9,891 | 10,474 | 1.3 | 43 | 75.2 | 72.4 | 24.6 | 27.3 | 0.1 | 0.2 |
| MONTGOMERY | 121 | 0000 | 573 | 73,913 | 77,259 | 78,604 | 0.4 | 81 | 92.0 | 89.8 | 3.8 | 4.4 | 3.8 | 5.3 |
| NELSON | 125 | 0000 | 573 | 12,778 | 14,409 | 15,521 | 1.2 | 45 | 80.2 | 77.2 | 18.8 | 21.5 | 0.2 | 0.3 |
| NEW KENT | 127 | 6760 | 556 | 10,445 | 13,517 | 15,041 | 2.5 | 12 | 77.3 | 70.3 | 20.6 | 27.4 | 0.3 | 0.5 |
| NORTHAMPTON | 131 | 0000 | 544 | 13,061 | 12,824 | 12,896 | -0.2 | 113 | 52.7 | 49.6 | 46.2 | 49.0 | 0.1 | 0.2 |
| NORTHUMBERLAND | 133 | 0000 | 556 | 10,524 | 11,819 | 12,564 | 1.1 | 49 | 70.2 | 67.6 | 29.4 | 32.0 | 0.2 | 0.3 |
| NOTTOWAY | 135 | 0000 | 556 | 14,993 | 15,319 | 15,474 | 0.2 | 90 | 58.3 | 54.3 | 41.1 | 44.9 | 0.3 | 0.4 |
| ORANGE | 137 | 0000 | 556 | 21,421 | 26,137 | 28,118 | 2.0 | 22 | 85.1 | 82.5 | 14.4 | 16.9 | 0.2 | 0.3 |
| PAGE | 139 | 0000 | 511 | 21,690 | 23,280 | 23,903 | 0.7 | 60 | 97.5 | 96.8 | 2.0 | 2.5 | 0.3 | 0.5 |
| PATRICK | 141 | 0000 | 518 | 17,473 | 18,659 | 19,305 | 0.6 | 66 | 92.3 | 90.9 | 7.2 | 8.4 | 0.1 | 0.2 |
| PITTSYLVANIA | 143 | 1950 | 573 | 55,655 | 56,930 | 57,830 | 0.2 | 90 | 72.9 | 69.4 | 26.8 | 30.2 | 0.1 | 0.1 |
| POWHATAN | 145 | 6760 | 556 | 15,328 | 23,285 | 27,638 | 4.2 | 5 | 78.0 | 73.7 | 21.5 | 25.5 | 0.2 | 0.3 |
| PRINCE EDWARD | 147 | 0000 | 556 | 17,320 | 19,308 | 19,655 | 1.1 | 49 | 63.1 | 59.2 | 36.2 | 39.8 | 0.4 | 0.6 |
| PRINCE GEORGE | 149 | 6760 | 556 | 27,394 | 29,113 | 30,613 | 0.6 | 66 | 66.7 | 62.7 | 29.1 | 31.4 | 2.2 | 3.0 |
| PRINCE WILLIAM | 153 | 8840 | 511 | 215,686 | 278,554 | 316,738 | 2.5 | 12 | 83.3 | 79.6 | 11.6 | 13.0 | 3.0 | 4.5 |
| PULASKI | 155 | 0000 | 573 | 34,496 | 34,427 | 34,531 | 0.0 | 106 | 93.8 | 92.6 | 5.8 | 6.9 | 0.2 | 0.3 |
| RAPPAHANNOCK | 157 | 0000 | 511 | 6,622 | 7,698 | 7,907 | 1.5 | 37 | 92.0 | 90.6 | 7.4 | 8.6 | 0.2 | 0.3 |
| RICHMOND | 159 | 0000 | 556 | 7,273 | 8,784 | 8,974 | 1.9 | 26 | 69.1 | 59.2 | 30.2 | 39.7 | 0.3 | 0.5 |
| ROANOKE | 161 | 6800 | 573 | 79,332 | 81,185 | 81,310 | 0.2 | 90 | 96.5 | 95.5 | 2.5 | 3.0 | 0.8 | 1.2 |
| VIRGINIA | | | | | | | 1.1 | | 77.4 | 74.8 | 18.8 | 19.9 | 2.6 | 3.8 |
| UNITED STATES | | | | | | | 1.0 | | 80.3 | 77.9 | 12.1 | 12.4 | 2.9 | 3.9 |

# POPULATION COMPOSITION

| COUNTY | % HISPANIC ORIGIN | | 2000 AGE DISTRIBUTION (%) | | | | | | | | | | MEDIAN AGE | | 2000 Males/ Females (×100) |
|---|---|---|---|---|---|---|---|---|---|---|---|---|---|---|---|
| | 1990 | 2000 | 0-4 | 5-9 | 10-14 | 15-19 | 20-24 | 25-44 | 45-64 | 65-84 | 85+ | 18+ | 1990 | 2000 | |
| ACCOMACK | 1.4 | 2.2 | 6.0 | 6.5 | 6.8 | 6.5 | 5.5 | 25.7 | 24.1 | 16.3 | 2.5 | 76.5 | 37.6 | 40.2 | 91.4 |
| ALBEMARLE | 1.2 | 2.1 | 5.8 | 6.3 | 6.2 | 9.9 | 8.9 | 30.6 | 21.8 | 9.3 | 1.2 | 78.1 | 31.7 | 34.4 | 94.3 |
| ALLEGHANY | 0.4 | 1.2 | 5.1 | 6.0 | 6.8 | 7.0 | 5.0 | 27.5 | 28.4 | 13.0 | 1.3 | 77.9 | 37.2 | 40.6 | 100.0 |
| AMELIA | 0.5 | 1.1 | 6.4 | 6.9 | 7.3 | 7.1 | 5.5 | 28.4 | 25.2 | 11.8 | 1.5 | 75.0 | 34.5 | 38.0 | 98.0 |
| AMHERST | 0.8 | 1.4 | 5.7 | 6.1 | 6.5 | 7.9 | 6.7 | 28.5 | 25.0 | 12.2 | 1.4 | 77.3 | 35.0 | 37.8 | 96.7 |
| APPOMATTOX | 0.2 | 0.7 | 6.0 | 6.3 | 6.7 | 6.7 | 5.7 | 27.8 | 25.7 | 13.4 | 1.8 | 77.1 | 35.8 | 39.3 | 92.5 |
| ARLINGTON | 13.5 | 19.5 | 5.0 | 4.6 | 4.6 | 4.4 | 6.9 | 40.5 | 23.4 | 9.2 | 1.3 | 83.5 | 33.8 | 37.2 | 95.7 |
| AUGUSTA | 0.4 | 1.0 | 5.6 | 6.4 | 6.9 | 6.7 | 5.7 | 30.2 | 26.3 | 11.1 | 1.1 | 76.9 | 34.9 | 38.2 | 102.3 |
| BATH | 0.5 | 1.0 | 4.8 | 5.4 | 5.8 | 6.4 | 5.1 | 26.5 | 29.3 | 14.9 | 1.7 | 80.2 | 39.3 | 42.3 | 103.0 |
| BEDFORD | 0.4 | 1.0 | 5.8 | 6.4 | 6.8 | 6.2 | 5.0 | 30.8 | 26.6 | 11.2 | 1.2 | 77.2 | 35.7 | 38.7 | 99.7 |
| BLAND | 0.4 | 1.0 | 4.5 | 5.5 | 6.1 | 6.4 | 5.5 | 31.2 | 26.7 | 12.5 | 1.7 | 80.0 | 36.5 | 39.6 | 115.7 |
| BOTETOURT | 0.6 | 1.3 | 5.0 | 5.8 | 6.5 | 6.5 | 5.1 | 29.5 | 27.9 | 12.5 | 1.3 | 78.7 | 36.8 | 40.3 | 100.0 |
| BRUNSWICK | 0.3 | 0.6 | 5.4 | 6.1 | 6.6 | 8.3 | 8.4 | 29.0 | 22.0 | 13.0 | 1.3 | 78.3 | 34.2 | 35.9 | 102.7 |
| BUCHANAN | 0.8 | 1.6 | 4.7 | 6.2 | 7.4 | 7.9 | 6.4 | 31.2 | 25.2 | 10.1 | 0.9 | 76.8 | 32.2 | 36.9 | 100.3 |
| BUCKINGHAM | 0.3 | 0.6 | 5.6 | 5.8 | 6.2 | 6.9 | 7.0 | 32.9 | 22.1 | 11.9 | 1.6 | 78.1 | 35.1 | 36.3 | 123.4 |
| CAMPBELL | 0.5 | 1.0 | 6.0 | 6.4 | 6.8 | 6.2 | 5.5 | 31.0 | 25.2 | 11.7 | 1.1 | 77.0 | 34.1 | 37.6 | 97.3 |
| CAROLINE | 0.5 | 1.0 | 7.0 | 7.4 | 7.6 | 6.8 | 5.6 | 30.1 | 23.5 | 10.9 | 1.2 | 74.0 | 33.2 | 36.3 | 98.1 |
| CARROLL | 0.6 | 1.2 | 4.9 | 5.4 | 6.0 | 5.9 | 5.2 | 28.1 | 27.5 | 15.1 | 2.0 | 80.0 | 37.8 | 41.4 | 98.1 |
| CHARLES CITY | 0.4 | 0.6 | 5.3 | 6.3 | 6.8 | 6.7 | 5.5 | 30.4 | 26.2 | 11.4 | 1.2 | 77.6 | 35.2 | 38.7 | 95.0 |
| CHARLOTTE | 0.3 | 0.7 | 5.9 | 6.3 | 7.3 | 7.0 | 5.5 | 25.9 | 24.4 | 15.8 | 1.9 | 76.3 | 36.5 | 39.3 | 94.0 |
| CHESTERFIELD | 1.2 | 2.2 | 6.9 | 7.9 | 8.1 | 7.8 | 5.6 | 33.8 | 23.3 | 6.2 | 0.5 | 72.4 | 31.9 | 34.6 | 95.5 |
| CLARKE | 0.7 | 1.4 | 5.6 | 6.2 | 6.9 | 6.6 | 5.2 | 28.1 | 26.1 | 13.4 | 1.9 | 77.4 | 36.5 | 39.8 | 97.5 |
| CRAIG | 0.1 | 0.6 | 5.5 | 6.1 | 6.7 | 6.3 | 4.9 | 29.5 | 26.9 | 12.5 | 1.6 | 78.0 | 36.4 | 39.8 | 104.1 |
| CULPEPER | 0.7 | 1.3 | 6.8 | 7.3 | 7.4 | 6.8 | 6.3 | 31.1 | 22.2 | 10.5 | 1.6 | 74.3 | 33.0 | 35.5 | 98.5 |
| CUMBERLAND | 0.6 | 1.1 | 6.3 | 6.8 | 7.4 | 7.1 | 5.9 | 27.2 | 24.7 | 12.8 | 1.9 | 75.1 | 35.3 | 37.9 | 93.7 |
| DICKENSON | 0.3 | 1.0 | 5.2 | 6.4 | 7.4 | 7.6 | 6.0 | 28.3 | 25.4 | 12.2 | 1.5 | 76.2 | 34.0 | 38.1 | 96.3 |
| DINWIDDIE | 0.6 | 1.0 | 6.1 | 6.6 | 6.9 | 6.3 | 5.6 | 29.7 | 25.4 | 12.2 | 1.2 | 76.7 | 34.7 | 38.0 | 97.3 |
| ESSEX | 0.3 | 0.8 | 5.6 | 6.3 | 6.6 | 6.3 | 5.3 | 26.7 | 25.4 | 15.1 | 2.7 | 77.8 | 37.6 | 40.6 | 91.1 |
| FAIRFAX | 6.3 | 9.6 | 6.2 | 6.6 | 6.9 | 6.3 | 5.9 | 34.9 | 25.1 | 7.4 | 0.7 | 76.4 | 33.1 | 36.3 | 96.9 |
| FAUQUIER | 1.2 | 2.3 | 7.1 | 7.6 | 7.8 | 6.7 | 5.7 | 31.0 | 23.8 | 9.2 | 1.1 | 73.4 | 33.1 | 35.9 | 99.2 |
| FLOYD | 0.5 | 1.2 | 5.0 | 5.8 | 6.6 | 6.3 | 5.3 | 27.6 | 27.5 | 13.8 | 2.2 | 78.7 | 37.8 | 41.0 | 98.5 |
| FLUVANNA | 0.6 | 1.2 | 6.5 | 7.0 | 7.3 | 6.2 | 5.2 | 29.2 | 24.4 | 12.8 | 1.2 | 75.4 | 34.4 | 38.1 | 96.4 |
| FRANKLIN | 0.3 | 0.8 | 5.4 | 6.0 | 6.5 | 7.4 | 6.0 | 28.3 | 26.2 | 12.7 | 1.5 | 78.4 | 35.1 | 39.0 | 97.0 |
| FREDERICK | 0.6 | 1.4 | 6.8 | 7.4 | 7.5 | 6.8 | 5.3 | 31.3 | 23.9 | 9.9 | 1.1 | 74.0 | 33.0 | 36.4 | 98.9 |
| GILES | 0.3 | 1.0 | 5.0 | 5.5 | 6.3 | 6.3 | 5.5 | 27.3 | 26.7 | 15.6 | 1.8 | 79.4 | 38.1 | 41.2 | 95.6 |
| GLOUCESTER | 1.0 | 1.9 | 6.8 | 7.4 | 7.6 | 6.8 | 5.3 | 30.8 | 23.9 | 10.0 | 1.4 | 73.9 | 33.5 | 36.5 | 97.6 |
| GOOCHLAND | 0.2 | 0.6 | 5.1 | 5.6 | 5.9 | 5.7 | 5.0 | 34.8 | 25.4 | 11.1 | 1.4 | 80.0 | 35.9 | 38.7 | 95.6 |
| GRAYSON | 0.5 | 1.1 | 5.1 | 5.7 | 6.2 | 6.8 | 4.9 | 27.2 | 26.8 | 15.3 | 2.0 | 78.6 | 38.0 | 41.1 | 96.4 |
| GREENE | 0.5 | 1.1 | 7.2 | 7.5 | 8.0 | 6.3 | 5.3 | 32.0 | 23.8 | 8.9 | 0.9 | 73.4 | 32.5 | 36.0 | 97.5 |
| GREENSVILLE | 0.7 | 1.9 | 5.4 | 5.9 | 6.7 | 7.3 | 7.4 | 31.7 | 22.9 | 11.4 | 1.2 | 77.5 | 34.9 | 36.4 | 114.9 |
| HALIFAX | 0.6 | 4.8 | 5.2 | 6.2 | 6.8 | 7.0 | 5.7 | 27.2 | 25.7 | 14.4 | 1.9 | 77.5 | 36.9 | 40.1 | 94.1 |
| HANOVER | 0.5 | 1.1 | 5.9 | 6.7 | 7.2 | 7.3 | 5.5 | 29.1 | 25.9 | 11.2 | 1.2 | 76.1 | 34.5 | 37.9 | 94.7 |
| HENRICO | 1.0 | 1.8 | 6.0 | 6.4 | 6.4 | 6.1 | 6.3 | 33.2 | 22.8 | 11.2 | 1.7 | 77.5 | 33.9 | 36.9 | 86.3 |
| HENRY | 0.4 | 1.0 | 5.6 | 6.1 | 6.7 | 6.0 | 5.1 | 29.4 | 26.7 | 12.9 | 1.4 | 78.0 | 35.2 | 39.4 | 93.0 |
| HIGHLAND | 0.2 | 0.8 | 4.8 | 5.6 | 6.5 | 5.4 | 4.0 | 25.6 | 28.7 | 17.2 | 2.3 | 79.9 | 40.7 | 44.0 | 99.2 |
| ISLE OF WIGHT | 0.7 | 1.3 | 6.7 | 7.3 | 7.5 | 6.9 | 5.5 | 29.4 | 24.7 | 11.0 | 1.1 | 74.3 | 33.7 | 37.3 | 98.3 |
| JAMES CITY | 1.1 | 2.0 | 6.2 | 6.8 | 6.7 | 6.1 | 5.6 | 30.8 | 23.6 | 12.8 | 1.4 | 76.6 | 34.3 | 37.5 | 93.9 |
| KING AND QUEEN | 0.4 | 0.9 | 6.4 | 6.8 | 7.4 | 6.4 | 5.6 | 27.5 | 24.4 | 14.2 | 1.4 | 75.4 | 35.3 | 38.3 | 96.4 |
| KING GEORGE | 1.2 | 2.0 | 8.0 | 8.2 | 8.1 | 6.7 | 5.7 | 32.1 | 21.2 | 9.0 | 1.0 | 71.6 | 31.1 | 34.2 | 98.0 |
| KING WILLIAM | 0.6 | 1.1 | 6.8 | 7.4 | 7.5 | 7.0 | 5.9 | 28.7 | 24.3 | 10.8 | 1.5 | 73.8 | 34.1 | 36.5 | 92.6 |
| LANCASTER | 0.7 | 1.3 | 4.5 | 5.6 | 5.6 | 5.8 | 4.0 | 21.2 | 25.7 | 23.7 | 3.9 | 80.7 | 45.5 | 47.6 | 88.2 |
| LEE | 0.5 | 1.2 | 5.7 | 6.4 | 7.4 | 7.2 | 5.7 | 27.5 | 25.1 | 13.2 | 1.9 | 76.0 | 35.4 | 38.7 | 92.7 |
| LOUDOUN | 2.5 | 4.3 | 7.7 | 7.9 | 7.6 | 6.2 | 5.2 | 36.3 | 22.5 | 5.8 | 0.7 | 72.9 | 31.6 | 34.5 | 97.4 |
| LOUISA | 0.5 | 1.1 | 6.1 | 6.8 | 7.2 | 6.8 | 5.3 | 29.4 | 24.9 | 12.0 | 1.5 | 75.7 | 34.8 | 38.0 | 97.0 |
| LUNENBURG | 0.7 | 1.6 | 5.5 | 6.4 | 7.0 | 6.9 | 5.7 | 27.2 | 24.4 | 15.3 | 1.6 | 76.7 | 37.2 | 39.3 | 102.8 |
| MADISON | 0.3 | 0.8 | 6.2 | 6.9 | 7.1 | 7.2 | 5.5 | 27.2 | 24.7 | 13.1 | 2.1 | 75.3 | 35.6 | 38.7 | 95.9 |
| MATHEWS | 0.6 | 1.3 | 4.2 | 5.2 | 5.7 | 5.9 | 4.5 | 24.1 | 27.9 | 19.2 | 3.3 | 81.1 | 43.1 | 45.3 | 92.7 |
| MECKLENBURG | 0.4 | 0.8 | 5.3 | 6.0 | 6.7 | 6.4 | 5.6 | 27.4 | 24.8 | 15.9 | 1.8 | 78.0 | 37.4 | 40.1 | 93.3 |
| MIDDLESEX | 0.6 | 1.1 | 5.0 | 5.6 | 5.9 | 5.3 | 4.2 | 24.0 | 27.3 | 19.9 | 2.9 | 80.2 | 42.8 | 45.0 | 93.5 |
| MONTGOMERY | 1.1 | 1.9 | 4.9 | 4.9 | 4.9 | 12.9 | 18.7 | 28.1 | 17.2 | 7.3 | 1.1 | 82.5 | 25.6 | 27.7 | 106.6 |
| NELSON | 0.9 | 1.6 | 5.8 | 6.5 | 6.9 | 6.7 | 5.1 | 26.4 | 26.0 | 14.7 | 1.9 | 76.6 | 37.1 | 40.5 | 94.5 |
| NEW KENT | 0.7 | 1.4 | 5.7 | 6.4 | 6.8 | 6.6 | 5.1 | 32.9 | 25.9 | 9.7 | 0.9 | 76.8 | 34.6 | 37.9 | 105.6 |
| NORTHAMPTON | 2.0 | 2.8 | 6.0 | 7.1 | 7.2 | 6.9 | 5.1 | 24.7 | 22.5 | 17.7 | 2.7 | 75.4 | 37.5 | 40.1 | 87.0 |
| NORTHUMBERLAND | 0.5 | 1.1 | 4.8 | 5.6 | 5.8 | 5.3 | 4.0 | 22.0 | 26.6 | 23.2 | 2.6 | 80.5 | 45.4 | 46.9 | 89.5 |
| NOTTOWAY | 0.6 | 1.0 | 5.2 | 5.8 | 6.1 | 6.4 | 7.0 | 29.6 | 22.3 | 15.2 | 2.3 | 78.9 | 36.7 | 38.3 | 108.0 |
| ORANGE | 0.7 | 1.4 | 5.7 | 6.4 | 6.8 | 6.9 | 5.0 | 27.5 | 25.1 | 14.6 | 1.9 | 76.9 | 36.4 | 39.9 | 94.8 |
| PAGE | 0.5 | 1.2 | 5.8 | 6.3 | 6.7 | 6.4 | 5.1 | 28.3 | 25.5 | 14.0 | 1.7 | 77.3 | 36.2 | 39.4 | 95.3 |
| PATRICK | 0.7 | 1.4 | 4.9 | 5.6 | 6.2 | 6.5 | 5.1 | 27.1 | 27.3 | 15.0 | 2.3 | 79.4 | 38.0 | 41.6 | 96.6 |
| PITTSYLVANIA | 0.4 | 0.9 | 5.3 | 6.3 | 6.8 | 6.8 | 5.4 | 29.2 | 26.2 | 12.6 | 1.4 | 77.4 | 35.5 | 39.2 | 96.6 |
| POWHATAN | 0.4 | 0.9 | 5.3 | 5.8 | 6.4 | 7.7 | 5.9 | 35.6 | 24.1 | 8.3 | 0.8 | 77.8 | 33.7 | 36.1 | 129.7 |
| PRINCE EDWARD | 0.7 | 1.2 | 5.2 | 5.6 | 5.9 | 13.2 | 14.4 | 23.1 | 18.6 | 11.8 | 2.0 | 79.8 | 28.6 | 30.5 | 93.1 |
| PRINCE GEORGE | 3.9 | 5.9 | 7.0 | 7.3 | 6.6 | 7.6 | 8.6 | 34.9 | 20.8 | 6.7 | 0.5 | 75.5 | 30.1 | 32.1 | 113.0 |
| PRINCE WILLIAM | 4.5 | 7.2 | 8.3 | 8.5 | 8.1 | 7.0 | 7.0 | 36.4 | 20.3 | 4.1 | 0.3 | 70.8 | 29.0 | 31.5 | 102.0 |
| PULASKI | 0.4 | 1.0 | 5.1 | 5.7 | 6.2 | 5.6 | 5.3 | 29.6 | 26.9 | 13.7 | 1.9 | 79.7 | 36.6 | 40.0 | 94.8 |
| RAPPAHANNOCK | 1.0 | 1.9 | 5.7 | 6.7 | 7.3 | 5.7 | 4.5 | 26.7 | 29.1 | 12.9 | 1.4 | 76.8 | 37.3 | 40.7 | 99.5 |
| RICHMOND | 0.7 | 1.4 | 5.0 | 5.8 | 6.2 | 6.1 | 7.6 | 28.5 | 22.2 | 15.2 | 3.2 | 79.2 | 37.9 | 38.8 | 112.3 |
| ROANOKE | 0.6 | 1.3 | 4.7 | 5.6 | 6.2 | 6.7 | 5.5 | 29.1 | 27.5 | 12.8 | 1.9 | 79.5 | 37.3 | 40.5 | 89.3 |
| VIRGINIA | 2.6 | 4.1 | 6.5 | 6.7 | 6.8 | 6.9 | 7.0 | 32.2 | 22.6 | 10.1 | 1.3 | 76.2 | 32.6 | 35.7 | 95.5 |
| UNITED STATES | 9.0 | 11.8 | 6.9 | 7.2 | 7.2 | 7.2 | 6.7 | 29.9 | 22.2 | 11.1 | 1.6 | 74.6 | 32.9 | 35.7 | 95.6 |

# HOUSEHOLDS

| COUNTY | HOUSEHOLDS 1990 | HOUSEHOLDS 2000 | HOUSEHOLDS 2005 | % Annual Rate 1990-2000 | 2000 Average HH Size | FAMILIES 1990 | FAMILIES 2000 | % Annual Rate 1990-2000 | MEDIAN HOUSEHOLD INCOME 2000 | MEDIAN HOUSEHOLD INCOME 2005 | 2000 National Rank | 2000 State Rank |
|---|---|---|---|---|---|---|---|---|---|---|---|---|
| ACCOMACK | 12,653 | 13,450 | 13,713 | 0.7 | 2.34 | 8,780 | 8,926 | 0.2 | 28,268 | 33,419 | 2405 | 109 |
| ALBEMARLE | 24,433 | 29,668 | 32,017 | 2.4 | 2.48 | 17,031 | 19,915 | 1.9 | 47,651 | 52,252 | 251 | 24 |
| ALLEGHANY | 4,942 | 4,717 | 4,732 | -0.6 | 2.53 | 3,849 | 3,557 | -1.0 | 35,557 | 39,665 | 1160 | 58 |
| AMELIA | 3,131 | 4,014 | 4,508 | 3.1 | 2.69 | 2,428 | 3,034 | 2.7 | 33,543 | 39,086 | 1457 | 74 |
| AMHERST | 9,827 | 11,153 | 11,853 | 1.5 | 2.59 | 7,676 | 8,448 | 1.2 | 34,361 | 37,766 | 1338 | 67 |
| APPOMATTOX | 4,531 | 5,166 | 5,578 | 1.6 | 2.58 | 3,567 | 3,943 | 1.2 | 31,074 | 34,301 | 1918 | 88 |
| ARLINGTON | 78,520 | 81,219 | 82,307 | 0.4 | 2.12 | 37,327 | 37,306 | 0.0 | 61,577 | 73,304 | 62 | 5 |
| AUGUSTA | 19,781 | 23,681 | 25,765 | 2.2 | 2.56 | 15,602 | 18,217 | 1.9 | 36,257 | 40,316 | 1073 | 53 |
| BATH | 1,895 | 2,024 | 2,093 | 0.8 | 2.42 | 1,389 | 1,428 | 0.3 | 33,819 | 39,320 | 1418 | 73 |
| BEDFORD | 17,292 | 22,582 | 24,563 | 3.3 | 2.57 | 13,678 | 17,380 | 2.9 | 43,031 | 49,487 | 456 | 34 |
| BLAND | 2,244 | 2,394 | 2,418 | 0.8 | 2.60 | 1,740 | 1,801 | 0.4 | 31,161 | 36,438 | 1897 | 86 |
| BOTETOURT | 9,148 | 11,169 | 12,270 | 2.4 | 2.59 | 7,298 | 8,647 | 2.1 | 49,534 | 59,298 | 210 | 22 |
| BRUNSWICK | 5,499 | 6,023 | 6,355 | 1.1 | 2.56 | 3,959 | 4,170 | 0.6 | 28,485 | 35,996 | 2368 | 106 |
| BUCHANAN | 11,061 | 10,267 | 9,751 | -0.9 | 2.62 | 9,108 | 8,234 | -1.2 | 23,466 | 26,849 | 2943 | 133 |
| BUCKINGHAM | 4,341 | 4,961 | 5,330 | 1.6 | 2.57 | 3,229 | 3,559 | 1.2 | 35,387 | 43,544 | 1186 | 59 |
| CAMPBELL | 17,952 | 20,276 | 21,369 | 1.5 | 2.48 | 13,811 | 15,135 | 1.1 | 33,153 | 36,384 | 1512 | 76 |
| CAROLINE | 6,631 | 8,177 | 8,782 | 2.6 | 2.69 | 5,188 | 6,215 | 2.2 | 38,535 | 47,674 | 804 | 45 |
| CARROLL | 10,463 | 11,531 | 11,860 | 1.2 | 2.38 | 8,067 | 8,570 | 0.7 | 29,425 | 33,869 | 2231 | 101 |
| CHARLES CITY | 2,161 | 2,685 | 2,985 | 2.7 | 2.74 | 1,735 | 2,098 | 2.3 | 38,560 | 44,684 | 801 | 43 |
| CHARLOTTE | 4,312 | 4,790 | 5,059 | 1.3 | 2.58 | 3,243 | 3,451 | 0.8 | 30,604 | 37,994 | 2008 | 94 |
| CHESTERFIELD | 73,441 | 90,976 | 97,521 | 2.6 | 2.78 | 58,395 | 70,371 | 2.3 | 56,568 | 64,335 | 108 | 10 |
| CLARKE | 4,236 | 4,569 | 4,886 | 0.9 | 2.78 | 3,256 | 3,392 | 0.5 | 49,196 | 63,553 | 218 | 23 |
| CRAIG | 1,676 | 1,955 | 2,067 | 1.9 | 2.54 | 1,305 | 1,479 | 1.5 | 36,976 | 43,819 | 983 | 49 |
| CULPEPER | 9,757 | 12,049 | 13,232 | 2.6 | 2.69 | 7,431 | 8,921 | 2.2 | 45,589 | 54,162 | 326 | 28 |
| CUMBERLAND | 2,813 | 2,982 | 3,094 | 0.7 | 2.63 | 2,103 | 2,139 | 0.2 | 30,341 | 34,876 | 2072 | 98 |
| DICKENSON | 6,457 | 6,439 | 6,274 | 0.0 | 2.55 | 5,127 | 4,955 | -0.4 | 23,426 | 28,531 | 2949 | 135 |
| DINWIDDIE | 7,492 | 8,992 | 9,507 | 2.2 | 2.74 | 5,869 | 6,829 | 1.9 | 35,121 | 37,361 | 1231 | 63 |
| ESSEX | 3,258 | 3,557 | 3,604 | 1.1 | 2.52 | 2,359 | 2,488 | 0.6 | 36,040 | 42,038 | 1099 | 55 |
| FAIRFAX | 292,345 | 354,120 | 388,430 | 2.4 | 2.68 | 213,547 | 249,886 | 1.9 | 76,469 | 85,414 | 8 | 1 |
| FAUQUIER | 16,509 | 19,838 | 22,234 | 2.3 | 2.81 | 13,266 | 15,461 | 1.9 | 61,136 | 74,552 | 65 | 6 |
| FLOYD | 4,763 | 5,532 | 5,953 | 1.8 | 2.41 | 3,549 | 3,953 | 1.3 | 30,877 | 36,386 | 1954 | 89 |
| FLUVANNA | 4,518 | 7,736 | 9,450 | 6.7 | 2.59 | 3,558 | 5,969 | 6.5 | 49,669 | 60,496 | 206 | 21 |
| FRANKLIN | 14,655 | 18,027 | 19,750 | 2.5 | 2.47 | 11,307 | 13,479 | 2.2 | 34,547 | 40,612 | 1312 | 66 |
| FREDERICK | 16,470 | 21,279 | 23,362 | 3.2 | 2.68 | 13,034 | 16,349 | 2.8 | 41,210 | 47,560 | 568 | 38 |
| GILES | 6,461 | 6,742 | 6,958 | 0.5 | 2.41 | 4,861 | 4,876 | 0.0 | 32,017 | 35,954 | 1712 | 81 |
| GLOUCESTER | 10,966 | 13,609 | 14,958 | 2.7 | 2.62 | 8,505 | 10,232 | 2.3 | 43,098 | 53,759 | 451 | 33 |
| GOOCHLAND | 4,880 | 6,520 | 7,312 | 3.6 | 2.54 | 3,883 | 5,026 | 3.2 | 50,749 | 55,041 | 190 | 19 |
| GRAYSON | 6,468 | 6,690 | 6,838 | 0.4 | 2.43 | 4,875 | 4,844 | -0.1 | 28,006 | 32,235 | 2442 | 113 |
| GREENE | 3,749 | 5,689 | 6,846 | 5.2 | 2.68 | 2,949 | 4,346 | 4.8 | 38,238 | 44,459 | 836 | 47 |
| GREENSVILLE | 3,150 | 3,121 | 3,201 | -0.1 | 2.57 | 2,434 | 2,333 | -0.5 | 28,047 | 34,975 | 2433 | 111 |
| HALIFAX | 10,728 | 11,478 | 11,775 | 0.8 | 2.55 | 8,199 | 8,451 | 0.4 | 23,524 | 28,612 | 2938 | 132 |
| HANOVER | 22,628 | 32,798 | 38,925 | 4.6 | 2.64 | 18,090 | 25,531 | 4.3 | 55,226 | 63,810 | 123 | 12 |
| HENRICO | 89,138 | 107,400 | 115,161 | 2.3 | 2.28 | 59,729 | 69,179 | 1.8 | 43,348 | 47,628 | 436 | 32 |
| HENRY | 21,771 | 22,243 | 22,345 | 0.3 | 2.46 | 16,699 | 16,488 | -0.2 | 29,457 | 32,235 | 2228 | 100 |
| HIGHLAND | 1,081 | 1,054 | 1,036 | -0.3 | 2.33 | 784 | 737 | -0.7 | 27,179 | 29,468 | 2550 | 121 |
| ISLE OF WIGHT | 9,032 | 11,494 | 12,714 | 3.0 | 2.61 | 7,087 | 8,770 | 2.6 | 40,527 | 45,241 | 624 | 39 |
| JAMES CITY | 12,968 | 18,017 | 20,710 | 4.1 | 2.59 | 9,613 | 12,905 | 3.6 | 55,239 | 61,415 | 121 | 11 |
| KING AND QUEEN | 2,339 | 2,563 | 2,705 | 1.1 | 2.57 | 1,750 | 1,846 | 0.6 | 39,145 | 47,747 | 743 | 41 |
| KING GEORGE | 4,736 | 6,557 | 7,467 | 4.0 | 2.72 | 3,622 | 4,863 | 3.6 | 46,654 | 55,948 | 287 | 26 |
| KING WILLIAM | 3,834 | 4,831 | 5,359 | 2.8 | 2.73 | 3,003 | 3,668 | 2.5 | 44,088 | 52,632 | 390 | 30 |
| LANCASTER | 4,564 | 4,999 | 5,164 | 1.1 | 2.23 | 3,253 | 3,421 | 0.6 | 34,206 | 36,366 | 1355 | 68 |
| LEE | 9,231 | 9,297 | 9,287 | 0.1 | 2.53 | 7,029 | 6,848 | -0.3 | 23,053 | 26,183 | 2969 | 136 |
| LOUDOUN | 30,490 | 60,559 | 80,994 | 8.7 | 2.75 | 23,278 | 44,446 | 8.2 | 68,169 | 79,413 | 19 | 3 |
| LOUISA | 7,427 | 9,967 | 11,366 | 3.6 | 2.55 | 5,628 | 7,300 | 3.2 | 38,578 | 44,941 | 795 | 42 |
| LUNENBURG | 4,423 | 4,384 | 4,230 | -0.1 | 2.40 | 3,216 | 3,060 | -0.6 | 24,796 | 29,042 | 2828 | 129 |
| MADISON | 4,144 | 4,670 | 4,921 | 1.5 | 2.67 | 3,201 | 3,501 | 1.1 | 38,339 | 48,502 | 827 | 46 |
| MATHEWS | 3,530 | 4,035 | 4,293 | 1.6 | 2.30 | 2,501 | 2,749 | 1.2 | 34,786 | 38,317 | 1285 | 65 |
| MECKLENBURG | 11,244 | 12,574 | 13,000 | 1.4 | 2.38 | 8,164 | 8,783 | 0.9 | 29,188 | 33,386 | 2268 | 102 |
| MIDDLESEX | 3,530 | 4,165 | 4,493 | 2.0 | 2.31 | 2,578 | 2,940 | 1.6 | 38,546 | 46,942 | 802 | 44 |
| MONTGOMERY | 26,241 | 28,496 | 29,491 | 1.0 | 2.41 | 15,851 | 16,528 | 0.5 | 31,271 | 35,588 | 1875 | 85 |
| NELSON | 4,807 | 5,576 | 6,089 | 1.8 | 2.56 | 3,581 | 4,018 | 1.4 | 35,206 | 42,963 | 1219 | 62 |
| NEW KENT | 3,718 | 4,898 | 5,554 | 3.4 | 2.68 | 3,056 | 3,924 | 3.1 | 53,234 | 65,824 | 147 | 15 |
| NORTHAMPTON | 5,129 | 5,142 | 5,228 | 0.0 | 2.44 | 3,516 | 3,387 | -0.5 | 23,429 | 25,301 | 2948 | 134 |
| NORTHUMBERLAND | 4,492 | 5,240 | 5,675 | 1.9 | 2.25 | 3,229 | 3,634 | 1.4 | 31,971 | 34,521 | 1720 | 82 |
| NOTTOWAY | 5,244 | 5,399 | 5,523 | 0.4 | 2.52 | 3,781 | 3,754 | -0.1 | 28,115 | 33,234 | 2425 | 110 |
| ORANGE | 7,930 | 10,057 | 11,070 | 2.9 | 2.56 | 6,103 | 7,502 | 2.5 | 46,966 | 59,282 | 275 | 25 |
| PAGE | 8,055 | 8,888 | 9,218 | 1.2 | 2.59 | 6,117 | 6,496 | 0.7 | 34,062 | 41,896 | 1382 | 71 |
| PATRICK | 6,908 | 7,826 | 8,333 | 1.5 | 2.36 | 5,274 | 5,698 | 0.9 | 28,908 | 34,700 | 2312 | 103 |
| PITTSYLVANIA | 20,613 | 22,169 | 23,080 | 0.9 | 2.55 | 16,161 | 16,785 | 0.5 | 32,591 | 37,821 | 1612 | 77 |
| POWHATAN | 4,672 | 7,659 | 9,471 | 6.2 | 2.71 | 3,896 | 6,229 | 5.9 | 52,363 | 62,984 | 164 | 16 |
| PRINCE EDWARD | 5,373 | 6,307 | 6,615 | 2.0 | 2.46 | 3,714 | 4,136 | 1.3 | 30,501 | 35,604 | 2031 | 97 |
| PRINCE GEORGE | 8,250 | 9,332 | 10,115 | 1.5 | 2.79 | 6,936 | 7,651 | 1.2 | 42,218 | 47,488 | 491 | 36 |
| PRINCE WILLIAM | 69,709 | 91,376 | 104,620 | 3.3 | 3.01 | 56,289 | 71,780 | 3.0 | 58,050 | 68,006 | 91 | 8 |
| PULASKI | 13,349 | 14,057 | 14,398 | 0.6 | 2.37 | 9,903 | 10,085 | 0.2 | 30,597 | 35,323 | 2010 | 95 |
| RAPPAHANNOCK | 2,496 | 2,905 | 3,068 | 1.9 | 2.51 | 1,908 | 2,159 | 1.5 | 41,834 | 51,122 | 527 | 37 |
| RICHMOND | 2,645 | 2,808 | 2,930 | 0.7 | 2.53 | 1,964 | 2,019 | 0.3 | 30,787 | 35,969 | 1973 | 91 |
| ROANOKE | 30,355 | 32,235 | 32,843 | 0.7 | 2.45 | 22,935 | 23,597 | 0.3 | 46,054 | 49,696 | 306 | 27 |
| VIRGINIA | | | | 1.8 | 2.53 | | | 1.5 | 44,048 | 51,389 | | |
| UNITED STATES | | | | 1.4 | 2.59 | | | 1.1 | 41,914 | 49,127 | | |

| COUNTY | 2000 Per Capita Income | 2000 HH Income Base | 2000 HOUSEHOLD INCOME DISTRIBUTION (%) | | | | | | 2000 AVERAGE DISPOSABLE INCOME BY AGE OF HOUSEHOLDER | | | | | |
|---|---|---|---|---|---|---|---|---|---|---|---|---|---|---|
| | | | Less than $15,000 | $15,000 to $24,999 | $25,000 to $49,999 | $50,000 to $99,999 | $100,000 to $149,999 | $150,000 or More | All Ages | <35 | 35-44 | 45-54 | 55-64 | 65+ |
| ACCOMACK | 15,365 | 13,450 | 23.6 | 19.6 | 36.0 | 18.2 | 1.9 | 0.7 | 27,373 | 26,109 | 30,293 | 33,045 | 30,764 | 20,948 |
| ALBEMARLE | 24,730 | 29,668 | 9.7 | 11.0 | 32.4 | 33.4 | 9.3 | 4.3 | 44,835 | 33,563 | 47,243 | 54,321 | 49,350 | 35,925 |
| ALLEGHANY | 15,741 | 4,716 | 17.4 | 15.4 | 38.7 | 25.5 | 2.8 | 0.2 | 30,980 | 29,254 | 34,371 | 39,385 | 33,071 | 18,566 |
| AMELIA | 15,658 | 4,014 | 16.1 | 17.4 | 40.2 | 22.9 | 2.3 | 1.0 | 31,252 | 29,226 | 35,115 | 38,275 | 33,070 | 20,211 |
| AMHERST | 14,884 | 11,153 | 17.5 | 15.8 | 40.1 | 24.4 | 1.7 | 0.5 | 30,538 | 29,136 | 36,041 | 36,737 | 30,469 | 20,247 |
| APPOMATTOX | 13,152 | 5,166 | 21.6 | 18.9 | 39.8 | 17.9 | 1.7 | 0.1 | 26,974 | 25,951 | 32,856 | 31,682 | 29,502 | 16,734 |
| ARLINGTON | 40,083 | 81,219 | 4.9 | 7.0 | 26.4 | 38.2 | 15.1 | 8.3 | 56,950 | 44,871 | 57,028 | 64,349 | 60,256 | 49,385 |
| AUGUSTA | 16,948 | 23,681 | 13.7 | 15.4 | 42.4 | 25.0 | 2.8 | 0.8 | 32,450 | 29,034 | 36,279 | 40,696 | 31,918 | 21,449 |
| BATH | 18,458 | 2,024 | 18.2 | 13.3 | 37.6 | 23.6 | 4.6 | 2.6 | 34,325 | 24,904 | 38,878 | 38,668 | 42,209 | 28,552 |
| BEDFORD | 21,811 | 22,582 | 10.3 | 12.9 | 36.3 | 32.1 | 6.4 | 2.1 | 38,874 | 34,426 | 43,020 | 46,090 | 40,580 | 26,369 |
| BLAND | 13,268 | 2,394 | 22.3 | 16.8 | 40.0 | 18.5 | 2.2 | 0.2 | 27,613 | 30,865 | 36,108 | 32,266 | 25,565 | 15,004 |
| BOTETOURT | 23,359 | 11,169 | 7.7 | 9.4 | 33.5 | 37.9 | 9.4 | 2.0 | 42,978 | 37,484 | 50,378 | 51,937 | 43,978 | 29,688 |
| BRUNSWICK | 12,954 | 6,023 | 26.5 | 16.0 | 34.9 | 18.9 | 2.8 | 0.9 | 28,155 | 24,773 | 31,750 | 34,732 | 32,455 | 20,788 |
| BUCHANAN | 11,960 | 10,267 | 31.6 | 21.7 | 32.1 | 12.3 | 1.5 | 0.7 | 24,208 | 23,153 | 29,866 | 26,250 | 21,648 | 16,830 |
| BUCKINGHAM | 13,915 | 4,961 | 20.7 | 12.7 | 37.8 | 24.8 | 3.2 | 0.8 | 31,411 | 30,323 | 35,703 | 36,975 | 33,047 | 23,567 |
| CAMPBELL | 15,882 | 20,276 | 18.1 | 17.0 | 39.2 | 22.4 | 2.6 | 0.7 | 30,370 | 27,455 | 34,895 | 37,941 | 30,141 | 20,486 |
| CAROLINE | 17,757 | 8,177 | 16.2 | 11.7 | 38.5 | 27.0 | 5.0 | 1.6 | 35,030 | 34,855 | 39,086 | 41,071 | 37,271 | 22,205 |
| CARROLL | 13,744 | 11,531 | 22.8 | 17.8 | 40.5 | 17.7 | 1.2 | 0.0 | 26,341 | 26,010 | 31,633 | 31,613 | 26,357 | 18,263 |
| CHARLES CITY | 16,937 | 2,685 | 15.4 | 12.0 | 38.4 | 28.8 | 4.6 | 0.8 | 34,204 | 31,162 | 34,802 | 42,146 | 34,180 | 23,109 |
| CHARLOTTE | 14,145 | 4,790 | 21.3 | 18.8 | 36.5 | 20.4 | 2.9 | 0.2 | 28,618 | 25,636 | 33,804 | 35,916 | 29,873 | 21,465 |
| CHESTERFIELD | 25,085 | 90,976 | 4.8 | 6.4 | 29.5 | 44.3 | 11.4 | 3.7 | 49,281 | 39,921 | 52,030 | 57,070 | 50,891 | 33,640 |
| CLARKE | 25,221 | 4,569 | 9.7 | 7.3 | 33.9 | 33.5 | 11.2 | 4.4 | 46,767 | 39,584 | 49,516 | 57,781 | 46,603 | 33,037 |
| CRAIG | 16,368 | 1,955 | 12.5 | 17.4 | 40.8 | 25.6 | 3.6 | 0.2 | 32,418 | 28,629 | 36,383 | 40,820 | 29,730 | 23,227 |
| CULPEPER | 22,030 | 12,049 | 11.2 | 10.0 | 35.2 | 32.2 | 8.9 | 2.5 | 41,254 | 37,308 | 47,569 | 47,679 | 39,184 | 29,402 |
| CUMBERLAND | 14,080 | 2,982 | 25.2 | 17.4 | 32.1 | 20.8 | 3.8 | 0.6 | 28,627 | 28,404 | 36,739 | 33,739 | 31,327 | 16,498 |
| DICKENSON | 11,956 | 6,439 | 31.3 | 20.8 | 31.4 | 14.1 | 2.2 | 0.2 | 24,099 | 23,959 | 29,685 | 26,794 | 21,907 | 18,080 |
| DINWIDDIE | 14,627 | 8,989 | 17.5 | 16.5 | 38.6 | 23.4 | 2.6 | 1.4 | 31,899 | 29,046 | 36,212 | 38,031 | 32,807 | 21,374 |
| ESSEX | 16,960 | 3,557 | 16.3 | 15.7 | 37.6 | 25.8 | 4.1 | 0.7 | 32,693 | 30,059 | 39,805 | 36,976 | 32,294 | 26,331 |
| FAIRFAX | 37,452 | 354,120 | 2.8 | 3.3 | 17.8 | 44.7 | 20.8 | 10.7 | 66,370 | 49,873 | 62,786 | 72,472 | 71,310 | 56,157 |
| FAUQUIER | 31,727 | 19,838 | 5.1 | 6.6 | 25.8 | 40.8 | 14.4 | 7.3 | 55,466 | 45,589 | 54,758 | 64,429 | 54,252 | 42,032 |
| FLOYD | 15,448 | 5,532 | 19.0 | 18.5 | 39.0 | 20.3 | 2.7 | 0.5 | 29,070 | 28,727 | 32,615 | 34,644 | 28,756 | 21,564 |
| FLUVANNA | 23,701 | 7,736 | 9.9 | 7.1 | 33.5 | 36.0 | 10.7 | 2.8 | 44,238 | 39,761 | 49,403 | 49,997 | 47,531 | 34,264 |
| FRANKLIN | 17,510 | 18,027 | 16.7 | 14.5 | 39.2 | 24.6 | 3.9 | 1.0 | 32,456 | 28,813 | 36,975 | 38,796 | 35,006 | 22,042 |
| FREDERICK | 18,428 | 21,278 | 11.3 | 11.0 | 40.8 | 31.2 | 4.6 | 1.1 | 36,430 | 34,034 | 39,892 | 43,569 | 35,774 | 25,008 |
| GILES | 15,952 | 6,742 | 19.4 | 17.9 | 37.7 | 22.0 | 2.3 | 0.7 | 29,625 | 26,752 | 33,900 | 37,307 | 32,043 | 20,997 |
| GLOUCESTER | 19,646 | 13,609 | 11.1 | 10.5 | 38.1 | 33.3 | 6.0 | 1.1 | 37,914 | 32,241 | 43,018 | 45,164 | 40,203 | 27,538 |
| GOOCHLAND | 31,301 | 6,520 | 9.0 | 9.3 | 30.9 | 30.4 | 11.4 | 9.1 | 54,307 | 44,495 | 53,210 | 60,818 | 54,056 | 34,295 |
| GRAYSON | 13,038 | 6,690 | 23.3 | 20.5 | 38.8 | 16.7 | 0.8 | 0.0 | 25,387 | 26,102 | 30,689 | 31,073 | 26,096 | 16,424 |
| GREENE | 17,385 | 5,689 | 15.1 | 12.1 | 40.4 | 27.2 | 3.9 | 1.3 | 34,627 | 30,559 | 39,114 | 41,203 | 38,449 | 21,376 |
| GREENSVILLE | 10,071 | 3,121 | 24.6 | 17.6 | 38.5 | 16.7 | 1.7 | 0.9 | 27,324 | 25,470 | 30,808 | 36,243 | 27,524 | 15,231 |
| HALIFAX | 10,443 | 11,473 | 31.1 | 21.5 | 35.9 | 10.8 | 0.7 | 0.0 | 22,285 | 22,589 | 26,754 | 28,153 | 21,810 | 13,935 |
| HANOVER | 25,155 | 32,798 | 7.3 | 7.0 | 28.3 | 43.8 | 10.6 | 3.0 | 47,032 | 42,086 | 51,495 | 56,653 | 50,676 | 28,769 |
| HENRICO | 24,924 | 107,400 | 9.7 | 12.9 | 35.9 | 32.7 | 6.2 | 2.7 | 40,319 | 33,532 | 44,757 | 48,234 | 42,432 | 29,762 |
| HENRY | 13,501 | 22,243 | 22.2 | 18.6 | 41.1 | 16.9 | 1.2 | 0.1 | 26,278 | 23,115 | 30,713 | 32,723 | 26,780 | 18,106 |
| HIGHLAND | 14,089 | 1,054 | 28.2 | 16.0 | 39.3 | 14.5 | 1.4 | 0.6 | 25,371 | 23,954 | 30,256 | 33,101 | 20,707 | 19,087 |
| ISLE OF WIGHT | 17,974 | 11,494 | 13.6 | 13.3 | 36.6 | 31.7 | 4.2 | 0.6 | 34,890 | 32,043 | 40,640 | 41,436 | 35,180 | 23,286 |
| JAMES CITY | 27,576 | 18,017 | 7.2 | 9.5 | 27.6 | 37.7 | 12.2 | 5.9 | 50,843 | 36,174 | 54,687 | 57,578 | 56,025 | 46,292 |
| KING AND QUEEN | 18,103 | 2,563 | 14.9 | 13.5 | 37.1 | 28.9 | 4.1 | 1.6 | 35,006 | 33,251 | 38,125 | 44,206 | 37,867 | 23,663 |
| KING GEORGE | 21,761 | 6,557 | 6.6 | 12.7 | 36.3 | 35.4 | 6.8 | 2.3 | 41,462 | 34,212 | 42,834 | 51,957 | 41,168 | 34,694 |
| KING WILLIAM | 20,520 | 4,831 | 10.9 | 11.0 | 36.0 | 32.7 | 6.9 | 2.5 | 40,588 | 38,136 | 43,732 | 50,732 | 41,316 | 24,257 |
| LANCASTER | 28,146 | 4,999 | 19.3 | 14.3 | 35.1 | 18.7 | 6.5 | 6.1 | 40,991 | 26,972 | 37,286 | 45,965 | 47,333 | 35,490 |
| LEE | 12,572 | 9,297 | 33.0 | 20.8 | 29.7 | 13.4 | 2.2 | 1.0 | 24,627 | 22,551 | 32,425 | 28,335 | 22,637 | 17,513 |
| LOUDOUN | 30,936 | 60,559 | 4.0 | 3.2 | 20.0 | 49.1 | 17.5 | 6.2 | 57,727 | 50,425 | 59,471 | 64,455 | 59,613 | 38,685 |
| LOUISA | 19,086 | 9,967 | 16.5 | 13.8 | 35.8 | 27.0 | 4.9 | 2.0 | 35,309 | 33,374 | 40,697 | 43,134 | 34,714 | 22,208 |
| LUNENBURG | 28,547 | 4,384 | 28.7 | 21.8 | 35.6 | 12.7 | 0.8 | 0.4 | 23,848 | 23,004 | 27,735 | 32,404 | 21,131 | 16,998 |
| MADISON | 19,846 | 4,670 | 14.2 | 13.4 | 36.6 | 27.3 | 6.4 | 2.1 | 36,980 | 35,036 | 38,710 | 44,842 | 39,880 | 27,700 |
| MATHEWS | 18,367 | 4,035 | 20.8 | 13.3 | 34.8 | 26.5 | 3.5 | 1.1 | 32,472 | 33,046 | 32,534 | 36,161 | 37,292 | 27,140 |
| MECKLENBURG | 15,286 | 12,574 | 24.8 | 18.2 | 35.3 | 18.6 | 2.3 | 0.8 | 28,112 | 27,017 | 33,224 | 36,330 | 28,641 | 18,712 |
| MIDDLESEX | 23,952 | 4,165 | 15.6 | 16.2 | 32.6 | 26.2 | 6.4 | 3.1 | 37,416 | 32,121 | 38,551 | 50,491 | 39,029 | 28,184 |
| MONTGOMERY | 15,778 | 28,494 | 22.7 | 17.5 | 31.6 | 23.1 | 3.9 | 1.2 | 30,822 | 22,146 | 38,705 | 42,628 | 41,132 | 23,729 |
| NELSON | 17,569 | 5,576 | 18.3 | 16.1 | 35.2 | 23.5 | 5.1 | 1.8 | 33,528 | 30,038 | 36,771 | 44,326 | 36,812 | 21,663 |
| NEW KENT | 22,986 | 4,898 | 6.6 | 7.8 | 31.5 | 41.6 | 10.3 | 2.3 | 45,126 | 41,412 | 49,564 | 49,308 | 47,270 | 33,001 |
| NORTHAMPTON | 13,609 | 5,142 | 33.7 | 19.5 | 28.7 | 13.9 | 2.9 | 1.2 | 25,560 | 23,867 | 31,260 | 31,925 | 25,286 | 18,813 |
| NORTHUMBERLAND | 20,677 | 5,240 | 20.5 | 17.0 | 34.7 | 19.9 | 4.7 | 3.2 | 34,108 | 28,470 | 35,927 | 41,507 | 39,407 | 27,688 |
| NOTTOWAY | 12,900 | 5,399 | 24.8 | 19.0 | 36.9 | 16.7 | 2.0 | 0.6 | 26,704 | 23,022 | 32,632 | 32,813 | 30,163 | 19,369 |
| ORANGE | 21,647 | 10,057 | 9.4 | 9.8 | 35.4 | 34.2 | 9.4 | 1.7 | 41,235 | 36,812 | 46,469 | 46,834 | 46,730 | 32,058 |
| PAGE | 16,467 | 8,888 | 16.9 | 16.7 | 38.9 | 23.3 | 3.5 | 0.8 | 31,494 | 30,060 | 34,066 | 38,601 | 33,532 | 22,775 |
| PATRICK | 14,031 | 7,826 | 26.4 | 16.0 | 39.1 | 16.6 | 1.8 | 0.1 | 25,971 | 24,545 | 32,124 | 33,551 | 24,505 | 17,206 |
| PITTSYLVANIA | 15,341 | 22,164 | 19.9 | 16.2 | 38.3 | 22.3 | 2.5 | 0.8 | 30,001 | 27,553 | 36,274 | 36,566 | 29,105 | 19,633 |
| POWHATAN | 24,879 | 7,659 | 5.2 | 7.2 | 34.7 | 39.8 | 9.5 | 3.6 | 46,803 | 39,680 | 51,917 | 54,632 | 44,726 | 31,638 |
| PRINCE EDWARD | 13,379 | 6,307 | 24.2 | 16.4 | 36.3 | 19.7 | 2.9 | 0.5 | 28,508 | 23,802 | 36,769 | 33,658 | 29,928 | 20,100 |
| PRINCE GEORGE | 16,927 | 9,330 | 8.0 | 14.0 | 39.6 | 33.8 | 3.8 | 0.8 | 36,803 | 31,254 | 39,473 | 44,609 | 36,988 | 30,372 |
| PRINCE WILLIAM | 22,232 | 91,371 | 3.5 | 5.2 | 29.6 | 49.2 | 10.6 | 2.0 | 48,022 | 40,502 | 49,021 | 57,032 | 51,927 | 35,169 |
| PULASKI | 15,099 | 14,057 | 21.0 | 19.3 | 37.3 | 19.8 | 2.3 | 0.3 | 28,225 | 25,803 | 33,316 | 33,661 | 29,792 | 19,250 |
| RAPPAHANNOCK | 28,829 | 2,905 | 12.4 | 11.2 | 34.8 | 30.5 | 7.1 | 4.1 | 42,710 | 32,650 | 44,731 | 45,213 | 49,294 | 34,008 |
| RICHMOND | 12,505 | 2,808 | 22.4 | 16.2 | 36.5 | 20.3 | 3.8 | 0.8 | 29,603 | 26,935 | 33,975 | 34,545 | 32,648 | 22,198 |
| ROANOKE | 23,233 | 32,235 | 9.6 | 10.8 | 35.4 | 34.4 | 7.4 | 2.4 | 41,159 | 34,480 | 45,877 | 48,758 | 44,756 | 27,907 |
| VIRGINIA | 22,934 | | 12.8 | 11.9 | 32.0 | 31.8 | 8.2 | 3.3 | 41,578 | 34,181 | 45,367 | 50,467 | 43,935 | 29,069 |
| UNITED STATES | 22,162 | | 14.5 | 12.5 | 32.3 | 29.8 | 7.4 | 3.5 | 40,748 | 34,503 | 44,969 | 49,579 | 43,409 | 27,339 |

| COUNTY | FINANCIAL SERVICES | | | | THE HOME | | | | | | ENTERTAINMENT | | | | | | PERSONAL | | | |
|---|---|---|---|---|---|---|---|---|---|---|---|---|---|---|---|---|---|---|---|---|
| | | | | | Home Improvements | | | Furnishings | | | | | | | | | | | | |
| | Auto Loan | Home Loan | Invest-ments | Retire-ment Plans | Home Repair | Lawn & Garden | Remodel-ing | Appli-ances | Elec-tronics | Furni-ture | Restau-rants | Sport-ing Goods | Theater & Concerts | Toys & Hobbies | Travel | Video Rental | Apparel | Auto After-market | Health Insur-ance | Pets & Supplies |
| ACCOMACK | 97 | 68 | 79 | 78 | 94 | 93 | 112 | 96 | 92 | 78 | 81 | 94 | 81 | 95 | 71 | 96 | 81 | 88 | 102 | 97 |
| ALBEMARLE | 101 | 106 | 101 | 103 | 102 | 103 | 104 | 100 | 102 | 102 | 107 | 103 | 102 | 104 | 91 | 100 | 105 | 103 | 99 | 104 |
| ALLEGHANY | 99 | 74 | 81 | 82 | 95 | 92 | 115 | 97 | 93 | 83 | 85 | 96 | 85 | 99 | 72 | 98 | 85 | 90 | 102 | 100 |
| AMELIA | 98 | 70 | 76 | 79 | 94 | 91 | 115 | 97 | 93 | 80 | 82 | 97 | 82 | 97 | 70 | 97 | 82 | 89 | 101 | 99 |
| AMHERST | 98 | 74 | 82 | 81 | 95 | 92 | 113 | 96 | 93 | 83 | 85 | 95 | 85 | 97 | 73 | 97 | 84 | 90 | 101 | 98 |
| APPOMATTOX | 97 | 69 | 76 | 77 | 94 | 91 | 113 | 96 | 92 | 80 | 81 | 95 | 82 | 96 | 70 | 96 | 81 | 88 | 101 | 97 |
| ARLINGTON | 103 | 133 | 127 | 122 | 116 | 119 | 103 | 103 | 109 | 117 | 120 | 109 | 117 | 105 | 114 | 102 | 120 | 116 | 102 | 107 |
| AUGUSTA | 100 | 80 | 85 | 86 | 96 | 93 | 115 | 98 | 95 | 87 | 89 | 98 | 88 | 101 | 75 | 98 | 89 | 93 | 101 | 101 |
| BATH | 97 | 72 | 81 | 81 | 96 | 93 | 112 | 96 | 91 | 81 | 83 | 94 | 84 | 96 | 74 | 97 | 83 | 89 | 103 | 97 |
| BEDFORD | 101 | 86 | 85 | 89 | 95 | 94 | 112 | 99 | 98 | 91 | 94 | 100 | 91 | 102 | 77 | 99 | 93 | 96 | 100 | 102 |
| BLAND | 98 | 69 | 76 | 79 | 93 | 91 | 114 | 96 | 93 | 79 | 81 | 96 | 82 | 97 | 70 | 97 | 82 | 89 | 102 | 98 |
| BOTETOURT | 101 | 90 | 92 | 93 | 99 | 97 | 110 | 99 | 99 | 95 | 97 | 101 | 96 | 103 | 81 | 100 | 97 | 98 | 101 | 103 |
| BRUNSWICK | 96 | 65 | 72 | 75 | 93 | 90 | 111 | 95 | 91 | 77 | 78 | 94 | 79 | 94 | 68 | 96 | 79 | 87 | 99 | 96 |
| BUCHANAN | 97 | 64 | 68 | 73 | 92 | 90 | 112 | 95 | 91 | 76 | 77 | 95 | 79 | 94 | 66 | 95 | 78 | 87 | 101 | 96 |
| BUCKINGHAM | 97 | 68 | 75 | 77 | 93 | 91 | 113 | 96 | 92 | 79 | 81 | 95 | 81 | 95 | 69 | 96 | 81 | 88 | 101 | 97 |
| CAMPBELL | 97 | 80 | 84 | 83 | 95 | 92 | 109 | 96 | 94 | 87 | 89 | 96 | 87 | 98 | 75 | 97 | 87 | 92 | 99 | 99 |
| CAROLINE | 98 | 76 | 79 | 81 | 94 | 92 | 111 | 97 | 94 | 84 | 86 | 97 | 85 | 98 | 72 | 97 | 85 | 91 | 100 | 99 |
| CARROLL | 97 | 64 | 68 | 73 | 93 | 91 | 112 | 96 | 91 | 76 | 77 | 96 | 79 | 94 | 67 | 95 | 78 | 87 | 102 | 96 |
| CHARLES CITY | 99 | 73 | 77 | 81 | 94 | 91 | 109 | 98 | 92 | 84 | 83 | 97 | 85 | 98 | 72 | 99 | 88 | 93 | 98 | 99 |
| CHARLOTTE | 98 | 66 | 71 | 76 | 92 | 91 | 114 | 96 | 92 | 77 | 79 | 96 | 80 | 96 | 67 | 96 | 79 | 87 | 102 | 97 |
| CHESTERFIELD | 104 | 112 | 99 | 108 | 101 | 104 | 103 | 103 | 107 | 110 | 115 | 108 | 107 | 108 | 92 | 102 | 113 | 109 | 99 | 106 |
| CLARKE | 99 | 87 | 96 | 90 | 100 | 98 | 108 | 98 | 95 | 92 | 95 | 97 | 93 | 101 | 82 | 98 | 93 | 95 | 101 | 100 |
| CRAIG | 100 | 74 | 80 | 83 | 95 | 92 | 117 | 98 | 94 | 83 | 86 | 98 | 85 | 100 | 71 | 98 | 86 | 91 | 102 | 101 |
| CULPEPER | 98 | 87 | 88 | 87 | 98 | 95 | 107 | 97 | 95 | 91 | 94 | 96 | 91 | 99 | 79 | 98 | 92 | 94 | 99 | 100 |
| CUMBERLAND | 95 | 70 | 76 | 75 | 94 | 91 | 106 | 94 | 90 | 79 | 81 | 92 | 82 | 94 | 71 | 95 | 80 | 87 | 100 | 95 |
| DICKENSON | 97 | 63 | 68 | 73 | 92 | 90 | 111 | 95 | 91 | 75 | 77 | 94 | 78 | 94 | 66 | 95 | 78 | 86 | 102 | 96 |
| DINWIDDIE | 97 | 77 | 80 | 82 | 95 | 92 | 107 | 96 | 93 | 85 | 86 | 96 | 86 | 97 | 73 | 97 | 86 | 91 | 99 | 98 |
| ESSEX | 99 | 75 | 85 | 85 | 96 | 95 | 117 | 98 | 94 | 83 | 86 | 97 | 86 | 99 | 74 | 98 | 87 | 91 | 104 | 101 |
| FAIRFAX | 107 | 133 | 117 | 125 | 111 | 119 | 105 | 107 | 114 | 120 | 128 | 115 | 120 | 111 | 109 | 104 | 127 | 120 | 103 | 110 |
| FAUQUIER | 102 | 106 | 99 | 102 | 101 | 102 | 104 | 101 | 105 | 106 | 110 | 104 | 104 | 106 | 90 | 101 | 108 | 106 | 99 | 105 |
| FLOYD | 98 | 68 | 73 | 77 | 93 | 91 | 114 | 96 | 93 | 78 | 80 | 97 | 81 | 97 | 68 | 96 | 81 | 88 | 102 | 98 |
| FLUVANNA | 100 | 84 | 100 | 93 | 102 | 104 | 114 | 101 | 94 | 91 | 93 | 97 | 93 | 101 | 85 | 98 | 93 | 95 | 106 | 101 |
| FRANKLIN | 99 | 72 | 79 | 81 | 95 | 92 | 116 | 97 | 92 | 81 | 83 | 97 | 84 | 98 | 72 | 97 | 84 | 90 | 102 | 100 |
| FREDERICK | 101 | 92 | 88 | 92 | 97 | 96 | 110 | 100 | 100 | 95 | 99 | 101 | 95 | 103 | 80 | 100 | 97 | 98 | 100 | 103 |
| GILES | 95 | 75 | 85 | 79 | 100 | 95 | 104 | 96 | 88 | 85 | 85 | 93 | 87 | 95 | 78 | 95 | 83 | 88 | 101 | 95 |
| GLOUCESTER | 99 | 84 | 85 | 86 | 95 | 92 | 111 | 97 | 96 | 90 | 93 | 97 | 89 | 100 | 76 | 99 | 91 | 94 | 99 | 101 |
| GOOCHLAND | 103 | 98 | 104 | 103 | 103 | 104 | 110 | 102 | 103 | 103 | 105 | 105 | 103 | 106 | 89 | 101 | 106 | 104 | 101 | 105 |
| GRAYSON | 97 | 67 | 74 | 76 | 94 | 92 | 111 | 96 | 92 | 78 | 79 | 96 | 81 | 95 | 69 | 95 | 80 | 88 | 102 | 97 |
| GREENE | 100 | 83 | 84 | 86 | 95 | 92 | 114 | 98 | 96 | 89 | 92 | 98 | 89 | 101 | 75 | 99 | 91 | 94 | 100 | 102 |
| GREENSVILLE | 98 | 67 | 73 | 77 | 93 | 91 | 113 | 96 | 92 | 78 | 80 | 97 | 81 | 96 | 68 | 96 | 81 | 88 | 102 | 98 |
| HALIFAX | 97 | 67 | 75 | 76 | 94 | 92 | 112 | 96 | 92 | 78 | 80 | 95 | 81 | 95 | 69 | 96 | 80 | 88 | 101 | 97 |
| HANOVER | 103 | 105 | 101 | 103 | 103 | 104 | 104 | 102 | 104 | 107 | 111 | 105 | 105 | 106 | 91 | 101 | 109 | 106 | 100 | 105 |
| HENRICO | 99 | 103 | 100 | 98 | 102 | 102 | 97 | 99 | 98 | 101 | 104 | 100 | 100 | 101 | 90 | 99 | 102 | 101 | 98 | 101 |
| HENRY | 97 | 67 | 73 | 76 | 94 | 91 | 112 | 96 | 91 | 78 | 80 | 96 | 81 | 95 | 69 | 96 | 80 | 87 | 101 | 97 |
| HIGHLAND | 98 | 66 | 73 | 80 | 92 | 91 | 116 | 96 | 91 | 74 | 78 | 96 | 79 | 96 | 69 | 97 | 80 | 88 | 105 | 98 |
| ISLE OF WIGHT | 98 | 80 | 84 | 84 | 95 | 92 | 111 | 96 | 93 | 86 | 88 | 96 | 87 | 99 | 74 | 97 | 87 | 92 | 100 | 100 |
| JAMES CITY | 103 | 107 | 102 | 105 | 103 | 106 | 103 | 102 | 103 | 106 | 110 | 105 | 104 | 105 | 92 | 101 | 109 | 106 | 100 | 105 |
| KING AND QUEEN | 97 | 69 | 76 | 77 | 95 | 92 | 111 | 96 | 91 | 80 | 81 | 96 | 83 | 96 | 70 | 96 | 81 | 88 | 101 | 97 |
| KING GEORGE | 100 | 92 | 93 | 92 | 98 | 96 | 110 | 99 | 98 | 95 | 98 | 100 | 94 | 102 | 81 | 100 | 96 | 98 | 99 | 103 |
| KING WILLIAM | 98 | 86 | 83 | 85 | 96 | 93 | 106 | 97 | 96 | 91 | 93 | 96 | 90 | 99 | 78 | 98 | 91 | 95 | 98 | 99 |
| LANCASTER | 99 | 81 | 102 | 93 | 101 | 104 | 109 | 99 | 94 | 87 | 90 | 95 | 91 | 98 | 84 | 97 | 90 | 93 | 106 | 99 |
| LEE | 96 | 65 | 70 | 74 | 92 | 90 | 111 | 95 | 91 | 76 | 77 | 94 | 79 | 94 | 67 | 96 | 79 | 87 | 101 | 96 |
| LOUDOUN | 105 | 115 | 98 | 108 | 102 | 106 | 102 | 104 | 109 | 113 | 119 | 110 | 109 | 108 | 94 | 103 | 116 | 111 | 99 | 107 |
| LOUISA | 99 | 73 | 80 | 82 | 95 | 92 | 116 | 97 | 94 | 82 | 85 | 97 | 84 | 99 | 72 | 98 | 85 | 90 | 102 | 100 |
| LUNENBURG | 97 | 63 | 66 | 73 | 92 | 90 | 112 | 96 | 91 | 75 | 77 | 96 | 78 | 95 | 66 | 95 | 78 | 86 | 102 | 96 |
| MADISON | 100 | 80 | 86 | 86 | 98 | 94 | 115 | 98 | 94 | 87 | 90 | 98 | 89 | 101 | 76 | 99 | 90 | 93 | 102 | 102 |
| MATHEWS | 97 | 72 | 84 | 81 | 95 | 93 | 111 | 96 | 93 | 80 | 83 | 93 | 83 | 96 | 73 | 97 | 83 | 90 | 103 | 98 |
| MECKLENBURG | 97 | 70 | 76 | 77 | 95 | 92 | 111 | 96 | 90 | 80 | 81 | 95 | 82 | 95 | 71 | 96 | 81 | 88 | 101 | 97 |
| MIDDLESEX | 101 | 77 | 92 | 91 | 98 | 100 | 120 | 100 | 94 | 84 | 88 | 99 | 88 | 101 | 79 | 98 | 88 | 93 | 107 | 102 |
| MONTGOMERY | 96 | 90 | 93 | 90 | 97 | 93 | 105 | 92 | 91 | 84 | 90 | 92 | 86 | 96 | 79 | 94 | 89 | 92 | 97 | 98 |
| NELSON | 99 | 74 | 81 | 82 | 94 | 92 | 116 | 97 | 94 | 82 | 85 | 96 | 84 | 99 | 72 | 98 | 85 | 91 | 102 | 100 |
| NEW KENT | 101 | 91 | 93 | 95 | 98 | 98 | 111 | 100 | 100 | 96 | 99 | 101 | 96 | 104 | 82 | 100 | 98 | 99 | 101 | 103 |
| NORTHAMPTON | 95 | 67 | 75 | 76 | 93 | 90 | 109 | 95 | 90 | 77 | 78 | 91 | 79 | 92 | 70 | 96 | 79 | 87 | 100 | 95 |
| NORTHUMBERLAND | 100 | 73 | 89 | 89 | 97 | 99 | 119 | 99 | 93 | 81 | 84 | 97 | 86 | 99 | 77 | 98 | 86 | 91 | 107 | 101 |
| NOTTOWAY | 94 | 74 | 80 | 77 | 96 | 92 | 104 | 94 | 89 | 82 | 83 | 90 | 83 | 93 | 75 | 95 | 82 | 88 | 99 | 95 |
| ORANGE | 101 | 84 | 97 | 92 | 101 | 101 | 114 | 100 | 96 | 90 | 94 | 99 | 93 | 103 | 82 | 99 | 94 | 95 | 105 | 103 |
| PAGE | 98 | 75 | 83 | 82 | 98 | 94 | 110 | 97 | 91 | 84 | 86 | 96 | 86 | 98 | 75 | 97 | 85 | 90 | 102 | 98 |
| PATRICK | 97 | 65 | 70 | 74 | 92 | 90 | 113 | 96 | 92 | 76 | 78 | 96 | 79 | 95 | 67 | 95 | 79 | 87 | 101 | 97 |
| PITTSYLVANIA | 98 | 68 | 74 | 77 | 94 | 91 | 113 | 96 | 92 | 79 | 81 | 97 | 82 | 96 | 69 | 96 | 81 | 88 | 102 | 98 |
| POWHATAN | 101 | 93 | 93 | 94 | 99 | 98 | 109 | 100 | 100 | 97 | 101 | 101 | 97 | 104 | 83 | 100 | 100 | 100 | 100 | 104 |
| PRINCE EDWARD | 94 | 75 | 83 | 79 | 94 | 90 | 101 | 92 | 88 | 78 | 80 | 90 | 81 | 91 | 73 | 93 | 82 | 88 | 96 | 94 |
| PRINCE GEORGE | 98 | 94 | 84 | 89 | 94 | 92 | 102 | 98 | 99 | 95 | 100 | 98 | 93 | 100 | 79 | 100 | 96 | 99 | 96 | 102 |
| PRINCE WILLIAM | 103 | 113 | 94 | 105 | 99 | 102 | 100 | 102 | 106 | 109 | 115 | 108 | 105 | 106 | 91 | 102 | 112 | 108 | 97 | 106 |
| PULASKI | 97 | 75 | 83 | 81 | 97 | 93 | 111 | 96 | 92 | 84 | 85 | 95 | 86 | 97 | 74 | 97 | 85 | 90 | 101 | 98 |
| RAPPAHANNOCK | 100 | 77 | 84 | 85 | 96 | 93 | 116 | 98 | 94 | 84 | 88 | 98 | 87 | 101 | 74 | 99 | 88 | 92 | 102 | 102 |
| RICHMOND | 97 | 70 | 78 | 79 | 93 | 92 | 116 | 96 | 93 | 79 | 82 | 94 | 82 | 96 | 71 | 97 | 82 | 89 | 102 | 98 |
| ROANOKE | 101 | 102 | 104 | 100 | 104 | 103 | 104 | 100 | 101 | 103 | 105 | 102 | 102 | 104 | 90 | 100 | 104 | 103 | 100 | 103 |
| VIRGINIA | 100 | 102 | 100 | 101 | 102 | 102 | 103 | 99 | 101 | 100 | 103 | 102 | 101 | 102 | 90 | 100 | 102 | 102 | 99 | 102 |
| UNITED STATES | 100 | 100 | 100 | 100 | 100 | 100 | 100 | 100 | 100 | 100 | 100 | 100 | 100 | 100 | 100 | 100 | 100 | 100 | 100 | 100 |

| COUNTY | FIPS Code | MSA Code | DMA Code | POPULATION 1990 | POPULATION 2000 | POPULATION 2005 | 1990-2000 ANNUAL CHANGE % Rate | 1990-2000 ANNUAL CHANGE State Rank | RACE (%) White 1990 | White 2000 | Black 1990 | Black 2000 | Asian/Pacific 1990 | Asian/Pacific 2000 |
|---|---|---|---|---|---|---|---|---|---|---|---|---|---|---|
| ROCKBRIDGE | 163 | 0000 | 573 | 18,350 | 19,779 | 20,906 | 0.7 | 60 | 96.3 | 95.7 | 3.1 | 3.6 | 0.3 | 0.4 |
| ROCKINGHAM | 165 | 0000 | 569 | 57,482 | 63,085 | 63,133 | 0.9 | 56 | 97.7 | 97.1 | 1.5 | 1.8 | 0.2 | 0.4 |
| RUSSELL | 167 | 0000 | 531 | 28,667 | 28,619 | 28,080 | 0.0 | 106 | 98.8 | 98.5 | 1.1 | 1.3 | 0.1 | 0.1 |
| SCOTT | 169 | 3660 | 531 | 23,204 | 22,388 | 21,804 | -0.3 | 114 | 99.3 | 99.1 | 0.6 | 0.8 | 0.0 | 0.0 |
| SHENANDOAH | 171 | 0000 | 511 | 31,636 | 35,660 | 38,118 | 1.2 | 45 | 98.2 | 97.7 | 1.1 | 1.4 | 0.3 | 0.5 |
| SMYTH | 173 | 0000 | 531 | 32,370 | 32,619 | 32,221 | 0.1 | 96 | 97.6 | 97.4 | 2.0 | 2.2 | 0.2 | 0.3 |
| SOUTHAMPTON | 175 | 0000 | 544 | 17,550 | 17,780 | 18,210 | 0.1 | 96 | 54.9 | 50.6 | 44.8 | 49.0 | 0.1 | 0.1 |
| SPOTSYLVANIA | 177 | 8840 | 511 | 57,403 | 90,690 | 107,548 | 4.6 | 3 | 87.5 | 84.9 | 10.8 | 12.6 | 1.1 | 1.6 |
| STAFFORD | 179 | 8840 | 511 | 61,236 | 96,835 | 115,107 | 4.6 | 3 | 90.7 | 88.8 | 7.0 | 8.0 | 1.2 | 1.8 |
| SURRY | 181 | 0000 | 544 | 6,145 | 6,514 | 6,634 | 0.6 | 66 | 44.3 | 40.1 | 55.5 | 59.7 | 0.0 | 0.0 |
| SUSSEX | 183 | 0000 | 556 | 10,248 | 12,312 | 12,149 | 1.8 | 28 | 41.5 | 37.7 | 58.1 | 61.8 | 0.2 | 0.2 |
| TAZEWELL | 185 | 0000 | 559 | 45,960 | 46,144 | 45,129 | 0.0 | 106 | 96.7 | 95.8 | 2.6 | 3.2 | 0.5 | 0.8 |
| WARREN | 187 | 8840 | 511 | 26,142 | 30,946 | 32,729 | 1.7 | 32 | 94.3 | 92.9 | 4.9 | 5.9 | 0.3 | 0.4 |
| WASHINGTON | 191 | 3660 | 531 | 45,887 | 50,072 | 51,554 | 0.9 | 56 | 98.2 | 97.9 | 1.5 | 1.8 | 0.2 | 0.2 |
| WESTMORELAND | 193 | 0000 | 511 | 15,480 | 16,235 | 16,116 | 0.5 | 74 | 66.3 | 62.6 | 33.0 | 36.4 | 0.4 | 0.6 |
| WISE | 195 | 0000 | 531 | 39,573 | 40,125 | 39,790 | 0.1 | 96 | 97.7 | 97.2 | 1.8 | 2.2 | 0.3 | 0.5 |
| WYTHE | 197 | 0000 | 573 | 25,466 | 26,639 | 27,287 | 0.4 | 81 | 96.1 | 95.2 | 3.5 | 4.2 | 0.3 | 0.4 |
| YORK | 199 | 5720 | 544 | 42,422 | 59,416 | 64,469 | 3.3 | 7 | 81.3 | 78.3 | 15.6 | 17.3 | 2.3 | 3.3 |
| ALEXANDRIA CITY | 510 | 8840 | 511 | 111,183 | 119,130 | 127,481 | 0.7 | 60 | 69.1 | 64.6 | 21.9 | 22.9 | 4.2 | 5.9 |
| BEDFORD CITY | 515 | 4640 | 573 | 6,073 | 6,808 | 7,436 | 1.1 | 49 | 77.2 | 74.6 | 22.0 | 24.4 | 0.5 | 0.7 |
| BRISTOL CITY | 520 | 3660 | 531 | 18,426 | 16,460 | 15,247 | -1.1 | 132 | 93.6 | 92.5 | 5.8 | 6.7 | 0.5 | 0.6 |
| BUENA VISTA CITY | 530 | 0000 | 573 | 6,406 | 6,390 | 6,018 | 0.0 | 106 | 95.1 | 94.5 | 4.4 | 5.0 | 0.3 | 0.4 |
| CHARLOTTESVILLE CITY | 540 | 1540 | 584 | 40,341 | 36,557 | 35,229 | -1.0 | 131 | 76.1 | 72.2 | 21.2 | 24.1 | 2.3 | 3.2 |
| CHESAPEAKE CITY | 550 | 5720 | 544 | 151,976 | 206,316 | 224,509 | 3.0 | 9 | 70.7 | 66.3 | 27.4 | 31.0 | 1.2 | 1.8 |
| CLIFTON FORGE CITY | 560 | 0000 | 573 | 4,679 | 4,149 | 3,881 | -1.2 | 134 | 84.8 | 82.3 | 14.9 | 17.2 | 0.2 | 0.2 |
| COLONIAL HGHTS CITY | 570 | 6760 | 556 | 16,064 | 16,163 | 15,806 | 0.1 | 96 | 96.5 | 95.1 | 0.8 | 0.9 | 2.2 | 3.3 |
| COVINGTON CITY | 580 | 0000 | 573 | 6,991 | 6,747 | 6,274 | -0.3 | 114 | 85.2 | 82.2 | 13.9 | 16.5 | 0.7 | 1.0 |
| DANVILLE CITY | 590 | 1950 | 573 | 53,056 | 50,076 | 46,633 | -0.6 | 123 | 62.7 | 59.4 | 36.6 | 39.7 | 0.5 | 0.7 |
| EMPORIA CITY | 595 | 0000 | 556 | 5,306 | 5,580 | 5,624 | 0.5 | 74 | 53.7 | 50.2 | 45.6 | 49.0 | 0.5 | 0.5 |
| FAIRFAX CITY | 600 | 8840 | 511 | 19,622 | 20,715 | 20,795 | 0.5 | 74 | 85.8 | 81.6 | 4.9 | 5.1 | 7.2 | 10.3 |
| FALLS CHURCH CITY | 610 | 8840 | 511 | 9,578 | 10,086 | 10,822 | 0.5 | 74 | 89.1 | 85.3 | 3.1 | 3.4 | 4.8 | 6.9 |
| FRANKLIN CITY | 620 | 0000 | 544 | 7,864 | 7,934 | 7,697 | 0.1 | 96 | 46.2 | 42.8 | 53.4 | 56.8 | 0.3 | 0.3 |
| FREDERICKSBURG CITY | 630 | 8840 | 511 | 19,027 | 18,374 | 17,913 | -0.3 | 114 | 76.0 | 72.3 | 21.6 | 24.5 | 1.1 | 1.5 |
| GALAX CITY | 640 | 0000 | 573 | 6,670 | 6,393 | 5,957 | -0.4 | 120 | 93.2 | 92.2 | 5.8 | 6.5 | 0.2 | 0.4 |
| HAMPTON CITY | 650 | 5720 | 544 | 133,793 | 137,069 | 136,332 | 0.2 | 90 | 58.4 | 53.8 | 38.9 | 42.5 | 1.7 | 2.5 |
| HARRISONBURG CITY | 660 | 0000 | 569 | 30,707 | 34,376 | 35,615 | 1.1 | 49 | 91.1 | 89.0 | 6.6 | 7.7 | 1.5 | 2.2 |
| HOPEWELL CITY | 670 | 6760 | 556 | 23,101 | 22,453 | 21,435 | -0.3 | 114 | 72.2 | 68.8 | 25.6 | 28.2 | 1.3 | 1.9 |
| LEXINGTON CITY | 678 | 0000 | 573 | 6,959 | 7,393 | 7,525 | 0.6 | 66 | 86.6 | 84.5 | 11.7 | 13.4 | 1.3 | 1.6 |
| LYNCHBURG CITY | 680 | 4640 | 573 | 66,049 | 63,622 | 62,002 | -0.4 | 120 | 72.5 | 69.2 | 26.4 | 29.3 | 0.8 | 1.0 |
| MANASSAS CITY | 683 | 8840 | 511 | 27,957 | 34,099 | 37,126 | 2.0 | 22 | 83.5 | 79.3 | 10.3 | 11.8 | 3.1 | 4.6 |
| MANASSAS PARK CITY | 685 | 8840 | 511 | 6,734 | 8,066 | 8,933 | 1.8 | 28 | 88.2 | 84.8 | 7.3 | 8.4 | 2.5 | 3.8 |
| MARTINSVILLE CITY | 690 | 0000 | 573 | 16,162 | 14,757 | 14,096 | -0.9 | 130 | 62.7 | 60.2 | 36.8 | 39.3 | 0.2 | 0.2 |
| NEWPORT NEWS CITY | 700 | 5720 | 544 | 170,045 | 179,671 | 182,413 | 0.5 | 74 | 62.6 | 57.8 | 33.6 | 36.7 | 2.3 | 3.4 |
| NORFOLK CITY | 710 | 5720 | 544 | 261,229 | 223,565 | 212,157 | -1.5 | 136 | 56.7 | 51.1 | 39.1 | 43.3 | 2.6 | 3.8 |
| NORTON CITY | 720 | 0000 | 531 | 4,247 | 3,974 | 3,808 | -0.6 | 123 | 92.4 | 90.8 | 6.3 | 7.6 | 0.8 | 1.0 |
| PETERSBURG CITY | 730 | 6760 | 556 | 38,386 | 34,064 | 32,400 | -1.2 | 134 | 26.6 | 24.1 | 72.1 | 74.2 | 0.8 | 1.1 |
| POQUOSON CITY | 735 | 5720 | 544 | 11,005 | 11,644 | 12,041 | 0.6 | 66 | 97.5 | 96.6 | 0.8 | 0.9 | 1.5 | 2.2 |
| PORTSMOUTH CITY | 740 | 5720 | 544 | 103,907 | 97,452 | 93,306 | -0.6 | 123 | 51.2 | 47.0 | 47.3 | 51.0 | 0.8 | 1.1 |
| RADFORD CITY | 750 | 0000 | 573 | 15,940 | 15,703 | 15,796 | -0.1 | 112 | 91.9 | 89.8 | 6.0 | 7.4 | 1.7 | 2.3 |
| RICHMOND CITY | 760 | 6760 | 556 | 203,056 | 188,911 | 184,797 | -0.7 | 127 | 43.4 | 39.9 | 55.2 | 58.3 | 0.9 | 1.2 |
| ROANOKE CITY | 770 | 6800 | 573 | 96,397 | 92,707 | 89,523 | -0.4 | 120 | 74.6 | 71.0 | 24.3 | 27.5 | 0.7 | 1.1 |
| SALEM CITY | 775 | 6800 | 573 | 23,756 | 23,988 | 23,712 | 0.1 | 96 | 94.6 | 93.6 | 4.5 | 5.2 | 0.7 | 1.0 |
| SOUTH BOSTON CITY | 780 | 0000 | 573 | 6,997 | 7,070 | 7,101 | 0.1 | 96 | 62.5 | 59.7 | 36.7 | 39.3 | 0.5 | 0.7 |
| STAUNTON CITY | 790 | 0000 | 569 | 24,461 | 24,419 | 24,035 | 0.0 | 106 | 86.6 | 84.6 | 12.6 | 14.3 | 0.4 | 0.6 |
| SUFFOLK CITY | 800 | 5720 | 544 | 52,141 | 66,845 | 76,834 | 2.5 | 12 | 54.7 | 50.4 | 44.6 | 48.7 | 0.4 | 0.5 |
| VIRGINIA BEACH CITY | 810 | 5720 | 544 | 393,069 | 435,329 | 444,622 | 1.0 | 55 | 80.5 | 76.5 | 13.9 | 15.4 | 4.3 | 6.4 |
| WAYNESBORO CITY | 820 | 0000 | 569 | 18,549 | 19,372 | 19,859 | 0.4 | 81 | 89.9 | 88.3 | 9.4 | 10.8 | 0.2 | 0.3 |
| WILLIAMSBURG CITY | 830 | 5720 | 544 | 11,530 | 12,537 | 12,747 | 0.8 | 59 | 81.2 | 78.7 | 15.2 | 16.9 | 2.9 | 3.7 |
| WINCHESTER CITY | 840 | 0000 | 511 | 21,947 | 22,576 | 22,934 | 0.3 | 87 | 88.6 | 86.5 | 10.0 | 11.6 | 1.0 | 1.5 |
| VIRGINIA | | | | | | | 1.1 | | 77.4 | 74.8 | 18.8 | 19.9 | 2.6 | 3.8 |
| UNITED STATES | | | | | | | 1.0 | | 80.3 | 77.9 | 12.1 | 12.4 | 2.9 | 3.9 |

# POPULATION COMPOSITION

| COUNTY | % HISPANIC ORIGIN 1990 | % HISPANIC ORIGIN 2000 | 2000 AGE DISTRIBUTION (%) 0-4 | 5-9 | 10-14 | 15-19 | 20-24 | 25-44 | 45-64 | 65-84 | 85+ | 18+ | MEDIAN AGE 1990 | MEDIAN AGE 2000 | 2000 Males/ Females (×100) |
|---|---|---|---|---|---|---|---|---|---|---|---|---|---|---|---|
| ROCKBRIDGE | 0.3 | 0.9 | 5.5 | 6.0 | 6.4 | 6.7 | 4.8 | 28.1 | 26.0 | 14.9 | 1.4 | 77.8 | 36.7 | 40.2 | 98.5 |
| ROCKINGHAM | 0.9 | 1.9 | 6.0 | 6.6 | 7.0 | 7.0 | 6.1 | 28.9 | 24.7 | 11.9 | 1.8 | 76.5 | 34.5 | 37.8 | 96.9 |
| RUSSELL | 0.3 | 0.8 | 5.0 | 6.0 | 6.9 | 7.3 | 5.7 | 30.0 | 26.4 | 11.3 | 1.4 | 77.6 | 34.6 | 38.5 | 96.2 |
| SCOTT | 0.3 | 0.9 | 4.7 | 5.1 | 5.7 | 5.8 | 5.4 | 28.2 | 27.7 | 15.1 | 2.1 | 80.8 | 38.2 | 41.6 | 93.4 |
| SHENANDOAH | 0.9 | 1.8 | 5.6 | 6.1 | 6.5 | 6.2 | 4.9 | 27.6 | 25.6 | 15.1 | 2.2 | 78.1 | 37.4 | 40.6 | 94.7 |
| SMYTH | 0.3 | 0.9 | 5.2 | 5.7 | 6.2 | 6.4 | 5.7 | 28.7 | 25.7 | 14.5 | 1.9 | 79.0 | 36.5 | 39.9 | 92.8 |
| SOUTHAMPTON | 0.4 | 0.8 | 5.7 | 6.2 | 6.5 | 7.3 | 8.0 | 29.3 | 22.8 | 12.7 | 1.5 | 77.4 | 33.8 | 36.8 | 113.3 |
| SPOTSYLVANIA | 1.5 | 2.7 | 7.8 | 8.4 | 8.4 | 7.1 | 5.5 | 33.9 | 21.2 | 6.9 | 0.7 | 70.9 | 30.9 | 33.4 | 98.0 |
| STAFFORD | 2.0 | 3.5 | 7.5 | 8.1 | 8.2 | 7.1 | 7.8 | 33.8 | 21.4 | 5.5 | 0.6 | 71.8 | 29.9 | 32.2 | 106.6 |
| SURRY | 0.3 | 0.7 | 6.5 | 7.3 | 7.8 | 7.0 | 5.6 | 28.7 | 23.5 | 12.2 | 1.4 | 74.3 | 34.4 | 37.0 | 92.7 |
| SUSSEX | 0.2 | 0.4 | 6.4 | 6.8 | 7.2 | 6.4 | 5.7 | 27.1 | 23.6 | 14.8 | 2.1 | 76.0 | 35.3 | 38.4 | 94.0 |
| TAZEWELL | 0.3 | 0.9 | 5.1 | 6.0 | 6.9 | 7.3 | 5.7 | 28.3 | 25.7 | 13.4 | 1.6 | 77.5 | 35.4 | 39.2 | 93.6 |
| WARREN | 0.9 | 1.9 | 7.0 | 7.5 | 7.7 | 6.6 | 5.4 | 29.3 | 23.3 | 11.7 | 1.5 | 73.9 | 34.0 | 36.9 | 96.4 |
| WASHINGTON | 0.3 | 0.9 | 4.8 | 5.5 | 6.3 | 6.8 | 5.9 | 28.1 | 27.6 | 13.5 | 1.6 | 79.6 | 36.8 | 40.5 | 94.5 |
| WESTMORELAND | 0.6 | 1.2 | 6.0 | 6.7 | 6.7 | 6.2 | 5.0 | 25.3 | 25.1 | 17.0 | 1.9 | 76.7 | 38.4 | 40.8 | 93.2 |
| WISE | 0.3 | 0.9 | 5.4 | 6.5 | 7.3 | 8.0 | 6.3 | 28.3 | 24.7 | 11.8 | 1.5 | 76.0 | 33.9 | 37.3 | 94.4 |
| WYTHE | 0.2 | 0.7 | 5.3 | 5.9 | 6.6 | 6.7 | 5.6 | 28.0 | 25.8 | 14.2 | 2.0 | 78.3 | 36.3 | 39.8 | 90.9 |
| YORK | 1.7 | 2.9 | 6.3 | 7.7 | 7.9 | 6.7 | 5.4 | 32.3 | 24.2 | 8.7 | 0.7 | 73.7 | 32.8 | 35.6 | 97.4 |
| ALEXANDRIA CITY | 9.7 | 13.6 | 5.0 | 4.4 | 4.5 | 4.2 | 7.0 | 40.6 | 22.6 | 10.1 | 1.6 | 83.8 | 33.5 | 37.4 | 88.3 |
| BEDFORD CITY | 0.9 | 1.8 | 5.6 | 6.1 | 6.0 | 5.8 | 5.3 | 25.4 | 22.0 | 19.0 | 4.8 | 78.9 | 39.9 | 41.9 | 91.3 |
| BRISTOL CITY | 0.3 | 0.9 | 5.2 | 5.6 | 6.0 | 6.8 | 6.3 | 25.4 | 23.7 | 17.8 | 3.2 | 79.8 | 37.6 | 41.2 | 80.9 |
| BUENA VISTA CITY | 0.2 | 0.6 | 4.6 | 5.1 | 5.9 | 8.6 | 6.9 | 26.2 | 25.2 | 15.2 | 2.2 | 80.5 | 36.5 | 39.9 | 83.5 |
| CHARLOTTESVILLE CITY | 1.2 | 2.0 | 5.4 | 5.1 | 5.0 | 7.2 | 18.1 | 29.5 | 16.6 | 11.2 | 1.9 | 82.2 | 28.9 | 30.8 | 87.3 |
| CHESAPEAKE CITY | 1.3 | 2.2 | 7.6 | 7.9 | 7.9 | 7.2 | 6.2 | 32.5 | 21.5 | 8.3 | 0.9 | 72.3 | 31.3 | 33.8 | 94.3 |
| CLIFTON FORGE CITY | 0.5 | 1.2 | 5.2 | 5.8 | 6.2 | 6.0 | 5.1 | 24.4 | 22.8 | 19.7 | 4.8 | 79.7 | 41.2 | 43.1 | 82.5 |
| COLONIAL HGHTS CITY | 1.0 | 1.9 | 5.0 | 5.4 | 6.0 | 6.3 | 5.5 | 27.0 | 27.3 | 15.9 | 1.7 | 79.9 | 38.5 | 41.7 | 87.9 |
| COVINGTON CITY | 0.4 | 0.9 | 5.5 | 5.6 | 6.1 | 5.7 | 5.8 | 26.8 | 24.0 | 17.8 | 2.5 | 79.6 | 39.6 | 41.1 | 88.9 |
| DANVILLE CITY | 0.5 | 1.0 | 5.6 | 6.1 | 6.3 | 6.6 | 5.9 | 26.6 | 23.5 | 16.9 | 2.4 | 78.2 | 37.4 | 40.2 | 85.0 |
| EMPORIA CITY | 1.1 | 1.7 | 6.6 | 6.7 | 7.1 | 6.3 | 5.9 | 25.4 | 21.6 | 17.6 | 2.8 | 75.5 | 37.2 | 39.1 | 90.8 |
| FAIRFAX CITY | 5.9 | 9.0 | 5.3 | 5.3 | 5.7 | 5.1 | 5.6 | 37.2 | 22.8 | 11.9 | 1.4 | 81.2 | 33.6 | 37.5 | 94.3 |
| FALLS CHURCH CITY | 6.3 | 9.9 | 4.5 | 4.9 | 5.9 | 5.6 | 6.0 | 30.1 | 29.4 | 11.5 | 2.0 | 80.8 | 38.0 | 41.2 | 92.9 |
| FRANKLIN CITY | 0.2 | 0.4 | 6.9 | 7.1 | 7.5 | 7.7 | 6.5 | 25.5 | 22.8 | 13.8 | 2.1 | 73.7 | 34.9 | 37.2 | 85.2 |
| FREDERICKSBURG CITY | 2.4 | 3.8 | 6.2 | 5.4 | 5.0 | 9.5 | 12.7 | 29.7 | 17.1 | 12.3 | 2.1 | 81.0 | 28.9 | 32.1 | 84.3 |
| GALAX CITY | 1.0 | 1.7 | 6.0 | 6.0 | 6.3 | 5.6 | 5.0 | 25.4 | 24.3 | 17.4 | 3.9 | 78.4 | 39.3 | 41.9 | 83.2 |
| HAMPTON CITY | 2.0 | 3.1 | 7.3 | 7.3 | 7.1 | 7.3 | 7.1 | 33.0 | 20.1 | 9.8 | 1.0 | 74.7 | 30.8 | 34.0 | 93.7 |
| HARRISONBURG CITY | 1.6 | 2.6 | 4.4 | 4.3 | 4.1 | 16.1 | 22.6 | 22.5 | 15.0 | 9.6 | 1.5 | 84.9 | 24.4 | 24.7 | 85.6 |
| HOPEWELL CITY | 1.8 | 3.0 | 7.2 | 7.2 | 7.3 | 6.8 | 6.6 | 29.3 | 21.4 | 12.5 | 1.7 | 74.4 | 32.5 | 35.5 | 90.0 |
| LEXINGTON CITY | 0.9 | 1.6 | 2.5 | 3.0 | 3.3 | 18.9 | 23.9 | 15.4 | 17.0 | 13.4 | 2.6 | 88.6 | 24.3 | 24.7 | 141.0 |
| LYNCHBURG CITY | 0.7 | 1.3 | 6.0 | 6.1 | 6.4 | 9.2 | 9.1 | 25.6 | 20.5 | 14.5 | 2.8 | 78.0 | 33.1 | 36.1 | 82.4 |
| MANASSAS CITY | 5.7 | 8.6 | 8.8 | 8.7 | 7.6 | 6.3 | 6.8 | 38.2 | 17.4 | 5.4 | 0.7 | 71.3 | 28.8 | 31.5 | 101.6 |
| MANASSAS PARK CITY | 4.7 | 7.7 | 8.8 | 8.9 | 8.1 | 7.6 | 7.1 | 36.2 | 17.5 | 5.5 | 0.3 | 69.6 | 27.6 | 30.2 | 95.8 |
| MARTINSVILLE CITY | 0.4 | 0.8 | 5.5 | 5.9 | 6.4 | 6.0 | 5.5 | 26.3 | 23.8 | 18.4 | 2.3 | 78.5 | 38.2 | 41.3 | 83.0 |
| NEWPORT NEWS CITY | 2.8 | 4.4 | 9.0 | 8.0 | 7.1 | 6.3 | 7.7 | 35.3 | 17.0 | 8.6 | 1.0 | 72.4 | 29.5 | 31.6 | 94.8 |
| NORFOLK CITY | 2.9 | 3.8 | 8.1 | 7.0 | 6.1 | 7.6 | 13.0 | 31.5 | 15.6 | 9.9 | 1.2 | 76.3 | 27.4 | 29.6 | 103.2 |
| NORTON CITY | 0.7 | 1.7 | 5.6 | 6.6 | 7.0 | 7.7 | 6.4 | 28.7 | 23.1 | 13.3 | 1.5 | 76.4 | 34.0 | 37.2 | 86.7 |
| PETERSBURG CITY | 1.2 | 1.8 | 6.7 | 6.8 | 6.8 | 6.6 | 7.1 | 29.1 | 21.1 | 14.0 | 1.8 | 76.1 | 33.7 | 36.3 | 85.5 |
| POQUOSON CITY | 0.9 | 1.8 | 5.4 | 6.6 | 7.7 | 7.5 | 5.2 | 30.3 | 28.5 | 7.8 | 1.1 | 75.5 | 35.2 | 38.0 | 99.7 |
| PORTSMOUTH CITY | 1.3 | 2.1 | 7.5 | 7.5 | 7.4 | 7.1 | 7.3 | 29.7 | 19.5 | 12.5 | 1.5 | 73.6 | 31.7 | 34.1 | 90.6 |
| RADFORD CITY | 1.1 | 1.9 | 3.2 | 3.3 | 3.9 | 19.8 | 26.5 | 18.2 | 15.3 | 8.9 | 0.8 | 87.9 | 23.2 | 23.7 | 79.7 |
| RICHMOND CITY | 0.9 | 1.5 | 6.0 | 5.9 | 5.8 | 7.0 | 8.7 | 31.4 | 19.3 | 13.7 | 2.3 | 79.3 | 33.2 | 36.1 | 84.0 |
| ROANOKE CITY | 0.7 | 1.3 | 6.2 | 6.2 | 6.3 | 6.1 | 6.2 | 30.3 | 21.9 | 14.4 | 2.5 | 77.9 | 35.2 | 38.1 | 87.2 |
| SALEM CITY | 0.5 | 1.1 | 4.5 | 5.1 | 5.6 | 7.8 | 7.1 | 27.5 | 25.2 | 15.0 | 2.2 | 81.4 | 37.1 | 40.1 | 90.6 |
| SOUTH BOSTON CITY | 0.6 | 4.9 | 5.7 | 6.1 | 6.5 | 6.6 | 6.3 | 25.9 | 23.4 | 16.0 | 3.3 | 77.5 | 38.2 | 39.8 | 80.4 |
| STAUNTON CITY | 0.7 | 1.5 | 4.8 | 5.3 | 5.6 | 7.4 | 6.9 | 27.9 | 23.5 | 16.2 | 2.4 | 80.5 | 36.8 | 39.7 | 89.6 |
| SUFFOLK CITY | 0.6 | 1.1 | 6.8 | 7.4 | 7.7 | 7.1 | 5.9 | 29.2 | 23.5 | 11.1 | 1.3 | 73.6 | 33.6 | 36.2 | 91.1 |
| VIRGINIA BEACH CITY | 3.1 | 4.9 | 8.1 | 7.9 | 7.3 | 6.5 | 8.1 | 36.3 | 18.0 | 7.0 | 0.7 | 73.0 | 28.9 | 31.5 | 99.1 |
| WAYNESBORO CITY | 0.8 | 1.7 | 6.1 | 6.4 | 6.4 | 6.8 | 5.3 | 26.9 | 24.2 | 15.8 | 2.0 | 77.1 | 36.4 | 39.7 | 90.1 |
| WILLIAMSBURG CITY | 1.3 | 2.1 | 2.2 | 2.3 | 2.2 | 19.8 | 29.0 | 17.1 | 11.2 | 14.1 | 2.2 | 91.6 | 23.8 | 24.1 | 86.4 |
| WINCHESTER CITY | 1.0 | 1.8 | 6.2 | 5.9 | 6.1 | 6.5 | 7.5 | 30.1 | 21.3 | 14.2 | 2.1 | 78.7 | 33.8 | 36.9 | 91.8 |
| VIRGINIA | 2.6 | 4.1 | 6.5 | 6.7 | 6.8 | 6.9 | 7.0 | 32.2 | 22.6 | 10.1 | 1.3 | 76.2 | 32.6 | 35.7 | 95.5 |
| UNITED STATES | 9.0 | 11.8 | 6.9 | 7.2 | 7.2 | 7.2 | 6.7 | 29.9 | 22.2 | 11.1 | 1.6 | 74.6 | 32.9 | 35.7 | 95.6 |

| COUNTY | HOUSEHOLDS | | | | | FAMILIES | | | MEDIAN HOUSEHOLD INCOME | | | |
|---|---|---|---|---|---|---|---|---|---|---|---|---|
| | 1990 | 2000 | 2005 | % Annual Rate 1990-2000 | 2000 Average HH Size | 1990 | 2000 | % Annual Rate 1990-2000 | 2000 | 2005 | 2000 National Rank | 2000 State Rank |
| ROCKBRIDGE | 7,202 | 8,178 | 8,852 | 1.6 | 2.40 | 5,378 | 5,899 | 1.1 | 32,241 | 36,124 | 1676 | 78 |
| ROCKINGHAM | 20,750 | 23,816 | 24,339 | 1.7 | 2.57 | 16,077 | 17,839 | 1.3 | 37,525 | 42,647 | 895 | 48 |
| RUSSELL | 10,641 | 11,316 | 11,445 | 0.7 | 2.50 | 8,434 | 8,700 | 0.4 | 23,922 | 26,308 | 2909 | 131 |
| SCOTT | 8,966 | 9,098 | 9,073 | 0.2 | 2.44 | 6,971 | 6,801 | -0.3 | 27,704 | 31,457 | 2474 | 117 |
| SHENANDOAH | 12,452 | 14,633 | 15,959 | 2.0 | 2.40 | 9,106 | 10,259 | 1.5 | 35,117 | 43,801 | 1234 | 64 |
| SMYTH | 12,234 | 12,946 | 13,078 | 0.7 | 2.43 | 9,422 | 9,646 | 0.3 | 28,286 | 31,894 | 2400 | 108 |
| SOUTHAMPTON | 6,009 | 6,122 | 6,323 | 0.2 | 2.65 | 4,526 | 4,446 | -0.2 | 34,083 | 37,136 | 1378 | 70 |
| SPOTSYLVANIA | 18,945 | 30,707 | 36,851 | 6.0 | 2.94 | 15,654 | 24,667 | 5.7 | 53,788 | 63,117 | 138 | 13 |
| STAFFORD | 19,415 | 30,046 | 35,226 | 5.4 | 3.16 | 16,205 | 24,533 | 5.2 | 60,568 | 75,734 | 68 | 7 |
| SURRY | 2,283 | 2,553 | 2,654 | 1.4 | 2.55 | 1,715 | 1,849 | 0.9 | 30,656 | 32,171 | 1995 | 93 |
| SUSSEX | 3,795 | 3,847 | 3,866 | 0.2 | 2.52 | 2,779 | 2,712 | -0.3 | 29,495 | 32,002 | 2222 | 99 |
| TAZEWELL | 17,309 | 18,423 | 18,560 | 0.8 | 2.48 | 13,352 | 13,742 | 0.3 | 25,328 | 27,918 | 2776 | 127 |
| WARREN | 9,879 | 11,918 | 12,734 | 2.3 | 2.56 | 7,280 | 8,510 | 1.9 | 42,625 | 52,653 | 471 | 35 |
| WASHINGTON | 17,483 | 19,805 | 20,798 | 1.5 | 2.46 | 13,485 | 14,795 | 1.1 | 30,531 | 33,633 | 2027 | 96 |
| WESTMORELAND | 6,057 | 6,627 | 6,718 | 1.1 | 2.44 | 4,393 | 4,626 | 0.6 | 35,378 | 44,818 | 1187 | 60 |
| WISE | 14,513 | 14,589 | 14,598 | 0.1 | 2.62 | 11,269 | 10,998 | -0.3 | 27,869 | 31,834 | 2459 | 115 |
| WYTHE | 9,852 | 10,635 | 11,061 | 0.9 | 2.47 | 7,380 | 7,631 | 0.4 | 28,347 | 32,559 | 2390 | 107 |
| YORK | 14,474 | 21,924 | 24,646 | 5.2 | 2.69 | 11,851 | 17,327 | 4.7 | 52,069 | 57,967 | 169 | 17 |
| ALEXANDRIA CITY | 53,280 | 59,702 | 65,306 | 1.4 | 1.96 | 24,149 | 26,091 | 0.9 | 50,946 | 58,013 | 184 | 18 |
| BEDFORD CITY | 2,475 | 2,646 | 2,830 | 0.8 | 2.41 | 1,643 | 1,663 | 0.1 | 35,345 | 42,056 | 1192 | 61 |
| BRISTOL CITY | 7,591 | 7,545 | 7,328 | -0.1 | 2.09 | 5,116 | 4,832 | -0.7 | 27,266 | 29,828 | 2540 | 119 |
| BUENA VISTA CITY | 2,404 | 2,518 | 2,427 | 0.6 | 2.39 | 1,779 | 1,779 | 0.0 | 31,682 | 34,074 | 1781 | 83 |
| CHARLOTTESVILLE CITY | 16,009 | 15,785 | 15,838 | -0.2 | 2.17 | 8,228 | 7,648 | -0.9 | 32,221 | 35,852 | 1681 | 79 |
| CHESAPEAKE CITY | 51,965 | 73,713 | 82,083 | 4.3 | 2.75 | 41,474 | 57,133 | 4.0 | 50,386 | 59,299 | 197 | 20 |
| CLIFTON FORGE CITY | 1,930 | 1,847 | 1,788 | -0.5 | 2.10 | 1,228 | 1,106 | -1.3 | 28,570 | 30,461 | 2353 | 105 |
| COLONIAL HGHTS CITY | 6,363 | 7,102 | 7,293 | 1.3 | 2.25 | 4,699 | 5,037 | 0.8 | 40,250 | 43,753 | 653 | 40 |
| COVINGTON CITY | 2,998 | 3,055 | 2,917 | 0.2 | 2.20 | 2,009 | 1,946 | -0.4 | 27,680 | 30,330 | 2482 | 118 |
| DANVILLE CITY | 21,712 | 21,388 | 20,315 | -0.2 | 2.27 | 14,520 | 13,741 | -0.7 | 26,126 | 29,210 | 2699 | 126 |
| EMPORIA CITY | 2,031 | 2,131 | 2,155 | 0.6 | 2.51 | 1,412 | 1,435 | 0.2 | 28,023 | 35,018 | 2440 | 112 |
| FAIRFAX CITY | 7,362 | 8,244 | 8,508 | 1.4 | 2.46 | 4,999 | 5,342 | 0.8 | 64,734 | 74,908 | 36 | 4 |
| FALLS CHURCH CITY | 4,195 | 4,591 | 5,018 | 1.1 | 2.19 | 2,484 | 2,578 | 0.5 | 68,246 | 80,474 | 18 | 2 |
| FRANKLIN CITY | 3,006 | 3,507 | 3,642 | 1.9 | 2.23 | 2,155 | 2,454 | 1.6 | 26,754 | 29,344 | 2613 | 123 |
| FREDERICKSBURG CITY | 7,450 | 9,260 | 9,697 | 2.7 | 1.74 | 4,137 | 4,851 | 1.9 | 36,869 | 45,084 | 996 | 52 |
| GALAX CITY | 2,750 | 2,919 | 2,848 | 0.7 | 2.09 | 1,864 | 1,925 | 0.4 | 31,157 | 39,442 | 1902 | 87 |
| HAMPTON CITY | 49,673 | 53,042 | 53,660 | 0.8 | 2.49 | 35,186 | 36,306 | 0.4 | 36,932 | 41,765 | 987 | 51 |
| HARRISONBURG CITY | 10,310 | 11,302 | 11,697 | 1.1 | 2.44 | 5,677 | 5,836 | 0.3 | 31,605 | 35,773 | 1800 | 84 |
| HOPEWELL CITY | 9,014 | 9,118 | 8,969 | 0.1 | 2.36 | 6,376 | 6,195 | -0.3 | 34,199 | 38,070 | 1356 | 69 |
| LEXINGTON CITY | 2,172 | 2,414 | 2,547 | 1.3 | 2.06 | 1,160 | 1,231 | 0.7 | 27,917 | 32,985 | 2452 | 114 |
| LYNCHBURG CITY | 25,143 | 26,273 | 26,509 | 0.5 | 2.21 | 16,380 | 16,365 | 0.0 | 28,806 | 31,318 | 2327 | 104 |
| MANASSAS CITY | 9,481 | 13,017 | 15,014 | 3.9 | 2.56 | 7,103 | 9,327 | 3.4 | 53,528 | 62,434 | 143 | 14 |
| MANASSAS PARK CITY | 2,182 | 3,148 | 3,798 | 4.5 | 2.56 | 1,747 | 2,408 | 4.0 | 44,702 | 51,726 | 365 | 29 |
| MARTINSVILLE CITY | 6,839 | 6,923 | 6,954 | 0.1 | 2.11 | 4,519 | 4,408 | -0.3 | 27,860 | 30,695 | 2461 | 116 |
| NEWPORT NEWS CITY | 63,952 | 69,977 | 72,078 | 1.1 | 2.51 | 45,250 | 47,908 | 0.7 | 33,956 | 38,581 | 1401 | 72 |
| NORFOLK CITY | 89,478 | 81,317 | 78,141 | -1.2 | 2.45 | 57,640 | 50,644 | -1.6 | 30,722 | 37,505 | 1983 | 92 |
| NORTON CITY | 1,697 | 1,726 | 1,721 | 0.2 | 2.29 | 1,185 | 1,176 | -0.1 | 24,375 | 27,117 | 2872 | 130 |
| PETERSBURG CITY | 14,730 | 14,387 | 14,075 | -0.3 | 2.32 | 9,338 | 8,762 | -0.8 | 26,736 | 29,867 | 2615 | 124 |
| POQUOSON CITY | 3,769 | 4,111 | 4,315 | 1.1 | 2.81 | 3,178 | 3,383 | 0.8 | 56,895 | 61,417 | 104 | 9 |
| PORTSMOUTH CITY | 38,741 | 37,759 | 36,906 | -0.3 | 2.50 | 27,493 | 25,937 | -0.7 | 30,817 | 37,010 | 1967 | 90 |
| RADFORD CITY | 5,207 | 5,369 | 5,489 | 0.4 | 2.41 | 2,599 | 2,457 | -0.7 | 26,972 | 29,429 | 2584 | 122 |
| RICHMOND CITY | 85,337 | 85,581 | 86,763 | 0.0 | 2.08 | 46,795 | 44,961 | -0.5 | 26,514 | 29,745 | 2650 | 125 |
| ROANOKE CITY | 41,030 | 40,943 | 40,317 | 0.0 | 2.21 | 25,603 | 24,398 | -0.6 | 27,250 | 30,403 | 2543 | 120 |
| SALEM CITY | 9,161 | 10,036 | 10,239 | 1.1 | 2.20 | 6,361 | 6,653 | 0.5 | 36,947 | 42,251 | 986 | 50 |
| SOUTH BOSTON CITY | 2,795 | 2,926 | 2,990 | 0.6 | 2.34 | 1,910 | 1,919 | 0.1 | 25,120 | 28,393 | 2802 | 128 |
| STAUNTON CITY | 9,432 | 9,306 | 9,129 | -0.2 | 2.30 | 6,132 | 5,761 | -0.8 | 32,080 | 35,110 | 1702 | 80 |
| SUFFOLK CITY | 18,516 | 24,528 | 28,706 | 3.5 | 2.69 | 14,168 | 18,289 | 3.1 | 35,713 | 39,556 | 1133 | 57 |
| VIRGINIA BEACH CITY | 135,566 | 156,385 | 162,174 | 1.7 | 2.73 | 102,201 | 114,101 | 1.3 | 43,473 | 50,482 | 428 | 31 |
| WAYNESBORO CITY | 7,568 | 7,969 | 8,201 | 0.6 | 2.38 | 5,263 | 5,290 | 0.1 | 33,482 | 38,141 | 1466 | 75 |
| WILLIAMSBURG CITY | 3,468 | 3,779 | 3,927 | 1.0 | 2.06 | 1,602 | 1,578 | -0.2 | 35,821 | 41,740 | 1121 | 56 |
| WINCHESTER CITY | 9,084 | 9,845 | 10,306 | 1.0 | 2.18 | 5,495 | 5,675 | 0.4 | 36,105 | 43,112 | 1091 | 54 |
| VIRGINIA | | | | 1.8 | 2.53 | | | 1.5 | 44,048 | 51,389 | | |
| UNITED STATES | | | | 1.4 | 2.59 | | | 1.1 | 41,914 | 49,127 | | |

| COUNTY | | | 2000 HOUSEHOLD INCOME DISTRIBUTION (%) | | | | | | 2000 AVERAGE DISPOSABLE INCOME BY AGE OF HOUSEHOLDER | | | | | |
|---|---|---|---|---|---|---|---|---|---|---|---|---|---|---|
| | 2000 Per Capita Income | 2000 HH Income Base | Less than $15,000 | $15,000 to $24,999 | $25,000 to $49,999 | $50,000 to $99,999 | $100,000 to $149,999 | $150,000 or More | All Ages | <35 | 35-44 | 45-54 | 55-64 | 65+ |
| ROCKBRIDGE | 16,743 | 8,178 | 19.1 | 15.2 | 39.0 | 22.2 | 3.5 | 1.0 | 30,952 | 26,977 | 32,700 | 40,085 | 34,238 | 23,060 |
| ROCKINGHAM | 17,146 | 23,816 | 12.8 | 14.9 | 39.7 | 28.1 | 3.7 | 0.8 | 33,917 | 30,946 | 39,198 | 40,712 | 34,406 | 23,715 |
| RUSSELL | 12,057 | 11,316 | 32.6 | 19.6 | 31.9 | 13.6 | 1.9 | 0.4 | 24,062 | 22,378 | 30,004 | 27,261 | 23,256 | 16,455 |
| SCOTT | 13,591 | 9,093 | 28.4 | 17.1 | 33.8 | 18.3 | 2.0 | 0.3 | 26,334 | 26,616 | 32,706 | 32,086 | 26,789 | 17,039 |
| SHENANDOAH | 18,348 | 14,633 | 17.2 | 14.7 | 38.3 | 25.2 | 3.5 | 1.1 | 32,623 | 29,404 | 36,300 | 41,610 | 34,970 | 23,078 |
| SMYTH | 13,361 | 12,946 | 24.2 | 19.2 | 39.0 | 16.0 | 1.6 | 0.1 | 25,851 | 23,815 | 30,995 | 32,384 | 26,610 | 17,865 |
| SOUTHAMPTON | 14,847 | 6,122 | 22.7 | 12.0 | 35.0 | 26.4 | 3.6 | 0.5 | 31,163 | 30,652 | 35,309 | 38,968 | 33,210 | 20,110 |
| SPOTSYLVANIA | 22,131 | 30,707 | 5.9 | 6.0 | 32.5 | 43.2 | 9.7 | 2.6 | 46,298 | 42,010 | 50,037 | 52,905 | 43,778 | 30,835 |
| STAFFORD | 22,958 | 30,046 | 4.9 | 4.9 | 26.7 | 46.1 | 13.8 | 3.7 | 50,813 | 43,496 | 54,022 | 59,287 | 51,400 | 33,153 |
| SURRY | 15,272 | 2,553 | 20.8 | 18.8 | 35.4 | 22.0 | 1.9 | 1.1 | 29,701 | 28,438 | 37,473 | 35,938 | 28,314 | 18,147 |
| SUSSEX | 13,221 | 3,847 | 27.6 | 15.9 | 34.3 | 18.6 | 3.3 | 0.3 | 27,007 | 23,965 | 33,346 | 34,953 | 27,427 | 18,547 |
| TAZEWELL | 13,480 | 18,423 | 30.0 | 19.4 | 32.9 | 15.1 | 1.8 | 0.8 | 25,474 | 22,057 | 32,796 | 29,954 | 24,417 | 17,627 |
| WARREN | 20,277 | 11,918 | 12.3 | 10.8 | 37.1 | 32.9 | 5.7 | 1.2 | 37,186 | 36,811 | 40,798 | 41,567 | 40,375 | 26,415 |
| WASHINGTON | 15,650 | 19,805 | 21.2 | 18.8 | 35.7 | 19.8 | 3.5 | 1.0 | 29,699 | 26,608 | 35,674 | 34,476 | 30,481 | 21,243 |
| WESTMORELAND | 18,597 | 6,627 | 17.0 | 17.2 | 34.1 | 26.1 | 3.9 | 1.7 | 33,516 | 27,750 | 42,635 | 39,097 | 36,173 | 25,389 |
| WISE | 13,623 | 14,589 | 26.5 | 18.5 | 33.1 | 17.9 | 2.9 | 1.1 | 28,165 | 24,768 | 34,473 | 33,960 | 27,948 | 18,436 |
| WYTHE | 14,225 | 10,635 | 23.6 | 20.5 | 34.6 | 19.1 | 1.6 | 0.6 | 27,284 | 25,601 | 30,486 | 33,598 | 27,457 | 20,382 |
| YORK | 23,193 | 21,919 | 6.7 | 9.2 | 31.2 | 41.7 | 8.9 | 2.3 | 44,391 | 35,057 | 46,633 | 54,223 | 47,162 | 33,569 |
| ALEXANDRIA CITY | 35,644 | 59,702 | 6.2 | 7.9 | 34.6 | 36.1 | 10.6 | 4.6 | 47,787 | 39,310 | 49,177 | 55,519 | 52,217 | 40,638 |
| BEDFORD CITY | 17,362 | 2,646 | 18.6 | 12.9 | 38.2 | 23.2 | 6.5 | 0.7 | 33,166 | 30,055 | 37,830 | 39,406 | 36,554 | 28,003 |
| BRISTOL CITY | 15,294 | 7,545 | 30.4 | 15.8 | 33.6 | 17.9 | 2.1 | 0.3 | 25,981 | 25,113 | 32,603 | 32,747 | 25,731 | 18,641 |
| BUENA VISTA CITY | 14,043 | 2,518 | 18.6 | 17.7 | 43.5 | 17.8 | 2.3 | 0.1 | 27,954 | 26,195 | 33,124 | 34,308 | 25,639 | 20,901 |
| CHARLOTTESVILLE CITY | 19,811 | 15,782 | 21.7 | 16.1 | 34.0 | 21.7 | 4.3 | 2.3 | 32,938 | 23,680 | 39,986 | 44,723 | 43,958 | 29,479 |
| CHESAPEAKE CITY | 21,674 | 73,713 | 7.2 | 8.9 | 33.4 | 40.4 | 8.5 | 1.7 | 42,939 | 36,556 | 47,053 | 52,048 | 44,591 | 29,141 |
| CLIFTON FORGE CITY | 17,895 | 1,847 | 25.7 | 17.7 | 36.3 | 14.0 | 4.4 | 2.0 | 29,089 | 24,264 | 30,623 | 37,982 | 41,306 | 17,843 |
| COLONIAL HGHTS CITY | 20,815 | 7,102 | 12.2 | 14.1 | 37.2 | 31.7 | 3.8 | 1.1 | 35,439 | 31,582 | 38,901 | 45,475 | 40,658 | 24,296 |
| COVINGTON CITY | 15,366 | 3,055 | 21.6 | 21.7 | 39.8 | 14.8 | 1.9 | 0.2 | 26,251 | 27,570 | 29,692 | 31,429 | 26,092 | 20,155 |
| DANVILLE CITY | 15,208 | 21,387 | 29.5 | 18.6 | 32.5 | 16.4 | 1.9 | 1.2 | 26,781 | 21,508 | 30,784 | 34,589 | 31,053 | 19,355 |
| EMPORIA CITY | 13,769 | 2,131 | 24.9 | 18.8 | 36.4 | 16.9 | 2.3 | 0.6 | 27,049 | 22,458 | 30,178 | 36,404 | 31,127 | 19,906 |
| FAIRFAX CITY | 34,769 | 8,244 | 3.7 | 5.5 | 22.2 | 47.0 | 15.9 | 5.7 | 55,429 | 45,477 | 57,685 | 60,323 | 62,278 | 50,254 |
| FALLS CHURCH CITY | 42,831 | 4,591 | 5.6 | 6.2 | 20.1 | 41.0 | 16.7 | 10.5 | 62,356 | 46,604 | 60,716 | 73,147 | 59,978 | 42,808 |
| FRANKLIN CITY | 16,680 | 3,507 | 30.0 | 17.2 | 29.6 | 18.3 | 3.6 | 1.2 | 28,150 | 21,496 | 33,210 | 34,299 | 30,448 | 21,215 |
| FREDERICKSBURG CITY | 24,578 | 9,260 | 14.7 | 16.3 | 34.7 | 27.3 | 4.9 | 2.1 | 35,604 | 31,026 | 38,720 | 50,057 | 35,508 | 28,495 |
| GALAX CITY | 17,790 | 2,919 | 21.8 | 16.2 | 38.1 | 20.0 | 3.2 | 0.8 | 29,619 | 27,372 | 36,834 | 31,535 | 31,061 | 23,552 |
| HAMPTON CITY | 17,282 | 53,041 | 14.2 | 14.9 | 39.0 | 27.8 | 3.4 | 0.7 | 33,337 | 28,418 | 36,143 | 41,745 | 37,159 | 25,127 |
| HARRISONBURG CITY | 15,528 | 11,302 | 21.3 | 16.3 | 35.5 | 20.5 | 3.8 | 2.6 | 32,893 | 23,698 | 40,848 | 47,652 | 38,789 | 26,026 |
| HOPEWELL CITY | 16,494 | 9,118 | 18.3 | 15.8 | 38.9 | 23.8 | 2.9 | 0.2 | 30,474 | 26,303 | 35,063 | 36,851 | 36,067 | 21,865 |
| LEXINGTON CITY | 13,174 | 2,414 | 31.1 | 14.0 | 31.2 | 20.5 | 3.1 | 0.2 | 27,263 | 15,758 | 37,974 | 38,549 | 34,640 | 21,938 |
| LYNCHBURG CITY | 17,658 | 26,270 | 24.5 | 19.3 | 32.2 | 19.0 | 3.1 | 1.8 | 30,051 | 24,332 | 34,165 | 38,108 | 34,969 | 22,466 |
| MANASSAS CITY | 24,825 | 13,017 | 4.6 | 6.6 | 33.0 | 45.2 | 8.5 | 2.1 | 45,682 | 40,418 | 48,670 | 51,807 | 49,487 | 32,368 |
| MANASSAS PARK CITY | 18,926 | 3,147 | 5.0 | 7.9 | 45.1 | 39.8 | 2.2 | 0.0 | 38,201 | 38,402 | 37,689 | 47,366 | 34,435 | 26,468 |
| MARTINSVILLE CITY | 19,816 | 6,923 | 25.8 | 20.0 | 31.4 | 17.5 | 2.7 | 2.5 | 30,459 | 23,082 | 36,528 | 38,151 | 33,987 | 21,885 |
| NEWPORT NEWS CITY | 16,735 | 69,977 | 17.6 | 16.9 | 37.5 | 23.9 | 3.1 | 0.9 | 31,707 | 26,357 | 34,900 | 41,008 | 37,154 | 24,610 |
| NORFOLK CITY | 15,802 | 81,313 | 20.2 | 19.7 | 35.8 | 20.4 | 2.9 | 1.0 | 29,784 | 25,209 | 33,853 | 37,716 | 33,370 | 25,016 |
| NORTON CITY | 14,486 | 1,724 | 35.3 | 15.7 | 30.1 | 15.3 | 2.6 | 1.1 | 25,522 | 19,512 | 28,897 | 31,514 | 27,408 | 21,031 |
| PETERSBURG CITY | 14,341 | 14,387 | 28.6 | 18.0 | 33.2 | 17.4 | 2.2 | 0.6 | 26,390 | 20,805 | 29,811 | 33,981 | 29,933 | 21,586 |
| POQUOSON CITY | 23,769 | 4,111 | 5.9 | 8.3 | 27.2 | 45.6 | 10.1 | 2.9 | 46,992 | 38,107 | 49,580 | 56,558 | 48,639 | 26,388 |
| PORTSMOUTH CITY | 14,708 | 37,758 | 21.3 | 18.5 | 36.5 | 21.0 | 2.2 | 0.5 | 28,688 | 24,544 | 32,815 | 36,600 | 30,557 | 22,232 |
| RADFORD CITY | 14,860 | 5,369 | 28.1 | 18.6 | 32.4 | 15.2 | 3.2 | 2.5 | 29,479 | 19,032 | 39,269 | 42,188 | 43,485 | 22,732 |
| RICHMOND CITY | 17,567 | 85,572 | 28.5 | 18.8 | 31.8 | 16.6 | 2.8 | 1.5 | 28,083 | 22,911 | 32,174 | 35,397 | 30,084 | 22,290 |
| ROANOKE CITY | 15,731 | 40,934 | 26.1 | 19.4 | 35.6 | 15.8 | 2.3 | 0.9 | 26,892 | 24,217 | 30,651 | 32,179 | 28,640 | 20,749 |
| SALEM CITY | 21,518 | 10,029 | 14.5 | 14.9 | 38.0 | 26.0 | 4.6 | 2.0 | 35,057 | 28,741 | 39,549 | 44,312 | 38,007 | 25,375 |
| SOUTH BOSTON CITY | 16,240 | 2,926 | 27.6 | 22.3 | 28.4 | 16.8 | 3.4 | 1.5 | 27,903 | 21,966 | 28,073 | 38,197 | 34,397 | 19,997 |
| STAUNTON CITY | 16,583 | 9,306 | 20.2 | 16.9 | 38.1 | 21.2 | 2.6 | 1.0 | 30,183 | 27,935 | 35,303 | 37,997 | 31,818 | 22,098 |
| SUFFOLK CITY | 17,337 | 24,528 | 19.9 | 15.4 | 32.6 | 25.2 | 4.6 | 2.3 | 34,559 | 29,748 | 38,608 | 42,470 | 35,792 | 22,162 |
| VIRGINIA BEACH CITY | 19,730 | 156,385 | 6.7 | 12.6 | 39.6 | 33.7 | 5.6 | 1.8 | 39,625 | 31,970 | 41,503 | 49,701 | 46,214 | 33,284 |
| WAYNESBORO CITY | 17,107 | 7,969 | 16.6 | 19.7 | 36.8 | 22.5 | 3.6 | 0.9 | 31,397 | 26,240 | 34,937 | 38,517 | 36,303 | 25,380 |
| WILLIAMSBURG CITY | 17,457 | 3,777 | 15.5 | 16.9 | 32.6 | 24.9 | 7.2 | 2.9 | 37,868 | 23,475 | 42,901 | 53,252 | 49,180 | 44,397 |
| WINCHESTER CITY | 21,150 | 9,845 | 14.9 | 15.7 | 36.8 | 26.3 | 4.6 | 1.8 | 34,950 | 28,980 | 39,517 | 44,069 | 40,038 | 26,943 |
| VIRGINIA | 22,934 | | 12.8 | 11.9 | 32.0 | 31.8 | 8.2 | 3.3 | 41,578 | 34,181 | 45,367 | 50,467 | 43,935 | 29,069 |
| UNITED STATES | 22,162 | | 14.5 | 12.5 | 32.3 | 29.8 | 7.4 | 3.5 | 40,748 | 34,503 | 44,969 | 49,579 | 43,409 | 27,339 |

| COUNTY | FINANCIAL SERVICES | | | | THE HOME | | | | | | ENTERTAINMENT | | | | | | PERSONAL | | | |
|---|---|---|---|---|---|---|---|---|---|---|---|---|---|---|---|---|---|---|---|---|
| | | | | | Home Improvements | | | Furnishings | | | | | | | | | | | | |
| | Auto Loan | Home Loan | Invest-ments | Retire-ment Plans | Home Repair | Lawn & Garden | Remodel-ing | Appli-ances | Elec-tronics | Furni-ture | Restau-rants | Sport-ing Goods | Theater & Concerts | Toys & Hobbies | Travel | Video Rental | Apparel | Auto After-market | Health Insur-ance | Pets & Supplies |
| ROCKBRIDGE | 98 | 76 | 83 | 84 | 95 | 93 | 112 | 97 | 94 | 84 | 86 | 96 | 86 | 98 | 74 | 98 | 86 | 91 | 101 | 99 |
| ROCKINGHAM | 99 | 80 | 88 | 86 | 97 | 95 | 113 | 98 | 95 | 87 | 89 | 98 | 89 | 100 | 76 | 98 | 89 | 93 | 102 | 101 |
| RUSSELL | 97 | 66 | 72 | 76 | 93 | 91 | 112 | 96 | 92 | 77 | 79 | 96 | 80 | 95 | 68 | 96 | 79 | 87 | 102 | 97 |
| SCOTT | 97 | 65 | 71 | 74 | 94 | 91 | 110 | 96 | 90 | 77 | 78 | 95 | 80 | 94 | 69 | 95 | 79 | 87 | 101 | 96 |
| SHENANDOAH | 98 | 78 | 88 | 85 | 98 | 95 | 112 | 97 | 93 | 86 | 88 | 96 | 88 | 99 | 76 | 98 | 88 | 92 | 102 | 99 |
| SMYTH | 97 | 71 | 80 | 79 | 95 | 93 | 109 | 96 | 92 | 81 | 82 | 95 | 84 | 95 | 72 | 96 | 82 | 89 | 101 | 97 |
| SOUTHAMPTON | 98 | 73 | 79 | 82 | 94 | 93 | 111 | 97 | 95 | 82 | 83 | 98 | 85 | 97 | 72 | 97 | 84 | 90 | 101 | 98 |
| SPOTSYLVANIA | 103 | 103 | 89 | 99 | 97 | 99 | 105 | 102 | 105 | 105 | 110 | 106 | 101 | 106 | 86 | 102 | 107 | 105 | 98 | 106 |
| STAFFORD | 104 | 110 | 96 | 106 | 100 | 103 | 104 | 103 | 107 | 109 | 114 | 108 | 105 | 107 | 90 | 102 | 111 | 108 | 99 | 106 |
| SURRY | 97 | 67 | 71 | 75 | 92 | 90 | 113 | 96 | 92 | 78 | 80 | 96 | 80 | 95 | 67 | 96 | 80 | 87 | 101 | 97 |
| SUSSEX | 96 | 66 | 71 | 74 | 93 | 90 | 110 | 95 | 91 | 77 | 78 | 94 | 79 | 93 | 69 | 95 | 79 | 87 | 100 | 96 |
| TAZEWELL | 97 | 74 | 83 | 81 | 95 | 93 | 108 | 96 | 93 | 82 | 84 | 94 | 85 | 95 | 74 | 97 | 84 | 90 | 101 | 97 |
| WARREN | 97 | 84 | 85 | 85 | 97 | 93 | 106 | 97 | 94 | 89 | 91 | 95 | 89 | 98 | 78 | 98 | 89 | 93 | 99 | 99 |
| WASHINGTON | 98 | 73 | 80 | 81 | 95 | 92 | 112 | 96 | 93 | 82 | 83 | 96 | 84 | 97 | 72 | 97 | 84 | 90 | 101 | 98 |
| WESTMORELAND | 98 | 75 | 88 | 84 | 98 | 97 | 112 | 97 | 92 | 84 | 86 | 94 | 86 | 97 | 77 | 97 | 85 | 90 | 103 | 98 |
| WISE | 97 | 68 | 75 | 77 | 93 | 91 | 112 | 95 | 92 | 78 | 80 | 94 | 81 | 95 | 69 | 96 | 81 | 88 | 101 | 97 |
| WYTHE | 97 | 72 | 82 | 80 | 96 | 94 | 108 | 96 | 92 | 82 | 83 | 95 | 85 | 96 | 73 | 96 | 83 | 89 | 102 | 97 |
| YORK | 103 | 110 | 104 | 107 | 104 | 106 | 100 | 103 | 105 | 110 | 113 | 107 | 107 | 106 | 95 | 102 | 113 | 108 | 99 | 105 |
| ALEXANDRIA CITY | 101 | 127 | 118 | 114 | 110 | 112 | 99 | 101 | 105 | 111 | 115 | 105 | 110 | 103 | 106 | 101 | 113 | 111 | 99 | 106 |
| BEDFORD CITY | 94 | 83 | 99 | 85 | 104 | 99 | 98 | 96 | 89 | 91 | 89 | 91 | 91 | 94 | 85 | 94 | 87 | 91 | 100 | 95 |
| BRISTOL CITY | 95 | 85 | 100 | 87 | 103 | 98 | 100 | 97 | 91 | 91 | 89 | 93 | 91 | 95 | 85 | 96 | 88 | 92 | 98 | 96 |
| BUENA VISTA CITY | 93 | 83 | 92 | 82 | 103 | 97 | 97 | 95 | 88 | 91 | 89 | 91 | 91 | 95 | 84 | 94 | 87 | 90 | 100 | 94 |
| CHARLOTTESVILLE CITY | 93 | 96 | 104 | 93 | 102 | 96 | 94 | 90 | 90 | 88 | 90 | 89 | 89 | 93 | 86 | 93 | 91 | 93 | 94 | 95 |
| CHESAPEAKE CITY | 101 | 104 | 93 | 98 | 99 | 100 | 98 | 100 | 103 | 105 | 107 | 103 | 101 | 103 | 88 | 101 | 106 | 104 | 96 | 103 |
| CLIFTON FORGE CITY | 94 | 77 | 94 | 82 | 100 | 98 | 100 | 95 | 90 | 85 | 86 | 89 | 88 | 93 | 80 | 96 | 85 | 90 | 103 | 94 |
| COLONIAL HGHTS CITY | 97 | 97 | 108 | 96 | 107 | 104 | 98 | 98 | 95 | 100 | 101 | 97 | 100 | 100 | 92 | 97 | 98 | 98 | 102 | 99 |
| COVINGTON CITY | 92 | 79 | 91 | 79 | 104 | 98 | 98 | 95 | 85 | 89 | 87 | 90 | 89 | 94 | 83 | 94 | 84 | 88 | 101 | 93 |
| DANVILLE CITY | 93 | 83 | 94 | 83 | 102 | 95 | 96 | 96 | 89 | 90 | 86 | 91 | 89 | 94 | 83 | 95 | 87 | 91 | 95 | 95 |
| EMPORIA CITY | 93 | 80 | 94 | 82 | 101 | 95 | 98 | 95 | 89 | 88 | 86 | 89 | 88 | 93 | 82 | 95 | 85 | 90 | 96 | 94 |
| FAIRFAX CITY | 103 | 130 | 126 | 120 | 115 | 119 | 102 | 103 | 111 | 116 | 123 | 108 | 119 | 109 | 111 | 103 | 122 | 118 | 104 | 108 |
| FALLS CHURCH CITY | 104 | 132 | 129 | 122 | 117 | 121 | 103 | 104 | 112 | 119 | 124 | 109 | 120 | 108 | 114 | 103 | 123 | 119 | 104 | 109 |
| FRANKLIN CITY | 93 | 81 | 93 | 85 | 99 | 92 | 95 | 96 | 92 | 89 | 82 | 91 | 88 | 92 | 82 | 97 | 88 | 92 | 90 | 96 |
| FREDERICKSBURG CITY | 95 | 99 | 95 | 91 | 99 | 97 | 92 | 95 | 93 | 95 | 98 | 94 | 93 | 96 | 86 | 97 | 95 | 97 | 95 | 98 |
| GALAX CITY | 97 | 73 | 81 | 80 | 96 | 92 | 112 | 96 | 92 | 83 | 84 | 94 | 84 | 96 | 73 | 96 | 84 | 89 | 101 | 98 |
| HAMPTON CITY | 96 | 96 | 90 | 89 | 98 | 95 | 91 | 96 | 95 | 97 | 97 | 95 | 94 | 97 | 84 | 98 | 97 | 98 | 93 | 98 |
| HARRISONBURG CITY | 92 | 95 | 93 | 87 | 97 | 92 | 94 | 90 | 90 | 86 | 91 | 89 | 86 | 92 | 82 | 93 | 88 | 91 | 94 | 96 |
| HOPEWELL CITY | 93 | 89 | 94 | 85 | 102 | 96 | 93 | 95 | 91 | 94 | 91 | 91 | 92 | 94 | 85 | 96 | 91 | 93 | 95 | 95 |
| LEXINGTON CITY | 93 | 94 | 109 | 94 | 104 | 98 | 92 | 91 | 88 | 87 | 89 | 89 | 89 | 92 | 87 | 92 | 89 | 92 | 95 | 94 |
| LYNCHBURG CITY | 95 | 90 | 102 | 91 | 103 | 99 | 96 | 96 | 92 | 94 | 92 | 93 | 93 | 95 | 87 | 96 | 92 | 94 | 96 | 96 |
| MANASSAS CITY | 104 | 114 | 91 | 105 | 99 | 102 | 98 | 103 | 107 | 111 | 118 | 109 | 105 | 107 | 91 | 102 | 114 | 108 | 97 | 106 |
| MANASSAS PARK CITY | 97 | 100 | 95 | 92 | 100 | 99 | 93 | 97 | 97 | 101 | 105 | 98 | 99 | 102 | 87 | 98 | 101 | 100 | 97 | 100 |
| MARTINSVILLE CITY | 97 | 89 | 107 | 95 | 106 | 103 | 100 | 98 | 92 | 96 | 93 | 96 | 97 | 97 | 90 | 97 | 94 | 95 | 100 | 97 |
| NEWPORT NEWS CITY | 93 | 93 | 93 | 87 | 98 | 93 | 91 | 94 | 93 | 91 | 92 | 92 | 91 | 93 | 83 | 97 | 92 | 95 | 92 | 97 |
| NORFOLK CITY | 91 | 91 | 92 | 84 | 98 | 92 | 88 | 93 | 91 | 89 | 89 | 89 | 89 | 91 | 82 | 96 | 89 | 93 | 90 | 95 |
| NORTON CITY | 92 | 68 | 74 | 73 | 94 | 90 | 103 | 92 | 89 | 78 | 78 | 85 | 78 | 88 | 72 | 95 | 78 | 86 | 100 | 92 |
| PETERSBURG CITY | 92 | 83 | 98 | 83 | 101 | 93 | 87 | 95 | 89 | 91 | 83 | 89 | 89 | 91 | 84 | 96 | 89 | 92 | 89 | 93 |
| POQUOSON CITY | 106 | 108 | 103 | 108 | 103 | 106 | 108 | 104 | 108 | 110 | 115 | 108 | 108 | 110 | 93 | 103 | 115 | 110 | 101 | 108 |
| PORTSMOUTH CITY | 92 | 87 | 92 | 83 | 100 | 94 | 88 | 95 | 89 | 92 | 87 | 90 | 90 | 92 | 84 | 97 | 91 | 94 | 91 | 94 |
| RADFORD CITY | 94 | 97 | 101 | 95 | 100 | 96 | 101 | 89 | 91 | 86 | 92 | 90 | 87 | 94 | 84 | 93 | 91 | 93 | 96 | 97 |
| RICHMOND CITY | 92 | 89 | 99 | 88 | 101 | 95 | 87 | 94 | 89 | 91 | 85 | 89 | 89 | 90 | 87 | 95 | 91 | 94 | 90 | 93 |
| ROANOKE CITY | 92 | 86 | 98 | 84 | 103 | 96 | 92 | 95 | 88 | 92 | 87 | 89 | 90 | 92 | 86 | 95 | 89 | 92 | 94 | 94 |
| SALEM CITY | 97 | 94 | 103 | 93 | 103 | 101 | 101 | 97 | 95 | 96 | 97 | 95 | 96 | 99 | 87 | 97 | 95 | 96 | 100 | 98 |
| SOUTH BOSTON CITY | 90 | 83 | 89 | 78 | 101 | 94 | 96 | 93 | 86 | 88 | 86 | 87 | 87 | 91 | 82 | 93 | 84 | 88 | 96 | 92 |
| STAUNTON CITY | 95 | 89 | 101 | 90 | 102 | 99 | 100 | 96 | 93 | 92 | 93 | 93 | 93 | 96 | 85 | 96 | 91 | 93 | 100 | 96 |
| SUFFOLK CITY | 97 | 84 | 90 | 86 | 99 | 94 | 103 | 97 | 94 | 91 | 89 | 95 | 91 | 97 | 80 | 98 | 91 | 94 | 96 | 98 |
| VIRGINIA BEACH CITY | 99 | 105 | 95 | 98 | 99 | 99 | 97 | 99 | 101 | 101 | 106 | 101 | 99 | 101 | 88 | 100 | 102 | 102 | 96 | 103 |
| WAYNESBORO CITY | 97 | 89 | 105 | 92 | 105 | 102 | 101 | 97 | 93 | 94 | 94 | 95 | 95 | 98 | 88 | 96 | 92 | 94 | 101 | 98 |
| WILLIAMSBURG CITY | 95 | 104 | 107 | 97 | 103 | 99 | 94 | 93 | 92 | 92 | 96 | 93 | 93 | 95 | 89 | 95 | 95 | 97 | 96 | 98 |
| WINCHESTER CITY | 96 | 99 | 102 | 95 | 102 | 100 | 97 | 96 | 95 | 97 | 98 | 96 | 97 | 98 | 88 | 97 | 96 | 97 | 97 | 98 |
| VIRGINIA | 100 | 102 | 100 | 101 | 102 | 102 | 103 | 99 | 101 | 100 | 103 | 102 | 101 | 102 | 90 | 100 | 102 | 102 | 99 | 102 |
| UNITED STATES | 100 | 100 | 100 | 100 | 100 | 100 | 100 | 100 | 100 | 100 | 100 | 100 | 100 | 100 | 100 | 100 | 100 | 100 | 100 | 100 |

# POPULATION CHANGE

| COUNTY | FIPS Code | MSA Code | DMA Code | POPULATION 1990 | POPULATION 2000 | POPULATION 2005 | 1990-2000 ANNUAL CHANGE % Rate | 1990-2000 ANNUAL CHANGE State Rank | RACE (%) White 1990 | White 2000 | Black 1990 | Black 2000 | Asian/Pacific 1990 | Asian/Pacific 2000 |
|---|---|---|---|---|---|---|---|---|---|---|---|---|---|---|
| ADAMS | 001 | 0000 | 881 | 13,603 | 15,218 | 15,133 | 1.1 | 31 | 66.9 | 56.2 | 0.2 | 0.2 | 0.7 | 0.8 |
| ASOTIN | 003 | 0000 | 881 | 17,605 | 21,314 | 21,919 | 1.9 | 17 | 97.3 | 96.9 | 0.2 | 0.2 | 0.6 | 0.9 |
| BENTON | 005 | 6740 | 810 | 112,560 | 139,241 | 146,596 | 2.1 | 16 | 91.4 | 88.0 | 1.0 | 1.1 | 2.0 | 2.8 |
| CHELAN | 007 | 0000 | 819 | 52,250 | 61,487 | 64,918 | 1.6 | 22 | 92.5 | 89.3 | 0.2 | 0.2 | 0.7 | 1.0 |
| CLALLAM | 009 | 0000 | 819 | 56,464 | 65,181 | 67,777 | 1.4 | 25 | 93.0 | 92.2 | 0.6 | 0.6 | 1.1 | 1.5 |
| CLARK | 011 | 6440 | 820 | 238,053 | 346,277 | 395,921 | 3.7 | 1 | 94.6 | 92.9 | 1.3 | 1.5 | 2.4 | 3.4 |
| COLUMBIA | 013 | 0000 | 881 | 4,024 | 4,145 | 4,096 | 0.3 | 38 | 96.3 | 95.1 | 0.0 | 0.0 | 0.4 | 0.5 |
| COWLITZ | 015 | 0000 | 820 | 82,119 | 92,652 | 96,220 | 1.2 | 30 | 95.6 | 94.5 | 0.4 | 0.4 | 1.4 | 2.0 |
| DOUGLAS | 017 | 0000 | 819 | 26,205 | 34,817 | 37,970 | 2.8 | 4 | 92.9 | 90.9 | 0.2 | 0.2 | 0.6 | 0.8 |
| FERRY | 019 | 0000 | 881 | 6,295 | 7,199 | 7,253 | 1.3 | 28 | 80.8 | 79.4 | 0.3 | 0.4 | 0.4 | 0.5 |
| FRANKLIN | 021 | 6740 | 810 | 37,473 | 47,296 | 49,849 | 2.3 | 13 | 71.8 | 64.3 | 3.5 | 3.7 | 2.3 | 2.7 |
| GARFIELD | 023 | 0000 | 881 | 2,248 | 2,354 | 2,432 | 0.5 | 36 | 98.8 | 98.5 | 0.0 | 0.0 | 0.3 | 0.4 |
| GRANT | 025 | 0000 | 881 | 54,758 | 73,598 | 81,490 | 2.9 | 3 | 85.8 | 80.6 | 1.1 | 1.2 | 1.2 | 1.5 |
| GRAYS HARBOR | 027 | 0000 | 819 | 64,175 | 66,886 | 65,817 | 0.4 | 37 | 93.9 | 92.9 | 0.2 | 0.2 | 1.1 | 1.6 |
| ISLAND | 029 | 7600 | 819 | 60,195 | 75,099 | 82,729 | 2.2 | 15 | 91.4 | 89.6 | 2.4 | 2.1 | 4.2 | 5.9 |
| JEFFERSON | 031 | 0000 | 819 | 20,146 | 27,195 | 29,552 | 3.0 | 2 | 95.6 | 94.5 | 0.4 | 0.7 | 1.0 | 1.4 |
| KING | 033 | 7600 | 819 | 1,507,319 | 1,680,747 | 1,756,949 | 1.1 | 31 | 84.8 | 80.5 | 5.1 | 5.8 | 7.9 | 10.9 |
| KITSAP | 035 | 1150 | 819 | 189,731 | 239,295 | 253,526 | 2.3 | 13 | 90.2 | 87.8 | 2.7 | 2.8 | 4.4 | 6.1 |
| KITTITAS | 037 | 0000 | 810 | 26,725 | 32,513 | 34,958 | 1.9 | 17 | 95.5 | 94.4 | 0.6 | 0.6 | 1.8 | 2.1 |
| KLICKITAT | 039 | 0000 | 820 | 16,616 | 19,829 | 21,282 | 1.7 | 21 | 92.6 | 91.0 | 0.2 | 0.2 | 0.8 | 1.1 |
| LEWIS | 041 | 0000 | 819 | 59,358 | 69,225 | 72,334 | 1.5 | 24 | 97.1 | 96.3 | 0.3 | 0.3 | 0.6 | 0.9 |
| LINCOLN | 043 | 0000 | 881 | 8,864 | 9,809 | 10,047 | 1.0 | 34 | 97.7 | 97.3 | 0.2 | 0.2 | 0.4 | 0.5 |
| MASON | 045 | 0000 | 819 | 38,341 | 50,966 | 54,131 | 2.8 | 4 | 93.3 | 92.2 | 0.9 | 1.0 | 1.2 | 1.7 |
| OKANOGAN | 047 | 0000 | 881 | 33,350 | 38,640 | 39,788 | 1.4 | 25 | 82.8 | 80.7 | 0.2 | 0.2 | 0.5 | 0.7 |
| PACIFIC | 049 | 0000 | 819 | 18,882 | 20,737 | 20,583 | 0.9 | 35 | 93.7 | 92.3 | 0.3 | 0.3 | 2.5 | 3.5 |
| PEND OREILLE | 051 | 0000 | 881 | 8,915 | 11,752 | 12,558 | 2.7 | 6 | 96.9 | 96.5 | 0.1 | 0.2 | 0.3 | 0.4 |
| PIERCE | 053 | 8200 | 819 | 586,203 | 700,858 | 760,658 | 1.8 | 19 | 85.1 | 81.8 | 7.2 | 7.8 | 5.0 | 6.9 |
| SAN JUAN | 055 | 0000 | 819 | 10,035 | 13,215 | 14,818 | 2.7 | 6 | 97.8 | 97.3 | 0.2 | 0.2 | 0.9 | 1.2 |
| SKAGIT | 057 | 0000 | 819 | 79,555 | 103,097 | 112,654 | 2.6 | 10 | 93.2 | 91.0 | 0.4 | 0.4 | 1.0 | 1.4 |
| SKAMANIA | 059 | 0000 | 820 | 8,289 | 9,981 | 10,670 | 1.8 | 19 | 96.4 | 95.7 | 0.1 | 0.1 | 0.6 | 0.9 |
| SNOHOMISH | 061 | 7600 | 819 | 465,642 | 611,962 | 685,714 | 2.7 | 6 | 93.3 | 91.1 | 1.0 | 1.4 | 3.5 | 5.0 |
| SPOKANE | 063 | 7840 | 881 | 361,364 | 411,377 | 420,561 | 1.3 | 28 | 94.6 | 93.3 | 1.4 | 1.6 | 1.8 | 2.5 |
| STEVENS | 065 | 0000 | 881 | 30,948 | 40,652 | 43,383 | 2.7 | 6 | 92.9 | 92.2 | 0.2 | 0.2 | 0.6 | 0.8 |
| THURSTON | 067 | 5910 | 819 | 161,238 | 208,511 | 224,233 | 2.5 | 11 | 91.9 | 89.6 | 1.8 | 2.1 | 3.8 | 5.3 |
| WAHKIAKUM | 069 | 0000 | 820 | 3,327 | 3,851 | 3,898 | 1.4 | 25 | 96.7 | 95.9 | 0.1 | 0.1 | 0.5 | 0.8 |
| WALLA WALLA | 071 | 0000 | 810 | 48,439 | 53,981 | 54,777 | 1.1 | 31 | 89.4 | 85.4 | 1.5 | 2.0 | 1.3 | 1.7 |
| WHATCOM | 073 | 0860 | 819 | 127,780 | 163,004 | 176,861 | 2.4 | 12 | 93.3 | 91.8 | 0.5 | 0.6 | 1.8 | 2.6 |
| WHITMAN | 075 | 0000 | 881 | 38,775 | 38,166 | 37,031 | -0.2 | 39 | 91.9 | 89.8 | 1.3 | 1.4 | 5.4 | 7.2 |
| YAKIMA | 077 | 9260 | 810 | 188,823 | 222,962 | 234,146 | 1.6 | 22 | 73.9 | 66.8 | 1.0 | 1.1 | 1.0 | 1.3 |
| WASHINGTON | | | | | | | 1.8 | | 88.5 | 85.7 | 3.1 | 3.4 | 4.3 | 5.9 |
| UNITED STATES | | | | | | | 1.0 | | 80.3 | 77.9 | 12.1 | 12.4 | 2.9 | 3.9 |

| COUNTY | % HISPANIC ORIGIN | | 2000 AGE DISTRIBUTION (%) | | | | | | | | | | MEDIAN AGE | | 2000 Males/ Females (×100) |
|---|---|---|---|---|---|---|---|---|---|---|---|---|---|---|---|
| | 1990 | 2000 | 0-4 | 5-9 | 10-14 | 15-19 | 20-24 | 25-44 | 45-64 | 65-84 | 85+ | 18+ | 1990 | 2000 | |
| ADAMS | 32.8 | 44.1 | 8.5 | 9.1 | 9.4 | 9.1 | 7.3 | 24.2 | 21.1 | 10.0 | 1.4 | 67.0 | 30.7 | 30.8 | 101.9 |
| ASOTIN | 1.6 | 2.8 | 6.7 | 7.4 | 7.8 | 8.0 | 5.9 | 26.4 | 22.8 | 12.6 | 2.3 | 72.8 | 34.9 | 37.3 | 93.9 |
| BENTON | 7.7 | 11.8 | 7.3 | 7.9 | 8.4 | 8.4 | 6.2 | 28.8 | 22.9 | 9.0 | 1.1 | 71.1 | 32.1 | 34.4 | 98.8 |
| CHELAN | 9.2 | 14.3 | 7.0 | 7.5 | 7.9 | 8.0 | 5.9 | 27.6 | 23.6 | 10.6 | 1.9 | 72.8 | 35.1 | 36.3 | 100.2 |
| CLALLAM | 2.0 | 3.2 | 5.6 | 6.2 | 6.7 | 7.3 | 5.9 | 23.6 | 24.7 | 17.4 | 2.6 | 76.9 | 38.4 | 41.4 | 100.8 |
| CLARK | 2.5 | 4.2 | 6.9 | 7.3 | 7.8 | 7.7 | 6.5 | 29.2 | 24.3 | 9.2 | 1.2 | 73.2 | 32.9 | 35.4 | 97.5 |
| COLUMBIA | 11.5 | 16.6 | 4.8 | 5.9 | 7.0 | 7.7 | 5.4 | 25.0 | 26.2 | 15.1 | 2.8 | 77.0 | 39.0 | 41.3 | 99.2 |
| COWLITZ | 2.0 | 3.4 | 6.4 | 7.0 | 7.8 | 8.0 | 5.9 | 27.5 | 24.1 | 11.5 | 1.7 | 74.0 | 34.3 | 37.1 | 99.1 |
| DOUGLAS | 10.4 | 14.2 | 6.8 | 7.4 | 8.1 | 8.1 | 5.7 | 26.9 | 22.7 | 12.7 | 1.6 | 72.8 | 33.5 | 36.6 | 101.8 |
| FERRY | 1.4 | 2.3 | 6.8 | 7.6 | 8.8 | 10.2 | 5.9 | 26.0 | 24.1 | 9.6 | 1.1 | 70.1 | 32.8 | 35.3 | 109.8 |
| FRANKLIN | 30.2 | 40.3 | 9.3 | 9.0 | 8.9 | 9.6 | 7.9 | 27.6 | 18.4 | 8.4 | 1.0 | 66.9 | 28.7 | 28.7 | 105.8 |
| GARFIELD | 1.0 | 2.1 | 4.6 | 6.2 | 7.3 | 7.5 | 3.9 | 22.2 | 26.4 | 18.5 | 3.4 | 75.5 | 41.1 | 43.9 | 98.3 |
| GRANT | 17.2 | 25.1 | 8.0 | 8.5 | 8.9 | 9.0 | 6.2 | 25.9 | 21.3 | 11.0 | 1.3 | 69.1 | 31.9 | 33.3 | 103.9 |
| GRAYS HARBOR | 1.8 | 3.1 | 6.7 | 7.1 | 7.5 | 7.7 | 6.2 | 25.4 | 24.4 | 13.0 | 2.0 | 73.9 | 35.4 | 37.8 | 100.9 |
| ISLAND | 3.3 | 5.1 | 7.5 | 7.2 | 7.0 | 6.4 | 7.0 | 29.5 | 21.4 | 12.7 | 1.3 | 74.6 | 32.2 | 35.6 | 101.2 |
| JEFFERSON | 1.2 | 2.5 | 4.6 | 5.6 | 6.6 | 6.5 | 4.3 | 24.1 | 28.1 | 18.2 | 2.0 | 78.8 | 41.1 | 44.0 | 99.8 |
| KING | 2.9 | 4.7 | 5.9 | 6.2 | 6.8 | 6.7 | 6.5 | 33.9 | 23.5 | 9.2 | 1.4 | 77.4 | 33.7 | 36.8 | 97.7 |
| KITSAP | 3.3 | 5.1 | 7.0 | 7.4 | 7.9 | 7.9 | 7.1 | 30.1 | 22.3 | 9.0 | 1.3 | 73.0 | 31.8 | 34.4 | 103.3 |
| KITTITAS | 2.6 | 4.3 | 5.2 | 5.6 | 5.7 | 10.2 | 14.3 | 25.3 | 21.3 | 10.7 | 1.7 | 79.9 | 30.2 | 33.0 | 98.7 |
| KLICKITAT | 5.6 | 8.4 | 6.7 | 7.4 | 7.9 | 8.3 | 6.5 | 24.9 | 25.8 | 11.0 | 1.5 | 72.4 | 34.5 | 37.0 | 101.4 |
| LEWIS | 2.3 | 3.9 | 6.3 | 7.3 | 8.2 | 8.5 | 5.7 | 25.7 | 23.8 | 12.4 | 2.1 | 72.8 | 34.9 | 37.2 | 98.6 |
| LINCOLN | 0.9 | 1.9 | 5.2 | 6.8 | 7.7 | 7.6 | 3.9 | 22.8 | 27.0 | 16.1 | 3.0 | 74.7 | 39.3 | 42.5 | 102.1 |
| MASON | 2.3 | 3.6 | 5.5 | 6.4 | 7.2 | 7.4 | 5.6 | 25.9 | 25.7 | 14.6 | 1.6 | 76.1 | 36.9 | 39.9 | 107.7 |
| OKANOGAN | 8.3 | 11.4 | 6.9 | 7.4 | 8.0 | 8.4 | 6.1 | 24.0 | 25.3 | 12.2 | 1.8 | 72.2 | 35.0 | 37.5 | 102.1 |
| PACIFIC | 2.3 | 3.5 | 5.6 | 6.1 | 7.0 | 7.3 | 4.6 | 22.7 | 25.6 | 18.6 | 2.6 | 76.4 | 40.3 | 42.7 | 99.4 |
| PEND OREILLE | 1.3 | 2.5 | 6.2 | 7.2 | 8.7 | 8.1 | 4.6 | 24.4 | 27.1 | 11.9 | 1.7 | 72.1 | 36.1 | 39.2 | 99.4 |
| PIERCE | 3.5 | 5.6 | 7.6 | 7.5 | 7.5 | 7.7 | 7.6 | 30.7 | 21.0 | 9.2 | 1.3 | 73.2 | 31.3 | 33.6 | 99.9 |
| SAN JUAN | 1.2 | 2.2 | 4.2 | 5.3 | 6.3 | 5.6 | 3.2 | 23.6 | 31.5 | 18.2 | 2.1 | 80.2 | 42.7 | 46.0 | 99.0 |
| SKAGIT | 5.4 | 8.7 | 6.4 | 7.0 | 7.5 | 8.0 | 5.9 | 25.9 | 24.6 | 12.8 | 1.9 | 74.3 | 35.6 | 38.0 | 97.9 |
| SKAMANIA | 2.1 | 3.7 | 6.6 | 7.7 | 8.6 | 8.4 | 5.2 | 28.2 | 25.3 | 9.1 | 1.0 | 71.9 | 33.7 | 36.5 | 105.0 |
| SNOHOMISH | 2.3 | 4.1 | 7.3 | 7.9 | 8.3 | 7.5 | 5.8 | 31.4 | 22.4 | 8.2 | 1.1 | 71.9 | 32.2 | 34.9 | 99.2 |
| SPOKANE | 1.9 | 3.4 | 6.7 | 6.8 | 7.2 | 8.0 | 7.6 | 28.9 | 22.4 | 10.7 | 1.7 | 74.8 | 33.0 | 35.3 | 96.0 |
| STEVENS | 1.6 | 2.7 | 6.6 | 7.3 | 7.7 | 8.9 | 6.9 | 23.6 | 26.8 | 10.7 | 1.5 | 72.2 | 34.5 | 37.2 | 99.9 |
| THURSTON | 3.0 | 5.0 | 6.3 | 6.8 | 7.3 | 7.8 | 6.8 | 29.2 | 24.3 | 9.9 | 1.6 | 74.9 | 33.7 | 36.2 | 95.4 |
| WAHKIAKUM | 2.1 | 3.6 | 5.3 | 6.2 | 7.5 | 7.3 | 4.6 | 23.3 | 27.0 | 16.1 | 2.6 | 76.2 | 40.2 | 42.4 | 100.7 |
| WALLA WALLA | 9.7 | 14.1 | 6.1 | 6.5 | 7.2 | 9.0 | 8.4 | 27.3 | 21.1 | 12.0 | 2.3 | 75.9 | 33.5 | 35.3 | 104.8 |
| WHATCOM | 2.9 | 4.9 | 6.1 | 6.5 | 6.9 | 8.2 | 9.1 | 28.6 | 22.6 | 10.3 | 1.6 | 76.2 | 32.7 | 35.2 | 97.5 |
| WHITMAN | 1.8 | 2.9 | 4.7 | 4.6 | 4.5 | 13.6 | 23.8 | 24.6 | 15.5 | 7.4 | 1.3 | 83.2 | 24.5 | 24.7 | 105.9 |
| YAKIMA | 23.9 | 32.9 | 8.1 | 8.4 | 8.6 | 8.3 | 7.1 | 27.0 | 20.8 | 9.9 | 1.7 | 69.9 | 31.5 | 32.4 | 100.1 |
| WASHINGTON | 4.4 | 6.8 | 6.7 | 7.0 | 7.4 | 7.6 | 6.9 | 30.3 | 22.9 | 9.9 | 1.5 | 74.5 | 33.1 | 35.7 | 98.9 |
| UNITED STATES | 9.0 | 11.8 | 6.9 | 7.2 | 7.2 | 7.2 | 6.7 | 29.9 | 22.2 | 11.1 | 1.6 | 74.6 | 32.9 | 35.7 | 95.6 |

# HOUSEHOLDS

| COUNTY | HOUSEHOLDS 1990 | HOUSEHOLDS 2000 | HOUSEHOLDS 2005 | % Annual Rate 1990-2000 | 2000 Average HH Size | FAMILIES 1990 | FAMILIES 2000 | % Annual Rate 1990-2000 | MEDIAN HOUSEHOLD INCOME 2000 | MEDIAN HOUSEHOLD INCOME 2005 | 2000 National Rank | 2000 State Rank |
|---|---|---|---|---|---|---|---|---|---|---|---|---|
| ADAMS | 4,586 | 5,207 | 5,215 | 1.6 | 2.90 | 3,518 | 3,930 | 1.4 | 34,967 | 41,301 | 1257 | 30 |
| ASOTIN | 7,003 | 8,845 | 9,273 | 2.9 | 2.38 | 4,892 | 6,006 | 2.5 | 34,996 | 40,132 | 1251 | 29 |
| BENTON | 42,227 | 52,785 | 55,838 | 2.7 | 2.63 | 30,503 | 37,188 | 2.4 | 53,041 | 60,874 | 152 | 3 |
| CHELAN | 20,645 | 24,361 | 25,747 | 2.0 | 2.49 | 14,111 | 16,120 | 1.6 | 37,833 | 44,940 | 866 | 19 |
| CLALLAM | 22,837 | 26,940 | 28,314 | 2.0 | 2.36 | 15,902 | 18,149 | 1.6 | 35,587 | 39,490 | 1158 | 27 |
| CLARK | 88,440 | 131,684 | 152,169 | 4.9 | 2.61 | 63,895 | 92,957 | 4.6 | 50,894 | 57,848 | 186 | 4 |
| COLUMBIA | 1,582 | 1,650 | 1,638 | 0.5 | 2.41 | 1,070 | 1,070 | 0.0 | 33,715 | 42,024 | 1435 | 33 |
| COWLITZ | 31,640 | 36,540 | 38,376 | 1.8 | 2.50 | 22,611 | 25,281 | 1.4 | 39,604 | 45,260 | 701 | 14 |
| DOUGLAS | 9,687 | 13,051 | 14,323 | 3.7 | 2.65 | 7,316 | 9,642 | 3.4 | 41,839 | 52,049 | 526 | 12 |
| FERRY | 2,247 | 2,622 | 2,662 | 1.9 | 2.66 | 1,635 | 1,848 | 1.5 | 33,912 | 43,630 | 1406 | 32 |
| FRANKLIN | 12,196 | 15,242 | 16,045 | 2.7 | 3.05 | 9,306 | 11,440 | 2.5 | 37,770 | 45,716 | 868 | 20 |
| GARFIELD | 922 | 991 | 1,037 | 0.9 | 2.34 | 647 | 670 | 0.4 | 35,927 | 43,234 | 1110 | 25 |
| GRANT | 19,745 | 26,959 | 30,074 | 3.8 | 2.70 | 14,467 | 19,244 | 3.5 | 35,752 | 42,071 | 1129 | 26 |
| GRAYS HARBOR | 25,514 | 27,422 | 27,377 | 0.9 | 2.41 | 17,423 | 18,047 | 0.4 | 32,531 | 37,375 | 1620 | 36 |
| ISLAND | 21,787 | 27,912 | 30,733 | 3.0 | 2.63 | 16,608 | 20,689 | 2.7 | 46,439 | 58,328 | 293 | 7 |
| JEFFERSON | 8,627 | 11,742 | 12,870 | 3.8 | 2.27 | 5,886 | 7,727 | 3.4 | 38,226 | 43,797 | 837 | 17 |
| KING | 615,792 | 702,161 | 741,660 | 1.6 | 2.35 | 378,290 | 414,322 | 1.1 | 54,339 | 61,903 | 131 | 1 |
| KITSAP | 69,267 | 87,874 | 93,070 | 2.9 | 2.66 | 50,100 | 61,680 | 2.6 | 47,077 | 57,791 | 271 | 6 |
| KITTITAS | 10,460 | 13,021 | 14,036 | 2.7 | 2.34 | 6,270 | 7,474 | 2.2 | 32,231 | 37,280 | 1678 | 37 |
| KLICKITAT | 6,210 | 7,581 | 8,226 | 2.4 | 2.59 | 4,534 | 5,363 | 2.1 | 33,236 | 37,543 | 1500 | 35 |
| LEWIS | 22,478 | 26,678 | 28,102 | 2.1 | 2.56 | 16,224 | 18,658 | 1.7 | 37,160 | 45,289 | 951 | 22 |
| LINCOLN | 3,605 | 4,096 | 4,246 | 1.6 | 2.37 | 2,603 | 2,864 | 1.2 | 37,614 | 43,566 | 888 | 21 |
| MASON | 14,565 | 19,672 | 21,091 | 3.7 | 2.48 | 10,688 | 14,056 | 3.4 | 40,131 | 48,423 | 663 | 13 |
| OKANOGAN | 12,654 | 14,948 | 15,532 | 2.0 | 2.54 | 9,062 | 10,355 | 1.6 | 30,070 | 35,221 | 2139 | 39 |
| PACIFIC | 7,896 | 8,839 | 8,844 | 1.4 | 2.31 | 5,412 | 5,807 | 0.9 | 30,825 | 36,466 | 1964 | 38 |
| PEND OREILLE | 3,395 | 4,695 | 5,133 | 4.0 | 2.49 | 2,518 | 3,377 | 3.6 | 33,370 | 37,839 | 1480 | 34 |
| PIERCE | 214,652 | 259,924 | 283,128 | 2.3 | 2.62 | 151,672 | 178,355 | 2.0 | 45,167 | 56,487 | 350 | 9 |
| SAN JUAN | 4,392 | 5,748 | 6,424 | 3.3 | 2.27 | 2,915 | 3,663 | 2.8 | 46,426 | 52,793 | 294 | 8 |
| SKAGIT | 30,573 | 40,128 | 44,066 | 3.4 | 2.53 | 21,768 | 27,586 | 2.9 | 43,869 | 52,958 | 404 | 11 |
| SKAMANIA | 3,066 | 3,842 | 4,187 | 2.8 | 2.59 | 2,304 | 2,803 | 2.4 | 39,274 | 44,149 | 730 | 16 |
| SNOHOMISH | 171,713 | 230,727 | 261,983 | 3.6 | 2.62 | 124,139 | 160,663 | 3.2 | 53,581 | 65,270 | 141 | 2 |
| SPOKANE | 141,619 | 164,029 | 169,130 | 1.8 | 2.44 | 93,982 | 106,098 | 1.5 | 39,551 | 45,311 | 705 | 15 |
| STEVENS | 11,241 | 14,996 | 16,127 | 3.6 | 2.69 | 8,509 | 11,070 | 3.2 | 36,850 | 46,937 | 1000 | 23 |
| THURSTON | 62,150 | 81,505 | 88,207 | 3.3 | 2.53 | 43,336 | 54,867 | 2.9 | 47,624 | 57,301 | 253 | 5 |
| WAHKIAKUM | 1,321 | 1,617 | 1,681 | 2.5 | 2.35 | 972 | 1,150 | 2.1 | 36,458 | 39,747 | 1049 | 24 |
| WALLA WALLA | 17,623 | 19,646 | 20,040 | 1.3 | 2.48 | 11,992 | 12,952 | 0.9 | 37,845 | 45,629 | 864 | 18 |
| WHATCOM | 48,543 | 62,504 | 68,098 | 3.1 | 2.53 | 32,198 | 40,079 | 2.7 | 44,235 | 54,711 | 385 | 10 |
| WHITMAN | 13,546 | 13,989 | 13,700 | 0.4 | 2.31 | 7,549 | 7,318 | -0.4 | 34,112 | 41,482 | 1372 | 31 |
| YAKIMA | 65,985 | 77,832 | 81,656 | 2.0 | 2.82 | 48,107 | 55,411 | 1.7 | 35,455 | 41,682 | 1179 | 28 |
| WASHINGTON | | | | 2.4 | 2.51 | | | 2.1 | 46,940 | 55,472 | | |
| UNITED STATES | | | | 1.4 | 2.59 | | | 1.1 | 41,914 | 49,127 | | |

| COUNTY | 2000 Per Capita Income | 2000 HH Income Base | 2000 HOUSEHOLD INCOME DISTRIBUTION (%) | | | | | | 2000 AVERAGE DISPOSABLE INCOME BY AGE OF HOUSEHOLDER | | | | | |
|---|---|---|---|---|---|---|---|---|---|---|---|---|---|---|
| | | | Less than $15,000 | $15,000 to $24,999 | $25,000 to $49,999 | $50,000 to $99,999 | $100,000 to $149,999 | $150,000 or More | All Ages | <35 | 35-44 | 45-54 | 55-64 | 65+ |
| ADAMS | 14,848 | 5,207 | 16.2 | 16.0 | 39.1 | 23.4 | 4.2 | 1.1 | 34,167 | 26,570 | 38,423 | 42,421 | 38,679 | 25,801 |
| ASOTIN | 18,543 | 8,845 | 17.2 | 16.0 | 36.8 | 23.4 | 4.6 | 2.0 | 35,466 | 25,860 | 40,766 | 44,730 | 40,717 | 25,189 |
| BENTON | 24,935 | 52,783 | 9.6 | 8.0 | 28.7 | 39.6 | 11.1 | 3.0 | 48,228 | 38,775 | 52,787 | 60,072 | 54,156 | 32,432 |
| CHELAN | 20,102 | 24,361 | 15.6 | 15.4 | 32.8 | 28.2 | 5.6 | 2.4 | 38,649 | 31,172 | 42,120 | 46,703 | 44,257 | 26,216 |
| CLALLAM | 19,525 | 26,940 | 16.4 | 15.2 | 37.2 | 24.8 | 4.8 | 1.6 | 35,706 | 29,125 | 41,170 | 42,117 | 40,920 | 28,786 |
| CLARK | 24,870 | 131,684 | 8.0 | 8.6 | 32.2 | 37.4 | 10.4 | 3.5 | 48,313 | 40,865 | 51,968 | 57,633 | 51,066 | 33,095 |
| COLUMBIA | 17,537 | 1,650 | 17.9 | 18.6 | 36.9 | 21.4 | 3.8 | 1.4 | 33,335 | 28,827 | 36,854 | 38,505 | 44,837 | 22,846 |
| COWLITZ | 19,267 | 36,537 | 16.2 | 11.7 | 36.0 | 29.5 | 5.4 | 1.3 | 37,255 | 31,890 | 41,278 | 48,213 | 41,623 | 23,692 |
| DOUGLAS | 19,367 | 13,051 | 11.8 | 13.1 | 36.8 | 30.7 | 6.0 | 1.7 | 39,550 | 33,103 | 45,032 | 48,943 | 43,436 | 28,208 |
| FERRY | 14,579 | 2,622 | 18.8 | 12.4 | 39.4 | 26.7 | 2.4 | 0.2 | 32,156 | 31,533 | 34,818 | 35,373 | 39,837 | 19,487 |
| FRANKLIN | 16,765 | 15,239 | 16.4 | 14.3 | 32.8 | 28.3 | 6.1 | 2.2 | 38,420 | 30,201 | 43,531 | 46,225 | 43,022 | 30,057 |
| GARFIELD | 19,315 | 991 | 14.9 | 14.1 | 42.3 | 24.7 | 3.3 | 0.6 | 33,927 | 27,083 | 37,320 | 43,875 | 39,077 | 24,045 |
| GRANT | 16,591 | 26,959 | 15.2 | 17.2 | 36.1 | 25.8 | 4.4 | 1.3 | 35,372 | 29,363 | 39,548 | 44,101 | 38,728 | 25,286 |
| GRAYS HARBOR | 17,938 | 27,422 | 19.9 | 16.8 | 37.1 | 20.7 | 3.8 | 1.8 | 33,441 | 29,101 | 37,665 | 39,476 | 37,220 | 23,260 |
| ISLAND | 22,039 | 27,912 | 5.9 | 12.6 | 36.4 | 35.4 | 7.4 | 2.3 | 43,812 | 35,230 | 45,133 | 56,587 | 51,197 | 36,187 |
| JEFFERSON | 22,623 | 11,742 | 13.5 | 14.9 | 37.6 | 25.0 | 6.4 | 2.6 | 39,192 | 34,800 | 38,064 | 45,187 | 43,980 | 33,291 |
| KING | 33,190 | 702,161 | 7.2 | 8.4 | 29.5 | 35.6 | 11.9 | 7.4 | 55,940 | 43,466 | 56,215 | 65,131 | 60,992 | 37,965 |
| KITSAP | 22,527 | 87,874 | 8.1 | 10.4 | 35.0 | 35.9 | 8.0 | 2.7 | 45,130 | 36,026 | 47,577 | 55,541 | 49,117 | 33,059 |
| KITTITAS | 17,369 | 13,021 | 21.2 | 16.5 | 35.3 | 21.0 | 4.2 | 2.0 | 33,664 | 23,401 | 38,533 | 45,013 | 43,303 | 25,062 |
| KLICKITAT | 17,664 | 7,581 | 16.7 | 16.8 | 38.9 | 21.8 | 4.3 | 1.6 | 34,228 | 26,709 | 41,091 | 36,067 | 39,886 | 26,681 |
| LEWIS | 18,070 | 26,678 | 15.5 | 14.4 | 38.6 | 24.5 | 5.3 | 1.8 | 36,283 | 30,945 | 42,906 | 46,245 | 37,952 | 23,225 |
| LINCOLN | 19,995 | 4,096 | 13.1 | 14.4 | 38.5 | 26.8 | 5.7 | 1.6 | 37,284 | 30,975 | 40,319 | 46,622 | 44,364 | 28,113 |
| MASON | 19,865 | 19,672 | 12.0 | 13.0 | 38.8 | 28.4 | 5.9 | 1.9 | 38,913 | 34,197 | 42,387 | 49,408 | 42,843 | 27,339 |
| OKANOGAN | 17,364 | 14,948 | 19.8 | 20.3 | 36.1 | 18.9 | 3.4 | 1.6 | 31,913 | 27,100 | 35,619 | 37,886 | 36,262 | 21,524 |
| PACIFIC | 17,474 | 8,839 | 20.8 | 18.7 | 33.9 | 20.9 | 4.1 | 1.6 | 32,557 | 27,897 | 40,541 | 41,007 | 34,422 | 23,497 |
| PEND OREILLE | 16,715 | 4,695 | 16.5 | 17.9 | 37.6 | 23.2 | 3.8 | 1.0 | 33,302 | 29,547 | 37,678 | 39,626 | 33,608 | 24,687 |
| PIERCE | 21,268 | 259,923 | 10.8 | 11.3 | 33.9 | 33.9 | 7.8 | 2.3 | 42,909 | 35,924 | 45,762 | 53,337 | 48,157 | 30,456 |
| SAN JUAN | 36,224 | 5,748 | 10.5 | 9.2 | 35.5 | 26.0 | 10.1 | 8.7 | 54,740 | 38,909 | 45,447 | 56,168 | 52,679 | 50,196 |
| SKAGIT | 22,348 | 40,128 | 10.6 | 12.7 | 35.1 | 31.7 | 7.5 | 2.4 | 42,368 | 37,306 | 46,547 | 50,467 | 46,820 | 29,891 |
| SKAMANIA | 18,912 | 3,842 | 15.5 | 9.9 | 39.8 | 27.7 | 5.4 | 1.8 | 37,867 | 34,770 | 42,808 | 41,433 | 41,946 | 22,199 |
| SNOHOMISH | 25,485 | 230,727 | 6.4 | 7.4 | 31.2 | 41.2 | 10.8 | 3.1 | 49,567 | 43,853 | 51,815 | 59,013 | 53,673 | 31,742 |
| SPOKANE | 22,082 | 164,029 | 14.4 | 13.7 | 35.1 | 27.0 | 6.7 | 3.1 | 40,805 | 31,691 | 45,053 | 50,067 | 44,919 | 29,294 |
| STEVENS | 16,848 | 14,990 | 18.0 | 11.8 | 36.8 | 27.8 | 4.6 | 0.9 | 35,229 | 29,794 | 38,997 | 44,432 | 37,531 | 23,123 |
| THURSTON | 23,319 | 81,505 | 8.6 | 10.4 | 33.6 | 36.6 | 8.6 | 2.3 | 44,560 | 36,049 | 47,691 | 55,383 | 48,469 | 33,611 |
| WAHKIAKUM | 19,628 | 1,617 | 16.0 | 12.2 | 40.3 | 24.9 | 4.0 | 2.7 | 36,873 | 31,856 | 39,850 | 44,237 | 50,117 | 22,126 |
| WALLA WALLA | 19,085 | 19,646 | 16.1 | 13.7 | 35.3 | 26.6 | 6.0 | 2.4 | 38,076 | 28,992 | 42,579 | 47,716 | 43,043 | 30,581 |
| WHATCOM | 22,376 | 62,504 | 11.1 | 12.5 | 33.6 | 32.0 | 8.0 | 2.9 | 43,383 | 34,279 | 45,801 | 54,491 | 48,174 | 31,189 |
| WHITMAN | 17,196 | 13,987 | 21.6 | 15.0 | 30.7 | 25.9 | 5.1 | 1.8 | 35,372 | 22,611 | 42,019 | 51,517 | 52,672 | 32,935 |
| YAKIMA | 16,116 | 77,832 | 17.2 | 16.2 | 35.1 | 25.4 | 4.5 | 1.6 | 35,421 | 29,644 | 39,769 | 43,204 | 38,874 | 25,462 |
| WASHINGTON | 25,073 | | 10.2 | 10.7 | 32.6 | 33.5 | 9.0 | 4.0 | 46,762 | 37,920 | 49,676 | 56,367 | 50,973 | 31,996 |
| UNITED STATES | 22,162 | | 14.5 | 12.5 | 32.3 | 29.8 | 7.4 | 3.5 | 40,748 | 34,503 | 44,969 | 49,579 | 43,409 | 27,339 |

# SPENDING POTENTIAL INDEXES

| COUNTY | FINANCIAL SERVICES | | | | THE HOME | | | | | | ENTERTAINMENT | | | | | | PERSONAL | | | |
|---|---|---|---|---|---|---|---|---|---|---|---|---|---|---|---|---|---|---|---|---|
| | | | | | Home Improvements | | | Furnishings | | | | | | | | | | | | |
| | Auto Loan | Home Loan | Investments | Retirement Plans | Home Repair | Lawn & Garden | Remodeling | Appliances | Electronics | Furniture | Restaurants | Sporting Goods | Theater & Concerts | Toys & Hobbies | Travel | Video Rental | Apparel | Auto Aftermarket | Health Insurance | Pets & Supplies |
| ADAMS | 96 | 77 | 79 | 79 | 92 | 92 | 105 | 98 | 95 | 83 | 83 | 86 | 79 | 88 | 76 | 92 | 80 | 90 | 99 | 93 |
| ASOTIN | 98 | 82 | 85 | 88 | 98 | 95 | 109 | 99 | 97 | 91 | 88 | 89 | 85 | 91 | 81 | 93 | 88 | 92 | 98 | 93 |
| BENTON | 99 | 99 | 94 | 97 | 101 | 100 | 103 | 101 | 101 | 101 | 100 | 93 | 93 | 95 | 89 | 94 | 98 | 98 | 96 | 95 |
| CHELAN | 98 | 89 | 96 | 93 | 101 | 100 | 108 | 100 | 98 | 95 | 93 | 90 | 89 | 93 | 86 | 93 | 92 | 94 | 99 | 93 |
| CLALLAM | 99 | 83 | 97 | 91 | 101 | 102 | 110 | 101 | 96 | 91 | 90 | 90 | 87 | 93 | 85 | 92 | 88 | 92 | 103 | 93 |
| CLARK | 100 | 95 | 91 | 94 | 100 | 99 | 104 | 101 | 101 | 99 | 99 | 93 | 91 | 95 | 86 | 94 | 97 | 98 | 97 | 95 |
| COLUMBIA | 95 | 73 | 78 | 80 | 95 | 92 | 110 | 97 | 94 | 82 | 82 | 85 | 78 | 88 | 75 | 92 | 82 | 88 | 100 | 90 |
| COWLITZ | 98 | 88 | 92 | 90 | 101 | 98 | 106 | 100 | 97 | 95 | 92 | 90 | 88 | 92 | 85 | 93 | 92 | 94 | 98 | 93 |
| DOUGLAS | 99 | 91 | 90 | 92 | 98 | 97 | 107 | 100 | 100 | 96 | 95 | 92 | 89 | 94 | 84 | 94 | 94 | 96 | 97 | 95 |
| FERRY | 98 | 76 | 78 | 83 | 94 | 92 | 116 | 99 | 94 | 84 | 84 | 91 | 80 | 92 | 75 | 92 | 84 | 90 | 100 | 93 |
| FRANKLIN | 97 | 93 | 87 | 89 | 96 | 95 | 99 | 99 | 98 | 92 | 93 | 89 | 87 | 91 | 84 | 93 | 90 | 95 | 97 | 94 |
| GARFIELD | 98 | 63 | 69 | 79 | 92 | 92 | 112 | 97 | 92 | 73 | 76 | 89 | 73 | 89 | 70 | 92 | 78 | 86 | 103 | 91 |
| GRANT | 97 | 80 | 82 | 83 | 95 | 93 | 109 | 98 | 95 | 88 | 87 | 88 | 82 | 90 | 78 | 92 | 86 | 91 | 98 | 92 |
| GRAYS HARBOR | 96 | 75 | 82 | 82 | 98 | 95 | 110 | 98 | 94 | 86 | 83 | 87 | 81 | 89 | 78 | 91 | 83 | 89 | 99 | 91 |
| ISLAND | 99 | 95 | 98 | 98 | 102 | 106 | 106 | 103 | 100 | 97 | 99 | 92 | 91 | 94 | 90 | 94 | 97 | 98 | 102 | 96 |
| JEFFERSON | 100 | 84 | 97 | 94 | 102 | 105 | 114 | 103 | 97 | 92 | 91 | 91 | 88 | 94 | 86 | 93 | 92 | 94 | 104 | 95 |
| KING | 102 | 116 | 106 | 111 | 107 | 110 | 102 | 104 | 108 | 111 | 111 | 99 | 103 | 98 | 101 | 96 | 110 | 107 | 98 | 98 |
| KITSAP | 99 | 98 | 92 | 95 | 100 | 99 | 102 | 101 | 102 | 101 | 101 | 93 | 92 | 95 | 88 | 94 | 99 | 99 | 97 | 95 |
| KITTITAS | 96 | 80 | 83 | 85 | 95 | 92 | 108 | 94 | 92 | 81 | 83 | 85 | 78 | 88 | 77 | 89 | 83 | 88 | 98 | 91 |
| KLICKITAT | 97 | 71 | 76 | 80 | 95 | 92 | 113 | 98 | 94 | 83 | 81 | 88 | 78 | 90 | 74 | 92 | 82 | 88 | 100 | 92 |
| LEWIS | 98 | 76 | 81 | 83 | 96 | 93 | 113 | 99 | 96 | 86 | 85 | 89 | 81 | 91 | 76 | 93 | 85 | 90 | 99 | 92 |
| LINCOLN | 99 | 65 | 71 | 81 | 92 | 92 | 115 | 98 | 93 | 75 | 78 | 90 | 75 | 90 | 70 | 93 | 80 | 87 | 104 | 92 |
| MASON | 100 | 79 | 88 | 89 | 99 | 99 | 119 | 102 | 95 | 87 | 87 | 92 | 84 | 94 | 81 | 93 | 88 | 92 | 103 | 95 |
| OKANOGAN | 97 | 71 | 76 | 80 | 94 | 92 | 113 | 98 | 94 | 82 | 81 | 87 | 78 | 89 | 73 | 92 | 82 | 88 | 100 | 91 |
| PACIFIC | 98 | 74 | 86 | 83 | 98 | 96 | 114 | 100 | 94 | 83 | 83 | 89 | 81 | 91 | 78 | 92 | 83 | 89 | 102 | 92 |
| PEND OREILLE | 99 | 70 | 74 | 83 | 94 | 93 | 121 | 100 | 95 | 80 | 81 | 91 | 78 | 92 | 73 | 93 | 82 | 89 | 102 | 93 |
| PIERCE | 99 | 99 | 96 | 96 | 102 | 101 | 102 | 100 | 101 | 101 | 100 | 92 | 93 | 94 | 90 | 94 | 98 | 98 | 97 | 94 |
| SAN JUAN | 106 | 97 | 111 | 111 | 109 | 118 | 115 | 109 | 102 | 103 | 104 | 98 | 99 | 100 | 99 | 95 | 105 | 101 | 110 | 100 |
| SKAGIT | 99 | 87 | 94 | 92 | 101 | 100 | 110 | 101 | 98 | 94 | 93 | 91 | 88 | 94 | 85 | 93 | 92 | 94 | 100 | 94 |
| SKAMANIA | 100 | 78 | 81 | 85 | 96 | 93 | 117 | 100 | 97 | 89 | 87 | 91 | 83 | 94 | 76 | 93 | 88 | 91 | 99 | 95 |
| SNOHOMISH | 101 | 103 | 93 | 99 | 101 | 101 | 102 | 102 | 104 | 105 | 105 | 95 | 95 | 96 | 90 | 95 | 103 | 101 | 96 | 96 |
| SPOKANE | 98 | 96 | 97 | 95 | 102 | 100 | 101 | 99 | 99 | 98 | 96 | 90 | 91 | 93 | 89 | 93 | 95 | 96 | 97 | 93 |
| STEVENS | 99 | 76 | 78 | 84 | 95 | 93 | 114 | 100 | 97 | 86 | 85 | 90 | 82 | 92 | 75 | 93 | 86 | 91 | 100 | 94 |
| THURSTON | 99 | 97 | 94 | 95 | 100 | 100 | 104 | 101 | 101 | 101 | 100 | 93 | 92 | 95 | 88 | 94 | 98 | 98 | 97 | 95 |
| WAHKIAKUM | 98 | 70 | 77 | 81 | 94 | 93 | 115 | 98 | 94 | 80 | 81 | 89 | 78 | 91 | 73 | 93 | 82 | 88 | 102 | 92 |
| WALLA WALLA | 97 | 91 | 98 | 93 | 102 | 100 | 103 | 99 | 97 | 95 | 93 | 88 | 88 | 91 | 87 | 92 | 91 | 94 | 99 | 92 |
| WHATCOM | 99 | 92 | 91 | 94 | 99 | 97 | 107 | 99 | 98 | 94 | 94 | 91 | 88 | 93 | 85 | 93 | 94 | 95 | 98 | 94 |
| WHITMAN | 95 | 88 | 91 | 91 | 97 | 94 | 103 | 93 | 93 | 84 | 86 | 85 | 81 | 88 | 81 | 89 | 87 | 91 | 97 | 91 |
| YAKIMA | 97 | 88 | 91 | 88 | 99 | 97 | 104 | 99 | 97 | 93 | 91 | 88 | 86 | 91 | 84 | 92 | 89 | 93 | 98 | 93 |
| WASHINGTON | 100 | 101 | 98 | 100 | 102 | 103 | 104 | 101 | 102 | 102 | 101 | 94 | 95 | 95 | 92 | 94 | 100 | 100 | 98 | 95 |
| UNITED STATES | 100 | 100 | 100 | 100 | 100 | 100 | 100 | 100 | 100 | 100 | 100 | 100 | 100 | 100 | 100 | 100 | 100 | 100 | 100 | 100 |

| COUNTY | FIPS Code | MSA Code | DMA Code | POPULATION 1990 | 2000 | 2005 | 1990-2000 ANNUAL CHANGE % Rate | State Rank | RACE (%) White 1990 | White 2000 | Black 1990 | Black 2000 | Asian/Pacific 1990 | Asian/Pacific 2000 |
|---|---|---|---|---|---|---|---|---|---|---|---|---|---|---|
| BARBOUR | 001 | 0000 | 598 | 15,699 | 15,935 | 15,699 | 0.1 | 25 | 97.7 | 97.7 | 0.9 | 0.9 | 0.2 | 0.3 |
| BERKELEY | 003 | 8840 | 511 | 59,253 | 74,587 | 83,273 | 2.3 | 1 | 95.4 | 95.2 | 3.7 | 3.8 | 0.5 | 0.6 |
| BOONE | 005 | 0000 | 564 | 25,870 | 26,326 | 26,443 | 0.2 | 22 | 98.9 | 98.8 | 0.8 | 0.9 | 0.1 | 0.1 |
| BRAXTON | 007 | 0000 | 564 | 12,998 | 13,393 | 13,305 | 0.3 | 14 | 99.3 | 99.2 | 0.4 | 0.4 | 0.2 | 0.2 |
| BROOKE | 009 | 8080 | 554 | 26,992 | 25,744 | 24,998 | -0.5 | 44 | 98.8 | 98.6 | 0.7 | 0.9 | 0.2 | 0.2 |
| CABELL | 011 | 3400 | 564 | 96,827 | 92,883 | 89,571 | -0.4 | 42 | 95.1 | 94.9 | 4.1 | 4.3 | 0.6 | 0.7 |
| CALHOUN | 013 | 0000 | 564 | 7,885 | 7,996 | 8,089 | 0.1 | 25 | 99.4 | 99.2 | 0.0 | 0.1 | 0.4 | 0.4 |
| CLAY | 015 | 0000 | 564 | 9,983 | 10,692 | 11,085 | 0.7 | 10 | 99.8 | 99.9 | 0.0 | 0.0 | 0.1 | 0.1 |
| DODDRIDGE | 017 | 0000 | 598 | 6,994 | 7,486 | 7,625 | 0.7 | 10 | 99.4 | 99.4 | 0.0 | 0.0 | 0.1 | 0.2 |
| FAYETTE | 019 | 0000 | 559 | 47,952 | 46,447 | 44,760 | -0.3 | 40 | 93.2 | 92.0 | 6.3 | 7.4 | 0.3 | 0.4 |
| GILMER | 021 | 0000 | 598 | 7,669 | 7,134 | 7,077 | -0.7 | 49 | 99.0 | 98.9 | 0.4 | 0.5 | 0.4 | 0.5 |
| GRANT | 023 | 0000 | 511 | 10,428 | 11,157 | 11,263 | 0.7 | 10 | 98.5 | 98.4 | 1.0 | 1.1 | 0.2 | 0.3 |
| GREENBRIER | 025 | 0000 | 559 | 34,693 | 35,250 | 34,949 | 0.2 | 22 | 96.0 | 95.7 | 3.7 | 3.9 | 0.2 | 0.2 |
| HAMPSHIRE | 027 | 0000 | 511 | 16,498 | 19,679 | 20,993 | 1.7 | 4 | 98.9 | 98.9 | 0.7 | 0.6 | 0.1 | 0.1 |
| HANCOCK | 029 | 8080 | 554 | 35,233 | 33,479 | 32,203 | -0.5 | 44 | 96.9 | 96.8 | 2.6 | 2.6 | 0.3 | 0.3 |
| HARDY | 031 | 0000 | 511 | 10,977 | 12,086 | 12,617 | 0.9 | 8 | 97.9 | 97.6 | 1.9 | 2.1 | 0.0 | 0.0 |
| HARRISON | 033 | 0000 | 598 | 69,371 | 70,010 | 68,461 | 0.1 | 25 | 98.1 | 97.7 | 1.4 | 1.7 | 0.3 | 0.4 |
| JACKSON | 035 | 0000 | 564 | 25,938 | 28,613 | 30,206 | 1.0 | 7 | 99.5 | 99.5 | 0.1 | 0.1 | 0.2 | 0.3 |
| JEFFERSON | 037 | 8840 | 511 | 35,926 | 42,953 | 46,374 | 1.8 | 3 | 91.7 | 91.3 | 7.4 | 7.7 | 0.4 | 0.5 |
| KANAWHA | 039 | 1480 | 564 | 207,619 | 197,481 | 188,685 | -0.5 | 44 | 92.5 | 92.2 | 6.6 | 6.8 | 0.6 | 0.8 |
| LEWIS | 041 | 0000 | 598 | 17,223 | 17,414 | 17,167 | 0.1 | 25 | 99.2 | 99.3 | 0.3 | 0.1 | 0.3 | 0.3 |
| LINCOLN | 043 | 0000 | 564 | 21,382 | 22,447 | 22,952 | 0.5 | 13 | 99.8 | 99.8 | 0.0 | 0.0 | 0.1 | 0.1 |
| LOGAN | 045 | 0000 | 564 | 43,032 | 39,604 | 36,833 | -0.8 | 51 | 96.2 | 96.0 | 3.2 | 3.2 | 0.4 | 0.5 |
| MCDOWELL | 047 | 0000 | 559 | 35,233 | 28,652 | 25,499 | -2.0 | 55 | 86.3 | 86.1 | 13.5 | 13.7 | 0.1 | 0.1 |
| MARION | 049 | 0000 | 598 | 57,249 | 55,497 | 53,339 | -0.3 | 40 | 96.2 | 95.9 | 3.2 | 3.5 | 0.3 | 0.3 |
| MARSHALL | 051 | 9000 | 554 | 37,356 | 35,651 | 34,340 | -0.5 | 44 | 99.1 | 99.0 | 0.5 | 0.5 | 0.2 | 0.3 |
| MASON | 053 | 0000 | 564 | 25,178 | 26,096 | 26,493 | 0.3 | 14 | 99.1 | 99.0 | 0.4 | 0.4 | 0.3 | 0.4 |
| MERCER | 055 | 0000 | 559 | 64,980 | 63,902 | 62,766 | -0.2 | 37 | 93.0 | 92.9 | 6.4 | 6.5 | 0.5 | 0.5 |
| MINERAL | 057 | 1900 | 511 | 26,697 | 27,078 | 27,100 | 0.1 | 25 | 96.9 | 96.7 | 2.8 | 2.9 | 0.3 | 0.3 |
| MINGO | 059 | 0000 | 564 | 33,739 | 31,044 | 28,952 | -0.8 | 51 | 97.2 | 96.9 | 2.4 | 2.7 | 0.2 | 0.3 |
| MONONGALIA | 061 | 0000 | 508 | 75,509 | 76,662 | 74,969 | 0.1 | 25 | 95.0 | 94.8 | 2.4 | 2.5 | 2.1 | 2.3 |
| MONROE | 063 | 0000 | 559 | 12,406 | 13,397 | 13,875 | 0.8 | 9 | 98.4 | 98.4 | 1.3 | 1.3 | 0.1 | 0.1 |
| MORGAN | 065 | 0000 | 511 | 12,128 | 14,078 | 14,981 | 1.5 | 5 | 98.8 | 98.8 | 0.8 | 0.8 | 0.1 | 0.2 |
| NICHOLAS | 067 | 0000 | 564 | 26,775 | 27,516 | 27,486 | 0.3 | 14 | 99.6 | 99.6 | 0.0 | 0.0 | 0.2 | 0.3 |
| OHIO | 069 | 9000 | 554 | 50,871 | 47,271 | 45,052 | -0.7 | 49 | 95.9 | 95.6 | 3.3 | 3.5 | 0.6 | 0.8 |
| PENDLETON | 071 | 0000 | 569 | 8,054 | 8,033 | 7,999 | 0.0 | 33 | 97.7 | 97.6 | 2.1 | 2.2 | 0.2 | 0.1 |
| PLEASANTS | 073 | 0000 | 597 | 7,546 | 7,542 | 7,633 | 0.0 | 33 | 99.6 | 99.7 | 0.2 | 0.1 | 0.0 | 0.0 |
| POCAHONTAS | 075 | 0000 | 573 | 9,008 | 9,071 | 9,086 | 0.1 | 25 | 99.0 | 97.9 | 0.8 | 1.8 | 0.0 | 0.1 |
| PRESTON | 077 | 0000 | 508 | 29,037 | 29,825 | 29,880 | 0.3 | 14 | 99.5 | 99.4 | 0.3 | 0.3 | 0.1 | 0.1 |
| PUTNAM | 079 | 1480 | 564 | 42,835 | 52,744 | 56,784 | 2.1 | 2 | 99.2 | 99.2 | 0.3 | 0.3 | 0.3 | 0.4 |
| RALEIGH | 081 | 0000 | 559 | 76,819 | 79,240 | 79,173 | 0.3 | 14 | 91.6 | 91.2 | 7.7 | 7.9 | 0.5 | 0.7 |
| RANDOLPH | 083 | 0000 | 598 | 27,803 | 28,633 | 28,537 | 0.3 | 14 | 98.7 | 98.4 | 0.8 | 1.0 | 0.3 | 0.3 |
| RITCHIE | 085 | 0000 | 598 | 10,233 | 10,569 | 11,011 | 0.3 | 14 | 99.8 | 99.8 | 0.1 | 0.1 | 0.1 | 0.1 |
| ROANE | 087 | 0000 | 564 | 15,120 | 15,449 | 15,653 | 0.2 | 22 | 99.6 | 99.5 | 0.0 | 0.0 | 0.2 | 0.2 |
| SUMMERS | 089 | 0000 | 559 | 14,204 | 13,854 | 13,787 | -0.2 | 37 | 93.9 | 96.8 | 5.1 | 2.6 | 0.2 | 0.2 |
| TAYLOR | 091 | 0000 | 598 | 15,144 | 15,376 | 15,424 | 0.1 | 25 | 99.0 | 98.6 | 0.6 | 1.0 | 0.2 | 0.2 |
| TUCKER | 093 | 0000 | 598 | 7,728 | 7,438 | 7,073 | -0.4 | 42 | 99.7 | 99.2 | 0.1 | 0.5 | 0.2 | 0.2 |
| TYLER | 095 | 0000 | 554 | 9,796 | 9,631 | 9,212 | -0.2 | 37 | 99.6 | 99.5 | 0.0 | 0.0 | 0.1 | 0.2 |
| UPSHUR | 097 | 0000 | 598 | 22,867 | 23,526 | 23,433 | 0.3 | 14 | 99.0 | 98.9 | 0.5 | 0.5 | 0.2 | 0.3 |
| WAYNE | 099 | 3400 | 564 | 41,636 | 41,749 | 41,200 | 0.0 | 33 | 99.6 | 99.6 | 0.0 | 0.1 | 0.1 | 0.1 |
| WEBSTER | 101 | 0000 | 598 | 10,729 | 9,907 | 9,286 | -0.8 | 51 | 99.8 | 99.7 | 0.0 | 0.0 | 0.1 | 0.1 |
| WETZEL | 103 | 0000 | 554 | 19,258 | 18,100 | 17,510 | -0.6 | 48 | 99.6 | 99.5 | 0.1 | 0.1 | 0.2 | 0.3 |
| WIRT | 105 | 0000 | 564 | 5,192 | 5,814 | 6,087 | 1.1 | 6 | 99.8 | 99.8 | 0.1 | 0.1 | 0.1 | 0.1 |
| WOOD | 107 | 6020 | 597 | 86,915 | 85,992 | 84,287 | -0.1 | 36 | 98.5 | 98.3 | 0.9 | 1.0 | 0.4 | 0.5 |
| WYOMING | 109 | 0000 | 559 | 28,990 | 26,679 | 25,191 | -0.8 | 51 | 98.9 | 98.9 | 0.8 | 0.8 | 0.1 | 0.1 |
| WEST VIRGINIA | | | | | | | 0.1 | | 96.2 | 96.1 | 3.1 | 3.2 | 0.4 | 0.5 |
| UNITED STATES | | | | | | | 1.0 | | 80.3 | 77.9 | 12.1 | 12.4 | 2.9 | 3.9 |

# POPULATION COMPOSITION

| COUNTY | % HISPANIC ORIGIN | | 2000 AGE DISTRIBUTION (%) | | | | | | | | | | MEDIAN AGE | | 2000 Males/ Females (×100) |
|---|---|---|---|---|---|---|---|---|---|---|---|---|---|---|---|
| | 1990 | 2000 | 0-4 | 5-9 | 10-14 | 15-19 | 20-24 | 25-44 | 45-64 | 65-84 | 85+ | 18+ | 1990 | 2000 | |
| BARBOUR | 0.6 | 1.1 | 5.6 | 6.2 | 6.5 | 7.8 | 7.3 | 26.1 | 25.4 | 12.9 | 2.2 | 77.3 | 34.9 | 38.5 | 93.6 |
| BERKELEY | 0.7 | 1.1 | 6.8 | 6.8 | 6.7 | 6.4 | 7.0 | 29.8 | 24.7 | 10.6 | 1.1 | 75.8 | 33.3 | 36.6 | 98.0 |
| BOONE | 0.2 | 0.6 | 5.2 | 5.9 | 6.8 | 7.2 | 7.0 | 28.0 | 27.0 | 11.7 | 1.3 | 77.5 | 34.5 | 38.9 | 95.2 |
| BRAXTON | 0.3 | 0.7 | 6.0 | 6.7 | 6.9 | 6.8 | 6.1 | 25.7 | 25.8 | 13.9 | 2.3 | 76.0 | 36.4 | 39.6 | 96.9 |
| BROOKE | 0.3 | 0.8 | 4.5 | 5.1 | 5.6 | 7.2 | 7.8 | 25.4 | 27.1 | 15.4 | 1.8 | 80.8 | 37.3 | 41.3 | 91.9 |
| CABELL | 0.5 | 0.9 | 5.0 | 5.3 | 5.6 | 7.4 | 8.8 | 26.2 | 25.3 | 14.2 | 2.1 | 80.6 | 35.8 | 39.3 | 88.1 |
| CALHOUN | 0.2 | 0.6 | 6.1 | 6.6 | 6.7 | 7.7 | 6.6 | 25.3 | 26.2 | 12.8 | 2.0 | 75.5 | 35.6 | 38.9 | 97.9 |
| CLAY | 0.1 | 0.6 | 6.7 | 7.2 | 7.4 | 7.8 | 7.3 | 26.5 | 24.4 | 11.3 | 1.4 | 73.8 | 32.9 | 35.9 | 96.1 |
| DODDRIDGE | 0.2 | 0.6 | 5.7 | 6.6 | 6.7 | 7.3 | 6.3 | 26.7 | 25.9 | 13.0 | 1.7 | 76.4 | 35.4 | 39.1 | 98.5 |
| FAYETTE | 0.5 | 1.4 | 4.9 | 5.7 | 6.3 | 7.3 | 7.1 | 25.9 | 25.8 | 14.8 | 2.1 | 78.7 | 36.2 | 40.4 | 91.9 |
| GILMER | 0.3 | 0.7 | 5.5 | 6.0 | 6.0 | 9.0 | 9.3 | 24.9 | 23.9 | 13.0 | 2.4 | 78.9 | 33.2 | 36.9 | 97.7 |
| GRANT | 0.3 | 0.7 | 5.5 | 6.0 | 6.6 | 6.3 | 6.0 | 27.1 | 27.5 | 12.8 | 2.2 | 78.0 | 35.7 | 40.1 | 97.1 |
| GREENBRIER | 0.4 | 0.9 | 5.1 | 5.7 | 6.0 | 6.7 | 6.0 | 26.1 | 27.0 | 15.0 | 2.4 | 79.2 | 37.3 | 41.6 | 92.6 |
| HAMPSHIRE | 0.6 | 1.0 | 6.4 | 6.6 | 6.9 | 6.8 | 6.6 | 26.6 | 26.1 | 12.7 | 1.4 | 76.1 | 34.5 | 38.4 | 97.5 |
| HANCOCK | 0.6 | 1.0 | 4.9 | 5.3 | 5.6 | 6.2 | 6.2 | 26.9 | 27.4 | 15.7 | 1.8 | 80.3 | 37.7 | 41.9 | 91.5 |
| HARDY | 0.5 | 0.9 | 5.9 | 6.0 | 6.3 | 6.1 | 6.3 | 27.5 | 26.8 | 13.4 | 1.6 | 78.0 | 36.1 | 40.0 | 96.9 |
| HARRISON | 1.2 | 1.7 | 5.5 | 6.0 | 6.4 | 7.2 | 6.3 | 26.2 | 25.4 | 14.8 | 2.3 | 77.7 | 36.9 | 40.1 | 91.2 |
| JACKSON | 0.3 | 0.7 | 5.9 | 6.3 | 6.5 | 6.6 | 6.2 | 25.7 | 28.0 | 13.1 | 1.8 | 77.3 | 35.7 | 40.4 | 95.1 |
| JEFFERSON | 1.2 | 1.8 | 6.4 | 6.9 | 7.2 | 7.8 | 7.2 | 28.5 | 24.4 | 10.5 | 1.1 | 75.4 | 32.7 | 36.0 | 95.8 |
| KANAWHA | 0.4 | 0.9 | 5.3 | 5.8 | 6.3 | 6.4 | 6.4 | 27.0 | 26.4 | 14.5 | 1.9 | 78.8 | 36.7 | 40.7 | 90.2 |
| LEWIS | 0.4 | 0.8 | 5.4 | 5.8 | 6.2 | 6.5 | 6.5 | 27.2 | 26.8 | 13.4 | 2.2 | 78.5 | 36.5 | 40.3 | 94.6 |
| LINCOLN | 0.2 | 0.6 | 5.7 | 6.4 | 6.9 | 7.5 | 7.1 | 27.7 | 26.1 | 11.2 | 1.3 | 76.3 | 33.4 | 37.6 | 95.4 |
| LOGAN | 0.7 | 1.2 | 5.2 | 6.0 | 7.0 | 7.4 | 7.3 | 27.9 | 25.7 | 12.2 | 1.3 | 77.2 | 33.9 | 38.2 | 92.6 |
| MCDOWELL | 0.5 | 0.9 | 6.0 | 6.3 | 6.5 | 7.3 | 7.9 | 26.4 | 24.6 | 13.3 | 1.6 | 76.3 | 34.0 | 37.9 | 88.9 |
| MARION | 0.5 | 1.0 | 5.1 | 5.4 | 5.7 | 6.8 | 6.7 | 26.8 | 25.9 | 15.3 | 2.4 | 80.2 | 37.3 | 40.8 | 88.9 |
| MARSHALL | 0.6 | 1.1 | 5.4 | 5.8 | 6.1 | 6.6 | 6.5 | 27.1 | 26.7 | 14.1 | 1.8 | 78.6 | 36.6 | 40.5 | 94.9 |
| MASON | 0.2 | 0.6 | 5.4 | 5.9 | 6.1 | 7.0 | 6.8 | 26.3 | 27.3 | 13.6 | 1.6 | 78.1 | 35.8 | 40.6 | 95.1 |
| MERCER | 0.4 | 0.8 | 5.0 | 5.5 | 5.8 | 7.1 | 7.2 | 26.6 | 26.0 | 14.6 | 2.1 | 79.6 | 36.4 | 40.1 | 90.0 |
| MINERAL | 0.4 | 0.8 | 5.8 | 6.1 | 6.4 | 7.6 | 6.8 | 26.3 | 26.7 | 12.7 | 1.6 | 77.7 | 35.3 | 39.1 | 94.6 |
| MINGO | 0.4 | 0.8 | 6.2 | 7.0 | 7.5 | 8.0 | 7.9 | 28.7 | 23.8 | 9.8 | 1.1 | 74.2 | 31.1 | 34.8 | 95.1 |
| MONONGALIA | 0.8 | 1.4 | 5.0 | 4.9 | 4.9 | 11.0 | 15.0 | 28.1 | 20.3 | 9.5 | 1.3 | 82.1 | 29.2 | 31.4 | 98.2 |
| MONROE | 0.3 | 0.8 | 5.6 | 6.1 | 6.5 | 6.5 | 5.9 | 25.4 | 26.9 | 15.2 | 2.0 | 77.9 | 37.5 | 40.9 | 94.1 |
| MORGAN | 0.4 | 0.8 | 5.2 | 5.5 | 5.9 | 5.6 | 6.0 | 26.0 | 27.9 | 16.1 | 2.0 | 80.1 | 38.0 | 42.4 | 93.7 |
| NICHOLAS | 0.2 | 0.6 | 5.9 | 6.4 | 6.7 | 7.0 | 6.8 | 26.5 | 26.2 | 12.7 | 1.6 | 76.4 | 34.7 | 38.8 | 95.6 |
| OHIO | 0.3 | 0.7 | 5.3 | 5.5 | 5.6 | 7.3 | 7.5 | 24.9 | 25.4 | 15.9 | 2.5 | 79.9 | 37.7 | 40.9 | 87.0 |
| PENDLETON | 0.3 | 0.7 | 6.1 | 6.2 | 6.4 | 6.0 | 6.4 | 26.2 | 25.7 | 14.6 | 2.3 | 77.8 | 36.6 | 40.3 | 98.3 |
| PLEASANTS | 0.1 | 0.5 | 5.4 | 5.8 | 6.1 | 7.2 | 6.1 | 29.0 | 25.7 | 12.7 | 1.9 | 78.0 | 34.9 | 39.2 | 96.3 |
| POCAHONTAS | 0.3 | 1.2 | 5.3 | 5.9 | 6.4 | 5.9 | 5.6 | 25.2 | 27.8 | 15.2 | 2.7 | 78.7 | 38.5 | 42.3 | 100.7 |
| PRESTON | 0.3 | 0.7 | 6.0 | 6.4 | 6.8 | 7.3 | 6.6 | 26.9 | 26.0 | 12.4 | 1.7 | 76.2 | 34.5 | 38.6 | 98.3 |
| PUTNAM | 0.3 | 0.8 | 6.1 | 6.6 | 6.8 | 6.6 | 6.0 | 29.5 | 26.8 | 10.3 | 1.2 | 76.2 | 34.2 | 38.2 | 95.4 |
| RALEIGH | 0.4 | 0.9 | 5.2 | 5.9 | 6.6 | 7.0 | 6.5 | 26.9 | 26.6 | 13.5 | 1.8 | 77.7 | 36.1 | 40.2 | 90.0 |
| RANDOLPH | 0.5 | 0.9 | 5.4 | 5.9 | 6.3 | 7.4 | 7.0 | 26.9 | 26.2 | 12.8 | 2.2 | 78.2 | 35.4 | 39.3 | 97.8 |
| RITCHIE | 0.1 | 0.5 | 5.4 | 6.1 | 6.3 | 6.7 | 6.5 | 27.1 | 26.9 | 12.7 | 2.3 | 78.1 | 36.4 | 40.1 | 94.2 |
| ROANE | 0.2 | 0.6 | 5.2 | 6.2 | 6.8 | 7.1 | 6.6 | 26.1 | 27.6 | 12.5 | 1.9 | 77.2 | 36.0 | 40.0 | 96.9 |
| SUMMERS | 1.5 | 1.0 | 5.0 | 5.6 | 6.0 | 6.6 | 6.7 | 26.0 | 25.8 | 15.9 | 2.3 | 79.2 | 37.3 | 41.0 | 88.4 |
| TAYLOR | 0.4 | 0.8 | 6.0 | 6.5 | 6.8 | 7.0 | 6.0 | 26.8 | 25.0 | 13.8 | 2.1 | 76.5 | 35.7 | 39.1 | 94.2 |
| TUCKER | 0.2 | 0.6 | 5.2 | 5.6 | 6.0 | 7.1 | 5.7 | 25.8 | 28.1 | 14.0 | 2.5 | 78.8 | 37.2 | 41.3 | 93.7 |
| TYLER | 0.2 | 0.6 | 5.7 | 6.1 | 6.4 | 6.7 | 6.2 | 26.0 | 27.5 | 13.6 | 1.8 | 77.5 | 36.3 | 40.5 | 94.7 |
| UPSHUR | 0.5 | 0.9 | 5.8 | 6.1 | 6.4 | 8.9 | 9.1 | 25.5 | 24.8 | 11.6 | 2.0 | 77.4 | 33.4 | 36.7 | 96.0 |
| WAYNE | 0.3 | 0.7 | 5.4 | 5.8 | 6.2 | 6.8 | 6.5 | 27.6 | 27.0 | 13.1 | 1.5 | 78.5 | 35.3 | 39.7 | 93.0 |
| WEBSTER | 0.3 | 0.7 | 6.0 | 6.4 | 6.8 | 7.0 | 6.7 | 26.9 | 25.5 | 12.8 | 1.9 | 76.4 | 34.8 | 38.6 | 93.9 |
| WETZEL | 0.2 | 0.6 | 5.7 | 6.2 | 6.3 | 7.0 | 6.3 | 25.7 | 27.6 | 13.3 | 1.9 | 77.5 | 36.1 | 40.3 | 92.7 |
| WIRT | 0.1 | 0.4 | 6.3 | 6.7 | 6.7 | 7.1 | 6.2 | 27.7 | 26.6 | 11.4 | 1.4 | 75.6 | 34.5 | 38.2 | 96.8 |
| WOOD | 0.3 | 0.7 | 5.7 | 6.0 | 6.2 | 6.5 | 6.4 | 27.2 | 27.1 | 13.0 | 2.0 | 78.1 | 36.0 | 40.1 | 90.4 |
| WYOMING | 0.3 | 0.7 | 5.3 | 6.1 | 7.1 | 7.5 | 6.9 | 27.9 | 26.5 | 11.7 | 1.0 | 76.7 | 33.6 | 38.4 | 94.5 |
| WEST VIRGINIA | 0.5 | 0.9 | 5.5 | 5.9 | 6.3 | 7.1 | 7.2 | 27.0 | 25.9 | 13.3 | 1.8 | 78.2 | 35.4 | 39.2 | 92.9 |
| UNITED STATES | 9.0 | 11.8 | 6.9 | 7.2 | 7.2 | 7.2 | 6.7 | 29.9 | 22.2 | 11.1 | 1.6 | 74.6 | 32.9 | 35.7 | 95.6 |

| COUNTY | HOUSEHOLDS 1990 | HOUSEHOLDS 2000 | HOUSEHOLDS 2005 | % Annual Rate 1990-2000 | 2000 Average HH Size | FAMILIES 1990 | FAMILIES 2000 | % Annual Rate 1990-2000 | MEDIAN HOUSEHOLD INCOME 2000 | 2005 | 2000 National Rank | 2000 State Rank |
|---|---|---|---|---|---|---|---|---|---|---|---|---|
| BARBOUR | 5,835 | 6,311 | 6,407 | 1.0 | 2.46 | 4,293 | 4,497 | 0.6 | 20,531 | 24,544 | 3083 | 49 |
| BERKELEY | 22,350 | 29,126 | 32,972 | 3.3 | 2.53 | 16,220 | 20,550 | 2.9 | 35,916 | 41,792 | 1112 | 3 |
| BOONE | 9,656 | 10,156 | 10,364 | 0.6 | 2.59 | 7,428 | 7,552 | 0.2 | 23,321 | 26,136 | 2953 | 38 |
| BRAXTON | 4,950 | 5,193 | 5,242 | 0.6 | 2.52 | 3,679 | 3,727 | 0.2 | 22,122 | 24,759 | 3020 | 44 |
| BROOKE | 10,131 | 10,120 | 10,037 | 0.0 | 2.45 | 7,560 | 7,306 | -0.4 | 33,056 | 36,559 | 1529 | 5 |
| CABELL | 39,146 | 39,057 | 38,406 | 0.0 | 2.29 | 26,252 | 25,198 | -0.5 | 27,722 | 30,451 | 2472 | 17 |
| CALHOUN | 2,978 | 3,102 | 3,178 | 0.5 | 2.57 | 2,238 | 2,248 | 0.1 | 19,172 | 21,136 | 3119 | 52 |
| CLAY | 3,627 | 4,043 | 4,274 | 1.3 | 2.64 | 2,793 | 3,006 | 0.9 | 19,088 | 21,468 | 3120 | 53 |
| DODDRIDGE | 2,623 | 3,016 | 3,180 | 1.7 | 2.48 | 1,956 | 2,173 | 1.3 | 24,725 | 31,748 | 2836 | 31 |
| FAYETTE | 18,292 | 18,792 | 18,561 | 0.3 | 2.42 | 13,189 | 13,084 | -0.1 | 22,200 | 24,819 | 3017 | 43 |
| GILMER | 2,717 | 2,648 | 2,668 | -0.3 | 2.53 | 1,975 | 1,867 | -0.7 | 19,365 | 21,485 | 3110 | 51 |
| GRANT | 3,925 | 4,368 | 4,487 | 1.3 | 2.52 | 2,985 | 3,199 | 0.8 | 29,697 | 35,974 | 2201 | 13 |
| GREENBRIER | 13,775 | 14,641 | 14,833 | 0.7 | 2.37 | 9,896 | 10,112 | 0.3 | 25,839 | 28,659 | 2731 | 26 |
| HAMPSHIRE | 6,182 | 7,558 | 8,159 | 2.5 | 2.57 | 4,608 | 5,445 | 2.0 | 27,992 | 34,827 | 2443 | 15 |
| HANCOCK | 13,781 | 13,742 | 13,564 | 0.0 | 2.42 | 10,219 | 9,800 | -0.5 | 31,159 | 34,738 | 1900 | 7 |
| HARDY | 4,286 | 4,863 | 5,152 | 1.5 | 2.47 | 3,185 | 3,486 | 1.1 | 30,179 | 37,074 | 2110 | 10 |
| HARRISON | 27,009 | 28,226 | 28,164 | 0.5 | 2.42 | 19,415 | 19,538 | 0.1 | 27,435 | 31,551 | 2517 | 19 |
| JACKSON | 9,645 | 11,096 | 11,951 | 1.7 | 2.55 | 7,634 | 8,516 | 1.3 | 30,449 | 34,122 | 2046 | 8 |
| JEFFERSON | 12,914 | 15,673 | 17,145 | 2.4 | 2.62 | 9,487 | 11,223 | 2.1 | 39,576 | 45,714 | 704 | 1 |
| KANAWHA | 84,713 | 85,157 | 83,578 | 0.1 | 2.28 | 58,957 | 56,968 | -0.4 | 30,405 | 32,935 | 2057 | 9 |
| LEWIS | 6,615 | 7,050 | 7,094 | 0.8 | 2.43 | 4,736 | 4,839 | 0.3 | 23,469 | 26,627 | 2942 | 36 |
| LINCOLN | 7,647 | 8,299 | 8,619 | 1.0 | 2.70 | 6,100 | 6,425 | 0.6 | 21,044 | 23,355 | 3066 | 48 |
| LOGAN | 15,425 | 15,257 | 14,687 | -0.1 | 2.58 | 12,087 | 11,598 | -0.5 | 23,081 | 25,629 | 2966 | 41 |
| MCDOWELL | 12,880 | 11,220 | 10,323 | -1.7 | 2.54 | 9,773 | 8,250 | -2.0 | 16,441 | 18,173 | 3139 | 55 |
| MARION | 22,667 | 22,895 | 22,433 | 0.1 | 2.37 | 15,841 | 15,334 | -0.4 | 26,211 | 29,343 | 2688 | 25 |
| MARSHALL | 14,051 | 13,862 | 13,636 | -0.2 | 2.47 | 10,480 | 9,997 | -0.6 | 28,838 | 31,861 | 2322 | 14 |
| MASON | 9,603 | 10,276 | 10,600 | 0.8 | 2.51 | 7,262 | 7,551 | 0.5 | 26,527 | 29,460 | 2649 | 23 |
| MERCER | 25,390 | 25,812 | 25,830 | 0.2 | 2.41 | 18,427 | 18,069 | -0.2 | 24,783 | 27,198 | 2831 | 30 |
| MINERAL | 9,981 | 10,332 | 10,434 | 0.4 | 2.57 | 7,496 | 7,541 | 0.1 | 27,471 | 31,887 | 2516 | 18 |
| MINGO | 11,830 | 11,512 | 11,037 | -0.3 | 2.68 | 9,312 | 8,823 | -0.7 | 21,286 | 23,515 | 3060 | 47 |
| MONONGALIA | 29,087 | 30,755 | 30,643 | 0.7 | 2.30 | 17,634 | 17,841 | 0.1 | 30,169 | 34,001 | 2114 | 11 |
| MONROE | 4,749 | 5,338 | 5,636 | 1.4 | 2.48 | 3,557 | 3,853 | 1.0 | 24,304 | 27,591 | 2880 | 34 |
| MORGAN | 4,731 | 5,654 | 6,102 | 2.2 | 2.46 | 3,554 | 4,115 | 1.8 | 31,716 | 40,854 | 1773 | 6 |
| NICHOLAS | 9,970 | 10,733 | 10,958 | 0.9 | 2.55 | 7,700 | 8,012 | 0.5 | 24,382 | 27,881 | 2871 | 32 |
| OHIO | 20,646 | 20,105 | 19,591 | -0.3 | 2.24 | 13,481 | 12,608 | -0.8 | 30,029 | 32,096 | 2148 | 12 |
| PENDLETON | 3,061 | 3,136 | 3,217 | 0.3 | 2.52 | 2,321 | 2,320 | 0.0 | 27,273 | 30,802 | 2539 | 20 |
| PLEASANTS | 2,769 | 2,925 | 3,013 | 0.7 | 2.52 | 2,075 | 2,134 | 0.3 | 27,155 | 29,963 | 2555 | 21 |
| POCAHONTAS | 3,628 | 3,838 | 3,942 | 0.7 | 2.31 | 2,556 | 2,608 | 0.2 | 21,667 | 23,213 | 3045 | 45 |
| PRESTON | 10,619 | 11,301 | 11,548 | 0.8 | 2.61 | 8,146 | 8,406 | 0.4 | 25,007 | 29,346 | 2809 | 29 |
| PUTNAM | 15,695 | 20,079 | 22,021 | 3.0 | 2.61 | 12,626 | 15,740 | 2.7 | 39,545 | 43,238 | 706 | 2 |
| RALEIGH | 29,483 | 31,775 | 32,421 | 0.9 | 2.45 | 21,828 | 22,741 | 0.5 | 26,398 | 29,308 | 2666 | 24 |
| RANDOLPH | 10,366 | 11,112 | 11,311 | 0.8 | 2.43 | 7,516 | 7,757 | 0.4 | 25,639 | 30,129 | 2743 | 27 |
| RITCHIE | 3,928 | 4,157 | 4,380 | 0.7 | 2.51 | 2,932 | 2,979 | 0.2 | 23,105 | 27,780 | 2965 | 40 |
| ROANE | 5,740 | 6,032 | 6,199 | 0.6 | 2.55 | 4,308 | 4,378 | 0.2 | 20,474 | 24,255 | 3086 | 50 |
| SUMMERS | 5,240 | 5,356 | 5,440 | 0.3 | 2.41 | 3,807 | 3,754 | -0.2 | 22,303 | 25,122 | 3008 | 42 |
| TAYLOR | 5,741 | 5,977 | 6,080 | 0.5 | 2.50 | 4,249 | 4,277 | 0.1 | 24,363 | 29,391 | 2876 | 33 |
| TUCKER | 3,017 | 3,065 | 2,990 | 0.2 | 2.38 | 2,182 | 2,134 | -0.3 | 23,419 | 26,935 | 2950 | 37 |
| TYLER | 3,709 | 3,845 | 3,771 | 0.4 | 2.49 | 2,846 | 2,857 | 0.0 | 26,827 | 32,800 | 2607 | 22 |
| UPSHUR | 8,245 | 8,728 | 8,812 | 0.7 | 2.54 | 6,070 | 6,216 | 0.3 | 23,113 | 27,279 | 2964 | 39 |
| WAYNE | 15,626 | 16,379 | 16,517 | 0.6 | 2.54 | 12,100 | 12,295 | 0.2 | 25,503 | 29,138 | 2756 | 28 |
| WEBSTER | 3,996 | 3,937 | 3,803 | -0.2 | 2.50 | 3,076 | 2,924 | -0.6 | 17,936 | 20,943 | 3128 | 54 |
| WETZEL | 7,303 | 7,130 | 7,027 | -0.3 | 2.51 | 5,437 | 5,108 | -0.8 | 27,813 | 30,469 | 2468 | 16 |
| WIRT | 1,942 | 2,242 | 2,382 | 1.8 | 2.59 | 1,480 | 1,648 | 1.3 | 24,029 | 28,580 | 2898 | 35 |
| WOOD | 34,168 | 35,312 | 35,349 | 0.4 | 2.41 | 24,965 | 24,935 | 0.0 | 33,964 | 36,906 | 1400 | 4 |
| WYOMING | 10,474 | 10,293 | 10,029 | -0.2 | 2.58 | 8,330 | 7,946 | -0.6 | 21,302 | 23,312 | 3059 | 46 |
| WEST VIRGINIA | | | | 0.6 | 2.44 | | | 0.2 | 27,663 | 31,361 | | |
| UNITED STATES | | | | 1.4 | 2.59 | | | 1.1 | 41,914 | 49,127 | | |

| COUNTY | 2000 Per Capita Income | 2000 HH Income Base | 2000 HOUSEHOLD INCOME DISTRIBUTION (%) | | | | | | 2000 AVERAGE DISPOSABLE INCOME BY AGE OF HOUSEHOLDER | | | | | |
|---|---|---|---|---|---|---|---|---|---|---|---|---|---|---|
| | | | Less than $15,000 | $15,000 to $24,999 | $25,000 to $49,999 | $50,000 to $99,999 | $100,000 to $149,999 | $150,000 or More | All Ages | <35 | 35-44 | 45-54 | 55-64 | 65+ |
| BARBOUR | 11,066 | 6,311 | 37.6 | 21.1 | 28.0 | 11.8 | 1.2 | 0.3 | 22,368 | 19,959 | 27,072 | 26,854 | 22,929 | 16,682 |
| BERKELEY | 16,322 | 29,126 | 16.1 | 14.5 | 40.4 | 24.6 | 3.8 | 0.6 | 33,171 | 28,920 | 38,587 | 41,557 | 34,376 | 21,326 |
| BOONE | 12,476 | 10,156 | 34.0 | 18.6 | 28.2 | 16.7 | 1.8 | 0.7 | 25,881 | 24,567 | 31,219 | 29,471 | 24,764 | 18,691 |
| BRAXTON | 11,254 | 5,193 | 34.2 | 21.0 | 30.6 | 13.0 | 1.1 | 0.1 | 23,185 | 21,226 | 30,721 | 27,824 | 24,601 | 15,621 |
| BROOKE | 15,624 | 10,120 | 19.8 | 15.7 | 37.3 | 24.3 | 2.2 | 0.6 | 31,195 | 28,366 | 38,033 | 40,351 | 30,295 | 21,567 |
| CABELL | 17,258 | 39,057 | 28.2 | 16.8 | 32.1 | 17.7 | 3.2 | 2.1 | 30,670 | 23,020 | 38,040 | 37,482 | 34,105 | 21,965 |
| CALHOUN | 9,250 | 3,102 | 41.5 | 21.1 | 28.1 | 8.6 | 0.6 | 0.1 | 20,274 | 16,967 | 25,854 | 23,796 | 19,666 | 15,384 |
| CLAY | 8,978 | 4,043 | 41.2 | 19.7 | 29.3 | 9.2 | 0.5 | 0.1 | 20,129 | 18,093 | 24,728 | 22,807 | 19,571 | 15,750 |
| DODDRIDGE | 13,013 | 3,016 | 26.4 | 24.3 | 31.9 | 14.8 | 2.0 | 0.6 | 26,243 | 24,274 | 31,239 | 31,114 | 28,364 | 18,538 |
| FAYETTE | 11,591 | 18,792 | 33.3 | 21.4 | 31.2 | 12.8 | 1.1 | 0.1 | 23,296 | 20,054 | 30,280 | 27,009 | 25,010 | 17,325 |
| GILMER | 10,967 | 2,648 | 40.0 | 20.2 | 27.3 | 10.1 | 1.6 | 0.8 | 22,752 | 19,396 | 27,673 | 27,980 | 25,029 | 15,947 |
| GRANT | 14,900 | 4,368 | 22.9 | 18.6 | 38.3 | 17.1 | 2.2 | 0.9 | 28,806 | 27,103 | 35,071 | 33,830 | 31,652 | 18,944 |
| GREENBRIER | 13,499 | 14,641 | 26.7 | 21.6 | 33.0 | 16.5 | 2.2 | 0.1 | 26,224 | 22,517 | 31,547 | 33,314 | 25,359 | 20,392 |
| HAMPSHIRE | 14,145 | 7,558 | 24.4 | 18.5 | 37.3 | 17.0 | 1.8 | 0.9 | 28,100 | 25,045 | 33,309 | 36,133 | 29,398 | 17,710 |
| HANCOCK | 16,363 | 13,742 | 22.0 | 16.9 | 35.0 | 23.2 | 2.2 | 0.8 | 30,602 | 24,287 | 38,437 | 39,599 | 34,143 | 20,263 |
| HARDY | 15,005 | 4,863 | 23.1 | 17.2 | 39.4 | 17.9 | 1.9 | 0.5 | 28,505 | 27,737 | 34,129 | 35,678 | 31,028 | 17,724 |
| HARRISON | 14,528 | 28,226 | 26.1 | 19.3 | 33.5 | 17.6 | 2.7 | 0.9 | 28,262 | 24,962 | 35,010 | 34,336 | 29,941 | 20,290 |
| JACKSON | 13,999 | 11,096 | 23.6 | 18.0 | 36.5 | 19.6 | 1.9 | 0.5 | 28,589 | 25,039 | 32,968 | 35,537 | 32,431 | 18,741 |
| JEFFERSON | 19,370 | 15,673 | 14.0 | 11.7 | 38.9 | 27.2 | 5.5 | 2.6 | 38,942 | 32,345 | 42,939 | 47,558 | 39,402 | 26,812 |
| KANAWHA | 17,956 | 85,157 | 23.7 | 17.7 | 33.1 | 20.4 | 3.4 | 1.8 | 31,538 | 26,317 | 37,226 | 38,830 | 33,230 | 22,440 |
| LEWIS | 11,338 | 7,050 | 34.2 | 19.2 | 33.0 | 12.8 | 0.8 | 0.0 | 23,048 | 20,566 | 29,378 | 28,069 | 22,096 | 16,483 |
| LINCOLN | 10,122 | 8,299 | 38.1 | 18.4 | 30.7 | 12.0 | 0.8 | 0.1 | 22,392 | 19,659 | 27,728 | 26,312 | 21,194 | 17,219 |
| LOGAN | 11,957 | 15,257 | 33.7 | 19.3 | 31.4 | 13.4 | 1.5 | 0.7 | 24,648 | 21,255 | 29,532 | 28,140 | 26,632 | 17,938 |
| MCDOWELL | 9,469 | 11,220 | 46.2 | 20.6 | 23.6 | 8.2 | 1.2 | 0.2 | 19,749 | 16,611 | 24,262 | 22,314 | 20,505 | 16,449 |
| MARION | 13,908 | 22,895 | 29.4 | 18.7 | 33.3 | 16.1 | 1.9 | 0.6 | 26,590 | 22,437 | 32,276 | 34,937 | 28,937 | 19,304 |
| MARSHALL | 14,770 | 13,862 | 24.8 | 18.9 | 33.4 | 19.7 | 2.4 | 0.8 | 28,853 | 25,572 | 35,566 | 37,567 | 28,972 | 18,474 |
| MASON | 13,268 | 10,276 | 28.9 | 18.1 | 35.1 | 15.6 | 1.8 | 0.5 | 26,455 | 22,947 | 33,506 | 30,791 | 27,661 | 18,619 |
| MERCER | 13,894 | 25,812 | 30.2 | 20.2 | 32.5 | 14.4 | 1.9 | 0.8 | 26,159 | 22,361 | 32,447 | 32,837 | 27,417 | 18,412 |
| MINERAL | 13,002 | 10,332 | 24.4 | 20.7 | 37.2 | 16.0 | 1.2 | 0.6 | 27,039 | 23,329 | 33,495 | 32,942 | 30,538 | 17,684 |
| MINGO | 12,021 | 11,512 | 38.0 | 18.0 | 27.5 | 13.2 | 2.3 | 0.9 | 24,634 | 21,908 | 31,127 | 27,305 | 24,011 | 17,214 |
| MONONGALIA | 18,093 | 30,755 | 24.9 | 16.3 | 32.1 | 20.4 | 3.9 | 2.4 | 32,841 | 21,733 | 41,166 | 46,667 | 37,574 | 25,042 |
| MONROE | 11,729 | 5,338 | 28.9 | 22.3 | 33.8 | 13.9 | 1.1 | 0.1 | 24,218 | 23,708 | 29,401 | 30,461 | 25,362 | 16,288 |
| MORGAN | 16,062 | 5,654 | 18.7 | 17.7 | 38.8 | 21.6 | 2.6 | 0.7 | 30,854 | 27,017 | 36,046 | 38,722 | 34,358 | 21,271 |
| NICHOLAS | 12,045 | 10,733 | 29.2 | 21.9 | 31.7 | 15.1 | 1.9 | 0.2 | 25,285 | 22,039 | 30,870 | 30,014 | 26,568 | 18,653 |
| OHIO | 17,014 | 20,105 | 25.6 | 16.5 | 34.5 | 18.6 | 3.5 | 1.4 | 30,231 | 24,620 | 36,319 | 38,171 | 33,669 | 21,970 |
| PENDLETON | 13,082 | 3,136 | 24.2 | 21.0 | 34.5 | 18.4 | 1.7 | 0.2 | 26,936 | 25,493 | 31,274 | 33,861 | 29,385 | 19,036 |
| PLEASANTS | 13,256 | 2,925 | 27.3 | 18.8 | 33.8 | 16.9 | 2.7 | 0.6 | 27,503 | 21,814 | 34,753 | 34,544 | 31,846 | 18,512 |
| POCAHONTAS | 12,332 | 3,838 | 31.8 | 27.2 | 29.1 | 10.0 | 1.6 | 0.3 | 22,628 | 18,604 | 28,780 | 26,299 | 25,089 | 17,317 |
| PRESTON | 11,335 | 11,301 | 29.4 | 20.6 | 34.7 | 13.9 | 1.3 | 0.1 | 24,543 | 23,101 | 30,558 | 29,030 | 24,559 | 16,093 |
| PUTNAM | 18,709 | 20,079 | 14.1 | 13.7 | 37.0 | 28.1 | 5.2 | 1.9 | 37,363 | 35,491 | 44,051 | 44,531 | 36,139 | 21,802 |
| RALEIGH | 14,789 | 31,775 | 27.7 | 20.0 | 32.5 | 16.0 | 2.6 | 1.2 | 28,150 | 23,641 | 34,907 | 34,387 | 28,444 | 19,563 |
| RANDOLPH | 13,119 | 11,112 | 26.8 | 21.9 | 32.9 | 15.9 | 2.0 | 0.6 | 26,599 | 23,025 | 30,880 | 31,866 | 28,672 | 19,483 |
| RITCHIE | 11,786 | 4,157 | 30.7 | 22.8 | 31.6 | 13.3 | 1.5 | 0.1 | 24,218 | 20,938 | 26,399 | 32,256 | 26,077 | 16,474 |
| ROANE | 10,675 | 6,032 | 35.6 | 23.4 | 29.9 | 9.6 | 1.0 | 0.5 | 22,274 | 19,981 | 25,748 | 28,489 | 21,543 | 14,642 |
| SUMMERS | 11,955 | 5,356 | 31.9 | 22.7 | 30.7 | 12.8 | 1.6 | 0.3 | 23,989 | 21,028 | 32,223 | 28,056 | 26,041 | 17,151 |
| TAYLOR | 11,494 | 5,977 | 30.9 | 20.3 | 34.2 | 13.3 | 1.2 | 0.2 | 24,129 | 22,475 | 28,137 | 30,607 | 24,527 | 17,369 |
| TUCKER | 12,038 | 3,065 | 30.4 | 22.3 | 34.2 | 11.7 | 0.9 | 0.6 | 23,866 | 24,199 | 29,134 | 29,146 | 23,443 | 15,321 |
| TYLER | 12,422 | 3,845 | 29.7 | 17.6 | 34.7 | 16.9 | 1.0 | 0.1 | 25,918 | 23,848 | 31,385 | 33,692 | 27,524 | 16,841 |
| UPSHUR | 10,662 | 8,728 | 32.3 | 21.4 | 32.9 | 12.5 | 0.9 | 0.1 | 23,317 | 19,872 | 27,974 | 28,381 | 24,577 | 16,865 |
| WAYNE | 12,779 | 16,379 | 30.1 | 19.1 | 32.0 | 16.3 | 2.1 | 0.4 | 26,187 | 23,796 | 32,518 | 32,467 | 25,911 | 17,779 |
| WEBSTER | 9,319 | 3,937 | 42.9 | 21.7 | 27.1 | 7.4 | 0.8 | 0.1 | 19,761 | 18,670 | 25,684 | 21,842 | 19,373 | 14,518 |
| WETZEL | 13,575 | 7,130 | 31.6 | 15.1 | 33.0 | 17.7 | 1.9 | 0.8 | 27,300 | 23,333 | 32,963 | 34,955 | 30,258 | 17,114 |
| WIRT | 10,975 | 2,242 | 31.6 | 20.2 | 35.4 | 12.0 | 0.8 | 0.0 | 23,359 | 20,317 | 26,631 | 32,860 | 21,557 | 16,226 |
| WOOD | 16,778 | 35,312 | 20.9 | 15.2 | 36.1 | 23.8 | 3.1 | 0.8 | 31,849 | 27,490 | 38,899 | 39,507 | 34,633 | 20,754 |
| WYOMING | 10,884 | 10,293 | 36.0 | 20.2 | 29.1 | 13.1 | 1.4 | 0.2 | 23,388 | 19,426 | 28,731 | 26,780 | 22,640 | 18,389 |
| WEST VIRGINIA | 14,694 | | 27.0 | 18.3 | 33.4 | 17.8 | 2.5 | 1.0 | 28,436 | 24,166 | 34,601 | 35,109 | 29,773 | 19,746 |
| UNITED STATES | 22,162 | | 14.5 | 12.5 | 32.3 | 29.8 | 7.4 | 3.5 | 40,748 | 34,503 | 44,969 | 49,579 | 43,409 | 27,339 |

| COUNTY | FINANCIAL SERVICES | | | | THE HOME | | | | | | ENTERTAINMENT | | | | | | PERSONAL | | | |
|---|---|---|---|---|---|---|---|---|---|---|---|---|---|---|---|---|---|---|---|---|
| | | | | | Home Improvements | | | Furnishings | | | | | | | | | | | | |
| | Auto Loan | Home Loan | Investments | Retirement Plans | Home Repair | Lawn & Garden | Remodeling | Appliances | Electronics | Furniture | Restaurants | Sporting Goods | Theater & Concerts | Toys & Hobbies | Travel | Video Rental | Apparel | Auto Aftermarket | Health Insurance | Pets & Supplies |
| BARBOUR | 96 | 65 | 72 | 75 | 92 | 91 | 111 | 95 | 92 | 76 | 78 | 93 | 79 | 93 | 68 | 96 | 79 | 87 | 102 | 96 |
| BERKELEY | 98 | 82 | 89 | 86 | 97 | 94 | 110 | 97 | 94 | 89 | 90 | 96 | 89 | 99 | 77 | 98 | 89 | 93 | 99 | 100 |
| BOONE | 97 | 66 | 72 | 75 | 93 | 91 | 111 | 95 | 91 | 77 | 79 | 94 | 80 | 94 | 68 | 96 | 79 | 87 | 101 | 96 |
| BRAXTON | 95 | 63 | 70 | 73 | 92 | 90 | 109 | 94 | 91 | 75 | 77 | 91 | 77 | 92 | 68 | 96 | 77 | 86 | 102 | 94 |
| BROOKE | 97 | 82 | 93 | 85 | 102 | 97 | 106 | 97 | 91 | 90 | 90 | 95 | 91 | 98 | 81 | 97 | 88 | 92 | 101 | 98 |
| CABELL | 96 | 87 | 99 | 90 | 102 | 99 | 103 | 96 | 93 | 91 | 91 | 94 | 92 | 97 | 84 | 96 | 90 | 93 | 100 | 98 |
| CALHOUN | 97 | 63 | 67 | 73 | 92 | 90 | 111 | 95 | 91 | 75 | 77 | 95 | 78 | 94 | 66 | 95 | 78 | 86 | 102 | 96 |
| CLAY | 97 | 64 | 69 | 74 | 92 | 90 | 113 | 96 | 92 | 76 | 77 | 96 | 79 | 95 | 67 | 95 | 78 | 87 | 101 | 97 |
| DODDRIDGE | 96 | 67 | 75 | 76 | 93 | 91 | 112 | 95 | 92 | 78 | 80 | 92 | 80 | 94 | 69 | 96 | 80 | 88 | 101 | 96 |
| FAYETTE | 94 | 66 | 76 | 75 | 94 | 92 | 107 | 94 | 91 | 77 | 79 | 90 | 79 | 91 | 71 | 96 | 79 | 87 | 101 | 94 |
| GILMER | 95 | 66 | 71 | 73 | 92 | 90 | 108 | 93 | 90 | 75 | 77 | 90 | 78 | 91 | 68 | 95 | 78 | 86 | 101 | 94 |
| GRANT | 96 | 65 | 71 | 75 | 92 | 91 | 111 | 95 | 92 | 76 | 78 | 93 | 79 | 94 | 68 | 96 | 79 | 87 | 102 | 96 |
| GREENBRIER | 96 | 70 | 80 | 78 | 94 | 92 | 109 | 95 | 92 | 79 | 81 | 92 | 82 | 94 | 72 | 97 | 81 | 88 | 102 | 96 |
| HAMPSHIRE | 98 | 68 | 74 | 78 | 93 | 91 | 116 | 96 | 92 | 77 | 80 | 96 | 81 | 96 | 69 | 97 | 81 | 88 | 102 | 98 |
| HANCOCK | 96 | 83 | 98 | 86 | 103 | 99 | 102 | 97 | 91 | 91 | 91 | 93 | 92 | 97 | 83 | 96 | 89 | 92 | 102 | 97 |
| HARDY | 97 | 64 | 68 | 73 | 92 | 90 | 113 | 96 | 91 | 76 | 77 | 96 | 79 | 95 | 66 | 95 | 78 | 87 | 101 | 97 |
| HARRISON | 96 | 77 | 91 | 85 | 100 | 97 | 106 | 96 | 91 | 86 | 86 | 93 | 88 | 95 | 79 | 96 | 86 | 90 | 101 | 96 |
| JACKSON | 97 | 72 | 80 | 79 | 95 | 92 | 111 | 96 | 92 | 82 | 83 | 95 | 84 | 96 | 72 | 97 | 83 | 89 | 101 | 97 |
| JEFFERSON | 99 | 87 | 92 | 90 | 98 | 95 | 111 | 98 | 96 | 92 | 94 | 98 | 92 | 101 | 80 | 98 | 93 | 95 | 100 | 101 |
| KANAWHA | 97 | 87 | 101 | 91 | 103 | 100 | 104 | 97 | 94 | 93 | 92 | 96 | 94 | 98 | 85 | 97 | 92 | 94 | 101 | 98 |
| LEWIS | 95 | 65 | 73 | 74 | 93 | 91 | 108 | 94 | 91 | 76 | 78 | 91 | 79 | 92 | 69 | 96 | 79 | 87 | 101 | 94 |
| LINCOLN | 97 | 64 | 69 | 74 | 92 | 90 | 112 | 96 | 92 | 76 | 78 | 95 | 79 | 95 | 67 | 96 | 78 | 87 | 102 | 97 |
| LOGAN | 96 | 66 | 73 | 74 | 93 | 91 | 109 | 95 | 91 | 77 | 78 | 93 | 79 | 93 | 69 | 96 | 79 | 87 | 101 | 95 |
| MCDOWELL | 94 | 64 | 70 | 72 | 93 | 89 | 105 | 95 | 90 | 77 | 75 | 91 | 78 | 91 | 68 | 95 | 78 | 86 | 97 | 94 |
| MARION | 94 | 78 | 93 | 82 | 101 | 97 | 101 | 95 | 89 | 86 | 86 | 91 | 88 | 94 | 80 | 96 | 85 | 90 | 101 | 95 |
| MARSHALL | 96 | 76 | 87 | 82 | 99 | 95 | 107 | 96 | 91 | 85 | 86 | 93 | 87 | 96 | 77 | 96 | 85 | 90 | 101 | 97 |
| MASON | 96 | 68 | 74 | 76 | 94 | 91 | 110 | 95 | 91 | 79 | 79 | 94 | 81 | 94 | 70 | 96 | 80 | 87 | 101 | 96 |
| MERCER | 96 | 74 | 86 | 81 | 96 | 94 | 108 | 95 | 92 | 83 | 84 | 93 | 85 | 95 | 75 | 96 | 83 | 89 | 101 | 96 |
| MINERAL | 97 | 75 | 83 | 81 | 97 | 93 | 111 | 96 | 92 | 83 | 85 | 94 | 85 | 97 | 74 | 97 | 85 | 90 | 101 | 98 |
| MINGO | 96 | 66 | 71 | 74 | 94 | 91 | 110 | 95 | 91 | 77 | 78 | 94 | 80 | 93 | 69 | 95 | 78 | 87 | 101 | 96 |
| MONONGALIA | 96 | 89 | 97 | 90 | 99 | 95 | 106 | 93 | 92 | 87 | 91 | 94 | 88 | 96 | 81 | 95 | 89 | 93 | 99 | 98 |
| MONROE | 96 | 63 | 68 | 73 | 92 | 90 | 111 | 95 | 91 | 75 | 77 | 94 | 78 | 93 | 66 | 95 | 78 | 86 | 102 | 96 |
| MORGAN | 99 | 76 | 83 | 84 | 97 | 94 | 116 | 98 | 93 | 84 | 86 | 97 | 86 | 100 | 75 | 98 | 87 | 91 | 103 | 101 |
| NICHOLAS | 96 | 66 | 71 | 74 | 92 | 90 | 111 | 95 | 92 | 77 | 79 | 94 | 79 | 94 | 68 | 96 | 79 | 87 | 101 | 96 |
| OHIO | 96 | 90 | 104 | 92 | 105 | 101 | 100 | 97 | 92 | 95 | 93 | 95 | 95 | 97 | 88 | 96 | 92 | 94 | 99 | 97 |
| PENDLETON | 97 | 65 | 71 | 74 | 92 | 91 | 112 | 95 | 92 | 76 | 78 | 94 | 79 | 94 | 68 | 95 | 79 | 87 | 101 | 96 |
| PLEASANTS | 98 | 69 | 76 | 79 | 93 | 91 | 113 | 96 | 93 | 79 | 81 | 95 | 82 | 96 | 70 | 97 | 82 | 89 | 102 | 98 |
| POCAHONTAS | 97 | 67 | 73 | 79 | 92 | 91 | 116 | 96 | 92 | 76 | 79 | 94 | 79 | 95 | 69 | 97 | 80 | 88 | 103 | 97 |
| PRESTON | 97 | 67 | 73 | 76 | 93 | 91 | 112 | 96 | 92 | 78 | 79 | 95 | 80 | 95 | 69 | 96 | 80 | 88 | 101 | 97 |
| PUTNAM | 101 | 87 | 89 | 91 | 97 | 96 | 111 | 99 | 99 | 92 | 95 | 101 | 93 | 102 | 79 | 99 | 94 | 97 | 101 | 103 |
| RALEIGH | 97 | 72 | 83 | 82 | 95 | 93 | 111 | 96 | 93 | 81 | 83 | 94 | 84 | 96 | 73 | 97 | 83 | 90 | 102 | 97 |
| RANDOLPH | 97 | 69 | 78 | 78 | 95 | 92 | 111 | 95 | 92 | 79 | 81 | 94 | 82 | 95 | 71 | 96 | 81 | 88 | 101 | 97 |
| RITCHIE | 98 | 65 | 70 | 75 | 92 | 90 | 113 | 96 | 92 | 76 | 78 | 96 | 79 | 95 | 67 | 96 | 79 | 87 | 102 | 97 |
| ROANE | 97 | 64 | 69 | 74 | 92 | 90 | 112 | 95 | 92 | 76 | 77 | 95 | 79 | 94 | 67 | 96 | 78 | 87 | 102 | 96 |
| SUMMERS | 96 | 67 | 75 | 77 | 93 | 91 | 111 | 95 | 91 | 77 | 79 | 92 | 80 | 93 | 70 | 97 | 80 | 88 | 101 | 96 |
| TAYLOR | 96 | 69 | 77 | 77 | 93 | 91 | 110 | 95 | 92 | 79 | 81 | 92 | 81 | 94 | 70 | 97 | 81 | 88 | 101 | 96 |
| TUCKER | 97 | 67 | 74 | 77 | 93 | 91 | 113 | 95 | 92 | 77 | 79 | 94 | 80 | 95 | 69 | 97 | 80 | 88 | 102 | 97 |
| TYLER | 97 | 68 | 73 | 77 | 94 | 91 | 112 | 96 | 92 | 79 | 80 | 95 | 81 | 95 | 69 | 96 | 80 | 88 | 101 | 97 |
| UPSHUR | 97 | 74 | 84 | 81 | 96 | 93 | 109 | 96 | 92 | 82 | 83 | 94 | 84 | 96 | 74 | 96 | 83 | 89 | 101 | 97 |
| WAYNE | 97 | 72 | 80 | 79 | 96 | 93 | 110 | 96 | 92 | 82 | 83 | 94 | 84 | 96 | 73 | 96 | 83 | 89 | 101 | 97 |
| WEBSTER | 97 | 63 | 68 | 73 | 92 | 90 | 112 | 95 | 91 | 75 | 77 | 95 | 78 | 94 | 66 | 95 | 78 | 86 | 102 | 96 |
| WETZEL | 97 | 68 | 78 | 78 | 95 | 93 | 110 | 96 | 92 | 79 | 80 | 95 | 82 | 95 | 71 | 96 | 81 | 88 | 102 | 97 |
| WIRT | 97 | 63 | 66 | 73 | 92 | 90 | 112 | 96 | 91 | 75 | 77 | 96 | 78 | 95 | 66 | 95 | 78 | 86 | 102 | 96 |
| WOOD | 97 | 84 | 96 | 89 | 101 | 98 | 106 | 97 | 94 | 91 | 91 | 95 | 92 | 98 | 82 | 97 | 90 | 93 | 101 | 98 |
| WYOMING | 97 | 63 | 68 | 73 | 92 | 90 | 112 | 95 | 91 | 75 | 77 | 95 | 78 | 94 | 66 | 95 | 78 | 86 | 102 | 96 |
| WEST VIRGINIA | 97 | 77 | 88 | 84 | 98 | 95 | 108 | 96 | 92 | 85 | 86 | 94 | 87 | 96 | 77 | 96 | 85 | 90 | 101 | 97 |
| UNITED STATES | 100 | 100 | 100 | 100 | 100 | 100 | 100 | 100 | 100 | 100 | 100 | 100 | 100 | 100 | 100 | 100 | 100 | 100 | 100 | 100 |

# POPULATION CHANGE

| COUNTY | FIPS Code | MSA Code | DMA Code | POPULATION | | | 1990-2000 ANNUAL CHANGE | | RACE (%) | | | | | |
|---|---|---|---|---|---|---|---|---|---|---|---|---|---|---|
| | | | | | | | | | White | | Black | | Asian/Pacific | |
| | | | | 1990 | 2000 | 2005 | % Rate | State Rank | 1990 | 2000 | 1990 | 2000 | 1990 | 2000 |
| ADAMS | 001 | 0000 | 705 | 15,682 | 19,049 | 20,588 | 1.9 | 6 | 95.7 | 95.5 | 2.4 | 2.1 | 0.4 | 0.5 |
| ASHLAND | 003 | 0000 | 676 | 16,307 | 16,341 | 16,100 | 0.0 | 67 | 90.4 | 89.7 | 0.1 | 0.2 | 0.3 | 0.4 |
| BARRON | 005 | 0000 | 613 | 40,750 | 44,353 | 45,691 | 0.8 | 37 | 99.0 | 98.8 | 0.1 | 0.2 | 0.2 | 0.3 |
| BAYFIELD | 007 | 0000 | 676 | 14,008 | 15,480 | 16,094 | 1.0 | 29 | 90.7 | 90.1 | 0.2 | 0.3 | 0.2 | 0.2 |
| BROWN | 009 | 3080 | 658 | 194,594 | 217,941 | 225,288 | 1.1 | 25 | 95.9 | 94.9 | 0.5 | 0.6 | 1.3 | 1.9 |
| BUFFALO | 011 | 0000 | 702 | 13,584 | 14,329 | 14,573 | 0.5 | 52 | 99.5 | 99.4 | 0.0 | 0.1 | 0.2 | 0.4 |
| BURNETT | 013 | 0000 | 613 | 13,084 | 15,116 | 16,147 | 1.4 | 13 | 95.5 | 95.1 | 0.2 | 0.3 | 0.2 | 0.2 |
| CALUMET | 015 | 0460 | 658 | 34,291 | 39,542 | 42,112 | 1.4 | 13 | 98.9 | 98.4 | 0.1 | 0.1 | 0.5 | 0.8 |
| CHIPPEWA | 017 | 2290 | 702 | 52,360 | 54,935 | 55,940 | 0.5 | 52 | 99.0 | 98.7 | 0.1 | 0.1 | 0.5 | 0.8 |
| CLARK | 019 | 0000 | 702 | 31,647 | 33,628 | 34,691 | 0.6 | 43 | 99.3 | 99.2 | 0.1 | 0.1 | 0.1 | 0.2 |
| COLUMBIA | 021 | 0000 | 669 | 45,088 | 52,421 | 55,644 | 1.5 | 10 | 98.6 | 98.2 | 0.5 | 0.7 | 0.3 | 0.5 |
| CRAWFORD | 023 | 0000 | 637 | 15,940 | 16,525 | 16,508 | 0.4 | 59 | 99.1 | 98.9 | 0.3 | 0.3 | 0.4 | 0.5 |
| DANE | 025 | 4720 | 669 | 367,085 | 432,873 | 454,296 | 1.6 | 8 | 93.9 | 92.0 | 2.9 | 3.6 | 2.4 | 3.2 |
| DODGE | 027 | 0000 | 617 | 76,559 | 84,175 | 87,522 | 0.9 | 33 | 97.6 | 96.9 | 1.5 | 1.8 | 0.3 | 0.4 |
| DOOR | 029 | 0000 | 658 | 25,690 | 27,152 | 27,546 | 0.5 | 52 | 98.8 | 98.6 | 0.1 | 0.2 | 0.2 | 0.3 |
| DOUGLAS | 031 | 2240 | 676 | 41,758 | 42,942 | 42,759 | 0.3 | 62 | 96.9 | 96.3 | 0.4 | 0.5 | 0.6 | 0.9 |
| DUNN | 033 | 0000 | 613 | 35,909 | 39,452 | 40,675 | 0.9 | 33 | 97.3 | 96.4 | 0.5 | 0.6 | 1.8 | 2.5 |
| EAU CLAIRE | 035 | 2290 | 702 | 85,183 | 90,129 | 92,087 | 0.6 | 43 | 96.5 | 95.3 | 0.3 | 0.3 | 2.5 | 3.6 |
| FLORENCE | 037 | 0000 | 553 | 4,590 | 5,107 | 4,963 | 1.0 | 29 | 99.4 | 99.2 | 0.1 | 0.2 | 0.1 | 0.1 |
| FOND DU LAC | 039 | 0000 | 658 | 90,083 | 95,002 | 96,182 | 0.5 | 52 | 98.5 | 98.0 | 0.3 | 0.4 | 0.5 | 0.7 |
| FOREST | 041 | 0000 | 705 | 8,776 | 9,698 | 9,891 | 1.0 | 29 | 89.4 | 88.9 | 1.4 | 1.3 | 0.2 | 0.3 |
| GRANT | 043 | 0000 | 669 | 49,264 | 49,341 | 49,359 | 0.0 | 67 | 99.1 | 98.7 | 0.2 | 0.3 | 0.5 | 0.7 |
| GREEN | 045 | 0000 | 669 | 30,339 | 34,242 | 36,173 | 1.2 | 23 | 99.5 | 99.3 | 0.1 | 0.1 | 0.2 | 0.3 |
| GREEN LAKE | 047 | 0000 | 658 | 18,651 | 19,617 | 19,930 | 0.5 | 52 | 98.6 | 98.1 | 0.1 | 0.1 | 0.6 | 0.8 |
| IOWA | 049 | 0000 | 669 | 20,150 | 23,010 | 24,535 | 1.3 | 19 | 99.7 | 99.7 | 0.0 | 0.1 | 0.1 | 0.1 |
| IRON | 051 | 0000 | 676 | 6,153 | 6,252 | 6,027 | 0.2 | 64 | 99.5 | 99.5 | 0.0 | 0.0 | 0.0 | 0.0 |
| JACKSON | 053 | 0000 | 702 | 16,588 | 17,994 | 18,734 | 0.8 | 37 | 95.3 | 94.7 | 0.3 | 0.4 | 0.2 | 0.3 |
| JEFFERSON | 055 | 0000 | 617 | 67,783 | 74,436 | 76,397 | 0.9 | 33 | 98.4 | 97.9 | 0.3 | 0.3 | 0.4 | 0.6 |
| JUNEAU | 057 | 0000 | 669 | 21,650 | 24,246 | 25,092 | 1.1 | 25 | 98.4 | 98.0 | 0.1 | 0.2 | 0.4 | 0.6 |
| KENOSHA | 059 | 3800 | 617 | 128,181 | 148,041 | 156,788 | 1.4 | 13 | 93.0 | 90.8 | 4.1 | 5.1 | 0.5 | 0.8 |
| KEWAUNEE | 061 | 0000 | 658 | 18,878 | 20,083 | 20,696 | 0.6 | 43 | 99.4 | 99.2 | 0.1 | 0.2 | 0.1 | 0.2 |
| LA CROSSE | 063 | 3870 | 702 | 97,904 | 102,566 | 103,332 | 0.5 | 52 | 96.3 | 95.0 | 0.4 | 0.5 | 2.7 | 4.0 |
| LAFAYETTE | 065 | 0000 | 669 | 16,076 | 15,896 | 15,295 | -0.1 | 70 | 99.6 | 99.4 | 0.1 | 0.2 | 0.1 | 0.2 |
| LANGLADE | 067 | 0000 | 705 | 19,505 | 20,606 | 20,830 | 0.5 | 52 | 98.9 | 98.7 | 0.1 | 0.2 | 0.1 | 0.1 |
| LINCOLN | 069 | 0000 | 705 | 26,993 | 30,159 | 31,233 | 1.1 | 25 | 99.0 | 98.6 | 0.3 | 0.5 | 0.3 | 0.5 |
| MANITOWOC | 071 | 0000 | 658 | 80,421 | 83,091 | 84,113 | 0.3 | 62 | 97.9 | 97.1 | 0.1 | 0.2 | 1.3 | 2.0 |
| MARATHON | 073 | 8940 | 705 | 115,400 | 124,245 | 127,544 | 0.7 | 41 | 97.2 | 96.2 | 0.1 | 0.1 | 2.2 | 3.1 |
| MARINETTE | 075 | 0000 | 658 | 40,548 | 43,108 | 43,570 | 0.6 | 43 | 99.3 | 99.2 | 0.0 | 0.1 | 0.2 | 0.2 |
| MARQUETTE | 077 | 0000 | 669 | 12,321 | 15,620 | 16,975 | 2.3 | 2 | 98.8 | 98.5 | 0.3 | 0.3 | 0.1 | 0.2 |
| MENOMINEE | 078 | 0000 | 658 | 3,890 | 5,088 | 5,374 | 2.7 | 1 | 10.7 | 10.8 | 0.0 | 0.0 | 0.0 | 0.0 |
| MILWAUKEE | 079 | 5080 | 617 | 959,275 | 900,446 | 870,311 | -0.6 | 72 | 74.9 | 69.7 | 20.4 | 24.1 | 1.6 | 2.2 |
| MONROE | 081 | 0000 | 702 | 36,633 | 40,026 | 41,491 | 0.9 | 33 | 98.2 | 97.7 | 0.4 | 0.6 | 0.4 | 0.6 |
| OCONTO | 083 | 0000 | 658 | 30,226 | 34,897 | 37,462 | 1.4 | 13 | 99.0 | 98.8 | 0.1 | 0.1 | 0.1 | 0.2 |
| ONEIDA | 085 | 0000 | 705 | 31,679 | 36,307 | 37,624 | 1.3 | 19 | 98.9 | 98.8 | 0.2 | 0.2 | 0.2 | 0.3 |
| OUTAGAMIE | 087 | 0460 | 658 | 140,510 | 160,501 | 170,612 | 1.3 | 19 | 96.8 | 95.8 | 0.1 | 0.2 | 1.4 | 2.0 |
| OZAUKEE | 089 | 5080 | 617 | 72,831 | 82,722 | 86,359 | 1.3 | 19 | 98.4 | 97.7 | 0.7 | 1.0 | 0.6 | 0.9 |
| PEPIN | 091 | 0000 | 613 | 7,107 | 7,405 | 7,855 | 0.4 | 59 | 99.5 | 99.3 | 0.0 | 0.1 | 0.1 | 0.2 |
| PIERCE | 093 | 5120 | 613 | 32,765 | 36,495 | 38,696 | 1.1 | 25 | 98.8 | 98.5 | 0.3 | 0.3 | 0.5 | 0.7 |
| POLK | 095 | 0000 | 613 | 34,773 | 39,901 | 42,596 | 1.4 | 13 | 98.8 | 98.6 | 0.1 | 0.1 | 0.1 | 0.2 |
| PORTAGE | 097 | 0000 | 705 | 61,405 | 65,192 | 66,099 | 0.6 | 43 | 97.7 | 96.9 | 0.3 | 0.3 | 1.3 | 1.7 |
| PRICE | 099 | 0000 | 705 | 15,600 | 15,465 | 14,999 | -0.1 | 70 | 99.2 | 99.1 | 0.0 | 0.1 | 0.2 | 0.2 |
| RACINE | 101 | 6600 | 617 | 175,034 | 186,190 | 188,286 | 0.6 | 43 | 86.9 | 83.0 | 9.7 | 12.2 | 0.6 | 0.8 |
| RICHLAND | 103 | 0000 | 669 | 17,521 | 17,692 | 17,416 | 0.1 | 66 | 99.4 | 99.2 | 0.1 | 0.1 | 0.2 | 0.3 |
| ROCK | 105 | 3620 | 669 | 139,510 | 151,528 | 153,921 | 0.8 | 37 | 93.8 | 91.9 | 4.8 | 6.1 | 0.7 | 1.0 |
| RUSK | 107 | 0000 | 702 | 15,079 | 15,030 | 14,692 | 0.0 | 67 | 98.3 | 97.9 | 0.2 | 0.3 | 0.8 | 1.0 |
| ST. CROIX | 109 | 5120 | 613 | 50,251 | 61,671 | 68,556 | 2.0 | 4 | 99.3 | 98.9 | 0.1 | 0.2 | 0.3 | 0.5 |
| SAUK | 111 | 0000 | 669 | 46,975 | 55,055 | 58,904 | 1.6 | 8 | 98.9 | 98.5 | 0.1 | 0.3 | 0.2 | 0.3 |
| SAWYER | 113 | 0000 | 676 | 14,181 | 16,344 | 16,971 | 1.4 | 13 | 84.4 | 83.4 | 0.1 | 0.2 | 0.1 | 0.1 |
| SHAWANO | 115 | 0000 | 658 | 37,157 | 39,490 | 40,983 | 0.6 | 43 | 94.9 | 94.4 | 0.1 | 0.1 | 0.2 | 0.3 |
| SHEBOYGAN | 117 | 7620 | 617 | 103,877 | 110,361 | 111,635 | 0.6 | 43 | 96.6 | 95.2 | 0.4 | 0.6 | 2.0 | 2.9 |
| TAYLOR | 119 | 0000 | 705 | 18,901 | 19,266 | 19,300 | 0.2 | 64 | 99.5 | 99.2 | 0.0 | 0.2 | 0.2 | 0.3 |
| TREMPEALEAU | 121 | 0000 | 702 | 25,263 | 26,869 | 27,774 | 0.6 | 43 | 99.6 | 99.4 | 0.0 | 0.1 | 0.2 | 0.3 |
| VERNON | 123 | 0000 | 702 | 25,617 | 27,906 | 28,983 | 0.8 | 37 | 99.6 | 99.4 | 0.0 | 0.1 | 0.2 | 0.2 |
| VILAS | 125 | 0000 | 705 | 17,707 | 22,064 | 23,895 | 2.2 | 3 | 91.0 | 90.9 | 0.1 | 0.1 | 0.2 | 0.3 |
| WALWORTH | 127 | 0000 | 617 | 75,000 | 87,691 | 93,333 | 1.5 | 10 | 97.0 | 95.8 | 0.6 | 0.7 | 0.7 | 0.9 |
| WASHBURN | 129 | 0000 | 676 | 13,772 | 16,020 | 17,300 | 1.5 | 10 | 98.6 | 98.5 | 0.2 | 0.3 | 0.2 | 0.3 |
| WASHINGTON | 131 | 5080 | 617 | 95,328 | 117,268 | 125,354 | 2.0 | 4 | 99.1 | 98.8 | 0.1 | 0.2 | 0.4 | 0.5 |
| WAUKESHA | 133 | 5080 | 617 | 304,715 | 363,571 | 389,473 | 1.7 | 7 | 97.9 | 97.1 | 0.4 | 0.4 | 0.9 | 1.3 |
| WAUPACA | 135 | 0000 | 658 | 46,104 | 51,198 | 53,078 | 1.0 | 29 | 99.1 | 98.8 | 0.0 | 0.1 | 0.2 | 0.3 |
| WAUSHARA | 137 | 0000 | 658 | 19,385 | 22,013 | 22,984 | 1.2 | 23 | 98.5 | 98.0 | 0.1 | 0.2 | 0.2 | 0.4 |
| WINNEBAGO | 139 | 0460 | 658 | 140,320 | 151,089 | 153,710 | 0.7 | 41 | 97.5 | 96.5 | 0.5 | 0.7 | 1.2 | 1.8 |
| WOOD | 141 | 0000 | 705 | 73,605 | 76,329 | 76,951 | 0.4 | 59 | 98.0 | 97.4 | 0.1 | 0.2 | 1.0 | 1.4 |
| WISCONSIN | | | | | | | 0.7 | | 92.3 | 91.0 | 5.0 | 5.4 | 1.1 | 1.5 |
| UNITED STATES | | | | | | | 1.0 | | 80.3 | 77.9 | 12.1 | 12.4 | 2.9 | 3.9 |

| COUNTY | % HISPANIC ORIGIN | | 2000 AGE DISTRIBUTION (%) | | | | | | | | | | MEDIAN AGE | | 2000 Males/ Females (×100) |
|---|---|---|---|---|---|---|---|---|---|---|---|---|---|---|---|
| | 1990 | 2000 | 0-4 | 5-9 | 10-14 | 15-19 | 20-24 | 25-44 | 45-64 | 65-84 | 85+ | 18+ | 1990 | 2000 | |
| ADAMS | 2.0 | 2.9 | 4.4 | 5.1 | 6.2 | 6.2 | 4.7 | 26.6 | 26.9 | 18.0 | 1.9 | 80.3 | 40.2 | 42.9 | 115.1 |
| ASHLAND | 0.7 | 1.2 | 6.1 | 6.9 | 8.0 | 8.9 | 6.8 | 26.4 | 21.0 | 13.1 | 2.7 | 74.1 | 33.7 | 36.1 | 97.5 |
| BARRON | 0.4 | 0.9 | 6.3 | 7.0 | 7.7 | 8.1 | 5.4 | 26.9 | 23.0 | 13.1 | 2.5 | 74.0 | 34.5 | 37.7 | 100.1 |
| BAYFIELD | 0.4 | 0.8 | 5.3 | 6.6 | 8.0 | 7.5 | 4.6 | 25.9 | 25.8 | 14.3 | 2.0 | 75.2 | 37.2 | 40.4 | 105.0 |
| BROWN | 0.8 | 1.5 | 6.6 | 7.1 | 7.9 | 7.7 | 6.6 | 31.8 | 21.7 | 9.2 | 1.4 | 74.1 | 31.4 | 34.8 | 95.2 |
| BUFFALO | 0.3 | 0.8 | 6.5 | 7.2 | 7.9 | 7.6 | 4.9 | 26.8 | 22.9 | 13.6 | 2.6 | 73.4 | 34.9 | 38.5 | 101.0 |
| BURNETT | 0.3 | 0.8 | 5.0 | 5.9 | 7.4 | 7.1 | 4.2 | 24.0 | 26.2 | 17.8 | 2.5 | 77.0 | 39.2 | 42.6 | 99.2 |
| CALUMET | 0.4 | 1.1 | 6.9 | 7.8 | 9.1 | 8.2 | 5.4 | 31.0 | 21.3 | 9.0 | 1.4 | 70.9 | 31.3 | 34.5 | 99.4 |
| CHIPPEWA | 0.3 | 0.8 | 6.1 | 7.0 | 8.3 | 8.0 | 5.3 | 28.6 | 22.5 | 12.1 | 2.1 | 73.5 | 33.4 | 36.9 | 97.9 |
| CLARK | 0.4 | 0.9 | 6.9 | 7.8 | 8.3 | 8.5 | 5.3 | 25.0 | 22.1 | 13.4 | 2.6 | 71.3 | 33.9 | 36.9 | 102.0 |
| COLUMBIA | 0.8 | 1.6 | 6.2 | 6.8 | 7.6 | 7.6 | 5.5 | 27.4 | 24.0 | 12.8 | 2.2 | 74.7 | 35.2 | 38.0 | 99.1 |
| CRAWFORD | 0.4 | 0.9 | 6.1 | 7.1 | 8.6 | 8.5 | 4.8 | 25.6 | 23.2 | 13.7 | 2.4 | 72.5 | 34.9 | 37.9 | 99.9 |
| DANE | 1.6 | 2.6 | 5.7 | 6.3 | 7.2 | 8.2 | 9.5 | 32.4 | 21.3 | 8.1 | 1.3 | 77.3 | 30.7 | 34.2 | 95.8 |
| DODGE | 1.2 | 2.2 | 6.0 | 6.7 | 7.9 | 7.8 | 5.8 | 29.9 | 22.3 | 11.4 | 2.1 | 74.6 | 33.8 | 36.5 | 107.4 |
| DOOR | 0.6 | 1.2 | 5.6 | 6.4 | 7.3 | 7.3 | 5.5 | 25.8 | 25.7 | 13.7 | 2.6 | 75.8 | 36.5 | 40.3 | 98.6 |
| DOUGLAS | 0.5 | 1.0 | 5.9 | 6.3 | 7.1 | 7.7 | 6.6 | 27.4 | 24.1 | 12.8 | 2.3 | 76.3 | 34.8 | 37.9 | 96.6 |
| DUNN | 0.5 | 1.1 | 5.5 | 6.2 | 7.2 | 10.4 | 13.3 | 26.5 | 19.4 | 9.6 | 1.8 | 76.9 | 28.5 | 31.4 | 99.3 |
| EAU CLAIRE | 0.5 | 1.1 | 5.9 | 6.2 | 7.2 | 9.9 | 10.7 | 28.0 | 20.1 | 10.4 | 1.7 | 76.6 | 30.3 | 33.3 | 92.8 |
| FLORENCE | 0.2 | 0.7 | 5.6 | 6.3 | 7.1 | 8.0 | 4.9 | 26.0 | 25.7 | 14.1 | 2.3 | 75.2 | 36.2 | 40.0 | 103.8 |
| FOND DU LAC | 1.0 | 1.9 | 5.8 | 6.6 | 7.9 | 8.2 | 6.3 | 28.6 | 22.4 | 12.1 | 2.2 | 74.8 | 33.4 | 36.7 | 95.0 |
| FOREST | 0.3 | 0.7 | 6.3 | 6.7 | 8.0 | 8.8 | 5.1 | 24.3 | 23.1 | 15.4 | 2.2 | 73.3 | 35.7 | 38.2 | 101.4 |
| GRANT | 0.3 | 0.8 | 5.7 | 6.5 | 8.0 | 9.6 | 8.7 | 25.9 | 20.9 | 12.5 | 2.2 | 75.1 | 31.5 | 34.9 | 102.9 |
| GREEN | 0.4 | 1.0 | 6.2 | 7.0 | 7.7 | 7.6 | 5.5 | 27.4 | 24.2 | 12.2 | 2.1 | 74.1 | 34.4 | 37.9 | 98.5 |
| GREEN LAKE | 1.0 | 1.9 | 5.8 | 6.4 | 7.0 | 7.9 | 5.4 | 25.8 | 23.7 | 15.0 | 3.1 | 75.7 | 36.8 | 39.9 | 96.4 |
| IOWA | 0.2 | 0.7 | 6.7 | 7.5 | 8.3 | 7.9 | 5.2 | 27.8 | 22.9 | 11.8 | 1.8 | 72.3 | 33.2 | 36.9 | 101.1 |
| IRON | 0.1 | 0.6 | 4.4 | 5.1 | 5.8 | 6.1 | 5.6 | 24.0 | 25.2 | 20.0 | 3.6 | 80.6 | 42.1 | 44.3 | 97.0 |
| JACKSON | 0.9 | 1.5 | 6.3 | 7.0 | 7.7 | 7.7 | 5.8 | 25.7 | 23.7 | 13.9 | 2.3 | 74.2 | 35.5 | 38.4 | 104.7 |
| JEFFERSON | 1.7 | 2.9 | 5.7 | 6.3 | 7.6 | 9.5 | 6.7 | 28.7 | 23.0 | 10.9 | 1.7 | 75.8 | 32.8 | 36.1 | 98.2 |
| JUNEAU | 0.7 | 1.4 | 6.0 | 6.7 | 8.1 | 7.6 | 4.8 | 26.0 | 23.6 | 14.8 | 2.3 | 74.1 | 35.5 | 38.8 | 98.0 |
| KENOSHA | 4.4 | 6.8 | 6.8 | 7.2 | 7.9 | 7.6 | 6.5 | 29.5 | 22.1 | 10.8 | 1.6 | 73.8 | 32.5 | 35.5 | 96.6 |
| KEWAUNEE | 0.3 | 0.8 | 5.9 | 6.9 | 8.3 | 8.2 | 5.4 | 28.1 | 22.3 | 12.8 | 2.1 | 73.6 | 33.7 | 37.0 | 101.7 |
| LA CROSSE | 0.7 | 1.3 | 5.8 | 6.3 | 7.2 | 9.3 | 9.5 | 29.1 | 20.5 | 10.5 | 1.9 | 76.5 | 31.2 | 34.2 | 93.4 |
| LAFAYETTE | 0.2 | 0.7 | 6.9 | 7.7 | 8.1 | 8.5 | 5.0 | 26.2 | 21.9 | 13.6 | 2.1 | 71.9 | 33.6 | 37.4 | 99.1 |
| LANGLADE | 0.5 | 1.2 | 5.6 | 6.4 | 8.0 | 7.6 | 5.0 | 25.6 | 23.8 | 15.5 | 2.5 | 74.9 | 36.6 | 39.7 | 96.8 |
| LINCOLN | 0.4 | 1.0 | 5.9 | 6.5 | 7.2 | 8.4 | 5.7 | 27.0 | 23.3 | 13.7 | 2.4 | 74.8 | 34.9 | 38.4 | 98.9 |
| MANITOWOC | 0.7 | 1.4 | 5.9 | 6.6 | 7.9 | 7.6 | 5.6 | 28.0 | 22.9 | 13.4 | 2.3 | 75.0 | 34.6 | 37.9 | 96.6 |
| MARATHON | 0.4 | 0.9 | 6.5 | 7.1 | 7.8 | 7.7 | 5.9 | 29.5 | 23.1 | 10.8 | 1.6 | 73.9 | 32.7 | 36.3 | 98.4 |
| MARINETTE | 0.4 | 0.9 | 6.1 | 6.6 | 7.3 | 7.9 | 6.1 | 25.5 | 23.8 | 13.9 | 2.6 | 74.8 | 35.6 | 38.8 | 97.8 |
| MARQUETTE | 1.2 | 2.1 | 4.9 | 5.9 | 7.4 | 7.0 | 4.5 | 24.6 | 25.1 | 18.3 | 2.3 | 77.1 | 39.1 | 42.1 | 98.3 |
| MENOMINEE | 1.4 | 2.1 | 11.1 | 10.9 | 11.6 | 9.9 | 7.7 | 24.4 | 16.0 | 7.7 | 0.6 | 59.8 | 24.5 | 24.1 | 95.2 |
| MILWAUKEE | 4.7 | 6.8 | 6.5 | 6.7 | 7.7 | 7.5 | 7.0 | 30.5 | 20.5 | 11.6 | 1.9 | 74.9 | 32.3 | 35.4 | 90.8 |
| MONROE | 0.6 | 1.3 | 6.6 | 7.4 | 8.7 | 8.1 | 5.2 | 27.5 | 22.7 | 11.9 | 1.8 | 72.0 | 33.7 | 36.5 | 101.8 |
| OCONTO | 0.4 | 0.9 | 6.3 | 7.1 | 7.8 | 7.5 | 5.4 | 26.7 | 23.5 | 13.6 | 2.1 | 73.8 | 35.0 | 38.1 | 100.4 |
| ONEIDA | 0.3 | 0.8 | 4.9 | 5.7 | 7.0 | 6.8 | 4.4 | 25.7 | 27.2 | 16.1 | 2.2 | 77.9 | 38.7 | 42.2 | 98.3 |
| OUTAGAMIE | 0.7 | 1.4 | 7.1 | 7.6 | 8.3 | 7.8 | 6.4 | 30.9 | 21.3 | 9.3 | 1.4 | 72.4 | 31.4 | 34.6 | 98.2 |
| OZAUKEE | 0.7 | 1.5 | 5.6 | 6.6 | 8.1 | 7.7 | 5.3 | 28.8 | 25.4 | 11.1 | 1.4 | 75.0 | 34.6 | 38.3 | 98.3 |
| PEPIN | 0.3 | 0.9 | 6.6 | 7.3 | 7.9 | 8.3 | 5.3 | 24.5 | 23.0 | 13.7 | 3.3 | 72.7 | 35.1 | 38.5 | 95.7 |
| PIERCE | 0.6 | 1.3 | 6.5 | 7.0 | 7.4 | 9.8 | 9.3 | 29.8 | 20.0 | 8.7 | 1.5 | 74.8 | 29.3 | 32.4 | 100.8 |
| POLK | 0.4 | 0.9 | 6.4 | 7.2 | 7.9 | 8.1 | 5.4 | 26.0 | 24.2 | 12.4 | 2.3 | 73.1 | 34.6 | 38.1 | 99.5 |
| PORTAGE | 0.9 | 1.8 | 6.1 | 6.5 | 7.1 | 9.7 | 10.3 | 29.2 | 20.6 | 9.1 | 1.4 | 76.0 | 29.3 | 32.8 | 99.7 |
| PRICE | 0.4 | 0.9 | 5.5 | 6.3 | 7.9 | 7.5 | 5.0 | 25.7 | 23.7 | 15.5 | 2.8 | 75.0 | 36.8 | 39.8 | 101.0 |
| RACINE | 5.2 | 7.8 | 6.7 | 7.0 | 7.9 | 7.6 | 6.3 | 29.3 | 22.8 | 10.9 | 1.5 | 73.7 | 32.9 | 35.9 | 96.2 |
| RICHLAND | 0.3 | 0.8 | 6.3 | 7.2 | 7.9 | 7.6 | 5.3 | 25.9 | 23.2 | 14.1 | 2.5 | 74.2 | 35.3 | 38.1 | 98.1 |
| ROCK | 1.3 | 2.2 | 6.3 | 6.7 | 8.0 | 7.8 | 6.3 | 29.0 | 23.2 | 10.9 | 1.7 | 74.3 | 33.0 | 36.3 | 96.1 |
| RUSK | 0.6 | 1.2 | 5.9 | 6.8 | 8.2 | 8.2 | 5.1 | 25.7 | 22.8 | 14.9 | 2.5 | 73.9 | 35.2 | 38.4 | 99.0 |
| ST. CROIX | 0.4 | 1.0 | 7.0 | 7.7 | 8.6 | 7.9 | 5.6 | 30.4 | 22.8 | 8.4 | 1.6 | 71.5 | 31.6 | 35.1 | 100.1 |
| SAUK | 0.4 | 1.1 | 6.5 | 7.2 | 8.0 | 7.5 | 5.4 | 27.8 | 23.3 | 12.3 | 2.2 | 73.6 | 34.2 | 37.4 | 98.8 |
| SAWYER | 0.7 | 1.2 | 6.0 | 6.6 | 7.5 | 7.5 | 5.4 | 23.2 | 24.5 | 16.6 | 2.6 | 74.7 | 38.2 | 40.7 | 102.0 |
| SHAWANO | 0.3 | 0.9 | 5.9 | 6.7 | 8.0 | 7.7 | 5.0 | 26.5 | 23.3 | 14.4 | 2.5 | 74.3 | 35.3 | 38.6 | 99.7 |
| SHEBOYGAN | 1.6 | 2.8 | 6.3 | 6.8 | 7.5 | 7.6 | 6.3 | 28.7 | 22.9 | 11.8 | 2.1 | 74.6 | 33.8 | 36.9 | 98.5 |
| TAYLOR | 0.2 | 0.7 | 7.3 | 7.9 | 8.6 | 8.3 | 5.4 | 27.7 | 20.9 | 11.7 | 2.2 | 70.8 | 32.3 | 35.7 | 102.5 |
| TREMPEALEAU | 0.2 | 0.7 | 6.1 | 6.9 | 7.7 | 7.2 | 4.8 | 27.1 | 23.4 | 13.8 | 3.0 | 74.7 | 35.7 | 38.6 | 99.9 |
| VERNON | 0.4 | 1.0 | 6.3 | 7.2 | 8.0 | 7.8 | 4.8 | 24.5 | 23.6 | 14.8 | 2.9 | 73.3 | 36.2 | 39.6 | 97.1 |
| VILAS | 0.3 | 0.8 | 4.9 | 5.7 | 6.7 | 6.5 | 4.2 | 21.5 | 27.1 | 20.7 | 2.8 | 78.4 | 42.9 | 45.4 | 101.6 |
| WALWORTH | 2.7 | 4.5 | 5.7 | 6.2 | 7.0 | 8.0 | 9.2 | 27.0 | 23.2 | 11.6 | 1.9 | 76.9 | 33.1 | 36.4 | 97.9 |
| WASHBURN | 0.2 | 0.8 | 5.6 | 6.3 | 7.3 | 7.5 | 5.2 | 23.4 | 26.1 | 16.1 | 2.5 | 75.8 | 38.0 | 41.4 | 100.9 |
| WASHINGTON | 0.7 | 1.4 | 6.5 | 7.1 | 8.0 | 7.4 | 5.8 | 30.8 | 23.5 | 9.6 | 1.5 | 73.9 | 32.5 | 35.9 | 99.1 |
| WAUKESHA | 1.8 | 3.0 | 5.5 | 6.4 | 8.1 | 7.7 | 5.2 | 30.0 | 25.3 | 10.3 | 1.4 | 75.1 | 34.0 | 37.9 | 98.1 |
| WAUPACA | 0.9 | 1.6 | 6.3 | 6.9 | 7.6 | 7.5 | 5.5 | 27.1 | 22.8 | 13.3 | 2.9 | 74.4 | 35.0 | 38.1 | 98.6 |
| WAUSHARA | 2.0 | 3.2 | 5.6 | 6.3 | 7.0 | 6.9 | 5.2 | 24.4 | 24.9 | 16.9 | 2.7 | 76.6 | 38.6 | 41.4 | 100.7 |
| WINNEBAGO | 0.8 | 1.6 | 6.0 | 6.4 | 7.2 | 8.3 | 7.7 | 29.7 | 22.0 | 10.9 | 1.8 | 76.3 | 32.5 | 35.9 | 96.6 |
| WOOD | 0.5 | 1.1 | 6.2 | 7.0 | 8.2 | 7.8 | 5.6 | 29.0 | 22.4 | 11.9 | 2.0 | 73.8 | 33.3 | 36.7 | 96.2 |
| WISCONSIN | 1.9 | 3.0 | 6.2 | 6.7 | 7.7 | 7.9 | 6.7 | 29.2 | 22.4 | 11.3 | 1.8 | 74.8 | 32.9 | 36.2 | 96.7 |
| UNITED STATES | 9.0 | 11.8 | 6.9 | 7.2 | 7.2 | 7.2 | 6.7 | 29.9 | 22.2 | 11.1 | 1.6 | 74.6 | 32.9 | 35.7 | 95.6 |

# HOUSEHOLDS

| COUNTY | HOUSEHOLDS | | | | | FAMILIES | | | MEDIAN HOUSEHOLD INCOME | | | |
|---|---|---|---|---|---|---|---|---|---|---|---|---|
| | 1990 | 2000 | 2005 | % Annual Rate 1990-2000 | 2000 Average HH Size | 1990 | 2000 | % Annual Rate 1990-2000 | 2000 | 2005 | 2000 National Rank | 2000 State Rank |
| ADAMS | 5,972 | 7,506 | 8,251 | 2.8 | 2.38 | 4,373 | 5,337 | 2.4 | 32,962 | 40,569 | 1545 | 56 |
| ASHLAND | 6,255 | 6,406 | 6,388 | 0.3 | 2.44 | 4,083 | 4,031 | -0.2 | 30,500 | 34,327 | 2033 | 68 |
| BARRON | 15,435 | 17,174 | 17,890 | 1.3 | 2.55 | 11,052 | 11,893 | 0.9 | 33,650 | 41,252 | 1444 | 53 |
| BAYFIELD | 5,515 | 6,140 | 6,403 | 1.3 | 2.50 | 3,871 | 4,155 | 0.9 | 32,205 | 39,452 | 1684 | 61 |
| BROWN | 72,280 | 83,173 | 87,147 | 1.7 | 2.55 | 50,504 | 56,607 | 1.4 | 45,848 | 51,570 | 318 | 17 |
| BUFFALO | 5,123 | 5,585 | 5,774 | 1.1 | 2.53 | 3,742 | 3,942 | 0.6 | 35,353 | 42,471 | 1189 | 45 |
| BURNETT | 5,242 | 6,147 | 6,605 | 1.9 | 2.42 | 3,715 | 4,204 | 1.5 | 33,893 | 42,873 | 1408 | 52 |
| CALUMET | 11,772 | 13,811 | 14,837 | 2.0 | 2.84 | 9,269 | 10,615 | 1.7 | 52,192 | 64,164 | 168 | 7 |
| CHIPPEWA | 19,077 | 20,632 | 21,290 | 1.0 | 2.61 | 13,992 | 14,603 | 0.5 | 38,830 | 46,489 | 770 | 31 |
| CLARK | 11,209 | 12,078 | 12,545 | 0.9 | 2.74 | 8,204 | 8,557 | 0.5 | 31,919 | 38,347 | 1732 | 63 |
| COLUMBIA | 16,868 | 19,960 | 21,401 | 2.1 | 2.56 | 12,217 | 13,973 | 1.6 | 43,505 | 52,568 | 423 | 22 |
| CRAWFORD | 5,914 | 6,317 | 6,393 | 0.8 | 2.57 | 4,252 | 4,374 | 0.3 | 32,181 | 39,559 | 1692 | 62 |
| DANE | 142,786 | 172,164 | 182,411 | 2.3 | 2.42 | 87,363 | 102,334 | 1.9 | 52,352 | 61,091 | 166 | 6 |
| DODGE | 26,853 | 30,409 | 32,234 | 1.5 | 2.62 | 20,079 | 22,009 | 1.1 | 45,906 | 58,255 | 314 | 16 |
| DOOR | 10,066 | 10,887 | 11,159 | 1.0 | 2.46 | 7,192 | 7,538 | 0.6 | 38,140 | 43,837 | 842 | 36 |
| DOUGLAS | 16,374 | 17,255 | 17,360 | 0.6 | 2.41 | 11,013 | 11,220 | 0.2 | 34,085 | 38,326 | 1377 | 51 |
| DUNN | 12,250 | 13,918 | 14,508 | 1.6 | 2.64 | 8,289 | 8,954 | 0.9 | 38,480 | 47,475 | 808 | 34 |
| EAU CLAIRE | 31,282 | 33,650 | 34,650 | 0.9 | 2.54 | 20,660 | 21,454 | 0.5 | 40,019 | 46,186 | 672 | 27 |
| FLORENCE | 1,755 | 2,025 | 1,999 | 1.7 | 2.48 | 1,296 | 1,446 | 1.3 | 36,771 | 45,901 | 1010 | 39 |
| FOND DU LAC | 32,644 | 35,316 | 36,200 | 1.0 | 2.60 | 23,665 | 24,808 | 0.6 | 43,604 | 50,203 | 419 | 21 |
| FOREST | 3,290 | 3,809 | 3,968 | 1.8 | 2.46 | 2,383 | 2,671 | 1.4 | 28,807 | 32,264 | 2326 | 71 |
| GRANT | 17,169 | 17,586 | 17,784 | 0.3 | 2.63 | 12,251 | 12,153 | -0.1 | 35,478 | 44,568 | 1175 | 44 |
| GREEN | 11,541 | 13,210 | 14,051 | 1.7 | 2.56 | 8,249 | 9,117 | 1.2 | 39,872 | 48,839 | 685 | 28 |
| GREEN LAKE | 7,189 | 7,651 | 7,814 | 0.8 | 2.53 | 5,176 | 5,301 | 0.3 | 38,590 | 46,353 | 793 | 33 |
| IOWA | 7,406 | 8,632 | 9,292 | 1.9 | 2.64 | 5,397 | 6,095 | 1.5 | 38,273 | 46,397 | 831 | 35 |
| IRON | 2,602 | 2,718 | 2,654 | 0.5 | 2.26 | 1,747 | 1,761 | 0.1 | 29,539 | 34,544 | 2216 | 70 |
| JACKSON | 6,253 | 6,927 | 7,290 | 1.2 | 2.53 | 4,439 | 4,773 | 0.9 | 31,659 | 37,652 | 1788 | 64 |
| JEFFERSON | 24,019 | 26,727 | 27,598 | 1.3 | 2.64 | 17,601 | 18,938 | 0.9 | 46,684 | 56,882 | 285 | 13 |
| JUNEAU | 8,265 | 9,313 | 9,671 | 1.5 | 2.57 | 5,917 | 6,446 | 1.0 | 35,752 | 43,996 | 1129 | 42 |
| KENOSHA | 47,029 | 55,106 | 58,792 | 1.9 | 2.64 | 33,926 | 38,277 | 1.5 | 46,292 | 53,822 | 297 | 14 |
| KEWAUNEE | 6,756 | 7,354 | 7,656 | 1.0 | 2.70 | 5,053 | 5,334 | 0.7 | 38,773 | 46,051 | 773 | 32 |
| LA CROSSE | 36,662 | 39,429 | 40,228 | 0.9 | 2.48 | 23,899 | 25,132 | 0.6 | 39,676 | 43,907 | 694 | 29 |
| LAFAYETTE | 5,876 | 6,049 | 5,935 | 0.4 | 2.61 | 4,273 | 4,251 | -0.1 | 32,458 | 40,530 | 1632 | 59 |
| LANGLADE | 7,563 | 8,136 | 8,295 | 0.9 | 2.50 | 5,341 | 5,547 | 0.5 | 31,113 | 35,733 | 1912 | 66 |
| LINCOLN | 10,159 | 11,539 | 12,071 | 1.6 | 2.55 | 7,465 | 8,233 | 1.2 | 40,934 | 50,496 | 594 | 24 |
| MANITOWOC | 30,112 | 31,677 | 32,388 | 0.6 | 2.57 | 21,563 | 21,863 | 0.2 | 42,819 | 50,179 | 465 | 23 |
| MARATHON | 41,547 | 45,843 | 47,634 | 1.2 | 2.68 | 31,002 | 33,427 | 0.9 | 47,296 | 56,538 | 264 | 11 |
| MARINETTE | 15,542 | 16,857 | 17,301 | 1.0 | 2.49 | 11,080 | 11,644 | 0.6 | 34,095 | 38,890 | 1376 | 50 |
| MARQUETTE | 4,831 | 6,301 | 6,941 | 3.3 | 2.46 | 3,546 | 4,458 | 2.8 | 33,139 | 40,253 | 1514 | 54 |
| MENOMINEE | 1,079 | 1,418 | 1,501 | 3.4 | 3.56 | 905 | 1,170 | 3.2 | 21,859 | 24,702 | 3034 | 72 |
| MILWAUKEE | 373,048 | 356,121 | 346,972 | -0.6 | 2.46 | 239,289 | 219,949 | -1.0 | 40,251 | 44,454 | 652 | 26 |
| MONROE | 13,144 | 14,903 | 15,625 | 1.5 | 2.64 | 9,605 | 10,546 | 1.1 | 35,857 | 41,265 | 1120 | 41 |
| OCONTO | 11,283 | 13,461 | 14,692 | 2.2 | 2.56 | 8,368 | 9,694 | 1.8 | 34,477 | 40,172 | 1319 | 48 |
| ONEIDA | 12,666 | 14,738 | 15,421 | 1.9 | 2.40 | 9,049 | 10,209 | 1.5 | 36,775 | 40,730 | 1008 | 38 |
| OUTAGAMIE | 50,527 | 58,916 | 63,334 | 1.9 | 2.67 | 37,232 | 42,370 | 1.6 | 53,487 | 61,966 | 144 | 5 |
| OZAUKEE | 25,707 | 29,681 | 31,281 | 1.8 | 2.74 | 20,487 | 22,996 | 1.4 | 64,655 | 71,150 | 39 | 2 |
| PEPIN | 2,612 | 2,685 | 2,824 | 0.3 | 2.71 | 1,900 | 1,884 | -0.1 | 33,080 | 40,632 | 1526 | 55 |
| PIERCE | 11,011 | 12,567 | 13,469 | 1.6 | 2.73 | 7,958 | 8,735 | 1.1 | 46,855 | 58,705 | 282 | 12 |
| POLK | 13,056 | 15,237 | 16,404 | 1.9 | 2.58 | 9,567 | 10,788 | 1.5 | 37,764 | 47,118 | 870 | 37 |
| PORTAGE | 21,306 | 23,179 | 23,730 | 1.0 | 2.67 | 14,883 | 15,803 | 0.7 | 44,800 | 53,204 | 361 | 19 |
| PRICE | 6,054 | 6,258 | 6,211 | 0.4 | 2.43 | 4,292 | 4,257 | -0.1 | 35,731 | 42,015 | 1131 | 43 |
| RACINE | 63,736 | 68,980 | 70,665 | 1.0 | 2.63 | 47,011 | 49,553 | 0.6 | 47,430 | 52,779 | 260 | 10 |
| RICHLAND | 6,593 | 6,843 | 6,839 | 0.5 | 2.55 | 4,760 | 4,795 | 0.1 | 35,307 | 43,909 | 1199 | 46 |
| ROCK | 52,252 | 57,654 | 59,184 | 1.2 | 2.56 | 37,520 | 39,918 | 0.8 | 45,012 | 51,323 | 354 | 18 |
| RUSK | 5,693 | 5,897 | 5,875 | 0.4 | 2.49 | 4,073 | 4,095 | 0.1 | 29,822 | 36,853 | 2177 | 69 |
| ST. CROIX | 17,638 | 22,117 | 24,882 | 2.8 | 2.75 | 13,316 | 16,162 | 2.4 | 55,574 | 66,440 | 116 | 4 |
| SAUK | 17,703 | 20,915 | 22,489 | 2.0 | 2.59 | 12,701 | 14,506 | 1.6 | 39,637 | 44,709 | 697 | 30 |
| SAWYER | 5,569 | 6,578 | 6,907 | 2.0 | 2.44 | 3,996 | 4,516 | 1.5 | 30,767 | 36,342 | 1976 | 67 |
| SHAWANO | 13,775 | 14,822 | 15,483 | 0.9 | 2.61 | 10,189 | 10,607 | 0.5 | 36,709 | 45,751 | 1018 | 40 |
| SHEBOYGAN | 38,592 | 41,835 | 42,818 | 1.0 | 2.56 | 28,006 | 29,494 | 0.6 | 47,867 | 57,897 | 241 | 8 |
| TAYLOR | 6,692 | 6,973 | 7,077 | 0.5 | 2.72 | 5,014 | 5,090 | 0.2 | 34,453 | 40,777 | 1320 | 49 |
| TREMPEALEAU | 9,495 | 10,322 | 10,784 | 1.0 | 2.54 | 6,770 | 7,080 | 0.5 | 34,753 | 42,236 | 1288 | 47 |
| VERNON | 9,725 | 10,635 | 11,067 | 1.1 | 2.58 | 6,895 | 7,257 | 0.6 | 31,541 | 39,486 | 1811 | 65 |
| VILAS | 7,294 | 9,250 | 10,100 | 2.9 | 2.36 | 5,319 | 6,525 | 2.5 | 32,290 | 36,727 | 1662 | 60 |
| WALWORTH | 27,620 | 33,031 | 35,534 | 2.2 | 2.55 | 18,938 | 21,935 | 1.8 | 47,452 | 57,807 | 259 | 9 |
| WASHBURN | 5,456 | 6,377 | 6,905 | 1.9 | 2.48 | 3,801 | 4,284 | 1.5 | 32,772 | 39,103 | 1576 | 57 |
| WASHINGTON | 32,977 | 41,520 | 44,863 | 2.8 | 2.80 | 25,949 | 31,728 | 2.5 | 58,379 | 67,873 | 85 | 3 |
| WAUKESHA | 105,990 | 129,723 | 140,740 | 2.5 | 2.76 | 84,074 | 100,106 | 2.1 | 66,398 | 74,832 | 28 | 1 |
| WAUPACA | 17,037 | 19,380 | 20,330 | 1.6 | 2.56 | 12,350 | 13,551 | 1.1 | 40,923 | 49,573 | 596 | 25 |
| WAUSHARA | 7,616 | 8,807 | 9,271 | 1.8 | 2.48 | 5,567 | 6,206 | 1.3 | 32,684 | 41,135 | 1595 | 58 |
| WINNEBAGO | 53,216 | 58,389 | 59,971 | 1.1 | 2.47 | 36,292 | 38,440 | 0.7 | 46,287 | 53,315 | 298 | 15 |
| WOOD | 27,473 | 29,066 | 29,620 | 0.7 | 2.60 | 19,957 | 20,493 | 0.3 | 44,078 | 49,198 | 391 | 20 |
| WISCONSIN | | | | 1.2 | 2.56 | | | 0.8 | 44,486 | 51,618 | | |
| UNITED STATES | | | | 1.4 | 2.59 | | | 1.1 | 41,914 | 49,127 | | |

| COUNTY | 2000 Per Capita Income | 2000 HH Income Base | 2000 HOUSEHOLD INCOME DISTRIBUTION (%) Less than $15,000 | $15,000 to $24,999 | $25,000 to $49,999 | $50,000 to $99,999 | $100,000 to $149,999 | $150,000 or More | 2000 AVERAGE DISPOSABLE INCOME BY AGE OF HOUSEHOLDER All Ages | <35 | 35-44 | 45-54 | 55-64 | 65+ |
|---|---|---|---|---|---|---|---|---|---|---|---|---|---|---|
| ADAMS | 18,385 | 7,506 | 15.2 | 18.8 | 38.7 | 21.9 | 4.1 | 1.2 | 28,965 | 28,702 | 36,999 | 39,013 | 29,917 | 17,912 |
| ASHLAND | 16,290 | 6,406 | 18.9 | 21.5 | 37.3 | 17.3 | 3.4 | 1.7 | 27,774 | 24,358 | 34,241 | 38,185 | 28,930 | 15,742 |
| BARRON | 16,550 | 17,174 | 16.8 | 16.9 | 39.5 | 21.6 | 4.1 | 1.2 | 29,231 | 27,745 | 34,778 | 40,368 | 31,276 | 16,457 |
| BAYFIELD | 16,086 | 6,140 | 18.1 | 17.3 | 38.9 | 21.4 | 3.2 | 1.0 | 27,904 | 26,028 | 33,229 | 37,189 | 28,900 | 17,081 |
| BROWN | 22,818 | 83,170 | 11.3 | 9.1 | 34.9 | 33.8 | 8.0 | 2.8 | 38,799 | 32,360 | 43,691 | 50,911 | 42,639 | 22,566 |
| BUFFALO | 16,880 | 5,585 | 16.2 | 16.1 | 38.5 | 24.6 | 3.7 | 0.9 | 29,657 | 28,000 | 35,885 | 39,698 | 29,885 | 18,128 |
| BURNETT | 16,713 | 6,147 | 16.3 | 16.2 | 39.8 | 23.7 | 3.4 | 0.6 | 28,548 | 27,883 | 34,316 | 36,290 | 32,645 | 18,666 |
| CALUMET | 22,628 | 13,811 | 7.0 | 5.5 | 34.6 | 39.6 | 10.9 | 2.4 | 42,550 | 38,383 | 47,707 | 51,370 | 48,594 | 25,480 |
| CHIPPEWA | 17,409 | 20,626 | 16.3 | 11.4 | 38.1 | 28.8 | 4.5 | 1.0 | 31,806 | 29,129 | 38,245 | 41,088 | 32,742 | 18,699 |
| CLARK | 14,323 | 12,078 | 18.4 | 18.2 | 39.1 | 20.9 | 2.8 | 0.8 | 27,455 | 26,771 | 33,565 | 34,604 | 30,801 | 16,572 |
| COLUMBIA | 20,132 | 19,960 | 9.9 | 10.4 | 38.7 | 33.8 | 6.1 | 1.2 | 35,365 | 32,004 | 40,207 | 46,363 | 37,756 | 23,619 |
| CRAWFORD | 15,742 | 6,317 | 17.1 | 18.3 | 40.2 | 20.5 | 3.2 | 0.8 | 27,727 | 27,047 | 32,201 | 36,793 | 27,434 | 17,942 |
| DANE | 27,428 | 172,164 | 7.9 | 8.5 | 30.5 | 37.4 | 11.2 | 4.4 | 44,251 | 33,455 | 48,962 | 56,129 | 50,936 | 31,907 |
| DODGE | 20,703 | 30,409 | 9.1 | 9.2 | 36.9 | 35.8 | 7.4 | 1.5 | 37,334 | 33,885 | 43,452 | 48,396 | 40,932 | 22,734 |
| DOOR | 18,718 | 10,887 | 15.0 | 13.1 | 38.0 | 28.6 | 4.4 | 1.0 | 31,471 | 28,552 | 34,443 | 40,905 | 35,495 | 20,737 |
| DOUGLAS | 17,077 | 17,255 | 17.9 | 15.8 | 39.4 | 22.6 | 3.5 | 0.9 | 28,748 | 24,927 | 33,675 | 38,112 | 32,057 | 17,839 |
| DUNN | 17,759 | 13,918 | 13.4 | 14.1 | 37.5 | 27.2 | 5.8 | 2.0 | 33,551 | 27,190 | 40,463 | 44,285 | 39,284 | 20,874 |
| EAU CLAIRE | 18,858 | 33,650 | 14.0 | 13.0 | 36.2 | 29.4 | 5.8 | 1.5 | 33,631 | 27,706 | 39,862 | 44,750 | 36,126 | 22,190 |
| FLORENCE | 17,289 | 2,025 | 15.3 | 14.7 | 39.1 | 26.2 | 4.1 | 0.7 | 30,243 | 30,455 | 34,769 | 37,629 | 30,951 | 19,702 |
| FOND DU LAC | 19,907 | 35,316 | 11.1 | 9.9 | 38.2 | 33.3 | 6.1 | 1.5 | 35,627 | 31,992 | 40,540 | 46,339 | 40,083 | 21,475 |
| FOREST | 15,014 | 3,809 | 20.6 | 22.1 | 36.8 | 16.1 | 3.3 | 1.2 | 26,116 | 24,475 | 31,074 | 36,614 | 25,916 | 16,095 |
| GRANT | 16,306 | 17,586 | 14.7 | 16.3 | 38.0 | 25.8 | 4.2 | 1.1 | 30,628 | 26,470 | 35,491 | 41,681 | 34,518 | 20,312 |
| GREEN | 19,029 | 13,210 | 11.0 | 13.7 | 40.4 | 29.3 | 4.5 | 1.2 | 33,038 | 30,071 | 36,869 | 41,257 | 37,039 | 21,805 |
| GREEN LAKE | 18,432 | 7,651 | 13.6 | 12.4 | 40.5 | 28.4 | 4.1 | 1.0 | 31,514 | 29,554 | 36,609 | 41,303 | 34,575 | 21,213 |
| IOWA | 17,228 | 8,632 | 13.7 | 13.7 | 39.5 | 27.9 | 4.3 | 1.0 | 31,515 | 29,303 | 36,160 | 39,588 | 32,804 | 20,062 |
| IRON | 16,107 | 2,718 | 18.8 | 22.3 | 36.6 | 18.4 | 3.5 | 0.4 | 26,006 | 27,207 | 33,792 | 33,972 | 30,427 | 16,481 |
| JACKSON | 17,205 | 6,927 | 15.9 | 18.4 | 41.2 | 19.1 | 3.7 | 1.7 | 29,005 | 26,649 | 35,077 | 37,176 | 31,953 | 17,754 |
| JEFFERSON | 20,805 | 26,727 | 9.7 | 8.5 | 36.3 | 35.6 | 8.1 | 1.9 | 38,199 | 34,024 | 43,268 | 48,970 | 43,451 | 23,054 |
| JUNEAU | 16,686 | 9,313 | 15.1 | 15.6 | 40.0 | 24.6 | 3.8 | 0.9 | 29,793 | 29,300 | 35,343 | 38,387 | 31,226 | 19,079 |
| KENOSHA | 22,474 | 55,106 | 9.3 | 10.6 | 35.2 | 35.0 | 7.7 | 2.3 | 38,022 | 33,047 | 43,482 | 48,688 | 40,792 | 23,927 |
| KEWAUNEE | 17,497 | 7,354 | 15.6 | 12.9 | 37.7 | 26.8 | 5.3 | 1.8 | 32,944 | 30,090 | 38,295 | 44,934 | 40,709 | 16,760 |
| LA CROSSE | 19,797 | 39,421 | 13.8 | 12.4 | 38.0 | 27.5 | 6.0 | 2.3 | 34,566 | 27,481 | 40,949 | 45,983 | 40,125 | 21,809 |
| LAFAYETTE | 14,762 | 6,049 | 16.7 | 18.5 | 40.7 | 20.8 | 2.9 | 0.5 | 27,200 | 25,780 | 30,969 | 35,057 | 29,774 | 18,487 |
| LANGLADE | 16,222 | 8,136 | 17.2 | 19.3 | 39.4 | 18.2 | 4.2 | 1.7 | 28,624 | 26,539 | 34,341 | 38,578 | 31,783 | 16,855 |
| LINCOLN | 18,779 | 11,539 | 14.0 | 10.9 | 38.1 | 31.2 | 4.9 | 1.0 | 32,887 | 32,586 | 40,403 | 41,641 | 33,856 | 20,150 |
| MANITOWOC | 19,886 | 31,677 | 12.2 | 10.3 | 37.7 | 32.6 | 5.8 | 1.4 | 34,890 | 31,309 | 40,858 | 45,354 | 40,524 | 21,670 |
| MARATHON | 21,359 | 45,843 | 10.7 | 9.3 | 33.4 | 36.3 | 8.3 | 2.0 | 38,382 | 34,212 | 44,437 | 49,841 | 41,923 | 21,780 |
| MARINETTE | 16,191 | 16,857 | 16.8 | 16.3 | 40.8 | 21.9 | 3.4 | 0.9 | 28,687 | 28,461 | 34,326 | 37,053 | 30,400 | 16,428 |
| MARQUETTE | 16,398 | 6,301 | 16.2 | 18.4 | 38.6 | 23.2 | 2.9 | 0.8 | 28,168 | 29,214 | 35,128 | 36,626 | 30,324 | 17,925 |
| MENOMINEE | 8,749 | 1,417 | 34.4 | 19.8 | 28.0 | 14.7 | 2.7 | 0.5 | 22,542 | 16,359 | 25,458 | 30,033 | 30,121 | 17,020 |
| MILWAUKEE | 21,062 | 356,113 | 15.2 | 12.5 | 35.4 | 28.6 | 6.0 | 2.4 | 34,703 | 29,582 | 39,176 | 43,915 | 38,936 | 23,749 |
| MONROE | 15,897 | 14,903 | 15.2 | 15.3 | 40.7 | 25.1 | 3.1 | 0.6 | 29,260 | 26,501 | 33,496 | 36,180 | 32,456 | 18,887 |
| OCONTO | 16,646 | 13,461 | 16.6 | 15.2 | 41.7 | 20.8 | 4.1 | 1.6 | 29,979 | 29,515 | 37,792 | 37,906 | 30,504 | 16,472 |
| ONEIDA | 20,313 | 14,738 | 10.8 | 15.9 | 41.5 | 23.6 | 5.4 | 2.8 | 33,635 | 28,477 | 38,181 | 46,302 | 36,597 | 20,505 |
| OUTAGAMIE | 24,601 | 58,916 | 7.6 | 6.3 | 31.7 | 40.0 | 11.4 | 3.1 | 43,313 | 38,597 | 48,124 | 54,304 | 47,006 | 26,133 |
| OZAUKEE | 33,593 | 29,681 | 4.1 | 4.8 | 25.5 | 39.1 | 15.5 | 11.0 | 58,856 | 44,327 | 60,404 | 69,680 | 59,891 | 37,273 |
| PEPIN | 15,488 | 2,685 | 21.5 | 14.6 | 37.2 | 22.3 | 3.4 | 0.9 | 27,949 | 25,177 | 33,730 | 39,067 | 30,518 | 15,965 |
| PIERCE | 21,489 | 12,567 | 9.7 | 9.3 | 35.3 | 33.0 | 9.1 | 3.6 | 40,654 | 34,197 | 46,064 | 52,438 | 44,242 | 23,745 |
| POLK | 18,720 | 15,237 | 15.0 | 14.6 | 35.7 | 27.3 | 5.5 | 2.0 | 32,952 | 31,162 | 39,387 | 42,582 | 34,385 | 17,878 |
| PORTAGE | 20,019 | 23,179 | 11.4 | 10.1 | 35.1 | 33.1 | 7.7 | 2.6 | 37,861 | 31,324 | 43,186 | 50,692 | 42,830 | 22,428 |
| PRICE | 17,850 | 6,258 | 17.1 | 13.8 | 39.3 | 23.9 | 4.8 | 1.3 | 30,337 | 31,001 | 37,237 | 40,246 | 33,644 | 16,935 |
| RACINE | 23,023 | 68,980 | 10.6 | 9.1 | 33.5 | 35.2 | 8.5 | 3.1 | 39,725 | 32,184 | 44,465 | 51,948 | 44,952 | 25,104 |
| RICHLAND | 16,916 | 6,843 | 15.6 | 16.8 | 38.2 | 24.5 | 3.9 | 1.1 | 29,842 | 27,613 | 36,901 | 38,887 | 31,622 | 18,643 |
| ROCK | 21,830 | 57,654 | 11.1 | 10.4 | 35.3 | 34.0 | 7.2 | 2.0 | 36,873 | 32,193 | 41,817 | 47,940 | 39,931 | 22,572 |
| RUSK | 14,641 | 5,897 | 19.4 | 21.1 | 38.2 | 17.7 | 2.9 | 0.7 | 25,983 | 24,508 | 31,877 | 33,635 | 29,203 | 15,822 |
| ST. CROIX | 25,276 | 22,117 | 7.4 | 6.8 | 28.7 | 41.0 | 11.9 | 4.1 | 45,064 | 40,265 | 49,777 | 55,863 | 47,588 | 22,859 |
| SAUK | 17,705 | 20,915 | 12.4 | 13.5 | 39.9 | 29.1 | 4.2 | 0.9 | 32,124 | 29,930 | 36,934 | 40,427 | 34,708 | 20,684 |
| SAWYER | 16,733 | 6,578 | 18.5 | 20.1 | 36.8 | 18.9 | 4.1 | 1.6 | 28,187 | 25,422 | 35,641 | 34,734 | 31,839 | 18,236 |
| SHAWANO | 16,589 | 14,822 | 16.3 | 13.5 | 39.1 | 26.8 | 3.7 | 0.7 | 30,177 | 29,542 | 35,531 | 39,468 | 32,379 | 18,975 |
| SHEBOYGAN | 22,422 | 41,835 | 9.6 | 8.7 | 34.8 | 36.4 | 8.5 | 2.1 | 38,991 | 35,270 | 44,254 | 50,022 | 44,296 | 23,413 |
| TAYLOR | 15,038 | 6,973 | 16.9 | 16.9 | 39.0 | 22.6 | 3.6 | 0.9 | 28,955 | 27,904 | 33,998 | 37,930 | 31,663 | 16,242 |
| TREMPEALEAU | 16,121 | 10,322 | 16.2 | 15.3 | 41.0 | 24.0 | 3.1 | 0.5 | 28,676 | 28,077 | 34,539 | 36,864 | 32,123 | 16,807 |
| VERNON | 15,539 | 10,635 | 20.0 | 18.4 | 36.5 | 20.2 | 3.8 | 1.2 | 27,783 | 25,231 | 32,416 | 37,384 | 30,865 | 17,725 |
| VILAS | 19,014 | 9,250 | 16.2 | 19.6 | 36.6 | 21.5 | 4.2 | 1.9 | 29,681 | 26,679 | 35,746 | 39,329 | 32,506 | 20,770 |
| WALWORTH | 23,306 | 33,031 | 8.9 | 10.9 | 33.6 | 35.1 | 8.6 | 2.9 | 39,532 | 32,454 | 45,288 | 49,857 | 45,871 | 25,964 |
| WASHBURN | 16,382 | 6,377 | 18.2 | 17.9 | 37.8 | 21.4 | 3.9 | 0.8 | 27,999 | 26,245 | 33,499 | 36,977 | 30,672 | 18,021 |
| WASHINGTON | 26,192 | 41,519 | 5.2 | 4.7 | 29.5 | 42.9 | 13.7 | 4.0 | 47,174 | 41,590 | 50,973 | 56,860 | 51,858 | 29,552 |
| WAUKESHA | 32,030 | 129,723 | 4.3 | 3.8 | 22.7 | 44.2 | 17.0 | 8.0 | 55,559 | 45,342 | 57,484 | 66,180 | 59,826 | 34,789 |
| WAUPACA | 18,347 | 19,380 | 13.4 | 12.0 | 37.6 | 31.2 | 5.0 | 0.8 | 32,951 | 32,647 | 38,896 | 41,750 | 34,426 | 19,798 |
| WAUSHARA | 15,806 | 8,807 | 18.3 | 17.2 | 38.5 | 22.6 | 2.8 | 0.6 | 27,563 | 26,782 | 33,608 | 36,333 | 30,695 | 17,851 |
| WINNEBAGO | 22,110 | 58,389 | 11.3 | 9.7 | 34.0 | 35.4 | 7.6 | 2.0 | 37,701 | 32,077 | 43,230 | 49,910 | 42,192 | 23,450 |
| WOOD | 23,339 | 29,066 | 11.6 | 10.0 | 36.2 | 30.7 | 7.9 | 3.6 | 39,095 | 31,960 | 45,447 | 50,954 | 43,587 | 22,899 |
| WISCONSIN | 22,127 | | 11.7 | 10.8 | 34.5 | 32.4 | 7.8 | 2.8 | 37,949 | 32,304 | 43,189 | 48,841 | 41,897 | 23,477 |
| UNITED STATES | 22,162 | | 14.5 | 12.5 | 32.3 | 29.8 | 7.4 | 3.5 | 40,748 | 34,503 | 44,969 | 49,579 | 43,409 | 27,339 |

# SPENDING POTENTIAL INDEXES

| COUNTY | FINANCIAL SERVICES | | | | THE HOME | | | | | | ENTERTAINMENT | | | | | | PERSONAL | | | |
|---|---|---|---|---|---|---|---|---|---|---|---|---|---|---|---|---|---|---|---|---|
| | | | | | Home Improvements | | | Furnishings | | | | | | | | | | | | |
| | Auto Loan | Home Loan | Invest-ments | Retire-ment Plans | Home Repair | Lawn & Garden | Remodel-ing | Appli-ances | Elec-tronics | Furni-ture | Restau-rants | Sport-ing Goods | Theater & Concerts | Toys & Hobbies | Travel | Video Rental | Apparel | Auto After-market | Health Insur-ance | Pets & Supplies |
| ADAMS | 100 | 71 | 76 | 86 | 93 | 92 | 123 | 99 | 92 | 76 | 82 | 98 | 85 | 99 | 80 | 102 | 82 | 92 | 108 | 101 |
| ASHLAND | 95 | 78 | 84 | 84 | 96 | 93 | 105 | 95 | 92 | 84 | 85 | 92 | 89 | 94 | 86 | 99 | 83 | 92 | 101 | 96 |
| BARRON | 98 | 72 | 78 | 83 | 92 | 91 | 111 | 96 | 91 | 79 | 83 | 96 | 85 | 97 | 80 | 100 | 82 | 91 | 104 | 98 |
| BAYFIELD | 99 | 72 | 76 | 84 | 93 | 91 | 117 | 97 | 92 | 79 | 83 | 96 | 85 | 98 | 80 | 101 | 82 | 92 | 105 | 99 |
| BROWN | 99 | 99 | 94 | 97 | 100 | 98 | 100 | 98 | 98 | 99 | 102 | 99 | 101 | 101 | 96 | 102 | 98 | 101 | 99 | 100 |
| BUFFALO | 97 | 71 | 77 | 82 | 93 | 91 | 109 | 96 | 90 | 78 | 83 | 95 | 85 | 96 | 80 | 100 | 81 | 91 | 104 | 97 |
| BURNETT | 100 | 71 | 76 | 86 | 93 | 92 | 121 | 98 | 93 | 78 | 83 | 98 | 85 | 99 | 80 | 102 | 83 | 92 | 107 | 101 |
| CALUMET | 101 | 91 | 85 | 93 | 96 | 94 | 109 | 100 | 100 | 95 | 100 | 101 | 98 | 103 | 89 | 104 | 96 | 100 | 101 | 103 |
| CHIPPEWA | 98 | 79 | 82 | 85 | 95 | 92 | 107 | 97 | 93 | 85 | 89 | 95 | 90 | 98 | 84 | 101 | 86 | 93 | 102 | 98 |
| CLARK | 98 | 66 | 72 | 81 | 91 | 90 | 111 | 96 | 90 | 73 | 80 | 96 | 82 | 96 | 76 | 100 | 79 | 90 | 106 | 97 |
| COLUMBIA | 99 | 78 | 82 | 85 | 95 | 91 | 112 | 97 | 93 | 84 | 88 | 96 | 89 | 99 | 83 | 101 | 86 | 93 | 103 | 100 |
| CRAWFORD | 97 | 70 | 76 | 81 | 92 | 90 | 111 | 96 | 91 | 78 | 83 | 95 | 84 | 96 | 78 | 100 | 81 | 91 | 104 | 97 |
| DANE | 100 | 107 | 99 | 103 | 101 | 101 | 99 | 98 | 100 | 101 | 107 | 100 | 103 | 102 | 100 | 102 | 102 | 104 | 99 | 102 |
| DODGE | 98 | 82 | 86 | 87 | 97 | 93 | 110 | 97 | 94 | 88 | 91 | 96 | 92 | 99 | 86 | 101 | 88 | 94 | 102 | 100 |
| DOOR | 99 | 79 | 84 | 88 | 95 | 93 | 116 | 98 | 93 | 84 | 88 | 97 | 90 | 100 | 84 | 101 | 86 | 94 | 104 | 101 |
| DOUGLAS | 96 | 83 | 88 | 86 | 98 | 94 | 105 | 96 | 92 | 88 | 89 | 93 | 92 | 96 | 88 | 100 | 87 | 93 | 101 | 97 |
| DUNN | 96 | 78 | 81 | 84 | 93 | 90 | 107 | 94 | 91 | 80 | 86 | 93 | 86 | 95 | 81 | 99 | 83 | 92 | 101 | 97 |
| EAU CLAIRE | 97 | 93 | 92 | 92 | 97 | 95 | 102 | 96 | 95 | 91 | 96 | 95 | 95 | 98 | 91 | 100 | 92 | 97 | 99 | 99 |
| FLORENCE | 100 | 74 | 78 | 86 | 93 | 91 | 119 | 98 | 94 | 80 | 85 | 97 | 87 | 99 | 80 | 102 | 84 | 93 | 105 | 101 |
| FOND DU LAC | 99 | 89 | 92 | 91 | 99 | 95 | 107 | 98 | 95 | 93 | 96 | 97 | 96 | 100 | 90 | 101 | 92 | 97 | 101 | 100 |
| FOREST | 99 | 69 | 73 | 83 | 92 | 91 | 120 | 98 | 92 | 76 | 81 | 97 | 83 | 97 | 78 | 101 | 81 | 91 | 106 | 99 |
| GRANT | 97 | 74 | 79 | 83 | 93 | 90 | 108 | 95 | 91 | 79 | 84 | 94 | 86 | 96 | 81 | 100 | 82 | 91 | 103 | 97 |
| GREEN | 97 | 77 | 82 | 84 | 95 | 92 | 107 | 96 | 91 | 83 | 87 | 95 | 89 | 97 | 83 | 100 | 84 | 92 | 103 | 98 |
| GREEN LAKE | 98 | 75 | 80 | 84 | 95 | 92 | 112 | 97 | 92 | 82 | 86 | 95 | 88 | 98 | 82 | 101 | 84 | 92 | 103 | 99 |
| IOWA | 99 | 73 | 77 | 83 | 92 | 90 | 111 | 96 | 91 | 79 | 85 | 97 | 86 | 98 | 79 | 101 | 83 | 92 | 104 | 99 |
| IRON | 97 | 74 | 79 | 84 | 95 | 92 | 113 | 96 | 90 | 81 | 83 | 94 | 87 | 96 | 83 | 100 | 82 | 91 | 104 | 97 |
| JACKSON | 98 | 69 | 75 | 82 | 92 | 91 | 112 | 96 | 91 | 77 | 81 | 96 | 84 | 96 | 78 | 100 | 80 | 90 | 104 | 98 |
| JEFFERSON | 98 | 85 | 88 | 88 | 97 | 93 | 107 | 97 | 94 | 89 | 93 | 95 | 93 | 99 | 87 | 101 | 89 | 95 | 101 | 99 |
| JUNEAU | 97 | 71 | 76 | 82 | 92 | 90 | 112 | 96 | 91 | 78 | 83 | 95 | 84 | 96 | 79 | 100 | 81 | 91 | 104 | 98 |
| KENOSHA | 97 | 94 | 96 | 93 | 101 | 98 | 100 | 97 | 95 | 96 | 98 | 96 | 99 | 99 | 95 | 101 | 94 | 98 | 100 | 99 |
| KEWAUNEE | 98 | 77 | 82 | 84 | 96 | 92 | 111 | 97 | 92 | 84 | 88 | 96 | 90 | 99 | 83 | 101 | 85 | 93 | 103 | 99 |
| LA CROSSE | 97 | 96 | 94 | 94 | 99 | 96 | 101 | 96 | 96 | 95 | 98 | 96 | 97 | 98 | 94 | 101 | 94 | 98 | 99 | 99 |
| LAFAYETTE | 98 | 66 | 73 | 81 | 91 | 90 | 111 | 96 | 90 | 73 | 80 | 96 | 82 | 96 | 77 | 100 | 79 | 90 | 106 | 98 |
| LANGLADE | 97 | 71 | 76 | 82 | 93 | 91 | 111 | 96 | 91 | 78 | 82 | 94 | 85 | 96 | 80 | 100 | 81 | 90 | 104 | 97 |
| LINCOLN | 97 | 77 | 83 | 84 | 95 | 93 | 111 | 97 | 93 | 84 | 87 | 94 | 89 | 97 | 84 | 101 | 85 | 92 | 103 | 98 |
| MANITOWOC | 97 | 86 | 91 | 89 | 99 | 95 | 106 | 97 | 94 | 91 | 93 | 95 | 95 | 98 | 90 | 101 | 89 | 95 | 101 | 99 |
| MARATHON | 99 | 88 | 91 | 92 | 98 | 96 | 105 | 98 | 95 | 92 | 95 | 97 | 96 | 100 | 90 | 101 | 92 | 97 | 101 | 100 |
| MARINETTE | 98 | 76 | 80 | 84 | 95 | 92 | 112 | 97 | 92 | 82 | 86 | 95 | 88 | 97 | 83 | 100 | 84 | 92 | 103 | 98 |
| MARQUETTE | 99 | 71 | 76 | 84 | 93 | 91 | 118 | 97 | 93 | 79 | 83 | 96 | 85 | 98 | 79 | 101 | 82 | 92 | 105 | 99 |
| MENOMINEE | 89 | 80 | 77 | 76 | 100 | 90 | 98 | 93 | 86 | 86 | 82 | 86 | 86 | 87 | 90 | 95 | 80 | 89 | 95 | 92 |
| MILWAUKEE | 95 | 98 | 103 | 96 | 104 | 100 | 94 | 96 | 94 | 98 | 97 | 94 | 100 | 96 | 100 | 100 | 95 | 98 | 98 | 97 |
| MONROE | 98 | 76 | 80 | 84 | 94 | 91 | 111 | 97 | 92 | 82 | 87 | 96 | 88 | 98 | 81 | 101 | 84 | 92 | 103 | 99 |
| OCONTO | 99 | 73 | 76 | 83 | 93 | 91 | 114 | 97 | 94 | 81 | 85 | 97 | 86 | 98 | 79 | 101 | 83 | 92 | 104 | 99 |
| ONEIDA | 99 | 75 | 81 | 87 | 95 | 93 | 118 | 98 | 93 | 81 | 85 | 97 | 88 | 99 | 83 | 101 | 84 | 93 | 106 | 100 |
| OUTAGAMIE | 99 | 96 | 92 | 94 | 99 | 97 | 102 | 99 | 98 | 97 | 101 | 99 | 100 | 101 | 94 | 102 | 97 | 100 | 100 | 101 |
| OZAUKEE | 105 | 115 | 113 | 117 | 108 | 112 | 107 | 104 | 108 | 113 | 118 | 109 | 117 | 109 | 112 | 105 | 116 | 112 | 104 | 106 |
| PEPIN | 97 | 63 | 70 | 79 | 90 | 89 | 109 | 95 | 90 | 72 | 78 | 94 | 80 | 94 | 75 | 100 | 77 | 89 | 106 | 96 |
| PIERCE | 98 | 87 | 84 | 89 | 95 | 92 | 106 | 96 | 95 | 88 | 93 | 96 | 92 | 98 | 86 | 101 | 90 | 96 | 100 | 99 |
| POLK | 98 | 74 | 78 | 84 | 93 | 91 | 114 | 97 | 93 | 80 | 85 | 95 | 86 | 97 | 80 | 101 | 83 | 92 | 104 | 99 |
| PORTAGE | 98 | 88 | 88 | 90 | 97 | 93 | 105 | 96 | 95 | 90 | 94 | 96 | 93 | 99 | 88 | 101 | 91 | 96 | 100 | 100 |
| PRICE | 98 | 75 | 82 | 84 | 97 | 94 | 111 | 97 | 91 | 83 | 86 | 96 | 89 | 97 | 84 | 100 | 83 | 92 | 104 | 98 |
| RACINE | 97 | 96 | 99 | 95 | 102 | 99 | 99 | 98 | 96 | 98 | 98 | 96 | 100 | 99 | 97 | 101 | 95 | 99 | 100 | 98 |
| RICHLAND | 98 | 69 | 75 | 81 | 91 | 90 | 110 | 96 | 91 | 76 | 82 | 96 | 84 | 96 | 78 | 100 | 80 | 90 | 105 | 98 |
| ROCK | 98 | 91 | 93 | 92 | 100 | 96 | 103 | 97 | 95 | 94 | 96 | 96 | 97 | 99 | 93 | 101 | 93 | 97 | 100 | 99 |
| RUSK | 98 | 68 | 73 | 81 | 91 | 90 | 113 | 96 | 92 | 75 | 81 | 96 | 83 | 96 | 77 | 101 | 80 | 90 | 105 | 98 |
| ST. CROIX | 101 | 96 | 93 | 98 | 99 | 98 | 106 | 100 | 101 | 98 | 102 | 101 | 101 | 103 | 94 | 104 | 99 | 102 | 101 | 103 |
| SAUK | 98 | 76 | 80 | 84 | 93 | 91 | 112 | 97 | 92 | 82 | 86 | 96 | 88 | 98 | 81 | 101 | 84 | 92 | 103 | 99 |
| SAWYER | 98 | 72 | 75 | 84 | 93 | 91 | 118 | 97 | 92 | 78 | 82 | 96 | 85 | 97 | 80 | 101 | 82 | 91 | 105 | 99 |
| SHAWANO | 98 | 70 | 75 | 82 | 92 | 90 | 113 | 96 | 92 | 78 | 82 | 95 | 84 | 97 | 78 | 101 | 81 | 91 | 104 | 98 |
| SHEBOYGAN | 98 | 88 | 90 | 90 | 99 | 95 | 106 | 97 | 94 | 92 | 95 | 96 | 95 | 99 | 90 | 101 | 91 | 96 | 100 | 99 |
| TAYLOR | 98 | 72 | 77 | 83 | 92 | 90 | 111 | 96 | 92 | 79 | 84 | 96 | 85 | 97 | 79 | 101 | 82 | 91 | 104 | 99 |
| TREMPEALEAU | 98 | 74 | 81 | 84 | 95 | 92 | 110 | 97 | 92 | 81 | 86 | 95 | 88 | 97 | 82 | 101 | 83 | 92 | 104 | 98 |
| VERNON | 97 | 66 | 72 | 80 | 91 | 90 | 110 | 95 | 91 | 74 | 79 | 94 | 81 | 95 | 76 | 100 | 79 | 90 | 105 | 97 |
| VILAS | 99 | 71 | 78 | 86 | 93 | 93 | 121 | 98 | 91 | 77 | 82 | 97 | 85 | 98 | 81 | 101 | 82 | 92 | 107 | 100 |
| WALWORTH | 98 | 86 | 90 | 90 | 97 | 94 | 110 | 97 | 94 | 88 | 92 | 96 | 93 | 99 | 88 | 101 | 89 | 95 | 102 | 100 |
| WASHBURN | 98 | 69 | 73 | 83 | 92 | 91 | 117 | 97 | 92 | 76 | 81 | 96 | 83 | 97 | 78 | 101 | 80 | 91 | 106 | 99 |
| WASHINGTON | 102 | 100 | 95 | 100 | 100 | 99 | 105 | 101 | 102 | 102 | 106 | 102 | 104 | 104 | 96 | 104 | 102 | 104 | 101 | 103 |
| WAUKESHA | 105 | 114 | 110 | 115 | 107 | 110 | 104 | 104 | 108 | 113 | 118 | 108 | 116 | 109 | 110 | 105 | 115 | 112 | 104 | 106 |
| WAUPACA | 98 | 77 | 81 | 85 | 95 | 92 | 111 | 97 | 94 | 84 | 87 | 95 | 89 | 98 | 83 | 101 | 85 | 93 | 103 | 99 |
| WAUSHARA | 99 | 72 | 78 | 85 | 93 | 92 | 117 | 98 | 93 | 79 | 83 | 97 | 86 | 98 | 80 | 101 | 82 | 92 | 105 | 100 |
| WINNEBAGO | 98 | 95 | 95 | 94 | 100 | 97 | 100 | 97 | 96 | 96 | 99 | 97 | 99 | 100 | 95 | 101 | 95 | 99 | 100 | 99 |
| WOOD | 98 | 88 | 90 | 91 | 98 | 95 | 106 | 98 | 95 | 92 | 95 | 96 | 96 | 99 | 90 | 101 | 91 | 97 | 101 | 99 |
| WISCONSIN | 98 | 93 | 95 | 95 | 99 | 98 | 104 | 98 | 96 | 94 | 97 | 98 | 98 | 100 | 94 | 101 | 94 | 98 | 101 | 100 |
| UNITED STATES | 100 | 100 | 100 | 100 | 100 | 100 | 100 | 100 | 100 | 100 | 100 | 100 | 100 | 100 | 100 | 100 | 100 | 100 | 100 | 100 |

| COUNTY | FIPS Code | MSA Code | DMA Code | POPULATION 1990 | POPULATION 2000 | POPULATION 2005 | 1990-2000 ANNUAL CHANGE % Rate | 1990-2000 ANNUAL CHANGE State Rank | RACE (%) White 1990 | White 2000 | Black 1990 | Black 2000 | Asian/Pacific 1990 | Asian/Pacific 2000 |
|---|---|---|---|---|---|---|---|---|---|---|---|---|---|---|
| ALBANY | 001 | 0000 | 751 | 30,797 | 28,743 | 27,182 | -0.7 | 21 | 93.6 | 92.7 | 0.8 | 0.9 | 2.1 | 2.6 |
| BIG HORN | 003 | 0000 | 756 | 10,525 | 11,222 | 11,261 | 0.6 | 13 | 97.0 | 96.8 | 0.0 | 0.0 | 0.2 | 0.3 |
| CAMPBELL | 005 | 0000 | 751 | 29,370 | 33,014 | 34,547 | 1.1 | 4 | 97.6 | 97.2 | 0.1 | 0.1 | 0.3 | 0.4 |
| CARBON | 007 | 0000 | 751 | 16,659 | 15,301 | 14,637 | -0.8 | 22 | 90.7 | 89.8 | 0.6 | 0.7 | 0.5 | 0.7 |
| CONVERSE | 009 | 0000 | 767 | 11,128 | 12,492 | 12,971 | 1.1 | 4 | 96.3 | 96.0 | 0.1 | 0.1 | 0.3 | 0.4 |
| CROOK | 011 | 0000 | 764 | 5,294 | 5,781 | 5,817 | 0.9 | 7 | 99.3 | 99.4 | 0.0 | 0.0 | 0.1 | 0.1 |
| FREMONT | 013 | 0000 | 767 | 33,662 | 36,273 | 36,719 | 0.7 | 11 | 79.5 | 78.6 | 0.2 | 0.2 | 0.3 | 0.4 |
| GOSHEN | 015 | 0000 | 759 | 12,373 | 12,577 | 12,214 | 0.2 | 17 | 95.0 | 94.6 | 0.2 | 0.2 | 0.1 | 0.1 |
| HOT SPRINGS | 017 | 0000 | 767 | 4,809 | 4,389 | 4,222 | -0.9 | 23 | 96.9 | 97.0 | 0.3 | 0.4 | 0.0 | 0.0 |
| JOHNSON | 019 | 0000 | 751 | 6,145 | 6,910 | 7,186 | 1.2 | 3 | 98.6 | 98.6 | 0.0 | 0.0 | 0.1 | 0.2 |
| LARAMIE | 021 | 1580 | 759 | 73,142 | 79,068 | 80,169 | 0.8 | 9 | 90.6 | 89.7 | 3.0 | 2.9 | 1.1 | 1.5 |
| LINCOLN | 023 | 0000 | 758 | 12,625 | 14,053 | 14,429 | 1.1 | 4 | 98.5 | 98.4 | 0.1 | 0.0 | 0.3 | 0.3 |
| NATRONA | 025 | 1350 | 767 | 61,226 | 63,021 | 62,346 | 0.3 | 16 | 96.9 | 96.5 | 0.7 | 0.8 | 0.5 | 0.6 |
| NIOBRARA | 027 | 0000 | 764 | 2,499 | 2,687 | 2,718 | 0.7 | 11 | 98.0 | 98.0 | 0.3 | 0.3 | 0.1 | 0.1 |
| PARK | 029 | 0000 | 756 | 23,178 | 25,479 | 25,368 | 0.9 | 7 | 97.4 | 97.2 | 0.1 | 0.1 | 0.5 | 0.7 |
| PLATTE | 031 | 0000 | 751 | 8,145 | 8,657 | 8,868 | 0.6 | 13 | 98.9 | 99.0 | 0.1 | 0.0 | 0.1 | 0.1 |
| SHERIDAN | 033 | 0000 | 764 | 23,562 | 25,082 | 25,054 | 0.6 | 13 | 98.0 | 97.8 | 0.2 | 0.1 | 0.4 | 0.6 |
| SUBLETTE | 035 | 0000 | 770 | 4,843 | 5,887 | 6,275 | 1.9 | 2 | 98.1 | 98.1 | 0.1 | 0.1 | 0.3 | 0.3 |
| SWEETWATER | 037 | 0000 | 770 | 38,823 | 39,041 | 37,663 | 0.1 | 18 | 94.2 | 93.6 | 0.7 | 0.7 | 0.7 | 0.9 |
| TETON | 039 | 0000 | 758 | 11,172 | 14,853 | 16,448 | 2.8 | 1 | 98.4 | 98.1 | 0.2 | 0.2 | 0.4 | 0.6 |
| UINTA | 041 | 0000 | 770 | 18,705 | 20,304 | 20,333 | 0.8 | 9 | 97.7 | 97.5 | 0.1 | 0.1 | 0.4 | 0.5 |
| WASHAKIE | 043 | 0000 | 767 | 8,388 | 8,496 | 8,273 | 0.1 | 18 | 93.8 | 93.5 | 0.2 | 0.2 | 0.5 | 0.6 |
| WESTON | 045 | 0000 | 764 | 6,518 | 6,343 | 6,053 | -0.3 | 20 | 98.0 | 97.7 | 0.0 | 0.0 | 0.2 | 0.2 |
| WYOMING | | | | | | | 0.5 | | 94.2 | 93.7 | 0.8 | 0.8 | 0.6 | 0.8 |
| UNITED STATES | | | | | | | 1.0 | | 80.3 | 77.9 | 12.1 | 12.4 | 2.9 | 3.9 |

# POPULATION COMPOSITION

## B

| COUNTY | % HISPANIC ORIGIN 1990 | % HISPANIC ORIGIN 2000 | 2000 AGE DISTRIBUTION (%) 0-4 | 5-9 | 10-14 | 15-19 | 20-24 | 25-44 | 45-64 | 65-84 | 85+ | 18+ | MEDIAN AGE 1990 | MEDIAN AGE 2000 | 2000 Males/ Females (×100) |
|---|---|---|---|---|---|---|---|---|---|---|---|---|---|---|---|
| ALBANY | 6.5 | 7.6 | 5.1 | 4.7 | 5.1 | 11.6 | 19.7 | 26.6 | 18.5 | 7.5 | 1.0 | 81.4 | 26.5 | 27.6 | 107.9 |
| BIG HORN | 5.2 | 6.1 | 5.9 | 6.4 | 8.0 | 9.1 | 6.0 | 19.7 | 27.5 | 14.8 | 2.6 | 73.4 | 36.1 | 41.4 | 100.8 |
| CAMPBELL | 3.0 | 4.1 | 7.4 | 8.0 | 9.2 | 9.8 | 7.5 | 30.4 | 22.1 | 5.0 | 0.6 | 68.7 | 29.2 | 31.3 | 104.3 |
| CARBON | 13.9 | 15.4 | 5.4 | 6.0 | 7.5 | 8.9 | 7.5 | 26.9 | 26.1 | 10.3 | 1.4 | 75.1 | 32.8 | 37.6 | 114.3 |
| CONVERSE | 5.1 | 5.8 | 6.2 | 6.9 | 8.5 | 9.4 | 6.7 | 25.1 | 26.3 | 9.7 | 1.2 | 71.8 | 31.9 | 36.9 | 95.8 |
| CROOK | 0.5 | 0.9 | 6.3 | 6.9 | 8.8 | 8.8 | 6.1 | 22.4 | 27.7 | 11.6 | 1.4 | 71.8 | 33.4 | 38.8 | 101.6 |
| FREMONT | 4.0 | 4.8 | 6.4 | 6.9 | 8.1 | 9.2 | 6.9 | 23.1 | 26.2 | 11.7 | 1.5 | 72.5 | 32.9 | 37.7 | 99.7 |
| GOSHEN | 8.7 | 9.7 | 5.4 | 5.9 | 7.3 | 9.3 | 6.8 | 22.3 | 26.0 | 14.6 | 2.3 | 75.6 | 34.6 | 40.4 | 95.1 |
| HOT SPRINGS | 1.4 | 1.8 | 3.9 | 4.9 | 6.6 | 8.2 | 5.5 | 21.0 | 29.0 | 17.3 | 3.5 | 79.0 | 38.6 | 44.9 | 97.4 |
| JOHNSON | 1.3 | 1.6 | 4.8 | 5.3 | 6.8 | 8.4 | 6.0 | 21.5 | 29.1 | 15.4 | 2.7 | 77.6 | 37.6 | 43.2 | 98.3 |
| LARAMIE | 10.0 | 11.6 | 6.4 | 6.1 | 7.1 | 8.3 | 8.4 | 26.9 | 25.3 | 10.3 | 1.3 | 75.5 | 31.9 | 36.6 | 99.6 |
| LINCOLN | 2.0 | 2.5 | 7.5 | 8.2 | 10.0 | 10.6 | 6.5 | 22.6 | 23.9 | 9.9 | 0.9 | 66.6 | 29.8 | 32.8 | 103.7 |
| NATRONA | 3.7 | 4.5 | 6.0 | 6.4 | 7.6 | 8.8 | 7.2 | 25.7 | 25.4 | 11.4 | 1.4 | 74.6 | 32.8 | 37.7 | 96.3 |
| NIOBRARA | 1.4 | 1.9 | 4.5 | 5.0 | 6.5 | 7.6 | 5.4 | 22.2 | 29.7 | 15.9 | 3.2 | 78.7 | 38.6 | 44.2 | 87.5 |
| PARK | 3.6 | 4.0 | 5.8 | 6.2 | 7.4 | 9.4 | 7.0 | 23.6 | 26.6 | 12.2 | 1.9 | 75.3 | 33.9 | 39.1 | 98.2 |
| PLATTE | 5.0 | 5.5 | 5.6 | 6.1 | 7.6 | 8.4 | 6.0 | 21.8 | 28.6 | 13.7 | 2.2 | 74.9 | 36.3 | 41.5 | 99.7 |
| SHERIDAN | 1.9 | 2.4 | 4.8 | 5.4 | 6.8 | 8.9 | 6.6 | 23.6 | 28.4 | 13.4 | 2.0 | 77.5 | 36.3 | 41.6 | 99.2 |
| SUBLETTE | 1.2 | 1.8 | 5.4 | 5.9 | 7.5 | 8.0 | 5.5 | 24.6 | 29.8 | 11.4 | 1.8 | 75.8 | 35.4 | 41.3 | 109.1 |
| SWEETWATER | 8.9 | 9.8 | 6.6 | 7.2 | 8.8 | 10.1 | 7.8 | 27.2 | 24.2 | 7.1 | 1.0 | 70.8 | 30.4 | 33.5 | 102.5 |
| TETON | 1.4 | 1.9 | 5.8 | 6.7 | 7.8 | 6.4 | 5.6 | 31.5 | 28.2 | 7.3 | 0.7 | 75.7 | 33.5 | 38.5 | 107.5 |
| UINTA | 4.1 | 4.9 | 8.3 | 8.8 | 10.2 | 10.8 | 7.9 | 27.6 | 20.0 | 5.6 | 0.7 | 65.0 | 27.1 | 28.0 | 103.8 |
| WASHAKIE | 9.5 | 10.3 | 5.6 | 6.2 | 7.7 | 9.4 | 6.1 | 22.5 | 27.5 | 13.3 | 1.8 | 74.0 | 34.6 | 40.5 | 103.1 |
| WESTON | 1.3 | 1.9 | 5.1 | 6.2 | 7.6 | 8.7 | 6.4 | 23.4 | 28.0 | 12.9 | 1.7 | 75.3 | 34.4 | 40.7 | 101.3 |
| WYOMING | 5.7 | 6.5 | 6.1 | 6.5 | 7.8 | 9.2 | 7.9 | 25.6 | 25.2 | 10.3 | 1.4 | 73.9 | 32.0 | 36.5 | 101.0 |
| UNITED STATES | 9.0 | 11.8 | 6.9 | 7.2 | 7.2 | 7.2 | 6.7 | 29.9 | 22.2 | 11.1 | 1.6 | 74.6 | 32.9 | 35.7 | 95.6 |

| COUNTY | HOUSEHOLDS | | | | | FAMILIES | | | MEDIAN HOUSEHOLD INCOME | | | |
|---|---|---|---|---|---|---|---|---|---|---|---|---|
| | 1990 | 2000 | 2005 | % Annual Rate 1990-2000 | 2000 Average HH Size | 1990 | 2000 | % Annual Rate 1990-2000 | 2000 | 2005 | 2000 National Rank | 2000 State Rank |
| ALBANY | 11,957 | 11,736 | 11,264 | -0.2 | 2.26 | 6,855 | 6,503 | -0.6 | 28,438 | 32,277 | 2373 | 18 |
| BIG HORN | 3,905 | 4,519 | 4,710 | 1.8 | 2.44 | 2,865 | 3,202 | 1.4 | 28,920 | 34,455 | 2310 | 17 |
| CAMPBELL | 9,968 | 11,550 | 12,268 | 1.8 | 2.83 | 7,611 | 8,527 | 1.4 | 51,366 | 62,945 | 180 | 2 |
| CARBON | 6,001 | 5,748 | 5,635 | -0.5 | 2.48 | 4,335 | 4,011 | -0.9 | 35,631 | 43,328 | 1147 | 8 |
| CONVERSE | 4,046 | 4,789 | 5,103 | 2.1 | 2.59 | 3,051 | 3,505 | 1.7 | 32,586 | 37,680 | 1613 | 12 |
| CROOK | 1,892 | 2,172 | 2,231 | 1.7 | 2.63 | 1,453 | 1,625 | 1.4 | 27,096 | 30,315 | 2566 | 19 |
| FREMONT | 12,002 | 13,603 | 14,077 | 1.5 | 2.61 | 8,936 | 9,780 | 1.1 | 26,941 | 29,830 | 2591 | 20 |
| GOSHEN | 4,790 | 5,154 | 5,151 | 0.9 | 2.39 | 3,437 | 3,574 | 0.5 | 24,449 | 28,644 | 2859 | 22 |
| HOT SPRINGS | 1,943 | 2,014 | 2,055 | 0.4 | 2.09 | 1,326 | 1,335 | 0.1 | 31,937 | 36,220 | 1727 | 13 |
| JOHNSON | 2,397 | 2,814 | 2,986 | 2.0 | 2.40 | 1,717 | 1,945 | 1.5 | 30,033 | 32,389 | 2147 | 15 |
| LARAMIE | 28,092 | 31,509 | 32,448 | 1.4 | 2.47 | 19,816 | 21,450 | 1.0 | 37,386 | 43,728 | 917 | 6 |
| LINCOLN | 4,137 | 4,690 | 4,860 | 1.5 | 3.00 | 3,232 | 3,574 | 1.2 | 40,592 | 51,175 | 621 | 4 |
| NATRONA | 23,837 | 25,762 | 26,155 | 0.9 | 2.41 | 16,657 | 17,312 | 0.5 | 35,627 | 39,093 | 1148 | 9 |
| NIOBRARA | 1,032 | 1,180 | 1,233 | 1.6 | 2.16 | 686 | 752 | 1.1 | 26,016 | 30,777 | 2711 | 21 |
| PARK | 8,757 | 10,259 | 10,526 | 1.9 | 2.41 | 6,292 | 7,161 | 1.6 | 36,980 | 43,550 | 982 | 7 |
| PLATTE | 3,179 | 3,587 | 3,775 | 1.5 | 2.39 | 2,281 | 2,490 | 1.1 | 24,449 | 27,019 | 2859 | 22 |
| SHERIDAN | 9,426 | 10,569 | 10,818 | 1.4 | 2.31 | 6,365 | 6,854 | 0.9 | 28,982 | 31,774 | 2298 | 16 |
| SUBLETTE | 1,834 | 2,358 | 2,581 | 3.1 | 2.46 | 1,331 | 1,659 | 2.7 | 33,588 | 40,544 | 1453 | 11 |
| SWEETWATER | 13,616 | 14,307 | 14,146 | 0.6 | 2.70 | 10,077 | 10,269 | 0.2 | 51,581 | 62,278 | 177 | 1 |
| TETON | 4,568 | 6,151 | 6,854 | 3.7 | 2.40 | 2,803 | 3,558 | 2.9 | 40,420 | 45,210 | 634 | 5 |
| UINTA | 5,885 | 6,629 | 6,734 | 1.5 | 3.03 | 4,584 | 5,007 | 1.1 | 44,486 | 53,211 | 373 | 3 |
| WASHAKIE | 3,156 | 3,447 | 3,487 | 1.1 | 2.42 | 2,300 | 2,437 | 0.7 | 33,595 | 38,655 | 1451 | 10 |
| WESTON | 2,419 | 2,469 | 2,416 | 0.2 | 2.51 | 1,815 | 1,798 | -0.1 | 31,875 | 34,938 | 1740 | 14 |
| WYOMING | | | | 1.3 | 2.51 | | | 0.8 | 35,870 | 41,325 | | |
| UNITED STATES | | | | 1.4 | 2.59 | | | 1.1 | 41,914 | 49,127 | | |

| COUNTY | 2000 Per Capita Income | 2000 HH Income Base | 2000 HOUSEHOLD INCOME DISTRIBUTION (%) Less than $15,000 | $15,000 to $24,999 | $25,000 to $49,999 | $50,000 to $99,999 | $100,000 to $149,999 | $150,000 or More | 2000 AVERAGE DISPOSABLE INCOME BY AGE OF HOUSEHOLDER All Ages | <35 | 35-44 | 45-54 | 55-64 | 65+ |
|---|---|---|---|---|---|---|---|---|---|---|---|---|---|---|
| ALBANY | 17,631 | 11,734 | 27.6 | 17.1 | 31.2 | 19.3 | 3.4 | 1.4 | 31,429 | 18,547 | 39,928 | 47,875 | 47,427 | 31,900 |
| BIG HORN | 13,961 | 4,519 | 23.5 | 18.3 | 39.2 | 17.0 | 1.6 | 0.4 | 28,578 | 25,209 | 33,232 | 37,369 | 30,438 | 19,703 |
| CAMPBELL | 20,851 | 11,543 | 9.6 | 6.3 | 31.7 | 41.8 | 9.0 | 1.6 | 46,829 | 37,822 | 55,776 | 55,235 | 48,822 | 24,773 |
| CARBON | 15,970 | 5,707 | 16.0 | 15.1 | 37.4 | 27.9 | 3.1 | 0.5 | 34,405 | 27,524 | 41,439 | 43,023 | 39,205 | 22,766 |
| CONVERSE | 14,872 | 4,779 | 20.2 | 17.5 | 39.1 | 19.4 | 2.9 | 1.0 | 32,127 | 24,348 | 39,876 | 39,494 | 33,941 | 19,732 |
| CROOK | 12,737 | 2,172 | 24.0 | 20.8 | 36.1 | 17.2 | 1.7 | 0.2 | 28,128 | 23,457 | 33,467 | 36,722 | 28,498 | 17,477 |
| FREMONT | 12,226 | 13,603 | 26.6 | 19.3 | 35.5 | 16.6 | 1.5 | 0.5 | 27,296 | 19,986 | 33,070 | 34,510 | 30,075 | 19,572 |
| GOSHEN | 12,669 | 5,154 | 28.9 | 22.4 | 34.3 | 12.7 | 0.7 | 1.0 | 26,067 | 19,039 | 31,632 | 33,767 | 31,084 | 18,221 |
| HOT SPRINGS | 18,112 | 2,011 | 18.8 | 18.1 | 38.7 | 19.5 | 4.0 | 0.9 | 32,547 | 27,445 | 39,974 | 40,614 | 34,721 | 22,719 |
| JOHNSON | 15,783 | 2,814 | 24.5 | 19.8 | 33.5 | 17.1 | 3.7 | 1.4 | 31,132 | 23,942 | 33,768 | 35,677 | 38,544 | 24,938 |
| LARAMIE | 18,227 | 31,509 | 14.4 | 15.9 | 36.9 | 27.7 | 4.0 | 1.2 | 36,918 | 26,689 | 43,678 | 47,975 | 42,952 | 26,628 |
| LINCOLN | 15,983 | 4,690 | 12.1 | 13.0 | 38.2 | 31.9 | 4.1 | 0.8 | 38,419 | 31,785 | 43,778 | 49,089 | 42,584 | 23,831 |
| NATRONA | 18,461 | 25,734 | 17.2 | 14.5 | 38.2 | 24.7 | 4.1 | 1.4 | 35,896 | 26,695 | 43,442 | 42,228 | 42,097 | 26,774 |
| NIOBRARA | 15,808 | 1,180 | 27.5 | 20.3 | 32.3 | 15.8 | 3.0 | 1.2 | 29,172 | 26,654 | 32,838 | 33,394 | 30,401 | 23,518 |
| PARK | 18,740 | 10,259 | 14.6 | 16.0 | 38.0 | 25.5 | 4.4 | 1.5 | 36,750 | 26,746 | 43,295 | 47,209 | 38,845 | 27,734 |
| PLATTE | 12,515 | 3,587 | 32.8 | 17.8 | 35.2 | 12.2 | 1.6 | 0.4 | 25,348 | 22,243 | 34,845 | 27,538 | 27,418 | 16,682 |
| SHERIDAN | 15,549 | 10,569 | 23.1 | 19.7 | 36.9 | 17.4 | 2.2 | 0.8 | 29,744 | 22,365 | 36,418 | 38,853 | 29,972 | 20,739 |
| SUBLETTE | 17,419 | 2,358 | 16.5 | 18.3 | 38.2 | 20.7 | 4.3 | 2.0 | 35,382 | 28,383 | 36,712 | 43,133 | 37,002 | 27,273 |
| SWEETWATER | 24,934 | 14,283 | 10.2 | 6.5 | 30.9 | 40.2 | 10.1 | 2.1 | 48,198 | 37,288 | 54,995 | 59,190 | 52,591 | 33,289 |
| TETON | 23,242 | 6,151 | 8.9 | 13.7 | 41.1 | 29.1 | 5.3 | 2.0 | 41,424 | 30,545 | 43,657 | 49,824 | 42,899 | 30,667 |
| UINTA | 18,715 | 6,627 | 10.6 | 8.5 | 39.2 | 34.0 | 6.2 | 1.4 | 42,242 | 35,032 | 46,507 | 53,123 | 45,002 | 24,781 |
| WASHAKIE | 15,938 | 3,431 | 17.8 | 17.6 | 43.3 | 18.3 | 2.3 | 0.7 | 31,734 | 24,631 | 38,949 | 38,292 | 34,154 | 24,332 |
| WESTON | 14,493 | 2,469 | 17.4 | 18.5 | 43.7 | 18.1 | 1.6 | 0.7 | 30,654 | 24,505 | 36,745 | 38,540 | 29,931 | 23,051 |
| WYOMING | 17,650 | | 17.7 | 15.1 | 36.3 | 25.4 | 4.3 | 1.2 | 35,762 | 27,008 | 43,177 | 45,031 | 39,383 | 24,696 |
| UNITED STATES | 22,162 | | 14.5 | 12.5 | 32.3 | 29.8 | 7.4 | 3.5 | 40,748 | 34,503 | 44,969 | 49,579 | 43,409 | 27,339 |

| COUNTY | FINANCIAL SERVICES | | | | THE HOME | | | | | | ENTERTAINMENT | | | | | | PERSONAL | | | |
|---|---|---|---|---|---|---|---|---|---|---|---|---|---|---|---|---|---|---|---|---|
| | | | | | Home Improvements | | | Furnishings | | | | | | | | | | | | |
| | Auto Loan | Home Loan | Invest-ments | Retire-ment Plans | Home Repair | Lawn & Garden | Remodel-ing | Appli-ances | Elec-tronics | Furni-ture | Restau-rants | Sport-ing Goods | Theater & Concerts | Toys & Hobbies | Travel | Video Rental | Apparel | Auto After-market | Health Insur-ance | Pets & Supplies |
| ALBANY | 95 | 99 | 95 | 97 | 98 | 94 | 102 | 93 | 94 | 89 | 91 | 86 | 83 | 89 | 85 | 89 | 91 | 93 | 94 | 91 |
| BIG HORN | 96 | 66 | 72 | 78 | 93 | 92 | 111 | 97 | 94 | 78 | 78 | 86 | 75 | 87 | 71 | 92 | 79 | 87 | 101 | 89 |
| CAMPBELL | 100 | 97 | 81 | 92 | 95 | 95 | 103 | 102 | 103 | 102 | 102 | 95 | 91 | 95 | 83 | 95 | 99 | 99 | 94 | 96 |
| CARBON | 98 | 83 | 83 | 85 | 95 | 93 | 110 | 99 | 97 | 91 | 90 | 89 | 84 | 92 | 78 | 93 | 89 | 92 | 98 | 93 |
| CONVERSE | 99 | 83 | 77 | 85 | 94 | 92 | 108 | 100 | 99 | 90 | 90 | 91 | 84 | 93 | 76 | 94 | 89 | 93 | 98 | 94 |
| CROOK | 100 | 75 | 79 | 84 | 94 | 92 | 118 | 100 | 95 | 85 | 85 | 93 | 81 | 94 | 74 | 93 | 85 | 90 | 101 | 95 |
| FREMONT | 96 | 78 | 81 | 83 | 96 | 93 | 109 | 98 | 95 | 87 | 85 | 87 | 82 | 90 | 77 | 92 | 85 | 90 | 98 | 91 |
| GOSHEN | 98 | 72 | 78 | 81 | 94 | 92 | 114 | 98 | 95 | 82 | 82 | 89 | 79 | 90 | 74 | 92 | 83 | 89 | 100 | 92 |
| HOT SPRINGS | 95 | 73 | 78 | 79 | 94 | 92 | 108 | 97 | 94 | 83 | 82 | 85 | 78 | 88 | 74 | 92 | 82 | 88 | 99 | 90 |
| JOHNSON | 98 | 81 | 87 | 88 | 97 | 97 | 110 | 99 | 97 | 88 | 87 | 90 | 84 | 91 | 80 | 93 | 88 | 92 | 101 | 93 |
| LARAMIE | 98 | 96 | 96 | 95 | 102 | 100 | 102 | 100 | 100 | 100 | 98 | 91 | 92 | 93 | 89 | 93 | 96 | 97 | 97 | 93 |
| LINCOLN | 100 | 81 | 80 | 87 | 95 | 94 | 113 | 100 | 98 | 88 | 89 | 93 | 84 | 94 | 77 | 94 | 89 | 93 | 100 | 95 |
| NATRONA | 98 | 93 | 89 | 92 | 99 | 97 | 102 | 100 | 100 | 98 | 97 | 91 | 90 | 93 | 85 | 94 | 95 | 96 | 97 | 93 |
| NIOBRARA | 97 | 68 | 77 | 80 | 93 | 93 | 114 | 98 | 94 | 78 | 80 | 88 | 76 | 89 | 73 | 92 | 81 | 88 | 102 | 91 |
| PARK | 99 | 84 | 85 | 88 | 96 | 96 | 110 | 100 | 98 | 91 | 90 | 90 | 85 | 93 | 80 | 94 | 90 | 93 | 99 | 93 |
| PLATTE | 98 | 74 | 77 | 82 | 94 | 92 | 112 | 98 | 95 | 83 | 83 | 88 | 80 | 91 | 74 | 93 | 84 | 89 | 100 | 92 |
| SHERIDAN | 97 | 83 | 87 | 87 | 98 | 96 | 109 | 99 | 96 | 90 | 88 | 89 | 85 | 91 | 81 | 93 | 88 | 91 | 99 | 92 |
| SUBLETTE | 99 | 75 | 77 | 83 | 94 | 92 | 116 | 99 | 96 | 84 | 85 | 91 | 80 | 93 | 74 | 93 | 85 | 90 | 101 | 94 |
| SWEETWATER | 98 | 92 | 86 | 90 | 97 | 96 | 104 | 100 | 100 | 98 | 97 | 91 | 89 | 94 | 83 | 94 | 95 | 96 | 96 | 93 |
| TETON | 102 | 104 | 88 | 99 | 99 | 101 | 104 | 103 | 104 | 105 | 106 | 97 | 95 | 97 | 90 | 96 | 104 | 102 | 98 | 98 |
| UINTA | 100 | 96 | 79 | 91 | 94 | 94 | 104 | 101 | 103 | 101 | 101 | 94 | 89 | 95 | 82 | 95 | 97 | 98 | 94 | 95 |
| WASHAKIE | 98 | 75 | 78 | 82 | 95 | 92 | 112 | 98 | 95 | 84 | 84 | 88 | 80 | 91 | 75 | 93 | 84 | 89 | 100 | 92 |
| WESTON | 99 | 74 | 78 | 83 | 95 | 92 | 115 | 99 | 96 | 84 | 84 | 90 | 80 | 92 | 74 | 93 | 85 | 90 | 100 | 93 |
| WYOMING | 98 | 89 | 87 | 90 | 97 | 96 | 106 | 99 | 99 | 94 | 93 | 91 | 87 | 93 | 82 | 93 | 92 | 94 | 97 | 93 |
| UNITED STATES | 100 | 100 | 100 | 100 | 100 | 100 | 100 | 100 | 100 | 100 | 100 | 100 | 100 | 100 | 100 | 100 | 100 | 100 | 100 | 100 |

# SUMMARY DATA SECTION

# STATE SUMMARY DATA

COUNTY

13th EDITION

# POPULATION CHANGE
## STATE AND U.S. TOTALS

**A**

| STATE | STATE Fips Code | POPULATION 1990 | POPULATION 2000 | POPULATION 2005 | 1990-2000 ANNUAL CHANGE % Rate | 1990-2000 ANNUAL CHANGE National Rank | RACE (%) White 1990 | White 2000 | Black 1990 | Black 2000 | Asian/Pacific 1990 | Asian/Pacific 2000 |
|---|---|---|---|---|---|---|---|---|---|---|---|---|
| ALABAMA | 01 | 4,040,587 | 4,395,481 | 4,520,532 | 0.8 | 23 | 73.7 | 73.1 | 25.3 | 25.8 | 0.5 | 0.7 |
| ALASKA | 02 | 550,043 | 624,523 | 649,680 | 1.2 | 15 | 75.5 | 74.1 | 4.1 | 3.8 | 3.6 | 4.5 |
| ARIZONA | 04 | 3,665,228 | 4,894,006 | 5,470,735 | 2.9 | 2 | 80.9 | 78.6 | 3.0 | 3.4 | 1.5 | 2.0 |
| ARKANSAS | 05 | 2,350,725 | 2,566,938 | 2,642,789 | 0.9 | 20 | 82.7 | 82.3 | 15.9 | 15.8 | 0.5 | 0.7 |
| CALIFORNIA | 06 | 29,760,021 | 33,603,430 | 35,801,342 | 1.2 | 15 | 69.0 | 64.3 | 7.4 | 7.1 | 9.6 | 11.8 |
| COLORADO | 08 | 3,294,394 | 4,139,027 | 4,552,480 | 2.3 | 3 | 88.2 | 86.9 | 4.0 | 4.1 | 1.8 | 2.4 |
| CONNECTICUT | 09 | 3,287,116 | 3,289,062 | 3,321,459 | 0.0 | 48 | 87.0 | 84.6 | 8.3 | 9.0 | 1.5 | 2.5 |
| DELAWARE | 10 | 666,168 | 762,227 | 805,899 | 1.3 | 13 | 80.3 | 76.7 | 16.9 | 19.3 | 1.4 | 2.1 |
| DISTRICT OF COLUMBIA | 11 | 606,900 | 513,618 | 486,620 | -1.6 | 51 | 29.6 | 31.7 | 65.8 | 61.8 | 1.9 | 3.0 |
| FLORIDA | 12 | 12,937,926 | 15,341,185 | 16,441,601 | 1.7 | 9 | 83.1 | 80.3 | 13.6 | 15.1 | 1.2 | 1.8 |
| GEORGIA | 13 | 6,478,216 | 7,950,119 | 8,705,974 | 2.0 | 6 | 71.0 | 68.5 | 27.0 | 28.1 | 1.2 | 2.0 |
| HAWAII | 15 | 1,108,229 | 1,184,688 | 1,181,325 | 0.7 | 27 | 33.4 | 31.5 | 2.5 | 2.8 | 61.8 | 63.0 |
| IDAHO | 16 | 1,006,749 | 1,273,309 | 1,380,571 | 2.3 | 3 | 94.4 | 93.1 | 0.3 | 0.5 | 0.9 | 1.1 |
| ILLINOIS | 17 | 11,430,602 | 12,187,552 | 12,482,167 | 0.6 | 33 | 78.3 | 76.1 | 14.8 | 15.0 | 2.5 | 3.4 |
| INDIANA | 18 | 5,544,159 | 5,979,311 | 6,157,321 | 0.7 | 27 | 90.6 | 89.6 | 7.8 | 8.2 | 0.7 | 1.0 |
| IOWA | 19 | 2,776,755 | 2,877,060 | 2,914,191 | 0.3 | 42 | 96.6 | 95.7 | 1.7 | 2.0 | 0.9 | 1.3 |
| KANSAS | 20 | 2,477,574 | 2,672,387 | 2,761,987 | 0.7 | 27 | 90.1 | 88.9 | 5.8 | 5.7 | 1.3 | 1.8 |
| KENTUCKY | 21 | 3,685,296 | 3,988,695 | 4,123,759 | 0.8 | 23 | 92.0 | 91.8 | 7.1 | 7.2 | 0.5 | 0.7 |
| LOUISIANA | 22 | 4,219,973 | 4,386,033 | 4,443,297 | 0.4 | 40 | 67.3 | 65.7 | 30.8 | 32.1 | 1.0 | 1.3 |
| MAINE | 23 | 1,227,928 | 1,257,219 | 1,277,551 | 0.2 | 44 | 98.4 | 98.2 | 0.4 | 0.5 | 0.5 | 0.7 |
| MARYLAND | 24 | 4,781,468 | 5,212,902 | 5,419,269 | 0.8 | 23 | 71.0 | 66.9 | 24.9 | 27.5 | 2.9 | 4.1 |
| MASSACHUSETTS | 25 | 6,016,425 | 6,206,482 | 6,354,477 | 0.3 | 42 | 89.8 | 87.0 | 5.0 | 5.8 | 2.4 | 3.7 |
| MICHIGAN | 26 | 9,295,297 | 9,907,530 | 10,126,504 | 0.6 | 33 | 83.4 | 82.6 | 13.9 | 14.0 | 1.1 | 1.6 |
| MINNESOTA | 27 | 4,375,099 | 4,820,250 | 5,042,023 | 0.9 | 20 | 94.4 | 92.5 | 2.2 | 2.9 | 1.8 | 2.7 |
| MISSISSIPPI | 28 | 2,573,216 | 2,788,415 | 2,882,592 | 0.8 | 23 | 63.5 | 62.5 | 35.6 | 36.3 | 0.5 | 0.7 |
| MISSOURI | 29 | 5,117,073 | 5,502,243 | 5,670,963 | 0.7 | 27 | 87.7 | 87.0 | 10.7 | 11.0 | 0.8 | 1.1 |
| MONTANA | 30 | 799,065 | 885,795 | 904,153 | 1.0 | 19 | 92.8 | 92.2 | 0.3 | 0.3 | 0.5 | 0.6 |
| NEBRASKA | 31 | 1,578,385 | 1,672,199 | 1,704,953 | 0.6 | 33 | 93.8 | 92.0 | 3.6 | 4.0 | 0.8 | 1.3 |
| NEVADA | 32 | 1,201,833 | 1,879,204 | 2,224,769 | 4.5 | 1 | 84.3 | 79.0 | 6.6 | 7.5 | 3.2 | 4.7 |
| NEW HAMPSHIRE | 33 | 1,109,252 | 1,215,100 | 1,284,313 | 0.9 | 20 | 98.0 | 97.5 | 0.7 | 0.7 | 0.8 | 1.2 |
| NEW JERSEY | 34 | 7,730,188 | 8,192,386 | 8,420,928 | 0.6 | 33 | 79.3 | 75.3 | 13.4 | 14.1 | 3.5 | 5.7 |
| NEW MEXICO | 35 | 1,515,069 | 1,750,921 | 1,811,534 | 1.4 | 12 | 75.6 | 73.8 | 2.0 | 2.3 | 0.9 | 1.3 |
| NEW YORK | 36 | 17,990,455 | 18,223,519 | 18,348,422 | 0.1 | 45 | 74.4 | 71.3 | 15.9 | 16.4 | 3.9 | 5.5 |
| NORTH CAROLINA | 37 | 6,628,637 | 7,762,819 | 8,315,774 | 1.6 | 10 | 75.6 | 74.5 | 22.0 | 22.0 | 0.8 | 1.4 |
| NORTH DAKOTA | 38 | 638,800 | 631,032 | 624,572 | -0.1 | 49 | 94.6 | 93.4 | 0.6 | 0.6 | 0.5 | 0.8 |
| OHIO | 39 | 10,847,115 | 11,281,851 | 11,399,561 | 0.4 | 40 | 87.8 | 86.6 | 10.7 | 11.4 | 0.8 | 1.2 |
| OKLAHOMA | 40 | 3,145,585 | 3,383,158 | 3,492,422 | 0.7 | 27 | 82.1 | 81.3 | 7.4 | 7.7 | 1.1 | 1.3 |
| OREGON | 41 | 2,842,321 | 3,356,108 | 3,552,515 | 1.6 | 10 | 92.8 | 90.8 | 1.6 | 1.8 | 2.4 | 3.3 |
| PENNSYLVANIA | 42 | 11,881,643 | 11,986,139 | 11,942,109 | 0.1 | 45 | 88.5 | 87.4 | 9.2 | 9.5 | 1.2 | 1.7 |
| RHODE ISLAND | 44 | 1,003,464 | 992,011 | 997,723 | -0.1 | 49 | 91.4 | 89.4 | 3.9 | 4.5 | 1.8 | 2.3 |
| SOUTH CAROLINA | 45 | 3,486,703 | 3,935,123 | 4,171,206 | 1.2 | 15 | 69.0 | 68.7 | 29.8 | 29.7 | 0.6 | 0.9 |
| SOUTH DAKOTA | 46 | 696,004 | 734,993 | 748,458 | 0.5 | 38 | 91.6 | 90.1 | 0.5 | 0.7 | 0.5 | 0.6 |
| TENNESSEE | 47 | 4,877,185 | 5,539,577 | 5,817,773 | 1.3 | 13 | 83.0 | 82.1 | 16.0 | 16.4 | 0.7 | 1.0 |
| TEXAS | 48 | 16,986,510 | 20,398,490 | 22,099,571 | 1.8 | 7 | 75.2 | 72.3 | 11.9 | 11.9 | 1.9 | 2.8 |
| UTAH | 49 | 1,722,850 | 2,164,175 | 2,335,941 | 2.2 | 5 | 93.8 | 92.2 | 0.7 | 0.8 | 1.9 | 2.6 |
| VERMONT | 50 | 562,758 | 596,714 | 610,534 | 0.6 | 33 | 98.6 | 98.2 | 0.4 | 0.5 | 0.6 | 0.8 |
| VIRGINIA | 51 | 6,187,358 | 6,945,067 | 7,306,804 | 1.1 | 18 | 77.4 | 74.8 | 18.8 | 19.9 | 2.6 | 3.8 |
| WASHINGTON | 53 | 4,866,692 | 5,835,089 | 6,225,232 | 1.8 | 7 | 88.5 | 85.7 | 3.1 | 3.4 | 4.3 | 5.9 |
| WEST VIRGINIA | 54 | 1,793,477 | 1,804,812 | 1,787,726 | 0.1 | 45 | 96.2 | 96.1 | 3.1 | 3.2 | 0.4 | 0.5 |
| WISCONSIN | 55 | 4,891,769 | 5,277,833 | 5,414,897 | 0.7 | 27 | 92.3 | 91.0 | 5.0 | 5.4 | 1.1 | 1.5 |
| WYOMING | 56 | 453,588 | 479,673 | 480,753 | 0.5 | 38 | 94.2 | 93.7 | 0.8 | 0.8 | 0.6 | 0.8 |
| UNITED STATES | | | | | 1.0 | | 80.3 | 77.9 | 12.1 | 12.4 | 2.9 | 3.9 |

# POPULATION COMPOSITION

## STATE AND U.S. TOTALS

# B

| STATE | % HISPANIC ORIGIN | | 2000 AGE DISTRIBUTION (%) | | | | | | | | | | MEDIAN AGE | | 2000 Males/ Females (×100) |
|---|---|---|---|---|---|---|---|---|---|---|---|---|---|---|---|
| | 1990 | 2000 | 0-4 | 5-9 | 10-14 | 15-19 | 20-24 | 25-44 | 45-64 | 65-84 | 85+ | 18+ | 1990 | 2000 | |
| ALABAMA | 0.6 | 1.3 | 6.6 | 6.6 | 6.6 | 7.2 | 7.2 | 29.6 | 23.2 | 11.5 | 1.5 | 76.0 | 33.0 | 36.2 | 92.2 |
| ALASKA | 3.2 | 4.2 | 7.8 | 8.8 | 9.4 | 9.3 | 8.1 | 27.6 | 23.3 | 5.4 | 0.4 | 68.4 | 29.4 | 31.1 | 110.2 |
| ARIZONA | 18.8 | 23.0 | 8.0 | 7.8 | 7.6 | 7.3 | 6.8 | 28.1 | 21.2 | 11.7 | 1.4 | 72.4 | 32.2 | 34.7 | 97.9 |
| ARKANSAS | 0.9 | 2.4 | 6.9 | 6.9 | 7.3 | 7.6 | 7.0 | 27.3 | 22.9 | 12.3 | 1.8 | 74.5 | 33.8 | 36.2 | 93.5 |
| CALIFORNIA | 25.8 | 31.7 | 7.4 | 8.1 | 7.2 | 7.1 | 7.1 | 31.9 | 20.2 | 9.7 | 1.3 | 73.3 | 31.5 | 33.7 | 100.0 |
| COLORADO | 12.9 | 15.1 | 7.0 | 7.0 | 7.5 | 7.7 | 6.8 | 29.3 | 24.7 | 8.8 | 1.2 | 74.1 | 32.5 | 36.0 | 98.3 |
| CONNECTICUT | 6.5 | 8.7 | 6.6 | 7.2 | 7.5 | 6.4 | 5.4 | 30.3 | 22.3 | 12.4 | 2.0 | 75.2 | 34.4 | 37.2 | 94.3 |
| DELAWARE | 2.4 | 3.9 | 6.5 | 6.7 | 6.8 | 6.7 | 6.4 | 32.0 | 21.7 | 11.7 | 1.4 | 76.5 | 32.9 | 36.2 | 94.6 |
| DISTRICT OF COLUMBIA | 5.4 | 7.3 | 5.1 | 6.0 | 4.5 | 4.7 | 6.3 | 35.1 | 24.3 | 12.1 | 1.8 | 82.4 | 33.5 | 38.0 | 88.1 |
| FLORIDA | 12.2 | 15.7 | 6.2 | 6.7 | 6.8 | 6.3 | 5.8 | 27.6 | 22.4 | 15.9 | 2.2 | 76.6 | 36.4 | 38.9 | 94.2 |
| GEORGIA | 1.7 | 3.3 | 7.4 | 7.3 | 7.3 | 7.3 | 7.1 | 32.3 | 21.8 | 8.6 | 1.1 | 74.0 | 31.6 | 34.1 | 94.9 |
| HAWAII | 7.3 | 8.3 | 6.6 | 7.1 | 6.4 | 7.0 | 7.2 | 28.4 | 23.4 | 12.4 | 1.5 | 75.8 | 32.6 | 37.4 | 99.3 |
| IDAHO | 5.3 | 7.8 | 7.3 | 7.2 | 7.7 | 9.0 | 8.2 | 26.7 | 22.6 | 9.8 | 1.5 | 72.3 | 31.5 | 33.7 | 99.6 |
| ILLINOIS | 7.9 | 10.7 | 7.2 | 7.5 | 7.2 | 7.2 | 6.6 | 30.2 | 21.9 | 10.7 | 1.6 | 74.1 | 32.8 | 35.4 | 95.3 |
| INDIANA | 1.8 | 2.9 | 6.9 | 7.0 | 7.2 | 7.4 | 6.8 | 29.7 | 22.5 | 10.9 | 1.5 | 74.8 | 32.8 | 35.7 | 94.8 |
| IOWA | 1.2 | 2.5 | 6.3 | 6.5 | 7.3 | 7.9 | 6.8 | 27.4 | 22.9 | 12.6 | 2.3 | 75.5 | 34.0 | 37.1 | 95.0 |
| KANSAS | 3.8 | 5.9 | 6.8 | 6.8 | 7.6 | 8.1 | 7.2 | 28.5 | 21.7 | 11.3 | 2.0 | 74.1 | 32.9 | 35.6 | 96.8 |
| KENTUCKY | 0.6 | 1.2 | 6.5 | 6.5 | 6.7 | 7.4 | 7.3 | 29.5 | 23.7 | 10.9 | 1.5 | 76.1 | 33.0 | 36.4 | 94.4 |
| LOUISIANA | 2.2 | 2.9 | 7.1 | 7.2 | 7.6 | 8.5 | 7.7 | 28.0 | 22.4 | 10.2 | 1.3 | 73.2 | 31.0 | 34.4 | 92.7 |
| MAINE | 0.6 | 1.1 | 5.2 | 6.0 | 7.2 | 7.2 | 6.2 | 30.3 | 24.0 | 12.2 | 1.8 | 77.5 | 33.9 | 38.1 | 95.3 |
| MARYLAND | 2.6 | 4.1 | 6.6 | 7.2 | 7.4 | 6.7 | 5.9 | 32.4 | 22.2 | 10.3 | 1.3 | 75.1 | 33.0 | 36.0 | 94.5 |
| MASSACHUSETTS | 4.8 | 6.6 | 6.3 | 6.8 | 6.9 | 6.2 | 5.7 | 32.0 | 22.2 | 12.0 | 1.9 | 76.9 | 33.6 | 36.8 | 93.2 |
| MICHIGAN | 2.2 | 3.1 | 6.5 | 7.2 | 7.6 | 7.4 | 6.6 | 30.0 | 22.4 | 10.9 | 1.5 | 74.5 | 32.6 | 35.8 | 94.8 |
| MINNESOTA | 1.2 | 2.3 | 6.6 | 7.0 | 8.0 | 8.0 | 6.6 | 29.7 | 22.0 | 10.4 | 1.8 | 73.8 | 32.5 | 35.7 | 97.2 |
| MISSISSIPPI | 0.6 | 1.1 | 7.2 | 7.3 | 7.4 | 8.2 | 7.7 | 28.5 | 21.5 | 10.5 | 1.5 | 73.4 | 31.2 | 33.9 | 92.0 |
| MISSOURI | 1.2 | 2.0 | 6.5 | 6.9 | 7.4 | 7.6 | 6.7 | 29.1 | 22.3 | 11.7 | 1.8 | 74.8 | 33.6 | 36.3 | 94.0 |
| MONTANA | 1.5 | 2.2 | 5.8 | 6.4 | 7.6 | 8.5 | 7.1 | 25.5 | 25.9 | 11.4 | 1.8 | 75.0 | 33.8 | 38.2 | 98.8 |
| NEBRASKA | 2.3 | 5.0 | 6.8 | 6.9 | 7.8 | 8.3 | 7.2 | 27.6 | 21.9 | 11.5 | 2.1 | 73.7 | 33.0 | 35.7 | 95.7 |
| NEVADA | 10.4 | 17.3 | 7.9 | 7.6 | 7.5 | 6.8 | 6.1 | 29.5 | 23.1 | 10.6 | 0.9 | 73.0 | 33.3 | 35.5 | 103.7 |
| NEW HAMPSHIRE | 1.0 | 1.9 | 6.0 | 6.9 | 8.0 | 7.0 | 5.6 | 33.0 | 21.6 | 10.6 | 1.5 | 75.4 | 32.8 | 36.1 | 96.9 |
| NEW JERSEY | 9.6 | 12.9 | 6.6 | 7.1 | 7.0 | 6.3 | 5.8 | 30.7 | 22.9 | 11.9 | 1.7 | 75.7 | 34.5 | 37.2 | 94.1 |
| NEW MEXICO | 38.2 | 41.2 | 7.4 | 7.7 | 8.0 | 8.3 | 7.1 | 27.5 | 22.4 | 10.3 | 1.3 | 71.9 | 31.3 | 34.8 | 96.8 |
| NEW YORK | 12.3 | 14.9 | 6.6 | 7.1 | 6.7 | 6.5 | 6.3 | 30.6 | 22.8 | 11.6 | 1.7 | 76.0 | 33.9 | 36.6 | 93.1 |
| NORTH CAROLINA | 1.2 | 2.5 | 6.9 | 7.2 | 7.2 | 6.7 | 6.6 | 30.3 | 22.6 | 11.1 | 1.4 | 75.1 | 33.1 | 35.7 | 94.1 |
| NORTH DAKOTA | 0.7 | 1.5 | 6.0 | 6.3 | 7.5 | 8.5 | 7.6 | 27.2 | 22.4 | 12.2 | 2.4 | 75.4 | 32.4 | 36.5 | 98.8 |
| OHIO | 1.3 | 2.0 | 6.5 | 6.9 | 7.3 | 7.4 | 6.7 | 29.5 | 22.6 | 11.8 | 1.6 | 75.2 | 33.3 | 36.3 | 93.6 |
| OKLAHOMA | 2.7 | 4.4 | 6.9 | 6.9 | 7.5 | 8.0 | 7.3 | 27.1 | 23.2 | 11.6 | 1.7 | 74.2 | 33.2 | 36.0 | 95.4 |
| OREGON | 4.0 | 6.8 | 6.5 | 6.6 | 7.2 | 7.4 | 6.7 | 28.1 | 24.6 | 11.3 | 1.7 | 75.4 | 34.5 | 37.1 | 97.6 |
| PENNSYLVANIA | 2.0 | 3.0 | 5.8 | 6.6 | 7.1 | 6.8 | 5.9 | 28.9 | 23.0 | 13.9 | 2.0 | 76.8 | 35.0 | 38.2 | 92.6 |
| RHODE ISLAND | 4.6 | 7.1 | 6.2 | 7.0 | 7.2 | 6.5 | 5.8 | 30.8 | 20.9 | 13.4 | 2.2 | 76.5 | 34.0 | 36.8 | 92.6 |
| SOUTH CAROLINA | 0.9 | 1.6 | 6.4 | 6.8 | 6.9 | 7.2 | 7.2 | 30.2 | 23.1 | 11.0 | 1.3 | 75.9 | 32.0 | 35.9 | 93.1 |
| SOUTH DAKOTA | 0.8 | 1.6 | 6.6 | 7.0 | 7.9 | 8.8 | 7.4 | 26.6 | 21.5 | 12.1 | 2.2 | 73.3 | 32.5 | 35.7 | 96.7 |
| TENNESSEE | 0.7 | 1.5 | 6.6 | 6.7 | 6.8 | 7.0 | 6.7 | 30.2 | 23.7 | 10.9 | 1.5 | 76.0 | 33.6 | 36.4 | 93.3 |
| TEXAS | 25.6 | 30.4 | 8.1 | 7.8 | 7.7 | 8.0 | 7.4 | 29.6 | 21.4 | 8.8 | 1.2 | 71.8 | 30.8 | 33.2 | 97.3 |
| UTAH | 4.9 | 7.5 | 9.8 | 8.5 | 8.6 | 10.0 | 10.5 | 26.5 | 17.5 | 7.7 | 1.0 | 67.0 | 26.2 | 26.8 | 98.8 |
| VERMONT | 0.7 | 1.3 | 5.2 | 6.1 | 7.3 | 7.3 | 6.1 | 31.2 | 24.5 | 10.6 | 1.7 | 77.6 | 33.0 | 37.5 | 96.9 |
| VIRGINIA | 2.6 | 4.1 | 6.5 | 6.7 | 6.8 | 6.9 | 7.0 | 32.2 | 22.6 | 10.1 | 1.3 | 76.2 | 32.6 | 35.7 | 95.5 |
| WASHINGTON | 4.4 | 6.8 | 6.7 | 7.0 | 7.4 | 7.6 | 6.9 | 30.3 | 22.9 | 9.9 | 1.5 | 74.5 | 33.1 | 35.7 | 98.9 |
| WEST VIRGINIA | 0.5 | 0.9 | 5.5 | 5.9 | 6.3 | 7.1 | 7.2 | 27.0 | 25.9 | 13.3 | 1.8 | 78.2 | 35.4 | 39.2 | 92.9 |
| WISCONSIN | 1.9 | 3.0 | 6.2 | 6.7 | 7.7 | 7.9 | 6.7 | 29.2 | 22.4 | 11.3 | 1.8 | 74.8 | 32.9 | 36.2 | 96.7 |
| WYOMING | 5.7 | 6.5 | 6.1 | 6.5 | 7.8 | 9.2 | 7.9 | 25.6 | 25.2 | 10.3 | 1.4 | 73.9 | 32.0 | 36.5 | 101.0 |
| UNITED STATES | 9.0 | 11.8 | 6.9 | 7.2 | 7.2 | 7.2 | 6.7 | 29.9 | 22.2 | 11.1 | 1.6 | 74.6 | 32.9 | 35.7 | 95.6 |

# HOUSEHOLDS

## STATE AND U.S. TOTALS



| STATE | HOUSEHOLDS | | | | | FAMILIES | | | MEDIAN HOUSEHOLD INCOME | | |
|---|---|---|---|---|---|---|---|---|---|---|---|
| | 1990 | 2000 | 2005 | % Annual Rate 1990-2000 | 2000 Average HH Size | 1990 | 2000 | % Annual Rate 1990-2000 | 2000 | 2005 | 2000 National Rank |
| ALABAMA | 1,506,790 | 1,691,374 | 1,765,565 | 1.4 | 2.54 | 1,103,835 | 1,204,000 | 1.1 | 35,938 | 40,905 | 40 |
| ALASKA | 188,915 | 218,455 | 228,403 | 1.8 | 2.78 | 132,837 | 147,699 | 1.3 | 61,318 | 74,930 | 1 |
| ARIZONA | 1,368,843 | 1,859,700 | 2,097,596 | 3.8 | 2.58 | 940,106 | 1,246,874 | 3.5 | 39,067 | 45,710 | 30 |
| ARKANSAS | 891,179 | 990,647 | 1,028,622 | 1.3 | 2.53 | 651,555 | 702,083 | 0.9 | 30,582 | 35,648 | 50 |
| CALIFORNIA | 10,381,206 | 11,848,976 | 12,694,606 | 1.6 | 2.77 | 7,139,394 | 7,996,740 | 1.4 | 47,551 | 58,616 | 9 |
| COLORADO | 1,282,489 | 1,629,529 | 1,802,167 | 3.0 | 2.49 | 854,214 | 1,061,443 | 2.7 | 48,112 | 55,833 | 7 |
| CONNECTICUT | 1,230,479 | 1,248,798 | 1,269,064 | 0.2 | 2.56 | 864,493 | 847,569 | -0.2 | 53,506 | 61,897 | 4 |
| DELAWARE | 247,497 | 293,197 | 315,627 | 2.1 | 2.53 | 175,867 | 201,216 | 1.7 | 47,219 | 54,184 | 10 |
| DISTRICT OF COLUMBIA | 249,634 | 224,159 | 218,341 | -1.3 | 2.12 | 122,087 | 106,192 | -1.7 | 40,143 | 45,439 | 25 |
| FLORIDA | 5,134,869 | 6,059,612 | 6,481,506 | 2.0 | 2.48 | 3,511,825 | 4,027,108 | 1.7 | 38,118 | 45,132 | 34 |
| GEORGIA | 2,366,615 | 2,965,764 | 3,279,895 | 2.8 | 2.62 | 1,713,072 | 2,108,021 | 2.6 | 43,179 | 51,136 | 19 |
| HAWAII | 356,267 | 407,716 | 419,968 | 1.7 | 2.81 | 263,456 | 299,285 | 1.6 | 50,350 | 59,490 | 5 |
| IDAHO | 360,723 | 469,643 | 515,928 | 3.3 | 2.66 | 263,194 | 332,925 | 2.9 | 39,372 | 46,555 | 28 |
| ILLINOIS | 4,202,240 | 4,494,471 | 4,611,882 | 0.8 | 2.64 | 2,924,880 | 3,049,135 | 0.5 | 46,248 | 53,055 | 13 |
| INDIANA | 2,065,355 | 2,264,713 | 2,351,479 | 1.1 | 2.56 | 1,480,351 | 1,578,807 | 0.8 | 42,096 | 48,409 | 22 |
| IOWA | 1,064,325 | 1,110,517 | 1,128,806 | 0.5 | 2.50 | 740,819 | 744,631 | 0.1 | 37,579 | 43,070 | 37 |
| KANSAS | 944,726 | 1,016,017 | 1,048,281 | 0.9 | 2.55 | 658,600 | 686,553 | 0.5 | 39,174 | 46,093 | 29 |
| KENTUCKY | 1,379,782 | 1,519,046 | 1,583,173 | 1.2 | 2.56 | 1,015,998 | 1,086,994 | 0.8 | 34,473 | 39,332 | 43 |
| LOUISIANA | 1,499,269 | 1,622,714 | 1,677,289 | 1.0 | 2.63 | 1,089,882 | 1,148,984 | 0.6 | 31,622 | 35,502 | 48 |
| MAINE | 465,312 | 501,972 | 522,708 | 0.9 | 2.43 | 328,685 | 343,205 | 0.5 | 37,175 | 43,579 | 39 |
| MARYLAND | 1,748,991 | 1,945,979 | 2,042,232 | 1.3 | 2.62 | 1,245,814 | 1,348,907 | 1.0 | 54,427 | 63,444 | 3 |
| MASSACHUSETTS | 2,247,110 | 2,386,401 | 2,480,785 | 0.7 | 2.51 | 1,514,746 | 1,557,491 | 0.3 | 48,636 | 56,863 | 6 |
| MICHIGAN | 3,419,331 | 3,752,696 | 3,891,698 | 1.1 | 2.58 | 2,439,171 | 2,603,657 | 0.8 | 43,403 | 49,028 | 18 |
| MINNESOTA | 1,647,853 | 1,830,553 | 1,922,495 | 1.3 | 2.57 | 1,130,683 | 1,226,626 | 1.0 | 47,612 | 54,787 | 8 |
| MISSISSIPPI | 911,374 | 1,018,519 | 1,069,985 | 1.4 | 2.66 | 674,378 | 732,900 | 1.0 | 31,144 | 36,358 | 49 |
| MISSOURI | 1,961,206 | 2,122,566 | 2,193,984 | 1.0 | 2.52 | 1,368,334 | 1,440,535 | 0.6 | 38,422 | 44,218 | 33 |
| MONTANA | 306,163 | 353,199 | 367,103 | 1.8 | 2.44 | 211,666 | 235,433 | 1.3 | 32,474 | 36,874 | 46 |
| NEBRASKA | 602,363 | 641,542 | 655,819 | 0.8 | 2.53 | 415,427 | 428,168 | 0.4 | 37,925 | 43,544 | 36 |
| NEVADA | 466,297 | 730,903 | 865,184 | 5.6 | 2.54 | 307,400 | 475,900 | 5.4 | 46,090 | 54,726 | 14 |
| NEW HAMPSHIRE | 411,186 | 464,999 | 499,580 | 1.5 | 2.54 | 292,601 | 319,986 | 1.1 | 46,866 | 55,884 | 12 |
| NEW JERSEY | 2,794,711 | 2,997,218 | 3,100,047 | 0.9 | 2.67 | 2,021,346 | 2,106,448 | 0.5 | 55,149 | 64,448 | 2 |
| NEW MEXICO | 542,709 | 644,015 | 674,388 | 2.1 | 2.67 | 391,487 | 454,914 | 1.8 | 35,131 | 41,077 | 42 |
| NEW YORK | 6,639,322 | 6,825,090 | 6,918,272 | 0.3 | 2.59 | 4,489,312 | 4,502,436 | 0.0 | 42,807 | 50,643 | 20 |
| NORTH CAROLINA | 2,517,026 | 2,972,124 | 3,197,957 | 2.0 | 2.53 | 1,812,053 | 2,072,403 | 1.6 | 38,498 | 44,239 | 32 |
| NORTH DAKOTA | 240,878 | 248,462 | 250,906 | 0.4 | 2.44 | 166,270 | 164,529 | -0.1 | 32,300 | 37,344 | 47 |
| OHIO | 4,087,546 | 4,330,947 | 4,416,316 | 0.7 | 2.54 | 2,895,223 | 2,978,835 | 0.4 | 38,607 | 43,591 | 31 |
| OKLAHOMA | 1,206,135 | 1,304,842 | 1,350,648 | 1.0 | 2.52 | 855,321 | 896,531 | 0.6 | 33,255 | 39,070 | 45 |
| OREGON | 1,103,313 | 1,320,956 | 1,406,531 | 2.2 | 2.49 | 750,844 | 870,570 | 1.8 | 39,843 | 46,114 | 26 |
| PENNSYLVANIA | 4,495,966 | 4,619,386 | 4,644,657 | 0.3 | 2.52 | 3,155,989 | 3,142,712 | -0.1 | 40,344 | 46,169 | 24 |
| RHODE ISLAND | 377,977 | 378,089 | 382,404 | 0.0 | 2.53 | 258,886 | 249,877 | -0.4 | 42,500 | 50,661 | 21 |
| SOUTH CAROLINA | 1,258,044 | 1,493,431 | 1,621,449 | 2.1 | 2.56 | 928,206 | 1,070,554 | 1.7 | 37,975 | 43,472 | 35 |
| SOUTH DAKOTA | 259,034 | 277,307 | 283,649 | 0.8 | 2.56 | 180,306 | 186,394 | 0.4 | 34,164 | 40,407 | 44 |
| TENNESSEE | 1,853,725 | 2,159,580 | 2,295,135 | 1.9 | 2.50 | 1,348,019 | 1,533,132 | 1.6 | 37,221 | 42,289 | 38 |
| TEXAS | 6,070,937 | 7,353,082 | 8,014,923 | 2.4 | 2.71 | 4,343,878 | 5,159,984 | 2.1 | 39,535 | 46,148 | 27 |
| UTAH | 537,273 | 702,807 | 773,032 | 3.3 | 3.03 | 410,862 | 529,151 | 3.1 | 44,395 | 52,426 | 16 |
| VERMONT | 210,650 | 237,022 | 249,554 | 1.4 | 2.43 | 144,895 | 157,534 | 1.0 | 40,913 | 48,538 | 23 |
| VIRGINIA | 2,291,830 | 2,658,141 | 2,839,450 | 1.8 | 2.53 | 1,629,490 | 1,841,739 | 1.5 | 44,048 | 51,389 | 17 |
| WASHINGTON | 1,872,431 | 2,280,005 | 2,450,058 | 2.4 | 2.51 | 1,264,934 | 1,495,979 | 2.1 | 46,940 | 55,472 | 11 |
| WEST VIRGINIA | 688,557 | 722,607 | 730,197 | 0.6 | 2.44 | 500,259 | 507,508 | 0.2 | 27,663 | 31,361 | 51 |
| WISCONSIN | 1,822,118 | 2,003,695 | 2,075,676 | 1.2 | 2.56 | 1,275,172 | 1,362,217 | 0.8 | 44,486 | 51,618 | 15 |
| WYOMING | 168,839 | 187,016 | 191,513 | 1.3 | 2.51 | 119,825 | 128,328 | 0.8 | 35,870 | 41,325 | 41 |
| UNITED STATES | | | | 1.4 | 2.59 | | | 1.1 | 41,914 | 49,127 | |

D

# INCOME

## STATE AND U.S. TOTALS

| STATE | 2000 Per Capita Income | 2000 HH Income Base | 2000 HOUSEHOLD INCOME DISTRIBUTION (%) | | | | | | 2000 AVERAGE DISPOSABLE INCOME BY AGE OF HOUSEHOLDER | | | | | |
|---|---|---|---|---|---|---|---|---|---|---|---|---|---|---|
| | | | Less than $15,000 | $15,000 to $24,999 | $25,000 to $49,999 | $50,000 to $99,999 | $100,000 to $149,999 | $150,000 or More | All Ages | <35 | 35-44 | 45-54 | 55-64 | 65+ |
| ALABAMA | 18,753 | 1,691,328 | 19.6 | 14.3 | 32.9 | 25.7 | 5.4 | 2.1 | 36,364 | 31,258 | 42,625 | 45,673 | 37,541 | 23,609 |
| ALASKA | 28,723 | 218,446 | 7.3 | 7.3 | 24.0 | 39.8 | 14.3 | 7.2 | 58,298 | 42,559 | 59,022 | 68,415 | 57,596 | 40,357 |
| ARIZONA | 20,150 | 1,859,632 | 14.9 | 14.5 | 33.7 | 28.2 | 6.2 | 2.4 | 38,777 | 32,856 | 43,804 | 47,838 | 40,193 | 29,132 |
| ARKANSAS | 15,500 | 990,637 | 22.3 | 18.1 | 34.7 | 20.6 | 3.3 | 1.1 | 30,169 | 26,250 | 36,993 | 38,283 | 31,856 | 20,464 |
| CALIFORNIA | 24,644 | 11,848,927 | 11.9 | 10.8 | 29.7 | 32.6 | 9.5 | 5.5 | 46,445 | 39,081 | 48,623 | 54,321 | 49,552 | 33,400 |
| COLORADO | 26,360 | 1,629,490 | 10.2 | 10.9 | 30.9 | 33.3 | 10.0 | 4.7 | 45,968 | 35,367 | 50,661 | 54,594 | 47,779 | 30,712 |
| CONNECTICUT | 29,921 | 1,248,792 | 10.0 | 8.1 | 27.7 | 36.6 | 10.6 | 7.0 | 50,081 | 41,488 | 50,857 | 59,429 | 54,470 | 31,943 |
| DELAWARE | 24,474 | 293,197 | 10.2 | 10.3 | 32.5 | 34.6 | 8.9 | 3.5 | 43,151 | 36,896 | 47,294 | 52,745 | 46,227 | 30,023 |
| DISTRICT OF COLUMBIA | 28,952 | 224,159 | 16.2 | 14.3 | 29.3 | 26.4 | 8.2 | 5.5 | 40,393 | 33,612 | 42,112 | 47,326 | 41,037 | 31,092 |
| FLORIDA | 21,473 | 6,059,480 | 14.8 | 15.2 | 34.4 | 26.9 | 5.9 | 2.9 | 40,198 | 34,749 | 44,201 | 47,664 | 43,025 | 31,150 |
| GEORGIA | 22,304 | 2,965,717 | 13.9 | 11.8 | 31.9 | 30.9 | 8.0 | 3.5 | 41,548 | 35,922 | 45,313 | 49,959 | 41,633 | 25,795 |
| HAWAII | 23,519 | 407,713 | 9.1 | 10.7 | 29.7 | 36.1 | 9.9 | 4.4 | 42,024 | 31,905 | 41,983 | 50,720 | 48,703 | 35,728 |
| IDAHO | 19,275 | 469,617 | 12.8 | 14.6 | 36.3 | 28.4 | 5.9 | 2.0 | 37,085 | 30,971 | 42,209 | 45,831 | 37,897 | 25,545 |
| ILLINOIS | 24,170 | 4,494,410 | 12.6 | 10.6 | 31.0 | 32.3 | 9.1 | 4.4 | 43,984 | 37,679 | 47,254 | 53,608 | 47,357 | 28,025 |
| INDIANA | 21,043 | 2,264,683 | 12.6 | 12.5 | 34.8 | 31.1 | 6.5 | 2.4 | 39,887 | 33,966 | 44,886 | 50,043 | 42,864 | 25,630 |
| IOWA | 18,653 | 1,110,481 | 14.8 | 14.5 | 37.4 | 27.0 | 4.8 | 1.6 | 33,931 | 28,488 | 40,263 | 43,264 | 36,563 | 23,029 |
| KANSAS | 20,105 | 1,015,987 | 14.5 | 14.0 | 35.0 | 28.1 | 5.9 | 2.4 | 37,751 | 30,612 | 43,142 | 47,811 | 41,695 | 25,693 |
| KENTUCKY | 17,910 | 1,519,039 | 20.3 | 15.1 | 33.7 | 24.1 | 4.9 | 1.9 | 34,208 | 29,344 | 40,489 | 41,778 | 33,655 | 22,337 |
| LOUISIANA | 16,391 | 1,622,662 | 24.2 | 15.7 | 32.0 | 21.9 | 4.3 | 1.9 | 33,918 | 28,008 | 39,291 | 41,400 | 34,336 | 22,821 |
| MAINE | 18,925 | 501,961 | 15.4 | 14.7 | 37.4 | 26.5 | 4.6 | 1.5 | 33,487 | 30,671 | 39,210 | 40,548 | 34,953 | 21,724 |
| MARYLAND | 27,573 | 1,945,941 | 8.5 | 8.3 | 28.1 | 37.8 | 11.9 | 5.4 | 48,317 | 40,836 | 50,237 | 56,712 | 50,186 | 34,105 |
| MASSACHUSETTS | 25,526 | 2,386,381 | 13.5 | 9.1 | 28.8 | 34.4 | 9.5 | 4.7 | 43,224 | 38,730 | 46,636 | 53,180 | 48,358 | 26,556 |
| MICHIGAN | 22,281 | 3,752,653 | 14.8 | 11.2 | 31.6 | 31.5 | 7.6 | 3.4 | 40,429 | 33,253 | 45,056 | 52,082 | 45,156 | 24,635 |
| MINNESOTA | 24,804 | 1,830,550 | 10.5 | 10.0 | 32.2 | 33.5 | 9.5 | 4.3 | 43,593 | 36,990 | 48,415 | 54,568 | 46,928 | 26,595 |
| MISSISSIPPI | 15,620 | 1,018,513 | 24.1 | 16.2 | 32.7 | 21.6 | 4.0 | 1.5 | 32,177 | 28,646 | 37,129 | 39,522 | 32,438 | 20,720 |
| MISSOURI | 19,444 | 2,122,493 | 15.8 | 14.1 | 34.4 | 28.2 | 5.6 | 1.9 | 36,824 | 32,026 | 42,273 | 46,089 | 39,038 | 23,886 |
| MONTANA | 16,982 | 353,179 | 19.5 | 17.2 | 36.6 | 21.9 | 3.6 | 1.2 | 30,753 | 24,090 | 35,624 | 37,665 | 32,967 | 22,582 |
| NEBRASKA | 19,393 | 641,532 | 14.3 | 14.9 | 36.6 | 27.0 | 5.2 | 2.0 | 35,837 | 29,458 | 42,366 | 44,678 | 38,685 | 24,332 |
| NEVADA | 24,115 | 730,885 | 9.8 | 11.4 | 33.5 | 33.7 | 8.4 | 3.2 | 45,641 | 39,906 | 49,413 | 54,160 | 47,414 | 32,251 |
| NEW HAMPSHIRE | 23,086 | 464,999 | 10.2 | 9.9 | 33.7 | 35.2 | 8.1 | 2.8 | 42,879 | 41,111 | 47,248 | 51,660 | 46,004 | 25,721 |
| NEW JERSEY | 28,926 | 2,997,205 | 9.9 | 7.9 | 26.5 | 36.6 | 12.1 | 7.0 | 48,859 | 44,187 | 51,112 | 56,303 | 53,799 | 30,415 |
| NEW MEXICO | 17,428 | 643,981 | 18.7 | 15.7 | 33.5 | 25.1 | 5.3 | 1.8 | 35,040 | 28,013 | 39,399 | 43,150 | 38,690 | 26,905 |
| NEW YORK | 24,235 | 6,824,962 | 16.2 | 11.5 | 29.7 | 29.5 | 8.1 | 5.0 | 40,926 | 35,448 | 42,934 | 47,623 | 44,515 | 27,215 |
| NORTH CAROLINA | 19,736 | 2,972,111 | 15.4 | 14.1 | 34.9 | 27.7 | 5.8 | 2.1 | 36,471 | 31,935 | 41,916 | 45,251 | 37,794 | 23,975 |
| NORTH DAKOTA | 16,189 | 248,457 | 19.3 | 17.7 | 37.0 | 21.9 | 3.3 | 0.9 | 31,496 | 26,663 | 38,247 | 39,642 | 34,148 | 22,008 |
| OHIO | 19,315 | 4,330,904 | 16.1 | 13.6 | 34.9 | 28.0 | 5.4 | 2.0 | 35,978 | 30,645 | 41,145 | 45,889 | 39,280 | 23,523 |
| OKLAHOMA | 17,482 | 1,304,811 | 19.8 | 16.6 | 34.3 | 23.3 | 4.3 | 1.7 | 33,043 | 26,989 | 38,466 | 41,397 | 36,423 | 23,614 |
| OREGON | 20,754 | 1,320,919 | 13.7 | 13.8 | 35.4 | 28.8 | 6.2 | 2.2 | 35,484 | 30,078 | 40,209 | 44,693 | 38,211 | 23,703 |
| PENNSYLVANIA | 21,645 | 4,619,293 | 14.8 | 13.1 | 34.1 | 28.4 | 6.5 | 3.1 | 38,768 | 34,429 | 43,367 | 48,861 | 42,361 | 24,642 |
| RHODE ISLAND | 21,898 | 378,089 | 15.1 | 11.1 | 32.9 | 30.7 | 7.1 | 3.2 | 39,112 | 35,424 | 44,276 | 48,870 | 44,309 | 24,614 |
| SOUTH CAROLINA | 18,998 | 1,493,401 | 16.3 | 13.8 | 34.8 | 27.6 | 5.6 | 1.9 | 35,928 | 31,758 | 40,040 | 43,833 | 37,442 | 24,491 |
| SOUTH DAKOTA | 16,386 | 277,307 | 17.4 | 16.7 | 37.2 | 23.8 | 3.8 | 1.1 | 32,328 | 27,818 | 37,662 | 41,463 | 36,537 | 21,847 |
| TENNESSEE | 19,874 | 2,159,539 | 17.1 | 14.4 | 34.0 | 26.4 | 5.7 | 2.4 | 39,053 | 34,053 | 44,876 | 48,417 | 39,984 | 24,353 |
| TEXAS | 20,236 | 7,353,015 | 16.2 | 13.9 | 31.8 | 28.0 | 6.9 | 3.2 | 41,217 | 33,340 | 45,769 | 49,732 | 43,451 | 28,369 |
| UTAH | 18,462 | 702,788 | 10.0 | 11.3 | 35.7 | 33.4 | 7.4 | 2.2 | 39,988 | 32,718 | 44,911 | 50,872 | 45,507 | 27,888 |
| VERMONT | 21,048 | 237,022 | 12.8 | 12.6 | 36.7 | 29.5 | 6.1 | 2.3 | 37,144 | 33,498 | 41,652 | 45,856 | 40,530 | 22,952 |
| VIRGINIA | 22,934 | 2,658,064 | 12.8 | 11.9 | 32.0 | 31.8 | 8.2 | 3.3 | 41,578 | 34,181 | 45,367 | 50,467 | 43,935 | 29,069 |
| WASHINGTON | 25,073 | 2,279,988 | 10.2 | 10.7 | 32.6 | 33.5 | 9.0 | 4.0 | 46,762 | 37,920 | 49,676 | 56,367 | 50,973 | 31,996 |
| WEST VIRGINIA | 14,694 | 722,607 | 27.0 | 18.3 | 33.4 | 17.8 | 2.5 | 1.0 | 28,436 | 24,166 | 34,601 | 35,109 | 29,773 | 19,746 |
| WISCONSIN | 22,127 | 2,003,668 | 11.7 | 10.8 | 34.5 | 32.4 | 7.8 | 2.8 | 37,949 | 32,304 | 43,189 | 48,841 | 41,897 | 23,477 |
| WYOMING | 17,650 | 186,883 | 17.7 | 15.1 | 36.3 | 25.4 | 4.3 | 1.2 | 35,762 | 27,008 | 43,177 | 45,031 | 39,383 | 24,696 |
| UNITED STATES | 22,162 | | 14.5 | 12.5 | 32.3 | 29.8 | 7.4 | 3.5 | 40,748 | 34,503 | 44,969 | 49,579 | 43,409 | 27,339 |

# SPENDING POTENTIAL INDEXES

## STATE AND U.S. TOTALS

# E

| STATE | FINANCIAL SERVICES | | | | THE HOME | | | | | | ENTERTAINMENT | | | | | | PERSONAL | | | |
|---|---|---|---|---|---|---|---|---|---|---|---|---|---|---|---|---|---|---|---|---|
| | | | | | Home Improvements | | | Furnishings | | | | | | | | | | | | |
| | Auto Loan | Home Loan | Investments | Retirement Plans | Home Repair | Lawn & Garden | Remodeling | Appliances | Electronics | Furniture | Restaurants | Sporting Goods | Theater & Concerts | Toys & Hobbies | Travel | Video Rental | Apparel | Auto Aftermarket | Health Insurance | Pets & Supplies |
| ALABAMA | 98 | 85 | 92 | 90 | 98 | 96 | 105 | 98 | 95 | 91 | 90 | 98 | 91 | 98 | 80 | 98 | 91 | 94 | 98 | 99 |
| ALASKA | 102 | 108 | 93 | 103 | 100 | 102 | 103 | 104 | 107 | 107 | 108 | 98 | 97 | 97 | 92 | 96 | 106 | 104 | 96 | 98 |
| ARIZONA | 100 | 101 | 97 | 99 | 101 | 103 | 102 | 102 | 101 | 102 | 101 | 94 | 94 | 95 | 91 | 94 | 98 | 99 | 99 | 96 |
| ARKANSAS | 97 | 81 | 89 | 86 | 97 | 95 | 107 | 97 | 94 | 87 | 88 | 96 | 88 | 97 | 78 | 97 | 88 | 92 | 99 | 98 |
| CALIFORNIA | 101 | 118 | 106 | 110 | 106 | 109 | 99 | 103 | 108 | 108 | 109 | 97 | 102 | 95 | 102 | 97 | 106 | 107 | 98 | 99 |
| COLORADO | 101 | 104 | 97 | 103 | 102 | 103 | 103 | 103 | 104 | 105 | 104 | 96 | 96 | 96 | 92 | 95 | 103 | 101 | 98 | 96 |
| CONNECTICUT | 103 | 110 | 112 | 110 | 100 | 102 | 94 | 101 | 103 | 109 | 110 | 106 | 111 | 106 | 107 | 101 | 113 | 105 | 103 | 105 |
| DELAWARE | 99 | 99 | 102 | 98 | 103 | 102 | 102 | 99 | 98 | 99 | 101 | 100 | 99 | 101 | 89 | 99 | 100 | 100 | 100 | 101 |
| DISTRICT OF COLUMBIA | 96 | 106 | 109 | 101 | 106 | 103 | 88 | 99 | 96 | 105 | 95 | 98 | 101 | 94 | 99 | 101 | 105 | 105 | 90 | 98 |
| FLORIDA | 99 | 98 | 104 | 98 | 103 | 104 | 102 | 100 | 96 | 99 | 99 | 100 | 98 | 100 | 90 | 98 | 97 | 99 | 101 | 101 |
| GEORGIA | 99 | 96 | 94 | 96 | 99 | 98 | 103 | 99 | 99 | 98 | 98 | 101 | 97 | 101 | 85 | 99 | 98 | 99 | 97 | 101 |
| HAWAII | 97 | 133 | 104 | 113 | 94 | 104 | 89 | 96 | 117 | 96 | 116 | 92 | 96 | 85 | 102 | 112 | 99 | 107 | 96 | 97 |
| IDAHO | 99 | 89 | 88 | 92 | 98 | 97 | 108 | 100 | 99 | 94 | 93 | 92 | 88 | 93 | 83 | 94 | 93 | 95 | 98 | 94 |
| ILLINOIS | 99 | 103 | 103 | 103 | 103 | 103 | 99 | 100 | 100 | 102 | 103 | 100 | 105 | 100 | 103 | 103 | 101 | 104 | 100 | 101 |
| INDIANA | 98 | 92 | 94 | 94 | 99 | 97 | 103 | 98 | 96 | 95 | 97 | 98 | 98 | 100 | 93 | 101 | 94 | 98 | 100 | 100 |
| IOWA | 97 | 86 | 90 | 90 | 97 | 95 | 104 | 96 | 94 | 89 | 92 | 96 | 94 | 98 | 89 | 101 | 89 | 95 | 102 | 98 |
| KANSAS | 98 | 93 | 93 | 95 | 98 | 97 | 102 | 97 | 97 | 94 | 97 | 97 | 98 | 99 | 93 | 101 | 93 | 98 | 100 | 99 |
| KENTUCKY | 98 | 84 | 91 | 89 | 98 | 96 | 106 | 97 | 95 | 89 | 90 | 97 | 91 | 98 | 80 | 97 | 90 | 93 | 100 | 99 |
| LOUISIANA | 97 | 87 | 92 | 90 | 98 | 95 | 101 | 97 | 95 | 92 | 90 | 97 | 92 | 97 | 82 | 98 | 92 | 95 | 95 | 98 |
| MAINE | 100 | 85 | 90 | 90 | 90 | 89 | 100 | 97 | 95 | 91 | 92 | 99 | 93 | 101 | 86 | 99 | 95 | 93 | 102 | 102 |
| MARYLAND | 101 | 109 | 107 | 107 | 105 | 107 | 101 | 101 | 103 | 107 | 108 | 105 | 106 | 104 | 96 | 101 | 108 | 106 | 99 | 103 |
| MASSACHUSETTS | 101 | 107 | 109 | 106 | 99 | 100 | 93 | 100 | 101 | 106 | 106 | 104 | 107 | 104 | 104 | 101 | 109 | 103 | 103 | 104 |
| MICHIGAN | 98 | 96 | 98 | 98 | 101 | 99 | 102 | 99 | 97 | 97 | 98 | 98 | 101 | 100 | 97 | 102 | 96 | 100 | 99 | 100 |
| MINNESOTA | 100 | 98 | 94 | 98 | 99 | 99 | 102 | 99 | 99 | 97 | 101 | 100 | 101 | 101 | 96 | 102 | 97 | 101 | 101 | 101 |
| MISSISSIPPI | 97 | 81 | 87 | 86 | 97 | 94 | 105 | 97 | 94 | 88 | 87 | 96 | 88 | 96 | 78 | 97 | 88 | 93 | 97 | 98 |
| MISSOURI | 98 | 92 | 94 | 95 | 99 | 97 | 102 | 98 | 97 | 94 | 96 | 98 | 98 | 99 | 93 | 101 | 94 | 98 | 100 | 99 |
| MONTANA | 98 | 84 | 87 | 89 | 98 | 96 | 107 | 99 | 97 | 90 | 89 | 89 | 85 | 91 | 81 | 93 | 89 | 92 | 99 | 92 |
| NEBRASKA | 98 | 91 | 92 | 94 | 97 | 96 | 102 | 97 | 96 | 92 | 95 | 97 | 96 | 98 | 92 | 101 | 92 | 97 | 101 | 99 |
| NEVADA | 100 | 104 | 92 | 99 | 101 | 101 | 100 | 102 | 103 | 104 | 103 | 95 | 94 | 95 | 91 | 95 | 101 | 100 | 96 | 96 |
| NEW HAMPSHIRE | 102 | 97 | 94 | 98 | 92 | 92 | 96 | 99 | 100 | 100 | 102 | 103 | 100 | 105 | 93 | 101 | 104 | 99 | 101 | 104 |
| NEW JERSEY | 103 | 111 | 111 | 111 | 100 | 103 | 93 | 102 | 104 | 110 | 110 | 107 | 111 | 106 | 109 | 102 | 114 | 107 | 103 | 105 |
| NEW MEXICO | 98 | 96 | 94 | 94 | 100 | 99 | 103 | 101 | 99 | 99 | 96 | 91 | 90 | 92 | 88 | 94 | 94 | 97 | 97 | 94 |
| NEW YORK | 100 | 105 | 107 | 103 | 99 | 98 | 92 | 99 | 99 | 106 | 103 | 103 | 105 | 101 | 105 | 101 | 107 | 102 | 101 | 102 |
| NORTH CAROLINA | 98 | 88 | 92 | 91 | 98 | 97 | 106 | 98 | 96 | 92 | 93 | 98 | 92 | 99 | 81 | 98 | 93 | 95 | 99 | 100 |
| NORTH DAKOTA | 97 | 86 | 85 | 88 | 94 | 93 | 101 | 95 | 94 | 87 | 91 | 95 | 92 | 96 | 87 | 100 | 88 | 95 | 100 | 98 |
| OHIO | 98 | 94 | 98 | 96 | 101 | 99 | 101 | 98 | 96 | 96 | 97 | 97 | 100 | 99 | 96 | 101 | 95 | 99 | 100 | 99 |
| OKLAHOMA | 97 | 88 | 92 | 90 | 98 | 96 | 104 | 97 | 95 | 91 | 93 | 96 | 92 | 98 | 81 | 98 | 92 | 95 | 99 | 99 |
| OREGON | 99 | 94 | 95 | 95 | 101 | 100 | 105 | 100 | 99 | 97 | 96 | 92 | 91 | 94 | 87 | 93 | 95 | 96 | 98 | 94 |
| PENNSYLVANIA | 99 | 92 | 100 | 96 | 95 | 94 | 94 | 98 | 95 | 97 | 96 | 100 | 99 | 101 | 94 | 99 | 100 | 96 | 102 | 101 |
| RHODE ISLAND | 99 | 98 | 104 | 98 | 97 | 96 | 92 | 98 | 96 | 101 | 100 | 100 | 102 | 102 | 99 | 99 | 102 | 98 | 102 | 101 |
| SOUTH CAROLINA | 98 | 88 | 93 | 91 | 98 | 97 | 105 | 98 | 96 | 92 | 93 | 98 | 93 | 99 | 81 | 98 | 93 | 95 | 99 | 100 |
| SOUTH DAKOTA | 97 | 85 | 86 | 89 | 95 | 93 | 104 | 96 | 94 | 87 | 91 | 95 | 92 | 97 | 87 | 100 | 88 | 95 | 101 | 98 |
| TENNESSEE | 98 | 88 | 92 | 91 | 99 | 97 | 105 | 98 | 96 | 92 | 92 | 98 | 93 | 99 | 82 | 98 | 93 | 95 | 99 | 100 |
| TEXAS | 99 | 100 | 96 | 98 | 99 | 99 | 101 | 99 | 99 | 98 | 100 | 100 | 97 | 100 | 87 | 99 | 98 | 100 | 98 | 102 |
| UTAH | 100 | 99 | 91 | 97 | 100 | 99 | 102 | 101 | 102 | 101 | 101 | 93 | 92 | 95 | 88 | 94 | 99 | 99 | 96 | 95 |
| VERMONT | 100 | 88 | 89 | 92 | 90 | 89 | 99 | 97 | 95 | 92 | 94 | 99 | 94 | 102 | 87 | 99 | 96 | 94 | 102 | 102 |
| VIRGINIA | 100 | 102 | 100 | 101 | 102 | 102 | 103 | 99 | 101 | 100 | 103 | 102 | 101 | 102 | 90 | 100 | 102 | 102 | 99 | 102 |
| WASHINGTON | 100 | 101 | 98 | 100 | 102 | 103 | 104 | 101 | 102 | 102 | 101 | 94 | 95 | 95 | 92 | 94 | 100 | 100 | 98 | 95 |
| WEST VIRGINIA | 97 | 77 | 88 | 84 | 98 | 95 | 108 | 96 | 92 | 85 | 86 | 94 | 87 | 96 | 77 | 96 | 85 | 90 | 101 | 97 |
| WISCONSIN | 98 | 93 | 95 | 95 | 99 | 98 | 104 | 98 | 96 | 94 | 97 | 98 | 98 | 100 | 94 | 101 | 94 | 98 | 101 | 100 |
| WYOMING | 98 | 89 | 87 | 90 | 97 | 96 | 106 | 99 | 99 | 94 | 93 | 91 | 87 | 93 | 82 | 93 | 92 | 94 | 97 | 93 |
| UNITED STATES | 100 | 100 | 100 | 100 | 100 | 100 | 100 | 100 | 100 | 100 | 100 | 100 | 100 | 100 | 100 | 100 | 100 | 100 | 100 | 100 |

# MSA SUMMARY DATA

13th EDITION

# POPULATION CHANGE

## MSA AND U.S. TOTALS



| MSA | MSA Code | POPULATION 1990 | POPULATION 2000 | POPULATION 2005 | 1990-2000 ANNUAL CHANGE % Rate | 1990-2000 ANNUAL CHANGE National Rank | RACE (%) White 1990 | RACE (%) White 2000 | RACE (%) Black 1990 | RACE (%) Black 2000 | RACE (%) Asian/Pacific 1990 | RACE (%) Asian/Pacific 2000 |
|---|---|---|---|---|---|---|---|---|---|---|---|---|
| ABILENE, TX | 0040 | 119,655 | 124,780 | 126,362 | 0.4 | 226 | 83.8 | 80.8 | 6.3 | 6.5 | 1.2 | 1.9 |
| AKRON, OH | 0080 | 657,575 | 691,795 | 700,678 | 0.5 | 212 | 88.8 | 87.2 | 9.9 | 11.1 | 0.9 | 1.3 |
| ALBANY, GA | 0120 | 112,561 | 118,341 | 118,750 | 0.5 | 212 | 53.3 | 50.4 | 45.8 | 48.4 | 0.4 | 0.7 |
| ALBANY-SCH.-TROY, NY | 0160 | 861,424 | 868,003 | 859,142 | 0.1 | 262 | 93.4 | 92.1 | 4.6 | 5.1 | 1.2 | 1.9 |
| ALBUQUERQUE, NM | 0200 | 589,131 | 682,903 | 703,467 | 1.5 | 73 | 76.0 | 73.2 | 2.5 | 3.0 | 1.4 | 2.0 |
| ALEXANDRIA, LA | 0220 | 131,556 | 127,051 | 128,153 | -0.3 | 297 | 70.7 | 68.1 | 28.0 | 30.2 | 0.7 | 0.9 |
| ALLENTWN-BETH-EASTON | 0240 | 595,081 | 620,529 | 630,324 | 0.4 | 226 | 94.2 | 92.4 | 2.0 | 2.3 | 1.1 | 1.6 |
| ALTOONA, PA | 0280 | 130,542 | 129,421 | 126,866 | -0.1 | 283 | 98.7 | 98.4 | 0.8 | 1.0 | 0.3 | 0.4 |
| AMARILLO, TX | 0320 | 187,547 | 210,157 | 217,716 | 1.1 | 129 | 84.5 | 81.4 | 5.2 | 5.5 | 1.7 | 2.4 |
| ANCHORAGE, AK | 0380 | 226,338 | 260,161 | 271,496 | 1.4 | 80 | 80.7 | 78.5 | 6.4 | 6.2 | 4.8 | 6.3 |
| ANN ARBOR, MI | 0440 | 490,058 | 566,656 | 612,576 | 1.4 | 80 | 89.0 | 87.7 | 6.9 | 7.1 | 2.6 | 3.5 |
| ANNISTON, AL | 0450 | 116,034 | 116,316 | 115,200 | 0.0 | 270 | 80.0 | 78.9 | 18.6 | 19.4 | 0.7 | 0.9 |
| APPLTN-OSHKSH-NEENAH | 0460 | 315,121 | 351,132 | 366,434 | 1.1 | 129 | 97.4 | 96.4 | 0.3 | 0.4 | 1.2 | 1.8 |
| ASHEVILLE, NC | 0480 | 191,774 | 217,170 | 227,341 | 1.2 | 110 | 91.6 | 90.8 | 7.5 | 7.8 | 0.4 | 0.7 |
| ATHENS, GA | 0500 | 126,262 | 141,769 | 148,828 | 1.1 | 129 | 76.9 | 73.0 | 20.7 | 23.3 | 1.8 | 2.9 |
| ATLANTA, GA | 0520 | 2,959,950 | 3,972,438 | 4,520,521 | 2.9 | 10 | 72.1 | 70.4 | 25.2 | 25.3 | 1.8 | 2.9 |
| ATLANTIC-CAPE MAY,NJ | 0560 | 319,416 | 339,275 | 347,539 | 0.6 | 200 | 81.5 | 77.2 | 13.9 | 15.8 | 1.7 | 2.9 |
| AUBURN-OPELIKA, AL | 0580 | 87,146 | 104,274 | 114,397 | 1.8 | 49 | 74.5 | 72.0 | 23.4 | 25.6 | 1.8 | 2.1 |
| AUGUSTA-AIKEN, GA-SC | 0600 | 415,184 | 463,774 | 478,423 | 1.1 | 129 | 66.1 | 63.7 | 31.8 | 32.9 | 1.3 | 2.3 |
| AUSTIN-SAN MARCOS,TX | 0640 | 846,227 | 1,183,948 | 1,373,243 | 3.3 | 6 | 76.6 | 73.2 | 9.4 | 9.5 | 2.2 | 3.0 |
| BAKERSFIELD, CA | 0680 | 543,477 | 649,311 | 683,572 | 1.8 | 49 | 69.6 | 62.8 | 5.5 | 5.9 | 3.0 | 3.9 |
| BALTIMORE, MD | 0720 | 2,382,172 | 2,500,977 | 2,555,185 | 0.5 | 212 | 71.8 | 69.3 | 25.9 | 27.3 | 1.8 | 2.6 |
| BANGOR, ME | 0733 | 146,601 | 144,122 | 142,526 | -0.2 | 290 | 98.0 | 97.8 | 0.4 | 0.5 | 0.6 | 0.8 |
| BARNSTABLE-YARMOUTH | 0743 | 186,605 | 216,032 | 233,725 | 1.4 | 80 | 96.2 | 95.3 | 1.5 | 1.9 | 0.5 | 0.8 |
| BATON ROUGE, LA | 0760 | 528,264 | 583,561 | 606,306 | 1.0 | 149 | 68.8 | 67.3 | 29.6 | 30.9 | 1.1 | 1.3 |
| BEAUMONT-P.ARTHUR,TX | 0840 | 361,226 | 376,942 | 380,319 | 0.4 | 226 | 73.2 | 70.9 | 23.4 | 24.6 | 1.6 | 2.2 |
| BELLINGHAM, WA | 0860 | 127,780 | 163,004 | 176,861 | 2.4 | 22 | 93.3 | 91.8 | 0.5 | 0.6 | 1.8 | 2.6 |
| BENTON HARBOR, MI | 0870 | 161,378 | 159,495 | 158,243 | -0.1 | 283 | 82.6 | 81.0 | 15.4 | 16.5 | 0.9 | 1.3 |
| BERGEN-PASSAIC, NJ | 0875 | 1,278,440 | 1,347,041 | 1,371,074 | 0.5 | 212 | 81.6 | 75.2 | 8.3 | 9.6 | 5.2 | 8.5 |
| BILLINGS, MT | 0880 | 113,419 | 127,939 | 131,708 | 1.2 | 110 | 95.2 | 94.4 | 0.5 | 0.5 | 0.5 | 0.6 |
| BILOXI-GULFPORT-PAS. | 0920 | 312,368 | 357,861 | 377,927 | 1.3 | 91 | 78.9 | 76.7 | 18.8 | 20.1 | 1.8 | 2.5 |
| BINGHAMTON, NY | 0960 | 264,497 | 245,567 | 236,357 | -0.7 | 315 | 96.2 | 95.1 | 1.8 | 2.0 | 1.5 | 2.3 |
| BIRMINGHAM, AL | 1000 | 840,140 | 921,864 | 955,172 | 0.9 | 166 | 70.5 | 70.7 | 28.7 | 28.5 | 0.5 | 0.6 |
| BISMARCK, ND | 1010 | 83,831 | 92,537 | 95,564 | 1.0 | 149 | 97.0 | 96.3 | 0.1 | 0.1 | 0.3 | 0.5 |
| BLOOMINGTON, IN | 1020 | 108,978 | 117,343 | 119,507 | 0.7 | 188 | 94.3 | 93.0 | 2.6 | 2.9 | 2.5 | 3.3 |
| BLOOMINGTN-NORMAL,IL | 1040 | 129,180 | 147,251 | 156,125 | 1.3 | 91 | 93.7 | 92.6 | 4.3 | 4.8 | 1.3 | 1.7 |
| BOISE CITY, ID | 1080 | 295,851 | 419,681 | 479,022 | 3.5 | 4 | 94.4 | 92.7 | 0.4 | 0.5 | 1.3 | 1.6 |
| BOSTON-WOR-LAW-LW-BR | 1123 | 5,685,998 | 5,939,496 | 6,125,499 | 0.4 | 226 | 90.6 | 88.0 | 4.6 | 5.3 | 2.5 | 3.7 |
| BOULDER-LONGMONT, CO | 1125 | 225,339 | 278,798 | 307,073 | 2.1 | 34 | 93.3 | 91.8 | 0.9 | 0.9 | 2.4 | 3.2 |
| BRAZORIA, TX | 1145 | 191,707 | 239,649 | 266,040 | 2.2 | 29 | 80.8 | 77.6 | 8.3 | 8.5 | 1.0 | 1.6 |
| BREMERTON, WA | 1150 | 189,731 | 239,295 | 253,526 | 2.3 | 25 | 90.2 | 87.8 | 2.7 | 2.8 | 4.4 | 6.1 |
| BRWNSVL-HARL-S.BENIT | 1240 | 260,120 | 334,853 | 363,711 | 2.5 | 16 | 82.4 | 81.6 | 0.3 | 0.3 | 0.3 | 0.4 |
| BRYAN-COLLEGE STA,TX | 1260 | 121,862 | 135,403 | 141,106 | 1.0 | 149 | 77.8 | 73.7 | 11.2 | 12.0 | 3.5 | 4.9 |
| BUFFALO-NIAGARA FLLS | 1280 | 1,189,288 | 1,132,858 | 1,087,237 | -0.5 | 309 | 87.2 | 85.1 | 10.3 | 11.6 | 0.9 | 1.4 |
| BURLINGTON, VT | 1303 | 177,059 | 196,550 | 205,657 | 1.0 | 149 | 97.9 | 97.3 | 0.5 | 0.8 | 0.9 | 1.3 |
| CANTON-MASSILLON, OH | 1320 | 394,106 | 402,567 | 403,065 | 0.2 | 250 | 92.8 | 91.8 | 6.4 | 7.2 | 0.4 | 0.6 |
| CASPER, WY | 1350 | 61,226 | 63,021 | 62,346 | 0.3 | 240 | 96.9 | 96.5 | 0.7 | 0.8 | 0.5 | 0.6 |
| CEDAR RAPIDS, IA | 1360 | 168,767 | 186,658 | 195,442 | 1.0 | 149 | 96.7 | 95.9 | 2.0 | 2.2 | 0.8 | 1.1 |
| CHAMPAIGN-URBANA, IL | 1400 | 173,025 | 170,414 | 171,298 | -0.1 | 283 | 84.7 | 81.9 | 9.6 | 10.6 | 4.6 | 6.3 |
| CHARLESTON-N.CHARLES | 1440 | 506,875 | 562,713 | 608,879 | 1.0 | 149 | 67.8 | 66.4 | 30.2 | 31.0 | 1.2 | 1.8 |
| CHARLESTON, WV | 1480 | 250,454 | 250,225 | 245,469 | 0.0 | 270 | 93.6 | 93.7 | 5.6 | 5.4 | 0.6 | 0.7 |
| CHARLOTTE-GAST-ROCK | 1520 | 1,162,093 | 1,451,305 | 1,617,194 | 2.2 | 29 | 78.5 | 76.9 | 19.9 | 20.5 | 1.0 | 1.7 |
| CHARLOTTESVILLE, VA | 1540 | 131,107 | 153,301 | 163,720 | 1.5 | 73 | 83.2 | 80.8 | 14.4 | 16.0 | 2.0 | 2.7 |
| CHATTANOOGA, TN-GA | 1560 | 424,347 | 454,477 | 466,754 | 0.7 | 188 | 85.2 | 84.0 | 13.7 | 14.4 | 0.7 | 1.0 |
| CHEYENNE, WY | 1580 | 73,142 | 79,068 | 80,169 | 0.8 | 175 | 90.6 | 89.7 | 3.0 | 2.9 | 1.1 | 1.5 |
| CHICAGO, IL | 1600 | 7,410,858 | 8,066,815 | 8,358,052 | 0.8 | 175 | 71.0 | 68.7 | 19.3 | 18.9 | 3.4 | 4.5 |
| CHICO-PARADISE, CA | 1620 | 182,120 | 196,641 | 201,336 | 0.8 | 175 | 90.7 | 88.1 | 1.3 | 1.4 | 2.8 | 3.9 |
| CINCINNATI, OH-KY-IN | 1640 | 1,526,092 | 1,638,563 | 1,691,658 | 0.7 | 188 | 86.4 | 86.0 | 12.5 | 12.6 | 0.8 | 1.0 |
| CLARKSVLL-HOPKINSVLL | 1660 | 169,439 | 203,730 | 215,945 | 1.8 | 49 | 75.9 | 74.2 | 20.5 | 20.6 | 1.6 | 2.5 |
| CLEVELAND-LORAIN-ELY | 1680 | 2,202,069 | 2,218,280 | 2,202,936 | 0.1 | 262 | 80.5 | 78.8 | 17.3 | 18.3 | 1.0 | 1.4 |
| COLORADO SPRINGS, CO | 1720 | 397,014 | 509,408 | 557,497 | 2.5 | 16 | 86.0 | 83.9 | 7.2 | 7.5 | 2.5 | 3.4 |
| COLUMBIA, MO | 1740 | 112,379 | 131,788 | 138,949 | 1.6 | 67 | 89.0 | 86.4 | 7.5 | 8.9 | 2.8 | 3.9 |
| COLUMBIA, SC | 1760 | 453,331 | 522,991 | 556,768 | 1.4 | 80 | 67.8 | 68.2 | 30.4 | 29.4 | 1.1 | 1.5 |
| COLUMBUS, GA-AL | 1800 | 260,860 | 271,509 | 271,292 | 0.4 | 226 | 60.3 | 55.6 | 36.8 | 40.0 | 1.2 | 1.9 |
| COLUMBUS, OH | 1840 | 1,345,450 | 1,505,610 | 1,585,095 | 1.1 | 129 | 85.8 | 84.2 | 12.1 | 13.2 | 1.6 | 2.1 |
| CORPUS CHRISTI, TX | 1880 | 349,894 | 388,758 | 397,003 | 1.0 | 149 | 75.7 | 72.8 | 3.9 | 3.9 | 0.8 | 1.1 |
| CORVALLIS, OR | 1890 | 70,811 | 77,187 | 77,073 | 0.8 | 175 | 92.0 | 90.1 | 0.9 | 1.0 | 5.5 | 6.7 |
| CUMBERLAND, MD-WV | 1900 | 101,643 | 97,510 | 93,927 | -0.4 | 301 | 97.2 | 96.5 | 2.2 | 2.8 | 0.4 | 0.5 |
| DALLAS, TX | 1920 | 2,676,248 | 3,362,473 | 3,763,222 | 2.3 | 25 | 73.3 | 71.3 | 15.8 | 15.1 | 2.5 | 3.8 |
| DANVILLE, VA | 1950 | 108,711 | 107,006 | 104,463 | -0.2 | 290 | 67.9 | 64.7 | 31.6 | 34.6 | 0.3 | 0.4 |
| DVNPRT-MOL.-R.ISLAND | 1960 | 350,861 | 359,472 | 362,757 | 0.2 | 250 | 92.0 | 90.4 | 5.4 | 6.0 | 0.7 | 1.0 |
| DAYTON-SPRINGFLD, OH | 2000 | 951,270 | 957,069 | 948,492 | 0.1 | 262 | 85.3 | 83.6 | 13.3 | 14.6 | 1.0 | 1.4 |
| DAYTONA BEACH, FL | 2020 | 399,413 | 482,085 | 517,949 | 1.9 | 44 | 88.7 | 86.0 | 9.0 | 10.7 | 0.8 | 1.2 |
| DECATUR, AL | 2030 | 131,556 | 144,391 | 149,027 | 0.9 | 166 | 86.4 | 86.0 | 11.3 | 12.2 | 0.3 | 0.4 |
| DECATUR, IL | 2040 | 117,206 | 112,630 | 109,734 | -0.4 | 301 | 87.2 | 85.9 | 12.1 | 13.1 | 0.4 | 0.6 |
| DENVER, CO | 2080 | 1,622,980 | 2,018,969 | 2,217,775 | 2.2 | 29 | 85.6 | 84.4 | 5.9 | 5.9 | 2.3 | 3.0 |
| DES MOINES, IA | 2120 | 392,928 | 449,038 | 477,135 | 1.3 | 91 | 93.8 | 92.3 | 3.8 | 4.2 | 1.6 | 2.2 |
| UNITED STATES | | | | | 1.0 | | 80.3 | 77.9 | 12.1 | 12.4 | 2.9 | 3.9 |

# POPULATION COMPOSITION

## MSA AND U.S. TOTALS

# B

| MSA | % HISPANIC ORIGIN | | 2000 AGE DISTRIBUTION (%) | | | | | | | | | | MEDIAN AGE | | 2000 Males/ Females (×100) |
|---|---|---|---|---|---|---|---|---|---|---|---|---|---|---|---|
| | 1990 | 2000 | 0-4 | 5-9 | 10-14 | 15-19 | 20-24 | 25-44 | 45-64 | 65-84 | 85+ | 18+ | 1990 | 2000 | |
| ABILENE, TX | 14.6 | 18.7 | 8.1 | 7.5 | 7.0 | 9.1 | 9.5 | 27.1 | 19.7 | 10.3 | 1.7 | 72.8 | 30.2 | 31.8 | 96.0 |
| AKRON, OH | 0.6 | 1.1 | 6.1 | 6.5 | 6.9 | 7.4 | 7.0 | 29.9 | 22.7 | 12.0 | 1.5 | 76.6 | 33.4 | 36.7 | 92.5 |
| ALBANY, GA | 0.8 | 1.6 | 7.8 | 7.8 | 7.8 | 8.8 | 7.8 | 29.2 | 20.7 | 8.9 | 1.1 | 71.4 | 29.9 | 31.9 | 91.4 |
| ALBANY-SCH.-TROY, NY | 1.7 | 2.6 | 6.2 | 7.0 | 6.7 | 7.0 | 6.6 | 29.5 | 22.9 | 12.2 | 1.9 | 76.5 | 33.9 | 37.0 | 93.9 |
| ALBUQUERQUE, NM | 37.1 | 40.2 | 7.1 | 7.3 | 7.5 | 7.6 | 6.8 | 29.6 | 22.8 | 10.1 | 1.2 | 73.6 | 32.0 | 35.8 | 95.7 |
| ALEXANDRIA, LA | 1.2 | 1.7 | 6.9 | 7.1 | 7.5 | 8.3 | 7.5 | 27.2 | 22.8 | 11.2 | 1.5 | 73.5 | 31.4 | 35.2 | 90.6 |
| ALLENTWN-BETH-EASTON | 4.6 | 6.8 | 5.7 | 6.4 | 7.0 | 6.7 | 5.8 | 28.7 | 23.6 | 14.1 | 2.0 | 77.2 | 35.5 | 38.9 | 94.0 |
| ALTOONA, PA | 0.3 | 0.8 | 5.6 | 6.2 | 6.6 | 7.1 | 6.0 | 27.2 | 23.9 | 15.2 | 2.3 | 77.6 | 36.2 | 39.3 | 90.1 |
| AMARILLO, TX | 13.5 | 17.4 | 8.1 | 7.8 | 7.7 | 7.9 | 7.1 | 27.9 | 22.3 | 9.9 | 1.4 | 72.0 | 31.8 | 34.3 | 93.9 |
| ANCHORAGE, AK | 4.1 | 5.4 | 7.7 | 8.4 | 8.7 | 8.2 | 7.6 | 30.5 | 23.4 | 5.1 | 0.3 | 70.4 | 29.8 | 32.6 | 105.6 |
| ANN ARBOR, MI | 2.5 | 3.4 | 6.0 | 6.6 | 7.0 | 8.3 | 9.1 | 31.6 | 22.0 | 8.2 | 1.1 | 76.4 | 30.6 | 33.9 | 97.9 |
| ANNISTON, AL | 1.1 | 2.1 | 5.9 | 6.1 | 6.1 | 7.7 | 8.3 | 29.2 | 23.4 | 11.9 | 1.4 | 78.0 | 32.7 | 36.3 | 93.1 |
| APPLTN-OSHKSH-NEENAH | 0.7 | 1.5 | 6.6 | 7.1 | 7.9 | 8.0 | 6.8 | 30.4 | 21.6 | 10.0 | 1.6 | 73.9 | 31.9 | 35.2 | 97.7 |
| ASHEVILLE, NC | 0.7 | 1.8 | 6.2 | 6.5 | 6.9 | 6.3 | 5.4 | 28.2 | 24.6 | 13.8 | 2.1 | 76.8 | 36.8 | 39.1 | 91.9 |
| ATHENS, GA | 1.5 | 2.9 | 6.5 | 6.2 | 6.1 | 9.5 | 13.7 | 30.8 | 18.4 | 7.7 | 1.2 | 77.8 | 27.6 | 30.4 | 92.4 |
| ATLANTA, GA | 2.0 | 3.8 | 7.4 | 7.2 | 7.2 | 6.8 | 6.6 | 35.1 | 21.8 | 7.0 | 0.9 | 74.3 | 31.5 | 34.1 | 94.9 |
| ATLANTIC-CAPE MAY,NJ | 5.6 | 8.4 | 6.9 | 7.2 | 6.7 | 6.2 | 5.6 | 29.9 | 21.9 | 13.5 | 2.1 | 75.8 | 34.9 | 37.5 | 93.3 |
| AUBURN-OPELIKA, AL | 0.6 | 1.3 | 6.0 | 5.6 | 5.4 | 10.1 | 16.9 | 28.7 | 18.4 | 7.9 | 0.9 | 79.6 | 26.2 | 29.0 | 96.7 |
| AUGUSTA-AIKEN, GA-SC | 1.4 | 2.7 | 7.2 | 7.5 | 7.5 | 7.7 | 7.0 | 30.7 | 22.0 | 9.4 | 1.0 | 73.4 | 31.3 | 34.2 | 95.1 |
| AUSTIN-SAN MARCOS,TX | 20.9 | 26.5 | 7.9 | 7.5 | 7.1 | 8.2 | 9.4 | 32.6 | 19.8 | 6.7 | 0.9 | 73.5 | 29.6 | 31.9 | 98.7 |
| BAKERSFIELD, CA | 28.0 | 36.1 | 8.8 | 10.1 | 8.1 | 7.7 | 6.9 | 30.3 | 18.1 | 8.9 | 1.0 | 68.4 | 29.7 | 30.7 | 104.6 |
| BALTIMORE, MD | 1.3 | 2.2 | 6.5 | 7.2 | 7.4 | 6.8 | 5.8 | 31.7 | 22.4 | 10.9 | 1.4 | 75.1 | 33.4 | 36.4 | 94.0 |
| BANGOR, ME | 0.5 | 1.0 | 4.8 | 5.6 | 6.9 | 8.2 | 7.7 | 30.7 | 23.2 | 11.4 | 1.5 | 78.9 | 32.5 | 37.1 | 95.7 |
| BARNSTABLE-YARMOUTH | 1.2 | 2.0 | 5.6 | 6.4 | 6.6 | 5.3 | 4.1 | 26.3 | 24.6 | 18.2 | 2.9 | 78.3 | 39.5 | 42.2 | 91.4 |
| BATON ROUGE, LA | 1.4 | 2.0 | 7.0 | 7.3 | 7.6 | 8.8 | 8.2 | 29.6 | 22.0 | 8.5 | 1.0 | 73.4 | 29.9 | 33.1 | 93.0 |
| BEAUMONT-P.ARTHUR,TX | 4.2 | 5.8 | 6.9 | 7.3 | 7.6 | 7.8 | 6.4 | 26.8 | 23.9 | 11.8 | 1.5 | 73.6 | 33.3 | 36.7 | 95.1 |
| BELLINGHAM, WA | 2.9 | 4.9 | 6.1 | 6.5 | 6.9 | 8.2 | 9.1 | 28.6 | 22.6 | 10.3 | 1.6 | 76.2 | 32.7 | 35.2 | 97.5 |
| BENTON HARBOR, MI | 1.7 | 2.4 | 6.3 | 7.2 | 7.7 | 7.4 | 6.1 | 28.2 | 22.8 | 12.5 | 1.8 | 74.4 | 33.6 | 36.7 | 92.4 |
| BERGEN-PASSAIC, NJ | 11.6 | 16.5 | 6.2 | 6.6 | 6.8 | 6.1 | 5.6 | 30.1 | 24.0 | 12.8 | 1.8 | 76.8 | 36.1 | 38.5 | 93.3 |
| BILLINGS, MT | 2.8 | 3.8 | 5.8 | 6.2 | 7.5 | 8.2 | 7.0 | 26.8 | 25.6 | 11.1 | 1.7 | 75.5 | 33.5 | 37.9 | 94.8 |
| BILOXI-GULFPORT-PAS. | 1.5 | 2.4 | 7.3 | 7.3 | 7.3 | 7.5 | 7.3 | 29.6 | 22.0 | 10.6 | 1.1 | 73.8 | 31.4 | 34.4 | 98.0 |
| BINGHAMTON, NY | 1.1 | 1.8 | 6.5 | 7.3 | 6.7 | 7.0 | 6.3 | 28.7 | 22.4 | 13.1 | 2.0 | 75.9 | 33.9 | 37.2 | 94.9 |
| BIRMINGHAM, AL | 0.4 | 1.0 | 6.5 | 6.7 | 6.8 | 6.9 | 6.6 | 30.6 | 23.3 | 11.2 | 1.5 | 76.0 | 33.7 | 36.8 | 90.6 |
| BISMARCK, ND | 0.5 | 1.1 | 5.8 | 6.4 | 7.8 | 8.5 | 6.3 | 28.5 | 23.8 | 11.1 | 1.8 | 74.9 | 32.3 | 37.1 | 94.7 |
| BLOOMINGTON, IN | 1.3 | 2.2 | 5.2 | 5.1 | 5.1 | 11.9 | 17.4 | 28.8 | 17.4 | 8.0 | 1.0 | 81.9 | 26.4 | 28.6 | 92.5 |
| BLOOMINGTN-NORMAL,IL | 1.3 | 2.2 | 6.4 | 6.6 | 6.3 | 9.9 | 12.7 | 28.6 | 19.2 | 8.9 | 1.5 | 77.1 | 28.8 | 31.5 | 91.7 |
| BOISE CITY, ID | 5.9 | 8.8 | 7.2 | 7.0 | 7.5 | 8.4 | 8.3 | 29.0 | 22.4 | 8.7 | 1.4 | 73.1 | 31.8 | 33.8 | 97.6 |
| BOSTON-WOR-LAW-LW-BR | 4.3 | 6.0 | 6.3 | 6.8 | 7.1 | 6.2 | 5.6 | 32.8 | 22.0 | 11.3 | 1.8 | 76.6 | 33.2 | 36.5 | 93.8 |
| BOULDER-LONGMONT, CO | 6.7 | 8.7 | 6.1 | 6.5 | 7.0 | 8.1 | 8.6 | 31.1 | 24.7 | 6.9 | 1.0 | 76.7 | 31.6 | 35.4 | 99.3 |
| BRAZORIA, TX | 17.6 | 22.6 | 7.9 | 7.9 | 7.8 | 7.7 | 6.8 | 30.9 | 22.1 | 8.1 | 0.8 | 71.7 | 31.1 | 33.6 | 105.7 |
| BREMERTON, WA | 3.3 | 5.1 | 7.0 | 7.4 | 7.9 | 7.9 | 7.1 | 30.1 | 22.3 | 9.0 | 1.3 | 73.0 | 31.8 | 34.4 | 103.3 |
| BRWNSVL-HARL-S.BENIT | 81.9 | 85.8 | 9.6 | 9.0 | 9.1 | 9.7 | 8.5 | 25.7 | 18.6 | 8.9 | 1.1 | 66.2 | 27.4 | 28.0 | 92.3 |
| BRYAN-COLLEGE STA,TX | 13.7 | 18.1 | 7.0 | 6.3 | 5.7 | 12.4 | 21.2 | 25.0 | 15.2 | 6.3 | 0.9 | 78.0 | 24.2 | 24.4 | 104.4 |
| BUFFALO-NIAGARA FLLS | 2.0 | 3.0 | 6.4 | 7.0 | 6.8 | 6.6 | 6.0 | 28.7 | 22.6 | 13.9 | 2.0 | 76.1 | 34.7 | 37.8 | 92.1 |
| BURLINGTON, VT | 0.8 | 1.4 | 5.4 | 6.1 | 7.2 | 7.8 | 7.4 | 33.7 | 22.7 | 8.5 | 1.2 | 77.8 | 30.7 | 35.3 | 95.9 |
| CANTON-MASSILLON, OH | 0.7 | 1.3 | 6.1 | 6.6 | 7.1 | 7.1 | 6.0 | 28.2 | 24.1 | 13.1 | 1.8 | 76.1 | 34.9 | 38.0 | 92.4 |
| CASPER, WY | 3.7 | 4.5 | 6.0 | 6.4 | 7.6 | 8.8 | 7.2 | 25.7 | 25.4 | 11.4 | 1.4 | 74.6 | 32.8 | 37.7 | 96.3 |
| CEDAR RAPIDS, IA | 0.9 | 2.1 | 6.3 | 6.5 | 7.2 | 7.4 | 6.6 | 30.3 | 23.5 | 10.6 | 1.6 | 76.0 | 33.1 | 36.4 | 94.9 |
| CHAMPAIGN-URBANA, IL | 2.0 | 2.8 | 6.2 | 6.4 | 6.2 | 10.7 | 14.7 | 29.2 | 17.5 | 8.0 | 1.2 | 78.2 | 27.8 | 29.1 | 101.2 |
| CHARLESTON-N.CHARLES | 1.5 | 2.5 | 7.6 | 7.6 | 7.0 | 6.7 | 7.7 | 33.0 | 20.3 | 9.1 | 1.0 | 74.1 | 29.5 | 33.1 | 95.0 |
| CHARLESTON, WV | 0.4 | 0.9 | 5.5 | 6.0 | 6.4 | 6.4 | 6.3 | 27.5 | 26.5 | 13.6 | 1.7 | 78.2 | 36.3 | 40.2 | 91.3 |
| CHARLOTTE-GAST-ROCK | 0.9 | 2.2 | 7.2 | 7.5 | 7.4 | 6.5 | 5.9 | 31.6 | 22.7 | 9.9 | 1.2 | 74.3 | 32.8 | 35.4 | 93.4 |
| CHARLOTTESVILLE, VA | 1.1 | 1.9 | 6.0 | 6.2 | 6.3 | 8.4 | 10.2 | 30.3 | 21.1 | 10.2 | 1.3 | 78.2 | 31.1 | 34.3 | 93.1 |
| CHATTANOOGA, TN-GA | 0.6 | 1.4 | 6.2 | 6.5 | 6.9 | 6.8 | 6.3 | 29.1 | 24.8 | 11.8 | 1.6 | 76.4 | 34.5 | 37.6 | 91.7 |
| CHEYENNE, WY | 10.0 | 11.6 | 6.4 | 6.1 | 7.1 | 8.3 | 8.4 | 26.9 | 25.3 | 10.3 | 1.3 | 75.5 | 31.9 | 36.6 | 99.6 |
| CHICAGO, IL | 11.4 | 14.9 | 7.5 | 7.7 | 7.3 | 7.0 | 6.4 | 31.4 | 21.7 | 9.8 | 1.4 | 73.6 | 32.3 | 34.9 | 95.0 |
| CHICO-PARADISE, CA | 7.5 | 10.9 | 6.3 | 7.6 | 6.3 | 7.8 | 9.7 | 25.5 | 19.9 | 14.9 | 2.0 | 76.1 | 33.8 | 35.6 | 97.9 |
| CINCINNATI, OH-KY-IN | 0.5 | 1.0 | 7.1 | 7.3 | 7.7 | 7.4 | 6.5 | 30.4 | 21.8 | 10.5 | 1.5 | 73.6 | 32.4 | 35.3 | 93.5 |
| CLARKSVLL-HOPKINSVLL | 3.3 | 5.6 | 9.1 | 7.3 | 6.3 | 7.0 | 11.2 | 32.6 | 18.0 | 7.4 | 1.0 | 73.8 | 28.2 | 29.8 | 104.2 |
| CLEVELAND-LORAIN-ELY | 2.3 | 3.2 | 6.3 | 6.7 | 7.3 | 6.9 | 5.9 | 29.0 | 23.1 | 12.9 | 1.8 | 75.5 | 34.4 | 37.6 | 91.5 |
| COLORADO SPRINGS, CO | 8.7 | 11.3 | 7.9 | 7.2 | 7.4 | 7.9 | 8.4 | 29.7 | 22.9 | 7.7 | 0.9 | 73.1 | 30.2 | 33.1 | 99.1 |
| COLUMBIA, MO | 1.1 | 1.8 | 6.4 | 6.4 | 6.4 | 10.0 | 13.8 | 31.8 | 17.0 | 7.1 | 1.1 | 77.5 | 27.7 | 29.8 | 93.7 |
| COLUMBIA, SC | 1.3 | 2.3 | 6.0 | 6.4 | 6.5 | 7.6 | 8.2 | 32.7 | 22.5 | 9.1 | 1.0 | 77.1 | 31.2 | 34.9 | 93.8 |
| COLUMBUS, GA-AL | 2.9 | 5.1 | 7.6 | 7.3 | 7.1 | 7.6 | 8.6 | 30.5 | 20.0 | 10.0 | 1.2 | 74.0 | 30.4 | 32.8 | 98.5 |
| COLUMBUS, OH | 0.8 | 1.4 | 6.6 | 6.8 | 7.1 | 7.3 | 7.8 | 32.4 | 21.4 | 9.4 | 1.2 | 75.7 | 31.5 | 34.5 | 95.0 |
| CORPUS CHRISTI, TX | 52.0 | 59.2 | 8.5 | 8.2 | 8.0 | 8.3 | 7.2 | 28.3 | 21.1 | 9.3 | 1.1 | 70.3 | 30.5 | 32.4 | 96.3 |
| CORVALLIS, OR | 2.5 | 4.2 | 5.6 | 5.7 | 6.0 | 10.2 | 13.8 | 27.9 | 21.0 | 8.6 | 1.2 | 79.0 | 29.3 | 31.6 | 102.5 |
| CUMBERLAND, MD-WV | 0.4 | 1.0 | 5.4 | 6.1 | 6.5 | 7.8 | 6.7 | 25.5 | 24.3 | 15.4 | 2.3 | 78.1 | 36.9 | 39.4 | 92.1 |
| DALLAS, TX | 14.0 | 17.2 | 8.1 | 7.7 | 7.5 | 7.3 | 6.9 | 32.4 | 21.9 | 7.2 | 0.9 | 72.4 | 30.7 | 33.8 | 96.9 |
| DANVILLE, VA | 0.5 | 1.0 | 5.5 | 6.2 | 6.6 | 6.7 | 5.6 | 27.9 | 24.9 | 14.6 | 1.9 | 77.8 | 36.4 | 39.6 | 91.0 |
| DVNPRT-MOL.-R.ISLAND | 3.7 | 6.1 | 6.8 | 7.1 | 7.3 | 7.4 | 6.5 | 28.0 | 23.2 | 11.8 | 1.8 | 74.4 | 33.9 | 36.5 | 94.2 |
| DAYTON-SPRINGFLD, OH | 0.8 | 1.3 | 6.3 | 6.7 | 7.1 | 7.4 | 6.6 | 29.3 | 23.2 | 12.0 | 1.5 | 75.8 | 33.4 | 36.7 | 92.8 |
| DAYTONA BEACH, FL | 4.0 | 6.0 | 5.4 | 5.8 | 6.0 | 6.0 | 5.5 | 25.2 | 23.0 | 20.5 | 2.6 | 79.6 | 39.8 | 42.4 | 94.8 |
| DECATUR, AL | 0.5 | 1.3 | 6.5 | 6.7 | 6.8 | 6.7 | 6.1 | 30.4 | 24.4 | 11.0 | 1.3 | 75.9 | 33.3 | 37.0 | 94.5 |
| DECATUR, IL | 0.5 | 1.0 | 6.5 | 6.9 | 6.9 | 7.4 | 6.8 | 26.8 | 23.8 | 13.0 | 2.0 | 75.4 | 35.0 | 37.5 | 91.9 |
| DENVER, CO | 13.0 | 15.2 | 7.1 | 7.1 | 7.7 | 7.2 | 5.9 | 30.4 | 24.9 | 8.6 | 1.1 | 73.8 | 32.8 | 36.5 | 96.5 |
| DES MOINES, IA | 1.7 | 3.4 | 6.6 | 6.7 | 7.4 | 7.3 | 6.4 | 31.0 | 22.9 | 10.0 | 1.6 | 75.1 | 32.6 | 35.9 | 92.5 |
| UNITED STATES | 9.0 | 11.8 | 6.9 | 7.2 | 7.2 | 7.2 | 6.7 | 29.9 | 22.2 | 11.1 | 1.6 | 74.6 | 32.9 | 35.7 | 95.6 |

# HOUSEHOLDS

## MSA AND U.S. TOTALS



| MSA | HOUSEHOLDS | | | | | FAMILIES | | | MEDIAN HOUSEHOLD INCOME | | |
|---|---|---|---|---|---|---|---|---|---|---|---|
| | 1990 | 2000 | 2005 | % Annual Rate 1990-2000 | 2000 Average HH Size | 1990 | 2000 | % Annual Rate 1990-2000 | 2000 | 2005 | 2000 National Rank |
| ABILENE, TX | 43,301 | 44,683 | 45,382 | 0.4 | 2.60 | 31,027 | 30,968 | 0.0 | 34,425 | 41,260 | 266 |
| AKRON, OH | 249,227 | 270,039 | 276,994 | 1.0 | 2.51 | 174,996 | 183,720 | 0.6 | 41,128 | 45,956 | 129 |
| ALBANY, GA | 39,362 | 42,771 | 43,673 | 1.0 | 2.66 | 29,394 | 31,358 | 0.8 | 35,691 | 40,099 | 235 |
| ALBANY-SCH.-TROY, NY | 330,484 | 342,947 | 343,880 | 0.4 | 2.44 | 221,031 | 221,214 | 0.0 | 43,608 | 50,012 | 99 |
| ALBUQUERQUE, NM | 221,619 | 263,639 | 274,946 | 2.1 | 2.56 | 153,400 | 178,885 | 1.9 | 40,980 | 47,406 | 135 |
| ALEXANDRIA, LA | 45,941 | 46,149 | 47,287 | 0.1 | 2.65 | 34,195 | 33,441 | -0.3 | 28,028 | 30,772 | 316 |
| ALLENTWN-BETH-EASTON | 225,831 | 238,867 | 244,455 | 0.7 | 2.52 | 162,345 | 166,719 | 0.3 | 44,689 | 52,682 | 84 |
| ALTOONA, PA | 50,332 | 50,979 | 50,585 | 0.2 | 2.47 | 35,787 | 34,963 | -0.3 | 31,380 | 35,053 | 301 |
| AMARILLO, TX | 71,897 | 80,798 | 84,237 | 1.4 | 2.53 | 50,387 | 55,127 | 1.1 | 35,893 | 41,053 | 232 |
| ANCHORAGE, AK | 82,702 | 96,171 | 101,012 | 1.8 | 2.65 | 56,503 | 63,052 | 1.3 | 63,105 | 76,082 | 4 |
| ANN ARBOR, MI | 175,050 | 207,686 | 227,154 | 2.1 | 2.60 | 119,500 | 139,727 | 1.9 | 55,019 | 63,126 | 16 |
| ANNISTON, AL | 42,983 | 44,935 | 45,257 | 0.5 | 2.49 | 31,718 | 32,221 | 0.2 | 31,771 | 36,580 | 298 |
| APPLTN-OSHKSH-NEENAH | 115,515 | 131,116 | 138,142 | 1.5 | 2.60 | 82,793 | 91,425 | 1.2 | 50,044 | 58,530 | 34 |
| ASHEVILLE, NC | 77,290 | 87,847 | 92,331 | 1.6 | 2.39 | 54,141 | 59,601 | 1.2 | 37,053 | 42,266 | 213 |
| ATHENS, GA | 47,066 | 53,332 | 56,165 | 1.5 | 2.50 | 29,203 | 32,599 | 1.3 | 36,187 | 41,475 | 228 |
| ATLANTA, GA | 1,102,578 | 1,499,443 | 1,717,216 | 3.8 | 2.61 | 778,182 | 1,048,938 | 3.7 | 51,962 | 61,353 | 27 |
| ATLANTIC-CAPE MAY,NJ | 122,979 | 131,416 | 134,927 | 0.8 | 2.52 | 82,243 | 83,909 | 0.2 | 43,394 | 52,366 | 102 |
| AUBURN-OPELIKA, AL | 33,097 | 40,935 | 45,632 | 2.6 | 2.44 | 20,115 | 24,420 | 2.4 | 32,662 | 38,081 | 290 |
| AUGUSTA-AIKEN, GA-SC | 149,093 | 170,459 | 178,134 | 1.6 | 2.63 | 109,862 | 123,264 | 1.4 | 40,422 | 46,275 | 140 |
| AUSTIN-SAN MARCOS,TX | 325,995 | 459,293 | 533,546 | 4.2 | 2.51 | 203,994 | 285,947 | 4.2 | 46,107 | 54,540 | 61 |
| BAKERSFIELD, CA | 181,480 | 213,227 | 225,611 | 2.0 | 2.91 | 135,925 | 156,312 | 1.7 | 38,806 | 48,543 | 176 |
| BALTIMORE, MD | 880,145 | 945,892 | 975,962 | 0.9 | 2.59 | 620,591 | 650,519 | 0.6 | 51,572 | 61,002 | 29 |
| BANGOR, ME | 54,063 | 55,813 | 56,522 | 0.4 | 2.45 | 38,125 | 38,206 | 0.0 | 34,565 | 39,967 | 262 |
| BARNSTABLE-YARMOUTH | 77,586 | 91,913 | 100,741 | 2.1 | 2.30 | 52,006 | 59,059 | 1.6 | 43,269 | 50,276 | 107 |
| BATON ROUGE, LA | 188,377 | 216,226 | 228,537 | 1.7 | 2.64 | 135,962 | 153,442 | 1.5 | 37,852 | 42,122 | 190 |
| BEAUMONT-P.ARTHUR,TX | 134,238 | 140,408 | 142,787 | 0.5 | 2.61 | 98,499 | 100,504 | 0.2 | 35,958 | 39,675 | 229 |
| BELLINGHAM, WA | 48,543 | 62,504 | 68,098 | 3.1 | 2.53 | 32,198 | 40,079 | 2.7 | 44,235 | 54,711 | 91 |
| BENTON HARBOR, MI | 61,025 | 62,290 | 62,642 | 0.2 | 2.52 | 43,845 | 43,271 | -0.2 | 39,136 | 43,816 | 167 |
| BERGEN-PASSAIC, NJ | 464,149 | 496,310 | 508,931 | 0.8 | 2.68 | 340,323 | 353,690 | 0.5 | 58,881 | 67,267 | 9 |
| BILLINGS, MT | 44,689 | 51,830 | 54,089 | 1.8 | 2.43 | 30,500 | 34,097 | 1.4 | 37,406 | 42,224 | 202 |
| BILOXI-GULFPORT-PAS. | 111,828 | 131,791 | 141,127 | 2.0 | 2.64 | 83,221 | 95,722 | 1.7 | 35,569 | 40,743 | 241 |
| BINGHAMTON, NY | 100,681 | 96,107 | 93,872 | -0.6 | 2.47 | 69,289 | 63,974 | -1.0 | 36,275 | 40,949 | 226 |
| BIRMINGHAM, AL | 319,774 | 358,732 | 375,563 | 1.4 | 2.52 | 230,088 | 252,338 | 1.1 | 42,265 | 47,718 | 114 |
| BISMARCK, ND | 31,361 | 35,795 | 37,579 | 1.6 | 2.51 | 22,178 | 24,509 | 1.2 | 38,034 | 43,305 | 187 |
| BLOOMINGTON, IN | 39,351 | 44,252 | 45,940 | 1.4 | 2.31 | 22,953 | 25,045 | 1.1 | 39,621 | 45,330 | 159 |
| BLOOMINGTN-NORMAL,IL | 46,796 | 53,943 | 57,349 | 1.7 | 2.53 | 30,305 | 33,510 | 1.2 | 49,638 | 58,949 | 38 |
| BOISE CITY, ID | 108,759 | 158,026 | 182,416 | 4.6 | 2.61 | 77,896 | 110,544 | 4.3 | 45,615 | 53,351 | 70 |
| BOSTON-WOR-LAW-LW-BR | 2,111,440 | 2,272,501 | 2,380,110 | 0.9 | 2.53 | 1,432,816 | 1,496,434 | 0.5 | 50,707 | 59,358 | 33 |
| BOULDER-LONGMONT, CO | 88,402 | 111,573 | 123,933 | 2.9 | 2.42 | 54,375 | 66,973 | 2.6 | 55,678 | 63,746 | 15 |
| BRAZORIA, TX | 64,019 | 81,241 | 90,946 | 2.9 | 2.83 | 50,044 | 61,841 | 2.6 | 46,891 | 54,833 | 54 |
| BREMERTON, WA | 69,267 | 87,874 | 93,070 | 2.9 | 2.66 | 50,100 | 61,680 | 2.6 | 47,077 | 57,791 | 53 |
| BRWNSVL-HARL-S.BENIT | 73,278 | 97,214 | 107,026 | 3.5 | 3.39 | 60,178 | 79,515 | 3.4 | 26,185 | 30,126 | 317 |
| BRYAN-COLLEGE STA,TX | 43,725 | 49,463 | 51,923 | 1.5 | 2.49 | 24,903 | 26,837 | 0.9 | 32,909 | 40,140 | 286 |
| BUFFALO-NIAGARA FLLS | 461,803 | 457,276 | 446,943 | -0.1 | 2.42 | 314,204 | 300,247 | -0.5 | 38,432 | 42,057 | 181 |
| BURLINGTON, VT | 64,783 | 77,029 | 83,276 | 2.1 | 2.45 | 43,525 | 50,209 | 1.7 | 47,681 | 55,622 | 46 |
| CANTON-MASSILLON, OH | 149,240 | 155,710 | 157,585 | 0.5 | 2.53 | 108,971 | 109,927 | 0.1 | 38,426 | 43,291 | 182 |
| CASPER, WY | 23,837 | 25,762 | 26,155 | 0.9 | 2.41 | 16,657 | 17,312 | 0.5 | 35,627 | 39,093 | 239 |
| CEDAR RAPIDS, IA | 65,501 | 72,400 | 75,762 | 1.2 | 2.52 | 45,039 | 48,115 | 0.8 | 44,351 | 49,072 | 89 |
| CHAMPAIGN-URBANA, IL | 63,900 | 63,582 | 64,028 | -0.1 | 2.42 | 38,604 | 36,825 | -0.6 | 36,714 | 41,263 | 220 |
| CHARLESTON-N.CHARLES | 177,668 | 208,184 | 229,173 | 1.9 | 2.65 | 129,792 | 147,434 | 1.6 | 40,277 | 46,970 | 144 |
| CHARLESTON, WV | 100,408 | 105,236 | 105,599 | 0.6 | 2.35 | 71,583 | 72,708 | 0.2 | 32,000 | 35,218 | 294 |
| CHARLOTTE-GAST-ROCK | 440,670 | 553,239 | 618,076 | 2.8 | 2.58 | 317,636 | 387,614 | 2.4 | 44,885 | 51,100 | 80 |
| CHARLOTTESVILLE, VA | 48,709 | 58,878 | 64,151 | 2.3 | 2.43 | 31,766 | 37,878 | 2.2 | 42,355 | 48,110 | 112 |
| CHATTANOOGA, TN-GA | 163,117 | 179,222 | 186,300 | 1.1 | 2.49 | 119,123 | 127,770 | 0.9 | 36,495 | 40,589 | 224 |
| CHEYENNE, WY | 28,092 | 31,509 | 32,448 | 1.4 | 2.47 | 19,816 | 21,450 | 1.0 | 37,386 | 43,728 | 203 |
| CHICAGO, IL | 2,671,540 | 2,916,286 | 3,025,489 | 1.1 | 2.72 | 1,852,128 | 1,982,129 | 0.8 | 51,938 | 59,592 | 28 |
| CHICO-PARADISE, CA | 71,665 | 78,127 | 80,487 | 1.1 | 2.45 | 46,125 | 48,085 | 0.5 | 34,959 | 42,199 | 254 |
| CINCINNATI, OH-KY-IN | 574,602 | 627,076 | 651,837 | 1.1 | 2.56 | 400,931 | 430,687 | 0.9 | 41,085 | 46,724 | 132 |
| CLARKSVLL-HOPKINSVLL | 55,981 | 72,552 | 78,456 | 3.2 | 2.64 | 43,565 | 55,288 | 2.9 | 36,875 | 46,570 | 216 |
| CLEVELAND-LORAIN-ELY | 845,186 | 868,667 | 871,321 | 0.3 | 2.51 | 585,787 | 583,895 | 0.0 | 39,770 | 43,947 | 156 |
| COLORADO SPRINGS, CO | 146,965 | 192,463 | 212,709 | 3.3 | 2.56 | 104,095 | 131,942 | 2.9 | 49,098 | 58,970 | 39 |
| COLUMBIA, MO | 41,937 | 50,457 | 53,762 | 2.3 | 2.40 | 25,573 | 29,666 | 1.8 | 40,163 | 45,121 | 147 |
| COLUMBIA, SC | 163,223 | 198,654 | 216,880 | 2.4 | 2.50 | 114,878 | 136,147 | 2.1 | 44,305 | 50,243 | 90 |
| COLUMBUS, GA-AL | 92,695 | 99,388 | 100,480 | 0.8 | 2.59 | 67,700 | 70,661 | 0.5 | 35,794 | 41,326 | 233 |
| COLUMBUS, OH | 513,498 | 581,609 | 615,366 | 1.5 | 2.51 | 346,124 | 381,712 | 1.2 | 41,910 | 47,579 | 122 |
| CORPUS CHRISTI, TX | 118,516 | 133,603 | 137,761 | 1.5 | 2.85 | 89,144 | 98,470 | 1.2 | 34,725 | 40,275 | 258 |
| CORVALLIS, OR | 26,126 | 29,859 | 30,242 | 1.6 | 2.40 | 16,353 | 18,001 | 1.2 | 42,211 | 48,684 | 116 |
| CUMBERLAND, MD-WV | 39,615 | 38,948 | 37,881 | -0.2 | 2.42 | 27,899 | 26,339 | -0.7 | 29,537 | 33,078 | 310 |
| DALLAS, TX | 1,001,750 | 1,274,789 | 1,435,537 | 3.0 | 2.60 | 683,612 | 858,161 | 2.8 | 48,479 | 55,695 | 40 |
| DANVILLE, VA | 42,325 | 43,557 | 43,395 | 0.3 | 2.41 | 30,681 | 30,526 | -0.1 | 29,562 | 33,841 | 309 |
| DVNPRT-MOL.-R.ISLAND | 136,269 | 140,174 | 141,822 | 0.3 | 2.51 | 94,694 | 93,679 | -0.1 | 39,023 | 42,805 | 168 |
| DAYTON-SPRINGFLD, OH | 364,300 | 368,960 | 366,594 | 0.2 | 2.54 | 257,962 | 252,866 | -0.2 | 40,402 | 45,715 | 141 |
| DAYTONA BEACH, FL | 165,296 | 198,895 | 213,364 | 2.3 | 2.36 | 112,048 | 131,371 | 1.9 | 35,330 | 43,756 | 248 |
| DECATUR, AL | 49,209 | 55,739 | 58,451 | 1.5 | 2.55 | 37,683 | 41,526 | 1.2 | 39,988 | 44,690 | 151 |
| DECATUR, IL | 45,996 | 44,547 | 43,664 | -0.4 | 2.46 | 32,330 | 30,323 | -0.8 | 37,769 | 41,229 | 194 |
| DENVER, CO | 649,404 | 813,427 | 895,353 | 2.8 | 2.45 | 420,379 | 518,207 | 2.6 | 52,660 | 60,442 | 23 |
| DES MOINES, IA | 153,100 | 174,966 | 185,947 | 1.6 | 2.51 | 104,094 | 115,415 | 1.3 | 43,701 | 49,602 | 98 |
| UNITED STATES | | | | 1.4 | 2.59 | | | 1.1 | 41,914 | 49,127 | |

# D

# INCOME

## MSA AND U.S. TOTALS

| MSA | 2000 Per Capita Income | 2000 HH Income Base | 2000 HOUSEHOLD INCOME DISTRIBUTION (%) Less than $15,000 | $15,000 to $24,999 | $25,000 to $49,999 | $50,000 to $99,999 | $100,000 to $149,999 | $150,000 or More | 2000 AVERAGE DISPOSABLE INCOME BY AGE OF HOUSEHOLDER All Ages | <35 | 35-44 | 45-54 | 55-64 | 65+ |
|---|---|---|---|---|---|---|---|---|---|---|---|---|---|---|
| ABILENE, TX | 16,691 | 44,679 | 17.7 | 16.5 | 35.6 | 25.1 | 3.8 | 1.4 | 34,967 | 28,084 | 41,285 | 42,781 | 40,803 | 25,608 |
| AKRON, OH | 21,492 | 270,038 | 14.4 | 12.7 | 33.7 | 29.9 | 6.8 | 2.5 | 38,489 | 31,933 | 43,055 | 49,941 | 43,689 | 25,213 |
| ALBANY, GA | 16,523 | 42,771 | 20.5 | 14.7 | 32.5 | 25.6 | 5.1 | 1.6 | 33,809 | 27,790 | 37,782 | 42,323 | 36,007 | 22,392 |
| ALBANY-SCH.-TROY, NY | 22,380 | 342,933 | 12.3 | 11.9 | 33.7 | 32.3 | 7.2 | 2.7 | 37,806 | 33,785 | 42,682 | 47,786 | 41,403 | 23,984 |
| ALBUQUERQUE, NM | 20,786 | 263,637 | 13.6 | 13.3 | 33.7 | 30.2 | 6.9 | 2.3 | 39,237 | 31,435 | 43,144 | 47,938 | 43,771 | 30,392 |
| ALEXANDRIA, LA | 14,162 | 46,147 | 26.3 | 18.1 | 32.6 | 18.8 | 2.9 | 1.3 | 30,417 | 25,044 | 35,573 | 36,582 | 33,532 | 21,249 |
| ALLENTWN-BETH-EASTON | 22,383 | 238,863 | 11.0 | 11.2 | 34.9 | 33.2 | 7.3 | 2.5 | 40,368 | 37,355 | 45,586 | 52,225 | 43,185 | 25,116 |
| ALTOONA, PA | 15,719 | 50,973 | 20.6 | 17.4 | 38.2 | 20.7 | 2.5 | 0.7 | 28,867 | 26,564 | 34,500 | 36,017 | 32,913 | 18,900 |
| AMARILLO, TX | 18,355 | 80,798 | 17.0 | 15.2 | 35.6 | 26.0 | 4.4 | 1.8 | 36,352 | 29,003 | 41,055 | 43,856 | 40,295 | 27,327 |
| ANCHORAGE, AK | 31,147 | 96,171 | 5.9 | 7.3 | 24.0 | 39.8 | 14.8 | 8.1 | 60,753 | 42,355 | 60,763 | 70,778 | 61,389 | 46,613 |
| ANN ARBOR, MI | 27,378 | 207,686 | 9.0 | 8.3 | 26.8 | 38.3 | 12.0 | 5.7 | 49,752 | 37,079 | 53,456 | 63,196 | 56,540 | 31,957 |
| ANNISTON, AL | 15,324 | 44,927 | 21.3 | 15.7 | 38.1 | 21.7 | 2.6 | 0.7 | 30,825 | 27,200 | 36,693 | 38,369 | 32,060 | 20,683 |
| APPLTN-OSHKSH-NEENAH | 23,307 | 131,116 | 9.2 | 7.8 | 33.0 | 37.9 | 9.7 | 2.5 | 40,733 | 35,655 | 46,005 | 52,101 | 44,997 | 24,777 |
| ASHEVILLE, NC | 19,589 | 87,847 | 16.0 | 14.2 | 36.6 | 26.8 | 5.0 | 1.5 | 34,702 | 30,935 | 39,907 | 42,849 | 36,284 | 25,013 |
| ATHENS, GA | 20,067 | 53,332 | 20.6 | 14.5 | 30.3 | 25.0 | 6.5 | 3.1 | 36,956 | 25,977 | 42,846 | 48,801 | 42,278 | 26,595 |
| ATLANTA, GA | 26,922 | 1,499,427 | 9.1 | 9.0 | 29.6 | 36.2 | 10.9 | 5.2 | 48,593 | 40,950 | 50,607 | 56,825 | 48,425 | 30,555 |
| ATLANTIC-CAPE MAY,NJ | 23,564 | 131,416 | 12.9 | 11.5 | 33.0 | 31.3 | 7.6 | 3.8 | 39,159 | 37,471 | 43,637 | 47,829 | 44,035 | 24,069 |
| AUBURN-OPELIKA, AL | 19,263 | 40,935 | 26.8 | 12.3 | 29.8 | 22.8 | 5.4 | 2.9 | 35,322 | 23,303 | 46,815 | 50,370 | 41,360 | 26,022 |
| AUGUSTA-AIKEN, GA-SC | 19,712 | 170,458 | 16.1 | 12.8 | 33.1 | 29.0 | 6.8 | 2.4 | 37,905 | 33,018 | 41,365 | 46,135 | 39,936 | 24,344 |
| AUSTIN-SAN MARCOS,TX | 25,170 | 459,290 | 12.3 | 11.8 | 30.2 | 32.0 | 9.5 | 4.3 | 46,840 | 34,596 | 51,738 | 57,843 | 50,903 | 37,090 |
| BAKERSFIELD, CA | 17,559 | 213,224 | 16.2 | 14.0 | 33.7 | 27.7 | 5.8 | 2.6 | 37,386 | 32,740 | 41,660 | 46,220 | 40,061 | 25,114 |
| BALTIMORE, MD | 26,289 | 945,876 | 10.2 | 9.0 | 28.9 | 36.2 | 10.9 | 4.8 | 45,851 | 39,496 | 48,968 | 54,881 | 47,754 | 30,676 |
| BANGOR, ME | 16,830 | 55,811 | 17.8 | 16.6 | 37.2 | 23.8 | 3.4 | 1.2 | 31,077 | 27,628 | 36,675 | 38,439 | 32,893 | 19,470 |
| BARNSTABLE-YARMOUTH | 24,369 | 91,913 | 12.8 | 12.0 | 33.3 | 31.6 | 7.4 | 3.0 | 38,289 | 35,878 | 43,015 | 48,384 | 42,910 | 27,021 |
| BATON ROUGE, LA | 18,840 | 216,226 | 19.0 | 13.1 | 32.5 | 27.2 | 5.8 | 2.5 | 38,652 | 30,263 | 44,126 | 47,370 | 39,845 | 26,648 |
| BEAUMONT-P.ARTHUR,TX | 17,907 | 140,393 | 20.1 | 14.5 | 33.5 | 25.2 | 4.7 | 2.0 | 36,136 | 30,180 | 42,039 | 44,344 | 37,833 | 25,262 |
| BELLINGHAM, WA | 22,376 | 62,504 | 11.1 | 12.5 | 33.6 | 32.0 | 8.0 | 2.9 | 43,383 | 34,279 | 45,801 | 54,491 | 48,174 | 31,189 |
| BENTON HARBOR, MI | 20,284 | 62,289 | 15.7 | 12.7 | 35.6 | 27.2 | 6.1 | 2.6 | 36,633 | 30,551 | 41,380 | 48,550 | 42,728 | 23,284 |
| BERGEN-PASSAIC, NJ | 32,746 | 496,307 | 9.1 | 7.3 | 24.7 | 36.5 | 13.1 | 9.3 | 53,476 | 46,910 | 53,527 | 60,166 | 59,004 | 34,580 |
| BILLINGS, MT | 18,702 | 51,830 | 15.6 | 14.3 | 36.7 | 27.1 | 5.0 | 1.4 | 34,238 | 27,405 | 39,120 | 41,767 | 37,057 | 25,273 |
| BILOXI-GULFPORT-PAS. | 16,801 | 131,791 | 18.3 | 14.9 | 35.2 | 25.9 | 4.4 | 1.2 | 34,474 | 29,855 | 39,014 | 41,287 | 36,287 | 24,409 |
| BINGHAMTON, NY | 17,713 | 96,107 | 17.6 | 14.8 | 35.7 | 26.6 | 4.0 | 1.3 | 31,553 | 28,426 | 36,581 | 41,544 | 35,039 | 19,462 |
| BIRMINGHAM, AL | 23,080 | 358,732 | 15.1 | 12.2 | 31.0 | 29.9 | 8.0 | 3.8 | 43,119 | 36,538 | 50,053 | 52,062 | 42,988 | 27,669 |
| BISMARCK, ND | 18,218 | 35,795 | 14.2 | 15.5 | 37.1 | 27.0 | 4.7 | 1.4 | 35,851 | 29,891 | 41,606 | 46,142 | 38,526 | 22,978 |
| BLOOMINGTON, IN | 20,923 | 44,252 | 16.7 | 12.7 | 32.8 | 28.0 | 7.2 | 2.6 | 38,687 | 27,717 | 44,210 | 51,704 | 47,341 | 29,625 |
| BLOOMINGTN-NORMAL,IL | 25,661 | 53,941 | 9.9 | 9.5 | 31.0 | 35.0 | 10.1 | 4.5 | 45,788 | 35,878 | 51,076 | 59,244 | 50,031 | 31,432 |
| BOISE CITY, ID | 22,798 | 158,014 | 8.9 | 12.3 | 34.1 | 33.6 | 8.2 | 2.9 | 42,046 | 34,829 | 46,676 | 51,264 | 41,697 | 29,794 |
| BOSTON-WOR-LAW-LW-BR | 26,234 | 2,272,489 | 12.4 | 8.5 | 28.2 | 35.8 | 10.1 | 4.9 | 44,907 | 40,454 | 48,167 | 54,784 | 49,697 | 27,222 |
| BOULDER-LONGMONT, CO | 32,760 | 111,573 | 7.7 | 8.4 | 27.5 | 36.3 | 12.5 | 7.6 | 53,700 | 37,372 | 56,307 | 64,778 | 57,454 | 36,661 |
| BRAZORIA, TX | 19,618 | 81,241 | 10.8 | 10.8 | 32.3 | 36.6 | 7.5 | 2.1 | 43,294 | 37,140 | 48,062 | 52,500 | 44,471 | 29,469 |
| BREMERTON, WA | 22,527 | 87,874 | 8.1 | 10.4 | 35.0 | 35.9 | 8.0 | 2.7 | 45,130 | 36,026 | 47,577 | 55,541 | 49,117 | 33,059 |
| BRWNSVL-HARL-S.BENIT | 11,074 | 97,214 | 29.6 | 18.4 | 29.8 | 18.0 | 3.1 | 1.2 | 29,258 | 25,006 | 31,594 | 33,534 | 31,153 | 24,430 |
| BRYAN-COLLEGE STA,TX | 19,707 | 49,463 | 24.5 | 14.2 | 29.5 | 22.8 | 5.6 | 3.4 | 37,408 | 24,753 | 47,844 | 52,998 | 53,621 | 32,314 |
| BUFFALO-NIAGARA FLLS | 20,404 | 457,268 | 17.0 | 13.2 | 34.6 | 27.4 | 5.6 | 2.3 | 34,142 | 30,079 | 39,636 | 43,996 | 38,329 | 21,785 |
| BURLINGTON, VT | 24,283 | 77,029 | 10.4 | 9.7 | 32.7 | 35.3 | 8.6 | 3.3 | 42,444 | 37,316 | 46,696 | 52,166 | 45,825 | 25,419 |
| CANTON-MASSILLON, OH | 19,095 | 155,710 | 14.6 | 13.3 | 37.7 | 28.1 | 4.9 | 1.5 | 35,357 | 31,016 | 40,005 | 44,839 | 38,820 | 23,747 |
| CASPER, WY | 18,461 | 25,734 | 17.2 | 14.5 | 38.2 | 24.7 | 4.1 | 1.4 | 35,896 | 26,695 | 43,442 | 42,228 | 42,097 | 26,774 |
| CEDAR RAPIDS, IA | 22,424 | 72,399 | 11.2 | 10.8 | 36.0 | 32.9 | 6.8 | 2.4 | 38,744 | 32,468 | 44,877 | 48,175 | 42,438 | 24,888 |
| CHAMPAIGN-URBANA, IL | 18,691 | 63,574 | 17.9 | 15.0 | 34.1 | 25.9 | 5.2 | 1.9 | 34,795 | 24,724 | 39,627 | 46,204 | 43,982 | 28,518 |
| CHARLESTON-N.CHARLES | 19,455 | 208,174 | 13.4 | 13.5 | 35.4 | 29.8 | 5.8 | 2.1 | 37,646 | 32,255 | 40,809 | 45,760 | 40,675 | 27,419 |
| CHARLESTON, WV | 18,115 | 105,236 | 21.9 | 16.9 | 33.9 | 21.8 | 3.7 | 1.8 | 32,649 | 28,201 | 38,620 | 40,048 | 33,790 | 22,346 |
| CHARLOTTE-GAST-ROCK | 22,754 | 553,233 | 11.1 | 11.7 | 33.3 | 33.0 | 7.9 | 3.0 | 41,420 | 36,550 | 46,389 | 50,438 | 42,749 | 25,988 |
| CHARLOTTESVILLE, VA | 22,688 | 58,875 | 13.4 | 12.0 | 33.7 | 30.0 | 7.6 | 3.3 | 40,581 | 30,125 | 45,053 | 50,466 | 46,781 | 32,526 |
| CHATTANOOGA, TN-GA | 19,843 | 179,210 | 17.1 | 14.8 | 34.7 | 25.4 | 5.3 | 2.7 | 38,315 | 33,214 | 44,318 | 47,330 | 39,698 | 23,186 |
| CHEYENNE, WY | 18,227 | 31,509 | 14.4 | 15.9 | 36.9 | 27.7 | 4.0 | 1.2 | 36,918 | 26,689 | 43,678 | 47,975 | 42,952 | 26,628 |
| CHICAGO, IL | 26,908 | 2,916,269 | 10.5 | 8.8 | 28.4 | 35.1 | 11.3 | 5.9 | 48,974 | 41,798 | 50,537 | 57,931 | 52,580 | 31,562 |
| CHICO-PARADISE, CA | 20,434 | 78,127 | 16.2 | 16.8 | 35.4 | 23.1 | 5.3 | 3.2 | 36,436 | 27,997 | 42,539 | 47,862 | 39,719 | 28,342 |
| CINCINNATI, OH-KY-IN | 20,938 | 627,070 | 15.2 | 12.6 | 33.2 | 29.7 | 6.6 | 2.7 | 38,827 | 32,480 | 44,191 | 48,767 | 41,135 | 24,783 |
| CLARKSVLL-HOPKINSVLL | 16,615 | 72,547 | 12.7 | 16.7 | 38.3 | 28.0 | 3.7 | 0.7 | 35,488 | 31,156 | 40,931 | 44,743 | 37,718 | 24,072 |
| CLEVELAND-LORAIN-ELY | 20,632 | 868,659 | 16.3 | 12.8 | 33.5 | 29.0 | 6.0 | 2.4 | 37,243 | 31,775 | 41,739 | 46,957 | 41,631 | 24,683 |
| COLORADO SPRINGS, CO | 24,165 | 192,463 | 7.7 | 11.4 | 32.0 | 36.1 | 9.7 | 3.3 | 44,537 | 34,631 | 48,930 | 53,319 | 47,404 | 34,620 |
| COLUMBIA, MO | 20,734 | 50,457 | 15.9 | 13.5 | 31.9 | 29.5 | 6.7 | 2.5 | 38,629 | 28,249 | 45,059 | 50,274 | 47,814 | 30,281 |
| COLUMBIA, SC | 21,789 | 198,651 | 11.3 | 11.6 | 33.9 | 33.4 | 7.6 | 2.3 | 40,241 | 33,890 | 43,531 | 49,442 | 42,674 | 28,644 |
| COLUMBUS, GA-AL | 18,218 | 99,372 | 18.4 | 15.4 | 33.6 | 25.5 | 5.3 | 1.9 | 34,920 | 29,827 | 38,617 | 43,711 | 37,308 | 24,307 |
| COLUMBUS, OH | 21,301 | 581,603 | 13.0 | 12.8 | 34.2 | 31.0 | 6.6 | 2.4 | 38,874 | 32,357 | 44,229 | 49,176 | 41,849 | 25,679 |
| CORPUS CHRISTI, TX | 16,239 | 133,598 | 20.5 | 15.1 | 33.7 | 24.3 | 4.5 | 1.9 | 35,438 | 29,964 | 38,909 | 42,448 | 37,800 | 25,996 |
| CORVALLIS, OR | 22,396 | 29,859 | 14.7 | 12.4 | 31.6 | 29.4 | 8.1 | 3.9 | 39,086 | 26,802 | 43,114 | 52,860 | 47,409 | 32,302 |
| CUMBERLAND, MD-WV | 16,257 | 38,948 | 22.5 | 19.7 | 35.4 | 18.3 | 2.7 | 1.5 | 28,755 | 24,851 | 35,428 | 36,906 | 30,975 | 19,232 |
| DALLAS, TX | 26,207 | 1,274,786 | 10.0 | 11.1 | 30.4 | 33.2 | 10.0 | 5.3 | 49,894 | 39,250 | 52,999 | 58,890 | 51,763 | 33,601 |
| DANVILLE, VA | 15,279 | 43,551 | 24.7 | 17.4 | 35.4 | 19.4 | 2.2 | 1.0 | 28,420 | 24,487 | 33,708 | 35,694 | 30,027 | 19,480 |
| DVNPRT-MOL.-R.ISLAND | 19,594 | 140,174 | 15.5 | 13.9 | 34.6 | 28.6 | 5.5 | 1.9 | 35,497 | 28,423 | 41,385 | 46,001 | 38,667 | 23,801 |
| DAYTON-SPRINGFLD, OH | 19,711 | 368,951 | 14.8 | 12.9 | 34.9 | 30.1 | 5.6 | 1.8 | 36,737 | 31,099 | 41,390 | 47,549 | 40,081 | 24,700 |
| DAYTONA BEACH, FL | 19,346 | 198,893 | 15.4 | 17.0 | 36.7 | 24.9 | 4.5 | 1.5 | 35,903 | 32,737 | 40,605 | 43,360 | 39,502 | 29,271 |
| DECATUR, AL | 19,811 | 55,739 | 16.7 | 12.1 | 33.6 | 29.9 | 5.9 | 1.8 | 38,104 | 34,877 | 43,959 | 49,048 | 39,219 | 21,860 |
| DECATUR, IL | 19,703 | 44,547 | 17.4 | 13.7 | 35.2 | 26.7 | 4.9 | 2.2 | 35,281 | 28,424 | 40,850 | 44,633 | 38,871 | 24,442 |
| DENVER, CO | 29,721 | 813,416 | 8.5 | 9.3 | 29.1 | 35.3 | 11.8 | 5.9 | 50,051 | 38,013 | 53,453 | 58,115 | 52,599 | 33,619 |
| DES MOINES, IA | 22,296 | 174,963 | 11.1 | 11.6 | 35.4 | 32.5 | 7.0 | 2.5 | 38,950 | 32,734 | 44,763 | 48,413 | 40,703 | 25,722 |
| UNITED STATES | 22,162 | | 14.5 | 12.5 | 32.3 | 29.8 | 7.4 | 3.5 | 40,748 | 34,503 | 44,969 | 49,579 | 43,409 | 27,339 |

# SPENDING POTENTIAL INDEXES

## MSA AND U.S. TOTALS



| MSA | FINANCIAL SERVICES | | | | THE HOME | | | | | | ENTERTAINMENT | | | | | | PERSONAL | | | |
|---|---|---|---|---|---|---|---|---|---|---|---|---|---|---|---|---|---|---|---|---|
| | | | | | Home Improvements | | | Furnishings | | | | | | | | | | | | |
| | Auto Loan | Home Loan | Invest-ments | Retire-ment Plans | Home Repair | Lawn & Garden | Remodel-ing | Appli-ances | Elec-tronics | Furni-ture | Restau-rants | Sport-ing Goods | Theater & Concerts | Toys & Hobbies | Travel | Video Rental | Apparel | Auto After-market | Health Insur-ance | Pets & Supplies |
| ABILENE, TX | 97 | 96 | 96 | 94 | 100 | 98 | 99 | 97 | 96 | 94 | 97 | 96 | 94 | 98 | 85 | 97 | 94 | 97 | 98 | 100 |
| AKRON, OH | 98 | 98 | 103 | 99 | 104 | 101 | 98 | 98 | 96 | 99 | 100 | 97 | 102 | 100 | 100 | 101 | 97 | 100 | 100 | 99 |
| ALBANY, GA | 96 | 90 | 92 | 90 | 98 | 94 | 97 | 97 | 95 | 95 | 91 | 96 | 92 | 96 | 83 | 98 | 94 | 96 | 92 | 98 |
| ALBANY-SCH.-TROY, NY | 99 | 96 | 100 | 97 | 95 | 94 | 93 | 98 | 96 | 99 | 99 | 100 | 100 | 102 | 95 | 99 | 101 | 97 | 101 | 102 |
| ALBUQUERQUE, NM | 99 | 101 | 96 | 98 | 101 | 101 | 101 | 102 | 102 | 102 | 101 | 93 | 93 | 94 | 91 | 94 | 98 | 99 | 97 | 95 |
| ALEXANDRIA, LA | 96 | 83 | 89 | 86 | 97 | 93 | 101 | 96 | 93 | 89 | 87 | 94 | 89 | 95 | 79 | 97 | 89 | 93 | 95 | 97 |
| ALLENTWN-BETH-EASTON | 100 | 94 | 101 | 98 | 96 | 95 | 95 | 99 | 96 | 99 | 99 | 101 | 101 | 103 | 96 | 99 | 101 | 97 | 103 | 102 |
| ALTOONA, PA | 96 | 80 | 89 | 84 | 92 | 89 | 95 | 96 | 90 | 89 | 88 | 95 | 91 | 97 | 87 | 97 | 90 | 90 | 102 | 98 |
| AMARILLO, TX | 97 | 97 | 97 | 94 | 100 | 98 | 99 | 97 | 96 | 96 | 98 | 97 | 95 | 98 | 86 | 98 | 95 | 97 | 97 | 100 |
| ANCHORAGE, AK | 103 | 114 | 96 | 109 | 102 | 105 | 102 | 105 | 109 | 111 | 112 | 100 | 100 | 99 | 96 | 96 | 110 | 107 | 96 | 99 |
| ANN ARBOR, MI | 102 | 109 | 104 | 108 | 103 | 104 | 104 | 100 | 103 | 104 | 109 | 103 | 107 | 104 | 103 | 103 | 106 | 107 | 101 | 104 |
| ANNISTON, AL | 97 | 82 | 89 | 86 | 98 | 94 | 106 | 97 | 93 | 88 | 88 | 96 | 89 | 97 | 78 | 97 | 88 | 92 | 98 | 99 |
| APPLTN-OSHKSH-NEENAH | 99 | 95 | 93 | 94 | 99 | 97 | 102 | 98 | 97 | 97 | 100 | 98 | 99 | 101 | 94 | 102 | 96 | 100 | 100 | 100 |
| ASHEVILLE, NC | 98 | 86 | 97 | 90 | 100 | 98 | 108 | 98 | 94 | 91 | 92 | 97 | 92 | 99 | 82 | 98 | 92 | 94 | 101 | 100 |
| ATHENS, GA | 96 | 92 | 93 | 91 | 97 | 94 | 101 | 94 | 94 | 89 | 92 | 94 | 89 | 96 | 81 | 96 | 91 | 94 | 96 | 99 |
| ATLANTA, GA | 101 | 107 | 97 | 103 | 101 | 102 | 102 | 101 | 103 | 105 | 107 | 105 | 103 | 104 | 90 | 101 | 107 | 105 | 97 | 104 |
| ATLANTIC-CAPE MAY,NJ | 99 | 91 | 96 | 94 | 93 | 93 | 94 | 99 | 95 | 97 | 96 | 100 | 97 | 101 | 93 | 100 | 100 | 96 | 102 | 102 |
| AUBURN-OPELIKA, AL | 96 | 89 | 90 | 91 | 93 | 89 | 102 | 92 | 92 | 85 | 88 | 91 | 86 | 94 | 87 | 94 | 89 | 92 | 95 | 96 |
| AUGUSTA-AIKEN, GA-SC | 98 | 93 | 94 | 93 | 99 | 97 | 102 | 98 | 97 | 96 | 96 | 99 | 95 | 99 | 83 | 99 | 96 | 97 | 97 | 100 |
| AUSTIN-SAN MARCOS,TX | 100 | 106 | 95 | 101 | 99 | 99 | 100 | 98 | 100 | 100 | 104 | 101 | 98 | 101 | 88 | 99 | 102 | 102 | 97 | 102 |
| BAKERSFIELD, CA | 98 | 97 | 90 | 92 | 98 | 98 | 99 | 100 | 100 | 97 | 97 | 91 | 90 | 92 | 87 | 94 | 94 | 97 | 96 | 94 |
| BALTIMORE, MD | 100 | 105 | 105 | 104 | 105 | 105 | 99 | 101 | 101 | 105 | 105 | 103 | 104 | 103 | 94 | 100 | 106 | 104 | 97 | 102 |
| BANGOR, ME | 98 | 84 | 89 | 87 | 89 | 87 | 98 | 96 | 93 | 89 | 91 | 97 | 91 | 100 | 85 | 98 | 92 | 92 | 101 | 101 |
| BARNSTABLE-YARMOUTH | 103 | 92 | 103 | 101 | 95 | 100 | 101 | 102 | 97 | 97 | 100 | 103 | 101 | 105 | 97 | 100 | 102 | 98 | 109 | 105 |
| BATON ROUGE, LA | 98 | 95 | 94 | 95 | 99 | 97 | 101 | 98 | 97 | 97 | 96 | 99 | 95 | 99 | 84 | 99 | 97 | 98 | 95 | 100 |
| BEAUMONT-P.ARTHUR,TX | 97 | 87 | 93 | 89 | 99 | 95 | 102 | 97 | 94 | 92 | 91 | 96 | 92 | 97 | 82 | 98 | 92 | 95 | 96 | 98 |
| BELLINGHAM, WA | 99 | 92 | 91 | 94 | 99 | 97 | 107 | 99 | 98 | 94 | 94 | 91 | 88 | 93 | 85 | 93 | 94 | 95 | 98 | 94 |
| BENTON HARBOR, MI | 96 | 88 | 95 | 90 | 100 | 96 | 103 | 97 | 93 | 92 | 93 | 95 | 96 | 97 | 93 | 100 | 90 | 96 | 100 | 97 |
| BERGEN-PASSAIC, NJ | 105 | 123 | 123 | 121 | 106 | 110 | 95 | 103 | 108 | 116 | 118 | 111 | 120 | 108 | 119 | 104 | 122 | 113 | 106 | 107 |
| BILLINGS, MT | 99 | 95 | 96 | 95 | 101 | 100 | 103 | 100 | 100 | 99 | 97 | 92 | 91 | 94 | 88 | 93 | 96 | 96 | 98 | 94 |
| BILOXI-GULFPORT-PAS. | 98 | 88 | 94 | 90 | 99 | 97 | 103 | 98 | 95 | 93 | 93 | 97 | 93 | 98 | 82 | 98 | 93 | 96 | 98 | 99 |
| BINGHAMTON, NY | 98 | 89 | 96 | 91 | 93 | 91 | 94 | 97 | 94 | 94 | 95 | 97 | 96 | 101 | 91 | 98 | 96 | 94 | 101 | 100 |
| BIRMINGHAM, AL | 99 | 95 | 99 | 98 | 101 | 100 | 102 | 99 | 98 | 98 | 97 | 101 | 98 | 100 | 87 | 99 | 99 | 99 | 97 | 101 |
| BISMARCK, ND | 98 | 94 | 91 | 92 | 97 | 95 | 101 | 97 | 97 | 95 | 98 | 97 | 97 | 99 | 92 | 102 | 94 | 99 | 99 | 99 |
| BLOOMINGTON, IN | 96 | 97 | 97 | 97 | 99 | 95 | 101 | 93 | 94 | 90 | 95 | 94 | 94 | 97 | 93 | 98 | 92 | 97 | 98 | 98 |
| BLOOMINGTN-NORMAL,IL | 99 | 98 | 95 | 98 | 99 | 97 | 102 | 97 | 98 | 96 | 100 | 98 | 98 | 100 | 95 | 101 | 96 | 100 | 99 | 100 |
| BOISE CITY, ID | 100 | 96 | 92 | 96 | 100 | 99 | 105 | 101 | 102 | 100 | 99 | 94 | 92 | 95 | 87 | 94 | 98 | 98 | 97 | 95 |
| BOSTON-WOR-LAW-LW-BR | 102 | 108 | 109 | 107 | 99 | 100 | 93 | 100 | 102 | 107 | 108 | 105 | 108 | 105 | 105 | 101 | 111 | 104 | 102 | 105 |
| BOULDER-LONGMONT, CO | 103 | 113 | 101 | 110 | 104 | 107 | 104 | 104 | 108 | 110 | 110 | 99 | 100 | 99 | 97 | 96 | 110 | 106 | 98 | 98 |
| BRAZORIA, TX | 100 | 97 | 92 | 95 | 97 | 97 | 105 | 99 | 100 | 98 | 101 | 101 | 96 | 102 | 83 | 100 | 99 | 100 | 98 | 102 |
| BREMERTON, WA | 99 | 98 | 92 | 95 | 100 | 99 | 102 | 101 | 102 | 101 | 101 | 93 | 92 | 95 | 88 | 94 | 99 | 99 | 97 | 95 |
| BRWNSVL-HARL-S.BENIT | 94 | 93 | 95 | 85 | 95 | 96 | 96 | 97 | 95 | 88 | 92 | 91 | 90 | 93 | 82 | 97 | 85 | 95 | 99 | 102 |
| BRYAN-COLLEGE STA,TX | 95 | 101 | 95 | 96 | 96 | 93 | 97 | 90 | 92 | 86 | 93 | 92 | 87 | 94 | 82 | 94 | 91 | 94 | 94 | 97 |
| BUFFALO-NIAGARA FLLS | 97 | 91 | 100 | 93 | 95 | 93 | 89 | 97 | 93 | 97 | 95 | 97 | 98 | 100 | 95 | 98 | 98 | 94 | 100 | 99 |
| BURLINGTON, VT | 101 | 97 | 92 | 97 | 91 | 90 | 94 | 98 | 99 | 97 | 101 | 102 | 98 | 103 | 91 | 100 | 102 | 99 | 100 | 104 |
| CANTON-MASSILLON, OH | 97 | 91 | 96 | 92 | 102 | 98 | 101 | 98 | 94 | 95 | 96 | 96 | 98 | 98 | 95 | 100 | 92 | 97 | 100 | 98 |
| CASPER, WY | 98 | 93 | 89 | 92 | 99 | 97 | 102 | 100 | 100 | 98 | 97 | 91 | 90 | 93 | 85 | 94 | 95 | 96 | 97 | 93 |
| CEDAR RAPIDS, IA | 98 | 98 | 98 | 97 | 101 | 99 | 100 | 98 | 98 | 99 | 102 | 98 | 101 | 100 | 97 | 101 | 97 | 100 | 100 | 100 |
| CHAMPAIGN-URBANA, IL | 97 | 99 | 98 | 97 | 99 | 97 | 99 | 95 | 96 | 94 | 99 | 96 | 97 | 98 | 96 | 100 | 95 | 99 | 98 | 99 |
| CHARLESTON-N.CHARLES | 98 | 96 | 92 | 93 | 98 | 97 | 99 | 98 | 98 | 97 | 98 | 98 | 95 | 99 | 84 | 99 | 97 | 98 | 96 | 100 |
| CHARLESTON, WV | 98 | 87 | 98 | 91 | 102 | 99 | 106 | 98 | 95 | 93 | 93 | 97 | 94 | 99 | 84 | 98 | 92 | 95 | 101 | 99 |
| CHARLOTTE-GAST-ROCK | 99 | 96 | 95 | 96 | 100 | 99 | 104 | 99 | 98 | 98 | 99 | 100 | 97 | 101 | 85 | 99 | 98 | 99 | 98 | 101 |
| CHARLOTTESVILLE, VA | 99 | 99 | 100 | 99 | 101 | 101 | 104 | 97 | 97 | 96 | 100 | 99 | 96 | 101 | 87 | 98 | 99 | 99 | 99 | 101 |
| CHATTANOOGA, TN-GA | 98 | 89 | 96 | 92 | 100 | 98 | 104 | 98 | 96 | 94 | 93 | 98 | 94 | 99 | 83 | 98 | 94 | 96 | 99 | 99 |
| CHEYENNE, WY | 98 | 96 | 96 | 95 | 102 | 100 | 102 | 100 | 100 | 100 | 98 | 91 | 92 | 93 | 89 | 93 | 96 | 97 | 97 | 93 |
| CHICAGO, IL | 100 | 111 | 107 | 108 | 106 | 106 | 98 | 101 | 102 | 107 | 108 | 103 | 110 | 102 | 109 | 104 | 106 | 108 | 99 | 102 |
| CHICO-PARADISE, CA | 96 | 89 | 99 | 90 | 101 | 100 | 101 | 97 | 93 | 90 | 89 | 86 | 85 | 89 | 86 | 90 | 87 | 91 | 99 | 91 |
| CINCINNATI, OH-KY-IN | 98 | 98 | 99 | 98 | 101 | 100 | 100 | 99 | 98 | 99 | 100 | 99 | 102 | 100 | 98 | 102 | 97 | 101 | 99 | 100 |
| CLARKSVLL-HOPKINSVLL | 94 | 87 | 83 | 83 | 94 | 90 | 99 | 94 | 93 | 87 | 91 | 93 | 88 | 94 | 77 | 97 | 88 | 93 | 94 | 98 |
| CLEVELAND-LORAIN-ELY | 98 | 99 | 105 | 100 | 105 | 103 | 98 | 99 | 97 | 101 | 100 | 98 | 104 | 99 | 102 | 101 | 98 | 101 | 99 | 99 |
| COLORADO SPRINGS, CO | 100 | 106 | 96 | 102 | 102 | 103 | 100 | 102 | 104 | 106 | 106 | 96 | 96 | 96 | 93 | 95 | 104 | 102 | 96 | 96 |
| COLUMBIA, MO | 99 | 100 | 92 | 98 | 97 | 96 | 101 | 97 | 98 | 96 | 101 | 98 | 98 | 99 | 94 | 101 | 97 | 101 | 98 | 100 |
| COLUMBIA, SC | 100 | 100 | 98 | 99 | 101 | 100 | 101 | 99 | 99 | 101 | 102 | 101 | 99 | 102 | 88 | 100 | 102 | 101 | 97 | 102 |
| COLUMBUS, GA-AL | 96 | 91 | 97 | 91 | 101 | 97 | 97 | 97 | 94 | 95 | 92 | 96 | 94 | 97 | 85 | 98 | 95 | 96 | 95 | 98 |
| COLUMBUS, OH | 99 | 102 | 98 | 100 | 101 | 100 | 99 | 99 | 99 | 100 | 102 | 100 | 102 | 100 | 99 | 102 | 99 | 102 | 99 | 100 |
| CORPUS CHRISTI, TX | 97 | 98 | 93 | 92 | 97 | 97 | 98 | 98 | 98 | 96 | 99 | 97 | 95 | 98 | 84 | 99 | 94 | 98 | 98 | 102 |
| CORVALLIS, OR | 99 | 103 | 102 | 103 | 99 | 98 | 100 | 97 | 98 | 97 | 100 | 98 | 97 | 100 | 98 | 97 | 100 | 99 | 99 | 99 |
| CUMBERLAND, MD-WV | 95 | 81 | 94 | 84 | 102 | 97 | 102 | 95 | 90 | 88 | 88 | 92 | 89 | 95 | 82 | 95 | 87 | 90 | 101 | 96 |
| DALLAS, TX | 101 | 109 | 100 | 105 | 101 | 103 | 100 | 101 | 103 | 104 | 108 | 104 | 103 | 103 | 92 | 100 | 106 | 104 | 98 | 104 |
| DANVILLE, VA | 96 | 75 | 84 | 80 | 98 | 93 | 105 | 96 | 91 | 84 | 83 | 94 | 86 | 95 | 76 | 96 | 84 | 89 | 99 | 97 |
| DVNPRT-MOL.-R.ISLAND | 97 | 93 | 96 | 93 | 100 | 97 | 99 | 97 | 95 | 95 | 97 | 95 | 98 | 98 | 95 | 100 | 93 | 97 | 100 | 98 |
| DAYTON-SPRINGFLD, OH | 97 | 97 | 100 | 97 | 102 | 100 | 98 | 98 | 96 | 98 | 99 | 97 | 101 | 99 | 98 | 101 | 96 | 100 | 99 | 99 |
| DAYTONA BEACH, FL | 99 | 92 | 106 | 97 | 104 | 106 | 104 | 100 | 94 | 94 | 96 | 98 | 96 | 100 | 89 | 97 | 94 | 97 | 104 | 101 |
| DECATUR, AL | 99 | 84 | 88 | 88 | 97 | 95 | 107 | 98 | 96 | 90 | 91 | 98 | 91 | 99 | 78 | 98 | 91 | 94 | 100 | 100 |
| DECATUR, IL | 97 | 91 | 95 | 92 | 100 | 97 | 100 | 98 | 95 | 95 | 96 | 96 | 98 | 98 | 94 | 101 | 93 | 98 | 99 | 98 |
| DENVER, CO | 102 | 109 | 99 | 106 | 104 | 105 | 101 | 104 | 106 | 109 | 108 | 98 | 99 | 97 | 96 | 95 | 107 | 104 | 97 | 97 |
| DES MOINES, IA | 99 | 100 | 96 | 98 | 100 | 99 | 99 | 98 | 98 | 99 | 103 | 99 | 102 | 100 | 97 | 102 | 98 | 101 | 99 | 100 |
| UNITED STATES | 100 | 100 | 100 | 100 | 100 | 100 | 100 | 100 | 100 | 100 | 100 | 100 | 100 | 100 | 100 | 100 | 100 | 100 | 100 | 100 |

# POPULATION CHANGE

## MSA AND U.S. TOTALS

| MSA | MSA Code | POPULATION 1990 | POPULATION 2000 | POPULATION 2005 | 1990-2000 ANNUAL CHANGE % Rate | 1990-2000 ANNUAL CHANGE National Rank | RACE (%) White 1990 | White 2000 | Black 1990 | Black 2000 | Asian/Pacific 1990 | Asian/Pacific 2000 |
|---|---|---|---|---|---|---|---|---|---|---|---|---|
| DETROIT, MI | 2160 | 4,266,654 | 4,481,651 | 4,519,816 | 0.5 | 212 | 75.4 | 74.5 | 22.1 | 22.2 | 1.3 | 2.0 |
| DOTHAN, AL | 2180 | 130,964 | 135,722 | 138,112 | 0.3 | 240 | 77.0 | 75.4 | 21.2 | 22.5 | 0.9 | 1.1 |
| DOVER, DE | 2190 | 110,993 | 127,518 | 134,868 | 1.4 | 80 | 78.7 | 75.1 | 18.6 | 20.9 | 1.3 | 2.1 |
| DUBUQUE, IA | 2200 | 86,403 | 88,126 | 88,211 | 0.2 | 250 | 98.8 | 98.5 | 0.4 | 0.4 | 0.5 | 0.7 |
| DULUTH-SUPERIOR | 2240 | 239,971 | 236,053 | 233,934 | -0.2 | 290 | 96.9 | 96.2 | 0.5 | 0.7 | 0.6 | 0.9 |
| DUTCHESS COUNTY, NY | 2281 | 259,462 | 270,448 | 281,033 | 0.4 | 226 | 88.3 | 86.1 | 8.4 | 9.1 | 2.2 | 3.5 |
| EAU CLAIRE, WI | 2290 | 137,543 | 145,064 | 148,027 | 0.5 | 212 | 97.5 | 96.6 | 0.2 | 0.2 | 1.7 | 2.5 |
| EL PASO, TX | 2320 | 591,610 | 710,795 | 754,282 | 1.8 | 49 | 76.5 | 75.1 | 3.7 | 3.3 | 1.1 | 1.4 |
| ELKHART-GOSHEN, IN | 2330 | 156,198 | 176,634 | 186,489 | 1.2 | 110 | 93.8 | 92.5 | 4.5 | 5.2 | 0.6 | 0.9 |
| ELMIRA, NY | 2335 | 95,195 | 91,248 | 88,856 | -0.4 | 301 | 92.8 | 91.7 | 5.5 | 6.1 | 0.7 | 1.1 |
| ENID, OK | 2340 | 56,735 | 56,993 | 57,122 | 0.0 | 270 | 92.4 | 91.7 | 3.6 | 3.7 | 1.0 | 1.3 |
| ERIE, PA | 2360 | 275,572 | 275,921 | 270,638 | 0.0 | 270 | 93.6 | 92.1 | 5.2 | 6.2 | 0.5 | 0.7 |
| EUGENE-SPRINGFLD, OR | 2400 | 282,912 | 317,460 | 329,798 | 1.1 | 129 | 95.4 | 94.3 | 0.7 | 0.8 | 2.0 | 2.5 |
| EVANSVILLE-HENDERSON | 2440 | 278,990 | 291,955 | 295,742 | 0.4 | 226 | 93.5 | 92.8 | 5.8 | 6.3 | 0.4 | 0.6 |
| FARGO-MOORHEAD,ND-MN | 2520 | 153,296 | 171,860 | 180,451 | 1.1 | 129 | 97.2 | 96.2 | 0.3 | 0.4 | 0.9 | 1.4 |
| FAYETTEVILLE, NC | 2560 | 274,566 | 283,175 | 280,616 | 0.3 | 240 | 61.9 | 59.2 | 31.9 | 30.9 | 2.1 | 3.5 |
| FAYETTEVL-SPRNGD-ROG | 2580 | 210,908 | 290,966 | 321,072 | 3.2 | 7 | 96.6 | 95.7 | 0.9 | 1.0 | 0.7 | 1.0 |
| FLAGSTAFF, AZ-UT | 2620 | 101,760 | 121,387 | 125,198 | 1.7 | 61 | 65.7 | 64.1 | 1.4 | 1.6 | 0.9 | 1.1 |
| FLINT, MI | 2640 | 430,459 | 438,296 | 443,303 | 0.2 | 250 | 78.2 | 76.4 | 19.6 | 20.9 | 0.7 | 1.0 |
| FLORENCE, AL | 2650 | 131,327 | 136,886 | 137,016 | 0.4 | 226 | 87.1 | 86.2 | 12.4 | 13.2 | 0.2 | 0.3 |
| FLORENCE, SC | 2655 | 114,344 | 125,880 | 129,114 | 0.9 | 166 | 60.8 | 60.2 | 38.7 | 39.2 | 0.3 | 0.4 |
| FT. COLLINS-LOVELAND | 2670 | 186,136 | 242,402 | 269,498 | 2.6 | 13 | 94.5 | 93.4 | 0.6 | 0.6 | 1.5 | 1.9 |
| FORT LAUDERDALE, FL | 2680 | 1,255,488 | 1,565,639 | 1,714,670 | 2.2 | 29 | 81.7 | 77.4 | 15.4 | 18.2 | 1.4 | 2.2 |
| FT. MYERS-CAPE CORAL | 2700 | 335,113 | 407,688 | 443,457 | 1.9 | 44 | 91.4 | 89.2 | 6.6 | 7.8 | 0.6 | 0.9 |
| FT.PIERCE-P.ST.LUCIE | 2710 | 251,071 | 304,555 | 327,477 | 1.9 | 44 | 85.3 | 82.2 | 12.2 | 14.2 | 0.6 | 1.0 |
| FORT SMITH, AR-OK | 2720 | 175,911 | 197,241 | 205,903 | 1.1 | 129 | 88.4 | 87.0 | 3.9 | 4.3 | 2.1 | 2.9 |
| FORT WALTON BEACH,FL | 2750 | 143,776 | 171,619 | 179,604 | 1.7 | 61 | 87.1 | 83.8 | 9.0 | 10.3 | 2.5 | 4.0 |
| FORT WAYNE, IN | 2760 | 456,281 | 487,606 | 503,846 | 0.6 | 200 | 91.6 | 90.1 | 6.7 | 7.5 | 0.7 | 0.9 |
| FT. WORTH-ARLINGTON | 2800 | 1,361,034 | 1,666,115 | 1,847,987 | 2.0 | 40 | 80.7 | 77.5 | 10.6 | 10.9 | 2.2 | 3.3 |
| FRESNO, CA | 2840 | 755,580 | 888,134 | 930,057 | 1.6 | 67 | 64.3 | 58.4 | 4.8 | 4.6 | 7.7 | 9.1 |
| GADSDEN, AL | 2880 | 99,840 | 103,549 | 103,720 | 0.4 | 226 | 85.4 | 84.5 | 13.8 | 14.7 | 0.4 | 0.4 |
| GAINESVILLE, FL | 2900 | 181,596 | 199,047 | 202,042 | 0.9 | 166 | 77.5 | 72.6 | 19.0 | 22.3 | 2.5 | 3.7 |
| GALVESTON-TEXAS CITY | 2920 | 217,399 | 251,546 | 267,018 | 1.4 | 80 | 75.5 | 72.5 | 17.6 | 18.3 | 1.6 | 2.5 |
| GARY, IN | 2960 | 604,526 | 629,687 | 636,331 | 0.4 | 226 | 76.2 | 73.9 | 19.4 | 20.0 | 0.6 | 0.9 |
| GLENS FALLS, NY | 2975 | 118,539 | 121,598 | 121,644 | 0.2 | 250 | 97.1 | 96.9 | 2.0 | 2.0 | 0.3 | 0.6 |
| GOLDSBORO, NC | 2980 | 104,666 | 111,718 | 111,994 | 0.6 | 200 | 66.1 | 64.5 | 32.3 | 32.8 | 0.8 | 1.4 |
| GRAND FORKS, ND-MN | 2985 | 103,181 | 93,269 | 88,082 | -1.0 | 318 | 95.2 | 94.0 | 1.5 | 1.6 | 0.9 | 1.3 |
| GRAND JUNCTION, CO | 2995 | 93,145 | 117,425 | 128,745 | 2.3 | 25 | 94.7 | 93.7 | 0.4 | 0.4 | 0.7 | 0.9 |
| GR.RAPIDS-MSKGN-HOLL | 3000 | 937,891 | 1,064,260 | 1,125,224 | 1.2 | 110 | 90.0 | 88.8 | 6.9 | 7.2 | 0.9 | 1.4 |
| GREAT FALLS, MT | 3040 | 77,691 | 77,903 | 75,961 | 0.0 | 270 | 93.1 | 92.2 | 1.4 | 1.6 | 1.0 | 1.1 |
| GREELEY, CO | 3060 | 131,821 | 171,203 | 197,136 | 2.6 | 13 | 88.9 | 86.8 | 0.4 | 0.5 | 0.9 | 1.1 |
| GREEN BAY, WI | 3080 | 194,594 | 217,941 | 225,288 | 1.1 | 129 | 95.9 | 94.9 | 0.5 | 0.6 | 1.3 | 1.9 |
| G'BORO-W.SLM-H.PT,NC | 3120 | 1,050,304 | 1,192,326 | 1,257,256 | 1.2 | 110 | 79.4 | 78.6 | 19.3 | 19.5 | 0.7 | 1.1 |
| GREENVILLE, NC | 3150 | 107,924 | 129,773 | 138,769 | 1.8 | 49 | 65.5 | 63.6 | 33.3 | 34.2 | 0.7 | 1.1 |
| GREENVL-SPAR'BG-ANDR | 3160 | 830,563 | 941,074 | 998,621 | 1.2 | 110 | 81.6 | 80.8 | 17.4 | 17.9 | 0.6 | 0.9 |
| HAGERSTOWN, MD | 3180 | 121,393 | 128,198 | 130,136 | 0.5 | 212 | 92.9 | 91.4 | 6.0 | 7.0 | 0.7 | 1.0 |
| HAMILTON-MIDDLETOWN | 3200 | 291,479 | 336,522 | 351,724 | 1.4 | 80 | 94.3 | 93.3 | 4.5 | 5.2 | 0.9 | 1.3 |
| HARR'BG-LEBANON-CARL | 3240 | 587,986 | 620,097 | 627,984 | 0.5 | 212 | 91.3 | 89.6 | 6.7 | 7.6 | 1.1 | 1.6 |
| HARTFORD, CT | 3283 | 1,123,678 | 1,116,754 | 1,130,090 | -0.1 | 283 | 86.2 | 83.7 | 8.5 | 9.1 | 1.5 | 2.5 |
| HATTIESBURG, MS | 3285 | 98,738 | 114,729 | 123,145 | 1.5 | 73 | 74.2 | 72.5 | 25.0 | 26.4 | 0.6 | 0.8 |
| HICKRY-MRGNTN-LENOIR | 3290 | 292,409 | 329,776 | 349,338 | 1.2 | 110 | 91.7 | 90.6 | 7.3 | 7.7 | 0.6 | 1.1 |
| HONOLULU, HI | 3320 | 836,231 | 861,359 | 845,492 | 0.3 | 240 | 31.6 | 29.1 | 3.1 | 3.5 | 63.0 | 64.6 |
| HOUMA, LA | 3350 | 182,842 | 196,690 | 204,100 | 0.7 | 188 | 80.6 | 78.8 | 14.6 | 16.2 | 0.7 | 1.0 |
| HOUSTON, TX | 3360 | 3,322,025 | 4,096,257 | 4,502,811 | 2.1 | 34 | 66.4 | 62.7 | 18.5 | 18.3 | 3.8 | 5.5 |
| HUNTINGTON-ASHLAND | 3400 | 312,529 | 311,351 | 306,022 | 0.0 | 270 | 97.3 | 97.2 | 2.2 | 2.3 | 0.3 | 0.4 |
| HUNTSVILLE, AL | 3440 | 293,047 | 347,365 | 367,135 | 1.7 | 61 | 78.8 | 77.3 | 18.9 | 20.0 | 1.5 | 1.8 |
| INDIANAPOLIS, IN | 3480 | 1,380,491 | 1,553,630 | 1,635,322 | 1.2 | 110 | 85.5 | 84.8 | 13.2 | 13.4 | 0.8 | 1.1 |
| IOWA CITY, IA | 3500 | 96,119 | 104,754 | 109,439 | 0.8 | 175 | 93.3 | 91.5 | 2.1 | 2.3 | 4.0 | 5.2 |
| JACKSON, MI | 3520 | 149,756 | 158,219 | 162,835 | 0.5 | 212 | 90.5 | 89.9 | 8.0 | 8.2 | 0.4 | 0.6 |
| JACKSON, MS | 3560 | 395,396 | 436,246 | 454,055 | 1.0 | 149 | 56.9 | 56.1 | 42.5 | 43.1 | 0.4 | 0.6 |
| JACKSON, TN | 3580 | 90,801 | 102,730 | 108,377 | 1.2 | 110 | 71.3 | 69.3 | 28.2 | 30.1 | 0.3 | 0.5 |
| JACKSONVILLE, FL | 3600 | 906,727 | 1,074,363 | 1,152,803 | 1.7 | 61 | 77.4 | 73.8 | 20.0 | 22.3 | 1.7 | 2.7 |
| JACKSONVILLE, NC | 3605 | 149,838 | 142,291 | 141,253 | -0.5 | 309 | 74.7 | 72.3 | 19.9 | 18.6 | 2.0 | 3.4 |
| JAMESTOWN, NY | 3610 | 141,895 | 136,435 | 131,542 | -0.4 | 301 | 96.1 | 94.9 | 1.7 | 2.1 | 0.4 | 0.6 |
| JANESVILLE-BELOIT,WI | 3620 | 139,510 | 151,528 | 153,921 | 0.8 | 175 | 93.8 | 91.9 | 4.8 | 6.1 | 0.7 | 1.0 |
| JERSEY CITY, NJ | 3640 | 553,099 | 554,254 | 554,446 | 0.0 | 270 | 68.8 | 63.3 | 14.4 | 14.4 | 6.6 | 9.7 |
| J.CITY-KNGSPRT-BRIST | 3660 | 436,047 | 464,538 | 473,435 | 0.6 | 200 | 97.4 | 97.0 | 2.0 | 2.3 | 0.3 | 0.4 |
| JOHNSTOWN, PA | 3680 | 241,247 | 231,964 | 223,070 | -0.4 | 301 | 98.0 | 97.5 | 1.6 | 2.0 | 0.2 | 0.3 |
| JONESBORO, AR | 3700 | 68,956 | 78,349 | 81,831 | 1.3 | 91 | 93.5 | 92.3 | 5.5 | 6.2 | 0.6 | 0.7 |
| JOPLIN, MO | 3710 | 134,910 | 151,516 | 158,476 | 1.1 | 129 | 96.4 | 96.1 | 1.0 | 1.2 | 0.6 | 0.7 |
| KALAMAZOO-BATTLE CRK | 3720 | 429,453 | 448,603 | 455,464 | 0.4 | 226 | 88.3 | 86.9 | 9.1 | 9.8 | 1.0 | 1.5 |
| KANKAKEE, IL | 3740 | 96,255 | 103,121 | 104,996 | 0.7 | 188 | 83.3 | 81.2 | 15.0 | 16.5 | 0.7 | 0.9 |
| KANSAS CITY, MO-KS | 3760 | 1,582,875 | 1,775,860 | 1,873,609 | 1.1 | 129 | 84.4 | 83.3 | 12.7 | 13.0 | 1.1 | 1.6 |
| KENOSHA, WI | 3800 | 128,181 | 148,041 | 156,788 | 1.4 | 80 | 93.0 | 90.8 | 4.1 | 5.1 | 0.5 | 0.8 |
| KILLEEN-TEMPLE, TX | 3810 | 255,301 | 296,841 | 300,331 | 1.5 | 73 | 71.0 | 67.2 | 19.5 | 19.6 | 2.8 | 4.4 |
| KNOXVILLE, TN | 3840 | 585,960 | 678,506 | 709,119 | 1.4 | 80 | 92.7 | 91.8 | 6.1 | 6.5 | 0.8 | 1.2 |
| KOKOMO, IN | 3850 | 96,946 | 100,475 | 101,139 | 0.3 | 240 | 94.3 | 93.2 | 4.5 | 5.2 | 0.5 | 0.7 |
| UNITED STATES | | | | | 1.0 | | 80.3 | 77.9 | 12.1 | 12.4 | 2.9 | 3.9 |

# POPULATION COMPOSITION

## MSA AND U.S. TOTALS

# B

| MSA | % HISPANIC ORIGIN | | 2000 AGE DISTRIBUTION (%) | | | | | | | | | | MEDIAN AGE | | 2000 Males/ Females (×100) |
|---|---|---|---|---|---|---|---|---|---|---|---|---|---|---|---|
| | 1990 | 2000 | 0-4 | 5-9 | 10-14 | 15-19 | 20-24 | 25-44 | 45-64 | 65-84 | 85+ | 18+ | 1990 | 2000 | |
| DETROIT, MI | 2.0 | 2.8 | 6.5 | 7.1 | 7.6 | 6.8 | 5.8 | 30.9 | 22.7 | 11.2 | 1.5 | 74.8 | 33.0 | 36.4 | 92.8 |
| DOTHAN, AL | 1.3 | 2.4 | 7.4 | 7.1 | 6.8 | 6.9 | 7.3 | 30.5 | 21.8 | 10.8 | 1.4 | 74.6 | 31.5 | 34.6 | 93.5 |
| DOVER, DE | 2.3 | 3.8 | 7.5 | 7.3 | 6.9 | 6.9 | 6.6 | 33.1 | 20.5 | 9.9 | 1.2 | 74.5 | 31.1 | 34.0 | 95.5 |
| DUBUQUE, IA | 0.5 | 1.2 | 6.2 | 6.5 | 7.4 | 8.5 | 7.0 | 27.5 | 22.6 | 12.3 | 2.1 | 75.2 | 33.1 | 36.4 | 94.5 |
| DULUTH-SUPERIOR | 0.5 | 1.1 | 5.5 | 5.8 | 6.6 | 7.9 | 7.0 | 26.6 | 24.2 | 14.0 | 2.5 | 77.8 | 35.6 | 38.8 | 96.2 |
| DUTCHESS COUNTY, NY | 3.8 | 5.0 | 6.4 | 7.2 | 7.1 | 7.0 | 6.1 | 30.7 | 23.3 | 10.6 | 1.6 | 75.6 | 33.4 | 36.5 | 100.8 |
| EAU CLAIRE, WI | 0.4 | 1.0 | 6.0 | 6.5 | 7.6 | 9.2 | 8.6 | 28.2 | 21.0 | 11.1 | 1.8 | 75.4 | 31.5 | 34.8 | 94.7 |
| EL PASO, TX | 69.6 | 75.4 | 9.4 | 8.6 | 8.2 | 9.0 | 8.4 | 28.4 | 19.1 | 8.0 | 0.9 | 68.4 | 27.9 | 29.4 | 93.7 |
| ELKHART-GOSHEN, IN | 1.9 | 3.3 | 7.9 | 8.0 | 8.2 | 7.2 | 5.9 | 29.3 | 22.4 | 9.8 | 1.4 | 71.6 | 31.8 | 34.6 | 96.7 |
| ELMIRA, NY | 1.5 | 2.2 | 6.6 | 7.7 | 7.0 | 6.9 | 6.3 | 27.7 | 22.4 | 13.3 | 2.1 | 74.8 | 34.2 | 36.9 | 96.1 |
| ENID, OK | 1.9 | 3.3 | 6.7 | 6.8 | 7.4 | 7.5 | 6.9 | 25.9 | 23.7 | 13.0 | 2.2 | 74.5 | 34.2 | 37.4 | 92.7 |
| ERIE, PA | 1.2 | 2.1 | 6.3 | 7.0 | 7.3 | 8.1 | 7.1 | 28.0 | 21.9 | 12.6 | 1.7 | 75.3 | 32.9 | 35.8 | 93.7 |
| EUGENE-SPRINGFLD, OR | 2.4 | 4.3 | 6.1 | 6.2 | 6.6 | 7.8 | 8.3 | 28.1 | 24.2 | 11.1 | 1.7 | 77.0 | 33.9 | 36.6 | 95.2 |
| EVANSVILLE-HENDERSON | 0.5 | 1.1 | 6.6 | 6.8 | 7.1 | 7.1 | 6.0 | 29.9 | 22.9 | 11.8 | 1.8 | 75.4 | 34.1 | 37.1 | 93.1 |
| FARGO-MOORHEAD,ND-MN | 1.2 | 2.3 | 6.0 | 6.0 | 7.0 | 9.1 | 10.8 | 29.8 | 20.4 | 9.1 | 1.7 | 77.0 | 29.7 | 33.2 | 97.0 |
| FAYETTEVILLE, NC | 4.8 | 9.4 | 9.7 | 8.3 | 7.0 | 7.0 | 10.6 | 34.4 | 15.8 | 6.7 | 0.6 | 71.7 | 27.3 | 28.8 | 104.1 |
| FAYETTEVL-SPRNGD-ROG | 1.4 | 3.9 | 6.9 | 6.8 | 7.0 | 7.7 | 8.2 | 28.1 | 22.2 | 11.7 | 1.5 | 75.4 | 33.1 | 35.2 | 96.0 |
| FLAGSTAFF, AZ-UT | 9.6 | 12.5 | 8.4 | 8.6 | 8.5 | 10.5 | 11.8 | 27.6 | 18.2 | 5.8 | 0.6 | 70.5 | 26.4 | 26.7 | 99.8 |
| FLINT, MI | 2.1 | 2.9 | 6.8 | 7.2 | 7.6 | 7.4 | 6.5 | 29.9 | 22.9 | 10.4 | 1.2 | 73.9 | 32.0 | 35.4 | 91.8 |
| FLORENCE, AL | 0.4 | 1.0 | 6.0 | 6.0 | 6.0 | 6.6 | 6.7 | 28.7 | 25.0 | 13.3 | 1.6 | 78.2 | 35.1 | 38.6 | 91.5 |
| FLORENCE, SC | 0.4 | 0.9 | 6.3 | 6.9 | 7.4 | 7.6 | 7.1 | 29.5 | 23.6 | 10.4 | 1.1 | 74.9 | 32.2 | 35.8 | 88.3 |
| FT. COLLINS-LOVELAND | 6.6 | 8.6 | 6.7 | 6.8 | 7.0 | 8.5 | 9.1 | 29.6 | 23.0 | 8.0 | 1.2 | 75.3 | 31.1 | 34.1 | 98.2 |
| FORT LAUDERDALE, FL | 8.6 | 13.1 | 6.1 | 6.5 | 6.6 | 5.8 | 5.3 | 29.4 | 22.6 | 15.1 | 2.6 | 77.3 | 37.7 | 39.3 | 93.0 |
| FT. MYERS-CAPE CORAL | 4.5 | 7.0 | 5.5 | 6.0 | 6.1 | 5.2 | 4.2 | 24.1 | 23.1 | 23.2 | 2.7 | 79.3 | 42.0 | 44.2 | 93.9 |
| FT.PIERCE-P.ST.LUCIE | 4.3 | 6.5 | 5.9 | 6.5 | 6.4 | 5.6 | 4.4 | 24.2 | 22.4 | 22.3 | 2.3 | 77.8 | 40.3 | 42.9 | 96.4 |
| FORT SMITH, AR-OK | 1.2 | 3.2 | 7.3 | 7.1 | 7.7 | 7.4 | 6.6 | 27.9 | 23.5 | 10.9 | 1.6 | 73.4 | 33.4 | 35.8 | 94.7 |
| FORT WALTON BEACH,FL | 3.1 | 4.9 | 7.7 | 7.5 | 6.7 | 6.1 | 6.9 | 32.7 | 20.5 | 11.0 | 0.8 | 74.5 | 31.5 | 34.4 | 99.8 |
| FORT WAYNE, IN | 1.7 | 2.9 | 7.5 | 7.6 | 7.7 | 7.2 | 6.2 | 30.2 | 21.8 | 10.2 | 1.5 | 72.7 | 32.2 | 34.9 | 95.0 |
| FT. WORTH-ARLINGTON | 11.1 | 14.7 | 8.1 | 7.8 | 7.5 | 7.3 | 6.8 | 31.4 | 22.1 | 8.1 | 1.0 | 72.4 | 30.8 | 34.1 | 97.6 |
| FRESNO, CA | 35.3 | 43.2 | 8.7 | 9.9 | 8.0 | 8.0 | 7.6 | 29.0 | 18.0 | 9.5 | 1.3 | 68.7 | 29.6 | 30.6 | 101.1 |
| GADSDEN, AL | 0.3 | 0.9 | 5.6 | 5.8 | 6.0 | 6.6 | 6.3 | 28.1 | 25.3 | 14.2 | 1.9 | 78.6 | 36.0 | 39.5 | 90.7 |
| GAINESVILLE, FL | 3.7 | 5.5 | 6.2 | 6.7 | 6.4 | 10.3 | 14.3 | 29.0 | 17.6 | 8.4 | 1.1 | 77.3 | 28.3 | 29.3 | 95.6 |
| GALVESTON-TEXAS CITY | 14.2 | 18.7 | 7.3 | 7.4 | 7.4 | 7.5 | 6.7 | 28.7 | 23.6 | 10.4 | 1.1 | 73.3 | 32.6 | 35.9 | 96.2 |
| GARY, IN | 8.0 | 11.5 | 6.9 | 7.0 | 7.3 | 7.4 | 6.7 | 29.3 | 22.8 | 11.2 | 1.3 | 74.3 | 32.9 | 35.9 | 92.8 |
| GLENS FALLS, NY | 1.5 | 2.2 | 6.5 | 7.5 | 7.0 | 6.6 | 5.9 | 29.4 | 23.3 | 12.0 | 1.8 | 75.2 | 33.7 | 36.7 | 100.7 |
| GOLDSBORO, NC | 1.3 | 2.8 | 7.4 | 7.3 | 7.1 | 6.5 | 7.2 | 31.8 | 21.1 | 10.4 | 1.1 | 74.2 | 31.8 | 33.8 | 101.0 |
| GRAND FORKS, ND-MN | 2.1 | 3.8 | 6.7 | 6.5 | 7.2 | 9.3 | 10.7 | 29.0 | 19.0 | 9.7 | 2.0 | 75.5 | 29.0 | 31.7 | 101.9 |
| GRAND JUNCTION, CO | 8.1 | 10.4 | 6.5 | 6.7 | 7.5 | 8.3 | 6.1 | 24.6 | 26.1 | 12.5 | 1.8 | 74.4 | 34.7 | 38.7 | 94.7 |
| GR.RAPIDS-MSKGN-HOLL | 3.1 | 4.4 | 7.5 | 8.0 | 8.3 | 7.9 | 6.4 | 30.3 | 20.6 | 9.5 | 1.5 | 71.7 | 31.1 | 33.8 | 95.6 |
| GREAT FALLS, MT | 1.8 | 2.5 | 6.5 | 6.5 | 7.4 | 7.7 | 7.3 | 26.1 | 25.2 | 11.4 | 1.8 | 74.9 | 32.7 | 37.3 | 97.0 |
| GREELEY, CO | 20.9 | 25.5 | 7.6 | 7.4 | 7.5 | 8.9 | 8.7 | 27.9 | 22.3 | 8.4 | 1.3 | 72.9 | 30.5 | 32.9 | 97.9 |
| GREEN BAY, WI | 0.8 | 1.5 | 6.6 | 7.1 | 7.9 | 7.7 | 6.6 | 31.8 | 21.7 | 9.2 | 1.4 | 74.1 | 31.4 | 34.8 | 95.2 |
| G'BORO-W.SLM-H.PT,NC | 0.7 | 1.8 | 6.5 | 6.8 | 7.0 | 6.5 | 6.0 | 30.4 | 23.8 | 11.6 | 1.6 | 76.3 | 34.2 | 37.1 | 91.7 |
| GREENVILLE, NC | 0.9 | 2.0 | 6.9 | 7.1 | 7.0 | 8.6 | 10.6 | 30.4 | 19.5 | 8.8 | 1.0 | 75.3 | 29.5 | 31.6 | 91.3 |
| GREENVL-SPAR'BG-ANDR | 0.7 | 1.5 | 5.9 | 6.4 | 6.8 | 7.2 | 6.8 | 29.4 | 24.7 | 11.5 | 1.4 | 77.2 | 33.5 | 37.4 | 93.2 |
| HAGERSTOWN, MD | 0.7 | 1.5 | 6.1 | 6.5 | 6.7 | 6.4 | 6.4 | 30.9 | 22.4 | 12.9 | 1.8 | 77.1 | 34.4 | 36.9 | 102.7 |
| HAMILTON-MIDDLETOWN | 0.5 | 1.0 | 6.6 | 7.1 | 7.4 | 8.3 | 8.0 | 29.5 | 21.9 | 10.1 | 1.2 | 74.7 | 31.5 | 34.7 | 93.6 |
| HARR'BG-LEBANON-CARL | 1.7 | 2.8 | 5.6 | 6.4 | 6.9 | 6.7 | 5.9 | 30.1 | 23.5 | 13.0 | 1.8 | 77.4 | 34.8 | 38.1 | 93.4 |
| HARTFORD, CT | 6.8 | 9.0 | 6.4 | 7.1 | 7.4 | 6.4 | 5.6 | 30.5 | 22.2 | 12.4 | 2.0 | 75.6 | 34.2 | 37.1 | 93.7 |
| HATTIESBURG, MS | 0.7 | 1.2 | 7.1 | 7.0 | 6.9 | 8.7 | 10.6 | 29.2 | 19.8 | 9.3 | 1.3 | 74.6 | 29.3 | 31.6 | 89.5 |
| HICKRY-MRGNTN-LENOIR | 0.6 | 1.7 | 6.4 | 6.8 | 7.2 | 6.5 | 5.4 | 29.7 | 24.9 | 11.7 | 1.4 | 75.7 | 34.6 | 37.6 | 96.1 |
| HONOLULU, HI | 6.8 | 7.6 | 6.6 | 6.9 | 6.1 | 6.8 | 7.6 | 29.0 | 23.1 | 12.5 | 1.5 | 76.8 | 32.2 | 37.3 | 99.1 |
| HOUMA, LA | 1.4 | 2.2 | 7.8 | 7.9 | 8.1 | 8.7 | 7.0 | 29.1 | 21.7 | 8.7 | 0.9 | 71.0 | 29.3 | 33.0 | 96.0 |
| HOUSTON, TX | 21.3 | 26.0 | 8.3 | 8.0 | 7.8 | 7.7 | 6.9 | 31.7 | 21.8 | 7.0 | 0.8 | 71.2 | 30.4 | 33.1 | 98.3 |
| HUNTINGTON-ASHLAND | 0.4 | 0.9 | 5.5 | 5.8 | 6.1 | 7.2 | 7.2 | 27.5 | 25.7 | 13.2 | 1.7 | 78.5 | 35.3 | 38.9 | 91.9 |
| HUNTSVILLE, AL | 1.1 | 2.2 | 6.7 | 6.5 | 6.1 | 6.6 | 7.1 | 33.3 | 23.0 | 9.6 | 1.1 | 77.1 | 32.0 | 35.7 | 96.1 |
| INDIANAPOLIS, IN | 0.9 | 1.6 | 7.2 | 7.2 | 7.2 | 6.8 | 6.2 | 31.9 | 22.3 | 9.9 | 1.4 | 74.3 | 32.5 | 35.5 | 93.4 |
| IOWA CITY, IA | 1.5 | 3.0 | 5.7 | 5.4 | 5.5 | 10.1 | 16.7 | 32.1 | 17.2 | 6.4 | 1.0 | 80.3 | 27.3 | 29.0 | 96.7 |
| JACKSON, MI | 1.5 | 2.3 | 6.4 | 7.0 | 7.3 | 7.0 | 6.4 | 30.5 | 22.6 | 11.3 | 1.6 | 75.2 | 33.4 | 36.2 | 103.6 |
| JACKSON, MS | 0.5 | 0.9 | 7.1 | 7.2 | 7.4 | 8.1 | 7.4 | 30.6 | 21.5 | 9.3 | 1.3 | 73.8 | 31.0 | 34.1 | 89.5 |
| JACKSON, TN | 0.5 | 1.0 | 6.8 | 7.1 | 7.1 | 7.8 | 7.4 | 29.2 | 22.0 | 10.9 | 1.7 | 75.1 | 32.9 | 35.3 | 90.4 |
| JACKSONVILLE, FL | 2.5 | 4.0 | 7.3 | 7.9 | 7.9 | 7.1 | 6.4 | 30.4 | 21.7 | 10.2 | 1.2 | 72.9 | 32.1 | 35.0 | 94.4 |
| JACKSONVILLE, NC | 5.4 | 9.9 | 10.3 | 8.3 | 6.6 | 7.3 | 17.3 | 31.3 | 12.3 | 6.0 | 0.6 | 72.4 | 24.6 | 25.1 | 132.2 |
| JAMESTOWN, NY | 2.9 | 4.3 | 6.4 | 7.7 | 7.0 | 7.4 | 6.4 | 26.8 | 22.3 | 13.6 | 2.3 | 75.0 | 34.3 | 37.0 | 95.3 |
| JANESVILLE-BELOIT,WI | 1.3 | 2.2 | 6.3 | 6.7 | 8.0 | 7.8 | 6.3 | 29.0 | 23.2 | 10.9 | 1.7 | 74.3 | 33.0 | 36.3 | 96.1 |
| JERSEY CITY, NJ | 33.2 | 41.6 | 6.8 | 6.5 | 6.3 | 6.0 | 7.1 | 34.7 | 20.9 | 10.3 | 1.4 | 77.0 | 33.1 | 35.4 | 96.4 |
| J.CITY-KNGSPRT-BRIST | 0.4 | 1.1 | 5.4 | 5.7 | 6.1 | 6.4 | 6.0 | 29.0 | 26.3 | 13.3 | 1.8 | 79.2 | 36.3 | 39.6 | 93.4 |
| JOHNSTOWN, PA | 0.5 | 1.1 | 5.3 | 6.0 | 6.3 | 6.8 | 6.2 | 26.9 | 23.7 | 16.3 | 2.3 | 78.3 | 37.0 | 40.1 | 93.0 |
| JONESBORO, AR | 0.6 | 1.8 | 6.9 | 6.6 | 6.9 | 8.1 | 9.3 | 28.6 | 22.1 | 10.2 | 1.4 | 75.8 | 31.6 | 34.1 | 92.7 |
| JOPLIN, MO | 0.9 | 1.6 | 6.4 | 6.8 | 7.3 | 7.6 | 6.4 | 28.0 | 22.9 | 12.6 | 1.9 | 75.2 | 34.3 | 36.9 | 93.8 |
| KALAMAZOO-BATTLE CRK | 2.0 | 3.0 | 6.5 | 6.9 | 7.3 | 8.2 | 8.2 | 28.3 | 22.3 | 10.7 | 1.6 | 75.0 | 32.3 | 35.0 | 94.0 |
| KANKAKEE, IL | 2.0 | 3.2 | 7.4 | 8.0 | 7.7 | 7.7 | 6.5 | 28.0 | 21.7 | 11.4 | 1.6 | 72.3 | 32.9 | 35.1 | 94.9 |
| KANSAS CITY, MO-KS | 2.9 | 4.3 | 6.8 | 7.0 | 7.7 | 7.3 | 6.2 | 31.0 | 22.5 | 10.2 | 1.5 | 74.2 | 32.9 | 35.9 | 93.7 |
| KENOSHA, WI | 4.4 | 6.8 | 6.8 | 7.2 | 7.9 | 7.6 | 6.5 | 29.5 | 22.1 | 10.8 | 1.6 | 73.8 | 32.5 | 35.5 | 96.6 |
| KILLEEN-TEMPLE, TX | 12.2 | 16.8 | 10.1 | 8.0 | 6.5 | 7.5 | 11.9 | 32.8 | 15.4 | 6.8 | 1.0 | 71.9 | 27.2 | 28.0 | 106.9 |
| KNOXVILLE, TN | 0.5 | 1.3 | 6.1 | 6.2 | 6.2 | 6.7 | 6.9 | 30.2 | 24.6 | 11.7 | 1.5 | 77.9 | 34.6 | 37.6 | 92.2 |
| KOKOMO, IN | 1.2 | 2.2 | 6.6 | 6.7 | 7.1 | 6.9 | 5.7 | 28.9 | 25.0 | 11.5 | 1.5 | 75.3 | 34.3 | 37.6 | 92.5 |
| UNITED STATES | 9.0 | 11.8 | 6.9 | 7.2 | 7.2 | 7.2 | 6.7 | 29.9 | 22.2 | 11.1 | 1.6 | 74.6 | 32.9 | 35.7 | 95.6 |

# HOUSEHOLDS

## MSA AND U.S. TOTALS

| MSA | HOUSEHOLDS | | | | | FAMILIES | | | MEDIAN HOUSEHOLD INCOME | | |
|---|---|---|---|---|---|---|---|---|---|---|---|
| | 1990 | 2000 | 2005 | % Annual Rate 1990-2000 | 2000 Average HH Size | 1990 | 2000 | % Annual Rate 1990-2000 | 2000 | 2005 | 2000 National Rank |
| DETROIT, MI | 1,580,063 | 1,715,135 | 1,758,158 | 1.0 | 2.58 | 1,120,599 | 1,182,257 | 0.7 | 46,570 | 51,445 | 56 |
| DOTHAN, AL | 48,418 | 51,885 | 53,510 | 0.8 | 2.57 | 35,962 | 37,412 | 0.5 | 34,796 | 39,631 | 257 |
| DOVER, DE | 39,655 | 47,211 | 50,723 | 2.1 | 2.62 | 29,343 | 33,796 | 1.7 | 41,669 | 50,793 | 123 |
| DUBUQUE, IA | 30,799 | 31,508 | 31,625 | 0.3 | 2.66 | 22,150 | 21,902 | -0.1 | 39,775 | 43,185 | 155 |
| DULUTH-SUPERIOR | 95,275 | 95,638 | 95,495 | 0.0 | 2.40 | 62,916 | 60,836 | -0.4 | 38,090 | 41,677 | 186 |
| DUTCHESS COUNTY, NY | 89,567 | 95,192 | 99,803 | 0.7 | 2.66 | 64,757 | 66,536 | 0.3 | 49,921 | 59,550 | 35 |
| EAU CLAIRE, WI | 50,359 | 54,282 | 55,940 | 0.9 | 2.57 | 34,652 | 36,057 | 0.5 | 39,521 | 46,303 | 161 |
| EL PASO, TX | 178,366 | 220,611 | 236,814 | 2.6 | 3.18 | 142,854 | 175,636 | 2.5 | 30,494 | 35,140 | 304 |
| ELKHART-GOSHEN, IN | 56,713 | 65,051 | 69,188 | 1.7 | 2.67 | 41,751 | 46,631 | 1.3 | 45,196 | 54,137 | 76 |
| ELMIRA, NY | 35,275 | 34,675 | 34,211 | -0.2 | 2.49 | 24,808 | 23,529 | -0.6 | 35,495 | 40,813 | 246 |
| ENID, OK | 22,460 | 22,766 | 22,877 | 0.2 | 2.44 | 15,738 | 15,327 | -0.3 | 33,003 | 36,923 | 281 |
| ERIE, PA | 101,564 | 103,566 | 102,708 | 0.2 | 2.55 | 71,125 | 70,295 | -0.1 | 38,400 | 43,045 | 183 |
| EUGENE-SPRINGFLD, OR | 110,799 | 127,342 | 133,810 | 1.7 | 2.43 | 73,498 | 81,206 | 1.2 | 35,516 | 40,344 | 245 |
| EVANSVILLE-HENDERSON | 108,663 | 114,735 | 117,105 | 0.7 | 2.48 | 76,611 | 78,802 | 0.3 | 41,112 | 46,064 | 130 |
| FARGO-MOORHEAD,ND-MN | 57,771 | 66,686 | 70,917 | 1.8 | 2.46 | 37,140 | 40,820 | 1.2 | 38,373 | 43,654 | 184 |
| FAYETTEVILLE, NC | 91,500 | 95,949 | 95,284 | 0.6 | 2.75 | 69,966 | 71,580 | 0.3 | 37,288 | 44,881 | 206 |
| FAYETTEVL-SPRNGD-ROG | 80,927 | 110,926 | 122,400 | 3.9 | 2.55 | 58,962 | 78,300 | 3.5 | 34,924 | 39,863 | 256 |
| FLAGSTAFF, AZ-UT | 31,642 | 39,120 | 40,891 | 2.6 | 2.92 | 22,486 | 25,012 | 1.3 | 37,266 | 42,448 | 209 |
| FLINT, MI | 161,296 | 169,438 | 174,036 | 0.6 | 2.56 | 115,849 | 118,061 | 0.2 | 45,205 | 50,531 | 75 |
| FLORENCE, AL | 51,001 | 55,237 | 56,297 | 1.0 | 2.45 | 38,140 | 40,143 | 0.6 | 35,933 | 39,457 | 230 |
| FLORENCE, SC | 40,217 | 46,683 | 49,086 | 1.8 | 2.64 | 30,175 | 34,095 | 1.5 | 35,524 | 39,585 | 243 |
| FT. COLLINS-LOVELAND | 70,472 | 93,407 | 104,606 | 3.5 | 2.53 | 47,247 | 61,031 | 3.2 | 49,808 | 57,664 | 37 |
| FORT LAUDERDALE, FL | 528,442 | 651,888 | 709,903 | 2.6 | 2.38 | 335,022 | 398,711 | 2.1 | 40,269 | 47,132 | 145 |
| FT. MYERS-CAPE CORAL | 140,124 | 167,954 | 181,376 | 2.2 | 2.40 | 99,698 | 116,156 | 1.9 | 38,522 | 46,997 | 179 |
| FT.PIERCE-P.ST.LUCIE | 101,196 | 121,294 | 129,722 | 2.2 | 2.47 | 73,377 | 85,782 | 1.9 | 41,102 | 49,260 | 131 |
| FORT SMITH, AR-OK | 66,884 | 75,525 | 79,083 | 1.5 | 2.58 | 49,413 | 54,249 | 1.1 | 31,610 | 36,479 | 299 |
| FORT WALTON BEACH,FL | 53,313 | 63,615 | 66,393 | 2.2 | 2.62 | 39,703 | 45,699 | 1.7 | 38,463 | 43,141 | 180 |
| FORT WAYNE, IN | 168,806 | 183,804 | 191,746 | 1.0 | 2.61 | 121,885 | 129,524 | 0.7 | 44,967 | 50,524 | 79 |
| FT. WORTH-ARLINGTON | 506,281 | 625,871 | 697,455 | 2.6 | 2.63 | 360,454 | 433,503 | 2.3 | 47,152 | 56,579 | 52 |
| FRESNO, CA | 249,303 | 292,164 | 307,570 | 1.9 | 2.95 | 184,316 | 212,377 | 1.7 | 37,522 | 44,882 | 198 |
| GADSDEN, AL | 38,675 | 41,461 | 42,206 | 0.8 | 2.47 | 28,585 | 29,852 | 0.5 | 32,308 | 36,650 | 292 |
| GAINESVILLE, FL | 71,258 | 77,781 | 78,840 | 1.1 | 2.41 | 41,151 | 43,289 | 0.6 | 30,368 | 33,671 | 306 |
| GALVESTON-TEXAS CITY | 81,451 | 95,461 | 101,997 | 1.9 | 2.61 | 58,178 | 66,337 | 1.6 | 43,390 | 49,326 | 103 |
| GARY, IN | 215,907 | 228,503 | 232,881 | 0.7 | 2.72 | 160,395 | 165,089 | 0.4 | 44,562 | 49,821 | 86 |
| GLENS FALLS, NY | 42,815 | 45,239 | 45,829 | 0.7 | 2.59 | 30,811 | 31,447 | 0.2 | 38,897 | 45,689 | 173 |
| GOLDSBORO, NC | 36,889 | 39,598 | 39,918 | 0.9 | 2.62 | 27,577 | 28,747 | 0.5 | 34,948 | 41,246 | 255 |
| GRAND FORKS, ND-MN | 37,324 | 35,269 | 33,967 | -0.7 | 2.45 | 25,364 | 22,970 | -1.2 | 34,560 | 40,290 | 263 |
| GRAND JUNCTION, CO | 36,250 | 46,717 | 51,792 | 3.1 | 2.46 | 25,419 | 31,687 | 2.7 | 37,891 | 44,456 | 189 |
| GR.RAPIDS-MSKGN-HOLL | 333,911 | 385,981 | 412,126 | 1.8 | 2.69 | 245,075 | 276,697 | 1.5 | 45,859 | 52,506 | 65 |
| GREAT FALLS, MT | 30,133 | 31,554 | 31,352 | 0.6 | 2.41 | 21,037 | 21,238 | 0.1 | 31,811 | 35,503 | 297 |
| GREELEY, CO | 47,470 | 61,534 | 70,806 | 3.2 | 2.71 | 33,763 | 42,693 | 2.9 | 38,270 | 46,189 | 185 |
| GREEN BAY, WI | 72,280 | 83,173 | 87,147 | 1.7 | 2.55 | 50,504 | 56,607 | 1.4 | 45,848 | 51,570 | 66 |
| G'BORO-W.SLM-H.PT,NC | 414,793 | 473,373 | 500,806 | 1.6 | 2.46 | 293,261 | 324,725 | 1.2 | 39,189 | 44,177 | 166 |
| GREENVILLE, NC | 40,491 | 49,511 | 53,340 | 2.5 | 2.50 | 26,434 | 30,942 | 1.9 | 35,552 | 39,873 | 242 |
| GREENVL-SPAR'BG-ANDR | 312,740 | 371,660 | 403,592 | 2.1 | 2.47 | 228,567 | 264,268 | 1.8 | 39,481 | 44,633 | 163 |
| HAGERSTOWN, MD | 44,762 | 48,208 | 49,432 | 0.9 | 2.49 | 32,349 | 33,780 | 0.5 | 41,059 | 49,074 | 133 |
| HAMILTON-MIDDLETOWN | 104,535 | 124,647 | 132,094 | 2.2 | 2.61 | 77,931 | 90,946 | 1.9 | 45,953 | 52,437 | 62 |
| HARR'BG-LEBANON-CARL | 226,353 | 242,527 | 247,810 | 0.8 | 2.47 | 157,924 | 163,775 | 0.4 | 43,304 | 48,599 | 105 |
| HARTFORD, CT | 423,651 | 426,333 | 433,719 | 0.1 | 2.53 | 294,375 | 285,804 | -0.4 | 51,217 | 59,674 | 32 |
| HATTIESBURG, MS | 36,033 | 42,854 | 46,581 | 2.1 | 2.56 | 25,223 | 29,289 | 1.8 | 30,891 | 35,590 | 302 |
| HICKRY-MRGNTN-LENOIR | 112,387 | 127,330 | 135,320 | 1.5 | 2.54 | 84,189 | 92,462 | 1.1 | 37,094 | 41,740 | 211 |
| HONOLULU, HI | 265,304 | 292,879 | 296,902 | 1.2 | 2.82 | 197,294 | 216,777 | 1.1 | 52,209 | 61,436 | 26 |
| HOUMA, LA | 60,672 | 68,355 | 72,685 | 1.5 | 2.84 | 48,110 | 52,845 | 1.1 | 31,931 | 35,800 | 296 |
| HOUSTON, TX | 1,193,305 | 1,472,369 | 1,620,381 | 2.6 | 2.75 | 835,457 | 1,017,709 | 2.4 | 43,292 | 49,839 | 106 |
| HUNTINGTON-ASHLAND | 119,640 | 123,047 | 122,824 | 0.3 | 2.47 | 88,354 | 88,144 | 0.0 | 28,548 | 31,561 | 314 |
| HUNTSVILLE, AL | 110,893 | 136,779 | 147,407 | 2.6 | 2.48 | 80,752 | 96,530 | 2.2 | 45,443 | 50,951 | 74 |
| INDIANAPOLIS, IN | 529,814 | 602,823 | 637,403 | 1.6 | 2.53 | 368,546 | 409,586 | 1.3 | 45,706 | 51,639 | 68 |
| IOWA CITY, IA | 36,067 | 39,208 | 40,988 | 1.0 | 2.43 | 20,317 | 21,143 | 0.5 | 40,361 | 46,914 | 142 |
| JACKSON, MI | 53,660 | 58,578 | 61,241 | 1.1 | 2.55 | 38,878 | 41,255 | 0.7 | 40,997 | 47,499 | 134 |
| JACKSON, MS | 140,157 | 159,649 | 169,178 | 1.6 | 2.64 | 101,558 | 112,888 | 1.3 | 39,235 | 45,847 | 165 |
| JACKSON, TN | 34,167 | 39,598 | 42,308 | 1.8 | 2.50 | 24,806 | 28,036 | 1.5 | 36,347 | 41,301 | 225 |
| JACKSONVILLE, FL | 343,526 | 408,368 | 437,028 | 2.1 | 2.59 | 240,414 | 277,449 | 1.8 | 42,338 | 50,026 | 113 |
| JACKSONVILLE, NC | 40,658 | 41,002 | 40,950 | 0.1 | 2.79 | 32,971 | 32,616 | -0.1 | 32,286 | 40,783 | 293 |
| JAMESTOWN, NY | 53,696 | 52,768 | 51,527 | -0.2 | 2.47 | 37,203 | 35,191 | -0.7 | 32,870 | 37,549 | 288 |
| JANESVILLE-BELOIT,WI | 52,252 | 57,654 | 59,184 | 1.2 | 2.56 | 37,520 | 39,918 | 0.8 | 45,012 | 51,323 | 78 |
| JERSEY CITY, NJ | 208,739 | 212,031 | 213,634 | 0.2 | 2.57 | 136,143 | 137,005 | 0.1 | 40,632 | 49,862 | 136 |
| J.CITY-KNGSPRT-BRIST | 170,569 | 189,356 | 196,608 | 1.3 | 2.40 | 126,603 | 135,973 | 0.9 | 32,680 | 36,160 | 289 |
| JOHNSTOWN, PA | 91,578 | 89,748 | 87,581 | -0.2 | 2.47 | 66,236 | 62,518 | -0.7 | 30,102 | 33,108 | 308 |
| JONESBORO, AR | 26,285 | 30,773 | 32,638 | 1.9 | 2.46 | 18,877 | 21,493 | 1.6 | 31,414 | 36,363 | 300 |
| JOPLIN, MO | 53,020 | 60,090 | 63,151 | 1.5 | 2.47 | 37,568 | 41,179 | 1.1 | 32,943 | 37,434 | 284 |
| KALAMAZOO-BATTLE CRK | 160,916 | 173,077 | 178,055 | 0.9 | 2.51 | 110,832 | 115,650 | 0.5 | 39,925 | 44,090 | 153 |
| KANKAKEE, IL | 34,623 | 37,367 | 38,170 | 0.9 | 2.66 | 24,922 | 26,102 | 0.6 | 41,558 | 48,645 | 125 |
| KANSAS CITY, MO-KS | 608,459 | 683,197 | 720,719 | 1.4 | 2.55 | 421,893 | 461,245 | 1.1 | 45,665 | 52,142 | 69 |
| KENOSHA, WI | 47,029 | 55,106 | 58,792 | 1.9 | 2.64 | 33,926 | 38,277 | 1.5 | 46,292 | 53,822 | 60 |
| KILLEEN-TEMPLE, TX | 83,927 | 101,350 | 103,786 | 2.3 | 2.69 | 63,983 | 75,396 | 2.0 | 35,707 | 43,699 | 234 |
| KNOXVILLE, TN | 231,254 | 272,026 | 286,195 | 2.0 | 2.44 | 164,123 | 188,678 | 1.7 | 37,799 | 42,196 | 193 |
| KOKOMO, IN | 37,549 | 39,353 | 39,862 | 0.6 | 2.52 | 27,283 | 27,642 | 0.2 | 46,607 | 51,873 | 55 |
| UNITED STATES | | | | 1.4 | 2.59 | | | 1.1 | 41,914 | 49,127 | |

| MSA | 2000 Per Capita Income | 2000 HH Income Base | 2000 HOUSEHOLD INCOME DISTRIBUTION (%) | | | | | | 2000 AVERAGE DISPOSABLE INCOME BY AGE OF HOUSEHOLDER | | | | | |
|---|---|---|---|---|---|---|---|---|---|---|---|---|---|---|
| | | | Less than $15,000 | $15,000 to $24,999 | $25,000 to $49,999 | $50,000 to $99,999 | $100,000 to $149,999 | $150,000 or More | All Ages | <35 | 35-44 | 45-54 | 55-64 | 65+ |
| DETROIT, MI | 24,656 | 1,715,111 | 15.1 | 9.7 | 28.9 | 33.1 | 8.7 | 4.5 | 43,556 | 35,625 | 46,834 | 54,618 | 48,602 | 26,796 |
| DOTHAN, AL | 17,682 | 51,885 | 18.6 | 15.1 | 35.4 | 25.2 | 4.3 | 1.4 | 34,528 | 30,058 | 40,198 | 44,818 | 37,110 | 21,507 |
| DOVER, DE | 19,567 | 47,211 | 11.7 | 12.5 | 36.6 | 31.2 | 6.1 | 1.9 | 37,892 | 31,426 | 41,892 | 47,592 | 41,616 | 26,807 |
| DUBUQUE, IA | 18,210 | 31,504 | 13.4 | 13.2 | 37.8 | 28.5 | 5.2 | 1.8 | 35,322 | 28,007 | 41,595 | 46,331 | 37,376 | 24,278 |
| DULUTH-SUPERIOR | 19,837 | 95,638 | 16.5 | 12.8 | 36.6 | 26.8 | 5.5 | 1.9 | 34,229 | 28,729 | 41,147 | 45,264 | 37,298 | 22,655 |
| DUTCHESS COUNTY, NY | 21,988 | 95,192 | 10.6 | 9.4 | 30.1 | 39.6 | 7.9 | 2.4 | 40,060 | 37,661 | 43,845 | 48,995 | 44,867 | 23,749 |
| EAU CLAIRE, WI | 18,309 | 54,276 | 14.9 | 12.4 | 36.9 | 29.2 | 5.3 | 1.3 | 32,938 | 28,160 | 39,241 | 43,289 | 34,731 | 20,729 |
| EL PASO, TX | 12,891 | 220,608 | 22.1 | 18.5 | 33.2 | 21.2 | 3.6 | 1.3 | 32,323 | 26,167 | 33,819 | 38,646 | 36,678 | 26,283 |
| ELKHART-GOSHEN, IN | 21,332 | 65,048 | 8.4 | 10.7 | 37.4 | 34.4 | 7.0 | 2.0 | 41,489 | 35,756 | 44,775 | 51,560 | 46,259 | 27,725 |
| ELMIRA, NY | 17,597 | 34,674 | 16.9 | 15.8 | 37.6 | 23.9 | 4.2 | 1.6 | 31,416 | 28,238 | 37,520 | 40,215 | 33,439 | 19,959 |
| ENID, OK | 16,644 | 22,766 | 17.9 | 16.9 | 38.2 | 22.2 | 3.8 | 1.0 | 31,738 | 27,199 | 36,651 | 39,416 | 34,279 | 24,575 |
| ERIE, PA | 18,894 | 103,566 | 15.2 | 13.2 | 37.3 | 27.7 | 5.1 | 1.6 | 35,189 | 30,211 | 39,791 | 46,292 | 40,073 | 22,594 |
| EUGENE-SPRINGFLD, OR | 18,245 | 127,331 | 17.3 | 15.6 | 35.9 | 25.3 | 4.4 | 1.4 | 31,669 | 25,212 | 36,517 | 41,602 | 35,215 | 21,753 |
| EVANSVILLE-HENDERSON | 21,858 | 114,733 | 13.9 | 12.7 | 34.9 | 29.3 | 6.7 | 2.6 | 39,315 | 33,663 | 45,486 | 48,704 | 42,044 | 25,096 |
| FARGO-MOORHEAD,ND-MN | 19,047 | 66,682 | 15.5 | 13.4 | 36.7 | 27.4 | 5.3 | 1.8 | 36,130 | 27,904 | 42,478 | 46,930 | 41,064 | 26,876 |
| FAYETTEVILLE, NC | 16,561 | 95,949 | 12.9 | 16.7 | 37.2 | 27.7 | 4.4 | 1.2 | 34,680 | 29,525 | 39,742 | 43,472 | 37,356 | 25,701 |
| FAYETTEVL-SPRNGD-ROG | 16,997 | 110,926 | 15.5 | 17.1 | 38.0 | 24.6 | 3.8 | 1.1 | 33,176 | 27,379 | 39,542 | 41,977 | 36,114 | 25,104 |
| FLAGSTAFF, AZ-UT | 16,024 | 39,105 | 17.9 | 14.1 | 33.4 | 27.4 | 5.6 | 1.7 | 36,320 | 27,579 | 42,779 | 46,161 | 39,482 | 28,084 |
| FLINT, MI | 21,520 | 169,425 | 16.6 | 9.8 | 29.4 | 34.4 | 7.5 | 2.2 | 39,077 | 30,852 | 44,905 | 52,374 | 42,707 | 24,694 |
| FLORENCE, AL | 19,375 | 55,223 | 18.7 | 14.9 | 34.2 | 25.2 | 5.1 | 1.8 | 35,637 | 30,755 | 43,283 | 44,881 | 37,559 | 23,476 |
| FLORENCE, SC | 17,461 | 46,683 | 20.5 | 14.1 | 33.9 | 24.7 | 4.8 | 2.0 | 33,960 | 30,447 | 37,035 | 42,684 | 33,322 | 21,543 |
| FT. COLLINS-LOVELAND | 26,696 | 93,407 | 10.0 | 10.4 | 29.8 | 34.6 | 10.3 | 5.0 | 46,705 | 35,169 | 52,948 | 57,487 | 49,795 | 31,200 |
| FORT LAUDERDALE, FL | 24,450 | 651,888 | 14.1 | 14.5 | 32.9 | 28.0 | 6.7 | 3.8 | 43,079 | 38,441 | 47,454 | 50,510 | 45,330 | 30,528 |
| FT. MYERS-CAPE CORAL | 21,636 | 167,913 | 11.5 | 16.0 | 37.3 | 27.1 | 5.7 | 2.4 | 39,813 | 36,600 | 44,373 | 46,174 | 44,786 | 33,012 |
| FT.PIERCE-P.ST.LUCIE | 23,894 | 121,294 | 11.9 | 13.5 | 35.4 | 28.9 | 6.8 | 3.5 | 43,369 | 39,227 | 46,367 | 49,365 | 46,763 | 36,758 |
| FORT SMITH, AR-OK | 15,899 | 75,525 | 20.1 | 17.9 | 36.3 | 21.4 | 3.3 | 1.1 | 30,817 | 26,931 | 37,071 | 38,040 | 32,578 | 20,721 |
| FORT WALTON BEACH,FL | 18,353 | 63,614 | 10.7 | 16.8 | 37.6 | 29.2 | 4.4 | 1.4 | 37,941 | 30,369 | 40,099 | 47,722 | 42,511 | 32,613 |
| FORT WAYNE, IN | 21,553 | 183,802 | 9.5 | 11.5 | 35.9 | 34.1 | 6.9 | 2.1 | 41,180 | 35,674 | 45,424 | 51,946 | 45,345 | 26,338 |
| FT. WORTH-ARLINGTON | 23,458 | 625,870 | 10.2 | 11.1 | 31.9 | 34.5 | 8.9 | 3.5 | 46,210 | 37,802 | 50,358 | 55,888 | 49,301 | 31,414 |
| FRESNO, CA | 18,279 | 292,164 | 16.5 | 14.8 | 33.4 | 25.9 | 6.2 | 3.3 | 38,151 | 31,303 | 42,083 | 46,239 | 42,569 | 27,919 |
| GADSDEN, AL | 16,808 | 41,461 | 22.5 | 15.1 | 35.4 | 22.3 | 3.5 | 1.2 | 32,123 | 28,463 | 39,538 | 41,110 | 34,424 | 20,332 |
| GAINESVILLE, FL | 17,475 | 77,777 | 24.9 | 17.2 | 30.1 | 20.9 | 4.6 | 2.3 | 34,131 | 22,566 | 40,706 | 46,930 | 42,777 | 28,346 |
| GALVESTON-TEXAS CITY | 22,788 | 95,461 | 15.4 | 11.5 | 30.6 | 30.9 | 7.7 | 3.9 | 44,001 | 35,093 | 47,972 | 54,283 | 46,712 | 28,925 |
| GARY, IN | 20,840 | 228,497 | 13.8 | 10.8 | 32.3 | 32.8 | 7.3 | 2.9 | 41,472 | 34,805 | 46,164 | 51,027 | 45,308 | 26,748 |
| GLENS FALLS, NY | 19,387 | 45,239 | 14.0 | 13.2 | 38.2 | 28.0 | 4.7 | 1.9 | 34,215 | 31,456 | 39,695 | 42,095 | 36,251 | 22,183 |
| GOLDSBORO, NC | 16,288 | 39,598 | 17.2 | 16.2 | 37.4 | 24.8 | 3.6 | 0.9 | 32,136 | 28,299 | 38,143 | 40,303 | 34,017 | 20,846 |
| GRAND FORKS, ND-MN | 16,645 | 35,266 | 16.9 | 16.1 | 38.6 | 23.9 | 3.7 | 0.8 | 32,253 | 26,096 | 38,457 | 42,553 | 37,960 | 23,275 |
| GRAND JUNCTION, CO | 19,423 | 46,717 | 15.0 | 14.9 | 36.2 | 27.6 | 4.8 | 1.6 | 35,066 | 28,826 | 41,397 | 42,507 | 36,580 | 25,369 |
| GR.RAPIDS-MSKGN-HOLL | 21,766 | 385,979 | 10.4 | 10.1 | 34.9 | 33.7 | 8.2 | 2.7 | 41,242 | 35,713 | 45,998 | 52,819 | 45,907 | 24,420 |
| GREAT FALLS, MT | 16,912 | 31,549 | 18.7 | 19.3 | 36.8 | 20.9 | 3.3 | 1.1 | 30,142 | 23,316 | 35,527 | 36,251 | 32,478 | 23,702 |
| GREELEY, CO | 16,985 | 61,534 | 15.4 | 14.2 | 35.9 | 28.1 | 5.1 | 1.4 | 35,012 | 28,287 | 40,967 | 44,568 | 37,091 | 22,954 |
| GREEN BAY, WI | 22,818 | 83,170 | 11.3 | 9.1 | 34.9 | 33.8 | 8.0 | 2.8 | 38,799 | 32,360 | 43,691 | 50,911 | 42,639 | 22,566 |
| G'BORO-W.SLM-H.PT,NC | 21,070 | 473,372 | 14.3 | 14.0 | 35.6 | 27.8 | 5.9 | 2.5 | 37,471 | 32,134 | 42,689 | 46,452 | 39,319 | 24,365 |
| GREENVILLE, NC | 18,477 | 49,511 | 21.0 | 14.8 | 31.7 | 24.9 | 5.2 | 2.4 | 34,623 | 28,141 | 40,004 | 45,876 | 36,459 | 21,973 |
| GREENVL-SPAR'BG-ANDR | 20,563 | 371,658 | 15.0 | 13.2 | 35.3 | 28.2 | 6.0 | 2.3 | 37,241 | 33,182 | 42,372 | 46,066 | 38,314 | 23,167 |
| HAGERSTOWN, MD | 19,415 | 48,206 | 13.3 | 11.4 | 37.7 | 30.7 | 5.6 | 1.4 | 35,663 | 32,899 | 41,347 | 44,617 | 37,204 | 24,084 |
| HAMILTON-MIDDLETOWN | 22,050 | 124,646 | 11.8 | 10.9 | 32.0 | 34.3 | 8.0 | 3.1 | 41,952 | 34,559 | 47,326 | 53,313 | 45,004 | 26,354 |
| HARR'BG-LEBANON-CARL | 21,289 | 242,526 | 10.4 | 11.9 | 36.8 | 32.9 | 6.2 | 1.8 | 38,652 | 34,746 | 43,363 | 48,753 | 42,222 | 25,142 |
| HARTFORD, CT | 25,816 | 426,327 | 10.6 | 8.8 | 29.0 | 38.0 | 9.5 | 4.2 | 44,641 | 38,893 | 47,483 | 55,364 | 49,530 | 28,030 |
| HATTIESBURG, MS | 17,497 | 42,852 | 24.1 | 16.7 | 30.7 | 21.2 | 4.8 | 2.6 | 34,128 | 27,112 | 39,040 | 42,919 | 35,848 | 22,435 |
| HICKRY-MRGNTN-LENOIR | 17,489 | 127,330 | 14.4 | 14.0 | 39.6 | 27.4 | 3.6 | 1.0 | 33,746 | 30,794 | 38,894 | 42,068 | 35,600 | 21,616 |
| HONOLULU, HI | 24,093 | 292,876 | 8.2 | 10.4 | 28.7 | 37.3 | 10.6 | 4.8 | 43,380 | 31,931 | 43,018 | 52,950 | 50,711 | 37,873 |
| HOUMA, LA | 15,072 | 68,349 | 22.2 | 16.3 | 34.1 | 22.5 | 3.8 | 1.2 | 32,891 | 28,213 | 38,050 | 40,768 | 31,949 | 21,880 |
| HOUSTON, TX | 22,475 | 1,472,365 | 13.7 | 12.6 | 30.8 | 30.5 | 8.3 | 4.2 | 45,278 | 35,263 | 48,361 | 52,461 | 47,810 | 31,735 |
| HUNTINGTON-ASHLAND | 15,162 | 123,047 | 27.5 | 16.9 | 32.8 | 18.7 | 2.9 | 1.3 | 29,124 | 23,815 | 35,578 | 36,335 | 30,996 | 19,572 |
| HUNTSVILLE, AL | 23,540 | 136,777 | 12.6 | 10.6 | 31.7 | 33.6 | 8.3 | 3.1 | 43,787 | 37,245 | 47,242 | 54,884 | 48,525 | 27,890 |
| INDIANAPOLIS, IN | 24,354 | 602,815 | 11.4 | 11.6 | 32.0 | 33.0 | 8.1 | 3.9 | 44,179 | 36,739 | 48,217 | 54,291 | 46,799 | 27,765 |
| IOWA CITY, IA | 22,010 | 39,207 | 15.1 | 13.5 | 32.0 | 27.4 | 7.5 | 4.5 | 40,007 | 27,167 | 47,050 | 55,462 | 55,386 | 31,478 |
| JACKSON, MI | 19,654 | 58,578 | 14.1 | 12.2 | 35.0 | 30.2 | 6.4 | 2.2 | 37,208 | 31,551 | 42,819 | 49,009 | 41,624 | 23,168 |
| JACKSON, MS | 19,686 | 159,648 | 17.6 | 13.3 | 31.9 | 27.9 | 6.5 | 2.8 | 39,044 | 33,583 | 43,075 | 46,906 | 39,134 | 25,094 |
| JACKSON, TN | 18,347 | 39,598 | 17.4 | 14.7 | 34.8 | 25.8 | 5.4 | 1.9 | 37,430 | 33,400 | 43,322 | 47,890 | 38,879 | 23,331 |
| JACKSONVILLE, FL | 21,718 | 408,363 | 12.2 | 12.7 | 34.3 | 31.4 | 6.8 | 2.7 | 42,326 | 35,689 | 45,978 | 50,989 | 45,486 | 30,627 |
| JACKSONVILLE, NC | 14,852 | 41,002 | 12.4 | 22.2 | 40.8 | 22.2 | 2.0 | 0.5 | 30,428 | 25,937 | 35,985 | 38,813 | 35,674 | 23,625 |
| JAMESTOWN, NY | 16,417 | 52,768 | 19.7 | 16.6 | 37.8 | 21.4 | 3.4 | 1.1 | 29,164 | 25,571 | 34,671 | 37,941 | 32,080 | 19,135 |
| JANESVILLE-BELOIT,WI | 21,830 | 57,654 | 11.1 | 10.4 | 35.3 | 34.0 | 7.2 | 2.0 | 36,873 | 32,193 | 41,817 | 47,940 | 39,931 | 22,572 |
| JERSEY CITY, NJ | 20,807 | 212,030 | 17.0 | 11.8 | 32.2 | 29.3 | 7.1 | 2.7 | 36,115 | 37,215 | 38,510 | 40,693 | 40,037 | 22,770 |
| J.CITY-KNGSPRT-BRIST | 17,597 | 189,345 | 21.1 | 16.4 | 34.8 | 22.4 | 4.0 | 1.4 | 33,571 | 30,006 | 39,802 | 41,870 | 34,899 | 21,677 |
| JOHNSTOWN, PA | 14,983 | 89,743 | 21.1 | 19.2 | 37.2 | 19.4 | 2.4 | 0.8 | 28,085 | 26,290 | 33,859 | 36,314 | 30,382 | 19,145 |
| JONESBORO, AR | 16,627 | 30,773 | 21.1 | 17.2 | 35.3 | 21.8 | 3.2 | 1.4 | 31,284 | 25,833 | 38,435 | 40,045 | 35,367 | 19,456 |
| JOPLIN, MO | 16,742 | 60,090 | 18.1 | 17.6 | 36.8 | 23.0 | 3.4 | 1.0 | 31,845 | 28,631 | 37,248 | 40,733 | 33,288 | 20,766 |
| KALAMAZOO-BATTLE CRK | 20,118 | 173,075 | 15.7 | 12.8 | 34.4 | 28.7 | 5.9 | 2.5 | 36,864 | 29,255 | 42,332 | 48,720 | 42,172 | 23,044 |
| KANKAKEE, IL | 19,833 | 37,367 | 14.6 | 11.4 | 35.3 | 29.9 | 6.5 | 2.3 | 38,028 | 33,064 | 43,160 | 49,563 | 38,779 | 24,720 |
| KANSAS CITY, MO-KS | 23,092 | 683,157 | 11.3 | 11.1 | 32.8 | 33.7 | 8.0 | 3.2 | 42,792 | 35,653 | 47,243 | 52,923 | 44,559 | 28,115 |
| KENOSHA, WI | 22,474 | 55,106 | 9.3 | 10.6 | 35.2 | 35.0 | 7.7 | 2.3 | 38,022 | 33,047 | 43,482 | 48,688 | 40,792 | 23,927 |
| KILLEEN-TEMPLE, TX | 15,930 | 101,350 | 13.4 | 18.2 | 37.5 | 25.8 | 4.0 | 1.0 | 35,293 | 29,521 | 40,336 | 45,733 | 41,532 | 26,612 |
| KNOXVILLE, TN | 21,549 | 272,024 | 16.8 | 14.2 | 33.3 | 26.9 | 5.9 | 3.0 | 40,427 | 33,147 | 45,930 | 49,990 | 43,059 | 26,168 |
| KOKOMO, IN | 24,267 | 39,353 | 11.4 | 9.4 | 33.1 | 35.2 | 8.0 | 2.9 | 43,016 | 35,227 | 47,675 | 55,519 | 47,442 | 26,636 |
| UNITED STATES | 22,162 | | 14.5 | 12.5 | 32.3 | 29.8 | 7.4 | 3.5 | 40,748 | 34,503 | 44,969 | 49,579 | 43,409 | 27,339 |

# SPENDING POTENTIAL INDEXES

## MSA AND U.S. TOTALS

| MSA | FINANCIAL SERVICES | | | | THE HOME | | | | | | ENTERTAINMENT | | | | | | PERSONAL | | | |
|---|---|---|---|---|---|---|---|---|---|---|---|---|---|---|---|---|---|---|---|---|
| | | | | | Home Improvements | | | Furnishings | | | | | | | | | | | | |
| | Auto Loan | Home Loan | Invest-ments | Retire-ment Plans | Home Repair | Lawn & Garden | Remodel-ing | Appli-ances | Elec-tronics | Furni-ture | Restau-rants | Sport-ing Goods | Theater & Concerts | Toys & Hobbies | Travel | Video Rental | Apparel | Auto After-market | Health Insur-ance | Pets & Supplies |
| DETROIT, MI | 99 | 102 | 104 | 103 | 104 | 103 | 98 | 100 | 99 | 103 | 102 | 100 | 105 | 101 | 103 | 102 | 101 | 103 | 98 | 100 |
| DOTHAN, AL | 98 | 88 | 90 | 89 | 97 | 95 | 104 | 97 | 96 | 92 | 93 | 97 | 92 | 98 | 80 | 98 | 92 | 95 | 97 | 99 |
| DOVER, DE | 97 | 89 | 91 | 86 | 97 | 94 | 104 | 96 | 94 | 92 | 94 | 95 | 91 | 98 | 80 | 97 | 91 | 94 | 97 | 99 |
| DUBUQUE, IA | 97 | 89 | 95 | 91 | 100 | 97 | 102 | 97 | 94 | 92 | 95 | 95 | 96 | 98 | 93 | 100 | 91 | 96 | 101 | 98 |
| DULUTH-SUPERIOR | 96 | 86 | 93 | 89 | 99 | 96 | 103 | 96 | 93 | 90 | 92 | 93 | 94 | 97 | 91 | 100 | 88 | 94 | 101 | 97 |
| DUTCHESS COUNTY, NY | 102 | 105 | 105 | 105 | 97 | 98 | 94 | 100 | 102 | 106 | 108 | 105 | 107 | 106 | 101 | 101 | 110 | 103 | 102 | 106 |
| EAU CLAIRE, WI | 97 | 88 | 88 | 90 | 97 | 94 | 104 | 96 | 94 | 89 | 93 | 95 | 93 | 98 | 89 | 100 | 89 | 95 | 100 | 99 |
| EL PASO, TX | 96 | 101 | 92 | 91 | 96 | 96 | 93 | 98 | 98 | 93 | 98 | 96 | 94 | 96 | 85 | 99 | 92 | 99 | 97 | 102 |
| ELKHART-GOSHEN, IN | 99 | 89 | 92 | 92 | 98 | 96 | 107 | 98 | 97 | 93 | 96 | 97 | 97 | 100 | 90 | 102 | 93 | 98 | 100 | 100 |
| ELMIRA, NY | 97 | 87 | 96 | 90 | 94 | 91 | 92 | 96 | 92 | 94 | 93 | 96 | 95 | 99 | 91 | 97 | 94 | 92 | 101 | 99 |
| ENID, OK | 97 | 85 | 91 | 88 | 98 | 96 | 103 | 96 | 94 | 89 | 91 | 94 | 90 | 97 | 81 | 97 | 89 | 93 | 100 | 98 |
| ERIE, PA | 98 | 87 | 94 | 91 | 93 | 90 | 95 | 97 | 93 | 93 | 93 | 97 | 95 | 100 | 90 | 98 | 95 | 93 | 101 | 100 |
| EUGENE-SPRINGFLD, OR | 98 | 94 | 95 | 94 | 101 | 99 | 103 | 99 | 98 | 96 | 95 | 90 | 89 | 93 | 87 | 92 | 94 | 95 | 97 | 93 |
| EVANSVILLE-HENDERSON | 98 | 92 | 94 | 94 | 100 | 97 | 103 | 98 | 96 | 95 | 97 | 97 | 98 | 99 | 94 | 101 | 93 | 98 | 100 | 99 |
| FARGO-MOORHEAD,ND-MN | 97 | 98 | 91 | 94 | 97 | 95 | 96 | 96 | 96 | 95 | 99 | 96 | 97 | 98 | 94 | 100 | 94 | 98 | 98 | 99 |
| FAYETTEVILLE, NC | 94 | 91 | 86 | 85 | 94 | 91 | 95 | 94 | 94 | 89 | 93 | 93 | 89 | 94 | 79 | 97 | 90 | 95 | 93 | 98 |
| FAYETTEVL-SPRNGD-ROG | 99 | 87 | 94 | 91 | 99 | 98 | 109 | 98 | 95 | 90 | 93 | 97 | 91 | 100 | 81 | 97 | 92 | 95 | 101 | 101 |
| FLAGSTAFF, AZ-UT | 98 | 97 | 89 | 96 | 97 | 97 | 103 | 99 | 99 | 96 | 95 | 91 | 88 | 92 | 86 | 92 | 94 | 96 | 96 | 94 |
| FLINT, MI | 96 | 94 | 97 | 94 | 101 | 98 | 97 | 97 | 95 | 98 | 96 | 96 | 99 | 98 | 97 | 101 | 95 | 99 | 97 | 98 |
| FLORENCE, AL | 97 | 81 | 91 | 87 | 99 | 96 | 107 | 97 | 94 | 88 | 88 | 96 | 90 | 98 | 79 | 97 | 89 | 93 | 100 | 98 |
| FLORENCE, SC | 98 | 85 | 92 | 89 | 98 | 95 | 104 | 97 | 95 | 91 | 90 | 97 | 91 | 98 | 80 | 98 | 91 | 94 | 97 | 99 |
| FT. COLLINS-LOVELAND | 102 | 105 | 95 | 103 | 102 | 102 | 104 | 102 | 104 | 104 | 104 | 96 | 95 | 96 | 91 | 94 | 103 | 101 | 97 | 97 |
| FORT LAUDERDALE, FL | 100 | 104 | 108 | 102 | 105 | 107 | 100 | 100 | 98 | 103 | 104 | 101 | 102 | 102 | 94 | 99 | 101 | 102 | 101 | 102 |
| FT. MYERS-CAPE CORAL | 100 | 94 | 107 | 99 | 104 | 108 | 105 | 102 | 96 | 97 | 99 | 100 | 98 | 102 | 91 | 98 | 96 | 98 | 106 | 102 |
| FT.PIERCE-P.ST.LUCIE | 101 | 96 | 107 | 101 | 104 | 109 | 106 | 103 | 97 | 98 | 100 | 101 | 99 | 103 | 91 | 99 | 98 | 99 | 106 | 103 |
| FORT SMITH, AR-OK | 98 | 83 | 89 | 87 | 98 | 95 | 107 | 97 | 94 | 89 | 90 | 97 | 90 | 98 | 79 | 97 | 89 | 93 | 100 | 99 |
| FORT WALTON BEACH,FL | 98 | 98 | 96 | 94 | 100 | 99 | 100 | 98 | 98 | 97 | 101 | 99 | 97 | 100 | 86 | 99 | 98 | 99 | 98 | 101 |
| FORT WAYNE, IN | 99 | 93 | 92 | 94 | 98 | 96 | 103 | 98 | 97 | 96 | 98 | 98 | 99 | 100 | 93 | 102 | 95 | 99 | 99 | 100 |
| FT. WORTH-ARLINGTON | 101 | 105 | 97 | 101 | 100 | 101 | 100 | 100 | 101 | 103 | 106 | 103 | 101 | 103 | 89 | 100 | 104 | 103 | 98 | 103 |
| FRESNO, CA | 98 | 101 | 93 | 96 | 99 | 99 | 98 | 100 | 101 | 98 | 98 | 91 | 91 | 92 | 89 | 94 | 95 | 98 | 96 | 95 |
| GADSDEN, AL | 97 | 77 | 89 | 84 | 99 | 95 | 107 | 97 | 92 | 86 | 86 | 95 | 87 | 97 | 77 | 96 | 86 | 91 | 100 | 97 |
| GAINESVILLE, FL | 96 | 98 | 96 | 97 | 98 | 95 | 100 | 93 | 94 | 90 | 94 | 95 | 90 | 96 | 83 | 95 | 93 | 96 | 95 | 98 |
| GALVESTON-TEXAS CITY | 98 | 96 | 96 | 95 | 100 | 98 | 100 | 98 | 97 | 98 | 98 | 99 | 96 | 99 | 86 | 99 | 97 | 99 | 96 | 100 |
| GARY, IN | 98 | 95 | 97 | 96 | 101 | 98 | 98 | 99 | 97 | 99 | 99 | 98 | 101 | 100 | 97 | 102 | 98 | 101 | 98 | 99 |
| GLENS FALLS, NY | 99 | 83 | 88 | 88 | 91 | 88 | 100 | 97 | 93 | 89 | 91 | 98 | 92 | 101 | 86 | 99 | 93 | 92 | 103 | 101 |
| GOLDSBORO, NC | 96 | 83 | 86 | 84 | 96 | 93 | 104 | 96 | 93 | 89 | 89 | 95 | 88 | 97 | 77 | 97 | 89 | 93 | 96 | 98 |
| GRAND FORKS, ND-MN | 95 | 89 | 86 | 88 | 94 | 92 | 98 | 94 | 93 | 88 | 92 | 93 | 92 | 95 | 88 | 99 | 88 | 95 | 98 | 97 |
| GRAND JUNCTION, CO | 99 | 91 | 95 | 95 | 101 | 100 | 107 | 101 | 100 | 97 | 95 | 92 | 90 | 94 | 87 | 93 | 95 | 96 | 99 | 94 |
| GR.RAPIDS-MSKGN-HOLL | 98 | 94 | 93 | 94 | 99 | 96 | 102 | 98 | 97 | 96 | 99 | 97 | 98 | 100 | 93 | 101 | 95 | 99 | 99 | 100 |
| GREAT FALLS, MT | 97 | 90 | 93 | 91 | 101 | 98 | 102 | 99 | 97 | 95 | 93 | 89 | 89 | 92 | 86 | 92 | 92 | 94 | 97 | 92 |
| GREELEY, CO | 99 | 91 | 88 | 92 | 97 | 96 | 106 | 100 | 99 | 94 | 94 | 91 | 87 | 93 | 83 | 93 | 93 | 95 | 97 | 95 |
| GREEN BAY, WI | 99 | 99 | 94 | 97 | 100 | 98 | 100 | 98 | 98 | 99 | 102 | 99 | 101 | 101 | 96 | 102 | 98 | 101 | 99 | 100 |
| G'BORO-W.SLM-H.PT,NC | 99 | 91 | 96 | 93 | 100 | 98 | 105 | 98 | 97 | 94 | 95 | 99 | 95 | 100 | 84 | 98 | 95 | 97 | 99 | 100 |
| GREENVILLE, NC | 95 | 89 | 85 | 86 | 95 | 91 | 99 | 94 | 93 | 89 | 91 | 94 | 88 | 95 | 78 | 96 | 90 | 94 | 93 | 98 |
| GREENVL-SPAR'BG-ANDR | 99 | 88 | 94 | 92 | 99 | 97 | 107 | 98 | 96 | 92 | 93 | 99 | 93 | 100 | 82 | 98 | 93 | 95 | 99 | 100 |
| HAGERSTOWN, MD | 97 | 87 | 96 | 88 | 101 | 97 | 105 | 97 | 93 | 91 | 92 | 95 | 92 | 98 | 82 | 97 | 91 | 94 | 100 | 99 |
| HAMILTON-MIDDLETOWN | 100 | 102 | 98 | 102 | 101 | 101 | 101 | 100 | 100 | 101 | 104 | 101 | 104 | 102 | 99 | 102 | 100 | 103 | 100 | 101 |
| HARR'BG-LEBANON-CARL | 100 | 92 | 99 | 96 | 94 | 93 | 95 | 98 | 96 | 97 | 98 | 100 | 99 | 103 | 93 | 99 | 100 | 96 | 102 | 102 |
| HARTFORD, CT | 101 | 104 | 106 | 104 | 97 | 98 | 92 | 100 | 100 | 106 | 106 | 104 | 106 | 105 | 102 | 101 | 109 | 102 | 102 | 104 |
| HATTIESBURG, MS | 97 | 87 | 92 | 89 | 98 | 94 | 102 | 96 | 94 | 89 | 90 | 95 | 89 | 97 | 80 | 97 | 90 | 94 | 96 | 98 |
| HICKRY-MRGNTN-LENOIR | 99 | 78 | 86 | 85 | 96 | 94 | 113 | 97 | 94 | 85 | 87 | 97 | 87 | 99 | 75 | 97 | 87 | 92 | 101 | 100 |
| HONOLULU, HI | 97 | 134 | 105 | 114 | 94 | 104 | 89 | 95 | 117 | 96 | 116 | 91 | 96 | 85 | 102 | 112 | 99 | 107 | 95 | 97 |
| HOUMA, LA | 97 | 78 | 83 | 83 | 95 | 92 | 107 | 96 | 93 | 86 | 86 | 96 | 87 | 97 | 75 | 97 | 86 | 91 | 98 | 98 |
| HOUSTON, TX | 100 | 108 | 99 | 103 | 100 | 102 | 99 | 100 | 102 | 103 | 106 | 104 | 102 | 102 | 91 | 100 | 105 | 104 | 97 | 104 |
| HUNTINGTON-ASHLAND | 97 | 78 | 89 | 84 | 99 | 95 | 107 | 96 | 92 | 86 | 86 | 95 | 88 | 96 | 78 | 96 | 86 | 91 | 101 | 97 |
| HUNTSVILLE, AL | 101 | 102 | 101 | 103 | 102 | 103 | 104 | 101 | 101 | 102 | 104 | 104 | 102 | 104 | 90 | 100 | 104 | 102 | 100 | 103 |
| INDIANAPOLIS, IN | 99 | 101 | 98 | 101 | 101 | 100 | 100 | 100 | 99 | 101 | 103 | 100 | 103 | 101 | 99 | 102 | 100 | 102 | 99 | 101 |
| IOWA CITY, IA | 96 | 102 | 94 | 97 | 97 | 94 | 97 | 93 | 95 | 91 | 98 | 94 | 94 | 96 | 93 | 98 | 94 | 98 | 96 | 99 |
| JACKSON, MI | 98 | 89 | 95 | 92 | 100 | 97 | 104 | 98 | 95 | 94 | 95 | 96 | 97 | 99 | 93 | 101 | 92 | 97 | 100 | 99 |
| JACKSON, MS | 99 | 96 | 96 | 96 | 100 | 98 | 99 | 99 | 98 | 99 | 98 | 100 | 97 | 100 | 86 | 99 | 99 | 99 | 95 | 101 |
| JACKSON, TN | 98 | 88 | 90 | 91 | 98 | 96 | 103 | 98 | 96 | 93 | 92 | 98 | 93 | 98 | 82 | 98 | 93 | 95 | 97 | 99 |
| JACKSONVILLE, FL | 98 | 98 | 95 | 95 | 99 | 99 | 99 | 98 | 98 | 99 | 100 | 99 | 97 | 100 | 86 | 99 | 98 | 99 | 96 | 100 |
| JACKSONVILLE, NC | 91 | 87 | 77 | 77 | 89 | 85 | 94 | 92 | 92 | 84 | 90 | 89 | 84 | 91 | 74 | 96 | 85 | 92 | 91 | 97 |
| JAMESTOWN, NY | 96 | 79 | 88 | 83 | 91 | 88 | 95 | 95 | 90 | 88 | 88 | 94 | 90 | 97 | 85 | 97 | 89 | 89 | 102 | 98 |
| JANESVILLE-BELOIT,WI | 98 | 91 | 93 | 92 | 100 | 96 | 103 | 97 | 95 | 94 | 96 | 96 | 97 | 99 | 93 | 101 | 93 | 97 | 100 | 99 |
| JERSEY CITY, NJ | 96 | 102 | 96 | 90 | 100 | 93 | 85 | 95 | 91 | 108 | 96 | 98 | 100 | 91 | 107 | 102 | 101 | 98 | 96 | 97 |
| J.CITY-KNGSPRT-BRIST | 98 | 79 | 88 | 85 | 98 | 95 | 109 | 97 | 93 | 87 | 88 | 96 | 88 | 98 | 77 | 97 | 87 | 92 | 101 | 99 |
| JOHNSTOWN, PA | 96 | 77 | 90 | 84 | 93 | 90 | 95 | 96 | 90 | 88 | 87 | 94 | 91 | 97 | 86 | 97 | 89 | 89 | 103 | 98 |
| JONESBORO, AR | 97 | 84 | 91 | 88 | 97 | 95 | 106 | 96 | 94 | 88 | 90 | 95 | 89 | 97 | 79 | 97 | 89 | 93 | 99 | 98 |
| JOPLIN, MO | 97 | 81 | 87 | 86 | 97 | 94 | 107 | 97 | 93 | 87 | 89 | 94 | 91 | 97 | 86 | 100 | 86 | 93 | 101 | 98 |
| KALAMAZOO-BATTLE CRK | 97 | 94 | 95 | 94 | 100 | 97 | 101 | 97 | 95 | 95 | 96 | 96 | 98 | 98 | 94 | 100 | 93 | 98 | 99 | 99 |
| KANKAKEE, IL | 96 | 90 | 93 | 91 | 99 | 95 | 100 | 97 | 95 | 94 | 94 | 95 | 96 | 97 | 93 | 101 | 92 | 97 | 98 | 98 |
| KANSAS CITY, MO-KS | 99 | 102 | 98 | 101 | 101 | 101 | 99 | 100 | 100 | 102 | 104 | 101 | 104 | 101 | 100 | 103 | 101 | 103 | 99 | 101 |
| KENOSHA, WI | 97 | 94 | 96 | 93 | 101 | 98 | 100 | 97 | 95 | 96 | 98 | 96 | 99 | 99 | 95 | 101 | 94 | 98 | 100 | 99 |
| KILLEEN-TEMPLE, TX | 94 | 93 | 87 | 87 | 95 | 92 | 97 | 95 | 95 | 90 | 95 | 94 | 90 | 95 | 80 | 97 | 91 | 95 | 94 | 99 |
| KNOXVILLE, TN | 99 | 91 | 96 | 93 | 100 | 99 | 105 | 98 | 96 | 94 | 95 | 98 | 94 | 100 | 84 | 98 | 94 | 96 | 100 | 100 |
| KOKOMO, IN | 98 | 89 | 95 | 92 | 100 | 97 | 103 | 98 | 95 | 94 | 96 | 96 | 98 | 99 | 93 | 101 | 92 | 97 | 101 | 99 |
| UNITED STATES | 100 | 100 | 100 | 100 | 100 | 100 | 100 | 100 | 100 | 100 | 100 | 100 | 100 | 100 | 100 | 100 | 100 | 100 | 100 | 100 |

# POPULATION CHANGE

## MSA AND U.S. TOTALS

A

| MSA | MSA Code | POPULATION 1990 | POPULATION 2000 | POPULATION 2005 | 1990-2000 ANNUAL CHANGE % Rate | 1990-2000 ANNUAL CHANGE National Rank | RACE (%) White 1990 | RACE (%) White 2000 | RACE (%) Black 1990 | RACE (%) Black 2000 | RACE (%) Asian/Pacific 1990 | RACE (%) Asian/Pacific 2000 |
|---|---|---|---|---|---|---|---|---|---|---|---|---|
| LA CROSSE, WI-MN | 3870 | 116,401 | 122,184 | 123,612 | 0.5 | 212 | 96.8 | 95.6 | 0.4 | 0.5 | 2.3 | 3.4 |
| LAFAYETTE, LA | 3880 | 344,953 | 380,067 | 394,108 | 1.0 | 149 | 71.7 | 69.2 | 27.2 | 29.5 | 0.6 | 0.8 |
| LAFAYETTE, IN | 3920 | 161,572 | 176,214 | 180,297 | 0.8 | 175 | 94.5 | 93.0 | 1.7 | 1.9 | 3.0 | 4.0 |
| LAKE CHARLES, LA | 3960 | 168,134 | 181,361 | 185,326 | 0.7 | 188 | 76.2 | 73.9 | 22.9 | 25.0 | 0.4 | 0.5 |
| LAKELND-WINTER HAVEN | 3980 | 405,382 | 462,856 | 489,919 | 1.3 | 91 | 84.4 | 81.1 | 13.4 | 15.6 | 0.6 | 1.0 |
| LANCASTER, PA | 4000 | 422,822 | 463,301 | 479,792 | 0.9 | 166 | 94.1 | 92.2 | 2.4 | 2.7 | 1.1 | 1.6 |
| LANSING-E.LANSING,MI | 4040 | 432,674 | 451,921 | 455,405 | 0.4 | 226 | 88.1 | 86.6 | 7.2 | 7.6 | 1.9 | 2.7 |
| LAREDO, TX | 4080 | 133,239 | 199,480 | 230,933 | 4.0 | 2 | 70.3 | 69.8 | 0.1 | 0.1 | 0.4 | 0.5 |
| LAS CRUCES, NM | 4100 | 135,510 | 172,519 | 183,394 | 2.4 | 22 | 91.1 | 90.2 | 1.6 | 1.8 | 0.9 | 1.3 |
| LAS VEGAS, NV-AZ | 4120 | 852,737 | 1,442,896 | 1,749,297 | 5.3 | 1 | 83.0 | 78.1 | 8.4 | 9.0 | 3.1 | 4.6 |
| LAWRENCE, KS | 4150 | 81,798 | 100,135 | 108,967 | 2.0 | 40 | 89.1 | 87.9 | 4.1 | 4.3 | 3.2 | 3.9 |
| LAWTON, OK | 4200 | 111,486 | 105,572 | 100,338 | -0.5 | 309 | 71.5 | 69.5 | 17.9 | 17.8 | 2.7 | 3.5 |
| LEWISTON-AUBURN, ME | 4243 | 105,259 | 101,289 | 100,909 | -0.4 | 301 | 98.5 | 98.2 | 0.5 | 0.6 | 0.5 | 0.7 |
| LEXINGTON, KY | 4280 | 405,936 | 461,353 | 489,356 | 1.3 | 91 | 88.6 | 88.0 | 9.9 | 10.0 | 1.1 | 1.5 |
| LIMA, OH | 4320 | 154,340 | 153,688 | 151,943 | 0.0 | 270 | 91.0 | 89.8 | 8.0 | 8.9 | 0.5 | 0.7 |
| LINCOLN, NE | 4360 | 213,641 | 239,742 | 250,114 | 1.1 | 129 | 94.9 | 92.9 | 2.2 | 2.4 | 1.6 | 2.5 |
| LITTLE ROCK-N.LITTLE | 4400 | 513,117 | 564,430 | 587,510 | 0.9 | 166 | 78.9 | 77.5 | 19.9 | 20.8 | 0.7 | 0.9 |
| LONGVIEW-MARSHALL,TX | 4420 | 193,801 | 210,818 | 217,307 | 0.8 | 175 | 77.1 | 75.0 | 20.6 | 21.9 | 0.3 | 0.5 |
| LOS ANGELES-L.BEACH | 4480 | 8,863,164 | 9,424,833 | 9,879,261 | 0.6 | 200 | 56.8 | 51.8 | 11.2 | 10.5 | 10.8 | 13.0 |
| LOUISVILLE, KY-IN | 4520 | 948,829 | 1,011,888 | 1,041,824 | 0.6 | 200 | 86.2 | 85.9 | 12.9 | 12.9 | 0.6 | 0.8 |
| LUBBOCK, TX | 4600 | 222,636 | 227,339 | 224,460 | 0.2 | 250 | 79.1 | 75.4 | 7.7 | 8.0 | 1.2 | 1.7 |
| LYNCHBURG, VA | 4640 | 193,928 | 210,120 | 216,137 | 0.8 | 175 | 81.2 | 79.4 | 18.1 | 19.6 | 0.5 | 0.6 |
| MACON, GA | 4680 | 290,909 | 324,609 | 339,362 | 1.1 | 129 | 63.8 | 59.0 | 35.0 | 39.0 | 0.7 | 1.2 |
| MADISON, WI | 4720 | 367,085 | 432,873 | 454,296 | 1.6 | 67 | 93.9 | 92.0 | 2.9 | 3.6 | 2.4 | 3.2 |
| MANSFIELD, OH | 4800 | 174,007 | 176,724 | 177,345 | 0.2 | 250 | 93.4 | 92.0 | 5.9 | 7.0 | 0.4 | 0.6 |
| MCALLN-EDNBG-MISSION | 4880 | 383,545 | 549,938 | 625,504 | 3.6 | 3 | 74.8 | 73.8 | 0.2 | 0.2 | 0.3 | 0.4 |
| MEDFORD-ASHLAND, OR | 4890 | 146,389 | 178,400 | 191,404 | 1.9 | 44 | 95.8 | 94.4 | 0.2 | 0.3 | 1.0 | 1.3 |
| MELBRN-TITUSVL-P.BAY | 4900 | 398,978 | 476,045 | 504,234 | 1.7 | 61 | 89.8 | 87.3 | 7.9 | 9.3 | 1.3 | 2.1 |
| MEMPHIS, TN-AR-MS | 4920 | 1,007,306 | 1,115,981 | 1,171,229 | 1.0 | 149 | 58.0 | 56.3 | 40.7 | 41.9 | 0.8 | 1.2 |
| MERCED, CA | 4940 | 178,403 | 204,109 | 220,046 | 1.3 | 91 | 67.4 | 61.6 | 4.8 | 4.6 | 8.5 | 10.3 |
| MIAMI, FL | 5000 | 1,937,094 | 2,198,826 | 2,318,135 | 1.2 | 110 | 72.9 | 72.3 | 20.5 | 19.9 | 1.4 | 1.8 |
| MID'SX-SOMER'T-HUNT. | 5015 | 1,019,835 | 1,144,645 | 1,212,143 | 1.1 | 129 | 84.8 | 79.9 | 6.9 | 7.5 | 5.6 | 9.0 |
| MILWAUKEE-WAUKESHA | 5080 | 1,432,149 | 1,464,007 | 1,471,497 | 0.2 | 250 | 82.6 | 80.4 | 13.8 | 15.0 | 1.3 | 1.8 |
| MINNEAPOLIS-ST. PAUL | 5120 | 2,538,834 | 2,910,649 | 3,101,921 | 1.3 | 91 | 92.3 | 89.8 | 3.5 | 4.6 | 2.6 | 3.8 |
| MISSOULA, MT | 5140 | 78,687 | 89,724 | 91,829 | 1.3 | 91 | 96.1 | 95.6 | 0.2 | 0.3 | 1.1 | 1.2 |
| MOBILE, AL | 5160 | 476,923 | 540,121 | 562,980 | 1.2 | 110 | 71.2 | 70.5 | 27.4 | 27.9 | 0.8 | 0.9 |
| MODESTO, CA | 5170 | 370,522 | 445,583 | 486,764 | 1.8 | 49 | 80.2 | 75.2 | 1.7 | 1.8 | 5.2 | 6.7 |
| MONMOUTH-OCEAN, NJ | 5190 | 986,327 | 1,124,765 | 1,199,603 | 1.3 | 91 | 90.8 | 88.2 | 6.0 | 6.8 | 1.9 | 3.3 |
| MONROE, LA | 5200 | 142,191 | 146,669 | 146,646 | 0.3 | 240 | 68.1 | 65.5 | 31.0 | 33.4 | 0.5 | 0.7 |
| MONTGOMERY, AL | 5240 | 292,517 | 324,208 | 333,051 | 1.0 | 149 | 63.0 | 62.3 | 36.0 | 36.5 | 0.6 | 0.7 |
| MUNCIE, IN | 5280 | 119,659 | 114,744 | 111,045 | -0.4 | 301 | 93.0 | 91.8 | 6.0 | 6.9 | 0.5 | 0.8 |
| MYRTLE BEACH, SC | 5330 | 144,053 | 183,239 | 206,483 | 2.4 | 22 | 81.3 | 80.8 | 17.5 | 17.5 | 0.8 | 1.1 |
| NAPLES, FL | 5345 | 152,099 | 214,106 | 248,907 | 3.4 | 5 | 91.4 | 89.1 | 4.6 | 5.5 | 0.4 | 0.6 |
| NASHVILLE, TN | 5360 | 985,026 | 1,190,023 | 1,281,156 | 1.9 | 44 | 83.1 | 82.5 | 15.5 | 15.4 | 1.0 | 1.5 |
| NASSAU-SUFFOLK, NY | 5380 | 2,609,212 | 2,702,524 | 2,769,214 | 0.3 | 240 | 88.4 | 85.8 | 7.4 | 8.2 | 2.4 | 3.7 |
| N.HAVEN-BRDGPRT.,CT | 5483 | 1,631,864 | 1,638,450 | 1,656,770 | 0.0 | 270 | 85.0 | 82.3 | 10.0 | 10.8 | 1.7 | 2.8 |
| NEW LONDON-NORWICH | 5523 | 254,957 | 245,057 | 239,839 | -0.4 | 301 | 91.9 | 90.0 | 4.8 | 5.2 | 1.3 | 2.2 |
| NEW ORLEANS, LA | 5560 | 1,285,270 | 1,305,253 | 1,302,998 | 0.2 | 250 | 62.2 | 61.9 | 34.8 | 34.5 | 1.7 | 2.2 |
| NEW YORK, NY | 5600 | 8,546,846 | 8,744,344 | 8,897,467 | 0.2 | 250 | 56.5 | 52.3 | 26.3 | 26.4 | 6.5 | 9.1 |
| NEWARK, NJ | 5640 | 1,915,928 | 1,960,240 | 1,988,045 | 0.2 | 250 | 71.5 | 68.7 | 22.1 | 22.1 | 2.8 | 4.6 |
| NEWBURGH, NY-PA | 5660 | 335,613 | 380,436 | 404,360 | 1.2 | 110 | 89.7 | 88.1 | 6.7 | 7.1 | 1.1 | 1.7 |
| NRFOLK-VA BCH-N.NEWS | 5720 | 1,443,244 | 1,571,466 | 1,616,198 | 0.8 | 175 | 68.1 | 64.9 | 28.3 | 30.2 | 2.4 | 3.5 |
| OAKLAND, CA | 5775 | 2,082,914 | 2,387,893 | 2,573,999 | 1.3 | 91 | 65.9 | 60.2 | 14.6 | 14.8 | 12.9 | 16.7 |
| OCALA, FL | 5790 | 194,833 | 251,138 | 276,818 | 2.5 | 16 | 85.8 | 83.2 | 12.8 | 14.6 | 0.5 | 0.8 |
| ODESSA-MIDLAND, TX | 5800 | 225,545 | 243,728 | 247,275 | 0.8 | 175 | 79.0 | 75.6 | 6.1 | 6.5 | 0.7 | 1.0 |
| OKLAHOMA CITY, OK | 5880 | 958,839 | 1,056,331 | 1,098,993 | 0.9 | 166 | 81.1 | 80.0 | 10.5 | 10.7 | 1.9 | 2.3 |
| OLYMPIA, WA | 5910 | 161,238 | 208,511 | 224,233 | 2.5 | 16 | 91.9 | 89.6 | 1.8 | 2.1 | 3.8 | 5.3 |
| OMAHA, NE-IA | 5920 | 639,580 | 705,149 | 736,776 | 1.0 | 149 | 89.4 | 87.3 | 8.0 | 8.5 | 1.0 | 1.6 |
| ORANGE COUNTY, CA | 5945 | 2,410,556 | 2,810,321 | 3,047,014 | 1.5 | 73 | 78.6 | 73.6 | 1.8 | 1.7 | 10.3 | 13.3 |
| ORLANDO, FL | 5960 | 1,224,852 | 1,572,022 | 1,750,503 | 2.5 | 16 | 83.6 | 79.9 | 12.0 | 13.8 | 1.7 | 2.7 |
| OWENSBORO, KY | 5990 | 87,189 | 91,353 | 92,296 | 0.5 | 212 | 95.4 | 95.1 | 4.2 | 4.3 | 0.3 | 0.4 |
| PANAMA CITY, FL | 6015 | 126,994 | 149,113 | 155,109 | 1.6 | 67 | 86.3 | 82.9 | 10.8 | 12.8 | 1.8 | 2.8 |
| PARKERSBURG-MARIETTA | 6020 | 149,169 | 148,800 | 146,011 | 0.0 | 270 | 98.3 | 98.1 | 1.1 | 1.2 | 0.3 | 0.5 |
| PENSACOLA, FL | 6080 | 344,406 | 407,859 | 428,853 | 1.7 | 61 | 80.6 | 77.9 | 16.2 | 17.6 | 1.7 | 2.7 |
| PEORIA-PEKIN, IL | 6120 | 339,172 | 346,750 | 348,136 | 0.2 | 250 | 91.2 | 90.1 | 7.4 | 8.1 | 0.8 | 1.1 |
| PHILADELPHIA, PA-NJ | 6160 | 4,922,175 | 4,952,449 | 4,965,870 | 0.1 | 262 | 76.6 | 74.6 | 19.1 | 19.5 | 2.1 | 3.2 |
| PHOENIX-MESA, AZ | 6200 | 2,238,480 | 3,099,797 | 3,530,356 | 3.2 | 7 | 84.3 | 81.4 | 3.5 | 3.9 | 1.6 | 2.2 |
| PINE BLUFF, AR | 6240 | 85,487 | 80,092 | 76,719 | -0.6 | 313 | 56.0 | 52.5 | 43.1 | 46.3 | 0.4 | 0.6 |
| PITTSBURGH, PA | 6280 | 2,394,811 | 2,319,118 | 2,253,649 | -0.3 | 297 | 91.5 | 90.2 | 7.5 | 8.5 | 0.7 | 1.0 |
| PITTSFIELD, MA | 6323 | 139,352 | 131,557 | 128,088 | -0.6 | 313 | 97.0 | 96.0 | 1.8 | 2.3 | 0.7 | 1.1 |
| POCATELLO, ID | 6340 | 66,026 | 75,394 | 78,057 | 1.3 | 91 | 93.5 | 92.0 | 0.7 | 1.0 | 1.1 | 1.3 |
| PORTLAND, ME | 6403 | 243,135 | 258,514 | 268,517 | 0.6 | 200 | 98.1 | 97.7 | 0.6 | 0.8 | 0.9 | 1.1 |
| PORTLAND-VANCOUVER | 6440 | 1,515,452 | 1,875,745 | 2,023,324 | 2.1 | 34 | 91.5 | 89.3 | 2.8 | 2.9 | 3.5 | 4.7 |
| PROVID.-WARWICK-PAW. | 6483 | 916,270 | 908,799 | 913,811 | -0.1 | 283 | 91.2 | 89.1 | 3.9 | 4.5 | 1.9 | 2.4 |
| PROVO-OREM, UT | 6520 | 263,590 | 355,170 | 396,568 | 3.0 | 9 | 96.2 | 95.0 | 0.1 | 0.2 | 1.5 | 2.0 |
| PUEBLO, CO | 6560 | 123,051 | 139,071 | 149,424 | 1.2 | 110 | 84.8 | 82.7 | 1.8 | 2.1 | 0.6 | 0.7 |
| PUNTA GORDA, FL | 6580 | 110,975 | 139,272 | 150,605 | 2.2 | 29 | 95.0 | 93.5 | 3.8 | 4.6 | 0.7 | 1.2 |
| UNITED STATES | | | | | 1.0 | | 80.3 | 77.9 | 12.1 | 12.4 | 2.9 | 3.9 |

# POPULATION COMPOSITION

## MSA AND U.S. TOTALS

# B

| MSA | % HISPANIC ORIGIN | | 2000 AGE DISTRIBUTION (%) | | | | | | | | | | MEDIAN AGE | | 2000 Males/ Females (×100) |
|---|---|---|---|---|---|---|---|---|---|---|---|---|---|---|---|
| | 1990 | 2000 | 0-4 | 5-9 | 10-14 | 15-19 | 20-24 | 25-44 | 45-64 | 65-84 | 85+ | 18+ | 1990 | 2000 | |
| LA CROSSE, WI-MN | 0.6 | 1.2 | 6.0 | 6.4 | 7.5 | 9.0 | 8.7 | 28.6 | 20.8 | 10.9 | 2.0 | 75.8 | 31.7 | 34.7 | 94.3 |
| LAFAYETTE, LA | 1.2 | 1.8 | 7.6 | 7.7 | 8.0 | 8.7 | 7.8 | 28.2 | 21.7 | 9.3 | 1.1 | 71.7 | 30.0 | 33.0 | 92.2 |
| LAFAYETTE, IN | 1.6 | 2.7 | 6.2 | 6.0 | 6.0 | 10.7 | 14.1 | 28.0 | 18.5 | 9.0 | 1.5 | 78.5 | 28.1 | 30.2 | 100.7 |
| LAKE CHARLES, LA | 1.1 | 1.7 | 6.8 | 7.2 | 7.6 | 8.4 | 7.3 | 27.6 | 23.6 | 10.5 | 1.1 | 73.5 | 31.6 | 35.3 | 93.9 |
| LAKELND-WINTER HAVEN | 4.1 | 6.3 | 6.6 | 7.2 | 7.4 | 6.9 | 5.5 | 25.0 | 22.4 | 16.9 | 2.0 | 74.7 | 36.5 | 39.0 | 95.0 |
| LANCASTER, PA | 3.7 | 5.6 | 6.9 | 7.6 | 7.9 | 7.3 | 5.9 | 29.1 | 21.7 | 11.7 | 1.9 | 73.5 | 32.8 | 35.9 | 94.2 |
| LANSING-E.LANSING,MI | 3.9 | 5.3 | 6.3 | 6.9 | 7.2 | 8.9 | 9.5 | 30.7 | 21.0 | 8.3 | 1.2 | 75.5 | 29.8 | 33.0 | 93.4 |
| LAREDO, TX | 93.9 | 95.4 | 10.4 | 10.1 | 9.6 | 9.4 | 8.7 | 28.1 | 16.5 | 6.4 | 0.8 | 64.1 | 25.5 | 26.1 | 95.4 |
| LAS CRUCES, NM | 56.4 | 59.2 | 8.1 | 7.9 | 8.0 | 9.4 | 9.7 | 27.1 | 19.8 | 8.8 | 1.0 | 71.0 | 27.9 | 30.5 | 98.8 |
| LAS VEGAS, NV-AZ | 10.4 | 17.2 | 7.7 | 7.6 | 7.4 | 6.5 | 5.9 | 29.4 | 23.1 | 11.5 | 0.9 | 73.4 | 33.8 | 35.9 | 102.2 |
| LAWRENCE, KS | 2.6 | 4.1 | 5.7 | 5.2 | 5.6 | 11.5 | 18.5 | 29.6 | 16.0 | 6.7 | 1.2 | 80.3 | 25.8 | 27.4 | 98.4 |
| LAWTON, OK | 6.2 | 9.6 | 8.3 | 7.5 | 7.5 | 8.7 | 11.0 | 28.9 | 18.5 | 8.5 | 0.9 | 72.2 | 28.2 | 29.4 | 105.9 |
| LEWISTON-AUBURN, ME | 0.7 | 1.3 | 5.4 | 6.2 | 7.4 | 7.5 | 6.6 | 30.4 | 22.6 | 12.0 | 1.9 | 76.7 | 32.8 | 37.0 | 94.5 |
| LEXINGTON, KY | 0.8 | 1.5 | 6.3 | 6.1 | 6.2 | 7.7 | 9.4 | 31.9 | 22.1 | 9.0 | 1.2 | 77.7 | 31.4 | 34.6 | 92.6 |
| LIMA, OH | 1.0 | 1.6 | 6.8 | 7.3 | 7.8 | 7.6 | 6.3 | 29.0 | 21.3 | 12.0 | 1.8 | 73.6 | 32.9 | 35.5 | 98.7 |
| LINCOLN, NE | 1.8 | 4.1 | 6.4 | 6.3 | 6.8 | 8.7 | 10.0 | 30.8 | 20.3 | 9.3 | 1.5 | 76.7 | 30.7 | 33.2 | 95.6 |
| LITTLE ROCK-N.LITTLE | 0.8 | 2.2 | 7.1 | 7.0 | 7.3 | 7.5 | 7.3 | 30.5 | 22.1 | 9.8 | 1.3 | 74.1 | 32.2 | 34.7 | 92.4 |
| LONGVIEW-MARSHALL,TX | 2.9 | 4.2 | 7.1 | 7.4 | 7.6 | 8.3 | 6.6 | 26.1 | 23.7 | 11.4 | 1.8 | 73.1 | 33.0 | 36.3 | 93.4 |
| LOS ANGELES-L.BEACH | 37.8 | 44.5 | 7.8 | 8.1 | 7.3 | 7.1 | 7.6 | 33.0 | 19.4 | 8.6 | 1.2 | 73.0 | 30.7 | 32.6 | 100.2 |
| LOUISVILLE, KY-IN | 0.6 | 1.2 | 6.3 | 6.5 | 6.9 | 6.9 | 6.4 | 30.1 | 24.0 | 11.3 | 1.5 | 76.2 | 33.8 | 37.2 | 92.1 |
| LUBBOCK, TX | 22.9 | 28.9 | 7.6 | 7.3 | 7.0 | 8.8 | 9.7 | 30.3 | 19.1 | 9.0 | 1.2 | 74.1 | 28.8 | 31.7 | 96.8 |
| LYNCHBURG, VA | 0.6 | 1.2 | 5.9 | 6.3 | 6.6 | 7.3 | 6.6 | 28.8 | 24.0 | 12.7 | 1.8 | 77.5 | 34.5 | 37.7 | 92.9 |
| MACON, GA | 1.0 | 2.1 | 7.4 | 7.3 | 7.4 | 7.5 | 6.9 | 30.4 | 22.0 | 9.8 | 1.2 | 73.5 | 31.8 | 34.5 | 91.1 |
| MADISON, WI | 1.6 | 2.6 | 5.7 | 6.3 | 7.2 | 8.2 | 9.5 | 32.4 | 21.3 | 8.1 | 1.3 | 77.3 | 30.7 | 34.2 | 95.8 |
| MANSFIELD, OH | 0.7 | 1.2 | 6.3 | 6.7 | 7.2 | 7.1 | 6.6 | 27.9 | 24.0 | 12.6 | 1.6 | 75.6 | 34.4 | 37.3 | 96.0 |
| MCALLN-EDNBG-MISSION | 85.2 | 88.6 | 9.7 | 9.4 | 8.8 | 9.4 | 9.4 | 26.8 | 17.1 | 8.4 | 1.1 | 66.2 | 26.1 | 27.0 | 95.2 |
| MEDFORD-ASHLAND, OR | 4.1 | 6.9 | 6.2 | 6.4 | 7.1 | 7.3 | 6.0 | 25.8 | 25.9 | 13.6 | 1.9 | 76.0 | 36.7 | 39.5 | 96.3 |
| MELBRN-TITUSVL-P.BAY | 3.1 | 5.0 | 6.1 | 6.7 | 6.7 | 6.0 | 5.2 | 27.4 | 23.0 | 17.2 | 1.7 | 77.1 | 36.2 | 39.8 | 97.0 |
| MEMPHIS, TN-AR-MS | 0.8 | 1.5 | 7.8 | 7.8 | 7.5 | 7.4 | 7.0 | 31.2 | 21.3 | 8.8 | 1.2 | 72.7 | 31.3 | 33.7 | 91.3 |
| MERCED, CA | 32.6 | 40.5 | 9.8 | 11.1 | 8.8 | 8.4 | 7.1 | 28.4 | 17.0 | 8.5 | 1.0 | 65.2 | 27.9 | 28.5 | 101.7 |
| MIAMI, FL | 49.2 | 57.9 | 6.9 | 7.1 | 7.3 | 7.0 | 6.5 | 29.4 | 22.2 | 11.8 | 1.8 | 74.6 | 34.2 | 36.2 | 92.4 |
| MID'SX-SOMER'T-HUNT. | 7.0 | 9.8 | 6.4 | 6.9 | 6.7 | 6.2 | 5.9 | 32.3 | 23.2 | 11.0 | 1.3 | 76.6 | 33.9 | 37.2 | 96.4 |
| MILWAUKEE-WAUKESHA | 3.6 | 5.1 | 6.2 | 6.7 | 7.8 | 7.6 | 6.4 | 30.3 | 22.2 | 11.1 | 1.7 | 74.9 | 32.8 | 36.2 | 93.6 |
| MINNEAPOLIS-ST. PAUL | 1.5 | 2.6 | 6.9 | 7.1 | 8.1 | 7.5 | 6.5 | 32.4 | 21.7 | 8.5 | 1.3 | 73.5 | 31.7 | 35.0 | 96.6 |
| MISSOULA, MT | 1.2 | 1.9 | 5.7 | 6.0 | 7.0 | 8.8 | 9.6 | 28.9 | 23.7 | 8.9 | 1.4 | 76.9 | 31.6 | 35.6 | 97.3 |
| MOBILE, AL | 0.9 | 1.8 | 7.1 | 7.2 | 7.2 | 7.2 | 6.8 | 28.8 | 22.8 | 11.5 | 1.4 | 74.2 | 32.6 | 35.8 | 91.0 |
| MODESTO, CA | 21.8 | 28.7 | 8.6 | 9.3 | 8.2 | 7.9 | 6.8 | 29.1 | 19.2 | 9.5 | 1.3 | 69.1 | 30.5 | 31.7 | 96.4 |
| MONMOUTH-OCEAN, NJ | 3.7 | 5.7 | 6.5 | 7.4 | 7.0 | 6.0 | 4.9 | 28.4 | 22.4 | 14.9 | 2.4 | 75.4 | 36.4 | 38.9 | 92.6 |
| MONROE, LA | 0.8 | 1.3 | 7.1 | 7.1 | 7.6 | 9.2 | 8.9 | 26.8 | 21.9 | 10.1 | 1.4 | 73.1 | 30.2 | 33.3 | 88.5 |
| MONTGOMERY, AL | 0.7 | 1.4 | 7.0 | 7.1 | 7.1 | 7.5 | 7.2 | 30.6 | 22.1 | 10.2 | 1.4 | 74.6 | 31.9 | 34.6 | 93.1 |
| MUNCIE, IN | 0.7 | 1.4 | 5.8 | 5.7 | 5.9 | 9.7 | 11.1 | 26.6 | 22.0 | 11.6 | 1.6 | 79.1 | 31.4 | 34.4 | 90.4 |
| MYRTLE BEACH, SC | 0.9 | 1.6 | 5.9 | 6.2 | 6.2 | 5.9 | 6.1 | 30.2 | 24.1 | 14.2 | 1.1 | 78.2 | 33.8 | 38.4 | 93.7 |
| NAPLES, FL | 13.6 | 18.9 | 5.6 | 6.0 | 6.0 | 5.2 | 4.7 | 24.4 | 23.2 | 22.4 | 2.4 | 79.2 | 40.7 | 43.5 | 96.0 |
| NASHVILLE, TN | 0.8 | 1.7 | 7.0 | 7.0 | 6.9 | 7.0 | 7.0 | 32.0 | 22.9 | 9.0 | 1.2 | 75.2 | 32.5 | 35.2 | 93.5 |
| NASSAU-SUFFOLK, NY | 6.3 | 8.5 | 6.0 | 6.9 | 7.1 | 6.0 | 5.0 | 30.3 | 24.4 | 12.7 | 1.6 | 76.6 | 34.9 | 38.4 | 94.4 |
| N.HAVEN-BRDGPRT.,CT | 7.5 | 10.0 | 6.5 | 7.2 | 7.7 | 6.2 | 5.2 | 30.1 | 22.5 | 12.6 | 2.0 | 75.1 | 34.8 | 37.5 | 93.4 |
| NEW LONDON-NORWICH | 3.3 | 4.8 | 7.1 | 7.3 | 7.1 | 6.5 | 6.4 | 31.4 | 21.2 | 11.4 | 1.6 | 75.1 | 32.5 | 35.6 | 100.7 |
| NEW ORLEANS, LA | 4.2 | 5.3 | 6.9 | 7.0 | 7.4 | 8.0 | 7.1 | 29.3 | 22.8 | 10.3 | 1.2 | 74.0 | 31.8 | 35.4 | 91.0 |
| NEW YORK, NY | 22.1 | 25.8 | 6.8 | 7.0 | 6.5 | 6.0 | 6.4 | 32.1 | 22.6 | 10.9 | 1.7 | 76.4 | 34.0 | 36.2 | 90.4 |
| NEWARK, NJ | 9.9 | 13.3 | 6.6 | 7.2 | 7.2 | 6.4 | 5.7 | 30.7 | 23.6 | 11.1 | 1.6 | 75.3 | 34.4 | 37.2 | 92.8 |
| NEWBURGH, NY-PA | 6.6 | 8.7 | 7.6 | 8.3 | 7.9 | 7.1 | 6.1 | 29.6 | 22.3 | 9.7 | 1.4 | 72.1 | 32.2 | 34.8 | 100.4 |
| NRFOLK-VA BCH-N.NEWS | 2.3 | 3.4 | 7.7 | 7.6 | 7.2 | 7.0 | 8.1 | 33.1 | 19.3 | 9.1 | 1.0 | 73.9 | 29.8 | 32.7 | 96.8 |
| OAKLAND, CA | 13.1 | 17.4 | 6.5 | 7.6 | 7.0 | 6.8 | 6.4 | 31.8 | 22.5 | 10.0 | 1.4 | 75.1 | 33.2 | 36.0 | 96.1 |
| OCALA, FL | 3.0 | 4.8 | 5.9 | 6.6 | 6.8 | 6.1 | 4.8 | 23.2 | 22.9 | 21.7 | 2.0 | 77.0 | 40.0 | 42.5 | 93.6 |
| ODESSA-MIDLAND, TX | 26.6 | 32.6 | 9.1 | 8.9 | 8.4 | 8.2 | 6.4 | 27.7 | 21.0 | 9.3 | 1.0 | 68.5 | 30.6 | 32.5 | 95.2 |
| OKLAHOMA CITY, OK | 3.6 | 5.6 | 7.1 | 7.0 | 7.4 | 8.0 | 7.7 | 29.4 | 22.3 | 9.9 | 1.3 | 74.0 | 32.0 | 34.7 | 95.3 |
| OLYMPIA, WA | 3.0 | 5.0 | 6.3 | 6.8 | 7.3 | 7.8 | 6.8 | 29.2 | 24.3 | 9.9 | 1.6 | 74.9 | 33.7 | 36.2 | 95.4 |
| OMAHA, NE-IA | 2.6 | 5.5 | 7.2 | 7.2 | 8.0 | 7.7 | 6.9 | 30.4 | 21.6 | 9.6 | 1.4 | 73.0 | 31.6 | 34.5 | 94.5 |
| ORANGE COUNTY, CA | 23.4 | 29.3 | 7.0 | 7.7 | 6.6 | 6.9 | 7.1 | 33.3 | 20.8 | 9.3 | 1.4 | 74.9 | 31.4 | 34.3 | 100.3 |
| ORLANDO, FL | 8.2 | 12.3 | 6.8 | 7.2 | 7.3 | 6.6 | 6.4 | 30.6 | 21.6 | 12.0 | 1.5 | 74.9 | 33.1 | 36.0 | 95.5 |
| OWENSBORO, KY | 0.4 | 0.9 | 7.0 | 7.0 | 6.8 | 7.4 | 6.7 | 28.5 | 23.5 | 11.6 | 1.5 | 74.8 | 33.2 | 36.5 | 92.1 |
| PANAMA CITY, FL | 1.8 | 3.0 | 6.7 | 7.4 | 7.6 | 6.8 | 5.9 | 29.0 | 23.1 | 12.5 | 1.1 | 74.4 | 33.2 | 36.7 | 96.9 |
| PARKERSBURG-MARIETTA | 0.3 | 0.8 | 5.8 | 6.2 | 6.5 | 6.9 | 6.4 | 27.5 | 26.0 | 12.9 | 1.9 | 77.4 | 35.4 | 39.3 | 91.6 |
| PENSACOLA, FL | 1.8 | 3.0 | 6.9 | 7.5 | 7.7 | 7.5 | 6.9 | 28.7 | 22.4 | 11.3 | 1.2 | 73.9 | 32.4 | 35.5 | 95.8 |
| PEORIA-PEKIN, IL | 1.1 | 1.9 | 6.6 | 7.2 | 7.2 | 7.4 | 6.4 | 28.0 | 23.1 | 12.2 | 2.0 | 74.8 | 34.2 | 36.9 | 94.5 |
| PHILADELPHIA, PA-NJ | 3.6 | 5.0 | 6.5 | 7.1 | 7.4 | 6.7 | 5.9 | 30.3 | 22.1 | 12.3 | 1.8 | 75.2 | 33.7 | 36.8 | 92.0 |
| PHOENIX-MESA, AZ | 17.0 | 21.4 | 8.2 | 7.9 | 7.6 | 7.1 | 6.5 | 29.2 | 21.1 | 10.9 | 1.4 | 72.2 | 32.1 | 34.6 | 97.9 |
| PINE BLUFF, AR | 0.5 | 1.3 | 7.2 | 7.2 | 7.5 | 9.1 | 7.9 | 27.0 | 21.6 | 10.9 | 1.6 | 73.0 | 31.9 | 33.4 | 93.5 |
| PITTSBURGH, PA | 0.6 | 1.1 | 5.3 | 6.1 | 6.7 | 6.5 | 5.6 | 28.2 | 23.8 | 15.6 | 2.1 | 78.3 | 36.8 | 40.1 | 90.6 |
| PITTSFIELD, MA | 1.0 | 1.8 | 5.5 | 6.5 | 6.8 | 6.6 | 5.2 | 28.4 | 23.0 | 15.3 | 2.5 | 77.7 | 35.9 | 39.2 | 93.1 |
| POCATELLO, ID | 4.1 | 6.6 | 8.0 | 7.8 | 7.8 | 9.1 | 9.1 | 28.5 | 20.3 | 8.2 | 1.2 | 70.9 | 29.5 | 30.7 | 99.2 |
| PORTLAND, ME | 0.6 | 1.2 | 5.0 | 5.6 | 6.8 | 6.8 | 6.4 | 32.8 | 23.2 | 11.6 | 1.8 | 78.9 | 33.7 | 37.7 | 92.9 |
| PORTLAND-VANCOUVER | 3.3 | 5.8 | 6.7 | 6.8 | 7.3 | 7.2 | 6.5 | 30.0 | 24.4 | 9.6 | 1.5 | 74.9 | 33.8 | 36.3 | 96.9 |
| PROVID.-WARWICK-PAW. | 4.8 | 7.5 | 6.2 | 7.0 | 7.2 | 6.6 | 5.9 | 30.6 | 20.9 | 13.5 | 2.2 | 76.5 | 34.0 | 36.8 | 92.3 |
| PROVO-OREM, UT | 3.2 | 5.2 | 10.3 | 7.7 | 8.2 | 12.5 | 18.1 | 22.3 | 13.9 | 6.2 | 0.9 | 67.2 | 22.5 | 23.1 | 96.8 |
| PUEBLO, CO | 35.8 | 41.4 | 6.7 | 6.6 | 7.4 | 8.1 | 6.5 | 24.6 | 25.3 | 12.9 | 1.8 | 74.4 | 34.7 | 38.1 | 94.5 |
| PUNTA GORDA, FL | 2.5 | 4.3 | 4.2 | 4.8 | 5.1 | 4.5 | 3.5 | 19.3 | 24.7 | 30.7 | 3.3 | 83.3 | 53.6 | 52.7 | 94.0 |
| UNITED STATES | 9.0 | 11.8 | 6.9 | 7.2 | 7.2 | 7.2 | 6.7 | 29.9 | 22.2 | 11.1 | 1.6 | 74.6 | 32.9 | 35.7 | 95.6 |

# HOUSEHOLDS
## MSA AND U.S. TOTALS

C

| MSA | HOUSEHOLDS | | | | | FAMILIES | | | MEDIAN HOUSEHOLD INCOME | | |
|---|---|---|---|---|---|---|---|---|---|---|---|
| | 1990 | 2000 | 2005 | % Annual Rate 1990-2000 | 2000 Average HH Size | 1990 | 2000 | % Annual Rate 1990-2000 | 2000 | 2005 | 2000 National Rank |
| LA CROSSE, WI-MN | 43,506 | 46,712 | 47,767 | 0.9 | 2.50 | 28,952 | 30,324 | 0.6 | 39,815 | 44,351 | 154 |
| LAFAYETTE, LA | 121,807 | 141,861 | 151,039 | 1.9 | 2.63 | 89,586 | 101,127 | 1.5 | 28,973 | 31,914 | 312 |
| LAFAYETTE, IN | 57,068 | 62,927 | 64,838 | 1.2 | 2.51 | 37,352 | 39,734 | 0.8 | 42,039 | 49,749 | 120 |
| LAKE CHARLES, LA | 60,328 | 68,024 | 71,059 | 1.5 | 2.62 | 45,035 | 49,591 | 1.2 | 35,254 | 38,450 | 250 |
| LAKELND-WINTER HAVEN | 155,969 | 176,911 | 186,630 | 1.5 | 2.56 | 114,554 | 126,161 | 1.2 | 36,864 | 45,275 | 217 |
| LANCASTER, PA | 150,956 | 167,716 | 174,854 | 1.3 | 2.68 | 112,106 | 121,388 | 1.0 | 47,611 | 57,863 | 48 |
| LANSING-E.LANSING,MI | 156,887 | 168,724 | 172,071 | 0.9 | 2.56 | 106,053 | 110,708 | 0.5 | 44,463 | 51,549 | 87 |
| LAREDO, TX | 34,438 | 52,067 | 60,521 | 5.1 | 3.79 | 29,469 | 44,833 | 5.2 | 30,477 | 37,879 | 305 |
| LAS CRUCES, NM | 45,029 | 59,353 | 64,098 | 3.4 | 2.83 | 33,228 | 43,154 | 3.2 | 29,240 | 34,541 | 311 |
| LAS VEGAS, NV-AZ | 330,490 | 559,962 | 677,911 | 6.6 | 2.55 | 220,027 | 369,960 | 6.5 | 44,847 | 53,728 | 82 |
| LAWRENCE, KS | 30,138 | 36,018 | 38,554 | 2.2 | 2.54 | 17,291 | 19,879 | 1.7 | 37,826 | 45,658 | 192 |
| LAWTON, OK | 37,569 | 38,016 | 36,536 | 0.1 | 2.65 | 28,724 | 28,381 | -0.1 | 32,960 | 38,916 | 283 |
| LEWISTON-AUBURN, ME | 40,017 | 40,537 | 41,324 | 0.2 | 2.42 | 28,047 | 27,613 | -0.2 | 37,357 | 45,181 | 204 |
| LEXINGTON, KY | 154,089 | 178,003 | 190,185 | 1.8 | 2.47 | 105,755 | 118,629 | 1.4 | 40,075 | 44,248 | 150 |
| LIMA, OH | 55,384 | 55,882 | 55,760 | 0.1 | 2.63 | 41,233 | 40,322 | -0.3 | 37,193 | 42,282 | 210 |
| LINCOLN, NE | 82,759 | 93,055 | 97,307 | 1.4 | 2.44 | 52,985 | 57,730 | 1.0 | 43,777 | 50,536 | 96 |
| LITTLE ROCK-N.LITTLE | 195,437 | 217,663 | 227,935 | 1.3 | 2.54 | 138,788 | 150,747 | 1.0 | 37,531 | 42,975 | 197 |
| LONGVIEW-MARSHALL,TX | 72,092 | 79,886 | 83,097 | 1.3 | 2.58 | 52,593 | 56,519 | 0.9 | 33,876 | 39,164 | 274 |
| LOS ANGELES-L.BEACH | 2,989,552 | 3,199,899 | 3,367,195 | 0.8 | 2.89 | 2,013,926 | 2,137,362 | 0.7 | 42,060 | 52,502 | 119 |
| LOUISVILLE, KY-IN | 366,364 | 395,106 | 409,162 | 0.9 | 2.52 | 258,803 | 272,235 | 0.6 | 41,141 | 45,766 | 128 |
| LUBBOCK, TX | 81,534 | 85,237 | 84,983 | 0.5 | 2.56 | 55,462 | 56,304 | 0.2 | 35,679 | 40,299 | 236 |
| LYNCHBURG, VA | 72,689 | 82,930 | 87,124 | 1.6 | 2.43 | 53,188 | 58,991 | 1.3 | 34,461 | 38,606 | 264 |
| MACON, GA | 106,478 | 122,650 | 130,141 | 1.7 | 2.58 | 77,832 | 87,768 | 1.5 | 38,904 | 42,839 | 172 |
| MADISON, WI | 142,786 | 172,164 | 182,411 | 2.3 | 2.42 | 87,363 | 102,334 | 1.9 | 52,352 | 61,091 | 24 |
| MANSFIELD, OH | 65,956 | 66,921 | 67,246 | 0.2 | 2.57 | 48,104 | 47,159 | -0.2 | 34,660 | 40,116 | 259 |
| MCALLN-EDNBG-MISSION | 103,479 | 150,047 | 171,679 | 4.6 | 3.63 | 87,912 | 126,800 | 4.5 | 23,020 | 26,332 | 318 |
| MEDFORD-ASHLAND, OR | 57,238 | 70,839 | 76,500 | 2.6 | 2.47 | 40,141 | 47,909 | 2.2 | 35,300 | 39,401 | 249 |
| MELBRN-TITUSVL-P.BAY | 161,365 | 191,058 | 201,487 | 2.1 | 2.46 | 113,149 | 128,838 | 1.6 | 39,480 | 45,832 | 164 |
| MEMPHIS, TN-AR-MS | 365,450 | 412,196 | 436,352 | 1.5 | 2.65 | 261,463 | 290,037 | 1.3 | 38,988 | 44,323 | 171 |
| MERCED, CA | 55,331 | 64,525 | 70,044 | 1.9 | 3.13 | 43,246 | 49,762 | 1.7 | 32,920 | 41,289 | 285 |
| MIAMI, FL | 692,355 | 782,447 | 822,975 | 1.5 | 2.77 | 481,263 | 541,788 | 1.4 | 35,093 | 42,124 | 253 |
| MID'SX-SOMER'T-HUNT. | 365,085 | 419,181 | 448,654 | 1.7 | 2.66 | 270,114 | 300,566 | 1.3 | 65,101 | 76,403 | 3 |
| MILWAUKEE-WAUKESHA | 537,722 | 557,045 | 563,856 | 0.4 | 2.57 | 369,799 | 374,779 | 0.2 | 48,093 | 53,936 | 44 |
| MINNEAPOLIS-ST. PAUL | 960,170 | 1,104,376 | 1,179,736 | 1.7 | 2.59 | 648,958 | 735,846 | 1.5 | 54,974 | 62,754 | 17 |
| MISSOULA, MT | 30,782 | 36,319 | 37,786 | 2.0 | 2.39 | 19,847 | 22,577 | 1.6 | 32,986 | 36,078 | 282 |
| MOBILE, AL | 173,943 | 203,786 | 216,029 | 1.9 | 2.61 | 128,956 | 147,086 | 1.6 | 35,908 | 40,814 | 231 |
| MODESTO, CA | 125,375 | 150,664 | 164,648 | 2.3 | 2.92 | 94,306 | 110,467 | 1.9 | 43,727 | 54,871 | 97 |
| MONMOUTH-OCEAN, NJ | 365,717 | 420,839 | 450,610 | 1.7 | 2.63 | 266,675 | 296,236 | 1.3 | 56,481 | 66,144 | 11 |
| MONROE, LA | 50,518 | 54,045 | 54,955 | 0.8 | 2.62 | 36,482 | 38,111 | 0.5 | 30,718 | 33,584 | 303 |
| MONTGOMERY, AL | 105,531 | 120,351 | 125,372 | 1.6 | 2.59 | 76,074 | 84,536 | 1.3 | 38,766 | 43,592 | 178 |
| MUNCIE, IN | 45,177 | 44,634 | 43,723 | -0.1 | 2.40 | 30,186 | 28,743 | -0.6 | 35,135 | 38,167 | 251 |
| MYRTLE BEACH, SC | 55,764 | 76,909 | 89,939 | 4.0 | 2.34 | 40,450 | 54,153 | 3.6 | 37,298 | 42,832 | 205 |
| NAPLES, FL | 61,703 | 96,238 | 117,132 | 5.5 | 2.19 | 43,795 | 66,513 | 5.2 | 45,472 | 50,925 | 72 |
| NASHVILLE, TN | 375,831 | 463,708 | 503,712 | 2.6 | 2.50 | 264,570 | 321,636 | 2.4 | 46,509 | 52,982 | 58 |
| NASSAU-SUFFOLK, NY | 856,234 | 905,032 | 935,640 | 0.7 | 2.94 | 685,095 | 702,266 | 0.3 | 66,269 | 77,683 | 2 |
| N.HAVEN-BRDGPRT.,CT | 609,741 | 620,718 | 631,936 | 0.2 | 2.57 | 428,919 | 422,581 | -0.2 | 56,347 | 63,926 | 12 |
| NEW LONDON-NORWICH | 93,245 | 92,087 | 90,819 | -0.2 | 2.54 | 66,385 | 63,204 | -0.6 | 51,542 | 61,159 | 30 |
| NEW ORLEANS, LA | 469,823 | 498,116 | 507,823 | 0.7 | 2.57 | 327,669 | 338,367 | 0.4 | 34,305 | 38,291 | 270 |
| NEW YORK, NY | 3,252,399 | 3,347,821 | 3,416,475 | 0.4 | 2.55 | 2,051,867 | 2,078,167 | 0.2 | 40,164 | 48,079 | 146 |
| NEWARK, NJ | 686,032 | 709,112 | 723,121 | 0.4 | 2.71 | 496,224 | 500,937 | 0.1 | 55,952 | 64,337 | 13 |
| NEWBURGH, NY-PA | 112,042 | 128,398 | 136,989 | 1.7 | 2.86 | 85,115 | 94,776 | 1.3 | 51,221 | 63,636 | 31 |
| NRFOLK-VA BCH-N.NEWS | 511,136 | 580,667 | 607,291 | 1.6 | 2.61 | 371,603 | 412,444 | 1.3 | 40,086 | 46,726 | 149 |
| OAKLAND, CA | 779,806 | 910,530 | 989,244 | 1.9 | 2.58 | 521,515 | 594,573 | 1.6 | 60,619 | 73,709 | 7 |
| OCALA, FL | 78,177 | 100,443 | 110,423 | 3.1 | 2.46 | 57,039 | 70,838 | 2.7 | 32,896 | 38,047 | 287 |
| ODESSA-MIDLAND, TX | 81,242 | 90,681 | 93,589 | 1.3 | 2.66 | 60,122 | 65,100 | 1.0 | 37,933 | 44,788 | 188 |
| OKLAHOMA CITY, OK | 367,775 | 404,773 | 421,294 | 1.2 | 2.54 | 254,582 | 271,475 | 0.8 | 37,271 | 44,104 | 207 |
| OLYMPIA, WA | 62,150 | 81,505 | 88,207 | 3.3 | 2.53 | 43,336 | 54,867 | 2.9 | 47,624 | 57,301 | 47 |
| OMAHA, NE-IA | 240,149 | 266,001 | 278,635 | 1.2 | 2.60 | 167,244 | 180,214 | 0.9 | 43,881 | 50,053 | 93 |
| ORANGE COUNTY, CA | 827,066 | 983,013 | 1,075,339 | 2.1 | 2.82 | 583,162 | 676,832 | 1.8 | 61,136 | 74,735 | 5 |
| ORLANDO, FL | 465,275 | 597,468 | 665,261 | 3.1 | 2.57 | 323,858 | 403,233 | 2.7 | 42,000 | 51,024 | 121 |
| OWENSBORO, KY | 33,036 | 35,236 | 35,908 | 0.8 | 2.53 | 23,980 | 24,828 | 0.4 | 36,247 | 41,168 | 227 |
| PANAMA CITY, FL | 48,938 | 56,923 | 58,898 | 1.8 | 2.57 | 35,608 | 39,787 | 1.4 | 35,659 | 41,782 | 237 |
| PARKERSBURG-MARIETTA | 57,804 | 59,966 | 59,968 | 0.4 | 2.44 | 42,386 | 42,500 | 0.0 | 33,982 | 37,275 | 272 |
| PENSACOLA, FL | 128,508 | 152,209 | 160,355 | 2.1 | 2.59 | 93,404 | 107,856 | 1.8 | 37,024 | 42,834 | 214 |
| PEORIA-PEKIN, IL | 129,363 | 132,586 | 133,574 | 0.3 | 2.54 | 91,728 | 90,674 | -0.1 | 42,968 | 47,897 | 108 |
| PHILADELPHIA, PA-NJ | 1,801,159 | 1,841,551 | 1,859,915 | 0.3 | 2.62 | 1,259,166 | 1,249,505 | -0.1 | 48,289 | 56,202 | 42 |
| PHOENIX-MESA, AZ | 846,714 | 1,189,000 | 1,365,833 | 4.2 | 2.56 | 576,998 | 792,183 | 3.9 | 42,431 | 50,123 | 111 |
| PINE BLUFF, AR | 30,001 | 28,612 | 27,669 | -0.6 | 2.64 | 21,972 | 20,435 | -0.9 | 28,395 | 33,558 | 315 |
| PITTSBURGH, PA | 947,248 | 940,872 | 925,965 | -0.1 | 2.40 | 656,278 | 628,954 | -0.5 | 36,784 | 40,219 | 219 |
| PITTSFIELD, MA | 54,315 | 53,511 | 53,160 | -0.2 | 2.35 | 36,622 | 34,538 | -0.7 | 38,834 | 44,374 | 174 |
| POCATELLO, ID | 23,412 | 26,990 | 28,122 | 1.7 | 2.75 | 16,794 | 18,729 | 1.3 | 38,805 | 44,668 | 177 |
| PORTLAND, ME | 94,512 | 105,909 | 112,640 | 1.4 | 2.38 | 63,087 | 68,566 | 1.0 | 43,509 | 50,063 | 100 |
| PORTLAND-VANCOUVER | 589,441 | 736,770 | 798,889 | 2.7 | 2.51 | 394,237 | 480,746 | 2.4 | 46,484 | 53,747 | 59 |
| PROVID.-WARWICK-PAW. | 345,290 | 345,833 | 349,721 | 0.0 | 2.53 | 236,552 | 228,563 | -0.4 | 42,129 | 50,236 | 117 |
| PROVO-OREM, UT | 70,168 | 93,210 | 103,185 | 3.5 | 3.71 | 56,511 | 74,013 | 3.3 | 45,839 | 55,045 | 67 |
| PUEBLO, CO | 47,057 | 54,202 | 58,851 | 1.7 | 2.51 | 33,248 | 37,426 | 1.4 | 34,449 | 37,912 | 265 |
| PUNTA GORDA, FL | 48,433 | 60,462 | 65,110 | 2.7 | 2.26 | 35,325 | 42,993 | 2.4 | 38,999 | 49,742 | 170 |
| UNITED STATES | | | | 1.4 | 2.59 | | | 1.1 | 41,914 | 49,127 | |

# INCOME

## MSA AND U.S. TOTALS

| MSA | 2000 Per Capita Income | 2000 HH Income Base | 2000 HOUSEHOLD INCOME DISTRIBUTION (%) Less than $15,000 | $15,000 to $24,999 | $25,000 to $49,999 | $50,000 to $99,999 | $100,000 to $149,999 | $150,000 or More | 2000 AVERAGE DISPOSABLE INCOME BY AGE OF HOUSEHOLDER All Ages | <35 | 35-44 | 45-54 | 55-64 | 65+ |
|---|---|---|---|---|---|---|---|---|---|---|---|---|---|---|
| LA CROSSE, WI-MN | 19,664 | 46,704 | 13.6 | 12.5 | 38.0 | 27.8 | 6.0 | 2.1 | 34,664 | 28,045 | 40,783 | 46,071 | 39,953 | 21,923 |
| LAFAYETTE, LA | 15,291 | 141,851 | 27.7 | 16.1 | 31.4 | 19.1 | 3.9 | 1.9 | 31,998 | 26,996 | 37,424 | 38,114 | 31,346 | 21,607 |
| LAFAYETTE, IN | 21,083 | 62,927 | 11.9 | 13.2 | 34.5 | 30.0 | 7.4 | 3.1 | 41,005 | 30,068 | 48,339 | 53,655 | 46,868 | 29,428 |
| LAKE CHARLES, LA | 17,125 | 68,024 | 21.5 | 14.3 | 33.3 | 24.5 | 4.7 | 1.7 | 35,300 | 28,803 | 40,850 | 44,517 | 35,953 | 23,676 |
| LAKELND-WINTER HAVEN | 18,572 | 176,910 | 14.4 | 15.5 | 36.9 | 26.7 | 5.0 | 1.5 | 37,143 | 33,844 | 43,021 | 45,112 | 40,684 | 28,031 |
| LANCASTER, PA | 21,665 | 167,709 | 8.2 | 9.3 | 35.6 | 36.7 | 8.1 | 2.2 | 42,070 | 38,520 | 45,800 | 52,956 | 46,023 | 27,886 |
| LANSING-E.LANSING,MI | 21,419 | 168,724 | 12.6 | 11.3 | 32.9 | 33.2 | 7.4 | 2.7 | 39,980 | 30,764 | 44,727 | 52,453 | 46,820 | 25,690 |
| LAREDO, TX | 11,462 | 52,067 | 24.9 | 16.8 | 31.4 | 20.3 | 4.7 | 2.0 | 33,408 | 30,468 | 35,833 | 38,652 | 34,146 | 23,838 |
| LAS CRUCES, NM | 13,354 | 59,353 | 24.6 | 17.8 | 34.0 | 19.6 | 3.0 | 1.1 | 29,862 | 23,026 | 33,637 | 38,165 | 35,022 | 24,779 |
| LAS VEGAS, NV-AZ | 23,435 | 559,939 | 10.3 | 12.2 | 33.7 | 32.9 | 8.0 | 3.0 | 44,527 | 39,719 | 48,983 | 53,061 | 45,432 | 31,303 |
| LAWRENCE, KS | 18,800 | 36,018 | 18.9 | 12.6 | 33.2 | 25.9 | 6.2 | 3.2 | 37,543 | 25,890 | 44,595 | 54,813 | 48,253 | 31,798 |
| LAWTON, OK | 15,157 | 38,003 | 16.2 | 18.8 | 38.4 | 22.7 | 3.0 | 0.8 | 31,328 | 25,597 | 34,624 | 38,847 | 35,654 | 26,884 |
| LEWISTON-AUBURN, ME | 18,817 | 40,537 | 15.3 | 13.5 | 38.3 | 26.9 | 4.6 | 1.3 | 33,592 | 31,150 | 40,342 | 41,152 | 35,430 | 20,207 |
| LEXINGTON, KY | 22,421 | 178,002 | 15.6 | 13.1 | 33.1 | 27.5 | 7.0 | 3.7 | 40,506 | 31,156 | 46,005 | 49,595 | 41,862 | 26,524 |
| LIMA, OH | 16,276 | 55,881 | 15.7 | 14.6 | 38.5 | 26.5 | 3.8 | 0.9 | 33,111 | 28,931 | 38,627 | 43,188 | 36,156 | 21,579 |
| LINCOLN, NE | 22,285 | 93,055 | 11.5 | 11.7 | 35.0 | 32.3 | 7.3 | 2.2 | 39,610 | 30,370 | 46,683 | 50,157 | 45,750 | 28,675 |
| LITTLE ROCK-N.LITTLE | 18,694 | 217,655 | 15.7 | 15.0 | 35.3 | 27.2 | 5.2 | 1.7 | 35,701 | 29,433 | 42,082 | 44,810 | 38,030 | 23,959 |
| LONGVIEW-MARSHALL,TX | 16,696 | 79,886 | 21.3 | 15.1 | 34.3 | 23.5 | 4.3 | 1.5 | 34,259 | 29,528 | 39,441 | 41,986 | 36,307 | 23,984 |
| LOS ANGELES-L.BEACH | 21,973 | 3,199,884 | 15.0 | 12.5 | 30.7 | 29.1 | 7.6 | 5.1 | 43,185 | 36,409 | 44,111 | 49,754 | 46,185 | 31,679 |
| LOUISVILLE, KY-IN | 21,468 | 395,102 | 14.2 | 12.8 | 33.7 | 30.0 | 6.7 | 2.6 | 39,467 | 32,542 | 44,587 | 48,430 | 40,426 | 26,569 |
| LUBBOCK, TX | 18,563 | 85,237 | 19.2 | 14.9 | 32.8 | 25.6 | 5.4 | 2.1 | 37,085 | 27,694 | 43,286 | 48,288 | 41,425 | 29,897 |
| LYNCHBURG, VA | 17,972 | 82,927 | 17.9 | 16.3 | 36.3 | 24.3 | 3.8 | 1.4 | 32,696 | 28,453 | 37,290 | 40,386 | 34,726 | 22,874 |
| MACON, GA | 19,514 | 122,650 | 17.4 | 12.7 | 33.9 | 28.3 | 5.4 | 2.3 | 36,788 | 30,857 | 40,107 | 45,532 | 37,973 | 24,769 |
| MADISON, WI | 27,428 | 172,164 | 7.9 | 8.5 | 30.5 | 37.4 | 11.2 | 4.4 | 44,251 | 33,455 | 48,962 | 56,129 | 50,936 | 31,907 |
| MANSFIELD, OH | 16,071 | 66,921 | 17.3 | 16.4 | 38.2 | 24.3 | 2.9 | 0.9 | 31,515 | 27,630 | 36,253 | 41,020 | 34,787 | 20,154 |
| MCALLN-EDNBG-MISSION | 9,342 | 150,047 | 33.5 | 19.7 | 28.2 | 15.1 | 2.5 | 1.1 | 26,855 | 22,906 | 29,616 | 30,692 | 28,851 | 22,096 |
| MEDFORD-ASHLAND, OR | 18,135 | 70,839 | 17.7 | 15.2 | 37.4 | 24.4 | 4.0 | 1.2 | 31,022 | 26,296 | 35,632 | 39,169 | 33,419 | 21,998 |
| MELBRN-TITUSVL-P.BAY | 19,872 | 191,046 | 13.3 | 14.6 | 35.9 | 29.7 | 5.0 | 1.4 | 38,219 | 34,013 | 42,065 | 47,617 | 42,775 | 29,590 |
| MEMPHIS, TN-AR-MS | 19,688 | 412,190 | 17.3 | 13.3 | 32.4 | 27.9 | 6.4 | 2.7 | 40,254 | 34,495 | 45,079 | 49,766 | 40,715 | 24,750 |
| MERCED, CA | 14,751 | 64,525 | 18.2 | 18.7 | 35.0 | 22.1 | 4.0 | 2.0 | 33,294 | 28,190 | 37,602 | 40,861 | 37,667 | 23,177 |
| MIAMI, FL | 19,686 | 782,446 | 20.5 | 15.0 | 31.1 | 23.6 | 5.8 | 3.9 | 39,949 | 34,011 | 41,986 | 44,832 | 41,639 | 29,056 |
| MID'SX-SOMER'T-HUNT. | 32,493 | 419,180 | 6.1 | 5.1 | 22.4 | 42.0 | 16.1 | 8.4 | 55,505 | 50,890 | 56,884 | 62,802 | 59,463 | 33,692 |
| MILWAUKEE-WAUKESHA | 24,905 | 557,036 | 11.3 | 9.5 | 31.5 | 33.8 | 9.6 | 4.3 | 41,776 | 33,841 | 45,718 | 52,767 | 46,944 | 27,204 |
| MINNEAPOLIS-ST. PAUL | 28,900 | 1,104,375 | 7.7 | 7.5 | 28.9 | 37.7 | 12.2 | 6.0 | 49,519 | 40,553 | 52,304 | 60,116 | 53,332 | 30,681 |
| MISSOULA, MT | 18,412 | 36,319 | 20.1 | 16.6 | 35.1 | 22.1 | 4.3 | 1.8 | 32,025 | 22,517 | 37,111 | 41,423 | 35,158 | 24,102 |
| MOBILE, AL | 18,232 | 203,778 | 19.0 | 14.9 | 32.9 | 25.9 | 5.4 | 2.0 | 36,364 | 29,802 | 40,707 | 44,838 | 38,139 | 27,047 |
| MODESTO, CA | 20,987 | 150,663 | 12.8 | 11.3 | 33.5 | 30.7 | 7.8 | 3.9 | 42,096 | 36,602 | 46,045 | 51,408 | 43,726 | 28,620 |
| MONMOUTH-OCEAN, NJ | 29,930 | 420,838 | 8.8 | 7.8 | 26.1 | 38.0 | 12.2 | 7.2 | 49,498 | 47,571 | 54,705 | 60,019 | 54,694 | 28,522 |
| MONROE, LA | 16,082 | 54,045 | 25.3 | 16.4 | 31.2 | 21.2 | 4.1 | 1.8 | 33,054 | 25,775 | 38,403 | 42,386 | 35,457 | 22,247 |
| MONTGOMERY, AL | 18,649 | 120,351 | 17.1 | 13.7 | 33.1 | 28.5 | 5.6 | 2.0 | 37,690 | 32,183 | 42,662 | 47,112 | 39,143 | 25,805 |
| MUNCIE, IN | 19,603 | 44,634 | 20.4 | 14.6 | 33.8 | 24.7 | 4.7 | 1.8 | 34,300 | 26,356 | 39,658 | 46,561 | 38,562 | 22,774 |
| MYRTLE BEACH, SC | 20,509 | 76,909 | 14.2 | 15.2 | 36.7 | 27.2 | 5.2 | 1.6 | 35,431 | 30,705 | 39,647 | 41,367 | 37,299 | 29,457 |
| NAPLES, FL | 35,615 | 96,238 | 8.2 | 12.6 | 34.0 | 28.6 | 9.3 | 7.3 | 53,371 | 39,374 | 48,330 | 54,351 | 56,485 | 50,793 |
| NASHVILLE, TN | 25,089 | 463,706 | 10.9 | 10.8 | 32.3 | 33.0 | 8.9 | 4.1 | 47,767 | 39,474 | 52,825 | 57,654 | 49,762 | 30,710 |
| NASSAU-SUFFOLK, NY | 32,087 | 905,031 | 6.5 | 5.4 | 20.9 | 40.9 | 16.1 | 10.2 | 57,860 | 49,909 | 56,450 | 65,373 | 62,996 | 38,996 |
| N.HAVEN-BRDGPRT.,CT | 34,015 | 620,718 | 9.9 | 7.6 | 25.6 | 35.3 | 11.7 | 9.8 | 55,533 | 44,281 | 54,444 | 63,567 | 58,952 | 35,547 |
| NEW LONDON-NORWICH | 25,527 | 92,087 | 8.4 | 8.1 | 31.4 | 38.5 | 9.9 | 3.7 | 44,614 | 38,793 | 46,634 | 56,089 | 49,422 | 29,559 |
| NEW ORLEANS, LA | 18,598 | 498,111 | 21.8 | 14.7 | 31.6 | 24.1 | 5.1 | 2.6 | 36,865 | 30,026 | 41,303 | 44,016 | 37,365 | 25,145 |
| NEW YORK, NY | 25,166 | 3,347,741 | 19.7 | 12.0 | 28.3 | 26.6 | 7.7 | 5.8 | 40,982 | 36,074 | 41,338 | 44,878 | 43,355 | 28,226 |
| NEWARK, NJ | 30,077 | 709,107 | 10.9 | 7.9 | 25.0 | 35.5 | 12.5 | 8.2 | 50,634 | 43,644 | 51,479 | 56,578 | 55,846 | 32,623 |
| NEWBURGH, NY-PA | 22,065 | 128,397 | 10.7 | 8.5 | 29.2 | 38.2 | 10.0 | 3.5 | 42,550 | 39,900 | 46,422 | 51,655 | 46,153 | 24,300 |
| NRFOLK-VA BCH-N.NEWS | 18,789 | 580,654 | 12.6 | 14.1 | 36.5 | 30.1 | 5.2 | 1.5 | 36,570 | 29,932 | 40,030 | 46,063 | 40,596 | 28,146 |
| OAKLAND, CA | 32,171 | 910,528 | 8.5 | 6.6 | 24.0 | 38.5 | 14.2 | 8.2 | 55,476 | 46,040 | 57,258 | 63,224 | 57,896 | 39,098 |
| OCALA, FL | 17,276 | 100,442 | 16.4 | 19.2 | 37.2 | 22.5 | 3.6 | 1.2 | 33,700 | 31,776 | 39,634 | 41,741 | 36,395 | 26,388 |
| ODESSA-MIDLAND, TX | 21,228 | 90,681 | 16.8 | 14.9 | 32.3 | 26.3 | 6.1 | 3.6 | 41,007 | 31,557 | 44,708 | 47,678 | 43,439 | 31,761 |
| OKLAHOMA CITY, OK | 19,109 | 404,759 | 16.0 | 14.9 | 34.6 | 27.4 | 5.2 | 1.9 | 35,866 | 28,255 | 40,879 | 44,920 | 40,792 | 26,154 |
| OLYMPIA, WA | 23,319 | 81,505 | 8.6 | 10.4 | 33.6 | 36.6 | 8.6 | 2.3 | 44,560 | 36,049 | 47,691 | 55,383 | 48,469 | 33,611 |
| OMAHA, NE-IA | 22,436 | 265,992 | 10.5 | 12.2 | 35.0 | 31.8 | 7.3 | 3.3 | 41,123 | 32,108 | 46,593 | 50,884 | 43,428 | 28,000 |
| ORANGE COUNTY, CA | 31,077 | 983,013 | 6.1 | 6.9 | 25.3 | 38.7 | 14.1 | 8.9 | 57,207 | 48,171 | 58,016 | 64,843 | 60,604 | 39,768 |
| ORLANDO, FL | 21,417 | 597,468 | 10.6 | 13.7 | 35.5 | 31.2 | 6.7 | 2.4 | 41,984 | 37,446 | 46,247 | 50,199 | 44,832 | 30,146 |
| OWENSBORO, KY | 17,628 | 35,233 | 17.9 | 14.1 | 36.4 | 25.9 | 4.5 | 1.3 | 33,970 | 28,672 | 39,961 | 43,211 | 35,294 | 21,937 |
| PANAMA CITY, FL | 17,898 | 56,913 | 16.4 | 15.8 | 36.3 | 26.0 | 4.2 | 1.3 | 35,585 | 30,519 | 38,696 | 43,745 | 38,863 | 27,266 |
| PARKERSBURG-MARIETTA | 16,548 | 59,966 | 20.4 | 15.6 | 36.4 | 23.6 | 3.2 | 0.8 | 31,469 | 27,682 | 37,534 | 39,745 | 34,355 | 20,267 |
| PENSACOLA, FL | 18,102 | 152,202 | 16.2 | 15.2 | 35.4 | 26.8 | 5.0 | 1.5 | 36,609 | 30,167 | 39,951 | 45,309 | 40,004 | 28,603 |
| PEORIA-PEKIN, IL | 21,165 | 132,568 | 14.1 | 11.8 | 32.7 | 32.0 | 7.1 | 2.4 | 38,961 | 31,875 | 44,480 | 50,417 | 42,419 | 25,745 |
| PHILADELPHIA, PA-NJ | 25,816 | 1,841,502 | 12.3 | 9.9 | 29.6 | 33.3 | 9.7 | 5.3 | 45,781 | 39,682 | 48,226 | 55,101 | 50,144 | 29,605 |
| PHOENIX-MESA, AZ | 22,199 | 1,188,985 | 12.1 | 13.1 | 33.4 | 31.0 | 7.4 | 2.9 | 41,820 | 35,669 | 46,615 | 51,087 | 42,947 | 30,757 |
| PINE BLUFF, AR | 13,555 | 28,611 | 28.0 | 16.5 | 31.9 | 19.8 | 2.9 | 1.0 | 28,584 | 23,908 | 34,740 | 36,768 | 31,263 | 18,998 |
| PITTSBURGH, PA | 21,314 | 940,865 | 17.5 | 14.7 | 34.0 | 25.5 | 5.5 | 2.9 | 36,311 | 32,014 | 41,596 | 46,368 | 39,788 | 23,285 |
| PITTSFIELD, MA | 20,792 | 53,511 | 17.0 | 13.1 | 34.2 | 28.2 | 5.2 | 2.4 | 34,681 | 31,354 | 38,516 | 45,412 | 39,901 | 22,602 |
| POCATELLO, ID | 16,777 | 26,981 | 16.2 | 12.4 | 37.1 | 28.3 | 4.9 | 1.2 | 35,014 | 28,160 | 40,982 | 45,139 | 36,159 | 23,763 |
| PORTLAND, ME | 23,546 | 105,906 | 11.5 | 11.5 | 35.0 | 32.0 | 7.4 | 2.7 | 39,207 | 35,359 | 45,031 | 46,938 | 41,914 | 25,501 |
| PORTLAND-VANCOUVER | 24,211 | 736,762 | 9.9 | 11.0 | 33.3 | 34.0 | 8.6 | 3.2 | 41,472 | 34,827 | 45,556 | 50,778 | 44,594 | 27,532 |
| PROVID.-WARWICK-PAW. | 21,607 | 345,833 | 15.4 | 11.2 | 33.0 | 30.3 | 7.0 | 3.2 | 38,739 | 35,297 | 43,868 | 48,479 | 43,914 | 24,251 |
| PROVO-OREM, UT | 15,807 | 93,210 | 9.4 | 10.5 | 35.4 | 34.2 | 8.1 | 2.5 | 41,187 | 32,408 | 47,764 | 54,899 | 50,463 | 30,527 |
| PUEBLO, CO | 16,686 | 54,190 | 18.7 | 15.8 | 35.4 | 25.2 | 4.0 | 0.9 | 31,920 | 24,977 | 38,901 | 40,529 | 33,566 | 23,153 |
| PUNTA GORDA, FL | 21,785 | 60,458 | 9.2 | 17.0 | 38.4 | 28.6 | 5.2 | 1.6 | 39,201 | 38,479 | 45,805 | 47,448 | 41,137 | 33,990 |
| UNITED STATES | 22,162 | | 14.5 | 12.5 | 32.3 | 29.8 | 7.4 | 3.5 | 40,748 | 34,503 | 44,969 | 49,579 | 43,409 | 27,339 |

# SPENDING POTENTIAL INDEXES

## MSA AND U.S. TOTALS

E

| MSA | FINANCIAL SERVICES | | | | THE HOME: Home Improvements | | | THE HOME: Furnishings | | | ENTERTAINMENT | | | | | | PERSONAL | | | |
|---|---|---|---|---|---|---|---|---|---|---|---|---|---|---|---|---|---|---|---|---|
| | Auto Loan | Home Loan | Investments | Retirement Plans | Home Repair | Lawn & Garden | Remodeling | Appliances | Electronics | Furniture | Restaurants | Sporting Goods | Theater & Concerts | Toys & Hobbies | Travel | Video Rental | Apparel | Auto Aftermarket | Health Insurance | Pets & Supplies |
| LA CROSSE, WI-MN | 98 | 94 | 93 | 94 | 98 | 96 | 102 | 97 | 96 | 93 | 97 | 96 | 96 | 99 | 92 | 101 | 93 | 98 | 100 | 99 |
| LAFAYETTE, LA | 97 | 85 | 87 | 88 | 96 | 93 | 102 | 97 | 95 | 90 | 89 | 96 | 90 | 96 | 79 | 97 | 90 | 94 | 95 | 98 |
| LAFAYETTE, IN | 98 | 96 | 96 | 96 | 99 | 97 | 101 | 96 | 96 | 94 | 98 | 96 | 97 | 99 | 94 | 100 | 94 | 98 | 99 | 99 |
| LAKE CHARLES, LA | 97 | 85 | 92 | 88 | 98 | 95 | 103 | 97 | 94 | 92 | 90 | 96 | 91 | 97 | 81 | 98 | 91 | 94 | 96 | 98 |
| LAKELND-WINTER HAVEN | 97 | 86 | 101 | 89 | 100 | 99 | 104 | 98 | 93 | 91 | 92 | 96 | 92 | 98 | 83 | 97 | 89 | 94 | 101 | 99 |
| LANCASTER, PA | 100 | 89 | 93 | 93 | 91 | 90 | 99 | 98 | 96 | 94 | 96 | 100 | 96 | 103 | 89 | 99 | 98 | 95 | 102 | 103 |
| LANSING-E.LANSING,MI | 98 | 97 | 95 | 95 | 99 | 97 | 100 | 97 | 97 | 96 | 100 | 97 | 98 | 99 | 95 | 101 | 96 | 99 | 98 | 99 |
| LAREDO, TX | 95 | 93 | 89 | 85 | 93 | 93 | 97 | 97 | 96 | 89 | 92 | 92 | 89 | 94 | 81 | 98 | 85 | 96 | 98 | 102 |
| LAS CRUCES, NM | 96 | 93 | 90 | 88 | 96 | 95 | 100 | 98 | 97 | 92 | 92 | 87 | 86 | 89 | 84 | 92 | 88 | 94 | 96 | 94 |
| LAS VEGAS, NV-AZ | 101 | 103 | 93 | 99 | 101 | 102 | 100 | 102 | 103 | 104 | 103 | 95 | 94 | 95 | 91 | 95 | 101 | 100 | 97 | 96 |
| LAWRENCE, KS | 95 | 93 | 88 | 90 | 94 | 90 | 99 | 92 | 92 | 86 | 93 | 91 | 89 | 94 | 88 | 97 | 88 | 94 | 96 | 97 |
| LAWTON, OK | 95 | 92 | 87 | 87 | 96 | 93 | 96 | 95 | 95 | 91 | 94 | 94 | 91 | 95 | 81 | 97 | 91 | 95 | 95 | 98 |
| LEWISTON-AUBURN, ME | 98 | 84 | 89 | 87 | 90 | 88 | 96 | 96 | 93 | 90 | 91 | 96 | 92 | 99 | 86 | 98 | 93 | 91 | 101 | 100 |
| LEXINGTON, KY | 99 | 97 | 98 | 97 | 100 | 99 | 103 | 98 | 98 | 96 | 98 | 99 | 96 | 100 | 86 | 98 | 98 | 98 | 98 | 101 |
| LIMA, OH | 97 | 87 | 92 | 89 | 99 | 95 | 104 | 97 | 94 | 91 | 93 | 95 | 95 | 98 | 90 | 100 | 90 | 95 | 100 | 98 |
| LINCOLN, NE | 98 | 101 | 97 | 97 | 100 | 98 | 97 | 97 | 97 | 97 | 101 | 97 | 99 | 99 | 97 | 101 | 97 | 100 | 98 | 100 |
| LITTLE ROCK-N.LITTLE | 98 | 93 | 95 | 93 | 99 | 97 | 103 | 98 | 97 | 95 | 96 | 98 | 94 | 99 | 84 | 98 | 95 | 97 | 97 | 100 |
| LONGVIEW-MARSHALL,TX | 97 | 85 | 90 | 87 | 97 | 95 | 105 | 97 | 95 | 90 | 90 | 96 | 90 | 97 | 79 | 97 | 90 | 94 | 98 | 99 |
| LOS ANGELES-L.BEACH | 100 | 125 | 109 | 112 | 107 | 109 | 95 | 103 | 109 | 108 | 110 | 97 | 103 | 93 | 106 | 98 | 107 | 109 | 97 | 99 |
| LOUISVILLE, KY-IN | 98 | 96 | 102 | 97 | 103 | 101 | 101 | 99 | 97 | 99 | 99 | 99 | 98 | 100 | 89 | 98 | 98 | 99 | 99 | 100 |
| LUBBOCK, TX | 97 | 97 | 96 | 93 | 99 | 97 | 99 | 96 | 96 | 95 | 97 | 96 | 94 | 98 | 85 | 97 | 95 | 97 | 97 | 100 |
| LYNCHBURG, VA | 98 | 84 | 90 | 87 | 98 | 95 | 106 | 97 | 94 | 90 | 91 | 96 | 90 | 98 | 79 | 97 | 90 | 93 | 99 | 99 |
| MACON, GA | 98 | 93 | 95 | 93 | 100 | 97 | 101 | 98 | 96 | 96 | 94 | 98 | 95 | 99 | 85 | 98 | 96 | 97 | 95 | 100 |
| MADISON, WI | 100 | 107 | 99 | 103 | 101 | 101 | 99 | 98 | 100 | 101 | 107 | 100 | 103 | 102 | 100 | 102 | 102 | 104 | 99 | 102 |
| MANSFIELD, OH | 97 | 84 | 91 | 88 | 99 | 95 | 104 | 97 | 93 | 90 | 91 | 94 | 94 | 97 | 90 | 100 | 88 | 94 | 101 | 98 |
| MCALLN-EDNBG-MISSION | 94 | 92 | 92 | 84 | 94 | 94 | 96 | 97 | 95 | 88 | 91 | 91 | 89 | 93 | 81 | 97 | 84 | 95 | 98 | 102 |
| MEDFORD-ASHLAND, OR | 99 | 89 | 94 | 92 | 101 | 99 | 107 | 100 | 98 | 94 | 93 | 91 | 88 | 93 | 85 | 93 | 92 | 94 | 99 | 94 |
| MELBRN-TITUSVL-P.BAY | 100 | 101 | 104 | 99 | 104 | 105 | 100 | 100 | 98 | 101 | 104 | 101 | 101 | 102 | 91 | 99 | 101 | 100 | 102 | 102 |
| MEMPHIS, TN-AR-MS | 98 | 97 | 95 | 96 | 100 | 98 | 98 | 99 | 98 | 99 | 97 | 100 | 97 | 99 | 87 | 99 | 99 | 100 | 94 | 100 |
| MERCED, CA | 97 | 96 | 88 | 90 | 96 | 96 | 98 | 100 | 100 | 94 | 95 | 89 | 88 | 90 | 85 | 94 | 90 | 96 | 96 | 95 |
| MIAMI, FL | 97 | 106 | 104 | 98 | 106 | 103 | 99 | 98 | 94 | 109 | 99 | 101 | 100 | 94 | 100 | 100 | 100 | 102 | 95 | 97 |
| MID'SX-SOMER'T-HUNT. | 105 | 117 | 111 | 116 | 100 | 105 | 94 | 103 | 108 | 113 | 118 | 111 | 115 | 109 | 110 | 103 | 120 | 110 | 104 | 108 |
| MILWAUKEE-WAUKESHA | 99 | 104 | 106 | 103 | 104 | 103 | 99 | 99 | 99 | 103 | 104 | 100 | 106 | 101 | 103 | 102 | 101 | 103 | 100 | 100 |
| MINNEAPOLIS-ST. PAUL | 101 | 107 | 98 | 103 | 101 | 102 | 100 | 100 | 102 | 104 | 108 | 102 | 106 | 103 | 101 | 103 | 104 | 105 | 100 | 102 |
| MISSOULA, MT | 97 | 93 | 92 | 92 | 100 | 97 | 103 | 98 | 97 | 95 | 93 | 89 | 87 | 91 | 85 | 92 | 92 | 94 | 96 | 93 |
| MOBILE, AL | 98 | 87 | 93 | 90 | 99 | 97 | 105 | 98 | 95 | 92 | 91 | 98 | 92 | 99 | 82 | 98 | 93 | 95 | 98 | 100 |
| MODESTO, CA | 99 | 97 | 91 | 94 | 99 | 98 | 101 | 101 | 101 | 99 | 98 | 92 | 91 | 93 | 87 | 94 | 95 | 98 | 97 | 95 |
| MONMOUTH-OCEAN, NJ | 104 | 107 | 110 | 110 | 98 | 102 | 96 | 103 | 103 | 107 | 110 | 108 | 110 | 108 | 104 | 102 | 112 | 105 | 105 | 106 |
| MONROE, LA | 97 | 88 | 95 | 90 | 99 | 95 | 101 | 97 | 94 | 92 | 90 | 96 | 91 | 97 | 82 | 98 | 92 | 95 | 95 | 98 |
| MONTGOMERY, AL | 98 | 93 | 95 | 94 | 99 | 98 | 101 | 98 | 97 | 97 | 96 | 99 | 95 | 100 | 84 | 99 | 97 | 98 | 96 | 100 |
| MUNCIE, IN | 96 | 91 | 96 | 93 | 101 | 97 | 100 | 96 | 93 | 92 | 94 | 94 | 96 | 97 | 94 | 99 | 91 | 96 | 99 | 98 |
| MYRTLE BEACH, SC | 99 | 88 | 98 | 93 | 100 | 101 | 110 | 100 | 95 | 92 | 94 | 98 | 93 | 100 | 84 | 98 | 93 | 95 | 102 | 101 |
| NAPLES, FL | 102 | 102 | 110 | 106 | 106 | 113 | 107 | 104 | 99 | 101 | 105 | 102 | 103 | 104 | 95 | 99 | 103 | 102 | 107 | 104 |
| NASHVILLE, TN | 100 | 100 | 97 | 99 | 101 | 100 | 103 | 99 | 100 | 100 | 101 | 102 | 99 | 102 | 88 | 99 | 101 | 100 | 98 | 102 |
| NASSAU-SUFFOLK, NY | 106 | 120 | 121 | 120 | 104 | 110 | 96 | 105 | 110 | 116 | 120 | 111 | 121 | 112 | 116 | 104 | 125 | 114 | 107 | 109 |
| N.HAVEN-BRDGPRT.,CT | 104 | 117 | 118 | 118 | 103 | 107 | 96 | 103 | 106 | 113 | 114 | 110 | 116 | 108 | 113 | 102 | 119 | 109 | 105 | 107 |
| NEW LONDON-NORWICH | 100 | 99 | 102 | 99 | 95 | 95 | 92 | 99 | 99 | 101 | 103 | 101 | 102 | 104 | 97 | 100 | 105 | 99 | 102 | 103 |
| NEW ORLEANS, LA | 98 | 97 | 99 | 97 | 102 | 99 | 97 | 99 | 97 | 99 | 97 | 99 | 97 | 99 | 88 | 99 | 99 | 99 | 94 | 100 |
| NEW YORK, NY | 100 | 112 | 108 | 105 | 102 | 99 | 89 | 98 | 98 | 111 | 104 | 104 | 107 | 97 | 112 | 103 | 109 | 104 | 98 | 102 |
| NEWARK, NJ | 104 | 116 | 117 | 116 | 103 | 106 | 93 | 103 | 106 | 114 | 112 | 109 | 115 | 107 | 113 | 103 | 118 | 110 | 102 | 106 |
| NEWBURGH, NY-PA | 102 | 98 | 99 | 100 | 94 | 95 | 96 | 100 | 100 | 102 | 103 | 104 | 103 | 105 | 96 | 101 | 106 | 100 | 102 | 105 |
| NRFOLK-VA BCH-N.NEWS | 97 | 98 | 94 | 93 | 99 | 97 | 96 | 97 | 97 | 97 | 99 | 98 | 96 | 99 | 86 | 99 | 98 | 99 | 95 | 100 |
| OAKLAND, CA | 104 | 127 | 114 | 119 | 110 | 115 | 101 | 106 | 113 | 116 | 117 | 102 | 109 | 99 | 109 | 99 | 116 | 114 | 100 | 101 |
| OCALA, FL | 98 | 86 | 104 | 90 | 101 | 102 | 105 | 99 | 93 | 91 | 93 | 97 | 93 | 99 | 84 | 97 | 88 | 94 | 103 | 100 |
| ODESSA-MIDLAND, TX | 99 | 100 | 98 | 97 | 100 | 100 | 101 | 99 | 99 | 99 | 102 | 99 | 98 | 101 | 87 | 99 | 98 | 100 | 98 | 102 |
| OKLAHOMA CITY, OK | 98 | 97 | 95 | 95 | 100 | 98 | 99 | 97 | 97 | 97 | 99 | 98 | 96 | 99 | 86 | 98 | 97 | 98 | 97 | 100 |
| OLYMPIA, WA | 99 | 97 | 94 | 95 | 100 | 100 | 104 | 101 | 101 | 101 | 100 | 93 | 92 | 95 | 88 | 94 | 98 | 98 | 97 | 95 |
| OMAHA, NE-IA | 99 | 102 | 97 | 100 | 101 | 100 | 99 | 99 | 99 | 100 | 103 | 99 | 102 | 100 | 99 | 102 | 99 | 102 | 99 | 100 |
| ORANGE COUNTY, CA | 104 | 129 | 111 | 118 | 109 | 114 | 100 | 106 | 113 | 114 | 118 | 102 | 108 | 99 | 107 | 98 | 115 | 114 | 100 | 102 |
| ORLANDO, FL | 99 | 100 | 95 | 96 | 99 | 100 | 99 | 99 | 99 | 100 | 102 | 100 | 98 | 101 | 87 | 99 | 99 | 100 | 98 | 101 |
| OWENSBORO, KY | 97 | 89 | 97 | 90 | 101 | 98 | 103 | 97 | 95 | 93 | 94 | 96 | 94 | 99 | 84 | 97 | 93 | 95 | 99 | 99 |
| PANAMA CITY, FL | 97 | 89 | 95 | 90 | 99 | 98 | 106 | 98 | 94 | 93 | 94 | 96 | 92 | 99 | 83 | 98 | 93 | 95 | 99 | 100 |
| PARKERSBURG-MARIETTA | 98 | 83 | 93 | 87 | 100 | 97 | 107 | 97 | 94 | 89 | 90 | 95 | 91 | 98 | 80 | 97 | 90 | 93 | 101 | 99 |
| PENSACOLA, FL | 98 | 94 | 94 | 92 | 99 | 97 | 102 | 98 | 97 | 96 | 97 | 98 | 95 | 99 | 84 | 99 | 96 | 98 | 97 | 100 |
| PEORIA-PEKIN, IL | 97 | 93 | 97 | 94 | 101 | 98 | 100 | 98 | 95 | 96 | 98 | 96 | 99 | 99 | 96 | 101 | 94 | 98 | 100 | 99 |
| PHILADELPHIA, PA-NJ | 101 | 102 | 106 | 105 | 97 | 98 | 92 | 100 | 100 | 105 | 104 | 104 | 106 | 104 | 102 | 101 | 108 | 101 | 100 | 103 |
| PHOENIX-MESA, AZ | 101 | 105 | 96 | 101 | 102 | 104 | 101 | 103 | 103 | 104 | 104 | 96 | 95 | 96 | 92 | 94 | 102 | 101 | 98 | 96 |
| PINE BLUFF, AR | 96 | 80 | 89 | 85 | 98 | 93 | 102 | 96 | 92 | 88 | 85 | 94 | 88 | 95 | 79 | 97 | 88 | 92 | 94 | 97 |
| PITTSBURGH, PA | 98 | 91 | 102 | 96 | 96 | 95 | 92 | 98 | 94 | 97 | 96 | 98 | 99 | 101 | 96 | 98 | 99 | 95 | 102 | 100 |
| PITTSFIELD, MA | 98 | 90 | 100 | 93 | 95 | 93 | 93 | 97 | 93 | 96 | 95 | 97 | 97 | 101 | 94 | 98 | 97 | 94 | 102 | 100 |
| POCATELLO, ID | 98 | 93 | 89 | 92 | 98 | 96 | 103 | 99 | 99 | 96 | 95 | 90 | 88 | 92 | 84 | 93 | 94 | 95 | 96 | 93 |
| PORTLAND, ME | 101 | 98 | 102 | 100 | 95 | 95 | 95 | 99 | 98 | 100 | 101 | 102 | 101 | 104 | 96 | 100 | 104 | 99 | 102 | 104 |
| PORTLAND-VANCOUVER | 100 | 101 | 97 | 99 | 102 | 102 | 103 | 101 | 102 | 102 | 101 | 94 | 94 | 95 | 91 | 94 | 100 | 99 | 97 | 95 |
| PROVID.-WARWICK-PAW. | 99 | 97 | 104 | 98 | 97 | 96 | 91 | 98 | 96 | 101 | 100 | 100 | 102 | 101 | 98 | 99 | 102 | 97 | 102 | 101 |
| PROVO-OREM, UT | 99 | 97 | 88 | 94 | 98 | 96 | 102 | 99 | 100 | 97 | 98 | 91 | 89 | 94 | 85 | 93 | 97 | 98 | 95 | 94 |
| PUEBLO, CO | 96 | 88 | 92 | 88 | 101 | 98 | 102 | 99 | 96 | 95 | 91 | 88 | 88 | 91 | 85 | 92 | 90 | 93 | 97 | 92 |
| PUNTA GORDA, FL | 103 | 93 | 116 | 105 | 108 | 116 | 110 | 105 | 95 | 96 | 100 | 100 | 100 | 104 | 95 | 97 | 97 | 98 | 112 | 104 |
| UNITED STATES | 100 | 100 | 100 | 100 | 100 | 100 | 100 | 100 | 100 | 100 | 100 | 100 | 100 | 100 | 100 | 100 | 100 | 100 | 100 | 100 |

# POPULATION CHANGE

## MSA AND U.S. TOTALS

| MSA | MSA Code | POPULATION 1990 | POPULATION 2000 | POPULATION 2005 | 1990-2000 ANNUAL CHANGE % Rate | 1990-2000 ANNUAL CHANGE National Rank | RACE (%) White 1990 | White 2000 | Black 1990 | Black 2000 | Asian/Pacific 1990 | Asian/Pacific 2000 |
|---|---|---|---|---|---|---|---|---|---|---|---|---|
| RACINE, WI | 6600 | 175,034 | 186,190 | 188,286 | 0.6 | 200 | 86.9 | 83.0 | 9.7 | 12.2 | 0.6 | 0.8 |
| RALEIGH-DURHAM-CH.H. | 6640 | 855,545 | 1,133,318 | 1,271,731 | 2.8 | 11 | 73.4 | 72.0 | 24.2 | 23.9 | 1.6 | 2.8 |
| RAPID CITY, SD | 6660 | 81,343 | 88,677 | 91,380 | 0.8 | 175 | 89.5 | 87.0 | 1.6 | 2.3 | 1.1 | 1.5 |
| READING, PA | 6680 | 336,523 | 360,479 | 371,653 | 0.7 | 188 | 93.5 | 91.5 | 3.0 | 3.4 | 0.8 | 1.2 |
| REDDING, CA | 6690 | 147,036 | 165,415 | 169,812 | 1.2 | 110 | 93.8 | 92.7 | 0.7 | 0.8 | 1.8 | 2.5 |
| RENO, NV | 6720 | 254,667 | 326,967 | 362,512 | 2.5 | 16 | 88.4 | 83.9 | 2.2 | 2.5 | 3.9 | 5.7 |
| RICHLAND-K'WCK-PASCO | 6740 | 150,033 | 186,537 | 196,445 | 2.1 | 34 | 86.5 | 82.0 | 1.6 | 1.7 | 2.1 | 2.8 |
| RICHMOND-PETERSBURG | 6760 | 865,640 | 970,282 | 1,015,546 | 1.1 | 129 | 68.8 | 67.4 | 29.2 | 29.8 | 1.4 | 2.0 |
| RIVERSIDE-SAN BERN. | 6780 | 2,588,793 | 3,272,183 | 3,627,526 | 2.3 | 25 | 74.6 | 69.8 | 6.9 | 6.8 | 3.9 | 5.0 |
| ROANOKE, VA | 6800 | 224,477 | 227,548 | 226,638 | 0.1 | 262 | 86.7 | 85.1 | 12.3 | 13.5 | 0.7 | 1.0 |
| ROCHESTER, MN | 6820 | 106,470 | 121,226 | 131,096 | 1.3 | 91 | 95.7 | 93.5 | 0.7 | 1.0 | 3.0 | 4.9 |
| ROCHESTER, NY | 6840 | 1,062,470 | 1,077,595 | 1,069,799 | 0.1 | 262 | 87.9 | 85.8 | 8.9 | 9.9 | 1.3 | 2.0 |
| ROCKFORD, IL | 6880 | 329,676 | 360,422 | 369,796 | 0.9 | 166 | 90.0 | 88.5 | 7.1 | 7.6 | 1.0 | 1.3 |
| ROCKY MOUNT, NC | 6895 | 133,235 | 148,175 | 153,850 | 1.0 | 149 | 57.4 | 58.0 | 41.9 | 41.0 | 0.2 | 0.4 |
| SACRAMENTO, CA | 6920 | 1,340,010 | 1,613,512 | 1,752,516 | 1.8 | 49 | 79.4 | 75.8 | 7.4 | 7.2 | 7.7 | 10.1 |
| SAGINAW-B.CITY-MIDL. | 6960 | 399,320 | 400,043 | 396,650 | 0.0 | 270 | 86.8 | 85.5 | 9.7 | 10.2 | 0.6 | 0.9 |
| ST. CLOUD, MN | 6980 | 148,976 | 166,591 | 174,923 | 1.1 | 129 | 98.6 | 98.0 | 0.3 | 0.5 | 0.6 | 1.0 |
| ST. JOSEPH, MO | 7000 | 97,715 | 97,212 | 97,040 | -0.1 | 283 | 96.1 | 95.3 | 2.7 | 3.2 | 0.3 | 0.4 |
| ST. LOUIS, MO-IL | 7040 | 2,492,525 | 2,576,352 | 2,612,851 | 0.3 | 240 | 81.5 | 80.9 | 17.0 | 17.3 | 1.0 | 1.3 |
| SALEM, OR | 7080 | 278,024 | 340,586 | 367,334 | 2.0 | 40 | 91.8 | 88.9 | 0.8 | 0.9 | 1.7 | 2.3 |
| SALINAS, CA | 7120 | 355,660 | 377,527 | 398,038 | 0.6 | 200 | 63.8 | 57.8 | 6.4 | 6.0 | 7.8 | 9.7 |
| SALT LAKE CITY-OGDEN | 7160 | 1,072,227 | 1,289,736 | 1,361,989 | 1.8 | 49 | 93.3 | 91.0 | 1.0 | 1.2 | 2.4 | 3.2 |
| SAN ANGELO, TX | 7200 | 98,458 | 102,330 | 102,375 | 0.4 | 226 | 80.8 | 76.9 | 4.2 | 4.3 | 1.0 | 1.4 |
| SAN ANTONIO, TX | 7240 | 1,324,749 | 1,589,702 | 1,714,294 | 1.8 | 49 | 75.3 | 73.0 | 6.7 | 6.3 | 1.2 | 1.6 |
| SAN DIEGO, CA | 7320 | 2,498,016 | 2,872,950 | 3,125,152 | 1.4 | 80 | 74.9 | 69.9 | 6.4 | 6.0 | 7.9 | 10.5 |
| SAN FRANCISCO, CA | 7360 | 1,603,678 | 1,694,652 | 1,735,277 | 0.5 | 212 | 66.0 | 59.9 | 7.6 | 7.3 | 20.6 | 25.7 |
| SAN JOSE, CA | 7400 | 1,497,577 | 1,662,097 | 1,732,406 | 1.0 | 149 | 68.9 | 62.6 | 3.8 | 3.6 | 17.5 | 21.8 |
| S.LUIS O.-ATASC-PASO | 7460 | 217,162 | 239,701 | 253,311 | 1.0 | 149 | 89.2 | 86.7 | 2.6 | 2.8 | 2.9 | 3.8 |
| S.BARB-S.MARIA-LOMP. | 7480 | 369,608 | 393,737 | 406,078 | 0.6 | 200 | 77.2 | 72.2 | 2.8 | 2.9 | 4.4 | 5.6 |
| SANTA CRUZ-WATSONVLL | 7485 | 229,734 | 247,902 | 260,754 | 0.7 | 188 | 83.9 | 79.4 | 1.1 | 1.2 | 3.7 | 4.9 |
| SANTA FE, NM | 7490 | 117,043 | 144,329 | 153,407 | 2.1 | 34 | 82.4 | 80.6 | 0.6 | 0.8 | 0.8 | 1.1 |
| SANTA ROSA, CA | 7500 | 388,222 | 447,119 | 479,889 | 1.4 | 80 | 90.6 | 87.9 | 1.4 | 1.5 | 2.8 | 3.9 |
| SARASOTA-BRADENTON | 7510 | 489,483 | 558,242 | 593,430 | 1.3 | 91 | 92.6 | 90.4 | 5.8 | 7.1 | 0.5 | 0.9 |
| SAVANNAH, GA | 7520 | 258,060 | 292,525 | 306,121 | 1.2 | 110 | 64.1 | 60.4 | 34.3 | 37.2 | 1.0 | 1.6 |
| SCRANTON-W.BARRE-HAZ | 7560 | 638,466 | 606,886 | 583,984 | -0.5 | 309 | 98.3 | 98.0 | 0.9 | 1.0 | 0.5 | 0.7 |
| SEATTLE-BELLEV-EV'TT | 7600 | 2,033,156 | 2,367,808 | 2,525,392 | 1.5 | 73 | 87.0 | 83.5 | 4.1 | 4.5 | 6.8 | 9.2 |
| SHARON, PA | 7610 | 121,003 | 121,201 | 119,922 | 0.0 | 270 | 94.6 | 93.5 | 4.9 | 5.8 | 0.3 | 0.5 |
| SHEBOYGAN, WI | 7620 | 103,877 | 110,361 | 111,635 | 0.6 | 200 | 96.6 | 95.2 | 0.4 | 0.6 | 2.0 | 2.9 |
| SHERMAN-DENISON, TX | 7640 | 95,021 | 105,315 | 113,115 | 1.0 | 149 | 90.0 | 88.5 | 6.9 | 7.6 | 0.4 | 0.7 |
| SHREVEPRT-BOS'R CITY | 7680 | 376,330 | 378,719 | 377,924 | 0.1 | 262 | 64.3 | 62.1 | 34.6 | 36.6 | 0.6 | 0.8 |
| SIOUX CITY, IA-NE | 7720 | 115,018 | 120,727 | 121,419 | 0.5 | 212 | 93.5 | 91.6 | 1.7 | 1.8 | 1.4 | 2.1 |
| SIOUX FALLS, SD | 7760 | 139,236 | 167,507 | 182,666 | 1.8 | 49 | 97.5 | 96.5 | 0.6 | 0.8 | 0.5 | 0.8 |
| SOUTH BEND, IN | 7800 | 247,052 | 258,862 | 260,685 | 0.5 | 212 | 87.8 | 85.7 | 9.8 | 11.0 | 1.0 | 1.4 |
| SPOKANE, WA | 7840 | 361,364 | 411,377 | 420,561 | 1.3 | 91 | 94.6 | 93.3 | 1.4 | 1.6 | 1.8 | 2.5 |
| SPRINGFIELD, IL | 7880 | 189,550 | 204,539 | 205,565 | 0.7 | 188 | 91.3 | 90.1 | 7.6 | 8.4 | 0.7 | 1.0 |
| SPRINGFIELD, MO | 7920 | 264,346 | 312,095 | 330,974 | 1.6 | 67 | 97.0 | 96.6 | 1.5 | 1.7 | 0.6 | 0.9 |
| SPRINGFIELD, MA | 8003 | 602,878 | 589,514 | 585,376 | -0.2 | 290 | 87.1 | 83.7 | 6.1 | 7.4 | 1.4 | 2.1 |
| STATE COLLEGE, PA | 8050 | 123,786 | 132,407 | 133,604 | 0.7 | 188 | 94.2 | 92.3 | 2.3 | 2.6 | 3.1 | 4.5 |
| STEUBENVILLE-WEIRTON | 8080 | 142,523 | 131,852 | 124,881 | -0.8 | 316 | 95.5 | 95.0 | 3.9 | 4.3 | 0.3 | 0.4 |
| STOCKTON-LODI, CA | 8120 | 480,628 | 574,605 | 631,219 | 1.8 | 49 | 73.5 | 68.6 | 5.6 | 5.6 | 12.4 | 15.6 |
| SUMTER, SC | 8140 | 102,637 | 112,842 | 115,172 | 0.9 | 166 | 55.3 | 54.2 | 43.2 | 43.9 | 0.9 | 1.2 |
| SYRACUSE, NY | 8160 | 742,177 | 730,234 | 715,788 | -0.2 | 290 | 92.2 | 90.9 | 5.7 | 6.2 | 1.1 | 1.6 |
| TACOMA, WA | 8200 | 586,203 | 700,858 | 760,658 | 1.8 | 49 | 85.1 | 81.8 | 7.2 | 7.8 | 5.0 | 6.9 |
| TALLAHASSEE, FL | 8240 | 233,598 | 261,884 | 267,637 | 1.1 | 129 | 67.8 | 63.2 | 30.1 | 33.7 | 1.2 | 1.8 |
| TAMPA-ST.PETE-CLEARW | 8280 | 2,067,959 | 2,307,399 | 2,438,175 | 1.1 | 129 | 88.4 | 85.5 | 9.0 | 10.5 | 1.1 | 1.8 |
| TERRE HAUTE, IN | 8320 | 147,585 | 147,796 | 145,728 | 0.0 | 270 | 94.6 | 93.9 | 4.1 | 4.4 | 0.8 | 1.1 |
| TEXARKANA, TX-AR | 8360 | 120,132 | 123,517 | 123,559 | 0.3 | 240 | 76.9 | 74.7 | 22.0 | 23.9 | 0.3 | 0.5 |
| TOLEDO, OH | 8400 | 614,128 | 608,251 | 604,593 | -0.1 | 283 | 85.7 | 84.0 | 11.4 | 12.3 | 1.0 | 1.3 |
| TOPEKA, KS | 8440 | 160,976 | 171,444 | 174,671 | 0.6 | 200 | 87.7 | 86.0 | 8.3 | 8.7 | 0.7 | 1.1 |
| TRENTON, NJ | 8480 | 325,824 | 335,522 | 343,737 | 0.3 | 240 | 75.1 | 70.1 | 18.9 | 20.8 | 3.1 | 5.0 |
| TUCSON, AZ | 8520 | 666,880 | 816,221 | 880,397 | 2.0 | 40 | 78.7 | 75.3 | 3.1 | 3.5 | 1.8 | 2.3 |
| TULSA, OK | 8560 | 708,954 | 797,152 | 847,729 | 1.2 | 110 | 83.3 | 82.6 | 8.2 | 8.5 | 0.9 | 1.1 |
| TUSCALOOSA, AL | 8600 | 150,522 | 162,444 | 167,107 | 0.7 | 188 | 72.7 | 70.7 | 26.2 | 28.0 | 0.8 | 0.9 |
| TYLER, TX | 8640 | 151,309 | 171,832 | 181,486 | 1.2 | 110 | 75.1 | 72.6 | 20.9 | 22.2 | 0.4 | 0.6 |
| UTICA-ROME, NY | 8680 | 316,633 | 290,454 | 277,747 | -0.8 | 316 | 94.0 | 92.7 | 4.4 | 5.1 | 0.7 | 1.1 |
| VALLEJO-FAIRFLD-NAPA | 8720 | 451,186 | 515,564 | 558,385 | 1.3 | 91 | 72.2 | 66.8 | 10.4 | 10.6 | 10.4 | 13.9 |
| VENTURA, CA | 8735 | 669,016 | 758,411 | 816,948 | 1.2 | 110 | 79.1 | 74.3 | 2.3 | 2.3 | 5.2 | 6.7 |
| VICTORIA, TX | 8750 | 74,361 | 82,629 | 85,479 | 1.0 | 149 | 79.7 | 76.5 | 6.6 | 7.0 | 0.3 | 0.5 |
| VINELND-M'VLE-BRDGTN | 8760 | 138,053 | 139,808 | 138,286 | 0.1 | 262 | 73.5 | 68.2 | 16.9 | 18.5 | 0.8 | 1.4 |
| VISALIA-TULARE-P'VLE | 8780 | 311,921 | 362,474 | 381,984 | 1.5 | 73 | 65.7 | 59.1 | 1.5 | 1.4 | 4.3 | 5.2 |
| WACO, TX | 8800 | 189,123 | 205,331 | 210,795 | 0.8 | 175 | 77.3 | 74.3 | 15.6 | 16.4 | 0.7 | 1.1 |
| WASHINGTON, DC | 8840 | 4,223,485 | 4,810,569 | 5,159,072 | 1.3 | 91 | 67.3 | 65.3 | 25.4 | 24.8 | 4.8 | 6.7 |
| WATERLOO-CEDAR FALLS | 8920 | 123,798 | 119,540 | 116,012 | -0.3 | 297 | 91.8 | 90.7 | 6.9 | 7.5 | 0.8 | 1.1 |
| WAUSAU, WI | 8940 | 115,400 | 124,245 | 127,544 | 0.7 | 188 | 97.2 | 96.2 | 0.1 | 0.1 | 2.2 | 3.1 |
| W.PALM BEACH-B.RATON | 8960 | 863,518 | 1,067,555 | 1,157,553 | 2.1 | 34 | 84.8 | 81.5 | 12.5 | 14.5 | 1.0 | 1.6 |
| WHEELING, WV-OH | 9000 | 159,301 | 153,738 | 148,042 | -0.3 | 297 | 97.5 | 97.2 | 2.0 | 2.2 | 0.3 | 0.4 |
| WICHITA, KS | 9040 | 485,270 | 555,602 | 588,967 | 1.3 | 91 | 87.3 | 85.5 | 7.6 | 7.9 | 1.9 | 2.5 |
| UNITED STATES | | | | | 1.0 | | 80.3 | 77.9 | 12.1 | 12.4 | 2.9 | 3.9 |

# POPULATION COMPOSITION

## MSA AND U.S. TOTALS

# B

| MSA | % HISPANIC ORIGIN | | 2000 AGE DISTRIBUTION (%) | | | | | | | | | | MEDIAN AGE | | 2000 Males/ Females (×100) |
|---|---|---|---|---|---|---|---|---|---|---|---|---|---|---|---|
| | 1990 | 2000 | 0-4 | 5-9 | 10-14 | 15-19 | 20-24 | 25-44 | 45-64 | 65-84 | 85+ | 18+ | 1990 | 2000 | |
| RACINE, WI | 5.2 | 7.8 | 6.7 | 7.0 | 7.9 | 7.6 | 6.3 | 29.3 | 22.8 | 10.9 | 1.5 | 73.7 | 32.9 | 35.9 | 96.2 |
| RALEIGH-DURHAM-CH.H. | 1.3 | 2.9 | 7.0 | 7.1 | 7.0 | 6.8 | 7.5 | 33.8 | 21.3 | 8.3 | 1.1 | 75.6 | 31.7 | 34.3 | 93.7 |
| RAPID CITY, SD | 2.2 | 3.8 | 7.6 | 7.0 | 7.7 | 7.9 | 8.5 | 30.0 | 20.4 | 9.6 | 1.3 | 73.1 | 30.1 | 33.3 | 97.4 |
| READING, PA | 5.1 | 7.5 | 5.8 | 6.5 | 7.1 | 6.9 | 5.6 | 28.5 | 23.5 | 14.0 | 2.1 | 76.7 | 35.4 | 38.6 | 93.9 |
| REDDING, CA | 3.8 | 5.8 | 6.8 | 8.4 | 7.4 | 7.3 | 5.5 | 26.4 | 23.2 | 13.5 | 1.6 | 72.9 | 34.9 | 37.3 | 97.1 |
| RENO, NV | 9.0 | 14.9 | 7.6 | 7.1 | 7.0 | 7.0 | 6.6 | 29.6 | 23.9 | 10.1 | 1.1 | 74.5 | 33.6 | 36.2 | 104.8 |
| RICHLAND-K'WCK-PASCO | 13.3 | 19.0 | 7.8 | 8.2 | 8.5 | 8.7 | 6.6 | 28.5 | 21.7 | 8.9 | 1.1 | 70.0 | 31.3 | 32.9 | 100.6 |
| RICHMOND-PETERSBURG | 1.1 | 1.9 | 6.2 | 6.7 | 6.9 | 6.9 | 6.5 | 32.3 | 22.7 | 10.4 | 1.4 | 76.3 | 33.2 | 36.2 | 91.4 |
| RIVERSIDE-SAN BERN. | 26.5 | 34.3 | 8.8 | 9.4 | 8.1 | 7.5 | 6.7 | 30.1 | 18.2 | 10.0 | 1.3 | 69.4 | 30.3 | 31.8 | 99.2 |
| ROANOKE, VA | 0.6 | 1.3 | 5.3 | 5.8 | 6.2 | 6.5 | 5.9 | 29.5 | 25.0 | 13.6 | 2.1 | 78.9 | 36.4 | 39.5 | 89.9 |
| ROCHESTER, MN | 0.9 | 1.8 | 7.2 | 7.7 | 8.6 | 7.5 | 5.7 | 31.7 | 21.3 | 8.7 | 1.6 | 72.1 | 31.6 | 35.2 | 94.7 |
| ROCHESTER, NY | 3.0 | 4.3 | 6.7 | 7.5 | 7.3 | 7.2 | 6.4 | 29.1 | 22.9 | 11.0 | 1.7 | 74.7 | 33.0 | 36.1 | 93.9 |
| ROCKFORD, IL | 3.4 | 5.2 | 7.1 | 7.5 | 7.5 | 7.0 | 5.8 | 29.1 | 23.2 | 11.2 | 1.6 | 73.7 | 33.5 | 36.3 | 94.7 |
| ROCKY MOUNT, NC | 0.6 | 1.4 | 6.9 | 7.5 | 7.8 | 6.7 | 5.9 | 29.6 | 23.2 | 11.1 | 1.4 | 73.7 | 33.3 | 36.0 | 89.1 |
| SACRAMENTO, CA | 10.8 | 14.5 | 7.2 | 8.0 | 7.2 | 7.0 | 6.4 | 30.9 | 21.4 | 10.5 | 1.3 | 73.4 | 32.6 | 35.1 | 95.6 |
| SAGINAW-B.CITY-MIDL. | 4.4 | 5.9 | 6.4 | 7.2 | 7.7 | 7.5 | 6.2 | 29.2 | 23.1 | 11.2 | 1.6 | 74.2 | 33.0 | 36.2 | 93.6 |
| ST. CLOUD, MN | 0.4 | 1.1 | 7.2 | 7.3 | 7.8 | 10.0 | 10.0 | 28.9 | 18.4 | 9.0 | 1.5 | 73.1 | 28.2 | 30.9 | 100.0 |
| ST. JOSEPH, MO | 1.9 | 3.0 | 6.6 | 7.0 | 7.5 | 7.6 | 6.5 | 28.0 | 21.8 | 12.7 | 2.3 | 74.5 | 34.3 | 36.6 | 92.4 |
| ST. LOUIS, MO-IL | 1.1 | 1.8 | 6.9 | 7.3 | 7.7 | 7.3 | 6.1 | 30.0 | 22.1 | 11.0 | 1.6 | 73.8 | 33.2 | 36.0 | 92.7 |
| SALEM, OR | 7.6 | 12.3 | 6.9 | 7.0 | 7.4 | 7.8 | 7.0 | 27.5 | 22.6 | 11.6 | 2.1 | 74.1 | 33.8 | 35.8 | 98.6 |
| SALINAS, CA | 33.6 | 41.3 | 8.1 | 8.8 | 7.2 | 7.3 | 7.9 | 31.9 | 17.8 | 9.7 | 1.3 | 71.9 | 29.6 | 31.8 | 107.2 |
| SALT LAKE CITY-OGDEN | 5.8 | 9.0 | 9.7 | 8.7 | 8.6 | 9.2 | 8.9 | 28.4 | 18.2 | 7.4 | 1.0 | 67.3 | 27.4 | 28.3 | 98.9 |
| SAN ANGELO, TX | 25.9 | 32.5 | 7.9 | 7.7 | 7.3 | 8.6 | 7.9 | 26.9 | 21.0 | 11.0 | 1.7 | 73.0 | 31.2 | 33.7 | 94.3 |
| SAN ANTONIO, TX | 47.4 | 54.5 | 8.1 | 8.0 | 7.9 | 8.0 | 7.2 | 29.6 | 20.7 | 9.4 | 1.2 | 71.5 | 30.4 | 32.8 | 95.0 |
| SAN DIEGO, CA | 20.4 | 26.8 | 7.3 | 7.7 | 6.7 | 6.8 | 7.7 | 33.5 | 19.1 | 9.8 | 1.3 | 74.8 | 30.9 | 33.6 | 101.9 |
| SAN FRANCISCO, CA | 14.5 | 18.2 | 5.1 | 5.8 | 5.6 | 5.5 | 6.0 | 33.4 | 24.4 | 12.3 | 1.9 | 80.4 | 35.8 | 38.9 | 98.1 |
| SAN JOSE, CA | 21.0 | 26.1 | 6.7 | 7.5 | 6.6 | 6.9 | 6.8 | 33.9 | 21.4 | 9.1 | 1.1 | 75.5 | 31.9 | 35.0 | 101.7 |
| S.LUIS O.-ATASC-PASO | 13.3 | 17.8 | 5.7 | 7.0 | 6.0 | 7.7 | 9.0 | 29.6 | 20.0 | 13.3 | 1.7 | 77.9 | 33.1 | 35.6 | 107.0 |
| S.BARB-S.MARIA-LOMP. | 26.6 | 33.8 | 6.8 | 7.3 | 6.6 | 7.8 | 8.4 | 31.1 | 19.4 | 10.8 | 1.7 | 75.9 | 31.6 | 33.8 | 100.5 |
| SANTA CRUZ-WATSONVLL | 20.4 | 27.1 | 6.5 | 7.6 | 6.5 | 7.6 | 7.3 | 32.8 | 20.8 | 9.3 | 1.6 | 75.7 | 33.0 | 35.1 | 99.8 |
| SANTA FE, NM | 43.5 | 47.1 | 6.1 | 6.4 | 7.1 | 7.4 | 6.2 | 28.4 | 27.2 | 10.1 | 1.1 | 75.8 | 34.9 | 38.7 | 96.6 |
| SANTA ROSA, CA | 10.6 | 14.8 | 6.3 | 7.3 | 7.0 | 7.0 | 5.7 | 29.1 | 24.3 | 11.4 | 1.9 | 75.4 | 34.8 | 37.3 | 96.0 |
| SARASOTA-BRADENTON | 3.1 | 5.1 | 4.8 | 5.4 | 5.6 | 5.0 | 4.1 | 22.5 | 23.7 | 25.0 | 4.0 | 81.2 | 46.4 | 47.0 | 90.8 |
| SAVANNAH, GA | 1.2 | 2.3 | 7.5 | 7.5 | 7.6 | 7.5 | 7.2 | 30.1 | 21.2 | 10.1 | 1.3 | 73.1 | 31.8 | 34.1 | 94.2 |
| SCRANTON-W.BARRE-HAZ | 0.6 | 1.2 | 5.2 | 6.0 | 6.6 | 6.8 | 5.7 | 27.4 | 23.3 | 16.6 | 2.4 | 78.7 | 37.4 | 40.2 | 90.4 |
| SEATTLE-BELLEV-EV'TT | 2.8 | 4.6 | 6.3 | 6.6 | 7.2 | 6.9 | 6.3 | 33.1 | 23.1 | 9.0 | 1.4 | 75.9 | 33.3 | 36.3 | 98.2 |
| SHARON, PA | 0.4 | 0.9 | 5.3 | 6.3 | 7.0 | 7.3 | 6.1 | 26.6 | 23.4 | 15.8 | 2.4 | 77.5 | 36.4 | 39.6 | 94.2 |
| SHEBOYGAN, WI | 1.6 | 2.8 | 6.3 | 6.8 | 7.5 | 7.6 | 6.3 | 28.7 | 22.9 | 11.8 | 2.1 | 74.6 | 33.8 | 36.9 | 98.5 |
| SHERMAN-DENISON, TX | 2.9 | 4.4 | 6.6 | 6.8 | 7.1 | 7.6 | 6.1 | 25.6 | 24.7 | 13.3 | 2.2 | 75.1 | 35.0 | 38.6 | 92.3 |
| SHREVEPRT-BOS'R CITY | 1.2 | 1.8 | 6.9 | 7.0 | 7.4 | 8.1 | 7.3 | 27.0 | 23.3 | 11.4 | 1.7 | 73.9 | 32.4 | 35.9 | 89.0 |
| SIOUX CITY, IA-NE | 3.2 | 6.1 | 7.1 | 7.1 | 8.0 | 8.3 | 6.9 | 27.8 | 21.6 | 11.3 | 1.9 | 72.9 | 32.7 | 35.0 | 95.2 |
| SIOUX FALLS, SD | 0.5 | 1.3 | 6.8 | 7.2 | 8.0 | 7.9 | 6.9 | 30.4 | 21.3 | 10.0 | 1.7 | 73.4 | 31.6 | 35.2 | 93.4 |
| SOUTH BEND, IN | 2.1 | 3.5 | 6.8 | 7.0 | 7.2 | 8.1 | 7.8 | 28.1 | 21.5 | 11.8 | 1.8 | 75.0 | 32.8 | 35.2 | 94.3 |
| SPOKANE, WA | 1.9 | 3.4 | 6.7 | 6.8 | 7.2 | 8.0 | 7.6 | 28.9 | 22.4 | 10.7 | 1.7 | 74.8 | 33.0 | 35.3 | 96.0 |
| SPRINGFIELD, IL | 0.7 | 1.3 | 6.6 | 7.1 | 7.2 | 6.9 | 5.9 | 29.3 | 23.6 | 11.4 | 1.9 | 74.8 | 34.3 | 37.2 | 90.9 |
| SPRINGFIELD, MO | 0.8 | 1.5 | 6.1 | 6.5 | 7.0 | 8.0 | 7.7 | 30.2 | 22.1 | 10.8 | 1.6 | 76.5 | 32.6 | 35.5 | 94.2 |
| SPRINGFIELD, MA | 8.2 | 11.0 | 6.3 | 6.8 | 6.9 | 7.7 | 7.2 | 29.7 | 21.0 | 12.5 | 1.9 | 76.7 | 32.7 | 35.7 | 91.6 |
| STATE COLLEGE, PA | 1.1 | 1.9 | 4.8 | 5.2 | 5.3 | 9.9 | 18.1 | 28.8 | 17.8 | 8.9 | 1.2 | 82.0 | 27.0 | 29.6 | 105.4 |
| STEUBENVILLE-WEIRTON | 0.5 | 1.0 | 5.0 | 5.5 | 5.9 | 6.8 | 6.7 | 26.1 | 26.2 | 15.8 | 1.9 | 79.6 | 37.6 | 41.1 | 90.8 |
| STOCKTON-LODI, CA | 23.4 | 29.5 | 8.2 | 9.5 | 7.9 | 7.9 | 6.8 | 29.5 | 19.0 | 9.9 | 1.4 | 69.8 | 30.9 | 32.1 | 102.4 |
| SUMTER, SC | 1.2 | 1.9 | 7.4 | 7.4 | 7.0 | 7.0 | 8.4 | 32.9 | 19.8 | 9.0 | 1.1 | 74.2 | 29.6 | 32.4 | 98.0 |
| SYRACUSE, NY | 1.4 | 2.1 | 6.9 | 7.6 | 7.2 | 7.9 | 7.0 | 28.8 | 21.7 | 11.4 | 1.7 | 74.5 | 32.3 | 35.4 | 94.7 |
| TACOMA, WA | 3.5 | 5.6 | 7.6 | 7.5 | 7.5 | 7.7 | 7.6 | 30.7 | 21.0 | 9.2 | 1.3 | 73.2 | 31.3 | 33.6 | 99.9 |
| TALLAHASSEE, FL | 2.4 | 3.5 | 6.3 | 7.0 | 7.1 | 9.4 | 11.6 | 30.1 | 19.3 | 8.2 | 1.0 | 75.8 | 29.3 | 31.2 | 92.5 |
| TAMPA-ST.PETE-CLEARW | 6.7 | 10.3 | 5.7 | 6.2 | 6.4 | 5.8 | 5.3 | 27.1 | 23.1 | 17.8 | 2.7 | 78.4 | 38.6 | 40.8 | 92.2 |
| TERRE HAUTE, IN | 0.8 | 1.4 | 6.1 | 6.2 | 6.5 | 8.2 | 7.7 | 28.7 | 21.9 | 12.5 | 2.1 | 77.3 | 33.7 | 36.3 | 96.5 |
| TEXARKANA, TX-AR | 1.4 | 2.4 | 6.9 | 7.1 | 7.6 | 7.6 | 6.5 | 26.9 | 23.5 | 12.0 | 1.8 | 73.7 | 33.6 | 36.6 | 94.2 |
| TOLEDO, OH | 3.3 | 4.6 | 6.8 | 7.1 | 7.5 | 7.9 | 7.7 | 29.4 | 21.2 | 11.0 | 1.6 | 74.6 | 31.9 | 34.7 | 91.7 |
| TOPEKA, KS | 4.8 | 7.7 | 6.5 | 6.5 | 7.3 | 7.6 | 6.5 | 29.3 | 23.1 | 11.4 | 1.7 | 75.0 | 33.8 | 36.6 | 94.5 |
| TRENTON, NJ | 6.0 | 8.6 | 6.4 | 7.1 | 6.7 | 7.1 | 6.7 | 30.3 | 22.5 | 11.5 | 1.6 | 76.2 | 34.1 | 36.7 | 94.0 |
| TUCSON, AZ | 24.5 | 29.9 | 7.3 | 7.1 | 7.0 | 7.3 | 7.4 | 28.7 | 21.2 | 12.4 | 1.6 | 74.7 | 32.8 | 35.3 | 96.4 |
| TULSA, OK | 2.1 | 3.5 | 7.0 | 7.1 | 7.8 | 7.7 | 6.7 | 28.2 | 23.6 | 10.5 | 1.4 | 73.5 | 33.0 | 36.0 | 94.4 |
| TUSCALOOSA, AL | 0.6 | 1.3 | 6.1 | 6.1 | 6.0 | 8.4 | 11.0 | 29.9 | 20.8 | 10.4 | 1.3 | 78.2 | 30.6 | 33.3 | 92.4 |
| TYLER, TX | 5.9 | 8.0 | 7.2 | 7.2 | 7.4 | 7.8 | 6.5 | 27.0 | 23.4 | 11.9 | 1.7 | 73.9 | 33.2 | 36.5 | 93.2 |
| UTICA-ROME, NY | 1.9 | 3.0 | 6.4 | 7.5 | 6.7 | 6.8 | 6.1 | 28.5 | 21.8 | 14.0 | 2.2 | 75.7 | 34.1 | 37.0 | 98.9 |
| VALLEJO-FAIRFLD-NAPA | 13.6 | 17.9 | 7.3 | 8.6 | 7.4 | 7.1 | 6.4 | 31.4 | 20.7 | 9.8 | 1.3 | 72.6 | 32.0 | 34.3 | 101.3 |
| VENTURA, CA | 26.4 | 33.7 | 7.3 | 8.2 | 7.7 | 7.2 | 6.4 | 31.6 | 21.5 | 8.8 | 1.2 | 72.6 | 31.7 | 34.2 | 101.5 |
| VICTORIA, TX | 34.1 | 41.5 | 8.3 | 8.3 | 8.3 | 8.2 | 6.4 | 27.5 | 21.8 | 10.0 | 1.2 | 70.1 | 31.6 | 33.9 | 95.6 |
| VINELND-M'VLE-BRDGTN | 13.3 | 18.6 | 7.3 | 8.0 | 7.5 | 6.9 | 6.1 | 29.5 | 21.3 | 11.7 | 1.6 | 73.1 | 33.3 | 35.3 | 97.0 |
| VISALIA-TULARE-P'VLE | 38.8 | 47.4 | 9.1 | 10.6 | 8.7 | 8.5 | 6.9 | 27.6 | 18.1 | 9.3 | 1.3 | 66.5 | 29.2 | 29.7 | 100.1 |
| WACO, TX | 12.5 | 16.6 | 7.5 | 7.2 | 7.2 | 9.0 | 9.5 | 25.6 | 21.3 | 11.0 | 1.7 | 73.8 | 31.1 | 33.4 | 94.2 |
| WASHINGTON, DC | 5.4 | 7.7 | 6.5 | 6.9 | 6.9 | 6.3 | 6.2 | 34.8 | 22.9 | 8.5 | 1.0 | 76.1 | 32.5 | 35.7 | 95.0 |
| WATERLOO-CEDAR FALLS | 0.7 | 1.6 | 5.9 | 6.2 | 7.1 | 8.7 | 9.1 | 26.9 | 22.5 | 11.9 | 1.8 | 76.6 | 32.8 | 35.9 | 91.6 |
| WAUSAU, WI | 0.4 | 0.9 | 6.5 | 7.1 | 7.8 | 7.7 | 5.9 | 29.5 | 23.1 | 10.8 | 1.6 | 73.9 | 32.7 | 36.3 | 98.4 |
| W.PALM BEACH-B.RATON | 7.7 | 11.4 | 5.7 | 6.3 | 6.5 | 5.4 | 4.5 | 26.1 | 22.1 | 19.8 | 3.7 | 78.3 | 39.9 | 42.2 | 91.6 |
| WHEELING, WV-OH | 0.4 | 0.8 | 5.3 | 5.7 | 6.2 | 6.9 | 6.4 | 26.7 | 25.0 | 15.5 | 2.2 | 78.8 | 37.5 | 40.5 | 91.6 |
| WICHITA, KS | 4.1 | 6.4 | 7.5 | 7.4 | 8.0 | 7.8 | 6.5 | 29.7 | 21.1 | 10.4 | 1.5 | 72.4 | 32.1 | 34.8 | 96.0 |
| UNITED STATES | 9.0 | 11.8 | 6.9 | 7.2 | 7.2 | 7.2 | 6.7 | 29.9 | 22.2 | 11.1 | 1.6 | 74.6 | 32.9 | 35.7 | 95.6 |

# HOUSEHOLDS

## MSA AND U.S. TOTALS

| MSA | HOUSEHOLDS | | | | | FAMILIES | | | MEDIAN HOUSEHOLD INCOME | | |
|---|---|---|---|---|---|---|---|---|---|---|---|
| | 1990 | 2000 | 2005 | % Annual Rate 1990-2000 | 2000 Average HH Size | 1990 | 2000 | % Annual Rate 1990-2000 | 2000 | 2005 | 2000 National Rank |
| RACINE, WI | 63,736 | 68,980 | 70,665 | 1.0 | 2.63 | 47,011 | 49,553 | 0.6 | 47,430 | 52,779 | 49 |
| RALEIGH-DURHAM-CH.H. | 334,506 | 447,326 | 504,472 | 3.6 | 2.45 | 221,142 | 289,360 | 3.3 | 48,423 | 55,303 | 41 |
| RAPID CITY, SD | 30,553 | 33,449 | 34,532 | 1.1 | 2.61 | 21,762 | 23,109 | 0.7 | 39,015 | 47,044 | 169 |
| READING, PA | 127,649 | 138,397 | 143,495 | 1.0 | 2.54 | 91,268 | 96,092 | 0.6 | 45,547 | 53,660 | 71 |
| REDDING, CA | 55,966 | 64,270 | 66,616 | 1.7 | 2.53 | 40,473 | 44,866 | 1.3 | 36,860 | 42,064 | 218 |
| RENO, NV | 102,294 | 131,530 | 145,812 | 3.1 | 2.44 | 64,311 | 80,073 | 2.7 | 45,888 | 52,482 | 64 |
| RICHLAND-K'WCK-PASCO | 54,423 | 68,027 | 71,883 | 2.7 | 2.72 | 39,809 | 48,628 | 2.5 | 49,914 | 57,293 | 36 |
| RICHMOND-PETERSBURG | 331,824 | 387,448 | 413,651 | 1.9 | 2.43 | 228,797 | 261,793 | 1.6 | 42,851 | 48,675 | 109 |
| RIVERSIDE-SAN BERN. | 866,804 | 1,099,082 | 1,220,236 | 2.9 | 2.92 | 647,718 | 798,734 | 2.6 | 43,314 | 54,155 | 104 |
| ROANOKE, VA | 89,694 | 94,383 | 95,669 | 0.6 | 2.34 | 62,197 | 63,295 | 0.2 | 36,602 | 41,033 | 222 |
| ROCHESTER, MN | 40,058 | 45,925 | 49,878 | 1.7 | 2.58 | 27,737 | 30,628 | 1.2 | 52,841 | 60,388 | 22 |
| ROCHESTER, NY | 396,089 | 411,952 | 414,075 | 0.5 | 2.53 | 273,830 | 275,890 | 0.1 | 44,422 | 50,080 | 88 |
| ROCKFORD, IL | 124,809 | 138,001 | 142,384 | 1.2 | 2.57 | 89,953 | 97,055 | 0.9 | 44,865 | 51,135 | 81 |
| ROCKY MOUNT, NC | 49,360 | 55,004 | 57,400 | 1.3 | 2.63 | 36,309 | 39,184 | 0.9 | 34,584 | 39,989 | 261 |
| SACRAMENTO, CA | 505,476 | 604,703 | 654,396 | 2.2 | 2.63 | 345,702 | 402,130 | 1.8 | 47,181 | 56,407 | 51 |
| SAGINAW-B.CITY-MIDL. | 148,235 | 154,192 | 156,005 | 0.5 | 2.55 | 108,719 | 109,748 | 0.1 | 39,953 | 43,496 | 152 |
| ST. CLOUD, MN | 50,711 | 57,729 | 61,125 | 1.6 | 2.76 | 35,328 | 38,965 | 1.2 | 42,729 | 50,116 | 110 |
| ST. JOSEPH, MO | 37,915 | 38,090 | 38,171 | 0.1 | 2.48 | 26,504 | 25,633 | -0.4 | 33,540 | 38,439 | 278 |
| ST. LOUIS, MO-IL | 942,119 | 978,975 | 995,424 | 0.5 | 2.59 | 659,696 | 669,134 | 0.2 | 43,787 | 50,358 | 94 |
| SALEM, OR | 101,661 | 126,682 | 137,402 | 2.7 | 2.59 | 71,379 | 86,210 | 2.3 | 40,107 | 47,461 | 148 |
| SALINAS, CA | 112,965 | 123,110 | 131,243 | 1.0 | 2.91 | 83,015 | 89,128 | 0.9 | 43,478 | 54,582 | 101 |
| SALT LAKE CITY-OGDEN | 347,531 | 441,383 | 478,237 | 2.9 | 2.88 | 260,479 | 326,310 | 2.8 | 46,550 | 54,251 | 57 |
| SAN ANGELO, TX | 35,408 | 37,564 | 37,859 | 0.7 | 2.59 | 25,212 | 25,991 | 0.4 | 35,592 | 42,775 | 240 |
| SAN ANTONIO, TX | 458,502 | 558,919 | 608,217 | 2.4 | 2.78 | 335,617 | 400,165 | 2.2 | 37,414 | 42,988 | 201 |
| SAN DIEGO, CA | 887,403 | 1,048,142 | 1,152,222 | 2.0 | 2.65 | 599,428 | 689,842 | 1.7 | 45,892 | 56,513 | 63 |
| SAN FRANCISCO, CA | 642,504 | 693,510 | 717,567 | 0.9 | 2.38 | 362,319 | 382,336 | 0.7 | 54,833 | 63,683 | 18 |
| SAN JOSE, CA | 520,180 | 594,597 | 628,414 | 1.6 | 2.74 | 359,677 | 401,908 | 1.4 | 68,026 | 81,445 | 1 |
| S.LUIS O.-ATASC-PASO | 80,281 | 89,950 | 95,860 | 1.4 | 2.51 | 52,320 | 56,453 | 0.9 | 45,447 | 56,747 | 73 |
| S.BARB-S.MARIA-LOMP. | 129,802 | 140,830 | 146,599 | 1.0 | 2.68 | 86,077 | 91,382 | 0.7 | 44,603 | 53,764 | 85 |
| SANTA CRUZ-WATSONVLL | 83,566 | 91,830 | 97,558 | 1.1 | 2.61 | 53,752 | 56,741 | 0.7 | 54,579 | 68,100 | 19 |
| SANTA FE, NM | 45,053 | 57,387 | 61,947 | 3.0 | 2.46 | 30,359 | 37,601 | 2.6 | 48,191 | 54,150 | 43 |
| SANTA ROSA, CA | 149,011 | 173,402 | 187,195 | 1.9 | 2.53 | 99,876 | 111,282 | 1.3 | 52,917 | 65,703 | 21 |
| SARASOTA-BRADENTON | 216,553 | 243,636 | 257,469 | 1.4 | 2.25 | 145,391 | 157,307 | 1.0 | 40,440 | 48,054 | 139 |
| SAVANNAH, GA | 94,940 | 108,675 | 114,383 | 1.7 | 2.61 | 67,935 | 76,580 | 1.5 | 40,462 | 47,825 | 138 |
| SCRANTON-W.BARRE-HAZ | 246,491 | 239,738 | 233,334 | -0.3 | 2.44 | 170,867 | 159,820 | -0.8 | 33,919 | 39,324 | 273 |
| SEATTLE-BELLEV-EV'TT | 809,292 | 960,800 | 1,034,376 | 2.1 | 2.42 | 519,037 | 595,674 | 1.7 | 53,864 | 62,692 | 20 |
| SHARON, PA | 45,591 | 46,706 | 46,783 | 0.3 | 2.47 | 33,275 | 32,921 | -0.1 | 33,653 | 38,536 | 276 |
| SHEBOYGAN, WI | 38,592 | 41,835 | 42,818 | 1.0 | 2.56 | 28,006 | 29,494 | 0.6 | 47,867 | 57,897 | 45 |
| SHERMAN-DENISON, TX | 36,847 | 41,261 | 44,360 | 1.4 | 2.51 | 26,534 | 28,691 | 1.0 | 33,854 | 39,585 | 275 |
| SHREVEPRT-BOS'R CITY | 139,815 | 145,488 | 147,742 | 0.5 | 2.54 | 100,012 | 101,023 | 0.1 | 31,940 | 35,698 | 295 |
| SIOUX CITY, IA-NE | 42,934 | 45,222 | 45,524 | 0.6 | 2.60 | 30,151 | 30,646 | 0.2 | 37,615 | 43,608 | 196 |
| SIOUX FALLS, SD | 53,142 | 63,684 | 69,196 | 2.2 | 2.56 | 36,159 | 42,013 | 1.8 | 42,227 | 49,447 | 115 |
| SOUTH BEND, IN | 92,365 | 98,506 | 100,129 | 0.8 | 2.50 | 63,629 | 65,732 | 0.4 | 39,722 | 43,494 | 158 |
| SPOKANE, WA | 141,619 | 164,029 | 169,130 | 1.8 | 2.44 | 93,982 | 106,098 | 1.5 | 39,551 | 45,311 | 160 |
| SPRINGFIELD, IL | 76,345 | 82,877 | 83,538 | 1.0 | 2.43 | 50,736 | 52,991 | 0.5 | 41,648 | 46,815 | 124 |
| SPRINGFIELD, MO | 101,791 | 120,942 | 128,430 | 2.1 | 2.49 | 70,604 | 82,616 | 1.9 | 37,470 | 42,647 | 199 |
| SPRINGFIELD, MA | 219,958 | 220,467 | 221,890 | 0.0 | 2.51 | 151,080 | 145,693 | -0.4 | 39,506 | 46,865 | 162 |
| STATE COLLEGE, PA | 42,683 | 46,525 | 47,530 | 1.1 | 2.49 | 26,359 | 27,741 | 0.6 | 37,017 | 41,171 | 215 |
| STEUBENVILLE-WEIRTON | 55,223 | 53,185 | 51,418 | -0.5 | 2.42 | 40,382 | 37,481 | -0.9 | 30,282 | 33,019 | 307 |
| STOCKTON-LODI, CA | 158,156 | 190,570 | 210,297 | 2.3 | 2.93 | 116,878 | 137,595 | 2.0 | 42,117 | 52,807 | 118 |
| SUMTER, SC | 32,723 | 35,807 | 36,365 | 1.1 | 2.95 | 25,673 | 27,456 | 0.8 | 33,160 | 40,565 | 280 |
| SYRACUSE, NY | 272,974 | 275,413 | 273,153 | 0.1 | 2.54 | 187,569 | 182,942 | -0.3 | 39,742 | 44,652 | 157 |
| TACOMA, WA | 214,652 | 259,924 | 283,128 | 2.3 | 2.62 | 151,672 | 178,355 | 2.0 | 45,167 | 56,487 | 77 |
| TALLAHASSEE, FL | 88,233 | 98,736 | 100,436 | 1.4 | 2.52 | 55,257 | 60,118 | 1.0 | 38,818 | 44,592 | 175 |
| TAMPA-ST.PETE-CLEARW | 869,481 | 960,285 | 1,009,180 | 1.2 | 2.35 | 574,378 | 611,431 | 0.8 | 36,532 | 43,387 | 223 |
| TERRE HAUTE, IN | 55,824 | 56,922 | 56,578 | 0.2 | 2.43 | 38,190 | 37,656 | -0.2 | 34,590 | 40,056 | 260 |
| TEXARKANA, TX-AR | 44,868 | 46,748 | 47,169 | 0.5 | 2.56 | 32,879 | 33,248 | 0.1 | 33,305 | 39,587 | 279 |
| TOLEDO, OH | 230,681 | 233,628 | 234,720 | 0.2 | 2.53 | 157,754 | 154,453 | -0.3 | 37,663 | 41,951 | 195 |
| TOPEKA, KS | 63,768 | 65,544 | 65,467 | 0.3 | 2.56 | 43,046 | 42,942 | 0.0 | 43,973 | 50,468 | 92 |
| TRENTON, NJ | 116,941 | 120,657 | 123,765 | 0.4 | 2.65 | 82,447 | 81,968 | -0.1 | 57,353 | 66,076 | 10 |
| TUCSON, AZ | 261,792 | 324,895 | 352,631 | 2.7 | 2.46 | 169,666 | 205,449 | 2.3 | 34,130 | 38,841 | 271 |
| TULSA, OK | 277,202 | 313,157 | 333,720 | 1.5 | 2.50 | 193,707 | 213,214 | 1.2 | 37,268 | 43,466 | 208 |
| TUSCALOOSA, AL | 55,354 | 62,068 | 64,681 | 1.4 | 2.49 | 37,355 | 40,622 | 1.0 | 34,423 | 40,211 | 267 |
| TYLER, TX | 56,800 | 65,751 | 70,108 | 1.8 | 2.57 | 41,184 | 46,194 | 1.4 | 37,080 | 42,971 | 212 |
| UTICA-ROME, NY | 117,498 | 110,460 | 106,920 | -0.7 | 2.49 | 81,311 | 73,793 | -1.2 | 35,658 | 40,389 | 238 |
| VALLEJO-FAIRFLD-NAPA | 154,741 | 178,463 | 193,591 | 1.7 | 2.80 | 114,668 | 128,180 | 1.4 | 55,840 | 68,747 | 14 |
| VENTURA, CA | 217,298 | 248,181 | 268,257 | 1.6 | 3.00 | 164,773 | 183,999 | 1.3 | 59,849 | 74,683 | 8 |
| VICTORIA, TX | 26,228 | 29,728 | 31,057 | 1.5 | 2.75 | 19,820 | 21,940 | 1.2 | 40,338 | 45,999 | 143 |
| VINELND-M'VLE-BRDGTN | 47,118 | 48,019 | 47,708 | 0.2 | 2.76 | 34,966 | 34,646 | -0.1 | 40,597 | 48,628 | 137 |
| VISALIA-TULARE-P'VLE | 97,861 | 115,735 | 122,824 | 2.1 | 3.08 | 76,529 | 88,934 | 1.8 | 32,542 | 41,165 | 291 |
| WACO, TX | 70,208 | 77,235 | 79,748 | 1.2 | 2.56 | 47,862 | 51,370 | 0.9 | 36,607 | 43,878 | 221 |
| WASHINGTON, DC | 1,566,134 | 1,818,253 | 1,967,723 | 1.8 | 2.59 | 1,051,112 | 1,204,844 | 1.7 | 61,080 | 70,400 | 6 |
| WATERLOO-CEDAR FALLS | 46,932 | 46,310 | 45,322 | -0.2 | 2.46 | 32,143 | 30,433 | -0.7 | 37,426 | 41,124 | 200 |
| WAUSAU, WI | 41,547 | 45,843 | 47,634 | 1.2 | 2.68 | 31,002 | 33,427 | 0.9 | 47,296 | 56,538 | 50 |
| W.PALM BEACH-B.RATON | 365,558 | 449,634 | 486,101 | 2.5 | 2.34 | 242,273 | 288,081 | 2.1 | 41,391 | 45,063 | 126 |
| WHEELING, WV-OH | 62,858 | 61,895 | 60,717 | -0.2 | 2.37 | 44,180 | 41,861 | -0.7 | 28,963 | 31,589 | 313 |
| WICHITA, KS | 186,640 | 215,215 | 229,217 | 1.7 | 2.54 | 129,919 | 145,521 | 1.4 | 41,155 | 48,060 | 127 |
| UNITED STATES | | | | 1.4 | 2.59 | | | 1.1 | 41,914 | 49,127 | |

# INCOME

## MSA AND U.S. TOTALS

| MSA | 2000 Per Capita Income | 2000 HH Income Base | 2000 HOUSEHOLD INCOME DISTRIBUTION (%) Less than $15,000 | $15,000 to $24,999 | $25,000 to $49,999 | $50,000 to $99,999 | $100,000 to $149,999 | $150,000 or More | 2000 AVERAGE DISPOSABLE INCOME BY AGE OF HOUSEHOLDER All Ages | <35 | 35-44 | 45-54 | 55-64 | 65+ |
|---|---|---|---|---|---|---|---|---|---|---|---|---|---|---|
| RACINE, WI | 23,023 | 68,980 | 10.6 | 9.1 | 33.5 | 35.2 | 8.5 | 3.1 | 39,725 | 32,184 | 44,465 | 51,948 | 44,952 | 25,104 |
| RALEIGH-DURHAM-CH.H. | 25,523 | 447,323 | 10.8 | 10.2 | 30.7 | 34.6 | 9.8 | 4.0 | 44,515 | 36,667 | 49,231 | 54,785 | 46,359 | 29,722 |
| RAPID CITY, SD | 18,969 | 33,449 | 11.0 | 16.0 | 37.7 | 28.1 | 5.5 | 1.7 | 36,889 | 29,991 | 41,679 | 47,181 | 43,110 | 25,967 |
| READING, PA | 22,412 | 138,397 | 10.9 | 10.5 | 34.9 | 33.5 | 7.7 | 2.6 | 40,894 | 38,356 | 46,503 | 52,441 | 44,604 | 25,407 |
| REDDING, CA | 19,384 | 64,270 | 16.6 | 14.7 | 36.0 | 25.0 | 5.1 | 2.7 | 36,311 | 31,474 | 40,364 | 46,017 | 38,945 | 24,474 |
| RENO, NV | 24,884 | 131,530 | 9.7 | 11.9 | 33.5 | 33.1 | 8.4 | 3.5 | 45,730 | 38,238 | 49,048 | 54,482 | 48,102 | 32,922 |
| RICHLAND-K'WCK-PASCO | 22,864 | 68,022 | 11.1 | 9.4 | 29.6 | 37.1 | 10.0 | 2.8 | 46,031 | 36,632 | 50,663 | 57,325 | 51,966 | 31,878 |
| RICHMOND-PETERSBURG | 22,435 | 387,434 | 13.5 | 12.3 | 32.8 | 32.0 | 6.8 | 2.6 | 39,553 | 32,328 | 43,997 | 48,598 | 41,934 | 27,201 |
| RIVERSIDE-SAN BERN. | 19,525 | 1,099,076 | 13.6 | 11.7 | 32.7 | 32.1 | 6.9 | 3.1 | 40,667 | 36,736 | 44,672 | 48,817 | 42,870 | 28,384 |
| ROANOKE, VA | 20,012 | 94,367 | 17.1 | 14.8 | 35.5 | 25.9 | 5.1 | 1.7 | 34,537 | 28,993 | 39,278 | 42,562 | 37,780 | 24,513 |
| ROCHESTER, MN | 25,888 | 45,925 | 8.3 | 7.6 | 30.1 | 37.6 | 11.4 | 4.9 | 47,003 | 38,549 | 50,750 | 59,701 | 51,224 | 29,793 |
| ROCHESTER, NY | 21,623 | 411,947 | 12.9 | 11.0 | 33.0 | 33.4 | 7.3 | 2.5 | 37,821 | 33,293 | 42,208 | 48,120 | 41,192 | 23,588 |
| ROCKFORD, IL | 21,919 | 138,001 | 11.6 | 10.5 | 34.5 | 33.8 | 7.3 | 2.3 | 40,256 | 35,025 | 45,067 | 50,731 | 43,451 | 25,304 |
| ROCKY MOUNT, NC | 16,567 | 55,004 | 19.2 | 15.9 | 35.0 | 24.6 | 4.1 | 1.2 | 32,442 | 29,631 | 37,101 | 40,498 | 33,397 | 20,277 |
| SACRAMENTO, CA | 24,178 | 604,701 | 10.8 | 10.5 | 31.8 | 34.0 | 8.8 | 4.2 | 44,421 | 37,388 | 47,970 | 53,385 | 48,167 | 31,305 |
| SAGINAW-B.CITY-MIDL. | 19,693 | 154,192 | 18.1 | 12.3 | 32.4 | 29.3 | 5.9 | 2.2 | 36,154 | 28,625 | 41,294 | 48,933 | 41,108 | 21,973 |
| ST. CLOUD, MN | 19,336 | 57,729 | 10.6 | 11.7 | 37.4 | 31.2 | 7.1 | 2.1 | 38,043 | 33,236 | 43,998 | 48,810 | 42,707 | 24,163 |
| ST. JOSEPH, MO | 16,238 | 38,072 | 20.2 | 14.9 | 37.2 | 23.2 | 3.6 | 0.9 | 31,784 | 27,825 | 37,492 | 39,937 | 34,711 | 21,328 |
| ST. LOUIS, MO-IL | 21,663 | 978,935 | 12.7 | 11.5 | 33.3 | 32.6 | 7.2 | 2.7 | 40,917 | 35,244 | 44,966 | 50,849 | 43,894 | 26,320 |
| SALEM, OR | 19,219 | 126,673 | 12.4 | 14.3 | 36.7 | 29.3 | 5.7 | 1.6 | 34,761 | 29,243 | 39,818 | 44,395 | 38,117 | 24,518 |
| SALINAS, CA | 20,548 | 123,109 | 10.0 | 12.8 | 34.8 | 31.7 | 7.3 | 3.5 | 42,071 | 34,741 | 42,895 | 50,601 | 46,296 | 36,985 |
| SALT LAKE CITY-OGDEN | 20,256 | 441,382 | 8.8 | 10.5 | 35.0 | 35.2 | 8.1 | 2.4 | 41,408 | 33,747 | 45,750 | 52,080 | 47,281 | 29,069 |
| SAN ANGELO, TX | 17,071 | 37,564 | 17.0 | 16.0 | 35.6 | 25.7 | 4.4 | 1.4 | 35,598 | 29,300 | 41,117 | 44,355 | 38,959 | 26,110 |
| SAN ANTONIO, TX | 18,054 | 558,915 | 16.3 | 15.1 | 33.6 | 27.0 | 5.8 | 2.2 | 38,446 | 30,963 | 41,706 | 46,470 | 41,787 | 30,356 |
| SAN DIEGO, CA | 24,123 | 1,048,139 | 10.9 | 11.8 | 31.9 | 32.3 | 8.4 | 4.7 | 44,652 | 37,196 | 47,404 | 52,881 | 48,441 | 33,823 |
| SAN FRANCISCO, CA | 34,886 | 693,510 | 9.5 | 8.5 | 27.1 | 34.0 | 12.1 | 8.8 | 54,345 | 46,092 | 54,423 | 58,945 | 56,421 | 40,554 |
| SAN JOSE, CA | 34,200 | 594,597 | 5.9 | 5.0 | 21.1 | 40.9 | 17.3 | 9.8 | 60,801 | 51,345 | 61,221 | 68,586 | 62,903 | 43,312 |
| S.LUIS O.-ATASC-PASO | 25,660 | 89,950 | 11.0 | 11.7 | 32.6 | 31.3 | 8.8 | 4.7 | 44,593 | 34,942 | 49,058 | 55,306 | 49,268 | 34,770 |
| S.BARB-S.MARIA-LOMP. | 24,620 | 140,830 | 12.0 | 12.1 | 31.6 | 30.7 | 8.2 | 5.4 | 45,167 | 34,641 | 46,844 | 54,069 | 50,837 | 36,915 |
| SANTA CRUZ-WATSONVLL | 28,851 | 91,829 | 9.1 | 8.6 | 27.3 | 35.9 | 12.2 | 6.9 | 51,214 | 42,716 | 53,355 | 60,834 | 54,069 | 34,161 |
| SANTA FE, NM | 26,909 | 57,387 | 10.2 | 11.9 | 29.7 | 33.4 | 10.0 | 4.8 | 46,591 | 33,598 | 47,167 | 54,242 | 51,629 | 38,414 |
| SANTA ROSA, CA | 29,200 | 173,402 | 8.1 | 8.4 | 29.6 | 37.2 | 10.9 | 5.7 | 49,452 | 42,946 | 51,513 | 58,303 | 51,761 | 35,822 |
| SARASOTA-BRADENTON | 24,795 | 243,633 | 11.0 | 15.0 | 36.0 | 28.1 | 6.8 | 3.1 | 42,556 | 36,728 | 46,509 | 49,594 | 46,944 | 36,679 |
| SAVANNAH, GA | 19,973 | 108,675 | 15.8 | 12.3 | 33.4 | 29.5 | 6.6 | 2.4 | 38,057 | 32,921 | 41,902 | 45,776 | 40,865 | 26,842 |
| SCRANTON-W.BARRE-HAZ | 18,538 | 239,732 | 19.0 | 15.8 | 36.8 | 22.4 | 4.2 | 1.9 | 32,656 | 30,667 | 38,752 | 43,460 | 36,488 | 20,335 |
| SEATTLE-BELLEV-EV'TT | 30,845 | 960,800 | 7.0 | 8.3 | 30.1 | 37.0 | 11.5 | 6.2 | 54,057 | 43,306 | 54,879 | 63,432 | 58,860 | 36,452 |
| SHARON, PA | 16,338 | 46,706 | 17.3 | 16.5 | 38.7 | 23.3 | 3.4 | 0.8 | 30,982 | 27,956 | 35,324 | 40,078 | 36,275 | 20,932 |
| SHEBOYGAN, WI | 22,422 | 41,835 | 9.6 | 8.7 | 34.8 | 36.4 | 8.5 | 2.1 | 38,991 | 35,270 | 44,254 | 50,022 | 44,296 | 23,413 |
| SHERMAN-DENISON, TX | 18,052 | 41,261 | 18.7 | 15.6 | 36.3 | 22.9 | 4.5 | 2.0 | 35,340 | 29,954 | 41,982 | 43,985 | 37,801 | 23,648 |
| SHREVEPRT-BOS'R CITY | 16,721 | 145,476 | 23.3 | 15.7 | 33.0 | 22.2 | 4.1 | 1.7 | 33,648 | 27,500 | 39,500 | 41,447 | 35,038 | 22,982 |
| SIOUX CITY, IA-NE | 18,190 | 45,205 | 15.3 | 14.4 | 37.0 | 27.1 | 4.7 | 1.6 | 34,080 | 28,889 | 40,205 | 43,104 | 37,269 | 22,592 |
| SIOUX FALLS, SD | 20,202 | 63,684 | 10.6 | 12.2 | 37.6 | 32.1 | 5.9 | 1.7 | 38,825 | 33,224 | 43,764 | 49,002 | 42,536 | 25,293 |
| SOUTH BEND, IN | 19,451 | 98,506 | 14.0 | 14.1 | 35.9 | 29.0 | 5.3 | 1.7 | 36,952 | 32,187 | 42,223 | 47,977 | 39,942 | 23,303 |
| SPOKANE, WA | 22,082 | 164,029 | 14.4 | 13.7 | 35.1 | 27.0 | 6.7 | 3.1 | 40,805 | 31,691 | 45,053 | 50,067 | 44,919 | 29,294 |
| SPRINGFIELD, IL | 21,590 | 82,877 | 13.1 | 13.1 | 34.5 | 31.3 | 6.0 | 2.0 | 37,731 | 31,775 | 42,148 | 47,310 | 41,613 | 25,282 |
| SPRINGFIELD, MO | 18,792 | 120,942 | 15.1 | 14.4 | 36.4 | 27.4 | 5.0 | 1.6 | 35,960 | 30,212 | 41,901 | 44,296 | 39,462 | 24,111 |
| SPRINGFIELD, MA | 19,229 | 220,459 | 17.8 | 12.0 | 33.9 | 28.8 | 5.5 | 2.1 | 34,653 | 30,548 | 38,823 | 44,778 | 40,248 | 21,886 |
| STATE COLLEGE, PA | 18,387 | 46,523 | 16.5 | 15.0 | 33.6 | 26.2 | 6.0 | 2.7 | 36,578 | 25,962 | 42,403 | 51,732 | 46,434 | 26,138 |
| STEUBENVILLE-WEIRTON | 15,441 | 53,185 | 23.7 | 17.0 | 35.5 | 20.9 | 2.2 | 0.6 | 28,836 | 24,905 | 35,465 | 37,442 | 31,403 | 19,238 |
| STOCKTON-LODI, CA | 18,885 | 190,564 | 14.5 | 12.2 | 32.9 | 30.7 | 7.0 | 2.8 | 39,504 | 35,669 | 43,775 | 47,051 | 41,875 | 27,844 |
| SUMTER, SC | 14,395 | 35,804 | 18.6 | 17.4 | 35.7 | 24.0 | 3.5 | 0.9 | 31,460 | 27,641 | 34,810 | 39,066 | 33,543 | 21,635 |
| SYRACUSE, NY | 19,096 | 275,412 | 15.3 | 13.0 | 35.1 | 29.3 | 5.4 | 1.8 | 34,310 | 30,892 | 39,637 | 43,110 | 37,595 | 21,235 |
| TACOMA, WA | 21,268 | 259,923 | 10.8 | 11.3 | 33.9 | 33.9 | 7.8 | 2.3 | 42,909 | 35,924 | 45,762 | 53,337 | 48,157 | 30,456 |
| TALLAHASSEE, FL | 20,515 | 98,735 | 17.4 | 13.9 | 30.8 | 28.3 | 6.6 | 3.0 | 40,361 | 28,468 | 47,276 | 51,756 | 47,617 | 30,336 |
| TAMPA-ST.PETE-CLEARW | 20,844 | 960,271 | 14.9 | 16.4 | 35.7 | 25.7 | 5.1 | 2.2 | 37,860 | 34,023 | 43,600 | 46,458 | 40,291 | 28,276 |
| TERRE HAUTE, IN | 18,805 | 56,916 | 17.5 | 16.3 | 36.6 | 23.4 | 4.5 | 1.9 | 34,189 | 28,685 | 40,579 | 44,745 | 36,922 | 22,104 |
| TEXARKANA, TX-AR | 16,747 | 46,748 | 22.1 | 15.3 | 33.3 | 23.4 | 4.3 | 1.7 | 33,747 | 28,515 | 40,259 | 42,292 | 34,757 | 23,081 |
| TOLEDO, OH | 19,172 | 233,624 | 17.9 | 13.7 | 34.1 | 26.7 | 5.2 | 2.3 | 35,689 | 29,122 | 41,136 | 46,602 | 39,761 | 22,849 |
| TOPEKA, KS | 20,933 | 65,537 | 10.8 | 12.1 | 34.8 | 33.2 | 7.1 | 2.2 | 40,119 | 31,929 | 44,793 | 50,958 | 44,396 | 29,347 |
| TRENTON, NJ | 30,226 | 120,657 | 8.7 | 8.1 | 25.9 | 36.7 | 12.7 | 8.0 | 51,142 | 44,893 | 53,475 | 59,467 | 54,620 | 32,462 |
| TUCSON, AZ | 18,569 | 324,895 | 19.0 | 16.4 | 34.0 | 24.1 | 4.8 | 1.8 | 34,817 | 26,975 | 39,001 | 43,521 | 38,477 | 29,152 |
| TULSA, OK | 20,116 | 313,154 | 16.4 | 14.8 | 34.0 | 26.8 | 5.5 | 2.5 | 36,861 | 29,543 | 41,605 | 45,016 | 40,750 | 25,630 |
| TUSCALOOSA, AL | 18,453 | 62,068 | 22.7 | 14.0 | 31.7 | 24.3 | 5.4 | 2.0 | 35,285 | 26,237 | 42,047 | 47,650 | 38,280 | 24,196 |
| TYLER, TX | 19,538 | 65,749 | 17.3 | 14.7 | 33.3 | 26.5 | 5.8 | 2.4 | 38,295 | 31,594 | 43,079 | 47,303 | 41,379 | 27,487 |
| UTICA-ROME, NY | 17,114 | 110,450 | 17.4 | 15.4 | 36.4 | 25.6 | 4.0 | 1.2 | 31,111 | 28,795 | 36,376 | 40,033 | 35,255 | 20,046 |
| VALLEJO-FAIRFLD-NAPA | 24,866 | 178,461 | 7.8 | 7.2 | 27.7 | 41.4 | 11.6 | 4.3 | 48,941 | 42,957 | 52,328 | 57,890 | 51,714 | 34,554 |
| VENTURA, CA | 26,343 | 248,180 | 7.2 | 7.0 | 24.7 | 41.3 | 13.4 | 6.5 | 53,165 | 46,276 | 54,867 | 61,422 | 55,799 | 36,137 |
| VICTORIA, TX | 19,911 | 29,728 | 17.2 | 12.5 | 32.4 | 28.3 | 6.5 | 3.0 | 40,842 | 32,534 | 45,799 | 50,240 | 41,123 | 28,040 |
| VINELND-M'VLE-BRDGTN | 18,416 | 48,019 | 16.3 | 11.4 | 34.4 | 30.2 | 5.9 | 1.9 | 34,529 | 32,797 | 39,167 | 42,556 | 37,576 | 22,275 |
| VISALIA-TULARE-P'VLE | 14,944 | 115,735 | 20.0 | 17.3 | 34.0 | 22.2 | 4.2 | 2.4 | 33,783 | 27,705 | 37,054 | 41,857 | 37,016 | 24,897 |
| WACO, TX | 18,696 | 77,231 | 19.6 | 13.6 | 32.7 | 26.6 | 5.6 | 2.0 | 37,161 | 28,274 | 43,724 | 48,472 | 41,683 | 27,797 |
| WASHINGTON, DC | 31,232 | 1,818,241 | 6.1 | 6.7 | 25.4 | 40.6 | 14.4 | 6.9 | 54,093 | 43,184 | 53,979 | 61,759 | 56,521 | 42,424 |
| WATERLOO-CEDAR FALLS | 19,198 | 46,310 | 17.6 | 14.2 | 34.1 | 26.8 | 5.3 | 2.0 | 34,146 | 24,329 | 42,290 | 47,186 | 34,983 | 23,359 |
| WAUSAU, WI | 21,359 | 45,843 | 10.7 | 9.3 | 33.4 | 36.3 | 8.3 | 2.0 | 38,382 | 34,212 | 44,437 | 49,841 | 41,923 | 21,780 |
| W.PALM BEACH-B.RATON | 27,929 | 449,634 | 13.3 | 13.5 | 32.9 | 27.7 | 7.5 | 5.1 | 46,442 | 40,086 | 47,791 | 52,828 | 49,665 | 37,268 |
| WHEELING, WV-OH | 15,105 | 61,895 | 25.0 | 18.4 | 34.9 | 18.4 | 2.7 | 0.8 | 28,310 | 24,460 | 34,256 | 36,540 | 30,201 | 19,752 |
| WICHITA, KS | 20,773 | 215,212 | 13.2 | 12.9 | 35.5 | 30.5 | 5.9 | 2.0 | 38,036 | 31,342 | 42,279 | 47,264 | 43,177 | 27,137 |
| UNITED STATES | 22,162 | | 14.5 | 12.5 | 32.3 | 29.8 | 7.4 | 3.5 | 40,748 | 34,503 | 44,969 | 49,579 | 43,409 | 27,339 |

# SPENDING POTENTIAL INDEXES

## MSA AND U.S. TOTALS

# E

| MSA | FINANCIAL SERVICES | | | | THE HOME | | | | | | ENTERTAINMENT | | | | | | PERSONAL | | | |
|---|---|---|---|---|---|---|---|---|---|---|---|---|---|---|---|---|---|---|---|---|
| | | | | | Home Improvements | | | Furnishings | | | | | | | | | | | | |
| | Auto Loan | Home Loan | Investments | Retirement Plans | Home Repair | Lawn & Garden | Remodeling | Appliances | Electronics | Furniture | Restaurants | Sporting Goods | Theater & Concerts | Toys & Hobbies | Travel | Video Rental | Apparel | Auto Aftermarket | Health Insurance | Pets & Supplies |
| RACINE, WI | 97 | 96 | 99 | 95 | 102 | 99 | 99 | 98 | 96 | 98 | 98 | 96 | 100 | 99 | 97 | 101 | 95 | 99 | 100 | 98 |
| RALEIGH-DURHAM-CH.H. | 100 | 102 | 96 | 100 | 100 | 100 | 102 | 99 | 100 | 100 | 103 | 102 | 99 | 102 | 87 | 99 | 102 | 101 | 97 | 102 |
| RAPID CITY, SD | 98 | 97 | 93 | 95 | 98 | 96 | 101 | 97 | 98 | 96 | 100 | 97 | 98 | 99 | 94 | 101 | 95 | 100 | 98 | 100 |
| READING, PA | 100 | 89 | 98 | 93 | 95 | 93 | 97 | 98 | 95 | 96 | 96 | 99 | 97 | 102 | 92 | 99 | 98 | 95 | 103 | 102 |
| REDDING, CA | 97 | 88 | 89 | 89 | 98 | 97 | 105 | 99 | 97 | 93 | 92 | 89 | 87 | 91 | 83 | 93 | 90 | 93 | 98 | 92 |
| RENO, NV | 100 | 106 | 98 | 102 | 103 | 103 | 101 | 101 | 103 | 104 | 104 | 95 | 95 | 95 | 93 | 94 | 102 | 101 | 97 | 96 |
| RICHLAND-K'WCK-PASCO | 99 | 97 | 93 | 96 | 100 | 99 | 102 | 101 | 101 | 99 | 98 | 92 | 91 | 94 | 88 | 94 | 96 | 98 | 97 | 95 |
| RICHMOND-PETERSBURG | 99 | 101 | 99 | 99 | 101 | 101 | 99 | 99 | 99 | 101 | 102 | 101 | 99 | 101 | 89 | 99 | 102 | 101 | 97 | 101 |
| RIVERSIDE-SAN BERN. | 100 | 101 | 91 | 96 | 99 | 100 | 100 | 102 | 102 | 101 | 101 | 94 | 93 | 94 | 89 | 94 | 97 | 99 | 97 | 96 |
| ROANOKE, VA | 97 | 94 | 100 | 93 | 102 | 99 | 100 | 97 | 95 | 97 | 96 | 96 | 96 | 99 | 87 | 98 | 96 | 97 | 98 | 99 |
| ROCHESTER, MN | 101 | 106 | 101 | 104 | 102 | 103 | 102 | 101 | 102 | 104 | 108 | 103 | 106 | 104 | 102 | 103 | 104 | 105 | 101 | 103 |
| ROCHESTER, NY | 99 | 94 | 98 | 95 | 94 | 92 | 93 | 98 | 96 | 98 | 98 | 100 | 99 | 102 | 93 | 99 | 101 | 96 | 101 | 102 |
| ROCKFORD, IL | 98 | 96 | 96 | 96 | 100 | 98 | 101 | 98 | 97 | 98 | 99 | 98 | 100 | 100 | 96 | 102 | 96 | 100 | 100 | 100 |
| ROCKY MOUNT, NC | 98 | 82 | 86 | 86 | 97 | 94 | 106 | 97 | 95 | 89 | 89 | 97 | 89 | 98 | 78 | 98 | 89 | 93 | 98 | 99 |
| SACRAMENTO, CA | 100 | 105 | 96 | 100 | 102 | 102 | 100 | 102 | 103 | 104 | 104 | 95 | 95 | 95 | 92 | 95 | 102 | 101 | 97 | 96 |
| SAGINAW-B.CITY-MIDL. | 97 | 92 | 96 | 93 | 101 | 97 | 101 | 98 | 95 | 95 | 96 | 96 | 98 | 99 | 94 | 101 | 93 | 97 | 99 | 98 |
| ST. CLOUD, MN | 97 | 90 | 86 | 90 | 95 | 93 | 101 | 96 | 95 | 90 | 95 | 96 | 93 | 98 | 88 | 101 | 90 | 96 | 100 | 99 |
| ST. JOSEPH, MO | 96 | 84 | 89 | 88 | 99 | 95 | 103 | 96 | 93 | 90 | 91 | 94 | 93 | 96 | 90 | 100 | 87 | 94 | 100 | 97 |
| ST. LOUIS, MO-IL | 99 | 99 | 99 | 100 | 102 | 101 | 100 | 99 | 98 | 101 | 101 | 100 | 103 | 101 | 99 | 102 | 99 | 102 | 99 | 100 |
| SALEM, OR | 98 | 93 | 94 | 93 | 100 | 99 | 103 | 100 | 99 | 97 | 95 | 91 | 90 | 93 | 87 | 93 | 94 | 96 | 98 | 94 |
| SALINAS, CA | 101 | 122 | 106 | 110 | 106 | 109 | 97 | 104 | 110 | 107 | 111 | 98 | 103 | 96 | 102 | 97 | 107 | 109 | 99 | 100 |
| SALT LAKE CITY-OGDEN | 100 | 103 | 94 | 99 | 102 | 101 | 100 | 102 | 103 | 105 | 104 | 95 | 95 | 96 | 91 | 95 | 102 | 101 | 96 | 96 |
| SAN ANGELO, TX | 97 | 95 | 94 | 92 | 98 | 97 | 100 | 97 | 97 | 95 | 97 | 97 | 94 | 99 | 84 | 98 | 94 | 97 | 98 | 101 |
| SAN ANTONIO, TX | 99 | 100 | 96 | 96 | 98 | 99 | 99 | 99 | 99 | 98 | 101 | 99 | 97 | 100 | 87 | 99 | 97 | 100 | 98 | 102 |
| SAN DIEGO, CA | 100 | 114 | 102 | 106 | 104 | 106 | 98 | 102 | 106 | 106 | 107 | 96 | 99 | 95 | 98 | 96 | 104 | 105 | 98 | 98 |
| SAN FRANCISCO, CA | 103 | 135 | 119 | 122 | 112 | 117 | 101 | 104 | 115 | 115 | 119 | 100 | 109 | 96 | 114 | 102 | 115 | 114 | 100 | 100 |
| SAN JOSE, CA | 105 | 138 | 121 | 127 | 113 | 121 | 103 | 107 | 118 | 118 | 124 | 104 | 114 | 100 | 115 | 100 | 121 | 119 | 102 | 103 |
| S.LUIS O.-ATASC-PASO | 100 | 101 | 101 | 100 | 103 | 104 | 104 | 101 | 100 | 100 | 100 | 92 | 93 | 94 | 92 | 93 | 98 | 99 | 100 | 95 |
| S.BARB-S.MARIA-LOMP. | 101 | 119 | 113 | 114 | 109 | 112 | 101 | 103 | 108 | 108 | 110 | 97 | 104 | 97 | 104 | 95 | 108 | 108 | 100 | 99 |
| SANTA CRUZ-WATSONVLL | 103 | 122 | 112 | 115 | 109 | 112 | 102 | 105 | 110 | 112 | 113 | 100 | 105 | 99 | 105 | 97 | 111 | 110 | 100 | 100 |
| SANTA FE, NM | 102 | 112 | 105 | 107 | 106 | 107 | 104 | 104 | 106 | 111 | 108 | 98 | 100 | 97 | 99 | 96 | 107 | 106 | 98 | 98 |
| SANTA ROSA, CA | 102 | 112 | 105 | 108 | 106 | 109 | 103 | 104 | 107 | 110 | 110 | 98 | 101 | 98 | 99 | 96 | 108 | 106 | 100 | 98 |
| SARASOTA-BRADENTON | 100 | 94 | 113 | 100 | 106 | 110 | 104 | 102 | 94 | 96 | 98 | 99 | 99 | 102 | 92 | 97 | 95 | 97 | 107 | 102 |
| SAVANNAH, GA | 97 | 93 | 96 | 93 | 100 | 98 | 100 | 98 | 96 | 96 | 95 | 97 | 95 | 98 | 85 | 99 | 96 | 97 | 95 | 99 |
| SCRANTON-W.BARRE-HAZ | 97 | 83 | 94 | 87 | 94 | 91 | 94 | 96 | 90 | 92 | 91 | 95 | 93 | 99 | 90 | 97 | 92 | 91 | 102 | 98 |
| SEATTLE-BELLEV-EV'TT | 102 | 112 | 103 | 108 | 105 | 108 | 102 | 103 | 106 | 109 | 109 | 98 | 100 | 97 | 98 | 96 | 108 | 105 | 98 | 98 |
| SHARON, PA | 97 | 80 | 92 | 84 | 93 | 90 | 94 | 96 | 90 | 89 | 88 | 95 | 91 | 98 | 87 | 97 | 90 | 90 | 102 | 98 |
| SHEBOYGAN, WI | 98 | 88 | 90 | 90 | 99 | 95 | 106 | 97 | 94 | 92 | 95 | 96 | 95 | 99 | 90 | 101 | 91 | 96 | 100 | 99 |
| SHERMAN-DENISON, TX | 97 | 83 | 91 | 87 | 98 | 96 | 107 | 96 | 94 | 88 | 90 | 95 | 90 | 97 | 79 | 97 | 89 | 93 | 100 | 98 |
| SHREVEPRT-BOS'R CITY | 96 | 89 | 94 | 90 | 99 | 96 | 98 | 97 | 94 | 94 | 91 | 96 | 92 | 96 | 83 | 98 | 93 | 95 | 94 | 98 |
| SIOUX CITY, IA-NE | 96 | 91 | 95 | 92 | 100 | 97 | 101 | 96 | 94 | 93 | 95 | 94 | 96 | 97 | 94 | 100 | 91 | 96 | 100 | 98 |
| SIOUX FALLS, SD | 99 | 97 | 92 | 96 | 98 | 97 | 100 | 98 | 98 | 97 | 101 | 98 | 99 | 100 | 94 | 102 | 96 | 100 | 99 | 100 |
| SOUTH BEND, IN | 97 | 95 | 98 | 95 | 101 | 99 | 99 | 98 | 96 | 97 | 98 | 97 | 100 | 99 | 97 | 101 | 95 | 99 | 100 | 99 |
| SPOKANE, WA | 98 | 96 | 97 | 95 | 102 | 100 | 101 | 99 | 99 | 98 | 96 | 90 | 91 | 93 | 89 | 93 | 95 | 96 | 97 | 93 |
| SPRINGFIELD, IL | 99 | 98 | 99 | 98 | 102 | 100 | 101 | 98 | 98 | 99 | 100 | 98 | 101 | 100 | 98 | 102 | 97 | 101 | 100 | 100 |
| SPRINGFIELD, MO | 99 | 92 | 92 | 94 | 98 | 96 | 105 | 98 | 97 | 93 | 97 | 98 | 97 | 100 | 91 | 101 | 93 | 98 | 101 | 100 |
| SPRINGFIELD, MA | 98 | 94 | 101 | 95 | 96 | 94 | 90 | 97 | 94 | 99 | 97 | 98 | 99 | 100 | 96 | 98 | 100 | 96 | 101 | 100 |
| STATE COLLEGE, PA | 99 | 95 | 97 | 99 | 92 | 91 | 96 | 95 | 95 | 92 | 96 | 99 | 94 | 101 | 91 | 97 | 99 | 96 | 101 | 102 |
| STEUBENVILLE-WEIRTON | 95 | 82 | 93 | 86 | 102 | 97 | 101 | 97 | 90 | 90 | 90 | 93 | 94 | 96 | 91 | 99 | 86 | 93 | 101 | 96 |
| STOCKTON-LODI, CA | 99 | 104 | 95 | 98 | 101 | 101 | 98 | 101 | 103 | 101 | 102 | 93 | 94 | 93 | 91 | 96 | 98 | 100 | 97 | 96 |
| SUMTER, SC | 96 | 86 | 89 | 87 | 96 | 94 | 101 | 97 | 95 | 91 | 91 | 96 | 90 | 96 | 79 | 97 | 91 | 94 | 95 | 99 |
| SYRACUSE, NY | 98 | 91 | 96 | 92 | 93 | 91 | 93 | 97 | 95 | 95 | 96 | 98 | 96 | 101 | 91 | 98 | 98 | 95 | 101 | 101 |
| TACOMA, WA | 99 | 99 | 96 | 96 | 102 | 101 | 102 | 100 | 101 | 101 | 100 | 92 | 93 | 94 | 90 | 94 | 98 | 98 | 97 | 94 |
| TALLAHASSEE, FL | 98 | 102 | 96 | 99 | 99 | 98 | 100 | 97 | 98 | 97 | 99 | 99 | 95 | 99 | 86 | 98 | 99 | 99 | 95 | 101 |
| TAMPA-ST.PETE-CLEARW | 98 | 95 | 106 | 96 | 103 | 104 | 101 | 99 | 95 | 97 | 98 | 98 | 97 | 100 | 89 | 97 | 95 | 97 | 102 | 100 |
| TERRE HAUTE, IN | 97 | 86 | 93 | 90 | 100 | 96 | 105 | 97 | 94 | 91 | 92 | 95 | 95 | 97 | 91 | 100 | 89 | 95 | 101 | 98 |
| TEXARKANA, TX-AR | 96 | 82 | 88 | 86 | 97 | 93 | 104 | 96 | 93 | 88 | 87 | 95 | 88 | 96 | 78 | 97 | 88 | 92 | 97 | 98 |
| TOLEDO, OH | 97 | 96 | 99 | 97 | 101 | 99 | 100 | 97 | 96 | 97 | 97 | 97 | 99 | 98 | 97 | 101 | 95 | 99 | 99 | 99 |
| TOPEKA, KS | 98 | 100 | 99 | 98 | 102 | 100 | 99 | 98 | 97 | 100 | 101 | 98 | 102 | 100 | 99 | 101 | 97 | 101 | 99 | 100 |
| TRENTON, NJ | 103 | 109 | 111 | 111 | 100 | 102 | 92 | 102 | 103 | 109 | 109 | 107 | 111 | 106 | 107 | 102 | 113 | 105 | 102 | 105 |
| TUCSON, AZ | 99 | 100 | 100 | 98 | 102 | 102 | 101 | 101 | 99 | 99 | 98 | 92 | 92 | 93 | 91 | 93 | 96 | 97 | 98 | 95 |
| TULSA, OK | 99 | 96 | 97 | 96 | 100 | 99 | 102 | 98 | 98 | 97 | 98 | 99 | 96 | 100 | 86 | 98 | 97 | 98 | 98 | 100 |
| TUSCALOOSA, AL | 97 | 92 | 97 | 93 | 99 | 96 | 102 | 95 | 94 | 91 | 93 | 95 | 91 | 97 | 83 | 97 | 93 | 95 | 96 | 99 |
| TYLER, TX | 99 | 91 | 95 | 93 | 99 | 98 | 104 | 98 | 96 | 94 | 95 | 98 | 94 | 99 | 83 | 98 | 95 | 97 | 98 | 100 |
| UTICA-ROME, NY | 97 | 86 | 96 | 89 | 93 | 91 | 94 | 96 | 93 | 93 | 93 | 96 | 95 | 99 | 90 | 98 | 94 | 92 | 101 | 100 |
| VALLEJO-FAIRFLD-NAPA | 101 | 110 | 98 | 104 | 102 | 104 | 99 | 103 | 106 | 107 | 108 | 97 | 98 | 96 | 95 | 96 | 105 | 104 | 97 | 97 |
| VENTURA, CA | 106 | 128 | 113 | 122 | 110 | 116 | 104 | 108 | 115 | 118 | 120 | 105 | 111 | 102 | 108 | 98 | 119 | 115 | 102 | 103 |
| VICTORIA, TX | 99 | 100 | 98 | 99 | 99 | 99 | 102 | 99 | 100 | 98 | 100 | 100 | 97 | 101 | 86 | 99 | 97 | 100 | 99 | 103 |
| VINELND-M'VLE-BRDGTN | 96 | 86 | 91 | 86 | 93 | 89 | 93 | 96 | 91 | 95 | 92 | 95 | 94 | 98 | 90 | 98 | 94 | 92 | 100 | 98 |
| VISALIA-TULARE-P'VLE | 97 | 92 | 88 | 89 | 97 | 96 | 100 | 100 | 99 | 93 | 93 | 89 | 87 | 90 | 84 | 93 | 89 | 95 | 97 | 94 |
| WACO, TX | 96 | 92 | 97 | 92 | 100 | 97 | 101 | 96 | 94 | 92 | 93 | 95 | 92 | 97 | 84 | 97 | 93 | 95 | 97 | 98 |
| WASHINGTON, DC | 103 | 119 | 111 | 114 | 107 | 111 | 102 | 103 | 107 | 112 | 115 | 108 | 111 | 106 | 101 | 102 | 115 | 112 | 99 | 106 |
| WATERLOO-CEDAR FALLS | 96 | 93 | 99 | 93 | 102 | 98 | 98 | 96 | 94 | 94 | 96 | 94 | 98 | 97 | 96 | 99 | 92 | 97 | 100 | 97 |
| WAUSAU, WI | 99 | 88 | 91 | 92 | 98 | 96 | 105 | 98 | 95 | 92 | 95 | 97 | 96 | 100 | 90 | 101 | 92 | 97 | 101 | 100 |
| W.PALM BEACH-B.RATON | 101 | 105 | 110 | 106 | 106 | 110 | 103 | 102 | 99 | 103 | 105 | 103 | 104 | 103 | 96 | 99 | 103 | 102 | 104 | 103 |
| WHEELING, WV-OH | 95 | 81 | 94 | 85 | 101 | 97 | 103 | 96 | 91 | 89 | 88 | 93 | 90 | 96 | 82 | 96 | 87 | 91 | 100 | 96 |
| WICHITA, KS | 98 | 97 | 94 | 95 | 99 | 97 | 99 | 98 | 97 | 97 | 100 | 97 | 99 | 99 | 95 | 101 | 95 | 99 | 99 | 99 |
| UNITED STATES | 100 | 100 | 100 | 100 | 100 | 100 | 100 | 100 | 100 | 100 | 100 | 100 | 100 | 100 | 100 | 100 | 100 | 100 | 100 | 100 |

# POPULATION CHANGE

## MSA AND U.S. TOTALS

**A**

| MSA | MSA Code | POPULATION 1990 | POPULATION 2000 | POPULATION 2005 | 1990-2000 ANNUAL CHANGE % Rate | 1990-2000 ANNUAL CHANGE National Rank | RACE (%) White 1990 | RACE (%) White 2000 | RACE (%) Black 1990 | RACE (%) Black 2000 | RACE (%) Asian/Pacific 1990 | RACE (%) Asian/Pacific 2000 |
|---|---|---|---|---|---|---|---|---|---|---|---|---|
| WICHITA FALLS, TX | 9080 | 130,351 | 136,391 | 135,825 | 0.4 | 226 | 84.6 | 81.0 | 8.6 | 9.8 | 1.4 | 2.2 |
| WILLIAMSPORT, PA | 9140 | 118,710 | 116,016 | 112,610 | -0.2 | 290 | 96.9 | 96.3 | 2.4 | 2.7 | 0.4 | 0.6 |
| WILMINGTON-NEWARK | 9160 | 513,293 | 577,417 | 607,316 | 1.2 | 110 | 82.4 | 78.9 | 14.8 | 16.9 | 1.4 | 2.2 |
| WILMINGTON, NC | 9200 | 171,269 | 226,889 | 250,815 | 2.8 | 11 | 79.5 | 78.6 | 19.4 | 19.9 | 0.4 | 0.7 |
| YAKIMA, WA | 9260 | 188,823 | 222,962 | 234,146 | 1.6 | 67 | 73.9 | 66.8 | 1.0 | 1.1 | 1.0 | 1.3 |
| YOLO, CA | 9270 | 141,092 | 157,835 | 168,199 | 1.1 | 129 | 75.9 | 70.4 | 2.2 | 2.3 | 8.4 | 10.3 |
| YORK, PA | 9280 | 339,574 | 379,431 | 393,835 | 1.1 | 129 | 95.2 | 94.0 | 3.2 | 3.8 | 0.6 | 0.9 |
| YOUNGSTOWN-WARREN,OH | 9320 | 600,895 | 585,970 | 569,818 | -0.2 | 290 | 89.6 | 88.4 | 9.4 | 10.3 | 0.4 | 0.5 |
| YUBA CITY, CA | 9340 | 122,643 | 139,371 | 143,915 | 1.3 | 91 | 77.5 | 72.0 | 2.8 | 2.7 | 9.0 | 11.9 |
| YUMA, AZ | 9360 | 106,895 | 139,742 | 157,398 | 2.6 | 13 | 75.5 | 72.5 | 2.9 | 2.9 | 1.3 | 1.6 |
| UNITED STATES | | | | | 1.0 | | 80.3 | 77.9 | 12.1 | 12.4 | 2.9 | 3.9 |

# POPULATION COMPOSITION

MSA AND U.S. TOTALS

B

| MSA | % HISPANIC ORIGIN | | 2000 AGE DISTRIBUTION (%) | | | | | | | | | | MEDIAN AGE | | 2000 Males/ Females (×100) |
|---|---|---|---|---|---|---|---|---|---|---|---|---|---|---|---|
| | 1990 | 2000 | 0-4 | 5-9 | 10-14 | 15-19 | 20-24 | 25-44 | 45-64 | 65-84 | 85+ | 18+ | 1990 | 2000 | |
| WICHITA FALLS, TX | 8.2 | 11.4 | 7.4 | 7.2 | 6.9 | 8.8 | 7.9 | 27.2 | 21.7 | 11.2 | 1.8 | 74.6 | 31.9 | 34.5 | 98.5 |
| WILLIAMSPORT, PA | 0.5 | 1.1 | 6.1 | 6.6 | 7.1 | 7.1 | 6.1 | 28.1 | 23.3 | 13.6 | 2.0 | 76.2 | 34.8 | 37.9 | 93.8 |
| WILMINGTON-NEWARK | 2.4 | 4.0 | 6.5 | 6.8 | 6.9 | 7.0 | 6.7 | 32.4 | 21.7 | 10.7 | 1.3 | 76.2 | 32.5 | 35.7 | 94.9 |
| WILMINGTON, NC | 0.8 | 1.8 | 6.1 | 6.5 | 6.7 | 6.6 | 6.1 | 29.0 | 24.5 | 13.2 | 1.3 | 77.2 | 34.8 | 37.9 | 91.7 |
| YAKIMA, WA | 23.9 | 32.9 | 8.1 | 8.4 | 8.6 | 8.3 | 7.1 | 27.0 | 20.8 | 9.9 | 1.7 | 69.9 | 31.5 | 32.4 | 100.1 |
| YOLO, CA | 20.0 | 26.4 | 6.9 | 7.3 | 6.4 | 9.0 | 11.0 | 31.5 | 18.1 | 8.7 | 1.1 | 76.0 | 28.9 | 31.2 | 97.5 |
| YORK, PA | 1.5 | 2.5 | 5.8 | 6.7 | 7.3 | 6.4 | 5.0 | 31.1 | 23.9 | 12.1 | 1.7 | 76.4 | 34.5 | 38.1 | 95.9 |
| YOUNGSTOWN-WARREN,OH | 1.3 | 2.0 | 6.0 | 6.4 | 6.9 | 6.9 | 6.0 | 27.7 | 23.9 | 14.5 | 1.8 | 76.5 | 35.8 | 38.7 | 91.9 |
| YUBA CITY, CA | 14.1 | 19.0 | 8.5 | 9.5 | 7.8 | 7.5 | 6.7 | 27.6 | 20.4 | 10.8 | 1.2 | 69.7 | 30.9 | 32.5 | 99.0 |
| YUMA, AZ | 40.6 | 46.6 | 8.4 | 7.9 | 7.3 | 7.6 | 8.7 | 25.6 | 18.6 | 14.5 | 1.3 | 71.8 | 30.5 | 32.3 | 101.7 |
| UNITED STATES | 9.0 | 11.8 | 6.9 | 7.2 | 7.2 | 7.2 | 6.7 | 29.9 | 22.2 | 11.1 | 1.6 | 74.6 | 32.9 | 35.7 | 95.6 |

# HOUSEHOLDS

## MSA AND U.S. TOTALS

C

| MSA | HOUSEHOLDS | | | | | FAMILIES | | | MEDIAN HOUSEHOLD INCOME | | |
|---|---|---|---|---|---|---|---|---|---|---|---|
| | 1990 | 2000 | 2005 | % Annual Rate 1990-2000 | 2000 Average HH Size | 1990 | 2000 | % Annual Rate 1990-2000 | 2000 | 2005 | 2000 National Rank |
| WICHITA FALLS, TX | 48,228 | 50,146 | 50,325 | 0.5 | 2.52 | 34,546 | 34,822 | 0.1 | 35,099 | 42,493 | 252 |
| WILLIAMSPORT, PA | 44,949 | 44,838 | 43,999 | 0.0 | 2.50 | 32,165 | 31,023 | -0.4 | 34,420 | 41,945 | 268 |
| WILMINGTON-NEWARK | 188,886 | 219,573 | 234,864 | 1.8 | 2.55 | 133,775 | 150,477 | 1.4 | 52,344 | 60,338 | 25 |
| WILMINGTON, NC | 68,208 | 92,025 | 102,591 | 3.7 | 2.42 | 47,691 | 62,806 | 3.4 | 37,847 | 42,037 | 191 |
| YAKIMA, WA | 65,985 | 77,832 | 81,656 | 2.0 | 2.82 | 48,107 | 55,411 | 1.7 | 35,455 | 41,682 | 247 |
| YOLO, CA | 50,972 | 58,211 | 62,480 | 1.6 | 2.61 | 32,184 | 35,053 | 1.0 | 43,781 | 54,442 | 95 |
| YORK, PA | 128,666 | 145,890 | 152,634 | 1.5 | 2.56 | 94,919 | 104,825 | 1.2 | 44,823 | 51,586 | 83 |
| YOUNGSTOWN-WARREN,OH | 227,967 | 228,428 | 225,540 | 0.0 | 2.52 | 166,603 | 161,346 | -0.4 | 33,613 | 37,065 | 277 |
| YUBA CITY, CA | 42,887 | 49,153 | 50,925 | 1.7 | 2.78 | 31,910 | 35,656 | 1.4 | 35,523 | 44,862 | 244 |
| YUMA, AZ | 35,791 | 47,750 | 54,062 | 3.6 | 2.86 | 27,671 | 36,669 | 3.5 | 34,377 | 44,755 | 269 |
| UNITED STATES | | | | 1.4 | 2.59 | | | 1.1 | 41,914 | 49,127 | |

# INCOME

## MSA AND U.S. TOTALS

D

| MSA | 2000 Per Capita Income | 2000 HH Income Base | 2000 HOUSEHOLD INCOME DISTRIBUTION (%) | | | | | | 2000 AVERAGE DISPOSABLE INCOME BY AGE OF HOUSEHOLDER | | | | | |
|---|---|---|---|---|---|---|---|---|---|---|---|---|---|---|
| | | | Less than $15,000 | $15,000 to $24,999 | $25,000 to $49,999 | $50,000 to $99,999 | $100,000 to $149,999 | $150,000 or More | All Ages | <35 | 35-44 | 45-54 | 55-64 | 65+ |
| WICHITA FALLS, TX | 17,264 | 50,132 | 18.1 | 15.7 | 35.2 | 25.1 | 4.4 | 1.4 | 35,176 | 29,822 | 39,889 | 44,039 | 38,320 | 26,001 |
| WILLIAMSPORT, PA | 16,121 | 44,838 | 16.8 | 16.4 | 40.0 | 23.4 | 2.9 | 0.7 | 30,682 | 27,731 | 35,823 | 38,884 | 34,425 | 20,340 |
| WILMINGTON-NEWARK | 26,697 | 219,573 | 8.4 | 8.1 | 30.6 | 38.2 | 10.6 | 4.2 | 46,465 | 39,399 | 49,626 | 56,536 | 49,525 | 32,623 |
| WILMINGTON, NC | 21,186 | 92,025 | 16.2 | 14.4 | 34.4 | 26.7 | 5.7 | 2.6 | 36,618 | 29,960 | 41,414 | 45,917 | 38,730 | 26,243 |
| YAKIMA, WA | 16,116 | 77,832 | 17.2 | 16.2 | 35.1 | 25.4 | 4.5 | 1.6 | 35,421 | 29,644 | 39,769 | 43,204 | 38,874 | 25,462 |
| YOLO, CA | 23,111 | 58,210 | 13.9 | 12.4 | 30.8 | 30.2 | 8.3 | 4.4 | 42,960 | 32,329 | 48,457 | 55,375 | 49,726 | 33,087 |
| YORK, PA | 21,008 | 145,889 | 9.6 | 10.6 | 37.6 | 34.5 | 6.1 | 1.6 | 39,071 | 36,305 | 43,873 | 49,124 | 42,619 | 23,962 |
| YOUNGSTOWN-WARREN,OH | 16,610 | 228,422 | 19.7 | 16.2 | 36.1 | 23.6 | 3.4 | 1.0 | 31,303 | 26,588 | 36,529 | 41,100 | 34,467 | 20,794 |
| YUBA CITY, CA | 18,057 | 49,153 | 16.5 | 16.6 | 34.7 | 24.6 | 5.0 | 2.6 | 35,688 | 29,666 | 39,617 | 44,446 | 39,567 | 26,200 |
| YUMA, AZ | 15,464 | 47,750 | 16.6 | 17.6 | 34.5 | 25.9 | 4.3 | 1.1 | 34,114 | 32,031 | 37,157 | 44,748 | 35,243 | 26,156 |
| UNITED STATES | 22,162 | | 14.5 | 12.5 | 32.3 | 29.8 | 7.4 | 3.5 | 40,748 | 34,503 | 44,969 | 49,579 | 43,409 | 27,339 |

# SPENDING POTENTIAL INDEXES

## MSA AND U.S. TOTALS

# E

| MSA | FINANCIAL SERVICES | | | | THE HOME | | | | | | ENTERTAINMENT | | | | | | PERSONAL | | | |
|---|---|---|---|---|---|---|---|---|---|---|---|---|---|---|---|---|---|---|---|---|
| | | | | | Home Improvements | | | Furnishings | | | | | | | | | | | | |
| | Auto Loan | Home Loan | Invest-ments | Retire-ment Plans | Home Repair | Lawn & Garden | Remodel-ing | Appli-ances | Elec-tronics | Furni-ture | Restau-rants | Sport-ing Goods | Theater & Concerts | Toys & Hobbies | Travel | Video Rental | Apparel | Auto After-market | Health Insur-ance | Pets & Supplies |
| WICHITA FALLS, TX | 97 | 90 | 96 | 92 | 99 | 97 | 101 | 97 | 95 | 92 | 94 | 96 | 93 | 98 | 84 | 98 | 93 | 96 | 98 | 99 |
| WILLIAMSPORT, PA | 98 | 81 | 91 | 86 | 92 | 89 | 96 | 96 | 91 | 89 | 89 | 96 | 91 | 99 | 86 | 97 | 91 | 90 | 102 | 99 |
| WILMINGTON-NEWARK | 100 | 104 | 105 | 102 | 104 | 105 | 100 | 100 | 100 | 103 | 105 | 102 | 103 | 103 | 92 | 99 | 104 | 103 | 99 | 102 |
| WILMINGTON, NC | 99 | 92 | 97 | 95 | 100 | 99 | 107 | 99 | 96 | 95 | 96 | 99 | 94 | 100 | 85 | 98 | 95 | 97 | 100 | 101 |
| YAKIMA, WA | 97 | 88 | 91 | 88 | 99 | 97 | 104 | 99 | 97 | 93 | 91 | 88 | 86 | 91 | 84 | 92 | 89 | 93 | 98 | 93 |
| YOLO, CA | 97 | 100 | 94 | 95 | 100 | 98 | 98 | 97 | 98 | 95 | 96 | 89 | 88 | 91 | 88 | 92 | 93 | 96 | 96 | 93 |
| YORK, PA | 100 | 88 | 93 | 92 | 92 | 90 | 98 | 98 | 96 | 94 | 96 | 100 | 96 | 103 | 89 | 99 | 98 | 95 | 102 | 102 |
| YOUNGSTOWN-WARREN,OH | 96 | 86 | 95 | 88 | 102 | 97 | 100 | 97 | 92 | 92 | 92 | 94 | 96 | 97 | 93 | 100 | 89 | 95 | 100 | 97 |
| YUBA CITY, CA | 96 | 92 | 89 | 88 | 99 | 96 | 99 | 99 | 97 | 94 | 93 | 88 | 88 | 90 | 85 | 93 | 90 | 94 | 96 | 93 |
| YUMA, AZ | 97 | 94 | 97 | 90 | 99 | 101 | 99 | 101 | 97 | 93 | 94 | 89 | 89 | 91 | 87 | 93 | 88 | 95 | 100 | 95 |
| UNITED STATES | 100 | 100 | 100 | 100 | 100 | 100 | 100 | 100 | 100 | 100 | 100 | 100 | 100 | 100 | 100 | 100 | 100 | 100 | 100 | 100 |

# DMA SUMMARY DATA

COUNTY

13th EDITION

# POPULATION CHANGE

## DMA AND U.S. TOTALS

**A**

| DMA | DMA Code | POPULATION 1990 | POPULATION 2000 | POPULATION 2005 | 1990-2000 ANNUAL CHANGE % Rate | 1990-2000 ANNUAL CHANGE National Rank | RACE (%) White 1990 | RACE (%) White 2000 | RACE (%) Black 1990 | RACE (%) Black 2000 | RACE (%) Asian/Pacific 1990 | RACE (%) Asian/Pacific 2000 |
|---|---|---|---|---|---|---|---|---|---|---|---|---|
| ABILENE-SWEETWATER | 662 | 277,315 | 285,237 | 285,116 | 0.3 | 158 | 86.1 | 82.4 | 4.6 | 5.6 | 0.6 | 1.0 |
| ALBANY, GA | 525 | 360,527 | 392,756 | 405,718 | 0.8 | 96 | 62.6 | 58.7 | 36.3 | 39.8 | 0.3 | 0.5 |
| ALBANY-SCHENEC.-TROY | 532 | 1,322,351 | 1,326,334 | 1,313,065 | 0.0 | 181 | 94.6 | 93.4 | 3.8 | 4.2 | 1.0 | 1.5 |
| ALBUQUERQUE-SANTA FE | 790 | 1,428,893 | 1,650,267 | 1,708,099 | 1.4 | 46 | 72.2 | 70.4 | 1.7 | 2.0 | 0.9 | 1.2 |
| ALEXANDRIA, LA | 644 | 250,202 | 238,369 | 238,790 | -0.5 | 206 | 72.7 | 70.2 | 25.1 | 27.2 | 1.0 | 1.3 |
| ALPENA | 583 | 40,750 | 41,887 | 42,573 | 0.3 | 159 | 99.1 | 99.0 | 0.2 | 0.2 | 0.3 | 0.4 |
| AMARILLO | 634 | 477,282 | 501,005 | 504,665 | 0.5 | 135 | 83.7 | 80.4 | 3.6 | 4.3 | 1.1 | 1.5 |
| ANCHORAGE, AK | 743 | 306,823 | 369,660 | 394,065 | 1.8 | 27 | 83.7 | 82.2 | 4.9 | 4.6 | 3.8 | 4.8 |
| ATLANTA | 524 | 3,729,657 | 4,896,502 | 5,535,592 | 2.7 | 10 | 74.1 | 72.0 | 23.5 | 24.0 | 1.5 | 2.6 |
| AUGUSTA, GA | 520 | 584,495 | 640,217 | 657,265 | 0.9 | 88 | 62.0 | 59.5 | 36.4 | 37.8 | 1.0 | 1.7 |
| AUSTIN | 635 | 922,879 | 1,282,718 | 1,484,011 | 3.3 | 4 | 77.7 | 74.2 | 9.0 | 9.1 | 2.1 | 2.8 |
| BAKERSFIELD | 800 | 543,477 | 649,311 | 683,572 | 1.8 | 31 | 69.6 | 62.8 | 5.5 | 5.9 | 3.0 | 3.9 |
| BALTIMORE | 512 | 2,559,181 | 2,700,043 | 2,765,962 | 0.5 | 127 | 72.7 | 70.2 | 25.1 | 26.6 | 1.7 | 2.5 |
| BANGOR | 537 | 330,295 | 337,077 | 336,948 | 0.2 | 164 | 98.3 | 98.2 | 0.2 | 0.3 | 0.4 | 0.5 |
| BATON ROUGE | 716 | 727,698 | 786,161 | 810,097 | 0.8 | 107 | 65.6 | 63.8 | 33.0 | 34.4 | 0.9 | 1.2 |
| BEAUMONT-PORT ARTHUR | 692 | 422,543 | 445,607 | 450,644 | 0.5 | 127 | 74.3 | 72.1 | 22.6 | 23.8 | 1.4 | 1.9 |
| BEND, OR | 821 | 74,958 | 115,342 | 137,164 | 4.3 | 2 | 97.8 | 97.2 | 0.1 | 0.1 | 0.6 | 0.8 |
| BILLINGS | 756 | 227,200 | 250,784 | 256,029 | 1.0 | 83 | 92.6 | 91.9 | 0.3 | 0.3 | 0.4 | 0.5 |
| BILOXI-GULFPORT | 746 | 291,358 | 328,996 | 344,896 | 1.2 | 61 | 77.6 | 75.1 | 20.0 | 21.6 | 1.9 | 2.6 |
| BINGHAMTON | 502 | 363,490 | 342,086 | 330,175 | -0.6 | 207 | 96.8 | 95.9 | 1.5 | 1.7 | 1.2 | 1.8 |
| BIRMINGHAM | 630 | 1,613,950 | 1,745,624 | 1,798,596 | 0.8 | 105 | 75.5 | 75.0 | 23.8 | 24.1 | 0.4 | 0.5 |
| BLUEFLD-BECKLEY-OAK. | 559 | 367,751 | 360,360 | 351,921 | -0.2 | 196 | 93.6 | 93.4 | 5.9 | 6.0 | 0.3 | 0.4 |
| BOISE | 757 | 409,766 | 557,868 | 625,299 | 3.1 | 7 | 93.1 | 91.3 | 0.5 | 0.6 | 1.4 | 1.6 |
| BOSTON | 506 | 5,664,859 | 5,956,673 | 6,162,922 | 0.5 | 132 | 90.8 | 88.3 | 4.6 | 5.2 | 2.4 | 3.7 |
| BOWLING GREEN | 736 | 178,273 | 200,053 | 208,171 | 1.1 | 65 | 93.6 | 93.1 | 5.7 | 6.0 | 0.4 | 0.6 |
| BUFFALO | 514 | 1,674,148 | 1,616,275 | 1,561,516 | -0.3 | 205 | 89.8 | 88.0 | 7.9 | 8.9 | 0.8 | 1.2 |
| BURLINGTON-PLATTSBGH | 523 | 768,507 | 802,593 | 816,330 | 0.4 | 139 | 97.4 | 96.8 | 1.1 | 1.3 | 0.6 | 0.9 |
| BUTTE-BOZEMAN, MT | 754 | 126,972 | 145,870 | 151,670 | 1.4 | 49 | 97.3 | 96.9 | 0.1 | 0.2 | 0.5 | 0.6 |
| CASPER-RIVERTON | 767 | 119,213 | 124,671 | 124,531 | 0.4 | 137 | 91.7 | 91.1 | 0.5 | 0.5 | 0.4 | 0.5 |
| C. RAPIDS-W'LOO-DUB. | 637 | 774,531 | 807,166 | 818,875 | 0.4 | 142 | 96.6 | 95.9 | 1.9 | 2.1 | 1.0 | 1.3 |
| CHAMPN.-S'FIELD-DEC. | 648 | 896,450 | 905,472 | 900,583 | 0.1 | 173 | 91.8 | 90.6 | 6.4 | 7.0 | 1.3 | 1.7 |
| CHARLESTON, SC | 519 | 624,369 | 693,680 | 746,524 | 1.0 | 77 | 64.3 | 63.2 | 34.0 | 34.5 | 1.0 | 1.5 |
| CHARLESTON-HUNTINGTN | 564 | 1,249,722 | 1,261,208 | 1,248,438 | 0.1 | 174 | 97.0 | 96.9 | 2.3 | 2.4 | 0.4 | 0.5 |
| CHARLOTTE | 517 | 1,951,195 | 2,344,561 | 2,568,820 | 1.8 | 30 | 80.4 | 79.1 | 18.3 | 18.8 | 0.8 | 1.3 |
| CHARLOTTESVILLE | 584 | 130,627 | 145,595 | 152,472 | 1.1 | 73 | 84.0 | 81.9 | 13.6 | 14.8 | 2.0 | 2.8 |
| CHATTANOOGA | 575 | 775,369 | 861,898 | 901,972 | 1.0 | 75 | 89.9 | 88.9 | 9.0 | 9.3 | 0.5 | 0.8 |
| CHEYEN-SCTSBLF-STERL | 759 | 121,540 | 127,652 | 128,035 | 0.5 | 133 | 91.2 | 89.2 | 1.9 | 1.9 | 0.8 | 1.2 |
| CHICAGO | 602 | 8,364,129 | 9,064,800 | 9,368,078 | 0.8 | 102 | 72.3 | 69.9 | 18.8 | 18.5 | 3.1 | 4.1 |
| CHICO-REDDING | 868 | 416,642 | 455,337 | 464,686 | 0.9 | 92 | 91.7 | 89.7 | 0.9 | 1.0 | 2.2 | 3.0 |
| CINCINNATI | 515 | 2,008,586 | 2,191,899 | 2,271,873 | 0.9 | 94 | 88.7 | 88.3 | 10.3 | 10.4 | 0.7 | 1.0 |
| CLARKSBURG-WESTON | 598 | 268,709 | 268,925 | 264,132 | 0.0 | 184 | 98.2 | 98.0 | 1.3 | 1.5 | 0.2 | 0.3 |
| CLEVELAND | 510 | 3,778,813 | 3,873,166 | 3,879,191 | 0.2 | 161 | 85.3 | 84.0 | 13.0 | 13.9 | 0.9 | 1.2 |
| COLORADO SPR.-PUEBLO | 752 | 626,929 | 782,204 | 848,820 | 2.2 | 17 | 86.7 | 84.8 | 5.1 | 5.6 | 1.8 | 2.4 |
| COLUMBIA, SC | 546 | 799,477 | 896,381 | 938,760 | 1.1 | 67 | 60.8 | 61.0 | 37.8 | 37.1 | 0.8 | 1.1 |
| COLUMBIA-JEFF. CITY | 604 | 370,325 | 410,348 | 425,359 | 1.0 | 81 | 92.8 | 91.2 | 5.6 | 6.7 | 1.0 | 1.5 |
| COLUMBUS, GA | 522 | 485,384 | 518,328 | 528,360 | 0.6 | 119 | 61.2 | 57.4 | 36.7 | 39.6 | 1.0 | 1.5 |
| COLUMBUS, OH | 535 | 1,823,652 | 2,027,241 | 2,121,637 | 1.0 | 75 | 88.7 | 87.3 | 9.6 | 10.5 | 1.2 | 1.7 |
| COLUMBUS-TUPELO-W.PT | 673 | 450,725 | 477,268 | 487,002 | 0.6 | 125 | 71.1 | 69.4 | 28.2 | 29.8 | 0.4 | 0.5 |
| CORPUS CHRISTI | 600 | 505,097 | 557,493 | 567,715 | 1.0 | 83 | 76.2 | 73.6 | 3.3 | 3.3 | 0.8 | 1.1 |
| DALLAS-FT.WORTH | 623 | 4,482,380 | 5,531,894 | 6,146,770 | 2.1 | 19 | 76.9 | 74.4 | 13.5 | 13.3 | 2.2 | 3.3 |
| DAVENPORT-R.ISL-MOL. | 682 | 788,031 | 795,587 | 795,453 | 0.1 | 174 | 94.5 | 93.2 | 3.2 | 3.6 | 0.6 | 0.8 |
| DAYTON | 542 | 1,324,225 | 1,348,370 | 1,345,521 | 0.2 | 168 | 88.7 | 87.5 | 10.0 | 10.9 | 0.8 | 1.1 |
| DENVER | 751 | 2,627,700 | 3,269,585 | 3,595,529 | 2.2 | 18 | 88.7 | 87.4 | 3.8 | 3.8 | 1.9 | 2.4 |
| DES MOINES-AMES | 679 | 941,768 | 998,677 | 1,026,682 | 0.6 | 124 | 96.3 | 95.2 | 1.9 | 2.2 | 1.3 | 1.7 |
| DETROIT | 505 | 4,705,164 | 4,991,396 | 5,072,638 | 0.6 | 123 | 76.7 | 75.8 | 20.7 | 20.7 | 1.5 | 2.2 |
| DOTHAN | 606 | 231,089 | 240,762 | 244,185 | 0.4 | 142 | 76.5 | 74.7 | 22.1 | 23.7 | 0.7 | 0.8 |
| DULUTH-SUPERIOR | 676 | 435,573 | 444,253 | 446,014 | 0.2 | 166 | 96.0 | 95.3 | 0.4 | 0.5 | 0.4 | 0.6 |
| EL PASO | 765 | 733,442 | 889,574 | 943,969 | 1.9 | 26 | 79.2 | 78.0 | 3.3 | 3.0 | 1.0 | 1.4 |
| ELMIRA | 565 | 254,071 | 249,667 | 246,309 | -0.2 | 194 | 96.2 | 95.5 | 2.7 | 2.9 | 0.5 | 0.9 |
| ERIE | 516 | 406,791 | 408,284 | 401,477 | 0.0 | 180 | 95.2 | 94.1 | 3.8 | 4.6 | 0.4 | 0.6 |
| EUGENE | 801 | 508,645 | 558,048 | 569,993 | 0.9 | 87 | 95.2 | 94.2 | 0.6 | 0.7 | 2.1 | 2.7 |
| EUREKA | 802 | 142,578 | 147,392 | 144,956 | 0.3 | 153 | 89.8 | 88.4 | 1.3 | 1.5 | 1.9 | 2.7 |
| EVANSVILLE | 649 | 686,681 | 710,587 | 718,614 | 0.3 | 152 | 95.2 | 94.8 | 4.2 | 4.5 | 0.3 | 0.4 |
| FAIRBANKS | 745 | 83,633 | 90,530 | 91,966 | 0.8 | 104 | 81.8 | 80.3 | 7.0 | 6.3 | 2.5 | 3.2 |
| FARGO-VALLEY CITY | 724 | 570,970 | 574,593 | 574,589 | 0.1 | 176 | 96.5 | 95.7 | 0.4 | 0.4 | 0.6 | 0.9 |
| FLINT-SAGINAW-B.CITY | 513 | 1,169,321 | 1,194,254 | 1,203,648 | 0.2 | 163 | 86.8 | 85.7 | 10.7 | 11.3 | 0.6 | 0.8 |
| FLORENCE-MYRTL BEACH | 570 | 551,555 | 623,308 | 656,851 | 1.2 | 60 | 59.1 | 59.1 | 32.3 | 31.6 | 0.4 | 0.6 |
| FRESNO-VISALIA | 866 | 1,361,675 | 1,594,751 | 1,678,128 | 1.6 | 42 | 65.3 | 59.3 | 4.2 | 4.1 | 6.7 | 7.9 |
| FT. MYERS-NAPLES | 571 | 655,416 | 824,128 | 907,215 | 2.3 | 14 | 90.7 | 88.5 | 6.5 | 7.4 | 0.5 | 0.9 |
| FT.SMITH-FAY-SPRNGDL | 670 | 487,366 | 597,320 | 638,361 | 2.0 | 21 | 92.8 | 92.2 | 2.1 | 2.2 | 1.1 | 1.5 |
| FT. WAYNE | 509 | 629,137 | 669,896 | 690,063 | 0.6 | 120 | 93.5 | 92.3 | 5.0 | 5.6 | 0.6 | 0.8 |
| GAINESVILLE | 592 | 227,771 | 259,624 | 268,652 | 1.3 | 54 | 79.7 | 75.8 | 17.[illegible] | 19.9 | 2.1 | 3.0 |
| GLENDIVE | 798 | 10,888 | 9,915 | 9,368 | -0.9 | 209 | 98.6 | 98.4 | 0.0 | 0.0 | 0.3 | 0.4 |
| GRAND JCT.-MONTROSE | 773 | 119,863 | 153,107 | 168,368 | 2.4 | 12 | 95.0 | 94.0 | 0.4 | 0.4 | 0.6 | 0.8 |
| G.RAPIDS-K'ZOO-B.CRK | 563 | 1,688,555 | 1,875,289 | 1,956,928 | 1.0 | 77 | 90.8 | 89.7 | 6.5 | 6.9 | 0.8 | 1.2 |
| GREAT FALLS | 755 | 167,458 | 165,888 | 161,439 | -0.1 | 192 | 87.8 | 86.5 | 0.7 | 0.8 | 0.6 | 0.7 |
| GREEN BAY-APPLETON | 658 | 945,668 | 1,034,261 | 1,068,091 | 0.9 | 90 | 97.1 | 96.3 | 0.3 | 0.3 | 0.9 | 1.3 |
| UNITED STATES | | | | | 1.0 | | 80.3 | 77.9 | 12.1 | 12.4 | 2.9 | 3.9 |

# POPULATION COMPOSITION

## DMA AND U.S. TOTALS

# B

| DMA | % HISPANIC ORIGIN | | 2000 AGE DISTRIBUTION (%) | | | | | | | | | | MEDIAN AGE | | 2000 Males/ Females (×100) |
|---|---|---|---|---|---|---|---|---|---|---|---|---|---|---|---|
| | 1990 | 2000 | 0-4 | 5-9 | 10-14 | 15-19 | 20-24 | 25-44 | 45-64 | 65-84 | 85+ | 18+ | 1990 | 2000 | |
| ABILENE-SWEETWATER | 14.8 | 19.2 | 7.3 | 7.2 | 7.1 | 8.5 | 7.5 | 25.0 | 22.0 | 13.0 | 2.4 | 73.6 | 33.7 | 36.0 | 96.9 |
| ALBANY, GA | 1.6 | 2.6 | 7.8 | 7.8 | 7.9 | 8.3 | 7.2 | 28.1 | 21.5 | 10.0 | 1.4 | 71.6 | 31.2 | 33.1 | 91.8 |
| ALBANY-SCHENEC.-TROY | 1.6 | 2.5 | 6.2 | 6.9 | 6.8 | 6.9 | 6.2 | 29.0 | 23.2 | 12.7 | 2.0 | 76.5 | 34.3 | 37.4 | 95.1 |
| ALBUQUERQUE-SANTA FE | 34.8 | 37.4 | 7.5 | 7.9 | 8.2 | 8.3 | 6.8 | 27.3 | 22.6 | 10.2 | 1.3 | 71.4 | 31.4 | 34.9 | 96.8 |
| ALEXANDRIA, LA | 2.3 | 3.0 | 7.2 | 7.0 | 7.2 | 8.5 | 10.0 | 27.1 | 21.0 | 10.5 | 1.4 | 73.9 | 29.4 | 32.5 | 98.7 |
| ALPENA | 0.5 | 1.0 | 5.6 | 6.4 | 6.6 | 7.0 | 5.5 | 25.9 | 24.8 | 16.0 | 2.2 | 77.1 | 37.2 | 40.6 | 96.1 |
| AMARILLO | 18.4 | 22.4 | 7.8 | 7.8 | 7.9 | 8.3 | 6.7 | 26.2 | 22.4 | 11.3 | 1.7 | 71.5 | 32.3 | 35.0 | 96.6 |
| ANCHORAGE, AK | 3.5 | 4.6 | 7.4 | 8.5 | 9.2 | 8.9 | 7.3 | 28.8 | 24.1 | 5.4 | 0.3 | 69.4 | 30.1 | 32.7 | 107.4 |
| ATLANTA | 1.8 | 3.6 | 7.3 | 7.2 | 7.1 | 6.9 | 6.8 | 34.0 | 22.0 | 7.8 | 1.0 | 74.5 | 31.7 | 34.3 | 95.0 |
| AUGUSTA, GA | 1.1 | 2.2 | 7.2 | 7.5 | 7.5 | 7.8 | 7.0 | 29.8 | 21.9 | 9.9 | 1.2 | 73.3 | 31.5 | 34.2 | 94.6 |
| AUSTIN | 20.0 | 25.5 | 7.7 | 7.4 | 7.0 | 8.1 | 9.0 | 31.8 | 20.2 | 7.6 | 1.1 | 73.7 | 30.1 | 32.5 | 98.4 |
| BAKERSFIELD | 28.0 | 36.1 | 8.8 | 10.1 | 8.1 | 7.7 | 6.9 | 30.3 | 18.1 | 8.9 | 1.0 | 68.4 | 29.7 | 30.7 | 104.6 |
| BALTIMORE | 1.2 | 2.2 | 6.5 | 7.2 | 7.4 | 6.8 | 5.7 | 31.5 | 22.4 | 11.1 | 1.4 | 75.1 | 33.5 | 36.4 | 94.2 |
| BANGOR | 0.5 | 1.0 | 5.0 | 5.9 | 7.1 | 7.6 | 6.5 | 29.1 | 24.5 | 12.4 | 1.8 | 77.7 | 33.9 | 38.3 | 96.5 |
| BATON ROUGE | 1.4 | 2.0 | 7.1 | 7.3 | 7.7 | 8.7 | 8.1 | 29.3 | 21.9 | 8.8 | 1.1 | 73.1 | 30.2 | 33.2 | 94.9 |
| BEAUMONT-PORT ARTHUR | 3.8 | 5.5 | 6.9 | 7.3 | 7.5 | 7.8 | 6.3 | 26.3 | 24.1 | 12.2 | 1.6 | 73.7 | 33.6 | 37.1 | 95.3 |
| BEND, OR | 2.0 | 3.8 | 6.2 | 6.5 | 7.4 | 7.1 | 5.5 | 27.6 | 26.8 | 11.6 | 1.3 | 75.5 | 35.9 | 38.9 | 100.2 |
| BILLINGS | 2.5 | 3.3 | 5.9 | 6.4 | 7.8 | 8.5 | 6.5 | 25.0 | 26.1 | 11.9 | 1.9 | 74.6 | 34.1 | 38.7 | 96.8 |
| BILOXI-GULFPORT | 1.4 | 2.3 | 7.4 | 7.4 | 7.3 | 7.6 | 7.5 | 29.9 | 21.7 | 10.2 | 1.1 | 73.6 | 31.1 | 33.8 | 97.9 |
| BINGHAMTON | 1.1 | 1.8 | 6.5 | 7.5 | 6.9 | 7.1 | 5.9 | 28.0 | 22.7 | 13.3 | 2.1 | 75.4 | 34.1 | 37.4 | 95.8 |
| BIRMINGHAM | 0.5 | 1.1 | 6.3 | 6.5 | 6.6 | 7.1 | 7.0 | 29.7 | 23.5 | 11.7 | 1.6 | 76.6 | 33.6 | 36.8 | 91.6 |
| BLUEFLD-BECKLEY-OAK. | 0.5 | 0.9 | 5.2 | 5.8 | 6.4 | 7.1 | 6.7 | 26.8 | 26.1 | 14.0 | 1.9 | 78.2 | 35.9 | 40.0 | 91.7 |
| BOISE | 7.0 | 10.0 | 7.3 | 7.1 | 7.6 | 8.4 | 8.0 | 28.1 | 22.7 | 9.4 | 1.5 | 72.9 | 32.1 | 34.1 | 98.7 |
| BOSTON | 4.1 | 5.7 | 6.2 | 6.8 | 7.1 | 6.2 | 5.6 | 32.7 | 22.2 | 11.5 | 1.8 | 76.7 | 33.4 | 36.7 | 94.0 |
| BOWLING GREEN | 0.4 | 1.0 | 6.1 | 6.2 | 6.4 | 7.9 | 7.6 | 28.6 | 24.1 | 11.5 | 1.6 | 77.1 | 33.5 | 36.7 | 92.8 |
| BUFFALO | 1.9 | 2.9 | 6.4 | 7.2 | 6.9 | 7.0 | 6.0 | 28.4 | 22.5 | 13.5 | 2.0 | 75.6 | 34.4 | 37.3 | 94.0 |
| BURLINGTON-PLATTSBGH | 1.0 | 1.7 | 5.5 | 6.4 | 7.2 | 7.5 | 6.6 | 31.0 | 23.3 | 10.8 | 1.6 | 77.1 | 32.6 | 36.6 | 99.6 |
| BUTTE-BOZEMAN, MT | 1.6 | 2.2 | 5.3 | 5.8 | 6.8 | 8.9 | 9.5 | 26.7 | 24.7 | 10.7 | 1.6 | 77.5 | 33.3 | 36.8 | 104.4 |
| CASPER-RIVERTON | 4.2 | 5.0 | 6.0 | 6.5 | 7.8 | 9.0 | 6.9 | 24.5 | 26.0 | 11.7 | 1.5 | 73.8 | 33.1 | 38.1 | 97.7 |
| C. RAPIDS-W'LOO-DUB. | 0.7 | 1.7 | 6.2 | 6.4 | 7.1 | 8.3 | 8.0 | 27.7 | 22.4 | 11.8 | 2.0 | 75.9 | 33.0 | 36.0 | 95.7 |
| CHAMPN.-S'FIELD-DEC. | 1.0 | 1.7 | 6.5 | 6.9 | 6.8 | 8.1 | 8.2 | 27.8 | 21.9 | 11.8 | 2.0 | 75.8 | 33.1 | 35.7 | 95.3 |
| CHARLESTON, SC | 1.3 | 2.2 | 7.4 | 7.5 | 7.1 | 6.9 | 7.5 | 31.9 | 20.8 | 9.7 | 1.0 | 74.0 | 29.9 | 33.6 | 94.0 |
| CHARLESTON-HUNTINGTN | 0.4 | 0.8 | 5.7 | 6.2 | 6.7 | 7.5 | 7.3 | 27.8 | 25.0 | 12.2 | 1.6 | 77.1 | 34.2 | 37.8 | 93.7 |
| CHARLOTTE | 0.8 | 1.9 | 6.9 | 7.2 | 7.3 | 6.7 | 6.0 | 30.5 | 23.3 | 10.7 | 1.3 | 74.8 | 33.3 | 36.0 | 93.7 |
| CHARLOTTESVILLE | 1.0 | 1.9 | 5.9 | 6.2 | 6.2 | 8.6 | 10.5 | 30.2 | 21.0 | 10.1 | 1.4 | 78.4 | 31.1 | 34.1 | 92.9 |
| CHATTANOOGA | 0.8 | 1.9 | 6.3 | 6.5 | 6.8 | 6.9 | 6.4 | 29.3 | 24.8 | 11.5 | 1.5 | 76.3 | 34.3 | 37.3 | 93.4 |
| CHEYEN-SCTSBLF-STERL | 11.2 | 15.3 | 6.3 | 6.2 | 7.2 | 8.4 | 7.9 | 25.8 | 24.8 | 11.8 | 1.7 | 75.2 | 33.0 | 37.2 | 97.3 |
| CHICAGO | 10.7 | 14.2 | 7.4 | 7.6 | 7.3 | 7.0 | 6.4 | 31.1 | 21.8 | 10.0 | 1.4 | 73.6 | 32.4 | 35.0 | 95.0 |
| CHICO-REDDING | 7.1 | 10.2 | 6.6 | 8.0 | 6.9 | 7.5 | 7.4 | 25.6 | 21.7 | 14.3 | 1.8 | 74.2 | 34.5 | 36.6 | 97.9 |
| CINCINNATI | 0.5 | 1.0 | 7.0 | 7.3 | 7.6 | 7.5 | 6.7 | 30.0 | 21.9 | 10.6 | 1.5 | 73.8 | 32.4 | 35.3 | 93.8 |
| CLARKSBURG-WESTON | 0.6 | 1.1 | 5.5 | 5.9 | 6.2 | 7.3 | 6.8 | 26.4 | 25.7 | 13.9 | 2.2 | 78.2 | 36.1 | 39.6 | 93.0 |
| CLEVELAND | 1.6 | 2.4 | 6.3 | 6.8 | 7.3 | 7.1 | 6.2 | 28.9 | 23.1 | 12.6 | 1.7 | 75.5 | 34.2 | 37.3 | 92.4 |
| COLORADO SPR.-PUEBLO | 16.0 | 18.5 | 7.3 | 6.9 | 7.4 | 7.9 | 7.7 | 28.1 | 23.9 | 9.4 | 1.3 | 73.8 | 31.9 | 35.0 | 100.2 |
| COLUMBIA, SC | 1.0 | 1.8 | 6.2 | 6.7 | 6.7 | 7.6 | 7.9 | 31.5 | 22.4 | 9.8 | 1.1 | 76.2 | 31.3 | 35.0 | 93.5 |
| COLUMBIA-JEFF. CITY | 0.7 | 1.3 | 6.3 | 6.6 | 7.0 | 8.5 | 9.1 | 29.2 | 20.5 | 10.9 | 1.8 | 75.9 | 32.1 | 34.3 | 98.6 |
| COLUMBUS, GA | 1.8 | 3.2 | 7.1 | 6.9 | 6.8 | 8.1 | 9.8 | 29.6 | 20.2 | 10.1 | 1.3 | 75.1 | 30.3 | 32.6 | 95.9 |
| COLUMBUS, OH | 0.7 | 1.3 | 6.5 | 6.8 | 7.1 | 7.4 | 7.5 | 31.6 | 21.8 | 9.9 | 1.3 | 75.5 | 32.0 | 35.0 | 96.0 |
| COLUMBUS-TUPELO-W.PT | 0.5 | 1.0 | 7.0 | 7.0 | 7.1 | 8.0 | 7.9 | 28.4 | 21.9 | 11.1 | 1.7 | 74.5 | 31.8 | 34.6 | 91.9 |
| CORPUS CHRISTI | 54.3 | 60.7 | 8.4 | 8.1 | 7.9 | 8.3 | 7.3 | 27.7 | 21.1 | 9.9 | 1.2 | 70.5 | 30.7 | 32.6 | 97.8 |
| DALLAS-FT.WORTH | 12.3 | 15.7 | 8.0 | 7.6 | 7.5 | 7.3 | 6.8 | 31.4 | 22.2 | 8.0 | 1.1 | 72.6 | 31.0 | 34.2 | 97.4 |
| DAVENPORT-R.ISL-MOL. | 3.2 | 5.3 | 6.5 | 6.9 | 7.1 | 7.4 | 6.3 | 27.2 | 23.6 | 12.7 | 2.1 | 74.9 | 34.7 | 37.4 | 95.2 |
| DAYTON | 0.7 | 1.2 | 6.5 | 6.8 | 7.3 | 7.4 | 6.4 | 29.0 | 23.1 | 12.0 | 1.6 | 75.2 | 33.4 | 36.6 | 93.8 |
| DENVER | 11.8 | 14.0 | 6.9 | 7.0 | 7.5 | 7.6 | 6.7 | 29.8 | 24.7 | 8.5 | 1.2 | 74.2 | 32.5 | 36.1 | 98.2 |
| DES MOINES-AMES | 1.1 | 2.3 | 6.2 | 6.4 | 7.2 | 7.8 | 6.9 | 27.8 | 23.0 | 12.4 | 2.3 | 75.9 | 34.0 | 37.1 | 94.6 |
| DETROIT | 2.0 | 2.7 | 6.4 | 7.0 | 7.6 | 7.0 | 6.2 | 31.0 | 22.6 | 10.8 | 1.4 | 74.9 | 32.8 | 36.2 | 93.3 |
| DOTHAN | 1.3 | 2.2 | 7.0 | 6.8 | 6.7 | 6.9 | 7.0 | 29.6 | 22.6 | 11.7 | 1.6 | 75.3 | 32.7 | 35.8 | 93.1 |
| DULUTH-SUPERIOR | 0.5 | 1.0 | 5.5 | 6.0 | 6.9 | 7.8 | 6.4 | 25.6 | 24.6 | 14.7 | 2.5 | 75.9 | 36.2 | 39.7 | 98.1 |
| EL PASO | 67.1 | 72.2 | 9.2 | 8.4 | 8.2 | 9.1 | 8.7 | 28.1 | 19.3 | 8.2 | 0.9 | 68.9 | 28.0 | 29.5 | 94.8 |
| ELMIRA | 0.9 | 1.5 | 6.6 | 7.6 | 7.2 | 7.2 | 6.0 | 26.9 | 23.3 | 13.2 | 2.0 | 74.5 | 34.3 | 37.3 | 96.9 |
| ERIE | 0.9 | 1.7 | 6.2 | 6.9 | 7.2 | 7.9 | 6.7 | 27.6 | 22.5 | 13.0 | 1.9 | 75.5 | 33.6 | 36.6 | 93.9 |
| EUGENE | 2.4 | 4.2 | 6.1 | 6.2 | 6.7 | 8.0 | 8.2 | 26.9 | 24.4 | 11.8 | 1.7 | 76.8 | 34.1 | 36.9 | 97.3 |
| EUREKA | 5.2 | 7.5 | 6.4 | 8.1 | 6.9 | 7.7 | 7.5 | 29.2 | 21.3 | 11.6 | 1.4 | 74.6 | 33.0 | 35.4 | 103.0 |
| EVANSVILLE | 0.4 | 1.0 | 6.6 | 6.8 | 7.0 | 7.3 | 6.1 | 28.8 | 23.5 | 12.1 | 1.9 | 75.3 | 34.2 | 37.2 | 94.1 |
| FAIRBANKS | 3.7 | 5.0 | 8.0 | 8.7 | 9.1 | 9.9 | 11.3 | 27.2 | 21.0 | 4.5 | 0.4 | 68.9 | 27.7 | 27.6 | 113.3 |
| FARGO-VALLEY CITY | 1.0 | 2.0 | 6.1 | 6.4 | 7.5 | 8.7 | 7.9 | 26.5 | 22.0 | 12.4 | 2.6 | 75.5 | 32.7 | 36.3 | 99.4 |
| FLINT-SAGINAW-B.CITY | 2.7 | 3.8 | 6.5 | 7.1 | 7.6 | 7.7 | 6.8 | 28.9 | 22.7 | 11.2 | 1.5 | 74.4 | 32.4 | 35.7 | 93.7 |
| FLORENCE-MYRTL BEACH | 0.6 | 1.2 | 6.7 | 7.1 | 7.4 | 7.1 | 6.7 | 29.1 | 23.3 | 11.5 | 1.2 | 74.5 | 32.2 | 35.8 | 90.4 |
| FRESNO-VISALIA | 35.3 | 43.4 | 8.9 | 10.2 | 8.2 | 8.1 | 7.5 | 28.9 | 17.8 | 9.2 | 1.2 | 67.9 | 29.2 | 30.0 | 102.0 |
| FT. MYERS-NAPLES | 7.2 | 10.6 | 5.5 | 5.9 | 6.1 | 5.3 | 4.4 | 23.5 | 23.2 | 23.6 | 2.6 | 79.4 | 42.4 | 44.6 | 95.3 |
| FT.SMITH-FAY-SPRNGDL | 1.2 | 3.3 | 7.0 | 6.9 | 7.3 | 7.6 | 7.3 | 27.6 | 23.0 | 11.6 | 1.6 | 74.4 | 33.6 | 35.8 | 95.8 |
| FT. WAYNE | 1.6 | 2.8 | 7.4 | 7.5 | 7.7 | 7.3 | 6.2 | 29.7 | 22.1 | 10.5 | 1.6 | 73.0 | 32.4 | 35.2 | 95.4 |
| GAINESVILLE | 3.3 | 4.9 | 6.2 | 6.8 | 6.7 | 9.6 | 12.3 | 27.8 | 19.2 | 10.3 | 1.2 | 76.9 | 29.7 | 31.4 | 96.4 |
| GLENDIVE | 0.7 | 1.3 | 5.1 | 5.8 | 7.5 | 8.3 | 5.4 | 23.3 | 27.0 | 14.9 | 2.6 | 76.5 | 36.4 | 41.6 | 100.2 |
| GRAND JCT.-MONTROSE | 8.7 | 11.0 | 6.3 | 6.7 | 7.5 | 8.1 | 5.9 | 24.1 | 26.9 | 12.7 | 1.8 | 74.5 | 35.2 | 39.4 | 95.2 |
| G.RAPIDS-K'ZOO-B.CRK | 2.6 | 3.7 | 7.1 | 7.7 | 8.0 | 8.0 | 6.8 | 29.5 | 21.3 | 10.0 | 1.5 | 72.7 | 31.6 | 34.3 | 96.6 |
| GREAT FALLS | 1.2 | 1.8 | 6.4 | 6.9 | 8.0 | 8.2 | 6.6 | 24.7 | 25.1 | 12.1 | 2.0 | 73.4 | 33.3 | 37.8 | 98.1 |
| GREEN BAY-APPLETON | 0.7 | 1.5 | 6.3 | 6.9 | 7.8 | 7.8 | 6.3 | 29.2 | 22.3 | 11.4 | 1.9 | 74.3 | 33.1 | 36.3 | 97.2 |
| UNITED STATES | 9.0 | 11.8 | 6.9 | 7.2 | 7.2 | 7.2 | 6.7 | 29.9 | 22.2 | 11.1 | 1.6 | 74.6 | 32.9 | 35.7 | 95.6 |

# HOUSEHOLDS

## DMA AND U.S. TOTALS

| DMA | HOUSEHOLDS | | | | | FAMILIES | | | MEDIAN HOUSEHOLD INCOME | | |
|---|---|---|---|---|---|---|---|---|---|---|---|
| | 1990 | 2000 | 2005 | % Annual Rate 1990-2000 | 2000 Average HH Size | 1990 | 2000 | % Annual Rate 1990-2000 | 2000 | 2005 | 2000 National Rank |
| ABILENE-SWEETWATER | 104,336 | 106,106 | 106,663 | 0.2 | 2.52 | 74,728 | 73,576 | -0.2 | 30,195 | 36,036 | 189 |
| ALBANY, GA | 127,220 | 142,766 | 149,707 | 1.4 | 2.67 | 95,412 | 104,444 | 1.1 | 31,930 | 35,796 | 177 |
| ALBANY-SCHENEC.-TROY | 504,649 | 521,296 | 523,201 | 0.4 | 2.45 | 342,625 | 341,123 | -0.1 | 41,582 | 47,939 | 47 |
| ALBUQUERQUE-SANTA FE | 509,126 | 603,042 | 631,416 | 2.1 | 2.69 | 367,386 | 425,752 | 1.8 | 35,812 | 41,718 | 109 |
| ALEXANDRIA, LA | 84,793 | 82,878 | 84,441 | -0.3 | 2.68 | 64,547 | 61,290 | -0.6 | 26,736 | 30,338 | 206 |
| ALPENA | 16,099 | 17,180 | 17,783 | 0.8 | 2.41 | 11,649 | 11,994 | 0.4 | 30,944 | 33,896 | 183 |
| AMARILLO | 178,456 | 189,624 | 193,111 | 0.7 | 2.56 | 129,965 | 134,421 | 0.4 | 32,788 | 37,624 | 156 |
| ANCHORAGE, AK | 110,346 | 133,812 | 143,213 | 2.4 | 2.71 | 76,800 | 89,665 | 1.9 | 63,248 | 76,738 | 2 |
| ATLANTA | 1,385,104 | 1,845,405 | 2,100,847 | 3.5 | 2.61 | 986,152 | 1,297,916 | 3.4 | 48,957 | 57,961 | 15 |
| AUGUSTA, GA | 208,075 | 234,204 | 243,916 | 1.4 | 2.64 | 153,807 | 169,200 | 1.2 | 36,819 | 42,225 | 99 |
| AUSTIN | 356,908 | 499,329 | 578,606 | 4.2 | 2.50 | 226,171 | 313,662 | 4.0 | 44,849 | 53,154 | 29 |
| BAKERSFIELD | 181,480 | 213,227 | 225,611 | 2.0 | 2.91 | 135,925 | 156,312 | 1.7 | 38,806 | 48,543 | 82 |
| BALTIMORE | 946,349 | 1,021,165 | 1,056,137 | 0.9 | 2.59 | 669,326 | 704,209 | 0.6 | 50,968 | 60,388 | 6 |
| BANGOR | 123,945 | 133,682 | 137,202 | 0.9 | 2.44 | 88,393 | 92,233 | 0.5 | 32,311 | 37,831 | 172 |
| BATON ROUGE | 252,676 | 284,360 | 298,677 | 1.4 | 2.68 | 185,373 | 204,279 | 1.2 | 35,549 | 40,023 | 116 |
| BEAUMONT-PORT ARTHUR | 157,034 | 165,645 | 168,908 | 0.7 | 2.61 | 115,879 | 119,083 | 0.3 | 35,207 | 39,282 | 121 |
| BEND, OR | 29,217 | 44,750 | 53,119 | 5.3 | 2.56 | 21,202 | 31,346 | 4.9 | 41,120 | 46,905 | 53 |
| BILLINGS | 87,104 | 99,881 | 103,786 | 1.7 | 2.46 | 60,710 | 67,186 | 1.2 | 34,768 | 40,161 | 130 |
| BILOXI-GULFPORT | 103,696 | 120,335 | 127,865 | 1.8 | 2.66 | 77,300 | 87,664 | 1.5 | 35,966 | 41,412 | 107 |
| BINGHAMTON | 137,468 | 132,902 | 130,082 | -0.4 | 2.49 | 95,484 | 89,303 | -0.8 | 35,196 | 40,007 | 122 |
| BIRMINGHAM | 608,122 | 676,224 | 705,317 | 1.3 | 2.53 | 443,506 | 480,385 | 1.0 | 37,021 | 42,066 | 97 |
| BLUEFLD-BECKLEY-OAK. | 139,836 | 144,044 | 144,051 | 0.4 | 2.45 | 103,899 | 103,352 | -0.1 | 23,986 | 26,752 | 209 |
| BOISE | 150,272 | 210,100 | 238,394 | 4.2 | 2.60 | 108,829 | 148,128 | 3.8 | 41,442 | 49,317 | 48 |
| BOSTON | 2,114,512 | 2,291,541 | 2,408,565 | 1.0 | 2.51 | 1,427,837 | 1,500,612 | 0.6 | 50,758 | 59,167 | 8 |
| BOWLING GREEN | 67,665 | 77,324 | 81,326 | 1.6 | 2.50 | 49,598 | 54,991 | 1.3 | 31,055 | 35,226 | 182 |
| BUFFALO | 636,988 | 635,529 | 623,864 | 0.0 | 2.46 | 439,835 | 423,640 | -0.5 | 37,148 | 41,456 | 93 |
| BURLINGTON-PLATTSBGH | 282,334 | 310,248 | 323,676 | 1.2 | 2.46 | 195,297 | 207,214 | 0.7 | 39,914 | 46,668 | 67 |
| BUTTE-BOZEMAN, MT | 48,953 | 58,668 | 62,168 | 2.2 | 2.37 | 32,424 | 37,561 | 1.8 | 33,002 | 36,968 | 154 |
| CASPER-RIVERTON | 44,984 | 49,615 | 50,877 | 1.2 | 2.47 | 32,270 | 34,369 | 0.8 | 32,502 | 35,960 | 166 |
| C. RAPIDS-W'LOO-DUB. | 291,529 | 306,219 | 311,803 | 0.6 | 2.52 | 201,104 | 203,288 | 0.1 | 38,443 | 43,528 | 83 |
| CHAMPN.-S'FIELD-DEC. | 343,769 | 349,074 | 348,359 | 0.2 | 2.46 | 233,078 | 227,858 | -0.3 | 37,709 | 42,847 | 86 |
| CHARLESTON, SC | 218,091 | 255,554 | 280,255 | 1.9 | 2.66 | 160,928 | 182,815 | 1.6 | 38,331 | 44,595 | 85 |
| CHARLESTON-HUNTINGTN | 469,409 | 491,140 | 494,431 | 0.6 | 2.51 | 349,431 | 354,286 | 0.2 | 27,386 | 30,781 | 205 |
| CHARLOTTE | 739,072 | 893,818 | 982,757 | 2.3 | 2.57 | 540,439 | 634,368 | 2.0 | 41,051 | 46,901 | 56 |
| CHARLOTTESVILLE | 48,335 | 55,812 | 59,622 | 1.8 | 2.43 | 31,409 | 35,410 | 1.5 | 41,263 | 46,310 | 50 |
| CHATTANOOGA | 294,666 | 335,328 | 355,136 | 1.6 | 2.52 | 220,197 | 244,368 | 1.3 | 35,474 | 40,268 | 119 |
| CHEYEN-SCTSBLF-STERL | 46,938 | 50,768 | 51,589 | 1.0 | 2.47 | 33,135 | 34,593 | 0.5 | 33,982 | 39,351 | 141 |
| CHICAGO | 3,015,208 | 3,281,015 | 3,397,409 | 1.0 | 2.71 | 2,105,099 | 2,242,864 | 0.8 | 50,864 | 58,191 | 7 |
| CHICO-REDDING | 160,312 | 177,720 | 182,727 | 1.3 | 2.51 | 110,478 | 117,928 | 0.8 | 35,117 | 41,626 | 123 |
| CINCINNATI | 749,067 | 832,691 | 870,101 | 1.3 | 2.58 | 531,754 | 581,042 | 1.1 | 41,129 | 47,047 | 52 |
| CLARKSBURG-WESTON | 102,759 | 107,122 | 107,322 | 0.5 | 2.44 | 74,241 | 74,535 | 0.1 | 24,812 | 28,805 | 207 |
| CLEVELAND | 1,434,403 | 1,500,820 | 1,518,328 | 0.6 | 2.53 | 1,011,708 | 1,026,587 | 0.2 | 39,407 | 44,060 | 71 |
| COLORADO SPR.-PUEBLO | 234,195 | 296,736 | 325,830 | 2.9 | 2.53 | 165,779 | 203,817 | 2.5 | 43,138 | 51,165 | 37 |
| COLUMBIA, SC | 280,531 | 328,844 | 352,310 | 1.9 | 2.59 | 204,526 | 233,016 | 1.6 | 39,317 | 45,363 | 72 |
| COLUMBIA-JEFF. CITY | 137,664 | 154,542 | 161,449 | 1.4 | 2.48 | 94,282 | 101,963 | 1.0 | 36,442 | 41,869 | 104 |
| COLUMBUS, GA | 175,368 | 193,037 | 199,756 | 1.2 | 2.56 | 124,206 | 132,469 | 0.8 | 33,096 | 38,479 | 152 |
| COLUMBUS, OH | 687,107 | 774,262 | 815,942 | 1.5 | 2.53 | 476,226 | 521,782 | 1.1 | 40,068 | 45,694 | 66 |
| COLUMBUS-TUPELO-W.PT | 164,820 | 180,248 | 186,890 | 1.1 | 2.58 | 121,782 | 128,612 | 0.7 | 30,343 | 35,151 | 188 |
| CORPUS CHRISTI | 171,222 | 190,886 | 196,595 | 1.3 | 2.84 | 129,298 | 141,391 | 1.1 | 32,565 | 38,411 | 164 |
| DALLAS-FT.WORTH | 1,673,085 | 2,087,167 | 2,332,134 | 2.7 | 2.61 | 1,164,688 | 1,423,775 | 2.5 | 46,399 | 54,419 | 21 |
| DAVENPORT-R.ISL-MOL. | 303,952 | 308,240 | 309,181 | 0.2 | 2.52 | 214,947 | 209,950 | -0.3 | 37,411 | 42,093 | 88 |
| DAYTON | 499,898 | 513,901 | 514,957 | 0.3 | 2.57 | 360,677 | 359,497 | 0.0 | 40,122 | 45,754 | 65 |
| DENVER | 1,032,500 | 1,298,400 | 1,433,442 | 2.8 | 2.48 | 675,858 | 832,534 | 2.5 | 49,637 | 57,260 | 13 |
| DES MOINES-AMES | 365,653 | 389,787 | 401,682 | 0.8 | 2.47 | 251,442 | 258,482 | 0.3 | 38,915 | 44,980 | 79 |
| DETROIT | 1,738,136 | 1,904,190 | 1,965,573 | 1.1 | 2.58 | 1,226,900 | 1,307,765 | 0.8 | 47,363 | 52,583 | 19 |
| DOTHAN | 86,078 | 92,980 | 95,817 | 0.9 | 2.55 | 64,171 | 67,171 | 0.6 | 32,697 | 37,200 | 160 |
| DULUTH-SUPERIOR | 171,449 | 178,323 | 180,516 | 0.5 | 2.43 | 116,558 | 117,020 | 0.1 | 36,274 | 40,290 | 106 |
| EL PASO | 225,417 | 282,044 | 303,042 | 2.8 | 3.11 | 177,661 | 220,405 | 2.7 | 30,184 | 34,982 | 190 |
| ELMIRA | 94,366 | 95,251 | 95,118 | 0.1 | 2.53 | 67,383 | 65,734 | -0.3 | 35,032 | 39,816 | 126 |
| ERIE | 150,993 | 154,511 | 153,654 | 0.3 | 2.54 | 106,680 | 105,726 | -0.1 | 36,417 | 40,788 | 105 |
| EUGENE | 196,931 | 222,158 | 229,685 | 1.5 | 2.44 | 133,482 | 144,806 | 1.0 | 34,868 | 39,361 | 129 |
| EUREKA | 54,407 | 56,935 | 56,402 | 0.6 | 2.47 | 35,824 | 36,028 | 0.1 | 35,034 | 41,885 | 125 |
| EVANSVILLE | 262,259 | 275,520 | 281,083 | 0.6 | 2.52 | 190,948 | 194,859 | 0.3 | 37,061 | 42,078 | 96 |
| FAIRBANKS | 28,602 | 31,737 | 32,461 | 1.3 | 2.74 | 20,505 | 21,839 | 0.8 | 58,764 | 72,827 | 4 |
| FARGO-VALLEY CITY | 214,973 | 223,296 | 226,473 | 0.5 | 2.46 | 146,943 | 146,008 | -0.1 | 34,203 | 39,387 | 137 |
| FLINT-SAGINAW-B.CITY | 431,159 | 455,470 | 467,025 | 0.7 | 2.57 | 314,579 | 322,420 | 0.3 | 40,144 | 44,878 | 64 |
| FLORENCE-MYRTL BEACH | 197,787 | 236,034 | 255,906 | 2.2 | 2.59 | 147,544 | 170,729 | 1.8 | 33,407 | 38,050 | 148 |
| FRESNO-VISALIA | 437,181 | 513,612 | 544,020 | 2.0 | 3.00 | 331,001 | 382,305 | 1.8 | 35,632 | 43,285 | 112 |
| FT. MYERS-NAPLES | 269,769 | 345,777 | 385,060 | 3.1 | 2.34 | 193,516 | 241,108 | 2.7 | 39,874 | 47,938 | 68 |
| FT.SMITH-FAY-SPRNGDL | 185,304 | 227,770 | 243,945 | 2.5 | 2.57 | 136,838 | 162,811 | 2.1 | 32,326 | 37,370 | 171 |
| FT. WAYNE | 231,727 | 251,340 | 261,303 | 1.0 | 2.62 | 169,340 | 178,905 | 0.7 | 43,526 | 50,062 | 35 |
| GAINESVILLE | 88,537 | 100,584 | 104,013 | 1.6 | 2.44 | 54,016 | 59,728 | 1.2 | 30,003 | 33,830 | 193 |
| GLENDIVE | 4,259 | 4,128 | 4,015 | -0.4 | 2.36 | 3,026 | 2,818 | -0.9 | 32,263 | 37,265 | 174 |
| GRAND JCT.-MONTROSE | 46,602 | 60,868 | 67,672 | 3.3 | 2.47 | 33,069 | 41,856 | 2.9 | 37,491 | 43,585 | 87 |
| G.RAPIDS-K'ZOO-B.CRK | 607,947 | 688,266 | 726,371 | 1.5 | 2.64 | 441,951 | 487,970 | 1.2 | 42,665 | 48,994 | 42 |
| GREAT FALLS | 62,813 | 65,157 | 64,714 | 0.5 | 2.46 | 44,306 | 44,346 | 0.0 | 30,457 | 34,247 | 186 |
| GREEN BAY-APPLETON | 350,660 | 391,864 | 409,185 | 1.4 | 2.57 | 251,259 | 272,468 | 1.0 | 43,747 | 50,747 | 33 |
| UNITED STATES | | | | 1.4 | 2.59 | | | 1.1 | 41,914 | 49,127 | |

# D

# INCOME

## DMA AND U.S. TOTALS

| DMA | 2000 Per Capita Income | 2000 HH Income Base | 2000 HOUSEHOLD INCOME DISTRIBUTION (%) Less than $15,000 | $15,000 to $24,999 | $25,000 to $49,999 | $50,000 to $99,999 | $100,000 to $149,999 | $150,000 or More | 2000 AVERAGE DISPOSABLE INCOME BY AGE OF HOUSEHOLDER All Ages | <35 | 35-44 | 45-54 | 55-64 | 65+ |
|---|---|---|---|---|---|---|---|---|---|---|---|---|---|---|
| ABILENE-SWEETWATER | 15,377 | 106,102 | 23.0 | 18.3 | 33.9 | 20.4 | 3.2 | 1.2 | 31,441 | 26,837 | 37,795 | 39,488 | 35,016 | 22,039 |
| ALBANY, GA | 15,344 | 142,759 | 23.1 | 16.2 | 32.9 | 22.4 | 4.1 | 1.3 | 31,237 | 27,165 | 36,174 | 38,420 | 32,858 | 20,626 |
| ALBANY-SCHENEC.-TROY | 21,501 | 521,281 | 13.5 | 12.5 | 34.7 | 30.4 | 6.5 | 2.5 | 36,570 | 32,845 | 41,503 | 46,237 | 40,043 | 23,268 |
| ALBUQUERQUE-SANTA FE | 17,662 | 602,991 | 18.4 | 15.2 | 33.3 | 25.7 | 5.5 | 1.9 | 35,552 | 28,733 | 39,879 | 43,404 | 38,683 | 27,010 |
| ALEXANDRIA, LA | 13,031 | 82,876 | 27.0 | 19.7 | 33.0 | 17.0 | 2.5 | 1.0 | 28,815 | 24,672 | 34,428 | 35,527 | 30,224 | 19,591 |
| ALPENA | 16,255 | 17,180 | 20.0 | 19.1 | 37.6 | 19.1 | 3.0 | 1.3 | 29,253 | 26,738 | 34,360 | 40,229 | 33,093 | 18,230 |
| AMARILLO | 16,564 | 189,621 | 19.7 | 16.9 | 35.3 | 22.9 | 3.8 | 1.3 | 33,497 | 27,533 | 38,695 | 40,736 | 37,456 | 24,646 |
| ANCHORAGE, AK | 30,532 | 133,812 | 6.6 | 7.0 | 23.3 | 40.2 | 15.0 | 8.0 | 60,472 | 43,732 | 60,843 | 70,098 | 58,996 | 43,010 |
| ATLANTA | 25,339 | 1,845,386 | 10.6 | 10.0 | 30.5 | 34.4 | 9.9 | 4.6 | 46,190 | 39,391 | 49,139 | 54,587 | 45,889 | 28,581 |
| AUGUSTA, GA | 18,124 | 234,196 | 19.1 | 13.8 | 33.0 | 26.3 | 5.8 | 2.0 | 35,367 | 31,418 | 39,044 | 43,254 | 37,118 | 22,491 |
| AUSTIN | 24,728 | 499,326 | 12.9 | 12.2 | 30.5 | 31.1 | 9.1 | 4.2 | 45,882 | 34,454 | 51,068 | 56,680 | 49,415 | 34,964 |
| BAKERSFIELD | 17,559 | 213,224 | 16.2 | 14.0 | 33.7 | 27.7 | 5.8 | 2.6 | 37,386 | 32,740 | 41,660 | 46,220 | 40,061 | 25,114 |
| BALTIMORE | 25,999 | 1,021,149 | 10.4 | 9.2 | 29.2 | 35.9 | 10.7 | 4.6 | 45,377 | 39,160 | 48,614 | 54,423 | 47,224 | 30,449 |
| BANGOR | 16,604 | 133,677 | 19.3 | 17.5 | 37.3 | 21.5 | 3.3 | 1.2 | 29,898 | 27,007 | 35,446 | 36,674 | 31,377 | 19,311 |
| BATON ROUGE | 17,335 | 284,343 | 20.9 | 14.0 | 32.5 | 25.3 | 5.2 | 2.1 | 36,565 | 29,672 | 42,071 | 44,496 | 36,929 | 24,815 |
| BEAUMONT-PORT ARTHUR | 17,428 | 165,630 | 20.4 | 14.9 | 33.7 | 24.8 | 4.5 | 1.8 | 35,406 | 30,044 | 41,366 | 43,411 | 37,128 | 24,670 |
| BEND, OR | 20,511 | 44,750 | 10.6 | 13.5 | 37.2 | 30.0 | 6.7 | 2.1 | 36,410 | 31,201 | 40,357 | 45,160 | 39,344 | 23,862 |
| BILLINGS | 17,170 | 99,881 | 18.0 | 16.0 | 36.8 | 24.1 | 4.0 | 1.1 | 32,299 | 26,406 | 37,200 | 39,372 | 34,297 | 23,633 |
| BILOXI-GULFPORT | 16,783 | 120,335 | 17.5 | 15.1 | 35.6 | 26.3 | 4.4 | 1.2 | 34,670 | 30,044 | 39,129 | 41,447 | 36,588 | 24,429 |
| BINGHAMTON | 17,165 | 132,902 | 17.6 | 15.9 | 36.3 | 25.2 | 3.8 | 1.2 | 30,839 | 28,011 | 36,041 | 39,793 | 34,134 | 19,379 |
| BIRMINGHAM | 19,885 | 676,216 | 18.6 | 13.9 | 32.7 | 26.3 | 6.0 | 2.6 | 37,957 | 32,559 | 45,002 | 47,218 | 38,148 | 24,172 |
| BLUEFLD-BECKLEY-OAK. | 12,961 | 144,044 | 31.2 | 20.5 | 31.6 | 14.3 | 1.9 | 0.6 | 25,318 | 21,811 | 31,649 | 30,688 | 25,689 | 18,276 |
| BOISE | 21,096 | 210,084 | 11.1 | 14.1 | 35.2 | 30.2 | 7.0 | 2.4 | 39,073 | 32,703 | 44,080 | 48,006 | 39,061 | 27,105 |
| BOSTON | 26,501 | 2,291,530 | 11.9 | 8.6 | 28.5 | 35.8 | 10.2 | 5.0 | 45,147 | 40,661 | 48,310 | 54,895 | 49,949 | 27,808 |
| BOWLING GREEN | 16,583 | 77,324 | 23.8 | 16.0 | 34.1 | 21.0 | 3.8 | 1.4 | 31,044 | 27,652 | 38,344 | 38,647 | 29,154 | 19,810 |
| BUFFALO | 19,116 | 635,520 | 17.0 | 14.1 | 35.8 | 26.3 | 5.0 | 1.9 | 33,061 | 29,362 | 38,480 | 42,544 | 36,876 | 21,092 |
| BURLINGTON-PLATTSBGH | 19,954 | 310,248 | 13.8 | 13.1 | 36.7 | 28.6 | 5.8 | 2.0 | 36,119 | 32,912 | 41,122 | 44,594 | 39,492 | 22,301 |
| BUTTE-BOZEMAN, MT | 19,442 | 58,663 | 19.5 | 16.4 | 35.8 | 22.1 | 4.2 | 2.1 | 32,485 | 23,646 | 37,784 | 41,110 | 35,826 | 23,215 |
| CASPER-RIVERTON | 16,103 | 49,558 | 20.2 | 16.5 | 37.9 | 21.3 | 3.2 | 1.0 | 32,748 | 24,658 | 39,978 | 39,437 | 36,775 | 23,755 |
| C. RAPIDS-W'LOO-DUB. | 19,106 | 306,213 | 14.8 | 14.0 | 36.6 | 27.4 | 5.2 | 2.0 | 34,861 | 28,107 | 41,460 | 45,222 | 37,750 | 23,346 |
| CHAMPN.-S'FIELD-DEC. | 18,822 | 349,066 | 16.0 | 14.5 | 36.0 | 27.0 | 4.9 | 1.7 | 34,833 | 28,491 | 39,952 | 44,852 | 39,182 | 23,961 |
| CHARLESTON, SC | 18,546 | 255,539 | 15.4 | 14.0 | 35.2 | 28.1 | 5.5 | 1.9 | 36,296 | 31,583 | 39,432 | 44,155 | 38,920 | 26,078 |
| CHARLESTON-HUNTINGTN | 14,430 | 491,140 | 28.1 | 17.8 | 32.5 | 17.7 | 2.7 | 1.1 | 28,237 | 24,069 | 34,176 | 34,445 | 29,088 | 19,465 |
| CHARLOTTE | 20,514 | 893,811 | 13.4 | 12.9 | 34.9 | 30.2 | 6.4 | 2.3 | 38,151 | 34,103 | 43,492 | 47,050 | 39,399 | 23,758 |
| CHARLOTTESVILLE | 22,298 | 55,809 | 14.0 | 12.8 | 34.0 | 28.9 | 7.1 | 3.2 | 39,773 | 29,549 | 43,992 | 50,043 | 45,885 | 31,635 |
| CHATTANOOGA | 18,231 | 335,316 | 17.8 | 15.3 | 35.6 | 24.8 | 4.6 | 1.9 | 35,938 | 32,371 | 41,609 | 44,358 | 36,675 | 21,903 |
| CHEYEN-SCTSBLF-STERL | 16,787 | 50,768 | 17.8 | 17.2 | 36.8 | 24.0 | 3.3 | 1.1 | 33,562 | 25,516 | 40,234 | 43,089 | 38,958 | 23,285 |
| CHICAGO | 26,183 | 3,280,992 | 10.9 | 9.1 | 29.0 | 34.8 | 10.8 | 5.5 | 47,967 | 41,084 | 49,978 | 57,002 | 51,465 | 30,784 |
| CHICO-REDDING | 19,199 | 177,720 | 17.1 | 16.3 | 35.6 | 23.5 | 4.9 | 2.6 | 35,406 | 29,217 | 40,252 | 45,282 | 38,531 | 25,946 |
| CINCINNATI | 20,665 | 832,684 | 15.1 | 12.5 | 33.3 | 29.9 | 6.6 | 2.6 | 38,693 | 32,589 | 44,156 | 48,740 | 40,841 | 24,609 |
| CLARKSBURG-WESTON | 12,822 | 107,122 | 30.1 | 20.2 | 32.5 | 14.8 | 1.8 | 0.5 | 25,620 | 22,472 | 31,082 | 31,587 | 26,988 | 18,509 |
| CLEVELAND | 20,033 | 1,500,811 | 15.6 | 13.2 | 34.6 | 28.7 | 5.7 | 2.1 | 36,729 | 31,319 | 41,337 | 46,646 | 40,987 | 24,281 |
| COLORADO SPR.-PUEBLO | 21,658 | 296,724 | 11.8 | 13.2 | 33.0 | 31.6 | 7.8 | 2.6 | 40,216 | 32,266 | 45,934 | 49,071 | 41,659 | 28,664 |
| COLUMBIA, SC | 18,827 | 328,838 | 15.4 | 13.4 | 34.4 | 29.2 | 6.0 | 1.7 | 36,437 | 31,693 | 40,052 | 44,736 | 38,224 | 24,975 |
| COLUMBIA-JEFF. CITY | 18,247 | 154,539 | 16.4 | 15.1 | 35.8 | 26.3 | 4.9 | 1.5 | 34,993 | 29,226 | 40,930 | 44,437 | 39,064 | 23,416 |
| COLUMBUS, GA | 17,355 | 193,021 | 22.4 | 15.1 | 32.6 | 23.3 | 4.7 | 1.9 | 33,490 | 27,191 | 39,065 | 42,801 | 36,186 | 22,786 |
| COLUMBUS, OH | 19,852 | 774,255 | 14.3 | 13.5 | 35.1 | 29.3 | 5.8 | 2.0 | 37,021 | 31,464 | 42,501 | 46,783 | 39,487 | 24,192 |
| COLUMBUS-TUPELO-W.PT | 14,880 | 180,245 | 24.3 | 16.4 | 35.1 | 20.2 | 3.0 | 1.0 | 30,364 | 27,733 | 36,010 | 38,028 | 30,420 | 18,843 |
| CORPUS CHRISTI | 15,648 | 190,880 | 22.3 | 16.0 | 32.8 | 22.9 | 4.3 | 1.8 | 34,189 | 28,904 | 37,924 | 41,364 | 36,392 | 25,334 |
| DALLAS-FT.WORTH | 24,476 | 2,087,163 | 11.1 | 11.6 | 31.2 | 32.6 | 9.1 | 4.4 | 47,317 | 38,204 | 51,296 | 56,705 | 49,208 | 31,039 |
| DAVENPORT-R.ISL-MOL. | 18,318 | 308,240 | 15.7 | 14.4 | 36.7 | 27.3 | 4.5 | 1.4 | 33,809 | 28,522 | 39,736 | 43,322 | 36,368 | 22,842 |
| DAYTON | 19,047 | 513,892 | 14.4 | 13.2 | 36.0 | 29.8 | 5.2 | 1.6 | 36,207 | 31,398 | 41,086 | 46,646 | 39,259 | 24,033 |
| DENVER | 27,594 | 1,298,335 | 9.9 | 10.3 | 30.2 | 33.8 | 10.6 | 5.3 | 47,514 | 35,945 | 51,854 | 56,132 | 49,898 | 31,490 |
| DES MOINES-AMES | 19,512 | 389,783 | 14.0 | 13.8 | 37.1 | 28.2 | 5.3 | 1.7 | 34,940 | 29,723 | 41,294 | 44,204 | 37,429 | 23,677 |
| DETROIT | 24,983 | 1,904,166 | 14.5 | 9.6 | 28.6 | 33.6 | 9.1 | 4.7 | 44,211 | 35,791 | 47,553 | 55,512 | 49,419 | 27,202 |
| DOTHAN | 16,591 | 92,980 | 20.7 | 16.0 | 34.9 | 23.4 | 3.8 | 1.2 | 32,714 | 29,151 | 38,688 | 42,532 | 34,868 | 20,253 |
| DULUTH-SUPERIOR | 18,749 | 178,323 | 16.9 | 14.6 | 36.9 | 25.1 | 4.9 | 1.6 | 32,677 | 28,438 | 39,520 | 43,248 | 35,441 | 21,079 |
| EL PASO | 12,966 | 282,041 | 22.7 | 18.4 | 33.3 | 20.8 | 3.5 | 1.3 | 31,763 | 25,348 | 33,767 | 38,474 | 36,363 | 25,912 |
| ELMIRA | 17,183 | 95,250 | 16.4 | 16.7 | 37.6 | 24.0 | 4.0 | 1.3 | 31,143 | 27,957 | 36,983 | 40,080 | 33,768 | 19,783 |
| ERIE | 17,857 | 154,511 | 16.2 | 14.7 | 37.9 | 25.6 | 4.3 | 1.4 | 33,462 | 29,084 | 38,129 | 43,841 | 37,681 | 21,529 |
| EUGENE | 17,943 | 222,139 | 17.7 | 16.0 | 36.3 | 24.2 | 4.3 | 1.5 | 31,435 | 25,401 | 36,105 | 41,222 | 34,666 | 21,669 |
| EUREKA | 19,108 | 56,935 | 18.7 | 16.2 | 35.0 | 23.3 | 4.7 | 2.2 | 34,231 | 27,565 | 36,890 | 43,447 | 39,371 | 25,836 |
| EVANSVILLE | 18,766 | 275,515 | 17.2 | 14.2 | 35.8 | 26.0 | 5.1 | 1.7 | 35,274 | 31,031 | 41,676 | 43,805 | 36,794 | 22,709 |
| FAIRBANKS | 27,128 | 31,736 | 6.8 | 8.1 | 25.8 | 40.6 | 13.0 | 5.7 | 54,838 | 37,776 | 56,509 | 69,127 | 58,811 | 40,047 |
| FARGO-VALLEY CITY | 17,049 | 223,289 | 17.5 | 16.3 | 37.7 | 23.4 | 3.9 | 1.2 | 32,313 | 27,004 | 38,624 | 41,418 | 36,468 | 22,538 |
| FLINT-SAGINAW-B.CITY | 19,377 | 455,457 | 17.5 | 12.5 | 32.4 | 29.7 | 5.9 | 1.9 | 35,955 | 28,986 | 41,769 | 48,779 | 40,113 | 22,090 |
| FLORENCE-MYRTL BEACH | 16,623 | 236,034 | 20.3 | 16.0 | 34.9 | 23.3 | 4.2 | 1.4 | 32,166 | 28,521 | 36,341 | 38,927 | 32,896 | 23,240 |
| FRESNO-VISALIA | 16,749 | 513,608 | 17.5 | 16.0 | 34.0 | 24.4 | 5.3 | 2.8 | 36,175 | 29,884 | 40,031 | 44,192 | 40,221 | 26,362 |
| FT. MYERS-NAPLES | 24,709 | 345,732 | 10.7 | 15.5 | 36.4 | 27.4 | 6.5 | 3.5 | 42,947 | 37,007 | 45,148 | 48,069 | 46,512 | 37,520 |
| FT.SMITH-FAY-SPRNGDL | 15,872 | 227,770 | 18.6 | 18.0 | 37.0 | 22.1 | 3.3 | 1.0 | 31,193 | 26,812 | 37,584 | 38,896 | 33,220 | 22,310 |
| FT. WAYNE | 20,488 | 251,338 | 10.0 | 11.6 | 37.2 | 33.3 | 6.3 | 1.7 | 39,845 | 34,999 | 44,364 | 50,414 | 43,188 | 25,571 |
| GAINESVILLE | 16,686 | 100,575 | 24.8 | 17.6 | 31.5 | 20.0 | 4.2 | 1.9 | 32,970 | 23,203 | 39,541 | 43,954 | 38,639 | 25,942 |
| GLENDIVE | 15,454 | 4,128 | 20.4 | 17.3 | 38.7 | 20.6 | 2.7 | 0.3 | 28,315 | 24,309 | 33,925 | 34,387 | 32,342 | 19,085 |
| GRAND JCT.-MONTROSE | 19,388 | 60,868 | 14.9 | 15.1 | 36.2 | 26.9 | 5.1 | 1.7 | 35,203 | 29,145 | 41,358 | 42,980 | 37,125 | 24,624 |
| G.RAPIDS-K'ZOO-B.CRK | 20,396 | 688,262 | 12.6 | 11.5 | 35.3 | 31.3 | 6.9 | 2.4 | 38,733 | 33,114 | 43,952 | 50,237 | 43,072 | 23,178 |
| GREAT FALLS | 15,462 | 65,151 | 21.2 | 19.2 | 36.4 | 19.3 | 3.0 | 0.9 | 28,721 | 22,713 | 33,872 | 33,781 | 31,709 | 22,342 |
| GREEN BAY-APPLETON | 20,864 | 391,860 | 12.0 | 10.3 | 35.9 | 32.7 | 7.1 | 2.0 | 36,482 | 32,712 | 42,099 | 47,224 | 39,973 | 21,567 |
| UNITED STATES | 22,162 | | 14.5 | 12.5 | 32.3 | 29.8 | 7.4 | 3.5 | 40,748 | 34,503 | 44,969 | 49,579 | 43,409 | 27,339 |

# SPENDING POTENTIAL INDEXES

## DMA AND U.S. TOTALS

# E

| DMA | FINANCIAL SERVICES | | | | THE HOME | | | | | | ENTERTAINMENT | | | | | | PERSONAL | | | |
|---|---|---|---|---|---|---|---|---|---|---|---|---|---|---|---|---|---|---|---|---|
| | | | | | Home Improvements | | | Furnishings | | | | | | | | | | | | |
| | Auto Loan | Home Loan | Invest-ments | Retire-ment Plans | Home Repair | Lawn & Garden | Remodel-ing | Appli-ances | Elec-tronics | Furni-ture | Restau-rants | Sport-ing Goods | Theater & Concerts | Toys & Hobbies | Travel | Video Rental | Apparel | Auto After-market | Health Insur-ance | Pets & Supplies |
| ABILENE-SWEETWATER | 96 | 83 | 88 | 86 | 96 | 94 | 105 | 96 | 94 | 86 | 88 | 94 | 88 | 96 | 78 | 97 | 87 | 92 | 100 | 98 |
| ALBANY, GA | 96 | 79 | 85 | 83 | 95 | 92 | 105 | 96 | 93 | 87 | 85 | 95 | 86 | 95 | 76 | 97 | 87 | 92 | 96 | 97 |
| ALBANY-SCHENEC.-TROY | 99 | 92 | 97 | 95 | 94 | 92 | 95 | 98 | 95 | 96 | 97 | 99 | 98 | 102 | 93 | 99 | 99 | 95 | 102 | 102 |
| ALBUQUERQUE-SANTA FE | 98 | 96 | 94 | 94 | 100 | 99 | 103 | 101 | 99 | 99 | 96 | 92 | 90 | 92 | 88 | 94 | 94 | 97 | 97 | 94 |
| ALEXANDRIA, LA | 95 | 79 | 83 | 81 | 94 | 91 | 102 | 95 | 92 | 85 | 85 | 93 | 85 | 94 | 75 | 97 | 85 | 91 | 95 | 96 |
| ALPENA | 98 | 77 | 83 | 86 | 96 | 93 | 112 | 97 | 93 | 83 | 86 | 95 | 89 | 97 | 84 | 101 | 84 | 93 | 104 | 99 |
| AMARILLO | 97 | 87 | 92 | 89 | 97 | 96 | 103 | 96 | 95 | 90 | 92 | 95 | 91 | 97 | 81 | 98 | 90 | 94 | 100 | 99 |
| ANCHORAGE, AK | 103 | 111 | 93 | 106 | 101 | 103 | 103 | 104 | 108 | 110 | 111 | 100 | 99 | 99 | 94 | 96 | 109 | 106 | 96 | 99 |
| ATLANTA | 101 | 102 | 96 | 101 | 100 | 101 | 103 | 100 | 101 | 102 | 104 | 104 | 100 | 103 | 88 | 100 | 103 | 102 | 97 | 103 |
| AUGUSTA, GA | 98 | 87 | 90 | 90 | 97 | 95 | 104 | 98 | 96 | 92 | 91 | 98 | 92 | 98 | 80 | 98 | 92 | 95 | 97 | 99 |
| AUSTIN | 100 | 104 | 95 | 100 | 99 | 99 | 101 | 98 | 100 | 99 | 103 | 101 | 97 | 101 | 87 | 99 | 100 | 101 | 98 | 102 |
| BAKERSFIELD | 98 | 97 | 90 | 92 | 98 | 98 | 99 | 100 | 100 | 97 | 97 | 91 | 90 | 92 | 87 | 94 | 94 | 97 | 96 | 94 |
| BALTIMORE | 100 | 104 | 104 | 103 | 104 | 104 | 99 | 100 | 100 | 105 | 104 | 103 | 103 | 103 | 93 | 100 | 105 | 103 | 98 | 102 |
| BANGOR | 99 | 77 | 83 | 84 | 88 | 86 | 102 | 96 | 93 | 85 | 87 | 97 | 88 | 99 | 81 | 98 | 89 | 90 | 103 | 101 |
| BATON ROUGE | 98 | 89 | 92 | 91 | 98 | 95 | 102 | 97 | 96 | 94 | 92 | 98 | 92 | 98 | 82 | 98 | 94 | 96 | 95 | 99 |
| BEAUMONT-PORT ARTHUR | 97 | 84 | 91 | 88 | 98 | 95 | 103 | 97 | 94 | 90 | 89 | 95 | 90 | 97 | 80 | 97 | 90 | 94 | 97 | 98 |
| BEND, OR | 100 | 91 | 92 | 93 | 99 | 99 | 110 | 101 | 100 | 96 | 95 | 92 | 89 | 95 | 85 | 94 | 94 | 96 | 99 | 95 |
| BILLINGS | 98 | 85 | 89 | 90 | 98 | 97 | 107 | 99 | 98 | 92 | 91 | 90 | 86 | 92 | 82 | 93 | 90 | 93 | 99 | 93 |
| BILOXI-GULFPORT | 97 | 90 | 94 | 90 | 99 | 96 | 102 | 97 | 96 | 94 | 94 | 97 | 93 | 98 | 83 | 98 | 94 | 96 | 97 | 99 |
| BINGHAMTON | 98 | 85 | 92 | 89 | 92 | 90 | 97 | 97 | 93 | 91 | 92 | 97 | 93 | 100 | 88 | 98 | 94 | 92 | 102 | 101 |
| BIRMINGHAM | 98 | 87 | 93 | 92 | 99 | 97 | 104 | 98 | 95 | 92 | 91 | 98 | 92 | 98 | 82 | 98 | 93 | 95 | 98 | 99 |
| BLUEFLD-BECKLEY-OAK. | 96 | 70 | 80 | 79 | 95 | 92 | 109 | 95 | 92 | 80 | 81 | 93 | 82 | 94 | 72 | 96 | 81 | 88 | 101 | 96 |
| BOISE | 99 | 92 | 89 | 93 | 98 | 98 | 107 | 101 | 100 | 96 | 96 | 93 | 90 | 94 | 84 | 94 | 95 | 96 | 98 | 95 |
| BOSTON | 102 | 108 | 108 | 107 | 98 | 100 | 94 | 100 | 102 | 107 | 108 | 105 | 108 | 105 | 104 | 101 | 111 | 104 | 103 | 105 |
| BOWLING GREEN | 98 | 78 | 85 | 85 | 96 | 94 | 108 | 96 | 94 | 85 | 86 | 96 | 87 | 97 | 75 | 97 | 86 | 91 | 100 | 98 |
| BUFFALO | 97 | 88 | 96 | 90 | 94 | 91 | 92 | 97 | 93 | 94 | 93 | 96 | 95 | 99 | 91 | 98 | 95 | 93 | 100 | 99 |
| BURLINGTON-PLATTSBGH | 99 | 86 | 89 | 91 | 90 | 88 | 99 | 97 | 95 | 91 | 93 | 99 | 93 | 101 | 86 | 99 | 95 | 94 | 102 | 102 |
| BUTTE-BOZEMAN, MT | 97 | 86 | 88 | 90 | 98 | 96 | 106 | 98 | 97 | 90 | 89 | 88 | 85 | 90 | 82 | 92 | 89 | 92 | 98 | 92 |
| CASPER-RIVERTON | 98 | 87 | 85 | 88 | 97 | 95 | 105 | 99 | 98 | 93 | 92 | 90 | 86 | 92 | 81 | 93 | 91 | 93 | 97 | 93 |
| C. RAPIDS-W'LOO-DUB. | 97 | 87 | 91 | 91 | 97 | 95 | 103 | 96 | 94 | 89 | 93 | 95 | 94 | 98 | 90 | 100 | 89 | 96 | 101 | 98 |
| CHAMPN.-S'FIELD-DEC. | 98 | 90 | 94 | 93 | 99 | 96 | 103 | 97 | 95 | 92 | 95 | 96 | 96 | 98 | 92 | 101 | 92 | 97 | 100 | 99 |
| CHARLESTON, SC | 98 | 92 | 92 | 92 | 98 | 97 | 101 | 98 | 97 | 95 | 96 | 98 | 94 | 98 | 83 | 98 | 95 | 97 | 96 | 100 |
| CHARLESTON-HUNTINGTN | 97 | 75 | 86 | 82 | 97 | 94 | 108 | 96 | 92 | 84 | 84 | 95 | 86 | 96 | 75 | 96 | 84 | 90 | 101 | 97 |
| CHARLOTTE | 99 | 89 | 92 | 92 | 98 | 97 | 107 | 98 | 97 | 93 | 94 | 99 | 93 | 100 | 82 | 98 | 94 | 96 | 99 | 101 |
| CHARLOTTESVILLE | 99 | 99 | 99 | 98 | 101 | 100 | 104 | 97 | 97 | 96 | 100 | 99 | 96 | 101 | 87 | 98 | 99 | 99 | 98 | 101 |
| CHATTANOOGA | 98 | 83 | 90 | 88 | 98 | 96 | 107 | 97 | 95 | 89 | 90 | 97 | 90 | 98 | 79 | 97 | 90 | 93 | 100 | 99 |
| CHEYEN-SCTSBLF-STERL | 98 | 91 | 94 | 92 | 100 | 99 | 104 | 100 | 98 | 96 | 94 | 90 | 89 | 92 | 86 | 93 | 93 | 95 | 98 | 93 |
| CHICAGO | 100 | 109 | 106 | 107 | 105 | 105 | 98 | 101 | 102 | 106 | 107 | 102 | 109 | 101 | 107 | 104 | 105 | 107 | 99 | 102 |
| CHICO-REDDING | 96 | 86 | 93 | 88 | 99 | 98 | 104 | 98 | 95 | 90 | 89 | 88 | 85 | 90 | 83 | 91 | 88 | 92 | 99 | 92 |
| CINCINNATI | 99 | 96 | 98 | 98 | 101 | 99 | 101 | 99 | 97 | 98 | 99 | 99 | 101 | 100 | 97 | 102 | 96 | 100 | 100 | 100 |
| CLARKSBURG-WESTON | 96 | 73 | 84 | 80 | 97 | 94 | 107 | 95 | 91 | 82 | 83 | 93 | 84 | 94 | 75 | 96 | 83 | 89 | 101 | 96 |
| CLEVELAND | 98 | 96 | 102 | 98 | 103 | 101 | 99 | 98 | 96 | 99 | 99 | 97 | 102 | 99 | 99 | 101 | 96 | 100 | 100 | 99 |
| COLORADO SPR.-PUEBLO | 99 | 99 | 94 | 98 | 101 | 101 | 102 | 101 | 102 | 101 | 100 | 94 | 93 | 94 | 89 | 94 | 98 | 99 | 97 | 95 |
| COLUMBIA, SC | 99 | 92 | 94 | 94 | 99 | 97 | 103 | 98 | 97 | 95 | 96 | 99 | 95 | 99 | 83 | 99 | 96 | 97 | 97 | 100 |
| COLUMBIA-JEFF. CITY | 99 | 88 | 89 | 92 | 96 | 95 | 106 | 97 | 96 | 90 | 94 | 97 | 94 | 99 | 89 | 101 | 91 | 97 | 101 | 100 |
| COLUMBUS, GA | 96 | 85 | 92 | 87 | 98 | 94 | 101 | 95 | 93 | 89 | 89 | 95 | 89 | 96 | 80 | 96 | 90 | 93 | 96 | 97 |
| COLUMBUS, OH | 99 | 96 | 96 | 97 | 100 | 98 | 101 | 98 | 97 | 97 | 99 | 99 | 100 | 100 | 96 | 101 | 96 | 100 | 99 | 100 |
| COLUMBUS-TUPELO-W.PT | 97 | 75 | 81 | 82 | 95 | 92 | 108 | 96 | 93 | 83 | 83 | 96 | 85 | 96 | 73 | 96 | 84 | 90 | 99 | 98 |
| CORPUS CHRISTI | 97 | 95 | 93 | 91 | 96 | 97 | 99 | 98 | 97 | 94 | 97 | 96 | 93 | 98 | 83 | 98 | 92 | 97 | 98 | 101 |
| DALLAS-FT.WORTH | 101 | 105 | 98 | 102 | 100 | 102 | 101 | 100 | 102 | 102 | 105 | 103 | 101 | 102 | 90 | 100 | 103 | 103 | 98 | 103 |
| DAVENPORT-R.ISL-MOL. | 97 | 87 | 92 | 90 | 99 | 96 | 103 | 97 | 94 | 91 | 93 | 95 | 95 | 98 | 91 | 100 | 89 | 95 | 101 | 98 |
| DAYTON | 98 | 92 | 96 | 94 | 101 | 98 | 102 | 98 | 96 | 95 | 97 | 97 | 99 | 99 | 95 | 101 | 94 | 98 | 100 | 99 |
| DENVER | 101 | 106 | 97 | 104 | 102 | 104 | 103 | 103 | 105 | 106 | 105 | 97 | 97 | 97 | 93 | 95 | 104 | 102 | 98 | 97 |
| DES MOINES-AMES | 98 | 89 | 91 | 92 | 97 | 96 | 103 | 97 | 95 | 91 | 94 | 96 | 95 | 98 | 91 | 101 | 91 | 97 | 101 | 99 |
| DETROIT | 99 | 103 | 104 | 103 | 104 | 103 | 99 | 100 | 99 | 103 | 103 | 101 | 106 | 101 | 103 | 102 | 101 | 104 | 98 | 100 |
| DOTHAN | 97 | 82 | 86 | 86 | 96 | 94 | 106 | 97 | 94 | 88 | 88 | 96 | 89 | 97 | 77 | 97 | 88 | 93 | 98 | 99 |
| DULUTH-SUPERIOR | 97 | 80 | 87 | 87 | 97 | 94 | 108 | 97 | 93 | 86 | 88 | 94 | 91 | 97 | 87 | 100 | 86 | 93 | 103 | 98 |
| EL PASO | 96 | 100 | 92 | 91 | 96 | 95 | 94 | 97 | 97 | 92 | 97 | 95 | 93 | 96 | 84 | 98 | 91 | 98 | 97 | 102 |
| ELMIRA | 98 | 80 | 89 | 86 | 91 | 88 | 98 | 96 | 92 | 89 | 89 | 97 | 91 | 99 | 85 | 98 | 91 | 91 | 102 | 100 |
| ERIE | 98 | 83 | 91 | 88 | 92 | 89 | 97 | 97 | 93 | 91 | 91 | 97 | 93 | 100 | 87 | 98 | 93 | 92 | 102 | 100 |
| EUGENE | 98 | 91 | 93 | 92 | 100 | 98 | 105 | 99 | 98 | 94 | 93 | 90 | 88 | 92 | 85 | 92 | 92 | 94 | 98 | 93 |
| EUREKA | 95 | 86 | 89 | 86 | 98 | 95 | 103 | 97 | 94 | 90 | 89 | 86 | 84 | 90 | 82 | 91 | 88 | 91 | 97 | 91 |
| EVANSVILLE | 98 | 84 | 88 | 89 | 98 | 95 | 106 | 97 | 95 | 90 | 91 | 96 | 94 | 98 | 88 | 101 | 89 | 95 | 101 | 99 |
| FAIRBANKS | 100 | 105 | 90 | 100 | 99 | 99 | 100 | 102 | 105 | 104 | 105 | 95 | 94 | 95 | 89 | 95 | 103 | 102 | 94 | 97 |
| FARGO-VALLEY CITY | 97 | 83 | 84 | 88 | 94 | 92 | 103 | 95 | 93 | 85 | 90 | 95 | 90 | 96 | 86 | 100 | 86 | 94 | 101 | 98 |
| FLINT-SAGINAW-B.CITY | 97 | 89 | 93 | 91 | 99 | 96 | 103 | 97 | 94 | 93 | 93 | 96 | 96 | 98 | 92 | 101 | 91 | 96 | 99 | 98 |
| FLORENCE-MYRTL BEACH | 98 | 80 | 90 | 87 | 97 | 96 | 108 | 98 | 94 | 88 | 88 | 97 | 89 | 97 | 79 | 97 | 88 | 92 | 99 | 99 |
| FRESNO-VISALIA | 97 | 98 | 91 | 93 | 98 | 98 | 98 | 100 | 100 | 96 | 96 | 90 | 90 | 91 | 87 | 94 | 92 | 97 | 97 | 95 |
| FT. MYERS-NAPLES | 101 | 96 | 109 | 101 | 105 | 110 | 106 | 103 | 96 | 97 | 100 | 100 | 99 | 102 | 92 | 98 | 97 | 99 | 107 | 103 |
| FT.SMITH-FAY-SPRNGDL | 98 | 83 | 90 | 88 | 97 | 96 | 109 | 97 | 94 | 88 | 90 | 97 | 89 | 98 | 79 | 97 | 89 | 93 | 101 | 99 |
| FT. WAYNE | 99 | 90 | 90 | 92 | 98 | 95 | 105 | 98 | 96 | 93 | 96 | 98 | 96 | 100 | 90 | 102 | 93 | 98 | 100 | 100 |
| GAINESVILLE | 96 | 93 | 96 | 93 | 97 | 95 | 102 | 94 | 93 | 89 | 92 | 94 | 89 | 96 | 82 | 95 | 91 | 94 | 97 | 98 |
| GLENDIVE | 98 | 79 | 87 | 87 | 97 | 97 | 108 | 99 | 96 | 87 | 87 | 90 | 84 | 92 | 79 | 93 | 87 | 91 | 101 | 92 |
| GRAND JCT.-MONTROSE | 99 | 88 | 92 | 92 | 100 | 98 | 108 | 100 | 99 | 94 | 93 | 91 | 88 | 93 | 84 | 93 | 92 | 94 | 99 | 94 |
| G.RAPIDS-K'ZOO-B.CRK | 98 | 91 | 92 | 92 | 98 | 96 | 103 | 98 | 96 | 94 | 96 | 97 | 97 | 99 | 92 | 101 | 93 | 98 | 100 | 99 |
| GREAT FALLS | 97 | 82 | 87 | 87 | 98 | 96 | 105 | 98 | 95 | 89 | 87 | 89 | 85 | 90 | 81 | 92 | 88 | 91 | 99 | 91 |
| GREEN BAY-APPLETON | 98 | 89 | 90 | 92 | 98 | 95 | 105 | 98 | 96 | 93 | 96 | 97 | 96 | 100 | 90 | 101 | 92 | 97 | 101 | 100 |
| UNITED STATES | 100 | 100 | 100 | 100 | 100 | 100 | 100 | 100 | 100 | 100 | 100 | 100 | 100 | 100 | 100 | 100 | 100 | 100 | 100 | 100 |

# POPULATION CHANGE

## DMA AND U.S. TOTALS

A

| DMA | DMA Code | POPULATION 1990 | POPULATION 2000 | POPULATION 2005 | 1990-2000 ANNUAL CHANGE % Rate | 1990-2000 ANNUAL CHANGE National Rank | RACE (%) White 1990 | White 2000 | Black 1990 | Black 2000 | Asian/Pacific 1990 | Asian/Pacific 2000 |
|---|---|---|---|---|---|---|---|---|---|---|---|---|
| GR'NSBORO-H.PT-W.SLM | 518 | 1,344,845 | 1,508,110 | 1,584,520 | 1.1 | 67 | 80.8 | 79.9 | 18.0 | 18.3 | 0.6 | 1.0 |
| GREENVL.-N.BERN-WAS. | 545 | 636,383 | 680,643 | 697,898 | 0.7 | 115 | 68.5 | 67.0 | 29.3 | 29.5 | 0.8 | 1.3 |
| GRNVL-SPR'BG-ASH-AND | 567 | 1,698,730 | 1,917,351 | 2,023,618 | 1.2 | 61 | 84.4 | 83.6 | 14.5 | 14.9 | 0.5 | 0.7 |
| GREENWOOD-GREENVILLE | 647 | 241,733 | 234,246 | 225,557 | -0.3 | 204 | 41.7 | 39.2 | 57.7 | 60.0 | 0.3 | 0.4 |
| HARLIN-W'LCO-B'VL-MC | 636 | 701,888 | 962,263 | 1,073,097 | 3.1 | 6 | 77.0 | 75.8 | 0.2 | 0.3 | 0.3 | 0.3 |
| HARRISBG-LAN-LEB-YRK | 566 | 1,495,478 | 1,620,671 | 1,664,998 | 0.8 | 102 | 93.7 | 92.2 | 4.1 | 4.7 | 0.9 | 1.3 |
| HARRISONBURG, VA | 569 | 193,930 | 211,206 | 216,336 | 0.8 | 96 | 94.0 | 93.0 | 5.1 | 5.7 | 0.5 | 0.7 |
| HARTFORD & NEW HAVEN | 533 | 2,459,471 | 2,444,048 | 2,458,998 | -0.1 | 189 | 87.8 | 85.6 | 7.8 | 8.4 | 1.4 | 2.2 |
| HATTIESBURG-LAUREL | 710 | 250,336 | 273,802 | 286,182 | 0.9 | 90 | 70.8 | 68.7 | 28.7 | 30.6 | 0.3 | 0.4 |
| HELENA | 766 | 47,495 | 54,400 | 56,268 | 1.3 | 51 | 96.8 | 96.4 | 0.1 | 0.2 | 0.5 | 0.6 |
| HONOLULU | 744 | 1,108,229 | 1,184,688 | 1,181,325 | 0.7 | 116 | 33.4 | 31.5 | 2.5 | 2.8 | 61.8 | 63.0 |
| HOUSTON | 618 | 4,021,279 | 4,930,720 | 5,403,746 | 2.0 | 20 | 68.2 | 64.6 | 17.8 | 17.7 | 3.3 | 4.9 |
| HUNTSVILLE-DECATUR | 691 | 785,180 | 880,822 | 913,458 | 1.1 | 65 | 86.4 | 85.3 | 12.0 | 13.0 | 0.7 | 0.9 |
| IDAHO FLS.-POCATELLO | 758 | 282,967 | 323,590 | 336,196 | 1.3 | 52 | 94.1 | 92.6 | 0.3 | 0.5 | 0.8 | 0.9 |
| INDIANAPOLIS | 527 | 2,315,598 | 2,521,848 | 2,609,784 | 0.8 | 96 | 89.8 | 88.9 | 8.9 | 9.4 | 0.7 | 1.0 |
| JACKSON, MS | 718 | 810,669 | 857,120 | 875,037 | 0.6 | 126 | 55.1 | 53.8 | 44.3 | 45.4 | 0.3 | 0.4 |
| JACKSON, TN | 639 | 149,973 | 168,043 | 177,150 | 1.1 | 67 | 79.5 | 77.8 | 20.1 | 21.6 | 0.2 | 0.3 |
| JACKSONVILLE,BRUNSWK | 561 | 1,213,370 | 1,434,043 | 1,529,235 | 1.6 | 39 | 77.6 | 73.8 | 20.2 | 22.7 | 1.4 | 2.2 |
| JOHNSTOWN-ALTOONA | 574 | 757,431 | 759,635 | 748,034 | 0.0 | 181 | 97.7 | 97.0 | 1.3 | 1.7 | 0.7 | 1.1 |
| JONESBORO | 734 | 190,658 | 212,296 | 220,319 | 1.1 | 74 | 97.1 | 96.3 | 2.2 | 2.6 | 0.3 | 0.4 |
| JOPLIN-PITTSBURG | 603 | 354,441 | 376,324 | 383,866 | 0.6 | 122 | 95.0 | 94.8 | 1.2 | 1.3 | 0.5 | 0.6 |
| JUNEAU, AK | 747 | 26,751 | 30,282 | 30,773 | 1.2 | 56 | 80.6 | 78.2 | 1.1 | 1.1 | 4.3 | 5.5 |
| KANSAS CITY | 616 | 1,937,522 | 2,162,333 | 2,275,062 | 1.1 | 72 | 86.3 | 85.1 | 10.9 | 11.3 | 1.1 | 1.6 |
| KNOXVILLE | 557 | 1,030,161 | 1,176,718 | 1,233,158 | 1.3 | 53 | 94.8 | 94.1 | 4.4 | 4.7 | 0.5 | 0.8 |
| LA CROSSE-EAU CLAIRE | 702 | 466,183 | 490,638 | 499,266 | 0.5 | 130 | 97.8 | 97.0 | 0.3 | 0.3 | 1.3 | 1.9 |
| LAFAYETTE, IN | 582 | 138,774 | 151,666 | 156,091 | 0.9 | 92 | 93.8 | 92.2 | 1.9 | 2.1 | 3.5 | 4.6 |
| LAFAYETTE, LA | 642 | 527,301 | 572,614 | 591,343 | 0.8 | 101 | 73.1 | 70.5 | 25.7 | 28.0 | 0.7 | 0.9 |
| LAKE CHARLES, LA | 643 | 228,703 | 247,116 | 252,551 | 0.8 | 107 | 78.0 | 75.5 | 21.0 | 23.2 | 0.3 | 0.5 |
| LANSING | 551 | 625,861 | 657,596 | 667,729 | 0.5 | 133 | 89.5 | 88.3 | 6.9 | 7.2 | 1.5 | 2.0 |
| LAREDO | 749 | 142,518 | 211,012 | 242,987 | 3.9 | 3 | 70.4 | 69.8 | 0.1 | 0.1 | 0.3 | 0.4 |
| LAS VEGAS | 839 | 763,015 | 1,309,964 | 1,600,974 | 5.4 | 1 | 81.6 | 76.5 | 9.3 | 9.9 | 3.4 | 5.0 |
| LEXINGTON | 541 | 1,002,293 | 1,123,585 | 1,181,048 | 1.1 | 67 | 93.8 | 93.4 | 5.3 | 5.5 | 0.5 | 0.8 |
| LIMA | 558 | 109,755 | 106,435 | 104,159 | -0.3 | 203 | 87.6 | 85.7 | 11.2 | 12.8 | 0.5 | 0.7 |
| LINCOLN-HAST'GS-KRNY | 722 | 644,788 | 669,599 | 674,181 | 0.4 | 147 | 97.4 | 96.1 | 0.9 | 1.0 | 0.7 | 1.3 |
| LITTLE ROCK-PINE BLF | 693 | 1,199,074 | 1,290,705 | 1,324,861 | 0.7 | 111 | 81.1 | 80.3 | 17.8 | 18.2 | 0.4 | 0.6 |
| LOS ANGELES | 803 | 13,379,397 | 14,709,345 | 15,597,820 | 0.9 | 86 | 63.6 | 59.1 | 8.7 | 8.1 | 9.7 | 11.8 |
| LOUISVILLE | 529 | 1,402,505 | 1,526,882 | 1,591,750 | 0.8 | 99 | 88.6 | 88.4 | 10.4 | 10.2 | 0.6 | 0.9 |
| LUBBOCK | 651 | 410,743 | 410,115 | 401,635 | 0.0 | 186 | 77.5 | 73.7 | 6.1 | 6.5 | 0.8 | 1.1 |
| MACON | 503 | 531,173 | 581,900 | 602,030 | 0.9 | 88 | 62.2 | 57.4 | 36.9 | 41.1 | 0.5 | 0.9 |
| MADISON | 669 | 765,979 | 871,924 | 907,610 | 1.3 | 55 | 95.6 | 94.2 | 2.3 | 2.9 | 1.3 | 1.9 |
| MANKATO | 737 | 127,193 | 124,310 | 122,162 | -0.2 | 198 | 98.1 | 97.2 | 0.2 | 0.3 | 0.8 | 1.3 |
| MARQUETTE | 553 | 224,492 | 218,624 | 215,493 | -0.3 | 200 | 96.7 | 96.0 | 0.7 | 1.2 | 0.6 | 0.9 |
| MEDFORD-KLAMATH FLS. | 813 | 346,462 | 398,849 | 416,828 | 1.4 | 47 | 94.8 | 93.8 | 0.5 | 0.5 | 0.8 | 1.1 |
| MEMPHIS | 640 | 1,620,347 | 1,742,326 | 1,803,732 | 0.7 | 112 | 61.5 | 59.6 | 37.5 | 39.0 | 0.6 | 0.9 |
| MERIDIAN | 711 | 180,507 | 185,393 | 185,367 | 0.3 | 160 | 60.2 | 58.1 | 37.1 | 38.7 | 0.3 | 0.4 |
| MIAMI-FT. LAUDERDALE | 528 | 3,270,606 | 3,843,959 | 4,109,929 | 1.6 | 40 | 76.8 | 74.7 | 18.2 | 18.9 | 1.3 | 1.9 |
| MILWAUKEE | 617 | 2,058,583 | 2,154,901 | 2,185,458 | 0.5 | 136 | 85.9 | 84.0 | 10.8 | 11.7 | 1.1 | 1.6 |
| MINNEAPOLIS-ST. PAUL | 613 | 3,582,027 | 4,037,526 | 4,266,607 | 1.2 | 63 | 93.9 | 91.8 | 2.6 | 3.4 | 2.0 | 2.9 |
| MINOT-BISMK.-DICK'SN | 687 | 362,780 | 354,166 | 347,155 | -0.2 | 199 | 90.5 | 88.8 | 0.5 | 0.5 | 0.4 | 0.6 |
| MISSOULA | 762 | 198,488 | 242,763 | 254,506 | 2.0 | 22 | 94.9 | 94.2 | 0.2 | 0.2 | 0.6 | 0.7 |
| MOBILE-PENSACOLA | 686 | 1,109,472 | 1,274,062 | 1,329,053 | 1.4 | 49 | 75.6 | 74.1 | 22.1 | 22.8 | 1.2 | 1.8 |
| MONROE-EL DORADO | 628 | 479,325 | 481,977 | 478,066 | 0.1 | 179 | 66.5 | 63.9 | 32.8 | 35.3 | 0.3 | 0.4 |
| MONTEREY-SALINAS | 828 | 622,091 | 679,175 | 724,082 | 0.9 | 94 | 71.6 | 66.2 | 4.1 | 3.8 | 6.0 | 7.4 |
| MONTGOMERY | 698 | 588,175 | 620,220 | 626,770 | 0.5 | 127 | 58.2 | 57.7 | 41.1 | 41.6 | 0.4 | 0.5 |
| NASHVILLE | 659 | 1,838,622 | 2,183,386 | 2,331,316 | 1.7 | 34 | 86.4 | 85.5 | 12.2 | 12.6 | 0.8 | 1.2 |
| NEW ORLEANS | 622 | 1,667,480 | 1,736,635 | 1,760,432 | 0.4 | 142 | 65.9 | 65.5 | 31.2 | 31.0 | 1.4 | 1.8 |
| NEW YORK | 501 | 18,566,988 | 19,310,336 | 19,776,410 | 0.4 | 145 | 70.7 | 67.2 | 17.9 | 18.1 | 4.7 | 6.9 |
| NORFOLK-P'MTH-N.NEWS | 544 | 1,635,296 | 1,779,950 | 1,831,598 | 0.8 | 99 | 67.4 | 64.5 | 29.4 | 31.1 | 2.2 | 3.2 |
| NORTH PLATTE | 740 | 36,713 | 37,945 | 38,934 | 0.3 | 153 | 96.8 | 94.4 | 0.3 | 0.3 | 0.3 | 0.5 |
| ODESSA-MIDLAND | 633 | 363,291 | 377,303 | 377,882 | 0.4 | 147 | 78.9 | 75.3 | 4.7 | 5.2 | 0.6 | 0.8 |
| OKLAHOMA CITY | 650 | 1,483,805 | 1,585,716 | 1,627,372 | 0.7 | 116 | 83.7 | 82.5 | 7.8 | 8.2 | 1.4 | 1.8 |
| OMAHA | 652 | 920,629 | 987,735 | 1,017,275 | 0.7 | 113 | 92.3 | 90.6 | 5.7 | 6.1 | 0.8 | 1.3 |
| ORLANDO-D.BEACH-MEL. | 534 | 2,249,653 | 2,825,243 | 3,099,356 | 2.3 | 15 | 85.8 | 82.4 | 10.9 | 12.7 | 1.4 | 2.1 |
| OTTUMWA-KIRKSVILLE | 631 | 123,548 | 124,371 | 124,124 | 0.1 | 176 | 98.3 | 97.9 | 0.8 | 0.9 | 0.5 | 0.6 |
| PADUC-CG-HARR-MTVERN | 632 | 920,481 | 954,858 | 961,480 | 0.4 | 149 | 93.0 | 92.0 | 6.1 | 6.9 | 0.5 | 0.7 |
| PALM SPRINGS | 804 | 1,170,413 | 1,574,240 | 1,790,181 | 2.9 | 8 | 76.4 | 71.5 | 5.4 | 5.5 | 3.6 | 4.6 |
| PANAMA CITY | 656 | 265,877 | 315,765 | 329,649 | 1.7 | 34 | 84.4 | 80.9 | 13.4 | 16.0 | 1.0 | 1.6 |
| PARKERSBURG, WV | 597 | 156,715 | 156,342 | 153,644 | 0.0 | 187 | 98.4 | 98.2 | 1.0 | 1.1 | 0.3 | 0.4 |
| PEORIA-BLOOMINGTON | 675 | 587,112 | 614,251 | 624,511 | 0.4 | 137 | 92.8 | 91.9 | 5.7 | 6.2 | 0.8 | 1.1 |
| PHILADELPHIA | 504 | 7,133,165 | 7,308,039 | 7,385,757 | 0.2 | 161 | 79.1 | 76.7 | 16.6 | 17.3 | 1.9 | 2.9 |
| PHOENIX | 753 | 2,702,562 | 3,715,691 | 4,201,992 | 3.2 | 5 | 83.0 | 80.7 | 3.0 | 3.4 | 1.5 | 2.0 |
| PITTSBURGH | 508 | 2,927,843 | 2,850,194 | 2,775,420 | -0.3 | 200 | 92.7 | 91.5 | 6.4 | 7.2 | 0.7 | 1.0 |
| PORTLAND, OR | 820 | 2,206,193 | 2,686,661 | 2,878,091 | 1.9 | 25 | 92.2 | 90.1 | 2.0 | 2.2 | 2.8 | 3.8 |
| PORTLAND-AUBURN | 500 | 880,935 | 918,646 | 946,104 | 0.4 | 141 | 98.6 | 98.4 | 0.4 | 0.5 | 0.6 | 0.8 |
| PRESQUE ISLE | 552 | 86,936 | 74,909 | 70,448 | -1.4 | 210 | 97.3 | 97.1 | 1.1 | 1.2 | 0.5 | 0.6 |
| PROVIDENCE-N.BEDFORD | 521 | 1,509,789 | 1,514,859 | 1,533,485 | 0.0 | 181 | 92.7 | 90.9 | 3.1 | 3.7 | 1.5 | 2.0 |
| QUINCY-HAN'BL-KEOKUK | 717 | 290,674 | 290,847 | 287,794 | 0.0 | 184 | 96.7 | 95.9 | 2.3 | 2.9 | 0.5 | 0.7 |
| UNITED STATES | | | | | 1.0 | | 80.3 | 77.9 | 12.1 | 12.4 | 2.9 | 3.9 |

# POPULATION COMPOSITION

## DMA AND U.S. TOTALS

# B

| DMA | % HISPANIC ORIGIN 1990 | % HISPANIC ORIGIN 2000 | 2000 AGE DISTRIBUTION (%) 0-4 | 5-9 | 10-14 | 15-19 | 20-24 | 25-44 | 45-64 | 65-84 | 85+ | 18+ | MEDIAN AGE 1990 | MEDIAN AGE 2000 | 2000 Males/ Females (×100) |
|---|---|---|---|---|---|---|---|---|---|---|---|---|---|---|---|
| GR'NSBORO-H.PT-W.SLM | 0.8 | 1.9 | 6.4 | 6.7 | 7.0 | 6.5 | 5.8 | 30.0 | 24.1 | 12.0 | 1.6 | 76.4 | 34.5 | 37.4 | 92.3 |
| GREENVL.-N.BERN-WAS. | 2.1 | 4.0 | 7.7 | 7.5 | 7.1 | 7.1 | 9.4 | 29.4 | 20.0 | 10.7 | 1.2 | 74.2 | 30.1 | 32.5 | 100.2 |
| GRNVL-SPR'BG-ASH-AND | 0.7 | 1.5 | 5.9 | 6.4 | 6.7 | 6.9 | 6.2 | 28.4 | 24.8 | 13.0 | 1.7 | 77.2 | 34.9 | 38.4 | 92.9 |
| GREENWOOD-GREENVILLE | 0.6 | 0.9 | 8.0 | 8.0 | 8.1 | 9.2 | 8.7 | 27.1 | 19.3 | 10.0 | 1.7 | 70.5 | 29.3 | 30.7 | 91.7 |
| HARLIN-W'LCO-B'VL-MC | 84.7 | 88.1 | 9.7 | 9.3 | 9.0 | 9.5 | 9.0 | 26.2 | 17.7 | 8.5 | 1.1 | 66.0 | 26.5 | 27.2 | 94.3 |
| HARRISBG-LAN-LEB-YRK | 2.2 | 3.4 | 6.1 | 6.9 | 7.3 | 6.8 | 5.7 | 29.9 | 23.1 | 12.4 | 1.8 | 75.9 | 34.1 | 37.5 | 94.3 |
| HARRISONBURG, VA | 0.8 | 1.6 | 5.5 | 6.0 | 6.3 | 8.4 | 8.7 | 27.9 | 23.5 | 12.2 | 1.6 | 78.6 | 33.5 | 36.7 | 95.0 |
| HARTFORD & NEW HAVEN | 5.8 | 7.8 | 6.6 | 7.3 | 7.5 | 6.4 | 5.6 | 30.4 | 21.8 | 12.4 | 2.0 | 75.2 | 34.1 | 36.8 | 94.4 |
| HATTIESBURG-LAUREL | 0.5 | 0.9 | 7.1 | 7.2 | 7.2 | 8.4 | 8.4 | 28.3 | 21.2 | 10.6 | 1.5 | 73.8 | 31.1 | 33.6 | 91.2 |
| HELENA | 1.2 | 1.8 | 5.6 | 6.3 | 7.5 | 8.6 | 6.6 | 26.7 | 27.1 | 10.0 | 1.5 | 75.4 | 34.1 | 38.5 | 96.1 |
| HONOLULU | 7.3 | 8.3 | 6.6 | 7.1 | 6.4 | 7.0 | 7.2 | 28.4 | 23.4 | 12.4 | 1.5 | 75.8 | 32.6 | 37.4 | 99.3 |
| HOUSTON | 20.4 | 24.9 | 8.2 | 7.9 | 7.8 | 7.7 | 6.9 | 31.1 | 22.0 | 7.6 | 0.9 | 71.6 | 30.7 | 33.4 | 99.1 |
| HUNTSVILLE-DECATUR | 0.7 | 1.5 | 6.4 | 6.4 | 6.3 | 6.6 | 6.5 | 30.8 | 24.3 | 11.4 | 1.4 | 77.2 | 33.5 | 37.1 | 94.2 |
| IDAHO FLS.-POCATELLO | 5.0 | 7.5 | 8.1 | 8.1 | 8.7 | 10.6 | 8.9 | 25.4 | 20.7 | 8.5 | 1.1 | 68.9 | 28.3 | 29.5 | 100.7 |
| INDIANAPOLIS | 0.9 | 1.7 | 6.8 | 6.9 | 7.0 | 7.2 | 6.9 | 30.5 | 22.6 | 10.6 | 1.5 | 75.2 | 32.7 | 35.7 | 93.8 |
| JACKSON, MS | 0.4 | 0.8 | 7.2 | 7.4 | 7.5 | 8.4 | 7.4 | 28.7 | 21.5 | 10.4 | 1.5 | 73.1 | 31.4 | 34.2 | 89.6 |
| JACKSON, TN | 0.5 | 1.1 | 6.5 | 6.8 | 6.9 | 7.2 | 6.6 | 28.4 | 23.6 | 12.1 | 1.8 | 75.8 | 34.5 | 37.0 | 91.7 |
| JACKSONVILLE,BRUNSWK | 2.2 | 3.7 | 7.3 | 7.8 | 7.8 | 7.1 | 6.5 | 30.1 | 21.6 | 10.6 | 1.2 | 72.9 | 32.3 | 34.9 | 96.3 |
| JOHNSTOWN-ALTOONA | 0.5 | 1.1 | 5.5 | 6.1 | 6.4 | 7.4 | 8.0 | 27.7 | 22.7 | 14.2 | 2.0 | 78.2 | 34.6 | 37.6 | 96.2 |
| JONESBORO | 0.5 | 1.6 | 6.4 | 6.4 | 6.9 | 7.4 | 7.0 | 26.2 | 24.0 | 13.7 | 2.0 | 76.2 | 35.5 | 37.7 | 93.0 |
| JOPLIN-PITTSBURG | 1.0 | 1.8 | 6.3 | 6.6 | 7.2 | 7.9 | 6.4 | 26.4 | 23.0 | 13.7 | 2.4 | 75.4 | 35.2 | 37.7 | 94.2 |
| JUNEAU, AK | 2.8 | 3.4 | 6.6 | 8.0 | 9.1 | 8.7 | 6.4 | 27.0 | 27.8 | 5.8 | 0.6 | 71.0 | 31.9 | 35.9 | 103.5 |
| KANSAS CITY | 2.6 | 3.9 | 6.7 | 6.9 | 7.5 | 7.6 | 6.9 | 30.3 | 22.1 | 10.5 | 1.6 | 74.6 | 32.8 | 35.7 | 94.1 |
| KNOXVILLE | 0.5 | 1.2 | 6.1 | 6.2 | 6.4 | 6.8 | 6.6 | 29.5 | 25.0 | 12.0 | 1.5 | 77.5 | 34.6 | 37.8 | 93.3 |
| LA CROSSE-EAU CLAIRE | 0.5 | 1.1 | 6.1 | 6.7 | 7.7 | 8.9 | 7.6 | 27.3 | 21.6 | 11.9 | 2.1 | 74.8 | 32.6 | 35.7 | 96.9 |
| LAFAYETTE, IN | 1.5 | 2.7 | 6.0 | 5.7 | 5.8 | 11.3 | 15.4 | 28.0 | 18.1 | 8.4 | 1.3 | 79.4 | 27.2 | 29.3 | 102.2 |
| LAFAYETTE, LA | 1.2 | 1.8 | 7.6 | 7.8 | 8.0 | 8.7 | 7.5 | 27.5 | 21.9 | 9.8 | 1.2 | 71.5 | 30.3 | 33.3 | 92.4 |
| LAKE CHARLES, LA | 1.3 | 2.1 | 6.8 | 7.1 | 7.6 | 8.3 | 7.2 | 28.0 | 23.4 | 10.5 | 1.2 | 73.5 | 31.6 | 35.3 | 96.6 |
| LANSING | 3.1 | 4.3 | 6.4 | 6.9 | 7.3 | 8.4 | 8.5 | 30.4 | 21.5 | 9.2 | 1.3 | 75.3 | 30.9 | 33.9 | 96.0 |
| LAREDO | 93.0 | 94.9 | 10.4 | 10.1 | 9.6 | 9.4 | 8.6 | 27.8 | 16.7 | 6.6 | 0.8 | 64.1 | 25.7 | 26.2 | 95.5 |
| LAS VEGAS | 11.0 | 18.3 | 7.9 | 7.7 | 7.5 | 6.6 | 6.0 | 30.1 | 22.7 | 10.6 | 0.9 | 73.0 | 33.2 | 35.3 | 102.5 |
| LEXINGTON | 0.5 | 1.1 | 6.3 | 6.3 | 6.5 | 7.7 | 8.0 | 30.1 | 23.5 | 10.2 | 1.4 | 76.8 | 32.4 | 35.8 | 94.3 |
| LIMA | 1.1 | 1.8 | 6.7 | 7.1 | 7.6 | 7.7 | 6.7 | 29.2 | 21.3 | 11.9 | 1.8 | 74.3 | 33.0 | 35.3 | 100.2 |
| LINCOLN-HAST'GS-KRNY | 1.5 | 3.5 | 6.3 | 6.4 | 7.3 | 8.5 | 7.8 | 26.4 | 22.1 | 12.6 | 2.5 | 75.3 | 33.9 | 36.5 | 95.9 |
| LITTLE ROCK-PINE BLF | 0.7 | 2.1 | 6.8 | 6.8 | 7.2 | 7.6 | 7.0 | 27.9 | 22.9 | 12.1 | 1.7 | 74.8 | 33.8 | 36.2 | 93.4 |
| LOS ANGELES | 33.4 | 39.8 | 7.7 | 8.2 | 7.3 | 7.2 | 7.4 | 32.7 | 19.7 | 8.7 | 1.2 | 72.8 | 30.7 | 32.8 | 100.1 |
| LOUISVILLE | 0.7 | 1.3 | 6.6 | 6.7 | 6.9 | 7.1 | 6.6 | 30.0 | 23.7 | 11.1 | 1.5 | 75.7 | 33.3 | 36.7 | 93.7 |
| LUBBOCK | 28.8 | 35.0 | 8.1 | 7.9 | 7.6 | 8.8 | 8.4 | 27.7 | 19.9 | 10.1 | 1.4 | 71.7 | 29.8 | 32.0 | 98.2 |
| MACON | 0.8 | 1.7 | 7.3 | 7.2 | 7.4 | 7.7 | 7.0 | 29.8 | 22.0 | 10.3 | 1.4 | 73.6 | 32.1 | 34.6 | 92.6 |
| MADISON | 1.1 | 2.1 | 6.0 | 6.6 | 7.6 | 8.1 | 7.7 | 30.0 | 22.3 | 10.3 | 1.6 | 75.7 | 32.2 | 35.6 | 97.1 |
| MANKATO | 1.1 | 2.1 | 5.8 | 6.3 | 7.5 | 9.5 | 9.7 | 24.8 | 20.7 | 13.2 | 2.6 | 76.0 | 32.4 | 35.4 | 97.1 |
| MARQUETTE | 0.5 | 1.0 | 5.7 | 6.5 | 7.0 | 8.2 | 7.4 | 27.0 | 22.2 | 13.7 | 2.2 | 76.5 | 34.2 | 37.1 | 102.6 |
| MEDFORD-KLAMATH FLS. | 4.2 | 6.9 | 6.1 | 6.5 | 7.1 | 7.2 | 5.5 | 24.7 | 26.1 | 14.8 | 2.0 | 75.8 | 37.3 | 40.4 | 97.9 |
| MEMPHIS | 0.7 | 1.5 | 7.6 | 7.6 | 7.6 | 7.7 | 7.2 | 29.7 | 21.5 | 9.7 | 1.4 | 72.8 | 31.5 | 33.9 | 91.2 |
| MERIDIAN | 0.5 | 0.9 | 7.1 | 7.2 | 7.2 | 8.3 | 7.5 | 27.6 | 21.7 | 11.6 | 1.9 | 73.8 | 32.1 | 34.7 | 90.2 |
| MIAMI-FT. LAUDERDALE | 32.8 | 38.8 | 6.6 | 6.8 | 7.0 | 6.4 | 5.9 | 29.4 | 22.5 | 13.2 | 2.1 | 75.9 | 35.7 | 37.7 | 93.0 |
| MILWAUKEE | 3.5 | 5.1 | 6.2 | 6.7 | 7.8 | 7.7 | 6.5 | 29.9 | 22.4 | 11.1 | 1.7 | 74.8 | 32.9 | 36.2 | 95.1 |
| MINNEAPOLIS-ST. PAUL | 1.3 | 2.3 | 6.7 | 7.1 | 8.1 | 7.9 | 6.6 | 30.6 | 21.8 | 9.7 | 1.6 | 73.5 | 32.0 | 35.3 | 97.3 |
| MINOT-BISMK.-DICK'SN | 0.7 | 1.3 | 6.3 | 6.7 | 8.0 | 8.4 | 6.2 | 25.9 | 23.2 | 13.0 | 2.3 | 73.5 | 33.1 | 37.4 | 97.7 |
| MISSOULA | 1.3 | 1.9 | 5.6 | 6.2 | 7.6 | 8.5 | 7.1 | 25.7 | 26.7 | 11.0 | 1.7 | 75.5 | 34.1 | 38.6 | 98.6 |
| MOBILE-PENSACOLA | 1.4 | 2.5 | 7.1 | 7.3 | 7.2 | 7.2 | 6.9 | 29.3 | 22.4 | 11.3 | 1.3 | 74.2 | 32.3 | 35.4 | 94.3 |
| MONROE-EL DORADO | 0.8 | 1.3 | 6.8 | 7.0 | 7.6 | 9.1 | 8.4 | 25.2 | 22.5 | 11.6 | 1.7 | 73.4 | 31.5 | 34.6 | 90.6 |
| MONTEREY-SALINAS | 29.4 | 37.2 | 7.5 | 8.4 | 7.0 | 7.5 | 7.6 | 32.0 | 19.0 | 9.5 | 1.4 | 73.1 | 30.9 | 32.9 | 103.8 |
| MONTGOMERY | 0.5 | 1.0 | 7.0 | 7.1 | 7.0 | 7.8 | 7.3 | 29.0 | 22.0 | 11.2 | 1.6 | 74.4 | 32.2 | 34.8 | 90.9 |
| NASHVILLE | 0.9 | 1.9 | 6.9 | 6.8 | 6.8 | 7.0 | 7.1 | 30.7 | 23.2 | 10.2 | 1.4 | 75.5 | 32.9 | 35.7 | 95.0 |
| NEW ORLEANS | 3.5 | 4.5 | 7.0 | 7.1 | 7.5 | 8.2 | 7.2 | 28.9 | 22.7 | 10.3 | 1.2 | 73.6 | 31.5 | 35.1 | 91.9 |
| NEW YORK | 15.1 | 18.3 | 6.6 | 7.0 | 6.8 | 6.1 | 5.9 | 31.2 | 23.1 | 11.6 | 1.7 | 76.1 | 34.4 | 37.0 | 92.6 |
| NORFOLK-P'MTH-N.NEWS | 2.1 | 3.2 | 7.6 | 7.5 | 7.2 | 7.0 | 7.8 | 32.4 | 19.7 | 9.7 | 1.1 | 74.0 | 30.3 | 33.2 | 96.3 |
| NORTH PLATTE | 4.5 | 9.2 | 6.5 | 6.9 | 8.2 | 8.7 | 6.0 | 24.8 | 23.8 | 13.0 | 2.1 | 72.7 | 34.9 | 37.7 | 95.9 |
| ODESSA-MIDLAND | 32.9 | 38.7 | 8.9 | 8.7 | 8.3 | 8.4 | 6.5 | 26.8 | 21.3 | 9.9 | 1.2 | 68.9 | 30.8 | 32.7 | 97.4 |
| OKLAHOMA CITY | 3.2 | 5.1 | 6.9 | 6.9 | 7.4 | 8.1 | 7.7 | 27.9 | 22.5 | 11.0 | 1.7 | 74.4 | 32.7 | 35.3 | 95.4 |
| OMAHA | 2.0 | 4.4 | 6.9 | 7.1 | 7.9 | 7.8 | 6.5 | 28.7 | 22.1 | 11.1 | 1.9 | 73.4 | 32.8 | 35.8 | 95.1 |
| ORLANDO-D.BEACH-MEL. | 6.0 | 9.2 | 6.3 | 6.8 | 6.9 | 6.4 | 5.9 | 28.4 | 22.2 | 15.3 | 1.8 | 76.3 | 35.2 | 38.2 | 95.7 |
| OTTUMWA-KIRKSVILLE | 0.6 | 1.3 | 5.6 | 6.0 | 6.9 | 8.5 | 7.3 | 25.9 | 23.0 | 14.0 | 2.7 | 77.4 | 35.9 | 38.3 | 93.1 |
| PADUC-CG-HARR-MTVERN | 0.6 | 1.2 | 6.0 | 6.4 | 6.6 | 7.5 | 7.3 | 27.2 | 23.5 | 13.4 | 2.2 | 77.0 | 35.1 | 37.7 | 95.7 |
| PALM SPRINGS | 26.3 | 34.1 | 8.5 | 9.1 | 7.8 | 7.1 | 6.3 | 29.5 | 18.1 | 12.0 | 1.6 | 70.5 | 31.5 | 33.1 | 99.5 |
| PANAMA CITY | 1.6 | 2.8 | 6.2 | 6.9 | 7.4 | 7.1 | 6.2 | 27.8 | 23.5 | 13.4 | 1.5 | 75.3 | 34.4 | 37.4 | 101.7 |
| PARKERSBURG, WV | 0.3 | 0.8 | 5.7 | 6.2 | 6.4 | 6.9 | 6.4 | 27.6 | 26.0 | 12.9 | 1.9 | 77.4 | 35.4 | 39.3 | 91.8 |
| PEORIA-BLOOMINGTON | 1.1 | 2.0 | 6.4 | 7.0 | 6.9 | 7.9 | 7.9 | 28.0 | 22.2 | 11.8 | 2.0 | 75.6 | 33.3 | 35.9 | 94.7 |
| PHILADELPHIA | 4.1 | 5.8 | 6.4 | 7.0 | 7.3 | 6.7 | 6.0 | 30.3 | 22.2 | 12.4 | 1.8 | 75.6 | 33.9 | 36.9 | 92.7 |
| PHOENIX | 15.8 | 19.9 | 8.1 | 7.9 | 7.6 | 7.2 | 6.6 | 28.2 | 21.4 | 11.6 | 1.4 | 72.3 | 32.3 | 34.9 | 98.1 |
| PITTSBURGH | 0.5 | 1.1 | 5.4 | 6.1 | 6.7 | 6.9 | 6.0 | 28.0 | 23.6 | 15.2 | 2.1 | 78.2 | 36.3 | 39.6 | 91.2 |
| PORTLAND, OR | 3.8 | 6.5 | 6.7 | 6.8 | 7.3 | 7.3 | 6.5 | 28.9 | 24.3 | 10.4 | 1.7 | 74.8 | 34.1 | 36.6 | 97.5 |
| PORTLAND-AUBURN | 0.6 | 1.1 | 5.2 | 6.1 | 7.3 | 7.0 | 5.8 | 30.7 | 23.8 | 12.3 | 1.8 | 77.4 | 34.1 | 38.2 | 94.6 |
| PRESQUE ISLE | 0.6 | 1.1 | 5.0 | 5.7 | 7.1 | 6.9 | 6.7 | 29.8 | 23.2 | 13.6 | 1.9 | 78.1 | 33.3 | 38.1 | 100.5 |
| PROVIDENCE-N.BEDFORD | 3.9 | 6.1 | 6.3 | 7.1 | 7.3 | 6.3 | 5.6 | 30.9 | 21.3 | 13.2 | 2.1 | 76.2 | 33.9 | 36.8 | 92.6 |
| QUINCY-HAN'BL-KEOKUK | 0.7 | 1.4 | 6.1 | 6.7 | 6.9 | 8.1 | 7.2 | 25.9 | 22.5 | 13.8 | 2.8 | 76.0 | 35.1 | 37.5 | 96.1 |
| UNITED STATES | 9.0 | 11.8 | 6.9 | 7.2 | 7.2 | 7.2 | 6.7 | 29.9 | 22.2 | 11.1 | 1.6 | 74.6 | 32.9 | 35.7 | 95.6 |

# HOUSEHOLDS

## DMA AND U.S. TOTALS

C

| DMA | HOUSEHOLDS | | | | | FAMILIES | | | MEDIAN HOUSEHOLD INCOME | | |
|---|---|---|---|---|---|---|---|---|---|---|---|
| | 1990 | 2000 | 2005 | % Annual Rate 1990-2000 | 2000 Average HH Size | 1990 | 2000 | % Annual Rate 1990-2000 | 2000 | 2005 | 2000 National Rank |
| GR'NSBORO-H.PT-W.SLM | 528,540 | 595,552 | 627,804 | 1.5 | 2.47 | 378,803 | 413,510 | 1.1 | 37,252 | 42,234 | 91 |
| GREENVL.-N.BERN-WAS. | 223,705 | 244,550 | 252,380 | 1.1 | 2.60 | 164,587 | 173,449 | 0.6 | 32,482 | 37,869 | 167 |
| GRNVL-SPR'BG-ASH-AND | 651,790 | 760,376 | 816,047 | 1.9 | 2.46 | 477,554 | 540,575 | 1.5 | 36,781 | 41,802 | 101 |
| GREENWOOD-GREENVILLE | 79,928 | 79,426 | 77,880 | -0.1 | 2.81 | 58,440 | 56,442 | -0.4 | 24,506 | 27,883 | 208 |
| HARLIN-W'LCO-B'VL-MC | 192,137 | 268,094 | 301,474 | 4.1 | 3.55 | 161,435 | 224,439 | 4.1 | 23,826 | 27,222 | 210 |
| HARRISBG-LAN-LEB-YRK | 559,337 | 615,330 | 637,128 | 1.2 | 2.56 | 404,787 | 432,891 | 0.8 | 44,196 | 51,213 | 31 |
| HARRISONBURG, VA | 70,902 | 79,210 | 82,348 | 1.4 | 2.50 | 51,072 | 55,263 | 1.0 | 35,008 | 39,257 | 128 |
| HARTFORD & NEW HAVEN | 925,468 | 932,633 | 944,068 | 0.1 | 2.54 | 645,462 | 627,234 | -0.4 | 50,677 | 59,589 | 9 |
| HATTIESBURG-LAUREL | 90,051 | 100,869 | 106,696 | 1.4 | 2.64 | 66,430 | 72,293 | 1.0 | 28,813 | 33,369 | 198 |
| HELENA | 18,649 | 21,949 | 23,014 | 2.0 | 2.41 | 12,610 | 14,289 | 1.5 | 37,169 | 42,641 | 92 |
| HONOLULU | 356,267 | 407,716 | 419,968 | 1.7 | 2.81 | 263,456 | 299,285 | 1.6 | 50,350 | 59,490 | 10 |
| HOUSTON | 1,440,940 | 1,772,097 | 1,947,082 | 2.5 | 2.74 | 1,017,495 | 1,232,227 | 2.4 | 42,487 | 49,155 | 43 |
| HUNTSVILLE-DECATUR | 299,583 | 348,245 | 367,480 | 1.8 | 2.49 | 224,031 | 252,356 | 1.5 | 38,923 | 43,441 | 78 |
| IDAHO FLS.-POCATELLO | 93,403 | 108,496 | 113,612 | 1.8 | 2.94 | 70,051 | 79,011 | 1.5 | 39,279 | 46,035 | 74 |
| INDIANAPOLIS | 880,387 | 975,471 | 1,017,155 | 1.3 | 2.51 | 619,277 | 667,769 | 0.9 | 43,109 | 49,448 | 38 |
| JACKSON, MS | 286,563 | 313,354 | 325,537 | 1.1 | 2.66 | 210,195 | 223,379 | 0.7 | 32,000 | 37,335 | 176 |
| JACKSON, TN | 57,589 | 65,951 | 70,306 | 1.7 | 2.49 | 42,413 | 47,185 | 1.3 | 34,701 | 39,683 | 131 |
| JACKSONVILLE,BRUNSWK | 452,786 | 537,185 | 573,270 | 2.1 | 2.60 | 321,951 | 371,002 | 1.7 | 40,862 | 48,028 | 59 |
| JOHNSTOWN-ALTOONA | 283,008 | 288,345 | 287,252 | 0.2 | 2.50 | 200,795 | 197,015 | -0.2 | 31,823 | 35,877 | 179 |
| JONESBORO | 74,707 | 85,017 | 89,258 | 1.6 | 2.44 | 54,812 | 60,334 | 1.2 | 27,583 | 32,384 | 203 |
| JOPLIN-PITTSBURG | 139,977 | 149,688 | 153,182 | 0.8 | 2.45 | 97,598 | 100,810 | 0.4 | 30,001 | 34,547 | 194 |
| JUNEAU, AK | 9,902 | 11,309 | 11,570 | 1.6 | 2.62 | 6,628 | 7,193 | 1.0 | 69,036 | 85,789 | 1 |
| KANSAS CITY | 743,580 | 829,733 | 872,316 | 1.3 | 2.54 | 513,135 | 556,107 | 1.0 | 43,038 | 49,956 | 39 |
| KNOXVILLE | 397,248 | 465,007 | 492,681 | 1.9 | 2.48 | 292,152 | 333,027 | 1.6 | 33,926 | 38,583 | 142 |
| LA CROSSE-EAU CLAIRE | 171,437 | 184,585 | 189,720 | 0.9 | 2.56 | 118,661 | 123,801 | 0.5 | 37,099 | 43,193 | 94 |
| LAFAYETTE, IN | 48,633 | 53,533 | 55,420 | 1.2 | 2.50 | 31,120 | 32,993 | 0.7 | 41,925 | 49,132 | 46 |
| LAFAYETTE, LA | 184,880 | 211,420 | 223,831 | 1.6 | 2.67 | 137,914 | 152,984 | 1.3 | 27,999 | 31,129 | 202 |
| LAKE CHARLES, LA | 80,923 | 90,443 | 94,437 | 1.4 | 2.64 | 61,069 | 66,582 | 1.1 | 33,994 | 37,499 | 140 |
| LANSING | 226,184 | 244,787 | 251,778 | 1.0 | 2.56 | 156,690 | 164,765 | 0.6 | 42,956 | 50,331 | 40 |
| LAREDO | 37,300 | 55,755 | 64,443 | 5.0 | 3.75 | 31,837 | 47,846 | 5.1 | 30,166 | 37,432 | 191 |
| LAS VEGAS | 295,014 | 506,911 | 618,559 | 6.8 | 2.56 | 194,284 | 332,418 | 6.7 | 46,206 | 55,347 | 22 |
| LEXINGTON | 373,759 | 426,417 | 452,238 | 1.6 | 2.55 | 274,572 | 303,468 | 1.2 | 32,300 | 37,064 | 173 |
| LIMA | 39,408 | 38,587 | 38,084 | -0.3 | 2.61 | 28,973 | 27,432 | -0.7 | 35,593 | 40,162 | 113 |
| LINCOLN-HAST'GS-KRNY | 250,514 | 261,289 | 263,777 | 0.5 | 2.46 | 169,805 | 170,647 | 0.1 | 35,557 | 41,018 | 114 |
| LITTLE ROCK-PINE BLF | 454,869 | 499,446 | 517,301 | 1.1 | 2.51 | 329,904 | 351,930 | 0.8 | 31,619 | 36,885 | 180 |
| LOS ANGELES | 4,506,218 | 4,999,092 | 5,326,383 | 1.3 | 2.89 | 3,118,614 | 3,417,022 | 1.1 | 46,598 | 57,877 | 20 |
| LOUISVILLE | 529,274 | 583,668 | 612,134 | 1.2 | 2.56 | 384,280 | 413,240 | 0.9 | 38,974 | 44,036 | 77 |
| LUBBOCK | 145,984 | 148,811 | 147,478 | 0.2 | 2.65 | 105,162 | 104,504 | -0.1 | 32,506 | 37,403 | 165 |
| MACON | 190,119 | 215,255 | 226,120 | 1.5 | 2.61 | 139,822 | 154,281 | 1.2 | 35,491 | 40,039 | 117 |
| MADISON | 291,290 | 338,627 | 355,998 | 1.8 | 2.50 | 194,194 | 218,046 | 1.4 | 46,015 | 54,194 | 24 |
| MANKATO | 47,718 | 47,298 | 46,763 | -0.1 | 2.50 | 31,784 | 30,149 | -0.6 | 38,365 | 44,436 | 84 |
| MARQUETTE | 85,295 | 85,219 | 85,291 | 0.0 | 2.43 | 58,907 | 56,693 | -0.5 | 32,719 | 36,606 | 158 |
| MEDFORD-KLAMATH FLS. | 136,753 | 160,641 | 169,392 | 2.0 | 2.44 | 96,482 | 109,399 | 1.5 | 32,761 | 37,162 | 157 |
| MEMPHIS | 586,534 | 645,436 | 675,960 | 1.2 | 2.63 | 424,843 | 456,673 | 0.9 | 34,491 | 39,678 | 134 |
| MERIDIAN | 65,690 | 69,765 | 70,914 | 0.7 | 2.59 | 48,014 | 49,354 | 0.3 | 28,828 | 33,085 | 197 |
| MIAMI-FT. LAUDERDALE | 1,254,380 | 1,469,460 | 1,567,181 | 1.9 | 2.58 | 836,883 | 961,204 | 1.7 | 37,364 | 44,646 | 90 |
| MILWAUKEE | 765,571 | 813,133 | 831,497 | 0.7 | 2.58 | 535,360 | 554,985 | 0.4 | 47,699 | 54,455 | 18 |
| MINNEAPOLIS-ST. PAUL | 1,341,770 | 1,523,507 | 1,616,218 | 1.6 | 2.59 | 921,130 | 1,024,542 | 1.3 | 50,060 | 57,710 | 12 |
| MINOT-BISMK.-DICK'SN | 134,829 | 137,474 | 137,510 | 0.2 | 2.51 | 96,897 | 95,502 | -0.2 | 30,797 | 35,998 | 185 |
| MISSOULA | 76,858 | 97,523 | 104,014 | 2.9 | 2.44 | 52,952 | 64,925 | 2.5 | 32,390 | 36,175 | 169 |
| MOBILE-PENSACOLA | 406,655 | 475,055 | 500,211 | 1.9 | 2.62 | 300,808 | 341,583 | 1.6 | 35,961 | 41,162 | 108 |
| MONROE-EL DORADO | 170,063 | 177,014 | 178,506 | 0.5 | 2.62 | 124,628 | 125,875 | 0.1 | 27,542 | 31,634 | 204 |
| MONTEREY-SALINAS | 207,953 | 231,778 | 249,329 | 1.3 | 2.81 | 145,846 | 158,967 | 1.1 | 48,047 | 60,442 | 16 |
| MONTGOMERY | 212,334 | 231,058 | 237,048 | 1.0 | 2.60 | 153,466 | 162,137 | 0.7 | 32,605 | 37,540 | 162 |
| NASHVILLE | 693,735 | 847,080 | 915,178 | 2.5 | 2.51 | 505,936 | 604,302 | 2.2 | 40,321 | 46,621 | 63 |
| NEW ORLEANS | 601,210 | 653,060 | 675,722 | 1.0 | 2.61 | 428,391 | 453,802 | 0.7 | 32,994 | 37,049 | 155 |
| NEW YORK | 6,790,358 | 7,137,005 | 7,346,290 | 0.6 | 2.65 | 4,674,647 | 4,808,608 | 0.3 | 50,290 | 59,399 | 11 |
| NORFOLK-P'MTH-N.NEWS | 583,732 | 661,176 | 691,569 | 1.5 | 2.60 | 424,065 | 468,569 | 1.2 | 38,892 | 45,459 | 81 |
| NORTH PLATTE | 14,311 | 14,673 | 14,993 | 0.3 | 2.55 | 10,105 | 10,019 | -0.1 | 35,021 | 38,194 | 127 |
| ODESSA-MIDLAND | 127,817 | 136,909 | 139,510 | 0.8 | 2.69 | 95,830 | 99,721 | 0.5 | 35,235 | 41,961 | 120 |
| OKLAHOMA CITY | 570,309 | 609,713 | 626,621 | 0.8 | 2.52 | 397,532 | 411,142 | 0.4 | 34,451 | 40,564 | 135 |
| OMAHA | 349,110 | 376,845 | 389,357 | 0.9 | 2.56 | 243,942 | 255,374 | 0.6 | 40,443 | 46,457 | 61 |
| ORLANDO-D.BEACH-MEL. | 882,232 | 1,103,372 | 1,208,255 | 2.8 | 2.50 | 614,987 | 745,221 | 2.4 | 39,306 | 47,283 | 73 |
| OTTUMWA-KIRKSVILLE | 48,743 | 49,762 | 49,986 | 0.3 | 2.38 | 33,208 | 32,591 | -0.2 | 28,631 | 32,719 | 200 |
| PADUC-CG-HARR-MTVERN | 359,314 | 375,938 | 381,052 | 0.6 | 2.43 | 253,487 | 256,170 | 0.1 | 30,164 | 34,289 | 192 |
| PALM SPRINGS | 402,067 | 538,585 | 611,949 | 3.6 | 2.87 | 296,028 | 384,683 | 3.2 | 43,898 | 54,441 | 32 |
| PANAMA CITY | 100,391 | 116,626 | 121,507 | 1.8 | 2.56 | 73,297 | 81,850 | 1.4 | 32,718 | 38,507 | 159 |
| PARKERSBURG, WV | 60,573 | 62,891 | 62,981 | 0.5 | 2.44 | 44,461 | 44,634 | 0.1 | 33,635 | 36,936 | 145 |
| PEORIA-BLOOMINGTON | 220,747 | 231,791 | 236,308 | 0.6 | 2.53 | 154,312 | 155,759 | 0.1 | 42,953 | 49,230 | 41 |
| PHILADELPHIA | 2,623,504 | 2,731,957 | 2,782,381 | 0.5 | 2.60 | 1,840,309 | 1,857,694 | 0.1 | 47,967 | 56,059 | 17 |
| PHOENIX | 1,011,925 | 1,415,679 | 1,616,277 | 4.2 | 2.58 | 697,277 | 951,020 | 3.8 | 40,968 | 47,974 | 58 |
| PITTSBURGH | 1,145,455 | 1,143,002 | 1,127,008 | 0.0 | 2.42 | 797,715 | 768,012 | -0.5 | 35,551 | 38,912 | 115 |
| PORTLAND, OR | 851,938 | 1,049,820 | 1,130,841 | 2.6 | 2.52 | 579,926 | 694,853 | 2.2 | 43,465 | 50,805 | 36 |
| PORTLAND-AUBURN | 338,053 | 369,288 | 388,655 | 1.1 | 2.43 | 236,327 | 249,904 | 0.7 | 39,814 | 46,499 | 69 |
| PRESQUE ISLE | 31,366 | 29,124 | 28,417 | -0.9 | 2.41 | 23,439 | 21,188 | -1.2 | 28,285 | 32,861 | 201 |
| PROVIDENCE-N.BEDFORD | 565,645 | 576,852 | 588,717 | 0.2 | 2.54 | 394,542 | 389,015 | -0.2 | 42,221 | 50,953 | 44 |
| QUINCY-HAN'BL-KEOKUK | 111,122 | 111,719 | 110,959 | 0.1 | 2.46 | 77,295 | 74,896 | -0.4 | 32,597 | 37,764 | 163 |
| UNITED STATES | | | | 1.4 | 2.59 | | | 1.1 | 41,914 | 49,127 | |

# INCOME

## DMA AND U.S. TOTALS



| DMA | 2000 Per Capita Income | 2000 HH Income Base | 2000 HOUSEHOLD INCOME DISTRIBUTION (%) Less than $15,000 | $15,000 to $24,999 | $25,000 to $49,999 | $50,000 to $99,999 | $100,000 to $149,999 | $150,000 or More | 2000 AVERAGE DISPOSABLE INCOME BY AGE OF HOUSEHOLDER All Ages | <35 | 35-44 | 45-54 | 55-64 | 65+ |
|---|---|---|---|---|---|---|---|---|---|---|---|---|---|---|
| GR'NSBORO-H.PT-W.SLM | 19,814 | 595,551 | 15.7 | 14.5 | 36.0 | 26.4 | 5.2 | 2.2 | 35,817 | 31,418 | 41,277 | 44,403 | 37,238 | 22,973 |
| GREENVL.-N.BERN-WAS. | 16,126 | 244,550 | 19.9 | 17.1 | 35.7 | 22.6 | 3.5 | 1.2 | 31,305 | 27,021 | 36,440 | 40,032 | 33,305 | 21,972 |
| GRNVL-SPR'BG-ASH-AND | 19,043 | 760,374 | 16.7 | 14.3 | 36.2 | 26.2 | 5.0 | 1.7 | 34,774 | 31,457 | 39,961 | 43,162 | 36,111 | 23,108 |
| GREENWOOD-GREENVILLE | 13,086 | 79,425 | 33.5 | 17.2 | 28.8 | 15.7 | 3.1 | 1.6 | 28,068 | 23,767 | 32,977 | 34,389 | 28,781 | 18,239 |
| HARLIN-W'LCO-B'VL-MC | 9,912 | 268,094 | 32.7 | 19.1 | 28.5 | 15.9 | 2.7 | 1.1 | 27,477 | 23,343 | 29,989 | 31,431 | 29,578 | 22,885 |
| HARRISBG-LAN-LEB-YRK | 20,917 | 615,321 | 9.9 | 11.2 | 37.0 | 33.7 | 6.5 | 1.8 | 39,154 | 35,853 | 43,688 | 49,265 | 42,712 | 25,183 |
| HARRISONBURG, VA | 16,602 | 79,210 | 16.0 | 16.2 | 39.2 | 24.3 | 3.2 | 1.1 | 32,364 | 27,653 | 37,374 | 40,702 | 33,646 | 23,069 |
| HARTFORD & NEW HAVEN | 25,573 | 932,627 | 10.7 | 8.6 | 29.7 | 37.4 | 9.4 | 4.1 | 44,306 | 38,696 | 47,203 | 55,016 | 49,254 | 28,017 |
| HATTIESBURG-LAUREL | 15,382 | 100,867 | 25.6 | 18.0 | 31.5 | 19.5 | 3.7 | 1.6 | 31,039 | 26,628 | 36,123 | 38,721 | 31,560 | 20,104 |
| HELENA | 17,877 | 21,949 | 15.5 | 14.5 | 37.8 | 27.6 | 3.8 | 0.9 | 32,863 | 24,921 | 36,785 | 41,276 | 34,711 | 24,822 |
| HONOLULU | 23,534 | 407,713 | 9.1 | 10.7 | 29.7 | 36.1 | 9.9 | 4.4 | 42,024 | 31,905 | 41,983 | 50,720 | 48,703 | 35,728 |
| HOUSTON | 21,901 | 1,772,092 | 14.3 | 12.7 | 31.0 | 30.2 | 8.0 | 3.9 | 44,313 | 34,975 | 47,877 | 51,981 | 46,584 | 30,385 |
| HUNTSVILLE-DECATUR | 20,166 | 348,229 | 16.7 | 13.3 | 33.6 | 28.4 | 6.0 | 2.0 | 38,126 | 34,215 | 43,985 | 48,082 | 40,136 | 23,247 |
| IDAHO FLS.-POCATELLO | 16,673 | 108,487 | 13.2 | 13.9 | 37.5 | 29.0 | 5.0 | 1.5 | 36,377 | 29,626 | 41,636 | 45,585 | 39,107 | 24,606 |
| INDIANAPOLIS | 22,602 | 975,461 | 12.5 | 12.3 | 33.5 | 31.6 | 7.1 | 3.1 | 41,499 | 34,567 | 46,223 | 51,983 | 44,300 | 26,467 |
| JACKSON, MS | 16,484 | 313,353 | 24.1 | 15.7 | 30.9 | 22.7 | 4.7 | 2.0 | 33,729 | 29,862 | 38,421 | 41,215 | 33,201 | 21,714 |
| JACKSON, TN | 18,049 | 65,951 | 18.3 | 15.8 | 35.5 | 24.1 | 4.8 | 1.6 | 35,919 | 33,210 | 41,885 | 46,529 | 36,217 | 21,873 |
| JACKSONVILLE,BRUNSWK | 20,631 | 537,180 | 13.4 | 13.3 | 34.6 | 30.0 | 6.3 | 2.4 | 40,557 | 34,656 | 44,530 | 49,232 | 43,217 | 29,005 |
| JOHNSTOWN-ALTOONA | 15,727 | 288,325 | 19.6 | 17.6 | 37.4 | 21.3 | 3.0 | 1.0 | 29,886 | 26,747 | 35,704 | 38,663 | 33,398 | 19,654 |
| JONESBORO | 14,516 | 85,017 | 25.2 | 19.7 | 34.6 | 17.5 | 2.3 | 0.8 | 27,561 | 25,121 | 34,640 | 35,229 | 29,019 | 18,119 |
| JOPLIN-PITTSBURG | 15,319 | 149,688 | 21.6 | 19.2 | 36.2 | 19.4 | 2.8 | 0.8 | 29,142 | 26,158 | 34,806 | 37,108 | 31,656 | 19,535 |
| JUNEAU, AK | 30,802 | 11,309 | 4.2 | 6.1 | 20.1 | 44.4 | 18.8 | 6.5 | 61,026 | 44,953 | 61,166 | 74,096 | 63,301 | 38,430 |
| KANSAS CITY | 21,928 | 829,693 | 12.8 | 12.1 | 33.4 | 31.7 | 7.3 | 2.9 | 40,920 | 33,871 | 46,007 | 51,312 | 43,024 | 26,813 |
| KNOXVILLE | 18,586 | 465,005 | 19.7 | 16.0 | 33.8 | 23.8 | 4.6 | 2.1 | 36,249 | 30,939 | 41,841 | 44,343 | 38,115 | 23,915 |
| LA CROSSE-EAU CLAIRE | 17,742 | 184,571 | 15.3 | 14.2 | 38.2 | 26.1 | 4.8 | 1.4 | 31,962 | 27,684 | 37,883 | 41,841 | 35,302 | 19,908 |
| LAFAYETTE, IN | 21,059 | 53,533 | 12.2 | 13.4 | 34.0 | 29.6 | 7.5 | 3.3 | 41,243 | 29,432 | 48,451 | 54,237 | 47,983 | 30,474 |
| LAFAYETTE, LA | 14,546 | 211,410 | 28.4 | 16.6 | 31.6 | 18.3 | 3.5 | 1.6 | 30,900 | 26,628 | 36,283 | 36,693 | 30,722 | 20,832 |
| LAKE CHARLES, LA | 16,346 | 90,443 | 22.1 | 15.0 | 33.3 | 23.7 | 4.4 | 1.5 | 34,365 | 28,883 | 39,995 | 43,064 | 34,449 | 22,945 |
| LANSING | 20,846 | 244,787 | 13.0 | 11.6 | 33.9 | 32.0 | 7.0 | 2.5 | 38,963 | 30,971 | 44,049 | 51,172 | 44,761 | 24,511 |
| LAREDO | 11,444 | 55,755 | 25.3 | 16.9 | 31.3 | 20.0 | 4.6 | 1.9 | 33,047 | 30,068 | 35,543 | 38,346 | 34,047 | 23,693 |
| LAS VEGAS | 24,111 | 506,910 | 9.7 | 11.5 | 33.3 | 33.9 | 8.4 | 3.2 | 45,771 | 40,293 | 49,641 | 54,183 | 47,116 | 32,406 |
| LEXINGTON | 17,514 | 426,416 | 22.4 | 15.9 | 32.8 | 22.1 | 4.7 | 2.1 | 33,436 | 28,288 | 39,820 | 40,018 | 32,735 | 21,836 |
| LIMA | 15,902 | 38,586 | 17.9 | 15.4 | 37.4 | 24.9 | 3.5 | 1.0 | 32,195 | 27,135 | 38,075 | 41,668 | 35,601 | 21,150 |
| LINCOLN-HAST'GS-KRNY | 17,984 | 261,279 | 15.9 | 16.0 | 37.6 | 25.0 | 4.3 | 1.2 | 33,198 | 27,990 | 39,919 | 41,653 | 36,794 | 23,291 |
| LITTLE ROCK-PINE BLF | 16,221 | 499,437 | 21.5 | 17.2 | 34.4 | 21.9 | 3.7 | 1.2 | 31,253 | 26,995 | 38,235 | 39,678 | 32,828 | 20,937 |
| LOS ANGELES | 23,506 | 4,999,072 | 12.7 | 11.1 | 29.6 | 31.9 | 9.1 | 5.6 | 45,997 | 38,930 | 47,297 | 53,186 | 49,028 | 32,840 |
| LOUISVILLE | 19,757 | 583,664 | 15.2 | 13.8 | 34.9 | 28.3 | 5.8 | 2.1 | 37,390 | 31,440 | 42,717 | 45,852 | 37,982 | 25,238 |
| LUBBOCK | 16,793 | 148,811 | 21.3 | 16.6 | 32.7 | 23.0 | 4.6 | 1.8 | 34,691 | 27,297 | 40,333 | 43,901 | 38,349 | 26,411 |
| MACON | 17,457 | 215,253 | 20.2 | 14.0 | 33.9 | 25.3 | 4.7 | 1.9 | 34,177 | 29,512 | 38,153 | 42,407 | 35,063 | 22,468 |
| MADISON | 23,234 | 338,627 | 10.2 | 10.7 | 34.1 | 33.8 | 8.3 | 2.9 | 38,960 | 32,172 | 44,148 | 49,949 | 42,781 | 25,336 |
| MANKATO | 18,178 | 47,298 | 13.7 | 14.0 | 38.7 | 27.3 | 4.9 | 1.4 | 34,086 | 28,490 | 39,499 | 44,791 | 39,206 | 24,926 |
| MARQUETTE | 16,901 | 85,218 | 19.7 | 16.6 | 37.2 | 21.6 | 3.7 | 1.1 | 30,392 | 26,779 | 37,731 | 41,675 | 34,837 | 17,956 |
| MEDFORD-KLAMATH FLS. | 17,354 | 160,641 | 19.5 | 16.7 | 37.1 | 21.7 | 3.8 | 1.3 | 29,945 | 25,931 | 34,450 | 38,408 | 32,109 | 21,082 |
| MEMPHIS | 17,486 | 645,430 | 20.9 | 15.0 | 32.7 | 24.3 | 5.1 | 2.0 | 36,074 | 31,925 | 41,322 | 45,197 | 36,127 | 21,956 |
| MERIDIAN | 15,555 | 69,763 | 26.5 | 17.3 | 32.1 | 19.5 | 3.3 | 1.3 | 30,360 | 27,957 | 36,573 | 36,926 | 29,901 | 19,653 |
| MIAMI-FT. LAUDERDALE | 21,816 | 1,469,458 | 17.4 | 14.8 | 32.0 | 25.7 | 6.3 | 3.9 | 41,469 | 35,901 | 44,413 | 47,402 | 43,334 | 30,083 |
| MILWAUKEE | 24,077 | 813,124 | 10.8 | 9.5 | 32.5 | 34.4 | 9.2 | 3.7 | 40,830 | 33,666 | 45,220 | 51,876 | 45,811 | 26,208 |
| MINNEAPOLIS-ST. PAUL | 25,944 | 1,523,506 | 9.5 | 9.2 | 31.2 | 34.9 | 10.4 | 4.8 | 45,360 | 38,178 | 49,633 | 56,213 | 48,778 | 27,380 |
| MINOT-BISMK.-DICK'SN | 14,874 | 137,474 | 21.2 | 18.6 | 36.4 | 20.3 | 2.8 | 0.7 | 29,743 | 26,064 | 35,918 | 36,966 | 31,026 | 20,885 |
| MISSOULA | 17,294 | 97,514 | 19.5 | 17.3 | 36.5 | 21.6 | 3.8 | 1.3 | 30,846 | 23,591 | 35,572 | 38,459 | 32,545 | 22,350 |
| MOBILE-PENSACOLA | 17,643 | 475,038 | 17.8 | 15.4 | 34.3 | 26.0 | 4.9 | 1.6 | 35,913 | 29,805 | 39,908 | 44,344 | 38,394 | 27,193 |
| MONROE-EL DORADO | 14,547 | 177,014 | 28.7 | 17.1 | 31.1 | 18.3 | 3.4 | 1.5 | 30,211 | 24,490 | 36,430 | 38,785 | 31,652 | 19,971 |
| MONTEREY-SALINAS | 23,741 | 231,776 | 9.4 | 10.9 | 31.5 | 33.7 | 9.5 | 5.0 | 46,164 | 38,060 | 47,832 | 55,565 | 49,868 | 35,751 |
| MONTGOMERY | 16,315 | 231,058 | 23.0 | 15.4 | 32.1 | 23.6 | 4.4 | 1.5 | 33,408 | 29,086 | 39,016 | 42,058 | 34,809 | 22,577 |
| NASHVILLE | 21,268 | 847,054 | 14.4 | 13.4 | 34.2 | 28.9 | 6.5 | 2.7 | 41,438 | 36,001 | 47,689 | 50,856 | 42,389 | 25,718 |
| NEW ORLEANS | 17,562 | 653,049 | 22.8 | 15.2 | 31.9 | 23.1 | 4.8 | 2.3 | 35,519 | 29,257 | 40,195 | 42,726 | 35,799 | 24,153 |
| NEW YORK | 28,328 | 7,136,912 | 14.0 | 9.4 | 26.3 | 32.4 | 10.7 | 7.3 | 47,264 | 40,766 | 47,950 | 53,046 | 51,098 | 31,275 |
| NORFOLK-P'MTH-N.NEWS | 18,441 | 661,163 | 13.8 | 14.5 | 36.3 | 29.0 | 5.0 | 1.5 | 35,768 | 29,676 | 39,444 | 45,005 | 39,188 | 26,899 |
| NORTH PLATTE | 17,388 | 14,673 | 19.5 | 13.9 | 37.0 | 24.5 | 3.9 | 1.2 | 32,128 | 25,548 | 39,106 | 39,976 | 36,018 | 22,318 |
| ODESSA-MIDLAND | 18,830 | 136,909 | 19.2 | 15.7 | 32.7 | 24.4 | 5.1 | 2.8 | 37,799 | 30,202 | 42,168 | 44,139 | 40,694 | 28,049 |
| OKLAHOMA CITY | 17,822 | 609,699 | 18.8 | 16.0 | 34.6 | 24.5 | 4.5 | 1.6 | 33,623 | 26,995 | 39,183 | 42,280 | 37,820 | 24,353 |
| OMAHA | 20,559 | 376,836 | 12.4 | 13.8 | 36.4 | 29.0 | 5.9 | 2.5 | 37,822 | 30,828 | 43,997 | 47,021 | 39,791 | 25,319 |
| ORLANDO-D.BEACH-MEL. | 20,319 | 1,103,357 | 12.6 | 15.0 | 35.9 | 28.8 | 5.7 | 1.9 | 39,315 | 35,713 | 44,130 | 47,729 | 42,425 | 29,241 |
| OTTUMWA-KIRKSVILLE | 15,335 | 49,762 | 23.3 | 20.0 | 35.5 | 17.4 | 2.7 | 1.0 | 27,794 | 22,942 | 33,191 | 36,818 | 30,538 | 18,966 |
| PADUC-CG-HARR-MTVERN | 16,044 | 375,932 | 24.7 | 17.0 | 33.8 | 19.8 | 3.4 | 1.4 | 30,085 | 26,172 | 36,728 | 39,080 | 31,259 | 19,343 |
| PALM SPRINGS | 20,906 | 538,583 | 13.3 | 11.8 | 32.2 | 31.7 | 7.2 | 3.8 | 42,024 | 38,138 | 45,765 | 49,900 | 45,269 | 30,628 |
| PANAMA CITY | 16,311 | 116,606 | 19.6 | 17.4 | 35.0 | 23.1 | 3.8 | 1.2 | 33,347 | 29,001 | 37,680 | 40,812 | 36,646 | 24,671 |
| PARKERSBURG, WV | 16,389 | 62,891 | 20.7 | 15.8 | 36.3 | 23.2 | 3.2 | 0.8 | 31,284 | 27,410 | 37,407 | 39,511 | 34,238 | 20,182 |
| PEORIA-BLOOMINGTON | 21,526 | 231,771 | 13.4 | 12.0 | 33.2 | 31.5 | 7.2 | 2.7 | 39,460 | 32,627 | 45,353 | 50,745 | 42,497 | 26,259 |
| PHILADELPHIA | 25,373 | 2,731,904 | 11.8 | 9.9 | 30.5 | 33.6 | 9.4 | 4.8 | 44,842 | 39,267 | 47,902 | 54,489 | 48,922 | 28,886 |
| PHOENIX | 21,159 | 1,415,616 | 13.3 | 13.8 | 33.7 | 29.7 | 6.8 | 2.7 | 40,363 | 34,687 | 45,596 | 49,565 | 41,274 | 29,672 |
| PITTSBURGH | 20,145 | 1,142,995 | 18.3 | 15.3 | 34.4 | 24.4 | 5.0 | 2.5 | 34,994 | 30,366 | 40,400 | 44,826 | 38,390 | 22,662 |
| PORTLAND, OR | 22,455 | 1,049,799 | 11.4 | 12.1 | 34.4 | 31.9 | 7.5 | 2.7 | 39,054 | 33,124 | 43,616 | 48,389 | 41,944 | 25,915 |
| PORTLAND-AUBURN | 20,095 | 369,285 | 13.5 | 13.3 | 37.4 | 28.9 | 5.2 | 1.7 | 35,329 | 32,664 | 40,915 | 42,356 | 37,291 | 23,161 |
| PRESQUE ISLE | 14,224 | 29,121 | 23.7 | 20.2 | 38.2 | 16.0 | 1.5 | 0.5 | 25,601 | 24,109 | 31,502 | 32,515 | 26,619 | 15,249 |
| PROVIDENCE-N.BEDFORD | 21,097 | 576,851 | 15.8 | 10.8 | 32.8 | 31.0 | 6.7 | 2.8 | 37,914 | 35,234 | 43,186 | 47,681 | 42,786 | 23,094 |
| QUINCY-HAN'BL-KEOKUK | 15,777 | 111,719 | 19.9 | 16.3 | 37.7 | 22.1 | 3.2 | 0.8 | 30,327 | 27,163 | 35,527 | 38,663 | 33,012 | 20,995 |
| UNITED STATES | 22,162 | | 14.5 | 12.5 | 32.3 | 29.8 | 7.4 | 3.5 | 40,748 | 34,503 | 44,969 | 49,579 | 43,409 | 27,339 |

# E

# SPENDING POTENTIAL INDEXES

## DMA AND U.S. TOTALS

| DMA | FINANCIAL SERVICES | | | | THE HOME | | | | | | ENTERTAINMENT | | | | | | PERSONAL | | | |
|---|---|---|---|---|---|---|---|---|---|---|---|---|---|---|---|---|---|---|---|---|
| | | | | | Home Improvements | | | Furnishings | | | | | | | | | | | | |
| | Auto Loan | Home Loan | Investments | Retirement Plans | Home Repair | Lawn & Garden | Remodeling | Appliances | Electronics | Furniture | Restaurants | Sporting Goods | Theater & Concerts | Toys & Hobbies | Travel | Video Rental | Apparel | Auto Aftermarket | Health Insurance | Pets & Supplies |
| GR'NSBORO-H.PT-W.SLM | 99 | 87 | 93 | 91 | 99 | 97 | 107 | 98 | 96 | 92 | 93 | 98 | 93 | 99 | 81 | 98 | 93 | 95 | 99 | 100 |
| GREENVL.-N.BERN-WAS. | 96 | 82 | 85 | 84 | 95 | 92 | 105 | 96 | 93 | 86 | 88 | 94 | 87 | 96 | 77 | 97 | 87 | 92 | 97 | 98 |
| GRNVL-SPR'BG-ASH-AND | 99 | 83 | 91 | 89 | 98 | 97 | 109 | 98 | 95 | 89 | 90 | 98 | 91 | 99 | 79 | 97 | 90 | 93 | 100 | 100 |
| GREENWOOD-GREENVILLE | 94 | 76 | 87 | 82 | 97 | 91 | 97 | 96 | 91 | 87 | 79 | 92 | 85 | 92 | 77 | 96 | 86 | 91 | 90 | 95 |
| HARLIN-W'LCO-B'VL-MC | 94 | 92 | 93 | 84 | 94 | 95 | 96 | 97 | 95 | 88 | 91 | 91 | 89 | 93 | 82 | 97 | 84 | 95 | 99 | 102 |
| HARRISBG-LAN-LEB-YRK | 100 | 89 | 95 | 93 | 92 | 91 | 98 | 98 | 96 | 95 | 96 | 100 | 96 | 102 | 90 | 99 | 98 | 95 | 102 | 102 |
| HARRISONBURG, VA | 98 | 83 | 91 | 87 | 98 | 95 | 109 | 96 | 94 | 88 | 90 | 96 | 89 | 98 | 79 | 97 | 89 | 93 | 100 | 99 |
| HARTFORD & NEW HAVEN | 101 | 103 | 105 | 103 | 97 | 97 | 92 | 100 | 100 | 105 | 105 | 103 | 105 | 104 | 101 | 100 | 108 | 101 | 102 | 103 |
| HATTIESBURG-LAUREL | 97 | 77 | 85 | 83 | 96 | 93 | 106 | 96 | 93 | 84 | 84 | 95 | 86 | 96 | 75 | 96 | 86 | 91 | 98 | 98 |
| HELENA | 99 | 94 | 94 | 94 | 101 | 99 | 105 | 100 | 99 | 99 | 97 | 92 | 91 | 94 | 87 | 94 | 96 | 96 | 98 | 94 |
| HONOLULU | 97 | 133 | 104 | 113 | 94 | 104 | 89 | 96 | 117 | 96 | 116 | 92 | 96 | 85 | 102 | 112 | 99 | 107 | 96 | 97 |
| HOUSTON | 100 | 105 | 98 | 102 | 100 | 101 | 100 | 100 | 101 | 102 | 104 | 103 | 101 | 102 | 90 | 100 | 103 | 103 | 97 | 103 |
| HUNTSVILLE-DECATUR | 99 | 88 | 93 | 93 | 99 | 98 | 107 | 98 | 97 | 93 | 94 | 100 | 94 | 100 | 82 | 98 | 94 | 96 | 100 | 101 |
| IDAHO FLS.-POCATELLO | 99 | 90 | 88 | 92 | 98 | 96 | 107 | 100 | 99 | 94 | 94 | 92 | 88 | 94 | 83 | 93 | 93 | 95 | 98 | 94 |
| INDIANAPOLIS | 99 | 95 | 96 | 97 | 100 | 98 | 102 | 99 | 97 | 97 | 99 | 99 | 100 | 100 | 95 | 102 | 96 | 100 | 100 | 100 |
| JACKSON, MS | 97 | 85 | 91 | 90 | 98 | 95 | 102 | 97 | 95 | 91 | 89 | 97 | 91 | 97 | 81 | 98 | 91 | 95 | 96 | 98 |
| JACKSON, TN | 98 | 80 | 84 | 85 | 96 | 94 | 106 | 97 | 94 | 87 | 87 | 97 | 88 | 97 | 77 | 97 | 88 | 92 | 99 | 98 |
| JACKSONVILLE,BRUNSWK | 98 | 95 | 94 | 93 | 99 | 98 | 101 | 98 | 97 | 96 | 97 | 98 | 95 | 99 | 85 | 98 | 96 | 98 | 97 | 100 |
| JOHNSTOWN-ALTOONA | 97 | 79 | 88 | 85 | 91 | 88 | 97 | 96 | 91 | 87 | 87 | 96 | 90 | 98 | 84 | 97 | 90 | 90 | 102 | 99 |
| JONESBORO | 97 | 74 | 84 | 82 | 95 | 94 | 109 | 96 | 93 | 82 | 84 | 95 | 84 | 96 | 74 | 96 | 83 | 90 | 101 | 97 |
| JOPLIN-PITTSBURG | 96 | 76 | 83 | 84 | 95 | 92 | 107 | 96 | 93 | 83 | 86 | 93 | 88 | 95 | 83 | 100 | 83 | 92 | 102 | 97 |
| JUNEAU, AK | 104 | 111 | 98 | 106 | 103 | 106 | 104 | 105 | 108 | 112 | 112 | 100 | 101 | 100 | 96 | 97 | 110 | 107 | 98 | 99 |
| KANSAS CITY | 99 | 99 | 96 | 99 | 100 | 99 | 100 | 99 | 99 | 99 | 101 | 99 | 101 | 100 | 97 | 102 | 98 | 101 | 99 | 100 |
| KNOXVILLE | 98 | 83 | 91 | 88 | 98 | 96 | 107 | 97 | 95 | 89 | 90 | 97 | 90 | 98 | 79 | 97 | 90 | 93 | 100 | 99 |
| LA CROSSE-EAU CLAIRE | 97 | 83 | 86 | 88 | 96 | 93 | 106 | 96 | 94 | 86 | 90 | 95 | 91 | 97 | 86 | 100 | 87 | 94 | 102 | 98 |
| LAFAYETTE, IN | 98 | 99 | 97 | 97 | 100 | 97 | 100 | 96 | 96 | 95 | 99 | 96 | 98 | 99 | 95 | 100 | 95 | 99 | 99 | 100 |
| LAFAYETTE, LA | 96 | 81 | 85 | 85 | 95 | 92 | 104 | 96 | 94 | 88 | 86 | 96 | 88 | 96 | 77 | 97 | 88 | 92 | 96 | 98 |
| LAKE CHARLES, LA | 97 | 83 | 89 | 86 | 97 | 94 | 105 | 97 | 94 | 89 | 88 | 95 | 89 | 97 | 79 | 97 | 89 | 93 | 97 | 98 |
| LANSING | 98 | 94 | 94 | 94 | 99 | 96 | 102 | 97 | 96 | 95 | 98 | 97 | 98 | 99 | 93 | 101 | 94 | 98 | 99 | 99 |
| LAREDO | 95 | 92 | 90 | 85 | 93 | 94 | 97 | 97 | 96 | 89 | 92 | 92 | 89 | 94 | 81 | 98 | 85 | 95 | 98 | 102 |
| LAS VEGAS | 101 | 105 | 91 | 99 | 101 | 101 | 99 | 102 | 103 | 105 | 104 | 96 | 95 | 95 | 91 | 95 | 102 | 101 | 96 | 96 |
| LEXINGTON | 98 | 82 | 89 | 88 | 97 | 95 | 107 | 97 | 95 | 88 | 89 | 97 | 89 | 98 | 78 | 97 | 89 | 93 | 100 | 99 |
| LIMA | 96 | 90 | 95 | 91 | 100 | 96 | 101 | 97 | 94 | 93 | 94 | 95 | 96 | 98 | 93 | 100 | 91 | 96 | 100 | 98 |
| LINCOLN-HAST'GS-KRNY | 97 | 85 | 88 | 90 | 96 | 94 | 103 | 96 | 94 | 87 | 91 | 95 | 92 | 97 | 88 | 100 | 88 | 95 | 102 | 98 |
| LITTLE ROCK-PINE BLF | 97 | 83 | 90 | 87 | 97 | 95 | 106 | 97 | 94 | 88 | 89 | 96 | 89 | 97 | 79 | 97 | 89 | 93 | 99 | 99 |
| LOS ANGELES | 101 | 123 | 108 | 112 | 107 | 109 | 97 | 104 | 109 | 109 | 111 | 98 | 103 | 95 | 104 | 97 | 108 | 109 | 98 | 99 |
| LOUISVILLE | 98 | 90 | 97 | 93 | 101 | 99 | 104 | 98 | 96 | 94 | 95 | 98 | 95 | 99 | 84 | 98 | 94 | 96 | 99 | 100 |
| LUBBOCK | 97 | 92 | 94 | 90 | 97 | 96 | 100 | 97 | 95 | 91 | 94 | 95 | 92 | 97 | 82 | 97 | 91 | 96 | 99 | 100 |
| MACON | 97 | 85 | 90 | 88 | 98 | 95 | 103 | 97 | 95 | 91 | 89 | 97 | 91 | 97 | 80 | 98 | 91 | 94 | 96 | 99 |
| MADISON | 99 | 94 | 93 | 96 | 98 | 97 | 103 | 97 | 97 | 94 | 98 | 98 | 98 | 100 | 93 | 101 | 94 | 99 | 101 | 100 |
| MANKATO | 97 | 80 | 87 | 87 | 95 | 93 | 105 | 95 | 92 | 83 | 88 | 94 | 89 | 96 | 85 | 99 | 85 | 93 | 102 | 97 |
| MARQUETTE | 96 | 79 | 84 | 85 | 96 | 93 | 107 | 95 | 92 | 84 | 87 | 93 | 89 | 95 | 85 | 100 | 84 | 92 | 102 | 97 |
| MEDFORD-KLAMATH FLS. | 98 | 82 | 90 | 88 | 99 | 97 | 108 | 99 | 96 | 90 | 88 | 89 | 85 | 91 | 81 | 92 | 88 | 92 | 100 | 93 |
| MEMPHIS | 97 | 88 | 91 | 91 | 98 | 96 | 101 | 98 | 96 | 93 | 91 | 98 | 93 | 97 | 82 | 98 | 93 | 96 | 95 | 99 |
| MERIDIAN | 96 | 74 | 83 | 81 | 96 | 92 | 107 | 96 | 92 | 83 | 82 | 94 | 85 | 95 | 74 | 96 | 84 | 90 | 98 | 97 |
| MIAMI-FT. LAUDERDALE | 99 | 105 | 106 | 100 | 106 | 105 | 100 | 99 | 96 | 106 | 101 | 101 | 101 | 98 | 97 | 100 | 101 | 102 | 98 | 99 |
| MILWAUKEE | 99 | 100 | 102 | 100 | 103 | 101 | 100 | 99 | 98 | 100 | 101 | 99 | 103 | 100 | 100 | 102 | 98 | 101 | 100 | 100 |
| MINNEAPOLIS-ST. PAUL | 100 | 100 | 95 | 100 | 99 | 99 | 102 | 99 | 100 | 99 | 103 | 101 | 102 | 101 | 97 | 103 | 99 | 102 | 101 | 102 |
| MINOT-BISMK.-DICK'SN | 97 | 82 | 82 | 86 | 94 | 92 | 103 | 96 | 94 | 86 | 89 | 95 | 90 | 96 | 85 | 101 | 86 | 94 | 101 | 97 |
| MISSOULA | 98 | 83 | 85 | 87 | 97 | 95 | 110 | 99 | 97 | 90 | 89 | 89 | 84 | 91 | 80 | 93 | 88 | 92 | 98 | 93 |
| MOBILE-PENSACOLA | 98 | 89 | 92 | 90 | 99 | 97 | 103 | 98 | 96 | 93 | 93 | 98 | 93 | 99 | 82 | 98 | 93 | 96 | 98 | 100 |
| MONROE-EL DORADO | 96 | 76 | 86 | 83 | 96 | 92 | 104 | 96 | 92 | 85 | 83 | 94 | 86 | 94 | 76 | 96 | 85 | 91 | 96 | 97 |
| MONTEREY-SALINAS | 102 | 121 | 108 | 111 | 107 | 110 | 99 | 104 | 109 | 109 | 111 | 98 | 103 | 97 | 103 | 97 | 109 | 109 | 99 | 100 |
| MONTGOMERY | 97 | 83 | 88 | 87 | 97 | 94 | 103 | 97 | 94 | 90 | 88 | 96 | 90 | 96 | 79 | 98 | 90 | 93 | 96 | 98 |
| NASHVILLE | 99 | 89 | 92 | 92 | 98 | 97 | 106 | 98 | 97 | 93 | 94 | 99 | 93 | 99 | 82 | 98 | 93 | 96 | 99 | 100 |
| NEW ORLEANS | 97 | 92 | 96 | 93 | 100 | 98 | 100 | 98 | 96 | 96 | 94 | 98 | 95 | 98 | 85 | 98 | 95 | 97 | 95 | 99 |
| NEW YORK | 102 | 114 | 113 | 112 | 102 | 103 | 93 | 101 | 103 | 112 | 110 | 107 | 112 | 103 | 112 | 103 | 114 | 107 | 102 | 105 |
| NORFOLK-P'MTH-N.NEWS | 97 | 96 | 93 | 92 | 98 | 97 | 98 | 97 | 97 | 96 | 97 | 98 | 95 | 98 | 84 | 99 | 96 | 98 | 96 | 100 |
| NORTH PLATTE | 97 | 82 | 86 | 87 | 95 | 93 | 106 | 96 | 93 | 87 | 89 | 95 | 91 | 97 | 86 | 100 | 86 | 94 | 101 | 98 |
| ODESSA-MIDLAND | 98 | 96 | 97 | 94 | 98 | 98 | 102 | 98 | 98 | 96 | 98 | 98 | 95 | 99 | 85 | 98 | 95 | 98 | 99 | 101 |
| OKLAHOMA CITY | 97 | 91 | 92 | 91 | 98 | 97 | 102 | 97 | 96 | 92 | 94 | 96 | 93 | 98 | 82 | 98 | 93 | 95 | 99 | 99 |
| OMAHA | 98 | 94 | 94 | 96 | 99 | 97 | 101 | 98 | 97 | 95 | 98 | 98 | 99 | 99 | 94 | 102 | 94 | 99 | 100 | 100 |
| ORLANDO-D.BEACH-MEL. | 99 | 98 | 100 | 96 | 101 | 102 | 101 | 99 | 97 | 98 | 100 | 100 | 97 | 101 | 88 | 98 | 97 | 99 | 100 | 101 |
| OTTUMWA-KIRKSVILLE | 96 | 76 | 82 | 84 | 94 | 92 | 106 | 95 | 92 | 82 | 85 | 93 | 87 | 95 | 83 | 100 | 83 | 92 | 103 | 97 |
| PADUC-CG-HARR-MTVERN | 97 | 76 | 86 | 84 | 96 | 94 | 109 | 96 | 93 | 83 | 85 | 94 | 86 | 96 | 75 | 97 | 85 | 90 | 101 | 98 |
| PALM SPRINGS | 100 | 101 | 93 | 97 | 100 | 102 | 100 | 103 | 102 | 102 | 102 | 94 | 93 | 95 | 90 | 94 | 98 | 99 | 99 | 96 |
| PANAMA CITY | 97 | 81 | 91 | 87 | 97 | 97 | 108 | 97 | 93 | 88 | 89 | 95 | 89 | 97 | 79 | 97 | 88 | 92 | 101 | 99 |
| PARKERSBURG, WV | 98 | 82 | 92 | 87 | 99 | 97 | 107 | 97 | 94 | 89 | 90 | 95 | 90 | 98 | 80 | 97 | 89 | 93 | 101 | 99 |
| PEORIA-BLOOMINGTON | 98 | 92 | 95 | 93 | 100 | 97 | 102 | 97 | 95 | 94 | 96 | 96 | 97 | 99 | 94 | 101 | 93 | 97 | 100 | 99 |
| PHILADELPHIA | 101 | 101 | 104 | 103 | 97 | 97 | 92 | 100 | 99 | 103 | 103 | 103 | 104 | 104 | 100 | 100 | 107 | 100 | 101 | 103 |
| PHOENIX | 101 | 102 | 96 | 100 | 102 | 104 | 102 | 103 | 102 | 103 | 102 | 95 | 94 | 95 | 92 | 94 | 100 | 100 | 99 | 96 |
| PITTSBURGH | 98 | 89 | 100 | 94 | 95 | 93 | 93 | 97 | 93 | 95 | 94 | 98 | 97 | 100 | 93 | 98 | 97 | 94 | 102 | 100 |
| PORTLAND, OR | 99 | 97 | 95 | 96 | 101 | 100 | 104 | 101 | 100 | 99 | 98 | 93 | 92 | 94 | 89 | 94 | 97 | 97 | 98 | 95 |
| PORTLAND-AUBURN | 100 | 87 | 92 | 92 | 91 | 90 | 100 | 98 | 96 | 93 | 94 | 100 | 95 | 102 | 88 | 99 | 97 | 94 | 103 | 103 |
| PRESQUE ISLE | 97 | 73 | 78 | 80 | 86 | 84 | 100 | 95 | 92 | 82 | 84 | 95 | 85 | 97 | 78 | 98 | 86 | 88 | 102 | 99 |
| PROVIDENCE-N.BEDFORD | 99 | 97 | 102 | 97 | 96 | 95 | 91 | 98 | 96 | 100 | 100 | 100 | 101 | 101 | 98 | 99 | 101 | 97 | 101 | 101 |
| QUINCY-HAN'BL-KEOKUK | 97 | 77 | 85 | 85 | 96 | 93 | 107 | 96 | 92 | 83 | 87 | 94 | 89 | 96 | 84 | 100 | 84 | 92 | 103 | 97 |
| UNITED STATES | 100 | 100 | 100 | 100 | 100 | 100 | 100 | 100 | 100 | 100 | 100 | 100 | 100 | 100 | 100 | 100 | 100 | 100 | 100 | 100 |

# POPULATION CHANGE

## DMA AND U.S. TOTALS

**A**

| DMA | DMA Code | POPULATION 1990 | POPULATION 2000 | POPULATION 2005 | 1990-2000 ANNUAL CHANGE % Rate | 1990-2000 ANNUAL CHANGE National Rank | RACE (%) White 1990 | White 2000 | Black 1990 | Black 2000 | Asian/Pacific 1990 | Asian/Pacific 2000 |
|---|---|---|---|---|---|---|---|---|---|---|---|---|
| RALEIGH-DURHAM | 560 | 1,902,672 | 2,291,803 | 2,470,822 | 1.8 | 27 | 67.2 | 66.4 | 30.1 | 29.3 | 1.2 | 2.0 |
| RAPID CITY | 764 | 222,473 | 234,116 | 235,814 | 0.5 | 130 | 88.0 | 85.6 | 0.9 | 1.2 | 0.6 | 0.9 |
| RENO | 811 | 433,144 | 556,231 | 608,962 | 2.5 | 11 | 89.0 | 85.0 | 2.1 | 2.5 | 2.8 | 4.1 |
| RICHMOND-PETERSBURG | 556 | 1,115,880 | 1,263,026 | 1,322,689 | 1.2 | 56 | 67.7 | 65.7 | 30.6 | 31.9 | 1.1 | 1.6 |
| ROANOKE-LYNCHBURG | 573 | 1,001,388 | 1,034,125 | 1,043,724 | 0.3 | 156 | 83.5 | 81.7 | 15.5 | 17.0 | 0.7 | 0.9 |
| ROCHESTER, NY | 538 | 960,564 | 972,276 | 965,328 | 0.1 | 171 | 87.2 | 85.0 | 9.5 | 10.4 | 1.4 | 2.2 |
| ROCH.-MAS.CTY-AUSTIN | 611 | 330,702 | 341,848 | 349,738 | 0.3 | 153 | 97.7 | 96.4 | 0.4 | 0.5 | 1.3 | 2.2 |
| ROCKFORD | 610 | 412,120 | 444,760 | 453,267 | 0.8 | 109 | 90.7 | 89.2 | 6.7 | 7.3 | 0.9 | 1.2 |
| SACRAM-STOCKTN-MODES | 862 | 3,023,651 | 3,589,372 | 3,889,913 | 1.7 | 34 | 77.9 | 73.7 | 6.2 | 6.2 | 8.3 | 10.7 |
| SALISBURY | 576 | 246,036 | 291,758 | 311,833 | 1.7 | 38 | 77.5 | 72.8 | 21.1 | 25.4 | 0.6 | 0.9 |
| SALT LAKE CITY | 770 | 1,846,823 | 2,307,442 | 2,481,228 | 2.2 | 16 | 93.7 | 92.1 | 0.7 | 0.8 | 1.8 | 2.4 |
| SAN ANGELO | 661 | 134,348 | 138,504 | 138,279 | 0.3 | 157 | 82.7 | 79.2 | 3.3 | 3.5 | 0.8 | 1.1 |
| SAN ANTONIO | 641 | 1,682,797 | 2,025,855 | 2,182,909 | 1.8 | 27 | 75.9 | 73.6 | 5.8 | 5.6 | 1.0 | 1.4 |
| SAN DIEGO | 825 | 2,498,016 | 2,872,950 | 3,125,152 | 1.4 | 48 | 74.9 | 69.9 | 6.4 | 6.0 | 7.9 | 10.5 |
| S.FRAN-OAKLND-S.JOSE | 807 | 5,814,132 | 6,454,363 | 6,794,403 | 1.0 | 80 | 69.4 | 63.8 | 8.4 | 8.5 | 15.1 | 18.9 |
| S.BARB.-S.MARIA-SLO | 855 | 586,770 | 633,438 | 659,389 | 0.8 | 109 | 81.6 | 77.7 | 2.7 | 2.8 | 3.9 | 4.9 |
| SAVANNAH | 507 | 641,162 | 745,018 | 785,219 | 1.5 | 44 | 66.0 | 62.5 | 32.1 | 34.5 | 0.8 | 1.3 |
| SEATTLE-TACOMA | 819 | 3,523,519 | 4,192,282 | 4,481,224 | 1.7 | 33 | 88.1 | 85.2 | 3.8 | 4.2 | 5.3 | 7.3 |
| SHERMAN,TX-ADA,OK | 657 | 278,023 | 297,745 | 309,389 | 0.7 | 114 | 84.7 | 84.3 | 5.4 | 5.7 | 0.3 | 0.5 |
| SHREVEPORT | 612 | 978,109 | 993,229 | 993,182 | 0.2 | 169 | 69.1 | 66.8 | 29.0 | 30.8 | 0.3 | 0.5 |
| SIOUX CITY | 624 | 390,725 | 398,413 | 395,339 | 0.2 | 166 | 96.5 | 95.5 | 0.6 | 0.7 | 0.7 | 1.0 |
| SIOUX FLS.(MITCHELL) | 725 | 584,917 | 608,008 | 615,104 | 0.4 | 145 | 95.1 | 94.1 | 0.2 | 0.4 | 0.4 | 0.6 |
| SOUTH BEND-ELKHART | 588 | 805,288 | 856,590 | 876,507 | 0.6 | 121 | 90.6 | 89.5 | 7.5 | 8.1 | 0.7 | 1.0 |
| SPOKANE | 881 | 821,933 | 975,496 | 1,016,785 | 1.7 | 34 | 93.6 | 92.2 | 0.8 | 0.9 | 1.4 | 1.8 |
| SPRINGFIELD, MO | 619 | 810,422 | 948,336 | 1,001,004 | 1.6 | 42 | 97.2 | 97.1 | 1.3 | 1.3 | 0.6 | 0.8 |
| SPRINGFIELD-HOLYOKE | 543 | 672,970 | 660,339 | 656,285 | -0.2 | 195 | 88.3 | 85.1 | 5.5 | 6.7 | 1.3 | 2.0 |
| ST. JOSEPH, MO | 638 | 145,999 | 144,792 | 144,393 | -0.1 | 191 | 96.2 | 95.3 | 2.6 | 3.1 | 0.4 | 0.5 |
| ST. LOUIS | 609 | 2,863,759 | 2,969,647 | 3,012,209 | 0.4 | 150 | 83.6 | 82.9 | 15.1 | 15.4 | 0.9 | 1.2 |
| SYRACUSE | 555 | 941,730 | 932,475 | 918,441 | -0.1 | 193 | 92.6 | 91.3 | 4.9 | 5.4 | 1.5 | 2.1 |
| TALLAHASSEE-THOMASVL | 530 | 532,524 | 602,774 | 623,580 | 1.2 | 56 | 67.8 | 63.2 | 30.6 | 34.5 | 0.7 | 1.1 |
| TAMPA-ST.PETE,S'SOTA | 539 | 3,144,270 | 3,542,945 | 3,747,667 | 1.2 | 63 | 88.7 | 86.0 | 8.9 | 10.4 | 0.9 | 1.5 |
| TERRE HAUTE | 581 | 402,750 | 411,233 | 407,626 | 0.2 | 164 | 97.5 | 96.8 | 1.8 | 2.3 | 0.4 | 0.6 |
| TOLEDO | 547 | 1,094,352 | 1,107,387 | 1,109,093 | 0.1 | 171 | 90.3 | 89.0 | 6.9 | 7.4 | 0.7 | 1.0 |
| TOPEKA | 605 | 422,821 | 428,382 | 427,263 | 0.1 | 170 | 89.0 | 88.1 | 6.8 | 6.5 | 1.4 | 1.7 |
| TRAVERSE CITY-CAD'LC | 540 | 500,441 | 581,736 | 617,599 | 1.5 | 44 | 96.2 | 96.0 | 1.1 | 1.3 | 0.3 | 0.4 |
| TRI-CITIES, TN-VA | 531 | 724,614 | 756,133 | 763,475 | 0.4 | 139 | 97.8 | 97.2 | 1.7 | 2.2 | 0.2 | 0.4 |
| TUCSON (NOGALES), AZ | 789 | 794,180 | 969,876 | 1,042,576 | 2.0 | 23 | 78.9 | 75.6 | 3.3 | 3.6 | 1.8 | 2.3 |
| TULSA | 671 | 1,148,572 | 1,268,112 | 1,333,325 | 1.0 | 83 | 81.3 | 80.7 | 7.1 | 7.4 | 0.7 | 0.9 |
| TWIN FALLS | 760 | 136,104 | 159,475 | 166,942 | 1.6 | 41 | 93.3 | 91.4 | 0.1 | 0.2 | 0.7 | 0.8 |
| TYLER-LONGVIEW, TX | 709 | 575,049 | 635,593 | 660,652 | 1.0 | 82 | 78.3 | 75.8 | 18.1 | 19.4 | 0.4 | 0.6 |
| UTICA | 526 | 377,150 | 351,028 | 337,983 | -0.7 | 208 | 94.6 | 93.5 | 3.9 | 4.4 | 0.7 | 1.1 |
| VICTORIA | 626 | 74,361 | 82,629 | 85,479 | 1.0 | 77 | 79.7 | 76.5 | 6.6 | 7.0 | 0.3 | 0.5 |
| WACO-TEMPLE-BRYAN | 625 | 704,075 | 787,641 | 805,731 | 1.1 | 71 | 75.0 | 71.6 | 16.5 | 16.9 | 1.9 | 2.8 |
| WASHINGTON, DC | 511 | 4,850,543 | 5,491,203 | 5,861,505 | 1.2 | 56 | 70.8 | 68.7 | 22.8 | 22.5 | 4.3 | 6.0 |
| WATERTOWN | 549 | 249,713 | 248,451 | 240,628 | -0.1 | 188 | 94.5 | 92.7 | 3.3 | 4.1 | 0.7 | 1.1 |
| WAUSAU-RHINELANDER | 705 | 405,253 | 438,380 | 448,954 | 0.8 | 105 | 97.4 | 96.8 | 0.3 | 0.3 | 1.1 | 1.5 |
| W.PALM BCH-FT.PIERCE | 548 | 1,234,424 | 1,506,313 | 1,626,722 | 2.0 | 24 | 85.3 | 82.0 | 12.0 | 14.0 | 0.9 | 1.4 |
| WHEELING-STEUBENVLLE | 554 | 412,820 | 400,892 | 388,597 | -0.3 | 202 | 97.1 | 96.8 | 2.4 | 2.6 | 0.3 | 0.4 |
| WICHITA FALLS-LAWTON | 627 | 411,186 | 408,474 | 400,436 | -0.1 | 189 | 82.6 | 80.3 | 9.3 | 9.6 | 1.4 | 1.9 |
| WICHITA-HUTCHINSON | 678 | 1,085,730 | 1,160,841 | 1,191,587 | 0.7 | 116 | 91.0 | 88.9 | 4.2 | 4.6 | 1.2 | 1.7 |
| WILKES BARRE- SCRAN. | 577 | 1,434,255 | 1,443,186 | 1,424,698 | 0.1 | 176 | 98.3 | 97.6 | 1.0 | 1.4 | 0.4 | 0.6 |
| WILMINGTON, NC | 550 | 278,374 | 352,762 | 385,047 | 2.3 | 13 | 74.0 | 73.3 | 24.6 | 24.8 | 0.3 | 0.5 |
| YAKIMA-PAS-RICH-KENN | 810 | 480,894 | 574,730 | 606,265 | 1.8 | 31 | 82.7 | 77.6 | 1.2 | 1.3 | 1.4 | 1.8 |
| YOUNGSTOWN | 536 | 721,898 | 707,171 | 689,740 | -0.2 | 196 | 90.4 | 89.2 | 8.6 | 9.6 | 0.4 | 0.5 |
| YUMA,AZ-EL CENTRO,CA | 771 | 216,198 | 286,506 | 311,777 | 2.8 | 9 | 71.4 | 68.3 | 2.6 | 2.7 | 1.6 | 1.9 |
| ZANESVILLE | 596 | 82,068 | 84,960 | 85,773 | 0.3 | 151 | 95.2 | 94.4 | 4.2 | 4.9 | 0.2 | 0.3 |
| UNITED STATES | | | | | 1.0 | | 80.3 | 77.9 | 12.1 | 12.4 | 2.9 | 3.9 |

# POPULATION COMPOSITION

## DMA AND U.S. TOTALS

# B

| DMA | % HISPANIC ORIGIN | | 2000 AGE DISTRIBUTION (%) | | | | | | | | | | MEDIAN AGE | | |
|---|---|---|---|---|---|---|---|---|---|---|---|---|---|---|---|
| | 1990 | 2000 | 0-4 | 5-9 | 10-14 | 15-19 | 20-24 | 25-44 | 45-64 | 65-84 | 85+ | 18+ | 1990 | 2000 | 2000 Males/ Females (×100) |
| RALEIGH-DURHAM | 1.7 | 3.4 | 7.3 | 7.4 | 7.2 | 6.8 | 7.4 | 32.0 | 21.1 | 9.6 | 1.2 | 74.5 | 31.7 | 34.1 | 94.7 |
| RAPID CITY | 1.9 | 3.3 | 7.0 | 7.1 | 8.0 | 8.7 | 7.4 | 26.7 | 22.3 | 11.2 | 1.6 | 72.6 | 31.9 | 35.2 | 99.0 |
| RENO | 9.0 | 14.5 | 7.5 | 7.3 | 7.2 | 7.0 | 6.5 | 28.7 | 23.8 | 10.9 | 1.1 | 74.0 | 33.8 | 36.2 | 108.4 |
| RICHMOND-PETERSBURG | 1.0 | 1.7 | 6.1 | 6.6 | 6.8 | 7.0 | 6.5 | 31.3 | 22.9 | 11.2 | 1.5 | 76.5 | 33.7 | 36.6 | 93.0 |
| ROANOKE-LYNCHBURG | 0.6 | 1.3 | 5.4 | 5.9 | 6.3 | 7.5 | 7.2 | 28.2 | 24.5 | 13.3 | 1.8 | 78.8 | 35.0 | 38.3 | 93.5 |
| ROCHESTER, NY | 3.1 | 4.5 | 6.7 | 7.5 | 7.3 | 7.2 | 6.5 | 29.1 | 22.9 | 11.0 | 1.7 | 74.8 | 33.0 | 36.1 | 93.6 |
| ROCH.-MAS.CTY-AUSTIN | 1.2 | 2.3 | 6.5 | 7.0 | 8.0 | 7.7 | 5.3 | 27.4 | 22.7 | 12.9 | 2.5 | 74.0 | 34.4 | 37.7 | 95.0 |
| ROCKFORD | 3.0 | 4.6 | 7.0 | 7.4 | 7.4 | 7.0 | 5.8 | 28.9 | 23.1 | 11.5 | 1.7 | 73.9 | 33.7 | 36.4 | 95.4 |
| SACRAM-STOCKTN-MODES | 14.8 | 19.4 | 7.5 | 8.5 | 7.4 | 7.3 | 6.6 | 30.2 | 20.7 | 10.5 | 1.3 | 72.3 | 32.0 | 34.1 | 98.5 |
| SALISBURY | 1.1 | 1.8 | 6.0 | 6.5 | 6.6 | 6.6 | 5.8 | 28.9 | 22.7 | 15.1 | 1.7 | 77.3 | 35.3 | 38.4 | 96.6 |
| SALT LAKE CITY | 5.1 | 7.8 | 9.7 | 8.5 | 8.6 | 10.0 | 10.3 | 26.5 | 17.8 | 7.6 | 1.0 | 67.0 | 26.5 | 27.0 | 99.3 |
| SAN ANGELO | 27.3 | 33.7 | 7.7 | 7.6 | 7.3 | 8.4 | 7.3 | 25.9 | 21.8 | 11.9 | 2.0 | 72.9 | 32.4 | 35.0 | 95.3 |
| SAN ANTONIO | 47.6 | 54.1 | 8.1 | 8.0 | 7.9 | 8.0 | 7.1 | 28.5 | 21.0 | 10.1 | 1.4 | 71.4 | 30.8 | 33.1 | 95.5 |
| SAN DIEGO | 20.4 | 26.8 | 7.3 | 7.7 | 6.7 | 6.8 | 7.7 | 33.5 | 19.1 | 9.8 | 1.3 | 74.8 | 30.9 | 33.6 | 101.9 |
| S.FRAN-OAKLND-S.JOSE | 15.3 | 19.6 | 6.2 | 7.0 | 6.5 | 6.5 | 6.3 | 32.3 | 23.0 | 10.7 | 1.5 | 76.6 | 33.8 | 36.7 | 98.1 |
| S.BARB.-S.MARIA-SLO | 21.7 | 27.7 | 6.4 | 7.2 | 6.3 | 7.8 | 8.6 | 30.5 | 19.6 | 11.8 | 1.7 | 76.6 | 32.2 | 34.5 | 102.9 |
| SAVANNAH | 1.8 | 3.3 | 7.7 | 7.4 | 7.3 | 7.9 | 8.6 | 29.5 | 20.1 | 10.2 | 1.2 | 73.5 | 30.3 | 32.6 | 97.0 |
| SEATTLE-TACOMA | 3.1 | 5.0 | 6.5 | 6.9 | 7.3 | 7.3 | 6.6 | 31.2 | 23.0 | 9.8 | 1.4 | 75.1 | 33.2 | 36.0 | 98.9 |
| SHERMAN,TX-ADA,OK | 2.0 | 3.3 | 6.4 | 6.6 | 7.3 | 7.9 | 6.6 | 24.8 | 24.4 | 13.8 | 2.3 | 75.1 | 35.3 | 38.4 | 93.8 |
| SHREVEPORT | 1.7 | 2.7 | 6.9 | 7.1 | 7.5 | 8.2 | 6.9 | 25.9 | 23.5 | 12.3 | 1.9 | 73.7 | 33.3 | 36.5 | 91.8 |
| SIOUX CITY | 1.3 | 2.8 | 6.8 | 7.1 | 7.9 | 8.4 | 6.3 | 25.5 | 22.1 | 13.4 | 2.6 | 73.3 | 34.1 | 36.8 | 95.6 |
| SIOUX FLS.(MITCHELL) | 0.4 | 1.1 | 6.3 | 6.8 | 7.8 | 8.7 | 7.0 | 25.9 | 21.9 | 13.1 | 2.6 | 74.1 | 33.6 | 36.8 | 96.0 |
| SOUTH BEND-ELKHART | 1.8 | 3.0 | 7.2 | 7.5 | 7.7 | 7.6 | 6.4 | 28.3 | 22.2 | 11.4 | 1.6 | 73.3 | 32.8 | 35.5 | 95.3 |
| SPOKANE | 3.6 | 5.7 | 6.5 | 6.8 | 7.2 | 8.5 | 8.0 | 26.9 | 23.4 | 11.1 | 1.7 | 74.6 | 33.3 | 35.8 | 98.9 |
| SPRINGFIELD, MO | 0.9 | 1.6 | 6.0 | 6.4 | 6.9 | 7.5 | 6.6 | 26.9 | 23.6 | 14.1 | 2.0 | 76.5 | 35.3 | 38.0 | 96.2 |
| SPRINGFIELD-HOLYOKE | 7.5 | 10.0 | 6.4 | 6.8 | 6.9 | 7.5 | 7.0 | 29.7 | 21.4 | 12.4 | 1.9 | 76.6 | 32.9 | 35.9 | 91.9 |
| ST. JOSEPH, MO | 1.5 | 2.5 | 6.2 | 6.7 | 7.2 | 8.4 | 7.8 | 27.6 | 21.0 | 12.7 | 2.5 | 75.6 | 33.8 | 35.8 | 97.2 |
| ST. LOUIS | 1.0 | 1.7 | 6.8 | 7.2 | 7.6 | 7.3 | 6.1 | 29.7 | 22.1 | 11.4 | 1.7 | 74.0 | 33.4 | 36.1 | 93.7 |
| SYRACUSE | 1.4 | 2.2 | 6.7 | 7.4 | 7.0 | 8.4 | 7.8 | 28.6 | 21.3 | 11.1 | 1.6 | 75.2 | 31.8 | 34.8 | 95.0 |
| TALLAHASSEE-THOMASVL | 1.8 | 2.9 | 6.9 | 7.3 | 7.4 | 8.5 | 9.1 | 29.3 | 20.6 | 9.7 | 1.2 | 74.0 | 30.7 | 32.7 | 94.5 |
| TAMPA-ST.PETE,S'SOTA | 5.8 | 8.8 | 5.7 | 6.2 | 6.4 | 5.8 | 5.1 | 25.6 | 23.1 | 19.4 | 2.8 | 78.5 | 39.7 | 41.9 | 92.5 |
| TERRE HAUTE | 0.5 | 1.2 | 6.3 | 6.6 | 6.8 | 7.7 | 6.4 | 27.6 | 22.8 | 13.5 | 2.4 | 76.2 | 34.9 | 37.5 | 95.8 |
| TOLEDO | 3.7 | 5.1 | 6.7 | 7.2 | 7.5 | 7.8 | 7.1 | 29.0 | 21.8 | 11.2 | 1.6 | 74.2 | 32.4 | 35.3 | 93.9 |
| TOPEKA | 3.7 | 5.9 | 6.8 | 6.5 | 7.1 | 8.5 | 9.4 | 27.9 | 20.4 | 11.2 | 2.1 | 75.0 | 31.3 | 33.9 | 99.8 |
| TRAVERSE CITY-CAD'LC | 0.7 | 1.3 | 6.1 | 7.0 | 7.4 | 7.5 | 6.1 | 26.9 | 23.5 | 13.7 | 1.8 | 75.1 | 34.8 | 37.9 | 99.5 |
| TRI-CITIES, TN-VA | 0.4 | 1.0 | 5.4 | 5.9 | 6.4 | 6.7 | 6.0 | 29.0 | 26.0 | 12.9 | 1.7 | 78.4 | 35.5 | 39.1 | 94.2 |
| TUCSON (NOGALES), AZ | 27.1 | 32.6 | 7.5 | 7.3 | 7.2 | 7.4 | 7.3 | 28.2 | 21.3 | 12.2 | 1.5 | 74.0 | 32.6 | 35.0 | 97.0 |
| TULSA | 1.7 | 2.9 | 6.8 | 6.9 | 7.6 | 7.8 | 6.5 | 26.7 | 24.0 | 12.0 | 1.7 | 74.0 | 34.0 | 36.9 | 94.7 |
| TWIN FALLS | 8.9 | 12.4 | 7.5 | 7.5 | 8.1 | 8.8 | 7.1 | 25.6 | 22.7 | 11.0 | 1.7 | 71.1 | 32.4 | 34.8 | 100.4 |
| TYLER-LONGVIEW, TX | 5.1 | 7.0 | 6.9 | 7.1 | 7.3 | 8.1 | 7.0 | 25.8 | 23.4 | 12.4 | 1.9 | 74.1 | 33.4 | 36.7 | 95.0 |
| UTICA | 1.8 | 2.8 | 6.3 | 7.5 | 6.7 | 7.2 | 6.5 | 27.9 | 21.8 | 13.8 | 2.2 | 75.9 | 33.9 | 36.9 | 97.8 |
| VICTORIA | 34.1 | 41.5 | 8.3 | 8.3 | 8.3 | 8.2 | 6.4 | 27.5 | 21.8 | 10.0 | 1.2 | 70.1 | 31.6 | 33.9 | 95.6 |
| WACO-TEMPLE-BRYAN | 12.4 | 16.6 | 8.3 | 7.4 | 6.7 | 8.8 | 11.8 | 27.9 | 18.4 | 9.2 | 1.5 | 73.7 | 28.6 | 29.7 | 101.7 |
| WASHINGTON, DC | 4.8 | 6.9 | 6.5 | 6.9 | 6.9 | 6.3 | 6.2 | 34.1 | 23.0 | 9.0 | 1.1 | 76.1 | 32.7 | 35.8 | 95.2 |
| WATERTOWN | 1.8 | 3.2 | 7.4 | 7.8 | 6.8 | 8.2 | 9.0 | 29.0 | 19.9 | 10.3 | 1.6 | 74.2 | 30.1 | 32.5 | 104.7 |
| WAUSAU-RHINELANDER | 0.6 | 1.2 | 6.0 | 6.6 | 7.6 | 7.9 | 6.1 | 27.8 | 23.3 | 12.7 | 1.9 | 75.0 | 33.8 | 37.4 | 99.3 |
| W.PALM BCH-FT.PIERCE | 6.8 | 10.1 | 5.8 | 6.3 | 6.5 | 5.5 | 4.5 | 25.4 | 22.2 | 20.6 | 3.3 | 78.2 | 40.1 | 42.5 | 93.0 |
| WHEELING-STEUBENVLLE | 0.4 | 0.8 | 5.4 | 5.9 | 6.3 | 7.0 | 6.4 | 26.7 | 25.4 | 15.0 | 2.0 | 78.3 | 37.0 | 40.2 | 92.4 |
| WICHITA FALLS-LAWTON | 7.2 | 10.3 | 7.4 | 7.2 | 7.2 | 8.3 | 8.0 | 26.5 | 21.6 | 11.9 | 2.0 | 73.8 | 32.2 | 34.8 | 98.6 |
| WICHITA-HUTCHINSON | 4.7 | 7.3 | 7.1 | 7.1 | 7.8 | 8.1 | 6.3 | 27.8 | 21.6 | 12.0 | 2.1 | 73.2 | 33.4 | 36.0 | 97.0 |
| WILKES BARRE- SCRAN. | 0.7 | 1.5 | 5.5 | 6.3 | 6.9 | 6.9 | 5.7 | 27.9 | 23.3 | 15.3 | 2.2 | 77.5 | 36.5 | 39.2 | 93.7 |
| WILMINGTON, NC | 0.7 | 1.7 | 6.3 | 6.8 | 7.1 | 6.7 | 5.8 | 28.5 | 24.5 | 13.0 | 1.4 | 76.1 | 34.8 | 37.8 | 92.0 |
| YAKIMA-PAS-RICH-KENN | 15.9 | 22.5 | 7.5 | 7.8 | 8.2 | 8.6 | 7.4 | 27.4 | 21.5 | 10.0 | 1.5 | 71.4 | 31.8 | 33.2 | 101.1 |
| YOUNGSTOWN | 1.2 | 1.8 | 5.9 | 6.4 | 6.9 | 6.9 | 6.0 | 27.5 | 23.8 | 14.7 | 1.9 | 76.7 | 35.9 | 38.9 | 92.3 |
| YUMA,AZ-EL CENTRO,CA | 53.3 | 60.6 | 8.4 | 8.9 | 7.8 | 8.2 | 8.5 | 27.5 | 17.8 | 11.9 | 1.1 | 69.9 | 29.7 | 30.5 | 103.7 |
| ZANESVILLE | 0.3 | 0.7 | 6.6 | 6.9 | 7.2 | 7.7 | 6.6 | 28.2 | 22.8 | 12.3 | 1.8 | 74.9 | 33.5 | 36.4 | 91.8 |
| UNITED STATES | 9.0 | 11.8 | 6.9 | 7.2 | 7.2 | 7.2 | 6.7 | 29.9 | 22.2 | 11.1 | 1.6 | 74.6 | 32.9 | 35.7 | 95.6 |

# HOUSEHOLDS

## DMA AND U.S. TOTALS

C

| DMA | HOUSEHOLDS | | | | | FAMILIES | | | MEDIAN HOUSEHOLD INCOME | | |
|---|---|---|---|---|---|---|---|---|---|---|---|
| | 1990 | 2000 | 2005 | % Annual Rate 1990-2000 | 2000 Average HH Size | 1990 | 2000 | % Annual Rate 1990-2000 | 2000 | 2005 | 2000 National Rank |
| RALEIGH-DURHAM | 711,143 | 868,619 | 943,195 | 2.5 | 2.54 | 502,160 | 594,361 | 2.1 | 41,083 | 47,593 | 55 |
| RAPID CITY | 81,377 | 87,920 | 89,470 | 0.9 | 2.60 | 58,295 | 61,015 | 0.6 | 33,104 | 39,383 | 151 |
| RENO | 168,547 | 216,670 | 238,204 | 3.1 | 2.48 | 111,002 | 138,125 | 2.7 | 45,030 | 52,396 | 27 |
| RICHMOND-PETERSBURG | 422,792 | 494,717 | 529,126 | 1.9 | 2.45 | 296,465 | 339,127 | 1.6 | 41,238 | 47,217 | 51 |
| ROANOKE-LYNCHBURG | 384,160 | 414,880 | 427,187 | 0.9 | 2.40 | 274,602 | 286,764 | 0.5 | 32,210 | 36,549 | 175 |
| ROCHESTER, NY | 360,047 | 374,340 | 376,381 | 0.5 | 2.51 | 247,095 | 248,906 | 0.1 | 45,119 | 50,488 | 26 |
| ROCH.-MAS.CTY-AUSTIN | 128,176 | 133,728 | 137,396 | 0.5 | 2.49 | 89,599 | 89,961 | 0.1 | 40,627 | 47,035 | 60 |
| ROCKFORD | 156,204 | 170,376 | 174,638 | 1.1 | 2.56 | 112,185 | 119,192 | 0.7 | 43,556 | 50,033 | 34 |
| SACRAM-STOCKTN-MODES | 1,083,252 | 1,288,025 | 1,395,594 | 2.1 | 2.72 | 770,834 | 891,329 | 1.8 | 46,097 | 56,387 | 23 |
| SALISBURY | 93,572 | 113,902 | 123,645 | 2.4 | 2.46 | 66,906 | 78,017 | 1.9 | 36,503 | 40,748 | 103 |
| SALT LAKE CITY | 579,669 | 753,736 | 825,662 | 3.2 | 3.02 | 442,318 | 565,798 | 3.0 | 44,627 | 52,670 | 30 |
| SAN ANGELO | 48,876 | 51,572 | 51,998 | 0.7 | 2.57 | 35,070 | 35,988 | 0.3 | 33,072 | 40,045 | 153 |
| SAN ANTONIO | 580,120 | 706,900 | 768,854 | 2.4 | 2.79 | 428,771 | 511,631 | 2.2 | 35,665 | 41,234 | 111 |
| SAN DIEGO | 887,403 | 1,048,142 | 1,152,222 | 2.0 | 2.65 | 599,428 | 689,842 | 1.7 | 45,892 | 56,513 | 25 |
| S.FRAN-OAKLND-S.JOSE | 2,184,037 | 2,473,784 | 2,628,622 | 1.5 | 2.55 | 1,407,242 | 1,557,430 | 1.2 | 59,566 | 71,273 | 3 |
| S.BARB.-S.MARIA-SLO | 210,083 | 230,780 | 242,459 | 1.2 | 2.61 | 138,397 | 147,835 | 0.8 | 44,961 | 54,879 | 28 |
| SAVANNAH | 227,298 | 271,700 | 290,800 | 2.2 | 2.62 | 166,425 | 194,508 | 1.9 | 36,541 | 42,890 | 102 |
| SEATTLE-TACOMA | 1,371,118 | 1,657,188 | 1,784,037 | 2.3 | 2.48 | 913,988 | 1,070,110 | 1.9 | 49,331 | 58,622 | 14 |
| SHERMAN,TX-ADA,OK | 107,503 | 116,049 | 120,804 | 0.9 | 2.50 | 77,373 | 80,735 | 0.5 | 28,775 | 33,260 | 199 |
| SHREVEPORT | 362,496 | 377,939 | 382,969 | 0.5 | 2.56 | 263,972 | 266,544 | 0.1 | 29,846 | 33,880 | 195 |
| SIOUX CITY | 146,501 | 150,848 | 150,384 | 0.4 | 2.55 | 103,733 | 103,034 | -0.1 | 35,081 | 40,577 | 124 |
| SIOUX FLS.(MITCHELL) | 221,221 | 232,805 | 236,446 | 0.6 | 2.52 | 153,006 | 155,091 | 0.2 | 33,845 | 39,915 | 143 |
| SOUTH BEND-ELKHART | 296,354 | 321,096 | 331,450 | 1.0 | 2.60 | 214,929 | 226,085 | 0.6 | 41,312 | 47,942 | 49 |
| SPOKANE | 314,999 | 383,172 | 403,795 | 2.4 | 2.48 | 216,264 | 256,659 | 2.1 | 37,084 | 43,489 | 95 |
| SPRINGFIELD, MO | 314,700 | 373,440 | 395,824 | 2.1 | 2.47 | 227,610 | 261,734 | 1.7 | 31,175 | 36,406 | 181 |
| SPRINGFIELD-HOLYOKE | 247,598 | 248,892 | 250,720 | 0.1 | 2.50 | 169,431 | 163,785 | -0.4 | 39,467 | 46,913 | 70 |
| ST. JOSEPH, MO | 55,140 | 54,754 | 54,734 | -0.1 | 2.48 | 38,333 | 36,636 | -0.6 | 32,464 | 37,595 | 168 |
| ST. LOUIS | 1,080,262 | 1,125,648 | 1,145,307 | 0.5 | 2.58 | 760,749 | 772,745 | 0.2 | 42,093 | 48,622 | 45 |
| SYRACUSE | 344,263 | 348,446 | 346,816 | 0.2 | 2.54 | 233,515 | 228,452 | -0.3 | 38,893 | 43,746 | 80 |
| TALLAHASSEE-THOMASVL | 194,223 | 220,765 | 229,140 | 1.6 | 2.60 | 134,235 | 148,432 | 1.2 | 34,509 | 39,638 | 133 |
| TAMPA-ST.PETE,S'SOTA | 1,318,511 | 1,470,607 | 1,547,889 | 1.3 | 2.36 | 890,476 | 958,605 | 0.9 | 36,818 | 43,828 | 100 |
| TERRE HAUTE | 154,474 | 159,771 | 159,855 | 0.4 | 2.45 | 108,938 | 108,863 | 0.0 | 33,634 | 39,685 | 146 |
| TOLEDO | 403,397 | 416,627 | 421,747 | 0.4 | 2.59 | 287,857 | 288,050 | 0.0 | 39,095 | 44,473 | 76 |
| TOPEKA | 158,438 | 159,033 | 157,540 | 0.1 | 2.56 | 109,198 | 106,192 | -0.3 | 37,370 | 44,216 | 89 |
| TRAVERSE CITY-CAD'LC | 188,152 | 226,351 | 244,109 | 2.3 | 2.50 | 136,209 | 159,052 | 1.9 | 33,779 | 38,434 | 144 |
| TRI-CITIES, TN-VA | 277,733 | 301,270 | 310,286 | 1.0 | 2.45 | 210,131 | 220,448 | 0.6 | 30,378 | 33,969 | 187 |
| TUCSON (NOGALES), AZ | 305,146 | 378,090 | 409,016 | 2.6 | 2.51 | 202,144 | 244,544 | 2.3 | 33,368 | 38,180 | 149 |
| TULSA | 446,030 | 494,063 | 520,518 | 1.3 | 2.51 | 316,564 | 340,388 | 0.9 | 34,112 | 39,962 | 139 |
| TWIN FALLS | 48,924 | 58,842 | 62,422 | 2.3 | 2.67 | 35,843 | 41,692 | 1.9 | 34,421 | 39,710 | 136 |
| TYLER-LONGVIEW, TX | 214,578 | 241,123 | 252,845 | 1.4 | 2.56 | 154,848 | 168,677 | 1.0 | 32,632 | 38,183 | 161 |
| UTICA | 139,223 | 132,651 | 129,180 | -0.6 | 2.49 | 96,079 | 88,334 | -1.0 | 35,478 | 40,425 | 118 |
| VICTORIA | 26,228 | 29,728 | 31,057 | 1.5 | 2.75 | 19,820 | 21,940 | 1.2 | 40,338 | 45,999 | 62 |
| WACO-TEMPLE-BRYAN | 249,046 | 283,999 | 293,045 | 1.6 | 2.59 | 173,245 | 192,129 | 1.3 | 34,132 | 41,360 | 138 |
| WASHINGTON, DC | 1,800,563 | 2,079,151 | 2,240,343 | 1.8 | 2.58 | 1,223,391 | 1,390,538 | 1.6 | 57,638 | 66,663 | 5 |
| WATERTOWN | 85,068 | 86,120 | 84,529 | 0.2 | 2.63 | 62,003 | 60,966 | -0.2 | 32,361 | 37,694 | 170 |
| WAUSAU-RHINELANDER | 150,016 | 166,297 | 172,378 | 1.3 | 2.58 | 109,078 | 117,592 | 0.9 | 41,100 | 47,820 | 54 |
| W.PALM BCH-FT.PIERCE | 515,025 | 623,870 | 671,415 | 2.4 | 2.37 | 350,527 | 410,951 | 2.0 | 41,028 | 45,550 | 57 |
| WHEELING-STEUBENVLLE | 159,989 | 159,102 | 156,964 | -0.1 | 2.43 | 115,758 | 110,977 | -0.5 | 29,205 | 32,310 | 196 |
| WICHITA FALLS-LAWTON | 151,569 | 154,229 | 152,625 | 0.2 | 2.53 | 111,178 | 109,766 | -0.2 | 31,838 | 38,434 | 178 |
| WICHITA-HUTCHINSON | 418,043 | 447,589 | 460,102 | 0.8 | 2.53 | 293,059 | 303,851 | 0.4 | 36,882 | 43,107 | 98 |
| WILKES BARRE- SCRAN. | 546,292 | 557,168 | 555,054 | 0.2 | 2.49 | 387,285 | 382,031 | -0.2 | 34,587 | 40,874 | 132 |
| WILMINGTON, NC | 108,539 | 139,649 | 153,830 | 3.1 | 2.47 | 77,882 | 97,380 | 2.8 | 35,706 | 40,065 | 110 |
| YAKIMA-PAS-RICH-KENN | 173,314 | 207,708 | 219,434 | 2.2 | 2.70 | 123,883 | 144,624 | 1.9 | 39,114 | 45,988 | 75 |
| YOUNGSTOWN | 273,558 | 275,134 | 272,323 | 0.1 | 2.51 | 199,878 | 194,267 | -0.3 | 33,620 | 37,302 | 147 |
| YUMA,AZ-EL CENTRO,CA | 68,633 | 89,863 | 98,747 | 3.3 | 3.03 | 53,674 | 70,118 | 3.3 | 30,910 | 38,343 | 184 |
| ZANESVILLE | 30,753 | 32,449 | 33,077 | 0.7 | 2.56 | 22,494 | 22,970 | 0.3 | 33,118 | 38,815 | 150 |
| UNITED STATES | | | | 1.4 | 2.59 | | | 1.1 | 41,914 | 49,127 | |

# INCOME

## DMA AND U.S. TOTALS

| DMA | 2000 Per Capita Income | 2000 HH Income Base | 2000 HOUSEHOLD INCOME DISTRIBUTION (%) | | | | | | 2000 AVERAGE DISPOSABLE INCOME BY AGE OF HOUSEHOLDER | | | | | |
|---|---|---|---|---|---|---|---|---|---|---|---|---|---|---|
| | | | Less than $15,000 | $15,000 to $24,999 | $25,000 to $49,999 | $50,000 to $99,999 | $100,000 to $149,999 | $150,000 or More | All Ages | <35 | 35-44 | 45-54 | 55-64 | 65+ |
| RALEIGH-DURHAM | 20,852 | 868,614 | 14.4 | 13.1 | 33.3 | 29.7 | 7.0 | 2.6 | 38,655 | 33,170 | 43,939 | 47,650 | 39,845 | 25,777 |
| RAPID CITY | 16,121 | 87,920 | 17.7 | 17.9 | 37.0 | 22.7 | 3.7 | 1.1 | 32,156 | 26,624 | 37,139 | 41,276 | 35,381 | 22,326 |
| RENO | 23,688 | 216,653 | 10.4 | 11.7 | 34.2 | 32.8 | 7.9 | 3.0 | 44,389 | 37,991 | 48,104 | 53,197 | 47,135 | 31,381 |
| RICHMOND-PETERSBURG | 21,398 | 494,703 | 14.6 | 12.7 | 33.5 | 30.4 | 6.4 | 2.4 | 38,317 | 31,979 | 42,931 | 46,984 | 40,484 | 26,482 |
| ROANOKE-LYNCHBURG | 16,792 | 414,847 | 20.5 | 16.9 | 36.2 | 21.9 | 3.4 | 1.1 | 30,805 | 26,174 | 35,843 | 38,338 | 33,225 | 21,614 |
| ROCHESTER, NY | 22,116 | 374,335 | 12.8 | 10.7 | 32.4 | 33.8 | 7.6 | 2.7 | 38,337 | 33,504 | 42,636 | 48,738 | 41,848 | 24,035 |
| ROCH.-MAS.CTY-AUSTIN | 20,383 | 133,728 | 12.8 | 12.8 | 36.4 | 29.4 | 6.3 | 2.3 | 36,899 | 32,399 | 43,076 | 46,550 | 40,316 | 24,198 |
| ROCKFORD | 21,196 | 170,376 | 11.9 | 11.2 | 35.3 | 32.8 | 6.7 | 2.1 | 39,196 | 34,356 | 44,119 | 49,473 | 42,530 | 24,888 |
| SACRAM-STOCKTN-MODES | 22,462 | 1,288,014 | 11.7 | 10.9 | 32.0 | 33.3 | 8.5 | 3.7 | 43,114 | 36,990 | 47,165 | 52,003 | 46,070 | 30,448 |
| SALISBURY | 18,677 | 113,888 | 15.9 | 15.1 | 36.7 | 25.8 | 4.9 | 1.7 | 33,743 | 30,892 | 40,111 | 41,159 | 35,929 | 23,393 |
| SALT LAKE CITY | 18,719 | 753,691 | 10.1 | 11.1 | 35.6 | 33.5 | 7.4 | 2.3 | 40,356 | 33,080 | 45,284 | 51,175 | 45,705 | 27,992 |
| SAN ANGELO | 16,629 | 51,572 | 19.9 | 16.9 | 34.0 | 23.5 | 4.2 | 1.6 | 34,320 | 28,625 | 39,861 | 43,098 | 36,997 | 24,836 |
| SAN ANTONIO | 17,189 | 706,896 | 18.4 | 15.7 | 33.1 | 25.4 | 5.4 | 2.1 | 36,977 | 30,183 | 40,477 | 44,703 | 40,095 | 28,752 |
| SAN DIEGO | 24,123 | 1,048,139 | 10.9 | 11.8 | 31.9 | 32.3 | 8.4 | 4.7 | 44,652 | 37,196 | 47,404 | 52,881 | 48,441 | 33,823 |
| S.FRAN-OAKLND-S.JOSE | 32,846 | 2,473,780 | 8.4 | 7.1 | 24.9 | 37.3 | 13.9 | 8.4 | 55,448 | 46,897 | 56,728 | 62,392 | 57,619 | 39,607 |
| S.BARB.-S.MARIA-SLO | 25,014 | 230,780 | 11.6 | 12.0 | 32.0 | 30.9 | 8.4 | 5.2 | 44,943 | 34,754 | 47,702 | 54,533 | 50,239 | 35,997 |
| SAVANNAH | 18,153 | 271,698 | 18.1 | 14.3 | 34.0 | 26.1 | 5.5 | 2.1 | 35,343 | 30,303 | 38,678 | 42,658 | 37,991 | 26,696 |
| SEATTLE-TACOMA | 26,775 | 1,657,187 | 8.8 | 9.9 | 32.1 | 34.9 | 9.7 | 4.6 | 49,019 | 39,861 | 51,195 | 58,682 | 53,330 | 33,459 |
| SHERMAN,TX-ADA,OK | 15,669 | 116,049 | 25.6 | 17.7 | 33.6 | 18.2 | 3.4 | 1.5 | 30,121 | 25,580 | 36,307 | 38,013 | 32,651 | 20,697 |
| SHREVEPORT | 15,366 | 377,927 | 25.6 | 16.7 | 32.6 | 20.3 | 3.5 | 1.3 | 31,291 | 26,707 | 37,538 | 39,208 | 32,583 | 20,980 |
| SIOUX CITY | 16,706 | 150,831 | 15.8 | 16.3 | 38.8 | 24.5 | 3.7 | 1.0 | 31,786 | 27,862 | 37,669 | 39,965 | 35,199 | 22,260 |
| SIOUX FLS.(MITCHELL) | 16,465 | 232,805 | 17.6 | 16.7 | 37.6 | 23.4 | 3.7 | 1.0 | 31,866 | 27,872 | 37,345 | 41,066 | 35,876 | 21,597 |
| SOUTH BEND-ELKHART | 19,818 | 321,092 | 12.3 | 12.4 | 36.9 | 30.8 | 5.9 | 1.8 | 38,070 | 33,253 | 42,716 | 48,657 | 42,159 | 24,538 |
| SPOKANE | 19,690 | 383,164 | 15.7 | 14.9 | 35.8 | 25.9 | 5.5 | 2.2 | 37,140 | 29,694 | 41,789 | 45,946 | 39,990 | 26,446 |
| SPRINGFIELD, MO | 16,007 | 373,440 | 20.0 | 18.8 | 35.7 | 21.1 | 3.3 | 1.0 | 30,751 | 27,436 | 36,844 | 38,698 | 32,554 | 21,164 |
| SPRINGFIELD-HOLYOKE | 19,200 | 248,884 | 17.5 | 12.1 | 34.2 | 28.8 | 5.4 | 2.0 | 34,467 | 30,451 | 38,559 | 44,390 | 39,959 | 21,843 |
| ST. JOSEPH, MO | 15,449 | 54,736 | 20.9 | 15.3 | 37.2 | 22.2 | 3.5 | 0.8 | 31,071 | 27,070 | 36,754 | 39,715 | 34,380 | 20,965 |
| ST. LOUIS | 20,862 | 1,125,608 | 13.6 | 12.1 | 33.9 | 31.2 | 6.7 | 2.4 | 39,548 | 34,445 | 43,949 | 49,455 | 42,248 | 25,248 |
| SYRACUSE | 18,635 | 348,445 | 15.8 | 13.5 | 35.3 | 28.4 | 5.3 | 1.9 | 33,937 | 29,636 | 39,194 | 42,894 | 37,713 | 21,416 |
| TALLAHASSEE-THOMASVL | 17,737 | 220,764 | 19.8 | 15.5 | 32.7 | 24.7 | 5.2 | 2.1 | 35,615 | 28,368 | 41,535 | 44,638 | 38,954 | 24,520 |
| TAMPA-ST.PETE,S'SOTA | 20,949 | 1,470,580 | 14.4 | 16.4 | 35.9 | 26.0 | 5.3 | 2.2 | 38,187 | 34,148 | 43,717 | 46,495 | 41,104 | 29,863 |
| TERRE HAUTE | 17,366 | 159,765 | 18.1 | 16.8 | 37.3 | 22.8 | 3.8 | 1.3 | 32,320 | 28,405 | 38,492 | 41,643 | 34,883 | 21,584 |
| TOLEDO | 18,737 | 416,623 | 15.6 | 13.1 | 36.2 | 28.3 | 5.0 | 1.8 | 35,755 | 30,287 | 41,156 | 46,390 | 39,716 | 22,701 |
| TOPEKA | 17,813 | 159,024 | 14.9 | 15.1 | 36.3 | 27.3 | 5.0 | 1.4 | 35,113 | 27,832 | 40,805 | 46,395 | 40,164 | 25,660 |
| TRAVERSE CITY-CAD'LC | 16,929 | 226,351 | 17.5 | 17.0 | 37.1 | 23.2 | 4.0 | 1.2 | 31,466 | 27,771 | 38,137 | 41,513 | 34,664 | 19,922 |
| TRI-CITIES, TN-VA | 15,793 | 301,257 | 23.6 | 17.5 | 34.6 | 19.9 | 3.3 | 1.1 | 30,934 | 28,224 | 36,710 | 37,723 | 31,690 | 20,426 |
| TUCSON (NOGALES), AZ | 17,809 | 378,090 | 19.7 | 16.6 | 34.2 | 23.4 | 4.5 | 1.7 | 34,124 | 26,775 | 38,339 | 42,611 | 37,649 | 28,105 |
| TULSA | 18,300 | 494,059 | 19.1 | 16.3 | 34.0 | 23.8 | 4.7 | 2.1 | 34,161 | 27,960 | 39,380 | 42,455 | 37,143 | 24,066 |
| TWIN FALLS | 17,868 | 58,841 | 15.6 | 17.8 | 37.2 | 23.1 | 4.4 | 1.9 | 33,934 | 28,796 | 38,893 | 41,679 | 35,243 | 22,249 |
| TYLER-LONGVIEW, TX | 17,005 | 241,121 | 21.7 | 15.8 | 33.9 | 22.5 | 4.4 | 1.7 | 34,177 | 28,704 | 39,768 | 42,958 | 36,545 | 23,823 |
| UTICA | 17,056 | 132,637 | 17.3 | 15.7 | 36.4 | 25.4 | 4.0 | 1.2 | 31,062 | 28,471 | 36,375 | 40,063 | 35,129 | 20,125 |
| VICTORIA | 19,911 | 29,728 | 17.2 | 12.5 | 32.4 | 28.3 | 6.5 | 3.0 | 40,842 | 32,534 | 45,799 | 50,240 | 41,123 | 28,040 |
| WACO-TEMPLE-BRYAN | 17,122 | 283,995 | 19.8 | 15.9 | 33.8 | 24.2 | 4.6 | 1.7 | 35,172 | 27,927 | 41,660 | 45,852 | 40,373 | 25,967 |
| WASHINGTON, DC | 29,644 | 2,079,136 | 7.1 | 7.6 | 26.9 | 39.0 | 13.2 | 6.2 | 51,601 | 41,889 | 52,454 | 59,625 | 53,538 | 38,764 |
| WATERTOWN | 14,583 | 86,119 | 19.7 | 17.0 | 37.5 | 22.2 | 2.9 | 0.8 | 28,634 | 26,208 | 34,261 | 36,114 | 31,311 | 17,749 |
| WAUSAU-RHINELANDER | 20,210 | 166,297 | 12.7 | 12.5 | 36.4 | 29.5 | 6.6 | 2.2 | 35,266 | 31,424 | 41,604 | 46,604 | 38,145 | 20,568 |
| W.PALM BCH-FT.PIERCE | 26,693 | 623,870 | 13.1 | 13.8 | 33.5 | 27.8 | 7.2 | 4.7 | 45,470 | 39,366 | 47,307 | 51,712 | 48,626 | 37,183 |
| WHEELING-STEUBENVLLE | 14,547 | 159,102 | 25.0 | 17.8 | 35.6 | 18.9 | 2.2 | 0.6 | 27,896 | 24,400 | 33,596 | 36,024 | 30,247 | 18,967 |
| WICHITA FALLS-LAWTON | 15,900 | 154,202 | 20.4 | 17.4 | 35.8 | 21.8 | 3.6 | 1.1 | 31,950 | 27,272 | 36,982 | 40,186 | 35,474 | 23,416 |
| WICHITA-HUTCHINSON | 18,413 | 447,586 | 15.2 | 15.3 | 37.0 | 26.5 | 4.6 | 1.5 | 34,651 | 29,557 | 39,756 | 43,134 | 39,213 | 24,216 |
| WILKES BARRE- SCRAN. | 17,566 | 557,162 | 17.9 | 15.6 | 37.7 | 23.3 | 4.0 | 1.5 | 32,328 | 30,848 | 38,465 | 42,321 | 35,338 | 19,848 |
| WILMINGTON, NC | 19,264 | 139,649 | 18.5 | 15.2 | 34.1 | 25.1 | 5.0 | 2.1 | 34,482 | 29,099 | 40,094 | 43,041 | 35,574 | 24,060 |
| YAKIMA-PAS-RICH-KENN | 18,575 | 207,703 | 15.5 | 14.0 | 33.7 | 28.6 | 6.2 | 2.0 | 38,121 | 30,735 | 43,174 | 47,634 | 42,252 | 26,966 |
| YOUNGSTOWN | 16,564 | 275,128 | 19.3 | 16.2 | 36.5 | 23.5 | 3.4 | 1.0 | 31,248 | 26,798 | 36,335 | 40,926 | 34,768 | 20,820 |
| YUMA,AZ-EL CENTRO,CA | 13,329 | 89,863 | 22.1 | 17.7 | 33.0 | 22.3 | 3.7 | 1.2 | 31,490 | 29,143 | 34,578 | 39,428 | 32,851 | 24,048 |
| ZANESVILLE | 15,186 | 32,449 | 20.6 | 15.5 | 38.1 | 22.1 | 2.9 | 0.8 | 30,146 | 27,193 | 35,319 | 38,540 | 31,779 | 20,259 |
| UNITED STATES | 22,162 | | 14.5 | 12.5 | 32.3 | 29.8 | 7.4 | 3.5 | 40,748 | 34,503 | 44,969 | 49,579 | 43,409 | 27,339 |

# SPENDING POTENTIAL INDEXES

## DMA AND U.S. TOTALS

**E**

| DMA | FINANCIAL SERVICES | | | | THE HOME | | | | | | ENTERTAINMENT | | | | | | PERSONAL | | | |
|---|---|---|---|---|---|---|---|---|---|---|---|---|---|---|---|---|---|---|---|---|
| | | | | | Home Improvements | | | Furnishings | | | | | | | | | | | | |
| | Auto Loan | Home Loan | Invest-ments | Retire-ment Plans | Home Repair | Lawn & Garden | Remodel-ing | Appli-ances | Elec-tronics | Furni-ture | Restau-rants | Sport-ing Goods | Theater & Concerts | Toys & Hobbies | Travel | Video Rental | Apparel | Auto After-market | Health Insur-ance | Pets & Supplies |
| RALEIGH-DURHAM | 98 | 93 | 93 | 94 | 98 | 97 | 104 | 98 | 97 | 94 | 96 | 99 | 94 | 99 | 83 | 98 | 95 | 97 | 97 | 100 |
| RAPID CITY | 97 | 85 | 86 | 88 | 95 | 93 | 104 | 96 | 94 | 88 | 91 | 95 | 92 | 97 | 87 | 101 | 88 | 95 | 100 | 98 |
| RENO | 100 | 101 | 95 | 98 | 101 | 101 | 103 | 101 | 101 | 102 | 101 | 94 | 93 | 95 | 90 | 94 | 99 | 99 | 97 | 95 |
| RICHMOND-PETERSBURG | 99 | 96 | 96 | 96 | 100 | 99 | 101 | 99 | 98 | 98 | 98 | 100 | 97 | 100 | 86 | 99 | 98 | 99 | 98 | 101 |
| ROANOKE-LYNCHBURG | 97 | 81 | 90 | 86 | 98 | 95 | 106 | 96 | 93 | 88 | 88 | 95 | 89 | 97 | 79 | 97 | 88 | 92 | 99 | 98 |
| ROCHESTER, NY | 99 | 95 | 99 | 96 | 94 | 93 | 92 | 98 | 97 | 99 | 99 | 100 | 99 | 102 | 94 | 99 | 101 | 97 | 100 | 102 |
| ROCH.-MAS.CTY-AUSTIN | 99 | 89 | 93 | 94 | 98 | 97 | 104 | 98 | 96 | 92 | 95 | 98 | 97 | 99 | 92 | 101 | 92 | 97 | 102 | 99 |
| ROCKFORD | 98 | 94 | 95 | 95 | 100 | 98 | 102 | 98 | 96 | 96 | 98 | 98 | 99 | 100 | 95 | 101 | 95 | 99 | 100 | 100 |
| SACRAM-STOCKTN-MODES | 100 | 102 | 95 | 99 | 101 | 101 | 100 | 102 | 103 | 102 | 102 | 94 | 94 | 94 | 91 | 95 | 99 | 100 | 97 | 96 |
| SALISBURY | 98 | 83 | 94 | 89 | 99 | 98 | 111 | 98 | 94 | 89 | 90 | 97 | 90 | 99 | 80 | 97 | 90 | 93 | 102 | 100 |
| SALT LAKE CITY | 100 | 98 | 91 | 96 | 100 | 99 | 103 | 101 | 102 | 101 | 100 | 93 | 92 | 95 | 88 | 94 | 99 | 99 | 96 | 95 |
| SAN ANGELO | 97 | 89 | 91 | 89 | 97 | 96 | 103 | 97 | 96 | 91 | 94 | 96 | 92 | 98 | 81 | 98 | 91 | 95 | 100 | 100 |
| SAN ANTONIO | 98 | 97 | 95 | 94 | 98 | 98 | 100 | 99 | 98 | 96 | 98 | 98 | 95 | 99 | 85 | 99 | 94 | 98 | 99 | 102 |
| SAN DIEGO | 100 | 114 | 102 | 106 | 104 | 106 | 98 | 102 | 106 | 106 | 107 | 96 | 99 | 95 | 98 | 96 | 104 | 105 | 98 | 98 |
| S.FRAN-OAKLND-S.JOSE | 103 | 130 | 116 | 121 | 111 | 116 | 102 | 105 | 114 | 115 | 118 | 102 | 109 | 98 | 111 | 99 | 116 | 114 | 100 | 101 |
| S.BARB.-S.MARIA-SLO | 101 | 112 | 109 | 109 | 107 | 109 | 102 | 103 | 105 | 105 | 106 | 95 | 100 | 96 | 100 | 95 | 105 | 104 | 100 | 97 |
| SAVANNAH | 97 | 86 | 91 | 89 | 97 | 96 | 104 | 97 | 94 | 90 | 91 | 96 | 90 | 97 | 81 | 97 | 91 | 94 | 97 | 99 |
| SEATTLE-TACOMA | 101 | 105 | 100 | 103 | 103 | 104 | 103 | 102 | 104 | 104 | 104 | 95 | 97 | 96 | 94 | 95 | 103 | 101 | 98 | 96 |
| SHERMAN,TX-ADA,OK | 96 | 77 | 86 | 84 | 96 | 94 | 108 | 96 | 93 | 84 | 85 | 94 | 86 | 96 | 76 | 97 | 85 | 91 | 100 | 97 |
| SHREVEPORT | 96 | 80 | 87 | 84 | 97 | 93 | 104 | 96 | 93 | 87 | 86 | 95 | 87 | 95 | 77 | 97 | 87 | 92 | 97 | 97 |
| SIOUX CITY | 97 | 80 | 85 | 87 | 95 | 93 | 106 | 96 | 93 | 84 | 88 | 95 | 90 | 96 | 85 | 100 | 85 | 93 | 103 | 97 |
| SIOUX FLS.(MITCHELL) | 97 | 82 | 86 | 88 | 95 | 93 | 104 | 96 | 93 | 85 | 89 | 95 | 91 | 97 | 86 | 100 | 86 | 94 | 102 | 98 |
| SOUTH BEND-ELKHART | 98 | 88 | 92 | 91 | 99 | 96 | 106 | 98 | 95 | 92 | 94 | 97 | 96 | 99 | 91 | 101 | 91 | 97 | 101 | 99 |
| SPOKANE | 98 | 87 | 90 | 90 | 99 | 97 | 106 | 99 | 97 | 92 | 91 | 90 | 87 | 92 | 83 | 93 | 90 | 93 | 98 | 93 |
| SPRINGFIELD, MO | 98 | 80 | 87 | 87 | 96 | 95 | 108 | 97 | 94 | 85 | 88 | 96 | 91 | 97 | 86 | 100 | 86 | 94 | 103 | 98 |
| SPRINGFIELD-HOLYOKE | 98 | 94 | 101 | 94 | 96 | 93 | 91 | 97 | 94 | 98 | 97 | 98 | 99 | 100 | 96 | 98 | 99 | 96 | 101 | 100 |
| ST. JOSEPH, MO | 96 | 82 | 87 | 87 | 97 | 94 | 104 | 96 | 93 | 87 | 89 | 94 | 91 | 96 | 87 | 100 | 86 | 93 | 101 | 97 |
| ST. LOUIS | 99 | 96 | 98 | 98 | 101 | 100 | 101 | 99 | 98 | 98 | 99 | 99 | 101 | 100 | 97 | 102 | 97 | 100 | 100 | 100 |
| SYRACUSE | 98 | 90 | 95 | 92 | 93 | 91 | 94 | 97 | 95 | 94 | 95 | 98 | 96 | 101 | 91 | 98 | 97 | 94 | 101 | 101 |
| TALLAHASSEE-THOMASVL | 97 | 89 | 91 | 90 | 96 | 94 | 104 | 96 | 95 | 91 | 91 | 97 | 90 | 97 | 80 | 97 | 91 | 95 | 96 | 99 |
| TAMPA-ST.PETE,S'SOTA | 98 | 93 | 107 | 96 | 103 | 105 | 102 | 99 | 94 | 95 | 97 | 98 | 97 | 100 | 89 | 97 | 93 | 97 | 103 | 100 |
| TERRE HAUTE | 97 | 78 | 85 | 85 | 97 | 94 | 107 | 96 | 93 | 85 | 87 | 94 | 90 | 96 | 85 | 100 | 85 | 93 | 102 | 97 |
| TOLEDO | 98 | 90 | 94 | 93 | 100 | 97 | 104 | 98 | 95 | 93 | 95 | 97 | 97 | 99 | 93 | 101 | 92 | 97 | 100 | 99 |
| TOPEKA | 97 | 90 | 90 | 91 | 97 | 94 | 101 | 96 | 95 | 90 | 94 | 95 | 94 | 97 | 90 | 100 | 90 | 96 | 100 | 98 |
| TRAVERSE CITY-CAD'LC | 99 | 79 | 84 | 88 | 95 | 94 | 114 | 98 | 94 | 84 | 88 | 97 | 90 | 99 | 85 | 101 | 86 | 94 | 104 | 100 |
| TRI-CITIES, TN-VA | 97 | 75 | 84 | 82 | 96 | 94 | 110 | 96 | 93 | 84 | 85 | 96 | 86 | 97 | 75 | 96 | 85 | 90 | 101 | 98 |
| TUCSON (NOGALES), AZ | 98 | 98 | 98 | 97 | 102 | 102 | 101 | 100 | 99 | 98 | 98 | 91 | 91 | 93 | 90 | 93 | 95 | 97 | 98 | 95 |
| TULSA | 98 | 89 | 94 | 92 | 99 | 97 | 105 | 97 | 96 | 92 | 93 | 97 | 93 | 99 | 82 | 98 | 93 | 95 | 99 | 99 |
| TWIN FALLS | 99 | 84 | 86 | 92 | 97 | 97 | 110 | 100 | 98 | 90 | 90 | 92 | 86 | 93 | 81 | 93 | 90 | 93 | 100 | 94 |
| TYLER-LONGVIEW, TX | 97 | 83 | 90 | 87 | 97 | 95 | 106 | 97 | 94 | 88 | 89 | 95 | 89 | 97 | 79 | 97 | 89 | 93 | 99 | 99 |
| UTICA | 98 | 85 | 94 | 89 | 93 | 90 | 95 | 96 | 93 | 92 | 92 | 96 | 94 | 99 | 89 | 98 | 94 | 92 | 102 | 100 |
| VICTORIA | 99 | 100 | 98 | 99 | 99 | 99 | 102 | 99 | 100 | 98 | 100 | 100 | 97 | 101 | 86 | 99 | 97 | 100 | 99 | 103 |
| WACO-TEMPLE-BRYAN | 95 | 89 | 90 | 89 | 96 | 93 | 100 | 94 | 94 | 88 | 91 | 93 | 89 | 95 | 80 | 96 | 90 | 94 | 96 | 98 |
| WASHINGTON, DC | 102 | 116 | 109 | 111 | 106 | 109 | 102 | 102 | 106 | 110 | 112 | 107 | 109 | 105 | 99 | 102 | 112 | 109 | 99 | 105 |
| WATERTOWN | 97 | 78 | 82 | 83 | 88 | 85 | 99 | 95 | 91 | 85 | 86 | 95 | 87 | 98 | 81 | 97 | 88 | 89 | 101 | 100 |
| WAUSAU-RHINELANDER | 98 | 82 | 86 | 89 | 96 | 94 | 110 | 97 | 94 | 87 | 91 | 96 | 92 | 99 | 87 | 101 | 88 | 95 | 103 | 99 |
| W.PALM BCH-FT.PIERCE | 101 | 102 | 109 | 104 | 105 | 110 | 104 | 102 | 99 | 102 | 104 | 102 | 102 | 103 | 94 | 99 | 102 | 101 | 104 | 103 |
| WHEELING-STEUBENVLLE | 96 | 78 | 90 | 83 | 100 | 96 | 104 | 96 | 90 | 87 | 87 | 93 | 88 | 96 | 79 | 96 | 86 | 90 | 101 | 96 |
| WICHITA FALLS-LAWTON | 96 | 84 | 89 | 87 | 97 | 94 | 103 | 96 | 94 | 88 | 90 | 94 | 89 | 96 | 79 | 97 | 89 | 93 | 99 | 98 |
| WICHITA-HUTCHINSON | 97 | 88 | 90 | 91 | 97 | 95 | 102 | 97 | 95 | 91 | 94 | 96 | 95 | 98 | 90 | 101 | 90 | 96 | 101 | 98 |
| WILKES BARRE- SCRAN. | 98 | 82 | 91 | 87 | 93 | 90 | 97 | 97 | 91 | 90 | 90 | 97 | 93 | 99 | 87 | 98 | 92 | 91 | 103 | 100 |
| WILMINGTON, NC | 99 | 86 | 94 | 91 | 98 | 98 | 109 | 98 | 95 | 91 | 92 | 98 | 92 | 99 | 81 | 98 | 92 | 95 | 100 | 100 |
| YAKIMA-PAS-RICH-KENN | 97 | 90 | 91 | 91 | 99 | 97 | 104 | 99 | 98 | 94 | 93 | 90 | 88 | 92 | 84 | 93 | 91 | 94 | 97 | 93 |
| YOUNGSTOWN | 96 | 86 | 94 | 88 | 101 | 97 | 100 | 97 | 92 | 92 | 92 | 94 | 95 | 96 | 93 | 100 | 89 | 94 | 100 | 97 |
| YUMA,AZ-EL CENTRO,CA | 96 | 95 | 94 | 90 | 98 | 99 | 96 | 100 | 98 | 92 | 93 | 88 | 88 | 89 | 87 | 93 | 88 | 95 | 98 | 95 |
| ZANESVILLE | 97 | 82 | 88 | 86 | 99 | 95 | 105 | 97 | 92 | 89 | 89 | 94 | 92 | 96 | 88 | 100 | 86 | 93 | 101 | 97 |
| UNITED STATES | 100 | 100 | 100 | 100 | 100 | 100 | 100 | 100 | 100 | 100 | 100 | 100 | 100 | 100 | 100 | 100 | 100 | 100 | 100 | 100 |

# BUSINESS DATA BY COUNTY

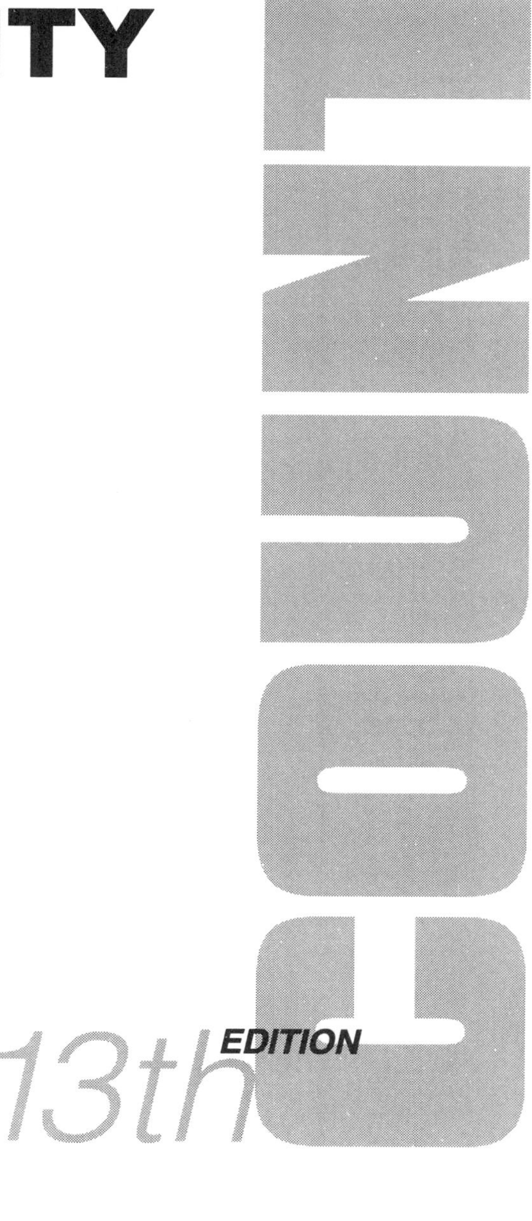

| COUNTY | 2000 Total Firms | 2000 Total Employ-ees | TOP INDUSTRY RANKED on 2000 EMPLOYMENT | COUNTY | 2000 Total Firms | 2000 Total Employ-ees | TOP INDUSTRY RANKED on 2000 EMPLOYMENT |
|---|---|---|---|---|---|---|---|
| AUTAUGA, AL | 1031 | 9598 | EATING AND DRINKING PLACES | MATANUSKA-SUSITNA, AK | 2890 | 14670 | EDUCATIONAL SERVICES |
| BALDWIN, AL | 6347 | 47331 | EATING AND DRINKING PLACES | NOME, AK | 450 | 2759 | EDUCATIONAL SERVICES |
| BARBOUR, AL | 882 | 10174 | LUMBER & WOOD PRODS, EXC FURN. | NORTH SLOPE, AK | 417 | 3844 | EXECUTIVE, LEGISLATIVE GOVT. |
| BIBB, AL | 435 | 4067 | HEALTH SERVICES | NORTHWEST ARCTIC, AK | 284 | 1966 | EDUCATIONAL SERVICES |
| BLOUNT, AL | 1035 | 9279 | FOOD AND KINDRED PRODUCTS | PR OF WALES-OUT KTCH, AK | 404 | 2369 | EDUCATIONAL SERVICES |
| BULLOCK, AL | 348 | 3971 | FOOD AND KINDRED PRODUCTS | SITKA, AK | 661 | 4060 | EDUCATIONAL SERVICES |
| BUTLER, AL | 632 | 6317 | LUMBER & WOOD PRODS, EXC FURN. | SKAGWAY-YAKUTAT-ANGO, AK | 509 | 2777 | EDUCATIONAL SERVICES |
| CALHOUN, AL | 3486 | 40626 | EDUCATIONAL SERVICES | SOUTHEAST FAIRBANKS, AK | 449 | 1924 | NATIONAL SECURITY/INT AFFAIRS |
| CHAMBERS, AL | 1062 | 10598 | EDUCATIONAL SERVICES | VALDEZ-CORDOVA, AK | 1012 | 6179 | FOOD AND KINDRED PRODUCTS |
| CHEROKEE, AL | 713 | 5107 | TEXTILE MILL PRODUCTS | WADE HAMPTON, AK | 266 | 1596 | EDUCATIONAL SERVICES |
| CHILTON, AL | 1017 | 8135 | GENERAL MERCHANDISE STORES | WRANGELL-PETERSBURG, AK | 651 | 3474 | FOOD AND KINDRED PRODUCTS |
| CHOCTAW, AL | 577 | 5417 | PAPER AND ALLIED PRODUCTS | YUKON-KOYUKUK, AK | 645 | 3487 | HOTELS, ROOMING HOUSES, CAMPS |
| CLARKE, AL | 969 | 9838 | LUMBER & WOOD PRODS, EXC FURN. | APACHE, AZ | 1421 | 12594 | EDUCATIONAL SERVICES |
| CLAY, AL | 426 | 6497 | CONSTRUCT: SPEC TRADE CONTRACT | COCHISE, AZ | 3422 | 26420 | EATING AND DRINKING PLACES |
| CLEBURNE, AL | 340 | 3389 | APPAREL, FINISHED PRODUCTS | COCONINO, AZ | 4286 | 50595 | EATING AND DRINKING PLACES |
| COFFEE, AL | 1249 | 14870 | FOOD AND KINDRED PRODUCTS | GILA, AZ | 1816 | 15303 | MINING AND QUARRYING EXC FUELS |
| COLBERT, AL | 1882 | 20303 | EDUCATIONAL SERVICES | GRAHAM, AZ | 954 | 9636 | EDUCATIONAL SERVICES |
| CONECUH, AL | 391 | 3924 | MOTOR FREIGHT TRANSPORTATION | GREENLEE, AZ | 239 | 4157 | MINING AND QUARRYING EXC FUELS |
| COOSA, AL | 206 | 2156 | FURNITURE AND FIXTURES | LA PAZ, AZ | 939 | 6520 | EXECUTIVE, LEGISLATIVE GOVT. |
| COVINGTON, AL | 1329 | 12345 | APPAREL, FINISHED PRODUCTS | MARICOPA, AZ | 75612 | 1156902 | EATING AND DRINKING PLACES |
| CRENSHAW, AL | 379 | 3294 | APPAREL, FINISHED PRODUCTS | MOHAVE, AZ | 5472 | 40191 | EDUCATIONAL SERVICES |
| CULLMAN, AL | 2289 | 25640 | GENERAL MERCHANDISE STORES | NAVAJO, AZ | 2864 | 27942 | EDUCATIONAL SERVICES |
| DALE, AL | 1296 | 13692 | TRANSPORTATION BY AIR | PIMA, AZ | 23197 | 333329 | EDUCATIONAL SERVICES |
| DALLAS, AL | 1413 | 17171 | EDUCATIONAL SERVICES | PINAL, AZ | 3351 | 39646 | EDUCATIONAL SERVICES |
| DEKALB, AL | 2111 | 24374 | TEXTILE MILL PRODUCTS | SANTA CRUZ, AZ | 1508 | 12181 | FOOD STORES |
| ELMORE, AL | 1500 | 12747 | EDUCATIONAL SERVICES | YAVAPAI, AZ | 6476 | 48157 | EATING AND DRINKING PLACES |
| ESCAMBIA, AL | 1258 | 13621 | EDUCATIONAL SERVICES | YUMA, AZ | 3166 | 52573 | NATIONAL SECURITY/INT AFFAIRS |
| ETOWAH, AL | 2981 | 35702 | HEALTH SERVICES | ARKANSAS, AR | 832 | 8316 | INDUSTRIAL & COMM. MACHINERY |
| FAYETTE, AL | 524 | 6279 | APPAREL, FINISHED PRODUCTS | ASHLEY, AR | 861 | 8201 | LUMBER & WOOD PRODS, EXC FURN. |
| FRANKLIN, AL | 888 | 11235 | FOOD AND KINDRED PRODUCTS | BAXTER, AR | 1723 | 12688 | MESR/ANLYZ/CNTRL INSTRMNTS |
| GENEVA, AL | 692 | 5731 | EDUCATIONAL SERVICES | BENTON, AR | 4439 | 70397 | GENERAL MERCHANDISE STORES |
| GREENE, AL | 271 | 1653 | EDUCATIONAL SERVICES | BOONE, AR | 1550 | 14787 | EDUCATIONAL SERVICES |
| HALE, AL | 394 | 4129 | FOOD AND KINDRED PRODUCTS | BRADLEY, AR | 419 | 3543 | LUMBER & WOOD PRODS, EXC FURN. |
| HENRY, AL | 490 | 4484 | APPAREL, FINISHED PRODUCTS | CALHOUN, AR | 180 | 1411 | CHEMICALS AND ALLIED PRODUCTS |
| HOUSTON, AL | 3669 | 47213 | EATING AND DRINKING PLACES | CARROLL, AR | 1442 | 11709 | FOOD AND KINDRED PRODUCTS |
| JACKSON, AL | 1481 | 15460 | TEXTILE MILL PRODUCTS | CHICOT, AR | 489 | 3999 | APPAREL, FINISHED PRODUCTS |
| JEFFERSON, AL | 21098 | 291120 | HEALTH SERVICES | CLARK, AR | 790 | 9163 | EDUCATIONAL SERVICES |
| LAMAR, AL | 483 | 5700 | APPAREL, FINISHED PRODUCTS | CLAY, AR | 625 | 6407 | FURNITURE AND FIXTURES |
| LAUDERDALE, AL | 2634 | 29950 | HEALTH SERVICES | CLEBURNE, AR | 891 | 6559 | EDUCATIONAL SERVICES |
| LAWRENCE, AL | 825 | 7450 | PAPER AND ALLIED PRODUCTS | CLEVELAND, AR | 223 | 1462 | EDUCATIONAL SERVICES |
| LEE, AL | 2700 | 38116 | EDUCATIONAL SERVICES | COLUMBIA, AR | 948 | 9917 | EDUCATIONAL SERVICES |
| LIMESTONE, AL | 1566 | 18992 | TRANSPORTATION EQUIPMENT | CONWAY, AR | 630 | 6133 | EDUCATIONAL SERVICES |
| LOWNDES, AL | 250 | 2564 | EDUCATIONAL SERVICES | CRAIGHEAD, AR | 3272 | 39852 | EDUCATIONAL SERVICES |
| MACON, AL | 528 | 6838 | EDUCATIONAL SERVICES | CRAWFORD, AR | 1499 | 14304 | FOOD AND KINDRED PRODUCTS |
| MADISON, AL | 9077 | 128873 | EATING AND DRINKING PLACES | CRITTENDEN, AR | 1492 | 17609 | MOTOR FREIGHT TRANSPORTATION |
| MARENGO, AL | 766 | 7506 | LUMBER & WOOD PRODS, EXC FURN. | CROSS, AR | 593 | 4709 | LEATHER AND LEATHER PRODUCTS |
| MARION, AL | 1049 | 13574 | WHOLESALE TRADE: DURABLE GOODS | DALLAS, AR | 380 | 3113 | BUILDING MATRIALS/GARDEN SUPPL |
| MARSHALL, AL | 2957 | 35514 | FOOD AND KINDRED PRODUCTS | DESHA, AR | 615 | 5373 | EDUCATIONAL SERVICES |
| MOBILE, AL | 12769 | 168309 | HEALTH SERVICES | DREW, AR | 669 | 6406 | EDUCATIONAL SERVICES |
| MONROE, AL | 768 | 8063 | PAPER AND ALLIED PRODUCTS | FAULKNER, AR | 2401 | 29284 | BUSINESS SERVICES |
| MONTGOMERY, AL | 7917 | 126137 | HEALTH SERVICES | FRANKLIN, AR | 523 | 4341 | FOOD AND KINDRED PRODUCTS |
| MORGAN, AL | 3554 | 47353 | EDUCATIONAL SERVICES | FULTON, AR | 360 | 2499 | EDUCATIONAL SERVICES |
| PERRY, AL | 308 | 3059 | EDUCATIONAL SERVICES | GARLAND, AR | 3577 | 33796 | HEALTH SERVICES |
| PICKENS, AL | 602 | 4776 | EDUCATIONAL SERVICES | GRANT, AR | 443 | 4016 | EDUCATIONAL SERVICES |
| PIKE, AL | 892 | 10568 | EDUCATIONAL SERVICES | GREENE, AR | 1223 | 15156 | TRANSPORTATION EQUIPMENT |
| RANDOLPH, AL | 707 | 6143 | APPAREL, FINISHED PRODUCTS | HEMPSTEAD, AR | 729 | 9987 | FOOD AND KINDRED PRODUCTS |
| RUSSELL, AL | 1309 | 12606 | TEXTILE MILL PRODUCTS | HOT SPRING, AR | 864 | 7331 | EDUCATIONAL SERVICES |
| ST. CLAIR, AL | 1542 | 12831 | EATING AND DRINKING PLACES | HOWARD, AR | 512 | 9271 | FOOD AND KINDRED PRODUCTS |
| SHELBY, AL | 3970 | 45965 | WHOLESALE TRADE: DURABLE GOODS | INDEPENDENCE, AR | 1194 | 15490 | FOOD AND KINDRED PRODUCTS |
| SUMTER, AL | 447 | 3910 | EDUCATIONAL SERVICES | IZARD, AR | 453 | 3239 | EDUCATIONAL SERVICES |
| TALLADEGA, AL | 2124 | 24152 | EDUCATIONAL SERVICES | JACKSON, AR | 643 | 5468 | HEALTH SERVICES |
| TALLAPOOSA, AL | 1236 | 11211 | HEALTH SERVICES | JEFFERSON, AR | 2452 | 29362 | EDUCATIONAL SERVICES |
| TUSCALOOSA, AL | 4506 | 64489 | EDUCATIONAL SERVICES | JOHNSON, AR | 677 | 8386 | FOOD AND KINDRED PRODUCTS |
| WALKER, AL | 1929 | 15056 | EDUCATIONAL SERVICES | LAFAYETTE, AR | 290 | 1971 | FURNITURE AND FIXTURES |
| WASHINGTON, AL | 470 | 5123 | CHEMICALS AND ALLIED PRODUCTS | LAWRENCE, AR | 693 | 5564 | EDUCATIONAL SERVICES |
| WILCOX, AL | 385 | 3713 | PAPER AND ALLIED PRODUCTS | LEE, AR | 292 | 2187 | JUSTICE, PUBLIC ORDER/SAFETY |
| WINSTON, AL | 756 | 11811 | WHOLESALE TRADE: DURABLE GOODS | LINCOLN, AR | 300 | 3049 | EXECUTIVE, LEGISLATIVE GOVT. |
| ALEUTIANS EAST, AK | 139 | 2248 | FOOD AND KINDRED PRODUCTS | LITTLE RIVER, AR | 461 | 4743 | PAPER AND ALLIED PRODUCTS |
| ALEUTIANS WEST, AK | 273 | 3206 | FOOD AND KINDRED PRODUCTS | LOGAN, AR | 682 | 6168 | FOOD AND KINDRED PRODUCTS |
| ANCHORAGE, AK | 10822 | 127599 | TRANSPORTATION BY AIR | LONOKE, AR | 1287 | 9736 | FABRICATED METAL PRODUCTS |
| BETHEL, AK | 729 | 4738 | EDUCATIONAL SERVICES | MADISON, AR | 416 | 2663 | FOOD AND KINDRED PRODUCTS |
| BRISTOL BAY, AK | 270 | 3083 | FOOD STORES | MARION, AR | 559 | 4829 | TRANSPORTATION EQUIPMENT |
| DILLINGHAM, AK | 333 | 1898 | EDUCATIONAL SERVICES | MILLER, AR | 1251 | 12791 | RUBBER & MISC PLASTIC PRODUCTS |
| FAIRBANKS NORTH STAR, AK | 3630 | 38714 | NATIONAL SECURITY/INT AFFAIRS | MISSISSIPPI, AR | 1772 | 22204 | EDUCATIONAL SERVICES |
| HAINES, AK | 315 | 1129 | HEAVY CONSTRUCTION: EXC BUILD | MONROE, AR | 451 | 2978 | EDUCATIONAL SERVICES |
| JUNEAU, AK | 1804 | 15517 | ADMIN: HUMAN RESOURCE PROGRAM | MONTGOMERY, AR | 304 | 1936 | HOTELS, ROOMING HOUSES, CAMPS |
| KENAI PENINSULA, AK | 3608 | 20246 | FOOD AND KINDRED PRODUCTS | NEVADA, AR | 254 | 1964 | EDUCATIONAL SERVICES |
| KETCHIKAN GATEWAY, AK | 1203 | 8627 | FOOD AND KINDRED PRODUCTS | NEWTON, AR | 264 | 1375 | EDUCATIONAL SERVICES |
| KODIAK ISLAND, AK | 859 | 6844 | FOOD AND KINDRED PRODUCTS | OUACHITA, AR | 954 | 9336 | PAPER AND ALLIED PRODUCTS |
| LAKE AND PENINSULA, AK | 169 | 722 | FOOD AND KINDRED PRODUCTS | PERRY, AR | 277 | 1374 | EDUCATIONAL SERVICES |

# BUSINESS DATA

| COUNTY | 2000 Total Firms | 2000 Total Employ-ees | TOP INDUSTRY RANKED on 2000 EMPLOYMENT |
|---|---|---|---|
| PHILLIPS, AR | 866 | 7622 | EDUCATIONAL SERVICES |
| PIKE, AR | 507 | 3414 | LUMBER & WOOD PRODS, EXC FURN. |
| POINSETT, AR | 991 | 7007 | EDUCATIONAL SERVICES |
| POLK, AR | 768 | 5993 | EDUCATIONAL SERVICES |
| POPE, AR | 1953 | 21784 | EDUCATIONAL SERVICES |
| PRAIRIE, AR | 285 | 1686 | EDUCATIONAL SERVICES |
| PULASKI, AR | 14644 | 225563 | HEALTH SERVICES |
| RANDOLPH, AR | 473 | 5037 | LUMBER & WOOD PRODS, EXC FURN. |
| ST. FRANCIS, AR | 934 | 8673 | EDUCATIONAL SERVICES |
| SALINE, AR | 1977 | 16056 | EATING AND DRINKING PLACES |
| SCOTT, AR | 320 | 3439 | FOOD AND KINDRED PRODUCTS |
| SEARCY, AR | 324 | 1717 | EDUCATIONAL SERVICES |
| SEBASTIAN, AR | 4432 | 69021 | FOOD AND KINDRED PRODUCTS |
| SEVIER, AR | 500 | 6120 | FOOD AND KINDRED PRODUCTS |
| SHARP, AR | 745 | 4666 | EDUCATIONAL SERVICES |
| STONE, AR | 505 | 3607 | HOTELS, ROOMING HOUSES, CAMPS |
| UNION, AR | 1765 | 21262 | FOOD AND KINDRED PRODUCTS |
| VAN BUREN, AR | 632 | 4361 | EDUCATIONAL SERVICES |
| WASHINGTON, AR | 5281 | 66335 | EDUCATIONAL SERVICES |
| WHITE, AR | 2123 | 20585 | EDUCATIONAL SERVICES |
| WOODRUFF, AR | 313 | 2269 | WHOLESALE TRADE: NONDURABLE |
| YELL, AR | 708 | 5884 | WHOLESALE TRADE: NONDURABLE |
| ALAMEDA, CA | 45234 | 553788 | EDUCATIONAL SERVICES |
| ALPINE, CA | 72 | 519 | EXECUTIVE, LEGISLATIVE GOVT. |
| AMADOR, CA | 1697 | 11293 | EDUCATIONAL SERVICES |
| BUTTE, CA | 7567 | 63278 | EDUCATIONAL SERVICES |
| CALAVERAS, CA | 1870 | 8751 | EDUCATIONAL SERVICES |
| COLUSA, CA | 722 | 6402 | EDUCATIONAL SERVICES |
| CONTRA COSTA, CA | 27554 | 248082 | EDUCATIONAL SERVICES |
| DEL NORTE, CA | 986 | 6463 | EDUCATIONAL SERVICES |
| EL DORADO, CA | 6338 | 42411 | HOTELS, ROOMING HOUSES, CAMPS |
| FRESNO, CA | 22413 | 250374 | EDUCATIONAL SERVICES |
| GLENN, CA | 1081 | 7439 | EDUCATIONAL SERVICES |
| HUMBOLDT, CA | 5711 | 44596 | EDUCATIONAL SERVICES |
| IMPERIAL, CA | 3981 | 47977 | AGRICULTURAL SERVICES |
| INYO, CA | 1081 | 15540 | NATIONAL SECURITY/INT AFFAIRS |
| KERN, CA | 17351 | 200496 | EDUCATIONAL SERVICES |
| KINGS, CA | 2691 | 36416 | NATIONAL SECURITY/INT AFFAIRS |
| LAKE, CA | 2514 | 14979 | EDUCATIONAL SERVICES |
| LASSEN, CA | 905 | 7667 | EDUCATIONAL SERVICES |
| LOS ANGELES, CA | 284772 | 3210941 | EDUCATIONAL SERVICES |
| MADERA, CA | 3296 | 33546 | EDUCATIONAL SERVICES |
| MARIN, CA | 13888 | 98754 | BUSINESS SERVICES |
| MARIPOSA, CA | 771 | 5854 | AUTO DEALERS & GAS SERV STA. |
| MENDOCINO, CA | 4717 | 32972 | EDUCATIONAL SERVICES |
| MERCED, CA | 4554 | 59702 | WHOLESALE TRADE: NONDURABLE |
| MODOC, CA | 601 | 3107 | EDUCATIONAL SERVICES |
| MONO, CA | 1131 | 9561 | HOTELS, ROOMING HOUSES, CAMPS |
| MONTEREY, CA | 13675 | 138660 | WHOLESALE TRADE: NONDURABLE |
| NAPA, CA | 5225 | 47611 | FOOD AND KINDRED PRODUCTS |
| NEVADA, CA | 4834 | 28567 | EDUCATIONAL SERVICES |
| ORANGE, CA | 95583 | 1117532 | EATING AND DRINKING PLACES |
| PLACER, CA | 8838 | 89101 | HOME FURNITURE/EQUIPMENT STORE |
| PLUMAS, CA | 1448 | 6758 | LUMBER & WOOD PRODS, EXC FURN. |
| RIVERSIDE, CA | 36496 | 390274 | EDUCATIONAL SERVICES |
| SACRAMENTO, CA | 34564 | 423971 | EDUCATIONAL SERVICES |
| SAN BENITO, CA | 1466 | 13932 | WHOLESALE TRADE: NONDURABLE |
| SAN BERNARDINO, CA | 42577 | 441372 | EDUCATIONAL SERVICES |
| SAN DIEGO, CA | 91061 | 1092274 | NATIONAL SECURITY/INT AFFAIRS |
| SAN FRANCISCO, CA | 38855 | 450757 | EATING AND DRINKING PLACES |
| SAN JOAQUIN, CA | 14147 | 182086 | EDUCATIONAL SERVICES |
| SAN LUIS OBISPO, CA | 10760 | 79778 | EATING AND DRINKING PLACES |
| SAN MATEO, CA | 26040 | 300164 | HOME FURNITURE/EQUIPMENT STORE |
| SANTA BARBARA, CA | 13871 | 138849 | EATING AND DRINKING PLACES |
| SANTA CLARA, CA | 55377 | 825063 | BUSINESS SERVICES |
| SANTA CRUZ, CA | 9992 | 89762 | EATING AND DRINKING PLACES |
| SHASTA, CA | 6167 | 54193 | EDUCATIONAL SERVICES |
| SIERRA, CA | 222 | 1296 | EDUCATIONAL SERVICES |
| SISKIYOU, CA | 2110 | 12983 | EDUCATIONAL SERVICES |
| SOLANO, CA | 9979 | 110390 | NATIONAL SECURITY/INT AFFAIRS |
| SONOMA, CA | 17589 | 157078 | EDUCATIONAL SERVICES |
| STANISLAUS, CA | 11766 | 144613 | FOOD AND KINDRED PRODUCTS |
| SUTTER, CA | 2483 | 23307 | EDUCATIONAL SERVICES |
| TEHAMA, CA | 2026 | 17067 | GENERAL MERCHANDISE STORES |
| TRINITY, CA | 637 | 3905 | EDUCATIONAL SERVICES |
| TULARE, CA | 10090 | 105528 | WHOLESALE TRADE: NONDURABLE |
| TUOLUMNE, CA | 2637 | 16869 | EATING AND DRINKING PLACES |
| VENTURA, CA | 22468 | 252512 | EATING AND DRINKING PLACES |
| YOLO, CA | 4822 | 59180 | WHOLESALE TRADE: NONDURABLE |
| YUBA, CA | 1564 | 16221 | HEALTH SERVICES |

| COUNTY | 2000 Total Firms | 2000 Total Employ-ees | TOP INDUSTRY RANKED on 2000 EMPLOYMENT |
|---|---|---|---|
| ADAMS, CO | 9470 | 130424 | WHOLESALE TRADE: DURABLE GOODS |
| ALAMOSA, CO | 810 | 6424 | EDUCATIONAL SERVICES |
| ARAPAHOE, CO | 16207 | 216196 | BUSINESS SERVICES |
| ARCHULETA, CO | 1029 | 3728 | HOTELS, ROOMING HOUSES, CAMPS |
| BACA, CO | 207 | 1039 | EDUCATIONAL SERVICES |
| BENT, CO | 170 | 1852 | HEALTH SERVICES |
| BOULDER, CO | 11087 | 137828 | BUSINESS SERVICES |
| CHAFFEE, CO | 1039 | 6770 | EATING AND DRINKING PLACES |
| CHEYENNE, CO | 155 | 1016 | EDUCATIONAL SERVICES |
| CLEAR CREEK, CO | 497 | 3578 | HOTELS, ROOMING HOUSES, CAMPS |
| CONEJOS, CO | 222 | 1392 | EDUCATIONAL SERVICES |
| COSTILLA, CO | 147 | 902 | EDUCATIONAL SERVICES |
| CROWLEY, CO | 124 | 987 | JUSTICE, PUBLIC ORDER/SAFETY |
| CUSTER, CO | 134 | 617 | EDUCATIONAL SERVICES |
| DELTA, CO | 1176 | 6543 | HEALTH SERVICES |
| DENVER, CO | 22939 | 340427 | BUSINESS SERVICES |
| DOLORES, CO | 125 | 436 | EXECUTIVE, LEGISLATIVE GOVT. |
| DOUGLAS, CO | 4069 | 41218 | EATING AND DRINKING PLACES |
| EAGLE, CO | 3032 | 30397 | AMUSEMENT/RECREATION SERVICES |
| ELBERT, CO | 589 | 2720 | EDUCATIONAL SERVICES |
| EL PASO, CO | 16355 | 215754 | EATING AND DRINKING PLACES |
| FREMONT, CO | 1410 | 11884 | JUSTICE, PUBLIC ORDER/SAFETY |
| GARFIELD, CO | 2528 | 15269 | CONSTRUCT: SPEC TRADE CONTRACT |
| GILPIN, CO | 194 | 7301 | ADMIN: ECONOMIC PROGRAMS |
| GRAND, CO | 1112 | 8530 | HOTELS, ROOMING HOUSES, CAMPS |
| GUNNISON, CO | 1098 | 11086 | HOTELS, ROOMING HOUSES, CAMPS |
| HINSDALE, CO | 91 | 381 | HOTELS, ROOMING HOUSES, CAMPS |
| HUERFANO, CO | 327 | 2428 | EATING AND DRINKING PLACES |
| JACKSON, CO | 141 | 632 | EDUCATIONAL SERVICES |
| JEFFERSON, CO | 16511 | 193974 | EATING AND DRINKING PLACES |
| KIOWA, CO | 156 | 653 | HEALTH SERVICES |
| KIT CARSON, CO | 484 | 2642 | EDUCATIONAL SERVICES |
| LAKE, CO | 336 | 1789 | EDUCATIONAL SERVICES |
| LA PLATA, CO | 3661 | 27459 | CONSTRUCT: SPEC TRADE CONTRACT |
| LARIMER, CO | 9584 | 106637 | EDUCATIONAL SERVICES |
| LAS ANIMAS, CO | 661 | 4213 | EDUCATIONAL SERVICES |
| LINCOLN, CO | 359 | 2425 | JUSTICE, PUBLIC ORDER/SAFETY |
| LOGAN, CO | 939 | 7668 | HEALTH SERVICES |
| MESA, CO | 4677 | 47166 | EDUCATIONAL SERVICES |
| MINERAL, CO | 83 | 286 | HOTELS, ROOMING HOUSES, CAMPS |
| MOFFAT, CO | 608 | 4100 | EDUCATIONAL SERVICES |
| MONTEZUMA, CO | 1518 | 10172 | AMUSEMENT/RECREATION SERVICES |
| MONTROSE, CO | 1746 | 11998 | EATING AND DRINKING PLACES |
| MORGAN, CO | 1137 | 10221 | FOOD AND KINDRED PRODUCTS |
| OTERO, CO | 768 | 6635 | EDUCATIONAL SERVICES |
| OURAY, CO | 320 | 1211 | EATING AND DRINKING PLACES |
| PARK, CO | 576 | 1993 | EDUCATIONAL SERVICES |
| PHILLIPS, CO | 340 | 1717 | HEALTH SERVICES |
| PITKIN, CO | 1940 | 16723 | HOTELS, ROOMING HOUSES, CAMPS |
| PROWERS, CO | 602 | 4861 | WHOLESALE TRADE: DURABLE GOODS |
| PUEBLO, CO | 4183 | 50993 | EATING AND DRINKING PLACES |
| RIO BLANCO, CO | 397 | 2775 | MINING AND QUARRYING EXC FUELS |
| RIO GRANDE, CO | 645 | 4319 | WHOLESALE TRADE: NONDURABLE |
| ROUTT, CO | 1513 | 13057 | HOTELS, ROOMING HOUSES, CAMPS |
| SAGUACHE, CO | 241 | 1414 | WHOLESALE TRADE: NONDURABLE |
| SAN JUAN, CO | 149 | 379 | EATING AND DRINKING PLACES |
| SAN MIGUEL, CO | 766 | 4970 | HOTELS, ROOMING HOUSES, CAMPS |
| SEDGWICK, CO | 173 | 725 | EDUCATIONAL SERVICES |
| SUMMIT, CO | 2157 | 22858 | HOTELS, ROOMING HOUSES, CAMPS |
| TELLER, CO | 795 | 6109 | AMUSEMENT/RECREATION SERVICES |
| WASHINGTON, CO | 238 | 1271 | EDUCATIONAL SERVICES |
| WELD, CO | 5206 | 64722 | EDUCATIONAL SERVICES |
| YUMA, CO | 536 | 2940 | EDUCATIONAL SERVICES |
| FAIRFIELD, CT | 35786 | 399040 | EDUCATIONAL SERVICES |
| HARTFORD, CT | 27147 | 455937 | INSURANCE CARRIERS |
| LITCHFIELD, CT | 7114 | 61234 | EDUCATIONAL SERVICES |
| MIDDLESEX, CT | 5774 | 55342 | EDUCATIONAL SERVICES |
| NEW HAVEN, CT | 25595 | 298852 | EDUCATIONAL SERVICES |
| NEW LONDON, CT | 8297 | 112487 | AMUSEMENT/RECREATION SERVICES |
| TOLLAND, CT | 3334 | 34089 | EDUCATIONAL SERVICES |
| WINDHAM, CT | 3283 | 34609 | EDUCATIONAL SERVICES |
| KENT, DE | 4041 | 59618 | NATIONAL SECURITY/INT AFFAIRS |
| NEW CASTLE, DE | 16656 | 225186 | EDUCATIONAL SERVICES |
| SUSSEX, DE | 6443 | 56179 | EATING AND DRINKING PLACES |
| DISTRICT OF COLUMBIA, DC | 32747 | 475285 | EDUCATIONAL SERVICES |
| ALACHUA, FL | 6563 | 94991 | EDUCATIONAL SERVICES |
| BAKER, FL | 528 | 4024 | JUSTICE, PUBLIC ORDER/SAFETY |
| BAY, FL | 5609 | 56235 | EATING AND DRINKING PLACES |
| BRADFORD, FL | 518 | 4038 | EDUCATIONAL SERVICES |
| BREVARD, FL | 15710 | 170504 | ADMIN: ECONOMIC PROGRAMS |

| COUNTY | 2000 Total Firms | 2000 Total Employees | TOP INDUSTRY RANKED on 2000 EMPLOYMENT |
|---|---|---|---|
| BROWARD, FL | 54215 | 551069 | EATING AND DRINKING PLACES |
| CALHOUN, FL | 395 | 3859 | JUSTICE, PUBLIC ORDER/SAFETY |
| CHARLOTTE, FL | 4428 | 41393 | HEALTH SERVICES |
| CITRUS, FL | 4015 | 26289 | EATING AND DRINKING PLACES |
| CLAY, FL | 3388 | 36624 | EATING AND DRINKING PLACES |
| COLLIER, FL | 12764 | 107274 | HEALTH SERVICES |
| COLUMBIA, FL | 1622 | 19290 | HEALTH SERVICES |
| DADE, FL | 74595 | 808780 | EDUCATIONAL SERVICES |
| DE SOTO, FL | 934 | 8181 | AGRICULTURAL SERVICES |
| DIXIE, FL | 449 | 2874 | JUSTICE, PUBLIC ORDER/SAFETY |
| DUVAL, FL | 23967 | 366535 | HEALTH SERVICES |
| ESCAMBIA, FL | 8985 | 124933 | NATIONAL SECURITY/INT AFFAIRS |
| FLAGLER, FL | 1237 | 10830 | EATING AND DRINKING PLACES |
| FRANKLIN, FL | 571 | 3034 | JUSTICE, PUBLIC ORDER/SAFETY |
| GADSDEN, FL | 1166 | 15345 | HEALTH SERVICES |
| GILCHRIST, FL | 293 | 3911 | JUSTICE, PUBLIC ORDER/SAFETY |
| GLADES, FL | 296 | 1922 | EXECUTIVE, LEGISLATIVE GOVT. |
| GULF, FL | 503 | 3458 | JUSTICE, PUBLIC ORDER/SAFETY |
| HAMILTON, FL | 308 | 3777 | CHEMICALS AND ALLIED PRODUCTS |
| HARDEE, FL | 758 | 6866 | HEALTH SERVICES |
| HENDRY, FL | 1062 | 11156 | AGRICULTURAL - CROPS |
| HERNANDO, FL | 3172 | 27598 | HEALTH SERVICES |
| HIGHLANDS, FL | 3225 | 24196 | HEALTH SERVICES |
| HILLSBOROUGH, FL | 30450 | 402292 | EATING AND DRINKING PLACES |
| HOLMES, FL | 428 | 2853 | EDUCATIONAL SERVICES |
| INDIAN RIVER, FL | 4315 | 39374 | WHOLESALE TRADE: NONDURABLE |
| JACKSON, FL | 1345 | 11848 | HEALTH SERVICES |
| JEFFERSON, FL | 448 | 2796 | JUSTICE, PUBLIC ORDER/SAFETY |
| LAFAYETTE, FL | 159 | 1472 | JUSTICE, PUBLIC ORDER/SAFETY |
| LAKE, FL | 8430 | 65595 | HEALTH SERVICES |
| LEE, FL | 16711 | 161738 | EATING AND DRINKING PLACES |
| LEON, FL | 7713 | 108350 | EATING AND DRINKING PLACES |
| LEVY, FL | 1192 | 7704 | EDUCATIONAL SERVICES |
| LIBERTY, FL | 162 | 1560 | JUSTICE, PUBLIC ORDER/SAFETY |
| MADISON, FL | 552 | 4087 | JUSTICE, PUBLIC ORDER/SAFETY |
| MANATEE, FL | 8215 | 88516 | EATING AND DRINKING PLACES |
| MARION, FL | 9846 | 86429 | HEALTH SERVICES |
| MARTIN, FL | 4860 | 43642 | HEALTH SERVICES |
| MONROE, FL | 5732 | 41818 | HOTELS, ROOMING HOUSES, CAMPS |
| NASSAU, FL | 1793 | 15256 | HOTELS, ROOMING HOUSES, CAMPS |
| OKALOOSA, FL | 8257 | 69158 | EATING AND DRINKING PLACES |
| OKEECHOBEE, FL | 1182 | 8889 | EATING AND DRINKING PLACES |
| ORANGE, FL | 30152 | 434605 | EATING AND DRINKING PLACES |
| OSCEOLA, FL | 5336 | 52086 | EATING AND DRINKING PLACES |
| PALM BEACH, FL | 40022 | 408399 | EATING AND DRINKING PLACES |
| PASCO, FL | 8883 | 77885 | EDUCATIONAL SERVICES |
| PINELLAS, FL | 30669 | 349668 | EATING AND DRINKING PLACES |
| POLK, FL | 14490 | 152497 | EDUCATIONAL SERVICES |
| PUTNAM, FL | 2108 | 16941 | EDUCATIONAL SERVICES |
| ST. JOHNS, FL | 4334 | 33716 | EATING AND DRINKING PLACES |
| ST. LUCIE, FL | 4851 | 50686 | EDUCATIONAL SERVICES |
| SANTA ROSA, FL | 3579 | 23165 | EDUCATIONAL SERVICES |
| SARASOTA, FL | 13811 | 119305 | EATING AND DRINKING PLACES |
| SEMINOLE, FL | 12646 | 121742 | EATING AND DRINKING PLACES |
| SUMTER, FL | 1281 | 9060 | JUSTICE, PUBLIC ORDER/SAFETY |
| SUWANNEE, FL | 967 | 7790 | HEALTH SERVICES |
| TAYLOR, FL | 660 | 6748 | LUMBER & WOOD PRODS, EXC FURN. |
| UNION, FL | 207 | 3585 | HEALTH SERVICES |
| VOLUSIA, FL | 14414 | 139469 | EATING AND DRINKING PLACES |
| WAKULLA, FL | 552 | 3647 | EDUCATIONAL SERVICES |
| WALTON, FL | 1760 | 12427 | EATING AND DRINKING PLACES |
| WASHINGTON, FL | 566 | 5555 | JUSTICE, PUBLIC ORDER/SAFETY |
| APPLING, GA | 597 | 4687 | EDUCATIONAL SERVICES |
| ATKINSON, GA | 202 | 2504 | WHOLESALE TRADE: DURABLE GOODS |
| BACON, GA | 423 | 3258 | LUMBER & WOOD PRODS, EXC FURN. |
| BAKER, GA | 75 | 344 | EXECUTIVE, LEGISLATIVE GOVT. |
| BALDWIN, GA | 1212 | 21479 | HEALTH SERVICES |
| BANKS, GA | 440 | 3361 | MISCELLANEOUS RETAIL |
| BARROW, GA | 1038 | 11679 | ELECTRIC, GAS & SANITARY SERV. |
| BARTOW, GA | 2210 | 25140 | WHOLESALE TRADE: DURABLE GOODS |
| BEN HILL, GA | 639 | 8775 | LUMBER & WOOD PRODS, EXC FURN. |
| BERRIEN, GA | 391 | 3811 | APPAREL, FINISHED PRODUCTS |
| BIBB, GA | 5100 | 74913 | EDUCATIONAL SERVICES |
| BLECKLEY, GA | 323 | 3650 | WHOLESALE TRADE: DURABLE GOODS |
| BRANTLEY, GA | 305 | 1748 | EDUCATIONAL SERVICES |
| BROOKS, GA | 383 | 3246 | HEALTH SERVICES |
| BRYAN, GA | 555 | 3794 | EDUCATIONAL SERVICES |
| BULLOCH, GA | 1833 | 18056 | EDUCATIONAL SERVICES |
| BURKE, GA | 599 | 4621 | EDUCATIONAL SERVICES |
| BUTTS, GA | 460 | 4409 | EXECUTIVE, LEGISLATIVE GOVT. |

| COUNTY | 2000 Total Firms | 2000 Total Employees | TOP INDUSTRY RANKED on 2000 EMPLOYMENT |
|---|---|---|---|
| CALHOUN, GA | 221 | 1363 | APPAREL, FINISHED PRODUCTS |
| CAMDEN, GA | 1193 | 18920 | NATIONAL SECURITY/INT AFFAIRS |
| CANDLER, GA | 328 | 2609 | HEALTH SERVICES |
| CARROLL, GA | 2519 | 32344 | WHOLESALE TRADE: DURABLE GOODS |
| CATOOSA, GA | 1367 | 14394 | HEALTH SERVICES |
| CHARLTON, GA | 293 | 1747 | EDUCATIONAL SERVICES |
| CHATHAM, GA | 8034 | 114002 | EATING AND DRINKING PLACES |
| CHATTAHOOCHEE, GA | 150 | 28084 | NATIONAL SECURITY/INT AFFAIRS |
| CHATTOOGA, GA | 601 | 7440 | TEXTILE MILL PRODUCTS |
| CHEROKEE, GA | 4104 | 29238 | EATING AND DRINKING PLACES |
| CLARKE, GA | 3598 | 53238 | EDUCATIONAL SERVICES |
| CLAY, GA | 88 | 769 | HOTELS, ROOMING HOUSES, CAMPS |
| CLAYTON, GA | 5578 | 102665 | TRANSPORTATION BY AIR |
| CLINCH, GA | 223 | 2495 | FABRICATED METAL PRODUCTS |
| COBB, GA | 21341 | 244941 | EATING AND DRINKING PLACES |
| COFFEE, GA | 1086 | 12786 | FOOD AND KINDRED PRODUCTS |
| COLQUITT, GA | 1181 | 13375 | APPAREL, FINISHED PRODUCTS |
| COLUMBIA, GA | 2081 | 21148 | EDUCATIONAL SERVICES |
| COOK, GA | 468 | 4449 | EATING AND DRINKING PLACES |
| COWETA, GA | 2174 | 19312 | WHOLESALE TRADE: DURABLE GOODS |
| CRAWFORD, GA | 245 | 1219 | EDUCATIONAL SERVICES |
| CRISP, GA | 853 | 8967 | EATING AND DRINKING PLACES |
| DADE, GA | 417 | 3420 | EDUCATIONAL SERVICES |
| DAWSON, GA | 704 | 4608 | MISCELLANEOUS RETAIL |
| DECATUR, GA | 910 | 9392 | CHEMICALS AND ALLIED PRODUCTS |
| DEKALB, GA | 20048 | 283742 | EDUCATIONAL SERVICES |
| DODGE, GA | 457 | 4393 | EDUCATIONAL SERVICES |
| DOOLY, GA | 351 | 2420 | EDUCATIONAL SERVICES |
| DOUGHERTY, GA | 3362 | 46191 | EDUCATIONAL SERVICES |
| DOUGLAS, GA | 2585 | 24241 | EATING AND DRINKING PLACES |
| EARLY, GA | 494 | 4681 | PAPER AND ALLIED PRODUCTS |
| ECHOLS, GA | 24 | 128 | EDUCATIONAL SERVICES |
| EFFINGHAM, GA | 678 | 6876 | PAPER AND ALLIED PRODUCTS |
| ELBERT, GA | 791 | 6842 | WHOLESALE TRADE: DURABLE GOODS |
| EMANUEL, GA | 707 | 6527 | EDUCATIONAL SERVICES |
| EVANS, GA | 324 | 3558 | FOOD AND KINDRED PRODUCTS |
| FANNIN, GA | 863 | 5503 | APPAREL, FINISHED PRODUCTS |
| FAYETTE, GA | 2654 | 26607 | EATING AND DRINKING PLACES |
| FLOYD, GA | 2702 | 34131 | EDUCATIONAL SERVICES |
| FORSYTH, GA | 3318 | 33200 | WHOLESALE TRADE: DURABLE GOODS |
| FRANKLIN, GA | 722 | 6824 | HEALTH SERVICES |
| FULTON, GA | 33294 | 534832 | BUSINESS SERVICES |
| GILMER, GA | 799 | 6125 | FOOD AND KINDRED PRODUCTS |
| GLASCOCK, GA | 72 | 311 | EDUCATIONAL SERVICES |
| GLYNN, GA | 3018 | 32145 | HOTELS, ROOMING HOUSES, CAMPS |
| GORDON, GA | 1421 | 20776 | TEXTILE MILL PRODUCTS |
| GRADY, GA | 692 | 5430 | EDUCATIONAL SERVICES |
| GREENE, GA | 435 | 4324 | TEXTILE MILL PRODUCTS |
| GWINNETT, GA | 15115 | 219559 | WHOLESALE TRADE: DURABLE GOODS |
| HABERSHAM, GA | 1648 | 15245 | JUSTICE, PUBLIC ORDER/SAFETY |
| HALL, GA | 4468 | 57203 | FOOD AND KINDRED PRODUCTS |
| HANCOCK, GA | 202 | 1511 | EDUCATIONAL SERVICES |
| HARALSON, GA | 690 | 5956 | EDUCATIONAL SERVICES |
| HARRIS, GA | 526 | 5223 | HOTELS, ROOMING HOUSES, CAMPS |
| HART, GA | 638 | 6847 | TRANSPORTATION EQUIPMENT |
| HEARD, GA | 192 | 1753 | APPAREL, FINISHED PRODUCTS |
| HENRY, GA | 2561 | 23240 | EDUCATIONAL SERVICES |
| HOUSTON, GA | 2526 | 44436 | NATIONAL SECURITY/INT AFFAIRS |
| IRWIN, GA | 264 | 2185 | WHOLESALE TRADE: DURABLE GOODS |
| JACKSON, GA | 1297 | 13649 | FOOD AND KINDRED PRODUCTS |
| JASPER, GA | 238 | 2233 | LUMBER & WOOD PRODS, EXC FURN. |
| JEFF DAVIS, GA | 437 | 4931 | APPAREL, FINISHED PRODUCTS |
| JEFFERSON, GA | 581 | 5324 | EDUCATIONAL SERVICES |
| JENKINS, GA | 236 | 2702 | MISCELLANEOUS RETAIL |
| JOHNSON, GA | 216 | 1763 | APPAREL, FINISHED PRODUCTS |
| JONES, GA | 439 | 2795 | EDUCATIONAL SERVICES |
| LAMAR, GA | 403 | 4519 | APPAREL, FINISHED PRODUCTS |
| LANIER, GA | 140 | 1075 | HEALTH SERVICES |
| LAURENS, GA | 1522 | 18000 | HEALTH SERVICES |
| LEE, GA | 413 | 3176 | EDUCATIONAL SERVICES |
| LIBERTY, GA | 1328 | 32937 | NATIONAL SECURITY/INT AFFAIRS |
| LINCOLN, GA | 351 | 1820 | FOOD AND KINDRED PRODUCTS |
| LONG, GA | 117 | 795 | EDUCATIONAL SERVICES |
| LOWNDES, GA | 2996 | 31475 | EATING AND DRINKING PLACES |
| LUMPKIN, GA | 826 | 5878 | EDUCATIONAL SERVICES |
| MCDUFFIE, GA | 699 | 7569 | EDUCATIONAL SERVICES |
| MCINTOSH, GA | 451 | 2380 | EATING AND DRINKING PLACES |
| MACON, GA | 377 | 3726 | FOOD AND KINDRED PRODUCTS |
| MADISON, GA | 484 | 3092 | EDUCATIONAL SERVICES |
| MARION, GA | 137 | 896 | EDUCATIONAL SERVICES |

| COUNTY | 2000 Total Firms | 2000 Total Employ-ees | TOP INDUSTRY RANKED on 2000 EMPLOYMENT | COUNTY | 2000 Total Firms | 2000 Total Employ-ees | TOP INDUSTRY RANKED on 2000 EMPLOYMENT |
|---|---|---|---|---|---|---|---|
| MERIWETHER, GA | 612 | 6584 | MISC. MANUFACTURING INDUSTRIES | CARIBOU, ID | 307 | 2475 | CHEMICALS AND ALLIED PRODUCTS |
| MILLER, GA | 217 | 1202 | HEALTH SERVICES | CASSIA, ID | 941 | 8206 | FOOD AND KINDRED PRODUCTS |
| MITCHELL, GA | 608 | 7140 | FOOD AND KINDRED PRODUCTS | CLARK, ID | 61 | 379 | EDUCATIONAL SERVICES |
| MONROE, GA | 604 | 4599 | EDUCATIONAL SERVICES | CLEARWATER, ID | 455 | 2844 | LUMBER & WOOD PRODS, EXC FURN. |
| MONTGOMERY, GA | 202 | 1382 | EDUCATIONAL SERVICES | CUSTER, ID | 294 | 1558 | HOTELS, ROOMING HOUSES, CAMPS |
| MORGAN, GA | 635 | 5474 | EATING AND DRINKING PLACES | ELMORE, ID | 789 | 13706 | NATIONAL SECURITY/INT AFFAIRS |
| MURRAY, GA | 713 | 11496 | TEXTILE MILL PRODUCTS | FRANKLIN, ID | 320 | 2042 | EDUCATIONAL SERVICES |
| MUSCOGEE, GA | 5291 | 69915 | EATING AND DRINKING PLACES | FREMONT, ID | 399 | 2589 | EDUCATIONAL SERVICES |
| NEWTON, GA | 1566 | 14706 | EDUCATIONAL SERVICES | GEM, ID | 455 | 3038 | ELECTRIC, GAS & SANITARY SERV. |
| OCONEE, GA | 750 | 5669 | EDUCATIONAL SERVICES | GOODING, ID | 547 | 3448 | EDUCATIONAL SERVICES |
| OGLETHORPE, GA | 245 | 1185 | EDUCATIONAL SERVICES | IDAHO, ID | 811 | 4137 | LUMBER & WOOD PRODS, EXC FURN. |
| PAULDING, GA | 1306 | 9810 | EDUCATIONAL SERVICES | JEFFERSON, ID | 505 | 4092 | FOOD AND KINDRED PRODUCTS |
| PEACH, GA | 696 | 7824 | TRANSPORTATION EQUIPMENT | JEROME, ID | 641 | 5549 | MOTOR FREIGHT TRANSPORTATION |
| PICKENS, GA | 518 | 5263 | EDUCATIONAL SERVICES | KOOTENAI, ID | 4537 | 38951 | EATING AND DRINKING PLACES |
| PIERCE, GA | 487 | 3084 | EDUCATIONAL SERVICES | LATAH, ID | 1368 | 11757 | EDUCATIONAL SERVICES |
| PIKE, GA | 287 | 1298 | EDUCATIONAL SERVICES | LEMHI, ID | 517 | 2902 | FORESTRY |
| POLK, GA | 901 | 7195 | EDUCATIONAL SERVICES | LEWIS, ID | 146 | 700 | EDUCATIONAL SERVICES |
| PULASKI, GA | 353 | 2888 | APPAREL, FINISHED PRODUCTS | LINCOLN, ID | 143 | 1130 | HEAVY CONSTRUCTION: EXC BUILD |
| PUTNAM, GA | 477 | 4625 | LUMBER & WOOD PRODS, EXC FURN. | MADISON, ID | 704 | 8860 | EDUCATIONAL SERVICES |
| QUITMAN, GA | 57 | 236 | EXECUTIVE, LEGISLATIVE GOVT. | MINIDOKA, ID | 704 | 6323 | FOOD AND KINDRED PRODUCTS |
| RABUN, GA | 712 | 5875 | TEXTILE MILL PRODUCTS | NEZ PERCE, ID | 1787 | 18532 | HEALTH SERVICES |
| RANDOLPH, GA | 278 | 2048 | EDUCATIONAL SERVICES | ONEIDA, ID | 144 | 756 | EDUCATIONAL SERVICES |
| RICHMOND, GA | 5944 | 88155 | EXECUTIVE, LEGISLATIVE GOVT. | OWYHEE, ID | 323 | 2226 | EDUCATIONAL SERVICES |
| ROCKDALE, GA | 2213 | 25488 | EATING AND DRINKING PLACES | PAYETTE, ID | 664 | 5073 | LUMBER & WOOD PRODS, EXC FURN. |
| SCHLEY, GA | 112 | 1107 | LUMBER & WOOD PRODS, EXC FURN. | POWER, ID | 310 | 3944 | FOOD AND KINDRED PRODUCTS |
| SCREVEN, GA | 482 | 3678 | TEXTILE MILL PRODUCTS | SHOSHONE, ID | 672 | 4560 | HOTELS, ROOMING HOUSES, CAMPS |
| SEMINOLE, GA | 330 | 2332 | APPAREL, FINISHED PRODUCTS | TETON, ID | 202 | 852 | HOTELS, ROOMING HOUSES, CAMPS |
| SPALDING, GA | 1589 | 16753 | EDUCATIONAL SERVICES | TWIN FALLS, ID | 2953 | 27445 | FOOD AND KINDRED PRODUCTS |
| STEPHENS, GA | 829 | 8943 | EDUCATIONAL SERVICES | VALLEY, ID | 686 | 4004 | EATING AND DRINKING PLACES |
| STEWART, GA | 166 | 1165 | LUMBER & WOOD PRODS, EXC FURN. | WASHINGTON, ID | 371 | 2656 | FOOD STORES |
| SUMTER, GA | 1085 | 13337 | EDUCATIONAL SERVICES | ADAMS, IL | 2524 | 30027 | EDUCATIONAL SERVICES |
| TALBOT, GA | 151 | 753 | EXECUTIVE, LEGISLATIVE GOVT. | ALEXANDER, IL | 349 | 2077 | EDUCATIONAL SERVICES |
| TALIAFERRO, GA | 79 | 279 | EDUCATIONAL SERVICES | BOND, IL | 497 | 3596 | EDUCATIONAL SERVICES |
| TATTNALL, GA | 541 | 4656 | APPAREL, FINISHED PRODUCTS | BOONE, IL | 1036 | 9897 | EDUCATIONAL SERVICES |
| TAYLOR, GA | 316 | 2140 | WHOLESALE TRADE: NONDURABLE | BROWN, IL | 199 | 2369 | WHOLESALE TRADE: NONDURABLE |
| TELFAIR, GA | 419 | 3996 | INDUSTRIAL & COMM. MACHINERY | BUREAU, IL | 1430 | 12358 | EDUCATIONAL SERVICES |
| TERRELL, GA | 316 | 2302 | WHOLESALE TRADE: NONDURABLE | CALHOUN, IL | 206 | 963 | EATING AND DRINKING PLACES |
| THOMAS, GA | 1581 | 21404 | HEALTH SERVICES | CARROLL, IL | 762 | 5787 | INDUSTRIAL & COMM. MACHINERY |
| TIFT, GA | 1548 | 17735 | GENERAL MERCHANDISE STORES | CASS, IL | 544 | 5293 | FOOD AND KINDRED PRODUCTS |
| TOOMBS, GA | 997 | 11680 | APPAREL, FINISHED PRODUCTS | CHAMPAIGN, IL | 5544 | 98043 | EDUCATIONAL SERVICES |
| TOWNS, GA | 591 | 2955 | EDUCATIONAL SERVICES | CHRISTIAN, IL | 1311 | 11252 | WHOLESALE TRADE: DURABLE GOODS |
| TREUTLEN, GA | 188 | 1145 | TEXTILE MILL PRODUCTS | CLARK, IL | 609 | 4428 | EATING AND DRINKING PLACES |
| TROUP, GA | 2071 | 26134 | TEXTILE MILL PRODUCTS | CLAY, IL | 600 | 3814 | EDUCATIONAL SERVICES |
| TURNER, GA | 330 | 3067 | BUSINESS SERVICES | CLINTON, IL | 1146 | 10930 | EDUCATIONAL SERVICES |
| TWIGGS, GA | 204 | 1885 | STONE/CLAY/GLASS PRODUCTS | COLES, IL | 2020 | 25106 | EDUCATIONAL SERVICES |
| UNION, GA | 937 | 4870 | EDUCATIONAL SERVICES | COOK, IL | 161418 | 2272710 | EDUCATIONAL SERVICES |
| UPSON, GA | 865 | 8451 | TEXTILE MILL PRODUCTS | CRAWFORD, IL | 675 | 6502 | EDUCATIONAL SERVICES |
| WALKER, GA | 1434 | 17567 | TEXTILE MILL PRODUCTS | CUMBERLAND, IL | 317 | 1780 | EDUCATIONAL SERVICES |
| WALTON, GA | 1479 | 11539 | EDUCATIONAL SERVICES | DEKALB, IL | 2858 | 33488 | EDUCATIONAL SERVICES |
| WARE, GA | 1361 | 13222 | EDUCATIONAL SERVICES | DE WITT, IL | 591 | 6040 | ELECTRIC, GAS & SANITARY SERV. |
| WARREN, GA | 156 | 1134 | EDUCATIONAL SERVICES | DOUGLAS, IL | 900 | 7876 | LUMBER & WOOD PRODS, EXC FURN. |
| WASHINGTON, GA | 606 | 7576 | STONE/CLAY/GLASS PRODUCTS | DUPAGE, IL | 36528 | 512666 | WHOLESALE TRADE: DURABLE GOODS |
| WAYNE, GA | 809 | 7554 | WHOLESALE TRADE: DURABLE GOODS | EDGAR, IL | 674 | 5571 | EDUCATIONAL SERVICES |
| WEBSTER, GA | 54 | 222 | EDUCATIONAL SERVICES | EDWARDS, IL | 284 | 3059 | TRANSPORTATION EQUIPMENT |
| WHEELER, GA | 134 | 693 | EDUCATIONAL SERVICES | EFFINGHAM, IL | 1461 | 19266 | PRINTING AND PUBLISHING |
| WHITE, GA | 1253 | 6842 | EATING AND DRINKING PLACES | FAYETTE, IL | 768 | 6981 | JUSTICE, PUBLIC ORDER/SAFETY |
| WHITFIELD, GA | 3150 | 52477 | TEXTILE MILL PRODUCTS | FORD, IL | 648 | 4840 | HEALTH SERVICES |
| WILCOX, GA | 242 | 2043 | APPAREL, FINISHED PRODUCTS | FRANKLIN, IL | 1606 | 10937 | TRANSPORTATION EQUIPMENT |
| WILKES, GA | 578 | 4064 | WHOLESALE TRADE: DURABLE GOODS | FULTON, IL | 1190 | 8672 | EDUCATIONAL SERVICES |
| WILKINSON, GA | 285 | 3212 | MINING AND QUARRYING EXC FUELS | GALLATIN, IL | 251 | 1466 | EDUCATIONAL SERVICES |
| WORTH, GA | 466 | 3765 | EDUCATIONAL SERVICES | GREENE, IL | 423 | 2465 | EDUCATIONAL SERVICES |
| HAWAII, HI | 6623 | 53066 | HOTELS, ROOMING HOUSES, CAMPS | GRUNDY, IL | 1270 | 10650 | EDUCATIONAL SERVICES |
| HONOLULU, HI | 24924 | 323170 | EATING AND DRINKING PLACES | HAMILTON, IL | 295 | 1361 | EDUCATIONAL SERVICES |
| KALAWAO, HI | 8 | 56 | EXECUTIVE, LEGISLATIVE GOVT. | HANCOCK, IL | 872 | 6777 | ELECTRONIC/ELCTRCL EQPMNT |
| KAUAI, HI | 2990 | 25474 | HOTELS, ROOMING HOUSES, CAMPS | HARDIN, IL | 155 | 1056 | HEALTH SERVICES |
| MAUI, HI | 7371 | 64903 | HOTELS, ROOMING HOUSES, CAMPS | HENDERSON, IL | 269 | 1652 | EDUCATIONAL SERVICES |
| ADA, ID | 11644 | 146199 | EATING AND DRINKING PLACES | HENRY, IL | 1939 | 15381 | EDUCATIONAL SERVICES |
| ADAMS, ID | 191 | 1208 | LUMBER & WOOD PRODS, EXC FURN. | IROQUOIS, IL | 1255 | 8966 | EDUCATIONAL SERVICES |
| BANNOCK, ID | 2544 | 28465 | EDUCATIONAL SERVICES | JACKSON, IL | 1984 | 19304 | EATING AND DRINKING PLACES |
| BEAR LAKE, ID | 236 | 1395 | EDUCATIONAL SERVICES | JASPER, IL | 376 | 2566 | EDUCATIONAL SERVICES |
| BENEWAH, ID | 397 | 2857 | LUMBER & WOOD PRODS, EXC FURN. | JEFFERSON, IL | 1592 | 18844 | AUTO DEALERS & GAS SERV STA. |
| BINGHAM, ID | 1250 | 11079 | FOOD AND KINDRED PRODUCTS | JERSEY, IL | 634 | 4223 | EDUCATIONAL SERVICES |
| BLAINE, ID | 1393 | 9349 | HOTELS, ROOMING HOUSES, CAMPS | JO DAVIESS, IL | 1185 | 9578 | HOTELS, ROOMING HOUSES, CAMPS |
| BOISE, ID | 237 | 1171 | LUMBER & WOOD PRODS, EXC FURN. | JOHNSON, IL | 409 | 3241 | JUSTICE, PUBLIC ORDER/SAFETY |
| BONNER, ID | 1911 | 11877 | MISCELLANEOUS RETAIL | KANE, IL | 12144 | 160140 | EDUCATIONAL SERVICES |
| BONNEVILLE, ID | 3174 | 33429 | EATING AND DRINKING PLACES | KANKAKEE, IL | 3662 | 43596 | EDUCATIONAL SERVICES |
| BOUNDARY, ID | 513 | 3420 | EDUCATIONAL SERVICES | KENDALL, IL | 1559 | 12253 | EDUCATIONAL SERVICES |
| BUTTE, ID | 145 | 643 | HEALTH SERVICES | KNOX, IL | 1947 | 21350 | EDUCATIONAL SERVICES |
| CAMAS, ID | 58 | 196 | FORESTRY | LAKE, IL | 20597 | 291551 | WHOLESALE TRADE: DURABLE GOODS |
| CANYON, ID | 3805 | 43285 | EDUCATIONAL SERVICES | LA SALLE, IL | 4285 | 43695 | EDUCATIONAL SERVICES |

| COUNTY | 2000 Total Firms | 2000 Total Employ-ees | TOP INDUSTRY RANKED on 2000 EMPLOYMENT | COUNTY | 2000 Total Firms | 2000 Total Employ-ees | TOP INDUSTRY RANKED on 2000 EMPLOYMENT |
|---|---|---|---|---|---|---|---|
| LAWRENCE, IL | 568 | 4598 | HEALTH SERVICES | HAMILTON, IN | 5032 | 71772 | WHOLESALE TRADE: DURABLE GOODS |
| LEE, IL | 1248 | 13652 | EDUCATIONAL SERVICES | HANCOCK, IN | 1451 | 12903 | EDUCATIONAL SERVICES |
| LIVINGSTON, IL | 1355 | 14505 | PRINTING AND PUBLISHING | HARRISON, IN | 860 | 8308 | EDUCATIONAL SERVICES |
| LOGAN, IL | 1059 | 9671 | EDUCATIONAL SERVICES | HENDRICKS, IN | 2497 | 25153 | EATING AND DRINKING PLACES |
| MCDONOUGH, IL | 1231 | 15133 | EDUCATIONAL SERVICES | HENRY, IN | 1456 | 14040 | EDUCATIONAL SERVICES |
| MCHENRY, IL | 8372 | 86706 | INDUSTRIAL & COMM. MACHINERY | HOWARD, IN | 2537 | 41812 | ELECTRONIC/ELCTRCL EQPMNT |
| MCLEAN, IL | 4498 | 68675 | EDUCATIONAL SERVICES | HUNTINGTON, IN | 1154 | 15333 | ELECTRONIC/ELCTRCL EQPMNT |
| MACON, IL | 3665 | 53142 | EDUCATIONAL SERVICES | JACKSON, IN | 1518 | 17558 | TRANSPORTATION EQUIPMENT |
| MACOUPIN, IL | 1548 | 12031 | EDUCATIONAL SERVICES | JASPER, IN | 987 | 8438 | EATING AND DRINKING PLACES |
| MADISON, IL | 7821 | 84210 | EDUCATIONAL SERVICES | JAY, IN | 658 | 7287 | STONE/CLAY/GLASS PRODUCTS |
| MARION, IL | 1542 | 17490 | HEALTH SERVICES | JEFFERSON, IN | 1135 | 12866 | EDUCATIONAL SERVICES |
| MARSHALL, IL | 460 | 3562 | EDUCATIONAL SERVICES | JENNINGS, IN | 743 | 7347 | BUILDING MATRIALS/GARDEN SUPPL |
| MASON, IL | 582 | 3752 | EDUCATIONAL SERVICES | JOHNSON, IN | 2978 | 33284 | EATING AND DRINKING PLACES |
| MASSAC, IL | 597 | 7409 | AMUSEMENT/RECREATION SERVICES | KNOX, IN | 1481 | 16991 | EDUCATIONAL SERVICES |
| MENARD, IL | 405 | 2490 | EDUCATIONAL SERVICES | KOSCIUSKO, IN | 2520 | 35176 | MESR/ANLYZ/CNTRL INSTRMNTS |
| MERCER, IL | 567 | 3318 | EDUCATIONAL SERVICES | LAGRANGE, IN | 927 | 12173 | LUMBER & WOOD PRODS, EXC FURN. |
| MONROE, IL | 883 | 6099 | EATING AND DRINKING PLACES | LAKE, IN | 12466 | 174442 | PRIMARY METAL INDUSTRIES |
| MONTGOMERY, IL | 1226 | 10594 | HEALTH SERVICES | LA PORTE, IN | 3459 | 47866 | EATING AND DRINKING PLACES |
| MORGAN, IL | 1316 | 14731 | EDUCATIONAL SERVICES | LAWRENCE, IN | 1365 | 15690 | WHOLESALE TRADE: DURABLE GOODS |
| MOULTRIE, IL | 515 | 4116 | CONSTRUCT: SPEC TRADE CONTRACT | MADISON, IN | 3821 | 45207 | EATING AND DRINKING PLACES |
| OGLE, IL | 1677 | 18648 | FOOD STORES | MARION, IN | 26273 | 494581 | EATING AND DRINKING PLACES |
| PEORIA, IL | 6865 | 102736 | HEALTH SERVICES | MARSHALL, IN | 1642 | 21024 | FABRICATED METAL PRODUCTS |
| PERRY, IL | 758 | 6414 | ELECTRONIC/ELCTRCL EQPMNT | MARTIN, IN | 392 | 12829 | NATIONAL SECURITY/INT AFFAIRS |
| PIATT, IL | 599 | 3577 | EDUCATIONAL SERVICES | MIAMI, IN | 885 | 9582 | EATING AND DRINKING PLACES |
| PIKE, IL | 637 | 4434 | EDUCATIONAL SERVICES | MONROE, IN | 3643 | 50897 | EATING AND DRINKING PLACES |
| POPE, IL | 122 | 836 | SOCIAL SERVICES | MONTGOMERY, IN | 1322 | 16849 | PRINTING AND PUBLISHING |
| PULASKI, IL | 211 | 1517 | EDUCATIONAL SERVICES | MORGAN, IN | 1577 | 13439 | EDUCATIONAL SERVICES |
| PUTNAM, IL | 252 | 2315 | PRIMARY METAL INDUSTRIES | NEWTON, IN | 482 | 3577 | RUBBER & MISC PLASTIC PRODUCTS |
| RANDOLPH, IL | 1241 | 12105 | FOOD AND KINDRED PRODUCTS | NOBLE, IN | 1242 | 20615 | TRANSPORTATION EQUIPMENT |
| RICHLAND, IL | 699 | 7610 | TRANSPORTATION EQUIPMENT | OHIO, IN | 186 | 824 | EDUCATIONAL SERVICES |
| ROCK ISLAND, IL | 4807 | 71581 | INDUSTRIAL & COMM. MACHINERY | ORANGE, IN | 665 | 6826 | FURNITURE AND FIXTURES |
| ST. CLAIR, IL | 7194 | 81242 | EATING AND DRINKING PLACES | OWEN, IN | 454 | 5107 | MESR/ANLYZ/CNTRL INSTRMNTS |
| SALINE, IL | 1127 | 9659 | HEALTH SERVICES | PARKE, IN | 457 | 4178 | RUBBER & MISC PLASTIC PRODUCTS |
| SANGAMON, IL | 7185 | 111851 | EDUCATIONAL SERVICES | PERRY, IN | 608 | 6044 | EDUCATIONAL SERVICES |
| SCHUYLER, IL | 299 | 1926 | HEALTH SERVICES | PIKE, IN | 326 | 2911 | ELECTRIC, GAS & SANITARY SERV. |
| SCOTT, IL | 222 | 1926 | HEAVY CONSTRUCTION: EXC BUILD | PORTER, IN | 3875 | 49487 | PRIMARY METAL INDUSTRIES |
| SHELBY, IL | 788 | 8614 | ENGINEERING, ACCOUNTING, ETC. | POSEY, IN | 795 | 9662 | RUBBER & MISC PLASTIC PRODUCTS |
| STARK, IL | 246 | 1279 | EDUCATIONAL SERVICES | PULASKI, IN | 505 | 5180 | EDUCATIONAL SERVICES |
| STEPHENSON, IL | 1829 | 23011 | ELECTRONIC/ELCTRCL EQPMNT | PUTNAM, IN | 1058 | 11440 | JUSTICE, PUBLIC ORDER/SAFETY |
| TAZEWELL, IL | 3886 | 45377 | EDUCATIONAL SERVICES | RANDOLPH, IN | 832 | 7185 | EDUCATIONAL SERVICES |
| UNION, IL | 669 | 4831 | EDUCATIONAL SERVICES | RIPLEY, IN | 1020 | 11636 | MESR/ANLYZ/CNTRL INSTRMNTS |
| VERMILION, IL | 2864 | 32567 | WHOLESALE TRADE: DURABLE GOODS | RUSH, IN | 547 | 5002 | FABRICATED METAL PRODUCTS |
| WABASH, IL | 488 | 3990 | FABRICATED METAL PRODUCTS | ST. JOSEPH, IN | 8801 | 122950 | EDUCATIONAL SERVICES |
| WARREN, IL | 682 | 6219 | WHOLESALE TRADE: NONDURABLE | SCOTT, IN | 685 | 6870 | RUBBER & MISC PLASTIC PRODUCTS |
| WASHINGTON, IL | 610 | 5344 | TRANSPORTATION EQUIPMENT | SHELBY, IN | 1218 | 15677 | STONE/CLAY/GLASS PRODUCTS |
| WAYNE, IL | 635 | 4678 | TRANSPORTATION EQUIPMENT | SPENCER, IN | 629 | 7003 | AMUSEMENT/RECREATION SERVICES |
| WHITE, IL | 707 | 4903 | EDUCATIONAL SERVICES | STARKE, IN | 673 | 4822 | HEALTH SERVICES |
| WHITESIDE, IL | 1989 | 22446 | WHOLESALE TRADE: DURABLE GOODS | STEUBEN, IN | 1261 | 15385 | TRANSPORTATION EQUIPMENT |
| WILL, IL | 12190 | 130881 | EDUCATIONAL SERVICES | SULLIVAN, IN | 567 | 4759 | HEALTH SERVICES |
| WILLIAMSON, IL | 2591 | 29000 | EDUCATIONAL SERVICES | SWITZERLAND, IN | 195 | 1311 | LEATHER AND LEATHER PRODUCTS |
| WINNEBAGO, IL | 9030 | 135127 | INDUSTRIAL & COMM. MACHINERY | TIPPECANOE, IN | 3477 | 72113 | EDUCATIONAL SERVICES |
| WOODFORD, IL | 1092 | 10841 | EDUCATIONAL SERVICES | TIPTON, IN | 491 | 3620 | FABRICATED METAL PRODUCTS |
| ADAMS, IN | 1041 | 14112 | TRANSPORTATION EQUIPMENT | UNION, IN | 212 | 1185 | EATING AND DRINKING PLACES |
| ALLEN, IN | 9365 | 167115 | EATING AND DRINKING PLACES | VANDERBURGH, IN | 6183 | 111073 | HEALTH SERVICES |
| BARTHOLOMEW, IN | 2335 | 34084 | WHOLESALE TRADE: DURABLE GOODS | VERMILLION, IN | 451 | 4537 | CHEMICALS AND ALLIED PRODUCTS |
| BENTON, IN | 386 | 2698 | EDUCATIONAL SERVICES | VIGO, IN | 3145 | 49087 | EDUCATIONAL SERVICES |
| BLACKFORD, IN | 402 | 4591 | PAPER AND ALLIED PRODUCTS | WABASH, IN | 1111 | 13254 | EDUCATIONAL SERVICES |
| BOONE, IN | 1553 | 13119 | EATING AND DRINKING PLACES | WARREN, IN | 188 | 1429 | EDUCATIONAL SERVICES |
| BROWN, IN | 607 | 3731 | HOTELS, ROOMING HOUSES, CAMPS | WARRICK, IN | 1348 | 12777 | PRIMARY METAL INDUSTRIES |
| CARROLL, IN | 624 | 5809 | FOOD AND KINDRED PRODUCTS | WASHINGTON, IN | 804 | 6594 | EDUCATIONAL SERVICES |
| CASS, IN | 1182 | 16008 | FOOD AND KINDRED PRODUCTS | WAYNE, IN | 2469 | 30929 | EATING AND DRINKING PLACES |
| CLARK, IN | 2977 | 40048 | EATING AND DRINKING PLACES | WELLS, IN | 816 | 10640 | WHOLESALE TRADE: NONDURABLE |
| CLAY, IN | 774 | 7208 | TRANSPORTATION EQUIPMENT | WHITE, IN | 936 | 10403 | TRANSPORTATION EQUIPMENT |
| CLINTON, IN | 993 | 12961 | WHOLESALE TRADE: NONDURABLE | WHITLEY, IN | 915 | 11018 | TRANSPORTATION EQUIPMENT |
| CRAWFORD, IN | 269 | 1705 | MINING AND QUARRYING EXC FUELS | ADAIR, IA | 344 | 2721 | STONE/CLAY/GLASS PRODUCTS |
| DAVIESS, IN | 1036 | 10053 | FOOD AND KINDRED PRODUCTS | ADAMS, IA | 230 | 1382 | HEALTH SERVICES |
| DEARBORN, IN | 1291 | 14305 | AMUSEMENT/RECREATION SERVICES | ALLAMAKEE, IA | 654 | 5291 | FOOD AND KINDRED PRODUCTS |
| DECATUR, IN | 861 | 12023 | TRANSPORTATION EQUIPMENT | APPANOOSE, IA | 551 | 4225 | EDUCATIONAL SERVICES |
| DE KALB, IN | 1175 | 20389 | RUBBER & MISC PLASTIC PRODUCTS | AUDUBON, IA | 347 | 2323 | EDUCATIONAL SERVICES |
| DELAWARE, IN | 3883 | 48136 | EATING AND DRINKING PLACES | BENTON, IA | 849 | 5983 | EDUCATIONAL SERVICES |
| DUBOIS, IN | 1524 | 26448 | FURNITURE AND FIXTURES | BLACK HAWK, IA | 3851 | 73022 | INDUSTRIAL & COMM. MACHINERY |
| ELKHART, IN | 5744 | 116244 | TRANSPORTATION EQUIPMENT | BOONE, IA | 811 | 7781 | HEALTH SERVICES |
| FAYETTE, IN | 758 | 11064 | WHOLESALE TRADE: DURABLE GOODS | BREMER, IA | 893 | 8562 | EDUCATIONAL SERVICES |
| FLOYD, IN | 2035 | 26290 | EDUCATIONAL SERVICES | BUCHANAN, IA | 793 | 5680 | EDUCATIONAL SERVICES |
| FOUNTAIN, IN | 594 | 6361 | TRANSPORTATION EQUIPMENT | BUENA VISTA, IA | 842 | 8795 | FOOD AND KINDRED PRODUCTS |
| FRANKLIN, IN | 604 | 4535 | EATING AND DRINKING PLACES | BUTLER, IA | 597 | 3737 | EDUCATIONAL SERVICES |
| FULTON, IN | 796 | 7823 | EDUCATIONAL SERVICES | CALHOUN, IA | 512 | 3512 | HEALTH SERVICES |
| GIBSON, IN | 1103 | 9349 | EATING AND DRINKING PLACES | CARROLL, IA | 1064 | 9936 | EDUCATIONAL SERVICES |
| GRANT, IN | 2103 | 27501 | WHOLESALE TRADE: DURABLE GOODS | CASS, IA | 763 | 6140 | EDUCATIONAL SERVICES |
| GREENE, IN | 979 | 7730 | EDUCATIONAL SERVICES | CEDAR, IA | 701 | 4871 | EDUCATIONAL SERVICES |

| COUNTY | 2000 Total Firms | 2000 Total Employees | TOP INDUSTRY RANKED on 2000 EMPLOYMENT |
|---|---|---|---|
| CERRO GORDO, IA | 2033 | 21435 | EATING AND DRINKING PLACES |
| CHEROKEE, IA | 628 | 5819 | FOOD AND KINDRED PRODUCTS |
| CHICKASAW, IA | 539 | 4974 | FOOD AND KINDRED PRODUCTS |
| CLARKE, IA | 323 | 3180 | ELECTRONIC/ELCTRCL EQPMNT |
| CLAY, IA | 889 | 10194 | HEALTH SERVICES |
| CLAYTON, IA | 840 | 7312 | EDUCATIONAL SERVICES |
| CLINTON, IA | 1751 | 19181 | EDUCATIONAL SERVICES |
| CRAWFORD, IA | 758 | 7354 | FOOD AND KINDRED PRODUCTS |
| DALLAS, IA | 1034 | 12140 | NONDEPOSITORY CREDIT INSTITUT. |
| DAVIS, IA | 343 | 2015 | HEALTH SERVICES |
| DECATUR, IA | 361 | 3201 | EDUCATIONAL SERVICES |
| DELAWARE, IA | 654 | 5740 | ELECTRONIC/ELCTRCL EQPMNT |
| DES MOINES, IA | 1688 | 23093 | EATING AND DRINKING PLACES |
| DICKINSON, IA | 937 | 7114 | EATING AND DRINKING PLACES |
| DUBUQUE, IA | 3232 | 51975 | EDUCATIONAL SERVICES |
| EMMET, IA | 472 | 4181 | EDUCATIONAL SERVICES |
| FAYETTE, IA | 911 | 8125 | EDUCATIONAL SERVICES |
| FLOYD, IA | 650 | 5915 | SOCIAL SERVICES |
| FRANKLIN, IA | 480 | 3201 | EDUCATIONAL SERVICES |
| FREMONT, IA | 300 | 2931 | FABRICATED METAL PRODUCTS |
| GREENE, IA | 544 | 3331 | EDUCATIONAL SERVICES |
| GRUNDY, IA | 490 | 3650 | EDUCATIONAL SERVICES |
| GUTHRIE, IA | 519 | 3052 | EDUCATIONAL SERVICES |
| HAMILTON, IA | 671 | 8360 | ELECTRONIC/ELCTRCL EQPMNT |
| HANCOCK, IA | 513 | 6792 | LUMBER & WOOD PRODS, EXC FURN. |
| HARDIN, IA | 821 | 7720 | EDUCATIONAL SERVICES |
| HARRISON, IA | 560 | 3887 | EDUCATIONAL SERVICES |
| HENRY, IA | 786 | 10423 | GENERAL MERCHANDISE STORES |
| HOWARD, IA | 437 | 3582 | WHOLESALE TRADE: DURABLE GOODS |
| HUMBOLDT, IA | 468 | 4209 | INDUSTRIAL & COMM. MACHINERY |
| IDA, IA | 397 | 3374 | INDUSTRIAL & COMM. MACHINERY |
| IOWA, IA | 721 | 10793 | ELECTRONIC/ELCTRCL EQPMNT |
| JACKSON, IA | 857 | 6360 | EDUCATIONAL SERVICES |
| JASPER, IA | 1213 | 12901 | ELECTRONIC/ELCTRCL EQPMNT |
| JEFFERSON, IA | 918 | 7650 | EDUCATIONAL SERVICES |
| JOHNSON, IA | 3197 | 42714 | EATING AND DRINKING PLACES |
| JONES, IA | 743 | 5547 | EDUCATIONAL SERVICES |
| KEOKUK, IA | 426 | 2250 | HEALTH SERVICES |
| KOSSUTH, IA | 843 | 5854 | EDUCATIONAL SERVICES |
| LEE, IA | 1484 | 18971 | EATING AND DRINKING PLACES |
| LINN, IA | 6109 | 99089 | EATING AND DRINKING PLACES |
| LOUISA, IA | 389 | 3637 | FOOD AND KINDRED PRODUCTS |
| LUCAS, IA | 341 | 4217 | FOOD STORES |
| LYON, IA | 506 | 3209 | EDUCATIONAL SERVICES |
| MADISON, IA | 444 | 3373 | EATING AND DRINKING PLACES |
| MAHASKA, IA | 821 | 8047 | EDUCATIONAL SERVICES |
| MARION, IA | 1041 | 15537 | FABRICATED METAL PRODUCTS |
| MARSHALL, IA | 1391 | 18495 | FOOD AND KINDRED PRODUCTS |
| MILLS, IA | 377 | 2647 | EDUCATIONAL SERVICES |
| MITCHELL, IA | 414 | 3296 | TEXTILE MILL PRODUCTS |
| MONONA, IA | 477 | 3466 | EDUCATIONAL SERVICES |
| MONROE, IA | 290 | 2268 | HEALTH SERVICES |
| MONTGOMERY, IA | 537 | 4826 | FABRICATED METAL PRODUCTS |
| MUSCATINE, IA | 1310 | 16742 | EDUCATIONAL SERVICES |
| O'BRIEN, IA | 767 | 6779 | EDUCATIONAL SERVICES |
| OSCEOLA, IA | 285 | 2250 | PAPER AND ALLIED PRODUCTS |
| PAGE, IA | 738 | 6492 | EDUCATIONAL SERVICES |
| PALO ALTO, IA | 501 | 4294 | EDUCATIONAL SERVICES |
| PLYMOUTH, IA | 927 | 7799 | EDUCATIONAL SERVICES |
| POCAHONTAS, IA | 396 | 3166 | INDUSTRIAL & COMM. MACHINERY |
| POLK, IA | 13018 | 242105 | HEALTH SERVICES |
| POTTAWATTAMIE, IA | 2474 | 32911 | AMUSEMENT/RECREATION SERVICES |
| POWESHIEK, IA | 781 | 7687 | EDUCATIONAL SERVICES |
| RINGGOLD, IA | 210 | 1344 | HEALTH SERVICES |
| SAC, IA | 648 | 3666 | EDUCATIONAL SERVICES |
| SCOTT, IA | 5212 | 82156 | EATING AND DRINKING PLACES |
| SHELBY, IA | 653 | 5379 | EDUCATIONAL SERVICES |
| SIOUX, IA | 1298 | 14286 | APPAREL, FINISHED PRODUCTS |
| STORY, IA | 2427 | 40409 | EDUCATIONAL SERVICES |
| TAMA, IA | 729 | 4962 | EDUCATIONAL SERVICES |
| TAYLOR, IA | 356 | 1958 | EDUCATIONAL SERVICES |
| UNION, IA | 513 | 5592 | EDUCATIONAL SERVICES |
| VAN BUREN, IA | 361 | 2398 | INDUSTRIAL & COMM. MACHINERY |
| WAPELLO, IA | 1273 | 16219 | SOCIAL SERVICES |
| WARREN, IA | 986 | 7742 | EDUCATIONAL SERVICES |
| WASHINGTON, IA | 953 | 7503 | EDUCATIONAL SERVICES |
| WAYNE, IA | 288 | 1636 | EDUCATIONAL SERVICES |
| WEBSTER, IA | 1833 | 18600 | EDUCATIONAL SERVICES |
| WINNEBAGO, IA | 571 | 5275 | EDUCATIONAL SERVICES |
| WINNESHIEK, IA | 805 | 8677 | EDUCATIONAL SERVICES |
| WOODBURY, IA | 3576 | 54700 | HEALTH SERVICES |
| WORTH, IA | 319 | 2167 | LUMBER & WOOD PRODS, EXC FURN. |
| WRIGHT, IA | 648 | 6432 | FABRICATED METAL PRODUCTS |
| ALLEN, KS | 642 | 5623 | EDUCATIONAL SERVICES |
| ANDERSON, KS | 363 | 1961 | EDUCATIONAL SERVICES |
| ATCHISON, KS | 591 | 7245 | EDUCATIONAL SERVICES |
| BARBER, KS | 368 | 1987 | HEALTH SERVICES |
| BARTON, KS | 1474 | 12824 | EDUCATIONAL SERVICES |
| BOURBON, KS | 608 | 6388 | WHOLESALE TRADE: NONDURABLE |
| BROWN, KS | 548 | 3506 | EDUCATIONAL SERVICES |
| BUTLER, KS | 1829 | 15067 | EDUCATIONAL SERVICES |
| CHASE, KS | 143 | 732 | EDUCATIONAL SERVICES |
| CHAUTAUQUA, KS | 206 | 1032 | HEALTH SERVICES |
| CHEROKEE, KS | 814 | 7243 | EDUCATIONAL SERVICES |
| CHEYENNE, KS | 216 | 863 | EDUCATIONAL SERVICES |
| CLARK, KS | 167 | 879 | EDUCATIONAL SERVICES |
| CLAY, KS | 421 | 2908 | EDUCATIONAL SERVICES |
| CLOUD, KS | 568 | 4141 | HEALTH SERVICES |
| COFFEY, KS | 400 | 2695 | EDUCATIONAL SERVICES |
| COMANCHE, KS | 139 | 637 | HEALTH SERVICES |
| COWLEY, KS | 1457 | 10115 | EDUCATIONAL SERVICES |
| CRAWFORD, KS | 1587 | 16427 | EDUCATIONAL SERVICES |
| DECATUR, KS | 210 | 1018 | HEALTH SERVICES |
| DICKINSON, KS | 841 | 5442 | GENERAL MERCHANDISE STORES |
| DONIPHAN, KS | 356 | 3166 | INDUSTRIAL & COMM. MACHINERY |
| DOUGLAS, KS | 2994 | 38174 | EDUCATIONAL SERVICES |
| EDWARDS, KS | 205 | 957 | EDUCATIONAL SERVICES |
| ELK, KS | 152 | 609 | EDUCATIONAL SERVICES |
| ELLIS, KS | 1430 | 14782 | EDUCATIONAL SERVICES |
| ELLSWORTH, KS | 328 | 2581 | HEALTH SERVICES |
| FINNEY, KS | 1519 | 20272 | FOOD AND KINDRED PRODUCTS |
| FORD, KS | 1288 | 15903 | FOOD AND KINDRED PRODUCTS |
| FRANKLIN, KS | 838 | 5421 | EDUCATIONAL SERVICES |
| GEARY, KS | 977 | 22539 | NATIONAL SECURITY/INT AFFAIRS |
| GOVE, KS | 248 | 1575 | EDUCATIONAL SERVICES |
| GRAHAM, KS | 218 | 999 | EDUCATIONAL SERVICES |
| GRANT, KS | 440 | 3363 | OIL AND GAS EXTRACTION |
| GRAY, KS | 317 | 2156 | EDUCATIONAL SERVICES |
| GREELEY, KS | 158 | 643 | HEALTH SERVICES |
| GREENWOOD, KS | 419 | 2119 | HEALTH SERVICES |
| HAMILTON, KS | 203 | 1089 | HEALTH SERVICES |
| HARPER, KS | 388 | 2436 | EDUCATIONAL SERVICES |
| HARVEY, KS | 1203 | 12466 | INDUSTRIAL & COMM. MACHINERY |
| HASKELL, KS | 228 | 1475 | EDUCATIONAL SERVICES |
| HODGEMAN, KS | 109 | 493 | MOTOR FREIGHT TRANSPORTATION |
| JACKSON, KS | 478 | 3736 | AMUSEMENT/RECREATION SERVICES |
| JEFFERSON, KS | 587 | 3437 | EDUCATIONAL SERVICES |
| JEWELL, KS | 178 | 988 | EDUCATIONAL SERVICES |
| JOHNSON, KS | 14418 | 212398 | EATING AND DRINKING PLACES |
| KEARNY, KS | 204 | 1030 | EDUCATIONAL SERVICES |
| KINGMAN, KS | 371 | 2466 | HEALTH SERVICES |
| KIOWA, KS | 194 | 1082 | EDUCATIONAL SERVICES |
| LABETTE, KS | 877 | 8962 | EDUCATIONAL SERVICES |
| LANE, KS | 163 | 870 | EDUCATIONAL SERVICES |
| LEAVENWORTH, KS | 1555 | 18742 | EXECUTIVE, LEGISLATIVE GOVT. |
| LINCOLN, KS | 204 | 1034 | HEALTH SERVICES |
| LINN, KS | 399 | 2142 | ELECTRIC, GAS & SANITARY SERV. |
| LOGAN, KS | 236 | 1558 | EDUCATIONAL SERVICES |
| LYON, KS | 1235 | 16174 | FOOD AND KINDRED PRODUCTS |
| MCPHERSON, KS | 1209 | 11407 | EDUCATIONAL SERVICES |
| MARION, KS | 558 | 4103 | EDUCATIONAL SERVICES |
| MARSHALL, KS | 603 | 4292 | TRANSPORTATION EQUIPMENT |
| MEADE, KS | 236 | 1477 | EDUCATIONAL SERVICES |
| MIAMI, KS | 892 | 5985 | EDUCATIONAL SERVICES |
| MITCHELL, KS | 403 | 3356 | INDUSTRIAL & COMM. MACHINERY |
| MONTGOMERY, KS | 1632 | 17012 | EDUCATIONAL SERVICES |
| MORRIS, KS | 309 | 1753 | EDUCATIONAL SERVICES |
| MORTON, KS | 257 | 1889 | AGRICULTURAL - CROPS |
| NEMAHA, KS | 536 | 4792 | MOTOR FREIGHT TRANSPORTATION |
| NEOSHO, KS | 785 | 8444 | EDUCATIONAL SERVICES |
| NESS, KS | 316 | 1392 | HEALTH SERVICES |
| NORTON, KS | 340 | 2475 | COMMUNICATIONS |
| OSAGE, KS | 507 | 3361 | EDUCATIONAL SERVICES |
| OSBORNE, KS | 300 | 1585 | EDUCATIONAL SERVICES |
| OTTAWA, KS | 271 | 1419 | HEALTH SERVICES |
| PAWNEE, KS | 333 | 2255 | JUSTICE, PUBLIC ORDER/SAFETY |
| PHILLIPS, KS | 334 | 2508 | EDUCATIONAL SERVICES |
| POTTAWATOMIE, KS | 809 | 7489 | HEALTH SERVICES |
| PRATT, KS | 637 | 3985 | EDUCATIONAL SERVICES |
| RAWLINS, KS | 191 | 873 | EDUCATIONAL SERVICES |

| COUNTY | 2000 Total Firms | 2000 Total Employ-ees | TOP INDUSTRY RANKED on 2000 EMPLOYMENT | COUNTY | 2000 Total Firms | 2000 Total Employ-ees | TOP INDUSTRY RANKED on 2000 EMPLOYMENT |
|---|---|---|---|---|---|---|---|
| RENO, KS | 2392 | 29597 | WHOLESALE TRADE: DURABLE GOODS | HICKMAN, KY | 135 | 1330 | EDUCATIONAL SERVICES |
| REPUBLIC, KS | 348 | 2112 | RUBBER & MISC PLASTIC PRODUCTS | HOPKINS, KY | 1607 | 16276 | EDUCATIONAL SERVICES |
| RICE, KS | 481 | 3263 | EDUCATIONAL SERVICES | JACKSON, KY | 339 | 3179 | ELECTRONIC/ELCTRCL EQPMNT |
| RILEY, KS | 1828 | 20833 | EDUCATIONAL SERVICES | JEFFERSON, KY | 20492 | 372228 | EATING AND DRINKING PLACES |
| ROOKS, KS | 396 | 2154 | EDUCATIONAL SERVICES | JESSAMINE, KY | 1018 | 11910 | EDUCATIONAL SERVICES |
| RUSH, KS | 253 | 1330 | HEALTH SERVICES | JOHNSON, KY | 723 | 5794 | EDUCATIONAL SERVICES |
| RUSSELL, KS | 504 | 2656 | EATING AND DRINKING PLACES | KENTON, KY | 3660 | 42364 | EATING AND DRINKING PLACES |
| SALINE, KS | 2263 | 29425 | INDUSTRIAL & COMM. MACHINERY | KNOTT, KY | 412 | 3694 | COAL MINING |
| SCOTT, KS | 336 | 1981 | AGRICULTURAL - LIVESTOCK SPEC | KNOX, KY | 949 | 10933 | EATING AND DRINKING PLACES |
| SEDGWICK, KS | 14281 | 221587 | TRANSPORTATION EQUIPMENT | LARUE, KY | 325 | 2130 | APPAREL, FINISHED PRODUCTS |
| SEWARD, KS | 1010 | 11948 | FOOD AND KINDRED PRODUCTS | LAUREL, KY | 1506 | 17020 | BUSINESS SERVICES |
| SHAWNEE, KS | 6476 | 100239 | HEALTH SERVICES | LAWRENCE, KY | 370 | 2570 | HEALTH SERVICES |
| SHERIDAN, KS | 167 | 835 | HEALTH SERVICES | LEE, KY | 208 | 1799 | EDUCATIONAL SERVICES |
| SHERMAN, KS | 423 | 2298 | EDUCATIONAL SERVICES | LESLIE, KY | 329 | 2516 | COAL MINING |
| SMITH, KS | 258 | 1480 | HEALTH SERVICES | LETCHER, KY | 658 | 5623 | EDUCATIONAL SERVICES |
| STAFFORD, KS | 260 | 1445 | EDUCATIONAL SERVICES | LEWIS, KY | 249 | 1773 | LEATHER AND LEATHER PRODUCTS |
| STANTON, KS | 157 | 718 | EDUCATIONAL SERVICES | LINCOLN, KY | 425 | 3290 | EDUCATIONAL SERVICES |
| STEVENS, KS | 292 | 1651 | EDUCATIONAL SERVICES | LIVINGSTON, KY | 237 | 2070 | MINING AND QUARRYING EXC FUELS |
| SUMNER, KS | 994 | 6868 | EDUCATIONAL SERVICES | LOGAN, KY | 849 | 10013 | FABRICATED METAL PRODUCTS |
| THOMAS, KS | 574 | 2970 | EDUCATIONAL SERVICES | LYON, KY | 271 | 2196 | JUSTICE, PUBLIC ORDER/SAFETY |
| TREGO, KS | 221 | 1413 | HEALTH SERVICES | MCCRACKEN, KY | 2865 | 34820 | EATING AND DRINKING PLACES |
| WABAUNSEE, KS | 248 | 1136 | EDUCATIONAL SERVICES | MCCREARY, KY | 365 | 4389 | HEALTH SERVICES |
| WALLACE, KS | 171 | 616 | EDUCATIONAL SERVICES | MCLEAN, KY | 267 | 1854 | ELECTRIC, GAS & SANITARY SERV. |
| WASHINGTON, KS | 352 | 1736 | EDUCATIONAL SERVICES | MADISON, KY | 1871 | 23968 | EDUCATIONAL SERVICES |
| WICHITA, KS | 178 | 863 | AGRICULTURAL - LIVESTOCK SPEC | MAGOFFIN, KY | 352 | 2456 | EDUCATIONAL SERVICES |
| WILSON, KS | 435 | 3833 | TRANSPORTATION EQUIPMENT | MARION, KY | 431 | 5549 | HEALTH SERVICES |
| WOODSON, KS | 171 | 852 | EDUCATIONAL SERVICES | MARSHALL, KY | 1021 | 8701 | CHEMICALS AND ALLIED PRODUCTS |
| WYANDOTTE, KS | 4146 | 75834 | EDUCATIONAL SERVICES | MARTIN, KY | 309 | 2979 | COAL MINING |
| ADAIR, KY | 436 | 3914 | HEALTH SERVICES | MASON, KY | 664 | 10414 | INDUSTRIAL & COMM. MACHINERY |
| ALLEN, KY | 408 | 4687 | ELECTRONIC/ELCTRCL EQPMNT | MEADE, KY | 665 | 3571 | CHEMICALS AND ALLIED PRODUCTS |
| ANDERSON, KY | 398 | 3186 | WHOLESALE TRADE: DURABLE GOODS | MENIFEE, KY | 167 | 928 | EDUCATIONAL SERVICES |
| BALLARD, KY | 347 | 3056 | PAPER AND ALLIED PRODUCTS | MERCER, KY | 621 | 5165 | EDUCATIONAL SERVICES |
| BARREN, KY | 1340 | 13781 | PRINTING AND PUBLISHING | METCALFE, KY | 274 | 2544 | ELECTRONIC/ELCTRCL EQPMNT |
| BATH, KY | 246 | 2035 | APPAREL, FINISHED PRODUCTS | MONROE, KY | 374 | 3767 | APPAREL, FINISHED PRODUCTS |
| BELL, KY | 898 | 9185 | EDUCATIONAL SERVICES | MONTGOMERY, KY | 728 | 8011 | FOOD AND KINDRED PRODUCTS |
| BOONE, KY | 2899 | 52812 | TRANSPORTATION BY AIR | MORGAN, KY | 325 | 2830 | JUSTICE, PUBLIC ORDER/SAFETY |
| BOURBON, KY | 602 | 5985 | EDUCATIONAL SERVICES | MUHLENBERG, KY | 855 | 8074 | EDUCATIONAL SERVICES |
| BOYD, KY | 1745 | 23758 | HEALTH SERVICES | NELSON, KY | 1123 | 12223 | FOOD STORES |
| BOYLE, KY | 990 | 13337 | HEALTH SERVICES | NICHOLAS, KY | 136 | 1661 | WHOLESALE TRADE: NONDURABLE |
| BRACKEN, KY | 207 | 1068 | RUBBER & MISC PLASTIC PRODUCTS | OHIO, KY | 555 | 5167 | EDUCATIONAL SERVICES |
| BREATHITT, KY | 332 | 3117 | EDUCATIONAL SERVICES | OLDHAM, KY | 1056 | 9591 | JUSTICE, PUBLIC ORDER/SAFETY |
| BRECKINRIDGE, KY | 556 | 3268 | EDUCATIONAL SERVICES | OWEN, KY | 196 | 1569 | HEALTH SERVICES |
| BULLITT, KY | 1278 | 11626 | PRINTING AND PUBLISHING | OWSLEY, KY | 135 | 1049 | EDUCATIONAL SERVICES |
| BUTLER, KY | 285 | 3053 | PRIMARY METAL INDUSTRIES | PENDLETON, KY | 314 | 2561 | EDUCATIONAL SERVICES |
| CALDWELL, KY | 418 | 3540 | FOOD AND KINDRED PRODUCTS | PERRY, KY | 1025 | 11277 | EDUCATIONAL SERVICES |
| CALLOWAY, KY | 1143 | 12866 | EDUCATIONAL SERVICES | PIKE, KY | 2058 | 18962 | COAL MINING |
| CAMPBELL, KY | 2160 | 25301 | EDUCATIONAL SERVICES | POWELL, KY | 353 | 3166 | INDUSTRIAL & COMM. MACHINERY |
| CARLISLE, KY | 191 | 867 | STONE/CLAY/GLASS PRODUCTS | PULASKI, KY | 1861 | 20698 | EDUCATIONAL SERVICES |
| CARROLL, KY | 352 | 5308 | CHEMICALS AND ALLIED PRODUCTS | ROBERTSON, KY | 60 | 255 | HEALTH SERVICES |
| CARTER, KY | 673 | 5510 | EDUCATIONAL SERVICES | ROCKCASTLE, KY | 377 | 3151 | EDUCATIONAL SERVICES |
| CASEY, KY | 342 | 3089 | APPAREL, FINISHED PRODUCTS | ROWAN, KY | 698 | 7661 | EDUCATIONAL SERVICES |
| CHRISTIAN, KY | 1862 | 49777 | NATIONAL SECURITY/INT AFFAIRS | RUSSELL, KY | 683 | 4949 | APPAREL, FINISHED PRODUCTS |
| CLARK, KY | 957 | 12379 | ELECTRIC, GAS & SANITARY SERV. | SCOTT, KY | 955 | 22567 | TRANSPORTATION EQUIPMENT |
| CLAY, KY | 520 | 4209 | EDUCATIONAL SERVICES | SHELBY, KY | 904 | 9822 | EDUCATIONAL SERVICES |
| CLINTON, KY | 286 | 3043 | WHOLESALE TRADE: NONDURABLE | SIMPSON, KY | 540 | 6445 | PRINTING AND PUBLISHING |
| CRITTENDEN, KY | 253 | 2377 | HEALTH SERVICES | SPENCER, KY | 201 | 998 | EDUCATIONAL SERVICES |
| CUMBERLAND, KY | 204 | 1568 | HEALTH SERVICES | TAYLOR, KY | 768 | 9934 | TEXTILE MILL PRODUCTS |
| DAVIESS, KY | 2881 | 41296 | HEALTH SERVICES | TODD, KY | 327 | 3184 | APPAREL, FINISHED PRODUCTS |
| EDMONSON, KY | 196 | 1434 | AMUSEMENT/RECREATION SERVICES | TRIGG, KY | 340 | 3167 | CONSTRUCT: SPEC TRADE CONTRACT |
| ELLIOTT, KY | 132 | 766 | EDUCATIONAL SERVICES | TRIMBLE, KY | 126 | 702 | EDUCATIONAL SERVICES |
| ESTILL, KY | 360 | 2580 | EDUCATIONAL SERVICES | UNION, KY | 459 | 4175 | TRANSPORTATION EQUIPMENT |
| FAYETTE, KY | 8234 | 141630 | INDUSTRIAL & COMM. MACHINERY | WARREN, KY | 3009 | 42503 | EATING AND DRINKING PLACES |
| FLEMING, KY | 349 | 2771 | EDUCATIONAL SERVICES | WASHINGTON, KY | 293 | 2734 | RUBBER & MISC PLASTIC PRODUCTS |
| FLOYD, KY | 1227 | 12099 | HEALTH SERVICES | WAYNE, KY | 445 | 5440 | TRANSPORTATION EQUIPMENT |
| FRANKLIN, KY | 1858 | 39637 | EXECUTIVE, LEGISLATIVE GOVT. | WEBSTER, KY | 407 | 3821 | COAL MINING |
| FULTON, KY | 337 | 3488 | APPAREL, FINISHED PRODUCTS | WHITLEY, KY | 839 | 9474 | EDUCATIONAL SERVICES |
| GALLATIN, KY | 177 | 1198 | WHOLESALE TRADE: DURABLE GOODS | WOLFE, KY | 226 | 1436 | EDUCATIONAL SERVICES |
| GARRARD, KY | 330 | 2782 | SOCIAL SERVICES | WOODFORD, KY | 708 | 8183 | PRINTING AND PUBLISHING |
| GRANT, KY | 544 | 3969 | EDUCATIONAL SERVICES | ACADIA, LA | 1583 | 14169 | EDUCATIONAL SERVICES |
| GRAVES, KY | 1117 | 12237 | WHOLESALE TRADE: NONDURABLE | ALLEN, LA | 640 | 6778 | AMUSEMENT/RECREATION SERVICES |
| GRAYSON, KY | 665 | 6503 | WHOLESALE TRADE: NONDURABLE | ASCENSION, LA | 2322 | 24496 | CHEMICALS AND ALLIED PRODUCTS |
| GREEN, KY | 269 | 1601 | HEALTH SERVICES | ASSUMPTION, LA | 467 | 9280 | HEALTH SERVICES |
| GREENUP, KY | 833 | 6510 | EDUCATIONAL SERVICES | AVOYELLES, LA | 1096 | 10526 | AMUSEMENT/RECREATION SERVICES |
| HANCOCK, KY | 163 | 4182 | PRIMARY METAL INDUSTRIES | BEAUREGARD, LA | 903 | 7653 | EDUCATIONAL SERVICES |
| HARDIN, KY | 2639 | 30174 | EATING AND DRINKING PLACES | BIENVILLE, LA | 421 | 3839 | WHOLESALE TRADE: NONDURABLE |
| HARLAN, KY | 922 | 8686 | EDUCATIONAL SERVICES | BOSSIER, LA | 2656 | 42455 | AMUSEMENT/RECREATION SERVICES |
| HARRISON, KY | 447 | 4748 | PRIMARY METAL INDUSTRIES | CADDO, LA | 8188 | 102760 | HEALTH SERVICES |
| HART, KY | 532 | 4712 | RUBBER & MISC PLASTIC PRODUCTS | CALCASIEU, LA | 5871 | 71691 | EDUCATIONAL SERVICES |
| HENDERSON, KY | 1356 | 20141 | PRIMARY METAL INDUSTRIES | CALDWELL, LA | 295 | 2136 | FOOD STORES |
| HENRY, KY | 368 | 3248 | GENERAL MERCHANDISE STORES | CAMERON, LA | 396 | 3478 | AMUSEMENT/RECREATION SERVICES |

# BUSINESS DATA

| COUNTY | 2000 Total Firms | 2000 Total Employ-ees | TOP INDUSTRY RANKED on 2000 EMPLOYMENT |
|---|---|---|---|
| CATAHOULA, LA | 356 | 2136 | WHOLESALE TRADE: NONDURABLE |
| CLAIBORNE, LA | 503 | 4079 | JUSTICE, PUBLIC ORDER/SAFETY |
| CONCORDIA, LA | 635 | 4735 | EDUCATIONAL SERVICES |
| DE SOTO, LA | 689 | 5757 | EDUCATIONAL SERVICES |
| EAST BATON ROUGE, LA | 14072 | 199995 | EATING AND DRINKING PLACES |
| EAST CARROLL, LA | 267 | 1913 | EDUCATIONAL SERVICES |
| EAST FELICIANA, LA | 429 | 3884 | HEALTH SERVICES |
| EVANGELINE, LA | 856 | 7494 | HEALTH SERVICES |
| FRANKLIN, LA | 632 | 5915 | HEALTH SERVICES |
| GRANT, LA | 344 | 2425 | EDUCATIONAL SERVICES |
| IBERIA, LA | 2241 | 26119 | EDUCATIONAL SERVICES |
| IBERVILLE, LA | 893 | 13959 | CHEMICALS AND ALLIED PRODUCTS |
| JACKSON, LA | 454 | 3441 | PAPER AND ALLIED PRODUCTS |
| JEFFERSON, LA | 14629 | 192217 | BUSINESS SERVICES |
| JEFFERSON DAVIS, LA | 965 | 7369 | EDUCATIONAL SERVICES |
| LAFAYETTE, LA | 8082 | 103015 | OIL AND GAS EXTRACTION |
| LAFOURCHE, LA | 2517 | 25105 | EDUCATIONAL SERVICES |
| LA SALLE, LA | 434 | 3487 | LUMBER & WOOD PRODS, EXC FURN. |
| LINCOLN, LA | 1340 | 16585 | EDUCATIONAL SERVICES |
| LIVINGSTON, LA | 1838 | 12992 | EDUCATIONAL SERVICES |
| MADISON, LA | 371 | 2994 | EDUCATIONAL SERVICES |
| MOREHOUSE, LA | 928 | 7296 | HEALTH SERVICES |
| NATCHITOCHES, LA | 1177 | 11721 | EDUCATIONAL SERVICES |
| ORLEANS, LA | 13691 | 222842 | HEALTH SERVICES |
| OUACHITA, LA | 5202 | 61310 | HEALTH SERVICES |
| PLAQUEMINES, LA | 937 | 16072 | EDUCATIONAL SERVICES |
| POINTE COUPEE, LA | 633 | 5110 | EDUCATIONAL SERVICES |
| RAPIDES, LA | 4256 | 53378 | HEALTH SERVICES |
| RED RIVER, LA | 297 | 2096 | EDUCATIONAL SERVICES |
| RICHLAND, LA | 659 | 5209 | HEALTH SERVICES |
| SABINE, LA | 720 | 5672 | LUMBER & WOOD PRODS, EXC FURN. |
| ST. BERNARD, LA | 1497 | 13484 | EATING AND DRINKING PLACES |
| ST. CHARLES, LA | 1058 | 20429 | PETROLEUM REFINING INDUSTRIES |
| ST. HELENA, LA | 264 | 1784 | HEALTH SERVICES |
| ST. JAMES, LA | 501 | 7318 | CHEMICALS AND ALLIED PRODUCTS |
| ST. JOHN THE BAPTIST, LA | 1002 | 12305 | EDUCATIONAL SERVICES |
| ST. LANDRY, LA | 2244 | 18050 | EDUCATIONAL SERVICES |
| ST. MARTIN, LA | 1098 | 12472 | TEXTILE MILL PRODUCTS |
| ST. MARY, LA | 2203 | 24542 | WATER TRANSPORTATION |
| ST. TAMMANY, LA | 6177 | 48001 | EATING AND DRINKING PLACES |
| TANGIPAHOA, LA | 2811 | 29353 | EDUCATIONAL SERVICES |
| TENSAS, LA | 265 | 1468 | EDUCATIONAL SERVICES |
| TERREBONNE, LA | 3492 | 43925 | OIL AND GAS EXTRACTION |
| UNION, LA | 542 | 5552 | FOOD AND KINDRED PRODUCTS |
| VERMILION, LA | 1560 | 13123 | EDUCATIONAL SERVICES |
| VERNON, LA | 1133 | 9435 | EDUCATIONAL SERVICES |
| WASHINGTON, LA | 1237 | 10507 | EDUCATIONAL SERVICES |
| WEBSTER, LA | 1352 | 11797 | EDUCATIONAL SERVICES |
| WEST BATON ROUGE, LA | 675 | 9629 | CONSTRUCT: SPEC TRADE CONTRACT |
| WEST CARROLL, LA | 356 | 2872 | HEALTH SERVICES |
| WEST FELICIANA, LA | 316 | 6323 | JUSTICE, PUBLIC ORDER/SAFETY |
| WINN, LA | 482 | 4474 | LUMBER & WOOD PRODS, EXC FURN. |
| ANDROSCOGGIN, ME | 3419 | 42624 | HEALTH SERVICES |
| AROOSTOOK, ME | 2958 | 28609 | EDUCATIONAL SERVICES |
| CUMBERLAND, ME | 13254 | 146459 | EDUCATIONAL SERVICES |
| FRANKLIN, ME | 1274 | 10509 | PAPER AND ALLIED PRODUCTS |
| HANCOCK, ME | 2909 | 23860 | EDUCATIONAL SERVICES |
| KENNEBEC, ME | 4542 | 61138 | HEALTH SERVICES |
| KNOX, ME | 2020 | 15142 | EDUCATIONAL SERVICES |
| LINCOLN, ME | 1778 | 11292 | EDUCATIONAL SERVICES |
| OXFORD, ME | 1985 | 19659 | HOTELS, ROOMING HOUSES, CAMPS |
| PENOBSCOT, ME | 5783 | 65493 | EDUCATIONAL SERVICES |
| PISCATAQUIS, ME | 630 | 5297 | TEXTILE MILL PRODUCTS |
| SAGADAHOC, ME | 1149 | 16231 | TRANSPORTATION EQUIPMENT |
| SOMERSET, ME | 1796 | 16621 | EDUCATIONAL SERVICES |
| WALDO, ME | 1375 | 8294 | EDUCATIONAL SERVICES |
| WASHINGTON, ME | 1321 | 12567 | HEALTH SERVICES |
| YORK, ME | 7824 | 64330 | EATING AND DRINKING PLACES |
| ALLEGANY, MD | 2456 | 26539 | EDUCATIONAL SERVICES |
| ANNE ARUNDEL, MD | 14151 | 160470 | EATING AND DRINKING PLACES |
| BALTIMORE, MD | 21019 | 283839 | EDUCATIONAL SERVICES |
| CALVERT, MD | 2099 | 15416 | EATING AND DRINKING PLACES |
| CAROLINE, MD | 1050 | 8924 | EDUCATIONAL SERVICES |
| CARROLL, MD | 4539 | 41723 | EDUCATIONAL SERVICES |
| CECIL, MD | 2545 | 25311 | EDUCATIONAL SERVICES |
| CHARLES, MD | 3707 | 36992 | EATING AND DRINKING PLACES |
| DORCHESTER, MD | 1194 | 12994 | FOOD AND KINDRED PRODUCTS |
| FREDERICK, MD | 5869 | 72711 | EDUCATIONAL SERVICES |
| GARRETT, MD | 1243 | 11767 | EATING AND DRINKING PLACES |
| HARFORD, MD | 5724 | 50919 | EATING AND DRINKING PLACES |
| HOWARD, MD | 7054 | 98394 | BUSINESS SERVICES |
| KENT, MD | 1006 | 7756 | EDUCATIONAL SERVICES |
| MONTGOMERY, MD | 25009 | 362939 | EDUCATIONAL SERVICES |
| PRINCE GEORGE'S, MD | 19695 | 262464 | EDUCATIONAL SERVICES |
| QUEEN ANNE'S, MD | 1808 | 10765 | EATING AND DRINKING PLACES |
| ST. MARY'S, MD | 2643 | 27438 | EDUCATIONAL SERVICES |
| SOMERSET, MD | 678 | 6292 | JUSTICE, PUBLIC ORDER/SAFETY |
| TALBOT, MD | 2159 | 17451 | EATING AND DRINKING PLACES |
| WASHINGTON, MD | 4469 | 56850 | BUSINESS SERVICES |
| WICOMICO, MD | 3205 | 40770 | EDUCATIONAL SERVICES |
| WORCESTER, MD | 3205 | 29776 | EATING AND DRINKING PLACES |
| BALTIMORE CITY, MD | 17710 | 246555 | EDUCATIONAL SERVICES |
| BARNSTABLE, MA | 12679 | 87830 | EATING AND DRINKING PLACES |
| BERKSHIRE, MA | 5801 | 56952 | EDUCATIONAL SERVICES |
| BRISTOL, MA | 16754 | 197818 | EDUCATIONAL SERVICES |
| DUKES, MA | 1631 | 8005 | EATING AND DRINKING PLACES |
| ESSEX, MA | 24171 | 283726 | EDUCATIONAL SERVICES |
| FRANKLIN, MA | 2650 | 25578 | EDUCATIONAL SERVICES |
| HAMPDEN, MA | 14213 | 184272 | EDUCATIONAL SERVICES |
| HAMPSHIRE, MA | 5106 | 52381 | EDUCATIONAL SERVICES |
| MIDDLESEX, MA | 53005 | 700296 | EDUCATIONAL SERVICES |
| NANTUCKET, MA | 990 | 5109 | EATING AND DRINKING PLACES |
| NORFOLK, MA | 21918 | 266866 | EDUCATIONAL SERVICES |
| PLYMOUTH, MA | 15720 | 151794 | EDUCATIONAL SERVICES |
| SUFFOLK, MA | 23918 | 428355 | EDUCATIONAL SERVICES |
| WORCESTER, MA | 24744 | 292922 | EDUCATIONAL SERVICES |
| ALCONA, MI | 429 | 2057 | EDUCATIONAL SERVICES |
| ALGER, MI | 557 | 3911 | JUSTICE, PUBLIC ORDER/SAFETY |
| ALLEGAN, MI | 3564 | 43318 | CHEMICALS AND ALLIED PRODUCTS |
| ALPENA, MI | 1312 | 12828 | SOCIAL SERVICES |
| ANTRIM, MI | 1023 | 7731 | HOTELS, ROOMING HOUSES, CAMPS |
| ARENAC, MI | 599 | 4989 | EATING AND DRINKING PLACES |
| BARAGA, MI | 404 | 3774 | EATING AND DRINKING PLACES |
| BARRY, MI | 1385 | 11145 | EDUCATIONAL SERVICES |
| BAY, MI | 3908 | 41812 | EDUCATIONAL SERVICES |
| BENZIE, MI | 740 | 4558 | HOTELS, ROOMING HOUSES, CAMPS |
| BERRIEN, MI | 6268 | 68724 | EDUCATIONAL SERVICES |
| BRANCH, MI | 1299 | 11466 | EDUCATIONAL SERVICES |
| CALHOUN, MI | 4481 | 59915 | EATING AND DRINKING PLACES |
| CASS, MI | 1365 | 11333 | EDUCATIONAL SERVICES |
| CHARLEVOIX, MI | 1292 | 10009 | EATING AND DRINKING PLACES |
| CHEBOYGAN, MI | 1339 | 8808 | EATING AND DRINKING PLACES |
| CHIPPEWA, MI | 1488 | 16162 | AMUSEMENT/RECREATION SERVICES |
| CLARE, MI | 1119 | 7430 | EDUCATIONAL SERVICES |
| CLINTON, MI | 1980 | 17359 | EDUCATIONAL SERVICES |
| CRAWFORD, MI | 621 | 5035 | EATING AND DRINKING PLACES |
| DELTA, MI | 1604 | 14876 | PAPER AND ALLIED PRODUCTS |
| DICKINSON, MI | 1272 | 12701 | WHOLESALE TRADE: DURABLE GOODS |
| EATON, MI | 3369 | 33391 | EATING AND DRINKING PLACES |
| EMMET, MI | 1822 | 16891 | HOTELS, ROOMING HOUSES, CAMPS |
| GENESEE, MI | 13623 | 155041 | TRANSPORTATION EQUIPMENT |
| GLADWIN, MI | 811 | 5525 | INDUSTRIAL & COMM. MACHINERY |
| GOGEBIC, MI | 774 | 7293 | HOTELS, ROOMING HOUSES, CAMPS |
| GRAND TRAVERSE, MI | 4523 | 47552 | HEALTH SERVICES |
| GRATIOT, MI | 1236 | 12099 | TRANSPORTATION EQUIPMENT |
| HILLSDALE, MI | 1545 | 16062 | TRANSPORTATION EQUIPMENT |
| HOUGHTON, MI | 1267 | 12915 | EDUCATIONAL SERVICES |
| HURON, MI | 1442 | 13468 | FABRICATED METAL PRODUCTS |
| INGHAM, MI | 10924 | 145174 | EDUCATIONAL SERVICES |
| IONIA, MI | 1591 | 16705 | JUSTICE, PUBLIC ORDER/SAFETY |
| IOSCO, MI | 1271 | 10072 | TRANSPORTATION EQUIPMENT |
| IRON, MI | 592 | 3899 | EDUCATIONAL SERVICES |
| ISABELLA, MI | 1815 | 26206 | EATING AND DRINKING PLACES |
| JACKSON, MI | 5073 | 59149 | ELECTRIC, GAS & SANITARY SERV. |
| KALAMAZOO, MI | 8178 | 116936 | EDUCATIONAL SERVICES |
| KALKASKA, MI | 636 | 5504 | OIL AND GAS EXTRACTION |
| KENT, MI | 19681 | 332035 | HEALTH SERVICES |
| KEWEENAW, MI | 172 | 1272 | HOTELS, ROOMING HOUSES, CAMPS |
| LAKE, MI | 365 | 1914 | EATING AND DRINKING PLACES |
| LAPEER, MI | 2677 | 23306 | EDUCATIONAL SERVICES |
| LEELANAU, MI | 1169 | 6904 | EATING AND DRINKING PLACES |
| LENAWEE, MI | 3021 | 34364 | EDUCATIONAL SERVICES |
| LIVINGSTON, MI | 5460 | 44122 | EATING AND DRINKING PLACES |
| LUCE, MI | 303 | 2674 | HEALTH SERVICES |
| MACKINAC, MI | 807 | 6615 | HOTELS, ROOMING HOUSES, CAMPS |
| MACOMB, MI | 22017 | 310452 | EATING AND DRINKING PLACES |
| MANISTEE, MI | 990 | 6593 | EDUCATIONAL SERVICES |
| MARQUETTE, MI | 2561 | 27939 | EDUCATIONAL SERVICES |
| MASON, MI | 1092 | 11232 | EDUCATIONAL SERVICES |
| MECOSTA, MI | 1155 | 10850 | EDUCATIONAL SERVICES |

| COUNTY | 2000 Total Firms | 2000 Total Employ-ees | TOP INDUSTRY RANKED on 2000 EMPLOYMENT | COUNTY | 2000 Total Firms | 2000 Total Employ-ees | TOP INDUSTRY RANKED on 2000 EMPLOYMENT |
|---|---|---|---|---|---|---|---|
| MENOMINEE, MI | 815 | 9536 | EXECUTIVE, LEGISLATIVE GOVT. | NICOLLET, MN | 806 | 12120 | EDUCATIONAL SERVICES |
| MIDLAND, MI | 2748 | 30694 | HEALTH SERVICES | NOBLES, MN | 857 | 9300 | FOOD AND KINDRED PRODUCTS |
| MISSAUKEE, MI | 491 | 2594 | EDUCATIONAL SERVICES | NORMAN, MN | 436 | 2795 | EDUCATIONAL SERVICES |
| MONROE, MI | 3879 | 41178 | EDUCATIONAL SERVICES | OLMSTED, MN | 3614 | 56908 | HEALTH SERVICES |
| MONTCALM, MI | 1875 | 17999 | ELECTRONIC/ELCTRCL EQPMNT | OTTER TAIL, MN | 2242 | 20632 | HEALTH SERVICES |
| MONTMORENCY, MI | 327 | 2118 | FABRICATED METAL PRODUCTS | PENNINGTON, MN | 531 | 7615 | TRANSPORTATION EQUIPMENT |
| MUSKEGON, MI | 4839 | 60097 | EDUCATIONAL SERVICES | PINE, MN | 710 | 8636 | AMUSEMENT/RECREATION SERVICES |
| NEWAYGO, MI | 1232 | 9448 | EDUCATIONAL SERVICES | PIPESTONE, MN | 453 | 3842 | EDUCATIONAL SERVICES |
| OAKLAND, MI | 45148 | 601860 | EATING AND DRINKING PLACES | POLK, MN | 1312 | 12398 | EDUCATIONAL SERVICES |
| OCEANA, MI | 831 | 7614 | HOTELS, ROOMING HOUSES, CAMPS | POPE, MN | 409 | 3789 | HEALTH SERVICES |
| OGEMAW, MI | 915 | 6112 | EATING AND DRINKING PLACES | RAMSEY, MN | 15902 | 305721 | EDUCATIONAL SERVICES |
| ONTONAGON, MI | 409 | 2241 | EDUCATIONAL SERVICES | RED LAKE, MN | 211 | 1596 | EDUCATIONAL SERVICES |
| OSCEOLA, MI | 726 | 7283 | TRANSPORTATION EQUIPMENT | REDWOOD, MN | 757 | 6486 | EDUCATIONAL SERVICES |
| OSCODA, MI | 416 | 3120 | HOTELS, ROOMING HOUSES, CAMPS | RENVILLE, MN | 745 | 7233 | FOOD AND KINDRED PRODUCTS |
| OTSEGO, MI | 1140 | 11261 | EATING AND DRINKING PLACES | RICE, MN | 1691 | 20389 | EDUCATIONAL SERVICES |
| OTTAWA, MI | 7745 | 105559 | TRANSPORTATION EQUIPMENT | ROCK, MN | 369 | 3551 | HEALTH SERVICES |
| PRESQUE ISLE, MI | 542 | 3356 | EDUCATIONAL SERVICES | ROSEAU, MN | 557 | 6000 | TRANSPORTATION EQUIPMENT |
| ROSCOMMON, MI | 1021 | 7075 | EATING AND DRINKING PLACES | ST. LOUIS, MN | 8039 | 93457 | HEALTH SERVICES |
| SAGINAW, MI | 7481 | 98067 | TRANSPORTATION EQUIPMENT | SCOTT, MN | 2498 | 43042 | AMUSEMENT/RECREATION SERVICES |
| ST. CLAIR, MI | 5242 | 50284 | EATING AND DRINKING PLACES | SHERBURNE, MN | 1678 | 17183 | EATING AND DRINKING PLACES |
| ST. JOSEPH, MI | 2161 | 22893 | TRANSPORTATION EQUIPMENT | SIBLEY, MN | 458 | 4015 | FOOD AND KINDRED PRODUCTS |
| SANILAC, MI | 1491 | 13995 | BUILDING MATRIALS/GARDEN SUPPL | STEARNS, MN | 5010 | 68175 | EDUCATIONAL SERVICES |
| SCHOOLCRAFT, MI | 416 | 2969 | HEALTH SERVICES | STEELE, MN | 1194 | 17292 | FABRICATED METAL PRODUCTS |
| SHIAWASSEE, MI | 2104 | 18235 | EDUCATIONAL SERVICES | STEVENS, MN | 486 | 4537 | EDUCATIONAL SERVICES |
| TUSCOLA, MI | 1612 | 14322 | EDUCATIONAL SERVICES | SWIFT, MN | 490 | 4482 | INDUSTRIAL & COMM. MACHINERY |
| VAN BUREN, MI | 2402 | 21318 | EDUCATIONAL SERVICES | TODD, MN | 713 | 5999 | HEALTH SERVICES |
| WASHTENAW, MI | 10957 | 191928 | EDUCATIONAL SERVICES | TRAVERSE, MN | 212 | 1291 | EDUCATIONAL SERVICES |
| WAYNE, MI | 51750 | 699985 | EDUCATIONAL SERVICES | WABASHA, MN | 762 | 7834 | EDUCATIONAL SERVICES |
| WEXFORD, MI | 1281 | 16173 | RUBBER & MISC PLASTIC PRODUCTS | WADENA, MN | 687 | 5940 | HEALTH SERVICES |
| AITKIN, MN | 628 | 4041 | EDUCATIONAL SERVICES | WASECA, MN | 629 | 7625 | PRINTING AND PUBLISHING |
| ANOKA, MN | 6232 | 110965 | MESR/ANLYZ/CNTRL INSTRMNTS | WASHINGTON, MN | 4564 | 53786 | EATING AND DRINKING PLACES |
| BECKER, MN | 1243 | 11934 | EDUCATIONAL SERVICES | WATONWAN, MN | 508 | 4617 | FOOD AND KINDRED PRODUCTS |
| BELTRAMI, MN | 1695 | 16004 | EDUCATIONAL SERVICES | WILKIN, MN | 294 | 2272 | HEALTH SERVICES |
| BENTON, MN | 1125 | 15011 | EATING AND DRINKING PLACES | WINONA, MN | 1653 | 24788 | EDUCATIONAL SERVICES |
| BIG STONE, MN | 307 | 2288 | EDUCATIONAL SERVICES | WRIGHT, MN | 2791 | 27061 | EDUCATIONAL SERVICES |
| BLUE EARTH, MN | 2380 | 27526 | EDUCATIONAL SERVICES | YELLOW MEDICINE, MN | 479 | 3959 | HEALTH SERVICES |
| BROWN, MN | 1171 | 15623 | EDUCATIONAL SERVICES | ADAMS, MS | 1560 | 14288 | HEALTH SERVICES |
| CARLTON, MN | 1073 | 11353 | EDUCATIONAL SERVICES | ALCORN, MS | 1258 | 15048 | HEALTH SERVICES |
| CARVER, MN | 1967 | 25357 | EDUCATIONAL SERVICES | AMITE, MS | 320 | 2195 | LUMBER & WOOD PRODS, EXC FURN. |
| CASS, MN | 1520 | 9458 | EDUCATIONAL SERVICES | ATTALA, MS | 588 | 5558 | HEALTH SERVICES |
| CHIPPEWA, MN | 645 | 5950 | EDUCATIONAL SERVICES | BENTON, MS | 156 | 1308 | WHOLESALE TRADE: DURABLE GOODS |
| CHISAGO, MN | 1229 | 14269 | HEALTH SERVICES | BOLIVAR, MS | 1098 | 11215 | EDUCATIONAL SERVICES |
| CLAY, MN | 1681 | 18154 | EDUCATIONAL SERVICES | CALHOUN, MS | 524 | 4007 | APPAREL, FINISHED PRODUCTS |
| CLEARWATER, MN | 383 | 3038 | HEALTH SERVICES | CARROLL, MS | 170 | 864 | EDUCATIONAL SERVICES |
| COOK, MN | 483 | 3572 | HOTELS, ROOMING HOUSES, CAMPS | CHICKASAW, MS | 672 | 9410 | FURNITURE AND FIXTURES |
| COTTONWOOD, MN | 563 | 5126 | HEALTH SERVICES | CHOCTAW, MS | 263 | 2052 | EDUCATIONAL SERVICES |
| CROW WING, MN | 2652 | 27101 | AMUSEMENT/RECREATION SERVICES | CLAIBORNE, MS | 243 | 2017 | LUMBER & WOOD PRODS, EXC FURN. |
| DAKOTA, MN | 8199 | 135111 | EATING AND DRINKING PLACES | CLARKE, MS | 465 | 4728 | TEXTILE MILL PRODUCTS |
| DODGE, MN | 445 | 4835 | EDUCATIONAL SERVICES | CLAY, MS | 653 | 7853 | FOOD AND KINDRED PRODUCTS |
| DOUGLAS, MN | 1649 | 15389 | HEALTH SERVICES | COAHOMA, MS | 1010 | 12642 | HEALTH SERVICES |
| FARIBAULT, MN | 882 | 6764 | EDUCATIONAL SERVICES | COPIAH, MS | 678 | 6839 | EDUCATIONAL SERVICES |
| FILLMORE, MN | 950 | 6258 | EDUCATIONAL SERVICES | COVINGTON, MS | 499 | 5000 | FOOD AND KINDRED PRODUCTS |
| FREEBORN, MN | 1177 | 12046 | EATING AND DRINKING PLACES | DESOTO, MS | 2471 | 28848 | EATING AND DRINKING PLACES |
| GOODHUE, MN | 1670 | 21790 | APPAREL AND ACCESSORY STORES | FORREST, MS | 2412 | 32727 | EDUCATIONAL SERVICES |
| GRANT, MN | 357 | 2426 | EDUCATIONAL SERVICES | FRANKLIN, MS | 252 | 1879 | EDUCATIONAL SERVICES |
| HENNEPIN, MN | 37137 | 749639 | BUSINESS SERVICES | GEORGE, MS | 522 | 3699 | EDUCATIONAL SERVICES |
| HOUSTON, MN | 729 | 5301 | EDUCATIONAL SERVICES | GREENE, MS | 254 | 1285 | EDUCATIONAL SERVICES |
| HUBBARD, MN | 777 | 4959 | FOOD AND KINDRED PRODUCTS | GRENADA, MS | 908 | 10843 | CONSTRUCT: SPEC TRADE CONTRACT |
| ISANTI, MN | 786 | 8064 | EDUCATIONAL SERVICES | HANCOCK, MS | 1083 | 8297 | EDUCATIONAL SERVICES |
| ITASCA, MN | 1872 | 15144 | EDUCATIONAL SERVICES | HARRISON, MS | 6098 | 79542 | AMUSEMENT/RECREATION SERVICES |
| JACKSON, MN | 451 | 5150 | INDUSTRIAL & COMM. MACHINERY | HINDS, MS | 8748 | 132337 | EDUCATIONAL SERVICES |
| KANABEC, MN | 464 | 4077 | EDUCATIONAL SERVICES | HOLMES, MS | 513 | 4510 | EDUCATIONAL SERVICES |
| KANDIYOHI, MN | 1727 | 20658 | HEALTH SERVICES | HUMPHREYS, MS | 405 | 3509 | FOOD AND KINDRED PRODUCTS |
| KITTSON, MN | 323 | 1829 | HEALTH SERVICES | ISSAQUENA, MS | 34 | 151 | SOCIAL SERVICES |
| KOOCHICHING, MN | 621 | 6013 | PAPER AND ALLIED PRODUCTS | ITAWAMBA, MS | 604 | 5429 | CONSTRUCT: SPEC TRADE CONTRACT |
| LAC QUI PARLE, MN | 377 | 2709 | HEALTH SERVICES | JACKSON, MS | 3318 | 44206 | TRANSPORTATION EQUIPMENT |
| LAKE, MN | 441 | 4270 | MINING AND QUARRYING EXC FUELS | JASPER, MS | 401 | 4565 | FOOD AND KINDRED PRODUCTS |
| LAKE OF THE WOODS, MN | 237 | 1480 | HOTELS, ROOMING HOUSES, CAMPS | JEFFERSON, MS | 178 | 1977 | EDUCATIONAL SERVICES |
| LE SUEUR, MN | 811 | 8755 | EDUCATIONAL SERVICES | JEFFERSON DAVIS, MS | 302 | 2362 | EDUCATIONAL SERVICES |
| LINCOLN, MN | 349 | 1575 | EDUCATIONAL SERVICES | JONES, MS | 2035 | 26232 | EDUCATIONAL SERVICES |
| LYON, MN | 1065 | 14342 | FOOD AND KINDRED PRODUCTS | KEMPER, MS | 233 | 1969 | TRANSPORTATION EQUIPMENT |
| MCLEOD, MN | 1428 | 22992 | INDUSTRIAL & COMM. MACHINERY | LAFAYETTE, MS | 1225 | 14482 | EDUCATIONAL SERVICES |
| MAHNOMEN, MN | 217 | 1777 | EDUCATIONAL SERVICES | LAMAR, MS | 1218 | 13601 | GENERAL MERCHANDISE STORES |
| MARSHALL, MN | 466 | 2977 | EDUCATIONAL SERVICES | LAUDERDALE, MS | 2706 | 32669 | HEALTH SERVICES |
| MARTIN, MN | 1007 | 10561 | EDUCATIONAL SERVICES | LAWRENCE, MS | 346 | 3014 | PAPER AND ALLIED PRODUCTS |
| MEEKER, MN | 749 | 7260 | EDUCATIONAL SERVICES | LEAKE, MS | 492 | 6392 | FOOD AND KINDRED PRODUCTS |
| MILLE LACS, MN | 890 | 9967 | AMUSEMENT/RECREATION SERVICES | LEE, MS | 3147 | 53174 | HEALTH SERVICES |
| MORRISON, MN | 1093 | 11665 | TRANSPORTATION EQUIPMENT | LEFLORE, MS | 1269 | 15503 | EDUCATIONAL SERVICES |
| MOWER, MN | 1263 | 14561 | WHOLESALE TRADE: NONDURABLE | LINCOLN, MS | 1068 | 10132 | EDUCATIONAL SERVICES |
| MURRAY, MN | 395 | 2834 | EDUCATIONAL SERVICES | LOWNDES, MS | 2225 | 26286 | EDUCATIONAL SERVICES |

# BUSINESS DATA

| COUNTY | 2000 Total Firms | 2000 Total Employ-ees | TOP INDUSTRY RANKED on 2000 EMPLOYMENT | COUNTY | 2000 Total Firms | 2000 Total Employ-ees | TOP INDUSTRY RANKED on 2000 EMPLOYMENT |
|---|---|---|---|---|---|---|---|
| MADISON, MS | 2453 | 25409 | EATING AND DRINKING PLACES | HICKORY, MO | 290 | 1375 | EDUCATIONAL SERVICES |
| MARION, MS | 785 | 7881 | GENERAL MERCHANDISE STORES | HOLT, MO | 337 | 1801 | EDUCATIONAL SERVICES |
| MARSHALL, MS | 764 | 6364 | EDUCATIONAL SERVICES | HOWARD, MO | 362 | 2584 | EDUCATIONAL SERVICES |
| MONROE, MS | 1218 | 11006 | EDUCATIONAL SERVICES | HOWELL, MO | 1644 | 14251 | EDUCATIONAL SERVICES |
| MONTGOMERY, MS | 373 | 3290 | HEALTH SERVICES | IRON, MO | 430 | 2797 | HEALTH SERVICES |
| NESHOBA, MS | 748 | 13617 | AMUSEMENT/RECREATION SERVICES | JACKSON, MO | 20492 | 353235 | EDUCATIONAL SERVICES |
| NEWTON, MS | 645 | 7726 | HOME FURNITURE/EQUIPMENT STORE | JASPER, MO | 4036 | 47887 | EATING AND DRINKING PLACES |
| NOXUBEE, MS | 345 | 3714 | WHOLESALE TRADE: NONDURABLE | JEFFERSON, MO | 4739 | 43046 | HEALTH SERVICES |
| OKTIBBEHA, MS | 1130 | 15525 | EDUCATIONAL SERVICES | JOHNSON, MO | 1427 | 18603 | NATIONAL SECURITY/INT AFFAIRS |
| PANOLA, MS | 947 | 10130 | EDUCATIONAL SERVICES | KNOX, MO | 227 | 1110 | EDUCATIONAL SERVICES |
| PEARL RIVER, MS | 1278 | 8687 | EDUCATIONAL SERVICES | LACLEDE, MO | 1346 | 14100 | WHOLESALE TRADE: DURABLE GOODS |
| PERRY, MS | 293 | 2889 | LUMBER & WOOD PRODS, EXC FURN. | LAFAYETTE, MO | 1265 | 9459 | EDUCATIONAL SERVICES |
| PIKE, MS | 1471 | 13829 | FOOD AND KINDRED PRODUCTS | LAWRENCE, MO | 1152 | 8792 | EDUCATIONAL SERVICES |
| PONTOTOC, MS | 731 | 9988 | FURNITURE AND FIXTURES | LEWIS, MO | 383 | 2763 | EDUCATIONAL SERVICES |
| PRENTISS, MS | 800 | 8370 | INDUSTRIAL & COMM. MACHINERY | LINCOLN, MO | 859 | 7026 | EDUCATIONAL SERVICES |
| QUITMAN, MS | 303 | 2092 | EDUCATIONAL SERVICES | LINN, MO | 602 | 5835 | PRINTING AND PUBLISHING |
| RANKIN, MS | 3327 | 43426 | HEALTH SERVICES | LIVINGSTON, MO | 673 | 6699 | HEALTH SERVICES |
| SCOTT, MS | 752 | 11361 | WHOLESALE TRADE: NONDURABLE | MCDONALD, MO | 631 | 5880 | FOOD AND KINDRED PRODUCTS |
| SHARKEY, MS | 227 | 1815 | EDUCATIONAL SERVICES | MACON, MO | 620 | 5885 | ELECTRONIC/ELCTRCL EQPMNT |
| SIMPSON, MS | 761 | 5937 | HEALTH SERVICES | MADISON, MO | 368 | 3582 | HEALTH SERVICES |
| SMITH, MS | 266 | 3722 | LUMBER & WOOD PRODS, EXC FURN. | MARIES, MO | 283 | 1721 | EDUCATIONAL SERVICES |
| STONE, MS | 430 | 3292 | EDUCATIONAL SERVICES | MARION, MO | 1227 | 12461 | EDUCATIONAL SERVICES |
| SUNFLOWER, MS | 829 | 8867 | INDUSTRIAL & COMM. MACHINERY | MERCER, MO | 159 | 953 | EDUCATIONAL SERVICES |
| TALLAHATCHIE, MS | 348 | 2490 | EDUCATIONAL SERVICES | MILLER, MO | 810 | 6239 | EDUCATIONAL SERVICES |
| TATE, MS | 600 | 6743 | EDUCATIONAL SERVICES | MISSISSIPPI, MO | 477 | 3519 | EDUCATIONAL SERVICES |
| TIPPAH, MS | 598 | 6696 | FURNITURE AND FIXTURES | MONITEAU, MO | 472 | 4407 | FOOD AND KINDRED PRODUCTS |
| TISHOMINGO, MS | 571 | 5773 | WHOLESALE TRADE: DURABLE GOODS | MONROE, MO | 335 | 3790 | WHOLESALE TRADE: DURABLE GOODS |
| TUNICA, MS | 350 | 13904 | AMUSEMENT/RECREATION SERVICES | MONTGOMERY, MO | 502 | 2750 | HEALTH SERVICES |
| UNION, MS | 665 | 7967 | INDUSTRIAL & COMM. MACHINERY | MORGAN, MO | 784 | 4793 | EDUCATIONAL SERVICES |
| WALTHALL, MS | 320 | 2384 | HEALTH SERVICES | NEW MADRID, MO | 713 | 8223 | PRIMARY METAL INDUSTRIES |
| WARREN, MS | 1634 | 22048 | AMUSEMENT/RECREATION SERVICES | NEWTON, MO | 1844 | 20257 | HEALTH SERVICES |
| WASHINGTON, MS | 2101 | 22855 | EDUCATIONAL SERVICES | NODAWAY, MO | 907 | 8278 | EDUCATIONAL SERVICES |
| WAYNE, MS | 600 | 5307 | EDUCATIONAL SERVICES | OREGON, MO | 354 | 2310 | EDUCATIONAL SERVICES |
| WEBSTER, MS | 292 | 3612 | APPAREL, FINISHED PRODUCTS | OSAGE, MO | 410 | 3012 | EDUCATIONAL SERVICES |
| WILKINSON, MS | 252 | 1855 | EDUCATIONAL SERVICES | OZARK, MO | 379 | 1995 | EDUCATIONAL SERVICES |
| WINSTON, MS | 559 | 5878 | INDUSTRIAL & COMM. MACHINERY | PEMISCOT, MO | 704 | 4931 | EDUCATIONAL SERVICES |
| YALOBUSHA, MS | 354 | 3792 | TRANSPORTATION EQUIPMENT | PERRY, MO | 519 | 8061 | TRANSPORTATION EQUIPMENT |
| YAZOO, MS | 755 | 6152 | EDUCATIONAL SERVICES | PETTIS, MO | 1542 | 16810 | EDUCATIONAL SERVICES |
| ADAIR, MO | 889 | 10751 | HEALTH SERVICES | PHELPS, MO | 1615 | 14384 | EDUCATIONAL SERVICES |
| ANDREW, MO | 371 | 2358 | EDUCATIONAL SERVICES | PIKE, MO | 672 | 5622 | EDUCATIONAL SERVICES |
| ATCHISON, MO | 415 | 2308 | EDUCATIONAL SERVICES | PLATTE, MO | 1971 | 33769 | TRANSPORTATION BY AIR |
| AUDRAIN, MO | 908 | 6916 | STONE/CLAY/GLASS PRODUCTS | POLK, MO | 948 | 6936 | EDUCATIONAL SERVICES |
| BARRY, MO | 1352 | 14588 | PRIMARY METAL INDUSTRIES | PULASKI, MO | 1206 | 8807 | EDUCATIONAL SERVICES |
| BARTON, MO | 463 | 5307 | FURNITURE AND FIXTURES | PUTNAM, MO | 223 | 1069 | HEALTH SERVICES |
| BATES, MO | 606 | 3911 | EDUCATIONAL SERVICES | RALLS, MO | 325 | 3033 | WHOLESALE TRADE: NONDURABLE |
| BENTON, MO | 743 | 3886 | EDUCATIONAL SERVICES | RANDOLPH, MO | 854 | 10322 | TRANSPORTATION EQUIPMENT |
| BOLLINGER, MO | 265 | 1759 | EDUCATIONAL SERVICES | RAY, MO | 537 | 3764 | EDUCATIONAL SERVICES |
| BOONE, MO | 4353 | 65997 | EDUCATIONAL SERVICES | REYNOLDS, MO | 303 | 2440 | MINING AND QUARRYING EXC FUELS |
| BUCHANAN, MO | 2856 | 37692 | EATING AND DRINKING PLACES | RIPLEY, MO | 460 | 2401 | EDUCATIONAL SERVICES |
| BUTLER, MO | 1575 | 17841 | HEALTH SERVICES | ST. CHARLES, MO | 6058 | 81546 | ELECTRONIC/ELCTRCL EQPMNT |
| CALDWELL, MO | 333 | 1600 | EDUCATIONAL SERVICES | ST. CLAIR, MO | 323 | 2051 | EDUCATIONAL SERVICES |
| CALLAWAY, MO | 1123 | 9689 | EDUCATIONAL SERVICES | STE. GENEVIEVE, MO | 529 | 5770 | CHEMICALS AND ALLIED PRODUCTS |
| CAMDEN, MO | 2519 | 18296 | HOTELS, ROOMING HOUSES, CAMPS | ST. FRANCOIS, MO | 1830 | 18518 | HEALTH SERVICES |
| CAPE GIRARDEAU, MO | 2738 | 34857 | EATING AND DRINKING PLACES | ST. LOUIS, MO | 32111 | 506787 | EATING AND DRINKING PLACES |
| CARROLL, MO | 425 | 2504 | EDUCATIONAL SERVICES | SALINE, MO | 923 | 9591 | FOOD AND KINDRED PRODUCTS |
| CARTER, MO | 270 | 1440 | EDUCATIONAL SERVICES | SCHUYLER, MO | 183 | 841 | EDUCATIONAL SERVICES |
| CASS, MO | 2148 | 16251 | EDUCATIONAL SERVICES | SCOTLAND, MO | 261 | 1490 | HEALTH SERVICES |
| CEDAR, MO | 586 | 3502 | EDUCATIONAL SERVICES | SCOTT, MO | 1496 | 14626 | EDUCATIONAL SERVICES |
| CHARITON, MO | 363 | 1999 | EDUCATIONAL SERVICES | SHANNON, MO | 299 | 1553 | EDUCATIONAL SERVICES |
| CHRISTIAN, MO | 1646 | 11965 | EDUCATIONAL SERVICES | SHELBY, MO | 339 | 2139 | EDUCATIONAL SERVICES |
| CLARK, MO | 312 | 1397 | EDUCATIONAL SERVICES | STODDARD, MO | 1109 | 9693 | WHOLESALE TRADE: NONDURABLE |
| CLAY, MO | 5092 | 77944 | AMUSEMENT/RECREATION SERVICES | STONE, MO | 1107 | 6029 | EDUCATIONAL SERVICES |
| CLINTON, MO | 598 | 3743 | HEALTH SERVICES | SULLIVAN, MO | 246 | 2124 | FOOD AND KINDRED PRODUCTS |
| COLE, MO | 2940 | 50788 | EXECUTIVE, LEGISLATIVE GOVT. | TANEY, MO | 2832 | 25457 | HOTELS, ROOMING HOUSES, CAMPS |
| COOPER, MO | 664 | 5840 | EDUCATIONAL SERVICES | TEXAS, MO | 874 | 5738 | EDUCATIONAL SERVICES |
| CRAWFORD, MO | 792 | 5124 | EDUCATIONAL SERVICES | VERNON, MO | 783 | 7313 | HEALTH SERVICES |
| DADE, MO | 263 | 2036 | WHOLESALE TRADE: NONDURABLE | WARREN, MO | 601 | 6129 | FABRICATED METAL PRODUCTS |
| DALLAS, MO | 472 | 2715 | EDUCATIONAL SERVICES | WASHINGTON, MO | 553 | 4413 | EDUCATIONAL SERVICES |
| DAVIESS, MO | 373 | 2241 | EDUCATIONAL SERVICES | WAYNE, MO | 485 | 2692 | EDUCATIONAL SERVICES |
| DE KALB, MO | 338 | 2691 | JUSTICE, PUBLIC ORDER/SAFETY | WEBSTER, MO | 857 | 6540 | EDUCATIONAL SERVICES |
| DENT, MO | 564 | 5109 | WHOLESALE TRADE: NONDURABLE | WORTH, MO | 121 | 654 | EDUCATIONAL SERVICES |
| DOUGLAS, MO | 364 | 1964 | EDUCATIONAL SERVICES | WRIGHT, MO | 651 | 4823 | EDUCATIONAL SERVICES |
| DUNKLIN, MO | 1217 | 9954 | HEALTH SERVICES | ST. LOUIS CITY, MO | 11531 | 266438 | HEALTH SERVICES |
| FRANKLIN, MO | 3279 | 35957 | EDUCATIONAL SERVICES | BEAVERHEAD, MT | 554 | 3125 | EDUCATIONAL SERVICES |
| GASCONADE, MO | 655 | 5389 | PRINTING AND PUBLISHING | BIG HORN, MT | 440 | 4142 | EXECUTIVE, LEGISLATIVE GOVT. |
| GENTRY, MO | 332 | 2102 | WHOLESALE TRADE: DURABLE GOODS | BLAINE, MT | 317 | 1809 | EDUCATIONAL SERVICES |
| GREENE, MO | 9387 | 134319 | EATING AND DRINKING PLACES | BROADWATER, MT | 202 | 1030 | WHOLESALE TRADE: NONDURABLE |
| GRUNDY, MO | 481 | 3814 | FOOD AND KINDRED PRODUCTS | CARBON, MT | 511 | 2249 | HOTELS, ROOMING HOUSES, CAMPS |
| HARRISON, MO | 525 | 2991 | EDUCATIONAL SERVICES | CARTER, MT | 90 | 358 | HEALTH SERVICES |
| HENRY, MO | 1017 | 8616 | HEALTH SERVICES | CASCADE, MT | 3087 | 27321 | EATING AND DRINKING PLACES |

| COUNTY | 2000 Total Firms | 2000 Total Employ-ees | TOP INDUSTRY RANKED on 2000 EMPLOYMENT | COUNTY | 2000 Total Firms | 2000 Total Employ-ees | TOP INDUSTRY RANKED on 2000 EMPLOYMENT |
|---|---|---|---|---|---|---|---|
| CHOUTEAU, MT | 272 | 1303 | EDUCATIONAL SERVICES | FRONTIER, NE | 173 | 870 | EDUCATIONAL SERVICES |
| CUSTER, MT | 609 | 4625 | EATING AND DRINKING PLACES | FURNAS, NE | 324 | 1984 | HEALTH SERVICES |
| DANIELS, MT | 141 | 903 | COMMUNICATIONS | GAGE, NE | 954 | 8443 | HEALTH SERVICES |
| DAWSON, MT | 410 | 3622 | EDUCATIONAL SERVICES | GARDEN, NE | 141 | 598 | HEALTH SERVICES |
| DEER LODGE, MT | 387 | 2969 | HEALTH SERVICES | GARFIELD, NE | 153 | 733 | EDUCATIONAL SERVICES |
| FALLON, MT | 176 | 1117 | HEALTH SERVICES | GOSPER, NE | 75 | 348 | HEALTH SERVICES |
| FERGUS, MT | 652 | 4588 | HEALTH SERVICES | GRANT, NE | 108 | 357 | AGRICULTURAL - LIVESTOCK SPEC |
| FLATHEAD, MT | 4475 | 32110 | EATING AND DRINKING PLACES | GREELEY, NE | 161 | 744 | EDUCATIONAL SERVICES |
| GALLATIN, MT | 3594 | 29548 | EATING AND DRINKING PLACES | HALL, NE | 2115 | 30597 | FOOD AND KINDRED PRODUCTS |
| GARFIELD, MT | 90 | 350 | EDUCATIONAL SERVICES | HAMILTON, NE | 537 | 3265 | EDUCATIONAL SERVICES |
| GLACIER, MT | 530 | 4646 | EDUCATIONAL SERVICES | HARLAN, NE | 230 | 1078 | EDUCATIONAL SERVICES |
| GOLDEN VALLEY, MT | 35 | 200 | AGRICULTURAL - LIVESTOCK SPEC | HAYES, NE | 45 | 190 | EDUCATIONAL SERVICES |
| GRANITE, MT | 125 | 553 | LUMBER & WOOD PRODS, EXC FURN. | HITCHCOCK, NE | 144 | 748 | EDUCATIONAL SERVICES |
| HILL, MT | 730 | 6726 | EDUCATIONAL SERVICES | HOLT, NE | 663 | 3991 | WHOLESALE TRADE: NONDURABLE |
| JEFFERSON, MT | 330 | 2014 | EXECUTIVE, LEGISLATIVE GOVT. | HOOKER, NE | 73 | 375 | AMUSEMENT/RECREATION SERVICES |
| JUDITH BASIN, MT | 109 | 388 | EDUCATIONAL SERVICES | HOWARD, NE | 187 | 925 | EDUCATIONAL SERVICES |
| LAKE, MT | 1335 | 8214 | EXECUTIVE, LEGISLATIVE GOVT. | JEFFERSON, NE | 400 | 3507 | STONE/CLAY/GLASS PRODUCTS |
| LEWIS AND CLARK, MT | 2638 | 27856 | ADMIN: ECONOMIC PROGRAMS | JOHNSON, NE | 214 | 1113 | EDUCATIONAL SERVICES |
| LIBERTY, MT | 132 | 744 | EDUCATIONAL SERVICES | KEARNEY, NE | 257 | 2010 | HEALTH SERVICES |
| LINCOLN, MT | 997 | 5774 | LUMBER & WOOD PRODS, EXC FURN. | KEITH, NE | 537 | 3901 | EATING AND DRINKING PLACES |
| MCCONE, MT | 117 | 752 | EDUCATIONAL SERVICES | KEYA PAHA, NE | 47 | 99 | EDUCATIONAL SERVICES |
| MADISON, MT | 426 | 1706 | EDUCATIONAL SERVICES | KIMBALL, NE | 257 | 1509 | ELECTRONIC/ELCTRCL EQPMNT |
| MEAGHER, MT | 125 | 623 | AGRICULTURAL - LIVESTOCK SPEC | KNOX, NE | 484 | 2669 | HEALTH SERVICES |
| MINERAL, MT | 174 | 1091 | EATING AND DRINKING PLACES | LANCASTER, NE | 7560 | 130772 | EDUCATIONAL SERVICES |
| MISSOULA, MT | 3898 | 40437 | EATING AND DRINKING PLACES | LINCOLN, NE | 1466 | 13051 | EATING AND DRINKING PLACES |
| MUSSELSHELL, MT | 220 | 1046 | EDUCATIONAL SERVICES | LOGAN, NE | 48 | 210 | EDUCATIONAL SERVICES |
| PARK, MT | 879 | 5248 | HOTELS, ROOMING HOUSES, CAMPS | LOUP, NE | 34 | 97 | EDUCATIONAL SERVICES |
| PETROLEUM, MT | 37 | 91 | EDUCATIONAL SERVICES | MCPHERSON, NE | 30 | 70 | EDUCATIONAL SERVICES |
| PHILLIPS, MT | 231 | 1273 | EDUCATIONAL SERVICES | MADISON, NE | 1417 | 18193 | WHOLESALE TRADE: NONDURABLE |
| PONDERA, MT | 326 | 2209 | EDUCATIONAL SERVICES | MERRICK, NE | 318 | 2173 | LUMBER & WOOD PRODS, EXC FURN. |
| POWDER RIVER, MT | 115 | 423 | EDUCATIONAL SERVICES | MORRILL, NE | 218 | 1421 | EDUCATIONAL SERVICES |
| POWELL, MT | 268 | 2029 | JUSTICE, PUBLIC ORDER/SAFETY | NANCE, NE | 162 | 788 | HEALTH SERVICES |
| PRAIRIE, MT | 82 | 298 | EDUCATIONAL SERVICES | NEMAHA, NE | 318 | 3238 | CHEMICALS AND ALLIED PRODUCTS |
| RAVALLI, MT | 1547 | 9835 | EDUCATIONAL SERVICES | NUCKOLLS, NE | 302 | 1723 | HEALTH SERVICES |
| RICHLAND, MT | 502 | 2897 | EDUCATIONAL SERVICES | OTOE, NE | 642 | 5815 | WHOLESALE TRADE: DURABLE GOODS |
| ROOSEVELT, MT | 428 | 3873 | EXECUTIVE, LEGISLATIVE GOVT. | PAWNEE, NE | 138 | 827 | EDUCATIONAL SERVICES |
| ROSEBUD, MT | 444 | 3725 | EDUCATIONAL SERVICES | PERKINS, NE | 212 | 1236 | HEALTH SERVICES |
| SANDERS, MT | 460 | 2303 | EDUCATIONAL SERVICES | PHELPS, NE | 437 | 4770 | MESR/ANLYZ/CNTRL INSTRMNTS |
| SHERIDAN, MT | 271 | 1301 | HEALTH SERVICES | PIERCE, NE | 307 | 1547 | EDUCATIONAL SERVICES |
| SILVER BOW, MT | 1542 | 16981 | CONSTRUCT: SPEC TRADE CONTRACT | PLATTE, NE | 1247 | 18892 | EDUCATIONAL SERVICES |
| STILLWATER, MT | 351 | 2896 | MINING AND QUARRYING EXC FUELS | POLK, NE | 246 | 1468 | HEALTH SERVICES |
| SWEET GRASS, MT | 219 | 1061 | MISCELLANEOUS RETAIL | RED WILLOW, NE | 604 | 5255 | EDUCATIONAL SERVICES |
| TETON, MT | 317 | 1968 | EDUCATIONAL SERVICES | RICHARDSON, NE | 461 | 2692 | EDUCATIONAL SERVICES |
| TOOLE, MT | 357 | 1916 | EDUCATIONAL SERVICES | ROCK, NE | 103 | 607 | HEALTH SERVICES |
| TREASURE, MT | 51 | 164 | EDUCATIONAL SERVICES | SALINE, NE | 500 | 6028 | FOOD AND KINDRED PRODUCTS |
| VALLEY, MT | 435 | 2369 | EDUCATIONAL SERVICES | SARPY, NE | 2463 | 35967 | MOTOR FREIGHT TRANSPORTATION |
| WHEATLAND, MT | 116 | 624 | HEALTH SERVICES | SAUNDERS, NE | 634 | 4540 | EDUCATIONAL SERVICES |
| WIBAUX, MT | 39 | 142 | EDUCATIONAL SERVICES | SCOTTS BLUFF, NE | 1751 | 15207 | EATING AND DRINKING PLACES |
| YELLOWSTONE, MT | 6059 | 59047 | EATING AND DRINKING PLACES | SEWARD, NE | 576 | 5903 | EDUCATIONAL SERVICES |
| ADAMS, NE | 1291 | 14608 | EDUCATIONAL SERVICES | SHERIDAN, NE | 358 | 1969 | EDUCATIONAL SERVICES |
| ANTELOPE, NE | 422 | 2293 | HEALTH SERVICES | SHERMAN, NE | 127 | 699 | EDUCATIONAL SERVICES |
| ARTHUR, NE | 38 | 83 | AGRICULTURAL - LIVESTOCK SPEC | SIOUX, NE | 35 | 107 | EDUCATIONAL SERVICES |
| BANNER, NE | 25 | 145 | EDUCATIONAL SERVICES | STANTON, NE | 145 | 793 | EDUCATIONAL SERVICES |
| BLAINE, NE | 42 | 119 | EDUCATIONAL SERVICES | THAYER, NE | 353 | 2296 | HEALTH SERVICES |
| BOONE, NE | 322 | 2107 | EDUCATIONAL SERVICES | THOMAS, NE | 78 | 316 | EDUCATIONAL SERVICES |
| BOX BUTTE, NE | 529 | 4282 | EDUCATIONAL SERVICES | THURSTON, NE | 279 | 3173 | EXECUTIVE, LEGISLATIVE GOVT. |
| BOYD, NE | 152 | 743 | EDUCATIONAL SERVICES | VALLEY, NE | 272 | 1481 | HEALTH SERVICES |
| BROWN, NE | 239 | 1329 | EDUCATIONAL SERVICES | WASHINGTON, NE | 651 | 5898 | HEALTH SERVICES |
| BUFFALO, NE | 1645 | 23136 | EDUCATIONAL SERVICES | WAYNE, NE | 331 | 3449 | EDUCATIONAL SERVICES |
| BURT, NE | 359 | 1855 | EDUCATIONAL SERVICES | WEBSTER, NE | 236 | 1216 | EDUCATIONAL SERVICES |
| BUTLER, NE | 270 | 1985 | EDUCATIONAL SERVICES | WHEELER, NE | 42 | 208 | WHOLESALE TRADE: NONDURABLE |
| CASS, NE | 666 | 5174 | EDUCATIONAL SERVICES | YORK, NE | 718 | 7200 | MOTOR FREIGHT TRANSPORTATION |
| CEDAR, NE | 390 | 2493 | EDUCATIONAL SERVICES | CHURCHILL, NV | 965 | 7278 | HEALTH SERVICES |
| CHASE, NE | 282 | 1578 | EDUCATIONAL SERVICES | CLARK, NV | 33723 | 630007 | AMUSEMENT/RECREATION SERVICES |
| CHERRY, NE | 357 | 1798 | EDUCATIONAL SERVICES | DOUGLAS, NV | 2030 | 27413 | AMUSEMENT/RECREATION SERVICES |
| CHEYENNE, NE | 514 | 5383 | WHOLESALE TRADE: DURABLE GOODS | ELKO, NV | 1911 | 23105 | AMUSEMENT/RECREATION SERVICES |
| CLAY, NE | 339 | 2285 | EDUCATIONAL SERVICES | ESMERALDA, NV | 52 | 254 | MINING AND QUARRYING EXC FUELS |
| COLFAX, NE | 366 | 4368 | FOOD AND KINDRED PRODUCTS | EUREKA, NV | 80 | 837 | MINING AND QUARRYING EXC FUELS |
| CUMING, NE | 498 | 3665 | FOOD AND KINDRED PRODUCTS | HUMBOLDT, NV | 649 | 9353 | MINING AND QUARRYING EXC FUELS |
| CUSTER, NE | 609 | 3356 | EDUCATIONAL SERVICES | LANDER, NV | 246 | 1960 | MINING AND QUARRYING EXC FUELS |
| DAKOTA, NE | 711 | 6266 | EDUCATIONAL SERVICES | LINCOLN, NV | 252 | 1089 | EDUCATIONAL SERVICES |
| DAWES, NE | 431 | 3106 | EDUCATIONAL SERVICES | LYON, NV | 1018 | 7782 | EDUCATIONAL SERVICES |
| DAWSON, NE | 1026 | 10596 | FOOD AND KINDRED PRODUCTS | MINERAL, NV | 214 | 1965 | ENGINEERING, ACCOUNTING, ETC. |
| DEUEL, NE | 113 | 703 | EDUCATIONAL SERVICES | NYE, NV | 916 | 6380 | MINING AND QUARRYING EXC FUELS |
| DIXON, NE | 219 | 1723 | WHOLESALE TRADE: NONDURABLE | PERSHING, NV | 193 | 1923 | MINING AND QUARRYING EXC FUELS |
| DODGE, NE | 1522 | 15253 | WHOLESALE TRADE: NONDURABLE | STOREY, NV | 155 | 645 | EATING AND DRINKING PLACES |
| DOUGLAS, NE | 14855 | 278242 | BUSINESS SERVICES | WASHOE, NV | 11255 | 156811 | AMUSEMENT/RECREATION SERVICES |
| DUNDY, NE | 163 | 894 | EDUCATIONAL SERVICES | WHITE PINE, NV | 413 | 3962 | JUSTICE, PUBLIC ORDER/SAFETY |
| FILLMORE, NE | 367 | 2505 | EDUCATIONAL SERVICES | CARSON CITY, NV | 2382 | 33228 | NATIONAL SECURITY/INT AFFAIRS |
| FRANKLIN, NE | 191 | 769 | EDUCATIONAL SERVICES | BELKNAP, NH | 2964 | 24904 | EATING AND DRINKING PLACES |

| COUNTY | 2000 Total Firms | 2000 Total Employ-ees | TOP INDUSTRY RANKED on 2000 EMPLOYMENT | COUNTY | 2000 Total Firms | 2000 Total Employ-ees | TOP INDUSTRY RANKED on 2000 EMPLOYMENT |
|---|---|---|---|---|---|---|---|
| CARROLL, NH | 2747 | 19402 | HOTELS, ROOMING HOUSES, CAMPS | FULTON, NY | 1914 | 17686 | EDUCATIONAL SERVICES |
| CHESHIRE, NH | 3038 | 27942 | EDUCATIONAL SERVICES | GENESEE, NY | 1863 | 24608 | EDUCATIONAL SERVICES |
| COOS, NH | 1527 | 14238 | HOTELS, ROOMING HOUSES, CAMPS | GREENE, NY | 1824 | 12661 | HOTELS, ROOMING HOUSES, CAMPS |
| GRAFTON, NH | 4089 | 46804 | EDUCATIONAL SERVICES | HAMILTON, NY | 506 | 2494 | HOTELS, ROOMING HOUSES, CAMPS |
| HILLSBOROUGH, NH | 14076 | 160471 | EDUCATIONAL SERVICES | HERKIMER, NY | 1876 | 18597 | EDUCATIONAL SERVICES |
| MERRIMACK, NH | 5847 | 66070 | EDUCATIONAL SERVICES | JEFFERSON, NY | 3261 | 33249 | EDUCATIONAL SERVICES |
| ROCKINGHAM, NH | 13305 | 111954 | EATING AND DRINKING PLACES | KINGS, NY | 50062 | 395425 | EDUCATIONAL SERVICES |
| STRAFFORD, NH | 3475 | 40609 | EDUCATIONAL SERVICES | LEWIS, NY | 848 | 6709 | EDUCATIONAL SERVICES |
| SULLIVAN, NH | 1668 | 13820 | EDUCATIONAL SERVICES | LIVINGSTON, NY | 1683 | 16801 | EDUCATIONAL SERVICES |
| ATLANTIC, NJ | 10585 | 139866 | AMUSEMENT/RECREATION SERVICES | MADISON, NY | 2104 | 30709 | MISC. MANUFACTURING INDUSTRIES |
| BERGEN, NJ | 33093 | 389195 | EDUCATIONAL SERVICES | MONROE, NY | 21764 | 310617 | EDUCATIONAL SERVICES |
| BURLINGTON, NJ | 11921 | 160054 | HEALTH SERVICES | MONTGOMERY, NY | 1579 | 15689 | EDUCATIONAL SERVICES |
| CAMDEN, NJ | 15023 | 175139 | EDUCATIONAL SERVICES | NASSAU, NY | 41450 | 433078 | EDUCATIONAL SERVICES |
| CAPE MAY, NJ | 6019 | 41129 | EATING AND DRINKING PLACES | NEW YORK, NY | 97458 | 1590131 | SECURITY/COMMODITY BROKERS |
| CUMBERLAND, NJ | 4112 | 52828 | EXECUTIVE, LEGISLATIVE GOVT. | NIAGARA, NY | 6025 | 75344 | EDUCATIONAL SERVICES |
| ESSEX, NJ | 25335 | 291887 | EDUCATIONAL SERVICES | ONEIDA, NY | 7258 | 98571 | EDUCATIONAL SERVICES |
| GLOUCESTER, NJ | 7189 | 79175 | EDUCATIONAL SERVICES | ONONDAGA, NY | 17295 | 242328 | EDUCATIONAL SERVICES |
| HUDSON, NJ | 15529 | 216339 | RUBBER & MISC PLASTIC PRODUCTS | ONTARIO, NY | 3752 | 41925 | EDUCATIONAL SERVICES |
| HUNTERDON, NJ | 5771 | 53203 | ENGINEERING, ACCOUNTING, ETC. | ORANGE, NY | 11726 | 110607 | EDUCATIONAL SERVICES |
| MERCER, NJ | 10400 | 162872 | EDUCATIONAL SERVICES | ORLEANS, NY | 1075 | 11476 | EDUCATIONAL SERVICES |
| MIDDLESEX, NJ | 20510 | 298209 | EDUCATIONAL SERVICES | OSWEGO, NY | 3381 | 32488 | EDUCATIONAL SERVICES |
| MONMOUTH, NJ | 25801 | 207695 | EDUCATIONAL SERVICES | OTSEGO, NY | 2144 | 20427 | EDUCATIONAL SERVICES |
| MORRIS, NJ | 18249 | 266497 | CHEMICALS AND ALLIED PRODUCTS | PUTNAM, NY | 2954 | 19416 | EDUCATIONAL SERVICES |
| OCEAN, NJ | 16338 | 130939 | HEALTH SERVICES | QUEENS, NY | 40572 | 363430 | EDUCATIONAL SERVICES |
| PASSAIC, NJ | 15397 | 160632 | EDUCATIONAL SERVICES | RENSSELAER, NY | 3961 | 44518 | EDUCATIONAL SERVICES |
| SALEM, NJ | 2050 | 21855 | ELECTRIC, GAS & SANITARY SERV. | RICHMOND, NY | 8348 | 72373 | EDUCATIONAL SERVICES |
| SOMERSET, NJ | 9490 | 134696 | COMMUNICATIONS | ROCKLAND, NY | 9915 | 92625 | EDUCATIONAL SERVICES |
| SUSSEX, NJ | 5699 | 37794 | EDUCATIONAL SERVICES | ST. LAWRENCE, NY | 3073 | 36186 | EDUCATIONAL SERVICES |
| UNION, NJ | 18697 | 222372 | WHOLESALE TRADE: NONDURABLE | SARATOGA, NY | 5983 | 54809 | EDUCATIONAL SERVICES |
| WARREN, NJ | 4297 | 31859 | EDUCATIONAL SERVICES | SCHENECTADY, NY | 4451 | 54636 | EDUCATIONAL SERVICES |
| BERNALILLO, NM | 19831 | 245576 | EATING AND DRINKING PLACES | SCHOHARIE, NY | 1099 | 8708 | EDUCATIONAL SERVICES |
| CATRON, NM | 125 | 562 | EDUCATIONAL SERVICES | SCHUYLER, NY | 664 | 4685 | EDUCATIONAL SERVICES |
| CHAVES, NM | 1985 | 17312 | EDUCATIONAL SERVICES | SENECA, NY | 1095 | 11136 | INDUSTRIAL & COMM. MACHINERY |
| CIBOLA, NM | 640 | 6931 | EDUCATIONAL SERVICES | STEUBEN, NY | 3006 | 41351 | NONCLASSIFIABLE ESTABLISHMENT |
| COLFAX, NM | 779 | 5958 | SOCIAL SERVICES | SUFFOLK, NY | 54867 | 507718 | EDUCATIONAL SERVICES |
| CURRY, NM | 1545 | 13131 | EDUCATIONAL SERVICES | SULLIVAN, NY | 3009 | 21929 | HOTELS, ROOMING HOUSES, CAMPS |
| DE BACA, NM | 86 | 441 | EDUCATIONAL SERVICES | TIOGA, NY | 1356 | 15688 | MESR/ANLYZ/CNTRL INSTRMNTS |
| DONA ANA, NM | 3553 | 45354 | EDUCATIONAL SERVICES | TOMPKINS, NY | 2870 | 33935 | EDUCATIONAL SERVICES |
| EDDY, NM | 1874 | 18835 | EDUCATIONAL SERVICES | ULSTER, NY | 6679 | 61294 | EDUCATIONAL SERVICES |
| GRANT, NM | 1056 | 9588 | MINING AND QUARRYING EXC FUELS | WARREN, NY | 3105 | 32268 | HOTELS, ROOMING HOUSES, CAMPS |
| GUADALUPE, NM | 270 | 1740 | EATING AND DRINKING PLACES | WASHINGTON, NY | 1588 | 14471 | EDUCATIONAL SERVICES |
| HARDING, NM | 56 | 187 | EDUCATIONAL SERVICES | WAYNE, NY | 2620 | 28861 | EDUCATIONAL SERVICES |
| HIDALGO, NM | 188 | 1878 | PRIMARY METAL INDUSTRIES | WESTCHESTER, NY | 31835 | 325935 | EDUCATIONAL SERVICES |
| LEA, NM | 2303 | 19041 | OIL AND GAS EXTRACTION | WYOMING, NY | 1123 | 13288 | JUSTICE, PUBLIC ORDER/SAFETY |
| LINCOLN, NM | 1262 | 7215 | EDUCATIONAL SERVICES | YATES, NY | 834 | 7245 | EDUCATIONAL SERVICES |
| LOS ALAMOS, NM | 703 | 23778 | EDUCATIONAL SERVICES | ALAMANCE, NC | 3968 | 55972 | TEXTILE MILL PRODUCTS |
| LUNA, NM | 656 | 5516 | EDUCATIONAL SERVICES | ALEXANDER, NC | 756 | 10971 | FURNITURE AND FIXTURES |
| MCKINLEY, NM | 1751 | 19535 | EDUCATIONAL SERVICES | ALLEGHANY, NC | 535 | 4112 | APPAREL, FINISHED PRODUCTS |
| MORA, NM | 143 | 772 | EDUCATIONAL SERVICES | ANSON, NC | 730 | 7810 | APPAREL, FINISHED PRODUCTS |
| OTERO, NM | 1785 | 17065 | HOTELS, ROOMING HOUSES, CAMPS | ASHE, NC | 937 | 7528 | EATING AND DRINKING PLACES |
| QUAY, NM | 463 | 3347 | EATING AND DRINKING PLACES | AVERY, NC | 732 | 6320 | HOTELS, ROOMING HOUSES, CAMPS |
| RIO ARRIBA, NM | 1132 | 9824 | EXECUTIVE, LEGISLATIVE GOVT. | BEAUFORT, NC | 1889 | 18279 | TEXTILE MILL PRODUCTS |
| ROOSEVELT, NM | 511 | 4814 | EDUCATIONAL SERVICES | BERTIE, NC | 593 | 7287 | FOOD AND KINDRED PRODUCTS |
| SANDOVAL, NM | 1938 | 15241 | EDUCATIONAL SERVICES | BLADEN, NC | 930 | 12761 | WHOLESALE TRADE: NONDURABLE |
| SAN JUAN, NM | 3846 | 41803 | OIL AND GAS EXTRACTION | BRUNSWICK, NC | 2438 | 21372 | CHEMICALS AND ALLIED PRODUCTS |
| SAN MIGUEL, NM | 868 | 7135 | EDUCATIONAL SERVICES | BUNCOMBE, NC | 7678 | 94539 | EATING AND DRINKING PLACES |
| SANTA FE, NM | 6766 | 64256 | EATING AND DRINKING PLACES | BURKE, NC | 2381 | 33580 | TEXTILE MILL PRODUCTS |
| SIERRA, NM | 595 | 3087 | HEALTH SERVICES | CABARRUS, NC | 3793 | 41799 | EDUCATIONAL SERVICES |
| SOCORRO, NM | 511 | 4438 | EDUCATIONAL SERVICES | CALDWELL, NC | 2017 | 28828 | FURNITURE AND FIXTURES |
| TAOS, NM | 1781 | 10903 | HOTELS, ROOMING HOUSES, CAMPS | CAMDEN, NC | 183 | 1060 | MEMBERSHIP ORGANIZATIONS |
| TORRANCE, NM | 417 | 2850 | EDUCATIONAL SERVICES | CARTERET, NC | 2817 | 21536 | EATING AND DRINKING PLACES |
| UNION, NM | 199 | 1148 | EDUCATIONAL SERVICES | CASWELL, NC | 399 | 2916 | EDUCATIONAL SERVICES |
| VALENCIA, NM | 1319 | 10642 | EDUCATIONAL SERVICES | CATAWBA, NC | 5042 | 100267 | FURNITURE AND FIXTURES |
| ALBANY, NY | 11319 | 201972 | EDUCATIONAL SERVICES | CHATHAM, NC | 1460 | 14216 | TEXTILE MILL PRODUCTS |
| ALLEGANY, NY | 1421 | 14480 | EDUCATIONAL SERVICES | CHEROKEE, NC | 920 | 8159 | APPAREL, FINISHED PRODUCTS |
| BRONX, NY | 18273 | 196722 | EDUCATIONAL SERVICES | CHOWAN, NC | 558 | 5616 | HEALTH SERVICES |
| BROOME, NY | 6760 | 92257 | HEALTH SERVICES | CLAY, NC | 326 | 1723 | HEALTH SERVICES |
| CATTARAUGUS, NY | 2454 | 32178 | EDUCATIONAL SERVICES | CLEVELAND, NC | 2790 | 34786 | TEXTILE MILL PRODUCTS |
| CAYUGA, NY | 2369 | 21607 | EDUCATIONAL SERVICES | COLUMBUS, NC | 1905 | 18449 | EDUCATIONAL SERVICES |
| CHAUTAUQUA, NY | 4892 | 57057 | EDUCATIONAL SERVICES | CRAVEN, NC | 2964 | 32428 | MISCELLANEOUS REPAIR SERVICES |
| CHEMUNG, NY | 2721 | 35713 | EDUCATIONAL SERVICES | CUMBERLAND, NC | 8217 | 93370 | EDUCATIONAL SERVICES |
| CHENANGO, NY | 1775 | 17922 | EDUCATIONAL SERVICES | CURRITUCK, NC | 760 | 4559 | FOOD STORES |
| CLINTON, NY | 2637 | 30331 | EDUCATIONAL SERVICES | DARE, NC | 2763 | 15580 | EATING AND DRINKING PLACES |
| COLUMBIA, NY | 2498 | 19546 | EDUCATIONAL SERVICES | DAVIDSON, NC | 4532 | 48929 | FURNITURE AND FIXTURES |
| CORTLAND, NY | 1528 | 19487 | EDUCATIONAL SERVICES | DAVIE, NC | 1001 | 7333 | MISCELLANEOUS RETAIL |
| DELAWARE, NY | 2005 | 17863 | EDUCATIONAL SERVICES | DUPLIN, NC | 1719 | 18876 | FOOD AND KINDRED PRODUCTS |
| DUTCHESS, NY | 8631 | 92536 | EDUCATIONAL SERVICES | DURHAM, NC | 6917 | 159935 | EDUCATIONAL SERVICES |
| ERIE, NY | 26014 | 397800 | EDUCATIONAL SERVICES | EDGECOMBE, NC | 1574 | 21837 | INDUSTRIAL & COMM. MACHINERY |
| ESSEX, NY | 1834 | 15847 | HOTELS, ROOMING HOUSES, CAMPS | FORSYTH, NC | 9903 | 149740 | HEALTH SERVICES |
| FRANKLIN, NY | 1560 | 18437 | EDUCATIONAL SERVICES | FRANKLIN, NC | 1130 | 10065 | EDUCATIONAL SERVICES |

| COUNTY | 2000 Total Firms | 2000 Total Employ-ees | TOP INDUSTRY RANKED on 2000 EMPLOYMENT |
|---|---|---|---|
| GASTON, NC | 5472 | 73248 | TEXTILE MILL PRODUCTS |
| GATES, NC | 217 | 1367 | EDUCATIONAL SERVICES |
| GRAHAM, NC | 263 | 2407 | FURNITURE AND FIXTURES |
| GRANVILLE, NC | 1182 | 15216 | CHEMICALS AND ALLIED PRODUCTS |
| GREENE, NC | 393 | 3568 | EDUCATIONAL SERVICES |
| GUILFORD, NC | 17055 | 251652 | EATING AND DRINKING PLACES |
| HALIFAX, NC | 1797 | 17411 | EDUCATIONAL SERVICES |
| HARNETT, NC | 2388 | 22826 | EDUCATIONAL SERVICES |
| HAYWOOD, NC | 1932 | 15691 | EATING AND DRINKING PLACES |
| HENDERSON, NC | 2840 | 32726 | HOTELS, ROOMING HOUSES, CAMPS |
| HERTFORD, NC | 794 | 8037 | EDUCATIONAL SERVICES |
| HOKE, NC | 602 | 6246 | FOOD AND KINDRED PRODUCTS |
| HYDE, NC | 310 | 1811 | WHOLESALE TRADE: NONDURABLE |
| IREDELL, NC | 4021 | 51046 | TEXTILE MILL PRODUCTS |
| JACKSON, NC | 1124 | 12074 | EDUCATIONAL SERVICES |
| JOHNSTON, NC | 3438 | 32555 | EATING AND DRINKING PLACES |
| JONES, NC | 249 | 1617 | APPAREL, FINISHED PRODUCTS |
| LEE, NC | 1980 | 23967 | FOOD AND KINDRED PRODUCTS |
| LENOIR, NC | 2164 | 24769 | EDUCATIONAL SERVICES |
| LINCOLN, NC | 1678 | 18247 | TEXTILE MILL PRODUCTS |
| MCDOWELL, NC | 1109 | 18945 | TEXTILE MILL PRODUCTS |
| MACON, NC | 1460 | 9481 | EATING AND DRINKING PLACES |
| MADISON, NC | 386 | 3833 | EDUCATIONAL SERVICES |
| MARTIN, NC | 964 | 8297 | EDUCATIONAL SERVICES |
| MECKLENBURG, NC | 25617 | 371158 | EATING AND DRINKING PLACES |
| MITCHELL, NC | 517 | 5435 | FURNITURE AND FIXTURES |
| MONTGOMERY, NC | 742 | 10460 | TEXTILE MILL PRODUCTS |
| MOORE, NC | 2927 | 28715 | SOCIAL SERVICES |
| NASH, NC | 3096 | 39085 | WHOLESALE TRADE: NONDURABLE |
| NEW HANOVER, NC | 8091 | 78790 | EATING AND DRINKING PLACES |
| NORTHAMPTON, NC | 509 | 4497 | EDUCATIONAL SERVICES |
| ONSLOW, NC | 3345 | 30432 | EATING AND DRINKING PLACES |
| ORANGE, NC | 3257 | 40559 | EDUCATIONAL SERVICES |
| PAMLICO, NC | 429 | 3349 | HOTELS, ROOMING HOUSES, CAMPS |
| PASQUOTANK, NC | 1451 | 14207 | EDUCATIONAL SERVICES |
| PENDER, NC | 1151 | 7124 | EDUCATIONAL SERVICES |
| PERQUIMANS, NC | 401 | 2156 | EDUCATIONAL SERVICES |
| PERSON, NC | 1056 | 12252 | TEXTILE MILL PRODUCTS |
| PITT, NC | 4084 | 50798 | EDUCATIONAL SERVICES |
| POLK, NC | 662 | 4398 | HEALTH SERVICES |
| RANDOLPH, NC | 4203 | 49654 | FURNITURE AND FIXTURES |
| RICHMOND, NC | 1435 | 16982 | HEALTH SERVICES |
| ROBESON, NC | 3140 | 40852 | EDUCATIONAL SERVICES |
| ROCKINGHAM, NC | 2774 | 31149 | TEXTILE MILL PRODUCTS |
| ROWAN, NC | 3536 | 46428 | TEXTILE MILL PRODUCTS |
| RUTHERFORD, NC | 2402 | 29832 | TEXTILE MILL PRODUCTS |
| SAMPSON, NC | 1930 | 16852 | EDUCATIONAL SERVICES |
| SCOTLAND, NC | 978 | 14574 | TEXTILE MILL PRODUCTS |
| STANLY, NC | 1922 | 21237 | TEXTILE MILL PRODUCTS |
| STOKES, NC | 977 | 7611 | EDUCATIONAL SERVICES |
| SURRY, NC | 2459 | 34048 | TEXTILE MILL PRODUCTS |
| SWAIN, NC | 723 | 7124 | EXECUTIVE, LEGISLATIVE GOVT. |
| TRANSYLVANIA, NC | 1160 | 13406 | EATING AND DRINKING PLACES |
| TYRRELL, NC | 169 | 1205 | AGRICULTURAL - CROPS |
| UNION, NC | 3498 | 42803 | CONSTRUCT: SPEC TRADE CONTRACT |
| VANCE, NC | 1429 | 17082 | TEXTILE MILL PRODUCTS |
| WAKE, NC | 21894 | 292828 | EDUCATIONAL SERVICES |
| WARREN, NC | 455 | 3668 | EDUCATIONAL SERVICES |
| WASHINGTON, NC | 523 | 5946 | PAPER AND ALLIED PRODUCTS |
| WATAUGA, NC | 2426 | 22019 | EDUCATIONAL SERVICES |
| WAYNE, NC | 2933 | 33927 | EDUCATIONAL SERVICES |
| WILKES, NC | 1864 | 22104 | BUILDING MATRIALS/GARDEN SUPPL |
| WILSON, NC | 2375 | 34784 | AUTO DEALERS & GAS SERV STA. |
| YADKIN, NC | 1073 | 9918 | TEXTILE MILL PRODUCTS |
| YANCEY, NC | 529 | 4582 | TEXTILE MILL PRODUCTS |
| ADAMS, ND | 170 | 809 | EDUCATIONAL SERVICES |
| BARNES, ND | 635 | 4708 | EDUCATIONAL SERVICES |
| BENSON, ND | 285 | 1944 | EDUCATIONAL SERVICES |
| BILLINGS, ND | 92 | 1127 | SOCIAL SERVICES |
| BOTTINEAU, ND | 503 | 2501 | EDUCATIONAL SERVICES |
| BOWMAN, ND | 265 | 1483 | EDUCATIONAL SERVICES |
| BURKE, ND | 161 | 553 | EDUCATIONAL SERVICES |
| BURLEIGH, ND | 3300 | 43163 | HEALTH SERVICES |
| CASS, ND | 5513 | 74136 | EATING AND DRINKING PLACES |
| CAVALIER, ND | 359 | 1776 | HEALTH SERVICES |
| DICKEY, ND | 286 | 1795 | EDUCATIONAL SERVICES |
| DIVIDE, ND | 130 | 573 | HEALTH SERVICES |
| DUNN, ND | 159 | 821 | EDUCATIONAL SERVICES |
| EDDY, ND | 152 | 894 | SOCIAL SERVICES |
| EMMONS, ND | 180 | 1333 | EDUCATIONAL SERVICES |
| FOSTER, ND | 306 | 1787 | FOOD AND KINDRED PRODUCTS |
| GOLDEN VALLEY, ND | 113 | 638 | EDUCATIONAL SERVICES |
| GRAND FORKS, ND | 2391 | 34250 | EDUCATIONAL SERVICES |
| GRANT, ND | 152 | 659 | EDUCATIONAL SERVICES |
| GRIGGS, ND | 396 | 1521 | HEALTH SERVICES |
| HETTINGER, ND | 156 | 675 | EDUCATIONAL SERVICES |
| KIDDER, ND | 145 | 600 | EDUCATIONAL SERVICES |
| LAMOURE, ND | 292 | 1436 | EDUCATIONAL SERVICES |
| LOGAN, ND | 147 | 588 | EDUCATIONAL SERVICES |
| MCHENRY, ND | 309 | 1572 | EDUCATIONAL SERVICES |
| MCINTOSH, ND | 198 | 1325 | HEALTH SERVICES |
| MCKENZIE, ND | 265 | 1310 | EDUCATIONAL SERVICES |
| MCLEAN, ND | 472 | 3135 | EDUCATIONAL SERVICES |
| MERCER, ND | 380 | 3990 | ELECTRIC, GAS & SANITARY SERV. |
| MORTON, ND | 1128 | 9053 | EDUCATIONAL SERVICES |
| MOUNTRAIL, ND | 379 | 2710 | EXECUTIVE, LEGISLATIVE GOVT. |
| NELSON, ND | 251 | 1259 | HEALTH SERVICES |
| OLIVER, ND | 61 | 519 | ELECTRIC, GAS & SANITARY SERV. |
| PEMBINA, ND | 621 | 3594 | HEALTH SERVICES |
| PIERCE, ND | 333 | 2024 | HEALTH SERVICES |
| RAMSEY, ND | 700 | 6308 | SOCIAL SERVICES |
| RANSOM, ND | 266 | 1709 | HEALTH SERVICES |
| RENVILLE, ND | 187 | 882 | EDUCATIONAL SERVICES |
| RICHLAND, ND | 748 | 7449 | EDUCATIONAL SERVICES |
| ROLETTE, ND | 435 | 6721 | EXECUTIVE, LEGISLATIVE GOVT. |
| SARGENT, ND | 299 | 1094 | EDUCATIONAL SERVICES |
| SHERIDAN, ND | 90 | 337 | GENL CONTRACT/OPERAT BUILDERS |
| SIOUX, ND | 72 | 1495 | EXECUTIVE, LEGISLATIVE GOVT. |
| SLOPE, ND | 39 | 74 | WHOLESALE TRADE: DURABLE GOODS |
| STARK, ND | 1193 | 11192 | HEALTH SERVICES |
| STEELE, ND | 115 | 541 | EDUCATIONAL SERVICES |
| STUTSMAN, ND | 1344 | 9550 | EATING AND DRINKING PLACES |
| TOWNER, ND | 191 | 1135 | EDUCATIONAL SERVICES |
| TRAILL, ND | 435 | 2977 | HEALTH SERVICES |
| WALSH, ND | 674 | 4421 | HEALTH SERVICES |
| WARD, ND | 2465 | 37488 | NATIONAL SECURITY/INT AFFAIRS |
| WELLS, ND | 562 | 1858 | AGRICULTURAL - CROPS |
| WILLIAMS, ND | 1193 | 8615 | EDUCATIONAL SERVICES |
| ADAMS, OH | 718 | 5217 | EDUCATIONAL SERVICES |
| ALLEN, OH | 3635 | 55145 | HEALTH SERVICES |
| ASHLAND, OH | 1485 | 19901 | EDUCATIONAL SERVICES |
| ASHTABULA, OH | 3483 | 38522 | RUBBER & MISC PLASTIC PRODUCTS |
| ATHENS, OH | 1690 | 19203 | EDUCATIONAL SERVICES |
| AUGLAIZE, OH | 1442 | 18253 | INDUSTRIAL & COMM. MACHINERY |
| BELMONT, OH | 2341 | 22020 | EATING AND DRINKING PLACES |
| BROWN, OH | 987 | 8543 | EDUCATIONAL SERVICES |
| BUTLER, OH | 8842 | 116217 | EDUCATIONAL SERVICES |
| CARROLL, OH | 738 | 5804 | EDUCATIONAL SERVICES |
| CHAMPAIGN, OH | 1093 | 11204 | EDUCATIONAL SERVICES |
| CLARK, OH | 3897 | 53412 | HEALTH SERVICES |
| CLERMONT, OH | 4579 | 52952 | EATING AND DRINKING PLACES |
| CLINTON, OH | 1285 | 23735 | TRANSPORTATION BY AIR |
| COLUMBIANA, OH | 3409 | 34322 | EATING AND DRINKING PLACES |
| COSHOCTON, OH | 1030 | 13665 | PRIMARY METAL INDUSTRIES |
| CRAWFORD, OH | 1438 | 16334 | INDUSTRIAL & COMM. MACHINERY |
| CUYAHOGA, OH | 50454 | 741980 | EATING AND DRINKING PLACES |
| DARKE, OH | 1617 | 18648 | RUBBER & MISC PLASTIC PRODUCTS |
| DEFIANCE, OH | 1297 | 18183 | TRANSPORTATION EQUIPMENT |
| DELAWARE, OH | 3022 | 34487 | NONDEPOSITORY CREDIT INSTITUT. |
| ERIE, OH | 2978 | 52282 | AMUSEMENT/RECREATION SERVICES |
| FAIRFIELD, OH | 3295 | 34442 | EDUCATIONAL SERVICES |
| FAYETTE, OH | 1023 | 11765 | RUBBER & MISC PLASTIC PRODUCTS |
| FRANKLIN, OH | 34176 | 615605 | EDUCATIONAL SERVICES |
| FULTON, OH | 1445 | 20090 | FURNITURE AND FIXTURES |
| GALLIA, OH | 917 | 8785 | EDUCATIONAL SERVICES |
| GEAUGA, OH | 2834 | 31045 | RUBBER & MISC PLASTIC PRODUCTS |
| GREENE, OH | 4045 | 48743 | EDUCATIONAL SERVICES |
| GUERNSEY, OH | 1382 | 15270 | HEALTH SERVICES |
| HAMILTON, OH | 33742 | 504957 | HEALTH SERVICES |
| HANCOCK, OH | 2424 | 36696 | EATING AND DRINKING PLACES |
| HARDIN, OH | 883 | 8261 | EDUCATIONAL SERVICES |
| HARRISON, OH | 476 | 3736 | WHOLESALE TRADE: DURABLE GOODS |
| HENRY, OH | 959 | 11856 | FOOD AND KINDRED PRODUCTS |
| HIGHLAND, OH | 1122 | 10406 | EDUCATIONAL SERVICES |
| HOCKING, OH | 790 | 6722 | AUTO DEALERS & GAS SERV STA. |
| HOLMES, OH | 1157 | 13825 | LUMBER & WOOD PRODS, EXC FURN. |
| HURON, OH | 1788 | 25529 | INDUSTRIAL & COMM. MACHINERY |
| JACKSON, OH | 972 | 10689 | WHOLESALE TRADE: NONDURABLE |
| JEFFERSON, OH | 2334 | 25225 | PRIMARY METAL INDUSTRIES |
| KNOX, OH | 1654 | 17245 | EDUCATIONAL SERVICES |

# BUSINESS DATA

| COUNTY | 2000 Total Firms | 2000 Total Employ-ees | TOP INDUSTRY RANKED on 2000 EMPLOYMENT | COUNTY | 2000 Total Firms | 2000 Total Employ-ees | TOP INDUSTRY RANKED on 2000 EMPLOYMENT |
|---|---|---|---|---|---|---|---|
| LAKE, OH | 8760 | 106251 | EATING AND DRINKING PLACES | JOHNSTON, OK | 377 | 3313 | TRANSPORTATION EQUIPMENT |
| LAWRENCE, OH | 1463 | 13258 | EDUCATIONAL SERVICES | KAY, OK | 1911 | 21933 | PIPELINES, EXCEPT NATURAL GAS |
| LICKING, OH | 4364 | 49146 | EDUCATIONAL SERVICES | KINGFISHER, OK | 741 | 6000 | WHOLESALE TRADE: DURABLE GOODS |
| LOGAN, OH | 1458 | 16883 | TRANSPORTATION EQUIPMENT | KIOWA, OK | 486 | 2989 | EDUCATIONAL SERVICES |
| LORAIN, OH | 7026 | 102473 | HEALTH SERVICES | LATIMER, OK | 346 | 2737 | EDUCATIONAL SERVICES |
| LUCAS, OH | 13679 | 211650 | HEALTH SERVICES | LE FLORE, OK | 1578 | 11552 | EDUCATIONAL SERVICES |
| MADISON, OH | 1067 | 10749 | JUSTICE, PUBLIC ORDER/SAFETY | LINCOLN, OK | 929 | 6716 | EDUCATIONAL SERVICES |
| MAHONING, OH | 9244 | 113860 | HEALTH SERVICES | LOGAN, OK | 1056 | 6857 | EDUCATIONAL SERVICES |
| MARION, OH | 1932 | 22071 | HEALTH SERVICES | LOVE, OK | 285 | 2160 | FOOD AND KINDRED PRODUCTS |
| MEDINA, OH | 4347 | 48226 | EATING AND DRINKING PLACES | MCCLAIN, OK | 976 | 6472 | EDUCATIONAL SERVICES |
| MEIGS, OH | 611 | 3924 | EDUCATIONAL SERVICES | MCCURTAIN, OK | 1385 | 11285 | EDUCATIONAL SERVICES |
| MERCER, OH | 1221 | 13337 | EDUCATIONAL SERVICES | MCINTOSH, OK | 711 | 4226 | HEALTH SERVICES |
| MIAMI, OH | 3123 | 45639 | INDUSTRIAL & COMM. MACHINERY | MAJOR, OK | 399 | 2110 | OIL AND GAS EXTRACTION |
| MONROE, OH | 423 | 5326 | PRIMARY METAL INDUSTRIES | MARSHALL, OK | 523 | 4375 | TRANSPORTATION EQUIPMENT |
| MONTGOMERY, OH | 17847 | 273203 | EATING AND DRINKING PLACES | MAYES, OK | 1522 | 13621 | INDUSTRIAL & COMM. MACHINERY |
| MORGAN, OH | 378 | 2917 | HEALTH SERVICES | MURRAY, OK | 563 | 3897 | HEALTH SERVICES |
| MORROW, OH | 714 | 5795 | EDUCATIONAL SERVICES | MUSKOGEE, OK | 2548 | 26796 | HEALTH SERVICES |
| MUSKINGUM, OH | 2787 | 32412 | HEALTH SERVICES | NOBLE, OK | 481 | 4240 | INDUSTRIAL & COMM. MACHINERY |
| NOBLE, OH | 325 | 2814 | MEMBERSHIP ORGANIZATIONS | NOWATA, OK | 345 | 2656 | EDUCATIONAL SERVICES |
| OTTAWA, OH | 1706 | 16933 | EATING AND DRINKING PLACES | OKFUSKEE, OK | 372 | 2192 | EDUCATIONAL SERVICES |
| PAULDING, OH | 560 | 5194 | EDUCATIONAL SERVICES | OKLAHOMA, OK | 25814 | 368626 | TRANSPORTATION EQUIPMENT |
| PERRY, OH | 791 | 6582 | EDUCATIONAL SERVICES | OKMULGEE, OK | 1187 | 9311 | EDUCATIONAL SERVICES |
| PICKAWAY, OH | 1265 | 17250 | AMUSEMENT/RECREATION SERVICES | OSAGE, OK | 1217 | 8543 | EDUCATIONAL SERVICES |
| PIKE, OH | 699 | 11929 | LUMBER & WOOD PRODS, EXC FURN. | OTTAWA, OK | 1150 | 9441 | EDUCATIONAL SERVICES |
| PORTAGE, OH | 4113 | 56076 | EDUCATIONAL SERVICES | PAWNEE, OK | 549 | 3072 | EDUCATIONAL SERVICES |
| PREBLE, OH | 1096 | 11343 | WHOLESALE TRADE: DURABLE GOODS | PAYNE, OK | 2676 | 34936 | EDUCATIONAL SERVICES |
| PUTNAM, OH | 1097 | 11315 | ELECTRONIC/ELCTRCL EQPMNT | PITTSBURG, OK | 1628 | 14981 | EDUCATIONAL SERVICES |
| RICHLAND, OH | 4119 | 59032 | EATING AND DRINKING PLACES | PONTOTOC, OK | 1460 | 13068 | EDUCATIONAL SERVICES |
| ROSS, OH | 2030 | 27520 | HEALTH SERVICES | POTTAWATOMIE, OK | 1986 | 17385 | EDUCATIONAL SERVICES |
| SANDUSKY, OH | 1887 | 24813 | ELECTRONIC/ELCTRCL EQPMNT | PUSHMATAHA, OK | 493 | 2590 | HEALTH SERVICES |
| SCIOTO, OH | 2213 | 27939 | HEALTH SERVICES | ROGER MILLS, OK | 220 | 1031 | EDUCATIONAL SERVICES |
| SENECA, OH | 1706 | 19900 | EDUCATIONAL SERVICES | ROGERS, OK | 2096 | 20720 | EDUCATIONAL SERVICES |
| SHELBY, OH | 1389 | 30187 | INDUSTRIAL & COMM. MACHINERY | SEMINOLE, OK | 1021 | 7843 | EDUCATIONAL SERVICES |
| STARK, OH | 11860 | 153964 | EATING AND DRINKING PLACES | SEQUOYAH, OK | 1121 | 8691 | EDUCATIONAL SERVICES |
| SUMMIT, OH | 17212 | 251755 | EATING AND DRINKING PLACES | STEPHENS, OK | 1804 | 14236 | INDUSTRIAL & COMM. MACHINERY |
| TRUMBULL, OH | 6821 | 98849 | TRANSPORTATION EQUIPMENT | TEXAS, OK | 885 | 8544 | AGRICULTURAL - CROPS |
| TUSCARAWAS, OH | 3073 | 31660 | EATING AND DRINKING PLACES | TILLMAN, OK | 389 | 2147 | EDUCATIONAL SERVICES |
| UNION, OH | 1072 | 23932 | TRANSPORTATION EQUIPMENT | TULSA, OK | 21740 | 273046 | EDUCATIONAL SERVICES |
| VAN WERT, OH | 930 | 12482 | RUBBER & MISC PLASTIC PRODUCTS | WAGONER, OK | 1097 | 8201 | EDUCATIONAL SERVICES |
| VINTON, OH | 252 | 2697 | WHOLESALE TRADE: DURABLE GOODS | WASHINGTON, OK | 1701 | 18543 | OIL AND GAS EXTRACTION |
| WARREN, OH | 3953 | 58027 | AMUSEMENT/RECREATION SERVICES | WASHITA, OK | 512 | 2776 | EDUCATIONAL SERVICES |
| WASHINGTON, OH | 2235 | 23224 | EDUCATIONAL SERVICES | WOODS, OK | 542 | 3689 | EDUCATIONAL SERVICES |
| WAYNE, OH | 3473 | 46659 | EDUCATIONAL SERVICES | WOODWARD, OK | 1060 | 8707 | OIL AND GAS EXTRACTION |
| WILLIAMS, OH | 1279 | 19414 | RUBBER & MISC PLASTIC PRODUCTS | BAKER, OR | 821 | 5457 | EDUCATIONAL SERVICES |
| WOOD, OH | 3772 | 51019 | EATING AND DRINKING PLACES | BENTON, OR | 2468 | 26276 | EDUCATIONAL SERVICES |
| WYANDOT, OH | 770 | 11633 | RUBBER & MISC PLASTIC PRODUCTS | CLACKAMAS, OR | 11242 | 116495 | HEALTH SERVICES |
| ADAIR, OK | 589 | 5419 | FOOD AND KINDRED PRODUCTS | CLATSOP, OR | 2337 | 16202 | EATING AND DRINKING PLACES |
| ALFALFA, OK | 345 | 1835 | JUSTICE, PUBLIC ORDER/SAFETY | COLUMBIA, OR | 1388 | 8554 | EDUCATIONAL SERVICES |
| ATOKA, OK | 430 | 3483 | EDUCATIONAL SERVICES | COOS, OR | 2721 | 18600 | EDUCATIONAL SERVICES |
| BEAVER, OK | 331 | 1830 | EDUCATIONAL SERVICES | CROOK, OR | 638 | 5419 | LUMBER & WOOD PRODS, EXC FURN. |
| BECKHAM, OK | 1046 | 6476 | OIL AND GAS EXTRACTION | CURRY, OR | 1231 | 6291 | LUMBER & WOOD PRODS, EXC FURN. |
| BLAINE, OK | 671 | 4008 | HEALTH SERVICES | DESCHUTES, OR | 5819 | 45689 | HOTELS, ROOMING HOUSES, CAMPS |
| BRYAN, OK | 1421 | 11667 | EDUCATIONAL SERVICES | DOUGLAS, OR | 4160 | 36215 | LUMBER & WOOD PRODS, EXC FURN. |
| CADDO, OK | 1282 | 7830 | EDUCATIONAL SERVICES | GILLIAM, OR | 151 | 554 | EDUCATIONAL SERVICES |
| CANADIAN, OK | 2343 | 23580 | INDUSTRIAL & COMM. MACHINERY | GRANT, OR | 505 | 2831 | LUMBER & WOOD PRODS, EXC FURN. |
| CARTER, OK | 2110 | 18821 | RUBBER & MISC PLASTIC PRODUCTS | HARNEY, OR | 466 | 3230 | TRANSPORTATION EQUIPMENT |
| CHEROKEE, OK | 1337 | 13677 | EDUCATIONAL SERVICES | HOOD RIVER, OR | 1181 | 10076 | HOTELS, ROOMING HOUSES, CAMPS |
| CHOCTAW, OK | 588 | 4666 | EDUCATIONAL SERVICES | JACKSON, OR | 7378 | 66793 | EATING AND DRINKING PLACES |
| CIMARRON, OK | 189 | 723 | EDUCATIONAL SERVICES | JEFFERSON, OR | 588 | 5581 | LUMBER & WOOD PRODS, EXC FURN. |
| CLEVELAND, OK | 5494 | 60518 | EDUCATIONAL SERVICES | JOSEPHINE, OR | 3016 | 21649 | EDUCATIONAL SERVICES |
| COAL, OK | 190 | 1501 | HEALTH SERVICES | KLAMATH, OR | 2307 | 22097 | EDUCATIONAL SERVICES |
| COMANCHE, OK | 3247 | 32822 | EDUCATIONAL SERVICES | LAKE, OR | 489 | 2379 | LUMBER & WOOD PRODS, EXC FURN. |
| COTTON, OK | 231 | 1119 | EDUCATIONAL SERVICES | LANE, OR | 12835 | 133779 | EDUCATIONAL SERVICES |
| CRAIG, OK | 605 | 5552 | HEALTH SERVICES | LINCOLN, OR | 2998 | 19025 | EATING AND DRINKING PLACES |
| CREEK, OK | 2135 | 20651 | EDUCATIONAL SERVICES | LINN, OR | 3972 | 37690 | EDUCATIONAL SERVICES |
| CUSTER, OK | 1243 | 10671 | EDUCATIONAL SERVICES | MALHEUR, OR | 1227 | 11350 | FOOD AND KINDRED PRODUCTS |
| DELAWARE, OK | 1414 | 8556 | EDUCATIONAL SERVICES | MARION, OR | 8792 | 110754 | FOOD AND KINDRED PRODUCTS |
| DEWEY, OK | 382 | 1619 | EDUCATIONAL SERVICES | MORROW, OR | 340 | 2829 | WHOLESALE TRADE: NONDURABLE |
| ELLIS, OK | 280 | 1111 | EDUCATIONAL SERVICES | MULTNOMAH, OR | 25574 | 374622 | EDUCATIONAL SERVICES |
| GARFIELD, OK | 2380 | 20619 | EDUCATIONAL SERVICES | POLK, OR | 1473 | 14307 | EDUCATIONAL SERVICES |
| GARVIN, OK | 1141 | 9533 | EDUCATIONAL SERVICES | SHERMAN, OR | 113 | 694 | EATING AND DRINKING PLACES |
| GRADY, OK | 1428 | 12286 | EDUCATIONAL SERVICES | TILLAMOOK, OR | 1377 | 8052 | EDUCATIONAL SERVICES |
| GRANT, OK | 291 | 1427 | EDUCATIONAL SERVICES | UMATILLA, OR | 2630 | 25825 | FOOD AND KINDRED PRODUCTS |
| GREER, OK | 268 | 1695 | JUSTICE, PUBLIC ORDER/SAFETY | UNION, OR | 1204 | 9774 | EDUCATIONAL SERVICES |
| HARMON, OK | 145 | 963 | EDUCATIONAL SERVICES | WALLOWA, OR | 490 | 2332 | EDUCATIONAL SERVICES |
| HARPER, OK | 146 | 858 | EDUCATIONAL SERVICES | WASCO, OR | 1115 | 8799 | EATING AND DRINKING PLACES |
| HASKELL, OK | 417 | 2566 | EDUCATIONAL SERVICES | WASHINGTON, OR | 12483 | 168423 | ELECTRONIC/ELCTRCL EQPMNT |
| HUGHES, OK | 486 | 3106 | EDUCATIONAL SERVICES | WHEELER, OR | 118 | 283 | EDUCATIONAL SERVICES |
| JACKSON, OK | 1030 | 13161 | NATIONAL SECURITY/INT AFFAIRS | YAMHILL, OR | 2760 | 28463 | EDUCATIONAL SERVICES |
| JEFFERSON, OK | 315 | 1724 | EDUCATIONAL SERVICES | ADAMS, PA | 2941 | 28858 | EDUCATIONAL SERVICES |

| COUNTY | 2000 Total Firms | 2000 Total Employ-ees | TOP INDUSTRY RANKED on 2000 EMPLOYMENT |
|---|---|---|---|
| ALLEGHENY, PA | 39786 | 560893 | EDUCATIONAL SERVICES |
| ARMSTRONG, PA | 2110 | 16407 | EDUCATIONAL SERVICES |
| BEAVER, PA | 4973 | 47615 | EDUCATIONAL SERVICES |
| BEDFORD, PA | 1877 | 17146 | EATING AND DRINKING PLACES |
| BERKS, PA | 11923 | 162089 | EDUCATIONAL SERVICES |
| BLAIR, PA | 4240 | 54603 | EDUCATIONAL SERVICES |
| BRADFORD, PA | 2245 | 21663 | HEALTH SERVICES |
| BUCKS, PA | 22045 | 226188 | EATING AND DRINKING PLACES |
| BUTLER, PA | 6396 | 71123 | HEALTH SERVICES |
| CAMBRIA, PA | 4657 | 51702 | HEALTH SERVICES |
| CAMERON, PA | 243 | 2973 | CHEMICALS AND ALLIED PRODUCTS |
| CARBON, PA | 1920 | 16978 | APPAREL, FINISHED PRODUCTS |
| CENTRE, PA | 4537 | 50877 | EATING AND DRINKING PLACES |
| CHESTER, PA | 14933 | 187173 | EDUCATIONAL SERVICES |
| CLARION, PA | 1498 | 15775 | EDUCATIONAL SERVICES |
| CLEARFIELD, PA | 2737 | 28712 | HEALTH SERVICES |
| CLINTON, PA | 1141 | 12205 | MISCELLANEOUS RETAIL |
| COLUMBIA, PA | 2190 | 23245 | EDUCATIONAL SERVICES |
| CRAWFORD, PA | 3333 | 31284 | INDUSTRIAL & COMM. MACHINERY |
| CUMBERLAND, PA | 7040 | 94905 | HEALTH SERVICES |
| DAUPHIN, PA | 8761 | 147512 | SOCIAL SERVICES |
| DELAWARE, PA | 15063 | 164777 | EDUCATIONAL SERVICES |
| ELK, PA | 1366 | 16523 | CHEMICALS AND ALLIED PRODUCTS |
| ERIE, PA | 8556 | 122477 | EDUCATIONAL SERVICES |
| FAYETTE, PA | 4356 | 35332 | EATING AND DRINKING PLACES |
| FOREST, PA | 260 | 1896 | EDUCATIONAL SERVICES |
| FRANKLIN, PA | 4287 | 46171 | INDUSTRIAL & COMM. MACHINERY |
| FULTON, PA | 461 | 5448 | INDUSTRIAL & COMM. MACHINERY |
| GREENE, PA | 1159 | 9890 | COAL MINING |
| HUNTINGDON, PA | 1159 | 9918 | JUSTICE, PUBLIC ORDER/SAFETY |
| INDIANA, PA | 2577 | 25357 | EDUCATIONAL SERVICES |
| JEFFERSON, PA | 1741 | 15494 | INDUSTRIAL & COMM. MACHINERY |
| JUNIATA, PA | 673 | 5808 | FOOD AND KINDRED PRODUCTS |
| LACKAWANNA, PA | 8248 | 96595 | HEALTH SERVICES |
| LANCASTER, PA | 15050 | 198818 | EATING AND DRINKING PLACES |
| LAWRENCE, PA | 3053 | 32934 | HEALTH SERVICES |
| LEBANON, PA | 3507 | 37268 | HEALTH SERVICES |
| LEHIGH, PA | 9751 | 145347 | EDUCATIONAL SERVICES |
| LUZERNE, PA | 11127 | 125741 | HEALTH SERVICES |
| LYCOMING, PA | 4031 | 46119 | EDUCATIONAL SERVICES |
| MCKEAN, PA | 1602 | 16570 | EDUCATIONAL SERVICES |
| MERCER, PA | 4057 | 43192 | EATING AND DRINKING PLACES |
| MIFFLIN, PA | 1485 | 18224 | WHOLESALE TRADE: DURABLE GOODS |
| MONROE, PA | 5074 | 44487 | HOTELS, ROOMING HOUSES, CAMPS |
| MONTGOMERY, PA | 27336 | 377249 | HEALTH SERVICES |
| MONTOUR, PA | 551 | 6156 | EDUCATIONAL SERVICES |
| NORTHAMPTON, PA | 7468 | 78774 | EDUCATIONAL SERVICES |
| NORTHUMBERLAND, PA | 2939 | 29085 | EDUCATIONAL SERVICES |
| PERRY, PA | 1296 | 6852 | EDUCATIONAL SERVICES |
| PHILADELPHIA, PA | 37723 | 490446 | EDUCATIONAL SERVICES |
| PIKE, PA | 1217 | 9114 | HOTELS, ROOMING HOUSES, CAMPS |
| POTTER, PA | 726 | 6380 | HEALTH SERVICES |
| SCHUYLKILL, PA | 4819 | 49341 | HEALTH SERVICES |
| SNYDER, PA | 1427 | 14909 | LUMBER & WOOD PRODS, EXC FURN. |
| SOMERSET, PA | 2609 | 25823 | EDUCATIONAL SERVICES |
| SULLIVAN, PA | 301 | 1766 | EDUCATIONAL SERVICES |
| SUSQUEHANNA, PA | 921 | 7412 | EDUCATIONAL SERVICES |
| TIOGA, PA | 1763 | 15438 | HEALTH SERVICES |
| UNION, PA | 1391 | 13560 | EDUCATIONAL SERVICES |
| VENANGO, PA | 1887 | 17221 | INDUSTRIAL & COMM. MACHINERY |
| WARREN, PA | 1486 | 15857 | FABRICATED METAL PRODUCTS |
| WASHINGTON, PA | 6207 | 63925 | EDUCATIONAL SERVICES |
| WAYNE, PA | 2078 | 15791 | HOTELS, ROOMING HOUSES, CAMPS |
| WESTMORELAND, PA | 12131 | 127896 | EATING AND DRINKING PLACES |
| WYOMING, PA | 1144 | 9870 | PAPER AND ALLIED PRODUCTS |
| YORK, PA | 11179 | 153488 | HEALTH SERVICES |
| BRISTOL, RI | 1477 | 13021 | EDUCATIONAL SERVICES |
| KENT, RI | 5835 | 71634 | EATING AND DRINKING PLACES |
| NEWPORT, RI | 3594 | 30098 | EATING AND DRINKING PLACES |
| PROVIDENCE, RI | 19275 | 255841 | EDUCATIONAL SERVICES |
| WASHINGTON, RI | 4231 | 39138 | EDUCATIONAL SERVICES |
| ABBEVILLE, SC | 667 | 8067 | TEXTILE MILL PRODUCTS |
| AIKEN, SC | 3469 | 56874 | ELECTRIC, GAS & SANITARY SERV. |
| ALLENDALE, SC | 333 | 3285 | EDUCATIONAL SERVICES |
| ANDERSON, SC | 4623 | 58275 | EATING AND DRINKING PLACES |
| BAMBERG, SC | 457 | 4206 | EDUCATIONAL SERVICES |
| BARNWELL, SC | 742 | 8470 | INDUSTRIAL & COMM. MACHINERY |
| BEAUFORT, SC | 4783 | 42765 | EATING AND DRINKING PLACES |
| BERKELEY, SC | 2899 | 32321 | EDUCATIONAL SERVICES |
| CALHOUN, SC | 366 | 3101 | WHOLESALE TRADE: DURABLE GOODS |

| COUNTY | 2000 Total Firms | 2000 Total Employ-ees | TOP INDUSTRY RANKED on 2000 EMPLOYMENT |
|---|---|---|---|
| CHARLESTON, SC | 12301 | 144720 | EATING AND DRINKING PLACES |
| CHEROKEE, SC | 1379 | 19310 | TEXTILE MILL PRODUCTS |
| CHESTER, SC | 1077 | 11935 | APPAREL, FINISHED PRODUCTS |
| CHESTERFIELD, SC | 1433 | 14168 | TEXTILE MILL PRODUCTS |
| CLARENDON, SC | 1148 | 8067 | EDUCATIONAL SERVICES |
| COLLETON, SC | 1140 | 10585 | TEXTILE MILL PRODUCTS |
| DARLINGTON, SC | 1897 | 23273 | CHEMICALS AND ALLIED PRODUCTS |
| DILLON, SC | 872 | 10047 | FOOD AND KINDRED PRODUCTS |
| DORCHESTER, SC | 2302 | 24119 | TRANSPORTATION EQUIPMENT |
| EDGEFIELD, SC | 518 | 5450 | APPAREL, FINISHED PRODUCTS |
| FAIRFIELD, SC | 645 | 6712 | TRANSPORTATION EQUIPMENT |
| FLORENCE, SC | 4716 | 54923 | EATING AND DRINKING PLACES |
| GEORGETOWN, SC | 2082 | 17269 | EATING AND DRINKING PLACES |
| GREENVILLE, SC | 13179 | 188600 | EATING AND DRINKING PLACES |
| GREENWOOD, SC | 2175 | 29464 | TEXTILE MILL PRODUCTS |
| HAMPTON, SC | 677 | 5770 | PAPER AND ALLIED PRODUCTS |
| HORRY, SC | 9947 | 101340 | EATING AND DRINKING PLACES |
| JASPER, SC | 567 | 4202 | EATING AND DRINKING PLACES |
| KERSHAW, SC | 1623 | 14936 | CHEMICALS AND ALLIED PRODUCTS |
| LANCASTER, SC | 1952 | 17571 | APPAREL, FINISHED PRODUCTS |
| LAURENS, SC | 1536 | 19948 | TEXTILE MILL PRODUCTS |
| LEE, SC | 440 | 4078 | JUSTICE, PUBLIC ORDER/SAFETY |
| LEXINGTON, SC | 6809 | 77872 | EATING AND DRINKING PLACES |
| MCCORMICK, SC | 330 | 2950 | JUSTICE, PUBLIC ORDER/SAFETY |
| MARION, SC | 1002 | 11371 | APPAREL, FINISHED PRODUCTS |
| MARLBORO, SC | 742 | 7072 | EDUCATIONAL SERVICES |
| NEWBERRY, SC | 1088 | 13236 | FOOD AND KINDRED PRODUCTS |
| OCONEE, SC | 1885 | 19549 | EDUCATIONAL SERVICES |
| ORANGEBURG, SC | 2856 | 32788 | EDUCATIONAL SERVICES |
| PICKENS, SC | 2558 | 38516 | EDUCATIONAL SERVICES |
| RICHLAND, SC | 10911 | 162688 | EDUCATIONAL SERVICES |
| SALUDA, SC | 460 | 4389 | FOOD AND KINDRED PRODUCTS |
| SPARTANBURG, SC | 7956 | 116125 | EATING AND DRINKING PLACES |
| SUMTER, SC | 3181 | 38180 | EDUCATIONAL SERVICES |
| UNION, SC | 821 | 9730 | TEXTILE MILL PRODUCTS |
| WILLIAMSBURG, SC | 1140 | 11220 | APPAREL, FINISHED PRODUCTS |
| YORK, SC | 4980 | 71628 | TEXTILE MILL PRODUCTS |
| AURORA, SD | 163 | 844 | EDUCATIONAL SERVICES |
| BEADLE, SD | 775 | 6640 | EDUCATIONAL SERVICES |
| BENNETT, SD | 100 | 815 | EDUCATIONAL SERVICES |
| BON HOMME, SD | 310 | 2085 | JUSTICE, PUBLIC ORDER/SAFETY |
| BROOKINGS, SD | 995 | 14444 | EDUCATIONAL SERVICES |
| BROWN, SD | 1608 | 17944 | EDUCATIONAL SERVICES |
| BRULE, SD | 341 | 2515 | EDUCATIONAL SERVICES |
| BUFFALO, SD | 67 | 611 | EXECUTIVE, LEGISLATIVE GOVT. |
| BUTTE, SD | 313 | 2243 | EDUCATIONAL SERVICES |
| CAMPBELL, SD | 68 | 407 | FOOD AND KINDRED PRODUCTS |
| CHARLES MIX, SD | 369 | 3375 | EDUCATIONAL SERVICES |
| CLARK, SD | 139 | 1174 | EDUCATIONAL SERVICES |
| CLAY, SD | 422 | 5153 | EDUCATIONAL SERVICES |
| CODINGTON, SD | 1195 | 15053 | ELECTRONIC/ELCTRCL EQPMNT |
| CORSON, SD | 109 | 787 | EDUCATIONAL SERVICES |
| CUSTER, SD | 265 | 2915 | HOTELS, ROOMING HOUSES, CAMPS |
| DAVISON, SD | 865 | 10021 | EATING AND DRINKING PLACES |
| DAY, SD | 246 | 1791 | EDUCATIONAL SERVICES |
| DEUEL, SD | 270 | 1461 | EDUCATIONAL SERVICES |
| DEWEY, SD | 284 | 2451 | EXECUTIVE, LEGISLATIVE GOVT. |
| DOUGLAS, SD | 194 | 1235 | HEALTH SERVICES |
| EDMUNDS, SD | 158 | 947 | HEALTH SERVICES |
| FALL RIVER, SD | 248 | 1986 | HEALTH SERVICES |
| FAULK, SD | 124 | 592 | EDUCATIONAL SERVICES |
| GRANT, SD | 362 | 3382 | WHOLESALE TRADE: DURABLE GOODS |
| GREGORY, SD | 233 | 1372 | EDUCATIONAL SERVICES |
| HAAKON, SD | 116 | 1046 | HEALTH SERVICES |
| HAMLIN, SD | 192 | 1268 | HEALTH SERVICES |
| HAND, SD | 207 | 1108 | HEALTH SERVICES |
| HANSON, SD | 105 | 428 | EDUCATIONAL SERVICES |
| HARDING, SD | 95 | 405 | EDUCATIONAL SERVICES |
| HUGHES, SD | 1036 | 11421 | EXECUTIVE, LEGISLATIVE GOVT. |
| HUTCHINSON, SD | 296 | 2412 | HEALTH SERVICES |
| HYDE, SD | 105 | 1268 | EDUCATIONAL SERVICES |
| JACKSON, SD | 137 | 790 | EDUCATIONAL SERVICES |
| JERAULD, SD | 115 | 1083 | WHOLESALE TRADE: NONDURABLE |
| JONES, SD | 95 | 509 | AUTO DEALERS & GAS SERV STA. |
| KINGSBURY, SD | 250 | 1672 | EDUCATIONAL SERVICES |
| LAKE, SD | 465 | 5027 | EDUCATIONAL SERVICES |
| LAWRENCE, SD | 859 | 9506 | HOTELS, ROOMING HOUSES, CAMPS |
| LINCOLN, SD | 754 | 6345 | HEALTH SERVICES |
| LYMAN, SD | 206 | 1316 | EDUCATIONAL SERVICES |
| MCCOOK, SD | 203 | 1471 | EDUCATIONAL SERVICES |

# BUSINESS DATA

| COUNTY | 2000 Total Firms | 2000 Total Employ-ees | TOP INDUSTRY RANKED on 2000 EMPLOYMENT |
|---|---|---|---|
| MCPHERSON, SD | 106 | 589 | EDUCATIONAL SERVICES |
| MARSHALL, SD | 180 | 1319 | WHOLESALE TRADE: DURABLE GOODS |
| MEADE, SD | 696 | 9746 | NATIONAL SECURITY/INT AFFAIRS |
| MELLETTE, SD | 69 | 516 | EDUCATIONAL SERVICES |
| MINER, SD | 132 | 660 | EDUCATIONAL SERVICES |
| MINNEHAHA, SD | 5717 | 87333 | EATING AND DRINKING PLACES |
| MOODY, SD | 217 | 1933 | AMUSEMENT/RECREATION SERVICES |
| PENNINGTON, SD | 4366 | 49406 | EATING AND DRINKING PLACES |
| PERKINS, SD | 199 | 1164 | EDUCATIONAL SERVICES |
| POTTER, SD | 208 | 1445 | HEALTH SERVICES |
| ROBERTS, SD | 414 | 2849 | EDUCATIONAL SERVICES |
| SANBORN, SD | 120 | 801 | STONE/CLAY/GLASS PRODUCTS |
| SHANNON, SD | 273 | 3558 | EDUCATIONAL SERVICES |
| SPINK, SD | 301 | 2291 | EXECUTIVE, LEGISLATIVE GOVT. |
| STANLEY, SD | 144 | 1247 | EDUCATIONAL SERVICES |
| SULLY, SD | 92 | 510 | EDUCATIONAL SERVICES |
| TODD, SD | 207 | 3348 | EXECUTIVE, LEGISLATIVE GOVT. |
| TRIPP, SD | 314 | 2258 | HEALTH SERVICES |
| TURNER, SD | 410 | 2293 | HEALTH SERVICES |
| UNION, SD | 480 | 17555 | INDUSTRIAL & COMM. MACHINERY |
| WALWORTH, SD | 301 | 2260 | EDUCATIONAL SERVICES |
| YANKTON, SD | 936 | 13843 | HEALTH SERVICES |
| ZIEBACH, SD | 49 | 239 | EDUCATIONAL SERVICES |
| ANDERSON, TN | 2429 | 41245 | ENGINEERING, ACCOUNTING, ETC. |
| BEDFORD, TN | 1147 | 13485 | MISC. MANUFACTURING INDUSTRIES |
| BENTON, TN | 551 | 4530 | EATING AND DRINKING PLACES |
| BLEDSOE, TN | 363 | 3149 | TRANSPORTATION EQUIPMENT |
| BLOUNT, TN | 3092 | 36057 | TRANSPORTATION EQUIPMENT |
| BRADLEY, TN | 2867 | 36702 | ELECTRONIC/ELCTRCL EQPMNT |
| CAMPBELL, TN | 1046 | 10637 | HEALTH SERVICES |
| CANNON, TN | 362 | 1848 | EDUCATIONAL SERVICES |
| CARROLL, TN | 908 | 9428 | APPAREL, FINISHED PRODUCTS |
| CARTER, TN | 1347 | 13955 | EDUCATIONAL SERVICES |
| CHEATHAM, TN | 695 | 6465 | ELECTRONIC/ELCTRCL EQPMNT |
| CHESTER, TN | 420 | 3059 | FABRICATED METAL PRODUCTS |
| CLAIBORNE, TN | 363 | 5400 | EDUCATIONAL SERVICES |
| CLAY, TN | 271 | 2116 | HEALTH SERVICES |
| COCKE, TN | 805 | 8409 | EATING AND DRINKING PLACES |
| COFFEE, TN | 1728 | 21295 | NATIONAL SECURITY/INT AFFAIRS |
| CROCKETT, TN | 489 | 4300 | WHOLESALE TRADE: NONDURABLE |
| CUMBERLAND, TN | 1432 | 12903 | EATING AND DRINKING PLACES |
| DAVIDSON, TN | 26571 | 371879 | EATING AND DRINKING PLACES |
| DECATUR, TN | 438 | 4072 | WHOLESALE TRADE: DURABLE GOODS |
| DEKALB, TN | 527 | 5180 | TRANSPORTATION EQUIPMENT |
| DICKSON, TN | 1247 | 12841 | HEALTH SERVICES |
| DYER, TN | 1307 | 15480 | PRINTING AND PUBLISHING |
| FAYETTE, TN | 718 | 5589 | RUBBER & MISC PLASTIC PRODUCTS |
| FENTRESS, TN | 566 | 4501 | APPAREL, FINISHED PRODUCTS |
| FRANKLIN, TN | 1033 | 9446 | EDUCATIONAL SERVICES |
| GIBSON, TN | 1646 | 20548 | FABRICATED METAL PRODUCTS |
| GILES, TN | 906 | 9275 | PRIMARY METAL INDUSTRIES |
| GRAINGER, TN | 432 | 3449 | WHOLESALE TRADE: DURABLE GOODS |
| GREENE, TN | 1756 | 22540 | EDUCATIONAL SERVICES |
| GRUNDY, TN | 422 | 2243 | EDUCATIONAL SERVICES |
| HAMBLEN, TN | 1787 | 29614 | EATING AND DRINKING PLACES |
| HAMILTON, TN | 11742 | 145824 | EATING AND DRINKING PLACES |
| HANCOCK, TN | 140 | 1099 | ELECTRONIC/ELCTRCL EQPMNT |
| HARDEMAN, TN | 765 | 7264 | HEALTH SERVICES |
| HARDIN, TN | 882 | 7811 | FABRICATED METAL PRODUCTS |
| HAWKINS, TN | 1114 | 13328 | TRANSPORTATION EQUIPMENT |
| HAYWOOD, TN | 564 | 6311 | RUBBER & MISC PLASTIC PRODUCTS |
| HENDERSON, TN | 816 | 8131 | TRANSPORTATION EQUIPMENT |
| HENRY, TN | 1133 | 11483 | RUBBER & MISC PLASTIC PRODUCTS |
| HICKMAN, TN | 437 | 3534 | EXECUTIVE, LEGISLATIVE GOVT. |
| HOUSTON, TN | 281 | 1960 | EDUCATIONAL SERVICES |
| HUMPHREYS, TN | 588 | 5360 | CHEMICALS AND ALLIED PRODUCTS |
| JACKSON, TN | 283 | 2643 | HEALTH SERVICES |
| JEFFERSON, TN | 962 | 10876 | EDUCATIONAL SERVICES |
| JOHNSON, TN | 456 | 4500 | ENGINEERING, ACCOUNTING, ETC. |
| KNOX, TN | 14235 | 186042 | EDUCATIONAL SERVICES |
| LAKE, TN | 233 | 2025 | JUSTICE, PUBLIC ORDER/SAFETY |
| LAUDERDALE, TN | 694 | 7622 | FABRICATED METAL PRODUCTS |
| LAWRENCE, TN | 1267 | 14842 | INDUSTRIAL & COMM. MACHINERY |
| LEWIS, TN | 348 | 2472 | RUBBER & MISC PLASTIC PRODUCTS |
| LINCOLN, TN | 952 | 8189 | HOME FURNITURE/EQUIPMENT STORE |
| LOUDON, TN | 1053 | 11207 | TRANSPORTATION EQUIPMENT |
| MCMINN, TN | 1421 | 19236 | TRANSPORTATION EQUIPMENT |
| MCNAIRY, TN | 767 | 6584 | ELECTRONIC/ELCTRCL EQPMNT |
| MACON, TN | 551 | 4587 | EDUCATIONAL SERVICES |
| MADISON, TN | 3580 | 49294 | EATING AND DRINKING PLACES |
| MARION, TN | 853 | 7236 | EATING AND DRINKING PLACES |
| MARSHALL, TN | 747 | 11396 | INDUSTRIAL & COMM. MACHINERY |
| MAURY, TN | 2229 | 28536 | TRANSPORTATION EQUIPMENT |
| MEIGS, TN | 209 | 1684 | TEXTILE MILL PRODUCTS |
| MONROE, TN | 888 | 10018 | TRANSPORTATION EQUIPMENT |
| MONTGOMERY, TN | 2956 | 34053 | EATING AND DRINKING PLACES |
| MOORE, TN | 144 | 1081 | FOOD AND KINDRED PRODUCTS |
| MORGAN, TN | 356 | 3518 | APPAREL, FINISHED PRODUCTS |
| OBION, TN | 1133 | 14912 | AUTO DEALERS & GAS SERV STA. |
| OVERTON, TN | 571 | 5327 | FURNITURE AND FIXTURES |
| PERRY, TN | 251 | 2420 | TRANSPORTATION EQUIPMENT |
| PICKETT, TN | 162 | 875 | WHOLESALE TRADE: NONDURABLE |
| POLK, TN | 428 | 3324 | AUTO DEALERS & GAS SERV STA. |
| PUTNAM, TN | 2254 | 29364 | FOOD AND KINDRED PRODUCTS |
| RHEA, TN | 891 | 10633 | HOME FURNITURE/EQUIPMENT STORE |
| ROANE, TN | 1373 | 18178 | ENGINEERING, ACCOUNTING, ETC. |
| ROBERTSON, TN | 1339 | 12797 | INDUSTRIAL & COMM. MACHINERY |
| RUTHERFORD, TN | 4501 | 63220 | TRANSPORTATION EQUIPMENT |
| SCOTT, TN | 681 | 7293 | LUMBER & WOOD PRODS, EXC FURN. |
| SEQUATCHIE, TN | 401 | 3055 | INDUSTRIAL & COMM. MACHINERY |
| SEVIER, TN | 3353 | 34679 | EATING AND DRINKING PLACES |
| SHELBY, TN | 27358 | 415010 | EDUCATIONAL SERVICES |
| SMITH, TN | 500 | 5464 | TRANSPORTATION EQUIPMENT |
| STEWART, TN | 288 | 1830 | EDUCATIONAL SERVICES |
| SULLIVAN, TN | 5109 | 68695 | HEALTH SERVICES |
| SUMNER, TN | 3383 | 35595 | EDUCATIONAL SERVICES |
| TIPTON, TN | 860 | 10090 | EDUCATIONAL SERVICES |
| TROUSDALE, TN | 217 | 1435 | EDUCATIONAL SERVICES |
| UNICOI, TN | 425 | 4763 | CHEMICALS AND ALLIED PRODUCTS |
| UNION, TN | 306 | 3223 | BUILDING MATRIALS/GARDEN SUPPL |
| VAN BUREN, TN | 98 | 958 | FABRICATED METAL PRODUCTS |
| WARREN, TN | 1666 | 16090 | INDUSTRIAL & COMM. MACHINERY |
| WASHINGTON, TN | 3681 | 53521 | HEALTH SERVICES |
| WAYNE, TN | 523 | 4998 | JUSTICE, PUBLIC ORDER/SAFETY |
| WEAKLEY, TN | 494 | 12695 | EDUCATIONAL SERVICES |
| WHITE, TN | 699 | 7099 | WHOLESALE TRADE: DURABLE GOODS |
| WILLIAMSON, TN | 4194 | 49006 | EATING AND DRINKING PLACES |
| WILSON, TN | 1915 | 22682 | HEALTH SERVICES |
| ANDERSON, TX | 1551 | 17755 | JUSTICE, PUBLIC ORDER/SAFETY |
| ANDREWS, TX | 573 | 4130 | OIL AND GAS EXTRACTION |
| ANGELINA, TX | 2970 | 31379 | EDUCATIONAL SERVICES |
| ARANSAS, TX | 1031 | 4792 | EATING AND DRINKING PLACES |
| ARCHER, TX | 284 | 1368 | EDUCATIONAL SERVICES |
| ARMSTRONG, TX | 82 | 470 | EDUCATIONAL SERVICES |
| ATASCOSA, TX | 986 | 6734 | EDUCATIONAL SERVICES |
| AUSTIN, TX | 945 | 6290 | EDUCATIONAL SERVICES |
| BAILEY, TX | 372 | 2409 | EDUCATIONAL SERVICES |
| BANDERA, TX | 638 | 3027 | EDUCATIONAL SERVICES |
| BASTROP, TX | 1482 | 9382 | EDUCATIONAL SERVICES |
| BAYLOR, TX | 231 | 1142 | EDUCATIONAL SERVICES |
| BEE, TX | 839 | 9081 | EXECUTIVE, LEGISLATIVE GOVT. |
| BELL, TX | 6312 | 64283 | EDUCATIONAL SERVICES |
| BEXAR, TX | 40097 | 496259 | EDUCATIONAL SERVICES |
| BLANCO, TX | 420 | 2084 | SOCIAL SERVICES |
| BORDEN, TX | 37 | 208 | EDUCATIONAL SERVICES |
| BOSQUE, TX | 617 | 4342 | HEALTH SERVICES |
| BOWIE, TX | 3222 | 30113 | EDUCATIONAL SERVICES |
| BRAZORIA, TX | 6558 | 72426 | CHEMICALS AND ALLIED PRODUCTS |
| BRAZOS, TX | 4231 | 54284 | EDUCATIONAL SERVICES |
| BREWSTER, TX | 569 | 3574 | EDUCATIONAL SERVICES |
| BRISCOE, TX | 99 | 372 | EDUCATIONAL SERVICES |
| BROOKS, TX | 308 | 2124 | EDUCATIONAL SERVICES |
| BROWN, TX | 1375 | 14883 | EDUCATIONAL SERVICES |
| BURLESON, TX | 504 | 3051 | OIL AND GAS EXTRACTION |
| BURNET, TX | 1542 | 9259 | HOTELS, ROOMING HOUSES, CAMPS |
| CALDWELL, TX | 974 | 6607 | EDUCATIONAL SERVICES |
| CALHOUN, TX | 795 | 9121 | CHEMICALS AND ALLIED PRODUCTS |
| CALLAHAN, TX | 541 | 2508 | EDUCATIONAL SERVICES |
| CAMERON, TX | 8305 | 95540 | EDUCATIONAL SERVICES |
| CAMP, TX | 380 | 2816 | HEALTH SERVICES |
| CARSON, TX | 284 | 1393 | EDUCATIONAL SERVICES |
| CASS, TX | 1013 | 8528 | HEALTH SERVICES |
| CASTRO, TX | 354 | 2031 | EDUCATIONAL SERVICES |
| CHAMBERS, TX | 922 | 9015 | WHOLESALE TRADE: NONDURABLE |
| CHEROKEE, TX | 1471 | 13192 | EDUCATIONAL SERVICES |
| CHILDRESS, TX | 315 | 1791 | ADMIN: ECONOMIC PROGRAMS |
| CLAY, TX | 304 | 1695 | EDUCATIONAL SERVICES |
| COCHRAN, TX | 153 | 909 | EDUCATIONAL SERVICES |
| COKE, TX | 147 | 848 | EDUCATIONAL SERVICES |
| COLEMAN, TX | 476 | 2518 | EDUCATIONAL SERVICES |

| COUNTY | 2000 Total Firms | 2000 Total Employ-ees | TOP INDUSTRY RANKED on 2000 EMPLOYMENT |
|---|---|---|---|
| COLLIN, TX | 12378 | 167277 | BUSINESS SERVICES |
| COLLINGSWORTH, TX | 161 | 991 | EDUCATIONAL SERVICES |
| COLORADO, TX | 924 | 7269 | WHOLESALE TRADE: DURABLE GOODS |
| COMAL, TX | 3134 | 28572 | HOTELS, ROOMING HOUSES, CAMPS |
| COMANCHE, TX | 646 | 4335 | HEALTH SERVICES |
| CONCHO, TX | 135 | 668 | EDUCATIONAL SERVICES |
| COOKE, TX | 1447 | 12978 | EDUCATIONAL SERVICES |
| CORYELL, TX | 1344 | 14547 | HEALTH SERVICES |
| COTTLE, TX | 113 | 532 | EDUCATIONAL SERVICES |
| CRANE, TX | 191 | 1363 | OIL AND GAS EXTRACTION |
| CROCKETT, TX | 235 | 1289 | OIL AND GAS EXTRACTION |
| CROSBY, TX | 254 | 1537 | EDUCATIONAL SERVICES |
| CULBERSON, TX | 216 | 1168 | HOTELS, ROOMING HOUSES, CAMPS |
| DALLAM, TX | 507 | 3095 | AGRICULTURAL - CROPS |
| DALLAS, TX | 81057 | 1138734 | BUSINESS SERVICES |
| DAWSON, TX | 558 | 3813 | EDUCATIONAL SERVICES |
| DEAF SMITH, TX | 684 | 6429 | EDUCATIONAL SERVICES |
| DELTA, TX | 185 | 1034 | ELECTRONIC/ELCTRCL EQPMNT |
| DENTON, TX | 9552 | 105075 | EDUCATIONAL SERVICES |
| DEWITT, TX | 705 | 5920 | EDUCATIONAL SERVICES |
| DICKENS, TX | 173 | 820 | EDUCATIONAL SERVICES |
| DIMMIT, TX | 312 | 2420 | EDUCATIONAL SERVICES |
| DONLEY, TX | 197 | 806 | EDUCATIONAL SERVICES |
| DUVAL, TX | 417 | 3582 | EDUCATIONAL SERVICES |
| EASTLAND, TX | 929 | 6439 | EDUCATIONAL SERVICES |
| ECTOR, TX | 4586 | 43330 | EDUCATIONAL SERVICES |
| EDWARDS, TX | 123 | 491 | EDUCATIONAL SERVICES |
| ELLIS, TX | 3232 | 30683 | EDUCATIONAL SERVICES |
| EL PASO, TX | 17132 | 233093 | EDUCATIONAL SERVICES |
| ERATH, TX | 1448 | 11664 | EDUCATIONAL SERVICES |
| FALLS, TX | 506 | 4015 | JUSTICE, PUBLIC ORDER/SAFETY |
| FANNIN, TX | 919 | 8254 | EDUCATIONAL SERVICES |
| FAYETTE, TX | 938 | 6828 | EDUCATIONAL SERVICES |
| FISHER, TX | 147 | 1054 | EDUCATIONAL SERVICES |
| FLOYD, TX | 281 | 1972 | EDUCATIONAL SERVICES |
| FOARD, TX | 93 | 477 | EDUCATIONAL SERVICES |
| FORT BEND, TX | 7335 | 83817 | EDUCATIONAL SERVICES |
| FRANKLIN, TX | 281 | 1835 | EDUCATIONAL SERVICES |
| FREESTONE, TX | 683 | 4550 | EXECUTIVE, LEGISLATIVE GOVT. |
| FRIO, TX | 444 | 3464 | EDUCATIONAL SERVICES |
| GAINES, TX | 536 | 4072 | EDUCATIONAL SERVICES |
| GALVESTON, TX | 7725 | 70370 | EATING AND DRINKING PLACES |
| GARZA, TX | 255 | 1236 | OIL AND GAS EXTRACTION |
| GILLESPIE, TX | 1158 | 7140 | EATING AND DRINKING PLACES |
| GLASSCOCK, TX | 65 | 376 | EDUCATIONAL SERVICES |
| GOLIAD, TX | 214 | 982 | EDUCATIONAL SERVICES |
| GONZALES, TX | 714 | 5155 | EDUCATIONAL SERVICES |
| GRAY, TX | 1141 | 8583 | OIL AND GAS EXTRACTION |
| GRAYSON, TX | 4045 | 41298 | EDUCATIONAL SERVICES |
| GREGG, TX | 5626 | 60650 | EATING AND DRINKING PLACES |
| GRIMES, TX | 855 | 10548 | AMUSEMENT/RECREATION SERVICES |
| GUADALUPE, TX | 2489 | 23108 | EDUCATIONAL SERVICES |
| HALE, TX | 1292 | 12573 | FOOD AND KINDRED PRODUCTS |
| HALL, TX | 208 | 1022 | EDUCATIONAL SERVICES |
| HAMILTON, TX | 285 | 1784 | EDUCATIONAL SERVICES |
| HANSFORD, TX | 303 | 2118 | HEALTH SERVICES |
| HARDEMAN, TX | 233 | 1154 | STONE/CLAY/GLASS PRODUCTS |
| HARDIN, TX | 1428 | 8948 | EDUCATIONAL SERVICES |
| HARRIS, TX | 114069 | 1505448 | EDUCATIONAL SERVICES |
| HARRISON, TX | 2076 | 20850 | EDUCATIONAL SERVICES |
| HARTLEY, TX | 113 | 651 | EDUCATIONAL SERVICES |
| HASKELL, TX | 300 | 1517 | EDUCATIONAL SERVICES |
| HAYS, TX | 3403 | 30443 | EDUCATIONAL SERVICES |
| HEMPHILL, TX | 245 | 1370 | OIL AND GAS EXTRACTION |
| HENDERSON, TX | 2327 | 15123 | EDUCATIONAL SERVICES |
| HIDALGO, TX | 12593 | 143029 | EDUCATIONAL SERVICES |
| HILL, TX | 1246 | 9296 | EDUCATIONAL SERVICES |
| HOCKLEY, TX | 866 | 7361 | OIL AND GAS EXTRACTION |
| HOOD, TX | 1517 | 9027 | EDUCATIONAL SERVICES |
| HOPKINS, TX | 1217 | 10897 | WHOLESALE TRADE: NONDURABLE |
| HOUSTON, TX | 803 | 7011 | EDUCATIONAL SERVICES |
| HOWARD, TX | 1307 | 11694 | HEALTH SERVICES |
| HUDSPETH, TX | 154 | 860 | EDUCATIONAL SERVICES |
| HUNT, TX | 2366 | 26161 | TRANSPORTATION EQUIPMENT |
| HUTCHINSON, TX | 993 | 7845 | PETROLEUM REFINING INDUSTRIES |
| IRION, TX | 75 | 459 | EDUCATIONAL SERVICES |
| JACK, TX | 348 | 2106 | EDUCATIONAL SERVICES |
| JACKSON, TX | 552 | 8052 | PAPER AND ALLIED PRODUCTS |
| JASPER, TX | 1338 | 11395 | EDUCATIONAL SERVICES |
| JEFF DAVIS, TX | 126 | 1105 | WHOLESALE TRADE: NONDURABLE |
| JEFFERSON, TX | 9112 | 112515 | HEALTH SERVICES |
| JIM HOGG, TX | 238 | 1309 | EDUCATIONAL SERVICES |
| JIM WELLS, TX | 1360 | 12434 | OIL AND GAS EXTRACTION |
| JOHNSON, TX | 3469 | 29727 | EDUCATIONAL SERVICES |
| JONES, TX | 670 | 5110 | JUSTICE, PUBLIC ORDER/SAFETY |
| KARNES, TX | 545 | 3728 | EDUCATIONAL SERVICES |
| KAUFMAN, TX | 2402 | 20005 | EDUCATIONAL SERVICES |
| KENDALL, TX | 1026 | 6507 | EDUCATIONAL SERVICES |
| KENEDY, TX | 15 | 106 | AGRICULTURAL - LIVESTOCK SPEC |
| KENT, TX | 76 | 247 | EDUCATIONAL SERVICES |
| KERR, TX | 2233 | 15387 | EATING AND DRINKING PLACES |
| KIMBLE, TX | 241 | 1361 | EDUCATIONAL SERVICES |
| KING, TX | 27 | 131 | AGRICULTURAL - LIVESTOCK SPEC |
| KINNEY, TX | 111 | 498 | ELECTRIC, GAS & SANITARY SERV. |
| KLEBERG, TX | 1020 | 9169 | EDUCATIONAL SERVICES |
| KNOX, TX | 248 | 1272 | HEALTH SERVICES |
| LAMAR, TX | 1811 | 17660 | FOOD AND KINDRED PRODUCTS |
| LAMB, TX | 610 | 4489 | EDUCATIONAL SERVICES |
| LAMPASAS, TX | 642 | 3348 | EDUCATIONAL SERVICES |
| LA SALLE, TX | 240 | 1333 | EDUCATIONAL SERVICES |
| LAVACA, TX | 749 | 8300 | LEATHER AND LEATHER PRODUCTS |
| LEE, TX | 574 | 4897 | EDUCATIONAL SERVICES |
| LEON, TX | 718 | 5104 | EDUCATIONAL SERVICES |
| LIBERTY, TX | 1890 | 14176 | EDUCATIONAL SERVICES |
| LIMESTONE, TX | 794 | 6924 | EDUCATIONAL SERVICES |
| LIPSCOMB, TX | 183 | 925 | EDUCATIONAL SERVICES |
| LIVE OAK, TX | 363 | 2309 | AUTO DEALERS & GAS SERV STA. |
| LLANO, TX | 777 | 3766 | HEALTH SERVICES |
| LOVING, TX | 15 | 18 | PUBLIC FINANCE, TAXATION |
| LUBBOCK, TX | 9148 | 94092 | EATING AND DRINKING PLACES |
| LYNN, TX | 286 | 1923 | EDUCATIONAL SERVICES |
| MCCULLOCH, TX | 467 | 2872 | EDUCATIONAL SERVICES |
| MCLENNAN, TX | 7987 | 96739 | EDUCATIONAL SERVICES |
| MCMULLEN, TX | 63 | 294 | EDUCATIONAL SERVICES |
| MADISON, TX | 379 | 3399 | JUSTICE, PUBLIC ORDER/SAFETY |
| MARION, TX | 426 | 2333 | EDUCATIONAL SERVICES |
| MARTIN, TX | 176 | 1032 | EDUCATIONAL SERVICES |
| MASON, TX | 207 | 884 | EDUCATIONAL SERVICES |
| MATAGORDA, TX | 1348 | 10113 | EDUCATIONAL SERVICES |
| MAVERICK, TX | 1118 | 10153 | EDUCATIONAL SERVICES |
| MEDINA, TX | 1003 | 6982 | EDUCATIONAL SERVICES |
| MENARD, TX | 132 | 672 | HEALTH SERVICES |
| MIDLAND, TX | 5686 | 51404 | OIL AND GAS EXTRACTION |
| MILAM, TX | 810 | 6427 | PRIMARY METAL INDUSTRIES |
| MILLS, TX | 288 | 1410 | HEALTH SERVICES |
| MITCHELL, TX | 318 | 2233 | EXECUTIVE, LEGISLATIVE GOVT. |
| MONTAGUE, TX | 905 | 4621 | HEALTH SERVICES |
| MONTGOMERY, TX | 8509 | 79839 | EDUCATIONAL SERVICES |
| MOORE, TX | 726 | 10702 | FOOD AND KINDRED PRODUCTS |
| MORRIS, TX | 439 | 4231 | PRIMARY METAL INDUSTRIES |
| MOTLEY, TX | 89 | 293 | EDUCATIONAL SERVICES |
| NACOGDOCHES, TX | 1983 | 21769 | EDUCATIONAL SERVICES |
| NAVARRO, TX | 1562 | 15957 | GENERAL MERCHANDISE STORES |
| NEWTON, TX | 393 | 2452 | EDUCATIONAL SERVICES |
| NOLAN, TX | 713 | 5658 | EDUCATIONAL SERVICES |
| NUECES, TX | 11515 | 126843 | EDUCATIONAL SERVICES |
| OCHILTREE, TX | 498 | 4004 | OIL AND GAS EXTRACTION |
| OLDHAM, TX | 126 | 1015 | EDUCATIONAL SERVICES |
| ORANGE, TX | 2739 | 24396 | CHEMICALS AND ALLIED PRODUCTS |
| PALO PINTO, TX | 1202 | 8758 | SOCIAL SERVICES |
| PANOLA, TX | 771 | 6404 | OIL AND GAS EXTRACTION |
| PARKER, TX | 2496 | 17851 | EDUCATIONAL SERVICES |
| PARMER, TX | 286 | 3759 | FOOD AND KINDRED PRODUCTS |
| PECOS, TX | 717 | 5299 | EDUCATIONAL SERVICES |
| POLK, TX | 1455 | 10295 | EXECUTIVE, LEGISLATIVE GOVT. |
| POTTER, TX | 6123 | 73608 | HEALTH SERVICES |
| PRESIDIO, TX | 322 | 1718 | EDUCATIONAL SERVICES |
| RAINS, TX | 311 | 1214 | EDUCATIONAL SERVICES |
| RANDALL, TX | 3438 | 27281 | EDUCATIONAL SERVICES |
| REAGAN, TX | 201 | 1582 | OIL AND GAS EXTRACTION |
| REAL, TX | 221 | 861 | EDUCATIONAL SERVICES |
| RED RIVER, TX | 461 | 3714 | EDUCATIONAL SERVICES |
| REEVES, TX | 487 | 4402 | FOOD AND KINDRED PRODUCTS |
| REFUGIO, TX | 349 | 2495 | OIL AND GAS EXTRACTION |
| ROBERTS, TX | 56 | 179 | EDUCATIONAL SERVICES |
| ROBERTSON, TX | 570 | 3750 | EDUCATIONAL SERVICES |
| ROCKWALL, TX | 1321 | 10204 | EATING AND DRINKING PLACES |
| RUNNELS, TX | 493 | 3615 | EDUCATIONAL SERVICES |
| RUSK, TX | 1389 | 11959 | EDUCATIONAL SERVICES |
| SABINE, TX | 408 | 2780 | HEALTH SERVICES |

| COUNTY | 2000 Total Firms | 2000 Total Employ-ees | TOP INDUSTRY RANKED on 2000 EMPLOYMENT |
|---|---|---|---|
| SAN AUGUSTINE, TX | 277 | 1883 | EDUCATIONAL SERVICES |
| SAN JACINTO, TX | 433 | 2231 | EDUCATIONAL SERVICES |
| SAN PATRICIO, TX | 1842 | 14023 | EDUCATIONAL SERVICES |
| SAN SABA, TX | 345 | 1581 | EDUCATIONAL SERVICES |
| SCHLEICHER, TX | 147 | 931 | EDUCATIONAL SERVICES |
| SCURRY, TX | 713 | 6077 | OIL AND GAS EXTRACTION |
| SHACKELFORD, TX | 181 | 881 | OIL AND GAS EXTRACTION |
| SHELBY, TX | 903 | 7564 | FOOD AND KINDRED PRODUCTS |
| SHERMAN, TX | 141 | 639 | AGRICULTURAL - LIVESTOCK SPEC |
| SMITH, TX | 7915 | 82687 | HEALTH SERVICES |
| SOMERVELL, TX | 320 | 3736 | ELECTRIC, GAS & SANITARY SERV. |
| STARR, TX | 926 | 8873 | EDUCATIONAL SERVICES |
| STEPHENS, TX | 545 | 2613 | OIL AND GAS EXTRACTION |
| STERLING, TX | 88 | 452 | ELECTRIC, GAS & SANITARY SERV. |
| STONEWALL, TX | 127 | 694 | HEAVY CONSTRUCTION: EXC BUILD |
| SUTTON, TX | 277 | 1700 | OIL AND GAS EXTRACTION |
| SWISHER, TX | 375 | 2317 | EDUCATIONAL SERVICES |
| TARRANT, TX | 46431 | 610612 | EATING AND DRINKING PLACES |
| TAYLOR, TX | 5110 | 49647 | EDUCATIONAL SERVICES |
| TERRELL, TX | 136 | 297 | EDUCATIONAL SERVICES |
| TERRY, TX | 501 | 3568 | EDUCATIONAL SERVICES |
| THROCKMORTON, TX | 120 | 499 | EDUCATIONAL SERVICES |
| TITUS, TX | 1066 | 13480 | FOOD AND KINDRED PRODUCTS |
| TOM GREEN, TX | 3772 | 36801 | EDUCATIONAL SERVICES |
| TRAVIS, TX | 30609 | 447987 | EDUCATIONAL SERVICES |
| TRINITY, TX | 507 | 2866 | EDUCATIONAL SERVICES |
| TYLER, TX | 543 | 2693 | EDUCATIONAL SERVICES |
| UPSHUR, TX | 984 | 5793 | EDUCATIONAL SERVICES |
| UPTON, TX | 193 | 1576 | EDUCATIONAL SERVICES |
| UVALDE, TX | 990 | 8793 | FOOD AND KINDRED PRODUCTS |
| VAL VERDE, TX | 1396 | 12266 | EDUCATIONAL SERVICES |
| VAN ZANDT, TX | 1532 | 8776 | EDUCATIONAL SERVICES |
| VICTORIA, TX | 3095 | 34322 | HEALTH SERVICES |
| WALKER, TX | 1471 | 22059 | EXECUTIVE, LEGISLATIVE GOVT. |
| WALLER, TX | 992 | 8626 | EDUCATIONAL SERVICES |
| WARD, TX | 486 | 3202 | OIL AND GAS EXTRACTION |
| WASHINGTON, TX | 1297 | 15233 | EDUCATIONAL SERVICES |
| WEBB, TX | 5605 | 58884 | EDUCATIONAL SERVICES |
| WHARTON, TX | 1564 | 12823 | EDUCATIONAL SERVICES |
| WHEELER, TX | 335 | 1877 | EDUCATIONAL SERVICES |
| WICHITA, TX | 5079 | 47929 | EATING AND DRINKING PLACES |
| WILBARGER, TX | 623 | 4652 | FOOD AND KINDRED PRODUCTS |
| WILLACY, TX | 465 | 3064 | EDUCATIONAL SERVICES |
| WILLIAMSON, TX | 6638 | 59846 | EDUCATIONAL SERVICES |
| WILSON, TX | 664 | 4556 | EDUCATIONAL SERVICES |
| WINKLER, TX | 329 | 2196 | OIL AND GAS EXTRACTION |
| WISE, TX | 1542 | 11407 | EDUCATIONAL SERVICES |
| WOOD, TX | 1577 | 9150 | EDUCATIONAL SERVICES |
| YOAKUM, TX | 388 | 2896 | OIL AND GAS EXTRACTION |
| YOUNG, TX | 1071 | 5905 | HEALTH SERVICES |
| ZAPATA, TX | 380 | 3141 | EDUCATIONAL SERVICES |
| ZAVALA, TX | 250 | 2250 | EDUCATIONAL SERVICES |
| BEAVER, UT | 324 | 2683 | RAILROAD TRANSPORTATION |
| BOX ELDER, UT | 1210 | 15034 | TRANSPORTATION EQUIPMENT |
| CACHE, UT | 2614 | 41227 | EDUCATIONAL SERVICES |
| CARBON, UT | 877 | 8467 | HEALTH SERVICES |
| DAGGETT, UT | 76 | 392 | UNITED STATES POSTAL SERVICE |
| DAVIS, UT | 6389 | 70458 | EDUCATIONAL SERVICES |
| DUCHESNE, UT | 667 | 5058 | EDUCATIONAL SERVICES |
| EMERY, UT | 442 | 3179 | MINING AND QUARRYING EXC FUELS |
| GARFIELD, UT | 432 | 3142 | HOTELS, ROOMING HOUSES, CAMPS |
| GRAND, UT | 672 | 4320 | EATING AND DRINKING PLACES |
| IRON, UT | 1436 | 12017 | EDUCATIONAL SERVICES |
| JUAB, UT | 351 | 2656 | EATING AND DRINKING PLACES |
| KANE, UT | 518 | 3030 | EATING AND DRINKING PLACES |
| MILLARD, UT | 523 | 3801 | ELECTRIC, GAS & SANITARY SERV. |
| MORGAN, UT | 241 | 1495 | EDUCATIONAL SERVICES |
| PIUTE, UT | 75 | 279 | EDUCATIONAL SERVICES |
| RICH, UT | 150 | 952 | HOTELS, ROOMING HOUSES, CAMPS |
| SALT LAKE, UT | 32317 | 461192 | BUSINESS SERVICES |
| SAN JUAN, UT | 442 | 4028 | EDUCATIONAL SERVICES |
| SANPETE, UT | 752 | 6897 | EDUCATIONAL SERVICES |
| SEVIER, UT | 772 | 6251 | EDUCATIONAL SERVICES |
| SUMMIT, UT | 1677 | 16130 | HOTELS, ROOMING HOUSES, CAMPS |
| TOOELE, UT | 807 | 7079 | ENGINEERING, ACCOUNTING, ETC. |
| UINTAH, UT | 1062 | 8217 | EDUCATIONAL SERVICES |
| UTAH, UT | 9463 | 118676 | EDUCATIONAL SERVICES |
| WASATCH, UT | 616 | 3799 | EATING AND DRINKING PLACES |
| WASHINGTON, UT | 3683 | 30910 | EATING AND DRINKING PLACES |
| WAYNE, UT | 148 | 907 | EDUCATIONAL SERVICES |
| WEBER, UT | 5709 | 86974 | HEALTH SERVICES |
| ADDISON, VT | 1470 | 12416 | EDUCATIONAL SERVICES |
| BENNINGTON, VT | 1832 | 17136 | HEALTH SERVICES |
| CALEDONIA, VT | 1226 | 10465 | EDUCATIONAL SERVICES |
| CHITTENDEN, VT | 7035 | 110933 | ENGINEERING, ACCOUNTING, ETC. |
| ESSEX, VT | 207 | 1654 | FURNITURE AND FIXTURES |
| FRANKLIN, VT | 1373 | 11947 | EDUCATIONAL SERVICES |
| GRAND ISLE, VT | 258 | 1122 | HOTELS, ROOMING HOUSES, CAMPS |
| LAMOILLE, VT | 1182 | 10657 | HOTELS, ROOMING HOUSES, CAMPS |
| ORANGE, VT | 964 | 6982 | EDUCATIONAL SERVICES |
| ORLEANS, VT | 1051 | 9171 | EDUCATIONAL SERVICES |
| RUTLAND, VT | 2925 | 26249 | HOTELS, ROOMING HOUSES, CAMPS |
| WASHINGTON, VT | 2736 | 29285 | EDUCATIONAL SERVICES |
| WINDHAM, VT | 2312 | 23396 | HOTELS, ROOMING HOUSES, CAMPS |
| WINDSOR, VT | 3007 | 23829 | HOTELS, ROOMING HOUSES, CAMPS |
| ACCOMACK, VA | 1362 | 13422 | WHOLESALE TRADE: NONDURABLE |
| ALBEMARLE, VA | 2276 | 26548 | EDUCATIONAL SERVICES |
| ALLEGHANY, VA | 340 | 4142 | HEALTH SERVICES |
| AMELIA, VA | 328 | 2046 | EDUCATIONAL SERVICES |
| AMHERST, VA | 814 | 8654 | HEALTH SERVICES |
| APPOMATTOX, VA | 402 | 3821 | FURNITURE AND FIXTURES |
| ARLINGTON, VA | 5561 | 99183 | BUSINESS SERVICES |
| AUGUSTA, VA | 1603 | 19966 | EDUCATIONAL SERVICES |
| BATH, VA | 267 | 3061 | HOTELS, ROOMING HOUSES, CAMPS |
| BEDFORD, VA | 1378 | 9372 | EDUCATIONAL SERVICES |
| BLAND, VA | 136 | 1609 | WHOLESALE TRADE: NONDURABLE |
| BOTETOURT, VA | 846 | 8196 | EDUCATIONAL SERVICES |
| BRUNSWICK, VA | 457 | 4431 | EDUCATIONAL SERVICES |
| BUCHANAN, VA | 766 | 7539 | COAL MINING |
| BUCKINGHAM, VA | 301 | 2855 | JUSTICE, PUBLIC ORDER/SAFETY |
| CAMPBELL, VA | 1495 | 16180 | FURNITURE AND FIXTURES |
| CAROLINE, VA | 545 | 4684 | EATING AND DRINKING PLACES |
| CARROLL, VA | 620 | 6111 | APPAREL, FINISHED PRODUCTS |
| CHARLES CITY, VA | 163 | 1272 | EDUCATIONAL SERVICES |
| CHARLOTTE, VA | 382 | 2991 | TEXTILE MILL PRODUCTS |
| CHESTERFIELD, VA | 6609 | 96845 | EXECUTIVE, LEGISLATIVE GOVT. |
| CLARKE, VA | 426 | 3522 | PRINTING AND PUBLISHING |
| CRAIG, VA | 133 | 620 | EDUCATIONAL SERVICES |
| CULPEPER, VA | 1166 | 11328 | EDUCATIONAL SERVICES |
| CUMBERLAND, VA | 254 | 1396 | EDUCATIONAL SERVICES |
| DICKENSON, VA | 409 | 2960 | EDUCATIONAL SERVICES |
| DINWIDDIE, VA | 553 | 5003 | HEALTH SERVICES |
| ESSEX, VA | 446 | 4446 | TRANSPORTATION EQUIPMENT |
| FAIRFAX, VA | 24829 | 382123 | BUSINESS SERVICES |
| FAUQUIER, VA | 1893 | 13501 | EDUCATIONAL SERVICES |
| FLOYD, VA | 307 | 1887 | EDUCATIONAL SERVICES |
| FLUVANNA, VA | 470 | 2610 | EDUCATIONAL SERVICES |
| FRANKLIN, VA | 1475 | 12315 | LUMBER & WOOD PRODS, EXC FURN. |
| FREDERICK, VA | 1445 | 16783 | EDUCATIONAL SERVICES |
| GILES, VA | 537 | 5982 | CHEMICALS AND ALLIED PRODUCTS |
| GLOUCESTER, VA | 1051 | 8475 | EDUCATIONAL SERVICES |
| GOOCHLAND, VA | 519 | 5823 | HOME FURNITURE/EQUIPMENT STORE |
| GRAYSON, VA | 404 | 3711 | EDUCATIONAL SERVICES |
| GREENE, VA | 355 | 2432 | EDUCATIONAL SERVICES |
| GREENSVILLE, VA | 205 | 4551 | FOOD AND KINDRED PRODUCTS |
| HALIFAX, VA | 799 | 6811 | EDUCATIONAL SERVICES |
| HANOVER, VA | 2964 | 41499 | AMUSEMENT/RECREATION SERVICES |
| HENRICO, VA | 7948 | 129893 | WHOLESALE TRADE: DURABLE GOODS |
| HENRY, VA | 1792 | 28885 | APPAREL, FINISHED PRODUCTS |
| HIGHLAND, VA | 115 | 556 | EDUCATIONAL SERVICES |
| ISLE OF WIGHT, VA | 776 | 9070 | FOOD AND KINDRED PRODUCTS |
| JAMES CITY, VA | 1535 | 20598 | HOTELS, ROOMING HOUSES, CAMPS |
| KING AND QUEEN, VA | 130 | 758 | EDUCATIONAL SERVICES |
| KING GEORGE, VA | 508 | 5063 | ENGINEERING, ACCOUNTING, ETC. |
| KING WILLIAM, VA | 386 | 3795 | PAPER AND ALLIED PRODUCTS |
| LANCASTER, VA | 617 | 3968 | HOTELS, ROOMING HOUSES, CAMPS |
| LEE, VA | 554 | 4500 | EDUCATIONAL SERVICES |
| LOUDOUN, VA | 5000 | 56525 | EDUCATIONAL SERVICES |
| LOUISA, VA | 607 | 4869 | ELECTRIC, GAS & SANITARY SERV. |
| LUNENBURG, VA | 296 | 2009 | EDUCATIONAL SERVICES |
| MADISON, VA | 370 | 2463 | EDUCATIONAL SERVICES |
| MATHEWS, VA | 337 | 1742 | EATING AND DRINKING PLACES |
| MECKLENBURG, VA | 1216 | 12002 | TEXTILE MILL PRODUCTS |
| MIDDLESEX, VA | 517 | 2984 | EDUCATIONAL SERVICES |
| MONTGOMERY, VA | 2341 | 33148 | EDUCATIONAL SERVICES |
| NELSON, VA | 469 | 3113 | HOTELS, ROOMING HOUSES, CAMPS |
| NEW KENT, VA | 336 | 2384 | FOOD STORES |
| NORTHAMPTON, VA | 525 | 4610 | TRANSPORTATION SERVICES |
| NORTHUMBERLAND, VA | 470 | 2343 | FOOD AND KINDRED PRODUCTS |
| NOTTOWAY, VA | 499 | 4269 | JUSTICE, PUBLIC ORDER/SAFETY |

| COUNTY | 2000 Total Firms | 2000 Total Employ-ees | TOP INDUSTRY RANKED on 2000 EMPLOYMENT | COUNTY | 2000 Total Firms | 2000 Total Employ-ees | TOP INDUSTRY RANKED on 2000 EMPLOYMENT |
|---|---|---|---|---|---|---|---|
| ORANGE, VA | 788 | 7190 | RUBBER & MISC PLASTIC PRODUCTS | FERRY, WA | 310 | 2087 | EDUCATIONAL SERVICES |
| PAGE, VA | 707 | 6436 | APPAREL, FINISHED PRODUCTS | FRANKLIN, WA | 1594 | 19638 | EDUCATIONAL SERVICES |
| PATRICK, VA | 552 | 5647 | TEXTILE MILL PRODUCTS | GARFIELD, WA | 130 | 883 | HEALTH SERVICES |
| PITTSYLVANIA, VA | 1422 | 12236 | TEXTILE MILL PRODUCTS | GRANT, WA | 2581 | 25504 | FOOD AND KINDRED PRODUCTS |
| POWHATAN, VA | 445 | 2353 | EDUCATIONAL SERVICES | GRAYS HARBOR, WA | 2774 | 22533 | EDUCATIONAL SERVICES |
| PRINCE EDWARD, VA | 624 | 6261 | EDUCATIONAL SERVICES | ISLAND, WA | 2447 | 24201 | NATIONAL SECURITY/INT AFFAIRS |
| PRINCE GEORGE, VA | 474 | 4922 | EDUCATIONAL SERVICES | JEFFERSON, WA | 1581 | 7917 | EATING AND DRINKING PLACES |
| PRINCE WILLIAM, VA | 5363 | 58315 | EATING AND DRINKING PLACES | KING, WA | 65157 | 868152 | EDUCATIONAL SERVICES |
| PULASKI, VA | 1133 | 19299 | TRANSPORTATION EQUIPMENT | KITSAP, WA | 6835 | 52516 | EDUCATIONAL SERVICES |
| RAPPAHANNOCK, VA | 277 | 1364 | MEMBERSHIP ORGANIZATIONS | KITTITAS, WA | 1555 | 10493 | EATING AND DRINKING PLACES |
| RICHMOND, VA | 340 | 2603 | JUSTICE, PUBLIC ORDER/SAFETY | KLICKITAT, WA | 824 | 5272 | EDUCATIONAL SERVICES |
| ROANOKE, VA | 2592 | 38025 | DEPOSITORY INSTITUTIONS | LEWIS, WA | 2917 | 23642 | EDUCATIONAL SERVICES |
| ROCKBRIDGE, VA | 621 | 8278 | TEXTILE MILL PRODUCTS | LINCOLN, WA | 454 | 2635 | EDUCATIONAL SERVICES |
| ROCKINGHAM, VA | 1311 | 22157 | FOOD AND KINDRED PRODUCTS | MASON, WA | 1528 | 10332 | EDUCATIONAL SERVICES |
| RUSSELL, VA | 647 | 6665 | APPAREL, FINISHED PRODUCTS | OKANOGAN, WA | 1800 | 14440 | WHOLESALE TRADE: NONDURABLE |
| SCOTT, VA | 565 | 4119 | EDUCATIONAL SERVICES | PACIFIC, WA | 1140 | 5890 | EDUCATIONAL SERVICES |
| SHENANDOAH, VA | 1492 | 14227 | FOOD AND KINDRED PRODUCTS | PEND OREILLE, WA | 385 | 1983 | EDUCATIONAL SERVICES |
| SMYTH, VA | 980 | 14079 | TRANSPORTATION EQUIPMENT | PIERCE, WA | 17588 | 208161 | HEALTH SERVICES |
| SOUTHAMPTON, VA | 464 | 3633 | JUSTICE, PUBLIC ORDER/SAFETY | SAN JUAN, WA | 1383 | 5953 | HOTELS, ROOMING HOUSES, CAMPS |
| SPOTSYLVANIA, VA | 2080 | 22163 | EDUCATIONAL SERVICES | SKAGIT, WA | 4099 | 40673 | EATING AND DRINKING PLACES |
| STAFFORD, VA | 1901 | 17575 | EDUCATIONAL SERVICES | SKAMANIA, WA | 393 | 2289 | EDUCATIONAL SERVICES |
| SURRY, VA | 158 | 1926 | ELECTRIC, GAS & SANITARY SERV. | SNOHOMISH, WA | 15104 | 197287 | TRANSPORTATION EQUIPMENT |
| SUSSEX, VA | 392 | 2863 | EATING AND DRINKING PLACES | SPOKANE, WA | 13354 | 175624 | HEALTH SERVICES |
| TAZEWELL, VA | 1402 | 14358 | EDUCATIONAL SERVICES | STEVENS, WA | 1316 | 9166 | EDUCATIONAL SERVICES |
| WARREN, VA | 1072 | 7772 | EATING AND DRINKING PLACES | THURSTON, WA | 6501 | 82014 | ADMIN: ENV QUALITY & HOUSING |
| WASHINGTON, VA | 1720 | 16565 | EDUCATIONAL SERVICES | WAHKIAKUM, WA | 185 | 854 | LUMBER & WOOD PRODS, EXC FURN. |
| WESTMORELAND, VA | 502 | 3326 | EDUCATIONAL SERVICES | WALLA WALLA, WA | 1820 | 20515 | FOOD AND KINDRED PRODUCTS |
| WISE, VA | 1257 | 11259 | EDUCATIONAL SERVICES | WHATCOM, WA | 6461 | 61574 | EDUCATIONAL SERVICES |
| WYTHE, VA | 1000 | 10734 | EATING AND DRINKING PLACES | WHITMAN, WA | 1261 | 14819 | EDUCATIONAL SERVICES |
| YORK, VA | 1432 | 15067 | EATING AND DRINKING PLACES | YAKIMA, WA | 6510 | 77426 | WHOLESALE TRADE: NONDURABLE |
| ALEXANDRIA CITY, VA | 4924 | 69026 | EATING AND DRINKING PLACES | BARBOUR, WV | 393 | 3036 | EDUCATIONAL SERVICES |
| BEDFORD CITY, VA | 371 | 4832 | CHEMICALS AND ALLIED PRODUCTS | BERKELEY, WV | 1929 | 20924 | HEALTH SERVICES |
| BRISTOL CITY, VA | 860 | 12106 | EATING AND DRINKING PLACES | BOONE, WV | 570 | 6624 | PETROLEUM REFINING INDUSTRIES |
| BUENA VISTA CITY, VA | 210 | 2171 | FABRICATED METAL PRODUCTS | BRAXTON, WV | 437 | 3461 | EDUCATIONAL SERVICES |
| CHARLOTTESVILLE CITY, VA | 2188 | 46128 | EDUCATIONAL SERVICES | BROOKE, WV | 601 | 10614 | PRIMARY METAL INDUSTRIES |
| CHESAPEAKE CITY, VA | 4926 | 69590 | EDUCATIONAL SERVICES | CABELL, WV | 3168 | 45540 | EATING AND DRINKING PLACES |
| CLIFTON FORGE CITY, VA | 158 | 1145 | RAILROAD TRANSPORTATION | CALHOUN, WV | 162 | 954 | HEALTH SERVICES |
| COLONIAL HGHTS CITY, VA | 790 | 7616 | GENERAL MERCHANDISE STORES | CLAY, WV | 203 | 1611 | COAL MINING |
| COVINGTON CITY, VA | 393 | 3230 | APPAREL, FINISHED PRODUCTS | DODDRIDGE, WV | 196 | 1256 | EDUCATIONAL SERVICES |
| DANVILLE CITY, VA | 2082 | 26706 | AUTO DEALERS & GAS SERV STA. | FAYETTE, WV | 1211 | 12264 | EDUCATIONAL SERVICES |
| EMPORIA CITY, VA | 369 | 4437 | HEALTH SERVICES | GILMER, WV | 188 | 1758 | EDUCATIONAL SERVICES |
| FAIRFAX CITY, VA | 1752 | 22335 | JUSTICE, PUBLIC ORDER/SAFETY | GRANT, WV | 354 | 3532 | HEALTH SERVICES |
| FALLS CHURCH CITY, VA | 885 | 7795 | HEALTH SERVICES | GREENBRIER, WV | 1317 | 12437 | HOTELS, ROOMING HOUSES, CAMPS |
| FRANKLIN CITY, VA | 361 | 4200 | HEALTH SERVICES | HAMPSHIRE, WV | 454 | 4200 | HOTELS, ROOMING HOUSES, CAMPS |
| FREDERICKSBURG CITY, VA | 1267 | 13961 | EATING AND DRINKING PLACES | HANCOCK, WV | 909 | 10676 | STONE/CLAY/GLASS PRODUCTS |
| GALAX CITY, VA | 399 | 6938 | FURNITURE AND FIXTURES | HARDY, WV | 388 | 5425 | FOOD AND KINDRED PRODUCTS |
| HAMPTON CITY, VA | 3397 | 44006 | EATING AND DRINKING PLACES | HARRISON, WV | 2451 | 28739 | JUSTICE, PUBLIC ORDER/SAFETY |
| HARRISONBURG CITY, VA | 1751 | 30680 | EDUCATIONAL SERVICES | JACKSON, WV | 739 | 9083 | PRIMARY METAL INDUSTRIES |
| HOPEWELL CITY, VA | 715 | 7848 | EDUCATIONAL SERVICES | JEFFERSON, WV | 975 | 12111 | INDUSTRIAL & COMM. MACHINERY |
| LEXINGTON CITY, VA | 345 | 2847 | HEALTH SERVICES | KANAWHA, WV | 6848 | 96671 | EATING AND DRINKING PLACES |
| LYNCHBURG CITY, VA | 2480 | 78103 | HEALTH SERVICES | LEWIS, WV | 396 | 4910 | HEALTH SERVICES |
| MANASSAS CITY, VA | 1121 | 15751 | BUSINESS SERVICES | LINCOLN, WV | 352 | 2420 | EDUCATIONAL SERVICES |
| MANASSAS PARK CITY, VA | 259 | 2541 | CONSTRUCT: SPEC TRADE CONTRACT | LOGAN, WV | 1215 | 10709 | GENERAL MERCHANDISE STORES |
| MARTINSVILLE CITY, VA | 752 | 8523 | FURNITURE AND FIXTURES | MCDOWELL, WV | 611 | 4313 | EDUCATIONAL SERVICES |
| NEWPORT NEWS CITY, VA | 4542 | 77684 | TRANSPORTATION EQUIPMENT | MARION, WV | 1711 | 18421 | EDUCATIONAL SERVICES |
| NORFOLK CITY, VA | 6468 | 111869 | EDUCATIONAL SERVICES | MARSHALL, WV | 787 | 7163 | EDUCATIONAL SERVICES |
| NORTON CITY, VA | 346 | 3833 | COAL MINING | MASON, WV | 548 | 5499 | EDUCATIONAL SERVICES |
| PETERSBURG CITY, VA | 1288 | 12641 | BUSINESS SERVICES | MERCER, WV | 1905 | 22856 | HEALTH SERVICES |
| POQUOSON CITY, VA | 277 | 1778 | EDUCATIONAL SERVICES | MINERAL, WV | 706 | 5977 | EDUCATIONAL SERVICES |
| PORTSMOUTH CITY, VA | 2309 | 37730 | HEALTH SERVICES | MINGO, WV | 843 | 8056 | COAL MINING |
| RADFORD CITY, VA | 418 | 10842 | WHOLESALE TRADE: NONDURABLE | MONONGALIA, WV | 2505 | 28234 | EATING AND DRINKING PLACES |
| RICHMOND CITY, VA | 8012 | 152634 | EDUCATIONAL SERVICES | MONROE, WV | 272 | 1574 | TRANSPORTATION EQUIPMENT |
| ROANOKE CITY, VA | 4204 | 67532 | DEPOSITORY INSTITUTIONS | MORGAN, WV | 324 | 2517 | HOTELS, ROOMING HOUSES, CAMPS |
| SALEM CITY, VA | 1212 | 25899 | HEALTH SERVICES | NICHOLAS, WV | 794 | 7299 | GENERAL MERCHANDISE STORES |
| SOUTH BOSTON CITY, VA | 496 | 5954 | HEALTH SERVICES | OHIO, WV | 2060 | 26744 | EATING AND DRINKING PLACES |
| STAUNTON CITY, VA | 1083 | 10100 | EATING AND DRINKING PLACES | PENDLETON, WV | 195 | 2134 | APPAREL AND ACCESSORY STORES |
| SUFFOLK CITY, VA | 1458 | 20522 | EXECUTIVE, LEGISLATIVE GOVT. | PLEASANTS, WV | 192 | 1791 | CHEMICALS AND ALLIED PRODUCTS |
| VIRGINIA BEACH CITY, VA | 10945 | 133958 | EATING AND DRINKING PLACES | POCAHONTAS, WV | 336 | 4724 | HOTELS, ROOMING HOUSES, CAMPS |
| WAYNESBORO CITY, VA | 958 | 11359 | INDUSTRIAL & COMM. MACHINERY | PRESTON, WV | 744 | 6095 | EDUCATIONAL SERVICES |
| WILLIAMSBURG CITY, VA | 547 | 14392 | ENGINEERING, ACCOUNTING, ETC. | PUTNAM, WV | 1344 | 13522 | EATING AND DRINKING PLACES |
| WINCHESTER CITY, VA | 1504 | 20743 | RUBBER & MISC PLASTIC PRODUCTS | RALEIGH, WV | 2620 | 26861 | HEALTH SERVICES |
| ADAMS, WA | 633 | 5179 | FOOD AND KINDRED PRODUCTS | RANDOLPH, WV | 952 | 9330 | LUMBER & WOOD PRODS, EXC FURN. |
| ASOTIN, WA | 715 | 4609 | EATING AND DRINKING PLACES | RITCHIE, WV | 346 | 2730 | FABRICATED METAL PRODUCTS |
| BENTON, WA | 3762 | 39888 | EATING AND DRINKING PLACES | ROANE, WV | 355 | 3278 | APPAREL, FINISHED PRODUCTS |
| CHELAN, WA | 2980 | 29796 | WHOLESALE TRADE: NONDURABLE | SUMMERS, WV | 315 | 2223 | EATING AND DRINKING PLACES |
| CLALLAM, WA | 2681 | 19085 | EATING AND DRINKING PLACES | TAYLOR, WV | 368 | 3118 | HEALTH SERVICES |
| CLARK, WA | 8184 | 88607 | EDUCATIONAL SERVICES | TUCKER, WV | 273 | 3082 | HOTELS, ROOMING HOUSES, CAMPS |
| COLUMBIA, WA | 223 | 1273 | HOTELS, ROOMING HOUSES, CAMPS | TYLER, WV | 208 | 1955 | CHEMICALS AND ALLIED PRODUCTS |
| COWLITZ, WA | 3393 | 38802 | LUMBER & WOOD PRODS, EXC FURN. | UPSHUR, WV | 798 | 6901 | EDUCATIONAL SERVICES |
| DOUGLAS, WA | 826 | 8433 | WHOLESALE TRADE: NONDURABLE | WAYNE, WV | 789 | 9609 | COAL MINING |

# BUSINESS DATA

| COUNTY | 2000 Total Firms | 2000 Total Employ-ees | TOP INDUSTRY RANKED on 2000 EMPLOYMENT |
|---|---|---|---|
| WEBSTER, WV | 235 | 1865 | COAL MINING |
| WETZEL, WV | 593 | 6476 | CHEMICALS AND ALLIED PRODUCTS |
| WIRT, WV | 115 | 748 | RUBBER & MISC PLASTIC PRODUCTS |
| WOOD, WV | 2824 | 39036 | HEALTH SERVICES |
| WYOMING, WV | 601 | 3651 | EDUCATIONAL SERVICES |
| ADAMS, WI | 597 | 4068 | EATING AND DRINKING PLACES |
| ASHLAND, WI | 781 | 6905 | EDUCATIONAL SERVICES |
| BARRON, WI | 1859 | 20612 | FOOD AND KINDRED PRODUCTS |
| BAYFIELD, WI | 950 | 4390 | EDUCATIONAL SERVICES |
| BROWN, WI | 7466 | 127964 | EATING AND DRINKING PLACES |
| BUFFALO, WI | 519 | 3678 | EDUCATIONAL SERVICES |
| BURNETT, WI | 732 | 4886 | INDUSTRIAL & COMM. MACHINERY |
| CALUMET, WI | 1050 | 13725 | INDUSTRIAL & COMM. MACHINERY |
| CHIPPEWA, WI | 2031 | 20766 | HEALTH SERVICES |
| CLARK, WI | 1131 | 11524 | EDUCATIONAL SERVICES |
| COLUMBIA, WI | 1991 | 21271 | EDUCATIONAL SERVICES |
| CRAWFORD, WI | 633 | 7254 | BUSINESS SERVICES |
| DANE, WI | 15668 | 252148 | EDUCATIONAL SERVICES |
| DODGE, WI | 2515 | 33184 | INDUSTRIAL & COMM. MACHINERY |
| DOOR, WI | 1935 | 13377 | HOTELS, ROOMING HOUSES, CAMPS |
| DOUGLAS, WI | 1685 | 16679 | EDUCATIONAL SERVICES |
| DUNN, WI | 1286 | 12428 | EATING AND DRINKING PLACES |
| EAU CLAIRE, WI | 3139 | 45393 | EATING AND DRINKING PLACES |
| FLORENCE, WI | 205 | 1336 | EDUCATIONAL SERVICES |
| FOND DU LAC, WI | 3185 | 46426 | INDUSTRIAL & COMM. MACHINERY |
| FOREST, WI | 545 | 3527 | EDUCATIONAL SERVICES |
| GRANT, WI | 1980 | 16562 | EDUCATIONAL SERVICES |
| GREEN, WI | 1373 | 17149 | MISCELLANEOUS RETAIL |
| GREEN LAKE, WI | 877 | 7064 | PRIMARY METAL INDUSTRIES |
| IOWA, WI | 837 | 9734 | MISCELLANEOUS RETAIL |
| IRON, WI | 429 | 3085 | EATING AND DRINKING PLACES |
| JACKSON, WI | 622 | 6292 | EATING AND DRINKING PLACES |
| JEFFERSON, WI | 2596 | 33523 | EDUCATIONAL SERVICES |
| JUNEAU, WI | 941 | 9698 | EDUCATIONAL SERVICES |
| KENOSHA, WI | 3965 | 53054 | EATING AND DRINKING PLACES |
| KEWAUNEE, WI | 714 | 6400 | LUMBER & WOOD PRODS, EXC FURN. |
| LA CROSSE, WI | 3775 | 67995 | HEALTH SERVICES |
| LAFAYETTE, WI | 579 | 3845 | EDUCATIONAL SERVICES |
| LANGLADE, WI | 850 | 7428 | EATING AND DRINKING PLACES |
| LINCOLN, WI | 1008 | 11954 | FABRICATED METAL PRODUCTS |
| MANITOWOC, WI | 2614 | 33815 | EDUCATIONAL SERVICES |
| MARATHON, WI | 3966 | 61234 | FABRICATED METAL PRODUCTS |
| MARINETTE, WI | 1618 | 16648 | EDUCATIONAL SERVICES |
| MARQUETTE, WI | 546 | 4357 | FOOD AND KINDRED PRODUCTS |
| MENOMINEE, WI | 159 | 4099 | EXECUTIVE, LEGISLATIVE GOVT. |
| MILWAUKEE, WI | 25301 | 460903 | EDUCATIONAL SERVICES |
| MONROE, WI | 1550 | 14860 | HEALTH SERVICES |
| OCONTO, WI | 1244 | 9231 | EDUCATIONAL SERVICES |
| ONEIDA, WI | 2152 | 17503 | HEALTH SERVICES |
| OUTAGAMIE, WI | 5439 | 87412 | PAPER AND ALLIED PRODUCTS |
| OZAUKEE, WI | 3237 | 37303 | EDUCATIONAL SERVICES |
| PEPIN, WI | 328 | 2472 | EDUCATIONAL SERVICES |
| PIERCE, WI | 1060 | 9306 | EDUCATIONAL SERVICES |
| POLK, WI | 1641 | 15126 | EDUCATIONAL SERVICES |
| PORTAGE, WI | 2303 | 27625 | EATING AND DRINKING PLACES |
| PRICE, WI | 727 | 7250 | INDUSTRIAL & COMM. MACHINERY |
| RACINE, WI | 5784 | 87993 | HEALTH SERVICES |
| RICHLAND, WI | 683 | 5901 | ELECTRONIC/ELCTRCL EQPMNT |
| ROCK, WI | 4831 | 71758 | TRANSPORTATION EQUIPMENT |
| RUSK, WI | 613 | 5406 | EDUCATIONAL SERVICES |
| ST. CROIX, WI | 2367 | 23017 | EATING AND DRINKING PLACES |
| SAUK, WI | 2309 | 30280 | EATING AND DRINKING PLACES |
| SAWYER, WI | 1042 | 6603 | EATING AND DRINKING PLACES |
| SHAWANO, WI | 1518 | 12573 | EATING AND DRINKING PLACES |
| SHEBOYGAN, WI | 3348 | 59833 | FABRICATED METAL PRODUCTS |
| TAYLOR, WI | 786 | 7231 | FOOD AND KINDRED PRODUCTS |
| TREMPEALEAU, WI | 1029 | 11956 | FURNITURE AND FIXTURES |
| VERNON, WI | 1086 | 7714 | EDUCATIONAL SERVICES |
| VILAS, WI | 1661 | 8567 | HOTELS, ROOMING HOUSES, CAMPS |
| WALWORTH, WI | 3809 | 38055 | EATING AND DRINKING PLACES |
| WASHBURN, WI | 800 | 5250 | EXECUTIVE, LEGISLATIVE GOVT. |
| WASHINGTON, WI | 3573 | 47311 | EATING AND DRINKING PLACES |
| WAUKESHA, WI | 13544 | 208546 | BUSINESS SERVICES |
| WAUPACA, WI | 2031 | 22431 | HEALTH SERVICES |
| WAUSHARA, WI | 911 | 6237 | EDUCATIONAL SERVICES |
| WINNEBAGO, WI | 5046 | 92469 | PAPER AND ALLIED PRODUCTS |
| WOOD, WI | 2823 | 41384 | PAPER AND ALLIED PRODUCTS |
| ALBANY, WY | 1181 | 16581 | EDUCATIONAL SERVICES |
| BIG HORN, WY | 551 | 4067 | EDUCATIONAL SERVICES |
| CAMPBELL, WY | 1523 | 17751 | COAL MINING |
| CARBON, WY | 834 | 5925 | JUSTICE, PUBLIC ORDER/SAFETY |
| CONVERSE, WY | 544 | 3945 | EDUCATIONAL SERVICES |
| CROOK, WY | 216 | 1873 | EDUCATIONAL SERVICES |
| FREMONT, WY | 1925 | 14808 | EDUCATIONAL SERVICES |
| GOSHEN, WY | 567 | 4357 | EDUCATIONAL SERVICES |
| HOT SPRINGS, WY | 296 | 1817 | EDUCATIONAL SERVICES |
| JOHNSON, WY | 419 | 2244 | HOTELS, ROOMING HOUSES, CAMPS |
| LARAMIE, WY | 3312 | 37221 | HEALTH SERVICES |
| LINCOLN, WY | 694 | 4234 | EDUCATIONAL SERVICES |
| NATRONA, WY | 3504 | 29850 | EATING AND DRINKING PLACES |
| NIOBRARA, WY | 149 | 665 | EDUCATIONAL SERVICES |
| PARK, WY | 1579 | 12369 | HOTELS, ROOMING HOUSES, CAMPS |
| PLATTE, WY | 441 | 2925 | EDUCATIONAL SERVICES |
| SHERIDAN, WY | 1335 | 10443 | EDUCATIONAL SERVICES |
| SUBLETTE, WY | 601 | 2403 | EDUCATIONAL SERVICES |
| SWEETWATER, WY | 1774 | 18588 | CHEMICALS AND ALLIED PRODUCTS |
| TETON, WY | 1578 | 14505 | HOTELS, ROOMING HOUSES, CAMPS |
| UINTA, WY | 1047 | 8513 | EDUCATIONAL SERVICES |
| WASHAKIE, WY | 494 | 4113 | FOOD AND KINDRED PRODUCTS |
| WESTON, WY | 258 | 1830 | EDUCATIONAL SERVICES |

# APPENDICES

*APPENDIX I* **STATE CODES**

13th **EDITION**

# STATE CODES

| State Name | State Code | State Name | State Code |
|---|---|---|---|
| Alabama | 01 | Montana | 30 |
| Alaska | 02 | Nebraska | 31 |
| Arizona | 04 | Nevada | 32 |
| Arkansas | 05 | New Hampshire | 33 |
| California | 06 | New Jersey | 34 |
| Colorado | 08 | New Mexico | 35 |
| Connecticut | 09 | New York | 36 |
| Delaware | 10 | North Carolina | 37 |
| District of Columbia | 11 | North Dakota | 38 |
| Florida | 12 | Ohio | 39 |
| Georgia | 13 | Oklahoma | 40 |
| Hawaii | 15 | Oregon | 41 |
| Idaho | 16 | Pennsylvania | 42 |
| Illinois | 17 | Rhode Island | 44 |
| Indiana | 18 | South Carolina | 45 |
| Iowa | 19 | South Dakota | 46 |
| Kansas | 20 | Tennessee | 47 |
| Kentucky | 21 | Texas | 48 |
| Louisiana | 22 | Utah | 49 |
| Maine | 23 | Vermont | 50 |
| Maryland | 24 | Virginia | 51 |
| Massachusetts | 25 | Washington | 53 |
| Michigan | 26 | West Virginia | 54 |
| Minnesota | 27 | Wisconsin | 55 |
| Mississippi | 28 | Wyoming | 56 |
| Missouri | 29 | | |

*APPENDIX II* **MSA CODES**

13th **EDITION**

# MSA CODES

| MSA NAME | MSA CODE |
|---|---|
| Abilene, TX | 0040 |
| Akron, OH | 0080 |
| Albany, GA | 0120 |
| Albany-Schenectady-Troy, NY | 0160 |
| Albuquerque, NM | 0200 |
| Alexandria, LA | 0220 |
| Allentown-Bethlehem-Easton, PA | 0240 |
| Altoona, PA | 0280 |
| Amarillo, TX | 0320 |
| Anchorage, AK | 0380 |
| Ann Arbor, MI | 0440 |
| Anniston, AL | 0450 |
| Appleton-Oshkosh-Neenah, WI | 0460 |
| Asheville, NC | 0480 |
| Athens, GA | 0500 |
| Atlanta, GA | 0520 |
| Atlantic-Cape May, NJ | 0560 |
| Auburn-Opelika, AL | 0580 |
| Augusta-Aiken, GA-SC | 0600 |
| Austin-San Marcos, TX | 0640 |
| Bakersfield, CA | 0680 |
| Baltimore, MD | 0720 |
| Bangor, ME | 0733 |
| Barnstable-Yarmouth, MA | 0743 |
| Baton Rouge, LA | 0760 |
| Beaumont-Port Arthur, TX | 0840 |
| Bellingham, WA | 0860 |
| Benton Harbor, MI | 0870 |
| Bergen-Passaic, NJ | 0875 |
| Billings, MT | 0880 |
| Biloxi-Gulfport-Pascagoula, MS | 0920 |
| Binghamton, NY | 0960 |
| Birmingham, AL | 1000 |
| Bismarck, ND | 1010 |
| Bloomington, IN | 1020 |
| Bloomington-Normal, IL | 1040 |
| Boise City, ID | 1080 |
| Boston-Worcester-Lawrence-Lowell-Brockton, MA-NH | 1123 |
| Boulder-Longmont, CO | 1125 |
| Brazoria, TX | 1145 |
| Bremerton, WA | 1150 |

| MSA NAME | MSA CODE |
|---|---|
| Brownsville-Harlingen-San Benito, TX | 1240 |
| Bryan-College Station, TX | 1260 |
| Buffalo-Niagara Falls, NY | 1280 |
| Burlington, VT | 1303 |
| Canton-Massillon, OH | 1320 |
| Casper, WY | 1350 |
| Cedar Rapids, IA | 1360 |
| Champaign-Urbana, IL | 1400 |
| Charleston-North Charleston, SC | 1440 |
| Charleston, WV | 1480 |
| Charlotte-Gastonia-Rock Hill, NC-SC | 1520 |
| Charlottesville, VA | 1540 |
| Chattanooga, TN-GA | 1560 |
| Cheyenne, WY | 1580 |
| Chicago, IL | 1600 |
| Chico-Paradise, CA | 1620 |
| Cincinnati, OH-KY-IN | 1640 |
| Clarksville-Hopkinsville, TN-KY | 1660 |
| Cleveland-Lorain-Elyria, OH | 1680 |
| Colorado Springs, CO | 1720 |
| Columbia, MO | 1740 |
| Columbia, SC | 1760 |
| Columbus, GA-AL | 1800 |
| Columbus, OH | 1840 |
| Corpus Christi, TX | 1880 |
| Corvallis, OR | 1890 |
| Cumberland, MD-WV | 1900 |
| Dallas, TX | 1920 |
| Danville, VA | 1950 |
| Davenport-Moline-Rock Island, IA-IL | 1960 |
| Dayton-Springfield, OH | 2000 |
| Daytona Beach, FL | 2020 |
| Decatur, AL | 2030 |
| Decatur, IL | 2040 |
| Denver, CO | 2080 |
| Des Moines, IA | 2120 |
| Detroit, MI | 2160 |
| Dothan, AL | 2180 |
| Dover, DE | 2190 |
| Dubuque, IA | 2200 |

| MSA NAME | MSA CODE |
|---|---|
| Duluth-Superior, MN-WI | 2240 |
| Dutchess County, NY | 2281 |
| Eau Claire, WI | 2290 |
| El Paso, TX | 2320 |
| Elkhart-Goshen, IN | 2330 |
| Elmira, NY | 2335 |
| Enid, OK | 2340 |
| Erie, PA | 2360 |
| Eugene-Springfield, OR | 2400 |
| Evansville-Henderson, IN-KY | 2440 |
| Fargo-Moorhead, ND-MN | 2520 |
| Fayetteville, NC | 2560 |
| Fayetteville-Springdale-Rogers, AR | 2580 |
| Flagstaff, AZ-UT | 2620 |
| Flint, MI | 2640 |
| Florence, AL | 2650 |
| Florence, SC | 2655 |
| Fort Collins-Loveland, CO | 2670 |
| Fort Lauderdale, FL | 2680 |
| Fort Myers-Cape Coral, FL | 2700 |
| Fort Pierce-Port St. Lucie, FL | 2710 |
| Fort Smith, AR-OK | 2720 |
| Fort Walton Beach, FL | 2750 |
| Fort Wayne, IN | 2760 |
| Fort Worth-Arlington, TX | 2800 |
| Fresno, CA | 2840 |
| Gadsden, AL | 2880 |
| Gainesville, FL | 2900 |
| Galveston-Texas City, TX | 2920 |
| Gary, IN | 2960 |
| Glens Falls, NY | 2975 |
| Goldsboro, NC | 2980 |
| Grand Forks, ND-MN | 2985 |
| Grand Junction, CO | 2995 |
| Grand Rapids-Muskegon-Holland, MI | 3000 |
| Great Falls, MT | 3040 |
| Greeley, CO | 3060 |
| Green Bay, WI | 3080 |
| Greensboro-Winston-Salem-High Point, NC | 3120 |

| MSA NAME | MSA CODE |
|---|---|
| Greenville, NC | 3150 |
| Greenville-Spartanburg-Anderson, SC | 3160 |
| Hagerstown, MD | 3180 |
| Hamilton-Middletown, OH | 3200 |
| Harrisburg-Lebanon-Carlisle, PA | 3240 |
| Hartford, CT | 3283 |
| Hattiesburg, MS | 3285 |
| Hickory-Morganton-Lenoir, NC | 3290 |
| Honolulu, HI | 3320 |
| Houma, LA | 3350 |
| Houston, TX | 3360 |
| Huntington-Ashland, WV-KY-OH | 3400 |
| Huntsville, AL | 3440 |
| Indianapolis, IN | 3480 |
| Iowa City, IA | 3500 |
| Jackson, MI | 3520 |
| Jackson, MS | 3560 |
| Jackson, TN | 3580 |
| Jacksonville, FL | 3600 |
| Jacksonville, NC | 3605 |
| Jamestown, NY | 3610 |
| Janesville-Beloit, WI | 3620 |
| Jersey City, NJ | 3640 |
| Johnson City-Kingsport-Bristol, TN-VA | 3660 |
| Johnstown, PA | 3680 |
| Jonesboro, AR | 3700 |
| Joplin, MO | 3710 |
| Kalamazoo-Battle Creek, MI | 3720 |
| Kankakee, IL | 3740 |
| Kansas City, MO-KS | 3760 |
| Kenosha, WI | 3800 |
| Killeen-Temple, TX | 3810 |
| Knoxville, TN | 3840 |
| Kokomo, IN | 3850 |
| La Crosse, WI-MN | 3870 |
| Lafayette, LA | 3880 |
| Lafayette, IN | 3920 |
| Lake Charles, LA | 3960 |
| Lakeland-Winter Haven, FL | 3980 |

| MSA NAME | MSA CODE |
|---|---|
| Lancaster, PA | 4000 |
| Lansing-East Lansing, MI | 4040 |
| Laredo, TX | 4080 |
| Las Cruces, NM | 4100 |
| Las Vegas, NV-AZ | 4120 |
| Lawrence, KS | 4150 |
| Lawton, OK | 4200 |
| Lewiston-Auburn, ME | 4243 |
| Lexington, KY | 4280 |
| Lima, OH | 4320 |
| Lincoln, NE | 4360 |
| Little Rock-North Little Rock, AR | 4400 |
| Longview-Marshall, TX | 4420 |
| Los Angeles-Long Beach, CA | 4480 |
| Louisville, KY-IN | 4520 |
| Lubbock, TX | 4600 |
| Lynchburg, VA | 4640 |
| Macon, GA | 4680 |
| Madison, WI | 4720 |
| Mansfield, OH | 4800 |
| McAllen-Edinburg-Mission, TX | 4880 |
| Medford-Ashland, OR | 4890 |
| Melbourne-Titusville-Palm Bay, FL | 4900 |
| Memphis, TN-AR-MS | 4920 |
| Merced, CA | 4940 |
| Miami, FL | 5000 |
| Middlesex-Somerset-Hunterdon, NJ | 5015 |
| Milwaukee-Waukesha, WI | 5080 |
| Minneapolis-St. Paul, MN-WI | 5120 |
| Missoula, MT | 5140 |
| Mobile, AL | 5160 |
| Modesto, CA | 5170 |
| Monmouth-Ocean, NJ | 5190 |
| Monroe, LA | 5200 |
| Montgomery, AL | 5240 |
| Muncie, IN | 5280 |
| Myrtle Beach, SC | 5330 |
| Naples, FL | 5345 |
| Nashville, TN | 5360 |

| MSA NAME | MSA CODE |
|---|---|
| Nassau-Suffolk, NY | 5380 |
| New Haven-Bridgeport-Stamford-Waterbury, Danbury, CT | 5483 |
| New London-Norwich, CT | 5523 |
| New Orleans, LA | 5560 |
| New York, NY | 5600 |
| Newark, NJ | 5640 |
| Newburgh, NY-PA | 5660 |
| Norfolk-Virginia Beach-Newport News, VA-NC | 5720 |
| Oakland, CA | 5775 |
| Ocala, FL | 5790 |
| Odessa-Midland, TX | 5800 |
| Oklahoma City, OK | 5880 |
| Olympia, WA | 5910 |
| Omaha, NE-IA | 5920 |
| Orange County, CA | 5945 |
| Orlando, FL | 5960 |
| Owensboro, KY | 5990 |
| Panama City, FL | 6015 |
| Parkersburg-Marietta, WV-OH | 6020 |
| Pensacola, FL | 6080 |
| Peoria-Pekin, IL | 6120 |
| Philadelphia, PA-NJ | 6160 |
| Phoenix-Mesa, AZ | 6200 |
| Pine Bluff, AR | 6240 |
| Pittsburgh, PA | 6280 |
| Pittsfield, MA | 6323 |
| Pocatello, ID | 6340 |
| Portland, ME | 6403 |
| Portland-Vancouver, OR-WA | 6440 |
| Providence-Warwick-Pawtucket, RI | 6483 |
| Provo-Orem, UT | 6520 |
| Pueblo, CO | 6560 |
| Punta Gorda, FL | 6580 |
| Racine, WI | 6600 |
| Raleigh-Durham-Chapel Hill, NC | 6640 |
| Rapid City, SD | 6660 |
| Reading, PA | 6680 |
| Redding, CA | 6690 |
| Reno, NV | 6720 |

| MSA NAME | MSA CODE |
|---|---|
| Richland-Kennewick-Pasco, WA | 6740 |
| Richmond-Petersburg, VA | 6760 |
| Riverside-San Bernardino, CA | 6780 |
| Roanoke, VA | 6800 |
| Rochester, MN | 6820 |
| Rochester, NY | 6840 |
| Rockford, IL | 6880 |
| Rocky Mount, NC | 6895 |
| Sacramento, CA | 6920 |
| Saginaw-Bay City-Midland, MI | 6960 |
| St. Cloud, MN | 6980 |
| St. Joseph, MO | 7000 |
| St. Louis, MO-IL | 7040 |
| Salem, OR | 7080 |
| Salinas, CA | 7120 |
| Salt Lake City-Ogden, UT | 7160 |
| San Angelo, TX | 7200 |
| San Antonio, TX | 7240 |
| San Diego, CA | 7320 |
| San Francisco, CA | 7360 |
| San Jose, CA | 7400 |
| San Luis Obispo-Atascadero-Paso Robles, CA | 7460 |
| Santa Barbara-Santa Maria-Lompoc, CA | 7480 |
| Santa Cruz-Watsonville, CA | 7485 |
| Santa Fe, NM | 7490 |
| Santa Rosa, CA | 7500 |
| Sarasota-Bradenton, FL | 7510 |
| Savannah, GA | 7520 |
| Scranton-Wilkes Barre-Hazleton, PA | 7560 |
| Seattle-Bellevue-Everett, WA | 7600 |
| Sharon, PA | 7610 |
| Sheboygan, WI | 7620 |
| Sherman-Denison, TX | 7640 |
| Shreveport-Bossier City, LA | 7680 |
| Sioux City, IA-NE | 7720 |
| Sioux Falls, SD | 7760 |
| South Bend, IN | 7800 |
| Spokane, WA | 7840 |
| Springfield, IL | 7880 |
| Springfield, MO | 7920 |

| MSA NAME | MSA CODE |
|---|---|
| Springfield, MA | 8003 |
| State College, PA | 8050 |
| Steubenville-Weirton, OH-WV | 8080 |
| Stockton-Lodi, CA | 8120 |
| Sumter, SC | 8140 |
| Syracuse, NY | 8160 |
| Tacoma, WA | 8200 |
| Tallahassee, FL | 8240 |
| Tampa-St. Petersburg-Clearwater, FL | 8280 |
| Terre Haute, IN | 8320 |
| Texarkana, TX-Texarkana, AR | 8360 |
| Toledo, OH | 8400 |
| Topeka, KS | 8440 |
| Trenton, NJ | 8480 |
| Tucson, AZ | 8520 |
| Tulsa, OK | 8560 |
| Tuscaloosa, AL | 8600 |
| Tyler, TX | 8640 |
| Utica-Rome, NY | 8680 |
| Vallejo-Fairfield-Napa, CA | 8720 |
| Ventura, CA | 8735 |
| Victoria, TX | 8750 |
| Vineland-Millville-Bridgeton, NJ | 8760 |
| Visalia-Tulare-Porterville, CA | 8780 |
| Waco, TX | 8800 |
| Washington, DC-MD-VA-WV | 8840 |
| Waterloo-Cedar Falls, IA | 8920 |
| Wausau, WI | 8940 |
| West Palm Beach-Boca Raton, FL | 8960 |
| Wheeling, WV-OH | 9000 |
| Wichita, KS | 9040 |
| Wichita Falls, TX | 9080 |
| Williamsport, PA | 9140 |
| Wilmington-Newark, DE-MD | 9160 |
| Wilmington, NC | 9200 |
| Yakima, WA | 9260 |
| Yolo, CA | 9270 |
| York, PA | 9280 |
| Youngstown-Warren, OH | 9320 |
| Yuba City, CA | 9340 |
| Yuma, AZ | 9360 |

*APPENDIX III* **MSA DEFINITIONS**

COUNTY

13th **EDITION**

# MSA DEFINITIONS

| MSA (MSA Code) County | | | FIPS Codes |
|---|---|---|---|
| **Abilene, TX (0040)** | | | |
| Taylor | TX | 48 | 441 |
| **Akron, OH (0080)** | | | |
| Portage | OH | 39 | 133 |
| Summit | | | 153 |
| **Albany, GA (0120)** | | | |
| Dougherty | GA | 13 | 095 |
| Lee | | | 177 |
| **Albany-Schenectady-Troy, NY (0160)** | | | |
| Albany | NY | 36 | 001 |
| Montgomery | | | 057 |
| Rensselaer | | | 083 |
| Saratoga | | | 091 |
| Schenectady | | | 093 |
| Schoharie | | | 095 |
| **Albuquerque, NM (0200)** | | | |
| Bernalillo | NM | 35 | 001 |
| Sandoval | | | 043 |
| Valencia | | | 061 |
| **Alexandria, LA (0220)** | | | |
| Rapides | LA | 22 | 079 |
| **Allentown-Bethlehem-Easton, PA (0240)** | | | |
| Carbon | PA | 42 | 025 |
| Lehigh | | | 077 |
| Northampton | | | 095 |
| **Altoona, PA (0280)** | | | |
| Blair | PA | 42 | 013 |
| **Amarillo, TX (0320)** | | | |
| Potter | TX | 48 | 375 |
| Randall | | | 381 |
| **Anchorage, AK (0380)** | | | |
| Anchorage | AK | 02 | 020 |
| **Ann Arbor, MI (0440)** | | | |
| Lenawee | MI | 26 | 091 |
| Livingston | | | 093 |
| Washtenaw | | | 161 |

| MSA (MSA Code) County | | | FIPS Codes |
|---|---|---|---|
| **Anniston, AL (0450)** | | | |
| Calhoun | AL | 01 | 015 |
| **Appleton-Oshkosh-Neenah, WI (0460)** | | | |
| Calumet | WI | 55 | 015 |
| Outagamie | | | 087 |
| Winnebago | | | 139 |
| **Asheville, NC (0480)** | | | |
| Buncombe | NC | 37 | 021 |
| Madison | | | 115 |
| **Athens, GA (0500)** | | | |
| Clarke | GA | 13 | 059 |
| Madison | | | 195 |
| Oconee | | | 219 |
| **Atlanta, GA (0520)** | | | |
| Barrow | GA | 13 | 013 |
| Bartow | | | 015 |
| Carroll | | | 045 |
| Cherokee | | | 057 |
| Clayton | | | 063 |
| Cobb | | | 067 |
| Coweta | | | 077 |
| DeKalb | | | 089 |
| Douglas | | | 097 |
| Fayette | | | 113 |
| Forsyth | | | 117 |
| Fulton | | | 121 |
| Gwinnett | | | 135 |
| Henry | | | 151 |
| Newton | | | 217 |
| Paulding | | | 223 |
| Pickens | | | 227 |
| Rockdale | | | 247 |
| Spalding | | | 255 |
| Walton | | | 297 |
| **Atlantic-Cape May, NJ (0560)** | | | |
| Atlantic | NJ | 34 | 001 |
| Cape May | | | 009 |
| **Auburn-Opelika, AL (0580)** | | | |
| Lee | AL | 01 | 081 |

# MSA DEFINITIONS

| MSA (MSA Code) County | | | FIPS Codes |
|---|---|---|---|
| **Augusta-Aiken, GA-SC (0600)** | | | |
| Columbia | GA | 13 | 073 |
| McDuffie | | | 189 |
| Richmond | | | 245 |
| Aiken | SC | 45 | 003 |
| Edgefield | | | 037 |
| **Austin-San Marcos, TX (0640)** | | | |
| Bastrop | TX | 48 | 021 |
| Caldwell | | | 055 |
| Hays | | | 209 |
| Travis | | | 453 |
| Williamson | | | 491 |
| **Bakersfield, CA (0680)** | | | |
| Kern | CA | 06 | 029 |
| **Baltimore, MD (0720)** | | | |
| Anne Arundel | MD | 24 | 003 |
| Baltimore | | | 005 |
| Carroll | | | 013 |
| Harford | | | 025 |
| Howard | | | 027 |
| Queen Anne's | | | 035 |
| Baltimore City | | | 510 |
| **Bangor, ME (0733)** | | | |
| Penobscot | ME | 23 | 019 |
| **Barnstable-Yarmouth, MA (0743)** | | | |
| Barnstable | MA | 25 | 001 |
| **Baton Rouge, LA (0760)** | | | |
| Ascension | LA | 22 | 005 |
| East Baton Rouge | | | 033 |
| Livingston | | | 063 |
| West Baton Rouge | | | 121 |
| **Beaumont-Port Arthur, TX (0840)** | | | |
| Hardin | TX | 48 | 199 |
| Jefferson | | | 245 |
| Orange | | | 361 |
| **Bellingham, WA (0860)** | | | |
| Whatcom | WA | 53 | 073 |
| **Benton Harbor, MI (0870)** | | | |
| Berrien | MI | 26 | 021 |

| MSA (MSA Code) County | | | FIPS Codes |
|---|---|---|---|
| **Bergen-Passaic, NJ (0875)** | | | |
| Bergen | NJ | 34 | 003 |
| Passaic | | | 031 |
| **Billings, MT (0880)** | | | |
| Yellowstone | MT | 30 | 111 |
| **Biloxi-Gulfport-Pascagoula, MS (0920)** | | | |
| Hancock | MS | 28 | 045 |
| Harrison | | | 047 |
| Jackson | | | 059 |
| **Binghamton, NY (0960)** | | | |
| Broome | NY | 36 | 007 |
| Tioga | | | 107 |
| **Birmingham, AL (1000)** | | | |
| Blount | AL | 01 | 009 |
| Jefferson | | | 073 |
| St. Clair | | | 115 |
| Shelby | | | 117 |
| **Bismarck, ND (1010)** | | | |
| Burleigh | ND | 38 | 015 |
| Morton | | | 059 |
| **Bloomington, IN (1020)** | | | |
| Monroe | IN | 18 | 105 |
| **Bloomington-Normal, IL (1040)** | | | |
| Mclean | IL | 17 | 113 |
| **Boise City, ID (1080)** | | | |
| Ada | ID | 16 | 001 |
| Canyon | | | 027 |
| **Boston-Worcester-Lawrence-Lowell-Brockton, MA-NH (1123)** | | | |
| Bristol | MA | 25 | 005 |
| Essex | | | 009 |
| Middlesex | | | 017 |
| Norfolk | | | 021 |
| Plymouth | | | 023 |
| Suffolk | | | 025 |
| Worcester | | | 027 |
| Hillsborough | NH | 33 | 011 |

| MSA (MSA Code) County | | | FIPS Codes |
|---|---|---|---|
| **Boston-Worcester-Lawrence-Lowell-Brockton, MA-NH (1123) Cont.** | | | |
| Rockingham | | | 015 |
| Strafford | | | 017 |
| **Boulder-Longmont, CO (1125)** | | | |
| Boulder | CO | 08 | 013 |
| **Brazoria, TX (1145)** | | | |
| Brazoria | TX | 48 | 039 |
| **Bremerton, WA (1150)** | | | |
| Kitsap | WA | 53 | 035 |
| **Brownsville-Harlingen-San Benito, TX (1240)** | | | |
| Cameron | TX | 48 | 061 |
| **Bryan-College Station, TX (1260)** | | | |
| Brazos | TX | 48 | 041 |
| **Buffalo-Niagara Falls, NY (1280)** | | | |
| Erie | NY | 36 | 029 |
| Niagara | | | 063 |
| **Burlington, VT (1303)** | | | |
| Chittenden | VT | 50 | 007 |
| Franklin | | | 011 |
| Grand Isle | | | 013 |
| **Canton-Massillon, OH (1320)** | | | |
| Carroll | OH | 39 | 019 |
| Stark | | | 151 |
| **Casper, WY (1350)** | | | |
| Natrona | WY | 56 | 025 |
| **Cedar Rapids, IA (1360)** | | | |
| Linn | IA | 19 | 113 |
| **Champaign-Urbana, IL (1400)** | | | |
| Champaign | IL | 17 | 019 |
| **Charleston-North Charleston, SC (1440)** | | | |
| Berkeley | SC | 45 | 015 |
| Charleston | | | 019 |
| Dorchester | | | 035 |

| MSA (MSA Code) County | | | FIPS Codes |
|---|---|---|---|
| **Charleston, WV (1480)** | | | |
| Kanawha | WV | 54 | 039 |
| Putnam | | | 079 |
| **Charlotte-Gastonia-Rock Hill, NC-SC (1520)** | | | |
| Cabarrus | NC | 37 | 025 |
| Gaston | | | 071 |
| Lincoln | | | 109 |
| Mecklenburg | | | 119 |
| Rowan | | | 159 |
| Union | | | 179 |
| York | SC | 45 | 091 |
| **Charlottesville, VA (1540)** | | | |
| Albemarle | VA | 51 | 003 |
| Fluvanna | | | 065 |
| Greene | | | 079 |
| Charlottesville City | | | 540 |
| **Chattanooga, TN-GA (1560)** | | | |
| Catoosa | GA | 13 | 047 |
| Dade | | | 083 |
| Walker | | | 295 |
| Hamilton | TN | 47 | 065 |
| Marion | | | 115 |
| **Cheyenne, WY (1580)** | | | |
| Laramie | WY | 56 | 021 |
| **Chicago, IL (1600)** | | | |
| Cook | IL | 17 | 031 |
| DeKalb | | | 037 |
| DuPage | | | 043 |
| Grundy | | | 063 |
| Kane | | | 089 |
| Kendall | | | 093 |
| Lake | | | 097 |
| Mchenry | | | 111 |
| Will | | | 197 |
| **Chico-Paradise, CA (1620)** | | | |
| Butte | CA | 06 | 007 |
| **Cincinnati, OH-KY-IN (1640)** | | | |
| Dearborn | IN | 18 | 029 |
| Ohio | | | 115 |
| Boone | KY | 21 | 015 |
| Campbell | | | 037 |

| MSA (MSA Code) County | | | FIPS Codes |
|---|---|---|---|
| **Cincinnati, OH-KY-IN (1640 Cont.** | | | |
| Gallatin | | | 077 |
| Grant | | | 081 |
| Kenton | | | 117 |
| Pendleton | | | 191 |
| Brown | OH | 39 | 015 |
| Clermont | | | 025 |
| Hamilton | | | 061 |
| Warren | | | 165 |
| **Clarksville-Hopkinsville, TN-KY (1660)** | | | |
| Christian | KY | 21 | 047 |
| Montgomery | TN | 47 | 125 |
| **Cleveland-Lorain-Elyria, OH (1680)** | | | |
| Ashtabula | OH | 39 | 007 |
| Cuyahoga | | | 035 |
| Geauga | | | 055 |
| Lake | | | 085 |
| Lorain | | | 093 |
| Medina | | | 103 |
| **Colorado Springs, CO (1720)** | | | |
| El Paso | CO | 08 | 041 |
| **Columbia, MO (1740)** | | | |
| Boone | MO | 29 | 019 |
| **Columbia, SC (1760)** | | | |
| Lexington | SC | 45 | 063 |
| Richland | | | 079 |
| **Columbus, GA-AL (1800)** | | | |
| Russell | AL | 01 | 113 |
| Chattahoochee | GA | 13 | 053 |
| Harris | | | 145 |
| Muscogee | | | 215 |
| **Columbus, OH (1840)** | | | |
| Delaware | OH | 39 | 041 |
| Fairfield | | | 045 |
| Franklin | | | 049 |
| Licking | | | 089 |
| Madison | | | 097 |
| Pickaway | | | 129 |

| MSA (MSA Code) County | | | FIPS Codes |
|---|---|---|---|
| **Corpus Christi, TX (1880)** | | | |
| Nueces | TX | 48 | 355 |
| San Patricio | | | 409 |
| **Corvallis, OR (1890)** | | | |
| Benton | OR | 41 | 003 |
| **Cumberland, MD-WV (1900)** | | | |
| Allegany | MD | 24 | 001 |
| Mineral | WV | 54 | 057 |
| **Dallas, TX (1920)** | | | |
| Collin | TX | 48 | 085 |
| Dallas | | | 113 |
| Denton | | | 121 |
| Ellis | | | 139 |
| Henderson | | | 213 |
| Hunt | | | 231 |
| Kaufman | | | 257 |
| Rockwall | | | 397 |
| **Danville, VA (1950)** | | | |
| Pittsylvania | VA | 51 | 143 |
| Danville City | | | 590 |
| **Davenport-Moline-Rock Island, IA-IL (1960)** | | | |
| Henry | IL | 17 | 073 |
| Rock Island | | | 161 |
| Scott | IA | 19 | 163 |
| **Dayton-Springfield, OH (2000)** | | | |
| Clark | OH | 39 | 023 |
| Greene | | | 057 |
| Miami | | | 109 |
| Montgomery | | | 113 |
| **Daytona Beach, FL (2020)** | | | |
| Flagler | FL | 12 | 035 |
| Volusia | | | 127 |
| **Decatur, AL (2030)** | | | |
| Lawrence | AL | 01 | 079 |
| Morgan | | | 103 |

# MSA DEFINITIONS

| MSA (MSA Code) County | | | FIPS Codes |
|---|---|---|---|
| **Decatur, IL (2040)** | | | |
| Macon | IL | 17 | 115 |
| **Denver, CO (2080)** | | | |
| Adams | CO | 08 | 001 |
| Arapahoe | | | 005 |
| Denver | | | 031 |
| Douglas | | | 035 |
| Jefferson | | | 059 |
| **Des Moines, IA (2120)** | | | |
| Dallas | IA | 19 | 049 |
| Polk | | | 153 |
| Warren | | | 181 |
| **Detroit, MI (2160)** | | | |
| Lapeer | MI | 26 | 087 |
| Macomb | | | 099 |
| Monroe | | | 115 |
| Oakland | | | 125 |
| St. Clair | | | 147 |
| Wayne | | | 163 |
| **Dothan, AL (2180)** | | | |
| Dale | AL | 01 | 045 |
| Houston | | | 069 |
| **Dover, DE (2190)** | | | |
| Kent | DE | 10 | 001 |
| **Dubuque, IA (2200)** | | | |
| Dubuque | IA | 19 | 061 |
| **Duluth-Superior, MN-WI (2240)** | | | |
| St. Louis | MN | 27 | 137 |
| Douglas | WI | 55 | 031 |
| **Dutchess County, NY (2281)** | | | |
| Dutchess | NY | 36 | 027 |
| **Eau Claire, WI (2290)** | | | |
| Chippewa | WI | 55 | 017 |
| Eau Claire | | | 035 |
| **El Paso, TX (2320)** | | | |
| El Paso | TX | 48 | 141 |
| **Elkhart-Goshen, IN (2330)** | | | |
| Elkhart | IN | 18 | 039 |

| MSA (MSA Code) County | | | FIPS Codes |
|---|---|---|---|
| **Elmira, NY (2335)** | | | |
| Chemung | NY | 36 | 015 |
| **Enid, OK (2340)** | | | |
| Garfield | OK | 40 | 047 |
| **Erie, PA (2360)** | | | |
| Erie | PA | 42 | 049 |
| **Eugene-Springfield, OR (2400)** | | | |
| Lane | OR | 41 | 039 |
| **Evansville-Henderson, IN-KY (2440)** | | | |
| Posey | IN | 18 | 129 |
| Vanderburgh | | | 163 |
| Warrick | | | 173 |
| Henderson | KY | 21 | 101 |
| **Fargo-Moorhead, ND-MN (2520)** | | | |
| Clay | MN | 27 | 027 |
| Cass | ND | 38 | 017 |
| **Fayetteville, NC (2560)** | | | |
| Cumberland | NC | 37 | 051 |
| **Fayetteville-Springdale-Rogers, AR (2580)** | | | |
| Benton | AR | 05 | 007 |
| Washington | | | 143 |
| **Flagstaff, AZ-UT (2620)** | | | |
| Coconino | AZ | 04 | 005 |
| Kane | UT | 49 | 025 |
| **Flint, MI (2640)** | | | |
| Genesee | MI | 26 | 049 |
| **Florence, AL (2650)** | | | |
| Colbert | AL | 01 | 033 |
| Lauderdale | | | 077 |
| **Florence, SC (2655)** | | | |
| Florence | SC | 45 | 041 |
| **Fort Collins-Loveland, CO (2670)** | | | |
| Larimer | CO | 08 | 069 |

| MSA (MSA Code) County | | | FIPS Codes |
|---|---|---|---|

**Fort Lauderdale, FL (2680)**

| Broward | FL | 12 | 011 |
|---|---|---|---|

**Fort Myers-Cape Coral, FL (2700)**

| Lee | FL | 12 | 071 |
|---|---|---|---|

**Fort Pierce-Port St. Lucie, FL (2710)**

| Martin | FL | 12 | 085 |
|---|---|---|---|
| St. Lucie | | | 111 |

**Fort Smith, AR-OK (2720)**

| Crawford | AR | 05 | 033 |
|---|---|---|---|
| Sebastian | | | 131 |
| Sequoyah | OK | 40 | 135 |

**Fort Walton Beach, FL (2750)**

| Okaloosa | FL | 12 | 091 |
|---|---|---|---|

**Fort Wayne, IN (2760)**

| Adams | IN | 18 | 001 |
|---|---|---|---|
| Allen | | | 003 |
| De Kalb | | | 033 |
| Huntington | | | 069 |
| Wells | | | 179 |
| Whitley | | | 183 |

**Fort Worth-Arlington, TX (2800)**

| Hood | TX | 48 | 221 |
|---|---|---|---|
| Johnson | | | 251 |
| Parker | | | 367 |
| Tarrant | | | 439 |

**Fresno, CA (2840)**

| Fresno | CA | 06 | 019 |
|---|---|---|---|
| Madera | | | 039 |

**Gadsden, AL (2880)**

| Etowah | AL | 01 | 055 |
|---|---|---|---|

**Gainesville, FL (2900)**

| Alachua | FL | 12 | 001 |
|---|---|---|---|

**Galveston-Texas City, TX (2920)**

| Galveston | TX | 48 | 167 |
|---|---|---|---|

**Gary, IN (2960)**

| Lake | IN | 18 | 089 |
|---|---|---|---|
| Porter | | | 127 |

**Glens Falls, NY (2975)**

| Warren | NY | 36 | 113 |
|---|---|---|---|
| Washington | | | 115 |

**Goldsboro, NC (2980)**

| Wayne | NC | 37 | 191 |
|---|---|---|---|

**Grand Forks, ND-MN (2985)**

| Polk | MN | 27 | 119 |
|---|---|---|---|
| Grand Forks | ND | 38 | 035 |

**Grand Junction, CO (2995)**

| Mesa | CO | 08 | 077 |
|---|---|---|---|

**Grand Rapids-Muskegon-Holland, MI (3000)**

| Allegan | MI | 26 | 005 |
|---|---|---|---|
| Kent | | | 081 |
| Muskegon | | | 121 |
| Ottawa | | | 139 |

**Great Falls, MT (3040)**

| Cascade | MT | 30 | 013 |
|---|---|---|---|

**Greeley, CO (3060)**

| Weld | CO | 08 | 123 |
|---|---|---|---|

**Green Bay, WI (3080)**

| Brown | WI | 55 | 009 |
|---|---|---|---|

**Greensboro-Winston Salem-High Point, NC (3120)**

| Alamance | NC | 37 | 001 |
|---|---|---|---|
| Davidson | | | 057 |
| Davie | | | 059 |
| Forsyth | | | 067 |
| Guilford | | | 081 |
| Randolph | | | 151 |
| Stokes | | | 169 |
| Yadkin | | | 197 |

**Greenville, NC (3150)**

| Pitt | NC | 37 | 147 |
|---|---|---|---|

**Greenville-Spartanburg-Anderson, SC (3160)**

| Anderson | SC | 45 | 007 |
|---|---|---|---|
| Cherokee | | | 021 |

# MSA DEFINITIONS

| MSA (MSA Code) County | | | FIPS Codes |
|---|---|---|---|
| **Greenville-Spartanburg-Anderson, SC (3160) Cont.** | | | |
| Greenville | | | 045 |
| Pickens | | | 077 |
| Spartanburg | | | 083 |
| **Hagerstown, MD (3180)** | | | |
| Washington | MD | 24 | 043 |
| **Hamilton-Middletown, OH (3200)** | | | |
| Butler | OH | 39 | 017 |
| **Harrisburg-Lebanon-Carlisle, PA (3240)** | | | |
| Cumberland | PA | 42 | 041 |
| Dauphin | | | 043 |
| Lebanon | | | 075 |
| Perry | | | 099 |
| **Hartford, CT (3283)** | | | |
| Hartford | CT | 09 | 003 |
| Middlesex | | | 007 |
| Tolland | | | 013 |
| **Hattiesburg, MS (3285)** | | | |
| Forrest | MS | 28 | 035 |
| Lamar | | | 073 |
| **Hickory-Morganton-Lenoir, NC (3290)** | | | |
| Alexander | NC | 37 | 003 |
| Burke | | | 023 |
| Caldwell | | | 027 |
| Catawba | | | 035 |
| **Honolulu, HI (3320)** | | | |
| Honolulu | HI | 15 | 003 |
| **Houma, LA (3350)** | | | |
| Lafourche | LA | 22 | 057 |
| Terrebonne | | | 109 |
| **Houston, TX (3360)** | | | |
| Chambers | TX | 48 | 071 |
| Fort Bend | | | 157 |
| Harris | | | 201 |
| Liberty | | | 291 |
| Montgomery | | | 339 |
| Waller | | | 473 |

| MSA (MSA Code) County | | | FIPS Codes |
|---|---|---|---|
| **Huntington-Ashland,WV-KY-OH (3400)** | | | |
| Boyd | KY | 21 | 019 |
| Carter | | | 043 |
| Greenup | | | 089 |
| Lawrence | OH | 39 | 087 |
| Cabell | WV | 54 | 011 |
| Wayne | | | 099 |
| **Huntsville, AL (3440)** | | | |
| Limestone | AL | 01 | 083 |
| Madison | | | 089 |
| **Indianapolis, IN (3480)** | | | |
| Boone | IN | 18 | 011 |
| Hamilton | | | 057 |
| Hancock | | | 059 |
| Hendricks | | | 063 |
| Johnson | | | 081 |
| Madison | | | 095 |
| Marion | | | 097 |
| Morgan | | | 109 |
| Shelby | | | 145 |
| **Iowa City, IA (3500)** | | | |
| Johnson | IA | 19 | 103 |
| **Jackson, MI (3520)** | | | |
| Jackson | MI | 26 | 075 |
| **Jackson, MS (3560)** | | | |
| Hinds | MS | 28 | 049 |
| Madison | | | 089 |
| Rankin | | | 121 |
| **Jackson, TN (3580)** | | | |
| Chester | TN | 47 | 023 |
| Madison | | | 113 |
| **Jacksonville, FL (3600)** | | | |
| Clay | FL | 12 | 019 |
| Duval | | | 031 |
| Nassau | | | 089 |
| St. Johns | | | 109 |
| **Jacksonville, NC (3605)** | | | |
| Onslow | NC | 37 | 133 |

| MSA (MSA Code) County | | | FIPS Codes |
|---|---|---|---|
| **Jamestown, NY (3610)** | | | |
| Chautauqua | NY | 36 | 013 |
| **Janesville-Beloit, WI (3620)** | | | |
| Rock | WI | 55 | 105 |
| **Jersey City, NJ (3640)** | | | |
| Hudson | NJ | 34 | 017 |
| **Johnson City-Kingsport-Bristol, TN-VA (3660)** | | | |
| Carter | TN | 47 | 019 |
| Hawkins | | | 073 |
| Sullivan | | | 163 |
| Unicoi | | | 171 |
| Washington | | | 179 |
| Scott | VA | 51 | 169 |
| Washington | | | 191 |
| Bristol City | | | 520 |
| **Johnstown, PA (3680)** | | | |
| Cambria | PA | 42 | 021 |
| Somerset | | | 111 |
| **Jonesboro, AR (3700)** | | | |
| Craighead | AR | 05 | 031 |
| **Joplin, MO (3710)** | | | |
| Jasper | MO | 29 | 097 |
| Newton | | | 145 |
| **Kalamazoo-Battle Creek, MI (3720)** | | | |
| Calhoun | MI | 26 | 025 |
| Kalamazoo | | | 077 |
| Van Buren | | | 159 |
| **Kankakee, IL (3740)** | | | |
| Kankakee | IL | 17 | 091 |
| **Kansas City, MO-KS (3760)** | | | |
| Johnson | KS | 20 | 091 |
| Leavenworth | | | 103 |
| Miami | | | 121 |
| Wyandotte | | | 209 |
| Cass | MO | 29 | 037 |
| Clay | | | 047 |
| Clinton | | | 049 |
| Jackson | | | 095 |
| Lafayette | | | 107 |

| MSA (MSA Code) County | | | FIPS Codes |
|---|---|---|---|
| **Kansas City, MO-KS (3760) Cont.** | | | |
| Platte | | | 165 |
| Ray | | | 177 |
| **Kenosha, WI (3800)** | | | |
| Kenosha | WI | 55 | 059 |
| **Killeen-Temple, TX (3810)** | | | |
| Bell | TX | 48 | 027 |
| Coryell | | | 099 |
| **Knoxville, TN (3840)** | | | |
| Anderson | TN | 47 | 001 |
| Blount | | | 009 |
| Knox | | | 093 |
| Loudon | | | 105 |
| Sevier | | | 155 |
| Union | | | 173 |
| **Kokomo, IN (3850)** | | | |
| Howard | IN | 18 | 067 |
| Tipton | | | 159 |
| **La Crosse, WI-MN (3870)** | | | |
| Houston | MN | 27 | 055 |
| La Crosse | WI | 55 | 063 |
| **Lafayette, LA (3880)** | | | |
| Acadia | LA | 22 | 001 |
| Lafayette | | | 055 |
| St. Landry | | | 097 |
| St. Martin | | | 099 |
| **Lafayette, IN (3920)** | | | |
| Clinton | IN | 18 | 023 |
| Tippecanoe | | | 157 |
| **Lake Charles, LA (3960)** | | | |
| Calcasieu | LA | 22 | 019 |
| **Lakeland-Winter Haven, FL (3980)** | | | |
| Polk | FL | 12 | 105 |
| **Lancaster, PA (4000)** | | | |
| Lancaster | PA | 42 | 071 |

# MSA DEFINITIONS

| MSA (MSA Code)<br>County | | | FIPS<br>Codes |
|---|---|---|---|
| **Lansing-East Lansing, MI (4040)** | | | |
| Clinton | MI | 26 | 037 |
| Eaton | | | 045 |
| Ingham | | | 065 |
| **Laredo, TX (4080)** | | | |
| Webb | TX | 48 | 479 |
| **Las Cruces, NM (4100)** | | | |
| Dona Ana | NM | 35 | 013 |
| **Las Vegas, NV-AZ (4120)** | | | |
| Mohave | AZ | 04 | 015 |
| Clark | NV | 32 | 003 |
| Nye | | | 023 |
| **Lawrence, KS (4150)** | | | |
| Douglas | KS | 20 | 045 |
| **Lawton, OK (4200)** | | | |
| Comanche | OK | 40 | 031 |
| **Lewiston-Auburn, ME (4243)** | | | |
| Androscoggin | ME | 23 | 001 |
| **Lexington, KY (4280)** | | | |
| Bourbon | KY | 21 | 017 |
| Clark | | | 049 |
| Fayette | | | 067 |
| Jessamine | | | 113 |
| Madison | | | 151 |
| Scott | | | 209 |
| Woodford | | | 239 |
| **Lima, OH (4320)** | | | |
| Allen | OH | 39 | 003 |
| Auglaize | | | 011 |
| **Lincoln, NE (4360)** | | | |
| Lancaster | NE | 31 | 109 |
| **Little Rock-North Little Rock, AR (4400)** | | | |
| Faulkner | AR | 05 | 045 |
| Lonoke | | | 085 |
| Pulaski | | | 119 |
| Saline | | | 125 |

| MSA (MSA Code)<br>County | | | FIPS<br>Codes |
|---|---|---|---|
| **Longview-Marshall, TX (4420)** | | | |
| Gregg | TX | 48 | 183 |
| Harrison | | | 203 |
| Upshur | | | 459 |
| **Los Angeles-Long Beach, CA (4480)** | | | |
| Los Angeles | CA | 06 | 037 |
| **Louisville, KY-IN (4520)** | | | |
| Clark | IN | 18 | 019 |
| Floyd | | | 043 |
| Harrison | | | 061 |
| Scott | | | 143 |
| Bullitt | KY | 21 | 029 |
| Jefferson | | | 111 |
| Oldham | | | 185 |
| **Lubbock, TX (4600)** | | | |
| Lubbock | TX | 48 | 303 |
| **Lynchburg, VA (4640)** | | | |
| Amherst | VA | 51 | 009 |
| Bedford | | | 019 |
| Campbell | | | 031 |
| Bedford City | | | 515 |
| Lynchburg City | | | 680 |
| **Macon, GA (4680)** | | | |
| Bibb | GA | 13 | 021 |
| Houston | | | 153 |
| Jones | | | 169 |
| Peach | | | 225 |
| Twiggs | | | 289 |
| **Madison, WI (4720)** | | | |
| Dane | WI | 55 | 025 |
| **Mansfield, OH (4800)** | | | |
| Crawford | OH | 39 | 033 |
| Richland | | | 139 |
| **McAllen-Edinburg-Mission, TX (4880)** | | | |
| Hidalgo | TX | 48 | 215 |
| **Medford-Ashland, OR (4890)** | | | |
| Jackson | OR | 41 | 029 |

# MSA DEFINITIONS

| MSA (MSA Code) County | | | FIPS Codes |
|---|---|---|---|
| **Melbourne-Titusville-Palm Bay, FL (4900)** | | | |
| Brevard | FL | 12 | 009 |
| **Memphis, TN-AR-MS (4920)** | | | |
| Crittenden | AR | 05 | 035 |
| DeSoto | MS | 28 | 033 |
| Fayette | TN | 47 | 047 |
| Shelby | | | 157 |
| Tipton | | | 167 |
| **Merced, CA (4940)** | | | |
| Merced | CA | 06 | 047 |
| **Miami, FL (5000)** | | | |
| Dade | FL | 12 | 025 |
| **Middlesex-Somerset-Hunterdon, NJ (5015)** | | | |
| Hunterdon | NJ | 34 | 019 |
| Middlesex | | | 023 |
| Somerset | | | 035 |
| **Milwaukee-Waukesha, WI (5080)** | | | |
| Milwaukee | WI | 55 | 079 |
| Ozaukee | | | 089 |
| Washington | | | 131 |
| Waukesha | | | 133 |
| **Minneapolis-St. Paul, MN-WI (5120)** | | | |
| Anoka | MN | 27 | 003 |
| Carver | | | 019 |
| Chisago | | | 025 |
| Dakota | | | 037 |
| Hennepin | | | 053 |
| Isanti | | | 059 |
| Ramsey | | | 123 |
| Scott | | | 139 |
| Sherburne | | | 141 |
| Washington | | | 163 |
| Wright | | | 171 |
| Pierce | WI | 55 | 093 |
| St. Croix | | | 109 |
| **Missoula, MT (5140)** | | | |
| Missoula | MT | 30 | 063 |
| **Mobile, AL (5160)** | | | |
| Baldwin | AL | 01 | 003 |
| Mobile | | | 097 |
| **Modesto, CA (5170)** | | | |
| Stanislaus | CA | 06 | 099 |
| **Monmouth-Ocean, NJ (5190)** | | | |
| Monmouth | NJ | 34 | 025 |
| Ocean | | | 029 |
| **Monroe, LA (5200)** | | | |
| Ouachita | LA | 22 | 073 |
| **Montgomery, AL (5240)** | | | |
| Autauga | AL | 01 | 001 |
| Elmore | | | 051 |
| Montgomery | | | 101 |
| **Muncie, IN (5280)** | | | |
| Delaware | IN | 18 | 035 |
| **Myrtle Beach, SC (5330)** | | | |
| Horry | SC | 45 | 051 |
| **Naples, FL (5345)** | | | |
| Collier | FL | 12 | 021 |
| **Nashville, TN (5360)** | | | |
| Cheatham | TN | 47 | 021 |
| Davidson | | | 037 |
| Dickson | | | 043 |
| Robertson | | | 147 |
| Rutherford | | | 149 |
| Sumner | | | 165 |
| Williamson | | | 187 |
| Wilson | | | 189 |
| **Nassau-Suffolk, NY (5380)** | | | |
| Nassau | NY | 36 | 059 |
| Suffolk | | | 103 |
| **New Haven-Bridgeport-Stamford-Waterbury-Danbury, CT (5483)** | | | |
| Fairfield | CT | 09 | 001 |
| New Haven | | | 009 |

# MSA DEFINITIONS

| MSA (MSA Code) County | | | FIPS Codes |
|---|---|---|---|
| **New London-Norwich, CT (5523)** | | | |
| New London | CT | 09 | 011 |
| **New Orleans, LA (5560)** | | | |
| Jefferson | LA | 22 | 051 |
| Orleans | | | 071 |
| Plaquemines | | | 075 |
| St. Bernard | | | 087 |
| St. Charles | | | 089 |
| St. James | | | 093 |
| St. John the Baptist | | | 095 |
| St. Tammany | | | 103 |
| **New York, NY (5600)** | | | |
| Bronx | NY | 36 | 005 |
| Kings | | | 047 |
| New York | | | 061 |
| Putnam | | | 079 |
| Queens | | | 081 |
| Richmond | | | 085 |
| Rockland | | | 087 |
| Westchester | | | 119 |
| **Newark, NJ (5640)** | | | |
| Essex | NJ | 34 | 013 |
| Morris | | | 027 |
| Sussex | | | 037 |
| Union | | | 039 |
| Warren | | | 041 |
| **Newburgh, NY-PA (5660)** | | | |
| Orange | NY | 36 | 071 |
| Pike | PA | 42 | 103 |
| **Norfolk-Virginia Beach-Newport News, VA-NC (5720)** | | | |
| Currituck | NC | 37 | 053 |
| Gloucester | VA | 51 | 073 |
| Isle of Wight | | | 093 |
| James City | | | 095 |
| Mathews | | | 115 |
| York | | | 199 |
| Chesapeake City | | | 550 |
| Hampton City | | | 650 |
| Newport News City | | | 700 |
| Norfolk City | | | 710 |
| Poquoson City | | | 735 |
| Portsmouth City | | | 740 |
| Suffolk City | | | 800 |

| MSA (MSA Code) County | | | FIPS Codes |
|---|---|---|---|
| **Norfolk-Virginia Beach-Newport News, VA-NC (5720) Cont.** | | | |
| Virginia Beach City | | | 810 |
| Williamsburg City | | | 830 |
| **Oakland, CA (5775)** | | | |
| Alameda | CA | 06 | 001 |
| Contra Costa | | | 013 |
| **Ocala, FL (5790)** | | | |
| Marion | FL | 12 | 083 |
| **Odessa-Midland, TX (5800)** | | | |
| Ector | TX | 48 | 135 |
| Midland | | | 329 |
| **Oklahoma City, OK (5880)** | | | |
| Canadian | OK | 40 | 017 |
| Cleveland | | | 027 |
| Logan | | | 083 |
| Mcclain | | | 087 |
| Oklahoma | | | 109 |
| Pottawatomie | | | 125 |
| **Olympia, WA (5910)** | | | |
| Thurston | WA | 53 | 067 |
| **Omaha, NE-IA (5920)** | | | |
| Pottawattamie | IA | 19 | 155 |
| Cass | NE | 31 | 025 |
| Douglas | | | 055 |
| Sarpy | | | 153 |
| Washington | | | 177 |
| **Orange County, CA (5945)** | | | |
| Orange | CA | 06 | 059 |
| **Orlando, FL (5960)** | | | |
| Lake | FL | 12 | 069 |
| Orange | | | 095 |
| Osceola | | | 097 |
| Seminole | | | 117 |
| **Owensboro, KY (5990)** | | | |
| Daviess | KY | 21 | 059 |
| **Panama City, FL (6015)** | | | |
| Bay | FL | 12 | 005 |

# MSA DEFINITIONS

| MSA (MSA Code) County | | | FIPS Codes |
|---|---|---|---|
| **Parkersburg-Marietta,WV-OH (6020)** | | | |
| Washington | OH | 39 | 167 |
| Wood | WV | 54 | 107 |
| **Pensacola, FL (6080)** | | | |
| Escambia | FL | 12 | 033 |
| Santa Rosa | | | 113 |
| **Peoria-Pekin, IL (6120)** | | | |
| Peoria | IL | 17 | 143 |
| Tazewell | | | 179 |
| Woodford | | | 203 |
| **Philadelphia, PA-NJ (6160)** | | | |
| Burlington | NJ | 34 | 005 |
| Camden | | | 007 |
| Gloucester | | | 015 |
| Salem | | | 033 |
| Bucks | PA | 42 | 017 |
| Chester | | | 029 |
| Delaware | | | 045 |
| Montgomery | | | 091 |
| Philadelphia | | | 101 |
| **Phoenix-Mesa, AZ (6200)** | | | |
| Maricopa | AZ | 04 | 013 |
| Pinal | | | 021 |
| **Pine Bluff, AR (6240)** | | | |
| Jefferson | AR | 05 | 069 |
| **Pittsburgh, PA (6280)** | | | |
| Allegheny | PA | 42 | 003 |
| Beaver | | | 007 |
| Butler | | | 019 |
| Fayette | | | 051 |
| Washington | | | 125 |
| Westmoreland | | | 129 |
| **Pittsfield, MA (6323)** | | | |
| Berkshire | MA | 25 | 003 |
| **Pocatello, ID (6340)** | | | |
| Bannock | ID | 16 | 005 |
| **Portland, ME (6403)** | | | |
| Cumberland | ME | 23 | 005 |

| MSA (MSA Code) County | | | FIPS Codes |
|---|---|---|---|
| **Portland-Vancouver, OR-WA (6440)** | | | |
| Clackamas | OR | 41 | 005 |
| Columbia | | | 009 |
| Multnomah | | | 051 |
| Washington | | | 067 |
| Yamhill | | | 071 |
| Clark | WA | 53 | 011 |
| **Providence-Warwick-Pawtucket, RI (6483)** | | | |
| Bristol | RI | 44 | 001 |
| Kent | | | 003 |
| Providence | | | 007 |
| Washington | | | 009 |
| **Provo-Orem, UT (6520)** | | | |
| Utah | UT | 49 | 049 |
| **Pueblo, CO (6560)** | | | |
| Pueblo | CO | 08 | 101 |
| **Punta Gorda, FL (6580)** | | | |
| Charlotte | FL | 12 | 015 |
| **Racine, WI (6600)** | | | |
| Racine | WI | 55 | 101 |
| **Raleigh-Durham-Chapel Hill, NC (6640)** | | | |
| Chatham | NC | 37 | 037 |
| Durham | | | 063 |
| Franklin | | | 069 |
| Johnston | | | 101 |
| Orange | | | 135 |
| Wake | | | 183 |
| **Rapid City, SD (6660)** | | | |
| Pennington | SD | 46 | 103 |
| **Reading, PA (6680)** | | | |
| Berks | PA | 42 | 011 |
| **Redding, CA (6690)** | | | |
| Shasta | CA | 06 | 089 |
| **Reno, NV (6720)** | | | |
| Washoe | NV | 32 | 031 |

# MSA DEFINITIONS

| MSA (MSA Code) County | | | FIPS Codes |
|---|---|---|---|
| **Richland-Kennewick-Pasco, WA (6740)** | | | |
| Benton | WA | 53 | 005 |
| Franklin | | | 021 |
| **Richmond-Petersburg, VA (6760)** | | | |
| Charles City | VA | 51 | 036 |
| Chesterfield | | | 041 |
| Dinwiddie | | | 053 |
| Goochland | | | 075 |
| Hanover | | | 085 |
| Henrico | | | 087 |
| New Kent | | | 127 |
| Powhatan | | | 145 |
| Prince George | | | 149 |
| Colonial Heights City | | | 570 |
| Hopewell City | | | 670 |
| Petersburg City | | | 730 |
| Richmond City | | | 760 |
| **Riverside-San Bernardino, CA (6780)** | | | |
| Riverside | CA | 06 | 065 |
| San Bernardino | | | 071 |
| **Roanoke, VA (6800)** | | | |
| Botetourt | VA | 51 | 023 |
| Roanoke | | | 161 |
| Roanoke City | | | 770 |
| Salem City | | | 775 |
| **Rochester, MN (6820)** | | | |
| Olmsted | MN | 27 | 109 |
| **Rochester, NY (6840)** | | | |
| Genesee | NY | 36 | 037 |
| Livingston | | | 051 |
| Monroe | | | 055 |
| Ontario | | | 069 |
| Orleans | | | 073 |
| Wayne | | | 117 |
| **Rockford, IL (6880)** | | | |
| Boone | IL | 17 | 007 |
| Ogle | | | 141 |
| Winnebago | | | 201 |

| MSA (MSA Code) County | | | FIPS Codes |
|---|---|---|---|
| **Rocky Mount, NC (6895)** | | | |
| Edgecombe | NC | 37 | 065 |
| Nash | | | 127 |
| **Sacramento, CA (6920)** | | | |
| El Dorado | CA | 06 | 017 |
| Placer | | | 061 |
| Sacramento | | | 067 |
| **Saginaw-Bay City-Midland, MI (6960)** | | | |
| Bay | MI | 26 | 017 |
| Midland | | | 111 |
| Saginaw | | | 145 |
| **St. Cloud, MN (6980)** | | | |
| Benton | MN | 27 | 009 |
| Stearns | | | 145 |
| **St. Joseph, MO (7000)** | | | |
| Andrew | MO | 29 | 003 |
| Buchanan | | | 021 |
| **St. Louis, MO-IL (7040)** | | | |
| Clinton | IL | 17 | 027 |
| Jersey | | | 083 |
| Madison | | | 119 |
| Monroe | | | 133 |
| St. Clair | | | 163 |
| Franklin | MO | 29 | 071 |
| Jefferson | | | 099 |
| Lincoln | | | 113 |
| St. Charles | | | 183 |
| St. Louis | | | 189 |
| Warren | | | 219 |
| St. Louis City | | | 510 |
| **Salem, OR (7080)** | | | |
| Marion | OR | 41 | 047 |
| Polk | | | 053 |
| **Salinas, CA (7120)** | | | |
| Monterey | CA | 06 | 053 |
| **Salt Lake City-Ogden, UT (7160)** | | | |
| Davis | UT | 49 | 011 |
| Salt Lake | | | 035 |
| Weber | | | 057 |

| MSA (MSA Code) County | | | FIPS Codes |
|---|---|---|---|
| **San Angelo, TX (7200)** | | | |
| Tom Green | TX | 48 | 451 |
| **San Antonio, TX (7240)** | | | |
| Bexar | TX | 48 | 029 |
| Comal | | | 091 |
| Guadalupe | | | 187 |
| Wilson | | | 493 |
| **San Diego, CA (7320)** | | | |
| San Diego | CA | 06 | 073 |
| **San Francisco, CA (7360)** | | | |
| Marin | CA | 06 | 041 |
| San Francisco | | | 075 |
| San Mateo | | | 081 |
| **San Jose, CA (7400)** | | | |
| Santa Clara | CA | 06 | 085 |
| **San Luis Obispo-Atascadero-Paso Robles, CA (7460)** | | | |
| San Luis Obispo | CA | 06 | 079 |
| **Santa Barbara-Santa Maria-Lompoc, CA (7480)** | | | |
| Santa Barbara | CA | 06 | 083 |
| **Santa Cruz-Watsonville, CA (7485)** | | | |
| Santa Cruz | CA | 06 | 087 |
| **Santa Fe, NM (7490)** | | | |
| Los Alamos | NM | 35 | 028 |
| Santa Fe | | | 049 |
| **Santa Rosa, CA (7500)** | | | |
| Sonoma | CA | 06 | 097 |
| **Sarasota-Bradenton, FL (7510)** | | | |
| Manatee | FL | 12 | 081 |
| Sarasota | | | 115 |
| **Savannah, GA (7520)** | | | |
| Bryan | GA | 13 | 029 |
| Chatham | | | 051 |
| Effingham | | | 103 |

| MSA (MSA Code) County | | | FIPS Codes |
|---|---|---|---|
| **Scranton-Wilkes-Barre-Hazleton, PA (7560)** | | | |
| Columbia | PA | 42 | 037 |
| Lackawanna | | | 069 |
| Luzerne | | | 079 |
| Wyoming | | | 131 |
| **Seattle-Bellevue-Everett, WA (7600)** | | | |
| Island | WA | 53 | 029 |
| King | | | 033 |
| Snohomish | | | 061 |
| **Sharon, PA (7610)** | | | |
| Mercer | PA | 42 | 085 |
| **Sheboygan, WI (7620)** | | | |
| Sheboygan | WI | 55 | 117 |
| **Sherman-Denison, TX (7640)** | | | |
| Grayson | TX | 48 | 181 |
| **Shreveport-Bossier City, LA (7680)** | | | |
| Bossier | LA | 22 | 015 |
| Caddo | | | 017 |
| Webster | | | 119 |
| **Sioux City, IA-NE (7720)** | | | |
| Woodbury | IA | 19 | 193 |
| Dakota | NE | 31 | 043 |
| **Sioux Falls, SD (7760)** | | | |
| Lincoln | SD | 46 | 083 |
| Minnehaha | | | 099 |
| **South Bend, IN (7800)** | | | |
| St. Joseph | IN | 18 | 141 |
| **Spokane, WA (7840)** | | | |
| Spokane | WA | 53 | 063 |
| **Springfield, IL (7880)** | | | |
| Menard | IL | 17 | 129 |
| Sangamon | | | 167 |
| **Springfield, MO (7920)** | | | |
| Christian | MO | 29 | 043 |
| Greene | | | 077 |
| Webster | | | 225 |

# MSA DEFINITIONS

| MSA (MSA Code) County | | | FIPS Codes |
|---|---|---|---|
| **Springfield, MA (8003)** | | | |
| Hampden | MA | 25 | 013 |
| Hampshire | | | 015 |
| **State College, PA (8050)** | | | |
| Centre | PA | 42 | 027 |
| **Steubenville-Weirton, OH-WV (8080)** | | | |
| Jefferson | OH | 39 | 081 |
| Brooke | WV | 54 | 009 |
| Hancock | | | 029 |
| **Stockton-Lodi, CA (8120)** | | | |
| San Joaquin | CA | 06 | 077 |
| **Sumter, SC (8140)** | | | |
| Sumter | SC | 45 | 085 |
| **Syracuse, NY (8160)** | | | |
| Cayuga | NY | 36 | 011 |
| Madison | | | 053 |
| Onondaga | | | 067 |
| Oswego | | | 075 |
| **Tacoma, WA (8200)** | | | |
| Pierce | WA | 53 | 053 |
| **Tallahassee, FL (8240)** | | | |
| Gadsden | FL | 12 | 039 |
| Leon | | | 073 |
| **Tampa-St. Petersburg-Clearwater, FL (8280)** | | | |
| Hernando | FL | 12 | 053 |
| Hillsborough | | | 057 |
| Pasco | | | 101 |
| Pinellas | | | 103 |
| **Terre Haute, IN (8320)** | | | |
| Clay | IN | 18 | 021 |
| Vermillion | | | 165 |
| Vigo | | | 167 |
| **Texarkana, TX-Texarkana, AR (8360)** | | | |
| Miller | AR | 05 | 091 |
| Bowie | TX | 48 | 037 |

| MSA (MSA Code) County | | | FIPS Codes |
|---|---|---|---|
| **Toledo, OH (8400)** | | | |
| Fulton | OH | 39 | 051 |
| Lucas | | | 095 |
| Wood | | | 173 |
| **Topeka, KS (8440)** | | | |
| Shawnee | KS | 20 | 177 |
| **Trenton, NJ (8480)** | | | |
| Mercer | NJ | 34 | 021 |
| **Tucson, AZ (8520)** | | | |
| Pima | AZ | 04 | 019 |
| **Tulsa, OK (8560)** | | | |
| Creek | OK | 40 | 037 |
| Osage | | | 113 |
| Rogers | | | 131 |
| Tulsa | | | 143 |
| Wagoner | | | 145 |
| **Tuscaloosa, AL (8600)** | | | |
| Tuscaloosa | AL | 01 | 125 |
| **Tyler, TX (8640)** | | | |
| Smith | TX | 48 | 423 |
| **Utica-Rome, NY (8680)** | | | |
| Herkimer | NY | 36 | 043 |
| Oneida | | | 065 |
| **Vallejo-Fairfield-Napa, CA (8720)** | | | |
| Napa | CA | 06 | 055 |
| Solano | | | 095 |
| **Ventura, CA (8735)** | | | |
| Ventura | CA | 06 | 111 |
| **Victoria, TX (8750)** | | | |
| Victoria | TX | 48 | 469 |
| **Vineland-Millville-Bridgeton, NJ (8760)** | | | |
| Cumberland | NJ | 34 | 011 |
| **Visalia-Tulare-Porterville, CA (8780)** | | | |
| Tulare | CA | 06 | 107 |

| MSA (MSA Code) County | | | FIPS Codes |
|---|---|---|---|
| **Waco, TX (8800)** | | | |
| Mclennan | TX | 48 | 309 |
| **Washington, DC-MD-VA-WV (8840)** | | | |
| District of Col. | DC | 11 | 001 |
| Calvert | MD | 24 | 009 |
| Charles | | | 017 |
| Frederick | | | 021 |
| Montgomery | | | 031 |
| Prince George's | | | 033 |
| Arlington | VA | 51 | 013 |
| Clarke | | | 043 |
| Culpeper | | | 047 |
| Fairfax | | | 059 |
| Fauquier | | | 061 |
| King George | | | 099 |
| Loudoun | | | 107 |
| Prince William | | | 153 |
| Spotsylvania | | | 177 |
| Stafford | | | 179 |
| Warren | | | 187 |
| Alexandria City | | | 510 |
| Fairfax City | | | 600 |
| Falls Church City | | | 610 |
| Fredericksburg City | | | 630 |
| Manassas City | | | 683 |
| Manassas Park City | | | 685 |
| Berkeley | WV | 54 | 003 |
| Jefferson | | | 037 |
| **Waterloo-Cedar Falls, IA (8920)** | | | |
| Black Hawk | IA | 19 | 013 |
| **Wausau, WI (8940)** | | | |
| Marathon | WI | 55 | 073 |
| **West Palm Beach-Boca Raton, FL (8960)** | | | |
| Palm Beach | FL | 12 | 099 |
| **Wheeling, WV-OH (9000)** | | | |
| Belmont | OH | 39 | 013 |
| Marshall | WV | 54 | 051 |
| Ohio | | | 069 |

| MSA (MSA Code) County | | | FIPS Codes |
|---|---|---|---|
| **Wichita, KS (9040)** | | | |
| Butler | KS | 20 | 015 |
| Harvey | | | 079 |
| Sedgwick | | | 173 |
| **Wichita Falls, TX (9080)** | | | |
| Archer | TX | 48 | 009 |
| Wichita | | | 485 |
| **Williamsport, PA (9140)** | | | |
| Lycoming | PA | 42 | 081 |
| **Wilmington-Newark, DE-MD (9160)** | | | |
| New Castle | DE | 10 | 003 |
| Cecil | MD | 24 | 015 |
| **Wilmington, NC (9200)** | | | |
| Brunswick | NC | 37 | 019 |
| New Hanover | | | 129 |
| **Yakima, WA (9260)** | | | |
| Yakima | WA | 53 | 077 |
| **Yolo, CA (9270)** | | | |
| Yolo | CA | 06 | 113 |
| **York, PA (9280)** | | | |
| York | PA | 42 | 133 |
| **Youngstown-Warren, OH (9320)** | | | |
| Columbiana | OH | 39 | 029 |
| Mahoning | | | 099 |
| Trumbull | | | 155 |
| **Yuba City, CA (9340)** | | | |
| Sutter | CA | 06 | 101 |
| Yuba | | | 115 |
| **Yuma, AZ (9360)** | | | |
| Yuma | AZ | 04 | 027 |

*APPENDIX IV* **DMA CODES**

# DMA CODES - ALPHABETICAL ORDER

| DMA NAME | DMA CODE |
|---|---|
| Abilene-Sweetwater | 662 |
| Albany, GA | 525 |
| Albany-Schenectady-Troy | 532 |
| Albuquerque-Santa Fe | 790 |
| Alexandria, LA | 644 |
| Alpena | 583 |
| Amarillo | 634 |
| Anchorage, AK | 743 |
| Atlanta | 524 |
| Augusta, GA | 520 |
| Austin | 635 |
| Bakersfield | 800 |
| Baltimore | 512 |
| Bangor | 537 |
| Baton Rouge | 716 |
| Beaumont-Port Arthur | 692 |
| Bend, OR | 821 |
| Billings | 756 |
| Biloxi-Gulfport | 746 |
| Binghamton | 502 |
| Birmingham (Anniston & Tuscaloosa), AL | 630 |
| Bluefield-Beckley-Oak Hill | 559 |
| Boise | 757 |
| Boston, MA (Manchester, NH) | 506 |
| Bowling Green | 736 |
| Buffalo | 514 |
| Burlington, VT-Plattsburgh, NY | 523 |
| Butte-Bozeman, MT | 754 |
| Casper-Riverton | 767 |
| Cedar Rapids- Waterloo & Dubuque, IA | 637 |
| Champaign & Springfield-Decatur, IL | 648 |
| Charleston, SC | 519 |
| Charleston-Huntington | 564 |
| Charlotte | 517 |
| Charlottesville | 584 |
| Chattanooga | 575 |
| Cheyenne, WY-Scottsbluff, NE | 759 |
| Chicago | 602 |
| Chico-Redding | 868 |
| Cincinnati | 515 |
| Clarksburg-Weston | 598 |
| Cleveland | 510 |
| Colorado Springs-Pueblo | 752 |
| Columbia, SC | 546 |
| Columbia-Jefferson City | 604 |
| Columbus, GA | 522 |
| Columbus, OH | 535 |
| Columbus-Tupelo-West Point | 673 |
| Corpus Christi | 600 |
| Dallas-Ft.Worth | 623 |
| Davenport, IA-Rock Island-Moline, IL | 682 |
| Dayton | 542 |
| Denver | 751 |
| Des Moines-Ames | 679 |
| Detroit | 505 |
| Dothan | 606 |
| Duluth, MN-Superior, WI | 676 |
| El Paso | 765 |
| Elmira | 565 |
| Erie | 516 |
| Eugene | 801 |
| Eureka | 802 |
| Evansville | 649 |
| Fairbanks | 745 |
| Fargo-Valley City | 724 |
| Flint-Saginaw-Bay City | 513 |
| Florence-Myrtle Beach, SC | 570 |
| Fresno-Visalia | 866 |
| Ft. Myers-Naples | 571 |
| Ft. Smith-Fayetteville-Springdale-Rogers | 670 |
| Ft. Wayne | 509 |
| Gainesville | 592 |
| Glendive | 798 |
| Grand Junction-Montrose | 773 |
| Grand Rapids-Kalamazoo-Battle Creek | 563 |
| Great Falls | 755 |
| Green Bay-Appleton | 658 |

# DMA CODES - ALPHABETICAL ORDER

| DMA NAME | DMA CODE |
|---|---|
| Greensboro-High Point-Winston Salem | 518 |
| Greenville-New Bern-Washington | 545 |
| Greenville-Spartanburg, SC-Asheville, NC-Anderson, SC | 567 |
| Greenwood-Greenville | 647 |
| Harlingen-Weslaco-Brownsville-McAllen | 636 |
| Harrisburg-Lancaster-Lebanon-York | 566 |
| Harrisonburg, VA | 569 |
| Hartford & New Haven, CT | 533 |
| Hattiesburg-Laurel | 710 |
| Helena | 766 |
| Honolulu | 744 |
| Houston | 618 |
| Huntsville-Decatur (Florence), AL | 691 |
| Idaho Falls-Pocatello | 758 |
| Indianapolis | 527 |
| Jackson, MS | 718 |
| Jackson, TN | 639 |
| Jacksonville, FL | 561 |
| Johnstown-Altoona | 574 |
| Jonesboro | 734 |
| Joplin, MO-Pittsburg, KS | 603 |
| Juneau, AK | 747 |
| Kansas City | 616 |
| Knoxville | 557 |
| La Crosse-Eau Claire | 702 |
| Lafayette, IN | 582 |
| Lafayette, LA | 642 |
| Lake Charles, LA | 643 |
| Lansing | 551 |
| Laredo | 749 |
| Las Vegas | 839 |
| Lexington | 541 |
| Lima | 558 |
| Lincoln & Hastings-Kearney, NE | 722 |
| Little Rock-Pine Bluff | 693 |
| Los Angeles | 803 |
| Louisville | 529 |

| DMA NAME | DMA CODE |
|---|---|
| Lubbock | 651 |
| Macon | 503 |
| Madison | 669 |
| Mankato | 737 |
| Marquette | 553 |
| Medford-Klamath Falls | 813 |
| Memphis | 640 |
| Meridian | 711 |
| Miami-Ft. Lauderdale | 528 |
| Milwaukee | 617 |
| Minneapolis-St. Paul | 613 |
| Minot-Bismarck-Dickinson (Williston), ND | 687 |
| Missoula | 762 |
| Mobile, AL-Pensacola (Ft. Walton Beach), FL | 686 |
| Monroe, LA-El Dorado, AR | 628 |
| Monterey-Salinas | 828 |
| Montgomery (Selma), AL | 698 |
| Nashville | 659 |
| New Orleans | 622 |
| New York | 501 |
| Norfolk-Portsmouth-Newport News | 544 |
| North Platte | 740 |
| Odessa-Midland | 633 |
| Oklahoma City | 650 |
| Omaha | 652 |
| Orlando-Daytona Beach-Melbourne | 534 |
| Ottumwa, IA-Kirksville, MO | 631 |
| Paducah, KY-Cape Girardeau, MO-Harrisburg-Mt. Vernon, IL | 632 |
| Palm Springs | 804 |
| Panama City | 656 |
| Parkersburg, WV | 597 |
| Peoria-Bloomington | 675 |
| Philadelphia | 504 |
| Phoenix | 753 |
| Pittsburgh | 508 |
| Portland, OR | 820 |
| Portland-Auburn | 500 |

# DMA CODES - ALPHABETICAL ORDER

| DMA NAME | DMA CODE |
|---|---|
| Presque Isle | 552 |
| Providence, RI- New Bedford, MA | 521 |
| Quincy, IL-Hannibal, MO-<br>Keokuk, IA | 717 |
| Raleigh-Durham (Fayetteville), NC | 560 |
| Rapid City | 764 |
| Reno | 811 |
| Richmond-Petersburg | 556 |
| Roanoke-Lynchburg | 573 |
| Rochester, MN-Mason City, IA-<br>Austin, MN | 611 |
| Rochester, NY | 538 |
| Rockford | 610 |
| Sacramento-Stockton-Modesto | 862 |
| Salisbury | 576 |
| Salt Lake City | 770 |
| San Angelo | 661 |
| San Antonio | 641 |
| San Diego | 825 |
| San Francisco-Oakland-San Jose | 807 |
| Santa Barbara-Santa Maria-<br>San Luis Obispo | 855 |
| Savannah | 507 |
| Seattle-Tacoma | 819 |
| Sherman, TX -Ada, OK | 657 |
| Shreveport | 612 |
| Sioux City | 624 |
| Sioux Falls (Mitchell), SD | 725 |
| South Bend-Elkhart | 588 |
| Spokane | 881 |
| Springfield, MO | 619 |
| Springfield-Holyoke, MA | 543 |
| St. Joseph, MO | 638 |
| St. Louis | 609 |
| Syracuse | 555 |
| Tallahassee, FL-Thomasville, GA | 530 |
| Tampa-St. Petersburg<br>(Sarasota), FL | 539 |
| Terre Haute | 581 |
| Toledo | 547 |
| Topeka | 605 |
| Traverse City-Cadillac | 540 |

| DMA NAME | DMA CODE |
|---|---|
| Tri-Cities, TN-VA | 531 |
| Tucson (Sierra Vista), AZ | 789 |
| Tulsa | 671 |
| Twin Falls | 760 |
| Tyler-Longview (Lufkin &<br>Nacogdoches), TX | 709 |
| Utica | 526 |
| Victoria | 626 |
| Waco-Temple-Bryan | 625 |
| Washington, DC (Hagerstown MD) | 511 |
| Watertown | 549 |
| Wausau-Rhinelander | 705 |
| West Palm Beach-Fort Pierce | 548 |
| Wheeling, WV-Steubenville, OH | 554 |
| Wichita Falls, TX &<br>Lawton, OK | 627 |
| Wichita-Hutchinson, KS Plus | 678 |
| Wilkes Barre-Scranton | 577 |
| Wilmington, NC | 550 |
| Yakima-Pasco-Richland-<br>Kennewick | 810 |
| Youngstown | 536 |
| Yuma, AZ-El Centro, CA | 771 |
| Zanesville | 596 |

# DMA CODES - NUMERICAL ORDER

| DMA NAME | DMA CODE |
|---|---|
| Portland-Auburn | 500 |
| New York | 501 |
| Binghamton | 502 |
| Macon | 503 |
| Philadelphia | 504 |
| Detroit | 505 |
| Boston, MA (Manchester, NH) | 506 |
| Savannah | 507 |
| Pittsburgh | 508 |
| Ft. Wayne | 509 |
| Cleveland | 510 |
| Washington, DC (Hagerstown MD) | 511 |
| Baltimore | 512 |
| Flint-Saginaw-Bay City | 513 |
| Buffalo | 514 |
| Cincinnati | 515 |
| Erie | 516 |
| Charlotte | 517 |
| Greensboro-High Point-Winston Salem | 518 |
| Charleston, SC | 519 |
| Augusta, GA | 520 |
| Providence, RI-New Bedford, MA | 521 |
| Columbus, GA | 522 |
| Burlington, VT-Plattsburgh, NY | 523 |
| Atlanta | 524 |
| Albany, GA | 525 |
| Utica | 526 |
| Indianapolis | 527 |
| Miami-Ft. Lauderdale | 528 |
| Louisville | 529 |
| Tallahassee, FL-Thomasville, GA | 530 |
| Tri-Cities, TN-VA | 531 |
| Albany-Schenectady-Troy | 532 |
| Hartford & New Haven, CT | 533 |
| Orlando-Daytona Beach-Melbourne | 534 |
| Columbus, OH | 535 |
| Youngstown | 536 |
| Bangor | 537 |
| Rochester, NY | 538 |

| DMA NAME | DMA CODE |
|---|---|
| Tampa-St. Petersburg (Sarasota), FL | 539 |
| Traverse City-Cadillac | 540 |
| Lexington | 541 |
| Dayton | 542 |
| Springfield-Holyoke, MA | 543 |
| Norfolk-Portsmouth-Newport News | 544 |
| Greenville-New Bern-Washington | 545 |
| Columbia, SC | 546 |
| Toledo | 547 |
| West Palm Beach-Fort Pierce | 548 |
| Watertown | 549 |
| Wilmington, NC | 550 |
| Lansing | 551 |
| Presque Isle | 552 |
| Marquette | 553 |
| Wheeling, WV-Steubenville, OH | 554 |
| Syracuse | 555 |
| Richmond-Petersburg | 556 |
| Knoxville | 557 |
| Lima | 558 |
| Bluefield-Beckley-Oak Hill | 559 |
| Raleigh-Durham (Fayetteville), NC | 560 |
| Jacksonville, FL | 561 |
| Grand Rapids-Kalamazoo-Battle Creek | 563 |
| Charleston-Huntington | 564 |
| Elmira | 565 |
| Harrisburg-Lancaster-Lebanon-York | 566 |
| Greenville-Spartanburg, SC-Asheville, NC-Anderson, SC | 567 |
| Harrisonburg, VA | 569 |
| Florence-Myrtle Beach, SC | 570 |
| Ft. Myers-Naples | 571 |
| Roanoke-Lynchburg | 573 |
| Johnstown-Altoona | 574 |
| Chattanooga | 575 |
| Salisbury | 576 |
| Wilkes Barre-Scranton | 577 |
| Terre Haute | 581 |

# DMA CODES - NUMERICAL ORDER

| DMA NAME | DMA CODE |
|---|---|
| Lafayette, IN | 582 |
| Alpena | 583 |
| Charlottesville | 584 |
| South Bend-Elkhart | 588 |
| Gainesville | 592 |
| Zanesville | 596 |
| Parkersburg, WV | 597 |
| Clarksburg-Weston | 598 |
| Corpus Christi | 600 |
| Chicago | 602 |
| Joplin, MO-Pittsburg, KS | 603 |
| Columbia-Jefferson City | 604 |
| Topeka | 605 |
| Dothan | 606 |
| St. Louis | 609 |
| Rockford | 610 |
| Rochester, MN-Mason City, IA-Austin, MN | 611 |
| Shreveport | 612 |
| Minneapolis-St. Paul | 613 |
| Kansas City | 616 |
| Milwaukee | 617 |
| Houston | 618 |
| Springfield, MO | 619 |
| New Orleans | 622 |
| Dallas-Ft. Worth | 623 |
| Sioux City | 624 |
| Waco-Temple-Bryan | 625 |
| Victoria | 626 |
| Wichita Falls, TX & Lawton, OK | 627 |
| Monroe, LA-El Dorado, AR | 628 |
| Birmingham (Anniston & Tuscaloosa), AL | 630 |
| Ottumwa, IA-Kirksville, MO | 631 |
| Paducah, KY-Cape Girardeau, MO-Harrisburg-Mt. Vernon, IL | 632 |
| Odessa-Midland | 633 |
| Amarillo | 634 |
| Austin | 635 |
| Harlingen-Weslaco-Brownsville-McAllen | 636 |
| Cedar Rapids-Waterloo & Dubuque, IA | 637 |
| St. Joseph, MO | 638 |
| Jackson, TN | 639 |
| Memphis | 640 |
| San Antonio | 641 |
| Lafayette, LA | 642 |
| Lake Charles, LA | 643 |
| Alexandria, LA | 644 |
| Greenwood-Greenville | 647 |
| Champaign & Springfield-Decatur, IL | 648 |
| Evansville | 649 |
| Oklahoma City | 650 |
| Lubbock | 651 |
| Omaha | 652 |
| Panama City | 656 |
| Sherman, TX -Ada, OK | 657 |
| Green Bay-Appleton | 658 |
| Nashville | 659 |
| San Angelo | 661 |
| Abilene-Sweetwater | 662 |
| Madison | 669 |
| Ft. Smith-Fayetteville-Springdale-Rogers | 670 |
| Tulsa | 671 |
| Columbus-Tupelo-West Point | 673 |
| Peoria-Bloomington | 675 |
| Duluth, MN-Superior, WI | 676 |
| Wichita-Hutchinson, KS Plus | 678 |
| Des Moines-Ames | 679 |
| Davenport, IA-Rock Island-Moline, IL | 682 |
| Mobile, AL-Pensacola (FT. Walton Beach), FL | 686 |
| Minot-Bismarck-Dickinson (Williston), ND | 687 |
| Huntsville-Decatur (Florence), AL | 691 |
| Beaumont-Port Arthur | 692 |
| Little Rock-Pine Bluff | 693 |
| Montgomery (Selma), AL | 698 |

# DMA CODES - NUMERICAL ORDER

| DMA NAME | DMA CODE |
|---|---|
| La Crosse-Eau Claire | 702 |
| Wausau-Rhinelander | 705 |
| Tyler-Longview (Lufkin & Nacogdoches), TX | 709 |
| Hattiesburg-Laurel | 710 |
| Meridian | 711 |
| Baton Rouge | 716 |
| Quincy, IL-Hannibal, MO-Keokuk, IA | 717 |
| Jackson, MS | 718 |
| Lincoln & Hastings-Kearney, NE | 722 |
| Fargo-Valley City | 724 |
| Sioux Falls (Mitchell), SD | 725 |
| Jonesboro | 734 |
| Bowling Green | 736 |
| Mankato | 737 |
| North Platte | 740 |
| Anchorage, AK | 743 |
| Honolulu | 744 |
| Fairbanks | 745 |
| Biloxi-Gulfport | 746 |
| Juneau, AK | 747 |
| Laredo | 749 |
| Denver | 751 |
| Colorado Springs-Pueblo | 752 |
| Phoenix | 753 |
| Butte-Bozeman, MT | 754 |
| Great Falls | 755 |
| Billings | 756 |
| Boise | 757 |
| Idaho Falls-Pocatello | 758 |
| Cheyenne, WY-Scottsbluff, NE | 759 |
| Twin Falls | 760 |
| Missoula | 762 |
| Rapid City | 764 |
| El Paso | 765 |
| Helena | 766 |
| Casper-Riverton | 767 |
| Salt Lake City | 770 |
| Yuma, AZ-El Centro, CA | 771 |
| Grand Junction-Montrose | 773 |
| Tucson (Sierra Vista), AZ | 789 |

| DMA NAME | DMA CODE |
|---|---|
| Albuquerque-Santa Fe | 790 |
| Glendive | 798 |
| Bakersfield | 800 |
| Eugene | 801 |
| Eureka | 802 |
| Los Angeles | 803 |
| Palm Springs | 804 |
| San Francisco-Oakland-San Jose | 807 |
| Yakima-Pasco-Richland-Kennewick | 810 |
| Reno | 811 |
| Medford-Klamath Falls | 813 |
| Seattle-Tacoma | 819 |
| Portland, OR | 820 |
| Bend, OR | 821 |
| San Diego | 825 |
| Monterey-Salinas | 828 |
| Las Vegas | 839 |
| Santa Barbara-Santa Maria-San Luis Obispo | 855 |
| Sacramento-Stockton-Modesto | 862 |
| Fresno-Visalia | 866 |
| Chico-Redding | 868 |
| Spokane | 881 |

*APPENDIX V*

# DMA DEFINITIONS

COUNTY

13th **EDITION**

# DMA DEFINITIONS

| DMA (DMA Code) County | | | FIPS Codes |
|---|---|---|---|
| **Abilene-Sweetwater (662)** | | | |
| Brown | TX | 48 | 049 |
| Callahan | | | 059 |
| Coleman | | | 083 |
| Eastland | | | 133 |
| Fisher | | | 151 |
| Haskell | | | 207 |
| Jones | | | 253 |
| Knox | | | 275 |
| Mitchell | | | 335 |
| Nolan | | | 353 |
| Runnels | | | 399 |
| Shackelford | | | 417 |
| Stephens | | | 429 |
| Stonewall | | | 433 |
| Taylor | | | 441 |
| **Albany, GA (525)** | | | |
| Atkinson | GA | 13 | 003 |
| Baker | | | 007 |
| Ben Hill | | | 017 |
| Berrien | | | 019 |
| Calhoun | | | 037 |
| Coffee | | | 069 |
| Colquitt | | | 071 |
| Cook | | | 075 |
| Crisp | | | 081 |
| Dougherty | | | 095 |
| Irwin | | | 155 |
| Lee | | | 177 |
| Mitchell | | | 205 |
| Terrell | | | 273 |
| Tift | | | 277 |
| Turner | | | 287 |
| Worth | | | 321 |
| **Albany-Schenectady-Troy (532)** | | | |
| Berkshire | MA | 25 | 003 |
| Albany | NY | 36 | 001 |
| Columbia | | | 021 |
| Fulton | | | 035 |
| Greene | | | 039 |
| Hamilton | | | 041 |
| Montgomery | | | 057 |
| Rensselaer | | | 083 |
| Saratoga | | | 091 |
| Schenectady | | | 093 |
| Schoharie | | | 095 |
| Warren | | | 113 |

| DMA (DMA Code) County | | | FIPS Codes |
|---|---|---|---|
| **Albany-Schenectady-Troy (532) Cont.** | | | |
| Washington | | | 115 |
| Bennington | VT | 50 | 003 |
| **Albuquerque-Santa Fe (790)** | | | |
| Apache | AZ | 04 | 001 |
| Conejos | CO | 08 | 021 |
| Costilla | | | 023 |
| La Plata | | | 067 |
| Montezuma | | | 083 |
| Bernalillo | NM | 35 | 001 |
| Catron | | | 003 |
| Chaves | | | 005 |
| Cibola | | | 006 |
| Colfax | | | 007 |
| De Baca | | | 011 |
| Eddy | | | 015 |
| Grant | | | 017 |
| Guadalupe | | | 019 |
| Harding | | | 021 |
| Hidalgo | | | 023 |
| Lea | | | 025 |
| Lincoln | | | 027 |
| Los Alamos | | | 028 |
| Luna | | | 029 |
| McKinley | | | 031 |
| Mora | | | 033 |
| Otero | | | 035 |
| Rio Arriba | | | 039 |
| Sandoval | | | 043 |
| San Juan | | | 045 |
| San Miguel | | | 047 |
| Santa Fe | | | 049 |
| Sierra | | | 051 |
| Socorro | | | 053 |
| Taos | | | 055 |
| Torrance | | | 057 |
| Valencia | | | 061 |
| **Alexandria, LA (644)** | | | |
| Avoyelles | LA | 22 | 009 |
| Grant | | | 043 |
| Rapides | | | 079 |
| Vernon | | | 115 |
| **Alpena (583)** | | | |
| Alcona | MI | 26 | 001 |
| Alpena | | | 007 |

| DMA (DMA Code) County | | | FIPS Codes |
|---|---|---|---|
| **Amarillo (634)** | | | |
| Morton | KS | 20 | 129 |
| Curry | NM | 35 | 009 |
| Quay | | | 037 |
| Roosevelt | | | 041 |
| Union | | | 059 |
| Beaver | OK | 40 | 007 |
| Cimarron | | | 025 |
| Texas | | | 139 |
| Armstrong | TX | 48 | 011 |
| Briscoe | | | 045 |
| Carson | | | 065 |
| Castro | | | 069 |
| Childress | | | 075 |
| Collingsworth | | | 087 |
| Cottle | | | 101 |
| Dallam | | | 111 |
| Deaf Smith | | | 117 |
| Donley | | | 129 |
| Gray | | | 179 |
| Hall | | | 191 |
| Hansford | | | 195 |
| Hartley | | | 205 |
| Hemphill | | | 211 |
| Hutchinson | | | 233 |
| Lipscomb | | | 295 |
| Moore | | | 341 |
| Ochiltree | | | 357 |
| Oldham | | | 359 |
| Parmer | | | 369 |
| Potter | | | 375 |
| Randall | | | 381 |
| Roberts | | | 393 |
| Sherman | | | 421 |
| Swisher | | | 437 |
| Wheeler | | | 483 |
| **Anchorage, AK (743)** | | | |
| Anchorage | AK | 02 | 020 |
| Kenai Peninsula | | | 122 |
| Matanuska-Susitna | | | 170 |
| **Atlanta (524)** | | | |
| Cleburne | AL | 01 | 029 |
| Randolph | | | 111 |
| Banks | GA | 13 | 011 |
| Barrow | | | 013 |
| Bartow | | | 015 |

| DMA (DMA Code) County | | | FIPS Codes |
|---|---|---|---|
| **Atlanta (524) Cont.** | | | |
| Butts | | | 035 |
| Carroll | | | 045 |
| Cherokee | | | 057 |
| Clarke | | | 059 |
| Clayton | | | 063 |
| Cobb | | | 067 |
| Coweta | | | 077 |
| Dawson | | | 085 |
| DeKalb | | | 089 |
| Douglas | | | 097 |
| Fayette | | | 113 |
| Floyd | | | 115 |
| Forsyth | | | 117 |
| Fulton | | | 121 |
| Gilmer | | | 123 |
| Gordon | | | 129 |
| Greene | | | 133 |
| Gwinnett | | | 135 |
| Habersham | | | 137 |
| Hall | | | 139 |
| Haralson | | | 143 |
| Heard | | | 149 |
| Henry | | | 151 |
| Jackson | | | 157 |
| Jasper | | | 159 |
| Lamar | | | 171 |
| Lumpkin | | | 187 |
| Meriwether | | | 199 |
| Morgan | | | 211 |
| Newton | | | 217 |
| Oconee | | | 219 |
| Paulding | | | 223 |
| Oglethorpe | | | 221 |
| Pickens | | | 227 |
| Pike | | | 231 |
| Polk | | | 233 |
| Putnam | | | 237 |
| Rabun | | | 241 |
| Rockdale | | | 247 |
| Spalding | | | 255 |
| Towns | | | 281 |
| Troup | | | 285 |
| Union | | | 291 |
| Upson | | | 293 |
| Walton | | | 297 |
| White | | | 311 |
| Clay | NC | 37 | 043 |

# DMA DEFINITIONS

| DMA (DMA Code) County | | | FIPS Codes |
|---|---|---|---|
| **Augusta, GA (520)** | | | |
| Burke | GA | 13 | 033 |
| Columbia | | | 073 |
| Emanuel | | | 107 |
| Glascock | | | 125 |
| Jefferson | | | 163 |
| Jenkins | | | 165 |
| Lincoln | | | 181 |
| McDuffie | | | 189 |
| Richmond | | | 245 |
| Taliaferro | | | 265 |
| Warren | | | 301 |
| Wilkes | | | 317 |
| Aiken | SC | 45 | 003 |
| Allendale | | | 005 |
| Bamberg | | | 009 |
| Barnwell | | | 011 |
| Edgefield | | | 037 |
| McCormick | | | 065 |
| Saluda | | | 081 |
| **Austin (635)** | | | |
| Bastrop | TX | 48 | 021 |
| Blanco | | | 031 |
| Burnet | | | 053 |
| Caldwell | | | 055 |
| Fayette | | | 149 |
| Hays | | | 209 |
| Lee | | | 287 |
| Llano | | | 299 |
| Mason | | | 319 |
| Travis | | | 453 |
| Williamson | | | 491 |
| **Bakersfield (800)** | | | |
| Kern | CA | 06 | 029 |
| **Baltimore (512)** | | | |
| Anne Arundel | MD | 24 | 003 |
| Baltimore | | | 005 |
| Caroline | | | 011 |
| Carroll | | | 013 |
| Cecil | | | 015 |
| Dorchester | | | 019 |
| Harford | | | 025 |
| Howard | | | 027 |
| Kent | | | 029 |
| Queen Anne's | | | 035 |

| DMA (DMA Code) County | | | FIPS Codes |
|---|---|---|---|
| **Baltimore (512) Cont.** | | | |
| Talbot | | | 041 |
| Baltimore City | | | 510 |
| **Bangor (537)** | | | |
| Hancock | ME | 23 | 009 |
| Penobscot | | | 019 |
| Piscataquis | | | 021 |
| Somerset | | | 025 |
| Waldo | | | 027 |
| Washington | | | 029 |
| **Baton Rouge (716)** | | | |
| Ascension | LA | 22 | 005 |
| Assumption | | | 007 |
| East Baton Rouge | | | 033 |
| East Feliciana | | | 037 |
| Iberville | | | 047 |
| Livingston | | | 063 |
| Pointe Coupee | | | 077 |
| St. Helena | | | 091 |
| St. Mary | | | 101 |
| West Baton Rouge | | | 121 |
| West Feliciana | | | 125 |
| Amite | MS | 28 | 005 |
| Wilkinson | | | 157 |
| **Beaumont-Port Arthur (692)** | | | |
| Hardin | TX | 48 | 199 |
| Jasper | | | 241 |
| Jefferson | | | 245 |
| Newton | | | 351 |
| Orange | | | 361 |
| Tyler | | | 457 |
| **Bend, OR (821)** | | | |
| Deschutes | OR | 41 | 017 |
| **Billings (756)** | | | |
| Big Horn | MT | 30 | 003 |
| Carbon | | | 009 |
| Custer | | | 017 |
| Garfield | | | 033 |
| Golden Valley | | | 037 |
| Meagher | | | 059 |
| Musselshell | | | 065 |
| Park | | | 067 |
| Petroleum | | | 069 |

| DMA (DMA Code) County | | | FIPS Codes |
|---|---|---|---|
| **Billings (756) Cont.** | | | |
| Powder River | | | 075 |
| Rosebud | | | 087 |
| Stillwater | | | 095 |
| Sweet Grass | | | 097 |
| Treasure | | | 103 |
| Wheatland | | | 107 |
| Yellowstone | | | 111 |
| Yellowstone Natl Park | | | 113 |
| Big Horn | WY | 56 | 003 |
| Park | | | 029 |
| **Biloxi-Gulfport (746)** | | | |
| Harrison | MS | 28 | 047 |
| Jackson | | | 059 |
| Stone | | | 131 |
| **Binghamton (502)** | | | |
| Broome | NY | 36 | 007 |
| Chenango | | | 017 |
| Delaware | | | 025 |
| Tioga | | | 107 |
| **Birmingham (Anniston & Tuscaloosa), AL (630)** | | | |
| Bibb | AL | 01 | 007 |
| Blount | | | 009 |
| Calhoun | | | 015 |
| Cherokee | | | 019 |
| Chilton | | | 021 |
| Clarke | | | 025 |
| Clay | | | 027 |
| Cullman | | | 043 |
| Etowah | | | 055 |
| Fayette | | | 057 |
| Greene | | | 063 |
| Hale | | | 065 |
| Jefferson | | | 073 |
| Marion | | | 093 |
| Pickens | | | 107 |
| St. Clair | | | 115 |
| Shelby | | | 117 |
| Talladega | | | 121 |
| Walker | | | 127 |
| Winston | | | 133 |

| DMA (DMA Code) County | | | FIPS Codes |
|---|---|---|---|
| **Bluefield-Beckley-Oak Hill (559)** | | | |
| Bland | VA | 51 | 021 |
| Tazewell | | | 185 |
| Fayette | WV | 54 | 019 |
| Greenbrier | | | 025 |
| McDowell | | | 047 |
| Mercer | | | 055 |
| Monroe | | | 063 |
| Raleigh | | | 081 |
| Summers | | | 089 |
| Wyoming | | | 109 |
| **Boise (757)** | | | |
| Ada | ID | 16 | 001 |
| Adams | | | 003 |
| Boise | | | 015 |
| Camas | | | 025 |
| Canyon | | | 027 |
| Elmore | | | 039 |
| Gem | | | 045 |
| Owyhee | | | 073 |
| Payette | | | 075 |
| Valley | | | 085 |
| Washington | | | 087 |
| Grant | OR | 41 | 023 |
| Malheur | | | 045 |
| **Boston, MA (Manchester, NH) (506)** | | | |
| Barnstable | MA | 25 | 001 |
| Dukes | | | 007 |
| Essex | | | 009 |
| Middlesex | | | 017 |
| Nantucket | | | 019 |
| Norfolk | | | 021 |
| Plymouth | | | 023 |
| Suffolk | | | 025 |
| Worcester | | | 027 |
| Belknap | NH | 33 | 001 |
| Cheshire | | | 005 |
| Hillsborough | | | 011 |
| Merrimack | | | 013 |
| Rockingham | | | 015 |
| Strafford | | | 017 |
| Windham | VT | 50 | 025 |

# DMA DEFINITIONS

| DMA (DMA Code) County | | | FIPS Codes |
|---|---|---|---|
| **Bowling Green (736)** | | | |
| Adair | KY | 21 | 001 |
| Barren | | | 009 |
| Butler | | | 031 |
| Cumberland | | | 057 |
| Edmonson | | | 061 |
| Hart | | | 099 |
| Metcalfe | | | 169 |
| Warren | | | 227 |
| **Buffalo (514)** | | | |
| Allegany | NY | 36 | 003 |
| Cattaraugus | | | 009 |
| Chautauqua | | | 013 |
| Erie | | | 029 |
| Genesee | | | 037 |
| Niagara | | | 063 |
| Orleans | | | 073 |
| Wyoming | | | 121 |
| McKean | PA | 42 | 083 |
| Potter | | | 105 |
| **Burlington, VT-Plattsburgh, NY (523)** | | | |
| Grafton | NH | 33 | 009 |
| Sullivan | | | 019 |
| Clinton | NY | 36 | 019 |
| Essex | | | 031 |
| Franklin | | | 033 |
| Addison | VT | 50 | 001 |
| Caledonia | | | 005 |
| Chittenden | | | 007 |
| Essex | | | 009 |
| Franklin | | | 011 |
| Grand Isle | | | 013 |
| Lamoille | | | 015 |
| Orange | | | 017 |
| Orleans | | | 019 |
| Rutland | | | 021 |
| Washington | | | 023 |
| Windsor | | | 027 |
| **Butte-Bozeman, MT (754)** | | | |
| Beaverhead | MT | 30 | 001 |
| Broadwater | | | 007 |
| Deer Lodge | | | 023 |
| Gallatin | | | 031 |
| Jefferson | | | 043 |
| Madison | | | 057 |

| DMA (DMA Code) County | | | FIPS Codes |
|---|---|---|---|
| **Butte-Bozeman, MT (754) Cont.** | | | |
| Powell | | | 077 |
| Silver Bow | | | 093 |
| **Casper-Riverton (767)** | | | |
| Converse | WY | 56 | 009 |
| Fremont | | | 013 |
| Hot Springs | | | 017 |
| Natrona | | | 025 |
| Washakie | | | 043 |
| **Cedar Rapids-Waterloo & Dubuque, IA (637)** | | | |
| Allamakee | IA | 19 | 005 |
| Benton | | | 011 |
| Black Hawk | | | 013 |
| Bremer | | | 017 |
| Buchanan | | | 019 |
| Butler | | | 023 |
| Chickasaw | | | 037 |
| Clayton | | | 043 |
| Delaware | | | 055 |
| Dubuque | | | 061 |
| Fayette | | | 065 |
| Grundy | | | 075 |
| Iowa | | | 095 |
| Johnson | | | 103 |
| Jones | | | 105 |
| Keokuk | | | 107 |
| Linn | | | 113 |
| Tama | | | 171 |
| Washington | | | 183 |
| Winneshiek | | | 191 |
| Crawford | WI | 55 | 023 |
| **Champaign & Springfield-Decatur, IL (648)** | | | |
| Champaign | IL | 17 | 019 |
| Christian | | | 021 |
| Coles | | | 029 |
| Cumberland | | | 035 |
| De Witt | | | 039 |
| Douglas | | | 041 |
| Effingham | | | 049 |
| Ford | | | 053 |
| Iroquois | | | 075 |
| Logan | | | 107 |
| Macon | | | 115 |

| DMA (DMA Code) County | | | FIPS Codes |
|---|---|---|---|
| **Champaign & Springfield-Decatur, IL (648) Cont.** | | | |
| Menard | | | 129 |
| Morgan | | | 137 |
| Moultrie | | | 139 |
| Piatt | | | 147 |
| Sangamon | | | 167 |
| Shelby | | | 173 |
| Vermilion | | | 183 |
| **Charleston, SC (519)** | | | |
| Berkeley | SC | 45 | 015 |
| Charleston | | | 019 |
| Colleton | | | 029 |
| Dorchester | | | 035 |
| Georgetown | | | 043 |
| Williamsburg | | | 089 |
| **Charleston-Huntington (564)** | | | |
| Boyd | KY | 21 | 019 |
| Carter | | | 043 |
| Elliott | | | 063 |
| Floyd | | | 071 |
| Greenup | | | 089 |
| Johnson | | | 115 |
| Lawrence | | | 127 |
| Lewis | | | 135 |
| Magoffin | | | 153 |
| Martin | | | 159 |
| Pike | | | 195 |
| Athens | OH | 39 | 009 |
| Gallia | | | 053 |
| Jackson | | | 079 |
| Lawrence | | | 087 |
| Meigs | | | 105 |
| Scioto | | | 145 |
| Vinton | | | 163 |
| Boone | WV | 54 | 005 |
| Braxton | | | 007 |
| Cabell | | | 011 |
| Calhoun | | | 013 |
| Clay | | | 015 |
| Jackson | | | 035 |
| Kanawha | | | 039 |
| Lincoln | | | 043 |
| Logan | | | 045 |
| Mason | | | 053 |
| Mingo | | | 059 |

| DMA (DMA Code) County | | | FIPS Codes |
|---|---|---|---|
| **Charleston-Huntington (564) Cont.** | | | |
| Nicholas | | | 067 |
| Putnam | | | 079 |
| Roane | | | 087 |
| Wayne | | | 099 |
| Wirt | | | 105 |
| **Charlotte (517)** | | | |
| Alexander | NC | 37 | 003 |
| Anson | | | 007 |
| Ashe | | | 009 |
| Avery | | | 011 |
| Burke | | | 023 |
| Cabarrus | | | 025 |
| Caldwell | | | 027 |
| Catawba | | | 035 |
| Cleveland | | | 045 |
| Gaston | | | 071 |
| Iredell | | | 097 |
| Lincoln | | | 109 |
| Mecklenburg | | | 119 |
| Richmond | | | 153 |
| Rowan | | | 159 |
| Stanly | | | 167 |
| Union | | | 179 |
| Watauga | | | 189 |
| Chester | SC | 45 | 023 |
| Chesterfield | | | 025 |
| Lancaster | | | 057 |
| York | | | 091 |
| **Charlottesville (584)** | | | |
| Albemarle | VA | 51 | 003 |
| Greene | | | 079 |
| Madison | | | 113 |
| Charlottesville City | | | 540 |
| **Chattanooga (575)** | | | |
| Catoosa | GA | 13 | 047 |
| Chattooga | | | 055 |
| Dade | | | 083 |
| Fannin | | | 111 |
| Murray | | | 213 |
| Walker | | | 295 |
| Whitfield | | | 313 |
| Cherokee | NC | 37 | 039 |
| Bledsoe | TN | 47 | 007 |
| Bradley | | | 011 |

# DMA DEFINITIONS

| DMA (DMA Code) County | | | FIPS Codes |
|---|---|---|---|
| **Chattanooga (575) Cont.** | | | |
| Grundy | | | 061 |
| Hamilton | | | 065 |
| McMinn | | | 107 |
| Marion | | | 115 |
| Meigs | | | 121 |
| Polk | | | 139 |
| Rhea | | | 143 |
| Sequatchie | | | 153 |
| **Cheyenne, WY-Scottsbluff, NE (759)** | | | |
| Scotts Bluff | NE | 31 | 157 |
| Goshen | WY | 56 | 015 |
| Laramie | | | 021 |
| **Chicago (602)** | | | |
| Cook | IL | 17 | 031 |
| DeKalb | | | 037 |
| DuPage | | | 043 |
| Grundy | | | 063 |
| Kane | | | 089 |
| Kankakee | | | 091 |
| Kendall | | | 093 |
| Lake | | | 097 |
| La Salle | | | 099 |
| McHenry | | | 111 |
| Will | | | 197 |
| Jasper | IN | 18 | 073 |
| Lake | | | 089 |
| La Porte | | | 091 |
| Newton | | | 111 |
| Porter | | | 127 |
| **Chico-Redding (868)** | | | |
| Butte | CA | 06 | 007 |
| Glenn | | | 021 |
| Shasta | | | 089 |
| Tehama | | | 103 |
| Trinity | | | 105 |
| **Cincinnati (515)** | | | |
| Dearborn | IN | 18 | 029 |
| Franklin | | | 047 |
| Ohio | | | 115 |
| Ripley | | | 137 |
| Switzerland | | | 155 |
| Union | | | 161 |
| Boone | KY | 21 | 015 |

| DMA (DMA Code) County | | | FIPS Codes |
|---|---|---|---|
| **Cincinnati (515) Cont.** | | | |
| Bracken | | | 023 |
| Campbell | | | 037 |
| Gallatin | | | 077 |
| Grant | | | 081 |
| Kenton | | | 117 |
| Mason | | | 161 |
| Owen | | | 187 |
| Pendleton | | | 191 |
| Robertson | | | 201 |
| Adams | OH | 39 | 001 |
| Brown | | | 015 |
| Butler | | | 017 |
| Clermont | | | 025 |
| Clinton | | | 027 |
| Hamilton | | | 061 |
| Highland | | | 071 |
| Warren | | | 165 |
| **Clarksburg-Weston (598)** | | | |
| Barbour | WV | 54 | 001 |
| Doddridge | | | 017 |
| Gilmer | | | 021 |
| Harrison | | | 033 |
| Lewis | | | 041 |
| Marion | | | 049 |
| Randolph | | | 083 |
| Ritchie | | | 085 |
| Taylor | | | 091 |
| Tucker | | | 093 |
| Upshur | | | 097 |
| Webster | | | 101 |
| **Cleveland (510)** | | | |
| Ashland | OH | 39 | 005 |
| Ashtabula | | | 007 |
| Carroll | | | 019 |
| Cuyahoga | | | 035 |
| Erie | | | 043 |
| Geauga | | | 055 |
| Holmes | | | 075 |
| Huron | | | 077 |
| Lake | | | 085 |
| Lorain | | | 093 |
| Medina | | | 103 |
| Portage | | | 133 |
| Richland | | | 139 |
| Stark | | | 151 |

# DMA DEFINITIONS

| DMA (DMA Code) County | | | FIPS Codes |
|---|---|---|---|
| **Cleveland (510) Cont.** | | | |
| Summit | | | 153 |
| Tuscarawas | | | 157 |
| Wayne | | | 169 |
| **Colorado Springs-Pueblo (752)** | | | |
| Baca | CO | 08 | 009 |
| Bent | | | 011 |
| Cheyenne | | | 017 |
| Crowley | | | 025 |
| El Paso | | | 041 |
| Fremont | | | 043 |
| Huerfano | | | 055 |
| Kiowa | | | 061 |
| Las Animas | | | 071 |
| Lincoln | | | 073 |
| Otero | | | 089 |
| Pueblo | | | 101 |
| Teller | | | 119 |
| **Columbia, SC (546)** | | | |
| Calhoun | SC | 45 | 017 |
| Clarendon | | | 027 |
| Fairfield | | | 039 |
| Kershaw | | | 055 |
| Lee | | | 061 |
| Lexington | | | 063 |
| Newberry | | | 071 |
| Orangeburg | | | 075 |
| Richland | | | 079 |
| Sumter | | | 085 |
| **Columbia-Jefferson City, MO (604)** | | | |
| Audrain | MO | 29 | 007 |
| Boone | | | 019 |
| Callaway | | | 027 |
| Chariton | | | 041 |
| Cole | | | 051 |
| Cooper | | | 053 |
| Howard | | | 089 |
| Maries | | | 125 |
| Miller | | | 131 |
| Moniteau | | | 135 |
| Montgomery | | | 139 |
| Morgan | | | 141 |
| Osage | | | 151 |
| Randolph | | | 175 |

| DMA (DMA Code) County | | | FIPS Codes |
|---|---|---|---|
| **Columbus, GA (522)** | | | |
| Barbour | AL | 01 | 005 |
| Chambers | | | 017 |
| Lee | | | 081 |
| Russell | | | 113 |
| Chattahoochee | GA | 13 | 053 |
| Clay | | | 061 |
| Harris | | | 145 |
| Marion | | | 197 |
| Muscogee | | | 215 |
| Quitman | | | 239 |
| Randolph | | | 243 |
| Schley | | | 249 |
| Stewart | | | 259 |
| Sumter | | | 261 |
| Talbot | | | 263 |
| Taylor | | | 269 |
| Webster | | | 307 |
| **Columbus, OH (535)** | | | |
| Coshocton | OH | 39 | 031 |
| Crawford | | | 033 |
| Delaware | | | 041 |
| Fairfield | | | 045 |
| Fayette | | | 047 |
| Franklin | | | 049 |
| Hardin | | | 065 |
| Hocking | | | 073 |
| Knox | | | 083 |
| Licking | | | 089 |
| Madison | | | 097 |
| Marion | | | 101 |
| Morgan | | | 115 |
| Morrow | | | 117 |
| Perry | | | 127 |
| Pickaway | | | 129 |
| Pike | | | 131 |
| Ross | | | 141 |
| Union | | | 159 |
| **Columbus-Tupelo-West Point (673)** | | | |
| Lamar | AL | 01 | 075 |
| Calhoun | MS | 28 | 013 |
| Chickasaw | | | 017 |
| Choctaw | | | 019 |
| Clay | | | 025 |
| Itawamba | | | 057 |
| Lee | | | 081 |

| DMA (DMA Code) County | | | FIPS Codes |
|---|---|---|---|
| **Columbus-Tupelo-West Point (673) Cont.** | | | |
| Lowndes | | | 087 |
| Monroe | | | 095 |
| Montgomery | | | 097 |
| Noxubee | | | 103 |
| Oktibbeha | | | 105 |
| Pontotoc | | | 115 |
| Prentiss | | | 117 |
| Tishomingo | | | 141 |
| Union | | | 145 |
| Webster | | | 155 |
| Winston | | | 159 |
| Yalobusha | | | 161 |
| **Corpus Christi (600)** | | | |
| Aransas | TX | 48 | 007 |
| Bee | | | 025 |
| Brooks | | | 047 |
| Duval | | | 131 |
| Jim Hogg | | | 247 |
| Jim Wells | | | 249 |
| Kenedy | | | 261 |
| Kleberg | | | 273 |
| Live Oak | | | 297 |
| Nueces | | | 355 |
| Refugio | | | 391 |
| San Patricio | | | 409 |
| **Dallas-Ft. Worth (623)** | | | |
| Anderson | TX | 48 | 001 |
| Bosque | | | 035 |
| Collin | | | 085 |
| Comanche | | | 093 |
| Cooke | | | 097 |
| Dallas | | | 113 |
| Delta | | | 119 |
| Denton | | | 121 |
| Ellis | | | 139 |
| Erath | | | 143 |
| Fannin | | | 147 |
| Freestone | | | 161 |
| Hamilton | | | 193 |
| Henderson | | | 213 |
| Hill | | | 217 |
| Hood | | | 221 |
| Hopkins | | | 223 |
| Hunt | | | 231 |

| DMA (DMA Code) County | | | FIPS Codes |
|---|---|---|---|
| **Dallas-Ft. Worth (623) Cont.** | | | |
| Jack | | | 237 |
| Johnson | | | 251 |
| Kaufman | | | 257 |
| Lamar | | | 277 |
| Navarro | | | 349 |
| Palo Pinto | | | 363 |
| Parker | | | 367 |
| Rains | | | 379 |
| Rockwall | | | 397 |
| Somervell | | | 425 |
| Tarrant | | | 439 |
| Van Zandt | | | 467 |
| Wise | | | 497 |
| **Davenport, IA-Rock Island-Moline, IL (682)** | | | |
| Bureau | IL | 17 | 011 |
| Carroll | | | 015 |
| Henderson | | | 071 |
| Henry | | | 073 |
| Jo Daviess | | | 085 |
| Knox | | | 095 |
| Mercer | | | 131 |
| Rock Island | | | 161 |
| Warren | | | 187 |
| Whiteside | | | 195 |
| Cedar | IA | 19 | 031 |
| Clinton | | | 045 |
| Des Moines | | | 057 |
| Henry | | | 087 |
| Jackson | | | 097 |
| Louisa | | | 115 |
| Muscatine | | | 139 |
| Scott | | | 163 |
| **Dayton (542)** | | | |
| Wayne | IN | 18 | 177 |
| Auglaize | OH | 39 | 011 |
| Champaign | | | 021 |
| Clark | | | 023 |
| Darke | | | 037 |
| Greene | | | 057 |
| Logan | | | 091 |
| Mercer | | | 107 |
| Miami | | | 109 |
| Montgomery | | | 113 |

# DMA DEFINITIONS

| DMA (DMA Code) County | | | FIPS Codes |
|---|---|---|---|
| **Dayton (542) Cont.** | | | |
| Preble | | | 135 |
| Shelby | | | 149 |
| **Denver (751)** | | | |
| Adams | CO | 08 | 001 |
| Alamosa | | | 003 |
| Arapahoe | | | 005 |
| Archuleta | | | 007 |
| Boulder | | | 013 |
| Chaffee | | | 015 |
| Clear Creek | | | 019 |
| Custer | | | 027 |
| Delta | | | 029 |
| Denver | | | 031 |
| Dolores | | | 033 |
| Douglas | | | 035 |
| Eagle | | | 037 |
| Elbert | | | 039 |
| Garfield | | | 045 |
| Gilpin | | | 047 |
| Grand | | | 049 |
| Gunnison | | | 051 |
| Hinsdale | | | 053 |
| Jackson | | | 057 |
| Jefferson | | | 059 |
| Kit Carson | | | 063 |
| Lake | | | 065 |
| Larimer | | | 069 |
| Logan | | | 075 |
| Mineral | | | 079 |
| Moffat | | | 081 |
| Morgan | | | 087 |
| Park | | | 093 |
| Phillips | | | 095 |
| Pitkin | | | 097 |
| Prowers | | | 099 |
| Rio Blanco | | | 103 |
| Rio Grande | | | 105 |
| Routt | | | 107 |
| Saguache | | | 109 |
| San Juan | | | 111 |
| San Miguel | | | 113 |
| Sedgwick | | | 115 |
| Summit | | | 117 |
| Washington | | | 121 |
| Weld | | | 123 |
| Yuma | | | 125 |

| DMA (DMA Code) County | | | FIPS Codes |
|---|---|---|---|
| **Denver (751) Cont.** | | | |
| Box Butte | NE | 31 | 013 |
| Cheyenne | | | 033 |
| Dawes | | | 045 |
| Deuel | | | 049 |
| Garden | | | 069 |
| Keith | | | 101 |
| Kimball | | | 105 |
| Eureka | NV | 32 | 011 |
| Albany | WY | 56 | 001 |
| Campbell | | | 005 |
| Carbon | | | 007 |
| Johnson | | | 019 |
| Platte | | | 031 |
| **Des Moines-Ames (679)** | | | |
| Adair | IA | 19 | 001 |
| Appanoose | | | 007 |
| Audubon | | | 009 |
| Boone | | | 015 |
| Calhoun | | | 025 |
| Carroll | | | 027 |
| Clarke | | | 039 |
| Dallas | | | 049 |
| Decatur | | | 053 |
| Franklin | | | 069 |
| Greene | | | 073 |
| Guthrie | | | 077 |
| Hamilton | | | 079 |
| Hardin | | | 083 |
| Humboldt | | | 091 |
| Jasper | | | 099 |
| Kossuth | | | 109 |
| Lucas | | | 117 |
| Madison | | | 121 |
| Mahaska | | | 123 |
| Marion | | | 125 |
| Marshall | | | 127 |
| Monroe | | | 135 |
| Pocahontas | | | 151 |
| Polk | | | 153 |
| Poweshiek | | | 157 |
| Ringgold | | | 159 |
| Story | | | 169 |
| Taylor | | | 173 |
| Union | | | 175 |
| Warren | | | 181 |
| Wayne | | | 185 |

# DMA DEFINITIONS

| DMA (DMA Code) County | | | FIPS Codes |
|---|---|---|---|
| **Des Moines-Ames (679) Cont.** | | | |
| Webster | | | 187 |
| Wright | | | 197 |
| Mercer | MO | 29 | 129 |
| **Detroit (505)** | | | |
| Lapeer | MI | 26 | 087 |
| Livingston | | | 093 |
| Macomb | | | 099 |
| Monroe | | | 115 |
| Oakland | | | 125 |
| St. Clair | | | 147 |
| Sanilac | | | 151 |
| Washtenaw | | | 161 |
| Wayne | | | 163 |
| **Dothan (606)** | | | |
| Coffee | AL | 01 | 031 |
| Dale | | | 045 |
| Geneva | | | 061 |
| Henry | | | 067 |
| Houston | | | 069 |
| Early | GA | 13 | 099 |
| Seminole | | | 253 |
| **Duluth, MN-Superior, WI (676)** | | | |
| Gogebic | MI | 26 | 053 |
| Aitkin | MN | 27 | 001 |
| Carlton | | | 017 |
| Cook | | | 031 |
| Itasca | | | 061 |
| Koochiching | | | 071 |
| Lake | | | 075 |
| St. Louis | | | 137 |
| Ashland | WI | 55 | 003 |
| Bayfield | | | 007 |
| Douglas | | | 031 |
| Iron | | | 051 |
| Sawyer | | | 113 |
| Washburn | | | 129 |
| **El Paso (765)** | | | |
| Dona Ana | NM | 35 | 013 |
| Culberson | TX | 48 | 109 |
| El Paso | | | 141 |
| Hudspeth | | | 229 |

| DMA (DMA Code) County | | | FIPS Codes |
|---|---|---|---|
| **Elmira (565)** | | | |
| Chemung | NY | 36 | 015 |
| Schuyler | | | 097 |
| Steuben | | | 101 |
| Tioga | PA | 42 | 117 |
| **Erie (516)** | | | |
| Crawford | PA | 42 | 039 |
| Erie | | | 049 |
| Warren | | | 123 |
| **Eugene (801)** | | | |
| Benton | OR | 41 | 003 |
| Coos | | | 011 |
| Douglas | | | 019 |
| Lane | | | 039 |
| **Eureka (802)** | | | |
| Del Norte | CA | 06 | 015 |
| Humboldt | | | 023 |
| **Evansville (649)** | | | |
| Edwards | IL | 17 | 047 |
| Wabash | | | 185 |
| Wayne | | | 191 |
| White | | | 193 |
| Dubois | IN | 18 | 037 |
| Gibson | | | 051 |
| Perry | | | 123 |
| Pike | | | 125 |
| Posey | | | 129 |
| Spencer | | | 147 |
| Vanderburgh | | | 163 |
| Warrick | | | 173 |
| Daviess | KY | 21 | 059 |
| Hancock | | | 091 |
| Henderson | | | 101 |
| Hopkins | | | 107 |
| McLean | | | 149 |
| Muhlenberg | | | 177 |
| Ohio | | | 183 |
| Union | | | 225 |
| Webster | | | 233 |
| **Fairbanks (745)** | | | |
| Fairbanks-N. Star | AK | 02 | 090 |
| Southeast Fairbanks | | | 240 |

# DMA DEFINITIONS

| DMA (DMA Code) County | | | FIPS Codes |
|---|---|---|---|
| **Fargo-Valley City (724)** | | | |
| Becker | MN | 27 | 005 |
| Clay | | | 027 |
| Clearwater | | | 029 |
| Kittson | | | 069 |
| Lake of the Woods | | | 077 |
| Mahnomen | | | 087 |
| Marshall | | | 089 |
| Norman | | | 107 |
| Otter Tail | | | 111 |
| Pennington | | | 113 |
| Polk | | | 119 |
| Red Lake | | | 125 |
| Roseau | | | 135 |
| Wilkin | | | 167 |
| Barnes | ND | 38 | 003 |
| Benson | | | 005 |
| Cass | | | 017 |
| Cavalier | | | 019 |
| Dickey | | | 021 |
| Eddy | | | 027 |
| Foster | | | 031 |
| Grand Forks | | | 035 |
| Griggs | | | 039 |
| LaMoure | | | 045 |
| Nelson | | | 063 |
| Pembina | | | 067 |
| Ramsey | | | 071 |
| Ransom | | | 073 |
| Richland | | | 077 |
| Sargent | | | 081 |
| Steele | | | 091 |
| Stutsman | | | 093 |
| Towner | | | 095 |
| Traill | | | 097 |
| Walsh | | | 099 |
| **Flint-Saginaw-Bay City (513)** | | | |
| Arenac | MI | 26 | 011 |
| Bay | | | 017 |
| Genesee | | | 049 |
| Gladwin | | | 051 |
| Gratiot | | | 057 |
| Huron | | | 063 |
| Iosco | | | 069 |
| Isabella | | | 073 |
| Midland | | | 111 |
| Ogemaw | | | 129 |

| DMA (DMA Code) County | | | FIPS Codes |
|---|---|---|---|
| **Flint-Saginaw-Bay City (513) Cont.** | | | |
| Saginaw | | | 145 |
| Shiawassee | | | 155 |
| Tuscola | | | 157 |
| **Florence-Myrtle Beach, SC (570)** | | | |
| Robeson | NC | 37 | 155 |
| Scotland | | | 165 |
| Darlington | SC | 45 | 031 |
| Dillon | | | 033 |
| Florence | | | 041 |
| Horry | | | 051 |
| Marion | | | 067 |
| Marlboro | | | 069 |
| **Fresno-Visalia (866)** | | | |
| Fresno | CA | 06 | 019 |
| Kings | | | 031 |
| Madera | | | 039 |
| Mariposa | | | 043 |
| Merced | | | 047 |
| Tulare | | | 107 |
| **Ft. Myers-Naples (571)** | | | |
| Charlotte | FL | 12 | 015 |
| Collier | | | 021 |
| De Soto | | | 027 |
| Glades | | | 043 |
| Hendry | | | 051 |
| Lee | | | 071 |
| **Ft. Smith-Fayetteville-Springdale-Rogers (670)** | | | |
| Benton | AR | 05 | 007 |
| Crawford | | | 033 |
| Franklin | | | 047 |
| Logan | | | 083 |
| Madison | | | 087 |
| Scott | | | 127 |
| Sebastian | | | 131 |
| Washington | | | 143 |
| Le Flore | OK | 40 | 079 |
| Sequoyah | | | 135 |
| **Ft. Wayne (509)** | | | |
| Adams | IN | 18 | 001 |
| Allen | | | 003 |
| De Kalb | | | 033 |

# DMA DEFINITIONS

| DMA (DMA Code) County | | | FIPS Codes |
|---|---|---|---|
| **Ft. Wayne (509) Cont.** | | | |
| Huntington | | | 069 |
| Jay | | | 075 |
| Noble | | | 113 |
| Steuben | | | 151 |
| Wabash | | | 169 |
| Wells | | | 179 |
| Whitley | | | 183 |
| Paulding | OH | 39 | 125 |
| Van Wert | | | 161 |
| **Gainesville (592)** | | | |
| Alachua | FL | 12 | 001 |
| Dixie | | | 029 |
| Gilchrist | | | 041 |
| Levy | | | 075 |
| **Glendive (798)** | | | |
| Dawson | MT | 30 | 021 |
| Prairie | | | 079 |
| **Grand Junction-Montrose (773)** | | | |
| Mesa | CO | 08 | 077 |
| Montrose | | | 085 |
| Ouray | | | 091 |
| **Grand Rapids-Kalamazoo-Battle Creek (563)** | | | |
| Allegan | MI | 26 | 005 |
| Barry | | | 015 |
| Branch | | | 023 |
| Calhoun | | | 025 |
| Ionia | | | 067 |
| Kalamazoo | | | 077 |
| Kent | | | 081 |
| Montcalm | | | 117 |
| Muskegon | | | 121 |
| Newaygo | | | 123 |
| Oceana | | | 127 |
| Ottawa | | | 139 |
| St. Joseph | | | 149 |
| Van Buren | | | 159 |
| **Great Falls (755)** | | | |
| Blaine | MT | 30 | 005 |
| Cascade | | | 013 |
| Chouteau | | | 015 |
| Fergus | | | 027 |

| DMA (DMA Code) County | | | FIPS Codes |
|---|---|---|---|
| **Great Falls (755) Cont.** | | | |
| Glacier | | | 035 |
| Hill | | | 041 |
| Judith Basin | | | 045 |
| Liberty | | | 051 |
| Phillips | | | 071 |
| Pondera | | | 073 |
| Teton | | | 099 |
| Toole | | | 101 |
| Valley | | | 105 |
| **Green Bay-Appleton (658)** | | | |
| Menominee | MI | 26 | 109 |
| Brown | WI | 55 | 009 |
| Calumet | | | 015 |
| Door | | | 029 |
| Fond du Lac | | | 039 |
| Green Lake | | | 047 |
| Kewaunee | | | 061 |
| Manitowoc | | | 071 |
| Marinette | | | 075 |
| Menominee | | | 078 |
| Oconto | | | 083 |
| Outagamie | | | 087 |
| Shawano | | | 115 |
| Waupaca | | | 135 |
| Waushara | | | 137 |
| Winnebago | | | 139 |
| **Greensboro-High Point-Winston Salem (518)** | | | |
| Alamance | NC | 37 | 001 |
| Alleghany | | | 005 |
| Caswell | | | 033 |
| Davidson | | | 057 |
| Davie | | | 059 |
| Forsyth | | | 067 |
| Guilford | | | 081 |
| Montgomery | | | 123 |
| Randolph | | | 151 |
| Rockingham | | | 157 |
| Stokes | | | 169 |
| Surry | | | 171 |
| Wilkes | | | 193 |
| Yadkin | | | 197 |
| Grayson | VA | 51 | 077 |
| Patrick | | | 141 |

# DMA DEFINITIONS

| DMA (DMA Code) County | | | FIPS Codes |
|---|---|---|---|
| **Greenville-New Bern-Washington (545)** | | | |
| Beaufort | NC | 37 | 013 |
| Bertie | | | 015 |
| Carteret | | | 031 |
| Craven | | | 049 |
| Duplin | | | 061 |
| Greene | | | 079 |
| Hyde | | | 095 |
| Jones | | | 103 |
| Lenoir | | | 107 |
| Martin | | | 117 |
| Onslow | | | 133 |
| Pamlico | | | 137 |
| Pitt | | | 147 |
| Tyrrell | | | 177 |
| Washington | | | 187 |
| **Greenville-Spartanburg, SC-Asheville, NC-Anderson, SC (567)** | | | |
| Elbert | GA | 13 | 105 |
| Franklin | | | 119 |
| Hart | | | 147 |
| Madison | | | 195 |
| Stephens | | | 257 |
| Buncombe | NC | 37 | 021 |
| Graham | | | 075 |
| Haywood | | | 087 |
| Henderson | | | 089 |
| Jackson | | | 099 |
| McDowell | | | 111 |
| Macon | | | 113 |
| Madison | | | 115 |
| Mitchell | | | 121 |
| Polk | | | 149 |
| Rutherford | | | 161 |
| Swain | | | 173 |
| Transylvania | | | 175 |
| Yancey | | | 199 |
| Abbeville | SC | 45 | 001 |
| Anderson | | | 007 |
| Cherokee | | | 021 |
| Greenville | | | 045 |
| Greenwood | | | 047 |
| Laurens | | | 059 |
| Oconee | | | 073 |

| DMA (DMA Code) County | | | FIPS Codes |
|---|---|---|---|
| **Greenville-Spartanburg, SC-Asheville, NC-Anderson, SC (567) Cont.** | | | |
| Pickens | | | 077 |
| Spartanburg | | | 083 |
| Union | | | 087 |
| **Greenwood-Greenville (647)** | | | |
| Chicot | AR | 05 | 017 |
| Bolivar | MS | 28 | 011 |
| Carroll | | | 015 |
| Grenada | | | 043 |
| Leflore | | | 083 |
| Sunflower | | | 133 |
| Tallahatchie | | | 135 |
| Washington | | | 151 |
| **Harlingen-Weslaco-Brownsville-McAllen (636)** | | | |
| Cameron | TX | 48 | 061 |
| Hidalgo | | | 215 |
| Starr | | | 427 |
| Willacy | | | 489 |
| **Harrisburg-Lancaster-Lebanon-York (566)** | | | |
| Adams | PA | 42 | 001 |
| Cumberland | | | 041 |
| Dauphin | | | 043 |
| Juniata | | | 067 |
| Lancaster | | | 071 |
| Lebanon | | | 075 |
| Mifflin | | | 087 |
| Perry | | | 099 |
| York | | | 133 |
| **Harrisonburg, VA (569)** | | | |
| Augusta | VA | 51 | 015 |
| Rockingham | | | 165 |
| Harrisonburg City | | | 660 |
| Staunton City | | | 790 |
| Waynesboro City | | | 820 |
| Pendleton | WV | 54 | 071 |
| **Hartord & New Haven, CT (533)** | | | |
| Hartford | CT | 09 | 003 |
| Litchfield | | | 005 |
| Middlesex | | | 007 |

# DMA DEFINITIONS

| DMA (DMA Code) County | | | FIPS Codes |
|---|---|---|---|
| **Hartord & New Haven, CT (533) Cont.** | | | |
| New Haven | | | 009 |
| New London | | | 011 |
| Tolland | | | 013 |
| Windham | | | 015 |
| **Hattiesburg-Laurel (710)** | | | |
| Covington | MS | 28 | 031 |
| Forrest | | | 035 |
| Jasper | | | 061 |
| Jones | | | 067 |
| Lamar | | | 073 |
| Marion | | | 091 |
| Perry | | | 111 |
| Wayne | | | 153 |
| **Helena (766)** | | | |
| Lewis and Clark | MT | 30 | 049 |
| **Honolulu (744)** | | | |
| Hawaii | HI | 15 | 001 |
| Honolulu | | | 003 |
| Kalawao | | | 005 |
| Kauai | | | 007 |
| Maui | | | 009 |
| **Houston (618)** | | | |
| Austin | TX | 48 | 015 |
| Brazoria | | | 039 |
| Calhoun | | | 057 |
| Chambers | | | 071 |
| Colorado | | | 089 |
| Fort Bend | | | 157 |
| Galveston | | | 167 |
| Grimes | | | 185 |
| Harris | | | 201 |
| Jackson | | | 239 |
| Liberty | | | 291 |
| Matagorda | | | 321 |
| Montgomery | | | 339 |
| Polk | | | 373 |
| San Jacinto | | | 407 |
| Walker | | | 471 |
| Waller | | | 473 |
| Washington | | | 477 |
| Wharton | | | 481 |

| DMA (DMA Code) County | | | FIPS Codes |
|---|---|---|---|
| **Huntsville-Decatur (Florence), AL (691)** | | | |
| Colbert | AL | 01 | 033 |
| DeKalb | | | 049 |
| Franklin | | | 059 |
| Jackson | | | 071 |
| Lauderdale | | | 077 |
| Lawrence | | | 079 |
| Limestone | | | 083 |
| Madison | | | 089 |
| Marshall | | | 095 |
| Morgan | | | 103 |
| Lincoln | TN | 47 | 103 |
| **Idaho Falls-Pocatello (758)** | | | |
| Bannock | ID | 16 | 005 |
| Bingham | | | 011 |
| Bonneville | | | 019 |
| Butte | | | 023 |
| Caribou | | | 029 |
| Clark | | | 033 |
| Custer | | | 037 |
| Fremont | | | 043 |
| Jefferson | | | 051 |
| Lemhi | | | 059 |
| Madison | | | 065 |
| Power | | | 077 |
| Teton | | | 081 |
| Lincoln | WY | 56 | 023 |
| Teton | | | 039 |
| **Indianapolis (527)** | | | |
| Bartholomew | IN | 18 | 005 |
| Benton | | | 007 |
| Blackford | | | 009 |
| Boone | | | 011 |
| Brown | | | 013 |
| Carroll | | | 015 |
| Cass | | | 017 |
| Clinton | | | 023 |
| Decatur | | | 031 |
| Delaware | | | 035 |
| Fayette | | | 041 |
| Fountain | | | 045 |
| Grant | | | 053 |
| Hamilton | | | 057 |
| Hancock | | | 059 |
| Hendricks | | | 063 |

# DMA DEFINITIONS

| DMA (DMA Code) County | | | FIPS Codes |
|---|---|---|---|
| **Indianapolis (527) Cont.** | | | |
| Henry | | | 065 |
| Howard | | | 067 |
| Johnson | | | 081 |
| Lawrence | | | 093 |
| Madison | | | 095 |
| Marion | | | 097 |
| Miami | | | 103 |
| Monroe | | | 105 |
| Montgomery | | | 107 |
| Morgan | | | 109 |
| Owen | | | 119 |
| Putnam | | | 133 |
| Randolph | | | 135 |
| Rush | | | 139 |
| Shelby | | | 145 |
| Tipton | | | 159 |
| White | | | 181 |
| **Jackson, MS (718)** | | | |
| Adams | MS | 28 | 001 |
| Attala | | | 007 |
| Claiborne | | | 021 |
| Copiah | | | 029 |
| Franklin | | | 037 |
| Hinds | | | 049 |
| Holmes | | | 051 |
| Humphreys | | | 053 |
| Issaquena | | | 055 |
| Jefferson | | | 063 |
| Jefferson Davis | | | 065 |
| Lawrence | | | 077 |
| Leake | | | 079 |
| Lincoln | | | 085 |
| Madison | | | 089 |
| Pike | | | 113 |
| Rankin | | | 121 |
| Scott | | | 123 |
| Sharkey | | | 125 |
| Simpson | | | 127 |
| Smith | | | 129 |
| Walthall | | | 147 |
| Warren | | | 149 |
| Yazoo | | | 163 |

| DMA (DMA Code) County | | | FIPS Codes |
|---|---|---|---|
| **Jackson, TN (639)** | | | |
| Carroll | TN | 47 | 017 |
| Hardin | | | 071 |
| Henderson | | | 077 |
| Madison | | | 113 |
| **Jacksonville (561)** | | | |
| Baker | FL | 12 | 003 |
| Bradford | | | 007 |
| Clay | | | 019 |
| Columbia | | | 023 |
| Duval | | | 031 |
| Nassau | | | 089 |
| Putnam | | | 107 |
| St. Johns | | | 109 |
| Union | | | 125 |
| Camden | GA | 13 | 039 |
| Charlton | | | 049 |
| Glynn | | | 127 |
| Ware | | | 299 |
| Brantley | | | 025 |
| **Johnstown-Altoona (574)** | | | |
| Bedford | PA | 42 | 009 |
| Blair | | | 013 |
| Cambria | | | 021 |
| Cameron | | | 023 |
| Centre | | | 027 |
| Clearfield | | | 033 |
| Elk | | | 047 |
| Forest | | | 053 |
| Huntingdon | | | 061 |
| Jefferson | | | 065 |
| Somerset | | | 111 |
| **Jonesboro (734)** | | | |
| Clay | AR | 05 | 021 |
| Craighead | | | 031 |
| Greene | | | 055 |
| Izard | | | 065 |
| Lawrence | | | 075 |
| Randolph | | | 121 |
| Sharp | | | 135 |
| Ripley | MO | 29 | 181 |

| DMA (DMA Code) County | | | FIPS Codes |
|---|---|---|---|
| **Joplin, MO-Pittsburg, KS (603)** | | | |
| Allen | KS | 20 | 001 |
| Bourbon | | | 011 |
| Cherokee | | | 021 |
| Crawford | | | 037 |
| Labette | | | 099 |
| Neosho | | | 133 |
| Wilson | | | 205 |
| Woodson | | | 207 |
| Barton | MO | 29 | 011 |
| Jasper | | | 097 |
| McDonald | | | 119 |
| Newton | | | 145 |
| Vernon | | | 217 |
| Ottawa | OK | 40 | 115 |
| **Juneau, AK (747)** | | | |
| Juneau | AK | 02 | 110 |
| **Kansas City (616)** | | | |
| Anderson | KS | 20 | 003 |
| Atchison | | | 005 |
| Douglas | | | 045 |
| Franklin | | | 059 |
| Johnson | | | 091 |
| Leavenworth | | | 103 |
| Linn | | | 107 |
| Miami | | | 121 |
| Wyandotte | | | 209 |
| Bates | MO | 29 | 013 |
| Caldwell | | | 025 |
| Carroll | | | 033 |
| Cass | | | 037 |
| Clay | | | 047 |
| Clinton | | | 049 |
| Daviess | | | 061 |
| Gentry | | | 075 |
| Grundy | | | 079 |
| Harrison | | | 081 |
| Henry | | | 083 |
| Jackson | | | 095 |
| Johnson | | | 101 |
| Lafayette | | | 107 |
| Linn | | | 115 |
| Livingston | | | 117 |
| Pettis | | | 159 |
| **Kansas City (616) Cont.** | | | |
| Platte | | | 165 |
| Ray | | | 177 |
| Saline | | | 195 |
| **Knoxville (557)** | | | |
| Bell | KY | 21 | 013 |
| Harlan | | | 095 |
| McCreary | | | 147 |
| Anderson | TN | 47 | 001 |
| Blount | | | 009 |
| Campbell | | | 013 |
| Claiborne | | | 025 |
| Cocke | | | 029 |
| Cumberland | | | 035 |
| Fentress | | | 049 |
| Grainger | | | 057 |
| Hamblen | | | 063 |
| Hancock | | | 067 |
| Jefferson | | | 089 |
| Knox | | | 093 |
| Loudon | | | 105 |
| Monroe | | | 123 |
| Morgan | | | 129 |
| Roane | | | 145 |
| Scott | | | 151 |
| Sevier | | | 155 |
| Union | | | 173 |
| **La Crosse-Eau Claire (702)** | | | |
| Houston | MN | 27 | 055 |
| Winona | | | 169 |
| Buffalo | WI | 55 | 011 |
| Chippewa | | | 017 |
| Clark | | | 019 |
| Eau Claire | | | 035 |
| Jackson | | | 053 |
| La Crosse | | | 063 |
| Monroe | | | 081 |
| Rusk | | | 107 |
| Trempealeau | | | 121 |
| Vernon | | | 123 |
| **Lafayette, IN (582)** | | | |
| Tippecanoe | IN | 18 | 157 |
| Warren | | | 171 |

# DMA DEFINITIONS

| DMA (DMA Code) County | | | FIPS Codes |
|---|---|---|---|
| **Lafayette, LA (642)** | | | |
| Acadia | LA | 22 | 001 |
| Evangeline | | | 039 |
| Iberia | | | 045 |
| Jefferson Davis | | | 053 |
| Lafayette | | | 055 |
| St. Landry | | | 097 |
| St. Martin | | | 099 |
| Vermilion | | | 113 |
| **Lake Charles, LA (643)** | | | |
| Allen | LA | 22 | 003 |
| Beauregard | | | 011 |
| Calcasieu | | | 019 |
| Cameron | | | 023 |
| **Lansing (551)** | | | |
| Clinton | MI | 26 | 037 |
| Eaton | | | 045 |
| Hillsdale | | | 059 |
| Ingham | | | 065 |
| Jackson | | | 075 |
| **Laredo (749)** | | | |
| Webb | TX | 48 | 479 |
| Zapata | | | 505 |
| **Las Vegas (839)** | | | |
| Clark | NV | 32 | 003 |
| Lincoln | | | 017 |
| Nye | | | 023 |
| **Lexington (541)** | | | |
| Anderson | KY | 21 | 005 |
| Bath | | | 011 |
| Bourbon | | | 017 |
| Boyle | | | 021 |
| Breathitt | | | 025 |
| Casey | | | 045 |
| Clark | | | 049 |
| Clay | | | 051 |
| Estill | | | 065 |
| Fayette | | | 067 |
| Fleming | | | 069 |
| Franklin | | | 073 |
| Garrard | | | 079 |
| Harrison | | | 097 |
| Jackson | | | 109 |

| DMA (DMA Code) County | | | FIPS Codes |
|---|---|---|---|
| **Lexington (541) Cont.** | | | |
| Jessamine | | | 113 |
| Knott | | | 119 |
| Knox | | | 121 |
| Laurel | | | 125 |
| Lee | | | 129 |
| Lincoln | | | 137 |
| Madison | | | 151 |
| Menifee | | | 165 |
| Mercer | | | 167 |
| Montgomery | | | 173 |
| Morgan | | | 175 |
| Nicholas | | | 181 |
| Owsley | | | 189 |
| Perry | | | 193 |
| Powell | | | 197 |
| Pulaski | | | 199 |
| Rockcastle | | | 203 |
| Rowan | | | 205 |
| Russell | | | 207 |
| Scott | | | 209 |
| Wayne | | | 231 |
| Whitley | | | 235 |
| Wolfe | | | 237 |
| Woodford | | | 239 |
| **Lima (558)** | | | |
| Allen | OH | 39 | 003 |
| **Lincoln & Hastings-Kearney, NE (722)** | | | |
| Cloud | KS | 20 | 029 |
| Jewell | | | 089 |
| Phillips | | | 147 |
| Republic | | | 157 |
| Smith | | | 183 |
| Adams | NE | 31 | 001 |
| Antelope | | | 003 |
| Boone | | | 011 |
| Boyd | | | 015 |
| Brown | | | 017 |
| Buffalo | | | 019 |
| Chase | | | 029 |
| Clay | | | 035 |
| Custer | | | 041 |
| Dawson | | | 047 |
| Fillmore | | | 059 |
| Franklin | | | 061 |

| DMA (DMA Code) County | | | FIPS Codes |
|---|---|---|---|
| **Lincoln & Hastings-Kearney, NE (722) Cont.** | | | |
| Frontier | | | 063 |
| Furnas | | | 065 |
| Gage | | | 067 |
| Garfield | | | 071 |
| Gosper | | | 073 |
| Greeley | | | 077 |
| Hall | | | 079 |
| Hamilton | | | 081 |
| Harlan | | | 083 |
| Hayes | | | 085 |
| Hitchcock | | | 087 |
| Holt | | | 089 |
| Howard | | | 093 |
| Jefferson | | | 095 |
| Kearney | | | 099 |
| Keya Paha | | | 103 |
| Lancaster | | | 109 |
| Loup | | | 115 |
| Merrick | | | 121 |
| Nance | | | 125 |
| Nuckolls | | | 129 |
| Perkins | | | 135 |
| Phelps | | | 137 |
| Polk | | | 143 |
| Red Willow | | | 145 |
| Rock | | | 149 |
| Saline | | | 151 |
| Seward | | | 159 |
| Sherman | | | 163 |
| Thayer | | | 169 |
| Valley | | | 175 |
| Webster | | | 181 |
| Wheeler | | | 183 |
| York | | | 185 |
| **Little Rock-Pine Bluff (693)** | | | |
| Arkansas | AR | 05 | 001 |
| Bradley | | | 011 |
| Calhoun | | | 013 |
| Clark | | | 019 |
| Cleburne | | | 023 |
| Cleveland | | | 025 |
| Conway | | | 029 |
| Dallas | | | 039 |
| Desha | | | 041 |
| Drew | | | 043 |

| DMA (DMA Code) County | | | FIPS Codes |
|---|---|---|---|
| **Little Rock-Pine Bluff (693) Cont.** | | | |
| Faulkner | | | 045 |
| Garland | | | 051 |
| Grant | | | 053 |
| Hot Spring | | | 059 |
| Independence | | | 063 |
| Jackson | | | 067 |
| Jefferson | | | 069 |
| Johnson | | | 071 |
| Lincoln | | | 079 |
| Lonoke | | | 085 |
| Monroe | | | 095 |
| Montgomery | | | 097 |
| Ouachita | | | 103 |
| Perry | | | 105 |
| Pike | | | 109 |
| Polk | | | 113 |
| Pope | | | 115 |
| Prairie | | | 117 |
| Pulaski | | | 119 |
| Saline | | | 125 |
| Searcy | | | 129 |
| Stone | | | 137 |
| Van Buren | | | 141 |
| White | | | 145 |
| Woodruff | | | 147 |
| Yell | | | 149 |
| **Los Angeles (803)** | | | |
| Inyo | CA | 06 | 027 |
| Los Angeles | | | 037 |
| Orange | | | 059 |
| San Bernardino | | | 071 |
| Ventura | | | 111 |
| **Louisville (529)** | | | |
| Clark | IN | 18 | 019 |
| Crawford | | | 025 |
| Floyd | | | 043 |
| Harrison | | | 061 |
| Jackson | | | 071 |
| Jefferson | | | 077 |
| Jennings | | | 079 |
| Orange | | | 117 |
| Scott | | | 143 |
| Washington | | | 175 |
| Breckinridge | KY | 21 | 027 |
| Bullitt | | | 029 |

| DMA (DMA Code) County | | | FIPS Codes |
|---|---|---|---|
| **Louisville (529) Cont.** | | | |
| Carroll | | | 041 |
| Grayson | | | 085 |
| Green | | | 087 |
| Hardin | | | 093 |
| Henry | | | 103 |
| Jefferson | | | 111 |
| Larue | | | 123 |
| Marion | | | 155 |
| Meade | | | 163 |
| Nelson | | | 179 |
| Oldham | | | 185 |
| Shelby | | | 211 |
| Spencer | | | 215 |
| Taylor | | | 217 |
| Trimble | | | 223 |
| Washington | | | 229 |
| **Lubbock (651)** | | | |
| Bailey | TX | 48 | 017 |
| Borden | | | 033 |
| Cochran | | | 079 |
| Crosby | | | 107 |
| Dawson | | | 115 |
| Dickens | | | 125 |
| Floyd | | | 153 |
| Gaines | | | 165 |
| Garza | | | 169 |
| Hale | | | 189 |
| Hockley | | | 219 |
| Kent | | | 263 |
| Lamb | | | 279 |
| Lubbock | | | 303 |
| Lynn | | | 305 |
| Motley | | | 345 |
| Scurry | | | 415 |
| Terry | | | 445 |
| Yoakum | | | 501 |
| **Macon (503)** | | | |
| Baldwin | GA | 13 | 009 |
| Bibb | | | 021 |
| Bleckley | | | 023 |
| Crawford | | | 079 |
| Dodge | | | 091 |
| Dooly | | | 093 |
| Hancock | | | 141 |
| Houston | | | 153 |

| DMA (DMA Code) County | | | FIPS Codes |
|---|---|---|---|
| **Macon (503) Cont.** | | | |
| Johnson | | | 167 |
| Jones | | | 169 |
| Laurens | | | 175 |
| Macon | | | 193 |
| Monroe | | | 207 |
| Peach | | | 225 |
| Pulaski | | | 235 |
| Telfair | | | 271 |
| Treutlen | | | 283 |
| Twiggs | | | 289 |
| Washington | | | 303 |
| Wheeler | | | 309 |
| Wilcox | | | 315 |
| Wilkinson | | | 319 |
| **Madison (669)** | | | |
| Columbia | WI | 55 | 021 |
| Dane | | | 025 |
| Grant | | | 043 |
| Green | | | 045 |
| Iowa | | | 049 |
| Juneau | | | 057 |
| Lafayette | | | 065 |
| Marquette | | | 077 |
| Richland | | | 103 |
| Rock | | | 105 |
| Sauk | | | 111 |
| **Mankato (737)** | | | |
| Emmet | IA | 19 | 063 |
| Blue Earth | MN | 27 | 013 |
| Brown | | | 015 |
| Martin | | | 091 |
| Watonwan | | | 165 |
| **Marquette (553)** | | | |
| Alger | MI | 26 | 003 |
| Baraga | | | 013 |
| Delta | | | 041 |
| Dickinson | | | 043 |
| Houghton | | | 061 |
| Iron | | | 071 |
| Keweenaw | | | 083 |
| Marquette | | | 103 |
| Ontonagon | | | 131 |
| Schoolcraft | | | 153 |
| Florence | WI | 55 | 037 |

# DMA DEFINITIONS

| DMA (DMA Code) County | | | FIPS Codes |
|---|---|---|---|
| **Medford-Klamath Falls (813)** | | | |
| Modoc | CA | 06 | 049 |
| Siskiyou | | | 093 |
| Curry | OR | 41 | 015 |
| Jackson | | | 029 |
| Josephine | | | 033 |
| Klamath | | | 035 |
| Lake | | | 037 |
| **Memphis (640)** | | | |
| Crittenden | AR | 05 | 035 |
| Cross | | | 037 |
| Lee | | | 077 |
| Mississippi | | | 093 |
| Phillips | | | 107 |
| Poinsett | | | 111 |
| St. Francis | | | 123 |
| Alcorn | MS | 28 | 003 |
| Benton | | | 009 |
| Coahoma | | | 027 |
| DeSoto | | | 033 |
| Lafayette | | | 071 |
| Marshall | | | 093 |
| Panola | | | 107 |
| Quitman | | | 119 |
| Tate | | | 137 |
| Tippah | | | 139 |
| Tunica | | | 143 |
| Pemiscot | MO | 29 | 155 |
| Chester | TN | 47 | 023 |
| Crockett | | | 033 |
| Dyer | | | 045 |
| Fayette | | | 047 |
| Gibson | | | 053 |
| Hardeman | | | 069 |
| Haywood | | | 075 |
| Lauderdale | | | 097 |
| McNairy | | | 109 |
| Shelby | | | 157 |
| Tipton | | | 167 |
| **Meridian (711)** | | | |
| Choctaw | AL | 01 | 023 |
| Sumter | | | 119 |
| Clarke | MS | 28 | 023 |
| Kemper | | | 069 |

| DMA (DMA Code) County | | | FIPS Codes |
|---|---|---|---|
| **Meridian (711) Cont.** | | | |
| Lauderdale | | | 075 |
| Neshoba | | | 099 |
| Newton | | | 101 |
| **Miami-Ft. Lauderdale (528)** | | | |
| Broward | FL | 12 | 011 |
| Dade | | | 025 |
| Monroe | | | 087 |
| **Milwaukee (617)** | | | |
| Dodge | WI | 55 | 027 |
| Jefferson | | | 055 |
| Kenosha | | | 059 |
| Milwaukee | | | 079 |
| Ozaukee | | | 089 |
| Racine | | | 101 |
| Sheboygan | | | 117 |
| Walworth | | | 127 |
| Washington | | | 131 |
| Waukesha | | | 133 |
| **Minneapolis-St. Paul (613)** | | | |
| Anoka | MN | 27 | 003 |
| Beltrami | | | 007 |
| Benton | | | 009 |
| Big Stone | | | 011 |
| Carver | | | 019 |
| Cass | | | 021 |
| Chippewa | | | 023 |
| Chisago | | | 025 |
| Cottonwood | | | 033 |
| Crow Wing | | | 035 |
| Dakota | | | 037 |
| Douglas | | | 041 |
| Faribault | | | 043 |
| Goodhue | | | 049 |
| Grant | | | 051 |
| Hennepin | | | 053 |
| Hubbard | | | 057 |
| Isanti | | | 059 |
| Jackson | | | 063 |
| Kanabec | | | 065 |
| Kandiyohi | | | 067 |
| Lac qui Parle | | | 073 |
| Le Sueur | | | 079 |
| Lyon | | | 083 |
| McLeod | | | 085 |

| DMA (DMA Code) County | | | FIPS Codes |
|---|---|---|---|
| **Minneapolis-St. Paul (613) Cont.** | | | |
| Meeker | | | 093 |
| Mille Lacs | | | 095 |
| Morrison | | | 097 |
| Nicollet | | | 103 |
| Pine | | | 115 |
| Pope | | | 121 |
| Ramsey | | | 123 |
| Redwood | | | 127 |
| Renville | | | 129 |
| Rice | | | 131 |
| Scott | | | 139 |
| Sherburne | | | 141 |
| Sibley | | | 143 |
| Stearns | | | 145 |
| Steele | | | 147 |
| Stevens | | | 149 |
| Swift | | | 151 |
| Todd | | | 153 |
| Traverse | | | 155 |
| Wabasha | | | 157 |
| Wadena | | | 159 |
| Waseca | | | 161 |
| Washington | | | 163 |
| Wright | | | 171 |
| Yellow Medicine | | | 173 |
| Barron | WI | 55 | 005 |
| Burnett | | | 013 |
| Dunn | | | 033 |
| Pepin | | | 091 |
| Pierce | | | 093 |
| Polk | | | 095 |
| St. Croix | | | 109 |
| **Minot-Bismarck-Dickinson (Williston), ND (687)** | | | |
| Daniels | MT | 30 | 019 |
| Fallon | | | 025 |
| McCone | | | 055 |
| Richland | | | 083 |
| Roosevelt | | | 085 |
| Sheridan | | | 091 |
| Wibaux | | | 109 |
| Adams | ND | 38 | 001 |
| Billings | | | 007 |
| Bottineau | | | 009 |
| Bowman | | | 011 |
| Burke | | | 013 |

| DMA (DMA Code) County | | | FIPS Codes |
|---|---|---|---|
| **Minot-Bismarck-Dickinson (Williston), ND (687) Cont.** | | | |
| Burleigh | | | 015 |
| Divide | | | 023 |
| Dunn | | | 025 |
| Emmons | | | 029 |
| Golden Valley | | | 033 |
| Grant | | | 037 |
| Hettinger | | | 041 |
| Kidder | | | 043 |
| Logan | | | 047 |
| McHenry | | | 049 |
| McIntosh | | | 051 |
| McKenzie | | | 053 |
| McLean | | | 055 |
| Mercer | | | 057 |
| Morton | | | 059 |
| Mountrail | | | 061 |
| Oliver | | | 065 |
| Pierce | | | 069 |
| Renville | | | 075 |
| Rolette | | | 079 |
| Sheridan | | | 083 |
| Sioux | | | 085 |
| Slope | | | 087 |
| Stark | | | 089 |
| Ward | | | 101 |
| Wells | | | 103 |
| Williams | | | 105 |
| Campbell | SD | 46 | 021 |
| Corson | | | 031 |
| Dewey | | | 041 |
| Perkins | | | 105 |
| **Missoula (762)** | | | |
| Flathead | MT | 30 | 029 |
| Granite | | | 039 |
| Lake | | | 047 |
| Mineral | | | 061 |
| Missoula | | | 063 |
| Ravalli | | | 081 |
| Sanders | | | 089 |
| **Mobile, AL-Pensacola (Ft. Walton Beach), FL (686)** | | | |
| Baldwin | AL | 01 | 003 |
| Clarke | | | 025 |
| Conecuh | | | 035 |

# DMA DEFINITIONS

| DMA (DMA Code) County | | | FIPS Codes |
|---|---|---|---|
| **Mobile, AL-Pensacola (Ft. Walton Beach), FL (686) Cont.** | | | |
| Escambia | | | 053 |
| Mobile | | | 097 |
| Monroe | | | 099 |
| Washington | | | 129 |
| Escambia | FL | 12 | 033 |
| Okaloosa | | | 091 |
| Santa Rosa | | | 113 |
| George | MS | 28 | 039 |
| Greene | | | 041 |
| **Monroe, LA-El Dorado, AR (628)** | | | |
| Ashley | AR | 05 | 003 |
| Union | | | 139 |
| Caldwell | LA | 22 | 021 |
| Catahoula | | | 025 |
| Concordia | | | 029 |
| East Carroll | | | 035 |
| Franklin | | | 041 |
| Jackson | | | 049 |
| La Salle | | | 059 |
| Lincoln | | | 061 |
| Madison | | | 065 |
| Morehouse | | | 067 |
| Ouachita | | | 073 |
| Richland | | | 083 |
| Tensas | | | 107 |
| Union | | | 111 |
| West Carroll | | | 123 |
| Winn | | | 127 |
| **Monterey-Salinas (828)** | | | |
| Monterey | CA | 06 | 053 |
| San Benito | | | 069 |
| Santa Cruz | | | 087 |
| **Montgomery (Selma), AL (698)** | | | |
| Autauga | AL | 01 | 001 |
| Bullock | | | 011 |
| Butler | | | 013 |
| Coosa | | | 037 |
| Covington | | | 039 |
| Crenshaw | | | 041 |
| Dallas | | | 047 |
| Elmore | | | 051 |
| Lowndes | | | 085 |
| Macon | | | 087 |

| DMA (DMA Code) County | | | FIPS Codes |
|---|---|---|---|
| **Montgomery (Selma), AL (698) Cont.** | | | |
| Marengo | | | 091 |
| Montgomery | | | 101 |
| Perry | | | 105 |
| Pike | | | 109 |
| Tallapoosa | | | 123 |
| Wilcox | | | 131 |
| **Nashville (659)** | | | |
| Allen | KY | 21 | 003 |
| Christian | | | 047 |
| Clinton | | | 053 |
| Logan | | | 141 |
| Monroe | | | 171 |
| Simpson | | | 213 |
| Todd | | | 219 |
| Trigg | | | 221 |
| Bedford | TN | 47 | 003 |
| Benton | | | 005 |
| Cannon | | | 015 |
| Cheatham | | | 021 |
| Clay | | | 027 |
| Coffee | | | 031 |
| Davidson | | | 037 |
| Decatur | | | 039 |
| DeKalb | | | 041 |
| Dickson | | | 043 |
| Franklin | | | 051 |
| Giles | | | 055 |
| Henry | | | 079 |
| Hickman | | | 081 |
| Houston | | | 083 |
| Humphreys | | | 085 |
| Jackson | | | 087 |
| Lawrence | | | 099 |
| Lewis | | | 101 |
| Macon | | | 111 |
| Marshall | | | 117 |
| Maury | | | 119 |
| Montgomery | | | 125 |
| Moore | | | 127 |
| Overton | | | 133 |
| Perry | | | 135 |
| Pickett | | | 137 |
| Putnam | | | 141 |
| Robertson | | | 147 |
| Rutherford | | | 149 |
| Smith | | | 159 |

| DMA (DMA Code) County | | | FIPS Codes |
|---|---|---|---|
| **Nashville (659) Cont.** | | | |
| Stewart | | | 161 |
| Sumner | | | 165 |
| Trousdale | | | 169 |
| Van Buren | | | 175 |
| Warren | | | 177 |
| Wayne | | | 181 |
| White | | | 185 |
| Williamson | | | 187 |
| Wilson | | | 189 |
| **New Orleans (622)** | | | |
| Jefferson | LA | 22 | 051 |
| Lafourche | | | 057 |
| Orleans | | | 071 |
| Plaquemines | | | 075 |
| St. Bernard | | | 087 |
| St. Charles | | | 089 |
| St. James | | | 093 |
| St. John the Baptist | | | 095 |
| St. Tammany | | | 103 |
| Tangipahoa | | | 105 |
| Terrebonne | | | 109 |
| Washington | | | 117 |
| Hancock | MS | 28 | 045 |
| Pearl River | | | 109 |
| **New York (501)** | | | |
| Fairfield | CT | 09 | 001 |
| Bergen | NJ | 34 | 003 |
| Essex | | | 013 |
| Hudson | | | 017 |
| Hunterdon | | | 019 |
| Middlesex | | | 023 |
| Monmouth | | | 025 |
| Morris | | | 027 |
| Ocean | | | 029 |
| Passaic | | | 031 |
| Somerset | | | 035 |
| Sussex | | | 037 |
| Union | | | 039 |
| Warren | | | 041 |
| Bronx | NY | 36 | 005 |
| Dutchess | | | 027 |
| Kings | | | 047 |
| Nassau | | | 059 |
| New York | | | 061 |
| Orange | | | 071 |

| DMA (DMA Code) County | | | FIPS Codes |
|---|---|---|---|
| **New York (501) Cont.** | | | |
| Putnam | | | 079 |
| Queens | | | 081 |
| Richmond | | | 085 |
| Rockland | | | 087 |
| Suffolk | | | 103 |
| Sullivan | | | 105 |
| Ulster | | | 111 |
| Westchester | | | 119 |
| Pike | PA | 42 | 103 |
| **Norfolk-Portsmouth-Newport News (544)** | | | |
| Camden | NC | 37 | 029 |
| Chowan | | | 041 |
| Currituck | | | 053 |
| Dare | | | 055 |
| Gates | | | 073 |
| Hertford | | | 091 |
| Pasquotank | | | 139 |
| Perquimans | | | 143 |
| Accomack | VA | 51 | 001 |
| Gloucester | | | 073 |
| Isle of Wight | | | 093 |
| James City | | | 095 |
| Mathews | | | 115 |
| Northampton | | | 131 |
| Southampton | | | 175 |
| Surry | | | 181 |
| York | | | 199 |
| Chesapeake City | | | 550 |
| Franklin City | | | 620 |
| Hampton City | | | 650 |
| Newport News City | | | 700 |
| Norfolk City | | | 710 |
| Poquoson City | | | 735 |
| Portsmouth City | | | 740 |
| Suffolk City | | | 800 |
| Virginia Beach City | | | 810 |
| Williamsburg City | | | 830 |
| **North Platte (740)** | | | |
| Arthur | NE | 31 | 005 |
| Blaine | | | 009 |
| Hooker | | | 091 |
| Lincoln | | | 111 |

| DMA (DMA Code) County | | | FIPS Codes |
|---|---|---|---|
| **North Platte (740) Cont.** | | | |
| Logan | | | 113 |
| McPherson | | | 117 |
| Thomas | | | 171 |
| **Odessa-Midland (633)** | | | |
| Andrews | TX | 48 | 003 |
| Brewster | | | 043 |
| Crane | | | 103 |
| Ector | | | 135 |
| Glasscock | | | 173 |
| Howard | | | 227 |
| Jeff Davis | | | 243 |
| Loving | | | 301 |
| Martin | | | 317 |
| Midland | | | 329 |
| Pecos | | | 371 |
| Presidio | | | 377 |
| Reagan | | | 383 |
| Reeves | | | 389 |
| Terrell | | | 443 |
| Upton | | | 461 |
| Ward | | | 475 |
| Winkler | | | 495 |
| **Oklahoma City (650)** | | | |
| Alfalfa | OK | 40 | 003 |
| Beckham | | | 009 |
| Blaine | | | 011 |
| Caddo | | | 015 |
| Canadian | | | 017 |
| Cleveland | | | 027 |
| Custer | | | 039 |
| Dewey | | | 043 |
| Ellis | | | 045 |
| Garfield | | | 047 |
| Garvin | | | 049 |
| Grady | | | 051 |
| Grant | | | 053 |
| Greer | | | 055 |
| Harmon | | | 057 |
| Harper | | | 059 |
| Hughes | | | 063 |
| Kay | | | 071 |
| Kingfisher | | | 073 |
| Kiowa | | | 075 |
| Lincoln | | | 081 |
| Logan | | | 083 |

| DMA (DMA Code) County | | | FIPS Codes |
|---|---|---|---|
| **Oklahoma City (650) Cont.** | | | |
| McClain | | | 087 |
| Major | | | 093 |
| Murray | | | 099 |
| Noble | | | 103 |
| Oklahoma | | | 109 |
| Payne | | | 119 |
| Pottawatomie | | | 125 |
| Roger Mills | | | 129 |
| Seminole | | | 133 |
| Washita | | | 149 |
| Woods | | | 151 |
| Woodward | | | 153 |
| **Omaha (652)** | | | |
| Adams | IA | 19 | 003 |
| Cass | | | 029 |
| Crawford | | | 047 |
| Fremont | | | 071 |
| Harrison | | | 085 |
| Mills | | | 129 |
| Montgomery | | | 137 |
| Page | | | 145 |
| Pottawattamie | | | 155 |
| Shelby | | | 165 |
| Atchison | MO | 29 | 005 |
| Burt | NE | 31 | 021 |
| Butler | | | 023 |
| Cass | | | 025 |
| Colfax | | | 037 |
| Cuming | | | 039 |
| Dodge | | | 053 |
| Douglas | | | 055 |
| Johnson | | | 097 |
| Nemaha | | | 127 |
| Otoe | | | 131 |
| Pawnee | | | 133 |
| Platte | | | 141 |
| Richardson | | | 147 |
| Sarpy | | | 153 |
| Saunders | | | 155 |
| Washington | | | 177 |
| **Orlando-Daytona Beach-Melbourne (534)** | | | |
| Brevard | FL | 12 | 009 |
| Flagler | | | 035 |
| Lake | | | 069 |

| DMA (DMA Code) County | | | FIPS Codes |
|---|---|---|---|
| **Orlando-Daytona Beach-Melbourne (534) Cont.** | | | |
| Marion | | | 083 |
| Orange | | | 095 |
| Osceola | | | 097 |
| Seminole | | | 117 |
| Sumter | | | 119 |
| Volusia | | | 127 |
| **Ottumwa, IA-Kirksville, MO (631)** | | | |
| Davis | IA | 19 | 051 |
| Jefferson | | | 101 |
| Van Buren | | | 177 |
| Wapello | | | 179 |
| Adair | MO | 29 | 001 |
| Macon | | | 121 |
| Putnam | | | 171 |
| Schuyler | | | 197 |
| Sullivan | | | 211 |
| **Paducah, KY-Cape Girardeau, MO-Harrisburg-Mt. Vernon, IL (632)** | | | |
| Alexander | IL | 17 | 003 |
| Franklin | | | 055 |
| Gallatin | | | 059 |
| Hamilton | | | 065 |
| Hardin | | | 069 |
| Jackson | | | 077 |
| Jefferson | | | 081 |
| Johnson | | | 087 |
| Massac | | | 127 |
| Perry | | | 145 |
| Pope | | | 151 |
| Pulaski | | | 153 |
| Saline | | | 165 |
| Union | | | 181 |
| Williamson | | | 199 |
| Ballard | KY | 21 | 007 |
| Caldwell | | | 033 |
| Calloway | | | 035 |
| Carlisle | | | 039 |
| Crittenden | | | 055 |
| Fulton | | | 075 |
| Graves | | | 083 |
| Hickman | | | 105 |
| Livingston | | | 139 |
| Lyon | | | 143 |
| McCracken | | | 145 |

| DMA (DMA Code) County | | | FIPS Codes |
|---|---|---|---|
| **Paducah, KY-Cape Girardeau, MO-Harrisburg-Mt. Vernon, IL (632) Cont.** | | | |
| Marshall | | | 157 |
| Bollinger | MO | 29 | 017 |
| Butler | | | 023 |
| Cape Girardeau | | | 031 |
| Carter | | | 035 |
| Dunklin | | | 069 |
| Madison | | | 123 |
| Mississippi | | | 133 |
| New Madrid | | | 143 |
| Perry | | | 157 |
| Reynolds | | | 179 |
| Scott | | | 201 |
| Stoddard | | | 207 |
| Wayne | | | 223 |
| Lake | TN | 47 | 095 |
| Obion | | | 131 |
| Weakley | | | 183 |
| **Palm Springs (804)** | | | |
| Riverside | CA | 06 | 065 |
| **Panama City (656)** | | | |
| Bay | FL | 12 | 005 |
| Calhoun | | | 013 |
| Franklin | | | 037 |
| Gulf | | | 045 |
| Holmes | | | 059 |
| Jackson | | | 063 |
| Liberty | | | 077 |
| Walton | | | 131 |
| Washington | | | 133 |
| **Parkersburg, WV (597)** | | | |
| Washington | OH | 39 | 167 |
| Pleasants | WV | 54 | 073 |
| Wood | | | 107 |
| **Peoria-Bloomington (675)** | | | |
| Fulton | IL | 17 | 057 |
| Livingston | | | 105 |
| McLean | | | 113 |
| Marshall | | | 123 |
| Mason | | | 125 |
| Peoria | | | 143 |
| Putnam | | | 155 |

| DMA (DMA Code) County | | | FIPS Codes |
|---|---|---|---|
| **Peoria-Bloomington (675) Cont.** | | | |
| Stark | | | 175 |
| Tazewell | | | 179 |
| Woodford | | | 203 |
| **Philadelphia (504)** | | | |
| Kent | DE | 10 | 001 |
| New Castle | | | 003 |
| Atlantic | NJ | 34 | 001 |
| Burlington | | | 005 |
| Camden | | | 007 |
| Cape May | | | 009 |
| Cumberland | | | 011 |
| Gloucester | | | 015 |
| Mercer | | | 021 |
| Salem | | | 033 |
| Berks | PA | 42 | 011 |
| Bucks | | | 017 |
| Chester | | | 029 |
| Delaware | | | 045 |
| Lehigh | | | 077 |
| Montgomery | | | 091 |
| Northampton | | | 095 |
| Philadelphia | | | 101 |
| **Phoenix (753)** | | | |
| Coconino | AZ | 04 | 005 |
| Gila | | | 007 |
| Graham | | | 009 |
| Greenlee | | | 011 |
| La Paz | | | 012 |
| Maricopa | | | 013 |
| Mohave | | | 015 |
| Navajo | | | 017 |
| Pinal | | | 021 |
| Yavapai | | | 025 |
| **Pittsburgh (508)** | | | |
| Garrett | MD | 24 | 023 |
| Allegheny | PA | 42 | 003 |
| Armstrong | | | 005 |
| Beaver | | | 007 |
| Butler | | | 019 |
| Clarion | | | 031 |
| Fayette | | | 051 |
| Greene | | | 059 |
| Indiana | | | 063 |
| Lawrence | | | 073 |

| DMA (DMA Code) County | | | FIPS Codes |
|---|---|---|---|
| **Pittsburgh (508) Cont.** | | | |
| Venango | | | 121 |
| Washington | | | 125 |
| Westmoreland | | | 129 |
| Monongalia | WV | 54 | 061 |
| Preston | | | 077 |
| **Portland, OR (820)** | | | |
| Baker | OR | 41 | 001 |
| Clackamas | | | 005 |
| Clatsop | | | 007 |
| Columbia | | | 009 |
| Crook | | | 013 |
| Gilliam | | | 021 |
| Harney | | | 025 |
| Hood River | | | 027 |
| Jefferson | | | 031 |
| Lincoln | | | 041 |
| Linn | | | 043 |
| Marion | | | 047 |
| Multnomah | | | 051 |
| Polk | | | 053 |
| Sherman | | | 055 |
| Tillamook | | | 057 |
| Union | | | 061 |
| Wasco | | | 065 |
| Washington | | | 067 |
| Wheeler | | | 069 |
| Yamhill | | | 071 |
| Clark | WA | 53 | 011 |
| Cowlitz | | | 015 |
| Klickitat | | | 039 |
| Skamania | | | 059 |
| Wahkiakum | | | 069 |
| **Portland-Auburn (500)** | | | |
| Androscoggin | ME | 23 | 001 |
| Cumberland | | | 005 |
| Franklin | | | 007 |
| Kennebec | | | 011 |
| Knox | | | 013 |
| Lincoln | | | 015 |
| Oxford | | | 017 |
| Sagadahoc | | | 023 |
| York | | | 031 |
| Carroll | NH | 33 | 003 |
| Coos | | | 007 |

| DMA (DMA Code) County | | | FIPS Codes |
|---|---|---|---|

### Presque Isle (552)

|  |  | | |
|---|---|---|---|
| Aroostook | ME | 23 | 003 |

### Providence, RI-New Bedford, MA (521)

|  |  | | |
|---|---|---|---|
| Bristol | MA | 25 | 005 |
| Bristol | RI | 44 | 001 |
| Kent | | | 003 |
| Newport | | | 005 |
| Providence | | | 007 |
| Washington | | | 009 |

### Quincy, IL-Hannibal, MO-Keokuk, IA (717)

|  |  | | |
|---|---|---|---|
| Adams | IL | 17 | 001 |
| Brown | | | 009 |
| Cass | | | 017 |
| Hancock | | | 067 |
| McDonough | | | 109 |
| Pike | | | 149 |
| Schuyler | | | 169 |
| Scott | | | 171 |
| Lee | IA | 19 | 111 |
| Clark | MO | 29 | 045 |
| Knox | | | 103 |
| Lewis | | | 111 |
| Marion | | | 127 |
| Monroe | | | 137 |
| Ralls | | | 173 |
| Scotland | | | 199 |
| Shelby | | | 205 |

### Raleigh-Durham (Fayetteville), NC (560)

|  |  | | |
|---|---|---|---|
| Chatham | NC | 37 | 037 |
| Cumberland | | | 051 |
| Durham | | | 063 |
| Edgecombe | | | 065 |
| Franklin | | | 069 |
| Granville | | | 077 |
| Halifax | | | 083 |
| Harnett | | | 085 |
| Hoke | | | 093 |
| Johnston | | | 101 |
| Lee | | | 105 |
| Moore | | | 125 |
| Nash | | | 127 |
| Northampton | | | 131 |

### Raleigh-Durham (Fayetteville), NC (560) Cont.

|  |  | | |
|---|---|---|---|
| Orange | | | 135 |
| Person | | | 145 |
| Sampson | | | 163 |
| Vance | | | 181 |
| Wake | | | 183 |
| Warren | | | 185 |
| Wayne | | | 191 |
| Wilson | | | 195 |
| Mecklenburg | VA | 51 | 117 |

### Rapid City (764)

|  |  | | |
|---|---|---|---|
| Carter | MT | 30 | 011 |
| Banner | NE | 31 | 007 |
| Grant | | | 075 |
| Morrill | | | 123 |
| Sheridan | | | 161 |
| Sioux | | | 165 |
| Bennett | SD | 46 | 007 |
| Butte | | | 019 |
| Custer | | | 033 |
| Fall River | | | 047 |
| Haakon | | | 055 |
| Harding | | | 063 |
| Jackson | | | 071 |
| Lawrence | | | 081 |
| Meade | | | 093 |
| Pennington | | | 103 |
| Shannon | | | 113 |
| Ziebach | | | 137 |
| Crook | WY | 56 | 011 |
| Niobrara | | | 027 |
| Sheridan | | | 033 |
| Weston | | | 045 |

### Reno (811)

|  |  | | |
|---|---|---|---|
| Alpine | CA | 06 | 003 |
| Lassen | | | 035 |
| Mono | | | 051 |
| Churchill | NV | 32 | 001 |
| Douglas | | | 005 |
| Esmeralda | | | 009 |
| Humboldt | | | 013 |
| Lander | | | 015 |
| Lyon | | | 019 |
| Mineral | | | 021 |
| Pershing | | | 027 |

# DMA DEFINITIONS

| DMA (DMA Code) County | | | FIPS Codes |
|---|---|---|---|
| **Reno (811) Cont.** | | | |
| Storey | | | 029 |
| Washoe | | | 031 |
| Carson City | | | 510 |
| **Richmond-Petersburg (556)** | | | |
| Amelia | VA | 51 | 007 |
| Brunswick | | | 025 |
| Buckingham | | | 029 |
| Caroline | | | 033 |
| Charles City | | | 036 |
| Chesterfield | | | 041 |
| Cumberland | | | 049 |
| Dinwiddie | | | 053 |
| Essex | | | 057 |
| Fluvanna | | | 065 |
| Goochland | | | 075 |
| Greensville | | | 081 |
| Hanover | | | 085 |
| Henrico | | | 087 |
| King and Queen | | | 097 |
| King William | | | 101 |
| Lancaster | | | 103 |
| Louisa | | | 109 |
| Lunenburg | | | 111 |
| Middlesex | | | 119 |
| New Kent | | | 127 |
| Northumberland | | | 133 |
| Nottoway | | | 135 |
| Orange | | | 137 |
| Powhatan | | | 145 |
| Prince Edward | | | 147 |
| Prince George | | | 149 |
| Richmond | | | 159 |
| Sussex | | | 183 |
| Colonial Heights City | | | 570 |
| Emporia City | | | 595 |
| Hopewell City | | | 670 |
| Petersburg City | | | 730 |
| Richmond City | | | 760 |
| **Roanoke-Lynchburg (573)** | | | |
| Alleghany | VA | 51 | 005 |
| Amherst | | | 009 |
| Appomattox | | | 011 |
| Bath | | | 017 |
| Bedford | | | 019 |
| Botetourt | | | 023 |

| DMA (DMA Code) County | | | FIPS Codes |
|---|---|---|---|
| **Roanoke-Lynchburg (573) Cont.** | | | |
| Campbell | | | 031 |
| Carroll | | | 035 |
| Charlotte | | | 037 |
| Craig | | | 045 |
| Floyd | | | 063 |
| Franklin | | | 067 |
| Giles | | | 071 |
| Halifax | | | 083 |
| Henry | | | 089 |
| Highland | | | 091 |
| Montgomery | | | 121 |
| Nelson | | | 125 |
| Pittsylvania | | | 143 |
| Pulaski | | | 155 |
| Roanoke | | | 161 |
| Rockbridge | | | 163 |
| Wythe | | | 197 |
| Bedford City | | | 515 |
| Buena Vista City | | | 530 |
| Clifton Forge City | | | 560 |
| Covington City | | | 580 |
| Danville City | | | 590 |
| Galax City | | | 640 |
| Lexington City | | | 678 |
| Lynchburg City | | | 680 |
| Martinsville City | | | 690 |
| Radford City | | | 750 |
| Roanoke City | | | 770 |
| Salem City | | | 775 |
| South Boston City | | | 780 |
| Pocahontas | WV | 54 | 075 |
| **Rochester, MN-Mason City, IA-Austin, MN (611)** | | | |
| Cerro Gordo | IA | 19 | 033 |
| Floyd | | | 067 |
| Hancock | | | 081 |
| Howard | | | 089 |
| Mitchell | | | 131 |
| Winnebago | | | 189 |
| Worth | | | 195 |
| Dodge | MN | 27 | 039 |
| Fillmore | | | 045 |
| Freeborn | | | 047 |
| Mower | | | 099 |
| Olmsted | | | 109 |

| DMA (DMA Code) County | | | FIPS Codes |
|---|---|---|---|
| **Rochester, NY (538)** | | | |
| Livingston | NY | 36 | 051 |
| Monroe | | | 055 |
| Ontario | | | 069 |
| Wayne | | | 117 |
| **Rockford (610)** | | | |
| Boone | IL | 17 | 007 |
| Lee | | | 103 |
| Ogle | | | 141 |
| Stephenson | | | 177 |
| Winnebago | | | 201 |
| **Sacramento-Stockton-Modesto (862)** | | | |
| Amador | CA | 06 | 005 |
| Calaveras | | | 009 |
| Colusa | | | 011 |
| El Dorado | | | 017 |
| Nevada | | | 057 |
| Placer | | | 061 |
| Plumas | | | 063 |
| Sacramento | | | 067 |
| San Joaquin | | | 077 |
| Sierra | | | 091 |
| Solano | | | 095 |
| Stanislaus | | | 099 |
| Sutter | | | 101 |
| Tuolumne | | | 109 |
| Yolo | | | 113 |
| Yuba | | | 115 |
| **Salisbury (576)** | | | |
| Sussex | DE | 10 | 005 |
| Somerset | MD | 24 | 039 |
| Wicomico | | | 045 |
| Worcester | | | 047 |
| **Salt Lake City (770)** | | | |
| Bear Lake | ID | 16 | 007 |
| Franklin | | | 041 |
| Oneida | | | 071 |
| Elko | NV | 32 | 007 |
| White Pine | | | 033 |
| Beaver | UT | 49 | 001 |
| Box Elder | | | 003 |
| Cache | | | 005 |
| Carbon | | | 007 |
| Daggett | | | 009 |

| DMA (DMA Code) County | | | FIPS Codes |
|---|---|---|---|
| **Salt Lake City (770) Cont.** | | | |
| Davis | | | 011 |
| Duchesne | | | 013 |
| Emery | | | 015 |
| Garfield | | | 017 |
| Grand | | | 019 |
| Iron | | | 021 |
| Juab | | | 023 |
| Kane | | | 025 |
| Millard | | | 027 |
| Morgan | | | 029 |
| Piute | | | 031 |
| Rich | | | 033 |
| Salt Lake | | | 035 |
| San Juan | | | 037 |
| Sanpete | | | 039 |
| Sevier | | | 041 |
| Summit | | | 043 |
| Tooele | | | 045 |
| Uintah | | | 047 |
| Utah | | | 049 |
| Wasatch | | | 051 |
| Washington | | | 053 |
| Wayne | | | 055 |
| Weber | | | 057 |
| Sublette | WY | 56 | 035 |
| Washburn | | | 129 |
| Sweetwater | | | 037 |
| Teton | | | 039 |
| Uinta | | | 041 |
| **San Angelo (661)** | | | |
| Coke | TX | 48 | 081 |
| Concho | | | 095 |
| Crockett | | | 105 |
| Irion | | | 235 |
| Kimble | | | 267 |
| McCulloch | | | 307 |
| Menard | | | 327 |
| Schleicher | | | 413 |
| Sterling | | | 431 |
| Sutton | | | 435 |
| Tom Green | | | 451 |
| **San Antonio (641)** | | | |
| Atascosa | TX | 48 | 013 |
| Bandera | | | 019 |
| Bexar | | | 029 |

# DMA DEFINITIONS

| DMA (DMA Code) County | | | FIPS Codes |
|---|---|---|---|
| **San Antonio (641) Cont.** | | | |
| Comal | | | 091 |
| DeWitt | | | 123 |
| Dimmit | | | 127 |
| Edwards | | | 137 |
| Frio | | | 163 |
| Gillespie | | | 171 |
| Goliad | | | 175 |
| Gonzales | | | 177 |
| Guadalupe | | | 187 |
| Karnes | | | 255 |
| Kendall | | | 259 |
| Kerr | | | 265 |
| Kinney | | | 271 |
| La Salle | | | 283 |
| Lavaca | | | 285 |
| McMullen | | | 311 |
| Maverick | | | 323 |
| Medina | | | 325 |
| Real | | | 385 |
| Uvalde | | | 463 |
| Val Verde | | | 465 |
| Wilson | | | 493 |
| Zavala | | | 507 |
| **San Diego (825)** | | | |
| San Diego | CA | 06 | 073 |
| **San Francisco-Oakland-San Jose (807)** | | | |
| Alameda | CA | 06 | 001 |
| Contra Costa | | | 013 |
| Lake | | | 033 |
| Marin | | | 041 |
| Mendocino | | | 045 |
| Napa | | | 055 |
| San Francisco | | | 075 |
| San Mateo | | | 081 |
| Santa Clara | | | 085 |
| Sonoma | | | 097 |
| **Santa Barbara-Santa Maria-San Luis Obispo (855)** | | | |
| San Luis Obispo | CA | 06 | 079 |
| Santa Barbara | | | 083 |

| DMA (DMA Code) County | | | FIPS Codes |
|---|---|---|---|
| **Savannah (507)** | | | |
| Appling | GA | 13 | 001 |
| Bacon | | | 005 |
| Bryan | | | 029 |
| Bulloch | | | 031 |
| Candler | | | 043 |
| Chatham | | | 051 |
| Effingham | | | 103 |
| Evans | | | 109 |
| Jeff Davis | | | 161 |
| Liberty | | | 179 |
| Long | | | 183 |
| McIntosh | | | 191 |
| Montgomery | | | 209 |
| Pierce | | | 229 |
| Screven | | | 251 |
| Tattnall | | | 267 |
| Toombs | | | 279 |
| Wayne | | | 305 |
| Beaufort | SC | 45 | 013 |
| Hampton | | | 049 |
| Jasper | | | 053 |
| **Seattle-Tacoma (819)** | | | |
| Chelan | WA | 53 | 007 |
| Clallam | | | 009 |
| Douglas | | | 017 |
| Grays Harbor | | | 027 |
| Island | | | 029 |
| Jefferson | | | 031 |
| King | | | 033 |
| Kitsap | | | 035 |
| Lewis | | | 041 |
| Mason | | | 045 |
| Pacific | | | 049 |
| Pierce | | | 053 |
| San Juan | | | 055 |
| Skagit | | | 057 |
| Snohomish | | | 061 |
| Thurston | | | 067 |
| Whatcom | | | 073 |
| **Sherman, TX-Ada, OK (657)** | | | |
| Atoka | OK | 40 | 005 |
| Bryan | | | 013 |
| Carter | | | 019 |
| Choctaw | | | 023 |
| Coal | | | 029 |

# DMA DEFINITIONS

| DMA (DMA Code) County | | | FIPS Codes |
|---|---|---|---|
| **Sherman, TX-Ada, OK (657) Cont.** | | | |
| Johnston | | | 069 |
| Love | | | 085 |
| Marshall | | | 095 |
| Pontotoc | | | 123 |
| Pushmataha | | | 127 |
| Grayson | TX | 48 | 181 |
| **Shreveport (612)** | | | |
| Columbia | AR | 05 | 027 |
| Hempstead | | | 057 |
| Howard | | | 061 |
| Lafayette | | | 073 |
| Little River | | | 081 |
| Miller | | | 091 |
| Nevada | | | 099 |
| Sevier | | | 133 |
| Bienville | LA | 22 | 013 |
| Bossier | | | 015 |
| Caddo | | | 017 |
| Claiborne | | | 027 |
| De Soto | | | 031 |
| Natchitoches | | | 069 |
| Red River | | | 081 |
| Sabine | | | 085 |
| Webster | | | 119 |
| McCurtain | OK | 40 | 089 |
| Bowie | TX | 48 | 037 |
| Camp | | | 063 |
| Cass | | | 067 |
| Harrison | | | 203 |
| Marion | | | 315 |
| Morris | | | 343 |
| Panola | | | 365 |
| Red River | | | 387 |
| Sabine | | | 403 |
| Shelby | | | 419 |
| Titus | | | 449 |
| **Sioux City (624)** | | | |
| Buena Vista | IA | 19 | 021 |
| Cherokee | | | 035 |
| Clay | | | 041 |
| Dickinson | | | 059 |
| Ida | | | 093 |
| Monona | | | 133 |
| O'Brien | | | 141 |
| Palo Alto | | | 147 |

| DMA (DMA Code) County | | | FIPS Codes |
|---|---|---|---|
| **Sioux City (624) Cont.** | | | |
| Plymouth | | | 149 |
| Sac | | | 161 |
| Sioux | | | 167 |
| Woodbury | | | 193 |
| Cedar | NE | 31 | 027 |
| Dakota | | | 043 |
| Dixon | | | 051 |
| Knox | | | 107 |
| Madison | | | 119 |
| Pierce | | | 139 |
| Stanton | | | 167 |
| Thurston | | | 173 |
| Wayne | | | 179 |
| Union | SD | 46 | 127 |
| **Sioux Falls (Mitchell), SD (725)** | | | |
| Lyon | IA | 19 | 119 |
| Osceola | | | 143 |
| Lincoln | MN | 27 | 081 |
| Murray | | | 101 |
| Nobles | | | 105 |
| Pipestone | | | 117 |
| Rock | | | 133 |
| Cherry | NE | 31 | 031 |
| Aurora | SD | 46 | 003 |
| Beadle | | | 005 |
| Bon Homme | | | 009 |
| Brookings | | | 011 |
| Brown | | | 013 |
| Brule | | | 015 |
| Buffalo | | | 017 |
| Charles Mix | | | 023 |
| Clark | | | 025 |
| Clay | | | 027 |
| Codington | | | 029 |
| Davison | | | 035 |
| Day | | | 037 |
| Deuel | | | 039 |
| Douglas | | | 043 |
| Edmunds | | | 045 |
| Faulk | | | 049 |
| Grant | | | 051 |
| Gregory | | | 053 |
| Hamlin | | | 057 |
| Hand | | | 059 |
| Hanson | | | 061 |
| Hughes | | | 065 |

# DMA DEFINITIONS

| DMA (DMA Code) County | | | FIPS Codes |
|---|---|---|---|
| **Sioux Falls (Mitchell), SD (725) Cont.** | | | |
| Hutchinson | | | 067 |
| Hyde | | | 069 |
| Jerauld | | | 073 |
| Jones | | | 075 |
| Kingsbury | | | 077 |
| Lake | | | 079 |
| Lincoln | | | 083 |
| Lyman | | | 085 |
| McCook | | | 087 |
| McPherson | | | 089 |
| Marshall | | | 091 |
| Mellette | | | 095 |
| Miner | | | 097 |
| Minnehaha | | | 099 |
| Moody | | | 101 |
| Potter | | | 107 |
| Roberts | | | 109 |
| Sanborn | | | 111 |
| Spink | | | 115 |
| Stanley | | | 117 |
| Sully | | | 119 |
| Todd | | | 121 |
| Tripp | | | 123 |
| Turner | | | 125 |
| Walworth | | | 129 |
| Yankton | | | 135 |
| **South Bend-Elkhart (588)** | | | |
| Elkhart | IN | 18 | 039 |
| Fulton | | | 049 |
| Kosciusko | | | 085 |
| Lagrange | | | 087 |
| Marshall | | | 099 |
| Pulaski | | | 131 |
| St. Joseph | | | 141 |
| Starke | | | 149 |
| Berrien | MI | 26 | 021 |
| Cass | | | 027 |
| **Spokane (881)** | | | |
| Benewah | ID | 16 | 009 |
| Bonner | | | 017 |
| Boundary | | | 021 |
| Clearwater | | | 035 |
| Idaho | | | 049 |
| Kootenai | | | 055 |
| Latah | | | 057 |

| DMA (DMA Code) County | | | FIPS Codes |
|---|---|---|---|
| **Spokane (881) Cont.** | | | |
| Lewis | | | 061 |
| Nez Perce | | | 069 |
| Shoshone | | | 079 |
| Lincoln | MT | 30 | 053 |
| Wallowa | OR | 41 | 063 |
| Adams | WA | 53 | 001 |
| Asotin | | | 003 |
| Columbia | | | 013 |
| Ferry | | | 019 |
| Garfield | | | 023 |
| Grant | | | 025 |
| Lincoln | | | 043 |
| Okanogan | | | 047 |
| Pend Oreille | | | 051 |
| Spokane | | | 063 |
| Stevens | | | 065 |
| Whitman | | | 075 |
| **Springfield, MO (619)** | | | |
| Baxter | AR | 05 | 005 |
| Boone | | | 009 |
| Carroll | | | 015 |
| Fulton | | | 049 |
| Marion | | | 089 |
| Newton | | | 101 |
| Barry | MO | 29 | 009 |
| Benton | | | 015 |
| Camden | | | 029 |
| Cedar | | | 039 |
| Christian | | | 043 |
| Dade | | | 057 |
| Dallas | | | 059 |
| Dent | | | 065 |
| Douglas | | | 067 |
| Greene | | | 077 |
| Hickory | | | 085 |
| Howell | | | 091 |
| Laclede | | | 105 |
| Lawrence | | | 109 |
| Oregon | | | 149 |
| Ozark | | | 153 |
| Phelps | | | 161 |
| Polk | | | 167 |
| Pulaski | | | 169 |
| St. Clair | | | 185 |
| Shannon | | | 203 |
| Stone | | | 209 |

| DMA (DMA Code) County | | | FIPS Codes |
|---|---|---|---|
| **Springfield, MO (619) Cont.** | | | |
| Taney | | | 213 |
| Texas | | | 215 |
| Webster | | | 225 |
| Wright | | | 229 |
| **Springfield-Holyoke, MA (543)** | | | |
| Franklin | MA | 25 | 011 |
| Hampden | | | 013 |
| Hampshire | | | 015 |
| **St. Joseph, MO (638)** | | | |
| Doniphan | KS | 20 | 043 |
| Andrew | MO | 29 | 003 |
| Buchanan | | | 021 |
| De Kalb | | | 063 |
| Holt | | | 087 |
| Nodaway | | | 147 |
| Worth | | | 227 |
| **St. Louis (609)** | | | |
| Bond | IL | 17 | 005 |
| Calhoun | | | 013 |
| Clinton | | | 027 |
| Fayette | | | 051 |
| Greene | | | 061 |
| Jersey | | | 083 |
| Macoupin | | | 117 |
| Madison | | | 119 |
| Marion | | | 121 |
| Monroe | | | 133 |
| Montgomery | | | 135 |
| Randolph | | | 157 |
| St. Clair | | | 163 |
| Washington | | | 189 |
| Crawford | MO | 29 | 055 |
| Franklin | | | 071 |
| Gasconade | | | 073 |
| Iron | | | 093 |
| Jefferson | | | 099 |
| Lincoln | | | 113 |
| Pike | | | 163 |
| St. Charles | | | 183 |
| Ste. Genevieve | | | 186 |
| St. Francois | | | 187 |
| St. Louis | | | 189 |
| Warren | | | 219 |

| DMA (DMA Code) County | | | FIPS Codes |
|---|---|---|---|
| **St. Louis (609) Cont.** | | | |
| Washington | | | 221 |
| St. Louis City | | | 510 |
| **Syracuse (555)** | | | |
| Cayuga | NY | 36 | 011 |
| Cortland | | | 023 |
| Madison | | | 053 |
| Onondaga | | | 067 |
| Oswego | | | 075 |
| Seneca | | | 099 |
| Tompkins | | | 109 |
| Yates | | | 123 |
| **Tallahassee, FL-Thomasville, GA (530)** | | | |
| Gadsden | FL | 12 | 039 |
| Hamilton | | | 047 |
| Jefferson | | | 065 |
| Lafayette | | | 067 |
| Leon | | | 073 |
| Madison | | | 079 |
| Suwannee | | | 121 |
| Taylor | | | 123 |
| Wakulla | | | 129 |
| Brooks | GA | 13 | 027 |
| Clinch | | | 065 |
| Decatur | | | 087 |
| Echols | | | 101 |
| Grady | | | 131 |
| Lanier | | | 173 |
| Lowndes | | | 185 |
| Miller | | | 201 |
| Thomas | | | 275 |
| **Tampa-St. Petersburg (Sarasota), FL (539)** | | | |
| Citrus | FL | 12 | 017 |
| Hardee | | | 049 |
| Hernando | | | 053 |
| Highlands | | | 055 |
| Hillsborough | | | 057 |
| Manatee | | | 081 |
| Pasco | | | 101 |
| Pinellas | | | 103 |
| Polk | | | 105 |
| Sarasota | | | 115 |

# DMA DEFINITIONS

| DMA (DMA Code) County | | | FIPS Codes |
|---|---|---|---|
| **Terre Haute (581)** | | | |
| Clark | IL | 17 | 023 |
| Clay | | | 025 |
| Crawford | | | 033 |
| Edgar | | | 045 |
| Jasper | | | 079 |
| Lawrence | | | 101 |
| Richland | | | 159 |
| Clay | IN | 18 | 021 |
| Daviess | | | 027 |
| Greene | | | 055 |
| Knox | | | 083 |
| Martin | | | 101 |
| Parke | | | 121 |
| Sullivan | | | 153 |
| Vermillion | | | 165 |
| Vigo | | | 167 |
| **Toledo (547)** | | | |
| Lenawee | MI | 26 | 091 |
| Defiance | OH | 39 | 039 |
| Fulton | | | 051 |
| Hancock | | | 063 |
| Henry | | | 069 |
| Lucas | | | 095 |
| Ottawa | | | 123 |
| Putnam | | | 137 |
| Sandusky | | | 143 |
| Seneca | | | 147 |
| Williams | | | 171 |
| Wood | | | 173 |
| Wyandot | | | 175 |
| **Topeka (605)** | | | |
| Brown | KS | 20 | 013 |
| Clay | | | 027 |
| Coffey | | | 031 |
| Geary | | | 061 |
| Jackson | | | 085 |
| Jefferson | | | 087 |
| Lyon | | | 111 |
| Marshall | | | 117 |
| Morris | | | 127 |
| Nemaha | | | 131 |
| Osage | | | 139 |
| Pottawatomie | | | 149 |
| Riley | | | 161 |
| Shawnee | | | 177 |

| DMA (DMA Code) County | | | FIPS Codes |
|---|---|---|---|
| **Topeka (605) Cont.** | | | |
| Wabaunsee | | | 197 |
| Washington | | | 201 |
| **Traverse City-Cadillac (540)** | | | |
| Antrim | MI | 26 | 009 |
| Benzie | | | 019 |
| Charlevoix | | | 029 |
| Cheboygan | | | 031 |
| Chippewa | | | 033 |
| Clare | | | 035 |
| Crawford | | | 039 |
| Emmet | | | 047 |
| Grand Traverse | | | 055 |
| Kalkaska | | | 079 |
| Lake | | | 085 |
| Leelanau | | | 089 |
| Luce | | | 095 |
| Mackinac | | | 097 |
| Manistee | | | 101 |
| Mason | | | 105 |
| Mecosta | | | 107 |
| Missaukee | | | 113 |
| Montmorency | | | 119 |
| Osceola | | | 133 |
| Oscoda | | | 135 |
| Otsego | | | 137 |
| Presque Isle | | | 141 |
| Roscommon | | | 143 |
| Wexford | | | 165 |
| **Tri-Cities, TN-VA (531)** | | | |
| Leslie | KY | 21 | 131 |
| Letcher | | | 133 |
| Carter | TN | 47 | 019 |
| Greene | | | 059 |
| Hawkins | | | 073 |
| Johnson | | | 091 |
| Sullivan | | | 163 |
| Unicoi | | | 171 |
| Washington | | | 179 |
| Buchanan | VA | 51 | 027 |
| Dickenson | | | 051 |
| Lee | | | 105 |
| Russell | | | 167 |
| Scott | | | 169 |
| Smyth | | | 173 |
| Washington | | | 191 |

| DMA (DMA Code) County | | | FIPS Codes |
|---|---|---|---|
| **Tri-Cities, TN-VA (531) Cont.** | | | |
| Wise | | | 195 |
| Bristol City | | | 520 |
| Norton City | | | 720 |
| **Tucson (Sierra Vista), AZ (789)** | | | |
| Cochise | AZ | 04 | 003 |
| Pima | | | 019 |
| Santa Cruz | | | 023 |
| **Tulsa (671)** | | | |
| Chautauqua | KS | 20 | 019 |
| Montgomery | | | 125 |
| Adair | OK | 40 | 001 |
| Cherokee | | | 021 |
| Craig | | | 035 |
| Creek | | | 037 |
| Delaware | | | 041 |
| Haskell | | | 061 |
| Latimer | | | 077 |
| McIntosh | | | 091 |
| Mayes | | | 097 |
| Muskogee | | | 101 |
| Nowata | | | 105 |
| Okfuskee | | | 107 |
| Okmulgee | | | 111 |
| Osage | | | 113 |
| Pawnee | | | 117 |
| Pittsburg | | | 121 |
| Rogers | | | 131 |
| Tulsa | | | 143 |
| Wagoner | | | 145 |
| Washington | | | 147 |
| **Twin Falls (760)** | | | |
| Blaine | ID | 16 | 013 |
| Cassia | | | 031 |
| Gooding | | | 047 |
| Jerome | | | 053 |
| Lincoln | | | 063 |
| Minidoka | | | 067 |
| Twin Falls | | | 083 |
| **Tyler-Longview (Lufkin & Nacogdoches), TX (709)** | | | |
| Angelina | TX | 48 | 005 |
| Cherokee | | | 073 |
| Franklin | | | 159 |

| DMA (DMA Code) County | | | FIPS Codes |
|---|---|---|---|
| **Tyler-Longview (Lufkin & Nacogdoches), TX (709) Cont.** | | | |
| Gregg | | | 183 |
| Houston | | | 225 |
| Nacogdoches | | | 347 |
| Rusk | | | 401 |
| San Augustine | | | 405 |
| Smith | | | 423 |
| Trinity | | | 455 |
| Upshur | | | 459 |
| Wood | | | 499 |
| **Utica (526)** | | | |
| Herkimer | NY | 36 | 043 |
| Oneida | | | 065 |
| Otsego | | | 077 |
| **Victoria (626)** | | | |
| Victoria | TX | 48 | 469 |
| **Waco-Temple-Bryan (625)** | | | |
| Bell | TX | 48 | 027 |
| Brazos | | | 041 |
| Burleson | | | 051 |
| Coryell | | | 099 |
| Falls | | | 145 |
| Lampasas | | | 281 |
| Leon | | | 289 |
| Limestone | | | 293 |
| McLennan | | | 309 |
| Madison | | | 313 |
| Milam | | | 331 |
| Mills | | | 333 |
| Robertson | | | 395 |
| San Saba | | | 411 |
| **Washington, DC (Hagerstown, MD) (511)** | | | |
| District of Col. | DC | 11 | 001 |
| Allegany | MD | 24 | 001 |
| Calvert | | | 009 |
| Charles | | | 017 |
| Frederick | | | 021 |
| Montgomery | | | 031 |
| Prince George's | | | 033 |
| St. Mary's | | | 037 |
| Washington | | | 043 |
| Franklin | PA | 42 | 055 |

| DMA (DMA Code) County | | | FIPS Codes |
|---|---|---|---|
| **Washington, DC (Hagerstown, MD) (511) Cont.** | | | |
| Fulton | | | 057 |
| Arlington | VA | 51 | 013 |
| Clarke | | | 043 |
| Culpeper | | | 047 |
| Fairfax | | | 059 |
| Fauquier | | | 061 |
| Frederick | | | 069 |
| King George | | | 099 |
| Loudoun | | | 107 |
| Page | | | 139 |
| Prince William | | | 153 |
| Rappahannock | | | 157 |
| Shenandoah | | | 171 |
| Spotsylvania | | | 177 |
| Stafford | | | 179 |
| Warren | | | 187 |
| Westmoreland | | | 193 |
| Alexandria City | | | 510 |
| Fairfax City | | | 600 |
| Falls Church City | | | 610 |
| Fredericksburg City | | | 630 |
| Manassas City | | | 683 |
| Manassas Park City | | | 685 |
| Winchester City | | | 840 |
| Berkeley | WV | 54 | 003 |
| Grant | | | 023 |
| Hampshire | | | 027 |
| Hardy | | | 031 |
| Jefferson | | | 037 |
| Mineral | | | 057 |
| Morgan | | | 065 |
| **Watertown (549)** | | | |
| Jefferson | NY | 36 | 045 |
| Lewis | | | 049 |
| St. Lawrence | | | 089 |
| **Wausau-Rhinelander (705)** | | | |
| Adams | WI | 55 | 001 |
| Forest | | | 041 |
| Langlade | | | 067 |
| Lincoln | | | 069 |
| Marathon | | | 073 |
| Oneida | | | 085 |
| Portage | | | 097 |
| Price | | | 099 |

| DMA (DMA Code) County | | | FIPS Codes |
|---|---|---|---|
| **Wausau-Rhinelander (705) Cont.** | | | |
| Taylor | | | 119 |
| Vilas | | | 125 |
| Wood | | | 141 |
| **West Palm Beach-Fort Pierce (548)** | | | |
| Indian River | FL | 12 | 061 |
| Martin | | | 085 |
| Okeechobee | | | 093 |
| Palm Beach | | | 099 |
| St. Lucie | | | 111 |
| **Wheeling, WV-Steubenville, OH (554)** | | | |
| Belmont | OH | 39 | 013 |
| Guernsey | | | 059 |
| Harrison | | | 067 |
| Jefferson | | | 081 |
| Monroe | | | 111 |
| Noble | | | 121 |
| Brooke | WV | 54 | 009 |
| Hancock | | | 029 |
| Marshall | | | 051 |
| Ohio | | | 069 |
| Tyler | | | 095 |
| Wetzel | | | 103 |
| **Wichita Falls, TX & Lawton, OK(627)** | | | |
| Comanche | OK | 40 | 031 |
| Cotton | | | 033 |
| Jackson | | | 065 |
| Jefferson | | | 067 |
| Stephens | | | 137 |
| Tillman | | | 141 |
| Archer | TX | 48 | 009 |
| Baylor | | | 023 |
| Clay | | | 077 |
| Foard | | | 155 |
| Hardeman | | | 197 |
| King | | | 269 |
| Montague | | | 337 |
| Throckmorton | | | 447 |
| Wichita | | | 485 |
| Wilbarger | | | 487 |
| Young | | | 503 |

# DMA DEFINITIONS

| DMA (DMA Code) County | | | FIPS Codes |
|---|---|---|---|
| **Wichita-Hutchinson, KS Plus (678)** | | | |
| Barber | KS | 20 | 007 |
| Barton | | | 009 |
| Butler | | | 015 |
| Chase | | | 017 |
| Cheyenne | | | 023 |
| Clark | | | 025 |
| Comanche | | | 033 |
| Cowley | | | 035 |
| Decatur | | | 039 |
| Dickinson | | | 041 |
| Edwards | | | 047 |
| Elk | | | 049 |
| Ellis | | | 051 |
| Ellsworth | | | 053 |
| Finney | | | 055 |
| Ford | | | 057 |
| Gove | | | 063 |
| Graham | | | 065 |
| Grant | | | 067 |
| Gray | | | 069 |
| Greeley | | | 071 |
| Greenwood | | | 073 |
| Hamilton | | | 075 |
| Harper | | | 077 |
| Harvey | | | 079 |
| Haskell | | | 081 |
| Hodgeman | | | 083 |
| Kearny | | | 093 |
| Kingman | | | 095 |
| Kiowa | | | 097 |
| Lane | | | 101 |
| Lincoln | | | 105 |
| Logan | | | 109 |
| McPherson | | | 113 |
| Marion | | | 115 |
| Meade | | | 119 |
| Mitchell | | | 123 |
| Ness | | | 135 |
| Norton | | | 137 |
| Osborne | | | 141 |
| Ottawa | | | 143 |
| Pawnee | | | 145 |
| Pratt | | | 151 |
| Rawlins | | | 153 |
| Reno | | | 155 |
| Rice | | | 159 |
| Rooks | | | 163 |
| **Wichita-Hutchinson, KS Plus (678) Cont.** | | | |
| Rush | | | 165 |
| Russell | | | 167 |
| Saline | | | 169 |
| Scott | | | 171 |
| Sedgwick | | | 173 |
| Seward | | | 175 |
| Sheridan | | | 179 |
| Sherman | | | 181 |
| Stafford | | | 185 |
| Stanton | | | 187 |
| Stevens | | | 189 |
| Sumner | | | 191 |
| Thomas | | | 193 |
| Trego | | | 195 |
| Wallace | | | 199 |
| Wichita | | | 203 |
| Dundy | NE | 31 | 057 |
| **Wilkes Barre-Scranton (577)** | | | |
| Bradford | PA | 42 | 015 |
| Carbon | | | 025 |
| Clinton | | | 035 |
| Columbia | | | 037 |
| Lackawanna | | | 069 |
| Luzerne | | | 079 |
| Lycoming | | | 081 |
| Monroe | | | 089 |
| Montour | | | 093 |
| Northumberland | | | 097 |
| Schuylkill | | | 107 |
| Snyder | | | 109 |
| Sullivan | | | 113 |
| Susquehanna | | | 115 |
| Union | | | 119 |
| Wayne | | | 127 |
| Wyoming | | | 131 |
| **Wilmington, NC (550)** | | | |
| Bladen | NC | 37 | 017 |
| Brunswick | | | 019 |
| Columbus | | | 047 |
| New Hanover | | | 129 |
| Pender | | | 141 |

| DMA (DMA Code) County | | | FIPS Codes |
|---|---|---|---|
| **Yakima-Pasco-Richland-Kennewick (810)** | | | |
| Morrow | OR | 41 | 049 |
| Umatilla | | | 059 |
| Benton | WA | 53 | 005 |
| Franklin | | | 021 |
| Kittitas | | | 037 |
| Walla Walla | | | 071 |
| Yakima | | | 077 |
| **Youngstown (536)** | | | |
| Columbiana | OH | 39 | 029 |
| Mahoning | | | 099 |
| Trumbull | | | 155 |
| Mercer | PA | 42 | 085 |
| **Yuma, AZ-El Centro, CA (771)** | | | |
| Yuma | AZ | 04 | 027 |
| Imperial | CA | 06 | 025 |
| **Zanesville (596)** | | | |
| Muskingum | OH | 39 | 119 |

*APPENDIX VI* **SIC CODES**

# APPENDIX VI
# SIC Codes

01 Agricultural Production - Crops
02 Agricultural Production - Livestock and Animal Specialties
07 Agricultural Services
08 Forestry
09 Fishing, Hunting and Trapping
10 Metal Mining
12 Coal Mining
13 Oil and Gas Extraction
14 Mining and Quarrying of Nonmetallic Minerals, Except Fuels
15 Building Cnstrctn - General Contractors & Operative Builders
16 Heavy Cnstrctn, Except Building Construction - Contractors
17 Construction - Special Trade Contractors
20 Food and Kindred Products
21 Tobacco Products
22 Textile Mill Products
23 Apparel, Finished Prdcts from Fabrics & Similar Materials
24 Lumber and Wood Products, Except Furniture
25 Furniture and Fixtures
26 Paper and Allied Products
27 Printing, Publishing and Allied Industries
28 Chemicals and Allied Products
29 Petroleum Refining and Related Industries
30 Rubber and Miscellaneous Plastic Products
31 Leather and Leather Products
32 Stone, Clay, Glass, and Concrete Products
33 Primary Metal Industries
34 Fabricated Metal Prdcts, Except Machinery & Transport Eqpmnt
35 Industrial and Commercial Machinery and Computer Equipment
36 Electronic, Elctrcl Eqpmnt & Cmpnts, Excpt Computer Eqpmnt
37 Transportation Equipment
38 Mesr/Anlyz/Cntrl Instrmnts; Photo/Med/Opt Gds; Watchs/Clocks
39 Miscellaneous Manufacturing Industries
40 Railroad Transportation
41 Local, Suburban Transit & Interurbn Hgwy Passenger Transport
42 Motor Freight Transportation
43 United States Postal Service
44 Water Transportation
45 Transportation by Air
46 Pipelines, Except Natural Gas
47 Transportation Services
48 Communications
49 Electric, Gas and Sanitary Services
50 Wholesale Trade - Durable Goods
51 Wholesale Trade - Nondurable Goods
52 Building Matrials, Hrdwr, Garden Supply & Mobile Home Dealrs
53 General Merchandise Stores
54 Food Stores
55 Automotive Dealers and Gasoline Service Stations
56 Apparel and Accessory Stores
57 Home Furniture, Furnishings and Equipment Stores
58 Eating and Drinking Places
59 Miscellaneous Retail
60 Depository Institutions
61 Nondepository Credit Institutions
62 Security & Commodity Brokers, Dealers, Exchanges & Services
63 Insurance Carriers
64 Insurance Agents, Brokers and Service
65 Real Estate
67 Holding and Other Investment Offices
70 Hotels, Rooming Houses, Camps, and Other Lodging Places
72 Personal Services
73 Business Services
75 Automotive Repair, Services and Parking
76 Miscellaneous Repair Services
78 Motion Pictures
79 Amusement and Recreation Services
80 Health Services
81 Legal Services
82 Educational Services
83 Social Services
84 Museums, Art Galleries and Botanical and Zoological Gardens
86 Membership Organizations
87 Engineering, Accounting, Research, Management & Related Svcs
88 Private Households
89 Services, Not Elsewhere Classified
91 Executive, Legislative & General Government, Except Finance
92 Justice, Public Order and Safety
93 Public Finance, Taxation and Monetary Policy
94 Administration of Human Resource Programs
95 Administration of Environmental Quality and Housing Programs
96 Administration of Economic Programs
97 National Security and International Affairs
99 Nonclassifiable Establishments

# COUNTY MAPS

13th EDITION

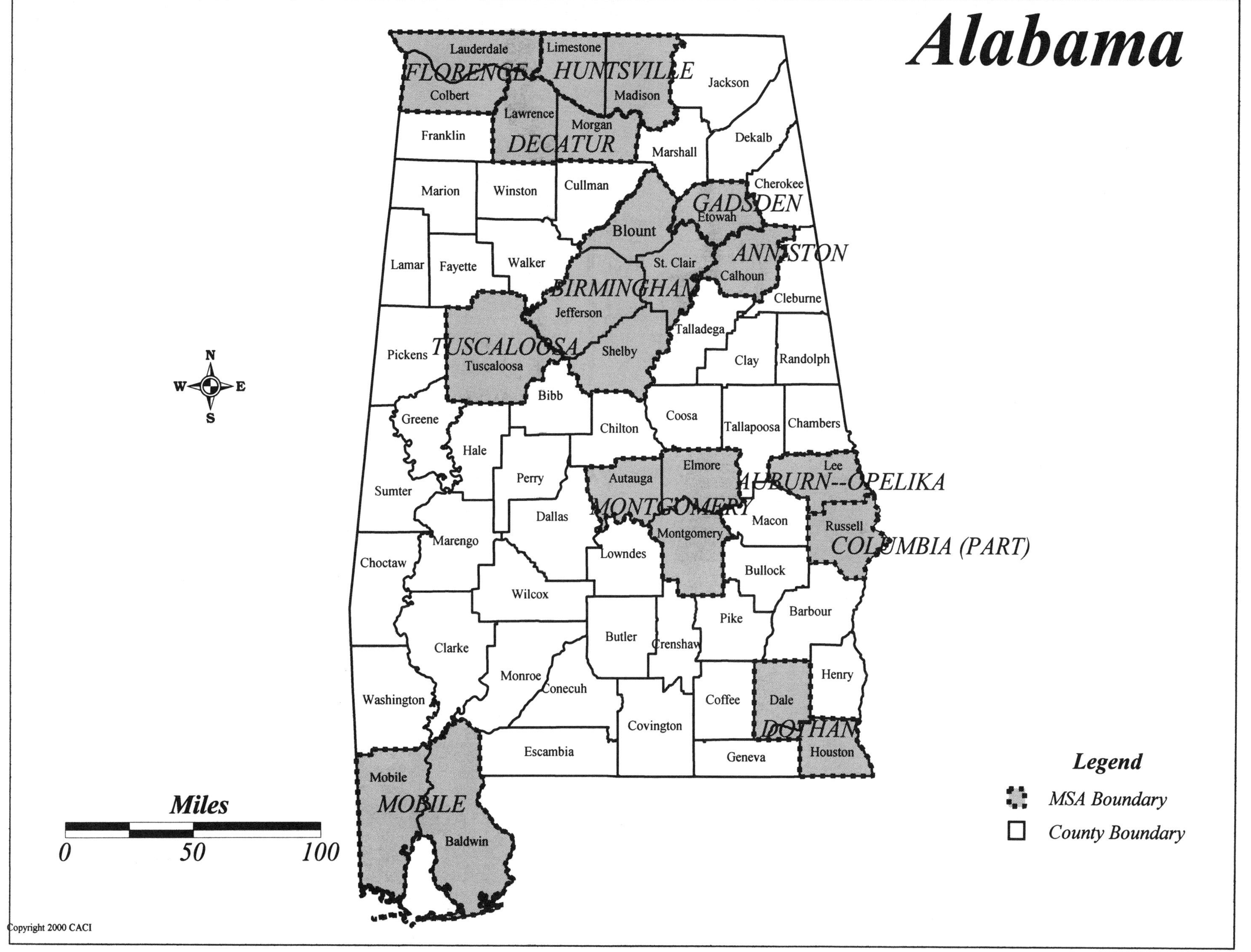

Alabama
Lauderdale
Limestone
FLORENCE
HUNTSVILLE
Colbert
Madison
Jackson
Lawrence
Morgan
Franklin
DECATUR
Dekalb
Marshall
Marion
Winston
Cullman
Cherokee
GADSDEN
Etowah
Blount
ANNISTON
Lamar
Fayette
Walker
St. Clair
Calhoun
BIRMINGHAM
Cleburne
Jefferson
Talladega
Pickens
TUSCALOOSA
Shelby
Clay
Randolph
Tuscaloosa
N
W
E
S
Bibb
Greene
Coosa
Chilton
Tallapoosa
Chambers
Hale
Elmore
Lee
Autauga
Perry
AUBURN--OPELIKA
Sumter
MONTGOMERY
Macon
Dallas
Russell
Montgomery
Marengo
COLUMBIA (PART)
Choctaw
Lowndes
Bullock
Wilcox
Barbour
Pike
Butler
Clarke
Crenshaw
Henry
Monroe
Conecuh
Washington
Coffee
Dale
Covington
DOTHAN
Escambia
Geneva
Houston
Legend
MSA Boundary
County Boundary
Mobile
Miles
MOBILE
Baldwin
0
50
100
Copyright 2000 CACI

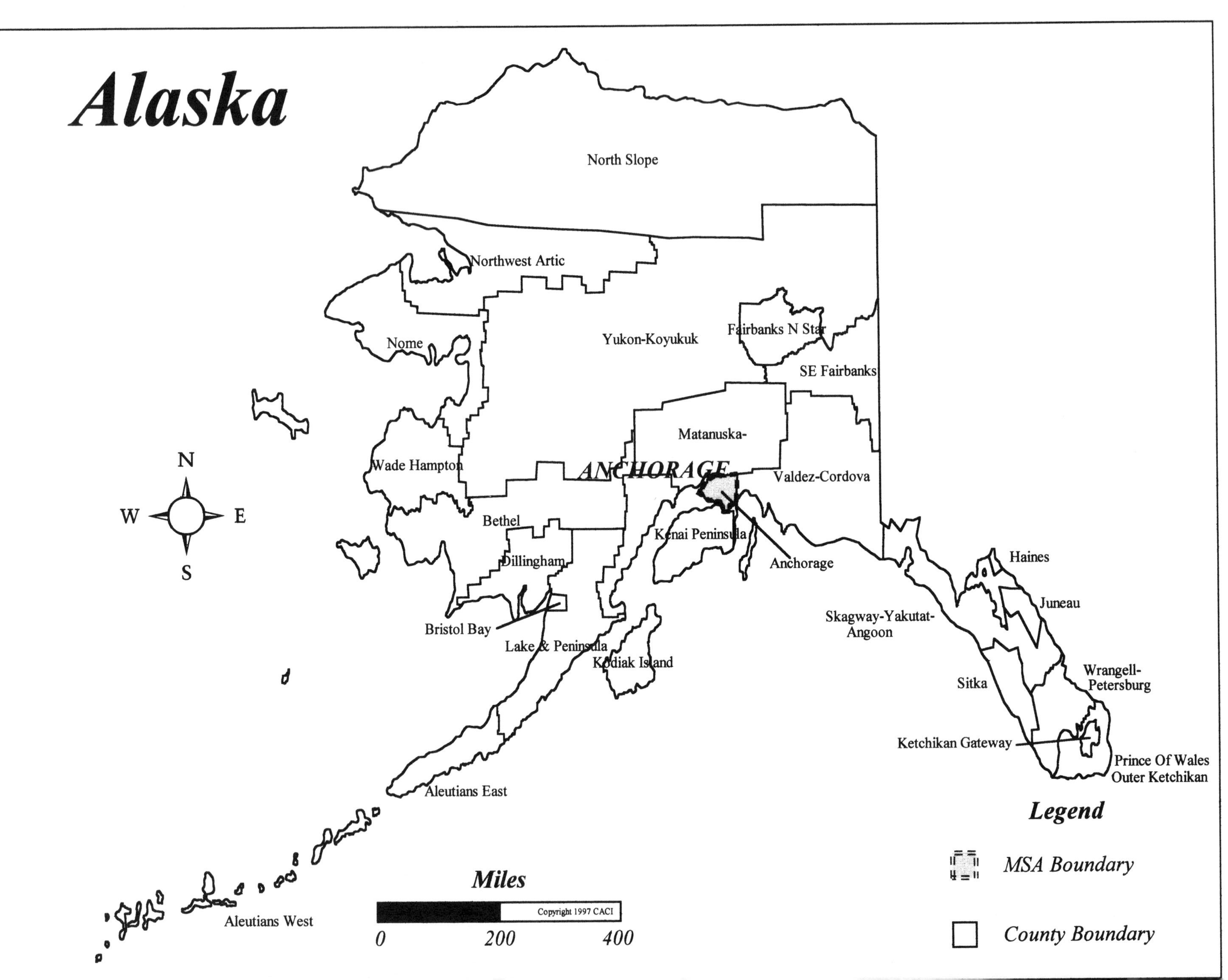

Alaska
North Slope
Northwest Artic
Nome
Yukon-Koyukuk
Fairbanks N Star
SE Fairbanks
Matanuska-
ANCHORAGE
Valdez-Cordova
Wade Hampton
Bethel
Kenai Peninsula
Anchorage
Dillingham
Bristol Bay
Lake & Peninsula
Kodiak Island
Aleutians East
Aleutians West
Skagway-Yakutat-Angoon
Haines
Juneau
Sitka
Wrangell-Petersburg
Ketchikan Gateway
Prince Of Wales Outer Ketchikan
Legend
MSA Boundary
County Boundary
Miles
0
200
400
Copyright 1997 CACI
N
W
E
S

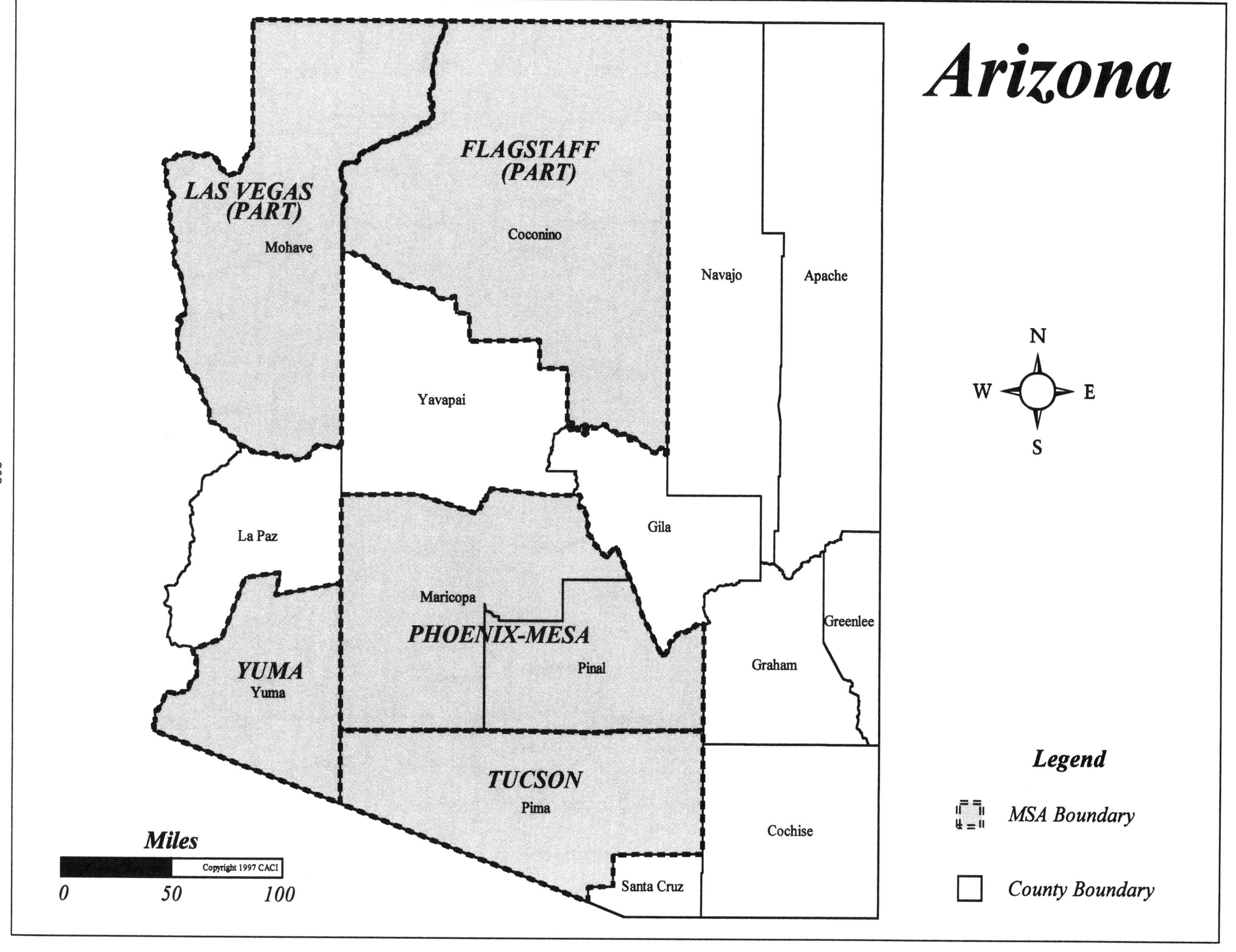
Arizona
LAS VEGAS (PART)
Mohave
FLAGSTAFF (PART)
Coconino
Navajo
Apache
N
W
E
S
Yavapai
La Paz
Gila
Maricopa
PHOENIX-MESA
Pinal
Greenlee
Graham
YUMA
Yuma
TUCSON
Pima
Cochise
Santa Cruz
Legend
MSA Boundary
County Boundary
Miles
0
50
100
Copyright 1997 CACI

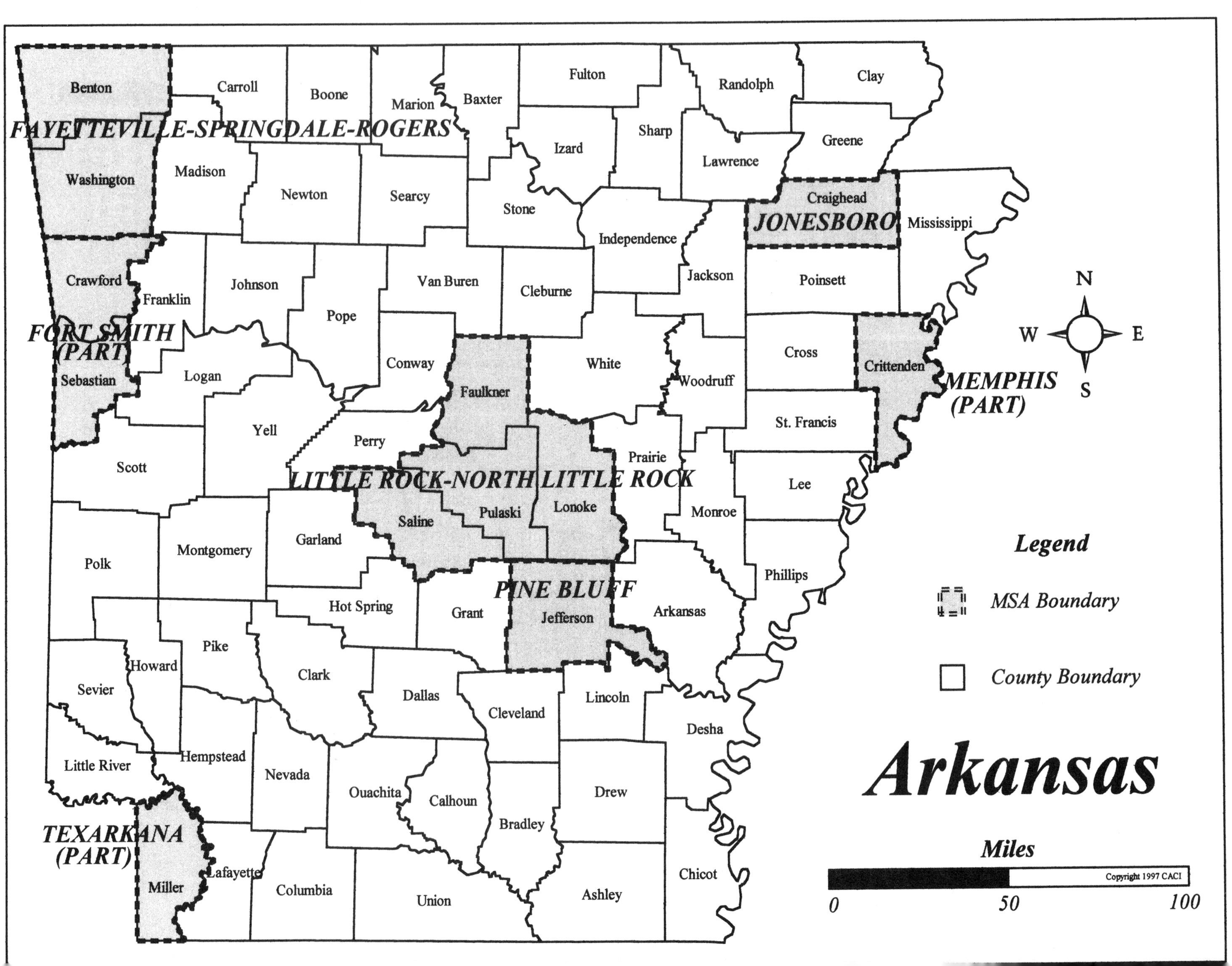
Arkansas
Legend
MSA Boundary
County Boundary
Miles
0
50
100
Copyright 1997 CACI
N
W
E
S
FAYETTEVILLE-SPRINGDALE-ROGERS
FORT SMITH (PART)
LITTLE ROCK-NORTH LITTLE ROCK
PINE BLUFF
JONESBORO
MEMPHIS (PART)
TEXARKANA (PART)
Benton
Carroll
Boone
Marion
Baxter
Fulton
Randolph
Clay
Washington
Madison
Newton
Searcy
Izard
Sharp
Lawrence
Greene
Stone
Independence
Craighead
Mississippi
Crawford
Franklin
Johnson
Pope
Van Buren
Cleburne
Jackson
Poinsett
Sebastian
Logan
Conway
Faulkner
White
Woodruff
Cross
Crittenden
Yell
Perry
Prairie
St. Francis
Scott
Saline
Pulaski
Lonoke
Monroe
Lee
Polk
Montgomery
Garland
Hot Spring
Grant
Jefferson
Arkansas
Phillips
Sevier
Howard
Pike
Clark
Dallas
Cleveland
Lincoln
Desha
Little River
Hempstead
Nevada
Ouachita
Calhoun
Bradley
Drew
Miller
Lafayette
Columbia
Union
Ashley
Chicot

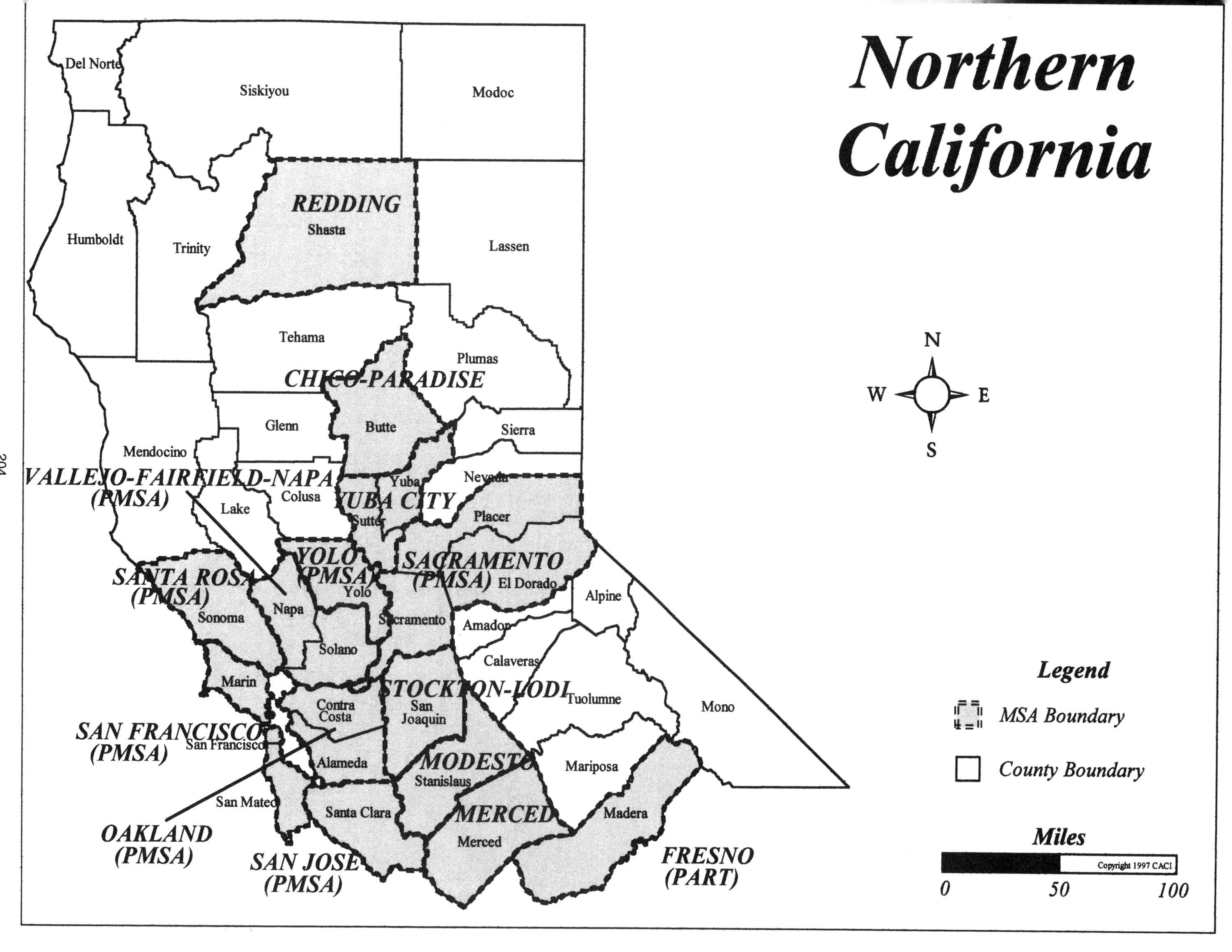

Northern California
N
W
E
S
Del Norte
Siskiyou
Modoc
REDDING
Shasta
Humboldt
Trinity
Lassen
Tehama
Plumas
CHICO-PARADISE
Glenn
Butte
Sierra
Mendocino
VALLEJO-FAIRFIELD-NAPA (PMSA)
Yuba
Nevada
Colusa
Lake
YUBA CITY
Sutter
Placer
YOLO (PMSA)
SACRAMENTO (PMSA)
SANTA ROSA (PMSA)
El Dorado
Yolo
Napa
Alpine
Sonoma
Sacramento
Amador
Solano
Calaveras
Marin
STOCKTON-LODI
Tuolumne
Contra Costa
San Joaquin
Mono
SAN FRANCISCO (PMSA)
San Francisco
Alameda
MODESTO
Mariposa
Stanislaus
San Mateo
Santa Clara
MERCED
Madera
OAKLAND (PMSA)
Merced
SAN JOSE (PMSA)
FRESNO (PART)
Legend
MSA Boundary
County Boundary
Miles
0
50
100
Copyright 1997 CACI

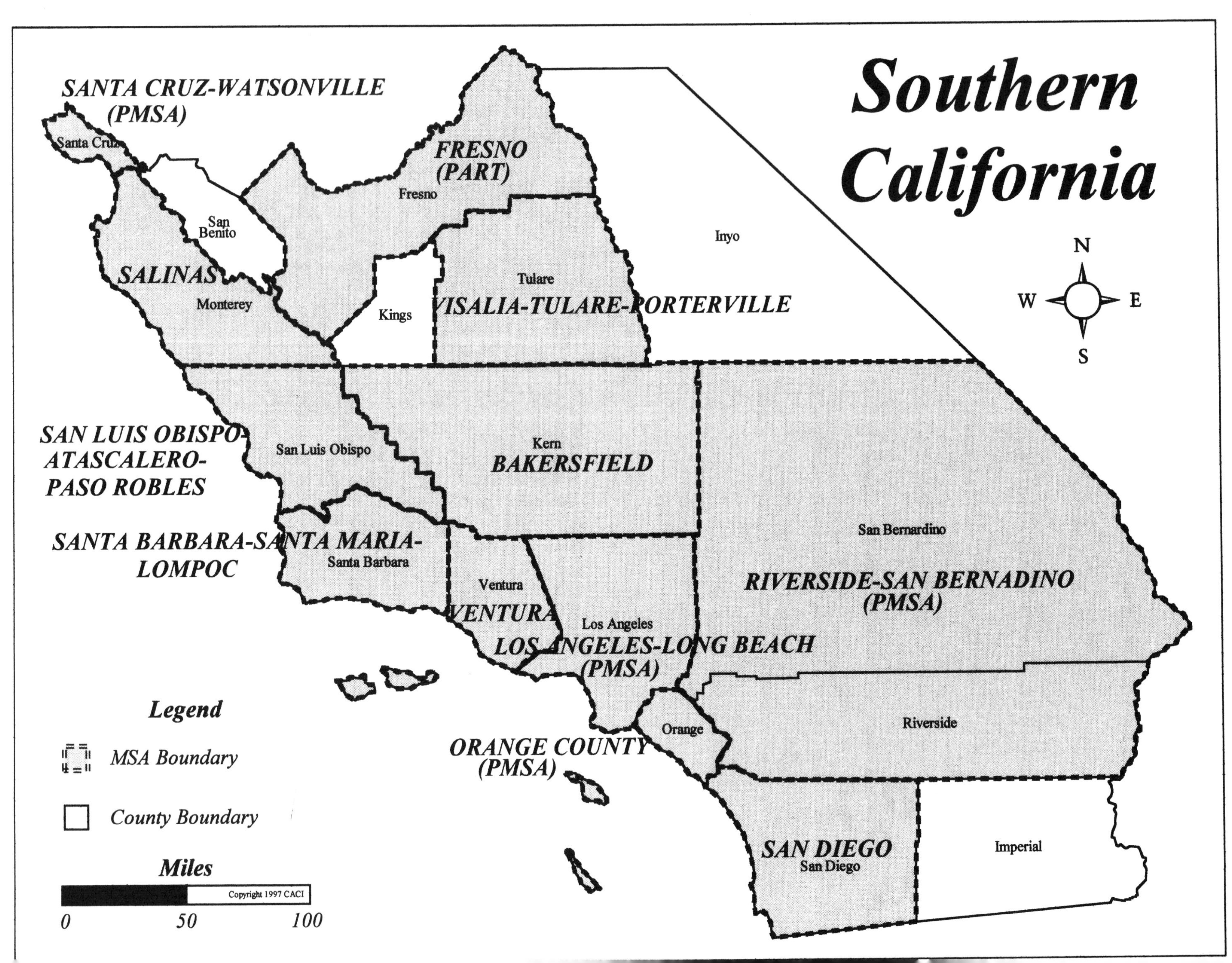

Southern California
N
W
E
S
SANTA CRUZ-WATSONVILLE (PMSA)
Santa Cruz
San Benito
FRESNO (PART)
Fresno
SALINAS
Monterey
Kings
Tulare
VISALIA-TULARE-PORTERVILLE
Inyo
SAN LUIS OBISPO-ATASCALERO-PASO ROBLES
San Luis Obispo
Kern
BAKERSFIELD
SANTA BARBARA-SANTA MARIA-LOMPOC
Santa Barbara
Ventura
VENTURA
Los Angeles
LOS ANGELES-LONG BEACH (PMSA)
San Bernardino
RIVERSIDE-SAN BERNADINO (PMSA)
Riverside
Orange
ORANGE COUNTY (PMSA)
SAN DIEGO
San Diego
Imperial
Legend
MSA Boundary
County Boundary
Miles
Copyright 1997 CACI
0
50
100

# Colorado

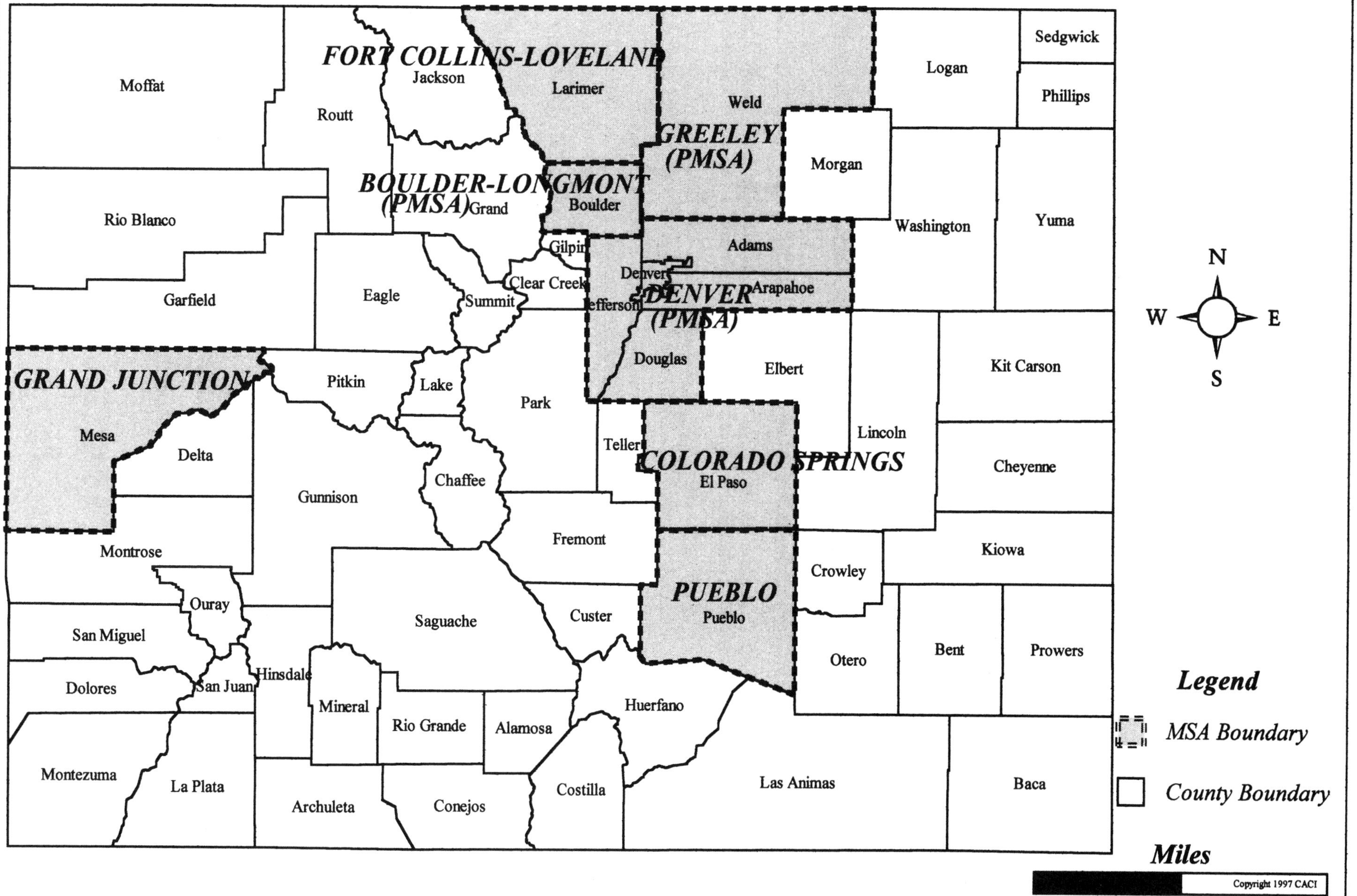

FORT COLLINS-LOVELAND
GREELEY (PMSA)
BOULDER-LONGMONT (PMSA)
DENVER (PMSA)
GRAND JUNCTION
COLORADO SPRINGS
PUEBLO
Moffat
Routt
Jackson
Larimer
Weld
Logan
Sedgwick
Phillips
Morgan
Rio Blanco
Grand
Boulder
Washington
Yuma
Gilpin
Adams
Garfield
Eagle
Summit
Clear Creek
Denver
Arapahoe
Jefferson
Douglas
Elbert
Kit Carson
Mesa
Pitkin
Lake
Park
Delta
Teller
Lincoln
Cheyenne
El Paso
Gunnison
Chaffee
Fremont
Montrose
Kiowa
Crowley
Ouray
Saguache
Custer
Pueblo
San Miguel
Otero
Bent
Prowers
Dolores
San Juan
Hinsdale
Mineral
Rio Grande
Alamosa
Huerfano
Montezuma
La Plata
Archuleta
Conejos
Costilla
Las Animas
Baca
N
W
E
S
Legend
MSA Boundary
County Boundary
Miles
Copyright 1997 CACI
0
50
100

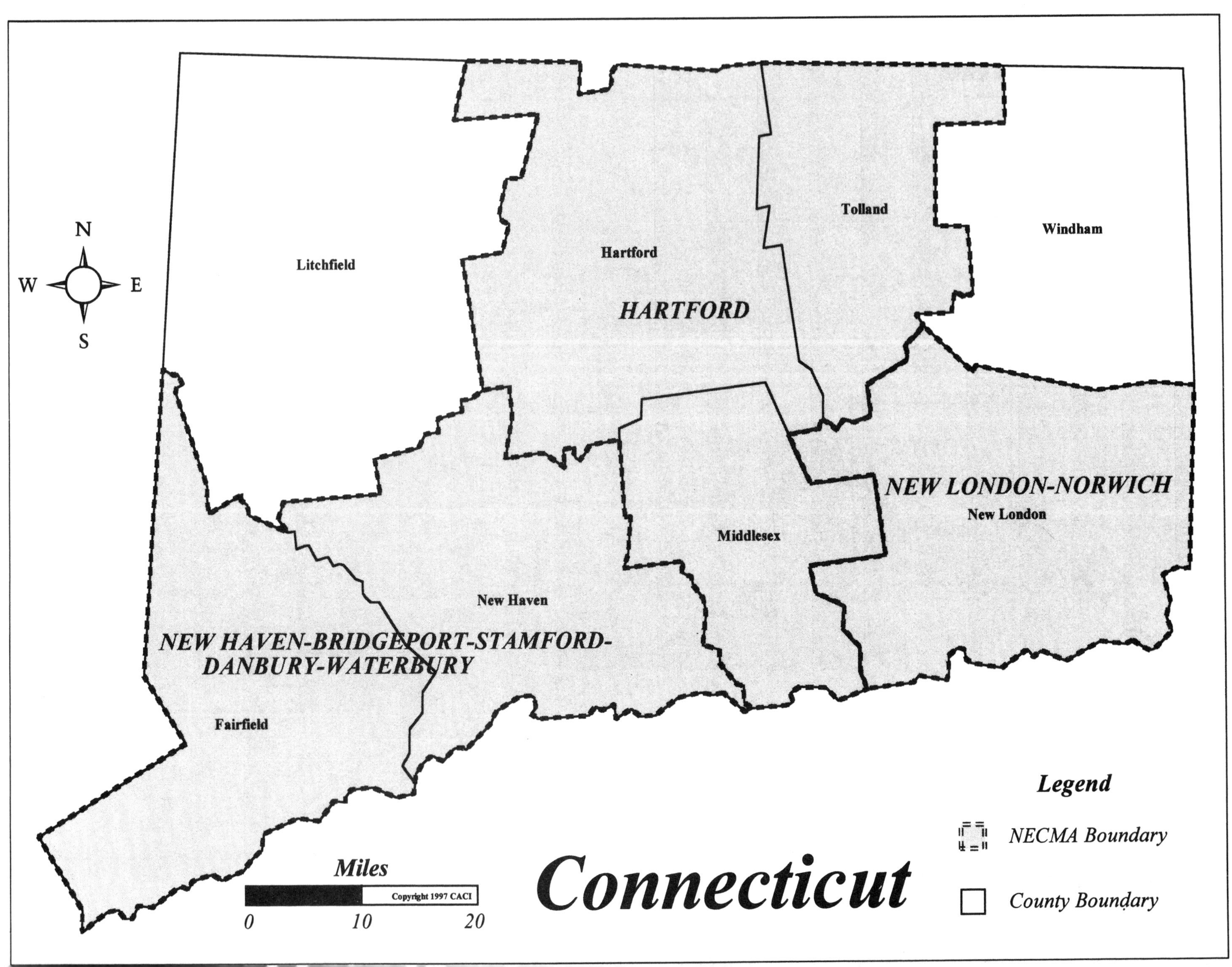

N
W
E
S
Litchfield
Hartford
HARTFORD
Tolland
Windham
NEW LONDON-NORWICH
New London
Middlesex
New Haven
NEW HAVEN-BRIDGEPORT-STAMFORD-
DANBURY-WATERBURY
Fairfield
Legend
NECMA Boundary
County Boundary
Miles
Copyright 1997 CACI
0
10
20
Connecticut

# Delaware

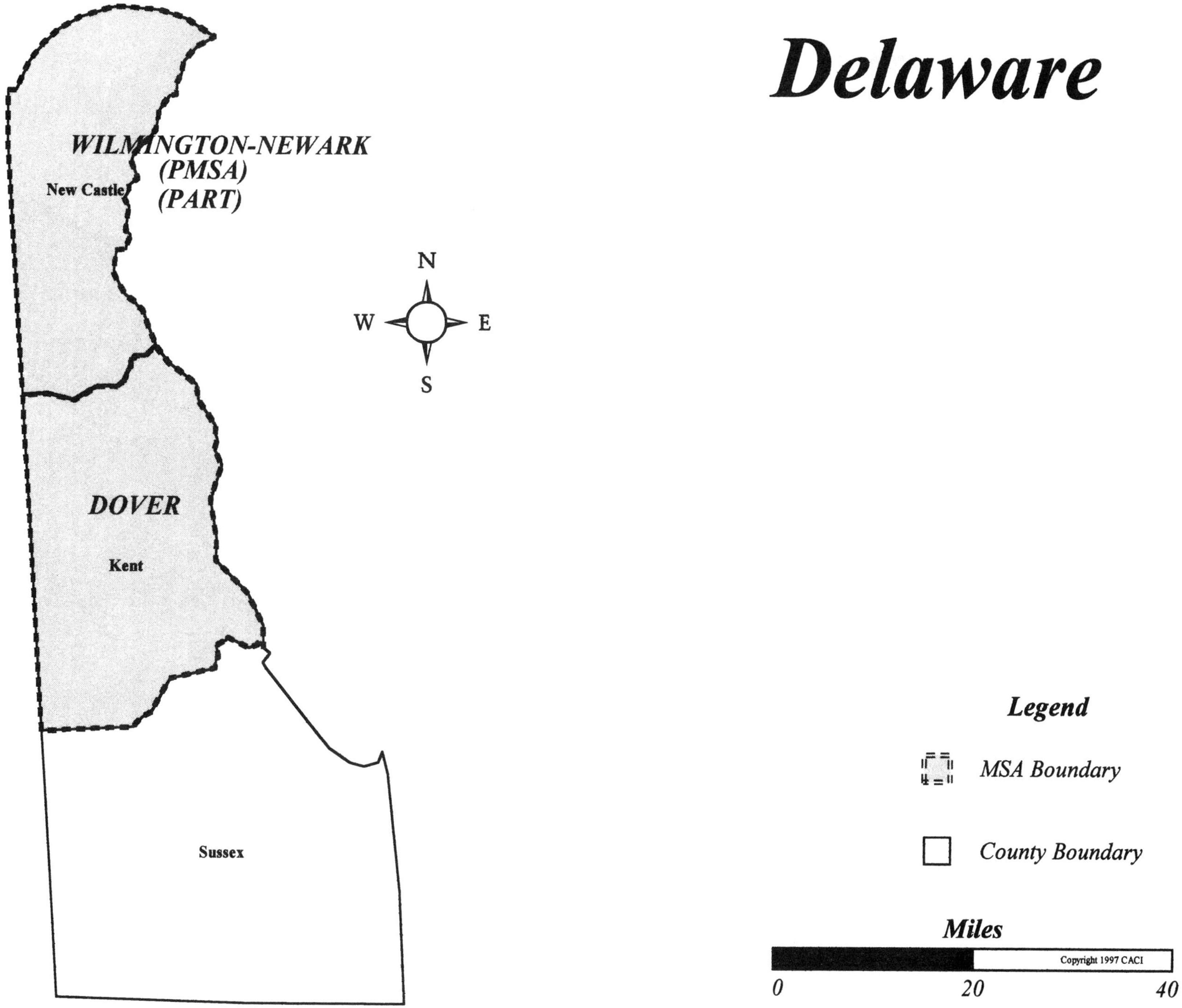

WILMINGTON-NEWARK
(PMSA)
(PART)
New Castle
N
W
E
S
DOVER
Kent
Sussex
Legend
MSA Boundary
County Boundary
Miles
Copyright 1997 CACI
0
20
40

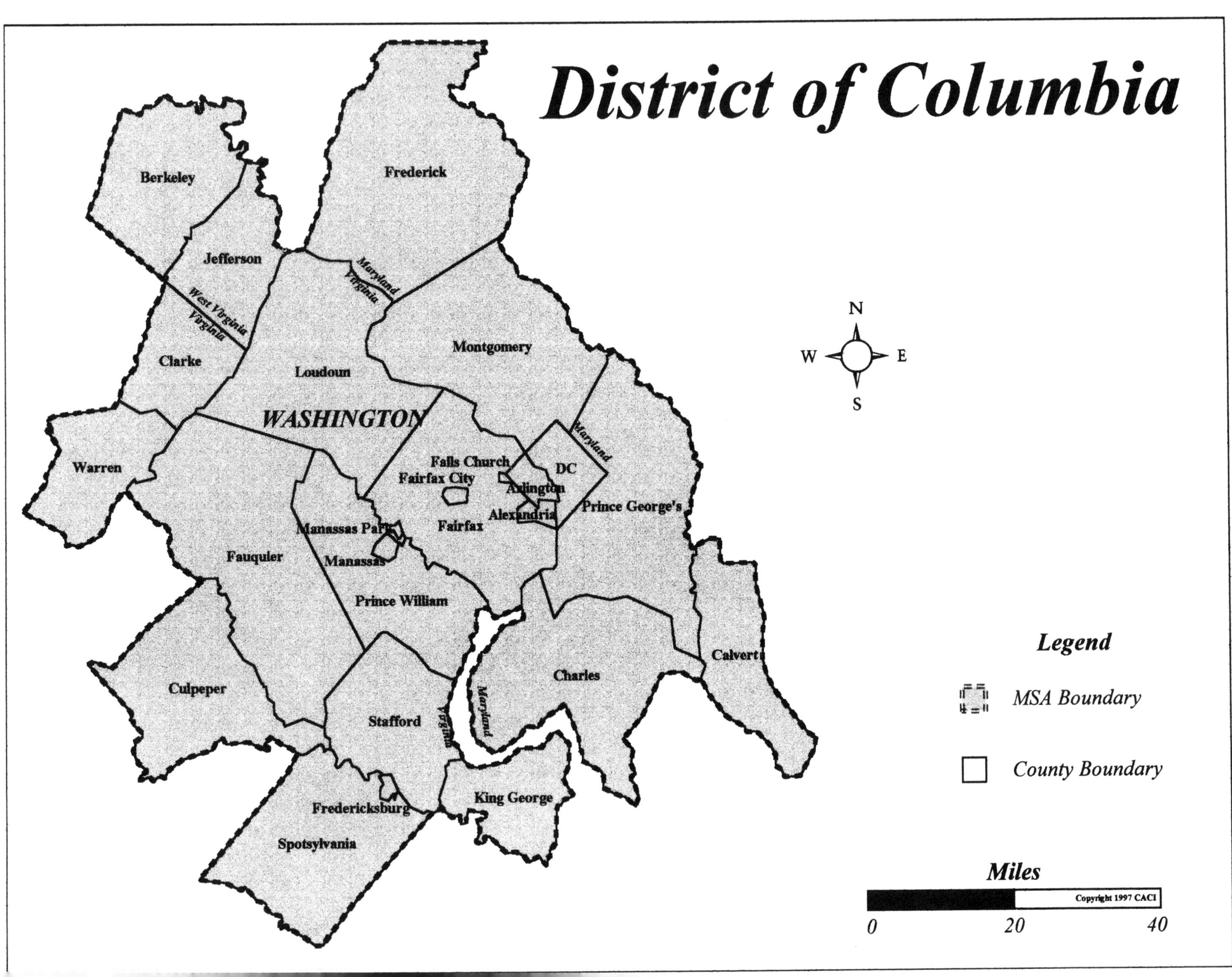

District of Columbia
Berkeley
Frederick
Jefferson
Maryland
Virginia
West Virginia
Virginia
Montgomery
Clarke
Loudoun
WASHINGTON
Warren
Falls Church
Fairfax City
DC
Maryland
Arlington
Alexandria
Prince George's
Fairfax
Manassas Park
Manassas
Fauquier
Prince William
Calvert
Charles
Culpeper
Maryland
Stafford
Virginia
King George
Fredericksburg
Spotsylvania
N
W
E
S
Legend
MSA Boundary
County Boundary
Miles
Copyright 1997 CACI
0
20
40

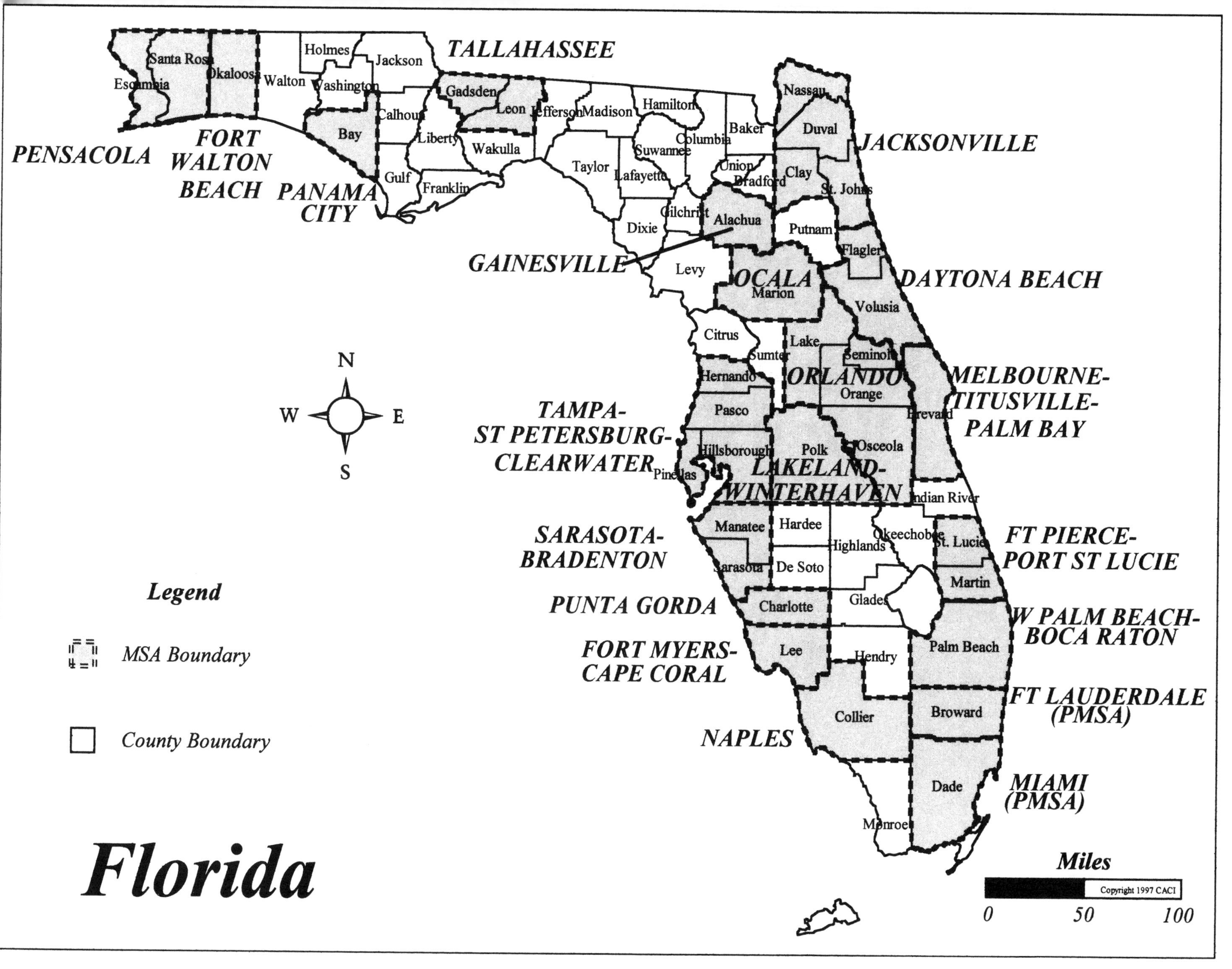

TALLAHASSEE
PENSACOLA
FORT WALTON BEACH
PANAMA CITY
JACKSONVILLE
GAINESVILLE
OCALA
DAYTONA BEACH
ORLANDO
MELBOURNE-TITUSVILLE-PALM BAY
TAMPA-ST PETERSBURG-CLEARWATER
LAKELAND-WINTERHAVEN
SARASOTA-BRADENTON
FT PIERCE-PORT ST LUCIE
PUNTA GORDA
W PALM BEACH-BOCA RATON
FORT MYERS-CAPE CORAL
FT LAUDERDALE (PMSA)
NAPLES
MIAMI (PMSA)
Escambia
Santa Rosa
Okaloosa
Walton
Holmes
Jackson
Washington
Bay
Calhoun
Gulf
Liberty
Franklin
Gadsden
Leon
Wakulla
Jefferson
Madison
Taylor
Hamilton
Suwannee
Lafayette
Columbia
Baker
Union
Bradford
Gilchrist
Dixie
Alachua
Levy
Nassau
Duval
Clay
St. Johns
Putnam
Flagler
Marion
Volusia
Citrus
Sumter
Lake
Seminole
Orange
Hernando
Pasco
Hillsborough
Pinellas
Polk
Osceola
Brevard
Indian River
Manatee
Hardee
Highlands
Okeechobee
St. Lucie
Sarasota
De Soto
Martin
Charlotte
Glades
Lee
Hendry
Palm Beach
Collier
Broward
Dade
Monroe
N
W
E
S
Legend
MSA Boundary
County Boundary
Florida
Miles
Copyright 1997 CACI
0
50
100

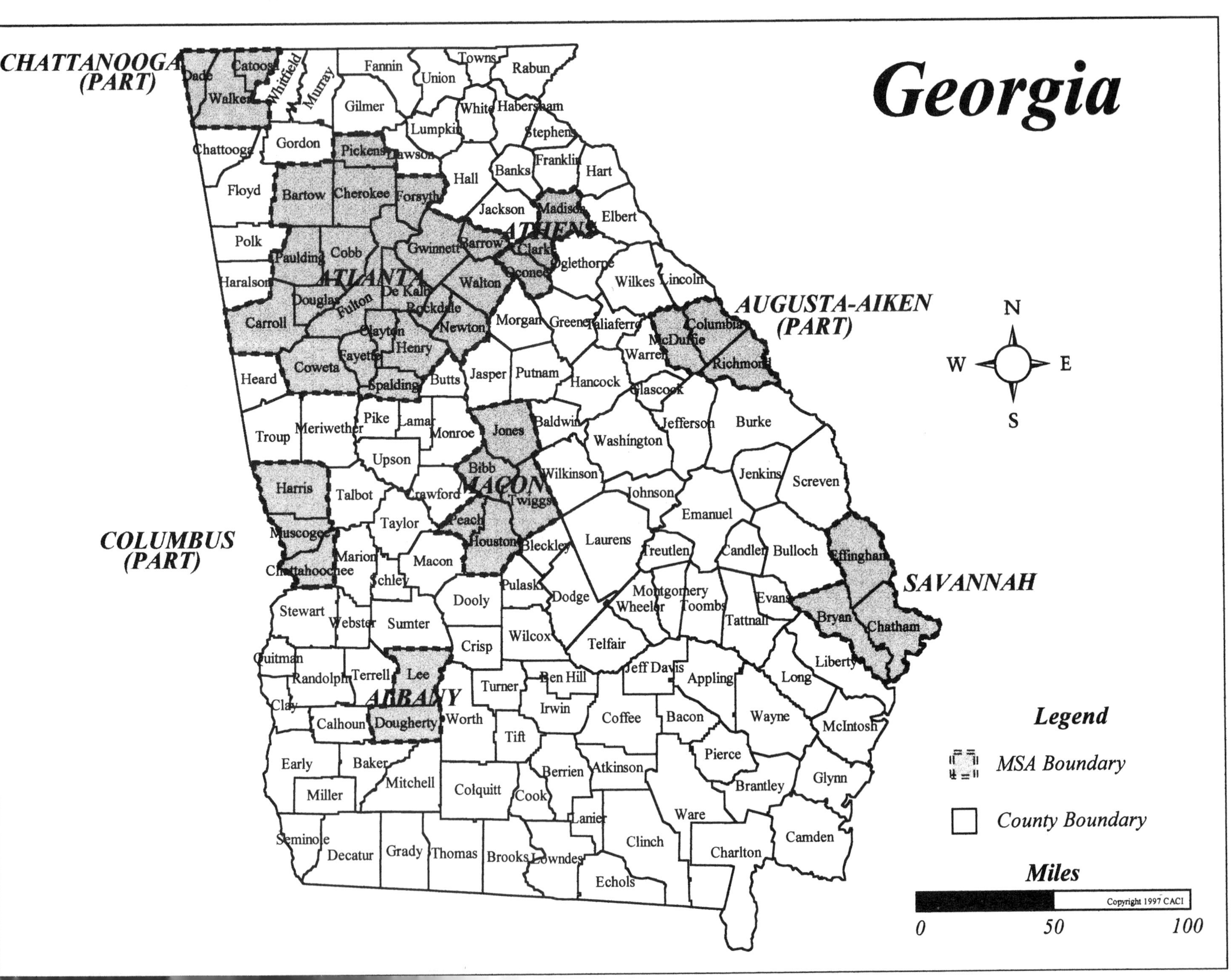
Georgia
CHATTANOOGA (PART)
ATLANTA
ATHENS
AUGUSTA-AIKEN (PART)
MACON
COLUMBUS (PART)
ALBANY
SAVANNAH
N
S
E
W
Dade
Catoosa
Walker
Whitfield
Murray
Fannin
Union
Towns
Rabun
Gilmer
White
Habersham
Lumpkin
Stephens
Chattooga
Gordon
Pickens
Dawson
Franklin
Hart
Banks
Hall
Floyd
Bartow
Cherokee
Forsyth
Jackson
Madison
Elbert
Polk
Paulding
Cobb
Gwinnett
Barrow
Clarke
Oglethorpe
Wilkes
Lincoln
Haralson
Douglas
Fulton
De Kalb
Walton
Oconee
Carroll
Rockdale
Newton
Morgan
Greene
Taliaferro
Columbia
McDuffie
Clayton
Henry
Fayette
Coweta
Warren
Richmond
Heard
Spalding
Butts
Jasper
Putnam
Hancock
Glascock
Troup
Meriwether
Pike
Lamar
Monroe
Jones
Baldwin
Washington
Jefferson
Burke
Upson
Bibb
Wilkinson
Jenkins
Screven
Harris
Talbot
Crawford
Twiggs
Johnson
Emanuel
Taylor
Peach
Houston
Bleckley
Laurens
Muscogee
Marion
Macon
Treutlen
Candler
Bulloch
Effingham
Chattahoochee
Schley
Pulaski
Dodge
Montgomery
Wheeler
Toombs
Evans
Stewart
Webster
Sumter
Dooly
Wilcox
Tattnall
Bryan
Chatham
Crisp
Telfair
Quitman
Randolph
Terrell
Lee
Jeff Davis
Appling
Long
Liberty
Turner
Ben Hill
Clay
Calhoun
Dougherty
Worth
Irwin
Coffee
Bacon
Wayne
McIntosh
Tift
Early
Baker
Pierce
Glynn
Miller
Mitchell
Colquitt
Cook
Berrien
Atkinson
Brantley
Lanier
Ware
Seminole
Decatur
Grady
Thomas
Brooks
Lowndes
Clinch
Charlton
Camden
Echols
Legend
MSA Boundary
County Boundary
Miles
0
50
100
Copyright 1997 CACI

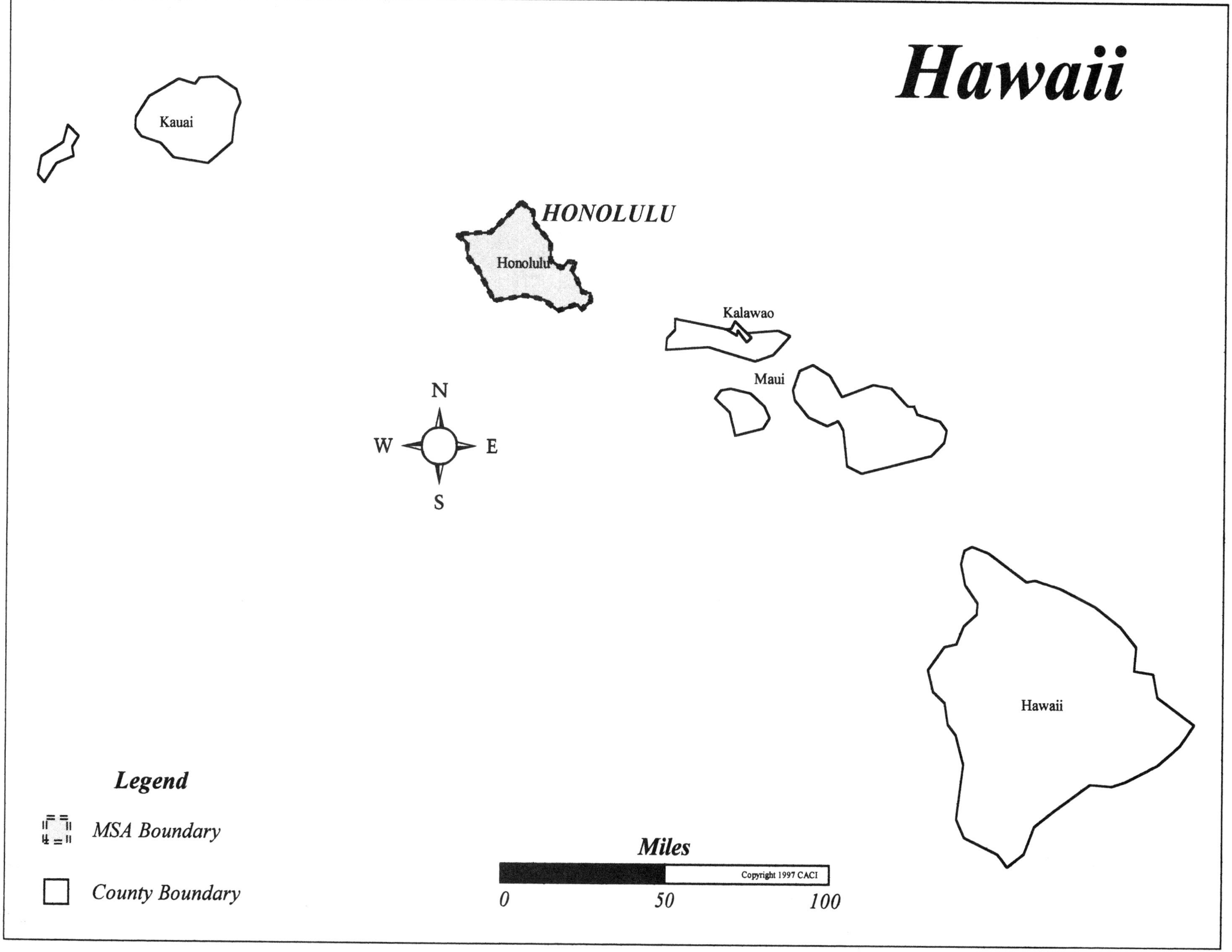

# Hawaii

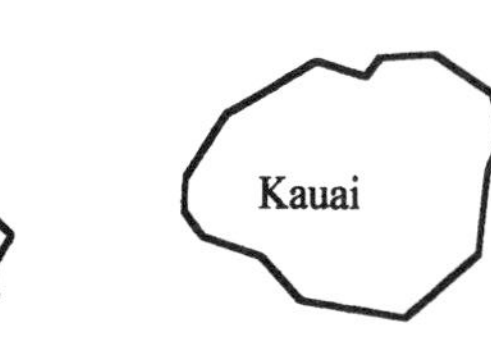
Kauai
HONOLULU
Honolulu
Kalawao
Maui
Hawaii
N
W
E
S
Legend
MSA Boundary
County Boundary
Miles
0
50
100
Copyright 1997 CACI

# Idaho

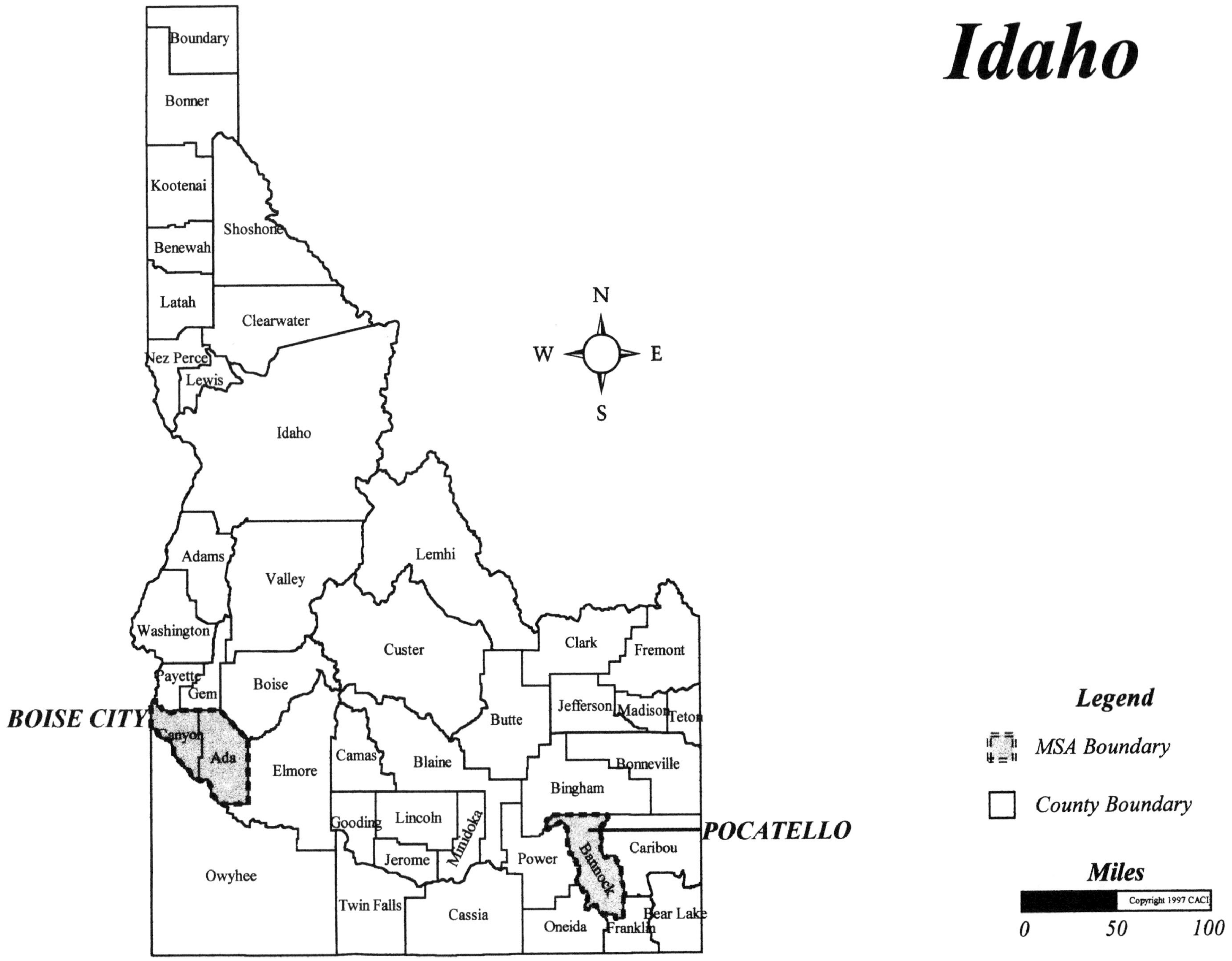
Boundary
Bonner
Kootenai
Shoshone
Benewah
Latah
Clearwater
Nez Perce
Lewis
Idaho
N
W
E
S
Adams
Valley
Lemhi
Washington
Custer
Clark
Fremont
Payette
Gem
Boise
Butte
Jefferson
Madison
Teton
BOISE CITY
Canyon
Ada
Elmore
Camas
Blaine
Bonneville
Bingham
Gooding
Lincoln
Minidoka
Jerome
Power
Bannock
Caribou
POCATELLO
Owyhee
Twin Falls
Cassia
Oneida
Franklin
Bear Lake
Legend
MSA Boundary
County Boundary
Miles
Copyright 1997 CACI
0
50
100

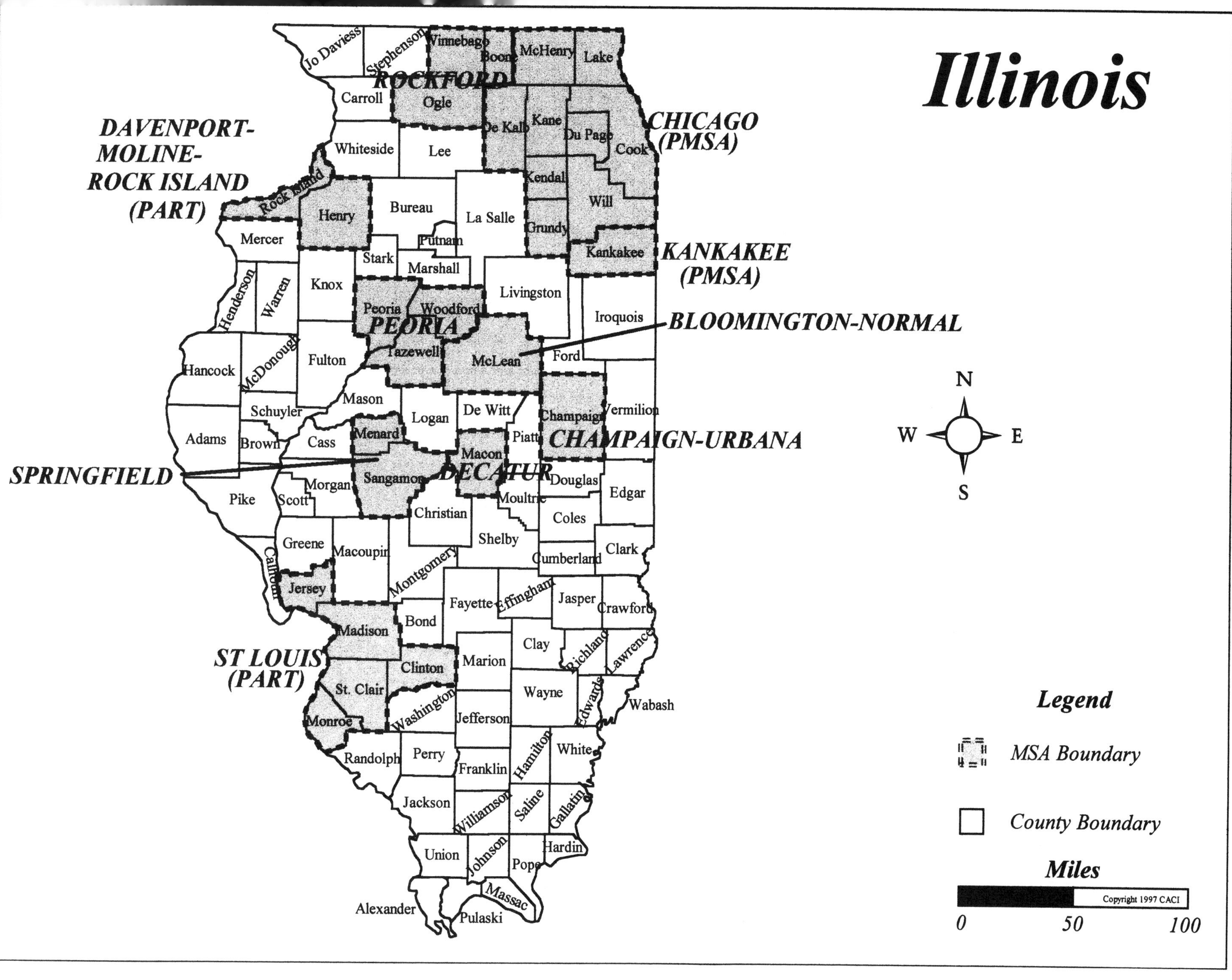

Illinois
CHICAGO (PMSA)
KANKAKEE (PMSA)
BLOOMINGTON-NORMAL
CHAMPAIGN-URBANA
DECATUR
PEORIA
ROCKFORD
SPRINGFIELD
DAVENPORT-MOLINE-ROCK ISLAND (PART)
ST LOUIS (PART)
N
W
E
S
Legend
MSA Boundary
County Boundary
Miles
0
50
100
Copyright 1997 CACI
Jo Daviess
Stephenson
Winnebago
Boone
McHenry
Lake
Carroll
Ogle
De Kalb
Kane
Du Page
Cook
Whiteside
Lee
Kendall
Will
Rock Island
Henry
Bureau
La Salle
Grundy
Mercer
Putnam
Stark
Marshall
Kankakee
Henderson
Warren
Knox
Peoria
Woodford
Livingston
Iroquois
Hancock
McDonough
Fulton
Tazewell
McLean
Ford
Schuyler
Mason
Logan
De Witt
Champaign
Vermilion
Adams
Brown
Cass
Menard
Piatt
Macon
Sangamon
Morgan
Pike
Scott
Douglas
Edgar
Moultrie
Christian
Coles
Greene
Macoupin
Shelby
Calhoun
Cumberland
Clark
Jersey
Montgomery
Fayette
Effingham
Jasper
Crawford
Bond
Madison
Clay
Richland
Lawrence
Marion
Clinton
St. Clair
Wayne
Edwards
Wabash
Washington
Jefferson
Monroe
Randolph
Perry
Hamilton
White
Franklin
Jackson
Williamson
Saline
Gallatin
Union
Johnson
Pope
Hardin
Massac
Alexander
Pulaski

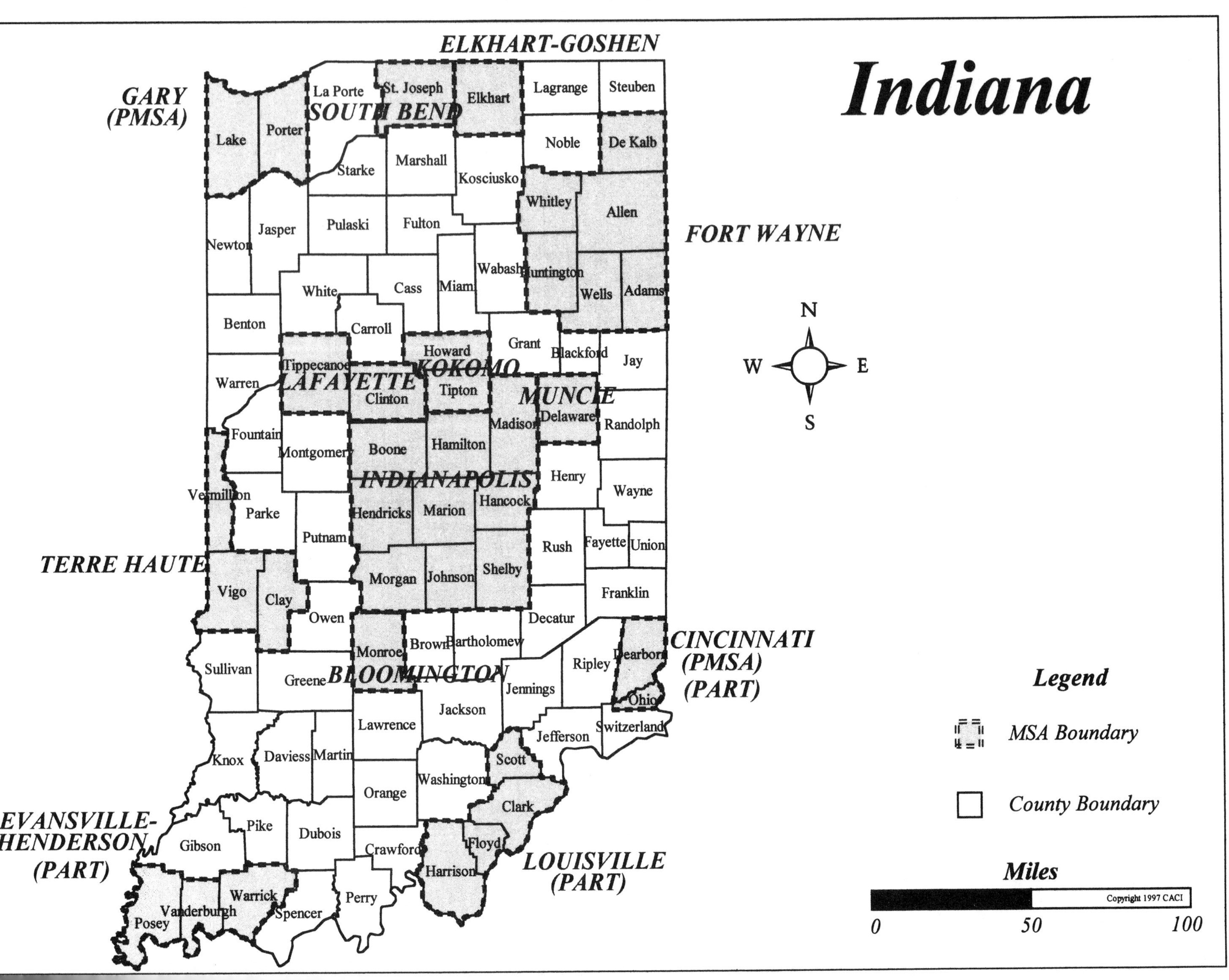
Indiana
ELKHART-GOSHEN
GARY (PMSA)
SOUTH BEND
FORT WAYNE
LAFAYETTE
KOKOMO
MUNCIE
INDIANAPOLIS
TERRE HAUTE
BLOOMINGTON
CINCINNATI (PMSA) (PART)
EVANSVILLE-HENDERSON (PART)
LOUISVILLE (PART)
N
W
E
S
Lake
Porter
La Porte
St. Joseph
Elkhart
Lagrange
Steuben
Noble
De Kalb
Starke
Marshall
Kosciusko
Whitley
Allen
Newton
Jasper
Pulaski
Fulton
Wabash
Huntington
Wells
Adams
White
Cass
Miami
Benton
Carroll
Grant
Blackford
Jay
Howard
Tippecanoe
Warren
Clinton
Tipton
Madison
Delaware
Randolph
Fountain
Montgomery
Boone
Hamilton
Henry
Wayne
Vermillion
Parke
Hendricks
Marion
Hancock
Putnam
Rush
Fayette
Union
Vigo
Clay
Morgan
Johnson
Shelby
Franklin
Owen
Decatur
Monroe
Brown
Bartholomew
Sullivan
Greene
Ripley
Dearborn
Ohio
Jennings
Jackson
Lawrence
Jefferson
Switzerland
Knox
Daviess
Martin
Scott
Washington
Orange
Clark
Pike
Dubois
Gibson
Crawford
Floyd
Harrison
Warrick
Perry
Spencer
Vanderburgh
Posey
Legend
MSA Boundary
County Boundary
Miles
0
50
100
Copyright 1997 CACI

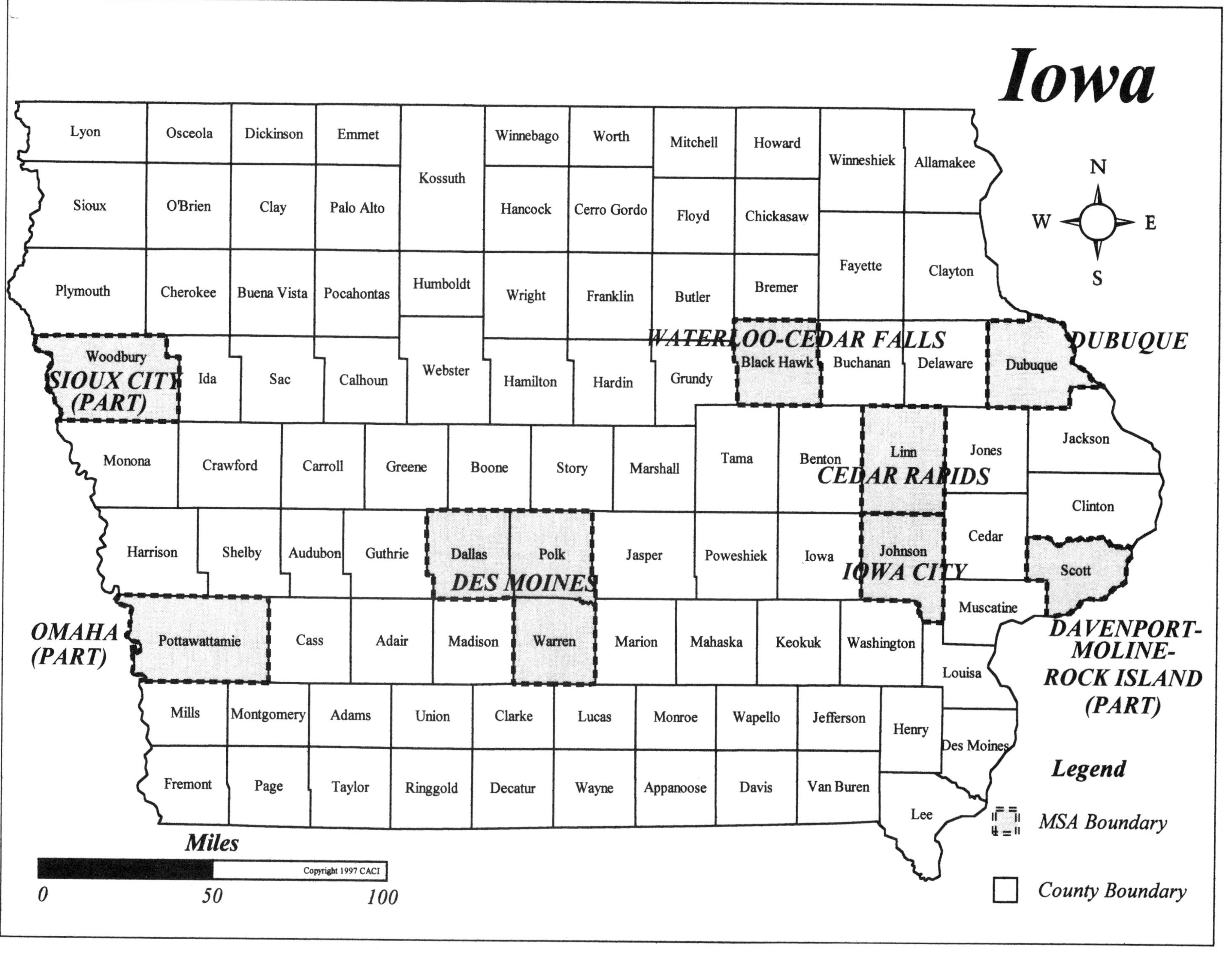
Iowa
N
W
E
S
Lyon
Osceola
Dickinson
Emmet
Kossuth
Winnebago
Worth
Mitchell
Howard
Winneshiek
Allamakee
Sioux
O'Brien
Clay
Palo Alto
Hancock
Cerro Gordo
Floyd
Chickasaw
Fayette
Clayton
Plymouth
Cherokee
Buena Vista
Pocahontas
Humboldt
Wright
Franklin
Butler
Bremer
WATERLOO-CEDAR FALLS
DUBUQUE
Woodbury
SIOUX CITY (PART)
Ida
Sac
Calhoun
Webster
Hamilton
Hardin
Grundy
Black Hawk
Buchanan
Delaware
Dubuque
Monona
Crawford
Carroll
Greene
Boone
Story
Marshall
Tama
Benton
Linn
CEDAR RAPIDS
Jones
Jackson
Clinton
Harrison
Shelby
Audubon
Guthrie
Dallas
Polk
DES MOINES
Jasper
Poweshiek
Iowa
Johnson
IOWA CITY
Cedar
Scott
Muscatine
OMAHA (PART)
Pottawattamie
Cass
Adair
Madison
Warren
Marion
Mahaska
Keokuk
Washington
Louisa
DAVENPORT-MOLINE-ROCK ISLAND (PART)
Mills
Montgomery
Adams
Union
Clarke
Lucas
Monroe
Wapello
Jefferson
Henry
Des Moines
Fremont
Page
Taylor
Ringgold
Decatur
Wayne
Appanoose
Davis
Van Buren
Lee
Legend
MSA Boundary
County Boundary
Miles
Copyright 1997 CACI
0
50
100

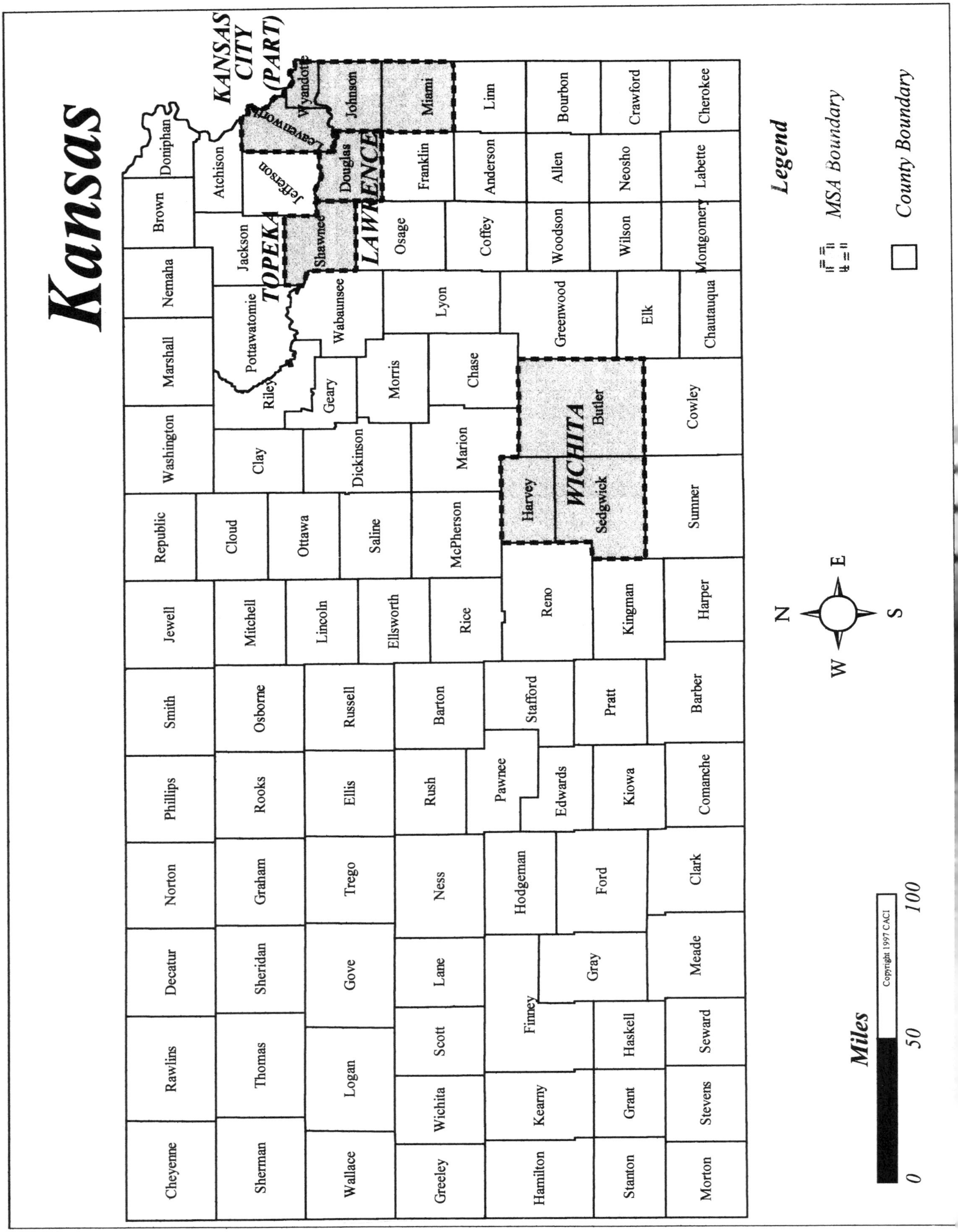

# Kansas

Cheyenne | Rawlins | Decatur | Norton | Phillips | Smith | Jewell | Republic | Washington | Marshall | Nemaha | Brown | Doniphan

Sherman | Thomas | Sheridan | Graham | Rooks | Osborne | Mitchell | Cloud | Clay | Riley | Pottawatomie | Jackson | Atchison

KANSAS CITY (PART)

TOPEKA

Jefferson | Leavenworth | Wyandotte

Wallace | Logan | Gove | Trego | Ellis | Russell | Lincoln | Ottawa | Dickinson | Geary | Wabaunsee | Shawnee | Douglas | Johnson

LAWRENCE

Greeley | Wichita | Scott | Lane | Ness | Rush | Barton | Ellsworth | Saline | Morris | Osage | Franklin | Miami

Rice | McPherson | Marion | Chase | Lyon | Coffey | Anderson | Linn

Hamilton | Kearny | Finney | Hodgeman | Pawnee | Stafford | Reno | Harvey | Greenwood | Woodson | Allen | Bourbon

Edwards

WICHITA

Stanton | Grant | Haskell | Gray | Ford | Kiowa | Pratt | Kingman | Sedgwick | Butler | Elk | Wilson | Neosho | Crawford

Morton | Stevens | Seward | Meade | Clark | Comanche | Barber | Harper | Sumner | Cowley | Chautauqua | Montgomery | Labette | Cherokee

N

W E

S

**Legend**

*MSA Boundary*

*County Boundary*

**Miles**

0 50 100

# Kentucky

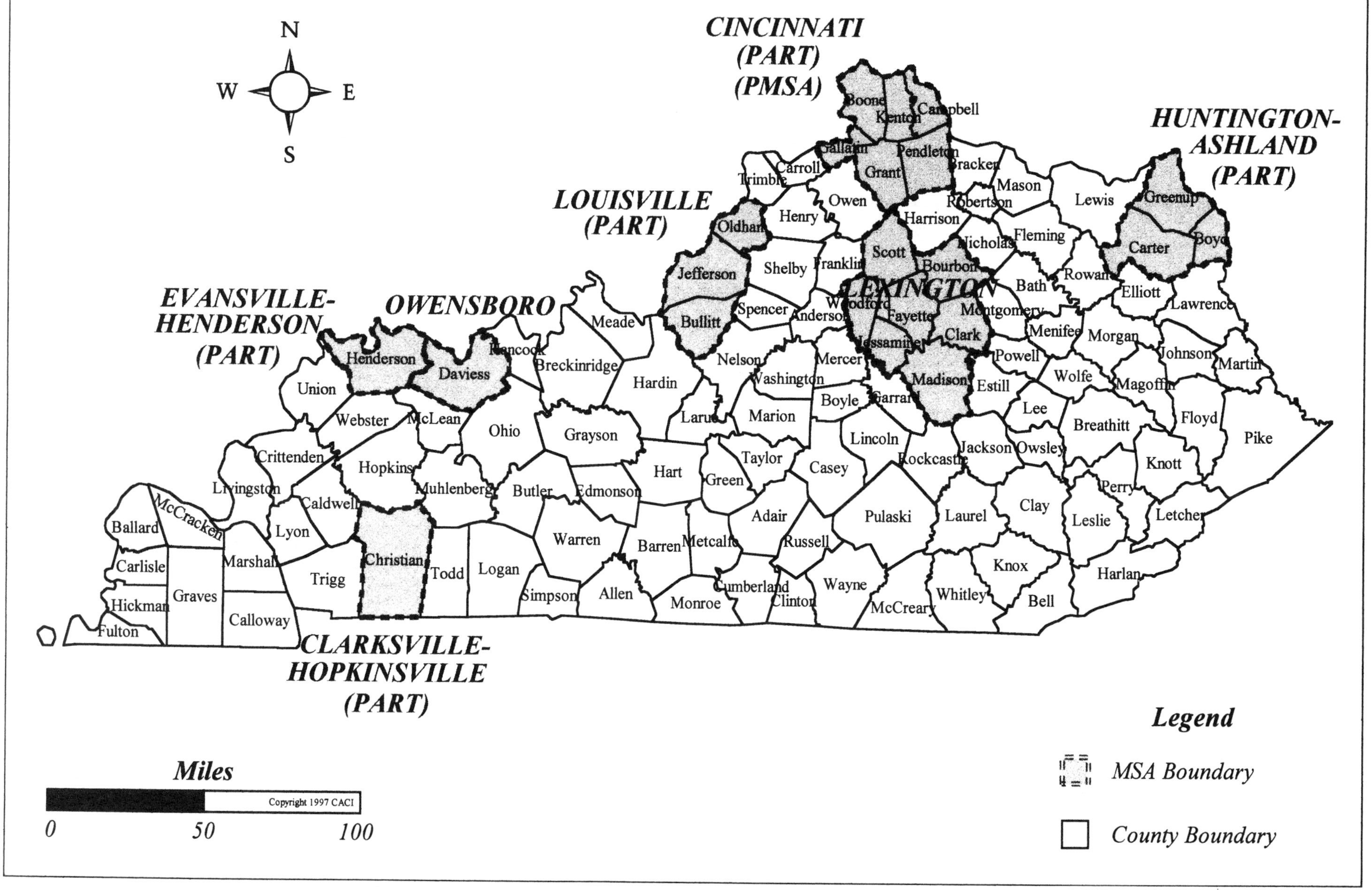

N
W E
S

CINCINNATI (PART) (PMSA)
HUNTINGTON-ASHLAND (PART)
LOUISVILLE (PART)
LEXINGTON
EVANSVILLE-HENDERSON (PART)
OWENSBORO
CLARKSVILLE-HOPKINSVILLE (PART)

Boone
Kenton
Campbell
Gallatin
Grant
Pendleton
Bracken
Carroll
Trimble
Owen
Mason
Robertson
Lewis
Greenup
Boyd
Carter
Henry
Oldham
Harrison
Nicholas
Fleming
Scott
Bourbon
Shelby
Franklin
Jefferson
Woodford
Fayette
Bath
Rowan
Elliott
Lawrence
Spencer
Anderson
Montgomery
Bullitt
Jessamine
Clark
Menifee
Morgan
Meade
Nelson
Mercer
Powell
Johnson
Martin
Hancock
Henderson
Daviess
Breckinridge
Washington
Madison
Wolfe
Magoffin
Union
Hardin
Boyle
Garrard
Estill
Lee
Breathitt
Floyd
Pike
Webster
McLean
Ohio
Grayson
Larue
Marion
Lincoln
Jackson
Owsley
Knott
Crittenden
Hopkins
Hart
Taylor
Casey
Rockcastle
Livingston
Muhlenberg
Butler
Edmonson
Green
Perry
Caldwell
McCracken
Ballard
Lyon
Adair
Pulaski
Laurel
Clay
Leslie
Letcher
Warren
Barren
Metcalfe
Russell
Carlisle
Marshall
Christian
Trigg
Todd
Logan
Knox
Harlan
Graves
Hickman
Fulton
Calloway
Simpson
Allen
Monroe
Cumberland
Clinton
Wayne
McCreary
Whitley
Bell

## Legend

MSA Boundary

County Boundary

Miles



0 50 100

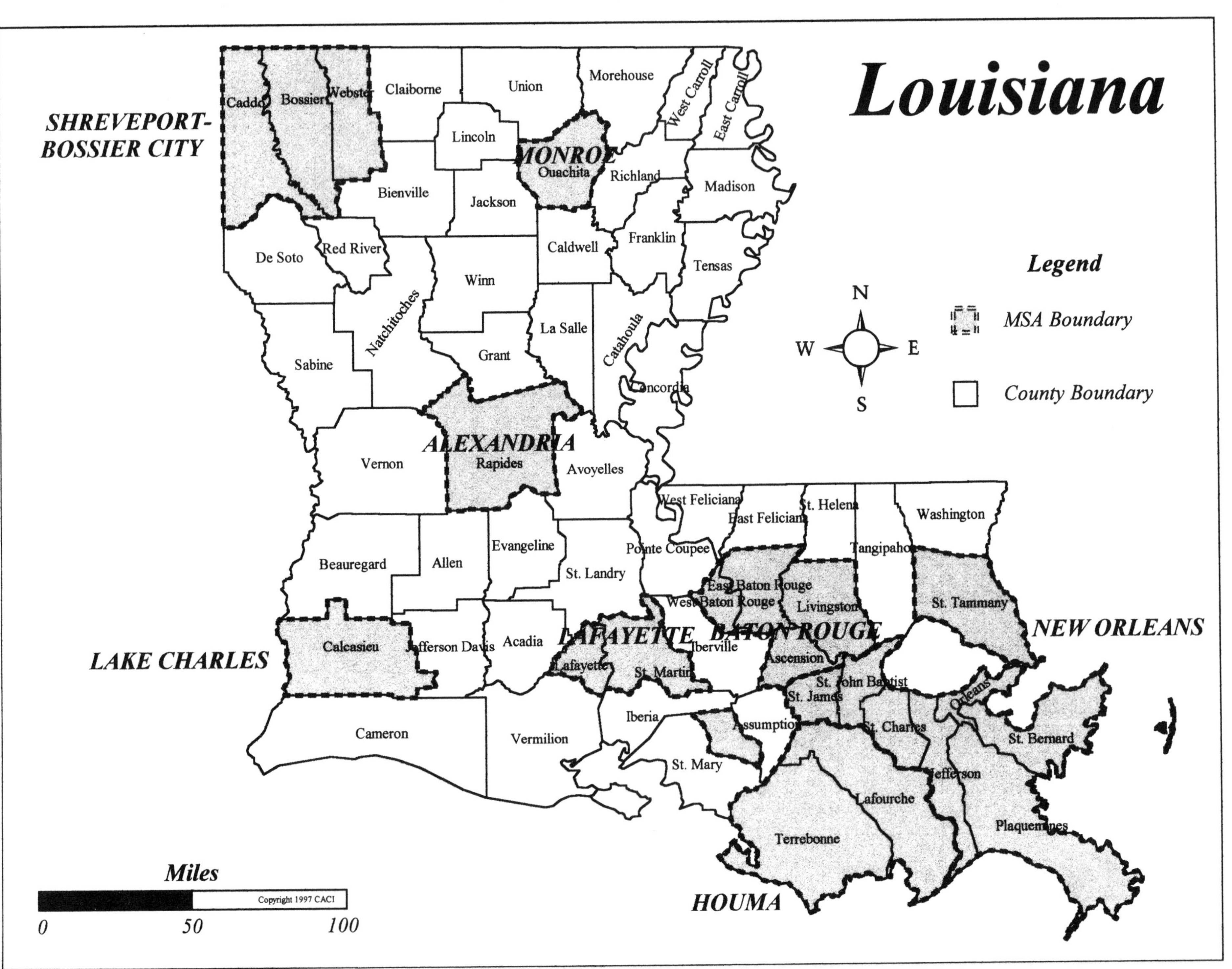

Louisiana
Legend
MSA Boundary
County Boundary
N
S
E
W
SHREVEPORT-
BOSSIER CITY
MONROE
ALEXANDRIA
LAFAYETTE
BATON ROUGE
NEW ORLEANS
LAKE CHARLES
HOUMA
Caddo
Bossier
Webster
Claiborne
Union
Morehouse
West Carroll
East Carroll
Lincoln
Ouachita
Richland
Madison
Bienville
Jackson
De Soto
Red River
Caldwell
Franklin
Tensas
Winn
Natchitoches
La Salle
Catahoula
Sabine
Grant
Concordia
Vernon
Rapides
Avoyelles
West Feliciana
East Feliciana
St. Helena
Washington
Tangipahoa
Beauregard
Allen
Evangeline
St. Landry
Pointe Coupee
East Baton Rouge
West Baton Rouge
Livingston
St. Tammany
Calcasieu
Jefferson Davis
Acadia
Lafayette
St. Martin
Iberville
Ascension
St. John Baptist
St. James
Orleans
Cameron
Vermilion
Iberia
Assumption
St. Charles
St. Bernard
St. Mary
Jefferson
Lafourche
Terrebonne
Plaquemines
Miles
0
50
100
Copyright 1997 CACI

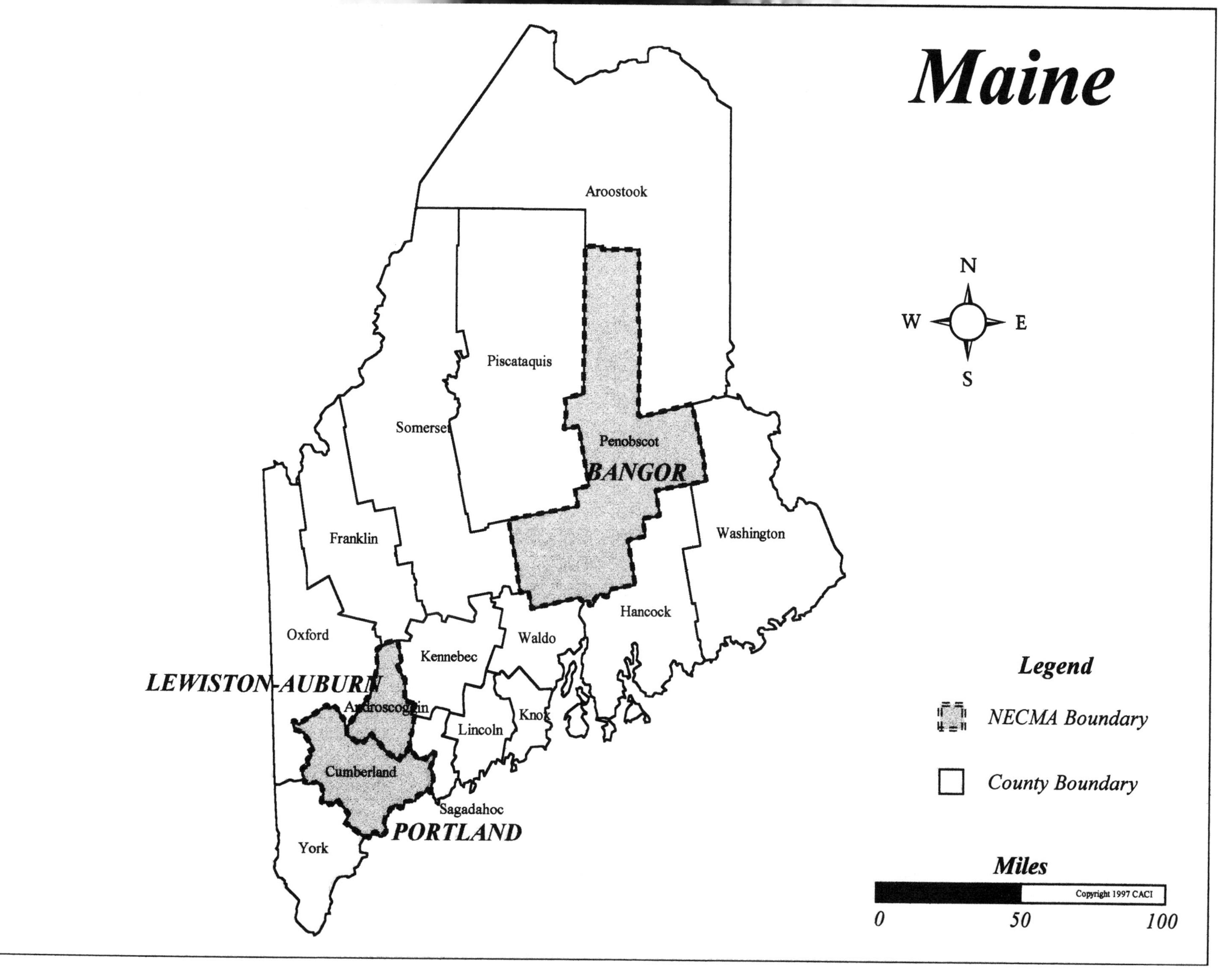

Maine
Aroostook
N
W
E
S
Piscataquis
Somerset
Penobscot
BANGOR
Franklin
Washington
Hancock
Oxford
Waldo
Kennebec
LEWISTON-AUBURN
Androscoggin
Knox
Lincoln
Cumberland
Sagadahoc
PORTLAND
York
Legend
NECMA Boundary
County Boundary
Miles
Copyright 1997 CACI
0
50
100

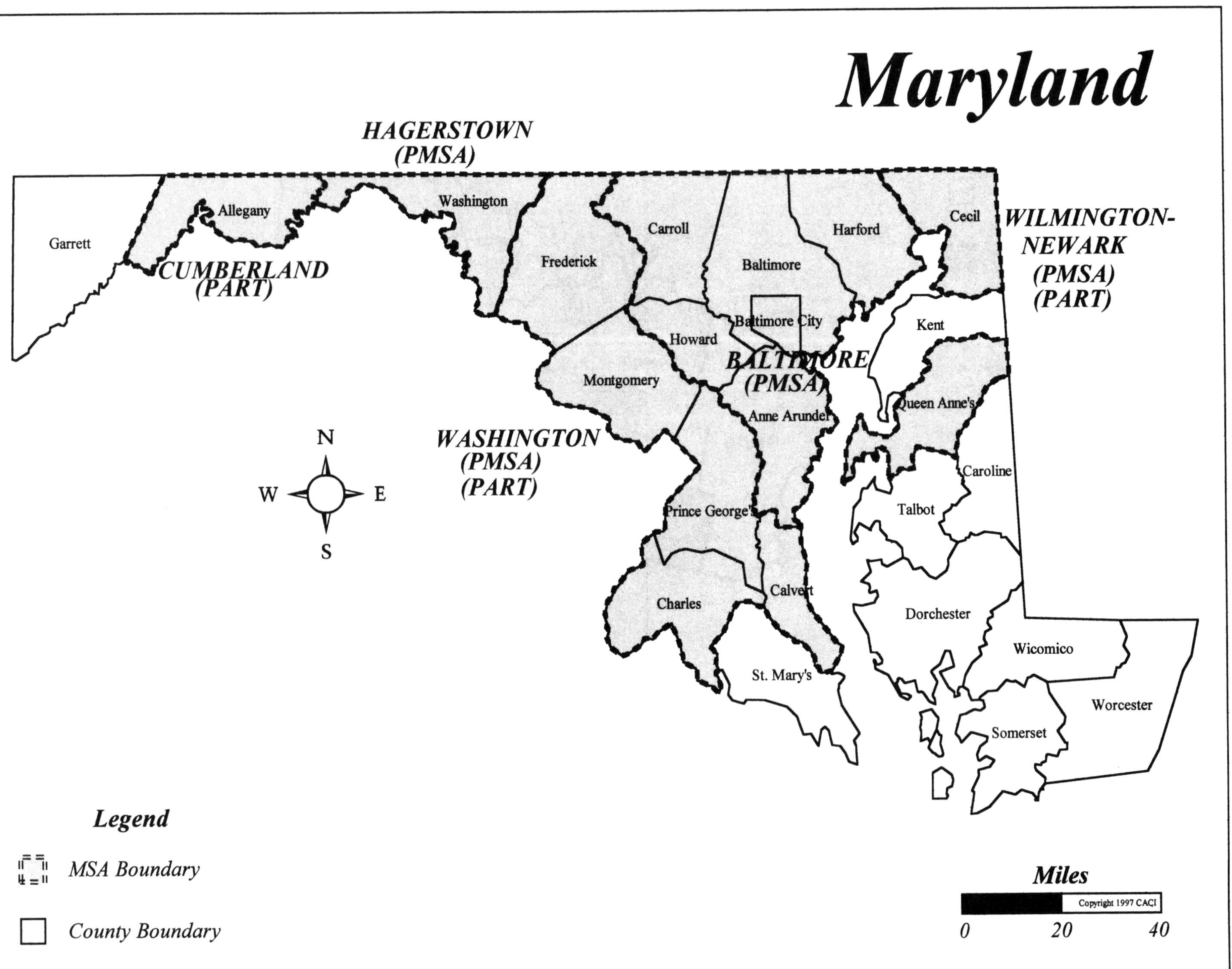
Maryland
HAGERSTOWN (PMSA)
CUMBERLAND (PART)
WILMINGTON-NEWARK (PMSA) (PART)
BALTIMORE (PMSA)
WASHINGTON (PMSA) (PART)
Garrett
Allegany
Washington
Frederick
Carroll
Baltimore
Harford
Cecil
Kent
Baltimore City
Howard
Montgomery
Anne Arundel
Queen Anne's
Caroline
Talbot
Prince George's
Calvert
Charles
St. Mary's
Dorchester
Wicomico
Worcester
Somerset
N
W
E
S
Legend
MSA Boundary
County Boundary
Miles
Copyright 1997 CACI
0
20
40

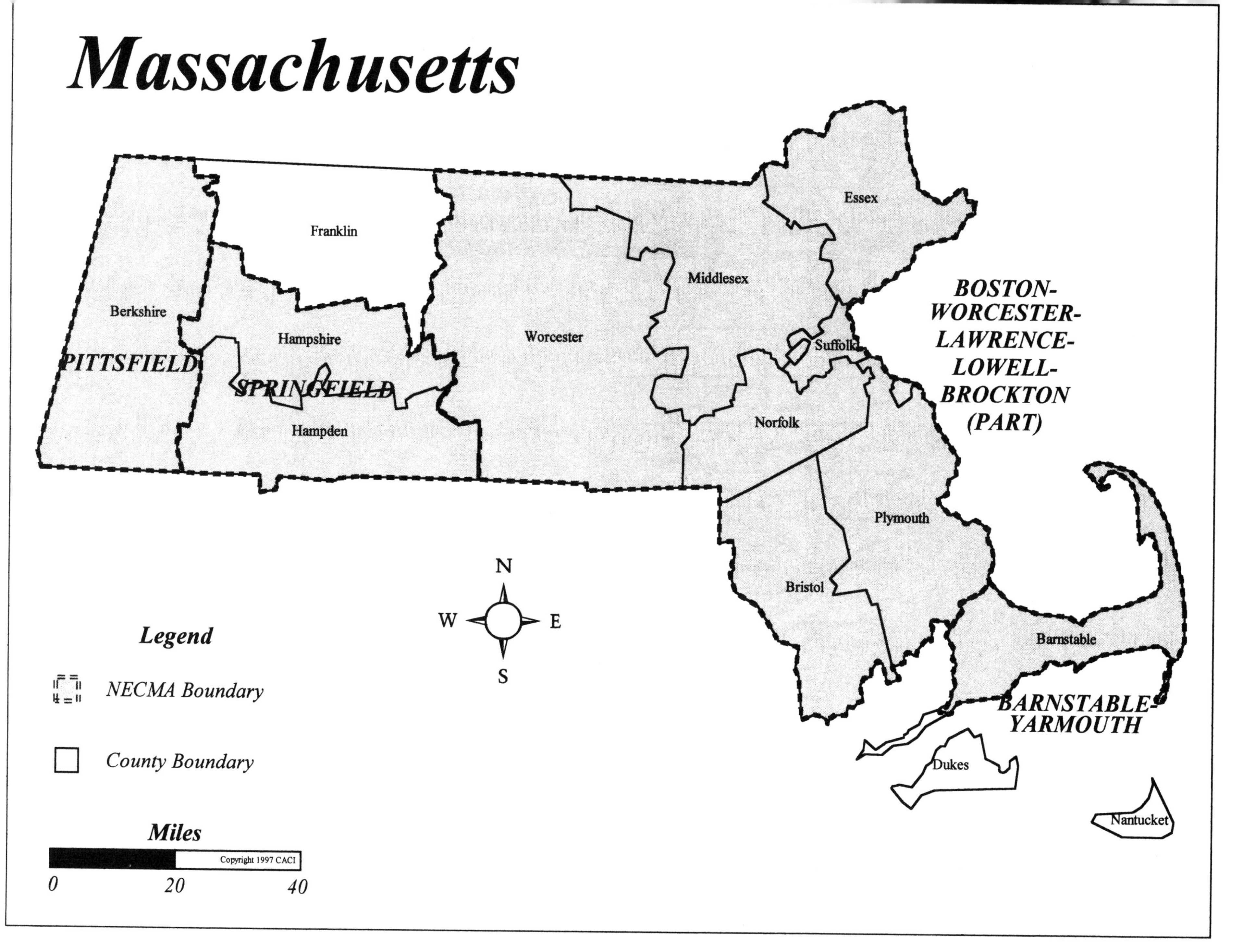

Massachusetts
Berkshire
PITTSFIELD
Franklin
Hampshire
SPRINGFIELD
Hampden
Worcester
Middlesex
Essex
Suffolk
Norfolk
BOSTON-
WORCESTER-
LAWRENCE-
LOWELL-
BROCKTON
(PART)
Plymouth
Bristol
Barnstable
BARNSTABLE-
YARMOUTH
Dukes
Nantucket
N
W
E
S
Legend
NECMA Boundary
County Boundary
Miles
Copyright 1997 CACI
0
20
40

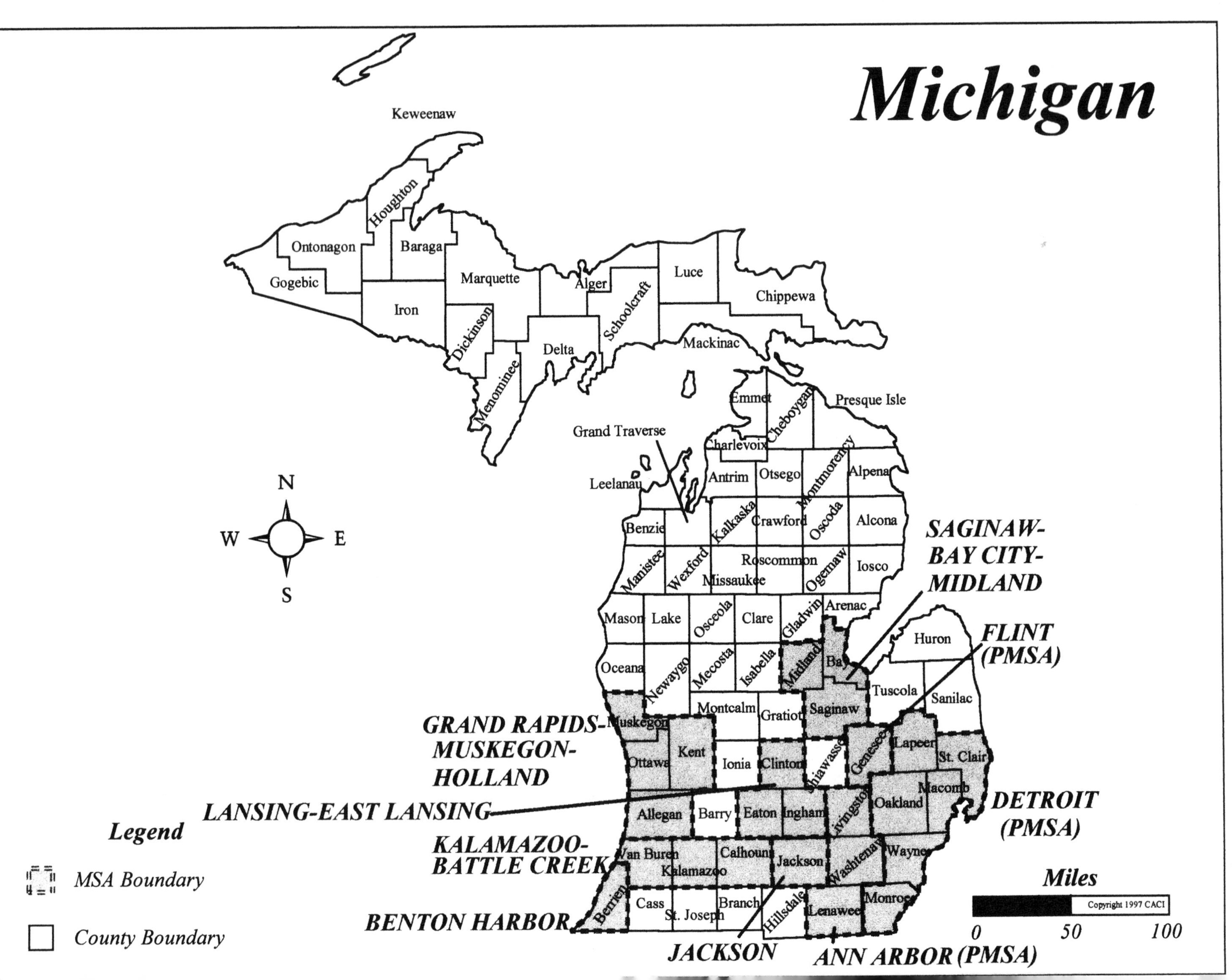
Michigan
Keweenaw
Houghton
Ontonagon
Baraga
Gogebic
Iron
Marquette
Dickinson
Menominee
Delta
Alger
Schoolcraft
Luce
Chippewa
Mackinac
Emmet
Cheboygan
Presque Isle
Grand Traverse
Leelanau
Charlevoix
Antrim
Otsego
Montmorency
Alpena
Benzie
Kalkaska
Crawford
Oscoda
Alcona
Manistee
Wexford
Missaukee
Roscommon
Ogemaw
Iosco
Mason
Lake
Osceola
Clare
Gladwin
Arenac
Huron
Oceana
Newaygo
Mecosta
Isabella
Midland
Bay
Tuscola
Sanilac
Muskegon
Kent
Montcalm
Gratiot
Saginaw
Ottawa
Ionia
Clinton
Shiawassee
Genesee
Lapeer
St. Clair
Allegan
Barry
Eaton
Ingham
Livingston
Oakland
Macomb
Van Buren
Kalamazoo
Calhoun
Jackson
Washtenaw
Wayne
Berrien
Cass
St. Joseph
Branch
Hillsdale
Lenawee
Monroe
SAGINAW-BAY CITY-MIDLAND
FLINT (PMSA)
GRAND RAPIDS-MUSKEGON-HOLLAND
LANSING-EAST LANSING
DETROIT (PMSA)
KALAMAZOO-BATTLE CREEK
BENTON HARBOR
JACKSON
ANN ARBOR (PMSA)
N
W
E
S
Legend
MSA Boundary
County Boundary
Miles
0
50
100
Copyright 1997 CACI

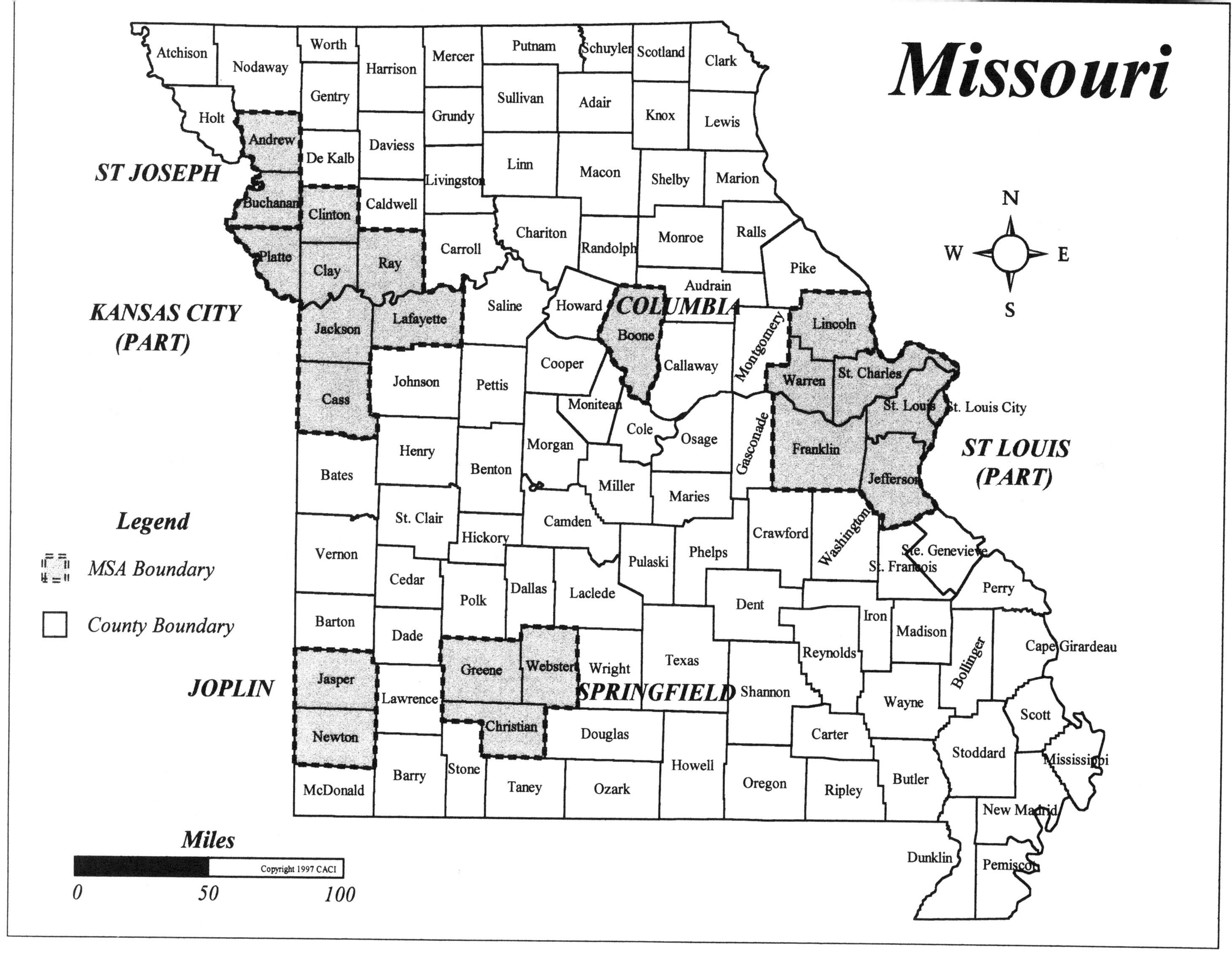

Missouri
N
W
E
S
ST JOSEPH
KANSAS CITY (PART)
COLUMBIA
ST LOUIS (PART)
SPRINGFIELD
JOPLIN
Legend
MSA Boundary
County Boundary
Miles
Copyright 1997 CACI
0
50
100
Atchison
Nodaway
Worth
Harrison
Mercer
Putnam
Schuyler
Scotland
Clark
Holt
Andrew
Gentry
Grundy
Sullivan
Adair
Knox
Lewis
De Kalb
Daviess
Livingston
Linn
Macon
Shelby
Marion
Buchanan
Clinton
Caldwell
Chariton
Randolph
Monroe
Ralls
Platte
Clay
Ray
Carroll
Pike
Audrain
Saline
Howard
Boone
Lincoln
Jackson
Lafayette
Cooper
Callaway
Montgomery
Warren
St. Charles
St. Louis
St. Louis City
Cass
Johnson
Pettis
Moniteau
Cole
Osage
Gasconade
Franklin
Jefferson
Bates
Henry
Benton
Morgan
Miller
Maries
St. Clair
Hickory
Camden
Crawford
Washington
Ste. Genevieve
St. Francois
Vernon
Cedar
Polk
Dallas
Laclede
Pulaski
Phelps
Dent
Iron
Madison
Perry
Barton
Dade
Greene
Webster
Wright
Texas
Reynolds
Bollinger
Cape Girardeau
Jasper
Lawrence
Christian
Shannon
Wayne
Scott
Newton
Douglas
Carter
Stoddard
Mississippi
McDonald
Barry
Stone
Taney
Ozark
Howell
Oregon
Ripley
Butler
New Madrid
Dunklin
Pemiscot

# Montana

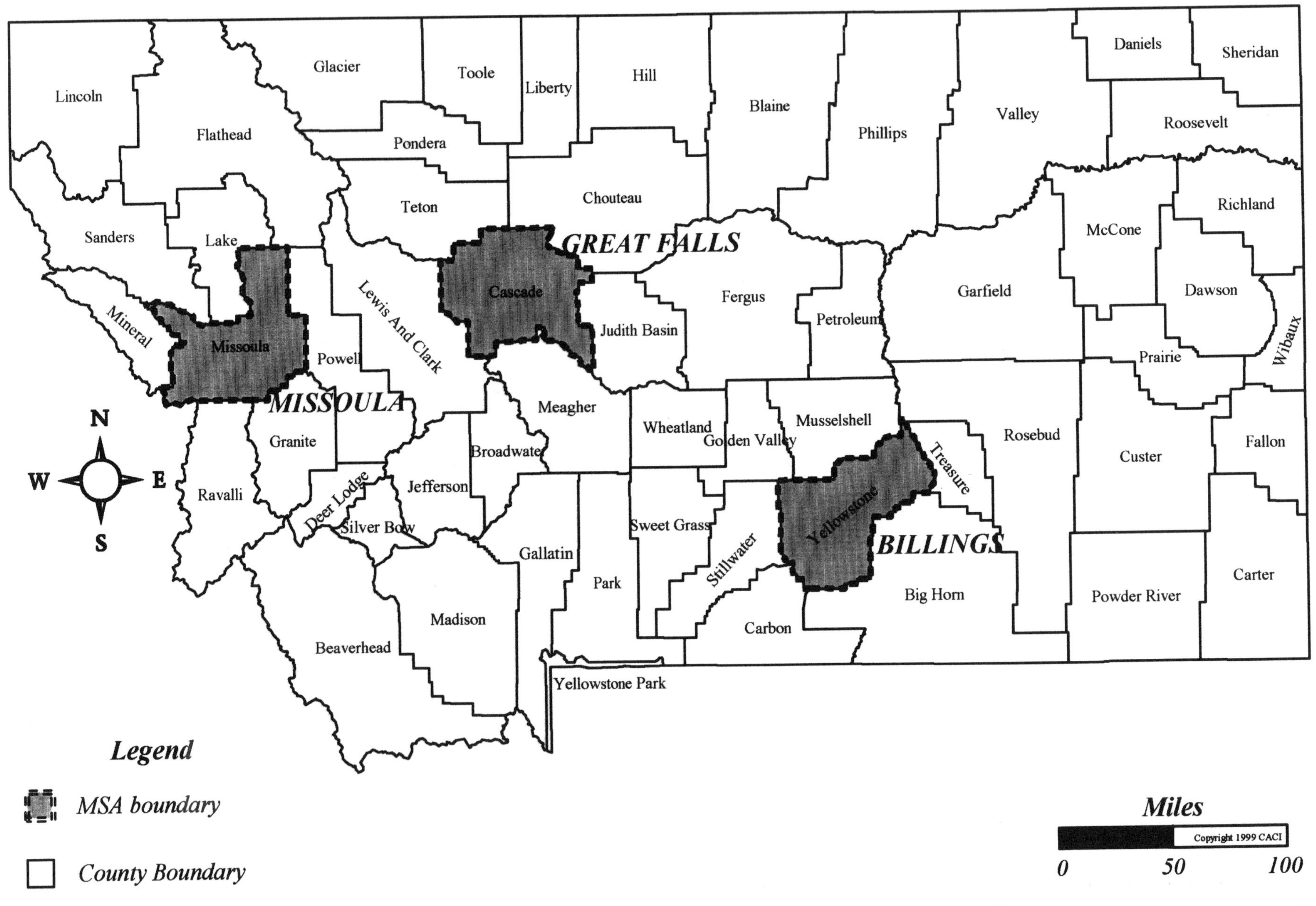
Lincoln
Flathead
Glacier
Toole
Liberty
Hill
Blaine
Phillips
Valley
Daniels
Sheridan
Roosevelt
Pondera
Teton
Chouteau
Sanders
Lake
Mineral
Missoula
Powell
Lewis And Clark
Cascade
GREAT FALLS
Judith Basin
Fergus
Petroleum
Garfield
McCone
Richland
Dawson
Prairie
Wibaux
MISSOULA
Granite
Ravalli
Deer Lodge
Silver Bow
Jefferson
Broadwater
Meagher
Wheatland
Golden Valley
Musselshell
Treasure
Rosebud
Custer
Fallon
Sweet Grass
Stillwater
Yellowstone
BILLINGS
Big Horn
Carbon
Gallatin
Park
Madison
Beaverhead
Yellowstone Park
Powder River
Carter
N
S
E
W
Legend
MSA boundary
County Boundary
Miles
0
50
100
Copyright 1999 CACI

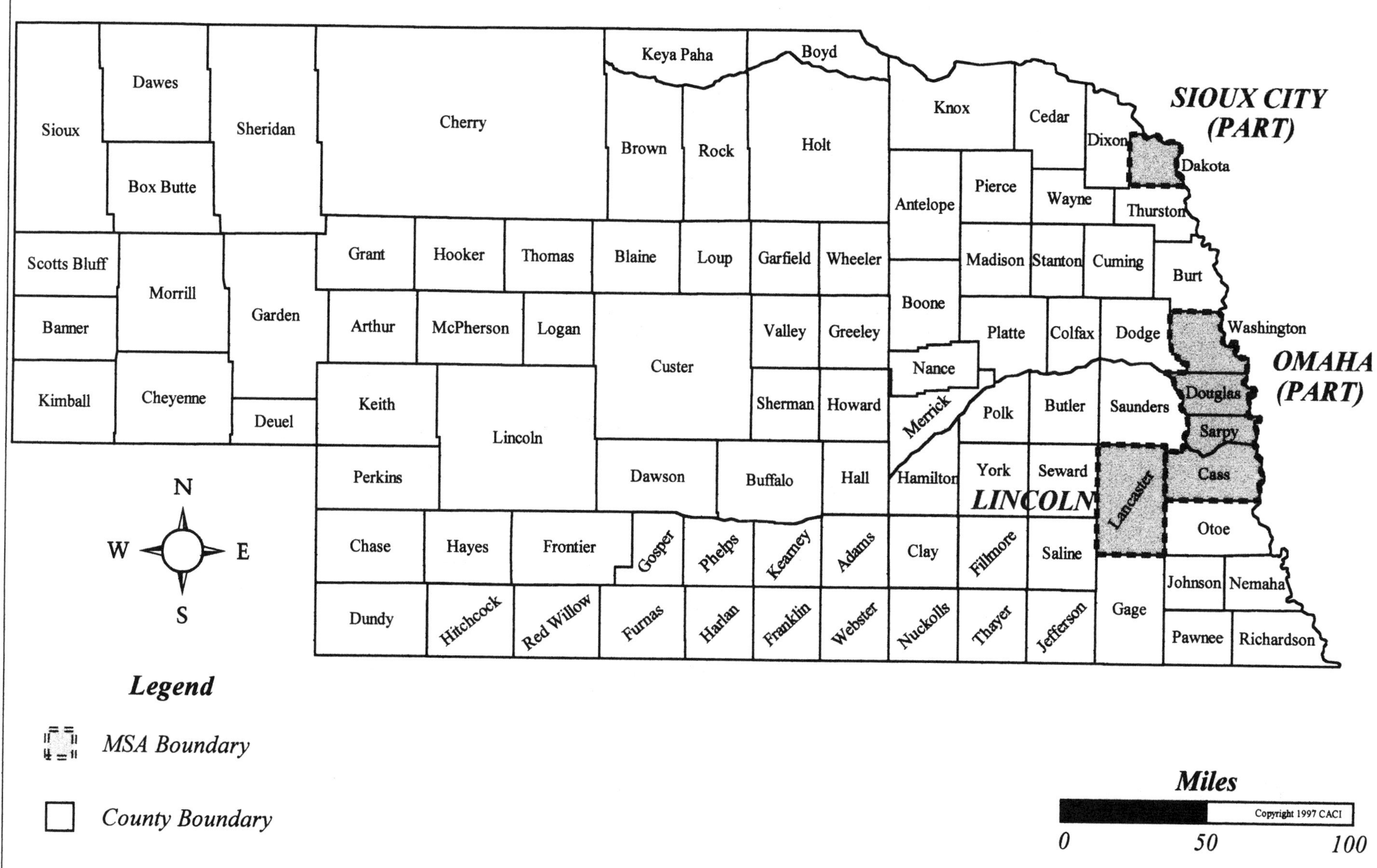
Nebraska
SIOUX CITY (PART)
OMAHA (PART)
LINCOLN
Sioux
Dawes
Box Butte
Sheridan
Cherry
Keya Paha
Boyd
Brown
Rock
Holt
Knox
Cedar
Dixon
Dakota
Antelope
Pierce
Wayne
Thurston
Scotts Bluff
Banner
Kimball
Morrill
Cheyenne
Garden
Deuel
Grant
Hooker
Thomas
Blaine
Loup
Garfield
Wheeler
Madison
Stanton
Cuming
Burt
Boone
Arthur
McPherson
Logan
Valley
Greeley
Platte
Colfax
Dodge
Washington
Nance
Custer
Keith
Lincoln
Sherman
Howard
Merrick
Polk
Butler
Saunders
Douglas
Sarpy
Perkins
Dawson
Buffalo
Hall
Hamilton
York
Seward
Lancaster
Cass
Otoe
Chase
Hayes
Frontier
Gosper
Phelps
Kearney
Adams
Clay
Fillmore
Saline
Johnson
Nemaha
Dundy
Hitchcock
Red Willow
Furnas
Harlan
Franklin
Webster
Nuckolls
Thayer
Jefferson
Gage
Pawnee
Richardson
N
W
E
S
Legend
MSA Boundary
County Boundary
Miles
Copyright 1997 CACI
0
50
100

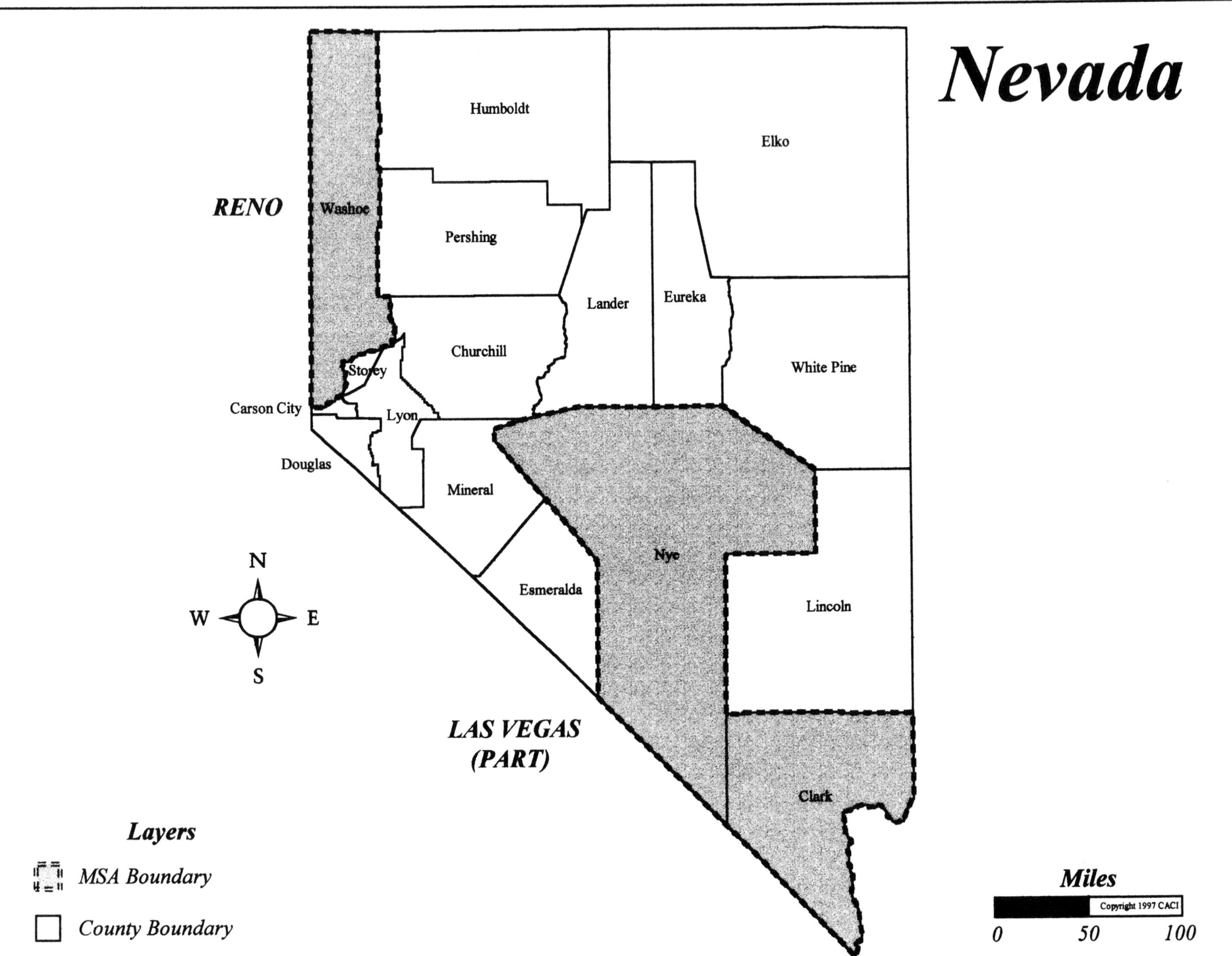
Nevada
RENO
Washoe
Humboldt
Elko
Pershing
Lander
Eureka
Churchill
White Pine
Storey
Carson City
Lyon
Douglas
Mineral
Nye
Esmeralda
Lincoln
N
W
E
S
LAS VEGAS
(PART)
Clark
Layers
MSA Boundary
County Boundary
Miles
Copyright 1997 CACI
0
50
100

# New Hampshire

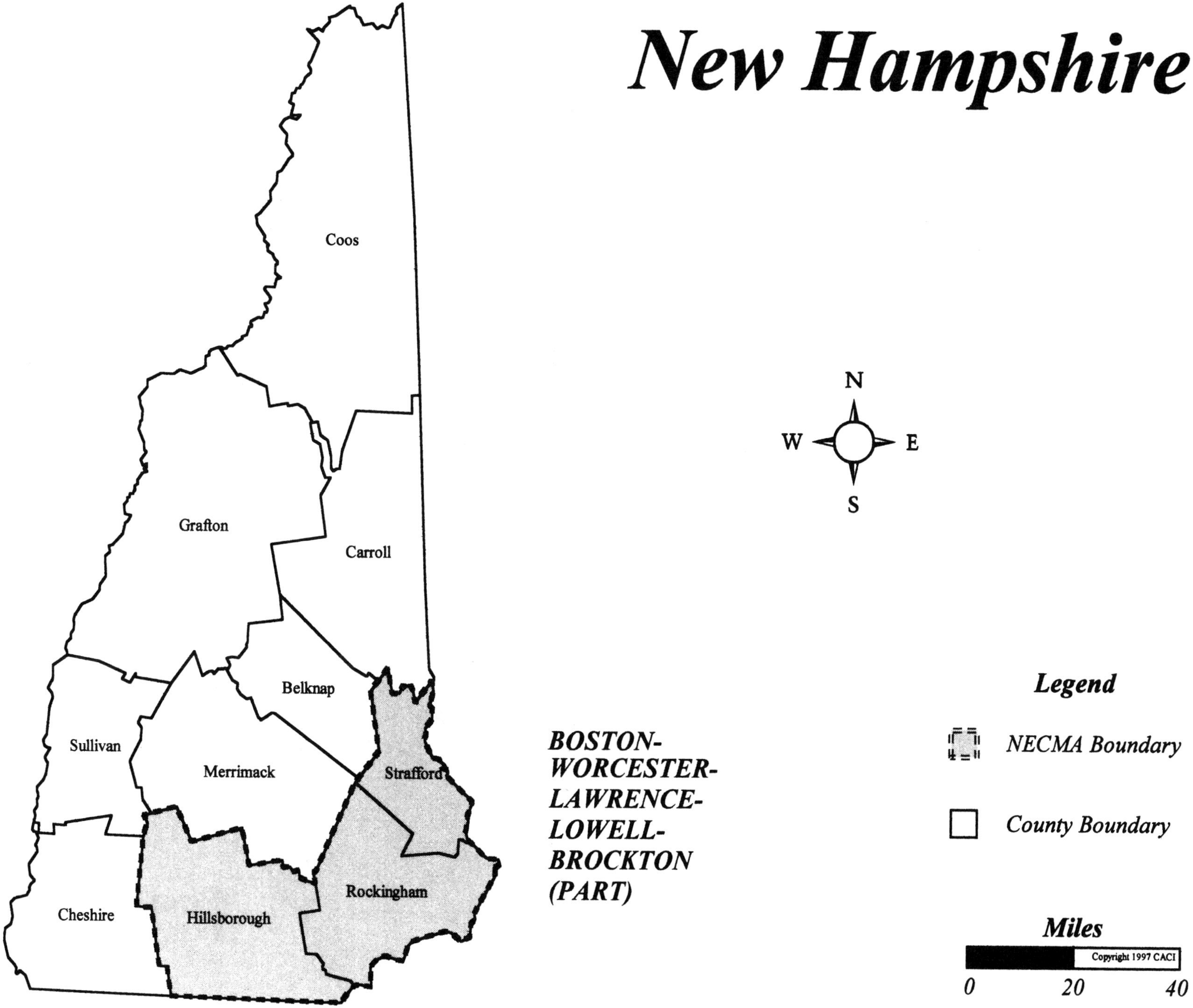

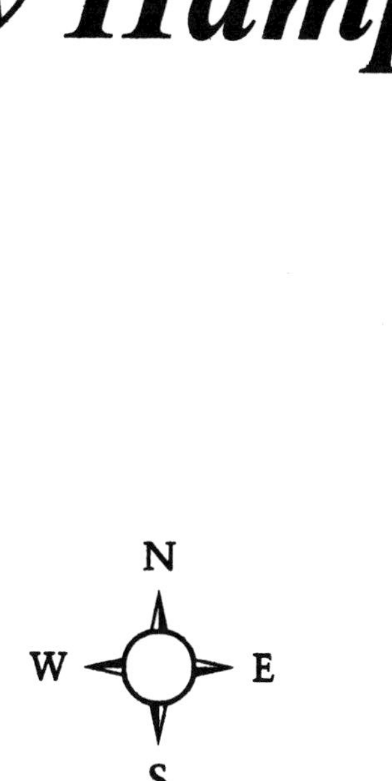


Coos

Grafton

Carroll

Belknap

Sullivan

Merrimack

Strafford

Cheshire

Hillsborough

Rockingham

*BOSTON-*
*WORCESTER-*
*LAWRENCE-*
*LOWELL-*
*BROCKTON*
*(PART)*

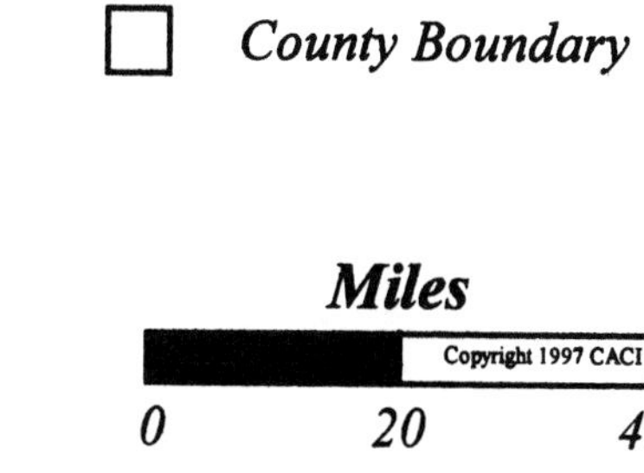

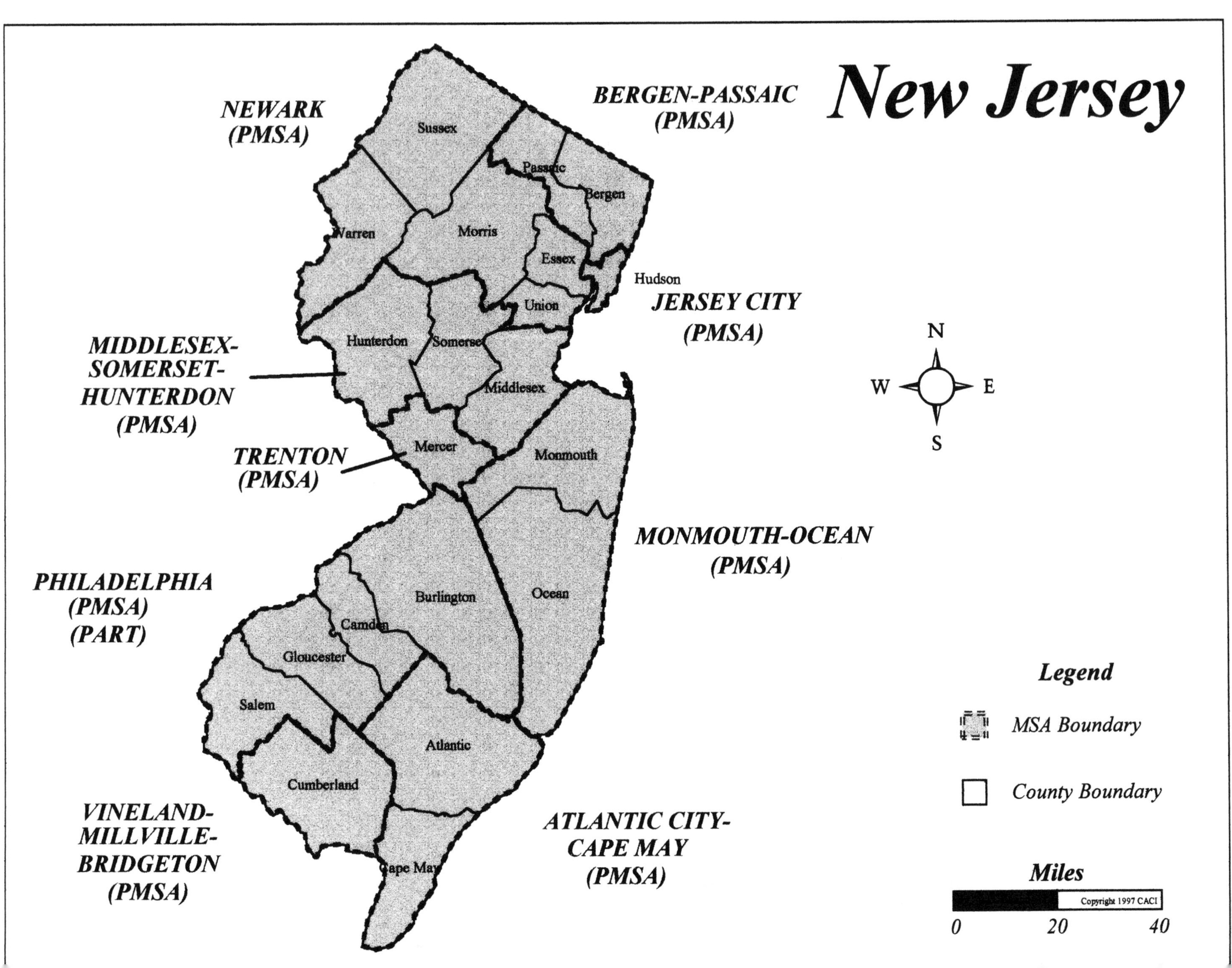
New Jersey
NEWARK (PMSA)
BERGEN-PASSAIC (PMSA)
JERSEY CITY (PMSA)
Hudson
MIDDLESEX-SOMERSET-HUNTERDON (PMSA)
TRENTON (PMSA)
MONMOUTH-OCEAN (PMSA)
PHILADELPHIA (PMSA) (PART)
VINELAND-MILLVILLE-BRIDGETON (PMSA)
ATLANTIC CITY-CAPE MAY (PMSA)
Sussex
Passaic
Bergen
Warren
Morris
Essex
Union
Hunterdon
Somerset
Middlesex
Mercer
Monmouth
Burlington
Ocean
Camden
Gloucester
Salem
Atlantic
Cumberland
Cape May
N
W
E
S
Legend
MSA Boundary
County Boundary
Miles
Copyright 1997 CACI
0
20
40

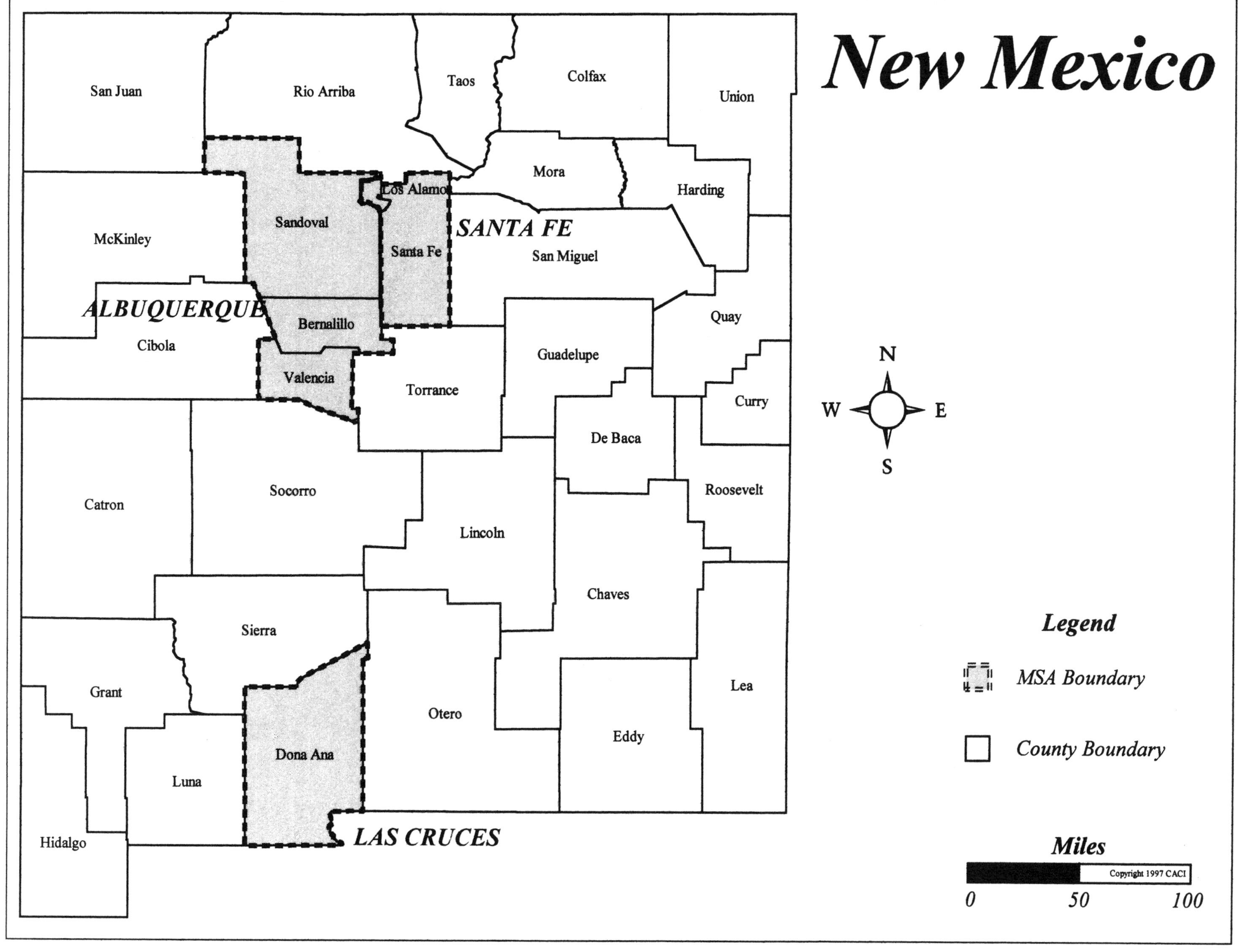
New Mexico
San Juan
Rio Arriba
Taos
Colfax
Union
Mora
Harding
Los Alamos
Sandoval
McKinley
Santa Fe
SANTA FE
San Miguel
ALBUQUERQUE
Bernalillo
Cibola
Quay
Guadelupe
Valencia
Torrance
Curry
De Baca
Catron
Socorro
Roosevelt
Lincoln
Chaves
Sierra
Grant
Lea
Otero
Eddy
Dona Ana
Luna
Hidalgo
LAS CRUCES
N
W
E
S
Legend
MSA Boundary
County Boundary
Miles
0
50
100
Copyright 1997 CACI

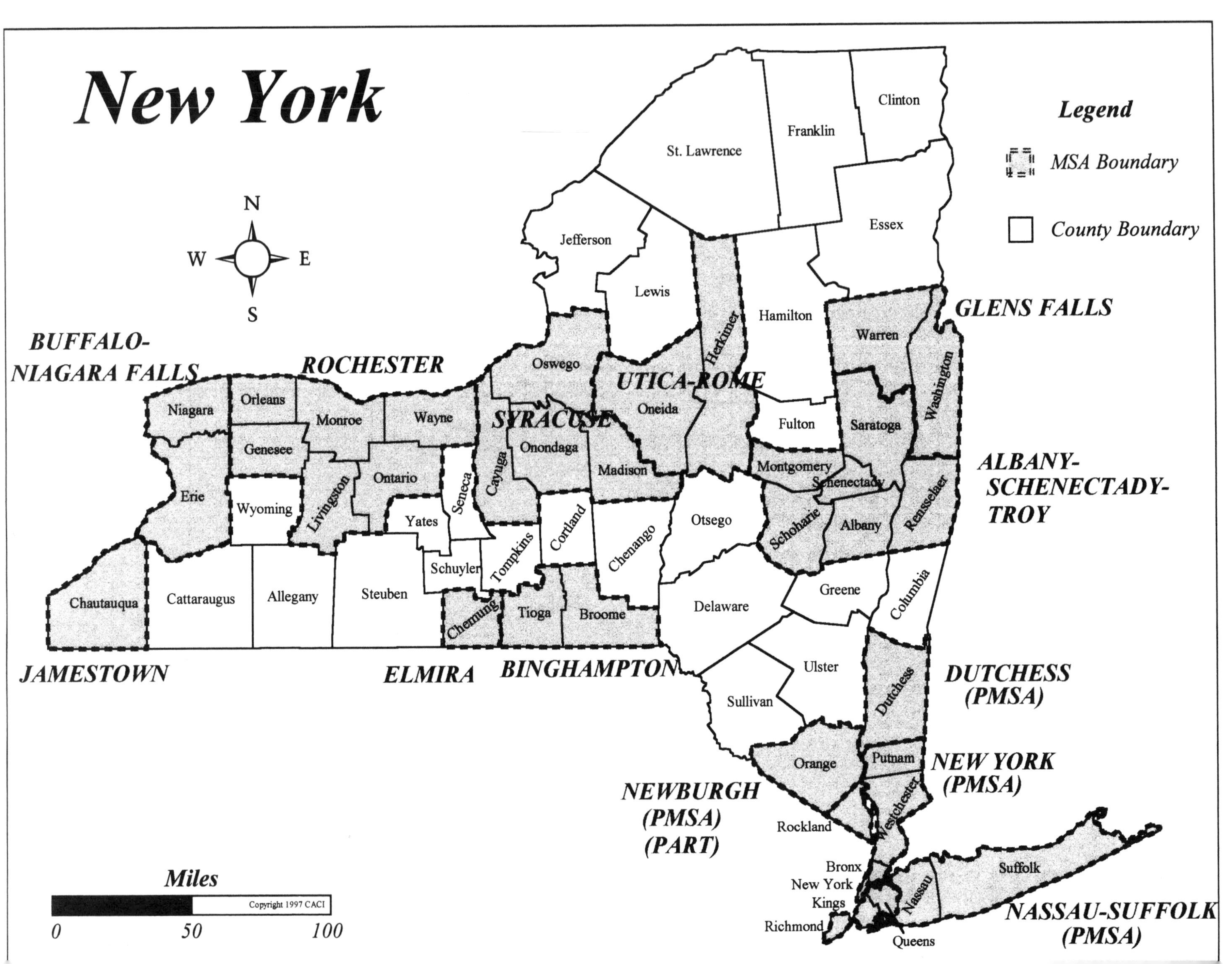

New York
N
W
E
S
Legend
MSA Boundary
County Boundary
BUFFALO-NIAGARA FALLS
ROCHESTER
SYRACUSE
UTICA-ROME
GLENS FALLS
ALBANY-SCHENECTADY-TROY
JAMESTOWN
ELMIRA
BINGHAMPTON
DUTCHESS (PMSA)
NEW YORK (PMSA)
NEWBURGH (PMSA) (PART)
NASSAU-SUFFOLK (PMSA)
St. Lawrence
Franklin
Clinton
Essex
Jefferson
Lewis
Herkimer
Hamilton
Warren
Washington
Niagara
Orleans
Monroe
Wayne
Oswego
Oneida
Fulton
Saratoga
Genesee
Onondaga
Madison
Montgomery
Schenectady
Erie
Wyoming
Livingston
Ontario
Yates
Seneca
Cayuga
Cortland
Chenango
Otsego
Schoharie
Albany
Rensselaer
Chautauqua
Cattaraugus
Allegany
Steuben
Schuyler
Tompkins
Chemung
Tioga
Broome
Delaware
Greene
Columbia
Ulster
Sullivan
Dutchess
Orange
Putnam
Westchester
Rockland
Bronx
New York
Kings
Richmond
Queens
Nassau
Suffolk
Miles
Copyright 1997 CACI
0
50
100

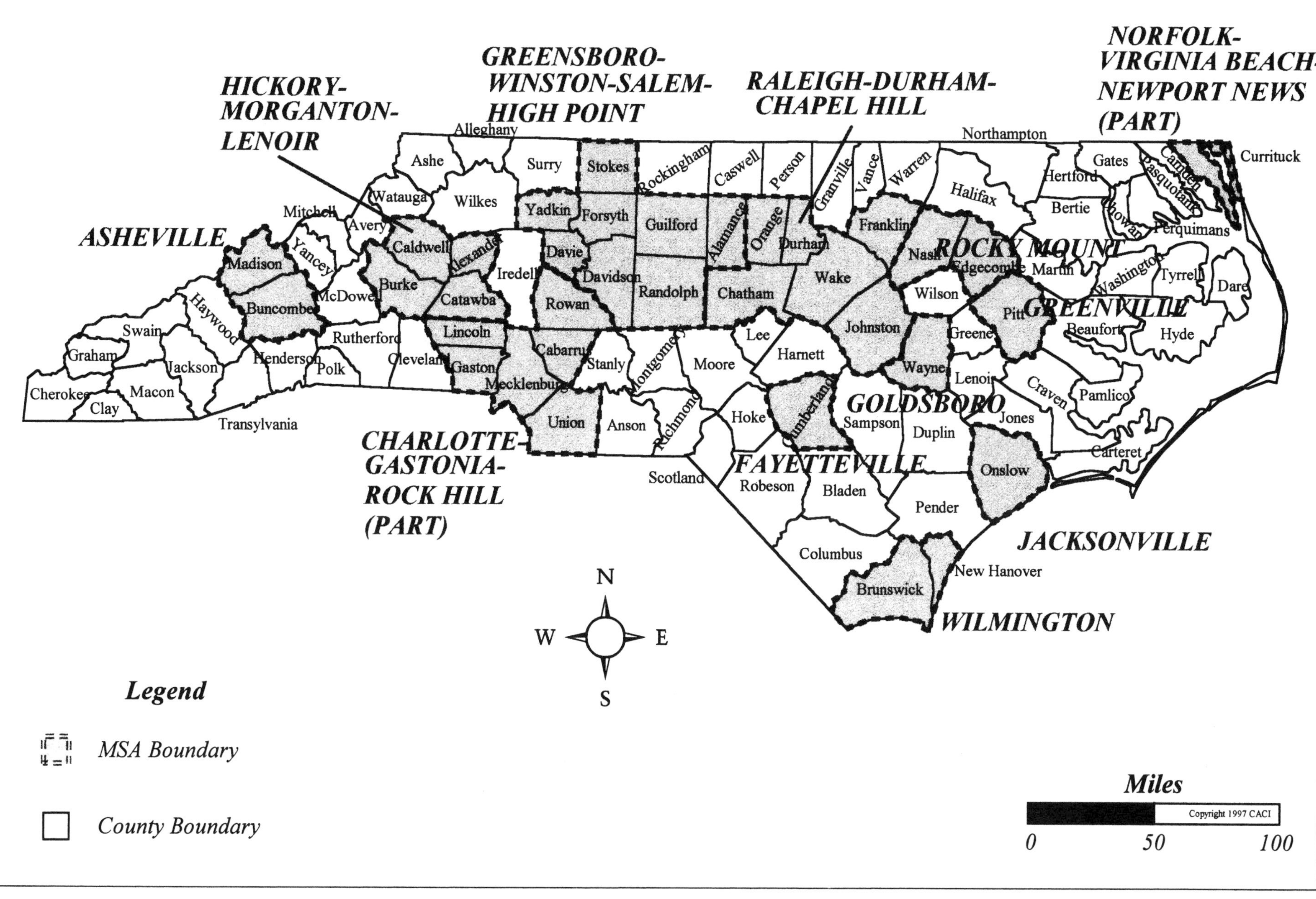

North Carolina
HICKORY-MORGANTON-LENOIR
GREENSBORO-WINSTON-SALEM-HIGH POINT
RALEIGH-DURHAM-CHAPEL HILL
NORFOLK-VIRGINIA BEACH-NEWPORT NEWS (PART)
ASHEVILLE
ROCKY MOUNT
GREENVILLE
GOLDSBORO
FAYETTEVILLE
CHARLOTTE-GASTONIA-ROCK HILL (PART)
JACKSONVILLE
WILMINGTON
Alleghany
Ashe
Surry
Stokes
Rockingham
Caswell
Person
Granville
Vance
Warren
Northampton
Halifax
Hertford
Gates
Camden
Pasquotank
Currituck
Perquimans
Chowan
Bertie
Watauga
Wilkes
Yadkin
Forsyth
Guilford
Alamance
Orange
Durham
Franklin
Nash
Edgecombe
Martin
Washington
Tyrrell
Dare
Mitchell
Avery
Yancey
Madison
Caldwell
Alexander
Iredell
Davie
Davidson
Randolph
Chatham
Wake
Wilson
Pitt
Beaufort
Hyde
Burke
McDowell
Buncombe
Catawba
Rowan
Haywood
Swain
Graham
Cherokee
Clay
Macon
Jackson
Henderson
Polk
Rutherford
Cleveland
Lincoln
Gaston
Mecklenburg
Cabarrus
Stanly
Montgomery
Moore
Lee
Harnett
Johnston
Greene
Wayne
Lenoir
Craven
Pamlico
Transylvania
Union
Anson
Richmond
Hoke
Cumberland
Sampson
Duplin
Jones
Carteret
Onslow
Scotland
Robeson
Bladen
Pender
Columbus
Brunswick
New Hanover
N
W
E
S
Legend
MSA Boundary
County Boundary
Miles
Copyright 1997 CACI
0
50
100

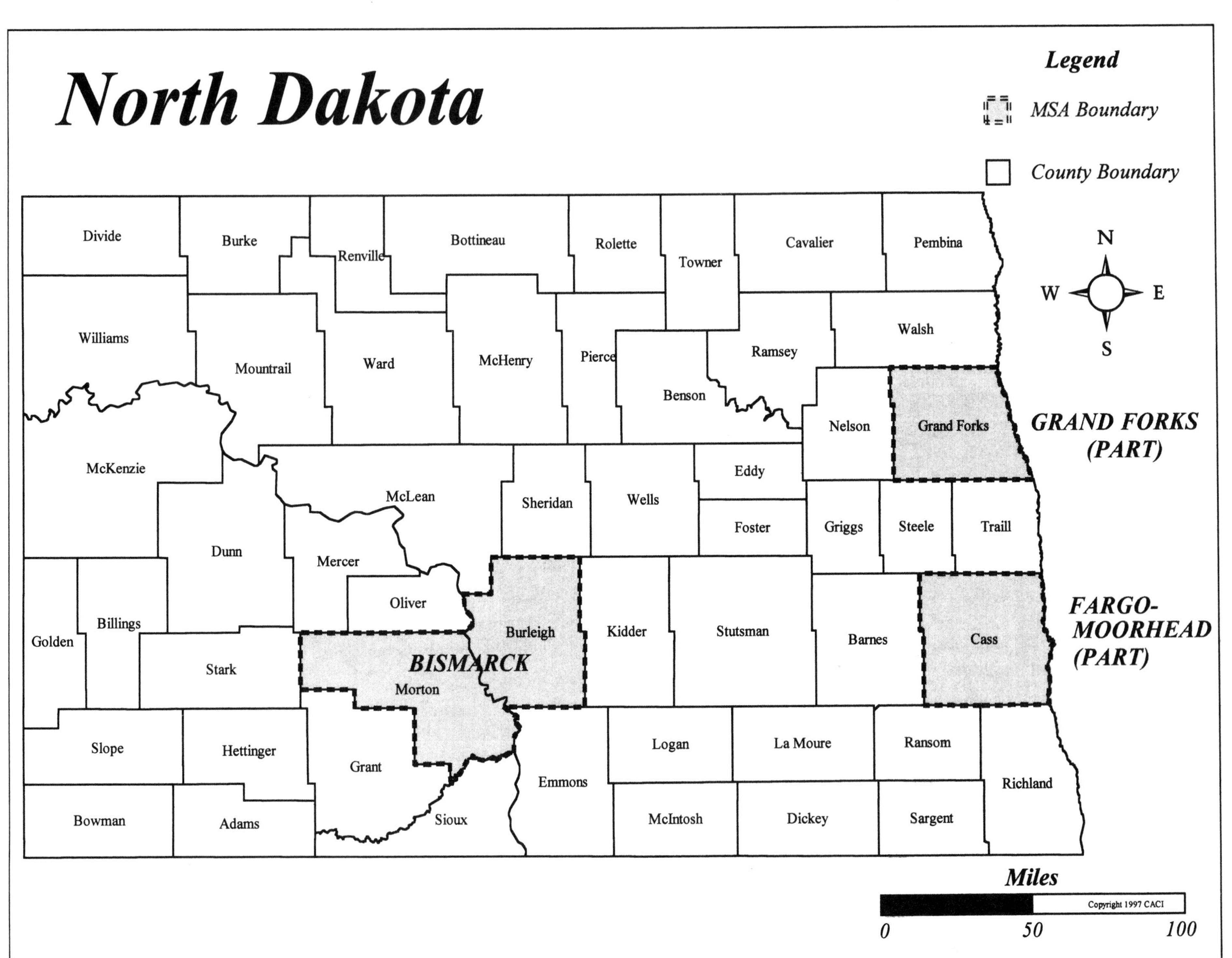

North Dakota
Legend
MSA Boundary
County Boundary
N
W
E
S
GRAND FORKS (PART)
FARGO-MOORHEAD (PART)
BISMARCK
Divide
Burke
Renville
Bottineau
Rolette
Towner
Cavalier
Pembina
Williams
Mountrail
Ward
McHenry
Pierce
Benson
Ramsey
Walsh
Nelson
Grand Forks
McKenzie
McLean
Sheridan
Wells
Eddy
Foster
Griggs
Steele
Traill
Dunn
Mercer
Oliver
Burleigh
Kidder
Stutsman
Barnes
Cass
Golden
Billings
Stark
Morton
Slope
Hettinger
Grant
Emmons
Logan
La Moure
Ransom
Richland
Bowman
Adams
Sioux
McIntosh
Dickey
Sargent
Miles
Copyright 1997 CACI
0
50
100

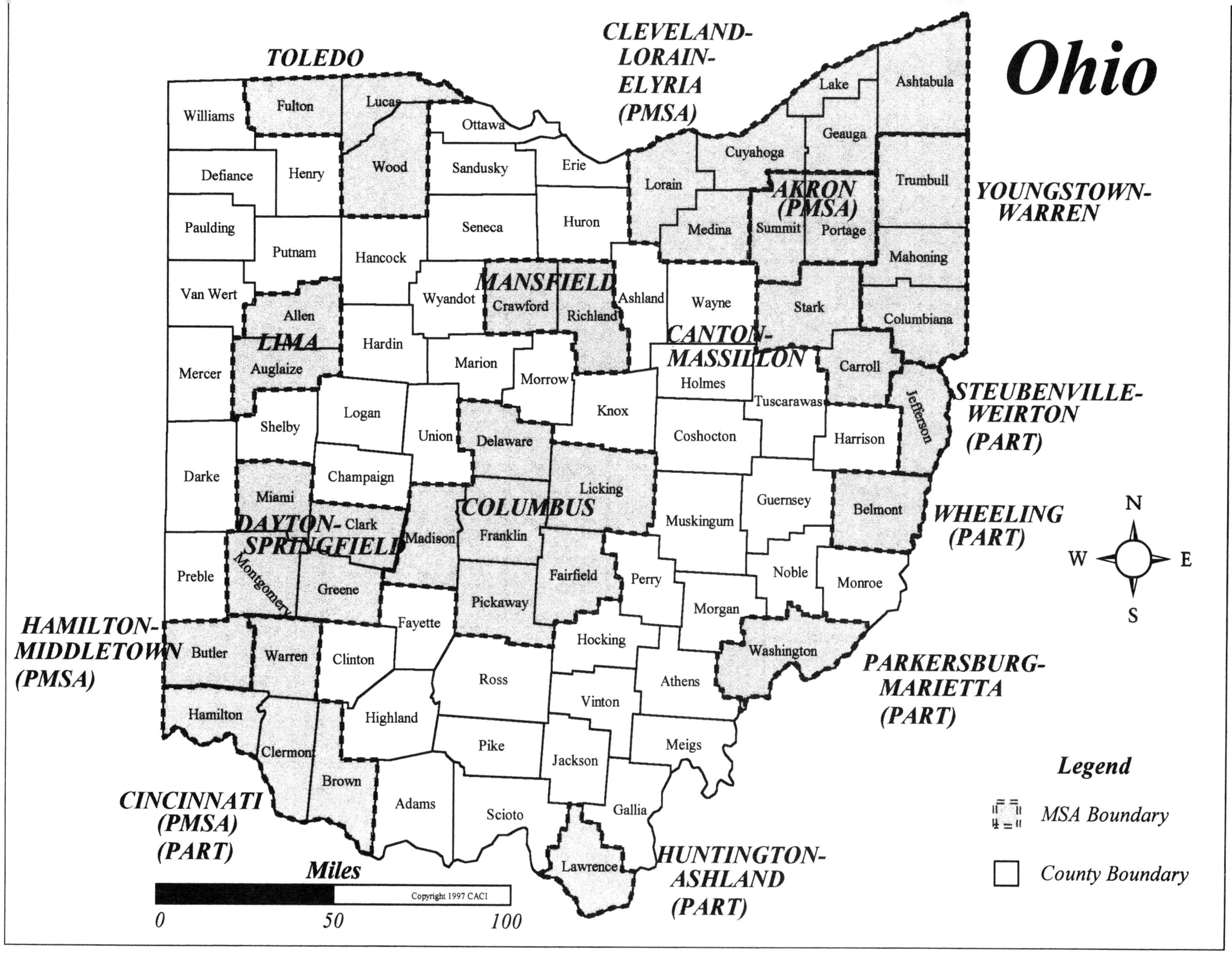
Ohio
TOLEDO
CLEVELAND-LORAIN-ELYRIA (PMSA)
YOUNGSTOWN-WARREN
AKRON (PMSA)
MANSFIELD
CANTON-MASSILLON
LIMA
STEUBENVILLE-WEIRTON (PART)
COLUMBUS
WHEELING (PART)
DAYTON-SPRINGFIELD
HAMILTON-MIDDLETOWN (PMSA)
PARKERSBURG-MARIETTA (PART)
CINCINNATI (PMSA) (PART)
HUNTINGTON-ASHLAND (PART)
Williams
Fulton
Lucas
Ottawa
Wood
Defiance
Henry
Sandusky
Erie
Lorain
Cuyahoga
Lake
Geauga
Ashtabula
Trumbull
Paulding
Putnam
Hancock
Seneca
Huron
Medina
Summit
Portage
Mahoning
Van Wert
Allen
Wyandot
Crawford
Richland
Ashland
Wayne
Stark
Columbiana
Mercer
Auglaize
Hardin
Marion
Morrow
Holmes
Carroll
Tuscarawas
Jefferson
Shelby
Logan
Union
Delaware
Knox
Coshocton
Harrison
Darke
Miami
Champaign
Licking
Guernsey
Belmont
Clark
Madison
Franklin
Muskingum
Preble
Montgomery
Greene
Pickaway
Fairfield
Perry
Noble
Monroe
Morgan
Fayette
Butler
Warren
Clinton
Hocking
Washington
Ross
Athens
Vinton
Hamilton
Highland
Pike
Jackson
Meigs
Clermont
Brown
Adams
Scioto
Gallia
Lawrence
Miles
0
50
100
Copyright 1997 CACI
N
S
E
W
Legend
MSA Boundary
County Boundary

# Oklahoma

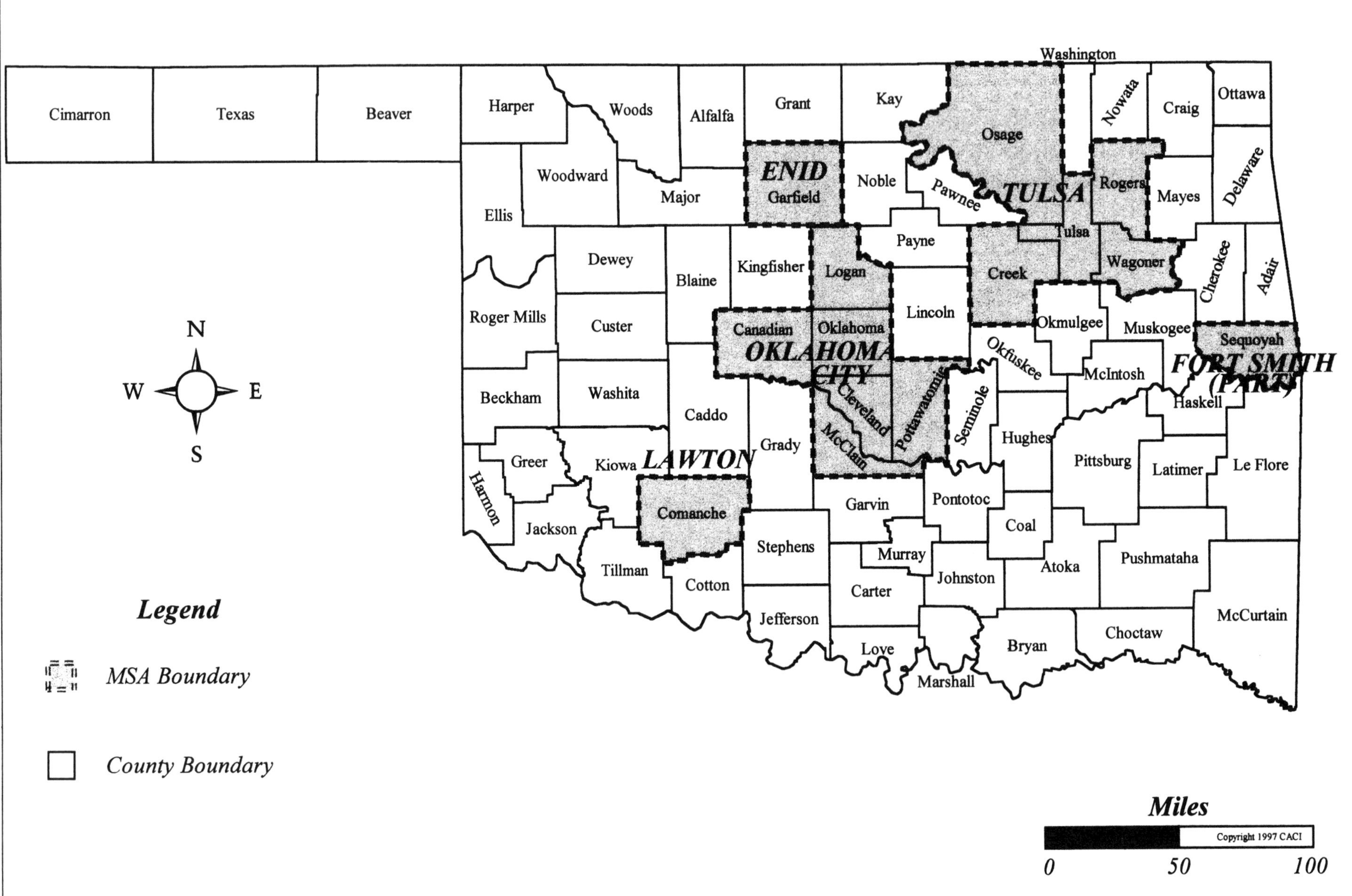
Cimarron
Texas
Beaver
Harper
Woods
Alfalfa
Grant
Kay
Osage
Washington
Nowata
Craig
Ottawa
Woodward
Major
ENID
Garfield
Noble
Pawnee
TULSA
Rogers
Mayes
Delaware
Ellis
Dewey
Blaine
Kingfisher
Logan
Payne
Creek
Tulsa
Wagoner
Cherokee
Adair
Roger Mills
Custer
Canadian
Oklahoma
OKLAHOMA CITY
Lincoln
Okmulgee
Muskogee
Sequoyah
FORT SMITH (PART)
Okfuskee
McIntosh
Beckham
Washita
Caddo
Cleveland
Pottawatomie
Seminole
Haskell
Hughes
Greer
Kiowa
LAWTON
Grady
McClain
Pittsburg
Latimer
Le Flore
Harmon
Comanche
Garvin
Pontotoc
Coal
Jackson
Stephens
Murray
Tillman
Cotton
Johnston
Atoka
Pushmataha
Carter
Jefferson
Love
Marshall
Bryan
Choctaw
McCurtain
N
W
E
S
Legend
MSA Boundary
County Boundary
Miles
0
50
100
Copyright 1997 CACI

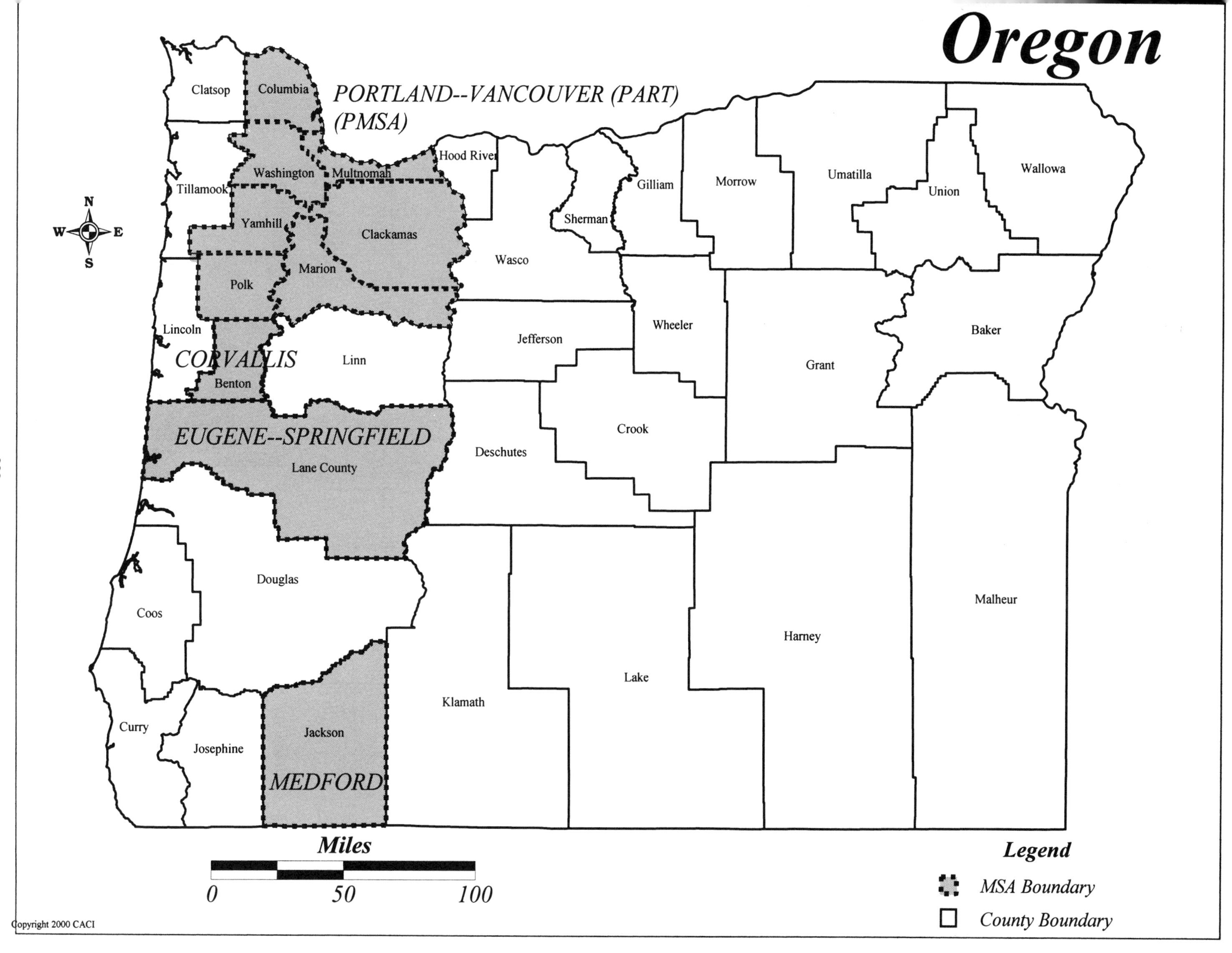
Oregon
PORTLAND--VANCOUVER (PART)
(PMSA)
CORVALLIS
EUGENE--SPRINGFIELD
MEDFORD
Clatsop
Columbia
Tillamook
Washington
Multnomah
Yamhill
Clackamas
Polk
Marion
Lincoln
Benton
Linn
Lane County
Hood River
Wasco
Sherman
Gilliam
Morrow
Umatilla
Union
Wallowa
Jefferson
Wheeler
Grant
Baker
Crook
Deschutes
Douglas
Coos
Curry
Josephine
Jackson
Klamath
Lake
Harney
Malheur
N
W
E
S
Miles
0
50
100
Legend
MSA Boundary
County Boundary
Copyright 2000 CACI

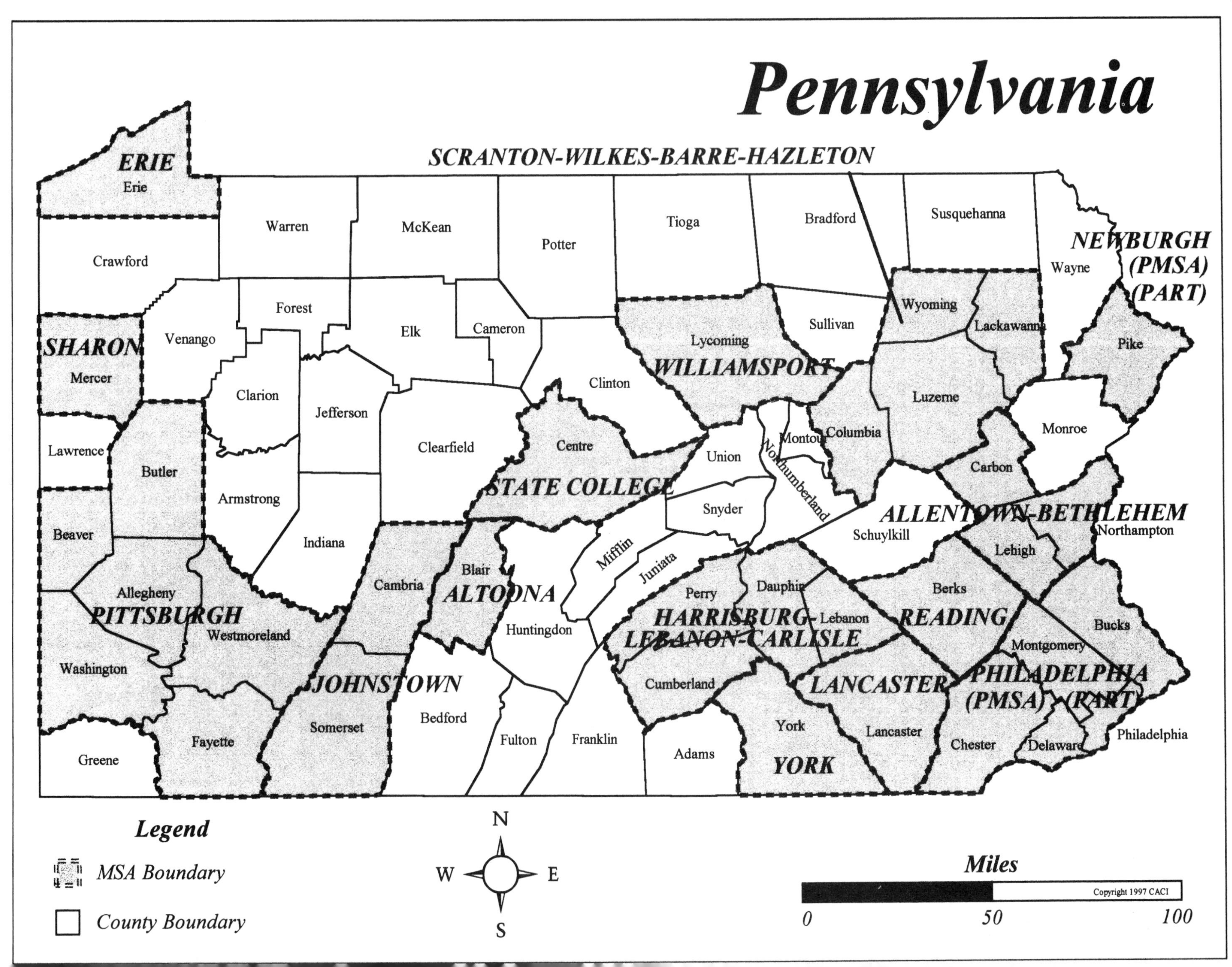
Pennsylvania
SCRANTON-WILKES-BARRE-HAZLETON
ERIE
Erie
Warren
McKean
Potter
Tioga
Bradford
Susquehanna
NEWBURGH (PMSA) (PART)
Wayne
Crawford
Forest
Elk
Cameron
Sullivan
Wyoming
Lackawanna
Pike
SHARON
Mercer
Venango
Lycoming
WILLIAMSPORT
Clarion
Jefferson
Clinton
Luzerne
Monroe
Lawrence
Butler
Clearfield
Centre
Union
Montour
Columbia
Northumberland
Carbon
Armstrong
STATE COLLEGE
Snyder
Beaver
Indiana
ALLENTOWN-BETHLEHEM
Northampton
Schuylkill
Lehigh
Mifflin
Juniata
Allegheny
Cambria
Blair
ALTOONA
Perry
Dauphin
Berks
PITTSBURGH
Westmoreland
Huntingdon
HARRISBURG-LEBANON-CARLISLE
Lebanon
READING
Bucks
Montgomery
Washington
JOHNSTOWN
Cumberland
LANCASTER
PHILADELPHIA (PMSA) (PART)
Bedford
Somerset
York
Lancaster
Chester
Delaware
Philadelphia
Fayette
Fulton
Franklin
Adams
Greene
YORK
Legend
MSA Boundary
County Boundary
N
W
E
S
Miles
0
50
100
Copyright 1997 CACI

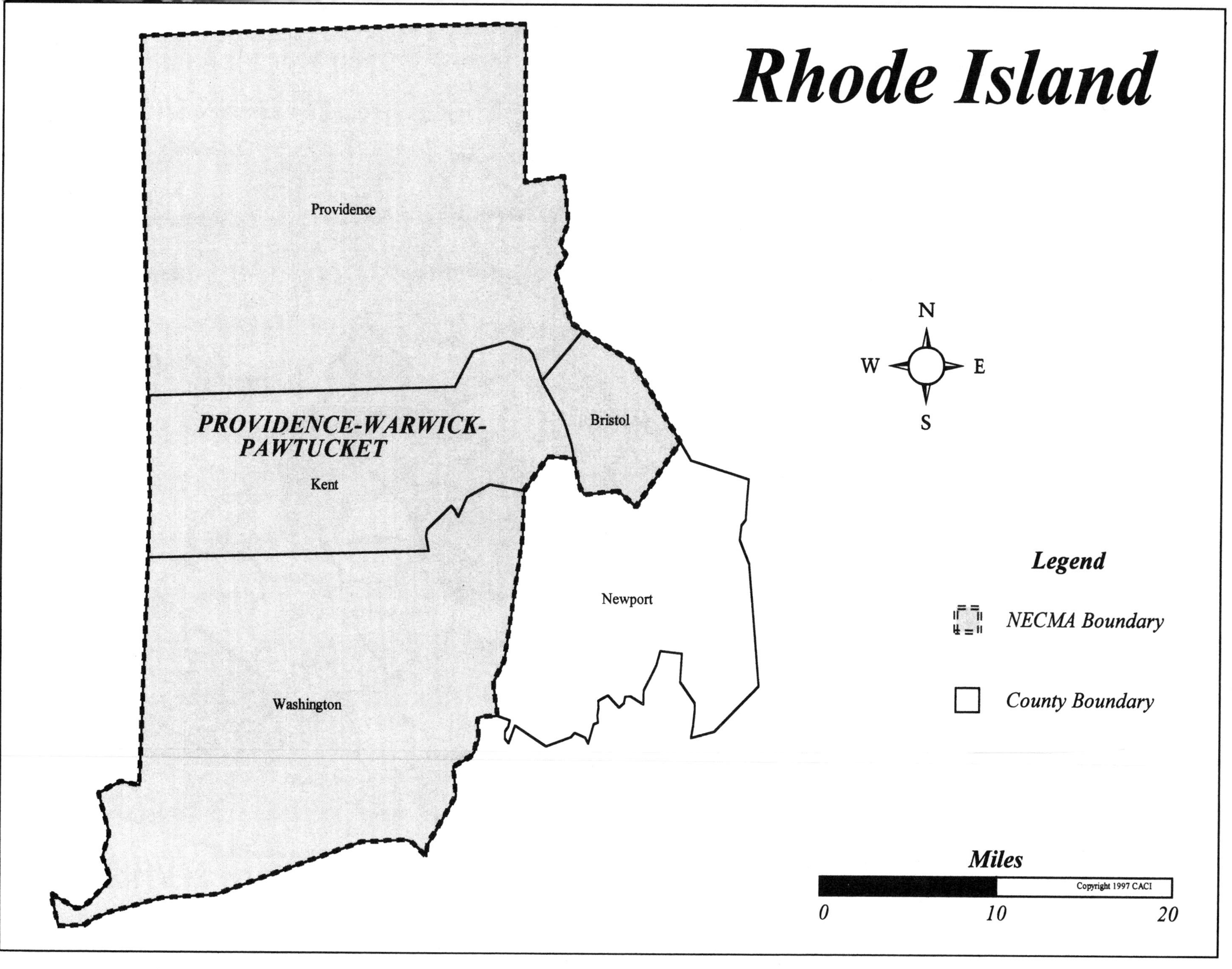
Rhode Island
Providence
PROVIDENCE-WARWICK-
PAWTUCKET
Kent
Bristol
Washington
Newport
N
W
E
S
Legend
NECMA Boundary
County Boundary
Miles
Copyright 1997 CACI
0
10
20

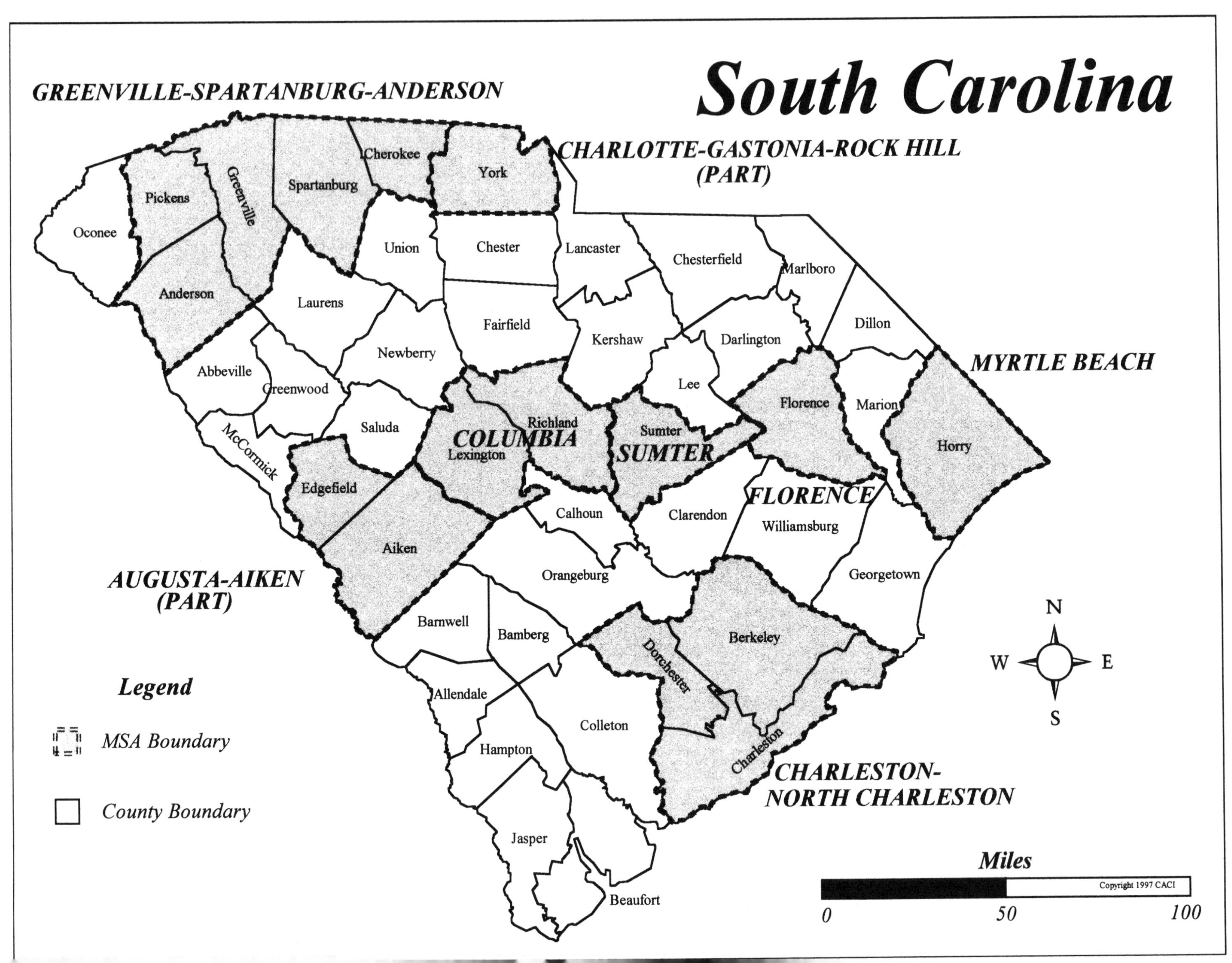

South Carolina
GREENVILLE-SPARTANBURG-ANDERSON
CHARLOTTE-GASTONIA-ROCK HILL
(PART)
MYRTLE BEACH
COLUMBIA
SUMTER
FLORENCE
AUGUSTA-AIKEN
(PART)
CHARLESTON-
NORTH CHARLESTON
Oconee
Pickens
Greenville
Spartanburg
Cherokee
York
Anderson
Laurens
Union
Chester
Lancaster
Chesterfield
Marlboro
Dillon
Fairfield
Kershaw
Darlington
Newberry
Abbeville
Greenwood
Saluda
McCormick
Edgefield
Aiken
Lexington
Richland
Lee
Sumter
Florence
Marion
Horry
Calhoun
Clarendon
Williamsburg
Georgetown
Orangeburg
Barnwell
Bamberg
Allendale
Hampton
Colleton
Dorchester
Berkeley
Charleston
Jasper
Beaufort
N
W
E
S
Legend
MSA Boundary
County Boundary
Miles
0
50
100
Copyright 1997 CACI

# Minnesota

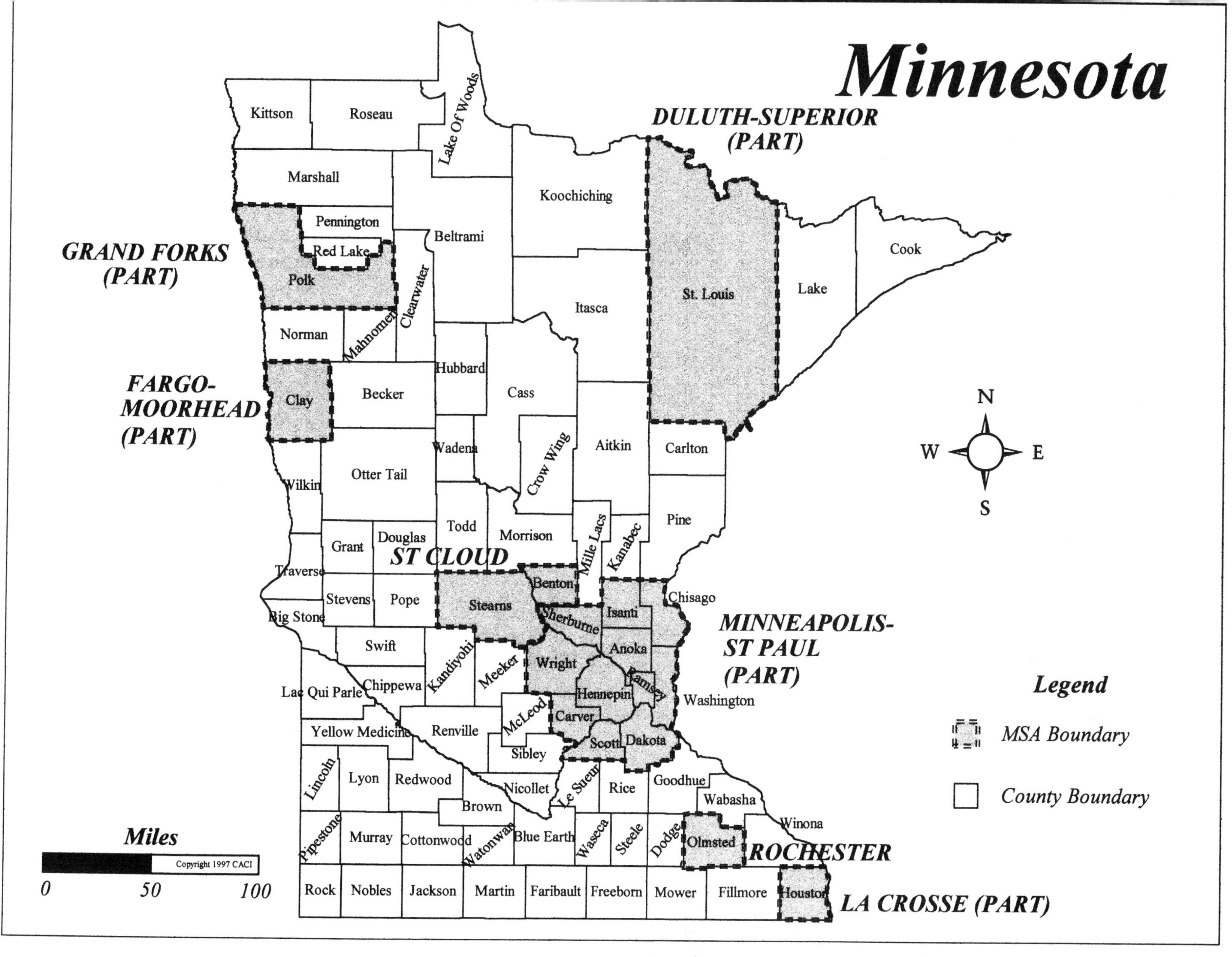

DULUTH-SUPERIOR (PART)
GRAND FORKS (PART)
FARGO-MOORHEAD (PART)
ST CLOUD
MINNEAPOLIS-ST PAUL (PART)
ROCHESTER
LA CROSSE (PART)
Kittson
Roseau
Lake Of Woods
Marshall
Koochiching
Pennington
Red Lake
Polk
Beltrami
Clearwater
Cook
Lake
St. Louis
Itasca
Norman
Mahnomen
Hubbard
Cass
Clay
Becker
Wadena
Crow Wing
Aitkin
Carlton
Otter Tail
Wilkin
Todd
Morrison
Mille Lacs
Kanabec
Pine
Grant
Douglas
Traverse
Stevens
Pope
Stearns
Benton
Chisago
Big Stone
Sherburne
Isanti
Anoka
Swift
Wright
Kandiyohi
Meeker
Hennepin
Ramsey
Washington
Lac Qui Parle
Chippewa
McLeod
Carver
Yellow Medicine
Renville
Scott
Dakota
Sibley
Lincoln
Lyon
Redwood
Nicollet
Le Sueur
Rice
Goodhue
Brown
Wabasha
Pipestone
Murray
Cottonwood
Watonwan
Blue Earth
Waseca
Steele
Dodge
Olmsted
Winona
Rock
Nobles
Jackson
Martin
Faribault
Freeborn
Mower
Fillmore
Houston
N
W
E
S
Legend
MSA Boundary
County Boundary
Miles
0
50
100
Copyright 1997 CACI

# Mississippi

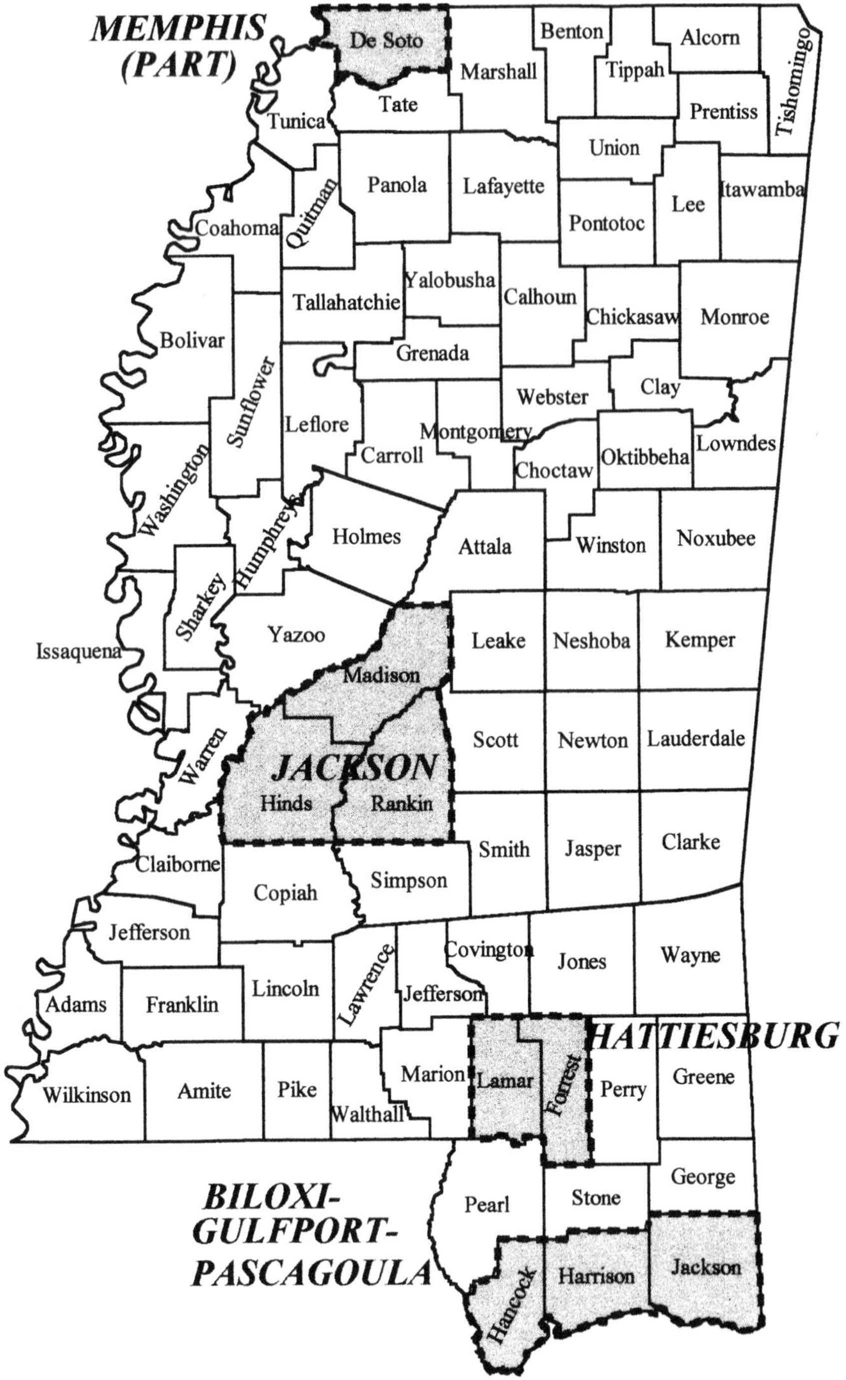

MEMPHIS (PART)

De Soto, Marshall, Benton, Tippah, Alcorn, Tishomingo, Tunica, Tate, Prentiss, Union, Panola, Lafayette, Lee, Itawamba, Coahoma, Quitman, Pontotoc, Tallahatchie, Yalobusha, Calhoun, Chickasaw, Monroe, Bolivar, Sunflower, Grenada, Leflore, Webster, Clay, Montgomery, Carroll, Choctaw, Oktibbeha, Lowndes, Washington, Humphreys, Holmes, Attala, Winston, Noxubee, Sharkey, Issaquena, Yazoo, Leake, Neshoba, Kemper, Madison, Scott, Newton, Lauderdale, Warren

JACKSON

Hinds, Rankin, Smith, Jasper, Clarke, Claiborne, Copiah, Simpson, Jefferson, Covington, Jones, Wayne, Lincoln, Lawrence, Adams, Franklin, Jefferson Davis

HATTIESBURG

Marion, Lamar, Forrest, Perry, Greene, Wilkinson, Amite, Pike, Walthall, Pearl River, Stone, George

BILOXI-GULFPORT-PASCAGOULA

Hancock, Harrison, Jackson

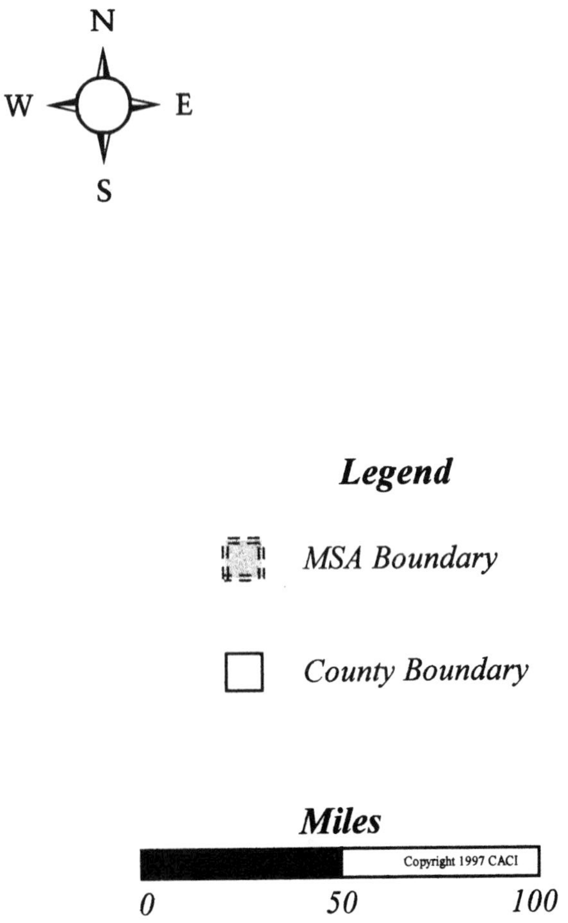

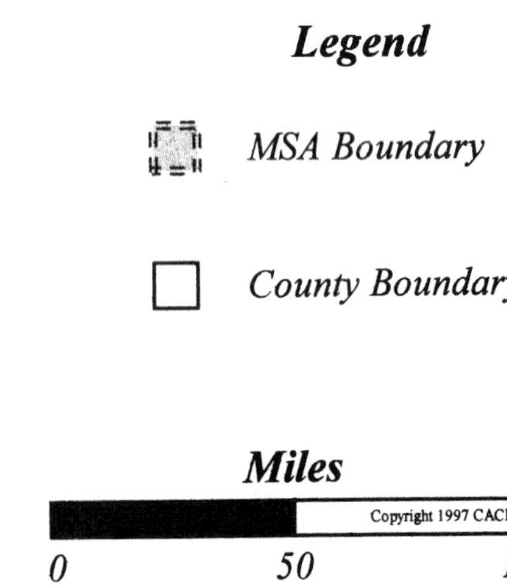

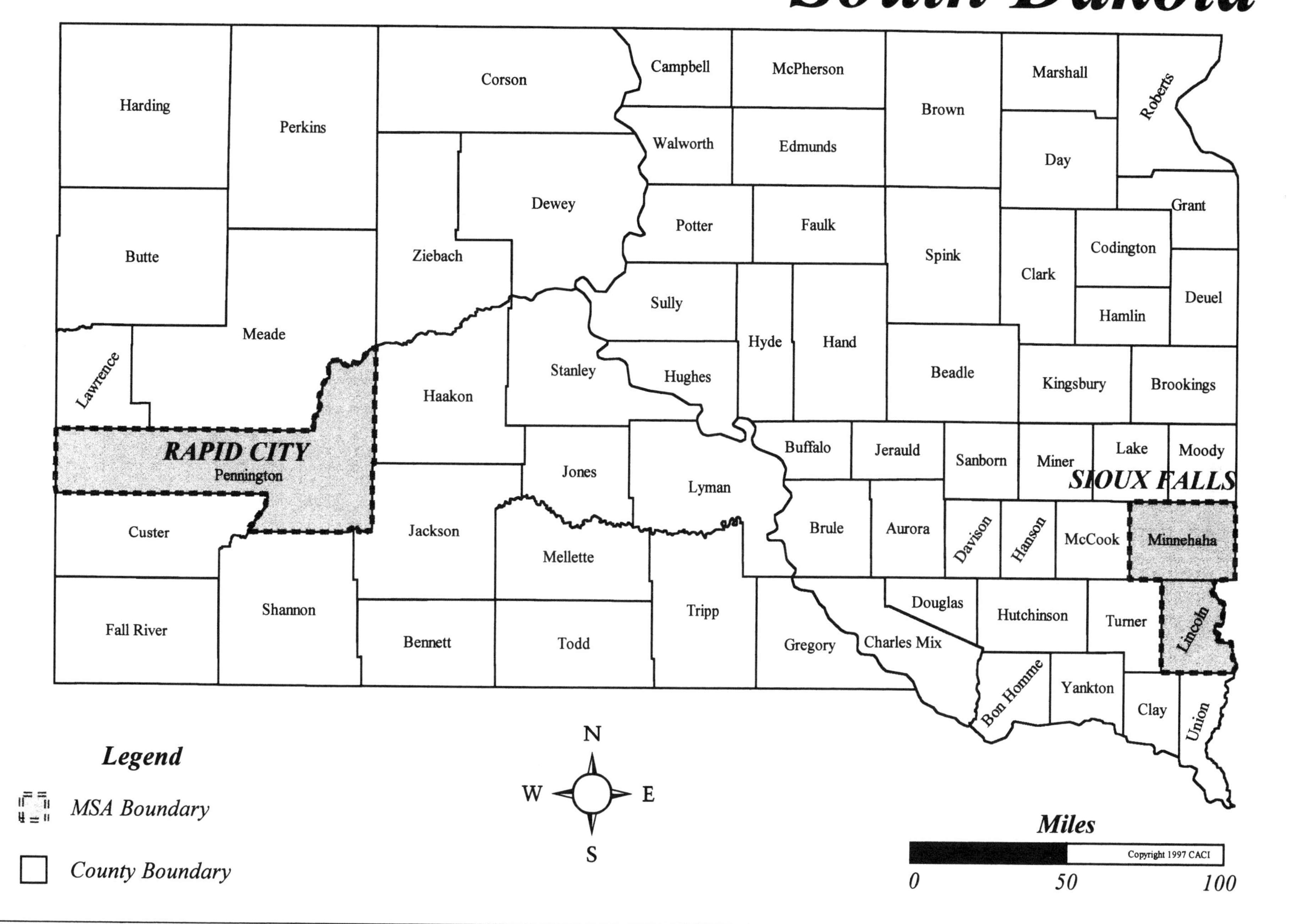
South Dakota
Harding
Perkins
Corson
Campbell
McPherson
Brown
Marshall
Roberts
Walworth
Edmunds
Day
Butte
Dewey
Potter
Faulk
Grant
Ziebach
Spink
Clark
Codington
Deuel
Sully
Hamlin
Meade
Lawrence
Hyde
Hand
Stanley
Hughes
Beadle
Kingsbury
Brookings
Haakon
RAPID CITY
Pennington
Buffalo
Jerauld
Sanborn
Miner
Lake
Moody
Jones
Lyman
SIOUX FALLS
Custer
Jackson
Brule
Aurora
Davison
Hanson
McCook
Minnehaha
Mellette
Shannon
Tripp
Douglas
Hutchinson
Turner
Lincoln
Fall River
Bennett
Todd
Gregory
Charles Mix
Bon Homme
Yankton
Clay
Union
Legend
MSA Boundary
County Boundary
N
W
E
S
Miles
Copyright 1997 CACI
0
50
100

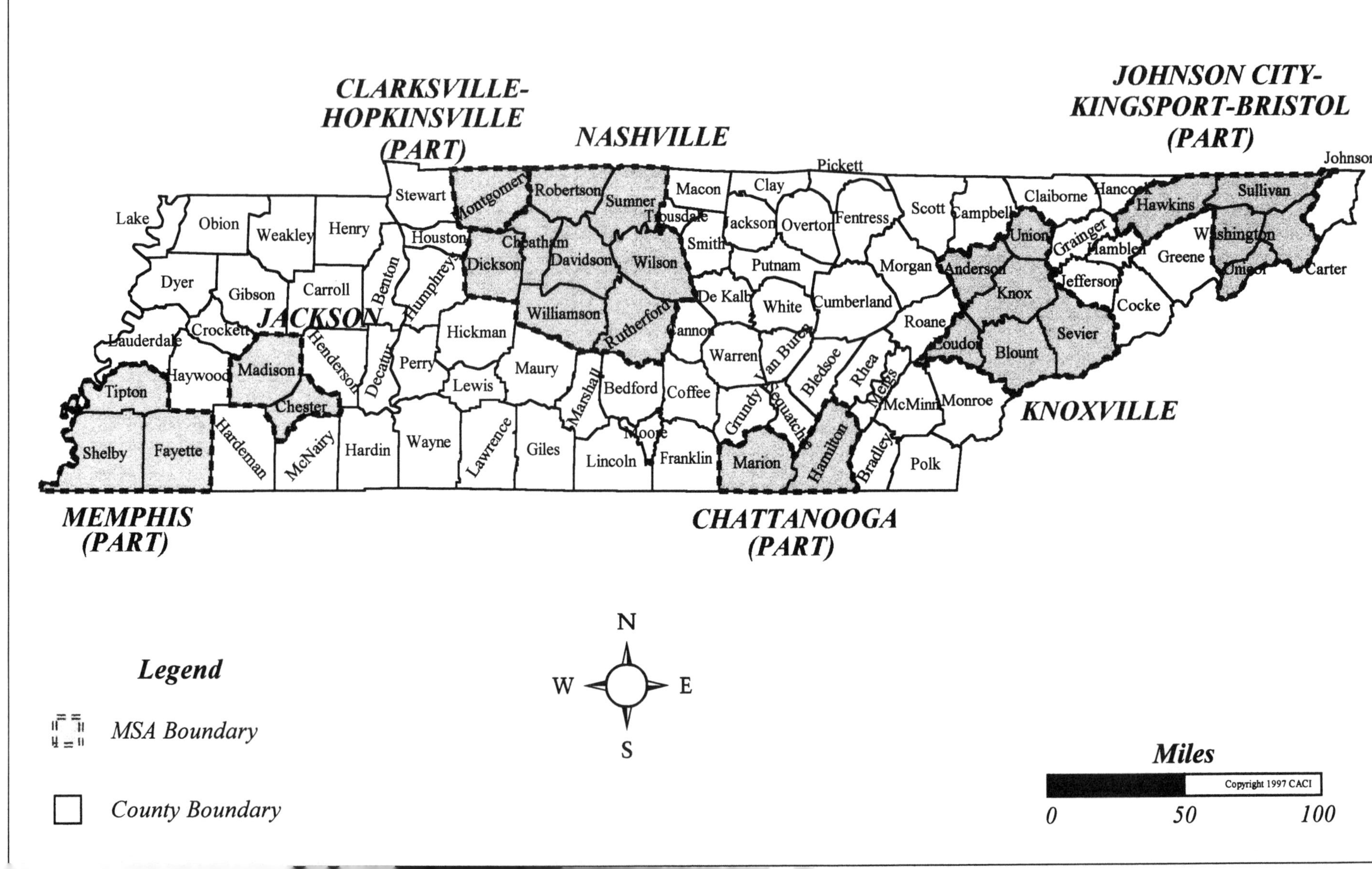
Tennessee
CLARKSVILLE-HOPKINSVILLE (PART)
NASHVILLE
JOHNSON CITY-KINGSPORT-BRISTOL (PART)
JACKSON
KNOXVILLE
MEMPHIS (PART)
CHATTANOOGA (PART)
Lake
Obion
Weakley
Henry
Stewart
Montgomery
Robertson
Sumner
Macon
Clay
Pickett
Scott
Campbell
Claiborne
Hancock
Hawkins
Sullivan
Johnson
Trousdale
Jackson
Overton
Fentress
Union
Grainger
Hamblen
Washington
Houston
Cheatham
Davidson
Wilson
Smith
Putnam
Morgan
Anderson
Greene
Unicoi
Carter
Dyer
Gibson
Carroll
Benton
Humphreys
Dickson
De Kalb
White
Cumberland
Knox
Jefferson
Cocke
Williamson
Rutherford
Roane
Crockett
Lauderdale
Hickman
Cannon
Loudon
Blount
Sevier
Haywood
Madison
Henderson
Decatur
Perry
Warren
Van Buren
Bledsoe
Rhea
Meigs
Tipton
Chester
Lewis
Maury
Marshall
Bedford
Coffee
Grundy
Sequatchie
McMinn
Monroe
Moore
Shelby
Fayette
Hardeman
McNairy
Hardin
Wayne
Lawrence
Giles
Lincoln
Franklin
Marion
Hamilton
Bradley
Polk
Legend
MSA Boundary
County Boundary
N
W
E
S
Miles
Copyright 1997 CACI
0
50
100

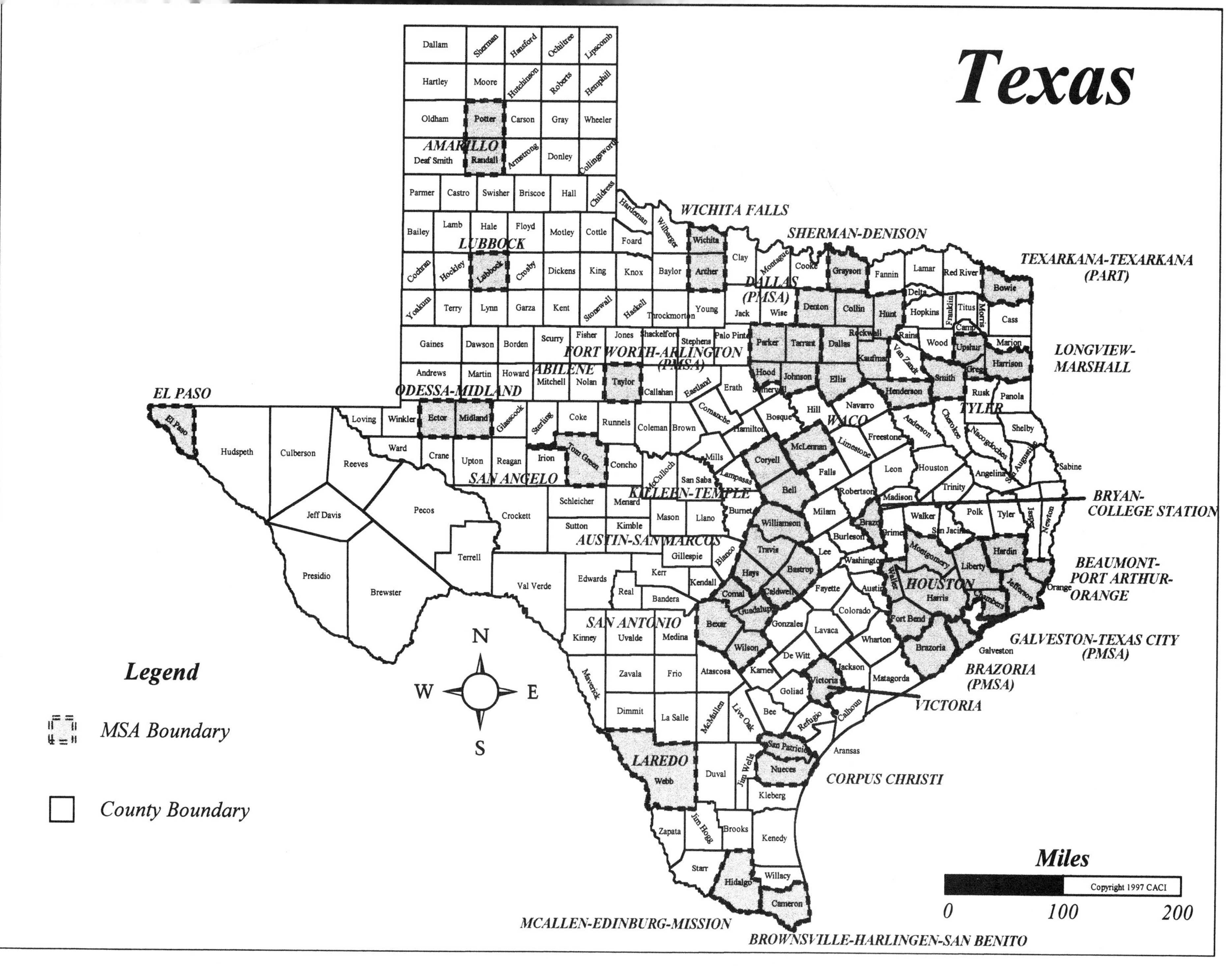

Texas
AMARILLO
LUBBOCK
WICHITA FALLS
SHERMAN-DENISON
TEXARKANA-TEXARKANA (PART)
DALLAS (PMSA)
FORT WORTH-ARLINGTON (PMSA)
LONGVIEW-MARSHALL
ABILENE
ODESSA-MIDLAND
EL PASO
TYLER
WACO
SAN ANGELO
KILLEEN-TEMPLE
BRYAN-COLLEGE STATION
AUSTIN-SAN MARCOS
BEAUMONT-PORT ARTHUR-ORANGE
HOUSTON
SAN ANTONIO
GALVESTON-TEXAS CITY (PMSA)
BRAZORIA (PMSA)
VICTORIA
LAREDO
CORPUS CHRISTI
MCALLEN-EDINBURG-MISSION
BROWNSVILLE-HARLINGEN-SAN BENITO
N
W
E
S
Legend
MSA Boundary
County Boundary
Miles
0
100
200
Copyright 1997 CACI

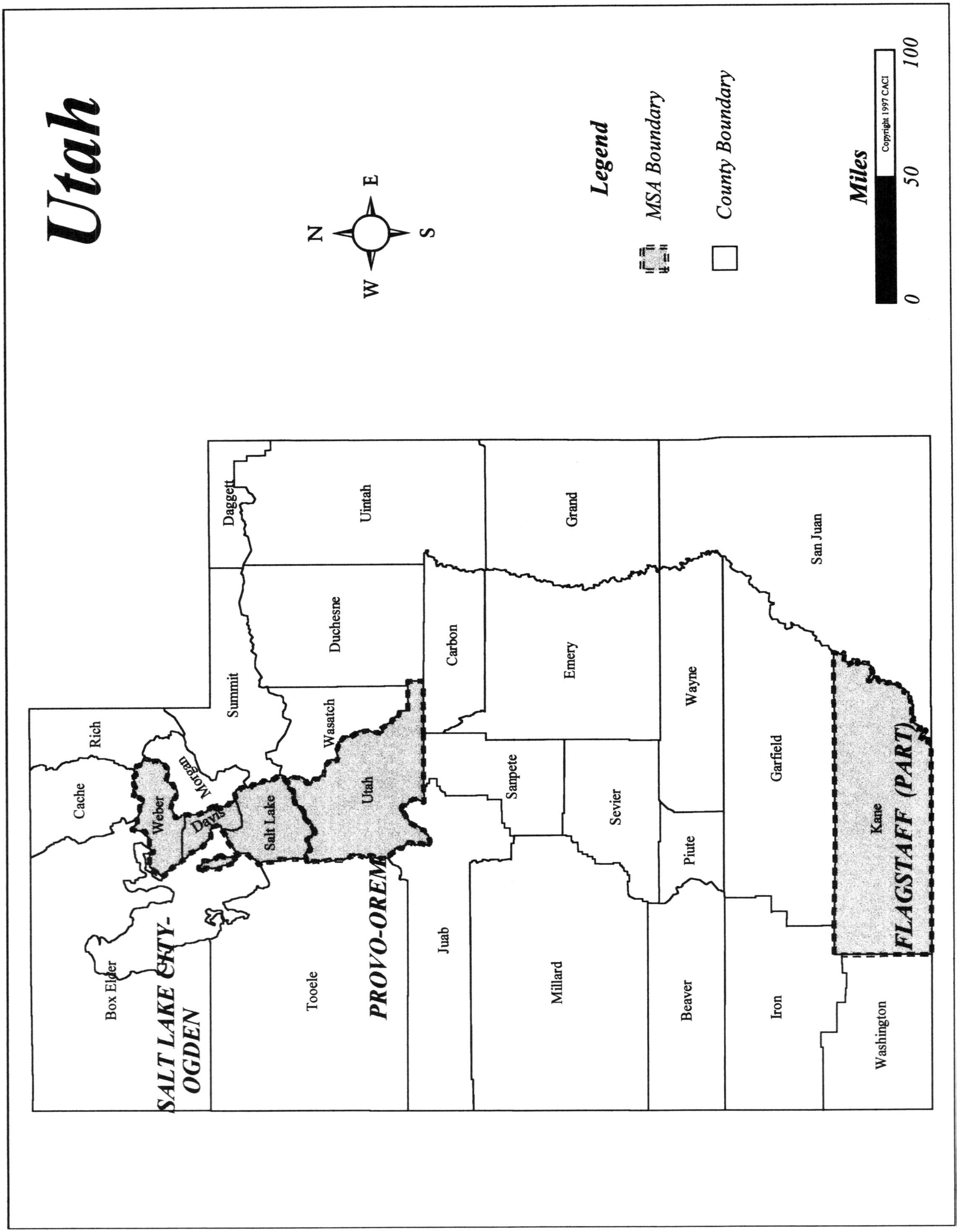

# Utah

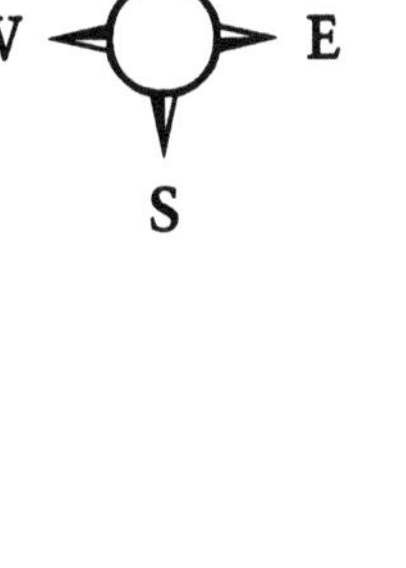
N
W
E
S

SALT LAKE CITY-
OGDEN
PROVO-OREM
FLAGSTAFF (PART)
Box Elder
Cache
Rich
Weber
Davis
Morgan
Summit
Daggett
Salt Lake
Tooele
Wasatch
Duchesne
Uintah
Utah
Juab
Carbon
Sanpete
Millard
Emery
Grand
Sevier
Beaver
Piute
Wayne
Iron
Garfield
San Juan
Washington
Kane

Legend
MSA Boundary
County Boundary

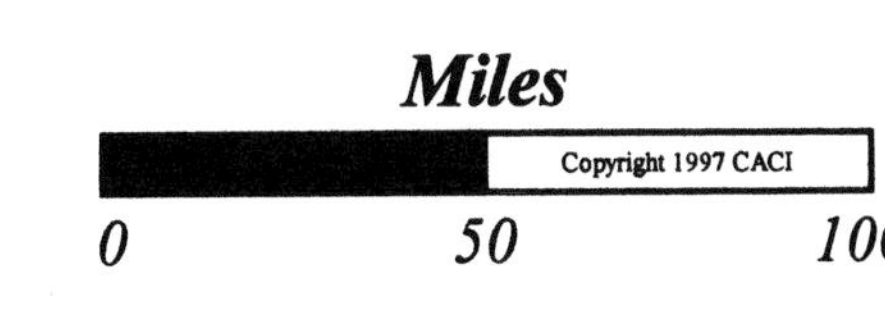
Miles
Copyright 1997 CACI
0
50
100

# Vermont

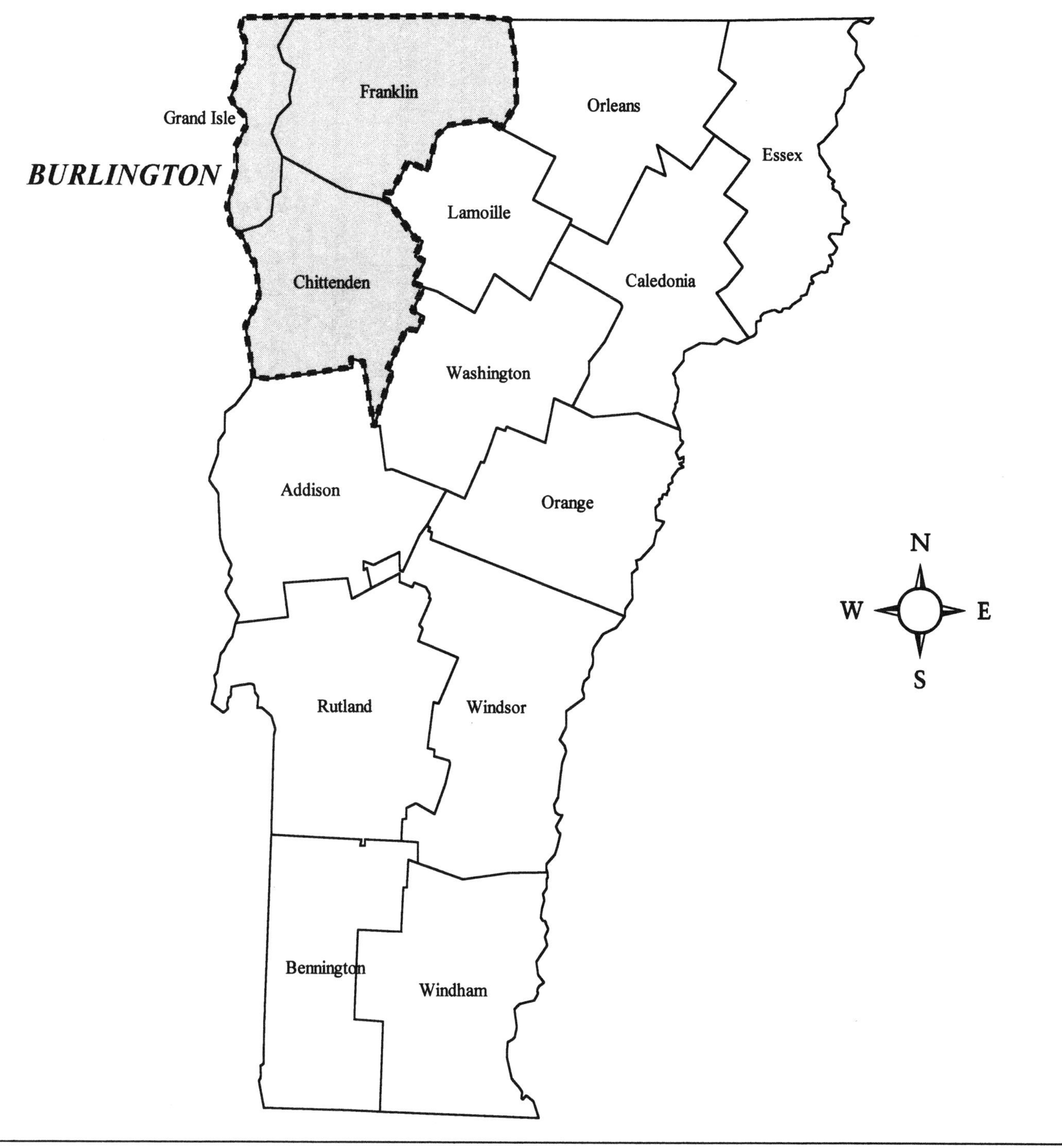
Franklin
Grand Isle
BURLINGTON
Orleans
Essex
Lamoille
Chittenden
Caledonia
Washington
Addison
Orange
N
W
E
S
Rutland
Windsor
Bennington
Windham
Legend
NECMA Boundary
County Boundary
Miles
Copyright 1997 CACI
0
20
40

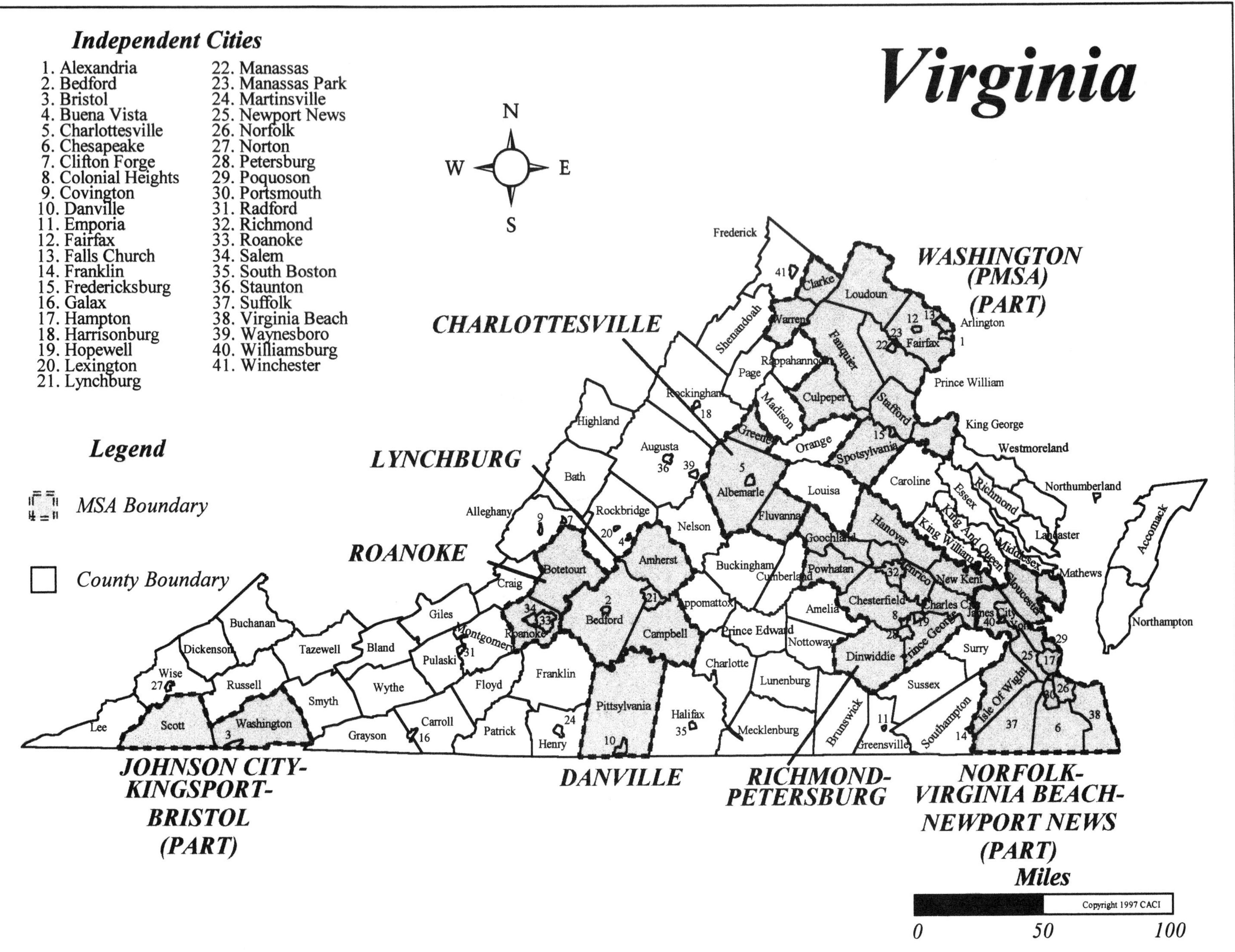

Virginia
Independent Cities
1. Alexandria
2. Bedford
3. Bristol
4. Buena Vista
5. Charlottesville
6. Chesapeake
7. Clifton Forge
8. Colonial Heights
9. Covington
10. Danville
11. Emporia
12. Fairfax
13. Falls Church
14. Franklin
15. Fredericksburg
16. Galax
17. Hampton
18. Harrisonburg
19. Hopewell
20. Lexington
21. Lynchburg
22. Manassas
23. Manassas Park
24. Martinsville
25. Newport News
26. Norfolk
27. Norton
28. Petersburg
29. Poquoson
30. Portsmouth
31. Radford
32. Richmond
33. Roanoke
34. Salem
35. South Boston
36. Staunton
37. Suffolk
38. Virginia Beach
39. Waynesboro
40. Williamsburg
41. Winchester
N
W
E
S
Legend
MSA Boundary
County Boundary
WASHINGTON (PMSA) (PART)
CHARLOTTESVILLE
LYNCHBURG
ROANOKE
JOHNSON CITY-KINGSPORT-BRISTOL (PART)
DANVILLE
RICHMOND-PETERSBURG
NORFOLK-VIRGINIA BEACH-NEWPORT NEWS (PART)
Frederick
Clarke
Loudoun
Arlington
Fairfax
Warren
Shenandoah
Fauquier
Rappahannock
Page
Prince William
Rockingham
Culpeper
Madison
Stafford
King George
Highland
Augusta
Greene
Orange
Spotsylvania
Westmoreland
Bath
Albemarle
Louisa
Caroline
Essex
Richmond
Northumberland
Accomack
Alleghany
Rockbridge
Fluvanna
Nelson
Goochland
Hanover
King William
King And Queen
Middlesex
Lancaster
Botetourt
Amherst
Buckingham
Cumberland
Powhatan
Henrico
New Kent
Gloucester
Mathews
Craig
Giles
Bedford
Campbell
Chesterfield
Charles City
James City
York
Northampton
Buchanan
Dickenson
Tazewell
Bland
Montgomery
Roanoke
Prince Edward
Amelia
Nottoway
Dinwiddie
Prince George
Surry
Pulaski
Charlotte
Wise
Russell
Franklin
Floyd
Wythe
Smyth
Lunenburg
Sussex
Isle Of Wight
Lee
Scott
Washington
Grayson
Carroll
Patrick
Henry
Pittsylvania
Halifax
Mecklenburg
Brunswick
Greensville
Southampton
Miles
Copyright 1997 CACI
0
50
100

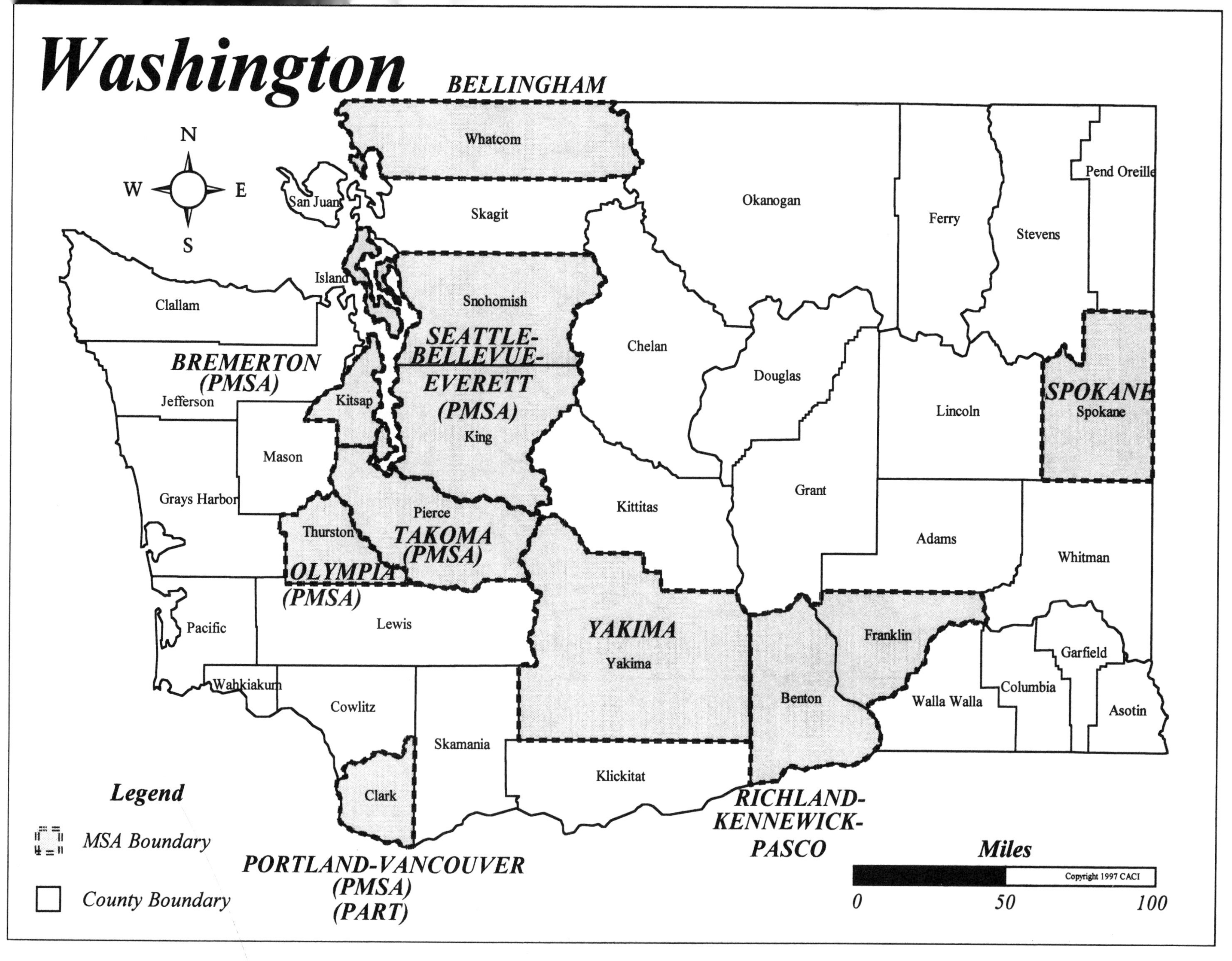
Washington
BELLINGHAM
N
W
E
S
Whatcom
San Juan
Skagit
Okanogan
Ferry
Stevens
Pend Oreille
Island
Clallam
Snohomish
SEATTLE-BELLEVUE-EVERETT (PMSA)
King
BREMERTON (PMSA)
Jefferson
Kitsap
Mason
Chelan
Douglas
Lincoln
SPOKANE
Spokane
Grays Harbor
Pierce
TAKOMA (PMSA)
Thurston
OLYMPIA (PMSA)
Kittitas
Grant
Adams
Whitman
Pacific
Lewis
YAKIMA
Yakima
Franklin
Benton
Walla Walla
Columbia
Garfield
Asotin
Wahkiakum
Cowlitz
Skamania
Klickitat
Clark
RICHLAND-KENNEWICK-PASCO
PORTLAND-VANCOUVER (PMSA) (PART)
Legend
MSA Boundary
County Boundary
Miles
0
50
100
Copyright 1997 CACI

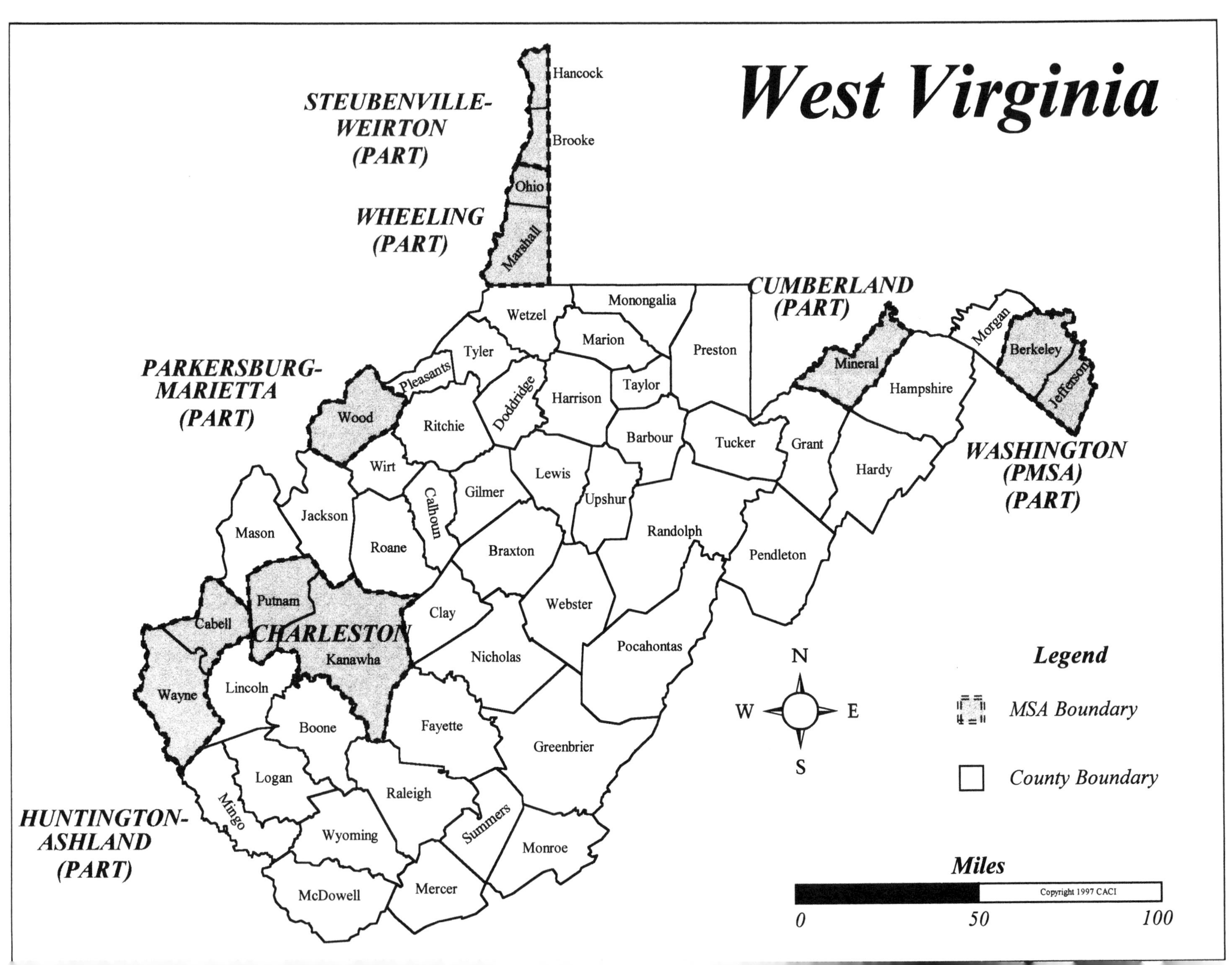
West Virginia
STEUBENVILLE-
WEIRTON
(PART)
WHEELING
(PART)
PARKERSBURG-
MARIETTA
(PART)
CUMBERLAND
(PART)
WASHINGTON
(PMSA)
(PART)
CHARLESTON
HUNTINGTON-
ASHLAND
(PART)
Hancock
Brooke
Ohio
Marshall
Wetzel
Monongalia
Marion
Preston
Tyler
Pleasants
Wood
Ritchie
Doddridge
Harrison
Taylor
Barbour
Tucker
Mineral
Hampshire
Morgan
Berkeley
Jefferson
Grant
Hardy
Wirt
Calhoun
Gilmer
Lewis
Upshur
Randolph
Pendleton
Jackson
Mason
Roane
Braxton
Webster
Pocahontas
Putnam
Cabell
Kanawha
Clay
Nicholas
Wayne
Lincoln
Boone
Fayette
Greenbrier
Logan
Mingo
Raleigh
Summers
Monroe
Wyoming
McDowell
Mercer
N
W
E
S
Legend
MSA Boundary
County Boundary
Miles
Copyright 1997 CACI
0
50
100

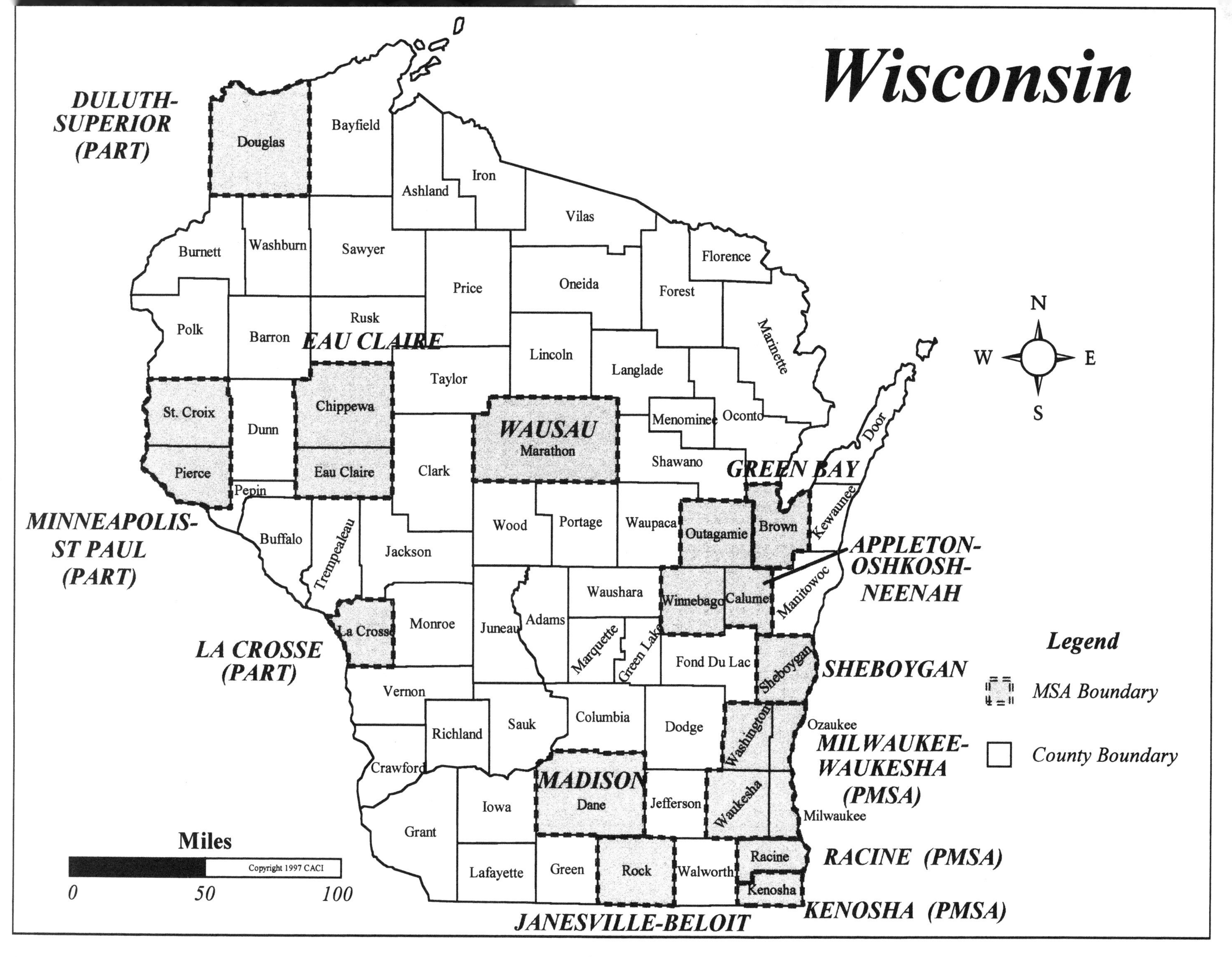

Wisconsin
DULUTH-SUPERIOR (PART)
Douglas
Bayfield
Ashland
Iron
Vilas
Burnett
Washburn
Sawyer
Florence
Price
Oneida
Forest
Polk
Barron
Rusk
EAU CLAIRE
Marinette
Lincoln
Langlade
Taylor
N
W
E
S
St. Croix
Dunn
Chippewa
WAUSAU
Marathon
Menominee
Oconto
Door
Pierce
Eau Claire
Clark
Shawano
GREEN BAY
Pepin
MINNEAPOLIS-ST PAUL (PART)
Buffalo
Trempealeau
Jackson
Wood
Portage
Waupaca
Outagamie
Brown
Kewaunee
APPLETON-OSHKOSH-NEENAH
Waushara
Winnebago
Calumet
Manitowoc
La Crosse
Monroe
Juneau
Adams
Marquette
Green Lake
Fond Du Lac
Sheboygan
LA CROSSE (PART)
SHEBOYGAN
Legend
MSA Boundary
County Boundary
Vernon
Richland
Sauk
Columbia
Dodge
Washington
Ozaukee
MILWAUKEE-WAUKESHA (PMSA)
Crawford
MADISON
Dane
Jefferson
Waukesha
Milwaukee
Grant
Iowa
Miles
Lafayette
Green
Rock
Walworth
Racine
RACINE (PMSA)
Kenosha
KENOSHA (PMSA)
0
50
100
Copyright 1997 CACI
JANESVILLE-BELOIT

# Wyoming

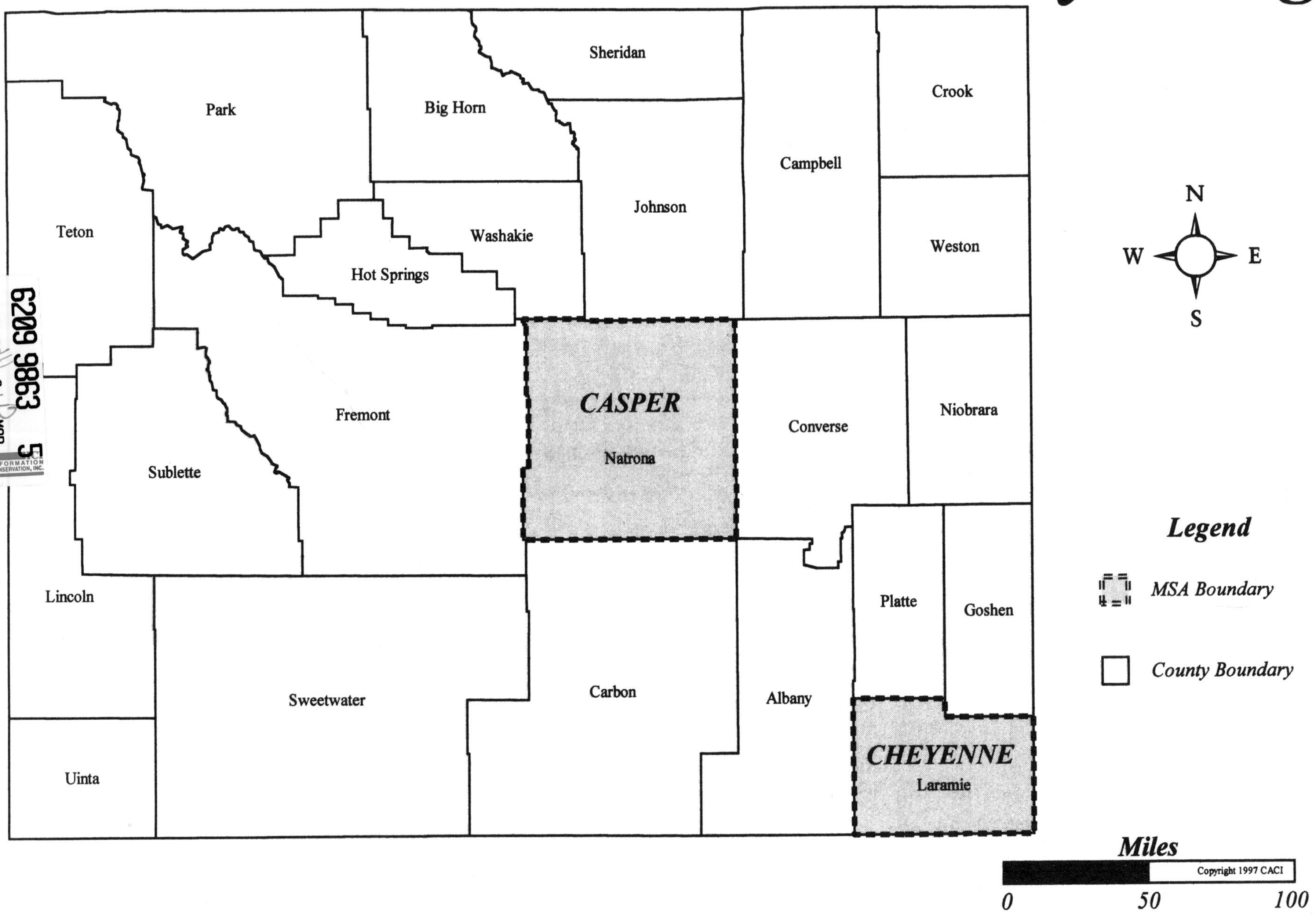

Park
Big Horn
Sheridan
Crook
Campbell
Teton
Johnson
Washakie
Hot Springs
Weston
N
W
E
S
CASPER
Natrona
Fremont
Converse
Niobrara
Sublette
Legend
MSA Boundary
County Boundary
Lincoln
Platte
Goshen
Sweetwater
Carbon
Albany
CHEYENNE
Laramie
Uinta
Miles
Copyright 1997 CACI
0
50
100